# THE HISTORY OF PARLIAMENT

# THE HOUSE OF COMMONS 1754-1790

# THE HISTORY OF PARLIAMENT

# THE
# HOUSE OF COMMONS
# 1754-1790

*Sir Lewis Namier and John Brooke*

II
MEMBERS
A–J

PUBLISHED FOR THE HISTORY OF PARLIAMENT TRUST
BY OXFORD UNIVERSITY PRESS, NEW YORK
1964

*© Crown copyright 1964*

Printed in Great Britain by Butler & Tanner, Ltd.

# Contributors

| | |
|---|---|
| J.B. | John Brooke |
| R.B. | Richard Brown |
| J.A.C. | J. A. Cannon |
| I.R.C. | I. R. Christie |
| E.C. | Eveline Cruickshanks |
| M.M.D. | Mary M. Drummond (Mrs. M. H. Port) |
| J.M.F. | J. M. Fewster |
| E.H.-G. | Edith, Lady Haden-Guest |
| B.H. | Brian Hayes |
| B.K. | Betty Kemp |
| R.M. | Rosemary Mitchison |
| L.B.N. | Sir Lewis Namier |
| A.N.N. | A. N. Newman |
| J.B.O. | J. B. Owen |
| M.H.P. | M. H. Port |
| R.R.S. | R. R. Sedgwick |
| E.A.S. | E. A. Smith |
| L.S.S. | Lucy S. Sutherland |
| P.D.G.T. | Peter D. G. Thomas |

# Abbreviations

In addition to standard and self-explanatory abbreviations, the following are used.

*In the preliminary paragraphs:*

| | |
|---|---|
| abp. | archbishop |
| adv. | advocate |
| bp. | bishop |
| called | called to the bar |
| ch. | children |
| c.j. | chief justice |
| commr. | commissioner |
| c.p. | common pleas |
| contr. | contract |
| da. | daughter, daughters |
| dep. | deputy |
| e. | elder, eldest |
| E.I. | East Indies, East India |
| ft. | regiment of foot |
| [GB] | Great Britain, British |
| g.s. | grammar school |
| gd.-s., etc. | grandson, etc. |
| h.s. | high school |
| [I] | Ireland, Irish |
| jt. | joint |
| l.c.j. | lord chief justice |
| *m.* | married |
| M.P. | a Member of the House of Commons whose entire term of membership lies outside the period 1754–1790 |
| Mq. | Marquess |
| ret. | retired |
| s. | son, sons |
| [S] | Scotland, Scottish |
| S.C.J. | Senator of the College of Justice |
| *suc.* | succeeded |
| w. | wife |
| W.I. | West Indies, West Indian |
| wid. | widow |

*In the footnotes:*

| | |
|---|---|
| Add. | Additional MSS, British Museum |
| *AHR* | *American Historical Review* |
| Almon | John Almon, *Parliamentary Register* (for reports of debates 1774–1780) |
| *APC Col* | *Acts of the Privy Council, Colonial series* |
| Bodl. | Bodleian Library, Oxford |
| *Burke LG* | Burke's *Landed Gentry* |
| *Burke PB* | Burke's *Peerage and Baronetage* |
| *CB* | *Complete Baronetage* |
| *CJ* | *Journals of the House of Commons* |
| *CP* | *Complete Peerage* |
| *DAm.B* | *Dictionary of American Biography* |
| Debrett | John Debrett, *History, Debates, and Proceedings of both Houses of Parliament* (for reports of debates 1754–1774), and *Parliamentary Register* (for reports of debates 1780–1790) |
| *DNB* | *Dictionary of National Biography* |
| *DWB* | *Dictionary of Welsh Biography* |
| Egerton | Egerton MSS, British Museum |
| *EHR* | *English Historical Review* |
| Fortescue | Hon. Sir John Fortescue, *Correspondence of King George III* |
| Grenville mss (Bodl.) | Grenville MSS, Bodleian Library |
| Grenville mss (HL) | Grenville MSS, Huntington Library |
| Grenville mss (JM) | Grenville MSS, in the possession of Sir John Murray, K.C.V.O. |
| Grenville letter bk. | George Grenville's letter books, Huntington Library |
| *HMC* | Historical Manuscripts Commission |
| *Jnl.* | *Journal* |
| Laprade | W. T. Laprade, *Parliamentary papers of John Robinson, 1774–1784* |
| Lib. | Library |
| *N. & Q.* | *Notes and Queries* |
| NLS | National Library of Scotland |
| NLW | National Library of Wales |
| *OR* | *[Official] Return of Members of Parliament* |
| PCC | Prerogative Court of Canterbury |
| PRO | Public Record Office (PRO documents are referred to by their class numbers only) |
| Ramsay of Ochtertyre | *Scotland and Scotsmen in the eighteenth century from the mss of John Ramsay of Ochtertyre*, edited by Alexander Allardyce |
| RO | Record Office |
| Sedgwick | Romney Sedgwick, *Letters from George III to Lord Bute, 1756–1766* |
| *SHR* | *Scottish Historical Review* |
| SRO | Public Record Office of Scotland |
| Stockdale | John Stockdale, *Parliamentary Register* (for reports of debates 1774–1780), and *Debates and Proceedings of the House of Commons* (for reports of debates 1784–1790) |
| UCNW | University College of North Wales |
| *VCH* | *Victoria County History* |
| WO | War Office |

# MEMBERS
# A-J

## ABDY, Sir Anthony Thomas, 5th Bt. (?1720–75), of Chobham Place, Surr. and Albyns, Essex.

KNARESBOROUGH   3 Feb. 1763–7 Apr. 1775

*b.* ?1720, 1st s. of Sir William Abdy, 4th Bt. (of the 1641 creation), of Chobham Place by Mary, da. and h. of Philip Stotherd of Terling, Essex. *educ.* Felsted; St. John's, Camb. 9 June 1738, aged 17; L. Inn 1738, called 1744, bencher 1758, K.C. 1765. *m.* 13 Aug. 1747, Catherine, da. and coh. of William Hamilton of Chancery Lane, London, *s.p. suc.* fa. 18 Jan. 1750; and to Albyns under will of his 3rd cos. Sir John Abdy (q.v.) 1759.

Abdy's practice was in chambers rather than at the bar and more akin to an attorney's than a barrister's: he specialized in family business and in cases concerning landed property. He was legal adviser to Lord Thanet and managed for him the borough of Appleby; and was legal agent to Lord Burlington whose daughter and heiress married the 4th Duke of Devonshire. His father had been London agent to the 3rd Earl of Ailesbury, uncle by marriage of Lady Burlington, and son of a prominent Jacobite exile. When in 1756 Lady Burlington solicited the chief justiceship of Chester for Abdy, Devonshire replied:[1]

Sir Anthony and his father's principles have been a little heretofore called in question, and his friends and the company he kept have been of that stamp; for which reason the King may find fault with me for recommending him, and therefore in order to obviate the difficulty, if Sir Anthony will make an avowal (which I am persuaded he will have no objection to) either to your Ladyship or Mr. Arundell [Richard Arundell, q.v.] of his loyalty and attachment to the King, I give your Ladyship or Mr. Arundell full powers to make use of my name in his behalf and shall wish him success.

Presumably Abdy made the required declaration, but his application was unsuccessful; as were also further ones on 29 Sept. 1756 and 15 Dec. 1761.[2]

In January 1763 a vacancy occurred at Knaresborough, a Burlington borough now controlled by Devonshire; who offered the seat to Abdy. Abdy replied on 20 Jan.:[3]

I am very desirous of making the earliest persona

acknowledgements for your very kind remembrance of my former inclination to come into Parliament. Those inclinations were founded in the countenance which I flattered myself your Grace's patronage and protection would afford me in public, and as the great opinion I had then formed of your character and politics . . . is much heightened from what hath since happened, my inclinations have kept pace with that opinion and are stronger than formerly for the object I then wished for.

Abdy voted consistently with the Cavendishes, and was always classed as belonging to the Rockingham party. Though he advised on legal points, he was not in the party's inner circle. He supervised the drafting of the nullum tempus bill, and spoke for it in the House on 17 Feb. and 15 Nov. 1768. Most of his speeches deal with legal questions, and are dry and colourless.

On 24 Aug. 1769 Abdy wrote to Rockingham about the Surrey petition on the Middlesex election:

My confinement with the gout has prevented my attending the meetings in Surrey . . . Indeed, their present method of proceeding is entirely against my opinion. I would have persuaded them to have petitioned the House of Commons and have addressed their Members . . . but numbers overpowered, and an address to the Crown was almost unanimously carried.

Rockingham was sufficiently impressed to ask Burke to go down to Albyns and consult further with Abdy, who then changed his mind; he wrote from Albyns to Rockingham on 10 Sept.:

I have now been drove to form some plan of a petition to the Crown to be ready in case any meeting should be had in this county . . . I think this petition should be confined to the freeholders' rights only . . . and then pray the Crown to give such constitutional relief as the law of the country hath put into his hands, this can be nothing but a removal of ministers and dissolution of Parliament.[4]

This was the procedure later adopted in Yorkshire, which produced the prototype petition for the other counties.

On 28 Feb. 1770 Bamber Gascoyne wrote to John Strutt (qq.v.):[5] 'Sir Anthony Abdy was near dying on Saturday, but do not be shocked he is now better.' But henceforth Abdy suffered increasingly from gout, and took much less part in politics. His last recorded speech was on 12 Dec. 1770, and no vote by him is known 1771–5. In Robinson's surveys on the royal marriage bill, March 1772, Abdy is classed as 'contra, sick, present'; and in that of September 1774 as 'contra'. He died 7 Apr. 1775.

[1] 25 Feb. 1756, Devonshire mss. [2] Devonshire mss. [3] Ibid.
[4] Rockingham mss. [5] Strutt mss.

J.B.

## ABDY, Sir John, 4th Bt. (?1714–59), of Albyns, Essex.

ESSEX 13 Dec. 1748–1 Apr. 1759

*b.* ?1714, 1st s. of Sir Robert Abdy, 3rd Bt. (of the 1660 creation), M.P., of Albyns by Theodosia, da. and h. of George Bramston, master of Trinity Hall, Camb. *educ.* M. Temple 1731; Trinity, Oxf. 11 July 1732, aged 18. *unm. suc.* fa. 27 Aug. 1748.

Abdy, on the death of his father, was returned unopposed for Essex, and again in 1754. In Dupplin's list of the Parliament of 1754 he was classed as Tory 'against'. He died 1 Apr. 1759.

J.B.

## ABERCROMBY, Burnet (?1738–92), of Brucefield, Clackmannan.

CLACKMANNANSHIRE 29 Nov. 1788–1790

*b.* ?1738, 2nd s. of George Abercromby of Tullibody, Clackmannan; bro. of Ralph and nephew of James Abercromby (qq.v.). *m.* Elizabeth, *s.p.*

The least distinguished of four brothers, Burnet Abercromby went to sea in the East India Company's service, and on his visits to Bengal gained the favour of Clive, to whom he appealed for help in July 1767 in getting 'a good voyage'.[1] Appointed to the command of the *Grenville*, he sailed for Bombay in 1768, but did not make the expected fortune. In May 1773 'Burnet Abercromby of Bury St., St. James's, mariner and merchant', was declared bankrupt.[2] On the death of his uncle James Abercromby in 1775, he and his father succeeded to the Brucefield estate. Thereafter his fortunes improved and by 1788 he was 'in opulent circumstances, connected with India shipping'.[3]

He was returned for Clackmannan through the interest of Henry Dundas, an intimate family friend. On 16 Dec. 1788 and on 11 Feb. 1789 he voted with Administration on the Regency. Dundas wrote to Col. Robert Abercromby in India, 8 Apr. 1789,[4] that Burnet 'gave a steady and cordial support in all our late struggles'.

Clackmannan was not represented in the 1790 Parliament and Abercromby does not appear to have sought election elsewhere. He died 24 Mar. 1792.

[1] Clive mss. [2] *London Gaz.*, 4–8 May 1773. [3] *Pol. State Scotland 1788*, p. 83. [4] H. Furber, *Hen. Dundas*, 71.

E.H.-G.

## ABERCROMBY, James (1707–75), of Brucefield, Clackmannan.

CLACKMANNANSHIRE 1761–1768

*b.* 1707, 3rd s. of Alexander Abercromby, M.P., of Tullibody by Mary, da. of Alexander Duff of Braco; uncle of Burnet and Ralph Abercromby (qq.v.). *educ.* Westminster 1720; Leyden 1724 or 1725; L. Inn 1726, called 1738. *unm.*

Attorney-gen. S. Carolina 1730–45; agent N. Carolina 1748–57; agent N. Carolina assembly 1758–60; agent Virginia 1754–61; agent Virginia gov. and council 1761–74; dep. auditor gen. of plantations 1757–65.

Purchased Brucefield estate 1758 or 1759.

The greater part of Abercromby's active life was spent in the Carolinas and Virginia, or on their business in London.[1] During his residence in South Carolina as attorney-general he acquired a plantation and other property in the colony, and in 1739 became a member of the assembly. Diligent in the conduct of affairs, he acquired a reputation for being 'very tenacious of his fees and perquisites';[2] and by 1761 his agency business was running down. The only agency he retained, that for the governor and council of Virginia, was more concerned with the raising of royal revenues than with the business of the colony.

Returned apparently unopposed for Clackmannan in 1761, he attached himself to Newcastle, to whom he sent on 4 Apr. 1762 a memorandum on sugar exports from Martinique and Guadeloupe. In a covering letter he wrote:[3]

His Grace . . . will be pleased to look upon this as an instance of Mr. Abercromby's inclination to serve his Grace in public or in private capacity on all occasions, in return for his Grace's favour about to be granted to Mr. Abercromby in the way of office (as others before him have enjoyed) upon the interposition of his friend Lord Kinnoull.

It is not known to what office this refers.

Abercromby, however, did not follow Newcastle into opposition, but in December 1762 was counted by Fox among those favourable to the peace preliminaries, and appears in no minority list during the Grenville Administration. In 1763 he was examined before the Board of Trade on the question of Virginia's paper currency and sterling debts,[4] but despite his expert knowledge, did not intervene in the debates of March 1764 on Grenville's budget and the American tax bill. Charles Stuart, a Scots Virginia merchant, reported on the third reading of the American bill:[5] 'The colonies mustered their forces. New England was pretty strong; Virginia made no figure at all.'

On 6 Jan. 1765 Abercromby wrote to Grenville:[6]

After many years service in plantation business, but of late years more particularly concerned in matters of his Majesty's personal revenue, I have . . . made some discoveries and observations whereby the King's particular revenues may be much improved, through the interposition of the Treasury alone; but while duty to the King leads me to lay such before you, on the other hand, I am restrained from doing anything whereby I may undo myself in the service of those upon whom at present is my sole depen[dence]. In this situation prudence directs me to remain silent, and thereupon I make the following proposal . . .

Finding that my conduct in Parliament with regard to plantation matters . . . may not correspond in many respects with the sentiments of my constituents in America, and moreover that public business and service in Parliament become too much for my health, but above all considering that my situation must prove extremely precarious, serving in office under the nomination and pleasure of the government of Virginia, whose administration in point of the King's revenues I must call in question . . . I am very much inclined to retire from the service and to resign my employment of solicitor or agent for the King's affairs in Virginia . . . The nomination . . . is from the lt.-governor and council in Virginia, the salary £400 sterling per annum (besides occasional perquisites), 200 whereof paid out of the 2s. hogshead tobacco, the additional 200 out of the quitrents. But as my circumstances do not admit of a resignation without obtaining an adequate income, in consideration therefore of my services and of the improvement of the King's personal revenue . . . I humbly propose that his Majesty do grant to me an addition of £300 to the £200 which I now have on the quitrents, so as to make up to me my present income by way of an annuity for life . . . which addition may be considered as a temporary reward to a person by whose means an additional and permanent revenue is acquired by the King and a revenue of such a nature as may be extended to all others of the King's colonies.

In return for the pension, Abercromby proposed to prepare a complete review of American royal revenues. If the offer were accepted, the King would receive the benefit 'of the labour of thirty years' service . . . and your Administration the merit of carrying into execution what may be found beneficial therein . . .' Abercrombie was apparently interviewed either by Grenville or Jenkinson, but received no pension, and of his revenue scheme nothing further is recorded. He remained agent for Virginia council until at least September 1774.[7]

Grenville so far interested himself in Abercromby's career as to make in June 1765 a tentative and obscure approach to Sir Lawrence Dundas (q.v.) and Lord Gower, with the apparent object of obtaining for Abercromby a seat in the next Parliament.[8]

Although listed 'pro' by Rockingham in July 1765, Abercromby followed Grenville into opposition, spoke 18 Dec. 1765 in support of Rigby's

and Grenville's motion for American papers,[9] and voted against the repeal of the Stamp Act, 7 Feb. 1766. Under the Chatham Administration he was listed by Rockingham as attached to Bute, by Townshend as 'doubtful', and by Newcastle as 'Administration', but he voted against the Government on the land tax, 27 Feb. 1767. He does not appear to have stood in 1768.

He died before November 1775.[10]

[1] For his work as colonial agent, see E. Lonn, *Col. Agents of Southern Cols., Bd. Trade Jnls., Col. Recs. of N.C.,* and *Recs. of Robert Dinwiddie* (Va. Hist. Coll.). [2] Robert to Andrew Pringle, 7 May and 9 June 1744, Pringle's letter bk. in possession of S.C. Hist. Soc. [3] Add. 32936, f. 329. [4] *Bd. Trade Jnl. 1759-63,* pp. 330-1, 1 and 2 Feb. 1763. [5] Stuart's letter bk. 23 Mar. 1764, Liverpool RO. [6] Add. 38204, f. 9. [7] Lonn, 66. [8] Sandwich to Grenville, 15 June 1765, Grenville mss (JM); Grenville to Sandwich, 16 June 1765, Sandwich mss. [9] Harris's 'Debates', 18 Dec. 1765. [10] *Comm. Recs. of Stirling,* i. *sub* 18 Nov. 1775.

E.H.-G.

**ABERCROMBY, Ralph** (1734–1801), of Tullibody, Clackmannan.

CLACKMANNANSHIRE 1774–1780, 1796–Feb. 1798

*b.* 7 Oct. 1734,[1] 1st s. of George Abercromby of Tullibody by Mary, da. of Ralph Dundas of Manour, Perth; bro. of Burnet and nephew of James Abercromby (qq.v.). *educ.* Alloa; Rugby 1748–52; Holland and Leipzig 1752–3. *m.* 17 Nov. 1767, Mary Anne, da. and coh. of John Menzies of Ferntower, Crieff, Perth, 4s. 3da. *cr.* K.B. 22 July 1795; *suc.* fa. 1800.

Cornet 3 Drag. Gds. 1756; capt. 3 Horse 1762, maj. 1770, lt.-col. 1773; col. 103 Ft. 1781–3; maj.-gen. 1787; col. 69 Ft. 1790–2, 6 Ft. 1792–5, 7 Drag. Gds. 1795–6, 2 Drag. 1796–*d.*; lt.-gen. 1797.

Lt.-gov. I.o.W. 1795–9; gov. Inverness 1798–*d.*

Intended for the bar, Abercromby[2] studied civil law at Edinburgh and Leipzig but in 1756, overcoming his father's objections, joined the army. Mentioned in 1760 as a candidate alternative to his uncle James Abercromby, he stood in 1774, with the support of Sir Lawrence Dundas (q.v.), a connexion by marriage, against James Francis Erskine and the Mar interest. After a violent contest (during which the candidates fought a duel), Abercromby, contrary to Robinson's expectations,[3] was returned, and Erskine's petition was dismissed by the House.

Although he owed his election to Dundas, Abercromby was unwilling to submit to his dictation in parliamentary affairs and eventually broke with him. According to his son, Abercromby, in his private opinions known only to his family and a few friends, sympathized with the Americans, admired Washington, and was only restrained from resigning his seat by a sense of obligation to his Clackmannan supporters, but 'was able to avoid a conflict between his duty as a soldier and his principles as a citizen' by remaining in Ireland, and not seeking military service in America until France entered the war. On the contractors bill, 12 Feb. 1779, he was listed 'pro, abroad', and his only recorded vote throughout the Parliament was on the motion against the prorogation, 24 Apr. 1780, when he divided with Administration. Clackmannan was not represented in the Parliament of 1780, and Abercromby did not stand elsewhere.

On the disbandment of his regiment in 1783, Abercromby retired to the Tullibody estates, unsuccessfully contested Clackmannan in 1784, and thereafter devoted himself to the agricultural and social improvement of the district. Differing in politics with the Orkney Dundasses, the Abercromby family were now close friends of Henry Dundas (q.v.) who supported their interest in the 1788 by-election; but Ralph, who genuinely disliked parliamentary life, again declined the nomination in favour of his brother Burnet (q.v.).

He died 28 Mar. 1801 in Aboukir Bay, from wounds received at the battle of Alexandria. On 28 May his widow was created Baroness Abercromby.

[1] CP gives 25 Oct. Other sources, e.g. Anderson, *Scottish Nation*, give 7 Oct. and bap. 27 Oct. [2] The following outline is based on *Mems. of Sir Ralph Abercromby* by his s. James, cr. Lord Dunfermline. [3] Laprade, 7, 20.

E.H.-G.

**ACLAND, John** (1756–1831), of Fairfield, nr. Bridgwater, Som.

BRIDGWATER    2 Mar. 1781–1784

*b.* 11 Feb. 1756, 1st s. of Arthur Acland of Fairfield by Elizabeth, da. of William Oxenham of Oxenham, Devon. *educ.* Eton 1765–73; Univ. Coll. Oxf. 1774. *m.* (1) 12 July 1781, Elizabeth, da. of Rev. Henry Fuller of Rose Hill, Suss., 3s. 3da.; (2) 5 Nov. 1818, Sarah Maria, da. of Robert Knipe of New Lodge, Herts., wid. of Philip Gibbes of Barbados, *s.p.  suc.* fa. 1771; *cr.* Bt. 9 Dec. 1818.

Acland stood at Bridgwater in 1780 with the support of the Powlett interest, was defeated, but seated on petition. There is no record of his having voted during North's Administration or on Shelburne's peace preliminaries. In Robinson's list of March 1783 he is classed as 'country gentleman, doubtful'. He voted against Fox's East India bill, 5 Dec. 1783, and supported Pitt. He did not stand in 1784.

He died 23 Feb. 1831.

J.B.

**ACLAND, John Dyke** (1746–78), of Pixton, Som.

CALLINGTON    1774–22 Nov. 1778

*b.* 18 Feb. 1746, 1st s. of Sir Thomas Dyke Acland, 7th Bt. (q.v.). *educ.* Eton 1763–4; Univ. Coll. Oxf. 1765; Grand Tour, with Thomas Townshend jun.

(q.v.). *m.* 3 June 1770, Lady Christiana Harriet Caroline Fox Strangways, da. of Stephen, 1st Earl of Ilchester, 1s. 1da.

Ensign 33 Ft. 1774, capt. 1775; maj. 20 Ft. 1775.

Returned for Callington on Lady Orford's interest, Acland made his first speech on 20 Feb. 1775 on North's motion to allow the colonies to tax themselves:[1]

I have supported Administration on every American step they have taken during the session, because I have approved them; and as long as I had continued to approve them, I should have continued to support them. But, Sir, I cannot approve this measure.

On 27 Feb.[2] he elaborated his argument: North's proposals neither satisfied America who denied the right of taxation, nor Britain who claimed it. He was not anti-American, but convinced of the justice of the British cause:

That which is generosity, which is magnanimity after victory, is timidity and foul disgrace before it. There may be situations in which states may be found where they cannot, without certain ruin, acquiesce even in just claims; there are situations too, in which states may grant more than is asked, and give more than is desired, with honour, security, and advantage.

In the summer of 1775 he asked permission to raise a regiment. North, 'convinced that the spirit which has been raised in the west has been almost entirely owing to Mr. Acland, and that some favour shown to him at present will be of considerable political use', recommended it:[3] 'The cause of Great Britain is not yet sufficiently popular', he wrote to the King on 25 Aug. 1775,[4] 'and it will derive great credit from such a public declaration of an independent gentleman of fortune.' But the King, although approving Acland's 'laudable sentiments' and 'the love he bears to the military profession', preferred to augment the old regiments.[5] Acland persisted until he made a nuisance of himself. On 28 Nov. the King wrote to North: 'I do not see the means of promoting him in Ireland'; his pretensions were 'so exorbitant'; but if he would 'take the civil line' something could be arranged for him.[6]

In moving the Address on 26 Oct. 1775 Acland said the issue was clear[7]:

Do gentlemen choose to acquiesce in the independence of America, or to enforce their submission to this country by vigorous measures . . . I must maintain that it would have been better for this country that America had never been known, than that a great consolidated American Empire should exist independent of Britain.

On 22 Nov., in an altercation with Charles James Fox, he described himself as 'no adventurer or place-hunter; he was a gentleman of independent fortune, who voted purely in conformity with his sentiments, without any sinister views whatever'.[8]

In November 1775 he left to join his regiment in America, where he was twice wounded, and captured at Saratoga. 'His behaviour', wrote Burgoyne to Sir William Howe on 25 Oct. 1777, 'has been that of a high-spirited soldier of fortune.'[9] On his return to England in May 1778 he was received by the King, who wished 'to hear his account of the different scenes he had been engaged in'.[10] 'The zeal he has shewn', the King wrote to North, 'made me think him deserving of this distinction.'

He died 22 Nov. 1778, 'by a fall on his head in a duel'.[11]

[1] Almon, i. 207. [2] Ibid. 237. [3] North to the King [14 Aug. 1775], Fortescue, iii. 246. [4] Ibid. 249. [5] The King to North, 18 Aug. 1775, ibid. 247. [6] Ibid. 297. [7] Almon, iii. 6. [8] Ibid. 207–8. [9] HMC Royal Institution, i. 144. [10] The King to North, 14 May 1778, Fortescue, iv. 142. [11] Lady Sarah Lennox to Duchess of Leinster, 12 Dec. 1778, Leinster Corresp. 265.

J.B.

**ACLAND, Sir Thomas Dyke,** 7th Bt. (1722–85), of Killerton, Devon, and Holnicote, Som.

DEVON      15 Apr. 1746–1747
SOMERSET      28 Jan. 1767–1768

b. 14 Aug. 1722, 1st s. of Sir Hugh Acland, 6th Bt., M.P., by Cicely, da. and h. of Sir Thomas Wroth, 3rd Bt., M.P., of Petherton Park, Som. educ. Balliol, Oxf. 1740. m. 7 Jan. 1745, Elizabeth Dyke, da. and h. of Thomas Dyke of Tetton, Som. and took add. name of Dyke, 2s. suc. fa. 29 July 1728.
Sheriff, Som. 1751–2.

Twice returned as a stop-gap, Acland is a rare example in the 18th century of a Member who served for two counties. His only known vote was given on 27 Feb. 1767 against Government on the land tax.

He died 24 Feb. 1785.

J.B.

**A'COURT, William** (c.1708–81), of Heytesbury, Wilts.

HEYTESBURY      25 Jan. 1751–2 Aug. 1781

b. c.1708, 2nd s. of Pierce A'Court, M.P., and bro. of Pierce A'Court Ashe (q.v.). m. 22 Feb. 1746, Annabella, da. and coh. of Thomas Vernon of Twickenham Park, Mdx., 1s. suc. bro. and took add. name of Ashe under will of his uncle Edward Ashe 1768.
Ensign 11 Ft. 1726; lt. 2 Ft. Gds. 1738; capt. and lt.-col. 1745; maj. and col. 1755; maj.-gen. 1759; lt.-col. 2 Ft. Gds. 1762–3; lt.-gen. Mar. 1765; col. 11 Ft. Aug. 1765–d.; gen. 1778.

In Dupplin's list of 1754 A'Court was classed 'for', and on 18 July 1754, in a memorial asking to be promoted to the rank of colonel, stated that his family and himself had 'ever been steady supporters of his Majesty's interest in Parliament'.[1] There is no record of his having spoken in the House.

On 5 Nov. 1762 Lord Harcourt wrote to Jenkinson:[2] 'General Acourt . . . is supposed to be so much displeased and disappointed in not getting the Regiment [55 Ft.] . . . that it is thought he will go into opposition . . . there are two brothers in Parliament, and I should imagine it might be no difficult matter to secure them.' But A'Court voted with Opposition in the divisions on the peace preliminaries, 9 and 10 Dec. 1762, and again in the division on Wilkes's case, 15 Nov. 1763, for which he was deprived of his commission as lieutenant-colonel of the 2nd Foot Guards. In August 1765 he was made colonel of the 11th Foot and given a pension of £800 p.a., which is not likely to have been continued after July 1766 when A'Court went with Rockingham into opposition. In Rockingham's lists of July 1765 and November 1766 and in Newcastle's of March 1767 he was classed as one of their party. He voted with the Opposition on nullum tempus, 17 Feb. 1768, but does not appear in further lists till 25 Feb. 1774 when he again voted with Opposition on Grenville's Election Act, and continued to do so until his death on 2 Aug. 1781.

[1] Add. 32736, f. 55. [2] Add. 38200, f. 95.

M.M.D.

**A'COURT, William Pierce Ashe** (c.1747–1817), of Heytesbury, Wilts.

HEYTESBURY      3 Sept. 1781–Dec. 1790, 1806–Jan. 1807

b. c.1747, 1st s. of Gen. William A'Court Ashe (q.v.). educ. Eton 1759–65. m. (1) 1769, Catherine (d.23 Sept. 1776), da. of Lt.-Col. John Bradford, s.p.; (2) 30 Oct. 1777, Letitia, da. of Henry Wyndham of The Close, Salisbury, 3s. 4da. suc. fa. 1781; cr. Bt. 4 July 1795.

A'Court was in opposition during North's Administration. He was classed 'doubtful' in Shelburne's list of November 1782, and voted against the peace preliminaries, 18 Feb. 1783. In Robinson's list of March 1783 he was described as of 'Mr. Fox's connection', but he did not vote on the East India bill. In Stockdale's list of 19 Mar. 1784 he was classed 'against Mr. Pitt', and during Pitt's Administration voted consistently in opposition. There is no record of his having spoken in the House in our period.

A'Court died 22 July 1817.[1]

[1] GEC Baronetage; Gent. Mag. 1817 ii. 185 gives 27 July.

M.M.D.

**A'COURT ASHE, Pierce** (?1707–68), of Ivy Church, Wilts.

HEYTESBURY      1734–1768

b. ?1707, 1st s. of Pierce A'Court, M.P., of Ivy Church

by Elizabeth, da. of William Ashe, M.P., of Heytesbury, Wilts. *educ.* Wadham, Oxf. 17 July 1725, aged 18. *m.* Janet, da. of Col. Robert Brown, sis. of Robiniana, Countess of Peterborough, *s.p.* *suc.* fa. 13 Apr. 1725; and to estates of his cos. William Ashe, M.P., 1750, and took add. name of Ashe.

Equerry to the King July 1739.

A'Court was returned for Heytesbury on the Ashe family interest which he later inherited. He supported Administration in all his recorded votes; and was listed for the Government in Dupplin's list of 1754. In 1753 he was granted a secret service pension of £500 p.a., but 'seems to have been so indifferent to money that sometimes for two years he did not trouble to draw it'.[1] His pension ceased in 1762 when he and his brother William A'Court (q.v.) remained with Newcastle in opposition. In 1765 he appears in Newcastle's list of 'persons particularly recommended to the Marquess of Rockingham', but nothing appears to have been done for him.

He died 6 Sept. 1768.

[1] Namier, *Structure*, 217, 218, 438.

M.M.D.

## ADAIR, James (?1743–98).

COCKERMOUTH     30 Jan. 1775–1780
HIGHAM FERRERS   13 Sept. 1793–21 July 1798

*b.* ?1743, 1st s. of James Adair, merchant and Irish factor, of Aldermanbury, London by his w. Margaret. *educ.* ?Eton 1753–9; Peterhouse, Camb. 10 Nov. 1759, aged 16; L. Inn 1761, called 1767. *m.* Elizabeth Spencer, 1s. 1da.

Serjeant-at-law 1774; recorder of London 1779–89; King's serjeant 1782; counsel to Board of Ordnance 1782–*d.*; c.j. Chester 1796–*d.*

During the ten years before he entered Parliament Adair was an active opponent of the court. According to Almon[1] he was the author of two pamphlets. The first, published in 1764, was *Thoughts on the Dismission of Officers*, which condemned the dismissal of an officer for voting against the court: 'To control his exercise of private judgment is to deprive him of that liberty without which he cannot discharge the duties he owes to the public.' The second, published in 1768, *Observations on the Power of Alienation in the Crown*, attacked the Treasury grant of Inglewood Forest to Sir James Lowther. Both were critical of all George III's Administrations except that of Rockingham.

Adair established his reputation by his fervent backing of Wilkes and the popular cause. In May 1769 he was counsel for the Middlesex freeholders petitioning against the seating of Luttrell, and was approached by Rockingham about publicising the Opposition case;[2] the following year he obtained useful notoriety by intervening in Wilkes's quarrel

with Horne Tooke, and in 1771 was counsel for the publishers of the Junius letters. During the East India Company crisis of 1772–3 Adair seems to have acted as intermediary between Rockingham, Richmond, and members of the Company opposed to increased Government control in India.

In 1775 Adair was returned for Cockermouth by Sir James Lowther, whom he had attacked in his pamphlet of 1768, but who had by now gone into opposition. In Parliament Adair consistently opposed North's Administration, and spoke fairly frequently. His first reported speech was in support of Wilkes's motion for expunging from the journals the resolution of 17 Feb. 1769. He was a vigorous opponent of the anti-American measures, describing them as 'the most violent, the most unjust and tyrannical, that ever disgraced the annals of any civilized nation'.[3] He supported the New York petition against the Declaratory Act, 15 May 1775, and after the outbreak of war, in a long speech, 27 Oct. 1775, declared:

> I am against the present war . . . because I think it unjust in its commencement, injurious to both countries in its prosecution, and ruinous in its event. It is staking the fate of a great empire against a shadow. The quarrel which occasioned it, took its rise from the assertion of a right, at best but doubtful in itself; a right from whence the warmest advocates for it have long been forced to admit that this country can never derive a single shilling of advantage.[4]

Adair made several speeches advocating Opposition measures of reform, and, as a Dissenter and advocate of the abolition of subscription to the 39 Articles, spoke for Sir Henry Hoghton's bill for the relief of Protestant Dissenters, 10 Mar. 1779. In the debate, 28 Apr. 1780, on Burke's economical reforms he 'urged the absolute necessity of complying with the prayers of the petitions in regard to economy', and he himself introduced a motion, 19 May, 'relative to giving satisfaction to the people respecting the grievances set forth in their petitions—no more sums of money granted for the public services till grievances stated in the petitions be redressed'. According to the *Parliamentary Register* he 'was up for nearly an hour, was very able, and remarkably well heard . . . and proved in a most able and convincing manner, the indispensable necessity there was of taking some effective step for the relief of the people'.[5] The *Public Ledger* wrote of Adair (1779): 'He is reckoned a good lawyer, but rather tedious in speaking.' The *City Biography*[6] states that 'his action was awkward, and his voice better suited to a rookery than a Senate'; nevertheless 'his talents . . . were strong, improved by labour and sharpened by practice; he was a correct, methodical, and plausible speaker'.

Adair was not returned by Lowther in 1780, and does not appear to have stood at the general election, but in September 1782 unsuccessfully contested Southwark. He adhered to Fox, and as Pitt gained support in the City, Adair gradually lost ground, eventually in 1789 resigning his recordership—possibly over the Regency. He broke with Fox in 1793 over the war with France.

Adair died 21 July 1798. The *Gentleman's Magazine* wrote (p. 721) in his obituary notice: 'Mr. A. was not distinguished for luminous talents; but he possessed a solid judgment, with rectitude of principle, and a deep knowledge of the laws of this country.'

[1] *Biog., Lit. & Political Anecs.* (1797) i. 83–91. [2] Adair to Rockingham, 17 and 18 May 1769, Rockingham mss. [3] Almon, iii. 65. [4] Ibid. [5] Debrett, xvii. 598, 708. [6] Anon. pamphlet, 1800.

M.M.D.

## ADAM, Robert (1728–92), of Dowhill, Kinross.

### KINROSS-SHIRE 1768–1774

*b.* 3 July 1728, 2nd s. of William Adam of Maryburgh, Kinross, architect and master mason to the Board of Ordnance in Scotland, by Mary, da. of William Robertson of Gladney, Fife; uncle of William Adam (q.v.). *educ.* Kirkcaldy; Edinburgh h.s.; Edinburgh Univ. 1743, *unm. suc.* to the ruined castle of Dowhill on *d.* of fa. 1748.

Jt. architect to Board of Works 1762–8.

Adam's father, having made a fortune in private practice and by Ordnance contracts, purchased a 4,000 acre estate in Kinross and an interest in the Pinkie coalfield. Robert, the most brilliant of four brothers, all architects, was a handsome, high-spirited, ambitious young man, the close friend of his cousin William Robertson, David Hume, John Home, Gilbert Elliot (q.v.), and other Edinburgh *literati*.[1] From 1754 to 1757 he travelled widely in Italy,[2] made a detailed study of Diocletian's palace at Spalato (Split) in Dalmatia, and on his return in January 1758 set up in practice in London.

Introduced to Bute by John Home in May 1758, he was mortified by his curt and haughty reception,[3] and as a 'free Scot' with a good conceit of his own 'infinite merit', strongly resented Bute's indifference.[4] With the assistance of Gilbert Elliot and Archibald, Duke of Argyll, Adam soon found other patrons. Admiral Boscawen (q.v.) and the Admiralty gave him important commissions (including the Admiralty House pillared screen, Whitehall), and the Adam style became the vogue, revolutionizing eighteenth-century taste. By 1760 Bute was won over and in 1761 presented him to George III, who appointed him and his rival, Sir William Chambers, royal architects. Joined in London by his two younger brothers, Adam numbered among his clients

and friends many of the Bute family connexions, Shelburne, Sir Lawrence Dundas, Lord Mansfield and Charles Townshend.

Inundated with lucrative commissions, but disappointed in his ambition to erect a royal palace or vast public building in 'pure style',[5] Adam sought the prestige of a parliamentary seat. In 1768 he relinquished his place as King's architect, which was given to his brother James; and at the general election defeated John Irwin (q.v.) in a contest for Kinross-shire.

A perfervid Scot,[6] and a regular Government supporter, he was chiefly connected in Parliament with the friends of Bute and Argyll in Administration, whose assistance he sought over his extravagant building project, the Adelphi. In 1768 the brothers obtained a lease of the Durham Yard river bank area, began operations in 1769, and, to complete their design, proposed to embank and reclaim the swampy foreshore. Their petition seeking parliamentary sanction was supported by the King and North, but opposed by the City of London and the companies of watermen and lightermen. It was managed chiefly by Adam's friends, Archibald Edmonstone, Lord Frederick Campbell, Sir George Colebrooke, and Jeremiah Dyson (qq.v.). The Adams's bill was backed by almost all their fellow Scots, of whom only Henry Dundas, otherwise friendly, demurred at the proposal of 6 Mar. 1771 to exclude additional Opposition evidence. During the stormy debates Adam himself spoke only once, on 20 Mar. 1771, when he repudiated the charge that the bill was being rushed through by 'parliamentary craft'.[7]

In June 1772 the brothers' speculative building schemes were halted by the general credit crisis. On 27 June David Hume wrote to Adam Smith:[8]

Of all the sufferers I am the most concerned for the Adams . . . But their undertakings were so rash that nothing could support them. They must dismiss 3,000 workmen, who, comprehending the materials, must have expended above £100,000 a year. They have great funds but if these must be disposed of in a hurry and to disadvantage, I am afraid the remainder will amount to little or nothing . . . If Sir George Colebrooke stop, it will probably disconcert all the plans of our friends, as it will diminish their patrons' influence, which is a new misfortune.

The brothers, having failed to raise sufficient funds by a loan on the family estate and a sale of their art collections, petitioned Parliament on 25 May 1773 for permission to dispose of all their assets (except the estate) by a lottery. After considerable debate, the bill, prepared by Thomas Walpole, William Pulteney, and other friends, passed both Houses. Horace Walpole commented:[9] 'What patronage of the arts in Parliament to vote the City's land to these brothers and then sanctify the sale by a bubble.' Two days before the draw, Robert wrote to William Mure, 28 Feb. 1774:[10]

> The lottery goes on most swimmingly . . . [and] bids fair to take off every ticket before the wheel turns round. We have this day paid the half of all our mortgages and whenever the deeds of assignment are ready will pay the whole. This is real felicity to honest minds.

Despite his preoccupation with finance, professional commissions, and the publication (July 1773) of the *Works in Architecture*, Adam was assiduous in attending the House. Kinross was not represented in the 1774 Parliament; Adam did not apparently seek a seat elsewhere, and for the rest of his life devoted himself to his profession.

Sensible, liberal-minded, somewhat vain, and a lively conversationalist, Adam retained the friendship and patronage of many of the leading men of his day, but, partly by the intrigues of Sir William Chambers, lost the favour of the King.[11] He died 3 Mar. 1792.

[1] For anecdotes of Adam's youth, see Carlyle, *Autobiog.* 285, 319 n. [2] Ibid. 375. A. T. Bolton, *Architecture of R. and J. Adam*, ii. 318. [3] Carlyle, 375. [4] Adam to Alex. Macmillan, 11 Aug. 1758, James Lees-Milne, *Age of Adam*, 24–25. [5] Adam to Lord Kames, 31 Mar. 1763, Bolton, i. 52–54. [6] Walpole, *Mems. Geo. III*, ii. 160. [7] Cavendish's 'Debates', Egerton 226, f. 212. [8] *Letters of D. Hume* ed. Greig, ii. 263. [9] Walpole to Rev. W. Mason, 17 Sept. 1773. [10] *Caldwell Pprs.* ii(2), p. 230. [11] The King to North, 5 June 1777, Fortescue, iii. 452; Adam to Lord Buchan, 19 Sept. 1781, Bolton, i. 123.

E.H.-G.

## ADAM, William (1751–1839), of Woodstone, Kincardine and Blair-Adam, Kinross.

| | |
|---|---|
| GATTON | 27 Dec. 1774–1780 |
| WIGTOWN BURGHS | 1780–1784 |
| ELGIN BURGHS | 1784–1790 |
| ROSS-SHIRE | 1790–Apr. 1794 |
| KINCARDINESHIRE | 1806–Jan. 1812 |

*b.* 2 Aug. 1751, o. surv. s. of John Adam of Blair-Adam, architect and master mason to the Board of Ordnance in Scotland, by Jean, da. and h. of John Ramsay of Woodstone. *educ.* Edinburgh Univ.; Ch. Ch. Oxf. 1769; L. Inn 1769; ?Grand Tour.[1] Adv. 1773; called to the English bar 1782. *m.* 7 May 1777, Eleanora, da. of Charles, 10th Lord Elphinstone, sis. of George Keith Elphinstone (q.v.), 5 s. 1 da. *suc.* fa. June 1792.

Treasurer of the Ordnance Sept. 1780–May 1782, Apr.–Dec. 1783; solicitor-gen. 1802–5, attorney-gen. 1805–6 to the Prince of Wales; chancellor of Duchy of Cornwall 1806–15; baron of the Scottish ct. of Exchequer 1814–19; P.C. 17 Mar. 1815; lord chief commr. of the Scottish jury ct. 1815–*d*. Ld. lt. Kinross 1802–*d*.

From his youth Adam, brought up among the Edinburgh *literati*, experienced recurring reverses in his family fortunes. In 1764 his father lost heavily by the failure of Fairholme's bank,[2] but by 1769 had recovered sufficiently to give his sons an English

education, and 'incur more hazards' in the Adelphi project.[3] After the 1772 crash the Blair estate was mortgaged, but William's own small Kincardineshire estate was not apparently involved. He abandoned the Scottish bar in 1774 when brought in for Gatton by Sir William Mayne (q.v.), a family friend.

He soon made his mark as a forceful speaker of independent views; on 6 Feb. 1775 he advocated strong measures against America; opposed North's conciliation proposal as 'waiving Britain's supremacy', yet voted with the Opposition on Wilkes, 22 Feb. 1775. On 27 Oct., supporting the Address, he praised North's ability, but lectured him on his indolence. North's deference to his 'candour' aroused suspicions that Adam was the mouthpiece of discontented ministerial Scots; but he pursued his independent course, attacked Government mismanagement, supported Fox's demand, 20 Feb. 1776, for an inquiry into the ill success of British arms, but remained adamant against conciliation. He supported Government on the suspension of the Habeas Corpus Act, 17 Feb. 1777, as a necessary measure long overdue; and on 16 Apr. justified with specious arguments the payment of the civil list debts. Walpole wrote: 'Young Adam, on this occasion, made a foolish speech of impudent paradoxes which the House received with every mark of ridicule and contempt.' Having opposed on 21 Nov. 1777 any negotiation with rebels still in arms, in February 1778 he acquiesced reluctantly in the conciliation mission, whose failure he predicted.[4]

In April 1778 Adam accepted a lieutenant's commission in Buccleuch's Southern Fencibles. Experience of the weakness of home defence convinced him of the Government's incapacity to make war against both America and France. On 27 Nov. 1778 he urged priority for the French war 'leaving America at rest', and strongly supported the Opposition's demand for an inquiry into ministerial mismanagement. Adam now began to vote with the Opposition; was listed 'contra, absent' on the contractors bill, 12 Feb. 1779; but in the March debates on Keppel he withheld his vote, maintaining that although he believed the Admiralty culpable, there was insufficient evidence for a vote of censure.[5]

During the recess Adam convinced himself that incompetent commanders were probably more to blame than ministers for the ill success of the war. On 25 Nov. 1779 he 'apprized the House of his intention to abandon the minority' and to vote against the motion for the removal of the ministry, who were at least preferable to an Opposition pledged to 'abject concessions' to the Americans.[6] Ridiculed by Fox and lampooned in the newspapers,

Adam challenged Fox to a duel in which, with a pistol borrowed from William Fullarton (q.v.), he slightly wounded his adversary.

From now on he spoke and voted for the Government, while still professing independence. On 22 Mar. 1780, after Fullarton's duel with Shelburne, he rose to defend his friend and to repudiate newspaper abuse of his own motives in challenging Fox:[7]

> He declared to God he had no motive whatever but [defence of his honour]. So far from being guilty of the base servility of hoping to please a minister by what he had done, he disclaimed any connexion whatever with the minister; he thanked God he could say he had never crossed the threshold of that minister's door, he had never asked him a favour, nor had he any favour to ask him.

Despite the efforts of his friend Charles Jenkinson, Adam had no promise of a seat in the next Parliament.[8] North and Robinson opened negotiations with Lord Stair to secure Wigtown Burghs for Adam, who, before leaving for Scotland in September, was unexpectedly offered a place as lord of Trade.[9] When the appointment was not gazetted, Jenkinson wrote to Adam, 20 Sept.:[10]

> Lord Lisburne was to have been comptroller of the Household which he has declined. This has prevented a removal from the Board of Trade which would have made a vacancy for you. I have reason to believe that they are endeavouring to contrive this in some other way.

When these endeavours failed, North nominated Adam treasurer of the Ordnance, and wrote to the King, 24 Sept.:[11]

> Mr. Adam does not know of this appointment and Lord North is afraid will not much like it as he expected to be a lord of Trade but . . . Lord North imagines he will prefer the treasurer of the Ordnance to remaining out of place.

'Curious' but not offended at the change, Adam accepted.[12]

Returned for Wigtown Burghs after a hard bargain with Stair,[13] he immediately went into action against the Opposition. On 13 Nov. he attacked the Westminster Association's pledge to guard Fox's life as an insinuation against himself. Repudiating newspaper vilification of his own character, Adam ridiculed Fox as 'the King of Westminster' whose dissipation he contrasted with his own 'private and retired' family life and 'strict domestic economy'.[14] Adam now became North's intimate friend and defender, frequently singled out for Opposition attack. On 26 Mar. 1781, in the debate on the Government loan, he denied he was the William Adam listed among the subscribers and protested his integrity:[15]

> He first came into that House . . . perfectly independent and unconnected. He opposed the minister as long

as he thought the American war was pursued for unjust purposes; but when the question changed, when the sole object was the maintaining the rights of the British legislature and preventing the independence of America, the question met with his entire approbation . . . But even now, if the noble lord's measures should appear to him more likely to do more harm than good, or adopt ideas of altering the British constitution, or listen to any visionary project of innovation, he would as steadily oppose as he now supported him . . . The place he held . . . was bestowed upon him unasked and unsought for. He had neither directly or indirectly a share in the loan.

He loyally supported North to the end.

Deprived of his place by North's resignation, Adam was also harassed by yet another crisis in his father's financial affairs. He decided to seek a career at the English bar, and for a while took little part in parliamentary debates. In October 1782 Shelburne, having already gained Dundas, sent for Adam who ignored his hints of preferment, being resolved to remain attached solely to North.[16] But when, over the peace, North and his friends were obliged to declare themselves, Adam and Jenkinson strongly favoured a conditional alliance with the ministry.[17] When Dundas insisted that, to placate Pitt, North must accept humiliating terms, Adam, 'incensed and provoked', concurred in the view that the only way to prevent the ruin of the North party was an immediate alliance with Fox. Adam thus bore a major responsibility for the Fox–North Coalition.[18] In the debate of 17–18 Feb. 1783 Adam accordingly spoke and voted against the peace,[19] and on the formation of the Portland Administration in April was restored to his place in the Ordnance.

Adam resented Dundas's retention of the lord advocate's office and control of Scottish patronage which he hoped to secure for himself, and on Dundas's removal sought to undermine his interest in Midlothian.[20]

Although now a successful barrister, 'overwhelmed with briefs',[21] Adam was still in financial difficulties. Early in November 1783 he sought permission to exchange places with John Anstruther, receiver of bishops' rents in Scotland—an appointment not so valuable as his treasurership but 'less in the hurricane latitudes'.[22] But before anything was done the Coalition was dismissed.

On 19 Dec. 1783 Adam spoke against a dissolution, eulogizing North and his union with Fox. With no chance of re-election in Wigtown Burghs, he transferred to Elgin Burghs on the Elphinstone interest, and immediately after the general election prepared a list of the new Parliament, indicating the political alignment of all its members. He immediately attacked the Government on the Address; opposed Pitt's East India bill, constituted himself the champion of reduced officers, and of Scottish grievances under the Distillery Act, and took a prominent part in the debates on Fox's Westminster election.[23]

From the spring of 1785 Adam was obliged to devote himself almost exclusively to his bar practice. The Adam brothers' partnership was now on the verge of bankruptcy, and the Blair estate had again to be mortgaged. Deeply distressed by 'this afflicting business' Adam wrote to his brother-in-law George Loch, 30 Apr. 1785:[24]

> My father's fortune is deeply involved in the concerns of my uncles ... there is much embarrassment and difficulty ... As for myself and Elie, we consider it only as a diminution of income for the time, which we must accommodate ourselves to, till by additional exertion of industry I can make it more.

Adam's concern with parliamentary affairs in the 1785–6 session was therefore perfunctory. Consistently opposed to innovation, he resisted proposals for the reform of Scottish burghs,[25] was a manager of the impeachment both of Hastings and of Impey, and acquired a great knowledge of Indian affairs. He was active throughout the Regency crisis in party management, organizing a comprehensive collection of confidential information on the electoral interests in the Scottish counties and the political affiliations of every freeholder, for use in the event of a change of Government.[26]

A warm hearted, popular man, exceptionally able in business management, he was a close personal friend of the Prince of Wales, and in later years of Sir Walter Scott. Despite financial stringency he sacrificed preferment to his political principles and personal loyalties. Comparatively late in life he was rewarded with high legal office in his native country, where he died 17 Feb. 1839.

[1] Adam to Mountstuart, 12 Nov. 1781, Add. 38774, f. 74, where he refers to M. Jacque (sec. to Lord Mountstuart in Turin) as an old friend and excellent tutor. [2] David Hume to Hugh Blair, 26 Apr. 1764, Greig, *Letters of Hume*, i. 436; Hume to James Edmonstone, Apr. 1764, Klibansky and Mossner, *New Letters of Hume*, 82. [3] Hume to Adam Smith, 27 June 1772, *Letters of Hume*, ii. 263. [4] Almon, i. 158, 207; iii. 58–59, 332; iv. 260–2; vii. 85–88; viii. 31; xi. 66–68; Walpole, *Last Jnls*. i. 529; ii. 21. [5] Almon, xi. 66–68; xii. 81–82. [6] Almon, xvi. 9–12. [7] Almon, xvii. 408. [8] Adam to Jenkinson, ? July 1780, Add. 38215, f. 70, and 4 Aug., Add. 38214, f. 126. [9] Adam to Jenkinson, 10 and 19 Sept. 1780, Add. 38214, ff. 169, 182; North to the King, 4 Sept. 1780, Fortescue, v. 114. [10] Add. 38308, f. 8b. [11] Fortescue, v. 132. [12] Adam to Jenkinson, 28 Sept. 1780, Add. 38214, f. 194. [13] Corresp. between Adam and Jenkinson, 9, 12 Dec. 1780, 13, 16 Jan. 1781, Add. 38215, ff. 23, 111, and 38308, ff. 59, 68. [14] Debrett, i. 82–84. [15] Ibid. ii. 335, 340. [16] *Mems. C. J. Fox*, ii. 31. [17] Adam to Jenkinson, 3 Jan. 1783, Add. 38218, f. 154; Jenkinson to Adam, 4 Jan., Add. 38309, f. 77. [18] *Mems. C. J. Fox*, ii. 28–39. [19] Debrett, ix. 289. [20] Adam to Portland, 24 July, 16 and 23 Sept. 1783, Portland mss; Alex Carlyle, *Autobiog*. 308. [21] Adam to W. Eden, 25 Sept. 1783, Add. 34419, f. 271. [22] Adam to Portland, 7 Nov. 1783, Portland mss. [23] Debrett, xii. 457; xv. 33–35; xvii. 30, 31, 35, 213, 366–7; Stockdale, iii. 188; vi. 494. [24] Add. 40885, f. 221. [25] Stockdale, xii. 177. [26] *Pol. State Scotland 1788* (pub. by his descendant Sir C. Elphinstone Adam, 1889).

E.H.-G.

## ADAMS, George (1731–89), of Sambrook, Salop, and Shugborough, Staffs.

| | |
|---|---|
| SALTASH | 1761–1768 |
| LICHFIELD | 31 Jan. 1770–27 Oct. 1789 |

*bap*. 25 July 1731, 1st s. of Sambrook Adams of Sambrook by Janet, da. of William Anson, sis. of Thomas (q.v.) and Adm. Lord Anson. *m*. 5 Jan. 1763, Hon. Mary Venables Vernon, da. of George, 1st Baron Vernon (q.v.), 8s. 3da. *suc*. to estates of his uncle Thomas Anson, and took name of Anson 1773.

Adams was returned for Saltash in 1761 through the influence of his uncle Lord Anson, then first lord of the Admiralty. In Parliament he followed the lead of his uncle Thomas Anson, and in February 1764 joined the Opposition. He supported the Rockingham Administration, but in November 1766 went back into opposition. In 1768 he could not expect to be returned again for an Admiralty borough, and he was out of Parliament until January 1770 when his uncle vacated the family seat at Lichfield.

Anson (as Adams became in 1773) consistently opposed North's Administration. He voted for Shelburne's peace preliminaries, 18 Feb. 1783, and was classed in Robinson's list as influenced by Lord Hardwicke (Lord Anson had married the sister of the 2nd Earl of Hardwicke). Anson voted for Fox's East India bill, 27 Nov. 1783, and on 16 Dec. Fox wrote to request his 'immediate attendance' in Parliament:[1]

> The indecent interference which has defeated the India bill in the House of Lords has alarmed the minds of all men ... I am sure you will do me the justice to believe that I should not write in this manner to a gentleman with whom I have so little the honour of acquaintance if the critical situation of things did not justify me.

Anson was classed by Robinson January 1784 as 'Opposition', and remained with them until his death, 27 Oct. 1789.

[1] Earl of Lichfield's mss.

J.B.

## ADAMS, James (1752–1816), of Doctors' Commons, London.

| | |
|---|---|
| WEST LOOE | 21 Aug. 1784–1790 |
| HINDON | 1790–1796 |
| BRAMBER | 1796–1802 |
| HARWICH | 7 Apr. 1803–1806, 9 Mar.–29 Apr. 1807 |

*b*. 5 June 1752, 1st s. of Sir Richard Adams, baron of the Exchequer 1753–73, by his w. née Molinier of Putney. *educ*. Univ. Coll. Oxf. 1769; I. Temple 1769; adv. Doctors' Commons. *m*. 10 Sept. 1796, Mary Anne Susanna, da. and coh. of Leonard Hammond of Cheam, Surr., *s.p.* Her sis. Ursula Mary, was 1st w. of

Henry Addington (q.v.), 1st Visct. Sidmouth. *suc.* fa. 1753.

Ld. of Admiralty 1801–4.

Adams's return for West Looe on the Buller interest was presumably arranged by Administration. His first recorded vote was with Opposition on Richmond's fortifications plan, 27 Feb. 1786, but he voted with Administration on the impeachment of Impey, 9 May 1788 and the Regency, 1788–9. His only reported speech during the Parliament of 1784–1790 was in the debate on the impeachment of Hastings, 11 Dec. 1787, when he said that he had voted against the inclusion of Philip Francis (q.v.) among the managers because 'it was not becoming the honour and dignity of their proceedings for that House to appoint for one of their managers . . . the only one of its Members who had . . . had a personal quarrel with Mr. Hastings'.[1]

He died 14 Sept. 1816.

[1] Stockdale, xiii. 89.

M.M.D.

## ADAMS, John (?1746–1817), of Peterwell, Card.

CARMARTHEN    1774–1780

*b.* ?1746, s. of John Adams of Whitland, Carm. by his 2nd w. Elizabeth, da. of Walter Lloyd, M.P., of Peterwell. *educ.* Queen's, Oxf. 23 Jan. 1766, aged 19; L. Inn 1765, called 1772. *suc.* uncle Sir Herbert Lloyd (q.v.) 19 Aug. 1769.

In 1767 John Adams gave £4,000 towards the rebuilding of Carmarthen guildhall. He was returned unopposed in 1774 on the interest of Griffith Philipps (q.v.). He had also purchased a seat of Lord Verney at Wendover, which he presumably sold after having been returned at Carmarthen. In the House he consistently supported North's Administration, and though Lord Lisburne (q.v.) wrote that Adams had 'an appetite for Parliament'[1] there is no indication that he ever took part in debate. When Philipps dropped him in 1780 Adams canvassed Cardigan, where his estate gave him an interest, but declined the poll.

He had found the Peterwell estate heavily mortgaged, and long before his death had spent his inheritance and sold the estate.[2] He died 2 June 1817.

[1] To W. Powell, 22 May 1780, Nanteos mss, NLW. [2] S. R. Meyrick, *Hist. Card.* 209.

P.D.G.T.

## ADAMSON, Robert (1753–1817), of Oaksey, Wilts.

CRICKLADE    13 Apr. 1784–4 Apr. 1785

*b.* 1753, s. of Benjamin Adamson of Henley, Oxon. and Oaksey by Alice, da. and coh. of Sir Robert Westley, ld. mayor of London 1744–5. *educ.* Eton 1761–70; Magdalen, Oxf. 1770. *m.* 19 Mar. 1790, Miss Bruce of Lower Grosvenor St., London.

In May 1782 Adamson announced his candidature for the reformed constituency of Cricklade, in opposition to G. R. St. John, Robert Nicholas, and Samuel Petrie. He was considered a supporter of Lord North. Finding himself the weakest of the contestants, he negotiated a compromise with St. John, and stood down in his favour.[1]

At the general election in 1784 he came forward again, in partnership with his cousin C. W. Coxe, and stood against Nicholas and J. W. Heneage, supporters of Pitt.[2] Adamson and Coxe were returned but unseated on petition. No vote or speech of Adamson's in the House is recorded.

Adamson does not appear to have sought to re-enter Parliament. He died 17 Sept. 1817.

[1] Nicholas to Shelburne, 31 May and 12 June 1782, Lansdowne mss. [2] *Glocester Jnl.* 12 Apr. 1784.

J.A.C.

## ADDINGTON, Henry (1757–1844), of Mortimer, Berks.

DEVIZES    1784–12 Jan. 1805

*b.* 30 May 1757, 1st s. of Anthony Addington, M.D., of Fringford, Oxon. by Mary, da. and h. of Rev. Haviland John Hiley of Reading. *educ.* Cheam; Winchester 1768; B.N.C. Oxf. 1774; L. Inn 1772; I. Temple 1780, called 1784. *m.* (1) 19 Sept. 1781, Ursula Mary (*d.*23 June 1811), da. and coh. of Leonard Hammond of Cheam, Surr., 2s. 4da.; (2) 29 July 1823, Mary Anne, da. and h. of William Scott, 1st Baron Stowell, wid. of Thomas Townshend of Honington, Warws., *s.p.* *suc.* fa. 22 Mar. 1790; *cr.* Visct. Sidmouth 12 Jan. 1805.

Recorder, Devizes 1784–*d.*; Speaker of House of Commons June 1789–Feb. 1801; P.C. 23 June 1789; first ld. of the Treasury Mar. 1801–May 1804; ld. president of the Council Jan.–July 1805; ld. privy seal Feb.–Oct. 1806; ld. president Oct. 1806–Mar. 1807, Apr.–June 1812; Home sec. June 1812–Jan. 1822; Cabinet minister without office Jan. 1822–Nov. 1824.

Addington had planned a legal career, but by 1782 he was developing a friendship with William Pitt; the two having first met in childhood when Addington's father had been Lord Chatham's physician. Their friendship was sufficiently advanced by the spring of 1783 for Charles Bragge to expect Addington to receive some official position 'under the auspices of your illustrious friend'; but Pitt's going out of office put an end to such hopes. These revived when Pitt returned to power: 'Secretary, either official or confidential, I should wish you', wrote Bragge on 30 Dec. 1783, but Addington received no appointment.[1]

About this time Addington was offered a seat in Parliament. 'Whoever the gentleman was who made you that unexpected offer', wrote his father, 'you judged right in my opinion to decline it. I believe you are an enemy to corruption in all shapes, and as such have good reason to depend on an unbought seat in Parliament in case of a dissolution.'[2] On 29 Jan. 1784 Addington wrote to Reginald Pole Carew (q.v.): 'If a dissolution had taken place, I had a flattering prospect of succeeding at ——. That event is deferred, but I trust . . . to no very remote period.' The blank may in all probability be filled in as Devizes. Addington's brother-in-law, James Sutton of New Park, had until 1780 shared its representation with its recorder, Charles Garth. In 1780 Addington had spent the summer there with the Suttons, and won general esteem; so much that, when Sutton decided to retire, 'several of Mr. Sutton's friends in the borough would indeed have preferred him as their representative to Sir James Long; but Mr. Sutton's influence being already pledged in the baronet's favour, Mr. Addington's claims were not prominently paraded until . . . 1784',[3] when, on the death of Garth, Addington was elected recorder,[4] and at the general election Member with Long. His opponent John Lubbock, after an unsuccessful canvass, declined a poll.[5]

When Addington entered the House, according to his own admission, he knew personally only three Members. He was not eager to answer the expectations of his friends by becoming a conspicuous figure, and there is no record of his speaking before Pitt persuaded him to second the Address at the opening of the 1786 session: 'I will not disguise that in asking this favour of you, I look beyond the immediate object of the first day's debate, from a persuasion that whatever induces you to take a part in public, will equally contribute to your personal credit, and to that of the system to which I have the pleasure of thinking you are so warmly attached.' Thomas Harley (q.v.) is reported to have said that 'he had never heard an address so well seconded'.[6] But Addington did not speak again until 2 May 1787.

Though a reluctant speaker in the House, Addington was a keen committee man; and it was generally expected that he would soon be given office. Still, his record was hardly such as to qualify him for the post of Speaker. Lord Graham, in proposing him to the House on 8 June 1789, remarked that although young, 'his judgment was of full maturity', and that his 'very superior' abilities were well-known to his friends.[7] But his opponent, Sir Gilbert Elliot, with greater candour wrote on 6 June:[8]

Pitt could not have made a more obnoxious choice than this one. This is Addington's first Parliament. He is son of Lord Chatham's physician, and is in fact a sort of dependant to the family. The chair has hitherto been filled by persons of quite a different description, either eminent for abilities, experience, or rank, or of independent situations and characters.

Pitt's friends allow that Addington is a very improper person for this office, and it has given great offence; but I do not believe this will make much difference to the event.

Addington's conduct as Speaker, however, won the approbation of his opponents. In the debate on a motion for settling a salary of £5000 on the Speaker, 15 Mar. 1790, an amendment for increasing the amount to £6000 was carried by a very considerable majority; and Welbore Ellis, who in 1789 had proposed Elliot, declared that Addington 'had completely fulfilled the expectations of his friends, and by his propriety and impartiality engaged and secured the general good opinion of the House'.[9] Still, his appointment to the conduct of affairs in 1801 was regarded as a mere stop-gap.

He died 15 Feb. 1844.

[1] Pellew, *Life of Sidmouth*, i. 30, 31. [2] Ibid., 32. [3] *Hist. Devizes* (anon. 1859), 462. [4] B. H. Cunnington, *Annals of Devizes 1555-1791*, p. 231. [5] Pellew, i. 34-35. [6] Ibid. 38, 40, 47. [7] Stockdale, xvii. 286-7. [8] Lady Minto, *Life of Elliot*, i. 321-2. [9] Stockdale, xix. 155.

M.H.P.

**ADDINGTON, John Hiley** (1759-1818), of Chetwood, Som.

| | |
|---|---|
| TRURO | 6 Mar. 1787-1790 |
| WINCHELSEA | 17 Feb. 1794-1796 |
| WENDOVER | 1796-1802 |
| BOSSINEY | 31 Aug.-Dec. 1802 |
| HARWICH | 4 Jan. 1803-11 June 1818 |

*b.* 1759, 2nd s. of Anthony Addington, M.D., and bro. of Henry (q.v.). *educ.* Cheam; Winchester 1769; B.N.C. Oxf. 1776. *m.* 25 Oct. 1785, Mary, da. and h. of Henry Unwin of Stock, Essex, 2s. 1da.

Ld. of Treasury Dec. 1800-Mar. 1801 and July 1802-Nov. 1803; sec. to Treasury Mar. 1801-2; jt. paymaster gen. Jan. 1803-July 1804; P.C. 16 Feb. 1803; commr. for Indian affairs Feb. 1806-Apr. 1807; under-sec. of state for Home affairs 1812-18.

High steward, Harwich 1803-*d.*

Hiley Addington 'while a boy, was left a considerable fortune by a relation'; and he acquired another by marriage.[1] His parliamentary career he owed to his brother Henry (q.v.), whose interests he looked after at Devizes in the general election of 1784.[2] Pitt wrote to Henry on 14 July 1786 proposing that Hiley might, at no expense to himself, come in for Berwick-on-Tweed, on Lord Delaval's interest.[3] Hiley, however, was defeated. Several months later he was returned on Lord Falmouth's interest at Truro. No speech of his is recorded before 1790; he voted with Pitt in the Regency crisis.

To his brother's regret, Hiley was not returned in

1790.[4] He subsequently held several minor ministerial posts, and died 11 June 1818.

[1] J. Wilson, *Biog. Index. to Commons*, 1806, p. 10. [2] Hiley to Hen. Addington, Apr. 1784, Sidmouth mss. [3] Sidmouth mss. [4] Hen. Addington to R. P. Carew, 10 July 1790, Sidmouth mss.

M.H.P.

## ADEANE, James Whorwood (1740–1802), of Babraham, Cambs. and Chalgrove, Oxon.

CAMBRIDGE                     1780–May 1789
CAMBRIDGESHIRE    19 May 1789–15 Apr. 1802

*bap.* 14 Dec. 1740, o.s. of Simon Adeane[1] of Chalgrove by Mary, da. of Hon. and Rev. Henry Brydges (bro. of James, 1st Duke of Chandos). *educ.* ?Westminster 1750–4. *m.* c.1763, Anne, da. and h. of Robert Jones (q.v.), 1s. 3da. *suc.* fa. 1747.
    Entered army 1755;[2] lt. 71 Ft. 1757; capt. 67 Ft. 1761; lt. and capt. 1st troop Horse Gren. Gds. 1763; maj. 1768; capt. and lt.-col. 1770; col. 1779; maj.-gen. 1782; col. 45 Ft. 1788–*d.*; lt.-gen. 1796; gen. 1801.
    Groom of the bedchamber 1784–*d.*

Adeane's own property lay in Oxfordshire and Buckinghamshire, but in 1774 his son, then a child, inherited the estate of Babraham (6½ miles outside Cambridge) under the will of his maternal grandfather, and in November 1776 Adeane announced his intention of standing for Cambridge at the next vacancy. He assiduously cultivated an interest there, and according to Dr. Ewin, a Cambridge correspondent of Lord Hardwicke, declared that he would spend £10,000 to secure his return.[3] By 16 Jan. 1780 Ewin reported[4] that Adeane obviously thought he was

> clear in his seat for this town, indeed the attention he pays to it by his almost constant weekly visits and making a point of buying everything he wants here, gains him many friends, and he makes himself all things to all men, rather too much so.

Nevertheless, a sudden demand for his qualification just before the poll so confused Adeane that, according to Ewin,[5] 'he was inclined to give it up', and was only saved by his wife producing the necessary information, whereupon he was returned at the head of the poll.

In Parliament Adeane seems at first to have supported North's Administration; was classed as 'pro' in Robinson's survey of February 1781,[6] and does not appear in the Opposition list on Lowther's motion against the war, 12 Dec. 1781; but he voted with Opposition on the censure motion against the Admiralty, 20 Feb. 1782, and in the four subsequent divisions for which lists are extant before the fall of North. Adeane voted for Shelburne's peace preliminaries, 18 Feb. 1783, for Pitt's parliamentary reform proposals, 7 May 1783, and against Fox's East India bill, 27 Nov. 1783. He was classed as

'pro' in Robinson's list of January 1784 and in Stockdale's of 19 Mar.

At the general election of 1784 Adeane was returned for Cambridge unopposed. During this Parliament his only reported votes were in favour of Pitt's parliamentary reform proposals, 18 Apr. 1785, and Richmond's fortifications plan, 27 Feb. 1786. In the debate of 18 May 1786, when John Mortlock, Adeane's fellow Member for Cambridge, was accused of altering several names in a list of commissioners for executing the Land Tax Act, Adeane, who had officially delivered the list, intervened several times to pursue the charges, and produced a resolution of 1780 'stating that any person's altering any paper belonging to that House, was to be deemed and considered as highly criminal'—his only reported speech before 1790.[7]

When in May 1789 the death of Sir Henry Peyton vacated one of the Cambridge county seats, Adeane used his appointment as groom of the bedchamber five years previously as a means to vacate his seat at Cambridge, and with the support of the Rutland family[8] was returned for the county unopposed.

Adeane died 15 Apr. 1802.

[1] I. R. Christie, 'Adeane of Babraham', *Gen. Mag.* xiii, pp. 385–6. [2] Adeane to Pitt, 9 Mar. 1788, Chatham mss. [3] Add. 35626, f. 22. [4] To Hardwicke, ibid. f. 107. [5] Ewin to Hardwicke, 7 Sept. 1780, ibid. f. 174; W. Cole's account of the election confirms this report. [6] Abergavenny mss. [7] Stockdale, viii. 307–8, 399, 403, 465. [8] Duchess of Rutland to Pitt, 27 Mar. 1789, Chatham mss.

M.M.D.

## AFFLECK, Edmund (1725–88), of Fingringhoe Hall, nr. Colchester, Essex.

COLCHESTER    4 Mar. 1782–19 Nov. 1788

*b.* 19 Apr. 1725, 9th s. of Gilbert Affleck, M.P., and bro. of John Affleck (q.v.). *m.* (1) Esther (*d.*15 Dec. 1787), da. of John Ruth, wid. of Peter Creffield of Ardleigh Hall, nr. Colchester, *s.p.*; (2) 14 May 1788, Margaret, née Burgess, wid. of Rev. William Smithers, vicar of St. Peter's, Colchester, *s.p.* *cr.* Bt. 10 July 1782, with sp. rem. to heirs male of his fa.
    Lt. R.N. 1745; capt. 1757; r.-adm. 1784.

Affleck was on active service 1778–83, most of the time in American waters, and, in 1782, was created a baronet for his part in the action off Dominica. He was abroad at the time of his election for Colchester, and 'totally ignorant of his having been set up as a candidate'.[1] The election was managed by Richard Rigby (q.v.), who obtained a promise of Government help not exceeding '£1,500 or £2,000 at the most'.[2] Affleck was defeated by Christopher Potter (q.v.), but returned on petition.

He did not take his seat until 23 Jan. 1784[3] and then cannot have played a prominent part in debates as he was still marked absent in Stockdale's list of 19 Mar. 1784. On 26 Mar. he wrote from

Colchester to John Robinson asking for his interest at the approaching election.[4] He was returned head of the poll.

He was classed by William Adam in May 1784 as 'doubtful', and does not appear in any division list for this Parliament. Two speeches by him are recorded, on 5 Mar. 1787 and 29 Apr. 1788,[5] both testifying to the conduct of naval officers with whom he had served.

He died 19 Nov. 1788.

[1] Debrett, v. 282. [2] North to John Robinson, 1 Oct. 1781, Abergavenny mss. [3] *Morning Chron.* 23 Jan. 1784. [4] Abergavenny mss. [5] Debrett, xxi. 374; xxii. 527.

J.B.

**AFFLECK, John** (1710–76), of Dalham, nr. Bury St. Edmunds, Suff.

SUFFOLK 23 Mar. 1743–1761
AMERSHAM 4 Dec. 1767–1768

*b.* 12 Feb. 1710, 1st s. of Gilbert Affleck, M.P., of Dalham by Anne, da. of John Dolben of Finedon, Northants. *educ.* Westminster 1722; Ch. Ch. Oxf. 1727; I. Temple 1728. *m.* 1736, Sarah, da. of James Metcalfe of Roxton, Beds., 3s. *suc.* fa. 12 Nov. 1764.

Affleck was present at the meeting convened on 14 Jan. 1757 by George Townshend (q.v.), apparently with Pitt's approval, to discuss how to proceed with the inquiry into the loss of Minorca. He declined to stand again in 1761 but, to preserve the peace of the county, seems to have taken a hand in fixing up the succession.[1]

At Amersham he sat on the Drake interest as a stop-gap until the general election of 1768. He died 17 Feb. 1776.

[1] See SUFFOLK constituency and BUNBURY, Thomas Charles.

L.B.N.

**AISLABIE, William** (?1699–1781), of Studley Royal, nr. Ripon, Yorks.

RIPON 1 Apr. 1721–17 May 1781

*b.* ?1699, 1st s. of John Aislabie, M.P., chancellor of the Exchequer 1718–21, by his 1st w. Anne, da. of Sir William Rawlinson of Hendon, Mdx. *m.* (1) c.1722, Lady Elizabeth Cecil (*d.*6 Apr. 1733), da. of John, 6th Earl of Exeter, 2s. (*d.v.p.*) 5da.; (2) 6 Sept. 1745, Elizabeth, da. of Sir Charles Vernon (q.v.), 1s. (*d.v.p.*) 1da. *suc.* fa. 1742.
Auditor of the imprest 1738–*d.*; registrar of consist. ct. of York 1749–*d.*

Aislabie controlled both seats at Ripon, and always returned a relation for the second seat. He had opposed Walpole, and under the Pelham Administration wavered a good deal. In Newcastle's list of 1754 he was classed as 'doubtful'. After 1754 he generally supported Government, but was tho-

roughly independent. He held his two places for life.

Aislabie does not appear in Fox's list of Members supporting the peace preliminaries, nor did he vote against them. His first recorded speech in the new reign was on the motion for a committee of accounts, 22 Feb. 1763. 'Speaking of his own office [as auditor of the imprest] as a profitable one', reports James Harris, '[he] said how much more so it had been made by the large and expensive schemes of certain honourable gentlemen, looking towards Beckford but hinting at (I imagine) Pitt.' And on 6 Apr. 1764 he criticized the pay office for their delay in passing the German accounts.

Aislabie voted with the Opposition on general warrants, 15 and 18 Feb. 1764. In Rockingham's list of July 1765 he was classed as 'doubtful', but he spoke for the repeal of the Stamp Act, 24 Feb. 1766. He voted with the Chatham Administration on the land tax, 27 Feb. 1767, but against them on nullum tempus, 17 Feb. 1768. Henceforth he regularly supported Government. His last recorded speech was on the Duke of Bridgwater's canal bill, 9 Mar. 1770, and his last recorded vote on the revived motion on the Middlesex election, 26 Apr. 1773. 'His age and infirmities do not allow him to attend,' wrote the *Public Ledger* in 1779.

He died 17 May 1781, aged 81. 'The contemplation of the beauties of nature and rural occupations formed his chief and unceasing delight',[1] and his claim to remembrance is that he restored Fountains abbey.

[1] J. R. Walbran, *Mem. Lords of Studley.*

J.B.

**ALDRIDGE, John Clater** (?1737–95), of New Lodge, St. Leonard's Forest, Suss.

QUEENBOROUGH 1784–1790
NEW SHOREHAM 1790–16 May 1795

*b.* ?1737, 1st s. of Abel Aldridge of Uxbridge, Mdx. by his w. Sarah Clater. *educ.* Merton, Oxf. 16 Dec. 1754, aged 17; L. Inn 1761. *m.* Henrietta Tomlinson, wid. of William Busby of Stoughton Grange, nr. Leicester, 3s. 2da. *suc.* fa. 1782.
Storekeeper of Ordnance Apr. 1782–Apr. 1783 and Dec. 1783–*d.*

Aldridge had considerable estates in West Sussex, and twice—1774 and 1784—contested New Shoreham after its representation had been thrown into the rape of Bramber. On both occasions he was bottom of the poll. He was a friend of the Duke of Richmond, who, when master-general of the Ordnance, appointed Aldridge to be storekeeper. In 1784 Aldridge was returned after a contest on the Ordnance interest for Queenborough. Six speeches by him are recorded before 1790: four on Ordnance business, and two on a complaint of Ordnance interference at Queenborough.

He died 16 May 1795.

M.M.D.

## ALDWORTH, Richard Neville (1717–93), of Stanlake and Billingbear, Berks.

| | |
|---|---|
| READING | 1747–1754 |
| WALLINGFORD | 1754–1761 |
| TAVISTOCK | 1761–1774 |

*b.* 3 Sept. 1717, o.s. of Richard Aldworth by Catherine, da. of Richard Neville, M.P., of Billingbear. *educ.* Eton 1728–32; Merton, Oxf. 1736; Grand Tour. *m.* 1748, Magdalen, da. of Francis Calandrini, first syndic of Geneva, 1s. 1da. *suc.* fa. 1738, and on *d.* of his aunt, Elizabeth, Countess of Portsmouth, to estates of his gd.-fa. Richard Neville of Billingbear 1762, and changed his name to Neville.

Under-sec. of state 1748–51; sec. to embassy at Paris Sept. 1762–May 1763; minister plenipotentiary, Paris, May–Nov. 1763; paymaster of pensions May 1763–July 1765.

Aldworth came of an old-established Berkshire family, and for most of his political life was a follower of the Duke of Bedford.

In June 1752 Aldworth informed Bedford that he expected an opposition at Reading at the next general election, which would involve him in an expense he could not afford.[1] In December Lord Fane, another of Bedford's followers, was unexpectedly applied to by 'the most considerable inhabitants of Wallingford', and immediately recommended Aldworth as a candidate, assuming that he would 'be well pleased to get in for a town in his own county, if it can be upon terms at least as easy as elsewhere'.[2] Aldworth stood jointly with John Hervey (q.v.) against two Administration candidates, and was returned after an expensive contest. He later wrote that he was 'much indebted' to Bedford for his seat[3] —presumably he received financial assistance.

In Dupplin's list Aldworth is classed as an Opposition Whig. When towards the end of 1755 Bedford became reconciled to Administration, Aldworth followed. He was anxious to obtain office, and on 8 Feb. 1757 wrote to Bedford that Lord Portsmouth had offered to return him for Whitchurch (where a vacancy seemed probable) 'if a secure and easy seat in Parliament might, through your Grace's influence, be instrumental in getting me a place at either of the Boards of Admiralty, or Trade'.[4] Aldworth was among the minority who voted for the Minorca inquiry, 26 Apr. 1757.[5] In 1761 he was returned by Bedford at Tavistock. Like the Duke he supported the Bute Administration. On 30 May

1762 he again applied to the Duke to recommend him for employment 'at the Board of Trade or for any other post becoming an old and faithful humble servant of your Grace's'.[6] Bedford was unable to do anything immediately, but when he went to Paris in September to start negotiations for peace, he took Aldworth as his secretary. In May 1763, at Bedford's recommendation, Neville (as Aldworth now was) was appointed paymaster of pensions, but instead of immediately returning to England remained in Paris as minister till the arrival of the new ambassador. He was described by David Hume,[7] who met him in Paris, as 'an honest, worthy English gentleman'.

Neville, who lost his post as paymaster on the formation of the Rockingham Administration, voted against the repeal of the Stamp Act, 22 Feb. 1766. During the unsuccessful negotiations of December 1766 between Chatham and Bedford, he was included by the Duke among 'friends who had suffered on our account to be replaced *pari passu*'.[8] He voted against the Administration on the land tax, 27 Feb. 1767, but at the end of 1767, with the other members of the Bedford group, went over to Administration. Returned again by Bedford for Tavistock in 1768, he wrote to the Duke on 23 Oct., asking to be recommended for postmaster general, should the position become vacant:

> What makes that post an objection to most Members of Parliament, to me enhances its value; a strict attendance in the House being too much for my state of health. And though this appointment would not only be an honourable retreat from Parliament, but an ample compensation for the loss of a place, which through your Grace's kind testimony and recommendation had been given as a reward for services, yet I have a consciousness about me, of not being totally undeserving of it.

Bedford replied that he was already under fire because of the number of his friends appointed to office, and must 'wait till some more proper opportunity may present itself . . . especially as you are in such circumstances as not to need any assistance'.[9] Neville voted with the Administration over Wilkes and the Middlesex election, 3 Feb., 15 Apr., and 8 May 1769, and on Brass Crosby, 27 Mar. 1771. Robinson counted him as 'doubtful, absent' in both his surveys on the royal marriage bill, March 1772; no other vote by him was reported, and he was classed as 'pro' by Robinson in his survey of September 1774. There is no record of his having spoken during his 27 years in the House.

Neville, who for many years had suffered from continual ill-health, did not stand again for Parliament. He died 17 July 1793.

[1] Bedford mss 28, ff. 41, 49. [2] Fane to Bedford, 6 Dec. 1752 (misdated Nov.), ibid. 28, f. 80. [3] Aldworth to Bedford, 8 Feb. 1757, ibid. 33, f. 7. [4] Ibid. [5] Add. 35877, f. 363. [6] Bedford mss 45, f. 178. [7] Letters, ed. Grieg, i. 409. [8] 'Precis of the conversation betwixt Lord Chatham and me', 1 Dec. 1766, Bedford mss 54, f. 132. [9] Ibid. 57, ff. 186, 190.

M.M.D.

## ALDWORTH NEVILLE, Richard (1750–1825), of Stanlake and Billingbear, Berks.

| GRAMPOUND | 1774–1780 |
| BUCKINGHAM | 1780–Feb. 1782 |
| READING | 21 Feb. 1782–25 May 1797 |

*bap.* 29 June 1750,[1] 1st s. of Richard Neville Aldworth afterwards Neville (q.v.). *educ.* Eton 1759–67; Merton, Oxf. 1768. *m.* 9 June 1780,[2] Catherine, da. of George Grenville (q.v.), 4s. 4da. *suc.* fa. to estates of Stanlake and Billingbear 1793; and his distant cos. John Griffin Griffin, Lord Braybrooke (q.v.), under sp. rem., as 2nd Lord Braybrooke, 25 May 1797, inheriting Audley End, Essex, and took the name of Griffin.

At the general election of 1774 Neville was returned for Grampound, which had been put at the disposal of Administration by Edward Eliot (q.v.) at a cost of £2,000 a seat. In Parliament Neville seems generally to have supported Administration; he does not appear in any of the minority lists, 1775–8, and on 31 Oct. 1776 (in his one reported speech before 1790) moved an Address commending the Administration's American measures.[3] In the list on the contractors bill, 12 Feb. 1779, Neville was classed as 'contra present', but with 'friend' added. He voted with Administration on the motion for an account of pensions, 21 Feb. 1780, but with Opposition on economical reform, 8 Mar. 1780; did not vote on the motion to abolish the Board of Trade, 13 Mar., but voted with Administration on Dunning's motion, 6 Apr., and the motion against prorogation, 24 Apr. 1780; and was classed by Robinson in July 1780 as 'pro'.

When at the general election of 1780 Edward Eliot, now in Opposition, refused to re-elect Administration supporters, Neville was returned for Buckingham on the interest of his brother-in-law, Lord Temple; but having political disagreements with Temple,[4] vacated his seat at Buckingham when a vacancy occurred at Reading, and was returned after an expensive contest. His first reported vote on re-entering the House was with Opposition on Conway's motion against the war, 27 Feb. 1782. Robinson in his survey for that division noted that Neville was 'friendly, but called on at Reading on his election to vote against the American war';[5] he did not however vote on John Cavendish's censure motion, 8 Mar. 1782, or on Rous's motion of no confidence, 15 Mar. 1782. Neville voted for Shelburne's peace preliminaries, 18 Feb. 1783, and against Fox's East India bill, 27 Nov. 1783. He

was classed as pro-Pitt in Robinson's list of January 1784, in Stockdale's of 19 Mar., and by Adam in May. At the general election of 1784 he was returned unopposed for Reading. He continued to support Pitt throughout this Parliament.

Braybrooke (as he became in 1797) died 28 Feb. 1825.

[1] New Windsor par. reg. [2] Neville to James Grenville, 13 June 1780, Braybrooke mss, Berks. RO. [3] Almon, vi. 6. [4] Braybrooke to Glastonbury, 12 Sept. 1806, Braybrooke mss. [5] Abergavenny mss.

M.M.D.

## ALEXANDER, William (c.1690–1761), of Edinburgh.

| EDINBURGH | 1754–1761 |

*b.* c.1690, 2nd s. of John Alexander, Glasgow merchant, by Janet, da. of Alexander Cuninghame of Craigends, Renfrew. *m.* bef. 1721, Marianne Louisa de la Croix, of a Huguenot fam., 3s. 1da.

Director, Royal Bank of Scotland 1730–60; burgess of Edinburgh 1733; trustee for fisheries and manufactures 1738; ld. prov. Edinburgh 1752–4; commr. for forfeited estates 1755–60.

William Alexander was an Edinburgh merchant and banker engaged in the continental trade, especially in the re-export of American tobacco to France. In 1754, after considerable experience in local politics, he came forward as candidate for Edinburgh with the support of the Argyll-Milton influence, and was unanimously elected.

He did not attend the short first session of the new Parliament, but in the following session 'gave close attendance . . . from the first to last day'.[1] He was a supporter of Newcastle. George Drummond, a leading Edinburgh politician, in a letter to Newcastle of 28 Oct. 1755[2] referred to Alexander's 'honest determination to support his Majesty's Administration'. There is no record of his having spoken in the House.

In failing health, he did not stand at the general election of 1761; and died 25 July 1761.

[1] Alexander to Newcastle, 27 May 1755, Add. 32855, f. 233. [2] Add. 32860 ,f. 218.

E.H.-G.

## ALLANSON, Charles (?1720–75), of Bramham Biggin, Yorks.

| RIPON | 1768–17 Sept. 1775 |

*b.* ?1720, 1st s. of William Allanson of Little Sion, Mdx. *educ.* Queen's, Oxf. 2 May 1739, aged 18; I. Temple 1738. *m.* (1) 30 Apr. 1757, Mary (*d.*14 Oct. 1762), da. of Daniel Turner, M.D., wid. of Col. Peters, *s.p.*; (2) 14 Feb. 1765, Elizabeth, da. and coh. of William Aislabie (q.v.), *s.p.*

Allanson was returned for Ripon on the interest of his father-in-law, William Aislabie, and like him followed an independent line in the House; voted with the Administration on the expulsion of Wilkes, 3 Feb. 1769, and the Middlesex election, 15 Apr. 1769, but with Opposition on the renewal of the Middlesex question, 25 Jan. 1770. He was listed as 'doubtful, present' in both Robinson's surveys on the royal marriage bill, March 1772; as a dissenting friend in the King's list on Grenville's Election Act, 25 Feb. 1774, and as 'pro' in Robinson's survey of September 1774. There is no record of his having spoken in the House.

He died 17 Sept. 1775.

M.M.D.

## ALLANSON WINN, Sir George, 1st Bt. (1725–1798), of Bramham Biggin, Yorks.

RIPON 1 Sept. 1789–9 Apr. 1798

*b.* 1725, o.s. of Pelham Winn of South Ferriby, Lincs. by Elizabeth, da. of Rev. Gilbert Wighton by Elizabeth, sis. of William Allanson of Bramham Biggin, Yorks. *educ.* L. Inn 1744, called 1755. *m.* (1) 12 Apr. 1765, Anne (*d.*9 Oct. 1774), da. of Sir Rowland Winn, 4th Bt., of Nostell, Yorks., 1da.; (2) 24 June 1783, Jane, da. and coh. of Arthur Blennerhassett of Ballyseedy, co. Kerry, 2s. 2da. *suc.* cos. Mark Winn of Little Warley, Essex 1763; and cos. Charles Allanson (q.v.) of Bramham Biggin and took name of Allanson before Winn 20 Feb. 1777; *cr.* Bt. 14 Sept. 1776; Lord Headley [I] 27 Nov. 1797.

Baron of the Exchequer in Scotland 1761–76.

Winn was returned for Ripon by William Lawrence (q.v.) to whom he was distantly related. No vote or speech by him is known during his first Parliament.

He died 9 Apr. 1798.

M.M.D.

## ALLARDICE, *see* BARCLAY ALLARDICE

## ALLEN, Benjamin (1731–91), of Bridgwater, Som.

BRIDGWATER 1768–2 Mar. 1781

*b.* ?1731, 2nd s. of John Allen, M.D., F.R.S., of Bridgwater.[1] *educ.* Bridgwater; Sidney Suss. Camb. 4 June 1751, aged 19; M. Temple 1749, called 1754. *m.* in or bef. 1760; at least 1s.[2]

Allen took advantage of his local connexions to cultivate an interest at Bridgwater. He became a member of the corporation, and in 1768 contested the borough against the powerful Poulett interest. In Parliament Allen voted regularly with Opposition. His only reported speech was on East India affairs, 24 Mar. 1773. In 1774 he was returned unopposed. The *Public Ledger* wrote of him in 1779: 'Seems to be a fair, well-meaning man. Votes on each side conformably to his opinion, but generally in opposition.' Charles James Fox wrote to John

Chubb, of Bridgwater, 8 Apr. 1780:[3] 'I think it my duty to let you know that Mr. Allen has attended and supported the cause of the people with the most unremitting diligence.' In 1780 Allen and Fox jointly contested the borough. He, though not Fox, was returned, but was unseated on petition. Allen continued his activities on the Bridgwater corporation, and, in spite of a quarrel with Fox and his Bridgwater friends in 1785, seems to have maintained an interest in the borough, continued by his son Jefferys Allen who was returned there in 1796.

Allen died before 1792,[4] and may be the Benjamin Allen whose death in Jamaica in October 1791 is reported by the *Gentleman's Magazine*.

[1] About him see *DNB*. [2] Jeffreys Allen adm. Pembroke, Camb., 20 Nov. 1778, aged 18. [3] T. B. Dilks, *C. J. Fox and Bridgwater*, 13. [4] Oldfield, *Boroughs* (1792), ii. 547, mentions 'the late Mr. Allen'.

M.M.D.

## ALLEN, Joshua, 5th Visct. Allen [I] (1728–1816).

EYE 1 Dec. 1762–Apr. 1770

*b.* 26 Apr. 1728, 4th s. of Hon. Richard Allen by Dorothy, da. and coh. of Maj. Samuel Green of Killaghy, co. Tipperary. *m.* 5 Aug. 1781, Frances, da. of Gaynor Barry of Dormstown, co. Meath, 1s. 2 da. *suc.* bro. as 5th Visct. 10 Nov. 1753.

Ensign 17 Ft. 1742, lt. 1745; half pay 1748; capt.–lt. 53 Ft. 1755; capt. 37 Ft. 1756; dep. q.m.g. to British forces in Portugal 1761; capt. 1 Ft. Gds. and lt.-col. 1765; ret. 1774.

Allen, who had served under Prince Ferdinand of Brunswick and been wounded at Minden, was a close friend of Lord Cornwallis (q.v.), who returned him for Eye. On 12 Nov. 1763 the Grenville Diary mentioned that 'Mr. Wilkes went out this morning with Lord Cornwallis, Lord Allen, and another gentleman';[1] and Allen appears in opposition in the four divisions on Wilkes and general warrants, November 1763–February 1764. He was classed 'pro' by Rockingham, July 1765, and on 14 Sept. Lord Barrington wrote to Newcastle: 'Lord Rockingham is most certainly Lord Allen's friend, and will I believe recommend him strongly to the King [for a company]'; while Newcastle, recommending him to Ligonier the same day, described him as 'a very honest fellow'.[2] Classed in Rockingham's list of November 1766 as a follower of Chatham, he voted with Administration on the land tax, 27 Feb. 1767; on nullum tempus, 17 Feb. 1768, and the Middlesex election, 8 May 1769. He is not known to have spoken in the House. On 26 Apr. 1770 he was given a pension of £600 a year on the Irish establishment, and about the same time vacated his seat.

He died 1 Feb. 1816.

[1] *Grenville Pprs.* ii. 159. [2] Add. 32969, ff. 386, 388.

M.M.D.

**ALSTON, Thomas** (c.1724–74), of Odell, Beds.

BEDFORDSHIRE 1747–1761

*b.* c.1724, 1st s. of Sir Rowland Alston, 4th Bt., M.P. for Beds., by Elizabeth, da. and h. of Capt. Thomas Raynes. *educ.* Westminster Jan. 1736, aged 11; Queens', Camb. 1740 *m.* 30 Aug. 1750, Catherine Davies, da. and h. of Rev. Thomas Davies Bovey of Longstowe, Cambs., *s.p. suc.* fa. as 5th Bt. 2 Jan. 1759.

Ensign 1 Ft. Gds. 1741, lt. and capt. 1743; ret. 1745.

On 5 Aug. 1753 Philip Yorke (q.v.) wrote to Lord Hardwicke about Alston, who had been for a short time in a madhouse:

> Sir R. Alston is very desirous that his son should come in again for the county. If the young man is in any tolerable state of sanity, I do not see any other choice can be made in order to keep up the Whig interest here.[1]

His re-election in 1754 was unopposed, and he was classed by Dupplin as an Opposition Whig connected with the Duke of Bedford. On 15 Nov. 1755 Horace Walpole, writing to Henry Seymour Conway of the debate on the subsidy treaties with Hesse and Russia, noted 'Poor Alston was mad, and spoke ten times to order'. On 30 Sept. 1758, Thomas Potter (q.v.), who himself thought of standing for Bedfordshire, wrote to the Duke of Bedford with regard to the next general election:

> I am pretty certain that if Mr. Alston should choose to be re-elected, the county will not choose to re-elect him.

Bedford replied on 2 Oct. 1758:[2]

> . . . whether, though Mr. Alston should be thought an improper person, his brother Lt.-Col. Alston, might not be thought a proper candidate, by many of the Whig gentlemen, and the Dissenting interest in this county (which is not an inconsiderable one) I cannot take upon me to determine.

Neither stood in 1761.

Thomas Alston, who had separated from his wife by mutual consent two years after their marriage, died 18 July 1774, leaving all his property to Margaret Lee, his housekeeper, through whom it eventually descended to his illegitimate son Thomas.[3]

[1] Add. 35351, ff. 248–51. [2] Bedford mss 37, f. 222; 38, f. 10. [3] Rev. F. S. Alston's mss, quoted Cresswell, *Stemmata Alstoniana*, 282.

L.B.N.

**ALTHORP, Visct.,** *see* **SPENCER, George John**

**AMBLER, Charles** (1721–94), of Stubbings Park, Bisham, Berks.

BRAMBER          14 Feb. 1769–1774
NEWTOWN I.o.W.   24 Apr. 1775–1780
BOROUGHBRIDGE    1780–1784
SALTASH          1784–1790

*b.* 19 Apr. 1721, 2nd s. of Humphrey Ambler, barrister, of Stubbings by his w. Ann Breame. *educ.* M. Temple 1736, called 1742; L. Inn 1757, bencher 1758; K.C.

1761. *m.* Anne, da. of Nicholas Paxton, solicitor to the Treasury, *s.p.*

Solicitor-gen. to the Queen 1771–82; attorney-gen. to the Queen 1782–*d.*

Ambler seems to have had an interest at Bramber. It is not clear when or how he acquired it, but on 4 Oct. 1767 Newcastle wrote to Lord Winterton:[1] 'I have been informed that the Marquess of Granby has bought all the Windsor votes in Bramber, of Mr. Ambler; and that my Lord Granby is to . . . bring in Mr. Ambler for Bramber at the next election.' Ambler and Thomas Thoroton, Granby's two candidates, were defeated but returned on petition. Unlike the rest of the Rutland group who in 1770 went into opposition, Ambler voted with the court throughout this Parliament except on Grenville's Election Act, 25 Feb. 1774, when he voted in opposition. He made several speeches on different subjects, usually of a legal character.

In 1774 Ambler was deprived of his seat at Bramber by a compromise restricting the Rutland family to one seat which was left to Thoroton, though John Baker in his diary (25 Apr.) calls Ambler a 'favourite' of Rutland. No other seat was found for him, but in 1775 he was returned for Newtown after Harcourt Powell had vacated his seat and conveyed his interest to Sir Richard Worsley (q.v.). Ambler again consistently supported Administration, and in 1780 the *English Chronicle* wrote that he was 'one of the *heaviest* and most steady of Lord North's phalanx, known by the nickname of Tully Ambler, an ironical title which he does not owe to his *abilities*'.

At the 1780 general election Ambler was returned unopposed on the Duke of Newcastle's interest at Boroughbridge. His name does not appear in any of the lists on the important divisions between December 1781 and March 1782, and he did not vote on Shelburne's peace preliminaries, 18 Feb. 1783. He is reported to have spoken only twice during this Parliament: in favour of retaining the Act for regulating marriages, 15 June 1781, and against the custom house reform bill, 21 May 1783.

On 23 Mar. 1784 William Pitt wrote to the Duke of Rutland: 'The Duke of Newcastle will positively not bring in Ambler; but we will certainly take care of him in the manner you wish.'[2] And Ambler was returned for Saltash on the Administration interest. His attendance seems again to have been irregular— his only reported vote was with Administration on the Regency, 16 Dec. 1788. No speech of his in this Parliament is known.

In 1790 he published *Reports on Cases in Chancery, 1737–83*. He died 28 Feb. 1794.

[1] Add. 32985, f. 345. [2] *Corresp. between Charles, Duke of Rutland and Wm. Pitt*, 10.

M.M.D.

**AMCOTTS, Charles** (1729–77), of Harrington and Kettlethorpe, Lincs.

BOSTON 1754–1761, 22 Dec. 1766–14 Apr. 1777

*bap.* 25 June 1729, 2nd but o. surv. s. of Vincent Amcotts by Elizabeth, da. of John Quincey of Aslackby, Lincs. *educ.* Trinity Hall, Camb. 1746–9. *unm. suc.* fa. 1733, and his fa.'s half-bro. Charles Hall, M.P., to Kettlethorpe estates 1743.

Sheriff, Lincs. 1753–4; alderman, Boston 1774.

Expelled from Cambridge for drinking the Pretender's health, Amcotts not surprisingly appears in Newcastle's election lists of 1754, and in Dupplin's list of Members, as a Tory. In October 1760 Newcastle described him as 'the head' of the Tory country gentlemen raising an opposition in the county. And on 20 Dec. 1760 Lord Monson wrote to Newcastle:[1] 'Yesterday Mr. Amcotts told me he has quite given up Boston, that I much fear he intends to disturb us at Lincoln.' He did not stand for either at the general election; but was again returned unopposed for Boston at the by-election of December 1766. In Rockingham's list of November 1766 he appears as 'Tory, Bute'; in Townshend's of January 1767 'Rockingham, country gentleman'; and in Newcastle's of 2 Mar. 1767 'Tory'. In two out of the three division lists on the land tax, 27 Feb. 1767, he is marked as voting against Administration. But in divisions between 1768 and his death, Amcotts appears in almost every list of Government supporters and never with Opposition; and is always classed as 'pro' by Robinson. John Lee wrote to William Eden (qq.v.), 11 Oct. 1772:[2] 'While I was at Harrogate I met with Mr. Amcotts, a Lincolnshire Member, a most furious courtier, I need not add, formerly a most notorious Jacobite.' Furious and notorious Amcotts may have been, but there is no record of his having spoken in the House. He died 14 Apr. 1777.[3]

[1] Add. 32916, f. 302. [2] Add. 34412, f. 189. [3] Maddison, *Lincs. Peds.*; *London Mag.* gives 20 Apr.

L.B.N.

**AMCOTTS, Wharton** (1740–1807), of East Retford, Notts., and Kettlethorpe, Lincs.

EAST RETFORD 1780–1790, 1796–1802

*b.* 23 Feb. 1740, 1st s. of Alexander Emerson of East Retford and Caister, Lincs. by Elizabeth, da. and coh. of Rev. Thomas Bosville, rector of Ufford, Northants. *m.* (1) 16 Apr. 1762, Anna Maria (*d.*1 July 1800), da. of Vincent Amcotts of Harrington and Aistrop, Lincs. and sis. and h. of Charles Amcotts (q.v.), 1da.; (2) 20 Oct. 1800, Amelia Campbell of Whitley, Northumb., 1da. *suc.* fa. c.1744; Charles Amcotts at Kettlethorpe, and took name of Amcotts 13 May 1777; *cr.* Bt. 11 May 1796.

Ensign 14 Ft. 1758, lt. 1759, left army shortly afterwards.

In January 1760 Emerson (as he then was) wrote to Newcastle stating that he had property at East Retford which gave him an interest in the borough, and asking to be made a captain in the army.[1] He was not applying for a livelihood, he subsequently informed Newcastle,[2] 'which I have no occasion to do, but . . . no young man can be blamed for endeavouring to advance himself'; even so, he would not ask for a favour were he not conscious of being able to return it, and he referred again to his future parliamentary interest—'I . . . thought upon that account your Grace might assist me'. Unsuccessful in his application, Amcotts apparently retired from the army soon afterwards, but does not seem to have played a major part in the politics of East Retford till shortly before the general election of 1780. Robinson, in his survey of July 1780, wrote against East Retford: 'An attempt will be made here to throw Sir Cecil Wray out by Mr. Amcotts' standing with Lord John Clinton. It will be fixed while the [2nd] Duke of Newcastle is in the country and known on his return. If it succeeds, we shall here gain.' The attempt was successful, and Amcotts was returned unopposed.

In Parliament he regularly supported North's Administration till its fall. He did not vote on Shelburne's peace preliminaries, 18 Feb. 1783, but on 5 Apr. wrote to congratulate Portland on his assumption of office, and on 14 Aug. promised his future support.[3] He voted for Fox's East India bill, 27 Nov. 1783, but on 5 Dec. 1783 he wrote again to Portland:

> Having received instructions from the bailiffs, aldermen, and burgesses of East Retford to vote for the repeal of the receipts tax, I found myself obliged to comply with the wishes of my constituents, though I confess it gave me great concern to oppose Government in any of their measures, being determined to support your Grace's administration upon every question whenever your Grace is pleased to call upon me.

In Robinson's list of January 1784 he was classed as 'doubtful', but in Stockdale's of 19 Mar. and Adam's of May as a Foxite. Though Robinson hoped that the Duke of Newcastle might secure the second seat at Retford for an Administration supporter,[4] Amcotts was returned unopposed on his own interest, and he regularly voted against Pitt's Administration. There is no record of his having spoken in the House.

Amcotts died 26 Sept. 1807.

[1] Add. 32901, f. 536. [2] 24 Feb. 1760, Add. 32902, f. 372. [3] Portland mss. [4] Laprade, 116.

L.B.N.

**AMHERST, William** (1732–81), of Troublefield, Hants.

HYTHE            17 Nov. 1766–1768
LAUNCESTON            1768–1774

*bap.* 5 Feb. 1732, 7th s. of Jeffery Amherst of River-head, Kent, barrister, by Elizabeth, da. of Thomas Kerrill of Hadlow, Kent, and bro. of Field Marshal Lord Amherst. *m.* 31 Mar. 1766, Elizabeth, da. of Thomas Paterson of London, 1s. 2da.

Ensign 1 Ft. Gds. 1755, lt. and capt. 1757, capt. and lt.-col. 1765; col. 1766; col. 32 Ft. 1775–*d.*; maj.-gen. 1777; lt.-gen. 1779.

In 1766 Hythe was disputed between the lord warden, Lord Holdernesse, with Government support, and Lord George Sackville (q.v.). Amherst was nominated as a candidate acceptable to both parties, being a personal friend of Sackville, but well inclined towards Administration. Lord Holdernesse, however, 'lest Col. Amherst should be supposed to come in on any interest of the Sackvilles', wished him 'removed to some other place'[1] at the general election. Amherst's position was summed up in a letter from Grafton to Chatham, 22 Jan. 1767:[2]

> The step which Lord Holdernesse has very properly resolved for the borough of Hythe lays Colonel Amherst under very peculiar difficulties, as his private friendship and some obligations cannot justify him in taking a part in opposition to Lord George Sackville in that borough, whatever his political opinion calls him to do in a more essential and public place.

Grafton asked for leave to 'tell Colonel Amherst that he should be a candidate at one of the Government boroughs at the general election'. On 28 Jan. Holdernesse wrote that he had dissuaded Amherst from standing at Hythe at the general election 'though there are few gentlemen whom . . . I would sooner have wished to have obliged.'[3]

Classed as a follower of Chatham in Rockingham's list of November 1766, Amherst's one recorded vote in this Parliament was with Administration on the land tax, 27 Feb. 1767.

In 1768 Amherst was nominated by Administration at Launceston and returned unopposed. He supported the Government over Wilkes (3 Feb., 15 Apr., 8 May 1769, 26 Apr. 1773), but appears in no other division list. His only recorded speech was on the fortification of Newfoundland, 10 Dec. 1770.

Amherst did not stand in 1774. Before the general election of 1780 Jenkinson suggested to John Robinson (24 Aug.) that there was 'no military man so proper for Bath as General Amherst, and I wish it the more as it will contribute to strengthen the army interest in the House of Commons',[4] but was afraid that Amherst would decline; and in fact he did not stand. He died 13 May 1781.

[1] G. Wilks, *Barons of Cinque Ports*, 165. [2] Chatham mss. [3] Wilks op. cit. 112–13. [4] Abergavenny mss.

M.M.D.

**AMYAND, Claudius** (1718–74), of Langleybury, Herts.

TREGONY            1747–1754
SANDWICH            1754–11 Dec. 1756

*b.* 10 Aug. 1718, 1st s. of Claudius Amyand, serjeant-surgeon to George II, by Marie, da. of Daniel Rabache. *educ.* Westminster 1726; Ch. Ch. Oxf. 1736; L. Inn 1734, called 1742. *m.* 26 Nov. 1761, Frances, da. of Rev. Thomas Payne, wid. of George Compton, 6th Earl of Northampton, 'a very amiable woman with a jointure of £2500 per annum',[1] *s.p. suc.* fa. 1740.

Keeper of the King's Lib. 1745; under-sec. of state 1750–6; commr. of customs 1756–65; receiver of land tax, Mdx. and London 1765–*d.*

Amyand was a Government official, of no consequence in Parliament. At the general election of 1754 he was offered a seat at Bossiney for £1,500, but declined, 'not being able to bear the expense';[2] and he was brought in on the Government interest at Sandwich. Retained in office by Robinson, and next 'on the same footing' by Fox,[3] he was removed in 1756 by Pitt to the Board of Customs, according to Chesterfield 'because nobody liked him'.[4] In 1765 he gave that up 'with great pleasure'[5] for the lucrative office of receiver of the land tax for Middlesex and London.

Amyand died 1 Apr. 1774.

[1] Geo. Amyand to Sir Jas. Porter, 8 Dec. 1761, Egerton 2157, f. 3. [2] Add. 32995, ff. 110–12. [3] Robinson to Edw. Weston, 30 Oct. 1755, *HMC 10th Rep. I*, 310. [4] Chesterfield to Dayrolles, 7 Jan. 1758, Add. 32877 f. 62. [5] Amyand to Bute, Jan. 1765, Add. 5726C, f. 5.

J.B.

**AMYAND, George** (1720–66), of Laurence Pountney Hill, London and Carshalton, Surr.

BARNSTAPLE            1754–16 Aug. 1766

*b.* 26 Sept. 1720, 2nd s. of Claudius Amyand, and bro. of Claudius Amyand (q.v.). *educ.* Westminster 1729–35. *m.* 9 Apr. 1746, Anna Maria, da. of John Abraham Corteen, a Hamburg merchant, 2s. 2da. *cr.* Bt. 9 Aug. 1764.

Asst. to Russia Co. 1756; director, E.I. Co. 1760, 1763–4. Partner in Amyand and Rucker, merchants, of Laurence Pountney Hill, and in Amyand, Staples and Mercer, bankers, of Cornhill.

Apprenticed to a London merchant in 1736, Amyand soon set up on his own, and rapidly acquired large interests in the German trade. In 1750 the appointment of his brother Claudius as under-secretary gave him a link with Administration, and in 1754 he was nominated at Barnstaple, where he received £2,000 from secret service funds through his brother's friend John Clevland (q.v.) 'to defray all expenses exceeding £1,500'.[1] Amyand seems by this time to have been connected with several companies, including the Emden East India Company,[2] and 'in partnership with Uhthoff, son-in-law of Sir

Joshua Vanneck'.[3] He subscribed £40,000 to the loan of 1757;[4] in April 1759 was included among 'the most known people in the City' whom Newcastle consulted on 'the present state of credit';[5] and in December was the third largest subscriber to the £8,000,000 loan which he with other 'principal and most responsible men in the City' had agreed to underwrite, his own firm and its customers taking £660,000 of the sum of £924,000 allotted to him.[6] In 1761 he subscribed £480,000 to the Government loan. But no very considerable amounts of Government stock were ever held by him for any length of time; nor any Bank stock after April 1760.[7] During the seven years' war Amyand obtained important Government contracts in Germany and by 1760 was remitting a large part of the money for the allied army there, and supplying it with grain.[8] His banking firm Amyand, Staples and Mercer acted as bankers for the diplomatic service in the supply of money abroad and the handling of individual accounts.

In 1761, after a 'slight opposition',[9] Amyand was again returned for Barnstaple. He continued to support Administration after Newcastle's resignation; retained his contracts in Germany; in April 1762 obtained new ones in Portugal; secured a subscription of £200,000 in the very profitable loan of 1763;[10] and in June 1763 was remitting money to Minorca, together with Nicholas Linwood (q.v.).[11] In May 1763 Amyand unsuccessfully solicited his fellow-merchants for an address of thanks to the King on the peace.

In March 1764 Amyand, who had been a director of the East India Company since 1763, and had 'quarrelled with Sulivan [q.v.] the leader of the faction to oppose Lord Clive, suddenly proposed to give the government of Bengal with powers over their affairs to that lord'.[12] An attempt was then made to put Amyand at the head of the direction in opposition to Sulivan, but on 6 Mar. Joseph Salvador wrote to Charles Jenkinson: 'my hopes are suspended by Mr. Amyand's informing me he has definitely agreed with Mr. Grenville not to stand [for the direction]',[13] an agreement to which Amyand adhered in spite of Salvador's pleas.

Amyand's connexion with Grenville became increasingly close: on 17 Mar. 1765 George Onslow wrote to Newcastle that Grenville was thought by the City to be 'governed' by Amyand and Peregrine Cust (q.v.); and a week later sarcastically described Amyand, Cust, and Touchet (q.v.) as Grenville's 'wise counsellors'.[14] Yet in July 1765 Amyand was classed by Rockingham as 'doubtful, pro' with the note 'has made applications'; nor did he vote against the repeal of the Stamp Act, 22 Feb. 1766. Amy-

and's speeches in the House were invariably on commercial matters.

He died 16 Aug. 1766. His friend Sir James Porter wrote:[15]

Sir George is no more. He has left clear £160,000 sterling and perhaps more, this pursuit, keen and arduous, worked the capillaries of the brain, wore them to a filament, distorted their whole construction and dissolved the whole frame at 46.

[1] Namier, *Structure*, 243. It is therefore astonishing to find Amyand in a list of Members who voted against the Address, 13 Nov. 1755 (Add. 33034, f. 206); which must be a mistake. James West, reporting that day to Newcastle (Add. 32860, f. 471), enumerates some noteworthy votes on the Opposition side, but does not mention Amyand. Perhaps 'George Amyand' should read 'George Colebrooke', who spoke that day against the Address. [2] Add. 35635, f. 97. [3] Thus marked in a list of Members, mainly merchants, in the Lowther mss; undated but compiled between Apr. 1754 and Mar. 1755. [4] Devonshire mss. [5] Add. 32890, f. 125. [6] Namier, *Structure*, 54, 55. The rest went to people billeted on him by Newcastle. [7] Bank of England recs. [8] See H. B. Legge to Newcastle, 15 July 1758, Add. 32881, ff. 327–8; Amyand to Newcastle, 27 Jan. 1762, Add. 32834, f. 37; T52/51/2, 52/53/286, 29/34/244. [9] Add. 32921, f. 111. [10] *Hist. Late Minority*, 94. [11] Add. 38338, ff. 109–11. [12] Walpole, *Mems. Geo. III*, i. 310. [13] Jucker, *Jenkinson Pprs*. 270. [14] Add. 32966, ff. 55–57, 96. [15] *HMC 9th Rep.* pt. 1, 401.

L.B.N.

## AMYAND, John (1751–80).

CAMELFORD  1774–5 June 1780

*b.* 6 Nov. 1751, 2nd s. of Sir George Amyand (q.v.), 1st Bt. *educ.* Eton 1758–65. *unm.* His sisters m. James Harris (q.v.), 1st Earl of Malmesbury, and Sir Gilbert Elliot, 4th Bt. (q.v.), 1st Earl of Minto.

Amyand was a merchant, carrying on his father's business. In 1774 he was returned unopposed, presumably as a Government candidate. His first recorded vote was with Opposition on Wilkes, 22 Feb. 1775, but his name does not appear in other minority lists, and in 1776 he obtained a contract for victualling 3000 men in North America. Eighteen months later, November 1777, he terminated the contract as the Treasury 'construction of the same has been different from what he conceived it to be'.[1] He voted with Administration against the contractors bill, 12 Feb. 1779, and continued to support North until 6 Apr. 1780 when he voted for Dunning's motion; on 24 Apr. 1780 he again voted in opposition on the motion against prorogation. Robinson in his survey of the 1780 election classed him as 'doubtful'. There is no record of his having spoken in the House. He died 5 June 1780.

[1] T29/46/411.

M.M.D.

## AMYAND, *see also* CORNEWALL, Sir George

## AMYATT, James (1734–1813), of Freemantle, Hants.

TOTNES          1774–1780
SOUTHAMPTON  1784–1806

*bap.* 18 July 1734, 2nd s. of Benjamin Amyatt of Totnes. *m.* Maria, da. of Rev. W. Wollaston of Norf., wid. of Peter Amyatt of the council of Calcutta, 2da.

Amyatt came of a prominent Totnes family; his father was mayor in 1739, and another relative, John Amyatt, in 1724, 1727, and 1735. On 27 June 1754 Charles Taylor wrote to his brother-in-law, Admiral Edward Vernon (q.v.), asking him to get 'a place in the India service, or in a merchant ship' for his young friend Amyatt who was 'esteemed a very sober young man and a good seaman'.[1] Amyatt is said to have become a captain in the East India Company's service, and also to have been a free merchant in India.[2]

In 1774 he successfully contested Totnes in opposition to the Duke of Bolton's interest. Amyatt was apparently an Administration supporter till April 1780; he does not appear in any of the Opposition lists which alone are extant for 1775–8; he was marked by Robinson as 'pro, present' on the contractors bill, 12 Feb. 1779; and voted with the Government till April 1780, when he joined the Opposition on Dunning's motion, 6 Apr., and the motion against prorogation, 24 Apr. He was classed as 'contra' by Robinson in July. There is no record of his having spoken during this Parliament.

Robinson, in his survey of 1780, noted that at the general election the combined Bolton and Buller interests would probably 'throw out Amyatt' at Totnes; in fact Amyatt did not seek re-election, nor does he seem to have attempted to re-enter Parliament elsewhere in 1780. In 1784 he successfully contested Southampton, apparently with Administration support. He voted for Pitt's proposals for parliamentary reform, 18 Apr. 1785, and regularly supported Pitt's Administration. His only reported speech during this Parliament was to press for the modification or repeal of the tax on retail shops, 2 Mar. 1786.[3]

Amyatt died 10 Jan. 1813.

[1] Add. 40776, f. 178. [2] Foster, *Coll. Gen., M.P.s England*, 42; Holzmann, *Nabobs in England*, 115. [3] Debrett, xix. 270.

M.M.D.

## ANCRAM, Earl of, *see* KERR

## ANDERSON, Charles, *see* ANDERSON PELHAM

## ANDERSON, Francis Evelyn (1752–1821)

| GREAT GRIMSBY | 1774–1780 |
| BEVERLEY | 1780–1784 |

*b.* 8 Apr. 1752, 2nd s. of Francis Anderson of Manby, and bro. of Charles Anderson Pelham (q.v.). *educ.* Eton 1763–9. *m.* Caroline, da. of Gen. James Johnstone, *s.p.*

Cornet 15 Lt. Drag. 1770, lt. 1779; lt. 1 Ft. Gds. and capt. 1780; maj. 85 Ft. 1783, lt.-col. 1794.

In 1774 Anderson was returned unopposed for Grimsby on his brother's interest, and in 1780 at Beverley. Like Charles Pelham he voted with the Opposition till the fall of North; voted against Shelburne's peace preliminaries, 18 Feb. 1783, and was classed by Robinson in March 1783 as a follower of Fox. He voted for Pitt's parliamentary reform proposals, 7 May 1783; for Fox's East India bill, 27 Nov. 1783, and was listed as a Foxite by Robinson in January 1784 and in Stockdale's list of March. George III wrote to Pitt on 30 Mar.:[1] 'I understand . . . Beverley is so offended with Major Anderson, that any fresh man would probably succeed there'; and Anderson was defeated at the general election. He does not appear to have attempted to re-enter Parliament. There is no record of his having spoken in the House.

Anderson died 12 Sept. 1821.

[1] Chatham mss.

M.M.D.

## ANDERSON PELHAM, Charles (1749–1823), of Brocklesby, Lincs.

| BEVERLEY | 1768–1774 |
| LINCOLNSHIRE | 1774–13 Aug. 1794 |

*b.* 3 Feb. 1749, 1st s. of Francis Anderson of Manby, Lincs. by Eleanor, da. of Thomas Carter of Bathavern, Denb. *educ.* Eton 1763–5. *m.* 21 July 1770, Sophia, da. and h. of George René Aufrère (q.v.); 2s. 5da. *suc.* fa. 1758; and to estates of his uncle Charles Pelham and took add. name of Pelham 1763; *cr.* Baron Yarborough 13 Aug. 1794.

Anderson Pelham, the owner of large estates in Lincolnshire, was said in 1780 to be 'one of the richest commoners in England'.[1] He had an interest at Grimsby and at Beverley, and in 1768, while still under age, was returned unopposed at Beverley. In 1774, and at all his subsequent elections, he was returned unopposed for Lincolnshire. In Parliament he voted with Opposition on the Middlesex election, 15 Apr. 1769; regularly opposed North's Administration till its fall; voted against Shelburne's peace preliminaries, 18 Feb. 1783, and was classed by Robinson in March 1783 as a follower of Fox. He voted for Pitt's parliamentary reform proposals, 7 May 1783; did not vote on Fox's East India Bill, 27 Nov. 1783, but was listed by Robinson in January 1784 as a Foxite. Sir John Sinclair, in a list drawn up early in January, notes about him: 'wants a peerage, which would secure him and his brother's vote'.[2] This was not forthcoming and Anderson Pelham opposed Pitt's Administration till the outbreak of war with France. He is reported to have spoken only once in the House, during a debate on Ireland, 7 Apr. 1778.

He died 22 Sept. 1823.

[1] *Eng. Chron.* 1780. [2] Sinclair mss. at Thurso East Mains.

M.M.D.

## ANNESLEY, Francis (1734–1812), of Reading, Berks.

READING 1774–1806

*b.* 2 May 1734, 1st s. of Rev. Martin Annesley of Bucklebury and Frilsham, Berks. by Mary, da. and coh. of William Hanbury of Little Marcle, Herefs. *educ.* Reading; G. Inn 1753. *unm. suc.* fa. 1749.

In 1772, when a by-election at Reading seemed imminent, Annesley was nominated by a large group of townspeople in opposition to the attempt by John Dodd, the other Member, to secure the seat for a friend. In 1774, and again in 1780, Annesley contested the borough and was returned head of the poll. In Parliament he voted consistently with the Opposition till the fall of North. The *Public Ledger* wrote of him in 1779: 'A very conscientious Member of Parliament, means well, votes with the Opposition, but not attached to any party.' He voted for Shelburne's peace preliminaries, 18 Feb. 1783; did not vote on Fox's East India bill, 27 Nov. 1783, and was classed by Robinson in January 1784 as 'hopeful, absent'. He belonged to the St. Alban's Tavern group, and was counted by Stockdale (19 Mar.) and Adam (May 1784) as a follower of Pitt. He voted against Richmond's fortifications plan, 27 Feb. 1786. There is no record of his having spoken in the House before 1790.

Annesley died 17 Apr. 1812.

M.M.D.

## ANSON, Thomas (?1695–1773), of Shugborough Hall, Staffs.

LICHFIELD 1747–Jan. 1770

*b.* ?1695, 1st s. of William Anson of Shugborough by Isabella, da. and coh. of Charles Carrier of Wirksworth, Derbys., and bro. of Adm. Lord Anson. *educ.* St. John's, Oxf. 2 June 1711, aged 15; I. Temple, called 1719. *unm. suc.* fa. 1720.

Bencher, I. Temple 1746.

Sir John Eardley Wilmot, the judge, wrote about Thomas Anson on the day of his death:[1] 'In the former part of his life [he] had lived many years abroad; was a very ingenious, polite, well bred man, and dignified . . . his accomplishments by his universal benevolence.' He entered Parliament late, and made no mark.

Under the Pelhams he was always classed as a Whig. He does not appear in Fox's list of Members secured for the peace preliminaries, early December 1762; voted for the motion to postpone their consideration,

1 Dec. 1762; but not against the preliminaries themselves. He seems to have joined the Opposition in February 1764: he did not vote with them in the division of 15 Nov. 1763, and was included by James Harris (q.v.) in a list, dated 18 Feb. 1764, of 'desertions this session'. He voted against general warrants in the divisions of 15 and 18 Feb. 1764, and was classed by Newcastle (10 May) as a 'sure friend'. He supported the Rockingham Administration, and opposed that of Chatham. His last recorded vote was for the nullum tempus bill, 17 Feb. 1768. His only recorded speech, 29 Mar. 1765, was on an enclosure bill which concerned the dean and chapter of Lichfield cathedral. In January 1770 he vacated his seat in favour of his nephew and heir, George Adams.

Anson died 30 Mar. 1773.

[1] J. Wilmot, *Life of Sir J. E. Wilmot*, 199.

J.B.

## ANSON, Thomas (1767–1818), of Shugborough Hall, Staffs.

LICHFIELD 5 Dec. 1789–17 Feb. 1806

*b.* 14 Feb. 1767, 1st s. of George Anson (q.v.) of Shugborough by Mary, da. of George Venables Vernon (q.v.). *educ.* Eton 1779; Oriel, Oxf. 1784. *m.* 15 Sept. 1794, Anne Margaret, da. of Thomas William Coke (q.v.), 6s. 4da. *suc.* fa. 1789; *cr.* Visct. Anson 17 Feb. 1806.

The death of Anson's father in 1789 opened a vacancy at Lichfield, then controlled jointly by the Leveson Gower and Anson families. Pitt wrote to Lord Stafford in the hope that there might be an opportunity to revive Rose's scheme of 1784 of an opposition to the Ansons and to secure the return of a friend of Government, but Stafford had already agreed to support Anson's return 'at this election':

> Independent of the feelings I had to a family, with which I have lived in friendship and connection for near half a century [he wrote to Pitt on 2 Nov.[1]] I think I did the best for the King and for his Administration . . . all circumstances considered. The young Mr. Anson is, I believe, a man of good character and good dispositions, he is at present, I hope, not linked with any party, he succeeds to an unencumbered landed estate of £16,000 *per annum*. Is it worth while to risk at the present moment the compelling this young man to connect himself with the enemies of the present Administration, when there is a probability of throwing that property into the other scale?

Anson was at Vienna when his father died and was elected during his absence. He returned shortly before the general election of 1790, but disappointed Stafford by adopting his father's political attitude. He became one of Fox's closest friends, and owed his peerage to Fox.

He died 31 July 1818.

[1] Chatham mss.

E.A.S.

**ANSON**, *see also* **ADAMS, George**

**ANSTRUTHER, Sir John,** 2nd Bt. (1718–99), of Anstruther and Elie, Fife.

ANSTRUTHER EASTER BURGHS  17 Jan. 1766–1774, 1780–Dec. 1782, 1790–Feb. 1793

*b.* 27 Dec. 1718, o. surv. s. of Sir John Anstruther, 1st Bt., M.P., by Lady Margaret Carmichael, da. of James, 2nd Earl of Hyndford [S]. *educ.* Glasgow Univ. 1733; ?Grand Tour. *m.* 4 Oct. 1750, Janet, da. of James Fall, M.P., merchant and provost of Dunbar, 3 surv. s. 1 surv. da. *suc.* fa. as 2nd Bt. 21 Sept. 1753; and cos. Gen. Philip Anstruther, M.P., 11 Nov. 1760.

Chief of an ancient Fife family, Sir John was known as a numismatist,[1] an agricultural improver, an exponent of drill husbandry, and the 'well drilled husband'[2] of the beautiful 'Jenny Faa', with whose brother Robert he founded in 1756 the Anstruther whale fishing company.[3]

In 1760 he inherited a great fortune and the Airdrie estate from the notorious Gen. Philip Anstruther, together with a share of his unpopularity, which was not lessened by his own arrogance, his extravagant building projects, and the ruthless removal of an entire village, reputedly at the whim of his wife, to improve the amenities of Elie House.[4]

On the death of Sir Henry Erskine (q.v.) in August 1765, Anstruther returned post haste from Spa, and, after consultation with Sir Alexander Gilmour (q.v.), who had already recommended him to Newcastle, stood with Government support for Anstruther Burghs.[5] His opponent was Robert Alexander, son of William Alexander (q.v.), banker and tobacco merchant, supported by Alexander Wedderburn and the Erskine interest. After a campaign unprecedented for bribery and chicanery, of which anecdotes were current for over a hundred years, Anstruther was returned.[6]

Anstruther supported the Rockingham Administration on the repeal of the Stamp Act. Under the Chatham Administration his allegiance was uncertain: in the winter of 1766–7 he was listed 'doubtful' by Rockingham and 'Government' by Townshend, and in March 1767 Newcastle counted him as 'doubtful or absent'. In the land tax division, 27 Feb. 1767, Almon records him as voting against Administration, but his name does not appear either in Meredith's list or in that printed in Paris.

In view of his local unpopularity and the litigation still proceeding over burgh council elections, his prospects of return in 1768 were doubtful. As early as October 1766 he was mentioned as a candidate for Fife, since 'in all appearances he would lose his

burghs'.[7] Nevertheless, with the assistance of Col. John Scott and the Erskines of Kellie (whose estates he purchased in 1769), he was re-elected, and supported the Grafton Administration over Wilkes and the Middlesex election. He also supported North, but seems to have been absent a good deal through ill health; and Robinson, in his 'Minutes as to Scotland', 13 Dec. 1773,[8] records: 'Sir John is abroad and query whether he will come in again.'

At the 1774 election Anstruther brought in his eldest son Philip for the Burghs, and devoted himself to the development of his estates, coalmines and saltpans. In 1780 he terminated the arrangement under which George Damer had replaced Philip Anstruther in the Burghs, and took back the representation into his own hands, with the intention of serving 'a session or two', and thereafter vacating in favour of his son.[9]

He consistently supported North, but did not vote on Cavendish's censure motion, 8 Mar. 1782, having apparently left London. Robinson sought the intervention of Henry Dundas, who replied, 9 Mar.:[10] 'I send you a letter from me to him which will certainly bring him up.' As a result Sir John returned, and voted with Administration on Rous's no confidence motion of 15 Mar.

In June Sir John returned to Scotland, and in December resigned his seat to his second son John, thereafter concerning himself mainly with his agricultural experiments[11] and the management of his estates. In 1783 he sold the Airdrie estate to Lt.-Col. James Moncrieff, who in 1784 stood as Government candidate against John Anstruther. Despite the defection of the Balcaskie branch of the Anstruther family, Sir John secured his son's return, but by 1788 had ceased to endorse his Opposition politics,[12] had reached agreement with Henry Dundas on burgh patronage, and become a Government supporter. In 1790 he refused John the nomination and was himself returned for the Burghs, but vacated his seat in February 1793 in favour of his third son Robert.

An ailing and emaciated old man,[13] he spent his last years in the preparation of his two treatises on agriculture, *Drill Husbandry* (1796) and *Hoeing Husbandry* (1798). He died 4 July 1799.

[1] *Pococke's Tours in Scotland* (S.H.S. 1887), 275. [2] W. Anderson, *Scottish Nation*, i. 142. [3] Sir Wm. Fraser, *Leven & Melville Pprs.* i. 340–1. [4] W. Wood, *East Neuk of Fife* (1887), 227–9. [5] Gilmour to Newcastle, 28 Aug. 1765, Add. 32960, f. 209. [6] For the story of Alexander's petition, see ANSTRUTHER EASTER BURGHS. [7] Geo. Chalmers to Geo. Grenville, 16 Oct. 1766, Grenville mss. (JM). [8] Laprade, 7. [9] Robinson's survey of 1780, Royal archives, Windsor. [10] Dundas to Robinson, Abergavenny mss. [11] *Scots Mag.* 1784, p. 210. [12] *Pol. State Scotland 1788*, p. 125; H. Furber, *Henry Dundas*, 245. [13] J. Fergusson, *Letters G. Dempster to Sir A. Fergusson*, 309.

E.H.-G.

**ANSTRUTHER, John** (1753–1811), of Anstruther, Fife.

ANSTRUTHER EASTER BURGHS 21 Jan. 1783–1790
COCKERMOUTH 1790–1796
ANSTRUTHER EASTER BURGHS 1796–July 1797
1806–26 June 1811

*b.* 27 Mar. 1753, 2nd s. of Sir John Anstruther (q.v.), 2nd Bt. *educ.?* St. Andrews 1766; Glasgow Univ. 1772; adv. 1774; L. Inn 1774, called 1779, bencher 1793, treasurer 1807. *m.* 1788, Maria Jane, da. of Edward Brice of Berners St., Marylebone, 2 surv. s. 1da. Kntd. 4 Oct. 1797; *cr.* Bt. 18 May 1798; *suc.* bro. Philip (q.v.) as 4th Bt. 5 Jan. 1808.

Receiver-gen. of bishops' rents in Scotland 1780; solicitor-gen. to Prince of Wales 1793–5; Welsh judge 1793–7; c.j. Bengal 1797–1806; P.C. 19 Nov. 1806.

After studying law at Glasgow under the radical Whig Professor John Millar, Anstruther, at the outset of a successful career at the English bar, became active in East India Company affairs, and in October 1782 as a member of the court of proprietors made an effective speech (subsequently printed) strenuously opposing the Commons resolution for the recall of Warren Hastings, whose administration he defended as mild, just and upright.[1] On his father's withdrawal, he entered Parliament in January 1783. While his father was thought to favour a Fox-North Opposition,[2] his own views, although he owed his place to North, were apparently uncertain. He did not vote on Shelburne's peace preliminaries, February 1783, and in March Robinson listed him under 'North—doubtful'. But on the formation of the Coalition he became their 'zealous supporter'.[3] In his maiden speech on 20 Nov. on Fox's East India bill, he established himself as an able speaker, and on 8 Dec. strongly attacked the Company's 'fluctuating unresponsible executive power, lodged in the hands of a multitude'.[4]

In December 1783, shortly before the fall of the Coalition, Robinson wrote:[5]

Mr. Anstruther at present takes the line of support of Government because he holds an office, but, if a change, in a future Parliament would, it is believed, support as he does now.

But Anstruther remained opposed to Pitt, and at the general election of 1784 Henry Dundas sponsored a Government candidate against him. Nevertheless, John Anstruther was returned.[6]

In the new Parliament he became a leading Opposition speaker, specializing in East India affairs and legal issues. On 4 Aug. 1784 he for once joined forces with Dundas to oppose, on behalf of his Scottish constituents, the duty on printed linens, commenting upon 'the dangerous spirit of emigration excited among the manufacturers'.[7] In 1785 he voted against Pitt's Irish propositions, became a contributor to the

*Rolliad,* and both in and out of the House directed his shafts against Dundas. During the East India debates of 1786 he strongly attacked Hastings, and had a violent altercation with Jenkinson on 26 Apr. on the question of supplying Hastings with copies of the charges against him. When on 2 June Dundas taunted him with his printed speech as an East India proprietor in 1782, Anstruther replied: he felt he should have had 'no reason to blush for inconsistency, when at one moment refusing to recall Mr. Hastings for supposed, not actual offences, and at the present time condemning him for his evident criminalities'.[8] He was appointed a manager for Hastings's impeachment, and in 1788 took a leading part in the attempt to impeach Impey.

A consistent opponent of reform, he rebutted the claim made on 23 May 1787 that Francis Charteris was not required to vacate his seat on becoming the eldest son of a Scottish peer, and when Lord Maitland threatened to bring in a bill to put English and Scottish peers' sons on a footing of equality, declared: 'It behoves the representatives of the boroughs and counties of Scotland and also . . . of England to reflect seriously before they gave consideration to any bill, the object of which was to alter the Act of Union.'[9] On 18 May he opposed Sheridan's motion for the internal reform of Scottish burghs.[10] Before the matter again came before Parliament in 1788, Anstruther wrote to the magistrates of Pittenweem, one of the burghs particularly attacked by the reformers, asking for a statement of their finances for 1765 and 1787–8.[11] When on 17 June 1788 Sheridan moved for a bill to reform the government of the royal burghs of Scotland and the manner of accounting for their property and revenue, Anstruther opposed it as leading 'effectually to a change in the election of representatives to serve in Parliament', denied that revenue grievances existed, and when Sir Thomas Dundas suggested that one of Anstruther's own burghs required investigation, asserted 'that the revenue of the burgh alluded to, so far from being decayed had within the last twenty years trebled its amount.' In April 1789 he again spoke strongly against Sheridan's bill for Scottish burgh reform.[12]

By this time he was aware that he would not be re-elected for Anstruther Burghs. The Opposition survey of the 'Political State of Scotland 1788–9' records:[13] 'Sir John Anstruther . . . It is said he will go with Administration against his son John.' General James Grant (q.v.) wrote to Lord Cornwallis in India, 3 Apr. 1790:[14] 'In Scotland the Opposition will certainly lose considerably . . . The unfortunate Anstruther who was to have gone out chief justice to India [presumably if the Prince of Wales had become Regent], will not be able to come into Parliament at the next election.' However, he found a seat at Cockermouth on the Lowther interest, and in 1793 became reunited in politics with his family.

He died 26 June 1811.

¹ See Hen. Dundas's speech, 2 June 1786, Debrett, xx. 327. ² Loughborough to W. Eden, 24 Aug. 1782, *Jnl. & Corresp. Ld. Auckland*, i. 32. ³ Wm. Adam to Portland, 7 Nov. 1783, Portland mss. ⁴ Debrett, xii, 81, 379-82. ⁵ Laprade, 99. ⁶ See ANSTRUTHER, Sir John, 2nd Bt. ⁷ Stockdale, iii. 391. ⁸ Debrett, xx. 120, 298-9, 327, 330-1. ⁹ Ibid. xxii. 395. ¹⁰ Ibid. 418; Stockdale, xii. 177. ¹¹ D. Cook, *Annals of Pittenweem* (1867), pp. 153-4. ¹² Stockdale, xv. 189-90, 191-2; xvii. 432. ¹³ *Pol. State Scotland*, 125. ¹⁴ *Cornwallis Corresp.* ii. 42-43.

E.H.-G.

**ANSTRUTHER, Philip** (1752-1808), of Anstruther and Elie, Fife.

ANSTRUTHER EASTER BURGHS 1774-Dec. 1777

*b.* 13 Jan. 1752, 1st s. of Sir John Anstruther (q.v.), 2nd Bt. *educ.* St. Andrews 1766. *m.* 17 Feb. 1778, Anne, da. and h. of Sir John Paterson (q.v.), 3rd Bt., of Eccles, *s.p.* Took add. name of Paterson c.1782. *suc.* fa. as 3rd Bt. 4 July 1799.

Cornet 1 Drag. Gds. 1770, lt. 1773; ret. 1775.

Anstruther was brought into Parliament by his father, and in February and March 1775 piloted through the House a bill permitting the burgh of Anstruther Easter to levy a twopenny duty on ale for the repair of its bridge and harbour.¹ Apart from this, little is known of his parliamentary activities, and no speech by him is recorded. In 1777 he vacated his seat in favour of George Damer, and did not subsequently attempt to re-enter Parliament.

He died 5 Jan. 1808.

¹ *CJ*, 20, 23 Feb. and 7, 15, 22, 27 Mar. 1775.

E.H.-G.

**APSLEY, Lord,** *see* BATHURST, Henry

**ARCEDECKNE, Chaloner** (?1743-1809), of Cockfield Hall and Glevering Park, Suff.

WALLINGFORD 1780-1784
WESTBURY 1784-Jan. 1786

*b.* ?1743, s. of Andrew Arcedeckne of Gurnamone, co. Galway, attorney-gen. of Jamaica. *educ.* Eton 1753-9; Ch. Ch. Oxf. 7 Dec. 1760, aged 17. *m.* 1777, Catherine, da. and coh. of John Leigh of North Court House, I.o.W., 3s. 2da. *suc.* fa. 1763.

Sheriff, Suff. 1797-8.

The Arcedecknes were Roman Catholics, and Andrew Arcedeckne was the first to conform. From him Chaloner Arcedeckne inherited large estates in Jamaica. Robinson notes against Wallingford in his survey of 1780 an opposition by 'Mr. Archdeacon, a Jamaica planter, supported by Lord Abingdon'; he was returned after a contest. Following Abingdon (who was his contemporary at Oxford) Arcedeckne

adhered to the Opposition, voting with them in each of the six divisions for which lists are available, 12 Dec. 1781-15 Mar. 1782. He similarly followed Abingdon in adhering to Shelburne, and voted for his peace preliminaries, 18 Feb. 1783; supported Pitt on parliamentary reform, 7 May 1783; voted against Fox's East India bill; and was classed as a follower of Pitt in all the lists of 1784. In 1784 he was returned unopposed for Abingdon's borough of Westbury; there is nothing to show why he resigned his seat in January 1786. No speech by him in the House is recorded.

Arcedeckne died 20 Dec. 1809.

L.B.N.

**ARCHER, Hon. Andrew** (1736-78), of Umberslade, Warws.

COVENTRY 1761-19 Oct. 1768

*b.* 29 July 1736, o.s. of Thomas Archer, M.P., 1st Lord Archer, by Catherine, da. and coh. of Sir Thomas Tipping, 1st Bt. *educ.* Eton 1747-53; Trinity, Oxf. 1754. *m.* 23 July 1761, Sarah, da. of James West (q.v.), 1s. *d.v.p.* 3da. *suc.* fa. as 2nd Lord 19 Oct. 1768.

Recorder, Coventry 1769-*d.*

Archer came of an old Warwickshire family with an interest at Warwick and Coventry. In 1761, when he faced a contest at Coventry, he reinsured himself by standing at Bramber, a borough rented by his father from Sir Henry Gough. Returned for both, he elected to sit for Coventry. In Parliament he was influenced by his father-in-law, James West, and followed Newcastle. Archer voted with the Opposition on the peace preliminaries, 9 and 10 Dec. 1762, and on general warrants, 6, 15, and 18 Feb. 1764; and was listed by Newcastle as a 'sure friend', 10 May 1764. He was classed by Rockingham, July 1765, as 'doubtful', but as 'Whig', November 1766, and he stayed with the Opposition till he left Parliament on succeeding to the peerage. There is no record of his having spoken in the House.

He died 18 or 25 Apr. 1778.

M.M.D.

**ARCHER, Henry** (1700-68), of Hale, Hants.

WARWICK 25 Feb. 1735-1768

*bap.* 18 Nov. 1700, 2nd s. of Andrew Archer, M.P., by Elizabeth, da. of Sir Samuel Dashwood, M.P., and bro. of Thomas, 1st Lord Archer. *educ.* Eton c.1716; Trinity, Oxf. 1718; M. Temple 1718; I. Temple 1723, called 1726. *m.* 22 Dec. 1743, Lady Elizabeth Montagu, da. of George, 1st Earl of Halifax, *s.p.* *suc.* uncle Thomas Archer 23 May 1743.

Archer sat for Warwick on the family interest. His only recorded speech after 1754 was on 18 Mar.

1761, when he proposed an address to the Crown to grant a pension to the Speaker.[1] He is not included in Fox's list of Members who favoured the peace preliminaries, nor is he known to have voted against them. On the division of 18 Feb. 1764 on general warrants he was classed by Jenkinson as an absent friend. On 20 Feb. 1765 he was excused attending the call of the House because of illness.[2] No vote by him is recorded in this Parliament, and the party leaders did not know what to make of him: Rockingham in July 1765 classed him as 'doubtful' and in November 1766 (incorrectly) as 'Bedford', Townshend in January 1767 (again incorrectly) as 'Rockingham', and Newcastle in March as 'doubtful or absent'. Probably he was absent a good deal during the last years of his life.

He died 16 Mar. 1768.

[1] Walpole, *Mems. Geo. III*, i. 40. [2] Harris's 'Debates'.

J.B.

## ARCHER, Michael, *see* NEWTON

## ARDEN, Baron, *see* PERCEVAL, Hon. Charles George

## ARDEN, Richard Pepper (1744–1804), of Alvanley, nr. Frodsham, Cheshire.

| | |
|---|---|
| NEWTOWN I.o.W. | 17 Jan. 1783–1784 |
| ALDBOROUGH | 1784–1790 |
| HASTINGS | 1790–Apr. 1794 |
| BATH | 3 May 1794–22 May 1801 |

*b.* 20 May 1744, 2nd s. of John Arden of Harden Hall, nr. Stockport by Mary, da. of Cuthbert Pepper of Pepper Hall, nr. Northallerton, Yorks., sis. and h. of Preston Pepper. *educ.* Manchester g.s. 1752; Trinity, Camb. 1761, fellow 1767; M. Temple 1762, called 1769. *m.* 9 Sept. 1784, Anne Dorothea, da. of Richard Wilbraham Bootle (q.v.), 3s. 4da. Kntd. 18 June 1788; *cr.* Baron Alvanley 22 May 1801.

A Welsh judge 1776–82; K.C. 1780; bencher, M. Temple 1780; solicitor-gen. July 1782–Apr. 1783, Dec. 1783–Mar. 1784; attorney-gen. and c.j. Chester Mar. 1784–June 1788; P.C. 18 June 1788; master of the rolls 1788–1801; c.j. of the common pleas 1801–*d.*

Arden, according to his obituary in the *Gentleman's Magazine* (1804, p. 384), after being called to the bar 'fixed his residence in Lincoln's Inn . . . and it is said he there lived on the same staircase' with Pitt, 'and they used to associate very much together'. Through Pitt's influence he was made solicitor-general and shortly afterwards brought into Parliament, and when Pitt resigned Arden followed him. 'There is great dissatisfaction in the House of Commons', he wrote to Lloyd Kenyon on 8 Apr. 1783, 'but what it will end in, no one can tell. For my part, I am heartily sick of politics, and should

be very glad never to set my foot in the House of Commons again.' And on 14 Apr.[1]: 'I am very well, in good spirits, and appeared in the House of Commons in boots, in the character of an independent country gentleman.'

He attacked Fox's East India bill, wrote Wraxall (iii. 180), 'through every stage with great pertinacity and spirit, not unaccompanied with legal ability'; it was, he told the House on 8 Dec. 1783, 'a private job'.[2] On the dismissal of the Coalition he resumed his old office. 'My constituents are so perfectly satisfied with my conduct in Parliament', he wrote to Kenyon on 9 Jan. 1784,[3] 'that they have unanimously re-elected me.'

He was one of Pitt's chief lieutenants on the Treasury bench, and his interventions in debate extended to subjects outside his judicial offices. On 18 Apr. 1785 he 'very ably' supported Pitt on parliamentary reform.[4] He was also a defender of Warren Hastings: 13 June 1786, he spoke against his impeachment, and on 9 May 1788 against the motion to impeach Impey; and on 4 May 1789 moved the previous question against a motion thanking Burke for his 'exertions and assiduity' in the prosecution of Hastings.

'Arden's merit', wrote Wraxall (iv. 151–2), 'seemed to consist principally in the strong predilection manifested towards him' by Pitt; without this 'never would Arden have reached the heights of the law'.

He died 19 Mar. 1804.

[1] *HMC Kenyon*, 515. [2] Debrett, xii. 404. [3] *HMC Kenyon*, 517. [4] Stockdale, v. 354.

J.B.

## ARMYTAGE, Sir George, 3rd Bt. (1734–83), of Kirklees Park, Yorks.

| | |
|---|---|
| YORK | 1761–1768 |

*b.* 25 Dec. 1734, 2nd s. of Sir Samuel Armytage, 1st Bt., and bro. of Sir John Armytage, 2nd Bt. (q.v.). *m.* 10 Apr. 1760, Anna Maria, da. and coh. of Godfrey Wentworth of Woolley Park, Yorks., 1s. and other issue. *suc.* bro. 10 Sept. 1758.

Armytage was returned unopposed at York as the candidate of Lord Rockingham, whom he followed in Parliament. Two speeches by him are recorded: 10 Dec. 1762, against the peace preliminaries;[1] and 23 Nov. 1763, on Wilkes's case.[2]

In the autumn of 1767 Armytage declared he would not stand at the general election, pleading ill health, and 'not being able to bear London'.[3] Rockingham, unable to find a suitable candidate, pressed him to change his mind but he refused— 'Mr. Wentworth, his father-in-law, anxiously wished him not to stand'.[4]

Armytage continued to support Rockingham in Yorkshire politics; he helped to organize the petition of 1769, was one of the deputation who presented it to the King, and was chairman of the county meeting in 1770. He died 21 Jan. 1783.

[1] Harris's 'Debates'. [2] His name appears in a list of speakers drawn up by Charles Jenkinson and sent to the King. Royal archives, Windsor. [3] John Fountayne to Rockingham, 28 Nov. 1767, Rockingham mss. [4] Rockingham to Newcastle, 16 Mar. 1768, Add. 32989, ff. 187-90.

J.B.

## ARMYTAGE, Sir John, 2nd Bt. (1732-58), of Kirklees Park, Yorks.

YORK 1754-10 Sept. 1758

b. 13 July 1732, 1st s. of Sir Samuel Armytage, 1st Bt., by Anne, da. of Thomas Griffith of Llanvyllan, Mont. educ. Eton, 1748; Trinity, Camb. 1751. unm. suc. fa. 19 Aug. 1747.

On 5 Dec. 1753 William Murray (q.v.) wrote to the Duke of Newcastle:[1]

Lord Rockingham desires me to acquaint your Grace that last Monday everything succeeded at York beyond his expectation. There was a most numerous appearance. They deputed a committee of 12 of the principal inhabitants to desire Lord Rockingham to recommend a candidate upon the Whig interest. He named Sir J. Armytage, and the recommendation was received unanimously.

Armytage supported Newcastle in Parliament. His only recorded speech was on the Minorca inquiry, 25 Apr. 1757.[2]

In 1758 he went as a volunteer on the expedition to St. Cas, and was killed 10 Sept.[3] At the time of his death he was engaged to be married to Mary, sister of George Augustus, 3rd Viscount Howe (q.v.).[4]

[1] Add. 32733, f. 367. [2] West to Newcastle [26 Apr. 1757], Add. 35877, f. 363. [3] London Mag. 1758, p. 518. But see also Walpole to Conway, 19 Sept. 1758, and London Chron. 19 Sept. 1758. [4] Walpole to Mann, 22 Sept. 1758.

J.B.

## ARUNDELL, Hon. Richard (c.1696-1758), of Allerton Mauleverer, Yorks.

KNARESBOROUGH 16 Apr. 1720-20 Jan. 1758

b. c.1696, 2nd s. of John, 2nd Baron Arundell of Trerice, by Barbara, da. of Sir Thomas Slingsby, M.P., 2nd Bt., of Scriven, nr. Knaresborough, Yorks., wid. of Sir Richard Mauleverer, 4th Bt., of Allerton Mauleverer. m. Aug. 1732, Lady Frances Manners, da. of John, 2nd Duke of Rutland, s.p. suc. to Allerton Mauleverer estate 1721.

Surveyor-gen. of works 1727-37; master of the mint 1737-44; ld. of Treasury 1744-6; treasurer of the chamber 1746-55; clerk of the pipe 1748-d.

Arundell was a close friend of Henry Pelham—they had married sisters—an intimate of Henry Fox and the Cavendish family, and a favourite of George

II. By 1754 he had almost reached the end of his active career as a placeman and parliamentarian. Newcastle, when reconstructing his Administration in November 1755, wrote to Lord Hartington:[1]

I have some reason to think, that our good friend Arundell would not be unwilling to retire upon the Irish establishment for his life. His present place brings him in above £2000 p.a. clear of all deductions, and therefore he would scarce like to accept less . . . You know how nice Arundell is, I write in fear and trembling lest he should be angry with me. I should not have troubled you upon this subject nor desired it of Arundell, if we were not so much distressed for places.

The offer was well received however, and Arundell retired from court with an Irish pension and a sinecure. He maintained his interest in the political scene, and was kept informed by Newcastle. 'You know the dependence I have upon your friendship and my regard for your judgment', wrote Newcastle on 30 Oct. 1756;[2] and in the negotiations of April 1757 Horace Walpole mentions Arundell as wishing to bring Fox and Newcastle together.[3]

Arundell died 20 Jan. 1758.

[1] 29 Nov. 1755, Add. 32861, f. 135. [2] Add. 32868, ff. 480-1 [3] Mems. Geo. II, iii. 6.

J.B.

## ARUNDELL, see also MONCKTON, William, and MONCKTON ARUNDELL

## ASHBURNHAM, William (1739-1823), of Broomham, nr. Hastings, Suss.

HASTINGS 1761-1774

b. 5 Mar. 1739, o. surv. s. of Rev. Sir William Ashburnham, 4th Bt., bp. of Chichester 1754-97, by Margaret, da. of Thomas Pelham of Lewes, Suss. educ. Corpus Christi, Camb. 1758. m. Apr. 1766, Alicia, da. of Rev. Francis Woodgate, rector of Mountfield, Suss., 4s. 1da. suc. fa. 4 Sept. 1797.

Dep. keeper of great wardrobe 12 July 1765-Mar. 1782.

Ashburnham, a distant cousin of Newcastle, was returned for Hastings on the Treasury interest. In Parliament he followed Newcastle, voted with the Opposition against Bute and Grenville, and was counted by Newcastle, 10 May 1764, as a 'sure friend'. Ashburnham was dependent on an allowance from his father, and on 24 Feb. 1765 wrote to an unnamed correspondent about his 'present very great want'. He was 'quite out of money', and concluded: 'If, therefore, Sir, you would be so kind to lend me ten pounds till Lady Day, I hope I shall then be able to return it to you again.'[1] In June 1765 he was considered for a post at the Ordnance,[2] but finally was appointed deputy keeper of the great wardrobe. Henceforth he supported successive

Administrations till he left Parliament. There is no record of his having spoken in the House.

He died 21 Aug. 1823.

[1] Add. 33068, f. 348. [2] Fortescue, i. 127.

M.M.D.

## ASHBY, Shukburgh (1724–92), of Quenby Hall, Leics.

LEICESTER  14 Feb.–25 Mar. 1784

*b.* 6 Oct. 1724, 1st s. of Skukburgh Ashby of Quenby by Mary, da. and h. of Nathaniel Cradock of Cossington, Leics. *educ.* Balliol, Oxf. 1 June 1742. *m.* c.1746, Elizabeth, da. and h. of Richard Hinde of Cold Ashby, Northants., 2da.

Sheriff, Leics. 1758–9.

Ashby was returned on the interest of the corporation and, in accordance with its inclination, supported Pitt. Although popular in the town he declined a contest in 1784.[1]

He died 28 Jan. 1792.

[1] *Northampton Merc.* 5 Apr. 1784.

I.R.C.

## ASHE, *see* A'COURT *and* A'COURT ASHE

## ASHLEY (ASHLEY COOPER), Cropley (1768–1851) of Wimborne St. Giles, Dorset.

DORCHESTER  30 Jan.–11 June 1790, 14 Apr. 1791–
14 May 1811

*b.* 21 Dec. 1768, 2nd s. of Anthony, 4th Earl of Shaftesbury, by his 2nd w. Hon. Mary Bouverie, da. of Jacob, 1st Visct. Folkestone. *educ.* Winchester 1778; Ch. Ch. Oxf. 1785–7. *m.* 10 Dec. 1796, Lady Anne Spencer, da. of George, 4th Duke of Marlborough, 6s. 4da. *suc.* bro. as 6th Earl of Shaftesbury 14 May 1811.

Clerk of deliveries of the Ordnance 1804–6, Mar.–July 1807; clerk of the Ordnance 1807–11; P.C. 22 July 1814; chairman of committees House of Lords 1814–51.

Ashley was returned on the family interest at Dorchester shortly before the dissolution. Defeated at the general election of 1790, he was returned on petition.

He died 2 June 1851.

E.A.S.

## ASSHETON SMITH, Thomas (c.1751–1828), of Vaenol, Caern. and Tidworth, Hants.

CAERNARVONSHIRE  1774–1780
ANDOVER  14 Dec. 1797–May 1821

*b.* c.1751, s. of Thomas Assheton of Ashley, Cheshire (who took name Smith on inheriting estates of his uncle) by his w. Mary Clayton, heiress of Brymbo

Hall, Denb. *educ.* Eton 1761. *m.* bef. 1776, Elizabeth, da. of Watkin Wynn of Voelas, Caern., 3s. 5da. *suc.* fa. 1774.

Sheriff, Caern. 1783–4; ld. lt. 1822–*d.*

Soon after succeeding to the family estates in 1774 Smith declared himself a candidate for Caernarvonshire in opposition to the sitting Member, Thomas Wynn. He received the support of Lord Bulkeley, who possessed the strongest interest in the county, and carried his election by 200 votes to 117.

In the House of Commons he voted consistently with Opposition. There is no record of his having spoken during his first Parliament. By 1780 Bulkeley had transferred his interest to another candidate, complaining that Smith had 'scandalously neglected both his friends and the country in general'.[1] Smith at once decided not to stand for re-election.

He died 12 May 1828.

[1] Baron Hill ms 5887.

P.D.G.T.

## ASTLEY, Sir John, 2nd Bt. (1687–1771), of Patshull, Staffs. and Everley, Wilts.

SHREWSBURY  1727–1734
SHROPSHIRE  1734–29 Dec. 1771

*bap.* 24 Jan. 1687, 1st surv. s. of Sir Richard Astley, 1st Bt., by his 2nd w. Henrietta, da. and coh. of William Borlase, M.P., of Great Marlow, Bucks. *m.* 27 May 1711, Mary, da. of Francis Prynce of Abbey Foregate, Shrewsbury, 1s. *d.v.p.* 6da. *suc.* fa. 24 Feb. 1688.

In 1754 a compromise existed in Shropshire whereby the county representation was left to the Tory country gentlemen, and Shrewsbury to Lord Powis's candidates. To this compromise Astley, a life-long Tory, strictly adhered,[1] even in 1760, though he was on friendly terms with Lord Bath.[2] His own elections for the county were unopposed. He is not in Fox's list of Members favourable to the peace preliminaries, but presumably voted for them. That Astley supported the Grenville Administration appears from a letter of 17 Mar. 1764,[3] in which Grenville thanks him for his offer of 'concurrence and support upon any emergent occasion'; but hopes to bring public business to a conclusion without asking friends 'now at a distance to return to town'; and refers to Astley's 'constant attendance throughout the course of this fatiguing session', and his 'cheerful and steady zeal . . . for the ease and quiet of the King's Government'. In the summer of 1765 Rockingham listed Astley as 'contra'; but he did not vote against the repeal of the Stamp Act, nor is any other vote of his recorded during his remaining years in Parliament. No speech of his in the House is mentioned during our period.

Dr. Richard Wilkes wrote in 1759 in his manuscript history of Staffordshire:[4]

Sir John Astley has lately pulled down the old church, house, stables, garden walls, etc. and in their stead erected those beautiful fabrics we now behold. . . . It is now the most beautiful place in the county; but neither this, nor affluence of fortune, makes happiness; for his lady has long lived at her own estate in Shrewsbury, and he the life of a recluse amidst an infinity of most delightful scenes.

He sold Patshull c. 1765 for £100,000 to Sir George Pigot (q.v.); and died 29 Dec. 1771.[5]

[1] See also HILL, Thomas. [2] Bath to Gen. Whitmore. 6 Nov. 1761, Powis mss at Powis Castle; Bath to Geo. Grenville, 7 Jan. 1764, Grenville mss (JM). [3] Grenville Letter Bk. [4] Quoted Stebbing Shaw, *Hist Staffs.* ii. 283. [5] Burke and *Gent. Mag.*; *GEC Baronetage* gives 29 Jan. 1772.

L.B.N.

**ASTLEY, Sir Edward,** 4th Bt. (1729–1802), of Melton Constable, Norf.[1]

NORFOLK 1768–1790

*bap.* 26 Dec. 1729, 1st s. of Sir Jacob Astley, 3rd Bt., of Melton Constable by Lucy, da. of Sir Nicholas L'Estrange, 4th Bt., of Hunstanton, Norf. and coh. of Sir Henry L'Estrange, 6th Bt. *educ.* Pembroke, Camb. 1747. *m.* (1) 23 May 1751, Rhoda (*d.*22 Oct. 1757), da. of Sir Francis Blake Delaval (q.v.), 3s.; (2) 24 Feb. 1759, Anne (*d.*23 July 1792), da. of Christopher Milles of Nackington, Kent, sis. of Richard Milles (q.v.), 1s.; (3) 30 July 1793, Elizabeth Bullen. *suc.* fa. 5 Jan. 1760.
Sheriff, Norf. 1763–4.

Astley, who came of an old and well-connected Norfolk family, canvassed the county at the by-election of 1764, but withdrew before the election. In 1768 he was returned for Norfolk after a very expensive contest.

Though, according to Wraxall, 'a man of no shining ability', Astley 'justly excited respect as an upright country gentleman' and 'was heard with much attention' by the House.[2] The *English Chronicle*, writing in 1780 or 1781, described him as

open and affable in his manner, unaffected in his conversation, and generous and liberal in his principles. He is fond of speaking in the House, for which, however, he is not exceedingly well calculated. His arguments are not indifferent, and his judgment is on all occasions above mediocrity, but he wants the easy *copia* of polished volubility.

Before his election Astley had privately expressed approval of the line taken by the Rockinghams.[3] In Parliament he was closely associated with them; in May 1769 he presided at the Opposition dinner at the Thatched House Tavern, and he regularly voted against the Grafton and North Administrations. Nevertheless he always considered himself a completely independent country gentleman, and on 12 Dec. 1770 declared:[4]

I do not propose myself to be of any party, or any side. I stand independent. . . . If every gentleman who stands up in this House to give a negative to Administration is to be termed a factious man, then, I say, a gentleman is intimidated from speaking his sentiments openly. I neither court the support of Administration, nor do I fear its favours, not of this, or any . . . I come with a desire to support it. If I have not done so often, I am not to blame.

On 5 Apr. 1770 he moved for an examination by the House of 'all pensions, additional salaries, and reversionary grants'[5] given during this Parliament, and in several of his other speeches, which covered a wide range of subjects, urged the need for economy. On 25 Feb. 1774, to prevent the House reverting to the 'very disagreeable and . . . very shameful' system of deciding election petitions, Astley moved to perpetuate Grenville's Election Act; and carried it against the Government.[6]

At the general election of 1774, and at all his subsequent elections, Astley, who had been forced to sell part of his estate to pay for the contest of 1768, and almost certainly could not have faced another,[7] was returned unopposed. He was hostile to the American war, and increasingly distrustful of North. On 5 Jan. 1781, after having complained of 'the growing burdens of this country', he asked ministers and placemen whether they would set an example of cheerful support by contributing to the public cause out of their 'great pensions and salaries', and on 12 June 1781, having lost one son in the war, he told the House he had 'still three more sons in the King's service', and he wished to know if any more of his blood 'was to be spilt in a war, which must end in our ruin, if pursued any longer?'[8]

After the fall of North, Astley supported the Rockingham Administration. He voted in favour of Shelburne's peace preliminaries, 18 Feb. 1783, and on 21 Feb. told the House that if the peace 'was not so good as gentlemen might think it ought to have been, the noble Lord in the blue riband, and not the present ministers, were to blame . . .' He lamented exceedingly that the inquiries into the noble Lord's conduct that were once talked of, 'had not been pursued'. His dislike of North made him oppose the Coalition: he told the House on 21 May 1783 that he had 'a great respect for several now in the Administration'. He had 'often voted with the right honourable secretary . . . [Fox]; his former Administration had done the country much service, and [he] should have been glad of continuing to support him, had he not coupled himself with others [he] could by no means approve'.[9] He spoke and voted against Fox's East India bill.[10]

Robinson, in his survey drawn up in December 1783, noted that Astley would 'often be for and perhaps sometimes against'. Astley himself told the House on 24 Dec. 1783 that though he had read in the papers that Sir Edward Astley had gone over to the Opposition, he must drink deep indeed of the water of Lethe before he should do that; he cared not indeed who was minister, he would support no man from influence but would always be guided by his opinion of the measure.[11] He was unable to be present at the meeting of country gentlemen at the St. Alban's Tavern in January 1784, but in the debate on Grosvenor's motion for a coalition, he said that he 'certainly would not concur with them in the resolution now under consideration of the House'. The country had 'already suffered greatly by the Coalition, the very name of which actually stank in the nation'.[12]

Astley consistently supported parliamentary reform; he voted for Pitt's reform proposals on 7 May 1783 and again on 18 Apr. 1785, and regularly endorsed Sawbridge's motion for annual Parliaments. Naturally concerned with agricultural interests, Astley on more than one occasion attempted to deflect taxes from them on to what he considered less desirable elements in the community. During the debate of 8 June 1785 on the tax on maid servants he owned he should

> be very well pleased to see both dogs and attornies subject to a duty. He thought them both articles of luxury, and had coupled them in this manner, because most of those who employed them ought, in his opinion, to pay for such an indulgence which he deemed in many ways exceptionable: indeed he had long wished to see a tax imposed on hairdressers, men milliners, and all others who dealt in effeminate occupations.[13]

On 7 Mar. 1788 Astley voted against Pitt on the East India declaratory bill, declaring that he had voted for his previous India bill because he thought it was the reverse of Fox's but now he found that 'it was almost as bad as the other'.[14] He went on to state that he had not withdrawn his confidence from Pitt, in fact he 'liked the right honourable gentleman', but wished he would keep better company; in other words he had 'a distrust of his colleagues'. He voted against Pitt over the Regency, 1788–9. He did not stand at the general election of 1790.

Astley died 27 Mar. 1802.

[1] This biography is based on a paper by Brian Hayes. [2] *Mems.* iii. 7; v. 74. [3] Rockingham to H. Harbord, 4 Oct. 1767, Suffield mss. [4] Cavendish's 'Debates', Egerton 223, f. 168. [5] Fortescue, ii. 139. [6] Cavendish's 'Debates', Egerton 252, ff. 113–16. [7] Lord Hastings, *Astley of Melton Constable*. See also E. Rolfe to T. W. Coke, 4 Apr. 1784, Leicester mss. [8] Debrett, i. 370; iii. 529. [9] Ibid. ix. 322; x. 62. [10] He does not appear in the division list for 27 Nov. but he told the House 7 Mar. 1788 (Stockdale, xiii. 333) that he had spoken and voted against. [11] Debrett, xii. 489. [12] Stockdale, xiii. 29. [13] Ibid. xviii. 491. [14] Ibid. xiii. 333.

M.M.D.

**ASTON, Sir Willoughby,** 5th Bt. (1714–72), of Risley, Derbys.

NOTTINGHAM  1754–1761

> *b.* 18 Feb. 1714, 1st s. of Richard Aston of Wadley, Berks. by Elizabeth, da. of John Warren of Wantage, Berks. *educ.* Oriel, Oxf. 1730, All Souls 1735; L. Inn 1731, called 1736. *m.* 14 May 1744, Elizabeth, da. of Henry Pye (q.v.) of Farringdon, Berks., 1s. 6da. *suc.* cos. as 5th Bt. 17 Feb. 1744.

In 1754 Aston stood for Nottingham on the Tory interest with the support of Lord Middleton, receiving financial support from him and 'divers other local gentlemen',[1] and was returned after a contest. In Dupplin's list of 1754 he was classed as Tory. There is no record of his having spoken in the House. He stood again in 1761, but without Lord Middleton's support or that of the local gentry,[2] and withdrew before the poll.

He died 24 Aug. 1772.

[1] John Clay to Newcastle, 24 Oct. 1753, Add. 32733, ff. 122–3. [2] Namier, *Structure*, 94; John Eggington to Newcastle, 4 Jan. 1761, Add. 32917, f. 121.

J.B.

**ATHERTON,** *see* **GWILLYM**

**ATKINSON, Christopher** (c.1738–1819), of Hales, Norf.

HEDON            1780–4 Dec. 1783, 1796–1806
OKEHAMPTON  1818–23 Apr. 1819

> *b.* c.1738. *m.* Jane, da. and coh. of John Savile of Enfield, Mdx., 1s. 2da. Her sis. m. Sir Thomas Hallifax (q.v.).

Christopher Atkinson was a corn factor, trading at 15 Mark Lane, London, and a contractor for wheat and malt to the Victualling Board. In 1775 he was defeated at Hedon, and in 1780 was returned after a contest. He supported North's Administration and voted against Shelburne's peace preliminaries, 18 Feb. 1783, but in March 1783 Robinson classed him as a doubtful friend of North. During his first period in Parliament he is not known to have spoken in the House.

On 31 Jan. 1781 a letter appeared in the *General Advertiser* accusing him of fraud in his dealings with the Victualling Board. Atkinson swore an affidavit that the charge was untrue, and was prosecuted for perjury. In July 1783 he was found guilty, and sentenced to stand in the pillory, to pay a fine of £2,000, and to be imprisoned for twelve months. In August he petitioned the Treasury that his transactions with the Victualling Board should be laid before the commission of public accounts, but his request was refused;[1] and 4 Dec. he was expelled the House.

He changed his name to Savile, 1798, and died 23 Apr. 1819.

[1] T29/54/302.

J.B.

**ATKINSON, Richard** (1738-85), of Fenchurch St., London.

NEW ROMNEY    14 June 1784–28 May 1785

*b.* 6 Mar. 1738, 3rd *s.* of Matthew Atkinson of Temple Sowerby, Westmld. by Margaret, *da.* of Richard Sutton of Kirkby Lonsdale, Westmld. *unm.*

Director, E.I. Co 1783–*d.*; alderman of London 1784–*d.*

The *Gentleman's Magazine* wrote in his obituary (1785, p. 570):

Mr. Atkinson when he came from the North was a mere adventurer, unsustained by any inheritance, by few family friends of any power, and by no acquisitions which education imparts but common penmanship and arithmetic. Thus circumstanced he came to London, and passing through different counting houses and experiments in trade, accumulated that prodigious wealth of which he died possessed, and which he had long enjoyed.

In 1774 he was a partner in the firm of Mure, Son, and Atkinson, of Nicholas Lane (and later of Fenchurch St.), West India merchants. During the American war he held a number of large government contracts for the supply of rum, victuals, and other necessities to the troops in North America and Gilbraltar.[1] Among his partners were Sir William James and Abel Smith (qq.v.). From about 1773 he was a minor member of the ministerial group in the court of East India proprietors. This, as well as his position as a government contractor, brought him into touch with John Robinson (also from Westmorland), and an intimate political friendship grew up between them.

In 1783 Atkinson took the lead in the Company against Fox's East India bill; and in 1784, seeking more power, pressed for reforms more drastic than Pitt and Dundas judged acceptable. At the general election he stood unsuccessfully for London as a supporter of Pitt; but two months later, at Pitt's request, was returned by Sir Edward Dering (q.v.) for New Romney, 'though much against Sir Edward's inclination, as not liking Mr. Atkinson's character'.[2] He spoke frequently in debates concerning the East India Company, and fiscal and commercial regulations. In debate, wrote Wraxall,[3] he was 'able and intelligent', speaking 'always with brevity, and never venturing to deviate into tracks with which he was unacquainted'. Daniel Pulteney (q.v.) wrote to the Duke of Rutland, 14 Feb. 1785:[4] 'It has for some time appeared to me that, for every purpose except entertaining the galleries, Jenkinson,

Atkinson . . . and Dundas possess almost all the good sense in the House.'

Atkinson died 28 May 1785, said to be worth over £300,000.

[1] T29/42/173–5, 322; T29/45/40, 103; T29/46/193. [2] Dering to Pitt, 24 Sept. [?1794], Chatham mss. [3] *Mems.* iii. 435. [4] *HMC Rutland*, iii. 180.

I.R.C.

**AUBREY, John** (1739-1826), of Boarstall and subsequently Dorton, Bucks.

| WALLINGFORD | 1768–1774 |
|---|---|
| AYLESBURY | 1774–1780 |
| WALLINGFORD | 1780–1784 |
| BUCKINGHAMSHIRE | 1784–1790 |
| CLITHEROE | 1790–1796 |
| ALDEBURGH | 1796–1812 |
| STEYNING | 1812–1820 |
| HORSHAM | 1820–14 Mar. 1826 |

*b.* 4 June 1739, 1st *s.* of Sir Thomas Aubrey, 5th Bt., of Boarstall, Bucks. and Llantrithyd, Glam. by Martha, *da.* of Richard Carter of Chilton, Bucks. *educ.* Westminster 1752; Ch. Ch. Oxf. 1758. *m.* (1) 9 Mar. 1771, Mary (*d.*14 June 1781), *da.* of Sir James Colebrooke, 1st Bt., (q.v.), 1s. *d.v.p.*; (2) 26 May 1783, his 1st cos. Martha Catherine, *da.* and *coh.* of George Richard Carter of Chilton, *s.p. suc.* fa. as 6th Bt. 4 Sept. 1786.

Ld. of Admiralty July 1782–Mar. 1783; ld. of Treasury Dec. 1783–Mar. 1789.

In 1768 Aubrey successfully contested Wallingford with the support of Lord Abingdon (with whom he had been at Westminster). Aubrey was a fervent admirer of Chatham, whom he described as 'the greatest minister this country knows',[1] and a close friend of Shelburne.[2] In Parliament he consistently voted against the Grafton and North Administrations. In his maiden speech on 17 Mar. 1769 he attacked the ministerial measures against Wilkes: 'proceedings . . . so violent and unconstitutional as power may for a time support, but nothing can justify'.[3] During the debate on the seating of Luttrell, 15 Apr. 1769, he pointed out the dangers of extending the privileges of the House to threaten the liberty of the constituents. On 25 Feb. 1774 he spoke in support of the motion to perpetuate the Grenville Act.

In 1774 Aubrey, having by the purchase of Dorton added considerably to his Buckinghamshire estates, decided to stand for the county at the general election;[4] but finding little support he withdrew several weeks before it. Finally he successfully contested Aylesbury, thereby enraging Lord Abingdon who, though already annoyed by Aubrey's threat to the peace of the county, had continued to support him at Wallingford. Abingdon wrote to Edmund Burke on 4 Oct.:[5]

Aubrey has used me most cruelly and treacherously, I had laboured through thick and thin to secure him a seat in Parliament . . . and after having procured him a clear majority, he slips away to Aylesbury and declares himself a candidate for that town, and flings the voters and all my party into the greatest consternation. . . . He is a most designing, wavering, unsteady chap.

Aubrey strongly opposed the Administration's American measures, and on 15 May 1775 declared that while the Government persisted in its attempts to tax America he would think himself 'justified in taking every opportunity of voting on the side of that oppressed, perhaps I might say, devoted people'.[6] During the debate of 11 Feb. 1778, supporting North's conciliatory proposals, he 'praised the conduct of the Americans, particularly their mode of making war, by which he showed the impossibility of success by our arms'.[7] He was increasingly critical of North; on 12 Mar. 1778 said that the Americans 'would never agree to any negotiation while the present ministers remained in power', and on 17 Mar. he urged North to resign to make way for Chatham,

> who had neither forced the Cabinet nor ever scrambled for a place . . . but who had once already conducted our public affairs with the perfect unanimity of the two Houses of Parliament, as well as that of the nation at large . . . his very name alone, were he in power, would more contribute to put a stop to the hostile designs of the House of Bourbon, than all the mighty preparations we had heard so much boasted of.[8]

Aubrey's liberal views extended also to Ireland, and during the second reading of the Irish bill, 18 Dec. 1779, he said that he 'wished to see not only their trade free but their constitution likewise'.[9]

By the summer of 1780 Aubrey had decided not to stand again for Aylesbury, and at the general election was returned once more for Wallingford, apparently unopposed and with Abingdon's support. After the formation of the Rockingham Administration in 1782 he wrote to Isaac Barré on 31 Mar. that though he was aware that all places were disposed of, he hoped for a distinction 'in another line'.[10] On 6 May 1782 he spoke in support of Burke's bill for abolishing various offices and sinecures, describing it as a

> perpetual monument to the honour of an Administration who availed themselves of power to no other purpose than to fulfil their promises when out of power; and would be received by the people of England as pledges of a farther and more effectual reformation in the state.[11]

Aubrey obtained office under Shelburne, but lost it on the formation of the Coalition. In December 1783 he accepted a lordship of the Treasury from Pitt, but 'avowed that with me office was not an object, and that an English peerage was what I

wished for'.[12] This ambition was to become an obsession, and during the next few years, convinced that he had obtained a definite promise of a peerage, he plied Pitt[13] with increasingly querulous letters reiterating his case.

At the general election of 1784 Aubrey successfully contested Buckinghamshire, his return undoubtedly being assisted by the absence of Lord Verney, his Coalition opponent, who was then living as a bankrupt in France. It was an expensive election; according to Aubrey himself, 'the expenses . . . were such, that they could have been endured by very few fortunes'.[14] During this Parliament Aubrey seems to have been frequently absent through illness—his only reported votes were in favour of Pitt's parliamentary reform proposals, 18 Apr. 1785, and of Richmond's fortifications plan, 27 Feb. 1786. Continued disappointment over his peerage embittered his relations with Pitt, though he denied[15] that this influenced him when in December 1788 he announced that he could not concur with the Administration in admitting the legality of a Parliament not summoned by the King or his proxy, in this case the Prince of Wales.

> Till this chasm in Parliament shall be filled [he declared on 22 Dec.[16]] I cannot assent to joining in any vote, or any other business of the House, beyond voting for a previous question, or some other question tending to prevent our further acting as a House. When this chasm shall be properly filled up, when the Parliament shall be full by a representation of the King, I shall cheerfully and heartily concur in the seemingly general sentiment of making the heir apparent *sole Regent*.

And though denying any connexion with the Opposition, he further declared that 'the argument for restriction of the Prince as a Regent seems more to favour of prejudice against a particular party in the state, than to concern the general and public welfare'.[17] An Administration supporter, Sir William Young, commented to the Marquess of Buckingham the following day:[18]

> Our rats . . . all showed their tails on last night's motion. . . . Sir John Aubrey, rat-major, receiving his emoluments of the Treasury for five years, and declaring himself unconnected with any, afforded a subject of a general laugh.

Aubrey himself professed surprise at the Administration's reaction to his defection, and when no longer summoned to meetings of the Treasury Board, wrote to Pitt on 3 March:[19]

> For this I can no otherwise account than by supposing that the explanation of my sentiments on the equally important and distressful Regency business, first to yourself in private, and afterwards to the House of Commons, was offensive to you. . . . But . . . neither the degree and kind of difference in sentiments between you and me, nor any circumstances attending

that difference, were such, as according to my view of the case could justify the least suspicion of my being influenced in my conduct by any bias towards the party in opposition to your Administration.

He then repeated at great length his arguments in the House, and denied that he had 'in any degree mixed the affair of the peerage with a consideration so entirely foreign'. Since his speech on the Regency he had adhered to his vow not to vote. He had refrained from resigning during the crisis, but the situation having now been restored by the King's recovery, he, though still unconnected with the Opposition, offered his resignation, which could 'be no longer delayed without seeming to acquiesce in the justice of your slight to me'. No further vote or speech by Aubrey is reported before 1790, but soon afterwards he went into opposition and voted with Fox during the French war.

He died 14 Mar. 1826.

¹ Almon, i. 471. ² Draft of letter from Shelburne to Temple, 18 Sept. 1779, refers to his 'particular regard and more than political friendship' for Aubrey, Lansdowne mss. ³ Cavendish's 'Debates', Egerton 219, pp. 110–12. ⁴ Burke to Rockingham, 18 Sept. 1774. ⁵ Sheffield City Lib., Burke mss. ⁶ Almon, i. 470–1. ⁷ Ibid. viii. 369. ⁸ Stockdale, viii. 131, 159. ⁹ Almon xvi. 222. ¹⁰ Lansdowne mss. ¹¹ Debrett, vii. 117–19. ¹² Aubrey to Pitt, 9 June 1787, Chatham mss. ¹³ There are in the Chatham papers nine letters from Aubrey to Pitt about his peerage. Most are long; all are tedious. ¹⁴ Aubrey to Pitt, 8 Apr. 1787, Chatham mss. ¹⁵ Aubrey to Pitt, 3 Mar. 1789, Chatham mss. ¹⁶ Stockdale, xvi. 146–8. ¹⁷ Ibid. ¹⁸ Buckingham, *Courts & Cabinets Geo. III*, ii. 72. ¹⁹ Chatham mss.

M.M.D.

**AUBREY, Thomas** (?1740–1814), of Savile Row, London.

WALLINGFORD    1784–1790

*b.* ?1740, 2nd s. of Sir Thomas Aubrey, 5th Bt., of Boarstall, Bucks. and Llantrithyd, Glam. and bro. of John Aubrey (q.v.). *educ.* Westminster, May 1752, aged 11; Jesus, Oxf. 15 Nov. 1756, aged 16. *m.* Elizabeth Twing, 1da.
Ensign 9 Ft. 1762; lt. 4 Ft 1766; capt. 47 Ft. 1771; maj. 1782; half pay as capt. 1788.

Aubrey was returned for Wallingford with his brother's support.¹ In William Adam's list of May 1784 he is classed as an Administration supporter; he voted for Pitt's parliamentary reform proposals, 18 Apr. 1785, and for Richmond's fortifications plan, 27 Feb. 1786. On 12 Sept. 1787 he unsuccessfully applied to Pitt for promotion in the army.² Like his brother, Aubrey did not vote on the Regency, 1788–9. There is no record of his having spoken in the House.

Aubrey died 15 Jan. 1814.

¹ Sir John Aubrey to Pitt, 8 Apr. 1787, Chatham mss. ² Ibid.

M.M.D.

**AUCKLAND, Baron,** *see* **EDEN, William**

**AUFRÈRE, George René** (1715–1801), of Chelsea, Mdx.

STAMFORD    21 Jan. 1765–1774

*b.* 7 Nov. 1715, 2nd s. of Israel Antoine Aufrère, a Huguenot clergyman, by Sarah Amsincq of a distinguished Dutch family. G. R. Aufrère's gd.-fa., Marquis de Colville in France, fled to Holland in 1683 and emigrated to England in 1700. *m.* 1746, Arabella, da. of William Bate of Foston Hall, Derbys., 1da. who m. Charles Anderson Pelham (q.v.).
Commr. for sale of French prizes 1756–64; director, London Assurance 1761–77; commr. for Liverpool on committee of the Africa Co. 1764–5.

Aufrère was a merchant, at first in partnership with Sir William Smith, linen draper in Cornhill; in 1743 with Smith and Peregrine Cust (q.v.); and in 1763 with John Sargent (q.v.). Before he entered Parliament he was a considerable subscriber to Government loans, but by 1765 his business activities had diminished a good deal and about 1770 he retired.

His wife was a cousin of Brownlow Cecil, 8th Earl of Exeter, and he was returned for Stamford on the Exeter interest. In July 1765 he was classed by Rockingham as 'pro' and was one of the merchants who dined with Rockingham 31 Dec. 1765 to discuss American policy.¹ In November 1766 Rockingham classed him as 'Whig', Townshend in January 1767 as 'Government', and Newcastle in March as 'friend'. He voted against Chatham's Administration on the land tax, 27 Feb. 1767, and nullum tempus, 17 Feb. 1768.

No vote by him is recorded in 1769, but he was against Administration on Glynn's motion, 6 Dec. 1770, and on three other divisions before the dissolution. His attendance seems to have been poor, and there is no record of his having spoken in the House. He did not stand in 1774.

He died, a wealthy man, 7 Jan. 1801. His widow at her death in 1804 left to her daughter Aufrère's pictures, 'one of the finest collections of paintings in the country'.²

¹ Rockingham to Newcastle, 2 Jan. 1766, Add. 32973, ff. 11–13. ² Agnew, *Protestant Exiles from France*, ii. 391.

J.B.

**AYTOUN,** *see* **COLVILE**

**BACKWELL, Barnaby** (*d.*1754), of Tyringham, Bucks.

BISHOP'S CASTLE    18 Apr.–3 Oct. 1754

2nd but 1st surv. s. of Tyringham Backwell of Tyringham, Bucks. by Elizabeth, da. of Sir Francis Child, ld. mayor of London, sis. of Samuel Child, M.P., banker. *m.* (1) 16 Apr. 1743, Margaret (*d.*1745), da. of Samuel Clarke, London merchant, *s.p.*; (2)

23 June 1747, Sarah Gibbon,[1] 1s. 3da. *suc.* fa. 19 July 1754.

Backwell was a partner in the bank of Samuel and Francis Child, and said to be 'possessed of £4,000 p.a.'.[2] In 1754 he stood for Bishop's Castle, a notoriously corrupt borough, which his uncle Samuel Child had represented 1747–52. The chief interest in it was held by the Walcot family who were heavily in debt to Child's bank. In Newcastle's 'state of elections', March 1754,[3] the note is placed against Bishop's Castle: 'strongly contested'. Backwell came out second on the poll. In Dupplin's list of 1754 he was classed as a Tory. He died 3 Oct. 1754.

[1] Lipscomb, *Bucks.* iv. 376; *Gent. Mag.* 1747, p. 296, gives her name as Gordon. [2] *Gent. Mag.* 1754, p. 483. [3] Add. 32995, ff. 138–41.

M.M.D.

## BACKWELL, Richard (?1695–1765), of Billing, nr. Northampton.

NORTHAMPTON    9 Dec. 1755–1761

*b.* ?1695, 1st s. of Richard Backwell by his w. Mary Banks. *m.* Catherine; their da. and h. m. 1753 Peregrine Bertie (q.v.). *suc.* fa. 1731.

Backwell purchased estates at Billing and Pattishall near Northampton, and in 1755 on the death of Charles Compton, whose heir was a minor, was returned there unopposed. No vote or speech by him is reported. He did not stand again in 1761 when Spencer Compton, now of age, came forward on the Compton interest.

Backwell died 12 Feb. 1765, aged 70.

M.M.D.

## BACON, Anthony (c.1717–86), of Woodford, Essex and Copthall Court, Throgmorton St., London.[1]

AYLESBURY    25 Jan. 1764–1784

Manxman; yr. bro. of Rev. Thomas Bacon of Maryland, compiler of Bacon's *Laws of Maryland*. *m.* bef. 1757, Elizabeth, 1s. *d.v.p.*

As a young man Bacon kept a store on Chesapeake Bay in Maryland. He left America about 1740, and for the next few years traded between England and the southern colonies as master of his own ship. About 1748 he settled as a merchant in London, importing tobacco from America, dealing in coal from Cumberland where he acquired mines, in Senegal gum, in slaves, etc. From 1758 onwards he held Government contracts; during the seven years' war for victualling and paying troops in West Africa, and from 1764 onwards in the West Indies; for the supply of slaves; for coal and shipping.

The most important chapter of his business career

was concerned with South Wales. In 1765 he took out a 99-year lease of some 4,000 acres of mineral bearing land around Merthyr Tydvil ('Bacon's Mineral Kingdom'), and set up furnaces and forges at Cyfarthfa and Hirwain. As a gun-founder he held Ordnance contracts from 1773 onwards, being among the first to use Wilkinson's invention of boring cannon from the solid. From 1775 he was one of the chief contractors for provisioning British troops in America. In 1782 he leased his works and retired from business.

In 1763 Bacon began to cultivate an interest at New Shoreham: in November he was defeated at Honiton after an expensive and riotous election; and in January 1764 returned for Aylesbury. Alexander Fall, a London merchant, wrote to Charles Jenkinson, 29 Jan.: 'They say . . . Bacon was obliged to get Member cost what it would, other ways he could not pass his accounts as contractor. He paid five guineas a man at Aylesbury, and £8000 it cost him opposing Yonge at Honiton.' Having made himself unpopular at New Shoreham, he henceforth stuck to Aylesbury, and, building up an interest of his own in a venal and expensive constituency, held his seat in contested elections in 1774 and 1780.

Bacon's first recorded speech in the House, 8 Mar. 1764, was for a bill to make Members liable to bankruptcy proceedings.[2] On 22 Mar. he spoke against Grenville's proposals for taxing American imports, and on 4 Apr. introduced a bill to prohibit paper currency in the colonies from becoming legal tender. He subsequently claimed to have opposed Grenville's Stamp Act. He 'was favoured with a long, though unsuccessful, conference with the minister', he wrote in 1775, ' . . . in the course of which all that has since happened in consequence of that ill-concerted measure was very nearly predicted'. His objections were against the mode of taxing the colonists, not against the right; still, though the Rockingham Administration opposed him at New Shoreham, he spoke for the third reading of the repeal bill, 4 Mar. 1766. Similarly he claimed to have been against the Townshend duties —'a more absurd or insufficient tax was never conceived, both with respect to the Americans or ourselves'—but nothing has been discovered of any opposition he made in the House of Commons.

Bacon consistently supported the Grafton and North Administrations—as a Government contractor for most of the period it was expected of him. About 1773, when his contracts were much reduced, he received a secret service pension of £600 per annum—which seems a small sum considering his wealth and standing, and which was presumably relinquished when he again became a contractor.

Few speeches by him are recorded—less than half a dozen for the period of the American war. On that war, his opinions are best seen in a pamphlet he published in 1775.[3] Taking his stand on his long association with America, he repeated every current cliché: the mother country should be lenient and tender and the children dutiful and obedient, but if ungrateful and obstreperous, should be treated 'with a little wholesome severity'; and he appealed for support of Lord North 'in every measure which may tend to bring back the Americans to their duty'.

In August 1782 John Robinson wrote in a memorandum for Shelburne: 'Mr Bacon had connexions with Government but they are all now put an end to, yet may be hopeful with attention.' But Bacon voted against Shelburne's peace preliminaries, 18 Feb. 1783, and supported the Coalition: his last speech in the House was a defence of their unpopular receipts tax;[4] he also voted for Fox's East India bill, 27 Nov. 1783, and in Stockdale's list of 19 Mar. 1784 is classed as an opponent of Pitt. He did not stand at the general election of 1784.

Bacon died 21 Jan. 1786. In contradistinction to most *nouveaux riches* of the period he does not seem to have risen socially, and little is known about his private life. His only legitimate child died in 1770, aged 12; but he left an illegitimate family by Mary Bushby of four sons and one daughter, to whom he bequeathed his property. When he drew up his will in 1785 his eldest son was at school at Gloucester 'by the name of William Addison'; another name used for him was Frankland, and for the other children Smith. In 1792 the eldest assumed the name of Bacon, and so apparently did the other children. Anthony Bacon's descendants in the male line died out in the second generation, and, though landowners, did not appear in Burke's *Landed Gentry*. He had done his best to hide his progeny, and in turn seems not to have been avowed by his descendants.

[1] This biography is based on Namier, 'Anthony Bacon, M.P., an 18th century merchant', *Jnl. Econ. & Business Hist.* 1929. [2] His speeches are reported in Harris's 'Debates'. [3] *A Short Address to the Government, the Merchants, Manufacturers, and the Colonists in America, and the Sugar Islands, on the present state of affairs, by a Member of Parliament.* [4] Debrett, x. 160, 163.

L.B.N.

**BACON, Edward** (?1712–86), of Earlham, nr. Norwich.

KING'S LYNN 25 Feb. 1742–1747
CALLINGTON 21 Apr. 1748–1754
NEWPORT 1754–June 1756
NORWICH 25 June 1756–1784

*b.* ?1712, 1st s. of Waller Bacon of Earlham, M.P. for Norwich, bencher of G. Inn, by his w. Frances. *educ.*

G. Inn 1731, called 1738, bencher 1755, treasurer 1764. *m.* 4 Sept. 1742, Elizabeth Knight of Southampton, *s.p.* *suc.* fa. 1734.

Steward of Norwich 1750, recorder 1752–83.

Ld. of Trade Dec. 1759–July 1765; chairman of committee of privileges and elections 1758–70.

Independent and diligent, Bacon was a highly respectable and apparently very dull Member. During his 41 years in the House he is not known to have spoken in any major debate, and altogether his interventions were exceedingly rare; his parliamentary activities centred on committee work, and he was an indefatigable representative of local interests. Horace Walpole described him as having 'more Whiggism than abilities'.[1]

Returned for King's Lynn, and next for Callington, on the Walpole interest, Bacon was a regular, though not a subservient, Government supporter. In 1754 he was invited to stand for Norwich. The following memorandum, dated 25 Mar. 1754, is among Newcastle's election papers:[2]

> Mr. Bacon says that Mr. Pelham pressed [him] to decline standing for Norwich, that to oblige Mr. Pelham he did decline (though it was to his own inclination to have stood) Mr. Pelham having promised to bring him into Parliament. Mr. Pelham acquainted him by letter this summer that he had fixed him at Newport, and that he should come in upon *easy and reasonable terms*. To which Mr. Bacon wrote an answer submitting to Mr. Pelham's pleasure as to his election, but declining contest or expense.
> Mr. Morice yesterday wrote to Mr. Bacon and Col. Lee that as he had been at an excessive expense at Newport they could not expect to come in for nothing, that he did not expect a reimbursement of his expenses, and that they should pay no more than what was agreed by Mr. Pelham. . .

And a further minute of 31 Mar.[3] reads: '*Mr. Bacon* of Norwich. Is willing to come in at Newport at an expense of £1000.' He was returned after a contest. When, however, toward the end of 1755 'Old Horace' Walpole, M.P. for Norwich, was about to be made a peer, Bacon would not stand down for his son Thomas (q.v.). This time Newcastle, apparently afraid that a dispute with Walpole might drive Bacon 'into measures of opposition', persuaded Walpole to give in: which did not surprise Bacon who had secured a 'steady and firm attachment' of 'gentlemen of all denominations' to his interest.[4] He was returned unopposed.

When on 2 May 1757, in the concluding debate on the loss of Minorca, George Townshend moved an amendment inculpating the Newcastle-Fox Administration, Bacon voted for it;[5] and in June, when a new Administration was being formed, Pitt insisted on his being appointed to the first vacancy at the Board of Trade; but because of a promise to Eliot (q.v.) that none should be disposed of till they both could be accommodated[6] he had to wait till December 1759. He then zealously applied himself to its work, his attendance at Board meetings during his 5½ years of office averaging nearly 80 per cent.[7]

At the general election of 1761 Bacon and Harbord were opposed by two Norwich aldermen whom they easily defeated. In October 1761 Newcastle sent Bacon his parliamentary whip through Lord Buckinghamshire; in Bute's list of December 1761, he is marked 'Government' and 'Orford'. In the choice of a new Speaker, Bacon was seriously considered by Newcastle[8] who, however, finding that he was 'not liked',[9] does not seem to have pressed his candidature. In November 1762 Newcastle still classed Bacon as 'pro', but Fox, in a list compiled at the beginning of December, more correctly included him among the Members favourable to the peace preliminaries. Not a single Opposition vote by Bacon is recorded under the Bute or the Grenville Administration. In March 1763 he was placed, as a safe man, on what was really a Treasury list for the select committee to inquire into the accounts of the late war. Only one single speech by Bacon is recorded in this Parliament (if it was a speech): on 29 Feb. 1764 he moved on behalf of his Board the estimates for the civil settlements of East and West Florida.[10]

Bacon's retention at the Board of Trade was never considered by the Rockinghams in June-July 1765; and he went into opposition with the Grenvilles; voted against the repeal of the Stamp Act, 7 and 22 Feb. 1766; and against the Chatham Administration over the land tax, 27 Feb. 1767. In January and March 1767 Townshend and Newcastle classed him as a follower of Grenville; but a letter from Lord Buckinghamshire to George Grenville, written from Norwich, 29 Feb. 1768,[11] suggests that he was veering toward the Government (his not voting on the nullum tempus bill may have been symptomatic):

> The county and city are in a high ferment, it does not appear to me that Bacon will lose his election, I could have wished his behaviour had lately been such as would have justified my interesting myself for him.

In the new Parliament Bacon's first recorded vote, on Wilkes's petition, 27 Jan. 1769, was still with Opposition; after which he appears in every extant division list as voting with Government, except on making permanent Grenville's Election Act—having long been chairman of the committee on elections, he appreciated the value of the Act; he appears in the King's list as a dissenting 'friend', and at the end of the Parliament was classed by Robinson as 'pro'. A few interventions in debate by Bacon in committees on the gunpowder bill and on the linen trade, 6 May 1772 and in March 1774, are reported in this Parliament (by Cavendish and Brickdale), the last to be recorded anywhere.

In 1774 Bacon's election was uncontested. In the new Parliament he remained an unwavering supporter of the North Administration: there are seven division lists in this Parliament giving the names of Government supporters, and from none was Bacon absent. The *Public Ledger*, an Opposition paper, wrote about him in 1779:

> Steadily attached to the ministry in all questions whatsoever. What his motives are, and what his objects (for he has not the appearance of being without them) does not fall to our knowledge.

But as he never held any office after 1765, it must be assumed that he acted from conviction—which the *English Chronicle*, though also an Opposition paper, acknowledged in a note on him in 1781:

> *Edward Bacon* . . . is an intelligent sensible man, perfectly conversant in the intricacies of committee business, and skilled in all the branches of commercial information. He is vulgarly denominated a *stickler*, but as this appellation appears in him to be only an ill-natured mode of conveying an idea of indefatigable attention to every subject that comes within his cognizance, it will rather operate as a compliment than otherwise. He is firmly attached to Lord North, and is of course his friend in Parliament.

The election of 1780 was warmly contested, and Bacon won by a narrow margin only. In the new Parliament no vote by him is recorded: he was too ill to attend. Robinson wrote about him in December 1783:[12]

> Mr. Bacon is so ill he can't attend and can't live long; perhaps may not wish to come in again.

He did not stand in 1784, and died 12 Mar. 1786.

[1] *Mems. Geo. III*, i. 68. [2] Add. 32995, f. 128. [3] Ibid. f. 134. [4] Walpole to Newcastle, 15 Nov. 1755, Add. 32861, f. 482; Newcastle to Bacon, 27 Nov., 1 Dec., Walpole to Newcastle, 2 Dec., Add. 32861, ff. 108, 161, 175. [5] J. West to Newcastle, 3 May, Add. 32871, f. 13. [6] Add. 32891, f. 235; 32896, f. 338; 32898, ff. 364-5. [7] Basye, *Board of Trade*, 223-5. [8] See list, n.d., Add. 32929, f. 319. [9] Newcastle to Bedford, 10 Oct., Bedford mss 44, f. 194. [10] Harris's 'Debates'. [11] Grenville mss (JM). [12] Laprade, 74.

L.B.N.

**BAGOT, Sir Walter Wagstaffe**, 5th Bt. (1702–68), of Blithfield, Staffs.

NEWCASTLE-UNDER-LYME 20 Nov 1724–1727
STAFFORDSHIRE 1727–1754
OXFORD UNIVERSITY 16 Dec. 1762–20 Jan. 1768

*b.* 3 Aug. 1702, 1st surv. s. of Sir Edward Bagot, 4th Bt., M.P. Staffs. 1698–1708, by Frances, da. and h. of Sir Thomas Wagstaffe of Tachbrook, Warws. *educ.* Isleworth and Colney Hatch schools, Mdx.; Magdalen, Oxf. 1720. *m.* 27 July 1724, Lady Barbara Legge, da. of William, 1st Earl of Dartmouth, 8s. 8da. *suc.* fa. 1712.

Trustee of Radcliffe Lib. Oxf. 1737.

Bagot, a Tory, consistently voted against the Walpole and Pelham Administrations. At the general election of 1754 he withdrew from Parliament in favour of his son, William.[1] But when on 30 Nov. 1762 he was urged by Thomas Jenner, president of Magdalen, to stand at the Oxford University by-election, he reluctantly agreed, though he felt

> unequal to undertake so high a trust, at my time of life; who have many years since . . .withdrawn myself from it; as knowing my health would not permit me to give that attendance to the House it was my duty to do.[2]

On 16 December Jenner informed him that his candidature had upheld 'the peace and honour of the University', and he had been returned unopposed. On the 18th Bagot himself wrote to the chancellor (Lord Lichfield) of the need to defend 'that great bulwark of the Church of England, who in these our days, has so many enemies to cope with; which makes me wish, now our constitution is at so ticklish a crisis, that the University had fixed on some person better qualified to serve them in Parliament, than it is in my power to do'.[3]

Bagot's first reported vote during this Parliament was with Administration, 10 Feb. 1764, against repealing the cider tax. And on 24 Apr. 1764 George Grenville wrote to Bagot's son, William: 'No man can have greater honour for Sir Walter or a more sincere desire to cultivate his friendship and his family than I have.'[4] In Rockingham's list of July 1765 he was classed as 'doubtful', and in that of November 1766 as 'Tory, Bute'. His only other reported vote was with Opposition on the land tax, 27 Feb. 1767. There is no record of any speech by him during his second period in the House.

Bagot died 20 Jan. 1768.

[1] W. R. Ward, *Georgian Oxford*, 224. [2] W. Bagot, *Mems. Bagot Fam.* 86–87. [3] Ibid. [4] Grenville mss (HL).

A.N.N.

**BAGOT, William** (1728–98), of Blithfield, Staffs.

STAFFORDSHIRE 1754–1780

*b.* 28 Feb. 1728, 1st surv. s. of Sir Walter Wagstaffe Bagot, 5th Bt. (q.v.). *educ.* Westminster 1739–46; Magdalen, Oxf. 1747; Grand Tour 1749–52. *m.* 20 Aug. 1760, Hon. Elizabeth Louisa St. John, da. of John, 2nd Visct. St. John, 6s. 4da. *suc.* fa. as 6th Bt. 20 Jan. 1768; *cr.* Baron Bagot 17 Oct. 1780.

In 1754 Bagot was returned for Staffordshire in place of his father. Classed in Dupplin's list as a Tory, he was one of the group who frequented the Cocoa Tree, Horn, and St. Alban's taverns.

In Bute's list of December 1761 he was classed 'Tory, Legge'; 'Legge' was later changed to 'Bute'. He did not receive Newcastle's whip in October

1761. But in November, when a commission of accounts was to be set up, Barrington suggested that he would 'make a proper commissioner'.[1] He appears in Fox's list of Members in favour of the peace preliminaries, and was offered a place at the Board of Trade: he 'seemed inclined to take it', wrote Newcastle to Devonshire on 23 Dec., 'but desired to consult his father . . . who . . . showed an inclination that his son should not accept it; upon which young Bagot refused it'.[2] His name does not appear in any of the minority lists between 1762 and 1764. In Rockingham's list of July 1765 he is classed as 'doubtful'. He voted against the repeal of the Stamp Act, 7 and 22 Feb. 1766; with Opposition on the land tax, 27 Feb. 1767; and with Administration on Wilkes's expulsion, 3 Feb. 1769 and the Middlesex election, 15 Apr. 1769. In the division list of 8 May 1769 he appears as voting with Opposition—almost certainly a mistake, since on 8 and 25 Jan. 1770 he again voted with Government over the Middlesex election.

Described by Walpole as 'Lord North's particular friend',[3] Bagot supported Government to the end of his time in the Commons. In April 1770 North offered him the office of treasurer of the chamber. In a long letter of refusal Bagot wrote:[4] 'Any little support it has been in my power to give you, was certainly due to you from every honest and unprejudiced man'; though flattered by the offer he 'declined it', for 'circumstanced so as not to be impatient for emoluments, I am confident this will be disposed of much more advantageously for his [Majesty's] service than if I had accepted it'. His only fear was that his refusal should offend the King. To this North replied: 'You need be under no apprehensions lest your refusal should be misinterpreted or misunderstood in any place; your principles are known to be honourable, loyal, and friendly towards Government.'

He was a frequent speaker in the House on both national and local issues, voluble, humourless, and a steady opponent of change. Supporting the royal marriage bill, 13 Mar. 1772, he declared that since it was impossible to draw a line defining the prerogative, he 'as a commoner' thought it 'safer to trust that line with the Crown than to trust that line anywhere else'.[5] He feared 'that without this bill the younger children of the Crown would intermarry with the great families, and the regal and aristocratical powers would oppress the commoners'.[6] He vigorously opposed all attempts to grant relief to the Dissenters, declaring (10 Mar. 1779) that such relief would be 'no less than an alteration of the constitution in this country', and 'that the toleration as it now stood was ample, and that under that toleration doctrines were delivered and disseminated of a very extraordinary nature'.[7] Even a bill to license a playhouse at Birmingham seemed to him a source of danger to the nation, 19 Apr. 1777:

> By way of proving the fatal tendency of establishing theatres indiscriminately in any kingdom, Sir William adverted to the times of the Romans, when he declared the giving theatres was the cause of the decline of the state; he declared, that to add to the dissipation of the people was always the maxim adopted by those who meant to enslave them . . . the Romans were also obliged to establish granaries of corn, and to give the people bread at the same time; this latter he feared would be the next step with Birmingham, if the House gave them a theatre.[8]

The *Public Ledger* wrote about Bagot in 1779: 'With very moderate abilities, and without any of those engaging qualities which attract men's regard, has continued to take a lead in the Cocoa Tree club . . . He wishes to be thought an unbiassed, independent man, but his conduct in Parliament shows the contrary.'

He did not stand in 1780, having been assured by North that he was to be created a peer. He died 22 Oct. 1798.

[1] Barrington to Newcastle, 1 Nov. 1761, Add. 32930, f. 257. [2] 23 Dec. 1762, Add. 32945, f. 338. [3] *Last Jnls.* ii. 22. [4] W. Bagot, *Mems. Bagot Fam.* 90. [5] Cavendish's 'Debates', Egerton 237, f. 118. [6] Lord John Cavendish to the Duke of Portland, 19 Mar. 1772, Portland mss. [7] Almon, xii. 101-2. [8] Ibid. vii. 136-7.

M.M.D.

## BAIKIE, Robert (d.1817), of Tankerness and Egilshay, Orkney.

ORKNEY AND SHETLAND 1780-23 Feb. 1781

1st s. of James Baikie of Tankerness by Janet, da. of William Douglas, and heiress of the Monteiths of Egilshay. *m.* 12 Feb. 1785, Mary, da. and coh. of Thomas Balfour of Huip, 4s. 3da. *suc.* fa. 1764.

Of an old Orkney family, influential both in the burgh of Kirkwall and in the county, Robert Baikie was connected through his mother with the Douglases, Earls of Morton. His father James Baikie, provost of Kirkwall during and after the '45, was a supporter of the Morton interest; and in 1760 received for his electoral services a pension of £200 p.a. continued after his death to his widow.[1]

In 1780 Robert Baikie stood as the Government sponsored candidate for Orkney and Shetland against Charles Dundas, then in opposition. Payments were made from the King's private account to assist Baikie: £300 on 22 Sept. 1779, £315 on 16 Feb. 1781, and £2300 on 26 July 1781 for 'Orkney and Edinburgh'.[2] He was returned by 11 votes to 5, but unseated on petition. In 1784 he was defeated at the poll by Thomas Dundas.

He died 4 Apr. 1817.

[1] Namier, *Structure*, 463. Mrs. Baikie's pension appears in a list delivered to Rockingham on 21 Apr. 1782 and to Shelburne on 17 July 1782, Royal archives, Windsor. [2] Laprade, 58-59.

E.H.-G.

## BAKER, Peter William (?1756-1815), of Ranston, nr. Blandford, Dorset.

| | |
|---|---|
| ARUNDEL | 26 Mar. 1781-1784 |
| WOOTTON BASSETT | 18 Dec. 1802-1806 |
| CORFE CASTLE | 1807-25 Aug. 1815 |

*b.* ?1756, o.s. of William Baker of Bromley, Salop and Wick House, Sion Hill, Mdx. by Martha, da. of Peter Storer of Highgate, Mdx. *educ.* Eton 1765-74; Trinity, Camb. 16 June 1774, aged 18; L. Inn 1773. *m.* 27 Nov. 1781, Jane, da. of James Clitherow of Boston House, Mdx., *s.p. suc.* fa. 1774.

Baker's father is reported to have been 'a great London builder, who made a large fortune'.[1] In 1781 Baker himself purchased the estate of Ranston in Dorset, and in March was returned unopposed for Arundel at his own expense, with the support of Lord Surrey (q.v.).

During February and March 1782 Baker voted with the Opposition in the first four of the five important divisions for which lists are extant, and paired in opposition on Rous's no confidence motion, 15 Mar. In August 1782 Robinson, in his survey drawn up for Shelburne, thought Baker might be reckoned 'hopeful with a little attention, as he was against the old Administration mostly when he attended, but indeed that was not much'.[2] Baker did not vote on Shelburne's peace preliminaries, 18 Feb. 1783; was classed by Robinson in March 1783 as a follower of Fox, but did not vote on Fox's East India bill, 27 Nov. In Robinson's list of January 1784 he was classed as 'very hopeful', and in Stockdale's of 19 Mar. as a supporter of Pitt. There is no record of his having spoken in the House during this Parliament. He did not stand again in 1784.

Baker died 25 Aug. 1815, aged 59.

[1] *Biog. List of Commons elected in Oct. 1812.* [2] Laprade, 44.

M.M.D.

## BAKER, William (1705-70), of Winchester St., London and Bayfordbury, Herts.

PLYMPTON ERLE 14 Dec. 1747-1768

*b.* 5 Nov. 1705, 1st s. of John Baker, draper, of Basinghall St. by his 2nd w. Maria, da. of William Cleeve of Hammersmith, Mdx. *m.* 19 Jan. 1742, Mary, da. of Jacob Tonson II, publisher, sis. of Richard Tonson (q.v.), 6s. 1da. *suc.* fa. 1727; purchased Bayfordbury 1757; kntd. 3 Nov. 1760.

Alderman of London 1739; director, E. I. Co. 1741-5, 1746-50, 1751-3; dep. chairman 1749, 1751-2; chairman 1749-50, 1752-3; dep. gov. Hudson's Bay Co. 1750-60, gov. 1760-d.

Baker was one of the foremost merchants trading with America; his interests, very considerable in the Carolinas[1] and New York,[2] extended over the whole length of the seaboard. He also made large land purchases in Georgia,[3] and at one time, together with Brice Fisher and Nicholas Linwood (qq.v.), held the 'Hobcaw Barony' in South Carolina.[4] From 1746 onwards he had contracts for victualling and paying troops in Nova Scotia;[5] that of March 1756 was for provisioning 12,000 men in America at 6*d*. per day, i.e., for nearly £110,000 a year; but he held none after March 1760. The circumstances of his dropping out of the East India directorate are not clear: possibly there was a connexion between it and the Brice Fisher affair, in which some of Baker's closest associates were involved: but while this may explain his not being elected to the directorate after 1755, it does not explain why he left it in 1753, before the matter had come up.[6] Baker was consulted by the Treasury on finance but was not one of its chief financiers; though at times he subscribed substantial sums to Government loans: in 1761 nearly £100,000. At his death the senior alderman, Baker was never sheriff or lord mayor; he was perhaps too much of a Pelhamite in Barnard's days, and too much against Pitt and Beckford in the '60s. The only Government post for which he is known to have applied was that of postmaster general.[7]

He was brought into Parliament by Administration in 1747 on the Edgumbe interest at Plympton. His re-election in 1754 was again arranged by the Treasury, Baker paying apparently £1,000, although £1,500 was usual at that general election. In 1761 he paid £2,000.[8] All his elections were unopposed.

In Parliament Baker was a steady but not a subservient Government supporter. Although Newcastle attached the utmost importance to the plate bill, on its second reading, 17 Mar. 1756, Baker went away without voting.[9] Horace Walpole calls him 'a man rather busy and confident than able';[10] Rigby, 'as shrewd a fellow as any in the world'.[11] When in Feb.-Mar. 1757 his victualling contract was violently attacked in the House by Charles Townshend, Baker's defence of it was generally acknowledged to have been clear and convincing, and on 14 Mar. the question of the contract passed without a division, 'and almost without a negative except the two Mr. Townshends and Alderman Beckford'.[12] There seems to have been a rooted dislike between Baker and Beckford. In April 1759 they clashed over East India affairs, Beckford indicting the Company as monopolists, and Baker defending them; and in the early 1760s they repeatedly followed each other in debate on opposite sides, although both were in opposition to the Bute and

Grenville Governments. A frequent subject of controversy between them was the militia, to which Baker was hostile.

Baker was repeatedly consulted by Newcastle on American affairs.[13] His reasoning on Canada *versus* Guadaloupe is noted on 14 Oct. 1760 in Newcastle's 'Memorandums for the King': then, as in a paper of 13 Apr. 1761,[14] Baker emphasized the value of Canada 'as a security to our other dominions in America, and as a means of wealth and power to Great Britain'—'if somewhat must be given up,' Guadaloupe 'seems the fittest'.[15]

In the House Baker was a frequent speaker: between December 1761 and April 1765, Harris notes 26 interventions by him in debate. While he took the Government side against Pitt, Harris had high praise for him: 'of all the citizens' no one spoke 'so well as Sir William Baker'; and on 25 Jan. 1762, when Baker defended the Government against Beckford: 'a very able speaker'. But a new note enters on 19 Mar. 1762: Baker 'was acute, and being a good natural logician, is sometimes pleased to ride in the regions of sophistry'; and on 13 Mar. 1763: 'Baker sophisticated, a task to which he often degrades his very acute parts'. Harris ends by calling him 'the Hippias or sophist of the House': but there are no reasonably full and coherent reports of his speeches to prove or disprove that contention.[16]

On Newcastle's dismissal Baker went into sharp opposition to the Government. 'He is a strong thinker and often a very free speaker', wrote Newcastle to Hardwicke, 16 July 1762,[17] 'and indeed he does not spare the present ministers or the present times.' Between December 1762 and July 1765 all Baker's recorded votes and most of his speeches were against Government: on Wilkes, 23 Nov. 1763, he spoke 'excellently',[18] and acted as teller for the Opposition; on the cider tax; 'on the monstrous profit' made by subscribers to the Government loan of 1763;[19] on the navy debt, 3 Feb. 1764, he 'had no regard to hurting public credit', wrote Harris, 'if it hurt Administration at the same time'; and Horace Walpole (to Lord Hertford, 6 Feb. 1765): Grenville 'was driven from entrenchment to entrenchment by Baker and Charles Townshend'.

On 9 Mar. 1764 Grenville opened his budget which contained proposals for taxing America. Baker, who rose immediately after him, according to Harris 'did not acquit himself with his usual acuteness, nor even with his usual sophistry'. Some of his argument is given in a fragmentary form in Nathaniel Ryder's notes:[20]

Agrees perfectly to our right to tax the colonies. Thinks the power of the Crown extends no further over the colonies than it does in England. And yet this power has been exerted as by orders passed here by the King in council which have gone to the plantations as kind of laws.

Stamps, does not dislike that duty in America but would have some regulations in England.

On 22 Mar. the American bill was debated 'for taxing the commodities of that country', writes Harris, 'that it might in some measure support itself. Baker, against the bill, particularly against taxing French indigo'; also for a lower duty on molasses. Grenville defended his proposals. 'Baker replied—Beckford for the measure.' Clearly Baker's objections as yet concerned detail rather than the principle of taxing America. When, however, on 6 Feb. 1765 Grenville brought in the American stamp bill, Baker opposed it, but, writes Harris, 'had less argument and less specious sophistry than I ever heard from him—rambled (like Beckford) . . . and acts the patriot, this rather awkwardly'. Again, when on 29 Mar. the secretary at war brought in the American mutiny bill, 'Beckford and Baker . . . objected to the quartering of men in private houses, and talked much for barracks.' An opposition to Grenville's American policy was forming.

Also outside the House, Baker between 1763 and 1765 played a leading part in attempts to organize opposition to the Government. In the City he 'acted strenuously against the Court'; and Charles Townshend, when sketching plans of action, wrote to Newcastle, 30 Apr. 1764: 'Sir William Baker should be desired to put the City in motion, both as an example to other counties, and as an attack nearest home.' Almon reported to Temple, 12 Nov. 1764: Fitzherbert (q.v.) and Baker are agreed 'that a weekly paper ought to be set up'. And when the Duke of Cumberland told Newcastle, 12 Dec., that since Charles Yorke had left them and Pitt would not work with them, 'all opposition would be in vain', Newcastle replied: 'that opposition there would certainly be from our zealous friends, Sir William Baker, etc.; and that I thought our friends must go with it'. Baker consistently pursued the Opposition line, and was indignant when in May 1764 Newcastle, to please Charles Yorke, recommended George Hay, a Government supporter, to the Archbishop of Canterbury for dean of the arches. 'I think I have great reason to complain of my old friend Sir William Baker', wrote Newcastle to Thomas Walpole, 20 July 1764, 'who is blowing up the party upon the silly point of Dr. Hay. . . . If I had done anything liable to objection, Sir William Baker is not the man who should first have sounded the trumpet upon it. I know it proceeds from his long hatred to Charles Yorke.' And in George Onslow's letter to Newcastle, 3 June 1765,

there is a somewhat cryptic reference to Baker's 'way of thinking and *publicly* talking of you'.[21]

Baker's not being too close to Newcastle recommended him to Rockingham, who did not want Newcastle to run the Treasury for him; and in a paper of June 1765,[22] dealing with the allocation of offices, Rockingham noted against Baker's name: 'Query—if proper to set at the head of the Board of Trade.' But the idea was not pursued any further. Newcastle attributed a great deal of Rockingham's behaviour 'to my old, ungrateful, *conceited* friend Sir William Baker, who thinks he can entirely govern these young men';[23] nevertheless, in a memorandum for Rockingham on who should be consulted on the Stamp Act, its repeal or modification, he himself named Baker.[24] Only too successfully: when during the next few weeks Rockingham settled his American policy not in the Cabinet but in 'a pretty mixed set of company'[25] whom he entertained to dinner, on one or two occasions Baker was of it (in these meetings, represented as merely exploratory, repeal was coupled with the Declaratory Act).[26] When on 18 Dec. Grenville moved an Address to the King for American papers, Baker treated him 'as the author of all the troubles in America';[27] and spoke again in the crucial debate of 24 Feb. 1766 in favour of repealing the Stamp Act.

Subsequently Baker went into opposition with Rockingham, and in 1767 was of the inner circle consulted on the proposal to take a shilling off the land tax.[28] He did not stand again in 1768, and Newcastle arranged with Edgcumbe for Baker's son to succeed him at Plympton. In the City election of 1768 Baker voted for Ladbroke, Trecothick and Wilkes, but not for Beckford. He died 23 Jan. 1770.

[1] Hawley to Bedford, 6 Nov. 1746, Bedford mss. [2] *Letter Bk. of John Watts*, (Colls. N.Y. Hist. Soc. 1928). [3] *Bd. Trade Jnl.* 29 May 1755; *APC*, 1766-83, pp. 295-6. [4] *S.C. Hist. and Gen. Mag.* Apr. 1913. [5] T27/26, 29/30-33, 52/43, 54/30, 37, 43. [6] See FISHER, Brice, and L. S. Sutherland, *A London Merchant.* [7] Baker to Newcastle, 21 Nov. 1758, Add. 32885, f. 478. [8] 'Lord Edgcumbe's list', Add. 32995, f. 100; Newcastle's 'Memorandums', 28 Feb. 1761, Add. 32919, f. 334; also Add. 32920, f. 103. [9] West to Newcastle, Add. 32863, f. 332. [10] *Mems. Geo. II*, i. 71. [11] *Bedford Corresp.* ii. 234-5. [12] Walpole, *Mems. Geo. II*, ii. 304; West to Newcastle, 14 Mar., Add. 32870, ff. 275-6. [13] See e.g. Baker's paper of 1754 on supporting a regular military force in America, Add. 32737, ff. 16-20. [14] Add. 33030, ff. 1-2; the paper is unsigned but in Baker's handwriting. [15] Add. 32922, f. 28; 32925, ff. 9-10, 26-29. [16] The fullest extant report is Newdigate's (Newdigate mss) of Baker's defence of his contract, but it consists of a mere collection of facts and figures. [17] Add. 32940, f. 372. [18] Onslow to Newcastle, Add. 32953, f. 16. [19] West to Newcastle, 18 Mar. 1763, Add. 32947, ff. 242-3. [20] Harrowby mss. [21] Walpole, *Mems. Geo. III*, i. 198; HMC *Townshend*, 400; *Grenville Pprs.* ii. 457; Add. 32960, f. 335; 32964, f. 257; 32967, f. 8. [22] Rockingham mss. [23] To John White, 3 Dec. 1765, M. Bateson, *Narrative of Changes in the Ministry*, 37. [24] 25 Dec., Add. 32972, f. 333. [25] So described by Lady Rockingham in a letter to Newcastle, 21 Jan. 1766, Add. 32973, f. 224, to explain why he was not included. [26] Add. 32972, f. 384; 32973, ff. 3, 11-13, 202, 224. [27] There is some discrepancy between Harris's and Horace Walpole's reports of Baker's speech. [28] Hardwicke to Chas. Yorke, 11 Feb. 1767, Add. 35362, ff. 61-62; Rockingham to Newcastle, 21 Feb., Add. 32980, ff. 138-9.

L.B.N.

**BAKER, William** (1743–1824), of Bayfordbury, Herts.

| | |
|---|---|
| PLYMPTON ERLE | 1768–1774 |
| ALDBOROUGH | 4 Mar. 1777–1780 |
| HERTFORD | 1780–1784 |
| HERTFORDSHIRE | 1790–1802, 11 Feb. 1805–1807 |

*b.* 3 Oct. 1743, 1st s. of Sir William Baker (q.v.). *educ.* Eton 1753–60; Clare, Camb. 1761; I. Temple 1761, called 1775. *m.* (1) 23 May 1771, Juliana (*d.* 23 Apr. 1772), da. of Thomas Penn of Stoke Park, Bucks., gd.-da. of William Penn, gov. of Pennsylvania, 1da.; (2) 7 Oct. 1775, Sophia, da. of John Conyers (q.v.) of Copt Hall, Essex, 9s. 6da. *suc.* fa. 1770.
Sheriff, London and Mdx. 1770–1; bencher, I. Temple 1808, reader 1818.

Baker, according to his obituary notice in the *Gentleman's Magazine* (1824, i. 183), 'was bred up as a country gentleman'; and from the London directories it appears that his younger brother Samuel took over their father's business. Yet in the lists of Members of the House of Commons printed in the *Royal Kalendar*, 1773, Baker was described as 'a merchant in London, and one of the committee of the Hudson's Bay Co.', and he was present at meetings of North American merchants in October 1775, helping to organize their petitions against the Government's American policy.[1]

In 1768 Baker's return for Plympton on the Edgcumbe interest was arranged by his father through the Duke of Newcastle.[2] And in Parliament he followed the same line as his father; attached himself to the Rockinghams, and voted constantly against the Grafton and North Administrations, though throughout his career he always put great emphasis on his independence. He wrote to his friend the Rev. Mr. Talbot on 13 Sept. 1770:[3] 'My political religion has but few tenets—perhaps they are rather unfashionable, but I am rather a bigot to them—to consult those whom I believe honest, and my own heart—to attend the advice of one, but to follow implicitly the dictates of the other.' Baker spoke fairly frequently in the House, particularly on City and American affairs. He vigorously attacked the Quebec bill and proposals to alter the Massachusetts government: 'I fought it through every stage almost alone when most of the Opposition were attending the Newmarket meeting or other occupations equally to be preferred to that duty',[4] he wrote to an American friend, Charles Lee.

In 1774 Baker, finding that Lord Edgcumbe would not return him again for Plympton, wrote to Rockingham on 14 Sept. to ask if he knew of 'any borough, for which, at a price not exorbitant, I may be elected with certainty, and have *free use of my vote* on all occasions'.[5] Rockingham, acting for Lord Galway, offered Baker a seat at Pontefract. What followed is by no means clear, but it seems that Henry, 2nd Duke of Newcastle persuaded Galway to return Charles Mellish, a common friend, promising a seat at one of his own boroughs for Baker as soon as a vacancy occurred.[6] In the meantime Baker unsuccessfully contested London, where he prejudiced his chances by refusing to commit himself to a definite plan for parliamentary and economical reform, though he favoured both: 'I must preserve my own judgment free on all subjects which may arise in Parliament', he wrote in an election address, 'I cannot with honour engage myself indefinitely and beforehand, to the fulfilling of instructions which I do not know.'[7] After his defeat Baker wrote to Charles Lee:[8] 'Though I should have thought it infamous to have deserted my post and not endeavoured to get in, yet I hardly can say that I much regret being out, there is so little prospect of doing good.' Nevertheless he continued to look for a seat, though he told Rockingham that he was reluctant to stand unless certain of election, his City contest having cost him £1500.[9] In December 1776 he was asked to stand for Westminster, but thinking his chances doubtful, refused.[10] In 1777, under the agreement with Newcastle, Baker was elected for Aldborough on the understanding that he was free to follow his own line in the House; and he continued to vote and speak against the Administration.

Baker's interventions in City politics were spasmodic, and, it seems, generally at the instigation of Rockingham who had hopes of using him to establish an interest in the City. When in September 1778 it seemed likely that Richard Oliver would vacate his seat, Baker considered resigning Aldborough and contesting London. Rockingham wrote to him on 18 Sept.:[11]

> Your reluctance or perhaps your *fixed resolution* of never taking upon you the load of a City gown, will be objected to you ... if it was possible that you could not only become one of the representatives for the City, but also at once take upon you the vacant aldermancy and instantly become *Lord Mayor* for the ensuing year, it would be a most important stroke in favour of the public, and would be perhaps the salvation and restoration of honour and dignity to the City of London.

But Oliver did not vacate his seat.

At the general election of 1780 Baker successfully contested Hertford on his own interest. After the fall of North, Baker voted against Shelburne's peace preliminaries, 18 Feb. 1783; supported Pitt's proposals for parliamentary reform, 7 May 1783, and voted for Fox's East India bill, 27 Nov. 1783. On 17 Dec. 1783 he moved that it was a breach of privilege to influence votes by reporting any 'opinion or pretended opinion of his Majesty'.[12] He was counted as a Foxite in Robinson's list of January 1784 and Stockdale's of 19 Mar. At the general election of 1784 he again contested Hertford but was defeated.

He died 20 Jan. 1824.

[1] Fortescue, iii. 263. [2] Add. 32989, f. 7. [3] Baker mss. [4] *Lee Pprs. i. 130–2, Colls. N.Y. Hist. Soc.* (1871). [5] Rockingham mss. [6] Rockingham to Baker, 18 Sept. 1778, Wm. Mellish to Rockingham, 4 Oct. 1778, 6 Oct. 1778, Rockingham mss. See also North to Newcastle, 7 Mar. 1775. Wm. Mellish to Newcastle, 8 Dec. 1776, Newcastle (Clumber) mss. [7] Baker mss. [8] *Lee Pprs.* loc. cit. [9] Rockingham mss. [10] Baker to Lady Juliana Penn, 15 Dec. 1776, Baker mss. [11] Rockingham mss. [12] Debrett, xii. 420–1.

M.M.D.

## BAKER HOLROYD, John (1735–1821), of Sheffield Place, Suss.

COVENTRY 15 Feb.–1 Sept. 1780, 27 Feb. 1781–1784

BRISTOL 1790–1802

*b.* 21 Dec. 1735, 1st surv. s. of Isaac Holroyd, of Dunamore, co. Meath by Dorothy, da. of Daniel Baker of Penn, Bucks. *m.* (1) 26 May 1767, Abigail (*d.*3 Apr. 1793), da. of Lewis Way of Richmond, sis. of Benjamin Way (q.v.), 1s. 2da. ; (2) 26 Dec. 1794, Hon. Lucy Pelham (*d.*18 Jan. 1797), da. of Thomas, 2nd Baron Pelham (q.v.), 1s.; (3) 20 Jan. 1798, Lady Anne North, da. of Frederick, 2nd Earl of Guilford (q.v.), 1s. 1da. *suc.* to estates of his uncle, Rev. Jones Baker 1768, and took name of Baker before Holroyd; *fa.* 1778; *cr.* Baron Sheffield [I] of Dunamore 9 Jan. 1781, Baron Sheffield [I] of Roscommon (with sp. rem. to his das.) 20 Sept. 1783; Baron Sheffield [GB] 20 July 1802; Earl of Sheffield [I] 22 Jan. 1816.

Cornet 21 Drag. 21 Apr. 1760, capt. 24 Dec. 1761; ret. 1763.

On the disbandment of his regiment in 1763 Holroyd travelled on the Continent, and at Lausanne met Gibbon, with whom he formed a life-long friendship. In 1769 he purchased Sheffield Place and settled down as a country gentleman. He considered standing for Sussex in 1774, but was advised by Gibbon against it. 'I cannot yet think you ripe for a county Member', Gibbon wrote on 20 Aug. 1774. 'Five years are very little to remove the obvious objection of a *novus homo*, and of all objections it is perhaps the most formidable.' In 1779 Holroyd raised a regiment (the 22nd Dragoons) of which he became lieutenant-colonel. It was stationed at Coventry; his stay there familiarized him with the politics of the borough, and he offered himself as candidate at the by-election of 1780. Gibbon wrote to him, 7 Feb.:

On this vacancy the celerity of your motions may probably prevent opposition; but at the general election, your enemy, the corporation, will not be asleep, and I wish, if it be not too late, to warn you against any promises or engagements which may terminate in a defeat, or at least a contest of ten thousand pounds.

Holroyd was returned unopposed.

But this caution was wise and necessary. At the general election of 1780 Holroyd and Edward Roe Yeo were opposed by Sir Thomas Hallifax and Thomas Rogers, who were backed by the corporation. A riotous, prolonged and expensive contest followed, involving two polls and a petition. Sheffield, as he had now become, was supported by Government who paid £2,000 towards his expenses.[1]

Sheffield supported North's Administration to the end. He spoke against Conway's motion to end the war, 22 Feb. 1782; voted against Shelburne's peace preliminaries, 18 Feb. 1783; supported the Fox-North Coalition; and opposed Pitt. At Coventry in 1784 he was opposed by both the corporation and Government, and after another expensive contest was defeated.

Sheffield's speeches in Parliament were frequent, well-informed and authoritative; though the work of Government interested him, he seems not to have aimed at office. He was particularly concerned with questions of trade and finance,—'I went last Thursday to my first play . . .', wrote his daughter Maria Josepha, on 1 Mar. 1786. 'Papa was too busy importing and exporting to think of such things'— and defended in speeches and pamphlets the commercial privileges of Britain.[2] Yet his title to fame rests on his friendship with Gibbon. Gibbon enjoyed his society, respected his knowledge, and felt at ease in his family circle. Sheffield placed himself at Gibbon's service: made himself responsible in Gibbon's lifetime for the disposal of his estates, and preserved and edited his papers after his death.

Sheffield died 30 May 1821.

[1] Laprade, 37. [2] *Girlhood of Maria Josepha Holroyd*, ed. Adeane, 12.

J.B.

## BALCH, Robert (1724–79), of Nether Stowey, Som.

BRIDGWATER 19 Jan. 1753–1761

*b.* 3 Jan. 1724, 1st s. of John Balch of Bridgwater by his w. Amy Bart. *m.* Susanna, da. of Robert Everard of Nether Stowey, Som., 4s. 5da. *suc.* fa. 14 Nov. 1732.

Balch's grandfather and great-grandfather had represented Bridgwater in the late seventeenth and early eighteenth centuries. At the general election of 1754 Balch stood on a joint interest with George Bubb Dodington (q.v.), supported by Administration, and was returned after a contest. In 1761, though again having Dodington's support, he was defeated, and seems to have made no further attempt to re-enter Parliament.

He died 15 Apr. 1779.

M.M.D.

44

**BALDWYN, Charles** (1729–1801), of Bockleton, Salop.

SHROPSHIRE  8 May 1766–1780

*bap.* 29 Sept. 1729, 1st s. of Charles Baldwyn of Bockleton by Elizabeth, da. of John Allgood of Newcastle-upon-Tyne, wid. of Sir Patrick Strachan of Aberdeen. *educ.* St. Mary Hall, Oxf. 1747. *m.* 14 May 1752, Catherine, da. and h. of William Lacon Childe, M.P. for Shropshire 1727–34, 2s. 1da. *suc.* fa. April 1751.

The Baldwyns were old Shropshire gentry;[1] and Charles Baldwyn's uncle, Acton Baldwyn, and before him three generations of the family, had sat for Ludlow.

In 1779, at the end of Charles Baldwyn's parliamentary career, the *Public Ledger* published a character sketch of him which, though adverse, comes near the truth: 'A puzzle-headed country gentleman, of Tory principles. Votes constantly with the minister, and avers that Kings and Governments, let their actions be what they will, must and ought to be supported.' Puzzle-headed he certainly appears in his autobiographical account in 1782; at the outset he was the choice of the Shropshire Tories and of Lord Powis, a ministerialist by preference under George III no less than under George II (and after having been threatened with a Whig opposition in 1766, Baldwyn was each time returned without a contest); but the degree of his compliance with Governments is somewhat exaggerated. On matters about which the country gentlemen felt strongly, Baldwyn would go against the Government—thus over the land tax, 27 Feb. 1767, and the motion for an account of pensions, 21 Feb. 1780. Otherwise his recorded votes, nine in all, were given on the Government side, and in Robinson's parliamentary surveys he is invariably classed as 'pro'.

Less than a dozen speeches by him are recorded during his 14 years in Parliament: the first in defence of Clive, against Burgoyne's motion of 19 May 1773.[2] 'He spoke (as well as he could )', wrote Lloyd Kenyon (q.v.), 'and voted as stoutly as anybody for Lord Clive'; 'in hopes, I fancy', wrote Kenyon in another letter, 'to have his interest at the next general election'.[3] Voicing the views of the less intelligent country gentlemen, Baldwyn spoke on 2 and 8 Mar. 1774 against a bill to prevent vexatious removals of the poor; he considered existing safeguards sufficient.[4] Over America Baldwyn opposed any weakening in Government policy. On 8 Nov. 1775, he said:[5]

he had always understood the dispute with America was for a revenue to be raised there to relieve the country gentlemen; but having since heard that the idea of taxation was given up . . . he thought . . . it was improper to expend any more money in the contest . . .

Being told by North 'that taxation is not nor ever was' out of the Government's view, Baldwyn 'was satisfied with this explanation'. But next, when North brought in his conciliatory propositions, 17 Feb. 1778, Baldwyn

declared he had been deceived by the minister; that three years ago he asked him whether a revenue was meant by the claim? That he was answered, it was; and upon that ground alone he had hitherto voted with the ministry.[6]

A rather different line was adopted by him on 17 June 1779 when, alone on the Government side, he spoke in favour of Lord John Cavendish's motion for employing all forces against the House of Bourbon, i.e. for withdrawing them from America.[7]

Robinson in his electoral survey of 1780 wrote against Shropshire: 'Mr. Baldwyn will not come in here again.' By that time his financial position was well-nigh desperate. He was in receipt of a secret service pension (which gives a curious twist to his vote for an account of pensions—presumably not secret ones); how long he had it is uncertain: in Robinson's accounts for 1779–80 three payments 'by order' are mentioned: 8 Mar. 1779, £800; 11 June 1779, £800; and 4 May 1780, £300; and under 15 July 1780 two quarters of an annual pension of £600 p.a.[8] This is also mentioned in April 1782 in the 'Account of pensions extinguished and not returned':[9] 'Mr. Baldwyn, on being out of Parliament, £600.' And on 27 Aug. 1782 Baldwyn wrote to Shelburne, then first lord of the Treasury:[10]

I little thought I should be under the necessity of ever becoming so humble a petitioner . . . being disappointed of assistance where I had the greatest reason to expect it, I have no prospect of being able to extricate myself from my difficulties, or even preserve my liberty, unless I . . . obtain some relief from Government . . . though an advocate for public economy, I am persuaded you wish to encourage such acts of royal benevolence, as are unmixed with corruption. . . .

He enclosed a printed leaflet of three pages, 'Case of Charles Baldwyn, Esq'. The gravamen of that 'case' is primarily against his eldest son, for whose sake he claimed to have ruined himself, and who now refused to come to his financial rescue. The story is hardly convincing: it is one of bad bargains with every member of the family he had to deal with; and while denying that he had gambled, he admits having speculated: he purchased 'estates when land sold very dear'; borrowed money 'the interest whereof is since raised'; and afterwards was 'under a necessity of selling estates very cheap'. Still, he claims that, while he 'impaired his finances

. . . he has served his son to whose welfare indeed he had in a great measure sacrificed his own fortune, his liberty, all the comforts of life, and perhaps his life itself, for as he finds his health much injured, he doubts not but his existence will be shortened by his uneasiness of mind.' He died nearly 20 years later, 28 Sept. 1801.

¹ E. H. Martin, 'The Baldwins', *Trans. Salop Arch. Soc.* (ser. 4), ii. 299–385. ² Cavendish's 'Debates', Egerton 247, ff. 45–46; 248, f. 87; Brickdale's 'Debates'; Fortescue, ii. 486. ³ 25 May and 8 June 1773, *HMC Kenyon*, 504, 505. ⁴ Cavendish's 'Debates', Egerton 253, ff. 97–100; 254, 4–6, 19; Brickdale's 'Debates'. ⁵ Almon, ii. 159, 160. ⁶ Ibid. viii. 387. ⁷ See list of speakers sent by North to the King, Fortescue, iv. 360. Baldwyn's speech is not mentioned in Almon, xiii. 446–7. ⁸ Add. 37836, ff. 58, 64, 76, 79. ⁹ Laprade, 49–50. ¹⁰ Lansdowne mss.

L.B.N.

## BAMPFYLDE, Charles Warwick (1753–1823), of Poltimore, Devon

EXETER 1774–1790, 1796–1812

*b.* 23 Jan. 1753, 1st surv. s. of Sir Richard Warwick Bampfylde, 4th Bt. (q.v.). *educ.* New Coll. Oxf. 1770. *m.* 9 Feb. 1776, Catherine, da. and coh. of Adm. Sir John Moore, 1st Bt., 2s. 1da. *suc.* fa. as 5th Bt. 15 July 1776.

Returned unopposed in 1774 and again in 1780, Bampfylde voted with Opposition in the two divisions on paying the civil list debts, 16 and 18 Apr. 1777, and next for the motion to inquire into pensions, 21 Feb. 1780. His attendance was irregular but till March 1782 all his recorded votes were with Opposition. After his election in 1780 the *English Chronicle* wrote:

> Before he succeeded to his estate, though scarcely twenty-five years of age, he had spent nearly two-thirds of it . . . Plundered by the most usurious contracts, and defrauded by every degree of rapacity and injustice, even reduced to the last extreme of necessity, Sir Charles Bampfylde has preserved the character of a fair and honourable man, and given a striking instance that the pride of an English gentleman, though it may reduce him to misfortune, will ever keep him above meanness . . . it is not likely that he will now change his political principles, since he has suffered all the consequences of the follies and extravagance of youth, without discovering any inclination to be converted by the prospect of relief from political apostacy.

He voted against Shelburne's peace preliminaries, 18 Feb. 1783, was classed by Robinson, March 1783, as 'Mr. Fox's connexion', and voted for the East India bill, 27 Nov. 1783.

Bampfylde was returned in 1784 after a contest, and was classed as Opposition in William Adam's list of the new Parliament; his only recorded votes were against Administration on Pitt's Irish commercial proposals, 13 May 1785, and the Duke of Richmond's fortifications plan, 27 Feb. 1786.

He is only known to have spoken twice before 1790: about presenting a petition against the receipts tax, 5 June 1783, and against the window tax, 10 Aug. 1784. He died 19 Apr. 1823.

J.B.

## BAMPFYLDE, Sir Richard Warwick, 4th Bt. (1722–76), of Poltimore, Devon.

EXETER 20 Dec. 1743–1747
DEVON 1747–15 July 1776

*bap.* 21 Nov. 1722, o.s. of Sir Coplestone Warwick Bampfylde, 3rd Bt., M.P., by Gertrude, da. of Sir John Carew, 3rd Bt., of Antony, Cornw., wid. of Sir Godfrey Copley, 2nd Bt., of Sprotborough, Yorks. *educ.* New Coll. Oxf. 1739. *m.* 8 Aug. 1742, Jane, da. and h. of John Codrington, M.P., of Wraxall, Som., 5s. 7da. *suc.* fa. 7 Oct. 1727.

Bampfylde voted against under George II, and under George III generally voted with the court. He appears in Fox's list of Members favourable to the peace preliminaries. But as Member for Devon he had to oppose the cider tax: he spoke against it on 13 Mar. 1763 and 'acquitted himself well'. 'Dick Bampfylde is in high credit both here and at London for his active opposition to the cider bill', wrote Philip Barton to Philip Rashleigh (q.v.) from Exeter on 17 Apr. 1763.¹ Yet he himself avowed in a later debate, on 24 Jan. 1764, that he 'spoke not his own sentiments . . . but those which the instructions and petitions of his constituents *forced* him to maintain'; he had 'endeavoured to keep the peace in his county', and praised Grenville for his 'politeness, open candour, plain integrity, and justice'.² Bampfylde is included in Newcastle's list of those 'supposed to have voted with us' on 15 Feb. 1764 over general warrants, but on 18 Feb. voted with Government. His lukewarm attitude over the cider tax now caused him trouble in Devon: he feared his constituents would instruct him to oppose 'every act of Government in general', and that an opposition was preparing for the next general election.³ But he continued to support Grenville, and on 16 Dec. 1764 wrote in reply to Grenville's whip:⁴

> The zeal I have for his Majesty's service, and for those who are at *present* entrusted with the management of public affairs, is not only an inducement for me to coincide with them in whatever shall be thought most beneficial for the community in general, but to testify my warmest endeavours for their permanency and success by an early attendance in Parliament.

Classed by Rockingham in July 1765 as 'doubtful', he voted against the repeal of the Stamp Act, 22 Feb. 1766; and in January 1767 Charles Townshend classed him as a follower of Grenville. He voted against Administration on the land tax, 27 Feb. 1767.

His name appears in no extant division list after 1767, and during this time he is only known to have made two speeches in the House—on 16 Jan. 1770, when presenting an address from his constituents, and on 17 Feb. 1774 on a motion for a committee on the linen industry.[5] In Robinson's first, undated, survey on the royal marriage bill, Bampfylde is classed 'doubtful'; in the second, 8 Mar. 1772, 'pro'; and in that of the Parliament of 1774 'hopeful'.

He died 15 July 1776.

[1] Rashleigh mss. [2] Harris's 'Debates'; Jas. Grenville to Lady Chatham, 27 Jan. 1764, *Chatham Corresp.* ii. 282. [3] Bampfylde to Bedford, 21 Sept. 1764, Bedford mss 50, f. 140. [4] Grenville mss (JM). [5] Cavendish's 'Debates', Egerton 252, f. 14.

J.B.

**BANKES, Henry** (1700–76), of Broadchalk, Salisbury, Wilts.

CORFE CASTLE    1741–Nov. 1762

*bap.* 2 Nov. 1700, 2nd s. of John Bankes, M.P., of Kingston Lacy, Dorset by Margaret, da. of Sir Henry Parker, 2nd Bt., of Honington, Warws. *educ.* Eton 1715–20; King's, Camb. 1720, fellow 1723–9; L. Inn 1720, called 1726, K.C. 1747. *m.* (1) Eleanor, da. of Richard Symonds of London, *s.p.*; (2) 11 June 1753, Margaret, da. of John Wynne, bp. of Bath and Wells, sis. and coh. of Sir W. Wynne, judge of the P.C.C., 2s. 1da. *suc.* bro. to Kingston Lacy estates 26 Jan. 1772.

K.C. to duchy of Lancaster 1738–61; dep.c.j. of S. Wales 1745–9; commr. of customs Dec. 1762–*d.*

The Bankes family controlled one seat at Corfe Castle. Returned on his brother's interest, Henry Bankes was classed 'pro' by Newcastle in 1747, 'doubtful' by Dupplin in 1754, and in Bute's list as 'Pitt, quaere'. In November 1762 he was offered, through his neighbour John Calcraft (q.v.), a commissionership of customs (at £1,000 p.a.), in return for his seat; and on 17 Nov. Henry Fox wrote to Bute:[1] 'We shall get his borough, and the nomination of it for your Lordship as long as he stays at the custom house. He was not yours when in the House. So surely this is a good bargain. He is gone down express to his brother to fix it.' On 4 Dec. Bankes was appointed commissioner of customs, and on 6 Dec. Bute's friend John Campbell of Calder was returned at Corfe Castle.

No speech by Bankes is reported, but on 3 Feb. 1762 James Harris noted him among 'all the lawyers' who spoke, 'some of one mind and some of another', on the Tamworth election debate.

Bankes died 23 Sept. 1776.

[1] Bute mss.

M.M.D.

**BANKES, Henry** (1756–1834), of Kingston Lacy, Dorset.

CORFE CASTLE        1780–Jan. 1826
DORSET              16 Feb. 1826–1831

*b.* 19 Dec. 1756,[1] 2nd but o. surv. s. of Henry Bankes (q.v.) by his 2nd w. Margaret Wynne. *educ.* Westminster 1767–73; Trinity Hall, Camb. 1773. *m.* 1784, Frances, da. of William Woodley (q.v.), 4s. 2da.

Robinson in his survey of 1780 expected Bankes to be a friend to Government, but about his first speech, 1 June 1781, Walpole wrote to H. S. Conway, 3 June: 'A still newer orator has appeared in the India business, a Mr. Bankes, and against Lord North too; and with a merit that the very last crop of orators left out of their rubric—modesty.' Bankes strongly opposed the American war: denied that it was a popular war—'The nation had been deceived into it, and the Americans had been compelled, on principles of self-defence, to have recourse to arms'; while the ministers who had promoted it had shown 'their total inability in carrying their own plans, crude . . . and defective as they were, into execution' (12 June 1781).[2] In each of the six extant division lists December 1781–March 1782 he appears as voting against Government. George Selwyn wrote to Lord Carlisle, 19 Feb. 1782: 'Young Pitt has formed a society of young ministers, who are to fight under his banner, and these are the Duke of Rutland, Mr. Bankes etc.'[3] On 5 Dec. 1782, seconding the Address, Bankes described peace as 'the only thing that could save us' and for which 'sacrifices must be made'; 'our debts were at all events to be discharged'; and 'in the concessions we should have to make, we ought to be anxious to put our pride out of the way'. Economy, even parsimony was required: 'nay it should be avarice, nothing short of it would do'. He voted for Shelburne's peace preliminaries, 18 Feb. 1783, as being 'highly favourable, and such as we have no reason to expect'. In December 1783, before Pitt's re-election on taking office, Bankes was authorized by him to tell the House that there would be no dissolution—a statement repeatedly quoted against him during the next few years, although Pitt declared, 12 Jan. 1784, that Bankes had spoken at his request.[4]

Bankes voted for Pitt's first parliamentary reform proposals, 7 May 1783, but against those of 18 Apr. 1785, for he disapproved 'of purchasing the boroughs with public money';[5] voted against Richmond's fortifications plan, 27 Feb. 1786; and in the debate on increases in army estimates, 10 Dec. 1787, asked for assurances that they were necessary.[6] He voted with Administration on the impeachment of Impey, 9 May 1788, and the Regency, 1788–9.

Wraxall wrote about Bankes:[7]

His talents compensated by their calm solidity for the want of brilliancy. His enunciation, slow, formal, precise, and not without some degree of embarrassment, was nevertheless always controlled by judgment, caution, and good sense. No man displayed more rectitude of intention, independence of mind, and superiority to every private object of interest or ambition.

His high principles were well known, and Daniel Pulteney (q.v.), a man of very different character, sarcastically refers to Bankes and Wilberforce and their influence on Pitt.[8]

Bankes was the author of a *Civil and Constitutional History of Rome*. A Member for over 50 years, mostly outside our period, he died 17 Dec. 1834. The *Gentleman's Magazine* wrote in his obituary:

> Mr. Bankes was an accomplished scholar, intimately acquainted with ancient and modern literature, and of a refined and acknowledged taste in the arts.

[1] Mem. bk. of Henry Bankes sen., 1757-61, Bankes mss. [2] Debrett, iii. 561. [3] *HMC Carlisle*, 581. [4] Debrett, iv. 4-7, 279; xii. 519, [5] Ibid. xviii. 83. [6] Stockdale, xiii. 59. [7] *Mems.* iv. 79. [8] *HMC Rutland*, iii. 217.

M.M.D.

## BARBOR, Robert (*d.*1761), of Somerford, Staffs.

STAMFORD     8 Dec. 1747-1761

*educ.* I. Temple 1725. *m.* bef. 1730, 1s.
Clerk of the privy seal and clerk of the court of requests 1754-*d.*

Barbor was Lord Exeter's chief agent, and was returned at Stamford on his interest. He was classed as 'doubtful' by Dupplin, and no vote or speech by him is reported. He died 22 July 1761.

M.M.D.

## BARCLAY ALLARDICE, Robert (1732-97), of Urie, Kincardine.

KINCARDINESHIRE     19 June 1788-8 Apr. 1797

*b.* 1732, 1st s. of Robert Barclay of Urie by Une, da. of Sir Ewen Cameron of Lochiel. *m.* (1) June 1756, his cos. Lucy (*d.* Mar. 1757), da. of David Barclay, linen draper, of Cheapside, London, 1da; (2) Dec. 1776, Sarah Anne, da. and h. of James Allardice of Allardice, Kincardine (div. Sept. 1793), 3s. 5da.[1] *suc.* fa. 1760.

This Member was the great-grandson of Robert Barclay, the Quaker 'Apologist' and colonizer of East New Jersey, and was connected by kinship and marriage with a number of wealthy London merchant families including Barclays the brewers. By his second marriage he acquired large estates and additional interest in Kincardineshire and Aberdeen Burghs,[2] and thereafter was known as Barclay Allardice of Urie and Allardice. 'Possessed of an enterprising spirit and extensive knowledge in agriculture, which he acquired by reading . . . and by his own observations in the different tours which he made on foot in his younger years through Scotland and a great part of England',[3] he was a pioneer of the new farming methods in the county.

A popular and philanthropic landlord, he laid out a new village adjoining Stonehaven,[4] and during the famine of 1783 organized 'a benevolent society for purchasing meal and grain to be retailed at an under-price'.[5] In 1785 his wife's claim for recognition as heir of line to her ancestor the Earl of Airth and Menteith, was successful and thereafter Barclay's 'great object' was to secure the peerage for his family.[6]

In 1788 Barclay was returned with the support of Henry Dundas, and voted with Pitt on the Regency bill. He is not known to have spoken in the House. He died 8 Apr. 1797.

[1] Barclay Allardice mss, SRO. [2] Barclay Allardice mss. 208. [3] *Statistical Account*, xii. 598. [4] Ibid. 598-60; xvii. 387. [5] Ibid. vi. 211. [6] Ms. notes, Barclay Allardice mss; *Scots Peerage*, i. 144; Adam, *Pol. State Scotland 1788*, p. 184.

E.H.-G.

## BARING, Francis (1740-1810), of Mincing Lane, London.

| | |
|---|---|
| GRAMPOUND | 1784-1790 |
| CHIPPING WYCOMBE | 1 Feb. 1794-1796 |
| CALNE | 1796-1802 |
| CHIPPING WYCOMBE | 1802-1806 |

*b.* 18 Apr. 1740, 3rd s. of John Baring of Larkbear, Devon, and bro. of John Baring (q.v.). *m.* 12 May 1767, Harriet, da. and coh. of William Herring of Croydon, Surr., 5s. 5da. *cr.* Bt. 29 May 1793.
     Director, Royal Exchange Assurance 1772-80; director, E. I. Co. 1779-82, 1784-7, 1789-91, 1794-7, 1799-1802, 1804-7, 1809-*d*; dep. chairman 1791-2; chairman 1792-3.

Baring did not enter the family woollen business, but was apprenticed as a merchant to the London firm of Boehm and Co. In 1763 he went into business in London with his brother John. He was an extremely able financier and soon obtained direction of the firm, which he made a financial house of European standing. By 1784 he was one of the principal merchants trading to America, the leader of the City interest in the East India Company,[1] and a recognized authority on trade and finance.

While Shelburne was at the Treasury, Baring acted as one of his chief financial advisers. 'Mr. Baring', wrote the King to Shelburne, 20 Sept. 1782,[2] 'by his account of Senegal and Goree fully answers the expectations in his favour Lord Shelburne has raised in my mind, and will I am confident prove very useful.' He remained attached to Shelburne after Shelburne left office, became connected with Pitt, and in 1784 was returned as an Administration candidate at Grampound.

Though handicapped as a debater by his deafness,[3] some 40 speeches by Baring are noted in the Parliament of 1784, every one on some aspect of trade or finance. 'Few individuals [in the House] could contend with him in financial knowledge and commercial information', wrote Wraxall.[4] He advised Pitt, and was appointed by him one of the commissioners for examining the regulation of public offices. Yet his real political allegiance was to Lansdowne (as Shelburne had become in 1784). On 22 Jan. 1789 at the time of the Regency crisis he wrote to Lansdowne:[5]

> I am inclined to think that *silence* of your Lordship's friends, whilst their votes have been firm and consistent, will be well understood by the great world, as conveying a sufficient disapprobation of some parts, although upon the whole it may not be thought proper to go further. And it may have an awkward appearance with regard to some of those friends if your Lordship should hold a language upon so delicate and important a subject as to contradict their conduct. At the same time it may appear particular if your Lordship is compelled to be in town about your private affairs and to keep away from the House, although I cannot think there was any positive pledge given for your attendance when the restriction came before the House.

Over the French Revolution he adhered to Lansdowne and broke with Pitt.

Baring died 12 Sept. 1810, 'unquestionably the first merchant in Europe, first in knowledge and talents, and first in character and opulence'.[6]

[1] C. H. Philips, *E. I. Co. 1784–1834.* [2] Fortescue, vi. 137. [3] Baring to Lansdowne, 10 May 1784, Lansdowne mss. [4] *Mems.* v. 72. [5] Lansdowne mss. [6] *Gent. Mag.* 1810, p. 293.

M.M.D.

## BARING, John (1730–1816), of Mount Radford, Exeter, Devon.

EXETER 9 Nov. 1776–1802

*b.* 5 Oct. 1730, 1st s. of John Baring of Larkbear, Devon by Elizabeth, da. of John Vowler, grocer, of Exeter; bro. of Francis Baring (q.v.). *educ.* Geneva. *m.* 24 Nov. 1757, Anne, da. of Francis Parker of Blagdon, Devon, 2s. 4da. *suc.* fa. 1748.
Sheriff, Devon 1776–7.

This Member's father, son of Franz Baring, minister of the Lutheran church of Bremen, settled as a clothier near Exeter in 1717; was naturalized in 1723; and left his son a flourishing Exeter cloth business, which the latter developed. In 1763 he extended his interests to London, and with his brother Francis (q.v.) established the firm of Baring and Co., initially to act as agency for the Exeter firm. They were particularly concerned with the financing of foreign trade, and though John Baring was originally the dominant figure in the firm, he gradually left its affairs to his brother Francis; while he himself returned to Devon, established the Plymouth bank, and in 1770 founded the Devonshire bank at Exeter. By 1776 his interests seem to have been principally financial. In 1774 he un-

successfully contested Honiton. His increasing wealth enabled him to purchase considerable property at Exeter; in 1776 he stood there in opposition to the corporation interest, and was returned after an expensive contest.

At first he supported Administration. In 1779 the *Public Ledger* wrote about him:

> He is a man of good fortune, and very respectable character. His brother, Mr. Francis Baring, is one of the East India directors; and from the influence, probably, of that connection, more than from any other circumstance, this Member is the avowed and steadfast friend of the present Administration.

But shortly afterwards, in his pre-election survey, Robinson wrote: 'Mr. Baring was a friend until Mr. Dunning married his sister.' In the critical divisions of 21 Feb. and 8, 13 Mar. 1780, Baring voted with the court; on 31 Mar. John Dunning (q.v.) and Elizabeth Baring were married; in the division of 6 Apr. Baring abstained, and on 24 Apr. he voted with the Opposition.

At the general election he was returned unopposed on the corporation interest at Exeter, and henceforth till the fall of North consistently voted with the Opposition. He voted for Shelburne's peace preliminaries, 18 Feb. 1783, for parliamentary reform, 7 May 1783, and against Fox's East India bill, 27 Nov. 1783; supported Pitt, but with his brother turned against him over the French Revolution.

There is no record of his having spoken in the House before 1790. He died 29 Jan. 1816[1].

[1] *Gent. Mag.* 1816, i. 278; Burke, *L.G.* gives 1 Feb. 1816.

M.M.D.

## BARKER, Sir Robert (?1732–89), of Busbridge, Surr.

WALLINGFORD 1774–1780

*b.* ?1732, o.s. of Robert Barker, M.D., of Hammersmith by his w. Hannah Whitehead, and 1st cos. of William Devaynes (q.v.). *m.* 4 Nov. 1780, Anne, da. and h. of Brabazon Hallowes of Glapwell, Derbys., *s.p. suc.* fa. 1745; kntd. 16 Apr. 1764; *cr.* Bt. 24 Mar. 1781.
Entered E.I. Co.'s military service c.1749; 2nd lt. Madras Artillery 1753, capt. lt. 1756, capt. 1757, maj. 1761; provincial c.-in-c. Bengal 1770–4.

In 1774 Barker resigned his post as provincial commander-in-chief, Bengal, after a disagreement with Hastings. Returning to England with, according to John Scott (q.v.), a 'very large fortune',[1] he was returned at the general election of 1774 for the corrupt and expensive borough of Wallingford. In Parliament he consistently supported North's Administration. There is no record of his having spoken in the House, and he does not seem to have stood again.

He died 14 Sept. 1789, aged 57. In his obituary notice, the *Gentleman's Magazine* writes (1789, p. 956), that he was 'no less distinguished in philosophy than in war', and lists several scientific papers communicated by him to the Royal Society, of which he was a member.

[1] Debrett, xvi. 102.

M.M.D.

**BARLOW, Hugh** (*d.*1763), of Lawrenny, Pemb.

PEMBROKE BOROUGHS  21 Dec. 1747–1761

2nd s. of John Barlow, M.P., of Lawrenny, by his 2nd w. Anne, da. of Sir Hugh Owen, 2nd Bt., M.P., of Orielton, Pemb. *m.* (1) Dec. 1733, Anne, da. of Richard Skrine of Wansley, Som., 1 da.; (2) his cos. Elizabeth, da. of Sir Arthur Owen, 3rd Bt., *s.p. suc.* bro. Oct. 1737.

Hugh Barlow sat for Pembroke Boroughs on the interest of his Owen relatives as a supporter of the Pelham and Newcastle Administrations. He died November 1763.

P.D.G.T.

**BARLOW, Hugh** (*d.*1809), *see* **OWEN** (afterwards **BARLOW**)

**BARNARD, Visct.**, *see* **VANE, Henry**, *and* **VANE, William Harry**

**BARNARD, Sir John** (c.1685–1764), of Clapham, Surr.

LONDON  1722–1761

*b.* c.1685, s. of John Barnard, merchant, of London, by Sarah, da. of Robert Payne of Play Hatch, Sonning, Berks.[1] *educ.* Wandsworth. *m.* 5 Oct. 1708, Jane, da. of John Godschall,[2] a Turkey merchant, 1s. 2da. Kntd. 29 Sept. 1732.
Alderman, London 1728–58, sheriff 1735–6, ld. mayor 1737–8; president Christ's Hospital 1740–58.

Of Quaker parentage, Barnard as a young man joined the Church of England. He entered his father's business c.1700 and later became a prominent insurer at Lloyd's, making a moderate fortune. Invited in 1722 to stand for the City in the popular Whig interest, he was for many years its unchallenged leader, and in 1754 still topped the poll in a hotly contested election. An extremely active independent, he was classed by Dupplin as 'doubtful'; yet was consulted by Newcastle on financial matters,[3] in which he enjoyed in many quarters a great reputation. In previous Parliaments a frequent speaker on economic subjects, he seems to have been much less prominent in that of 1754, only one speech of his—on a financial resolution

—being recorded.[4] His importance in the City also declined, Beckford taking his place as leader of its popular forces. In 1757 he played a prominent part in framing the unorthodox and unsuccessful method of raising the supplies adopted by H. B. Legge as chancellor of the Exchequer in the Devonshire-Pitt Administration.[5]

On grounds of health Barnard refused to stand again in 1761, and died 29 Aug. 1764.

[1] Reg. Oxfordshire Quarterly Meeting, Berks. RO. [2] Reg. St. Mary at Hill, London. [3] Jas. West to Newcastle, 11 Feb. 1758, Add. 32877, f. 422. [4] West to Newcastle, Add. 32861, f. 202. [5] See L. S. Sutherland, 'The City of London and the Devonshire–Pitt Administration, 1756–7', *Proc. Br. Acad.* xlvi.

L.B.N.

**BARNE, Barne** (1754–1828), of Sotterley Hall, Suff.

DUNWICH  10 Dec. 1777–Feb. 1791

*b.* 25 Aug. 1754, 2nd s. of Miles Barne (q.v.) by his 2nd w. Mary, da. of George Thornhill. *educ.* Westminster 1768; Trinity Hall, Camb. 1772; I. Temple 1770, called 1779. *unm.*
Fellow of Trinity Hall 1781–1814; bencher I. Temple 1811, reader 1820, treasurer 1820–1.
Commr. of taxes 9 Apr. 1791–1820.

Barne was returned for Dunwich on the family interest. In Parliament he constantly supported Administration till the fall of North; voted for Shelburne's peace preliminaries, 18 Feb. 1783, and against Fox's East India bill, 27 Nov. 1783. He was classed as an Administration supporter in Robinson's list of January 1784, Stockdale's of 19 Mar., and Adam's of May, and regularly supported Pitt's Administration. There is no record of his having spoken in the House. Barne applied to Pitt for a commissionership of customs or excise, but on 6 Nov. 1788 stated that he would be willing to accept a lesser office since he was anxious to marry and could not do so without employment.[1] Barne voted with Pitt on the Regency in December 1788. He wrote to his mother on 30 Dec. that in the likely event of Pitt being dismissed he could do nothing to get his brother excused from being sheriff:[2]

> I recollect giving it as my opinion . . . that it might be possible to have that favour granted even by Mr. Fox, but I remember adding likewise, provided I had an opportunity of voting with him occasionally, which I might do on some particular questions, although in general I was in opposition. In my present situation, however, having never shown the least favourable disposition to him, I could upon no account presume to request any favour from him, without being guilty of the greatest impropriety.

Barne voted with Pitt in the further divisions on the Regency, February 1789.

He died 19 June 1828.

[1] Chatham mss 111. [2] Ipswich and E. Suff. RO, Barne mss 359/128.

M.M.D.

**BARNE, Miles** (1718–80), of Sotterley Hall, Suff.

Dunwich 1747–1754, 18 Feb. 1764–Nov. 1777

*b.* Oct. 1718, o.s. of Miles Barne, London merchant, by Elizabeth, da. of Solomon Snowdon of York. *m.* (1) May 1745, Elizabeth (*d.*20 Sept. 1747), da. and h. of Nathaniel Elwick, gov. of Madras, of May Place, nr. Crayford, Kent, 1s. 1da.; (2) 23 Sept. 1752, Mary, da. of George Thornhill of Diddington, Hunts. 5s. 4da. *suc.* fa. 22 Mar. 1743.

Barne, who had purchased the Sotterley estate in Suffolk in 1744, and was returned for Dunwich on the interest of Sir George Downing in 1747, was dropped in 1754, but is reported to have declared then that should he outlive Downing he would stand again.[1] After Downing's death in 1764 he combined with the Vannecks to oust the Downing interest in the borough and was returned unopposed. He was classed in Newcastle's list of 10 May 1764 as a 'sure' friend; in Rockingham's of July 1765 as 'pro', and in that of November 1766 as 'Whig'. No vote or speech by him was reported during the 1761 Parliament. Barne voted with the Opposition on Wilkes's petition, 27 Jan. 1769; voted for the petition of the clergy on the 39 Articles, 6 Feb. 1772, and was marked as 'pro, present' in Robinson's first survey on the royal marriage bill, Mar. 1772, and as 'pro, present, query' in that of 9 Mar. He voted with the Administration on naval captains, 9 Feb. 1773; was marked in the King's list on Grenville's Election Act, 25 Feb. 1774, as a dissenting friend, and in Robinson's survey of 1774 was classed as 'pro'. No vote or speech of Barne's is reported during the Parliament of 1774. In 1777 he resigned his seat because of ill-health, and died 27 Dec. 1780.

[1] 'Memorandum respecting the borough of Dunwich', Barne mss, Ipswich & E. Suff. RO.

M.M.D.

**BARRÉ, Isaac** (1726–1802), of Manchester Buildings, Westminster.

Chipping Wycombe 5 Dec. 1761–1774
Calne 1774–1790

*b.* 15 Oct. 1726,[1] o.s. of Peter Barré of Dublin by Marie Madelaine Raboteau. *educ.* Trinity, Dublin 1740. *unm. suc.* fa. 1776.
  Ensign 32 Ft. 1746, lt. 1755, capt. 1758; capt. 28 Ft. 1760; lt.-col. 106 Ft. 1761–2; adjutant-gen. Mar.–Dec. 1763; gov. Stirling castle Apr.–Dec. 1763; ret. 1773.[2]
  P.C. 10 Sept. 1766; jt. vice-treasurer [I] Sept. 1766–Oct. 1768; treasurer of the navy Apr.–July 1782; paymaster gen. July 1782–Apr. 1783; clerk of the pells Jan. 1784–*d.*

Barré's father was a Huguenot refugee who settled as a merchant in Dublin c.1720, and his mother was also a Huguenot. In 1757 Barré served with James Wolfe and Lord Fitzmaurice (q.v.) on

the expedition to Rochfort. In 1758 he went to Canada with Wolfe, who appointed him adjutant-general; served at Louisbourg; and in the attack on Quebec (September 1759) was wounded and lost an eye. Though a major in America, his substantive rank was still only that of captain. 'For want of friends', he wrote to Pitt on 28 Apr. 1760,[3] asking for promotion, 'I had lingered a subaltern officer eleven years, when Mr. Wolfe's opinion of me rescued me from that obscurity.' In October 1760 he returned to England with despatches; and, after personally soliciting Pitt and Barrington, was promised the rank of lieutenant-colonel.[4]

He renewed his friendship with Fitzmaurice, who introduced him to Bute and recommended him for a seat in Parliament:[5] 'Barré . . . has parts which would certainly make a figure in a parliamentary way, and, what is not always the case of great parts, his are capable of very great attachment.' In May 1761, when Fitzmaurice succeeded his father in the Shelburne peerages, he offered to return Barré at Chipping Wycombe. In a letter to Shelburne of 15 May Barré professed to have doubts:

> I speak without reserve when I say that I may be an honest, but I fear greatly that a life of dissipation in my first setting out, has prevented me from being a very acceptable representative of your friends at Wycombe. I have not been sufficiently habituated to great objects to undertake this affair with ease to myself.

He was 'a good deal uneasy' about his qualification, and went over to Ireland to consult his father. From Dublin he wrote to Shelburne on 13 Aug.:

> My father . . . has by no means proved himself able in the management of his own affairs . . . His income arises from houses mostly . . . 'tis clear about £300 a year, and may (including a little lodge in the country, which I don't now estimate), sell at certain times for near £4,000.[6]

Presumably Shelburne provided him with a qualification, and on 5 Dec. 1761 he was returned to Parliament.[7] For more than twenty years he was Shelburne's closest friend, and chief spokesman in the House of Commons.

On 10 Dec. he made a sensational début. Walpole, who entered the House just as Barré was beginning to speak, writes:[8]

> My ear was struck with sounds I had little been accustomed to of late, virulent abuse on the last reign, and from a voice unknown to me. I turned, and saw a face equally new; a black, robust man, of a military figure, rather hard-favoured than not young, with a peculiar distortion on one side of his face, which it seems was owing to a bullet lodged loosely in his cheek, and which gave a savage glare to one eye. What I less expected from his appearance was very classic and eloquent diction, and as determined boldness as if accustomed to harangue in that place. He told the

House that in the late King's reign we had been governed solely by Hanoverian measures and councils; and . . . he proceeded with the same vociferous spirit to censure all ministers but Lord Bute; and for Mr. Pitt, who was not present, he received the appellation of a profligate minister, who had thrust himself into power on the shoulders of the mob.

The next day, when Pitt was present, Barré repeated his attack. 'Insult of language, terms, manner were addressed, and personally addressed, to Mr. Pitt by that bravo', writes Walpole;[9] and another eye-witness:[10]

He attacked Mr. Pitt's political principles, and said his life had been a series of change and contradiction from the beginning to the end; that after the most violent protestations against continental and Hanoverian connections, when he had thrust himself into the ministry, chameleon-like, he took the colour of the ground he stood on. He then ridiculed his figure and action, saying he was amazed to see the gentleman, with solemn looks, with eyes uplift to heaven, one hand beating on his breast, and formally contradicting and disowning the principles he had maintained the day before.

'You know I never was partial to Pitt', wrote Lord John Cavendish to the Duke of Devonshire,[11] 'but I am scandalized that such a creature as Lord Shelburne should dare to turn loose an Irish ruffian in the House of Commons to affront a man of Pitt's age and rank'; and opinion was general in condemning Barré.

Barré subsequently revealed in the House of Commons that he had been instigated to make these attacks on Pitt by Henry Fox.[12] He was 'pressed to go to court', was 'honoured with more than common attention',[13] and appointed lieutenant-colonel of the 106th Foot. In subsequent speeches that session he tried to maintain the style of his first. On the militia bill, 19 Mar. 1762, he was, writes Harris, 'strong, rough, and nervous'. On 12 May:[14]

Colonel Barré set out in a flaming, scurrilous speech as usual, but was discountenanced by the House. Many gentlemen as soon as he rose went out of the House; many of those who stayed shuffled about from their places, talked with one another, coughed, and would not hear him. And as he proceeded to talk in an unbecoming manner of the late King, abusing him for his German measures, Lord Barrington rose up in indignation and called him to order.

On the conclusion of peace Barré's regiment was disbanded, and Shelburne asked Bute to make him surveyor of the Ordnance:[15]

This would be rewarding him very nobly certainly, but upon weighing it I am clear he would be able to return it in the execution of the office and in the credit he would do your Lordship in a Board which, you may depend upon it, wants reformation more than any other.

Barré refused the offer because it would put him out of the way of promotion in the army—'what I cannot help calling my freehold'.[16] Appointed adjutant-general in March, he wrote to Shelburne on 18 Apr. complaining at not being properly rewarded.[17] 'Harsh usage may break my temper', he wrote, 'it shall not affect my spirit. Administration . . . may in some important hour want the assistance of one firm and honest man.' Bute, shortly before his retirement, obtained for Barré the governorship of Stirling castle.

On 25 Nov. 1763 Barré, together with Shelburne's other friends in the Commons, voted against Grenville's Administration over Wilkes; and was turned out of his military employments. He subsequently estimated that he lost £1500 a year,[18] and during the next twenty years frequently reminded the House that he had been dismissed because of his vote in Parliament. He became reconciled to Pitt, and took his place among the leading Opposition speakers. Walpole wrote to Mann on 11 Feb. 1765 about the debate of 29 Jan. on general warrants:

The hero of the day was the famous Colonel Barré, a man, or I am mistaken, whose fame will not stop here. He spoke with infinite wit and humour, and with that first of merits to me, novelty: his manner is original. He spoke too with extreme bitterness.

Harris described his speech as 'street dirt upon Lord Sandwich'; without doubt Barré excelled in virulence and abuse.

In 1764 he was engaged with Shelburne and Laurence Sulivan (q.v.) in East India Company affairs,[19] obtained a voting qualification and took part in the debates of the general court. Contemporaries believed that Barré was intended by Sulivan, had he proved victorious over Clive, to go out as governor of Bengal.[20] In the Commons on 14 Mar. 1765 Barré

made a full and masterly speech, and went at large into a state of the Company's affairs, showed and with plausibility the danger of changing the Company from a trading one into a fighting one, the motives it gave their servants to avarice and ambition, the experience and knowledge of war it taught the natives, the cruel incidents . . . to which it exposed our countrymen, opposed Lord Clive's party and their schemes, yet artfully contrived to give Lord Clive his due praise.[21]

He corresponded with friends in America and remained in touch with American affairs.[22] On 6 Feb. 1765 he seconded Beckford's motion against the stamp tax. 'There are gentlemen in this House from the West Indies', he said,[23] 'but there are very few who know the circumstances of North America . . . The tax intended is odious to all your colonies and they tremble at it.' It was, wrote Jared Ingersoll, agent to the governor of Connecticut, 'a very handsome and moving speech'; but it did not deny the right of Parliament, asserted by many Members in the debate, to tax the colonies. In reply to Charles Townshend (q.v.), who had described the colonies as 'children planted by our care, nourished by our indulgence . . . and protected by our arms', Barré delivered a second, impassioned, speech:

> They planted by your care? No! your oppressions planted them in America . . . They nourished by your indulgence? They grew by your neglect of them . . . They protected by your arms? They have nobly taken up arms in your defence . . . God knows I do not at this time speak from motives of party heat, what I deliver are the genuine sentiments of my heart . . . The people I believe are as truly loyal as any subjects the King has, but a people jealous of their liberties and who will vindicate them if ever they should be violated.

'These sentiments', wrote Ingersoll, 'were thrown out so entirely without premeditation, so forcibly and so firmly . . . that the whole House sat awhile as amazed, intently looking and without answering a word.'[24]

In the summer of 1765 Barré went to Italy, and while there the newly-formed Rockingham Administration sent him an offer, first of a seat at the Board of Trade, and next of the place of joint vice-treasurer of Ireland.[25] Barré wrote to Conway on 22 Oct., declining to join Administration:

> I have not the honour of knowing many others of his Majesty's new servants, and at this distance it cannot be supposed that I am well informed of the measures which they choose to adopt. Besides, in the very extensive change which has taken place I have not been able to find the names of those for whom (or rather for whose principles) I bear the highest respect.

'You know best, my Lord', he wrote to Shelburne on 23 Oct., 'whether I have acted sensibly as a politician, but *I* know I have acted as a gentleman and your friend.' A further offer in December 1765 of 'rank in the army or anything else added to the vice-treasurership' was also declined.[26]

On 3 Feb. 1766 he spoke against the declaratory bill,[27] taking Pitt's line that Parliament had no right to tax the colonies; yet in one point going beyond Pitt:

> All colonies have their date of independence. The wisdom or folly of our conduct may make it the sooner or later. If we act injudiciously this point may be reached in the life of many of the Members of this house.

On 24 Feb. he spoke for the repeal of the Stamp Act—'as well as I ever heard him', wrote George Onslow (q.v.) to Newcastle.[28]

Barré accepted from Chatham the vice-treasurership he had refused from Rockingham, and was sworn of the Privy Council. His silence during the early debates on Chatham's East India inquiry was unfavourably noticed by the King; who wrote to

Conway on 18 Feb. 1767:[29] 'I should imagine, considering the unmerited favours he has received, he ought to be zealous in supporting my Administration.' Barré spoke in the debate on printing the East India Company's papers on 6 Mar., and on 9 Mar. made 'a violent declamation on the undoubted right of the Crown to the possessions' in India.[30] Now that he had in the Company an antagonist he spoke much more frequently. But in the debates on America only one speech is recorded,[31] and of that no report is known: clearly he did not at the time realize the significance of the Townshend duties.

Barré resigned, following Chatham and Shelburne, on 31 Oct. 1768.[32] On 8 Nov. he spoke in the debate on the Address, and, writes Walpole,[33] 'made a better figure, as usual, in opposition'. He attacked the ministry's American policy, and on 17 Nov. criticized them for their supineness over Corsica. On 23 Nov. he said about Chatham: 'The sooner Heaven shall restore to health that proud assertor of the liberties of the country, the better it will be for that country.'[34] By January 1769, when Wilkes's case came into the Commons, Barré was in declared opposition, where he remained until the fall of North.

During the Parliament of 1768 Barré was one of the most frequent Opposition speakers. Two questions particularly concerned him: India and America.

On India he followed the line laid down by Chatham in 1766: the Company had no right to the territorial revenues, and should pay an annual tribute to the state.[35] In April 1772 he was elected to Burgoyne's select committee, and in October declined an invitation from the Company to go out to India to investigate and reform abuses.[36] He welcomed North's attempt in 1773 to regulate the Company's affairs in India, but said in the House on 23 Feb.:[37]

> If it was intended to take revenue and patronage into our own hands I should make my stand there, and resist such a step as highly dangerous to the constitution. The finger of Government to direct, aid, and control upon extraordinary occasions might be useful, but the strong hand of Government would ruin us all.

He spoke for Burgoyne's motion against Clive, 21 May 1773, and refused North's offer of a place on the Bengal council.[38]

His attitude towards America remained the same. The colonists, he said on 26 Jan. 1769,[39] 'will not submit to any law imposed upon them for the purposes of revenue'; if the Townshend duties are not repealed 'you run the risk of losing America'. Yet on 14 Mar. 1774 he supported the Boston port bill:[40]

The proposition before the House, he said, he could not help giving his hearty and proper affirmative to; that he liked it, harsh as it was . . . He wished . . . to see a unanimous vote in the first onset of this business, that when Boston saw this measure was carried by such a consent they would the more readily pay the sum of money to the India Company . . . Now is your time to try, in a civilized manner, your power over the Americans; other of your enemies are not in a condition to take part with them.

Contemporaries supposed that Shelburne and Barré were making overtures to the court,[41] which seems a natural conclusion to draw from the last sentences of Barré's speech:

I am not in office that my advice can be taken, if I was I should give it freely. If office comes to me it comes as an atonement for repeated and unmerited affronts. I shall at all times speak the language of a free and disinterested Member.

Barré, like Chatham, was not prepared to relinquish British supremacy over America. 'If it is necessary', he said on 23 Mar., 'I have no doubt but that a small part of our force would reduce the Americans.' But this situation should not be allowed to develop. 'As we are about to punish we should heal also', he said on 19 Apr.;[42] and he favoured the repeal of the tea duty, and fiercely opposed North's later punitive measures and the Quebec Act.[43]

Barré, contradicting many of the assertions he had previously made, was one of the severest critics of the American war. Even before Saratoga he warned Administration that the conquest of America was doubtful and 'the holding of it without the affection and goodwill of the natives' impossible;[44] should the war spread, 'we were by no means a match for the united forces of France and Spain'.[45] His criticism was not primarily directed against the conduct of the war (though he alleged that the troops 'misbehaved' at Bunker's Hill,[46] he never criticized the field commanders), but at what he regarded as governmental maladministration. Hoping to prove inefficiency and corruption he was constantly calling for returns of troops, ordnance, and ships (despite North's protests that such returns would give information to the enemy). He was very severe on contractors: 'their appetites for dishonest lucre and foul gain were as insatiable as their consciences were easily satisfied', he said on 17 Feb. 1777; and on 13 Mar. 1780 he accused North of having made a 'most corrupt and fraudulent' contract for rum with Richard Atkinson (q.v.).[47] In 1780 Barré moved for a commission of accounts,[48] and was considerably annoyed when North took up the idea but produced his own scheme.[49]

Jeremy Bentham wrote about Barré in 1781:[50]

Barré . . . abounds in stories that are well told and very entertaining. He really seems to have a great command of language; he states clearly and forcibly; and upon all points his words are fluent and well chosen.

'In his younger days', wrote Walpole,[51] 'he had acted plays with so much applause that it was said Garrick had offered him a thousand pounds a year to come upon the stage.' Gibbon described him in one debate as 'an actor equal to Garrick';[52] and Lord George Germain wrote of his speech of 26 Oct. 1775: 'very long, good acting, not much argument'.[53]

Melodramatic charges and threats abound in his speeches. Here are a few examples from one session: 15 Mar. 1779, he said that North and Sandwich had behaved 'like traitors to this country' and threatened them with impeachment; 22 Mar. 1779, he accused them of 'aiming like assassins at the life of Admiral Keppel'; 21 June 1779, he said of North that his crimes 'were black enough . . . to have warranted the suspicion of treachery'; etc.[54] Wedderburn said it was Barré's constant custom to be personal against him.[55] On 22 Feb. 1782 North, usually good-tempered, was roused by Barré's description of his conduct as 'scandalous, indecent, and insulting', to reply

that he supposed the large minority of that evening had inspired the right honourable gentleman with courage to abuse him. He had always held forth to him such language as was not decent, but now he had been insolent and brutal.

Barré, though professing to esteem North 'as a private gentleman', claimed that 'as a minister he had a right to use and treat him with as severe epithets as parliamentary form would allow'.[56]

On the formation of the Rockingham Administration Barré obtained a well-paid office, and a pension of £3200 p.a. if removed from his place. When the pension was criticized in Parliament, Barré defended it as compensation for being dismissed from his military offices in 1763.[57] During the Shelburne ministry he held the still more lucrative office of paymaster-general. In January 1784 he surrendered his pension for the sinecure of clerk of the pells.

Barré did not vote on Fox's East India bill, and in Robinson's list of January 1784 and Stockdale's of March is classed as 'absent'. About this time he became totally blind. On 14 Mar. 1785 he made his first speech since July 1782, in opposition to the extensive fortifications proposed in the Ordnance estimates. On 18 Apr. 1785 he voted for parliamentary reform. His last big speech in the House was on 27 Feb. 1786 against Richmond's fortifications plan.[58] He voted with Pitt on the Regency. He differed with Lansdowne on the French Revolution,[59] and was dropped in 1790.

Barré died 20 July 1802.

[1] *Reg. of the French Nonconformist Churches of Dublin* (Huguenot Soc.), 77. [2] Barré to Chatham, 21 Jan. 1773, *Chatham Corresp.* iv. 242–4. [3] Ibid. ii. 41–43. [4] See his letters to Pitt and Bute, Fortescue, i. 8–10; also Namier, *Add. and Corr.* 9. [5] Shelburne to Bute, Feb. 1761, Bute mss. [6] Lansdowne mss. [7] For his election, see CHIPPING WYCOMBE. [8] *Mems. Geo. III*, i. 86. [9] Ibid. 94. [10] John Milbanke to Rockingham, 28 Dec. 1761, *Rockingham Mems.* i. 81–82. [11] 12 Dec. 1761, Devonshire mss. [12] Walpole, *Mems. Geo. III*, iv. 194; *Cavendish's Debates*, ii. 426–7. [13] Barré to Shelburne, 18 Apr. 1763, Fitzmaurice, *Shelburne*, i. 102. [14] Robt. Symmers to Andrew Mitchell, 14 May 1762, Add. 6839, ff. 268–9. [15] Bute mss. [16] Barré to Shelburne, 23 Dec. 1762, Lansdowne mss. [17] Ibid. [18] Speech of 9 July 1782, Debrett, vii. 288–90. [19] Sutherland, *E. I. Co. in 18th Cent. Politics*, 121. [20] Walpole to Hertford, 20 Apr. 1764. [21] Harris's 'Debates'. [22] See corresp. of John Watts, a New York merchant and member of the Council, *Colls. N.Y. Hist. Soc.* (1928). [23] Ryder's 'Debates', Harrowby mss. [24] *Colls. Conn. Hist. Soc.* xviii. 322–3. [25] In the Lansdowne mss are copies of Conway's letter to Barré of 29 Aug. 1765 and Barré's reply of 22 Oct., enclosed in a letter to Shelburne of 23 Oct. [26] Shelburne to Pitt, 21 Dec. 1765, *Chatham Corresp.* ii. 355–6. [27] Ryder's 'Debates'. [28] Add. 32974, f. 79. [29] Fortescue, i. 451. See also Rigby's remark, reported in Walpole, *Mems. Geo. III*, ii. 296. [30] West to Newcastle, 9 Mar. 1767, Add. 32980, f. 248. [31] Ryder's 'Debates', 13 May 1767. [32] His letter of resignation is in the Grafton mss. [33] *Mems. Geo. III*, iii. 172. [34] *Cavendish's Debates*, i. 56–57, 63. [35] Speech of 27 Feb. 1769, ibid. 256–8. [36] Sutherland, 235. [37] Barré's account of this debate in the Lansdowne mss. Shelburne's letter to Chatham of 30 Mar. 1773 (*Chatham Corresp.* iv. 254–7) is based largely on this account. [38] Shelburne to Chatham, 12 June 1773, ibid. 273. [39] *Cavendish's Debates*. i. 205–7. [40] Debrett, vii. 74–75. [41] Walpole, *Last Jnls*, i. 314, 316. [42] Brickdale's 'Debates'. [43] See his speeches of 15 Apr., 2 May, and 26 May. [44] 10 Feb. 1777, Almon, vi. 173. [45] 31 Oct. 1776, ibid. 42. [46] 20 Feb. 1776, ibid. iii. 339. [47] Ibid. vii. 278; xvii. 290. [48] 14 Feb. 1780, ibid. 117, 120, 125. [49] 21 Mar. 1780, ibid. 398–402. [50] *Works*, x. 204. [51] *Mems. Geo. III*, ii. 87. [52] Gibbon to Holroyd, post 5 Dec. 1774. [53] *HMC Stopford-Sackville*, i. 137. [54] Almon, xii. 168, 254; xiii. 477. [55] 21 Feb. 1780, ibid. xvii. 142. [56] Debrett, vi. 281–2. [57] 9 July 1782, ibid. vii. 288–90. [58] Stockdale, v. 183–7, vii. 235–40. [59] Fitzmaurice, ii. 399.

J.B.

## BARRET, Thomas (?1743–1803), of Lee, Kent.

DOVER    2 Apr. 1773–1774

*b.* ?1743, *s.* of Thomas Barret of Lee by his 4th *w.* Catherine, *da.* of Humphrey Pudnor. *educ.* Trinity, Camb. 7 Mar. 1762, aged 18. *unm.*

Barret was a friend of Horace Walpole, who wrote to William Mason, 27 Mar. 1773: 'Mr. Barret stands for Dover, I suppose on the court interest, for Wilkes has sent down a remonstrating candidate.' But Barret, supported by Government, defeated John Trevanion (q.v.). He voted against perpetuating Grenville's Election Act, 25 Feb. 1774. He did not stand again in 1774, nor at any further election.

Walpole considered him 'a most worthy man'; he helped Barret to re-design Lee, and was especially proud of the library:

> It is [he wrote to Mary Berry, 17 Oct. 1794] the most perfect thing I ever saw, and has most the air it was intended to have . . . that of an abbot's library, supposing it could have been so exquisitely finished three hundred years ago.

He died 8 Jan. 1803. According to the *Gentleman's Magazine* (1803, p. 90),

> Mr. Barret was perfectly skilled in the arts, and warmly attached to them; his memory was powerful, and his knowledge of history, memoirs, and topography extensive and exact.

L.B.N.

## BARRINGTON, Sir John, 7th Bt. (*d.*1776), of Swainstown, I.o.W.

NEWTOWN I.o.W.    25 Apr. 1729–1734, 1741–Nov. 1775

*b.* by 1707,[1] 1st *s.* of Sir John Barrington, 6th Bt., of Swainstown, I.o.W. and Hitchin, Herts. by Susan, *da.* of George Draper of Hitchin. *m.* Mary, *da.* of Patricius Roberts, *s.p. suc. fa.* Aug. 1717.

The Barrington family owned a number of burgages at Newtown, and could usually claim one seat. In 1754 Sir John was returned unopposed, and was classed by Dupplin as 'doubtful'.

He voted with Opposition over the peace preliminaries, 9 Dec. 1762, Wilkes, 15 Nov. 1763, and general warrants, 6 and 15 Feb. 1764; was classed as a 'sure' friend by Newcastle on 10 May 1764, and as 'pro' by Rockingham in July 1765. But on 18 Aug. 1765 Newcastle wrote: 'Sir John Barrington, though generally with us, is in himself a wavering man.'[2] Listed as 'Government' by Charles Townshend in January 1767, he voted with them on the land tax, 27 Feb. 1767.

In 1768 Barrington had to fight a contested election at Newtown, standing jointly with Harcourt Powell (q.v.) against Sir Thomas Worsley and John Glynn (q.v.). Robinson noted him as 'pro, present' over the royal marriage bill, 1772, but his name appears in no division list for this Parliament. There is no record of his having spoken in the House.

In November 1775 he vacated his seat, and died 4 May 1776.

[1] His yr. bro. was *b.* 1708. [2] To the Duke of Cumberland, Add. 32969, f. 74.

M.M.D.

## BARRINGTON, John (1752–1818), of Swainstown, I.o.W.

NEWTOWN I.o.W.    1780–1796

*b.* 8 Dec. 1752, 1st surv. *s.* of Sir Fitzwilliam Barrington, 8th Bt., by Jane, *da.* of Mathew Hall of Horsham, Suss.; nephew of Sir John Barrington, 7th Bt. (q.v.). *educ.* Eton 1761–70; Trinity Hall, Camb. 1771. *unm. suc. fa.* as 9th Bt. 24 Sept. 1792.

Barrington was returned on the family interest at Newtown. 'It is hoped', Robinson noted in his survey for the general election of 1780, 'that he will be a friend.' But he voted with Opposition on Lowther's motion against the war, 12 Dec. 1781, and on Rous's no confidence motion, 15 Mar. 1782. He did not vote in the division on Shelburne's peace preliminaries, 18 Feb. 1783, but in Robinson's list of March 1783 was classed as a 'connexion of Lord Shelburne's Government'; voted against Fox's East India bill, 27 Nov. 1783; and in Stockdale's list of 19 Mar. 1784 was described as a supporter of Pitt. He voted for parliamentary reform, 18 Apr. 1785, but his name does not appear in any other list before 1789, when he voted with Pitt over the Regency. There is no record of his having spoken in the House in our period.

He died 5 Aug. 1818.

M.M.D.

**BARRINGTON, William Wildman**, 2nd Visct. Barrington [I] (1717–93), of Beckett, Berks.

BERWICK-UPON-TWEED  13 Mar. 1740–1754
PLYMOUTH  1754–24 May 1778

*b.* 15 Jan. 1717, 1st s. of John, 1st Visct. Barrington [I], M.P., of Beckett by Anne, da. and coh. of William Daines, M.P. *educ.* under James Graham,[1] schoolmaster at Dalston, Mdx.; Geneva 1735–8. *m.* 16 Sept. 1740, Mary, da. and coh. of Henry Lovell of Northampton, wid. of Hon. Samuel Grimston, *s.p.s. suc.* fa. 14 Dec. 1734.

Ld. of Admiralty Feb. 1746–Apr. 1754; master of the great wardrobe Apr. 1754–Oct. 1755; P.C. 11 Mar. 1755; sec. at war Oct. 1755–Mar. 1761; chancellor of the Exchequer Mar. 1761–May 1762; treasurer of navy June 1762–July 1765; sec. at war July 1765–Dec. 1778; jt. postmaster gen. Jan.–Apr. 1782.

In spite of 'a lisp and a tedious precision that prejudiced one against him', Horace Walpole named Barrington in 1755 among the 28 best speakers in the Commons,[2] and Newcastle among the half-dozen of the 'good second rank' on the Government side.[3] In March 1754, 'in return for eight years of laborious and useful service both in office and in Parliament',[4] he applied to Newcastle for a place at the Treasury, but when told that the King had destined him for master of the great wardrobe, said 'that he got more than he had solicited, expected, or deserved; and should never ask for any other employment'. He kept to this resolution: hardly another office-holder accepted with such good humour whatever was offered him; and he is almost unique among men of his rank during this period in never asking for a British peerage.

At Berwick Barrington was at loggerheads with Thomas Watson (q.v.), the Government manager; and after a good deal of strenuous 'parliamenteering', in October 1753 he 'gauged wisely to give up with them'.[5] Next he tried Bristol, which his father-in-law had represented and where Barrington had influential kinsmen 'powerfully seconded by the mob';[6] again, however, he found it advisable to decline. He then applied for an Admiralty borough, but when assigned Saltash,[7] wrote to Pelham that he would 'rather be chosen at Plymouth' as it was

'the cheapest, a consideration of some weight to a man who has already spent more to lose, than it ever cost him to carry, an election; and whose estate is under settlement, and burthened with jointures'. Moreover,

Plymouth affords business to its representative, and requires some nicety in the management of it; though I have been unfortunate at Berwick, I have still the vanity to think, that few *sea officers* understand the management of an interest in a corporation so well as myself.

When Barrington was moved from the Admiralty to the great wardrobe, one of his chief Plymouth supporters wrote to him, 2 Apr. 1754:

I congratulate you on the high dignity conferred by his Majesty on your Lordship and am sensible how much it will be in your power, both as to the corporation as well as particulars to favour them.

It will make no variation to our sentiments, as the borough is truly loyal, and from our knowledge of your Lordship, as well as the interest we have always espoused of the Admiralty.[8]

His election was unopposed, and so were all his re-elections. Masses of correspondence among his papers testify to his exertions on behalf of the borough and its electors ('Things done for people at Plymouth'); and so does a rebuke from Sandwich in 1774: 'I cannot acquiesce in their [the corporation] recommending to all employments that fall vacant at Plymouth . . . I must be allowed to be the proper judge what proportion of that favour is due to them.'[9] Barrington's sailor brother Samuel wrote to him from Plymouth, 9 Aug. 1771: 'I need not tell you what you already know, how much your constituents adore you.'

In September 1755 Newcastle picked Barrington, 'the most declared friend of mine', for the War Office, without Cumberland being consulted.[10] But Barrington gradually gained the favour of Cumberland who on 11 July 1762 signs himself in a letter to him 'your very affectionate friend'.[11]

When the Devonshire-Pitt Government was being formed, Temple wrote to Pitt, 9 Nov. 1756: 'Ellis the King will not make secretary at war, preferring Barrington.'[12] There followed years of extreme application to departmental duties: a competent executive, and self-confident within a comparatively narrow range but also acutely conscious of his own limitations, and no longer ambitious, Barrington shunned prominence. Not a strong personality, certainly no leader, he became submerged in his work. Still, though rather colourless and well-nigh anonymous, he was not 'flimsy and contemptible', fawning and servile, or 'little minded', descriptions attached to him by Horace Walpole and Fox. He repeatedly declared the principle on which he acted (more consonant with the avowed ideas of the period than party): he thought 'support of Government a duty, while an honest man could support it'.[13] From loyalty to his father he had attacked his father's enemy; but he was not cut out for opposition: by nature and choice he was a civil servant rather than a politician. He served the King and did his work; he was loyal and attentive to his friends, and much concerned never to lose one; and he looked after the interests of those in his charge, showing sympathy for officers without money or patrons to secure them promotion—'the poor, though deserving officer, should always find at the War Office a constant assertor of his rights, and a faithful guardian of his interests'.[14] He would not accept recommendations of army surgeons from colonels, or even from the commander-in-chief or Newcastle—'None but medical men', he wrote to H. S. Conway on 8 June 1759, 'can judge of medical men; and, in my opinion, it would be as preposterous to take the character of a surgeon from a colonel, as of an officer from the hospital board.'[15] He carefully scrutinized the financial demands of influential colonels—'You threaten me with the House of Commons', he wrote to Burgoyne (q.v.) on 27 Oct. 1759, '. . . This is not the way to influence me, and I am ready to give an account of my conduct, where ever any man has a right to question it.'[16] He put an absolute negative to Peter Taylor (q.v.), a crook employed by Fox and favoured by Calcraft (q.v.), when the Duke of Marlborough wanted to take him as commissary of stores on the expedition against Cherbourg and St. Malo. During his eighteen years at the War Office he struggled against the worst abuses of the prevailing system. When refusing a request of Lt.-Gen. Elliott on behalf of his son, he wrote on 25 Nov. 1767:[17]

> . . . what is once done innocently, will be often repeated inconveniently; especially in a country like this, with some hundred unreasonable Parliament men, supported by unreasonable but powerful patrons. Many years of my life have been spent in warfare against these gentlemen: and whenever I have success, it arises entirely from an invariable adherence to good general rules, without admitting one single exception.

When in 1776 he begged the King's leave to retire from the service, he stated as one of his reasons that 'conversation and correspondence with persons unreasonably soliciting military favours' had become too great a strain on his 'temper and civility'. It was the care which Barrington gave to the interests of the army that probably made George II and George III give preference to him when choosing a secretary at war.

By 1759 Charles Townshend was a claimant to the War Office. On 14 Dec. 1760 Newcastle, fearing

lest Bute, to secure Townshend, should sacrifice Barrington, wrote in his notes for a conference with Bute:[18] 'Lord Barrington is undoubtedly in all respects the best secretary at war that ever was, and a most steady and useful friend of mine in that office, and of great service to my friends.' Barrington, when shifted to the Exchequer, wrote to Andrew Mitchell, 23 Mar. 1761: 'my reason tells me it would have been more proper to have given me an employment of less consequence'; but his 'invariable rule' was 'to ask nothing, to refuse nothing, to let others place me, and to do my best wherever I am placed'.[19] On Pitt's resignation in October 1761, Barrington wrote to him,[20] as he did to other friends on their leaving office; Pitt replied, after five years' close co-operation with him in wartime:[21]

> I should certainly have had a particular pleasure in embracing you in a moment, when meeting as private friends only, I wished to renew to your Lordship the sincere assurances of esteem and affectionate regard for one I have known so long, and whose candour and honourable proceeding in all situations I truly value and applaud.

When Newcastle resigned in May 1762, his request to his friends to remain at court enabled Barrington to accept the treasurership of the navy, and combine attendance at Bute's levees with frequent visits to Claremont. But when after Devonshire's dismissal Newcastle was calling on his friends to resign, and Bute, pressed by Fox,[22] summoned Barrington (4 Nov.)[23] in order to inquire about his 'present way of thinking', Barrington replied that both his principles and inclinations induced him to support Government—

> which I had invariably done for seventeen years, ever since I had been in office, though I had sometimes disliked particular men and measures. That early in life I set out in opposition; but left it being sensible of the public mischiefs which it occasioned. That I did not say I would never oppose; but that I never would without very strong reason, and without resigning my employment.

Nor would he resign 'merely because others did, for that was faction'. Catechized on the subject of Newcastle, he declared he would defend him against all persons, and bear testimony to his 'disinterested zeal for his King and country', but felt not obliged to follow him when wrong.

From Bute Barrington went to Newcastle, who did not at first take kindly to the line adopted by Barrington; but assurances that where he was personally concerned Barrington 'would ever defend him to the utmost against all men, at all times' no doubt favourably affected Newcastle's anxious mind;[24] and Barrington kept his promise.[25] 'I never doubted your support and assistance whenever the measures should be attacked whether in your time, or before', wrote Newcastle to him on 12 Oct. 1763.[26] 'The Duke of Newcastle continues to treat me with friendship and kindness', Barrington wrote to Lord Buckinghamshire on 17 Dec. 1762.[27] And on 9 May 1764:[28] 'My old patron and friend the Duke of Newcastle . . . I have seen . . . often this last winter, and Abdiel as I am, have always been kindly received.'

After the crisis of August 1763 Halifax told Barrington that he had been proscribed by Pitt but that the King would not have him removed. Barrington thereupon wrote a letter on 1 Sept. 'to be delivered by Lord Halifax to the King'[29] begging him 'to deem the treasurership vacant' for his disposal.

> What I would not resign at the summons of faction, I can most cheerfully give up at the call of duty. I am not tired of being in your Majesty's service, of which I am extremely proud: I am not disgusted with office, which is very agreeable, and though not necessary, convenient to me . . . While your conveniency permits, I am happy to continue your servant; when it requires that my office should be in other hands, I should be miserable if it remained in mine.

The King replied that 'he should never see it with the same pleasure in any other hands'.[30] There is a great deal of selfconscious virtue in Barrington's letters or declarations—which does not prove them insincere: the eighteenth century revelled in tears of self-approbation.

When the Rockingham Administration 'was forming', in July 1765, Barrington went out of London— 'that I might not appear more solicitous about remaining in office than . . . I really am';[31] did not return till the 17th when things were settled; and went to the King's levee without knowing what was intended for him; again declared that he was devoted solely and personally to the King, and, in or out of office, would support any Administration he chose to appoint; and begged the King to dispose of his place if this would help to accommodate matters. But the King wanted Barrington 'again about his person, as secretary at war'. Barrington replied that he had 'not the least objection to return to the War Office', 'never preferred one employment to another', and would do his duty wherever placed; but would not accept anything 'which did not come directly from his Majesty and was not held solely under him'.

Next Barrington entreated the King not to believe reports to his disadvantage—

> that if he heard I frequented men under his displeasure, and possibly hereafter in opposition, he would hear truth for I should never give up intimacies with men I had loved from my early youth because

they were out of employment; but I entreated him never to believe any conclusions drawn from thence of my being in political concert or connexion with them. In like manner, that he would discredit all reports of another kind that I was in any cabals of his court because I frequented old friends of mine who were now come there, and with whom I had always lived in amity even while they were in an opposition I had disapproved. I assured the King that I detested faction equally in and out of court, and would never have anything to do with it.

He kissed hands on the 19th, and only after that communicated with Newcastle and Rockingham.

One curious feature of the transaction is that while an Administration was being formed for the King by Cumberland, the War Office was hardly mentioned. A question to Rockingham on 12 July[32]— 'Pray, does my Lord Barrington accept the secretary at war?'—is all that appears about it in Newcastle's voluminous documentation of those weeks. Probably Barrington, by whomever suggested, was readily accepted: a civil service rather than a political appointment. Under the Rockinghams, however, he for once voted against the Government on a major issue: over the repeal of the Stamp Act, 22 Feb. 1766; and yet this provoked no indignant discussions among the ministers, but presumably was accepted as the conscientious vote of an individual. For Barrington held strong views on America, as seen, e.g., in his 'Plan for the West', of 10 May 1766.[33] He proposed withdrawing a number of military outposts—'is it proper that this nation should be at such charge for that purpose, when the Americans contribute nothing to the maintenance . . . ?' The country westward 'was intended to be a desert for the Indians to hunt in and inhabit'; they fight only when wronged; 'we find no opposition there except from our own subjects'; which could best be countered by concentrating most of the troops in Nova Scotia: 'probably the insolence of their conduct last year proceeded from a knowledge that it was impossible to assemble such a force as might constrain them to duty and obedience.'

When Chatham replaced the Rockinghams, Barrington in a letter to him welcomed 'the happy prospect now opening'.[34] 'Barrington they say is to stay by virtue of his pliability', wrote John Yorke to Hardwicke on 24 July 1766.[35] So he did: again apparently without discussion or controversy.[36]

When, on the death of Charles Townshend, North at first refused the Exchequer, Grafton offered it to Barrington, who felt hesitant

> because I think I am not equal to the station. The office part of the business I have done when it was much more laborious, comprehensive and difficult; but to the parliamentary part (now much more important and nice . . .) I am not equal.

Still, if it was necessary for the King's service he would accept—

> having no political connexion with any man, being determined never to form one, and conceiving that in this age the country and its constitution is best served by an unbiased attachment to the Crown, I shall not . . . make any terms . . . for exchanging a situation which I may reasonably think permanent enough, for one the most precarious in the kingdom.

He could hardly have expressed more clearly his 'civil service' conception of his own position. And here is another definition given by him in the Commons on 9 Dec. 1770:[37]

> A secretary at war must obey the King's orders signified by a secretary of state or resign. The secretary at war is not a Cabinet councillor. He is only a ministerial officer. He is not a proper judge of the propriety of a measure.

Barrington's extensive correspondence with the King is almost entirely about military matters. But there are two significant letters, 27 and 28 Jan. 1770, in which the King, 'knowing the opinion Lord North has of your judgment', asks Barrington to go to North and encourage him to accept the Treasury.

In the House Barrington continued a fairly frequent speaker: during the years covered by James Harris's reports, November 1761 till April 1766, 34 speeches of his are noted, 109 in the Parliament of 1768–74 (the most fully reported), and 30 from 1774 to 1778. Most of them deal with departmental business (except during the Grenville Administration when he was in less active employment). While at the War Office he increasingly confined himself to the military field; in 1771 he strongly opposed the bill to assist the East India Company in raising military forces; but in 1773 defended the behaviour of its military officers including Clive; as also the military management of the St. Vincent expedition. Even his interventions in debates on America were usually concerned with military matters. He never spoke during the lengthy proceedings on the printers' case in 1771, and only once on the royal marriage bill in 1772. He took, however, a prominent part in the debates on Wilkes in 1769, and on 3 Feb. proposed the motion for his expulsion, which naturally made Barrington a target for attacks. Altogether, in spite of his caution and courtesy, at times he exposed himself by too frankly stating his views. Thus early in his official career: 'The Tories all attacked Lord Barrington', wrote Rigby to the Duke of Bedford, 23 Dec. 1756, 'for an imprudent and violent abuse of his yesterday of the addresses and instructions [against the Hessians] which he lumped with newspapers and pamphlets and said were full of falsehood and malice.'[38] Or again, when in 1768 he defended his own conduct

and the behaviour of the military in St. George's Fields. In December 1770 he showed too openly what he thought of British commanders; here is his own account of the incident in a letter to Lord Albemarle, on 20 Dec.:[39]

> I find my dear Lord that you have been informed, though not accurately, of something I said in the House of Commons the last day of the session: I will shortly state that matter to you. Barré lamented the death of Lord Granby and talked much of the necessity of a commander-in-chief at this juncture. I said I had always thought there should be one *at all times* . . . but I fairly confessed that so many requisites went to the appointment of a commander-in-chief and so many different circumstances must concur to make a man proper for such an office, that I did not know any man who could *at present* be proposed for it; though we had many excellent general officers . . . Neither General Conway or any other man took the least notice of this; but it was next day reported all over London I had said we had no general who could command an army. I believe no misrepresentation ever had less foundation or colour.

The fact remains that in 1771 he urged on Lord North 'the expediency of employing Prince Ferdinand of Brunswick, especially if there should be a war with any European power'; which advice he renewed in a letter to the King on 28 Mar. 1778.[40]

Although not a 'Cabinet councillor', in the absence of a commander-in-chief Barrington had to speak for the army, and his views came to differ from those of the Cabinet about measures to be adopted in America: in a letter to Lord Dartmouth, 12 Nov. 1774,[41] he reverts to the basic idea of his memorandum of 10 May 1766, and advises to remove the troops from Massachusetts to 'places not far distant' where they 'may remain in safety with convenience . . . till a proper juncture should offer for their return'; and meantime employ naval forces to 'reduce the colony to submission'. And again on 24 Dec.:[42] 'the contest in America will cost us more than we can ever gain by the success'; taxes cannot be levied 'against an universal opinion prevailing there'; 'our present contest is about the point of honour only'; troops in America might gain pitched battles but cannot subdue the country; naval action is preferable; the troops should be withdrawn to Canada, Nova Scotia, and East Florida.

> When three out of four taxes were repealed in the Duke of Grafton's ministry, I proposed in the House of Commons to repeal them *all*, where they had not been resisted, and to repeal *none* of them where they had been. I mentioned somewhat similar last year to a meeting at Lord North's . . .
> Pardon, my dear Lord, this liberty. I have accustomed myself for near thirty years, to lay my opinions before ministers; and as this was the only trouble I gave them, they took it in good part.

In January 1776 he warned against denuding this country of soldiers, because of danger of domestic trouble:[43]

> London is of all places in the island the most attentively to be watched, on account of the many actively desperate and ill-affected people who are in it. I need not say how little the magistracy of the city is to be trusted, or how much to be feared . . .
>
> If an insurrection in London should be attended with the least success, or even to continue unquelled for any time . . . it is highly probable, there would also be risings in many parts of the kingdom. The present apparent quiet should not make it [be] forgotten, that there is a very levelling spirit among the people.

In October 1775 he expressed to the King his desire to leave Parliament 'which had been growing more and more disagreeable to me';[44] but he left the time for it to the King's determination. He raised the matter once more on 7 June 1776, at the end of the session: 'in the 60th year of my age, and the 31st of my service of the Crown', he begged to be relieved of a burden which was becoming distressful to him—but again left the King 'master of the time of my dismission'. He reverted to the subject in September, but the King said 'that he found . . . much difficulty in fixing on a proper successor', and asked Barrington to stay on 'sometime longer'. Barrington replied that he would obey the King's commands, but that his difficulties 'in respect to the House of Commons were of the most serious kind': having to vote there contrary to opinions he had given to ministers in regard to the disputes with America. 'Why should you not remain for the present in the War Office, and quit the House of Commons . . .?' asked the King (he, too, taking the 'civil service' view of Barrington's position). Barrington replied he thought this feasible, and would 'open the matter to Lord North'. But North considered that 'a secretary at war must be in Parliament'. The question of Barrington's retirement was again discussed in January-February and June 1777, but with North's dilatoriness, Barrington's 'pliability', and the King's unwillingness to part with him, nothing was done. On 29 Oct., Barrington, from his 'great dislike of the House of Commons', again asked North for the Chiltern Hundreds though prepared to stay at the War Office as long as required. But when on 3 Dec. the news arrived of Burgoyne's surrender, he himself felt that this was not the time for withdrawing from business. Still, in March and May 1778 he again pressed to be released from Parliament: and on 21 May told the King 'that things were come to such a pass, that I could no longer reconcile my conduct in Parliament to my honour and duty. That disapproving many of the measures of Administration,

I could not support them with a good conscience, or oppose them without affecting my honour.' On 24 May he was given the Chiltern Hundreds, but remained at the War Office till the middle of December, Rigby, as paymaster, acting for the department in the Commons; and the King in a letter of 16 Dec., thanking Barrington for his services, settled on him, 'unsolicited by him', a pension of £2,000 'until he shall be appointed to some other employment'. 'I flatter myself', wrote Barrington to a friend, 'that no man ever died a more quiet, decent, or edifying *political* death.'[45] From January to April 1782 he was joint postmaster general; and when he lost the place on the fall of the North Administration, the previous pension was 'renewed and continued' to him.[46]

Barrington died 1 Feb. 1793.

[1] See *Pol. Life of Wm. Wildman Visct. Barrington*, compiled by his bro. Shute, bp. of Durham, 2. [2] *Mems. Geo. II*, ii. 143-4. [3] Newcastle to Wm. Murray, 28 Sept. 1754, Add. 32736, ff. 591-4. [4] Add. 32735, f. 229; Barrington to Grenville, 18 Mar. 1754, Grenville mss (JM). [5] T. Cockburn to Sir John Hall of Dunglass, Dunglass Pprs., SRO. [6] Robt. Nugent to Edw. Eliot, 27 Dec. 1753, Eliot mss. [7] Add. 32995, f. 63. [8] Barrington mss. [9] Ibid. 27 Dec. 1774. [10] Newcastle to Hardwicke, 26 Sept. 1755, Add. 32859, ff. 219-21. [11] Barrington mss; Ilchester, *Letters to Hen. Fox*, 116. [12] *Chatham Corresp.* i. 188. See also Symmer to And. Mitchell, 17 Dec. 1756, Add. 6839, ff. 26-27. [13] To And. Mitchell, 5 Dec. 1762, ibid. ff. 41-42. [14] See letter to Chas. Gould, adv. gen., 8 Feb. 1766, *Life*, 131-7. [15] Ibid. 48-50; see further letter to Lord Granby, 17 June 1760, ibid. 58-62. [16] Ibid. 57. [17] Ibid. 122-4. [18] Add. 32916, ff. 49-55. [19] *Chatham Corresp.* ii. 99. [20] 6 Oct. 1761, Chatham mss. [21] Barrington mss. [22] Shelburne to Bute, 2 Nov. 1762, Bute mss. [23] The following account is from a paper written by Barrington at the time, printed *Life*, 73-85. [24] Besides Barrington's account, see his letters to Newcastle, 4 and 5 Nov. 1762, Add. 32944, ff. 233 and 287. [25] Thus on 9 Dec. 1762 (Harris); 22 Feb. 1763 (Chas. Jenkinson's report in the Bodl. North mss); and 30 Mar. 1764 (Harris). [26] Barrington mss. [27] *HMC Lothian*, 245-6. [28] Ibid. 250. [29] *Life*, 91-93. There are two copies of it in the Barrington mss: one is the letter itself; and the other in an account of the transaction. [30] Halifax to Barrington, 5 Sept.; Barrington mss and *Life*, 94-95. [31] In a letter to Halifax, from Beckett, 12 July; for Barrington's account of the audience with the King, *Life*, 95-100. The quotations as given below are corrected from the original in the Barrington mss. [32] Add. 32967, f. 349. [33] Printed from a copy in the Lansdowne mss at the Clements Lib. by Alvord and Carter, *The New Regime 1765-7*, pp. 234-45; and from a copy in the Royal archives, Windsor by Fortescue, i. 432-41. Barrington was a friend and relation by marriage of Gov. Francis Bernard; see *Barrington-Bernard Corresp.* ed. Channing & Coolidge. [34] 26 July 1766, Chatham mss. [35] Add. 35374, f. 303. [36] See also Barrington to Sam. Martin, 24 July 1766, Add. 41354, f. 104. [37] Brickdale's 'Debates'. [38] Bedford mss. 32, f. 119. [39] Albemarle mss. [40] Quoted from a memorandum in Barrington's own hand, *Life*, 186-8. [41] *Life*, 140-2; see also the King to North, Fortescue, iii. 250. [42] *Life*, 142-8. [43] Ibid. 153-7. [44] This, and the account that follows, is taken from a memorandum by Barrington, written after his retirement in December 1778. The letter of October 1775 is neither in the Royal archives, Windsor nor among the Barrington mss. [45] *Life*, 184. [46] Rockingham to Barrington, 21 Apr. 1782, Rockingham mss.

L.B.N.

**BARROW, Charles** (1707-89), of Highgrove, Glos.

GLOUCESTER 19 Nov. 1751-10 Jan. 1789

*b.* 1707 in St. Kitts, o.s. of Charles Barrow, merchant, of St. Kitts by Elizabeth, da. of Lt.-Gov. Harris of the Leeward Islands. *m.* c.1728, Mary, da. of Daniel Randall of Gloucester, *s.p. cr.* Bt. with sp. rem. to Thomas Crawley Boevey of Flaxley Abbey, Glos., husband of his 1st cos. once removed, 22 Jan. 1784.

Barrow was returned unopposed for Gloucester in 1751 and 1754 on the Tory interest. In 1761 he joined a Whig, G. A. Selwyn (q.v.), against another Tory; and came out head of the poll. He appears in Fox's list of Members favourable to the peace preliminaries. On 11 Mar. 1763 he made his first reported speech, against the cider tax; and spoke on the same subject on 13 Mar.—'Barrow attempted wit without shewing much of it', wrote James Harris. He voted against Administration over general warrants, 15 and 18 Feb. 1764; and was classed by Newcastle on 10 May as a doubtful friend. He was brought into contact with the Rockingham group by William Dowdeswell (q.v.), his 'very particular friend';[1] and was described by the *Public Ledger* in 1779 as 'a constant attender of the House, and a most uniform zealous Oppositionist'.

Between 1764 and 1771 no speeches by him are recorded, but from 1771 until his death there are over 20. Three only dealt with important political questions: the printers' case of 1771, the East India Regulating Act of 1773, and Sawbridge's motion of 15 May 1783 for annual Parliaments.

Barrow had a strong interest at Gloucester, and after 1761 never had to face a poll. George Selwyn wrote of him on the eve of the general election of 1780:[2] 'Mr. Barrow . . . has established himself by an indefatigable attention for above thirty years in the goodwill of his constituents.'

Barrow voted for Shelburne's peace preliminaries, 18 Feb. 1783, and was classed by Robinson as a friend of Shelburne; yet he also voted for Fox's East India bill, 27 Nov. 1783, and was created a baronet on Fox's recommendation. In Stockdale's list of 19 Mar. 1784 Barrow was classed as an opponent of Pitt. No vote by him is recorded in the Parliament of 1784, and but one speech, 21 Feb. 1785, on a point of order.

On 16 July 1786 he wrote to the Prince of Wales:[3]

> I have often attempted to be introduced to your Royal Highness to have the honour of kissing your R. Highness's hand, and flattered myself about six weeks ago with the hopes of seeing you at Windsor and there to have requested that honour.
>
> I am sorry to hear that Parliament has not augmented your income to what your rank entitles you to, and what you justly merit. I have the sum of two thousand pounds at present by me, much at your Royal Highness's service, and if you will condescend to accept of it, I will immediately forward to you a draft on my banker (Child & Co.) for that sum.

Barrow died 10 Jan. 1789.

[1] Dowdeswell to Chas. Yorke, c. 4 Mar. 1767, Add. 35430, f. 49.
[2] Selwyn to Chas. Townshend, 31 Aug. 1780, Marsham-Townshend mss. [3] Royal archives, Windsor.

J.B.

**BARRY, Hon. Richard** (*c*.1720–87), of Marbury, Cheshire.

WIGAN 1747–1761

*b.* c.1720,[1] 2nd s. of James Barry, 4th Earl of Barrymore [I], M.P., by his 3rd w. Anne, da. of Arthur Chichester, 3rd Earl of Donegall [I]. *m.* 4 May 1749, Jane, da. and h. of Arthur Hyde of Castle Hyde, Ireland, 1s.
Lt. R.N. 1740; cdr. 1745.

In 1747 Barry was returned on the Tory interest at Wigan in place of his father. In 1754 a contest was threatened but there was no poll. Barry did not stand again in 1761; his influence at Wigan had been undermined by an opposition who, backed by Administration, had in 1759 established their predominance by having their candidate elected mayor.

Barry died 23 Nov. 1787.

[1] The 1st s., James 5th Earl of Barrymore, was b. 25 Apr. 1717, and the 4th, John, 28 July 1725.

J.B.

**BARWELL, Richard** (1741–1804), of Stansted Park, Suss.

| | |
|---|---|
| HELSTON | 12 Mar. 1781–1784 |
| ST. IVES | 1784–1790 |
| WINCHELSEA | 1790–1796 |

*b.* 8 Oct. 1741 at Calcutta, s. of William Barwell, later gov. of Fort William and director of E.I.Co., by his w. Elizabeth Pierce of Calcutta. *educ.* Westminster 1750. *m.* (1) 13 Sept. 1776 at Calcutta, Elizabeth Jane (*d.*1779), da. of Robert Sanderson, 2s. *d.v.p.*; (2) 24 June 1785, Catherine, da. of Nathaniel Coffin of Bristol, formerly cashier of customs, Boston, Mass., at least 10 surv. legit. ch.[1]
Writer in the E.I.Co. 1757; proceeded to Bengal 1758; 12th on council for Bengal 1770; 4th on the supreme council 1774; res. and returned to England 1780.

Barwell came of a family (originally from Kegworth, Leics.) which had East Indian connexions since at least 1682.[2] He had two brothers in the Company's civil service, and another a captain of an East Indiaman; his father, at one time a supporter of Laurence Sulivan (q.v.), got him his writership;[3] but he was the architect of his own fortune, amassed by private trade and by undertakings in the supply of timber and salt which were of very doubtful legality.[4] He was one of the first of the Company's servants to realize the advantage to his career of investing the money he remitted to England in East India stock, and of placing the votes in the Company so acquired at the disposal of the dominant faction.[5]

Barwell is best known for his support of Warren Hastings in the struggle against Philip Francis and his allies in the Supreme Council, 1774–80, though the alliance did not survive Hastings's return to England. Barwell was a calculating man, with strong family feelings but few close friends, despite his expansive hospitality; but he also avoided making enemies,[6] and Hastings spoke approvingly of his 'easy and pleasant' manners and his 'fertility of official resources'.[7] Nevertheless, while in Bengal he could not avoid the venom of Philip Francis, nor a duel with the bellicose General Clavering; and the laxity of his private morals made him vulnerable. His heavy gambling losses to Francis gained notoriety, and in the year of his return to England a disappointed blackmailer exposed some of his amorous exploits in a scurrilous pamphlet entitled *The Intrigues of a Nabob; or Bengal the Fittest Soil for Lust.*[8]

> While still in India he had distinguished between a servant of Government and a creature of the ministers. The former . . . a character which uninfluenced by a change in the Administration, invariably adheres to the court, and not . . . like the latter, attached to any personal interests of an individual.[9]

He kept in touch with John Robinson, secretary to the Treasury,[10] and in 1778, when planning to leave India, instructed his sister to tell Robinson that 'I shall be happy to hold a seat in the House under the countenance of the minister, and that I have commissioned you to be at any expense not exceeding £4,000 to enable me to render service in that line'.[11] In 1780 he stood for Wallingford on a joint interest with John Cator (q.v.) who felt 'sure of carrying the borough for both';[12] but they were defeated. In March 1781 Barwell was returned for Helston.

In the House he was one of the richest 'nabobs': he was believed to have returned with a fortune of more than £400,000. Though he was only 40 when elected to Parliament, his active career lay behind him. He sought a seat, no doubt partly for prestige, but partly to protect himself against attacks on the sources of his East India wealth. His three recorded interventions in parliamentary debate before 1790 were all in self-defence: 5 Mar. 1782 over his refusal to answer some questions put to him by the secret committee; 28 May, over the Rohilla war; and 19 Apr. 1787 in reply to a reference by Burke to him.[13] In his vulnerable position he exercised extreme caution: he tried to be politically inconspicuous, and preferred, whenever possible, to support the Government of the day. In the three divisions preceding the fall of the North Administration (27 Feb., 8 and 15 Mar. 1782) he voted with them. When Shelburne came into the Treasury, Barwell made a private approach to him;[14] but voted against the peace preliminaries, and in March 1783 was classed by Robinson 'North, doubtful'. He attended the general court of the East India

Company on 7 Nov., when it passed in defiance of the Fox-North Administration, a vote of thanks to Hastings.[15] But he kept neutral over Fox's India bill, 27 Nov. 1783; and John Sinclair (q.v.) wrote about him in a paper for Pitt, early in January 1784:[16] 'It would not be difficult to get his interest. He did not vote. Mr. Sinclair could speak to him if necessary.' By January 1784 he was classed by Robinson as a supporter of Pitt, and in 1784 was one of the candidates for whom Administration found seats—he is in the list of 'persons that will pay 2,000 or 2,500 or perhaps £3,000'; and the name Barwell usually appears twice, his brother James having also been considered for a seat.[17] Richard Barwell was finally returned by H. M. Praed for a seat at St. Ives which he had placed at the disposal of the Government for £3,500.[18]

Henceforth he was a consistent, though inert, supporter of Administration; voted with them against the impeachment of his former colleague, Sir Elijah Impey, 9 May 1788; and paired on their side in the divisions on the Regency. Shortly before the general election of 1790 Barwell and Lord Darlington purchased the estate of John Nesbitt (q.v.) at Winchelsea, the borough for which Barwell sat for the rest of his parliamentary life. He also purchased the borough of Tregony from Sir F. Basset (q.v.).

Barwell found adjustment to English life hard on his return from India, but seems to have overcome his difficulties.[19] In 1781 he purchased for about £100,000 the estate of Stansted Park, Sussex, from the trustees of the Earl of Halifax, and he occupied himself with the cares of his family and his fortune (he acquired large holdings in the funds by subscription and purchase between 1781 and 1784, but sold out all his holdings by March 1786),[20] with the purchase of land in Sussex, and the enlargement and beautification of his magnificent house and grounds at Stansted.[21] A lady visiting nearby wrote of him on 24 July 1785:[22]

> While I was at Uppark a marriage took place near there that surprised most people. Mr. Barwell, the great East Indian of Stansted, to Miss Coffin, a very pretty little girl not 16, of American extraction. Till a fortnight before this event he kept a very beautiful mistress close to his park, by whom he has several children, and till very lately he declared most strongly against matrimony. He seems a good-natured man, but the mogul prevails strongly, I think, in his way of life and conversation.

Barwell died 2 Sept. 1804.

[1] Ms ped. in possession of the Barwell family. [2] Nichols, *Leics.* iii (2), p. 853; J. M. Holzman, *Nabobs in England*, 39. [3] 'Letters of Mr. Richard Barwell', *Bengal Past & Present*, x. 242. [4] Ibid. ix. xi. and xii passim. [5] *Bengal Past & Present*, x. 248 and xi. 265. [6] See, e.g., ibid. ix. 92. [7] To. L. Sulivan, 6 Jan. 1780, Bodl. ms. Eng. Hist. C271, f. 37. [8] The author was Henry F. Thompson. [9] Barwell

to his sister Mary, 30 Mar. 1776, *Bengal Past & Present*, xiv. 223. [10] See letters from him to Barwell, 24 July and 25 Nov. 1776, Abergavenny mss. [11] *Bengal Past & Present*, xvii. 297. [12] Robinson's survey for the general election of 1780. [13] Debrett, vi. 326; vii. 197, 199; xxii. 126. [14] Barwell to Hastings, n.d. (recd. July 1783), Add. 29157 f. 330. [15] John Scott to Hastings, 10 Nov. 1783, Add. 29161, f. 301. [16] Thurso mss. [17] Laprade, 126–9. [18] Ibid. 108. [19] Hickey, *Mems*. ii. 306. [20] Bank of England recs. [21] J. Dallaway, *Western Division of Suss*. 159–60. [22] *Dear Miss Heber*, ed. Bamford, 18.

L.S.S.

## BASSET, Francis (1715–69), of Tehidy, nr. Redruth, Cornw.

### PENRYN 19 Nov. 1766–17 Nov. 1769

*b.* 1715, 2nd s. of Francis Basset, M.P., by his 2nd w. Mary, da. and h. of John Pendarves, and h. of her uncle, Alexander Pendarves, M.P. *educ.* Queen's, Oxf. Feb. 1733, aged 17. *m.* 19 Oct. 1756, Margaret, da. of Sir John St. Aubyn, 3rd Bt., M.P., sis. of Sir John St. Aubyn, 4th Bt. (q.v.), 2s. 5da. *suc.* at Tehidy his nephew, J. P. Basset 28 May 1756.

Basset was 'a Tory by tradition, estate, and connexions'.[1] In June 1760, Thomas Jones, Lord Edgcumbe's agent, wrote about Penryn: 'Mr. Basset, a neighbouring gentleman and a considerable landowner in the town, has been talked of for candidate, but at present there is not much probability that he will meddle.'[2] For reasons unascertained, he did not stand himself but put up two candidates nominated by Robert Clive (q.v.). Hardwicke, who tried to mediate with Clive, wrote to Bute, 5 Mar. 1761:[3]

> I happen to know that Mr. Basset has a great estate, and is full of money, and from copper mines, discovered and worked upon his estate, not many years ago. Under these circumstances, I doubt he will not be induced to let in a candidate upon Lord Falmouth's interest, which may occasion an expensive and troublesome contest.

Basset's candidates lost by a narrow margin, but on a vacancy in 1766 Basset was returned unopposed, as also in 1768. In December 1766 he was classed by Rockingham as 'Whig', possibly because like the truest Tories he was averse to all courts or administrations. Charles Townshend classed him in January 1767 as 'country gentleman, doubtful'. Only one vote of his is recorded; against Government on Wilkes's petition, 27 Jan. 1769. He is not known to have spoken in the House.

He died 17 Nov. 1769, aged 54.

[1] Namier, *Structure*, 311. [2] Add. 32907, ff. 461–2. [3] Bute mss.

L.B.N.

## BASSET, Francis (?1740–1802), of Heanton Court, nr. Barnstaple, Devon.

### BARNSTAPLE 1780–1784

*b.* ?1740, 2nd but o. surv. s. of John Francis Basset, M.P., by Eleanor, da. of Sir William Courtenay, 2nd Bt., M.P., sis. of Sir William Courtenay, 3rd Bt. (q.v.). *educ.* New Coll. Oxf. 22 Nov. 1758, aged 18. *unm. suc.* fa. 29 Sept. 1757.

The Bassets of Heanton Court were a junior branch of the Basset family of Tehidy. Francis Basset's grandfather sat for Barnstaple 1718–21 and his father 1740–1.

Francis Basset's name appears on the Government side in each of the six divisions 12 Dec. 1781–15 Mar. 1782 for which lists are available; he voted against Shelburne's peace preliminaries, 18 Feb. 1783; was classed by Robinson in March 1783 as 'North, doubtful'; voted in favour of Fox's East India bill; was classed as 'contra' by Robinson in January and as 'Opposition' in Stockdale's list of March 1784. He did not stand again at the general election of 1784. There is no record of his having spoken in the House.

He died November 1802.

L.B.N.

## BASSET, Sir Francis, 1st Bt. (1757–1835), of Tehidy, nr. Redruth, Cornw.

### PENRYN 1780–1796

*b.* 9 Aug. 1757, 1st s. of Francis Basset (*d.*1769, q.v.), *educ.* Harrow 1770; Eton 1771–4; King's Camb.. 1775; Grand Tour (France, Italy). *m.* (1) 16 Aug. 1780, Frances Susanna (*d.*14 June 1823), da. and eventually coh. of John Hippesley Coxe, sis. of Richard Hippesley Coxe (q.v.), 1da.; (2) 13 July 1824, Harriet, da. of Sir William Lemon (q.v.), 1st Bt., *s.p. suc.* fa. Nov. 1769; *cr.* Bt. 24 Nov. 1779; Baron de Dunstanville 17 June 1796; Baron Basset with sp. rem. to da. 30 Nov. 1797.

When in August 1779 a Franco-Spanish descent was expected on the Cornish coast 'the gentlemen of the county' raised a body of tin-miners for defence; and Lord Edgcumbe, lord lieutenant of Cornwall, on 14 Sept. successfully solicited the honour of a baronetcy for Basset,[1]

> whose services have been very essential in having marched near 70 miles at the head of 600 tinners, who are now actually working at the fortifications at Plymouth Dock. His subscription towards raising a regiment has been very liberal, and his activity to complete it will be as great.

In 1780, supporting local malcontents at Truro, Basset successfully attacked what had hitherto been considered an impregnable pocket borough of Lord Falmouth; and North and Robinson failed to make him agree to share the representation of Penryn with the Treasury whose interest was managed by Edgcumbe: their assurances how much they wished 'to be at all times on friendly terms' with him evoked no response. Virile, rigid, sensing infringement of his rights or offence where neither was meant, he seemed driven by an inner urge to fight, without much thought of the purpose: having carried both seats against Government, he, from the very first, adhered to them in the House, voting with them in favour of choosing a new Speaker.[2] After this, and till the fall of the North Administration, every recorded speech and vote of his was on their side; he appears in each of the six extant division lists, 12 Dec. 1781–15 Mar. 1782; on 26 Feb. 1781 he spoke against Burke's motion for regulating the civil list revenue, and on 8 May 1781 against Savile's motion reiterating that of Dunning on the influence of the Crown. Then, at the height of the crisis, he addressed some peremptory demands (so far untraced) to North, who wrote to Robinson, 15 Feb. 1782:[3]

> I enclose a summoning letter sent to me by Sir Francis Basset to give him the decisive answer I promised. I cannot give it him, but I have no right to expect him to remain undetermined, so that, I fear, I must let him take his course, the consequence of which will be the defection of himself and his three friends to the enemy. We can but ill spare them.

But the storm blew over, and Basset and his friends[4] continued with North to the end.

Under the Rockingham Administration Basset spoke against Crewe's bill disfranchising revenue officers, 15 Apr., and against Sawbridge's motion for shorter Parliaments, 16 May. He was a determined opponent of parliamentary reform, and in a pamphlet published anonymously in 1783, *Thoughts on Equal Representation*, argued that such representation 'never had a place in the British constitution', and that representation at all times was one 'of property, not of numbers'. W. J. Temple, vicar of Penryn and one of the anti-Basset party in the borough, wrote to Christopher Wyvill, on 9 Jan. 1783, to entertain no hopes of Penryn, for it was entirely in the hands of Basset, 'a forward, presuming young man, and of too interested and narrow a mind to wish for improvement of any kind'.[5] 'Interested and narrow' is hardly a correct description of Basset: he was egocentric, and lived in a world of his own preconceived, often contradictory, ideas.

Having gone into opposition with North, Basset voted against Shelburne's peace preliminaries, 18 Feb. 1783; and after that adhered to the Coalition, though not without occasional squalls—thus when Humphry Morice, long an absentee from England and no longer in Parliament, was replaced as warden of the stanneries by Lord Lewisham, Basset on 20 Nov. 1783 addressed the following letter to the Duke of Portland:[6]

> The ill usage my relative Mr. Morice has received . . . renders it impossible for me to act any longer with Administration. Something of this kind I own I had been taught to expect by some of my friends, but knowing and feeling the very honourable manner in

which I must say I have acted towards Administration I naturally expected the same conduct from them: ill usage to myself I could better have brooked than to my friends. As I consider my connexion with ministry as no longer subsisting I must beg leave to withdraw the various applications I have made to your Grace, as I cannot continue to receive favours where I mean to confer none.

Portland's reply is not extant; but a week later Basset voted for Fox's East India bill, and at the general election of 1784 Lewisham was his candidate in two constituencies.

That year he contested no less than five Cornish boroughs, attacking the Falmouth and the Edgcumbe interest: he tried to retain both seats at Penryn and Truro; put up two candidates at Tregony, and two at Mitchell; and one at Fowey, where Edgcumbe held one seat only. He also thought of putting up one candidate at Bossiney where the representation was shared by Edgcumbe and Lady Bute: the story is told in letters to her from her agent, Elford.[7] Thus on 22 Jan. 1784:

> Sir Francis Basset is certainly as formidable as any rival can be. He hath increased his borough interest prodigiously since he came of age, and the adding to it is his constant object. With the late ministry his interest was very great.

On 13 Feb., when told of assurances that Basset's attack was against the Edgcumbe interest only: 'Perhaps Sir Francis wishes to weaken the old interest by dividing it and to sap first the one and then the other.' And on 2 Apr.:

> I had great difficulty in prevailing on the under sheriff to let me have the precept for Bossiney, he being in Sir Francis Basset's interest, and having given all the trouble in his power to the boroughs where my Lord Mount Edgcumbe hath any interest.

'Our elections go on well', wrote Lord Sydney to the Duke of Rutland, 17 Apr. 1784, '. . . Sir Francis Basset is beat in two thirds of the places where he pushed his friends. He has returned but three, himself inclusive, and there is a petition against two of them, himself likewise inclusive.'[8] He returned himself and Sir John St. Aubyn at Penryn, and both retained their seats; so did David Howell at Mitchell, while Roger Wilbraham was unseated on petition;[9] he lost both seats at Truro by 11 votes to 12; both at Tregony, by 69 to 90; while at Fowey his candidate received 9 votes against 31 for Edgcumbe's candidate. Although but moderately successful, in four out of the five boroughs Basset had established an important interest. And what use did he make of it? In 1788 he purchased Falmouth's estate at Tregony,[10] but gave up all further claims to Truro; at Mitchell in 1790, Basset and Falmouth, whose interests were 'so much upon an equality', each contented himself 'with sending one Member';[11]

II—C*

Penryn was now Basset's; Fowey (and Bossiney) he never attempted again. And next? Before the next general election (1796) he had sold Tregony to Richard Barwell, and his share in Mitchell to Christopher Hawkins (qq.v.); and in 1803 voluntarily relinquished his hold on Penryn: a campaign on a scale greater than any other private individual had ever undertaken in Cornwall, with little value attached to its yield. 'Your turbulent nephew' with his 'moveable candidates', Frances Boscawen called him writing to Mrs. Delany in June 1784.[12] A similar turbulence Basset evinced in relations with neighbours: he engaged in disputes over mining rights with the Percevals of Pendarves, Thomas Pitt, and George Hunt (qq.v.). 'I could never yet learn' wrote to George Hunt his steward, William Jenkin, 24 Apr. 1798, 'by what right or grant that family [the Bassets] presumed to attack their neighbours' property . . . troublesome disturbers of the peace of the neighbourhood in which they reside' —'this all-grasping family'.[13]

In the Parliament of 1784–90 Basset steadily adhered to the Opposition, voting with them in every division for which lists are extant.[14] His speeches were similarly all on the Opposition side: over Mortlock (q.v.), 18 May 1784; against the commercial treaty with France, 6 and 15 Feb. 1787; and so were his interventions in debates on Indian affairs and the Regency.

In 1792 James Boswell, visiting W. J. Temple (by then obviously reconciled to Basset) records in his diary:[15]

My friend and I having a polite invitation from Sir Francis Basset, went to his seat at Tehidy Park . . . a large and splendid house; table, servants, every thing in style . . . Sir Francis . . . is a genteel, smart little man, well informed and lively . . . A great variety of dishes (and wines) delighted me and his high Tory talk crowned my satisfaction. He had three grand-uncles killed in battle for Charles I. His blue and buff dress and attachment to Charles Fox seemed not consistent with all this old aristocracy.

Basset went over to Pitt in 1793, and after the dissolution of Parliament in 1796 was created a peer. In his later years he published some books and pamphlets on agriculture.[16] He died 14 Feb. 1835.

[1] S.P. Dom. 41/33. [2] See his speech on 20 Nov. 1780, Debrett, i 110. [3] Laprade, 40; HMC 10th Rep. VI, 49. [4] John Rogers, Hen. Rosewarne and Fra. Basset (?1740–1802). [5] Wyvill Pprs. iv. 267. [6] Add. 21553, f. 122. [7] Wharncliffe mss, Sheffield City Lib. [8] HMC Rutland, iii. 89. [9] According to Sydney's calculation only Wilbraham was a Basset candidate; but he and Howell certainly stood on a joint interest, and Howell too, is treated by Oldfield as Basset's candidate; see 1816 ed., iii. 152; also by W. P. Courtney, Parlty. Rep. Cornw. 318. [10] See 28 Geo. III, c. 19. to enable Falmouth to sell it to Basset. [11] Oldfield (1792), i. 99. [12] Mrs. Delany, Autobiog. and Corresp. vi. 217–18. [13] A. K. Hamilton Jenkin, News from Cornw., 55–6. [14] D. Pulteney wrote to Rutland, 17 June 1784 (HMC Rutland iii. 111) that the previous night, over parliamentary reform, Pitt had been 'in the minority with Fox, Sir F. Basset, &c. &c.'; this of course was not a party question but Pulteney's statement ranging Basset on the side of reform can only be due to a misunderstanding; cf. his speech that

day in Debrett xv. 213, and Stockdale, ii. 69. [15] Private Pprs. xviii. 152. [16] Boase & Courtney, Bibliotheca Cornubiensis, i. 112–13.

L.B.N.

## BASTARD, Edmund (1758–1816), of Sharpham House, nr. Totnes, Devon.

DARTMOUTH   5 Oct. 1787–1812

b. 7 Feb. 1758, 2nd s. of William Bastard of Kitley, Devon, and bro. of John Pollexfen Bastard (q.v.). educ. Eton 1766–74; M. Temple 1775. m. Jane, da. and h. of Capt. Philemon Pownall, R.N., of Sharpham, 3s. suc. bro. 4 Apr. 1816.

On 26 Aug. 1787, a few weeks before the by-election at Dartmouth, George Rose wrote to William Pitt to know the 'determination' to be taken 'about the patronage of the borough, and the line you will follow with respect to the Bastards'.[1] Any opposition to Edmund Bastard 'would be fruitless':

It is therefore to be considered whether you will have him as a cool, doubtful friend, for the sake of recommending to the offices, or drive him at once, and his brother to be determined enemies; I am strongly inclined to wish for the latter as least mischievous to you.

Bastard was elected, as Rose had foreseen, without a contest.

Only two speeches by him are recorded before 1790: 26 and 28 May 1788, on a bill to regulate the Newfoundland fisheries (a matter which specially interested Dartmouth, one of the chief ports for the Newfoundland trade). The second, described in Stockdale's Debates (xv. 135–6) as 'a masterly detail of the nature of the fisheries at Newfoundland', concluded

with repeating the grounds of the anxiety felt by his constituents lest the bill should very materially affect the trade of the country; declaring, at the same time, that his constituents had nevertheless great confidence in the care and prudence of his Majesty's ministers.

He signed the third party circular of May 1788 and voted with Pitt on the Regency. He died June 1816.

[1] Chatham mss.

J.B.

## BASTARD, John Pollexfen (1756–1816), of Kitley, nr. Plymouth, Devon.

TRURO   8 July 1783–Jan. 1784
DEVON          1784–4 Apr. 1816

b. 18 Sept. 1756, 1st s. of William Bastard of Kitley by Anne, da. of Thomas Worsley (q.v.). educ. Eton 1766–74; M. Temple 1771. m (1) Sarah (d.26 Apr. 1808), wid. of Charles Wymondesoll of Lockinge, Berks., s.p.; (2) 1809, Judith Ann, da. of Sir Henry Martin, 1st Bt., M.P., s.p. suc. fa. 1782.

Bastard was returned for Truro on the interest of Sir Francis Basset (q.v.), who in 1780 had captured the borough from Lord Falmouth. No vote or speech by Bastard is recorded during his first term in Parliament, but he afterwards stated that he had disapproved of Fox's East India bill;[1] and it seems that Basset, a strong supporter of the Coalition, requested him to vacate his seat.

In 1784 he was defeated at Plymouth but was returned unopposed for Devon, and was classed by William Adam as a supporter of Pitt. On Pitt's motion for parliamentary reform, 18 Apr. 1785, he paired in favour of reform. He was a frequent speaker, generally for Administration, but was critical, independent, and pertinacious. In 1786 he pressed Pitt to deal with the problem of transportation of convicts, introduced a bill to reform the ecclesiastical courts, and opposed Pitt's excise on wines. In February 1786 he came out strongly against the Duke of Richmond's scheme to fortify the dockyards at Portsmouth and Plymouth, 'was proud to avow himself to have been its first opposer', and denounced fortresses as 'seminaries for soldiers and universities for Praetorian bands'. In a speech of 10 Dec. 1787, opposing an item in the army estimates, he summed up his attitude towards Administration: although 'he saw good grounds for reposing a confidence' in Pitt, he insisted on 'examining every proposition . . . and deciding upon it according to the best of his judgment'.[2]

In May 1788 he signed the third party circular, and later opposed Pitt's Regency bill. He died 4 Apr. 1816.

[1] Speech of 5 Mar. 1788, Stockdale, xiii. 302. [2] Ibid. vii. 227–8; xiii. 60.

J.B.

**BATEMAN, John,** 2nd Visct. Bateman [I] (1721–1802), of Shobdon, Herefs.

ORFORD 31 Jan. 1746–1747
NEW WOODSTOCK 1747–1768
LEOMINSTER 1768–1784

b. Apr. 1721, 1st s. of William, 1st Visct. Bateman [I], M.P., by Lady Anne Spencer, da. of Charles, 3rd Earl of Sunderland, and gd.-da. of John Churchill, 1st Duke of Marlborough. m. 2 July 1748, Elizabeth, da. and coh. of John Sambroke, M.P., bro. of Sir Jeremy Sambroke, 5th Bt., M.P., s.p. suc. fa. Dec. 1744.
Ld. lt. Herefs. 1747–d.; ld. of Admiralty 1755–6; P.C. 19 Nov. 1756; treasurer of the Household 1756–7; master of the buckhounds 1757–Mar. 1782; high steward, Leominster 1759–d.

Bateman inherited from his father property which gave him an interest at Leominster and on the Welsh borders; through his mother he was connected with the Marlborough, Bedford, and Pelham families.

In 1753, Bateman, then representing Woodstock on the interest of his uncle Charles, Duke of Marlborough, was nominated at St. Albans by the Duke, who was nursing the constituency for another nephew, John Spencer, then a minor. Bateman also seems to have acted as Marlborough's agent there, and was said to have 'given some umbrage by talking in a very high strain of preserving Mr. Spencer's interest for him till he came of age by weight of money against all opposers'.[1] A compromise was however reached, Bateman withdrew, and was again returned for Woodstock.

In Parliament Bateman supported Administration. In September 1755, Henry Fox included him in his list of persons to be promoted, adding 'the most useful man in the House who does not speak'.[2] He spoke in the debate on the Minorca inquiry, 26 Apr. 1757[3]—his only reported speech in the House—but no details are given. In 1761 he acted as one of Newcastle's agents in Radnorshire and the Welsh borders,[4] and Newcastle in October 1761 asked him to secure the attendance of five Members at the opening of the session.[5] After Newcastle's resignation he went with Fox, supporting the Bute and Grenville Administrations. Lady Holland wrote to her sister about Bateman, 6 Dec. 1764:[6] 'Though he is not a favourite with me, as he is not a pleasant body, yet I do value him for his constant disinterested attachment to Lord Holland.' On 11 July 1765, a few days after the formation of the Rockingham Administration, Bateman was sent by the Duke of Cumberland to attempt to dissuade the Duke of Marlborough from making his brother, Lord Charles Spencer, resign his office as comptroller of the Household.[7] But, Lord Digby wrote to Lord Holland, 18 July:[8] 'The Duke of Marlborough takes a hostile part, and I should think Lord Bateman would be in some danger.' Yet, though Bateman was counted as 'contra' by Rockingham in July 1765, and voted against the repeal of the Stamp Act (7 and 22 Feb. 1766), he retained his office worth more than £2,000 a year. At the same time he remained on good terms with Bute, to whom he wrote, 28 Oct. 1766:[9] 'To know if there is any business in the House of Commons at their first meeting that is agreeable to you that I should attend', and added that his obligations were to Bute alone. No vote of his is recorded during the Chatham Administration, but he was counted by Townshend in January 1767, and by Newcastle, 2 Mar. 1767, as a Government supporter.

In 1768 the seat at Woodstock was needed for Lord Robert Spencer, recently come of age, and Bateman was returned unopposed on his own interest at Leominster. He now constantly supported

Administration till the fall of North. On the formation of the second Rockingham Administration he lost his post as master of the buckhounds; does not appear in any division list before he left Parliament in 1784; and was classed as 'absent' by Robinson in January 1784. Wraxall, who knew him 'with great intimacy', writes:

No individual . . . was more personally regretted by the King than Lord Bateman . . . The frankness and gaiety of his disposition rendered him peculiarly agreeable to the Sovereign. At near seventy years[10] of age Lord Bateman preserved all the activity of youth, accompanied by an elasticity of mind and character which never forsook him. He might have been reinstated in the employment of master of the buckhounds under succeeding Administrations but he preferred the enjoyment of personal liberty, and passed the last years of his life principally at his seat of Shobdon. His understanding was good, though he loved pleasure of every description more than business, and he possessed that mediocrity of talents which never inspiring awe, forms the best recommendation to royal favour.[11]

He died 2 Mar. 1802.

[1] Add. 34734, f. 68. [2] Fox's proposals to Newcastle, Henry Fox mss. [3] Add. 35877, f. 363. [4] Namier, *Structure*, 268. [5] Add. 32930, ff. 37–42. [6] *Leinster Corresp.* i. 422. [7] Marlborough to Lord Gower, 11 July 1765, Bedford mss 52, f. 46. [8] Ilchester, *Letters to H. Fox*, 239. [9] Bute mss. [10] In 1782 Bateman was sixty-one. [11] *Mems.* ii. 275–6.

M.M.D.

### BATHURST, Benjamin (?1691–1767), of Mixbury Oxon., and Lydney, Glos.

| | |
|---|---|
| CIRENCESTER | 1713–1727 |
| GLOUCESTER | 16 Feb. 1728–1754 |
| MONMOUTH | 1754–5 Nov. 1767 |

*b.* ?1691, 3rd s. of Sir Benjamin Bathurst, M.P., by Frances, da. of Sir Allen Apsley; bro. of Allen, 1st Baron Bathurst. *educ.* Eton 1699; Trinity, Oxf. 30 June 1708, aged 16. *m.* (1) Finetta (*d.*1738), da. of Henry Poole of Kemble, Glos., 22 ch.; (2) 22 Oct. 1741, Catherine, da. of Rev. Lawrence Brodrick, wid. of William Whitfield, 14 ch.

Bathurst was a Tory. In 1754 he did not stand for Gloucester; was rebuffed at Shrewsbury; and finally was returned by the Duke of Beaufort at Monmouth. He does not appear in Fox's list of Members in favour of the peace preliminaries, early December 1762, nor did he vote against them. On general warrants he voted against the Grenville Administration, 15 and 18 Feb. 1764, and was classed by Newcastle, 10 May 1764, as a 'sure friend'. Yet on 30 Sept. 1764 Lord Botetourt, who managed the Beaufort interest during the minority of the 5th Duke, wrote to Grenville:[1]

Mr. B[athurst] having expressed some difficulties from his present engagements has proposed vacating his seat upon condition of a pension of five hundred a year being settled on his wife during her life. Have told

him that I would report his words, that I felt the approaching distress of his numerous family, and should be happy to serve him.

The nature of Grenville's reply can be gathered from Botetourt's letter to him of 6 Oct.:[2]

I entirely approve the determination against pensions *for life* and told it my friend when I read his words, which were put upon paper at my request in order to make mistake impossible. I likewise told him that the sum he asked was beyond what I had hopes of obtaining.

In July 1765 Bathurst was classed by Rockingham as 'pro', and he did not vote against the repeal of the Stamp Act. In over fifty years' parliamentary service he is not known to have spoken. He died 5 Nov. 1767.

[1] Grenville mss (JM). [2] Ibid.

J.B.

### BATHURST, Hon. Benjamin (1711–67), of Siddington, nr. Cirencester, Glos.

| | |
|---|---|
| GLOUCESTERSHIRE | 1734–1741 |
| CIRENCESTER | 1754–1761 |

*b.* 12 Aug. 1711, 1st s. of Allen, 1st Baron Bathurst, by Catherine, da. of Sir Peter Apsley. *educ.* Balliol, Oxf. 1725. *m.* 26 Nov. 1732, Lady Elizabeth Bruce, da. of Charles, 3rd Earl of Ailesbury, *s.p.*

Out-ranger of Windsor forest May 1763–July 1765.

Bathurst was returned unopposed for Cirencester in 1754, standing upon his own interest, independent of his family. He was classed by Dupplin as a Tory.

On accepting the office of out-ranger of Windsor forest he wrote to Bute:[1] 'The manner of giving it and the choice made of the employment, which was better and more suitable to me than anything my fondest wishes could hope for, is a great addition to his Majesty's bounty to me.' In 1765 he was removed by Rockingham and given a secret service pension of £500 a year. On 19 Aug. 1766 he wrote to remind Grafton of an offer to 'exchange the pension for any post in the excise, customs, greencloth, or anything else he might think me capable of'.[2]

He died 23 Jan. 1767.

[1] 20 Apr. 1763, Add. 5726 C, f. 20. [2] Grafton mss.

J.B.

### BATHURST, Henry, Lord Apsley (1762–1834).

| | |
|---|---|
| CIRENCESTER | 15 July 1783–6 Aug. 1794 |

*b.* 22 May 1762, 1st s. of Henry, 2nd Earl Bathurst, by his 2nd w. Tryphena, da. of Thomas Scawen of Maidwell, Northants. *educ.* Eton 1773–8; Ch. Ch. Oxf. 1779. *m.* 1 Apr. 1789, Georgiana, da. of Lord George Henry Lennox (q.v.), 4s. 2da. *suc.* fa. 6 Aug. 1794; K.G. 24 July 1817.

Ld. of Admiralty Dec. 1783–9; teller of the Exchequer 1790–1834; P.C. 21 June 1793; pres. Board of Trade 1807–12; master of the mint 1807–12; foreign sec. Oct.–Dec. 1809; sec. for war and colonies 1812–27; ld. pres. of Council 1828–30.

In April 1783, during the formation of the Coalition and before Apsley was in Parliament, North offered him a seat at the Admiralty Board.

> Lord Bathurst seemed most desirous of my accepting it, and I even went to court to kiss hands on Friday [Apsley wrote to R. M. Keith, 11 Apr.[1]], but some delay happening concerning the other members of the Board of Admiralty, I had time enough to prevail on my father to have his permission to write a refusal, not being willing so easily and so blindly to embrace any party, but more particularly one made up of such discordant principles as that which composes the present Administration.

He concluded: 'Such open prostitution and prevention of seduction by putting oneself up for sale was perhaps scarcely known in any country.'

In July Apsley was returned unopposed at Cirencester where the family seat was held for him by his uncle James Whitshed who resigned on Apsley's coming of age. In Parliament Apsley voted and spoke against Fox's East India bill, 27 Nov. 1783, and on the formation of Pitt's Administration in December 1783 accepted a seat at the Admiralty Board. He voted for parliamentary reform, 18 Apr. 1785. Only two speeches by him are reported in the 1784 Parliament, both on naval matters.

He died 27 July 1834.

[1] Add. 35525, f. 73.

M.M.D.

## BATHURST, Peter (1723–1801), of Clarendon Park, Wilts.

EYE   1784–1790, 11 Sept. 1792–Nov. 1795

*b.* 8 Jan. 1723, 1st s. of Peter Bathurst, M.P., by his 2nd w. Lady Selina Shirley, da. of Robert, 1st Earl Ferrers; nephew of Benjamin Bathurst of Mixbury (q.v.). *educ.* Univ. Coll. Oxf. 1741. *m.* 29 Oct. 1750, Elizabeth, da. of George Evelyn of Nutfield, Surr., *s.p. suc.* fa. 1748.

Capt. 85 Ft. 1759. On the disbandment of the regiment in 1762 he held no further active employment but continued on the army list, becoming lt.-col. 1762, col. 1777, maj.-gen. 1781, gen. 1798.

Bathurst contested Salisbury in 1765, and in 1775 canvassed Hindon but did not stand. In 1784 Lord Cornwallis, when pressed by Government to let his brother William contest Portsmouth, replaced him at Eye by Bathurst—he wrote to Lt.-Col. Ross, 5 Apr.:[1]

> I was very unwilling to part with my brother from Eye, and greatly at a loss whom to recommend. I had only an hour allowed me to decide, and I think I have chosen well, as Bathurst is a man of great honour, perfectly independent both in mind and fortune, and an eager and zealous friend to Pitt.

Bathurst voted with Pitt even over parliamentary reform, 18 Apr. 1785. There is no record of his having spoken in the House in our period.

He died 20 Dec. 1801.

[1] *Cornwallis Corresp.* i. 172.

L.B.N.

## BATTIE, *see* WRIGHTSON

## BAYHAM, Visct., *see* PRATT, Hon. John Jeffreys

## BAYLY, Nathaniel (c.1726–98), of Epsom, Surr. and Shipton House, Abingdon, Berks.

ABINGDON   8 Feb. 1770–1774
WESTBURY                  1774–Mar. 1779

*b.* c.1726. *m.* (1) 3 May 1767, Elizabeth, da. of Hon. Charles Ingram, M.P., sis. of Charles, 9th Visct. Irwin (q.v.) *s.p.*; (2) 18 Mar. 1773, Sophia Magdalena Lamack of Clapham, 2s. 4da.

The Baylys were already Jamaica planters early in the 18th century,[1] but retained their connexion with Westbury, where Nathaniel was born.[2] Bayly's nephew, Bryan Edwards, M.P., in an autobiographical sketch prefixed to his *History of the West Indies*, states that his uncle came to England in 1759, and settled in London 'in a high and elegant style of life'. With Abingdon Bayly had no previous connexion but was invited to contest it in 1768, obviously as one capable of bearing the expense; defeated on the poll by two votes, he was seated on petition, 8 Feb. 1770. In the House he acted with the Opposition; spoke on 19 Mar. 1770 against Clavering's motion attacking the City remonstrance;[3] and on 20 Mar. 1771, over the printers' case, for allowing counsel to the lord mayor.[4] His four recorded votes in this Parliament were all given on the Opposition side, and over the royal marriage bill, in March 1772, he was classed by Robinson as 'contra, present'; but, with undue optimism, as 'hopeful' in 1774, perhaps because of his connexion with Lord Irwin, a Government supporter.

In 1774 Bayly seemed to apprehend the defeat he was to suffer at Abingdon. According to the *London Chronicle* of 1 October, by 'a piece of ill-judged thrift' he withdrew his subscriptions to local celebrations and races; and he safeguarded himself by standing also at Westbury on Lord Abingdon's interest. Still, when the Abingdon election was declared void, Bayly applied for the Chiltern Hundreds in order to contest the borough once more, but was refused them by Lord North, to prevent 'vexatious opposition'. During the next four years the ruin which, according to him, the Government's American policy spelt for the West Indies and himself, and the neglect of the interests and safety of the islands, were the theme of most of Bayly's speeches, spiced with far-fetched imputations against ministers of shaping their measures with a view to enriching their favourites and dependants. He spoke repeatedly against the American prohibitory bill—it was 'madness in Administration to . . . put the nation to so immense an expense of blood and treasure' in order to establish an arbitrary right to tax America, 'which the minister confessed he never meant to make use of' (1 Dec. 1775). And on 11 Dec., criticizing the way in which the measure was sprung on those concerned—

> In order to wreak the revenge of a vindictive ministry on the Americans, you are now going to ruin all the plantations in the West-India islands, and to give their present produce up for plunder to your sailors, before the inhabitants can have any notice of your intentions.

On 21 Dec:

> He was well informed, nay he was fully convinced, that the inhabitants of those islands must be starved; and though they should not, their crops must be left, as they had not nearly lumber enough to save the present; that such being the case, the proprietors must be ruined, and the consequences would in the end reach the merchants, so as, he feared, to bring on a general bankruptcy among those in any manner concerned or interested in the West-India trade.[5]

In the budget debate, 15 May 1777, he criticized the terms of the Government's rum contract at 5s. 3d. per gallon, and offered to supply 'any quantity of Jamaica rum' at 2s. 2d. per gallon.[6] To his apparent indignation, the offer was not accepted.[7] On 26 Nov. 1777, alarmed at the weakness of the defence of Jamaica, he offered a wager to John Buller sen., a lord of the Admiralty, who denied it: to lay 23 or 2,300 guineas that there were not as many as 23 ships there. On 27 Nov. 1778 he returned to the same charge, warning the House that a French invasion of Jamaica was imminent, and that the ministry had shamefully neglected its defences.[8]

He made his last speech in the House of Commons on 1 Mar. 1779, when he objected to the additional tax on sugar imposed by the budget: he and his family paid duties to the value of £30,000 a year, and the additional tax of 5 per cent would affect his property very greatly.[9] But 'one circumstance which, with many others of a similar nature, might easily account for the great desire his Majesty's ministers had to continue the war' was that Lord George Germain's son, appointed by his father receiver general of Jamaica, was drawing 5 per cent on the public receipt which on a war footing amounted to £70,000 p.a. A month later, having to attend to 'affairs of consequence' to himself in the West Indies, Bayly resigned his seat as unable 'to

fulfil the duties of it'. He added: 'my conduct in Parliament has never been influenced by any person or party whatever.'[10] His name appears in six out of seven extant division lists, 1774-9, and always on the Opposition side; over the contractors bill, 12 Feb. 1779, he was classed by Robinson as 'contra, absent'. Subsequently he made several attempts to return to the House. In May 1783 he was reported to have declared his candidature at Abingdon but to have declined 'after a close canvass';[11] in January 1784, to be opposing the re-election of Sir George Yonge at Honiton;[12] and at the general election to be canvassing Abingdon once more—but he did not stand a poll.[13]

He died in Jamaica October 1798.

[1] N. & Q. cxcii. 16; J. H. Lawrence, *Monumental Inscriptions of Brit. W. Indies*, 238. [2] See his speech in the Commons, 15 Mar. 1775, Almon, i. 317. [3] Add. 35609, f. 163. [4] Cavendish's 'Debates', Egerton 226, ff. 341-3. [5] Almon, i. 317; iii. 246-7, 281, 286; vii. 150-1. [6] Ibid. vii. 213. [7] See Bayly's letter to his constituents, *Bath Jnl.* 5 Apr. 1779. [8] Almon, viii. 46-7; xi. 68. [9] Ibid. xii. 22-23. [10] *Bath Jnl.* 5 Apr. 1779. [11] *Glocester Jnl.* 11 May 1783. [12] *Bonner and Middleton's Bristol Jnl.* 3 Jan. 1784. [13] *Reading Merc. and Oxf. Gaz.*, 3 Apr. 1784.

J.A.C.

**BAYLY, Sir Nicholas,** 2nd Bt. (1709–82), of Plas Newydd, Anglesey.

ANGLESEY 1734–1741, 1747–1761, 12 Apr. 1770–1774

*b.* 1709, 1st s. of Sir Edward Bayly, 1st Bt., of Plas Newydd by Dorothy, da. of Hon. Oliver Lambart and gd.-da. of Charles, 1st Earl of Cavan [I]. *educ.* Trinity, Dublin 1726. *m* (1) 28 May 1736, Caroline (*d.*7 Feb. 1766), da. and h. of Brig.-Gen. Thomas Paget, 6s. 5da.; (2) Anne Hunter. *suc.* fa. 28 Sept. 1741.
Ld. lt. Anglesey 1761–82.

In 1754 Bayly was returned for Anglesey after a contest, and was classed by Dupplin as a Government supporter. In retrospect he wrote to Bute, 11 May 1764:[1]

> In the early part of my life I had the honour to be taken notice of and was sincerely attached to the late Prince of Wales on which account I was (as some others were) under a kind of proscription in the late reign and except when your Lordship was in Administration never honoured with any mark of royal favour.

By 1761 the gentlemen of the county were 'one and all for throwing out Sir Nicholas Bayly'[2] because of an occurrence thus related in Boswell's *Life of Johnson*:[3]

> Mrs. Thrale told me that a baronet lost an election in Wales, because he had debauched the sister of a gentleman in the county, whom he made one of his daughters invite as her companion at his seat in the county, when his lady and his other children were in London.

Bayly, who insisted on standing, was defeated. 'Although I am not in this Parliament', he wrote to Bute on 11 May 1764,[4] '[I] will be in the next whenever a new one is called.' But he did not succeed in re-entering the House until 1770. During his last four years in Parliament only one vote is recorded: 9 Feb. 1773, for the petition of the naval captains on half pay, when he was classed in the King's list as one who normally supported Government.[5] In Robinson's list of September 1774 he was also classed as a Government supporter. He did not stand at the general election.

On 14 July 1782 he wrote to Shelburne asking the King's permission to resign because of ill-health the lord lieutenancy of Anglesey, and that it should be conferred on his son, Lord Paget.[6] Bayly died 9 Dec. 1782.

[1] Bute mss. [2] Dowager Lady Bulkeley to Sir Hugh Williams, Baron Hill ms 5736, U.C.N.W. Lib. [3] Vol. iii. 350–1, and 528; Baron Hill ms 5738. [4] Bute mss. [5] His inclusion in the Opposition list of 26 Apr. 1773 is a duplication of Nathaniel Bayly's vote. [6] Lansdowne mss.

P.D.G.T.

## BAYLY, Nicholas (1749–1814), of Plas Newydd, Anglesey.

ANGLESEY 1784–1790

b. 1749, 3rd s. of Sir Nicholas Bayly, 2nd Bt. (q.v.). m. Frances Nettlefold, 1s. 1da.
Ensign 1 Ft. Gds. 1762, lt. and capt. 1770, capt. and lt.-col. 1777; retired 1780.

Bayly was returned for Anglesey after a fierce contest, on his brother's interest and at his expense. In Adam's list of May 1784 he was classed as an Administration supporter; he voted for Pitt's parliamentary reform proposals, 18 Apr. 1785; for Richmond's fortifications plan, 27 Feb. 1786, and with Pitt over the Regency, 1788–9. There is no record of his having spoken in the House. In 1790 the seat at Anglesey was required for his brother's son, and Bayly did not stand elsewhere. At the general election of 1796 he unsuccessfully contested Dover. He died 7 June 1814.

P.D.G.T.

## BAYNES GARFORTH, John (?1722–1808), of Steeton Hall, Yorks.

COCKERMOUTH 1780–1784
HASLEMERE 1784–1790
COCKERMOUTH 1790–1802

b. ?1722, 2nd s. of William Baynes of Mewith Head by Elizabeth, da. of Edmund Garforth of Steeton Hall, Yorks. m. bef. 1755, Miss Shrimpley of London, 1s. 2da. suc. to estates of his uncle Edward Garforth, and took add. name of Garforth.

Garforth, a London attorney, was steward and agent to Sir James Lowther, whom he naturally

followed in Parliament: he voted with the Opposition till the fall of North; for Shelburne's peace preliminaries, 18 Feb. 1783; against Fox's East India bill, 27 Nov. 1783; and supported Pitt till ordered by Sir James to vote against him on the Regency, 1788–9. There is no record of his having spoken in the House.

Oldfield wrote in 1792:

> The minister had a mind to compliment Mr. Garforth . . . with the place of collector of the customs in the city of Carlisle. Mr. Garforth on account of his situation was incapable of holding the office; and the place was *given in trust for him* to Mr. Fearon . . . A dispute, which was succeeded by a lawsuit, happened between Mr. Garforth and Mr. Fearon; and it was decided in the common pleas 'That the holding places in trust was illegal'.

Garforth died 15 Oct. 1808, aged 86.

[1] *Hist. Boroughs*, i. 197–8.

M.M.D.

## BAYNTUN ROLT, Andrew (c.1740–1816).

WEOBLEY 31 Mar. 1780–Apr. 1786

b. c.1740, 1st s. of Edward Bayntun Rolt (q.v.). m. (1) 28 June 1777, Lady Mary Alicia Coventry (div. 24 June 1783), da. of George William, 6th Earl of Coventry, 2da.; (2) Anna Maria Maude, 1s. d. v.p. suc. fa. as 2nd Bt. 3 Jan. 1800.

Bayntun Rolt was returned for Weobley on the interest of Lord Weymouth (there was an old family connexion between the Rolts and the Thynnes) as a supporter of Lord North. On Shelburne's peace preliminaries, 18 Feb. 1783, he voted with the Opposition; did not vote on Fox's East India bill; but in all parliamentary lists 1783–4 is classed as a supporter of Pitt. There is no record of his having spoken in the House. He vacated his seat when Weymouth's eldest son came of age.

Bayntun Rolt died 12 Aug. 1816.

J.B.

## BAYNTUN ROLT, Edward (1710–1800), of Spye Park, nr. Chippenham, Wilts.

CHIPPENHAM 22 June 1737–1780

b. 1710, 2nd s. of Edward Rolt of Sacombe, Herts. by Anne, da. of Henry Bayntun of Spye Park, sis. and h. of John Bayntun. m. Mary Poynter of Herriard, Hants, 3s. 2da. suc. uncle 1717, and took add. name of Bayntun; cr. Bt. 7 July 1762.
Groom of bedchamber to Prince of Wales 1745–6; surveyor gen. duchy of Cornwall 1751–96.

Bayntun Rolt inherited through his mother a considerable interest at Chippenham.

In 1747 and 1754 he received £800 from secret service funds towards his election expenses; and in 1761, when no Government money was issued for elections, Bute arranged for him a pension of £300 p.a. on the duchy of Cornwall.[1] In Bute's list he is classed as 'Granville and Bute', and he appears in Fox's list of Members favourable to the peace preliminaries. Henceforth he supported every Administration, and under George III is not known ever to have voted with Opposition. Only four speeches by him are recorded: three in 1765[2] and one in 1771,[3] all on minor matters.

Robinson in his survey for the general election of 1780 expected Bayntun Rolt to stand again but on 30 July noted: 'It is now said that there is some doubt whether Sir Edward Bayntun will come in.' Bayntun Rolt did not stand, but there is evidence to suggest that he tried to maintain his interest by sponsoring his son-in-law.[4] If so, it was the last effort he made in the borough; and before he died on 3 Jan. 1800 he had sold most of his property there.

[1] Lord Egremont to Bute, 8 and 10 Mar. 1761, Bute mss. [2] Harris's 'Debates', 21 Jan. 1765, and 14 and 20 Feb. 1765. [3] 22 Apr. 1771, Cavendish's 'Debates', Egerton 229. ff. 242–3. [4] J. A. Cannon, 'Parlty. Rep. Six Wilts. Boroughs, 1754–90' (Bristol Univ. Ph.D. thesis).

J.A.C.

**BEARCROFT, Edward** (1737–96), of Holland House, Kensington.[1]

Hindon 1784–1790
Saltash 1790–20 Nov. 1796

b. 30 Apr. 1737, 2nd s. of Rev. Philip Bearcroft, master of the Charterhouse, by his 1st w. Elizabeth Lovegrove. educ. Charterhouse; Peterhouse, Camb. 1752; I. Temple 1754, called 1758. m. (1) 31 Oct. 1758, Sarah Maria (d.28 Aug. 1759), da. of Hon. Walter Molesworth, 1s.; (2) Elizabeth (d.13 Oct. 1774), da. and coh. of Edward Rogers of Ockle Clifford, Glos., 1s. 1da.; (3) Dec. 1778, Clare St. George Wilson of Mortlake, 2s. 2da.

Counsel and steward of courts to the governors of the Charterhouse 1765; K.C. 1772; bencher, I. Temple 1772, reader 1780–1, treasurer 1781–2; c.j Chester 1788–d.

The *Gentleman's Magazine* in his obituary (1796, p. 972) wrote:

Mr. Bearcroft was an example of industry and perseverance at the bar. Many years he had hardly practice enough to support him with the severest economy, and thought of relinquishing the law in despair; but, in time his good sense and knowledge of the law excited confidence, and till his hearing was affected, he was one of the most successful of its professors.

Yet at 35 he was a K.C., and in the same year failed by only one vote to be elected recorder of London. By 1782 he was one of the leading lawyers in the country, much employed in election disputes, and estimated to be earning £2,000 a year.[2]

He was returned for Hindon on the Beckford interest, presumably on the recommendation of

Lord Chancellor Thurlow (William Beckford jun. had been a ward in Chancery); and soon became prominent in debate. In every recorded division he supported Pitt, and also voted with him for parliamentary reform and against the impeachment of Sir Elijah Impey. In the Parliament of 1784 sixteen speeches or interventions in debate by him are recorded, on a wide variety of subjects. According to Wraxall,[3] he 'possessed great intellectual powers, and looked forward confidently to the highest honours of his profession'.

He died 20 Nov. 1796.

[1] Leased by Bearcroft from the 3rd Lord Holland. [2] *Salisbury Jnl.* 25 Mar. 1782. [3] *Mems*, iv. 313.

J.B.

**BEAUCHAMP, Visct.,** *see* **SEYMOUR CONWAY, Francis**

**BEAUCHAMP PROCTOR, Sir William,** 1st Bt. (1722–73), of Tottenham, Mdx. and Langley, Norf.

Middlesex 1747–1768

bap. 11 May 1722, o.s. of Thomas Beauchamp of Tottenham by Anne, da. of William Proctor of Langley. educ. Magdalen, Oxf. 1738. m. (1) his cos. Jane (d.10 May 1761), da. of Christopher Towers of Huntsmoor Park, Bucks., 2s. 3da.; (2) 13 May 1762, Laetitia, da. and coh. of Henry Johnson of Great Berkhampstead, Herts., 4s. 2da. Her sis. Agneta m. 1762 Charles Yorke (q.v.). suc. fa. 15 June 1724, gd.-fa. Ephraim Beauchamp 16 Dec. 1728, uncle George Proctor of Langley 12 Sept. 1744, and took add. name of Proctor; cr. Bt. 20 Feb. 1745; K.B. 23 Mar. 1761.

Beauchamp Proctor successfully contested Middlesex in 1747, and was returned unopposed in 1754. He was classed by Dupplin in 1754 as a country gentleman supporting Administration, and in Bute's list of December 1761 as his supporter. But he voted against the peace preliminaries, 9 and 10 Dec. 1762; with Opposition on Wilkes and general warrants; and belonged to Wildman's Club. Rockingham in July 1765 classed him as 'pro', and in November 1766 as 'Whig'. He voted against the Chatham Administration on the land tax, 27 Feb. 1767.

At the general election of 1768 he was defeated for Middlesex, and stood again at the by-election in December. Rockingham wrote to Charles Yorke (q.v.) on 9 June 1768:[1]

Sir William on many occasions has acted handsomely (at least as *we* think, because it was on points in Parliament which were thought essential matters by *us*), and I thought I perceived an inclination among our friends to do him service.

Beauchamp Proctor was opposed by John Glynn

(q.v.), Wilkes's lawyer, and after a riotous and expensive contest was defeated. It was rumoured that the election cost him £10,000.[2] He did not attempt to contest the county again, nor, so far as is known, any other constituency.

He died 13 Sept. 1773.

[1] Add. 35430, ff. 118–19. [2] Jas. Harris's memorandum, 10 Dec. 1768, Malmesbury mss.

J.B.

## BEAUCLERK, Aubrey (1740–1802), of Hanwell, Mdx.

| THETFORD | 1761–1768 |
| ALDBOROUGH | 1768–1774 |

*b.* 3 June 1740, o. surv. s. of Lord Vere Beauclerk, M.P. (cr. 1750 Baron Vere of Hanworth), by Mary, da. and coh. of Thomas Chambers of Hanworth, Mdx.; gd.-s. of Charles, 1st Duke of Saint Albans. *educ.* Westminster 1746; Queen's, Oxf. 1758. *m.* 4 May 1763 Lady Catherine Ponsonby, da. of William, 2nd Earl of Bessborough [I] (q.v.), 4s. 3da. *suc.* fa. as 2nd Baron Vere 2 Oct. 1781; and his cos. as 5th Duke of Saint Albans 16 Feb. 1787.

The circumstances in which Beauclerk was returned for Thetford are described by Horace Walpole in a letter to Lady Suffolk:[1]

We are more successful, Madam, than I could flatter myself we should be. Mr. Conway . . . has negotiated so well, that the Duke of Grafton is disposed to bring Mr. Beauclerk in for Thetford. It will be expected, I believe, that Lord Vere should resign Windsor in a handsome manner to the Duke of Cumberland.

The Beauclerk family and the Duke of Cumberland both had influence at Windsor, and it seems clear that Grafton (who was closely connected with Cumberland) provided Beauclerk with a seat at Thetford in order to avoid a contest at Windsor.

Beauclerk's conduct in Parliament shows that he felt under no obligation to Grafton. In Bute's list of December 1761 he is marked 'pro', with the note 'Dorset'—there was an old connexion between his father and the Duke of Dorset;[2] and he is also included in Fox's list of Members favourable to the peace preliminaries. His marriage to a daughter of Lord Bessborough, brother-in-law of the 4th Duke of Devonshire, brought him into contact with the Opposition and seems to have changed his political allegiance. He voted against Grenville on general warrants, 6, 15, and 18 Feb. 1764, but in Newcastle's list of 10 May 1764 is classed as only a doubtful friend, nor did he belong to Wildman's Club. By the winter of 1766–7, however, both Rockingham and Newcastle counted him as of their party.

On 22 June 1767 Sir William Meredith (q.v.) suggested Beauclerk to Portland as 'an excellent man' to contest Leicester at the forthcoming general election. Beauclerk acknowledged, wrote Lord George Cavendish (q.v.) to Portland on 16 August, 'that he should like of all things to come into Parliament under your Grace's auspices, though perhaps he should not like to be beholden to any other person for a seat'; yet 'he was cautious of venturing where he could not see his way tolerably clearly', and 'could not be sure that he might not be drawn into an expense that would by no means agree with his circumstances'.[3] On 3 Nov. 1767 Newcastle wrote to Rockingham:[4]

The Duke of Grafton, as Lord Bessborough tells me, does not choose Mr. Beauclerk at Thetford because he votes constantly with us, and Lord Bessborough thinks with reason that we ought to take care of him.

Nothing had been done about finding a seat for Beauclerk when, at the beginning of February, Newcastle had from a friend the disposal of a safe seat for £2,000.[5] Rockingham consulted the Cavendishes, who told him 'that Lord Bessborough says he shall give Mr. Beauclerk £1,000 but will not allow that the Cavendishes should add anything by way of getting him a seat'.[6] In the end Newcastle agreed to choose Beauclerk at Aldborough, 'as a pure mark of attention to him and friendship and love to his father-in-law'.[7]

Beauclerk henceforth voted consistently with the Rockinghams, and attended the Opposition dinners at the Thatched House in May 1769 and January 1770. But he never belonged to the party's inner circle, and seems to have taken little interest in politics. There is no record of his having spoken in the House, and he did not stand in 1774.

Sir Henry Etherington, whose ward subsequently married Beauclerk's eldest son, wrote about Beauclerk on 29 Apr. 1788, after he had succeeded to the dukedom:[8]

I believe he can give his son nothing, his finances being in a ruined state that he was obliged to live abroad before he came to the title. He has been known at Newmarket. The Duke of Saint Albans is always hereditary Grand Falconer of England with a grant of £25,000 [sic] a year with it. This is all I believe that belongs to the title, and the Duke has nine children to provide for without any money to do it.

And from other correspondence it is clear that the lady's fortune was one of her chief recommendations in the Duke's eyes.

Saint Albans died 9 Feb. 1802.

[1] *Letters*, ed. Toynbee, v. 34–5. [2] See Henry Pelham's list of the House of Commons, 16 Oct. 1742, Add. 32699, f. 467, also Walpole to Hertford, 6 Feb. 1764. [3] Portland mss. [4] Add. 32986, ff. 234–5. [5] Newcastle to Rockingham, 6 Feb. 1768, Add. 32988, f. 196. [6] Rockingham to Newcastle, 10 Feb. 1768, ibid. f. 265. [7] Newcastle to James West, 26 May 1768, Add. 32990, f. 133. [8] A. M. W. Stirling, *Annals of a Yorkshire House*, ii. 207.

J.B.

## BEAUCLERK, Lord George (1704–68).

NEW WINDSOR  3 Dec. 1744–1754, 1768–11 May
1768

*b.* 26 Dec. 1704, 6th s. of Charles, 1st Duke of Saint
Albans, by Lady Diana de Vere, da. and h. of Aubrey,
20th Earl of Oxford. *m.* Margaret, da. of Thomas
Bainbridge, yeoman, of Slaley, Northumb. *s.p.*[1]
    Ensign 1 Ft. Gds. 1723; lt. 11 Hussars 1726; capt.
1 Ft. Gds. and lt.-col. 1736; col. 1745; col. 8 Marines
1747–8; col. 19 Ft. 1748–*d.*; gov. of Landguard Fort
1753–*d.*; maj.-gen. 1755; c.-in-c. Scotland 1756–67;
lt.-gen. 1758.

In 1756 Beauclerk was given a pension of £400
per annum on the Irish establishment. In 1768, supported by Government, he was returned unopposed
on his family interest at Windsor. He died 11 May
1768, the day after Parliament met.

[1] *Hist. Northumb.* vi. 274.

M.M.D.

## BEAUCLERK, Lord Henry (1701–61), of Wink-field, Berks.

PLYMOUTH  26 Nov. 1740–1741
THETFORD  29 Dec. 1741–5 Jan. 1761

*b.* 11 Aug. 1701, 4th s. of Charles, 1st Duke of Saint
Albans, and bro. of Lord George Beauclerk (q.v.). *m.*
25 June 1739, Hon. Martha Lovelace, da. of John,
4th Baron Lovelace, sis. and h. of Nevill, 6th Baron
Lovelace, 2s. 6da.
    Ensign 1 Ft. Gds. 1717; capt. 3 Ft. 1727; capt.
1 Ft. Gds. and lt.-col. 1735; col. 48 Ft. 1743–5; col.
31 Ft. 1745–9, when he left the army after a quarrel
with the Duke of Cumberland.

Beauclerk sat at Thetford on the interest of his
kinsman the Duke of Grafton. Dupplin's list of
1754 classes him as 'pro'. On 5 Nov. 1755 he wrote
to the Duke of Newcastle:[1]

> I am now very soon coming up to attend my duty at
> Westminster, but in prudence and justice to my
> numerous family can't help once more representing to
> your Grace that the unavoidable additional expense of
> being in town is what I can't nor must not continue
> unless some assistance is granted to me.

Beauclerk is reported to have spoken only once: in
committee on the Minorca inquiry, 26 Apr. 1757,[2]
when with other Members 'not expected to be
against'[3] he voted with the Opposition—his only
recorded vote during this Parliament.

On 3 Feb. 1759 Beauclerk's wife wrote to Newcastle asking him for financial assistance:[4]

> My son would be no trouble to the Crown nor would
> my daughters had Lord Henry Beauclerk had the
> common chances his rank demanded. But unless your
> Grace finds some employment he is worthy of I fear
> I must still be troublesome for myself and girls.

Beauclerk died 5 Jan. 1761, and on 16 Jan. his

widow was granted a pension of £400 per annum on
the Irish establishment.

[1] Add. 32860, f. 397. [2] Add. 35877, f. 363. [3] Hen. Fox to Devonshire, n.d., Devonshire mss. [4] Add. 32887, f. 489.

J.B.

## BEAUFOY, Henry (1750–95), of Great George St., Westminster.

MINEHEAD  11 Mar. 1783–1784
GREAT YARMOUTH  1784–17 May 1795

*b.* Nov. 1750, 1st s. of Mark Beaufoy, vinegar brewer,
of Cuper's Bridge, Lambeth by Elizabeth, da. of Capel
Hanbury of Bristol and Pontymoyle. *educ.* Hoxton
Acad. 1765–7; Warrington Acad. 1767–70; Edinburgh; Grand Tour (France, Italy). *m.* Elizabeth, da.
and coh. of William Jenks of Shifnal, Salop, *s.p.*  *suc.*
fa. 11 Feb. 1782. His sis. Maria m. 1773 George
Durant (q.v.) of Tong Castle, Salop.
    Sec. Bd. of Control [India Office] 1791–3.

Beaufoy, of a Quaker family, was sent to nonconformist schools, and though he joined the Established Church retained throughout life a close connexion with the Dissenters.[1] In 1775 he entered his
father's firm of vinegar distillers, but seems to have
taken no very active part in its business and
apparently severed his connexion with it after his
father's death.[2] Determined to enter Parliament, he
hoped to find a seat at the general election of 1780,
but, he wrote later:[3]

> Restricted to a line of cautious procedure by the
> smallness of my fortune, which, including the produce
> of my wife's estate, afforded but £1,600 a year; yet
> very desirous of representing a borough, in which the
> suffrages of honest men have at least a share, I resolved
> to ask the advice of some leader of a party, who might
> be willing to give me the assistance that is considered
> as due to a man, who will not indeed relinquish his
> independence, but from whom the sort of aid may be
> expected that similarity of principle affords.

He therefore asked his former tutor, Dr. Andrew
Kippis, to introduce him to Shelburne, to whom
Kippis wrote on 20 May 1780:

> From his earliest youth it has been his ambition to
> make a distinguished figure in Parliament, and to this
> end have all his studies been directed. His education
> has been liberal . . . With regard to the talents for
> public speaking which is his prime object, he has a
> copious invention, extensive knowledge and great
> readiness and force with correctness of language. The
> proprieties of elocution and language he has long
> learned under Mr. [Thomas] Sheridan, and three days
> in the week he speaks in my presence on some
> historical, constitutional or commercial subject. He
> is a true friend to religious and civil liberty and wholly
> disapproves of the measures of the present Administra-
> tion.

But though Shelburne suggested Beaufoy as a
candidate to an (unnamed) patron of a Cornish
borough, his application was too late, nor did a
meeting with Fox prove any more effectual, and

Beaufoy did not stand at the general election. During the next two years he continued to search impatiently but unsuccessfully for a seat. After Shelburne had taken office Kippis again wrote about Beaufoy, 20 July 1782:

Since I had the honour of introducing him to your Lordship he hath acquired a large accession of fortune by the death of his father and another relation, so that any expense attending an election would be a matter of no consequence to him. By the happy change of his Majesty's counsels Mr. Beaufoy would be an active and cheerful supporter of Government. . . . I would pawn my reputation on Mr. Beaufoy's making a figure in the House, both as a speaker and as a man of business.[4]

At length, in March 1783, Shelburne arranged that Beaufoy should pay £3,000 to Francis Fownes Luttrell to vacate his seat at Minehead. Beaufoy wrote subsequently:

No arguments were necessary to prove that this mode of obtaining a seat . . . however mortifying to my pride, or discordant to my ideas of the spirit of the constitution, was not only more consistent than any other plan I could possibly pursue with that perfect independence which I had always determined should form the basis of my political character, but was in fact the only way in which, in my unconnected situation, an independent seat was likely to be obtained at all.[5]

In Parliament Beaufoy opposed the Coalition, and his speeches show a strong dislike of North. In a maiden speech[6] on 7 May 1783, he supported Pitt's parliamentary reform proposals, and argued that the present advantages of the constitution were 'not the benefits of the ancient British constitution but of innovations on that constitution . . . No constitution can long remain unaltered that is not adapted to the circumstances of the times and the general disposition of the people.' He was one of the reforming group which surrounded Pitt and supported his Administration; but, according to Wraxall, though he was 'strongly attached' to Pitt 'he nevertheless preserved his independence of character, and might be esteemed rather a friend than a follower of the minister'.[7]

At the general election Beaufoy was invited to stand for Great Yarmouth in opposition to the Townshend interest. He was supported by a party of independent townsmen who were mostly Dissenters, and achieved such success on the canvass that he was returned unopposed. As a hedge he was re-elected for Minehead, but chose to sit for Yarmouth.

Beaufoy was a frequent speaker on a wide range of subjects, and, writes Wraxall, was 'among the Members who occupied throughout the session no inconsiderable portion of notice . . . On all subjects connected with commerce he displayed a great variety of information and his intentions were always directed to national benefit.'[8] As a member of a committee to inquire into the receipt and expenditure of public revenue he pointed out, 4 May 1786, the 'absurdity of employing persons in offices of great trouble and temptation without a salary adequate to the comforts or even support of life', and advocated the removal of corrupt officials and the addition of their salaries to those of the more deserving.[9] He spoke at length and with obvious knowledge on various commercial subjects, particularly the fishing industry, and in 1785 was chairman of a parliamentary committee to inquire into the state of the fisheries. He campaigned for a reform of the excise laws; condemned them in half a dozen speeches, and, 14 June 1785, introduced a bill to codify the existing laws and permit trial by jury for excise offences, emphasising the abuses arising from summary trials by magistrates.[10] In 1787 he was asked by the Dissenters to move the repeal of the Test and Corporation Acts. Wraxall writes that his speech of 28 Mar.

comprehended every argument which ingenuity or reason could suggest, clothed in language of no ordinary elegance and energy, tempered throughout by judgment as well as by moderation, and delivered with his characteristic oratorical cadence . . . I have indeed seen few more luminous displays of intellect in Parliament.[11]

He continued the campaign for repeal after this attempt had failed; moved for it again on 8 May 1789 and seconded Fox's motion of 3 Mar. 1790. He also introduced a bill to enforce the reading of the Bill of Rights in church in commemoration of the 1688 Revolution.[12] In a speech on 17 June 1788 he supported Sir William Dolben's measures for regulating the slave trade.[13]

He died 17 May 1795.

[1] G. Beaufoy, *Leaves from a Beech Tree*, 137, and Debrett, xxi. 530. [2] Debrett, xx. 335. [3] In a memoir about his entry into Parliament, excerpt in Aspinall & Smith, *English Hist. Docs*. xi. 242. [4] Lansdowne mss at Bowood. [5] *English Hist. Docs*. 241–3. [6] Debrett, ix. 714–22. [7] *Mems*. iv. 139. [8] Ibid. [9] Debrett, xx. 163–5. [10] Ibid. xvii. 502–13. [11] *Mems*. iv. 436. [12] 17 July 1789, Stockdale, xviii. 86–87. [13] Ibid. xv. 203–12.

M.M.D.

**BECKFORD, Julines** (?1717–64), of Steepleton Iwerne, Dorset.

SALISBURY 1754–27 Nov. 1764

*b*. ?1717, 7th s. of Peter Beckford of Jamaica, and yr. bro. of William Beckford (q.v.). *educ*. Westminster, June 1725, aged 7. *m*. 17 Jan. 1739, Elizabeth, da. of Solomon Ashley, M.P., of Ashby St. Ledgers, Northants., 1s. Sheriff, Dorset 1749–50.

Julines Beckford purchased Steepleton Iwerne in 1745 for £12,600,[1] and in 1759 added an estate at

Shillingstone. In a list of landholders in Jamaica, drawn up in 1754, he is noted as owning over 8000 acres.[2]

He sat at Salisbury on his brother's interest, and had to face a contest both in 1754 and 1761. Like his brother he was classed by Dupplin in 1754 as a Tory, and in 1761 was not sent Newcastle's parliamentary whip. He appears in none of the minority division lists 1762–4; and in the *Court and City Register* for 1764 is described as being in Jamaica, where he died 27 Nov. 1764.

[1] Hutchins, *Dorset*, i. 299. [2] CO 142/31; Add. 12436.

J.B.

## BECKFORD, Peter (?1739–1811), of Steepleton Iwerne, Dorset.

### MORPETH 1768–1774

*b.* ?1739, o.s. of Julines Beckford (q.v.). *educ.* Westminster Jan. 1748, aged 8; New Coll. Oxf. 12 Apr. 1757, aged 17; Grand Tour (France, Switzerland, Italy). *m.* 22 Mar. 1773, Louisa, da. of George Pitt (q.v.) of Strathfieldsaye, Hants, 2s. 3da. *suc.* fa. 1764.

Beckford stood for Morpeth in 1768 on the Carlisle interest, recommended by the Duke of Grafton; and was returned after a contest. No speech by him is recorded, and his name appears in only one division list: that of the minority on the Spanish convention, 13 Feb. 1771. In Robinson's first survey on the royal marriage bill he is classed as 'doubtful, present', in the second as 'pro, present'; and in Robinson's electoral survey of September 1774 as 'doubtful'. He did not stand in 1774.

He was more interested in hunting than in politics; and his book, *Thoughts upon Hare and Fox Hunting* (1781), is one of the classics of the sport He died 18 Feb. 1811, aged 71.

J.B.

## BECKFORD, Richard (1712–56).

### BRISTOL 1754–24 Jan. 1756

*b.* 1712, 3rd s. of Peter Beckford, and bro. of William (q.v.). *educ.* Westminster, July 1721, aged 9; Balliol, Oxf. 15 Jan. 1728, aged 15; Univ. Coll. Oxf., B.A. 1731; M. Temple 1730, called 1736. *unm.*
Alderman of London 1754.

Richard Beckford was one of the biggest planters in Jamaica, with an estate of 9,242 acres,[1] and was there at the time of the general election of 1754. The campaign at Bristol, where he stood as a Tory on a joint interest with Sir John Philipps (q.v.), was managed for him by his brother William, whom he followed in the House.

During his short term in a poorly reported

Parliament, three speeches by him are recorded. About the first, on the army estimates, 27 Nov. 1754, Walpole writes:[2]

> The younger Beckford, who had been announced for a genius, and had laid a foundation for being so by studying magazines and historical registers, made a tedious harangue against standing armies.

His second speech, during the debate on the Bristol night-watch bill, 17–19 Jan. 1755, dealt with the government of Bristol and the 'arbitrary power' of its magistrates' filling up vacancies by co-option;[3] while his third speech, on the Oxfordshire election, 23 Apr. 1755, drew arguments against the claim of copyholders in a county election from the composition of the Saxon armies which had conquered the country:[4]

> I have troubled you with so much of our ancient history to show how far we have already departed from the wise maxims of our ancestors; and the inconvenience of our having done so, is now felt by every gentleman who stands candidate at a county election.

Beckford died at Lyons 24 Jan. 1756.

[1] 'List of Landholders in Jamaica, 1754', CO142/31; also Add. 12436. [2] *Mems. Geo. II*, i. 410. [3] *Parl. Hist.* xv. 479–88. [4] Ibid. 450–8.

J.B.

## BECKFORD, Richard (d.1796), of Nicholas Lane, Lombard St., London.

### BRIDPORT 1780–1784
### ARUNDEL 14 June 1784–1790
### LEOMINSTER 28 Mar. 1791–1796

1st illegit. s. of Alderman William Beckford (q.v.). *unm.*

Beckford was a West India merchant, and by 1774 was established in partnership as Beckford and James, of Nicholas Lane, Lombard St., where he remained till his death.

In 1774 and again in 1776 he unsuccessfully contested Hindon, the interest of his father's widow and legitimate family going against him. In 1780 he was returned at Bridport with the support of Humphry Sturt (q.v.). The *English Chronicle* wrote in 1780 that he

> inherits his father's principles, though it is not probable that he will ever be actuated either by similar zeal, or be distinguished for similar influence. His vote, and good wishes, will be the only assistance the minority will derive from him in Parliament, he having got an impediment in his speech

and there is no record of his having spoken in the House. He voted in opposition in all the recorded divisions between December 1781 and March 1782 and against Shelburne's peace preliminaries, 18 Feb. 1783. He voted for parliamentary reform, 7 May 1783; and for Fox's East India bill, 27 Nov.

1783, being classed as a Foxite in Robinson's list of January 1784, and Stockdale's of 19 Mar. He did not stand at the general election, but in June 1784 was returned unopposed for Arundel, in place of Lord Surrey, who elected to sit for Carlisle. He voted for parliamentary reform, 18 Apr. 1785, and in general remained in opposition throughout this Parliament.

He died 12 Aug. 1796.

M.M.D.

## BECKFORD, William (1709-70), of Fonthill, Wilts.

SHAFTESBURY 8 Dec. 1747-1754
LONDON 1754-21 June 1770

*bap.* 19 Dec. 1709, in Jamaica, 2nd s. of Peter Beckford, sugar planter, Speaker of the Jamaica House of Assembly, and comptroller of customs, by Bathshua, da. and coh. of Julines Hering, also of Jamaica. *educ.* Westminster 1719; Balliol, Oxf. 1725; adm. Leyden as medical student 1731, and said afterwards to have studied, till 1735, at the Hôpital des Invalides in Paris.[1] *m.* 8 June 1756, Maria, da. of Hon. George Hamilton, 2nd s. of James, 6th Earl of Abercorn [S], wid. of Francis Marsh, 1 surv. s. 6 illegit. s. and 2da. recognized in his will. *suc.* bro. 1737.

Alderman of London 1752, sheriff 1755-6, ld. mayor 1762-3, 1769-70.

Beckford, who had inherited from his brother large estates in Jamaica,[2] sat for Shaftesbury on the interest of the 4th Earl of Shaftesbury, with whom he seems to have closely co-operated in politics for some time.[3]

In 1752 he took the step which was to condition his future career. With the support of Tory allies in the House and in the City of London, he took up by redemption the freedom of the Ironmongers' Company,[4] and a few days later was elected alderman of Billingsgate ward preliminary to standing for the City at the general election of 1754.[5] The City normally elected men who were not only citizens but intimately connected with its affairs. Though Beckford claimed to be a merchant on the strength of his business in buying and selling for his plantations, and later boasted that 'his family were new citizens, and some of them had borne the highest offices for a century past',[6] he was the first politician whose interests lay largely outside the City to seek to break through this custom. In 1754, returned third on the list after a hot contest, he thanked the electors for the trust which they had shown him despite the short time he had had the honour of being known to them, and the prejudices that had been laid against him.[7] He was in all very successful at this general election, boasting to Bedford that he had satisfied his ambition of having 'as many friends

elected into the new Parliament as I well could, with prudence in respect to my fortune', and that he had 'carried three cities and two boroughs'. (London for himself, Bristol, after a great struggle, for his brother Richard, and Salisbury for his brother Julines; Petersfield, for which he was returned, he handed on to Sir John Philipps, and at Hindon he brought in James Dawkins). His appeal to the Duke of Bedford for a seat for a third brother was, however, unsuccessful.[8]

An indefatigable speaker in the House from the beginning, he supported Tory measures; in March 1755 took a prominent part in meetings of the Tories at the Horn Tavern;[9] and as late as January 1760 acted as spokesman for them with Pitt.[10] But in 1754 a paragraph in the *Public Advertiser* alleged that at the Bristol election he had called himself a Whig;[11] on 7 Mar. 1763 he declared in the House: 'I am, Sir, a Whig, and have the utmost abhorrence of passive obedience';[12] and by 1769 could accuse others of 'rank Tory doctrines'.[13] Though working so closely in his earlier years with the Tory country gentlemen, and, like them repudiating any desire for office, he differed from them not only in his colonial and commercial interests, but in the urgency of his desire to find a leader who would implement the policies he supported, and in the steps he was prepared to take to this end. Disappointed, like others of his group, by the death of the Prince of Wales in 1751, in 1753-4 he went some way to enrolling himself under the banner of the Duke of Bedford; with his backing started a paper, the *Protestor* (run by Ralph till November 1753, when he went over to the Administration);[14] and on 4 June 1754 wrote to the Duke: 'As the eyes of most people are looking toward your Grace as the head of an Opposition founded on true patriot principles. . . .'[15] In 1755 he entertained hopes of the leadership of Henry Fox; even when speaking against the ministers on 21 Nov. he owned 'he had a great opinion of the abilities of Mr. Fox which if exerted well should have his support'.[16] Then—when the stress of war brought Pitt to the fore—he attached himself firmly and permanently to this new leader. 'I intend', he wrote on 6 Nov. 1756, 'to act as one of your private soldiers without commission.'[17]

In his enthusiastic support of Pitt as war minister from 1756 onwards, Beckford assisted him partly by frequent speeches (which were often ill-heard, and were described as 'rambling and irregular', but which also contained 'some things pertinent'),[18] partly by advice and the collection of expert opinions on America and the West Indies,[19] but mostly by the hold he gained over popular opinion in the City of London and by the skill he acquired in bringing it to bear on political questions. In return Pitt helped him in the House on matters concerning the West Indian interest—'without your presence', Beckford wrote to him, 19 Feb. 1760, 'I shall not dare to enter into the debate, for in this question I am the object of envy, hatred and all uncharitableness'.[20] Pitt rallied to his aid also on other occasions.[21] As early as 1758 Beckford began to press on Pitt his views as to a satisfactory peace: he urged the importance of retaining Canada—there is no evidence of his having favoured the return to France of the sugar islands in the interest of English sugar producers, as was alleged at the time.

In 1761 he made no further attempt to extend his parliamentary interest, which had suffered by the death of Richard, the most active of his brothers, but stood again for the City, where another contest took place. He described the nomination meeting of the livery as 'very troublesome and at the commencement a little tumultuous' where 'Mr. Beckford had the honour to have those for enemies who are not well-wishers of Mr. Pitt';[22] his appeal for assistance to Bedford was rejected, but he was said to have had some backing from Administration (for a rival candidate complained 'there is letters from the office of Ordnance and the Board of Works in Beckford's favour only');[23] and he was once again returned third of the four successful candidates.

Pitt's resignation in October 1761 brought Beckford back into the opposition to which he was accustomed, and presented him with the difficult task of reconciling the popular elements in the City to his leader's acceptance of a pension for himself and a title for his wife;[24] a letter from Pitt to Beckford explaining the situation was published in the press, and Beckford persuaded Pitt to attend the lord mayor's feast—a refusal 'would damp the ardour and public spirit of every well wisher to his country'.[25] It was said that 'mobs were hired by Mr. Beckford . . . to huzza and clap them as they passed along the streets'.[26] Beckford's campaign was so successful that when he was elected lord mayor in October 1762, it was considered 'a mark of their good-will to his friend Mr. Pitt',[27] though he owed it as much to his own adroitness. He carried out the formal duties of the lord mayor with splendour, made use of the position to support the views of his friends in Parliament, and fanned the fires of discontent in the City. He opposed the peace preliminaries; on 25 Nov. spoke vehemently against them, and, according to George Onslow, was heard as never in his life;[28] tried to speak again on 9 Dec.: he 'rose, but could not be heard';[29] and both on the 9th and 10th voted in the minority against them; and

in 1763, when addresses of thanks were being sought throughout the country, he refused to call the livery together in common hall to vote one.[30] When the majority of the court of aldermen voted an address on their own, he did not accompany them to present it.[31] And though he was personally unfriendly to Wilkes, whose *North Briton* attacked him in 1762–3,[32] he took up his cause, by the end of 1763 was outwardly at least on friendly terms with him[33] and spoke and voted on 17–18 Feb. 1764 against general warrants. It was at this time that Beckford began to earn the reputation of a demagogue, 'the scavenger . . . to throw dirt upon Government'.[34] On the other hand, his speech at the end of his mayoralty was said by Charles Townshend to be 'no bad speech. . . . It is composed upon good ideas of taste, and firm and explicit, without being indecent or warm.'[35]

In August–September 1763 he was employed as an intermediary in an attempt to persuade Pitt to return to power (a duty which he performed with goodwill and whose failure he openly deplored);[36] again in March 1764 an attempt by him to see Bute at Luton raised some speculation;[37] but with Pitt withdrawing from the political field in 1764–5, and the Wilkite agitation dying down in the City, Beckford's political importance declined. He was active in the House, however, on all matters concerning the West Indies and the militia (of which he had been an ardent supporter since 1759), and he could claim the somewhat rare distinction of opposing Grenville's Stamp Act both in 1764 when it was adumbrated, and in 1765 when it was introduced.[38] When Pitt re-emerged as a political force and supported the Rockinghams over the repeal of the Act, Beckford spoke and voted on their side;[39] but he viewed with much less favour their proposals for a free port in the West Indies, and persuaded Pitt to oppose it at first, though he did not succeed in carrying his leader very far with him in what proved an unpopular direction.[40]

The formation of the Chatham Administration gave him another experience of supporting Government, and even a short-lived prominence in the House when Chatham chose him to introduce his attack on the territorial rights of the East India Company in Bengal. The collapse and withdrawal of Chatham left him, however, without instructions, and without support except from Shelburne; and after May 1767 the matter was out of his hands.[41] In the debate on the embargo on the export of corn, 11 Nov. 1766, he supported Administration, making an unfortunate reference to the value of a 'dispensing power' which he never altogether lived down;[42] and he voted with them on the land tax, 27

Feb. 1767, because he considered 'that relief ought to be given to the poor man, in preference to the opulent land-holder'.[43] On the other hand he opposed them, 15 May 1767, on the measures to force the American Colonies to supply necessaries to the British troops there.[44]

In 1768 Beckford prepared for the forthcoming general election by introducing a bill on 26 Jan. to force Members to take an oath on their return that they had not used bribery in their elections, a measure viewed with favour by some country gentlemen, but attacked by Burke and Dowdeswell and abandoned in committee. He voted with Administration against the nullum tempus bill, 17 Feb. 1768, as he later maintained, on principle,[45] but during the general election of that year he was attacked in the press by the interests in the City usually associated with Administration, and after the resignation of Chatham and Shelburne was once more in opposition, especially on the American question. In the election for the City he was again returned third on the list. The contest was a confused one and made more so by the candidature of Wilkes, and while none of the candidates co-operated with him, Beckford and Barlow Trecothick (q.v.), both standing in the popular interest, found it wise to treat him 'with much civility'.[46]

Wilkes's triumphant return for Middlesex foreshadowed the rise of a new force in the City, where the measures taken by Administration raised a fury. Since Wilkes was serving a term of imprisonment and could not personally lead the following which had sprung up round him, Beckford was able for a time to enjoy the fruits of Wilkes's enterprise. Though he did not disguise his personal dislike of Wilkes,[47] and never joined the Supporters of the Bill of Rights Society, he soon found that an appearance of goodwill towards Wilkes was necessary. While as late as 14 Nov. 1768 he had declared in the House that he was 'tired of Wilkes and Liberty', on 23 Jan. 1769 he said, 'I shall move an address to his Majesty to pardon Mr. Wilkes'; and on 27 Jan., that 'no man has been more persecuted than he has been'.[48] Moreover his two new co-adjutors in the City, James Townsend and John Sawbridge (qq.v.), were at this time ardent Wilkites. On 10 Feb. 1769 Beckford assisted the livery to draw up instructions to their representatives;[49] and on 25 Apr. he supported in the court of aldermen the eligibility of Wilkes to sit in Parliament;[50] on 24 June he was received with acclamation by the livery,[51] when a petition to the Crown on the Middlesex election was brought forward; and on 6 July he was among those presenting it.

On 6 Oct. 1769 Beckford's supporters in the City put forward his name and that of Trecothick for lord mayor,[52] and the court of aldermen, believing his statement that he would not stand, elected him only to find to their indignation, that he withdrew his refusal at the instance of the livery.[53] His second mayoralty, though as splendid as his first, was thus stormy from its beginning, and entirely partisan in its character: the majority of the aldermen refused to attend the mayor's feast; of the Administration only Lord Chancellor Camden was present; the Opposition was there in force.

Beckford, backed by enthusiastic City supporters, enjoyed for the last few months of his life an unusual degree of independence from his leaders in politics. He even tried to force on them his own programme of parliamentary reform, based on the traditional aspirations of the 'country party' but reinforced with the somewhat sharper radicalism rising in the City. He arranged a grand dinner for the Opposition leaders of all parties on 22 Mar. 1770, at which he hoped to get their agreement to a scheme he had drawn up and given to Horne to put into shape. According to Horne, when Rockingham and his friends learnt this, they 'flatly refused any engagement; and Mr. Beckford as flatly swore they should then "eat none of his broth" '; but 'he was prevailed upon by—[Chatham]' to accept the position',[54] Chatham having written to him on the 10th that Rockingham, Temple, and himself were 'equally of opinion that no new matters should be opened or agitated at or after the convivium'.[55]

Apart from these attempts Beckford chiefly occupied himself in following up the City's petition to the Crown of 1769. On 6 Mar. 1770 he carried through the livery a strongly-worded remonstrance against the neglect of their petition,[56] from which the court of aldermen dissociated themselves[57] and which, when presented, called forth a rebuke from the King, and an address of disapprobation from both Houses of Parliament. In the Commons debate on this address Beckford defended himself and the City;[58] and, unabashed, organized a further remonstrance. It was more moderate in expression, but when presenting it on 23 May he took the unprecedented step of haranguing the King on the misdeeds of his ministers.[59] This speech, which called forth praise from both Chatham and Wilkes, marked the climax of Beckford's popularity. How he would have followed it up, and whether he would have been able to maintain his personal ascendancy now that Wilkes (since 18 Apr. 1770) was free and able to assert his influence, it is impossible to say. For Beckford, on 14 June reported ill of a neglected cold, died on 21 June.

His reputation in the City stood so high at his

death that a statue was voted him in Guildhall, inscribed with what was believed to be his speech to the King; and the slightest criticism in the eulogies lavished on him was resented.[60] His death was considered a grave blow to Chatham, and a rumour went round (quite unfounded) that he had 'forced himself into his [Beckford's] house and got away all the letters he had written to that demagogue'.[61] Hints in the press that Beckford had left money to Chatham and Wilkes were equally unfounded. So too was the popular estimate of the fortune he left, though it was large. Statements in the press estimated his son's inheritance at more than £48,000 p.a.;[62] he himself had boasted in 1770 that it would be over £40,000 p.a.;[63] it was in fact about £27,000 p.a.[64]

All his contemporaries agreed in judging Beckford a strange and contradictory character, and his enemies did not fail to point out the contrast between his declamations on liberty in England and his position as a great slave-owner in Jamaica,[65] and the irregularities of his private life (which he boastfully exaggerated) called forth some criticism. Walpole wrote in exasperation after his death: 'The papers make one sick with talking of that noisy vapouring fool, as they would of Algernon Sidney';[66] but his more considered verdict was also unfavourable:

> He had boldness, promptness, spirit, a heap of confused knowledge, displayed with the usual ostentation of his temper, and so uncorrected by judgment that his absurdities were made but more conspicuous by his vanity. Under a jovial style of good humour he was tyrannic in Jamaica . . . and under an appearance of prodigality, interested. On the other side, the excesses of his factious behaviour were founded neither on principle nor on rancour. Vainglory seemed to be the real motive of all his actions.[67]

On the other hand, he sought no private gain in politics, appears genuinely, if naïvely, to have believed in the shibboleths he propounded, and Chatham seems to have valued his support. Some years after his death Chatham told Beckford's son that his father had been 'an individual of great importance in politics, because of his uncommon popularity in the City of London, and the figure he made in the House of Commons', though he added that 'from the warmth of his character he was apt to overshoot himself in council'.[68] His career is of interest because it provides the link between the 'country party' of George II's reign and the radicalism of the City in the 1770s, between Sir John Barnard and John Wilkes.

¹ *London Chron.* 23–26 June 1770. ² See list of landholders in Jamaica 1754, CO142/31 and Add. 12436. ³ See e.g. Dodington, *Diary*, 22 Mar. 1751, and *Gent. Mag.* 1752, p. 89. ⁴ 22 June, *Gent. Mag.* 1752, p. 286. ⁵ 24 June, ibid. ⁶ *Public Advertiser*, 30 Sept. 1762. ⁷ Ibid. 8 May 1754. ⁸ *Bedford Corresp.* ii. 145. ⁹ Namier, 'Country Gentlemen in Parliament', *Personalities and Powers*, 68–71. ¹⁰ George to W. Lyttelton, 9 Dec. 1756, *Lyttelton Mems.* ii. 543; Newcastle to Hardwicke, 26 Jan. 1760, Add. 32901, f. 479. ¹¹ *Public Advertiser*, 25 Apr. 1754. See also Walpole, *Mems. Geo. II*, i. 357. ¹² Harris's 'Debates'. ¹³ 15 Apr. 1769, *Cavendish's Debates*, i. 370. ¹⁴ Dodington, *Diary*, 235–6, 243, 251; *Bedford Corresp.* ii. 127, 135; Walpole, *Mems. Geo. II*, i. 300–301. ¹⁵ *Bedford Corresp.* ii. 150. ¹⁶ Jas. West to Newcastle, Add. 32861, f. 55; see also *Lyttelton Mems.* ii. 543. ¹⁷ *Chatham Corresp.* i. 185–6. ¹⁸ Harris's 'Debates', 12 May 1762. ¹⁹ e.g. Beckford to Pitt, 11 Sept. 1758, *Chatham Corresp.* i. 352 seq.; mem. from M. Dzeganowski which Beckford offered to present, Chatham mss. ²⁰ Chatham mss. See also Walpole, *Mems. Geo. II*, ii. 350. ²¹ Climenson, *Eliz. Montagu*, ii. 127–8. ²² Beckford to Pitt, 5 Mar. [1761], Chatham mss. ²³ S. Fluyder to Kinnoull, 30 Mar. 1761, Add. 32921, f. 190. For Beckford's approach to Bedford, see Bedford mss 43, f. 178. ²⁴ See e.g. T. Birch to Royston, 27 Oct. 1761, *Rockingham Mems.* i. 49. ²⁵ Chatham mss. ²⁶ Narrative in Mrs. Grenville's hand, *Grenville Pprs.* i. 415; Walpole, *Mems. Geo. III*, i. 70. ²⁷ Walpole, *Mems. Geo. III*, i. 153. ²⁸ Newcastle to Hardwicke, 29 Nov.; Yorke, *Hardwicke*, iii. 438. ²⁹ Harris's 'Debates'. ³⁰ T. Walpole to Newcastle, 12 May 1763, Add. 32948, f. 269. ³¹ Repertory Bk. of the court of aldermen, vol. 167, pp. 280 seq. ³² e.g. on 13 Nov. 1762 and 26 Mar. 1763. ³³ *Grenville Pprs.* ii. 158. ³⁴ Harris's 'Debates', 16 Nov. 1763. ³⁵ Townshend to Temple, 3 Oct. 1763, *Grenville Pprs.* ii. 133. ³⁶ See *Chatham Corresp.* ii. 235–6; *Grenville Pprs.* ii. 201–2, 214–18. ³⁷ Grenville Diary, 7 Mar. 1764; ibid. i. 494. ³⁸ Harris's 'Debates'. ³⁹ For a report of his speech, 17 Jan. 1766, see report of debate in T1/446/134 and Harris's 'Debates'. ⁴⁰ Beckford to Pitt, 18 Apr. 1766, Chatham mss; Sackville to Irwin, 25 Apr. 1766, *HMC 9th Rep. pt. 3*, p. 24; Bateson, *Newcastle Letters*, 58–59. ⁴¹ See Sutherland, *E. I. Co. in 18th cent. Politics* ch. vi. ⁴² See Grenville to Temple, 18 Nov. 1766, *Grenville Pprs.* iii. 341–2. ⁴³ *Public Advertiser*, 22 Mar. 1768. ⁴⁴ Beckford to Chatham, 29 Apr. 1767, *Chatham Corresp.* iii. 225. ⁴⁵ *Cavendish's Debates*, i. 241. ⁴⁶ Walpole, *Mems. Geo. III*, iii. 127. ⁴⁷ *Cavendish's Debates*, i. 47 and 228. ⁴⁸ Ibid. 47, 117, 121. ⁴⁹ *Public Advertiser*, 11 Feb. 1769. ⁵⁰ W. P. Treloar, *Wilkes and the City*, 73. ⁵¹ *Rockingham Mems.* ii. 100–1. ⁵² Beckford to Shelburne, 24 Oct. 1769, Lansdowne mss. ⁵³ Common Hall Bk. 8 f. 148 seq. *Cf. Public Advertiser*. ⁵⁴ C. A. Stephens, *Mems. of John Horne Tooke*, i. 388. ⁵⁵ *Chatham Corresp.* iii. 431, n.i. ⁵⁶ *Public Advertiser*, 7–15 Mar. 1770. ⁵⁷ 14 Mar. 1770, ibid. ⁵⁸ 15 Mar. 1770, *Cavendish's Debates*, i. 520. ⁵⁹ The speech was impromptu, but what purported to be versions of it were printed widely in the press (e.g. *Public Advertiser*, 24 May); and some have attempted to deny that it was given at all —but of this there can be no doubt. ⁶⁰ e.g. the recorder's speech on 22 June at the meeting to elect a new mayor, *Public Advertiser*, 23 June 1770. ⁶¹ Walpole, *Mems. Geo. III*, iv. 104–5. ⁶² *London Chron.* 23–26 June 1770. ⁶³ *HMC 2nd Rep.* 25. ⁶⁴ *London Chron.* 1–4 June 1771. ⁶⁵ *Public Advertiser*, 18 Nov. 1769. ⁶⁶ 'To Lord Strafford, 9 July 1770. ⁶⁷ *Mems. Geo. III*, iv. 104. ⁶⁸ Cyrus Redding, *Mems. of Wm. Beckford [junior]* i. 87. Though this book is highly inaccurate on Wm. Beckford sen. this episode would seem to derive from Wm. Beckford jun. and to be worthy of credence.

L.S.S.

**BECKFORD, William** (1760–1844), of Fonthill, Wilts.

WELLS 1784–1790

HINDON 1790–Dec. 1794, 1806–1820

*b.* 29 Sept. 1760, o. legit. s. of William Beckford (q.v.). *educ.* private tutor; Grand Tour 1780–1. *m.* 5 May 1783, Lady Margaret Gordon, da. of Charles, 4th Earl of Aboyne [S], 2da.

On attaining his majority, Beckford was content to leave his parliamentary patronage in the hands of his guardian, Lord Chancellor Thurlow. He had no immediate wish to turn Lloyd Kenyon out of his Hindon seat, and so enter the Commons. 'What use can such a being as me be of in our boisterous Parliament? . . . Age will soon draw on, and the gay texture be shrivelled. Then I will mump, growl, snarl, bite, and be political', he wrote on 30 Aug. 1781.[1] The visit made by Lord Shelburne for his coming-of-age, 'in view of fixing or drawing young

Beckford into his party', was in vain.[2] He regarded politics with detachment, expressed only his loyalty to the King, and spent much of his time on the continent. In a draft letter, 19 Jan. 1784, he commented: 'England is in a glorious uproar. I do nothing but elect and re-elect Mr. Kenyon for Hindon—but feel no vocation to lift up my own voice in the land.'[3] Nevertheless, on 2 Apr. he wrote to Thurlow from Paris:'My health being greatly re-established, I am much inclined to sit in Parliament,' evidently with a view to obtaining a peerage, an 'object' already entrusted to Thurlow.[4] As arrangements had been made to return Edward Bearcroft for Hindon, Beckford came in for Wells (which his maternal grandfather had represented) in place of John Curtis nominated at Saltash, where Beckford was financing the attempt of John Buller jun. to break the Government's hold.[5]

Though it has been stated that Beckford did not take his seat before 1807,[6] there is evidence of earlier attendance: on 6 May 1784 he wrote to his cousin, Louisa Beckford, that he would visit her, 'if I can spare a few days from the joys of the House of Commons'.[7] Yet immediately he was elected, he pressed Thurlow about the peerage;[8] and newspapers already included his name in the list of forthcoming creations,[9] when in October 1784 accusations of homosexual behaviour ruined his prospects. He went abroad in July 1785, returned for two months in January 1787 after his wife's death, and, banished by his family, made a lengthy stay in Portugal and Spain.

In June 1788 the Buller-Beckford candidate for Saltash was seated on petition. This gave control of the borough to Buller, who had agreed with Beckford to let him have the the nomination to one seat during his lifetime.[10] Although Beckford was in England for the last eight months of the Parliament, there is no evidence of his having attended. No speech or vote of his is recorded before 1790. His nominees supported the Administration throughout this period.

He died 2 May 1844.

[1] L. Melville, *Life & Letters of Wm. Beckford*, 119. [2] *Mems. Bentham*, x. 107. [3] G. Chapman, *Beckford* (2nd ed.), 326, But on p. 171 Prof. Chapman gives a different version of the passage: 'I think it will not be long before I lift up my own voice in the land'. [4] J. W. Oliver, *Wm. Beckford*, 194. See also a letter from Thurlow in Melville, 185-7 (dated by Melville 'April 1784', but clearly December 1783). [5] I. R. Christie, 'Private Patronage versus Government Influence', *EHR*, 1056, pp. 249-55. [6] Chapman, 280. [7] *Cat. Autog. Letters Coll. Alfred Morrison* A-B, 189. [8] Thurlow to Beckford, 14 Apr. 1784, Melville, 229. [9] *Morning Intelligencer*, 1 Oct. 1784; *Morning Chron.* 9 Oct. 1784. [10] Christie, 225 n.

M.H.P.

**BELASYSE, Henry,** Lord Belasyse, (1743–1802), of Newburgh Hall, Yorks.

PETERBOROUGH 29 Nov. 1768–8 Feb. 1774

*b.* 13 Apr. 1743, o. surv. s. of Thomas, 1st Earl Fauconberg, by Catherine, da. and h. of John Betham of Rowington, Warws. *educ.* Eton 1757–63. *m.* (1) 29 May 1766, Charlotte (*d.*1 Apr. 1790), da. of Sir Matthew Lamb, 1st Bt. (q.v.), 4da.; (2) 5 Jan. 1791, Jane, da. of John Cheshyre of Bennington, Herts., *s.p. suc.* fa. as 2nd Earl Fauconberg 8 Feb. 1774.

Ld. of the bedchamber 1775–*d.*; ld. lt. N. R. Yorks. 1779–*d.*

Letters from Belasyse to his father before entering Parliament[1] show detachment from party and a high sense of duty. Thus on 24 Dec. 1767, about the Bedfords joining Administration:

> That unanimity and a steady perseverance to the public interest and welfare may appear in the measures of those who are to direct is my sincere wish; the only principle that prevails is self-interest, which evidently appears when a man will disapprove of measures when out of place, which very measures when in place he strongly supports.

On the death of Sir Matthew Lamb, 6 Nov. 1768, the dowager Lady Fitzwilliam (whose son, an old school-fellow of Belasyse, was on the grand tour) offered, from regard to the Lamb family, to return Belasyse for Peterborough free of all expense. His attendance at the House was constant and conscientious—he wrote on 20 Apr. 1769:

> Last Saturday I sat twelve hours in the House of Commons without moving, with which I was well satisfied, as it gave me the power from the various arguments on both sides of determining clearly by my vote my opinion.

And on 22 July 1769:

> The present prospect of home affairs are very disagreeable, wish the time may soon arrive that a great personage's eyes may be opened, and that he may listen to the complaints of his subjects. Then this ferment will subside, as measures will be taken after that in all probability they will restore tranquillity and promote respect.

Belasyse voted with Opposition in the divisions of 27 Jan. and 2 Feb. 1769 over Wilkes's libel, but in the (unreliable) list of 3 Feb. is marked as having voted for Wilkes's expulsion. On 15 Apr. and 8 May he voted with Opposition over the seating of Luttrell. In September he helped to promote the Yorkshire petition for a dissolution of Parliament; was one of the deputation who presented it to the King; and on 9 Jan. 1770 spoke for the first time in the House 'animatedly' in its favour.[2] 'I am so hearty in the cause', he wrote to his father, '. . .that I shall not be satisfied till something is done.'

On the debate on the repeal of the Townshend duties, 5 Mar. 1770, his comment to his father shows him still acting with the Rockinghams over America, critical of governmental half-measures, but basically in favour of coercion:

> *We* wished that the duty on teas . . . should likewise be taken off . . . This the ministry objected to, saying

they would leave that duty to show their power of taxing the colonies . . . As they leave this duty on tea, the bone of contention still continues. *Entre nous* my own private opinion is this, to first establish by proper means our undoubted right of taxing the colonies, and after they have submitted, then take into consideration what duties are necessary to remove, and what necessary to continue. Their behaviour to this country does not demand a mild, submissive treatment, but a firm determined conduct to compel them to obedience.

Henceforth his attitude became more detached. 'I flatter myself that those gentlemen whom I oppose now, will not think that I mean always to oppose them', he said on 15 Mar. 1770.[3] 'If I differ from the ministry I will tell them so in the language of a gentleman. I will tell the Opposition the same.' On Grenville's bill for trying disputed elections he wrote, 31 Mar. 1770: 'Being unwilling to be marked as one either approving or disapproving of the bill by my vote, I left the House before the division.' He praised Burke's speech censuring the conduct of Administration towards America, 7 May 1770, as 'very fine', but added:

After attending several hours to this interesting debate I determined to withdraw without giving my vote, for this reason, that I approved of the questions put by Mr. Burke, but much disapproved the language held in support and favour of the Bostonians by him, which he said was the excuse of these questions.

On 22 Nov. 1770 he supported the motion for papers on the dispute with Spain:[4]

Talked of his being an independent gentleman, without bias, who came to do his duty, but how could he do it, if some information was not given him? . . . After dinner he returned to the House, and, in a second speech said he had changed his mind, that having the papers he thought would be very improper; and therefore voted against having them.

He strongly opposed the royal marriage bill,[5] but in the King's list of the division of 9 Feb. 1773 was classed among the friends of the Government, and on 26 Apr. voted with them on renewal of the Wilkes issue.

As a peer he supported the American war, and in 1779 raised a regiment in Yorkshire for home service.

He died 23 Mar. 1802.

[1] In the possession of Capt. V. M. Wombwell. [2] Cavendish's 'Debates', Egerton 3711, p. 28. [3] Cavendish's 'Debates', Egerton 221, ff. 158–60. [4] Debrett, ix. 16. [5] See his speech of 11 Mar. 1772, Cavendish's 'Debates', Egerton 236, ff. 35–39.

L.B.N.

## BELCHIER, William (*d.*1772), of Epsom, Surr.

### SOUTHWARK    1747–1761

Prob. s. of James Belchier of the Castle Inn, Kingston-upon-Thames, Surr. by his w. Hannah. *m.* (1) 1 Dec. 1736, Jane (*d.* 11 Oct. 1738), da. of Edward Ironside,

banker, *s.p.*; (2) Frances Thomson of Hackthorn, Lincs., *s.p.*

Belchier was a banker in Lombard Street: 1729–56 the firm was Belchier and Ironside, and in 1757 it became Ironside, Belchier, and How. In 1747 he was returned for Southwark after a contest, and was classed by Newcastle as a supporter of Administration. He also cultivated an interest at Winchelsea: he had lent money to John Caryll, a considerable landowner at Winchelsea, on the security of his estates, and in 1754, partly by purchase and partly by foreclosure, was trying to get possession of them.[1] On 16 Mar. 1754 Newcastle noted about Winchelsea: 'Belcher gone down to oppose the election.'[2] But Belchier did not interfere, probably because the conveyance of Caryll's estate had not been completed. He was elected for Southwark, again after a contest, and was classed by Dupplin as against Administration.

His opposition, if it was serious, did not last long: in 1756 he applied through Henry Fox to be made banker to the commissioners for prizes,[3] and in 1760 subscribed £150,000 to the Government loan. This seems to have been mainly on behalf of his clients. According to Bank of England records his own purchases of stock between 1752 and 1760 amounted to about £60,000, which he bought for 'stagging'.

In December 1760 he went bankrupt. To John Caryll on 13 Dec. he wrote:[4] 'Your unkindness in this very long delay in your clearing up the title to the Winchelsea estate has in a great measure been the cause of my ruin'; and complained of the 'cruel, rash, and most outrageous act of my partner who would stop payment yesterday morn and did not give me half an hour's notice of it, nor could I prevail with him to forbear it'. And to Newcastle on 20 Dec.:[5]

The cruel and unexpected turn that has very lately befallen me in my fortune and credit has so far disabled me, that I cannot with honour and integrity appear in the character of a Member of Parliament as yet. I think it incumbent on me to give your Grace the earliest intelligence of my intention to decline being a candidate at the ensuing general election for Southwark . . . I shall be glad to receive your commands to know whom I shall oblige with my interest in that place, which I flatter myself is not inconsiderable.

And again to Newcastle on 17 Sept. 1761:[6]

Since the misfortune brought on me by the most unparalleled treachery of a partner, I would neither be in business or Parliament although I was offered both, until I had accomplished the desirable end of paying everyone his last shilling which I hope ere long to do. At present I have time on my hands and beg leave to tender my best services to your Grace in every assistance I am able, either in forming or the examination of plans for raising the supplies for the ensuing year;

my friends also are desirous and will be ready to subscribe.

Apparently Newcastle did not accept this offer.

In 1765 he resumed business in Lombard Street, but by 1767 he was once more in financial difficulties.[7] Perhaps it was the need to seek immunity from his creditors which led him in 1768 to stand again for Southwark, where he was bottom of the poll. In 1770 his business address is given as 34 Nicholas Lane, and he remained there until his death, 14 Dec. 1772.

[1] See his corresp. with Caryll in Add. 28231–5. [2] Add. 32995, f. 96. [3] Fox to Newcastle, 22 Sept. 1756, Add. 32867, f. 381. [4] Add. 28234, f. 132. [5] Add. 32916, f. 244. [6] Add. 32928, f. 213. [7] Belchier to Caryll, 10 Jan. 1767, Add. 28235, f. 327.

J.B.

## BELGRAVE, Visct., see GROSVENOR, Robert

## BELLINGHAM, William (?1755–1826), of Coleshill, Herts.

REIGATE 1784–Aug. 1789

b. ?1755, 4th s. of Alan Bellingham of Castle Bellingham, co. Louth, by Alice, da. and coh. of Rev. Hans Montgomery of Grey Abbey, co. Louth. educ. Trinity, Dublin, 2 Nov. 1773, aged 18. m. 3 Dec. 1783, Hester Frances, da. of Hon. & Rev. Robert Cholmondeley, gd.-da. of George, 3rd Earl of Cholmondeley, and through her mother a niece of Mrs. Woffington, the actress,[1] s.p. cr. Bt. with sp. rem. to heirs of his fa. 19 Apr. 1796.

Private sec. to William Pitt; commr. of victualling to the navy from 1789; sec. to Board of Ordnance 1807–10; receiver-gen. of land & assessed taxes for London.

Lord Hardwicke wrote to his nephew Philip Yorke (q.v.), 30 Mar. 1784:[2]

Our Reigate election is on Wednesday. But behold a change of scenery; Sir Charles [Cocks] has by Mr. Pitt's means got a peerage, and brings in that gentleman's secretary Mr. *Bellingham* for Reigate.

Bellingham received £125. 10s. from secret service funds for his expenses.[3] In the House he voted steadily with Pitt. No speech of his is reported, but Daniel Pulteney (q.v.) mentions his helping to carry on a long discussion on an adjournment, 7 Feb. 1787, after Sheridan's Begums of Oude speech, to give Pitt time to consider his reply.[4] Bellingham remained closely connected with the Pitt family. Lord Chatham wrote about him to Lord Grenville, 15 Feb. 1806,[5] as 'a very old and dear friend of mine, and very long attached to my poor brother'. A week later Bellingham was train-bearer to Chatham as chief mourner at Pitt's funeral.

He died 27 Oct. 1826.

[1] About her parents see *Farington Diary*, i. 140–1. [2] Add. 35362, f. 44. [3] G. Rose's accounts in Royal archives, Windsor. [4] *HMC Rutland*, iii. 370. [5] *HMC Fortescue*, vii. 32.

L.B.N.

## BENFIELD, Paul (1741–1810), of Wood Hall Park, Watton, Herts.

| | |
|---|---|
| CRICKLADE | 1780–1784 |
| MALMESBURY | 1 Feb. 1790–Feb. 1792 |
| SHAFTESBURY | 26 June 1793–1802 |

bap. 25 Jan. 1741, s. of John Benfield of Cheltenham, carpenter and joiner, by Anne, da. of Rev. Stephen Cull of Cranham, Glos. m. 7 Sept. 1793, Mary Frances, da. of Henry Swinburne, of Hamsterley, co. Durham, author and traveller, 1 da.

Benfield, one of the most notorious of the nabobs who sat in Parliament during this period, went out to India in 1764 as a civil architect at Madras with the rank of lieutenant in the East India Company's army. Five years later he resigned his commission, and became, still in the Company's service, a contractor for building ramparts at Black Town. Next, he began lending money,[1] was twice dismissed the service for disobedience, and twice restored. By 1774 he had become chief banker to the Nawab of the Carnatic, and was on the way to compiling an enormous fortune. The Nawab, after his invasion of the territories of his feudatory the Rajah of Tanjore, borrowed large sums from Benfield on the security of lands in Tanjore, which the Rajah, on being reinstated by Lord Pigot (q.v.) in 1776, refused to honour. 'Benfield's enmity against Lord Pigot is incredible', wrote George Smith to Robert Palk on 20 Sept. 1776.[2] A month later Benfield was threatening Pigot with charges of corruption, and declared 'he would spend one hundred thousand pounds to obtain satisfaction of him'.[3] The plot which resulted in Pigot's kidnapping and deposition as governor of Madras was hatched in Benfield's house. After Pigot's death the court of directors suspended Benfield and ordered him home.

Back in England, Benfield opened his campaign to secure reinstatement by procuring a seat in Parliament. In 1780 he bought John Nesbitt's Cricklade estate, and at the general election stood for the borough with another nabob, John Macpherson (q.v.). By wholesale bribery Benfield and Macpherson carried their election, but Macpherson was unseated and Benfield narrowly escaped being so. He now made up to Administration, and was able to engineer his return to India.

He arrived there in October 1781, and was soon on the worst of terms with the new governor of Madras, Lord Macartney (q.v.).[4] After Macartney's resignation in 1785, and while Macpherson was acting governor-general, Benfield continued his activities undisturbed, but the arrival of Cornwallis ended his Indian career. 'His conduct', wrote Cornwallis to the directors on 6 Nov. 1788,[5] had been 'far more offensive and exceptionable' than that of any other of the Nawab's creditors; and he was suspended from the service and ordered home. Again, on returning to England, his first step was to get himself into Parliament.

Benfield died bankrupt at Paris in April 1810.

¹ About his moneylending, see John Macpherson to Hastings, 27 Sept. 1774, Add. 29135, f. 234. ² *HMC Palk*, 291. ³ Geo. Baker to Palk, 6 Oct. 1776, ibid. 305. ⁴ Wraxall, *Mems.* iv. 92. ⁵ *Cornwallis Corresp.* i. 547.

J.A.C.

## BENNETT, Richard Henry Alexander (?1742–1814), of North Court, Shorwell, I.o.W.

NEWPORT, Cornw.    12 Feb. 1770–1774

*b.* ?1742, o.s. of Bennett Alexander Bennett by Mary, da. of Benjamin Ash of Ongar, Essex. She m. (2) Richard Bull (q.v.). *educ.* Westminster, June 1752, aged 9. *m.* 20 Jan. 1766, Elizabeth Amelia, da. of Peter Burrell II (q.v.), sis. of Sir Peter Burrell, 2nd Bt. (q.v.), 1s. 2da.

Bennett was introduced to Humphry Morice (q.v.), patron of Newport, by his stepfather, Richard Bull, who represented the borough 1756–80. In Parliament Bennett spoke on the Government side in the dispute with the Lords, 13 Dec. 1770; was classed as 'pro, present' in both Robinson's surveys on the royal marriage bill, March 1772; and appears in the King's lists on the naval captains, 9 Feb. 1773, and Grenville's Election Act, 25 Feb. 1774, as a friend voting in opposition. In 1774 Robinson classed him as 'pro'. He did not stand at the general election.

Bennett died 14 Mar. 1814.

M.M.D.

## BENTINCK, Lord Charles Edward (1744–1819).

| | |
|---|---|
| LEWES | 23 Dec. 1766–1768 |
| CARLISLE | 1768–1774 |
| NOTTINGHAMSHIRE | 11 Jan. 1775–1796 |
| CLITHEROE | 1796–1802 |

*b.* 3 Mar. 1744, 2nd s. of William, 2nd Duke of Portland, and bro. of William Henry, Marquess of Titchfield (q.v.). *educ.* Westminster 1754; Ch. Ch. Oxf. 1761; Grand Tour (France, Holland, and Germany) 1764–6. *m.* 28 Dec. 1782, Elizabeth, da. of Richard Cumberland, the dramatist, 2s. 2da.

Nicknamed 'Jolly Heart', Lord Edward Bentinck entered Parliament because he was the brother of a Duke, but had no liking for it. He was returned unopposed at Lewes on the Duke of Newcastle's interest, as a compliment to his brother. Portland soon had reason to complain of his slack attendance. He wrote to Bentinck, 28 Feb. 1767:

> In the midst of my joy last night on the question being carried for a reduction of the land tax, it was no small drawback upon me to recollect that your name was

not among those who had deserved well of their country.

'I have made the resolution', replied Bentinck, 6 Mar., 'of never accepting a seat or ever being in Parliament again.' And he wrote to Beaumont Hotham (q.v.), 16 Mar.:

> You mistake . . . if you think the attendance alone the great cause though it had some share of my saying I would not come into Parliament again. The real cause was of the trouble of coming in, the canvassing and the number of other disagreeable things one is obliged to do to gain admittance into that House.

In 1768 Bentinck fought a hot contest at Carlisle, part of the Portland-Lowther struggle, in which he had his fill of 'disagreeable things'. In November 1768 he went to Paris, and spent most of the next three years there. The struggle with Lowther had left Portland deep in debt, and Bentinck added to the amount. 'I should be infinitely obliged to you', he wrote to Portland on 26 Apr. 1769, 'if you could put me in the way of borrowing three or four thousand pounds, if it is five it will be the more agreeable provided I could have it soon.' And on 15 May, after he had received the money: 'Be assured that I shall live within bounds for the future.' In November 1771 he was short of cash again, and was soon making new resolutions. 'I mean to go to the very bottom of my affairs', he wrote to Portland on 19 Feb. 1772, 'and that if there only remains to me fifty pounds a year I will try to make it serve me.' But in April 1773 he asked Portland for £760 to repay a debt to Sir Charles Bunbury (q.v.), 'who wants it for Newmarket'. In December 1775 George Selwyn (q.v.) reported that Portland had agreed to pay Bentinck's debts, amounting to £27,000.¹

The only votes Bentinck is known to have given in Parliament before 1774 were for the nullum tempus bill, 17 Feb. 1768, and against the Spanish convention, 13 Feb. 1771. He was defeated at Nottingham at the general election of 1774, but in 1775 was returned unopposed for the county. Between 1775 and 1780 he voted with Opposition in seven out of the ten divisions for which lists are available, and was absent for the others; and on 6 Apr. 1780, when presenting the Nottinghamshire petition, made his only recorded speech in Parliament. Following Portland, he voted against Shelburne's peace preliminaries, 18 Feb. 1783, and for Fox's East India bill, 27 Nov. 1783.

A notice of Bentinck in the *English Chronicle* in 1780, inaccurate in fact and unfriendly in tone, concluded:

> In speaking of this nobleman's understanding, we cannot speak more justly, nor more emphatically, than in the words of the following quotation from a play; 'That a little wit goes a great way with a Lord'.

His father-in-law, Richard Cumberland, described him as 'one of the best and most amiable of men', and wrote of his marriage:[2]

> His choice was conspicuously disinterested; for if any thing like worldly wisdom could have found admittance to his generous heart, he might, and must, have sought *fortunam ex aliis*—neither could the lure of affluence and establishment be the motive that induced my child to share the fortunes of Lord Edward Bentinck.

Bentinck died at Brussels 8 Oct. 1819.

[1] Corresp. between Portland and Bentinck, Portland mss; *HMC Carlisle*, 313. [2] *Mems. Rich. Cumberland* (1807), ii. 331.

J.B.

## BENTINCK, Lord George (1715–59), of Hall Place, Heston, Mdx.

DROITWICH          4 Jan. 1742–1747
GRAMPOUND          1747–1754
MALMESBURY         1754–1 Mar. 1759

*b.* 24 Dec. 1715, 2nd s. of Henry, 1st Duke of Portland, by Lady Elizabeth Noel, da. and coh. of Wriothesley Baptist, 2nd Earl of Gainsborough. *educ.* Eton 1725–8. *m.* 29 June 1753, Mary Davies, *s.p.* Ensign 1 Ft. Gds. 1735, capt.-lt. and lt.-col. 1743, col. 1752; col. 5 Ft. 1754–*d.*

Bentinck was a regular Government supporter. In 1754, on Newcastle's recommendation,[1] he was returned for Malmesbury by Henry Fox who had the management of the borough and £1,000 of secret service money for the purpose, part of which 'H.M. need not, but chose to allow the candidates towards the election'.[2] Bentinck died 1 Mar. 1759; and on the 23rd his aunt Lady Sophia Egerton, sister of the 1st Duke of Portland and wife of the bishop of Durham, wrote about Lord George's widow to their Dutch cousin, Count William Bentinck:[3]

> I never heard that Lord George Bentinck had any children by this woman, who after having been quite common about town he took into his keeping, and of late years has married. The Duke and Duchess of Portland would never pretend to credit the match, on which Lord George disgusted, seldom, if ever, visited at the Duke's his brother—and neither he, or his matrimonialised mistress have ever been taken notice of in the family. It is reported that Lord George's grief on this account contributed as much, if not more, to his death than the gout, and that he has left £40,000 (the whole of his fortune) to the present Lady George Bentinck.

She married within four months on 24 June 1759.[4]

[1] Add. 32999, f. 119. [2] Fox to the Duke of Devonshire, 1 June 1758, Devonshire ms 330.225. But Newcastle's notes of 20 Mar. 1754, Add. 32995, f. 104, contain the entry: 'Lord George Bentinck £1,500.' It is not clear whether this is the entire cost or his contribution. See Namier, *Structure*, 444, n. 4. [3] Egerton 1719, f. 34. [4] *Gent. Mag.* 1759, p. 293.

L.B.N.

## BENTINCK, John Albert (1737–75), of Terrington St. Clement, Norf.

RYE    1761–1768

*b.* 29 Dec. 1737, 2nd s. of Count William Bentinck by Charlotte Sophia, da. and h. of Anthony II, Count of Aldenburg. *m.* 17 July 1763, Renira, da. of John, Baron de Tuyll de Serooskerken, 2s. 3da. Lt. R.N. 1757; cdr. May 1758; capt. Oct. 1758.

Bentinck's father, a count of the Holy Roman Empire, was a son of Hans William, 1st Earl of Portland; and though he owned property in England, he lived mostly in Holland, where he was politically prominent as leader of the pro-British party. John Bentinck entered the navy about 1752; distinguished himself in 1758 in an engagement with the French; took part in the expedition against St. Malo; and in 1759, as captain of a frigate, captured three French ships.

His father wrote to the Duke of Newcastle from The Hague, 27 May 1760:[1]

> I should reckon it a great honour, as well as a great advantage to him, if he could be elected for the next ensuing Parliament under your Grace's favour and protection. I will answer for his gratefulness.

Newcastle replied, 6 June 1760, that he would 'take care that Mr. Bentinck shall be chose at some sure and reasonable place'.[2] He named Bentinck for Rye, a Treasury borough where expenses were negligible but where preference was usually given to men with local connexions prepared to exert themselves on behalf of their constituents. Still, as Newcastle promised to assist Bentinck 'in his attention to the interest of the town and every member of it', his candidature was 'unanimously agreed to'.[3]

During the first two sessions of the new Parliament, Bentinck was probably away most of the time on active service. When on 6 June 1763 Sandwich, then at the Admiralty, offered Count Bentinck (with whom he had worked at the conference of Aix-la-Chapelle in 1748) a guardship for his son, the Count welcomed the chance of a post which in peace time would enable Bentinck to continue in the service and yet attend Parliament.[4] In further correspondence there seems to have been a good deal of sparring, Sandwich trying to pin down Bentinck politically, and the Count trying to evade the issue by saying that he could not undertake to answer for his son, 'much less to direct him in the detail of his conduct'.[5] But, he wrote on 7 Oct. 1763,[6]

> I am very much mistaken if he flings himself headlong into any party which would be equally contrary to his honour and to common prudence. I am sure your Lordship will find him perfectly disposed to give the attention due to what may be imparted to him by you . . . neither I nor my son will ever appear in the list of your enemies.

In fact, however, Bentinck had, early in September, connected himself with the Opposition,[7] and, to Sandwich's annoyance, joined them on his return to England in November.[8] He voted with them in the divisions over Wilkes and general warrants; was classed by Newcastle, 10 May 1764, as a 'sure friend'; and belonged to Wildman's Club. On 6 Mar. 1765 he made his only recorded speech in the House, in a debate on the proposals for discovering longitude at sea.[9]

On 9 Jan. 1765 Count Bentinck wrote to Newcastle from The Hague:[10]

This letter will be delivered to your Grace by my son, who has made me a visit . . . that he may receive from me the information necessary for his conduct . . . Resolved, as he is, to follow principally his profession, and making himself a point of duty and honour of keeping clear of all imputation or suspicion of feeling in point of gratefulness towards his protectors . . . he has hitherto made no use of, nor accepted, the advantages offered to him in his profession, fearing that his absence might be misinterpreted, notwithstanding those offers were made without any condition . . . Pray, my Lord, tell my son clearly and plainly whether his presence is absolutely necessary, and if his vote can be of any use to his friends. And if not, I believe your Grace will be enough his friend and mine to advise him to follow his profession and not to remain idle at his time of life, rather than plunge himself into another sort of affairs in which he can never satisfy himself nor be of any use to his friends.

Newcastle replied on 28 Feb.:[11]

Your son . . . is beloved, esteemed, and greatly commended by those who are at the head of his profession . . . There are few commands in time of peace that can be of service to him, and those few are, and must be, always given to older officers; and the commander of a guardship in time of peace can by no means be in view to Captain Bentinck. I therefore most sincerely concur in opinion with the Duke of Portland that it is by no means worth his while to think of it.

Bentinck supported the Rockingham Administration, by whom he was appointed to the command of a ship; and subsequently went with Rockingham into opposition. In a memorandum to Portland of 11 July 1767[12] he asked for a place of business at the Admiralty should Rockingham's negotiations for a new Administration be successful.

He did not take much interest in his Rye electors; 'he has never been here since his election, at which the freemen are not a little angry', wrote on 16 Aug. 1763 Thomas Lamb,[13] the Treasury manager at Rye, who adhered to Newcastle even after his resignation. In the much more difficult circumstances of 1768, Newcastle could not risk putting Bentinck up again, nor could he find another constituency for him. Meantime Portland had been induced, at considerable expense, to contest Callington, where he

had no 'natural' interest of his own; and his candidates were Bentinck and David Hartley (q.v.), both complete strangers to the borough. They were defeated, and Bentinck does not seem to have stood again for Parliament.

Bentinck continued in the navy. He is described in the *DNB* as having 'great ingenuity in mechanical pursuits', and is stated to have made some notable improvements in ships' pumps.

He died 23 Sept. 1775.

[1] Add. 32906, ff. 307–8. [2] Add. 32907, f. 28. [3] Mayor of Rye to Newcastle, 25 Mar. 1761, Add. 32921, f. 53. [4] Count Bentinck to Sandwich, 14 June 1763, Sandwich mss. [5] Same to same, 15 Sept. 1763, ibid. [6] Ibid. [7] Add. 32950, f. 315. [8] Greffier Fagel to Sandwich, Dec. 1763, Sandwich mss. [9] Harris's 'Debates'. [10] Add. 32965, ff. 107–8. [11] Ibid. ff. 406–7. [12] Portland mss. [13] Add. 32950, f. 148.

L.B.N.

**BENTINCK, William Henry Cavendish,** Mq. of Titchfield (1738–1809).

WEOBLEY 1761–1 May 1762

*b.* 14 Apr. 1738, 1st s. of William, 2nd Duke of Portland, by Lady Margaret Cavendish Harley, da. and h. of Edward, 2nd Earl of Oxford. *educ.* Westminster 1747–54; Ch. Ch. Oxf. 1755; Grand Tour (Poland, Germany, Italy) 1757–61. *m.* 8 Nov. 1766, Lady Dorothy Cavendish, da. of William, 4th Duke of Devonshire, 4s. 2da. *suc.* fa. as 3rd Duke 1 May 1762; K.G. 16 July 1794.

P.C. 10 July 1765; ld. chamberlain, July 1765–Dec. 1766; ld. lt. [I], Apr.–Aug. 1782; first ld. of Treasury, Apr.–Dec. 1783; Home sec. July 1794–July 1801; ld. president July 1801–Jan. 1805; first ld. of Treasury Mar. 1807–Oct. 1809.

Ld. lt. Notts. 1795–*d.*

'The Marquis of Titchfield', wrote Mrs. Delany to Mrs. Dewes, 16 Dec. 1757,[1] 'set out on Monday with Mr. Keith,[2] who is going as envoy to Russia'; he went via Hamburg to Warsaw, where he remained for over a year with Lord Stormont, envoy to Poland. In 1759–60 he travelled with Benjamin Langlois (q.v.) through Germany to Italy, spent a year in Turin, and then proceeded to Florence. 'Three and a half years I think a very long absence', wrote the Duchess of Portland on 15 June 1761;[3] in addition, Titchfield was spending more money than the family could afford.[4] On 17 Oct. 1761 Horace Mann wrote from Florence to Horace Walpole: 'Lord Titchfield leaves this place in a few days on his return home, without seeing Rome, so pressing are the Duke of Portland's entreaties to him.'

Titchfield in his absence had been returned for Weobley by his brother-in-law, Lord Weymouth. His career in the Commons was short and uneventful, and no vote or speech by him is recorded. As a peer he was a prominent member of the Rockingham group, close to Rockingham (who liked and trusted him), but by himself of no weight in the House.

For a Duke he was not rich, and both he and his

brother were extravagant. A document drawn up at the time of his marriage[5] shows that his estates (which were heavily mortgaged) brought in just over £9000 p.a.; from which had to be deducted a rent charge of £1600 p.a. to the dowager Duchess. Lady Dorothy Cavendish brought him £30,000. On the death of his mother in 1785 he inherited the Cavendish estates in Derbyshire and Nottingham-shire, estimated to be worth £12,000 p.a.[6]

The 2nd Duke of Portland had no electoral influence; the 3rd Duke showed a turn for elec-tioneering and made a success of it. In 1765 he captured Wigan; and in 1768, in the great fight with Sir James Lowther (q.v.), won both seats for Cumberland and Carlisle. He was at first ready to take risks (and also liable to be imposed upon),[7] but as he grew older became more cautious. By 1784 he had withdrawn from Carlisle and lost much of his influence at Wigan; while his position in Cumber-land was due to his being the leader of the anti-Lowther party rather than to his own interest.

On Rockingham's death he became the titular leader of the party. But Charles James Fox was the real driving force, and Portland would not have become head of the Coalition ministry had he not been content to be led by Fox. In 1794, strongly pressed by Burke and Windham and after much dithering, he led the bulk of his followers over to Pitt, protesting to the last that he remained a Whig.

He died 30 Oct. 1809.

[1] *Autobiog & Corresp. Mrs. Delany* (ser. 1), iii. 472. [2] Robert Murray Keith (q.v.). [3] To Wm. Bentinck, Egerton 1722, f. 181. [4] See letters quoted in A. S. Turberville, *Welbeck Abbey*, ii. 38–40. [5] Portland mss. [6] Walpole to Mann, 25 July 1785. [7] For Portland's unsuccessful electioneering, see CALLINGTON and COVENTRY constituencies.

J.B.

## BENYON, Richard (1746–96), of Gidea Hall, Essex.

PETERBOROUGH    16 Feb. 1774–22 Aug. 1796

*b.* 28 June 1746, o.s. of Richard Benyon, gov. of Fort St. George, by his 3rd w. Mary, da. of Francis Tyssen of Hackney, wid. of Powlett Wrighte of Englefield, Berks. *educ.* Eton 1759–62. *m.* 3 Sept. 1767, Hannah, da. of Sir Edward Hulse, 1st Bt., 3s. 3da. *suc.* fa. 27 Sept. 1774.

Benyon was a friend and contemporary at Eton of Lord Fitzwilliam, was returned on his interest at Peterborough, and followed him in politics. 'A well-meaning honest man', wrote the *Public Ledger* in 1779. He supported North, supported the Coalition, and opposed Pitt. There is no record of his having spoken in the House.

He died 22 Aug. 1796, leaving estates in Essex and Berkshire worth £8000 p.a.[1]

[1] *Gent. Mag.* 1797, p. 791.

J.B.

## BERKELEY, Hon. George Cranfield (1753–1818).

GLOUCESTERSHIRE    28 Apr. 1783–May 1810

*b.* 10 Aug. 1753, 3rd s. of Augustus, 4th Earl of Berkeley, by Elizabeth, da. of Henry Drax (q.v.) of Charborough, Dorset. *educ.* Eton 1761–6. *m.* 23 Aug. 1784, Emily Charlotte, da. of Lord George Lennox (q.v.), 2s. 3da. K.B. 1 Feb. 1813.

Entered R.N. 1766; lt. 1774; cdr. 1778; capt. 1780; r.-adm. 1799; v-adm. 1805; adm. 1810.

Surveyor gen. of the Ordnance 1789–95.

In December 1774 Berkeley was a candidate at Cricklade, but withdrew the day before the poll. In 1776 he contested Gloucestershire against W. B. Chester, who stood on the Beaufort interest; and after a very expensive campaign was narrowly defeated. At a by-election in 1783 he was returned unopposed.

Berkeley's first recorded vote was for parliamen-tary reform, 7 Apr. 1783. On 13 Oct. he replied to Fox's request to attend the forthcoming session of Parliament:[1] 'I . . . can assure you that I feel some satisfaction in giving my attendance in the House whenever *yourself* and the Whig interest demand it.' But he did not vote on Fox's East India bill. Robinson in January 1784 classed him as 'doubtful', and he was a member of the St. Alban's Tavern group which tried to unite Fox and Pitt. After their failure, Berkeley supported Pitt. There is no record before 1790 of his having spoken in the House.

He died 25 Feb. 1818.

[1] Add. 47568, f. 194.

J.B.

## BERKELEY, Norborne (?1717–70), of Stoke Gifford, Glos.

GLOUCESTERSHIRE    1741–Apr. 1763

*b.* ?1717, o.s. of John Symes Berkeley of Stoke Gifford, Glos. by Elizabeth, da. and coh. of Walter Norborne of Calne, Wilts., wid. of Edward Devereux, 8th Visct. Hereford. His sis. m. Charles Noel, 4th Duke of Beaufort, and he became guardian to the 5th Duke in 1756. *educ.* Westminster 1726 (aged 9)—1727. *unm.* Confirmed to barony of Botetourt 13 Apr. 1764.

Groom of the bedchamber 1760–4; lord of the bed-chamber 1767–*d.*; ld. lt. Glos. 1762–6; gov. Virginia 1768–*d.*

Berkeley was returned unopposed in 1754 and again in 1761. He was classed as a Tory in Dupplin's list of 1754, but on 31 May 1759 he seconded an address moved by Pitt.[1] In December 1760 Berkeley was one of the five Tories whose introduction into the bedchamber greatly upset Newcastle.[2] In Bute's list of December 1761 he was classed as 'Tory' and 'Bute'; and he appears in Fox's list of Members favourable to the peace preliminaries, December 1762. He was described in Grafton's *Autobiography*

(p. 184) as 'much attached to Lord Bute, and considered to be wholly devoted to his Majesty'. James Harris writes that Berkeley, supporting the cider bill, 22 Mar. 1762, told the House of his own independency—'that he had been for the jew-bill, and avowed it to his constituents, though the year before a general election—signified to us *now*, however, that he expected a seat among the peers'. In April 1763 he vacated his seat; claimed the Botetourt peerage which had been in abeyance for 250 years, and the following year established his claim.

In 1768 Botetourt was appointed governor of Virginia. Horace Walpole writes:[3]

Lord Botetourt, a very courtier, who was ruined in his fortune, was sent governor to Virginia, where resided some of the ablest of the American patriots; yet in the two years that he lived to govern them his soothing flattering manners had so wrought on the province, that his death was bewailed with the most general and affectionate concern.

He died 15 Oct. 1770.

[1] *Bedford Corresp.* ii. 383. [2] Newcastle to J. Yorke, 5 Dec. 1760 Add 32915, f. 308. [3] *Mems. Geo. III*, iv. 156.

M.M.D.

**BERKELEY, Rowland** (?1733–1805), of Cotheridge, nr. Worcester.

DROITWICH    31 May–30 Sept. 1774

*b.* ?1733, 1st s. of Rowland Berkeley of Cotheridge by Lucy, da. of Anthony Lechmere of Severn End, Worcs. *educ.* New Coll., Oxf. 29 Oct. 1750, aged 17. *m.* 28 June 1768, Sarah Carbonnel of Hampstead, *s.p. suc.* fa. 1759.
Sheriff, Worcs. 1764–5.

Berkeley was returned as a stop-gap on the Foley interest at Droitwich, and sat in Parliament for little more than a fortnight. No vote or speech by him is recorded. He died 1805.

J.B.

**BERNARD, Robert** (?1739–89), of Brampton, Hunts.

HUNTINGDONSHIRE    28 Dec. 1765–1768
WESTMINSTER    30 Apr. 1770–1774

*b.* ?1739, o.s. of Sir John Bernard, 4th Bt., of Brampton by Mary, da. and coh. of Sir Francis St. John, 1st Bt., of Longthorpe, Northants. *educ.* Westminster; Ch. Ch. Oxf. 10 May 1758, aged 18. *unm. suc.* fa. as 5th Bt. 15 Dec. 1766.
Recorder, Bedford 1771–*d.*

The Bernards were an old Huntingdonshire family, and in the 17th century had sat for Huntingdon. Sir Robert Bernard alone represented the county.

At the general election of 1761 the Duke of Manchester and Lord Sandwich agreed for the duration of that Parliament each to recommend one Member for the county; and on the retirement of Lord Charles Greville Montagu in 1765 Bernard was returned unopposed as Manchester's candidate. No vote or speech by him is recorded between 1765 and 1768; he was classed by Rockingham November 1766, as 'doubtful', by Townshend, January 1767 as 'country gentleman', and by Newcastle, March 1767, as 'Tory'. Probably he supported both the Rockingham and Chatham Administrations. Sandwich wrote to Newcastle, 29 Sept. 1767, that Bernard was 'in close connexion with Lord Shelburne',[1] but there is no correspondence from him in Shelburne's papers at Bowood.

In November 1766 Manchester and Bernard quarrelled,[2] and at the general election of 1768 Bernard stood against candidates supported by both Manchester and Sandwich. 'The Duke of Manchester intends writing to Sir Robert', wrote Lord Ludlow (q.v.) to Sandwich, 25 Mar. 1767,[3] 'to say that he is convinced his standing can answer no other end but that of making a disturbance in the county.' But Bernard persisted. 'Sir Robert . . . says', wrote Lady Sarah Osborn to her nephew, John, 29 Sept. 1767,[4] 'he has £45,000 in his banker's hands, and will spend it all in opposition to Hinchingbrooke and Carysfort for county Huntingdon'; and Manchester to Rockingham, 6 Dec. 1767:[5] 'His agents promise everything, land, money, places, and throw away sums without use or discretion.' Sandwich and Manchester rated him a formidable opponent, and were assiduous in their canvassing. Bernard obtained 666 votes, and was 138 behind his nearest opponent.

In 1769 Bernard helped to found the Bill of Rights Society, and henceforth belonged to the radical movement. In 1770, sponsored by Wilkes, he became a candidate for Westminster; the radical party in the city agreed to bear the expense of the election; and Bernard was returned unopposed. His only recorded speech (11 Mar. 1773, on a bill to restrain stock jobbing), was commonplace. In 1771 he voted for the dissolution of the Bill of Rights Society, joined the rival Constitutional Society, and broke with Wilkes. Hence in 1774 he was dropped by the Westminster radicals, nor is he known to have contested any other constituency.

In 1769 he had intervened at Bedford against the Duke of Bedford and had secured control of the corporation. In 1774 a candidate in his interest contested the borough, and another was elected in 1780 and 1784.[6] In Huntingdonshire he led the reform movement, closely associated with the 2nd Lord

Carysfort (q.v.), and was chairman of the Huntingdonshire Association of 1780. 'He was a warm supporter of the attempt . . . to procure an equal representation of the people in Parliament', wrote an obituary;[7] but 'violent attacks of the gout' compelled him to retire from politics.

He died 2 Jan. 1789.

[1] Add. 32985, ff. 270–1. [2] Sandwich to Gower, 14 Nov. 1766, PRO, Granville mss. [3] Sandwich mss. [4] *Social & Pol. Letters of Lady of 18th Cent.* ed. Osborn, 174. [5] Rockingham mss. [6] See BEDFORD constituency. [7] *Gent. Mag.* 1789, p. 88.

J.B.

**BERNARD, Scrope** (1758–1830), of Lower Winchendon, Bucks.

AYLESBURY        16 Feb. 1789–1802
ST. MAWES        1806–Apr. 1808, 28 Feb. 1809–18 Apr. 1830

*b.* 1 Oct. 1758, 3rd s. of Sir Francis Bernard, 1st Bt., gov. of Massachusetts Bay 1760–71, by Amelia, da. of Stephen Offley of Norton Hall, Derbys. *educ.* Harrow 1774–5; Ch. Ch. Oxf. 1775–81. *m.* 26 July 1785, Hannah, da. and h. of William Morland, M.P., of Lee, Kent, banker, 5s. 2da. *suc.* bro. as 4th Bt. 1 July 1818. Took add. name of Morland 1811.

Private sec. to ld. lt. [I] Sept. 1782–Apr. 1783 and 1787–9; usher of the black rod [I] 1787–9; under-sec. of state for Home affairs 1789–92; adv. Doctors' Commons 1789; judge of episcopal court of Durham 1795–*d.*

At Oxford, Bernard formed a close friendship with W. W. Grenville (q.v.), brother of Lord Temple, which was the foundation of his political career. He had intended to study medicine, but accepted Temple's offer to become his private secretary when he was appointed lord lieutenant of Ireland. After returning to England, he made two visits to France. In 1784 he canvassed Lincoln, where his family had an estate. Next Pitt, through Grenville, offered Bernard the secretaryship of a commission on public offices, on which he served 1785–6.

In 1787 he again served as private secretary to Lord Buckingham (as Temple now was) for his second viceroyalty; it had, however, been agreed with Buckingham that he should stand for Aylesbury when opportunity offered, and he successfully contested the borough in February 1789. In Ireland when the result was announced, he wrote: 'I think I ought to behave in the handsomest manner both in regard to personal attendance and expense to the borough as well as with a view to my next election, as for the general benefit of the party in that quarter.'[1] He proposed to spend £5,000 (of which Lord Buckingham was to provide £1,000) to consolidate his position.

After returning to England he accepted for

financial reasons an under-secretaryship at the Home Office under Grenville, though this kept him more in London than he wished. He spoke, 23 Apr. 1790, against the proposal to lay before the House part of the report of the commission on public offices.[2]

He died 18 Apr. 1830.

[1] *HMC Fortescue*, i. 417. [2] Debrett, xxvii. 484.

M.H.P.

**BERTIE, Lord Brownlow** (1729–1809), of Grimsthorpe and Swineshead, Lincs.

LINCOLNSHIRE        1761–8 July 1779

*b.* 1 May 1729, 3rd s. of Peregrine, 2nd Duke of Ancaster, by Jane, da. and coh. of Sir John Brownlow, 3rd Bt., M.P., of Humby, Lincs. His sis. m. Samuel Greatheed (q.v.). *educ.* Westminster 1743–6. *m.* (1) 11 Nov. 1762, Harriet (*d.*Apr. 1763), da. and h. of George Morton Pitt, M.P., gov. of Fort St. George, India, *s.p.*; (2) 2 Jan. 1769, Mary Anne, da. of Maj. Peter Layard of Canterbury, 1 da. *suc.* nephew as 5th Duke of Ancaster 8 July 1779.

P.C. 12 Feb. 1779; ld. lt. Lincs. 1779–*d.*

Bertie's name was listed by Dupplin in 1754 among 'Persons desirous to be brought into Parliament';[1] and the possibility of his standing for Coventry was discussed[2] but there is no evidence of his having stood anywhere at that general election. Nominated in 1761 for Lincolnshire by his brother, the Duke of Ancaster, Bertie was the first member of his family to stand for the county since their defeats of 1715 and 1720.[3] Ancaster seems to have been hesitant about putting him forward, but though an opposition was threatened it did not go to the poll, and he was returned unopposed. In December 1762 he was counted as a Government supporter in Henry Fox's list of Members favourable to the peace preliminaries, and by Jenkinson in the autumn of 1763. His only known vote in opposition was against the repeal of the Stamp Act, 22 Feb. 1766; he appears as a supporter of Administration in Townshend's and Newcastle's lists of 1767. In 1779 the *Public Ledger* wrote of him: 'though inclined to the ministry, he frequently quits the House when their questions are not such as he can vote for agreeable to his own feelings'. No speech by him is recorded.

He died 8 Feb. 1809.

[1] Add. 32995, f. 122. [2] See Lord Archer to Henry Pelham, 11 June 1753, Newcastle (Clumber) Pprs. [3] See LINCOLNSHIRE.

M.M.D.

**BERTIE, Peregrine** (1723–86), of Leyton, Essex.

WESTBURY        16 Jan. 1753–1774

*b.* 1723, 1st s. of Peregrine Bertie of Leyton by Elizabeth, da. of John Hungerford, of Doctors' Commons,

wid. of John Fisher of London, merchant. *educ.*
Magdalen, Oxf. 12 Dec. 1740, aged 17; M. Temple
1740, called 1745. *m.* (1) 17 Oct. 1753, Catherine
(*d.*2 July 1770), da. of Richard Backwell (q.v.) of
Great Billing, Northants., 2s. 4da.; (2) 16 Sept. 1771,
Elizabeth, da. of Joshua Peart of Lincoln, *s.p.   suc.*
fa. 9 Dec. 1743.

In 1753, and at all his subsequent elections,
Bertie was returned unopposed for Westbury on the
interest of his distant cousin Lord Abingdon. He
was generally described as a Tory, and is never once
known to have voted with Administration. His first
recorded vote was over general warrants, 15 Feb.
1764, and on 10 May 1764 Newcastle classed him as
a 'sure friend'. But Rockingham, July 1765, classed
him as 'doubtful', and he voted against the repeal of
the Stamp Act, 22 Feb. 1766. He voted against the
Chatham Administration on the land tax, 27 Feb.
1767, and the nullum tempus bill, 17 Feb. 1768;
and in the Parliament of 1768 appears in four out of
13 divisions always voting with Opposition. There
is no record of his having spoken in the House. He
did not stand in 1774.

He died 28 Dec. 1786, aged 63.

M.M.D.

## BERTIE, Hon. Peregrine (1741-90), of Weston-on-the-Green, Oxon.

OXFORD   1774-20 Aug. 1790

*b.* 13 Mar. 1741, 3rd s. of Willoughby, 3rd Earl of
Abingdon, by Anna Maria, da. of Sir John Collins.
*educ.* Westminster 1750. *m.* May 1790, Miss Hutchins
of Yattendon, Berks., *s.p.*
Lt. R.N. 1759; cdr. 1762; capt. 1762.

Bertie sat for Oxford on the family interest.
'Votes in opposition', wrote the *English Chronicle* in
1780, 'when he is brought to attend, which is but
very seldom'; and Robinson in his survey for the
general election of 1780: 'He is constantly against
and not a good attender.' He voted in only five out
of the twelve divisions 1774-80 for which lists are
extant, and in three out of the six between December
1781 and the fall of North—each time with Opposition. His brother Lord Abingdon, a strong supporter
of Shelburne's Administration, undertook to bring
up Bertie for the division on the peace preliminaries;[1] and on 18 Feb. 1783 Bertie voted with
Government. He did not vote on Fox's East India
bill.

Abingdon was a supporter of Pitt, and Bertie is so
classed in the lists compiled by Stockdale and
William Adam before and after the general election
of 1784. But his name appears in no division list
until that of the Regency. On 29 Apr. 1788 he made
his only recorded speech in the House, against
Administration on Bastard's motion on the promo-

tion of naval officers. And on the Regency he voted
with Opposition, although Abingdon remained faithful to Pitt.

Bertie died 20 Aug. 1790.

[1] Abingdon to Shelburne, 13 Feb. 1783, Lansdowne mss.

J.B.

## BERTIE, Lord Robert (1721-82), of Chislehurst, Kent.

WHITCHURCH   21 Nov. 1751-1754
BOSTON                    1754-10 Mar. 1782

*b.* 14 Nov. 1721, 5th[1] s. of Thomas, 1st Duke of
Ancaster, by his 2nd w. Albinia, da. of Maj.-Gen.
William Farrington of Chislehurst, Kent, and aunt of
G. A. Selwyn (q.v.). *educ.* Eton 1728. *m.* 5 Apr. 1762,
Mary Chetwynd, da. and coh. of Montagu, 1st Visct.
Blundell [I], wid. of Robert, 2nd Lord Raymond, *s.p.*
Ensign 2 Ft. Gds. 1737, lt. 1741, capt. 1744, col.
1752; col. 7 Ft. 1754-76; maj.-gen. 1758; lt.-gen.
1760; col. 2 Horse Gds. 1776-*d.*; gen. 1777.
Ld. of bedchamber to George III as Prince of Wales
and King 1751-*d.*; gov. Cork 1762-8, Duncannon
1768-*d.*

Returned in 1751 for Whitchurch on the Selwyn
interest, in 1754 Bertie was returned unopposed on
the Ancaster interest at Boston, and was classed
'for' by Dupplin.

He served at Gibraltar in 1756, and at Byng's
trial testified in his favour. On 28 Apr. 1757 he made
his only recorded speech in the House, declaring
that the ten ships under Byng were not fully manned
or provided with the necessary stores, and 'insisting
there was not a fire ship, tender, or hospital ship
with the fleet'.[2]

Bertie seems to have been uncertain about his
position at Boston, and on 21 July 1760 pressed
Newcastle for an office for one of his constituents
because 'the contest that I have at Boston makes it
very essential to my interest to oblige this gentleman in this particular affair'.[3] And on 1 Oct. 1760
it was reported that 'hot work is begun at Boston',
but Bertie was returned unopposed in 1761.

In December 1762 he was counted by Fox among
those favourable to the peace preliminaries, and in
the autumn of 1763 was classed as 'pro' by Jenkinson. But in a list of Members drawn up 15 Feb.
1764 by Augustus Hervey (q.v.) is the remark: 'is a
doubt if he stayed it out'.[4] In Rockingham's list
of July 1765 Bertie appears as 'pro', but he voted
against the repeal of the Stamp Act, 7 and 22 Feb.
1766, and in Rockingham's list of November 1766
is classed 'Bute'. He voted with the Government
on the land tax, 27 Feb. 1767, and nullum tempus,
17 Feb. 1768; and was listed by Newcastle and
Townshend as a Government supporter. This he
remained under North, but in the Parliament of

1768–74 he appears in only two out of seven division lists, and in none after February 1774. 'Lord Robert Bertie', wrote Mary Townshend to George Selwyn, 17 May 1779, '. . . has lately had an attack of St. Anthony's-fire in his leg, and he hurt himself whilst being reviewed at the head of his troop . . . the fatigue was too great for one who had been so long an invalid.'[5]

When in 1780 he had to stand a contest at Boston, he topped the poll. But again he was absent from all, even the most critical, divisions. On 28 May 1781 George Selwyn wrote to Lord Carlisle: 'Lord Robert Bertie is again relapsed as I hear, and if so will probably last but a very little time.'[6]

He died 10 Mar. 1782.

[1] Burke, *Peerage* (1931), Collins, *Peerage* gives 3rd s. [2] Jas. West to Newcastle, Add. 35877, f. 365. [3] Add. 32908, f. 406. [4] Grenville mss (JM). [5] Jesse, *Selwyn*, iv. 137. [6] HMC Carlisle, 487.

M.M.D.

## BEST, Thomas (?1713–95), of Chilston Park, Kent.

### CANTERBURY 1741–1754, 1761–1768

*b.* ?1713, 1st s. of Mawdistly Best by his w. Elizabeth Fearne. *educ.* Univ. Coll. Oxf. 8 June 1732, aged 18. *m.* 3 Jan. 1743, Caroline, da. of George Scot of Scot's Hall, Kent, *s.p.* *suc.* fa. 1744.

Lt. gov. Dover and dep. warden of Cinque Ports 1762–95.

Best, 'a man of fortune'[1] connected with many of the leading families in Kent, sought re-election for Canterbury at the general election of 1754, but withdrew before the poll. He told his uncle, Admiral Vernon (q.v.), 24 May 1754, that he would not have had to withdraw if his friends had 'declared themselves as much before the election as they have done since, however, I have the satisfaction to think I have saved my money'.[2] In 1761 he stood on a joint interest with Richard Milles (q.v.) in opposition to Newcastle's candidate, James Creed, and to William Mayne (qq.v.), who was backed by Bute. On 16 Mar. 1761, ten days before the poll, the archbishop of Canterbury wrote to Newcastle:[3]

Mr. Best . . . made me a visit this morning; and without asking for my interest, which he appeared sensible ought to be given the other side, earnestly desired me to assure your Grace in his name, that if he was chosen he would not enter into opposition, or put himself on a party footing, but concur with the Administration in everything, as far as he honestly could.

Best was returned second on the poll. In Bute's list of December 1761 he was classed as 'Tory' and 'Bute' with the note: 'Brother-in-law to Mr. Scot of the Princess's family',[4] and he appears in Henry Fox's list (December 1762) of Members favourable to the peace preliminaries. He was classed as 'doubtful' by Jenkinson in the autumn of 1763, and by Rockingham in his lists of July 1765 and Novem-

ber 1766. Best appears in two out of the three lists on the land tax, 27 Feb. 1767, as voting with Opposition, but does not appear in a third list; he was counted by Newcastle in March 1767 as 'Tory', and voted with Administration on nullum tempus, 17 Feb. 1768. He is not known to have spoken during this Parliament.

Before the general election of 1768 Charles Yorke feared that Best would stand against Sir Joseph Yorke at Dover,[5] but he once more contested Canterbury and was defeated. Best was included by North among a few 'very pressing' people still without seats on 5 Oct. 1774, and was put down as one of several possible candidates at Tregony; this was to have cost him £2,000,[6] but in the end he did not stand, and seems to have made no further attempt to re-enter Parliament.

He died 26 Mar. 1795.

[1] E. Climenson, *Eliz. Montagu*, i. 121. [2] Add. 40776, f. 152. [3] Add. 32920, f. 253. [4] G. L. Scott, who had been sub preceptor to Geo. III. [5] Add. 35385, ff. 196–9. [6] Laprade, 24, 35.

M.M.D.

## BETHELL, Hugh (1727–72), of Rise and Watton Abbey, Yorks.

### BEVERLEY 1768–8 May 1772

*b.* 17 Nov. 1727, 1st s. of Hugh Bethell of Rise and Watton Abbey by Anne, da. of Sir John Cope, 6th Bt., M.P., of Bramshill, Hants and Hanwell, Oxon. *educ.* Beverley; Sidney Sussex, Camb. 1746. *unm.* *suc.* fa. 25 Mar. 1752.

Sheriff, Yorks. 1762–3.

On 17 Dec. 1760 Rockingham asked Newcastle's support for his friend Bethell who had declared himself a candidate at Beverley. 'Lord Granby and I', he wrote, 'can either of us answer for the good disposition of Mr. Bethell, and I believe his merit is so well known in Beverley that I suppose every voter will give him one vote.' But on 20 Dec. Rockingham wrote again:

My friend Bethell has again changed his mind and has now wrote to me that after his having declared himself candidate at Beverley some of his friends there told him he had so often before declared that it was not his intention to stand this election, that they thought he could not now properly alter his mind. Unluckily they prevailed and a good Member of Parliament is lost.[1]

Bethell was returned in 1768 without a contest. His name does not appear in the division lists of 1769, but on 9 and 25 Jan. 1770 he voted with Opposition over Wilkes and on 13 Feb. 1771 he voted against the Spanish convention. He never spoke in the House.

Bethell died 8 May 1772.

[1] Add. 32916, ff. 158–9, 228.

J.B.

## BETHELL, Slingsby (1695–1758), of Tower Hill, London.

LONDON 1747–1 Nov. 1758

*bap.* 16 Mar. 1695, 3rd s. of William Bethell of Swindon, Yorks. (nephew of Slingsby Bethell, republican[1]) by Elizabeth, da. of Sir John Brooke, 1st Bt., M.P., of York, and a distant cos. of Hugh Bethell (q.v.). *unm. suc.* bro. Hugh Bethell, M.P., 7 Feb. 1747.
  Alderman of London 1749, sheriff 1751–2, ld. mayor 1755–6; pres. of British white herring fishery 1750–*d*.

Bethell as a young man went out to the West Indies, and c. 1720 was 'chief agent and manager' of all the Antigua plantations of his brother-in-law, Sir William Codrington.[2] He returned to England c.1730, and set up as a London merchant. Some information about his trade appears in the evidence he gave before the House of Commons on 16 Feb. 1736: he was sending 'great quantities' of English woollens to the Guinea coast, purchasing there negroes for the British plantations, and receiving in exchange 'the produce of the said islands, and particularly cotton'.[3]

In 1754 Bethell stood for London on a joint interest with William Beckford, and came out second on the poll, receiving only six votes less than Sir John Barnard. He was classed in Dupplin's lists as an Opposition Whig.

Bethell died 1 Nov. 1758, leaving most of his fortune, including his real estate in Antigua, to his Codrington nephews.[4]

[1] About him see *DNB.* [2] See C11/703/15, N. Barnardiston v. W. Codrington, 21 Jan. 1723. [3] *CJ*, xxii. 566. [4] V. L. Oliver, *Antigua.* 43.

J.B.

## BILSON LEGGE, see LEGGE, Hon. Henry

## BINDLEY, John (c.1735–86), of Whitefriars, London and Caversham, nr. Reading.

DOVER 23 Dec. 1766–1768

*b.* c.1735,[1] 1st s. of John Bindley of St. John's St., Smithfield, and Aldersgate, London. *educ.* ?Charterhouse.[2] *m.* Elizabeth, 1 surv. s. *suc.* fa. 1761.
  Sec. to Bd. of Excise Dec. 1761–Feb. 1763; commr. of Excise Feb. 1763–Dec. 1764.

Bindley started in business as a distiller in partnership with his father. Precluded from keeping on his business while connected with the Excise, he made it over to his brother James for a term of years, and appointed an employee William Wright as manager, reserving to himself £250 p.a. and the rest to his children.[3] When on 13 Feb. 1762 he asked his old friend Jenkinson for an introduction to Lord Bute, he claimed that he had been 'taken out of trade' which yielded a profit of £2–3,000 p.a., with a prospect of doubling in 10 or 12 years his 'not inconsiderable' fortune; that he meant to devote himself to the service of the public, with only a commissionership of the Excise in view; that he had already made considerable improvements in commerce and the revenue, and had others to suggest. And on 18 May,[4] a week before Bute replaced Newcastle at the Treasury:

> I can now put a plan into the hands of Government which will raise £5 or 600,000 the succeeding year, provided I am only removed from the post of secretary to the excise to commissioner . . . I find I am not to succeed by the assistance of those who promised me and tempted me out of trade.[5]

In November he was received by Bute and treated in a 'very gracious manner';[6] and in February 1763 was appointed commissioner of the Excise.

An early advantage which Bindley derived from his 'ministerial interest and connexions' was a share in subscriptions to Government loans: e.g., £76,000 to the short-term loan of 1762,[7] and £100,000 to the loan of 1763, on which, he stated, the profit was £12,000 or more.[8] According to Alexander Fordyce, since 1760 his banker, Bindley said he could, through influence, get a considerable sum in the 1763 subscription, 'but that he had neither money to make the necessary payments thereon, nor knowledge enough of the public funds . . . to conduct the same to the best advantage': in this loan certainly, and possibly also in others, Fordyce was his partner.

Bindley was a friend of Charles Townshend, and tried to make political capital by claiming to influence him. When on Bute's resignation Townshend hesitated whether to accept the Admiralty, Bindley wrote to Jenkinson, 8 Apr. 1763:[9]

> Mr. Townshend is to be at Mr. Burrell's [q.v.] at seven who will most strongly enforce his steady attachment to the Administration. The world say he will not accept. I am pretty confident he will. I shall call at 7 at Burrell's, and if anything occurs you shall hear from me.

Still looking on Bute as the minister, Bindley, on 3 June 1763, promised Jenkinson[10] 'some matters relative to *Claremont*'[11] for Bute's information: he is never suspected by them 'of consequence enough to convey anything to his *Lordship*', though they conceive he might to Townshend. 'They know Mr. Townshend loves me . . . and they keep telling me he only can preserve me or push my future fortune. But my obligations are due to my Lord.'

As early as January 1764 Townshend sent through Bindley messages to Halifax and Grenville expressing his high regard for them, and the little value he set on the Opposition.[12] On 15 June Bindley again reported to Jenkinson:[13]

My friend Townshend is in perfect health. He is at Adderbury. His letter of today says—*I am a free man, bound to no party, or system etc.* I hope therefore, dear sir, Government will find some means to engage and employ his talents.

It is not clear what share Bindley had in the tentative approaches between Townshend and Grenville through John Morton (q.v.) in the autumn of 1764. But when these broke down, Townshend's claims were stated for the first time in concrete terms by Bindley to Jenkinson who, when transmitting them to Grenville, 20 Nov. 1764, remarked:[14]

> You will judge how far all this is to be relied on, and what use should be made of it, but Bindley will call on you to-morrow between nine and ten, and if you admit him will tell you more.

By 1764 Bindley openly aspired to a seat in Parliament, and on 29 Mar. inquired through Jenkinson 'if Mr. Grenville chooses to gratify me in my wish . . . at a proper time'.[15] Next he saw Grenville who 'behaved in the most cordial and friendly manner . . . pressing me to remain in my present position till he can exchange it for a more honourable and more lucrative one'.[16] But on 25 July Bindley wrote to the Duke of Portland:[17]

> I do not think it is very probable I shall remain long in my present situation. I do not like it, I want to get into a walk more adapted to the principles I profess, liberty and independency, and where a man may at least show whether he has or has not abilities. I would however act with some caution lest I should not succeed in getting into Parliament.

And on 11 Dec. he joyfully reported to Portland that he had quitted his office, and was now full master of his own time—'I intend to be in Parliament but when or how I know not, but I am sure I shall never be in office again.'

In November 1764 Grenville recommended Bindley, 'a gentleman whom I have some time wished to see' in Parliament, to James Buller (q.v.), for a vacant seat at West Looe.[18] But Buller found serious difficulty in nominating him 'from the report which had been spread that he was the first proposer of the tax upon cider',[19] and Grenville was forced to name another. By that time Bindley had already another seat in view: on 23 Nov. he wrote to Jenkinson[20] about a vacancy at Berwick-upon-Tweed and a man with a considerable interest in the borough who 'is a great enemy to Administration but . . . loves me and my family'. Passed over in favour of J. H. Delaval, Bindley acquiesced with a show of devotion. But on 6 Jan. 1765:[21] Lord Tylney is believed dead (lived another 20 years), and Admiral Townsend is slow in dying (died 10 months later); he would therefore prefer Malmesbury to Rochester—'I cannot embark in the business I

propose [some revenue schemes] till I am in Parliament, having determined they shall take place together.'

When on the formation of the Rockingham Government Sir William Meredith had to seek re-election at Liverpool Bindley claimed to have been encouraged to stand but to have declined: which Townshend in a letter of 6 Aug. 1765 thought very prudent as it 'would certainly have been expensive, unpleasant to ministry, and offensive to the Crown'.[22]

> I think you are wise in concealing, I will not say in renouncing, your passion for a seat in Parliament, because, in this minute of arrangements, I conclude it would be difficult to promise it, even if it were practicable to do it, and the application itself might be used to engage and entangle you once more. It cannot be long before every impediment you have felt will be removed: you will *then* see your *fullest* wishes accomplished in the most pleasing manner, and in the meantime how large is your fortune, and how great your prospect. As to me, you know I have been invariably your advocate and . . . friend . . . and if you choose to take your fate with me . . . I am ready to become one with you upon this plan of joint communication and common interest. More than this I cannot say; you are to judge of the eligibleness of the offer.
>
> I wish I could prevail upon you to come here for a week: we would settle every thing.
>
> Lord Rockingham has a high opinion of you, and, I suppose, he will seek your aid when he begins to feel his wants in office . . .
>
> Be true to yourself; be sensible of your own consequence; be firm in your mind, and let not the minute darken the hour, nor the passing cloud of one hour give colour or gloom to so fair a day as you have before you. You will be great, if you will be explicit and patient . . . Forgive this. It is from love for you.

Gross flattery expressing in high-falutin language Bindley's half-avowed dreams—he replied on the 9th: 'I wish nothing so much as to take my fate with you. I never intended anything else when I expected to go into Parliament.' Before he ventured to treat with Grenville he had understood that Townshend had decided not to join in any opposition. 'My step was too hasty. He has deceived me most infamously and led me to the brink of losing your protection . . . I ask pardon for troubling you with his name. But I hate him so that I cannot help abusing him.' He had attended Rockingham's first levee; next was sent for; but was determined not to disclose to ministers his ideas concerning taxes 'till I am in a situation that may justify to the public my interfering in revenue matters.'[23]

Even before the change of Government Bindley had communicated with Portland about a vacancy at Ilchester;[24] on 21 July 1765 about Berwick at the next general election; and on 22 Jan. 1766 about a vacancy at Dartmouth. But Rockingham apparently was not keen on having him in the House.

When Townshend became paymaster general, Bindley had tried to make him 'lodge all the pay office money' in Fordyce's bank. And with Townshend a leading figure in the Chatham Administration, Bindley wrote to Fordyce, 7 Nov. 1766:

I now flatter myself with the prospect of being one day more useful to you, as at last it is settled that I go into Parliament at the beginning of the session. My push will be for some share in contracts . . . something may be struck for our joint concern and advantage . . . Perhaps the world . . . will blame me for quitting my Board for Parliament, but, besides the advantage I hope to gain by it and the great satisfaction I shall feel in being, if it becomes necessary, at liberty to superintend and to act at Whitefriars [his office], I profess my genius urged me to it and there is no resisting that.

Meantime he asked for Fordyce's 'assistance about my qualification [for Parliament]', and borrowed money for his election expenses from Richard Atkinson (q.v.) who at that time worked closely with Fordyce. When he was returned on the Government interest at Dover, on 23 Dec. 1766, Newcastle wrote to Rockingham: 'I see the excise man, and as some say, the *excise smuggler*, is chose for Dover.'[25]

There is no record of Bindley having spoken in the House; he was a Government supporter, and voted with them over the land tax, 27 Feb. 1767, but was absent from the division on nullum tempus, 17 Feb. 1768: Townshend was dead, and Bindley would not go against Portland. No Government contracts with him have been traced; and dealings in East India stock undertaken in May 1767 by Bindley and Fordyce on inside information from his ministerial friends resulted in losses. On leaving the Excise Bindley had resumed his business, making Wright a partner: they engaged in a variety of schemes with inadequate capital and heavy losses, and by August 1767 were very deep in debt to Fordyce. On 4 Sept. Townshend died. On the 25th, at a meeting with Fordyce and Wright, Bindley was beside himself, 'frequently burst into floods of tears, wrung his hands and walked about the room like a madman'. Fordyce offered him an annuity of £400 p.a. during his life and that of his wife, in return for an assignment of all his fortune; to which Bindley agreed. At the general election of 1768 Bindley stood for Reading—'all his . . . hope of being provided for in some office under Government', he told Fordyce, 'depended upon . . . getting into Parliament.' Fordyce therefore agreed to meet his 'common tavern expenses', and paid out £900. But Bindley was defeated, and his bankers refused to finance a petition to Parliament. His financial position deteriorated still further; and so did his relations with Fordyce who now denied the validity of the annuity agreement. Bindley fled to France; and when persuaded by Fordyce to return, was arrested for debt and made bankrupt.[26]

In 1771, 'to find immediate maintenance and future provision for my distressed family', Bindley entered the wine trade, with Portland for customer and, he hoped, also promoter of his venture.[27] In May 1772, again in danger of arrest, he escaped once more to France where he lived in penury, carrying on the wine trade (without having the necessary capital), spinning schemes for re-establishing himself; and pressing Lord North through Grey Cooper (q.v.) for some Government employment, but receiving only promises and occasional payments of £50 or £100 from secret service funds.[28] After a visit to England in 1776 he wrote to Portland (from Calais, 27 Nov.):

Lord North has put me off till another day, though he readily acknowledged he stood in need of my assistance. I was advised however not to throw away my talents; and to be out of the way of being cajoled, I again returned to the Continent.

Another payment of £50 appears in the secret service accounts for January–April 1779,[29] the first available for North's period at the Treasury. Those of Cooper, Bindley's paymaster, are missing for April 1779–October 1780, but when they restart Bindley is employed at the Exchequer at a salary of £500 p.a. In 1781 it rises to £700;[30] and in North's closing accounts stands at £1,000 p.a.; and is thus explained in a memorandum for the King:[31] 'Mr. Bindley has been much employed every year about the taxes, and his allowance has been annually increased. He receives his allowance till provided for.' His £1,000 was among the private pensions communicated to Rockingham, 21 Apr., and to Shelburne, 17 July 1782; and in a list, compiled for Pitt in the summer of 1782,[32] the remark is added: 'said to have been promised to be commissioner of the Excise—recommended much by Mr. Cooper, who reports also Lord North's high opinion of his services.' Apparently he now longed to return to the Board he had so uppishly left nearly 20 years earlier.

When he died, 18 Feb. 1786, the *Gentleman's Magazine* (1786, p. 183) described him as one 'to whose abilities the revenue . . . is considerably indebted, as well for its augmentation as improvement in several . . . branches'; and in an obituary memoir of his brother James in 1818 (1818, ii. 280):

His parents . . . brought up their children with strictness, and divided among them a moderate fortune. The eldest son had great talents, with a vivacious turn of mind, and united a peculiar aptitude for financial concerns to an ease and pleasantness of conversation, which . . . obtained for him many friends.

[1] His yr. bro. James (see *DNB*) was b. 16 Jan. 1737. [2] There is no list of Carthusians other than scholars before 1800, but James was at the Charterhouse 'on account of the vicinity to his father's dwelling' (see *Gent. Mag.* 1818, ii. 280); and John Bindley, writing to Charles Jenkinson, another Carthusian, 13 Feb. and 18 May 1762 (*Jenkinson Pprs.* ed. Jucker, 29, 40) refers to 'the intimacy that subsisted between us in our early days'. [3] A great deal of information concerning Bindley's financial affairs can be derived from an Exchequer case which he brought in 1770 against the banker A. Fordyce and his partners, E112/1614/1287. [4] *Jenkinson Pprs.* 40. [5] Presumably Newcastle. [6] Bindley to Jenkinson, 12 Nov., Add. 38200, f. 103. [7] Bute mss. [8] E112/1614/1287. [9] Add. 38200, f. 193. [10] Ibid. f. 355. [11] i.e. the Duke of Newcastle. [12] See Grenville Diary, 10 and 11 Jan. 1764, *Grenville Pprs.* ii. 482–3. [13] *Jenkinson Pprs.* 301; the letter is marked Friday, and misdated in the docket 'June 13'. For a further report on Townshend from Bindley see Jenkinson to Grenville, 28 Aug., Grenville mss (JM). [14] *Grenville Pprs.* ii. 465. [15] Add. 38202, f. 208. [16] To Fordyce, c. 17 Apr. 1764, E112/1614/1287. [17] This connexion may possibly have started through Chase Price (q.v.), a friend of Portland and Townshend, referred to by Bindley in a letter to Portland, 6 Dec. 1772, as 'my old friend Chase Price'. [18] Grenville to Buller, 1 and 17 Nov. 1764, Grenville Letter Bk. [19] Grenville to Buller, 11 Dec. 1764, ibid. [20] Add. 38203, f. 275. [21] Add. 38204, f. 3. [22] Buccleuch mss. [23] See also his letter to Portland, 21 July 1765. [24] See letter of 15 Apr. 1765. [25] 25 Dec., Add. 32978, f. 474. [26] *Gent. Mag.* 1769, p. 216. [27] Bindley to Portland, 3 Sept. 1771. [28] See his letters to Portland—there are more than a dozen covering the period 1772–6. [29] In the Royal mss, Windsor. [30] See also Bindley to Portland, 1 Aug. 1781. [31] Fortescue, v. 469. [32] Chatham mss.

L.B.N.

## BINGHAM, Charles, 1st Baron Lucan [I] (1735–1799), of Castlebar, co. Mayo.

NORTHAMPTON  26 Apr. 1782–1784

*b.* 22 Sept. 1735, 2nd s. of Sir John Bingham, 5th Bt., by Anne, da. of Agmondesham Vesey of Lucan, co. Dublin. *m.* 25 Aug. 1760, Margaret, da. and coh. of James Smith, M.P., of Cannons Leigh, Devon, 1s. 4da. *suc.* bro. as 7th Bt. 1752; *cr.* Baron Lucan of Castlebar [I] 25 July 1776; Earl of Lucan [I] 1 Oct. 1795.
M.P. [I] 1761–76.

Having become in 1781 the father-in-law of George John Spencer, Viscount Althorp (q.v.), Lucan was unexpectedly pressed into service as candidate for Northampton to preserve the Spencer interest when Althorp resigned to stand for Surrey.[1] He was returned unopposed. Following Althorp, he supported Rockingham's Government, voted against Shelburne's peace preliminaries, 18 Feb. 1783, and for Fox's East India bill, 27 Nov. 1783, and opposed Pitt. Very unpopular with his constituents, at the general election of 1784 he was defeated.

Sir John Blaquière described Lucan as 'in private life a respectable, amiable man—independent from fortune'.[2] Lucan was a zealous champion of the Irish claims to commercial and constitutional liberty put forward during the years 1779–83, and this interest, together with his connexion with Althorp and his fervent admiration for Fox, determined his political line.[3]

Lucan died 29 Mar. 1799.

[1] *HMC 14th Rep.* IX, 165. [2] *Irish Parlt.* 1775, ed. Hunt, 4. [3] *HMC 8th Rep.* pt. 1 (1881), p. 207; *HMC 14th Rep.* IX, 159, 163–4, 168; Lucan to Lady Spencer, 21 Feb. 1783, Spencer mss.

J.B.

## BISSHOPP, Sir Cecil, 6th Bt. (*d.*1778), of Parham Park, Suss.

PENRYN                     1727–1734
BOROUGHBRIDGE  15 Mar. 1755–1768

1st s. of Sir Cecil Bisshopp, 5th Bt., by Elizabeth, da. and h. of Henry Dunch of Newington, Oxon. *m.* 1726, Anne, da. of Hugh Boscawen, 1st Visct. Falmouth, 4s. 8da. *suc.* fa. 25 Oct. 1725.
Superintendent of foundries to the Board of Ordnance 1751–*d.*

Bisshopp began as an opponent of Newcastle in Sussex politics; became reconciled to him about 1746; and in 1751 was given a sinecure under the Ordnance. By 1754 Newcastle felt so sure of him as to return him for Boroughbridge.

You must be sensible [Newcastle wrote to Bisshopp on 6 Feb. 1755[1]] that it is a seat in Parliament entirely my own, and without one farthing of expense. But I am very cautious not to choose any one but such as I can entirely depend upon in everything. It is always my desire to choose persons of the first rank and distinction; and, as far as I can, to take them from our county. Nobody answers all these views so well as yourself and therefore I make you the first offer, as a proof of my entire dependence upon and affection for you.

Nor did Newcastle stop there, but between 1756 and 1761 found places for two of Bisshopp's sons; while on the accession of George III Bisshopp begged Newcastle 'that in the disposition of employments your Grace would think of me'.[2]

Newcastle, in a list of 13 Nov. 1762, classed Bisshopp as a friend, but Bisshopp did not vote against the peace preliminaries in December 1762 and soon broke with Newcastle. Jenkinson in the autumn of 1763 classed him as a Government supporter, and on 16 Feb. 1764, the day before the general warrants motion, Lord Harcourt wrote to Grenville:[3] 'I made inquiries yesterday about Sir Cecil Bisshopp, intending to have sent an express to him, but I was told that he would be in town today without fail.' He does not appear in the list of the minority on that division nor in Jenkinson's list of 'absent friends'. On 16 Jan. 1765, pressed by Jenkinson to attend the House, he replied:[4]

No one is, or can be, more desirous to support the present measures of Government than myself, but . . . I am not capable of taking a journey. I must now ask pardon . . . I take the liberty of doing it, hoping you will show the matter in its true light to Mr. Grenville.

Henceforth, no vote is recorded by him. In November 1766 he was classed by Rockingham as 'Swiss' and by Newcastle in March 1767 as 'Administration'; and obviously Newcastle had no intention of returning him in 1768.

Bisshopp died 15 June 1778.

[1] Add. 32852, ff. 367–8. [2] Add. 32914, f. 35. [3] Grenville mss (JM). [4] Add. 38204, f. 111.

J.B.

**BISSHOPP, Sir Cecil,** 8th Bt. (1753–1828), of Parham Park, Suss.

NEW SHOREHAM 1780–1790, 1796–1806

*b.* 29 Dec. 1753, 1st s. of Sir Cecil Bisshopp, 7th Bt., by Susanna, da. of Charles Hedges of Finchley, Mdx. *m.* 27 June 1782, Harriet Anne, da. and h. of William Southwell of Frampton, Glos. 2s. *d.v.p.* 3da. *suc.* fa. Sept. 1779; abeyance of the barony of Zouche terminated in his favour 11 Aug. 1815.

Returned without a contest in 1780, Bisshopp voted with Administration till the fall of North's Government; did not vote on Shelburne's peace preliminaries; and in Robinson's list of March 1783 was classed among 'Lord North's friends, doubtful'. He did not vote on Fox's East India bill. In Stockdale's list of 19 Mar. 1784 he was classed as a supporter of Pitt. There is no record of his having spoken in the House before 1790.

In 1784 Bisshopp stood a contested election, and came second on the poll. His only recorded vote in this Parliament was for Administration over the Regency, 1789.

He died 11 Nov. 1828.

L.B.N.

**BLACKBURNE, John** (1754–1833), of Orford Hall nr. Warrington, Lancs.

LANCASHIRE 1784–1830

*b.* 5 Aug. 1754, 1st s. of Thomas Blackburne of Orford Hall by Ireland, da. and coh. of Isaac Green of Childwall, Lancs. Her sis. Mary m. Bamber Gascoyne sen. (q.v.). *educ.* Harrow; Queen's, Oxf. 1772. *m.* 19 Apr. 1781, Anne, da. of Samuel Rodbard of Evercreech, Som., 3s. 4da. *suc.* fa. 1768.

Blackburne was elected in 1784 without a contest, and supported Pitt. His only known vote against Administration was on the Irish commercial propositions, 11 May 1785, where Pitt's policy ran contrary to the interests of Lancashire. Four speeches are recorded before 1790: two on the French commercial treaty of 1787, and two on the piece goods bill of 1789—both measures which affected Lancashire industry. 'Though not distinguished in debate', wrote the *Gentleman's Magazine* in his obituary (1833, i. 465), 'his attention to the interests of his constituents was assiduous.'

He died 11 Apr. 1833.

J.B.

**BLACKETT, Sir Edward,** 4th Bt. (1719–1804), of Matfen, Northumb. and Thorpe Lea, Surr.

NORTHUMBERLAND 1768–1774

*bap.* 9 Apr. 1719, 1st s. of John Blackett of Newby, Yorks. (3rd s. of Sir Edward, 2nd Bt.), by Patience, da. of Henry Wise of Brompton Park, Mdx. *educ.* Trinity, Oxf. 1737; L. Inn 1740. *m.* Sept. 1751, Anne,

da. and h. of Oley Douglas of Matfen, 3s. 2da. *suc.* fa. 1750, and his uncle as 4th Bt. 1 Mar. 1756.

In 1768 Blackett was proposed for Northumberland by Lord Percy and Sir Walter Blackett (qq.v.) and returned unopposed. In 1769 he voted with Administration over Wilkes and the Middlesex election, but in the division of 25 Jan. 1770 with Opposition. However, he had no sympathy with the radicalism of the City of London, and in the debate on its remonstrance, 19 Mar. 1770, he seconded a motion 'that to deny the validity of proceedings in Parliament was unwarrantable and tended to disturb the peace of the kingdom'.[1] He spoke at least a dozen times on various subjects between 1771 and 1773, and both in March 1772 and September 1774 was classed by Robinson as a Government supporter. He did not stand in 1774, declaring that his health would not permit him 'to give that due attendance which so great a trust demands'. But to his brother Henry he wrote on 15 Aug.:[2]

> I assure you I am as well pleased to be out, as any one can be to have me so. I shall be my own master, and accountable to nobody; why I do this, or why I do that: indeed I don't think that any prudent man should wish to represent a county who has not some private view of his own: I came in against my own inclinations, purely to preserve the peace of the county, having no private interests of my own to carry; no title, no place to accept of; and so no court would I pay to great people; I assure you I shall like my own country much better when I am a private man in it, and not accountable for my conduct to any one: and indeed I have not been so well as I could wish this twelvemonth. If the attendance in Parliament is not quite so agreeable, the attendance that I must give to all the public meetings when I am in the county is still more disagreeable: all these things determined me not to incur any fresh obligations, and not to give my friends any more trouble on my account.

He died 3 Feb. 1804.

Walpole, *Mems. Geo. III*, iv. 71. [2] Blackett mss at Matfen.

J.B.

**BLACKETT, Sir Walter,** 2nd Bt. (1707–77), of Calverley, nr. Leeds, Yorks. and Wallington Hall, Northumb.

NEWCASTLE-UPON-TYNE 1734–14 Feb. 1777

*b.* 18 Dec. 1707, o.s. of Sir Walter Calverley, 1st Bt., of Calverley, Yorks. by Julia, da. of Sir William Blackett, 1st Bt., M.P., of Wallington. *educ.* Westminster 1717; Balliol, Oxf. 1724. *m.* 29 Sept. 1729, Elizabeth Orde, natural da. and testamentary h. of his mat. uncle, Sir William Blackett, 2nd Bt., M.P., and assumed name of Blackett, 1da. *suc.* fa. 15 Oct. 1749.

Alderman of Newcastle 1729, mayor 1735, 1748, 1756, 1764, 1771; sheriff, Northumb. 1731–2.

The Blackett family had long been concerned in coal mining and the coal trade, and were leading men in the business community of Newcastle.

Walter Blackett's great-grandfather, grandfather, and uncle had represented the borough, and Blackett was a great benefactor to the town. Under George II he ranked as a Tory, but from 1747 onwards he stood on a joint interest with Matthew Ridley, a Whig. They were unopposed in 1754, 1761, and 1768, and at the contest of 1774 Blackett topped the poll.[1]

In the House he took the regular Tory line; appears as Tory in Dupplin's lists of 1754; and as such was not sent Newcastle's parliamentary whip in October 1761. In Bute's list of December 1761 Blackett is classed as a Tory and a 'Lowther opponent' (whatever that may mean); and on 13 Nov. 1762 as 'pro' by Newcastle who had been told by the Duke of Cumberland that Blackett 'had declared for us'.[2] He did vote with the Opposition on 1 Dec. for postponing consideration of the peace preliminaries; but during the next week was listed by Fox among the Members favourable to them; and he was not of the minority which voted against them. In the autumn of 1763 Jenkinson classed him as doubtful; but his name appears in none of the minority lists on general warrants. In July 1765 Rockingham, having first put him down as 'doubtful', next added: 'most probably pro, made application'. But Blackett voted against the repeal of the Stamp Act, 22 Feb. 1766. Charles Townshend listed him as doubtful in January 1767, and he voted against Government over the land tax, 27 Feb. 1767.

His first speech in the Parliament of 1761 is thus recorded by James Harris:

> Monday Mar. 29 [1762]—the game bill came on. The part first canvassed was the several times for killing game, what was too soon, what was too late, what the precise day. Then might you have heard a debate.
> *Of all such speakers, as did never speak*—Sir Blackett, Sir Codrington, Cornish knight Buller etc. The hares could obtain no Sabbath, the limitation for them upon a division of about 50 to 30 was rejected.

15 Dec. 1762: Blackett supported 'a strange petition about the high price of corn in the North compared with that of the West and praying the bounty for exportation might be taken off—the West [Harris's country] to be ruined, because the North suffers a present evil'. 25 Feb. 1763: about electoral qualifications. 13 Mar. 1763: against the cider tax. 1 Apr. 1765: against an export tax on coal. 23 Apr. 1765: defended Newcastle corporation from charges of neglecting Tyne navigation. 7 Mar. 1766: for a change in the cider tax.[3]

In the Parliament of 1768 Blackett voted with Opposition over Wilkes and the Middlesex election, 2, 3 Feb., 15 Apr. 1769; on the Address, and again on Middlesex, 9, 25 Jan. 1770; but refused to present a petition from Newcastle for the dissolu-

tion of Parliament. In the summer of 1770 he went abroad for his health; returned on 15 Nov. and went straight to the House; and surprised them 'exceedingly' by rising up 'when there was no question',[4] to speak, as he said,

> upon a point which for some months hath greatly disturbed me: and the only apology I can offer for thus abruptly troubling the House with a matter which merely concerns myself, is, that I am conscientiously compelled to it.
> Diffident of myself, forsaking my own judgment, and adopting the opinion of others, I voted last sessions that Mr. Wilkes was not incapacitated from sitting in this House, during this Parliament. Reconsidering that vote the night I had given it, and indeed ever since, hath occasioned the greatest uneasiness to me: and whilst I was abroad this summer ruminating upon what I had done, it appeared to me that the only satisfaction I could give to my mind, was, to acknowledge here the error, as I conceive, I had committed, and return to my own opinion, as I now do;—That Mr. Wilkes is incapacitated, constitutionally incapacitated, from sitting in this House during this Parliament.[5]

'The surprise of both sides of the House', reported Bradshaw to Grafton, 16 Nov., 'prevented a word being said by either party upon the occasion.'[6] And Hans Stanley to Lady Spencer: 'I did not happen to be present but it is said that he spoke admirably well, and affected all who heard him in the strongest manner.' But according to Walpole, 'Sir Walter's scruples were regarded as the effects of a weak head and sick body'.[7] Blackett subsequently appended the following postscript to the notes of his speech:

> N.B. There was a report at Calais that the House of Commons would be adjourned for some time which was an additional inducement to me to get to the House as soon as I could; and to make this acknowledgement was the principal inducement which brought me from France; for Sir John Pringle and Mr. Middleton had advised me to stay abroad for a year or longer; and this resolution I determined upon one morning when I was walking alone in the Tuileries.
> Newcastle July 23 1771.          Wr. Blackett.
> N.B.: executing the above resolution did set my mind at ease.

Over Brass Crosby, 27 Mar. 1771, and the Middlesex election, 26 Apr. 1773, Blackett is listed as voting with Administration; over the royal marriage bill, March 1772, was classed by Robinson first as 'pro, absent', and next as 'doubtful, present'; on Grenville's Act, as a friend voting with Opposition; and in the survey of September 1774 as 'pro'. His interventions in this Parliament were again on matters concerning his constituents; also on the Cumberland election. One was characteristic of the old Tory. When on 12 Feb. 1770 'Tommy' Townshend told Charles Jenkinson that his manner was 'not becoming a gentleman risen from the situation he had done', Blackett declared: 'Every man carries his honour in his own hand. Originality is nothing. It shall never strike me that originality signifies anything.'[8]

In the 1770s Blackett lost a great deal of his previous popularity. A radical movement was rising at Newcastle in favour of Wilkes and of America which he would not support. And what weighed even more, Blackett's espousing the unpopular side over the question of the town moor, hurt his interest at the 1774 election, and caused 'his princely benefactions to the town to be forgotten. This unfortunate business is said to have given him much uneasiness, and to have shortened his days.'[9] Both Blackett and Ridley declined in October 1775 to present to the King a petition against the American war, signed by 1,210 Newcastle burgesses, but presented one, signed by 169 persons, supporting the Government policy.[10] No speech or vote of Blackett's is recorded in the Parliament of 1774.

He died 14 Feb. 1777, bequeathing all his estates to his nephew Sir John Trevelyan (q.v.), and £40,000 to John's younger brother Walter.

[1] Namier, *Structure*, 95. [2] Add. 32944, ff. 213–14. [3] Fortescue, i. 278. All the other reports are from Harris's 'Debates'. [4] Hans Stanley to Lady Spencer, 18 Nov. 1770. [5] The notes of his speech, still preserved among the Trevelyan mss at Wallington, were printed by John Hodgson, *Hist. Northumb*. ii. (i), pp. 272–3, n. [6] Grafton mss. [7] *Mems. Geo. III*, iv. 133; Brickdale's 'Debates'. [8] Cavendish's 'Debates', Egerton 220, p. 67. The text, as amended in the printed version of *Cavendish's Debates* (i. 448), is probably closer to what Blackett actually said: 'Origin is nothing. It shall never have any weight with me.' [9] *Mems. Sir Walter Blackett* (Newcastle 1819) p. 28. [10] M. A. Richardson, *A Local Historian's Table Book*, ii. 240.

L.B.N.

**BLACKSTONE, William** (1723–80), of Wallingford, Berks.

HINDON          1761–1768
WESTBURY     1768–9 Feb. 1770

*b.* 10 July 1723, 3rd and posth. s. of Charles Blackstone, silkman and citizen of London by Mary, da. of Lovelace Bigg of Chilton Foliat, Wilts. *educ.* Charterhouse 1735–8; Pembroke, Oxf. 1738, Fellow, All Souls 1744; M. Temple 1741, called 1746. *m.* 6 May 1761, Sarah, da. of James Clitherow of Boston House, Brentford, 9 ch.[1] Kntd. 12 Feb. 1770.

Recorder, Wallingford 1749; Vinerian prof. Eng. law, Oxf. 1758–66; patent of precedence Apr. 1761; bencher M. Temple 1761; principal of New Inn Hall, Oxf. 1761–6; solicitor-gen. to the Queen 1763–70; j. common pleas 9 Feb.; j. King's bench 16 Feb. 1770; again j.c.p. 22 June 1770.

In 1750 Blackstone was a prominent Oxford Tory, and took the lead in proposing Sir Roger Newdigate as candidate for the university and in carrying his election in January 1751;[2] he also played an important part in the Oxfordshire election of 1754, and in the legal argument over the petition. But he did not at the time think of a parliamentary career for

himself; in 1753 he even decided to give up attending the courts at Westminster, and 'to pursue my profession . . . by residing at Oxford'. This resolution, he wrote to Newdigate on 3 July, had been growing upon him for some years:

> My temper, constitution, inclinations, and a thing called principle, have long quarrelled with active life . . . and have assured me I am not made to rise in it. Besides there are certain qualifications for being a public speaker, in which I am very sensible of my own deficiency; and happy that I am sensible so early.

But his Oxford lectures brought him back to an active life. Lord Fitzmaurice (q.v.) gave a 'book' of them to Bute for the Prince of Wales, and further copies were sent direct;[3] and in March 1761 Fitzmaurice recommended Blackstone to Bute for a seat at Hindon which had through Fox been placed at his disposal:[4]

> Blackstone is a man of business, and may be more so, and perhaps more useful. He is guardian or deeply connected with Ld. Suffolk and Ld. Abingdon, and may draw a certain part of that connexion with him. Such I take his merits to be, besides what your Lordship knows already of him.

Blackstone at first declined the offer;[5] but two days later, on 11 Mar.: he would accept if a way was found 'in which I can with honour and conscience satisfy the law in regard to a parliamentary qualification'. And on 12 Mar.: he sees a way, and will accept provided 'the expense . . . shall not be such as may injure my private fortune; which is confined within moderate bounds'. On 16 Mar. Blackstone's name was given by Fox to Calthorpe, the patron of Hindon, with £2,000;[6] and he was returned unopposed, apparently without any expense to himself (Shelburne wrote to Bute, 11 Dec. 1762: 'it cost you £2,500'). But Blackstone, when erroneously informed that he had not been elected, wrote to Fitzmaurice on 29 Mar. 1761 that he was easy under the disappointment: 'Your Lordship knows how little I expected or sought for a seat in Parliament.'

In the House Blackstone was an infrequent and 'an indifferent speaker':[7] during the seven years 1761–8 only 14 speeches by him are recorded, mostly on subjects of secondary importance. Very learned and original, over-subtle and ingenious, in major debates he showed a lack of political common sense. On 9 May 1765, when supporting Morton's motion to insert the name of the Princess of Wales in the Regency bill, he argued that the Regency Act of 1751 was 'not yet expired'; 'if the Crown should devolve on a minor son of the late Prince of Wales, she would be Regent'; and it would therefore be improper to exclude her from the new Act.[8] His speech of 3 Feb. 1766 against the repeal of the Stamp Act is recorded at considerable length by his friend Newdigate.[9] His contention was that obedience must be firmly enforced in dependent states—'if they can refuse any laws they are sovereign', and all other rights of sovereignty must be allowed to them. And here is a typical passage:

Journals 1623, House resolved our fishermen ought to have right to fish in New England and to take necessary wood and timber—a strong mark of superiority . . . any infringement upon the natural rights for mankind the same as taxing—exertion of power over property—if you have one you have the other. Penalty upon persons in New England cutting down trees under 5 inch—penalties are the same as taxes—no difference between a law with a pecuniary penalty and a tax. The Stamp Act is only a law with a penalty.

On 22 Feb. Blackstone voted against the repeal; and on the 24th moved a clause that the repeal should apply to those colonies only 'who expunge out of their Assembly the resolutions . . . derogatory from the honour and dignity of the Crown and Parliament'.[10] The motion 'was most childishly and peevishly supported', wrote George Onslow to Pitt, 'and, in about two hours, rejected without a division'.[11] On 21 Apr. 1766 Blackstone spoke against the new window tax—showed its futility, 'and how easy to be avoided':[12] 'If every person stops a window will take away the whole—46,000, if one half 23,000—will reduce the tax.'[13] On 5 Dec. 1766 Blackstone supported Grenville's motion for compensation for sufferers from the corn embargo; but in January 1767 was classed by Charles Townshend as a Government supporter, and similarly by Newcastle, 2 Mar. 1767. His name does not, however, appear in the division lists on the land tax, 27 Feb. 1767, and on nullum tempus, 17 Feb. 1768.

In 1768 Blackstone was returned for Westbury on Lord Abingdon's interest. In the new Parliament most of his speeches—and between November 1768 and January 1770 he intervened in 11 debates—were on Wilkes. On 1 Feb. 1769 he made the motion which condemned Wilkes's petition indicting Mansfield.[14] But the next day he spoke against the motion charging Wilkes with libel in his prefatory remarks to Weymouth's letter published in the *St. James's Chronicle*:[15]

I must give my reasons for voting against gentlemen, with whom I have usually voted, and may hereafter vote. You have information more than enough to cast the severest censure upon that unhappy man. This paper is not the cause of the public, but the cause of the minister.

On 3 Feb. however, he spoke and voted for Wilkes's expulsion because of the 'Essay on Woman':[16]

When I see all religion made a mockery and jest of, it behoves me to vindicate my God and my King.

On 8 May 1769 Blackstone gave it as his 'firm and unbiassed opinion' that Wilkes was disqualified by common law from sitting in the House, for 'the law and custom of Parliament is part of the common law'; and the House of Commons, with regard to its own privileges and Members, can declare law without appeal or review.[17] Over this he was 'severely confuted out of his own commentaries on the Law' by George Grenville who cited the passage enumerating nine cases of disqualification, of which expulsion was not one.[18] Blackstone made no reply, and was next attacked in pamphlets and newspapers.[19]

When on 31 Jan. 1770 Dowdeswell moved that no person eligible by law can be incapacitated by a vote or resolution of the House, but by Act of Parliament only, Blackstone is reported to have said:[20]

As to the question whether expulsion does of itself imply incapacity, I have never answered it in the affirmative, neither have I ever declared the contrary. I did not vote in the question last year, and I shall not, by any vote that I may now give, be included in that question.

This was Blackstone's last recorded speech in the House. On 9 Feb. his appointment to the Bench vacated his seat.

He died 14 Feb. 1780.

[1] According to the *Diary of John Baker* (ed. Yorke), 23 June 1775, 320, 'has 8 children besides 3 or 4 dead'. [2] See W. R. Ward, *Georgian Oxf.* and letters from Blackstone to Newdigate in the Newdigate mss, Warws. RO. [3] See Blackstone to Bute, 15 Mar. 1759, Bute mss. [4] Bute mss. [5] Blackstone to Fitzmaurice, 9 Mar., Lansdowne mss. [6] Fox to Fitzmaurice, Lansdowne mss; Fitzmaurice to Bute, Bute mss. [7] Walpole, *Mems. Geo. III*, ii. 198. [8] *Grenville Pprs.* iii. 30. [9] Newdigate ms B.2546/12–15. [10] Ryder's 'Debates', Harrowby mss. See also Harris's 'Debates', and Add. 35374, f. 287. [11] *Chatham Corresp.* ii. 395. [12] Harris. [13] Newdigate. [14] Cavendish's 'Debates', Egerton 217, pp. 12–17, 21, and 48. [15] Cavendish's 'Debates', Egerton 217, pp. 84–86. [16] Ibid. 128–9. [17] Egerton 219, pp. 361–9. [18] Walpole, *Mems. Geo. III*, iii. 241 and note by Le Marchant. [19] See letter addressed to him by Junius, 29 July 1769. [20] *Gent. Mag.* 1770, p. 548.

L.B.N.

**BLACKWELL, Samuel** (*d.*1785), of Williamstrip Park and Ampney Crucis, Glos.

CIRENCESTER 1774–30 Apr. 1785

*m.* 21 Nov. 1759[1] or 15 Jan. 1760,[2] Anne, da. of James Lennox Dutton of Sherborne, Glos., sis. of James Dutton (q.v.); issue, including one da. who m. W. H. Hartley (q.v.).

By the time Blackwell entered Parliament he had an established position in Gloucestershire. He was connected by marriage with the Duttons of Sherborne and the Masters of Cirencester, both old county families; since 1763 had commanded the Gloucestershire militia; and owned considerable property in the county.

His purchase of Ampney Crucis in 1765 gave him an interest at Cirencester. In 1768, standing against the Bathurst interest, he was defeated, but succeeded in 1774; and in 1780 and 1784 was returned without a contest.

Blackwell supported North's Administration to the end; voted for Shelburne's peace preliminaries, 18 Feb. 1783; and did not vote on Fox's East India bill. In Robinson's list of January 1784 he is classed as 'very hopeful'; but was included among the Opposition both by Stockdale, March 1784, and William Adam, May 1784. There is no record of his having spoken in the House, and hardly a reference to him in contemporary political correspondence.

Blackwell died 30 Apr. 1785.

[1] *Gent. Mag.* 1759, p. 550. [2] Ibid. 1760, p. 46.

J.B.

## BLAIR, see HUNTER BLAIR

## BLAKE, Patrick (?1742–84), of Langham, Suff.

SUDBURY 1768–1774, 22 Mar. 1775–1784

*b.* ?1742, 1st s. of Andrew Blake of St. Kitts and Montserrat by Marcella French of Ireland. *educ.* Eton 1758–60; St. John's, Camb. 18 Aug. 1760, aged 18. *m.* 14 Apr. 1762, Annabella (div. 1778), da. of Rev. Sir William Bunbury, sis. of T. C. Bunbury (q.v.), 2s. 3da. *suc.* gd.-fa. Patrick Blake of St. Kitts 1745; *cr.* Bt. 8 Oct. 1772.

Blake inherited considerable property in St. Kitts from his grandfather, but from his father '1s. only, because of his undutifullness . . . and following the advice of a parcel of Irish knaves who mean nothing but to plunder him'.[1]

He seems to have applied to Grafton for a seat at the general election of 1768. Sir William Musgrave wrote to Lord Carlisle, 1 Oct. 1767, that Grafton had proposed Blake for Morpeth 'and as you had directed me to take the Duke's nomination without exception, I immediately agreed'. But on 16 Oct.: 'Mr. Blake . . . has engaged himself in a contest at Sudbury, where it is thought he will be drawn into great expenses without success.'[2] Blake stood at Sudbury on a joint interest with Walden Hanmer, backed by Government. There was both expense and success, and a petition against the return. In Parliament he voted with Opposition on Wilkes's petition, 27 Jan. 1769, and expulsion, 3 Feb. 1769; with Administration on Brass Crosby, 27 Mar. 1771; was classed as 'pro, present' in Robinson's two surveys on the royal marriage bill, March 1772, and as 'pro' before the general election. In 1774 he was defeated at Sudbury but seated on petition. He does not appear in the five minority lists October 1775— December 1778, but was classed as 'contra, absent' on the contractors bill, 12 Feb. 1779. His only reported votes in this Parliament were with Opposition on the censure motion against the Admiralty,

8 Mar. 1779, Dunning's motion, 6 Apr. 1780, and the motion against prorogation 24 Apr. In 1780 he was re-elected at Sudbury at the head of the poll. The *English Chronicle* in 1780 or 1781 described him as 'attached to the cause of patriotism', and though he voted with Administration on Lowther's motion against the war, 12 Dec. 1781, he voted with Opposition on the censure motion against the Admiralty, 20 Feb. 1782, and on Conway's motion against the war, 22 Feb. No other vote by him is reported before he left Parliament. Robinson, March 1783, listed him as 'ill or cannot attend', and January 1784 as 'doubtful, absent'; Stockdale, 19 Mar. 1784, as 'Administration'. There is no record of his having spoken in the House. Blake did not stand again at the general election, and died 1 July 1784.

[1] Will of Andrew Blake, quoted Oliver, *Antigua*, i. 54. [2] *HMC Carlisle*, 216.

M.M.D.

## BLAND, Sir John, 6th Bt. (1722–55), of Kippax Park, Yorks. and Hulme, Lancs.

LUDGERSHALL 1754–3 Sept. 1755

*bap.* 13 Jan. 1722, 1st s. of Sir John Bland, 5th Bt., by Lady Frances Finch, da. of Heneage, 1st Earl of Aylesford. *educ.* Westminster 1735–9; St. John's, Oxf. 1740. *unm.* *suc.* fa. 14 Apr. 1743.

Bland was returned for Ludgershall on the interest of George Selwyn (q.v.) and in Dupplin's list of 1754 was classed as a follower of Henry Fox.

Bland was said 'by his wild dissipation and his unconquerable disposition to play' to have squandered 'immense estates and the whole of Manchester and its environs'.[1] Horace Walpole described him as 'good-natured and generous and well-bred', but added about his passion for gambling: 'never was such infatuation; I can call it by no term but *flirting* away his fortune'.[2] After an evening's play during which he lost £32,000, Bland, to escape his creditors, went to France, and lost further large sums to Theobald Taaffe (M.P. 1747–54), an Irish adventurer of infamous reputation. Unable to pay immediately, Bland gave post-dated bills which Taaffe at once presented and, on their being dishonoured, procured Bland's arrest under a *lettre de cachet*. 'To save him from the affront, and prevent him killing himself on the spot' Charles Selwyn, the English banker in Paris, advanced him £500. 'But', wrote Selwyn to Henry Fox, 6 Sept. 1755, 'his resentment was so great, as we had taken from him the power of procuring himself any satisfaction by engaging his honour that he would not see the person who had done him this injury till he had paid us this money, that he could not get over it',[3] and on

3 Sept. 1755 he committed suicide at Clermont-en-Beauvoisis.

¹ N. Carlisle, *Colls. Hist. Fam. of Bland*, 60. ² H. Walpole to Geo. Montagu, 20 Sept. 1755. ³ 6 Sept. 1755, quoted *Horace Walpole's Corresp.* (Yale ed.), 9, 172–3.

M.M.D.

**BLONDEAU, see HART**

**BLOXAM, Matthew** (1744–1822), of Highgate, Mdx.

MAIDSTONE    14 July 1788–1806

*bap.* 10 Aug. 1744, 1st s. of Rev. Matthew Bloxam, vicar of Comberton, Worcs. by Elizabeth, da. of Henry Turner, alderman of Gloucester. *m.* Kntd. 19 June 1800.

Sheriff of London 1787–8, alderman 1803–21; store-keeper to the stationery office 1818–21.

Bloxam was a partner in the firm of wholesale stationers, Foudrinier, Bloxam, and Walker, of Lombard Street; and in 1791 in the Southwark bank of Sanderson, Harrison, Brenchley, Bloxam, and Co. In 1780 he canvassed Cricklade, but withdrew before the poll; in 1788 he was returned after a contest on the Government interest at Maidstone (which was managed by John Brenchley, later his banking partner). Bloxam supported Pitt. There is no record before 1790 of his having spoken in the House.

He died 16 Oct. 1822.

J.B.

**BODVELL, William** (1694–1759), of Madryn, Caern.

CAERNARVONSHIRE    1741–1754
MONTGOMERY          1754–30 June 1759

*b.* Nov. 1694, 2nd but 1st surv. s. of Lloyd Bodvell of Bodvan, Caern. by Anne, da. and h. of Hugh Davies of Madryn. *m., s.p. suc.* bro. at Madryn 1711 and fa. at Bodvan Dec. 1731.

Constable of Beaumaris castle 1716–1725 and 1752–*d.*

Bodvell after representing Caernarvonshire for 13 years, again canvassed the county in 1754 against Sir John Wynn (q.v.). To prevent a contest, Lord Powis arranged a compromise and returned Bodvell for his pocket borough of Montgomery.

In 1755 Bodvell sought through Powis to obtain the office of custos rotulorum of Caernarvonshire for himself, and the chancellorship of Bangor for a kinsman. Powis, in supporting the application, wrote to Newcastle about him on 5 Sept. 1755: 'One thing is to be said; and that is that he is certainly your Grace's good friend . . .'¹

Although a Government supporter and one of Powis's group, Bodvell never sought to derive any

financial advantage from his membership of the House, and to that extent was independent. His epitaph claims that he remained 'unpensioned and unplaced, upon all occasions a real friend to the constitution of his country'.²

He died 30 June 1759.

¹ Add. 32858, f. 485. ² *Trans. Caern. Hist. Soc.* 1944, p. 53.

P.D.G.T.

**BOLD, Peter** (*d.*1762), of Bold Hall, Prescot, Lancs.

WIGAN          1727–1734
LANCASHIRE    4 May 1736–1741, 23 Jan. 1750–1761

s. of Richard Bold, M.P., by Elizabeth, da. of Thomas Norton of Barkisland, Yorks. *educ.* B.N.C. Oxf. 2 Feb. 1722. *m.* Anna Maria, da. and coh. of Godfrey Went-worth of Woolley Park, Yorks., wid. of Rev. Edward Sylvester of Barthwaite, 6da. *suc.* fa. 1704.

Bold came of an old Lancashire family, and his father and grand-father had both represented the county. He was a Tory, and was returned unopposed for Lancashire in 1754. He did not stand again in 1761, and died 12 Sept. 1762.

J.B.

**BOND, John** (1717–84), of Creech Grange, Dorset.

CORFE CASTLE    1747–1761, 2 Apr. 1764–1780

*b.* 11 May 1717, 1st s. of John Bond, M.P., of Tyne-ham, Dorset by Margaret, da. of John Williams of Herrington, Dorset. *educ.* Wadham, Oxf. 1736; I. Temple 1735, called 1740. *m.* 17 July 1749, Mary, da. of Edmund Dummer of Swaythling, Hants, 5s. 2da.; her sis. *m.* 1740 Valentine Knightley (q.v.). *suc.* fa. 21 June 1744, and uncle Denis Bond, M.P., at Creech Grange 30 Jan. 1747.

Recorder, Dorchester 1756–81, Poole 18 July 1772–*d.*

Bond practised a few years at the bar,¹ and only after having succeeded his uncle at Creech Grange was returned to Parliament for the seat which his uncle and father had held, 1715–44. In the House he ranked as an independent Government supporter—otherwise nothing is known about the part he took; nor why he did not stand at the general election of 1761. No speech of his is recorded during all the 30 years he sat in Parliament, and no vote during his first term for which no full division lists are extant, only occasional incomplete reports. His membership truly falls under the heading of 'honour with ease': he had to maintain his family's position in the county and its interest in the borough, which he nursed carefully, upholding the old alliance with the Bankes family. This was confirmed by letters exchanged with John Bankes in November 1757,² when John Calcraft (q.v.) was trying to break into Corfe Castle. Bond seems to have been popular in the neighbourhood: in October 1759 the mayor and burgesses of Poole asked their recorder, James West (q.v.), who could not regularly attend their sessions, to give up the post so that they might choose Bond in his place.[3]

When Lord Malpas, returned for Corfe Castle on Bond's interest in 1761, died on 15 Mar. 1764, Henry Bankes informed Bond of it, and asked him to come to London even 'if my sincere ally perseveres in his self denial, and declines public honour and parliamentary bustle, and chooses retirement, and rural quiet'. Bankes seems to have thought of recommending his cousin John Jenkinson (q.v.) to Bond. Bond replied: 'It would on many considerations have been more agreeable for me to have continued some little time longer out of Parliament. But it has long since been my resolution that in case any vacancy should happen with respect to this seat to stand myself.'[4] He was returned unopposed, as he was in all his elections. In July 1765 he was classed by Rockingham as 'doubtful', and in Newcastle's and Townshend's lists of 1767 as a Government supporter; but no vote of his is recorded. In the Parliament of 1768–74 he voted against the expulsion of Wilkes, 3 Feb. 1769; was classed as 'doubtful, present' in Robinson's surveys on the royal marriage bill, March 1772; voted with Government on the Middlesex resolution on 26 Apr. 1773 (which, if accurate, contradicts his vote of 1769); over Grenville's Act, 25 Feb. 1774, was marked in the King's list as a friend for once voting with Opposition; and was classed by Robinson as 'pro' in his survey of September 1774. For the period 1775–8 no majority lists are extant; but over the contractors bill Bond is listed by Robinson 'pro, present'; over Keppel he voted with Government, 3 Mar. 1779; and he appears as voting with Government in two of the six divisions, February— March 1780: on economical reform and on Dunning's motion. A packet of division lists preserved among his papers at Creech Grange bears witness to his interest in parliamentary proceedings. The *Public Ledger* wrote about him in 1779: 'A steady ministerialist . . . what is Lord North's hold upon him, he himself best knows.' Presumably it was his honest conviction.

In 1780 he stood down in favour of his son (q.v.), and died 30 May 1784. The *Gentleman's Magazine* wrote in his obituary notice:

He was particularly skilled in the writings of the best Greek and Roman authors. He had studied the constitution of his own country, which he thoroughly understood. He contributed greatly to the peace and happiness of the people in his neighbourhood, as from the general esteem in which he was held he was usually applied to as arbiter in their differences . . . Many of

his leisure hours were spent in improving and embellishing his estate.

[1] *Gent. Mag.* 1784, p. 476. [2] See CORFE CASTLE constituency. [3] West mss at Alscott, Glos. [4] Bond mss at Creech Grange.

L.B.N.

## BOND, John (1753–1824), of Creech Grange, Dorset.

CORFE CASTLE 1780–Feb. 1801

*b.* 24 July 1753, 1st s. of John Bond (q.v.). *educ.* Winchester; Magdalene, Camb. 1771; I. Temple 1773, called 1779. *m.* Aug. 1798, Elizabeth, da. and h. of John Lloyd of Cefn-y-Coed, Card., 2s. 2da. *suc.* fa. 30 May 1784.
Sheriff, Card. 1804–5.

Like his father, Bond was an independent country gentleman well disposed to the Government. In each of the six divisions, 12 Dec. 1781–15 Mar. 1782, he voted with them; voted against Shelburne's peace preliminaries, 18 Feb. 1783; was classed by Robinson in March as 'North, doubtful'; but voted against Fox's East India bill; and is classed as a supporter of Pitt both by Stockdale, 19 Mar. 1784, and William Adam, May 1784. He voted against Government on Richmond's fortifications plan, 27 Feb. 1786, but with them during the Regency crisis. There is no record of his having spoken in his first two Parliaments.

He died 12 May 1824.

L.B.N.

## BOND HOPKINS, Benjamin (?1745–94), of Painshill Park, Surr.

ILCHESTER 1784–1790
MALMESBURY 1790–30 Jan. 1794

*b.* ?1745, 1st s. of Benjamin Bond, Turkey merchant, of London by Elizabeth, da. of John Hopkins of Bretons, nr. Dagenham, Essex. *m.* (1) 8 Mar. 1770, Elizabeth Chamberlayn (*d.* 3 Jan. 1771) of Worcester, 1da.; (2) 20 May 1773, Alicia (*d.*28 Sept. 1788), da. of Capt. Tomkins, 1da.; (3) 23 Feb. 1791, Miss Knight, illegit. da. of Robert Knight, 1st Earl of Catherlough (q.v.), *s.p.* *suc.* to very considerable estates of his maternal gd.-mother's cos. John Hopkins the usurer, and took add. name of Hopkins 12 Dec. 1772. *suc.* fa. 20 Apr. 1785.

In 1772, when through the death of several intermediate branches of the Hopkins family[1] the inheritance from 'Vulture' Hopkins came to Benjamin Bond, he was clerk to a City attorney. In 1780 he became a candidate at Oxford, but withdrew during the poll. In 1783 he was nominated for Surrey where he had considerable property, but declined before the poll. In 1784 he successfully contested Ilchester on the Lockyer interest. He was classed as 'Opposition' by William Adam in May 1784, but apart from his vote in favour of parliamentary reform, 18 Apr. 1785, his only other recorded votes during this Parliament were with Administration over the Regency, 1788–9. There is no record of his having spoken in the House. He died 30 Jan. 1794.

[1] *Gent. Mag.* 1794, p. 183.

M.M.D.

**BOONE, Charles** (?1729–1819), of Barking Hall, Suff. and Lee Place, Kent.

| | |
|---|---|
| CASTLE RISING | 25 Feb. 1757–1768 |
| ASHBURTON | 1768–1784 |
| CASTLE RISING | 1784–1796 |

*b.* ?1729, s. of Charles Boone, M.P., by his 2nd w. Mary, da. of Col. Thomas Garth, wid. of George Evelyn of Rook's Nest, Surr., and half-bro. of Daniel Boone (q.v.). *educ.* Eton 1742–5; Trinity, Camb. 10 Feb. 1746, aged 16. *m.* (1) 22 Oct. 1762, Theodosia (*d.*9 Jan. 1765), da. of John Crowley, M.P., and gd.-da. of Sir Ambrose Crowley, M.P., of Barking Hall, Suff., 1da.; (2) 16 Jan. 1768, Harriet Wright of Roehampton, 1s. *d.v.p.* 1da.

In November 1756 George, 3rd Earl of Orford, with whom Charles Boone had been at Eton, tried to have him returned for Callington, but had to give way to the candidate of his mother, the Dowager Lady Orford. In February 1757, and at all his subsequent elections for Castle Rising and Ashburton, Boone was returned by Orford, to whom, according to Horace Walpole, he proved 'the single friend' that 'showed gratitude to him when he was no longer capable of serving anyone [i.e. when he was insane]'.[1]

In 1761 Boone was sent Newcastle's parliamentary whip direct. In November 1762 Henry Fox attempted to use him as an intermediary with Lord Orford.[2] Boone voted with the Administration on the division to postpone consideration of the peace preliminaries, 1 Dec. 1762, and in the autumn of 1763 was classed by Jenkinson as an Administration supporter; but in November 1763 Rigby wrote to Sandwich: 'Pray be as civil to him as possible, he has been wavering but is disposed to become quite steady.'[3] He did not vote against the Grenville Administration over Wilkes and general warrants. Rockingham in July 1765 classed him as 'pro' and in 1766 as 'Swiss' (prepared to vote with every Administration).

His first recorded vote in the Parliament of 1768 was with the Administration over Brass Crosby, 27 Mar. 1771. In both Robinson's surveys on the royal marriage bill, March 1772, he was listed as 'pro, present'; he voted with the Administration on the Middlesex election, 26 Apr. 1773; appears in the King's list of dissenting friends on the Grenville Election Act, 25 Feb. 1774; was classed by Robinson as 'pro' in September 1774; and henceforward

regularly supported Administration till the fall of North. In a survey drawn up for Shelburne in August 1782 Robinson noted about Boone: 'Is a very independent man. Was pretty closely attached to the old Administration and in long habits of friendship with Mr. Rigby and his friends; may be hopeful.'[4] Boone voted for Shelburne's peace preliminaries, 18 Feb. 1783, and against Fox's East India bill, 27 Nov. 1783. He regularly supported Pitt's Administration. There is no record of his having spoken in the House.

Boone died 3 Mar. 1819, aged 89.

[1] Walpole to Mann, 28 Apr. 1777. [2] *Mems. Geo. III*, i. 169. [3] Sandwich mss. [4] Laprade, 45.

L.B.N.

**BOONE, Daniel** (1710–70), of Rook's Nest, Surr.

| | |
|---|---|
| LUDGERSHALL | 1734–1741 |
| GRAMPOUND | 1741–1747 |
| STOCKBRIDGE | 1747–1754 |
| MINEHEAD | 1754–1761 |

*b.* Nov. 1710, 1st s. of Charles Boone, M.P., by his 1st w. Jane, da. of Daniel Chardin, merchant, of Fort St. George, and half-bro. of Charles Boone (q.v.). *educ.* prob. Eton 1725; Clare 1728 and Trinity, Camb. 1729; I. Temple 1727. *m.* 27 June 1736, his step-sis. Anne, da. and coh. of George Evelyn, M.P., of Rook's Nest, Surr., wid. of Thomas Gregg, 2da. *suc.* fa. 1735.

Commissary gen. of musters 1742–6; groom of the bedchamber to Frederick, Prince of Wales 1746–51; clerk of the Household to Dowager Princess of Wales 1751–*d.*

In 1754 Daniel Boone successfully contested Minehead on the interest of Lord Egremont and with the support of Administration. In 1757 his wife was given a secret service pension of £400 a year.[1]

Boone did not seek re-election in 1761 or subsequently. He died 20 May 1770, aged 60.

[1] Namier, *Structure*, 447.

**BOOTLE,** *see* **WILBRAHAM BOOTLE**

**BOSCAWEN FAMILY**

The Boscawens were one of the biggest of the Cornish borough-mongering families. In 1754 they controlled five seats in the House of Commons: two at Truro, one each at Tregony, Penryn, and St. Mawes. Truro was invariably reserved for members of the family, the other seats were sold to Administration.

Truro was lost in 1780 but regained in 1784; the seat at Penryn was lost by 1768; and in 1788 the Boscawen interest at Tregony and St. Mawes had been sold. By 1780 the family had gained two seats at Mitchell, one of which it lost by 1784. Thus in 1790 the Boscawen interest was limited to three seats: two at Truro, and one at Mitchell.

## BOSCAWEN, Hon. Edward (1711–61), of Hatchlands Park, Surr.

TRURO 21 June 1742–10 Jan. 1761

*b.* 19 Aug. 1711, 3rd s. of Hugh, 1st Visct. Falmouth, by Charlotte, da. of Col. Charles Godfrey, master of the jewel house, by Arabella, da. of Sir Winston Churchill, sis. of John, 1st Duke of Marlborough. *m.* 11 Dec. 1742, Frances, da. of William Evelyn Glanville (q.v.) of St. Clere, Ightham, Kent, 3s. 2da.
Entered R.N. 1726; lt. 1732; capt. 1737; r.-adm. 1747; v.-adm. 1755; adm. 1758; gen. of marines 1759; ld. of Admiralty 1751–*d.*; P.C. 2 Feb. 1759.

Boscawen sat at Truro on his family interest, reinforced by his own distinction as sailor and his popularity with the families whose sons he took to sea with him. 'Ready and decisive courage' was deemed the distinguishing feature of his character.[1] But the 'damn 'em, fight 'em' attitude of 'Old Dreadnought' (his nickname among his sailors) when transferred to politics was disconcerting for experts in that field, and perhaps most of all for his own allies. Horace Walpole describes him as 'attached to nothing but his own opinion'.[2] 'Odd as he is', writes Hardwicke about him to Newcastle in 1753;[3] and again in 1760: 'Your Grace knows he has a particular head.'[4] And Newcastle to Hardwicke, 17 Oct. 1753: 'My brother [Henry Pelham] says that Admiral Boscawen is a wild man, and he can do nothing with him.'[5] And even Lord Edgcumbe, allied as he was to the Boscawens, implies as much in a letter written to a friend, 7 Oct. 1753.[6]

Contrary to a tacit convention which for more than forty years had left the county representation of Cornwall uncontested to the Tory country gentlemen, in October 1753 Robert Hoblyn, a Cornish squire and mineowner, since 1742 M.P. for Bristol, decided to stand against the two sitting Members, John Molesworth and James Buller. Lord Edgcumbe strongly deprecated that move—'the Tories irritated by the opposition are very likely to endeavour at revenge in some of the boroughs' which so far were exceptionally quiet, and this 'for the sake only of a person, by whom there will be nothing gained [Hoblyn himself was a Tory], but the Admiral answers for his love to the ministry'.[7] The point appears even more clearly in a letter from Richard Edgcumbe (q.v.) who had attended the nomination meeting at Bodmin on 5 Oct. He wrote to Enys:[8]

Many people (and I confess myself among the rest) expected that a fourth would have *hoisted his flag*. But I fancy he knew that if he did, he should be followed by but a weak squadron, besides very much endangering the interest of his confederate which . . . is personally a strong one. All . . . are . . . much at a loss to see what will be gained by it . . . Thomas Pitt . . . urged that argument, which the Admiral answered only by

saying, 'that he liked the other better and that was reason sufficient for him to be for him.'

Apparently Boscawen was trying to make Hoblyn, the Tory, break through the traditional set-up in the county, reserving his own intervention to a future occasion. However, a week later Hoblyn withdrew his candidature.

'But although this incident be sufficiently provoking, yet the affair of Mitchell is far more vexatious to me', Lord Edgcumbe went on to say in his letter. Hardly in any other Cornish borough was the balance of electoral interests so complex and delicate as at Mitchell. Edgcumbe was as keen as the Boscawens to defend what he considered his due interest in the borough, but would have been satisfied with one candidate, Hussey (q.v.), whom they had already nominated. But

Mr. Hussey's counsellors have advised him rashly to propose a colleague one Mr. Lutterel, of whom I nothing know . . . he owes this step to the wild advice of those heroes who set up Hoblyn.

There is a mass of conflicting evidence concerning the interplay of interests and schemes at Mitchell. But so much seems clear: that Boscawen, in his decisive manner, had with his two brothers George and John started there a canvass on 29 Aug. 1753, visiting 'every house',[9] and this without giving the least notice to the Boscawens' partners in the borough; and subsequently acted in a manner unconducive to compromise. He managed both the election and the subsequent petition with great energy and ability, producing one of the worst parliamentary upheavals in the comparatively peaceful years of 1754–5.

In April 1755 Boscawen, in command of a squadron sailed for America, returning in November. Next, he commanded a squadron blockading Brest. He has been criticized for his part in the trial of Byng. But while there was little sympathy between the two, it is not clear that Boscawen did more than was incumbent on him as the senior member of the Admiralty Board, and its only sailor, barring Temple West, who had been Byng's second-in-command at Minorca. In a letter to him on 4 Oct. his wife remarks: 'I am vastly glad you have a scheme to avoid Byng's trial'[10]—which hardly bears out Walpole's story of Boscawen having shown open partisanship against Byng.[11]

In June 1757 Boscawen was placed once more in command of the fleet blockading Brest, but was soon recalled; expected to be employed on the expedition against Rochefort; but Knowles went as second-in-command to Hawke (q.v.). There were rumours that Boscawen was dismissed, and that he was 'extremely angry'.

He complains [wrote Jenkinson to Grenville on 4 Aug. 1757] that this is a private pique of Mr. Pitt's, and assigns as the cause thereof his opposition to the navy bill; he talks in short like a man who has lost a good cruise, and wants to raise a disturbance.[12]

Walpole had a similar story to tell[13]—and consequently, he wrote, 'his Boscawenhood is much more Boscawened; that is, surely in the deepest shade.'

But in October 1757 Boscawen was appointed second-in-command of the main fleet; and in February, as admiral of the Blue, sailed as naval commander of the expedition which captured Louisburg. On his return he received the thanks of the House of Commons, and was sworn a Privy Councillor. In April 1759 he sailed for the Mediterranean, and on 18 August won the victory of Lagos Bay over the French. On his return, he was appointed general of the marines, with a salary of £3,000 per annum.

At the height of his popularity and glory he now staged his second incursion into Cornish county politics. About the end of September 1760 there were rumours that he meant to stand for the county at the general election. Lord Edgcumbe, visibly disturbed, wrote to Newcastle on 28 Sept. that the admiral had not said a word to him about it although he had stayed with him two days during the past week; and while asking for the Duke's views, reminded him of the line taken by Walpole and Pelham on similar occasions.[14] The admiral had not said anything to him either, replied Newcastle on 2 Oct.; and 'I verily remember what was the opinion both of Sir Robert Walpole and my brother as to an opposition for your county'. Still, considering the admiral's 'rank and merit and the zeal of his family', he would have to be supported.[15]

In fact, at the county meeting at Bodmin, on 10 Oct., Boscawen declared his candidature; and the next day wrote to Newcastle asking for his support;[16] as he had not communicated with Lord Falmouth on the subject, he had not spoken about it to Newcastle and Edgcumbe either; he had hoped that one of the present Members would decline, but they were now standing on a joint interest. In short, Boscawen had once more acted entirely on his own, placing a *fait accompli* before his brother and friends, who would undoubtedly have tried to dissuade him. And at first he seemed likely to carry it: Molesworth declined on 16 Oct., and a junction between Boscawen and Buller seemed imminent. But these proceedings displeased a good many Tory country gentlemen who felt that their candidates before acting should have taken the opinion of the county; and a second county meeting was called at

Bodmin on 3 Nov., at which Sir John St. Aubyn stepped into Molesworth's place.[17] An end was put to the contest by Boscawen's death, after a short illness, at Hatchlands on 10 Jan. 1761. A friend and supporter of Buller's wrote to him on 17 Jan.:[17]

I had the honour of your letter by the last post, with an account of Adm. Boscawen's death: an event that greatly affects this county, there being a vast number of Cornishmen whose bread, and hopes of preferment depended entirely on him. The nation indeed must feel the loss of so great, so distinguished a commander, whose capacity, as well as courage enabled him to conduct naval expeditions better perhaps than any that are left behind him.

[1] Sir J. K. Laughton in *DNB*. [2] Walpole, *Mems. Geo. II*, i. 194. [3] Add. 32733, ff. 16-17, 4 Oct. 1753. [4] Add. 32911, f. 371. [5] Add. 32733, ff. 80-81. [6] To John Enys; in an autograph collection at the Royal Institution, Truro. [7] Ibid. [8] The first part of the letter is missing, but it was clearly enclosed in Lord Edgcumbe's letter of 7 Oct.: the two letters refer to each other. [9] Thos. Clarke to Lord Hardwicke, 10 Sept. 1753, Add. 35592, ff. 143-5. [10] C. Aspinall-Oglander, *Admiral's Wife*, 226. [11] *Mems. Geo. II*, ii. 286. [12] *Grenville Pprs.* i. 203-4. [13] See letters to Mann, 4 Aug. and 3 Sept. 1757. [14] Add. 32912, f. 195. [15] Ibid. ff. 297-8. [16] Add. 32913, ff. 63-64. [17] W. Stackhouse to Jas. Buller, Buller mss in the possession of Sir John Carew Pole at Antony, Cornw.

L.B.N.

## BOSCAWEN, Edward Hugh (1744-74).

TRURO    16 June 1767-17 July 1774

*b.* 13 Sept. 1744, 1st s. of Adm. Edward Boscawen (q.v.). *educ.* Eton 1753-61; Ch. Ch. Oxf. 1761. *unm.*

In Parliament Boscawen regularly supported Administration, except on Howe's motion for an increase of the half-pay of naval captains, 9 Feb. 1773, and Grenville's Election Act, 25 Feb. 1774, when he appears in the King's list of dissenting friends. His only reported speech was in support of Howe's motion.[1]

Always indifferent in health, Boscawen seems to have drifted into a rather unsatisfactory set, disapproved of by his family friends; he was described by Mrs. Delany as a 'coxcomb' and a 'fop'.[2]

In 1774, gravely ill, he was sent to Spa, where he died 17 July 1774.

[1] Fortescue, ii. 448. [2] C. Aspinall-Oglander, *Admiral's Widow*, 32.

M.M.D.

## BOSCAWEN, Hon. George (1712-75), of Charlton Forest, Oxford.

PENRYN    22 Feb. 1743-1761
TRURO               1761-1774

*b.* 1 Dec. 1712, 4th s. of Hugh, 1st Visct. Falmouth, and bro. of Hon. Edward and Hon. John Boscawen (qq.v.). *educ.* poss. Eton 1725-8. *m.* 3 Feb. 1743, Ann, da. of John Morley Trevor of Glynde, Suss., sis. and coh. of John Trevor of Trevalyn, Denb., 2s. 2da.

Ensign 1 Ft. Gds. 1729, lt. and capt. 1738, capt. and lt.-col. 1743, col. 1749; lt. gov. Scilly Isles 1750-*d.*; col. 29 Ft. 1752-61; maj.-gen. 1758; col. 23 Ft. 1761-*d.*; lt.-gen. 1760.

Boscawen throughout his parliamentary career supported each successive Administration: his name appears in almost all the majority lists, and his only known Opposition vote was for the repeal of the Cider Act, 10 Feb. 1764.[1] His first and last recorded intervention in debate during his 31 years in the House was on 12 Feb. 1770:[2]

I hope my honourable friend [Sir John Molesworth] will not take it amiss, if I cannot sit still and hear the county of Cornwall called the rotten part of the constitution. I remember his saying at the last general election that no adventurer was admitted into any of the boroughs, but that every one of them was carried by family interest.

He died 3 May 1775.

[1] Harris's 'Debates'. [2] Cavendish's 'Debates', Egerton 220, ff. 60–61.

M.M.D.

## BOSCAWEN, George (b.1745), of Trevalyn, Denb.

St. Mawes 1768–1774
Truro 1774–1780

b. 4 Sept. 1745, 1st s. of Hon. George Boscawen (q.v.). educ. Eton 1754–61. m. 1778 or after, Annabella, da. of Sir William Bunbury, 5th Bt., div. w. of Sir Patrick Blake, 1st Bt. (q.v.).
Ensign 4 Ft. 1774: no further mention in Army List.

Boscawen regularly supported Administration until 1776. In May of that year he eloped to France with Annabella, wife of Sir Patrick Blake (q.v.),[1] and remained abroad until 1779. On his return he voted with Opposition on the motion on sending Keppel to sea, 3 Mar. 1779, Dunning's motion, 6 Apr. 1780, and the motion against proroguing Parliament, 24 Apr. 1780. Before the general election of 1780 John Robinson wrote about Truro: 'It is hoped it will be two friends and not Mr. Boscawen again, and therefore it is canvassed hopeful.' Boscawen was not put up again. There is no record of his having spoken in the House.

[1] Diary of John Baker, ed. Yorke, 353.

L.B.N.

## BOSCAWEN, Hugh (d.1795), of Windlesham, Surr.

St. Mawes 1774–1790

Illegit. s. of Hugh, 2nd Visct. Falmouth. m. Anne, 3s. 1da.
Clerk of the charge to the yeomen of the guard 1772–d.; knight marshal of the Household and marshal of the Marshalsea 1792–d.

All Boscawen's recorded votes were with Administration, except in the division on economical reform, 8 Mar. 1780. He voted for Shelburne's peace preliminaries, 18 Feb. 1783; did not vote on Fox's East India bill; and Robinson wrote about

him in his survey for the general election of 1784: 'Mr. Boscawen may be made steady.' In Stockdale's list of 19 Mar. he appears as a supporter of Pitt.

From his father (who died 4 Feb. 1782) he inherited £30,000, the manor of St. Antony in Cornwall, and the Boscawen interest at St. Mawes. This he apparently sold to the Marquess of Buckingham, who controlled the other seat in the borough. Buckingham wrote to W. W. Grenville on 7 June 1788 that Boscawen's tenure of St. Mawes expired 'with the Parliament' where he had 'hitherto remained . . . for the object of a reversion [to the office of knight marshal] which Pitt has given him'.[1] In 1789 Boscawen voted with Pitt over the Regency, and in 1790 'relinquished' his seat.[2] There is no record of his having spoken in the House.

He died 4 Sept. 1795.

[1] HMC Fortescue, iii. 334. [2] Gent. Mag. 1795, p. 795.

L.B.N.

## BOSCAWEN, Hon. John (1714–67).

Truro 1747–30 Apr. 1767

b. 2 Jan. 1714, 5th s. of Hugh, 1st Visct. Falmouth, and bro. of Hon. Edward and Hon. George Boscawen (qq.v.). educ. poss. Eton 1728. m. 29 Dec. 1748, Thomasine da. of Robert Surman, merchant, of Valentine House, Essex, 1s.
Cornet 1 Horse 1736; page of honour to George II 1738; lt. 1742; capt. 1744; lt.-col. 1 Ft. Gds. 1748; col. 1758; col. 75 Ft. 1758–61; maj.-gen. 1761; col. 45 Ft. 1761–d.
Master of horse to Duke of Cumberland, 1747–57; groom of the bedchamber to same 1757–65; gov. Jersey 1760–d.

Classed 'for', as a follower of Cumberland, in Dupplin's list of 1754, Boscawen is described as a follower of Bute in Bute's list of December 1761, and in December 1762 appears in Henry Fox's list of Members favourable to the peace preliminaries. On 10 Feb. 1764 he voted for the repeal of the Cider Act,[1] but does not appear in any other division list. Rockingham counted him as 'pro' in July 1765, and as 'Swiss' (prepared to support every Administration) in November 1766. There is no record of his having spoken in the House.

He died 30 Apr. 1767.

[1] Harris's 'Debates'.

M.M.D.

## BOSCAWEN, William Augustus Spencer (1750–1828).

Truro 1784–Feb. 1792

b. 7 Jan. 1750, o. s. of Hon. John Boscawen (q.v.). m. 2s. 1da.
Ensign 2 Ft. Gds. 1769, lt. and capt. 1775, capt. and lt.-col. 1781; ret. 1790.

In 1780 Boscawen was an unsuccessful candidate at Truro. Returned after a contest in 1784, he voted against the Duke of Richmond's fortifications plan, 27 Feb. 1786, but with Administration over the Regency, 1789. His name appears in no other division list in this Parliament, and there is no record of his having spoken in the House.

He died 13 June 1828.

M.M.D.

**BOUGHTON ROUSE** (afterwards **ROUSE BOUGHTON**), **Charles William** (1747–1821), of Rouse Lench, Worcs.

EVESHAM 1780–1790
BRAMBER 1796–Jan. 1800

> *bap.* 16 Dec. 1747, 2nd s. of Shuckburgh Boughton of Poston Court, Herefs. by Mary, da. of Hon. Algernon Greville. *m.* 3 June 1782, Catherine, da. and h. of William Pearce Hall of Downton Hall, Salop, 1s. 3da. *suc.* to estates of his distant cos. Thomas Philips Rouse 1768, and took add. name of Rouse; *cr.* Bt. 28 July 1791; *suc.* bro. Sir Edward Boughton, 8th Bt., in the family baronetcy 26 Feb. 1794, and changed name to Rouse Boughton.

Sec. to the board of control for India 1784–91.

Boughton Rouse went out to India as a writer in 1765, and after holding judicial and administrative offices in the Company's service returned to England in 1778. He entered Parliament in 1780 after an expensive contest at Evesham; and until the fall of North voted with the Opposition. India was his main interest in politics, and the seven speeches which he is known to have made between 1780 and 1790 all deal with Indian affairs.

He voted for Shelburne's peace preliminaries, 18 Feb. 1783, for parliamentary reform, 7 May 1783, and for Fox's East India bill, 27 Nov. 1783. Yet in Robinson's list of January 1784 he is classed as 'very hopeful', and in Stockdale's of 19 Mar. 1784 as 'Administration'. He was a member of the St. Alban's Tavern group which tried to bring about a union between Pitt and Fox; but after having accepted office under Pitt, naturally voted consistently with his Administration. He opposed the impeachment of Warren Hastings—'He never thought Mr. Hastings a criminal, nor wished him to be so considered.'[1]

He died 26 Feb. 1821.

[1] Stockdale, vii. 165.

J.B.

**BOULTON,** *see* **CRABB BOULTON**

**BOURNE,** *see* **PAGE Francis**

**BOUVERIE, Hon. Bartholomew** (1753–1835).

DOWNTON 17 Dec. 1779–21 Feb. 1780, 1790–1796, 20 Feb. 1819–1826, 16 Dec. 1826–1830

> *b.* 29 Oct. 1753, 3rd s. of William Bouverie, 1st Earl of Radnor, bro. of Hon. William Henry Bouverie and half-bro. of Jacob Pleydell Bouverie, Visct. Folkestone (qq.v.). *educ.* Univ. Coll. Oxf. 1772. *m.* 9 Mar. 1779, Mary, da. of Hon. James Everard Arundell, sis. of James, 9th Lord Arundell of Wardour, 3s. 3da.

Bouverie unsuccessfully contested Shaftesbury in 1776 on Lord Shaftesbury's interest. In 1779 he was returned on his family interest at Downton after a contest, but unseated on petition.

He died 31 May 1835.

J.B.

**BOUVERIE, Hon. Edward** (1738–1810), of Delapré Abbey, Northants.

SALISBURY 1761–May 1771
NORTHAMPTON 1790–3 Sept. 1810

> *b.* 5 Sept. 1738, 2nd s. of Sir Jacob Bouverie, M.P., 1st Visct. Folkestone, by his 1st w. Mary, da. and h. of Bartholomew Clarke of Delapré Abbey and Hardingstone, Northants. *educ.* Eton 1753–6; Ch. Ch. Oxf. 1757. *m.* 30 June 1764, Harriet, da. of Sir Everard Fawkener, ambassador to the Porte, 3s. 5da.

Bouverie was returned for Salisbury on his family interest. In Parliament he seems to have followed an independent line. He was classed by Jenkinson in the autumn of 1763 as 'pro'; but voted with the Opposition on Wilkes, 15 Nov. 1763, and on general warrants, 15 and 18 Feb. 1764, and was listed by Newcastle, 10 May 1764 as a 'sure friend'. Rockingham classed him as 'pro', July 1765, and as 'Whig', November 1766; but Townshend put him down as 'Government', January 1767, and Newcastle, 2 Mar. 1767 as 'Tory'. No other vote by him is reported for this Parliament. In the next he voted with Administration on the expulsion of Wilkes, 3 Feb. 1769, and the Middlesex election, 15 Apr. and 8 May 1769, but with Opposition on the Spanish convention, 13 Feb. 1771. There is no record of his having spoken in the House during this period. In 1771 he resigned his seat in favour of his nephew Jacob Bouverie, Viscount Folkestone, now of age.

At the general election of 1774 Bouverie offered himself at Northampton, hoping for the support of the Compton interest, but withdrew without making a canvass.[1] At the by-election of 1782 he may also have considered standing.[2] Before the general election of 1784 Lord Spencer reported to his mother that Bouverie was to stand 'in avowed opposition to Lord Lucan, supported by a few of the malcontents of the Compton interest and all that description'; but next day he wrote again that 'the malcontents . . .

finding that Mr. Bouverie would only lend them his name, but not appear in person, they have set up Mr. Trotman'.[3] Bouverie successfully contested Northampton in 1790. He was a staunch supporter of Fox and voted with him consistently even after the outbreak of war with France.

He died 3 Sept. 1810.

[1] John Rowell, steward at Castle Ashby, to Lord Northampton, 'Christmas eve', 1774. Northampton mss. Ex inf. V. A. Hatley. [2] See advertisement in *Northampton Merc.* 8 Apr. 1782. [3] 29, 30 Mar. 1784, Spencer mss at Althorp.

M.M.D.

**BOUVERIE, Jacob,** *see* **PLEYDELL BOUVERIE**

**BOUVERIE, Hon. William** (1725–76), of Longford Castle, Wilts.

SALISBURY 1747–17 Feb. 1761

*b.* 26 Feb. 1725, 1st s. of Jacob, 1st Visct. Folkestone, and bro. of Hon. Edward Bouverie (q.v.). *educ.* Winchester; Univ. Coll. Oxf. 1743. *m.* (1) 18 Jan. 1748, Harriet (*d.*29 May 1750), da. and h. of Sir Mark Stewart Pleydell, 1st Bt., of Coleshill, Berks., 1s.; (2) 5 Sept. 1751, Rebecca (*d.*4 May 1764), da. of John Alleyne of Barbados, 4s. 2da.; (3) 22 July 1765 Anne, da. of Sir Thomas Hales, 3rd Bt. (q.v.), wid. of Anthony Duncombe, 1st Lord Feversham, 2da. *suc.* fa. 17 Feb. 1761; *cr.* Earl of Radnor 31 Oct. 1765.

In 1754 Bouverie was returned after a contest, and listed by Dupplin as a Tory.

He died 28 Jan. 1776.

M.M.D.

**BOUVERIE, Hon. William Henry** (1752–1806), of Betchworth House, Surr.

SALISBURY 19 Feb. 1776–1802

*b.* 30 Oct. 1752, 2nd s. of William Bouverie (q.v.), 1st Earl of Radnor; bro. of Hon. Bartholomew Bouverie, and half-bro. of Jacob, Visct. Folkestone (qq.v.). *educ.* Harrow c.1765; Univ. Coll. Oxf. 1771. *m.* 16 Aug. 1777, Lady Bridget Douglas, da. of James, 14th Earl of Morton[S], 1s. 2da.

Bouverie was regularly returned on the family interest at Salisbury without a contest. In Parliament he consistently voted with the Opposition till the fall of North. The *English Chronicle* wrote of him in 1781:

> He is a very constant attendant on his parliamentary duties, and as constantly divides with the Opposition. He has never attempted to display his abilities as an orator in the House . . . He possesses an estate of near two thousand pounds per annum, and with this fortune supports the consequence of his rank with great liberality and great respect.

Bouverie did not vote on Shelburne's peace preliminaries, 18 Feb. 1783, but was classed by Robinson in March as a follower of Shelburne. He voted for parliamentary reform, 7 May 1783;

against Fox's East India bill, 27 Nov. 1783; was a member of the St. Alban's Tavern group for a union of parties; and was classed by Robinson in January 1784 as a Pittite. But Stockdale on 18 Mar., and Adam in May, classed him as Opposition, and he usually voted against Pitt's Administration. He appears, however, as voting with them in the first extant division list on the Regency, 16 Dec. 1788, and on 27 Jan. 1789 said he supported the Address offering the Regency to the Prince of Wales 'provided no further restrictions were meant to be incorporated in the bill than the House had agreed to, but if any additional restrictions were intended he should vote against them'. But he voted with the Opposition in the division of 11 Feb., and appears with them in the consolidated list of votes on the Regency. Bouverie spoke several times during the Regency crisis, but few other speeches by him are reported (his first recorded speech was during a debate on taxing bricks on 22 July 1784—eight years after he entered Parliament). Bouverie objected to the House accepting a petition from Warren Hastings, 27 Apr. 1789, because he feared that such interference 'would materially affect the prosecution, perhaps prove its ruin. If the petition were entered upon farther . . . he really believed the loss of the cause would be the unfortunate consequence'. And on 4 May 1789 he moved 'That the thanks of the House be given to the Right Hon. Edmund Burke and the rest of the managers for their exertion and assiduity in the prosecution of Warren Hastings, Esq., and that they be desired to persevere in the same.' Bouverie continued to vote with the Opposition also after the outbreak of the war with France.[1]

He died 23 Aug. 1806. His obituary in the *Gentleman's Magazine* (1806, p. 877) paid tribute to the 'polished elegance of his manners', mentioned his interest in literature and medicine, and added that 'there were few subjects on which he was not intimately well informed'.

[1] Stockdale, xvi. 312; xvii. 106, 163.

M.M.D.

**BOWES, Andrew Robinson** (1747–1810), of Cold Pike Hill; Gibside, nr. Gateshead; and Streatlam Castle, co. Dur.

NEWCASTLE-UPON-TYNE 1780–1784

*b.* 19 Jan. 1747, 1st s. of George Stoney of Greyfort and Portland, co. Tipperary by Elizabeth, da. of James Johnston of Ballynockane. *m.* (1) 5 Nov. 1768,[1] Hannah, da. and h. of William Newton of Cold Pike Hill, Newcastle coal merchant, *s.p.*; (2) 17 Jan. 1777, Mary Eleanor, da. and h. of George Bowes (q.v.), wid. of John Lyon, 7th Earl of Strathmore [S], 1s. 1da. On marrying her Stoney took, under the terms of her father's will, the name of Bowes. She divorced him 3 Mar. 1789.

Ensign 4 Ft. 1764, lt. 1769; half-pay 1770.
Sheriff, Northumb. 1780-1.

Of Irish gentry and great-nephew of Maj.-Gen. Andrew Robinson (equerry to the Princess Dowager of Wales), this Member became connected with Newcastle through his first marriage. Hannah Newton had inherited Cold Pike Hill and a fortune of £20-30,000; he treated her abominably; but at her death retained her property. His second wife had inherited Gibside, Streatlam Castle, and a fortune of about £600,000, which, however, as 'the effect of a lucid interval' (as Lord Chancellor Thurlow put it) she had by pre-nuptial deeds conveyed to trustees; 'by the terrors of personal violence' he made her rescind them; even then his treatment of her grew more and more outrageous; and being 'of a very savage and tormenting disposition' he resorted to physical cruelty. The story of that marriage is fully told in contemporary and recent literature.[2]

A month after his marriage to Lady Strathmore a vacancy occurred at Newcastle, and Bowes (as he now was) declared his candidature.[3] Supported by the local radicals, he carried on a demagogical campaign, but lost by 95 votes on a poll of 2231. He stood again in 1780, described by Robinson as 'not adverse' to the Government. This time he won by 50 votes. 'Bowes is not the kind of colleague that a man would wish for', wrote Nicholas Ridley, brother of the other successful candidate, 25 Sept. 1780. '. . . On Thursday the new-elected Members are to give a joint ball; we have not much expectation of the brilliancy of it as many of the neighbouring people are so very much dissatisfied with Bowes that they will not even go to a ball of his giving though on occasion of an election.'[4] On 17 Feb. 1781 Charles Jenkinson wrote to John Robinson that the Duke of Northumberland could 'secure Mr. Bowes'.[5] But on 12 Dec. 1781, on Lowther's motion against the American war, he voted with Opposition; on the motion against the Admiralty, 20 Feb. 1782, he seems to have voted with Administration;[6] was absent from two divisions concerning America; and again voted with the Government over two motions directed against them, 8 and 15 Mar. In short, he would not vote for the American war but would not join in condemning the North Government as such. He was after an Irish peerage, and hoped to obtain it from North.

On 30 May 1782 Bowes wrote to Shelburne a long and verbose letter, disingenuous and empty, full of self-justification and in a high-falutin style. The winter of 1782-3 he spent in the north; and on 19 Feb. 1783 he wrote to Shelburne from Gibside: 'it has not been in my power this winter, on account of a severe indisposition, to attend my duty in Parliament'.[7] But to a friend he wrote, 15 Apr. 1783: 'A want of money, not a want of health, has detained me here so long.'[8] There is a good deal of bombast before the point is reached—'I wish your Lordship . . . to think me a moderate man who is so far endowed with common sense as not to be self sufficient . . . I am only prompted by my ardour to obtain an object to which my mind has been long attached': Lord North had absolutely promised him an Irish peerage; his application 'was supported and enforced by the Duke of Northumberland'; but there was procrastination; still, North, after he had resigned, assured the Duke 'that his Majesty approved of my wish; and that an Irish peerage would be conferred on me with the first opportunity'. He now repeats the request, 'stimulated by my own enterprising mind and by my strong idea of your Lordship's generosity'.

In March 1783 Robinson listed Bowes as connected with the Duke of Northumberland. On 7 May 1783 Bowes voted for Pitt's parliamentary reform proposals. He did not vote on Fox's East India bill; was listed by Robinson in January 1784 as 'doubtful, some hope'; and was expected by him to retain the seat. But Stockdale's list of 19 Mar. classed him as 'Opposition'; and according to a news report in the *Chelmsford Chronicle* of 9 Apr., he had entirely prejudiced his chances 'by his unfortunate attachment to Mr. Fox'. The election ended on 26 Apr., and on the 29th Nicholas Ridley wrote to his half-brother Richard:[9]

> As we were preparing to go to the hustings, a messenger arrived from Mr. Bowes to inform us that he declined the poll, but would meet us at the place of polling as he had something to say to people: he made a handsome farewell speech . . . Mr. B's leavetaking seemed to be *for ever*.

His only recorded speech in the House was on Lord Mahon's election bribery bill, 19 Mar. 1784: the laws, he said, were already too severe, and repugnant in particular 'to the interests of the lower class of constituents'; an honest mechanic, burgess of Newcastle, could not be expected to travel 300 miles at his own expense to vote at an election.

Bowes never stood for Parliament again. Lady Strathmore, unable to stand the ill-treatment any longer, escaped from him in February 1785, and took legal proceedings: exhibited articles of peace against him; a bill of complaint to re-establish the ante-nuptial trust deeds; and filed a suit for divorce. While these were proceeding, Bowes, on 10 Nov. 1786, had her kidnapped in Oxford Street and carried off to the north, his aim being by force to put a stop to the proceedings she had brought against him. Rescued from him, she won her suits; while he spent the remaining 23 years of his life in prison or 'within the prison rules', first for his crime, and next for debts. He died 16 Jan. 1810.

[1] *Gent. Mag.* 1768, p. 542. Burke's *Irish Landed Gentry* gives 1 Sept. 1769, but clearly the earlier date is more probable. [2] See foremost Jesse Foot, *Lives of A. R. Bowes and the Countess of Strathmore*, and R. Arnold, *Unhappy Countess*. [3] Before that he had thought of standing for Morpeth; see *HMC Carlisle*, 317, 319. [4] To his half-bro. Richard Ridley, Ridley mss at Blagdon. [5] Abergavenny ms 349. [6] Thus according to one list; in another he appears as absent. [7] Lansdowne mss. [8] Foot, op. cit. 78. [9] Ridley mss.

L.B.N.

**BOWES, George** (1701–60), of Streatlam Castle, co. Dur.

DURHAM CO.    1727–17 Sept. 1760

*b.* 21 Aug. 1701, 3rd s. of Sir William Bowes, M.P., of Streatlam Castle, da. and h. of Sir Francis Blakiston, 3rd Bt., of Gibside, co. Dur. *educ.* G. Inn 1719. *m.* (1) Oct. 1729, Eleanor (*d.*14 Dec. 1742), da. and h. of Hon. Thomas Verney (s. of George, 12th Lord Willoughby de Broke), *s.p.*; (2) 13 June 1743, Mary, da. and h. of Edward Gilbert of Paulswalden, Herts., 1da. who m. (1) John Lyon, 7th Earl of Strathmore [S], and (2) Andrew Robinson Stoney, afterwards Bowes (q.v.). *suc.* bro. 1722.
    Mayor, Durham 1739.

Bowes was one of the largest coal owners in Durham, and with the Wortleys and Liddells founded the 'Grand Alliance', a cartel which dominated the north country coal trade throughout the century.[1]

In Parliament the interests of the coal trade, vital to county Durham, were with him a dominant concern. Returned unopposed in 1754, he was classed by Dupplin as an Opposition Whig. During the debates on the Oxfordshire election petitions he spoke on the Tory side;[2] and at least one other speech of his in this Parliament is reported: 3 Mar. 1756, on the plate bill.[3]

He died 17 Sept. 1760, leaving a fortune estimated at £600,000.

[1] E. Hughes, *N. Country Life in 18th Cent.* 235–6. [2] R. J. Robson, *Oxfordshire Election of 1754*, p. 139. [3] Newdigate ms. B2549.

J.B.

**BOWLBY, Thomas** (1721–95), of Park St., London.

LAUNCESTON    1780–Jan. 1783

*bap.* 2 May 1721, 1st s. of Thomas Bowlby of Durham by his w. Mary Burrell of Durham. *educ.* Trinity Hall, Camb. 1740; M. Temple 1739. *m.* 20 June 1754, Lady Mary, da. of George Brudenell, 3rd Earl of Cardigan, wid. of Richard Powis of Hintlesham Hall, Suff., *d.s.p.*
    Commr. of Excise 1762–76; jt. comptroller of army accounts 1776–80; commissary gen. of musters 1780–d.

As a young man Bowlby spent some time in Italy, and in 1752 was buying Italian paintings for Lord Northumberland.[1] His marriage introduced him to court circles, and in 1762 Newcastle, when recommending him for a vacancy at the Excise, noted 'how much the King approved'.[2] On 3 Oct. 1776 Robinson suggested Bowlby to the King for a comptroller of army accounts: 'The Duke of Montagu, Lord Ailesbury, Mr. Bowlby and the Brudenell family have long and most earnestly solicited this office, and Lord North would wish to oblige them.'[3] But the change of office reduced Bowlby's salary by £200 a year which in January 1780 was made up by a secret service pension.[4] He seems to have been an able administrator, and according to his successor, Sir John Dick, much more vigorous and efficient than any of his immediate predecessors.[5] In May 1780 North proposed him as one of the commissioners to inquire into public accounts, describing him in the House as 'a man of as upright a heart, as clear a head, and as honest a mind as anyone living . . . whose talents, as well as the many recommendations he had received from various quarters, pointed him out as a very fit person to be a commissioner'. But Fox, though 'no man in that House, or out of it had a better opinion' of Bowlby than he had, condemned the attempt to introduce a placeman since placemen were specifically excluded by the bill; and the nomination was rejected by the House.[6]

On 4 September 1780 North wrote to Christopher D'Oyly (q.v.), commissary general of musters, who meant to retire from Parliament:[7]

> Mr. Bowlby is resolved to undertake a parliamentary life, and will be recommended by the Duke of Northumberland to one of his boroughs in the West. As you are changing your political situation, I do not see why you should not change places at the same time. The place he now fills is not tenable with a seat in the House of Commons, your place ought always to be held by a Member of Parliament.

The change of places was gazetted on the 6th, and a few days later Bowlby was returned on Northumberland's interest at Launceston. In Parliament he naturally supported Administration. His one reported speech in the House was in a debate on army accounts, 31 May 1781. In April 1782 North, in his observations on John Robinson's list of pensions, noted that Bowlby, 'who will be very grateful for the continuance in Lady Mary's name, does not wish to be continued in the list in his own name';[8] and a pension of £200 was still being paid to Lady Mary Bowlby in August 1782.[9] In 1783 Bowlby vacated his seat; his reasons for doing so have not been ascertained.

He died in October 1795.

[1] Mann to Walpole, 11 Aug. 1752. [2] Add. 32938, f. 365. [3] Add. 38833, f. 67. [4] 37836, f. 67. [5] Binney, *British Public Finance & Admini-*

stration, 12. ⁶Almon xvii. 609, 622. ⁷ Gent. Mag. 1829, 506. ⁸Fortescue, v. 469. ⁹Secret service accounts, Royal archives, Windsor.

M.M.D.

## BOWYER, George (1739–99), of Bracknell, Berks.

QUEENBOROUGH 1784–1790

*b.* 1739, 3rd s. of Sir William Bowyer, 3rd Bt., of Denham Place, Bucks. by Anne, da. of Sir John Stonhouse, 7th Bt., of Radley, Berks. *m.* (1) 11 Nov. 1768, Margaret (*d.*18 Sept. 1778), da. of Rev. John Price of Barrington, Glos., wid. of Sir Jacob Downing, 4th Bt. (q.v.), *s.p.*; (2) 4 June 1782, Henrietta, da. and h. of Adm. Sir Piercy Brett (q.v.), 3s. 2da. *cr.* Bt. 8 Sept. 1794. *suc.* bro. in the family baronetcy Apr. 1799. Lt. R.N. 1758; cdr. 1761; capt. 1762; r.-adm. 1793; v.-adm. 1794; adm. 1799.

Bowyer was returned after a contest on the Admiralty interest for Queenborough, and was a supporter of Pitt. On 18 June 1784 he made his maiden speech in defence of the state of the navy. Nine other speeches are reported, all on naval affairs. On 18 Apr. 1785 he voted for Pitt's motion on parliamentary reform.

He died 6 Dec. 1799.

J.B.

## BOYD, John (1750–1815), of Danson Park, Kent.

WAREHAM 1780–1784

*b.* 27 Oct. 1750, 1st s. of Sir John Boyd, 1st Bt., of Danson Park, London merchant and East India Co. director, by Mary, da. of William Bamstead of Upton, Warws. *educ.* Ch. Ch. Oxf. 1768. *m.* 26 Feb. 1784, Margaret, da. of Thomas Harley (q.v.), 2s. 1da. *suc.* fa. 24 Jan. 1800.

Boyd's seat for Wareham was probably purchased with the approval of the Treasury.[1] Up to March 1782 he supported North. On 18 Feb. 1783 he voted for Shelburne's peace preliminaries. Next month Robinson set him down as 'doubtful', among the 'country gentlemen and persons unconnected'. On 27 Nov. he voted against Fox's East India bill; and was classed in Stockdale's list of 19 Mar. 1784 as a supporter of Pitt, but did not stand at the general election. No speech by him is recorded.

He died 20 May 1815.

¹ Warren Lisle to Shelburne, 31 July 1782, A. L. Cross, *18th Cent. Docs. Rel. to Royal Forests, Sheriffs, and Smuggling*, 246.

I.R.C.

## BOYLE, Hamilton, Visct. Dungarvan (1730–64).

WARWICK 1761–23 Nov. 1762

*b.* 3 Feb. 1730, 2nd but 1st surv. s. of John, 5th Earl of Cork and Orrery [I], by his 1st w. Lady Henrietta Hamilton, da. of George, 1st Earl of Orkney [S]. *educ.* Westminster 1741; Ch. Ch. Oxf. 1748; I. Temple

1749. *unm. suc.* fa. as 6th Earl of Cork and Orrery [I] and 3rd Baron Boyle [GB] 23 Nov. 1762.
M.P. [I] 1759–60.
High steward, Oxford University 1762–*d.*

Lord Shelburne wrote in his autobiographical fragment:[1] 'I was . . . much connected during all the time I was at college with Mr. Hamilton Boyle.' Dungarvan, as Boyle had become in 1761, sat in Parliament on the interest of Lord Warwick, who was related to the Boyle family through the Hamiltons; and passed his brief career in the Commons under Shelburne's wing as a supporter of Bute. In Bute's list of 1761 he is described as 'well inclined to Lord Bute', and there was a suggestion that he should succeed James Stuart Mackenzie (q.v.) as envoy to Turin. Shelburne wrote to Bute in June 1761:[2] 'I saw Lord Dungarvan this day for two hours and have weighed the matter as much as I could without mentioning Turin to him. Upon the whole I think he is more fitted to try at the House of Commons. I therefore did not suggest it to him.' But there is no record of his having spoken in the Commons.

He died 17 Jan. 1764.

¹ Fitzmaurice, *Shelburne*, i. 15. ² Bute mss.

J.B.

## BOYLE, Hon. Robert, *see* WALSINGHAM

## BOYNTON, Sir Griffith, 6th Bt. (1745–78), of Burton Agnes, Yorks.

BEVERLEY 22 May 1772–1774

*b.* 22 Feb. 1745, o.s. of Sir Griffith Boynton, 5th Bt., of Burton Agnes, by Agnes, da. of Thomas White of Wallingwells, Notts. *educ.* Corpus Christi, Camb. 1760. *m.* (1) 9 May 1762, Charlotte (*d.*9 Sept. 1767), da. of Francis Topham, judge of the prerogative court of York, *s.p.*; (2) 1 Aug. 1768, Mary, da. of James Heblethwayte of Norton and Bridlington, Yorks., 3s. *suc.* fa. 22 Oct. 1761.

Boynton was returned for Beverley after a contest. His only known vote was for the motion to make Grenville's Election Act permanent, 25 Feb. 1774, and there is no record of his having spoken in Parliament. He did not stand at the general election of 1774.

He died 6 Jan. 1778.

J.B.

## BRADDYLL, Wilson (1756–1818), of Conishead Priory, Lancs.

| | |
|---|---|
| LANCASTER | 1780–1784 |
| HORSHAM | 1790–10 Mar. 1792 |
| CARLISLE | 3 Mar. 1791–1796 |

*bap.* 24 Feb. 1756, 1st s. of John Gale of Highhead Castle by Sarah, da. and coh. of Christopher Wilson of

Bardsea Hall, Lancs. *educ.* Queen's, Oxf. 1773. *m.* 29 Jan. 1776, Jane, da. and h. of Matthias Gale of Catgill Hall, Cumb., 1s. 4da. *suc.* to the Conishead estate of his 1st cos. Thomas Braddyll 1776 and took name of Braddyll; *suc. fa.* 19 Oct. 1814.

Sheriff, Lancs. 1778–9; groom of the bedchamber, 1812–*d.*

In 1780 Braddyll was returned unopposed for Lancaster, probably with Cavendish support. In Parliament he regularly voted against North's Administration; against Shelburne's peace preliminaries, 18 Feb. 1783; and for Fox's East India bill, 27 Nov. 1783. Robinson's list of January 1784 and Stockdale's of March both class him as a Foxite. There is no record of his having spoken in the House in this period. At the general election of 1784 he declined a contest.

Braddyll died 20 Nov. 1818.

I.R.C.

## BRADSHAW, Thomas (1733–74), of Hampton Court, Mdx.

HARWICH  30 Nov. 1767–1768
SALTASH  1768–May 1772, 8 June 1772–6 Nov. 1774

*b.* 25 Jan. 1733. *m.* Nov. 1757, Elizabeth, da. and coh. of Robert Wilson, London merchant, of Woodford, Essex, 4s. 2da. Her sis. m. Anthony Chamier (q.v.).

Clerk in the War Office c.1757–59, first clerk 1759–61; chief clerk at Treasury Dec. 1761–Feb. 1763; commr. of taxes Feb. 1763–Aug. 1767; sec. to Treasury Aug. 1767–Aug. 1770; ld. of Admiralty Apr. 1772–*d.*

Bradshaw began life in humble circumstances (according to Junius he was a 'clerk to a contractor for forage'[1]). His first patron was Lord Barrington (q.v.), his chief at the War Office, who, on becoming chancellor of the Exchequer in 1761, brought Bradshaw to the Treasury. During the following six years Bradshaw was an important civil servant, and formed connexions with several influential politicians, including the Duke of Grafton. It was Grafton who, as first lord of the Treasury, appointed Bradshaw its secretary,[2] and brought him into Parliament for the Government borough of Harwich.

Despite his experience in Government administration, Bradshaw henceforth regarded himself primarily as Grafton's confidential man of business for both public and private affairs. He assisted Grafton with the general election of 1768, and came to occupy a key post in Government as Grafton's link with North. He aided and encouraged Grafton in his wish to be rid of Shelburne; and in the summer of 1768, when Grafton wanted to divorce his duchess, he sent Bradshaw to obtain evidence of her adultery.

When Grafton resigned in January 1770 he obtained for Bradshaw the reversion for two lives of the office of auditor general of the plantations ('worth upwards of £2500 a year, and which may, and possibly will, be worth double that sum'[3]), and a pension of £1500 a year until it became vacant. Bradshaw remained at the Treasury, at Grafton's and North's request,[4] only to induct John Robinson (q.v.) into his new duties. He wrote to Grafton on 23 Aug. 1770:[5]

> You say, my Lord, that you wish me to remain in the Treasury *for my own sake*, for *that of my family*, and *even for yours*. Your bounty has made the two first reasons of no weight . . . All your Grace's friends, as well as mine, know from me that I leave the Treasury because you are no longer at the head of it. I have a high esteem for Lord North, but I cannot transfer that warmth of attachment which is necessary for my situation to whoever sits at that Board . . . I wish for no office but under you; and under you there is no employment, however trifling in value, of which I shall not be ambitious, whenever you return to the King's service.

Bradshaw remained in close touch with Government circles, and acted as Grafton's agent with Administration. In July 1770 he hinted to North, with Grafton's approval, that Grafton would like to go to the Admiralty; and he continued to watch over Grafton's interests in this matter.[6] In April 1772 he was made a lord of the Admiralty, and on standing for re-election at Saltash was defeated but returned on petition. He is not known to have spoken in debate.

William Hickey, who knew the family, wrote of Bradshaw's 'gay and social disposition' and his 'unbounded extravagance'.[7] And Bradshaw wrote to Robert Murray Keith on 11 Mar. 1773:[8] 'Some acts of friendship, and some of extravagancy, have distressed me for some months in money matters; but, I am growing a little fatter in the purse, and will soon pay my debt.'

He died 6 Nov. 1774. C. W. Cornwall (q.v.) wrote to Charles Jenkinson on 7 Nov.:[9] 'Poor Bradshaw died of a fever in town yesterday morning . . . His affairs, as you will easily imagine, are in a sad condition, and the distress of his family not to be described.' But according to Horace Walpole Bradshaw committed suicide,[10] and the story is repeated in the *Last Journals*:[11] 'His vanity had carried him to great excesses of profusion, and, being overwhelmed with debts, he shot himself.'

His will,[12] dated 19 May 1773, is a curious document. There is no mention of any real property, and all his personal property he left to his wife. The greater part of the will deals with the disposal of the profits of the auditorship-general of the plantations, an office he held only in reversion and to which he never succeeded. Trustees (one of whom was Anthony Chamier) were to pay allowances of £200 a year to Bradshaw's wife, his three younger sons, and his daughter; Elizabeth Worsley (probably an illegitimate daughter) was to receive £50 a year; and the remainder was to go to his eldest son. Shortly after his death his widow was given a secret service pension of £500 a year, and his two younger sons and daughter were given pensions of £100 a year.

Bradshaw left his papers to Anthony Chamier: their present location is unknown. A box of papers was to be delivered to the Duke of Grafton: there are letters from Bradshaw to Grafton in the Grafton manuscripts, but none of Bradshaw's papers.

[1] Junius to Grafton, 14 Feb. 1770. [2] Grafton to Chatham, 8 Jan. 1767, Chatham mss. [3] Bradshaw to R. M. Keith, 16 Apr. 1773, Add. 35505, f. 171. [4] Grafton, *Autobiog.* 257. [5] Grafton mss. [6] Bradshaw to Grafton, 24 July 1770, ibid. See also *Autobiog.* 260-3. [7] *Mems.* i. 319. [8] Add. 35505, f. 83. [9] Add. 38470, f. 146. [10] See Walpole's letters to Lord Strafford, 11 Nov. 1774, to Mann, 14 Nov., and to Lady Upper Ossory, 14 Nov. [11] Vol. i. 407. [12] PCC 387 Bargrave.

J.B.

## BRAMSTON, Thomas Berney (1733–1813), of Skreens, Essex.

ESSEX    11 May 1779–1802

*b.* 7 Dec. 1733, o.s. of Thomas Bramston, M.P. for Essex, by Elizabeth, da. of Richard Berney, recorder of Norwich. *educ.* Felsted; New Coll. Oxf. 1751; M. Temple 1742, called 1757. *m.* 10 Jan. 1764, Mary, da. and h. of Stephen Gardiner of Norwich, 3 surv. s. 1da. besides four children ob. inf.[1] *suc.* fa. 14 Nov. 1765.

Bencher, M. Temple 1783, reader 1791, treasurer 1795.

Bramston, of a Tory family and a close friend of John Strutt (q.v.), supported the 'old interest' in Essex county elections: Conyers in 1763; and Harvey and Houblon in 1768. He was active in county affairs but did not stand for Parliament till 1779, when he was returned for Essex unopposed; similarly in 1780 and 1784. In five out of six divisions for which lists are available, 21 Feb.–24 Apr. 1780, he voted with the Government: the one in which he does not appear was over Dunning's motion on the influence of the Crown, 6 Apr. The *English Chronicle*, although an Opposition paper, wrote about him after the general election of September 1780:

*Thomas Berney Bramston, Esq.* is universally respected by all distinctions of men as an honest, upright, well meaning man. He has often been solicited to accept a nomination, previous to his actual election for the county, but motives of domestic prudence induced him to decline it, as he had a large family and wished, from a just conception of parental duty, to avoid the great expense that inevitably attends a contest of this kind. He declined this honour, therefore, till the death of Mr. Harvey in 1779, when, being given to under-

stand that it was a point settled in the county, at a meeting of both parties, that each should introduce a Member of their own complexion without contention, repeated trials having taught them that the opposite interests were nearly equal, and that the difficulties of such a contest were therefore equally expensive and ineffectual, he was prevailed upon to offer himself a candidate, and was elected without opposition. He has since been returned with Mr. Luther. Mr. Bramston has a good estate and wants no favour from ministers at present, but he constantly votes with them.

In the new Parliament he appears on the Government side in each of the six division lists, 12 Dec. 1781–15 Mar. 1782. He voted against Shelburne's peace preliminaries,[2] was absent from the divisions on Fox's East India bill; and also at least from the first meetings of the House after the dismissal of the Coalition Government. Bamber Gascoyne sen. wrote to Strutt on Friday, 19 Dec. 1783 (Gascoyne and Bramston were life-long friends who at bottom disliked each other): 'As to Bramston the same motives which made him shrink from opposing the India bill may keep him quiet.' And in a postscript 'Come up on Monday. Force Bramston.'[3] John Sinclair (q.v.) wrote about Bramston in a paper of 'short hints of what he has collected with regard to some of the least known' Members, which he apparently sent to Pitt early in January 1784:[4]

A very worthy character insomuch that regret for the state of public affairs has affected his health. He did not vote, and will probably support the new ministers. Rigby has a good deal to say with him but Strutt, Sibthorp, and he, in general go together.

Robinson, in his list of January 1784 classed Bramston as 'very hopeful'; he belonged to the St. Alban's Tavern group which tried to bring about a union between Pitt and Fox; but after the breakdown of these negotiations Bramston apparently voted with the Government: he is listed among their supporters both by Stockdale, 19 March, and by William Adam, May 1784. A further letter from Gascoyne, 26 May 1784, again hints at Bramston's fitful attendance: he regrets Strutt's absence 'as you would have kept Bramston in the House'; and further: 'Bramston had Sir Robert Smyth's petition [for Colchester] which he deserted and left to Mr. Smith of Nottingham.' Bramston voted with Pitt during the Regency crisis. No speech of his in the House is recorded before 1790.

He died 12 Mar. 1813.

[1] See Bramston ped. in *Autobiog. of Sir John Bramston* (Cam. Soc. xxxii). [2] According to the list published by the *Morning Post*, 27 Feb. 1783, he voted for them, according to Robinson's list, against; the point is settled by a conversation between Barré and Rigby reported to Shelburne by T. Orde (q.v.), 17 July 1783 (Lansdowne mss). Rigby professed attachment and zeal for Shelburne, and insisted upon having given proofs of them 'though you had expressed chagrin against him for Bramston's vote on the peace, which however he could not help'. [3] Strutt mss. [4] Sinclair mss at Thurso.

L.B.N.

**BRAND, Thomas** (c.1717–70), of The Hoo, Kimpton, Herts.

NEW SHOREHAM    1741–1747
TAVISTOCK         1747–1754
GATTON            1754–1768
OKEHAMPTON        1768–22 Aug. 1770

*b.* c.1717, o.s. of Thomas Brand by Margaret, da. of John Nichol of Chipping Barnet, Herts. *educ.* Eton 1728;[1] prob. Queens', Camb. 1735.[2] *m.* 9 Jan. 1749, Lady Caroline Pierrepont (*d.*1753), da. of Evelyn, 1st Duke of Kingston, and half-sis. of Lady Evelyn Pierrepont, mother of Gertrude, Duchess of Bedford, 1s. 2da. On his marriage Thomas Brand settled estates worth £1,716 p.a.[3] *suc.* fa. 1718.

On 5 June 1754, when Brand was leaving England for a tour in Italy, Horace Walpole thus recommended him to Horace Mann:

His story is very melancholy: about six or seven years ago he married Lady Caroline Pierrepont . . . a match quite of esteem: she was rather older than he; but never were two people more completely, more reasonably happy. He is naturally all cheerfulness and laughter; she was very reserved, but quite sensible and faultless. She died about this time twelve-month of a fever, and left him, with two little children, the most unhappy man alive. He travels again to dissipate his grief: you will love him much, if he stays any time with you. His connexions are entirely with the Duke of Bedford.

Their connexion, established as early as 1747, when Brand was returned by Bedford for Tavistock, lasted till Brand's death. Before the general election of 1754 Brand agreed to contest Newport (Cornwall) at Bedford's expense,[4] but finally did not stand. Instead he was returned unopposed for Gatton through Bedford's influence in 1754 and again in 1761, and in 1768 was returned at Okehampton on Bedford's interest.

In Parliament Brand naturally followed Bedford's political line. There is no record of his having spoken in the House. His ambition was a peerage, and he hoped to obtain it through his political connexions. First Bute, and then Bedford, urged his claims, but found the King averse to increasing the peerage. In 1763, however, Bedford seems to have obtained a promise that Brand should be included in the next creation of peers.[5] Circumstances seemed more favourable to him when Chatham returned to office, and sought to strengthen his ministry by including the Bedfords. In the unsuccessful negotiations of December 1766 Bedford demanded a peerage for Brand, 'whenever any new peers should be made'. When Lord Lorne (q.v.) was created a British peer Brand wished to remind Chatham of the King's promise, but received no encouragement from Bedford.

I was so provoked [he wrote to Bedford on 18 Dec. 1766[6]] by the minister's behaviour . . . that I meant

if I could to distress them by making the claim of a promise at this time, to which they must have given some answer, and I could think of nothing more hostile than to reproach them with breach of their word in a proper manner. This was my intention, very far from thinking of profiting by this manner of proceeding, which would evidently produce ill will to me.

The promise of a peerage for Brand was confirmed when the Bedfords joined Administration in December 1767. On 28 Feb. 1768 Bedford informed him of a conversation with Grafton:[7]

He told me [Bedford wrote] that he had orders from the King to tell me, that he could not at this instant make any peers, but that he solemnly promised to make none without you, and that it should not be postponed beyond the end of the next winter sessions of Parliament.

But when in March 1769 Bedford raised the matter again, Grafton denied having mentioned a date, and contended that Brand 'was to be among the first of the peers to be created without a specification of time'.[8] He threatened to resign rather than agree to an immediate creation; but offered, in case of Brand's death, to extend the promise to his son.

Brand took this delay badly. Rigby wrote to Bedford on 11 Apr. 1769:

I hear from many quarters of Mr. Brand's great warmth of expression towards the Duke of Grafton upon the present *mal-entendre*. I am certain that can tend to no good end, and it is an ill-judged piece of resentment that will hurt nobody so much as himself. He is disappointed and angry, and is not aware that he is going to tramp it about the town more for Lord George Sackville's ill-humour than his own. He was with Lord George today at the House of Commons, and all last Saturday night at the opera; any prospect of a disagreement between your Grace and the Duke of Grafton will be nuts to Lord George and Lord Temple, and Brand, I am afraid, does not see that he will be the dupe to their malice.[9]

Brand's name does not appear in any of the division lists for 1769–70.

He died 22 or 23 Aug. 1770.[10]

[1] *Eton Coll. Reg. 1698–1752* suggests that the Brand who entered in 1728 was Thomas Brand Hollis (q.v.). But Horace Walpole, writing to Wm. Cole on 15 Nov. 1770, refers to Brand as 'our old school-fellow'. [2] Venn's suggestion that this was Thomas Brand Hollis is incorrect. [3] 'Proposals for a settlement on a marriage intended between Mr. B. and Lady C.P.', Oct. 1748, Bedford mss 22, f. 41. Bedford was one of the trustees of the marriage settlement. [4] Brand to Bedford, 19 Aug. 1747, ibid. 17, f. 90; Bedford to Brand, 9 Dec. 1753, ibid. 29, f. 127; Brand to Bedford, 19 Dec. 1753, ibid. f. 126. [5] Corresp. between Brand and Bedford, 2, 9 and 13 Oct. 1763, ibid. 48, ff. 142, 150 and 162. [6] Ibid. 54, f. 184. [7] Ibid. 57, f. 16. [8] Grafton to Bedford, 23 Mar. 1769, ibid. 58, f. 28. [9] Rigby to Bedford, 11 Apr. 1769, ibid. f. 36. [10] *Gent. Mag.* 1770, p. 441; Clutterbuck, *Herts.* iii. 75.

J.B.

**BRAND, Thomas** (1749–94), of The Hoo, Kimpton, Herts.

ARUNDEL    1774–1780

*b.* 17 Sept. 1749, 1st s. of Thomas Brand (q.v.). *educ.* Westminster (there 1764); Trinity, Camb. 1765. *m.*

20 Apr. 1771, Gertrude, da. of Charles Roper; she suc. her bro. as Baroness Dacre 4 July 1794, 2s. 1da. *suc.* fa. Aug. 1770.

Brand first attempted to enter Parliament at the Cambridgeshire by-election of 1770. Recommended to Lord Hardwicke by the Duke of Bedford as a promising 'Whig', and by Lord Temple as a 'young gentleman of great figure and fortune . . . and of a generous and independent spirit',[1] he himself wrote: 'A considerable part of my estate lies in that county [Cambridgeshire], and in the neighbourhood of it, which gives me a natural right to offer my services on the present occasion.'[2] But the county considered him as 'an entire stranger',[3] and Brand declined a few days before the poll, receiving £1000 compensation from Sir Sampson Gideon (q.v.).[4]

In 1774 Brand was returned unopposed at Arundel on the interest of the Duke of Norfolk.[5] He is known to have voted in only two divisions, on the Middlesex election, 22 Feb. 1775, and the Address, 26 Oct. 1775, each time in opposition. In a broadsheet published by J. Almon, 1780, recording 6 divisions between April 1777 and April 1780, he is described as 'out of the kingdom'. There is no record of his having spoken in the House, and he did not stand in 1780. He was a candidate at the Cambridgeshire by-election of 1789: 'I stand upon the most independent grounds', he wrote to Philip Yorke, 'and trust that I shall consequently be obnoxious to no party',[6] but there was 'such a unanimity'[7] of support for the other candidate, James Whorwood Adeane (q.v.), that Brand withdrew before the poll.

He died 21 Feb. 1794.

¹ Add. 35680, f. 267. ² Ibid. f. 257. ³ Sir John Hynde Cotton to Hardwicke, 28 Oct. 1770, ibid. f. 262. ⁴ Edw. Leeds to Hardwicke, 16 Nov. 1770, ibid. f. 283. ⁵ 'Tomkins Diary', 37 (*Suss. Arch. Colls.* lxxi). ⁶ 7 May 1789, Add. 35685, f. 51. ⁷ Sir John Hynde Cotton to Hardwicke, 4 May 1789.

M.M.D.

## BRAND HOLLIS, Thomas (c.1719–1804) of Ingatestone, Essex and Corscombe, Dorset.

HINDON 1774–23 Feb. 1775

*b.* c.1719, 1st s. of Timothy Brand of Ingatestone by Sarah, da. of Thomas Mitchell of Rickling, Essex. 1st cos. of Thomas Brand (c. 1717–70, q.v.). *educ.* Felsted; Glasgow Univ. 1738; I. Temple 1735. *unm. suc.* fa. 1735; to estates of his friend Thomas Hollis 1774, and took add. name of Hollis.

Brand's parents were Dissenters, and Brand at an early age formed a close friendship with Thomas Hollis, a celebrated and eccentric Radical. They travelled together in Europe 1748–50, and Hollis made Brand his heir. Brand held advanced views on religion and politics: was a member of the Essex Street group of Unitarians, a pro-American and

parliamentary reformer, and the friend of Joseph Priestley and Richard Price.

In 1774 he was offered a seat for Hindon on an independent interest run by John Stevens, a local butcher. The election was carried in his favour by heavy bribery, but on petition was declared void. Brand Hollis and his colleague, Richard Smith, were prosecuted, fined one thousand marks, and imprisoned for six months. According to the *Saturday Evening Post*, 7 Sept. 1776, Brand Hollis had not intended bribery, but 'was deluded and deceived by his agents'. If so, he must have been incredibly simple, for no attempt was made to hide the bribery. No vote or speech by him is recorded, and he made no further attempt to enter Parliament.

Brand Hollis died 2 Sept. 1804.

J.B.

## BRANDLING, Charles (1733–1802), of Gosforth, Northumb.

NEWCASTLE-UPON-TYNE 1784–Dec. 1797

*bap.* 5 July 1733, 1st surv. s. of Ralph Brandling of Felling, co. Dur. by Eleanor Ogle of Eglingham, Northumb. *m.* 3 Sept. 1756, Elizabeth, da. and h. of John Thompson of Shotton, co. Dur., 5s. 8da. *suc.* bro. 1751; removed the family seat to Gosforth in 1760.

Sheriff, Northumb. 1781–2.

The Brandlings were an established landed family who had sat in Parliament in the 16th and 17th centuries. The demand for coal and the rich deposits on their estates created a natural gravitation towards Newcastle: Charles Brandling, though not himself a banker, twice (in 1772 and 1793) gave financial support to Newcastle banks in danger of failing;[1] two daughters married Newcastle merchant bankers; and two sons became important in its commercial concerns. In contrast, his eldest son married into a local landed family.

At Newcastle in 1784 both the old Members were candidates, but Andrew Robinson Bowes (q.v.) withdrew at the poll and Brandling and Sir Matthew White Ridley were returned unopposed. Brandling was classed by William Adam as a supporter of Pitt, voted for parliamentary reform, 18 Apr. 1785, and for Richmond's fortifications plan, 27 Feb. 1786. Ridley wrote to his brother on 27 Feb. 1786 that most of the country gentlemen opposed these fortifications, 'but there are still some who professedly saying they do not understand them, think it right to let the ministers of the country judge for them, Charles Brandling of Gosforth to wit'.[2]

In his first recorded speech, 21 Feb. 1787, he commended the commercial treaty with France. Ten other speeches are reported in this Parliament, five of them on matters dealing with the coal trade. Over the Regency bill he was involved in a dispute when he described as 'reprehensible, pusillanimous, and contemptible' the conduct of the sheriff of Northumberland in opposing the Newcastle address of confidence in Pitt, for which he afterwards apologized. And on 14 Feb. 1789 he 'spoke in warm praise' of Pitt's conduct on the Regency question, and

> concluded with a declaration, that so satisfied was he in his conscience with the wisdom and rectitude of the measures he had supported during the late parliamentary discussions, that he should cheerfully submit his conduct to his constituents, and rest in hopes of their future favour on his confidence in their approbation.[3]

He died 29 June 1802.

[1] M. Phillips, *Banks, Bankers, and Banking in Northumb.* 29, 53.
[2] Ridley mss at Blagdon. [3] Stockdale, xvi. 311–13, 335–6, 474.

R.B.

**BRASSEY, Nathaniel** (?1697–1765), of Roxford, Hertingfordbury, Herts. and Lombard St., London.

HERTFORD    1734–1761

*b.* ?1697, 1st s. of John Brassey of Lombard St. by his w. Mary Lane. *m.* (1) Mary, 2s. *d.v.p.* 1da.; (2) 17 Oct. 1751, Martha Phillips, 1s. *suc.* fa. 1737.

Brassey, the son of a Quaker banker, joined his father's firm as a young man, and became a prominent banker himself. His father, by his purchase of the manor of Roxford, just outside Hertford, had established an interest in the borough where in 1754, Nathaniel was re-elected unopposed.

In Dupplin's list of 1754 Brassey was classed as an Administration supporter. He subscribed £10,000 to the loan of 1757.[1] He did not stand again in 1761 and died 29 Sept. 1765, aged 68.

[1] Devonshire mss.

M.M.D.

**BREBNER,** *see* **GORDON, James**

**BRERETON,** *see* **SALUSBURY** *and* **SALUSBURY BRERETON**

**BRETT, Charles** (c.1715–99), of Greenwich, Kent.

LOSTWITHIEL         1768–Nov. 1776
SANDWICH    25 Nov. 1776–1780
DARTMOUTH    16 Apr. 1782–1784
SANDWICH             1784–1790

*b.* c.1715, prob. s. of Capt Timothy Brett, R.N. *m.* 1753, Elizabeth Hooker of Greenwich, gd.-da. and h. of Sir William Hooker, *s.p.*
Paymaster of the navy July 1766–Jan. 1770; ld. of Admiralty Mar. 1782–Apr. 1783, Dec. 1783–July 1788.

Brett came of a naval family: both he and his brother, John, were naval officers, and another brother, Timothy, was comptroller of accounts in the Navy office. The stages of Charles Brett's naval promotions have not been ascertained. In 1747 he was flag lieutenant to Admiral Boscawen in the East Indies, and in 1755 was in charge of Portsmouth dockyard.[1] He probably left the navy soon after his marriage, by which he inherited property in London and Middlesex.

In his will[2], dated 24 Feb. 1795, he refers to Boscawen as 'my late worthy friend and patron'. After Boscawen's death he became connected with Lord Howe (q.v.), was appointed paymaster of the navy when Howe became its treasurer, and left office with him in January 1770. Possibly he also owed to Howe his seat at Lostwithiel, where he sat on Lord Edgcumbe's interest. During his first three years in the House no vote or speech by him is recorded; but later he became a frequent speaker, and his name appears in most division lists for the period. Nearly all his speeches were short and on points of business; he rarely spoke on political questions.

In Robinson's first survey on the royal marriage bill, March 1772, Brett was classed as 'doubtful, present'; in the second as 'pro, present'. For the remainder of this Parliament he was a Government supporter, although he voted against them on the naval captains' petition, 9 Feb. 1773, which Howe sponsored, and on Grenville's Act, 25 Feb. 1774. The first sign of his turning against Administration was on 11 Dec. 1775, when he spoke against extending the American prohibitory bill to Georgia.[3] In November 1776 he vacated his seat at Lostwithiel, and was returned on the Government interest for Sandwich—at that time the Howes were high in Government favour. But on 18 Apr. 1777 Brett voted with the Opposition on the civil list, as he did henceforth in every recorded division of this Parliament with one doubtful exception: in Robinson's list of the division on the contractors bill, 12 Feb. 1779, he is listed as 'pro, absent'—almost certainly a mistake. Brett did not speak on the inquiry into the conduct of the Howes in America, nor on any question concerning military or naval operations. At the general election of 1780 he stood at Sandwich against two Government candidates, and was defeated.

Brett was appointed to the Admiralty Board under the second Rockingham Administration, and brought into Parliament for Dartmouth at Howe's recommendation. He voted for Shelburne's peace preliminaries, 18 Feb. 1783, left office with Shelburne, and voted against Fox's East India bill, 27 Nov. 1783. In Pitt's Administration he was again at the Admiralty Board under Howe, and became one of its principal spokesmen in the Commons. He left office with Howe in 1788, but voted with Pitt on the Regency.

He died, 'far advanced in years',[4] on 10 Feb. 1799. He left his property to his nephew John, son of his brother John Brett; and in default of his heirs to the son of John Leveson Gower (q.v.), formerly his colleague at the Admiralty Board, who had married Boscawen's daughter.

[1] C. Aspinall-Oglander, *Admiral's Wife*, 57, 158. [2] PCC 94 Howe. [3] Almon, iii. 282. [4] *Gent. Mag.* 1799, p. 173.

J.B.

**BRETT, Sir Piercy** (c.1710–81), of Beckenham, Kent.

QUEENBOROUGH 1754–1774

*b.* c.1710, 1st s. of Piercy Brett, master attendant successively of Sheerness and Chatham dockyards, by his w. Ann Logan. *m.* Jan. 1745, Henrietta, da. of Thomas Colby, clerk of the cheque at Chatham dockyard, 2s. *d.v.p.*, 1da. who m. George Bowyer (q.v.). *suc.* fa. 4 June 1752; kntd. 2 Jan. 1753.

Lt. R.N. 1734; capt. 1743; r.-adm. 1762; v.-adm. 1770; adm. 1778.

Ld. of Admiralty Dec. 1766–Jan. 1770.

Brett and Charles Saunders (q.v.) were lieutenants on Anson's flag-ship, the *Centurion*, on his voyage round the world 1740–4. In 1745 Brett, in command of the *Lion*, fought the French ship *Elisabeth*, escorting the Young Pretender to Scotland; and in 1753 became captain of the royal yacht. In 1754 he was returned for Queenborough on the Admiralty interest.

During the seven years' war he served mostly in European waters, and was at sea when the peace preliminaries were debated in Parliament, December 1762. He seems at first to have supported the Grenville Administration,[1] but veered towards the Opposition over general warrants. He left the House before the division of 15 Feb. 1764,[2] voted against Administration on 18 Feb., and was classed by Newcastle on 10 May as a 'sure friend'. He was then associated politically with Saunders who, influenced by Augustus Keppel (q.v.) had gone over to Opposition.

Brett supported the Rockingham Administration, but did not go into opposition against Chatham. On 3 Dec. 1766 Newcastle wrote to Rockingham:[3] 'Sir Piercy Brett, who went with honest Admiral Keppel to dissuade Sir Edward Hawke from accepting, is to have one of the vacant seats in the Admiralty.' Brett voted with Administration on the land tax, 27 Feb. 1767, and the seating of Luttrell, 8 May 1769. In January 1770, after Chatham's re-emergence, he resigned his office; and henceforth voted regularly with Opposition. His only recorded speech was on the petition of the naval captains on half pay, 9 Feb. 1773. 'Four shillings a day is so small a sum of money that I think their case demands our assistance', is Cavendish's report.[4] He stood at Queenborough in 1774, opposed by two Government candidates, and was defeated.

He died 14 Oct. 1781.

[1] In Jas. Harris's report of the debate of 17–18 Feb. 1764 he is included in a 'list of desertions since this session'. [2] Augustus Hervey to Grenville, 15 Feb. 1764, Grenville mss (JM). [3] Add. 32978, ff. 151–2. [4] Cavendish's 'Debates', Egerton 242, f. 249.

J.B.

**BRICE,** *see* **KINGSMILL**

**BRICKDALE, Matthew** (1735–1831), of Clifton, Glos. and Taunton, Som.

BRISTOL 1768–1774, 1780–1790

*b.* 30 Apr. 1735, s. of John Brickdale, Bristol draper. *educ.* at Leicester.[1] *m.* bef. 1759,[2] Elizabeth, da. of Thomas Smith of Clifton, 2s. 1da. *suc.* fa. 1765.

Common councillor, Bristol 1767–84; elected mayor 1791 but refused to serve.

Brickdale, a Bristol clothier and undertaker,[3] was said to have inherited £100,000[4] on his father's death in 1765, and retired from business before entering Parliament. In 1768 he was returned unopposed for Bristol as candidate of the Tory Steadfast Society, of which his father had been a leading member.

In Parliament, while paying attention to the requirements of the Bristol commercial interest, Brickdale followed his own independent line. He voted with the Opposition over Wilkes, 29 Jan. 1769; the Middlesex election, 15 Apr. and 8 May 1769; on the Address, 9 Jan. 1770, and again on the Middlesex election, 25 Jan. 1770. His maiden speech on 28 Feb. 1770 was in support of Grenville's election bill, and though he spoke and voted for the attendance of the printers, 12 Mar. 1771,[5] he advocated leniency towards the City officials, and on 25 Mar. seconded an unsuccessful motion that Alderman Oliver should merely be reprimanded by the Speaker. He again voted with the Opposition on the Middlesex election motion, 26 Apr. 1773, but when on 25 Feb. 1774 he voted for making Grenville's Election Act permanent, he was included in the King's list of dissenting friends; and in Robinson's pre-electoral survey of 1774 he was classed as 'hopeful'.

An infrequent speaker himself, Brickdale, during this Parliament, kept a diary, of which eleven volumes, from November 1770 to the dissolution of 1774, are extant. These deal with the major debates such as the printers' case, which is very fully covered, and also more local matters in which Brickdale was particularly interested, as for example, the linen industry debates of 1774. Brickdale apparently took notes in the House in longhand, making no attempt at a verbatim report, and provides an intelligent summary of speeches.[6]

Brickdale stood again for Bristol in 1774, opposed by Burke who, on 1 July 1774, before deciding to stand, had written about Brickdale to his friend Dr. Thomas Wilson: '[He] does his duty very reputably and is a diligent and independent Member of Parliament.' In spite of Government support, Brickdale lost his seat to Burke by a narrow margin.

In July 1780 Brickdale was adopted as candidate for Bristol by the recently revived Steadfast Society, which with the Loyal and Constitutional Club, formed a nucleus of Government supporters, and at the general election was returned after a contest. He regularly voted with Administration till the fall of North; voted for Shelburne's peace preliminaries, 18 Feb. 1783, but did not vote on Fox's East India bill, 27 Nov. 1783. Brickdale was put down as 'hopeful' in Robinson's list of January 1784 but as 'Opposition' in Stockdale's of 19 Mar. In fact he seems once more to have followed his own independent line, influenced only by the instructions and interest of his constituents. About a dozen interventions by him in debate are recorded 1784–90, none at any length, and almost all on commercial matters, except for some concerned with regulations of polls and scrutiny, of interest to him and his constituency. He spoke and voted against Pitt's Irish commercial propositions, 13 May 1785, which were unpopular with most English trading communities; but voted with him over the Regency, 1788–9.

Brickdale did not stand again in 1790. According to W. R. Williams he 'spent enormous sums of money in his electoral contests, which left him in reduced circumstances in his old age'.[7] He died 8 Sept. 1831.

[1] Geo. Harry, 5th Earl of Stamford, educated at Leicester, in a letter to Portland, 26 Nov. 1768, refers to Brickdale as his 'old schoolfellow', Portland mss. [2] His son John matric. Ch. Ch. Oxf. March 1778, aged 18. [3] J. F. Nicholls and J. Taylor, *Bristol Past and Present*, iii. 183. [4] P. T. Underdown, 'Burke as M.P. for Bristol' (London Univ. Ph.D. thesis), 18, quoting *Bonner and Middleton's Bristol Jnl.* 8 Jan. 1785. [5] Cavendish's 'Debates', Egerton 226, p. 80; *CJ*, xxxiii. 251. [6] Now in Bristol Univ. Lib. For an analysis of the Diary see P. D. G. Thomas, 'Debates of the House of Commons, 1768–74' (London Univ. Ph.D. thesis). [7] *Members for Glos.* 128.

P.D.G.T.

**BRIDGEMAN, Henry** (1725–1800), of Weston Park, Staffs.

LUDLOW    7 Dec. 1748–1768
WENLOCK        1768–13 Aug. 1794

*b.* 7 Sept. 1725, 1st surv. s. of Sir Orlando Bridgeman, 4th Bt., of Castle Bromwich, Warws. by Anne, da. of Richard Newport, 2nd Earl of Bradford. *educ.* Queens', Camb. 1744; L. Inn 1744. *m.* 12 July 1755, Elizabeth, da. and h. of Rev. John Simpson of Stoke Hall, Derbys., 5s. 3da. *suc.* to Weston estate of his uncle Thomas, 4th Earl of Bradford, 1762; and fa. as 5th Bt. 25 July 1764; *cr.* Baron Bradford 13 Aug. 1794.

Clerk of the Household to the Prince of Wales 1756–60; clerk comptroller of the Board of Green Cloth 1761–Apr. 1764.

Recorder, Wenlock 1774–*d.*

Bridgeman sat at Ludlow on the interest of Lord Powis whom he followed as one of the 'Shropshire Gang'. On 23 Feb. 1756 he obtained through the Duke of Newcastle a place in the Household of the Prince of Wales;[1] and in the new reign was appointed to the Board of Green Cloth. Newcastle, in his list of 13 Nov. 1762, still classed him among his friends; on 20 Nov., when Powis's defection to the court had become clear, Newcastle wrote to the Duke of Devonshire that Bridgeman had 'been closeted, and . . . acted admirably well';[2] and on the 27th he still hoped he was sure of Bridgeman.[3] But Bridgeman voted with Administration on the motion to postpone consideration of the peace preliminaries, 1 Dec., and was listed by Fox among those supporting them. This seems, however, to have been a matter of honest conviction: by the autumn of 1763 Jenkinson classed Bridgeman as 'contra'; he voted with Opposition on 15 Nov., and again on 15 and 18 Feb.; and wrote on the 17th, in reply to a note from Powis,[4]

> that on the most mature and deliberate thinking and conversing on the subject his Lordship alludes to in his note, he thinks himself indispensably obliged to give his vote today as he did on Tuesday.[5] If it was a matter relative to any private affairs of his Lordship, Mr. Bridgeman would think himself not only guilty of a great breach of friendship, but of the highest ingratitude; this being an affair of national concern, he thinks, as he has already shewn his opinion upon it, his character might be justly called in question if he did not pursue it with steadiness and resolution.

Bridgeman was dismissed from his place at the Green Cloth for these votes;[6] was a member of Wildman's Club; and was classed by Newcastle as a 'sure friend', 10 May 1764. When the question of general warrants came up once more on 29 Jan. 1765, Powis wrote to George Grenville: 'I could not prevail with Sir Harry Bridgeman to be absent— though I tried all means to engage him to be so.'[7]

In a new Government under the aegis of the Duke of Cumberland, Bridgeman appears in Newcastle's list of 15 May among those to be restored to their places;[8] he re-appears in that of 26 June,[9] and in several later lists;[10] is crossed out in that of 2 July, and does not appear thereafter.[11] Presumably Bridgeman did not wish to be re-employed. But he was listed by Rockingham as 'pro' in the summer of

1765, and on 2 June 1766 is named by Newcastle among those 'Proposed to be made peers'.[12]

When Richard Lyster, M.P. for Shropshire, was dying, Bridgeman consulted Brooke Forester (q.v.) about standing for the county, and was advised to ask, among others, Powis's '*opinion* and friendship'; which, according to a note by Powis on an extract copied from Forester's letter, he never did.[13] Meeting with insufficient support, he gave up his candidature early in May. There was again some talk about his standing for the county in 1768.[14]

When the break came between Chatham and the Rockinghams over Edgcumbe's dismissal, Bridgeman talked to Newcastle 'very strongly against resignations; and hoped, the Duke of Portland would not resign'.[15] He himself continued to support Chatham; was classed accordingly by Rockingham, Townshend and Newcastle in their lists; and voted with the Government even on the land tax, 27 Feb. 1767, and on nullum tempus, 17 Feb. 1768. On 29 Jan. 1767 Nathaniel Ryder (q.v.) wrote in his diary:[16]

> Went to the Duke of Grafton's levee. Sir H. Bridgeman was there and took the Duke of Grafton aside. The conversation seemed by his countenance to be upon business of importance. I should probably think it was about a peerage, and as far as I could judge from Sir H. Bridgeman's looks the answer he received from the Duke of Grafton did not seem very favourable.

In 1768 he was returned for Wenlock together with George Forester, and in four divisions over Wilkes and the Middlesex election voted with the Opposition, 3 Feb., 15 Apr., and 8 May 1769, and 25 Jan. 1770; no other vote by him is recorded till 1773. In Robinson's first survey on the royal marriage bill in March 1772, Bridgeman was classed as 'doubtful, present', in the second as 'contra, present'. On the renewed motion over the Middlesex election, 26 Apr. 1773, he appears as voting with Government; and at the end of the Parliament was classed by Robinson as 'pro'. On 26 Mar. 1770 occurred Bridgeman's only recorded contribution to debate during his 46 years in the House—whether it amounted to a speech is uncertain: he seconded General Howard's motion to vote a copy of the *Whisperer* a libel, and call for its prosecution.[17]

In the next Parliament Bridgeman appears in three out of twelve division lists, each time voting with Opposition: on America, 26 Oct. 1775; on Dunning's motion, 6 Apr. 1780; and on the motion against prorogation, 24 Apr. 1780. Over the contractors bill, 12 Feb. 1779, he was listed by Robinson as 'pro, abroad'; and at the end of the Parliament, as 'con'. Absent abroad, he appears in none of the five division lists 12 Dec. 1781–15 Mar. 1782;

next, adhering to Fox, he voted against Shelburne's peace preliminaries and for Fox's East India bill; also for Pitt's scheme of electoral reform, which was not a party issue; and after the dismissal of the Coalition, continued with Opposition. He was created a peer, 13 Aug. 1794, and died 5 June 1800.

[1] Bridgeman to Newcastle, 23 Feb. 1756, Add. 32863, f. 61. [2] Add. 32945, ff. 90–91. [3] To Rockingham, ibid. f. 162. [4] Powis mss. [5] Tuesday was 14 Feb., but the vote was taken on the 15th at 4.30 a.m.; similarly the main division of the sitting of the 17th was not taken till the 18th at 5 a.m. [6] Walpole, *Mems. Geo. III*, i. 316. [7] Grenville mss (JM) [8] Fortescue, i. 92; Add. 32966, ff. 395–6. [9] Add. 32967, ff. 114–15. [10] Ibid. ff. 128–33 and 161–4; see also Fortescue, i. 127. [11] Ibid. i. 131, 143. [12] Add. 33001, f. 264. [13] Powis mss. [14] John Walsh to Geo. Clive, 18 Mar. 1768, Clive mss at India Office. [15] Newcastle to Rockingham, 25 Nov. 1766, Add. 32978, f. 62. [16] Harrowby mss. [17] J. Harris to Hardwicke, Add. 35609, f. 167.

L.B.N.

## BRIDGEMAN, Henry Simpson (1757–82).

### WIGAN 21 Aug. 1780–26 July 1782

*b.* 12 Apr. 1757, 1st s. of Henry Bridgeman (q.v.). *educ.* Hackney; Trinity, Camb. 1775. *unm.*

Bridgeman sat for Wigan on the family interest, supported by the Duke of Portland. Like his father he acted with the Rockingham party, opposing North's Government, but owing to poor health probably did not attend the House after the summer recess of 1781—in the early months of 1782 he was abroad.

He died *v.p.* 26 July 1782.

J.B.

## BRIDGEMAN (afterwards SIMPSON), John (1763–1850), of Babworth, Notts.

### WENLOCK 1784–July 1785, 9 Sept. 1794–1820

*b.* 13 May 1763, 4th but 2nd surv. s. of Henry Bridgeman (q.v.). *m.* (1) 23 June 1784, Henrietta Frances (*d.*25 July 1791), da. of Sir Thomas Worsley, 6th Bt., of Appuldurcombe, I.o.W., 1s. 2da.; (2) 27 Nov. 1793, Grace, da. of Samuel Estwicke (q.v.), 7s. 6da. *suc.* uncle Lindley Simpson 1785, and took name of Simpson.

Bridgeman sat for Wenlock, where his father was recorder, but gave up his seat when George Forester (q.v.) wished to re-enter Parliament. Bridgeman's only recorded vote in this period was against Pitt's Irish commercial propositions, and he is not known to have spoken.

He died 5 June 1850.

J.B.

## BRIDGEMAN, Orlando (1762–1825), of Weston Park, Staffs.

### WIGAN 1784–5 June 1800

*b.* 19 Mar. 1762, 3rd but 1st surv. s. of Henry Bridgeman (q.v.). *educ.* Harrow 1770–1; Hackney; Trinity, Camb. 1782. *m.* 29 May 1788, Hon. Lucy Elizabeth Byng, da. of George, 4th Visct. Torrington, 4s. 2da.

*suc.* fa. as 2nd Baron Bradford, 5 June 1800; *cr.* Earl of Bradford 30 Nov. 1815.

Bridgeman was returned unopposed on the family interest at Wigan, supported by the Duke of Portland. He voted with Opposition. There is no record of his having spoken in the House before 1790.

He died 7 Sept. 1825.

M.M.D.

**BRIDGES, Sir Brook,** 3rd Bt. (1733–91), of Goodnestone Park, Kent.

KENT    30 Nov. 1763–1774

*b.* 17 Sept. 1733, posth. s. of Sir Brook Bridges, 2nd Bt., by Anne, da. and coh. of Sir Thomas Palmer, 4th Bt., M.P., of Wingham, Kent. *educ.* Eton 1745–8; Trinity, Camb. 1752; Grand Tour. *m.* 11 June 1765, Fanny, da. and h. of Edmund Fowler of Baddow and Danbury, Essex, 4s. 4da. *suc.* to baronetcy at birth.

Bridges owned considerable property in Kent and was closely related to several important Kentish families, including the Finches; and when in 1763 a vacancy occurred for the county, Lord Gower wrote to the Duke of Bedford: 'Sir Brooke Bridges is chiefly talked of, he will be under the influence of the Finches, how they stand disposed at present Administration will, I suppose know.' [1] Bridges was supported by Newcastle and the Duke of Dorset. An opposition was threatened by John Sawbridge (q.v.), but a local man, Thomas Dilkes, wrote to the Duke of Portland, 30 Oct. 1763: 'Sawbridge has given up, as he says Sir B. is an honest fellow and thinks as he does of the ministry.'[2] In Parliament Bridges's first reported vote was with Administration on general warrants, 6 Feb. 1764, but in the division of 18 Feb. he voted with Opposition. Newcastle, 10 May 1764, classed him as 'doubtful', but Rockingham, July 1765, as 'pro', and November 1766, as 'Whig'. He voted with Opposition on the land tax, 27 Feb. 1767. In 1768 he was again returned unopposed. During this Parliament he voted regularly with Opposition, yet he appears as a friend voting with Opposition in the King's list of the division on Grenville's Act, 25 Feb. 1774, and was classed by Robinson in 1774 as 'doubtful'. There is no record of his having spoken in the House.

He died 4 Sept. 1791.

[1] Bedford mss 48, f. 134. [2] Portland mss.

M.M.D.

**BRISTOW, John** (1701–68), of Mark Lane, Fenchurch St., London and Quidenham, Norf.

| | |
|---|---|
| BERE ALSTON | 1734–1741 |
| ST. IVES | 1741–1754 |
| BERE ALSTON | 1754–1761 |
| ARUNDEL | 1761–1768 |

*b.* 25 Apr. 1701, 3rd surv. s. of Robert Bristow, M.P., by Catherine, da. of Robert Woolley, vintner, of London. *m.* 1733, Anne Judith, da. of Paul Foisin, East India merchant in Paris, 4s. 11da. His da. Anne Margaret m. 1761 Hon. Henry Hobart; Catherine m. Hon. Simon Fraser; and Caroline m. 1774 W. H. Lyttelton (qq.v.).

Director, South Sea Co., 1730–3, dep. gov. 1733–56, sub-gov. 1756–62.

By 1754 Bristow was perhaps the foremost British merchant in the Portugal trade which through Lisbon extended to Spain, South America, and the West Indies, and was one of the leading figures in the South Sea Company. In partnership with Peter Burrell I (q.v.) he held important Government contracts: 1740–56, for remitting money for the forces at Gibraltar and in Minorca (generally about £200,000 p.a.); and 1741–56, for provisioning the troops in Minorca. He was also a considerable underwriter of Government loans.

In Parliament Bristow sat as a regular Government supporter, from 1734 till 1761 on the interest of his brother-in-law, John, 1st Earl of Buckinghamshire (who died in 1756). Bristow's position was much impaired by the very severe losses which he suffered in the Lisbon earthquake of 1 Nov. 1755, and from which his firm never altogether recovered.[1] In November Burrell, Bristow and Gore (q.v.) were asked by the Treasury 'to procure provisions' for Portugal, and in December Bristow and Burrell were appointed to provide money for 'the relief of those distressed in Portugal, including British subjects', and were 'to be paid £100,000 to cover expenses'.[2] After the death of Peter Burrell in April 1756 Bristow was continued in his victualling contract for Minorca, but had Brice Fisher (q.v.) planted on him as partner; only the remittances were left solely to him. James West wrote to Newcastle, 8 May 1756: 'Mr. Bristow continues sullen and told me he could say nothing further . . . but as he has a favour to ask of your Grace for the late extra supply of beef to Minorca, I think . . . he will acquiesce in being joined with Mr. Fisher.'[3] After the loss of Minorca Bristow retained the remittance of money for the regiments transferred to Gibraltar, and received a share in the victualling of its garrison.

In 1761 he was returned for Arundel with Government support,[4] and jointly with Sir George Colebrooke; and in Bute's list of December 1761 he was classed 'Newcastle. Government', with the remark added: 'Hurt in circumstances.' Here is the minute of the Treasury Board, 1 Sept. 1761:[5]

Received a letter from Mr. Bristow to the Duke of Newcastle acknowledging his inability to supply the garrison [at Gibraltar] with the sums due from the money advanced to him for that service ... The money advanced to him and not remitted by him was reduced to about £18,000 but as probably the paymaster would draw more bills and he was not able to discharge the same he found himself obliged to apply ... for an indulgence of time.

A memorial from Bristow of 31 Aug.[6] stated that his estates in Norfolk, worth about £36,000, after payment of all encumbrances 'would produce clear more than sufficient to satisfy his debt due to the public'; while in Portugal sums were owing to him 'to the amount of £120,000 and upwards, and of that sum there is due from the Crown of Portugal more than treble what he stands indebted on account of his contract for remitting the garrison of Gibraltar'. If on his arrival in Portugal he was supported by H. M. ministers, he would 'soon be able to make up the deficiency on that account'. He went to Portugal; is not in Fox's list of Members favourable to the peace preliminaries but does not appear in the minority lists either; was marked by Jenkinson in the autumn of 1763 as absent; is silently treated as such over general warrants; and again appears as such in all the extant parliamentary lists, 1765–7. No record has been found of his having spoken in any parliamentary debate; but in the Parliament of 1761–8 not even a vote by him is recorded. In 1765 he wrote to Newcastle from Lisbon asking for the assistance of Government in securing his rights against the King of Portugal,[7] and in 1767 asked the Treasury to remit the payment of interest upon his debt of over £17,000; which was agreed to 'in consideration of the great losses which the memorialist has sustained by unavoidable misfortunes'.[8] He did not stand in April 1768, and died at Lisbon, 14 Nov. 1768.

[1] See Mrs. Delany to Mrs. Dewes, 29 Nov. 1755, *Autobiog.* (ser. 1), iii. 379. [2] T29/32/357, and 52/47, 9 Dec. 1755. [3] Add. 32864, f. 499. [4] Add. 32999, f. 19, and 32919, f. 58. [5] T29/34/160–1. [6] Add. 33055, f. 334. [7] 16 Nov. 1765, Add. 32971, f. 406. [8] T29/38/456.

L.B.N.

## BRISTOW, Robert (1712–76), of Micheldever, Hants.

| | |
|---|---|
| WINCHELSEA | 30 Jan. 1738–1741 |
| NEW SHOREHAM | 1747–1761 |

*b.* 1712, 1st s. of Robert Bristow, M.P., of Micheldever by Sarah, da. of Sir John Warde of Squerryes, Kent, a Portugal merchant, ld. mayor of London 1719–20; nephew of John Bristow (q.v.). *m.* (1) 7 June 1746, Susannah, da. and h. of John Phillipson (q.v.), 1da.; (2) Mary, da. of Rev. Richard Harding, vicar of Micheldever, 1s. 3da. *suc.* fa. 3 Nov. 1737.
Clerk of Board of Green Cloth 1738–c.1740.

In 1754 James West's paper on Pelham's election engagements, sent to Newcastle 13 Mar.,[1] notes

against Shoreham: 'Mr. Bristow to be brought in by Mr. Phillipson, receiving £1000, the remainder of the expense, which it is thought will amount to £1000, is to be furnished (as Mr. Phillipson proposed to have it done) amongst themselves or by Mr. Bristow.' £1000 was paid to Phillipson for Bristow's election from secret service funds on 2 May 1754.[2]

On 26 July 1760 Bristow is included in Newcastle's list of 'Persons to be brought into Parliament at the next election'; by 17 Feb. 1761 he is relegated to a concluding note on those for whom places were 'still wanted'; and by 1 Mar. he has disappeared from the list of 'Persons to be brought into Parliament'.[3] Bristow did not stand again, and died 9 Dec. 1776.

[1] Add. 32995, f. 71. [2] Namier, *Structure*, 340. [3] Add. 32999, f. 19; Add. 32919, ff. 58, 344.

L.B.N.

## BRODIE, Alexander (1748–1812).

| | |
|---|---|
| NAIRNSHIRE | 22 Dec. 1785–1790 |
| ELGIN BURGHS | 1790–1802 |

*b.* 3 Mar. 1748, 3rd s. of James Brodie of Spynie, Elginshire, adv., sheriff of Elgin, by his w. Emilia. *m.* 16 Aug. 1793, Elizabeth Margaret da. of Hon. James Wemyss of Wemyss (q.v.), 1da.

In 1759 Brodie's brother succeeded a 2nd cousin as laird of Brodie. The estates were heavily encumbered, and Alexander had to seek his fortune abroad as a writer in the East India Company's service in Madras. As a commissary and by private trade he amassed great wealth, narrowly escaped capture by Hyder Ali's troops in 1782, and returned home in 1783–4.[1]

The 'nabob' soon acquired considerable influence in the north as a leader of the Moray Association, independent of Lord Fife, the Duke of Gordon and other established interests. At the Nairnshire by-election of December 1785 he was returned as a Government supporter against a Coalition candidate. He voted with Administration on Richmond's fortifications plan, 27 Feb. 1786, and remained faithful throughout the Regency crisis. He is not known to have spoken in the House.

As Nairnshire was not to be represented in the 1790 Parliament, Brodie from 1786 was bargaining with several interests for another seat. His friendship with Henry Dundas, his extensive family connexions and 'oriental wealth' gave him a chance in Elgin Burghs, Elgin, and Cromarty.[2] In the event, as a result of Dundas's 'pacification' of the Fife, Gordon, Grant, and Findlater interests, he was returned unopposed for Elgin Burghs. 'A worthy friend' whom

Dundas wished 'at all times to oblige',[3] he died
15 Jan. 1812.

[1] H. D. Love, *Vestiges of Old Madras*, iii. 138, 164, 174, 240.
[2] See the Duke of Gordon's 'Fair Statement of Northern Politics' (1786), Melville mss, NLS; H. Furber, *Henry Dundas*, 229-30.
[3] Dundas to Pitt, 2 Oct. 1790, *HMC Fortescue*, i. 610.

E.H.-G.

**BRODNAX,** *see* **KNIGHT, Thomas**

**BRODRICK, George,** 3rd Visct. Midleton [I]
(1730-65), of Peper Harrow, Surr.

ASHBURTON            1754-1761
NEW SHOREHAM    1761-22 Aug. 1765

*b.* 3 Oct. 1730, 1st s. of Alan, 2nd Visct. Midleton, by
Mary, da. of Algernon Capel, 2nd Earl of Essex.
*educ.* Eton 1742-5. *m.* 1 May 1752, Albinia, da. of
Hon. Thomas Townshend (q.v.), sis. of Thomas, 1st
Visct. Sydney (q.v.), 6s. 3da. *suc.* fa. 8 June 1747.

Returned at Ashburton on the interest of John
Harris (q.v.), Midleton throughout his parliamentary career was a close follower of Newcastle.
In 1756 Newcastle offered him a place at the Board
of Trade which Midleton refused, fearing he might
not be returned again at Ashburton, where in any
case he was not 'very ambitious . . . of the honour
of a second recommendation from Mr. Harris'.[1] But
he was anxious for office, and in November 1758
applied for that of comptroller of the Household if
Lord Edgcumbe, who had just succeeded to the
peerage, should resign, pressing the application
'because I apprehend that there can be no great
difficulty in my being elected for the borough which
Lord Edgumbe must vacate by his peerage'.[2] This
application having failed, Midleton continued unsuccessfully to press for office, and on 17 Feb. 1761
wrote to Newcastle:[3]

> I do not imagine that your Grace would have given
> the same answers as you have given to me, to a person
> whom you really intended to serve, and therefore I
> look upon them to be meant to prevent any future
> application from me . . . These things which I have
> mentioned I have the vanity to think I had a right to
> ask for. And I think also that if my connexions had
> been with other persons I should not so frequently
> have failed in my applications.

Nevertheless: 'As a minister, and the head of that
set of men . . . whom I shall ever consider as the
truest friends to this country my respect for your
Grace can never fail.' He received no appointment,
but at the general election Newcastle introduced
him at New Shoreham where he was returned unopposed, and at Newcastle's request on 13 Nov.
1761 he moved the Address.

Midleton remained with Newcastle when he went
into opposition, and strongly opposed the peace

terms, introducing the motion to postpone consideration of the peace preliminaries, 1 Dec. 1762.
In January 1763 Newcastle wrote that Midleton,
with Lord Villiers and Thomas Pelham, was determined 'to cry aloud and spare not' in opposition.[4]
After Wilkes's arrest Midleton visited him at the
Tower, writing to Newcastle that it was 'very necessary for every honest and independent man to show
him all the countenance he can'.[5] He voted with the
minority in all the divisions on Wilkes, and though
in December 1764 thought that they had 'trifled
away the most favourable opportunities last year
with a very formidable party', yet believed that if 'all
the remaining persons . . . would act in harmony
and spirit' they might still rescue the country from
the 'present detestable ministry'.[6] Ill-health prevented him from attending the meeting at Claremont
to consider whether to take office, 30 June 1765, but
on July 2, 5 and 9 in lists submitted to the King
Midleton was suggested as treasurer of the navy.[7]
He preferred however 'the view of a peerage to any
other consideration', and on 21 July 1765 wrote to
Newcastle reminding him of a promise to apply for
one on his behalf, and on 24 July received the assurance from Newcastle: 'I have taken those steps
which I thought most proper to obtain it.'[8] But
Midleton died 22 Aug. 1765.

[1] Add. 32773, f. 327. [2] Add. 32885, f. 218. [3] Add. 32919, f. 84.
[4] Add. 32946, f. 194. [5] Add. 32948, f. 208. [6] Add. 32964, f. 225.
[7] *Fortescue*, i. 131, 137, 154. [8] Add. 32968, f. 220.

M.M.D.

**BRODRICK, George,** 4th Visct. Midleton [I]
(1754-1836), of Peper Harrow, Surr.

WHITCHURCH 1774-1796

*b.* 1 Nov. 1754, 1st s. of George, 3rd Visct. Midleton
(q.v.). *educ.* Eton 1766-71; St. John's, Camb. 1772.
*m.* (1) 4 Dec. 1778, Hon. Frances Pelham (*d.*28 June
1783), da. of Thomas, 2nd Lord Pelham (q.v.), 1da;
(2) 13 June 1797, Maria, da. of Richard Benyon (q.v.),
1s. 5da. *suc.* fa. 22 Aug. 1765; *cr.* Baron Brodrick
[GB] 11 June 1796.

Midleton was returned at Whitchurch on the
interest of his uncle Thomas Townshend (q.v.),
later Viscount Sydney, and followed his lead in
consistently opposing North's Administration. He
spoke several times on Irish affairs, and on 9 Apr.
1778 took the chair in committee on Irish trade and
commerce. On 18 Feb. 1783 he voted for Shelburne's peace preliminaries, possibly out of deference to his uncle, since in Robinson's list of March
1783 he was described as a follower of Fox. He did
not vote for parliamentary reform, 7 May 1783:
though 'not averse to reforming Parliament' he preferred 'continuing as we are' to a plan which would

new model us entirely'. The death of his wife in June 1783 deeply affected him, and in October he wrote to his brother-in-law Thomas Pelham (q.v.):

> I have been interrupted here by a messenger from the Duke of Portland who pressed me most strongly to offer myself for the county [Surrey] . . . That never was a scheme of mine, and I am now less inclined or rather more determined against it than ever. I am not equal to the fatigue of a canvass . . . I will venture to say that representing the county of Surrey cannot add to my ease, it may have a contrary effect.[1]

He was proposed by Portland as one of the commissioners to India under Fox's East India bill, but on North's demanding the appointment for one of his friends Midleton was offered a place at the Treasury Board. At first Midleton declined, fearing the strict attendance necessary would prevent him from devoting himself to 'the scrupulous discharge' of his duty to his motherless daughter.[2] He was persuaded by Portland to accept, but shortly afterwards the King dismissed the Coalition, and Midleton went into opposition.

Before the general election of 1784 Robinson noted about Whitchurch: 'Lord Sidney's borough and will return two friends.' Nevertheless Midleton was again returned, and continued to vote in opposition. In 1788 he signed the circular for a third party independent of Pitt and Fox. His last recorded vote in this Parliament was against Pitt over the Regency.

He died 12 Aug. 1836.

[1] Add. 33128, f. 216. [2] Ibid. f. 244.

M.M.D.

**BROME, Visct.,** see **CORNWALLIS, Charles**

**BROMLEY, Hon. Thomas** (1733–99), of Horseheath, Cambs.

CAMBRIDGE    1754–1 Jan. 1755

*b.* Jan. 1733, o.s. of Henry, 1st Baron Montfort, by Frances, da. of Thomas Wyndham of Trent, Som. *educ.* Eton 1742–8. *m.* 1 Mar. 1772, Mary Anne, da. of Andrew Blake of St. Kitts, sis. of Sir Patrick Blake, 1st Bt. (q.v.), 1s. *suc.* fa. as 2nd Baron Montfort 1 Jan. 1755 and as high steward of Cambridge, which office he retained till his death.

His father, who had sat for Cambridgeshire 1727–41, and had since about 1736 managed Cambridge elections in the Government interest, had in 1749 returned for the borough his son-in-law Charles Sloane Cadogan (q.v.), who in 1754 made room for Bromley, just come of age. Montfort,

> having entangled his circumstances very much, having an expensive and paltry fellow for his son, and some bodily complaints . . . shot himself on New Year's

Day [1755] in the morning, with all the premeditation and deliberation imaginable.[1]

Young Montfort reminded Newcastle on 11 May 1756 of a promise to give him a pension before the end of the session:[2]

> I hope his Majesty and your Grace will not think £1000 p.a. too much considering the condition I am left in, encumbered with debts to the amount of above £30,000, and my estate out of repair and in a very ruinous condition.

He was given a secret service pension of £800 (the equivalent of £1,000 because untaxed), starting from Christmas 1756, and he retained it at least till 1782, and presumably till the end of his life. He was for a long time the official manager of the Government interest at Cambridge (and also helped in county elections); but Dupplin (q.v.) till 1762, Soame Jenyns (q.v.), and the 2nd Lord Hardwicke had a considerable share in its management; and after Charles Sloane Cadogan had ceased to represent the borough, Montfort's influence declined still further. Absurdly extravagant, he was chronically in money difficulties, and in spite of his rich marriage in 1772 'having involved himself in embarrassments' he advertised in 1776 his estates for sale, and step by step sold his furniture, his pictures, the Hall itself for the materials, and finally his estates.[3]

He died 24 Oct. 1799.

[1] E. Pyle to S. Kerrich, 11 Jan. 1755, A. Hartshorne, *Mems. of a Royal Chaplain*, 225. See also H. Walpole to Rich. Bentley, 9 Jan. 1755. [2] Add. 32864, f. 524. [3] Walpole, *Corresp.* (Yale ed.), ii. 57, 113; *CP*.

L.B.N.

**BROMLEY, William Throckmorton** (?1726–69), of Baginton, nr. Coventry, Warws.

WARWICKSHIRE    6 Feb. 1765–3 Mar. 1769

*b.* ?1726, 1st s. of William Bromley, M.P., by Lucy, da. and h. of Sir Clement Throckmorton of Haseley, Warws. *educ.* Westminster, Apr. 1737, aged 10; Ch. Ch. Oxf. 16 June 1744, aged 17. *m.* May 1756, Bridget, da. of Richard Davenport, 1s. *suc.* fa. 1737.

On 13 Nov. 1764 Lord Hyde wrote to George Grenville about the by-election in Warwickshire:[1] 'Bromley and Sir F. Skipworth's son are the two candidates already talked of; both say they will stand by your Administration, both Tories.' Bromley was returned without a contest. In Rockingham's list of July 1765 he is classed as 'contra', and voted against the repeal of the Stamp Act. His only other known vote was for the nullum tempus bill, 17 Feb. 1768. No speech by him is recorded.

He died 3 Mar. 1769.

[1] Grenville mss (JM).

J.B.

## BROMLEY CHESTER, William (1738-80), of Cleve Hill, Glos.

GLOUCESTERSHIRE 6 May 1776-12 Dec. 1780

*bap.* 30 July 1738, o.s. of Rev. Francis Bromley, rector of Wickham, Hants by Rebecca, da. and h. of Dr. Francis Gastrell, bishop of Chester; gd.-s. of William Bromley, M.P., Speaker 1710-13. *educ.* Westminster; Ch. Ch. Oxf. 1757. *m.* 20 Apr. 1765, Elizabeth Lucy, da. and h. of Richard Howe Chester of Haseley, and heiress of her uncle Thomas Chester (q.v.), and took add. name of Chester, *s.p.*

Chester, supported by the Duke of Beaufort against G. C. Berkeley (q.v.), was returned in 1776 after a very expensive contest, and his election confirmed after a petition the following year. His election expenses were so great that in January 1780 there was 'still a large sum unpaid', and some of Chester's friends arranged a meeting to get 'gentlemen to subscribe some small or moderate sum annually for 3 years', for 'poor Chester' had paid 'so large a sum already, nearly £18,000 in defence of this common cause', that it would be 'hard upon him to pay much more'.[1]

Chester generally supported Administration, but on the contractors bill, 12 Feb. 1779, was noted by Robinson as a friend voting in opposition; and he again voted against Administration on the abolition of the Board of Trade, 13 Mar. 1780. His subsequent votes were for Administration, and he was listed as 'pro' in Robinson's 1780 survey. There is no record of his having spoken in the House: according to the family historian, Chester 'made no distinguished figure in Parliament' but 'took an active part in county business and was highly respected by his neighbours and constituents'.[2]

Returned without opposition at the general election, he died 12 Dec. 1780.

[1] J. Webb to John Parsons, 4 Jan. 1780, Gloucester Coll. Gloucester Pub. Lib. [2] R. E. C. Waters, *Fam. of Chester*, 46.

M.M.D.

## BROOKE, Thomas (1755-1820), of Ashton Hayes, nr. Chester.

NEWTON 10 Apr. 1786-1807

*b.* 1755, 2nd s. of Sir Richard Brooke, 4th Bt., of Norton Priory, Cheshire, by Frances, da. of Thomas Patten of Bank, Cheshire. *educ.* B.N.C. Oxf. 15 Nov. 1771, aged 16. *m.* 31 Dec. 1787, Margaret, da. of Sir Robert Cunliffe, 2nd Bt., 1s. 3da. Sheriff, Cheshire 1810-11.

Thomas Brooke was a neighbour and kinsman (second cousin twice removed) of Peter Legh (q.v.), and sat on his interest at Newton. Brooke's only recorded speech in his first Parliament was on

27 Nov. 1787 when he seconded the Address. He voted with Pitt on the Regency.

He died 20 June 1820.

M.H.P.

## BROWN, Lancelot (1748-1802), of Elsworth, Cambs.

| | |
|---|---|
| TOTNES | 1780-1784 |
| HUNTINGDON | 1784-Apr. 1787 |
| HUNTINGDONSHIRE | 15 May 1792-May 1794 |

*bap.* 13 Jan. 1748, 1st s. of Lancelot Brown ('Capability Brown'), head gardener to George III at Hampton Court, by his w. Bridget Wayet. *educ.* Eton 1761-5; Trinity, Oxf. 1766; L. Inn 1766, called 1772. *m.* c.1788, Frances, da. of Rev. Henry Fuller, sis. of John Fuller (q.v.), of Rose Hill, Suss. *suc.* fa. 1783.

Lord Sandwich wrote to Lord Gower, 19 Nov. 1769:[1]

Your friend Mr. Brown is I see one of three persons pricked as sheriff for this county, he will naturally apply to you to be off . . . it might not be amiss if you was to send Mr. Brown to apply to me, as it might occasion a beginning of a Huntingdonshire connexion between us; and the interest his estate will bring him is not contemptible.

And twenty years later, 19 Feb. 1789, Brown wrote to Sandwich, reviewing his political career:[2]

I flatter myself I need not repeat how long, how sincerely I have been attached to your Lordship, and that for a series of years I have consulted your interest more than my own; the best part of my life has been dedicated to your service, and my seats in Parliament, all taken at your request, have cost me much money.

Brown's first attempt to enter Parliament was in 1774 through Sir James Lowther;[3] his second, in December 1779, through Sandwich who recommended him to Lord Chesterfield for Aylesbury. 'This last instance of your friendship and attention', wrote Brown on 19 Dec.,[4] 'cannot but confirm me in the attachment I always had to your Lordship's person and interest. I fear my father will think the sum rather too much . . . your Lordship may perhaps see my father, and convince him that it will contribute very much to my advantage to close with the proposal.' And on 22 Dec., when about to see his father: 'I make no doubt that my persuasion added to your Lordship's influence will make him see the affair in a proper light; did the business depend upon myself alone, I should not hesitate a moment in accepting the proposal.' At the general election Brown stood for Totnes. Possibly his seat there was secured by Sandwich through John Buller, a lord of the Admiralty, uncle of Francis Yarde Buller, on whose interest Brown was returned. His election was unopposed, and he gave the corporation £1000 towards paying their debts.

There is no record of Brown having spoken in the

House. He supported North's Administration to the end, did not vote on Shelburne's peace preliminaries, 18 Feb. 1783, but was classed in Robinson's list of March 1783 as a follower of Sandwich. He hoped for office during the Coalition, but waived his claims 'because of the difficulties which attended its formation'.[5] He voted for Fox's East India bill, 27 Nov. 1783.

In 1784 Yarde Buller put the seat at Totnes at the disposal of Pitt, which ruled out Brown, now in opposition. He was returned by Sandwich at Huntingdon; voted against Pitt's Irish propositions, 13 May 1785; but in May 1787 resigned his seat, went abroad, and remained there at least two years. ('I am very sorry', wrote Lord Hinchingbrooke to Sandwich, 3 May, 'that Mr. Brown's determination to resign his seat in Parliament has got you under such difficulties.')[6] In February 1789, during the Regency crisis, while a change of ministry still seemed imminent, Brown wrote to Sandwich from Toulon reminding him of 'the steady part' he had always taken and asked for office:

> Your Lordship has frequently told me that you had no person whom you wished to push forward in a political line except myself, your weight is now considerable; surely then this is the time that I should have the greatest expectations.

He added:

> But at present I see nothing that will draw me towards England; and believe I shall pursue my former plan of staying in this place till the latter end of April, then go to Switzerland for the summer, and pass the ensuing winter in Italy. If I return home I have nothing to do, and here I find good climate, and amusement in seeing the various characters of different countries.

Brown died 28 Feb. 1802.

[1] PRO, Granville mss 30/29/1. [2] Sandwich mss. [3] See A. M. W. Stirling, *Annals of a Yorkshire House*, i. 310–12. [4] Sandwich mss. [5] Brown to Sandwich, 19 Feb. 1789. [6] Sandwich mss.

M.M.D.

**BROWNE, Francis John** (1754–1833), of Frampton, nr. Dorchester, Dorset.

DORSET 1784–1806

*b.* 4 Oct. 1754, 2nd but 1st surv. s. of George Browne of Frampton by his w. Mary Kingbury. *m.* 11 Aug. 1796, Frances, da. of Rev. John Richards of Long Bredy, Dorset, *s.p.* *suc.* fa. 1777.
    Sheriff, Dorset 1783–4.

Browne was returned for Dorset without a contest, and in William Adam's list is classed 'doubtful'. He voted for parliamentary reform, 18 Apr. 1785; against Richmond's fortifications plan, 27 Feb. 1786, but with Pitt over the Regency. No speech by him before 1790 is recorded.

He died 20 or 29 Mar. 1833.[1]

[1] Hutchins, *Dorset*, ii. 298; *Gent. Mag.* 1833, i. 46

**BROWNE, Isaac Hawkins** (1745–1818), of Badger, nr. Shifnal, Salop.

BRIDGNORTH 1784–1812

*b.* 7 Dec. 1745, o.s. of Isaac Hawkins Browne, M.P., by Jane, da. and coh. of Rev. David Trimnell, archdeacon of Leicester. *educ.* Westminster; Hertford, Oxf. 1763; Grand Tour (France, Switzerland, Italy, Germany). *m.* (1) 11 May 1788, Henrietta (*d.* 11 Apr. 1802), da. of Hon. Edward Hay, s. of George, 8th Earl of Kinnoull [S], *s.p.*; (2) 13 Dec. 1805, Elizabeth, da. of Thomas Boddington, of Clapton, *s.p.* *suc.* fa. 1760.

In 1774 Browne contested Milborne Port, where he seems to have been a stranger, and Tamworth, where he had property. In 1784 he stood at Bridgnorth, 'in consequence of an unsolicited and almost unanimous invitation from the resident burgesses'.[1] At first the three candidates, Browne, Thomas Whitmore, and Hugh Pigot (qq.v.) stood separately; but before the poll Whitmore came out in favour of Browne. Whitmore and Browne were returned, Browne being head of the poll.

On 27 May 1784 he wrote to Bishop Percy:[2] 'I have divided with three great majorities in support of Mr. Pitt; in whose favour, however, I have not pledged myself, and to whom or whose friends I am under no obligations.' In fact he voted with Pitt in all the important divisions of this Parliament; made his maiden speech (when he is reported to have spoken 'very shrewdly and forcefully') for Pitt's reform proposals, 18 Apr. 1785; and during a debate on the Regency, 7 Feb. 1789, 'delivered a very handsome panegyric on Mr. Pitt's Administration'.[3] About twenty speeches are reported: in defence of Hastings, hawkers and pedlars, the French commercial treaty, the Regency, the poor law, etc.

He died 30 May 1818. In a long and eulogistic obituary in the *Gentleman's Magazine* (1818, ii. 179–82) he is described as

> an honest, patriotic and independent country gentleman . . . attached . . . to no party further than was necessary to keep down the factious and preserve the constitution in Church and State . . . although friendly to improvement he was jealous of innovation. Few Members could surpass him in punctuality of attendance and universal diligence in the business of the House.

[1] Browne to Bp. Percy, 1 Mar. 1784; Nichols, *Literary Anecs.* viii. 227. [2] Ibid. [3] Stockdale, v. 346; xvi. 412.

J.B.

**BRUDENELL, Lord,** *see* **MONTAGU, John** (*d.*1770)

**BRUDENELL, George Bridges** (?1725–1801), of Ayston, nr. Uppingham, Rutland.

| | | |
|---|---|---|
| RUTLAND | 18 Dec. 1754–1761 | |
| STAMFORD | 1761–1768 | |
| RUTLAND | 1768–1790 | |

*b.* ?1725, 1st s. of James Brudenell, M.P. (bro. of George, 3rd Earl of Cardigan), by Susan, da. of Bartholomew Burton of North Luffenham, Rutland, sis. of Bartholomew Burton (q.v.); his sis. m. 1758 Sir Samuel Fluyder (q.v.). *educ.* Hackney; Peterhouse, Camb. 7 April 1743, aged 17. *unm.* *suc.* fa. 1746.

Equerry to the King 1746–61; clerk comptroller of the Household July 1765–8; clerk of the Board of Green Cloth 1768–Mar. 1782.

In 1754 Brudenell was returned unopposed for Rutland with Lord Exeter's support. In 1756 he received a secret service pension of £500 p.a., which he held throughout Newcastle's term at the Treasury. On George III's accession he was offered the renewal of his place as equerry, but told Thomas Worsley (q.v.)[1] that though 'he durst not presume to refuse a grace he had no pretension to expect without solicitation, knows how much his Majesty is pressed on all hands for favours, would trouble him for nothing at present, if in time he thinks him worthy he shall be happy to deserve his notice'.

In 1761 Exeter proposed his brother Thomas Cecil Chambers (q.v.) for Rutland, and Brudenell against his inclination was transferred to Exeter's borough of Stamford, where he was returned unopposed. Brudenell was a close friend of Lord Lincoln, and in October 1762 was mentioned by Newcastle as one who would follow Lincoln if he continued with the court.[2] He does not appear in Fox's list of Members favourable to the peace preliminaries, nor in any list of those voting against them; but to a memorandum of 11 Dec. 1762,[3] which notes, 'George Brudenell went away', Newcastle added in the margin: 'against'. Brudenell voted against Grenville's Administration over Wilkes, 15 Nov. 1763, and general warrants, 6 Feb. 1764; was classed by Newcastle as a 'sure friend', 10 May 1764, and given a good place by Rockingham. Henceforth he voted consistently with the court until the fall of North. He was returned unopposed for Rutland at all his subsequent elections, each time with the support of Lord Exeter.

Brudenell did not vote on Shelburne's peace preliminaries, 18 Feb. 1783; and was classed by Robinson as 'North, doubtful'. When the Coalition was being formed North considered him for the Admiralty Board, but it is not clear if the offer was ever made.[4] Brudenell voted against Fox's East India bill, 27 Nov. 1783, and supported Pitt. On 18 Apr. 1785 he voted for parliamentary reform. There is no record of his having spoken in the House.

He died 1 Feb. 1801.

[1] Worsley to Bute, n.d., Bute mss. [2] Add. 32943, f. 145. [3] Add. 33000, ff. 223–4. [4] Fortescue, vi. 335.

J.B.

## BRUDENELL, Hon. James (1725–1811).

| SHAFTESBURY | 1754–1761 |
| HASTINGS | 1761–1768 |
| GREAT BEDWYN | 19 Mar.–Nov. 1768 |
| MARLBOROUGH | 17 Nov. 1768–1780 |

*b.* 20 Apr. 1725, 2nd s. of George, 3rd Earl of Cardigan, by Lady Elizabeth Bruce, da. of Thomas, 2nd Earl of Ailesbury. *educ.* Winchester 1736; Oriel, Oxf. 1743. *m.* (1) 24 Nov. 1760, Anne (*d.*12 Jan. 1786), da. of George Legge, Visct. Lewisham, sis. of William, 2nd Earl of Dartmouth, *s.p.*; (2) 18 Apr. 1791, Lady Elizabeth Waldegrave, da. of John, 3rd Earl Waldegrave, *s.p.* *cr.* Baron Brudenell 17 Oct. 1780; *suc.* bro. as 5th Earl of Cardigan 23 May 1790.

Deputy cofferer 1755–60; master of the robes to the Prince of Wales and to the King 1758–90; constable of Windsor castle 1791–*d.*

In 1754 Brudenell was returned for Shaftesbury on Lord Shaftesbury's interest. Newcastle's pre-electoral survey noted that Brudenell would 'defray his own expenses'; and these were later reported to have amounted to more than £2000.[1] Brudenell, like the rest of his family, was interested in making a figure at court rather than in the House of Commons and politics, and naturally supported Administration. When on the accession of George III he was not continued deputy cofferer he received a compensatory secret service pension of £600 a year which was continued till the fall of North, though by 1779 it was reduced to £400.[2] In 1761 Brudenell was returned for Hastings on Newcastle's recommendation. In the autumn of 1762 when the Administration was seeking support for the peace preliminaries, Newcastle wrote to James Peachey (q.v.) on 27 Oct.:[3]

> They have begun with my two very good friends (as I thought) Mr. Brudenell and Mr. Offley; and they have prevailed so much with Mr. Brudenell, that he immediately assured my Lord Bute that he would support their measures in Parliament without knowing or inquiring what these measures were, or consulting or thinking of me, who gave him his seat there.

Brudenell faithfully supported each successive Administration throughout his parliamentary career, but his votes seem to have been mute for there is no record of his having spoken in the House. In 1768 he was returned for Great Bedwyn on the interest of his younger brother, Lord Bruce, to whom he wrote shortly afterwards:[4]

> It is no doubt my business to apply to the minister for favours for my Bedwyn friends, and more particularly so, considering the very handsome and generous manner in which you have chosen me, and which I shall at *all times* acknowledge, but if I don't succeed in my applications pray don't lay any blame on me, as my recommendation cannot have so much weight with the Duke of Grafton as *yours*, considering you are a peer, and I a poor younger brother of no consequence whatever.

On 30 Sept. 1774, sending news of the dissolution, he was less ceremonious:

> You will be so good as to let me know on *what day* the election is to be at Marlborough, and when you think it will be proper for me to come there . . . I had a letter some days ago from my friend Lord N[ort]h,[5] desiring to know if I could inform him who you intended choosing at Bedwyn, next Parliament . . . He says he hoped two Members who would be friends to Government.

Bruce replied:

> I should think that a little more ceremony is necessary about a seat in Parliament, even between brothers, than what you make use of upon the present occasion.
> Indeed your behaviour to your late constituents and me has been very unaccountable to
> Your affectionate brother,

Brudenell immediately apologized:

> I am very sorry . . . that you seem offended with the contents of my last to you. It was far from my intentions to say anything that could displease you. I wrote in the familiar manner that brothers generally do to each other. I certainly did not apply to you in form to choose me again at Marlborough, as I did not imagine you would expect it from me . . . but I now assure you, I shall think myself much obliged to you, if you will choose me again at Marlborough.

Brudenell's ambition was to obtain a peerage. North wrote to the King, 5 Sept. 1780:[6]

> The principal objection appears to be that he has no estate at present, and that he seeks for this dignity purely to avoid the trouble and fatigue of attending the House of Commons, on the other [hand] Mr. Brudenell is a man of a very noble family, very polite manners, much respected and generally beloved: his elder and his younger brethren are both peers. He will, probably, not have any progeny, and he will certainly succeed to a peerage, so that this creation will add to the House of Lords for a very short time.

Brudenell did not stand again at the general election of 1780 and a month later was created a peer.

He died 24 Feb. 1811.

[1] Add. 32995, ff. 63–67; 32913, ff. 16–17. [2] Namier, *Structure*, 473. [3] Add. 32944, ff. 105–6. [4] This letter and the three following are quoted by J. Wake, *Brudenells of Deene*, 293–4. [5] Brudenell's w. was North's step-sis. [6] Fortescue, v. 113.

M.M.D.

## BRUDENELL, Hon. Robert (1726–68).

GREAT BEDWYN    13 Dec. 1756–1761
MARLBOROUGH    1761–20 Oct. 1768

*b.* Oct. 1726, 3rd s. of George, 3rd Earl of Cardigan, and bro. of Hon. James Brudenell (q.v.). *educ.* Winchester; Oriel, Oxf. 1744. *m.* 27 Jan. 1759, Anne, da. of Sir Cecil Bisshopp (q.v.), 6th Bt., 1s. 2da.
   Ensign 1 Ft. Gds. 1748, lt. and capt. 1751; capt. 3 Ft. Gds. and lt.-col. 1758; col. 1762; col. 16 Ft. 1763–*d.*
   Lt.-gov. Windsor castle 1752; groom of the bedchamber to Duke of York 1760–7; vice-chamberlain to the Queen 1767–*d.*

Brudenell, like his brother James, took little interest in the House of Commons and politics. Promotion and military office were his main concern, and in Parliament he naturally supported Administration. On 6 Aug. 1760 he wrote to Newcastle that Col. Roger Townshend, governor of North Yarmouth castle, was dying, and asked to succeed him because, he wrote, 'though the income is but £182 10s. a year, it will be of great assistance to us'.[1] But the Townshend family had claims to Yarmouth, so Newcastle obtained for Brudenell the governorship of Cowes castle instead. Appointed aide-de-camp to the King, he wrote to his younger brother, Lord Bruce, on 20 July 1762:[2]

> I may safely say that I am exceedingly happy, and though it has always been the ill-humoured turn of the world to say I am never happy without a *grievance* . . . yet I may with great truth affirm that I never complained without apparent reason . . . I am glad to acknowledge myself in a very pleasing comfortable situation in life and am very grateful for it. But notwithstanding I am so, I hope by it I am not precluded from wishing to advance still further, and by aspiring to something greater, may not with any degree of propriety, be looked on as a grumbler and a discontented man.

In January 1763 he informed Bruce that he had written to Lord Bute 'telling him that I assumed no merit to myself, that I asked for no rewards, as most men did, but that my object, whenever the King thought me entitled to one, is a regiment'. He was gratified when four days later the King agreed to give him 'a good old regiment'.[3]

> Upon the whole, I have reasons to be happy and satisfied [he told Bruce], and am most truly so . . . I must observe to you that my regiment in Ireland, after the reduction, will be but a trifle better than my company and aide-de-campship together, but I am tired of having so many commanding officers over me in a regiment as six, and have pride and ambition enough to wish to command a fine body of men myself.

Brudenell voted against the repeal of the Stamp Act, 22 Feb. 1766, but otherwise appears to have supported each successive Administration with silent votes—there is no record of his having spoken in the House.

He died 20 Oct. 1768.

[1] Add. 32909, f. 294. [2] Quoted J. Wake, *Brudenells of Deene*, 283. [3] Ibid. 284.

M.M.D.

## BRYDGES, James, Mq. of Carnarvon[1] (1731–89).

WINCHESTER    1754–1761
RADNORSHIRE    1761–1768

*b.* 16 Dec. 1731, 1st s. of Henry, 2nd Duke of Chandos, by his 1st w. Lady Mary Bruce, da. and h. of Charles, 3rd Earl of Ailesbury. *educ.* Westminster 1742–9. *m.* (1) 22 Mar. 1753, Margaret (*d.* 14 Aug. 1768), da. and

h. of John Nicol of Minchenden House, Southgate, Mdx., *s.p.*; (2) 21 June 1777, Anne Eliza, da. of Richard Gamon of Datchworthbury, Herts., sis. of Richard Gamon jun. (q.v.), wid. of Roger Hope Elletson, 1da. *suc.* fa. as 3rd Duke of Chandos 28 Nov. 1771.

Ld. of the bedchamber 1760–4; ld. lt. Hants 1763–4, 1771–80; P.C. 12 May 1775; ld. steward of the Household Dec. 1783–*d.*

Carnarvon's grandfather, James, 1st Duke of Chandos, had been lord lieutenant of Radnorshire and steward of the King's manors, and Carnarvon tried to re-establish this interest. He meant to stand for Radnorshire in 1754; was supported by Lord Oxford and opposed by Howell Gwynne (q.v.); in the end transferred himself to Winchester where his father had inherited in 1751 a parliamentary interest from a distant cousin. He then promised his interest in Radnorshire 'to Lord Oxford's friend at the next vacancy', and refused to support Gwynne at the by-election of 1755.[2] Carnarvon's father, while holding office in the household of the Prince of Wales 1728–51, had incurred the King's displeasure; about 1754 Carnarvon solicited a pension for him who 'had spent £60,000 in elections, and never brought in a person who gave a vote against the ministry'[3]— a tall tale about one so long connected with the Prince. In June 1755, when a vacancy was expected in the lord lieutenancy of Radnorshire, Carnarvon applied for that office which, he wrote to Newcastle, 'would greatly strengthen my interest in the county, and I flatter myself, your Grace knows my attachments too well to think me capable of making a bad use of power lodged in my hands'.[4] But in the division on the Address, 13 Nov. 1755, he voted with the Opposition against the subsidy treaties.[5] Nevertheless, when the lieutenancy fell vacant, he renewed his application on 23 Dec., and received a snub from Newcastle: 'Mr. Gwynne, who is chosen for the county, was so strongly recommended to the King by the gentlemen who are friends to the Government in the county; and it was represented to be so much for his Majesty's service to have the lord lieutenant residing there, that his Majesty did think proper to appoint him.'[6] Carnarvon replied indignantly:[7] 'If it is more for his Majesty's honour and service to have Mr. Gwynne at the head of that county than myself I am very well content, but I may be able in a future election to show that that gentleman is not unanimously supported by the gentlemen of the county . . . I will make no apology for troubling your Grace with this second letter, but will promise that your Grace shall never be troubled with any other application.' Henceforth he banked on the 'reversionary resource' of the Prince of Wales. In 1759 he set up Simeon Stuart (q.v.) for

Hampshire against H. B. Legge (q.v.) and the Bolton interest, and secured for him Leicester House support. Perhaps because of his opposition to Legge and his friendship with Oxford he was looked on as a 'Tory' (but when in 1772 William Jolliffe told him so, he affirmed that 'he was the contrary, that he owed all his honours to the Whigs', and 'abominated the distinction').[8] Another difficulty arose over the Prince's wish to appoint Carnarvon a lord of his bedchamber, which he finally did in 1760 without previous notification to the King.[9]

On the accession of George III Carnarvon set out to deprive Gwynne both of his parliamentary seat and his lieutenancy.[10] In the end an agreement was concluded early in March 1761 which secured Carnarvon's unopposed return for the county but left its lieutenancy to Gwynne for a further five years. In Bute's parliamentary list Carnarvon naturally appears as one of his supporters, and he is included in Fox's list of Members favourable to the peace preliminaries. In July 1763 Carnarvon replaced the Duke of Bolton as lord lieutenant of Hampshire. Gibbon wrote to his stepmother on 6 Aug.: 'You may imagine how glad I am to hear of the fall of our tyrant and the accession of a just and righteous prince. Lord Carnarvon was always our utmost wish, and I have so very good an opinion of him as to believe he will not even plague our enemies to oblige us.' At the approach of the new session, on 25 Oct., Grenville asked Carnarvon to move the Address on the King's Speech;[11] Carnarvon replied on the 28th, he wished 'an abler person might be found out, than one who has sat nine years in the House, and never yet had the courage to open his mouth there';[12] but finally did so on 16 Nov., according to Grenville 'very well':[13] and this is Carnarvon's only recorded speech in the House. From the division of 18 Feb. 1764 on general warrants, when supreme efforts were made to bring up Members, Carnarvon was absent. Toward the end of January some unnamed interloper applied to Grenville for the stewardship of the King's manors in Radnorshire: Carnarvon in two letters, of 31 Jan. and 2 Feb., argued his own prior rights to them, and denied the claim of the applicant, 'even setting Lord Oxford and myself out of the question'. And next on 22 Nov. 1764 in a letter to Bute he renounced his own claim in favour of Oxford: being now settled in Hampshire he would find the execution of the office impracticable.[14] But even his ambitions with regard to Hampshire had met with a rebuff. For some time past Carnarvon had had an eye to capturing the Isle of Wight boroughs and supplanting the interest of the Holmes family by those of his own friends under the leadership of Sir Thomas Worsley, one of the foremost landowners in the island. Thus on 23 Jan. 1763 he applied to Bute for Worsley to succeed Holmes's nephew, Col. Troughear, as lieutenant-governor of the island;[15] and the letter from John White to Sir Harry Erskine, of 1 Feb.,[16] obviously for Bute to see, which hints at Carnarvon as successor to Lord Portsmouth in the governorship and describes him as a man much respected and 'beloved by the people in general', was another move in this direction. Lord Holmes was appointed on this occasion; but when Holmes was dying, Carnarvon, on 26 June, applied to Grenville to succeed him.[17] Grenville replied in a friendly but evasive letter; and, on 17 July, informed him that Hans Stanley (q.v.) was appointed.[18] Carnarvon replied on the 21st:[19] 'I very sincerely hope that this appointment may in every shape answer the expectations of Government . . . But as Mr. Stanley's connexions and mine are very different in the county, it will be impossible for me or my friends to co-operate with him, or to give him that assistance we should wish to any person employed by his Majesty.' He therefore asked permission to resign the lieutenancy of Hampshire and the bedchamber. Grenville asked him to reconsider the matter,[20] but Carnarvon replied that he could 'never consent to be placed at the head of a county, when the power is put into other hands'.[21]

It was perhaps this disagreement with Grenville which made Rockingham class Carnarvon in July 1765 as merely 'doubtful' and not as 'contra'; but on 22 Feb. 1766 Carnarvon voted against the repeal of the Stamp Act. Hence in November 1766 Rockingham listed him as 'Swiss', and Newcastle, in March 1767, as 'Administration'. But Carnarvon did not vote either on the land tax or the nullum tempus bill. In October 1765 he had informed Gwynne that he had 'no further thoughts of standing for the county';[22] and in a talk with Jolliffe in 1772 he said 'that the business of Parliament did not agree with him', and he would not offer himself as candidate for Hampshire in succession to Lord Henley, although 'he had been applied to by the gentlemen of the party who had put him at their head'.[23]

By this time Carnarvon was reconciled to the Government. When in 1771 Northington, a dying man, resigned the lieutenancy of Hampshire, Carnarvon was restored to it; and claimed to have been left by the Government 'to name whom he pleased' as candidate for the county on the vacancy which would follow Henley's succession to the peerage.[24] Having himself succeeded to the dukedom, 28 Nov. 1771, he supported Government in the Lords, where he was a frequent speaker. In the Hampshire by-election of December 1779 he took a prominent part

on the side of Sir Richard Worsley (q.v.) and the Government candidate.[25] But on Hans Stanley's death he greatly resented Worsley's being appointed governor of the Isle of Wight, North having been told that Chandos did not mean to apply for it. 'Lord Stormont brought me a letter . . . from the Duke of Chandos', wrote the King to North, 10 Feb., 'resigning the lieutenancy of Hampshire, alleging that the favours of the county were put into other hands . . . I have since heard that he is quite ruined and means to retire to Florence; if this is true, he will certainly not be prevailed upon to keep the lieutenancy.'[26] He did neither, but a short time later joined the Opposition; subsequently he supported Shelburne's Administration, opposed the Coalition, and was appointed lord steward by Pitt.

He died 10 Oct. 1789. Others beside Gibbon described him as 'a man of great sweetness of nature and good-breeding'.[27] The *Gentleman's Magazine* (1789, pp. 958-9) in its obituary calls him gentle and much beloved. 'If he had any defects, they arose from the excess of amiable qualities; from a want of firmness and resolution.' Chase Price spoke of his 'natural indolence'.[28]

[1] He always signed himself Carnarvan. [2] Carnarvon to Newcastle, 9 Feb. 1755, Add. 32852, f. 412. [3] Same to same, Add. 33055, f. 88. [4] Add. 32856, f. 571. [5] Add. 32860, f. 471. [6] Add. 32861, f. 481. [7] 1 Jan. 1756, Add. 32862, f. 3. [8] Jolliffe mss. [9] See R. Sedgwick, 'Letters from William Pitt to Bute', nos. 55 and 61-65, *Essays Presented to Sir Lewis Namier*; Bute to Pitt, 20 July 1758, *Chatham Corresp.* i. 170 (misdated '1756'). [10] For a fuller account of these transactions see RADNORSHIRE, and Namier, *Structure*, 268-78. [11] *Grenville Pprs.* ii. 145-6. [12] Grenville (Bodl.) mss. [13] Grenville to the King, 16 Nov., Fortescue, i. 58. [14] Bute mss. [15] Ibid. [16] Jucker, *Jenkinson Pprs.* 126-9. [17] Grenville mss (JM). [18] Grenville letter bk. [19] *Grenville Pprs.* ii. 399-401. [20] Ibid. 401-3. [21] Grenville mss (JM). [22] Rich. Price to Chase Price, 13 Oct., Portland mss. [23] Jolliffe mss. [24] Jolliffe's memorandum, Jolliffe mss. [25] For complaints of breach of privilege by so doing, see *CJ*, xxxvii. 557-8; for secret service payments see Fortescue, v. 467, 478. [26] Fortescue v. 17. [27] The father of Leigh Hunt as quoted in his son's *Autobiog.* [28] To Portland, 12 Sept. 1765, Portland mss.

L.B.N.

## BUBB, see DODINGTON

## BUDGEN, Thomas (d. 1772), of West Newdegate, Surr.

SURREY 8 May 1751–1761

5th s. but eventually h. of Edward Budgen of West Newdegate by Elizabeth, da. of James Ede of Cudworth, Surr. m. bef. 1741, Penelope, da. of Daniel Smith, governor of Nevis, 1s. 1da. suc. bro. Mar. 1731.

Returned unopposed in 1754 Budgen was classed by Dupplin as 'country gentleman, for'. He intended to stand again in 1761, and received support from Newcastle but at the county meeting there was such 'great discontent and dissatisfaction'[1] at his nomination that 'the whole ended in a scene of confusion',[2] and he was obliged to withdraw.

Budgen died 3 Mar. 1772.

[1] J. Shelley to Newcastle, 22 Jan. 1761, Add. 32918, f. 8. [2] Geo. Onslow to Newcastle, Jan. 1761, ibid. f. 6.

M.M.D.

**BULKELEY, Thomas James,** 7th Visct. Bulkeley [I] (1752–1822), of Baron Hill, Anglesey.

ANGLESEY 1774–1784

*b.* 12 Dec. 1752, posth. s. and h. of James, 6th Visct. Bulkeley, M.P., by Emma, da. and h. of Thomas Rowlands of Nant, Caern.; she m. 28 June 1760, Sir Hugh Williams, Bt. (q.v.). *educ.* Westminster 1764–9; Jesus, Oxf. 1769; Grand Tour, with George Grenville jun. (q.v.). *m.* 26 Apr. 1777, Elizabeth Harriet, da. and h. of Sir George Warren (q.v.), *s.p. cr.* Baron Bulkeley [GB] 14 May 1784. Took name of Warren before that of Bulkeley 20 Sept. 1802.

Chamberlain, N. Wales from 1771; ld. lt. Caern. Dec. 1781–*d.*; constable, Beaumaris castle 1795–*d.*

After his long minority Bulkeley tried to re-establish the parliamentary interest of his family. He first thought of standing for Caernarvonshire at the general election of 1774, but seeing that this might have let in Thomas Wynn (q.v.), he gave his interest to T. A. Smith (q.v.),[1] and was himself returned unopposed for Anglesey. In Parliament his earliest political connexions were with the young Grenvilles, based on his close personal friendship with George Grenville jun., who on 26 Mar. 1774 wrote about Bulkeley from Naples to his uncle Lord Temple:[2]

I am proud . . . of the choice I have made of my friend, for since I have travelled with him I have never found in him one quality which I did not admire. We are on the happiest terms, and mean to continue our intimacy in England, by seeing as much of each other in the country as we can make convenient to ourselves, and by living together when in London: a thing which he requested from me and which I love him too affectionately to refuse.

Bulkeley's first recorded vote in Parliament, 22 Feb. 1775, was for Wilkes's motion to expunge the resolution of 1769 on the Middlesex election, and his first speech, 15 Mar. 1775, was in support of George Grenville's motion (opposed by the Government) to enable Members to vacate their seats.[3] Still, he seems to have supported Administration more often than he opposed them; and if on 23 Feb. 1778 he 'quitted the majority' on a motion unpopular to them (to allow Parliament to nominate the conciliation commissioners), on 17 Mar. he spoke against an amendment to the Address calling for the removal of ministers.[4] It was the Government scheme to inquire into encroachments of private landowners on the royal domain in Wales which finally made him join the Opposition.

The first that took the alarm [wrote Horace Walpole[5]] was the young Lord Viscount Bulkeley. He immediately published a very warm advertisement against what he called the tyrannic intentions of the Administration, with which hitherto he had most commonly acted. He went farther, and infused the same spirit into his countrymen, especially young Sir Watkin Williams [Wynn, q.v.].

And John Robinson wrote to Charles Jenkinson, 5 Mar. 1779:[6]

Lord Bulkeley I doubt is gone and adverse, G. Grenville and the Welsh business carries him, although he told me on voting against us in the contractors bill [12 Feb.] that he was not going into opposition.

From now onwards Bulkeley seems to have voted steadily with the Opposition, gaining for them for a time the support of Glyn Wynn (q.v.) and securing the attendance of Hugh Williams (q.v.). He himself appears on their side in every extant division list February–April 1780.

Naturally Robinson would now have liked to raise an opposition to him in Anglesey, but failed. In Caernarvonshire the election of John Parry against Lord Newborough (q.v.) marks the re-assertion of the Bulkeley interest and the defeat of the Wynns of Glynllivon. At Beaumaris he returned his father-in-law Sir George Warren. On 8 Feb. 1781 he wrote to Hugh Williams, now out of Parliament:[7]

The power of the Crown has entirely routed us patriots, which, added to the division and animosity between the heads of the Opposition, renders the business of the House very lukewarm and insipid. The new Parliament consists much of moneyed men, who provided they get six instead of five per cent or seven instead of six care very little whether the land and the nation goes to the devil or not.

On 26 Feb. 1781 Bulkeley spoke for Burke's establishment bill;[8] and on 12 Dec. voted for the Opposition motion on the American war. When nevertheless he was that month appointed lord lieutenant of Caernarvonshire, James Hare (q.v.) wrote to Lord Carlisle,[9] 5 Jan. 1782, that Bulkeley 'though he has given a vote or two in opposition, is considered as a lost sheep'—which was wrong: he voted against the North Government in the divisions of February–March 1782 which brought about its fall.

On the formation of the Rockingham Government, Bulkeley, 'whose opinions and principles have coincided with the system of Administration which has now taken place',[10] adhered to it; waived his claim to the lord lieutenancy of Anglesey in favour of Paget; but deeply resented it when in some matters of patronage Glyn Wynn's recommendations seemed to have been preferred to his. After Rockingham's death Bulkeley adhered to Shelburne; and there are ten letters from him among the Shelburne mss at Bowood, July 1782—March 1783, mainly on patronage. That of 21 Feb. 1783 refers, however, to the vote on Shelburne's peace preliminaries:

> I am much concerned that Sir George Warren should have taken so active a part against the peace. But . . . I have no hold upon him although I bring him into Parliament. His having no hold upon me on this occasion will draw down upon me some marks of his dissatisfaction.

On the formation of the Coalition Government Bulkeley went into opposition and voted against Fox's East India bill. He next supported Pitt; and assured of a British peerage, did not himself stand again in 1784 but fought a bitter and expensive electoral battle both in Anglesey and in Caernarvonshire against another supporter of Pitt, Lord Paget, followed by a compromise which left Beaumaris and Caernarvonshire to Bulkeley, and Anglesey and Caernarvon to Paget. In the Parliament of 1784–90 Bulkeley and his nominees continued to support Pitt.

He died 3 June 1822.

¹ Bulkeley to Geo. Grenville, 9 Sept. 1774, Grenville mss (JM). ² Grenville Pprs. IV. 555. ³ Almon, i. 316. ⁴ Walpole, Last Jnls. ii. 122, 138. ⁵ Ibid. 213. ⁶ Add. 38210, f. 324. ⁷ Baron Hill ms 5894, Lib. Univ. Coll. N. Wales. ⁸ Debrett, ii. 39. ⁹ HMC Carlisle, 564. ¹⁰ Rockingham to Lord Paget, n.d., Rockingham mss.

P.D.G.T.

**BULKELEY, see also COVENTRY, John Bulkeley**

**BULL, Daniel** (c.1727–91), of Calne, Wilts.

CALNE    1761–Dec. 1762

*bap.* 18 Dec. 1727, s. of John and Elizabeth Bull of Calne. *unm. suc.* fa. 1 Jan. 1768.

Commr. of taxes 1762–d.; commr. of appeals in the Excise 1766–d.; vendue master of the Leeward Islands.¹

Daniel Bull's father was steward to John and William Petty (qq.v.), Lords Shelburne, and apparently also to William Northey and Thomas Duckett (qq.v.). He managed elections at Calne, and on 7 Feb. 1763 boasted to Lord Shelburne that he and his friends 'have carried every point for more than the last thirty years'.² In Bute's list of December 1761 Daniel Bull is described as 'inclinable to Lord Shelburne but elected against his Lordship's will by his father,—Bull who is steward to his Lordship and Mr. Northey'.

At first Daniel Bull made approaches to Newcastle. William Levinz wrote about him, 16 Dec. 1761:³ 'I know he is perfectly well-inclined to your Grace, and that he is a most worthy man.' On 7 Jan. 1762 he communicated a commission from Bull:⁴ 'he . . . has withstood . . . strong solicitations from others, resolving from the first to make your Grace

the only object of his attachment.' On 6 Feb. 1762: Bull 'is become very impatient: from a notion that he is not an object worthy of your consideration'.⁵ But on 19 Aug. Shelburne wrote to Henry Fox that Bute had been very obliging in assisting him essentially in regard to Calne:⁶ obviously by appointing Bull to an office which would vacate his seat; his actual appointment as commissioner of taxes was deferred till the Christmas recess, presumably so as not to lose a vote for the peace preliminaries.

Bull's father continued to act as Shelburne's election manager for Calne, assisted and succeeded by Daniel, who was given further offices during Shelburne's term as secretary of state, 1766–8. Between 1766 and 1769 Daniel Bull sold to Shelburne three farms near Calne for £11,134; and in 1789 his lands in Calne parish were still valued at nearly £9,000.

He died 29 Mar. 1791.

¹ He appears as holding it in a manuscript notebook of posts and sinecures in the colonies compiled in 1781, with the remark against it: 'When the fees are regulated, it may be worth £500 p.a.', Add. 22129, ff. 26–27. ² Lansdowne mss. ³ Add. 32932, f. 210. ⁴ Add. 32933, f. 94. ⁵ Add. 32934, f. 215; for fuller excerpts from these letters see L. B. Namier, 'Thomas Duckett and Daniel Bull, Members for Calne', Wilts. Arch. Mag. xliv. 3–4. ⁶ Ilchester, Letters to Hen. Fox, 157.

L.B.N.

**BULL, Frederick** (c.1714–84), of Leadenhall St., London.

LONDON    23 Dec. 1773–10 Jan. 1784

*b.* c.1714, 2nd s. of John Bull, 'gentleman', of London, by his w. Hannah. *m.* 26 Aug. 1737, Judith Dickinson of Ware. *suc.* his mother in property at Little Paxton, Hunts. 1746.

Sheriff, London 1771–2, alderman 1772, ld. mayor 1773–4.

From about 1744 Bull was in business on his own account as a tea merchant in Leadenhall Street, then from about 1757 in partnership with Samuel Moody. In 1760 and 1761 each of the partners was drawing a net profit of £1,000 p.a., and Bull's share of the capital was well over £11,000.¹ He retired from business about 1782.

Bull was a Dissenter—probably a Baptist, for he left a legacy of £1,000 to the British Education Society connected with the Baptist meeting house, Broad Mead, Bristol—and his politics were dominated by radicalism and anti-Popery. During most of his public career he was intimately connected with John Wilkes (in 1773 Horace Walpole called Bull 'entirely his creature'²). In 1771 he was acting as treasurer to the Society of Supporters of the Bill of Rights, and during the next two years he took a violently anti-ministerial line in City politics. In 1773 Bull stood at the London by-election, and on 9 Nov., in an election address to the livery, he set forth a modified version of the Bill of Rights Society programme, to which he was to adhere throughout his parliamentary career:[3]

> The shortening the duration of Parliaments is of indispensable necessity for the recovery of our ancient constitution and the integrity of the legislative body itself. Frequent appeals to the people are of the very essence of government founded on liberty and the surest means of calling to a speedy account all wicked and corrupt ministers . . . The exclusion of placemen and pensioners from sitting in Parliament, an equal representation of the people, a law to subject each candidate to an oath, that he has not used bribery, or any other illegal means of compassing his election, the restoration of the American liberties to our meritorious brethren in the new world, and relief to the oppressed condition of our fellow subjects in Ireland, are points of extreme importance . . . I will exert my poor abilities on this noble cause.

He concluded by promising not to take Crown money in any way. Bull was returned after a fierce contest, and both his subsequent elections were contested.

In Parliament he steadily opposed the North Administration. On 5 Apr. 1775, in a long speech on the third reading of the bill to restrain the trade of the southern colonies, he declared that the Government's policy with regard to the sale of East India Company tea in the colonies had been adopted less to relieve the Company than to assert a dictatorial authority, and with a side-blow at the Quebec Act, concluded: 'I hitherto have, and shall continue to the utmost of my power, to support the Americans, thus injured and oppressed by the cruel and vindictive measures of an Administration, whose whole conduct breathes the spirit of persecution and popery.'[4] 'I hope we shall have a confirmation of the American news and that Boston is cleared of the brutes that have too long been suffered to live there', he wrote to Wilkes, 5 Dec. 1775, when the first news of armed colonial resistance to Gage's troops had reached England.[5] On 29 Feb. 1776, in a debate on treaties for raising German mercenaries, he condemned

> the cruel and arbitrary measures . . . fatally carried into execution by . . . an unrelenting Administration, who have dared to abuse the throne by their wicked and sanguinary councils, and whose whole conduct has proved them entirely destitute of every principle of justice, humanity and the religion of their country. Their insatiable thirst for Protestant blood has been long evident; and it cries aloud to Heaven for vengeance, as well as for the just indignation of a long abused, insulted, oppressed people. To exult in the destruction of our most valuable commercial friends, and Protestant fellow-subjects; to pray that the same horrid scenes may be repeated; that war, desolation and bloodshed may pervade the whole continent of America, unless it shall bow its devoted head to Popery, to poverty, to the most abject and ignominious slavery, were not the fact on record, would be thought incredible! That record, Sir, to a nation

> professing a regard for liberty, and the rights of humanity, will remain an eternal monument of reproach.[6]

On 6 Mar. 1776 and several times subsequently, Bull spoke in support of Sawbridge's perennial motion for shorter Parliaments. In the debate on the Address, 18 Nov. 1777, he vigorously supported Granby's amendment calling for the cessation of hostilities and a declaration to assure the Americans of their rights: taxation without consent was mere robbery—

> Can there be any reason urged, why our brethren in America should not enjoy as fully all the privileges of the constitution as our brethren in Ireland? Can there be any reason urged, why our brethren in Ireland should not enjoy all the privileges to which Englishmen are entitled? I am confident there cannot.[7]

In April 1778 Bull signed an association 'for lawfully labouring to obtain a more equal parliamentary representation'.[8] In the spring of 1780 he was a conspicuous supporter of Lord George Gordon's Protestant crusade which gave rise to the riots of early June: on 19 June he made a vehement speech criticizing the Catholic Relief Act of 1778, expatiating with some violence upon the opening of Catholic schools and the fear of Catholic proselytising: 'opposition to a set of men holding such horrid opinions is not persecution, much less religious persecution . . . it is benevolence to ourselves and our connections'.[9]

In November 1782 Bull was reckoned as a supporter of the Shelburne ministry;[10] he did not vote on the peace preliminaries, 18 Feb. 1783, but in March was counted by Robinson as a supporter of Shelburne. His last recorded vote was in favour of parliamentary reform, 7 May 1783, and in his last reported speech, 16 May 1783, he once more seconded Sawbridge's motion for shorter Parliaments.

Bull died 10 Jan. 1784.

[1] Transcript from the firm's ledger for 1760 and 1761, Noble Coll. C. 78, Guildhall Lib. [2] *Last Jnls.* i. 250. [3] Noble Coll. C. 78. [4] Almon, i. 419–21. [5] Add. 30871, f. 228. [6] Almon, iii. 359. [7] Almon, viii. 14–15. [8] *General Evening Post*, 9–12 Sept. 1780. [9] Almon, xvii. 730. [10] List of the Parliament, Lansdowne mss.

I.R.C.

**BULL, Richard** (c.1725–1805), of Ongar, Essex and North Court, Shorwell, I.o.W.

NEWPORT, Cornw.   26 June 1756–1780

*b.* c.1725, s. of Sir John Bull of Chipping Ongar, Turkey merchant, by Elizabeth, da. of Richard Turner. *educ.* Westminster June 1735, aged 10; L. Inn. 1742; ?Trinity Hall, Camb. 1744. *m.* 1747 Mary, da. of Benjamin Ash, wid. of B. A. Bennett, by him mother of R. H. A. Bennett (q.v.) and of Lavinia, w. of John Luther (q.v.), 2 da.

Returned unopposed on the interest of his relative

and friend Humphry Morice, and presumably with Newcastle's support,[1] Bull early in 1761 pressed Newcastle for office; but in Newcastle's memoranda of 9 Mar. 1761 for a conference with Bute, and again on 13 Mar., only a 'private pension' of £600 p.a. is suggested.[2] To this offer Bull replied on 17 Mar. that he could not accept anything while Morice was neglected and disgraced;[3] moreover: 'Your kind offer to me being of an uncertain duration, and of rather too private a nature, I cannot consistent with my own and my friend's honour accept it.'[4] On 20 July, in Newcastle's list of applications 'relating to the family to be established for the Queen',[5] there is the entry: 'Mr. Bull, Mr. Morice's friend and chose by him, to have something.' In the end all he received was the secret service pension of £600, to start from Lady Day 1761.

Fox doubted whether over the peace preliminaries Morice could answer for Bull;[6] Bute replied that he himself would do so.[7] In fact, Bull during his 24 years in Parliament is not known to have ever voted against any Government measure (although in the Essex elections of 1763 and 1768 he gave his vote and interest to his step-son, John Luther); and his secret service pension appears in all the available lists under the different Administrations till 1780, when, after Morice had sold his boroughs, Bull left Parliament.[8] He seems to have attended divisions, but there is no record of his having spoken in the House.

Altogether Bull was an unpolitical figure, and is mainly remembered as a foremost collector of prints. The *Gentleman's Magazine* (1806, p. 289) wrote in its obituary notice: 'He early evinced an enthusiasm for the arts particularly that of engraving, which with much study he cultivated into a refined knowledge almost exclusively his own.' 'Through the greatest part of the century this venerable man . . . continued his favourite pursuit and . . . has erected for himself a monument of taste', to which the volumes of Bromley and Grange 'owe infinite obligation and bear honourable testimony'. Horace Walpole wrote to William Cole, 16 June 1781: 'Mr. Bull is honouring me, at least my *Anecdotes of Painting*, exceedingly. He has let every page into a pompous sheet, and is adding every print of portrait, building, etc., that I mention and that he can get, and specimens of all our engravers. It will make eight magnificent folios.' He was 'indefatigable' and by spending vast sums on prints helped to raise prices exceedingly. Cole described Bull's collection as 'delicate and choice'.[9]

Bull died 12 Dec. 1805.

[1] Chas. Phillips (q.v.) to Newcastle, 19 June 1756, Add. 32865, f. 371. [2] Add. 32920, ff. 19, 155. [3] See MORICE, Humphry. [4] Add. 32920, f. 308. [5] Add. 32925, f. 211. [6] To Bute, 23 Nov. 1762, Bute mss. [7] 23 Nov., Henry Fox mss. [8] Laprade, 50. [9] *Corresp.* (Yale ed.),

i. 287 n. 5, 313. On Bull's collections and their further fate see W. P. Courtney *N. & Q.* (ser. 2) vii. 171.

L.B.N.

## BULLER, Francis (1723–64), of Antony, Cornw.

### WEST LOOE    1761–31 Oct. 1764

*bap.* 31 Oct. 1723, 3rd s. of John Francis Buller, M.P., of Morval by Rebecca, da. and coh. of Sir Jonathan Trelawny, 3rd Bt., bp. of Winchester 1707–21; bro. of James and John Buller (qq.v.). *educ.* Balliol, Oxf. 1741; All Souls; M. Temple 1740, called 1748. *m.* 27 June 1749, Mary, da. of Sir Charles Bampfylde, 3rd Bt., M.P., sis. of Sir R. W. Bampfylde, 4th Bt. (q.v.), and wid. of Sir Coventry Carew, 6th and last Bt., of Antony, M.P., *s.p.*

Groom porter Dec. 1763–*d.*

Francis Gashry (q.v.), writing to Governor Trelawny on 25 July 1749 about Buller's marriage to Lady Carew, added, 'He is a worthy, hopeful young man, who designs to stick to the law.'[1] As the lawyer of the family Francis Buller was naturally active in his brothers' election affairs,[2] and in 1761 John Buller turned out John Frederick from the seat at West Looe he had held since 1743, and put in Francis. In Bute's list Francis Buller is marked 'Tory'—'Administration' would have been more correct: in October 1761 Newcastle sent him the parliamentary whip, which was not sent to James Buller or any other real Tory. On 13 Nov. 1762 Newcastle classed him as 'contra'; and of the three brothers Francis was the only one to appear in Fox's list of Members favourable to the peace preliminaries. On 7 Feb. 1763 James Buller wrote to Bute to second Francis's request to be 'put into some creditable office'—'I know his principles and disposition from the beginning have been strong in favour of the cause which your Lordship has undertaken. The sooner your Lordship would place him in some employment, the greater the obligation will be esteemed.'[3] He was made groom porter on 15 Dec. 1763; and again of the three brothers he was the only one never to vote against the Government over general warrants. But even he opposed the cider tax —a privileged occasion for Members from the Western counties: he is specifically mentioned by Harris on 10 Feb. 1764 as opposing it, and some of the speeches against it marked 'Buller' without initials may have been his, though most were probably John's.

He died 31 Oct. 1764, and the next day Grenville wrote to James Buller that his brother's 'sentiments in regard to the public business in general as well as his friendly dispositions towards me in particular, make me lament his loss very sincerely'.[4]

[1] Add. 19038, ff. 44–45. [2] Several letters from him of 1753 and 1760 dealing with them are among the Buller mss at Antony. [3] Add. 5726, f. 97. [4] Grenville letter bk.

L.B.N.

**BULLER, James** (1717-65), of Morval, Cornw.

EAST LOOE 1741-1747
CORNWALL 27 Apr. 1748-30 Apr. 1765

*bap.* 17 June 1717, 1st s. of John Francis Buller, M.P., and bro. of Francis and John Buller (qq.v.). *educ.* Balliol, Oxf. 1735. *m.* (1) 19 Nov. 1739, Elizabeth (*d.*Apr. 1742), da. and coh. of William Gould of Downes, Devon, 1s.; (2) Apr. 1744, Hon. Jane Bathurst, da. of Allen, 1st Lord Bathurst, 3s. 3da. *suc.* fa. June 1751.

James Buller was in a peculiar position: Cornish borough mongers required Government patronage, and therefore under George II had to be 'Whigs'; while the Cornish knights of the shire had to be 'Tories', and were therefore, as a rule, chosen from families under no such obligations to Government. James Buller was a Tory but had an important electoral interest in the two Looes; sat for East Looe 1741-7, and though returned at the request of Governor Trelawny and with the Government's consent, voted against them;[1] left Parliament in 1747 till returned for the county; and was replaced at East Looe by his younger brother John who in 1754 became Treasury manager for the two boroughs. But in 1764, with John Buller in opposition to the Government, it was James who on the death of their brother Francis offered Grenville to supply the vacancy with any person recommended by Grenville;[2] though even then it was John who managed the election. He wrote to James on 10 Jan. 1765:[3]

> The writ is moved for W. Looe, and I expect every hour to have it brought to me, and intend to set out with it early tomorrow morning . . . Mr. Sargent has charged me with the requisite for Bawden [a Buller agent], and seems so very well disposed that I cannot think you will in any event find your expectations unanswered by him.

And in a postscript: 'My nephew Francis and Mr. Sargent are this moment gone from here.' Each member of the Buller family followed his own individual line in Parliament, but the family interest at the Looes was a great common asset.

Buller was from the very outset well inclined to Bute,[4] and is marked accordingly in his list: but he is not in Fox's list of Members favourable to the peace preliminaries; still, he did not vote against them. In the autumn of 1763 Jenkinson classed him as 'pro'; he attended the Cockpit meeting on 14 Nov.; but in the decisive division on general warrants, 18 Feb. 1764, voted against the Government. He also opposed the cider tax, and when thanked by his constituents promised his best endeavours to secure its repeal.[5] Buller rarely spoke in the House. Over the game bill, 29 Mar. 1762, Harris, with some amusement, lists 'Cornish knight

Buller' among 'all such speakers, as did never speak'; and on 10 Feb. 1764 James Buller is specifically mentioned by him as speaking against the cider tax. But when the speaker on the cider tax appears merely as 'Mr. Buller'—three times in Harris's reports (24 Jan., 7 Feb. and 7 Mar. 1764), and once in Jenkinson's to Bute (11 Mar. 1763)[6]—it is uncertain which of the three brothers it was, though John seems the most likely: speaking came easier to him than to James, and opposition easier than to Francis.

James Buller died 30 Apr. 1765.

[1] See letter from Adm. Wager, first ld. of Admiralty, to the mayor of East Looe, 24 Mar. 1741, East Looe Town Trust. [2] Grenville to Jas. Buller, 1 Dec. 1764, Grenville letter bk. [3] Buller mss at Antony. [4] See his letter to Bute of 19 Feb. 1761, Add. 5726C. f. 96. [5] High Sheriff to Buller, 2 Aug. 1763, and Buller's reply, 3 Aug., Buller mss. [6] Bodl. North mss.

L.B.N.

**BULLER, John** (1721-86), of East Looe and Bake, Cornw.

EAST LOOE 1747-26 July 1786

*b.* 24 Jan. 1721, 2nd s. of John Francis Buller, M.P., and bro. of Francis and James Buller (qq.v.). *educ.* Balliol, Oxf. 1738; M. Temple 1740; I. Temple 1743, called Feb. 1747. *m.* (1) 3 Mar. 1760, Mary (*d.*14 Aug. 1767), da. of Sir John St. Aubyn, 3rd Bt., M.P., sis. of Sir John St. Aubyn, 4th Bt. (q.v.), 2s.; (2) 4 Nov. 1768, Elizabeth Caroline, da. of John Hunter, 1s. 1da. Comptroller of the mint 1754-*d.*; auditor of the duchy of Cornw. ?1772-?84; sec. to chancellor of the Exchequer 1759-61; ld. of Admiralty July 1765-Sept. 1780; ld. of Treasury Sept. 1780-Mar. 1782, Dec. 1783-*d.*

Recorder, East Looe 1754-*d.*; mayor 1746, 1754, 1772; mayor, West Looe by *mandamus* 1763, and 1764.

Buller wrote in a memorandum for Newcastle on the eve of the general election of 1761:[1]

> Upon the death of Governor Trelawny, Mr. Pelham thought Mr. John Buller a proper person to manage the interest at Looe, and promised he should be comptroller of the mint, and that the salary should be made up £500 a year, and ordered Gashry to assure him of some farther mark of the King's favour.
>
> My Lord Duke of Newcastle, succeeding to the Treasury, made good Mr. Pelham's engagement, by giving Lord Aylmer a pension of £500 a year;[2] and Mr. Buller, Mr. Noel, Mr. Frederick, and Mr. Gashry were chosen at the last general election, agreeable to his Grace's recommendation.
>
> The salary of the mint has never been worth more than £240 in any one year; the deficiency never paid but for one or two years.[3]
>
> What Mr. John Buller now desires is to receive some mark of the Duke of Newcastle's favour and confidence, in being made a commissioner of the excise or customs, by which his Grace may put in another Member at Looe, and Mr. Buller will have the satisfaction of knowing that his Grace has some regard for him. Mr. Buller promises the most zealous attachment to his Grace's interest, in this election, and in every future one.
>
> My Lord Duke will please to consider that six votes in the House depend on gratifying Mr. Buller in this

request. Captain Trelawny, Mr. Gashry and the person to be chosen in the room of Buller, will undoubtedly be his Grace's friends. Whereas should Mr. Buller continue a Member and choose a friend of his own, these two and Captain Trelawny, who will be awed and influenced by Buller, will most certainly not be his Grace's friends.

Buller's request was not gratified; he returned at the Looes himself, his brother Francis (ousting Frederick), his cousin William Trelawny, and his friend Gashry; and adhered to Legge, whose secretary he had been at the Exchequer—he did not follow his brothers James and Francis in paying homage to the new court. Early in 1762 Gashry's health was rapidly declining, and on 20 Feb. Legge wrote to Newcastle that 'Buller is ready to receive any friend of your nomination into the borough upon very easy terms':[4] £1,000 from the Member to be elected, and the succession to Gashry as treasurer of the Ordnance (£500 p.a.) for John Buller.[5] Newcastle spoke to Bute, and received an ambiguous reply.[6] When Gashry died, 19 May, a week before Newcastle was forced from office, Buller could have secured his succession by applying to Bute, but would not do so; and when 'examined about the borough' declared himself engaged to Newcastle's candidate, went with all haste to East Looe, and carried the election.[7] Henceforth Buller steadily adhered to the Opposition; voted against the peace preliminaries; appears on the Opposition side in every extant division list on Wilkes and general warrants; repeatedly spoke and voted against the cider tax; belonged to Wildman's Club and was reckoned a 'sure friend' by Newcastle. But even so, in January 1765 Buller managed at West Looe the election of the Government candidate accepted by his brother James.[8]

In February 1764 Legge named John Buller among the few friends whom he asked Newcastle to take care of should the Opposition return to power; and in his will—he died 23 Aug. 1764—named Buller a guardian to his son. When the Rockingham Administration was being formed, Legge's widow, Lady Stawell, wrote to Newcastle pressing Buller's claims to a seat at the Treasury or the Admiralty Board.[9] 'She lays it very strong upon the Duke of Newcastle, as due to the memory of poor Mr. Legge', he wrote in a memorandum for the Duke of Cumberland;[10] and added:

There are other political reasons which make the Duke of Newcastle wish that Mr. Buller may be provided for, which the Duke of Newcastle was ignorant of 'till yesterday morning.

Mr. Buller, upon the death of his two brothers, both friends of the last, or present ministers, has settled his affairs of the two Looes, that Mr. Buller can bring in *three Members*, without the least opposition.

As to his merit, he is a very honest man; has a family, with a small fortune; and has been a most firm friend; and refused the treasurer of Ordnance, offered to him, when it was given to Mr. Mackye.

And to Rockingham on 12 July:[11]

I hope, in regard to Mr. Legge's memory, in consideration of Mr. Buller's own merit, and the three Members of Parliament that he can choose, that no one will be preferred to him; if I find there was, I must take the liberty to speak to the King upon it. I hope therefore, your Lordship, and the other ministers, will make it unnecessary to trouble his Majesty upon these occasions.

Buller was made a lord of the Admiralty, and remained there 15 years, described by the *Public Ledger* in 1779 as 'a perfect office drudge, the routine of which he is well acquainted with, together with the profits'. Between July 1765 and March 1782 he is not known ever to have voted against any Government. His seat at East Looe he retained without a single contest till his death, accepting Government candidates for the other seat, as also for West Looe which he managed till, shortly before the general election of 1774, he ceded it under a family arrangement to his nephew, John Buller jun. (q.v.). From January 1771 till September 1780, as senior lord of the Admiralty in the House, he moved the naval estimates, and generally acted as spokesman for his department. But he was an undistinguished speaker: when in September 1780 his wish for a change of office[12] was gratified by a transfer to the Treasury Board, 'Lord North is much concerned', wrote his new chief to the King, 'that he can not have a more useful speaker than Mr. Buller.'[13] Buller adhered to North also after his resignation; voted against Shelburne's peace preliminaries, 18 Feb. 1783; but did not vote on Fox's East India bill; and in December 1783 was placed once more at the Treasury Board by Pitt, whose Administration he henceforth supported.

He died 26 July 1786.

[1] Add. 33055, f. 336. [2] For vacating the post of comptroller of the mint. [3] For payments to him from secret service funds see Namier, *Structure*, 437, 441. [4] Add. 32934, f. 490. [5] Add. 32936, f. 412. [6] Newcastle to Legge, 21 Apr., Add. 32937, f. 284. [7] For a more detailed account of these transactions see Namier, *Structure*, 329-31. [8] See BULLER, James. [9] 5 July 1765, Add. 32967, f. 225. [10] 7 July, ibid. f. 282. [11] Ibid. ff. 347-8. [12] See North to the King, [15] June 1779, Fortescue, iv. 352. [13] Fortescue, v. 115.

L.B.N.

**BULLER, John** (1745-93), of Morval, Cornw.

| | |
|---|---|
| EXETER | 1768-1774 |
| LAUNCESTON | 1774-1780 |
| WEST LOOE | 1780-March 1782, 3 Jan.-25 Mar. 1784 |

*bap.* 28 Feb. 1745, 2nd s. of James Buller (q.v.) by his 2nd w. *educ.* Balliol, Oxf. 1764. *m.* 3 Apr. 1770, Anne, da. of William Lemon of Carclew, sis. of Sir William Lemon (q.v.), 7s. 3da. *suc.* half-bro. 1772.

Commr. of Excise 1790–*d.*

In 1768 Buller was returned unopposed for Exeter on the corporation interest. 1769–70 he voted regularly with the Opposition, and attended their dinner of 9 May 1769. But in 1771 his attitude began to change: he did not vote with them on the Spanish Convention, 13 Feb. 1771, was classed 'doubtful' by Robinson on the royal marriage bill, and though he voted for Grenville's Act, 25 Feb. 1774, was classed by the King as a friend. On 19 Apr. 1774, 'fairly persuaded of the right of taxing America', he spoke against the repeal of the tea duty.[1] In September 1774 he was classed by Robinson as 'hopeful'.

Before the general election of 1774 (probably in 1772 on the death of his half-brother) he took over the management of West Looe, where he returned two Members friendly to Administration.[2] He himself did not stand again at Exeter, but contested Launceston against the Morice interest. Nor was this the end of his activities. Cory Carpenter, Lady Bute's agent at Bossiney, wrote to her from Launceston, 9 Oct. 1774, about the election for Cornwall:[3]

The most part of the gentlemen of property and influence are . . . unwilling to support Mr. Buller, whose ambition so early in life in business of elections requires a check, no old family interest nor any interest whatsoever being exempt from his attack. He hath opposed the Orford interest at Callington, the Morice interest at this place, and is moving heaven and earth for his brother [in] law for the county.

He was not at first a candidate for Cornwall, but when Sir John Molesworth and H. M. Praed (qq.v.) declared a union Buller joined Lemon—with the aim of drawing votes away from Lemon's opponents rather than of succeeding himself. At Callington in 1772 he had supported his half-brother James, and that in 1774 he still took an interest in the borough is shown by a letter to Buller of 3 Oct. 1774 from Francis Paynter, apparently employed in the office of the sheriff at Truro:[4] 'Now as I have no direction to whom to send the Callington writ, shall send it to you unless you give directions to the contrary.'

From 1774 to 1780 he voted regularly with Administration, and was a suitor for office. In a list of 1779 he was suggested for housekeeper at Whitehall,[5] and although North seems to have made him a promise[6] nothing was done for him.

He had inherited property at Saltash, and in 1780 contested the borough with Sir William James (q.v.) against the Government candidates Charles Jenkinson and Sir Grey Cooper. He was defeated but petitioned, and a committee of the House of Commons decided against him only by the chairman's casting vote. Buller's attack was not due to any change in his attitude towards North's Administration: according to Cooper he wanted the borough 'merely to have the merit of surrendering it' for the wardenship of the stannaries.[7] At West Looe he returned himself and James, who supported North to the end; while Buller voted with him on 20 Feb., but on 22 and 27 Feb. abstained. On 7 Mar. Lord Bathurst wrote to Robinson:[8]

My nephew Buller has desired me to ask his Majesty to give him the Chiltern Hundreds, as you have told him that Lord North will do nothing for him. I shall be under the necessity of telling a long story of repeated ill usage . . . I am not sure that I shall have interest enough with my nephew to prevail with him to bring in a friend to Government in his place.

North had resigned when Buller's successor J. S. Cocks was returned, but as the son of Sir Charles Cocks, clerk of the Ordnance in North's Administration, it is probable that he would have supported North.

In 1783 Buller again contested Saltash, with support from William Beckford jun. (q.v.); was defeated; and had his petition rejected. On James's death he returned himself for West Looe; appears in Stockdale's list as a supporter of Pitt; and at the general election of 1784 returned candidates friendly to Pitt. He himself was defeated at Exeter. Another defeat at Saltash in 1784 was followed by final victory in 1786, and an agreement between Buller and Beckford to divide the borough. In 1790 Buller was appointed a commissioner of Excise, and at the general election returned Government supporters both at Saltash and at West Looe.

He died 26 Nov. 1793.

[1] Cavendish's 'Debates', Egerton 255, p. 215. [2] Laprade, 22. [3] Wharncliffe mss, Sheffield City Lib. [4] Buller mss. [5] Fortescue, iv. 353. [6] Robinson to Jenkinson, 15 Jan. 1780, Add. 38567, f. 24. [7] Cooper to Jenkinson, 1 Oct. 1780, Add. 38214, ff. 198–9. [8] HMC 10th Rep. VI, 51.

J.B.

**BULLOCK, John** (1731–1809), of Faulkbourne Hall, nr. Witham, Essex.

| | |
|---|---|
| MALDON | 1754–1774 |
| STEYNING | 28 Nov. 1780–1784 |
| ESSEX | 1784–28 Dec. 1809 |

*b.* 31 Dec. 1731, 1st surv. s. of Josiah Bullock, Hamburg merchant, of Faulkbourne Hall by Hannah, da. of Sir Thomas Cooke, M.P., director E.I. Co. *educ.* Felsted; Clare, Camb. 1749; L. Inn 1750. *m.* 28 Nov. 1763, Elizabeth, da. and h. of Robert Lant of Putney, *s.p. suc.* fa. 1752.

At the turn of the century, Bullock's paternal grandfather had sat for Essex, a great-uncle for Maldon, and his maternal grandfather for Colchester.

In 1754 Bullock, supported by John Strutt (q.v.)

and other Essex Tories, contested Maldon against two Government candidates, and topped the poll. He was listed by Dupplin as an Opposition Whig; but next approached Newcastle through Sir John Ligonier and George Townshend (qq.v.) who, on 14 July 1755, recommended Bullock to the Duke as a man 'in whom you can deposit that confidence and power which every one who proposes to establish an interest in a corporation town is desirous of having on his side'.[1] His name does not appear in the list of Whigs who on 13 Nov. 1755 voted against the Address.[2]

Bullock also seemed desirous of standing well with his kinsman, the Duke of Bedford, who, after having been since June 1751 in opposition to the Pelhams, was now veering toward the Government. On 4 Dec. 1755, Rigby wrote to Bedford:[4]

Bullock was with me this morning, and very desirous to know your Grace's opinion of the treaties [with Russia and Hesse-Cassel]. I explained as well as I could to a very good-natured fox-hunting boy, your sentiments upon them . . . he seems as if he would be very well satisfied with your opinion only, and be glad to be of the same.[5]

In 1761 Bullock joined Colebrooke as a Government candidate. 'If this measure gives you offence', he wrote to Strutt on 15 Jan., 'I am sorry for it, but assure you I shall always remember the favours you shewed me last election.'[6] Gascoyne stood against them, and Colebrooke was defeated. In October Bullock was sent Newcastle's parliamentary whip through Bedford, and in Bute's list of December 1761 is marked 'Bedford and Government'. He is not in Fox's list of Members in favour of the peace preliminaries, December 1762, but did not vote against them. After 1763 he no longer had any connexion with Bedford, but drifted towards the Rockinghams. In the autumn of 1763 Jenkinson classed him as 'doubtful'; he voted against Government over general warrants, 15 and 18 Feb. 1764, belonged to Wildman's Club, and was counted among the 'sure friends' by Newcastle, 10 May 1764. He voted with Opposition on Meredith's motion on general warrants, 29–30 Jan. 1765[7]; was classed as 'pro' by Rockingham in July 1765, and probably voted for the repeal of the Stamp Act.[8] In November 1766 Rockingham listed him as 'Whig'; Charles Townshend in January 1767 as 'Government', but Newcastle in March 1767 as 'doubtful or absent'—which seems more nearly correct: he was absent from the division on the land tax, 27 Feb. 1767, and that on the nullum tempus bill, 17 Feb. 1768. But when at the Chelmsford assizes in Mar. 1767 an address was voted expressing satisfaction at the land tax having been reduced by a shilling, Bullock 'declared his sorrow for not attending and his hearty concurrence in . . . the address'.[9]

In 1768 Bullock fought his third contest at Maldon and won a decisive, though expensive, victory. When in the House, he voted with Opposition, but his name appears in only four out of 13 minority division lists in that Parliament.

He was averse to a fourth contest at Maldon. In 1774 the bills for the last election were still unpaid, and Bullock found that he was expected to pay also the share of John Huske (q.v.), his colleague in 1768 who had since died. Thomas Coe, one of the principal Dissenters at Maldon, told Bullock that 'he must not think of coming to Maldon unless he paid all the bills', to which Bullock replied 'that was damned hard indeed';[10] and on 28 Sept., 'foreseeing great trouble, expense, and uncertainty in so long a canvass', announced he would not stand.[11]

Two days later Parliament was dissolved.

Indeed I hoped [wrote Bullock to Portland[12]] to have got in somewhere else upon easier if not upon cheaper terms. I do not at this minute know what I can do, but will consult with my friends whether I can with propriety now offer myself but I fear not. If your Grace knows of any place that is to be got at I would most gladly comply with almost any proposal. Chase Price [q.v.] I believe hath an offer of Leominster, might I presume so far as to beg your Grace's interest with him?

He was willing to pay £3000;[13] and looked to Portland to find him a constituency.[14]

In 1780 he was suggested by Portland for one of the seats which Edward Eliot (q.v.) had placed at the disposal of the Opposition but, wrote Portland to Rockingham on 14 Aug.:[15] 'I am not satisfied . . . in respect to his being *prepared* in due time.' He was returned for Steyning on the Honywood interest; voted against North's Administration 12 Dec. 1781 and 20 Feb. 1782, paired on the Opposition side 27 Feb. 1782, and was absent from the division of 15 Mar. He did not vote on Shelburne's peace preliminaries, 18 Feb. 1783, but was classed by Robinson among 'Mr. Fox's connexions'. He voted for parliamentary reform, 7 May 1783, was absent from the division on Fox's East India bill, 27 Nov., but was classed by John Robinson in January, by Stockdale in March, and by Adam in May 1784, as in opposition to Pitt.

He was elected for Essex without a contest in 1784, voted for parliamentary reform, 18 Apr. 1785, but otherwise continued to vote against Pitt.

There is no record of his having spoken in any of the five Parliaments he sat in before 1790.

He died 28 Dec. 1809.

[1] Add. 32857, ff. 103–4. [2] Add. 33034, f. 208. [3] *Bedford Corresp.* ii. 177. [4] On 10 Dec. Bedford spoke for the treaties; see Walpole, *Mems. Geo. II*, ii. 104. [5] Strutt mss. [6] Bamber Gascoyne to John

Strutt, 31 Jan. 1765, Strutt mss. [7] Same to same, 8 Feb. 1766: 'I think Bullock . . . divided against us.' Ibid. [8] Same to same, 12 Mar. 1767, ibid. [9] Thomas Cooch to John Strutt [Sept. 1774], ibid. [10] Bullock to Portland, 30 Sept. 1774, Portland mss. [11] Ibid. [12] Same to same, 23 Oct. 1774, ibid. [13] Same to same, 19 Dec. 1774, ibid. [14] Rockingham mss.

J.B.

## BULLOCK, Joseph (1731–1808), of Caversfield, nr. Bicester, Oxon.

WENDOVER    6 Sept. 1770–Mar. 1775

*b.* 11 Dec. 1731, s. of Henry Bullock of Stanwell, Mdx. by his w. Mary. *educ.* Eton 1742–8; Merton, Oxf. 1749. *m.* Anne, da. of Peter Walter, M.P., of Stalbridge, Dorset, niece of Edward Walter (q.v.), 1da.

Bullock was a close friend of Lord Verney (q.v.), and in 1768 stood on his interest at Carmarthen. He was defeated and petitioned; Edmund Burke tried to rally the Rockingham party in his support; but on 8 Mar. 1770 the House determined against him by 101 votes to 30. Verney had him returned for Wendover on the first vacancy; and Burke wrote to Rockingham, 7 Sept. 1770: 'I wish your Lordship joy of another friend in Parliament.' There is no record that Bullock ever spoke in the House.

In 1774 Verney could no longer afford to return his friends gratis: Edmund Burke had to find a seat elsewhere, and presumably Bullock had to pay. If so, it is difficult to explain why six months later he vacated his seat. He remained on close terms with Verney, and in 1786 accepted the thankless task of trying to straighten out Verney's financial affairs.

Bullock died 13 Apr. 1808.

J.B.

## BUNBURY, Thomas Charles (1740–1821), of Barton, Suff. and Bunbury, Cheshire.

SUFFOLK    1761–1784, 1790–1812

*b.* May 1740, 1st s. of Rev. Sir William Bunbury, 5th Bt., by Eleanor, da. and coh. of Vere Graham of Wix Abbey, Essex. *educ.* Bury St. Edmunds 1747; Westminster c.1754; St. Catherine's Hall, Camb. 1757; Grand Tour ?1760–1. *m.* (1) 2 June 1762, Lady Sarah Lennox (divorced for desertion 1776), da. of Charles, 2nd Duke of Richmond, *s.p.*; (2) Margaret, *s.p.* His sis. Annabella m. (1) 14 Apr. 1762, Sir Patrick Blake, 1st Bt. (q.v.); (2) c.1778, George Boscawen (q.v.). *suc.* fa. 11 June 1764.

Sec. to Paris embassy, 4 Aug. 1764–May 1765; sec. to ld. lt. [I] May–July 1765; he did not discharge the duties of either office.

Sheriff, Suff. 1788–9.

The Bunburys were a Cheshire family, and Charles Bunbury's grandfather and uncle sat for Chester; but his father inherited the Suffolk estates of his maternal uncle, Sir Thomas Hanmer, Bt., M.P. for Suffolk, and at the general election of 1761 put up his son for the county. Before the county

meeting at Stowmarket Sir William met the other two candidates with a view to an agreement, and is reported to have said: 'I own I am anxious my son should have the honour this time; he is now upon his travels, and this will be the completest finishing of his education.'[1] (On 13 Sept. 1760, Horace Mann wrote from Florence to Horace Walpole: 'Your *recommandé* Mr. Bunbury is a very knowing, agreeable young man, but too retired out of complaisance to his companion, Lord Torrington, but not at all out of choice.') On a compromise Bunbury was returned unopposed, though still a month under age. 'His vanity is monstrously flattered by being Member for the county at his age', wrote Lady Holland to Lady Kildare, 22 June 1762, ' . . . he is chosen upon the Tory interest in Suffolk' (i.e. by the independent country gentlemen).[2]

'Mr. Bunbury is much attached to Lord Shelburne', wrote Lady Caroline Fox, 27 Jan. 1762.[3] On 10 Dec. 1761, the day Barré delivered his attack against Pitt and the German war, Bunbury, speaking first, did likewise in a much condemned maiden speech. 'Mr. Bunbury', reported George Onslow to Newcastle,[4] 'began by objecting in general to the German war; that he should never agree (as the last Parliament had done) from servile and mean unanimity to measures they could not approve.' And Lord John Cavendish to the Duke of Grafton: 'Mr. Bunbury stood up, and with a very theatrical tone and gesture made a flimsy kind of speech against the German war, and took the liberty of abusing Pitt heartily.'[5] John Milbanke described the speech as flashy, with 'no small assurance' and 'a great deal of bombast and false action';[6] Harris as 'vehement, abusive, and yet set and formal'; and Newcastle as 'most impertinent'.[7]

Bunbury's next parliamentary performance was equally immature. On 5 Feb. the Duke of Bedford, supported by Shelburne, moved for the recall of the troops from Germany, which embarrassed the King and Bute, though themselves opposed to the German war. On the 9th Bunbury gave notice that he would make a similar motion in the Commons on the 12th. But, discouraged by Fox, he only appeared when the House was about to adjourn, 'looking . . . rather awkwardly . . . All departed laughing at what had happened'.[8] Still, the next day he announced he would make the motion on Wednesday, the 17th. 'Pushing it now in the House of Commons will certainly be imputed to you', wrote Fox to Shelburne, the same day. ' . . . Mr. Bunbury has at Lady Caroline's desire put it off till Wednesday, which is very obliging.'[9] And on the 14th Fox wrote to Bute that Bunbury, dissuaded by Shelburne, had laid it aside altogether.[10] 'For a young man moving a question of so much import-ance . . . was at least ridiculous if not indecent', was Lady Caroline's comment.[11]

Since the autumn of 1761 Bunbury had been courting Lady Sarah Lennox, a younger sister of Lady Caroline Fox. Her family, who had enter-tained the most ambitious hopes for her, were not over-pleased. 'It's far from a good match', wrote Lady Caroline, 27 Jan. 1762; 'they are both young and in high life, they will not have the prudence to live within their income.' 9 Feb.: his father gives him £2,000 a year, 'a house in town and one in the country . . . 'tis in the county he is chose for, and where he must keep up an interest, which is very expensive'. 8 Apr.: 'The match . . . proves worse and worse, now the lawyers have examined it'—even after Sir William's death 'they will never see more than £2,500 in hard money probably'. 'A most miserable match in point of fortune', opined the Duke of Richmond. He also thought Bunbury 'a coxcomb'. Lady Caroline took a more favourable view of him: 'a very good character'; 'a grave young man of an elegant ingenious turn . . . a scholar and poet'. But even she wrote three days after the wedding: 'I own he don't take with me, neither Mr. Fox or I are more acquainted with him than we were the first week, though we have seen so much of him.' On 20 July 1762:

> I don't think Mr. Bunbury so great a coxcomb as he is reckoned, nor so very fond of himself; he seems to me a cold insipid disposition, loving Sarah better than anything else, very good tempered and indolent, having no pleasures, at least not seeming to enjoy them with the eagerness natural to his age.

And nearly four years later, 15 Mar. 1766: 'he mends upon long acquaintance. I think him a good man, not an agreeable one, but he makes her happy.'[12]

They settled at Barton; attended races (Bunbury was well known on the turf); and tried to make themselves popular with their county neighbours. But some better financial provision for them was required. 'Lord Shelburne', Lady Caroline had noted on 16 Feb. 1762, 'assures me Mr. Bunbury has such notions of independency he would not take a place for the world; this would vex me had I not seen so much of all that talk come to nothing.' Wherein she was right; by September Bunbury aspired to the post of secretary to the lord lieutenant of Ireland, worth £4,000 p.a. (which would not vacate his seat: the country gentleman might not wish to re-elect a placeman); while Fox, wrote Lady Sarah to Lady Kildare, 30 Sept.,[13] 'wants him to ask for a place immediately, but that he don't choose'.

Mr. Bunbury intends speaking for Lord Bute [she wrote]. Don't imagine . . . that he means to say, 'my Lord I am your creature'; for he dreads that more than anything in the world, and would not take a place but on condition he may speak as he pleases. Mr. Fox is trying to persuade him to be quite attached to Lord Bute, and has a notion that Mr. Bunbury is one of the wrong-headed, prating people that were in a set last winter—you heard of them, I don't doubt; Lord Shelburne is at the head of them—but he is vastly mistaken, for, to do my poor husband justice, he is the most right-headed person I ever saw . . . He has told me that his intentions are to be of Lord Bute's side in everything he approves of; but not to be tied to him or anybody else. He wishes to be independent as much as possible and yet wishes to be in business; and this place seems to answer both ends as much as any place can.

On 19 Oct., in a letter to Shelburne, Bunbury form-ally declared his support of Bute, and asked for the Irish post.[14] But it eluded him—'I am mad to think there is no likelihood of my being Madame la Secretaire', wrote Lady Sarah on 25 Nov.[15]

There is no record of Bunbury having spoken during the session of 1762–3; nor during the Gren-ville Administration: his only recorded intervention was on 25 Apr. 1765 when he divided the House and found himself in a minority of one against 124.[16] Early in April 1763 he was appointed secretary to the Paris embassy—'they like it', wrote Lady Holland, 'it's a step to farther preferment, will break into their expensive Barton life and suit them both very well.'[17] But the appointment was made without previous communication with Lord Hertford, the ambassador designate, who meantime had offered the post to David Hume. On 10 Apr. Hertford expressed to Bute his 'very sensible mortification'; disclaimed any personal objection to Bunbury, whom he hardly knew, but thought him 'a very young man from whom I can expect little assist-ance'; and feared that the manner of making the appointment, contrary to unvaried practice, would lower himself in the world's opinion.[18] 'I am sur-prised', wrote the King to Bute, 'Lord Egremont should commit so great a blunder as to send to Bunbury before he did to Lord Hertford'; and he told Hertford that the post had been promised to Bunbury before he 'had been pitched on as am-bassador'.[19] On 20 Oct. Hertford set out for Paris with Hume for private secretary,[20] and resolved never to see, nor do business with, his official secre-tary.[21] Meanwhile the meeting of Parliament sup-plied an excuse for retaining Bunbury in London. 'If Mr. Bunbury comes to Paris', wrote Sandwich to Holland, 26 Sept. 1763, 'I must depend on your taking care that he is over at the opening of the sessions, but we will endeavour to stop him here.'[22] 'Keep Bunbury with you, don't send him here for a month', replied Holland, 2 Oct.[23] And Sandwich to Holland, re-assuringly, 4 Oct.: 'Mr. Bunbury's detention has no meaning whatever in it but to add to our numbers in the House of Commons.'[24] But Hume to Adam Fergusson, from Fontainebleau, 9 Nov.:[25] 'Mr. Bunbury has been told that he must not go to Paris.' Hertford protested to George Grenville against his doing so;[26] Grenville spoke to the King who said 'he would not send Mr. Bunbury to Paris during the present session of Parliament'; and Grenville hoped that in the meantime another place would be found for him.

According to the pamphlet *The Four Last Suffolk Elections* (1772), Bunbury 'luckily escaped the question of general warrants, being not in town at the time' (he was at Newmarket); but his name is not in Jenkinson's list of friends absent from the division of 17–18 Feb. 1764; and while his mother's death on 14 Feb. may have kept him away from the division on the 15th, it seems improbable that anyone in his position would have absented himself from all the divisions on general warrants. In April 1764 Hume wrote from Paris:[27] 'I . . . do the business of the embassy without any character. Bunbury has the commission and appointments . . . above £1,000 a year.' Hertford continued to press for his removal: after having publicly on all occasions declared that he would not act with Bunbury, he wrote to Grenville, 28 July 1764, 'I cannot now depart from it without drawing on myself the imputation of levity or weakness.'[28] In March Bedford had urged Northumberland, then lord lieutenant of Ireland, to appoint Bunbury his secretary—he even quoted the King as 'desirous of obliging Mr. Bunbury'.[29] But Northumberland's reply was negative; it was essential to the comfort of a lord lieutenant that his first secretary should be his private friend.[30] At last, when in May 1765 Weymouth was appointed lord lieutenant of Ireland, Bunbury obtained the place he had so long desired, but now rendered less desirable by the feud between Weymouth and Bunbury's brother-in-law, Lord Kildare.[31] Anyhow six weeks later both Bunbury and his chief were out of office. Bunbury followed the Bedfords into opposition, and never again held a post.

On 17 Jan. 1766 Bunbury spoke on the Opposition side against rescinding the order to print the American papers;[32] he attended debates and divisions ('your nasty American business has kept him in town till now', wrote Lady Sarah to Lady Susan, 5 Feb.); voted against the repeal of the Stamp Act; and in 1766–7 was classed by all the parliamentary managers as a Bedford; but he did not vote either on the land tax, 27 Feb. 1767, or on nullum tempus, 17 Feb. 1768. At the general election of 1768 the

agreement of 1761 that either Bunbury or Holt should stand down for Rous was disregarded, and a contest was expected. Bunbury, wrote Whately to Grenville, 5 Nov. 1767,[33] 'does not seem much alarmed at the opposition to him in Suffolk, but is vexed at the expense.' And Lady Sarah to George Selwyn, the same day:[34]

> We talk and think of nothing but elections. Sir Charles's county meeting is to-morrow, where he expects an opposition, and the day after we both set out, he to go one side of the county, and I on the other, to canvass.

Sir William Musgrave to Lord Carlisle, 1 Dec.,[35] described her as 'an indefatigable canvasser'—'For the greater expedition she undertakes one district while he goes into another, and the other day she alone secured 94 out of 100 voters.' In the end he was returned unopposed.

In the summer of 1768 he went again 'jaunting to Paris'—'I believe', wrote Lady Holland, 30 June, 'because travelling is good for his disorders—the gravel, which is one, and change of place for his *ennui*, which is another.' What was worse, by that time Lady Sarah seems to have been bored with him. Mme. du Deffand's suspicions in February 1767, and Lauzun's claims[36] may have been unfounded; but the daughter to whom Lady Sarah gave birth, 19 Dec. 1768, was Lord William Gordon's;[37] and in February 1769 she left her husband and joined her lover. Bunbury, though greatly distressed, behaved toward her with much kindness and consideration—'she herself told me,' wrote Lady Holland, 27 Feb. 1769, 'Sir Charles made her as happy as she could be in her undone state.'[38] At times there were hopes of a reconciliation; and even after he had divorced her, his behaviour remained delicate and affectionate: when they met in 1778 he treated her 'like an old friend he was rejoiced to see' and assured her 'he had not a grain of resentment'.[39] Perhaps Mme. du Deffand's description of him, in her letter to Walpole, 6 Feb. 1767, was just: 'il me pârait le meilleur enfant du monde, doux et plein de candeur; il aime Milady à la folie.'

Politically Bunbury's role in the Parliament of 1768–74 was insignificant, and his attitude incoherent: it is difficult to discern any pattern in it. On 27 Jan. 1769 he voted for Wilkes's petition, but on 8 May for declaring Luttrell duly elected. Next, on 11 Mar. 1772, he voted with Opposition on the royal marriage bill; similarly on the petition of naval captains on half-pay, 9 Feb. 1773, but in the King's list was marked as one of those who normally were friends of Government. He voted with Government on Grenville's Act, 25 Feb. 1774, when again many regular supporters went against them; and at the end of the Parliament was classed by Robinson as 'hopeful'.

Nor do his interventions in debate explain his politics; they were not on major political issues, but were usually concerned with justice to individuals (the returning officer at New Shoreham, Clive, Horne, etc.), or with humanitarian causes. Bunbury supported Sir William Meredith, who on 27 Nov. 1770 moved for 'a committee to be appointed to consider of so much of the criminal laws as relate to capital offences', and on 6 May 1771 reported their conclusions. The committee, re-appointed on 31 Jan. 1772, on 14 Apr. was instructed to prepare and bring in a bill; besides Bunbury it included Meredith, Henry Herbert, Charles Fox, Sir George Savile, Serjeant Glynn, and Constantine Phipps.[40] Bunbury presented their bill; presided over the committee of the whole House which discussed it; and when it was passed on 21 May, carried it to the Lords (where it was rejected). Radzinowicz writes about Bunbury in his *History of English Criminal Law*:[41]

> Sir Charles Bunbury was very much interested in prison reform and the system of transportation, and took an active part in several debates on these matters in the House of Commons. Together with Eden, Howard and Blackstone, he was a member of the committee which framed 19 Geo. 3, c.74—one of the most important laws in the history of the prison system.

In 1774 Bunbury was returned unopposed. In the new House he seems at first to have sided with Government; his name does not appear in any of the four division lists 1775–7, which give the names of the minority only; nor is there any record of his having spoken before 8 May 1777 when he opposed the Government over a minor financial resolution. On 26 May, when moving an amendment to the tax on servants, he dragged in the subject of America (his speeches were often singularly inconsequential); declared that the American war 'was no longer justifiable'; and that he who 'had supported Government in this unhappy contest', was now convinced that its continuation 'must be disastrous to Great Britain'. 'I am not for lavishing more millions in search of a peppercorn, which perchance we never may be able to wring from them.' It was therefore hardly fair to Bunbury when Walpole described his speech of 4 Dec. in which, after Saratoga, he 'declared off the court', as a '*rati*fication of misfortune'. The experience of every campaign, said Bunbury, showed more and more that America 'was invincible'; 'all the laws enacted against them since the beginning of the disturbances' should be repealed; he could no longer vote for continuing measures 'which could be productive of no good' but would 'probably bring on ruin and destruction'.[42]

On 2 Feb. 1778 over America, and on 4 Dec., over the conciliatory mission, Bunbury voted with Opposition; over the contractors bill he was listed by Robinson as 'contra, absent' (12 Feb. 1779); and on 6 Apr. 1780 he presented the Suffolk petition in favour of economical reform.

His next political speech, 26 Jan. 1779 (he himself remarked on how rarely he asked for 'the indulgence and patience' of the House) was a plea in favour of union of 'all the men of abilities, let them be of what party they would'.[43] Lord John Cavendish wrote to Rockingham the same day: 'I believe Charles Fox knows more than he owns; his friend Sir C. Bunbury made a very odd speech today; the drift of which was the necessity of an union of all people of abilities; characters and panegyrics of Thurlow, Dunning, C. Fox and Lord North; though it was very absurd I do not think it was without a meaning.'[44]

Bunbury reverted to the subject on 22 June 1779, when speaking on the militia bill, critical of the Government though not hostile. Convinced that America could not be recovered by force, in a series of speeches he opposed the tendency 'to augment our land rather than our sea forces'; the armies asked for were 'too small for the conquest of America, too large for the defence of this island'; 'a large army to an Englishman was always disagreeable: a large army for no use was . . . disgustful'. It was insanity for this country to rely on any other security than a large naval force, and the condition of the fleet 'was truly deplorable'; etc. In September the news of the capture of Grenada by the French reached London: through inferiority at sea 'the valuable island of Grenada' was lost. And this was a very sore point with him: with engaging candour he admitted that he spoke as owner of property in the island. Thus on 27 Feb. 1782:[45]

> Sir Charles said, his sensibility was strong, which prevented him from speaking in public, and made him seldom trespass on their attention . . . He was, he acknowledged, much better calculated for a man of pleasure than politics; but his property in the West Indies compelled him to attend to those islands, however disagreeable and uncongenial the study might be.

During the critical years 1779–83 Grenada, and his property there, seems to have been an all-engrossing concern with Bunbury; and he was doubly sensitive to the alleged hardships inflicted on enemy civilians by the British commanders when St. Eustatius was captured in February 1781: he feared retaliation. In a speech of 21 Mar. Bunbury contrasted that capture, 'sullied by the seizure of private property', with 'the generosity' of the French King who had lately 'ordered the restitution of their property to the subjects of Grenada, as one of which he was happy to give this public testimony of his admiration and gratitude'.[46] A very long letter of 17 May to Thomas Walpole (q.v.) who, himself deeply engaged in Grenada, was in Paris carrying on dubious negotiations with the French, best describes Bunbury's attitude and activities:[47]

> If any apology were necessary for troubling you with this letter it would be sufficient to say that I am unfortunately *very deeply interested in the fate of Grenada* . . . You will conceive I have not been inactive in endeavouring to obtain redress for the French merchants, for I can truly assure you that not a day has elapsed, and hardly an hour . . . that I have not either in person, or by letter, solicited one, or other, of his Majesty's ministers in their behalf, and from the *gracious reception* I meet with from *some* of them (others being very well inclined), I have reason to believe my zeal in this business has rendered me as disgusting to their sight *as a messenger bringing bad tidings from Lord Cornwallis.* From the activity of my zeal upon this occasion however I can claim no merit, every man will struggle where his own interest is concerned, and I confess I have been stimulated by the mixed motives of compassion and self interest; compassion, for the unmerited sufferings of those French merchants who were settled at St. Eustatia, which however I believe have been greatly exaggerated in France, and the fear of having my property in Grenada seized, or grievously taxed in consequence of the violent and I fear unjustifiable behaviour of Sir G. Rodney and General Vaughan.

Governments changed but Bunbury's pre-occupation remained the same: Charles Fox, ten days after having assumed office, was writing to Thomas Walpole about Bunbury and Grenada;[48] and in September 1782 Bunbury was asking for an interview with Shelburne 'as an unfortunate proprietor . . . of lands in Grenada'.[49]

In 1780, when a contest seemed imminent in Suffolk between Holt, Bunbury, and Sir John Rous, Robinson thought that Bunbury 'probably . . . would fail'. But in the end Holt stood down, and the return was unopposed. In the new Parliament Bunbury voted regularly with Opposition. Next he followed his friend Fox; but did not vote on Shelburne's peace preliminaries; voted for Fox's East India bill; and presumably with him against Pitt after the Coalition had been dismissed—all political managers listed him as 'Opposition'; and as such, contrary to Robinson's forecast,[50] he was ignominiously defeated in April 1784. He re-entered Parliament in 1790 when 'all the gentlemen of the county' supported him.[51]

Bunbury retired in 1812, after having represented the county for 45 years, though never a politician. He was best known as a racing man, as the co-founder and first winner of the Derby in 1780 (and again in two other years), as a friend of Fox and his set, and a member of the Literary Club

(March 1774); he was one of the pall-bearers at Samuel Johnson's funeral.

Bunbury died 31 Mar. 1821.

[1] 'A Plain and True Narrative', E. Suff. RO, XLV/7; *Hist. Four Last Elections County of Suff.* (1772). [2] *Leinster Corresp.* i. 332–4. [3] Ibid. 311. [4] Add. 32932, ff. 107–8. [5] Grafton, *Autobiog.* 35. [6] *Rockingham Mems.* i. 81. [7] Add. 32932, f. 137. [8] Harris's 'Debates'; Add. 32934, f. 289. [9] Lansdowne mss. [10] Fitzmaurice, *Shelburne*, i. 105–6 (misdated); *Corresp. Sir Thos. Hanmer*, 370–1. [11] *Leinster Corresp.* i. 317. [12] Ibid. 311–34 passim. and 437. [13] Ibid. ii. 113. [14] Lansdowne mss. [15] *Life and Letters of Lady Sarah Lennox*, 126. [16] Harris's 'Debates'. [17] *Leinster Corresp.* i. 365. [18] Bute mss. [19] *Letters Geo. III to Bute*, 215, 217. [20] Ilchester, *Letters to H. Fox*, 186. [21] Klibansky and Mossner, *New Letters of Hume*, 77. [22] Ilchester, *Letters to H. Fox*, 184. [23] Sandwich mss. [24] Henry Fox mss. [25] Greig, *Letters of David Hume*, i. 411. [26] *Grenville Pprs.* ii. 186–7. [27] Klibansky and Mossner, 83–84. [28] *Grenville Pprs.* ii. 413. [29] Bedford mss 49, f. 70. [30] Ibid. f. 78. [31] *Grenville Pprs.* iii. 49; *Hanmer Corresp.* 373 (misdated); *Life and Letters of Lady Sarah Lennox*, 173. [32] Fortescue, i. 236. [33] *Grenville Pprs.* iv. 186. [34] Jesse, *Selwyn*, ii. 191. [35] HMC *Carlisle*, 221. [36] *Mémoires* (1858), 53–77. [37] *Leinster Corresp.* i. 569. [38] Ibid. i. 564. [39] Ibid. iii. 267–8; *Life and Letters*, 291–2. [40] *CJ*, xxxiii. 695. [41] i. 444 n.59, 473; Almon, vii. 175; xi. 235; Bunbury to Shelburne, Sept. 1782, Lansdowne mss. [42] Almon, vii. 155, 238–9; viii. 109–11. [43] Ibid. xi. 223–5. [44] Rockingham mss; Fortescue, iv. 263–7. [45] Debrett, vi. 317. [46] Debrett, ii. 304–8; vii. 161. [47] Walpole mss in possession of Mr. David Holland. [48] Ibid. [49] Lansdowne mss. [50] Laprade, 70. [51] HMC *Var.* vi. 353.

L.B.N.

**BURDETT, Sir Robert,** 4th Bt. (1716–97), of Bramcote, nr. Nuneaton, Warws. and Foremark, nr. Repton, Derbys.

TAMWORTH    12 Dec. 1748–1768

*b.* 28 May 1716, posth. s. and h. of Robert Burdett of Bramcote, by Hon. Elizabeth Tracy, da. of William, 4th Visct. Tracy [I]. *educ.* Westminster; New Coll. Oxf. 1733. *m.* (1) 6 Nov. 1739, Elizabeth (*d.*24 Aug. 1747), da. of Sir Charles Sedley, 1st Bt., sis. of Sir Charles Sedley, 2nd Bt. (q.v.), 3s. 2da.; (2) 17 July 1753, Lady Caroline, da. of John Manners, 2nd Duke of Rutland, wid. of Sir Henry Harpur, 5th Bt., M.P., and mother of Sir Henry Harpur, 6th Bt. (q.v.), *s.p. suc.* gd.-fa. as 4th Bt. at birth.

Burdett's grandfather had represented Warwickshire 1679–81, and he himself cultivated an interest at Tamworth. The family was Tory, and he himself was usually classed as such. In 1754 Burdett was returned unopposed; in 1761, after a contest in which he stood on a joint interest with Lord Weymouth's candidate. He was not included in Fox's list of Members in favour of the peace preliminaries, but did not vote against them; in the autumn of 1763 was marked by Jenkinson as 'pro'; and after the division on general warrants, 18 Feb. 1764, was listed by him among 'absent friends'. In July 1765 Rockingham classed him as 'contra'; and on 22 Feb. 1766 he voted against the repeal of the Stamp Act. On the land tax, 27 Feb. 1767, and the nullum tempus bill, 17 Feb. 1768, he voted against Administration. No speech of his is recorded. By 1768 he had surrendered his interest at Tamworth, and did not stand again.

He died 13 Feb. 1797.

J.B.

## BURGES, James Bland (1752–1824), of Nant-cribba, Mont.

HELSTON 27 Jan. 1787–1790

*b.* 8 June 1752, o.s. of George Burges, sec. of the Excise in Scotland, by the Hon. Anne Whichnor, da. of James, 12th Lord Somerville [S]. *educ.* Edinburgh Univ. 1765–7; Westminster 1767–9; Univ. Coll. Oxf. 1770–3; Grand Tour (Holland, Germany, Switzerland, France, Italy); L. Inn 1769, called 1777. *m.* (1) 19 June 1777, Hon. Elizabeth Noel (*d.*21 Jan. 1779), da. of Edward, 1st Visct. Wentworth, *s.p.*; (2) 16 Dec. 1780, Anne (*d.*17 Oct. 1810), da. of Lewis Charles Montolieu, Baron de St. Hypolite, 5s. 2da.; (3) 8 Sept. 1812, Lady Margaret Fordyce, da. of James Lindsay, 5th Earl of Balcarres [S], wid. of Alexander Fordyce, *s.p.* suc. fa. 1786; and John Lamb 1821, and took name of Lamb; *cr.* Bt. 21 Oct. 1795.

Bankruptcy commr. 1777–83; under-sec. of state for foreign affairs 1789–95; knight marshal of the Household 1795–*d.*

The *Gentleman's Magazine* (1825, i. 81), in its obituary notice of Burges wrote:

> In very early life he had formed a close intimacy with Mr. Pitt and the late Duke of Leeds, who, being anxious to attach to their party one so highly talented, prevailed upon him to embark in political affairs.

About 1778 Burges formed 'a very intimate and unreserved friendship' with Lord Carmarthen (q.v.), later 5th Duke of Leeds;[1] and in 1780 became acquainted with Pitt. At the general election of 1784 he claims to have received from Pitt 'an absolute promise of a seat in Parliament'.

> I was requested to go down to Totnes [Burges writes] where I should meet with no difficulties, and for which my return would be certain. I repaired thither, underwent all the horrors and fatigues of a twenty-one days' canvass, and lost my election. I was exhorted, however, not to be discouraged, as an opening would immediately occur, and everything be set right.[2]

This was written in 1818 and cannot be accepted as accurate. To begin with, Pitt could not provide Burges with a safe seat at Totnes: one seat was already earmarked for another Government candidate, and the other was under the patronage of the Duke of Bolton, who supported Fox. Next, Burges is unlikely to have undergone a 21 days' canvass, since only 11 days elapsed between the dissolution and the general election at Totnes; nor would he have required all that time to canvass a borough of only 100 voters. Lastly, there is no other evidence to support the story of a contest at Totnes in 1784. Robinson, in a memorandum he drew up shortly before the general election,[3] after noting that one seat was to go to Lord Mulgrave (q.v.), wrote: 'Mr. Rose to follow up a plan he has about the other seat.' What seems probable is that Rose suggested that Burges should stand, and Burges, after canvassing the borough, decided that he had no chance.

Pitt promised Carmarthen that at the first opportunity Burges should be brought into Parliament;[4] and, again according to his own account, Burges refused the offer of a seat at Seaford because £5000 was demanded for it—a figure, if correct, much above the normal price. He was finally brought in for Helston.

He had conceived a high opinion of Warren Hastings (although they had never met), and was convinced of 'the iniquity of the attack made upon him, and the propriety of opposing it'.[5] His first speech, in answer to Sheridan's oratory on the Begums of Oude charge, 7 Feb. 1787, was described by Daniel Pulteney (q.v.) as 'a long, insignificant speech of an hour for which he was coughed down',[6] while Burges himself wrote: 'I soon . . . found that the effervescence of the House was too great to admit of any calm attention to my arguments.' But he persisted, and next day rose again in defence of Hastings. So much so, that he quarrelled with Pitt about it. Before he took office the only subjects on which he spoke (and he spoke frequently) were the impeachment of Hastings and the relief of insolvent debtors. Three times he introduced a bill into the House providing for their relief. Unquestionably his biographer is right in saying that Burges 'seldom did things by halves', and when his opinions were formed 'he adhered to them tenaciously'.[7] He was undaunted alike by the oratory of his opponents and the indifference of the House, and consequently became a bore.

In 1789 Burges took office as Carmarthen's under-secretary of state, and at the general election of 1790 unsuccessfully contested Helston on his interest.

He died 11 Oct. 1824.

[1] James Hutton, *Sel. Letters & Corresp. Sir J. B. Burges*, 63. [2] Ibid. 74. [3] Laprade, 115. [4] Pitt to Carmarthen, 18 Apr. 1784, Egerton 3498, unfoliated. [5] Hutton, 81. [6] *HMC Rutland*, iii. 370. [7] Hutton, 84–85.

J.B.

## BURGHERSH, Lord, *see* FANE, John

## BURGHLEY, Lord, *see* CECIL, Brownlow

## BURGOYNE, John (1723–92).

MIDHURST 1761–1768
PRESTON 29 Nov. 1768–4 Aug. 1792

*b.* 4 Feb. 1723, 2nd s. of Capt. John Burgoyne, and gd.-s. of Sir John Burgoyne, 3rd Bt., of Sutton Park, Beds., by Anna Maria, da. of Charles Burneston of Hackney. *educ.* Westminster 1733–8. *m.* 1743, Lady Charlotte Stanley (*d.*1776), da. of Edward, 11th Earl of Derby, 1da. *d.v.p.* About 1780 Burgoyne took as his mistress Susan Caulfield, an actress, by whom he had 4 children.

Cornet 1 Royal Drag. 1744, lt. 1745, capt. 1745; sold out 1751; capt. 11 Drag. 1756; capt.-lt. 2 Ft. Gds. and lt-col. 1758; lt.-col. commandant 16 Lt. Drag. 1759; col. 1762; col. commandant 16 Lt. Drag. 1763–79; gov. of Fort William 1769–79; maj.-gen. 1772; lt.-gen. 1777; c.-in-c. Ireland 1782–4; col. 4 Ft. 1782–d.

Burgoyne is said to have formed a close friendship at Westminster School with Lord Strange (q.v.), with whose sister he made a runaway match. Her father disapproved, but Strange and Burgoyne remained fast friends; and Burgoyne later described him as 'the man of whose integrity and political judgment I had the highest veneration'.[1]

Burgoyne had little money of his own, and received none with his wife; in 1751 he sold his commission and retired to France to avoid his creditors. Having become reconciled with Lord Derby, in 1756 he returned to England and re-entered the army.

> I cannot help saying [he wrote to George Warde, major 11th Dragoons, 23 Nov. 1757[2]] that the circumstances of serving *under* so many men whom I had commanded appeared so disagreeable to me, when my friends proposed my entering a second time into the Army, that I should not have suffered any application to be made for me had I not had good assurances that I should not long continue a captain, and . . . that my situation would have procured me . . . as many indulgences as could be made consistently with the good of the service.

In 1758 he served on the expeditions to Cherbourg and St. Malo, and in 1759 raised a regiment of light dragoons of which he became lieutenant-colonel commandant. He drew up an elaborate set of instructions for his officers,[3] in which he forbade swearing and exhorted them to treat their men as 'thinking beings'. An officer should devote 'a short space of time . . . to reading each day'; should understand French; write English 'with swiftness and accuracy'; be 'well versed in figures'; have 'a competent knowledge of farriery'; etc. His biographer remarks: 'Burgoyne appears always to have been fond of writing' (in fact he let his pen run away with him).

In 1760 Sir William Peere Williams (q.v.), an officer in Burgoyne's regiment, offered to bring him into Parliament for Midhurst. Williams told Newcastle, who seemed not to approve; but Hans Stanley (q.v.) informed the Duke that 'Col. Burgoyne will honourably and steadily adhere to every assurance he gives your Grace on this occasion'.[4] He was returned unopposed.

In April 1761 he went as a volunteer on the expedition to Belle Isle, and in March 1762 was sent to Portugal in command of an Anglo-Portuguese brigade. In August he distinguished himself by capturing Valentia. Count la Lippe, the commander-in-chief, wrote to Bute of Burgoyne's 'remarkable valour, conduct, and presence of mind'; and recommended him as a 'most excellent' officer, 'extremely worthy of his Majesty's remembrance'.[5] In October he was promoted colonel—'out of regard to Lord Strange', wrote Bute, 'and your own merit';[6] and in January 1763 returned to England.

He supported Grenville's Administration, and applied for the post of chief secretary to the lord lieutenant of Ireland.[7] On 16 Feb. 1764 he wrote to Grenville about the coming debate on general warrants:[8]

> I take the liberty to communicate to you that I have considered the question of tomorrow's debate . . . and am very earnest in my wishes to avoid the decision of it at this juncture. I am also very desirous . . . to speak my sentiments in the House, and . . . I humbly offer myself to second any motion for postponing the question.

His offer was not accepted, and the very full reports of that debate by Walpole and Harris do not mention him; but he is named by Newdigate among the speakers.

In July 1765 Rockingham classed him as 'pro', but he voted against the repeal of the Stamp Act. 1765–8 only one speech by him is recorded: on 3 Feb. 1766 for the Declaratory Act. In the autumn of 1766 he visited Germany to study the battlefields of the seven years' war; attended the Austrian manoeuvres; and wrote a paper, 'Observations and reflections upon the present military state of Prussia, Austria, and France',[9] which he gave to Chatham. He supported Chatham's Administration, and voted with them over the land tax, 27 Feb. 1767.

In 1768 he contested Preston on Lord Derby's interest, and after one of the most violent elections of the century was seated on petition. In 1769 he was tried for incitement to violence at the election; and admitted that he had gone to the poll with a guard of soldiers and a loaded pistol in each hand. He was fined £1,000, and was fortunate to escape imprisonment.

On 29 Oct. 1768 Grafton wrote to Lord Granby recommending Burgoyne's 'fair pretensions' to 'an early mark of royal favour, on account of an expensive attack he has made in a part of the country the least affected to Government, and which has cost him a sum which I dare hardly name'.[10] Burgoyne's appointment to be governor of Fort William followed. To be colonel of a regiment and governor of a fort without having reached the rank of major-general in the army was unusual even for an officer with Burgoyne's good connexions. He was anxious to please and succeed in society; and took pride in being known as a wit, man of fashion, and successful dramatist (Walpole thought his play *The Heiress* 'the best modern comedy'[11]).

Burgoyne described his 'principles of acting in public' as 'to assist Government in my general line of conduct; but that in great national points . . . I would ever hold myself at liberty to maintain my own opinion'.[12] On at least three occasions between 1768 and 1774 he spoke and voted against the court: 13 Feb. 1771, the Spanish convention; 15 Feb. 1773, the expedition against St. Vincent; and 25 Feb. 1774, Grenville's Act. Over 70 speeches by him in the Parliament of 1768 are recorded, but he had no great reputation as a speaker: Walpole calls him 'a pompous man, whose speeches were studied and yet not striking',[13] and 'who had more reading than parts'.[14]

On 13 Apr. 1772, encouraged it is said by the Duke of Grafton,[15] he moved for a select committee to examine into the affairs of the East India Company; and became its chairman. It investigated events in India since 1757, and its revelations had considerable influence on parliamentary opinion, but it did not shape Government policy: Burgoyne was only the fly on the chariot wheel. He did not, however, intend to allow the reports of his committee to go unheeded: 'Not to proceed against persons who by the reports appear guilty', he said on 3 May 1773,[16] 'will be to give encouragement to others hereafter to offend. We should show that we have an eye to discern, a hand to correct.' Disclaiming all personal motive and acting independently of Government ('I have undertaken the work of a Hercules with the strength of a pigmy'[17]), he aimed to despoil Clive of his Indian wealth. On 10 May his resolutions condemning the conduct of the Company's servants in India were passed, but his vote of censure on Clive was defeated.

He resented the failure of Administration to support him and by 1774 was on bad terms with North. 'Nothing short of professed enmity', he wrote,[18] 'could place me further than I found myself from the confidence of this minister.' Yet he supported the Government's policy towards America. 'We have like an indulgent parent already ruined America by our lenity and tenderness', he said, 19 Apr. 1774, on Rose Fuller's motion to repeal the tea duty.[19] 'I am sure the tax is not the grievance but the power of laying it. That power I shall ever maintain exists in the Parliament of Great Britain.'

When in January 1775 he was offered a command in America he at first professed unwillingness to go but agreed when told he had been named by the King. Next, dissatisfied with 'the bare superintendence of a small brigade' and desirous of 'a principal or at least an active part', he asked to be made

governor of New York.[20] On 27 Feb. 1775, in a set speech, he delivered his creed on America:[21] 'Is there a man in England . . . who does not think the parliamentary rights of Great Britain a cause to fight for, to bleed and die for? . . . The reason of the nation has been long convinced; the trial now only is whether we have spirit to support our conviction.' 'I spoke from my heart', he wrote of this speech,[22] 'and to that cause I impute its success . . . Lord North professed . . . that it had done more essential service to Government than any speech of the year.' But it did not procure him the command at New York, which, though the King thought Burgoyne 'would best manage any negotiation',[23] had been promised to Howe.

Before leaving he obtained permission to return to England for the winter, 'unless he should have a separate command, or . . . should be employed in any service . . . beyond the common routine of military business'.[24] He also showed great concern for his wife in case he should be killed: 'To supply the requisites of her rank, to reward the virtues of her character', he wrote,[25] 'I could only bequeath her a legacy of my imprudences'; and he wrote a letter, to be delivered 'when the writer of it will be no more', recommending her to the King's charity.[26]

Hardly had he arrived at Boston before he complained to North that his situation was 'too humble . . . to promise . . . any hope of contributing essentially to his Majesty's service':[27] Gage, the c.-in-c., was 'unequal to his present station'; there was a 'want of capacity' in the administrative departments; money, food, and equipment were needed; the intelligence service was bad, etc.[28] After witnessing the battle of Bunker Hill he wrote to Lord Rochford:[29] 'You can have no probable prospect of bringing the war to a speedy conclusion with any force that Great Britain and Ireland can supply'; and recommended the use of foreign mercenaries, 'a large levy of Indians', 'a supply of arms for the blacks to awe the southern provinces', and 'a numerous fleet to sweep the whole coast'. And every letter contained a plea for greater responsibility for himself.

In 1776 he became second-in-command in Canada, and drew up a plan for an advance from Canada into the northern colonies. In March 1777 he was appointed commander of the expedition, and in June attained his first objective by the capture of Ticonderoga. This was received in England as a 'great and glorious success',[30] and the King announced his intention of making Burgoyne a Knight of the Bath, which Burgoyne declined—'From whim, caprice, or some other motive', wrote Lord Derby to Germain,[31] 'he has, I know, a strong objection to the honour.' At Ticonderoga on 30 June Burgoyne, brimful of confidence, issued a proclamation to the Americans which began with bombast ('The troops united to my command are designed to act in concert . . . with the numerous armies and fleets which already display in every quarter of America the power, the justice, and, when properly met, the mercy of the King') and ended with idle threats ('I have but to give stretch to the Indian forces under my direction, and they amount to thousands, to overtake the hardened enemies of Great Britain and America'—he had less than 500 Indians, and they were useless in battle).[32]

Burgoyne's plan had taken no account of the nature of the country; his administrative arrangements were bad; his troops were too few. In his proclamation he had described Congress as 'the completest system of tyranny that ever God in his displeasure suffered for a time to be exercised over a froward and stubborn generation'; but on 20 Aug. he wrote:[33] 'The great bulk of the country is undoubtedly with the Congress, in principle and in zeal.' Surrounded by superior forces, his retreat cut off, and his provisions exhausted, on 17 Oct. Burgoyne capitulated.

'My army would not fight and could not subsist', he wrote to Howe, 20 Oct. 1777,[34] 'and . . . I have made a treaty that saves them to the state for the next campaign.' But however pleased he felt with the terms of his capitulation, he was anxious about its reception in England. 'My honour and my life in great measure depends upon my return to England . . .', he wrote, 'I think it not impossible that the persons who are most bound to vindicate me will be the first to attack my reputation.' On 25 Oct. he sent another letter to Howe[35]—half an apology for his conduct, half a plea to be allowed to return; and when Congress refused to ratify the capitulation, Burgoyne, now a prisoner-of-war, obtained permission to give his parole.

He arrived in England on 13 May 1778 and requested an audience of the King, but was told that he should wait until a board of general officers had inquired into his conduct. He took offence at this refusal, which he professed to believe was to prevent him from telling the King the true state of affairs in America. On 26 May he delivered an oration in Parliament,[36] defending his conduct and demanding a parliamentary inquiry. This was refused, and on 28 May Burgoyne came out into open Opposition. 'The salvation of the country depends upon the confidence of the people in some part of the government', he said.[37] 'The ministry have it not; the whole nation see, or think they see, their insufficiency.' He considered himself 'a persecuted man . . . a marked victim to bear the sins that do not belong to me'; and ended by declaring his 'full support' for Hartley's motion for American independence.

The exact responsibility for Burgoyne's failure has never been determined, but so much is clear: Burgoyne, Howe, and Germain were each anxious to shift the responsibility from himself. Burgoyne by so precipitately going into opposition lost all sympathy at court; while his friendship with Fox made it clear that he intended to use his misfortunes and grievances as a weapon against Administration. On 5 June, after the War Office had decided that he could not be tried while on parole, he was ordered to rejoin his troops in America—'my ruin was made a measure of state', he wrote; but on pleading that 'repeated visits to Bath' were necessary to his health, was granted a respite.[38] Germain told him in the Commons on 26 Nov. 1778, after having listened to an harangue on his grievances, that he had 'no great cause to complain of intentional hard treatment' since the order had not been enforced 'notwithstanding he seemed to be in perfect health'—which only provoked another harangue, twice as long as the previous one.[39] Henceforth Burgoyne voted consistently with Opposition, believing, as he said on 14 Dec. 1778, that the war 'could never be terminated with success on our side'.[40] By 1781 he had convinced himself that 'he was ever of opinion that this country had no right to raise taxes upon America',[41] and that 'the American war was but part of a general design levelled against the constitution of this country and the general rights of mankind'.[42] His speeches were frequent, long, and tedious: filled with reiterations of his grievances and general censure of the incompetence of Administration; and almost every session he told the story of his campaign.

At last in May 1779 papers were laid before the House, and an inquiry was opened into the failure of his expedition. Burgoyne himself began the inquiry with a long speech[43] (17 pages in the printed debates) in which he told his tale complete with statistics, and took the lead in examining the witnesses. No resolutions were passed by the committee. On 24 Sept. he was informed that his failure to return to America was considered by the King 'a neglect of duty and disobedience of orders'. To this he replied in a long screed, full of the arguments he had used again and again, and ending with the demand for a court martial or the offer to resign his regiment and governorship.[44] 'Your Majesty's accepting the resignation', wrote Amherst, commander-in-chief, 'may be more than what the lieutenant-general intended, and what might be deemed severe usage'; but the King referred Burgoyne's 'very indecent answer' to the Cabinet, and replied to Amherst:[45] 'I am very far from clear what lenient measures he has left me room to employ without a total subversion of all military discipline.' His resignation was accepted. 'It is no less than £3,500 a year that he gives up', wrote Richard Fitzpatrick to Lord Upper Ossory (qq.v.),[46] 'and I suppose [he] has hardly anything left.'

Having burnt his boats he hastened to gain credit with the Opposition, sent copies of his correspondence with the War Office to Rockingham, and talked Opposition cant. 'I have ever thought with your Lordship', he wrote to Rockingham on 5 Nov. 1779,[47] 'that the prevalence of the term the *King's army* and the *King's fleet* in preference to their being called the forces of the state, was one among the many manifestations of the Tory doctrine of this reign.' Advised by Burke and Rockingham he published his correspondence with the War Office, and in 1780 a full account of his campaign and of his dealings with Administration[48] (there is nothing new in the practice of generals publishing their memoirs). He now ranked as an Opposition martyr second only to Keppel. But Horace Walpole, no supporter of the American war, wrote:[49] 'General Burgoyne flatters himself that everybody will forget their own sorrows to be occupied with his. I . . . beg to be excused myself. I cannot forget how ready he was to be a great favourite.'

When the Rockinghams took office Burgoyne was given a regiment and made commander-in-chief in Ireland. On Fox's resignation it was expected that Burgoyne would follow him; but his office, Portland wrote on 8 Dec. 1782,[50] was 'purely military'; and he continued: 'I could see no objection to your retaining it, and in carrying on the most violent opposition to the court at the same time in a political line'—a sentiment which Burgoyne himself then endorsed.[51] When the Coalition was formed he hoped to become lieutenant-general of the Ordnance,[52] but Fox could only secure for him the reversion of the 8th Dragoons[53]—which did not become vacant until 1787 when the engagement was forgotten.

He was summoned to England to vote for Fox's East India bill, and spoke on the third reading. On Fox's dismissal Burgoyne resigned: 'the trust of commander-in-chief', he now discovered, required 'the most confidential connexion with his Majesty's ministers on both sides the water';[54] and on 28 Feb. 1784 he denounced Pitt's Administration as unconstitutional. Henceforth his parliamentary career ceases to be of interest or importance: he was a regular follower of Fox (but never in the first rank),

and his many speeches are mostly concerned with details of military administration. He voted for parliamentary reform, 18 Apr. 1785; and was one of the managers for the impeachment of Warren Hastings, but did not speak during the trial.

Burgoyne died 4 Aug. 1792.

[1] E. B. de Fonblanque, *Life and Corresp. John Burgoyne*, 124. [2] Ibid. 11. [3] Ibid. 16–22. [4] Stanley to Newcastle, 21 Oct. 1760, Add. 32913, f. 257. [5] De Fonblanque, 45–46. [6] Ibid. 49. [7] Grenville to Burgoyne, 28 Jan. 1764, Grenville mss (HL). [8] Grenville mss (JM). [9] De Fonblanque, 62–82. [10] Rutland mss. [11] Walpole to Lady Upper Ossory, 14 June 1787. [12] De Fonblanque, 124. [13] *Last Jnls.* i. 80. [14] Ibid. 304. [15] L. S. Sutherland, *E. I. Co. in 18th Cent. Politics*, 231. [16] Brickdale's 'Debates'. [17] Ibid. [18] De Fonblanque, 123. [19] Brickdale's 'Debates'. [20] De Fonblanque, 124–7. [21] Almon, i. 252–3. [22] De Fonblanque, 130. [23] The King to North, 11 Apr. 1775, Fortescue, iii. 202. [24] North to the King, 14 Apr. 1775, ibid. 203. [25] De Fonblanque, 122. [26] Burgoyne to the King, 18 Apr. 1775, Fortescue, iii. 133–5. [27] Burgoyne to North, 14 June 1775, ibid. 137. [28] Burgoyne to Edw. Harvey, ibid. 140–1. [29] Ibid. 142–53. [30] Germain to the King, 23 Aug. 1777, Fortescue, iii. 471. [31] De Fonblanque, 249. [32] Ibid. 490–2. [33] Ibid. 274. [34] *HMC Royal Institution*, i. 140–2. [35] Ibid. 143–4. [36] Stockdale, viii. 308–24. [37] Ibid. 344–8. [38] Corresp. bet. Burgoyne and Ld. Barrington, June 1778, *Annual Reg.* 1779, pp. 302–4. [39] Almon, xi. 50. [40] Ibid. 154. [41] Debrett, iii. 551. [42] Ibid. v. 138–9. [43] Almon, xiii. 124–41. [44] This corresp. between Burgoyne and Chas. Jenkinson, secretary at war, is published in *Annual Reg.* for 1779, pp. 304–9. [45] Fortescue, iv. 456–7. [46] Add. 47579, f. 69. [47] Rockingham mss. [48] *State of the Expedition from Canada*. [49] To Mason, 16 Nov. 1779. [50] De Fonblanque, 415–16. [51] Ibid. 428. [52] Temple to W. W. Grenville, 28 Mar. 1783, *HMC Fortescue*, i. 206. [53] De Fonblanque, 429. [54] Burgoyne to Ld. Sidney, 4 Jan. 1784, ibid. 434.

J.B.

**BURKE, Edmund** (1729–97), of Beaconsfield, Bucks.

WENDOVER    23 Dec. 1765–1774
BRISTOL                        1774–1780
MALTON       7 Dec. 1780–11 July 1794

*b.* 12 Jan. 1729, 2nd surv. s. of Richard Burke, Dublin attorney, by Mary, da. of Peter Nagle of Ballyduff, co. Cork. *educ.* Ballitore sch. 1741–4; Trinity, Dublin 1744–50; M. Temple 1750. *m.* 12 Mar. 1757, Jane, da. of Christopher Nugent, physician, 2s., with *d.v.p.*

Private sec. to first lord of the Treasury July 1765–July 1766; P.C. 30 Mar. 1782; paymaster gen. Mar.–July 1782, Apr.–Dec. 1783.

Burke came of a middle-class Irish family, spent the best years of his life closely associated with English aristocrats, and ended as the political oracle of conservative Europe. In his early youth he imbibed a Catholic atmosphere without accepting Catholic doctrine, and his view of society was hierarchical and authoritarian. Yet as a young man he had known the life of the common people of Ireland, and one of the noblest traits in his character was his repeated defence of those who were too weak to defend themselves. Outstanding in the 18th century House of Commons for intellect, oratory, and drive, he lacked the ability either to lead or to conciliate men and never exerted an influence commensurate with his greatness. His career as a practical politician was a failure; as a political theorist he was for posterity.

Little is known of Burke's parents. His mother

suffered from what Burke called 'a cruel nervous disorder',[1] and his relations with his father were not happy. A boyhood friend, William Dennis, wrote in 1747:[2]

> My dear friend Burke leads a very unhappy life from his father's temper, and what is worse there is no prospect of bettering it. He must not stir out at night by any means, and if he stays at home there is some new subject for abuse. There is but one bright spirit in the family, and they'd willingly destroy it . . . Care, I believe, wears as many shapes as there are men, but that is the most intolerable which proceeds from want of liberty. This is my friend's case, who told me this morning he wants that jewel of life, 'peace of mind', and his trouble was so great that he often forms desperate resolutions.

Little trace of this unhappiness appears in the early letters Burke wrote to his school friend Richard Shackleton. He tried to hide his family life from even his closest friends; and later in England resented almost with frenzy any criticism of his dubious relatives. The unity of the family, which he had not known in boyhood, became an article of his adult creed.

In 1750 Burke crossed to England to study law at the Middle Temple. With what dreams did he come? For a brief period in 1748 he had published a series of essays in the manner of *The Spectator*, and on 24 Dec. 1747 had written to Shackleton about their common friend, Dennis:

> Don't you think had he money to bear his charges but 'twere his best course to go to London? I am told that a man who writes can't possibly miss there of getting some bread, and possibly good. I heard the other day of a gentleman who maintained himself in the study of the law by writing pamphlets in favour of the ministry.

The study of the law did not attract him; he had an unconscious resistance to his father's plans for him, and never became a lawyer. In 1755 he had the idea of applying for a post in the colonies, but dropped it when his father objected. In a fragment of a letter to his father, dated 11 Mar. 1755, he wrote: 'I shall be ready . . . to go to Ireland when you think proper, and the end for which you desire I should go can be answered.' But a little later he told Joseph Emin that he was 'a runaway son from a father',[3] and in 1757 described his 'manner of life' as 'chequered with various designs'.[4]

Marriage and parenthood marked Burke's independence from his father; the publication in 1756 of the *Vindication of Natural Society* and the *Sublime and the Beautiful* made his name known in London literary circles and seemed to open out a career for him. Horace Walpole met him in 1761 and wrote that 'he thinks there is nothing so charming as writers and to be one'.[5] He lived in a close family

circle with his father-in-law, his brother Richard, and his so-called 'cousin' William, whom he had known at least from his earliest days in England; and enjoyed in their society an ease and security he had never felt in his father's home.

Like planets in their orbits, the Burkes lived their lives without colliding with each other, yet moved by a common force: Edmund the literary man, Richard the business man, and William the politician. In 1759 Richard and William went to seek their fortunes in the West Indies, and Edmund, without a secure and regular income, applied for the consulship at Madrid. In 1759 or 1760 he entered the service of William Gerard Hamilton (q.v.) in a secretarial capacity—'a companion in your studies', he later described himself to Hamilton.[6] He seems to have received payment for his work, but probably in the form of occasional doles rather than a regular salary. In 1761 Hamilton went to Ireland as chief secretary to the lord lieutenant; Burke went with him, and in 1763 was granted a pension on the Irish establishment of £300 per annum.

William Burke came back to England in 1762, having lost his official position through the return of Guadeloupe to France. An intimate friend of Lord Verney (q.v.) and closely connected with Henry Fox and Lord Sandwich, he now looked forward to entering Parliament. Edmund still hoped for a literary career, despite the distractions of his work with Hamilton. In Ireland he had again become conscious of the depressed and persecuted position of the Catholics, had hoped to do something to relieve them, but had been disappointed by his chief's timidity. Back in England after Hamilton's dismissal in 1764, Burke was ill at ease and hoping for a change; early in 1765 he quarrelled violently with Hamilton and broke with him forever.

Necessity, not ambition, led him into politics, and his connexion with Rockingham began accidentally without either having much knowledge of the other. In July 1765, when the Rockingham Administration was being formed, William Fitzherbert recommended the Burkes to Lord John Cavendish, who in turn recommended them to Rockingham; and on 11 July Edmund wrote to his Irish friend, Charles O'Hara: 'I have got an employment of a kind humble enough . . . private secretary to Lord Rockingham, who has the reputation of a man of honour and with whom they say it is not difficult to live.' And on 14 Oct. he wrote about the new ministers: 'Newly, and almost as a stranger, I am come about these people.'

Returned to Parliament on Lord Verney's interest at Wendover (William Burke waiving his pretensions to the seat), Edmund was an almost instantaneous success in the House. When Rockingham left office in July 1766 Burke lost his employment, but there was nothing to stop him from taking another under the Chatham Administration. Grafton thought him 'the readiest man upon all points perhaps in the whole House . . . and one on whom the thoroughest dependence may be given', and wished to gain him for the new Administration.[7] Thanks to William Burke's speculations in East India stock, the Burkes were for the time being financially independent and had room to manœuvre. 'This joint stroke of providence and friendship', as Edmund described William's stock-jobbing, 'certainly leaves one with some freedom of action, but the time holds out nothing to guide that freedom.'[8] But in fact his decision had already been made. Hating Chatham, and already deeply attached to Rockingham, he replied to Conway's offer of employment:[9]

> That if the place which should be offered should prove in itself never so acceptable, I could take it only on condition that, in accepting it, and in holding it, I must be understood to belong not to the Administration but to those who were out; and that therefore if ever they should set up a standard, though spread for direct and personal opposition, I must be revocable into their party and join it.

When the East India inquiry came into the House of Commons, on 27 Nov. 1766, 'our friend Burke rose first in opposition', wrote Henry Flood;[10] and henceforth the story of his political career is bound up with that of the Rockingham group.

'I believe in any body of men in England I should have been in the minority', said Burke in 1778. 'I have always been in the minority.'[11] The outstanding trait in Burke's character was his aggression: there was a terrible need in him to fight, to argue, and to oppose; and to that was added enormous persistence, courage, concentration, and energy. His political life is a series of negative crusades: against the American war, Warren Hastings, the French Revolution; and his reputation as a statesman rests on his wisdom in Opposition, not on his achievements in office. Driven by the impulse to oppose, he was unable to stop or relax; no cause was for him hopeless; he always held on to the bitter end. With many of the qualities required for leadership, he lacked the ability to sense the feeling of others and always tried to impose his own.

Why did he attach himself to Rockingham? In his speech on American taxation, 19 Apr. 1774, he said of Rockingham:

> I did see in that noble person such sound principles, such an enlargement of mind, such clear and sagacious sense, and such unshaken fortitude, as have bound me, as well as others much better than me, by an inviolable attachment to him from that time forward.

This is wishful fantasy, rather than accurate appraisal of character. Rockingham's mind was commonplace and restricted, and wounded vanity rather than principle too often dictated his political conduct. Though ambitious, he lacked energy and vitality, and was perpetually anxious. Yet for Burke, Rockingham seemed at this time to possess every quality needed in a party leader.

Rockingham had a secure stake in the country and the right to share in its government through the possession of landed property not acquired but inherited—'the unbought grace of life'. O'Hara once told Burke that 'you . . . suppose that every void you feel would be agreeably filled up by property';[12] and Burke himself wrote in 1792 that the Rockingham party was:[13]

> A party, in its composition and in its principles, connected with the solid, permanent, long-possessed property of the country; a party which, by a temper derived from that species of property . . . was attached to the ancient tried usages of the kingdom; a party therefore essentially constructed upon a ground plot of stability and independence.

Burke, emotional and hysterical by temperament, without a profession or a secure income, an adventurer without standing in England, found stability and independence through attachment to Rockingham. Without shame or embarrassment he defended his position as a *novus homo*: 'Abilities cannot be settled with your estate', he told the House of Commons on 2 Apr. 1770.[14] '. . . All the wise governments have encouraged rising merit . . . we know not in what mountain of Scotland, what bog of Ireland, or what wild in America, that genius may now be rising who shall save this country.' Yet 'rising merit' must seek to better itself 'under the wings of established greatness' (social, rather than intellectual or political). And in a well-known letter to the Duke of Richmond in November 1772, he wrote:

> You people of great families and hereditary trusts and fortunes are not like such as I am, who, whatever we may be by the rapidity of our growth and of the fruit we bear . . . yet still we are but annual plants that perish with our season and leave no sort of traces behind us.

Burke received financial assistance from Rockingham, and after his death from Fitzwilliam, without feeling that he had in any way compromised his independence: their service was perfect freedom. Nor did Burke seek to assimilate himself to the society of his masters: he rarely visited their country houses, except for political consultations; shared few of their interests; and did not move in fashionable London society. His letters to them reveal a humility and obsequiousness which is no less unpleasant for being sincere. For them he sacrificed his material interests through sixteen long years of profitless opposition, and when his party at last came to power he failed to obtain any lasting advantage for himself or his family. The pension granted to him in 1794 compares unfavourably with the rewards received by others in comparable stations. In the famous passage on Marie Antoinette in the *Reflections on the French Revolution*, Burke, lamenting the departure of the 'age of chivalry', perhaps unconsciously described his own relations with the Whig aristocrats:

> Never, never more, shall we behold that generous loyalty to rank and sex, that proud submission, that dignified obedience, that subordination of the heart, which kept alive, even in servitude itself, the spirit of an exalted freedom.

Burke's theory of party was uncorrelated to the practice of his age, when the King still played an active part in politics and Members of Parliament took pride in their independence. The Rockingham group was a clique, rather than a party, without roots in the nation, which as yet had hardly begun to think along party lines. Burke profoundly distrusted the people, and believed in the divine right of the aristocracy to govern. 'All direction of public humour and opinion must originate in a few', he wrote to Rockingham on 23 Aug. 1775; and to Richmond on 26 Sept.: 'The people are not answerable for their present supine acquiescence . . . God and nature never meant them to think or to act without guidance or direction.' Nor did he ever advocate the party system, which takes from the Crown the choice of the prime minister. In his *Thoughts on the Cause of the Present Discontents*, published in 1770, Burke argued that since George III came to the throne an attempt had been made to govern unconstitutionally by means of a court cabal, 'totally separate from and independent of ostensible Administration', and a party of 'King's friends' in the House of Commons. Burke's distortions were the products of a mind prone to project on to reality its unconscious wishes; and the cause of the present discontents came to little more than Rockingham's failure to retain his situation as first minister. Yet in all Burke's political writings, despite their propagandist purposes, there are generalizations on human conduct of lasting value.

America was the outstanding political problem during the first ten years of Burke's parliamentary career. 'I do not look upon this as a common question', he wrote soon after entering Parliament; and again: 'Surely, since this monarchy, a more material point never came under the consideration of Parliament.'[15] Few in the House of Commons as yet understood the consequence of the American pro-

blem: a remarkable example of Burke's political prescience.

The Rockinghams proposed to repeal the Stamp Act and yet affirm the right of Great Britain to legislate for the colonies 'on all matters whatsoever'. Here was a source of difference with Pitt, who denied the right of the British Parliament to lay taxes upon America. Burke thought the right 'clear beyond contradiction, as an absolute and speculative opinion', but held that 'the system of government with respect to the plantations effectually excludes taxation'.[16] 'The power of taxing in Parliament', he said on 19 Apr. 1774, was 'an instrument of empire' not 'a means of supply'. Only a hair's breadth divided him from Pitt—whether or not Great Britain had a right which both agreed she should never enforce—and Burke 'hated the very sound' of 'these metaphysical distinctions'.[17] Yet he felt compelled to stand by the declaration of abstract right enunciated by the Rockingham Administration, and repeatedly declared his belief in the legislative supremacy of the British Parliament.

Again, it seems clear that Burke early recognized the implications of the Townshend duties. He said in Parliament on 8 Nov. 1768:[18]

> With regard to my own conduct when this proposition was made to the House, I expressed the little opinion I had, and I shall prove a true prophet. I said that you would never see a single shilling from America.

Yet when on 26 Jan. 1767 Townshend first declared his intention to raise a revenue from America, no follower of Rockingham rose to protest, nor did the party oppose the bill in its passage through the House. At that time Rockingham was hoping to form an Administration which should include both Grenville, author of the Stamp Act, and Townshend, author of the Townshend duties; and as late as August 1768, when news of fresh disturbances in America reached England, Dowdeswell, leader of the Rockingham party in the Commons, argued that to repeal the duties would be 'timidity, weakness, irresolution, and inconsistency' and would give the Americans 'a charter against being bound to any laws passed without their consent'.[19] This was precisely North's case for retaining the tea duty in 1774, against which Burke argued in his celebrated *Speech on American Taxation*. In short, while Burke saw earlier and clearer than most the significance of American taxation, he was unable to give a decisive lead to his party.

This was Burke's view of the relation between Great Britain and her colonies, as expressed in his speech of 19 Apr. 1774:

> The Parliament of Great Britain sits at the head of her extensive empire in two capacities: one as the local

legislature of this island, providing for all things at home, immediately, and by no other instrument than the executive power. The other, and I think her nobler capacity, is what I call her *imperial character*, in which, as from the throne of heaven, she superintends all the several inferior legislatures, and guides and controls them all, without annihilating any. As all these provincial legislatures are only co-ordinate with each other, they ought all to be subordinate to her; else they can neither preserve mutual peace nor hope for mutual justice nor effectually afford mutual assistance. It is necessary to coerce the negligent, to restrain the violent, and to aid the weak and deficient by the overruling plenitude of her power.

He saw the British empire in terms of the family, with the parent exercising a benevolent authority over the children; and, perhaps influenced by an earlier, personal, conflict, believed the British Government to have been harsh and tyrannical when it should have been lenient and forbearing. 'When any community is subordinately connected with another', he wrote in 1777,[20] 'the great danger of the connexion is the extreme pride and self-complacency of the superior.' Twice in 1775 (in March and November) he moved resolutions for conciliation with the colonies. On both occasions he found the origins of the conflict in taxation; and on the second occasion went further than he had ever gone before and proposed to renounce the right of parliamentary taxation, except for 'duties and taxes for the regulation of trade and commerce'. But he would not renounce the Declaratory Act, the shibboleth of the Rockingham party:[21]

He had always wished to preserve the legislative power of this kingdom entire in everything, and that it was with great grief he saw that even an odious and scarcely ever to be exercised part of it was to be abandoned . . . the repeal of the Declaratory Act was a thing impossible, for it was nothing less than to make legislature accuse itself of uttering propositions that were false and making claims that were groundless . . . the disgrace of an English Parliament could add nothing to the security of American liberty.

His conception of the British empire as an 'aggregate of many states under one common head' (wielding executive power, not a mere figurehead) came as near as was possible in the eighteenth century towards reconciling British authority with colonial autonomy. That the children should one day grow up and wish to throw off the authority of their parent was beyond Burke's understanding.

The American war tore Burke in two: he disliked American independence, yet could not relish the prospect of a British victory. Like most in Britain, he underestimated the ability of the Americans to resist and their urge towards independence. 'I look upon it as next to impossible that the present temper and unanimity of America can be kept up,' he wrote to Rockingham on 18 Sept. 1774. On 28 June 1775

he condemned the 'apparent want of system shown by the congress in suffering the King's forces to possess themselves of New York'.

They seem to have forgot that they are in rebellion . . . Their idea of a defensive war is quite ridiculous. Indeed, if this step of their's manifests a design of pacific measures, it is very happy and greatly to be applauded. But if it be the effect only of scrupulous timidity in the pursuit of violence, it is trifling and contradictory, and can hardly fail of bringing with it its own punishment. Whatever be done, God send us peace.

And on 11 Aug. 1776: 'I do not know how to wish success to those whose victory is to separate us from a large and noble part of our empire. Still less do I wish success to injustice, oppression, and absurdity . . . No good can come of any event in this war to any virtuous interest.'

In Ireland, his sympathies were with the persecuted Roman Catholics, 'reduced to beasts of burthen',[22] crying out for that elementary justice all subjects had a right to expect from their government, rather than with the Protestant Anglo-Irish who were striving to throw off the authority of the British Parliament. With Irish nationalism and its constitutional grievances he had no sympathy whatsoever. 'I am sure the people ought to eat whether they have septennial Parliaments or not', he wrote to O'Hara on 24 May 1766; and again on 20 Feb. 1768, after the Act had been changed into an octennial one:

The madness of the Government here which passed the Octennial Act is to be equalled only by the frenzy of your country which desired it and the tameness of this country which bore it. I consider that act as a virtual repeal of one of the most essential parts of Poynings's law, and I think it will necessarily draw on a change in other parts . . . However you have your day of joy and your drunken bout for the present.

'Ireland cannot be separated one moment from England without losing every source of her present prosperity and even hope of her future', he wrote towards the end of his life.[23] Despite his sympathy with the Irish Catholics, he always counselled moderation. 'I believe there are very few cases which will justify a revolt against the established Government of a country, let its constitution be what it will', he wrote to French Laurence on 12 May 1797. He disliked talk about the rights of man, whether from Americans or Frenchmen, but was solicitous for the rights of property and established government.

Burke always hated inaction: he could not remain a detached passive spectator of events, even when he knew that his efforts would come to naught. He was out to get things done, and would have scorned to be counted a mere political philosopher—one of the detested band of 'metaphysicians' and 'speculators'. But Rockingham was listless: strong, decisive action was not in his character. Burke wrote to him on 24 Jan. 1775:

> I cannot help continuing however with the deference I owe, and most cheerfully pay, to your Lordship's judgment, very strongly in opinion that a plan of in-action under our present circumstances is not at all in our power . . . There are others in the world who will not be inactive because we are so . . . The question then is whether your Lordship chooses to lead or be led . . . The only way to keep your Lordship in the public eye, and to keep you advantageously in it, must be to resolve to take the lead yourself.

On 4 Aug. 1775, when the news reached England of the outbreak of fighting in America, Burke wrote to Rockingham: 'We are called to rouse ourselves, each in his post, by a sound of a trumpet almost as loud as that which must awaken the dead.' He sug-gested that something should be done to stir up opinion in Yorkshire against the war. On 23 Aug. he tried again:

> I shall . . . make no apology for urging again and again how necessary it is for your Lordship and your great friends most seriously to take under immediate deliberation what you are to do in this crisis. Nothing like it has happened in your political life . . . This is no time for taking public business in its course and order, and only as a part in the scheme of life which comes and goes at its proper periods and is mixed in with other occupations and amusements.

On 14 Sept. he tried a third time, the 'sound of a trumpet almost as loud as that which must awaken the dead' having failed to waken Rockingham. He asked for

> early and vigorous steps, particularly that of calling the whole body of your Lordship's friends together as soon as possible, that they may not be, as they always are at the beginning of a session, utterly undetermined what part to take.

To Richmond he wrote:

> No regular or sustained endeavours of any kind have been used to dispose the people to a better sense of their condition. Any election must be lost, any family interest in a county would melt away, if greater pains . . . were not employed to carry on and support them than have ever been employed . . . in this most im-portant interest of the nation and of every individual in it.

On 24 Sept. Rockingham, having consulted some of his advisers at Wentworth, replied to these exhorta-tions:

> Upon the fullest discussion we could give to the matter in consideration it did not appear that anything essential could be done by me or by our friends in Parliament being immediately summoned to London . . . Nothing but a degree of experience of the evils can bring about a right judgment in the public at large.

Burke immediately submitted, and wrote to Rock-ingham on 1 Oct.:

> Nothing more than your Lordship's final determina-tion was required to satisfy my mind most perfectly on the prudence and propriety of the plan to which you adhere. I should have thoroughly acquiesced in it, although it were not confirmed, as it has been, by the joint opinion of the friends you consulted. I am sure I have a most unreserved deference to their judgment in all things.

On 8 Oct. 1777 he opened himself to Charles Fox about his leaders. 'A great deal of activity and enter-prise can scarcely ever be expected from such men, unless some horrible calamity is just over their heads, or unless they suffer some gross personal in-sults from power.' Rockingham, with a 'shattered constitution' and with an Opposition consisting of 'fleeting' and 'discordant' materials, had done better than Burke could have imagined. 'To act with any people with the least degree of comfort . . . we must contrive a little to assimilate to their character.' Still, the Rockinghams were 'indifferently qualified for storming a citadel'. And to William Baker, a fellow Rockinghamite, on 12 Oct. 1777:

> Alas, my dear friend, those whom you and I trust, and whom the public ought to love and trust, have not that trust and confidence in themselves which their merits authorize and which the necessities of the country absolutely demand. Ill success, ill health, minds too delicate for the rough and toilsome business of our time, a want of the stimulus of ambition, a degeneracy of the nation which they are not lofty enough to despise nor skilful enough to cure, have all together I am afraid contributed very much to weaken the spring of characters whose fault it never was to be too elastic and too firmly braced.

'We can do nothing essential unless the great change of sentiments arise in the public', wrote Rockingham on 26 Oct. 'I do most perfectly agree with your Lordship in every particular of your letter', replied Burke on 5 Nov. ' . . . To make our activity rational there must be some disposition in the minds of the many to co-operate, and something or other conspir-ing in the circumstances. None of these occur.'

In his letter to Fox of 8 Oct. 1777 Burke had complained of Rockingham's failure 'to guide and direct the public opinion'. It was an old complaint. In 1769 he had urged Rockingham to use his in-fluence in Yorkshire to procure a petition against the seating of Luttrell, but Rockingham would not move until he knew the sense of the county. 'I would not give any handle in Yorkshire', he wrote to Burke on 1 Sept. 1769, 'for Yorkshiremen to say that my politics had led them beyond their intentions or that I had checked their well-founded ardour.' Burke wanted the Whig magnates to use the influence given them by their property and wealth to further their political aims and to create public opinion.

'The public discontents', he wrote to Rockingham on 24 Jan. 1775, '. . . never did, do, or will ripen to any purpose unless they are matured by proper means.' Between 1774 and 1780 he tried to build up at Bristol a Rockingham party, opposed both to the supporters of Administration and to the radicals; but found it very hard going and was forced to abandon the attempt.[24] Burke was an Irishman and there was much both Catholic and feudal in his thought; he never really understood the Protestant and individualistic nature of English society. He never realized the essential independence of the English freeholder: that political ties were based on tradition rather than principle, and that no landlord, whatever his acreage, could mobilize his tenants for political action like a feudal lord his retainers. Rockingham, firmly rooted in English soil, was far wiser: he knew that his influence in Yorkshire came less from his property than from his always appearing to follow the bent of county opinion. He could assume the lead in a movement which had started spontaneously, but he could not stir up opinion himself.

Contrary to all Burke had ever said, public opinion was roused to action independently of the political leaders. The movement which began in Yorkshire in December 1779, and soon spread to other parts of the country, aimed at a reduction of Government expenditure through the suppression of unnecessary places and pensions. In 1780 it grew much wider in scope, and called for shorter Parliaments and parliamentary reform. Rockingham hastened to put himself at its head, to direct and channel it. Burke's economical reform bill, introduced on 11 Feb. 1780 with one of his finest speeches, was designed to reduce Government influence, 'the perennial spring of all prodigality and of all disorder', by a reformation of the King's household and of the holding of public accounts, and the abolition of a number of places tenable with a seat in the House of Commons. It was hoped to divert attention from parliamentary reform, which both Burke and Rockingham disliked; and it won the Rockinghams more support than they had ever previously received. North's Administration was twice defeated in committee, but eventually forced the bill's withdrawal. Economical reform henceforth became one of the main planks in the Rockingham platform; and in March 1782, when North resigned, the King was forced to accept it as a condition of Rockingham's taking office.

On the formation of the Rockingham ministry, Burke was appointed paymaster general with a salary of £4,000 per annum. At the same time he reformed the office: the cash balances, hitherto invested by the paymaster for his personal profit, were henceforth to be paid into the Treasury. His son was appointed deputy paymaster at £500 per annum; his brother secretary to the Treasury at £3,000 per annum; and a place in India under the pay office was created for William. Nor was this all: a sinecure for life was to be given to young Richard, as a secure income for himself and his mother. In a hasty memorandum for Rockingham, written before the ministry had taken office, Burke wrote:

> You need stipulate nothing for me except for my poor lad—even the office itself may keep cold and lie by for another time if arrangement should at all require it. I can readily consent to lie by, but having second rate pretensions, not to be put below others in that line.

No further explanation seems needed for his non-inclusion in the Cabinet.

In April Burke wrote to William:

> Oh! my dearest, oldest, best friend, you are far off indeed! May God of his infinite mercy preserve you. Your enemies, your cruel and unprovoked persecutors, are on the ground, suffering the punishment not of their villainy towards you, but of their other crimes, which are innumerable. I think the reign of Sulivan is over, the reign of Hastings is over . . . Resolutions will pass after the holidays to secure the Rajah of Tanjore and to limit the Nabob. Much good will happen. Indeed, my dear friend, your honest and humane labours have not been useless.

But while old enmities were remembered, old friendships were forgot. Poor Lord Verney was on the edge of bankruptcy. Verney had helped to finance William's speculations in India stock; had brought William and Edmund into Parliament gratis; and Edmund had written of him in 1779:[25] 'If I ever have been able to attempt anything in a public way . . . it is wholly owing to him.' Burke's brother, who never sat in Parliament, was given an office the duties of which he could hardly discharge without a seat in the House; yet Verney, who had been faithful to Rockingham for sixteen years, was given nothing.

Nor was Burke alone in forgetting past services. His son never received the 'something considerable' in the way of a sinecure which Burke had asked for him. Shelburne secured large pensions for Barré and Dunning; but Rockingham did nothing for Burke except cancel the debts which Burke owed him. It was a bitter disappointment, and provoked Burke into a foolish act. Shortly after Rockingham's death, he sent a proposal to Sir Edward Walpole, through his brother Horace, that Walpole should resign to Burke's son the valuable sinecure of clerk of the pells while retaining the profits for the rest of his life. Walpole was over 70 and not expected to live long; still, there was no reason why he should oblige

Burke, a man unknown to him.[26] This 'frantic' proposal, as Horace Walpole described it, came to nothing; how desperate must Burke have been to have even considered it.

Everything seemed to go wrong for Burke at this time, just when he seemed on the threshold of great achievements. Although his reform legislation passed the House with little difficulty, there were also serious political setbacks.

As long ago as 1769 Burke had laid down the conditions on which the Rockingham party should accept office.[27] Other parties were not proscribed, but the Cabinet was to be united in its opinions; and 'the great strongholds of Government' were to be held by reliable followers of Rockingham. In a letter to Rockingham of 22 Mar. 1782, Burke repeated this advice: 'I trust and hope that your Lordship will not let *one*, even but *one* branch of the state —neither army, navy, finance, Church, law, or anything else—out of your own hands or those which you can entirely rely on.' But Rockingham was in no position to make such demands. He could not prevent Thurlow, lord chancellor in the North ministry, from retaining his office; and the King accorded Shelburne, whom Burke disliked more than any other man, equal authority with Rockingham as first minister. But it was a culpable blunder on Rockingham's part to have allowed Shelburne to secure for his friend Dunning a seat in the Cabinet. The Cabinet of which Rockingham was the ostensible head was far from united; the two secretaries of state, in charge of peace negotiations, were each pursuing a separate policy; and on the immediate practical issue of the recognition of American independence, Dunning's inclusion in the Cabinet had put the Rockingham group in a minority.

There are signs that at this time the delicate balance of Burke's mind was disturbed. Sheridan, a political ally, thus reported his speech against Pitt's motion on parliamentary reform (7 May 1782):[28]

> Burke acquitted himself with the most magnanimous indiscretion, attacked W. Pitt in a scream of passion, and swore Parliament was and always had been precisely what it ought to be, and that all people who thought of reforming it wanted to overturn the constitution.

Horace Walpole wrote of him in his journal, under the date of 1 July 1782:[29]

> The enthusiasm of his luxuriant imagination presented every measure to him in the most vivid colours. In truth, it had been suspected for above a year that his intellects and sensations had mutually overheated each other: his behaviour in the ensuing year did not remove the supposition.

**Boswell** told Johnson in May 1783 that Burke had

been represented 'as actually mad'; to which Johnson replied: 'If a man will appear extravagant as he does, and cry, can he wonder that he is represented as mad?'[30] Rockingham's brief tenure of office had demonstrated his political inadequacy, but his death was a terrible and unexpected blow for Burke. The depth of his emotional reaction may be judged from his violent denunciation of Shelburne, in his resignation speech of 9 July:[31]

> He called heaven and earth to witness, so help him God, that he verily believed the present ministry would be fifty times worse than that of the noble lord who lately had been reprobated and removed [North] . . . If Lord Shelburne be not a Catiline or a Borgia in morals, it must not be ascribed to anything but his understanding.

Here, then, is a further reason why Burke never achieved the Cabinet.

During the Coalition Burke's insensitivity to outside opinion was a source of weakness to the Government. His reinstatement of two pay office clerks, Powell and Bembridge, who had been dismissed by his predecessor for embezzlement, raised a storm in the House. On 2 May 1783, 'rising in a violent fit of passion' to reply to James Martin, who had described Burke's action as 'a gross and daring insult to the public', he was pulled down by Sheridan, 'lest his heat should betray him into some intemperate expressions that might offend the House'.[32] On 19 May, after apologizing for 'the warmth he felt when this business was last before the House', he explained his reasons: Powell and Bembridge had been of great service, a criminal prosecution had been commenced against them, and until they were proved guilty he must presume their innocence. But he had failed to appreciate the temper of the House, extremely sensitive to any suggestion of corruption in Government officials; and Bembridge's conviction and Powell's suicide seemed to put Burke in the wrong. Again, in drafting the East India bill, he never sensed the indignation which was aroused by the attempt to take away patronage from both Company and Crown, and which did Fox so much harm with public opinion. Years later, Lord John Townshend recollected that the bill had been '*really* unpopular', and was made so by 'Burke's ungovernable temper'.[33] Nor was it a good bill from an administrative point of view. 'Burke's attempt to increase the governor general's subordination to a body sitting in England shows how little he understood the problems of Administration—the checking of abuses, not the government of a sub-continent, was what he still had chiefly in mind.'[34]

Ever since Rockingham had taken office, the punishment of those accused of corruption in India had been uppermost in Burke's mind. His strong aggressive instincts, sharpened by public and private disappointments, needed an enemy against which they could concentrate. Always inclined to compassionate the unfortunate, he became convinced that Hastings was the great source of misrule in India and that one striking example of retribution would deter other potential offenders. 'Impeachment', he had written in *Thoughts on the Cause of the Present Discontents*, 'that great guardian of the purity of the constitution, is in danger of being lost even to the idea of it.' With this in mind he listened eagerly to the accusations of Francis against Hastings: always a bad judge of character, Burke failed to allow for Francis's malice and hostility to the governor general. In Burke's disordered mind, Hastings appeared as a monster of iniquity, without one redeeming feature; he listened eagerly to any complaint against him; and the vehemence with which he prosecuted the impeachment gives some idea of the depth of his emotions. His violent language and intemperate charges alienated independent men and convinced his own party that he was a political liability. Nor did the impeachment achieve its effect: before Hastings had appeared at the bar of the Lords, Dundas and Cornwallis had begun the task of giving British India decent government.

Did Burke ever regret the part he had played in the impeachment of Hastings? Towards the end of his life he commissioned his friend French Laurence to write an account of the impeachment which would justify the part he had taken. On 10 Feb. 1797 only a few months before his death, he reminded Laurence of this:

I am as conscious as any person can be of the little value of the good or evil opinion of mankind to the part of me that shall remain, but I believe it is of some moment not to leave the fame of an evil example, of the expenditure of fourteen years labour, and of not less . . . than near £300,000. This is a terrible example, and it is not acquittance at all to a public man who, with all the means of undeceiving himself if he was wrong, has thus with such incredible pains both of himself and others persevered in the persecution of innocence and merit. It is, I say, no excuse at all to urge in his apology that he had enthusiastic good intentions . . . I have not even the other very bad excuse of acting from personal resentment or from the sense of private injury, never having received any; nor can I plead ignorance, no man ever having taken more pains to be informed. Therefore *I* say, *Remember*.

His crusade against the American war, against the influence of the Crown, against the French Revolution, required no apologia; there he felt sure he had been right. Only on the prosecution of Hastings did he feel the need for justification.

Burke was the first person to appreciate the significance of the French Revolution and to apply it to English conditions. On 27 Sept. 1789 he wrote to Windham that the French 'along with their political servitude' had thrown off 'the yoke of laws and morals'. On 9 Feb. 1790 he said in the House:[35]

In France a cruel, blind, and ferocious democracy had carried all before them; their conduct, marked with the most savage and unfeeling barbarity, had manifested no other system than a determination to destroy all order, subvert all arrangement, and reduce every rank and description of men to one common level.

Turning to Fox, he added: 'There were men in this kingdom . . . who favoured the wild theories of the times.' Fox managed to soothe him; but Sheridan attacked his view of the Revolution, and Burke declared their political separation. The split in the Whig party had begun.

Burke had England in mind when he wrote the *Reflections*: 'solicitous chiefly for the peace of my own country', he declared, and the full title of the book is *Reflections on the Revolution in France and on the proceedings of certain societies in London*. 'You seem in everything to have strayed out of the high road of nature', he wrote. 'The property of France does not govern it'; and in the *Letters on a Regicide Peace* he defined Jacobinism as 'the revolt of the enterprising talents of a country against its property'. If England, following the French example, were not to be governed by property, what would become of the principles Burke had proclaimed under Rockingham? Burke's *Reflections* is really his apologia for his devotion to Rockingham, and he spent the last years of his life fighting to make the world safe for future Rockinghams to rule.

Burke died 9 July 1797.

[1] Burke to Shackleton, 12 July 1746; to O'Hara, 30 Oct. 1762. [2] Copeland, *Corresp.* i. 66. [3] Ibid. 121. [4] Burke to Shackleton, 10 Aug. 1757. [5] Walpole to Montagu, 22 July 1761. [6] Burke to Hamilton, March 1763. [7] *Chatham Corresp.* iii. 110–11. [8] Burke to O'Hara, 21 Oct. 1766. [9] Burke to O'Hara, post 11 Nov. 1766. [10] *Chatham Corresp.* iii. 144. [11] Boswell, *Johnson*, iii. 235. [12] O'Hara to Burke, 10 Aug. 1762. [13] Burke to William Weddell, 31 Jan. 1792. [14] Sutherland, *Corresp.* ii. 128–9. [15] Burke to O'Hara, 31 Dec. 1765. [16] Speech on the Declaratory Act, 3 Feb. 1766, Ryder's 'Debates'. [17] *Speech on American Taxation*. [18] Cavendish's 'Debates', Egerton 215, ff. 110–18. [19] Dowdeswell to Rockingham, 14 Aug. 1768, Dowdeswell mss. [20] *Letter to Sheriffs of Bristol*. [21] Almon, iii. 170–86. [22] Burke to Fox, 8 Oct. 1777. [23] Burke to Laurence, 12 May 1797. [24] For Burke's relations with his constituency see BRISTOL constituency. [25] Burke to Portland, 24 Sept. 1779. [26] Burke to Horace Walpole, 7 July 1782, with copy of proposals; Richard Burke to Walpole, 7 July 1782; Walpole's notes of conversation with Richard Burke, in the possession of W. S. Lewis; *Last Jnls.* ii. 454. [27] *Observations on a late 'State of the Nation'*. [28] *Fox Corresp.* ii. 322. [29] *Last Jnls.* ii. 453. [30] Boswell, *Private Pprs.* xv. 234. [31] Debrett, vii. 312–15. [32] Ibid. ix. 681. [33] *Fox Corresp.* ii. 27. [34] Sutherland, *E. I. Co. in 18th Cent. Politics*, 401. [35] Stockdale, xix. 61–69.

J.B.

**BURKE, William** (1729–98), of Beaconsfield, Bucks.

GREAT BEDWYN 16 June 1766–1768, 20 May 1768–1774

*b.* 1729, 1st s. of John Burke, barrister, of St. Marylebone, London, by his 1st w. Elizabeth, da. of Thomas

Burke, vintner, of London. *educ.* Westminster, Sept. 1742, aged 13; Ch. Ch. Oxf. 26 June 1747, aged 18; M. Temple 1750, called 1755. *unm. suc.* fa. 1764.

Sec. and registrar of Guadeloupe 1759-63; undersec. of state 1765-7; dep. paymaster of the forces in India 1782-93.

William and Edmund Burke called each other cousin, but it seems doubtful whether they were related. Edmund, answering Lord Verney's bill in Chancery, 26 Nov. 1783, deposed[1]

> that he does not know nor can form any distinct opinion of what degree of relation (if any) William Burke . . . may stand to this defendant, but that he does believe that their fathers did sometimes call each other cousins, but has no other occasion to believe that they are of kindred.

When in 1750 Edmund entered the Middle Temple, William Burke's father acted as one of his sureties and the 'cousins' began a friendship which lasted until Edmund's death.

William Burke was first known as a political pamphleteer and the author of *An Account of the European Settlements in America*, published in 1757, and said to have been revised by Edmund. 1759-61 he was in Guadeloupe, and on his return to England lived in the closest intimacy with Edmund Burke and his family. Ambitious, anxious to please, and to become acquainted with celebrities, he was friendly with Garrick and Reynolds (but not apparently with Johnson—he is not mentioned in Boswell's *Life*); and in the political world, where he hoped to make his way, was known to Henry Fox, 1st Lord Holland. Of more immediate moment was his close friendship with Lord Verney (q.v.). 'He has', wrote Holland,[2] 'as great a sway with Lord Verney as I ever knew one man have with another.'

In 1762 he published a pamphlet, arguing for the retention of Guadeloupe; and sent a copy to Fox, now minister in the House of Commons.

> I waited upon Fox [Burke wrote to Charles O'Hara, 20 Nov. 1762[3]] who began with saying he was much displeased with my having wrote it . . . I said . . . that when I wrote he was not in the ministry, that my dependence was on him and him alone . . . and I had conceived that if I could draw the public attention I hoped that of the minister would follow. He did not, he said, suppose I meant to hurt my friends; owned that he was not then the minister. I thank God he now is.

Burke secured Verney for the peace preliminaries, and Fox promised to support his application for the governorship of Grenada. 'He is . . . a man to be depended upon', wrote Burke, 'and I have good hopes that something will be done.' Fox recommended him to Egremont, first for Grenada, then for Carolina;[4] next to Sandwich for the office of judge of the Admiralty at Grenada;[5] and wrote again to Sandwich, 12 Nov. 1763: 'Pray give Mr.

Burke a hearing. He is a very clever fellow, and I believe a very honest one.' But nothing was done for him.

He now hoped through Verney's influence to enter Parliament. On 17 Dec. 1763 Verney asked Grenville to appoint Verney Lovett (q.v.) to some military place which would vacate his seat at Wendover.[6] 'The gentleman I shall put into the major's seat', wrote Verney, 'will I am confident to his utmost support the measures I shall approve.' Grenville professed willingness to comply, but wrote to Verney, 18 Dec.:[7] 'There are some things in your Lordship's letter . . . which make it necessary for me to desire to see you in order to prevent any mistake and to explain my own intentions before any farther step is taken.'

Nothing came of this, and in April 1764 Burke raised the matter himself.[8] He assured Grenville that he was 'a man to be relied upon, and would retain a proper sense of an obligation'; promised a 'steady adherence' to Grenville consistent with his 'just attachment' to Verney; and concluded his appeal: 'I will not expect anything [from the seat] unless it should so happen that I should prove useful.' Grenville's carefully kept letter books contain no trace of a reply, nor is any further application known. But ever afterwards Burke referred to Grenville in terms of deep dislike.

The Burkes had no acquaintance with the Opposition leaders, but when the Rockingham Administration was being formed William Fitzherbert (q.v.) recommended them to Lord John Cavendish (q.v.). On 4 July Burke wrote to O'Hara: 'Lord John Cavendish . . . has mentioned us both as fit men to be employed to Lord Rockingham, who received it well, but what then? We have not a friend in the world to keep the impression alive. Something will I hope however turn up.'

Burke's appointment as under-secretary to Conway was followed by arrangements to vacate the seat at Wendover, which William now yielded to Edmund—an obligation Edmund never forgot and which he characteristically exaggerated: Verney expected shortly to be able to return William at Great Bedwyn. 'You can . . . form some judgment of the nature of that friendship', Edmund wrote to George Macartney (q.v.), 21 Dec. 1765, 'which could not only desire but press me to get upon his own ground.' William Burke, he wrote to William Markham, December 1771,

> has had the closest and longest friendship for me; and has pursued it with such nobleness in all respects, as has no example in these times, and would have dignified the best periods of history. Whenever I was in question, he has been not only ready, but earnest even, to annihilate himself . .. Looking back to the course

of my life, I remember no one considerable benefit in the whole of it, which I did not, mediately or immediately, derive from him.

In this style Edmund defended him at every stage of his career.

William had little political consciousness and was much slower than Edmund in attaching himself to Rockingham: as late as 21 Dec. 1765 in a letter to George Macartney he described Holland as 'my great north star to direct my political opinions'. He found his work dull—'much to do in what is called business, which is mostly attendance';[9] and, not being in Parliament or near the centre of affairs, did not have Edmund's opportunities. By the time a seat had been found for him (on Verney's interest at Great Bedwyn) Edmund had become a prominent politician, and henceforth took the lead.

William now became the man of business of the Burke family and addressed himself to the task of making their fortune. On 4 Oct. 1766 he wrote to O'Hara:

If Ned gets to you . . . he will tell you that our fortunes are in a condition to second our views of independency, and our resolution of acting in our public capacity with the same correctness as we have had the good fortune to observe in private life. You will be glad to know that in this we have no division of our obligation, all this like as the all before we owe to Lord Verney's wonderful goodness and friendship; in one word the necessary rise of values of East India stock was foreseen before the price rose or an increased dividend was talked of, but as that increase might possibly not be determined on in 3 or 6 or 9 or even 12 months those who bought on what they call speculation, that is who agreed to pay such a price for such a quantity at a particular day, ran the risk of losing if the price at that particular day happened not to answer his speculation; so that no one could with safety venture on buying with safety but those who could actually pay down their money, and keep their stock in their possession quietly till the dividend was increased. This Lord Verney could you know easily do and had he chosen to lay out a million that way, no one could have objected to his taking the consequential benefit of all the money he employed that way, but he considered this an opportunity of making us independent, and actually paid down of his own above £9,000 and engaged for above forty more for me. The dividend is come sooner than I expected, and though the accounts are not yet settled, I may within compass say that I have made £12,000 at least. It would be idle to use words to express what we owe to this man's disinterested unaffected worth and goodness to us. The season too is so critical, that surely we may think it providential, and without any superstitious vanity too, if the thought of it reminds us to endeavour to grow better men as we grow richer. It is our good fortune you see to have this advantage without even the imputation of stock jobbing, or the term of bull or bear being applicable to us.

That there was anything improper in an under-secretary of state speculating in East India stock when the Company was about to become the subject of parliamentary inquiry seems to have occurred to neither of the Burkes.

Naïve and optimistic, William Burke dreamt of their political future now they were financially independent.

Wherever we light now it must and in reason ought to be in the style of co-operation, not of personal attachment to any man or set of men, Ned's ability and Ld. Verney's weight may justly entitle us to our opinions, I think they never will be mean or base, and being what they ought to be, are to be pursued in a style of conduct suitable to them.

In Rockingham's list of the House of Commons, November 1766, William Burke is listed as 'Swiss' (presumably ready to follow any Administration for reward).

But Edmund was determined to remain with Rockingham, and fully concurred when in November 1766 Rockingham broke with Chatham and went into opposition; moreover, Chatham's projected inquiry into the East India Company impaired William's speculations, which depended for success on an increase in dividend. On 25 Nov. Edmund voted against Conway's motion for a committee of inquiry; which William, still in office as Conway's under-secretary, could hardly oppose.

On 23 Dec. Edmund wrote to O'Hara:

Will feels exactly as I do, that if Conway does not go out in a very short time indeed, he will get away from a situation of nicety, and fix himself upon more decided ground. He has stayed so long in Babylon, merely in compliance with the desires of his friends.

And on 15 Jan. 1767: 'Will is still in but how long so? the only difficulty is to separate without a quarrel; and that will be if possible.' He resigned in February. 'It so happened', he wrote to James Barry on 25 Feb., 'that consistent with propriety, I could not continue, and I thank God that my affairs are in that situation that I had no temptation from fear, to be backward in doing what I ought.' And in Rockingham's list the word 'Swiss' opposite his name was now changed to 'Whig'. 'Will feels easy in the freedom he has purchased at so good a price', wrote Edmund to O'Hara on 28 Feb.; and on 28 Mar.: 'Will . . . is beginning to be most active in the House . . . he will be an immense accession to the party.'

On 6 May 1767, when a settlement with the East India Company was in sight, the court of proprietors raised the dividend to 12½%. 'The indecency and insult of this proceeding', writes Walpole,[10] 'raised high resentment in the House of Commons'; on 7 May, when it was debated, 'Dempster and W. Burke . . . ventured to avow their own share of the criminality.' No other speech by

Burke on the dividend bill is known, while as yet his interest in the Company was purely financial and confined to keeping the dividend at as high a figure as possible.

In April 1768 Edmund Burke bought the estate of Gregories, near Beaconsfield—the high water mark of the Burkes' prosperity. It was also to be the home of William and Richard, Edmund's brother; but Edmund was the only one married and with a child and the purchase was concluded in his name. 'I have made a push with all I could collect of my own and the aid of my friends', he wrote,[11] 'to cast a little root into this country.' The estate cost £20,000, of which £14,000 was raised on mortgage; and it seems probable that William Burke was one of the friends who helped to provide the remainder.

The election of East India directors in 1769 was 'one of the most fiercely contested of the century'.[12] Laurence Sulivan (q.v.), in his bid to regain control of the Company, had built up a fund of stock to be used for making faggot votes. The subscribers, who included Verney and William and Richard Burke, borrowed stock which they pledged to return after the election at a price of 280. Hardly was the election over when there came the first great East India slump, in which the Burkes lost heavily. How much it is difficult to say; here is the estimate of Thomas Whateley (q.v.), a well-informed observer, not hostile to them:[13]

I find that on the opening of Mr. de la Fontaine's [Verney's broker] books the names of the Burkes stand against very large sums. Richard Burke £29,000 stock, upon which £10,745 is the difference.[14] Richard Burke and S. Dyer[15] £13,000 stock, upon which £4,870 is the difference. W. Burke £5,000 stock, upon which £1,900 is the difference.

In addition William had been engaged with Verney and Lauchlin Macleane (q.v.) in dealings in margins, which resulted in William owing large sums to Verney, and Macleane (who was ruined by the venture) owing over £6,000 to William. Finally, William and Verney had been conducting large-scale speculations on the Amsterdam market which left them with a joint liability of £47,000.[16]

In 1768 William Burke had been returned for Great Bedwyn on a compromise between Verney and Lord Bruce, who henceforth controlled the borough. His voting record is the same as Edmund Burke's: in every known division against Administration; and he said in the House, 19 Apr. 1769, of his connexion with the Rockingham party:[17] 'I am willing to be called a follower, the humblest and meanest of that set.' 173 interventions in debate are noted 1768–74, which puts him among the 20 most frequent speakers in that Parliament. 'As an orator', wrote Walpole,[18] he 'had neither manner nor

talents'; his speeches contain nothing original, and he was never regarded even in his own party as anything but Edmund Burke's jackal.

In 1774 Verney could no longer afford to bring the Burkes into Parliament gratis, nor could they pay for their seats. Edmund wrote to Rockingham on 25 Sept.:

I am not half so much concerned about my own seat as about that of my friend Burke, to whom I primarily owe my being a Member of Parliament, and who has for me sacrificed everything, and by his encouragement and example always made me act with proper resolution, if ever I have so acted. To him a seat is more essential [because of his debts]; and I could never, without grief and shame, see myself within the walls of that house, if he who first brought me within them, was to wait for me in the lobby.

Rockingham immediately offered Edmund a seat at Malton, his pocket borough, but could or would do nothing for William.

Your own feelings [he wrote to Edmund, 2 Oct.] in regard to Mr. William Burke are both natural and becoming your principles and actions in life, but I am sure both for Mr. William Burke and all your family concerns, yourself being in Parliament is the principal thing necessary.

Edmund now applied to Portland for a seat for William:[19]

He has been eminently useful and faithful to the cause, a constant friend to good men, and perfectly an enemy to their adversaries. Depend upon it if he is preserved he will pay it in real service. I have no other object more at heart. I can be neither easy nor happy without it. I fight this battle; I will fight any in England for the same prospect. I repeat it, the service he will do is beyond what I am sure is commonly imagined.

Apparently financed by Portland[20] William stood for Haslemere. He was defeated, but petitioned; and wrote to Portland, 12 Apr. 1775: 'On the whole I trust I might speak with confidence, but that which is *sub judice* is in its nature doubtful, so that I don't suffer my own mind to run the whole line of her expectations.' But his petition was rejected.

Out of Parliament, overwhelmed by debts (in 1774 judgments were entered against him in the King's bench for over £6,000[21]), and with no prospect of his party's speedy return to office, his future looked grim. India seemed to offer the only chance of re-establishing his fortunes, and in 1776 he hoped to succeed Lauchlin Macleane (q.v.) as commissary-general of musters in Bengal. This came to nothing, but in 1777, when news reached England of the imprisonment of Lord Pigot (q.v.) at Madras, Pigot's friends chose William Burke to carry the Company's orders for his release. Once in India it was expected that he would find some way of making his fortune, as others had done before him. Rockingham recommended him to Pigot, and Edmund Burke wrote about his departure to Philip Francis (q.v.), a member of the council of Bengal (9 June 1777):

> Indemnify me, my dear Sir, as well as you can, for such a loss, by contributing to the fortune of my friend. Bring him home with you an obliged person and at his ease, under the protection of your opulence. You know what his situation has been, and what things he might have surely kept, and infinitely increased, if he had not those feelings which make a man worthy of fortune, but do not put him in the way of securing it. Remember that he asks those favours which nothing but his sense of honour prevented his having it in his power to bestow. This will be a powerful recommendation to a heart like yours. Let Bengal protect a spirit and rectitude, which are no longer tolerated in England.

His 'rectitude' was rewarded, and he returned to England in 1778 as agent for the Rajah of Tanjore —an appointment which had unfortunate consequences. He plunged deep into the morass of Indian politics, and became Edmund Burke's adviser on Madras affairs as Francis was to be on Bengal; and the dispute between the Rajah of Tanjore and the Nawab of Arcot, in which the Burkes now took sides, became an issue in English party warfare.

When Parliament was dissolved in 1780 William Burke was on his way back to India, and on 8 Sept. he wrote from Paris to Portland:

> I have no doubt of my friend Lord Verney['s] serious intentions to serve me, free from all motives of interest or benefit to himself, but his Lordship is also deeply interested in the success of my fortune, which (if I can go out accredited with a seat in Parliament) is certain, easy and considerable . . .
>
> If this catches you in London, I am sure you will be so good to see Lord Verney; I know that the honour of your Grace's interference and expressing a wish to my being in Parliament will have its weight . . . As his Lordship knows you are apprised of the business and even a party (as far as the honour of your sanction to my promise of either paying down the £10,000[22] or relinquishing the seat immediately on my return) there will I trust be no unsurmountable awkwardness, in your Grace's writing to his Lordship.

No reply to this letter is known, but on 23 Sept. Burke wrote again:

> I learn today from my friend Mr. Adey,[23] the very kind manner in which your Grace received his late application concerning very material interests of mine. I am sure you do me the justice to believe me most sincerely sensible of your goodness to me on this and on the manifold other occasions wherein I have presumed to trouble you.

If Portland did anything it was of no avail. Verney had again to sell his seats at Wendover, but he seems to have tried to find a seat for William elsewhere.[24] However, neither William nor Edmund Burke was returned at the general election.[25]

In April 1782, after the Rockingham Administration had taken office, Edmund wrote to William:

> My dear, my ever dear friend, why were not you here to enjoy, and to partake in this great, and I trust, for the country, happy change. Be assured, that in the Indian arrangements, which I believe will take place, you will not be forgotten, at least I hope not . . . Oh! my dearest, oldest, best friend, you are far off indeed! May God of his infinite mercy preserve you. Your enemies, your cruel and unprovoked persecutors, are on the ground, suffering the punishment not of their villainy towards you, but of their other crimes, which are innumerable . . . Resolutions will pass after the holidays to secure the Rajah of Tanjore and to limit the Nabob. Much good will happen. Indeed, my dear friend, your honest and humane labours have not been useless . . . May God of his infinite mercy return you to us, happy and prosperous, and above all speedily.

Before the wiping out of old scores over India could begin, Rockingham was dead and his Administration had fallen to pieces; but Edmund had had time to appoint William deputy paymaster of the forces in India at a salary of £2,000 p.a. The office was 'created on purpose for him', wrote Walpole;[26] and Cornwallis, governor-general of Bengal, later declared 'that the sending William Burke to India was a most unnecessary job'.[27] He had at last got his hand into the government till and not before time, for Verney, on the edge of bankruptcy, was pressing the Burkes for repayment of their loans. In 1783 he sued Edmund for £6,000 which he alleged had been borrowed to pay off the mortgages on Gregories, but was non-suited.[28] In 1784 Verney estimated that Edmund owed him £11,000 and William £20,000, with 'no security except honour'.[29] Edmund was in no position to pay, and Verney's hopes were pinned on William's 'honour' and what he could plunder in India.

For his second period in India (1780–93) only one letter to Edmund survives (Edmund destroyed a considerable part of his correspondence), and it is not known how William set about making his fortune. His first efforts were not successful. In a letter to Richard Burke jun. of 30 Dec. 1785 he wrote: 'My last losses make my return speedily to haven not improbable.' Then he outlined a scheme to raise 'vast fortunes from the remittance of the public debt of near £600,000, which would without risk or the possibility of failure put six times £25,000 in my pocket'. If that did not materialize he hoped for the remittance of the pay for the Madras forces: from this he would clear £5,000 a year, deduct £3,000 for living expenses, add his salary of £2,000, and there would be a surplus of £4,000 a year— 'to be used of course for our common benefit'. And 'money made in remittance . . . is as fair as the product of a man's own acres'. '£4,000 a year for two or three years, if I last so long', he wrote, 'may clear me and clear Beaconsfield.' But it would hardly have cleared Verney's claims upon him.

These schemes depended upon the acquiescence of the pay office in London and the governor general in Calcutta. Had Edmund Burke remained paymaster general and had Fox's East India bill become law William Burke might have made his fortune, but the dismissal of the Coalition ruined his chances. He secured the remittance to Madras ('fixed at the scandalous exchange of 410 Arcot rupees for 100 pagodas' by John Macpherson (q.v.), acting governor general after Hastings's departure, 'in order to pay his court to Edmund Burke'[30]), but not to Bombay. Cornwallis, appointed governor general in 1786, objected that there was a 'positive order' from the Company against separate remittances, which would establish 'distinct funds, or rather treasuries . . . not subordinate to the respective governments'. This was one of the principles Edmund Burke when in opposition laid down in his plan of economical reform: 'That all subordinate treasuries . . . as naturally drawing to themselves as much money as they can, keeping it as long as they can, and accounting for it as late as they can, ought to be dissolved'.

Next, Burke put forward a plan, 'so extraordinary', wrote Cornwallis, 'that I had great difficulty to persuade myself he was in earnest'. He wished to remit to England the money owed by the Company to the Crown for the service of troops in India, 'about £800,000 . . . bearing interest at 8%', although this was a paper transaction which could easily be effected in London.

The times were no longer propitious for making fortunes out of public money. 'The folly and ignorance of my principals play the Devil with me', Burke wrote to his relation, William Cuppage, on 13 May 1792; 'if my dear Edmund cannot replace [William's office] on the bottom where he originally fixed it, it is impossible for me to hold with credit' —a Burkism, meaning that without Company remittances he could not make his fortune.

In 1793 he returned to England, broken in health, apparently a confirmed drunkard, and 'as much ruined as when he went':[31] worse, in fact, for there was a deficiency in his accounts as paymaster. Verney had died in 1791 without, as far as can be ascertained, having received anything from Burke, and his niece and heiress determined to prosecute him. On 16 Dec. 1795 Edmund Burke wrote to Cuppage:

Our worthy and unfortunate friend is arrested for ten thousand pound on a bond which he was cheated

into by Lord Verney. His niece Lady Fermanagh is the oppressor at present.

Lady Fermanagh, the last 'oppressor', fared no better than her uncle: her suggestion that William should convey his assets to trustees for the settlement of her claims was treated by Edmund as 'a deed palpably fraudulent . . . and directly against his public trust'. 'Where is the fund to answer the Crown balances', he asked, '. . . if everything he has in the world shall go to Lady Fermanagh?' In fact there was nothing for either.

William Burke's last years were spent in complete obscurity. He died in March 1798.

[1] Dixon Wecter, *Edmund Burke and his Kinsmen*, 7. [2] To Sandwich, 12 Nov. 1763, Sandwich mss. [3] Charles O'Hara was an Irish M.P. and a close friend of the Burkes. For their letters to him see Ross J. S. Hoffman, *Edmund Burke, New York Agent*. [4] 1 Mar. and 18 Apr. 1763, Egremont mss, PRO 30/47/29/3. [5] 30 Apr. 1763, Sandwich mss. [6] Grenville mss (JM). [7] Grenville letter bk. [8] Grenville mss (JM). [9] To Jas. Barry, 23 Mar. 1766. [10] *Mems. Geo. III*, iii. 16. [11] To Rich. Shackleton, 1 May 1768. [12] L. S. Sutherland, *E. I. Co. in 18th Cent. Politics*, 187–8. [13] Grenville mss (JM). [14] The difference between the price at which the stock then stood, and at which it had to be returned. [15] About Sam. Dyer see Wecter, 39. [16] See intro. to L. S. Sutherland, *Corresp. of Edmund Burke*, ii. (1768–74). [17] Cavendish's 'Debates', Egerton 219, ff. 293–4. [18] *Mems. Geo. III*, ii. 195. [19] ante 4 Oct. 1774. [20] W. Burke to Portland, 10 May 1775, Portland mss. [21] Dilke, *Papers of a Critic*, ii. 341. [22] Burke had given Verney a bond for £10,000 in part acknowledgment of his debts. [23] Stephen Addy, a London banker. [24] See Exchequer case, *Verney v. Weston*, E112/1718/4170. [25] Edmund was returned by Rockingham at Malton in Dec. 1780. [26] *Last Jnls.* ii. 453. [27] *Cornwallis Corresp.* i. 465. [28] See Appendix to Sutherland, *Corresp. Edmund Burke*, ii (1768–74). [29] *Verney Letters of 18th Cent.* ed. Verney, ii. 277–8. [30] Cornwallis to Lord Rawdon, 2 Dec. 1789, *Cornwallis Corresp.* ii. 463–5. [31] Sir Gilbert to Lady Elliot, 2 May 1793, *Life and Letters of Sir Gilbert Elliot*, ii. 136–8.

J.B.

**BURRARD, Harry** (?1707–1791), of Walhampton, nr. Lymington, Hants.

LYMINGTON 1741–Nov. 1778

*b.* ?1707, 1st s. of Paul Burrard, M.P., of Walhampton by Lucy, da. of Sir Thomas Dutton-Colt. *m* (1) 1731, Alicia (*d.*1737), da. of John Snape, *s.p.*; (2) 2 Mar. 1754, Mary Frances, da. of James Clarke of Wharton, Herefs. 1s. 1da., both *d.v.p. suc.* fa. 1735; *cr.* Bt. 3 Apr. 1769, with sp. rem. to his bros.

Gentlemen usher to the Prince of Wales 1728–36; collector of the customs of London 1731–*d.*; riding forester of the New Forest 1754–*d.*; gov. Calshot castle 1761–87.

The Burrard family had a very strong interest at Lymington, which usually gave them the recommendation to both seats.

In 1775 Sir Harry Burrard described himself as for 'five and thirty years a steady adherent to the Government'.[1] He is not known to have voted against any Administration, or ever to have spoken in the House; and, in exchange for support at Lymington, usually allowed Administration to recommend to one seat. Before 1754 he held a secret service pension of £500 p.a., which he gave up on being appointed riding forester:[2] at no time during his service in Parliament was he without provision from Administration. He died 12 Apr. 1791.

[1] Burrard to Duke of Chandos, 27 Mar. 1775, S. Burrard, *Annals of Walhampton*, 96. [2] Add. 33038, f. 415.

J.B.

## BURRARD, Harry (1755–1813).

LYMINGTON   1780–June   1788, 1790–Apr.   1791
                          9 July–Dec. 1802

*b.* 1 June 1755, 1st s. of George Burrard, bro. of Sir Harry Burrard (q.v.), by Madeline, da. of John Durell of Jersey. *m.* 20 Feb. 1789, Hannah, da. of Harry Darby, London merchant, 2s. *suc.* fa. 1777; *cr.* Bt. 12 Nov. 1807.

2nd lt. R.A. 1772; lt. 60 Ft. 1776, capt. 1777; maj. 14 Ft. 1786; capt. 1 Ft. Gds. and lt.-col. 1789; col. 1795; maj.-gen. 1798; lt.-col. 1 Ft. Gds. 1804; lt.-gen. 1805.

Gov. Calshot castle 1787–d.; riding forester of the New Forest 1791–d.

Burrard served in America 1778–83, and was probably absent when returned for Lymington. His first recorded vote was for Fox's East India bill, 27 Nov. 1783. In December 1783 Robinson wrote about him:[1]

> Mr. Burrard, an officer of service in America, Sir Harry's nephew and heir, has grievances in the army, at least Sir Harry used and has made complaint for him. Sir Harry was always attached to Government, and his nephew, notwithstanding complaints, goes with Administration. He will, it is apprehended, so continue, with civility and conversation with his uncle and him.

In January 1784 Robinson classed him as 'very hopeful', but in Stockdale's list of 19 March and William Adam's list of the new Parliament he is classed as Opposition. He appears in no division list of this Parliament nor is there any record of his having spoken in the House, and it is not clear when he came over to Pitt: presumably by 1787, when he succeeded his uncle as governor of Calshot castle. He vacated his seat in 1788 in favour of George Rose (q.v.), Pitt's secretary to the Treasury.

He died 17 Oct. 1813.

[1] Laprade, 89–90.

J.B.

## BURRELL, Merrick (1699–1787), of West Grinstead Park, Suss.

| | |
|---|---|
| GREAT MARLOW | 1747–1754 |
| GRAMPOUND | 1754–1768 |
| HASLEMERE | 11 May 1774–1780 |
| GREAT BEDWYN | 1780–1784 |

*b.* 3 Apr. 1699, 4th s. of Peter Burrell of Beckenham, Kent; yr. bro. of Peter Burrell I (q.v.). *educ.* Merchant Taylors' 1713–14. *unm.* *cr.* Bt. 15 July 1766, with sp. rem. to his nephew Peter Burrell II (q.v.).

II—F*

Director, Bank of England 1742–56, dep. gov. 1756–8, gov. 1758–60, director 1760–4.

Burrell was a very considerable merchant, a financier much consulted by the Treasury, and a steady Government supporter. Together with Thomas Walpole and the two Fonnereaus (qq.v.) he held since 1752 a victualling contract for Gibraltar. In 1754, he was put up by Pelham[1] at Grampound on the interest of Lord Edgcumbe, who demanded £3,000 for the two seats. While the other candidate, Simon Fanshawe, had been promised 'an easy election', Burrell told John Roberts (q.v.) that he was willing 'to pay £1500 without dispute'— 'but', added Newcastle's minute of 18 Mar.[2], 'on account of his late employment [i.e. his contract], he was not to boggle at £1800 or £2000.' In the end £1600 was paid by him,[3] £1000 by Fanshawe, and the rest from secret service money.

In 1761, after Grampound had placed itself under Edward Eliot and William Trevanion (qq.v.), Burrell was re-elected, presumably paying to the new patrons £2000 (as was done by Fanshawe).[4] In December 1762 he was marked by Fox as favourable to the peace preliminaries. Only once in all the years is he known to have voted against any Government: on 15 Feb. 1764 over general warrants. In the summer of 1765 Rockingham classed him as 'doubtful', but he must have supported the Rockingham Administration as his baronetcy, which appears in the warrant book under date of 26 June 1766,[5] was clearly their creation. Next he followed Chatham; in all the managerial lists of 1767 he is classed as a Government supporter, voting with them even on the land tax. In the House he was an infrequent speaker, and even the few occasions when he may have spoken are difficult to fix, as 'Mr. Burrell' in Harris's reports, 1761–5, may also denote his nephew Peter.

Merrick Burrell apparently did not stand for Parliament in 1768—possibly he felt too old at 69. Nevertheless he succeeded William Burrell in May 1774 on the family interest at Haslemere, where he was re-elected after a contest at the general election in October. When present, he again supported the Government; but over the contractors bill, 12 Feb. 1779, he is listed by Robinson as 'pro, absent'; and similarly he was absent from four out of six important divisions, between 3 Mar. 1779 and 24 Apr. 1780. By September 1780 the control of Haslemere had passed to Sir James Lowther, but Burrell secured his return for Great Bedwyn on Lord Ailesbury's interest. In the new Parliament he is not known ever to have voted, either before or after the fall of the North Administration: 'attends but little', Robinson wrote about Burrell in his electoral survey of August 1782;[6] and in the list of March 1783 places him among those 'ill or cannot attend'. In the list of 19 Mar. 1784, covering the preceding three months, Burrell again appears as 'absent'. He did not stand in 1784. There is no certain record of his having spoken during his second term in the House.[7] One may well wonder why he ever returned to it at the age of 75—presumably for the distinction conferred by its Membership.

The victualling contract for Gibraltar was renewed to Burrell and Fonnereau in 1763 and 1765,[8] and was terminated in 1778.[9] In the 1760s Burrell held at times considerable amounts of Government stock;[10] but both as merchant and financier he was much less active after 1768.

He died 6 Apr. 1787.

[1] See Pelham's 'Election Papers. Persons to be provided for', Add. 32995, f. 90; also f. 122. [2] Ibid. f. 98. [3] Ibid. f. 116. [4] Add. 32917, f. 359. [5] *Cal. Home Office Pprs. 1766-9*, p. 111. [6] Laprade, 46. [7] The only reference on 7 June 1781, Debrett, iii. 491, is to a 'Mr. Burrell', 15 years after he had been made a baronet; but as there was no other Burrell in Parliament at that date, a mistake in the names seems probable. [8] T54/39/200-205; T29/37/25-26. [9] T29/47/3. [10] Bank of England recs.

L.B.N.

## BURRELL, Peter I (1692–1756), of Langley Park, Beckenham, Kent.

HASLEMERE      1722–1754
DOVER      19 Apr. 1755–16 Apr. 1756

*b.* 6 Aug. 1692, 1st s. of Peter Burrell of Beckenham by Isabella, da. of John Merrick of Stubbers, North Ockenden, Essex; bro. of Merrick Burrell (q.v.). *educ.* Merchant Taylors' 1704–7. *m.* 14 Mar. 1723, Amy, da. of Hugh Raymond of Langley, Beckenham (a director of the South Sea Co. involved in the 'Bubble'), 4s. 2da. *suc.* fa. 1718.

Sheriff, Kent 1732–3; director, South Sea Co. 1724–33, sub-governor 1736–*d.*; director R. Exchange Ass. 1726–38.

Burrell, a steady supporter of Administration, held Haslemere for 32 years jointly with General James Oglethorpe, a Tory suspected of Jacobitism; never altogether secure, they were defeated in 1754. Hardwicke, who favoured Burrell's opponent, P. C. Webb, wrote disparagingly about him to Newcastle, 23 Nov. 1754: '. . . considering the little consequence of Mr. Burrell, otherwise than as sub-governor of the South Sea Company, and that he has brought this upon himself . . .'[1]

But in fact Burrell was a considerable merchant who, in partnership with John Bristow (q.v.), held important Government contracts for remittances and the victualling of troops;[2] and after the Lisbon earthquake of November 1755, in which they themselves suffered severely, for provisions and remittances to relieve 'those distressed in Portugal'.[3]

In April 1755 Burrell was returned for Dover on Newcastle's recommendation.[4] He died 16 Apr. 1756; two hours after his death, his son Peter wrote to Newcastle to claim the seat and contracts of his father who had served the Government for over 30 years 'in the most trying times;' was always ready to serve the public; 'and in assisting the distressed inhabitants of Lisbon, in whose calamities he has borne as large a share as any house in London, he has lost his life'[5]—which must not be taken literally, as he died at Beckenham.

[1] Add. 32737, f. 385. [2] See BRISTOW, John. [3] T52/47. [4] Add. 32854, f. 194. [5] Add. 32864, ff. 298-9, 320-1.

L.B.N.

## BURRELL, Peter II (1723–75), of Langley Park, Beckenham, Kent.

LAUNCESTON      21 Feb. 1759–1768
TOTNES      1768–1774

*b.* 6 Dec. 1723, 1st s. of Peter Burrell I (q.v.). *educ.* Merchant Taylors' 1737–8; St. John's, Camb. 1741; L. Inn 1742, called 1749. *m.* 28 Mar. 1748, Elizabeth, da. of John Lewis of Hackney, Mdx., 1s. 5da. His da. Elizabeth m. R. H. A. Bennett (q.v.); Isabella m. Lord Algernon Percy (q.v.), later 1st Earl of Beverley; Frances m. Hugh, Lord Percy (q.v.), later 2nd Duke of Northumberland; and Amelia m. Douglas, 8th Duke of Hamilton. *suc.* fa. 16 Apr. 1756.

Surveyor-gen. of Crown lands May 1769–*d.*

Burrell, having heard that the succession to his father's contracts was to go to Brice Fisher (q.v.) and the parliamentary seat to Thomas Sewell (q.v.), immediately on his father's death wrote a bitter letter to Newcastle[1] about Fisher and the emoluments heaped on him—'no one in the City of London would disapprove of a son's succeeding to his father'; and as for Dover, sending them a *congé d'élire* 'may be a dangerous experiment . . . there is some difference betwixt a lawyer or any other indifferent person and me, as my father has done services to many in that town, and I may justly call myself a countryman'.[2] 'Mr. Burrell, I think', wrote Newcastle to the Duke of Dorset, 17 Apr., 'seems to demand as a right to succeed his father everywhere . . . I own I have my doubts as to the prudence of bringing such a gentleman into Parliament.' Nonetheless he put Burrell on his list of parliamentary candidates,[3] and in September 1756 was willing to nominate him at Ilchester—but Burrell, wrote James West on 27 Sept.,[4] 'makes a good deal of difficulty about the expense, and apprehends your Grace intended to bring him into Parliament at little or no expense to himself'. In December, on a vacancy occurring in Newcastle's pocket borough of Boroughbridge, Burrell wrote to him:[5]

I am heartily sorry to be so obscure that even your own promise . . . could not call to your remembrance one who lost his seat at Haslemere to serve you, and withdrew his pretensions at Dover on the faith of your promise and on your earnest request ... What, my Lord, have I done to cancel it?

He asked: could he count on the Duke's promise or should he look out for himself? Newcastle replied[6] that promises given *qua* minister he could not be expected to fulfil in his own boroughs after having left employment.

At last in December 1758, after two other candidates had been considered, Burrell got his chance at Humphry Morice's borough of Launceston. Morice on 28 Dec. wrote to Newcastle[7] that he had put up Burrell, who thought himself unkindly treated by Newcastle; that he told Burrell he had done so at the Duke's request; and if the Duke confirmed this to Burrell 'he shall never know to the contrary from me'. Newcastle replied on 30 Dec.[8] approving of the choice: 'I know him to be a very honest man'; but did not believe Burrell thought any more 'of coming into Parliament by my means' —'as the merit to him is entirely your own, I think, I can take no other part in it but to approve extremely what you have done.' On 30 Dec. Burrell's opponent, Sir John St. Aubyn (q.v.), was returned, but Burrell was seated on petition, Charles Townshend, a close friend of his, acting for him in the House, and Newcastle and Pitt apparently favouring the petition.[9]

Although now provided for at Launceston, Burrell did not renounce the interest he had inherited at Haslemere. On the death of James More Molyneux he wrote to Newcastle, 27 June 1759,[10] that he was determined to back his pretensions and interest there 'at any expense, if ... pushed upon it', and asked for the Duke's support 'in an affair where I have the greatest reason to hope for success'. But he does not seem to have carried the issue to a poll. At the general election in 1761 Burrell was again returned for Launceston, but at Haslemere supported Muilman and Parker against Molyneux and Webb, and their petition when defeated. 'Mr. Burrell is outrageous with me on account of the Haslemere election, and talks very high upon taking his property from him by power', wrote Newcastle to Hardwicke, 21 Nov. 1761;[11] and when Newcastle peremptorily refused to support him, 'he made almost a disturbance in my levee room upon it'. In the end the petition was withdrawn: even Charles Townshend and Lord Carysfort, 'their chief friend', left them—'the cause came out such that he would have no more to do with it'.[12]

On 15 May 1761, Burrell wrote to the Duke of Bedford thanking him for 'the quiet election at Launceston'—'an opposition would have given me great uneasiness, and to your Grace I owe that there was none'. He referred to Bedford having told him that he thought of parting with his property at Newport—the twin borough to Launceston—'and would treat about it as soon as the hurry of elections should be over'.[13] The Duke sent the letter to his agent, John Butcher, for his opinion—'what method I had best proceed in the selling of the estate at Newport, and the price I can reasonably ask for it'; and on 17 May replied to Burrell: 'I am not yet at all determined, as to the parting with estates at Newport and Launceston, and therefore must decline for the present the treating with any person about them.'[14] It is not clear whether Burrell was acting on behalf of his friend Morice who, not being on good terms with the Duke, may have preferred not to appear openly in the matter, or whether he was out to establish an interest of his own in his friend's borough.

The friendship with Townshend was the lodestar of Burrell's political conduct, and his behaviour was as erratic as that of his leader. On 13 Nov. 1762, Newcastle classed both as 'doubtful'; next, Fox listed them as favourable to the peace preliminaries; and when on 9 Dec. Townshend left before the division, Burrell too abstained from voting. And next, on the formation of the Grenville Administration in April 1763, Burrell became involved through Townshend in the one incident which (barring his daughters' brilliant marriages) ever brought him into prominence. It was intended to move Townshend from the Board of Trade to the Admiralty, normally a promotion. But Townshend started his usual game of hanging back, accepting, and refusing, which was the more embarrassing as the Board of Trade was promised to Shelburne. John Bindley (q.v.), another friend of Townshend's, wrote to Charles Jenkinson (q.v.) on 8 Apr.: 'Mr. T. is to be at Mr. Burrell's at seven, who will most strongly enforce his steady attachment to the Administration. The world say he will not accept. I am pretty confident he will.'[15] At last, on the 14th, the King persuaded him to accept the Admiralty;[16] but the next day the King wrote to Bute at 12.27 p.m.:

Ch. Townshend begged to see me before I dressed, it was to push in the strongest manner for Burrell to be in the Admiralty; that he had no friend in that board; that it lowered his character which he knew I wished to support; I told him all the vacancies were filled up, that there was no room for his or any other man's friend.

At 1.15 p.m.:

Ch. Townshend has desired Ld. Halifax to tell me he cannot kiss hands without Burrell. I have sent Ld. Halifax out to tell him he yesterday accepted without conditions, and therefore expect he will kiss hands.

Next:

> Charles Townshend has refused because I won't promise him to vacate a seat in his board for Burrell.

At 3.50 p.m.:

> Ld. Halifax and Mr. Grenville promised him that any weight they could have should be used to gain the first vacancy in that board for Mr. Burrell; that he refused and returned to the first charge.[17]

To this James Harris adds (and the statement is confirmed by Walpole) that Townshend going to Court took 'his friend Peter Burrell (by virtue of his own right of entry) into the inner or second room, next the King's closet, that second room where his Majesty receives company, and where no one ever goes before the doors are opened, except persons peculiarly privileged by their offices'; and that there the two argued the matter with Halifax and Grenville—'neither he nor Burrell were satisfied, and Burrell 'twas remarked, took the lead in the remonstrance'.[18] After this they both naturally went into Opposition; joined Wildman's Club; and voted regularly with the minority. On 24 Jan. 1764 Burrell sharply attacked the Government over the Cider Act, and on 15 Feb., over Wilkes, acted as teller for the Opposition. A month later Newcastle listed them both as 'sure'; but when Townshend refused to take active office under Rockingham, Burrell was marked by Rockingham as 'doubtful'; and when Townshend took office under Chatham, Burrell became a regular follower of Administration, which he remained even after Townshend's death.

Although the Burrell hold on one seat at Haslemere was re-established in 1768, this was filled by William Burrell, while Peter was returned for Totnes on the Duke of Bolton's interest, probably at Grafton's request; but when in 1774 he stood again on the same interest, he was defeated.

As debater in the House Burrell was unimportant; and it is difficult to ascertain the frequency of his recorded speeches, as it is often impossible to distinguish him from Merrick Burrell, 1761–68, and from William Burrell, 1768–74. Nor did he apparently play any prominent part in finance though he continued his father's business—thus, for example, on John Bristow becoming practically insolvent, Burrell applied to Newcastle for Bristow's remittances to Gibraltar, 10 Sept. 1761[19]—'My correspondence at Lisbon gives me the same opportunities my father had, and my fortune and character in life a full security to the public'; and he can probably claim more merit than other applicants 'if constant attention to public service and the business of Parliament can give me any'. Similarly Samuel Martin (q.v.), reviewing for Bute engagements to contractors, 17 Apr. 1763,[20] mentions Peter

Burrell's application 'to be appointed remitter to Minorca'.

He died 6 Nov. 1775.

[1] Add. 32864, ff. 298–9. [2] The Dover people thought differently—see JONES, H. V. and DOVER constituency. [3] Add. 32884, ff. 397–8. [4] Add. 32867, f. 456. [5] 27 Dec. 1756, Add. 32869, f. 404. [6] Add. 32870, ff. 17–18. [7] Add. 32886, f. 505. [8] Ibid. f. 530. [9] See Townshend's report of the debate of 16 Jan. 1759 to Newcastle, Add. 32887, f. 197. [10] Add. 32892, f. 264. [11] Add. 32931, f. 195. [12] Same to same, 12 Feb. 1762, Add. 32934, f. 291. [13] Bedford mss 43, f. 260. [14] Ibid. f. 264. [15] Add. 38200, f. 293. [16] King to Bute, Sedgwick, 221. [17] For these four letters see ibid. 223–4. [18] James Harris's memorandum, Malmesbury mss. [19] Add. 32928, f. 76. [20] Bute mss.

L.B.N.

## BURRELL, Peter III (1754–1820), of Langley Park, Beckenham, Kent.

HASLEMERE 4 Nov. 1776–1780
BOSTON 23 Mar. 1782–1796

*b.* 16 June 1754, o.s. of Peter Burrell II (q.v.). *educ.* Eton 1761–70; St. John's, Camb. 1771. *m.* 23 Feb. 1779, Lady Priscilla Barbara Elizabeth Bertie, da. of Peregrine, 3rd Duke of Ancaster, 3s. 1da. *suc.* fa. 6 Nov. 1775. His wife suc. to a great part of the Ancaster estates 1779, to the barony of Willoughby of Eresby 18 Mar. 1780, and to the hereditary office of lord great chamberlain; Burrell was appointed her deputy, having previously been kntd. 6 July 1781. *suc.* uncle Sir Merrick Burrell (q.v.) as 2nd Bt. 6 Apr. 1787; *cr.* Baron Gwydir 16 June 1796.

Returned on the family interest at Haslemere, Burrell was independent, and on 18 Apr. 1777 voted with Opposition against payment of the King's debts; otherwise he usually supported the Government. Most of his recorded speeches are on America, in favour of coercion.[1] On 17 Feb. 1777 he 'spoke a few words' in favour of suspending the Habeas Corpus Act in cases of high treason in America.[2] Discussing North's conciliatory bills he said, 24 Feb. 1778, he had hitherto supported the Government 'because he had been persuaded they were fighting for the rights of Parliament; that taxation was the primary object of the contest; that therefore it was unwarrantable to give up that ground till some concessions had been made by America'; further, he objected to the bill leaving the commissioners free, as he thought, to treat with the Americans on the subject of independence.[3] He opposed, on 14 Dec. 1778, withdrawing the troops from America as being equivalent to an acknowledgment of her independence;[4] and, on 11 June 1779, Meredith's motion for restoring peace with America.[5] As for his votes: he was absent from the division on the contractors bill, 12 Feb. 1779, and from three of the six divisions March 1779–April 1780 for which lists are available; but when present he voted with the Government, including the division on Dunning's motion.

The control of Haslemere having passed to Sir James Lowther, Burrell did not seek re-election in 1780, but on 23 Mar. 1782 was returned for Boston on the Ancaster interest, apparently unopposed, though an opposition had been intended; and he was re-elected in 1784, in a contested election. On 21 Feb. 1783 he spoke against Shelburne's peace preliminaries, calling them 'one of the most disgraceful, the most infamous treaties that had ever insulted that or any other House of Parliament'; and advocated recourse to our 'power to resist' to avoid such 'humiliation and degradation of a great and powerful people'. 'He spoke . . . as an independent country gentlemen, who, unconnected with party . . . gave vent to his honest indignation'[6] (Burrell was emphatically the 'country gentleman' whenever occasion offered[7]). He supported the Coalition; voted for Fox's East India bill; attacked Pitt on 14 Jan. 1784 for remaining in office against the resolutions of the House; and in Adam's list of the Parliament of 1784 was classed as Opposition. Although on 7 May 1783 he had voted for Pitt's motion in favour of parliamentary reform, he was not one of its supporters in April 1785. He spoke and voted during the Regency crisis on the Opposition side (as he put it himself on 6 Jan. 1789, he spoke 'but seldom in the House'[8]). As deputy lord great chamberlain he officiated at the trial of Warren Hastings.

The luck of the Burrells became almost proverbial with contemporaries—the brilliant marriages of Peter Burrell's sisters and his own, which proved even more fortunate than could have been expected, when a few months later the sudden death of the 4th Duke of Ancaster left Burrell's wife the heiress to honours and riches. 'The fortune of the Burrells is powerful enough to baffle calculation', wrote Walpole to Lady Ailesbury, 10 July 1779; and A. M. Storer (q.v.) to William Eden, 14 Dec. 1787, 'Sir Peter Burrell's good luck is never failing'.[9] Wraxall describes Peter Burrell as 'a young man . . . of the most graceful person and the most engaging manners' and 'great elegance of deportment'.[10] Farington reported him as having £18,000 p.a.[11]

He died 29 June 1820.

[1] Evidence to the contrary is too uncertain to count. Walpole states (*Last Jnls.* ii. 122) that on North's conciliatory propositions (23 Feb. 1778) Burrell 'quitted the majority'—which may have been because he opposed the idea of conciliation. Further, on 6 Apr. he is reported by Stockdale (viii. 205) to have seconded Meredith's motion to repeal the Declaratory Act of 1766; *Parlty. Hist.* xviii. 1010 makes Sir G. Yonge second Meredith—which is much more likely. [2] Almon, vi. 259. [3] Almon, viii. 399; *Parlty. Hist.* xix. 784–5. [4] Almon, xi. 161. [5] Fortescue, iv. 352. [6] Debrett, ix. 307–9. [7] See e.g. 16, 21 June 1784, Stockdale, ii. 4–5, 9, and 119; and 10 Aug. 1784, Debrett, xvi. 383. [8] Stockdale, xvi. 189. [9] *Auckland Corresp.* i. 453. [10] *Mems.* iii. 353–4. [11] *Diary,* i. 7.

L.B.N.

**BURRELL, William** (1732–96), of Deepdene, nr. Dorking, Surr. and West Grinstead Park, Suss.

HASLEMERE 1768–May 1774

*b.* 10 Oct. 1732, 3rd s. of Peter Burrell I (q.v.). *educ.* Westminster 1743–9; St. John's, Camb. 1749; Doctors' Commons 1760. *m.* 13 Apr. 1773, Sophia, da. and coh. of Charles Raymond, banker, of Valentine House, Ilford, Essex, 5s. 2da. *suc.* fa.-in-law as 2nd Bt. 24 Aug. 1788.

Director, South Sea Co. 1763–75, Sun Fire Insurance 1773–95; chancellor, diocese of Rochester 1771–*d.*, of Worcester 1774–*d.*; commr. of the Excise 14 May 1774–90.

Burrell was a distinguished advocate and a notable antiquary. He practised chiefly in the Admiralty courts, and his manuscript reports of cases decided in them, 1766–74, were published in 1885. His collections for the history of Sussex[1] are in the British Museum, Add. 5670–5711. William Cole, the antiquary, described him as 'an active, stirring man; a good antiquary'. 'He is rather low, and squints a little; but very ingenious, and scholar-like.'[2]

Returned at Haslemere on the family interest, and jointly with Thomas More Molyneux, after a contest, Burrell steadily supported Administration in the House: he is not known to have ever voted against them, but was absent from the divisions on the naval captains, 9 Feb. 1773, and on Grenville's Act, 25 Feb. 1774. Twenty-one interventions in debate during this Parliament are attributed in Cavendish to 'Dr. Burrell'. He vacated his seat by accepting the commissionership of the Excise.

He died 20 Jan. 1796.

[1] See *DNB.* [2] Quoted Nichols, *Literary Anecs.* ix. 797.

L.B.N.

**BURT, William Mathew** (*d.*1781), of Maiden Erleigh, nr. Reading, Berks.

GREAT MARLOW 1761–1768

1st s. of William Pym Burt, chief justice of St. Kitts, by Louisa, da. of Sir William Mathew. *m.* 29 Aug. 1754, Sarah, da. of John Foster of Jamaica, sis. of Thomas Foster (q.v.), 1s. 2da. *suc.* fa. 1751.

Member of the council of St. Kitts 1748–55; gov. Leeward Is. 1776–*d.*

The Burts were an old West Indian family: William Mathew Burt's great-grandfather was in Nevis in 1670, and the family remained there until c.1725 when they moved to St. Kitts. William Mathew Burt seems to have spent his early years on the island, and to have gone to England between 1751 and 1755. He inherited estates both in St. Kitts and Nevis. In 1758 he was consulted by the Cabinet when planning the expedition to Martinique,[1] and in 1759 went as Crown Agent with the expedition which took Guadeloupe.

In 1761 he was returned after a contest for Great Marlow. His first recorded speech, 25 Nov. 1762, was in support of the peace preliminaries. James Harris described it as 'dull as far as could be heard', and had no better opinion of Burt's other speeches: 18 Apr. 1764 he wrote, 'I left Burt haranguing on the African trade'; and 12 Mar. 1765, 'Burt and Beckford rambled like Creolians from Africa to America, thence to East Indies, etc.' Only some half-dozen speeches by Burt are recorded, all except one (9 May 1765, against the proposal to appoint the Queen Regent) concerned with trade or the West Indies.

From the reports of his speeches Burt seems generally to have supported Grenville's Administration, but he voted against them over general warrants, 15 and 18 Feb. 1764. Newcastle classed him, 10 May 1764, as a 'doubtful friend'; and Rockingham, July 1765, as 'doubtful', which was afterwards altered to 'contra'. On 19 Dec. 1765 Burt spoke for Grenville's motion for American papers, and on 22 Feb. 1766 voted against the repeal of the Stamp Act. During the Chatham Administration he was usually classed as a supporter of Grenville; but though they were on friendly terms, Grenville himself never reckoned Burt as one of his followers. Burt voted against the Chatham Administration on the land tax, 27 Feb. 1767.

In 1768 he contested Great Marlow again, but was badly defeated.

He died in office as governor of the Leeward Islands, 27 Jan. 1781.

[1] Newcastle to Hardwicke, 5 Oct. 1758, Add. 32884, ff. 259–67.

J.B.

**BURTON, Bartholomew** (c.1695–1770), of King's Arms Yard, Coleman St., London and Petersham, Surr.

CAMELFORD 25 May 1759–1768

*b.* c.1695, 4th s. of Bartholomew Burton of North Luffenham, Rutland, by his 2nd w. Susanna, da. of George Gregory. *m.* (1) 1729 Hester Mansell; (2) Sept. 1733, Philadelphia (*d.*23 Apr. 1762), da. of Nathaniel Herne, M.P., 1da.; (3) Elizabeth, da. of John Marke. Director, Bank of England 1746–58, 1762–70; dep. gov. 1758–60; gov. 1760–2.

Burton, a London merchant and financier, dealt a good deal in Bank stock, holding at times amounts far in excess of what was required to qualify him for office. He was also a large dealer in Government stock, but seldom held any considerable balances. He appears as contributing £500,000 to the twelve million pound loan of 1762,[1] but since none of it appears in the Bank of England records, it must have been for clients or 'stagging'. In fact Burton was

foremost a financier, and does not appear to have held any of the typical Government contracts. But a man like Thomas Hill (q.v.) would consult him about investing in British or foreign stock.[2]

When in April 1759, at a time of acute financial crisis, a vacancy occurred at Camelford, James West (q.v.) in a review of candidates who could give the Treasury expert support in the House, wrote to Newcastle: 'Mr. Burton is a very good sensible man, but I do not think of any very great weight in the City'; he added, however, that 'if there is much difficulty or expense, it will not be easy to engage a proper person' so near the end of the Parliament. Newcastle fixed on Burton, and he was returned unopposed at a cost of about £500, of which £300 was paid by the Treasury from secret service funds.[3] In 1761 Burton was again returned unopposed.

Burton continued to adhere to Newcastle even out of office. He voted against the peace preliminaries, 9 and 10 Dec. 1762; voted with the Opposition on Wilkes, 15 Nov. 1763, and general warrants, 6, 15 and 18 Feb. 1764. In Rockingham's list of July 1765 he was classed as 'pro', and in a letter of 17 Dec. 1765 Newcastle refers to him as his 'great friend, that most zealous supporter of the Government, Mr. Burton'.[4] Newcastle continued even after July 1766 to regard him as a friend, although Burton supported Chatham over the East India inquiry and voted with Administration on the land tax motion, 27 Feb. 1767. In January 1768 James West reported to Newcastle that Burton did not mean to stand again.

As to my friend Mr. Burton [wrote Newcastle to Rockingham, 18 Jan.[5]] I am afraid there may be something in it; for his son-in-law, Captain Rowley, a very deserving man, is by a ridiculous will of his father's,[6] to aggrandize in time the Rowley family, left with little or no provision, but his employment in the Navy; and I believe Mr. Burton intends, in great measure, to support him himself.

Burton died in May 1770.

[1] Add. 33040, ff. 290–1. [2] See copy of his letter to Burton, 3 Sept. 1753, in vol. ii of his letter bks. at Salop RO. [3] See Namier, *Structure*, 341–3. [4] To Lord Egmont, Add. 32972, f. 265. [5] Add. 32988, f. 35–37. [6] Sir William Rowley (q.v.). See also Walpole to Mann, 17 Jan. 1768.

L.B.N.

**BURTON, Francis** (?1744–1832), of Edworth, Beds.

HEYTESBURY 4 Dec. 1780–1784
NEW WOODSTOCK 1784–1790
OXFORD 1790–1812

*b.*? 1744, s. of Col. Francis Burton of Westminster. *educ.* Westminster; Ch. Ch. Oxf. 9 Dec. 1760, aged 16; L. Inn 1761. called 1768. *m.* Jan. 1788, a da. of Nicholas Halhead of New Woodstock.

K.C. 1778; bencher, L. Inn 1778; recorder, New Woodstock 1780–1802; second justice of Chester 1788–1817; treasurer, L. Inn 1792; recorder, Oxford 1797–1801.

Burton was connected with the Duke of Marlborough, on whose interest he was returned at Heytesbury, Woodstock, and Oxford. His only recorded speech before 1790 was on 10 May 1781, when 'in sound, manly language' he defended the reports of North's commissioners on public accounts.[1] Marlborough supported North's Administration, but Burton's voting 1780–2 was erratic. On 12 Dec. 1781, on Lowther's motion against continuing the war, he voted with the court. But in the divisions of 20 and 22 Feb. 1782 he voted with Opposition; on 27 Feb. with the court (the division was on Conway's motion against the war—a repetition of that of 22 Feb.); and on 8 and 15 Mar. did not vote.

Burton voted for Shelburne's peace preliminaries, 18 Feb. 1783, and against Fox's East India bill, 27 Nov. 1783; and Robinson in January 1784 expected him to support Pitt. In Stockdale's list of March 1784 he is marked as absent. He accepted from Pitt judicial office tenable with a seat in the House, and voted with him on the Regency.

Burton died 28 Nov. 1832.

[1] Debrett, iii. 393.

J.B.

**BURTON, Ralph** (*d.*1768), of Hall Bank, Cottingham, Yorks.

WAREHAM        18 Mar.–29 Sept. 1768

s. of Richard Burton.[1] *m.* (1) 1750 Elizabeth (*d.*6 Aug. 1753), da. of Sir John St. Leger of Grangemellon, co. Kildare, niece of Arthur St. Leger, 1st Visct. Doneraile [I], sis. of Anthony St. Leger (q.v.), *s.p.*; (2) c. Oct. 1763, Marguerite,[2] da. of John Henry Lydius,[3] Baron de Quade of Albany, N.Y. and Kensington, London, 1s. 1da.
Lt.-gov. Quebec 1759; lt.-gov. Trois Rivières 1760. Addl. 2nd lt. 32 Ft. 1742; capt. 2 Horse Gren. Gds. 1745, maj. 1747; lt.-col. 48 Ft. 1754; col. (America only) 1758; col. 95 Ft. 1760–3; maj.-gen. 1763; col. 3 Ft. 1764–*d.*

Burton was a very close friend of John Calcraft (q.v.), whose letter-books contain a great number of letters to him; after Burton went out to America in 1755 Calcraft looked after his interests in England and kept him informed of political developments, military affairs and appointments. When at the end of 1757 Abercromby replaced Loudoun in the American command, and went out with ten blanks for appointing colonels, Calcraft attempted, apparently successfully, to secure one for Burton.[4] Burton was in the expedition against Louisbourg in 1758, and the following year served under Wolfe at

Quebec. In December 1760 he obtained a regiment on the recommendation of Amherst and through the intervention of Lord Bute.[5] After Burton's appointment in October 1760 as lieutenant governor of Trois Rivières, Calcraft wrote: 'I had great hopes of carrying the point of Canada for you and tried my utmost but the Scotch were too powerful and succeeded.'[6]

On 13 Nov. 1763 Calcraft wrote to General Amherst:[7]

Col. Maunsell gives me such a very melancholy account of Burton's health that I despair of ever seeing him and am most heartily concerned and affected. I have known and loved him many years and had figured to myself many happy hours of friendship on his return. If the worst happens I must take the liberty to entreat some attention to his family and I will answer your drafts for whatever may be wanted to bring them to England and defray their expenses in America.

Back in England Burton was returned on Calcraft's interest for Wareham at the general election of 1768, but died on 29 Sept. 1768.

[1] See Clutterbuck, *Herts.* i. 254. [2] About their marriage see letters from Calcraft, Add. 17493, f. 150; Add. 17496, ff. 29–30. [3] About Lydius see *Docs. relating to Colonial Hist. of the State of N.Y* and *Gent. Mag.* 1791, i. 383–5. [4] Add. 17493, ff. 131–2. [5] Add. 17495, f. 185. [6] Add. 17496, f. 12. [7] Ibid. f. 24.

L.B.N.

**BURTON** (afterwards **PHILLIPSON**), **Richard** (?1723–92).

EYE     1 Dec. 1762–1768, 14 Apr. 1770–18 Aug. 1792

*b.* ?1723, *s.* of William Burton of Herringswell, Suff. by his *w.* Grace Phillipson. *educ.* Eton 1732; Emmanuel, Camb. 28 Jan. 1742, aged 18; M. Temple 1741. *unm.* Took name of Phillipson 1766.
Cornet 1 Drag. 1744, lt. 1746, capt.-lt. 1750, capt 1751, maj. 1759; lt.-col. 1761; lt.-col. 1 Drag. 1771; col. 1775; col. 20 Lt. Drag. 1779–85; maj.-gen. 1779; col. 3 Drag. Gds. 1785–*d.*; lt.-gen. 1787.

Burton was returned for Eye on the interest of his friend, Lord Cornwallis. In the autumn of 1763 he was classed by Jenkinson as 'doubtful'; he voted with the Opposition over Wilkes on 15 Nov. 1763, and on general warrants, 18 Feb. 1764, but in Newcastle's division list of 6 Feb.[1] appears as voting with the Government, which is apparently a mistake as on 10 May Newcastle included him among his 'sure friends'. In the summer of 1765 Rockingham classed him as 'pro'. He supported the Chatham Administration, and voted with them on the land tax, 27 Feb. 1767, and the nullum tempus bill, 17 Feb. 1768.

In 1768 Phillipson (as he now was) unsuccessfully contested Winchelsea on the interest of Arnold Nesbitt, presumably with Government sanction and support. After his return to the House in 1770

Phillipson adhered to the North Government. Next he voted for Shelburne's peace preliminaries; against Fox's East India bill; and adhered to Pitt. There is no record of his having ever spoken during his 28 years in Parliament.

With age he grew very deaf and very stout. In 1784 Lord Cornwallis complained of Phillipson having 'most provokingly left all his trumpets in London, which is hard upon me in our têtes-à-tête';[2] and on 16 May 1790 Lord Brome wrote to his uncle, William Cornwallis, who was going to stand for Eye together with Phillipson:[3] 'If you are not here, he will very well do for *two*, and I think it will be no easy matter to chair him.'

He died 18 Aug. 1792.

[1] Add. 32955, ff. 405-7. [2] *Cornwallis Corresp.* i. 181. [3] *HMC Var.* vi. 354.

L.B.N.

**BURTON, Robert** (?1738–1810), of Gray's Inn.

WENDOVER 1784–1790

*b.* ?1738, yngst. s. of David Burton of Yarm, nr. Stockton, Yorks. *educ.* G. Inn 1757, called 1763, bencher 1781, treasurer 1781-2, 1800-1. *unm.* Kntd. 19 June 1800, on presenting an address from Gray's Inn congratulating the King on his escape from assassination.

Burton contested Wendover in 1784 with John Ord (q.v.) against Lord Verney's interest; their election is said to have cost them £6000. Burton was classed by William Adam as a supporter of Opposition, and voted with them over Richmond's fortifications plan, 27 Feb. 1786, and the Regency.

All the same he opposed the impeachment of Warren Hastings, in which all the prominent Opposition leaders took part; and voted against the impeachment of Impey, 9 May 1788. Four out of the eight speeches he is known to have made in the House were in defence of Hastings. On 26 Mar. 1786[1]

> he reprobated the sort of evidence which had been received in the course of the prosecution, and which, he said, the lowest courts of law would not have suffered to have been entertained a moment. He censured Mr. Burke for the intemperate manner in which throughout the prosecution he had talked of Mr. Hastings; a style of description, he said, which could only be justifiably held to convicts.

For this he was attacked by both Fox and Burke.

He did not stand in 1790, and died 2 Mar. 1810, aged 71.

[1] Stockdale, viii. 462.

J.B.

**BURY, Visct.,** *see* **KEPPEL, George**

**BUTLER, John** (1707–66), of Warminghurst Park, nr. Steyning, Suss.

EAST GRINSTEAD 23 Jan. 1742–1747
SUSSEX 1747–29 Dec. 1766

*b.* 19 Mar. 1707, 1st surv. s. of James Butler, M.P., of Warminghurst by Elizabeth, da. of Sir Charles Caesar of Bennington, Herts., wid. of Sir Richard Bennet, 3rd Bt. *educ.* St. John's, Camb. *m.* (1) Catherine (*d.* Oct. 1746), da. of John Morgan, M.P., of Tredegar, 2s.; (2) 14 Nov. 1749, Mary, da. of John Browne of Steyning, 1s. 2da. *suc.* fa. 1741.

John Butler succeeded his father as Member for Sussex, and as a faithful follower of the Duke of Newcastle; and before the removal of the Pelhamites in December 1762, was billeted for £700 p.a. on the office of comptroller of the Excise.[1] He voted against the peace preliminaries, 10 Dec. 1762, and appears against the Grenville Administration in every extant division list. He is not known to have spoken in the House. There are some 50 letters from him in the Newcastle papers, mostly on patronage matters or Sussex affairs—hardly one mentions general politics; and no clear picture of the man emerges.

Butler died 29 Dec. 1766.

[1] See Add. 38335, f. 51; 32950, f. 277.

J.B.

**BYDE, Thomas Plumer** (?1720–89), of Ware Park, Herts.

HERTFORDSHIRE 1761–1768

*b.* ?1720, 1st s. of Thomas Byde of Ware Park, Herts. by his 2nd w. Catherine, da. of John Plumer of Blakesware, Herts., sis. of William Plumer sen. (q.v.) who m. a da. of Thomas Byde by his 1st w. *educ.* Westminster Apr. 1735, aged 14; Pembroke, Camb. 30 Jan. 1738 aged 17; L. Inn 1740; G. Inn 1747. *m.* c.1750, Eleanor Hope, 2s. 1 da. *suc.* fa. 1732.

In the representation of Hertfordshire Byde was preceded by his cousin and brother-in-law William Plumer senior, and followed by his nephew William Plumer junior who sat for the county 1768–1807. How he came to intervene between them is not clear; but they both voted against him in the election.[1] Byde had the support of the Dissenters, and there seems to have been an element of popular support on his side. Almost one-third of his voters were plumpers, and he came out top of the poll although much fewer of the gentry voted for him than for the other two candidates.

Byde seems at no time to have been in direct touch with Newcastle, whose parliamentary whip was to be sent to him in October 1761 through James West (M.P. for St. Albans) and the Duke of Devonshire (a friend of the Plumers); and similarly in September 1762—even in November Newcastle still classed him as 'pro'. But in December he was included by Fox among Members favourable to the peace preliminaries. In Bute's list Byde is marked as primarily connected with Lord Harcourt, who wrote to Charles Jenkinson on 21 Nov. 1762:[2]

> I have cultivated an acquaintance with Mr. Byde because he is a worthy man, and because I wished to see him act with Lord Bute. There was something so singularly honourable in the manner of his election, that I thought him worth attending to. I brought him to Lord Bute's levee, the only one he was ever at, without being absolutely listed on any side. His general principle seems to be the support of the Crown, and as far as I can judge he is well disposed towards Lord Bute.

Byde was classed by Jenkinson in the autumn of 1763 as an Administration supporter, but he probably voted with the Opposition in the division of 6 Feb. 1764 on general warrants; and definitely did so on 15 Feb.[3] On 16 Feb. Harcourt wrote to George Grenville:[4]

> If I can think of any method to prevent Mr. Byde's attendance tomorrow in Parliament, I shall most readily make use of my good offices, though I doubt of the success.

Rightly so—Byde once more voted against the Government.[5]

In July 1765 Rockingham classed him as 'doubtful'; and though Byde did not vote against the repeal of the Stamp Act, Rockingham in November 1766 classed him as a 'Tory', whereas Newcastle in 1767 counted him among the 'Friends of the late [Rockingham] Administration.' In short, no one knew exactly where to place him, and he had best be considered an independent. On 27 Feb. 1767, over the land tax, Byde voted against the Government.

The reasons for Byde's withdrawal from the representation of Hertfordshire in 1768 have not been ascertained: but William Plumer junior, writing to Newcastle on 10 Oct. 1767 about the 'want of gentlemen here to be candidates',[6] does not even mention him as a possibility. In 1774 he contested Cambridge with the support of the 'New Party' whose nucleus was formed by the Dissenters, and on a joint interest with Samuel Meeke; and they both pledged themselves to oppose the Administration's American policy, and to support enlarged toleration of the Protestant Dissenters and parliamentary reform; and in a turbulent election described by their opponents as 'mob politics', obtained a majority of the votes of the resident freemen, and two-fifths of the total. Byde stood again for Cambridge at the by-election of November 1776, but was badly beaten, partly owing to dissensions between him and Meeke, who had also thought of standing at the by-election.[7]

He seems to have retained throughout a con-nexion with the business community: his younger brother John had been a merchant in Lisbon and 'a considerable sufferer' in the earthquake of 1755, after which he returned to England, settled as a merchant in the City, and became a director of the South Sea Company.[8] Byde himself never appears in the London commercial directories, but when in May 1779 he went bankrupt, he was described in the *Gentleman's Magazine* (p. 272) as a banker. William Baker (q.v.) wrote to his mother-in-law Lady Juliana Penn on 13 Nov. 1778:[9]

> By the folly, extravagance and knavery of my neighbour Mr. Byde our whole county, and particularly his own district, is involved in the utmost confusion and distress—indeed I suffer nothing personally, but trouble enough I shall have with others in our endeavours to retrieve the credit of our navigation trust, which, principally through his mismanagement has fallen in arrear to the amount of £2,800 annually. Hardly a farmer in his neighbourhood, but has suffered by placing money in his hands. In short it is easier to conceive than describe all the distress which this impudent and wicked man has occasioned.

Byde died at Naples 26 May 1789, 'reduced to the most abject condition, after all the visionary speculations in his own country, and the unjustified means he pursued to realize them.'[10]

[1] Herts. poll bk. 1761. [2] Jucker, *Jenkinson Pprs.* 93. [3] Add. 32955, ff. 370–3 and 483–5. [4] Grenville mss (JM). [5] Add. 38337, f. 193: Jenkinson's 'List of Persons who voted with the minority on the 17 Feb. 1764 who are friends or nearly so'. [6] Add. 32986, ff. 48–49. [7] See D. Cook, 'Rep. Hist. County, Town and University of Cambridge' (London Univ. Ph.D. thesis, 1935), p. 151. [8] About him see Jucker, 87–88, 93–94; also his letter to Bute, 21 Aug. 1762, Add. 5726, B. f. 14, C. f. 109. [9] See Namier, *England in the Age of the American Revolution*, 13, n. 2. Sir Lewis Namier saw that letter among the manuscripts then in the possession of Mr. H. Clinton-Baker, of Bayfordbury, Herts.; the letters from William Baker to Lady Juliana Penn are not among the Baker mss on deposit in the Herts. RO. [10] *Gent. Mag.* 1789, p. 669.

L.B.N.

## BYNG, George (?1735–89), of Wrotham Park, Mdx.

| | |
|---|---|
| WIGAN | 1768–1780 |
| MIDDLESEX | 1780–1784 |

*b.* ?1735, 1st s. of Hon. Robert Byng, 3rd s. of George, 1st Visct. Torrington, by Elizabeth, da. and coh. of Jonathan Forward. *educ.* Westminster Mar. 1743, aged 7. *m.* 5 Mar. 1761, Anne, da. of William Conolly, M.P., of Castletown, co. Kildare, sis. of Thomas Conolly (q.v.), 4s. 3da. *suc.* fa. 1740.

Ensign 24 Ft. 1753, lt. 1756; capt. 83 Ft. 1758; capt. 24 Ft. 1760; maj. commandant 99 Ft. 1761; seems to have left the army in 1773.

Byng was closely connected with the Duke of Portland, and in 1763 unsuccessfully contested Wigan on his interest. In 1765 Byng and Beaumont Hotham (q.v.), having cultivated the borough on Portland's behalf, concluded an agreement with Simon Luttrell and Sir Fletcher Norton (qq.v.), and were returned in 1768 after a contest with a local man.

Wraxall[1] describes Byng as 'a man of very honourable and upright intentions, but of an ardent temper, very limited talents, and devoted to the Rockingham party'. In Parliament he was one of the most active and dedicated members of the Rockingham group; a frequent speaker, he became an energetic and forceful party manager and 'whip'— 'muster master-general of the Opposition' was Wraxall's description. The *Public Ledger* wrote of him in 1779: 'An honest sanguine oppositionist . . . who devotes his whole thought to politics, and the House of Commons. On late days he counts the House and is generally appointed a teller on the side of the minority.' And Byng himself told the House on one occasion that 'he took shame to himself for having been one hour absent from his duty'. His speeches, ranging over many different topics, inevitably follow the usual Opposition line over the main political events, violently opposing the American war, and pressing for economical reform. Byng was particularly concerned with the need for tighter control of public expenditure; he deplored 'the careless manner in which supplies were usually granted', declaring, 9 Nov. 1780, that 'the indifference with which the House was treated by ministers, in points that peculiarly fell within the province of Parliament was astonishing: he heartily wished to see the good old custom of our ancestors revived, and that the House of Commons should do its duty, and insist on a redress of grievances previous to their voting a supply'. In a debate on resolutions of the committee of supply, 20 Feb. 1781, he complained that 'the noise and inattention in the House arose in proportion to the largeness of the sum voted'. He himself examined minutely the conditions of various government loans, and on 12 Mar. 1781 claimed that the loan for the present year 'had been managed by the minister in a way so suspicious and alarming that it merited the more serious consideration of the House', and he demanded an inquiry, pledging himself to prove 'the most profligate partiality' in drawing up the list of subscribers.[2]

In 1779 Byng, encouraged by a large number of Middlesex electors, wished to stand for the county at the by-election following the death of John Glynn. But when he applied for permission to vacate his seat, it was refused by North, who had already granted the Chiltern Hundreds to another member of the Opposition, George Forster Tuffnell. Byng, while angry at the refusal, and confident that he would have been elected, was glad to avoid a contest, for he wrote to Portland, 11 Oct. 1779:[3] 'I dare

not embark on a contest, my poverty will compel me to desist.' At a county meeting on 13 Oct. 'an amazing majority' voted for Byng's candidature and a deputation was sent to North, asking him to vacate Byng's seat.[4] North refused, but Tuffnell withdrew and Byng's chief supporter, Thomas Wood, was returned. At the general election of 1780 Byng was returned without a contest.

On the formation of the Rockingham Administration Byng, wrote the *Gentleman's Magazine* subsequently, 'took nothing to himself' although 'Mr. Byng's fortune was not in a very affluent condition at that time'.[5] On 18 Dec. 1782, during a debate on the peace provision, Byng 'spoke with great feeling of the division which had taken place between old and dear friends', then went on to attack the new ministry, who, he declared, had 'delivered themselves to vassalage and tuition'.[6] He was teller in the division against Shelburne's peace preliminaries, 18 Feb. 1783; he spoke and voted for Pitt's parliamentary reform proposals, 7 May 1783, though he did not consider they went far enough;[7] and voted for Fox's East India bill, 27 Nov. 1783. Byng contested Middlesex at the general election of 1784 as a follower of Fox, but was defeated.

He died 27 Oct. 1789.

[1] *Mems.* ii. 90. [2] Debrett, x. 296–7; i. 57, 517; ii. 224. [3] Portland mss. [4] Wm. Plumer to Portland, 13 Oct. 1779, Portland mss. [5] *Gent. Mag.* 1789, p. 1054. [6] Debrett, ix. 121. [7] Ibid. 707.

J.B.

**BYNG, George** (1764–1847), of Wrotham Park, Mdx.

NEWPORT I.o.W.     28 Jan.–11 June 1790
MIDDLESEX             1790–10 Jan. 1847

*b.* 17 May 1764, 1st s. of George Byng (q.v.). *educ.* Westminster 1773–80. *m.* Harriet, da. of Sir William Montgomery, 1st Bt., of Magbie Hill, Peebles, *s.p. suc.* fa. 27 Oct. 1789.

Byng unsuccessfully contested Maidstone in 1788; and, although a supporter of Fox, was returned unopposed for Newport in January 1790, in place of John Thomas Townshend (q.v.), appointed a lord of the Admiralty. There is no record of his speaking in the House before the general election of 1790, when he was returned for Middlesex, which he represented until his death on 10 Jan. 1847.

M.H.P.

**BYNG, Hon. John** (c.1704–57), of Wrotham Park, Mdx.

ROCHESTER     23 Jan. 1751–14 Mar. 1757

*b.* c.1704, 4th s. of George, 1st Visct. Torrington by Margaret, da. of James Master of East Langdon, Kent. *unm.*

Entered R.N. 1718, lt. 1724, capt. 1727, r-adm. 1745, v.-adm. 1746, adm. 1756.

Gov. and c.-in-c., Newfoundland 1741-4.

In September 1746 Byng was considered by Henry Pelham and the Duke of Bedford for a seat at Rochester but rejected in favour of Sir Chaloner Ogle, on whose death he was returned unopposed.

In April 1756 he was ordered to the Mediterranean to protect Gibraltar and Minorca; after the loss of Minorca he was court martialled, found guilty and recommended to mercy, but shot on the quarter deck of the *Monarque* in Portsmouth harbour, 14 Mar. 1757.

J.B.

## BYRNE, Michael (?1744-72), of Cabinteely, co. Dublin.

ST. MAWES    17 Jan. 1770-4 Nov. 1772

*b.* ?1744, 1st s. of George Byrne of Cabinteely by Clare, da. of Capt. Michael Nugent of Carlanstown, co. Westmeath, sis. of Robert, 1st Earl Nugent (q.v.). *educ.* Eton 1759-61; Queen's, Oxf. 13 Oct. 1761, aged 17; M. Temple 1764. *unm. suc.* fa. 1763.

Byrne was returned at the by-election of 1770 on the interest of his uncle Robert Nugent (q.v.). His only known vote was with Administration on the motion to commit Brass Crosby to the Tower, 27 Mar. 1771, though he is marked by Robinson as 'pro, present' in both his surveys on the royal marriage bill, March 1772. His one recorded speech was on 6 Feb. 1772 on the petition from some of the clergy for relief from the 39 Articles, which he opposed because 'some rule of conduct is essential to the preserving of every society, great or small, civil or religious'.[1]

Byrne died 4 Nov. 1772.[2]

[1] Cavendish's 'Debates', Egerton 232, ff. 130-2. [2] *Gent. Mag.* 1772, p. 543; Burke *L.G.* gives 7 Nov.

M.M.D.

## BYRNE, see also LEICESTER

## BYRON, Hon. William (1749-76).

MORPETH    28 Jan. 1775-22 June 1776

*b.* 27 Oct. 1749, 1st s. of William, 5th Baron Byron, by Elizabeth, da. and h. of Charles Shaw of Besthorpe Hall, Norf. *educ.* Eton 1763-6. *m.* his cos. Juliana Elizabeth, da. of Adm. John Byron, 1s.

At the general election of 1774 Byron contested Morpeth on the Carlisle interest, was defeated, but seated on petition. No vote or speech by him is recorded. He died 22 June 1776.

M.M.D.

## CADOGAN, Hon. Charles Sloane (1728-1807), of Caversham, Oxon.

CAMBRIDGE    31 Jan. 1749-1754, 13 Jan. 1755-24 Sept. 1776

*b.* 29 Sept. 1728, o.s. of Charles Cadogan, M.P., 2nd Baron Cadogan, by Elizabeth, da. and coh. of Sir Hans Sloane, 1st Bt. *educ.* Magdalen, Oxf. 1746. *m.* (1) 30 May 1747 Frances (*d.* 25 May 1768), da. of Henry Bromley, 1st Baron Montfort, sis. of Thomas Bromley (q.v.), 6s.; (2) 10 May 1777 Mary (div. 1796), da. of Charles Churchill (q.v.), 3s. 3da. *suc.* fa. 24 Sept. 1776; inherited under the will of Hans Stanley (q.v.) his half of the Sloane estate at Chelsea 1780; *cr.* Earl Cadogan 27 Dec. 1800.

Treasurer to Prince Edward (subsequently Duke of York) 1756-67; surveyor of the King's gardens, 1764-9; clerk of the venison warrant 1769-78; master of the mint 1769-84; Sloane trustee of the British Museum 1779-*d.*

Cadogan was returned for Cambridge in 1749 on the interest of Lord Montfort, supported by the Pelhams; in 1754 he made room for his brother-in-law, Thomas Bromley, and unsuccessfully contested Great Marlow; but he was again returned for Cambridge on Bromley's succeeding to the peerage; and till 1774 his elections at Cambridge were uncontested. The appointment in the Duke of York's 'family' in time created a new connexion, and as its senior member Cadogan naturally had to follow the Duke. In Bute's list of December 1761, 'Newcastle, Government' was first placed against Cadogan; but next 'Newcastle' was crossed out. He appears in Fox's list of Members in favour of the peace preliminaries; and writing to Bute, 30 Nov. 1762, Fox mentioned him among possible seconders of the Government motion.[1] In the autumn of 1763 Jenkinson marked him as 'pro', and towards the end of the year when vacancies were expected at the Boards of Trade and the Admiralty, the Duke of York seems to have pressed Cadogan's claims;[2] but finally he was appointed, in April 1764, surveyor of the King's gardens. In June 1765 some further 'arrangement in his favour' was discussed,[3] but the Grenvilles left office before it materialized.

In February 1766 Cadogan took a hand in trying to bring about a meeting and reconciliation between Grenville, Bedford, and Bute with a view to defeating the Rockinghams and the repeal of the Stamp Act[4] (their meeting, on 12 Feb. having proved of no avail, the Duke of York tried to obtain for Bedford an audience with the King for the same purpose[5]). No wonder then that Cadogan, on 22 Feb., voted against the repeal of the Stamp Act; and Rockingham, who in July 1765 had, mistakenly, classed him as 'pro', by November 1766 placed him among the 'Swiss', i.e. those prepared to serve any Administration. But after Cadogan had absented himself from the division on the land tax, Newcastle, in March 1767, counted him among the followers of 'Bedford and Grenville'. Horace Walpole ascribes responsibility to the Duke of York for 'Cadogan, his treasurer, attached to Grenville, and whose place of surveyor of Kensington garden had newly been increased to £1000 a year, absenting himself'.[6] This passage, in the 'foul' copy of the *Memoirs*, was written by Walpole in the second half of 1769. In the clean copy,[7] which he started after 1772 and continued to annotate till about 1785, he added the note:

> I have said he was attached to Grenville; it was because he thought Grenville likely to come into power again; but when deserted by the Bedfords, Cadogan paid his court to Lord Gower; and when Lord North became minister, became so servile to him, that being out shooting in Norfolk during the Newmarket season, it was a joke with the persons who returned thence to examine the game going to London, and at every inn was a parcel directed by Cadogan to Lord North.

By the beginning of 1768 Cadogan was back in the Government camp, towards which he had always gravitated; but more important than the failure of the negotiations for a united Opposition in July 1767, and the Bedfords' joining Administration, was the death of the Duke of York in September 1767, which set Cadogan free to follow his own inclinations—and a careful study of the various collections of Grenville and Bedford mss. shows that at no time was he really close to either. Henceforth he is never found voting against the Government.

In 1770, on Granby's death, Montfort thought of putting up Cadogan's eldest son, Captain Cadogan, for the county;[8] and before the general election of 1774, Cadogan, expecting soon to succeed to his father's peerage, would have liked to cede the seat at Cambridge to him, but in the end himself had to fight hard for it against a dangerous opposition encouraged by the 'parsimony and niggardliness' of the sitting Members.[9] 'In the autumn of 1775', writes the Cambridge scholar, William Cole, '. . . his eldest son, my dear friend Captain Charles Cadogan being fallen ill of a malady of which there was no great prospect of his getting the better of [insanity], he declined all interest at Cambridge'.[10]

Cadogan died 3 Apr. 1807.

[1] Bute mss. [2] See letters from Ld. Halifax to Geo. Grenville, 8 and 10 Nov. 1763, Grenville mss (JM). [3] Same to same, 27 June 1765, ibid. [4] See memorandum by Geo. Grenville, paper by Cadogan, 13 Feb. 1766. Printed *Grenville Pprs*, iii. 360, *n.* 1; Add. 34713, f. 265. [5] See Fortescue, i, 272-3, and Namier, *Add. & Corr.* 52-3. [6] *Mems. Geo. III*, ii. 300-1. [7] Both copies are in the possession of the Earl Waldegrave at Chewton House, Som. [8] See S. Jenyns to Ld. Hardwicke, 3 Nov. 1770, Add. 35631. ff. 93-94; and corresp. between Walpole and Cole, *Corresp. H. Walpole* (Yale ed.), i. 198-202.[9] Add. 5823, f. 100. [10] Ibid.

L.B.N.

**CALCRAFT, John** (1726-72), of Rempstone, Dorset and Ingress, Kent.

CALNE         22 Apr. 1766-1768
ROCHESTER       1768-23 Aug. 1772

*bap.* 4 Sept. 1726, 1st s. of John Calcraft, attorney, town clerk of Grantham, by his w. Christian Bursbie. *educ.* Leicester. *m.* 1744, Bridget,[1] *s.p. legit.*

Clerk in the pay office c.1745-57; clerk in the War Office 1747-56; paymaster of widows' pensions (W.O.) 1757-62; dep. commissary of musters 1756-Dec. 1763.

Calcraft set out under the patronage of Lord Granby, M.P. for Grantham, and still more under that of Henry Fox, to whom he was related—it is never stated how. At 19 he became deputy-paymaster to Cumberland's army, at 40s. a day for 476 days (25 Nov. 1745-15 Mar. 1747), besides £358 in extraordinary expenses[2]—i.e. at nearly £1,000 p.a., omitting less overt occasions for enrichment. When William Pitt succeeded Winnington as paymaster general, Calcraft wrote to him, 9 May 1746: 'As I am a relation to Mr. Fox he was so kind as to recommend me to Mr. Winnington and I flatter myself has now done to you.'[3] There is nothing to bear out the allegation that he was Fox's son,[4] but the terms in which the young man wrote about him were certainly remarkable. To general Wentworth, 16 May 1746: 'Mr. Fox who is my particular friend . . .' To Hesse of the pay office, 26 Aug. 1746, on differences with a senior official: 'I think it would be best for me to apply to my friend the secretary-at-war for an order from him.' On 23 Nov., to a colleague at the pay office: '. . . if I don't succeed Mr. Sawyer, [I] expect a transfer to the War Office which I wish may prove, as you say, to [be] a bishopric. I've to acquaint Mr. Fox . . .' On Calcraft's return to London a clerkship in the War Office was added to that at the pay office—Fox's private letter books as secretary-at-war, 1746-55, are still among Calcraft's papers at Rempstone. And he thus figures on 10 Sept. 1749 in Fox's semi-humorous record of sporting pursuits: 'Jack, alias Ld. William, alias Sportly, alias Vermin, alias Beau Calcraft, alias Squire Calcraft of the Grange, alias Mr. John Calcraft'; and on 10 Sept. 1750: 'Mr. Calcraft as bad . . . a companion a-shooting as he is clever in all other things'.[5]

Lucrative employments continued to come his way: the paymastership of widows' pensions (on 9 Mar. 1762 a letter from Calcraft was read at the Treasury Board 'giving reasons why he does not pay in the balance in his hands upon the widows' pensions'); he was employed in connexion with the rebuilding of the Horse Guards; held contracts for delivering coal to Gibraltar;[6] and in 1748 started on what was to be his chief concern, regimental agencies. He first acted as agent to some independent companies;[7] 1752-4, to one regiment; in 1754 to two. Now his progress became more rapid, helped also by the expansion of the army during the seven years' war—here is the number of his regimental agencies (besides those of independent companies and garrisons) during the years 1755-62: 19, 23, 28, 28, 37, 44, 52, 57—the last figure covers about half the army. Whenever a new colonel was appointed Calcraft would pull wires to obtain his agency, even approaching him through his superiors.[8] Or he would bargain beforehand: thus on 28 July 1757 he wrote to Lt.-Col. Oughton that he was likely to get a regiment soon, and asked him for a promise of his agency[9]—would it have been wise to refuse it to a man so close to Fox and Granby? 'Seniority or services promoted men slowly, unless they were disposed to employ Mr. Calcraft', wrote Horace Walpole.[10] The official duties of a regimental agent were administrative and financial; he arranged contracts for the regiment's clothing; dealt with the Board of Ordnance; had to draw the money due to the regiment and keep track of its expenditure. What his profits were it is difficult to ascertain, but they were such that a share in them was sometimes allowed to the colonel—thus Lord Blakeney billeted his late secretary on Calcraft for £100 p.a.[11] Mrs. Bellamy claimed to have secured four agencies for Calcraft, and in the balance sheet she drew up against him she put the value of two at £500 p.a. each and of the other two at £300.[12]

From official business there was an easy transition to the private business of the colonels. The agent would advance money to a needy client. Granby was heavily in debt to Calcraft (so much so that on 4 Nov. 1758 Calcraft, when asked to advance £3,000 more, wrote that he could not spare the money: 'I really distressed myself more than I will mention to lay down that sum which was so necessary for Lord Granby before he went abroad'[13]). Or to Brigadier-General Robert Monckton (q.v.), in Nova Scotia, 19 May 1759: 'By your account . . . you will see how considerably you are overpaid and that I could not with propriety go further'; this time he has managed to arrange matters but—'in future, do, dear Sir, pull up a little.'[14] Some friends he would advise how to carry on—thus Colonel Sandford, 1 June 1758: 'Don't let Mr. Wolfe's folly sway you to give up part of your profits, but make what you can properly and handsomely.' Of his 57 colonels in 1762, 17 were M.P.s ;in their absence he looked, if necessary, after their borough interests;[15] also after his colonels' wives and children, their mistresses and bastards.[16] He kept them informed of military vacancies; of changes in Government and in commands; and he tried to influence their politics in a sense favourable to Henry Fox. He advised colonels at a distance how to trim their sails to the prevailing wind, while those within easy reach of London he informed beforehand when their attendance in Parliament would be required. In short, he was the parliamentary whip of an army group. Besides, he had round him a group of army commissioners and army contractors;[17] and missed no chance of enrichment. On 6 May 1760 he asked Peter Taylor (q.v.) to find 'a well-informed and clever correspondent at The Hague' who would write Calcraft news directed to a friend in the Post Office, so that it might reach him early enough 'to be useful in the Alley'[18]—part of the news service which, with so many friends in the army administration, Fox and Calcraft were able to establish to help them in their speculations. These it is not easy to follow, especially as they were often undertaken under cover-names, and only investments of some duration, not 'stagging' operations, reached the Bank of England register. There Calcraft appears at various times for smaller though substantial sums; but on 12 Feb. 1761 he acquired 'by subscription' £160,000 of Government stock, to which he added between October 1762 and June 1763 £63,800 'by various purchases'. On 5 July 1763 he still held £192,900—which gives an idea of the wealth of the man who, moreover, during the preceding few years had laid out considerable sums in purchases of land. According to the *North Briton*, no. 42, March 1763, of the loan of that year Calcraft had £70,000, netting a profit of about £7,000. He also held notable amounts of East India stock, operating at India House, first in conjunction with Fox, and next with Shelburne—when creating votes for the election of April 1765, he split £15,000, one of the biggest holdings.[19]

In 1757 he purchased Rempstone, within walking distance from three parliamentary boroughs, Corfe Castle, Poole and Wareham, and at once set out to build up an interest in them: he managed to have his brother Thomas returned for Poole in 1761 and 1768; captured Wareham outright by 1768; but had to renounce his attempts and claims at Corfe Castle. Some of these transactions can be followed in his letter books: his drive and ruthless energy, his unflagging perseverance and robust self-confidence are as striking as is his brazen, insensitive egotism.[20] Allegations against him by Mrs. Bellamy must be treated with the utmost reserve; yet there is truth in the following passage:[21]

He had naturally a sound understanding. His mental faculties were strong. And, had they been properly cultivated, he would have been a dangerous member of society. For he was ambitious to a degree; and cared not at what expense or risk he carried his ambitious views into execution. In the same manner he gratified all his passions.

He had the makings of a modern dictator or financial buccaneer, and although he associated with the first statesmen, Fox, Shelburne, Pitt, Temple, etc., his most congenial companion was perhaps Richard Rigby (q.v.), another *homme d'affaires* who made politics and money his pursuit. 'You are . . . the best friend, and the best man in the world, there is absolutely nobody to equal you', wrote Calcraft to him, 26 Aug. 1760.[22]

In 1760 Calcraft bought Lord Bessborough's estate of Ingress, near Dartford, with 'house and furniture'; and during the next few years added further extensive purchases in the neighbourhood.[23] In the new reign Calcraft's politics changed with those of Fox. 'You will be happy to hear that the Duke [Cumberland] and his friends meet with the greatest civility from his Majesty', he assured Jeffrey Amherst, 13 Dec. 1760; but by 4 Dec. 1762: 'Opposition grows more and more violent, the Duke makes his servants in it, but notwithstanding all, things go most favourably for the court.'[24] When after Devonshire's dismissal both sides were seeking support, Newcastle wrote to Hardwicke, 9 Nov. 1762: 'The Duke [Cumberland] lays vast stress upon the Duke of Rutland's quitting. That devilish *Fox*, and *Calcraft* get in everywhere. The Duke apprehends Calcraft will do great hurt with Granby.'[25] On 13 Nov.: 'I hear both friend and foe put the whole upon the Duke of Rutland's quitting; and his Grace has certainly left it with the King, that he leaves *that* to be determined by my Lord Granby.'[26] Granby was about to return from Germany; and on 18 Nov. Thoroton (q.v.), Rutland's 'man of business', told Newcastle that Rutland advised him to have a letter delivered to Granby on landing,[27]

to desire him, however waylaid, to give no promise or answer till he sees his father. As Lord Granby's arrival is uncertain, I fear Calcraft would get much earlier intelligence of it than I possibly could, and would consequently out run me.

And the King, writing to Bute, 4 Nov., remarked on 'the weight Calcraft's language had with the Duchess [of Rutland]'.[28] Rutland and Granby were secured for the court.

'I am glad you like Lord Fitzmaurice [q.v.]', wrote Calcraft to a friend, 9 Dec. 1760. 'He is a great favourite of mine and is an acquisition to the army.'[29] In 1761–2 Fitzmaurice, by then Shelburne, closely collaborated with Fox and Bute, and when early in March 1763 Bute decided to relinquish the Treasury, Calcraft was much consulted and em-

ployed in the ensuing negotiations. During these a dislike of Fox creeps into Calcraft's letters to Shelburne: when Fox hesitated to accept the Treasury, Calcraft charged both Bute and Fox with thinking only of themselves 'without considering what becomes of those who supported them'.[30] He seconded Shelburne's endeavours to make Fox give up the pay office, 'a measure on which his credit so much depends'.[31] And when next Fox was trying to get the offer of the Treasury renewed through Shelburne, Calcraft wrote to Shelburne not as 'a man whose fortune is made by Mr. Fox, but as your well-wisher at this juncture', and begged him to think impartially 'on the good or bad consequences that may attend Mr. Fox's being minister'. 'We both know Mr. Fox in lights I should rejoice we did not.'[32] By the middle of April the breach between Fox and Calcraft was complete over the question whether Fox was pledged to leave the pay office when made a peer; and Fox, in his 'Narrative for Lord Kildare', asked himself what could have been Calcraft's view in the matter. Was he taken in 'by Lord Shelburne's romantic nonsense' of the lustre which quitting the pay office would add to Fox's character?

But then, when things turned out as they have done, why has he lived with Lord Shelburne ever since (they are inseparable), and hardly ever called upon me, and now quitted all acquaintance with me for ever? Can there be any other reason than that I am certainly for ever out of power or possibility of it, and that he can scheme with Lord Shelburne all day long? . . . indeed I do not know one man in the world so much obliged to another, as he has been to me. I loved him; I did not expect this, and I have not yet left off thinking of it.

For once opinion tended to side with Fox: 'this tool, this mushroom overdunged, rose against him', wrote Walpole.[33] 'Fox ordered Calcraft to make up his accounts, dismissed him worth near £300,000, and though so rich himself, grew almost justified; and though so hated, grew almost pitied.'[34] But Philip Francis (q.v.) wrote about the two: 'If either of them had common honesty, he could never have been the friend of the other.'[35] Nor of Francis.

While Shelburne was still being considered for a secretaryship of state in the new Government, Calcraft, writing to him on 15 March, claims to have told Fox: 'Was you [i.e. Shelburne] out of the question, I would carry all force I could to Hayes [i.e. to Pitt], but you and you only should be my standard'[36]—an accurate forecast of what was to follow. When in August 1763 Bute tried to form a new Government for the King, and Shelburne was employed in the attempt, Calcraft was sent to Pitt and the Bedfords.[37] On the failure of these tangled negotiations, Shelburne resigned from the Grenville

Government, while the Bedfords joined it; Calcraft, wrote Sandwich to Holland, 26 Sept. 1763, 'declares that he will stick to Lord Shelburne at all events, for which Rigby and Gower and all the rest of his friends give him up'.[38] But on the day after negotiations were broken off, Pitt and Temple, having attended the King's levee, 'went to visit Mr. Calcraft in Parliament Street'.[39] 'I never can forget the confidence you have placed in me', wrote Calcraft to Pitt, 2 Sept.,[40] 'or be insensible to your approbation of my conduct.' And at Ingress, about 12 miles from Hayes, he was henceforth a link between Shelburne and Pitt. Even while Shelburne still averred that he would 'support the Government out of employment', Sandwich thought he was underhand 'working with Calcraft to secure what followers he can';[41] and on 24 Nov., over Wilkes, the Shelburne group joined the Opposition. In the dismissals that followed Calcraft lost his place of deputy commissary of musters. 'I cannot help returning to the thought of getting some colonels to dismiss him from his agencies', wrote Holland to Sandwich, 8 Dec.[42]

Towards the end of November 1764 Calcraft informed his colonels that at Christmas he would retire from the agency business. 'He is supposed to have made half a million', wrote the *Public Advertiser* on 3 Dec., 'and wants to be a Member of Parliament.' On 21 Nov. 1765 a vacancy occurred at Rochester, where Calcraft had 'been laying on them for these three years';[43] he immediately came forward, 'most handsomely invited' and 'honourably supported' by his friends; by these he claimed he had to stand[44] when a letter from Shelburne conveyed to him the disapproval of Pitt, at that moment in secret talks with Rockingham. And Rockingham, complaining to his wife of the 'hurry of a contested election', in which his secretary to the Treasury was a candidate, added: 'Calcraft is the opponent—a less rich man would have no chance—and though it is reckoned a wild attempt in him I shall be glad to hear that he has found it so, and that he retires.'[45] He did not, but was defeated by a narrow margin. Next he was nibbling at the Cust interest in his native Grantham—'we have had much talk about Calcraft who is expected at Grantham tomorrow' wrote Francis Cust to his brother John in January 1766. 'I wish you could determine about the purchase of the houses: if you don't buy 'em Calcraft will get 'em.'[46]

On 22 Apr. 1766 Calcraft was returned by Shelburne for Calne; but no vote or speech by him is recorded during the remaining weeks of the Rockingham Administration. Under Chatham, he naturally voted with the Government, but again no

speech is recorded. In 1768 he stood for Rochester with Government support, jointly with Admiral Geary; he carefully organized his election and was returned, while his fellow-candidate was defeated by the independent interest. But on Shelburne's dismissal and Chatham's resignation, Calcraft went into Opposition.

Eight interventions in debate by Calcraft are recorded in the Parliament of 1768: mostly brief and none of importance; all on the Opposition side; the last on Sawbridge's motion for shorter Parliaments, 26 Apr. 1771.[47] Junius treated him as a mute: 'Even the silent vote of Mr. Calcraft is worth reckoning in a division.'[48] What now mattered was his endeavour to unite and consolidate the Opposition round Chatham, to whom he firmly adhered. 'I follow no man or set of men', Calcraft declared in the House on 22 Nov. 1770.[49] Much truer was what he said in letters to Chatham: 'Mr. Dowdeswell has desired me to attend a meeting at his house tomorrow . . . I presume your Lordship would wish me there', 23 Jan. 1771; 'My endeavour was to keep as much as possible to your Lordship's line', 26 Mar.; 'I opposed . . . on your Lordship's ground', 28 Mar.; 'if your Lordship has any hint to give . . . I will endeavour to get it adopted by every channel that has confidence in me', 8 Apr.[50] He was at Chatham's beck and call; was a link for him with the outer world; reported to him parliamentary debates, political events, etc.; promoted movements and actions which had Chatham's approval (e.g. the Kent petition of November 1769); co-operated with the City radicals, in fact with anyone he could enlist under Chatham's banner: his aim was to bring about Chatham's return to the head of affairs. It is difficult to assess the share he had in effecting the reconciliation between Chatham and Temple in November 1768—he certainly worked for it; also with George Grenville; even with the Rockinghams. 'The interest of all parties evidently required a coalition' wrote Philip Francis in his autobiography,[51] 'and Calcraft was again the mediator; at least he told me so.' He certainly played a considerable part in persuading Granby to resign in January 1770: the Opposition now seemed near to victory, but their fortunes ebbed, especially when the Falkland Islands dispute was settled without war. 'Opposition are in great want of a leader and a general system', wrote Calcraft to Chatham, 26 Mar. 1771. 'One set are so candid, another so violent, a third so dissatisfied, that the scene is dreadful.'[52] Even Calcraft's activities slackened; especially as he was by now a sick man.

The last years he had lived at Ingress with Mrs. Elizabeth Bride, and had by her four sons and one daughter. In his will of 9 July 1771 he made the eldest, John Calcraft (q.v.), his main heir; to each of the other four he left £10,000; to his children by Mrs. Bellamy, Henry Fox Calcraft and Elizabeth, £5,000 each. In a codicil of 23 Jan. 1772, he stated his intention, from the esteem he had for his friend Philip Francis and a sense 'of his real ability to be an useful representative in Parliament', to return him at Wareham, and bid his executors to do so should his own sons be still minors. In a second codicil he left Francis £1,000. In a memorandum of July 1772[53] Calcraft adds: 'At Rochester I hope to be chose: but I will also be elected with Mr. Francis at Wareham.'

On 17 Aug. Chatham wrote to congratulate Calcraft on his recovery 'from so tedious and anxious an illness'.[54]

> Do you still continue, my dear Sir, in your purpose of changing climate? If you leave England . . . you are . . . pretty sure not to meet a more corrupted people, or more contemptible country . . . You carry with you, within, an English heart—a more valuable collection than our boasted virtuosi ever import, with all their profusion of expense and waste of time.

Calcraft replied on the 21st:[55]

> Your Lordship's testimonial is the greatest, if not the only honour an Englishman has now to wish for; and I pity my poor countrymen, who can be deluded by such a court . . . My plan is to leave England the middle of next month, and winter at Naples.

He meant to join there Philip Francis. But he died at Ingress on 23 Aug. 'I knew what I had to expect', writes Francis in his autobiography, 'and was not much disappointed at hearing that he had left me nothing but a thousand pounds, and an injunction to his trustees to bring me into Parliament for Wareham during the minority of his sons.'[56] In lack of gratitude Calcraft was repaid by at least one member of Fox's deplorable set.

Contemporary sources allege that Calcraft aspired to an Irish peerage. Walpole, writing to Montagu, 14 Apr. 1763, treats the creation as imminent; Lady Mary Coke, in her *Journal* (i. 102), 17 Nov. 1766, recounts having heard at James Stuart Mackenzie's that Shelburne insisted on Calcraft being made an Irish peer; Walpole has it that Calcraft aspired by 'Grafton's favour to the title of Earl of Ormond';[57] and Junius, on 5 Oct. 1771, that Calcraft 'only determined to be a patriot, when he could not be a peer'. Yet the subject never appears in the voluminous correspondence of the people concerned.

[1] They seem to have separated soon; she survived him and made a successful claim against his estate (Calcraft Pprs. at Rempstone). He managed to keep dark his wife's existence: Lady Sarah Bunbury, a niece of H. Fox, writes on 24 Dec. 1762 about Miss Wriothesley being 'pert . . . upon Mr. Calcraft intending to marry her (which is my sister's intelligence)', *Life of Lady Sarah Lennox*, 128–9. Mrs. Bellamy, by whom he had his first illegitimate family, claims not to

have known that he was married when she agreed to live with him. [2] T52/45/42–3. [3] Calcraft's letter bk. 1745–6, at Rempstone. [4] See DNB. [5] Ilchester, *Henry Fox*, i. 57–9. [6] T52/49/166 (1758); T52/51/26 (1760); Add. 38340, ff. 26–39 (20 Aug. 1767). [7] T54/35/40; T52/45/176; *Court & City Reg.* 1749. [8] See e.g. his letters to Granby, 7 Oct. 1757, and to Loudoun, 8 Oct., Add. 17493, f. 98. [9] Ibid. f. 84. [10] *Mems. Geo. II*, ii. 42. [11] Add. 17494, f. 36. See also Add. 17493, ff. 175–6. [12] *Apology for the Life of Mrs. Bellamy*, v. 192. [13] To Thos. Thoroton, Add. 17494, f. 46. [14] Add. 17496, ff. 96–7. See also letter to Hale, ibid. ff. 97–8; a dunning letter to Col. Irwin for repayment; ibid. f. 107; etc. [15] See e.g. CRAUFURD, John, sen. and HARVEY, Edward. [16] See e.g. BURTON, Ralph. [17] See e.g. TAYLOR, Peter; TAYLOR, Robert Paris; LINWOOD, Nicholas; COCKBURN, Sir James. [18] Add. 17495, ff. 12–13. [19] L. S. Sutherland, *E. I. Co. in 18th Cent. Politics*, 121–2. [20] See e.g. for his attempts to purchase a burgage at Corfe Castle, Namier, 'So Come and Join the Dance', *In the Margin of History*. [21] *Apology*, iii. 80. [22] Add. 17495, f. 118. [23] See *London Chron.* 20–23 Dec. 1760; and Hasted, *Kent*. 2nd ed. ii, v. [24] PRO, Amherst Pprs. [25] Add. 32944, ff. 333–4. [26] Ibid. ff. 354–5; see also Newcastle to Devonshire, 16 Nov., Add. 32945, f. 51. [27] Ibid. f. 76. [28] Sedgwick, *Letters Geo. III to Bute*, 156. [29] Add. 17495, f. 183. [30] Calcraft to Shelburne, 15 Mar. 1763, Fitzmaurice, *Shelburne*, i. 147. [31] Ibid. 151, misdated 16 Mar. [32] Ibid. i. 159. [33] *Mems. Geo. III*: this passage, omitted in the printed text, is reproduced from the original at Chewton. [34] Ibid. i. 208. [35] Parkes & Merivale, *Mems. Philip Francis*, i. 359. [36] Fitzmaurice, i. 147. [37] See Fitzmaurice, i. 199–208; *Grenville Pprs.* iii. 90–92, 204; *Bedford Corresp.* iii. 236–7; Walpole, *Mems. Geo. III*, i. 228, 233. [38] Ilchester, *Letters to H. Fox*, 179. [39] Grenville Diary, *Grenville Pprs.* ii. 202; see also Sandwich to Holland, 6 Sept. 1763, Ilchester, 176. [40] *Chatham Corresp.* ii. 245. [41] Sandwich to Holland, 26 Sept., Ilchester, 179. [42] Sandwich mss. [43] G. Onslow to Newcastle, 30 Nov., Add. 32972, f. 84. [44] Calcraft to Pitt, Rochester, *Chatham Corresp.* ii. 337–8. [45] Rockingham mss. [46] *Recs. Cust Fam.* (ser. 3) ed. Cust, 84, 249. [47] Cavendish's 'Debates', Egerton 230, p. 230. [48] *Public Advertiser*, 5 Oct. 1771. [49] Brickdale's 'Debates'. [50] *Chatham Corresp.* iv. 81, 127, 138, 143. [51] Parkes & Merivale, *Mems. Philip Francis*, ii. 302. [52] *Chatham Corresp.* iv. 127. [53] Parkes & Merivale, i. 318. [54] *Chatham Corresp.* iv. 223–4. [55] Ibid. 224–6. [56] Parkes & Merivale, i. 365. [57] *Mems. Geo. III*, iii. 264–5, n. 3.

L.B.N.

**CALCRAFT, John** (1765–1831), of Rempstone, Dorset and Ingress, Kent.

| WAREHAM | 15 July 1786–1790 |
| | 16 June 1800–1806 |
| ROCHESTER | 1806–1818 |
| WAREHAM | 1818–1831 |
| DORSET | 16 May–11 Sept. 1831 |

*b.* 16 Oct. 1765, 1st (illegit.) s. of John Calcraft (q.v.) by Mrs. Elizabeth Bride, an actress. *educ.* Harrow 1774; Eton 1778–9. *m.* 5 Mar. 1790, Elizabeth, da. and coh. of Sir Thomas Pym Hales, 4th Bt. (q.v.), 2s. 3da. *suc.* fa. 23 Aug. 1772.

John Calcraft, chief heir to his father's estate, was returned for his pocket borough of Wareham three months before he came of age, Charles Lefebure, his step-father, vacating the seat. During his minority the electoral interest at Wareham was managed by his uncle Anthony Lucas, commissioner of Excise 1767–89, who in 1784 had returned two Members favourable to the Administration. But Calcraft joined the Opposition, voting with them on the Regency. There is no record of his having spoken in the House 1786–90. He did not stand in 1790; adhered to the Whigs 1800–28; and reverted to them over the reform bill in March 1831. He committed suicide 11 Sept. 1831.

L.B.N.

## CALCRAFT, Thomas (1738-83), of Ancaster, Lincs.

### POOLE 1761-1774

*bap.* 16 Mar. 1738, 6th s. of John Calcraft, attorney, town clerk of Grantham, and bro. of John Calcraft (*d.*1772, q.v.). *educ.* Leicester; academy in Soho Square.[1] *m.* 1764, Cecil Anne, da. of John Walker of Lyneham, Wilts., niece of the Colebrookes (qq.v.), 1s. 3da. *suc.* under John Calcraft's will to his Lincolnshire estates 1772.

Ensign 2 Ft. Gds. 1753; capt. 7 Ft. 1755; lt.-col. 91 Ft. Jan. 1760; col. 1772; maj.-gen. 1777; col. 65 Ft. 1779-*d.*; lt.-gen. 1782.

John Calcraft secured for his brother Thomas quick promotion, advantageously placing him with friends: he was aide-de-camp to Charles, 3rd Duke of Marlborough on the St. Malo expedition and in Germany, and after the Duke's death to Lord Granby. And Lord George Lennox (q.v.), though hostile to John Calcraft, allowed Thomas 'to be a very deserving young man, much liked in the army'.[2]

On 1 Nov. 1760 John Calcraft inquired from Lord Kildare whether, as Thomas was likely to continue on the Irish establishment, 'it might not be desirable for him to get into that Parliament'.[3] Next, he put up Thomas for Poole. Fox wrote to Newcastle, 29 Nov. 1760:[4]

Col. Calcraft is invited to Poole in the room of Sir Richard Lyttelton who is ill abroad and who does not stand there again, nor could carry it, if he did.

If your Grace will give your interest you will have no further trouble in it, and shall have a Member of Parliament as much devoted to you as any one of the very great majority which I hope will be so.

On the other side Fitzmaurice, whom Thomas had been directed to court,[5] applied to Bute in February 1761 to strengthen Calcraft's interest by continuing a pension to the Hydes, a family influential in the borough—'you'll greatly oblige him and his friends by it'.[6] Thomas was returned unopposed while on active service—it was John Calcraft who looked after the borough, then and later.

Thomas Calcraft was still in Germany when the peace preliminaries came before the House; and next, went over to Ireland as aide-de-camp to the new lord lieutenant, Lord Northumberland. They arrived in Dublin on 21 Sept. 1763, and on the 22nd George Grenville asked Northumberland to sound the dispositions of 'two gentlemen who I understand are gone over in your family to Ireland':[7]

The second is Colonel Calcraft, whose relation to Mr. Calcraft, and whose other habitudes and attachments, may render his opinions and conduct . . . uncertain. If his present situation and obligation to you cannot determine him, perhaps his stay where he is may be desirable; but if it can . . . I should be very glad if you could send him over here.

Northumberland replied on 3 Oct.: 'I find Colonel Calcraft is not yet at liberty to declare himself, not having received any instructions from his brother on whom he is entirely dependent; I shall however take such steps as I think most advisable for your service with him.'[8] And on 1 Nov. 1763, Sandwich wrote to Northumberland:[9]

I communicated to Mr. Grenville the contents of your letter as far as related to Colonel Calcraft, and we both join in opinion in begging of you to talk fully to him as a politician, and by all means to send him over by the meeting of the Parliament, for we are not to suppose after Lord Shelburne's declaration to the King of *his* intention to support Government, that Mr. Calcraft's brother, aide-de-camp to the lord lieutenant of Ireland and a lieutenant-colonel in the army, will venture to oppose the King's measures; and at all events it will be of great use if he does to fix the point of opposition upon that connexion.

Northumberland sent Calcraft who on 15 Nov. may have voted with the Government—he is not in the minority list. But in the division of 24 Nov., on the privilege of Parliament, 'the three people supposed to be influenced by Lord Shelburne, viz. Mr. Fitzmaurice, Colonel Barré, and Mr. Calcraft, were in the minority'.[10] Informed by Grenville 'of the defection', Northumberland dismissed Calcraft.[11]

Thomas Calcraft, following his brother, attached himself to Shelburne; voted with the Opposition in the divisions on Wilkes in February 1764; was classed as 'sure' in Newcastle's list of 10 May; but as 'doubtful' by Rockingham in July 1765; and adhered to the Chatham Administration, voting with them on the land tax and the nullum tempus bill. In the next Parliament Calcraft voted with Opposition. He did not stand again in 1774, and judging by John Calcraft's will, had already decided against doing so before his brother's death.[12] There is no record of his having spoken in the House.

Mrs. Bellamy writes about him:[13]

He was genteel in his figure, with a face which, had it not been for the ravages of the smallpox, would have been handsome. In his disposition he was generous, and . . . unlike his brother in every respect, except the love of the bottle.

He died 15 Feb. 1783.[14]

[1] Mrs. G. A. Bellamy attacking John Calcraft writes that he quarrelled with her 'for insisting that he [Thomas] should be placed, for some time, at the academy in Soho-square' (*Apology*, iii. 75); and in her financial reckoning with him: 'I expended upon your brother, Captain Calcraft, at the Academy, and for other necessaries, £350' (ibid. v. 193). For the mere fact of Thomas having been at the Academy her evidence seems acceptable. [2] Lady Caroline Fox to Lady Kildare, 8 Apr. 1760, *Leinster Corresp.* i. 278. [3] Add. 17495, f. 166. [4] Add. 32915, f. 172. [5] John to Thos. Calcraft, 11 Dec. 1760, Add. 17495, f. 184. [6] Bute mss. [7] *Grenville Pprs.* ii. 127-8. [8] Grenville mss. (Bodl.) [9] Sandwich mss. [10] Grenville Diary, *Grenville Pprs.* ii. 229. [11] Northumberland to Grenville, 20 Dec. 1763, Grenville mss. (Bodl.) [12] See 'Memorandum of Calcraft, 1772' in Parkes and Merivale, *Mems. Philip Francis*, i. 318. [13] *Apology*. iii. 75. [14] The date appears in his will (PCC 116 Cornwallis). As this was made by him but not properly attested, a friend was called in to prove his handwriting, and deposed that he 'has been informed and believes that Thomas Calcraft died on 15 Feb. 1783'.

L.B.N.

**CALL, John** (1732–1801), of Whiteford, nr. Callington, Cornw.

CALLINGTON 1784–1 Mar. 1801

*b.* 30 June 1732, s. of John Call of Prestacott, Cornw. by Jane, da. of John Mill. *educ.* 'under Mr. Daddo, at Tiverton' and 'Mr. Keate, of Somerton'.[1] *m.* 28 Mar. 1772, Philadelphia, da. and coh. of William Batty of Kingston-upon-Thames, Surr., 2s. 4da. *suc.* fa. 1766; *cr.* Bt. 28 July 1791.
    Sheriff, Cornw. 1771–2.

'Born of respectable though not affluent parents', Call 'was designed for the Church, but feeling a decided preference for an active life' went out in 1749 to India, became chief engineer first at Fort St. David, then at Madras, and eventually accountant general of the Madras presidency and a member of the council.[2] He worked closely with Clive; and, having amassed a fortune, returned in 1769 to England and settled down as a country gentleman.

On 1 Aug. 1770 Call wrote to Clive from Whiteford: 'Mr. Palk (q.v.) has already made an additional purchase for me near this place and I am looking out for other lands to enlarge my possessions.' On 5 Oct. he asked to consult Clive about his intended purchase from Humphry Morice (q.v.) of the Werrington Park estate and Morice's interest at Launceston and Newport: 'It would be a thing I should wish, as it would be exceedingly convenient, and keep me in my own country.' And again on 15 May 1771 about the Werrington estate: 'I should be vexed if after I had laid out £4,000 or £5,000 in adding to an old house, a better one and a good estate was to be sold in the neighbourhood.'[3] He now aimed only at Launceston, but for reasons not discovered the negotiations broke down.

Whiteford was only three miles from Callington, which offered a promising prospect to Call's parliamentary ambitions—Lady Orford, who had the chief interest there, lived mostly abroad and managed the borough through an agent. On 7 Nov. 1771 George Clive wrote to Lady Clive:[4] 'John Call is sorry he cannot be elected for Callington being sheriff of the county, though I believe Lady Orford's interest would have prevented him.' And in a letter to Shelburne of 27 Oct. 1782, after Lady Orford's death, Call claimed that in 1779 Lord Orford had promised to return him for Callington at the general election, 'but that Lord Sandwich and Lord Chesterfield forced him to adopt Mr. Morshead'.[5] 'At that juncture', Call added, 'I was not anxious to obtain a seat, and therefore declined any contest.'

In 1782 Shelburne appointed him a commissioner to inquire into the management of Crown lands, in which post he for many years did valuable work. When in October a by-election was expected at Callington, Call again thought of standing, and asked Shelburne to try to secure for him Orford's support; 'though', he wrote, 'perhaps I might carry the election with the opposite party'.[6]

In 1784 he became a partner in the bank of Pybus and Co., of 148 New Bond St. At the general election he was returned unopposed for Callington, probably on his own interest. He generally supported Pitt, and voted with him on parliamentary reform, 18 Apr. 1785, but against him on Richmond's fortifications plan, 27 Feb. 1786. There is no record before 1790 of his having spoken in the House.

He died 1 Mar. 1801.

[1] *GEC Baronetage.* [2] *Gent. Mag.* 1801, p. 469. [3] Clive mss. [4] Ibid. [5] Lansdowne mss. [6] Ibid.

J.B.

**CALTHORPE, James** (1699–1784), of Ampton, Suff.

HINDON 21 Jan. 1758–1761

*b.* 23 Mar. 1699, 1st s. of Christopher Calthorpe of Ampton by Elizabeth, da. and coh. of Gardiner Kettleborough of Elmswell, Suff. *educ.* Bishop's Stortford; Christ's, Camb. 1717; Grand Tour (France, Italy). *unm.*
    Gentleman usher in waiting 1731–42; yeoman of the removing wardrobe 1742–82.

Calthorpe entered court under the wing of Charles, 2nd Duke of Grafton, lord chamberlain 1724–51, and under him was given employment. At the general election of 1754 he was apparently a candidate for Hindon, where his cousin, Sir Henry Calthorpe, had an interest, but withdrew on a compromise. He again came forward on a vacancy in January 1756, but was kept out by William Mabbot, Henry Fox's candidate, endorsed by Newcastle. On the next vacancy at Hindon, in January 1758, he was returned unopposed.

Calthorpe did not stand again in 1761, but gave the nomination to Fox. 'Mr. Blackstone's name is given to Mr. Calthorpe with two thousand pounds', wrote Fitzmaurice (later Shelburne) to Bute about the middle of March.[1] And on 20 Feb. 1762 Fox sent Shelburne an account showing that Calthorpe 'paid for Blackstone's election £146 0s. 6d. more than he received. He is a very honest man, and you see he has been at other expenses which he does not reckon.' In 1774 Calthorpe stood once more for the borough, but was third on the poll. The House of Commons then declared the election void, and ordered the attorney-general to prosecute all four candidates for bribery. Calthorpe, however, was acquitted.

He died 11 Mar. 1784.

[1] Bute mss.

J.A.C.

## CALTHORPE, *see also* GOUGH

## CALVERLEY, *see* BLACKETT, Sir Walter

## CALVERT, John (1726–1804), of Albury Hall, Herts.

| | |
|---|---|
| WENDOVER | 25 Feb. 1754–1761 |
| HERTFORD | 1761–1780 |
| TAMWORTH | 27 Nov. 1780–1784 |
| HERTFORD | 1784–1802 |

*b.* 6 May 1726, 1st surv. s. of Felix Calvert, London brewer, of Albury Hall by his 2nd cos. Mary, da. of Felix Calvert of Nine Ashes, Herts. *m.* 8 Sept. 1757, Elizabeth, da. of Sir Edward Hulse, 1st Bt., 2s. *suc.* fa. 29 Apr. 1755.

Calvert inherited a partnership in the family brewery in Whitecross Street, and seems to have remained in the firm at least till 1784, when he was described by John Sinclair as 'a great brewer'.[1]

Calvert was returned for Wendover by Lord Verney. In Dupplin's list of 1754 he was classed as an Administration supporter. Returned unopposed for Hertford in 1761, he received the whip direct from Newcastle; in Bute's list of December 1761 he was first marked as a follower of Newcastle, and subsequently as 'doubtful'. He voted with the Administration in the first division on the peace preliminaries, 1 Dec. 1762, but with the Opposition in the divisions of 9 and 10 Dec. He was classed as 'contra' by Jenkinson in the autumn of 1763, and voted with the Opposition on Wilkes, 15 Nov. 1763, and general warrants, 6, 15 and 18 Feb. 1764. In July 1765 Rockingham classed him as 'pro', and in November 1766 as 'Whig'. Both Townshend, in January 1767, and Newcastle, in March, listed him as a supporter of Chatham's Administration, but he did not vote on the land tax, 27 Feb. 1767, or the nullum tempus bill, 17 Feb. 1768.

Calvert was again returned unopposed in 1768. During this Parliament his only reported votes were with Administration on the Middlesex election, 8 May 1769, and Grenville's Election Act, 25 Feb. 1774, though Robinson classed him as 'pro, present' in both his surveys of March 1772 on the royal marriage bill. Calvert is reported to have spoken four times during this Parliament: on 5 Mar. 1773 he opposed Dowdeswell's poor persons' annuity bill; on 2 and 8 Mar. 1774 he opposed the bill to prevent vexatious removals of the poor; and on 14

Mar. 1774, in the debate on the Boston port bill, he said: 'I would take away their charter and make the colony a royal government, for I do not think what we are about is punishment enough for their offences . . . I would stop the bounty, and lay burthens on their trade to pay the East India Co. Whatever we do we must do effectually.'[2]

Calvert does not appear in any of the minority lists 1775–8; was classed as 'pro, absent' on the contractors bill, 12 Feb. 1779; and henceforth voted regularly with Administration till the fall of North.

At the general election of 1780 Calvert unsuccessfully contested Hertford; in November 1780 he was returned by Lord Weymouth for Tamworth. He voted for Shelburne's peace preliminaries, 18 Feb. 1783; did not vote on Fox's East India bill, 27 Nov. 1783; and was classed as a follower of Pitt in Robinson's list of January 1784, in Stockdale's of 19 Mar., and by Adam in May. Calvert voted with Pitt on Richmond's fortification plans, 27 Feb. 1786, and over the Regency 1788–9.

He died 22 Feb. 1804.

[1] Sinclair mss, Thurso East Mains. [2] Cavendish's 'Debates', Egerton 244, f. 252; 253, ff. 53–54; 254, f. 21; Brickdale's 'Debates'.

J.B.

## CALVERT, John (?1758–1844), of Albury Hall, Herts.

| | |
|---|---|
| MALMESBURY | 28 Nov. 1780–1784 |
| TAMWORTH | 1784–1790 |
| ST. ALBANS | 1790–1796 |
| HUNTINGDON | 1796–1831 |

*b.* ?1758, 1st s. of John Calvert (q.v.). *educ.* Eton 1770–5; St. John's, Camb. 1776; L. Inn 1773. *unm.* Sec. to the lord chamberlain Dec. 1783–Nov. 1830.

Returned as a Government candidate at Malmesbury, Calvert voted with North's Administration until the end. He voted for Shelburne's peace preliminaries, 18 Feb. 1783, and, like his father, was classed by Robinson as a follower of Lord Weymouth; voted for Fox's East India bill, 27 Nov. 1783, but was classed in Stockdale's list of 19 Mar. 1784 as a follower of Pitt.

He was returned for Tamworth on Weymouth's interest in 1784, and supported Pitt. There is no record of his having spoken before 1790.

He died 2 June 1844.

J.B.

## CALVERT, Nicolson (?1724–93), of Hunsdon, Herts.

| | |
|---|---|
| TEWKESBURY | 1754–1774 |

*b.* ?1724, 1st surv. s. of Felix Calvert of Furneaux Pelham, Herts. by Christian, da. and coh. of Josiah

Nicolson, brewer, of Clapton, Essex. *educ.* Bury St. Edmunds g.s. 1735; Trinity, Camb. 27 Apr. 1743, aged 18. *m.* Rebecca, da. of Rev. John Goodwin, rector of Clapham, Surr., *s.p. suc.* fa. 1755.

Calvert was elected for Tewkesbury in 1754 after a contest, and was classed by Dupplin as a country gentleman supporting the court. 'With very great expense and trouble'[1] he established an interest in the borough, and was returned unopposed in 1761 and 1768.

In 1761 he received Newcastle's whip from James West, and was classed by Bute as a follower of Pitt. On 14 May 1762 when Newcastle was contemplating resignation, John Roberts (q.v.) wrote to him:[2]

> It is my duty to acquaint your Grace that Mr. Nicolson Calvert took me aside in the House of Commons today, and desired that I would take the first opportunity of assuring you in his name that he was steadily attached to your service, and that you might reckon upon him as a firm adherent to your interest upon all occasions, which declaration he had been induced now to make, as it was rumoured that your Grace was made uneasy at this time in your Administration, and might possibly stand in need of all those who professed themselves to be your well-wishers.

He regularly opposed Bute and Grenville and was a frequent speaker in the House.

Contemporaries were agreed about Nicolson Calvert: Walpole called him 'a mad volunteer, who always spoke what he thought';[3] Rigby, 'crazy Mr. Nicolson Calvert';[4] Burke, 'a mad Member';[5] and James Harris writes of his 'wild and odd way' of speaking.[6] His absurdity and eccentricity deprived him of all weight with the Opposition; and what would have been offensive in another man was only ludicrous in him. Walpole describes 'a very bold and extraordinary speech' pointed at Bute and the Princess Dowager, 1 Feb. 1763:[7]

> [Calvert] drew a picture of a fictitious family in Surrey, whom he called *the Steadys*, describing two old Steadys and a young one; with a very particular account of young Steady's mother, and of her improper intimacy with a Scotch gardener—he hoped the true friends of young *Steady* would advise him to recall his old friends, and turn away the Scotch gardener.

Here is another example, reported by Harris—a speech on the Regency bill, 7 May 1765:

> Calvert—wild—talked of Lord Chancellor and Lady Charlotte Finch[8] by name, taking down the young Prince (if he was to become King) in a post chaise to Edinburgh and then dissolving the Parliament—(Bedlam).

In July 1765 Newcastle recommended Calvert to Rockingham for an employment,[9] but no offer seems to have been made. In a debate of 14 Jan. 1766 on the Address, Calvert declared that since the previous year, when he had voted in favour of the Stamp Act as a reasonable way to make the Americans pay for their own defence, he had completely changed his opinion:

> To lay any tax upon a numerous people, situated as the Americans are, without consent is impossible . . . Can this be done, but by force? The thought of putting it to the trial, Sir, strikes me with horror! Let us not, Sir, drive them to despair . . . Notwithstanding the right is now so indubitably asserted by the legislature of this country, notwithstanding you were certain by force of arms to carry that resolution into execution, yet I for one should be of opinion that right, and that ability to exercise that right, is, at this time, neither proper nor expedient to be carried into execution.[10]

Calvert defined his attitude to the Rockingham ministry in a speech against the window tax, 18 Apr. 1766:[11]

> Calvert . . . said he had a budget of his own to open with debtor and creditor as to ministry. He had given them credit for cider, privilege, Canada bills, Manilla ransom, family compact, impeachment of the late ministry, and the never forsaking Mr. Pitt. Now as the per contra cider tax was gone, but that was totally balanced by the black attempt to annihilate the militia, privilege was not yet asserted, Canada bills not paid, Manilla ransom not settled, family compact had had nothing done to meet it, late ministers were very merry and under no apprehensions, Mr. Pitt was not in but kept out by his friends for the sake of his health —to which might be added no land tax reduced, as chancellor of Exchequer talked of last year, but on the contrary a new and perpetual land tax laid on.
>
> This was delivered with some humour, and received with great laughter and applause.

He supported Chatham's ministry, spoke for it on the Address, 11 Nov. 1766, and the East India inquiry, 9 Mar. 1767, and even voted with the court on the land tax, 27 Feb. 1767.

Calvert regularly voted against the Grafton and North Administrations, but only nine speeches by him are recorded 1768–74. During the debate of 13 Feb. 1771 on the Falkland Islands convention, Calvert declared that he had his own opinion of the dispute, different from both sides:[12]

> I look upon the whole of this affair that Great Britain is the aggressor . . . No sooner was your peace concluded, what did you do? You sent ships to take possession of the island . . . The islands were taken possibly for no other purpose but to annoy the Spaniards . . . When men vote for the liberties of their country, and things of that sort, I would go as far as any man: but when I come to run this country into a disorder of this sort, I declare I can't do it . . . I stand a free man. No man shall ever lead me.

He would heartily vote for Administration because there would be no war, but urged that the islands should be given up. He did not stand in 1774.

Calvert died 4 May 1793, aged 68.

[1] Calvert to Newcastle, 31 May 1760, Add. 32906, f. 399. [2] Add. 32938, f. 276. [3] *Mems. Geo. III,* i. 174. [4] Rigby to Bedford, 26 Nov.

1762, *Bedford Corresp.* iii. 161. ⁵ Burke to Chas. O'Hara, 25 Nov. 1762. ⁶ Harris's 'Debates', 25 Nov. 1762. ⁷ *Mems. Geo. III*, i. 191. ⁸ Governess to the King's children. ⁹ Newcastle to Rockingham, 12 July 1765, Add. 32967, f. 349. ¹⁰ *Parly. Hist.* xvi. 108. ¹¹ Harris's 'Debates'. ¹² Cavendish's 'Debates', Egerton 219, f. 110.

J.B.

## CALVERT, Sir William (?1703–61), of Mount Mascal, nr. Bexley, Kent.

LONDON 13 July 1742–1754
OLD SARUM 18 Mar. 1755–1761

*b.* ?1703, 3rd *s.* of William Calvert of Furneaux Pelham, Herts. by his 1st cos. Honor, da. of Peter Calvert of Nine Ashes, Herts. *educ.* Emmanuel, Camb. 1722. *m.* June 1732, Martha, da. of Samuel Smith and wid. of Charles Malyn of Southwark, brewer, *s.p.* Kntd. 18 Feb. 1744.

Alderman of London 1741, sheriff 1743–4, lord mayor 1748–9.

Calvert was head of the family brewery in London. During his first Parliament he voted in Opposition, but by 1747 had become an Administration supporter. In 1754 he stood again for London. 'I saw Sir William Calvert last night', wrote Newcastle to the King on 6 Apr., 'who told me he had the greatest appearance of merchants for him yesterday upon the exchange that ever was known; he seems confident of his success.'[1] Yet he was bottom of the poll, and Newcastle undertook to find him another seat. On 2 May 1754 Newcastle wrote to Robert Nugent (q.v.), who had elected to sit for Bristol, leaving a vacancy at St. Mawes: 'You now have an opportunity of doing a very agreeable thing to the King . . . by choosing at St. Mawes as worthy, as honourable, and as useful a friend to the Government as can come into Parliament—I mean Sir William Calvert.'[2] But Nugent returned his stepson, James Newsham. In the end Calvert was returned for Old Sarum without expense to himself.

On 19 Nov. 1758 he solicited from Newcastle the appointment of joint postmaster general:[3]

> My utmost ambition would be satisfied if peradventure I might some time or other arrive at the Post Office, because that had been frequently the honour and reward bestowed upon the most favoured citizens of London.

He applied again on 22 Apr. 1759, but was unsuccessful.

Calvert did not stand at the general election, and died 3 May 1761, aged 57.

¹ Add. 32835, ff. 48–49. ² C. Nugent, *Mem. Earl Nugent*, 203. ³ Add. 32885, f. 429.

A.N.N.

## CAMPBELL, Alexander (1756–85).

NAIRNSHIRE 1784–Nov. 1785

*b.* 14 Sept. 1756, 2nd *s.* of Pryse Campbell and bro. of John Campbell of Calder (qq.v.). *educ.* Eton 1766–8; Harrow 1770; Clare, Camb. 1774. *unm.*

Ensign 55 Ft. 1775, lt. 1777; capt. 75 Ft. 1778; half-pay 1783.

Campbell, while serving in America where he was wounded, was nominated one of the captains in a new Welsh regiment which his brother John and Thomas Johnes (qq.v.) offered to raise.

In 1780 he was enrolled as a freeholder of Inverness-shire on a qualification received from his brother,[1] who also provided a qualification in Nairnshire. In 1784 Campbell was returned for Nairnshire and was listed by William Adam in May 1784 among the Opposition. He is not known to have spoken in the House. He died during the recess in November 1785.

¹ SRO Bught mss 7/204.

E.H.-G.

## CAMPBELL, Archibald (1739–91), of Inverneil, Argyll.

STIRLING BURGHS 1774–1780, 21 Aug. 1789–31 Mar. 1791

*b.* 21 Aug. 1739, 2nd *s.* of James Campbell of Tuerechan, and bro. of James Campbell of Tuerechan (q.v.). *educ.* Glasgow Univ. 1753. *m.* 7 July 1779, Amelia, da. of Allan Ramsay, portrait painter, *s.p.* Purchased Inverneil 1775. K.B. 30 Sept. 1785.

Lt. 63 Ft. 1757, capt. 1760; sub-engineer and lt. Royal Engineers 1759; engineer extraordinary and capt.-lt. 1763; lt.-col. and chief engineer of Bengal 1768–72; lt.-col. 71 Ft. 1775; col. 1779; maj.-gen. 1782; col. 74 Ft. 1787–*d.*

Lt. gov. Jamaica 1781–2; gov. 1782–4; gov. Madras 1785–9; heritable usher of the white rod [S] 1790.

Campbell held commissions concurrently in the Royal Engineers and Fraser's Highlanders, served in America and was wounded at Quebec. After the peace he gained great reputation as a military engineer and expert on fortifications,[1] and in 1768, after declining an invitation 'to be chief engineer to the Venetians',[2] was seconded from the British army for three years to enter the East India Company's service as chief engineer in Bengal.[3] After reporting on Bombay's fortifications, he reorganized the Fort William defence system, and, as a private venture, initiated an ambitious scheme for obtaining a land grant and building extensive docks and shipyards at Raderpore. His proposal that, in return for a £500 annuity for life, he should apply for an extension of his three years' secondment was warmly recommended by the Bengal Council to the court of directors;[4] but later his ruthless expulsion of the native inhabitants from his dockyard area was strongly criticized.[5] He returned home in 1773 with a large fortune,[6] and a few years later sold his dockyard interest to his partner Colonel Henry Watson for a large sum.

In 1774, encouraged by his friend Robert Preston (q.v.), the East India captain, he stood for Stirling Burghs against the Lawrence Dundas interest, and by lavish use of his Indian wealth out-manoeuvred his opponents and was returned. Sir William Mayne (q.v.) estimated that for less than a third of his expenditure 'he might have secured an English borough, giving the highest price'.[7] A firm supporter of Administration, Campbell was highly regarded by James Boswell, his legal adviser, for his 'admirable parts, his activity, his application, his command of accurate expression';[8] but during his first year in the House, involved in numerous election lawsuits,[9] and with a petition pending against him, he seems to have been less concerned with his parliamentary career than with legal and military affairs.

Appointed in November 1775 to command the 2nd battalion of Fraser's new Highland regiment, he sailed for America in spring 1776, arrived in Boston harbour unaware of the British evacuation, was made prisoner, sent to Concord, and released on parole. When the British captured the American General Lee, Samuel Adams demanded that Campbell 'be secured . . . as one upon whom retaliation is to be made'. Campbell was then imprisoned in the common jail until released by Washington's intervention, but remained captive until exchanged in May 1778.[10]

Immediately resuming his command, he was appointed by Clinton in October 1778 to lead the expedition against Savannah and unite with Prevost's southern force.[11] Ably seconded by John Maitland (q.v.), Campbell accomplished his objectives, and after the capture of Savannah wrote to Lord Carlisle, 18 Jan. 1779:[12]

> I am not without the hope of being the first officer to take a stripe and star from the rebel flag of Congress . . . Your Lordship will see the necessity of sending out a governor immediately. I am merely a soldier and wish, when I can no longer render service to my Sovereign in that line, to retire from the bustle of public employ.

Leaving Prevost in command in Georgia, he sailed from Savannah in March and returned home a popular hero. While on leave in Scotland he proposed joining the Western Fencibles then raising. North wrote to the King, 30 Aug. 1779:[13]

> Lt.-Col. Campbell wishes to serve without pay with the irregulars and the new armed peasants, but Lord Amherst objects to it because he belongs to the army in America. Lord North . . . wishes as a public man that Mr. Campbell's talents, as they cannot in this instant be employed in America, might be made as useful as possible in Great Britain.

The King, however, agreed with Amherst, and by early 1780 Campbell was again out of the kingdom. At the general election of 1780 he stood down in favour of his brother James (q.v.); soon afterwards was appointed lieutenant governor of Jamaica; earned high praise for his reorganization of the island's defence;[14] and was commissioned governor on 10 July 1782.

On his return home he was knighted and appointed governor of Madras, through the friendship of Henry Dundas, who remained his constant correspondent and supporter to the end of his life.[15] An able, popular and enlightened administrator and military chief,[16] he was, however, strongly criticized by the East India Company board of directors, particularly for his agreement with the Nabob of Arcot on the settlement of his debts. Cornwallis wrote to Lord Sydney, 7 Jan. 1788:[17]

> I am astonished to hear that the court of directors seize every opportunity of attacking Sir Archibald Campbell . . . Nothing . . . could be more fatal to the British interest in India than his removal. He has shown great ability and the most perfect uprightness and integrity and possesses the esteem and confidence of the civil as well as the military part of the settlement.

Deeply hurt by the Company's 'illiberal treatment',[18] Campbell resigned, and, in poor health, returned home in June 1789. His brother James promptly vacated Stirling Burghs in his favour, and he was returned apparently unopposed. There is no record of his having spoken in the House. An acknowledged expert on Indian affairs, he was frequently consulted by Dundas.[19]

He died 31 Mar. 1791.

[1] H. Davison Love, *Vestiges of Old Madras*, iii. 19, 319. [2] Campbell's account of his career in conversation with James Boswell, 16 Oct. 1774, Boswell, *Private Pprs.* x. 29. [3] *Cal. Home Office Pprs.* 1773-5, no. 587. [4] *Fort William—India House Corresp.* 1767-9 (India Rec. Ser.), 97, 127; Bengal Council to Court, 28 Mar., 25 Sept. 1769, pp. 537, 580. [5] *Mems. Wm. Hickey*, ii. 121-2, 146-7. [6] Sir D. Campbell, *Recs. of Clan Campbell in E. I. Co.* 27-8. [7] Mayne to John Graham, 11 Jan. 1775, Kinross House mss, SRO. [8] Boswell, *Private Pprs.* x. 24, 29. [9] Ibid. 105; Boswell, *Johnson*, iii. 58-63. [10] *Warren-Adams Letters* (N.Y. Hist Colls.), i. 292; HMC *Royal Inst.* i. 90, 136, 164, 179, 217. [11] Clinton to Prevost, 8 Nov. 1778, ibid. 340. [12] HMC *Carlisle*, 413-14. [13] Fortescue, iv. 416-17. [14] *APC (Col.)* 1766-83, p. 503; HMC *Royal Inst.* ii. 415, 431, 474, 525, 526; HMC *Var.* vi. 184. [15] Holden Furber, *Henry Dundas*, 33, 42, 56-62. [16] HMC *Palk*, 386, 402; *Vestiges of Old Madras*, iii. 320-4, 341, 346-7, 368, 391; *Cornwallis Corresp.* i. 225, 281. Campbell's *Regulations for the Company's Troops on the Coast of Coromandel* and his *Horse Drill . . . for the Native Cavalry*, pub. in 1787. [17] *Cornwallis Corresp.* i. 322. [18] Dundas to Cornwallis, 13 July 1788, ibid. i. 406. [19] HMC *Fortescue*, i. 481, 518, ii. 11.

E.H.-G.

**CAMPBELL, Daniel** (c.1736-77), of Shawfield, Lanark and Islay, Argyll.

LANARKSHIRE       17 Jan. 1760-1768

*b.* c.1736, 1st s. of John Campbell of Shawfield (*d.v.p.* 1746), by Lady Henrietta Cunningham, da. of William 12th Earl of Glencairn [S]. *unm.* *suc.* gd.-fa. 1753.

In 1760 Campbell was returned unopposed for Lanarkshire on the united interest of the Dukes of

Douglas and Hamilton, with the support of the Duke of Argyll and Robert Dundas of Arniston.[1] In 1761 he was re-elected against an opponent supported by Lord Hyndford.

Argyll's death, followed by that of the Duke of Douglas, left Campbell without a patron. In December 1761 the dowager Duchess of Douglas recommended him to Bute as 'ready to oblige your Lordship'.[2] But in the division on the peace preliminaries, 9 Dec. 1762, he was a teller with John Wilkes for the Opposition. Furthermore, he was one of the few Scots who voted with the Opposition over Wilkes and general warrants, and was counted by Newcastle, 10 May 1764, as a 'sure' friend. During the debates on the repeal of the Stamp Act he appears in a list prepared by Sir Alexander Gilmour (q.v.), 18 Feb. 1766, as voting with the Government;[3] and he did not vote against them in the division of 22 Feb. Yet he is not known to have been closely connected with the leaders of the Newcastle-Rockingham group. Rockingham in November 1766 classed him as 'doubtful', Townshend in January 1767 as 'Government', and Newcastle in March as 'friend'; and he did not vote in the divisions on the land tax or nullum tempus.

As early as August 1766 Campbell opened his campaign for the 1768 general election.[4] Of his two opponents, Andrew Stuart stood on the Hamilton interest backed by the Argyll family, and Lockhart Ross had the friendship, if not the active support, of Stuart Mackenzie. Campbell's candidature seems to have had somewhat lukewarm Government approval. Patrick Craufurd of Auchenames wrote to Mure, 6 Dec. 1766: 'Ministry are more inclined to humour Shawfield than any other plan.'[5] In the end Lockhart Ross and Campbell united against Andrew Stuart, and Lockhart Ross having won the toss for the nomination, was elected.

At the general election of 1774 Campbell stood once more for Lanarkshire, regarded by the Argyll-Hamilton family as a dangerous opponent to Andrew Stuart. On 27 July 1773 William Mure warned the Duchess:[6]

Shawfield I hear is in play, I wish the Duke [Argyll] could throw an invitation in his way, to return by Inverary that you might have a conference with him. He is a great card as they are now shuffled.

The Duchess replied, 1 Aug.:[7]

What shall I say to Shawfield if he comes this way. I think the boroughs [Lanark, Linlithgow, etc.] might be offered to him. He was once too high and mighty to accept of such an offer and he may be so yet, but if they could keep him out of the county, I think it would be worthwhile.

Another compromise (rejected by Andrew Stuart as prejudicial to the Hamilton interest) proposed that Campbell should be adopted for the county and in return should pay Stuart's expenses for the Burghs, 'whatever sum that might amount to'.[8] In the end the Hamiltons prevented a coalition between their opponents by an alliance with Lockhart Ross and the interest of Lord President Dundas and his brother Henry Dundas. Campbell, left alone to oppose Stuart, was defeated.

He died 12 May 1777.

[1] Add. 33049, f. 307. [2] Bute mss. [3] Add. 32974, f. 24. [4] J. S. Mackenzie to W. Mure, 28 Aug. 1766, *Caldwell Pprs.* ii (2), p. 89. [5] Ibid. 96. [6] *Intimate Society Letters of the 18th Cent.* ed. Duke of Argyll, i. 154. [7] *Caldwell Pprs.* ii (2), p. 223. [8] Stuart to the Duchess of Argyll, 9 Oct. 1773, *Intimate Society Letters,* i. 178-86.

E.H.-G.

## CAMPBELL, Dugald (c.1710-64), of Ballimore, Argyll.

### ARGYLLSHIRE 1754-Dec. 1763

*b.* c.1710, 2nd s. of Archibald Campbell of Ballimore by Margaret, da. and h. of Dugald Campbell of Shirvan. *m.* ?1758, Christian Drummond, sis. of Alexander Drummond, sometime consul at Aleppo, and wid. of David Campbell of Dunloskine, 1s. 1da.

Lt. independent co. of Ft. 1725; capt. 42 Ft. 1739; half-pay 1749.

A half-pay captain, Campbell was brought into Parliament by Argyll,[1] to replace his ageing uncle Sir Duncan Campbell of Lochnell, whose secret service pension of £400 p.a. was transferred to him.[2] Entirely directed by Argyll, he voted 2 May 1757 with Henry Fox on the Minorca inquiry,[3] and was counted by Newcastle among the few who would remain faithful to Argyll whether in or out of power.[4] Sharing his patron's interest in science, he was consulted by Dr. John Pringle and others on scientific publications, as one who bought 'every work of reputation of that sort that comes out'.[5] Apparently he voted for the Scottish militia bill.[6]

Although he was re-elected in 1761 as a Government supporter,[7] his pension was discontinued. No vote of his is recorded in the new Parliament; he is not in Fox's list of those favourable to the peace preliminaries; and although not mentioned by Stuart Mackenzie as an absentee in the divisions of November 1763 on Wilkes,[8] he had by then been stricken by 'the great disorder of body and mind which rendered him quite incapable of business of any kind'.[9]

In December 1763 he vacated his seat on being given the sinecure of master of the revels. On his death, 30 Dec. 1764, his widow, 'through the interest of her husband's relations', received a pension of £200 p.a., half of which she allocated to the payment of his debts.[10]

[1] 'State of Elections in Scotland', 5 Apr. 1754, Add. 32995, f. 190; Dupplin's list 1754. [2] Namier, *Structure,* 217. [3] Add. 33034,

f. 232. [4] Add. 32995, f. 383. [5] John Pringle to Sir John Hall, 17 May 1755, Dunglass mss. [6] Leven to Chas. Macky, 1 Apr. 1760, Leven and Melville mss, SRO. [7] Note of the Elections in Scotland, 26 Apr. 1760, Add. 33049, f. 306. [8] Stuart Mackenzie to W. Mure, 17 Nov. 1763, Caldwell Pprs. ii(1), p. 190. [9] Clan Campbell, ed. Campbell and Paton, iii. 106, 108. [10] Ibid. 254.

E.H.-G.

**CAMPBELL, Lord Frederick** (1729–1816), of Ardencaple, Dunbarton, and Coombe Bank, Kent.

GLASGOW BURGHS 1761–1780
ARGYLLSHIRE 1780–Oct. 1799

b. 1729, 2nd surv. s. of John Campbell (d.1770, q.v.), 4th Duke of Argyll [S]; bro. of John, Lord Lorne, and Lord William Campbell (qq.v.). educ. Westminster 1743–6; Ch. Ch. Oxf. 1747; M. Temple 1751, called 1754. m. 28 Mar. 1769, Mary, da. of Amos Meredith, sis. of Sir William Meredith (q.v.), wid. of Laurence Shirley, 4th Earl Ferrers, 2da. suc. fa. to Coombe Bank estate 9 Nov. 1770.
M.P. [I] 1767–76.
Ld. privy seal [S] May–July 1765; P.C. 29 May 1765; chief sec. [I] 1767–8; ld. clerk register [S] 1768–d.; ld. of Trade 1786–1801; vice-treasurer [I] 1787–93; member Board of Control, India 1790–3.

Campbell, as a young lawyer, 'knew necessity' and 'squeezed with difficulty' 150 guineas from his patrimony to make a continental tour with his life-long friend Robert Murray Keith (q.v.)[1] and on his return owed much of his practice to the assistance of his brother-in-law Henry Seymour Conway.[2] In 1759 he became involved in the dispute over Ayr Burghs, which Argyll had intended for him, but when Bute set up Patrick Craufurd, Argyll gave his interest to Sir Adam Fergusson. When Bute, to settle the quarrel, offered to bring in Frederick as a candidate acceptable to them both, Argyll forbade him to stand unless Fergusson voluntarily withdrew.[3] Eventually, when Fergusson had been induced to stand down, Frederick was returned, but on the very same day (20 Apr.) his brother, Lord Lorne, the unopposed candidate for Glasgow Burghs, became ineligible by their father's accession as 4th Duke. Frederick was hastily brought in, in his brother's place, as a stop-gap, but chose to retain the seat and relinquish Ayr Burghs.

On good terms with Bute and Stuart Mackenzie, he soon made his mark as a Government speaker; opposed, 11 Dec. 1761, the motion for Spanish papers; seconded the Address on the war with Spain, 19 Jan. 1762, 'very handsomely both as to style and matter';[4] and in July was rewarded with the grant for life of the feu duty of the island of Islay, worth £450 p.a.[5]

He spoke 10 Dec. 1762 in favour of the Peace;[6]

continued to support Bute to the end of his Administration, but left him in autumn 1763 to attach himself to the Bedford party. Having seconded the Address, 16 Nov. 'with great approbation and propriety',[7] he distinguished himself by the 'warmth' and 'impetuosity' of his speeches, particularly on Wilkes and general warrants[8] and, violently disagreeing with Conway, made no protest against his dismissal. Walpole wrote:[9]

Lord Frederick was sensible, shrewd, and selfish; and on this and a subsequent crisis showed that no connexion or obligation could stand against the eagerness with which he pursued immediate fortune. Nothing else weighed with him, except the inveteracy of national prejudice. As Mr. Conway had acted in opposition to Scottish measures, Lord Frederick, forgetting Mr. Conway's friendship and kindness and his own youthful situation, and borne away by a hot temper, often and indecently attacked him in Parliament, though without any brilliancy of parts to colour over such improper behaviour.

He opposed, 29 Jan. 1765, Sir William Meredith's motion on general warrants, and, 5 Mar., Calvert's motion for restraining the powers of the attorney-general; spoke 15 Feb. against receiving colonial petitions against the Stamp Act; and on the Regency question on 9 May favoured leaving the choice of regent to the King.[10]

On 23 May, Grenville, having forced the King to agree to Stuart Mackenzie's dismissal, nominated Lord Frederick to the office of lord privy seal (which Lorne had declined in his brother's favour) together with the management of Scotland 'under certain limitations . . . but without access to the Closet'.[11] Seven weeks later Grenville's Administration was dismissed, and Lord Frederick, after consulting Lorne, on 23 July[12] resigned his office with its £3,000 p.a., and followed Grenville and Bedford into Opposition.

In the new session he spoke[13] and voted against the repeal of the Stamp Act, although, since many Glasgow merchants favoured repeal, it was thought 'he must leave his leader upon this question'.[14] He continued to act with the Bedford group until December 1766, when, with Lorne, he 'declared off' from Bedford, adhered to the Chatham Administration, and voted with them on the land tax, 27 Feb. 1767. Having in effect abandoned his legal practice, Campbell, with little money or property, except the Ardencaple estate (purchased for him by his father), now sought lucrative employment. He failed to obtain through Conway the office of vice-admiral of Scotland,[15] but accepted appointment as chief secretary to Lord Townshend, the new lord lieutenant of Ireland. He wrote to William Mure, 25 Sept. 1767:[16]

Nothing should at present have made me solicit this troublesome office, with all its advantages, but, finding it handsomely and heartily offered, I thought I owed it to myself not to decline service.

His services were rewarded in 1768 by the office of lord clerk register.

Henceforth he voted consistently with Administration. On 28 Nov. 1772 he was elected to the secret committee on East India affairs, but declined the chairmanship. Possessed of a lucrative office and a fine estate, Lord Frederick now had less incentive to distinguish himself in Parliament and rarely spoke. A member of a social group, 'the Gang', which included Henry Drummond, Richard Rigby, Thomas Bradshaw, and Thomas Harley he preferred retirement at Coombe Bank, and maintained a certain detachment in controversial issues. Deploring North's vacillation and the Cabinet's divided views in the heated debate of 10 May 1773[17] on East India affairs, he spoke and voted on 21 May against Burgoyne's motion condemning Clive.[18] On American affairs, he wrote to Robert Murray Keith, 3 Feb. 1775:[19] 'This conflict is terrible—however, the Administration is united, firm and confident, yet many good men doubt.' On 22 Mar. Campbell spoke against Burke's conciliatory propositions, and on 8 Nov. advocated 'vigorous armaments'.[20]

For financial reasons Campbell in autumn 1776 decided to reduce his London establishment and attend Parliament only some two days per week.[21] Having unsuccessfully applied for the office of keeper of the signet in 1776, he was compensated with the grant of his registership for life in February 1777.[22]

In 1780, Campbell, in ill health and tired of the burden of representing Glasgow Burghs, decided to seek a county constituency. Certain of return for Argyllshire, he also stood for Dunbartonshire where the Argyll interest was seriously threatened. After a violent contest he was returned, but did not seriously contest the petition which George Keith Elphinstone brought against him.

As Member for Argyll he could now indulge his 'idleness'.[23] A placeman 'attached to the Crown if not to the Government', he supported successive Administrations; spoke 15 May 1782 in favour of a Scottish militia; and 17 Feb. 1783 declared that 'he meant to vote honestly and fairly' for the peace.[24] Nonetheless he supported the Coalition, voted for Fox's East India bill, 27 Nov. 1783, and on the change of Administration took 'a warm and zealous part' in the address to the King against a dissolution.[25]

Listed 'hopeful' by Robinson in early January 1784, he spoke 12 Jan. in favour of considering Pitt's East India bill: 'He had voted for the other bill but whichever bill appeared to him to be the best . . . by that he would abide.'[26] On 20 Jan.[27] he pleaded for moderation and an 'accommodation between the parties in the present struggle for power'; thought the constitution was not in danger, but if the contrary was proved would join Fox. When Fox dispelled his 'sanguine hopes of union' Campbell went over to Pitt and by the end of the Parliament was counted 'Administration'. In the new Parliament he supported Pitt's measures, though strongly opposing his reform bill, 18 Apr. 1785.[28] He was now closely connected with Henry Dundas who appointed him to the Board of Trade in 1786, and in 1787 secured for him the place of vice treasurer of Ireland. Sacrificing his 'idleness', he became more active in parliamentary business, was chairman of the committee of the whole House in May 1787 on East India affairs, and on more than one occasion urged Members to learn from his example to restrain their 'warm tempers'.[29] To avoid violent controversy, he proposed the deferment of the slave trade bill, 21 May 1788.[30] A strong Government supporter in the Regency debate of 12 Dec. 1788, he had an acrimonious dispute with Fox who taunted him with time serving.[31] He remained faithful to Pitt until at the age of 70 he resigned his seat.

Wraxall describes him in 1785:[32]

Lord Frederick . . . still retained all the graces he had inherited from his mother. His figure united symmetry with elegance, and his manners, noble yet soft, dignified yet devoid of any pride or affectation, conciliated all who approached him. Devoid of shining talents, he nevertheless wanted not either ability or eloquence in a certain degree, both which were under the control of reason and temper.

He died 8 June 1816.

[1] Campbell to Keith, 11 Apr. 1773, *Mems. and Corresp. of Sir R. M. Keith*, i. 402. [2] Duke of Richmond to J. Caryll, 3 Jan. 1760, Add. 28233, f. 316. [3] Argyll to Sir H. Erskine, Mar. 1761, Bute mss; Sir H. Bellenden to W. Mure 26 Mar. 1761, *Caldwell Pprs.* ii (1), p. 150; Argyll to R. Campbell, 4, 7 Apr. 1761; Frederick's corresp. with Loudoun, Mar. and Apr. 1761, Loudoun mss. [4] Harris's 'Debates'. [5] Payable by Daniel Campbell of Shawfield, T17/18/213–5; see also Walpole *Mems. Geo. III*, ii. 127. [6] Harris's 'Debates'. [7] Grenville to the King, 16 Nov. 1763, Fortescue, i. 58. [8] Harris's 'Debates', 6, 14 Feb.; Onslow to Newcastle 13 Feb., Add. 32955, f. 462; Grenville to the King, 15 Feb., *Grenville Pprs.* ii. 262. [9] *Mems. Geo. III*, i. 322. [10] Harris's 'Debates'. [11] Gilbert Elliot's memorandum, *Jenkinson Pprs.* 372. [12] Campbell to Grenville, 23 July, Grenville to Campbell, 25 July 1765, Grenville mss (JM); *Jenkinson Pprs.* 379. [13] 17 Dec. 1765, Harris's 'Debates', 3, 5 Feb. 1766; Ryder's 'Debates', Harrowby mss. [14] W. Rouet to W. Mure, 10 Jan. 1766, *Caldwell Pprs.* ii (2), pp. 58–59. [15] Augustus Hervey to Grenville, 31 July 1767, T. Whateley to Grenville, 24 Aug., *Grenville Pprs.* iv. 131, 157. [16] *Caldwell Pprs.* ii (2), p. 124. [17] See his letter to R. M. Keith of 11 May 1773, *Mems. and Corresp. of Sir R. M. Keith*, i. 407–10. [18] Fortescue, ii. 489. [19] Add. 35508, f. 256. [20] Almon, i. 369; iii. 150. [21] Campbell to Keith, 1, 27 Nov. 1776, Add. 35511, ff. 47, 81. [22] Campbell to Keith, 7 Mar. 1777, ibid, f. 200. [23] Campbell to Keith, 13 Mar. 1781, Add. 35521, f. 211. [24] Debrett, vii. 165; ix. 288. [25] See Fox's attack upon him, 12 Dec. 1788, Stockdale, xvi. 38. [26] Debrett xii. 520. [27] Ibid. 608–9. [28] Ibid. xviii. 78. [29] e.g., 18 Apr. 1788, on naval promotions; Stockdale, xiv. 140. [30] Ibid. xv. 76. [31] Ibid. xvi. 38. [32] *Mems.* iv. 77–78.

E.H.-G.

## CAMPBELL, Ilay (1734–1823), of Succoth, Argyll.

GLASGOW BURGHS 1784–Oct. 1789

*b.* 25 Aug. 1734, 1st s. of Archibald Campbell of Succoth, writer to the signet, a principal clerk of session, by Helen, da. and h. of John Wallace of Elderslie, Renfrew. *educ.* Mundell's sch. Edinburgh; Glasgow Univ. 1751; adv. 1757. *m.* 14 Nov. 1766, Susan Mary, da. of Archibald Murray of Murrayfield, adv., sis. of Alexander Murray (q.v.), 2s. 6da. *suc.* fa. 1790; *cr.* Bt. 17 Sept. 1808.

Solicitor-gen. [S] Feb.–Aug. 1783; lord adv. Dec. 1783–Oct. 1789; trustee for fisheries and manufactures 1784; ld. pres. ct. of sess. Nov. 1789–1808.

Campbell was a brilliant lawyer, excelling in written argument rather than in oratory. In 1774, Boswell described him as 'the first writing lawyer' at the Scottish bar, earning £1,600 p.a.; and wrote in 1776: 'Ilay Campbell would cut off his thumbs rather than be pressed up to the bench.'[1]

A quiet man of simple tastes, he was often 'humdrum and ineffectual' in company. But his wide learning and legal subtlety were admired by Lord Chancellor Thurlow and Lord Advocate Dundas, through whom, in February 1783, he was offered the place of solicitor-general. He accepted without enthusiasm. Boswell describes a dinner in Edinburgh on 28 Feb.:

> Mr. Campbell was as usual silent and indifferent. But he gave a wonderful testimony of his confined Scottish views. He said Sir Gilbert Elliot and lord advocate . . . would have done better to have continued at the bar here.[2]

On Shelburne's fall Campbell remained in office until the Coalition dismissed Dundas in August, when he insisted upon resigning and, according to Dundas, even refused 'the advocate's gown'.[3] Alexander Wedderburn (q.v.) wrote:[4] 'Though I am sorry for the loss of Campbell's ability and plain good sense . . . his removal . . . will double the effect of the removal of Dundas.' Campbell wrote to Dundas, 1 Sept. 1783:[5]

> I should be sorry if you continued to differ with me about my resignation of the solicitor-generalship . . . The dismission of the Crown mandate from above will satisfy you that nothing less than a total change of system was the object in view . . . Had I continued in office, I must have had the appearance of aiding and countenancing every political scheme which the Whig party may choose to adopt in this country . . . In short I thought it much better to leave the field clear to them.

In the Pitt Administration Campbell was appointed lord advocate but had no parliamentary seat until the general election of 1784 when he defeated John Craufurd (q.v.) in Glasgow Burghs. In the House he was a frequent but unattractive speaker with a dry, legalistic manner.[6] His support of

Government was always tempered by his regard for Scottish and particularly Glasgow interests. Thus he opposed the duties on printed linens on 4 Aug. 1784; and in the debates on the Irish commercial propositions supported on 22 Feb. 1785 Sir William Cunynghame's plea for delay until Scottish representations were heard; and in April 1786 opposed the reduction of the bounty cn the Greenland fishery.[7]

He voted for parliamentary reform, 18 Apr. 1785. In the same month he took the lead in the proposed reduction of the number of Scottish judges from fifteen to ten, with a considerable increase in salary. Violent opposition in Scotland and in the House compelled Campbell to withdraw his resolution for diminution, but he carried that on salaries in the following year.[8]

An admirer of Warren Hastings, he protested on 3 Apr. 1786 against the plan to examine witnesses before bringing specific charges, and on 1 June spoke strongly in his support. On 9 May 1787 'he thought himself bound in conscience' to declare his favourable opinion of the accused, and that he intended 'to think, vote and act' according to his own judgment. In the Regency debate of 16 Dec. 1788 he argued 'that neither the Prince of Wales nor any other individual had a legal right in this case to be Regent, though in point of fitness and propriety he supposed not a man in the kingdom would think of any other than his Royal Highness'.[9]

On the death of Thomas Miller (q.v.), Dundas immediately recommended Campbell to succeed as president of the court of session, and wrote to W. W. Grenville on 18 Oct. 1789:[10]

> When the question of the Regency came forward last winter his adherence to our cause left him no prospect as then appeared, but that of retiring to the situation of a private barrister, in which he would have grown grey without the means or prospect of a dignified retirement . . . No one opportunity should be omitted of marking with favour and honour those whose conduct was distinguished with fidelity and firmness on that occasion.

As a judge 'he was inferior to none of his brethren in depth or learning and was greatly superior to them all in a genuine and liberal taste for the law's improvement'.[11] On his retirement in 1808 he received a baronetcy.

He died 28 Mar. 1823.

[1] *Private Pprs.* ix. 190–1; xii. 86. [2] Ibid. xiii. 104–6; xv. 162. [3] Dundas to W. W. Grenville, 18 Oct. 1789, *HMC Fortescue,* i. 535. [4] *Corresp. C. J. Fox,* ii. 203. [5] Holden Furber, *Henry Dundas,* 201–2. [6] Cockburn, *Memorials of his Time,* 127. [7] Stockdale, iii. 391; iv. 310; viii. 179. [8] Ibid. vi. 392–4, 427; viii. 101, 152–3; *Lord Advocates of Scotland,* ii. 175–6; Boswell, *Private Pprs.* xvi. 89, 158, 175–6. [9] Stockdale, viii. 112–13; ix. 39; xii. 41–48; xvi. 85–86. [10] *HMC Fortescue,* i. 524, 534–5. [11] Cockburn, 126.

E.H.-G.

**CAMPBELL** (formerly **LIVINGSTONE**), **James** (?1719–88), of Ardkinglass, Argyll and Glentirran, Stirling.

STIRLINGSHIRE  1747–1768

*b.* ?1719, 1st surv. s. of Sir James Livingstone, 2nd Bt. of Glentirran, by Helen, da. and h. of Sir James Campbell, M.P., 2nd Bt. of Ardkinglass; bro. of Adam Livingstone (q.v.). *educ.* Edinburgh. *m.* 18 June 1752, Catherine, da. and coh. of Walter Campbell, receiver-gen. of Scottish customs, and cos. of Daniel Campbell of Shawfield (q.v.), 1s. 1 da. *suc.* maternal gd.-fa. 5 July 1752, and fa. 30 Apr. 1771.
 Ensign 25 Ft. 1733, lt. 1740, capt. 1745, ret. 1754. Gov. Stirling castle 1763–*d.*

James Livingstone succeeded his brother Alexander as his grandfather's heir in December 1745, and, under the terms of the entail, took the name of Campbell. He entered the army, fought at Fontenoy, and under Cumberland at Culloden. As captain on guard he witnessed the Duke's cold reception of Duncan Forbes's 'well meant wishes for clemency',[1] and subsequently developed a strong aversion to Cumberland and Fox. He returned to Flanders, served at Laeffeld in June 1747,[2] and in July was returned unopposed for Stirlingshire.

At the 1754 election he was strongly opposed by Robert Haldane, supported by Lawrence Dundas (qq.v.) and the Duke of Montrose,[3] but after a close contest was returned. He was listed 'for' by Dupplin among the personal adherents of the Duke of Argyll, who at the opening of the new Parliament sent him to Newcastle with a letter recommending him to his protection in the petition proceedings brought by the Haldanes.[4] Newcastle, then intriguing against Argyll, made no final decision until the autumn of 1755 when, forced to admit Fox to the Administration, he became anxious to placate Fox's ally Argyll. Argyll wrote to Newcastle, October 1755:[5]

I am much obliged to your Grace for your declaring for Captain Campbell . . . that will heal a sore place I have felt for some time, and which, while Mr. Pelham lived, did not want a cure.

Meanwhile Campbell had shown himself willing to placate Newcastle by abstaining from voting on the Mitchell election. Admiral Boscawen wrote to Newcastle, 3 Mar. 1755:[6]

I have now with me a Scotsman who tells me, if your Grace will speak plain to his countrymen that dine with you to-day, many of them will not attend the committee to-night and in particular Sir Ludovick Grant, Captain Campbell and Mr. Mure who have agreed to go out of town to-morrow.

In politics Campbell was divided between his loyalty to Argyll and his dislike of Fox and Cumberland. When during the negotiations of March 1757 Fox proposed that 'the Duke of Newcastle should be minister for England . . . the Duke of Argyll for Scotland, professedly and independently',[7] Newcastle objected, and prepared a paper showing how the affiliations of Scots Members might be affected if Argyll were in or out of power.[8] He listed Campbell under those attached to Argyll 'while in power' but 'doubted if he will join Mr. Fox'. In the division of 2 May 1757 Campbell voted against Newcastle and Fox on the Minorca inquiry.[9]

In the 'Notes of the elections in Scotland' prepared for Newcastle in April 1760, the Stirlingshire situation was thus described:[10]

The present Member, Mr. Campbell, thinks himself sure of being re-elected, but there are some turbulent spirits in that county, and Mr. Campbell would find difficulty if the Duke of Argyll opposed him.

The evidence suggests that Campbell was about to transfer his allegiance to Bute. At the general election he was returned unopposed by agreement with Lawrence Dundas, and also took an active part in the Stirling Burghs election in support of Robert Haldane, against Argyll's candidate Admiral Holburne.[11]

In Parliament he remained an obscure Member. Although not listed by Fox among those favourable to the peace preliminaries in December 1762, he did not vote against them. Over-confident of Bute's support, he had by the summer of 1763 antagonized Dundas. Sir Harry Erskine wrote to Bute, 19 July 1763:[12]

Sir Lawrence . . . complains much of Mr. Campbell's conduct towards him. He says Mr. Campbell has boasted that he is master of the county in spite of Sir Lawrence and his friends, as sure as if he had it by burgage tenure . . . Sir Lawrence says that as he has £3,000 per annum in that county and Mr. Campbell but £300, and as a majority of the county has offered him the county in case of a vacancy it would be strange in him not to accept . . . That Mr. Campbell's boasting of his interest . . . has piqued him to convince him of his error. But that if Mr. Campbell should vacate his seat by the acceptance of an employment, if your Lordship desire him he will re-choose Mr. Campbell for the county for this Parliament. That your Lordship, he presumes, does not wish him to say that Mr. Campbell should represent that county as long as he lives. But if your Lordship shall desire it he will bring in Mr. Campbell for the borough of Richmond. That he flatters himself your Lordship can depend on him *at least as much as on Mr. Campbell* . . . Sir Lawrence informs me besides that Mr. Campbell's nearest relations and connexions all wish him to have an employment and to quit Parliament.

After the division of 15 Nov. 1763 on Wilkes, James Stuart Mackenzie commented:[13] 'Ardkinglass has not yet made his appearance; I am sorry for it.' Nonetheless when Isaac Barré was dismissed from the government of Stirling castle, Grenville gave the employment to Campbell 'to whom it was promised before'.[14] Naturally Campbell continued to support Grenville until his dismissal. Listed 'doubtful' by Rockingham in the summer of 1765, he voted against the Government on the repeal of the Stamp Act, 22 Feb. 1766. He was listed by Rockingham in November 1766 among the Bute connexion; and voted with Government on the land tax, 27 Feb. 1767, but not on nullum tempus in February 1768.

Although Dundas had apparently acquiesced in Campbell's re-election in 1763, the rivalry between the two interests in Stirlingshire had markedly increased, and at the 1768 general election the Dundases succeeded in wresting the county from Campbell.

In 1774 Campbell again opposed Thomas Dundas but was defeated;[15] he was also active in the Stirling Burghs election against the Dundas candidate.[16] Thereafter he seems to have abandoned political ambitions; throughout his parliamentary career of 20 years he is not recorded as having spoken in the House.

He died 21 Nov. 1788.

[1] Ramsay of Ochtertyre, i. 53–54. [2] *Mems. Sir James (Callander) Campbell* (Livingstone Campbell's nephew), 27, 71. [3] Argyll to Pelham, 5 Nov. 1753, Newcastle (Clumber) mss. [4] Add. 32737, f. 340. [5] Add. 32860, f. 262. [6] Add. 32853, f. 44. [7] Fox to Ilchester, 4 Mar. 1757, Ilchester, *Henry Fox*, ii. 36. [8] Add. 32995, f. 383. [9] Add. 33034, f. 232. [10] Add. 33049, f. 307. [11] Sir Harry Erskine to Bute, 30 Mar., 18 Apr. 1761, Bute mss. [12] Bute mss. [13] Mackenzie to W. Mure, 17 Nov. 1763, *Caldwell Pprs.* ii(2), p. 199. [14] Horace Walpole to Lord Hertford, 9 Dec. 1763. [15] Laprade, 7, 19. [16] Boswell, *Private Pprs.* x. 39–40, 46–47.

E.H.-G.

## CAMPBELL, James (1737–1805), of Tuerechan, Argyll.

STIRLING BURGHS    1780–22 July 1789

b. 16 Jan. 1737, 1st s. of James Campbell of Tuerechan, writer in Inverary, chamberlain of Argyll, by Elizabeth, da. of James Fisher of Durran, provost of Inverary; bro. of Archibald Campbell (q.v.). educ. Glasgow Univ. 1750. m. 16 July 1761, Jean, da. of John Campbell of Askomil, Argyll, 5s. 7da. suc. fa. 1760; and bro. in the Inverneil estate and as heritable usher of the white rod 1791. Kntd. 9 May 1788.
   Provost, Inverkeithing 1777–89.
   Ensign 30 Ft. 1755; lt. 60 Ft. 1756; capt. independent co. of ft. 1759; half pay 1763.

After his service in America,[1] Campbell seems to have lived in comparative obscurity until 1776 when, during his brother Archibald's absence abroad, he took charge of his electoral interests in Stirling Burghs, became provost of Inverkeithing in 1777,[2] and succeeded him as Member in 1780. In Parliament he consistently voted with every Administration: North, Shelburne, the Coalition, and the younger Pitt; and Robinson in January 1784 recognized that he would always support the party in power.[3]

He was returned in 1784 after a contest. He voted for parliamentary reform on 18 Apr. 1785, but did not vote on the Regency. There is no record of his having spoken in the House. When his brother Archibald, to whom he was under great obligation, returned from India in June 1789, James promptly vacated his seat in his favour.

He died 16 Mar. 1805.

[1] W. M. MacBean, *Biog. Reg. of St. Andrews Soc. of New York* (1922), i. no. 52. [2] W. Stephen, *Hist. Inverkeithing*, 227. [3] Laprade, 99.

E.H.-G.

## CAMPBELL, John (c.1693–1770), of Mamore, Dunbarton, and Coombe Bank, Kent.

| | |
|---|---|
| BUTESHIRE | 1713–1715 |
| ELGIN BURGHS | 7 Apr. 1715–1722 |
| | 25 Jan. 1725–1727 |
| DUNBARTONSHIRE | 1727–1761 |

b. c.1693, 1st s. of Hon. John Campbell, M.P.[S], of Mamore by Elizabeth, da. of John, 8th Lord Elphinstone [S]. m. 1720, Mary, da. of John, 2nd Lord Bellenden [S], 5s. 1da. suc. fa. 7 Apr. 1729, and cos. Archibald as 4th Duke of Argyll [S] 15 Apr. 1761; K.T. 7 Aug. 1765.
Ensign 3 Ft. Gds. 1710; capt.-lt. and lt-col. 1712; capt. and lt-col. 1715; col. 39 Ft. 1737–8; col. 21 Ft. 1738–52; maj.-gen. 1744; gov. Milford Haven 1746–61; lt.-gen. 1747; col. 2 Drag. 1752–d.; gov. Limerick Jan. 1761–d.; gen. 1765.
   Groom of the bedchamber 1727–61; P.C. 2 Jan. 1762; Scottish rep. peer 1761–d.

When Charles Townshend was intriguing to gain the leadership of Scottish affairs, his supporter John Dalrymple wrote to him, 5 Oct. 1759:[1]

General Campbell . . . has, I believe, no political views at all; he is a man of pleasure and his frequent topic is his astonishment at people's throwing away their lives in managing men and conducting measures . . . You used to think that he would be afraid of you taking a great part in this country and the measures concerning it out of his hands some future day. I believe he neither thinks of the country or its interests with these great views; he would rather see both the country and its measures at the devil than be so plagued with them.

Campbell owed his advancement to his cousins John, Duke of Argyll, and Archibald, Earl of Islay, who, on succeeding to the dukedom in 1743 treated Campbell as his heir. Elected for the fifth time for Dunbartonshire in 1754, he followed Argyll in supporting Newcastle's Administration and voted in its defence in the division on Minorca, 2 May 1757. He was Argyll's nominee for the governorship of Dumbarton castle in 1759 against Bute's nominee Lord Eglintoun,[2] and thus became involved in the Argyll-Bute quarrel of 1759–60, but was compensated with the governorship of Limerick.

Two days after his unopposed return for Dunbartonshire on 17 Apr. 1761, news arrived that by the death of Argyll on the 15th he had succeeded to the dukedom. His letter to Bute proposing candidates in the constituencies affected by the new situation was interpreted as an attempt to assume control of the 'viceroy's' interest. Gilbert Elliot wrote to Bute, May 1761:[3]

> It carries the most manifest marks of dotage and childish intoxication of new honours . . . I cannot help being persuaded that his Grace when advised by his real friends will drop all these vain pretensions.

An accommodation prevented any conflict with the easy-going Duke, whose politics thereafter followed those of his abler sons Lord Lorne and Lord Frederick Campbell (qq.v.). He died 9 Nov. 1770.

[1] Buccleuch mss. [2] Newcastle's memorandum for the King, 5 Dec. 1759, Add. 32899, f. 308; Newcastle to Hardwicke, 28 Feb. 1760, Add. 32902, f. 453. [3] Bute mss; see also Argyll to Bute, 6 May 1761, ibid.; Bute to Mure, 15 Apr. 1761, *Caldwell Pprs.* ii (1), p. 127.

E.H.-G.

## CAMPBELL, John (1695–1777), of Calder, Nairn, and Stackpole Court, Pemb.

| | |
|---|---|
| PEMBROKESHIRE | 1727–1747 |
| NAIRNSHIRE | 1747–1754 |
| INVERNESS BURGHS | 1754–1761 |
| CORFE CASTLE | 6 Dec. 1762–1768 |

*b.* 1695, 2nd s. of Sir Alexander Campbell, M.P. [S], of Calder, by Elizabeth, da. of Sir John Lort, 2nd Bt., of Stackpole Court and sis. and h. of Sir Gilbert, 3rd Bt. *educ.* L. Inn 1708; Clare, Camb. 1711. *m.* 30 Apr. 1726, Mary, da. and coh. of Lewis Pryse, M.P., of Gogerddan, Card., 3s. 3da. *suc.* mother in her Pembrokeshire estates 1714; and gd.-fa. Sir Hugh Campbell, M.P. [S] in his estates in Nairnshire, Inverness-shire and Argyll 11 Mar. 1716.
Ld. of Admiralty 1736–42, of Treasury 1746–54.

Campbell was related through his maternal grandmother to the Pelhams, and on his father's side to the Duke of Argyll. A year after his father's death in 1697 his mother inherited the Lort estates in Wales which became the family home. Campbell received an English education and resided little in Scotland.[1]

His parliamentary creed is summed up in a letter he wrote to Newcastle on 29 Sept. 1765, almost at the end of his active political life:[2]

> I have sat many years in Parliament during all which time it has been my opinion that though an honest man may often comply with things not quite agreeable to him, rather than give any advantage against an Administration which he approves, yet there are some things in which he must follow his own judgment such as he has, without regard to persons. In consequence of this opinion I did in some instances vote contrary to the inclinations of Sir Robert Walpole, of your Grace, and of your beloved brother, at the same time that I was firmly and warmly attached to those Administrations.

Nairnshire was not represented in the Parliament of 1754, and Campbell had not found a seat when Henry Pelham died. Newcastle, who wanted his place at the Treasury for Lord Dupplin, offered in exchange the place of Lyon King of Arms, worth £800 p.a. Campbell accepted on condition that the office was granted for the lives of his two younger sons; and Newcastle then recommended him for Inverness Burghs, where he was returned after a contest.[3]

Campbell was for many years a close friend of Henry Fox, and Newcastle, on joining Fox in October 1755, had him in mind for chancellor of the Exchequer. 'What think you of Campbell of Pembrokeshire?' he wrote to Hardwicke on 12 Oct.[4] 'He is an old corps man, but he is a Scotchman and a Campbell. The King will be uneasy.' The idea was soon dropped, nor did Fox press for a place for his friend. Campbell supported the Administration, voting with them even on the unpopular plate bill.[5]

During the debates on the trial of Admiral Byng, after Fox and Newcastle had left office, Campbell tried at first to fasten the responsibility for Byng's condemnation on the new Admiralty board, but, 'a most humane and honest man', unable to prefer 'the wrong side to the tender one' even for the sake of his friend Fox, he repudiated his former view and spoke for the bill to absolve members of the court martial from their oath of secrecy.[6] On 2 May 1757 he voted with Fox on the Minorca inquiry.

According to Horace Walpole, Campbell 'never forgave Pitt and the Grenvilles the share they had in overturning Sir Robert Walpole'. Certainly Campbell loathed Pitt, caustically referred to him as 'my lord Protector', and accused him of 'prevarication, self contradiction, and disregard of truth'. 'I have no very high opinion of his abilities as a minister', he wrote to Fox on 21 Oct. 1757;[7] and he blamed Pitt's 'mad ambition, mean popularity, pride, and the most intemperate passion' for the unsuccessful attacks on the French coast in 1758.[8]

During the Pitt-Newcastle Administration he grew weary of Parliament, and was unwilling to stand at the general election of 1761. Sir Harry Erskine wrote to Bute on 17 Mar.:[9]

> He is rather solicitous to retire to a corner in the country, than to sit in the House of Commons and see those who were mere children or at the university when he was in the Treasury, in high offices and making a figure in the House of Commons. But if your Lordship desire him he will accept of a seat for Inverness-shire, if it can be obtained. That is I presume he will accept of a seat, if he got a promise of somewhat lucrative. At least as that is the construction I put on those words . . .

On 21 Mar. Campbell placed himself and his family

at Bute's disposal—'however unwilling I am to come again into Parliament', he wrote,[10] '. . . I am much more unwilling to do anything displeasing to your Lordship.' His son Pryse was returned for Nairnshire, while he himself retired to Wales. But toward the end of 1762 Fox, anxious to have so good a friend in Parliament, arranged for his return at Corfe Castle.

When on 11 Feb. 1763 Sir John Philipps moved for a commission on public accounts, even the friends of Newcastle and Fox dared not oppose it: Campbell alone objected; and his was the 'single negative'.[11]

> Mr. Campbell of Pembrokeshire [reported West to Newcastle[12]] declared himself absolutely against the motion; that there had never been one of the kind that had not been made a job, first to obtain popularity and then preferments, and was against the question. Believed everything had been done honestly but that it was the nature of the war, the being principals in Germany, which he trusted we never should be again.

Campbell supported the Grenville Administration over general warrants—'I must confess', he wrote in retrospect on 3 Nov. 1765,[13] 'I have never yet been convinced by anything but *authority* . . . that general warrants, in the case of treasonable and seditious libels, are either illegal or inexpedient.' In December 1764 he sent through George Rice a message assuring Grenville of his support and offering to attend when 'any business of importance was expected to come on'.[14]

In July 1765 Rockingham listed Campbell as 'doubtful'. But on 29 Sept. 1765 he wrote to Newcastle:[15]

> If I was now able to attend the House of Commons, your Grace should find me . . . heartily and cheerfully supporting the King's Government conducted by your Grace and your friends, yet voting with those for whom I have far less esteem if questions were moved on which I have already declared my opinion, and not been convinced that it was mistaken.

Moreover he left his son Pryse free to choose his own line.

Incapacitated by a complaint which prevented his travelling, he remained at Stackpole Court. To Holland he wrote on 28 Jan. 1766:[16] 'I am glad Pitt has been too extravagant even for those who were grovelling in the dirt at his feet; glad I am of anything that may keep him from power.' And on 29 Apr.:[17]

> I do not wish a change, because I think frequent changes increase the weakness and confusion of this Government and country: and in truth I know not who to wish in their places. The appearance is very bad, but I resolve to make myself easy . . . I have wished myself in the House every time they have been overhauling what was done in former sessions, but I think that work is now pretty well finished.

Campbell does not seem to have attended the House again, and at the dissolution in 1768 withdrew from Parliament.

He died 6 Sept. 1777.

[1] G. Bain, *Hist Nairnshire*, 289–90. [2] Add. 32970, f. 103. [3] Leven to Chas. Mackie, 12, 23, 28, 30 Mar. 1754, Leven and Melville mss. SRO. [4] Add. 32860, f. 20. [5] West to Newcastle, 17 Mar. 1756, Add. 32863, f. 332. [6] Walpole, *Mems. Geo. II*, ii. 322–30. [7] Ilchester, *Letters to H. Fox*, 125. [8] Ibid. 135–6. [9] Bute mss. [10] Ibid. [11] Harris's 'Debates'. [12] Add. 32946, ff. 381–4. [13] *Letters to H. Fox*, 254–5. [14] Grenville's reply, 15 Dec. 1764, Grenville letter bk. [15] Add. 32970, f. 103. [16] *Letters to H. Fox*, 255–6. [17] Ibid. 257–8.

E.H.-G.

**CAMPBELL, John,** Mq. of Lorne (1723–1806), of Roseneath, Dunbarton.

GLASGOW BURGHS     26 Mar. 1744–1761
DOVER                      16 Jan. 1765–16 Dec. 1766

*bap.* June 1723, 1st surv. s. of John Campbell of Mamore (*d.*1770, q.v.), 4th Duke of Argyll [S]; bro. of Lords Frederick and William Campbell. *educ.* priv. sch. London.[1] *m.* 3 Mar. 1759, Elizabeth, da. of John Gunning of Castle Coote, co. Roscommon, Ireland, wid. of James, 6th Duke of Hamilton [S], 3s. 2da. From fa.'s succession as 4th Duke 15 Apr. 1761, styled Mq. of Lorne; *cr.* Baron Sundridge [G.B.] 16 Dec. 1766; *suc.* fa. as 5th Duke, 9 Nov. 1770.

2nd lt. 21 Ft. 1739, capt. 1741, brig. maj. 1743; lt.-col. 30 Ft. 1745–7; lt.-col. 42 Ft. 1749; adjutant-gen. [I] 1754; col. 1755; col. 56 Ft. 1755–57, 14 Drag. 1757–65; maj.-gen. 1759; lt.-gen. 1761; dep. c.-in-c. Scotland 1762–5; col. 1 Ft. 1765–82; c.-in-c. Scotland 1767–78; gen. 1778; col. 3 Ft. Gds. 1782–*d.*; f.m. 1796.

Campbell owed his advancement to Archibald, Duke of Argyll,[2] who, having secured his return for Glasgow Burghs, entirely directed his political conduct. In 1754 he was listed by Dupplin as a Government supporter. Extraordinarily handsome, Campbell in 1759 secured Argyll's consent to his marriage with a celebrated beauty, the widowed Duchess of Hamilton, thus uniting the Argyll and Hamilton interests during her son's minority. He was not personally involved in the Argyll-Bute dispute of 1759–60, and soon after George III's accession went abroad with his ailing wife for the winter.[3]

By the accession of his father as 4th Duke in April 1761, immediately before the Glasgow Burghs election, Campbell, now Marquess of Lorne, was disqualified, as the eldest son of a Scottish peer, from representing a Scottish constituency. When Bute excluded the new Duke from any share in the management of Scotland and offered Lorne neither an English seat nor any preferment (other than a temporary command in Scotland) the Marquess, thinking himself 'undervalued',[4] attached himself through Alexander Forrester (q.v.), a family friend, to the Duke of Bedford. Bute and Stuart Mackenzie (q.v.) further alienated him by their opposition to his stepson, the Duke of Hamilton, in the Douglas

Cause; but Lorne made no open declaration until Bute by his political intrigues in August-September 1763 violently antagonized Bedford. Lorne then submitted his claims to Bedford, who wrote to Welbore Ellis, secretary at war, 28 Nov. 1763:[5]

> As the Marquess of Lorne is thoroughly attached to the support of his Majesty's Government and extremely well intentioned to the present Administration, I cannot refuse interesting myself warmly in support of what he wishes, and I have the satisfaction to find his Majesty (to whom I have mentioned Ld. Lorne's desire of coming into Parliament, and of his and his father the Duke of Argyll's zeal for his service ...) very well disposed to show marks of favour to that family.

Lorne was disconcerted when his ingenuous father, disappointed by Bedford of a K.T., made a second application to Bute. He apologized to Bedford, 23 Jan. 1764:[6]

> Both myself and my brothers were totally ignorant of the step he has taken ... if we had known of it we should most earnestly have endeavoured to have dissuaded him from it as we have been all of us absolutely determined not to ask or expect any favour but by your Grace's intervention.

In his subsequent interview with Bedford, Lorne pressed for a British peerage for himself but got 'no encouragement to think of it'.[7]

In June Lorne secured from Grenville the Government interest at the Dover by-election, and, with the support of the Sackville and Yorke families, was returned unopposed in January 1765.[8] He is not known to have spoken in the House.

In May 1765 Grenville, having insisted with the King upon Stuart Mackenzie's dismissal, nominated Lorne his successor as lord privy seal for Scotland. Grenville's diary records, 23 May:[9]

> [Lord Lorne] was set out upon his journey to Scotland the day before and was fetched back express ... but declined the office in favour of Lord Frederick Campbell, his brother, but with all possible expressions of gratitude and attachment to Mr. Grenville.

When in July Grenville's Administration was dismissed, Lorne promptly wrote from Scotland renewing his professions to Grenville and Bedford,[10] and heartily concurred in his brother's decision to resign.[11] His loyalty was soon put to the test when, by the death of Sir Harry Erskine (q.v.), on 7 Aug., the colonelcy of the 1st Ft. (the Royals) fell vacant. According to Walpole, Lorne wrote to his brother-in-law Conway, now secretary of state, suggesting that although as a Bedford supporter he could ask nothing from the new Administration he would not refuse the King's offer of the regiment.[12] The evidence, however, supports Lorne's contention that 'he had not asked for the Royals, nor did he expect it'.[13] Rockingham, having consulted Conway

and Grafton, and obtained Cumberland's cordial consent, offered Lorne the regiment,[14] which he accepted but at once assured Grenville and Bedford that however 'extraordinary' his preferment might appear, he was 'not in the smallest degree obliged to any of the present Administration for it', but only to the King.[15] He wrote to Bedford, 6 Sept. 1765:[16]

> I hope your Grace could not suspect ... that I could think of joining any other persons in their public capacity however nearly I may lie otherwise connected with them ... I am and will remain as much attached to you with regard to my parliamentary conduct as any man of principle and conscience.

Lorne's appointment increased conjecture, already aroused by his father's acceptance of the K.T. from the new Administration. Lord George Sackville wrote to General Irwin, 14 Sept. 1765:[17]

> I ... look upon it as the second part of the Green Ribband, and I must now not be angry with his father for adorning his person since the son condescends to accept favours from Government in the particular situation in which his family stands relative to the late Administration ... What all this means I know not and we wait the event next session.

In the event Lorne and Lord Frederick remained attached to Bedford in opposition and voted against the repeal of the Stamp Act, 22 Feb. 1766, while their brother William adhered to the Rockinghams.

On the formation of the Chatham Administration, with Conway still in office and Stuart Mackenzie restored to the privy seal, Lorne, uneasy at the hostility between his wife and Mackenzie, discussed with William Mure (q.v.) in autumn 1766 a possible reconciliation with the Bute connexion.[18]

In November Bedford, during his negotiations with Chatham, included a peerage for Lorne among his terms for entering Administration.[19] When no agreement was reached Lorne, realizing that this might be his last chance before, by the death of his aged father, he became ineligible as a Scottish peer, applied directly to Chatham, who at once granted his request and thus 'took from the Duke of Bedford's scale the great Scottish interest of the Campbells'.[20] Lorne wrote to Bedford, 16 Dec.:[21]

> I am to kiss hands for a British peerage tomorrow. I own I should have had more satisfaction if I had owed this mark of his Majesty's favour to your Grace's interposition ... if it had been in your power. I hope therefore your Grace will not think I have done amiss to apply for it through the only channel by which in the present situation ... I thought it could be obtained.

In London the affair 'made a great noise and was universally blamed';[22] in Scotland it was welcomed as a step towards the reconciliation of the Argyll and Bute interests, and by February 1767 Lorne and Lord Frederick were known to be 'linked with Bute and his brother'.[23] Lorne sought to avoid entanglement in the continuing disputes between his Duchess and Mackenzie, and at the 1768 election gave the Argyll interest to Bute's son in Ayr Burghs.

Although despised by Walpole as 'sordidly covetous',[24] Lorne was generally considered an amiable, modest man without much force of personality,[25] who, backed by his astute wife and brother, usually achieved his ends by adroit diplomacy.

On succeeding to the dukedom he lived in magnificent style at Inveraray and became well known as an authority on agricultural improvement.[26]

He died 25 May 1806.

[1] Poss. Westminster (although unlisted); cf. John Campbell to Ld. Lovat, Aug. 1739, Sir W. Fraser, *Chiefs of Grant*, ii. 394. [2] Argyll to Duncan Forbes, 29 Nov. 1743, *More Culloden Pprs.* iii. 161–2. [3] H. Walpole to H. Mann, 1 Nov. 1760, 2 Jan. 1761. [4] Lorne to W. Mure, 27 Dec. 1766, *Caldwell Pprs.* ii.(2), p. 99. [5] Bedford mss 48, f. 190. [6] Ibid. 49, f. 34. [7] Bedford's endorsement on Lorne's letter of 23 Jan. [8] Grenville to Lorne, 18 June, and to Sir Joseph Yorke, 30 July 1764, Grenville letter bk.; Lorne to Grenville, 29 June, Grenville mss (JM). [9] *Grenville Pprs.* iii. 187; see also Walpole to Hertford, 25 May. [10] Lorne to Grenville, 16 July 1765, Grenville mss (JM); Lorne to Bedford, same date, Bedford mss 52, f. 62. [11] Lord F. Campbell to Grenville, 23 July 1765, Grenville mss (JM). [12] *Mems. Geo. III*, ii. 142. [13] James Abercrombie to Loudoun, 18 Sept. 1765, Loudoun mss. [14] Rockingham to Cumberland, bef. 13 Aug.; and Cumberland's reply, 23 Aug. 1765, Rockingham mss. [15] Lorne to Grenville, 6 Sept. 1765, Grenville mss (JM). [16] Bedford mss 52, f. 134. [17] *HMC Stopford-Sackville*, i. 102. [18] Mure to Mackenzie, 1 Dec. 1766, Caldwell mss (NLS); Lorne to Mure, 27 Dec. 1766, *Caldwell Pprs.* ii.(2), p. 99. [19] *Bedford Corresp.* iii. 359. [20] Walpole, *Mems. Geo. III*, ii. 291. [21] Bedford mss 54, f. 172. [22] Newcastle to Rockingham, 19 Dec. 1766, Add. 32978, f. 416. [23] W. Rouet to Mure, 10 Feb. 1767, *Caldwell Pprs.* ii.(2), p. 104. [24] Mure to Loudoun, 21 Feb. 1768, Loudoun mss; Bute to Mure, 3 May 1774, *Caldwell Pprs.* ii.(2), pp. 232–3. [25] *Mems. Geo. III*, i. 322. [26] Boswell, *Tour to the Hebrides*, 25 Oct. 1773; *Private Pprs.* xv. 225–6.

E.H.-G.

**CAMPBELL, John** (1755–1821), of Calder, Nairn; Stackpole Court, Pemb. and Llanvread, Card.

NAIRNSHIRE      18 Apr. 1777–May 1780
CARDIGAN BOROUGHS    12 June 1780–1796

*b.* 24 Apr. 1755, 1st s. of Pryse Campbell, and bro. of Alexander Campbell (qq.v.). *educ.* Eton 1763–7; Clare, Camb. 1772. *m.* 28 July 1789, Lady Isabella Caroline Howard, da. of Frederick, 5th Earl of Carlisle, 2s. *suc.* fa. 14 Dec. 1768 and gd.-fa. 6 Sept. 1777; *cr.* Baron Cawdor 21 June 1796.

'If my grandson sees with my eyes', wrote old John Campbell, 'nothing done here [at Stackpole Court] will make him insensible to the natural beauties of Calder, or slight that ancient, honourable and agreeable seat of the family.'[1] Brought up in Wales and England, young John knew little of Scotland when at the age of 21, and shortly before his grandfather's death, he was returned unopposed for Nairnshire.

In Parliament Campbell was a staunch supporter of North who in November 1778 asked him to second the Address.[2] 'The conduct of America', said Campbell, 'made vigorous measures necessary and unavoidable . . . however different opinions may have been respecting America, yet respecting France there could be but one opinion.'[3] This is the only time he is known to have spoken in the House. In 1777 he helped to raise a regiment of foot in South Wales, the 75th (Prince of Wales's) Regiment.[4]

As Nairnshire would not be represented in the next Parliament, Campbell had to find another seat. He thought of contesting Inverness-shire,[5] but a better opportunity occurred in May 1780 when Thomas Johnes vacated Cardigan Boroughs and transferred to Radnorshire. Campbell thereupon vacated Nairnshire, and was returned for Cardigan.

At the general election he was re-elected without opposition, and supported North to the end. On 18 Feb. 1783 he voted against Shelburne's peace preliminaries; did not vote on Fox's East India bill; and was marked absent by Robinson and Stockdale in their lists of January and March 1784. Robinson noted against Cardigan in the survey made in the second week of December 1783:

Mr. John Campbell is much inclined to support Government and it is thought might throughout be classed hopeful; was once strongly attached to Lord North. If he should desire to again stand for this place, might come [in], but had views on Pembrokeshire, and has a good interest in Scotland for the shire of Nairn which elects at the next election.

Campbell retained his Cardigan seat, and brought in his brother Alexander for Nairn, and in May 1784 both were listed by William Adam 'Opposition'. But Campbell did not vote against Pitt's Irish propositions in May 1785, and supported Administration on Richmond's fortifications plan, February 1786; but, after having been drawn into Lord Carlisle's circle, voted with Opposition on the Regency.

He died 1 June 1821.

[1] G. Bain, *Hist. Nairnshire*, 289. [2] North to the King, 10 Nov. 1778, Fortescue, iv. 215. [3] 26 Nov. 1778, Almon, xi. 3. [4] Ld. G. Germain to the King, 22 Dec. 1777; the King to North, 2 Jan. 1778; North to the King, 3 Jan.; the King to North, 3 Jan. 1778; Fortescue, iii. 518; iv. 2–4. [5] SRO Bught mss 7/204.

E.H.-G.

**CAMPBELL, Pryse** (1727–68), of Calder, Nairn; Stackpole Court, Pemb. and Llanvread, Card.

INVERNESS-SHIRE      1754–1761
NAIRNSHIRE          1761–1768
CARDIGAN BOROUGHS    24 Mar.–14 Dec. 1768

*b.* 1727, 1st s. of John Campbell of Calder (*d.*1777, q.v.). *educ.* Clare, Camb. 1745. *m.* 20 Sept. 1752, Sarah, da. and coh. of Sir Edmund Bacon, M.P., 6th Bt. of Garboldisham, Norf., 4s. 3da. Ld. of Treasury Aug. 1766–*d.*

Intended from youth for a parliamentary career, Pryse Campbell was mentioned as a possible candidate for Inverness-shire as early as December 1746.[1] When he came of age, large estates in Nairnshire and Inverness-shire were transferred to him by his father, who retained a life-rent interest.[2] In 1753 Argyll, anxious to secure seats for Pryse and his father, proposed that one of them should replace Lord Hyndford's brother James Carmichael in Linlithgow Burghs.[3] But the prospect of a costly contest with Lawrence Dundas (q.v.) deterred Campbell from accepting; eventually, after considerable negotiation, Pryse Campbell was returned unopposed for Inverness-shire.

In Parliament Pryse was at first regarded merely as an appendage of his father. But he soon showed his independence. While friendly with Fox, Pryse did not share his father's dislike of Pitt, and voted with him on the Minorca inquiry, 2 May 1757.[4] During the negotiations of 1757 Newcastle, while counting John Campbell among his personal supporters, listed Pryse among the Scots attached to the 'last ministry or Mr. Pitt'.[5]

Under the Newcastle-Pitt Coalition Pryse Campbell maintained his independence. In February and March 1759 he voted for allowing the free importation of Irish cattle, despite the petitions of his Inverness-shire constituents: on this he differed from his father and the majority of Scots Members, and incurred the displeasure of Argyll. Isolated from his friends, he sought to recommend himself to his kinsman Newcastle, to whom he wrote, 24 June 1759:[6]

A young man is not allowed to think for himself and your Grace may have been told that I am attached to a faction and will blindly follow wherever that leads, and though I have a better opinion of my own sense and honesty it is from my actions your Grace should form yours.

He returned to the Scottish fold over the militia, was a member of the committee nominated to prepare the bill, but is not mentioned as having spoken in the debates.

His cattle bill vote was not, however, forgotten. In February 1761 he learned from his friend Sir Harry Erskine that Argyll had 'put an absolute negative' upon him as candidate for Inverness-shire.[7] When George Ross (q.v.) suggested to Pryse that the 'offence' of his cattle bill vote would be 'got over' if he and his father procured for Simon Fraser (q.v.) a seat in Parliament or a colonial governorship,[8] Pryse categorically refused to make any such bargain.[9] When Argyll proved adamant and Newcastle did not intervene, Pryse and his father placed themselves unreservedly under Bute's direction,[10] but neither was acceptable to the Inverness-shire electors; and Pryse, replacing his brother Alexander as candidate, was returned for Nairnshire. He supported the Bute Administration,

and was listed by Fox as favourable to the peace preliminaries.

He voted with the Opposition on general warrants (6, 15 and 18 Feb. 1764), but was counted by Administration as a friend, and voted with them against the repeal of the cider tax.[11] A vehement critic of the Regency bill, he proposed provisos disqualifying any Regent who should marry a Catholic, or marry without the consent of Parliament; on 10 May 1765 he spoke in support of re-committing the bill, and was a teller in the subsequent division.[12]

Listed 'pro' by Rockingham in July 1765, he supported the repeal of the Stamp Act; but on 18 April 1766 voted against Dowdeswell's proposal for a new window tax.[13] In the militia debate of 22 Apr., Campbell intervened on behalf of a Scottish militia 'which he threatened to move next year'.[14] In the Chatham Administration he was appointed a lord of the Treasury; even so he did not vote on the land tax on 27 Feb. 1767.

As Nairnshire would not be represented in the next Parliament, Campbell thought at first of contesting Inverness-shire;[15] but in the event his Welsh interest secured his return for Cardigan Boroughs. In the new session he again took an independent line over Wilkes. At a meeting on 12 May 1768 of Government men of business he opposed the immediate expulsion of Wilkes.[16] By November his health, always indifferent, had broken down, and he was too ill to attend the Treasury Board.[17] He died 14 Dec. 1768.

[1] Ludovick Grant to H. Pelham, 31 July 1747, Pelham mss. [2] SRO, Bught mss 7/204. [3] Argyll to Pelham, 15 Oct. 1753, Pelham mss. [4] Add. 33034, f. 218. But he is not mentioned in Fox's list (Devonshire mss), nor in that in Add. 33034, f. 232. [5] Add. 32995, f. 383. [6] Add. 32892, f. 207. [7] Campbell to Bute, 18 Feb. 1761, Bute mss. [8] Pryse Campbell to Bute, 21 Feb. 1761; John Campbell to Bute, 14 Mar. 1761, ibid. [9] John Campbell to Newcastle, 20 Feb. 1761, Add. 32919, f. 153. [10] Pryse Campbell to Bute, 16 Apr. 1761, Bute mss. [11] Harris's 'Debates'. [12] Grenville to the King, 11 May, Fortescue, i. 87–91; Harris's 'Debates'. [13] Onslow to Newcastle, 18 Apr., Add. 32974, ff. 425–6. [14] Harris's 'Debates'. [15] T. Whateley to Geo. Grenville, 30 July 1766, Grenville mss (JM). [16] Newcastle to Rockingham, 16 May 1768, Add. 32990, f. 71. [17] Grafton to the King, 29 Nov. 1768, Fortescue, ii. 59.

E.H.-G.

**CAMPBELL, Robert** (c.1721–90), of Finab and Monzie, Perth and Inverawe, Argyll.

ARGYLLSHIRE    12 Dec. 1766–Nov. 1771

> b. c.1721, 1st s. of Col. Alexander Campbell of Finab by his 2nd w. Mary, da. of Sir John Home, 2nd Bt., of Blackadder, Berwicks. educ. Edinburgh Univ. c.1736. m. 26 Mar. 1749, Susanna, yst. da. of Charles Erskine of Tinwald, lord justice clerk, 1s. suc. fa. c.1741.
> Ensign 17 Ft. 1739; capt. 42 Ft. c.1742; ret. c.1749. Receiver gen. of Scottish customs 1771–d.; trustee for fisheries and manufactures 1776.

Campbell's father, a distinguished soldier, was a kinsman of the Duke of Argyll and the Earl of

Breadalbane, for both of whom he had acted as manager of their estates.[1]

During the seven years' war Robert Campbell served as major, and subsequently lieutenant-colonel of the Fencible Men of Argyll, a regiment raised by the Duke of Argyll. On its disbandment in 1763 he retired, purchased the estate of Inverawe from his niece Janet Campbell, and lived near Edinburgh on his estate of Drummore. Alexander Carlyle records:[2]

> Our neighbourhood was enriched by the residence of a very valuable man, Lieutenant-Colonel Robert Campbell of Finab, a man of first-rate understanding and ability. He had been in the Duke of Cumberland's war, and was captain of grenadiers in the 42nd regiment, but had been much disgusted with the Duke of Cumberland, and not having good health, he left the army . . . He was very sociable and liked golf . . . The Colonel had read very little but he had taken a more comprehensive view of men and affairs than almost any person I ever knew.

In the autumn of 1766 Campbell was selected by his former commander, the Marquess of Lorne, to replace Lord William Campbell as member for Argyll.[3] He divided with Administration on the land tax, 27 Feb. 1767; re-elected in 1768, he uniformly supported Government but is not known to have spoken in the House.

On the death in September 1771 of Sir Robert Murray, receiver general of customs, Mrs. Anderson, landlady of the British Coffee House, reported in her newsletter to her Scottish customers:[4] 'There will be scrambling for his place. Sir Lawrence Dundas has asked for it, we suppose for his brother.' But on 9 Oct.: 'The place of receiver general is given to the Argyll interest and is to be divided between Mr. Edmonstone of Duntreath and Col. Campbell of Finab who is to go out of Parliament; it is worth £1,500 and is burthened with £200 a year to a Mr. Stewart.'[5]

Campbell spent the rest of his life in Scotland, a very rich man, exercising considerable influence in the Argyll interest in Perthshire and Argyll.[6] He died 7 Apr. 1790.

[1] Campbell and Paton, *Clan Campbell*, i. 90–91, 157; iii. 31. [2] *Autobiog.* 385. [3] John Campbell of Innellan to Ld. Loudoun, 14 Oct. 1766, Loudoun mss. [4] Newsletter of 28 Sept. 1771, Loudoun mss. [5] Newsletter of 9 Oct. 1771, ibid. [6] *Pol. State of Scotland 1788*, pp. 45, 272.

E.H.-G.

## CAMPBELL, Lord William (c.1732–78).

ARGYLLSHIRE 17 Jan. 1764–July 1766

*b.* c.1732, 4th s . of John Campbell of Mamore (*d.*1770, q.v.), 4th Duke of Argyll [S]; bro. of John Campbell, Lord Lorne and Lord Frederick Campbell (qq.v.). *m.* 17 Apr. 1763, Sarah, da. and coh. of Ralph Izard of Burton or Fairspring plantation, St. George's, S. Carolina, 1s. 2da.

Lt. R.N. 1760; cdr. Jan. 1762; capt. Aug. 1762.
Gov. Nova Scotia 1766–73, South Carolina 1773–6.

During the latter part of his service in the seven years' war Campbell commanded H.M.S. *Nightingale*, based on Charleston, South Carolina, where he married a planter's daughter, 'esteemed one of the most considerable fortunes in the province'.[1] On his return home, late in 1763, he was nominated for the family seat in Argyllshire, and supported Grenville's Administration. Influenced by his Carolina connexions, he differed from his brothers Lorne and Lord Frederick on American affairs and shared the views of his brother-in-law H. S. Conway. He presumably voted with the Rockingham Administration on the repeal of the Stamp Act. He vacated his seat on being appointed, shortly before the Administration fell, governor of Nova Scotia.

In 1773, through the influence of his brother, the Duke of Argyll, Lord William was transferred to the governorship of South Carolina. When he reached Carolina in June 1773 the provincial congress and its committees had virtually displaced royal government. Personally popular, he sought at first to placate the revolutionary leaders, many of whom were his wife's connexions, but soon found the situation beyond his control. When the committee of safety, having obtained proof of Campbell's negotiations for a rising of back country loyalists, considered a proposal 'to take the governor into custody', Campbell dissolved the assembly and secretly went aboard a man-of-war in Charleston harbour. After strong points commanding his anchorage had been captured by the rebels, Campbell set sail on 10 Jan. 1776 to join the expedition under Clinton, intended for the reduction of the Southern colonies. On the junction with Sir Peter Parker's fleet, Campbell transferred to the flagship *Bristol* on which he served as a volunteer in the abortive attack on Charleston, and in the action at Sullivan's Island on 28 June 1776 received 'a contusion in his side'.[2]

After joining Howe's forces on Staten Island, New York, in August, Campbell left for England, arriving in December 1776. In March 1778 he was appointed to command a new ship, the *Lion*, but died at Southampton 4 Sept. 1778 of 'a painful and lingering consumption which the physicians thought proceeded from the wounds he received on Sullivan's island'.[3]

[1] *S.C. Hist. & Gen. Mag.* ii. 234–5. [2] For details of Campbell's activities in S. Carolina see E. McGrady, *S.C. in the Revolution*. [3] Mrs. Daniel Blake's letter, 5 Jan. 1779, quoted *S.C. Hist. and Gen. Mag.* ii. 235, n. 3. See also Horace Walpole to Lord Harcourt, 17 Sept. 1778.

E.H.-G.

**CAMPBELL,** *see also* **HUME CAMPBELL** *and* **MURE CAMPBELL**

**CAPEL** (afterwards **CAPEL CONINGSBY**), **George,** Visct. Malden (1757–1839).

WESTMINSTER     20 Apr. 1779–1780
LOSTWITHIEL     4 June 1781–1784
OKEHAMPTON     27 Apr. 1785–1790
RADNOR BOROUGHS  21 May 1794–4 Mar. 1799

*b.* 13 Nov. 1757, o.s. of William, 4th Earl of Essex by his 1st w. Frances, da. and coh. of Sir Charles Hanbury Williams (q.v.). *educ.* Westminster 1766–74; Corpus Christi, Camb. 1775. *m.* (1) 1786, Sarah, da. of Henry Bazett, wid. of Edward Stephenson, *s.p.*; (2) 1838, Catherine, da. of Edward Stephens, carver and gilder, *s.p. suc.* gd.-mother, Lady Frances Hanbury Williams (née Coningsby) 20 Dec. 1781, and took add. name of Coningsby; *suc.* fa. 4 Mar. 1799.

Malden's father, a nephew and political follower of the Duke of Bedford, being chronically in financial difficulties, relied on the royal bounty; in 1779 he had, among other things, a secret service pension of £900 p.a. Malden was returned for Westminster unopposed, but what expenses there were were probably paid by Government. The *Public Ledger* wrote about him: 'From the conduct and dependence of his father, we may presume that he will vote constantly with the ministry.' So he did in each of the five divisions for which lists are available between April 1779 and the dissolution. He did not stand at the general election of 1780. A man of fashion and a favourite of the Prince of Wales, he brought about the Prince's acquaintance with Mrs. Robinson, his own mistress.[1] Possibly it was not till the affair resulted in a scandal that the King learnt of it; for on 4 June 1781 Malden was returned on a vacancy at Lostwithiel, a borough which the Government leased from Edgcumbe, paying also for re-elections.[2] Next Malden went with the Duke of Gloucester to Bruges, where, wrote George Selwyn to Lord Carlisle, 18 June 1781, they 'passed two days with the Emperor' [Joseph II].[3] And on the 21st: 'I believe that his Imperial Majesty said very little of any importance *à nos deux vagabonds*, and the journey was made more out of ostentation than anything else.'[4] On 28 Aug. 1781 the King wrote to North:[5]

> My eldest son got last year into a very improper connexion with an actress and woman of indifferent character through the *friendly* assistance of Ld. Malden. A multitude of letters passed which she has threatened to publish unless he in short bought them of her . . . I have thought it right to authorize the getting them from her . . .

At the cost of £5,000 he got his son 'out of this shameful scrape'.

In Parliament Malden's attendance and voting were again most regular: in each of the six divisions, December 1781—15 Mar. 1782, his name appears on the Government side. He did not vote on Shelburne's peace preliminaries, 18 Feb. 1783, and in March 1783 was listed by Robinson 'abroad'; and when Fox was whipping up his friends before the opening of the session, he sent to the Duke of Manchester, ambassador in Paris, a letter for Malden 'whose direction I do not know'.[6] Malden returned and voted for Fox's East India bill; and continued with the Opposition. In 1784 he stood on the interest of the Duke of Bedford at Okehampton; went down with Robert Palmer, the Duke's estate agent; but met there with opposition and unexpected defeat. He immediately went back to Paris, as is shown by letters addressed to him there by Palmer in April and May 1784. When on 27 Apr. 1785 he was seated on petition, Palmer had to urge him 'to come immediately to England' to take his seat; and when in July he was 'very much wanted' for the action brought in his name and Minchin's (q.v.) against the mayor of Okehampton for a false return, he was again—or perhaps still—abroad. The first division in which his name appears is on the Regency. There is no record of his having spoken in the House before 1790.

He died 23 Apr. 1839.

[1] See H. Walpole, *Last Jnls*, ii. 350; and A. Storer to Ld. Carlisle, 28 June 1781, *HMC Carlisle*, 508–9. [2] Laprade, 58–59. [3] *HMC Carlisle*, 500. [4] Ibid. 504. [5] Fortescue, v. 269 (date corrected from original). See also Bessborough, *Georgiana*, 290. [6] *HMC 8th Rep.* pt. 2 (1881), p. 138a.

L.B.N.

**CAREW,** *see* **POLE CAREW**

**CAREY, Walter** (1685–1757), of West Sheen, Surr.

HELSTON     1722–1727
DARTMOUTH  1727–27 Apr. 1757

*b.* 17 Oct. 1685, 1st s. of Walter Carey of Everton, Beds. by Annabella, da. of Sir William Halford. *educ.* New Coll. Oxf. 1704. *m.* (1) c.1716, Elizabeth, da. of Anthony Stuart, M.P., of London, wid. of John Jeffreys, M.P., and mother of John Jeffreys (q.v.), *s.p.*; (2) 18 May 1738, Elizabeth, da. and coh. of Anthony Collins of Baddow Hall, Essex, *s.p. suc.* fa. 1714.

M.P. [I] 1731–*d.*

Clerk of the Council extraordinary 1717–29; ordinary 1729–*d.*; surveyor gen. to Prince of Wales 1723–5; warden of the mint 1725–7; ld. of Trade 1727–30; sec. to ld. lt. [I] 1730–7; P.C. [I] 1731; clerk of the Green Cloth 1738–*d.*

In 1754 Carey was returned for Dartmouth on the Government interest. He was then nearing the end of his career as a placeman, and no longer of consequence in Parliament.

He died 27 Apr. 1757.

J.B.

**CARHAMPTON, Earl of,** *see* **LUTTRELL, Henry Lawes,** *and* **LUTTRELL, Simon**

**CARHAMPTON, Visct.,** *see* **LUTTRELL, Simon**

**CARMARTHEN, Mq. of,** *see* **OSBORNE, Francis Godolphin**

**CARNAC, John** (?1720–1800), of Cams Hall, nr. Fareham, Hants.

LEOMINSTER    6 Feb. 1768–1774

b. ?1720, s. of Peter Carnac of Dublin, of Huguenot extraction. *educ.* Trinity, Dublin 15 May 1736, aged 15. *m.* (1) 7 Nov. 1765, Elizabeth (*d.* Oct. 1767), da. of Rev. W. Woollaston, *s.p.*; (2) 20 July 1769, Elizabeth, da. of Thomas Rivett, M.P., *s.p.*
2nd lt. 4 Marines 1739, lt. 1745; lt. 39 Ft. 1754; capt. Bengal army 1758; maj. 1760; brig.-gen. (local) 1764; col. 1765; res. Jan. 1767.
Member of the council at Bombay 1776–9.

Carnac went out to India with the 39th Foot in 1754, and when the regiment was sent home in 1758 he transferred to the East India Company's service. He became closely connected with Robert Clive (q.v.) and left India with him in 1760, but returned from St. Helena on receiving the news that he had been promoted by the Company and appointed military adviser to the Bengal council. In 1760 when he took up the command of the army at Patna he referred to Clive as 'the person to whom I owe everything'[1] and Clive after his return to England continued to support his cause. Carnac conducted two successful campaigns, but fell foul of Governor Vansittart (q.v.), on whose complaint he was dismissed by the Company in January 1764, but he was reinstated two months later. Clive wrote confidential letters to him, and as Clive's attorney he handled the Indian side of the dispute with the directors about Clive's 'jagir' in 1763. In 1764, when Clive was appointed governor, Carnac was made a member of the select committee and was closely associated with Clive throughout his governorship, returning home with him in February 1767, when he resigned the service. In 1765 he was given presents to the total of £32,000 by the Mogul and the Rajah of Benares, when they made peace with the Company. Clive, though opposing the presents taken by others about this time, strongly pressed the directors to permit Carnac to accept these sums since 'I found him the only officer of rank who had resisted the temptations to which, by his station, he was constantly subject, of acquiring an immense fortune'.[2]
On his return to England he purchased estates in Hampshire. He was determined to enter Parliament, and willing to go 'as far as £4000'[3] for a seat.

'He is a character that will reflect honour upon his friends' wrote John Walsh (q.v.) to Clive, 25 Nov. 1767.[4] Through Walsh Carnac seems to have met Chase Price (q.v.),[5] on whose interest he was returned unopposed for Leominster at the by-election in February 1768, and again at the general election. In Parliament Carnac voted with the Opposition, following Clive, whom he also supported at East India House. His speeches in Parliament were almost invariably on East India affairs. On 3 May 1773 he declared:

> I have not a shilling that causes me to blush. There should not be an universal brand of infamy put on every person who has been in India. Had I been rapacious I might have had four times the fortune I have.[6]

On 21 May 1773 he defended Clive, referring to his own special knowledge of the events discussed.[7] He gave evidence on several occasions before the select committee of 1772–3.
By the beginning of 1773 Carnac was seriously embarrassed financially owing to failure to have his fortune remitted to England; and on 6 Feb. Clive earnestly begged Warren Hastings to use his influence to 'get a part or the whole of his fortune sent him by every opportunity'.[8] Francis Sykes (q.v.) wrote on 20 Dec. 1774 that Carnac's 'circumstances are greatly shattered owing chiefly to the death of Francis Lister [in Bengal] who owed him a great deal of money'.[9] In 1774 Clive recommended him for the Bombay council, to which he was appointed in 1776 (a measure forced on the directors by a demand made in the general court by a group of his friends),[10] returning to India with the prospect of succeeding to the governorship. But, in spite of attempts by the second Lord Clive to save him,[11] he was dismissed on 10 Apr. 1780 for taking part in the convention of Wargaon with the Mahrattas in 1779. Nevertheless Carnac remained in Bombay for the rest of his life, selling his English estates in 1783.
He died at Bangalore 29 Nov. 1800.

[1] Carnac to Clive, 15 June 1760, Clive mss. [2] *Reports from Commons Committees 1715–1801*, iii. 392. [3] Geo. Clive to Ld. Clive, 17 Oct. 1767, Clive mss. [4] Ibid. [5] Walsh to Ld. Clive, 20 Nov. 1767, ibid. [6] Brickdale's 'Debates'. [7] Cavendish's 'Debates', Egerton 248, p. 341. [8] Add. 29131, f. 98. [9] F. Sykes to Warren Hastings, Add. 29135, ff. 393–5. [10] Court Bk. 84, 18 Mar. 1776. [11] Clive to North, 16 Jan. 1780, Clive mss.

L.S.S.

**CARNARVON, Mq. of,** *see* **BRYDGES**

**CARNEGIE, Sir David,** 4th Bt. (1753–1805), of Southesk.

ABERDEEN BURGHS    1784–1790
FORFARSHIRE          1796–25 May 1805

*b.* 22 Nov. 1753, 1st s. of Sir James Carnegie, 3rd Bt. (q.v.). *educ.* Eton 1765–9; St. Andrews; Ch. Ch. Oxf. 1771; Grand Tour. *m.* 30 Apr. 1783, Agnes Murray, da. of Andrew Elliot of Greenwells, Roxburgh, lt. gov. of N.Y. 1779–83 (bro. of Sir Gilbert Elliot, 3rd Bt. q.v.), 2s. 1oda. *suc.* fa. 30 Apr. 1765.

A boy of twelve when his father died, Carnegie was brought up under the guardianship of his mother and a number of trustees, including Sir Alexander Ramsay Irvine (q.v.), who completed the legal and financial business connected with the purchase of the Southesk forfeited estates, sold Pittarrow to his uncle George, a returned Jacobite, and by further land transactions paid off the entire debt.[1]

Ambitious from boyhood of 'restoring his family', he bought up former Southesk properties, selling some at a high profit,[2] and, having consolidated the estates of the ancient earldom, laid claim to the forfeited title, but dropped his case in 1782, when his English counsel advised that, although descended from a collateral branch, not attainted, he had no right to the forfeited honour.[3]

Active in Forfar and Kincardineshire affairs, and determined to increase his family prestige by entering Parliament, he unsuccessfully opposed Adam Dummond in Aberdeen Burghs in 1780 when Robinson counted both candidates 'friends'. 'A very pretty young man', according to Boswell, he was on friendly terms with Sir Lawrence Dundas, Lord Eglintoun, and other opponents of Henry Dundas.[4] Closely connected from 1783 with his wife's cousin Sir Gilbert Elliot and her sister's husband Lord Cathcart, he stood in 1784 for both Forfarshire and Aberdeen Burghs as Opposition candidate, although Robinson had previously expected him to support Pitt's Administration.[5] Defeated in Forfarshire but returned for Aberdeen Burghs, he voted against Pitt over the Irish commercial propositions, May 1785, and on the Regency, December 1788. Although no speech of his is reported in this Parliament, his attempt to speak on one occasion made him the butt of Dempster's ridicule. 'Mr. Speaker', began Sir David, 'I conceive, I conceive, I conceive', and could get no further. Dempster interposed: 'The honourable gentleman has conceived three times and has brought forth nothing. I therefore conceive we ought to be troubled no more with his abortive conceptions.'[6]

Carnegie died 25 May 1805.

[1] Sir W. Fraser, *Carnegies of Southesk*, i. 210 et seq., 215. [2] Ibid. 223. [3] Ibid. 224. Cf. Geo. Stewart's letter of Jan. 1772, p. 215. [4] Boswell, *Private Pprs.* xiv. 31, 222. [5] Laprade, 98. [6] J. Fergusson, *Letters of G. Dempster to Sir Adam Fergusson*, xix–xx, quoting A. Lowson, *Portrait Gallery of Forfar Notables.*

E.H.-G.

**CARNEGIE, Sir James,** 3rd Bt. (1715–65), of Pittarrow, Kincardine.

KINCARDINESHIRE    1741–30 Apr. 1765

*b.* 1715, 1st s. of Sir John Carnegie, 2nd Bt., by Mary, da. of Sir Thomas Burnett, 3rd Bt., of Leys, Aberdeen. *educ.* Glasgow Univ. 1730. *m.* 5 July 1752, Christian, da. and coh. of David Doig of Cookston, Angus, 4s. 2da. *suc.* fa. 3 Apr. 1729.
  Capt. 21 Ft. 1744; ret. 1755.
  Ld. lt. Kincardine 1746–d.

James Carnegie by the death in 1730 of his cousin, the attainted 5th Earl of Southesk, became heir male of the Southesk family, whose forfeited estates had been purchased by the York Buildings Company.

Directed in his political conduct by one ambition, the restoration of the Southesk title and estates, he consistently supported every Administration. He served at Fontenoy and returned with Cumberland's army to suppress the '45 rebellion. Although his brother was engaged in the Stuart cause, Carnegie's loyalty was so unquestioned that he was appointed lord lieutenant of Kincardine in April 1746. In 1748 he secured from the York Buildings Company a lease of the Southesk estates of Kinnaird, to the improvement of which he devoted himself after his return from army service in 1749.

In Pelham's election lists of 1754, Carnegie was classed as 'pro', 'supported by the Jacobite interest', and opposed by 'another Whig'; but when Argyll and Lord Milton secured for him Government support, his opponent Sir Alexander Ramsay Irvine withdrew and Carnegie was re-elected.[1] After leaving the army in 1755, Carnegie seemed wary of identifying himself with any particular political group. He was absent from the division of 2 May 1757 on the Minorca inquiry, and during the negotiations of 1757 Newcastle listed him among the Scots attached neither to Argyll nor himself, who were 'not to be relied on at present but to be treated with'.[2] Though not a leader in the Scottish militia agitation, he was nominated a member of the parliamentary committee to prepare the bill. Returned unopposed in 1761, Carnegie supported the Bute Administration on the peace preliminaries, 9 and 10 Dec. 1762, sending to Milton a full account of the debates in both Lords and Commons. 'This great, and I daresay unexpected, majority has given liberty to his Majesty, power to his minister and peace to his people—I hope even domestic peace . . . The Sons of Cakes have been steady.'[3]

In 1763 Carnegie achieved his goal. A bill introduced by Lord Panmure's friend Alexander Forrester passed both Houses empowering the court of session to sell those parts of the forfeited estates of Panmure, Southesk and Earl Marischal which had been leased by the York Buildings Company to Sir Archibald Grant and Alexander Garden of Troup (q.v.). The auction took place in Edinburgh on 20 Feb. 1764, and Carnegie and Panmure, both Government supporters, were thus absent from the division on general warrants on 18 Feb. The *Scots Magazine* described the scene in the crowded Parliament House:

> The Earl Marischal, the Earl of Panmure and Sir James Carnegie of Pitarrow, heir male of the family of Southesk, were there in person, attended by some of their friends; and each purchased what had formerly belonged to his family at the upset price, nobody offering against them. The people in the galleries could scarce forbear expressing their joy by acclamations.

To meet the purchase price of £36,870, Carnegie sold certain of his lands, and exchanged others for Panmure holdings, to form a compact estate.[4] But before negotiations were complete, he died of an apoplexy at Stamford, 30 Apr. 1765, while on his way home to Scotland after the parliamentary session.

[1] See Pelham mss. for Pelham's lists of 21 Mar. 1754 amended by Argyll; Add. 32995, f. 190 et seq., State of Elections in Scotland, 5 Apr. 1754. [2] Add. 32995, f. 383, undated. [3] Sir W. Fraser, *Carnegies of Southesk*, i. 208–9. [4] For details, see *Carnegies of Southesk*, i. 210 et seq.

E.H.-G.

## CARPENTER, George, 3rd Baron Carpenter [I] (1723–62), of Homme House, nr. Hereford.

TAUNTON 1754–9 Mar. 1762

*b.* 26 Aug. 1723, o.s. of George, 2nd Baron Carpenter [I], by Elizabeth, da. of David Petty of Wanstead, Essex. *m.* 23 Mar. 1748, Frances, da. of Sir Robert Clifton, 5th Bt., of Clifton, Notts., 3s. 3da. *suc.* fa. 12 July 1749; *cr.* Earl of Tyrconnel [I] 1 May 1761.

Carpenter stood in 1754 for Weobley on his own interest against that of Lord Weymouth, and was defeated. He was returned unopposed for Taunton on the interest of his brother-in-law Lord Egremont, whose politics he followed. Hence in the new reign he adhered to Bute, through whom he obtained his earldom.[1]

He died 9 Mar. 1762.

[1] Carpenter to Bute, 16 Mar. 1761, Bute mss.

L.B.N.

## CARPENTER, George, 2nd Earl of Tyrconnel [I] (1750–1805), of Homme House, nr. Hereford.

SCARBOROUGH 28 July 1772–1796
BERWICK-UPON-TWEED 1796–1802

*b.* 30 June 1750, 1st s. of George, 3rd Baron Carpenter [I], 1st Earl of Tyrconnel [I] (q.v.). *educ.* Westminster 1764–5; Ch. Ch. Oxf. 1767. *m.* (1) 9 July 1772, Frances, da. of John Manners, Mq. of Granby (q.v.); she was divorced Oct. 1777, having eloped with Charles Loraine Smith (q.v.), (2) 3 June 1780, Sarah

Hussey, da. of John Hussey Delaval (q.v.), 1 surv. da. *suc.* fa. as 2nd Earl of Tyrconnel [I] 9 Mar. 1762.

Tyrconnel was returned on the interest which his father-in-law, Lord Granby, had established at Scarborough. The election, though uncontested, seems to have been fairly expensive: in a memorandum, dated 1772, by John Calcraft (q.v.), who was connected with the Manners family, there is an entry: 'Sent £2,500 Scarborough'.[1] In the House Tyrconnel voted steadily with the Opposition, whom Granby had joined shortly before his death, and to whom his son adhered as soon as he entered the House. Tyrconnel's attendance seems to have been regular as his name appears in most of the extant division lists. Robinson in his survey of 1780 considered the question of putting up Sir Hugh Palliser (q.v.), who had a considerable following at Scarborough, in opposition to Tyrconnel, but feared that this might end by Constantine Phipps (q.v.) being knocked out; and apparently the idea was dropped. Tyrconnel, following the Duke of Rutland, voted for Shelburne's peace preliminaries, 18 Feb. 1783; but he was absent from the divisions on Fox's East India bill. In 1784 Tyrconnel came out top in a contested election at Scarborough. On 16 June 1784, when parliamentary reform was put off by the previous question, Tyrconnel voted with the majority;[2] but having received Rutland's 'sentiments respecting Pitt's reform',[3] on 18 Apr. 1785 voted for it. Daniel Pulteney (q.v.) wrote to Rutland on 15 July 1784:[4]

> I really think your Grace's Members are the most useful in the House, for I don't believe Pochin, Sutton, or myself have ever missed a single day, and Lord Tyrconnel is seldom or never absent at any expected business.

He voted for Richmond's fortifications plan, 27 Feb. 1786, and with Pitt over the Regency 1788–9. In May 1787, when the question of the Prince of Wales's debts was brought before Parliament, Pulteney informed Tyrconnel about the letter he had received from Rutland, and Tyrconnel was going to vote accordingly 'for the Prince.'[5] And Tyrconnel was returned on the Manners interest three times after he had divorced his first wife.

Tyrconnel died 15 Apr. 1805.

[1] *Mems. Philip Francis*, ed. Parkes and Merivale, i. 318. [2] D. Pulteney to Rutland, 17 June 1784; *HMC Rutland*, iii. 112. [3] Same to same, 27 Jan. 1785, ibid. 169. [4] Ibid. 125. [5] Pulteney to Rutland, 10 May 1787, ibid. 389–90.

L.B.N.

## CARRINGTON, Baron, see SMITH, Robert

## CARTERET, see THYNNE, Hon. Henry Frederick

## CARTWRIGHT, William (c.1704–68), of Aynho, Northants.

NORTHAMPTONSHIRE  26 Dec. 1754–1768

*b.* c.1704, 1st s. of Thomas Cartwright, M.P., by Hon. Armine Crew, da. and coh. of Thomas, 2nd Baron Crew of Stene. *educ.* Rugby, 1714; B.N.C. Oxf. 1721. *m.* (1) 16 June 1726, Byzantia (*d.* June 1738), da. of Ralph Lane of Woodbury, Cambs., 1s. 3da.; (2) 2 July 1748, Elizabeth, da. of Sir Clement Cottrell Dormer of Rowsham, Oxon., 2s. *suc.* fa. 1748.

Before the Northamptonshire by-election of 1754 Lord Northampton wrote to Cartwright, 4 May 1754:[1] 'Our eyes are . . . turned upon you. We think you have a right to expect an offer from the county, and it is the county's interest too to desire that you will consent to represent them in Parliament, as being the surest means we think to preserve the peace of the county.' Cartwright, professing reluctance, suggested Charles Compton (q.v.), Northampton's brother, but was persuaded to stand, and was returned unopposed.

No vote or speech of Cartwright's has been recorded. On 23 June 1757 Charles Townshend reported to his mother a conversation in which Cartwright, disgusted by Pitt's joining with Newcastle, had said he would 'go no more to Parliament in this incurable age, but turn planter and husbandman, to divert his mind from the recollection of his own credulity'.[2] Apparently he kept his word. Returned unopposed in 1761 he appears in no division list of this Parliament; was marked by Rockingham in July 1765 'not taken his seat' and in November 1766 'absent'; and by Newcastle in March 1767 'doubtful or absent'.

In December 1767 Cartwright declared his intention not to stand again 'on account of his ill state of health'.[3] He died 29 June 1768.

[1] E. G. Forrester, *Northants. County Elections and Electioneering*, 79. [2] Raynham mss. [3] Sir Wm. Dolben to Bedford, 6 Dec. 1767, Bedford mss.

M.M.D.

## CARY, Lucius Ferdinand, Master of Falkland (1735–80).

BRIDPORT  1774–20 Aug. 1780

*b.* 1735, o.s. of Lucius Charles, 7th Visct. Falkland [S], by his 1st w. Jane, da. and h. of Richard Butler of London, conveyancer, and wid. of James, Lord Villiers, 1st s. of the 1st Earl Grandison. *educ.* Westminster 1747–52. *m.* 28 Nov. 1757,[1] at Gibraltar, Anne, da. of Col. Alexander Leith, and sis. of Alexander Leith (q.v.), 2s. 5da.

Ensign 2 Ft. Gds. 1752; capt. 14 Ft. 1755; maj. 74 Ft. 1762; half pay 1763–5; maj. 60 Ft. 1765–8; again half pay 1768–79; lt.-col. commandant 89 Ft. 1779–*d.*

Henry Cary was created in 1620 a Scottish viscount, although the family had no connexion with Scotland, but had represented Devon in 12 Parliaments during the first half of the 15th century.

Lord North wrote to the King on 10 Oct. 1774:[2]

There are not many alterations but he is sorry to say that in general they are for the worse. Mr. Sambroke Freeman is replaced at Bridport by Mr. Cary . . . Mr. Cary may, however, be a friend to Government . . .

Cary voted 22 Feb. 1775 with the Opposition on Wilkes's motion for expunging the resolution on the Middlesex election. He did not vote in the five divisions February-April 1780, being out of the country. John Robinson classed him in his survey for the general election of 1780 as 'pro', but added: 'Mr. Cary can't come [in] again.' There is no record of his having spoken in the House.

He died *v.p.* in Tobago, 20 Aug. 1780. At his death he was in receipt of a secret service pension of £500 per annum.[3] The King, on the application of Lord Falkland, granted pensions of £100 per annum to each of Cary's five daughters, 'left in extreme indigence by their father'.[4]

[1] In the *Scots Peerage* the date is given as March 1760; but see *Augustus Hervey's Jnl.* ed. D. Erskine, 265. [2] Fortescue, iii. 137, should be dated 10 Oct. [3] Laprade, 50. [4] Fortescue, v. 204–5.

L.B.N.

## CARYSFORT, Baron, *see* PROBY, John

## CARYSFORT, Earl of, *see* PROBY, John Joshua

## CASWALL, Timothy (c. 1733–1802), of Sacombe Park, nr. Ware, Herts.

HERTFORD  1761–1768
BRACKLEY  4 Oct. 1771–Sept. 1789

*b.* c.1733, 1st s. of George Caswall of London and Weybridge by his w. Mary. Gd.-s. of Sir George Caswall, M.P., a London banker. *m.* 28 Jan. 1762, Mary Constantia, da. of Thomas Rolt of Sacombe Park, sis. and h. of Thomas Rolt, killed at St. Cas, 1758.

Ensign 2 Ft. Gds. 1750, lt. and capt. 1756; res. 1762. Dep. paymaster of the forces 1768–82; commr. of Excise 1789–*d.*

In 1758 at the battle of St. Cas, Caswall was 'wounded, and taken prisoner, being carried to St. Malo, he remained there four months in the most languishing condition, with both bones of his leg shattered by the ball. After great pain, and expense, he was brought to England, where his wound was healed.'[1] He now applied for promotion or an office. On 5 Oct. 1760 his uncle Nathaniel Brassey (q.v.) reminded Newcastle of his promise to do something for Caswall, and suggested a captaincy in the first Foot Guards.[2] On 8 Nov. Caswall himself asked Newcastle to be 'remembered in the establishment of his Majesty's family, or in some other way'.[3] The following year he was still pressing his case: finding himself 'a cripple, and suffering constantly great pain and inconvenience', he begged for the King's permission to 'retire from the service, with such a provision as his Majesty may think adequate',[4] or failing that for promotion to the first vacant company in the Guards. But he was again unsuccessful.

In 1761 Caswall was returned unopposed for Hertford on the interest of Nathaniel Brassey. On 29 July 1762 he wrote to Bute of his 'hearty desire' of being attached to him in Parliament, and begged him 'to obtain of his Majesty a salary of five hundred a year, with the title of gentleman of the Horse to the Queen'[5]—again without success. In November 1762 Bute recommended him as quarter master general in Ireland, but he had by that time sold his commission, and the King would not appoint an officer who had 'lately quitted for money'.[6] In Bute's list Caswall was classed as 'Government', and though not in Fox's list of Members favourable to the peace preliminaries, he does not appear in any of the minority lists 1762-4. Rockingham in July 1765 put him as 'contra'; and henceforth he was always classed as a member of the Bedford group. Whether his connexion was with Rigby or the Duke of Bridgwater is uncertain. In 1768 he was made by Rigby deputy paymaster of the forces. He did not stand at the general election of 1768, but in 1771 was returned by Bridgwater at Brackley. He supported Administration till the fall of North; voted against Shelburne's peace preliminaries, 18 Feb. 1783, and was classed by Robinson, March 1783, as 'North, doubtful, Bridgwater'. He voted for Fox's East India bill, 27 Nov. 1783, but under orders from the Duke of Bridgwater voted against the resolutions condemning the King's interference,[7] and was classed in all three lists of 1784 as 'Administration'. Still, his first recorded vote in this Parliament was with Opposition, over Pitt's Irish propositions, 13 May 1785, but he voted with Pitt on the Regency 1788-9.

Only a handful of speeches by Caswall are recorded during his 25 years in Parliament. On 14 Mar. and 7 June 1774 he spoke on motions to clear the House. On 11 Dec. 1787, he explained that he had voted against Philip Francis as manager for the impeachment of Hastings, because Francis 'had fought a duel with Mr. Hastings, and had consequently had a personal quarrel with him . . . Mr. Caswall said he was a plain man and told a plain story'.[8] His last speech, 7 May 1788, was in answer to Burke's attack on Impey.[9]

In September 1789 Caswall's seat was vacated by his appointment to a commissionership of Excise. He died 24 Aug. 1802.

[1] Undated memorandum from Caswall, Bodl. North b5, f. 68. From internal evidence it can be dated 1761. [2] Add. 32912, f. 387. [3] Add. 32914, f. 56. [4] Bodl. North b5, f. 68. [5] Bute mss. [6] Sedgwick, *Letters Geo. III to Bute*, 154. [7] Bamber Gascoyne to John Strutt, 19 Dec. 1783. Strutt mss. [8] Stockdale, xii. 88-89. [9] Ibid. xiv. 264.

M.M.D.

## CATHCART, Hon. Charles Allan (1759-88), of Sauchie, Clackmannan.

CLACKMANNANSHIRE 1784-10 June 1788

*b.* 28 Dec. 1759, 2nd s. of Charles Schaw, 9th Lord Cathcart [S], by Jean, da. of Lord Archibald Hamilton, M.P.; his sis. Louisa m. 1776 David, 7th Visct. Stormont [S]. *educ.* Eton 1767; Glasgow Univ. 1772. *unm.*

2nd lt. 23 Ft. Mar. 1777; capt. 77 Ft. Dec. 1777; maj. 98 Ft. 1780; lt.-col. (local rank in India) 1782.

Cathcart joined the army in America in 1776, serving as a volunteer until commissioned in the 23rd Foot. Sailing from New York to the 77th Foot in Ireland, he was captured by a French privateer, and on his release was commissioned in 1780 second in command of the 98th Foot then raising under William Fullarton (q.v.). From 1781 he served in India and in June 1783 distinguished himself against the French at Cuddalore.[1] Connected with Stormont and the Coalition, he stood at the general election of 1784 for Clackmannan as Opposition candidate with the support of Sir Thomas Dundas (q.v.), and contrary to Henry Dundas's forecast was returned.

In the House he spoke in the East India debates on 2 and 19 July 1784. He praised Hastings's ability and integrity, and, concentrating on military organization, urged a clear definition of the status of commanders-in-chief in relation to the civil administration.[2] Both Pitt and Henry Dundas complimented him on his contribution and agreed to incorporate some of his proposed reforms in the bill. He clearly had become a Government supporter before he left in 1784 or 1785 for India. In 1787 Dundas, impressed by his 'manners and good understanding',[3] sent him as special envoy to the Emperor of China to negotiate a commercial treaty,[4] but Cathcart died on the voyage there, 10 June 1788.

[1] See *Scots Mag.* 1783, p. 683. [2] Debrett, xv. 346-52; xvi. 118-24. [3] Dundas to Cornwallis, 21 July 1787, *Cornwallis Corresp.* i. 327. [4] See H. B. Morse, *E. I. Co. Trading to China*, ii. chap. XLIII.

E.H.-G.

## CATHERLOUGH, Earl of, *see* KNIGHT, Robert

## CATOR, John (1728-1806), of Bank Side, Southwark, and Beckenham, Kent.

WALLINGFORD 27 Jan. 1772-1780
IPSWICH 3 Apr.-18 June 1784
STOCKBRIDGE 1790-22 Feb. 1793

*b.* 12 Mar. 1728, 1st s. of John Cator of Southwark and Ross, Herefs. by Mary, da. of John Brough. *m.* 1753, Mary, da. of Peter Collinson, F.R.S., Quaker and friend of Benjamin Franklin. *suc.* fa. 21 July 1763.

Cator's father, of a prominent Herefordshire Quaker family, settled in London and established a timber business at Southwark. Cator joined the firm as a young man, and in 1763 took control. Shrewd and able, he seems early to have acquired a large fortune.

In 1768 he stood for Gloucester in opposition to George Selwyn, though he had no connexion with the borough. Selwyn's friends were indignant: 'I am heartily sorry, my dear George, that this d-d carpenter had made matters so serious with you', wrote Gilly Williams in March.[1] But William Dowdeswell, though he found it 'a very extraordinary opposition', told Charles Yorke that the arrival of 'this adventurer' had 'procured for Selwyn . . . the assistance of those who would have given him opposition if a gentleman of the neighbourhood had been proposed'.[2] And Cator was forced to withdraw. In 1772 he successfully contested the venal borough of Wallingford.

In Parliament he was inclined to support the Administration, but was sufficiently independent to follow his own line on several occasions: thus he voted with the Opposition on the naval captains' petition, 9 Feb. 1773, and Grenville's Election Act, 25 Feb. 1774, but is marked both times in the King's lists as a friend. While supporting the American war, he voted against the Administration on the civil list debts, 16 Apr. 1777, the contractors bill, 12 Feb. 1779, and on Keppel, 3 Mar. 1779. Still, Robinson in 1780 classed him as 'pro'. Half a dozen speeches by Cator on diverse subjects are reported during his first Parliament but only one after 1774.

Before the general election of 1780 Robinson, in his survey drawn up in July, expected an opposition at Wallingford—'But Mr. Cator [will] stand with another friend of Government and says that he is sure of carrying the borough for both.' Yet Cator and Richard Barwell (q.v.) after canvassing the borough withdrew before the election. Cator now showed a relentless determination to find another seat. Immediately after his defeat (8 Sept.) he wrote to Charles Jenkinson:[3]

I have informed our friend R[obinson] and have referred to his consideration that . . . when I should have compromised with the adversary, I have risked my seat and the expense to get a friend. I have signified a wish he would assist me in another seat at a moderate price.

And on 16 Sept:

I see there will be a vacancy for Aldborough, and

another for Rye if Mr. Onslow succeeds in Surrey. I hope Lord North will consider that I have lost my election by endeavouring to defeat Lord Abingdon, who sent and would have compromised me [sic] if I would.

A further letter with more suggestions followed on 27 Sept. and yet another on 6 Oct., contesting the prior claims of other defeated candidates—'I should expect that Lord North would prefer me to some others, who after they get in must be provided for, whereas I shall never trouble them.' And on 26 Oct.:

I have called on you last Saturday . . . to tell you of an offer I have had on very moderate terms, but to engage myself contrary to my present dispensation, since then the same was offered to me on condition of a loan on a good and sufficient security, which I would willingly have complied with to be *free*, but it is still insisted on as the *sine qua non* to attend when and to act as desired, and for that reason I have rejected the proposition.

This broad hint was followed on 31 Oct. by a further request and a list of fourteen vacant boroughs. But still no seat was forthcoming and the correspondence lapsed.[4]

After the fall of the Coalition Cator approached Lord Shelburne:[5]

Rejoicing at the fate of the India bill and the consequences thereon and wishing to support the new Administration, hoping you will be one, and as I find Lord Abingdon and myself are much of a mind I shall be glad to join any friend of his at Wallingford. I shall be much obliged to your Lordship to communicate this idea to his Lordship, or if your Lordship knows of a seat on moderate terms.

Cator appears in Robinson's lists of candidates for seats at the general election among 'persons that will pay £2,000 or £2,500, or perhaps £3,000'.[6] In the end no Administration seat was provided, but Cator was invited to contest Ipswich by the 'Yellow' party in the borough.[7] He paid £1,700 for his election, was returned, but on petition was found guilty of bribery and unseated. He also accepted an invitation from the town party at Lyme Regis to oppose the Fane interest, but was heavily defeated. In January 1785 he approached Jenkinson about a vacant seat at Ilchester,[8] but though Jenkinson seems to have been encouraging, nothing came of it. Nor did Hawkesbury (as Jenkinson had now become) offer him the seat at Ilchester when put at his disposal in October 1786, though Cator was still hoping to re-enter Parliament.

Cator was a friend of Henry Thrale, and with Dr. Johnson and Jeremiah Crutchley (q.v.) an executor of his will. Mrs. Thrale writes that when asked by her husband whom to appoint, she named Johnson, Sir Lucas Pepys, and Cator:

This was rather a testimony of good opinion . . . than of fondness, for who could be *fond* of Cator? and yet

I really think him as fit a man for the purpose as either of the other two. Rough in his manners, acute in his judgment, skilful in trade, and solid in property is John Cator Esq.

She thought it possible to 'gain great information from keeping him company; but his voice is so loud, and his manners so rough, that disgust gets the better of curiosity'.[9] And Fanny Burney: 'He prated so much, yet said so little, and pronounced his words so vulgarly, that I found it impossible to keep my countenance.'[10] But Dr. Johnson wrote to Mrs. Thrale: 'Cator has a rough, manly, independent understanding, and does not spoil it by complaisance, he never speaks merely to please and seldom is mistaken in things which he has any right to know.'[11] Cator seems to have been a conscientious trustee, and a good friend to the Thrales's daughters, and it was to his house that they went after their mother's second marriage. Boswell writes, June 1784,[12] that Johnson was

> pleased with the kindness of Mr. Cator, and thus describes him: 'There is much good in his character, and much usefulness in his knowledge'. He found a cordial solace at that gentleman's seat at Beckenham, in Kent, which is indeed one of the finest places at which I ever was a guest.

Cator died 21 Feb. 1806, 'immensely rich'.[13]

[1] J. H. Jesse, *Selwyn*, ii. 265. [2] Add. 35430, f. 230. [3] Abergavenny mss. [4] Add. 38458, ff. 131, 137; 38214, ff. 205, 250. [5] Lansdowne mss. [6] Laprade, 126. [7] See IPSWICH constituency. [8] Add. 38458, f. 153. [9] *Thraliana*, i. 220, 418. [10] *Diary*, i. 500. [11] *Letters*, ed. Chapman, no. 926. [12] *Life of Johnson*, iv. 313. [13] *Gent. Mag.* 1806, p. 285.

M.M.D.

**CAVE, Sir Thomas**, 5th Bt. (1712–78), of Stanford Hall, nr. Rugby, Leics.

LEICESTERSHIRE    1741–1747, 25 Mar. 1762–1774

*b.* 27 May 1712, 2nd s. of Sir Thomas Cave, 3rd Bt., M.P., by Hon. Margaret Verney, da. of John, 1st Visct. Fermanagh [I], M.P., and aunt of Ralph, 2nd Earl Verney [I] (q.v.). *educ.* Rugby 1720; Balliol, Oxf. 1729; I. Temple 1725, called 1735. *m.* Nov. 1735, Elizabeth, da. and h. of Griffith Davies, M.D., of Theddingworth, Leics., 2s. 6da. *suc.* bro. as 5th Bt. 13 Sept. 1734.

Cave was returned without a contest in 1762 and 1768.

He appears in Henry Fox's list of Members favourable to the peace preliminaries, December 1762. He voted against the Grenville Administration over general warrants, 15 and 18 Feb. 1764, but was classed by Jenkinson as normally a friend. In July 1765 Rockingham classed him as doubtful, but he seems to have supported the Rockingham Administration although he voted against the window tax, 18 Apr. 1766.[1] Classed either as Tory or country gentleman in the lists of 1766–7, he voted against Chatham's Administration over the land tax, 27

Feb. 1767, and the nullum tempus bill, 17 Feb. 1768.

He does not appear in any of the eleven division lists 1769–71. Robinson in the first survey on the royal marriage bill classed him as 'doubtful, present', and in the second as 'pro, present'. His only recorded speech was on 2 Mar. 1772 against the bill to abolish the observation of Charles I's execution. In this Parliament his only other known vote was against the court on the Middlesex resolution of 26 Apr. 1773. In 1774 he was again a candidate for Leicestershire but withdrew because of ill health.

Cave was well known as an antiquarian. He was chairman of the committee which sponsored the publication of Bridges's *History of Northamptonshire*, and collected materials which were afterwards used by John Nichols in his *History of Leicestershire*.

He died 7 Aug. 1778.

[1] Geo. Onslow to Newcastle, 18 Apr. 1766, Add. 32974, ff. 425–6.

J.B.

**CAVENDISH FAMILY**

Between 1754 and 1790 six Cavendishes sat in the House of Commons: three sons of the 3rd Duke of Devonshire, two sons of the 4th Duke, and a grandson of the 1st Duke. The family invariably occupied one seat for Derbyshire and one for Derby, for most of the period controlled the pocket borough of Knaresborough, and had considerable influence at Lancaster. They always voted together in politics; and among their associates were the Duke of Portland, Robert Boyle Walsingham, and the Ponsonbys (qq.v.).

The 4th Duke of Devonshire was outstanding for disinterestedness and integrity; and, while generally acting with the Pelhams, maintained his independence. On Newcastle's resignation in Nov. 1756 he became first lord of the Treasury, with Pitt as secretary of state; and on the formation of the Newcastle-Pitt coalition in July 1757 stepped down with relief to the office of lord chamberlain.

After the Duke's disgrace by George III in October 1762 the family went into Opposition, and for the next 20 years were pillars of the Newcastle-Rockingham group. The Duke died on 2 Oct. 1764 and Lord John Cavendish assumed the leadership of the family group, retaining it even after the 5th Duke came of age in 1769. After Rockingham's death in 1782 the Cavendishes followed Fox, but went over to Pitt with the Portland Whigs in 1794.

**CAVENDISH, Lord Frederick** (1729–1803).

DERBYSHIRE    27 June 1751–1754
DERBY                           1754–1780

*b.* Aug. 1729, 3rd s. of William, 3rd Duke of Devonshire, by Catherine, da. of John Hoskins of Oxted, Surr., and bro. of Lords George Augustus and John Cavendish (qq.v.). *unm.*

Ensign 1 Ft. Gds. 1749; lt. 2 Ft. Gds. 1752; lt.-col. 29 Ft. 1755; capt. 1 Ft. Gds. and lt.-col. 1756; col. 1758; col. 67 Ft. 1759–60; 34 Ft. 1760–97; maj.-gen. 1761; lt.-gen. 1770; gen. 1782; f.m. 1796.

Lord Frederick went out to Germany in April 1757 as aide-de-camp to the Duke of Cumberland; served on the expedition to St. Cas in September 1758, was wounded and taken prisoner, and afterwards exchanged; and from 1760 to 1763 served under Granby in Germany. He belonged to the group of officers politically connected with Cumberland. Horace Walpole wrote that he was 'by far the most agreeable and possessed the most useful sense of the whole family'.[1] But he was of less consequence in Parliament than either of his brothers, and only one speech by him is recorded: 24 Feb. 1780, on a bill to regulate the admission of honorary freemen in corporation boroughs.[2]

He died, 'immensely rich',[3] on 21 Oct. 1803.

[1] *Mems. Geo. III*, i. 17. [2] Almon, xvii. 168. [3] *Gent. Mag.* 1803, p. 995.

J.B.

## CAVENDISH, Lord George Augustus (?1727–94).

WEYMOUTH AND
MELCOMBE REGIS   28 Jan. 1751–1754
DERBYSHIRE          1754–1780
                   29 Nov. 1781–2 May 1794

*b.* ?1727, 2nd s. of William, 3rd Duke of Devonshire, and bro. of Lords Frederick and John Cavendish (qq.v.). *educ.* Chesterfield; St. John's, Camb. 29 May 1746, aged 18. *unm.  suc.* to Lancs. estates of cos. Sir William Lowther, 3rd Bt. (q.v.), 15 Apr. 1756.

Comptroller of the Household Nov. 1761–Oct. 1762; P.C. 15 Feb. 1762; ld. lt. Derbys. 1766–82.

At the general election of 1754 Lord George Cavendish was returned unopposed for Derbyshire. His conduct in Parliament conformed strictly to the family line. On 11 Dec. 1755 he wrote to his brother, the 4th Duke, who had recently succeeded to the title:[1]

I hope you will be so good when anything of consequence is foreseen in the House of Commons to signify your inclinations to me that I may act agreeably to them. You know that I always had the greatest regard for your advice, and now your opinion is the only guide that I can direct myself by, and all that I desire is to do what you should approve.

He told Horace Walpole in February 1783 that 'he liked an aristocracy, and thought it right that great families with great connexions should govern'.[2]

Lord George resigned on his brother's dismissal; and on 10 Dec. 1762, in what James Harris described as a 'rather cloudy' speech, attacked the

peace preliminaries. On the formation of the Rockingham Administration in July 1765 Newcastle suggested him for chancellor of the duchy of Lancaster or treasurer of the Household—'no one man can have more merit than his Lordship';[3] but Cavendish was indifferent to his own advancement. In the absence of Conway and Dowdeswell, who had to seek re-election on taking office, he read the speech at the Cockpit meeting, 16 Dec. 1765; and on 17 Dec. seconded the Address.

He attended regularly and spoke frequently, but was not a first-rate debater; and in party councils allowed his brother John to speak for the family. Wraxall wrote of him:[4]

Lord George . . . possessed very limited talents, but . . . the hereditary probity of the Cavendish family, which in no individual of that line was more recognized than in him, supplied the place of ability.

He died 2 May 1794, aged 66.

[1] *Devonshire mss.* [2] *Last Jnls.* ii. 488. [3] Newcastle to Rockingham, 12 July 1765, Add. 32967, f. 349. [4] *Mems.* iv. 381.

J.B.

## CAVENDISH, Lord George Augustus Henry (1754–1834).

KNARESBOROUGH   19 Apr. 1775–1780
DERBY            1780–1796
DERBYSHIRE       12 Jan. 1797–10 Sept. 1831

*b.* 21 Mar. 1754, 3rd s. of William, 4th Duke of Devonshire, by Charlotte, *suo jure* Baroness Clifford, da. and h. of Richard Boyle, 3rd Earl of Burlington. *educ.* Hackney; Trinity, Camb. 1770. *m.* 27 Feb. 1782, Lady Elizabeth Compton, da. and h. of Charles, 7th Earl of Northampton, 4s. 6da. *cr.* Earl of Burlington 10 Sept. 1831.

The *Public Ledger* wrote of Lord George Augustus Henry in 1779, in a long and eulogistic notice: 'As a senator . . . he is distinguished only for the known sincerity of his intentions'—which seems a fair summary of his career. Only two speeches by him are recorded before 1790: on 15 Mar. 1782 he seconded Rous's motion of no confidence in North's Administration; and on 12 Nov. 1783 moved an address of congratulation on the birth of a princess.

He died 4 May 1834.

J.B.

## CAVENDISH, Henry (1732–1804), of Doveridge Hall, Derbys. and Phoenix Park, Dublin.

LOSTWITHIEL   1768–1774

*b.* 29 Sept. 1732, 1st s. of Sir Henry Cavendish, 1st Bt. by his 1st w. Anne, da. and h. of Henry Pyne of Waterpark, co. Cork (by Anne, da. of Sir Richard Edgcumbe, K.B.). *educ.* Eton 1747–8; Trinity, Dublin 1750. *m.* 29 Aug. 1757, Sarah, da. and h. of Richard

Bradshaw of Cork, 4s. 4da. *suc.* fa. 31 Dec. 1776. His w. was *cr.* Baroness Waterpark [I] 15 June 1792.
M.P. [I] 1764–8, 1776–97, 1798–1800.
P.C. [I] 1 July 1779; commr. of the Treasury for Ireland 1793–5; receiver gen. for Ireland 1795–1801.

Henry Cavendish was descended from an illegitimate son of Henry, elder brother of William Cavendish, 1st Earl of Devonshire. The family had estates in Derbyshire, and Cavendish's father had some connexion with the 3rd Duke of Devonshire, who, after Cavendish had settled on his wife's estates in Ireland, returned him to the Irish House for Lismore, which Henry Cavendish also in turn represented.

In 1768 Cavendish was returned for Lostwithiel on the interest of his cousin, Lord Edgcumbe. From the beginning of the Parliament he took shorthand notes of the debates, which he intended one day to publish.[1] His pertinacity and industry were remarkable, yet the record he left has many gaps and omissions and is by no means a verbatim account of the debates.

In Parliament Cavendish regularly voted with the Opposition, and spoke against Administration on every political issue during his first years in the House. He vigorously attacked the Government's handling of the Middlesex election, and on 8 May 1769 declared:[2]

> I lay it down as a principle that no order of the House of Commons can make a minority a majority; that no resolution of the House of Commons can ever make Mr. Luttrell the legal representative of the county of Middlesex. For I do from my soul abhor, detest, and abjure, as unconstitutional and illegal that damnable doctrine and position that a resolution of the House of Commons can make, alter, suspend, abrogate or annihilate the law of the land. I think myself bound in duty to support the violated privileges of the freeholders. I will take every moderate, legal, and constitutional step for that purpose; if all these means will not succeed, rather than they should be thus wantonly and illegally torn from them, I would arm in their defence.

Cavendish, whom Horace Walpole described as 'hot-headed and odd',[3] was equally forthright on other matters. In the debate of 2 Mar. 1769 on the resolution to pay the civil list debt, he said: 'It seems to me an absurdity, notwithstanding all the precedents that have been mentioned, to pay first and examine accounts afterwards.'[4] Cavendish paid great attention to procedure and frequently spoke on points of order. On 3 May 1770, when Boyle Walsingham moved for papers relative to the sudden prorogation of the Irish Parliament, Cavendish argued that the House ought not to bring the affairs of Ireland before it, thus risking a censure of the Irish House;[5] and on Sawbridge's motion of 26 Apr. 1771 for shorter Parliaments, Cavendish,

'though believed to be a friend to the question, opposed it as improper, on account of the near conclusion of the session'.[6] During the proceedings against the printers in 1771 Cavendish's political views clashed with his regard for the dignity of the House; on 12 Mar. he voted with the small minority against the motions for the attendance of printers, but on 18 Mar., while protesting that the whole business had been 'wantonly introduced', he declared that since the problem was before the House he thought it his duty to vote for reprimanding the printers for their misrepresentations of the proceedings of the House,[7] but opposed any punishment of the City officials. Cavendish took an active part in opposing the royal marriage bill, March 1772, but subsequently took little part in debate till the following session, when East India affairs were debated by the House. During the debate of 10 May 1773, when Wedderburn, acting in defence of Clive, moved the order of the day, Horace Walpole reported that, just as it seemed the motion would fail for want of a seconder, 'young Mr. Cavendish . . . said he seconded Wedderburn's motion, but being a very absurd man, he only drew ridicule on what had no other support'.[8] When the East India regulating bill came before the Commons, Cavendish, like other Rockingham speakers, opposed it for depriving proprietors of their rights and for the increased patronage it put at the ministry's disposal.[9]

After the outbreak of disturbances in America, Cavendish, who had not previously spoken on American affairs, supported the Administration's punitive measures. On 14 Mar. 1774 he came out in favour of the motion for leave to bring in the Boston port bill,[10] and on 6 May during the last debate on the second Massachusetts bill said: 'I am happy to think that these measures have met with a large majority in this House; I am doubly happy to think that the greatest part of the nation approve them.'[11] Cavendish also apparently favoured the Quebec bill.[12] Though Cavendish had sided with the ministry on these measures, Robinson in his survey drawn up before the general election of 1774 still reckoned him an Opposition supporter. In 1774 Edgcumbe put his seats at the disposal of Administration, and Cavendish was not returned again.

During his term at Westminster, Cavendish paid considerable attention to Irish interests. But when on 11 Dec. 1770 his complaints about the high price of provisions in Ireland drew a taunt from Dempster, Cavendish at once answered: 'I rise as an English Member, though I am not ashamed to say I drew my first breath in Ireland; but my stake, such as it is, is much greater in England than in Ireland. I speak for the good of the community. I hope no distinctions will prevail as to English or Irish Members.'[13] Nevertheless, the rest of his political career was spent in Ireland, as Member of the Dublin Parliament, where he again kept a diary of debates. He was 'a perfect adept in the rules and orders of Parliament', countering arguments with precedents and raising points of order to interrupt opponents or merely to gain time. In a Government list of Members in 1783, the remark is placed against his name: 'A good shorthand writer but a tiresome speaker.'[14]

He died 3 Aug. 1804.

[1] A transcript of the major portion of these shorthand notes is in Egerton mss 215–262 and 3711. See also P. D. G. Thomas, *Sources for Debates of the House of Commons, 1768–74*. [2] Egerton 219, pp. 408–11. [3] *Mems. Geo. III*, iii. 145. [4] Egerton 218, pp. 294–6. [5] Egerton 222, pp. A165–6. [6] Almon, ix. 299. [7] Egerton 226, pp. 256–8. [8] *Last Jnls*. i. 201. [9] Egerton 239, pp. 123, 189. [10] Brickdale's 'Debates', x. 20. [11] Egerton 257, p. 142. [12] Egerton 262, p. 12. [13] Egerton 223, p. 313. [14] *Proc. R. Irish Acad*. lvi. 268.

P.D.G.T.

## CAVENDISH, Lord John (1732–96).

| | |
|---|---|
| WEYMOUTH AND MELCOMBE REGIS | 1754–1761 |
| KNARESBOROUGH | 1761–1768 |
| YORK | 1768–1784 |
| DERBYSHIRE | 23 May 1794–18 Nov. 1796 |

*b.* 22 Oct. 1732, 4th s. of William, 3rd Duke of Devonshire, and bro. of Lords George and Frederick Cavendish (qq.v.). *educ.* Hackney; Peterhouse, Camb. 1750. *unm.*

Ld. of Treasury July 1765–July 1766; P.C. 27 Mar. 1782; chancellor of the Exchequer Mar.–July 1782 and Apr.–Dec. 1783.

Lord John was by far the most important member of the Cavendish family who sat in the House of Commons during this period. Horace Walpole, who came up against him, wrote:[1]

He had read a good deal, and his eyes saw not faster than his memory retained . . . nor was he defective in quickness or reasoning. Under the appearance of virgin modesty he had a confidence in himself that nothing could equal and a thirst of dominion still more extraordinary . . . To be first in however small a circle was his wish . . . He was a kind of heresiarch that sought to be adored by his enthusiastic disciples without a view of extending his sect beyond that circle.

Still, Walpole 'honoured his integrity',[2] and Wraxall spoke of his 'high character for integrity and uprightness'.[3] Burke praised his judgment, disinterestedness, and sensibility; and declared his only fault to be 'the singular modesty and moderation of his nature'.[4]

In 1754 he was provided with a seat by Administration at Weymouth and Melcombe Regis, and in 1761 was returned on the family interest at Knaresborough. His rise to political importance began after Devonshire's dismissal in October 1762, but he did not become a first-rate political figure until after Devonshire's death. He spoke in the debate on the peace preliminaries, 10 Dec. 1762, only to move an amendment to the Address which passed unopposed; and like his brothers voted against the peace. He was one of the group of young men who pressed for an active Opposition in the winter of 1762–3, and began to make his reputation as a speaker. On the Regency bill he moved an Address for the King to name the Regent, 7 May 1765, and was foremost in opposing Morton's motion to include the Princess Dowager among those capable of the Regency—'this *damnable* design', as the Cavendish brothers described it in a letter to Newcastle.[5] ('Lord John . . . was inflexible to Bute', wrote Walpole.[6]) With his brothers and Robert Boyle Walsingham (q.v.) he attended the meeting at Claremont on 30 June 1765, and advocated taking office without Pitt.

During the Rockingham Administration Lord John favoured the attempt to bring in Pitt—the King, he wrote to Rockingham in January 1766,[7] 'must sooner or later swallow the pill' and 'the fewer wry faces he makes the better'. But when the Chatham Administration was being formed Lord John resigned from the Treasury Board. According to Walpole,[8] who was then in close touch with Grafton, 'he sent his resignation to the Duke of Grafton in a letter in which he told the Duke that he supposed his Grace did not desire to see a Cavendish at that Board'. No such letter survives among the Grafton mss, and this is Lord John's own explanation of his resignation:[9]

My reason for what I have done [he wrote to Newcastle on 26 July 1766] is that as I have always thought Mr. Pitt's style too high for my temper and I have been a long time tired of the confinement of my employment, it appeared to me I could not have a better opportunity of getting out than in company with those with whom I have been so long intimately connected, both in public and private life.

He once told Walpole that 'he wished the Opposition was reduced to six or seven who could depend on one another';[10] and said in the House on 2 Apr. 1770 that he 'wished all cursed distinctions of party to be done away'.[11] His conception of party was based on friendship and connexion rather than principle.

At the meeting of the chiefs of the Rockingham party on 19 Nov. 1766 Lord John pressed for resignations, apparently in the belief that Chatham would thus be compelled to yield to the Rockinghams.[12] In the East India debate of 25 Nov. he 'made a farewell speech to the Administration'.[13] He hoped to win back Conway, and during the negotiations of 1767 seems to have influenced Rockingham into making a stand on Conway's inclusion in any new Administration. Lord John, wrote Newcastle on 7 Sept.,[14] was 'not a friend or well-wisher to the union' between Bedford and Rockingham; and when Rockingham, in deference to Bedford, agreed to drop Conway, it was against Lord John's advice.[15]

In the autumn of 1767 he was invited by a group of merchants to contest Lancaster at the forthcoming general election. He canvassed strenuously: 'I don't think he likes it much', wrote Lord Frederick to Portland on 10 Nov.,[16] 'but he must now go through with it'; yet was forced to decline the poll, after having incurred heavy expenses.[17] On 14 Mar. 1768, on his way home from Lancaster, he called at Wentworth, and was pressed by Rockingham to stand for York. 'I desired to be excused', he wrote to Newcastle on 16 Mar.,[18]

> having so lately got out of one scrape, but I said I would go to Chatsworth, consult my brothers, and . . . if he [Rockingham] found York in the state he expected I would then go and offer myself, but would not engage in a second contest.

He was returned unopposed on the corporation, or old Tory, interest.

His influence in the Rockingham party was always against extreme measures. In his speeches he shows himself to have been much influenced by Burke, whose diagnosis of the 'present discontents' agreed with his own. In a debate of 2 Mar. 1769 Lord John said of the early years of George III's reign:[19]

> Did not France . . . at once see that those able counsellors whose advice had led to those successes were consulted and listened to no longer; that the system by which this country had been governed for the last fifty years was at once overturned; that no attention was paid to personal friendship; and that public virtue was disregarded.

In short, all would have gone well had Newcastle and Devonshire been retained in office—which agreed with what Rockingham thought. North, in March 1782, described Lord John as 'more in the confidence of Lord Rockingham than any other person',[20] which may well have been true then; though it is probable that until 1775 the more energetic Dowdeswell had the greatest influence with Rockingham. Lord John tended to be lukewarm in action, and became increasingly discouraged at the impotence of opposition—'I think our situation so unpleasant', he wrote to Rockingham on 26 Jan. 1779,[21] 'that I should be glad to get out of it at any rate.' Still, Rockingham at all times greatly trusted him, and never failed to consult him.

Lord John had no sympathy for Wilkes, but early realized the difficulties which would attend his expulsion. He said in the House on 3 Feb. 1769:[22]

> Let gentlemen consider that this is not the case of a little borough but of a large county put out of temper. If indeed he had been found incapable of being elected I should have been glad of it, for there are many very inconvenient circumstances in this man's situation.

And on 8 May:[23] 'I am sorry we have got into so unbecoming a contest with so unworthy an antagonist.' Neither then, nor in the printers' case of 1771, did he stress the constitutional issues: his concern was primarily for the dignity of Parliament.

'We must be as moderate towards the Americans as possible', he said in the House on 5 Dec. 1768;[24] and he was not one of those who believed the colonists could do no wrong. 'To be sure the Bostonians' behaviour is indefensible', he wrote to Rockingham on 29 Jan. 1774.[25] When the Boston port bill was introduced he 'doubted the efficacy of the measure',[26] and on 25 Mar. spoke against it:[27]

> I do not love to hear it said we must maintain national dignity when the measures proposed to maintain it are at the expense of national justice. This Act punishes the innocent and wealthy, the rabble remain as they were.

Towards the end of the American war he developed a constitutional theory like that of Chatham, which he projected back to the time of the Rockingham Administration. On 12 June 1781, during the debate on Fox's motion against the war, he replied to some remarks of Rigby on the Declaratory Act:[28]

> He should ever think there was a very material difference between stating and declaring a right presumed to be vested in Parliament, as the sovereign or supreme power, and employing methods of force and coercion in maintenance of that right. Besides, it was not fair to conclude that the declaratory law, which asserted a general, undefined right, namely 'to bind the colonies in all cases whatsoever', pointed to the exertion of a particular mode of exercising it, namely a right to tax, which claim had been renounced in the very same session by a repeal of the Stamp Act.

Such, however, had not been his opinion in 1766, when Pitt, almost alone in the House of Commons, had maintained that the British Parliament had no right to raise a revenue in America.

'I do not love general sweeping remedies', Lord John told the Commons on 12 Feb. 1770.[29] At the York meeting of 28 Mar. 1780 he refused to sign the plan of Association, and objected to the demands for increased county representation and shorter Parliaments 'as tending . . . to lessen the probability of success to the petition'.[30] In the Commons on 8 May 1780 he 'spoke against the principle of shortening the duration of Parliaments',[31] yet voted for it 'out of respect to the people'.[32] At the general election of 1780 there was a possibility that he would be opposed at York by a candidate more sympathetic to the Association's programme, and at one time he seemed inclined to retire. He wrote to Rockingham on 5 Sept.:[33] 'It is not the doubt of success nor the expense inclines me to have done so much as the disagreeableness here and hereafter. The House of Commons is no place for gentlemen of common sense.' During the second Rockingham Administration he opposed the plan for a committee on parliamentary reform,[34] yet voted for Pitt's scheme on 7 May 1783. In short, he trimmed a good deal, but his friends had no doubt of his real opinions.

In March 1782 he was only persuaded to take office out of respect for Rockingham, and on Rockingham's death is reported to have said 'that now . . . he cared no more about politics'.[35] Shelburne would have retained him in the new Cabinet, hoping to placate the followers of Rockingham; but Lord John would take no office. On 9 July he

> stated to the House his reasons for quitting the post of chancellor of the Exchequer, which, he said, were briefly that hearing a different system was meant to be pursued . . . he had determined to withdraw himself that he might not divide the Cabinet and render it a scene of confusion . . . for he always should be of opinion that a Cabinet unanimous in itself, although their measures might not be so good as could be wished, was much better for the country than a Cabinet which was divided.[36]

Fox regarded him as a valuable political asset, and drew him into opposition to the Shelburne Administration. On 17 Feb. Lord John moved the Opposition amendment to the address on the peace preliminaries, and on 21 Feb. the motion of censure. He described the treaty as 'degrading and disgusting'; talked of the 'formidable and truly respectable state of our navy', and the exhaustion of the Bourbon powers; and defended the coalition with North by comparing it with the Pitt-Newcastle Administration—'nothing but a union of great and able men could save the country'.[37]

Lord John's second tenure of the Exchequer was marked by his introduction of the unpopular receipts tax. His talents, wrote Wraxall,[38] 'were not eminently adapted for the discussion of measures of finance'. But the 'deserved and universal good opinion' entertained of him[39] more than made up for this weakness, and it is greatly to his credit that he withstood the extravagant demands of the Prince of Wales. He did not care for office: in November 1783 he seriously contemplated resigning,[40] and a few days before the Coalition fell was prepared to yield his place to Pitt if it would strengthen Administration.[41]

His adherence to the Coalition and his dislike of parliamentary reform led to his defeat at York in

1784. Burke wrote subsequently of this period of Lord John's life:[42]

> He retired from the world exceedingly irritated at the triumph of his enemies, which was carried pretty high against him personally; and somewhat disgusted with the coldness of his friends, who at that time showed little energy of mind and considered his retreat with too much indifference.

'Lord John', wrote John Hatsell, clerk of the House of Commons, to John Ley on 25 Apr. 1784, 'means to stay out of Parliament as long as he can';[43] and Sir Gilbert Elliot to his wife on 8 Jan. 1789:[44] 'Lord John Cavendish is very unwilling to engage again in public affairs.'

Henceforth he took little part in politics, and his friendship with Fox was severed by the French Revolution. He wrote to Burke on 14 Nov. 1790, after acknowledging the receipt of a copy of Burke's *Reflections*:

> All men of sense must I think feel obliged to you for showing in so forcible a manner that confusion is not the road to reformation. Though some of our allies have now and then run wild, our original set have always contended for that temperate resistance to the abuse of power as should not endanger the public peace or put all good order into hazard.

Lord John Cavendish died 18 Nov. 1796.

[1] *Mems. Geo. III*, ii. 17–18. [2] Walpole to Mann, 4 June 1780. [3] *Mems.* ii. 424. [4] *Corresp.* (1844), iv. 526–7. [5] Add. 32966, f. 355. [6] *Mems. Geo. III*, ii. 232. [7] *Rockingham mss.* [8] *Mems. Geo. III*, ii. 250. [9] Add. 32976, f. 269. [10] *Mems. Geo. III*, ii. 92. [11] Wm. Burke to Wm. Dennis, 6 Apr. 1770, Burke, *Corresp.* (1959), ii. 127. [12] Brooke, *Chatham Administration*, 55, 82. [13] Grenville Diary, 25 Nov. 1766, *Grenville Pprs*, iii. 389. [14] Add. 32985, ff. 45–51. [15] Portland to Newcastle, 20 Oct. 1767, Add. 32986, ff. 58–60. [16] Portland mss. [17] Wm. Mason to Chris. Alderson, 15 Mar. 1768, mss of Mr. C. J. Wilson of Godalming, Surr. [18] Add. 32989, ff. 191–2. [19] *Cavendish's Debates*, i. 301. [20] North to the King, 8 Mar. 1782, Fortescue, v. 381. [21] Rockingham mss. [22] *Cavendish's Debates*, i. 156. [23] Ibid. 414. [24] Ibid. 89–90. [25] Rockingham mss. [26] Walpole, *Last Jnls.* ii. 129. [27] Brickdale's 'Debates'. [28] Debrett, iii. 534. [29] *Cavendish's Debates*, i. 457. [30] Wyvill, *Political Pprs*, iii. [31] Almon, xvii. 681. [32] Savile to John Hewett, 9 May 1780, *HMC Foljambe*, 153. [33] Rockingham mss. [34] Richmond to Rockingham, 8 May 1782, *Rockingham Mems.* ii. 481. [35] Walpole, *Last Jnls.* ii. 446. [36] Debrett, vii. 311–12. [37] Ibid. ix. 297–302. [38] *Mems.* iv. 95. [39] Fox to Northington, 17 July 1783, *Corresp. C. J. Fox*, ii. 116. [40] Fitzwilliam to Portland, 16 Nov. 1783, Portland mss. [41] Dowager Lady Spencer to Ld. Spencer, 23 Dec. 1783, Spencer mss. [42] Burke to Wm. Windham, 23 Dec. 1796. [43] Ley mss. [44] *Life and Letters Sir G. Elliot*, i. 260.

J.B.

## CAVENDISH Richard (?1703–69).

### WENDOVER 1761–1768

b. ?1703, 1st s. of Dr. Edward Chandler, bp. of Durham 1730–50 by Barbara, da. of Sir Humphrey Brigges, 3rd Bt., of Haughton, Salop. *educ.* ?Eton 1718; Wadham, Oxf. 27 Apr. 1720, aged 16; L. Inn 1719, called 1726. *m.* Feb. 1732, Elizabeth, da. of Lord James Cavendish of Stayley Park, Derbys., s. of William, 1st Duke of Devonshire, *s.p. suc.* fa. 1750. Took name of Cavendish 1752, under terms of his fa.-in-law's will.

Prothonotary of common pleas for the county palatine 1737; chancellor of diocese of Durham, 1738; commr. of customs 1737–61.

Cavendish was on friendly terms with his wife's cousin, the Duke of Devonshire, and in 1760 was recommended by him to the Duke of Newcastle for a grant on the Irish establishment. When this was refused Cavendish himself wrote to Newcastle on 18 Dec. that he would ask for nothing else, preferring to continue in the commission of the customs.[1] In 1761, however, he was nominated as a Government candidate on the Verney interest at Wendover, and the Duke of Devonshire again approached Newcastle, pointing out on 7 Mar. that Cavendish must in consequence resign his commissionership of customs: 'If he can change it for no employment he would be glad of a pension. I am very sorry to be troublesome . . . but . . . this is a point I cannot possibly do without and therefore I hope you will get it done; is there nobody that has a pension that would exchange?'[2] No exchange took place, and Cavendish, who had been returned unopposed, was accommodated with a secret service pension of £800 a year. In April 1761 James Marriott (q.v.) reported to Newcastle that Cavendish was applying for an Irish peerage,[3] but nothing more appears about this application. In Bute's list Cavendish was classed a follower of Devonshire; with the rest of the Cavendish group he voted against the Bute and Grenville Administrations and lost his pension; supported Rockingham's; and opposed Chatham's. There is no record of his having spoken in the House. He did not stand again at the general election of 1768, and died 22 Nov. 1769.

[1] Add. 32916, f. 175. [2] Add. 32919, f. 501. [3] Add. 32921, f. 281.

M.M.D.

## CAVENDISH, Lord Richard (1752–81).

LANCASTER        15 Sept. 1773–1780
DERBYSHIRE                    1780–7 Sept. 1781

*b.* 19 June 1752, 2nd s. of William, 4th Duke of Devonshire, and bro. of Lord George Augustus Henry Cavendish (q.v.). *educ.* Hackney; Trinity, Camb. 1768. *unm.*

In September 1773, and again at the general election of 1774, Cavendish was returned unopposed for Lancaster. In Parliament, like the rest of his family, he voted regularly with the Opposition. In 1778–9, after the intervention of France in the war, he served afloat as a gentleman volunteer, under the command first of his kinsman Captain Robert (Boyle) Walsingham (q.v.) and then of Admiral Keppel (q.v.).[1] In 1780 he was returned for Derbyshire in place of his uncle Lord George Cavendish. There is no record of his having spoken in the House.

He died at Naples, 7 Sept. 1781.

[1] Rockingham to Portland, 27 June 1778, Portland mss.

I.R.C.

## CAWTHORNE, *see* FENTON CAWTHORNE

## CAYLEY, William (*d.*1768), of Scampton, Lincs.

DOVER      7 Feb. 1752–Apr. 1755

3rd s. of Simon Cayley (s. of Sir William Cayley, 2nd Bt.) of Brompton, Yorks. *m.*, 1 da.

Sec. to Sir Thomas Saunderson, minister to Lisbon, 1722; chargé d'affaires at Lisbon 1723–4, 1725; consul at Cadiz 1726–39; consul at Faro, Portugal 1739–46; commr. of Excise 1755–67.

In 1754 Cayley was returned on the Government interest. On 1 June 1754 he applied to Newcastle for an official appointment, claiming that Pelham had intended to make him a lord of Trade, or at least a commissioner of Excise. 'I have spent my best days in the King's service with the zeal and fidelity that are known to your Grace, and have hitherto had no advantages fall to my lot, that I am now, my Lord, making hasty approaches to the close of my humble part in life.'[1] Appointed to the Board of Excise in 1755, he resigned on account of ill-health in 1767 and died 14 Feb. 1768.

[1] Add. 32735, f. 355.

A.N.N.

## CECIL, Brownlow, Lord Burghley (1725–93).

RUTLAND     1747–3 Nov. 1754

*b.* 21 Sept. 1725, 1st surv. s. of Brownlow, 8th Earl of Exeter, by Hannah Sophia, da. and coh. of Thomas Chambers, citizen and merchant of London and Derby. *educ.* Winchester 1732; St. John's, Camb. 1744. *m.* (1) 27 July 1748, Letitia (*d.*17 Apr. 1756), da. and h. of Hon. Horatio Townshend, *s.p.*; (2) 23 Apr. 1770, Anna Maria, da. of Job Cheatham of Sodor Hall, Yorks., *s.p.*   *suc.* fa. 3 Nov. 1754.

Ld. lt. Rutland 1751–79.

Cecil was classed 'pro' by Newcastle in 1747, and again by Dupplin in 1754. He lived a 'retired life, preferring it to the tumult and bustle of a court from which he would never accept a place'. His time was largely spent in improving his seat at Burghley and collecting paintings, of which he left 'a superb collection from the hands of the most illustrious artists'.[1]

He died 23 Dec. 1793.

[1] *Gent. Mag.* 1793, p. 1213.

M.M.D.

## CECIL, Henry (1754–1804).

STAMFORD     1774–1790

*b.* 14 Mar. 1754, o.s. of Hon. Thomas Chambers Cecil (q.v.). *educ.* Eton 1764–70; St. John's, Camb. 1770. *m.* (1) 23 May 1776, Emma (div. 1791), da. of Thomas Vernon (q.v.) of Hanbury, Worcs., 2s. 1da.; (2) 3 Oct. 1791, Sarah (*d.*18 Jan. 1797), da. of Thomas Hoggins of Bolas Magna, Salop, 3s. 1da.; (3) 19 Aug. 1800, Elizabeth Anne, da. of Peter Burrell II (q.v.), div. w. of Douglas, 8th Duke of Hamilton [S], *s.p.*   *suc.* uncle as 10th Earl of Exeter, 26 Dec. 1793; *cr.* Mq. of Exeter 4 Feb. 1801.

Cecil was returned for Stamford on the family interest, and voted with Administration. But, after having been absent from the division on Conway's motion of 22 Feb. 1782, Sandwich wrote to Robinson:[1] 'Mr. Cecil is very slippery, but I think that with the aid of Lord Exeter I can get him up on any emergency if we have two days notice'; two days later, 27 Feb., Cecil voted with Administration on Conway's motion against the war, and 15 Mar. against Rous's motion of no confidence. He did not vote on Shelburne's peace preliminaries, 18 Feb. 1783; and in Robinson's list of March 1783 was among those listed 'ill or cannot attend'. He voted for parliamentary reform, 7 May 1783; did not vote on Fox's East India bill, 27 Nov. 1783; and in Stockdale's list of 19 Mar. 1784 was described as absent. Cecil again voted for parliamentary reform on 18 Apr. 1785; opposed Richmond's fortifications plan, 27 Feb. 1786, but supported Pitt on the Regency, 1788–9. There is no record of his having spoken in the House.

He died 1 May 1804.

[1] 25 Feb. 1782, Abergavenny mss.

M.M.D.

## CECIL, James, Visct. Cranborne (1748–1823).

GREAT BEDWYN 20 Dec. 1774–1780
LAUNCESTON 8 Sept.–19 Sept. 1780

*b.* 4 Sept. 1748, o.s. of James, 6th Earl of Salisbury, by Elizabeth, da. of Edward Keet of Canterbury, sis. of John Keet, rector of Hatfield. *educ.* Eton 1757–65. *m.* 2 Dec. 1773, Lady Emily Mary Hill, da. of Wills, 1st Earl of Hillsborough (q.v.), 1s. 2da. *suc.* fa. 19 Sept. 1780; *cr.* Mq. of Salisbury 25 Aug. 1789; K.G. 12 June 1793.

Ld. lt. Herts. 1771–*d.*; P.C. 27 Sept. 1780; treasurer of the Household 1780–2; ld. chamberlain Dec. 1783–1804; jt. postmaster general 1816–*d.*

Cranborne was returned on Lord Bruce's interest at Great Bedwyn, and voted regularly with Administration. In 1780 Robinson noted in his survey: 'Lord Cranborne will most likely be a peer very soon, and therefore desires to have only a temporary seat.' He was returned at Launceston on the interest of the Duke of Northumberland, and at Plympton on Lord Edgcumbe's interest, but almost immediately succeeded to the peerage. According to the *Gentleman's Magazine* (1833, i. 564) he was 'not . . . remarkable for any active part in Parliament', and his only recorded speech, 11 Feb. 1780, was against the Hertfordshire petition presented by William Plumer.[1]

He died 13 June 1823.

[1] Almon, xvii. 91.

M.M.D.

## CECIL, Hon. Thomas Chambers (1728–78).

RUTLAND 1761–1768

*b.* 25 June 1728, 2nd surv. s. of Brownlow, 8th Earl of Exeter, and bro. of Brownlow, Lord Burghley (q.v.). *m.* 20 Feb. 1751, Charlotte Garnier (or Gormiez), said to have been a Basque, 1s.

In June 1760 Cecil returned from abroad to stand for Rutland at the general election, but on 4 Dec. Lord Exeter told Lord Hardwicke that his brother was too ill 'to appear at the election, much less to attend Parliament', and would again have to go abroad.[1] There is no record of Cecil having spoken or voted, and he may never have taken his seat. In Bute's list he appears as 'absent'; he was still abroad in 1764;[2] and from Dinant, 30 May 1766, wrote a letter to Lord Winchilsea which suggests reasons for absence other than health:[3]

> I left England in conformity to the desires of my brother, your Lordship, and the rest of my friends; and should be very glad to oblige them by staying out of it; but alas! my former indiscretions and extravagancies not being properly provided for by my brother, will involuntarily compel me to act otherwise.

He had been ill for 'many months', and nothing would restore his health but 'spa water'—which he could not afford—or his 'native air', but he presumed his return would be contrary to his brother's wishes. His recent expenses had been so great that he was 'at a great loss what course to take . . . to avoid further reflections' on his conduct. He concluded:

> I think it very hard fate to have a seat in the British Parliament, and at the same time in such a situation subject to so many inconveniences and vicissitudes in life. I would not presume to dictate to any of my friends, whose knowledge and understanding . . . far exceeds mine . . . but nevertheless cannot help being of opinion that a little comfortable provision might be made for me in some employment or other.

There is no record of his receiving an appointment or returning to England while a Member. He did not stand again in 1768.

He died 14 Aug. 1778.[4]

[1] Hardwicke to G. Heathcote, 4 Dec. 1760, Add. 35596, ff. 197–201. [2] *Court and City Reg.* 1764. [3] Add. 29589B, f. 28. [4] *Annual Reg.* 1778, p. 226 gives 7 Aug.

M.M.D.

## CHAMIER, Anthony (1725–80), of Epsom, Surr.

TAMWORTH 10 June 1778–12 Oct. 1780

*b.* 6 Oct. 1725, 4th s. of Daniel Chamier by Susan de la Mejenelle. *m.* 3 Oct. 1753, Dorothy, da. and coh. of Robert Wilson, merchant, of Woodford, Essex, *s.p.* Her sis. Elizabeth m. Thomas Bradshaw (q.v.).

Sec. to commander-in-chief at the War Office 1763–72; dep. sec. at war 1772–5; under-sec. of state 1775–*d.*

Anthony Chamier's grandfather was a Calvinist minister at Neufchatel who came to England in 1691, and his mother's family were also Huguenots. His father, a London merchant, had been private secretary to the Earl of Stair on his embassy to France 1714–20. Anthony Chamier was a broker, conducting his business at Garraway's coffee house in Change Alley. By 1760 he had established himself as a leading City financier, and was one of Newcastle's advisers on monetary affairs. In a letter to Bute of 15 Jan. 1763,[1] asking for a share in the next Government loan, he wrote: 'I have never paid in less than £150,000 every year during the course of the late war.' He was also a man of wide cultural interests, and a foundation member of Samuel Johnson's literary club.

About 1763 he retired from business, and went into Government service. When in February 1763 Lord Sandwich was appointed ambassador to Spain he selected Chamier as his private secretary 'in consequence of a recommendation from Lord Barrington'.[2] Sandwich never went to Spain, and Chamier was appointed by Barrington to a place at the War Office. His introduction to Barrington he probably owed to his brother-in-law Bradshaw, who had been first clerk at the War Office. In a letter to Sandwich of 26 Sept. 1768[3] Robert Jones (q.v.), his man of business, wrote: 'I have told Mr. Chamier how favourably your Lordship speaks of him, and that he is the first person to be provided for when your Lordship has it in your power.' In December 1770 Sandwich was appointed secretary of state and offered Chamier the post of under-secretary;[4] but the following month Sandwich resigned to become first lord of the Admiralty, and Chamier remained at the War Office, becoming in 1772 its deputy head.

In 1775 Rigby recommended Chamier to Weymouth as under-secretary of state.[5] Three years later he was returned to Parliament on Weymouth's interest at Tamworth. There is no record of his having spoken in the House, and as a politician he was of little account.

Chamier was one of the few in Parliament to estimate correctly the difficulties the Government faced in prosecuting the American war. 'I am inclined to be a croaker in this business', he wrote about America to Sir Robert Murray Keith (q.v.), 21 July 1775.[6] And on 1 Jan. 1778, after the news of Burgoyne's surrender had reached England:[7] 'Stores of every sort and kind are now fitting out in France and Spain . . . for America; if they . . . arrive in their ports the submission of America is not to be obtained.' His letters to Keith show his poor opinion of North's Administration and his pessimism about

the future. 3 Apr. 1778: 'I do not think my present situation worth many years purchase';[8] 26 Feb. 1779: 'I . . . am sick of politics';[9] 16 July 1779: 'The public have very deservedly great contempt for the present Administration, but . . . still more . . . for the Opposition.'[10]

Chamier died 12 Oct. 1780.

[1] Add. 5726C, f. 127. [2] Sandwich to Grenville, 4 Aug. 1764, *Grenville Pprs.* ii. 415–16. [3] Sandwich mss. [4] Bradshaw to Grafton, 18 Dec. 1770, Grafton mss. [5] Chamier to Sir R. M. Keith, 23 Nov. 1775, Add. 35509, f. 248. [6] Ibid. f. 138. [7] Add. 35513, f. 1. [8] Ibid. f. 218. [9] Add. 35515, f. 262. [10] Add. 35517, f. 27.

J.B.

**CHAMPION, Anthony** (1725–1801), of Croydon, Surr.

| | |
|---|---|
| St. Germans | 1754–1761 |
| Liskeard | 1761–1768 |

*b.* 5 Feb. 1725, s. of Peter and Catherine Champion of Croydon, Surr. *educ.* Cheam; Eton 1739–43; St. Mary Hall, Oxf. 1743; M. Temple 1739, called 1749; bencher 1779; reader 1785. *unm. suc.* fa. 27 May 1758.

Champion's father, a rich Leghorn merchant, was of Cornish origin. Anthony, a contemporary of Edward Eliot (q.v.) at St. Mary Hall, Oxford, was returned by him for St. Germans—a friend, wrote Eliot to Newcastle, 18 Mar. 1754, 'whose attachment to his Majesty's person and family and Government I can be answerable for'.[1] When in the autumn of 1755 Eliot went to France for his health, Champion accompanied him, but returned home at Newcastle's request to Eliot, to attend Parliament. In 1761 he was returned by Eliot for Liskeard. In the divisions on the peace preliminaries, 1, 9, and 10 Dec. 1762, Champion voted with Opposition, while Eliot stayed away. In three divisions on Wilkes and general warrants (15 Nov. 1763, and 15 and 18 Feb. 1764) Champion again voted with Opposition, as did Eliot in the two February divisions; but on 6 Feb., when almost all the lawyers voted with the Government, Champion and Eliot did likewise. In the summer of 1765 both were listed 'pro' by Rockingham; and in 1766–7 were classed as supporters of the Chatham Administration—Champion voted with them even on the land tax, 27 Feb. 1767. There is no record of his having spoken in the House; and W. H. Lyttelton (q.v.) who, after Champion's death published a volume by him of *Miscellanies in Verse and Prose*, wrote in the preface that Champion sat in Parliament 'a mute observer of the scene'—

the same great modesty and reserve restrained him from displaying the powers of his very discerning and enlightened mind in that illustrious assembly, which prevented him also from communicating to the world those effusions of his rich and luxuriant vein of poetry that are now submitted to the judgment of the public.

Champion died 22 Feb. 1801.

[1] Add. 32734, f. 275; 32735, f. 599.

L.B.N.

## CHANDLER, see CAVENDISH, Richard

## CHAPLIN, John (?1728–64), of Blankney, Lincs.

LINCOLN   1754–1761
STAMFORD   1761–31 May 1764

*b.* ?1728, 1st s. of Thomas Chaplin by Diana, da. of Andrew Archer, M.P., sis. of Thomas, 1st Lord Archer. *educ.* Westminster Feb. 1744, aged 15, left 1745. *m.* 19 May 1757, Lady Elizabeth Cecil, da. of Brownlow, 8th Earl of Exeter, sis. of Thomas Chambers Cecil (q.v.), 1s. 1da. with other issue. Chaplin's sis. Diana m. 1749 Lord George Manners Sutton (q.v.). *suc.* fa. Jan. 1747.

At Lincoln, in 1754, Chaplin had the support of Lord Scarbrough and the Rutland family, and was returned in a warmly contested election. In Dupplin's list of 1754 he was classed as a Government supporter.

On 13 Jan. 1761 Thomas Thoroton wrote to Lord Granby (qq.v.):[1]

Mr. Chaplin declines [to stand for Lincoln] and Lord Scarbrough brings in Mr. Sibthorp in his place. Chaplin goes to Stamford.

There he was returned unopposed on the interest of his brother-in-law, Brownlow, 9th Earl of Exeter. In 1761 he was sent Newcastle's parliamentary whip through the Duke of Ancaster. In Bute's list the names of Lords Exeter and Granby are written against him; he voted for the peace preliminaries, 1 Dec. 1762, and on 10 Dec. 1762 spoke for them.[2] After that he presumably voted on the Government side. He never appears either as voting with the Opposition or as absent.

He died 31 May 1764.

[1] *HMC Rutland*, ii. 239. [2] Newcastle's 'Memorandums', 11 Dec. 1762, Add. 33000, ff. 223–4, and Harris's 'Debates'.

L.B.N.

## CHARLTON, Job Staunton (1700–78), of Staunton Hall, Notts.

NEWARK   1741–1761

*b.* 8 Feb. 1700, 1st s. of Gilbert Charlton (s. of Sir Job Charlton, 1st Bt., M.P.) by Anne, da. and h. of Harvey Staunton of Staunton Hall. *educ.* St. Catherine's, Camb. 1718; L. Inn 1718. *m.* 30 Dec. 1725, Mary, da. of Daniel Greenwood, M.D., of Northampton, 4da. *suc.* fa. 1703; and to his mother's Staunton estates 1732.

Clerk of deliveries in the Ordnance 1751–8; chairman of ways and means, House of Commons 1752–61.

Charlton was Newcastle's chief election agent in Nottinghamshire and his manager at Newark. For these services he received a place (not a sinecure) in the Ordnance at a salary of £400 p.a., which he exchanged in 1758 for a pension of £500 on Ireland; and in 1752 he was appointed chairman of committees with £500 p.a. out of secret service funds. In 1754 Newcastle procured a grant of £1,000 from secret service funds towards his election expenses, which appear to have amounted to about £1,700.[1]

In March 1761 Charlton, who had now become unpopular at Newark, applied to Newcastle for leave to retire on grounds of ill health. Still, he wrote on 5 Mar.,[2] 'If any untoward circumstances should make my continuing . . . necessary to your Grace's interest I must submit.' His resignation was accepted, but when he remained neutral in the contest of 1761 Newcastle thought it 'hard, after all the many great and permanent obligations he has to me'.[3]

Charlton died February 1778.

[1] Namier. *Structure*, 200, 228. [2] Add. 32919, f. 458. [3] Newcastle to John White, 25 Mar. 1761, Add. 32921, f. 59.

J.B.

## CHARLTON, see also LECHMERE

## CHARTERIS, Francis (1749–1808), of Amisfield, Haddington and Hornby, Lancs.

HADDINGTON BURGHS   23 Feb. 1780–23 May 1787

*b.* 31 Jan. 1749, o. s. of Hon. Francis Wemyss Charteris of Amisfield and Hornby (2nd s. of James, 4th Earl of Wemyss [S]) by Lady Catherine Gordon, da. of Alexander, 2nd Duke of Gordon [S]; nephew of Lord Adam Gordon and James Wemyss of Wemyss (qq.v.). *educ.* St. Andrews Univ. 1762; Grand Tour 1766.[1] *m.* 18 July 1771, Susan, da. of Anthony Tracy Keck (q.v.) of Great Tew, Oxon. and gd.-da. of James, 4th Duke of Hamilton [S], 1s. 4da.

Charteris's father inherited from Colonel Charteris, a notorious usurer and gambler, a vast fortune and great estates in Haddington, Lancashire and Westmorland, and by family agreements consequent upon the attainder in 1746 of the Jacobite Lord Elcho, Lord Wemyss's heir, obtained possession of the Elcho estates in Fife. He succeeded John Maitland in Haddington Burghs in February 1780 and consistently supported Administration to the end of the Parliament. He spoke, 11 Apr., in the debate on the grant for Scottish roads and bridges; on 24 Apr. against the motion to implement the vote of 6 Apr. on the influence of the Crown, and on 4 May in defence of Scotland's exemption from the malt tax.[2]

Although Charteris voted with Administration on 12 Dec. 1781 on Lowther's motion against the war, on 14 Dec. he expressed his satisfaction at their intention to limit American commitments. In the debate of 15 Mar. 1782 on Rous's motion of no confidence, he deplored reckless Opposition comment on Irish and American affairs. 'To the great latitude of speech . . . on the injustice of the American war were to be ascribed . . . many of those calamities which were now said to be the fruits of the present Administration.'[3]

He voted against Shelburne's peace preliminaries, 18 Feb. 1783; did not vote on Fox's East India bill; and in January 1784 was listed 'doubtful' by Robinson. On 23 Jan. 1784, when Pitt refused to state whether or not Parliament was to be dissolved,

> Mr. Charteris asserted his own independence. He was connected with no party. The conduct however of ministers struck him at present as being so affrontive of the dignity of the House that he would support any measures which conveyed censure on their conduct or tended to extort from them those informations which they were bound to give.[4]

Thereafter he was counted against Pitt. At the general election of 1784 he was returned after a contest, and voted with the Opposition on Pitt's Irish commercial propositions, 13 May 1785, and on Richmond's fortifications plan, 27 Feb. 1786.

On the death on 29 Apr. 1787 of David, Lord Elcho, owing to whose attainder the honours of Wemyss had been forfeited in 1756, Charteris's father as next heir assumed the title of 5th Earl of Wemyss, and Charteris himself that of Viscount Elcho. On 21 May, when Sir John Sinclair gave notice that he would move for a new writ for Haddington Burghs, Elcho declared he would oppose it as he had not vacated his seat. The question was fully debated on 23 May when Sinclair quoted precedents to prove that Elcho, having become the eldest son of a Scottish peer, was disqualified from representing a Scottish constituency. The Opposition disputed that interpretation of the Act of Union, and the discrimination between the eldest sons of Scottish and English peers, Elcho himself maintaining that he was at least entitled to retain his seat until the general election, when on his re-election a petition could be presented against him.[5] Sinclair's motion was carried without a division, Elcho had to vacate his seat, and did not accept Dundas's challenge to contest the by-election. Although in the event his father's title was not recognized, as being still under attainder, Elcho made no attempt to re-enter Parliament.

He died *v.p.* 20 Jan. 1808.

[1] See Hume to James Oswald, 1 Oct. 1766, *Letters of David Hume*, ii. 95 (Charteris is wrongly identified in the footnote). [2] Almon, xvii. 499, 556, 642. [3] Debrett, v. 183, vi. 458. [4] Ibid. xii. 643. [5] Stockdale, xii. 145–6, 149–54; *Scots Mag.* 1787, p. 334.

E.H.-G.

**CHAYTOR, William** (1732–1819), of Croft and Spennithorne, Yorks.

PENRYN 1774–1780
HEDON 1780–1790

*b.* 11 Jan. 1732, 1st s. of Henry Chaytor of Croft Hall, Darlington, Yorks. by Jane, da. and h. of Matthew Smales of Gilling, Yorks. *educ.* Appleby; Magdalene, Camb. 1750; L. Inn 1753; I. Temple 1755, called 1756. *m.* Jane Lee of Appleby, 3s. 5da. His bro. Rev. Henry Chaytor, prebendary of Durham m. 1765, Anne, sis. of John Robinson (q.v.). *suc.* fa. 9 Feb. 1774.

Bencher, I. Temple 1792, reader 1798, treasurer 1799; mayor, Appleby 1768, 1789, recorder 1793.

In 1774 Chaytor was returned for Penryn as a Government candidate. In 1780 he was defeated at Penryn but returned for Hedon. In the House he was a regular Government supporter, closely co-operating with Robinson 'whom', wrote the *Public Ledger* in 1779, 'he assists in counting the House upon late days, and for that purpose usually sits near the Bar'. There is no record of his having spoken in debate. He remained connected with Robinson after Robinson had left office; did not vote on Shelburne's peace preliminaries, 18 Feb. 1783, but voted for Fox's East India bill, 27 Nov. Robinson, in a list compiled in the second week of December 1783, counted Chaytor as 'pro', and noted against Hedon: 'Mr. Chaytor is well liked there and very likely will be elected again.' And a few days later, about securing also the second seat at Hedon:

> This to be attended to by sending to Mr. Chaytor in due time and having the proper manager up to town at the moment after the change [of Government].

But on 30 Mar. 1784 George Rose wrote to Robinson that Darell, the second Government candidate, was 'safe at Hedon, though he had no assistance from Chaytor'.[1]

In the Parliament of 1784 Chaytor steadily adhered to Pitt. He did not stand in 1790, but on 3 May, shortly before the general election, wrote to Pitt asking for an Irish peerage;[2] he claimed to have given all the help he could to Pitt's friends in co. Durham and Kent.

Chaytor died 15 May 1819.

[1] Laprade, 73, 112, 120. [2] Chatham ms 122.

I.R.C.

**CHESTER, Thomas** (1696–1763), of Almondsbury, nr. Bristol.

GLOUCESTER 1727–16 Feb. 1728
GLOUCESTERSHIRE 1734–1 Oct. 1763

*b.* 2 May 1696, 1st s. of Thomas Chester by Anne, da. and coh. of Sir Samuel Astry of Henbury, Glos. *educ.* Oriel, Oxf. 1713. *m.* (1) 25 Sept. 1721, Lady Sarah

Henrietta Howard (*d.*1722), da. of Henry, 6th Earl of Suffolk, *s.p.*; (2) 28 Feb. 1736, Mary, da. and h. of Jeremy Gough of London, wid. of George Guinnet, *s.p. suc.* fa. 1704.

Chester sat for Gloucestershire with Beaufort support and was returned unopposed in 1754 and again in 1761. He was classed as 'Tory' in Dupplin's list of 1754 and in Bute's of December 1761. He does not appear in Henry Fox's list of Members favourable to the peace preliminaries, December 1762, but did not vote against them. Jenkinson in the autumn of 1763 classed him as 'doubtful'. Chester is only once reported to have spoken in the House: on 13 Mar. 1763, during the debate on the cider tax, when, according to Harris, 'Old Chester . . . was seen to speak, but not heard, a gentle murmur on all sides filling the House as he spoke.'

He died 1 Oct. 1763.

M.M.D.

**CHESTER,** *see also* **BROMLEY CHESTER**

**CHETWYND, William Richard** (?1683–1770), of Ingestre Hall, Staffs.

STAFFORD      1715–1722
PLYMOUTH     1722–1727
STAFFORD      1734–3 Apr. 1770

*b.* ?1683, 3rd s. of John Chetwynd, M.P., of Ingestre Hall by Lucy, da. of Robert Roan of Chaldon, Surr.; uncle of Hon. W. R. Chetwynd (q.v.). *educ.* Westminster; Ch. Ch. Oxf. 8 June 1703, aged 19. *m.* (settlement dated 3 June 1715) Honora, da. of William Baker, consul at Algiers, 3s. 4da. *suc.* bro. as 3rd Visct. Chetwynd [I] 21 June 1767.

Envoy to Genoa 1708–12; ld. of Admiralty 1717–27; under-sec. of state 1745–8; master of the mint 1744–69.

The Chetwynds were an old Staffordshire family, who in the earlier part of the century usually held one seat at Stafford. On the death of John, 2nd Viscount, in 1767 the estates went to his daughter Catherine, who had married John Talbot (q.v.).

By 1754 William Richard Chetwynd's active political career was over and he had become a regular Government supporter, which he remained under George III. Horace Walpole wrote to Lord Hertford about the debate on general warrants of 14–15 Feb. 1764:

Old Will Chetwynd, now past eighty, and who had walked to the House, did not stir a single moment out of his place from three in the afternoon till the division at seven in the morning.

Chetwynd was returned for Stafford in 1768 after a contest; and died 3 Apr. 1770, aged 86.

J.B.

**CHETWYND, Hon. William Richard** (?1731–65).

STAFFORD      1754–Feb. 1765

*b.* ?1731, 2nd s. of John, 2nd Visct. Chetwynd [I], M.P., nephew of W. R. Chetwynd (q.v.). *educ.* Eton 1742; C.C.C. Oxf. 17 Jan. 1747, aged 15. *m.* 13 Mar. 1753, Elizabeth, da. of William Wollaston, M.P., sis. of William Wollaston (q.v.), 1da.

In Dupplin's list of 1754 Chetwynd was classed as a country gentleman supporting Administration. He appears in Fox's list of Members favourable to the peace preliminaries (early December 1762). In autumn 1763 Jenkinson first classed him as 'pro', then 'doubtful'. He voted against the Grenville Administration over general warrants, 15 and 18 Feb. 1764, and was classed by Newcastle, 10 May, as a doubtful friend. He died *v.p.* in the south of France, February 1765.

J.B.

**CHEWTON, Visct.,** *see* **WALDEGRAVE, George**

**CHICHESTER, Arthur,** 5th Earl of Donegall [I] (1739–99).

MALMESBURY      1768–1774

*b.* 13 June 1739, 1st s. of Hon. John Chichester of Abinger, Surr. (2nd s. of Arthur, 3rd Earl of Donegall), by Elizabeth, da. of Sir Richard Newdigate, 3rd Bt., of Arbury, Warws. *educ.* Westminster 1748; Trinity, Oxf. 1757. *m.* (1) 16 Nov. 1761, Lady Anne Hamilton (*d.* 11 Nov. 1780), da. of James, 5th Duke of Hamilton [S], 3s. 4da.; (2) 24 Oct. 1788, Charlotte (*d.* 28 Sept. 1789), da. of Conway Spencer of Tremary, co. Down, wid. of Thomas Moore of Barne, co. Tipperary, *s.p.*, (3) 12 Oct. 1790, Barbara, da. of Rev. Luke Godfrey, rector of Middleton, co. Cork, *s.p. suc.* uncle as 5th Earl of Donegall [I], 30 Sept. 1757; *cr.* Baron Fisherwick [GB] 3 July 1790; Mq. of Donegall [I] 4 July 1791.

Donegall was returned for Malmesbury by his friend Lord Suffolk, and at first followed Suffolk and the Grenville group. He voted against Administration over Wilkes on 2 Feb. 1769, but not in any other division of 1769; and again with Opposition on 8 and 25 Jan. 1770. On 13 Feb. 1771 he voted against the Spanish convention, although Suffolk had by then gone over to Administration. In Robinson's first survey on the royal marriage bill, Donegall is marked 'contra, present'; in the second 'pro, present'. He voted against Administration on the naval captains' petition, 9 Feb. 1773, and Grenville's Election Act, 25 Feb. 1774, but on both divisions was classed as basically friendly to Administration. He is not known to have spoken in the House, and did not stand in 1774.

He died 5 Jan. 1799.

J.B.

**CHILD, Francis** (c.1735–63), of Osterley Park, Mdx.

BISHOP'S CASTLE    1761–23 Sept. 1763

*b.* c. 1735, 1st surv. s. of Samuel Child, M.P., of Osterley Park, by Agatha, da. of Mileson Edward. *educ.* Westminster 1744; Magdalen, Oxf. 1753. *unm. suc.* fa. 1752.

In 1756 Francis Child became a partner in the family bank; and in 1761 was returned without a contest for Bishop's Castle, which his father had represented 1747–52. The election cost him £1200, and he had presumably the support of the Walcot family who were heavily in debt to Child's bank. In Bute's list of December 1761 Child is classed as a Tory. He is not in the list Fox drew up early in December 1762 of Members favourable to the peace preliminaries, but did not vote against them. Altogether no vote or speech by him is recorded. He died 23 Sept. 1763, shortly before he was to be married to a daughter of Robert Trevor Hampden (subsequently 4th Baron Trevor and 1st Viscount Hampden); he left her £50,000.

J.B.

**CHILD, Robert** (1739–82), of Osterley Park, Mdx.

WELLS    15 Jan. 1766–28 July 1782

*b.* Feb. 1739, 2nd surv. s. of Samuel Child, M.P., and bro. of Francis Child (q.v.). *educ.* Westminster, Feb. 1747, aged 8; Magdalen, Oxf. 9 Feb. 1758, aged 18. *m.* 6 Oct. 1763, Sarah, da. of Gilbert Jodrell of Ankerwyke, Bucks., 1da. *suc.* bro. 23 Sept. 1763.

Robert Child became a partner in the family banking business in 1760, and in 1763 succeeded his brother as titular head of the firm—it is not certain that he was ever an active partner.

At the by-election at Aylesbury in January 1764 Child came forward as a candidate with the support of the Grenville Administration, but owing to illness was forced to withdraw.[1] At Wells in December 1765 he stood on the interest of Clement Tudway, and after a contest was returned on petition.

His politics on entering Parliament are not known; he did not vote against the repeal of the Stamp Act. Rockingham in November 1766 and Townshend in January 1767 classed him as 'doubtful'. He voted against the Chatham Administration on the land tax, 27 Feb. 1767, and the nullum tempus bill, 17 Feb. 1768. At the general election of 1768 he fought another contest at Wells.

The *Public Ledger* wrote about him in 1779: 'attends but seldom, and votes in opposition'. The first statement seems correct: he appears in none of the 23 division lists between January 1769 and March 1780. But Robinson, in his lists on the royal marriage bill in 1772 and the contractors bill in

1779, classed him as a Government supporter. On Dunning's motion, 6 Apr. 1780, Child voted with Opposition; and was classed by Robinson in his survey for the general election of 1780 as 'doubtful'. In the divisions of February–March 1782 Child twice voted against North's Administration: 27 Feb. 1782, on Conway's motion against the war, and 15 Mar. 1782, on Rous's motion of no confidence. The large share which his firm had in the Government loan of February 1782 had no effect on his political conduct. There is no record of his having spoken in the House.

Child died 28 July 1782, aged 43. The *Gentleman's Magazine* (1782, p. 406), wrote in its obituary of him: 'He has died worth £15,000 per annum in landed property, exclusive of his seat at Osterley Park, which is deemed the most superb and elegant thing of its kind in England. His share of the profits in the banking business has never been estimated at less, for some years, than £30,000 per annum.' He was in addition a considerable holder of Government stock.[2]

[1] Grenville to Chas. Lowndes, 21 Jan. 1764, Grenville letter bk.
[2] Bank of England recs.

I.R.C.

**CHILD**, *see also* **TYLNEY**

**CHOLMLEY, Nathaniel** (1721–91), of Howsham and Whitby, Yorks.

ALDBOROUGH        11 Dec. 1756–1768
BOROUGHBRIDGE              1768–1774

*b.* 15 Nov. 1721, 1st surv. s. of Hugh Cholmley, M.P., by Catherine, da. of Sir John Wentworth, 1st Bt., of North Elmsall and Brodsworth, Yorks. *educ.* poss. Eton.[1] *m.* (1) 13 June 1750, Catherine (*d.*9 Apr. 1755), da. of Sir Rowland Winn, 4th Bt., of Nostell, Yorks., 2da.; (2) 10 Sept. 1757, Henrietta Catherine (*d.*22 Nov. 1769), da. of Stephen Croft of Stillington, Yorks., 1s. 2da.; (3) 22 Aug. 1774, Anne Jesse, da. of Leonard Smelt of Langton, Yorks., *s.p. suc.* fa. 1755.

When Pitt took office in November 1756 Newcastle, in search of a candidate at Aldborough, turned to Rockingham for advice. Rockingham first recommended Sir Rowland Winn, 4th Bt., who refused, and next Cholmley, Winn's son-in-law, whom he vouched for as 'a staunch and disinterested friend'.[2] Cholmley naturally followed Newcastle and Rockingham in politics: he voted against the peace preliminaries on 1, 9 and 10 Dec. 1762, and against general warrants, 6, 15 and 18 Feb. 1764; for the reduction of the land tax, 27 Feb. 1767, and for the nullum tempus bill, 17 Feb. 1768.

In 1768 Aldborough and Boroughbridge were the only boroughs on which Newcastle could absolutely depend to return his candidates; he seems to have preferred not to choose Cholmley again, but did not wish to offend Rockingham. In a list of candidates, dated 19 Dec. 1767, he put a query opposite Cholmley's name;[3] and wrote to Rockingham on 22 Dec.:[4]

> You know I choose four Members at my own boroughs. Honest West[5] I am engaged to, and to your Lordship, and to you only, and for your own reasons, to Cholmley.

Cholmley voted with the Opposition, 1768–74, and as a supporter of parliamentary reform, regularly voted for Sawbridge's motion for shorter Parliaments.[6] During this Parliament several speeches of his are reported, principally in opposition to the royal marriage bill, March 1772, and on the Selby canal bill, March–April 1773. At the general election of 1774 he stood little chance of remaining in Parliament: Henry, 2nd Duke of Newcastle supported Administration and would obviously not re-elect Cholmley, and his standing in the Rockingham party was not sufficient to procure him a seat. But he seems to have left Parliament without regret. In December 1779, apparently influenced by his father-in-law, Leonard Smelt, he opposed the petitioning movement: 'I do not think this is the proper time, when the nation is so engaged and has so many difficulties', he wrote to Wyvill, 5 Dec.; and anyway, he declared at the meeting on 30 Dec., he 'had sat far too long in the House to think that a petition would be productive of any good effect'.[7] In 1783 Mrs. Montagu visited the 'Elysian fields' of Howsham; here is the account she gave of Cholmley and his wife:[8]

> Mr. and Mrs. Cholmley wish not for any power but the power of doing good, nor contend for any superiority but that which transcendent virtue gives; and all they covet is to make those around them happy. They have built a village very near their house, and fitted up and furnished the houses with all the decent comforts humble life requires, and these habitations are bestowed on their old or married servants who are obliged to retire. The children of the latter are taught to read, write, cast accounts, sew, knit, spin, etc., at a school established by Mr. Cholmley, and well regulated and frequently inspected by Mrs. Cholmley. If in the golden age villages were built and inhabited, I dare say in their modes and their manners they resembled the village at Howsham in every respect.

Cholmley died 11 Mar. 1791.

[1] *Etoniana*, no. 65, p. 232. [2] Rockingham to Newcastle [2 Dec. 1756], Add. 32869, ff. 217–18. [3] Add. 32987, ff. 341–2. [4] Ibid. ff. 397–8. [5] James West sen. (q.v.). [6] *Wyvill Pprs.* iii. 130. [7] Ibid. i. 11. [8] Mrs. Montagu to the Dowager Duchess of Portland, 22 Nov. 1783, *HMC Bath*, i. 349.

J.B.

**CHOLMONDELEY, Charles** (1685–1756), of Vale Royal, Cheshire.

CHESHIRE 1710–1715
1722–30 Mar. 1756

*b.* 12 Jan. 1685, 1st s. of Thomas Cholmondeley, M.P., of Vale Royal by Anne, da. of Sir Walter St. John, 3rd Bt., M.P., of Lydiard Tregoze, Wilts. *educ.* St. John's, Camb. 1701; M. Temple 1709. *m.* 22 July 1714, Essex, da. of Governor Thomas Pitt, M.P., aunt of William Pitt, 3s. 5da. *suc.* fa. 1702.

Cholmondeley was a Tory, and voted in opposition. He died 30 Mar. 1756.

M.M.D.

**CHOLMONDELEY, George**, Visct. Malpas (1724–1764).

BRAMBER 1754–1761
CORFE CASTLE 1761–15 Mar. 1764

*b.* 17 Oct. 1724, 1st s. of George, 3rd Earl of Cholmondeley, by Mary, da. of Sir Robert Walpole, 1st Earl of Orford. *m.* 19 Jan. 1747, Hester, da. and h. of Sir Francis Edwardes, 3rd Bt., 1s. 1da.

Served as volunteer at Fontenoy; commanded as lt-col. regt. of Ft. raised by his fa. 1745–6; on half-pay as capt. of Ft. 1754–60; col. 65 Ft. Dec. 1760–d.

In March 1752 Malpas stood for Dorchester, and having lost by 118 to 113 votes, did not give up his 'endeavours to be chosen there'—writing to Newcastle, 6 Apr. 1754,[1] he claimed that the interest he had formed

> not only in the town but with the principal gentlemen of that country joined to an expense of upwards of a £1000 and a constant residence of upwards of two years left . . . little doubt of success.

As his opposition threatened primarily Joseph Damer, Lord Milton (q.v.), an Administration candidate, Henry Pelham offered to bring him into Parliament for Bramber, and Pelham's 'repeated solicitations' were reinforced by 'the commands' of Lord Cholmondeley. On 5 Jan. 1754 Malpas wrote to Pelham from Dorchester:[2]

> In consequence of what passed between us . . . I set out with a resolution to decline being a candidate for this borough. The difficulties I have met with, in order to effect this, have been much greater than I foresaw, as my poll was stronger than Lord Milton's, but not so strong as Mr. Pitt's. In these circumstances what arguments could I use? to mention it as *your request*, to most people would have been very improper; to intimate *my own fears* as to the *expense*, I thought not advisable . . . there is a discontented body here, who are much alarmed and displeased at my leaving them, and will be glad of any opportunity to foment an opposition.

Because of some 'invidious reports' spread by his opponents, he begged, 'both on my own account and that of my friends here', that his seat in Parliament 'may be for any borough sooner than Bramber'. As Damer had sat for Bramber 1747–54, an invidious interpretation might have been put on such an exchange against a seat in that borough of one where Malpas had appealed to a party of local malcontents. Other arrangements were therefore tried by Pelham, and after his death by Newcastle; but in the end Malpas was returned for Bramber. To compensate Malpas for his previous expenses, £1,000 was paid at Bramber from secret service money, to which he had to add £500 of his own.[3]

In 1755 Malpas was given a secret service pension of £600 p.a., of which the first instalment appears in Newcastle's accounts on 19 Mar. 1756 and the last on 21 Apr. 1761. What happened after that is not clear, but at the time of Bute's resignation, Malpas wrote to his secretary, Charles Jenkinson, 13 Apr. 1763,[4] about a pension given to him 'for three years *only*' and which expired on 25 Mar. 1763, but of which a year was 'yet unpaid'. And that he held one at the time of his death appears from Grenville's letter to his widow, 9 June 1764, refusing to recommend its continuance to her.[5]

In 1761 Malpas was returned for Corfe Castle on the interest of John Bond (q.v.). In the House he counted throughout as a supporter of Administration; was included in Fox's list of Members favourable to the peace preliminaries; and over the division on general warrants, 18 Feb. 1764, was placed by Jenkinson among 'friends absent'. He died 15 Mar. 1764.

I have just lost my nephew, Lord Malpas [wrote Walpole to Mann, 18 Mar.] a worthy amiable man, whom I have loved from his childhood. But my grief is light compared to that of poor Lady Malpas. He married her sixteen years ago, with no considerable portion of beauty, and less fortune, though of an exceedingly good family. As his father's profusion called for his restoring the estate, we lamented this match; but it proved a blessing: there never was a more prudent, estimable woman. They lived in the happiest union. Above two months ago he went to his regiment in Ireland and came away ill. He arrived in Town last Monday, grew immediately worse; it turned to an inflammation of his bowels, and carried him off in five days. There is but a slender provision for his widow, and less for his only daughter.

[1] Add. 32735, ff. 52–53. [2] Add. 32734, ff. 19–20. [3] See Newcastle's paper of 8 Apr. 1754, Add. 32995, f. 201. [4] Bute mss. [5] Grenville letter bk.

L.B.N.

## CHOLMONDELEY, Thomas (1726–79), of Vale Royal, Cheshire.

CHESHIRE    28 Apr. 1756–1768

*b.* 24 June 1726, 1st surv. s. of Charles Cholmondeley (q.v.). *educ.* Westminster 1740–3; St. John's, Camb. 1743. *m.* 29 Oct. 1764, Dorothy, da. and h. of Edmund Cowper of Overlegh, Cheshire, 6s. 3da. *suc.* fa. 30 Mar. 1756.

In 1756 and 1761 Cholmondeley was returned unopposed. In Bute's list he was classed 'Tory, Pitt'. He voted against the peace preliminaries, December 1762; in autumn 1763 was marked by

Jenkinson as 'contra', and voted with the Opposition on Wilkes, 15 Nov. 1763, and general warrants, February 1764; and was classed by Newcastle, 10 May 1764, as a 'sure friend'. Rockingham, July 1765, classed him as 'doubtful', but he did not vote against the repeal of the Stamp Act, and on 18 Apr. 1766 George Onslow (q.v.), in a letter to Newcastle, included Cholmondeley among 'our people' who had voted with the Administration on the budget.[1] Rockingham, November 1766, classed him as 'Whig'; Townshend, January 1767, as 'Rockingham'; Newcastle, 2 Mar. 1767, as 'Tory'. He voted against Administration on the land tax, 27 Feb. 1767,[2] and on the nullum tempus bill, 17 Feb. 1768.

Three speeches by Cholmondeley are recorded: when on 5 Mar. 1763 William Beckford, fulminating against standing armies, instanced Richard II's 'rabble from Cheshire', this 'drew up Cholmondeley to say a word for his Cheshire friends';[3] on 21 Mar. 1764 he spoke in support of the militia bill; and on 10 May 1765 for including the Princess Dowager in the Regency bill.

William Blackett wrote to his kinsman Sir Edward (q.v.) on 10 Dec. 1766 (in a letter of which the paper is torn):[4]

Mr. Cholmondeley's friends seem very confident he will . . . again for the county, if he stands on his own bottom . . . does not take that pains to ingratiate himself . . . gentlemen and freeholders of the county, so that his interest will decline daily as his estate is at rack rent, and the Stamford interest will gain ground in the county.

Cholmondeley did not stand in 1768, and died 2 June 1779.

[1] Add. 32974, ff. 425–6. [2] He appears in two out of the three lists of the majority in this division. [3] Harris's 'Debates'. [4] Blackett mss at Matfen, Northumb.

M.M.D.

## CHRISTIAN, John (1756–1828), of Ewanrigg and Workington Hall, Cumb.

| CARLISLE | 31 May 1786–1790 |
| | 3 Mar. 1791–1812 |
| | 8 Mar. 1816–1820 |
| CUMBERLAND | 1820–11 Dec. 1828 |

*b.* 12 July 1756, 1st surv. s. of John Christian by Jane, da. of Eldred Curwen, M.P., of Workington. *m.* (1) 10 Sept. 1775, Margaret (*d.* 1 Feb. 1778), da. of John Taubman, speaker of the House of Keys, of Castletown, I.o.M., 1s.; (2) 5 Oct. 1782, his cos. Isabella, da. and h. of Henry Curwen (q.v.), 5s. 3da. *suc.* fa. 1767; took add. name of Curwen 1790.

Sheriff, Cumb. 1784–5.

Christian traditionally belonged to the anti-Lowther party in Cumberland. His uncle Henry Curwen was the first man to lead the revolt against

Lowther in Cumberland, and his father had been one of Portland's supporters. He himself wrote from Brussels to Portland's friend, Lord Torrington, 27 Feb. 1780:

> I have long had a wish (foreseeing an opposition) to offer my services for Carlisle . . . I should think myself greatly indebted if your Lordship had no objections to name it to his Grace, at the same time explaining my sentiments: if his Grace would give me his full interest he should be put to no expense: that my principles as well as inclination would lead me in case of being successful to support the same his Grace does, that in all private affairs [I] must be left to act as I thought right.

Portland's reply was favourable, and Christian returned to England to begin his canvass. But he found Lord Surrey bent on establishing his interest at Carlisle, and unwilling to come to any definite arrangement, and by June, after keeping Christian on tenterhooks, Surrey announced that he would himself stand. Christian's nomination would now have embroiled Portland in a further struggle with Lowther, and to avoid it he recommended Christian to Edward Eliot (q.v.) for one of Eliot's Cornish boroughs. There was some confusion about informing Christian of this arrangement, and by the time the matter was cleared up Christian had made plans (probably to go abroad again) which prevented his accepting the offer. He deeply resented the part played by Surrey at this time, and wrote to Portland, 11 Aug:

> Lord Surrey's claim upon Carlisle, however unexpected it was to me, would have been readily concurred in by me had his Lordship taken the proper steps. It was the manner not the thing from which I felt myself so much hurt. It will not admit of my making any comments upon it—should his Lordship's seat prove a short one it is from your Grace only I can form any hopes of succeeding in what has been long an object of consequence with me.[1]

At the by-election of 1786 caused by the death of Lowther's Member, Edward Norton, Christian contested Carlisle with the support of Surrey, who had now taken Portland's place at the head of the anti-Lowther party in the city. Christian was defeated at the poll, but returned on petition.

Christian's first recorded vote was in favour of Pitt's motion that Parliament was competent to regulate the powers of the Regent, 16 Dec. 1788. In the debate three days later, he regretted that the question had been introduced at all, but since it had, he had thought 'it was the duty of that House to assert its rights and decide them for the benefit of posterity'. Now, however, he thought the House should 'declare the Prince of Wales Regent as our ancestors had declared the Prince of Orange King, and . . . he did not think it right to place any restrictions whatever on the Prince while acting as

Regent'. But later in the same debate he admitted he 'scarcely knew which way he ought to vote. He did not wish to shrink from his duty; but the possibility of voting away the rights of the Crown under the pretence of defending the rights of the people staggered him.'[2] On the second recorded division on the Regency, 11 Feb. 1789, he paired off in opposition. After the outbreak of the French war Christian voted regularly with Opposition.

Christian was well known for his agricultural improvements. He died 11 Dec. 1828.

[1] Portland mss. [2] Stockdale, xvi. 115, 138.

M.M.D.

**CHURCHILL, Charles** (?1720–1812), of Farleigh, nr. Basingstoke, Hants.

| | |
|---|---|
| STOCKBRIDGE | 1741–1747 |
| MILBORNE PORT | 2 Dec. 1747–1754 |
| GREAT MARLOW | 1754–1761 |

*b.* ?1720, illegit. s. of Charles Churchill, M.P., by Anne Oldfield, actress. *educ.* Westminster, adm. 1730 but withdrawn soon after; Geneva 1736–9. *m.* 23 Feb. 1746, Lady Mary Walpole (granted the style and precedence of an Earl's da.), illegit. da. of Robert, 1st Earl of Orford, 3s. 2da.

Lt. 6 Drag. Gds. 1736, lt. 2 Ft. Gds. 1739; ret. 1745.

Dep. ranger of St. James's and Hyde parks 1745–c.1751; searcher in port of London.[1] His wife was housekeeper of Windsor castle 1762–82.

Charles Churchill was closely attached to the Walpole family, married Sir Robert's favourite daughter, and in later years was a constant visitor to Strawberry Hill. In Parliament he was a regular Administration supporter. In 1754 he stood at Great Marlow on the Clayton interest against a candidate supported by his brother-in-law, Lord Cholmondeley, and was returned. He never stood again.

Without his knowledge, Horace Walpole wrote to the Duke of Devonshire, 18 Feb. 1760:[2]

> I have some suspicions . . . that Mr. Churchill and Lady Mary are far from easy in their affairs. He has been so unlucky in marrying a favourite daughter of Sir Robert Walpole, as to be involved in a lawsuit for her fortune and to be likely to lose part, if not the whole of it. He has had other losses; and the Duke of Newcastle was so unkind as to give away even the reversion of a place which she holds only for the life of another person. Your Grace knows the steadiness of his behaviour to the Government as a Member of Parliament, an opportunity of serving the King which he has always bought very dearly, without least recompense, and even without asking the least.

He died 'in his 92nd year'[3] on 13 Apr. 1812.

[1] He is so noted in a list of 'useless sinecures' compiled for Geo. III in 1782, Fortescue, vi. 178. [2] Devonshire mss. [3] *Gent. Mag.* 1812, i. 398.

A.N.N.

**CLANBRASSILL, Earl of,** *see* **HAMILTON, James**

**CLARE, Visct.,** *see* **NUGENT, Robert**

**CLARGES, Sir Thomas,** 3rd Bt. (1751–82), of Aston, Herts.

LINCOLN 1780–23 Dec. 1782

*b.* 4 Oct. 1751, s. of Thomas Clarges (*d.*1753) by Anne, da. of John Shute, 1st Visct. Barrington [I], and gd.-s. of Sir Thomas Clarges, 2nd Bt. *educ.* Eton 1765; Ch. Ch. Oxf. 1770. *m.* 20 Oct. 1777, Louisa, da. of William Skrine (q.v.), 1s. *suc.* gd.-fa. as 3rd Bt. 19 Feb. 1759.

Clarges successfully contested Lincoln at the general election of 1780. In Parliament, 'convinced of the justice of the American war', and believing ministerial declarations that America could be recovered, he at first regularly voted with the Administration. But he told the House on 12 June 1781 that he now

> saw that success by arms was beyond our reach . . . the justice of the war became an object of very little consequence when it was withheld, and we were no longer in a situation to enforce it . . . peace, upon almost any terms, was infinitely preferable to a war under such peculiar circumstances: he meant no other avowed or proposed object, but utter ruin of one or both parties, without the most distant prospect of advantage in the event to either.[1]

Henceforth he consistently voted with the Opposition till the fall of North. His only other reported speech was in favour of Sir John Rous's motion of no confidence, 15 Mar. 1782.[2]

Clarges died 23 Dec. 1782.

[1] Debrett, iii. 525–6. [2] Ibid. vi. 459.

M.M.D.

**CLARKE, Godfrey Bagnall** (c.1742–74), of Sutton, Derbys.

DERBYSHIRE 1768–26 Dec. 1774

*b.* c.1742, 1st s. of Godfrey Clarke by Anne, da. and h. of German Pole of Radbourne, Derbys. *educ.* Grand Tour (Italy) c.1764. *unm.* *suc.* fa. 30 Mar. 1774.

Clarke was a great friend of Gibbon, whom he first met at Lausanne in 1763. Supported by 'all the Tory gentlemen' and 'almost all the leading gentlemen' in the county,[1] he was returned for Derbyshire after a contest in 1768. In Parliament he voted consistently with Opposition, but does not appear to have spoken. In 1774 he was returned without a contest.

On 13 Apr. 1774 Gibbon wrote to J. B. Holroyd:

> If my esteem and friendship for Godfrey had been capable of any addition, it would have been very much increased by the manner in which he felt and

lamented his father's death . . . He is now in very different circumstances than before; instead of an easy and ample allowance, he has taken possession of a great estate, with low rents and high encumbrances.

Clarke fell ill in August 1774, made a partial recovery in September, but at the end of November was 'extremely ill'—in 'very great if not immediate danger'. 'I know not what to say about him', Gibbon wrote on 17 Dec., 'he is reduced to nothing, and his disorder is attended with every bad symptom.' He died 26 Dec. 1774.

[1] Ld. Frederick Cavendish to Devonshire, 17 Nov. 1767, Devonshire mss.

J.B.

**CLARKE** (afterwards **CLARKE JERVOISE**), **Jervoise** (?1733–1808), of Idsworth Park, Hants.

| | |
|---|---|
| YARMOUTH I.o.W. | 1768–19 Jan. 1769 |
| | 1774–Nov. 1779 |
| HAMPSHIRE | 13 Dec. 1779–1790 |
| YARMOUTH I.o.W. | 4 Jan. 1791–5 July 1808 |

*b.* ?1733, o.s. of Samuel Clarke of West Bromwich, Staffs. by Mary Elizabeth, da. of Thomas Jervoise, M.P., of Herriard Park, Hants. *educ.* Emmanuel, Camb. 10 Dec. 1751, aged 18. *m.* 12 July 1763, Kitty, da. and h. of Robert Warner of Bedhampton, Hants, 3s. *suc.* fa. 1767; took add. name of Jervoise in compliance with the will of his gd.-fa. c.1771.

Jervoise possessed estates said to be worth nearly £20,000 p.a. which included Hampshire property inherited from his maternal grandfather Thomas Jervoise. In 1768, with two other Hampshire gentlemen, Sir William Oglander and Sir Thomas Worsley, he attempted to overthrow the Holmes interest in the Isle of Wight boroughs. He successfully contested Yarmouth, but was unseated on petition. Before the next general election he concluded an agreement with the Holmes family by which each was to return one Member at Yarmouth, and in 1774 was himself returned there unopposed. In Parliament he voted consistently against North's Administration. In 1779 he vacated his seat at Yarmouth to stand for Hampshire where he was opposed by the whole weight of ministerial power, yet was returned by a large majority. The *English Chronicle* wrote about him in 1781: 'Though no active party man, he votes upon all occasions against Government, and is a constant attendant on his parliamentary duty.' Jervoise did not vote on Shelburne's peace preliminaries, 18 Feb. 1783; was classed by Robinson in March 1783 as a follower of Fox; voted for parliamentary reform, 7 May 1783, and for Fox's East India bill, 27 Nov. 1783. He consistently opposed Pitt's Administration from the start and throughout the 1784 Parliament. His only reported speech was during a debate on the bill for disfranchising voters employed by the Navy and Ordnance Boards, 30 Mar. 1786.

He died 5 July 1808.

M.M.D.

## CLARKE, Sir Thomas (1703–64), of Hampstead, Mdx.

MITCHELL 1747–1754
LOSTWITHIEL 1754–1761

*b.* 1703, 2nd s. of Thomas Clarke, carpenter of Holborn. *educ.* Westminster, 10 Jan. 1715, aged 11; Trinity, Camb. 10 June 1721, aged 18; fellow of Trinity 1727; G. Inn 1727, called 1729. *unm.* Kntd. 25 May 1754.
K.C. 1740; master of the rolls May 1754–*d.*; bencher, L. Inn 1754; P.C. 21 June 1754.

Clarke was a protégé of Lord Chancellor Macclesfield; and afterwards of Hardwicke, who in 1747 recommended him to a seat at Mitchell on the Scawen interest. When in 1753 it became clear that there would be a contest at Mitchell at the forthcoming general election, Clarke declined to stand because of the expense. 'I think a contested election one of the greatest evils that could befall me', he wrote on 2 Nov. 1753 to Hardwicke,[1] who arranged with Pelham for Clarke to come in at Lostwithiel on the Edgcumbe interest.

On 15 Mar. 1754 Lord Dupplin informed Newcastle 'that each man brought in by Lord Edgcumbe would cost near £1500 a Member'; Clarke, however, was to be brought in without expense to himself. On 21 Mar. Edgcumbe had reduced his price at Lostwithiel to £1000 a seat; Clarke was to pay £500 and Government the rest.[2]

Shortly after the general election Clarke was made master of the rolls at Hardwicke's recommendation. In November 1756 he declined to become a commissioner of the great seal, because it would conflict with his parliamentary duties; and in July 1757 refused the great seal itself. The 2nd Lord Hardwicke wrote that he was 'of no use in Parliament',[3] and there is no record of his having spoken in the House.

In December 1760 he informed Newcastle that an offer had been made to bring him in for Ashburton, 'without one sixpence of expense', at the forthcoming general election. Newcastle discouraged him from standing, and Clarke refused the offer. He expected to be returned again for Lostwithiel, but was indignant when he found the seat was to cost him £2000. In a letter of 16 Mar. 1761 he upbraided Newcastle, and claimed that by withdrawing at Ashburton he had earned the right to come in for nothing at Lostwithiel:

I will not comply with those terms and . . . if I was

to do so I should be so far from being fit to fill the station I have the honour to serve in, that on the contrary I should rather be a fit object for a commission of lunacy.[4]

And to Charles Yorke on 31 Mar. 1761:[5]

I suppose you know the Duke of Newcastle does not think of bringing me into Parliament . . . Are you able to account for this? I own I am not, though I can't avoid my conjectures.

He never stood again; and died on 13 Nov. 1764, said to be worth £200,000. He left the bulk of his fortune to the 3rd Earl of Macclesfield, the grandson of his first patron. The 2nd Earl of Hardwicke later wrote on the letter to his father in which Clarke had solicited the mastership of the rolls:[6] 'I cannot say that this (upon the whole) worthy man in the latter part of his life acted up to his obligations.'

[1] Add. 35592, f. 186. [2] Add. 32995, ff. 63–67, 116. [3] Add. 35423, f. 162. [4] Add. 32915, f. 405, and 32920, f. 245. [5] Add. 35636, f. 42. [6] Add. 35592, ff. 351–2.

J.B.

## CLARKE JERVOISE, Thomas (c.1765–1809), of Idsworth Park, Hants.

YARMOUTH I.O.W. 11 Apr. 1787–Dec. 1790

*b.* c.1765, 1st s. of Jervoise Clarke, afterwards Jervoise Clarke Jervoise (q.v.). *unm.* *suc.* fa. 5 July 1808.
Sheriff, Hants 1786–7.

Jervoise was returned unopposed for Yarmouth on his father's interest. Like his father he voted against Pitt over the Regency, 1788–9. There is no record of his having spoken in the House.

He died late in 1809.

M.M.D.

## CLAVERING, Sir Thomas, 7th Bt. (1719–94), of Axwell, co. Durham.

ST. MAWES 19 Jan. 1753–1754
SHAFTESBURY 1754–Nov. 1760
DURHAM CO. 1768–1790

*bap.* 19 June 1719, 1st surv. s. of Sir James Clavering, 6th Bt., by his 1st w. Catherine, da. of Thomas Yorke, M.P. of Richmond, Yorks. *educ.* C.C.C. Oxf. 1737. *m.* May 1746, Martha, da. of Joshua Douglas of Newcastle, *s.p.* *suc.* fa. 18 May 1748.

Clavering was of an old Durham family, settled at Axwell since the early 17th century. He was returned for Shaftesbury in 1754 on Lord Ilchester's interest. His expenses came to £2330, of which Clavering paid £2000 and the remainder came from secret service funds.[1] In December 1760 and at the general election of 1761 he unsuccessfully contested co. Durham. He was returned in 1768 and at every subsequent election unopposed.

In 1769 he voted against the court over Wilkes and the Middlesex election. But in March 1770, disgusted at the nonsense and bluster of the City of London, he turned away from the Opposition. On 15 Mar. he moved that the City remonstrance, which had been presented to the King the previous day, should be laid before the House; and on 19 Mar. proposed a resolution of censure against the remonstrance. In reply to Charles Wolfran Cornwall, who attacked him for changing his mind over the Middlesex election, he said:[2]

> It is a matter very indifferent to me who are the Administration. Those who do the business best are those I will support. I probably was hardly known to the minister. I had never spoke to the noble Lord [North] . . . The gentleman [Cornwall] has mentioned the acts of last year. I had the misfortune of voting in the minority. I think they [Administration] acted wrong, but when the majority of this House thought otherwise it was my duty to submit to it.

Henceforth he generally supported the court. On 'popular' measures—Grenville's Election Act (1774), economical reform (1780), and Dunning's motion (1780)—he went with the Opposition; but on motions of confidence or against the American war he voted with North to the end. On 25 Apr. 1782 he spoke against the bill disfranchising revenue officers.[3] He did not vote on Shelburne's peace preliminaries nor on Fox's East India bill; and in Stockdale's list of 19 Mar. 1784 is classed as absent. His name appears in no division list in the Parliament of 1784, and he did not stand in 1790.

He died 14 Oct. 1794.

[1] Namier, *Structure*, 429. [2] Cavendish's 'Debates', Egerton 221, f. 261. [3] Debrett, vii. 78.

J.B.

**CLAYTON, Courthorpe** (d.1762), of Shepherd's Bush, Mdx. and Mallow, co. Cork.

EYE 5 May 1749–1761

> 1st surv. s. of Laurence Clayton of Mallow by his 2nd w. Anne, da. and coh. of Sir Peter Courthorpe of Little Island, co. Cork. m. 6 Aug. 1745, Theodosia, da. of Edward Buckworth, 1da.
> M.P. [I] 1727–60.
> Ensign 2 Ft. Gds. 1725; cornet R. Horse Gds. 1727; lt. 1 Horse Gren. Gds. 1731, maj. 1751; lt.-col. 1756.
> Equerry to Prince of Wales 1726–7, and to the King 1727–60; avener and clerk marshal 1732–4, 1757–60. Pension of £500 p.a. during pleasure from January 1761.

Returned on Lord Cornwallis's interest, Clayton was classed as 'pro' by Dupplin in 1754. He is not known to have spoken or voted.

He died 22 Mar. 1762.

M.M.D.

**CLAYTON, Sir Kenrick,** 2nd Bt. (c.1715–69), of Marden, nr. Bletchingley, Surr.

BLETCHINGLEY 1734–10 Mar. 1769

> b. c.1715, 1st s. of Sir William Clayton, 1st Bt., M.P., of Marden, by Martha, da. of John Kenrick, London merchant of Flower, Surr. educ. Corpus Christi, Camb. 1732. m. 13 Feb. 1736, Henrietta Maria, da. of Henry Herring of London, director of the Bank of England, 1s. 2da. suc. fa. 28 Dec. 1744.

In 1754 Clayton was returned unopposed for Bletchingley, his family's pocket borough, and was classed by Dupplin as a country gentleman supporting Administration. On 10 Dec. 1761 he wrote to Newcastle that he was 'very unwilling to do anything against your Grace with whom I have acted without once deviating ever since the year thirty-four'.[1] But in Bute's list he is described as 'discontented with the Duke of Newcastle for the omission of some civilities'. His name appears neither in Fox's list of Members favourable to the peace preliminaries, December 1762, nor in the minority lists of 9 and 10 Dec. In the autumn of 1763 Jenkinson classed him as 'contra'; he voted with Opposition on Wilkes, 15 Nov. 1763, and general warrants, February 1764; and on 10 May 1764 was classed by Newcastle as a 'sure friend'. Rockingham in July 1765 listed him as 'pro' and in November 1766 as 'Whig'. He did not vote on the land tax, 27 Feb. 1767, and was classed by Newcastle, 2 Mar., as 'doubtful or absent'. There is no record of any other vote of his or of his having spoken in the House. He died 10 Mar. 1769.

[1] Add. 32932, f. 58.

M.M.D.

**CLAYTON, Robert** (?1740[1]–99), of Marden, Surr.

| | |
|---|---|
| BLETCHINGLEY | 1768–Nov. 1783 |
| SURREY | 19 Nov. 1783–1784 |
| BLETCHINGLEY | 20 Dec. 1787–1796 |
| ILCHESTER | 1796–10 May 1799 |

> b. ?1740, 1st s. of Sir Kenrick Clayton, 2nd Bt. (q.v.). educ. poss. Eton 1753–8; Clare, Camb. 1758. m. 1 June 1767, Mary, da. of Frederick Standert (q.v.), s.p. suc. fa. as 3rd Bt. 10 Mar. 1769.

In Parliament Clayton was closely associated with the Rockinghams, and consistently voted against the Grafton and North Administrations. His only reported speeches during his first Parliament were on the printers' case in March 1771, when he strongly criticized the proceedings,[2] and attacked George Onslow (q.v.).

Besides controlling both seats at Bletchingley, Clayton inherited large estates in Surrey and Buckinghamshire which gave him considerable influence in both counties. Nevertheless, by 1778 he seems to have been seriously embarrassed financially, and, having realized the timber on his estates, was forced to find other means of raising money. According to his cousin John Kenrick,[3] Clayton refused to sell any of his estates 'because he would not diminish his weight and influence arising from his great landed property', and instead contracted with Kenrick to sell for £10,000 the reversion at his death of the estate and borough of Bletchingley, the intrinsic value of which was about £100 p.a. Kenrick, in his account of the transaction drawn up ten years later,[4] concluded that an additional motive for selling the reversion was the fear that parliamentary reform might deprive Clayton of the value of the borough.

Before the general election of 1780 Clayton wrote to the Duke of Portland, 31 Aug.:

> Now if this Parliament is no more I will say it was the most profligate that ever was, has lost you thirteen fine colonies in America, ruined every branch of trade, shook public and private credit to his [sic] last breath. But I have no hopes for the next, because all people are ruined, and have no money to spend in elections so that the ministry will spend their money and have their elections, by that means the next will be as bad as this.[5]

Still, at the general election Clayton himself played an active part in supporting Keppel's candidature for Surrey, and on the strength of this, begged Keppel on 31 Mar. 1782 to recommend him to Rockingham for a place, putting forward the incredible claim that 'keeping the county free from ministerial power . . . at least has cost me £10,000'. His letter ended with characteristic exaggeration:

> If you would apply to Lord Rockingham for a place for me, I do not know how I would return it to you. The only way I could do would be to lay down my life to serve you, that I would do with pleasure, and at any time be subject to your calls; and any place given me I would lay down when you and the Marquis went out.[6]

To Rockingham the same day he wrote that having borne 'the whole weight' of keeping Surrey out of ministerial hands, he was much distressed financially: 'The favour I have to ask your Lordship is if you will grant me some place; it would not be right to dictate to your Lordship, what is vacant I believe is a vice-treasurer of Ireland, cofferer of his Majesty's Household, and master of the Household, as well as Board of Green Cloth.'[7] 'His conduct has been good', wrote Keppel on 1 April, 'and he is I believe honest and steadily devoted to me and your cause.'[8] But no office was forthcoming.

Clayton voted against Shelburne's peace preliminaries, 18 Feb. 1783. When in November 1783 one of the Surrey county seats became vacant he vacated his seat at Bletchingley and was returned

unopposed for Surrey. He voted for Fox's East India bill, 27 Nov. 1783, and was counted as a Foxite in Robinson's list of January 1784, and Stockdale's of 19 Mar.

On 12 Mar. 1784, during the debate on Sawbridge's motion for parliamentary reform, Clayton told the House that

> the motion should have his most hearty concurrence. He had voted indeed last year against a reform, but understanding that the sense of the county he had the honour to represent was friendly to it, he was ready to sacrifice not only his opinion, but his borough interest, to the wishes of his constituents.[9]

At the general election Clayton unsuccessfully contested Surrey. In June 1785 Clayton, urged on by his brother-in-law, Sir John Gresham, and, according to John Kenrick, influenced by the defeat of Pitt's proposals for parliamentary reform, attempted on very flimsy grounds to recover possession of the reversion of Bletchingley; but finally, in 1788, lost his Chancery suit against Kenrick.

In December 1787 John Nicholls, one of the Members for Bletchingley, vacated his seat in favour of Clayton, who voted with the Opposition on the impeachment of Impey, 9 May 1788, and over the Regency, 1788–9. His only reported speech during this Parliament was to oppose the bill to prevent the export of wool. Clayton continued in Opposition after the outbreak of the French war.

He died 10 May 1799.

[1] *A State of the Dispute between Sir R. Clayton Bt. . . . and J. Kenrick Esq. relative to . . . Bletchingley*, 17. [2] Cavendish's 'Debates', Egerton 226, ff. 35, 45, 366. [3] *A State of the Dispute*, 4. [4] Ibid. [5] Portland mss. [6] Rockingham mss. [7] Ibid. [8] Ibid. [9] *Gent. Mag.* 1784. i. 302.

M.M.D.

**CLAYTON, William** (c.1718–83), of Harleyford, nr. Great Marlow, Bucks.

| | |
|---|---|
| BLETCHINGLEY | 15 Jan. 1745–1761 |
| GREAT MARLOW | 1761–3 July 1783 |

*b.* c.1718, 2nd s. of Sir William Clayton, 1st Bt., M.P., and bro. of Sir Kenrick, 2nd Bt. (q.v.) *educ.* M. Temple 1737. *m.* (1) 30 May 1745, Mary (*d.*2 Jan. 1760), da. of John Warde of Squerryes, Kent, 1da.; (2) 3 May 1761, Caroline Mary (*d.*Dec. 1763), da. and coh. of Rice Lloyd of Alltycadno and Gwaelod-y-maes, Carm., 1s. 1da.; (3) 24 Sept. 1767, Lady Louisa Fermor, da. of Thomas, 1st Earl of Pomfret, 1s.

William Clayton generally followed the lead of his elder brother. He adhered to Newcastle, voted against the peace preliminaries, December 1762, and opposed the Grenville Administration. Rockingham in July 1765 classed him as 'pro' and in November 1766 as 'Whig', the same as his brother; like him, William Clayton did not vote on the land tax, 27 Feb. 1767, and on 2 Mar. was classed by Newcastle as 'doubtful or absent'.

He had a considerable interest at Great Marlow, an expensive and corrupt constituency, where he stood contests in 1768, 1774, and 1780. After his brother's death he supported the Grafton and North Administrations, and the only occasion on which he is known to have voted against the court was on Dunning's motion, 6 Apr. 1780. Only a few speeches by him are recorded: 21 Feb. 1771, on the Reading canal bill; 27 Mar. 1771, in the debate arising from the attack on North by a mob; 22 Apr. 1771, on the game bill; and three times in May 1780 when he moved for strangers to withdraw. The *English Chronicle* wrote in 1780 that he was 'not distinguished for any powers of oratory, or superiority of intellectual attainments'. On 18 Feb. 1783 he voted for Shelburne's peace preliminaries, and died 3 July 1783.

M.M.D.

## CLAYTON, William (1762–1834), of Harleyford, nr. Great Marlow, Bucks.

GREAT MARLOW        12 July 1783–1790

*b.* 16 Apr. 1762, 1st s. of William Clayton (q.v.) by his 2nd w. *educ.* Queen's, Oxf. 1780. *m.* 16 July 1785, Mary, da. of Sir William East, 1st Bt., of Hall Place, Berks., 5s. 2da. *suc.* fa. 3 July 1783 and cos. Sir Robert Clayton (q.v.) as 4th Bt. 10 May 1799.

Clayton, on his father's death, was returned unopposed for Great Marlow. He voted against Fox's East India bill, 27 Nov. 1783, and was classed by Robinson, January 1784, and Stockdale, 25 Mar., as a supporter of Pitt.

Robinson wrote in his survey for the general election of 1784: 'Mr. Clayton probably would be elected again'; and he was returned head of the poll. He was classed by William Adam in May 1784 as 'Administration', but his only known vote in this Parliament was against Pitt on the Regency, 16 Dec. 1788. There is no record of his having spoken in the House.

In 1787 he sold his property at Marlow, and did not stand at the general election of 1790. He died 26 Jan. 1834.

J.B.

## CLERKE, *see* JENNINGS, Philip

## CLEVLAND, John (c.1707–63), of Tapley, Devon.

SALTASH        1741–Mar. 1743
SANDWICH        1747–1761
SALTASH        1761–19 June 1763

*b.* c.1707, 1st s. of Capt. William Clevland, R.N., a commissioner of the navy, by Anne, da. of John Davie of Orleigh, Devon. *educ.* Westminster 1718; M. Temple 1723. *m.* (1) Elizabeth, da. of Sir Caesar Child, 2nd Bt., of Woodford, Essex, sis. of Sir Caesar Child, 3rd and last Bt., 2s. 2da.; (2) 1747,[1] Sarah, da. of Richard Shuckburgh of Longborough, Glos., sis. of Sir G. A. Shuckburgh, 6th Bt. (q.v.), 2s. 2da. *suc.* fa. 1715.

Clerk in the navy office c.1723–31; clerk of the cheque, Plymouth 1731–43; commr. of the navy Mar. 1743–6; second sec. to the Admiralty 1746–51, sec. 1751–*d.*

Clevland's father was a Scotsman by birth, a distinguished naval commander, and the first of the family to settle in Devon; his mother was of an old Devonshire family. John Clevland's career is best summed up in the 'Memorial' which some time in 1762 he presented to the King.[2]

That he has been near forty years in the naval service . . . That he was the active commissioner of the navy in the former Spanish war, and some time after the commencement of that with France, Mr. Corbett, then secretary of the Admiralty, being very infirm and frequently incapable of his duty, Mr. Clevland was made joint secretary with him, and carried on the business till the peace in 1748.

That the extensive and arduous operations of the present war have brought such an increase of business on the office of secretary of the Admiralty, that Mr. Clevland's health and eyesight is greatly impaired by incessant application to the faithful discharge of his trust, which he flatters himself to have done to the satisfaction of his superiors, and will not fail in his endeavours to continue the same whilst his health will permit.

But having a wife and great number of children, is very anxious to make some better provision for them than his own fortune will allow of after his death.

Therefore most ardently implores his Majesty, in consideration of his long and faithful services, to grant to Mrs. Clevland such pension as shall be thought proper, upon the Irish or any other establishment, which provision for his family will add greatly to his happiness, and be the means of prolonging a life entirely devoted to the public.

Clevland sat at Sandwich and Saltash on the Admiralty interest, and he managed both boroughs for the Government, besides Barnstaple where, with Tapley in its neighbourhood, he had an interest of his own. As an official he was in the House a regular Government supporter; while as the key man in his office, highly esteemed by successive chiefs, he enjoyed very nearly the permanency of a modern civil servant. Mrs. Edward Boscawen wrote on 4 Oct. 1756 to her husband, the Admiral (q.v.):[3]

It astonished me that Lord Anson should not have wrote to you. That Clevland is angry at your anger is very likely, but that his Lordship should adopt his secretary's resentment—that is surely very unworthy and would tend to confirm a vulgar opinion that Clevland is lord high admiral.

Clevland seemed indeed so closely identified with Anson's administration of the Admiralty that when Anson resigned in November 1756, his dismissal was expected.[4] But the new ministry knew better than to remove in the middle of a war the man best acquainted with naval business. Temple, now first lord, wrote on 14 Dec. 1756, to George Grenville, treasurer of the navy:[5] 'Will you be so kind as to call here tomorrow morning, that Mr. Clevland may explain to you some matters relating to the 55,000 men which are to be voted tomorrow?' And in September 1758 Pitt was concerting with Clevland 'an attempt on Martinico, if practicable'.[6] When Anson died, 6 June 1762, his successor, Lord Halifax, before accepting 'took care to be assured from Clevland that he would continue secretary during the war'.[7] Clevland himself reported to Newcastle, 16 June: 'Lord Halifax . . . has done me the honour to call upon me, and given me the strongest assurances of his friendship, and desired I would be upon the same footing with him as I was with Lord Anson.'[8] And Newcastle wrote to Hardwicke on 24 June: he has heard that Clevland is very pleased with Halifax—'I am sure it is wise in my Lord Halifax to make him so'.[9]

To Clevland Newcastle replied on 16 June:[10]

I am heartily glad of it [Halifax's appointment], upon your account, and indeed upon my own; for I dare say, he will receive most favourably any applications you shall make to him in behalf of my friends.

I long to have one hour's discourse with you. Come to me, whenever you can; you will always find the same affectionate friend, though a useless one in, Dear Clevland, your etc.

In October 1762, when Halifax was urging Bute to bring Newcastle back into office, Clevland kept the Duke informed of developments, possibly to prepare the ground for Halifax.[11] But when the break came between Newcastle and the court, Clevland naturally followed the official line, voted with the Government on 1 Dec. 1762, and was listed by Fox as supporting the peace preliminaries.

He died 19 June 1763. No evidence has been found of any pension to his widow; fairly ample provision had previously been made for his eldest son. His own salary as secretary of the Admiralty had been £800 p.a. but with fees and perquisites over £2,000 net;[12] in addition as secretary, since 1751, to the charity for the relief of poor widows of officers of the navy he had £200 p.a. In surviving lists he appears as subscriber to Government loans: thus in 1746 Sampson Gideon signed for him for £2,000;[13] in 1760 he was billeted for £10,000 on Amyand's list;[14] and at his death he left £17,000 in Government stock.[15] Yet he was, it seems, heavily in debt to the Admiralty—North wrote to Sandwich, 15 June 1778:[16]

It may not perhaps at first appear very becoming a lord of the Treasury to solicit for granting a longer

delay of payment for a public debtor, but as I really believe that it would be almost ruin to Mr. Clevland [jun.] if he were forced to discharge his father's debt by instalments of £4,000 a year, I most earnestly hope that you may be satisfy [sic] with smaller instalments. Mr. Clevland wished to have them reduced to £2,000 a year, and shall be very glad to hear that you are able to comply with his request, but whatever indulgence you can give him, your Lordship may set down to my account, as I am very desirous of giving him every reasonable degree of favour and assistance.

¹ Mrs. Edw. Boscawen to her husband, the Admiral, 29 Nov. 1747, C. Aspinall-Oglander, *Admiral's Wife*, 64. ² Add. 32945, f. 449; a copy of it is among the Townshend mss at Dalkeith House. Printed in Namier, *Structure*, 40–41. ³ Aspinall-Oglander, 209. ⁴ Symmer to A. Mitchell, 12 Nov., Add. 6839, f. 22; Mrs. Boscawen to her husband, 16 Nov., op. cit. 228. ⁵ *Grenville Pprs.* i. 187. ⁶ Newcastle to Hardwicke, 4 Sept. 1758, Add. 32883, f. 274. ⁷ Hardwicke to Newcastle, 17 June, Add. 32939, f. 384. ⁸ Ibid. f. 367. ⁹ Add. 32940, f. 58. ¹⁰ Add. 32939, f. 374. ¹¹ Add. 32943, ff. 143–4. ¹² *Reports on Emoluments in Public Offices*, 3rd Rep. 'Admiralty' (1786), p. 40. ¹³ T1/319. ¹⁴ Add. 32901, f. 242. ¹⁵ Bank of England recs. ¹⁶ Sandwich mss.

L.B.N.

**CLEVLAND, John** (1734–1817), of Tapley, Devon.

BARNSTAPLE 19 Nov. 1766–1802

*b.* 1734, 1st s. of John Clevland (q.v.). *m.* 3 Jan. 1782, Elizabeth, da. and h. of Richard Stevens (q.v.) of Winscott, Devon, wid. of Robert Awse of Horwood House, Frithelstock, Devon,[1] *s.p.* *suc.* fa. 19 June 1763.

Clerk at the Admiralty 1753–66; dep. judge of Admiralty 1757–63; agent for the marines, Plymouth 1761–6; commr. for the sale of French prizes 1756–63; commr. and accomptant of sixpeny office c.1764–1814.

John Clevland jun. wrote to the Duke of Newcastle, from Saltash, April 1754:[2] 'My father being uncertain when he might be here from Sandwich, sent me to conduct the affairs of the election at this place.' Although early employed in elections, he himself did not stand for Parliament in his father's lifetime. But subsequently he must have been known to intend doing so, for on the death of Sir George Amyand, M.P. for Barnstaple, 16 Aug. 1766, his brother Claudius Amyand (q.v.) immediately informed Clevland about it, thus enabling him to declare his candidature ahead of anyone else. Clevland now sent an express to the Duke of Grafton 'to prevent his sending any person, and also to desire the votes of the placemen', and in a second letter reported the 'very good success' he had met with; but he received no reply—'so I am going on entirely upon my own interest', he wrote to Thomas Pelham (q.v.),[3] '. . . the country gentlemen now will all support me, which they would not have done . . . upon any other footing . . . I have great hopes of succeeding and without much expense though there is 350 votes, and some very bad indeed.' He was returned unopposed. But before the general election of 1768 Clevland had 'a monstrous deal of trouble as well as expense', and electioneering which, he wrote to Pelham, 5 Jan., 'very near cost me my life';[4] and on 3 Apr. 1768: 'I have taken place of my brother Member, and he seemed very sensible of my assistance in bringing him into Parliament'[5]—the only evidence which so far has been found of there having been a poll. In 1774 and 1780 Clevland again topped the poll.

In his many and rather empty letters to Pelham, Clevland repeatedly dwells on his solitary turn of mind, his preference for rural retirement, and his indifference to politics: there is no record of his having spoken in the House, and up to December 1781 his attendance in divisions was poor. In November 1766 he was classed by Rockingham as 'Swiss', and in January 1767 by Townshend as 'Government': he voted with them on the land tax, 27 Feb. 1767. Not one vote of his is recorded 1768–72; in Robinson's two surveys on the royal marriage bill, March 1772, he is listed as 'pro, present', and he voted with the Government on the Middlesex resolution, 26 Apr. 1773, and even on Grenville's Act, 25 Feb. 1774. There are no majority lists for 1774–8, but on 12 Feb. 1779, over the contractors bill, he is listed by Robinson as one of the 'friends' who voted against the Government. There are eight division lists in March 1779 and February-April 1780, but Clevland appears only in that over the motion against prorogation, 24 Apr. 1780, voting on the Government side; and was classed by Robinson as 'pro' in his survey of 1780. In the new Parliament he voted with North in each of the six divisions December 1781–March 1782: possibly from a sense of gratitude for the service done him over his father's debt to the Admiralty he stood by North. Robinson wrote in a survey for Shelburne in August 1782:[6] 'Mr. Clevland comes in by his own interest, aided by the Government interest . . . He has always been connected with Government, and generally supported them, though sometimes shy. However, it is thought that he may be reckoned hopeful at least with attention.' But he voted against Shelburne's peace preliminaries, 18 Feb. 1783, and in March 1783 Robinson classed him as an office holder adhering to North. He was absent from the divisions on Fox's East India bill, and was again classed as 'pro' by Robinson in January 1784 and as 'Administration' by William Adam: yet in the ensuing Parliament he regularly voted with the Opposition; only over Impey's impeachment, which was not strictly a party question, he voted with Pitt.

He died in June 1817, aged 83.

[1] D. Drake, 'Members for Barnstaple', *Trans. Dev. Assn.* lxxiii. 187. [2] Add. 32735, f. 108. [3] 29 Aug. 1766, Add. 33088, f. 76. [4] Ibid. f. 129. [5] Ibid. f. 217. [6] Laprade, 45.

L.B.N.

## CLINTON, Hon. George (c.1685–1761).

SALTASH 1754–1761

*b.* c.1685, 2nd s. of Francis Fiennes, 6th Earl of Lincoln, by his 2nd w. Susan, da. of Anthony Penniston. *m.* Anne, da. and coh. of Gen. Peter Carle, 3s. 3da.
Capt. R.N. 1716; r.-adm. 1743; v.-adm. 1745; adm. 1747; adm. of the fleet 1757.
Gov. Newfoundland 1731–7, New York 1741–53.

Superseded as governor of New York without his 'knowledge, privity, or consent',[1] Clinton returned to England and was elected on the Admiralty interest at Saltash, paying 'the whole of the expense'[2] for his election. On 26 June 1755 he wrote to Newcastle recalling the manner of his dismissal, stating that he had never received his salary of £1200 a year as governor, and adding: 'I have been pointed at and greatly neglected since I came home, and for what reason I cannot conceive, unless it be owing to my unalterable attachment to your Grace (particularly on the Mitchell election, since which I have lost all manner of favour and correspondence with Lord Anson).'[3] On 21 July 1755 he pressed Newcastle for a naval appointment or a pension; and on 20 Nov. stated that for £1200 a year he was willing 'to resign his pretensions to all rank and service in the navy'. But he wished to have it for life since he would forfeit his half pay, and could not otherwise preserve his seat, and in Parliament might 'have an opportunity of being useful to his Grace'. Apparently there was an 'obstruction' to his having this sum for life, and on 30 Jan. 1756 he declared that he was 'the only officer, except another in the House of Commons, upon bare half pay', and asked if it 'could not be made up to him as full pay, in order to reimburse the expense of his election'. If Newcastle thought it 'absolutely necessary' that he should vacate his seat he expected 'that whoever succeeds him will refund the £500 he paid for coming in'.[4] Apparently he did not receive a pension, but in 1757 was appointed admiral of the fleet at £5 a day.

He died 10 July 1761.

[1] Clinton to Newcastle, 26 June 1755, Add. 32856, f. 225. [2] Namier, *Structure*, 197. [3] Add. 32856, f. 225. [4] Add. 32857, f. 285; 32861, f. 47; 32862, ff. 295–6.

M.M.D.

## CLINTON, Henry (1730–95).[1]

| | |
|---|---|
| BOROUGHBRIDGE | 27 July 1772–1774 |
| NEWARK | 1774–1784 |
| LAUNCESTON | 1790–July 1794 |

*b.* 4 June 1730, o. surv. s. of Hon. George Clinton (q.v.). *m.* Feb. 1767, Harriet, da. and coh. of Thomas Carter, 3s. 2da. *suc.* fa. 1761; K.B. 11 Apr. 1777.
Entered army in 1745; lt. and capt. 2 Ft. Gds. 1751; capt. and lt.-col. 1758; col. in army 1762; col.

12 Ft. 1766; maj.-gen. 1772; second-in-command in America 1776–8; lt.-gen. 1777; commander-in-chief in America 1778–82; col. 84 Ft. 1778–82; col. 7 Lt. Drag. 1779–*d.*; gen. 1793; gov. Gibraltar 1794–*d.*

Groom of the bedchamber to the Duke of Gloucester 1764–78.

Clinton served in Canada during the war of the Austrian succession and in Germany during the seven years' war. He was a cousin of Henry, 2nd Duke of Newcastle, and was returned on the Newcastle interest at Boroughbridge and Newark. In the House of Commons he was a regular Government supporter. From 1775 to 1782 he was in America, holding military posts of crucial importance. He seems to have been unequal to his responsibilities. 'Though I believe him . . . a brave and honest man', wrote G. B. Rodney (q.v.) to Germain, 22 Dec. 1780,[2] 'I am convinced nature has not given him an enterprizing and active spirit, capable of pushing the advantages he may have gained in battle.' Differences, first with Howe and then with Cornwallis, made his task no easier; and in April 1782, after repeated requests to resign his command, he was allowed to return to England.

Clinton voted against Shelburne's peace preliminaries, 18 Feb. 1783, and supported the Coalition. In July 1783 North applied to the King for an Irish viscountcy for Clinton, but could only obtain his agreement to a barony. Whereupon, William Windham reported to Lord Northington, the lord lieutenant, 17 July, Clinton 'was understood to have refused his peerage, not being able to succeed as to being a viscount'.[3] On 25 and 27 June 1783 he spoke for a motion to grant half pay to American Loyalist officers—his only recorded interventions in debate. He voted for Fox's East India bill, 27 Nov. 1783; was classed by Robinson in January 1784 as 'hopeful' and in Stockdale's list of 19 Mar. as 'absent'. Newcastle did not return him at the general election of 1784.

After his return to England Clinton pressed for an inquiry into his conduct as commander-in-chief in America; on this being refused him, he published a pamphlet for his own justification, and wrote but never published a more elaborate apologia.[4] Clinton died 23 Dec. 1795.

[1] Information about Clinton has been kindly supplied by W. B. Willcox, Univ. of California. [2] *HMC Stopford-Sackville*, ii. 192. [3] Add. 33100, ff. 189, 190, 205. [4] 'An Historical Detail of Seven Years Campaigns in North America'. Ed. 1954 by W. B. Willcox as *The American Rebellion*.

J.B.

**CLINTON,** *see also* **PELHAM CLINTON**

**CLIVE, Baron,** *see* **CLIVE, Hon. Edward,** *and* **CLIVE, Robert**

II—H*

**CLIVE, Hon. Edward** (1754–1839), of Oakley Park, Salop and Claremont, Surr.

LUDLOW 1774–13 Aug. 1794

*b.* 7 Mar. 1754, 1st s. of Robert, 1st Baron Clive (q.v.). *educ.* Eton 1762–70; Ch. Ch. Oxf. 1771. *m.* 7 May 1784, Lady Henrietta Antonia Herbert, da. of Henry Arthur, 1st Earl of Powis, and sis. and h. of George, 2nd Earl, 2s. 2da. *suc.* fa. as 2nd Baron Clive [I] 22 Nov. 1774; *cr.* Baron Clive of Walcot [GB] 13 Aug. 1794; Earl of Powis 14 May 1804.

Recorder, Shrewsbury from 1775; ld. lt. Salop 1775–98, 1804–*d.*; recorder Ludlow from 1801; ld. lt. Mont. 1804–30.

Gov. Madras 1798–1803; P.C. 21 Nov. 1805.

Returned unopposed for Ludlow on the Clive-Powis interest before he was of age, Edward Clive seems after his father's death to have been directed politically by his father's friends, Wedderburn and Strachey, voting with the North Administration in every division for which a list of its supporters is extant. At the opening of the session in November 1778 North asked him to second the Address, but Clive excused himself;[1] and there is no record of his having spoken in the House. The *Public Ledger* wrote about him in 1779:

Votes always with the ministry, and entirely under the direction of Mr. Wedderburn, who has the English peerage in view for him . . .

In 1780 he met with strong opposition at Ludlow. In the new House Clive again voted with the North Administration; but was abroad at the time of the division on Shelburne's peace preliminaries. When the Coalition Government was being formed Clive was apparently considered for some office;[2] voted for Fox's East India bill; and on the dismissal of the Coalition went into opposition. He died 16 May 1839.

[1] North to the King, 10 Nov. 1778, Fortescue, iv. 215. [2] Ibid. vi. 275.

L.B.N.

**CLIVE, George** (*d.*1779), of Wormbridge, Herefs.

BISHOP'S CASTLE 24 Nov. 1763–23 Mar. 1779

s. of Rev. Benjamin Clive by his w. Susan Floyer; cos. of Robert Clive (q.v.). *m.* 1 June 1763, Sydney, da. and h. of Thomas Bolton of Knock, co. Louth, 3s. 1da.

In 1755 George Clive, having on 19 Mar. obtained permission from the directors of the East India Company,[1] went out to India in the 'family' of Robert Clive. By 1757 he was acting as one of the agents for the army;[2] in that year Clive estimated George's probable fortune at between £15,000 and £20,000.[3] They returned in 1760, and in 1764 George joined the banking firm of Sir Francis Gosling and Co., of which he remained a partner till his death. The firm had already been handling a good deal of business in the 'splitting' of East India Company stock for Lord Clive, who in an undated letter to George wrote from India late in 1765: 'The business of your shop will be greatly increased by the gentlemen coming home, Carnac, Call, Turner, Swinton, Gregory, and Dr. Fullarton, all men of great fortune, have promised me to do business with Sir Francis Gosling.' George, replying on 16 May 1766, spoke well of his partners, but complained that the work was hard—he intended to give himself more leisure when in 'full possession of that easy fortune I am now entitled to'.[4] He remained a close friend of Clive; was one of his attorneys, transacting much of his business at East India House, and working in close touch with John Walsh (q.v.) and Luke Scrafton; and was an executor of, and a trustee under, Clive's will.

In 1761 George Clive unsuccessfully contested Penryn on the interest of Francis Basset sen. (q.v.), to whom he paid £2,000, advanced by Robert Clive;[5] and in 1763 he was returned, after a contest, on Clive's interest at Bishop's Castle. In the House he faithfully followed his cousin's lead; supported the Grenville Administration, and voted against the repeal of the Stamp Act, 22 Feb. 1766. He wrote to Clive, 16 Feb. 1768:[6]

> The parliamentary conduct you recommend has always been my wish to observe and which [sic] we have the same object in view there can be but little variety of sentiment; your honour and importance will ever be mine.

In 1768, and again in 1774, he was returned unopposed for Bishop's Castle. By 1769 he, like his cousin, had gone over to the Opposition, and he regularly voted against the Administration till the autumn of 1772, when with Clive he went back to Administration. When he voted with the Opposition on the naval captains' petition, 9 Feb. 1773, and Grenville's Election Act, 25 Feb. 1774, he was marked in the King's lists as a dissenting friend. He seems to have continued to support Administration after Lord Clive's death; was marked as 'pro, absent' on the contractors bill, 12 Feb. 1779; and voted with Administration on Keppel, 3 Mar. 1779. There is no record of his having spoken in the House. He died 23 Mar. 1779.

¹ Court Bk. 66, p. 329. ² Orme mss, xi. 25. ³ Malcolm, *Clive*, ii. 162, quoting a letter of 9 Aug. from Clive to his father and to W. Belchier, 21 Aug. 1757, Clive mss. ⁴ Clive mss. ⁵ G. Clive to Lord Clive, 13 Dec. 1765, Clive mss. ⁶ Ibid.

M.M.D.

## CLIVE, Richard (c.1693–1771), of Styche Hall, nr. Market Drayton, Salop.

MONTGOMERY    21 Nov. 1759–Apr. 1771

*b.* c. 1693,¹ 3rd but 1st surv. s. of George Clive of Styche by Elizabeth Amphlett of Four Ashes, Salop.

*m.* Rebecca, da. and coh. of Nathaniel Gaskell of Manchester, 6s. 7da.
  Bankruptcy commr. 1758 (?).

Richard Clive, of old Shropshire gentry and a descendant of Robert Clive, who sat for Bridgnorth in the Long Parliament, was a first cousin of Sir Edward Clive, M.P., a distinguished judge and a friend of Hardwicke's. Himself an attorney in the City, he had by 1757 practised 'above thirty years' in the court of Chancery, without much distinction: it was only his son's achievements which enabled him, from 1756 onwards, to press Newcastle for 'some preferment' in his own profession: the post of registrar of the Excise or of a master in Chancery —'for that purpose had I encouragement would put on the gown and might be called to the bar next term'.[2] All he obtained was a commissionership of bankrupts. Lord Kinnoull wrote about him to Newcastle, 16 Oct. 1758:[3]

> I believe he is an honest, hearty friend to you; but really the extraordinary success of his family seems almost to have overset his mind. It appeared so to people at Buxton this summer where he passed two or three days.

Unable to obtain a commission in the Guards for his son William (q.v.), Richard Clive wrote to Newcastle on 21 Mar. 1760 with engaging naïvety: 'I shall be much concerned when the Colonel comes to England (which I expect in a few months) to tell him I cannot prevail to get this young gentleman employed in his Majesty's service.'[4]

When Robert Clive started remitting home vast sums of money, his father acted for him: in the joint names of Sir Edward Clive, Richard Clive, William Belchier (q.v.), an intimate friend of Richard's, and William Smyth King, £78,750 of Government stock was acquired by subscription in January 1759, and £73,000 in February-March; after Clive's return, both holdings were transferred to him in March 1761.[5]

In November 1759 Richard Clive, by then in his middle sixties, was returned to Parliament by Lord Powis at Montgomery, obviously as a compliment to his son; and in the lists of Members in almanacs such as the *Court and City Kalendar*, Richard usually appears as father of Colonel (later Lord) Clive. No speech of his in the House is recorded; and his few recorded votes follow his son's line: he voted with the Opposition over Wilkes on 15 Nov. 1763, and again with the Opposition on the Middlesex election, 8 May 1769.

Richard Clive died in April 1771.

¹ His yr. bro. Benjamin was b. 27 Dec. 1695. ² See his letter to Newcastle, 14 Jan. 1757, Add. 32870, f. 80. ³ Add. 32884, ff. 397–8. ⁴ Add. 32903, f. 440. For anecdotes about the 'old rustic' (which he was not), see also Horace Walpole to Mann, 7 May 1760, and to Lord Hertford, 29 Dec. 1763. ⁵ Bank of England recs.

L.B.N.

**CLIVE, Robert** (1725–74), of Styche Hall, nr.
Market Drayton, Salop; subsequently of Walcot
Park, Salop; Claremont, Surr.; and Oakley Park,
Salop.

MITCHELL        1754–24 Mar. 1755
SHREWSBURY      1761–22 Nov. 1774

*b.* 29 Sept. 1725, 1st s. of Richard Clive (q.v.). *educ.*
Lostock, Cheshire; Market Drayton; Merchant Taylors', London; Hemel Hempstead, Herts. *m.* 18 Feb.
1753, at Fort St. George, Margaret, da. of Edmund
Maskelyne, 2s. 2da. *cr.* Baron Clive of Plassey [I]
15 Mar. 1762; K.B. 24 Apr. 1764.

   Writer, E.I. Co. at Fort St. George 1742; ensign in
their military service 1747; returned to civil establishment 1749; re-entered military service with brevet
rank of capt. 1751; left for England 23 Mar. 1753;
appointed 25 Mar. 1755 to the council of Fort St.
George, and dep. gov. of Fort St. David, with rank of
lt.-col.; sailed for India 23 Apr. 1755; appointed to
command of expedition to recapture Calcutta 21 Sept.
1756; gov. Bengal 1758–60. Having resigned the
service sailed for England 21 Feb. 1760, arriving
9 July 1760. Gov. and c.-in-c. Bengal 1764–7, with
rank of maj.-gen. in the Company's service; left England 4 June 1764, arriving Bengal 3 May 1765; left
Bengal 29 Jan. 1767, arriving in England 14 July
1767. Ld. lt. Salop, Mont. 1772–*d.*

Robert Clive arrived at Madras in 1743 at the
age of 17, poor, awkward, and without connexions.
In 1760 when he resigned the Company's service he
had by his exploits as a soldier and administrator
assured its predominance in India over its European
rivals, played a big part in consolidating its influence
in the Carnatic, and laid the basis of its rule in
Bengal. He had also made the first and greatest of
the large private fortunes acquired by the Company's servants in India, and his actions and example
had set in train the events which were to lead to the
gradual assumption by the state of responsibilities
become too great for a trading company.

The chance to show his natural military skill was
first given him by the struggles between the French
and English Companies in the Carnatic—before
1749 as part of the war between England and
France, after that, nominally at least, as allies of
Indian rulers competing for power. His heroic
defence of Arcot in 1751 and his share in the siege
of Trichinopoly in 1752 won him a high military
reputation, which his return to England in 1753, on
grounds of health, enabled him to exploit. He had
acquired by private trade, his military 'batta', and
prize money, a moderate fortune which he used to
establish his family in comfort, and he himself lived
in some style. Though he had every intention of
returning ultimately to India, in 1754 he stood for
Mitchell on the Scawen interest (on which his
cousin Edward Clive had sat 1741–51). He was
returned but unseated on petition, 24 Mar. 1755,

after long and exceedingly bitter wrangles in the
House. A proposal that he should stand for Dover
was not proceeded with.[1]

His return to India in 1755 was owing to the im-
minence of war between Britain and France, and the
knowledge that its outbreak would be followed by
hostilities in India. Royal land and naval forces had
already been sent to strengthen the Company's
arms; and the sudden assault on the Company's
factories and capture of Calcutta by Siraj-ud-daula,
the new Nawab of Bengal, gave him the opportunities
he needed. Placed by the Government of Fort St.
George in command of a strong force to retrieve the
situation in Bengal, he succeeded in recapturing
Calcutta, bringing the Nawab to terms, and in
seizing Chandernagore, the chief French stronghold
in Bengal. Evidence that Siraj-ud-daula was intriguing with the French led him to foment a conspiracy to replace him by Mir Jafar, and on 23 June
1757 Clive routed Siraj-ud-daula's forces at Plassey
and recognized Mir Jafar as Nawab. In 1758 the
council of the Bengal presidency invited Clive to act
as governor, and in 1759 he broke the power of
the Dutch Company in Bengal by defeating their
forces near Chinsura.

Mir Jafar confirmed the Company's rights in
Bengal, and made lavish gifts to Clive and others
concerned in the revolution. By the time Clive left
India he had acquired a fortune of nearly £300,000,
which he remitted to his attorneys in England,[2] and
in 1759 he was granted in addition by the Mogul a
'jagir' or quit-rent for an office of honour of some
£27,000 p.a. to be paid him by the Nawab.

In 1760 Clive left India, as he believed, for ever
and had ambitious though ill-defined plans for his
'future power', his 'future grandeur'[3] in his native
land. Clive's first claim was for a peerage and recognition by the Crown. He was discontented that
nothing was done for him until 1762 when the Duke
of Newcastle procured him an Irish barony, with
which he was by no means satisfied. He wrote to
Henry Vansittart that had he acquired a larger
fortune, 'I might have been an English Earl with a
Blue Ribbon, instead of an Irish Peer (with the
promise of a Red one). However the receipt of the
jagir money for a few years will do great things.'[4] A
small band of relatives and friends from India,
including John Walsh (q.v.), Luke Scrafton, his
father Richard Clive (q.v.), his cousin George Clive
(q.v.), his brother-in-law Edmund Maskelyne, and
after 1764 his secretary Henry Strachey (q.v.),
helped him in managing his affairs; his father, his
cousin Sir Edward Clive, William Belchier (q.v.),
and William Smyth King acted as his attorneys in
subscribing on his behalf £78,750 for Government

stock in January and £73,000 in Feb.-Mar. 1759, transferring the stock to his name in March 1761 (he sold most of it in March 1763);[5] John Walsh, Luke Scrafton, and his father later acted as his attorneys for the management of his considerable holdings of East India stock,[6] and he was always well served by them and others.

When in June 1759 Robert More, M.P. for Shrewsbury, declined to stand again at the general election, Clive's candidature was declared by his father with the support of Lord Powis, leader of the Shropshire Whigs, and was endorsed by the corporation in spite of Lord Bath's exertions on behalf of his son Lord Pulteney (q.v.), heir presumptive to very considerable estates in Shropshire. For a year Bath persisted, but after Clive's arrival in England Pulteney 'had really no chance of success',[7] and Bath withdrew his candidature.[8] Clive was returned unopposed; while his father, whom Powis, as a compliment to Clive, had returned for Montgomery in November 1759, was re-elected in 1761, and John Walsh secured for himself a seat at Worcester. This was the nucleus of a Clive group in Parliament, added to in 1763 when Clive bought at the inflated price of £92,000 Walcot Park, and thereby obtained the best interest at Bishop's Castle, the one notoriously venal borough in Shropshire; at a by-election in September he returned for it his cousin George Clive. Before the next general election his hold on Bishop's Castle was rendered complete by the purchase of two other adjoining estates, so that in 1768 and afterwards Clive nominated to both seats there; and the borough was his first and most lasting acquisition.

Early in his parliamentary career Clive had taken as a maxim 'No more struggles against the ministry; I choose to be with them'.[9] Nevertheless he did not think this aim inconsistent with a position of considerable political independence, and it was only for short periods, when his private needs were particularly urgent, that he was ever closely associated with the ministry of the day. After Newcastle had obtained the Irish peerage for him, Clive enrolled himself among his followers, rejecting Henry Fox's plea to support the new Administration in the debates on the peace preliminaries,[10] and voting with the minority on 1 and 9 Dec. 1762. The following year, however, the attack made on his 'jagir' by his enemies in the Company under the leadership of Laurence Sulivan (q.v.) led him to make a *volte face* and to offer his support to George Grenville in return for Grenville's good offices with the East India Company. 'My poor services, such as they are', Clive promised him, 'shall be dedicated for the rest of my days to the King, and my obliga-

tions to you always acknowledged, whether in or out of power.'[11] The Grenville Administration served him well, and while he was again abroad his parliamentary supporters considered themselves pledged to Grenville's support.[12] Still, on the fall of that Administration in July 1765, John Walsh, who was managing the political affairs of the Clive group, held that he was personally bound to Grenville but not to his allies in opposition; he therefore advocated a policy of 'independency',[13] but took pains to keep on good terms with first the Rockingham and then the Chatham Administration.[14]

In returning to Bengal in 1764 as governor and commander-in-chief Clive was largely moved by the disputes in which he was involved, by the need to protect his wealth against his enemies, and one of the results of his return was his success in securing the continuation of the 'jagir' for twenty years. He brought some order into the disorganized civil and military administration of Bengal (at the cost of raising up against himself new and dangerous enemies in the Company, in particular the formidable Johnstone family), and, obtaining a grant from the Mogul of the 'diwani' or financial administration of Bengal, he set up the so-called dual system of government which remained in force until superseded by the early reforms of Warren Hastings. The new grant caused still further disorganization in the East India Company by leading to violent speculation in its funds, in which Clive took part through his attorneys.

With the Parliament of 1761 in its seventh year, Clive's return to England in July 1767 produced a spate of election schemes: there seemed no need for him and his friends to hunt for boroughs—his fabulous wealth attracted offers from all over the country. A fortnight after his return he was invited to nominate one or two candidates for Colchester.[15] When in November he was negotiating a lease of Ball's Park, a mile from Hertford, people there were impatient to know whom he would 'recommend to represent them'.[16] He was approached through his father by a group of voters at Newcastle-under-Lyme—'if you refuse . . . as I believe you will', wrote Richard Clive on 23 Nov., 'it may serve as a compliment to Lord Gower'. At Leicester there was 'a warm contest and much money spent', and Lord Stamford's agent told George Clive that Booth Grey (q.v.) would be glad to join any candidate recommended by Clive, it being thought 'that your appearance quells every opposition'.[17]

'I have had three seats offered me for £7,000 which were engaged for Charles Townshend', wrote George Clive on 1 Oct. (Townshend had died on 4 Sept.). Names were withheld for some time by the intermediaries: the manager was the notorious Theobald Taaffe,[18] and the boroughs were Helston and Grampound; and the negotiation was broken off at the end of November when Taaffe insisted on handling the money before delivering the goods.[19]

On 26 Nov. Walsh wrote to Clive:

I imagine a perpetuity like mine at Pontefract will not be disagreeable to you. I am in close pursuit of one and for you, though it is a purchase I would like myself. Perfect secrecy on this head is necessary.

And the name of that 'perpetuity' nowhere appears.

Walsh also backed the schemes which Chase Price was pressing on Clive. These, as Price proved by returning Carnac for Leominster and himself for Radnorshire,[20] were perfectly feasible but were turned down by Clive, probably because they would have antagonized some of the leading men in mid-Wales and the border counties, including Lord Powis; and Clive, a very sick man, was averse to making new enemies.

In the end, besides defending his own seat at Shrewsbury, Clive actively engaged in two contests only: he supported the candidature of his brother-in-law Edmund Maskelyne at Cricklade, which was, however, abandoned a few days before the poll;[21] and pursuing a feud which originated at East India House, he unsuccessfully backed Robert Mackintosh in Perth Burghs against George Dempster, canvassing friends in his favour,[22] and helping him financially.[23] Dempster in turn reconnoitred Shrewsbury for William (Johnstone) Pulteney, when in March 1768 he decided to stand against Clive.[24] Clive stood jointly with Noel Hill, and was returned after a contest from which he was absent, having gone abroad for reasons of health. Thus in the end only three Members were added to the Clive group in 1768: John Carnac on Chase Price's interest at Leominster; Henry Strachey on Walsh's interest at Pontefract; and William Clive on Lord Clive's own interest at Bishop's Castle—a surprisingly meagre result of so much activity backed by such vast resources.

In March 1768, paying £43,000, Walsh bought for Clive V. Morris's Usk estate in Monmouthshire which carried considerable influence in the by-election of July 1771 but would not have sufficed to establish a new interest in the county. Some time after 1768 Clive bought Thomas Pitt's Okehampton estate, and returned in 1774 Wedderburn for the seat it carried (it was sold in 1778 to Lord Spencer); and further Oakley Park from Lord Powis with electoral influence at Ludlow. This is about the sum total of the parliamentary interests he acquired.

The personal friendship and trust which grew up between him and George Grenville after his return to England, and his annoyance with the Government over its East Indian policy led Clive into the parliamentary Opposition with which, by 1769, he was fully identified. On 9 May 1769 he was present at the dinner of Opposition Members at the Thatched House Tavern. When Alexander Wedderburn had to give up his seat at Richmond on account of the active part he took on the Middlesex election, Clive let Grenville know that he would return him for Bishop's Castle,[25] and did so on 16 Jan. 1770; and in the debate on the Address, 9 Jan. 1770, though Clive himself was absent, George Clive, Henry Strachey, and John Walsh voted in the minority. On 27 Feb. 1769 he himself made a vigorous and wide-ranging speech in opposition to the financial agreement concluded that year between the ministry and the Company.[26]

The death of Grenville on 13 Nov. 1770 left Clive without a leader, but though Grenville's followers, including Wedderburn (with whom Clive's relations had become increasingly close), soon made their terms with Administration, he himself received coldly tentative approaches made by the North Administration through Wedderburn in 1771. It was the events of 1772 that brought him into their fold. His new enemies in the Company joined with his old ones had for some time been encouraging attacks in the press against him and attributing to his second government of Bengal the economic and administrative disorders that continued to mount there. Early in 1772 the court of directors took up at their demand some charges against him. During a debate in the Commons, 30 Mar. 1772, Clive took the offensive and defended himself against these charges while vigorously attacking his opponents and the court of directors. The result was the setting up of a select committee of the House under the chairmanship of Colonel Burgoyne of which Clive and Henry Strachey were members but which, under the influence of Clive's enemies, began an investigation of his Indian career and that of other Company servants who had worked with him. The investigation, which threatened the confiscation of almost the whole of his fortune, aroused widespread and hostile interest. In the circumstances the value of good relations with the ministry became obvious, and in September 1772 Clive's appointment as lord lieutenant of Shropshire was generally and correctly taken as an indication that they had come to terms.[27] North stated on this occasion that 'an opportunity of manifesting my respect to his merit and my earnest desire of being well with him is what I have long wished to find'.[28] Though the minister studiously avoided reference to East Indian affairs in his talks with Clive, the results were satisfactory to both sides. Clive used his interest in the East India Company to help the ministry to achieve the reforms in the Company which accompanied the passing of the Regulating Act of 1773, and when the chairman of the select committee brought charges against Clive in the House of Commons on 19–21 May 1773, the ministry made no attempt to present a united front, and both North and the King were relieved when he was exonerated though North had divided against him.[29] In these debates Clive made several effective fighting speeches in his own defence, ending with a short speech on the night of 21 May, when he retired from the House begging them that 'when they come to decide upon my honour, they should not forget their own'.[30] Horace Walpole said of his defence that 'with the frankness of Julius Caesar he promised himself an escape like Verres'.[31]

For the few remaining months of his life Clive continued to support Administration though he by no means fully approved of the Regulating Act, and his influence and that of his circle in indoctrinating with their views on East India matters Philip Francis, appointed under the Act a member of the governor-general's council, may be said to have played a part in making the working of the Act impossible. Besides Clive's immediate followers certain 'nabobs' and others concerned with him in East India affairs tended to vote with him, but their numbers were not large. In 1774 Strachey considered the second seat at Worcester, in which Thomas Bates Rous had in 1773 tried to succeed Henry Crabb Boulton, as 'a great part of our parliamentary weight', and feared its loss when Rous's election being voided on petition, he refused for the moment to stand again, especially if 'Mr. Walsh should determine not to stand at the next election'.[32] Nevertheless he considered Clive's influence in Parliament to be considerable; and sharing the belief that the operation of Grenville's Act in the next election 'would prevent either King or minister from making the next Parliament so that those who have most members under their banner will command what they please', he wrote to Clive:

The only object you have in life [an English peerage] must be pushed for by weight at the next general election. It will certainly be the last effort, and most probably will succeed at that period.

But by this time Clive's health and spirits were undermined by anxiety and the excessive medical use of opium. His death on 22 Nov. 1774, before the new Parliament met, was by his own hand.

Clive's achievements in India were those of a soldier and man of action; his successes as an administrator were due rather to daemonic energy

and force of character than to grasp of long-range policy, but his part in the creation of British India was a great one. Ruthless and self-seeking, autocratic and violent, but capable of great exertion and fearless courage when set on a task, and of steady loyalty to those who befriended or served him, his qualities were more suited for the troubled scene in India in which he rose to fame, than to the political world of 18th century England. To this temperamental difficulties were added, moreover, the suspicions stimulated by his sudden and doubtfully gained wealth, and the enmities which he had aroused during his Indian career and in the Company after his return. For these reasons his part in the politics of the East India Company was on the whole damaging rather than useful, and in national politics his considerable talents and influence were confined almost wholly to the negative purpose of protecting his own position.

[1] Rich. Clive to Rob. Clive, 18 Apr. 1755, Sir G. W. Forrest, *Life of Clive*, i. 238. [2] Sir J. Malcolm, *Life of Clive*, ii. 187. [3] Clive to J. Pybus, 27 Feb. 1762, Malcolm, ii. 195. [4] 3 Feb. 1762, Clive mss. [5] Bank of England recs. [6] Sutherland, *E. I. Co. in 18th Cent. Politics*, 101–2. [7] Powis to Newcastle, 25 Sept. 1760, Add. 32912, ff. 106–7. [8] For the Shrewsbury election of 1761 see Namier, *Structure*, 257–68. [9] Robert to Rich. Clive, 19 Aug. 1757, Forrest, i. 36. [10] Namier, *Structure*, 288–9. [11] *Grenville Pprs*. ii. 183. [12] Malcolm, ii. 243–4. [13] Sutherland, 134, n. 3. [14] Malcolm, iii. 190. [15] John Cornel to Ld. Clive, 29 July 1767; all the following letters, unless otherwise marked, are to Ld. Clive and in the Clive mss. [16] Geo. Clive, 11 and 24 Nov. [17] Geo. Clive, 24 Nov.; see also SHIFFNER, Henry. [18] For Taaffe see TOWNSHEND, Hon. Charles. [19] On these negotiations see letters from G. Clive, 1, 17, 20, 24 Oct. and 13 Nov.; from Chase Price, 21 Oct.; from John Walsh, 26 Nov. and 1 Dec.; from T. Ryder and H. Mountfort, Taaffe's attorneys, 26, 27, 29 Nov.; from Taaffe himself, 28 Nov. [20] See PRICE, Chase. [21] For an account of Maskelyne's candidature see J. A. Cannon, 'Parlty. Rep. Six Wilts. Boroughs' (Bristol Univ. Ph.D. thesis), i. 55–61. [22] See e.g., letters to Clive from Lord Dupplin, 17 Sept., P. Craufurd, 23 Sept.; also from A. Austin, 8 and 16 Oct. [23] Walsh to Clive, 22 Apr. 1768; James Fergusson, *Letters of G. Dempster*, 65–68. [24] Dr. W. Adams to Rich. Clive, 9 Mar. 1768. [25] *Chatham Corresp*. iii. 358 n. [26] *Cavendish's Debates*, i. 260. [27] Burke to Rockingham, 29 Oct. 1772. [28] North to Wedderburn, 18 Sept. 1772, Forrest, ii. 395. [29] Sutherland, 255–8. [30] *Parlty. Hist.* xvii. 879. [31] *Last Jnls*. i. 198. [32] 8 Feb. 1774, Strachey mss.

L.S.S./L.B.N.

**CLIVE, William** (1745–1825), of Styche Hall, Salop.

BISHOP'S CASTLE 1768–Jan. 1770, 31 Mar. 1779–1820

*b.* 29 Aug. 1745, 6th s. of Richard Clive and bro. of Robert Clive (qq.v.). *educ.* Eton 1760–1. *m.* 25 Aug. 1790, his 2nd co. Elizabeth Clive, da. of John Rolton of Duffield, Derbys., 7s. 1da.

Cornet 1 Drag. 1764, lt. 1771; ret. 1776.

In the autumn of 1767 it was intended that William Clive should stand for Leominster at the next general election,[1] but the scheme was abandoned, possibly on Lord Clive's obtaining complete control of Bishop's Castle, where William was returned unopposed. In the House he followed his brother, and voted with the Opposition over Wilkes, 2 and 3 Feb. 1769, but apparently was absent from the later divisions; and vacated his seat when Lord Clive required it for Wedderburn. Returned again in 1779 by his nephew Edward, Lord Clive, William appears with him on the Government side in all the five extant division lists February–April 1780, and again in all the five lists of December 1781–March 1782; voted against Shelburne's peace preliminaries, 18 Feb. 1783; adhered to the Coalition, and voted for Fox's East India bill; and remained with them in opposition to Pitt till 1794. No speech by him is recorded before 1790. He died 23 June 1825.

[1] See PRICE, Chase.

L.B.N.

## COCKAYNE CUST, see CUST, Francis

## COCKBURN, Sir James, 8th Bt. (1729–1804), of Langton, Berwickshire and Petersham, Surr.

LINLITHGOW BURGHS 9 Jan. 1772–1784

*b.* 1729, 2nd s. of William Cockburn, merchant, of Ayton and Eyemouth, Berkwickshire, by his cos. Frances, da. of Dr. James Cockburn, physician in Jamaica. *m.* (1) 31 Mar. 1755, Mary (*d.*5 Apr. 1766), da. of Henry Douglas, London merchant, 1s. *d.v.p.* 3 da.; (2) 10 July 1769, Augusta Anne, da. of Rev. Francis Ayscough, dean of Bristol, 5s. 1da. *suc.* his cos. as 8th Bt. 30 Apr. 1745.

Commissary gen. to the army in Germany 1762–3; director E. I. Co. 1767–9, 1770–3; principal usher of the white rod in Scotland 1766.

When Cockburn unexpectedly succeeded to the baronetcy, the estates of the bankrupt Langton branch of the family had long been in the possession of their principal creditors, the Cockburns of Cockburn, who also claimed the hereditary office of principal usher. In 1755 James, after long litigation, failed to establish his right to the honour, which with all other Langton property was auctioned in 1757 and passed out of the ownership of both branches of the family.[1]

As a youth Cockburn entered business in London with Henry Douglas, a wealthy Scots-West Indian merchant, whose daughter (with a dowry of £10,000) he married. In May 1760 he was appointed a commissary under Prince Ferdinand,[2] and went to Germany with letters of introduction from his friend John Calcraft (q.v.).[3] Within a month he had succeeded as commissary of supply, 'without any other assistance than his own merit',[4] and by his energy and initiative earned the praise of Prince Ferdinand, Granby, and Conway.[5] He maintained close contact with Calcraft, Sir George Colebrooke and Nicholas Linwood (qq.v.) in London, to procure advancement for himself and contracts for his friends;[6] and in 1761 Gilbert Elliot (q.v.) wrote about him to Bute:[7] 'No commissary has given so

much satisfaction either to the Treasury or to the army in general as Sir James Cockburn.' In March 1762 he was appointed commissary general to the forces in Germany.[8]

After the war he was closely associated with Colebrooke in East India Company affairs; included in the House list of candidates for the court of directors in 1765, he was dropped at the insistence of Lawrence Dundas and Lord Holland,[9] and did not becomes a director until 1767. In 1765 Cockburn, his relation John Stewart (q.v.) and Colebrooke purchased extensive plantations in Dominica, and were active in obtaining a legislature and government separate from the Tobago-Grenada-group.[10] They were also concerned in the Colebrooke Bay Co., an undertaking to acquire two townships in New Hampshire.[11]

Cockburn was now a rich man and ambitious of restoring his family's prestige in Scotland. By 1766 he had bought back the office of heritable usher and in 1769 a portion of the Cockburn estates.[12] In 1771 Colebrooke, having purchased properties in Lanarkshire and attached himself to the Hamilton interest, recommended Cockburn to the Hamilton guardians as candidate at the by-election for Linlithgow Burghs; and he was returned unopposed.

Cockburn joined the East India group of M.P.s led by Laurence Sulivan and on 30 March seconded his motion for a bill (subsequently dropped) 'for the better regulation of the East India Company'.[13] During the crisis in the Company's affairs Cockburn, like Colebrooke, was known to have 'bulled' East India stock on the Amsterdam market; was accused 'of having withheld the true state of the Company's affairs from the proprietors';[14] and did not stand for the directorate in 1773.

Little affected by the financial crash of 1772, Cockburn lavished money on his burghs to counter the interest of Sir Lawrence Dundas.[15] Although given no guarantee in 1771 that he would be the Hamilton candidate at the general election, Cockburn felt aggrieved when Andrew Stuart, to split the opposition to the Hamilton interest in Lanarkshire, negotiated on behalf of the guardians an agreement with Buccleuch over Linlithgow Burghs. Anxious about the chances of his friend Sir Adam Fergusson in Ayrshire, Buccleuch authorized Henry Dundas to propose that the united Buccleuch-Hamilton interest should procure the burghs for Sir Adam, but that the election should be fought by the Hamilton nominee as 'ostensible candidate', who, if Fergusson lost Ayrshire, must resign in his favour. Cockburn, when informed, strongly objected, claiming that, with Hamilton support, he could defeat any combination against him.

It would not be suitable for him nor his situation in life to be the ostensible man in fighting the Burghs and afterwards retire, making his bow to them and desiring them to choose Sir Adam Fergusson or any other person whatever.

After numerous conferences, the Hamilton guardians pronounced their ultimatum: unless Cockburn accepted 'second place' the Hamilton interest would be given to another candidate. At a meeting on 23 Aug. at Colebrooke's house, attended by Stuart, Charles Fergusson (Sir Adam's brother), and John Fordyce, the Scottish receiver general, Cockburn swallowed his pride and agreed to the terms.[16] At the general election he was returned against the Dundas candidate; and, as Fergusson secured Ayrshire, retained the seat.

Cockburn uniformly supported Government in Parliament. In 1776 he and his partner Henry Douglas secured a valuable contract for supplying 100,000 gallons of Grenada rum to the troops in America;[17] and in the debate of 15 May 1777 on the cost of the war Cockburn rose to explain the circumstances of his contract and to justify the high price charged.[18] Cockburn and Douglas also acted as agents for the receiver general of the Scottish land tax who allowed them to retain vast sums in their hands.[19] By 1778 Cockburn was in serious financial trouble, although not apparently declared bankrupt until 1781. The major cause was his involvement in the transactions of Lauchlin Macleane and John Macpherson (qq.v.) with the Nawab of Arcot. Cockburn was persuaded to advance large sums and pledge his credit for a loan to the Nawab, but when Macleane was lost at sea in 1778 and the project fell into confusion, he found himself hopelessly in debt to his creditors, including the receiver general of the land tax.[20] North came to his rescue; by 1779 Cockburn was receiving a secret service pension of £600 p.a. in the name of his wife;[21] and until March 1782 his vote was naturally at North's disposal.

North wrote to the King soon after his resignation:[22]

> Sir James Cockburn is in the extremest distress. He has received the pension in the name of Lady Cockburn. His Majesty will consider whether it will be right to suppress this pension altogether or to leave Lady Cockburn in this, or to insert her in some other list, on account of her distress and the former connexions of her father with his Majesty and the Royal Family.

The King replied:[23] 'I will set down the name of his wife'; and included her in the list of private pensioners delivered on 21 Apr. to Rockingham, to whom Cockburn, in support of his claim, submitted a memorial recounting his services as commissary twenty years before.[24] Payment was continued under Shelburne, yet Cockburn voted against Shelburne's

peace preliminaries, 18 Feb. 1783. He voted for Fox's East India bill, 27 Nov. 1783, but was among the earliest converts to Pitt's Administration.[25]

In 1784 he had little chance of re-election; and, without money or influence, he was discarded by the combined Hamilton, Buccleuch and Queensberry interests.

In 1786 Cockburn, in desperate financial straits, sought refuge from his creditors by obtaining diplomatic immunity as secretary to the Prussian minister, an abuse of privilege against which Lord Carmarthen protested to the King.[26] When Cockburn in 1792 was trying to recover his Arcot debts, Henry Dundas commented:[27] 'I believe Sir James was the unfortunate dupe of others and therefore to be pitied.' During the last years of his life, when his sons had achieved distinction, Cockburn was apparently no longer in financial difficulties.

He died 26 July 1804.

[1] Sir R. Cockburn and H. A. Cockburn, *Cockburn Family Recs.* 54 et seq.; House of Lords Appeals, 14, 21 Mar. 1755, Add. 36159, ff. 349–418. [2] T52/50/479. [3] Add. 17495, ff. 12b, 14, 14b. [4] Calcraft to Lady Cockburn, 12 June 1760, ibid. f. 41. [5] See Cockburn's memorial of 1782 on his services, Rockingham mss, and his corresp. 1760–3 in *HMC Rutland*, ii. [6] Calcraft to Cockburn and to Peter Taylor, 3 Oct. 1760, Add. 17495. f. 150b. [7] Elliot to Bute, ?Aug, 1761, Bute mss. [8] T29/34/251; T52/53/349. [9] L. S. Sutherland. *E. I. Co. in 18th Cent. Politics*, 133; J. Walsh to Clive, 5 Apr. 1765. Powis mss. [10] T. Whately to G. Grenville, 25 Oct. 1765, Grenville mss (JM); *Bd. Trade Jnl.* 1764–7, pp. 425–6; *APC Col. Unbound Pprs.* 472; 1766–83, 14; T29/41/4. [11] John Nelson to Grenville, 4 Sept. 1769, Grenville mss (JM). [12] T. H. Cockburn Hood, *House of Cockburn*, 105. [13] Cavendish's 'Debates', Egerton 239, f. 184; Sutherland, 231. [14] Ibid. 228, 245. [15] Andrew Stuart to the Duchess of Argyll, 20 Aug. 1773, Duke of Argyll, *Intimate Society Letters of 18th Cent.* i. 169. Argyll to W. Mure, 24 Feb. 1774, *Caldwell Pprs.* ii (2), p. 230. [16] Corresp. between Dundas and A. Stuart, 7, 20, 25 June, 23 Aug. 1774; J. Lockhart Ross to Dundas, 15 July, and Dundas's reply, 29 Aug. 1774, Buccleuch mss. [17] T29/45/103; T54/42/187. [18] Almon, vii. 212–13. [19] W. R. Ward, 'Land Tax in Scotland 1707–98.' *Bulletin Rylands Lib.* xxxvii. 304. [20] Dundas to Lord Grenville, 5 Aug. 1792, *HMC Rutland*, ii. 297–8. [21] Royal archives, Windsor, secret service accs. [22] Fortescue, v. 469. [23] Ibid. 473. [24] Rockingham mss. [25] Laprade, 54. [26] Carmarthen to the King, 29 June 1786, Royal archives. [27] Dundas to Grenville, 5 Aug. 1792, *HMC Rutland*, ii. 207–8.

E.H.-G.

**COCKS, Charles** (1725–1806), of Castleditch, Herefs.

REIGATE     1747–1784

b. 29 June 1725, 1st s. of John Cocks, M.P., of Castleditch, Herefs. by his cos. Mary, da. and h. of Thomas Cocks of Castleditch; neph. of Philip, 1st Earl of Hardwicke. *educ.* Worcester, Oxf. 1742; L. Inn 1745, called 1750. *m.* (1) 8 Aug. 1759, Elizabeth (*d.* 1 Jan. 1771), da. of Richard Eliot, M.P., sis. of Edward Eliot (q.v.), 3s. 3da.; (2) 20 May 1772, Anne, da. of Reginald Pole of Stoke Damerel, Devon, sis. of Reginald Pole Carew (q.v.), 2s. 1da. *suc.* fa. 24 June 1771; *cr.* Bt. 7 Oct. 1772; Lord Sommers 17 May 1784.

Clerk of deliveries of Ordnance 1758–72; clerk of Ordnance 1772–82.

The Cocks family controlled one seat at Reigate which Charles Cocks held without opposition throughout his parliamentary career. As Hardwicke's nephew he adhered to the Pelhams, and on

12 Dec. 1755 spoke in defence of the Russian and Hessian subsidy treaties. On 14 Nov. 1757 Hardwicke wrote to Newcastle asking for an office for Cocks:[1] 'He has been in Parliament 10 or 11 years, and always behaved there very diligently and very steadily notwithstanding temptations to the contrary.' In December 1762 Cocks voted with the Administration over the peace preliminaries,[2] and after the dismissals was offered the post of storekeeper of the Ordnance but on Hardwicke's advice refused.[3] He was classed by Jenkinson in the autumn of 1763 as 'pro'; voted with the Administration on general warrants, 6 Feb. 1764, but with the Opposition on 15 and 18 Feb., and was counted by Newcastle on 10 May as a 'sure friend'. Like most west country gentlemen he voted for the repeal of the cider tax, 10 and 17 Feb. 1764. On the formation of the Rockingham Administration he wrote to Lord Granby on 21 July (and an almost identical letter to his cousin Charles Yorke on the 20th), recalling his previous refusal of the storekeeper's office, and concluding:[4]

> If removals are to be made, in order to introduce strangers, I presume your Lordship will think with me, that I have a right to the refusal of any place at the board under the rank of lieutenant-general which is military, as I have constantly supported his Majesty's Government ever since I have been in Parliament, now near twenty years.

When the former office holders were restored, and Cocks remained in the office he had held all through, he wrote to Yorke on 14 Sept.:[5] 'I . . . am perfectly satisfied as to myself with the intended restitution which is but just and honourable. It gives me great pleasure to see so many Whigs restored to his Majesty's service.' Rockingham in July 1765 classed him as 'pro', but in November 1766 as 'Swiss'. But Cocks voted with the Opposition on nullum tempus, 17 Feb. 1768. No vote by him is reported between 1769 and 1772. He was listed as 'pro, present' on the royal marriage bill, March 1772, and at this time was applying for a peerage, but only obtained a baronetcy. He voted with the Opposition on Grenville's election bill, 25 Feb. 1774, but otherwise appears to have regularly supported Administration. His only recorded speeches during this Parliament were to move the yearly Ordnance estimates. In 1780 he thought of standing at Worcester but decided against it. No further votes by him are reported; during the early part of 1782 he was abroad for reasons of health, and in January 1784 was listed by Robinson as 'absent'. But he was in the House on 20 Feb. 1784 when he 'praised the virtues and talents of the minister and wondered how it could be imagined he should be turned out of office before he had an opportunity of proving to his

country either his merits or his demerits'.[6] Cocks did not stand again at the general election, having been promised a peerage.

He died 30 Jan. 1806.

[1] Add. 32875, f. 501. [2] P. C. Yorke, *Hardwicke*, iii. 441. [3] Cocks to Chas. Yorke, 20 July 1765, Add. 35637, f. 198. [4] Rutland mss. [5] Add. 35637, f. 257. [6] Debrett, xiii. 182.

M.M.D.

### COCKS, John Sommers (1760-1841), of Castleditch, Herefs.

| | |
|---|---|
| WEST LOOE | 20 Feb. 1782–1784 |
| GRAMPOUND | 1784–1790 |
| REIGATE | 1790–30 Jan. 1806 |

*b.* 6 May 1760, 1st s. of Charles Cocks (q.v.) by his 1st w. Elizabeth, da. of Richard Eliot, M.P. *educ.* Harrow 1770–1; Westminster 1774; St. Alban Hall, Oxf. 1778. *m.* (1) 19 Mar. 1785, Margaret (*d.*9 Feb. 1831), da. of Rev. Treadway Russell Nash, historian of Worcs., 3s. 1da.; (2) 3 June 1834, his cos. Jane, da. of James Cocks, London banker, wid. of Rev. George Waddington, rector of Northwold, Norf. *suc.* fa. as 2nd Lord Sommers 30 Jan. 1806; *cr.* Earl Sommers 17 July 1821. Ld. lt. Herefs. 1817–*d.*

In 1782 Cocks was returned for West Looe on the interest of John Buller. In Parliament he supported Shelburne's Administration, and when on 18 Dec. 1782 Lord John Cavendish moved to lay before the House that part of the peace which recognized American independence, Cocks said (in his only reported speech before 1790) 'that in such a moment as the present we should have confidence in ministers and not call upon them to report progress, since it might materially affect the negotiations about which they were employed'.[1] Cocks voted against Fox's East India bill, 27 Nov. 1783. In Robinson's list of January 1784 and Stockdale's of 19 March he was classed as 'Administration'. At the general election he was returned on the interest of his uncle Edward Eliot (q.v.) at Grampound as a supporter of Administration. His only recorded vote during this Parliament was with Pitt on the Regency, 1788–9.

He died 5 Jan. 1841.

[1] Debrett, ix. 117.

M.M.D.

### CODRINGTON, Sir William, 2nd Bt. (1719-92), of Dodington, Glos.

| | |
|---|---|
| BEVERLEY | 1747–1761 |
| TEWKESBURY | 1761–11 Mar. 1792 |

*b.* 26 Oct. 1719, 1st s. of Sir William Codrington, 1st Bt., M.P., by Elizabeth, da. of William Bethell of Swindon, Yorks. and sis. and coh. of Slingsby Bethell (q.v.). Codrington's sis. m. William Dowdeswell (q.v.). *educ.* Westminster 1736; Univ. Coll. Oxf. 1736. *m.* 22 Feb. 1736, Anne Acton of Fulham, Mdx., 1s. 1da. *suc.* fa. 17 Dec. 1738.

It is probable that Codrington sat for Beverley on the interest of his uncle Slingsby Bethell who owned considerable property in that part of Yorkshire. At the contested election of 1754 Codrington was returned head of the poll and was listed by Dupplin as an Opposition Whig. He sat for Tewkesbury on the interest of his brother-in-law William Dowdeswell, supported by the corporation.

He did not receive Newcastle's whip in October 1761; was marked in Bute's list of December 1761 as 'Tory and West Indian' (he owned plantations in Barbados and Antigua); and voted against the peace preliminaries, 9 and 10 Dec. 1762. In the autumn of 1763 he was marked by Jenkinson as 'doubtful'.

In October 1763 he wished to stand against Edward Southwell (q.v.) at the by-election for Gloucestershire, and wrote to Grenville on 14 Oct.:[1]

> He [Southwell] is supported by the Beaufort family and Mr. [Norborne] Berkeley [q.v.] with the Tory interest. I have the assistance of Lord Chedworth, the influence of Berkeley Castle, and the Whig interest.

Codrington saw Grenville on 14 Oct. and 'desired earnestly' to have an office which would vacate his seat.[2] Grenville refused, having promised to give the Chiltern Hundreds to Southwell and not wishing to countenance an opposition against him. 'Had he been permitted to vacate his present seat in Parliament', wrote Samuel Rogers[3] to the Duke of Portland on 19 Oct.,[4] 'I think he would not have succeeded at Gloucester as Southwell's interest was so much bigger than his.'

Codrington voted against the Government over general warrants, 6, 15 and 18 Feb. 1764. Classed in November 1766 by Rockingham as 'Whig' and by Newcastle in March 1767 as 'friend', he voted regularly with the Rockinghams. He voted against Shelburne's peace preliminaries, 18 Feb. 1783, and was classed by Robinson, March 1783, as a friend of Fox; did not vote on the East India bill, 27 Nov. 1783, but was reckoned among the opponents of Pitt in Stockdale's list of 19 Mar. 1784. He voted against Pitt on the Irish commercial propositions, 13 May 1785, on the Duke of Richmond's fortifications plan, 27 Feb. 1786, and on the Regency.

His only recorded speech, 29 Mar. 1762, was on the game bill, when he is included by Harris in a list of 'all such speakers as did never speak'.

Codrington died 11 Mar. 1792.

¹ Grenville mss (Bodl.). ² Grenville to Norborne Berkeley, 20 Oct. 1763, Grenville mss (HL). ³ For Samuel Rogers, rector of St. Mary Magdalen, Oxford, and a Gloucestershire man, see Barker & Stenning, *Old Westminsters*. ⁴ Portland mss.

J.B.

**COGHILL** (formerly **MAYNE**), **John** (d.1785), of Richings Park, Bucks.

NEWPORT 1780–14 Nov. 1785

> m. in or after 1764, Hester, da. and h. of James Coghill, LL.D., wid. of Charles Moore, 1st Earl of Charleville [I], s.p. Assumed name of Coghill 6 Mar. 1779. cr. Bt. 24 Mar. 1781.
>   Cornet 14 Drag. (Ireland) 1734, capt. lt. 1754, maj. 1766; disappears from Army List 1771.

Coghill was returned unopposed for Newport on the Duke of Northumberland's interest. Shortly after his election in 1780 the *English Chronicle* wrote about him:

> He . . . went to Ireland in the *suite* of the Duke of Northumberland, when that nobleman was appointed the viceroy. Being remarkably handsome in his person, mild and engaging in his manners, he became in this situation not only an object of general regard amongst the men, but a peculiar favourite with the ladies. Amongst the rest, his personal accomplishments did not escape the attention of the Countess of *Charleville*, who became deeply enamoured with him, and of course soon yielded to his addresses, when he presented himself her suitor. He got a large fortune with this lady, and enjoys it with great esteem. His connexions in life will necessarily incline him to be ministerial in his political principles. He is not likely to make a distinguished figure as an orator in Parliament.

Coghill voted with the Administration on Lowther's motion against the war, 12 Dec. 1781, and the censure motion against the Admiralty, 20 Feb. 1782, but did not vote on the motions to end the war, 22 and 27 Feb. 1782, though he again supported North on the censure motions of 8 and 15 Mar. 1782. A letter from his wife to Shelburne, 6 Sept. 1782, states that Coghill believed that New York should be retained.[1] He did not vote on Shelburne's peace preliminaries, 18 Feb. 1783, nor on Fox's East India bill, 27 Nov. 1783. In Robinson's list of January 1784, Stockdale's of 19 Mar., and Adam's of May he is classed as a Pittite. There is no record of his having spoken in the House. He died 14 Nov. 1785.

¹ Lansdowne mss.

I.R.C.

**COKE, Daniel Parker** (1745–1825), of Derby.

DERBY 8 Feb. 1776–1780
NOTTINGHAM 1780–1802, 30 May 1803–1812

> b. 17 July 1745, o.s. of Thomas Coke, barrister, of Derby by Dorothy, da. and h. of Thomas Goodwin of Derby. educ. Queen's, Oxf. 1762; All Souls; L. Inn 1760, called 1768; M. Temple 1770. unm.
>   Commr. for settling American claims 1782–5; bencher M. Temple 1802, reader 1805.

Coke was a practising barrister, for many years attached to the Midland circuit. In 1775 he contested Derby on an independent interest in opposition to that of the corporation and the Devonshire family. He was defeated by 14 votes on a poll of 672, but was seated on petition.

Wraxall writes[1] that Coke was 'animated . . . by public spirited and honest . . . views of public benefit', and the *English Chronicle*, in about 1780, described him as 'a gentleman of small fortune . . . but as independent in his parliamentary conduct as any man in the House'. His first reported vote was with the Opposition on America, 2 Feb. 1778; he was listed as 'contra, present' on the contractors bill, 12 Feb. 1779; voted with the Opposition for an account of pensions, 21 Feb. 1780, and on Dunning's motion, 6 Apr. 1780. He spoke in support of the petitioning movement, 6 Apr., and on 13 Apr. voted for the motion to prevent prorogation till action had been taken about the petitions. Robinson wrote in his pre-electoral survey of July 1780: 'He has often gone with Government, but oftener against, and almost uniformly so in the late questions.'

At the general election he was invited to stand for Nottingham on the corporation interest, and was returned after a contest. On 27 Nov. 1780 Coke told the House that though 'he had been one of those who lamented the commencement of the American war, and disapproved many of the measures adopted in its prosecution', now that America was 'the confederate of the House of Bourbon . . . he saw no medium between unconditional submission to the enemy and the most spirited exertions',[2] and on 12 Dec. 1781 he voted with the Administration on Sir James Lowther's motion against the war. Coke voted with the Opposition on the censure motion against the Admiralty, 20 Feb. 1782; did not vote on Conway's motion against the war, 22 Feb. 1782, but again supported North on that of 27 Feb. In March he went off on circuit[3] and was absent from the censure motions of 8 and 15 Mar.

On 10 May 1782 Coke brought the Administration's proposal for arming the people before the House, and called on ministers 'to explain and justify a proceeding unauthorized previously by either branch of the legislature'. After an explanation by Fox, he said 'that if it ought to be generally adopted, nothing could contribute more to that end than by having it sanctified by Parliament'.[4] Coke was strongly opposed to the grant of a pension to Barré, and on 9 July 1782 demanded an inquiry as to which of the ministers had dared to recommend it.[5] He voted against Shelburne's peace preliminaries, 18 Feb. 1783, and for Fox's East India bill, 27 Nov. 1783. Coke was opposed to the Coalition's receipts tax, and on 4 Dec. declared that 'no man held the instructions of constituents, ordinarily considered, more cheap than he did', but when, as in the present case, he agreed with their views he would do his best to forward their wishes. However,

> he thought it incumbent on every gentleman who wished for the repeal of a tax in existence, when he moved such repeal, to come forward with another tax capable of supplying its place. He would propose two or three.

First, by which 'none but the rich would be affected', he suggested that private pews should be taxed. 'He would lay £5 a year on each of the stands of prebends, £10 on each of the stalls of deans, and £20 each on the stalls of bishops. Deans and prebends . . . were in his opinion, the most useless order of ecclesiastics in existence'; his other suggestions were for 40s. tax on grave stones marking burials in churches, which he disapproved of on health grounds; and a tax on dogs.[6]

In Robinson's list of January 1784, Stockdale's of 19 Mar. and Adam's of May, Coke is counted as a Foxite. At the general election of 1784 he again stood for Nottingham, declaring in his election address that he 'declined then entering into the discussion of political questions as they very often caused confusion'. He would 'vote and act as he was conscious he had heretofore done without any view of place or emolument, but from principle and a thorough conviction of the side he should take being right'.[7] He was returned unopposed.

He spoke and voted against Pitt's Irish commercial propositions, 13 May 1785; opposed Richmond's fortifications plan, 27 Feb. 1786; and on several occasions criticized tax proposals which he considered harmful to the interests of his constituents. On 5 May 1788 he introduced a bill to make the destruction of weaving frames a capital offence:[8] 'He wished not that any person should be hanged under the authority of the bill; God forbid that any should! But the bill was meant to operate upon the fears of the many, who would not otherwise abstain from practices so unjustifiable.' The same month Coke signed the third party circular. He voted against Pitt over the Regency 1788-9. During this Parliament he spoke several times in support of the claims of the American loyalists.

Coke died 4 Dec. 1825.

[1] *Mems.* ii. 310. [2] Debrett, i. 163. [3] *CJ*, xxxviii. 877. [4] Debrett, vii. 146, 153. [5] Wraxall, ii. 360. [6] Debrett, xii. 336-8. [7] Cresswell & Burbage's *Nottingham Journal*, quoted Christie, *End of North's Ministry*, 131. [8] Stockdale, xiv. 209-10.

M.M.D.

**COKE, Edward** (1758-1837), of Longford, Derbys.

| | |
|---|---|
| DERBY | 1780-Feb. 1807 |
| NORFOLK | 4 Mar.-29 Apr. 1807 |
| DERBY | 1807-1818 |

*b.* 1758, 2nd s. of Wenman Coke, and bro. of Thomas William Coke (qq.v.). *educ.* Harrow 1774–5. *m.* 9 Apr. 1792, Grace, da. of William Colhoun (q.v.), 2s. 1da. *suc.* fa. at Longford 1776.

Sheriff, Derbys. 1819–20.

Coke stood for Derby in 1780 as the corporation candidate, with the support of the Devonshire interest; and was returned after a contest. Like his brother Thomas, a friend of Fox, Edward Coke adhered first to Rockingham and then to Portland. He voted in opposition in all the last divisions against North's ministry, and with the Coalition on Shelburne's peace preliminaries and the East India bill. He remained in opposition with Fox throughout Pitt's ministry.

He died in 1837.[1]

[1] A. M. W. Stirling, *Coke of Norfolk*, 577.

I.R.C.

## COKE, Thomas William (1754–1842), of Holkham, Norf.

| NORFOLK | 8 May 1776–1784, 1790–19 Feb. 1807 |
| DERBY | 26 Feb. –29 Apr. 1807 |
| NORFOLK | 1807–1832 |

*b.* 6 May 1754, 1st s. of Wenman Coke, and bro. of Edward Coke (qq.v.). *educ.* Eton 1765–71; Grand Tour 1771–4. *m.* (1) 5 Oct. 1775, Jane (*d.*2 June 1800), da. of James Lennox Dutton of Loughcrew, Meath, sis. of James Dutton (q.v.), 3da.; (2) 26 Feb. 1822, Lady Anne Amelia Keppel, da. of William Charles, 4th Earl of Albemarle, 5s. 1da. *suc.* fa. 11 Apr. 1776; *cr.* Earl of Leicester 12 Aug. 1837.

In 1776 Coke inherited extensive Norfolk and Derbyshire estates from his father and was returned in his place for Norfolk. His real interests were in country pursuits, particularly in the improvement of his estates where his achievements were to bring him considerable fame; and of his first entry into Parliament he himself said many years later that he had stood[1]

> with great reluctance, for I had no wish to come into Parliament. I was no orator, no politician . . . But I was much solicited by Sir Harbord Harbord, Sir E. Astley, and Mr. Fellowes of Shottisham, who said . . . I owed it to my father's memory . . . and that if I did not, a Tory would come in. At the mention of a Tory . . . my blood chilled all over me from head to foot, and I came forward.

In Parliament Coke regularly voted against North's Administration till its fall:

> When I first went into Parliament, I attached myself to Fox, and I clung to him through life [he stated at his nomination meeting in 1830]. I lived in the closest bond of friendship with him. He was a friend of the people, the practiser of every kindness and generosity, the advocate of civil and religious liberty.[2]

Coke's strong dislike of the American war was voiced in his speech on 4 Dec. 1778[3] when he condemned the peace commissioners' declaration of 3 Oct. because it 'threatened the Americans with the horrors of a new system of hostilities, which every law, as well human as divine, equally reprobated'; and 'to express this detestation more fully, as well to vindicate this country in the eyes of the world from the character of barbarity it might gain by following the threatened system', he moved that the House condemn the manifesto.

Coke was one of the few great Norfolk landowners who supported the petitioning movement, and on 23 Feb. 1780 he presented the Norfolk petition to the House.[4] But on 2 Apr. 1781, during a debate on further county petitions, he said that though he was a 'firm friend of those constitutional petitions which had come in the last session from the counties', and that he 'highly approved their principle and object . . . things had sprung out of those petitions of which he did not approve, because he conceived them to be at once dangerous and unconstitutional—those were the associations and the congress of delegates . . . he could admit of no such characters in a legal and constitutional point of view'.[5]

On the fall of North, Coke naturally supported the Rockingham Administration, and in June 1782 it was reported that he would be included in the next creation of peers.[6] He voted against Shelburne's peace preliminaries, 18 Feb. 1783, and when after Shelburne's resignation no Administration had been formed by 21 Mar. he told the House that he would move for an Address to the King if a ministerial arrangement was not come to very soon; and on 24 Mar. declared that 'matters were so situated that it became the duty of Parliament to interfere, and to apply to the sovereign for redress'. Coke supported the Coalition; on its dismissal went into opposition, and on 2 Feb. 1784 moved 'that the continuance of the present ministers in power, after the resolution of this House, is an obstacle to a firm, efficient, extended, and united Administration, which alone could save this country'; and the following day, regretting that his motion had not yet produced any effect, called upon Members 'to take care that resolutions of the House should not remain a dead letter'.[7]

At the general election of 1784 Coke again stood for Norfolk, but his support of the Coalition had for the time being weakened his position in the county, and he was obliged to withdraw to avoid an expensive and probably unavailing contest. After 1790 he represented the county for the next forty years.

Coke died 30 June 1842.

[1] *Gent. Mag.* 1842, ii. 317. [2] *Norwich Merc.* 7 Aug. 1830, quoted by A. M. W. Stirling, *Coke of Norfolk*, i. 165. [3] Almon, xi. 105–7. [4] Almon, xvii. 155. [5] Debrett, iii. 137. [6] Edw. Malone to Charlemont, 8 June 1782, *HMC Charlemont*, i. 408. [7] Debrett, ix. 511, 512, 513; xii. 49, 61.

M.M.D.

## COKE, Wenman (c.1717–1776), of Longford, Derbys.

| | |
|---|---|
| HARWICH | 21 Nov. 1753–1761 |
| OKEHAMPTON | 1761–1768 |
| DERBY | 31 Jan. 1772–1774 |
| NORFOLK | 1774–11 Apr. 1776 |

*b.* c.1717, 1st s. of Philip Roberts by Anne, da. of Edward Coke of Holkham, Norf., sis. of Thomas, 1st Earl of Leicester. m. (2) bef. 1754, Elizabeth, da. of George Chamberlayne (afterwards Denton) M.P., of Hillesden, Bucks., 2s. 3da. *suc.* to Longford estate of uncle Robert Coke, M.P., 1750; to Holkham, the estate of Thomas, Earl of Leicester, on d. of his wid. 28 Feb. 1775.

Gent. usher to Prince of Wales 1738–51.

In 1753 Wenman Roberts, having on the death of his cousin Edward, Viscount Coke, become heir to the estates of his uncle, Thomas, Earl of Leicester, assumed the name of Coke, and was returned in place of his cousin at Harwich. When it became clear that Coke would not be returned by the Administration for Harwich in 1761, Leicester declared that he would find another seat for him. He wrote to the Duke of Devonshire: 'In these times of constant changes, I really think it better for him to be on his own legs than obliged to any.'[1] But he got his friend the Duke of Newcastle to arrange for Coke's return at Okehampton. In Parliament Coke followed Newcastle; voted with Opposition against Bute's and Grenville's Administrations, and supported Rockingham's. Newcastle described him, 17 Oct. 1767, as 'a particular friend of mine . . . who has constantly voted with us in Parliament'.[2] In 1768 Coke contested Norfolk but was defeated, and did not obtain another seat till 1772 when he was returned for Derby after a contest. He consistently voted against North's Administration. In 1774 he was returned unopposed for both Derby and Norfolk, and elected to sit for Norfolk. There is no record of his having spoken in the House.

He died 11 Apr. 1776.

[1] 11 Dec. 1757, Devonshire mss. [2] Add. 32986, f. 32.

M.M.D.

## COLEBROOKE, George (1729–1809), of Gatton, Surr.

| | |
|---|---|
| ARUNDEL | 1754–1774 |

*b.* 14 June 1729, 3rd s. of James Colebrooke, London banker; bro. of Robert and James Colebrooke (qq.v.). *educ.* Leyden Univ. 1747–9. *m.* 23 July 1754, Mary, da. and h. of Peter Gayner of Antigua, 3s. 3da. *suc.* bro. James as 2nd Bt. 10 May 1761.

Director, E. I. Co. 1767–71, 1772–3, dep. chairman 1768–9, chairman 1769–71, 1772–3.

George Colebrooke entered his father's bank, and after the death of his father and his brother James was left in sole control; he also inherited a large fortune from them. The family came from Arundel, and by 1754 had built up sufficient influence in the borough for George to be returned in a contested election. From 1761 to 1774 he effectively controlled both seats, while Gatton manor, which he inherited from his brother James, carried with it control of one seat at Gatton.

In 1754 George Colebrooke, like his two brothers, was listed by Dupplin as an Opposition Whig, and on 13 Nov. 1755 spoke, and probably voted, against the Address.[1] But four months later James Colebrooke was assuring Newcastle of his own and George's zealous support; and they were rewarded first with contracts, and next with a baronetcy for James with special remainder to George. But on 25 Feb. 1760 George Colebrooke, together with two other Government supporters, Baker and Amyand, voted against a proposed duty on spirits.[2]

In 1762, when Newcastle fell, Colebrooke held two contracts, one with Thomlinson, Nesbitt, and Hanbury for remitting money for the forces in America, the other with Nesbitt and Franks for victualling them. Though during the debate on the peace preliminaries, 10 Dec. 1762, he and Nesbitt 'were both in the House and went away to avoid voting',[3] he lost the first of these contracts shortly afterwards, and the second was not renewed when it expired in 1765.[4] When the Rockinghams took office in July 1765, compensation was considered due to him,[5] but he showed little enthusiasm when Newcastle spoke of contracts,[6] and on 10 Mar. 1766 accepted the place of chirographer to the court of common pleas with reversion to his sons. In the succeeding years he was brought from time to time into touch with Government by his outside interests, in particular those in East India House where he did not adhere to the Rockinghams, although he continued to support them in Parliament. Between January and May 1769 he voted with the Opposition in every one of the six divisions on Wilkes and the Middlesex election for which lists are extant; and attended the Opposition dinner at the end of the session (9 May). Between January 1770 and February 1771 his name again appears in every one of the four extant minority lists; over the royal marriage bill in March 1772 he was listed by Robinson as 'contra, present'; and he seconded an Opposition amendment to the bill on the 20th.[7] On

6 Feb. 1772 he voted for the petition asking for relief from subscription to the 39 Articles.

Colebrooke was not prominent in the House, though he sometimes spoke on commercial affairs and in East India debates between 1767 and 1772. Outside the House he was conspicuous by his wealth and ostentation, and the ambitious and speculative nature of his financial activities. In 1770 he was reported to be anxious to buy land in Scotland to the value of £140,000 'if estates could be found there such as would be an inducement to dispose of a very considerable land property in England, with a view either of getting better immediate returns, or getting estates capable by force of money of being greatly improved'.[8] In 1771 he bought large estates in Lanarkshire, including the lead mines of Leadhall. In 1773 his disastrous speculations in alum led to his taking over a number of alum mines in Yorkshire and Lancashire.[9] He also concerned himself in the purchase of colonial lands: added to his wife's plantations in Antigua, made large purchases in Grenada (valued in 1774 at £50,000) and Dominica,[10] and was one of the syndicate who projected the Vandalia settlement in the Ohio Valley in 1768.[11] He looked after the interests of the settlers in Dominica at the Board of Trade, and in 1769 was appointed agent by the assembly;[12] but the council vetoed the nomination.[13]

An active dealer in Government funds between 1762-4,[14] and a speculator in East India stock from c.1766 until 1772 on the London and Amsterdam markets, he received the subscriptions of jobbers and brokers for building the first London Stock Exchange in 1772.[15] In 1764 he became a partner with Nesbitt in a bank in Dublin which, after a chequered career, closed its doors in 1773.[16] He was chiefly notable, however, for his part in the affairs of the East India Company during their most troubled period, and for his ambitious speculations in raw materials.

He first concerned himself in the Company's affairs in 1764 in support of the Clive faction,[17] took a prominent part on the Company's side in negotiations with Government in 1767-8, and was one of their chief spokesmen in the House.

In 1767 he was elected a director of the Company, deputy chairman in 1768, and chairman in 1769, 1770 and 1772—after 1770 in a coalition with Laurence Sulivan (q.v.) engineered by Lord North. He was thus at the helm when the Company ran into the financial difficulties which led to the Regulating Act of 1773, and his last year of office was turbulent and unfortunate. His management of the Company's affairs was impugned; he was accused, with some justification, of jobbing its stock when in office; and he suffered severe financial loss over arrangements for procuring votes in the Company's elections, and by unsuccessful speculation. He was left a creditor of Lauchlin Macleane (q.v.), and heavily in debt, among others, to Laurence Sulivan and Mary, sister and agent of Richard Barwell (q.v.). He did not seek re-election to the direction in 1773, and ceased to be actively concerned in the Company's affairs.

The major cause of his downfall was, however, his speculations in raw materials[18] (hemp, flax, logwood, etc.). When in 1771 he had lost £190,000 on a speculation in hemp, he admitted that it would be improper for him as a banker to be suspected of having any further concern in ventures of this kind; yet he became so deeply involved in an attempt to corner the world supply of alum that the financial crisis of 1772 entangled him in hopeless difficulties. Though assistance from the Bank of England and private individuals (including Sir Thomas Rumbold, q.v.) enabled him to survive the first months of the crisis, his bank closed its doors on 31 Mar. 1773. On 5 May his creditors permitted him to resume business under the control of trustees, but on 7 Aug. 1776 he finally stopped payment, and on 21 Jan. 1777 a commission of bankruptcy was taken out against him. In 1774 much of his property, including Gatton Park, was sold, and consequently he did not stand again for Parliament.

After his bankruptcy he retired to Boulogne, so poor that in 1778 the East India Company voted him a pension of £200 p.a.[19] In 1781 he was appointed a senior merchant in their service, but did not take up the post.[20] In 1783 he applied unsuccessfully to the Duke of Portland for employment in the foreign service.[21] By 1789, however, he was back in Bath, in moderate but comfortable circumstances; part at least of his property was finally salvaged for his family, and his descendants claimed that his creditors were ultimately paid in full.[22] Mrs. Thrale, who called him 'a pretty little dapper man when at his best',[23] was scathing in her judgment of him at the time of his fall, but when she saw him in 1789 in Bath, admitted that 'no philosopher ever bore . . . vicissitudes with less loss of health, spirits and general animation than little Sir George Colebrooke'.[24] He died 5 Aug. 1809.

[1] For his speech see J. West to Newcastle, 13 Nov. 1755, Add. 32860, f. 471; for his vote see AMYAND, G. [2] J. West to Newcastle, 25 Feb. 1760, Add. 32902, f. 400. [3] Notes in Henry Fox's hand, Add. 40758, f. 279. [4] Colebrooke to Newcastle, 15 July 1765, Add. 32967, ff. 434-6. [5] Fortescue, i. 178. [6] See n. 4 above. [7] Walpole, Last Jnls. i. 64. [8] A. Stewart to Mure, 11 Sept. 1770, Caldwell Pprs. ii(2), p. 175. [9] L. S. Sutherland, 'Sir Geo. Colebrooke's World Corner in Alum, 1771-3', Econ. Jnl. Econ. Hist. Supp. Feb. 1936, p. 255. [10] PRO, Col. 106/9, f. 10; Memorandum by James Harris, 9 May 1763, Malmesbury mss. [11] APC Col. v. 210. See also FETHERSTONHAUGH, M. [12] Ibid. v. 12. [13] L. Penson, Colonial Agents of the West Indies, 112. [14] Bank of England recs. [15] St. James's

*Chronicle*, 19 Feb. 1771. ¹⁶ M. Dillon, *Hist. & Development of Banking in Ireland.* ¹⁷ L. S. Sutherland, *E. I. Co. in 18th Cent. Politics.* ¹⁸ For this and following see Sutherland, 'Sir Geo. Colebrooke's World Corner in Alum, 1771–3', loc. cit. ¹⁹ E. I. Co. Court Bks. 86, p. 605. ²⁰ Ibid. 90, p. 104, and 91, p. 76. ²¹ G. Colebrooke to Portland, 27 May 1783, Portland mss. ²² T. E. Colebrooke, *Life of H. T. Colebrooke*, 3–4. ²³ *Thraliana.* ed. Balderston, i. 334–5. ²⁴ Ibid. ii. 764.

L.S.S.

## COLEBROOKE, James (1722–61), of Gatton, Surr.

GATTON    27 Apr. 1751–10 May 1761

*b.* 21 July 1722, 2nd s. of James Colebrooke, London banker, and bro. of Robert and George Colebrooke (qq.v.). *educ.* Leyden Univ. 1738; I. Temple 1737. *m.* 7 May 1747, Mary, da. and coh. of Stephen Skinner of Leyton, Essex, 2da. *cr.* Bt. 12 Oct. 1759, with sp. rem. to his bro. George.

James Colebrooke in 1752 succeeded his father as head of the family bank, with his younger brother George as partner.

In 1751 he bought for £23,000 the manor of Gatton[1] which secured for him the uncontested control of one seat in the borough. In 1754 Dupplin classed him as an Opposition Whig; but on 8 Mar. 1756 Colebrooke wrote to Newcastle that he and his brother George would be for the (much contested) plate tax—'we shall be always happy to be able to support any measures of Government'.[2] In October 1758 Colebrooke, in partnership with Arnold Nesbitt, obtained a contract for victualling the garrisons at Louisbourg and St. John's,[3] and in November and December 1759, together with George Colebrooke and Moses Franks, further contracts for North America and the garrison at Guadeloupe.[4] In December 1759 Colebrooke was included by Newcastle among 'the principal and most responsible men in the City'[5] to be approached about a loan; and in the list of subscribers was put down for £480,000;[6] but at no time did he hold any considerable amount of Government stock.[7] On 6 June 1760 he wrote to Newcastle: 'My vote . . . is much your due for many favours received by me.'[8] There is no record of any speech by him in the House.

Colebrooke died on 10 May 1761, six weeks after being re-elected at Gatton.

¹ Manning and Bray, *Surr.* ii. 232. ² Add. 32919, f. 201. ³ T54/37/123–8. ⁴ T29/33/252, 260. ⁵ Add. 32893, f. 481. ⁶ Add. 32901, f. 238. ⁷ Bank of England recs. ⁸ Add. 32907, f. 48.

M.M.D.

## COLEBROOKE, Robert (1718–84), of Chilham, Kent.

MALDON    1741–1761

*b.* 24 June 1718, 1st s. of James Colebrooke, London banker, by his w. Mary Hudson; bro. of George and James Colebrooke (qq.v.). *m.* (1) 12 July 1741,

Henrietta (*d.*22 Dec. 1753), da. of Lord Harry Powlett (q.v.), *s.p.*; (2) 4 Aug. 1756, Anne, da. and h. of John Thresher of Bradford-on-Avon, Wilts., *s.p.* *suc.* fa. 18 Nov. 1752.

Minister to Switzerland 1762–4; appointed ambassador to Turkey 1765 but never went out.

Though classed as a Government supporter in 1747, for reasons unknown Colebrooke changed sides, and when re-elected in 1754 at Maldon after a contest, was listed by Dupplin among the Opposition Whigs (as were his younger brothers James and George). But by 1756 he held a secret service pension of £600 p.a., of which the first half-yearly instalment was paid to him on 13 Feb. In July 1760 Colebrooke unsuccessfully applied to Newcastle to be appointed resident at Hamburg, and before the general election of 1761 offered Government 'to bring in two Members at Maldon . . . and go out himself if he could get a consulship, or any other employment to live abroad'.[1] He seems to have made the same offer to Fox.[2] In the end he himself stood at Maldon, and when defeated, ascribed it to the support he had given to John Bullock (q.v.) by Newcastle's directions; and hoped the Duke would bring him in 'upon one of the double returns'.[3]

The secret service pension was continued to him till he kissed hands for minister to the Swiss Cantons; there he 'exhibited to a frugal people an unprecedented mode of splendour and profusion'.[4] Although on his return from Switzerland he received a pension of £500 p.a., which was doubled after he had resigned his appointment to Turkey, his financial circumstances remained 'deplorable'. Finally he 'decamped' to France, where he died, 10 May 1784.[5]

¹ Memorandum in Newcastle's handwriting, Add. 32915, f. 377. ² Fox to Fitzmaurice, 6 Jan. 1761, Lansdowne mss. ³ R. Colebrooke to Newcastle, 31 Mar. 1761, Add. 32920, f. 242. ⁴ Seymour, *Survey of Kent* (1776), p. 249. ⁵ Namier, *Structure*, 440, n. 2.

L.B.N.

## COLERAINE, Baron, *see* HANGER, Gabriel

## COLHOUN, William MacDowall (fl. 1773–1807), of Thorpe and Wretham, nr. Thetford, Norf. and St. Kitts, W.I.

BEDFORD    1784–1802

s. of Robert Colhoun, treasurer of St. Kitts 1754, by Frances, da. of John Mills of St. Kitts. *m.* a da. of one Parson of St. Kitts, 1 (poss. 2) s. 1da. (who m. 1792 Edward Coke, q.v.).[1]

Colhoun owned plantations in St. Kitts, Nevis, and St. Croix, besides two Norfolk estates, and the later financial entanglements of this 'lordly, evasive and muddle-headed' man are recounted and analysed by Richard Pares in *A West-India Fortune* (pp. 280–92). At first in his dealings with the house of Pinney and Tobin Colhoun did nothing 'downright dishonest', merely 'got himself into a horrid muddle'; but after about 1800, the 'rather shady patrician' was 'fast losing all pretence of decency', and 'lied and broke promises without shame'.

In politics he seems to have done so from the outset. In March 1773 he came forward as a candidate at Dover, supported by John Wilkes. His election address contained the usual radical promises:[2] never to accept a place and to support a bill for shortening the duration of Parliaments. In the end he did not stand, but made way for John Trevanion (q.v.). In 1780 he was a member of the Westminster committee of association, but dropped out before the end of 1782.

He is next heard of at Bedford in 1784. Bedford corporation had an old feud with the Duke, and next with Samuel Whitbread, one of the sitting Members, who was backed by the Woburn interest. In this fight the corporation were supported, or even directed, by Sir Robert Bernard (q.v.), and it was he who recommended Colhoun to the corporation. The radical John Horne Tooke acted as Bernard's agent, and his letters to Bernard tell the story of Colhoun's election in 1784.[3] An undated letter, which seems to be the first of the series, reports Colhoun's arrival at Huntingdon, 'he tells me ill with fatigue and fever'. And in a postscript: 'I have talked with Mr. Colhoun with the utmost openness, and have received the utmost satisfaction upon the points in question.' What these were is not stated. In a letter of 27 Mar. the corporation have unanimously pledged themselves to support Colhoun, and even the inhabitants, 'not hitherto . . . in our interest', finding that 'our political sentiments . . . agree with their own, id est, against the Coalition . . . declared utmost satisfaction'. But by 30 Mar. a report reached the town that Colhoun had said 'he reserved £2,000 to support Mr. Fox's election'. Colhoun, 'extremely mortified that (without the smallest reasonable foundation, and merely because he professes attachment to measures and not to men but as far as they pursue those measures) he should be so much mistaken', gave a laboured explanation. When a meeting of Bedford freeholders resident in London was held on 1 Apr., he did not attend, being 'very ill'; and when doubts were voiced concerning him, Horne Tooke had to fight his battle alone—'I had never fought a better battle in my life': 'the meeting finished . . . with an unanimous resolution to support Mr. Colhoun' provided he signed 'a certain test'—again what it was is not stated. On 5 Apr. Colhoun was returned unopposed with the support of warm adherents of Pitt; in May he was listed as a Foxite by

William Adam; and every recorded vote of his, 1784–90, was given on the Opposition side (he voted, however, with Pitt over parliamentary reform, 18 Apr. 1785, but so did Fox). There is no record of his having spoken before 1790.

The date of his death is unascertained.

[1] For the Colhoun or Colquhoun family of St. Kitts see Oliver, *Hist. Antigua*, iii. 258 and 418; see also Austen-Leigh, *Eton Coll. Reg.* for the sons of W. MacDowall Colhoun. John Horne Tooke, in an undated letter of March 1784, refers to William Parson, who in 1784 contested Thetford, as Colhoun's brother-in-law. [2] *Canterbury Jnl.* 16 Mar. 1773. [3] In the Duke of Manchester's mss, Hunts RO, ddM 12 bundle 2.

L.B.N.

## COLLETON, James Edward (c.1709–90), of Haines Hill, Berks.[1]

| | |
|---|---|
| LOSTWITHIEL | 1747–1768 |
| ST. MAWES | 4 Dec. 1772–1774 |

*b.* c.1709 at Barbados, 1st s. of John Colleton of Barbados and Haines Hill by Elizabeth, da. of Sir Edward Ernle, M.P., wid. of Thomas Drax; Henry Drax (q.v.) was his half-bro. *educ.* poss. Eton 1725; Clare, Camb. 1728. *m.* (1) 1731 Lady Anne Cowper (*d.*26 Mar. 1750), da. of William, 1st Earl Cowper, *s.p.*; (2) 30 Mar. 1754, Frances, da. of Philip Jennings, M.P., *s.p.  suc.* fa. Dec. 1755.

Colleton, who unsuccessfully contested Lyme Regis in 1734, was in 1747 returned as an Administration candidate for Lostwithiel. In 1754 he paid Lord Edgcumbe £1,000 for his seat, negotiated by Administration, and in 1761 £1,500. He held neither office nor pension. In Parliament, though not prominent, he seems to have been respected: in the autumn of 1761 Newcastle considered him a possible candidate for the Chair,[2] and when in November 1761 a commission of accounts was to be set up, Barrington thought that Colleton 'might guide the whole business'.[3] Up to May 1762 he adhered to Newcastle, but did not vote against the peace preliminaries in December 1762, and voted with Administration on general warrants, 6 Feb. 1764, having become connected with George Grenville. He followed Grenville into opposition and was the only Member with North American family affiliations who voted against the repeal of the Stamp Act, 22 Feb. 1766. Even after Robert Nugent (q.v.), with whom Colleton seems to have acted, had accepted office in December 1766, Colleton continued in opposition.

Colleton had no electoral interest of his own, and in 1768 could not have had at Lostwithiel either the support of Administration or of Lord Edgcumbe, who acted with the Rockinghams. He is not known to have stood in 1768, but in 1772 was returned by Nugent for St. Mawes as a Government supporter —in the division of 9 Feb. 1773 on the naval captains' petition he is placed among the 'friends' who voted against the Government. There is no record of his having spoken in the House, and he did not stand for re-election in 1774.

Colleton died 30 Aug. 1790. After his death Haines Hill and the Barbados plantations passed to the son of his cousin Charles Garth (q.v.).[4]

[1] See Namier, 'Charles Garth and his Connexions', *EHR*, July 1939. [2] Add 32929, f. 319. [3] Add. 32930, f. 257. [4] PCC 415 Bishop.

L.B.N.

## COLLIER, Sir George (1738–95), of West Hill, Surr.

HONITON 1784–1790

*b.* 11 May 1738, 1st s. of George Collier. *m.* (1) 3 Sept. 1763, Christiana (div. Mar. 1772), da. of Richard Gwynn of Midleton Hall, Carmarthen, 1s.; (2) 19 July 1781, Elizabeth, da. of William Fryer, merchant of Exeter, 2s. 4da. Kntd. 27 Jan. 1775.

Entered R.N. 1751; lt. 1754; cdr. 1761; capt. 1762; r.-adm. 1793; v.-adm. 1794.

Collier seems to have been sent to America some time in 1774, and knighted in 1775 after his return; but his services on this occasion were not stated. In 1776 he was sent out again; put in command of the Nova Scotia squadron, and in 1779, on the recall of Rear-Admiral Gambier, assumed temporary command of the British fleet in America. He at once took vigorous action against the Americans and scored several successes culminating in the capture and destruction of many ships at Penobscot. George III wrote to Sandwich, 29 Sept. 1779: 'It is rather remarkable that Sir G. Collier, with so scanty a force, should have been during the five months able to effect more objects against the rebels than the admirals that commanded such large fleets.'[1] Almost immediately after Penobscot Gambier's successor arrived and Collier returned to England. He hoped for official recognition of his services and twice unsuccessfully applied for a baronetcy; nor did he obtain promotion as he hoped. He served with the Channel fleet 1779–81, but seems to have resented the lack of recognition of his services in America, and in 1781 relinquished his command.

Collier unsuccessfully contested Shaftesbury in 1780, and in 1784 was returned for Honiton after a contest. He was classed by William Adam, May 1784, as 'Administration'; voted for parliamentary reform, 18 Apr. 1785, and for Richmond's fortifications plan, 27 Feb. 1786. In 1788 he signed the third party circular, and he voted with the Opposition on the Regency, 1788–9. Collier spoke several times in the House—almost invariably on naval matters. He urged that head-money should be paid the officers who took part in the Penobscot expedition, 6 Apr. 1785, and during the debate on Bastard's

motion about naval promotions, 21 Feb. 1788, said he considered the situation of the superannuated admiral as 'a disgraceful and very humiliating state to any officer who has served well, and has health and vigour still to serve his country'. He concluded:[2]

If this mode of partial promotion is pursued . . . the naval force of this kingdom must decline and be ruined by a measure so absurd and unjust . . . Will gentlemen be pleased to consider what *power* this gives a minister, or first lord of the Admiralty for (even) if a Member of this House happens to be in *Opposition*, he may from thence be disgraced and dishonoured by losing his promotion by his conduct in Parliament . . . With . . . miserable pay, a life of hardship and dangers, what besides honour does the sea officer aspire to? To a flag; yet, by this new regulation, his services and his merit go for nothing.

According to the *Naval Chronicle* (xiii. 381–3) Collier 'was much addicted to literary recreations; possessed a true taste, and his lighter pursuits in life were those of a refined gentleman, and elegant scholar. He translated the dramatic romance called *Selima and Azor*; which was brought out and played with success at Drury Lane Theatre 1776.'

He died 6 Apr. 1795.

[1] *Sandwich Pprs.* iii. 135. [2] Stockdale, xiii. 202–4.

M.M.D.

## COLMAN, Edward (c.1734–1815).[1]

ORFORD 1768–May 1771

*b.* c.1734, s. of William Colman of Gornhay, Tiverton, Devon by Jane, da. of Sir Edward Seymour, 5th Bt., and cos. of Francis Seymour Conway, 1st Earl of Hertford.[2] *m.* Martha, 2s. 2da.

Cornet 1 Drag. 1751, lt. 1754, maj. 1771, ret. 1775.

Clerk of the robes and wardrobes Sept. 1770–5; gent. usher of the privy chamber May 1771–5; serjeant-at-arms to House of Commons 1775–1805.

Colman was returned on Lord Hertford's interest at Orford, to act as a stop-gap till Hertford's son Robert Seymour Conway was of age. On 27 Jan. 1769 Hertford wrote to the King 'that his wishes and instructions have been expressed in the fullest manner to his sons and Mr. Colman in regard to Mr. Wilkes's case and expulsion';[3] and Colman voted regularly with Administration. There is no record of his having spoken in the House.

He died 29 July 1815.

[1] Thanks are due to Maj-Gen. I. T. P. Hughes, serjeant-at-arms to the House of Commons, and to Sir Owen Morshead for helping us from their records definitely to identify Edw. Colman, the Member and Court official, with Edw. Colman the serjeant-at-arms. [2] Vivian, *Vis. Devon* only mentions one son, Wm. Colman, but Wm. Colman, senior, refers in his will to his 'other children', though without naming them. In division lists Edw. Colman is described as 'a cousin of Lord Hertford', and his daughter's name was 'Jane Seymour Colman'. [3] Fortescue, ii. 73.

M.M.D.

## COLT, Robert (1756–97), of Auldhame, Haddington.

LYMINGTON 1784–1790

*b.* 22 Sept. 1756, 1st s. of Oliver Colt of Auldhame by Helen, da. of Robert Stewart, 7th Lord Blantyre [S]. *educ.* Elphinstone's acad. Kensington; Edinburgh Univ.; Glasgow Univ.;[1] adv. 1777. *m.* 22 Sept. 1778, Grizel, da. of Robert Dundas of Arniston, lord president of the court of session, and niece of Henry Dundas (q.v.), 1 surv. s. *suc.* fa. 1778.

In 1784 Colt seems at first to have been a candidate for Haddington Burghs; and John Robinson noted in his electoral survey:[2] 'If Mr. Colt shall succeed he will be pro.' Doubtless through the influence of Henry Dundas he was brought in for Lymington, where Sir Harry Burrard (q.v.) had placed a seat at the Government's disposal. The seat cost £2,000, of which the Government paid £500.[3] There is no record of Colt's having spoken in the House. He died 29 Dec. 1797.

[1] Alex. Carlyle, *Autobiog.* 493. But his name does not appear in the *Matric. Reg. of Glasgow Univ.* [2] Laprade, 103. [3] Geo. Roses's secret service accounts, Royal archives, Windsor.

J.B.

## COLVILE, Robert (*b.*1702), of Ochiltree, Ayr.

KINROSS-SHIRE 1754–1761

*b.* 1702, 1st s. of Sir John Aytoun of Aytoun, Fife by his 2nd w. Margaret, da. of Robert, 2nd Lord Colvill of Ochiltree [S]. *m.* (1) Janet (*d.*1739), da. of Sir Peter Wedderburn Halket, 1st Bt., of Gosford, 2s.; (2) 1740, Charles [sic],[1] da. of Sir George Preston, 3rd Bt., of Valleyfield, *s.p. suc.* to estates of his uncle Robert, 3rd Lord Colvill 1728, and assumed the name of Colvile.

Robert Aytoun, like his brother Andrew, later lord provost of Glasgow, was probably a merchant before succeeding in 1728 to the estates of his uncle. Thereafter he was known as Colvile of Ochiltree, although the family had little connexion with Ayrshire and their lands lay almost entirely in Fife and Kinross.

Connected by kinship and marriage with leading families, he was unexpectedly returned for Kinross in 1754, after both Pelham and Argyll had approved the candidature 'unopposed' of Colvile's kinsman, Sir John (Hope) Bruce of Kinross (M.P. Kinrossshire 1727–34, 1741–7),[2] who, however, seems to have stood down. Colvile was not connected with Argyll, and was listed by Dupplin among the 'Whigs —doubtful'. To attach him to the 'English ministry' Newcastle obtained for him a secret service pension of £300 p.a.,[3] and during the dispute with Argyll in 1755 named Colvile among the only three friends the Scottish 'viceroy' had left him in Scotland.

In June 1755 Colvile unsuccessfully applied to Newcastle for the appointment of his eldest son

Peter as gentleman of police:[4] 'Your Grace was pleased to say you would take the first opportunity of doing a service to my family . . . It is a place a member of Parliament can not have himself.'

While Newcastle was out of office 1756–7, Colvile's pension may have been discontinued. His political loyalties became uncertain. He was absent from the division of 2 May 1757 on the loss of Minorca; and during the negotiations for a new Administration which might not include Argyll, Newcastle listed him as attached neither to Argyll nor to himself, but among those Scots 'not to be relied on at present, but to be treated with'.[5] By March 1758 Colvile was again a Government pensioner.[6] He is not known to have spoken in the House, and did not stand in 1761.

The date of his death has not been ascertained. He may have died before the next Kinross election in 1768, and was almost certainly dead by 1777, when his son Peter was in possession of the Torryburn estate.

[1] *Scots Mag.* 1740, 142. [2] Election lists, March 1754, Newcastle (Clumber) mss. [3] See Newcastle's memorandum for the King, 21 Apr. 1755, proposing the pension (Add. 32854, f. 204) and Namier, *Structure*, 440. [4] Add. 32855, f. 387. [5] Add. 32995, f. 383. [6] Namier, *Structure*, 449.

E.H.-G.

## COMBE, Richard (?1728–80), of Earnshill, nr. Langport, Som.

MILBORNE PORT 7 Apr.–22 May 1772
ALDEBURGH 1774–1780

*b.* ?1728, o.s. of Henry Combe of Bristol, by his w. a da. of Richard Leversedge of Bristol. *educ.* Queen's, Oxf. 31 Oct. 1745, aged 17; I. Temple 1746. *m.* 14 July 1759, Ann Chamberlain of Bristol. Treasurer of the Ordnance Sept. 1780.

Combe's father was a successful Bristol merchant, warden and treasurer of the Society of Merchant Venturers, and a member of the common council; in 1739 he unsuccessfully contested Bristol, and in 1740 was elected mayor. Richard Combe, also a member of the Merchant Venturers, seems from the first to have concentrated on national rather than local politics, and in 1761 contested Ilchester. According to Lord Egmont, Member for Ilchester, the Duke of Newcastle arranged for Combe to stand in an attempt to upset Lockyer's control of the borough,[1] but Lord Fitzmaurice told Bute on 23 Mar. 1761 that Combe had gone 'to try three places merely with money and his person and no other recommendation—Ilchester against Lord Egmont one'.[2] There Combe was heavily defeated and does not seem to have gone to the poll in the other boroughs, nor does it appear which they were. In 1768 he was a candidate at Bristol, but retired on the eve of nomination, and does not seem to have stood elsewhere. In 1772 he contested Milborne Port on the interest of Edward Walter (q.v.), was returned, but unseated on petition. At the general election of 1774 he was returned unopposed for Aldeburgh on the Fonnereau interest.

In Parliament he consistently supported North's Administration. Only two speeches by him are reported: the first on the bill of 13 May 1777 'for the better securing and preserving the dockyards, magazines, ships, vessels . . . being the property of private persons', when he declared that numerous crimes punishable by death were much less heinous than the burning of ships, and added: 'I am surprised any gentleman should think it not high time to put to death such dangerous and wicked incendiaries.'[3] His other speech was in support of the militia bill, 22 June 1779.[4] When in 1779 Sandwich was attempting to raise seamen by a special press Combe was approached to exert his influence at Bristol. At the general election of 1780 he stood as the Administration candidate in opposition to Edmund Burke, was appointed treasurer of the Ordnance, and obtained £1,000 for the election from secret service funds.[5] But by the beginning of September he was a very sick man. Richard Champion, Burke's chief supporter, wrote to Portland on 1 Sept.:[6] 'The ill success which Mr. Combe has met with, added to his natural timidity and irresolution, and a dangerous fever from which he is not yet recovered, makes us hope he will resign his pretensions.' He died on 18 Sept. 1780—two days before the election.

[1] Egmont to Bute, 3 June 1762, Bute mss. [2] Bute mss. [3] Almon, vii. 175. [4] Ibid. xiii. 514. [5] Laprade, 57. [6] Portland mss.

M.M.D.

## COMPTON, Hon. Charles (1698-1755).

NORTHAMPTON     9 Dec. 1754–20 Nov. 1755

b. 30 Jan. 1698, 3rd s. of George, 4th Earl of Northampton, by his 1st w. Jane, da. of Sir Stephen Fox of Farley, Wilts. and half-sis. of Henry Fox (q.v.); bro. of Hon. George Compton (q.v.). educ. Eton 1706–7; Ch. Ch. Oxf. 1714; Grand Tour (France, Italy) 1718–20. m. 14 Aug. 1727, Mary, da. and h. of Sir Berkeley Lucy, 3rd Bt., of Broxbourne, Herts., 5s. 5da.
Consul at Lisbon 1727–42; envoy extraordinary 1742–5; paymaster of pensions 1745–d.

In 1734 Compton declined an invitation from his brother James, 5th Earl of Northampton, to return home and stand for Tamworth.[1] In December 1754, when his brother George succeeded to the peerage, he was returned on the family interest at Northampton, although 'so ill at the time of the election as not to be able to appear there'.[2] His daughter Jane wrote to her husband G. B. Rodney (q.v.), 30 Jan. 1755:[3]

'Papa came here last night at 12 from the House, seemed much tired. I wish he may not hurt himself by attending so constantly.'
Compton died 20 Nov. 1755.

[1] Marquess of Northampton, Comptons of Compton Wynyates. 180. [2] Ld. Northampton to Wm. Cartwright, 4 May 1755, Cartwright mss. quoted by Forrester, Northants, County Elections, 80. [3] Rodney Pprs. PRO 30/20/20.

L.B.N.

## COMPTON, Charles, Lord Compton (1760-1828).

NORTHAMPTON    1784–7 Apr. 1796

b. 21 Mar. 1760, o.s. of Spencer Compton (q.v.). educ. Westminster 1768–70; Ealing sch.; Trinity, Camb. 1776. m. 18 Aug. 1787, Maria, da. of Joshua Smith (q.v.) of Erlestoke Park, Wilts., 3s. 1da. suc. fa. as 9th Earl of Northampton 7 Apr. 1796; cr. Mq. of Northampton 7 Sept. 1812.
Ld. lt. Northants. 1796–d.

Lord Compton was meant to stand for Northampton at the general election which normally would have been held in the spring of 1781, by which time he would have been of age. When Parliament was suddenly dissolved on 1 Sept. 1780, he still canvassed the borough together with Lord Althorp (q.v.) on 4 and 5 Sept.;[1] but next it was obviously thought inadvisable for him to stand while still a minor, and on 9 Sept. his cousin George Rodney was returned in his place on the understanding that 'he is to resign whenever Lord Compton pleases'.[2]

At the contested election for Northampton in 1784 Lord Compton came out head of the poll. He was classed by William Adam as a supporter of Pitt, and on 23 Jan. 1787 moved the Address (his only recorded speech during his first Parliament). On 18 Apr. 1785 he voted for Pitt's motion for parliamentary reform, but does not appear in any other division list before 1790.

He died 24 May 1828.

[1] Canvass bk, Compton ms 1061, in the possession of the Marquess of Northampton. [2] Compton ms 1132.

L.B.N.

## COMPTON, Hon. George (1692-1758).

TAMWORTH       30 Jan. 1727–17 July 1727
NORTHAMPTON    1727– 3 Oct. 1754

b. 1692, 2nd s. of George, 4th Earl of Northampton; bro. of Hon. Charles Compton (q.v.). educ. Eton 1706–7. m. 5 Mar. 1748, Frances, da. of Rev. Thomas Payne, s.p. suc. bro. as 6th Earl 3 Oct. 1754.
Cornet, R. Horse Gds. 1707; maj. 1713; ret. 1715. Ld. of Treasury Feb. 1742–Dec. 1744.

George Compton was listed by Dupplin in 1754 as a Tory. But he played no part in the new Parliament which sat only one week (31 May–5 June) before he succeeded to the peerage. He died 6 Dec. 1758.

## COMPTON, Spencer (1738–96).

NORTHAMPTON    1761–18 Oct. 1763

*b.* 16 Aug. 1738, 2nd s. of the Hon. Charles Compton (q.v.). *educ.* Westminster 1746. *m.* (1) 23 July 1757, Jane (*d.*26 Nov. 1767), da. and h. of Henry Lawton of Northampton, 1s. 1da.; (2) 16 May 1769, Anne, da. and h. of Culpeper Hougham, linen-draper in St. Paul's Churchyard, *s.p.* *suc.* bro as 8th Earl of Northampton 18 Oct. 1763.

Ensign 2 Ft. Gds. 1756; capt. 31 Ft. 1757; retired 1760.

Groom of the bedchamber Nov. 1760–Apr. 1763; recorder, Northampton Dec. 1763–*d.*; ld. lt. Northants. 1771–*d.*

Spencer Compton was returned unopposed for Northampton in 1761. He did not receive Newcastle's parliamentary whip in Oct. 1761; was classed by him as 'contra' in the list of 13 Nov. 1762; is in Henry Fox's list of Members favourable to the peace preliminaries; and was marked 'pro' by Jenkinson in the autumn of 1763, but succeeded to the peerage before the opening of the session. There is no record of his having spoken in the House.

Extravagant and in debt even before the Northampton election of 1768, he was very nearly ruined by it. Some six years later he 'went to Switzerland for the rest of his life, partly for economy and partly because of his health'[1]; and died at Berne 7 Apr. 1796.

[1] Marquess of Northampton, *Comptons of Compton Wynyates*, 199.

L.B.N.

## CONGREVE, Ralph (?1721–75), of Aldermaston, Berks.

CARDIGAN BOROUGHS    13 Jan. 1769–1774

*b.* ?1721, o.s. of Col. Ralph Congreve, lt. gov. of Gibraltar, by his w. Anne Hanmer. *educ.* Worcester, Oxf. 3 Apr. 1738, aged 16. *m.* 29 June 1752, Charlotte, da. and h. of William, 3rd Baron Stawell, wid. of Ruishe Hassell, *s.p.* *suc.* fa. 1725.

Congreve was 'a person who was not so much as known' in Cardiganshire[1] when he stood for Cardigan in 1769 as the candidate of a party of local squires who were opposed to the unpopular Sir Herbert Lloyd (q.v.). He was returned after a hard-fought and expensive contest. Before 1773 his only recorded vote in the House was for Administration on the Middlesex petition, 8 May 1769. In Robinson's first survey on the royal marriage bill he is classed as 'pro, present'; in the second, 8 Mar. 1772, as 'contra, present'. He voted for the naval captains' petition, 9 Feb. 1773, and in the King's list is classed as a friend to Government; but voted against them on the renewal of the Middlesex question, 26 Apr. 1773. His only recorded speeches in the House were for the Reading canal bill, 21 Feb. 1771. He did not stand in 1774, and died December 1775.

[1] He is described as such by a group of his constituents in a petition presented against his return, *CJ*, 3 Feb. 1769.

P.D.G.T.

## CONINGSBY, *see* CAPEL

## CONOLLY, Thomas (?1737–1803), of Stretton Hall, Staffs., and Castletown, co. Kildare.

MALMESBURY    21 Mar. 1759–1768
CHICHESTER               1768–1780

*b.* ?1737, 1st s. of William Conolly, M.P., by Lady Anne Wentworth, da. of Thomas, 1st Earl of Strafford. *educ.* Westminster Jan. 1750, aged 12. *m.* 30 Dec. 1758, Lady Louisa Augusta Lennox, da. of Charles, 2nd Duke of Richmond, *s.p.* *suc.* fa. 1754.

M.P. [I] 1761–1800; P.C. [I] 1761.

Conolly's Irish estates were valued at £15,275 per annum in 1758; he proposed to settle on his wife lands 'of the yearly value of £6,178, free from all deductions and incumbrances subject to £2,500 a year jointure, £500 a year pin money, and £20,000 for younger children'.[1]

Lady Caroline Fox (later Lady Holland), the most discerning of Conolly's sisters-in-law, found him on first acquaintance 'free and easy and good-humoured' and, what pleased her more, in love with his wife: 'Mr. Conolly seems to be quite terrified when her finger aches. He seems immoderately fond of her, and of a very warm, affectionate temper.' And Louisa was fond of him.

> She is determined never to let Conolly be out of her sight [Lady Caroline wrote in Dec. 1759]. She told me last time I saw her, she thought it a bad custom to begin with ever to let him go anywhere without her.

On further acquaintance Lady Caroline noted another aspect of Conolly's character. She wrote to her sister Lady Kildare on 17 Apr. 1759:

> You must indeed be partial to Conolly not to think him immensely silly . . . sure he is a tiresome boy, and one feels sorry he is so, he seems so exceeding good-natured. I can but think how miserable I should have been at Louisa's age to have had such a husband.

In May 1759: 'People reckon poor Conolly such a fool'; and on 17 June: 'I look upon him as a boy of ten or eleven years old, and treat him as such. I only dread her feeling ashamed of him sometimes.' Soon she was referring to 'that boy Conolly' and 'Louisa and her little spouse'. And Lady Kildare wrote on 11 Nov. 1762:

> Conolly was in town yesterday . . . talked a vast deal of nonsense about politics in order to make me think him mighty cunning, and that he knew *the way of the world* as well as anybody.[2]

When Lord George Bentinck died in 1759, Henry

Fox considered returning Conolly for Malmesbury. Conolly was in Ireland, and Fox wished Devonshire to consult Lord Strafford.

> The expense will be upwards of £500 [he wrote to Devonshire on 4 Mar.[3]] which is too much [the Parliament had only two years to run]; but the election is sure and the candidate need never appear there . . . It strikes me strongly that Conolly would be very glad to find himself a Member of Parliament at his arrival, and that he will be sorry to find he might have been and is not.

Soon after his election Newcastle learnt that Lord Temple had tried 'to engage him to join their party'; Conolly replied: 'That he was a young man and could enter into no party'.[4] Fox in England, and Kildare in Ireland were his political mentors at this time; and his life was divided between the two countries.

Conolly received Newcastle's 'whip' in 1761 through Fox, and is classed as 'Fox' in Bute's list of the Parliament. He naturally appears among Fox's list of Members favourable to the peace preliminaries, but Lady Holland wrote to Lady Kildare on 9 Nov. 1762:

> Conolly has wrote to Mr. Fox, who was a little doubtful whether he should wish him to come or no. May not he be embarrassed about Lord Strafford, who I suppose will take part against the court with the Duke of Devonshire?

Conolly left Ireland on 16 Nov., and Lady Kildare wrote to her husband on 2 Dec.: 'I am glad for Mr. Conolly's own sake as well as his friends' that he is steady.'[5]

He supported the Grenville Administration but was classed by Rockingham in July 1765 as 'pro' and did not vote against the repeal of the Stamp Act. Probably he went over with Richmond to the Rockinghams: he is classed by Rockingham in Nov. 1766 as 'Whig' and by Newcastle in Mar. 1767, as 'friend'; yet he did not vote on the land tax, 27 Feb. 1767, or the nullum tempus bill, 17 Feb. 1768 (he was absent in Italy a good deal in 1767[6]). By 1768 Fox had lost control of Malmesbury, and was not in sympathy with Conolly's politics. Conolly was returned for Chichester on the Duke of Richmond's interest; and henceforth voted with the Rockinghams. He spoke occasionally in Parliament, mostly on Irish affairs, but made no mark in English politics.

In Ireland he was much more important. Here is the description of him in a list of the Irish Parliament in 1773:[7]

> Came in by his own interest which is very great as he had one of the largest estates in this kingdom. He is an Englishman married to the Duke of Richmond's sister and though in opposition to Government there yet he supports it here.

Another list of 1775,[8] probably drawn up by Sir John Blaquiere, chief secretary to the lord lieutenant of Ireland 1772–7, after recounting the favours he had received from Government, adds:

> He is so capricious and unsteady, that there is very little dependence to be had on him, and in my own opinion it would be better for Government that he was a declared opponent of its measures.

And in a list of 1782[9] he is described as 'inclined to Government but unsteady'.

He was particularly close to the Castle 1776–80, when his brother-in-law, Lord Buckinghamshire, was lord lieutenant; while supporting Irish demands for self-government, he wished to maintain a close connexion with England. He wrote to Rockingham on 8 Apr. 1782, at the end of a long letter on Irish affairs:[10]

> I have no motive in troubling you with this long detail, but that of duty to my country, and a love for your administration and its principles; the latter as they invigorate the constitution of Great Britain, and give independence to America, cannot consistently refuse the same, to a long neglected, loyal, spirited, and armed people.

But on 17 Apr. 1783 he wrote to Buckinghamshire:[11]

> I was always, as you know, a croaker, but the affairs of England have turned out more desperate than I ever imagined; nothing but a very strong, wise and upright Administration can preserve you from troubles which if once begun on your side will immediately kindle here, though Paddy has got everything he has asked, and more I am certain than is good for him, as I think it will be some time before his new constitution will begin to work to his expectation.

Henceforth his interest centred wholly in Irish politics. Sir Jonah Barrington, who disliked the part Conolly had taken in bringing about the Irish Union, described him as

> friendly—sincere—honourable—and munificent in disposition, but whimsical—wrong-headed, and positive,—his ideas and politics were limited and confined; he mistook obstinacy for independence—and singularity for patriotism—and fancied he was a Whig because he was not professedly a Tory.[12]

He added:

> Mr. Thomas Conolly never did or would accept of any office; the art of governing him seemed to be, by inducing him to think that nobody could influence him: in that he was mistaken.

He died 27 Apr. 1803.

[1] H. Fox to Newcastle, 19 Nov. 1758, Add. 32885, ff. 325–7. [2] *Leinster Corresp.* i. 134–268 passim. [3] Devonshire mss. [4] 4 Apr. 1759; Add. 32889, ff. 360–1. [5] *Leinster Corresp.* i. 84, 137, 144. [6] Lady Holland to Lady Kildare, 27 Aug. 1767, ibid. 517. [7] 'Notes on Irish Parlt. 1773' ed. Bodkin, *Proc. R. Irish Acad.* xlviii C/4. See also Walpole, *Last Jnls.* ii. 121. [8] *Irish Parlt. 1775* ed. Hunt. [9] 'Contemp. Sketches Members Irish Parlt. 1782', ed. Sayles, *Proc. R. Irish Acad.* lvi C/3. [10] Rockingham mss. [11] *HMC Lothian*, 417. [12] *Hist. Mems. Ire.* i. 165–6; see also Ld. Charlemont's opinion, *HMC 13th Rep. VII*, 243–4.

J.B.

## CONWAY, Hon. Henry Seymour (1719–95), of Park Place, Berks.

| | |
|---|---|
| HIGHAM FERRERS | 28 Dec. 1741–1747 |
| PENRYN | 1747–1754 |
| ST. MAWES | 1754–1761 |
| THETFORD | 1761–1774 |
| BURY ST. EDMUNDS | 27 Mar. 1775–1784 |

*bap.* 12 Aug. 1719, 2nd s. of Francis, 1st Lord Conway, by his 3rd w. Charlotte, da. of John Shorter of Bybrook, Kent; bro. of Francis, 1st Earl of Hertford, and cos. of Sir Edward and Horatio Walpole (qq.v.). *educ.* Eton 1732. *m.* 19 Dec. 1747, Caroline, da. of John Campbell (*d.*1770, q.v.), 4th Duke of Argyll [S], wid. of Charles Bruce, 3rd Earl of Ailesbury, 1da. who m. 1767 Hon. John Damer (q.v.).
Lt. 5 Drag. 1737; capt.-lt. 8 Drag. 1740; capt.-lt. 1 Ft. Gds. and lt.-col. 1741; capt. 1 Ft. Gds. 1742; col. 1746; col. 48 Ft. 1746–9, 34 Ft. 1749–51, 13 Drag. 1751–4, 4 Horse 1754–9; maj.-gen. 1756; lt.-gen. 1759; col. 1 Drag. 1759–64, 4 Drag. 1768–70, R. Horse Gds. 1770–*d.*; gen. 1772; gov. Jersey 1772–*d.*; f.m. 1793.
M.P. [I] 1741–61.
Groom of the bedchamber 1757–64; P.C. 10 July 1765; sec. of state, southern dept. July 1765–May 1766, northern dept. May 1766–Jan. 1768; lt.-gen. of Ordnance Aug. 1767–Oct. 1772; c.-in-c. army Mar. 1782–Dec. 1783.

Under George II Conway belonged to the old corps of Whigs, and in 1754 he was returned as a Government candidate on Lord Falmouth's interest at St. Mawes. From 1754 to 1765 his most important political connexions were with the Duke of Cumberland and the 4th Duke of Devonshire. He had been appointed aide-de-camp to Cumberland in 1745 and had served under him at Fontenoy and Culloden. Cumberland wrote about him to Devonshire on 23 May 1757:[1]

> The pleasure you express on the part Conway took in Parliament is so like the constant proofs of friendship you have always given . . . Harry knows the high opinion I have always had of him, and that his only fault is hiding his talents from too much modesty and a little indolence which with his good sense I am sure he can get the better of, and I hope he has already gained greatly upon it.

When Devonshire (then Lord Hartington) was appointed lord lieutenant of Ireland in 1755 he refused to go (according to Horace Walpole)[2] unless Conway, 'with whom he was scarce acquainted', went with him; and when he died in 1764 he left Conway a legacy of £5,000.

In 1757 Conway was made groom of the bedchamber (a post he had long desired), and appointed one of the commanders of the expedition to Rochfort. He was ambitious of military distinction, but the failure of the expedition brought him into disfavour with George II; nor was Cumberland, who had resigned his post of captain-general, in a posi-

tion to help him. In 1758 he asked leave to accompany the expedition to St. Malo but was refused. It was not until 1761, when he went to serve under Granby in Germany, that he again held military command. His reputation in the army was that of a brave soldier and an efficient staff officer, but he was neither a strategist nor a leader of men.

His closest friends were Horace Walpole and the Duke of Grafton. He sat for Thetford and Bury St. Edmunds on Grafton's interest, and was intimately associated with his private affairs: Grafton, by his will dated 12 June 1761, appointed Conway one of the guardians of his son;[3] and in 1764 it was Conway who negotiated on Grafton's behalf the terms of separation from the Duchess.[4] Walpole was proud and jealous of his influence over Conway; boosted his abilities, pushed his interest, and fought his battles; yet was continually hampered by his modesty and indecision.[5] The influence of Conway's brother Lord Hertford, a courtier whose sole allegiance was to the King, tended to keep him from close party connexion.

When Conway returned to England in March 1763 he found Walpole and Grafton in opposition. On 15 and 23 Nov. he voted against Grenville's ministry over Wilkes: the King proposed to dismiss him instantly, but was restrained by Grenville, who undertook to find out whether Conway considered himself in opposition or had voted against Government 'merely from opinion'. Conway denied that he intended to join the Opposition but would not give a pledge to support Government. On 6 and 18 Feb. 1764 he spoke and voted against them on general warrants, and when Parliament was prorogued in April was dismissed from his regiment and his place in the bedchamber.

'He neither complained', wrote Walpole, 'nor tried to instil a sense of his injuries into a single friend, though he wished they should take his part, and resent for him.' He acquired a martyr's reputation with the Opposition, and his dismissal was used as a stick with which to beat Grenville. In the negotiations for a new Administration in July 1765 he was considered for chancellor of the Exchequer, an office for which he knew himself to be unfit and which he was unwilling to take; but eventually, as Cumberland's choice, became secretary of state and leader of the House of Commons. As secretary of state he was hard-working and conscientious, but inclined to think in terms of routine administration rather than of policy. He was temperamentally unsuited to lead the Commons: 'could not be induced to traffic with Members', 'allowed too much to his scruples', and 'thought nothing a virtue but his own moderation'.[6] His failure to win the confidence of the House was one of the greatest weaknesses of the Rockingham ministry.

After Cumberland's death Conway formed with Rockingham and Grafton the junto of the Administration, in so far as any fixed lines can be discerned in it. But he did not believe that it could stand as it was, and together with Grafton wished to place Pitt at its head. In April 1766, when Rockingham made it clear that he would not stand down for Pitt, Conway considered resigning with Grafton. When Pitt came to power in July, Conway agreed to serve under him, though Pitt's projected northern alliance reversed Conway's pro-Austrian foreign policy. He hoped to act as mediator between Pitt and the Rockinghams, and they saw him as a guarantee of their influence in the new Administration. The dismissal of Lord Edgcumbe in December 1766 ended these hopes and occasioned the breach between Chatham and the Rockinghams: Conway tried to intervene on their behalf and talked of resignation, but, under pressure from Walpole and out of loyalty to Grafton, remained. He broke off relations with Chatham and gave the Rockinghams hope that he would soon resign.

During the session of 1767 he was in disagreement with his Cabinet colleagues on the fundamentals of their policy: he opposed Townshend's American plan, refused to introduce it in the Commons, and twice voted against it, 13 and 15 May; and he opposed Chatham's policy with respect to the East India Company and voted against the bill to restrain their dividends, 26 May. Yet Grafton, unable to replace him, begged him to remain in office: minister *malgré lui*, he was the main bulwark against an apparently united Opposition. Indeed, had he been ambitious or unscrupulous, he could have supplanted Grafton as effective minister; while the Rockinghams hoped for and expected his resignation as the prelude to Chatham's downfall. He feared the reproaches of Grafton if he resigned, and of Rockingham if he did not; 'dreaded its being said that he remained in place with all denominations of men';[7] yet declared himself independent of party. At last, in June 1767 he informed the King and Rockingham that he would resign at the end of the session.

Yet he delayed his resignation and persuaded the King to open negotiations with Rockingham, believing that the Rockinghams would be prepared to enter the Administration. After Rockingham had insisted that the negotiations should be extended to the Bedfords and Grenvilles, Conway, offended at the inclusion of Grenville and now conscious that his prime political allegiance was to the King, agreed to stay in office. On the failure of the negotiations

for a 'comprehensive Administration' Conway made a last effort to satisfy Rockingham and pressed him to accept office 'on his own bottom'; Rockingham's refusal freed Conway from his obligations to the party, but his failure to resign estranged him from them. 'Conway', wrote Burke on 18 Aug. 1767, 'is gone fairly to the Devil.'[8]

He remained unsettled and dissatisfied, searching for an excuse to shed his distasteful responsibilities as leader of the Commons and vaunt the purity and disinterestedness of his motives to the world. It was suggested that he might become secretary of state for America;[9] instead, in August 1767 he became lieutenant-general of the Ordnance and continued to do the work of secretary of state without drawing the salary. He made no objection to Grafton's negotiating with the Bedfords in November 1767 but saw their entry as the occasion for his own withdrawal. The Bedfords, sensing Conway's anxiety to retire and Grafton's weariness of his scruples, pressed for his resignation; and in January 1768 he gave up the seals to Weymouth and the lead in the Commons to North. At the King's request he remained in the Cabinet, and in February 1768 was appointed colonel of the 4th regiment of Dragoons.

Henceforth he adopted a detached attitude towards Government measures, and tried to avoid giving his opinion or accepting responsibility. Although not present at the Cabinet meeting which decided to expel Wilkes, 20 Apr. 1768, he did not contest their decision in principle, but held that expulsion should be deferred till next session. When the matter was reconsidered in January 1769, Conway was against expulsion, but went down to Parliament, wrote Hertford to the King on 27 Jan.,[10]

> without any prejudice upon his mind favourable to Mr. Wilkes and desirous of being convinced that the measure is right and that he may be able to support it with his opinion.

However he did not vote on the expulsion motion of 3 Feb., but said, 17 Mar., on the motion to declare Wilkes' third election void:[11]

> Originally, while it was a question of Mr. Wilkes's expulsion alone, I was one of those who took no part in it. I was not a friend of Mr. Wilkes: I considered his expulsion a very undesirable thing; but I did not care to be an advocate for him. As long as it was a question of Mr. Wilkes, I did not concern myself in it; but now it is become the case of the people at large . . . I say, that those who think to set up the liberty of the people against the liberty of Parliament, will find themselves mistaken.

He voted for the seating of Luttrell on 15 Apr. and 8 May 1769.

At the Cabinet meeting of 1 May 1769 Conway was in the minority who advocated the repeal of all the Townshend duties. When it was proposed in the Commons, 5 Mar. 1770, to repeal the duty on tea, he said: 'I did not know, till the day before yesterday, what determination the Administration had come to with regard to this matter.'[12] He then argued that it was impolitic to try to raise a revenue from America, and condemned the tea duty as 'an uncommercial measure'. In January 1770 he refused the post of master-general of the Ordnance but undertook to do the work of the office. In November he became colonel of the Royal Regt. of Horse Guards ('the most agreeable post in the Army', wrote Walpole),[13] withdrew from the Cabinet, but remained lieutenant-general of the Ordnance and its effective head. 'He had conceived a passion for his office', wrote Walpole 'and . . . was indefatigable in all the minute though necessary drudgery relating to the service of the artillery and all its branches.'[14]

From 1770 to 1775 he gave Government critical and unreliable support. He had objected to details in the royal marriage bill before its introduction, on second reading declared that he was 'a friend to the principle of the bill and to the minutest wish of the Crown',[15] and yet criticized it strongly in committee. In October 1772, piqued at the appointment of Lord Townshend, an officer junior to himself, to be master-general of the Ordnance, an office he could have had for the asking any time during the last two years, he resigned; but 'at the earnest solicitation' of Lord North[16] the King appointed him governor of Jersey. Early in 1774 he was still counted as a Government supporter, and voted on 25 Feb. against making Grenville's Election Act permanent. But on American affairs he wavered: spoke for the Boston port bill 23 Mar., but 19 Apr. voted for the repeal of the tea duty and 2 May spoke against the third reading of the Massachusetts Bay bill.

Conway was on the continent when Parliament was dissolved in September 1774. 'I had imagined', he wrote to Robert Murray Keith on 19 Nov., 'the Duke of Grafton, as he had said nothing to the contrary, purposed bringing me in as before.'[17] But Grafton, who had a contest at Bury St. Edmunds, could not propose a stranger who was out of the country. Conway would not ask a seat from Government, and was out of Parliament until returned by Grafton on the first vacancy in his boroughs.

Conway took a leading part against the American war, condemning it as 'cruel, unnecessary, and unnatural',[18] but without identifying himself with the Opposition parties or policies. Nor was he averse from speaking for Government when he considered they were unjustly attacked: thus he defended the Ordnance Board against Barré, 17 Dec. 1779, and spoke against postponing the grant of supplies,

27 Apr. 1780—though 'no great favourer of the measures of Administration' he was 'certainly no enemy to Government'.[19] His wish was 'that the offensive war with America should immediately cease':[20] on 22 Feb. 1782 he moved for an address against the war, which was defeated by 194 votes to 193; and on 27 Feb. moved a similar motion which was carried by 234 to 215.

Conway became commander-in-chief in the Rockingham Administration with a seat in the Cabinet. Grafton, Camden, and Conway, survivors from the Chatham Administration who had not resigned with Chatham, formed a group committed to neither Rockingham nor Shelburne. With them Conway remained in office under Shelburne, and defended his conduct against Fox in the Commons on 9 July 1782, using the clichés of twenty years earlier:[21] 'he looked to measures only, and not to men', and declared he would support Shelburne so long as he maintained the principles he had professed in opposition. He remained in office under the Coalition but at his own desire left the Cabinet. He resigned on the Coalition's fall in December 1783. On 19 Dec. he reported to Grafton that a dissolution of Parliament was looked upon as certain, and added: 'In regard to myself I have only to say that . . . I hope you will consider your own convenience and inclination in your future disposal of [the seat at Bury].'[22] He had no confidence in Pitt. 'A system of Administration . . . forced upon his Majesty', he wrote to Grafton on 4 Jan. 1784, 'I much dislike; but a system against the bent of the House of Commons, and supported only by the Crown, I take to be impracticable.'[23] On 23 Jan. he made a violent attack in the Commons on Pitt's Administration: they 'had endeavoured by every mean, sinister, and unworthy act to keep their places . . . their conduct was dark and intricate . . . they existed by corruption . . .'. Pitt's conduct with respect to the threatened dissolution was 'not only an insult, but an indecency'; Conway could not have imagined it possible 'that any man who stood upon his character could have treated the House of Commons in that manner'.[24] He had not spoken thus of the authors of the Coalition—the Administration 'forced upon his Majesty'; but then they had possessed a majority in the Commons and did not need a dissolution.

On 28 Mar. 1784 the King wrote to Pitt:[25]

Having heard this day that the Duke of Grafton has met with the repulse of his candidate General Conway at St. Edmundsbury and that the Duke to prevent the introduction of a stranger has been obliged to put up in his stead Captain George Fitzroy, I think it may be agreeable to Mr. Pitt to know of a certain friend instead of a determined enemy.

Conway had sat in Parliament for over forty years;

had worked at different times with different parties; yet at no time had he been a party man.

He died 9 July 1795.

¹ Devonshire mss. ² *Mems. Geo. II*, ii. 3. ³ Grafton mss. ⁴ Walpole to Hertford, 3 Dec. 1764. ⁵ *Mems. Geo. III*, i. 322. ⁶ Ibid. ii. 297–8, 321; iii. 91. ⁷ Ibid. iii. 29. ⁸ *Corresp.* (ed. Copeland), i. 321. ⁹ *Mems. Geo. III*, iii. 71. ¹⁰ Fortescue, ii. 73. ¹¹ *Cavendish's 'Debates'*, i. 351–2. ¹² Ibid. 497. ¹³ To Mann, 12 Nov. 1770. ¹⁴ *Last Jnls*, i. 146. ¹⁵ Ibid, 43. ¹⁶ Thos. Bradshaw to R. M. Keith, 20 Oct. 1772, Add. 35504, f. 106. ¹⁷ *Mems. & Corresp. Sir R. M. Keith*, ed. Gillespie Smith, ii. 29. ¹⁸ Almon, iii. 34. ¹⁹ Ibid. xvii. 584. ²⁰ Debrett, vi. 349. ²¹ Ibid. vii. 300. ²² Grafton, *Autobiog.* 386. ²³ Ibid. 388. ²⁴ Debrett, xii. 640–2. ²⁵ Chatham mss.

J.B.

## CONWAY, see also SEYMOUR CONWAY

## CONYERS, John (1717–75), of Copt Hall, Essex.

READING            1747–1754
ESSEX        25 Feb. 1772–8 Sept. 1775

*b.* 13 Dec. 1717, 1st s. of Edward Conyers, M.P., by Hon. Mathilda Fermor, da. of William, 1st Baron Leominster. *educ.* Univ. Coll. Oxf. 1735. *m.* (1) Hannah (*d.*4 Apr. 1745), da. of Richard Warner, of North Elmham, Norf., *s.p.*; (2) 1 Jan. 1747, his cos., Lady Henrietta Frances Fermor, da. of Thomas, 1st Earl of Pomfret, 13 ch. of whom 8 surv.¹ *suc.* fa. 23 Apr. 1742.

Conyers sat for Reading as a Tory; he did not stand again in 1754. He was talked of as a candidate for Essex on the vacancy in April 1759² but did not stand. In 1760 he was considering doing so; his sister, the wife of Sir Roger Newdigate (q.v.), wrote to her cousin, Sir Charles Mordaunt (q.v.), 9 July 1760,³ that her brother was 'in a hurry of spirits' about the Essex Assizes 'when tis supposed election business will be settled', and asked them to consult Jacob Houblon (q.v.); but Houblon thought that Conyers could not succeed, and he desisted. He did stand at the by-election of 1763, supported by the 'old interest' and by Sandwich; Grenville and Rigby remained neutral; and after an exceedingly expensive election, Conyers was defeated, 15 Dec., by a narrow margin of about 4 per cent of the votes cast. Some of his friends wanted him to petition. But Conyers feared 'the enormous expense' which, he wrote to John Strutt (q.v.) about the end of the year, 'notwithstanding your generous offer and those of some others will bring an additional blow upon my fortune and family'.⁴ And in another undated letter: on a further inspection of his affairs he found that the expense had so far exceeded his expectations that he could not take a share of the cost of a petition.

In December 1767 Strutt tried to persuade Conyers to stand: they must not deliver the county 'tamely to the enemy' while they have power to defend it. Conyers replied, 23 Dec.:

I am no longer in a condition to undertake the numberless uncertainties and the certain great ex-

penses; and the endless fatigues of body and mind, that I speak of with some experience and that in my present state would be utterly impracticable.

Maynard's offer to stand down for Conyers if this secured an uncontested election was not accepted. 'Conyers will never get courage for another battle', wrote Gascoyne to Strutt, 26 Dec. 1767. It was not until an unopposed return was secured for him in 1772⁵ that he declared himself once more a candidate for the county. In 1774 an unopposed return was again expected on a compromise between Conyers' and Luther's friends, but a contest was brought on at the last moment by an interloper.

In March 1772, over the royal marriage bill, Conyers was listed by Robinson as 'pro, present'; and on 26 Apr. 1773 he voted with the Government over the motion concerning the Middlesex election. This is his only recorded vote in the House. There is no record of his having spoken.

He died 8 Sept. 1775 'aged 57 years, 8 months, 3 weeks, and 5 days'.⁶

¹ Conyer's M.I., Epping (see Nichols, *Leics.* ii (2), p. 457). ² W. Salisbury to Newcastle, 18 Apr., Add. 32890, f. 200. ³ Mordaunt mss. ⁴ Strutt mss. ⁵ Gascoyne to Strutt, 30 Jan. 1772. ⁶ M.I. at Epping.

L.B.N.

## CONYNGHAM, Henry, 1st Baron Mount Charles [I] (c.1705–81), of Minster, Kent; Slane, co. Meath; and Mount Charles, co. Donegal.

TIVERTON      26 Dec. 1747–1754
SANDWICH     7 Dec. 1756–1774

*b.* c.1705, 2nd s. of Maj.-Gen. Henry Conyngham of Slane and Mount Charles by Mary, da. and h. of Sir John Williams, 2nd Bt., of Minster, wid. of Charles Petty, 1st Baron Shelburne [I]. *m.* Dec. 1744, Ellen, da. and h. of Solomon Merrett, London merchant, *s.p. suc.* bro. 26 Oct. 1738; *cr.* Baron Mount Charles [I] 3 Oct. 1753; Visct. Conyngham [I] 20 July 1756; Earl Conyngham [I] 4 Jan. 1781.
M.P. [I] 1727–53, P.C. [I] 27 May 1748.
Lt. 4 Drag. Gds. Jan. 1725; capt. Royal Irish Drags. Nov. 1725.

On 10 May 1754 Lord Mount Charles (as he then was) sent a memorandum to Newcastle in which, after mentioning his grandfather's and father's services in the army, he wrote:¹

Lord Mount Charles also served his present Majesty and his royal family above twenty years, but quit the service much against his inclinations on the decease of his elder brother. Since, he has spent several thousand pounds in elections, both in England and Ireland, to serve his Majesty and his ministry. He is the fifth in parliamentary interest in Ireland, and makes one Member in England.

The family were of Scottish origin, settled in Ireland; and Conyngham inherited from his mother property in Kent. In 1753 Arnold Nesbitt (q.v.)

II—I

recommended him to Thomas Scawen for a seat at Mitchell at the forthcoming general election,[2] but Conyngham was intent on establishing his interest at Sandwich, where he had been defeated in 1741.

On 18 Sept. 1753 the Duke of Dorset, lord lieutenant of Ireland, advised him against becoming a candidate at Sandwich:[3]

> Any opposition from your Lordship to those that are supported by the Government would appear extraordinary to the King, immediately after my representing you as a person most sincerely inclined to promote his service. Under these circumstances I should hope your Lordship, both for your own sake and mine, would not without the consent of Mr. Pelham, who knows his Majesty's intentions upon these affairs, disturb the unanimity which has lately subsisted at Sandwich.

'If you, sir, was out of the question', wrote Mount Charles to Pelham,[4] '. . . his Grace's letter would have determined me to do it, for I may not be treated in that manner.' He asked Pelham to remove John Clevland (q.v.), one of the sitting Members, to another constituency, and offered to contribute towards his expenses—'my interest at Sandwich is such as I would gladly establish in my family at any expense'. Even had he secured Pelham's consent, his success at Sandwich would have been doubtful without the support of Sir George Oxenden, who had no wish to strengthen a rival.

After Pelham's death, Mount Charles informed Newcastle that Pelham had promised to bring him into Parliament for one of the first vacancies on condition of his declining at Sandwich.[5] 'I find nothing in my brother's papers relating to the affair mentioned in your letter', wrote Newcastle on 25 Mar. 1754,[6] 'and . . . it is impossible for me to give any positive promise.' However, he was persuaded into doing so. Next, came an application from Mount Charles for the place of joint vice-treasurer of Ireland.[7] And on 17 Apr. 1755 he wrote to Lord Hartington, lord lieutenant of Ireland:[8]

> I asked the Duke of Dorset for the Ordnance of Ireland . . . and acquainted his Grace that the Duke of Newcastle had promised me for any favour I should request of his Majesty . . . but I never received any answer from the Duke of Dorset. I also desired to be made a viscount. I lay these my pretensions and requests before your Excellency to do what you think proper in my favour.

Hartington obtained for him the Irish viscountcy; and a few months later he was returned for Sandwich.

Once elected, Conyngham behaved as if he controlled the borough, and claimed credit for having returned a Government candidate in 1754. He wrote to Newcastle on 1 Apr. 1758:[9]

> At the last general election when I agreed to bring Mr.

Amyand into Parliament at your Grace's desire, you directed me to inform my friends at Sandwich that the Government interest and mine were to be united for the future, and that all favours they had to request of the ministry should be through me . . .

> I have no views but the Government interest, united with mine, and to convince your Grace of it, if you'll order the collector . . . and all others under the Government interest to unite warmly with my friends, I will undertake to choose two Members warmly attached to the Whig ministry, one of their recommending, the other of my family; and I will venture to say that if I do not interfere that the ministry, with all their power, cannot choose one Member.

When this failed to bring a favourable reply, he wrote again (22 Apr.):[10] 'It would give me great concern to be forced into another scene of acting for the rest of my life.' Newcastle did not comply —yet there is no evidence that Conyngham fulfilled his threat.

In the new reign he transferred his allegiance to Bute, and afterwards to Grenville. Grenville wrote to him on 31 Oct. 1763, in reply to a request for preferment for his nephew:[11]

> I am very sorry to see by your letter . . . that your Lordship thinks you have so many subjects of complaint from former ministers and lords lieutenant of Ireland, but however that may be it is utterly impossible for me to enter into it and to redress all the disappointments and causes of uneasiness that may have been given by my predecessors.

To which Conyngham replied (1 Nov.):[12]

> I received the favour of your very ministerial letter, but as I have not the disposition either of a minister or a courtier, when you canvass your friends in the House of Commons put me down in opposition to the present ministry, for I am determined not to be maltreated any longer.

Grenville's reaction is unknown, but Conyngham did not vote with the Opposition over Wilkes and general warrants. 'As I never gave a vote against Administration either in England or Ireland', he wrote to Grenville on 12 Feb. 1765, 'I should not think of it now if I was properly treated by the present ministry.' But on 3 May:

> I have been greatly indisposed these two months with a violent disorder on my nerves, which prevented my attendance in Parliament, but if you'll give me notice when anything material is to come before Parliament I will attend if possible.

On 17 June 1765 he applied for the place of master-general of the Ordnance in Ireland, and when Grenville referred him to Weymouth, newly-appointed lord lieutenant, wrote again (25 June):

> It is believed that a change of ministry will take place in a few days. If that should happen it is more than probable that Lord Weymouth will not go to Ireland. I therefore beg to know in the strictest confidence who will be our lord lieutenant in your opinion, that I may apply to him in time about the Ordnance,

if not disposed of, as it is one of the few employments that would suit me.[13]

'In the present situation of things', replied Grenville on 30 June,[14] 'I can only assure your Lordship that I do not know for whom the lieutenancy of Ireland is destined . . .' The Grenville Administration was on its last legs when Conyngham wrote again (2 July):[15]

I hope you will excuse my giving you so much trouble as there is at present no visible minister but you to apply to, and no time to be lost in my request of his Majesty, beside I am growing old and this is the critical time for me to expect success, and I should be sorry at the latter end of my life to be forced into opposition both in England and Ireland, which I can justify to the world if I do not succeed in my request.

Rockingham in July 1765 classed Conyngham as 'contra'; but he did not vote against the repeal of the Stamp Act—in spite of his frequent threats of opposition he is not known to have voted against any Administration. In November 1766 Rockingham classed him as 'absent', Townshend in January 1767 as 'doubtful', and Newcastle in March as 'doubtful or absent'. In the Parliament of 1768–74 two votes by him are recorded (both with Administration): on Brass Crosby's case, 27 Mar. 1771, and on the renewal of the Middlesex question, 26 Apr. 1773.

'The corporation of Sandwich . . . do me the honour to elect me and any friend of mine without expense', wrote Conyngham to Granby on 9 Apr. 1769.[16] This, like so much else in him, was all blague. At the general election of 1774 Government put up two candidates at Sandwich (hitherto they had been content with one seat). Conyngham received 68 votes, against 516 for Philip Stephens and 455 for William Hey.

Conyngham is not known to have spoken in the House.

He died 3 Apr. 1781.

[1] Add. 32735, ff. 252–3. [2] Thos. Clarke to Hardwicke, 13 Sept. 1753, Add. 35423, ff. 150–2. [3] Copy in Newcastle (Clumber) mss. [4] Enclosure to above. [5] Add. 32734, f. 330. [6] Ibid. f. 336. [7] Add. 32735, f. 248. [8] Devonshire mss. [9] Add. 32879, ff. 13–14. [10] Ibid. f. 267. [11] Grenville letter bk. [12] Grenville mss (Bodl.). [13] Grenville mss (JM). [14] Grenville letter bk. [15] Grenville mss (JM). [16] Rutland mss.

J.B.

**COOKE, George** (c.1705–68), of Harefield, Mdx.

TREGONY        28 Jan. 1742–1747
MIDDLESEX      8 Mar. 1750–5 June 1768

b. c.1705, o.s. of Sir George Cooke of Harefield, chief prothonotary in the court of common pleas, by Anne, da. of Edward Jennings of Dudleston, Salop. educ. I. Temple 1717, called 1728, bencher 1733, reader 1742, treasurer 1743. m. July 1735, Catherine, da. of Sir Thomas Twisden, 4th Bt., of East Peckham, Kent, 7s. suc. fa. 4 Nov. 1740.

Chief prothonotary in the court of common pleas 1732–d.; jt. paymaster gen. July 1766–d.

Cooke, the son of a distinguished barrister, practised at the bar at least until he succeeded to the family estate. The office of chief prothonotary, which he held for life, had also been held by his father and grandfather.

In 1754 he was returned unopposed for Middlesex, and under George II was a Tory—Horace Walpole called him 'a pompous Jacobite'.[1] By 1757 he had become attached to Pitt,[2] and henceforth remained his follower. This sometimes involved him in contradictions. Thus, on 9 Feb. 1761, true to his Tory principles, he spoke against an estimate of £300,000 due to the Hanoverian chancery;[3] but on 13 Nov. 'strongly supported the German war'.[4]

On 11 Dec. 1761 Cooke moved for papers on relations with Spain—'in a plain and decent manner' wrote Harris; and on 9 Dec. 1762 voted against the peace preliminaries. On 22 Feb. 1763 he supported Sir John Philipps's motion for a committee on public accounts. He voted with Opposition on Wilkes, and was carried to the House ill of the gout to attend the great debate on general warrants, 17-18 Feb. 1764.[5] Between 1761 and 1766 Harris reports over twenty speeches by him. On the prize bill, 3 Mar. 1762, he was 'not well heard', but otherwise seems to have been listened to with respect. Still, he owed most of his credit in the House to his connexion with Pitt.

When the Rockingham Administration met Parliament in December 1765 Cooke was asked to second the Address. Newcastle told him that Administration wished 'to have the sanction of an independent man at their setting out'[6]—but really much more to appear to have Pitt's approval. Cooke consulted Pitt:

I look up to you for the rule and conduct of my political life. Were you at the head of affairs the pride of my heart would be to be known and distinguished as your devoted friend. As the ministry are now composed I do not wish to take any part that has the appearance of *connexion*, where you are not *connected*.

Pitt disclaimed any tie with Administration, and Cooke declined Newcastle's request.

In the debate of 17 Dec. 1765 he 'treated the whole American affair as a mere mob';[7] on 14 Jan. 1766 'doubted the power of the legislature of this country to tax the colonies';[8] and on 17 Jan. 'declared against our right of taxing . . . in so gross a manner that Mr. Grenville called him to order'.[9] On 28 Jan. he presented the petition from the Stamp Act Congress against the measure. Harris notes him as one of the few Members who would have followed Pitt had there been a division on the Declaratory

Act; and in July 1766 he was given office in the Pitt Administration.

No speeches by Cooke are recorded during the last two years of his life. He voted against Administration on the land tax, 27 Feb. 1767, and apologized to Chatham for his vote:[10]

> My particular situation as Member for Middlesex, and being chose by the unanimous and affectionate voice of my constituents, rendered it impossible for me not to vote for the three shillings, as I am certain had I done otherwise I should at once have forfeited their good opinion . . . Under these circumstances I hope your Lordship will not take it amiss.

On nullum tempus, 17 Feb. 1768, he voted with Administration.

His interest in Middlesex was strong enough to ensure his return in the contested election of 1768, although he was ill in bed with gout on election day.[11] He 'never was well after the election, when he underwent a great deal of fatigue';[12] and died 5 June 1768.

[1] *Mems. Geo. II*, i. 13. [2] Rigby to Bedford, 28 June 1757, *Bedford Corresp.* ii. 256. [3] Walpole, *Mems. Geo. III*, i. 29. [4] Harris's 'Debates'. [5] West to Newcastle, 17 Feb. 1764, Yorke, *Life of Hardwicke*, iii. 563. [6] *Chatham Corresp.* ii. 338–42. [7] Harris's 'Debates'. [8] West to Newcastle, 14 Jan. 1766, Add. 32973, ff. 133–4. [9] Harris's 'Debates'. [10] *Chatham Corresp.* iii. 222–4. [11] Walpole to Mann, 31 Mar. 1768. [12] Dennys de Berdt to Richard Carey, 6 July 1768, *Colls. Col. Soc. Mass.* xiii. 335.

J.B.

**COOKE,** *see also* **FREEMAN, Sambrooke**

**COOPER, Grey** (c.1726–1801), of Worlington, Suff.

| | |
|---|---|
| ROCHESTER | 23 Dec. 1765–1768 |
| GRAMPOUND | 1768–1774 |
| SALTASH | 1774–1784 |
| RICHMOND | 7 Feb. 1786–1790 |

*b.* c.1726, 1st s. of William Cooper, M.D., of Newcastle-upon-Tyne, by Mary, da. of Edward Grey of Alnwick. *educ.* M. Temple 1747, called 1751. *m.* (1) 5 Oct. 1753, Margaret (*d.*1755), da. of Sir Henry Grey, 1st Bt., of Howick, Northumb., *s.p.*; (2) 19 July 1762, Elizabeth Kennedy of Newcastle-upon-Tyne, 2s. 2da. *suc.* fa. 5 May 1758; assumed, Aug. 1775, the baronetcy of Gogar [S] as heir male to the elder bro. of his gt.-gd.-fa., having been, at the sheriff's court at Edinburgh, served heir by a service which was however, 'never returned to Chancery, and [even] if it had been, could have conveyed no right to a title which had no existence'.[1]

Sec. to Treasury 1765–Mar. 1782; K.C. duchy of Lancaster 1765–*d.*; ld. of Treasury Apr.–Dec. 1783; P.C. 29 Apr. 1796.

In 1765 Cooper was making about £1,000 a year from his successful practice at the bar,[2] and he strengthened his reputation by his defence of the interests of the Duke and Duchess of Atholl during the hearing in the Commons of their petition regarding the sale of their sovereign rights in the Isle of Man to the Crown. Later in the year Cooper recommended himself to Rockingham by two pamphlets written in defence of Rockingham's newly-formed Administration—*A pair of Spectacles for Short-sighted Politicians* . . . and *The Merits of the New Administration truly stated.* In October he accepted Rockingham's offer of the post of secretary to the Treasury; but as this meant abandoning his career at the bar, demanded an adequate pension settlement as a recompense in case of loss of office. When the arrangement was almost completed, he suddenly jibbed at accepting promises which Rockingham might not later be in a position to fulfil and asked for the immediate grant of an income by letters patent under the Great Seal. In the extravagantly emotional language which he affected, he wrote to Rockingham:[3]

> My hand trembles whilst it lays before your Lordship the humble remonstrance of a heart anxious to do its duty and to perform its engagements of honour to your Lordship . . . [a friend] has stated my present most critical situation to me in a light which my eagerness to be connected with your Lordship and my ardent and disinterested love of the good cause which you conduct and support prevented me from seeing with my own eyes . . . Yet perhaps I could have had firmness enough to have resisted [these] attacks. But—the sight of my wife and children whose happiness, whose welfare, and even provision in the world depend upon my ultimate and final determination in this most important moment of my life, forces me with great reluctance, and after a severe and anxious conflict in my breast, to tell your Lordship, that the duty which I owe to myself and to my family will not permit me to enter upon the office which your Lordship destines for me before the security which has been promised to me in case of a removal be actually in my hands.

On this condition he gave assurances of 'constant zeal and unalterable fidelity' to the King and to Rockingham. In October he took up the appointment, and a grant of an annuity to him of £500 p.a. duly passed the Great Seal.[4] A seat in Parliament now had to be found, and on a vacancy at Rochester all the engines of Government, especially the Admiralty interest, were engaged to secure his election. Newcastle recommended him to one supporter as 'a very proper and a very ingenious man', who 'has at all times been a zealous Whig';[5] and his opponent complained:[6]

> Sir Charles Saunders, Admiral Keppel, and Sir William Meredith have been sitting three days in this city, as a board, to do any Admiralty favour that could procure a vote, as well as canvass for Mr. Cooper . . . My lord president of the council has been here also.

Once in the situation which he had accepted after much show of 'timidity' and *'feminine apprehensions of danger'*,[7] Cooper clung to it for over sixteen years. In 1768 by Treasury arrangement with Edward

Eliot he was returned for Grampound, and in 1774 and 1780 on the Admiralty interest for Saltash. As a junior minister, Cooper spoke frequently in the House, mainly on financial matters, sometimes on matters of procedure, and also to introduce and to forward Government business in general: but he did not take any part in the great political debates. He took notes of Opposition speeches with which to prime Lord North before his replies, and he wrote many of the brief reports on proceedings preserved among George III's papers. In the Treasury he took charge of the revenue side—where the conduct of affairs was described by his colleague in 1780 as 'slovenly'.[8] During the minority of the Prince of Wales he had the superintendence of the Government interest in the Cornish boroughs, and took a part in 1774 in settling the election arrangements,[9] but he does not appear to have continued these election activities in 1780. The *English Chronicle* described him in 1781 as 'a sort of man that every minister must have under him. He is a good drudge in business, is very important in his manner, and in his disposition very pleasant. He takes down notes in the House for Lord North, and both in public and private laughs most loudly at all his Lordship's jokes.' By 1782, in addition to his office as secretary, then worth about £5,000 p.a., and his annuity of £500 p.a., he had secured sinecures as searcher at Newcastle and as King's Counsel in the duchy of Lancaster, and for his sons the reversion of the post of auditor of the land revenue.

Cooper lost his place at the Treasury on the fall of the North Government. In November 1782 Shelburne hoped for his support,[10] but in the following months he was one of the men who urged North to join forces with Fox;[11] and he voted on 18 Feb. 1783 against Shelburne's peace preliminaries. He held office under the Coalition as a lord of the Treasury. After its fall he adhered to North in opposition, but only once entered prominently into the political debates of the early months of 1784. Ministerial election arrangements at the general election of 1784 involved his displacement from Saltash, and for the next two years he was out of Parliament. But by June 1785 he was looking forward to returning to the House;[12] in January 1786 it was rumoured he was to be brought in 'to make up for the loss of official knowledge' due to the defection to the Government of William Eden;[13] and in February he was provided with a seat at Richmond on the Dundas interest. For the next four years Cooper, still acting as a follower of North, took a prominent part in debate, speaking mainly on fiscal and commercial matters, ably and pertinaciously harassing Pitt. In 1787 he attacked the com-

mercial treaty with France and 'yielded to few in his accurate knowledge of the complicated interests which it included'.[14] When the Coalition hoped to return to office in 1789, during the King's illness, he was set down for reappointment to the Treasury Board.[15] But no seat was found for him at the general election of 1790.

Cooper's interest in public life was not yet ended. The excesses of the French Revolution led him to abandon opposition. Early in 1793, as soon as Alexander Wedderburn, Lord Loughborough, had been appointed lord chancellor, he offered his services to the Government through him, and told Portland, his nominal political chief, that had he been in the Commons he would have voted with Burke and Windham in support of the Government.[16] In February 1795 he suggested to Pitt that he might be appointed a commissioner in London to look after the loan to the Austrian Government.[17] In June he pressed Portland for the honour of appointment to the Privy Council, though without office or emolument:[18] this wish at least was granted in 1796, but his other applications were ignored.

Cooper died 30 July 1801.

[1] *GEC Baronetage*, ii. 446–7. [2] Ld. Geo. Sackville to John Irwin, 14 Sept. 1765, *HMC Stopford-Sackville*, i. 102–3. [3] Rockingham mss. [4] Add. 36133, f. 128; 33056, f. 148. [5] Newcastle to Chas. Polhill, 26 Nov. 1765, Polhill mss. [6] J. Calcraft to Pitt, 30 Nov. 1765, *Chatham Corresp.* ii. 338. [7] Cooper to Mellish, n.d. [Oct. 1765], Rockingham mss. [8] Robinson to Jenkinson, 6 Dec. 1780, Add. 38567, f. 89. [9] Wraxall, *Mems.* i. 428; North to Cooper, 5 Oct. 1774, to Robinson, 5 Oct., 19 Nov. 1774, Abergavenny mss. [10] Parlty. list, Lansdowne mss. [11] Robinson to Jenkinson, 22 Mar. 1783, Add. 38567, ff. 137–40. [12] Cooper to Sir R. M. Keith, 24 June 1785, Add. 35534, ff. 240–1. [13] Daniel Pulteney to Rutland, 23 Jan. [1786], *HMC Rutland*, iii. 277. [14] Wraxall, *Mems.* iv. 284. [15] *Fox Corresp.* iv. 398. [16] Cooper to Portland, 10 Feb. 1793, Portland mss. [17] 8 Feb. 1795, Chatham mss. [18] 10, 29 June 1795, Portland mss.

I.R.C.

**COOPER, John** (?1726–79), of Salisbury, Wilts.

DOWNTON      14 Feb. 1775–7 Aug. 1779

*b.* ?1726, *s.* of Thomas Cooper of Salisbury by his 2nd *w.* Sarah, *da.* of John Priaulx of Salisbury. *educ.* Queen's, Oxf. 13 Mar. 1744, aged 17. *m.* Rachel, *da.* of Edward Poore (q.v.).

In July 1774 Cooper, 'an eminent clothier in Salisbury',[1] declared himself a candidate for Salisbury;[2] but at the general election stood on the Radnor interest for Downton, was defeated, but was seated on petition. He voted regularly with the Opposition. There is no record of his having spoken in the House. He died 7 Aug. 1779.

[1] *English Chron.* 1780. [2] *London Chron.* 12 July 1774.

J.A.C.

**COOPER,** *see also* **ASHLEY (ASHLEY COOPER)**

**COOTE, Eyre** (1726–83), of West Park, nr. Rockbourn, Hants.

LEICESTER 1768–1774
POOLE 1774–1780

*b.* 1726, 4th s. of Rev. Chidley Coote of Ash Hill, co. Limerick by Jane, da. of George Evans of Bulgaden Hall, co. Limerick. *m.* 6 July 1763, a da. of Charles Hutchinson, gov. of St. Helena, *s.p.* K.B. 28 June 1770.

Went out to India 1754; capt. 39 Ft. 1755; lt.-col. 84 Ft. 1759; col. 1765; col. 27 Ft. 1771–3; col. 37 Ft. 1773–*d.*; maj.-gen. 1775; lt.-gen. 1777; c.-in-c. Madras 1769–70, Bengal 1777–*d.*

In 1762 Coote, after having served under Clive at Plassey and gained a considerable reputation by his own victories at Wandewash and Pondicherry, returned to England and bought the estate of West Park in Hampshire. Before the general election of 1768 he was encouraged by his friend Welbore Ellis (q.v.)[1] to stand at Aylesbury, but finding that he was to be opposed by John Durand (q.v.), who was 'determined to get into the House at any rate provided money can effect it', withdrew before an open declaration of his candidature was made.[2] Finally he successfully contested the expensive borough of Leicester jointly with Booth Grey, whose father Lord Stamford had an interest in that borough but was anxious to find a wealthy candidate to share the expenses. In November 1767 Lord Stamford's agent had approached Clive[3] about recommending one of his friends; whether Coote was his nominee is not certain.

No vote of Coote's appears in the year he had in Parliament before his departure to take up the appointment as commander-in-chief in Madras. Back in England again in 1771, he was classed in Robinson's surveys of March 1772 on the royal marriage bill as 'pro, present', but no vote of his was reported before 26 Apr. 1773 when he voted with Administration on the Middlesex election; his only other recorded vote was with Administration on Grenville's Election Act, 25 Feb. 1774. His only reported speech in the House was on 30 Mar. 1772 on a motion for an East India bill, when he declared that 'three times the number of troops now in India might be paid with the same money, but that the contractors and the *canaille* spent all the money'.[4]

In 1774 Coote successfully contested Poole. No vote or speech of his is reported before he left England to take up his post in Bengal. He did not stand again in 1780. He died at Madras on 26 Apr. 1783.

[1] Ld. Harcourt to Sir Wm. Lee, n.d. [prob. Dec. 1767], Lee pprs. Bucks. RO. [2] Coote to Lee, 23 Feb. 1768, ibid. [3] Geo. Clive to Lord Clive, 24 Nov. 1767, Clive mss. [4] Rob. Palk to W. M. Goodlad, 7 Apr. 1772, *HMC Palk.*

M.M.D.

**COPE, James** (c.1709–56).

DOWNTON 1754–1 Aug. 1756

*b.* c.1709, s. of Gen. Sir John Cope by Jane, da. of Anthony Duncombe, sis. of Anthony, 1st Lord Feversham. *unm.*

Sec. to Walter Titley at Danish court, 1729–37; sec. to commissioners to treat in Antwerp for a commercial treaty 1737–41; resident in Hamburg to the Hanse towns 1741–56. On leave 21 Aug. 1754–19 May 1755, and 21 Oct. 1755–*d.*[1]

Cope was brought in for Downton in 1754 by his uncle, Lord Feversham, who wrote to Newcastle, 16 May 1756, to demand that his nephew should be promoted at least to the rank of envoy:[2] 'It had been better for him not to have been in Parliament, than now he is there not to receive some mark of his Majesty's favour.' He died in England on 1 Aug. 1756, before anything could be done for him.

[1] D. B. Horn, *British Diplomatic Reps 1689–1789*, p. 71. [2] Add. 32865, f. 29.

J.A.C.

**CORBET, John** (1751–1817), of Sundorne, nr. Shrewsbury, Salop.

SHREWSBURY 17 Mar. 1775–1780

*b.* 1751, 1st s. of John Corbet of Sundorne by Barbara Letitia, da. of John Mytton of Halston, nr. Shrewsbury. *educ.* Pembroke, Oxf. 7 Jan. 1770 aged 18. *m.* (1) 15 Sept. 1774, his 2nd cos. Emma Elizabeth, da. of Sir Charlton Leighton, 3rd Bt., and sis. of Sir Charlton Leighton, 4th Bt. (q.v.), 1s. 1da.; (2) 19 Feb. 1806, Anne, da. of Rev. William Pigott of Edgmond, Newport, Salop, 4s. 1da.

Corbet came of a old Shropshire family with several branches in the county. His estate, within three miles of Shrewsbury, gave him a natural interest there, and in 1775, on the death of Lord Clive, he was returned unopposed. In Parliament he voted with the Opposition on America, 2 Feb. 1778, and was classed as 'contra, present' on the contractors bill, 12 Feb. 1779. His only other recorded votes were with the Opposition on Dunning's motion, 6 Apr. 1780, and the motion against prorogation, 24 Apr., and he appears as 'contra' in Robinson's survey of 1780. There is no record of his having spoken in the House. He did not stand again for Parliament in 1780.

Corbet died 19 May 1817. The *Gentleman's Magazine* (1817, i. 636–7) wrote that he was 'well known beyond the precincts of his own county, particularly in Warwickshire, where at his own expense, he kept a pack of fox hounds for nearly 30 years . . . [He] kept up the character of the independent country gentleman firmly attached to our glorious constitution . . . and always anxiously wishing his powerful interest in the borough of Shrewsbury to tend to its support.'

M.M.D.

**CORNEWALL, Frederick** (1706–88), of Delbury Hall, Diddlesbury, Salop.

MONTGOMERY 15 June 1771–1774

*bap.* 3 Aug. 1706, 3rd s. of Rev. Frederick Cornewall, vicar of Bromfield, Salop by his w. Elizabeth Trice. *m.* 2 May 1746, Mary, da. of Francis Herbert, M.P., of Oakley Park, Ludlow, a 2nd cos. of Lord Powis, 3s. Lt. R.N. 1734; capt. 1744; lost an arm off Toulon, Feb. 1744.

Cornewall was returned to Parliament on Lord Powis's interest. On 18 Oct. 1771 he wrote to his relative Charles Jenkinson (q.v.):[1]

The Parliament, the news say, will not meet till after Christmas which I hope is true as I am by no means fond of London. I trust when I make my appearance in St. Stephen's Chapel that you will take me by the hand.

On 5 Feb. 1773:[2]

The papers say there will be a call of the House in about a fortnight. If there is I beg you will excuse me. I cannot plead my health which is better than it has been for many years, which I attribute to the country air and exercise . . . Though if your friend on the Treasury bench should want me, I will cheerfully attend as I look upon him to be a very honest, worthy man.

On 3 Dec. 1773:[3]

By a letter I received last post from Lord North desiring my attendance at the beginning of the sessions as things of importance were expected to come under consideration. I fear a long attendance may be detrimental to my health, as I never am well in the smoke of London . . . If my coming for a few weeks will answer . . . I will come up at the opening of the Parliament but if you think I can be excused I should be happy.

And on 27 Jan. 1774:[4]

Last post brought me a summons to attend the House . . . I have pleaded want of health in answer to the sheriff's letter . . . If there is any occasion for my attendance I think it cannot be any ways detrimental to my health.

There is no record of his having spoken or voted in the House, but in Robinson's two surveys on the royal marriage bill, March 1772, he is listed as 'pro, present'.

Cornewall died 4 Aug. 1788.

[1] Add. 38469, f. 288. [2] Add. 38470, f. 116. [3] Ibid. f. 128. [4] Add. 38308, f. 33.

L.B.N.

**CORNEWALL, Frederick** (1752–83), of Delbury Hall, Diddlesbury, Salop.

LEOMINSTER 27 Sept. 1776–1780
LUDLOW 1780–Mar. 1783

*b.* 13 Apr. 1752, 1st s. of Frederick Cornewall (q.v.). *educ.* Eton 1765–9; St. John's, Camb. 1770; L. Inn.

1773. *unm.* Took name of Walker before Cornewall, 21 July 1781.

The circumstances of Cornewall's return for Leominster have not been ascertained, but it is probable that he had there the support of Lord Powis. Robinson wrote under Ludlow in his survey for the general election of 1780:

There is a contest here . . . a Mr. Beale is set up by the patriots and discontents of the town, though it is thought he can't succeed.

That the threat was taken seriously can be seen from the very extensive correspondence of the candidates and their agent trying to secure votes,[1] but it is not clear whether Beale stood the poll. Cornewall's name does not appear in the division list over James Lowther's motion on America, 12 Dec. 1781, but on Conway's, 27 Feb., and Rous's motion, 15 Mar. 1782, he voted with the Government. He did not vote on Shelburne's peace preliminaries, 18 Feb. 1783, and there is no record of his having ever spoken in the House. He died *v.p.* in March 1783.

[1] Clive mss, Salop RO.

L.B.N.

**CORNEWALL, Sir George,** 2nd Bt. (1748–1819), of Moccas Court, Herefs.

HEREFORDSHIRE 1774–1796, 1802–1807

*b.* 5 Nov. 1748, 1st s. of Sir George Amyand (q.v.) by Anna Maria, da. of John Abraham Corteen, a Hamburg merchant. *educ.* Eton 1758–64; Ch. Ch. Oxf. 1766. *m.* 18 July 1771, Catherine, da. and h. of Velters Cornewall (q.v.) of Moccas Court, Herefs., and assumed name of Cornewall, 2s. 5da. His sisters m. James Harris, 1st Earl of Malmesbury and Sir Gilbert Elliot, 4th Bt. (qq.v.). *suc.* fa. as 2nd Bt. 16 Aug. 1766.

Cornewall inherited his father's share in the banking firm Amyand (subsequently Cornewall), Staples, and Mercer, and seems to have been associated with it until 1776.

At the general election of 1774 he successfully contested Herefordshire (which his father-in-law had represented 1722–68). His first recorded vote was against Administration on Wilkes, 22 Feb. 1775, and he again voted in opposition on the civil list debts, 16 Apr. 1777. No further vote of his is recorded till 12 Feb. 1779, when he voted with Opposition on the contractors bill; after this he voted regularly against Administration until the fall of North. He supported Shelburne's peace preliminaries, 18 Feb. 1783, but did not vote on Fox's East India bill, 27 Nov. 1783. He was at the St. Alban's Tavern meeting of country gentlemen in January 1784 which advocated the union of parties.

In William Adam's list of the new Parliament Cornewall was classed as Opposition, and he voted against Pitt on the Regency. Two or three short speeches of Cornewall's on different subjects are recorded.

He died 26 Sept. 1819.

M.M.D.

**CORNEWALL, Velters** (?1697–1768), of Moccas Court, Herefs.

HEREFORDSHIRE 1722–3 Apr. 1768.

*b.* ?1697, 3rd s. of Gen. Henry Cornewall, M.P., of Moccas by Susanna, da. of Sir John Williams, 2nd Bt., of Minster, Kent. *educ.* Ch. Ch. Oxf. 8 July 1714, aged 17; L. Inn 1714. *m.* (1) 1722 (marriage licence 22 Apr.), Judith, da. of Sir James Herbert of Coldbrook, Mon., wid. of Sir Thomas Powell, 1st Bt., M.P., *s.p.s.*; (2) Oct. 1734, Jane (*d.* 10 Apr. 1735), da. of Edmund Bray of Barrington Court, Glos., *s.p.*; (3) 2 Apr. 1737, Catherine, yst. da. and coh. of William Hanbury of Byfleet, Surr., 1s. *d.v.p.*, 1da. who m. 1771 Sir George Amyand, 2nd Bt. (q.v.), who took name of Cornewall. *suc.* fa. in estates of Moccas and Bredwardine 1717.

Cornewall was a Tory. In 1754 his re-election was opposed—the first contest since 1722. Lady Grey wrote to her husband Lord Royston (q.v.) in April 1754:[1]

Nothing new I think has happened in the election trade since you left us, but a story out of Herefordshire . . . of Lord Bateman's and Mr. Fox having attempted to set up Mr. Price for the county a few days before the election, and to distress Mr. Cornewall, had got a writ served upon him in his own house for an old bond debt which he had forgot or neglected till by the interest it had accumulated to £2,500— This seems a very odd and not a very genteel way of attacking a man.

In the House Cornewall continued to rank as a member of the Tory Opposition, and had a reputation for whimsicality. Thus Horace Walpole, reporting the sitting of 18 Mar. 1761, at which Speaker Onslow took leave of the House, writes:[2]

Velters Cornewall made one of his absurd, ill-natured speeches, which the House was always so kind as to take for humour, teasing the Speaker under pretence of complimenting him; while the good old man sat overpowered with gratitude and weeping over the testimonies borne to his virtue.

And James Harris, in his notes on the debate on the cider bill, 11 Mar. 1763, having reported Glover's speech against it: 'Velters Cornewall got up, was of the same side, yet could not help ridiculing the tragic pomp of Glover, whom he hailed his melancholy friend.' Jenkinson in his report for Bute[3] says that Cornewall spoke 'in his usual odd manner'. Two days later, speaking after Thomas Chester, a man of his own age,

his old friend Velters Cornewall . . . gave us to understand that both himself and friend were grown old,

that the House were kind to hear them; that the concatenation of their ideas was hurt, etc. He himself however was well heard, having a share of humour so as to claim attention.[4]

And speaking again on the Cider Act, 2 Mar. 1764, Cornewall 'rambled, was friendly and hostile, regular and irregular, humorous and odd'.[5]

In the autumn of 1763 Jenkinson classed him as 'pro' Administration, and he did not vote against them over Wilkes and general warrants till 18 Feb. 1764 when Jenkinson marked him as a friend voting with the Opposition. In the summer of 1765 he appears in two lists of Rockingham as 'pro' and in one as 'con'. He did not vote against the repeal of the Stamp Act. Whether he voted for it is uncertain, but he seems to have been inclined that way; Lord Egmont told the King, 17 Feb. 1766,[6] that 'on Saturday last' (15 Feb.) Lord Temple 'in a long conversation' had tried to persuade Cornewall 'not to vote for the repeal of the Stamp Act'. As a Tory country gentleman he voted, 27 Feb. 1767, against the Government for the lower land tax; and on 17 Feb. 1768 he voted again with the Opposition on the nullum tempus bill.

He died on 3 Apr. 1768, when, in the words of his memorial in Hereford cathedral, 'his constituents were preparing to elect him to an eighth Parliament'.

[1] Add. 35376, f. 38. [2] *Mems. Geo. III*, i. 40–41. [3] Bodl. North mss. [4] Harris's 'Debates'. [5] Ibid. [6] Fortescue, i. 272.

L.B.N.

**CORNISH, Samuel** (c.1715–70), of Sharnbrook, Beds.

NEW SHOREHAM 23 Dec. 1765–30 Oct. 1770

*b.* c.1715. *m.* Susan, da. of James Gambier of Holborn, *s.p. cr.* Bt. 1 Feb. 1766.
Lt. R.N. 1739; capt. 1742; r.-adm. 1759; v.-adm. 1762.

Cornish is said to have been born of humble parentage, and to have entered the navy as an able seaman. He commanded a squadron in the East Indies 1759–62, and was naval c.-in-c. at the capture of the Philippine Islands. He returned to England a rich man, and in 1765 bought Sharnbrook.

In 1765 Cornish was recommended by his brother officers, Sir Charles Saunders and Augustus Keppel (qq.v.), to Newcastle for a seat at New Shoreham; which cost him 1000 guineas. In Parliament he was closely connected with Saunders and Keppel, and was always counted as of the Rockingham group. He gave evidence during the East Indian inquiry of 1767, but there is no record of his having spoken in the House. He died 30 Oct. 1770.

J.B.

**CORNWALL,**[1] **Charles Wolfran** (1735–89), of Barton Priors, nr. Winchester, Hants.

GRAMPOUND 1768–1774
WINCHELSEA 1774–1780
RYE 1780–2 Jan. 1789

*b.* 15 June 1735, o.s. of Jacobs Cornwall of Berrington, Herefs. by Rose, da. of Robert Fowler of Barton Priors. *educ.* Winchester 1748; L. Inn 1755; G. Inn 1757, called 1757. *m.* 17 Aug. 1764, his cos. Elizabeth, da. of Col. Charles Jenkinson, sis. of Charles and John Jenkinson (qq.v.), *s.p.*

Commr. for examining the German accounts 1763–1765,[2] bencher, G. Inn 1770, treasurer 1774; ld. of Treasury 1774–80; P.C. 8 Nov. 1780; Speaker of the House of Commons and chief justice in eyre north of Trent 1780–*d.*

Cornwall was first associated in politics with Charles Jenkinson, and their connexion was strengthened by his marriage to Jenkinson's sister. Although he had 'a very comfortable patrimonial fortune'[3] Jenkinson wished to obtain an office for him, but Cornwall raised objections: 'A seat in Parliament is my first object', he wrote,[4] 'without that I would not choose to engage in any department of public business.' However, his objections were overcome, and as commissioner for inquiring into the German accounts he did good work and gained a useful knowledge of Treasury procedure.

He remained on friendly terms with Jenkinson, but after 1765 began to drift away from him politically. By 1767 he was close to Rockingham, negotiating at Barnstaple a seat for a relative of Rockingham's. He had also become connected with Shelburne, who recommended him to Edward Eliot (q.v.) for a seat at Grampound, and who apparently paid at least part of his election expenses. On 19 Mar. 1768 Eliot wrote to inform Shelburne that Cornwall and Grey Cooper 'were chose unanimously':[5]

To bring matters to this degree of certainty has brought on a large expense. I must necessarily write to Mr. Cooper on this head who will of course communicate my letter to Mr. Cornwall: I cannot therefore prevent Mr. Cornwall being informed of the amount of the expense, nor ought I perhaps if I could. He shall be made acquainted with your Lordship's kindness towards him.

Cornwall soon became known as one of the most prominent speakers on the Opposition side. In Cavendish's reports 200 interventions of his in debate are noted for the years 1768–74, touching almost every political topic. While inclined to follow Shelburne and Chatham his friendship with Dowdeswell kept him also connected with Rockingham; and in the squabbles of the two parties he managed to keep on good terms with both and to act as a reconciling influence. But Dowdeswell wrote

about him to Rockingham, 20 Dec. 1772, in connexion with East India affairs:[6]

If he acquiesces in my opinion there is no certainty that he will not be turned by others with whom he associates more than he does with us. Where the opinion is not mine but his own I trust he will be more firm; and perhaps in that case the opinion may be not his own only but the opinion of others with whom he acts.

He made East India affairs his special concern. In 1769 he planned with Rockingham a coalition between Clive, Colebrooke, and Sulivan against ministerial influence at India House,[7] and in 1772 was invited by Clive and Colebrooke to go to India as one of the Company's supervisors.[8] But next he turned against Clive, was a member of Burgoyne's select committee and urged privately to North, and in the House that its reports should be acted upon. North offered him a place on the council to be set up in Bengal by the Regulating Act, but Cornwall refused. He told North:[9]

Though I very much approved the present plan, that circumstanced as I was I had rather take my chance at home, and that if I went entirely out of public life in consequence of what had been engaged for by his Lordship a few months ago I should be perfectly contented and easy.

What had North 'engaged for . . . a few months ago'? Was it the pension of £500 p.a. which in July 1773 was granted to Cornwall out of the revenues of the West Indian islands? On 18 July Dowdeswell wrote to Rockingham:[10]

I am much concerned at the loss of Cornwall if it prove true. It is a public loss. I think he will find himself no gainer, and I am sure I feel it a particular loss to myself . . . If the consideration is what your Lordship thinks it, his meritorious services in the liquidation of the German demands, it is a less defensible grant than Dyson's or Bradshaw's. For he has been rewarded for those services . . . But I really mistrust your information, for if Cornwall goes to the court he is too wise to take his reward in this manner.

When on 18 May 1774 the Opposition raised the matter in the House, Cornwall said: 'There was nothing but justice in my appointment'; and in reply to a question why the pension was not given when the German demands were liquidated: 'I am but a bad solicitor and believe it was my own fault. It came at last without any application, and [if] I thought I had not merited it I would not have taken it.'[11]

When in 1774 Cornwall was offered a place at the Treasury Board, Shelburne wrote to Chatham:[12]

Lord North . . . very frankly told Mr. Cornwall that he should not know how to turn himself if he refused it, and expressed himself in regard to Mr. Cornwall's principles and future conduct . . . in a very open liberal manner. Mr. Cornwall, however, remains truly undetermined. He has, I believe, mentioned it only to

Mr. Dunning, Colonel Barré, myself, and his brother-in-law, Mr. Jenkinson, who was totally ignorant of it; but I should imagine it will end in his acceptance; from the distracted, unexplained state of Opposition, as well as the several motives I had the honour of discussing with your Lordship in the summer.

What these were is not known, but there were political reasons which urged Cornwall to join Administration. He had no sympathy with the Opposition policy towards America. 'We ill hold the title of mother country', he said, 19 Apr. 1774,[13] 'if we are to do what America says we must do, or desist from doing what America says we must not do.'

He frequently defended North's American policy, but seems to have had doubts about the conduct of the war; and was much shaken by the news of Burgoyne's capitulation. On 29 Dec. 1777 he wrote about North to Jenkinson:[14] 'I am so much out of humour with his conduct, and see so little chance of things turning out tolerably well, that I endeavour to think as little as I can on the subject of America.' Jenkinson and Cornwall were consulted by North when he framed his conciliatory plan, and Cornwall was strongly for it. 'The fairest and clearest exposition of the conciliatory proposition', he wrote to Jenkinson on 4 Jan. 1778,[15] 'seems to me to be the only measure which can ever be productive of a proper reunion between the two countries.'

Henceforth his interventions in debate were confined to Treasury business, and his sphere more like that of a higher civil servant than of a politician. And when in October 1780 Frederick Montagu refused North's offer of the Chair, Cornwall accepted it without demur. He was, wrote the King,[16] 'a very respectable person for the office of Speaker'. Walpole too spoke well of him:[17] 'Cornwall was a comely sensible man, decent in his manner and matter, but of no great vivacity'; and according to Wraxall[18] he 'possessed every physical quality requisite to ornament the place'. His early promise had never matured, and as Speaker he was undistinguished. He died 2 Jan. 1789.

[1] His name is often spelt Cornewall—he was a first cousin once removed of Velters Cornewall (q.v.)—but he himself spelt it as above. [2] Whately to Jenkinson, 11 July 1766, *Jenkinson Pprs.* ed. Jucker, 415. [3] Jenkinson to J. S. Mackenzie, 11 Sept. 1764, ibid. 330. [4] Add. 38206, ff. 90–91, docketed 'winter 1768', but probably written before April 1763. [5] Lansdowne mss. [6] Rockingham mss. [7] Sutherland, *E. I. Co. in 18th Cent. Politics*, 193–4. [8] Ibid. 235. [9] Cornwall to Jenkinson, 4 May 1773, Add. 38207, ff. 358–9. [10] Dowdeswell mss, William L. Clements Lib. [11] Brickdale's 'Debates'. [12] *Chatham Corresp.* iv. 326. [13] Brickdale's 'Debates'. [14] Add. 38470, f. 236. [15] Add. 38210, f. 121. [16] The King to North, 25 Oct. 1780, Fortescue, v. 143. [17] *Last Jnls.* i. 80. [18] *Mems.* i. 260.

J.B.

## CORNWALLIS, Charles, Visct. Brome (1738–1805).

EYE   25 Jan. 1760–23 June 1762

*b.* 31 Dec. 1738, 1st s. of Charles, 1st Earl Cornwallis, by Hon. Elizabeth Townshend, da. of Charles, 2nd Visct. Townshend. *educ.* Eton 1753–4; Clare, Camb. 1755; Turin military acad. *m.* 14 July 1768, Jemima, da. of James Jones, sis. of Arnoldus Skelton Jones (q.v.), 1s. 1da. *suc.* fa. 23 June 1762; *cr.* Mq. 8 Oct. 1792.

Ensign 1 Ft. Gds. 1756; capt. 85 Ft. 1759; lt.-col. 12 Ft. 1761; col. 1764; col. 33 Ft. 1766–*d.*; maj.-gen. 1775; lt.-gen. 1777; gen. 1793.

Ld. of the bedchamber July–Aug. 1765; chief justice in eyre south of Trent 1766–9; jt. vice-treasurer [I] 1769–70; constable of the Tower of London 1770–1784; served in America 1776–82; envoy to Prussia Aug.–Sept. 1785; gov. gen. of Bengal 1786–93; master gen. of the Ordnance 1795–1801; 1797 appointed gov. gen. of Bengal but did not go out; ld. lt. [I] 1798–1801; plenipotentiary at Amiens 1801–2; gov. gen. of Bengal 1805.

Most of the time Cornwallis was a Member of Parliament he spent on active service in Germany. As a peer he at first followed Pitt, and was one of the five peers who voted against the Declaratory Act. Although opposed to the American war he served in America, and it was his surrender at Yorktown in October 1781 which ended the war. He voted against Fox's East India bill and supported the younger Pitt.

He died 5 Oct. 1805.

J.B.

## CORNWALLIS, Hon. Edward (1713–76), of Essington, Herts.

EYE              9 Dec. 1743–Apr. 1749
WESTMINSTER   16 Jan. 1753–18 Mar. 1762

*b.* 22 Feb. 1713, 6th s. of Charles, 4th Baron Cornwallis by Lady Charlotte Butler, da. and h. of Richard, 1st Earl of Arran [I]. *educ.* Eton 1725–8. *m.* 17 Mar. 1753, Hon. Mary Townshend, da. of Charles, 2nd Visct. Townshend, *s.p.*

Ensign 1730, lt. 1731; capt. 8 Ft. 1734; maj. 20 Ft. 1742; lt.-col. 1745; col. 1749; col. 40 Ft. 1749–52; col. 24 Ft. 1752–*d.*; maj.-gen. 1757; lt.-gen. 1760.

Groom of the bedchamber 1747–63; gov. Nova Scotia 1749–52, Gibraltar 1762–*d.*

Returned unopposed for Westminster in 1753, Cornwallis had to face a contest at the general election of 1754 and claimed that Government should pay his expenses. 'His reasons', wrote John Roberts to Newcastle, 18 July 1754,[1] 'seem indeed well-founded, as Mr. Hardinge is elected at Eye in his room by Lord Cornwallis.' They were met from secret service money.[2]

Cornwallis was with Byng's fleet in the expedition against Minorca, May 1756, and with Hawke and Mordaunt on the expedition against Rochfort, 1757, and came in for a good deal of criticism on that occasion. When in 1761 Sir George Vandeput, who had contested Westminster in 1749, once more threatened an opposition, Cornwallis wrote to Newcastle, 7 Mar.:[3]

> Indeed, my Lord, if some care is not taken of Westminster there will be trouble. I before told your Grace of what Sir George Vandeput said . . . I hear today a Mr. Scot, a brewer in Westminster, intends to declare himself a candidate. I can only say I am ready to support or willingly decline. It is the Government's interest to support this election and they only can do it.

According to Lord Fitzmaurice, Cornwallis was 'supposed to be disliked at Westminster'.[4] But in the end he and Lord Pulteney were returned unopposed. Cornwallis vacated his seat on being appointed governor of Gibraltar.

Only one speech by him in Parliament is recorded: on 29 Jan. 1762, in a confused debate on a technical point about the papers concerning the German musters. 'Generals Cornwallis and Griffin both spoke . . . twenty others spoke . . . Each had his own scheme, which came to nothing by the immediate proposal of a fresh one.'[5]

Cornwallis apparently was no favourite with George III. When in November 1762 Sir Richard Lyttelton's place was wanted, the King, while protesting that his removal 'would be cruel and unjust', added: 'if some great government were to be vacant he might indeed step into that: Cornwallis may be removed, but I believe Mr. Fox will cry out for he has always been his friend.'[6] Cornwallis was not removed from his post at Gibraltar, but on 9 Sept. 1764 Horace Walpole reported to Lord Hertford: 'Mrs. Cornwallis has found that her husband has been dismissed from the bedchamber this twelvemonth with no notice; his appointments were even paid; but on this discovery they were stopped.' This is confirmed by a letter from George Grenville to Lord Townshend, a nephew of Mrs. Cornwallis, 4 July 1764: on inquiring he found that upon some arrangement made before he became first lord of the Treasury, Cornwallis was removed—'I own I do not perfectly understand upon what foundation'.[7]

Cornwallis died 14 Jan. 1776.

[1] Add. 32736, ff. 53–54. [2] Namier, *Structure*, 200, 202; Add. 33055, f. 152. [3] Add. 32919, f. 513. [4] Fitzmaurice to Bute, 15 Feb. 1761, Bute mss. [5] Harris's *'Debates'*. [6] Sedgwick, *Letters Geo. III to Bute*, 166. [7] Grenville letter bk.

L.B.N.

## CORNWALLIS, Hon. Henry (1740–61).

EYE    30 Mar.–Apr. 1761

*b.* 10 Sept. 1740, 2nd s. of Charles, 1st Earl Cornwallis, and bro. of Charles, Visct. Brome (q.v.). *educ.* Eton 1753–4. *unm.*

Ensign 1 Ft. Gds. 1755; capt. 13 Ft. 1758.

Elected while still under age at the general elec-

tion, 30 Mar. 1761, Cornwallis never took his seat: he died in April, on the road from Germany.

L.B.N.

## CORNWALLIS, Hon. William (1744–1819).

EYE            1768–Mar. 1774, 3 Apr. 1782–1784
PORTSMOUTH    1784–1790
EYE            1790–Jan. 1807

*b.* 20 Feb. 1744, 4th s. of Charles, 1st Earl Cornwallis, and bro. of Charles, Visct. Brome and Hon. Henry Cornwallis (qq.v.). *educ.* Eton 1753. *unm.* G.C.B. 2 Jan. 1815.

Entered R.N. 1755; capt. 1765; on active service in the West Indies and North American waters 1776–82; c.-in-c. East Indies 1788–94; r.-adm. 1793; v.-adm. 1794; adm. 1799.

Cornwallis was returned by his brother Lord Cornwallis for the family borough of Eye; voted with Opposition over Wilkes, 27 Jan. 1769; but after this appears on neither side for four years, being most of the time away on service. Over the royal marriage bill, March 1772, he was classed by Robinson as 'pro, absent'; and on the renewed motion about the Middlesex election, 26 Apr. 1773, voted with Administration. He vacated his seat in March 1774 for Lord Carmarthen (q.v.) who writes in his *Political Memoranda* (p. 2): 'Captain Cornwallis, who wished as much to quit as I did to enter the House of Commons . . .'

A pension to 'Captain Cornwallis' of £400 p.a. appears in Robinson's secret service accounts, 1779–1781.[1] In the absence of earlier accounts the date at which it started is uncertain, and so is its origin. Bishop Cornwallis wrote to William, 1 Apr. 1782:[2] 'My secretary received what was *due* to you last Christmas; and there is an end of *that* business'—which reads like a reference to that pension. It is no longer in the lists communicated to Rockingham and Shelburne. The bishop goes on to say: 'You will be Member for Eye in a few days . . . You are at present without any appointment, but entirely at *liberty in Parliament* and I have no doubt will be honourably taken care of, although some time may be required for it.' And Lord Cornwallis wrote to him when informing him of his election, never to look

> to my conduct in the political line, but act entirely for yourself, and consider yourself, as you really are, as independent as any Member in the House of Commons.[3]

William Cornwallis was at that time in the West Indies where he greatly distinguished himself in Rodney's victory of 12 Apr. He returned home in October 1782, and on 18 Feb. 1783 voted for Shelburne's peace preliminaries; was again absent on service while Fox's India bill was before the House; and adhered to Pitt after the dismissal of the Coalition—in a letter to him, 25 Apr. 1796,[4] Cornwallis refers to his 'anxiety in support' of Pitt when there was a majority against him in the Commons.

Lord Cornwallis wrote to Lt.-Col. Ross, 5 Apr. 1784: 'My brother was pressed by Lord Howe [first lord of the Admiralty] to stand for Portsmouth, where Government was in great danger of being beat, and it was thought that his name and character would be of great use. I was very unwilling to part with my brother from Eye'[5]—still, they agreed; William received most vigorous support from the Admiralty;[6] and in the end was returned without a poll. There is no record of his having spoken in the House.

Lord Cornwallis wrote to William from Calcutta, 10 Mar. 1789:[7]

> In regard to Portsmouth you must judge for yourself . . . but I own I should be very sorry that you should decline Parliament altogether. Eye is entirely at your service, and need be no restraint upon you in point of attendance, or any other consideration.

But after William's election in 1802, he wrote to Ross, 13 July:[8]

> The Admiral got very drunk at the election, and the next day insisted upon my steward's taking £500 towards defraying the expenses. Without having given a vote in the House of Commons for many years past, and perhaps never intending to give one again, no youth of one-and-twenty was ever more pleased at coming into Parliament. What unaccountable creatures we are!

William Cornwallis died 5 July 1819.

[1] Royal archives, Windsor. [2] *HMC Var.* vi. 329. [3] Ibid. 333. [4] Chatham mss. [5] *Cornwallis Corresp.* i. 171-2. [6] Howe to Wm. Cornwallis, 31 Mar. 1784, *HMC Var.* vi. 339. [7] Ibid. 343. [8] *Cornwallis Corresp.* iii. 492.

L.B.N.

## COTES, John (?1750–1821), of Woodcote, Salop.

WIGAN                 7 Sept. 1782–1802
SHROPSHIRE            1806–24 Aug. 1821

*b.* ?1750, 1st s. of Rev. Shirley Cotes by Elizabeth, da. of Francis Chambre of Petton, Salop; nephew of Thomas Cotes (q.v.). *educ.* Eton 1759–67; Magdalen, Oxf. 26 Oct. 1767, aged 17; M. Temple 1770. *m.* 19 Oct. 1777, Hon. Lucy Courtenay (*d.*Dec. 1786), da. of William, 1st Visct. Courtenay (q.v.), 2da.; (2) 20 May 1794, Lady Maria Grey, da. of George, 5th Earl of Stamford (q.v.), 2s. 5da. *suc.* fa. 1775.

In 1782 and 1784 Cotes was returned unopposed on the Portland interest at Wigan. He voted with Opposition till Portland went over to Pitt in 1794. There is no record of his having spoken in the House before 1790.

He died 24 Aug. 1821.

M.M.D.

## COTES, Thomas (1712–67), of Woodcote, Salop.

GREAT BEDWYN    1761–16 July 1767

*b.* 4 June 1712, 4th s. of John Cotes of Woodcote by Lady Dorothy Shirley, da. of Robert, 1st Earl Ferrers. Humphry Cotes, the friend of Wilkes, was his yr. bro.; John Cotes (q.v.) his nephew. *m.* (1) Mary (*d.*1 Apr. 1754), wid. of N. Kendal of Pelyn, Cornw.; (2) Miss Ryder (apparently of the Ryders of Sandon),[1] *s.p. suc.* bro. 1766.

Lt. R.N. 1734; capt. 1740; r.-adm. 1755; v.-adm. 1758.

Cotes was returned for Great Bedwyn after a contest, on Lord Bruce's interest. He was then commander-in-chief in the West Indies, and probably did not return to England until after peace was declared. His only recorded vote was for the reduction of the land tax; and he seems in general to have supported all administrations. He died 16 July 1767.

[1] Nathaniel Ryder's diary, 13 Feb. 1767, Harrowby mss.

J.B.

## COTSFORD, Edward (1740–1810), of Winslade House, Clyst St. Mary, Devon.

MIDHURST    21 June 1784–1790

*b.* 6 Mar. 1740, s. of William Cotsford of Marylebone, London. *m.* 31 Oct. 1787, Lydia, da. of Rev. Henry Manning of Stoke, Devon, *s.p.* Sheriff, Devon 1792–3.

Cotsford was appointed a writer in the East India Company in 1757, and joined the Madras Engineers in 1758. He served in the Manila campaign of 1762, and in 1768 was appointed resident at Ganjam. He then transferred to the Company's civil service, and became a member of the council of Madras, and chief at Masulipatam. He wrote from Madras to Robert Palk (q.v.), 17 Oct. 1778:[1]

> If the state of things should put it in your power to serve me towards my promotion in this country, your assistance will always be very gratefully acknowledged by me. My presumption grows in seeing the small abilities of the present governor and council.

In 1781, however, he returned home, with a 'considerable fortune',[2] and though his name was apparently considered for the governorship of Madras,[3] he was not given further employment.

In November 1783 he received an increase to his fortune on the death of his mother,[4] and in December unsuccessfully contested Hindon. He came forward once more at the general election and was again defeated; but was returned at a by-election for Midhurst. He steadily voted against Pitt. There is no record of his having spoken in the House.

Cotsford died 25 May 1810.

[1] *HMC Palk*, 323. [2] Add. 19242, f. 191. [3] *Hickey's Bengal Gazette*, 24 June 1780. [4] *Gent. Mag.* 1783, p. 982.

J.A.C.

**COTTON, Sir John Hynde,** 4th Bt. (?1717–95), of Madingley Hall, Cambs.

| | |
|---|---|
| ST. GERMANS | 1741–1747 |
| MARLBOROUGH | 18 Feb. 1752–1761 |
| CAMBRIDGESHIRE | 22 Mar. 1764–1780 |

*b.* ?1717, o. surv. s. of Sir John Hynde Cotton, 3rd Bt., M.P., by Lettice, da. of Sir Ambrose Crowley, M.P., ironmaster. *educ.* Westminster Sept. 1727, aged 10; Emmanuel, Camb. 1736. *m.* 1 July 1745, his cos. Anne, da. and coh. of Humphrey Parsons, M.P., a London brewer, 6s. 3da. *suc.* fa. 4 Feb. 1752.

The Cottons of Madingley were an old-established and influential Cambridgeshire family with a long parliamentary tradition. Cotton's grandfather had represented Cambridge, and his father, one of the leading Tories in the House of Commons, both the borough and the county. The family had also for several generations married into City families, and Cotton himself, through his wife, inherited a share in the Red Lion brewery, Stepney, which after the death of his mother-in-law in 1759 he carried on for several years, continuing at the same time to play an active part in Cambridgeshire affairs.

Cotton was returned by Lord Bruce for Marlborough in place of his father. In Dupplin's list of 1754 he was classed as a Tory. No vote or speech by him is reported during this Parliament. In 1761 Bruce required both seats at Marlborough for members of his own family, and Cotton did not stand elsewhere. When in 1764 a seat for Cambridgeshire became vacant on Royston's succeeding as second Lord Hardwicke, Cotton was accepted as a compromise candidate by the Dukes of Rutland and Bedford and by Hardwicke, and was returned unopposed. He was classed by Rockingham in July 1765 as 'contra'; voted against the repeal of the Stamp Act, 22 Feb. 1766, and in November 1766 was counted by Rockingham as 'Tory'. Townshend's list of January 1767 puts him as a follower of Bedford. On 17 Apr. 1767 Bedford wrote that he had 'reason to be contented' with Cotton's political conduct, and assured him of 'steady adherence to his interest, on account of his steady conduct in Parliament'.[1] Cotton himself expressed 'his great regard and attachment'[2] for Bedford, but voted with the Opposition on nullum tempus, 17 Feb. 1768.

Before the general election of 1768 Soame Jenyns (q.v.) wrote to Hardwicke that Charles Yorke had proposed both Lord Granby and Cotton, 'to prevent drawing any party line between them . . . and take all nomination out of the hands of the Tories. Sir John was very desirous that it should be so, though I believe most of his old friends much disliked it, and were not a little disappointed.'[3] Cotton voted regularly with Administration, except on Grenville's Election Act, 25 Feb. 1774, when he is marked in the King's list as a dissenting friend. On 28 July 1774, Cotton, asking Hardwicke for his support at the general election, added: 'I have so great obligations to your Lordship that whenever your nephew Mr. Yorke is of age to take my seat in the county and your Lordship requires it, I shall most readily resign it to him.'[4] He subsequently declared that he had found it 'rather disagreable' to stand again, but had done so to preserve the peace of the county.[5] Meantime his health deteriorated, and in August 1777 he was reported to be seriously ill.[6] On 14 Nov. 1777, still in poor health and beset by financial worries, he wrote to ask Hardwicke to obtain for him 'something from Administration' when he resigned his seat, of which, he wrote,[7]

> I have been for some time most heartily tired, my circumstances not affording me to attend the duty in a manner agreable to me, and am indeed by this asthmatic cough which has now hung upon me many months at present not able . . . Worn out Members of Parliament . . . have been often indulged with the commissions in the excise or customs, and as my daughters have been for some years their whole time in the country, I should have no objection to change the scene as it might be an advantage to them.

On 10 Mar. 1779 he wrote to Hardwicke that he would vacate his seat whenever required, adding: 'When I am divested of it I have not lost the thoughts of making or rather renewing my application for something for myself . . . I flatter myself my conduct in Parliament deserves it, as well as many others who have gone before me.'[8] On 4 Nov. he told Hardwicke he was 'much like the nation, pretty near a conclusion'—

> He has been strongly solicited by more than one in Administration to come up to the meeting of Parliament but has wrote his inability to attend his duty there . . . he is in great dread this session of a fen bill which will not suit his heavy breath in a close committee room, however his constituents must now be contented with his former services as they can have no more from him.[9]

Cotton's only recorded vote during the remainder of the Parliament was with Administration on the motion for an account of pensions, 21 Feb. 1780. Early in 1780 a county meeting was called to consider a petition to the House for economical and parliamentary reform. Cotton and his fellow Member, Sir Sampson Gideon, attended, but since neither was enthusiastic, the meeting voted that Crisp Molineux, M.P. for King's Lynn, should present the county petition to Parliament.[10] On 6 Apr. 1780 Cotton, in his only reported speech 1754–80, declared that the meeting had been 'composed of market-folks, the townsmen, and the rabble of Cambridge', and 'could never be construed as conveying the sense of the county'.[11] After Cotton's retirement from Parliament, Hardwicke again wrote to North on his behalf, who replied on 7 July 1781:[12]

> There is no man living who I wish more to serve than Sir John Hynde Cotton. His worth, his amiable character, his long and honourable attachment to Government all speak in his favour, and are very materially supported by your Lordship's recommendation; the only thing against him has been the want of a favourable opportunity for assisting him, and the burthens under which the civil list has lately laboured: I will endeavour, however, to find out such some [sic] arrangement for him.

It is not known if any arrangement was made. Cotton in his letters to Hardwicke and Philip Yorke constantly referred to his very retired life, and on 14 Apr. 1784 he wrote to Hardwicke that in his life there had been 'incidents some that might, and many others that could not have been prevented which makes the evening of my life not to be envied'.[13]

He died 23 Jan. 1795.

[1] Bedford to Granby, Bedford mss 55, f. 72. [2] Lord Sandwich to Robert Palmer (Bedford's estate agent), 4 Nov. 1767, Bedford mss 56, f. 182. [3] 26 Sept. 1767, Add. 35631, f. 76. [4] Add. 35680, f. 343. [5] Add. 35681, f. 101. [6] Add. 35631, f. 162. [7] Add. 35681, f. 101. [8] Add. 35681, f. 130. [9] Ibid. f. 161. [10] Add. 35626, f. 130. [11] Almon, xvii, 445. [12] Add. 35424, ff. 31–32. [13] Add. 35682, f. 155.

M.M.D.

**COTTON, Sir Lynch Salusbury,** 4th Bt. (1705–1775), of Llewenny, Denb. and Combermere, Cheshire.

DENBIGHSHIRE 5 Dec. 1749–1774

*b.* 1705, 2nd s. of Sir Thomas Cotton, 2nd Bt., by Philadelphia, da. of Sir Thomas Lynch of Esher, Surr. *m.* Elizabeth, da. of Sir Rowland Cotton of Etwall, Derbys., 3s. *suc.* bro. as 4th Bt. 27 Aug. 1748.
Receiver of the land tax in N. Wales and Cheshire 1742–75.

By a compromise with Richard Myddelton of Chirk Castle, Cotton was returned unopposed for Denbighshire, while Myddelton represented the borough. Newcastle's 'Present State of Elections for England and Wales',[1] drawn up about the end of March 1754, marks against Denbighshire and its Members: 'County and town settled by agreement between them'. And this was continued in 1761 and 1768, preserving the peace of the county and the pockets of its two representatives.

Here is the description which Cotton's niece, Mrs. Thrale, gives of him in *Thraliana* (pp. 103–4):

> Sir Lynch Cotton . . . was an odd man as I have seen; impudent yet bashful, full of rusticity which offended, but had humour to divert one, he would say things nobody else thought on, and would be merry about his own fortune, his own children, and his own vices, with a sort of steady insensibility, that looked like archness.

He was harsh to his children; made one of his sons do his office business in North Wales, and gave him nothing for it; and was altogether miserly. After Cotton's return in 1768 Roger Kenyon wrote on 26 Apr. that his 'whole expense . . . amounted not to ten pounds, five of which was squeezed out of him, with prodigious reluctance, towards a ball for the Denbigh ladies'.[2] Johnson described him as 'gross'.[3]

In Bute's list Cotton is marked as 'Tory'; by Jenkinson in the autumn of 1763 as 'pro'. He voted with Administration on general warrants, 6 Feb. 1764, and was classed by Rockingham in July 1765 as 'doubtful'; he appears in Meredith's list as having voted with the Opposition in the second division on the repeal of the Stamp Act, 22 Feb. 1766, but not in the printed list. Rockingham in November 1766 classed him as 'Swiss'; he appears in two out of the three extant division lists on the land tax, 27 Feb. 1767, as voting with the Opposition. In 1774 he voluntarily withdrew from the representation of Denbighshire in favour of Sir Watkin Williams Wynn, 4th Bt., who had meantime come of age. There is no record of his having spoken in the House.

He died 14 Aug. 1775.

[1] Add. 32995, f. 82. [2] *HMC Kenyon*, 500. [3] *Tour in Wales*, ed. Broadley, 227.

L.B.N.

**COTTON, Sir Robert Salusbury,** 5th Bt. (c.1739–1809), of Combermere, Cheshire.

CHESHIRE 1 Mar. 1780–1796

*b.* c.1739, 1st s. of Sir Lynch Salusbury Cotton, 4th Bt. (q.v.). *educ.* Westminster; Trinity Hall, Camb. 1756. *m.* 1767, Frances, da. and coh. of James Russel Stapleton of Bodrhyddan, Flints., 4s. 4da. *suc.* fa. 14 Aug. 1775.

In March 1780, at the general election in September 1780, and again in 1784, Cotton was returned unopposed for Cheshire. He voted regularly with Opposition till the fall of North; for Shelburne's peace preliminaries, 18 Feb. 1783; for parliamentary reform, 7 May 1783; and against Fox's East India bill, 27 Nov. 1783. Robinson wrote of Cotton in his electoral survey of December 1783: 'might perhaps without reckoning too much be classed pro'.[1] In January 1784, when Pitt was rallying the country gentlemen, R. P. Arden (q.v.) wrote to Lloyd Kenyon (q.v.): 'Sir Robert Cotton has written a letter to Pitt, which does him much honour, in my opinion, and will certainly be here [for the debate of 20 Jan.]';[2] and in Robinson's list of January 1784 he was classed as 'pro'. Cotton was a member of the St. Alban's Tavern group, January 1784. He was classed in Stockdale's list, 19 Mar. 1784, and in Adam's, May 1784, as 'Administration', and supported Pitt till he left Parliament. There is no record of his having spoken in the House.

He died 24 Aug. 1809.

[1] Laprade, 66. [2] *HMC Kenyon*, 517.

M.M.D.

## COURTENAY, Henry Reginald (1714–63), of Aldershot, Hants.

HONITON  1741–1747, 1754–30 Apr. 1763

*b.* 8 June 1714, 4th s. of Sir William Courtenay, 2nd Bt., M.P., and bro. of Sir William Courtenay, 3rd Bt. (q.v.) *educ.* Westminster 1725; Magdalen, Oxf. 1731. *m.* 14 Apr. 1737, Hon. Catherine Bathurst, da. of Allen, 1st Baron Bathurst, 2s. 2da.

Courtenay was defeated at Honiton in 1747 and returned after a contest in 1754. He was invariably counted as a Tory. In Bute's list of December 1761 he is classed 'Tory—Bute'. But he does not appear in Fox's list of Members favourable to the peace preliminaries, December 1762, which must not, however, be taken to suggest that he was against them.

He died 30 Apr. 1763.

L.B.N.

## COURTENAY, John (1738–1816).[1]

TAMWORTH  1780–1796
APPLEBY  1796–1807, 9 Oct.–Dec. 1812

*b.* 22 Aug. 1738, 2nd s. of Henry Courtenay, a revenue officer in Ireland, by Mary, da. of Rev. William Major, prebendary of Ballymore, Armagh. *educ.* Dundalk g.s. *m.* c.1765, 2s. 5da.
Ensign 29 Ft. 1756, lt. 1759; sold out 1765.
Commissary of the musters [I] 1765–9; barrack master of Kinsale 1772; first sec. to the master gen. of the Ordnance 1773–82; surveyor gen. of the Ordnance Apr.–Dec. 1783; ld. of Treasury 1806–7.

In 1765, after selling his army commission, Courtenay purchased an appointment as one of the six commissaries of musters in Ireland. But in 1769, in order to pay increasing debts, he sold his office, and began writing for the *Batchelor*, a pro-Castle Administration journal. This brought him to the notice of Lord Townshend, the lord lieutenant, who obtained for him the sinecure place of barrack master of Kinsale, and when Townshend returned to England to become master general of the Ordnance, Courtenay accompanied him as his secretary.

In London Courtenay, who in 1773 published *The Rape of Poloma*, an elegiac poem, was introduced to the literary group frequented by Johnson and Boswell. He became a close friend and adviser of Boswell, who admired his work and found 'his conversation . . . excellent; it has so much litera-

ture, wit, and at the same time manly sense in it', and years later wrote of him as 'a friend to whom I have been much obliged'.[2]

At the general election of 1780 Courtenay was returned free of expense for a seat at Tamworth which Townshend had sold to Administration. 'Mr. Courtenay' wrote North in 1782, 'returned this favour to Government by supporting them always with great abilities and zeal'[3]—though from an unorthodox and highly personal viewpoint. He 'never was, nor never would be an advocate for the justice, wisdom, and expediency of the American war',[4] but the American alliance with France had convinced him of the necessity for its vigorous prosecution, and he urged this in the House on several occasions. Yet, he said, 28 Nov. 1781:[5]

> If there was a hope, a gleam of hope, that by acknowledging the independence of America, she could be detached from France, it would demand the serious attention of the House whether such terms should not be granted . . . great commercial and national advantages would be derived from a union between people naturally connected by the same language, manners, and religion . . . great and essential benefits might be mutually received by both countries connected by a federal union and Britain on such a liberal and enlarged system of policy might again become a great and flourishing nation.

In the House Courtenay was a frequent speaker, witty, and uninhibited. Wraxall writes[6] that he

> possessed a very uncommon and eccentric species of humour, original, classic, even Attic, allied to, and sustained by learning, inexhaustible and often irresistible, in its effects on the muscles, but always coarse, frequently licentious, or at least indecorous, and rarely under a becoming restraint. His wit seemed indeed more adapted to a tavern or to a convivial board than to the grave deliberations of such an assembly as the House of Commons.

He attacked the Opposition scathingly: during the debate of 26 Feb. 1781 on the bill for regulating the civil list revenue he ridiculed their proposals and threw doubts on their motives.[7] Horace Walpole writes that in reply Sheridan 'demolished Courtenay who old George Cavendish said well, is deputy buffoon to Lord North'.[8] Courtenay was undeterred —on a subsequent occasion he told the House that 'neither his temper, disposition, nor country inclined him to be intimidated, embarrassed or easily put out of countenance',[9] and on 8 May 1781, expressing his strong disapprobation of Sir George Savile's motion for diminishing the influence of the Crown, he said ironically that 'as the dangerous influence of the Crown would be increased by our victories, and diminished by our defeats, it was perfectly consistent . . . to hope for the improvement of the constitution, and the extinction of corruption by the ruin of the Empire'. Another example of

Courtenay's 'usual quaint style of serious ridicule and solemn jesting' was his speech of 31 May 1781 on Lord Beauchamp's bill to amend the Marriage Act, when he attacked the principle and tendency of the Act while elaborately pretending to defend it: 'the framers of the act . . . wisely threw as many obstacles as possible in the way of matrimony, and considering the miseries usually attending wedlock, the obvious purport of the act was judicious, salutary, and laudable'.[10]

Courtenay remained loyal to North till the end, and on 20 Mar. 1782, while the House was in an uproar, with the Opposition clamouring for the removal of ministers, he obstinately persevered in delivering a warm tribute to North, acknowledging[11]

the unfeigned respect he should ever bear for him . . . He could not form a more sanguine wish for the happiness of his country, than that in this day of difficulty, in this hour of calamity and distress, an Administration might be formed, as able and disinterested, as upright in their intention but more fortunate in the event than the noble Lord's.

After North's resignation he became an ally of Fox, with whom he had been on friendly terms for some time. He strongly disliked and distrusted Shelburne; in July 1782 rejected his suggestion for a meeting;[12] on 11 Dec. 1782 referred to his 'glorious, profitable, talent . . . so to contrive his measures as to make them palatable to all, his language was at all times such that he could explain it either this way or that way, and that every other man might do so too',[13] and subsequently to his 'specious, promising, deluding, janus-faced Administration'.[14] Courtenay did not vote for Pitt's proposals for parliamentary reform, 7 May 1783, though he had spoken in favour of reform on 7 May 1782, nor did he vote for it on 18 Apr. 1785.

He supported the Coalition, and after its dismissal was one of Pitt's most vigorous opponents. On 4 Aug. 1784, declaring that 'the public had very foolishly idolized' Pitt, he said he 'was determined in the most rapid possible manner to undeceive them';[15] and during the next few years harassed Pitt on numerous topics, particularly those concerning finance and the Ordnance. Drawing on his own experience in office, he discussed Ordnance affairs in minute detail, staunchly defended the measures of his former chief, Lord Townshend, while subjecting those of his successor, the Duke of Richmond, to vigorous criticism, repeatedly condemning his fortifications plans. Eventually, on 21 Apr. 1790, he moved for a committee to inquire into and report the expenditure of the money for the past four years, since 'every estimate presented by the noble Duke had . . . been false and fallacious'.[16] Though

Courtenay's caustic humour frequently 'kept the House in a roar of laughter'[17] he continually gave great offence, and on 9 May 1787, during a debate on the prosecution of Hastings, excelled himself in a speech which, writes Wraxall,[18]

as far as my parliamentary experience warrants me in asserting, stands alone in the annals of the House of Commons, exhibiting a violation of every form or principle which has been held sacred within these walls.

In it Courtenay referred to Hood (one of Hastings's defenders) as a 'spectator of the victorious feats of the brave Lord Rodney'; went on to lampoon Wilkes in forthright terms, and concluded with a hint that the King had taken bribes from Hastings. Though he retracted his words about Hood, Members were not satisfied, and on 14 May Pitt demanded a formal apology, pointing out that

those who knew the honourable gentleman would know that it was no very extraordinary supposition to be entertained that this explanation though it might appear an apology, might in fact be meant rather as an aggravation than an extenuation of the injury.[19]

Courtenay refused to be drawn that day, but on the next again averred that his words had been misunderstood, and concluded that Pitt

had said that it was hard to know when he was serious or ironical . . . lest the chancellor of the Exchequer should be at a loss for the future . . . Mr. Courtenay begged leave to assure him, whenever he paid him any compliments personally or politically, the right honourable gentleman might be persuaded that he was ironical.[20]

When, later in 1787, Courtenay's old friend and patron, Lord Townshend, went over to Pitt, Courtenay remained in opposition. By this time his financial position, never very sound, was seriously embarrassed. Boswell noted in his journal on 23 Feb. 1788 that Courtenay had lately told him 'that all that remained to him was an annuity of £40 a year which he was going to sell. I calculated it would yield him £240. It was wonderful to see with what spirit and serenity he lived with a wife and seven children, knowing his situation.'[21] 'He was in truth of the school of Diogenes' writes Wraxall,

I never remember a more complete cynic in his dress, manners, and general deportment, all which bespeak that inattention to external appearances or forms characteristic of the philosopher of Sinope. But under this neglected exterior lay concealed a classic mind, an understanding highly cultivated and a vast variety of information, and a vigorous intellect . . . Like Diogenes he was poor, but of a high and independent character, that seemed to despise wealth.[22]

He died 24 Mar. 1816.

[1] See J. Courtenay, *Incidental Anecs. & a Biog. Sketch* (1809). [2] *Boswell Pprs.* (Isham), xvii. 86; xviii. 171. [3] Fortescue. v. 466.

⁴ Debrett, ii. 36. ⁵ Ibid. v. 62–63. ⁶ *Mems.* ii. 85. ⁷ Ibid. ii. 36,
⁸ Walpole to Mason, 3 Mar. 1781. ⁹ Debrett, vi. 507–9. ¹⁰ Ibid. iii.
227–31, 337–9, 451. ¹¹ Ibid. vi. 507–9. ¹² To Shelburne, 25 July,
Lansdowne mss. ¹³ Debrett, ix. 83–84. ¹⁴ 4 July 1783, ibid. x. 276.
¹⁵ Ibid. xvi. 340. ¹⁶ Stockdale, xix. 256. ¹⁷ Debrect. vii. 135. ¹⁸ *Mems.*
v. 5. ¹⁹ Debrett, xxii. 341. ²⁰ Ibid. 353–5. ²¹ *Boswell Pprs.* xvii. 71.
²² *Mems.* iii. 453.

M.M.D.

## COURTENAY, Sir William, 3rd Bt. (1710–62), of Powderham Castle, Devon.

HONITON    1734–1741
DEVON      1741–6 May 1762

*b.* 11 Feb. 1710, 1st surv. s. of Sir William Courtenay, 2nd Bt., M.P. for Devon, by Lady Anne Bertie, da. of James, 1st Earl of Abingdon. *educ.* Westminster 1722; Magdalen, Oxf. 1729. *m.* 2 Apr. 1741, Lady Frances Finch, da. of Heneage, 2nd Earl of Aylesford, 1s. 5da. *suc.* fa. 1735; *cr.* Visct. Courtenay 6 May 1762.

Courtenay was a Tory. He appears in Newcastle's list of 1761 as 'against', but is not classed in Bute's list of December 1761—he was about to be created a peer.¹ He apparently owed his peerage to Bute who therefore could press him, against Courtenay's own inclination, to give his interest at the ensuing by-election for Devon to John Parker (q.v.).²

Courtenay died 16 May 1762.

¹ Jas. Buller to Bute, 20 Nov. 1761, Bute mss. ² Bute to Shelburne, 28 Apr. 1762, Lansdowne mss.

L.B.N.

## COURTOWN, Earl of, *see* STOPFORD, James

## COUTTS, James (1733–78), of Hampton, Mdx. and Whitsome Hill, Berwicks.

EDINBURGH   27 Feb. 1762–1768

*b.* 10 Mar. 1733, 3rd s. of John Coutts, merchant and banker of Edinburgh, by Jean, da. of Sir John Stuart, 2nd Bt., of Allanbank, Berwicks. *educ.* Edinburgh h.s. *m.* Apr. 1755, Mary, da. of John Peagrim or Peagrum of Elmstead, nr. Colchester, niece and h. of George Campbell, London banker, 1 surv. da.

When John Coutts, 'Patriot' lord provost of Edinburgh 1742–44, died in 1750, his four sons continued his banking and corn business; and in 1752 opened a London office under Patrick and Thomas, the eldest and youngest brothers, while John and James remained in Edinburgh. According to Sir William Forbes, an apprentice in the Edinburgh firm, James Coutts gave 'close application to business', but was not of an altogether amiable character: unpolished in manners, passionate, and resentful.¹ And in 1762 he himself wrote to David Hume:²

> With all pleasures there are great mixtures of mortification and every instant my limited education stares me more and more in the face. I have hardly looked on any but manuscript folios since I was 14. You'll say from idleness or want of taste. I say no, but from too much business and bad health. My constitution will

probably be always unfit for deep study; but pray is there no remedying this great defect a little without much study? . . . seriously I wish you would give me some advice on this head, what abridgements to read, etc.

On his marriage James Coutts was taken into partnership by George Campbell, head of the 'Whig' bank in the Strand (whose customers included Lord Bute); and on Campbell's death in 1761, James took into partnership his brother Thomas. The same year Patrick became insane, John died, and the Edinburgh and London branches of the old family business were reorganized, under, among others, John Hunter Blair and Robert Herries (qq.v.), and Sir William Forbes.

Bute, as privy purse to George III, placed the royal account at Coutts's bank. In the very profitable loan of 1762–3 Coutts received an allotment of £76,000,³ and Bute's patronage secured his return for Edinburgh. At first he 'dipped little into politics'; but, a devoted supporter of Bute, he thought the peace 'good and honourable';⁴ and on 5 Feb. 1763 he offered Bute advice on financial policy;⁵ and was distressed by his resignation.

That same year he was involved in a violent dispute which had arisen in Edinburgh over the council's claim to 'present' ministers to city churches.⁶ To William Mure's proposal that he should visit Edinburgh and influence the council elections he replied, 9 Aug. 1763:⁷

> My affairs will require my closest attention till the sitting of Parliament, when the burden must again fall chiefly on my brother . . . Indeed independent of this it would be very improper for me to visit Edinburgh on any political errand without being desired by my Lord Bute or Mr. Mackenzie . . . and I am determined on no consideration to think of it otherwise . . . I do not believe there can be the least occasion for my presence . . . I know my own little consequence in politics, but if my not asking anything for myself, a considerable necessary expense by my being in Parliament, and a very great avocation [sic] from business, can plead anything in my friends' favour, they ought in this case.

In the end Coutts reluctantly agreed to the demand of Mure and Lord Milton that he should 'lay his commands' on his business associates, Forbes and Hunter Blair, to accept nomination for the council, but on 9 Sept. confided to Mure, his 'father confessor in politics':⁸

> Notwithstanding I was so much obliged to Mr. Mackenzie for bringing me into Parliament, I do not think . . . that he has that opinion and confidence in me he ought . . . I have sometimes thought that his prejudices against, or want of attention to me . . . have arisen from some insidious suggestions of Lord Milton; as, though his Lordship expressed a very strong regard for me at my being proposed Member by my Lord Bute, he has constantly since behaved in a very different manner.

Coutts supported the Grenville Administration on Wilkes and general warrants. On 8 Mar. 1764 he spoke for the motion to limit parliamentary privilege by making merchant M.P.s liable to bankruptcy proceedings;[9] and on 19 Mar. on a motion to regulate Scottish banks he opposed any immediate change in the 'optional clause' in Scottish bank notes. But his language in the House was sometimes 'strange and incoherent',[10] and so occasionally was his behaviour.[11] His friends sent him an anonymous letter, whose draft is preserved in Caleb Whitefoord's papers:[12]

> I am going to offer you my advice on a delicate point, I mean speaking in the House . . . It was with great concern that I saw you rise up to speak several times during the last session—the first time you spoke it was in some degree necessary—Would to Heaven you had stopped there, for indeed my dear Sir you are by no means qualified for speaking . . . If you regard your own peace and quiet, if you regard your political interest, if you regard the opinion of many eminent and worthy persons you will give up all thought of speaking in the House . . . The fair character you bore with everybody and your very becoming deportment in business and in every other situation of life made me feel the most sensible concern to see you appear so unlike yourself.

Coutts continued to attend the House and its committees, but there is no record of any further speech by him. Listed 'pro, doubtful' by Rockingham in July 1765, he voted with Administration in the division on America, 7 Feb. 1766, but against the repeal of the Stamp Act, 22 Feb. He voted with Chatham's Administration on the land tax, 27 Feb. 1767, and on nullum tempus, 17 Feb. 1768.

Coutts consistently declined to allow political interest to influence his recommendations of the best qualified candidates for appointments.[13] Disliking intrigue and local power politics, he would not direct the opinions and votes of his friends, even when they had been 'plotted into the council' to strengthen his party.[14] He proved no match for the unscrupulous intrigues of Sir Lawrence Dundas when he made his bid for Edinburgh. In the autumn of 1767 Coutts went there to canvass for his re-election, supported by his business associate, Hunter Blair, 'a useful partisan'. Thomas Coutts still thought that if only James's health was good, matters 'will go there as he would wish as he is very strongly supported by the Duke of Grafton'. But Dundas, having won over the trades representatives, secured a majority on the council, and Coutts withdrew.

Next, he thought of standing for Morpeth on Lord Carlisle's interest. Sir William Musgrave, who was fixing candidates with the Duke of Grafton, reported on 29 Oct. to Carlisle, then in Paris, that Coutts 'will certainly be one . . . there can be no other objection to him than his being a Scotsman'; and on 10 Nov. that his being 'known to be worth £100,000' will deter others from giving disturbance. But after arrangements had been made for starting the canvass, Coutts, in one of his fits of 'flighty humour', retracted 'his most solemn promises'. Musgrave, indignant at 'Coutts's duplicity, folly and absurdity', felt obliged 'to put an end to every transaction with him and desire the Duke of Grafton to recommend some other person'.[15]

This was also the end of Coutts's parliamentary career; and as his fits of madness became more frequent, his brother Thomas, in 1774, on the expiry of the 12 years' partnership agreement, took steps to protect the bank's credit from James's irresponsible actions. Bute, Stuart Mackenzie, Sir John Pringle (the physician), and family friends signed a declaration that James was 'an improper person to be connected with such a business'; terms of a financial settlement were imposed by Bute and Rochford as arbitrators; James protested bitterly but in June 1775 was forced to sever his connexion with the bank. 'Ashamed of being treated like a madman', he went abroad in July 1775.[16] Next he toured English watering places and Scotland; and in November 1776 set out on another tour of the continent. At Turin in 1777–8 he became so violent that he was confined under military guard[17] and sent home by sea in the charge of keepers; but he died at Gibraltar, 15 Feb. 1778.

[1] Forbes, *Mems. of a Banking House*, 11. [2] *Letters of D. Hume to Wm. Strahan*, ed. Hill, 93. [3] List in Bute mss. [4] Coutts to Mure, 12 Oct. 1762, Caldwell mss. [5] Bute mss. [6] Memorandum on Edinburgh city affairs, July 1763, prepared by Provost G. Drummond or James Coutts, *Caldwell Pprs.* ii (1), p. 182. [7] Caldwell mss. [8] *Caldwell Pprs.* ii (1), p. 192. [9] Harris's 'Debates'. [10] See the pamphlet, *The Earl of Dundonald's answer to the Misstatements contained in the life of Thomas Coutts*, 1822. [11] Harris's 'Debates'. [12] Add. 36595, f. 283. [13] Coutts to Mure, 17 Dec. 1764, *Caldwell Pprs.* ii (1), p. 278; and to Provost Stewart, 13 May 1766, *HMC Laing*, ii. 450. [14] Coutts to Mure, 17 Dec. 1764. [15] *HMC Carlisle*, 217, 220–1. [16] See J. Macdonald, *Mems. of an 18th Cent. Footman*. [17] For an account of his last years, see Add. 37848, ff. 9–48.

E.H.-G.

**COVENTRY, John Bulkeley** (1724–1801), of Nether Burgate, Fordingbridge, Hants.

WORCESTERSHIRE 10 Apr. 1751–1761

*b.* 21 Mar. 1724, 3rd s. of William, 5th Earl of Coventry, by Elizabeth, da. of John Allen of Westminster, *educ.* Winchester 1731–40; University Coll. Oxf. 1740. *unm. suc.* to Nether Burgate estate on d. of his cos. James Coventry Bulkeley c.1764, and took add. name of Bulkeley.

In 1751 Coventry was returned for Worcestershire in place of his brother who vacated his seat on succeeding as 6th Earl of Coventry. In Dupplin's list of 1754 he was classed as a country gentleman supporting Administration. Coventry did not stand again in 1761, nor does he appear to have attempted to re-enter Parliament.

He died 16 Mar. 1801.

M.M.D.

## COVENTRY, Thomas (c.1713–97), of North Cray Place, Bexley, Kent.

BRIDPORT 1754–1780

*b.* c.1713, 2nd s. of Thomas Coventry, Russia merchant (bro. of William, 5th Earl of Coventry), by Mary, da. and h. of John Green of Hambleton, Bucks. *educ.* Magdalen Hall, Oxf. 1728; I. Temple 1732, called 1735, bencher 1766, reader 1777, treasurer 1778. *m.* c.1743, Margaret, da. and coh. of Thomas Savage of Elmley Castle, Worcs., *s.p. suc.* to estate of his kinsman William Hetherington 1778.

Director, South Sea Co. 1751–68; dep. gov. 1768–1771; sub gov. 1771–94.

Thomas Coventry was left 'one shilling and no more' by his father, but seems to have inherited considerable property from his mother. During the time he sat in Parliament he was a wealthy man: his purchases of Government stock between 1760 and 1796 amounted to nearly £400,000, and he died possessed of stock to the value of £185,000. In 1764 he began to buy Bank of England stock and at his death held £25,000 worth—a large amount for a man who never served as a Bank director.[1]

In 1754 Coventry was returned unopposed on the interest of his cousin Lord Coventry, and in Dupplin's list was classed as a country gentleman supporting Administration. Returned after a contest in 1761, and classed 'Newcastle and Government' in Bute's list, his first recorded vote was to postpone consideration of the peace preliminaries, 1 Dec. 1762. He voted against them on 9 Dec. 1762, and with the Opposition over Wilkes, 15 Nov. 1763, and general warrants, 15 and 18 Feb. 1764. Both Jenkinson and Newcastle in 1764 counted him as a friend. In July 1765 Rockingham classed him as 'pro', yet he opposed the repeal of the Stamp Act, 22 Feb. 1766. He voted against Government on the land tax, 27 Feb. 1767. Henceforth, he voted regularly with the Opposition, although he had no strong ties with any party leader.

Charles Lamb, who as a child had known Coventry, described him as 'the scarecrow of his inferiors, the browbeater of equals and superiors', with 'a rough spinous humour'.[2] 'Thomas Coventry', he wrote, 'passed his youth in contracted circumstances, which gave him early those parsimonious habits which in after life never forsook him; so that, with one windfall or another, about the time I knew him he was master of four or five hundred thousand pounds . . . a hoarder rather than a miser . . . Coventry gave away £30,000 at once in his life time to a blind charity.'[3]

Lamb's description is borne out by Coventry's speeches in Parliament. On 17 Mar. 1756, in the debate on the plate tax, Coventry

advised the proposer of the tax to consult the Acts of the Apostles, where he would find that St. Paul, by opposing the craft of the silversmiths, raised a great cry amongst the mob, and would hardly have escaped them but for one or two powerful friends and the assistance of the town clerk.[4]

And on 28 Feb. 1780, on a bill for the relief of insolvent debtors, he declared:[5]

It desired an entire alteration of the laws of the land, and was of infinitely too important a nature to be agreed to; that he objected to both its principle and to its provisions. That men now went to jail on purpose to enjoy the luxuries of a prison. That the King's Bench was crowded . . . and that the proposal of allowing debtors 2s. 4d. a week was highly improper. A soldier had but 6d. a day for being shot at, and should a rascal who had cheated industrious tradesmen and perhaps ruined many persons, be allowed 4d.?

Coventry died 21 May 1797.

[1] Bank of England recs. [2] *Old Benchers of I. Temple.* [3] See also Boswell, *Johnson*, ii. 509. [4] Jas. West to Newcastle, 17 Mar. 1756, Add. 32863, f. 332. [5] Almon, xvii. 178.

M.M.D.

## COWPER, George Nassau Clavering, Visct. Fordwich (1738–89).

HERTFORD 13 Dec. 1759–1761

*b.* 26 Aug. 1738, 1st s. of William, 2nd Earl Cowper, by Henrietta, da. of Henry Nassau de Auverquerque, 1st Earl of Grantham. *m.* 2 June 1775, Hannah Anne, da. and coh. of Charles Gore of Hockstow, Lincs., 3s. *suc.* to estates of maternal gd.-fa. in 1754; and fa. as 3rd Earl Cowper 18 Sept. 1765; *cr.* a prince of the Holy Roman Empire by Emperor Joseph II, 1777.

Cowper, sent abroad for his education, was by October 1757 'weary of Lausanne and wanting to ramble'.[1] A year later he went on a tour,[2] arrived at Venice 21 June 1759,[3] and eventually at Florence, where he remained. Elected to Parliament *in absentia* he never took his seat. 'We have Lord Fordwich', wrote Horace Mann to Horace Walpole, 14 June 1760, 'losing his whole time by acting the *cicisbeo* to the Marchesa [Corsi], and entertaining all her dependants.' On the eve of the general election of 1761, 13 Feb., Dean Cowper wrote to Lord Cowper: 'I don't think but Lord Fordwich in spite of his perverse negligence is still safe in, Brassey's [q.v.] interest being so closely connected with yours . . .' He was not even declared a candidate. On 17 Oct. 1761 Mann wrote to Walpole:

Lord Fordwich, who disobliged his father and lost his seat in Parliament by only not fixing the time of his departure, seems resolved to return to England soon.

He did not—even the earnest entreaties of his dying father failed to get him back from Florence. Still, his absence abroad did not stop him from applying in 1765 for the Order of the Bath, and the lord lieutenancy of Kent;[4] and in 1768 for the Garter or the Thistle.[5] In 1780, having tried through the Grand Duke of Tuscany to influence the King of Spain in favour of a general peace, he asked George III once more for the Garter to 'alleviate the mortification I am under . . . in having failed in my enterprise'; and offered the King Raphael's self-portrait and his 'Madonna and Child' (sold in 1928 for £175,000) for £2,500.[6] In August 1782 he applied to be created a duke;[7] and having at last returned to England in 1786, 'a very great stranger . . . in his native land and to it',[8] he asked to be made British minister at Florence; went back without it; and died at Florence 22 Dec. 1789; but was buried at Hertingfordbury in Hertfordshire.

[1] Spencer Cowper, Dean of Durham, to Earl Cowper, 23 Oct. 1757, *Letters of Spencer Cowper*, ed. Hughes. [2] Ibid. [3] Lady Mary Wortley Montagu to Lady Bute, 24 June 1759. [4] See letters from the Duke of Grafton to Cowper, 30 Aug. and 20 Nov. 1765, Herts. RO. Cowper mss. [5] See ibid. letters from Bute, 27 May, and from Grafton, 12 Dec. 1768. [6] Fortescue, v. 50. [7] Cowper to Shelburne, 5 Aug. 1782, Lansdowne mss. [8] Frances Boscawen to Mrs. Delany, 27 May 1786, *Autobiog. and Corresp.* vi. 356.

L.B.N.

**COWPER, William** (1721–69), of Hertingfordbury Park, Herts.

Hertford 1768–27 Aug. 1769

*b.* 1721, 1st s. of William Cowper, clerk of the Parliaments, by Jane, da. of John Budget of Chelsea. *educ.* Westminster, Apr. 1730, aged 8, left 1737; Worcester, Oxf. 1 Mar. 1739, aged 17; L. Inn 1740. *m.* 5 Aug. 1749, his cos. Maria Frances Cecilia, da. of Col. Martin Madan, M.P., 4s. 2da. *suc.* fa. 14 Feb. 1740.

Cowper had a natural interest at Hertford where he was returned unopposed in 1768. In Parliament he voted with Administration on Wilkes's expulsion, 3 Feb. 1769, and the Middlesex election, 8 May. There is no record of his having spoken in the House. He died 27 Aug. 1769, aged 48.

M.M.D.

**COX, Laurence** (*d.*1792), of Woolcombe, Dorset.

Honiton 1774–1780
Bere Alston 14 Feb. 1781–1784

Cox, a London merchant, bought an estate near Dorchester, and in 1768 unsuccessfully contested the borough. He did not again attempt a Dorset constituency, but in 1774 stood for Honiton where he was a 'perfect stranger', and was returned after a contest said to have cost him £5,000.[1] In Parliament he at first voted regularly with Opposition, but Robinson listed him as 'pro, present, gained' over the contractors bill, 12 Feb. 1779; he voted with Administration on the demand for an account of pensions, 21 Feb. 1780, against them on the abolition of the Board of Trade, 13 Mar. 1780, and with them on the motion against prorogation, 24 Apr. 1780; and was classed by Robinson in his survey for the general election of 1780 as 'pro'. In 1780 he once more contested Honiton, but was defeated. On 6 Feb. 1781 Cox was given a contract for victualling 1,000 men in New York.[2] He was returned on the Duke of Northumberland's interest at Bere Alston a few days later, and supported North's Administration till its fall. In January 1782 he obtained a further contract for victualling 1,500 men in America.[3] He voted for Shelburne's peace preliminaries, 18 Feb. 1783; for Fox's East India bill, 27 Nov. 1783; but was classed as a supporter of Pitt by Robinson, January 1784, and by Stockdale, 19 Mar. Cox did not stand again in 1784. There is no record of his having spoken in the House.

He was knighted 6 Sept. 1786, and died 26 Aug. 1792.

[1] W. H. Wilkins, 'Notes on Members for Honiton, 1640–1868' (*Trans. Dev. Assoc.* lxvi. 265). [2] T54/43/314. [3] Ibid. 435.

M.M.D.

**COXE, Charles Westley** (?1754–1806), of Kemble, nr. Cirencester, Glos.

Cricklade 13 Apr. 1784–4 Apr. 1785

*b.* ?1754, o.s. of Charles Coxe of Kemble by Elizabeth, da. and coh. of Sir Robert Westley, ld. mayor of London 1744–5. *educ.* C.C.C. Oxf. 9 July 1771, aged 17. *m.* 10 Dec. 1789, Anne, da. of Robert Gordon of Auchendolly, Kircudbright, 1da.

In 1784 Coxe and his cousin Robert Adamson stood jointly as supporters of the Coalition for the enlarged constituency of Cricklade. They were returned, but unseated on petition. No vote or speech by Coxe in the House is recorded.

Coxe does not appear to have sought to re-enter Parliament. He died 10 Mar. 1806.

J.A.C.

**COXE, Richard Hippisley** (1742–86), of Ston Easton, Som.

Somerset 1768–1784

*b.* 22 Sept. 1742, 1st s. of John Hippisley Coxe of Ston Easton by Mary, da. of Stephen Northleigh of Peamore, Devon. *educ.* Westminster 1754–9; Ch. Ch. Oxf. 1759–63. *unm. suc.* fa. 29 May 1769.

In 1768 Coxe stood jointly for Somerset with Sir Charles Kemys Tynte (q.v.) against John Trevelyan (q.v.), who declined the poll. Coxe's share of the election expenses came to over £2,600.[1]

In Parliament Coxe voted with the Rockinghams, although Rockingham had opposed him at his election.[2] He was active in the House, especially during his earlier years. On 12 Feb. 1770, as one who 'desires the character of a plain, honest country gentleman', he seconded Dowdeswell's motion to disfranchise revenue officers: 'if . . . Charles I had Government boroughs, if he had the disposal of so many lucrative boards, he would have died with his head upon his shoulders'; and on 2 Mar. 1772 Coxe seconded Montagu's motion against the observance of 30 Jan. (when Walpole, *Last Jnls.* i. 39, described him as 'a young man of very quick parts'). On 7 Feb. 1771 and 27 Feb. 1772 he seconded Savile's motions on the rights of electors; on 7 Mar. 1771 he supported Dowdeswell's motion on the rights of juries: etc.[3] He spoke on 15 Feb. 1775 against the army estimates; and on 11 Mar. 1778, having just returned from France, he averred that war was imminent.[4] He was re-elected without a contest in 1774 and 1780. About 1780 his health began to fail, and he is not known to have voted in any division after that year; but he spoke on two occasions: 16 Apr. 1782, for Crewe's bill to disfranchise revenue officers, and on 12 June, on Mahon's motion about election expenses.[5] In 1783 he was thought to be dying; and he did not stand in 1784. He was 'found to be lunatic under a writ *de lunatico inquirendo*', and his brothers were put in charge of his person and estates by an order of the court of Chancery, 9 Dec. 1784.[6]

He died 26 Aug. 1786.

[1] Kemys Tynte mss, Taunton RO. [2] Rockingham to Newcastle, 30 Oct. 1767, Add. 32986, ff. 173–4. [3] Cavendish's 'Debates', Egerton 220, pp. 55–58; 234, pp. 216–17; 224, p. 108; 225, pp. 420–2. [4] Stockdale, viii. 123. [5] Debrett, vii, 51, 228. [6] A. E. Hippisley, *Notes on Hippisley Fam.* ed. Fitzroy Jones, 118.

L.B.N.

**CRABB BOULTON, Henry** (c.1709–73), of Crosby Sq., Bishopsgate, and Thorncroft, nr. Leatherhead, Surr.

WORCESTER 1754–8 Oct. 1773

*b.* c.1709, s. of Hester Crabb, described in 1741 as 'of Tower Hill', wid., in will of her cos. Richard Boulton, director of E.I. Co. 1718–36; he, dying in 1746, left all his 'manors, messuages, lands etc.' to Henry Crabb who thereupon took add. name of Boulton. *unm.*

Entered office of E.I. Co. 1727;[1] clerk in the Company's pay office 1729; assistant to the paymaster 1730; jt. paymaster 1731; paymaster and clerk to the committee of shipping Aug. 1737–Apr. 1752.

Director E.I. Co. 1753–6, 1758–61, 1763–5, 1767–70, 1772–*d.*; dep. chairman 1764–5; chairman 1765–6, 1768–9, 1773–*d.*

Richard Boulton, Henry's patron, after some 20 years in the East India Company's marine service and 18 in its direction, retired a wealthy man to Worcestershire whence the family apparently derived. Henry's brother Richard Crabb similarly served some 20 years in the East India Company's marine, and on retiring from it in 1750 became one

of the most prominent managing owners or ship's husbands of Indiamen, who at this time dominated the monopoly East India shipping interest.[1] Henry Crabb Boulton, after his resignation from the Company's employment, concerned himself in his brother's shipping interests, and in 1753 became a director of the East India Company, primarily no doubt to further these interests. From 1755 on he is listed in the London directories as a merchant of Crosby Square, Bishopsgate.

At the general election of 1754 Boulton, possibly influenced by his family's Worcestershire interests, became a candidate for Worcester, and after an expensive campaign was returned unopposed. In Dupplin's list of 1754 he was classed as 'doubtful'; but on 24 Dec. 1755 Sandwich informed Newcastle that Boulton had 'attended and voted in every question in support of the measures of Government'.[2] In 1761 Boulton was re-elected at Worcester after a contest. Bute's list of December 1761 classes him as a supporter of Newcastle, and he voted with the Opposition on the peace preliminaries, 9 and 10 Dec. 1762; and on Wilkes, 15 Nov. 1763, and general warrants, 15 and 18 Feb. 1764.

Originally a follower of Laurence Sulivan in East India Company politics, Boulton later attached himself to Clive, and went over to Administration with him; Jenkinson reported to Grenville on 20 Apr. 1764 that Clive had said Boulton might be depended on, though 'a great rogue'.[3] Harris notes that during the debate of 1 Mar. 1765 on the bill to regulate splitting East India Company votes, Boulton was 'at the head of the government party'.[4] In Rockingham's list of July 1765 Boulton was classed as 'pro', and in that of November 1766 as 'Whig'. When, on 9 Dec. 1766 Beckford moved for an inquiry into East India Company affairs, Boulton voted for the motion, and though he 'said much against it, owned that the Company could not govern their servants, nor could Clive go on without the interposition of Government'.[5] No other votes by him are reported in this Parliament, but he spoke several times on East India affairs, and on 1 May 1767 when Beckford was again to move for an inquiry, Boulton, on behalf of the Company, informed the House that there 'was now a prospect of accommodation with the ministry'. In Townshend's list of January 1767 he was classed as 'doubtful', and in Newcastle's of 2 Mar. as 'doubtful or absent'. In 1768 Boulton was returned unopposed for Worcester.

He continued to play a considerable, though not a leading, part in the affairs of the East India Company in association with Lord Clive, George Wombwell, and Sir George Colebrooke (qq.v.), with the last of whom he engaged in speculative dealings in East

India stock in 1771, which received adverse comment in the report of the committee of secrecy 1773.[6] Despite his tendency to oppose Administration in the House, he was often in sympathy with their supporters in the Company, and after the debacle of 1772[7] he was with Government support elected chairman of the Company, as the most experienced director left to control its affairs. Generally following Clive's line, he may by then have drifted to the Government side also in Parliament, but the only vote recorded by him is with the Opposition on the motion concerning the Middlesex election, 26 Apr. 1773.

He died 8 Oct. 1773.

[1] For Richard Crabb's career see E. I. Co. ships' ledger receipt books 329E and 659E, ships' logs and ledgers 613 A–D, F–I, court minutes 10 and 17 Nov. 1738 and 14 Mar. 1739/40; and L. S. Sutherland, *London Merchant*. [2] Add. 32861, f. 427. [3] *Grenville Pprs.* ii. 46, misdated 1763. [4] 'Debates'. [5] Walpole, *Mems. Geo. III*, ii. 289. [6] See COLEBROOKE, Sir George. [7] SULIVAN, Laurence, and PURLING, John.

M.M.D.

## CRAGGS, *see* NEWSHAM

## CRAGGS NUGENT, *see* NUGENT, Robert

## CRANBORNE, Visct., *see* CECIL, James

## CRASTER, John (?1697–1763), of Craster, Alnwick, Northumb.

WEOBLEY    1754–1761

*b.* ?1697, 1st s. of John Craster of Craster by Mary, da. of John Ayton of Fawside, co. Dur. *educ.* Merton, Oxf. 4 July 1712, aged 15; C.C.C. Oxf.; G. Inn 1716, called 1721. *m.* 17 Jan. 1727, Catherine, da. of Col. Henry Villiers, 3s. 2da.
    Bencher, G. Inn 1742; lt.-gov. Tynemouth castle.

Craster was returned for Weobley by his wife's cousin Lord Weymouth. He was classed by Dupplin in 1754 as 'pro'. No vote or speech by him is reported. He did not stand in 1761 and died 31 Dec. 1763.

M.M.D.

## CRAUFURD, James (c.1744–1811).

HORSHAM    28 Nov. 1783–1784

*b.* c.1744, 2nd s. of Patrick Craufurd of Auchenames (q.v.), and bro. of John Craufurd (d. 1814, q.v.). *educ.* Eton 1755–8; Grand Tour 1760–1. *unm.*
    Entered army 1762; lt. 3 Ft. Gds. and capt. 1766; capt. and lt.-col. 1775; lt.-col. 73 Ft. 1780–3; equerry to Queen Charlotte 1766–94;[1] gov. Bermuda 1794–6.

Known at Eton as 'Flesh' to distinguish him from his elder brother 'Fish' Craufurd;[2] sometimes as the 'young Fish'. Georgiana, Duchess of Devonshire

describes him as 'very gallant' but lazy;[3] Mme du Deffand, as 'assez bon enfant'.[4] He was a reckless gambler. Lord March wrote to Selwyn, February 1773:[5] 'The Fish says that Colonel Craufurd continues to lose, and that he complains he has no money, nor anything now remaining of all his riches but bad debts.' And Selwyn to Lord Carlisle, 4 Aug. 1775:[6] Craufurd has 'paid another enormous sum for his brother, with which he torments or diverts everybody, while his brother does not seem to think himself obliged for a shilling'. In December 1774 John Craufurd applied to Lord Dartmouth for James to be made governor of East Florida.[7] In June 1779 James and Hare (q.v.), bracketed for 'foreign ministers' in the King's 'minutes of arrangements for consideration',[8] competed for the post of minister to Warsaw. Carlisle wrote to Selwyn, 21 May: 'The old Fish's importunity will beat me in my application for Hare, and the young Fish will go to Warsaw.' But to Fish's intense annoyance Hare won, and his brother was to go to Germany.[9] Then new complications arose: Craufurd asked 'that he might remain in the Guards during his mission to Munich'; Lord North dallied; Fish, losing patience, arranged for an exchange between James and an officer going out to India; and James reluctantly accepted the arrangement.[10] By the time North brought up the matter the King had already consented to the exchange—'more advantageous to Lt.-Col. Craufurd than going to Munich';[11] and when North, with a guilty feeling, reverted to the subject[12]—the Colonel foresaw 'little prospect of early advantage in India'—the King expressed disapproval of officers in the Guards being in wartime 'employed in foreign courts'—'if I was to advise him I should think in his situation no means so advisable as his going to the East Indies'.[13] When Craufurd was about to embark in May 1780, North obtained for him permission to retain during his absence the 'very genteel and distinguished' post he held 'in her Majesty's family'.[14]

When Craufurd was about to return to England, Lord Macartney wrote to John Macpherson (qq.v.) from Fort St. George, 11 Jan. 1782:[15]

Col. Craufurd is determined to go home and even grows a little angry at his friends attempting to dissuade him. He has £1,800 p.a., and yet says one reason for leaving us is that he cannot live upon it. He throws away in my opinion a brilliant fortune, whether considered in the light of affluence, or reputation.

Craufurd's return for Horsham in November 1783 on Lady Irwin's interest was arranged by her son-in-law Lord William Gordon (q.v.) who supported the Coalition Administration.[16] So did Craufurd; and on Gordon going over to Pitt he lost his seat in

1784. There is no record of his having spoken in the House.

He died in New York 22 Mar. 1811.

[1] P. Craufurd to Mure, 11 Dec. 1766, *Caldwell Pprs.* ii (2), p. 96. [2] *Eton Coll. Reg. 1753–90.* [3] Ld. Bessborough, *Georgiana,* 92. [4] To Horace Walpole, 29 Apr. 1772. [5] J. H. Jesse, *Selwyn,* iii. 27. Misdated '1772'; cf. Mme du Deffand to H. Walpole, 26 Feb. 1773. [6] *HMC Carlisle,* 284. [7] *HMC Dartmouth,* ii. 238. [8] Fortescue, iv. 353. [9] Jesse, iv. 156, 223. [10] North to the King, 17 Jan. 1780, Fortescue, v. 10–11. [11] The King to North, 17 Jan. ibid. 11. [12] North to the King, 28 Jan. ibid. 13–14. [13] The King to North, 3 Mar. 1780, ibid. 25. [14] North to the King, 20 May, and the King to North, 21 May, ibid. 63–64. [15] *Private Corresp. Lord Macartney,* ed. Davies, 19. [16] Laprade, 91, 101.

L.B.N.

## CRAUFURD, John (c.1725–64).

BERWICK-UPON-TWEED 1761–2 Aug. 1764

*b.* c.1725, 7th s. of Patrick Craufurd of Drumsoy, and bro. of Patrick Craufurd (q.v.). *unm.*
Ensign 13 Ft. 1738, capt. 1743, maj. 1747, lt.-col. 1749; col. 85 Ft. 1759–63; brig.-gen. 1760; served at Belle Isle Mar. 1761; in Portugal 1762–3; col. 3 Ft. 1763–d; lt. gov. Berwick Apr. 1764, Minorca June 1764–d.

As lieutenant-colonel of the 13th Ft. Craufurd served under General Pulteney, which may have played a part in his being selected for colonel of the regiment raised by Lord Bath for his son, Lord Pulteney (q.v.); so may the connexion between his brother Patrick and Bute, to whom Craufurd reported on the progress of his recruiting for the regiment. Thus on 20 Aug. 1759[1] when setting out for York

> where I shall meet Lord Northumberland, and some others who are zealous to serve the infant corps. From thence I shall go to Newcastle, where I have some friends, and will carry with me proper recommendations to Sir Walter Blackett, Mr. Ridley (qq.v.) and others.

There was another side to the northern recruiting tour—John Calcraft, regimental agent to the 85 Ft., wrote to Craufurd, 3 Sept.:[2]

> I do mightily approve your Newcastle scheme as well as your Berwick intentions, and think with you secrecy is necessary there at present as to election intentions, though I would do all I could consistent therewith and avoiding for the present public declaration . . .
> You will do well to please the Berwick gentry by bespeaking the gaiters there; is there any other matter we can help them in?

On 10 Sept.:[3] 'Berwick looks well indeed. But you can't have them too sure so I am by all means for the written invitation.' And on 16 Sept. to a common friend:[4] 'Craufurd has by invitation from the mayor, burgesses and a majority of freemen secured his election for Berwick and declared himself a candidate.'[5]

That Craufurd took the established interests at Berwick by surprise appears from a letter Thomas Watson (q.v.) wrote to the Duke of Newcastle,

30 Sept. 1759,[6] reporting the defeat of his own friend for mayor by 'the party that set Colonel Craufurd up'—'the first election of any sort I lost for above 35 years I have been in the magistracy of this corporation'.

Calcraft wrote to Craufurd, 30 Aug. 1760:[7]

> My advice to you is to go [to Berwick] as soon as you can for in cases of this sort storms rise which with management might be prevented, and your plan should be if possible to prevent any contest, for any will be more or less troublesome and expensive even to you, single or joined. Then comes another question, whether to keep single or join somebody . . . it is sometimes of as bad consequence to stand single against two, as to join a weak partner.

Craufurd decided to stand single:

> Mr. Delaval [wrote W. Temple, collector of customs at Berwick, 16 Sept. 1760][8] proposed to join Colonel Craufurd against Mr. Watson, the Colonel declined it, but gave leave to his single votes to split and give their second votes to either of the other candidates.

In Parliament Craufurd adhered to Bute, and afterwards to Grenville—he could be trusted, whenever present, to vote with the Government; thus for the peace preliminaries in December 1762. The rest of Craufurd's story appears in brief in Calcraft's letterbooks. To Edward Cornwallis, governor of Gibraltar,[9] 20 Nov. 1763: 'Your old friend Craufurd lives . . . in great ease'; 31 Jan. 1764: 'Craufurd has never spoke in the House though often threatened the attempt'; and 23 Apr. 1764: 'Craufurd is to be lieutenant governor of Berwick till Guise dies.' And to Sir John Mordaunt, 18 June 1764:[10] 'General Craufurd goes to Minorca.'

Craufurd died in Minorca 2 Aug. 1764.

[1] Bute mss. [2] Add. 17494, ff. 171–2. [3] Ibid. f. 178. [4] Ibid. f. 184. [5] See also Patrick Craufurd to Bute, 10 Sept., Bute mss; Argyll to Ld. Barrington, 13 Sept., Barrington mss. [6] Add. 32986, ff. 182–3. [7] Add. 17495, f. 125. [8] Add. 32912, f. 61. [9] Add. 17496, ff. 25, 32 and 34. [10] Ibid. f. 38.

L.B.N.

## CRAUFURD, John (?1742–1814), of Errol, Perth; Auchenames, Renfrew; and Drumsoy, Ayr.

| | |
|---|---|
| OLD SARUM | 1768–1774 |
| RENFREWSHIRE | 1774–1780 |
| GLASGOW BURGHS | 1780–1784, 26 Feb.–11 June 1790 |

*b.* ?1742, 1st s. of Patrick Craufurd, and bro. of James Craufurd (qq.v.). *educ.* Eton 1753–7; Glasgow Univ. 1757; Grand Tour 1760–1. *unm. suc.* fa. 10 Jan. 1778.
Chamberlain of Fife and Strathearn 1767–d.

Jack Craufurd, nicknamed at Eton 'The Fish' for his avid curiosity, was a schoolfellow of Stephen Fox through whom he became an intimate of the Holland House circle.[1] From 1760, when he began the grand tour with 'Ste', he made annual visits abroad and was as well known in French as in

English society. A little man of weak physique but exceptional intelligence, he had a mercurial temperament, in which gaiety, wit, and restless activity alternated with melancholy, hypochondria and indolence. Notorious as a gambler, he was one of the founders of Almacks in 1764.

Disappointed in his hopes of succeeding his uncle Col. John Craufurd as M.P. for Berwick,[2] he spent most of 1765 with Horace Walpole and David Hume in Paris, and formed an attachment to Madame du Deffand, whose devotion to her '*petit* Craufurd' lasted many years.[3] Early in 1766 he returned home, deeply in debt, to face an irate father, whom, however, he pacified by 'prudence, management and submission',[4] and persuaded to make over to him the revenues of the Errol estate. Bored by his father's society, and disliking Scotland as 'a vile country' where 'neither love nor wit can flourish',[5] Fish was soon immersed in fashionable London life, cultivating Grafton's favour for his father and himself at the next election.

When his scheme to secure a seat at Stockbridge fell through,[6] Craufurd, obsessed by his health, went to Bath and later with Lord March and G. A. Selwyn to Paris, in a bored and despondent mood.[7] Nevertheless he was kept informed of political changes,[8] and maintained contact with Shelburne and with Grafton, who, shortly after Craufurd's return home in December, offered him the place of chamberlain of Fife.[9] He also obtained from Thomas Pitt the promise of a seat at Old Sarum and in addition proposed to contest Renfrew in place of his father.

Shortly after his election Craufurd had a dispute with Grafton, thought of 'throwing up' his place, but was dissuaded by Hume, who wrote 29 Aug. 1768:[10]

His Grace passes for the most inflexible man in the world . . . And as his late coldness towards you proceeds more from a jealousy of friendship than anything else, it may rather be considered as obliging though unlucky.

Craufurd remained a Grafton supporter and voted with Administration on Wilkes and the Middlesex election. He next supported North's Administration, voting with them on Brass Crosby, 27 Mar. 1771. During the recess Fish for once remained at home, where he persuaded his father to give him full possession of Errol. Mme du Deffand commented:[11] '*Il n'en est pas plus riche mais son credit en augmente et il aura la satisfaction de se pouvoir ruiner.*'

When early in 1772 Fox disagreed with North and eventually resigned office, Mme du Deffand was alarmed lest Craufurd would join him in opposition.[12] But Fish wrote to Ossory, 21 Feb.:[13]

I think he [Fox] has been too hasty in a step of this consequence . . . It is better to err by too much spirit than by too little and as Charles does not mean to go into opposition, and is always worth a better place . . . it is my opinion that what he has done will . . . turn out to his advantage every way.

To this letter Fox added: 'I should not have resigned at this moment merely on account of my complaints against Lord North, if I had not determined to vote against this *Royal Family Bill.*' But Craufurd, in a competent maiden speech on 13 Mar. gave qualified support to the bill, and again, on 24 Mar., approved its principle.[14] On 18 Dec. he made his final appearance as an orator, in support of the Government's bill to restrain the East India Company from sending supervisors to India. He wrote to Stephen Fox:[15]

It was a prepared speech, ill-timed, ill-received, ill-delivered, languid, plaintive, and everything as bad as possible. Add to this, that it was very long, because being prepared and pompously begun, I did not know how the devil to get out of it . . . The only thing I said which was sensible or to the purpose, was misrepresented by Burke. Charles was not ashamed to acknowledge me in my distress. He explained and defended what I had said with spirit, warmth and great kindness to me . . . Certainly it was not the intention of nature that I should be a public speaker and I shall never attempt it any more.

He was less light-hearted over his father's determination to curb expenditure and entail all the family estates. He consulted William Mure on this and on his election prospects, particularly as Sir Lawrence Dundas had offered, if he failed in Renfrewshire, to bring him in elsewhere.[16] In the House his attendance was erratic. He did not vote on the naval captains' question on 9 Feb. 1773, but on 11 Feb. postponed a social visit to attend the debates on St. Vincent.[17] He wrote to Mure, 17 Feb.:[18]

Whether Administration has any settled plan with regard to [India] I cannot tell. Lord North is a very good Member of Parliament . . . but I believe he is not a great minister and that he has neither the extent of mind necessary to form large views nor the boldness to carry them into execution. Is he really and truly minister? Why was he beat the other day by a majority of near 100 on . . . the petition of the navy? Why did General Harvey, Sir Gilbert Elliot etc. vote and speak against him? I neither know nor care, but you, who are a greater politician than I am . . . may form your own conclusions.

Nevertheless he voted with North on the Middlesex election, 26 Apr. 1773, and on Grenville's Act, 25 Feb. 1774. By then he was actively making interest in Renfrewshire, and was extremely annoyed when, after he had induced 40 of his friends to attend the debate, the Renfrewshire petition against the Glasgow bridges bill was defeated through William MacDowall's mismanagement.[19]

He showed considerable skill in election intrigue in Renfrewshire, Ayrshire, and Perthshire, but embarrassed his friend Andrew Stuart by his well-intentioned attempt to negotiate on behalf of the Hamilton interest a compromise with Daniel Campbell of Shawfield in Lanarkshire and Selkirk Burghs.[20]

In 1775 Craufurd induced North to give him life tenure of his place, hitherto held at pleasure; shortly afterwards, when the ministry was under attack over American affairs and a change seemed imminent, George Selwyn wrote to Lord Carlisle, 25 Nov. 1775:[21]

> Fish is mightily embarrassed; he wants to be a patriot, to pay his court to Oss[ory] and Charles. But having just had a place made so for life he cannot *honnêtement as they tell him* pursue his own inclinations, which are to be well with the next Administration, but at present he has a merit with both. He votes with those who are in and loves cordially those who are out.

Craufurd's absurdities became as notorious as his gambling. He plagued his friends with his imaginary ailments, his 'ennui and jealousies', with requests to pay his debts '*pour le delivrer des Juifs*'; 'gate-crashed' parties, but when invited seldom attended. Selwyn wrote to Carlisle, 19 Dec. 1775:[22] 'I think verily he grows more tiresome every day, and everybody's patience is *à bout*.'

Nevertheless he retained his friends' affection, and sought to stand well with both Government and Opposition. 'Craufurdism' became a synonym for fulsome flattery. He never voted against Administration, but when possible avoided committing himself. On 5 Mar. 1779 Robinson wrote to Jenkinson:[23]

> Mr. Craufurd is a very ticklish blade and shirks. He is much attached to Charles Fox and he has been spoiled by Lord North's granting him some bishop's rents *for life*, which I protested against with all my might but it was afterwards carried when I was ill and he has ever since been captious and ruined.

He repeatedly solicited North for preferment for his brother. James Hare wrote to Selwyn, 18 May 1779:[24]

> The old Fish . . . has written Lord North the most . . . importunate letters; full of professions of inviolable attachment to the present Administration and of his claims on Government; though it is well known that after Keppel's trial, when Opposition seemed to be in a thriving way, the old Fish was wavering and actually kept away from the House when they were near run, that he might see whether they were likely to remain in their places or not . . . I daresay Lord North will give him what he asks merely to get rid of his solicitations.

Craufurd's voting record reflected the progress of the negotiations; he did not vote on the pensions question, 21 Feb. 1780, but when North, 'conscious that he had distressed both him and his brother',

again took up James's cause, Fish voted with the ministry in every recorded division to the end of the Parliament. At the general election, when faced by a combination against him, he was obliged to withdraw from Renfrewshire, and, with the support of the Hamilton and Argyll interest, transferred to Glasgow Burghs.

In the new Parliament he continued to keep a foot in each camp. Being now in funds himself by the sale of his estates of Errol and Drumsoy, he renewed his solicitations for his brother. He wrote to Jenkinson, 5 May 1781:[25]

> I don't love to talk of myself but I am now in my third Parliament, have been a steady friend to Government and . . . have never made a request for these eight or nine years except when my brother's distresses made me desire to have him sent minister to Munich. I am no man's competitor in anything but if I should be thought deserving of any favour, I would wish to have it shown to me in the person of my brother.

In May he was toadying to North,[26] but in July, when he had received nothing, he 'took occasion to say everything disagreeable to Lord North that one could well imagine'.[27] Selwyn wrote to Carlisle, 26 Oct. 1781:[28] 'That abominable cortigiano-ism with his affected disinterestedness and *noblesse d'âme* make him intolerable.' Craufurd did not vote on the Address (27 Nov.), 'which he was much impatient to discover to Charles with one of his fulsome compliments';[29] voted with Government on 12 Dec. on Lowther's motion against the war; but in the New Year was 'declaiming against Government with more than usual vehemence'.[30] When he was in a quandary Craufurd usually made illness his excuse. Before the motion of censure against the Admiralty of 20 Feb., Selwyn wrote to Carlisle:[31]

> It is thought that we shall be hard run in the House tomorrow . . . Absentees in the last question on both sides will now appear. I hope that Government will send two yeomen of the guard to carry the Fish down in his blankets, for he pretends to have the gout . . . He should be deposited . . . and be fairly asked his opinion and forced to give it one way or the other *en pleine assemblée*.

Craufurd, 'though he assured Lord Ossory in the morning that he would not vote at all . . . came down . . . and divided with the Government'.[32] But on the 22nd, on Conway's motion against the war, 'he retired before the division'. Selwyn commented:[33]

> At Brooks's he gave it as a reason that he *did not like the question*. I believe that it is not *questions* but *answers* to which he generally objects. But Lord North may thank himself for the Fish's system of acting. A place given for life to the scaly brood is sure to produce scruples at particular crises.

Anthony Storer was even more contemptuous: 'His own party, for so I call the Opposition, despise his conduct as much as we do; they laugh at him and abuse him for the most pitiful fellow that ever existed.' Craufurd again abstained on 27 Feb. on Conway's motion. On 1 Mar. Selwyn wrote to Carlisle: 'Fish, as I hear, doubles and trebles all his flattery to Charles and now and then throws in a compliment to Lord North, not being quite sure what may happen.' But he voted with Administration on Cavendish's motion of 8 Mar. and Rous's motion of no confidence on 15 Mar. While Selwyn suspected some ulterior motive, North himself was surprised at Craufurd's friendship in adversity; and for a time Fish fell 'greatly out of favour' with his Foxite friends at Brooks's.[34] But he soon transferred his allegiance to the new Administration, and remained faithful to Fox to the end of the Parliament; voted against Shelburne's peace preliminaries, 18 Feb. 1783; voted for Fox's East India bill, 27 Nov. 1783; and followed Fox into opposition.

On 6 Jan. 1784 Thomas Coutts wrote to Col. J. W. Crawford:[35]

> In case of a dissolution . . . J. Craufurd intends standing for Ayrshire as well as for Renfrewshire and Glasgow, and to put his brother in for the former and some friend I suppose for the latter. He assures me he will have such support as you can have no idea of.

When no immediate dissolution took place, Fish fell 'ill' and went to Bath. On his return Coutts wrote, 19 Mar. 1784:[36] 'I have seen Mr. Craufurd but once . . . I do not know what alteration his friends being out of office will make on his politics, or whether he still means the "Great Line" viz. Ayrshire, Renfrewshire, Glasgow etc.' Craufurd did not attempt Renfrewshire; in Ayrshire his chances were slight;[37] and at the general election he lost Glasgow Burghs.

Coutts wrote to Col. J. W. Crawford, 10 June 1784:[38]

> Jack Craufurd seems to bear his disappointments pretty well but I dare say he will pay his way into Parliament the first opportunity that offers. *It is the fashion* to be there and those he lives with are in it. He should buy a seat always, for his indolence will never do to keep up an interest even in a county.

Fish out of Parliament was a fish out of water.[39] He became more hypochondriac than ever, and spent much time abroad, but returned home during the Regency crisis. Coutts wrote from Paris to the Duchess of Devonshire, 24 Dec. 1788:[40] 'I have a great idea of our friend Mr. Craufurd's ability to fill some public employment and that his health would improve by having something to do. Where judgment is necessary I know no man superior.'

Craufurd did not contest the Ayrshire by-election of 1789. Coutts commented:[41] 'I do not imagine he thinks of Ayr or Renfrew *any more*. Politics is by

no means his natural bent; yet had he taken a public line early, few have better abilities.'

When Glasgow Burghs fell vacant, Craufurd won back his old seat for a few months, but lost it again at the general election of 1790, when his bid for Dysart Burghs also failed.[42]

Soon afterwards he fell seriously ill, and in 1792 went to Paris, returning horrified by revolutionary excesses. Thereafter he left his Foxite friends but did not seek to re-enter Parliament. After the Peace of Amiens he hastened to Paris 'very angry at being thought to . . . be in health . . . but delighted at being mistaken . . . for the English ambassador—determined . . . to be taken for an Emperor incog. next time' by the number of his carriages conveying him and his suite to the south of France.[43]

Always anxious to be on the winning side, The Fish turned Foxite[44] in 1806, but did not re-enter public life. He died 26 May 1814.

[1] Norman Pearsons' article on Fish Craufurd, *Nineteenth Century and After*, Feb. 1914. [2] Grenville to Patrick Craufurd, 11 Dec. 1764, Grenville letter bk. [3] See *Horace Walpole's Corresp. with Mme. du Deffand*. [4] Hume to Craufurd, 20 Dec. 1766, *New Letters of Hume*, ed. Klibansky & Mossner, 155. [5] Craufurd to Hume, 9 Dec. 1766, ibid. 154. [6] Chas. Fox to Craufurd, 15 Jan. 1767, *Corresp. C. J. Fox*, i. 35. [7] *Walpole-du Deffand Corresp.* i. 234, 265, 350, 355–6, 382–3. [8] Hume to Craufurd, 20 July 1767, *New Letters*, 173–5. [9] Mme. du Deffand to Walpole, 26 Dec. 1767; Selwyn to Carlisle, 29 Dec., *HMC Carlisle*, 225; T27/20/26. [10] *New Letters*, 184. [11] Mme du Deffand to Walpole, 10 Dec. 1771. [12] Same to same, 26 Feb. 1772. [13] *Corresp. C. J. Fox*, i. 72–74. [14] Cavendish's 'Debates', Egerton 237, pp. 33–35; 239, pp. 126–32; Walpole, *Last Jnls.* i. 50. [15] *Corresp. C. J. Fox*, i. 81–82. [16] *Caldwell Pprs.* ii (2), p. 216. [17] Walpole to Lady Ossory, 11 Feb. 1773. [18] *Caldwell Pprs.* ii. (2), p. 217. [19] Craufurd to Mure, 7 Apr. 1774, ibid. 231–2. [20] Duke of Argyll, *Intimate Society Letters*, i. 178–86. [21] *HMC Carlisle*, 749. [22] Ibid. 312. [23] Add. 38210, f. 325. [24] J. H. Jesse, *Geo. Selwyn and his Contemporaries*, iv. 141. [25] Add. 38216, f. 101. [26] Selwyn to Carlisle, 31 May 1781, *HMC Carlisle*, 490. [27] Anthony Storer to Carlisle, 18 July 1781, ibid. 514. [28] Ibid. 523. [29] Selwyn to Carlisle, 28 Nov. 1781, ibid. 538. [30] Hare to Carlisle, 11 Feb. 1781, ibid. 576. [31] Ibid. 580. [32] Storer to Carlisle, 24 Feb. 1782, ibid. 582. [33] Ibid. 583. [34] Ibid. 582, 585, 595, 600. [35] Ibid. 184. [36] Coutts to Col. Crawford, 30 Nov. 1784, ibid. 191. [37] E. H. Coleridge, *Life of T. Coutts*, i. 173. [38] Ibid. 177. [39] Ibid. 179. [40] Ibid. 264. [41] Ibid. 275. [42] H. Furber, *Hen. Dundas*, 228. [43] Ld. Granville Leveson Gower Corresp.* i. 366–7, Lady Bessborough quoting a letter from Jas. Hare in Paris. [44] *Corresp. C. J. Fox*, iv. 130.

E.H.-G.

## CRAUFURD, Patrick (c.1704–78), of Auchenames, Renfrew, and Crosbie and Drumsoy, Ayr.

| | |
|---|---|
| AYRSHIRE | 1741–1754 |
| RENFREWSHIRE | 1761–1768 |

*b.* c. 1704, 1st surv. s. of Patrick Craufurd, Edinburgh merchant, by his 2nd w. Jean, da. of Archibald Craufurd of Auchenames and Crosbie. *m.* (1) ?1740, Elizabeth (*d.*19 July 1746), da. and coh. of George Middleton of Errol, Perth, London banker, 2s.; (2) 22 Apr. 1750, Sarah, da. of Hew, 12th Lord Sempill[S], 1da. *suc.* fa. 1733. Burgess, Glasgow 1725, Edinburgh 1732.

Craufurd's father made a fortune in the Netherlands trade, purchased his wife's ancestral estates and his own family property of Drumsoy, and left them all to the eldest of his seven surviving sons. Patrick, or familiarly 'Peter', having begun life as a merchant, applied his business experience to the extension of his estates and electoral interest. He was a close friend of William Mure (q.v.), to whose judgment he deferred throughout his political life.

Through his marriage to Elizabeth Middleton he acquired another fortune and a life interest in the estate of Errol, where after his father-in-law's death in 1747 he chiefly resided. His wealth was his principal weapon in the Ayrshire election campaign of 1753–4 when he was opposed by James Mure Campbell (q.v.), cousin of Lord Loudoun, and Archibald Montgomerie (q.v.), brother of Lord Eglintoun. When Pelham and Argyll declared for Campbell, Col. John Craufurd (q.v.), sought an interview with Cumberland, 'in which he assured him that his brother was a person whose loyalty was not to be suspected, though it might appear so from the zeal of the court against him'.[1] Patrick resorted to extensive bribery, but was eventually obliged to accept a coalition with Eglintoun, who agreed to give him his interest on condition that at the next election Craufurd would support Montgomerie. On Pelham's death, Argyll hastened to prejudice Newcastle against Craufurd as one who 'votes always with the Tories',[2] and the joint Craufurd–Eglintoun interest was defeated.

Out of Parliament Craufurd divided his time between Scotland and London, where, through William Mure, he became connected with the Bute circle. When in 1758 Mure proposed that Craufurd should succeed Stuart Mackenzie (q.v.) in Ayr Burghs, Bute welcomed the idea and obtained Eglintoun's concurrence;[3] Craufurd was persuaded to 'quit his retreat' in Errol,[4] and begin the campaign under Mure's direction.[5] This resulted in a bitter quarrel between Bute and Argyll, who regarded Bute's intervention as a challenge to his own authority as 'Viceroy'.[6] On Bute's advice Craufurd tried to placate the angry Duke in an interview in Glasgow. Mure reported to Bute: 'I could make you laugh heartily at Peter's naïve account of it.'[7] When the Loudoun–Argyll interest sponsored the candidature of Sir Adam Fergusson (q.v.), Craufurd wrote to Bute, 10 Oct. 1759:[8]

It would be of great use to me . . . if Mr. Pitt would signify . . . that he believes me an honest disinterested person [and] wishes me success . . . as one favoured by your Lordship's interest . . . For my own part I say fairly and frankly my great motive to come into Parliament is to support your Lordship and Mr. Pitt.

When Pitt made no gesture and when Mure had to face a counter-attack in his own constituency, Craufurd, despite lavish expenditure and Eglintoun's assistance, met with little success. An opponent wrote to Loudoun from Ayr, 22 Jan. 1760:[9]

Mr. Craufurd left this place worse pleased than ever; all was spoke by Eglintoun, and Mr. Craufurd made up what he was deficient that way by most humble bows and squeezing the hand.

But in October 1760 the accession of George III turned the scales in Bute's favour and Argyll was obliged to negotiate a series of electoral compromises. When it was suggested that both Craufurd and Fergusson be 'laid aside' in favour of a third candidate for Ayr Burghs, Craufurd, an incorrigible busybody, immediately informed John Campbell of Stonefield, Bute's brother-in-law, and offered to recommend him.[10] But 'Peter's' views carried little weight either in this or in his attempt to obtain Inverness-shire for Bute's half-brother, young Fraser of Strichen.[11] Eventually, in the general settlement, Argyll reluctantly agreed to Bute's demand that on Mure's promotion to the Exchequer bench, Craufurd should be returned for Renfrewshire.

In Parliament an undemanding devotee of Bute, he quickly forgot his attachment to Pitt. He wrote to Mure, 17 Dec. 1761:[12] 'Col. Barré's attack, though rough and indecent, on Mr. Pitt will it's thought have no bad effect; and as he never spared others is the less regretted.' He considered the window tax 'an improper duty as it falls on the lower rank of people' but did not oppose it; favoured a Scottish militia but counselled patience 'till a plan can be properly digested for an universal British militia';[13] and continued to rely upon Mure for advice on Scottish affairs. He was greatly esteemed by Fox, never wavered in his allegiance to Bute, and was equally faithful to Grenville,[14] who however declined his proposal that his son John should succeed to Col. John Craufurd's seat at Berwick in 1764.[15] After Grenville's fall Rockingham listed him 'doubtful'. He voted with others of the Bute group against the repeal of the Stamp Act.

A thrifty Scot, Craufurd was angered by the reckless extravagance of his sons, who, as young men of fashion, were inclined to despise their pawky homespun father. In 1766 he took action to protect the Errol estate. David Hume wrote to John Craufurd, 15 Nov. 1766:[16]

I was told . . . that your father had taken out an inhibition against you by which he declared your obligation to entail your mother's estate and prohibited every one to lend you . . .

A reconciliation was however effected; he made over the Errol revenues to John, who in return assisted him in his Renfrewshire election affairs. Patrick wrote to Mure, 6 Dec. 1766:[17] 'I have reason to hope by Jack's means with the Duke of Grafton, I may have the disposal of all small offices that fall within the county . . . as I wish to support the King's measures and the present Administration.' Listed by Rockingham in November 1766 under 'Bute', he voted with the Chatham ministry on the land tax, 27 Feb. 1767, and on nullum tempus, 17 Feb. 1768.

His hold on Renfrewshire was insecure; he had no residence there except the ruined castle of Auchenames and was regarded as an Ayrshireman. In expectation of a costly campaign he raised his rents to 'bring in £10,000 clear'.[18] Loudoun, suspecting that he might make a bid for Ayrshire, wrote to Bute, 28 Aug. 1766:[19]

> I think your Lordship may carry any man of character in the county, except Mr. Peter Craufurd, to him I find a general objection, which may surprise your Lordship and possibly you may suspect that from his formerly opposing me I carry a rancour still against him, but it is not so, I do assure your Lordship, and in looking on him as a friend of yours I have advised such of my friends as have consulted me and have votes in Renfrew to give them to him.

Craufurd however was equally unwelcome in Renfrew, and when two opponents appeared against him seems to have handed over the management of the election to John.[20] After prolonged negotiations Patrick stood down and gave his interest to William McDowall (q.v.) on condition that John should be the candidate at the next general election.[21]

Thereafter he lived mainly in Edinburgh and in Bath. In 1771 he put John in possession of the Errol estate[22] but later, fearing the alienation of the family property, insisted upon safeguards. John wrote to Mure, 17 Feb. 1773, after a visit to his father at Bath:[23]

> He is much as you saw him in Scotland, but with the additional misfortune of being constantly deaf. Add to this that his temper or his mind are quite gone. He is grown anxious and attentive to money matters beyond what I ever saw an example of in anybody. I have been wearied by his persecutions into an entail of my estate along with his, which I know I shall repent all the rest of my life.

John begged Mure to assist him to 'undo what has been done' and was successful at the cost of a rift with his father. David Hume wrote to John from Edinburgh, 28 Jan. 1774:[24]

> I was told yesterday by Mr. Ross that he had just come from your father who regretted very feelingly his never hearing from you which he ascribed not to your indolence . . . but to your neglect of him and your prejudices against him. In the fullness of his heart he opened up all his friendly intentions towards you and declared that except a reasonable provision for your sister and a small annuity to your brother . . . he intended you to be the sole heir of all his remaining property. He wanted nothing from you except your friendship which he was sorry he could not obtain and it was the circumstance that embittered his remaining days.

Hume's intervention seems to have healed the breach, and old Patrick, despite failing powers, assisted John at the 1774 general election.[25]

He died in Edinburgh 10 Jan. 1778.

[1] Cathcart to Loudoun, 2 Oct. 1753, Loudoun mss. [2] Lists prepared by Pelham and Argyll, and annotated was the by Argyll for Newcastle's information, Newcastle (Clumber) mss. [3] Bute to Mure, 14 Jan. 1759, *Caldwell Pprs.* ii(1), p. 119. [4] Craufurd to Bute, 30 May 1759, Bute mss. [5] Mure to Bute, 10 and 22 Aug., Craufurd to Bute, 22 Aug. 1759, Bute mss. [6] Bute to Mure, 30 Aug. 1758, *Caldwell Pprs.* ii(1), p. 120. [7] Mure to Bute, 28 Sept. 1759, Bute mss. [8] Ibid. [9] Capt. D. Kennedy to Loudoun, Loudoun mss. [10] Campbell to Bute, 23 Apr. 1761, Bute mss. [11] Craufurd to Bute, 21 Feb. 1761; Ld. Strichen to Bute, 4 May 1761, ibid. [12] *Caldwell Pprs.* ii(1), p. 137. [13] Ibid. 138. [14] Craufurd to David Ross, 18 Feb. 1764, *Caldwell Pprs.* ii(1), pp. 237–8. [15] Grenville to Craufurd, 11 Dec. 1764, Grenville letter bk. [16] *New Letters of Hume*, 153. [17] *Caldwell Pprs.* ii(2), p. 95. [18] Chas. Dalrymple to Loudoun, 16 Jan. 1767, Loudoun mss. [19] Bute mss. [20] John Craufurd to Mure, 21 and 26 Feb. 1768, *Caldwell Pprs.* ii(2), pp. 132–4. [21] Ibid. 135–7. [22] Mme du Deffand to Horace Walpole, 10 Dec. 1771. [23] *Caldwell Pprs.* ii(2), pp. 216–17. [24] *Letters of Hume*, ii. 283–5. [25] *Caldwell Pprs.* ii(2), p. 236.

E.H.-G.

**CRAUFURD, Sir Patrick** (*d.*1782), of Piccadilly, London.

ARUNDEL 1780–12 Mar. 1781

1st s. of James Craufurd by his w. Elizabeth Andrews of Rotterdam. James Craufurd was the s. of Patrick Craufurd of Drumsoy, and bro. of Patrick Craufurd of Auchenames and Col. John Craufurd (qq.v.). Kntd. 2 May 1777.
Conservator of Scots privileges in Holland from 1760.[1]

Craufurd, like his father, was a merchant in Holland. At the general election of 1780 he successfully contested Arundel, a venal borough, but was unseated for bribery.

He died 24 Jan. 1782.

[1] John Craufurd to Bute, 12 Nov. 1760, Bute mss.

L.B.N.

**CRAVEN, Thomas** (c.1715–72), of Benham Park, nr. Newbury, Berks.

BERKSHIRE 2 Apr. 1766–14 Dec. 1772

*b.* c.1715, 4th s. of John Craven of Whitley, Warws. (bro. of William, 2nd Baron Craven), by Maria Rebecca da. of Henry Green of Wyken, Warws.; bro. of William Craven (q.v.). *unm.*
Lt. R.N. 1739; capt. 1746; r.-adm. 1770.

Craven was returned unopposed in 1766. He was classed by Rockingham and Newcastle as a Tory, and by Charles Townshend as a country gentleman; and he voted against the Government on the land tax, 27 Feb. 1767, and the nullum tempus bill, 17 Feb. 1768. At the poll for Berkshire in 1768 Craven came second, but with a comfortable majority. He voted with the court over Wilkes and the Middlesex election, and on the royal marriage bill Robinson classed him as a Government supporter. He is not known to have spoken in the House. He died 14 Dec. 1772.

J.B.

## CRAVEN, William (1705–1769), of Wyken, nr. Coventry, Warws.

WARWICKSHIRE 24 Dec. 1746–10 Nov. 1764

*b.* 19 Sept. 1705, 1st s. of John Craven, and bro. of Thomas Craven (q.v.). *educ.* Emmanuel, Camb. 1723. *m.* 27 Apr. 1749, Jane, da. of Rev. Rowland Berkeley of Cotheridge, Worcs., *s.p.* *suc.* fa. 1726; and cos. as 5th Baron Craven 10 Nov. 1764.

The Craven family had estates in both Warwickshire and Berkshire, and under George II were Tories. Little is known of William Craven's parliamentary activities: he represented the county without a contest, and is always classed as a Tory. He appears neither in Henry Fox's list of Members in favour of the peace preliminaries nor in the lists of those who voted against them. Absent from the division on general warrants, 18 Feb. 1764, he was classed by Jenkinson as a friend to Government. There is no record of his having spoken in the House.

He died 17 Mar. 1769.

J.B.

## CREED, Sir James (c.1695–1762), of Greenwich.

CANTERBURY 1754–1761

*b.* c.1695. *m.* (1), 1 da.; (2) July 1725, Mary, da. of Sir Henry Hankey, banker and alderman of London, 2s. 3da. Kntd. 21 Feb. 1744.
    Director, E.I. Co. 1755–8, 1761.

Described in the London directories as a lead merchant, Creed between 1755 and 1761 invested considerable sums in Government stock together with Samuel Touchet, John Major, Robert Bristow and Peter Burrell II (qq.v.).

He unsuccessfully contested Southwark in 1747. At Canterbury in 1754 he came forward at the last moment: his name does not appear in Newcastle's list drawn up in March, but when Creed declared himself a candidate Newcastle supported him. The nature of his interest at Canterbury is not known, but it must have been strong: Newcastle wrote to the King the day before the election, 'there is one certainly gained at Canterbury which was not expected';[1] and Creed was so far ahead after the first day's poll that Thomas Best (q.v.) withdrew.

Creed voted against Government on the plate bill, 17 Mar. 1756.[2]

In 1761 he stood again with support from Newcastle and Lord Sondes, but the juncture of the other candidates Thomas Best and Richard Milles, both local landowners, and the unpopularity of William Mayne (q.v.), whom he had joined at Newcastle's suggestion,[3] brought about his defeat at the poll. He died 7 Feb. 1762.

[1] Add. 32735, f. 92. [2] Add. 32863, ff. 332–3. [3] Namier, *Structure*, 99–102.

J.B.

## CRESPIGNY, Philip Champion (d.1803), of Burwood, nr. Cobham, Surr.

SUDBURY 12 Oct. 1774–22 Mar. 1775
ALDEBURGH 1780–1790

*b.* after 1731, 2nd s. of Philip Champion de Crespigny, proctor of the court of Admiralty, of Huguenot descent, by Anne, da. of Claude Fonnereau of Christ Church, Ipswich. *educ.* ?Eton 1748. *m* (1) 24 Nov. 1762, Sarah, da. and h. of Thomas Cocksedge of Thetford, ?3s. 2da.; (2) 1 July 1774, Clarissa (*d*.15 May 1782), da. of James Brooke, 1s. 2da.; (3) 20 Feb. 1783, Dorothy, da. of Richard Scott of Betton, Salop, *s.p.*
    Adv., Doctors' Commons 1759; King's proctor 1768–84.

In 1774 Crespigny was returned on the Fonnereau interest at Sudbury after a contest, but lost his seat on petition. In 1780 he was returned unopposed at Aldeburgh on the Fonnereau interest, and at Sudbury after a contest. He held both seats until 1781 when he lost Sudbury on petition, and continued to sit for Aldeburgh.

He supported North's Administration to the end. His one recorded speech was on 21 Mar. 1781 when he spoke against the bill for excluding contractors from the House of Commons.[1]

Crespigny's name appears in an 'Account of pensions added by Lord North which have ceased by death or otherwise', sent to the King in April 1782. It is not clear why the pension was given or why it ceased. It is mentioned but not explained in a letter from North to the King in March 1782:

> Mr. Crespigny, his Majesty's proctor, had, before his coming into Parliament, an annual payment of £200 a year. In consequence of election assistance he was to have had £400 but could not hold it in Parliament, and therefore has never received any since the general election, and therefore wished either to have a pension of £400 to his wife or to have the salary annexed to his office.[2]

On 19 Mar. 1782 his wife was granted a pension of £524 p.a. during pleasure.

Crespigny voted against Shelburne's peace preliminaries, 18 Feb. 1783, for Fox's East India bill, 27 Nov. 1783, and against Pitt.

The *English Chronicle* in 1781 wrote about him: 'His hauteur is so distinguished, that he is generally characterised . . . by the profane, though very applicable appellation, of *God Almighty*'; and his obituary in the *Gentleman's Magazine* (1803, p. 89) described him as 'very much a man of fashion in his person and demeanour, full of anecdote, and with a turn for satirical humour that rendered him a very amusing companion'.

He died 1 Jan. 1803.

[1] Debrett, ii. 296. [2] Fortescue, v. 417, 468.

M.M.D.

**CRESSETT,** *see* **PELHAM, Henry**

**CRESSWELL, Estcourt** (c.1745–1823), of Bibury, nr. Cirencester, Glos. and Pinkney Park, Wilts.

CIRENCESTER 1768–1774

*b.* c.1745, o.s. of Thomas Estcourt Cresswell (q.v.). *m.* (1) July 1771, Mary (*d.*30 Sept. 1772), da. and h. of Samuel Wotton of Speechwick Park, Devon, 1da.; (2) Mary Gregory of Sherston, Wilts., 5s. *suc.* fa. 1788.

Cresswell was returned at Cirencester after a contest against the Bathurst interest. In Parliament he voted regularly with Administration. There is no record of his having spoken in the House. In 1774 he was defeated at Cirencester.

He died 4 July 1823 'at a very advanced age, at Bath, whither he had been removed . . . by order of the lord chancellor'.[1]

[1] *Gent. Mag.* 1823, ii. 93.

M.M.D.

**CRESSWELL, Thomas Estcourt** (1712–88) of Pinkney Park, Wilts.

WOOTTON BASSETT 1754–1774

*bap.* 22 July 1712, 1st surv. s. of Richard Cresswell of Sidbury, Salop, and Barnehurst, Staffs. by Elizabeth, da. and h. of Sir Thomas Estcourt of Pinkney Park. *m.* c.1746, Anne, da. and h. of Edmund Warneford of Sevenhampton, Wilts. and Bibury Court, Glos., 1s. 1da. *suc.* fa. 1743.
Purveyor of Chelsea Hospital 1759–61.

Cresswell began his career as a free merchant trading to India and China, but soon gave this up and about 1732 began to lead a hand to mouth existence in England. He planned to marry an heiress, and when in 1742 he became entangled in an affair with his penniless cousin Elizabeth Scrope, he pacified her with a bogus Fleet marriage. About 1746, his financial difficulties being acute, he contracted a second marriage with Anne Warneford, an heiress whom he believed to be in poor health and unlikely to live more than a year. In 1747 the affair received publicity in a series of letters to the press, followed by Cresswell's extraordinarily candid *Narrative of the Affair* and Miss Scrope's *Answer*. Accused of bigamy and of attempting to murder both women, Cresswell counter-attacked vigorously; but contemporary opinion seems generally to have agreed with his distant cousin, Lord Ducie, in describing him as 'a very great villain'.

In 1754 Cresswell stood on the St. John interest for Wootton Bassett (which his grandfather had represented in 1713) and was returned after a violent and expensive contest. He was connected politically with Henry Fox; in 1754 he was classed by Dupplin

as an Opposition Whig, and in 1759 through Fox's influence was appointed purveyor of Chelsea Hospital. Returned unopposed in 1761 and 1768, Cresswell supported each successive Administration, but he did not stand in 1774, and there is no record of his having spoken in the House.

He died 14 Nov. 1788.

J.A.C.

**CREWE, John** (1742–1829), of Crewe Hall, Cheshire.

STAFFORD 4 Mar. 1765–1768
CHESHIRE 1768–1802

*b.* 27 Sept. 1742, 1st s. of John Crewe, M.P., of Crewe Hall by Anne, da. of Richard Shuttleworth, M.P., of Gawthorpe, Lancs. *educ.* Westminster; Ch. Ch. Oxf. 1760. *m.* 4 Apr. 1766, Frances, da. of Fulke Greville of Wilbury, Wilts., 1s. 1da. *cr.* Baron Crewe 25 Feb. 1806.

John Crewe's great-grandfather, John Offley of Madeley, Staffs., married Anne, daughter and heiress of John Crewe of Crewe Hall. Their eldest son inherited his mother's Cheshire property and took the name of Crewe; and between 1705 and 1802 he, his son and his grandson held one Cheshire seat for 62 years. William Crewe Offley, second son of John Offley and Anne Crewe, and father of John Offley (q.v.), inherited Madeley and sat for Newcastle-under-Lyme.

In 1765 John Crewe successfully contested Stafford, probably with the support of his friend Hugo Meynell (q.v.); and in 1768 and at all his subsequent elections he was returned unopposed for Cheshire. In Parliament he seems generally until 1784 to have followed the lead of his friend the Duke of Grafton, though between 1765 and 1774 only one vote by him is recorded: with the Administration on the Middlesex election, 26 Apr. 1773. When Grafton went into opposition over American affairs (26 Oct. 1775) Crewe followed him and henceforth voted consistently against the North Administration till the end. On 5 July 1782, immediately after the resignation of Fox, Grafton wrote to Shelburne, who was then trying to rally support:[1]

> In regard to Mr. Crewe I would take any step you would wish me: but, as he has so long since expressed to me that the only object he should ever look up to was an English peerage, and which I stated to your Lordship on our coming into office. I have no idea of his accepting any [office] under any ministry: but, as I may be mistaken, I would advise your Lordship to see him, mentioning to him your application to me, and that I have presumed to advise your seeing him.

He voted for Shelburne's peace preliminaries, 18 Feb. 1783, and for Fox's East India bill, 27 Nov. 1783. He had long been on intimate terms with

Fox: on 13 July 1773 Horace Walpole wrote to Horace Mann that Crewe was paying 'twelve hundred a year for him [Fox]—literally for him, being bound for him'; and according to George Selwyn, November 1773, he had 'such warm feelings' for Fox that he was willing to make further efforts to help him in his financial difficulties.[2] When Fox was dismissed in December 1783, Crewe followed him into opposition, and in February Fox, still hoping for an early return to office, included Crewe in a list of peers to be made then.[3] Crewe remained with Fox till the end, and in 1806, on Fox's return to office, received a peerage as his reward.

Crewe is reported to have spoken a dozen times in the House; seven times on the bill, with which his name is connected, to prevent revenue officers from voting at elections. He introduced the bill in 1780; proposed it again in 1781, and saw it through the House in 1782. His only other recorded speeches before 1790 were against a tax on maidservants, 10 May 1785, and on the County Election Act, 12 and 31 Mar. and 6 Apr. 1789.

He died 28 Apr. 1829.

[1] Lansdowne mss. [2] *HMC Carlisle*, 249. [3] J. C. Wedgwood, *Staffs. Parlty. Hist.* (Wm. Salt Arch. Soc.), ii (2), p. 306.

M.M.D.

## CRICKITT, Charles Alexander (1736–1803), of Smith's Hall, nr. Chipping Ongar, Essex.

IPSWICH    25 June 1784–16 Jan. 1803

*b.* 12 Jan. 1736, nephew of Capt. Charles Alexander, whom he *suc.* at Smith's Hall; and all his children were given Alexander as middle name. *educ.* Merchant Taylors' 1748–50. *m.* 24 Nov. 1767, Sarah Dolby of Brises, Kelvedon Hatch, Essex, 4s. 7da.
Recorder, Ipswich 1787–*d.*; receiver of the land tax for E. Suff. 1794–*d.*[1]

The Crickitt family were of Flemish extraction, settled at Colchester since the end of the 16th century.[2] In the 18th century they had a connexion with Doctors' Commons; Charles Alexander Crickitt is described in his marriage notice in the *Gentleman's Magazine* as of Doctors' Commons; and in his obituary notice[3] as 'a proctor in Doctors' Commons'; and his eldest son, also Charles Alexander Crickitt, was admitted to Trinity Hall, Cambridge in 1786.

Crickitt was a banker at Colchester from about 1774; on 10 Jan. 1786 the Ipswich Town and County Bank of Messrs. Crickitt, Truelove [?Truslow] and Kerridge was opened; he was also a partner in a Chelmsford bank with a branch at Maldon. Crickitt's bank at Ipswich was the bank of 'the Blues', while that of the Quaker family of Alexander and Cornwall was the bank of 'the Yellows'; and it was through their bank that the

financial side of the election of 1784 was transacted for the Yellows. The poll was fixed for Saturday, 3 April, and on Friday evening, in consequence of one of the Yellow candidates declining, the two parties agreed to join in support of Middleton ('Blue') and Cator ('Yellow') 'and no contest was expected till the arrival of Mr. Crickitt on that evening'; many of the voters 'did not hear of his arrival till the next morning'.[4] He obviously stood without any chance of immediate return, but to secure the basis for petitioning against Cator. Bamber Gascoyne sen., who was a friend of Crickitt's, managed his petition, and with Gascoyne's encouragement Crickitt applied to John Strutt to act as his nominee on the House of Commons committee.[5] Gascoyne wrote to Strutt, 26 May: 'I do believe he [Crickitt] will drive Cator out—nay it will not surprise me if Cator gives up, for I never saw a man so frightened in my life. Crickitt is in great spirits.' Cator was unseated; did not stand again; but there was a contest which Crickitt won easily.

In the House Crickitt adhered to Pitt; voted for his scheme of parliamentary reform, 18 Apr. 1785; for Richmond's fortifications plan, 27 Feb. 1786; and with Pitt during the Regency crisis, 1788–9. There is no record o his having spoken in his first Parliament.

He died 16 Jan. 1803.

[1] W. R. Ward. *English Land Tax*, 165, 173 n. 1; A. G. E. Jones, 'Early Banking in Ipswich', *N. & Q.* cxcvi. 402–5, dates his appointment 1795. [2] *Reg. of Baptisms in Dutch Church, Colchester, 1645–1728* (Huguenot Soc. xii). The name was spelled in many ways, e.g. Kriket. [3] *Gent. Mag.* 1803, p. 92. [4] A. Luders, *Controverted Elections*, i. 34–35. [5] Crickitt to Strutt, 24 and 30 May, 1 June 1784, Strutt mss.

L.B.N.

## CROFTES, Richard (c.1740–83), of Saxham, Suff.

| | |
|---|---|
| PETERSFIELD | 17 Dec. 1767–1768 |
| DOWNTON | 1768–Jan. 1771 |
| CAMBRIDGE UNIVERSITY | 4 Feb. 1771–1780 |

*b.* c.1740, 1st s. of William Croftes of Saxham by Mary, da. and coh. of Sir Matthew Decker, 1st Bt., M.P., London merchant. *educ.* Eton 1753–8; St. John's, Camb. 1758. *m.* 11 Feb. 1773, Harriet, da. and coh. of John Darell, 1da. *suc.* fa. 1770.

In 1760 Croftes's parents began negotiating for a seat for him, and on 9 June he appears in Newcastle's 'list of persons to be brought into Parliament', having been mentioned to him 'by the Duke of Grafton, at the request of Mr. Croftes, and by Mr. Page [q.v.] at the request of Mrs. Croftes'.[1] Though willing to pay for a seat, Croftes senior found Newcastle's suggestion of Sudbury 'impracticable' because 'it would be expensive and the success doubtful'.[2] But on 15 Feb. 1761 Mrs. Croftes wrote to Newcastle that her husband 'was willing to have parted with a large sum of money' to have his son returned, and she herself was 'greatly disappointed' that nothing had been arranged: 'What objections can your Grace have to serve my son? he is a worthy young man of great application, of good family, and likely to have a good fortune'; 'I flatter myself my son's behaviour will be such that you will not repent . . . bringing him into Parliament.'[3] In Newcastle's list of people to be brought in, he now appears as 'Mr. Croftes, somewhere with great expense'.[4] But a request from Croftes sen., 9 Mar., that he should be brought in for Newark was turned down;[5] and it was not till 1767 that at Grafton's recommendation,[6] a seat was found for him at Petersfield, where he was returned unopposed. In 1768 he transferred to Downton, and was again returned unopposed. He voted with the Administration on Wilkes, 3 Feb. 1769, and the Middlesex election, 8 May 1769.

In 1771, at the suggestion of Grafton, now chancellor of Cambridge University, Croftes vacated his seat at Downton to stand for the university. His nomination was not well received: 'sending down so young a man, and so little known, has given much offence', wrote the Bishop of Lincoln to Lord Hardwicke, 5 Feb. 1771;[7] and Richard Watson, regius professor of divinity, wrote to Grafton that the university were 'dissatisfied' with Croftes:[8]

> We have no particular objections to him as a private man; nay we believe him equal to transacting the business of *Downton*, but we by no means think him of consequence enough in life to be the representative, or of ability sufficient to support the interest of the *University of Cambridge*.

Although an independent section of the university put up their own candidate, Croftes was returned by 76 votes against 45. His only recorded votes in this Parliament were on the royal marriage bill, March 1772, and on the naval captains' petition, 9 Feb. 1773, when he was classed in the King's list as a friend voting with Opposition.

After an unopposed return in 1774, his first recorded vote, on the civil list debts, 18 Apr. 1777, was with the Opposition, with whom he henceforth regularly voted. There is no record of his having spoken in the House.

In 1780 he was defeated at Cambridge University, and did not stand again for Parliament. He died 5 July 1783.

[1] Memorandum from John Page, Add. 32907, f. 108. [2] Add. 32916, ff. 278–9. [3] Add. 32919, f. 19. [4] Add. 32919, f. 58. [5] Add. 32920, f. 29. [6] Jolliffe mss. [7] Add. 35658, f. 17. [8] *Anecdotes of the Life of Richard Watson, Bp. of Llandaff*, i. 76–77.

M.M.D.

**CROSBY, Brass** (1725–93), of Chelsfield, Kent.

HONITON   1768–1774

*b.* 8 May 1725, 1st s. of Hercules Crosby of Stockton-on-Tees by Mary, da. and coh. of John Brass of Blackhalls, Hesildon, Durham. *m.* (1) the wid. of one Walraven, 1da. *d.v.p.*; (2) the wid. of one Cooke, a 'collar-maker' to the Ordnance (*d.*20 Nov. 1767), *s.p.*; (3) 9 Feb. 1772, Mary, da. of James Maud, wine merchant of London, wid. of Rev. John Tattersall, rector of Gatton, *s.p.*

Member of common council of London 1758; 1760 purchased office of city remembrancer but sold it 1761; sheriff, London and Mdx. 1764–5; alderman, London 1765, ld. mayor 1770–1.

As a young man Crosby was apprenticed as an attorney in Sunderland, but soon moved to London where he practised successfully for several years.[1] According to the *Gentleman's Magazine* (1793, i. 188) 'he laid the foundation of his ample fortune by marrying the rich widow of a tailor and salesman'.

In 1768, already established in City politics, Crosby purchased his return for the corrupt and expensive borough of Honiton. From 1769 he was closely associated with Wilkes ('one of his most steady partizans',[2] writes Horace Walpole) and consistently opposed Administration both in the House and in City politics. As lord mayor he came into conflict with the Government over the use of press warrants, refusing to give any aid to the pressgangs and ordering the constables to prevent them from removing persons from the City limits. In 1771, influenced by Wilkes, he gave mayoral support to the London printers when the Commons attempted to enforce their privilege of secrecy of debate. Called to account by the House, he obstinately defended the chartered privileges of the City of London, and suffered a mild martyrdom by committal for the remainder of the session to the Tower, where he was lionized by the Opposition. Henceforth his parliamentary career was obscure, and his few speeches were on minor local matters.

In 1774 Crosby unsuccessfully contested London on a comprehensive radical programme. He did not stand at the general election of 1780, but at the by-election of January 1784 he again unsuccessfully contested the City. Probably because of ill-health, he did not stand at the general election. Throughout his life he maintained his interest in City affairs, particularly social and charitable work. His obituary describes him as 'possessed of an uncommon degree of patience, integrity, and sagacious penetration', and at his death on 14 Feb. 1793 he was still serving as chairman on the four principal City committees.

[1] *Mems. Brass Crosby* (1829). [2] *Mems. Geo. III*, iv. 131.

I.R.C.

**CROSSE, Sir John,** 2nd Bt. (?1700–62), of Westminster and Rainham, Essex.

| | |
|---|---|
| WOOTTON BASSETT | 1727–1734 |
| LOSTWITHIEL | 19 May 1735–1747 |
| WESTMINSTER | 1754–1761 |

*b.* ?1700, 2nd but o. surv. s. of Sir Thomas Crosse, 1st Bt., M.P., by Jane, da. of Patrick Lambe of Stoke Poges, Bucks. *educ.* Westminster 10 Jan. 1715, aged 14; Ch. Ch. Oxf. 21 Feb. 1717, aged 16. *m.* 15 July 1746, Mary Godfrey of Westminster, *s.p. suc.* fa. 27 May 1738.

Crosse had sat for Wootton Bassett and Lostwithiel as a Treasury candidate. In a letter to Bute of 18 Nov. 1761[1] he explained how he came to stand for Westminster:

It has been my lot, my Lord, ever since the year 1727 . . . to have taken a pretty considerable share in the conduct of the public business of Middlesex and Essex, the two counties where my estates lie, but more particularly of the City and Liberty which has the honour of being the place of his Majesty's birth and residence. As my late father had often been chosen for Westminster in his lifetime I was in consequence of that thought of as a proper person to be nominated as a candidate to represent them in the last Parliament, which I did with . . . the strongest approbation and protection of his late Majesty.

When asked by Henry Pelham to stand at the general election of 1754, Crosse 'declared he would not put up more than £500, and, as this was insufficient, Pelham tried to find someone who would go the length of £2000 but, having failed, accepted Crosse's offer'.[2] Crosse and Edward Cornwallis stood on a joint interest against Lord Middlesex (q.v.) and General Oglethorpe, put up solely 'to occasion money to be spent'; their expenses came to almost £2300, of which Crosse paid £500 and the remainder came from secret service money.

There is no record of any speech or vote by Crosse in this Parliament, but presumably he supported Administration. In 1761 he declined to stand because of ill health,[3] and he died 12 Mar. 1762.

[1] Bute mss. [2] Namier, *Structure*, 199. [3] Crosse to Newcastle, 28 Jan. 1761, Add. 32918, f. 106.

J.B.

**CROWLE, Charles John** (c.1738–1811), of Fryston Hall, Yorks.

RICHMOND 26 May 1769–1774

*b.* c.1738, o.s. of Richard Crowle (q.v.). *educ.* Westminster, adm. Jan. 1749, aged 8; Trinity, Camb. 30 July 1757, aged 19; I. Temple 1755. *unm. suc.* fa. 1757.

Lord Tavistock wrote to his father, 5 Nov. 1762, recommending Crowle to the Duke's protection 'during his stay at Paris':[1] 'I knew him at school

and he was afterwards very civil to me in Italy, he is not very wise but an inoffensive good humoured lad.'

Crowle was returned for Richmond in 1769 on the interest of Sir Lawrence Dundas (q.v.), in place of Alexander Wedderburn who had vacated his seat because of his vote on the Middlesex election. 'You will have heard that Richmond was offered to Raby Vane [q.v.]', wrote Sir James Lowther to Charles Jenkinson, 28 May 1769,[2] 'and he not taking it, then to Crowle, a great friend of young Dundas's.'

Crowle appears in no division list for this Parliament, but presumably as Dundas's Member he voted with Administration, and in Robinson's survey on the royal marriage bill, March 1772, is classed as 'pro, present'. His only recorded speech was on the Selby canal bill, 2 Apr. 1773.[3] He did not stand in 1774.

Crowle died 7 Mar. 1811, aged 73.

[1] Bedford mss 46, f. 96. [2] Add. 38206, f. 121. [3] Cavendish's 'Debates', Egerton 245, ff. 194–5.

J.B.

**CROWLE, Richard** (1699–1757), of Fryston Hall, Yorks.

KINGSTON-UPON-HULL 1754–21 June 1757

*b.* 15 July 1699, s. of William Crowle, Hull merchant, by Dorothy, da. of Richard Oates of Pontefract.[1] *educ.* at Beverley; St. John's, Camb. 1715; I. Temple 1716, called 1724, bencher 1754. *m.* Apr. 1735,[2] Elizabeth, da. of John Pearman, London timber merchant, 1s.

When Crowle's elder brother George retired from the representation of Hull in 1747, he gave his vote and interest to Lord Robert Manners against Richard, who was defeated.[3] In 1750–1 Richard Crowle acted as counsel to the Opposition on the Westminster by-election and, having given offence by certain remarks about the House of Commons, 'was reprimanded on his knees by the Speaker. As he rose from the ground he wiped his knees and said "it was the dirtiest house he had ever been in".'[4] 'Crowle was a noted punster', adds Walpole.

On 18 July 1753 Henry Pelham wrote to Newcastle:[5] 'Crowle the lawyer is making way at Hull . . . I had rather have another man than Crowle.' And on 7 Apr. 1754 Newcastle noted in his memoranda:[6] 'Mr. West to send a letter to the collector at Hull, to be singly for Lord Robert Manners with orders to give their second votes as he directs.' In Dupplin's list of 1754 Crowle is classed as an Opposition Whig, in Henry Fox's over the Mitchell election petition (February or March 1755) as a Tory;[7] and he attended the Tory meetings at the Horn Tavern over that petition.[8] He also sided with the Tories over the Oxfordshire election petitions;[9] and he spoke against the subsidy treaties on 10 Dec. 1755.[10]

Crowle died 21 June 1757.[11]

[1] 'Pedigree of Crowle Fam.' in *Charities of Hull.* [2] *Gent. Mag.* 1735, p. 218. The 'Pedigree' gives 1738 as the date of their marriage. [3] Poll book; and Thos. Hill's letter book, 24 July 1754, Attingham mss, Salop RO. [4] Walpole, *Mems. Geo. II*, i. 21. [5] Add. 32732, f. 303. [6] Add. 32995, f. 200. [7] Add. 33002, f. 438. [8] Sir Roger Newdigate's 'Diary', under 24 Mar. 1755, Newdigate mss, Warws. RO; and Namier, 'Country Gentlemen in Parlt.', *Personalities and Powers*, 69.[9] R. J. Robson, *Oxfordshire Election of 1754*, pp. 139, 166. [10] Fox to Devonshire, 11 Dec., Devonshire mss. [11] *Gent. Mag.* 1757, p. 290.

L.B.N.

## CRUGER, Henry (1739–1827), of Bristol.[1]

BRISTOL     1774–1780, 1784–1790

*b.* in New York 22 Nov. 1739, 2nd s. of Henry Cruger of New York by his w. Elizabeth Harris. *educ.* King's Coll. N.Y. (now Columbia Univ.). *m.* (1) Dec. 1765, Hannah (*d.*Feb. 1767), da. of Samuel Peach, Bristol merchant (a cos. of Samuel Peach [q.v.]), 1s.; (2) Elizabeth Blair (*d.*1790), 1da.; (3) 1799, Caroline Smith, an American, 4 ch.

Common councillor, Bristol 1766–90, sheriff 1766–7, ld. mayor 1781–2.

The Crugers were a family of New York merchants, prominent in provincial politics. Henry Cruger sen., a member of the provincial assembly 1745–59 and of the governor's council 1759–73, came to England in 1775, joined his son at Bristol, and died there in 1780. His brother John was mayor of New York in 1756, the first president of the New York chamber of commerce, a member of the Stamp Act congress, and Speaker of the New York assembly 1769–76. Henry Cruger's eldest son, John Harris Cruger, was a member of the governor's council of New York, served as a loyalist during the American war, and afterwards came to England. Two other sons settled in the West Indies.

Henry Cruger jun. came to England in 1757, and established himself as a merchant in Bristol. He married the daughter of a wealthy Bristol merchant and became active in local politics. In 1766 he was a member of the deputation of Bristol merchants which visited London to press for repeal of the Stamp Act. 'I was three weeks in London', he wrote to his father on 14 Feb. 1766,[2] 'and every day with some one Member of Parliament, talking as it were for my own life. It is surprising how ignorant some of them are on *trade and America*.' The non-importation agreement seriously affected his business, and during the remainder of his life in England he appears to have been financially embarrassed. In a letter to an American debtor, on 13 Feb. 1768,[3] he spoke of 'my pressing necessities', and on 14 July 1772 described himself as 'distressed for the

want of money more than ever man was'.[4] Edmund Burke in 1780 said that Cruger was 'not now worth a shilling'.[5]

Peach and Cruger were among the leaders of the radical movement, which grew rapidly in Bristol after 1768. Cruger presided over the meeting held at the Guildhall on 18 July 1769 to petition against the Middlesex election, and was the principal speaker at that of 20 Feb. 1772 to vote instructions to the Members.[6] He was present at the reception given to Wilkes on his visit to Bristol in January 1772,[7] and was described by North in September 1774 as 'a hot Wilkite'.[8] Well before the general election of 1774 he had been selected as the radical candidate at Bristol.

In 1773 Cruger went on a visit to America, returning to England in July 1774.[9] The committee of correspondence of the New York assembly wrote to their agent, Edmund Burke, on 31 May 1774:

> We beg leave to refer you for many particulars relative to the present situation of the colonies to Mr. Henry Cruger junior of Bristol, whose opportunities and means of information for a twelve month past have been extensive respecting a variety of matters of which you may be inclined to be informed.

At the general election in October he declined a union with Burke, and after a contest lasting 28 days was returned head of the poll. At its close (2 Nov.) he wrote to his brother-in-law, Jacob Walton, in New York:[10]

> Fum Hoam [Cruger's nickname in his family] is now, my dear Jacob, at the pinnacle of all human greatness —oh transitory joy!—he is exalted to the summit of all his earthly wishes, his foes are bending at his feet.
>   By the permission of providence I shall ascend the honourable car—the most magnificent chair that ever appeared in Bristol. Let the arrows of envy fly. I am fortified, I shall be protected against their malignant effects by the love and esteem of an hundred thousand people who will be assembled to attend my procession, and with shouts and acclamations of regard and approbation are determined to rend the air and shake the heavens.

At the declaration of the poll the next day he repeated a pledge he had given before the election:[11]

> It has ever been my opinion that the electors have a right to instruct their Members. For my part I shall always think it my duty in Parliament to be guided by your counsels and instructions.

The story that Cruger said 'I ditto to Mr. Burke' is an invention. As head of the poll Cruger spoke first.

'You may rely upon it', he wrote to Peter Van Schaack in New York on 5 Dec. 1774,[12] 'I will connect myself with none of the violent parties, but endeavour to temper my fire with prudence.' The American problem naturally concerned him most, and his first speech, 16 Dec. 1774, reflected the loyalty he felt for both Britain and America:[13]

I am far from approving all the proceedings in America. Many of their measures have been a dishonour to their cause. Their rights might have been asserted without violence, and their claims stated with temper as well as firmness. But . . . if they have erred, it may be considered as a failing of human nature. A people animated with a love of liberty, and alarmed with apprehensions of its being in danger, will unavoidably run into excesses . . .

I acknowledge that there must exist a power somewhere to superintend and regulate the movements of the whole for the attainment and preservation of our common happiness; this supreme power can be justly and adequately exercised only by the legislature of Great Britain . . .

When Great Britain derives from her colonies the most ample supplies of wealth by her commerce, is it not absurd to close up those channels for the sake of imposing taxes, which . . . never have and probably never will defray the expense of collecting them?

He was willing to believe that 'the impolicy and inexpediency of the late measures may reasonably be imputed to the difficulty of the occasion'. While pleading for forbearance towards America, he was not prepared to deny that the British Government had a case; and he had no confidence in the Opposition. He wrote to Van Schaack on 3 May 1775:[14]

The Opposition in the House of Commons flatter themselves that the confusion in *your* country will overthrow the ministry in this. But . . . let them come in when they will, they must adopt, and they know it, *nearly* the same measures with America that have been pursued by the present Administration, or they can not hold their places a single session. To get in is what we all want, and patriots in one station are great tyrants in another. America has long been made a cat's paw. On the ground of their calamities we fight our ambitious quarrels; and let who will gain the victory, New York will not be sixpence the gainer.

His second recorded speech, 2 Feb. 1775, was a failure.[15] In reply to a stupid tirade by James Grant on the cowardice of the Americans and their 'disagreeable manners',

he endeavoured to vindicate the Americans both as to their cowardice and gallantry . . . the latter he did with much good humour and pleasantry, but lost his temper in the former, became personal, and was called to order.

'I pant after peace between this country and its colonies', he said on 15 May;[16] and believed that only concessions on the part of America could bring it about. To his brother, John Harris Cruger, he wrote on 5 July:[17]

By one thing or other my heart is almost broke. Administration, finding everything in this country go to their liking, are bent upon carrying matters to the utmost extremities . . . Poor America will be utterly undone, unless some concession on their part is speedily made, which I am persuaded will be as speedily grasped at here, for all good men wish for a reconciliation.

In a speech of 20 Feb. 1776, on Fox's motion to

inquire into the conduct of the war, he reproached ministers for their treatment of the Loyalists:[18]

The friends of peace and good order in the province of New York did not deserve to be reproached with a shameful neutrality. They stood forth and opposed as long as they were able the increasing current of tumult and disorder, and exposed themselves . . . to the resentment and vengeance of their incensed neighbours. In a dutiful manner they submitted their grievances to the clemency of this House.. . . I shall not dwell on the contempt with which their zealous advances to a reconciliation were rejected . . . Administration not only neglected to aid them with a force sufficient to maintain their opposition against the zealots in their own province and the united powers of the adjacent colonies, but withdrew to Boston the few troops . . . which might have assisted in preserving order and the freedom and impartiality of public proceedings.

In private conversation with ministerial supporters he tried to put the American point of view. 'The answer always was', he wrote to Van Schaack on 17 June 1776, [19] 'that England would neither be intimidated by, nor receive laws from, America.'

Cruger did not vote for the Opposition amendment to the Address of 26 Oct. 1775, nor for their motion on the civil list debts of 16 Apr. 1777 (for neither division is a majority list extant). About this time he began to send to Charles Jenkinson reports from an agent in America on the state of affairs there. His first extant letter to Jenkinson is of 11 May 1777;[20] in it he wrote:

Let me entreat of you not to consider my attention in these small matters officious. You have been *peculiarly obliging to me*. I am sensibly grateful. And such is my natural turn of mind I shall always remain so.

How Jenkinson had obliged Cruger does not appear from their correspondence—possibly by services to his brother in America.

Only reluctantly did Cruger abandon the hope of an eventual reconciliation between Britain and America. On 10 Dec. 1777 he supported Wilkes's motion to repeal the Declaratory Act, and said:[21]

From my connections in America I have had an opportunity of collecting the sentiments of men of all orders and parties, and have reason to believe that independency is not yet the great object of the majority of the people; but a rooted and unconquerable aversion to those impolitic Acts prevail in every mind.

No further speech by Cruger on America is recorded until 5 May 1780,[22] when, in the debate on Conway's conciliation bill,

he said the American war . . . should be put an end to at all events; in order to do this the independency must be allowed, and the thirteen provinces treated as free states.

There is some ambiguity about Cruger's political attitude. Though elected as a professed radical, he is not known to have spoken for any radical measure. He did not attach himself to the Opposition, and seemed reluctant to break his links with the Government. One circumstance is particularly puzzling. In Robinson's 'Account of pensions extinguished', drawn up after the general election of 1780, is the entry of one of £500 per annum to Cruger, stopped when he left Parliament.[23] In Robinson's secret service accounts only one payment of this pension is recorded—on 19 May 1779;[24] but since these accounts are not extant before Jan. 1779 it is impossible to say when the pension started. Nor is it clear why it was given. £500 per annum was about the normal pension for a Member of Cruger's standing, and in the accounts it appears among those of Government supporters. Yet every one of Cruger's recorded votes was against Government, and in Robinson's survey for the general election of 1780 he was classed as against Administration. The sending of information such as he transmitted to Jenkinson was natural for a man in his position, but not a sufficient basis for such a pension.

Cruger and Burke were rivals at Bristol rather than colleagues; they disliked each other; and their enmity was aggravated by their supporters. Cruger had cultivated his constituents—according to Burke by 'a diligent attendance on *them*, and a total neglect of attendance in Parliament'.[25] In 1778 he obeyed instructions sent him from Bristol, and spoke and voted against removing the restrictions on Irish trade. He was popular with the poorer classes at Bristol, and in spite of strong opposition in 1780 from two Government candidates had a fair chance of success. The poor showing he made on the poll was due to deliberate abstention by Burke's supporters in revenge for Cruger's refusal to join with Burke. Cruger stood again at the by-election of 1781, but even with the support of Burke's friends was defeated. In both these contests he seems to have been financed mainly by his father-in-law.

On the conclusion of peace with America, Cruger wrote to John Hancock of Boston, 5 Mar. 1783:[26]

It is with heartfelt joy that I felicitate you on the channels of our intercourse being again opened by the accomplishment of our most sanguine wishes—the liberty and independence of America—an event on which I do most sincerely congratulate my countrymen. I embrace the earliest opportunity to inform my old friends and correspondents that I shall continue in this city in the American business, where I hope by receiving fresh marks of their favour and by redoubled industry to redeem the time lost in the late accursed war, and to repair the ravages which its influence has made on my fortune because of the steady principles which so strongly attached me to the just cause of America and mankind . . .

I purpose visiting my native land early the ensuing summer to participate in the joys and happiness which I hope to find resulting from the triumph of liberty and virtue.

Cruger was in America when the dissolution of 1784 took place, and the campaign at Bristol was conducted on his behalf by Peach and John Harris Cruger. He stood as a follower of Pitt, and was returned second on the poll.

His first speech in the new Parliament, 14 Feb. 1785,[27] was against the bill to restrain the United States from trading with Newfoundland. He

urged the expediency of encouraging the United States to continue their commercial intercourse with us as much as possible . . . He spoke . . . as a merchant, whose attachment was to Great Britain alone, and who regarded her prosperity as superior to every other consideration.

His further speeches were on subjects of interest to his constituents:[28] the Irish commercial propositions (he voted against Pitt on this question), the hawkers and pedlars bill, the shop tax, and the slave trade ('he considered a sudden and total abolition ruinous in the extreme'). He voted for parliamentary reform on 18 Apr. 1785; and supported Pitt on Richmond's fortifications plan and on the Regency.

On 17 Sept. 1789 Cruger applied to Pitt for a consular appointment in the United States, 'which would tend to rescue me and a large family from great difficulties'.[29] He was prepared to resign his seat at Bristol and support a candidate recommended by Pitt. But nothing came of this, and in March 1790 Cruger announced his intention of retiring to America. He sailed for New York on 8 Apr., still a Member of the British Parliament.

In 1792 he was elected to the senate of New York State, and died in New York on 24 Apr. 1827.

[1] In writing this biography use has been made of a paper by P. T. Underdown, and information supplied by Mr. A. H. Robertson, a descendant of Cruger. [2] 'Commerce of Rhode Island, 1726–1800', *Mass. Hist. Soc. Coll.* ser. 7, ix. 139–43. [3] Ibid. 219–20. [4] Ibid. 405. [5] Burke to Portland, 3 Sept. 1780. [6] *London Chron.* 25 July 1769, and *Bristol Gaz.* 27 Feb. 1772. [7] *Bristol Jnl.* 4 Jan. 1772. [8] Fortescue, iii. 137. [9] Rev. T. Wilson to Burke, 11 July 1774. [10] Ms in possession of Mr. A. H. Robertson. [11] *Bristol Jnl.* 5 Nov. 1774. [12] H. C. Van Schaack, *Henry Cruger*, 13. (New York, 1859; photostat copies in Bristol Univ. and Bristol Pub. Libs.) [13] Almon, i. 21–24. [14] Van Schaack, 16–17. [15] Almon, i. 136. [16] Ibid. 468. [17] Dartmouth mss. [18] Almon, iii. 333–9. [19] Van Schaack, 20. [20] Add. 38209, f. 120. [21] Almon, viii. 152–5. [22] Ibid. xvii. 658–9. [23] Laprade, 50. [24] Add. 37836, f. 63. [25] Burke to Portland, 3 Sept. 1780. [26] *New England Hist. & Geneal. Reg.* xxviii. 51. [27] Stockdale, iv. 168–9. [28] Stockdale, iv. 168–9; v. 233; vi. 437; xvii. 261–3, 275; Debrett, xix. 46. [29] Chatham mss.

J.B.

**CRUTCHLEY, Jeremiah** (1745–1805), of Sunninghill Park, Berks.

| | |
|---|---|
| HORSHAM | 1784–1790 |
| GRAMPOUND | 1790–1796 |
| ST. MAWES | 1796–1802 |

*b.* 20 Dec. 1745, o.s. of Jeremiah Crutchley of Sunninghill Park by his w. Alice née Jackson. *unm. suc. fa.* 1752.

In a list of candidates drawn up by John Robinson for the general election of 1784 Crutchley is included under the heading: 'Persons that will pay £2,000 or £2,500 or perhaps £3,000.'[1] He was provided with a seat at Horsham, placed by Lady Irwin at the disposal of Administration.[2] How much Crutchley paid is not known. Naturally, he supported Pitt. Before 1790 there is no record of his having spoken in the House.

Crutchley was a close friend of Henry Thrale (q.v.) and, with Samuel Johnson and John Cator (q.v.), an executor of his will. Mrs. Thrale, who disliked him, tells the story that he was Thrale's son, and calls him 'a mighty particular character . . . strangely mixed up of meanness and magnificence'. 'The sole comfort that fellow has in the world', she wrote in 1788, 'is doing his duty, which at last is done so disagreeably that he never gets even thanks for his pains.'[3] Her description is echoed by Fanny Burney:

> How strange, sad and perverse! With every possible means of happiness . . . to be thus unaccountably miserable. He has goodness, understanding, benevolence, riches, and independence, and with all these a something is wanting without which they are all as nothing.

She also writes of 'his never-ending oddities', and describes him as 'the least fathomable . . . of all the men I have seen'.[4]

Crutchley died 28 Dec. 1805.

[1] Laprade, 128. [2] About his election see Dr. Johnson to Mrs. Thrale, 15 Apr. 1784. [3] *Thraliana*, i. 496–7, 707. [4] *Diary and Letters of Mme d'Arblay*, ii. 3, 19, 42.

J.B.

**CUNINGHAME, James** (c.1731–88), of St. James's Place, London.

EAST GRINSTEAD 3 Mar. 1786–10 Sept. 1788

*b.* c.1731, 2nd s. of Col. David Cuninghame of Seabegs, Stirling, fort major of Stirling castle 1740–62, by Margaret, da. of John Callander of Craigforth, Stirling; bro. of Robert Cuninghame (q.v.). *unm.*

Capt. 45 Ft. 1755–75, lt.-col. 1758, col. 1772; half-pay 1775–80; maj.-gen. 1777; lt.-gen. 1782; col. 45 Ft. 1787–*d*.
Gov. Barbados 1780–2.

Cuninghame was closely connected with the Dorset family through his brother Robert (q.v.). He served in America under Loudoun and Wolfe,[1] and returned to England about 1760. In 1761 he was one of the officers selected to escort Queen Charlotte to England. After the peace he was stationed with his regiment in Ireland. In August 1773 the lord lieutenant, Lord Harcourt, forwarded to Rochford a memorial from Cuninghame mentioning his long service and asking for an appointment as lieutenant-colonel of a regiment of foot 'in any part of the world', or some other mark of favour.[2] His application was unsuccessful and in 1775 when his regiment was ordered to America, Cuninghame went on half pay, until in February 1780, through Germain's interest, he was appointed governor of Barbados.[3]

Here in February-March 1781 he initiated negotiations for the capitulation of the Dutch settlements at Demerara and Essequibo.[4] 'I flatter myself', he wrote to Germain on 25 Feb. 1781, 'that his Majesty will approve of the humanity to our old allies.'[5] But his humanity to the Barbadians was sharply challenged. From the beginning of his administration he was at odds with the colonial assembly, whose bill granting him a reduced salary he rejected in July 1780 in a truculent speech. He wrote to Germain, 10 Aug.:[6] 'This leaves me without income and I cannot hold out at my private expense.' Germain wrote to William Knox, 18 Sept. 1780:[7] 'I sincerely pity poor Cuninghame . . . I hope the Treasury will help the poor governor.' When Cuninghame proceeded to raise an income for himself by levying fees, the assembly raised the cry of 'No taxation without representation', refused to pass a supply bill, and through their agent Samuel Estwick (q.v.) petitioned for Cuninghame's removal.[8] Even when a devastating hurricane struck the island Cuninghame did not moderate his demands; he accepted an offer of £2,000 salary but insisted on retaining his fees and put in his personal claim for compensation for storm damage. His attitude shocked Horace Walpole:

> A governor writing on the ruins of a whole island levelled by the most fatal of all hurricanes, that his chief misery was the loss of what? his bracelets with the portraits of his idols—who would dare to bring such a revolting hyperbole on the stage?[9]

In February 1781 the assembly's charges against the governor came before the Board of Trade, who deferred consideration until receipt of Cuninghame's statement in defence.[10] Robert Cuninghame wrote to William Knox, 23 Aug. 1781, of his concern for his brother, 'who seems to have been intemperate and injudicious at setting out, but, since he began to recollect himself has done better'. Thankful that none of the governor's actions was considered censurable, Robert asked Knox to prompt North to remedy his brother's distress for money.[11]

But Cuninghame remained intransigent, continued to levy the disputed fees, delayed sending his defence, and the case was not heard until 13 Apr. 1782, after the fall of North and shortly before the abolition of the Board of Trade. When Estwick suggested that, in the circumstances, 'he supposed he should have no further occasion to trouble the Board', Cuninghame's counsel maintained that if there were no further proceedings, Cuninghame was entitled to an acquittal.[12] Cuninghame lost his governorship, but his conduct was regarded as vindicated.[13]

On his return home he settled in London. Although a supporter of North and the Coalition he, like his brother, went over to Pitt. He wrote to William Eden, 16 Dec. 1785:[14] 'I have now a transaction with [the Duke of Dorset] which I shall take an opportunity of communicating to you when you come to town.' This transaction was almost certainly the negotiation which led to his being returned on the Dorset interest for East Grinstead in March 1786. In the House, although assiduous in attendance, he is not known to have spoken.

His own precarious finances were improved by his appointment as colonel of his old regiment. Closely in touch with Irish as well as English political affairs and with the stock market, he kept Eden informed of events and opinions.[15] During the crisis of 1787 over Dutch affairs he wrote, 8 June:[16]

Opposition seem to be laying on their oars, thinking, I presume that they have a firm game to play. Our stocks fell one day for a quarter of an hour $3\frac{1}{2}$ per cent upon the report that Mr. Pitt was determined to resign —a flattering circumstance I think for him.

His loyalty to Pitt over the Regency question was not put to the test. He died 10 Sept. 1788.

[1] Cuninghame to Haldimand, 22 Nov. 1757, Add. 21728, f. 1; Cuninghame to Sackville, 30 May, 4 June 1758, HMC Stopford-Sackville, ii. 262. [2] Harcourt to Rochford, 10 Aug. 1773, Cal. Home Office Pprs. 1772–5, pp. 252, 279. [3] Bd. Trade Jnl. 1776–82, pp. 292–4. [4] APC Col. Unbound Pprs. 1006. [5] Ibid. 584. [6] HMC Stopford-Sackville, ii. 287. [7] HMC Var. vi. 172. [8] Bd. Trade Jnl. 1776–82, pp. 379, 392–3, 396. [9] Walpole to Lady Upper Ossory, 9 Jan. 1781; Cuninghame to Germain, 25 and 26 Nov. 1780, HMC Stopford-Sackville, ii. 290–1. [10] Bd. Trade Jnl. 1776–82, pp. 379, 392–6, 399–401. [11] HMC Var. vi. 179. [12] Bd. Trade Jnl. 1776–82, pp. 467–70. [13] Walpole to Lady Upper Ossory, 1 Oct. 1782. [14] Add. 34420, f. 259. [15] Auckland Corresp. i. 436–8. [16] Add. 34425, f. 92.

E.H.-G.

## CUNINGHAME, Robert (c.1728–1801), of Mount Kennedy, co. Wicklow.

EAST GRINSTEAD 8 Oct. 1788–Feb. 1789

b. c.1728, 1st s. of Col. David Cuninghame, and bro. of James Cuninghame (q.v.). educ. Edinburgh Univ. m. 29 May 1754, Elizabeth, da. and coh. of Col. John Murray, s.p.
Ensign 20 Ft. 1746; capt. 35 Ft. 1752–6, lt.-col. 1757, col. 1762; col. 58 Ft. 1767–75; gov. Kinsale Fort 1770–d.; maj.-gen. 1772; col. 14 Ft. 1775–87; lt.-gen. 1777; col. 5 Drag. 1787–99; gen. 1793; c.-in-c. [I] 1793–6.
M.P. [I] 1751–96; P.C. [I] 7 June 1782; cr. Baron Rossmore [I] 19 Oct. 1796.

In September 1745 Cuninghame joined the Edinburgh Volunteers in defence of the capital against the approaching rebel army, by whom he was captured while on a reconnoitring expedition. Alexander Carlyle writes:[1]

Bob Cunningham . . . was studying law; but his father being an officer . . . he had a military turn . . . He resented the bad usage his father's nephew, Murray of Broughton . . . had given him during the day he was captive, and was determined to become a volunteer in some regiment till the rebellion was suppressed.

He served at Culloden in the 14 Ft. and subsequently obtained a commission in Lord George Sackville's regiment. He early attracted the attention of his colonel, who, when Dorset was appointed lord lieutenant of Ireland, obtained for him a place in the household of Archbishop Stone and a seat in the Irish Parliament.[2]

In 1752 Cuninghame decided, with the backing of the Sackvilles, Argyll, and Loudoun, to oppose George Haldane (q.v.) in Stirling Burghs, but withdrew in 1754 after being 'outbid' by the Haldanes.[3]

Cuninghame's marriage in 1754 to a Scots-Irish heiress with influential family and parliamentary connexions determined his future career; he made his home in Ireland, where most of his military life was spent, and gained considerable reputation as an eloquent Government supporter in the Irish Parliament. He remained the lifelong friend and confidant of Lord George Sackville, and was on close terms with General Irwin and William Eden (qq.v.). 'Sufficiently affluent—happy at home',[4] he was not materially affected by the fall of North. Under the Coalition he was promised the command in Ireland,[5] but his hopes were disappointed by the change of ministry. Convinced at first that his Opposition friends must prevail, by February 1784 he was deeply disturbed by the situation. He wrote to Eden:[6] 'I did not know till now that I was so sincerely a patriot, for I ardently wish for any settlement rather than the present contest.' By 1785 he had gone over to Pitt, voted for his Irish propositions in the Irish Parliament, and congratulated Eden on accepting Government office.[7]

An able speaker, although 'much injured by a strong Scots accent',[8] Robert was in 1788 the obvious choice to succeed his brother James in the Sackville borough of East Grinstead. But within two months of his election, unwilling to commit himself on the Regency question, he wrote to the Duke of Dorset, then ambassador in Paris, asking leave to relinquish his seat. Hawkesbury reported to Pitt, 10 Dec. 1788:[9]

General Cuninghame . . . came to me yesterday and held a long conversation with me, which was not favourable. The most I could obtain was that he would give no vote till he heard from the Duke of Dorset . . . I have reason to think that [his brother-in-law] Lord Clermont (who lives at present with the Prince) is the General's adviser.

Cuninghame did not vote in the Regency divisions, and vacated his seat in February 1789. He resumed his career in Ireland, where he died 6 Aug. 1801.

[1] Carlyle, *Autobiog.* 136, 157-8. [2] Stone to Sackville, 20 May, 13 June 1751, *HMC Stopford-Sackville*, i. 172; Walpole to Mann, 13 May 1752. [3] Cuninghame to Loudoun, 14 Jan. 1753, Loudoun mss; Argyll to Pelham, 4 Sept. 1753, Newcastle (Clumber) mss. [4] Cuninghame to Eden, 20 Oct. 1782, Add. 34419, f. 61. [5] Ibid. f. 303. [6] Ibid. f. 359. [7] See his letters to Eden in Add. 34420. [8] Rev. John R. Scott, *A Review of the (Irish) House of Commons.* [9] Chatham mss.

E.H.-G.

**CUNLIFFE, Ellis** (1717–67), of Saighton Grange, nr. Chester.

LIVERPOOL 19 Dec. 1755–16 Oct. 1767

*b.* 12 Apr. 1717, 1st s. of Foster Cunliffe, merchant, of Liverpool and Saighton by Margaret, da. of Robert Carter, alderman of Lancaster. *m.* 19 Dec. 1760, Mary, da. of Henry Bennet of Moston, Cheshire, 2da. Kntd. 18 Apr. 1756; *suc.* fa. 1758; *cr.* Bt. 26 Mar. 1759, with spec. rem. to his bro. Robert.

Cunliffe, the son of a prosperous merchant and shipowner of Liverpool, seems to have made delicate health an excuse to avoid taking a very active part in the business, which he disliked, and during his father's lifetime spent much of his time in the south of England or travelling abroad.[1]

In 1755, helped by his father's popularity in Liverpool, he was returned unopposed on the corporation interest. In Parliament he supported Administration; in May 1758, his father having left him 'in possession of an affluent fortune',[2] he applied to Newcastle for a baronetcy; and in March 1759 had his request granted. In 1761 he successfully contested the borough, again on the corporation interest, jointly with the unsuccessful candidate Charles Pole (q.v.). According to their opponent Sir William Meredith (q.v.):[3]

No man ever stood better with his constituents, than Sir Ellis Cunliffe did at Liverpool, when I first went there. He sunk himself daily and gradually by supporting his colleague . . . the temper of the people was to choose a Member independent of the corporation; and by resisting that temper Sir Ellis Cunliffe's influence was lost entirely.

Yet Cunliffe topped the poll. Because of Newcastle's distrust of the 'Tory' Meredith, he obtained 'the disposal of everything'[4] at Liverpool on condition that he did not recommend any of Meredith's friends. In March 1762 he brought in a bill for erecting lights and building a new dock at Liverpool, and asked for Newcastle's help in getting it through the House. In Bute's list he was classed as 'Newcastle'; but he appears in Henry Fox's list of Members favourable to the peace preliminaries; and was noted by Newcastle as absent from the divisions of 9 and 10 Dec.[5] On 25 Oct. 1763 Meredith wrote to Charles Jenkinson: 'There is an idea of Sir Ellis

Cunliffe resigning his seat in Parliament; but I know no other presumption for it than his state of health, which is miserable.'[6] He was absent from the debates on general warrants, February 1764; and wrote to Newcastle, the same month, that he was 'under the care of Dr. James, the effects of whose medicines will by no means allow him to stir abroad'.[7] Newcastle, 10 May 1764, classed him as a 'sure friend', but Cunliffe continued to recommend to Government appointments at Liverpool. He was classed by Rockingham, July 1765, as 'pro', in November 1766 as 'Swiss', and by Townshend, January 1767, as 'Government'. He voted with the Administration on the land tax 27 Feb. 1767.

Cunliffe's one reported speech was on the prize bill, 4 May 1759. He died 16 Oct. 1767.

[1] Information from a family record written by Cunliffe's nephew, provided by Capt. R. L. Cunliffe, R.N. (retd.). [2] Add. 32879, ff. 442-3. [3] To E. Burke, 28 Oct. 1767. [4] *Jenkinson Pprs.* 214. [5] Add. 33000, ff. 278-9. [6] *Jenkinson Pprs.* 210. [7] Add. 32956, f. 13.

M.M.D.

**CUNYNGHAME, Sir William Augustus,** 4th Bt. (1747–1828), of Livingstone, Linlithgow and Milncraig, Ayr.

LINLITHGOWSHIRE 1774–1790

*b.* 19 Apr. 1747, o. surv. s. of Lt.-Gen. Sir David Cunynghame, 3rd Bt., by Lady Mary Montgomerie, da. of Alexander, 9th Earl of Eglintoun [S]. *educ.* Ch. Ch. Oxf. 1766; Grand Tour. *m.* (1) 21 Oct. 1768, Frances (*d.*14 Nov. 1771), da. and eventual h. of Sir Robert Myreton, 2nd Bt., of Gogar, Edinburghshire, 3s.; (2) 22 June 1785, Mary, da. and h. of Robert Udney of Udney, Aberdeen, 4s. 1da. *suc.* fa. 10 Oct. 1767.

Clerk comptroller of the Board of Green Cloth June 1779–Mar. 1782; receiver of the land tax in Scotland June 1806–Mar. 1807.

Cunynghame's father, a distinguished soldier, contested Linlithgowshire in 1761, and as early as 1764 announced his candidature against the Hopetoun interest at the next election.[1] William was originally intended for the army, but having been refused a vacant commission in his father's regiment, the 57th, apparently declined an unpaid ensigny in the 33rd.[2] On his father's death in 1767 he went abroad, returning shortly before the 1768 election to support James Dundas (q.v.) in Linlithgowshire. To 'void' his vote, his opponents made search for his 'birth brieve' and fixed the election date for 16 Apr., three days before he came of age.[3] Cunynghame's objections were a major factor in the success of Dundas's petition.

After the death of his wife in 1771 Cunynghame spent much time abroad, in Italy, Paris and Vienna,[4] until the general election of 1774, when by agreement with the Hopetoun interest he was returned for Linlithgowshire.[5] A wealthy young man of fashion, prone to 'rattle' of his 'fabulous gallantries', he was a close friend of his brother-in-law James Stuart and Lord Mountstuart,[6] whose politics he followed. As a faithful, though inconspicuous, Government supporter, he was given a lucrative place in the King's Household in June 1779, and made his first recorded speech in the debate of 22 June on doubling the militia.[7] On 3 Dec., in the debate on Scotland's defences, he denied the charges of his kinsman Lord George Gordon that Scotland was drained of men; and described from personal experience the 'respectable state of preparation' when Paul Jones was in the Firth of Forth.[8]

In the Parliament of 1780–4 no speech by him is recorded. He consistently voted with North to the end of his Administration; voted against Shelburne's peace preliminaries, 18 Feb. 1783; and for Fox's East India bill, 27 Nov. 1783. In December, shortly before Pitt took office, Robinson counted him 'contra', but possibly 'pro' in a new Parliament:[9]

Sir William Cunynghame is at present warm in support of the Administration. If he comes in he may not be quite steady, though most probably will be so, because he leans to Lord Mountstuart and affects to go as that family does; but a word from Lord Hopetoun might set this right both *now* and in *future*.

Nevertheless he remained against Pitt to the end of the Parliament, when Henry Dundas used all his influence without success to replace him in Linlithgowshire.[10] In the debate of 30 Mar. 1786 on Marsham's bill to disfranchise employees of the navy and ordnance boards, Cunynghame accused Dundas of having sent down dockyard placemen to 'interfere against him', an expedient which Dundas justified on party principles.[11]

Cunynghame, impervious to the ridicule of Pitt and Dundas, and even, on occasion, the admonitions of his friends, stood forth as the indefatigable champion of Scottish interests. Determined to 'give a brain blow' to the application of the coal tax in Scotland, he pressed a division on 1 July 1784; strongly supported the forfeited estates bill on 2 Aug. 1784; opposed, 4 Aug., on behalf of the Scots manufacturers, the new duties on cotton and linen, and was vehement against the window tax as oppressive to Scotland. In 1785 he campaigned in and outside the House against Pitt's Irish propositions as ruinous to the Scottish linen industry, corn trade, and fisheries. Strongly opposed to the abortive plan for reducing the number of Scottish judges, he actively supported in 1786 the proposed augmentation of their salaries, and unsuccessfully moved an amendment for a further increase commensurate

with the emoluments of English judges. He won great popularity in Scotland, and exasperated Pitt, by his vehement support of the Scots distilling interests in the measures of 1785, 1786 and 1788. He consistently voted against Administration.[12]

Defeated in 1790 by the Government-sponsored Hopetoun interest, he did not re-enter Parliament. He died 17 Jan. 1828.

[1] Sir David Cunynghame to W. Mure, 9 Apr. 1764, *Caldwell Pprs.* ii (2), p. 244. [2] Barrington to Granby, 18 and 29 Sept. 1766, Rutland mss. [3] Loudoun's corresp. with Ld. Cassillis and John Bell, Mar.-Apr. 1768, Loudoun mss. [4] See his letters to R. Murray Keith, Add. 35507, ff. 134, 222; also T. Heathcote to Keith, 5 Mar. 1774, ibid. f. 8. [5] Laprade, 8. [6] Boswell, *Private Pprs.* x. 163, 272–4; xi. 161, 254–5. [7] Fortescue, iv. 371. [8] Almon, xvi. 84–85. [9] Laprade, 103. [10] Dundas to Duke of Rutland, 13 Apr. 1784, *HMC Rutland*, iii. 88–89. [11] Debrett, xx. 45–46. [12] Stockdale, ii. 252–5, 263; iii. 368, 391, 447; iv. 310; v. 5–6, 7, 45–46, 49, 52, 217, 310; vi. 427; viii. 77–78, 153–4; xiii. 134, 183; xiv. 233; xv. 50.

E.H.-G.

**CURTIS, John** (?1751–1813), of Berkeley St., Berkeley Sq., London.

WELLS            31 Aug. 1782–1784
STEYNING      7 Mar. 1791–Jan. 1794

*b.* ?1751, s. of John Curtis of Bristol and Butcombe, Som. *m.* Susanna, *s.p.*

Curtis's father was a Bristol merchant who bought an estate at Butcombe in Somerset. Curtis successfully contested Wells on the interest of Clement Tudway (q.v.). In Parliament he voted against Shelburne's peace preliminaries, 18 Feb. 1783; for parliamentary reform, 7 May 1783; and against Fox's East India bill, 27 Nov. 1783. He was classed as 'pro' by Robinson, January 1784, and in Stockdale's list of 19 Mar.

In 1784 Curtis did not stand again at Wells, but unsuccessfully contested Saltash on the interest of William Beckford jun. (q.v.), who was returned for Wells.

Curtis died 30 Nov. 1813, aged 62.

M.M.D.

**CURWEN, Henry** (1728–78), of Workington, Cumb.

CARLISLE            1761–1768
CUMBERLAND    1768–1774

*bap.* 25 Nov. 1728, o.s. of Eldred Curwen, M.P., of Workington by his w. Julian Clenmoe. *educ.* Eton 1745; St. John's, Camb. 1746. *m.* Isabella, da. of William Gale of Whitehaven, 1 da., who m. John Christian (q.v.). *suc.* fa. 1745.
Sheriff, Cumb. 1753–4.

Curwen was a considerable coal proprietor at Workington: at his death his collieries were valued at about £5,000 a year.

He contested Carlisle in 1761 at the request of a group of independent freemen in opposition to Sir

James Lowther's interest. He was not sent New-castle's whip in 1761, and was noted by Bute as 'Tory' and 'contra'. Probably neither knew much about him and found him difficult to classify. He does not appear in Henry Fox's list of Members favourable to the peace preliminaries, but did not vote against them.

He was active in opposing the Lowther interest in Cumberland and became connected with the Duke of Portland. He voted against Administration on Wilkes, 15 Nov. 1763, and general warrants, 6, 15 and 18 Feb. 1764, and was classed by Rockingham in July 1765 as 'pro'. Both Rockingham in November 1766 and Newcastle in March 1767 counted him as a friend, and henceforth he voted with the Rockingham party. There is no record of his having spoken in Parliament.

He stood for Cumberland in 1768 on a joint interest with Henry Fletcher (q.v.), Portland's candidate, against Lowther and Humphrey Senhouse (q.v.). Curwen was returned head of the poll with 2139 votes—162 ahead of Lowther, who was returned with him. In November 1770 he told Portland that because of bad health, which had prevented him from attending Parliament regularly, he would retire at the next general election.[1]

He died 23 June 1778.

[1] Curwen to Portland, 19 Nov. 1770, Portland mss.

J.B.

## CURWEN, see also CHRISTIAN

## CURZON, Assheton (1730–1820), of Penn House, nr. Amersham, Bucks.

CLITHEROE   1754–1780, 28 Feb. 1792–13 Aug. 1794

*b.* 2 Feb. 1730, 2nd surv. s. of Sir Nathaniel Curzon, 4th Bt., M.P., by Mary, da. and coh. of Sir Ralph Assheton, 2nd Bt., M.P., of Middleton, Lancs.; bro. of Nathaniel Curzon (q.v.). *educ.* Westminster 1740–6; B.N.C. Oxf. 1747. *m.* (1) 23 Feb. 1756, Esther (*d.*21 July 1764), da. and h. of William Hanmer of Hanmer, Flints., 1s. 2da.; (2) 6 Feb. 1766, Dorothy (*d.*25 Feb. 1774), da. of Sir Robert Grosvenor, 6th Bt. (q.v.), 2s. 5da.; (3) 17 Apr. 1777, Anne, da. of Amos Meredith, sis. of Sir William Meredith, 3rd Bt. (q.v.), wid. of Barlow Trecothick (q.v.), *s.p.* *cr.* Baron Curzon 13 Aug. 1794; Visct. Curzon 27 Feb. 1802.

Curzon was a Tory. In 1754 he was returned for the family seat at Clitheroe. Recommended for Derbyshire by his brother in 1761, he declined to face a contest; refused an offer from the corporation of Derby to bring him in without expense;[1] and was returned again at Clitheroe. Henry Fox considered him for seconder of the Address on the King's Speech, 25 Nov. 1762,[2] and Jenkinson in the autumn of 1763 classed him as 'pro'. One speech by him is

reported during this Parliament: 13 Mar. 1764, on Rose Fuller's bill for converting statute labour into a rate. In July 1765 Rockingham classed him as 'contra', and he voted against the repeal of the Stamp Act. In January 1767 Townshend counted him as a follower of Grenville. He voted with Opposition on the land tax, 27 Feb. 1767, and the nullum tempus bill, 17 Feb. 1768.

Between 1768 and 1774 he spoke several times but does not appear in any division list. In Robinson's first survey on the royal marriage bill he is marked 'doubtful', in the second, 'pro'; but, 23 Mar., he spoke for Rose Fuller's clause to limit the duration of the bill. His next recorded vote was with Administration on the contractors bill, 12 Feb. 1779. In 1779 the *Public Ledger* wrote about him: 'A man of Tory principles, votes with the ministry, but sometimes affects to be conscientious by quitting the House when the minister's question is not agreeable to him.' He voted with the Opposition on the motion to abolish the Board of Trade, 13 Mar. 1780, but with the court on Dunning's motion, 6 Apr., and the motion against prorogation, 24 Apr. In July 1780 Robinson classed him as 'pro'.

In 1780 he stood again for Clitheroe, but was deprived of his share in its representation by his fellow Member, Thomas Lister, and defeated on the poll.[3]

He died 21 Mar. 1820.

[1] Scarsdale to Bute, 26 Aug. 1761, Bute mss. [2] Fox to Bute, 23 Nov. 1762, ibid. [3] See CLITHEROE constituency.

J.B.

## CURZON, Nathaniel (1726–1804), of Kedleston, Derbys.

CLITHEROE       2 Feb. 1748–1754
DERBYSHIRE      1754–1761

*b.* 23 Dec. 1726, 1st surv. s. of Sir Nathaniel Curzon, 4th Bt., M.P.; bro. of Assheton Curzon (q.v.). *educ.* Westminster 1740–4; Ch. Ch. Oxf. 1745; Grand Tour. *m.* 27 Oct. 1750, Lady Caroline Colyear, da. of Charles, 2nd Earl of Portmore [S], 5s. 2da. *suc.* fa. as 5th Bt. 18 Nov. 1758; *cr.* Baron Scarsdale 9 Apr. 1761.

Curzon's uncle and father had sat for Derbyshire as Tories 1701–27 and 1727–54, and he himself was classed by Dupplin in 1754 as 'Tory'. He was one of the Tories who on 12 Mar. 1755 over the Mitchell election petition voted on the Sandwich-Fox side.[1] Even under George II he was known to be bent on a peerage.[2] In the new reign, on 9 Nov. 1760, he wrote to Bute[3] claiming the barony of Powis, then in abeyance—

whatever favour his Majesty may be pleased to show me on this occasion will not be misplaced, and I shall always be happy in exerting on every occasion the influence of myself and family in the support of his Majesty's Government.

In February 1761 handbills appeared announcing that Curzon was 'soon to be made a peer'. Horace Walpole wrote to Horace Mann, 3 Mar. 1761:

Sir Nathaniel Curzon has struck a very novel stroke advertising that the King intended to make him a peer, and therefore, recommending his brother to the county of Derby for the same *independent* principles with himself. He takes a peerage to prove his independence, and recommends his brother to the Opposition to prove his gratitude!

But according to Curzon's own explanation to Bute[4]

the truth was that my friends through a mistaken zeal to serve me, got the hand bills printed and dispersed in my absence . . . I told my friends I had taken this advertisement upon myself but begged they would be careful it never appeared in a public paper, and when it did appear I sent express to London to stop it. And I do declare I never signed any one of them myself.

Curzon received his peerage on 9 Apr. 1761. On 2 Mar. 1764, disappointed in his claim to the lord lieutenancy of Derbyshire, he wrote to the King:[5]

I should wish indeed always to be considered as not building my interests on party combinations, but as choosing to rest my hopes on your Majesty's graciousness rather than ministerial favour.

He followed the Bedfords, and in December 1766 was included in the list of friends for whom they demanded office. After 1767 he voted with the court.

Curzon began to build a new house at Kedleston in 1759 or 1760. The main work took place in the years 1760–4 when at least £22,500 was spent; at least £42,000 was laid out from 1760 to 1777. This strained his resources—his rental income was about £8,000 to £9,000 a year—and the house was never completed. It seems that by 1779 he had alienated his Queen Square estate in London, which had brought in about £1,100 a year, in order to pay off debts incurred since he succeeded his father.[6]

Curzon died 5 Dec. 1804.

[1] E. Boscawen to Newcastle. Add. 32853, f. 260. [2] Egmont's parliamentary list c. 1750. [3] Fortescue, i. 5. [4] 17 Feb. 1761, Bute mss. [5] Fortescue, i. 67. [6] Ex inf. R. A. C. Parker, The Queen's College, Oxford.

L.B.N.

## CURZON, Hon. Nathaniel (1751–1837).

DERBYSHIRE    4 Feb. 1775–1784

*b.* 16 Sept. 1751, 1st s. of Nathaniel, 1st Baron Scarsdale (q.v.). *educ.* Westminster 1764–7; Ch. Ch. Oxf. 1768. *m.* (1) 11 Aug. 1777, Hon. Sophia Susanna Noel (*d.*28 June 1782), da. of Edward, 1st Visct. Wentworth, 1s. 1da.; (2) 18 Nov. 1798, Félicité Anne Josèphe, da. of François Josèphe des Wattines of Hesdin, France, 2s. 3da. *suc.* fa. as 2nd Lord Scarsdale 5 Dec. 1804.

Curzon apparently thought of standing at the general election of 1774. The Duchess of Devonshire wrote to Lady Spencer, 9 Oct. 1774: 'Lord Scarsdale intends to set up Mr. Curzon for the county.'[1] But he did not do so, nor did Curzon stand for a seat described as 'extremely eligible' and infinitely preferable 'to a contest for Derbyshire'[2] though costing £4,500, which was suggested to him. In February 1775 he was returned unopposed for Derbyshire.

Curzon consistently supported North till the end; voted against Shelburne's peace preliminaries, 18 Feb. 1783, and for Fox's East India bill, 27 Nov. 1783. Robinson noted in his survey for the general election of 1784 that Curzon would probably come in again, and that 'at present may vote con, but on a change, would it is apprehended, be for'; and in Stockdale's list of 19 Mar. 1784 he appears as a follower of Pitt. There is no record of his having spoken in the House—which confirms the statement of the *English Chronicle* in 1780 that 'he gives a *silent vote* always with the ministry'.

In 1784 Curzon canvassed for re-election, but met with 'a serious opposition'[3] in the county, and apparently withdrew before the poll.

He died 27 Jan. 1837.

[1] *Anglo-Saxon Review*, i. 226. [2] I. H. Browne to N. Curzon, n.d. 1774, Scarsdale mss. [3] Ld. Gower to Curzon, 9 Apr. 1784, ibid.

M.M.D.

## CURZON, Penn Assheton (1757–97), of Gopsall Hall, Leics.

LEOMINSTER         1784–1790
CLITHEROE          1790–Feb. 1792
LEICESTERSHIRE  27 Feb. 1792–3 Sept. 1797

*bap.* 31 Jan. 1757, 1st s. of Assheton Curzon (q.v.), by his 1st w. Esther Hanmer. *educ.* Westminster 1768; B.N.C. Oxf. 1774. *m.* 31 July 1787, Hon. Sophia Charlotte Howe, da. and h. of Richard, 4th Visct. Howe (q.v.), 3s. 1da. *suc.* uncle Charles Jennens, of Gopsall, Leics. 1773.

In 1784 Curzon successfully contested Leominster. He is listed by William Adam as a Government supporter. His only reported votes were with Opposition on Richmond's fortifications plan, 27 Feb. 1786, and with Administration on the Regency, 1788–9. There is no record of his having spoken in the House.

He died *v.p.* 3 Sept. 1797.

M.M.D.

## CUST, Sir Brownlow, 4th Bt. (1744–1807), of Belton, Lincs.

ILCHESTER   1768–1774
GRANTHAM   1774–20 May 1776

*b.* 5 Dec. 1744, 1st s. of Sir John Cust (q.v.). *educ.* at Stilton 1750; Eton 1758–60; Corpus Christi, Camb. 1762. *m.* (1) 16 Oct. 1770 ('with a large estate valued at £103,000'),[1] Jocosa Katherine (*d.*Feb. 1772), da. and coh. of Sir Thomas Drury, 1st Bt., of Overstone, Northants., 1da.; (2) 31 Aug. 1775, Frances, o. da. and h. of Sir Henry Bankes, London alderman, 6s. 5da. *suc.* fa. 24 Jan. 1770, and to Belton under the will of his gd.-m., Anne Lady Cust, 29 Dec. 1779; *cr.* (for his father's services) Baron Brownlow of Belton, 20 May 1776.

On coming of age Brownlow Cust took up the freedom of Grantham, and on 8 Jan. 1766 entertained the corporation and freemen at a big dinner, arranged by his uncles and attended by Lord Granby and Lord George Sutton (qq.v.).[2] This for the more distant future; but helping to find a seat for Brownlow before he succeeded to Grantham, Egmont, who had estates and connexions in Somerset, wrote to John Cust on 7 Aug. 1765:[3] 'I have spoken to Lockyer upon the subject we discoursed upon lately coming from Turnham Green, and I believe he will talk with you upon that business as soon as you come to town.' This is the beginning of the Custs' connexion with Ilchester, a borough managed by Thomas Lockyer (q.v.). Brownlow Cust wrote to his father from Ilchester, 16 Mar. 1768:[4]

> It is impossible that you even amongst our most valuable friends at Grantham can have today a more unanimous election than I have had here. There was scarce one of the opposite party to be seen and no interruption given to the poll: one man desired to vote for somebody else, but soon withdrew his vote, and gave us no opposition: insomuch that Mr. Leigh and I were in our chairs at half past eight. We were to give 'em a short harangue of thanks from the market cross, I concluded mine with a compliment to Mr. Lockyer.

In the House Brownlow regularly voted with the Government, his only vote against them being over Grenville's Election Act, 25 Feb. 1774; and this was treated by North as an exceptional deviation by a friend. There is no record of his having spoken in the House.

On being created a peer, Brownlow wrote to his grandmother, Anne Lady Cust, 18 May 1776, about the family being now 'possessed of that very fruit of my dear father's labours which was the great object of them'.[5]

He died 25 Dec. 1807.

[1] *Recs. Cust .Fam.* ii. 296. [2] Ibid. iii. 249–56. [3] Ibid. iii. 245. [4] Ibid. iii. 279. [5] Ibid. ii. 301.

L.B.N.

## CUST (afterwards COCKAYNE CUST), Francis (1722–91), of Cockayne Hatley, Beds.

| | |
|---|---|
| GRANTHAM | 2 Feb. 1770–1774 |
| HELSTON | 15 Mar. 1775–1780 |
| GRANTHAM | 1780–30 Nov. 1791 |

*bap.* 18 Mar. 1722, 3rd s. of Sir Richard Cust, 2nd Bt., by Anne, da. of Sir William Brownlow, 4th Bt., sis. and h. of John, 1st Visct. Tyrconnel [I]; bro. of Sir John and Peregrine Cust (qq.v.). *educ.* Grantham g.s.; Eton 1733; King's, Camb. 1738, fellow from 1742; M. Temple 1735, called 1742. *unm. suc.* to Cockayne Hatley estate of uncle Savile Cockayne Cust 27 Jan. 1772, and assumed name of Cockayne Cust.

Dep. recorder, Grantham 1752,[1] Boston 1760; recorder, Grantham 1780. Counsel to the Admiralty 1771–*d.*, also to university of Cambridge; bencher, M. Temple 1772, treasurer 1784.

In spite of deafness 'from which Francis Cust suffered so much and which interfered with his professional career',[2] he soon 'obtained good practice as a Chancery lawyer'.[3] He was much trusted by his family—'my brother Francis whom I never knew mistaken . . .' wrote John Cust to Lord Guilford in April 1754[4]—and he was regularly consulted in their affairs, although his irascible temper did not render dealings with him easy. 'It answers no end', he wrote to his brother John on one occasion, 'to debate any more on a subject, in which all that I have had to say has been answered either with levity, or with arrogance, or contempt' . . . 'It has been a constant maxim to drive me, and to require from me a tame submission to those who have no right to usurp such an arbitrary authority as has been exercised over me.'[5] Or again: 'You may be well assured that I will not search for your writings, if you cannot tell me where they are.'[6] But he thus opens that particular letter: 'I am sorry you think me in a scolding disposition . . .'

At the general election of 1761 Francis would have stood for Grantham had John contested the county—which added to Francis's annoyance at John's hesitations. But as John never left Grantham, Francis had to wait another ten years. After John's death in 1770, Lord William Manners planned an opposition at Grantham but 'the Duke's good sense has preserved the coalition between Belvoir and Belton entire'.[7] Francis Cust was returned unopposed. As counsel to the Admiralty, and, through the Brownlows, a cousin of Lord North, he adhered to Administration. In 1774 he had to withdraw from Grantham in favour of his nephew Brownlow. He was invited to stand at Helston by the party opposed to the Godolphin interest, on condition that if defeated he would petition. He and Philip Yorke of Erthig, a son-in-law of John Cust, were seated on a petition which impugned the working of the new charter given to the borough by the Government, 3 Sept. 1774. This did not, however, affect his line in the House—he voted with Administration whenever present. 'He is a heavy puzzle-headed gentleman', wrote the *Public Ledger* in 1779; while the *English Chronicle* spoke, in 1780, of his 'invariable attachment to Lord North'. Robinson, in his survey for the general election of 1780, first expected Peregrine to be re-elected at Grantham, but added on 30 July that Francis was to take his place, 'and he is equally a friend'. He voted with the North Government to the end.

Generally his attendance was irregular, and he seems to have taken no part in debate: both things may have been due to his deafness. Also after April 1782 he seems to have gone usually with the Government. In Shelburne's list of November 1782 he is classed as 'hopeful', and in Robinson's of March 1783 as a follower of Shelburne although he had not voted on the peace preliminaries, 18 Feb. And again although he had voted for Fox's India bill, in December 1783 Robinson classed him as 'hopeful'.[8] Next, in Stockdale's list of 19 Mar. 1784 he was classed as opposed to Pitt's Administration; but in William Adam's list of the new Parliament, as 'doubtful'. In short, neither side knew what to make of him. But in feeling, though perhaps not in action, he was with Opposition—thus in a letter to his nephew Philip Yorke, 23 Dec. 1784:[9] 'In such times what can Cato do? He can neither stoop to a Thurlotumbo of Law, nor bow to a boy in office who was made minister against the sense of the Commons.' Still, his only recorded vote in that Parliament was on the Government side, and that on Richmond's fortifications plan, on which a good many followers of Pitt voted with Opposition. He did not vote in the divisions on the Regency 1788-9.

Cust died 30 Nov. 1791. His will[10] starts: 'Whereas much trouble and inconvenience often arise from taking accounts of the goods and effects of persons dying intestate . . .'; but he omitted to have either the will or its codicil witnessed.

[1] *Recs. Cust Fam.* ii. 276. [2] Anne Lady Cust to John Cust, March 1750, ibid. 271. [3] Ibid. iii. 12. [4] Ibid. ii. 278; see also ibid. iii. 187. [5] Ibid. 194. [6] Ibid. 176-7. [7] Levett Blackborne to Geo. Vernon, 3 Feb. 1770, *HMC Rutland*, ii. 314. [8] Laprade, 74. [9] A. Cust. *Chrons. of Erthig*, ii. 234. [10] *Recs. Cust. Fam.* iii. 333.

L.B.N.

**CUST, Sir John,** 3rd Bt. (1718-70), of Belton, Lincs.

GRANTHAM    18 Apr. 1743-24 Jan. 1770

*b.* 12 Aug. 1718, 1st s. of Sir Richard Cust, 2nd Bt., M.P., and bro. of Francis and Peregrine Cust (qq.v.). *educ.* Grantham g.s.; Eton 1731-5; Corpus Christi, Camb. 1735-9; M. Temple 1735, called 1742. *m.* 8 Dec. 1743, Etheldred, da. and coh. of Thomas Payne of Hough, Lincs., 2s. 2da. *suc.* fa. 25 July 1734; his mother inherited Brownlow estates on d. of her bro. John, Visct. Tyrconnel, 27 Feb. 1754.
Clerk of the Household to the Prince of Wales 1747-51, to the Princess Dowager 1751-6; Speaker of the House of Commons 1761-19 Jan. 1770; P.C. 24 Jan. 1762.

Cust's elections at Grantham were all unopposed. His closest friends at Leicester House were Lord Egmont (q.v.), Henry Bathurst, and Sir Edmund Thomas (q.v.). After the Prince's death Cust joined the Pelhams, and in 1754 was listed by Dupplin as a Government supporter. But towards the end of 1755 he followed Pitt and Leicester House into opposition, and on 13 Nov. voted against the Address. Resenting, however (as did Egmont and George Lee), Bute's ascendancy at Leicester House, he resigned his appointment in 1756, and when in November 1756 Pitt came in 'upon his own terms'—'I don't find', wrote Cust to his mother, 'that he is at all acceptable to the generality of mankind.'[1] On 17 Mar. 1760 his brother Peregrine Cust (q.v.) wrote to him, then with the militia:[2]

> From what I learn there is a very strong opposition forming against Pitt and I am sorry you are out of the way. I think your presence at this time might be material and I would advise you to come up if possible directly. It seems your friend Lord Egmont has been often inquiring for you.

Conscientious but diffident, Cust did not carry much weight in the House: Newcastle included him in a rather indiscriminate list of 77 'speakers or efficient men' dated 30 May 1757;[3] Horace Walpole omitted him from a list of 28 front-rank speakers in that Parliament.[4] In January 1760 Cust thought of standing for the county at the next general election, and was scolded by his younger brothers for not taking 'the first requisite and necessary step.' Thus Peregrine in an undated letter:

> I am much obliged to you for being so open as to acknowledge it was the palpitation that prevented you from going to Ld. Scarbrough which I apprehended was the case and not the want of opportunity; all I can say in answer is I shall be sorry if you can't get the better of it when you return . . . the worst that can happen is being blanched . . . in short I think there is nothing in such a visit; but if you can't manage it you must let it alone and leave the county to chance.

And similarly Francis (who would have succeeded John at Grantham) on 17 Jan: '. . . a visit to Ld. Scarbrough does not appear to me to be the object of palpitation: especially as his Lordship is no great clerk in election matters, and his circumstances are so considerably affected by the election for the city which must engage his attention more than the county.' As for John not being able to leave his regiment of militia—'you seem to have changed places with your boy and to be more bound by the rules of a school than he is.' In the end Cust proved not to have 'resolution to go through with it'.[5]

Even in the new reign not much notice was at first taken of Cust—he had incurred the displeasure of the Princess of Wales by resigning his post in her

Household when this came under the control of Bute. The affair of the Speakership was managed for him by his brothers. Francis wrote on 8 Oct. 1761: 'I think it must be matter of speculation who is to be Speaker—why not you?' On the 13th Peregrine called on Richard Glover (q.v.), an old associate of Cust's at Leicester House: 'I . . . have had much conversation with him upon the subject of your being Speaker; he appears to approve it.' And on 14 Oct.:

> Mr. Glover has to-day put the business of Speaker into a proper tract, before this time Ld. Bute is acquainted with it, and to-morrow Mr. Glover is to be with him . . . Mr. Glover has behaved very friendly upon the occasion but I still fear Ld. Bute and the Princess won't forget your resignation.

Still, Peregrine pursued the matter with Glover, and through him with George Grenville. 'I desire you will immediately wait upon Mr. Grenville, if possibly on Wednesday morning', wrote Glover to John Cust from Grenville's house on Monday night, 19 Oct.[6] The next day Newcastle wrote to the Duke of Bedford: 'They have . . . determined to have Sir J. Cust, I doubt not a very bright one, but a sort of a plodding orderly man.'[7] And the same day to John White: 'He is not of my recommendation; and consequently am not answerable for his fitness for his office.'[8] And Horace Walpole, always severe on him, wrote in 1766: 'Cust . . . had nothing but industry; he was indeed a very poor creature.'[9] Besides an unblemished character, a friendly nature, and long service and regular attendance at the House, it was perhaps Cust's nondescript political record which recommended him for the post: the choice aroused no strong feelings anywhere, and his qualifications might have proved sufficient in normal times. But it fell to Cust to preside over the debates on Wilkes, 1763–4 and 1768–9, and other turbulent and very long sittings; and neither his firmness nor his health was equal to the task and strain. In 1766 and 1767, he himself wished to relinquish the Speakership for a peerage, and ignorant of the position at court, tried to approach the King through Bute and Egmont. 'I can only repeat', replied Bute on 28 June 1767, 'what I had the honour of expressing to you last year, my situation has given me no opportunity of learning ought that might be of service.' And Egmont, on 1 Sept: 'As I now stand circumstanced I can learn nothing, and therefore advise nothing.' When Cust applied through Grafton, he was told that 'from the present state of affairs the King's servants could not advise his Majesty to create any new peers'.[10]

Before the general election of 1768 difficulties arose at Grantham: John Calcraft (q.v.), son of its late town clerk and closely connected with the Rutland family, tried to build up an interest of his own in the borough; difficulties also arose in selecting the Rutland candidate; but in the end Granby and Brownlow Cust walked the town together on 25 Jan. 1768, and Lord George Manners Sutton and John Cust were returned unopposed. Even so the joint expenses amounted to nearly £1,200.[11]

Soon after the House had met in January 1770, John Cust suffered a paralytic stroke, resigned his post on the 19th, and died on the 24th. Walpole wrote about him as Speaker: 'His want of parts and spirit had been very prejudicial. He had no authority; and by his sufferance of Barré's, Burke's, and Savile's insults, which he ought to have checked, had endangered the country itself.'[12] Barring the flourish at the end, the verdict is borne out by Henry Cavendish's objective reports of the Parliament of 1768–74; Cust is seen instructing Members on precedents and rules of procedure, but seldom intervening to restore order; which his successor Norton, a less attractive character, did frequently and effectively.

[1] 16 Nov. *Recs. Cust. Fam.* iii. 164. [2] Ibid. 182. [3] Add. 32997, ff. 86–87. [4] *Mems. Geo. II,* ii. 143. [5] *Recs. Cust. Fam.* iii. 173, 175. [6] Ibid. iii. 63–64, 205, 207, 208. [7] *Bedford Corresp.* iii. 62. [8] Add. 32929, f. 409. [9] *Mems. Geo. III,* i. 68. [10] *Recs. Cust. Fam.* iii. 266–7. [11] Ibid. 89, 100–101, 249–57; Add. 17496, f. 43. [12] *Mems. Geo. III,* iv. 33.

L.B.N.

## CUST, Peregrine (1723–85), of Leadenhall St., London and Wanstead, Essex.

| | |
|---|---|
| BISHOP'S CASTLE | 1761–1768 |
| NEW SHOREHAM | 1768–1774 |
| ILCHESTER | 1774–4 Dec. 1775 |
| GRANTHAM | 20 May 1776–1780 |
| ILCHESTER | 1780–2 Jan. 1785 |

*bap.* 19 May 1723, 4th s. of Sir Richard Cust, 2nd Bt., M.P.; bro. of Sir John and Francis Cust (qq.v.). *educ.* Grantham g.s. *unm.*

Delegate for Bristol on the African committee 1755–65; director, E.I. Co. 1767–9, dep. chairman 1769–70.

In 1739, for a fee of £500, Peregrine Cust was apprenticed to William Smith, Aufrère (q.v.), and Co., linen drapers in Cornhill. Sent to Holland in 1743, he was ordered to learn 'many languages and other things'. 'I am now upon the High Dutch', he wrote to his brother John, 'and before I come home am to perfect myself in exchanges.'[1] The same year he was admitted partner with a capital of £3,000.

Cust was returned for Bishop's Castle at a cost of £1,200 on the interest of Charles Walcot (q.v.),[2] whose uncle and political mentor Sir Francis Dashwood (q.v.) was a Leicester House associate of

John Cust. But Peregrine's first frank and his first thanks went to his mother, whose grand-father, Sir Richard Mason, had represented the borough, and to whose assistance he chose to ascribe his having been elected 'not only without opposition but with the united hearts of the whole town'.[3] In the Commons he started by adhering to his brother's old Leicester House connexions, now the new court; and during the next 24 years he is not known ever to have voted against Government. Suffering from no hesitancy in debate, he spoke on the Address, 13 Nov. 1761, attacking the German war as too costly and risky—'all our success came from unforeseen accidents . . . we always shall be inferior on the continent'.[4] 'Mr. Cust', wrote Lord George Sackville, '. . . seemed in six sentences to answer the wild flights of Alderman Beckford.'[5] During the next 10 years his interventions in debate, not very frequent but almost always on subjects on which he had expert knowledge, received attention. Thus James Harris notes in reporting the debate on the peace preliminaries, 10 Dec. 1762: 'Cust . . . did laudably—gave the only good account of the African article, and of the great importance of Senegal, the little use of Goree, and all this from authentic vouchers.' And in March 1763, in the general court of the East India Company—'the first of the great general courts whose debates were sometimes to rival those of the House of Commons in the interest they aroused'[6]—Cust and Robert Wood (q.v.) were the chief spokesmen for the Government in the fight between Sulivan and Clive over the peace treaty.

By 1762 Cust was of sufficient standing in the City to be informed by Bute of 'the appointment of a minister to France'.[7] When a month later Government contracts were being transferred from Newcastle's friends to those of Bute, Cust, jointly with Touchet (q.v.), was employed 'to remit to Germany the subsistence of the troops';[8] and a year later, in money remittances to Gibraltar in partnership with Robert Jones (q.v.), Sandwich's 'man of business' in the Commons and in East India House. Cust was, in fact, one of the chief Government contractors under Bute's Treasury.[9] He remained close to the Grenville Administration; was ready to assist them in elections;[10] and together with Amyand and Touchet was supposed to advise, or even 'govern', Grenville on matters of finance.[11]

But on the advent of the Rockinghams, Cust did not follow Grenville into opposition; was not singled out by Newcastle among the 'contractors and remitters' to be removed;[12] did not vote against the repeal of the Stamp Act; and even in November 1766 was classed by Rockingham as merely 'doubt-

ful'. He now took a prominent part in debates on East India affairs: Conway, in his account of the opening debate on 9 Dec. 1766[13] classed him as 'pro', which he was to some extent: he admitted the Government's right to expect some return from the Company, but 'he was faithful too to the interests of the Company, and started many difficulties'.[14] Still, even over the land tax, 27 Feb. 1767, he voted with Administration, and was classed by Newcastle in his list of 2 Mar. among its followers.

Nevertheless, when in search of a seat before the general election of 1768, Cust managed to procure it for himself with Newcastle's approval. Here is the story as told by the Duke in a letter of 11 Nov. 1767.[15] Some time after Shoreham had in December 1765 returned Admiral Cornish at his recommendation, they proposed, he writes, that Cust

> should join Sir Samuel Cornish, which I very readily agreed to; and they now stand jointly as candidates for the next election.
> There are a number of Government votes; and Mr. Cust, as brother to the Speaker, has procured those votes to be for him, though they are not for Sir Samuel Cornish; and so they now stand: but that makes no alteration at all in their junction. There are some who will be for one of the candidates, though not for the other.

But when, on 17 Mar. 1768, the constable of Shoreham reported that the two had been returned 'on the recommendations of your Grace which I hope will still merit your approbation', Newcastle replied: 'As to Mr. Cust, he got his recommendation from me; and I have seen very little of him since.'[16]

The years 1767–70 were probably the culminating period in Peregrine Cust's public career. He was a director of the East India Company; in March 1767 took a prominent part in negotiations between them and the Government; similarly in the debates on the bill to limit dividends;[17] and in February 1768, with the permission of the Commons, gave evidence before the Lords on that bill. During those years he held also considerable amounts of Bank stock rising to about £10,000[18]—was it merely for investment or was it to qualify for office? But by August 1770 Cust had sold all his Bank stock; and dropped out of the East India directorate. Sir George Colebrooke wrote to Clive, September 1769, about Cust's 'curious resolution' to retire from the deputy chairmanship of the Company, which will cause disharmony in the directorate, 'but it's not to be wondered at that he is tired of conflicts'.[19]

When Alexander Fordyce's bankruptcy precipitated the severe credit crisis of 1772, Cust was a petitioning creditor, and managed the business with success for the creditors, consideration for Fordyce's partners, and civility to Fordyce himself. His conduct of the affair received general praise;[20] most significantly, from the court of Chancery.

After April 1771 Cust hardly ever spoke in Parliament, except to examine witnesses during the inquiry into the state of the linen industry, March-May 1774, and on 23 Feb. 1781 over a petition against his own return.

At the general election of 1774, Cust stood for Ilchester (Brownlow Cust having moved to the family seat at Grantham). His election was declared void, and he did not stand again; but when his nephew became a peer he succeeded to Grantham, 20 May 1776. Again he voted with the Administration, and was present in every recorded division, February-April 1780. After some hesitation for what borough he should stand,[21] he was once more returned on the Lockyer interest at Ilchester; was absent from divisions condemning the American war (12 Dec. 1781 and 27 Feb. 1782), but supported Government on motions of confidence (20 Feb. and 15 Mar. 1782). Again absent from the division on Shelburne's peace preliminaries, 18 Feb. 1783, in Robinson's list of March 1783 he is classed among 'Lord North's friends, doubtful'; voted for Fox's East India bill, 27 Nov., but apparently absented himself from the divisions after the dismissal of the Coalition. Robinson, in his list of December 1783, expected him to 'be *with*' Pitt's Government, in Adam's list of 1784 he is classed as Opposition—and there is no division list for the first session of the new Parliament to settle the point. Having been returned by a much reduced majority, Cust had to face a petition of which the circumstances harassed him 'more than was fitting in his ill state of health.'[22]

He died 2 Jan. 1785, leaving leasehold estates in Middlesex, Surrey and Sussex, and also one between Oxford Street and Piccadilly; and money legacies of nearly £30,000 besides a great many annuities. An illegitimate daughter born in 1769 and her mother are mentioned in the will.[23]

[1] *Recs. Cust. Fam.* ii. 257. [2] Letters from Cust to Walcot, in Walcot Pprs., Salop RO; also G. Grenville to Cust, 1 Dec. 1763, Grenville letter bk., Grenville mss (HL). [3] *Recs. Cust Fam.* ii. 290. [4] Horace Walpole's notes of that debate (the only ones of that kind which have been preserved) in the possession of W. S. Lewis. [5] To J. Irwin, 16 Nov. 1761, *HMC Stopford-Sackville*, i. 86. [6] Sutherland, *E. I. Co. in 18th Cent. Politics*, 108. [7] Cust to Jenkinson, 30 Aug. 1763, Bute mss. [8] Treasury Minute, 10 Sept. 1762, T29/34/342. [9] *Jenkinson Pprs.* 213-14; S. Martin to Bute, 17 Apr. 1763, Bute mss. [10] Grenville letter bk. 24, 27 Sept. 1763. [11] G. Onslow to Newcastle, 17 Mar. 1764, Add. 32966, f. 55. [12] Fortescue, i. 128. [13] Ibid. 425. [14] Walpole, *Mems. Geo. III*, ii. 288. [15] Add. 32986, f. 362. [16] Add. 32989, ff. 201, 280. [17] T. Bradshaw to Grafton, 14 May 1767, Grafton's *Autobiog.* 178. [18] Bank of England recs. [19] N.d. but endorsed 'received at Spa 4 Sept. 1769', Clive mss. [20] *London Chron.* 18 June, 24 Dec. 1772. [21] See CUST, Francis. [22] Ld. Brownlow to Philip Yorke of Erthig, 22 July 1784, Albinia Cust, *Chronicles of Erthig*, ii. 226. See ibid. 236, P. Cust to Yorke on his election, 8 Apr. 1784 (misdated 1786). [23] For an abstract see *Recs. Cust. Fam.* iii. 334.

L.B.N.

## DALRYMPLE, Sir Hew, 2nd Bt. (1712-90), of North Berwick, Haddington.

| | |
|---|---|
| HADDINGTON BURGHS | 27 Jan. 1742-1747 |
| HADDINGTONSHIRE | 1747-1761 |
| HADDINGTON BURGHS | 1761-1768 |

*b.* 12 Mar. 1712, 1st s. of Sir Robert Dalrymple of Castleton, adv., by his 1st w. Johanna, da. and h. of Hon. John Hamilton, master of Bargany; bro. of John Dalrymple, afterwards Hamilton (q.v.). *educ.* North Berwick g.s.; [1] ?Edinburgh Univ.; Leyden 1731. *m.* (1) contract 5 July 1743, Margaret (*d.*31 Dec. 1748), da. of Peter Sainthill of London, surgeon, 3s.; (2) 17 Aug. 1756, Martha, da. of Charles Edwin of London, barrister, *s.p. suc.* gd.-fa. as 2nd Bt. 1 Feb. 1737.

King's remembrancer in the Scottish Exchequer 1768-70.

Unlike his brother, who inherited the Bargany fortune, Sir Hew possessed no great wealth, and was chiefly concerned to obtain preferment for himself and his family. He was returned for Haddingtonshire in 1754 under an agreement with Argyll and Lord Milton, by which Dalrymple was to represent the county and Milton's son, Andrew Fletcher, the burghs. Having failed in 1754 to secure the office of Lord Lyon,[2] he unsuccessfully applied to Newcastle on 11 June 1755 for a place on the board of police.[3] Robert Dundas (q.v.), commenting on the death of Sir Hew's uncle Lord Drummore, S.C.J., warned Hardwicke against yielding to Dalrymple's solicitations:[4]

[Drummore] was at the head of what I must call the clan of Dalrymple which was in many respects too similar to a Highland clan . . . I hope this is the last in the low country, and if no new head is permitted to rise, the death of Lord Drummore will I hope break that cement.

Sir Hew's applications were unsuccessful until 1756, when he obtained for himself the reversion of the office of King's remembrancer,[5] and in September, by Argyll's interest, a judgeship for his cousin George Broun as Lord Coalston.[6]

Under the Pitt-Devonshire Administration, when his brother 'had much to say with the Grenvilles', Sir Hew apparently remained loyal to Newcastle on whose side he voted, 2 May 1757, in the Minorca debate. Although claiming that 'he had sacrificed every other political connexion and private friendship in adhering firm to Argyll',[7] Dalrymple, nevertheless, during the negotiations for a new Administration, was listed by Newcastle among the Scots who might desert 'the viceroy' if out of power. His loyalties were soon put to the test. From 1758 he was at feud with Milton who demanded that under their agreement Dalrymple should give up the county to Fletcher in 1761 and 'take his turn' of the burghs. Dalrymple, unwilling to admit the obligation, appealed for support to Newcastle who, when rallying his friends in March-April 1760 against the Scottish militia bill (of which Milton was a strong protagonist), counted Sir Hew among the Scots who might join Robert Dundas in opposing it.[8] Although in the division of 15 Apr. Dalrymple did not vote against the bill, he managed, with the assistance of Hans Stanley (q.v.), to placate Newcastle to whom he wrote, 9 May, asking him to intercede with Dundas (now lord president) for his interest in Haddingtonshire:[9]

> When I solicited his Lordship he made no other objection than that your Grace had formerly complained of me . . . I flatter myself that misrepresentation is now removed . . . by Mr. Stanley. As the president must still look upon me as a person ungrateful to your Grace, I hope you will remove the prejudice by writing to him.

And Newcastle wrote to Dundas, 20 June 1760:[10] 'Sir Hew Dalrymple is not only very zealous for his Majesty and his Government but a very particular friend of mine.' Dundas did not commit himself; but Argyll furiously protested against Newcastle's intervention,[11] and open conflict between the 'English' and 'Scotch' ministries was narrowly avoided by the arbitration of Bargany, Loudoun, Coalston, and other common friends. By the resulting compromise Dalrymple was obliged to surrender the county to Fletcher, and stood for the burghs on the united Argyll-Newcastle interest, with financial assistance from Milton and an anonymous subvention from Argyll. To his confidant, James Oswald, Sir Hew expressed resentment at the viceroy system, and 'gratitude and warmest zeal' for Newcastle.[12] But Lauderdale, who had been left out of the negotiations, warned Newcastle against strengthening Dalrymple's interest by the gift of Treasury places. 'Don't put the district out of your own power . . . for Sir Hew may probably desert you.'[13]

In the new Parliament Dalrymple spoke in the budget debate of 15 Dec. 1761. Harris records:

> Sir Hew . . . got up and opposed the measure, particularly . . . tax on windows . . . talked in the old style of taxes on luxury, post chaises, sugar etc . . . 'twas a dry debate.

On Newcastle's going into opposition, Dalrymple deserted him for Bute. Under Grenville's Administration he hoped for lucrative preferment. When his kinsman John Dalrymple proposed that Sir Hew be appointed a Scottish customs commissioner and transfer his burghs to him, James Stuart Mackenzie replied:[14]

> Neither his Majesty nor Mr. Grenville would think Sir Hew's conduct merited such a mark of favour as to give him who already had the reversion for life of one of the best offices in Scotland . . . another good place

> . . . which would put it out of his power to make any return to Government as a parliamentary man.

Although disappointed in his hopes, Dalrymple maintained his friendly relations with Grenville, followed him into opposition, and voted against the repeal of the Stamp Act, 22 Feb. 1766. Under the Chatham Administration he continued his connexion with Grenville, but made approaches to Government through the Bute connexion. In October 1766, 'under age, infirmities and entanglements',[15] finding himself opposed in the burghs by Lauderdale, he decided to withdraw in favour of his friend Patrick Warrender (q.v.) and stand for the county; he appealed for help to Grenville who wrote to Temple:[16] 'Both Sir Hew and his brother Mr. Hamilton acted constantly with us last year and I believe are more inclined to do so than those who oppose him.'

He voted with the Opposition on the land tax, 27 Feb. 1767, but in March was counted by Newcastle as an Administration supporter. When in the summer of 1767 Grafton dashed his hopes of Government support in his county election, Dalrymple turned once more to Grenville,[17] but also desperately tried to ingratiate himself with Bute's ministerial friends and voted with Government on the nullum tempus bill, 17 Feb. 1768. By every shift and intrigue he sought to divide his county opponents; while Grenville, at his request, interceded with Andrew Fletcher,[18] Dalrymple himself was preparing long statements for Loudoun, for submission to Bute and Grafton, placing himself at their disposal, apologizing for his Opposition connexion, and interpreting the Haddingtonshire contest in terms of the old political struggle between the Argyll part and the Squadrone as now represented by Lord President Dundas and his candidate.[19]

> Twenty-seven years in Parliament has pretty well satisfied my curiosity, during which time . . . I have been as little troublesome in solicitations and as constant in attendance as any man . . . If therefore Lord Bute or the Duke of Grafton want to have any other man . . . I am ready to . . . support their friend, or if they will accept of my son . . . I am willing to make him over to them . . . Let Lord Bute name the candidate from among the old friends of the Argathelians, I shall be the agent of his commands.

When Grafton proved obdurate Sir Hew withdrew and gave his interest to Fletcher's cousin, who was defeated.

In September 1768 he succeeded to the office of King's remembrancer, which two years later he sold to Andrew Stuart.[20] He lived partly in London but mainly in Scotland, improving his estates and rebuilding North Berwick House,[21] and exercising considerable influence in Scottish politics. In a whimsical and much publicized letter to Sir Lawrence Dundas on 24 May 1775 he wrote:[22] 'Having spent a long life in pursuit of pleasure and health, I am now retired from the world in poverty and with the gout; so . . . I go to church and say my prayers.' He died 24 Nov. 1790.

[1] The *Scots Peerage*, but not the records of the Faculty of Advocates, mentions him as adv. 1730. [2] Add. 32852, f. 156. [3] Add. 32855, f. 471. [4] Dundas to Hardwicke, 19 June 1755, Add. 35448, f. 267. [5] T17/16/470–1. [6] Add. 32867, f. 247. [7] Dalrymple to Argyll, c.Sept. 1760, Loudoun mss. [8] Newcastle's memorandum for the King, 3 Apr. 1760, Add. 32904, f. 176. [9] Add. 32905, f. 374. [10] Add. 32907, f. 316. [11] Argyll to Newcastle, 5 July 1760, Add. 32908, f. 108. [12] Dalrymple to Oswald, 30 July, 28 Aug., 18 Sept. 1760, *Memorials of Jas. Oswald*, 303–12. [13] Lauderdale to Newcastle, 20 Oct. 1760, Add. 32913, f. 230. [14] Mackenzie to G. Grenville, 27 Oct. 1763, Grenville mss (Bodl.). [15] Dalrymple to W. Mure, 15 Oct. 1766, *Caldwell Pprs*. ii(2), p. 92. [16] 24 Oct. 1766, Grenville mss (JM). [17] Grenville to Dalrymple, 26 Nov. 1767, Grenville letter bk. [18] Grenville to Fletcher, 16 Feb. 1768; Fletcher to Grenville, 9 Mar. 1768, Grenville mss (JM). [19] Dalrymple to Loudoun, 24, 26, 27 Feb. 1768, Loudoun mss. [20] T17/20/211; Col. Jas. Abercrombie to Loudoun, 9 June 1770, Loudoun mss. [21] Boswell, *Private Pprs*. xvi. 3–4. [22] *Statistical Account*, ii. 565–8.

E.H.-G.

**DALRYMPLE, Hew** (1746–1800), of North Berwick, Haddington.

HADDINGTONSHIRE   1780–July 1786

*b*. 26 Oct. 1746, 3rd but only surv. s. of Sir Hew Dalrymple, 2nd Bt. (q.v.), by his 1st w. Margaret, da. of Peter Sainthill. *m*. 26 Oct. 1770, his cos. Janet, da. of William Duff of Crombie, sheriff depute of Ayrshire, by Elizabeth, da. of Sir Robert Dalrymple of Castleton, 8s. 4da. *suc*. fa. 24 Nov. 1790 and uncle John Hamilton formerly Dalrymple (q.v.) in the Bargany estates and took name of Hamilton Dalrymple 1796. Ensign 31 Ft. 1763; capt. 1st Ft. 1768; capt. 92 Ft. 1779.

Auditor of the Excise in Scotland 1786–*d*.

In 1779 Dalrymple joined the new regiment raised by Bute's son, James Stuart (q.v.). Stuart's wife Margaret wrote on 27 Feb. 1780 to James Boswell:[1]

Capt. Hugh Dalrymple has a temper, heart, and manner really amiable. He has no gross or ungentlemanlike vices; is generous and compassionate even to female softness. His company adore him; he rebukes with gentleness and bestows both praises and rewards on those that do their duty well. But it is his excellent heart alone that renders him thus praiseworthy; his education has been cruelly neglected. He knows no language but his own and that not grammatically. He is not deficient in parts by any means.

A few months later he offered himself as candidate for Haddingtonshire, and owed his return mainly to his kinsmen of the Buchan family[2] and to Henry Dundas, with whom he remained associated throughout his parliamentary career. Faithful to the North Administration until its fall, he transferred his allegiance to Shelburne, and voted on 18 Feb. 1783 in favour of his peace preliminaries. With Dundas he

attached himself to Pitt and voted against Fox's East India bill.

Shortly after Pitt took office, Dalrymple became involved in a violent parliamentary controversy. On 14 Jan. 1784 Philip Yorke drew the attention of the House to information given him by a Scottish Member to whom during the Christmas recess an offer had been made that, if he would join the party of the Duke of Portland, he would, on their restoration to office, receive a place worth £500 p.a. Under pressure Yorke named as his informant Dalrymple who amid uproar rose in great agitation and in a singularly inept speech confirmed that the offer had been made in Portland's name by his uncle John Hamilton of Bargany. Fox, North, and others demanded a full investigation of this charge, which Portland was ready to answer. Dundas suggested that Hamilton 'might only have been amusing himself during the Christmas holidays with the credulity of the Hon. Member his relation' and Lord Frederick Campbell described the affair as a jest by a facetious old man 'to try the virtue of his friend'. Ridiculed and attacked on all sides, Dalrymple made matters worse by correcting his former statement: the place had been offered on the authority not of the Duke of Portland but of the Portland ministry. The honour of all the former ministers was now involved, and after a stormy debate a motion was carried that Hamilton be summoned to appear at the bar of the House. But on 29 Jan., after a letter from Hamilton had been read declaring on his honour that 'he had no authority from any of the late ministry to make any offer to Mr. Dalrymple', the order for his appearance was discharged and the affair was allowed to drop.[3]

Dalrymple remained firmly attached to Pitt, and in July 1786 vacated his seat on being appointed auditor of the Excise in Scotland.

He died 13 Feb. 1800.

[1] *Private Pprs*. xiv. 257. [2] *Pol. State of Scotland 1788*, p. 161. [3] Almon, xii. 562 et seq., 618; xiii. 15; *Scots Mag*. 1784, p. 23 et seq.

E.H.-G.

**DALRYMPLE, John,** *see* **HAMILTON** (formerly **DALRYMPLE**)

**DALRYMPLE, William** (1736–1807).

WIGTOWN BURGHS   1784–1790

*b*. 1736, 2nd s. of Hon. George Dalrymple of Dalmahoy, Edinburgh, M.P.[S], baron of Exchequer [S], by Euphame, da. of Sir Andrew Myreton, 1st Bt., of Gogar; bro. of John, 5th Earl of Stair [S]. *educ*. Glasgow Univ. 1749. *m*. 16 Sept. 1783, Marianne Dorothy, da. of Adm. Sir Robert Harland, 1st Bt., of Sproughton, Suff., 1s.

Ensign 52 Ft. 1756, lt. 1759; capt. 91 Ft. 1760, maj. 1762; half pay 1763; maj. 14 Ft. 1764, lt.-col. 1765; maj.-gen. (local, St. Vincent) 1772–3; quartermaster gen. (America) 1779–83; maj.-gen. 1782; lt.-gen. 1793; col. 47 Ft. 1794–*d.*; gen. 1798; lt.-gov. Chelsea Hospital 1798–*d.*

After service in Portugal (1762), Halifax (Nova Scotia), and Boston (1766–72), Dalrymple commanded the expedition sent to subdue the Caribs in St. Vincent, 1773.[1] In February 1773 he went home but kept in touch with American affairs through his Boston 'Tory' friends. News of the 'tea-party' caused him 'grief rather than surprise'; he offered his services and, failing to obtain promotion despite the friendship of Sandwich and Jenkinson, returned to Boston in October 1775 as a lieutenant-colonel.[2] In England again in 1777, he was mentioned as second choice for the colonelcy of the 82nd regiment.[3] On 7 June 1778 North wrote to the King:[4]

> Col. Dalrymple, having had hopes given him of a further payment to reimburse him for his expenses in the expedition against the Caribs, will in all probability desist from his claim upon obtaining the promotion he solicits.

He received nothing until the autumn of 1779, when he was appointed quartermaster general in America with the rank of brigadier-general.[5] He was sent home from New York in August 1780 to report on the gravity of the situation, returned in the summer of 1781, and after Yorktown took a major part in the negotiations with the Americans on the welfare and exchange of prisoners of war.[6]

In 1782 charges were brought against him concerning his accounts and profits; in his defence he quoted the comment of the commander-in-chief, Sir Henry Clinton:[7]

> Your acts have my complete approbation and ... the advantages that may have risen to yourself I am glad of. The public have been well served, and it is fit those who performed it so meritoriously should have their reward.

Dalrymple returned home in 1783, and at the 1784 election was returned after a contest, on Lord Stair's interest. Despite Stair's Opposition connexions, Dalrymple was listed 'doubtful' by William Adam in May 1784. He voted for parliamentary reform, 18 Apr. 1785, and with the Opposition on the Regency. No speech by him is recorded. He did not seek re-election in 1790.

'A man of the most amiable manners and temper',[8] he was a popular member of London society, and a close friend of John Courtenay and W. Gerard Hamilton (qq.v.).[9] He died 16 Feb. 1807.

[1] Jas. Abercrombie to Loudoun, 18 June 1764, Dalrymple to Loudoun, 22 June, 11 and 29 July 1765, Loudoun mss; *Gage Corresp.* ii. 38, 40, 388, 607–8, 614–15, 628, 633; Add. 38340, ff. 285, 309b; Hood to G. Grenville, 11 July, 18 Aug. 1768, *Grenville Pprs.* iv. 306–8, 332–4; *HMC Dartmouth*, ii. 97, 532; Fortescue, ii. 424; *H.O. Pprs.* 1770–2, nos. 1470, 1477. [2] Dalrymple to Loudoun, 22 Jan. 1774, Loudoun mss; *HMC Dartmouth*, ii. 192, 196, 209, 213, 304. [3] Fortescue, iii. 531. [4] Ibid. iv. 168. [5] See his 'Narrative of circumstances attending Gen. Dalrymple's ... employment as quartermaster general in America', Add. 33030, ff. 452–7. [6] *HMC Royal Institution*, ii. 170, 424, 441–4, 446–9, 455; *HMC Dartmouth*, ii. 477; Dalrymple's 'Narrative'. [7] His 'Narrative'. [8] *Gent. Mag.* 1807, p. 280. [9] Boswell, *Private Pprs.* xvi. 109, 116, 131; xviii. 7, 26.

E.H.-G.

## DALSTON, Sir George, 4th Bt. (1718–65), of Dalston Hall, Cumb.

WESTMORLAND 1754–1761

*bap.* 13 July 1718, 1st surv. s. of Sir Charles Dalston, 3rd Bt., by his 1st w., a da. and coh. of Sir Francis Blake of Witney, Oxon. *educ.* Westminster 1727–33. *m.* 28 Oct. 1742, Anne, da. of George Huxley, sometime commissary gen. of the musters, 1da. *suc.* fa. 5 Mar. 1723.

Volunteer with Adm. Haddock's squadron 1740.
Sheriff, Cumb. 1752–3.

The two branches of the Dalston family, the senior of Dalston Hall, and the junior of Acorn Bank, descended from a common ancestor in the reign of Henry VIII.

In 1754 Sir George was returned unopposed for Westmorland on the interest of the Lowthers, to whom he was related, and at their expense: in Mrs. Lowther's notebook there is an entry of £628 15s. 9d. paid for Dalston's election.[1] Dupplin classed him in 1754 as 'doubtful'. When in 1756, on behalf of Sir James Lowther, Dalston 'organized' Sir William Fleming's election for Cumberland, he was paid £200.[2] He did not stand again in 1761, by which time his financial difficulties were such that he sold Dalston Hall to a London grocer for £5,060. When in May 1762 Newcastle was about to relinquish office, Rockingham, also a relation of Dalston's, inquired: 'What will become of poor Sir George Dalston's £200 per annum?'[3] And Dalston himself inquired of Thomas Ramsden, 30 Dec. 1762,[4] how he stood to that 'small annuity' which he had been receiving since Christmas 1761; out of what it was paid he did not know, but thought it was 'quartered out of some place'.

> Small as it is, I should be very sorry to lose it; and more so at this time when I have lost by the [Yorkshire] militia being disembodied, the pay, which was pretty considerable, as I had the honour to be a lieutenant-colonel.

The loss of the £200, wrote Ramsden in a covering letter,[5] 'will totally break his back I fear', his finances being 'greatly *delabré*'.

Dalston died 7 Mar. 1765.

[1] B. Bonsall, *Sir James Lowther*, 15 n. 8. [2] Ibid. 37. [3] Add. 32938, f. 261. [4] *Jenkinson Pprs.*, 118. [5] Ramsden to Jenkinson, 3 Jan. 1763, ibid. 119.

L.B.N.

## DALSTON, John (1706–59), of Acorn Bank, Westmld.

WESTMORLAND 1747–25 May 1759

*bap.* 30 July 1706, 1st s. of John Dalston of Acorn Bank, by Lucy, da. of James Cook, Stockton merchant. *educ.* ?Queen's, Oxf. 1724. *unm. suc.* fa. 1707.

In 1754 Dalston was returned unopposed. Dupplin's list of that year classed him as 'doubtful'. Dalston died 25 May 1759.

L.B.N.

## DAMER, Hon. George (1746–1808).

| | |
|---|---|
| CRICKLADE | 1768–1774 |
| ANSTRUTHER EASTER BURGHS | 9 Jan. 1778–1780 |
| DORCHESTER | 1780–14 Apr. 1791 |
| MALTON | 7 May 1792–12 Jan. 1798 |

*b.* 28 Mar. 1746, 2nd s. of Joseph, 1st Lord Milton (q.v.), and bro. of Hon. John and Hon. Lionel Damer (qq.v.). *educ.* Eton 1755–63; Trinity, Camb. 1763; Grand Tour. *unm. suc.* fa. as 2nd Earl of Dorchester 12 Jan. 1798.
 M.P. [I] 1795–7.
 Maj. 87 Ft. 1779–85.
 P.C. 17 Dec. 1794; chief sec. to ld. lt. [I] 1794–5.

At Rome in 1765 George Damer and Sir Thomas Gascoigne (q.v.) were involved in a 'drunken riot' which had disgraceful consequences. 'Exacting such offices from their coachman as the *valets de place* only are used to render, and meeting with an opposition which wine and lust could not bear, a violent skirmish ensued in which the young gentlemen wounded four men', one of whom, said to have been shot by Damer, afterwards died.[1] Money, and the partiality of the governor of Rome, condoned their crime.

In 1768 Damer was elected for Cricklade, an expensive and corrupt borough, and voted consistently with the Opposition. In 1774 he canvassed but did not stand the poll. In 1776 he and his brothers had contracted debts to the amount of £70,000. Their father refused to pay them or to see his sons: the eldest, John, committed suicide, and George and Lionel 'retired to France'.[2]

On 27 May 1777 George wrote from Brussels to his uncle, Lord George Germain, 'expressing his gratitude for the friendly part taken by Lord George in his affairs and mentioning a letter received from Lord Milton, desiring him to remain abroad'.[3] It was probably Germain who arranged his rehabilitation, with a seat in Parliament and a commission in the army.

Damer voted with the court, 3 Mar. 1779, on the motion of censure against the Admiralty. From 1780 to 1782 he served with his regiment in the West Indies. He voted against Shelburne's peace pre-liminaries, 18 Feb. 1783, and for Fox's East India bill, 27 Nov. 1783. Milton and Sackville supported Pitt, but the younger Damers were closely connected with Lord Fitzwilliam and the Opposition: George, wrote Cornwallis to Lt-Col. Alexander Ross, 23 Feb. 1784, was 'grown a most violent party man'.[4] When Fitzwilliam in 1794, after having joined Pitt, went to Ireland with the avowed intention of reforming the government, he took George Damer as his chief secretary.

Damer died 7 Mar. 1808.

[1] Mann to Walpole, 23 Mar. 1765. [2] Walpole to Mann, 11 and 20 Aug. 1776. [3] *HMC Stopford-Sackville*, i. 72. [4] *Cornwallis Corresp.* i. 168.

J.B.

## DAMER, Hon. John (1744–76).

GATTON 1768–1774

*b.* 25 June 1744, 1st s. of Joseph, 1st Lord Milton (q.v.), and bro. of Hon. George and Hon. Lionel Damer (qq.v.). *educ.* Eton 1755–61; Trinity, Camb. 1762; Grand Tour. *m.* 11 June 1767, Anne, da. and h. of Hon. Henry Seymour Conway (q.v.), *s.p.*

Damer voted with the Opposition in Parliament. There is no record of his having spoken in the House.

He is described as 'of a turn rather too eccentric to be confined within the limits of any fortune'.[1] According to Gibbon, writing to Holroyd, 17 Aug. 1776, 'by his own indolence rather than extravagance his circumstances were embarrassed, and he had frequently declared himself tired of life'. On 15 Aug. 1776 he committed suicide 'in a most profligate and abandoned way'[2]—after having supped at a tavern in Covent Garden 'with four common women and a blind fiddler' till three o'clock in the morning. 'We are persuaded lunacy, not distress, was the sole cause of his fate', wrote Walpole to Mann, 20 Aug. 1776. 'He has often . . . hinted at such an exploit . . . His brothers have gamed, he never did. He was grave, cool, reasonable, and reserved; but passed his life as he died with troops of women and the blind fiddler.' Lord Milton insisted on selling Mrs. Damer's jewels to help to pay her husband's debts.

[1] *Gent. Mag.* 1776, p. 383; see also DAMER, Hon. George. [2] Lady Hertford to Horace Walpole, 15 Aug. 1776, Add. 23219, f. 82.

J.B.

## DAMER, John (1720–83), of Winterbourne Came, Dorset.

DORCHESTER 7 May 1762–1780

*b.* 27 Oct. 1720, 2nd s. of Joseph Damer, M.P., of Winterbourne Came, and bro. of Joseph, 1st Lord Milton (q.v.). *m.* 15 Apr. 1745, Martha, da. of Samuel Rush of Benhall, Suff., *s.p.*

John Damer followed his brother in politics. He appears in Henry Fox's list of Members favourable to the peace preliminaries, and at first supported Grenville but turned against him over general warrants. He was classed by Rockingham in July 1765 as 'doubtful', yet did not vote against the repeal of the Stamp Act. He was omitted by oversight from Rockingham's list of November 1766, was classed by Townshend, January 1767, as 'doubtful' and by Newcastle, March 1767, 'doubtful and absent'. He did not vote on the land tax, 27 Feb. 1767, or the nullum tempus bill, 17 Feb. 1768. Henceforth he supported Opposition, and attended the Opposition dinners at the Thatched House Tavern in 1769 and 1770. He was probably the 'Mr. Damer' who spoke for the Opposition on 19 Mar. 1770 and 5 Mar. 1771:[1] if so, these are his only recorded speeches. He voted for Wilkes's motion on the Middlesex election, 22 Feb. 1775, but no other vote is recorded.

John Robinson wrote about Dorchester in his survey for the general election of 1780:

> Whether Mr. John Damer may again come in is uncertain. He never attends. When he did attend formerly he was constantly against. Since Mr. G. Damer's attachment Mr. J. Damer has never voted against.

John Damer withdrew in 1780 in favour of his nephew.

He died 26 Dec. 1783.

[1] Cavendish's 'Debates', Egerton 221, ff. 187–8, 225, 249.

J.B.

**DAMER, Joseph,** 1st Baron Milton [I] (1718–98), of Milton Abbey, Dorset, and Shronell, co. Tipperary.

WEYMOUTH AND
 MELCOMBE REGIS    1741–1747
BRAMBER            1747–1754
DORCHESTER         1754–May 1762

*b.* 12 Mar. 1718, 1st s. of Joseph Damer, M.P., of Winterbourne Came, Dorset, by Mary, da. of John Churchill of Henbury, Dorset, and bro. of John Damer (q.v.). *educ.* Trinity, Dublin 1734–5. *m.* 27 July 1742, Lady Caroline Sackville, da. of Lionel, 1st Duke of Dorset, 3s. 1da. *suc.* fa. 1 Mar. 1737; and uncle John Damer of Shronell 1768; *cr.* Baron Milton [I] 3 July 1753; Baron Milton [GB] 10 May 1762; Earl of Dorchester [GB] 18 May 1792.

Joseph Damer, father of the 1st Lord Milton, married a niece of Awnsham Churchill, 'the greatest bookseller and stationer of his time',[1] who had considerable interest at Dorchester and represented the borough 1705–10. Joseph Damer sat for Dorchester 1722–7; and in the years 1750–1 and 1754–91 one Member was always a Damer.

Milton had Government support when a contest threatened at Dorchester in 1754. His career in the Commons was uneventful.

As a peer he was closely associated in politics with his brother-in-law, Lord George Sackville, and from 1768 to 1775 with Rockingham. Walpole wrote about him in 1778:[2]

> Lord Milton was in a kind of mad state, and had appeared nowhere since his wife's death, near two years before. He had been in opposition . . . till the breaking out of the American war, when he had taken up violent animosity to the Americans, probably instigated by his brother-in-law, Lord George Germain.

His income was variously estimated at between £15,000 and £30,000 a year. Walpole describes him as 'the most arrogant and proud of men',[3] and Wraxall writes:[4]

> At his seat of Milton Abbey in Dorsetshire, where he maintained a gloomy and sequestered splendour, analogous to his character and habits, he had made immense landed purchases, which, exhausting his pecuniary means, extensive as they were, reduced him to a species of temporary distress.

He died 12 Jan. 1798.

[1] James Granger, quoted by H. R. Plomer, *Dictionary of Printers & Booksellers, 1668–1725*, p. 69. [2] *Last Jnls.* ii. 125. [3] Ibid. i. 254. [4] *Mems.* iii. 249–50.

J.B.

**DAMER, Hon. Lionel** (1748–1807).

PETERBOROUGH    28 Feb. 1786–1802

*b.* 16 Sept. 1748, 3rd s. of Joseph, 1st Baron Milton (q.v.), and bro. of Hon. George and Hon. John Damer (qq.v.). *educ.* Eton 1755–65; Trinity, Camb. 1766. *m.* 16 Apr. 1778, Williamsa, da. of William Janssen, *s.p.*

Lionel Damer was considered for East Grinstead in 1783. On 9 May Lord Sackville wrote to General Irwin, who was leaving Parliament:[1] 'Your successor was to have been Mr. Lionel Damer, but his uncle did not approve of his being in Parliament.'

Like his brother George, Lionel Damer was closely connected with Lord Fitzwilliam. On 27 July 1784 he told Fitzwilliam he was willing to stand for Peterborough if a vacancy occurred, but could not pay more than £1,500 for his seat.[2] He was returned in 1786, but only after it had become clear that the town would not accept Lord John Cavendish (q.v.).[3] He voted in opposition with Fitzwilliam and his brother George. His one recorded speech before 1790 was on a private bill promoted by his father.[4]

He died 28 May 1807.

[1] *HMC Stopford-Sackville*, i. 144. [2] Fitzwilliam mss, Northants RO. [3] Bp. of Peterborough to Fitzwilliam, 29 Aug. 1785, ibid. [4] 5 May 1785, Stockdale, vi. 50.

J.B.

## DARBY, George (c.1720–90), of Newton, Hants.

PLYMOUTH   1780–1784

> b. c.1720. m. (1) 1768, Mary (d.5 Apr. 1773), da. of Sir William St. Quentin, 4th Bt., 2s.; (2) sis. of Richard Jackson (q.v.), wid. of Thomas Bridges.
> Lt. R.N. 1742; capt. 1747; r.-adm. 1778; v.-adm. 1779; c.-in-c. Western squadron 1780–2. Ld. of the Admiralty 1780–Mar. 1782.

Brought in on the Admiralty interest at Plymouth in 1780, Darby felt politically bound to Lord Sandwich, to whose favour he owed his professional advancement. He voted steadily in support of North's ministry, against Shelburne's peace preliminaries, 18 Feb. 1783, and for Fox's India bill, 27 Nov. 1783. As an adherent of the Fox-North opposition, he lost his seat at the general election of 1784.

Darby died 26 Mar. 1790.

I.R.C.

## DARCY, Sir Conyers (?1685–1758), of Aske, nr. Richmond, Yorks.

| YORKSHIRE | 3 Dec. 1707–1708 |
| NEWARK | 1715–1722 |
| RICHMOND | 1722–1727, 14 Mar. 1728–1747 |
| YORKSHIRE | 1747–1 Dec. 1758 |

> b. ?1685, 2nd surv. s. of Hon. John Darcy, M.P., by Hon. Bridget Sutton, da. of Robert, 1st Baron Lexinton; gd.-s. of Conyers Darcy, 2nd Earl of Holdernesse, and uncle of Robert, 4th Earl. educ. prob. Eton 1698; King's, Camb. 1703. m. (1) Aug. 1714, Mary (d.20 Aug. 1726), da. of Hans William Bentinck, 1st Earl of Portland, wid. of Algernon Capell, 2nd Earl of Essex, s.p.; (2) 12 Sept. 1728, Elizabeth, da. of John Rotherham of Much Waltham, Essex, wid. of Sir Theophilus Napier, 5th Bt., of Luton Hoo, Beds., and of Thomas Howard, 6th Lord Howard of Effingham, s.p. K.B. 27 May 1725.
> Commr. for the office of master of the horse 1712–1717; master of the Household 1720–30; ld. lt. N.R. Yorks. 1727–40; P.C. 11 June 1730; comptroller of the Household 1730–55.

Darcy belonged to the leading Whig family in the North Riding of Yorkshire, and had obvious claims to a county seat. In 1754 he was threatened with an opposition from a group of Yorkshire gentry, headed by Rockingham, who wished to have Sir George Savile (q.v.) as Member for the county. Darcy, wrote William Murray (q.v.) to Rockingham, 24 July 1753,[1] 'could not from age, purse and constitution have stood a poll'; but he had considerable credit in the county, and there was a general wish that he should not be disturbed. He was returned unopposed, and died 1 Dec. 1758.

[1] Rockingham mss.

J.B.

## DARELL, Lionel (1742–1803), of Richmond Hill, Surr.

HEDON   1784–1802

> b. 25 Sept. 1742 at Lisbon, 1st s. of Lionel Darell of Holborn by Honoria, da. of Humphrey Hardwicke, merchant and British vice-consul at Lisbon. m. 30 July 1766, Isabella, da. of Timothy Tullie, director of E.I. Co. 1750–63, 1s. 5da. suc. fa. 19 Oct. 1783; cr. Bt. 12 May 1795.
> Senior merchant, E.I. Co. 1768; keeper of account deposits 1770; director 1780–3, 1785–8, 1790–3, 1795–1798, 1800–d.

Darell entered the East India Company's service two years after his marriage to the daughter of a former director. In 1775, his fortune made, he left India. In 1780 he made an unsuccessful and expensive attempt to enter the House of Commons, contesting Lyme Regis on the interest of the independent householders in opposition to that of Lord Westmorland.

As one of the Sulivan faction in the Company, Darell was in close contact with John Robinson and Richard Atkinson, and became a friend of George Rose (qq.v.), who recommended him to Robinson in 1784 as one 'who will pay £2,000 or £2,500 or perhaps £3,000'[1] for a seat. Robinson proposed him for the second seat at Hedon, where he was returned after an expensive contest. In the House Darell supported Pitt. His only reported speech during this Parliament was in the debate of 5 May 1785 on East India Company finances, when he enumerated the various savings to be made in India, and pointed out the vast wealth available there.[2]

Darell died 30 Oct. 1803.

[1] Laprade, 126 ,128. [2] Debrett, xviii .188.

E.A.S.

## DARKER, John (?1722–84), of Clerkenwell, London, and Gayton, Northants.

LEICESTER   27 Jan. 1766–1768, 1774–8 Feb. 1784

> b. ?1722, s. of John Darker, merchant, of Clerkenwell. m. Mary, da. of John Parker of Retford, Notts., 3da. suc. fa. 1759.

Darker was born at Stoughton in Leicestershire, but by 1749 his father was established as a hop-merchant in Clerkenwell. Darker himself appears to have joined the firm shortly afterwards and remained in business till about 1773, building up a fortune and acquiring considerable property in Northamptonshire and Leicestershire.

In 1766 he successfully contested Leicester on the corporation interest.[1] In Parliament he seems to have been completely independent: according to John Nichols he 'was as free within the walls of the House as the passing air'.[2] His only recorded vote during this Parliament was with the Opposition on the land tax, 27 Feb. 1767.

In 1768 Darker again stood at Leicester as a corporation candidate, but was defeated after a fierce contest. In 1774 and 1780 he was returned unopposed on a compromise between the corporation and the independent interest.[3] He voted with the Opposition on America; was listed as 'pro, present' on the contractors bill, 12 Feb. 1779; again voted with the Opposition for an account of pensions, 21 Feb. 1780, and Dunning's motion, 6 Apr. 1780, but voted with Administration on the motion of 24 Apr. against prorogation. Robinson in his electoral survey of July 1780 noted: 'Mr. Darker shuffles and is a doubtful man especially on any trying question.' He voted with the Opposition on Conway's motion against the war, 22 Feb. 1782, but does not appear in any of the other extant lists of the critical divisions preceding the fall of North: he was reported to be away ill on 15 Mar. He voted against Shelburne's peace preliminaries, 18 Feb. 1783; did not vote on Fox's East India bill, 27 Nov. 1783, but in Robinson's list of January 1784 was classed as 'very hopeful'.

Darker, writes Nichols,[4] was 'particularly active in all committees relating to trade and commerce', but he is only reported to have spoken once in the House, on 12 May 1780, when he moved for the second reading of a bribery election bill.[5]

He died 8 Feb. 1784.

[1] R. W. Greaves, *Corporation of Leicester*, 103. [2] *Leics.* iv. 405. [3] Greaves, 104-5. [4] *Lit. Anecs.* iii. 622-3. [5] Almon, xvii. 698.

I.R.C.

**DARLING, Sir Robert** (*d.*1770), of Bethnal Green, London.

WENDOVER     1768—4 Aug. 1770

*unm.* Kntd. 8 Oct. 1766.
Sheriff, London and Mdx. 1766-7.

Darling, according to a local antiquary,[1] was

born at Chellington [Beds.] of humble parentage, where when a boy he used to keep cows on the hill on which the church stands. When of proper age, as we have been informed, he put himself apprentice to a lapidary, after which by great diligence and other means he acquired a large fortune.

In the London directories he appears as a merchant trading at Mile End; and in a list of the House of Commons, published in the *Gentleman's Magazine* for 1769,[2] as a 'contractor for cartouch boxes for the army'. His will[3] shows that he had property in London, the home counties, and Cumberland; and also at Wendover.

Darling was returned at Wendover with the support of Robert Atkins, a lace maker in the town, who

led an opposition to Lord Verney (q.v.), patron of the borough; according to Oldfield[4] 'no opposition [to Verney] was expected until the day of election'.

In the House, Darling supported Administration over Wilkes and the Middlesex election. There is no record of his having spoken. He died 4 Aug. 1770.

[1] Rev. T. O. Marsh, 'Colls. for a biog. of remarkable persons connected with the county of Bedford', Add. 21067, f. 62. [2] Supplement, p. 632. [3] *N. & Q.* (ser. 8), ii. 387. [4] *Hist. Boroughs*, i. 40.

J.B.

**DASHWOOD, Sir Francis,** 2nd Bt. (1708-81), of West Wycombe, Bucks.

NEW ROMNEY                1741-1761
WEYMOUTH AND
  MELCOMBE REGIS     1761-19 Apr. 1763

*b.* Dec. 1708, 1st s. of Sir Francis Dashwood, 1st Bt., M.P., of West Wycombe, by his 2nd w. Lady Mary Fane, da. of Vere, 4th Earl of Westmorland and 7th Lord le Despenser; gd.-s. of Francis Dashwood, Turkey merchant and alderman of London. *educ.* Eton 1725; Grand Tour (France, Italy) 1729-31. *m.* 19 Dec. 1745, Sarah, da. and coh. of George Gould of Iver, Bucks., wid. of Sir Richard Ellis, 3rd Bt., of Wyham, Lincs., *s.p. suc.* fa. 1724; the abeyance of the barony of le Despenser was terminated in his favour 19 Apr. 1763.

P.C. 20 Mar. 1761; treasurer of the chamber 1761-2; chancellor of the Exchequer 1762-3; ld. lt. Bucks. 1763-d.; keeper of the great wardrobe 1763-5; jt. postmaster gen. 1766-d.

Dashwood succeeded his brother-in-law, Sir Robert Austen, 4th Bt., as M.P. for New Romney, with the support of Henry Furnese (q.v.). In 1754 he was classed by Dupplin as an Opposition Whig, unconnected with any of the leading parties.

In September 1755 Pitt sounded Dashwood through Dodington about his attitude towards the subsidy treaties;[1] and in the debate of 13 Nov. Dashwood spoke and voted against them. About this time Horace Walpole ranked him among the thirty best speakers in the House.[2] In December, when Dodington and Furnese took office, an approach was made to Dashwood. On 16 Dec. Henry Fox, who had first intended him for the Admiralty, offered him the post of comptroller of the Household or 'an employment that shall, in your own eye and in that of the whole world, be at least as good'. Dashwood refused; it was, he said, his express opinion

that those would be unworthy of, and useless to, an Administration who should occasionally alter their opinions of any before adopted constitutional and great national points . . . Therefore I must entreat you, Sir, to be fully assured and convinced that neither the Admiralty nor the comptroller's staff, nor anything better, were ever of primary considerations with me.[3]

Instead, he threw in his lot with Bute and the Prince of Wales.

His papers contain a draft militia bill, 29 Dec. 1755, and two draft pamphlets: 'A Sketch for a National Militia', 29 Dec. 1755, and 'Reasons for the Speedy Regulation of a Formidable Militia', 18 Feb. 1756. He spoke in favour of the two militia bills of 1756 and 1757, and became the first colonel of the Bucks. militia.

Another matter which he had much at heart was the case of Admiral Byng. On 17 Feb. 1757, when Byng's sentence was notified to the House, Dashwood spoke against his expulsion and moved for 'the letter of the court martial'. 'His view, he said, was, by considering the warmth of their recommendation, to lead to some application for mercy.' On 23 Feb. he moved for the 12th Article of War, under which Byng had been condemned:

He said he had felt great animosity against the unhappy sufferer from the first representations; but his opinion was totally changed by the trial. That at most he could only impute misjudgment to Mr. Byng. To the court martial he must impute it more strongly, who, he thought, had condemned the admiral unjustly.

And on 25 Feb. he spoke on behalf of Augustus Keppel (q.v.) for a bill to enable the court martial 'to declare what had been their intention in pronouncing Mr. Byng guilty'. Horace Walpole, who described Dashwood as 'a man distinguished by no milkiness of temper', praises the humanity he showed towards Byng.[4]

In the struggle between Edward Dering and Rose Fuller (qq.v.) at New Romney, 1756–60, Dashwood took no part, and steadfastly refused to meddle in the affairs of the corporation. This cost him his seat, and in 1761 he was returned by Dodington for Weymouth and Melcombe Regis.

In the new reign Dashwood shared the fortunes of Bute. On 16 Jan. 1761 Bute told Dodington that he had refused to ally himself with Newcastle unless Dashwood, Charles Townshend, and Lord Talbot were offered 'such places as he wished'.[5] When Bute became secretary of state Dashwood was made treasurer of the chamber, and when Bute took the Treasury, chancellor of the Exchequer. The measure which marked his period at the Exchequer was the unpopular tax on cider; it aroused violent opposition and was never judged on its merits. He resigned with Bute, accepted court office, and was transferred to the Lords. As one of Bute's friends he was dismissed by the Rockinghams, but returned under Chatham. By then he was of little political significance.

Dashwood travelled widely, visiting Denmark and Russia, and was one of the founders of the Society of Dilettanti. His reputation has suffered greatly from the imputations of Horace Walpole,

and the hackneyed stories about the Medmenham Club are probably exaggerated. His tenure of the Post Office shows him to have been an honest and competent administrator.

He died 11 Dec. 1781.

[1] Dodington, *Diary*, 374. [2] *Mems. Geo. II*, ii. 144. [3] Dashwood mss. [4] Walpole, *Mems. Geo. II*, ii. 312, 318, 328. [5] *Diary*, 429.

B.K.

**DASHWOOD, Henry Watkin** (1745–1828), of Kirtlington Park, Oxon.

WIGTOWN BURGHS 23 Mar. 1775–1780
NEW WOODSTOCK 1784–1820

*b.* 30 Aug. 1745, 1st surv. s. of Sir James Dashwood, 2nd Bt. (q.v.). *educ.* B.N.C. Oxf. 1763; Grand Tour.[1] *m.* 17 July 1780, Helen Mary, da. of John Graham of Kinross, and niece of William and Robert Mayne (qq.v.),[2] 4s. 2da. *suc.* fa. as 3rd Bt. 10 Nov. 1779.

Gent. of privy chamber Mar. 1783–d.

In 1774 Dashwood contested Wigtown Burghs on the interest of his brother-in-law John Stewart, 7th Earl of Galloway, was defeated, but returned on petition. He voted with North's Administration. In 1780 he was defeated at Canterbury, where his uncle William Mayne had sat 1774–80.

In March 1783 the lord chamberlain, the Duke of Manchester, Dashwood's brother-in-law, tried to obtain for him the place of yeoman of the jewel office, worth only £50 p.a.;[3] instead, he was appointed gentleman of the privy chamber—an honorary appointment.

He was a friend of Lord Blandford (later 5th Duke of Marlborough), and in 1784 was returned for New Woodstock on the Marlborough interest. William Adam classed him as 'Opposition'; but the only vote he is known to have given in this Parliament, on the Regency, was for Administration. When soliciting a peerage in 1794 he pleaded his constant support of Government.[4]

He seems to have been very extravagant. In 1775 his father paid £25,000 to settle his debts, and Dashwood after he succeeded was forced to sell a large part of the family estates.

He died 10 June 1828.

[1] Dashwood to Sir Wm. Hamilton, 24 June 1768, Add. 41197, f. 55. [2] About her see Boswell, *Johnson*, iii. 407. [3] Manchester to the King, 18 Mar. 1783, Fortescue, vi. 288. [4] Dashwood to Pitt, 1 Aug. 1794, Chatham mss.

J.B.

**DASHWOOD, Sir James,** 2nd Bt. (1715–79), of Kirtlington Park, Oxon.

OXFORDSHIRE 30 Jan. 1740–1754, 1761–1768

*b.* 7 Aug. 1715, 1st. surv. s. of Robert Dashwood (1st surv. s. of Sir Robert Dashwood, 1st Bt., M.P.), by Dorothy, da. of Sir John Reade, 2nd Bt., of Brocket

Hall, Herts., sis. and coh. of Sir John Reade, 3rd Bt. *educ.* Abingdon g.s.; Grand Tour (France, Italy, Netherlands) 1732–6. *m.* 17 Feb. 1739, Elizabeth, da. and coh. of Edward Spencer of Rendlesham, Suff., 3s. 3da. His e. da. m. George Montagu, Visct. Mandeville (q.v.); the 2nd John Stewart, Lord Garlies (q.v.); the 3rd Lucy Knightley (q.v.). *suc.* fa. 29 Sept. 1728; gd.-fa. as 2nd Bt. 14 July 1734.

Sheriff, Oxon. 1738–9; high steward, Oxford 1759–*d.*

The family were Tory, and Sir James Dashwood's grandfather had represented Oxfordshire 1699–1700. Dashwood was a wealthy man, and built the house at Kirtlington at a cost of over £32,000. He was one of the two Tory candidates for Oxfordshire at the great contest of 1754. The Tories secured a majority on the poll, but a double return was made and the House of Commons seated the Whig candidates. The Tory expenses came to over £20,000, of which Dashwood and his colleague each paid £5,700.

In 1761 Dashwood was returned unopposed, on a compromise concluded with the Duke of Marlborough, the leading Oxfordshire Whig. He appears in Fox's list of Members favourable to the peace preliminaries, December 1762, and in the autumn of 1763 was classed by Jenkinson as 'pro'. He did not vote against the Grenville Administration over Wilkes and general warrants; in July 1765 was classed by Rockingham as 'contra'; and voted against the repeal of the Stamp Act, 22 Feb. 1766. Like most country gentlemen he voted to reduce the land tax, 27 Feb. 1767.

Dashwood rarely spoke in the House: 1754–61 no speeches by him are recorded, and 1761–8 only two —on the Lichfield election petition, 26 Jan. 1762, and on an enclosure bill, 8 Feb. 1762. He did not stand in 1768.

He died 10 Nov. 1779.

J.B.

**DASHWOOD,** *see also* **PEYTON**

**DASHWOOD KING, John** (1716–93), of Halton, Bucks.

BISHOP'S CASTLE    20 Jan. 1753–1761

*b.* 4 Aug. 1716, 2nd surv. s. of Sir Francis Dashwood, 1st Bt., of West Wycombe by his 3rd w. Mary, da. of Major King; half-bro. of Sir Francis Dashwood, 2nd Bt. (q.v.). *educ.* poss. Eton 1725–8; Queen's, Oxf. 1733; L. Inn 1732. *m.* 1761 Sarah, da. of Edmund Moore of Sayes House, Chertsey, Surr., 5s. 3da. *suc.* mother 1742 and took add. name of King; and half-bro. as 3rd Bt. 11 Dec. 1781.

Dashwood King sat at Bishop's Castle on the interest of his brother-in-law, John Walcot, M.P., and in 1754 was returned after a severe contest. He was listed by Dupplin as a Tory. No vote or speech

by him is reported during this Parliament. Before the general election of 1761 Shelburne noted that at Bishop's Castle the sitting Members were not wanted.[1] Dashwood King did not stand again.

He died 6 Dec. 1793.

[1] Lansdowne mss.

M.M.D.

**DAUBENY, George** (1742–1806), of Bristol and Cote, Glos.

BRISTOL    26 Feb. 1781–1784

*bap.* 21 Sept. 1742, s. of George Daubeny, Bristol merchant, by his w. Mary Jones. *m.* 21 Aug. 1766, Martha, da. of Slade Baker, Bristol merchant, *s.p.*

Member of common council, Bristol 1769; sheriff 1769–70; mayor 1786–7.

Daubeny was a leading business man in Bristol, and a prominent member of the society of merchant venturers, serving in 1784 as master of the hall. Engaged in sugar refining, he was also a partner in the firm of Stevens and Cave, glass manufacturers, and in 1786 helped to found the Bristol banking firm of Ames, Cave and Co.

In 1768 he became a member of the 'Steadfast Society', the organization of one of the two rival groups in Bristol politics. He took a leading part in re-animating the society after the defeat of its candidates in 1774, served as assistant president in 1775, and became president in 1781. On the death of Sir Henry Lippincott, in 1781, Daubeny was returned as its candidate after a contest in which he received £5,000 from Government towards his election expenses.[1] As an Administration supporter Daubeny spoke 'with great heat' in the House of Commons on 27 Nov. 1781 in favour of continuing the American war, and declared that the citizens of Bristol 'were willing to sacrifice half their fortune in the prosecution of it'.[2] He voted for Shelburne's peace preliminaries, 18 Feb. 1783, and for Fox's East India bill, 27 Nov. 1783. Stockdale's list of 19 Mar. 1784 classes him as a Foxite, though Robinson in January had counted him as 'hopeful', and in fact he seems not to have committed himself to the Opposition.[3] At the general election of 1784 he again contested Bristol, but was defeated.

He died 25 May 1806.

[1] Fortescue, v. 470. [2] Debrett, v. 44. [3] Ld. Sydney to Duke of Rutland, 3 Mar. 1784, *HMC Rutland*, iii. 77.

I.R.C.

**DAVENPORT, Thomas** (1734–86), of Hendon, Mdx.

NEWTON    1780–25 Mar. 1786

*b.* 14 Jan. 1734, 7th s. of Davies Davenport of Woodford, Cheshire by Penelope, da. and h. of John Ward of Capesthorne, Cheshire. *educ.* Westminster 1748–50; B.N.C. Oxf. 1751; I. Temple 1753, called 1754. *m.* Jane, da. of Robert Seel of Liverpool. Kntd. 27 June 1783.

Solicitor-gen. to the Queen 1781–2; serjeant-at-law June 1783.

Davenport was described by George III as 'a very creditable person in his profession',[1] but he was of little consequence in Parliament. He sat for Newton on the interest of Peter Legh (q.v.), a near neighbour of his family in Cheshire; and voted in Parliament with Lord North, both in office and in opposition. He spoke in the House on two subjects: in November and December 1783, when he pressed for the expulsion of Christopher Atkinson (q.v.), whom he had prosecuted for perjury; and in May and June 1784 for Fox on the Westminster scrutiny. He died 25 Mar. 1786.

[1] King to North, 8 Mar. 1781, Fortescue, v. 202.

J.B.

**DAVERS, Sir Charles,** 6th Bt. (1737–1806), of Rushbrooke, Suff.

WEYMOUTH AND MELCOME REGIS 1768–1774
BURY ST. EDMUNDS 1774–1802

*b.* 4 June 1737, 3rd s. of Sir Jermyn Davers, 4th Bt., M.P., of Rushbrooke by Margaret, da. of Rev. Edward Green. *educ.* Bury St. Edmunds g.s. 1744; Trinity, Camb. 1755. *unm.* 5s. 3da. by Frances Triece with whom he lived c.1768–d. *suc.* bro. as 6th Bt. June 1763.

Lt. 48 Ft. 1758, capt. Jan. 1761; capt. 44 Ft. Oct. 1761; served in America during seven years' war; ret. 1766.

The Davers family first sat for Bury St. Edmunds in 1689, and Sir Charles's father represented the borough 1722–7. In 1767 Davers concluded an agreement with the Duke of Grafton by which he promised to support Grafton's candidate for Bury St. Edmunds at the coming general election in return for a seat elsewhere. Grafton, through the Treasury, arranged a seat for him at Weymouth and Melcombe Regis.

Davers voted regularly against the court until the fall of North's Administration. In 1770 he thought of retiring from Parliament, and on 14 May 1770 his American friend Charles Lee wrote to dissuade him:[1]

I know your reasons, but cannot approve of them. You think that as you are no speaker and have no turn for business, that you can contribute but little to stem the torrent of corruption and villainy which at present seems to bear everything down before it . . . I conjure you . . . not in despair to quit the deck and get under the hatches.

In 1779 he was described in the *Public Ledger* as 'a

gentleman of a very ancient family, and independent fortune', who

has never taken a busy part in politics. Sir Charles may be esteemed, in the truest sense of the word, a respectable country gentleman. He is tolerably regular in his attendance in Parliament.

There is no record of his having spoken in the House.

He voted for Shelburne's peace preliminaries, 18 Feb. 1783, for parliamentary reform, 7 May 1783, and for Fox's East India bill, 27 Nov. 1783; and opposed Pitt.

He died 4 June 1806.

[1] *Lee Pprs.* (N.Y. Hist. Soc.) i. 371.

J.B.

**DAVIES, Somerset** (?1754–1817), of Wigmore Hall, Salop, and Croft Castle, Herefs.

LUDLOW 9 May 1783–1784

*b.* ?1754, o.s. of Somerset Davies, Ludlow mercer and alderman, receiver of the land tax 1758–87, of Wigmore Hall, Salop by Isabella, da. of Rev. John Lacy of Wellington Court, Herefs. *educ.* Eton 1765–7; St. John's, Camb. 24 June 1772, aged 18; L. Inn 1774. *m.* 6 Apr. 1786, Anne, da. and h. of Peter Hamond, 1da. *suc.* fa. 20 Feb. 1787.

Alderman, Ludlow, 1787–*d.*; sheriff, Herefs. 1805–6.

Davies was returned to Parliament by Lord Powis on the death of Frederick Cornewall (q.v.). He voted for Fox's East India bill, 27 Nov. 1783, and in Stockdale's list of 19 Mar. 1784 was classed as a Foxite. There is no record of his having spoken in the House, and he did not stand again in 1784.

He died 15 Oct. 1817.

L.B.N.

**DAWES, John** (*d.*1822), of Westminster.

TREGONY 1780–1784
HASTINGS 1784–1790

o.s. of John Dawes of Islington, an eminent London broker. *m.* 15 Mar. 1781, da. of Isaac Akerman, 1da. *suc.* fa. to a fortune estimated at over £60,000, 1788.

Dawes, a London banker, was from 1779 to 1810 partner in the firm of Croft, Roberts, Devaynes, and Dawes. He also seems to have financed mineral development in Wales.[1]

In 1780 he was returned unopposed at Tregony where both seats had been put at the Treasury's disposal. He supported North's Administration; did not vote on Shelburne's peace preliminaries, 18 Feb. 1783; but in Robinson's list of March 1783 appears among the M.P.s connected with Rigby, though the nature of their connexion has not been discovered. He voted for parliamentary reform, 7 May 1783; against Fox's East India bill, 27 Nov.

1783, and was classed by Robinson, January 1784, and Stockdale, 19 Mar., as a supporter of Pitt. He was a member of the St. Alban's Tavern group which tried to bring about a junction between Fox and Pitt. In 1784 Dawes successfully contested Hastings on the Government interest. He voted for parliamentary reform, 18 Apr. 1785, and supported Pitt till he left Parliament. There is no record of his having spoken in the House.

He died 23 Mar. 1822.

¹ G. W. J. Gyll, *Hist. Par. Wraysbury, Ankerwyke Priory*, 73.

M.M.D.

**DAWKINS, Henry** (1728–1814), of Over Norton, Oxon. and Standlynch, Wilts.

| | |
|---|---|
| SOUTHAMPTON | 29 Mar. 1760–1768 |
| CHIPPENHAM | 27 Mar. 1769–1774 |
| HINDON | 16 May 1776–1780 |
| CHIPPENHAM | 1780–1784 |

*b.* 24 May 1728, 2nd surv. s. of Henry Dawkins by Elizabeth, da. of Edward Pennant, c.j. of Jamaica; bro. of James Dawkins, who was cos. of Edward Morant and Richard Pennant (qq.v.). *educ.* St. Mary Hall, Oxf. 1745. *m.* 24 Nov. 1759, Lady Juliana Colyear, da. of Charles, 2nd Earl of Portmore [S], 8s. 3da. *suc.* bro. 1757.

Member of the Jamaica assembly 1752–8, of the council 1758–9.

Dawkins was a wealthy man, the owner of 20,000 acres in Jamaica and of estates in Wiltshire and Oxfordshire. He seems to have lived in Jamaica from c.1751 to 1759, when he left to reside permanently in England.

Southampton was a borough with a strong West Indian connexion, and Dawkins was first returned there on the death of Anthony Langley Swymmer, another West Indian. In Bute's list he is marked 'West Indian—son-in-law to Ld. Portmore—Tory'. His voting record in the Parliament of 1761 shows him to have been independent. He appears in Fox's list of Members favourable to the peace preliminaries; is known to have voted once against the Grenville Administration, 15 Feb. 1764; and though classed by Rockingham, July 1765, as 'doubtful', did not vote against the repeal of the Stamp Act. His attitude towards the Chatham Administration is not known: Rockingham and Newcastle both classed him as Tory, and Charles Townshend as 'doubtful'; and he does not appear in either of the two division lists for this Administration.

In 1766 he had bought the estate of Standlynch, five miles from Salisbury, and at the general election of 1768 contested the borough. Dawkins and Stephen Fox obtained the same number of votes, and when Fox petitioned, Dawkins informed the

House that he would not contest the petition. Six months later he was returned unopposed for Chippenham.

In the Parliament of 1768 his attendance seems to have been irregular—he appears in only four out of ten division lists, each time with the Opposition. Yet he belonged to neither of the two Opposition parties, and his name is hardly mentioned in contemporary correspondence. In 1774 he again stood for Salisbury but withdrew the day before the poll, and was out of Parliament until he found a seat on the Beckford interest at Hindon. In 1780 he was returned again for Chippenham, where he began buying property to secure his interest in the borough; and in 1784 was able to hand over his seat to his son.

During the period of the American war his attendance at the House became much more regular —he voted with the Opposition in each of the 11 divisions, March 1780–March 1782, for which lists are available. He did not vote on Shelburne's peace preliminaries or Fox's East India bill, yet in both Robinson's list of March 1783 and Stockdale's a year later he is classed as a follower of Fox. In over 20 years' membership of the House there is no record of his having spoken.

He died 19 June 1814.

J.B.

**DAWKINS, James** (1722–57), of Laverstoke, nr. Whitchurch, Hants.

| | |
|---|---|
| HINDON | 1754–Dec. 1757 |

*b.* 1722, 1st s. of Henry Dawkins, and bro. of Henry Dawkins (q.v.). *educ.* St. John's, Oxf. 1739; Grand Tour. *unm.* *suc.* fa. 1744.

James Dawkins was a great traveller, orientalist, and eccentric; 1751–3 he accompanied Robert Wood (q.v.) on his journeys in the East, and helped him in the preparation of his books *The Ruins of Palmyra* and *The Ruins of Balbec*. He was an active Jacobite even after the failure of the '45: he is said to have provided the Young Pretender with money, and in 1753 went on his behalf on a mission to Frederick of Prussia. The British Government issued a warrant for his arrest, and Dawkins abandoned Jacobitism. In 1754 he purchased Laverstoke for £9500.¹

He was probably the author of a pamphlet, published in 1756, entitled *Reflections Physical and Moral upon the various . . . Phenomena . . . which have happened from the Earthquake at Lima to the present time*. It argued that the Lisbon earthquake of 1755 was God's punishment for mankind's disobedience of the Mosaic law.²

He sat for Hindon on the interest of William

Beckford (q.v.), another West Indian, and was classed by Dupplin as a Tory. Nothing is known about his conduct in Parliament.

He died in Jamaica Dec. 1757.

¹ VCH Hants, iv. 209. ² Sir T. Kendrick, Lisbon Earthquake, 150.

J.A.C.

**DAWKINS, James** (?1760–1843), of Over Norton, Oxon. and Standlynch, Wilts.

CHIPPENHAM    1784–1806, 23 Feb. 1807–1812
HASTINGS        1812–1826
WILTON          1831–1832

b. ?1760, 1st s. of Henry Dawkins (q.v.). educ. Ch. Ch. Oxf. matric. 4 May 1779, aged 18. m. (1) 3 Sept. 1785, Hannah, da. of Thomas Phipps of Heywood, Wilts., wid. of Charles Long of Grittleton, Wilts., 2s. 1da.; (2) Maria, da. of Gen. Gordon Forbes, s.p. suc. fa. 1814, and to estates of his cos. Thomas, 4th Earl of Portmore [S] 1835, and took name of Colyear.

Dawkins succeeded his father as M.P. for Chippenham, and was returned unopposed. He was classed by William Adam as 'Opposition', and voted with them on Richmond's fortifications plan, 27 Feb. 1786, and on the Regency. There is no record of his having spoken in the House before 1790.

He died 13 Mar. 1843, aged 83.

J.A.C.

**DAWNAY, Henry Pleydell,** 3rd Visct. Downe [I] (1727–60), of Cowick Hall, Yorks.

YORKSHIRE    25 Apr. 1750–26 Dec. 1760

b. 8 Apr. 1727, 1st s. of Hon. John Dawnay, M.P. (1st s. of Henry, 2nd Visct. Downe, M.P.), by Charlotte Louisa, da. and h. of Robert Pleydell of Ampney Crucis, Glos. educ. Eton 1742; Ch. Ch. Oxf. 1745. unm. suc. gd.-fa. as 3rd Visct. May 1741.
Ld. of the bedchamber to Prince of Wales 1751–60.

Downe was closely connected with the Pelhams, who had proposed his standing for Yorkshire in 1750. He was returned in 1754 without a contest.¹

His one recorded speech (23 Mar. 1756, against the subsidy treaty with Hesse) is thus reported by Sir Roger Newdigate (q.v.) in his diary:²

Lord Downe with a truly British spirit expressed his indignation at calling in the Hessians, and called upon the Administration to arm the nation. That when the French landed the gentry and yeomanry might not be drove about the nation along with the herd of helpless women and children.

On 26 Apr. 1757 Downe voted against Newcastle and Fox on the Minorca inquiry.³ In May 1758 he went as a volunteer on the expedition to St. Malo; in 1759 commanded the 25th Foot in Germany; fought at Minden (1 Aug. 1759); was wounded at Campen (16 Oct. 1760), and died 26 Dec. 1760.⁴

Walpole wrote to Mann on 2 Jan. 1761:

We have lost poor Lord Downe, one of the most amiable men in the world. Frank, generous, spirited, and odd, with a large independent fortune, he had conceived a rage for the army. He received twelve wounds in the affair of Campen; and though one of them was in his knee, he was forced to walk five miles. This last wound was neglected and closed too soon, with a splinter in it, not being thought of consequence; and proved mortal. He bid the surgeons put him to as much pain as they pleased, so they did but make him fit for the next campaign. He languished ten weeks; and not a mouth is opened but in praise or regret of him.

¹ C. Collyer, 'The Rockinghams & Yorks. Politics, 1742–61', Thoresby Soc. xli. 360–1. ² Newdigate mss, Warws. RO. ³ Add. 35877, f. 363. ⁴ Gent. Mag. 1760, p. 594. CP, Lodge, and Burke give d. 9 Dec. but he was alive 18 Dec. (Granby to Ligonier, 18 Dec. 1760, HMC Rutland ,ii. 236).

J.B.

**DAWNAY, Hon. John** (1728–80), of Cowick Hall, Yorks.

CIRENCESTER    1754–1768
MALTON          1768–1774

b. 9 Apr. 1728, 2nd s. of Hon. John Dawnay, M.P., and bro. of Henry Pleydell Dawnay, 3rd Visct. Downe [I] (q.v.). educ. Eton 1742; Ch. Ch. Oxf. 1745. m. 20 May 1763, Laura, da. and h. of William Burton, commr. of Excise, of North Luffenham, Rutland, 5s. 2da. suc. bro. as 4th Visct. 26 Dec. 1760.

Dawnay stood for Cirencester on a joint interest with Benjamin Bathurst (q.v.) and was returned unopposed. His brother, Lord Downe, wrote to Newcastle on 3 Dec. 1753: 'Your Grace has gained a zealous friend in my brother and the Whigs a very steady man.'¹ At the contested election of 1761 he was head of the poll. In Bute's list of the 1761 Parliament he is classified as 'pro', with the comment 'Bathurst and Government'; and he also appears in Henry Fox's list of Members favourable to the peace preliminaries, December 1762. He appears in Jenkinson's list of Government supporters absent from the division on general warrants, 18 Feb. 1764. In Rockingham's list of July 1765 he is marked 'contra'; in another list he is first marked 'contra' then 'pro', and Rockingham noted: 'have seen him'. He did not vote against the repeal of the Stamp Act, and in June 1766 Rockingham recommended him for a British peerage.² Yet in Rockingham's list of the House of Commons, November 1766 he is classified as 'Bute'.

But by spring 1767 he had become a follower of Rockingham. He voted against the court on the land tax, 27 Feb. 1767, and wrote to Rockingham on 9 Mar. 1767, on receiving his whip for the East India inquiry:³

Your Lordship may depend on my attendance this day; and I wish my abilities were greater, that I might be more useful to your Lordship, that is, to my country, for no person living is more thoroughly persuaded than myself that all your Lordship's views . . . are directed to the benefit of that single object.

He voted for the nullum tempus bill, 17 Feb. 1768.

In 1765 he sold his Ampney Crucis estate, and with it his interest at Cirencester. In December 1767 Rockingham offered to bring him into Parliament at the general election,[4] which he at first declined. He seems to have been in poor health: his name does not appear in any division list for 1769, but he voted with the Rockinghams on 9 Jan. 1770. On 16 Oct. 1770 he repeated a request made to Rockingham the previous spring that he should be allowed to resign his seat because of his health;[5] and henceforth his attendance was poor. He did not stand at the general election of 1774.

He died 21 Dec. 1780.

[1] Add. 32733, f. 610. [2] Rockingham to the King, 5 June 1766, Fortescue, i. 355. [3] Rockingham mss. [4] Downe to Rockingham, 24 Dec. 1767, ibid. [5] Ibid.

J.B.

**DAWNAY, John Christopher Burton,** 5th Visct. Downe [I] (1764-1832), of Cowick Hall, Yorks.

PETERSFIELD            9 Feb. 1787-1790
WOOTTON BASSETT        1790-1796

*b.* 15 Nov. 1764, 1st s. of Hon. John Dawnay (q.v.). *educ.* Eton 1776-80. *m.* 31 Dec. 1815, Louisa Maria, da. of George Welsted of Apsley, Beds., *s.p.* *suc.* fa. as 5th Visct. 21 Dec. 1780; *cr.* Baron Dawnay [GB] 9 June 1796.

William Jolliffe (q.v.), patron of Petersfield and a steady adherent of the Coalition, returned Downe, who, like his father, followed the politics of Wentworth Woodhouse. Although he seems never to have spoken in the House, his rank and extensive estates in Yorkshire made Fitzwilliam propose to him, when Wilberforce fell seriously ill in 1788, to offer himself for the expected vacancy in the county.

At first Downe dissuaded Fitzwilliam from a declaration, fearing the resentment of Wilberforce's friends and the independent freeholders. On 29 Aug. Fitzwilliam, believing that a dissolution was imminent, asked Downe to confirm that he would stand, if necessary against Wilberforce. But Downe hesitated, confessed he was 'a novice' at electioneering, and concluded: 'Should Wilberforce's health induce him to resign I would readily come forward, though I could not think of standing against him.' Fitzwilliam was deeply disappointed: he believed Wilberforce to be equally reluctant to stand a contest and that it was only necessary to show determination, but Downe refused to reconsider his decision.[1]

Downe voted against Pitt on the Regency. He died 18 Feb. 1832.

[1] Corresp. in Fitzwilliam mss, Sheffield.

E.A.S.

**DEANE, Jocelyn** (1749-80).

HELSTON     12 Sept.-19 Nov. 1780

*bap.* 19 July 1749, 2nd s. of Sir Robert Deane, 5th Bt., of Muskerry, co. Cork by Charlotte, da. of Thomas Tilson of Dublin. *educ.* Ch. Ch. Oxf. 1766. *unm.*
M.P. [I] 1773-80.

Deane never took his seat in the British Parliament. He was returned on a double return for Helston at the general election of 1780, and died at Lyons, 19 Nov., before the House of Commons had determined the case in his favour.

J.B.

**DE CRESPIGNY,** *see* **CRESPIGNY**

**DE GREY, Thomas** (1717-81), of Merton, Norf.

NORFOLK     11 Apr. 1764-1774

*bap.* 29 Sept. 1717, 1st surv. s. of Thomas de Grey, M.P., of Merton, by Elizabeth, da. of William Windham of Felbrigg, Norf., and bro. of William de Grey (q.v.). *educ.* Bury St. Edmunds; Christ's, Camb. 1735. *m.* 1746, Elizabeth, da. and coh. of Samuel Fisher of Bury St. Edmunds, *s.p.*

The de Grey family, while not outstandingly wealthy, was of high standing in Norfolk. Thomas de Grey himself acquired a considerable estate on his marriage in 1746, and shortly afterwards seems to have taken over the management of his father's Norfolk estates.

When in 1764 George Townshend, Member for Norfolk, succeeded his father in the peerage, he recommended de Grey as his successor. De Grey at first professed reluctance to stand, but assured of the support of both the Townshend and the Walpole families, was even ready to face a contest.[1] Eventually, after some preliminary alarms, he was returned unopposed.

In Rockingham's list of July 1765 he was classed as 'contra'; he voted against the repeal of the Stamp Act, 22 Feb. 1766, and, writes James Harris, on 27 Feb. spoke 'for the first time and well' against repeal. In Rockingham's list of November 1766 he is classed as 'Swiss,' i.e. prepared to support every Administration. He voted against Administration on the land tax, 27 Feb. 1767.

At the general election of 1768 de Grey was returned again for Norfolk after a long and very expensive contest. During this Parliament he seems generally to have supported the Grafton and North

Administrations, though on 31 Jan. 1770 he told Members that he was 'not accountable to any one in this House'. He spoke in favour of annulling Wilkes's election for Middlesex, 17 Feb. 1769; voted with Administration on the Middlesex election, 8 May 1769, and spoke against inquiring into the causes of arrears in the civil list, 1 Mar. 1769. In the debate on the Address, 9 Jan. 1770, he denied that there was any substantial discontent in the country, attributing the Westminster petition to 'a few despicable mechanics, headed by base-born people, booksellers, and broken tradesmen'. In the debate of 31 Jan. 1770 he demanded whether 'the people' were not rather the 'men of great property' with 'a great stake to lose'. He voted for committing Brass Crosby to the Tower, 27 Mar. 1771, and on 16 Mar. 1772 spoke in favour of the royal marriage bill.[2]

Increasingly disabled by gout, and unwilling to face another contest, de Grey decided before February 1773 not to stand again.

He died 23 June 1781.

[1] Walsingham mss; draft of a speech in Thomas de Grey's hand. [2] Cavendish's 'Debates, Egerton 3711, ff. 212-13; 218, f. 250; *Parlty. Hist.* xvi. 696.

B.H.

## DE GREY, Thomas (1748-1818), of Merton, Norf.

| | |
|---|---|
| WAREHAM | 28 Jan.-30 Sept. 1774 |
| TAMWORTH | 1774-1780 |
| LOSTWITHIEL | 1780-9 May 1781 |

*b.* 14 July 1748, o. surv. s. of William de Grey (q.v.). *educ.* Eton 1760-5; Trinity Hall, Camb. 1766. *m.* 30 Apr. 1772, Hon. Augusta Georgiana Elizabeth Irby, da. of William, 1st Baron Boston (q.v.), 2s. 2da. *suc.* fa. as 2nd Baron Walsingham, 9 May 1781, and his uncle Thomas de Grey (q.v.) to his Merton estates, 23 June 1781.

Groom of the bedchamber 1771-7; ld. of Trade June 1777-81; under-sec. of state for American dept. Feb. 1778-Sept. 1780; vice-treasurer [I] 1784-7; jt. postmaster gen. 1787-94; chairman of committees, House of Lords, 1794-1814.

De Grey's return for Wareham on the interest of the late John Calcraft (q.v.) was negotiated by Lord North with Calcraft's executors and with Philip Francis.[1] He spoke and voted, 25 Feb. 1774, against making the Grenville Act permanent;[2] Lord Townshend described his speech as 'most able and well delivered';[3] and at the general election of 1774 returned him for Tamworth. At the opening of the new Parliament, 5 Dec. 1774, de Grey seconded the Address; and spoke several times in 1775, always on the Government side, and mostly on colonial problems. When on 5 June 1777 places were vacant at the Board of Trade and the Green Cloth, North offered Lord George Germain the choice of Sir Ralph Payne or de Grey. 'De Grey deserves to be

advanced', wrote the King next morning;[4] and he was to go to the Board of Trade. 'No office under Heaven . . . would I have accepted', wrote de Grey to Charles Hotham[5] (q.v.) on 16 June, 'if I was not at liberty to be as much about his Majesty's person as ever, though not officially. The office I have quitted is one of the most agreeable as well as one of the most honourable that any commoner can enjoy.' He speaks of his 'unalterable attachment' to the King—but he had to subordinate personal considerations to the interests of his family. 'I owe my appointment to *this* office entirely to Lord George Germain.' In February 1778 de Grey was appointed under-secretary to Germain, 'whose kindness to me', he wrote on 22 Sept. 1780, 'has always been more that of a parent than a principal in office'. He repeatedly spoke in the House on matters connected with his department. The *Public Ledger* described him in 1779 as 'a plodding, busy, persevering young man, and fit for such an employment of real business'; but his letters are fairly colourless, and his speeches as a rule received but short notice.

When the King asked North, on 27 Dec. 1780, to suggest some proper person for vice-chamberlain to the Queen (it was understood, replied North, that 'the person should be of a noble family . . . of genteel manners, good character, a married man, and not very young') North named de Grey as one of four possible candidates, adding however that he did believe de Grey would not wish 'to quit his seat at the Board of Trade'. The King replied the next day: 'Mr. de Grey would certainly not resign the Board of Trade for it, besides his manner is certainly not quite genteel and from his hurry he might fill the office but awkwardly.'[6]

Robinson wrote against Tamworth in his survey for the general election of 1780: 'Mr. de Grey will not come in again here. Who Lord Townshend will elect is not known.' The seat at Lostwithiel was bought for de Grey from Lord Edgcumbe by the Government for £3,000, to which de Grey's father contributed £1,000, the usual share for servants of the Crown.[7] When William de Grey was about to be created a peer Charles Sackville, on 21 Sept. 1780, wrote to Hotham about Thomas: 'de Grey as eldest son to a peer can no longer hold the under-secretaryship'; and when he succeeded as 2nd Lord Walsingham, a place at the Board of Trade was considered beneath his rank. But although by that time he had inherited two fortunes, according to Selwyn he got Robinson to 'job away' half a year's salary of his successor, A. M. Storer (q.v.),

in order to put one quarter more into the pocket of Lord Walsingham, who had the pride acquired by his title, of disdaining to be in a new patent, and so pressing that the old might not expire till he had received £200 more salary.[8]

In the House of Lords Walsingham was a frequent speaker, especially on colonial matters. On 17 Feb. 1783 he spoke against Shelburne's peace preliminaries; but on 30 June voted in favour of Pitt's proposals for parliamentary reform. Viscount Sackville wrote to William Knox on 4 July:

Lord Walsingham . . . has at last ventured to vote in opposition. I am glad he takes any decided part; it was too unbecoming in him to be suing to every minister, without attachment to any individual or any settled system. I think he cannot do wrong if he is admitted into Lord Thurlow's train, for Lord Temple and his Lordship will probably form the next Administration.

He also voted against Fox's East India bill, 15 Dec. 1783; and henceforth adhered to Pitt. A conscientious and able administrator, he was one of the best post masters general of the period and 'paid inveterate attention to business and accounts'.[9]

He died 16 Jan. 1818.

[1] North to Ld. March, 19 Jan. 1774, Cely-Trevelyan Coll. vi. f. 141, Soc. of Antiquaries of London; Parkes & Merivale, *Mems. of Francis*, i. 343. [2] Cavendish's 'Debates', Egerton 252, pp. 168-9. [3] To J. Hely-Hutchinson, 25 Feb. 1774, *HMC 12th Rep. IX*, 278. [4] Fortescue, iii. 452-3. [5] Hotham mss, E. Riding RO, Beverley. [6] Fortescue, v. 170-2. [7] Laprade, 24, 58-59. [8] Selwyn to Ld. Carlisle, 11 Dec. 1781, *HMC Carlisle*, 540; Storer to Carlisle, 11 Dec., ibid. 548; Walpole to Countess of Upper Ossory, 18 Dec. 1781. [9] K. L. Ellis, *Post Office in the 18th Cent.* 111.

L.B.N.

## DE GREY, William (1719-81).

NEWPORT 7 Dec. 1761–Jan. 1770
CAMBRIDGE UNIVERSITY 1 Feb. 1770–26 Jan. 1771

*b.* 7 July 1719, 3rd s. of Thomas de Grey, M.P., and bro. of Thomas de Grey (*d.* 1781, q.v.). *educ.* Trinity Hall, Camb. 1737; M. Temple 1738, called 1742. *m.* 12 Nov. 1743, Mary, da. of William Cowper of The Park, nr. Hertford, clerk of the Parliaments, 1s. Kntd. 28 Jan. 1771; *cr.* Baron Walsingham 17 Oct. 1780.

Solicitor-gen. to the Queen 1761-3; solicitor-gen. Dec. 1763-6 Aug. 1766; attorney-gen. 1766-71; l.c.j. common pleas 1771-80.

On 7 Dec. 1761 de Grey, solicitor-general to the Queen since September, was returned as an Administration candidate at Newport on Humphry Morice's interest, and on 16 Dec. applied to Bute for the post of solicitor-general to the King should it become vacant.[1] He appears to have had little interest in politics, entering Parliament merely to further his legal career, and in the House supported each successive Administration. In November 1763 he applied to Grenville for promotion, and the following month was appointed solicitor-general. De Grey's speeches were almost invariably to present the legal case for the Crown, and his political detachment enabled him to retain his office on each

change of Administration. Harris comments that on 17 Jan. 1766 de Grey 'declared strongly in favour' of the right of the British Commons to lay an internal tax on America, 'but had his doubts about the propriety of the Stamp Act (which last year as solicitor-general he had perused and approved)'.

In 1768 de Grey was again returned as a Government candidate at Newport, and also on the Townshend interest at Tamworth, but chose to sit for Newport. As attorney-general he presented the Government's case against Wilkes in 1769 and took a prominent part in the debates in the House.

After Camden's dismissal in Jan. 1770, Horace Walpole commenting on possible successors to the Great Seal, wrote that de Grey 'wanted health and weight, and yet asked too extravagant terms'.[2] Grafton writes:[3]

By the King's commands I saw Mr. de Grey, a most able and upright lawyer, and as perfect a gentleman . . . In a long conference we had at his house, he appeared inclined to undertake the situation in spite of his frequent attacks of gout.

But next day de Grey, discovering that Grafton soon intended to resign, declined the office. In February 1770, at Grafton's suggestion, he moved from Newport to Cambridge University and was returned there unopposed. On 12 Nov. 1770 Horace Walpole wrote to Horace Mann: 'We have . . . or shall by tomorrow have a lord chancellor. It is de Grey, the attorney-general, a very proper one, as often as the gout will let him be so.' But nothing came of this and in Jan. 1771 he became lord chief justice of the common pleas, which vacated his seat.

When in 1778 de Grey's office was required for Wedderburn who with Thurlow was also to have a peerage, North informed the King on 3 Apr. that de Grey refused to quit the chief justice's place without a peerage: he 'has a fortune in possession and expectation equal to a peerage, and . . . conceives himself well entitled to any honours that Mr. Thurlow or Mr. Wedderburn can pretend to. Both he and his son complain much of the slur intended to be thrown upon him.' The King replied the same day: 'As to the chief justice thinking himself ill-used . . . it has not the smallest foundation; I offered him the Great Seal and a peerage. He declined both.' And on 15 Apr. the King wrote that he had told de Grey that he could not now give three peerages to the legal profession; but would promise him one on the first promotion of others to peerages, or to his son in the case of his death. De Grey gave his 'hearty acquiescence' to this. He hoped in addition to obtain an annual pension of £2,500, but the whole arrangement was shelved by Wedderburn's remaining in the Commons.[4] De

Grey, who was described by Horace Walpole as 'a man of fair character and moderate principles',[5] resigned in June 1780, and was created a peer in October.

He died 9 May 1781.

[1] Bute mss. [2] *Mems. Geo. III*, iv. 33. [3] *Autobiog.* 246, 249. [4] Fortescue, iv. 95, 96, 110-11, 115. [5] *Mems. Geo. III*, i. 266.

M.M.D.

**DEHANY, Philip** (c.1720–1809), of Queen Anne St., London and Hayes Place, Kent.

ST. IVES 26 Dec. 1778–1780

*b.* c. 1720, 1st s. of David Dehany, merchant and planter of Jamaica, by Mary, da. of Matthew Gregory.[1] *m.* 1da.[2] *suc.* fa. 1754.

The *Public Ledger* in 1779 wrote about Dehany: 'Very lately come into Parliament, attached to the Duke of Bolton, and votes in the minority.' Dehany was friendly with Edward Morant (q.v.), also a West Indian and closely connected with the Duke of Bolton, and he was returned on Bolton's interest for St. Ives. In Robinson's list on the contractors bill, 12 Feb. 1779, he is marked 'contra, present', and in each of the six recorded divisions 1779–80 voted with Opposition. There is no record of his having spoken in the House. He did not stand in 1780.

Dehany died 27 Oct. 1809.

[1] *Caribbeana*, ii. 290. [2] *Gent. Mag.* 1759, p. 292.

J.B.

**DELAVAL, Francis Blake** (1727–71), of Ford Castle and Seaton Delaval, Northumb.

HINDON 4 May 1751–1754
ANDOVER 1754–1768

*b.* 16 Mar. 1727, 1st s. of Francis Blake Delaval, M.P., and bro. of John Hussey Delaval (q.v.). *educ.* Westminster 1737–44; Ch. Ch. Oxf. 1747. *m.* 8 Mar. 1750, Lady Isabella Powlett, wid. of Lord Nassau Powlett, M.P., da. and coh. of Thomas, 6th Earl of Thanet, *s.p. suc.* fa. 9 Dec. 1752; K.B. 23 Mar. 1761.

One of the 'gay Delavals', he was 'by his wit and gallantry, his dissipation and extravagance . . . conspicuous among the men of fashion'.[1] By 1755 his financial affairs had become so involved that a private act of Parliament was obtained (29 Geo. II, cap. 49)

for the sale or mortage of portions of his estates, and £45,000 was raised by mortgage on Ford castle for the payment of his debts. The management of his property was also placed in the hands of his brother John . . . who paid Sir Francis an annuity of £4,000 for the rest of his life.[2]

The mortgage was obtained from Henry Fox, though placed in the name of his nephew, Lord Digby (q.v.).[3]

Defeated in 1749 at Andover, Delaval stood again for the borough in 1754. Newcastle, attacked by the Delavals at Newark, tried in turn at Andover to keep out Delaval

who has no pretence to come thither. Mr. Delaval has attacked so many old and settled interests in other places, that I should imagine all those who have established interests in particular towns are concerned to prevent his succeeding wherever he makes his attack.[4]

And when Delaval was returned Dupplin classed his seat as a loss and him as an Opposition Whig. When Fox was appointed secretary of state, he sent J. H. Delaval his parliamentary whip; and presumably by then Francis also had joined the Government side: in 1763 he wrote of the 'zeal and alacrity' with which 'I served his late Majesty when once I professed it'.[5] In May 1758 he went as a volunteer with the expedition against St. Cas.

In 1760 Delaval, faced at Andover by 'seven candidates in array', turned to Newcastle, who on 23 Sept. wrote to Lord Portsmouth:[6]

I don't presume to interfere; but as Mr. Delaval only desired that I would acquaint your Lordship that his conduct in Parliament has been very zealous for the King's service, and such as I have entirely approved, I could not refuse doing him that justice.

In the House Delaval's interventions in debate were few and futile. Thus on 19 Nov. 1761, after the Queen's jointure had been voted, he 'made a panegyric' on her virtues, which, remarks Harris, was 'at least superfluous, as we all knew full as well of her Majesty's virtues as himself'. On 9 Dec., in the debate on the German war, Delaval 'with great hesitation and blundering' said he was against it, and attacked Pitt; and after Pitt had spoken, tried, in an impatient House, to explain himself, 'very faltering and bowing'.[7] After this he seems to have subsided as a speaker. In Bute's list of December 1761 he is marked 'Fox', yet on 13 Nov. 1762 Newcastle still classed him as a friend.

Provision for his brother Edward, fellow of Pembroke, Cambridge, a chemist and optician of distinction, and in 1762 candidate for the chair of modern history and languages, became for a time the pivot of Delaval's politics. Fox wrote to Bute, 4 Nov. 1762:[8]

Sir Francis Delaval very strangely got the Duke of Newcastle to write to Lord Egremont recommending his brother to the professorship of modern history in Cambridge,[9] which he deserves, and which Sir Francis is infinitely eager to procure for him. I have spoke to Lord Egremont and hope it was very properly refused only because of the recommendation.

Sir Francis is now very explicit with me, and indeed I have ever had reason to think he was inclined to me. If his Majesty should be so good as to give it him, I think it will secure his service.

And on 16 Nov.:[10]

> You'll see Sir Francis Delaval tomorrow, if you can oblige him you'll have a friend steady and more useful perhaps than a wiser man.

Bute, bound by a previous promise, assured Delaval that his brother should 'have something in the university equal to the professorship of modern languages'. On 1 Dec. 1762 Delaval voted with the Government against the motion to postpone the consideration of the peace preliminaries; and was counted by Fox among the Members in favour of them. Still, nothing was done for his brother: on 5 Apr. 1763 Delaval complained of Bute's behaviour as 'very inadequate';[11] and to George Grenville, 14 June, of 'the unequal returns' he had met with from ministers.[12] In the autumn of 1763 he was classed by Jenkinson as 'pro'; but to Grenville's letter inviting his attendance at the opening of Parliament he replied, 24 Oct.:[13]

> I have received your letter, in which you are pleased to say that 'many of my friends hope to see me in town'. I should be very glad to know who my friends are, having never in this Administration been able to find one.
> You persuade yourself that my zeal for the public service will induce me to give my attendance in the House at this critical conjuncture.
> My zeal for the public service has induced me to spend many thousand pounds in support of a parliamentary interest.
> My zeal for the public service did induce me to go in person against the enemies of his Majesty.
> My zeal for the public service did induce me to hazard and lose two brothers (very dear to their family) in the service of their country.[14]
> In consequence of this zeal I thought myself entitled, at this time last year, to ask a small favour of the ministry, and easily obtained an absolute promise. My services were then desired in a stronger manner than by a mere form. They never more thought of me 'till now that they have occasion to apply to me again for fresh services.
> It is for these reasons that I have taken the liberty to ask the favour of you to tell me whom, under these circumstances, you mean I should look upon as my friends.

Grenville replied the same day[15] that if Delaval

> will do him the honour to call upon him for a quarter of an hour this evening Mr. Grenville will endeavour to answer and explain to him the question which Sir Francis Delaval asks in his letter.

In a secret service list drawn up early in 1764, a pension of £300 p.a. appears against Edward Delaval;[16] it was continued during the Rockingham Administration;[17] and in Robinson's secret service accounts for 1779-82[18]—a hardy perennial on view whenever such a list is available.

Obviously mollified, Delaval did not vote against Government over general warrants;[19] nor against the Rockinghams over the repeal of the Stamp Act;

nor against the Chatham Administration over the reduction of the land tax. In the summer of 1765 Rockingham classed him as 'doubtful', at the end of 1766 as 'Swiss', Townshend in January 1767 as 'doubtful', and Newcastle, 2 Mar. 1767, as 'Administration'. In 1768 Delaval stood once more for Andover; the Duke and Duchess of Northumberland went to 'canvass the town' for him,[20] and the Duke tried to secure for him Grafton's support.[21] Delaval's friend the actor Foote, in a letter written to him about this time,[22] refers to 'the imminent political breach between you and the governor of Andover (possibly the mayor); and Delaval was defeated. Towards the close of his life he became a 'patriot', a supporter of Wilkes, and member of the Bill of Rights Society,[23] but was not trusted by them and thought by Wilkes a spy of the court.[24] In 1769 he was active in the north procuring petitions against the Middlesex election.

Delaval died on 7 Aug. 1771. Horace Walpole wrote to Mason, 9 Sept. 1771: ' . . . when there are columns in every paper on Sir Francis Delaval . . . who would be a hero of these times?'

[1] R. E. G. Cole, *Hist. Doddington*, 136. [2] Ibid. 140; Craster, *Hist. Northumb.* ix. 164. [3] Fox's 'Inventory of Personal Estate', 5 Jan. 1759, Bunbury papers, Bury St. Edmunds and W. Suff. RO. [4] To E. Hooper, 10 Apr. 1754, Add. 32725, f. 72. [5] To G. Grenville, 14 June 1763, Grenville mss (JM). [6] Add. 32911, f. 229. [7] Report by C. Jenkinson, Add. 38334, ff. 25-26; see also Harris's 'Debates' and *Rockingham Mems.* i. 75. [8] Bute mss. [9] Add. 32944, ff. 132, 145, 147-148. [10] Bute mss. [11] Ibid. [12] Grenville mss (JM). [13] *Grenville Pprs.* ii. 144-5. [14] Robert killed at the taking of Quebec, 1759; and Henry killed in India, 1760. [15] Grenville letter bk. Grenville mss. [16] In the King's handwriting, in the Royal archives, Windsor. [17] Rockingham mss. [18] Royal archives, Windsor. [19] In Newdigate ms B 2544 he is mentioned as having spoken, 17 Feb. 1764, for the Opposition motion, but his name appears in no other report of the debate. [20] Gilly Williams to G. Selwyn, n.d., J. H. Jesse, *Selwyn*, ii. 279. [21] Sir M. Fetherstonhaugh to Newcastle, 16 Feb. 1768, Add. 32988, f. 351. [22] Undated, *HMC 11th Rep. VII, Waterford*, 80. [23] Cole, op. cit. 142. [24] *Public Advertiser*, 12 Aug. 1771.

L.B.N.

## DELAVAL, George (1703–82), of Little Bavington, Northumb.

NORTHUMBERLAND    20 Dec. 1757–1774

*bap.* 28 Jan. 1703, 1st surv. s. of Edward Shafto of Hexham by Mary, da. of George Delaval of Dissington, sis. of Adm. George Delaval of Little Bavington; cos. of Francis Blake Delaval and John Hussey Delaval (qq.v.). *unm. suc.* his uncle at Little Bavington 1723 and took name of Delaval.

In 1757 Delaval applied to Newcastle for his support in the Northumberland election: 'My constant attachment to his Majesty and his family', he wrote to the Duke, 7 Oct., 'may, I hope, entitle me to the favour of those that have the honour to serve the Government in this county.'[1] He received Government support and was returned unopposed. On 10 May 1760 he complained to Newcastle:[2]

> I have not received the least mark of your Grace's regard for me since I have been in Parliament . . .

From the honour of being known to your Grace and the situation I am in of a representative of the county of Northumberland, I thought I had some claim to a share of the little employments that I always understood were disposed of at the solicitation of Members of Parliament. I assure your Grace my constituents think so, and often tell me I am not warm in their interest.

In 1761 and 1768 Delaval was again returned unopposed. In Bute's list of 1761 he is classed as 'Tory'. Though not listed by Henry Fox among Members favourable to the peace preliminaries, December 1762, he does not appear in the minority lists of 9 and 10 Dec. He voted with Opposition in three divisions on general warrants, February 1764, but in the list of 18 Feb. he is described by Jenkinson as a friend normally voting with Government. In Newcastle's list of 10 May 1764 he is marked 'doubtful'; in Rockingham's, July 1765, 'pro', but in November 1766 as 'doubtful', while Charles Townshend, January 1767, described him as 'Government'. He voted against Administration on the land tax, 27 Feb. 1767, and on nullum tempus, 17 Feb. 1768. He again voted with Opposition in two divisions on the Middlesex election, 15 Apr. and 8 May 1769; on the Address, 9 Jan. 1770, and again on the Middlesex election, 25 Jan. 1770. He does not appear as having voted in any other division, and there is no record of his having spoken in the House. On 12 July 1774 he wrote to his constituents: 'My late ill-state of health, which has prevented my attendance on my parliamentary duty, makes it necessary for me to decline offering myself at the general meeting.'[3]

He died January 1782.

[1] Add. 32874, f. 499. [2] Add. 32905, ff. 395-6. [3] *Coll. pprs. Northumb. election 1774.*

M.M.D.

## DELAVAL, John (1728–1808), of Doddington, Lincs. and Seaton Delaval, Northumb.

BERWICK-UPON-TWEED 1754–1761, 18 Jan. 1765– 1774, 1780–21 Aug. 1786

*b.* 17 Mar. 1728, 2nd s. of Francis Blake Delaval, M.P., by Rhoda, da. of Robert Apreece of Washingley, Hunts. and gd.-da. and h. of Sir Thomas Hussey, 2nd Bt., of Doddington; bro. of Sir Francis Blake Delaval (q.v.). *educ.* Westminster 1737–45; Pembroke, Camb. 1746. *m.* (1) 2 Apr. 1750, his cos. Susanna (*d.* 1 Oct. 1783), da. of R. Robinson of Gateshead, co. Dur. by Margaret, da. of Edward Delaval, wid. of John Potter, 1s. *d.v.p.* 6da.; (2) 5 Jan. 1803, Susanna Elizabeth Knight, *s.p. suc.* mother to Hussey estate of Doddington 9 Aug. 1759, and took add. name of Hussey before Delaval; bro. 7 Aug. 1771; *cr.* Bt. 1 July 1761; Baron Delaval [I] 17 Oct. 1783; Baron Delaval [GB] 21 Aug. 1786.

II—L

In 1754 Delaval successfully contested Berwick against John Wilkes who received Administration support from Newcastle, incensed by the Delavals' attack on his own interest at Newark. In Dupplin's lists Delaval was consequently classed as 'against', and Wilkes's defeat as a 'loss'. When in November 1754 Wilkes petitioned against the return on grounds of bribery, Delaval replied with a flippant speech 'full of wit, humour, and buffoonery, which kept the House in a roar', but brought him a sharp rebuke from Pitt.[1] Delaval's opposition was shortlived; and on Fox becoming secretary of state, he was sent Fox's parliamentary whip.[2]

In 1755, on a crisis in the financial affairs of Delaval's elder brother Francis, the management of his estate was placed in the hands of John Delaval who seems to have undertaken the task with energy and ability. In 1759 Thomas Watson wrote to Newcastle about the Berwick burgesses resenting Delaval's 'neglect of them since the last election',[3] and on 16 Sept. 1760 William Temple, collector of customs, reported[4] that Thomas Watson and Col. John Craufurd had offered themselves as candidates twelve months previously, but 'Mr. Delaval never appeared, nor was expected to appear'. Shortly after this Delaval approached Craufurd about standing jointly at Berwick, but withdrew when this suggestion was rejected. On 19 Jan. 1761 Lord Northumberland, Delaval's political patron, wrote to Newcastle that he was anxious to find a seat for him[5]—

and as I know him to be firmly attached to your Grace, and that no reasonable expense will be objected to, I should esteem it a particular favour if your Grace would be pleased to recommend him to a borough where he may be chosen till a vacancy happens at Berwick where his interest I believe is firmly established.

Delaval did not stand in 1761. After Newcastle's resignation, Northumberland approached Grenville about a seat for him; Grenville replied on 28 Oct. 1763 that he had heard from Francis Delaval that his brother did not think of leaving the north and was 'not much disposed to engage in any election that is likely to be contested'.[6] However, on the death of Col. Craufurd in 1764, Grenville suggested that there was a 'fair prospect' at Berwick for Delaval, to whom he would give his support.[7] Northumberland wrote back, 22 Nov.:[8]

I am certain I can answer for his being a steady and useful friend to Government and firmly attached to you, and I have no doubt but that the honour and weight of your support added to his own interest will procure him an easy and quiet election.

But Delaval was opposed by Wilmot Vaughan, nephew of Thomas Watson (who had long had the distribution of patronage in the borough), and according to Watson[9] secured his seat 'by the most notorious bribery' and 'many extraordinary exertions' of Government power and influence. The election, he claimed, cost Delaval 'not less than six or eight thousand pounds'.

Delaval's first reported vote in this Parliament was against the repeal of the Stamp Act, 22 Feb. 1766. He voted with the Chatham Administration on the land tax, 27 Feb. 1767, and nullum tempus, 17 Feb. 1768. In 1768 Delaval seems to have thought of standing for the county,[10] but finally stood again for Berwick where he was returned unopposed. He voted with Administration on Wilkes, 3 Feb. and 8 May 1769, but does not appear in any other division before 6 Mar. 1772 when he voted in favour of hearing the petition on the 39 Articles. Horace Walpole writes[11] that during the disgrace of the Duke of Cumberland after his marriage to Mrs. Horton, the Duke's 'intimates', Delaval and his wife, 'were the sole persons of a rank above the vulgar who went near'. In both Robinson's surveys on the royal marriage bill, March 1772, Delaval is marked as 'contra, present'; he voted with Opposition on the commitment of the royal marriage bill, 11 Mar. 1772; on the naval captains' petition, 9 Feb. 1773, and on the Middlesex election, 26 Apr. 1773. Only three interventions by Delaval in debate are reported during this Parliament, none of any note.

In 1774, while professing independence, Delaval stood for Northumberland with the support of the Duke of Northumberland, and was defeated, his candidature being looked upon in the county as an attempt by the Duke to nominate to both seats. He does not appear to have attempted to re-enter Parliament before 1780, when he was returned unopposed for Berwick. He constantly supported Administration till the fall of North. During the debate of 12 Dec. 1781 on Lowther's motion against the war he said that anxious as he was for the end of the war he had thought of abstaining, but North's answer to the motion had satisfied him; he hoped the House 'would not make so timid a declaration, as we will not any longer carry it on; he thought it was wise and necessary to abandon it, but it would be imprudent and impolitic to declare it by a vote of the House'. On 8 Mar. 1782, he 'rose . . . as a country gentleman just to say that he had a high opinion of his Majesty's ministers', and on 20 Mar., after North's resignation, he paid North a tribute, 'which would have, he said, a stronger effect from the obvious disinterestedness of panegyric pronounced on a minister in the moment of his retiring from power'. Delaval voted against Shelburne's peace preliminaries, 18 Feb. 1783; supported the

Coalition, which obtained for him an Irish peerage; did not vote on Fox's East India bill, 27 Nov. 1783, but during the debate of 16 Jan. 1784 on Pitt's bill 'spoke in favour of Lord North, and of the bill which had been rejected'. On 3 Feb. 1784 he supported a motion of censure against Pitt's Administration:

> It was folly to expect a ministry could stand when unsupported by the House of Commons, and it was equal folly in any set of men to expect support from that House, who owed their situations to means the most repugnant to every idea of the constitution. There was nothing in the motion which in the smallest degree affected the character of the right honourable gentleman over the way; it did not in any way exclude him from a future arrangement, let him . . . quit the situation that he owes to means which this House condemns, let him then come in at the door fairly and openly in the face of the world and not by dark passages and back stairs, and we will receive him with open arms.[12]

At the general election Delaval was again returned unopposed for Berwick. On 24 May, shortly after the House reassembled, he

> astonished a great many by a very warm, explicit declaration that he had, in the last Parliament, opposed Mr. Pitt as a supposed minister of secret influence, but having now heard so unequivocally from the people themselves that he was *their* minister, he should most heartily obey their voice, and give him all the support he deserved.[13]

Delaval's action was severely criticized by Opposition. On 16 July he replied in the House that what had been said

> as to his having altered an opinion, was true, and that he gloried in it; he should always hold himself open to conviction; that he voted with the majority of the present Parliament because he was sure they spoke the sense of the people . . . If the people of Great Britain were at any time, which he did not believe would be the case, to change their opinion concerning the right honourable gentlemen, he should think it incumbent upon him, as one of their representatives, to alter his.[14]

He voted for Pitt's parliamentary reform proposals, 18 Apr. 1785, and with Administration on Richmond's fortifications plan, 27 Feb. 1786.

Delaval, mentioned in the *Rolliad*, after obtaining a British peerage from Pitt in 1786, was the butt of an Opposition satire *The Delavaliad*.

He died 17 May 1808.

[1] H. Fox to Ld. Hartington, 26 Nov. 1754, *Mems. James, Earl Waldgrave*, 146–8. [2] 30 Sept. 1755, *HMC 11th Rep. VII*, 76. [3] E. Hughes, *North Country Life in 18th Cent.* 278, n. 1. [4] To E. Stanley, Add. 32912, f. 61. [5] Add. 32917, f. 404. [6] *Grenville Pprs.* ii. 149. [7] Grenville to Northumberland, 21 Nov. 1764, Grenville mss (JM). [8] Ibid. [9] To Newcastle, 22 July 1765, Add. 32968, f. 174. [10] Sir John Delaval to Sir Francis Blake Delaval, 5 Aug. 1767, Delaval pprs., Newcastle-upon-Tyne Lib. [11] *Mems. Geo. III*, iv. 241. [12] Debrett, v. 148; vi. 506; xii. 583; xiii. 63. [13] Daniel Pulteney (q.v.) to the Duke of Rutland, *HMC Rutland*, iii. 97. [14] Debrett, xvi. 94.

L.B.N.

**DELMÉ, Peter** (1748–89), of Titchfield, Hants; Braywick, Berks.; and Erlestoke, Wilts.

MORPETH    1774–15 Aug. 1789

*b.* 19 Dec. 1748, 1st surv. s. of Peter Delmé, M.P., by his 2nd w. Christiana Pain of Eltham, Kent. *m.* 16 Feb. 1769, Lady Elizabeth Howard, da. of Henry, 4th Earl of Carlisle, 4s. 1da. *suc.* fa. 1770.

Descended from a Flemish family settled in England *temp.* Elizabeth I, and grand-son of a lord mayor of London; cousin of Anne Duchess of Grafton (subsequently Lady Upper Ossory), Delmé belonged to the smart set, yet is not mentioned in Walpole's letters or *Memoirs*.

The description of him in the *English Chronicle*, 1780 or 1781, is ornate but not inaccurate:

He was born to a very large paternal estate . . . by the decease of an uncle, he succeeded to . . . the vast sum of £140,000 . . . By having indulged himself too freely in several of the fashionable vices . . . [he] considerably diminished the superabundance of that original affluence . . . His predominant propensity [was] a disposition for the turf . . . celebrated for a magnificence in his style of living . . . absurd pomp and superfluous ostentation . . . is known to have had near a hundred men servants at one time . . . As a senator . . . the Aye or the No have been the limits of his legislative eloquence, and this he has always pronounced with a most implicit acquiescence in the political sentiments of his patron and relation [Lord Carlisle].

Sir William Musgrave, Carlisle's step-father, writing to him, 12 Feb. 1768, about Delmé courting Lady Elizabeth, described him as 'a young gentleman, very plain in his person, . . . who has a very great commoner's estate'.[1] Returned for Morpeth by Carlisle in 1774 in a hotly contested election,[2] Delmé appears on the Government side in the major divisions 1774–82, but, judging by remarks in letters from George Selwyn to Carlisle, was perhaps not quite as assiduous in attendance as could be desired. 5 May 1781 (after a question had been carried against the Government on 3 May in a thin House): 'Delmé, I believe, thought he had had merit enough by attending on Lord Sandwich's motion'; and 25 Feb. 1782 (the Government having scraped through on 22 Feb. by a majority of 194 to 193 votes): 'Delmé was not to blame the other day in not coming down, for no messages had been sent.' By 1781 Delmé was in financial difficulties. 'Delmé has sold all his hunters', wrote Storer, his colleague at Morpeth, to Carlisle, 28 Feb. 1781, 'and sold them at very extraordinary prices; his hounds too sold excessively well.' And on 1 Mar.: 'With regard to Delmé's disappointing you respecting the payment of the money stipulated . . . I am surprised at nothing of that sort that he does'—the payment possibly refers to Morpeth expenses. And on 27 Apr. 1781:

Delmé keeps . . . Mrs. Smith, but, luckily for him, I believe she thinks that Sir John Lade[3] is a better keeper, and therefore gives him the preference . . . As he had got rid of a pack of hounds, he imagined he might indulge himself in some other extravagancy, and so he took a mistress . . . Sir John Lade seems his greatest friend; he takes all his follies from him, and does all he can to hinder Peter from completely ruining himself.

On 17 Nov. 1781, Selwyn, having mentioned that Francis Gregg (q.v.), Carlisle's legal and financial adviser, was much displeased by Delmé's conduct, added:

I am very sorry to hear such an account of the affairs of that family, and of so little disposition to do what is necessary to set them to rights. If the estate and the resources were forty times what they are, such dissipation and want of management must undo them.

Delmé voted against Shelburne's peace preliminaries, 18 Feb. 1783; and for Fox's East India bill, 27 Nov. 1783. In divisions 1784–9 his recorded votes were against Pitt. He died 15 Aug. 1789.

Selwyn wrote to Lady Carlisle, 21 Aug. 1789, that he hoped that 'Lady Betty will be reconciled to her change of life; there must have been one inevitably, and, perhaps that no less disagreeable'; and though her resources will be modest, that 'will be more comfortable than living in the constant dread of the consequences of a heedless dissipation'.

[1] All quotations in this biography are taken from *HMC Carlisle*. [2] About his expenses, see Selwyn to Carlisle, 8 Dec. 1775. [3] About Lade, see *Creevy Pprs.* ii. 335.

L.B.N.

**DEMPSTER, George** (1732–1818), of Dunnichen, Forfar.

PERTH BURGHS    1761–1768, 4 Apr. 1769–1790

*b.* 8 Dec. 1732, 1st s. of John Dempster of Dunnichen, Dundee merchant, by his 1st w. Isobel Ogilvie. *educ.* Dundee g.s., Leuchars; St. Andrews Univ.; Edinburgh Univ.; Academie Royale, Brussels; adv. 1755. *m.* 24 Sept. 1774, Rose, da. of Richard Heming of Jamaica, *s.p. suc.* fa. 3 Nov. 1754.
Sec. to the Order of the Thistle Aug. 1765–*d.*; director, E.I. Co. 1769, 1772–3.

Dempster inherited some 6,000 acres in Forfarshire (worth £769 p.a.) and a considerable fortune, founded by his grandfather, a grain merchant.[1] He began the Grand Tour with his life-long friend Adam Fergusson but, summoned home by family affairs, returned to Edinburgh to practise law. An attractive, humorous young man, of vigorous mind, much influenced by Hume, Rousseau and Montesquieu, Dempster was a member of the Select Society, an independent Whig, rating 'intrinsic merit' high above rank or wealth, a 'true blue Scot', dedicated to the encouragement of agriculture, industry and the arts, and to the establishment of a Scottish militia.[2]

In 1761 Dempster stood for Perth Burghs, and, after a contest which severely strained his finances, defeated Thomas Leslie, Newcastle's candidate. He at once made his mark in the House when on 13 Nov., in the debate on the Address, he spoke 'with an assurance that for its unexampled novelty gave great entertainment . . . pleaded the extension of the militia to Scotland . . . censured the German war . . . and condemned faction'.[3] Lord George Sackville wrote:[4]

A new Scotch Member, a Mr. Dempster, showed a strong desire of speaking and seems to have abilities sufficient to make him an object. In short, he promises well, and though he diverted the House by a becoming ignorance of its forms, yet he proved that he neither wanted language, manner, nor matter.

Dempster was now approached by Sir Harry Erskine, who wrote to Bute, 28 Nov. 1761:[5]

After showing him the necessity of attaching himself to some person or body of men, and entering on your Lordship's character, I asked him if he had made any connexion with any other person . . he declared he had not. I advised him if he meant to attach himself to you to tell you so . . . he said he chose to do it in writing . . . as an evidence to produce against him if he should act contrary to his professions.

Having affirmed his adherence Dempster, hostile to Pitt, on 11 Dec. attacked Beckford's motion for Spanish papers as 'foolish and factious'.[6] When, through the illness of Gilbert Elliot, the promised motion for a Scottish militia was delayed, Dempster was prepared to move for it himself. 'One ought to squeak when his toes are trod on', he wrote to Alexander Carlyle on 20 Jan. 1762.[7] Exasperated when, on Bute's advice, the scheme was dropped, he intervened in the English militia debate of 18 Mar. to accuse defecting counties of cowardice.[8] Dempster soon became restive in the Government camp and at variance with most of his Scots colleagues. His breach with Bute's friends became complete when on 9 and 10 Dec. he spoke and voted against the peace.

He was not, however, engrossed in politics; he collaborated with Boswell and Andrew Erskine in a critique of a play by Mallet; became active with his friends the Johnstones in East India Company affairs; and in summer 1763 founded the first Dundee bank, 'George Dempster & Co.' As a patriotic Scot he resented Wilkes's attacks in the *North Briton*, and voted 15 Nov. 1763 against him;[9] but, opposed in principle to general warrants, in February 1764 spoke and voted against Administration. Yet Dempster was still essentially unconnected; in May Newcastle listed him 'doubtful', and in June Robert Nugent sought to secure him for Grenville.[10] On 9 Jan. 1765 he attended the Cockpit meeting to hear the speech and address, but on 6 Feb. spoke and voted against the Stamp Act.[11] During the Regency bill debates Dempster on 9 May eulogized the King, deferring to his judgment in the selection of a Regent; but on 11 May he supported Pryse Campbell's motion against any female regent's marrying a Catholic.[12]

Under the Rockingham Administration Dempster accepted the office of secretary to the Thistle, though he had 'neither the head nor heart of a truly ambitious man'.[13] He spoke and voted for the repeal of the Stamp Act and, according to Boswell, acquired 'a real ministerial look'.[14]

On Rockingham's fall he expressed to Adam Fergusson his distrust of the new Administration under Chatham, whose wartime extravagance he had always deplored:[15]

Pitt is now sovereign arbiter . . . His object from the first moment of his former resignation was to attain this perch of power . . . I myself believe he will not pay off our debts . . . will not help the constitution and . . . will break his neck upon the backstairs.

When invited by Conway to attend the pre-Parliament meeting to hear the King's speech, Dempster sought direction from Rockingham:[16]

It will give me pleasure to regulate my parliamentary conduct in whatever shape is agreeable to you. Let me say even more pleasure now than when your Lordship was at the head of the Treasury. While in that situation the strongest declarations of attachment might admit of a double construction; at present your Lordship will not think I flatter when I express my very high esteem both of your public and private conduct.

Dempster therefore followed the Rockinghams into opposition and voted with them on the land tax, 27 Feb. 1767. Having opposed Beckford's motion in December 1766 for a parliamentary inquiry into East India Company affairs, Dempster in the court of proprietors on 12 Mar. 1767 followed Laurence Sulivan in objecting to the terms negotiated by the directors for the renewal of the charter: 'a letting the Government into a partnership with the Company would soon end in the absolute dependency and ruin of the latter'.[17] On 6 May he was a leader of the proprietors who in defiance of both ministry and the direction increased the dividend to $12\frac{1}{2}$%.[18]

Dempster's alliance with Sulivan and the Johnstones in the East India Company incurred the hostility of the Clive party, who now sent Robert Mackintosh to oppose him in his burghs. During the campaign Dempster was arrested for bribery, but on his plea of parliamentary privilege the case was adjourned. He returned to Parliament, voted with Opposition on nullum tempus, 17 Feb. 1768, but, with a criminal prosecution pending against him, withdrew his candidature in favour of his friend William (Johnstone) Pulteney, who was returned. Pulteney was also successful in Cromarty, for which he elected to sit, and Dempster, when the case against him had been dismissed, was returned again for his burghs. The campaign and litigation had cost him over £10,000; he was obliged to sell all his estates except Dunnichen and thereafter was justly reckoned poor.[19] In April 1769 the Sulivan party secured his election to the direction of the East India Company.

Faithful to the Rockinghams in opposition, he voted with them on the Middlesex election, 8 May 1769, and in November, when Sulivan went over to Administration, scotched rumours that he would follow suit. Burke wrote to Rockingham, 9 Nov. 1769:

Dempster thought as I do about Sulivan's coalition. He told me that it should make no difference in his line in India House; that there he would stand as firmly by him as he would continue to oppose his new friends in Parliament. That his political connexion was with your Lordship and would always be so; but that if Mr. Sulivan should find that course of conduct prejudicial to his interests in Leadenhall Street, that he would at an hour's notice disqualify for the directorship. This was what I expected from Dempster . . . not to sacrifice one duty to another; but to keep both if possible—if not, to put it out of his power to violate the principal.

Under North's Administration Dempster maintained his reputation for candour in opposition; strongly protested on 7 Dec. 1770 against the recruitment of German and Irish Catholic troops, advocating compulsory service, if necessary, and the creation of a Scottish militia; he was equally emphatic in the debates of 19 Feb. and 4 Mar. 1771 against the plan to raise German and Irish regiments for the service of the East India Company 'as increasing the influence of the Crown and creating a new standing army of foreigners'.[20]

During the debates on the printers' case in March 1771 he censured the Commons' 'avidity for prosecution' as below the dignity of Parliament: 'I see a new scene opened that affects the liberty of the press . . . I do not like to see people so passionately fond of privilege'; and he contended that the public had a right to printed reports of parliamentary proceedings.[21] In the heated debates over the conduct of Alderman Oliver and Brass Crosby he urged moderation, and voted against their commitment to the Tower.

In 1772 Dempster was elected a director of the East India Company, not on the house list but as the popular choice of the proprietors. He was closely concerned in the Company's proposed reforms and in the selection of supervisors to be sent out to India; when Parliament rejected the plan Dempster, strongly objecting to Government intervention, early in March 'disqualified as a director . . . that he might be more at liberty in Parliament';[22] with the Duke of Richmond and the Johnstones he headed a group of dissident proprietors[23] and was a frequent Opposition speaker in the debates of March–June 1773 on North's Regulating Act. 'I would rather return the territory to the Mogul than suffer it to be taken by the Crown.'[24] He opposed North's American policy, and spoke against the Boston port bill and the Quebec bill.

During the recess Dempster married, but got little money with his wife, and after his unopposed return at the general election decided, mainly for reasons of economy, not to attend the next parliamentary session. He wrote to Sir Adam Fergusson, 26 Jan. 1775:[25]

I have long thought . . . that unless one preserves a little freedom and independency in Parliament to act in every question and to vote agreeably to . . one's own mind, a seat in Parliament is a seat of thorns and rusty nails. That this cannot be attained without some ease in your affairs . . . either you must be very rich or very frugal . . . When single I lived on my salary in London the year round—as a married man this is impossible.

'Having discharged his duty last year to America very conscientiously and very fruitlessly',[26] he believed his attendance would not affect the issue. He wrote to Fergusson:[27]

The ministry are . . . determined to adhere to their system, the Americans to their natural rights . . . I foretell it will begin with bloodshed in America and end with a change of ministers and measures in England.

To his American friend Ralph Izard he wrote, 7 June 1775:[28]

In Scotland, myself and a very few more excepted, the whole body of the gentry and of the independent and enlightened class of people are to a man on the side of Administration . . . There is a principle against America as well as for her, insomuch that it would not be easy for a ministry more favourable to her to bring the bulk of the House over to their opinion.

Dempster returned to London for the autumn session of 1775, urged conciliation, opposed the prohibition of trade with America, and supported Fox's motion for an inquiry into the ill-success of British arms.[29] Believing that the American crisis might induce the Government to concede a Scottish militia, he assisted in drafting Lord Mountstuart's bill and strongly supported it in the debates of March 1776.[30] Dempster also favoured the extension of the Scottish franchise 'now engrossed by the great lords, the drunken laird and the drunkener baillie', and did not approve Dundas's abortive proposals for limiting the creation of county votes.[31] He wrote to Carlyle:[32]

Instead of curtailing the right by cutting off superiors, let it be extended to vassals and tenants . . . but I am Whig enough to think that the most beneficial law should not be crammed down the throats of any people, but their minds gradually prepared for the alteration.

Throughout 1777 Dempster maintained his opposition; demanded an inquiry into the civil list debts, 18 Apr.; criticized, 15 May, North's financial measures and the system of contracts; intervened in the East India debate on 22 May to attack the intrigues of the Nabob of Arcot; but affirmed his independent views on West India trade and the Scottish militia.[33]

Dempster's finances had now been augmented by £1,000 p.a. bequeathed to him under the will of Sir Robert Fletcher (q.v.).[34] In December 1777 he went to France, and did not return to Parliament until spring 1779. Convinced that 'the influence of the Crown is the true cause of the origin and absurd conduct of this American war', Dempster supported Burke on economical reform, 15 Dec. 1779, and was a prominent Opposition speaker in the debates on pensions and the civil list establishment.[35]

At the general election of 1780 Dempster, labelled by his opponents 'a traitor to Scotland' for his vote on Dunning's motion, was modestly surprised by 'the successful issue of his short campaign'.[36] In the new Parliament he took the lead in opposing concessions to Irish trade at the expense of Scotland; was prominent in the East India debates in support of the Company's rights, and maintained to the end his objections to the Bengal judicature bill. His 'proverbial candour' occasionally disconcerted his Opposition colleagues. When Fox on 21 June 1781 attacked George Johnstone for incompetence, suggesting that his naval command was a reward for going over to Administration, Dempster, who 'never framed his friendship on such sandy ground as party consideration,' joined North in defending Johnstone's ability and integrity.[37]

Dempster does not appear to have attended the winter session 1781–2; he did not vote in any of the divisions leading to North's fall. No speech of his is recorded until 18 Apr. 1782, when he intervened in the Bengal judicature debate in defence of his friend Sir Elijah Impey.[38] Although in general supporting the Rockingham Administration, Dempster maintained his independence in Indian, West Indian and Scottish affairs, and continued to press for a Scottish militia.

He voted for Shelburne's peace preliminaries, 18 Feb. 1783, 'as a thing absolutely necessary for the country'.[39] He supported the Coalition with considerable reserve and remained uncompromisingly hostile to North. Although in 1782 he had sup-

ported Pitt's motion for an inquiry into parliamentary representation and urged its extension to Scotland,[40] he did not approve his proposed reforms of 7 May 1783: 'As the representative of a borough he could not assent to give a vote that would lessen the influence of his constituents.'[41]

Seeking nothing for himself, he disliked soliciting for friends. He wrote to Fergusson on 22 Sept. 1783:[42]

When you ask a minister to do a favour . . . it founds an expectation that you will in return confer a favour upon him . . . But the true spirit of our constitution ought to make it criminal in a Member of Parliament to offer any constituent the smallest personal favour. We shall never sit quite at our ease in Parliament till it may be said . . . that we never obtained the slightest favour at court either for ourselves or others.

Over East India affairs Dempster during the long controversies had modified his views. He now wished to abandon all territorial claims and confine the Company's activities to commerce. On Fox's East India bill he expressed on 27 Nov. 1783 considerable misgivings:

All chartered rights should be held inviolable, one charter only excepted . . . The charter of the E.I. Co . . . ought to be destroyed for the sake of this country . . . of India . . . and of humanity. He . . . conjured ministers to abandon all idea of sovereignty in that quarter of the globe. It would be much wiser . . . to make some one of the native princes King . . . and to leave India to itself. [But] . . . he saw which way the House was inclined and therefore he should withdraw, as he would not vote, against his principles, for the throne of Delhi.

Shortly afterwards he left for Scotland, was absent during the change of Administration, and on his return in January 1784 was listed by Robinson as an opponent of Pitt. On 23 Jan. he strongly protested against a dissolution and welcomed Fox's motion to reintroduce his bill. 'He would now be able to modify it in respect of patronage and . . . make it generally palatable.' Dempster remained loyal to Fox, but as a member of the St. Alban's Tavern group favoured a union of parties and preached moderation so that 'something decisive' might be done for India.[43]

Returned unopposed at the general election, Dempster now became increasingly 'elevated above all party views'.[44] He was conciliatory to Pitt who, respecting his views on trade and finance, supported his motion for a committee on fisheries, which now became Dempster's major interest. Over India he maintained his individual view that he would rather see Indian affairs 'egregiously mismanaged' by the court of directors than well managed by the Crown, and that it was impracticable to govern India from

England. In the debate of 16 July 1784 he proposed:

> That his Majesty should be requested to send over one of his sons and make him King of that country; we might then make an alliance or federal union with him and then we could enjoy all the advantage that could be derived from the possession of the East Indies by Europeans—the benefit of commerce.

Dempster was critical of Opposition attacks on Warren Hastings 'to whom alone he imputed the salvation of India'.[45]

In the new session he supported Pitt's Irish propositions, although uneasy about their effect on Scottish trade and industry, and voted for them 13 May 1785; but in February 1786 he spoke and voted against Richmond's fortification plans as unnecessary and extravagant. During the East India debates of 1786-7 Dempster remained a vehement defender both of Warren Hastings and of Impey; rebutted all Opposition charges against a governor general whom he eulogized for his integrity as statesman, soldier and financier; and justified even his severities. But he joined with Opposition leaders in pressing the complaints of the East India Company servants in Bengal; on 19 Mar. he moved for the repeal of the East India Acts of 1784-6 and proposed a new system of government under a viceroy, council, and a representative assembly of resident Europeans. Although frequently an advocate of free institutions and better representation, especially in Scotland, Dempster now seems to have limited his proposals to county representation, and on 28 May 1787 declined to support petitions for the reform of Scottish burghs.[46]

In the House Dempster was respected as 'one of the most conscientious men who ever sat in Parliament',[47] particularly for his efforts to curb taxation and reduce the national debt, and for his championship of the distressed, whether famine-stricken Highlanders, poor hawkers, or American loyalists. In Scotland he was honoured for his exertions both in and out of Parliament to encourage Scottish trade, agriculture, manufactures and fisheries. In furtherance of his schemes he purchased in 1786 the estate of Skibo, and on his Angus estate embarked upon plans for building the new village of Letham. During the summer of 1788 he decided not to seek re-election, and in November informed his constituents. He wrote, 10 July 1788, to Alexander Carlyle:[48] 'It is now twenty years since I have found my opposition to any measure one of the necessary accompaniments of its success', and listed as examples the American war and Hastings's prosecution.

He returned to Parliament for the new session

and was a leading Opposition speaker in the Regency debates. On the King's recovery he resumed his customary strictures on Government expenditure, seconded the motion for toleration for Scottish Episcopalians, but opposed the abolition of the slave trade without full compensation to the planters and traders affected. He made his last recorded speech on 22 July in favour of supplying corn to revolutionary France.[49]

For the rest of his life he devoted himself to the development of Scottish fisheries, industries and communications, and the improvement of his own estates. He wrote to Adam Fergusson, 2 Aug. 1793:[50]

> I am full of occupation from morning till night . . . Although I don't get into debt, I am pretty near as bare of money as I used to be . . . I have . . . the satisfaction of considering that I am done with Parliament after a service of thirty years neither suited to my fortune nor genius, where I never was metaphysician enough to settle to my own satisfaction the bounds of the several duties a Member owes to his King, his country, to purity or Puritanism rather, and to party, to myself and those who depended upon my protection . . . but went on floundering like a blind horse in a deep road and a long journey.

He died 13 Feb. 1818.

[1] A. J. Warden, *Angus or Forfarshire*, iii. 197-8; J. Malcolm, *Parish of Monifieth*, 313. [2] Sir James Fergusson, *Letters of Geo. Dempster to Sir Adam Fergusson*, 25, 36, 346-7; Boswell, *Johnson*, i. 439-44; Boswell, *Letters*, i. 27; Carlyle, *Autobiog.* 338. [3] Harris's 'Debates'. [4] *HMC Stopford-Sackville*, i. 17. [5] Bute mss. [6] Harris's 'Debates'. [7] Carlyle mss, Edin. Univ. Lib. [8] Harris's 'Debates'. [9] *Caldwell Pprs.* ii (1), p. 199. [10] Nugent to Grenville, 28 June 1765, Grenville mss (JM). [11] Harris's 'Debates'; Fergusson, *Letters*, 85. [12] *Grenville Pprs.* iii. 27; Fortescue, i. 89. [13] Dempster's memorandum; Fergusson, *Letters*, 347. [14] Boswell, *Private Pprs.* vii. 77. [15] *Letters*, 63-4. [16] Dempster to Rockingham, 8 Nov. 1766, Rockingham mss. [17] J. West to Newcastle, 13 Mar. 1767, Add. 32980, f. 280. [18] L. S. Sutherland, *E. I. Co. in 18th cent. Politics*, 169-171. [19] *Letters*, 347; Boswell, *Private Pprs.* viii. 173. [20] Cavendish, *Debates*, ii. 190, 337, 352. [21] Ibid. 383-5, 389. [22] Ibid. 466; Brickdale's 'Debates', 27 Mar. 1771. [23] Sutherland, 157. [24] Brickdale's 'Debates'. [25] *Letters*, 84-85. [26] Dempster to Ralph Izard, 5 Mar. 1775, *Corresp. of Ralph Izard of S.C.*, ed. Anne I. Deas, 55. [27] *Letters*, 86. [28] *Corresp. of Ralph Izard*, 87-88. [29] Almon, iii. 70-73, 167, 249, 282, 331. [30] Dempster to Alex. Carlyle (early Dec. 1775), Carlyle mss; Almon, ii. 395. [31] *Scots Mag.* 1775, pp. 225, 289-91, 409-12, 566-9. [32] Carlyle mss. [33] Almon, vii. 106-7, 151, 209, 214, 233; xi. 129. [34] *Letters*, 100-104. [35] Almon, xvi. 37; xvii. 142, 385. [36] Rockingham to Sir Lawrence Dundas, Oct. 1780, Rockingham mss; *Letters*, 109. [37] Debrett, iii. 167-9, 193, 280, 377, 384, 653, 665. [38] Ibid. vii. 54, 263; Add. 16260, ff. 181b, 205b. [39] Debrett, ix. 206. [40] 7 May 1782, ibid. vii. 138. [41] Ibid. ix. 735. [42] *Letters*, 121. [43] Debrett, xii. 198-9, 640; xiii. 66, 90, 104, 251, 295. [44] Wraxall, *Mems.* iv. 339. [45] Debrett, xv. 381-2; xvi. 103, 309. [46] Ibid. xvii. 262; *Letters*, 141, 143-4; Stockdale, vii. 100; xi. 6-9; xii. 177. [47] Wraxall, *Mems.* iv. 339. [48] *Letters*, 193. [49] Stockdale, xvii. 227-8, 316; xviii. 99. [50] *Letters*, 232-3.

E.H.-G.


## DENHAM, see STEUART DENHAM


## DENIS, Peter (1713-78), of Westerham and Blackmanstone, Kent.

HEDON     1754-1768

*b.* 1713, 11th child of Rev. Jacob Denis, Huguenot minister expelled from France, by his w. Martha

Leach. *m.* 2 Sept. 1750, Elizabeth (known as 'Miss Pappet'), illegit. da. of John James Heidegger, manager of the opera in the Haymarket, *s.p. cr.* Bt. 28 Oct. 1767.

Lt. R.N. 1739; sailed round the world with Anson 1740–4; cdr. 1744; capt. 1745; member of Byng's court martial 1756; fought at Quiberon Bay 1759; r.-adm. 1770; v.-adm. 1775.

Denis was closely connected with Anson and sat on his interest at Hedon.

In 1762 he seems to have gone into opposition with Sir Charles Saunders (q.v.), who had succeeded Anson as patron of Hedon: though his name appears in no division list 1762–5 and he was absent from that on general warrants, 18 Feb. 1764, Newcastle on 10 May 1764 classed him as a 'sure friend'. He supported the Rockingham Administration, and in November 1766 Rockingham still counted him as a friend. In January 1767 Townshend classed him 'doubtful'; he voted with Administration over the land tax, 27 Feb. 1767; and was created a baronet at Grafton's recommendation. Saunders, who had remained in opposition with Rockingham, did not return Denis at Hedon in 1768, and Denis is not known to have stood elsewhere. There is no record of his having spoken in the House.

He died 11 June 1778.

J.B.

**DERING, Edward** (1732–98), of Surrenden Dering, nr. Ashford, Kent.

NEW ROMNEY 1761–Feb. 1770, 1774–Jan. 1787

*b.* 28 Sept. 1732, 1st s. of Sir Edward Dering, 5th Bt., M.P., of Surrenden Dering by his 1st w. Mary, da. and coh. of Edward Henshaw of Eltham, Kent. *educ.* King's School, Canterbury;[1] Westminster 1744–9; St. John's, Camb. 1751. *m.* (1) 8 Apr. 1755, Selina (*d.*29 Mar. 1757), da. of Sir Robert Furnese, 2nd Bt., M.P., of Waldershare, Kent, half-sis. and coh. of Sir Henry Furnese, 3rd Bt., 1s. 1da.; (2) 1 Jan. 1765, Deborah, da. of John Winchester, surgeon, 3s. 2da. *suc.* fa. as 6th Bt. 15 Apr. 1762.

The Derings were a very old Kentish family who first represented Kent in 1640: each of the first five baronets sat for the county. Under George II the family were Tories. Edward Dering inherited through his first wife the Furnese estates near New Romney. In 1756 he stood there but was forced to withdraw; 1756–60 fought and defeated Rose Fuller (q.v.) for control of the borough; and henceforth recommended to both seats.

In Bute's list of 1761 Dering is marked 'Tory'. He is not included in Henry Fox's list of Members favourable to the peace preliminaries, nor did he vote against them; but he seems to have supported Bute. James Harris (q.v.) wrote on 4 Nov. 1763:[2] 'Sir Edward Dering, a Tory, had been disgusted in

not obtaining from Lord Bute, and since from Mr. Grenville, a place for his brother.' He opposed Grenville's Administration, was classed by Newcastle as a 'sure friend', 10 May 1764, and was a member of Wildman's Club. In July 1765 Rockingham classed him 'pro' and in November 1766 'Whig'; Townshend in January 1767 'Government'; and Newcastle in March 1767 'Tory'. He voted with the court on the land tax, 27 Feb. 1767.

He was connected by marriage with Lord North (North's step-mother and Dering's first wife were sisters), and seems to have been prepared to accept his recommendations at New Romney while voting against him in Parliament. Altogether his voting record is extraordinary. In 1768 he returned Richard Jackson, who was closely connected with Administration; but in three divisions on Wilkes (2 and 3 Feb. and 15 Apr. 1769) he voted with the Opposition. In February 1770 he vacated his seat in favour of John Morton, a regular Government supporter. On 28 Feb. Bamber Gascoyne wrote to John Strutt: 'Sir Edward Dering hath lost £12,000, i.e. guineas, is selling his horses and equipage, going abroad immediately, resigned his seat in Parliament to Morton.' And on 6 Mar.: 'Your character of Edward Dering is just but he had a better estate than £4,000 p.a. I do not think his loss is much to the public nor will the lesson hurt him, for by this he will be cured, the total damage is £18,000.' Whether Dering's losses were by speculation or gambling is not known.

In 1774 Dering returned himself and Richard Jackson. Until 1779 he supported North's Administration: his first recorded vote against them was on the contractors bill, 12 Feb. 1779, when he was classed by Robinson as a friend normally voting with Government. Before 1779 only four speeches by him are reported, but 1779–82 he spoke in several of the big debates. In that of 3 Mar. 1779, censuring the Admiralty for sending Keppel to sea with insufficient forces, he mentioned the 'long acquaintance and personal obligations' which he had to Sandwich, then described Keppel as 'his honourable friend', and concluded by declaring Sandwich unfit to continue first lord of the Admiralty.[3] Yet his next speech, 21 June 1779, on the motion to increase the militia, was for Administration.[4]

On 21 Feb. 1780 he voted with the court on the motion for a list of pensions, but on 8 Mar. against them on Burke's economical reform bill. On 13 Mar. in the debate on the clause to abolish the Board of Trade, he attacked Rigby's argument that the House had no control over the civil list, and again voted against the court. On 20 Mar. he spoke against the clause to abolish the office of treasurer of the chamber, 'from a strong disapprobation of meddling or interfering with the management of any part of the King's Household'.[5] He voted against Dunning's motion, 6 Apr.; and against the motion to consider the petitions, 24 Apr.; and Robinson in his electoral survey of 1780 classed him as 'pro'.

He voted with the court on Lowther's motion to end the war, 12 Dec. 1781, and in four out of the five critical divisions of February–March (he was absent from that of 22 Feb.). He spoke on 7 Feb., 8 Mar., and 15 Mar. About the debate of 7 Feb. George Selwyn (q.v.) wrote to Lord Carlisle:[6]

Admiral Keppel spoke, and so did Sir E. Dering, drunk, *sicut suus mos est*; but he says in that *ivresse des verités vertes et piquantes*. He is a tiresome noisy fool, and I wish that he never spoke anywhere but in the House of Commons.

He voted for Shelburne's peace preliminaries, 18 Feb. 1783, for Fox's East India bill, 27 Nov. 1783, and supported Pitt. Robinson, in his electoral survey of 1784, wrote about Dering and New Romney: 'He will most likely return himself and Mr. Jackson again, and as things change, Sir Edward is not obstinate.' Jackson left Parliament, and at Pitt's request Dering returned John Smith, and when Smith vacated his seat, Richard Atkinson (though against his inclination 'as not liking Mr. Atkinson's character'[7]). In 1785, 1787 and 1790 he also returned candidates recommended by Pitt.

On going abroad in 1787 he vacated his seat, and because of ill-health did not stand in 1790. In 1794 he applied for a peerage, and included among the services he claimed to have rendered to Pitt the refusal of 'some very advantageous offers' made by the Opposition at the time of the Regency crisis.[8] He died 8 Dec. 1798.

Dering once described himself as 'one of the most virtuous, most honest, and independent members of the House'.[9] He seems to have been an odd character. Horace Walpole describes him as 'a foolish Kentish knight';[10] Lady Spencer wrote:[11] 'Sir Edward Dering's being disliked in the county is a natural consequence of his being very tenacious about game.' The obituary notice of him in the *Gentleman's Magazine* (1798, p. 1089) concludes: 'The large estate and honourable name which he inherited would have carried a vast command over his native county, had they not been unhappily sacrificed to his own imprudences.'

[1] Nichols, *Lit. Hist.* vi. 755. [2] Malmesbury mss. [3] Almon, xii. 43–44. [4] North to the King, 21 June 1779, Fortescue, iv. 365. Dering's speech is not reported in Almon. [5] Almon, xvii. 378. [6] *HMC Carlisle*, 572. [7] Dering's memorandum, 24 Sept. [1794], Chatham mss. [8] Ibid. [9] Almon, xvii. 317–18. [10] *Last Jnls.* ii. 280. [11] To Ld. Althorp, 28 Aug. 1781, Spencer mss.

J.B.

**DEVAYNES, William** (c.1730–1809), of Dover St. and Pall Mall, London.

| | |
|---|---|
| BARNSTAPLE | 1774–1780, 1784–1796 |
| WINCHELSEA | 13 Dec. 1796–1802 |
| BARNSTAPLE | 1802–1806 |

*b.* c.1730, 2nd s. of John Devaynes, a Huguenot, by Mary, o. surv. child of William Barker, City remembrancer. *m.* (1) Jane Wintle, 1s. 1da.; (2) 3 Feb. 1806, Mary, da. of William Wileman, *s.p. suc.* bro. 1801.[1]

London banker, of the firm Crofts, Roberts, Devaynes, and Dawes, 39 Pall Mall. Liverpool commr., Africa Co. 1772, 1776; director, E.I. Co. 1770–5, 1777–80, 1782–5, 1787–90, 1792–5, 1797–1800, 1802–5, chairman 1780–1, 1785–6, 1793–5; director, Globe Insurance Co.; director of the French Hospital 1770–*d.*

Devaynes was a big Government contractor, and between 1776 and 1782 held together with John Henniker, George Wombwell (qq.v.) and Edward Wheler army victualling contracts for 12–14,000 men in America.[2] All the partners except Henniker being directors of the East India Company, the friends of Hastings, whom Administration then meant to dismiss, feared that the contracts were part of Robinson's endeavours to gain control of the Company.[3] Devaynes held at various times considerable sums in Government stock: in 1783, £19,000; between 1783 and 1792 his purchases and sales of Government stock exceeded £100,000.

No previous connexion between Devaynes and Barnstaple has been traced: in all probability it was a cash nexus. He was defeated there in 1780 and 1796. In the House he voted invariably with the Government: with North in his first Parliament, and with Pitt in his second—'Devaynes to have *early* notice *vice* Bassett' (a supporter of the Coalition) Robinson had written in a paper of February–March 1784.[4] He spoke very rarely: on 26 May and 5 June 1777, when the Africa Company was charged by the Board of Trade with having 'set up and established a private trade, directly tending to a monopoly'[5] (and Devaynes was at that time the only commissioner of the Africa Company in the House); and in debates, 1788–90, he dealt with technical points concerning the East India Company. In the India House before 1782 he went with the Government side, directed by Sandwich and Robinson;[6] after 1782 he belonged to the so-called 'Old Party'. He is described as a 'self-seeking mediocrity'.[7] Richard Atkinson wrote to Henry Dundas, 31 Jan. 1785: 'As long as he gets his job, Devaynes will be all right.'[8]

He died 29 Nov. 1809. A 'mulatto daughter' is mentioned in his will, which suggests his having at one time resided in Africa.

[1] *Gent. Mag.* 1801, p. 93. [2] T29/45 seq., and 54/42–43. In Jan. 1782 Devaynes obtained a smaller separate contract. [3] F. Sykes to Hastings, 30 May 1776, and L. Macleane to same, 25 June 1776. Add. 29137, ff. 204, 249. [4] Laprade, 115. [5] Almon. vii. 234. [6] See e.g. Abergavenny mss 250, 265. [7] C. H. Philips, *E.I. Co. 1784–1834*, p. 26. [8] Ibid. 62n.

L.B.N.

## DEWAR, John (c.1746–95), of Clapham, Surr.

CRICKLADE    20 Feb. 1776–1780

*b.* c.1746, 1st s. of George Dewar of Antigua by Christina, da. and h. of John Panton of Basseterre, St. Kitts. *m.* 27 Aug. 1766, Caroline, da. of James Vernon of Hilton Park, Staffs.

John Dewar's grandfather was a merchant and postmaster of Edinburgh; his father emigrated to the West Indies, and on his return purchased an estate at Doles, near Enham, Hampshire.

Dewar was a stranger to Cricklade when he contested it at the general election of 1774. He declined during the poll. Nevertheless, on a vacancy in December 1774 he came forward once more, and was defeated apparently by the partiality of the returning officer, who closed the poll on the pretext of violence, and submitted a double return. The House of Commons declared the election void. In February 1775 he again contested the seat, in opposition to Samuel Peach (q.v.) and Samuel Petrie. Once again the returning officer intervened on Peach's behalf, and disqualified 108 of Dewar's votes. Peach was declared elected, but on petition the House seated Dewar. Dewar was absent at the time his petition came before the House, and his father sought leave to withdraw it. It was prosecuted, however, by Henry Herbert (q.v.) and Petrie, who between them seated Dewar despite himself.

In Robinson's list on the contractors bill, Dewar appears as 'pro, abroad'. His first recorded vote was over Keppel, 3 Mar. 1779, and in the four extant division lists, March–April 1780, he appears as voting with the Government. There is no record of his having spoken in the House.

Robinson's estimate for the 1780 election was that 'Mr. Dewar certainly will not come in again'. This was probably because he was in difficult financial circumstances. In 1784 his father made a will disinheriting John in favour of his younger brother, David.[1] He complained that his son had 'by a continued series of imprudences and extravagances, involved himself hopelessly in difficulties', and that he had sold an annuity of £400 p.a. which his father had settled on him.

Dewar died 9 Feb. 1795.

[1] PCC 371 Norfolk.

J.A.C.

## DICKER, Samuel (*d.*1760), of Walton-on-Thames, Surr.

PLYMOUTH    1754–1 Jan. 1760

1st s. of Philip Dicker of Exeter by Sarah, da. of John Reynell of North Tawton, Devon. *m.* Elizabeth, *s.p. suc.* fa. 1753.

Comptroller of customs at Jamaica 1740.

Dicker's family was connected with the Devon wool trade. He himself went to Jamaica as a young man; became an influential merchant, and acquired 'a very large estate there'.[1] In 1739 he was nominated to the Jamaica council, but, back in England, in 1747 resigned because he did 'not intend to return to the island'.[2] He bought an estate at Walton-on-Thames, and obtained a grant of arms, but continued in trade at Bristol, and in 1750 was chosen a Bristol representative on the committee of the Africa Company.

In 1754 he was returned at Plymouth with Government support. No vote or speech by him is reported.

Dicker maintained his connexion with the West Indies, and in 1757, together with William Beckford and Rose Fuller (qq.v.), was consulted by the Board of Trade about West Indian affairs.

Dicker spent large sums in building bridges over the Thames—according to Grosley's *A Tour to London*[3] 'by that means [he] became Pontifex Maximus.' Among these bridges that . . . at Walton makes a conspicuous figure: the building cost £10,000.' He died 1 Jan. 1760.

[1] *Gent. Mag.* 1824, ii. 223–4. [2] *APC Col.* App. II, 786. [3] Pub. as *Londres* at Lausanne, 1770. Trans. by Thomas Nugent, 1772.

M.M.D.

## DICKINS, Francis (1750–1833), of Wollaston, Northants. and Branches Park, Suff.

CAMBRIDGE              29 May 1788–1790
NORTHAMPTONSHIRE              1790–1806

*b.* 1750, o.s. of Ambrose Dickins, barrister, by Mary, da. of Sir William Abdy, 4th Bt., sis. of Sir Anthony Thomas Abdy, 5th Bt. (q.v.). *educ.* Westminster; Trinity Hall, Camb. 1767. *m.* 21 Apr. 1778, Diana, da. of Lord George Manners Sutton (q.v.), 2s.

Dickins first attempted to enter Parliament in 1784, when he contested Sudbury, but retired during the poll. Returned for Cambridge as a member of the Rutland group, he voted with Pitt on the Regency. There is no record of his having spoken in his first Parliament.

He died 23 Dec. 1833.

L.B.N.

**DICKINSON, Marshe** (?1703–65), of Cheapside, London, and Dunstable, Beds.

BRACKLEY    1754–6 Feb. 1765

*b*. ?1703, 3rd s. of John Dickinson, London merchant, by Elizabeth, da. of Thomas Powell, London merchant, gd.-da. and h. of Francis Marshe. *educ*. Westminster 1718, aged 15; I. Temple 1728. *m*., issue.
Common councillor, London 1738–43, alderman 1749–*d*., sheriff 1751–2, ld. mayor 1756–7.
Chairman of ways and mean Nov. 1761–*d*.

Dickinson seems to have been a City attorney—Dupplin in 1754 listed him as a practising lawyer. The Duke of Bedford wrote from Woburn on 5 Aug. 1753 to his nephew, the young Duke of Bridgwater, then on his Grand Tour: 'As he [Dickinson] is one for whom I have the greatest esteem and a near neighbour to me in this county, I was determined to bring him into Parliament and did intend him for the town of Bedford, but as our plan is altered there I take the liberty to recommend him to you for Brackley.'[1] Bridgwater accepted Bedford's recommendation, and after a contest Dickinson was returned, though not his colleague Henry Vernon (q.v.). Philip Yorke (q.v.) wrote to Lord Hardwicke, 5 Aug. 1753, that Dickinson 'is reckoned a moderate Tory';[2] in a parliamentary list, mainly of merchant M.P.s, 1754–5,[3] he is described as 'a friend of Sir William Calvert' (q.v.); by L. C. J. Willes as 'a particular friend' of the City recorder, Sir William Moreton (q.v.);[4] and by James West as 'the most intimate friend of Sir Robert Ladbroke' (q.v.).[5]

When on 20 Aug. 1756, after the loss of Minorca, the City address was presented to the King asking for 'the authors of our late losses and disappointments to be inquired into and punished', which the King told them would be done,[6] Hardwicke, who attended the King, wrote to Newcastle:[7] 'There were 15 aldermen but amongst them neither Sir John Barnard, nor any one of those who are called Whig-aldermen. Sir Robert Ladbroke and Alderman Dickinson were there. A great number of the common council attended.' Next year, at the time of Byng's trial and execution, Dickinson was lord mayor; and according to Walpole,[8] on 9 Mar. four Tory aldermen went to him 'to desire he would summon a common council, intending to promote a petition to the King to spare the admiral'; but Dickinson, 'unfeelingly formal', replied it was too late. And nothing more happened. Had such a petition been made, 'the King could not have pleaded his promise of severity pledged to the City'.

At a meeting of the livery at Guildhall, 4 Mar. 1761, Dickinson was 'put in nomination' for the general election, but failed to receive sufficient support.[9] On 10 Oct. 1761, Newcastle wrote to Bedford, discussing candidates for Speaker: 'I wish your Grace could suggest somebody. Alderman Dickinson has been named but his being an alderman is thought a great objection and your Grace knows he is designed for the money chair.'[10] Dickinson was duly elected chairman of the committee of ways and means (stipend: £500 p.a. from secret service funds). Three interventions of his in debate reported by Harris are on very secondary matters: 24 Nov. 1761, a clause to the Insolvent Debtors' Act; on 2 Feb. 1762, the toll on London Bridge; while on the third occasion, 29 Mar. 1762, he appears but too clearly as a Bedford agent in the House. Here is Harris's account:

> A bill had come to us from the Lords about certain trust lands at Tavistock, relating to the Duke of Bedford's affairs, and which he had brought in. There was a clause in it to declare that those lands were to convey no right of voting in that borough. This got among the Commons as a breach of their privileges, and the bill had certainly been flung out had not Alderman Dickinson moved that it be withdrawn. He was mistaken in the manner of doing this, by beginning that *he had authority from a noble duke*, etc. *We want no authority from noble dukes, nor from those greater than dukes, to empower us to do our acts.*

Similarly on 23 Mar., over 'excepting Covent Garden Market out of the fish bill'—'The commitment of the bill', wrote Dickinson to the Duke, 'I have got put off till to-morrow and shall be glad to receive your Grace's directions thereon that I may prevent opposition.'[11]

On one occasion Dickinson stood up to the Duke —for a short while. Lord Tavistock, a friend of Dickinson's son, John Marshe Dickinson, had obtained for young Dickinson the office of superintendent of his Majesty's gardens.[12] But when in April 1764, over a reshuffle in which Bedford wanted a place at the Board of the Green Cloth for Richard Vernon, John Dickinson was asked to surrender his place in exchange for a pension, old Dickinson took offence; looked upon it as a slur intended 'to be put on his family'; wrote a 'warm' and 'wrongheaded' note to the Duke; who even appealed to the King (only to be told 'that he must make his friends agree as they could, for that I [the King] had no part in this dispute'). In the end the Dickinsons agreed to the transaction, having received ample assurances that they should not suffer the least financial loss. Tavistock's comment on old Dickinson's behaviour was 'that those who have the least pretensions to pride have the most and that it was one of these fits that took him' on this occasion.[13]

In the House Dickinson naturally supported the peace treaty negotiated by Bedford, and exerted himself on the side of the Grenville-Bedford Government. When he died, 6 Feb. 1765, Mary Townshend wrote to her uncle, George Selwyn, that he 'died of general warrants'.[14]

[1] Bedford mss 29, f. 85, 103. [2] Add. 35351, ff. 248–51. [3] Lowther mss. [4] Willes to Bedford, 19 Mar. 1754, Bedford mss 30, f. 16. [5] West to Newcastle, 14 Aug. 1756, Add. 32866, ff. 448–9. [6] For text of the address and the King's reply, see *Gent. Mag.* 1756, p. 408. [7] Add. 32866, ff. 492–4; see also ff. 448–9. [8] *Mems. Geo. II*, ii. 368. [9] *British Chron.* 4 Mar.; see also Add. 32906, f. 488. [10] Bedford mss 44, f. 194. [11] Ibid. f. 54. [12] Tavistock to Bute, 11 May 1763, Bute mss and T52/55/18. [13] Bedford to Grenville, 14, 17, 25 Apr., Grenville mss (JM); Grenville to Bedford, 14 Apr. Bedford mss 49, f. 134; 17 Apr., Grenville letter bk.; 28 Apr., Bedford mss 49, f. 174; Tavistock to Bedford, 22 Apr.; ibid. 158; the King to Bute, c.18 and 19 Apr., Sedgwick, 237–8. [14] Jesse, *Selwyn*, i. 358.

L.B.N.

### DICKINSON, William (1745–1806), of Kingweston, Som.

| | |
|---|---|
| GREAT MARLOW | 1768–1774 |
| RYE | 20 May 1777–1790 |
| SOMERSET | 1796–26 May 1806 |

*b.* 13 July 1745, 1st s. of Caleb Dickinson, Bristol merchant, by Sarah, da. of Graffin Prankard, a Bristol iron merchant to whom Caleb Dickinson was apprenticed.[1] *m.* 1771, Philippa, da. of Stephen Fuller, niece of Rose Fuller (q.v.) 1s. 1da. and other issue. *suc.* fa. 6 Apr. 1783.

William Dickinson, despite his mercantile connexions, was not engaged in trade, except that arising from his West Indian plantations, in which he was closely associated with his wife's family, the Fullers, and with Hans Sloane (q.v.). He also had an East Indian connexion, and in 1780 supported Paul Benfield's candidature at Great Marlow.

How Dickinson came to stand for Marlow is not known. In 1768 he was returned after a contest, but in 1774 was defeated. He re-entered Parliament in 1777, succeeding Rose Fuller at Rye, a Treasury borough, where the Fullers had a good deal of influence.

Dickinson consistently supported North's Administration. His only recorded speech, 2 Feb. 1773, was on a bill concerning the West Indies.[2] He voted against Shelburne's peace preliminaries, 18 Feb. 1783, and for Fox's East India bill, 27 Nov. 1783. John Sinclair wrote of him in early January 1784:[3] 'Voted for the late bill, but *could* be converted.' And in Robinson's list he is classed as 'very hopeful'— presumably on the basis of Sinclair's information: which was misleading, for Dickinson went against Pitt, and remained in opposition in the Parliament of 1784. He voted for Pitt's parliamentary reform proposals of 13 May 1785.

Dickinson died 26 May 1806.

[1] *Ex inf.* W. E. Minchinton. [2] Cavendish's 'Debates', Egerton 242, f. 190. [3] Thurso mss.

J.B.

### DICKSON, James (c.1715–71), of Broughton, Peebles, and Ednam and Sydenham, Roxburgh.

LINLITHGOW BURGHS    29 Dec. 1768–14 Nov. 1771

*b.* c.1715, in the parish of Stitchell, Roxburgh; bro. of Archibald Dickson of Pontefract.

Of Dickson's parentage nothing has been ascertained except that the family had close ties with the Kelso district of Roxburghshire. On 24 Jan. 1760 George Ridpath, minister of Stitchell, recorded a visit from George Coventry, minister of the Secession Church[1]—

[He] had come to talk to me about distributing amongst the poor £5 that one Dickson, a native of this parish, and now a merchant in London where he is grown very rich, sent down to Smith of Jedburgh who is a relation of his. Smith wrote me about it, desiring me to distribute it in conjunction with Coventry.

Dickson had been established as a merchant in London from the early 1750s and apparently made his fortune in the West Indies during the seven years' war.[2]

In 1764 'Mr. Dickson of Havana' purchased the barony of Broughton, Peebles, from John ('Evidence') Murray for £16,000 sterling.[3] By further purchases he acquired practically the whole of the parish of Broughton adjoining the estates of John Dickson (q.v.) of Kilbucho.[4] He was active in agricultural improvements, rebuilt the village of Broughton 'after the English fashion', and interested himself in local antiquities.[5]

He also acquired the estates of Ednam and Sydenham in Roxburghshire, where he carried out even more elaborate 'improvements'. The Rev. David Dickson, minister of Ednam, wrote c.1790:[6]

When the late James Dickson Esq., M.P., became proprietor of Edenham, being a person of public spirit, he enclosed all his lands, planned and built a neat village, the houses being all of brick covered with pantile or slates; brought manufactures from England, and established woollen manufacturers for cloth, particularly for English blankets. He also erected a waulk mill to promote this useful undertaking, but his death marred the progress of these public-spirited schemes. He built also an extensive brewery . . . and great quantities of the ale and porter brewed in it are exported to England.

His wealth and enterprise commended him as a candidate for Parliament. In 1768 John Lockhart Ross was returned both for Lanarkshire and Linlithgow Burghs, and after considerable delay chose to sit for the county. In the burghs he had been opposed both by John Murray of Philiphaugh (q.v.) and the Hamilton interest. At the by-election the Hamilton interest was offered to Murray,[7] but he was in financial difficulties and does not seem to have contested the seat. On 29 Dec. James Dickson was elected apparently unopposed.

He supported Administration in the Wilkes debates, voting 3 Feb. 1769 for the expulsion of Wilkes, and on 15 Apr. and 8 May with the majority in the divisions on the Middlesex election.

He died 14 Nov. 1771.

[1] *Geo. Ridpath's Diary* (Sc. Hist. Soc.), 297–8. [2] Adam, *Pol. State of Scotland in 1788*, p. 309. [3] *Murray of Broughton's Memorials* (Sc. Hist. Soc.), p. xiii n. [4] Buchan and Paton, *Peeblesshire*, iii. 256, 266, 272. [5] Ibid. 258; *Stat. Acct.* vii. 156, 159. [6] *Stat. Acct.* xi. 305–6. [7] *Caldwell Pprs.* ii(2), pp. 147–8.

E.H.-G.

## DICKSON, John (c.1707–67), of Kilbucho, Peebles.

PEEBLESSHIRE    1747–2 Dec. 1767

*b.* c.1707, 1st s. of William Dickson of Kilbucho by Jean, da. of Sir William Menzies of St. Germains, E. Lothian. *educ.* Glasgow Univ. 1722; adv. 1728; Leyden 1729. *unm. suc.* fa. 6 Mar. 1762.

Burgess of Edinburgh 3 July 1765.

Dickson was returned for Peeblesshire in 1754 on the interest of the Earl of March, and was listed by Dupplin among the Scots friends of the Administration, 'of various connexions' (i.e. not specifically attached to the Duke of Argyll).[1] But during the negotiations on the change of ministry in the spring of 1757, Newcastle counted him among those 'not to be relied on at present but to be treated with'.[2] In the debates on the Minorca inquiry when, on the last day of the committee stage, 2 May 1757, the 'old ministry's triumphant majority' was seriously reduced, Henry Fox, enclosing a division list, wrote to the Duke of Devonshire, 3 May: 'You will see that some very unexpectedly left us.'[3] Among these was Dickson.

He supported the plan for a Scots militia and was nominated by the committee to prepare the abortive bill, 12 Mar. 1760. There is no record of his having spoken in the House.

In a 'Note of the Elections in Scotland', prepared for Newcastle on 26 Apr. 1760, there is the following about Peeblesshire:[4]

Mr. Dickson, the present Member, is extremely desirous of leaving Parliament if any (even small) office was bestowed upon him. Perhaps Lord March may think it hard to turn him out on any other condition, as the circumstances of his estate are very indifferent.

Other candidates had expectations in Peeblesshire. Shortly before the general election Alexander Wedderburn (q.v.) wrote to Sir Harry Erskine (q.v.):

If Lord March supported by Government were desirous to have me chosen in Dickson's place, there would be no difficulty in accomplishing it . . . Dickson, I am certain, will be very glad to retire and his pretensions I apprehend will not be very great, his

fortune is so narrow that he will not refuse a moderate place, and after serving two Parliaments he really has some sort of right to retire upon a decent provision.

Bute agreed to recommend Wedderburn to March, who on Bute's authority offered Dickson a place. But Dickson unaccountably would not accept, and declined to release the county freeholders from their promises to him. March wrote to Bute, 2 May 1761:

Mr. Dickson being unwilling to give up his seat in Parliament, which our assistance had alone secured, he was yesterday chose by those persons . . . who would otherwise have been better pleased at my request to have seconded your Lordship's recommendation . . . Even the gentlemen who were inclined to have given opposition to this proposal from a delicacy that the honour of the county would suffer from the representation of a stranger, could not have effected it at this time but by the extraordinary and ill-timed obstinacy of Mr. Dickson himself, to whom I had fairly stated the generous offer you had made to me for him. What may have been his secret motive for this conduct I cannot pretend to say, it being very certain he once seemed extremely desirous of having such an offer, which perhaps may still be the case, but that he thinks it will be more for his advantage to negotiate the point after his election and trust to his own ideas rather than to your Lordship's or mine for the execution of it.

In Parliament Dickson supported the Bute Administration, and in December 1762 Fox counted him as favourable to the peace preliminaries. After he succeeded as laird of Kilbucho he still desired a place but his pretensions rose, and when James Stuart Mackenzie did not support his claims, he transferred his allegiance to Grenville at a time when relations between Mackenzie and Grenville on the question of Scottish patronage were severely strained. He even aspired to succeed Lord Belhaven as general of the Scottish mint. Stuart Mackenzie wrote to Bute, 5 Sept. 1764:

I am a little apprehensive of Mr. Grenville's inclining that it should be given to Mr. Dickson, the Member, as he has paid a great deal of court to him of late, and has quarrelled with me because I did not obtain for him the office of conservator or that of solicitor to the customs; now I think I could cut out a place for Dickson that might serve him very well, whereas were he (from his character and turn and the idea people here have of him) to be made general of the mint, it would raise the laugh everywhere against me, for it would be placed to my account let who will have brought it about.[5]

The post was given to Mackenzie's stepfather, Lord Strichen, and Dickson was disappointed even of the minor place that Mackenzie might have 'cut out' for him. On the fall of the Grenville ministry Dickson followed him into opposition and voted against the repeal of the Stamp Act. On 2 Dec. 1766 he wrote to Grenville asking whether his attendance was required in the House. On 27 Feb. 1767 he voted against the Chatham Administration over the land tax. He died 2 Dec. 1767.

[1] Add. 33034, ff. 173-6. [2] Add. 32995, f. 283. [3] Devonshire mss. [4] Add. 33049, f. 307. [5] Bute mss.

E.H.-G.

**DIGBY, Edward,** 6th Baron Digby [I] (1730–57).

MALMESBURY 13 June 1751–1754
WELLS 1754–30 Nov. 1757

*b.* 5 July 1730, 1st s. of Hon. Edward Digby, M.P., by Charlotte, da. of Sir Stephen Fox, sis. of Henry Fox and Stephen, 1st Earl of Ilchester; gd.-s. of William Digby, 5th Baron Digby [I]. *educ.* Westminster 1739; Magdalen, Oxf. 1747. *unm. suc.* gd.-fa. as 6th Baron Digby 27 Nov. 1752.

Groom of the bedchamber to Prince of Wales 1751–3.

Digby's return for Malmesbury was arranged by his uncle Henry Fox, with whom he was on the closest terms. In 1754 he considered standing for Dorset where he had large estates, but withdrew when an expensive and exhausting contest seemed inevitable. He stood for Wells with Fox's support, and was returned at the head of the poll. In Parliament he naturally followed Fox, but, suffering from ill-health, he seems to have cared little about politics. His main ambition was to obtain either a British peerage or an Irish earldom. In March 1757, when Fox was attempting to form an Administration, he asked for a peerage for Digby[1] and appears to have obtained some kind of promise from the King.[2] But Digby, who had become a complete invalid after a gall-stone operation in 1756, died on 30 Nov. 1757 still only an Irish baron.

[1] Fox to Ilchester, 4 Mar. 1757, *Letters to H. Fox*, ed. Ilchester. [2] Fox to Duke of Devonshire, 29 May 1757, Devonshire mss.

M.M.D.

**DIGBY, Henry** (1731–93), of Minterne House, Cerne Abbas, Dorset.

LUDGERSHALL 21 Nov. 1755–1761
WELLS 1761–13 Aug. 1765

*b.* 21 July 1731, 2nd s. of Edward Digby, M.P., and bro. of Edward, 6th Baron Digby [I] and Robert Digby (qq.v.). *educ.* Westminster 1739, re-adm. 1743–8. *m.* (1) 4 Sept.[1] 1763, Elizabeth (*d.*19 Jan. 1765), da. of Hon. Charles Feilding, *s.p.*; (2) 10 Nov. 1770, Mary, da. and h. of John Knowles,[2] recorder of Canterbury, 3s. 2da. *suc.* bro. as 7th Baron Digby [I] 30 Nov. 1757; *cr.* Baron Digby [GB] 13 Aug. 1765; Earl Digby [GB] 1 Nov. 1790.

Under-sec. of state 1755–6; ld. of Admiralty Apr. 1763–July 1765; ld. lt. Dorset 1771–*d.*

Digby was closely connected with his uncle Henry Fox to whom he owed his political promotions. In May 1749 he became a clerk in the secretary of state's office under the Duke of Bedford, and in 1750 secretary to Fox's friend Sir Charles Hanbury

Williams (q.v.) with whom he travelled in Germany and Poland. In 1754, with Fox's support he was to stand for Wells, and Lord Digby for Dorset; but when the latter moved to Wells, Henry, left without a seat, wrote to him on 19 Mar.:

Things have turned out unlucky for me. I wish now I knew where to come into Parliament for fifteen hundred pound. For if I do not come in at the general election I am pretty sure I shall not come in at all till Mr. Fox comes into power and that must be very uncertain.

And next day, thanking his brother for an offered loan of £500:

I don't know where I can come in for fifteen hundred. I . . . would readily give that and hope in that case you would be so good as to help me proportionably. At all events you may be sure I will try all I can and be at the same time as careful of your money as if it was my own.[3]

In September 1755, on a vacancy at Tiverton, Fox unsuccessfully approached Newcastle on Digby's behalf;[4] but in November, as secretary of state, arranged for Digby's return for Ludgershall on the interest of George Selwyn (q.v.), and the same month appointed Digby his under-secretary. He left office with Fox who, while attempting to form an Administration, on 4 Mar. 1757 wrote to Lord Ilchester: 'I shall easily I fancy get Harry Digby the Board of Trade.'[5]

As part of Fox's reward in Apr. 1763, Digby was appointed a lord of the Admiralty with the promise of a British peerage 'in the next session';[6] which, however, he did not receive till after he lost his place in July 1765. There is no record of his having spoken in the Commons.

Lady Holland wrote to her sister, the Duchess of Leinster, 6 Dec. 1764:[7]

One thing I believe makes Holland House pleasant just now is all those poor dull Digbys being out of town. Lord Holland loves them, and they are good people, so I don't tell him so, but they give me an *ennui* I can't support.

The *Royal Register* in 1781 described Digby as 'the only man of sterling character whom Lord Holland was concerned in promoting'; and George Selwyn called him 'worthy', but wished for 'a little more sprightliness in his mind'.[8]

He died 25 Sept. 1793.

[1] *Gent. Mag.* 1763, p. 465; *CP* gives 5 Sept. [2] *Gent. Mag.* 1770, p. 487; *CP* and Collins, v. 385 give her name as Knowler. [3] Digby mss. [4] Add. 32858, ff. 386–7. [5] Ilchester, *Letters to H. Fox.* [6] Sedgwick, 214. [7] *Leinster Corresp.* i. 423. [8] *HMC Carlisle*, 584.

M.M.D.

**DIGBY, Robert** (1732–1815).

WELLS 15 Dec. 1757–1761

*b.* 20 Dec. 1732, 3rd s. of Edward Digby, M.P., and bro. of Edward and Henry (qq.v.). *m.* 19 Aug. 1784,

Eleanor, da. of Andrew Elliot, collector of customs at New York and lt.-gov. 1779–83, wid. of James Jauncey of N.Y., *s.p.*

Lt. R.N. 29 Oct. 1752; capt. 1755; r.-adm. 1779; v.-adm. 1787; adm. 1794.

Digby was returned at the by-election of 1757 presumably to hold the seat for his brother Henry, then representing Ludgershall. He does not appear to have made any other attempt to enter Parliament. He died 25 Feb. 1815.

M.M.D.

**DILLON, Hon. Charles** (1745–1813), of Loughlin House, Roscommon, and Ditchley, Oxon.

WESTBURY 21 Feb. 1770–1774

*b.* 6 Nov. 1745, 1st s. of Henry, 11th Visct. Dillon [I], by Lady Charlotte Lee, da. of George, 2nd Earl of Lichfield. *m.* (1) 19 Aug. 1776, Hon. Henrietta Maria Phipps (*d.*1782), da. of Constantine, 1st Lord Mulgrave [I], sis. of Constantine John Phipps (q.v.), 1s. 1da.; (2) 1787, Marie Rogier of Malines, Belgium, 1da. *suc.* to Oxon. estates of his gt.-uncle Robert, 4th Earl of Lichfield, 3 Nov. 1776, and assumed add. name of Lee. *suc.* fa. 15 Sept. 1787. K.P. 19 Mar. 1798.

P.C. [I] 22 Nov. 1774; dep. ranger of Hampton Court park 1773–4; sheriff, Mayo 1787, gov. 1788–*d.*; constable of Athlone castle 1797–*d.*

Brought up a Roman Catholic, Dillon conformed to the Church of England in 1767. In 1770 he was returned unopposed on Lord Abingdon's interest at Westbury. He voted with Administration over Brass Crosby, 27 Mar. 1771. On 22 Jan. 1772 he supported the Address in a 'short but elegant complimentary speech',[1] his only one on record. On 6 Feb. he voted against Sir William Meredith's motion for relief from subscription to the 39 Articles.[2] He was again with Administration over the royal marriage bill, March 1772, and the Middlesex election motion, 26 Apr. 1773; and when on 25 Feb. 1774 he voted with Opposition in favour of making Grenville's Election Act permanent he was classed in the King's list as one of those who 'generally vote with and are friends'. He does not appear to have sought re-election in 1774.

In 1789 he refused the offer of an Irish earldom but pressed for a British peerage.[3] He wrote to Pitt, 12 Feb. 1795:[4] 'I have constantly served the King as far as I was able in the English House of Commons, and in and out of Parliament, in this country [Ireland].' In 1799 his Irish estates were stated to be worth £20,000 p.a.[5]

Dillon died 9 Nov. 1813.

¹ Cavendish's 'Debates', Egerton 231, p. 205. ² Walpole, *Last Jnls*, i. p. 13, incorrectly dating the debate 7 Feb. ³ For his ambition to obtain 'a peerage one day or other', see Ld. Suffolk to the King. 4 Oct. 1772, Fortescue, ii. 398. ⁴ Chatham mss. ⁵ *CP*.

J.A.C.

**DIMSDALE, Thomas** (1712–1800), of The Priory, Hertford.

HERTFORD 1780–1790

*b.* 29 May 1712, 4th s. of John Dimsdale, surgeon, of Theydon Garnon, Essex by Susan, da. of Thomas Bowyer of Albury Hall, Herts. *educ.* pupil to his father; St. Thomas' Hospital. *m.* (1) July 1739, Mary (*d.*4 Feb. 1744), da. of Nathaniel Brassey (q.v.) of Roxford, Herts., *s.p.*; (2) 17 June 1746, Anne (*d.*1779), da. of John Iles, and 'a relation of his first wife',[1] 7s. 2da.; (3) 3 Nov. 1779, Elizabeth, da. of his cos. Joseph Dimsdale of Bishop's Stortford. *suc.* to Herts. estates of his cos. Sir John Dimsdale on d. of his wid. after 1745.

The Dimsdales were Quakers, and Thomas's grandfather Robert Dimsdale, surgeon, accompanied William Penn on a visit to America in 1684. Thomas himself set up in practice in 1734 at Hertford; and was a surgeon in the army during the rebellion of 1745. The fortune of his second wife and the inheritance he received from Lady Dimsdale enabled him to retire from practice, but his family becoming numerous, he resumed it, taking his degree of M.D. in 1761 at King's College, Aberdeen. In 1766 he published a treatise on inoculation for smallpox, and in 1768 he inoculated the Empress Catherine and her son, for which he received 'an annuity of £500, the rank of a baron of the Russian Empire . . . £10,000 and £2,000 for travelling charges, miniature pictures of the Empress and her son, and the same title to his son . . . The Baron inoculated numbers of people at Petersburg and Moscow; and, resisting the Empress's invitation to reside as her physician in Russia, he and his son . . . returned to England.'[2] He next opened his own 'inoculating house' at Hertford. About the same time he entered banking; and although he himself retired from the firm in 1776, the business was continued by his sons, and further descendants.[3]

In 1780 Dimsdale stood for Hertford, and his own popularity, the Dimsdale-Brassey interest, and the Quaker vote made him top of the poll, above William Baker and defeating John Calvert, both strong local candidates. The *English Chronicle* wrote about him in 1781:

> He is very much distinguished in his profession by the industrious and honest exercise of which he has acquired an independent fortune . . . He owes his seat entirely to the good opinion entertained of him by his electors, amongst whom he is an old and favourite resident. Oratory is not one of his talents, but it is believed, however, that he will at least pronounce the decisive monosyllable with eloquence, with the genuine eloquence of sincerity, and vote upon every subject from the unbiassed influence of his principles and conviction.

About his one recorded speech (on the receipts tax, 12 June 1783), the reporter writes that he 'spoke for some time, but in so low a tone, that we could not distinctly hear him'.[4]

As a Quaker Dimsdale naturally voted against the war, 12 Dec. 1781 and 22, 27 Feb. 1782, and, later on, for Shelburne's peace preliminaries, 18 Feb. 1783. But he was not in regular opposition to the North Government: he voted against the motion for removing them on 8 Mar. 1782, but for the 'no confidence' motion on the 15th. He voted against Fox's East India bill; belonged to the St. Alban's Tavern group which in January 1784 tried to bring about a coalition between Pitt and Fox; but after that must have supported Pitt, being classed as his supporter in Stockdale's list of 19 Mar. 1784. He was re-elected after a contest in April. In the new Parliament his only recorded vote was with Pitt over the Regency, 16 Dec. 1788. He did not stand in 1790, his son Nathaniel succeeding to his seat.

Dimsdale died 30 Dec. 1800.

[1] *Gent. Mag.* 1801, p. 669. [2] Ibid. [3] F. G. Hilton Price, *London Bankers*, 52–53. [4] Debrett, x. 161.

L.B.N.

**DODD, John** (1717–82), of Swallowfield, Berks.

READING 17 Feb.–27 Apr. 1741, 19 Nov. 1755–9 Feb. 1782

*b.* 24 Sept. 1717, s. of Randolph Dodd by Margaret, da. of William Glaseour. *educ.* Eton 1728–32; King's, Camb. 1735. *m.* (1) 4 Sept. 1739, Jane (*d.*13 Oct. 1741), da. of Henry Le Coq St. Leger of Shinfield, Berks., 3s. 1 da.; (2) 31 July 1753, Juliana, da. of Philip Jennings of Duddlestone Hall, Salop, sis. of Philip Jennings Clerke (q.v.) and sis.-in-law of J. E. Colleton and James Hayes (qq.v.), 1s. 3da. *suc.* 1722 under the will of Isabella Dodd, wid. of his gt.-uncle Samuel,[1] to the fortune amassed by him in legal practice.

William Cole, the antiquary, speaks of Dodd in *Athenae Cantabrigienses* as 'a man universally beloved; lively, generous, and sensible'. He 'was no scholar', writes John Nichols,[2] 'but he was a favourite of many ingenious, and clever men, as well as of others, who were exemplary in worth, and were of high rank. *Lord Fane described him as a fine horse ill broke-in.* He was generous, openhearted, and convivial, friendly, and hospitable to a fault.'

After having been returned for Reading on petition in February 1741, Dodd did not stand at the general election nor in 1747. At the general election of 1754 Dodd was encouraged by Administration once more to contest Reading, against a Bedford Whig and a Tory. After Henry Pelham's death, in a review of election engagements, the following appears on 18 Mar. 1754: '*Mr. Dodd.* Has received £1,000. Was promised £500 more and that it should

not be lost for £300 or £400 more.'[3] He received this further £900 on 21 Mar. and 11 and 12 Apr.[4] When the result was declared, with Strode, the Tory, top of the poll, and Dodd one vote behind Lord Fane (295 *v.* 296), he 'fainted away at the hustings'.[5] He petitioned against Fane's return. 'His canvass', wrote Ralph Shirley, 'this time cost (Lord Craven hears) £3,000, and what his appeal will come to . . . who can say?'[6] Another £100 was paid to him from secret service money in January 1755. Fane proposed an arrangement against Strode's expected death, but nothing seems to have been settled before it occurred on 29 Apr. 1755, and with Fane's friends uncommitted, although the Tories did not in the end put up any candidate, Dodd stood another costly canvass. On 29 Oct. Lord Barrington gave Newcastle 'previous notice' that Dodd intended to ask him 'for some cash for his approaching expenses at Reading, having probably none of his own'—he talked of £1,000 'to be deposited where he can draw for it on account'.[7] On 14 Nov. he received £500 from secret service funds. 'The election was over this morning at about 12 o'clock in my favour', wrote Dodd to Newcastle, 19 Nov. ' . . . Sir Crisp Gascoyne made an opposition last night, his poll was 17.'[8]

On 24 May 1758 Dodd received his first annual payment of a secret service pension of £500, which was continued to him till Newcastle left the Treasury in May 1762. Early in 1761 Dodd was reported not to intend to seek re-election unless it could be done 'without another great and ruinous expense'.[9] Still, after various manœuvres on the part of Fane, there was another contest in which Dodd headed the poll.

In 1761 Newcastle sent Dodd his parliamentary whip through his nephew and Dodd's close friend, Lord Lincoln; and in Bute's list of December 1761 Dodd is marked 'Old Whig, Newcastle', to whom he in fact remained faithful: he did not draw his pension during Bute's and Grenville's Administrations, and voted with the Opposition over the peace preliminaries and general warrants. He was also a member of Wildman's Club, and was counted by Newcastle, on 3 Mar. 1764, among his 'sure friends . . . to be sent to upon any occasion'.[10] After the Rockinghams had taken office, Dodd was classed by Rockingham in July 1765 as 'pro', and in November 1766 as 'Whig'. But Newcastle, possibly because of Lincoln's defection, in the list of his 'own particular friends in the House of Commons, as they stand now', 9 Jan. 1767, placed a query against Dodd's name; and after Dodd had voted with the Government on the land tax, 27 Feb. 1767, rightly classed him as 'Administration'. Henceforth whenever there is a list of those voting with the Government, Dodd's name appears in it, and never with the Opposition. His pension was continued to him till his death, and at some date before 1779 was raised to £750 p.a. He naturally had also the support of Government in his elections, each of them contested and each expensive. In 1780 Robinson, while expecting the candidature of 'a third man to create expenses', hoped that 'Mr. Dodd is safe against all attack'; and £1,600 was paid from secret service money 'on account of Reading'.[11]

The *English Chronicle* in 1780, in its 'Parliamentary Characters', wrote about the 'taciturn servility' of Dodd's acquiescence to the measures of Administration, and dilated on his 'inebriety . . . attended with . . . circumstances of degradation'. During nearly 30 years in the House he is not known to have spoken in political debate, and in the most fully reported Parliament, 1768–74, only two interventions of his are recorded: on 21 Feb. 1771 he introduced a scheme for a canal between Reading and Basingstoke; and on 2 Mar. 1772, at the desire of Reading corporation, moved for a writ in place of Henry Vansittart, supposed lost in the *Aurora*.[12]

He died 9 Feb. 1782. On 14 Feb. G. A. Selwyn wrote about him to Lord Carlisle: 'He . . . had had more wine of all sorts in his head, and less of any other furniture, than any man I knew, and [was] one of the most wrong-headed fellows that ever existed.'[13] And Horace Walpole, on the same day, to William Cole: 'My old friend and your acquaintance, Mr. Dodd, died last Sunday—not of cold water. He and I were born on the very same day, but took to different elements. I doubt he had hurt his fortune as well as health.' He left indeed his family in difficult financial circumstances (Swallowfield was sold in 1783), and his eldest son, Captain Dodd, on leaving the Guards was given a secret service pension of £150.[14]

¹ About him see *DNB*. ² *Lit. Illustrations*, i. 502. ³ Add. 32995, f. 98; see also Add. 32734, f. 237. ⁴ Namier, *Structure*, 427, 429. ⁵ J. Man, *Hist. Reading*, 241. ⁶ *HMC 5th Rep.* 364. ⁷ Add. 32860, f. 232. ⁸ Add. 32816, f. 31. ⁹ Fane to Bedford, 2 Feb. 1761, Bedford mss 43, f. 88. ¹⁰ Add. 32956, f. 190. ¹¹ Laprade, 57. ¹² Egerton 225, pp. 149, 153; 234, pp. 187, 204–5. ¹³ *HMC Carlisle*, 577. ¹⁴ Fortescue, v. 468; and 'List of private pensions and secret service money, August 1782', Chatham mss, PRO.

L.B.N.

## DODINGTON (formerly BUBB), George (?1691–1762), of Eastbury, Dorset.

| | |
|---|---|
| WINCHELSEA | 1715–1722 |
| BRIDGWATER | 1722–1754 |
| WEYMOUTH AND MELCOMBE REGIS | 1754–1761 |

*b.* ?1691, 1st s. of Jeremiah Bubb of Foy, Herefs. by Mary, da. of John Dodington of Dodington, Som. *educ.* Winchester 1703; Exeter, Oxf. 10 July 1707, aged 16; L. Inn 1711; Grand Tour. *m.* secretly c.1725,

Katherine Behan, *s.p.* Took name of Dodington 1717, and *suc.* uncle George Dodington, M.P., 1720; *cr.* Baron Melcombe 6 Apr. 1761.

Envoy to Spain 1715–17; clerk of the pells [I] 1720–*d.*; ld. lt. Som. 1721–44; ld. of Treasury 1724–1740; treasurer of the navy 1744–9; P.C. 3 Jan. 1745; treasurer of the chamber to the Prince of Wales 1749–1751; treasurer of the navy Dec. 1755–Nov. 1756.

Dodington was first given office by Walpole, whom he deserted shortly before his fall. He next served under Pelham, whom he deserted for Frederick, Prince of Wales. After the Prince's death he opened negotiations with Pelham for his return to Administration.

Dodington's parliamentary patronage extended to one seat at Bridgwater and, in association with John Tucker, four at Weymouth and Melcombe Regis. At the general election of 1754 he was defeated at Bridgwater but had insured himself at Weymouth, where he also placed two seats at the disposal of Administration.

On 21 Mar., after Henry Pelham's death, negotiations for Dodington's return to office re-opened with Newcastle. Dodington asked for his old place of treasurer of the navy, and Newcastle was all goodwill and friendship. 'He took me in his arms', wrote Dodington, 'and kissed me twice, with strong assurances of affection and service.'[1] But on 27 Mar. he learnt that, 'notwithstanding the fine conversation of last Thursday, all the employments were given away'. On 26 Apr. Dodington repeated to Newcastle 'my earnest desires to pass the rest of my life in his Grace's friendship and protection', and Newcastle made 'great professions of good wishes, goodwill, best endeavours, etc. . . . which', wrote Dodington, 'weigh with me as much as the breath they were composed of'. So the comedy went on.

In May 1755 Dodington professed to be convinced of the 'insufficiency, falseness, and meanness of the Duke of Newcastle's Administration'.[2] Opposed to the subsidy treaties with Russia and Hesse, he began to listen to overtures from Pitt. Then, in October 1755, Lord Halifax brought Dodington and Newcastle together again, and the bargain was quickly concluded: Dodington obtained office for himself and his friend, Henry Furnese, with 'full liberty to oppose the subsidies, honestly and fairly'.[3] What Newcastle got from the bargain is not easy to say.

Dodington was turned out by the Pitt-Devonshire Administration, and never held office again. For a brief period, in April 1757, it seemed that he might return, but Fox was unable to form a ministry and the advent of the Pitt-Newcastle Coalition finally extinguished his hopes. He now turned to Bute and the Prince of Wales, and waited for the King's death.

When that came Dodington was too old to take part in the game. But, standing on the touch-line, he encouraged Bute; offered him the nomination to two seats at Weymouth; and accepted a peerage. 'His coronet seems only calculated to adorn his tomb', wrote Horace Mann to Walpole on 25 Apr. 1761.

Dodington died 28 July 1762.

¹ Dodington, *Diary*, 273–89. ² Ibid. 331. ³ Ibid. 377–8, 492–500.

J.B.

**DOLBEN, Sir William,** 3rd Bt. (1727–1814), of Finedon, Northants.

| | |
|---|---|
| OXFORD UNIVERSITY | 3 Feb.–11 Mar. 1768 |
| NORTHAMPTONSHIRE | 1768–1774 |
| OXFORD UNIVERSITY | 1780–1806 |

*b.* 12 Jan. 1727, o.s. of Rev. Sir John Dolben, 2nd Bt., rector of Burton Latimer and vicar of Finedon, by Elizabeth, da. of William, 5th Baron Digby [I]. *educ.* Westminster 1734; Ch. Ch. Oxf. 1744. *m.* (1) 17 May 1758, Judith (*d.*1771), da. and h. of Somerset English, 1s. 1da.; (2) 14 Sept. 1789, his cos. Charlotte, da. of Gilbert Affleck, M.P., of Dalham Hall, Suff., and wid. of John Scotchmer, banker of Bury, *s.p. suc.* fa. 20 Nov. 1756.

Sheriff, Northants. 1760–1.

Some months before the general election of 1768 Dolben was nominated for Northamptonshire on the 'Tory' or country interest. Meanwhile, in February 1768 he was returned for Oxford University as a stop-gap on the old Tory interest. His only reported vote during the few weeks of this Parliament was with Opposition on nullum tempus, 17 Feb. 1768. At the general election Dolben was returned unopposed for Northamptonshire. Though essentially independent, his inclination was to support Administration, and he voted regularly with the Grafton and North ministries, but appears in the King's list of friends who voted with Opposition over the naval captains' petition, 26 Apr. 1773. He spoke several times during this Parliament; in the debate of 25 Feb. 1774 on the motion to perpetuate Grenville's Election Act he declared that though he was 'a great favourer' of the Act he believed it should not be perpetuated so soon and therefore would vote against the motion.¹

Dolben did not stand in 1774. At the general election of 1780, and again in 1784, he was returned unopposed for Oxford University. On 28 Feb. 1781, in his first recorded speech after his re-election, he opposed Burke's bill for regulating the civil list revenue, declaring:

If it were right to destroy the influence by which Members were returned to that House, it did not go far enough, for it ought also to have destroyed the influence of the aristocracy and of wealthy individuals as well as the influence of the Crown; and he said he should have no objection to a general and fair plan of

reform that went to the reduction of influence on both sides.

Though he considered that Lowther's motions of 12 Dec. 1781 against the war were 'moderate, temperate, and senatorial', he accepted North's assurances that the Government would no longer prosecute the war; otherwise 'he should certainly have voted for the motions, for he was heartily tired of the American war'. Speaking of the naval inquiry demanded by the Opposition, Dolben declared, 20 Dec. 1781, that not being 'one of those credulous men that were supposed on all occasions to vote with Administrations be the business what it might . . . when the examination they were now talking about should take place . . . he should endeavour to make it a sound one'. But on 20 Feb. 1782 he said that though he agreed mismanagement had been proved, he refused to support the demand for Sandwich's dismissal and trial; if the Opposition were to press it he would vote with the Administration on the whole question, and in fact did so. On 22 Feb. he voted with Opposition on Conway's motion against the war, but on the virtually identical motion of 27 Feb. he explained that he had decided to vote with Administration because he understood that a bill for a truce with America was to be introduced by the ministry, 'which in his opinion was by far the best mode offered'. He again voted with Administration on Cavendish's censure motion of 8 Mar. 1782, and Rous's of 15 Mar., when he said he hoped there would be a coalition between North and the Opposition leaders: 'the noble lord was an able minister, though he believed that conducting a war was not his forte; but in negotiations for peace, he was convinced would be found to have great abilities'. Opposition to American independence swayed his attitude to the war, and on 19 Dec. 1782, during the debate on negotiations for peace, he declared that 'a vigorous war with the house of Bourbon, crowned with success, would soon compel America to return to her duty'. During the debates of February and March 1783 on the peace preliminaries he complained incessantly that there was no authorization for granting American independence, and he naturally voted against Shelburne's peace preliminaries, 18 Feb. 1783. He voted for parliamentary reform, 7 May 1783, and for Fox's East India bill, 27 Nov. 1783. On 19 Dec. 1783 he called for a coalition between Fox and Pitt, but he disliked the Opposition's attempts to force the King to dismiss Pitt, and on 18 Feb. 1784 complained that 'the whole of the late conduct and proceedings of the House tended to abridge the prerogative of the Crown . . . He objected to all this violence . . . and hoped he should see the House returned again to moderation.' Henceforth he regularly supported Pitt.[2]

Dolben voted for Pitt's parliamentary reform proposals, 18 Apr. 1785; urged the abolition of pressing, 12 May 1786, and supported the debtors' relief bill, 11 Mar. 1788. During the trial of Warren Hastings he wrote, 8 Feb. 1787, that having heard Sheridan's 'brilliant and affecting' accusation, 'I dared not trust myself, under such a state of captivation to decide criminally against any man much less against one who undoubtedly had very great public merits, and therefore . . . I moved to adjourn'.[3] Convinced of the 'crying-evil' of the slave trade, Dolben on 21 May 1788 introduced a bill to improve the conditions of negroes being transported to the West Indies,[4] and by his vigorous efforts secured its passage through the House.

He died 20 Mar. 1814.

[1] Brickdale, 'Debates'. [2] Debrett, ii. 41; v. 139, 221; vi. 258-9, 328, 462-3; ix. 129; xiii. 158. [3] Dolben mss, Northants RO. [4] Stockdale, xv. 69-70, 71, 72, 75, 76.

M.M.D.

**DONEGALL, Earl of,** *see* **CHICHESTER, Arthur**

**DOUGLAS, Archibald** (1707–78), of Kirktoun, Dumfries and Witham, Essex.

DUMFRIES BURGHS 1754–1761
DUMFRIESSHIRE 1761–1774

*b.* 1707, 1st s. of William Douglas of Finland, Kirkcudbright Stewartry by Elizabeth, da. and coh. of Capt. Alexander Clerk of Glendorch, Lanark, an Edinburgh merchant. *m.* 1746, Elizabeth, da. of Edmund Burchard of Witham, Essex, 6s. 5da.
Cornet 4 Drag. 1739, lt. 1742, capt. 1745, maj. 1746, lt.-col. 1746, col. 1756; col. 13 Drag. 1758–*d.*; maj.-gen. 1759; lt.-gen. 1761. Served at Dettingen and Minden.

When his father, a former Jacobite, was obliged to sell the family estate of Finland in 1721, Douglas seems to have sought a military career abroad. His rapid promotion on entering the British army at the age of 32 suggests considerable previous military experience.[1]

His family had close connexions with Charles, 3rd Duke of Queensberry, for whom Douglas's younger brother Charles acted as chamberlain. In 1754 Douglas was returned for Dumfries Burghs on the interest of Queensberry, who on 18 Aug. 1754 recommended him to Newcastle for appointment as aide-de-camp to the King:[2]

He served abroad during all the last war, and is now the only officer of that rank and service who has not in some shape or other received some mark of his Majesty's favour since the peace. He wishes to owe that obligation to your Grace only, for he does not mean to apply through any other channel.

Douglas was not appointed aide-de-camp until June 1756. He voted against Newcastle on the Minorca inquiry, 2 May 1757.[3]

His politics were directed by Queensberry, who helped to get him his regiment in 1758.[4] In 1761 he was returned for Dumfriesshire on Queensberry's interest, apparently unopposed.

In the new reign Queensberry, an old friend of Bute, gained high office, and under his patronage Douglas became well known as a place hunter of considerable influence. In 1762 young James Boswell discussed with James Murray of Broughton (q.v.) his scheme for obtaining a commission in the Guards—

He told me [writes Boswell[5]] General Douglas was the most proper man that I could get to push the thing for me; for that he was indefatigable in business and being a man not much taken up with the gay world and enervated with scenes of dissipation, he could call upon a great man again and again and wait an hour in his parlour till he came down. Besides as he was a great military man, that a character from him as an officer might be very beneficial.

A loyal supporter of Bute's Administration, Douglas was equally faithful to Grenville. On a letter to Grenville from Douglas in February 1764, asking for a commission in the Guards for his son, Jenkinson wrote: 'This is the request of a very good friend.'[6] He was constantly in attendance during the debates on Wilkes and general warrants, and even when ill declined to absent himself without Grenville's permission.[7] When, overcome by illness and the fatigue of late sittings, he was obliged to go home to Witham on 24 Mar., he wrote to Jenkinson, offering to return after a few days rest, if his presence was required.[8]

At the change of Administration Douglas followed Grenville into opposition, voting against the Government on the repeal of the Stamp Act, 22 Feb. 1766. He voted against the Chatham Administration on the land tax, 27 Feb. 1767.

Re-elected in 1768, his military duties in Ireland prevented his close attendance in Parliament, but he returned to vote with the Administration in the divisions on Wilkes and Middlesex, 3 Feb., 15 Apr., and 8 May 1769. He supported the North Administration over the Middlesex election and on the royal marriage bill of 1772, but seems to have been absent from the division of 25 Feb. 1774 on the Grenville Election Act.

Douglas does not appear to have sought re-election in 1774, and died in Dublin on 8 Nov. 1778.

[1] P. W. L. Adams, *Hist. Douglas Fam. of Morton*, 335, 343, 360-1. [2] Add. 32734, f. 302. [3] Add. 33034, f. 232. [4] Add. 32880, f. 313. [5] *Private Pprs.* i. 73-74. [6] Add. 38202, f. 87. [7] Douglas to Jenkinson, 15 Mar. 1764, ibid. f. 161. [8] Ibid. f. 189.

E.H.-G.

**DOUGLAS** (formerly **STEUART**), **Archibald James Edward** (1748–1827), of Douglas, Lanark.

FORFARSHIRE    11 Feb. 1782–1790

*b.* 10 July 1748, 2nd surv. s. of Sir John Steuart, 3rd Bt., of Grandtully, Perth by his 2nd w. Lady Jane Douglas, o. sis. of Archibald, 1st Duke of Douglas [S]. *educ.* Rugby 1759–61, Westminster 1761–5. *m.* (1) 13 June 1771, Lady Lucy Graham (*d.*13 Feb. 1780), da. of William, 2nd Duke of Montrose [S], and sis. of James, Mq. of Graham (q.v.), 3s. 1da.; (2) 13 May 1783, Lady Frances Scott, da. of Francis, Earl of Dalkeith, sis. of Henry, 3rd Duke of Buccleuch [S], 5s. 3da.  *suc.* uncle in the Douglas estates 21 July 1761, and assumed name of Douglas; and the Duke of Queensberry in the Amesbury estate 1778; *cr.* Baron Douglas 8 July 1790.

In 1748 Lady Jane Douglas, then aged 50, announced the birth in Paris of twin sons by her secret marriage with an elderly bankrupt, formerly a colonel in the Swedish service. The Duke of Douglas suspecting fraud, refused to recognize the children as his nephews, disinherited his sister, and entailed his estates upon his heir male the Duke of Hamilton. Lady Jane died in 1753, shortly after the death of the younger twin, and Archibald, left destitute, with his putative father in a debtors' jail, was brought up by Lady Schaw (widow of Sir John Schaw of Greenock), on whose decease in 1757 the Duke of Queensberry assumed the responsibility.

From 1759 his fortunes improved; his father succeeded to the Grandtully baronetcy; the Duke of Douglas was persuaded to revoke the Hamilton settlement in 1760, and shortly before his death in 1761 recognized Archibald as his nephew and heir.[1] Archibald's principal guardian, Queensberry, and the Duchess of Douglas obtained confirmation of his rights of succession from the court of session in 1762, against the claims of the young Duke of Hamilton, whose guardians now began proceedings, directed by Andrew Stuart (q.v.) to prove that Archibald was not Douglas's nephew but the son of French peasants. The celebrated 'Douglas Cause' provoked violent controversy in all ranks of society, divided families, and considerably affected electoral alliances. When in 1767 Douglas lost his case in the court of session by the casting vote of Lord President Robert Dundas (q.v.), he appealed to the Lords, who on 27 Feb. 1769, by an overwhelming majority decided in his favour. Now established as 'the true son of Lady Jane', he returned in triumph to Scotland, the idol of the Edinburgh mob, celebrated his majority, became, with Queensberry, Buccleuch, Patrick Heron and others, a director of Douglas, Heron and Co., the ill-fated Bank of Ayr, and proceeded to develop the long dormant Douglas interest in the counties of Lanark, Angus, Roxburgh, and Perth.

The financial catastrophe of 1772 and the winding up of the Ayr Bank in 1773 obliged him to encumber his estates, but did not seriously affect his great fortune and interest. Allied by his marriage with the Montrose interest in Perthshire, he intervened at the by-election of 1773, and again in 1774, in support of Thomas Graham of Balgowan against James Murray (q.v.) and the Atholl interest.[2] At the general election he opposed the Hamilton interest both in Linlithgow Burghs and in Lanarkshire, where he stood against Andrew Stuart but eventually joined Daniel Campbell (q.v.), who was defeated.

His ambition now centred on obtaining a peerage either by establishing his right to the earldom of Angus or by a new creation. 'He has flattered himself', wrote Boswell in 1776, 'with being created Earl of Douglas.'[3]

Disappointed of a seat in either House, Douglas offered with his brother-in-law Lord Graham to raise a regiment in 1778, but was refused.[4] Finally relieved, in March 1779 by decision of the House of Lords, of harassing lawsuits by the Hamiltons against his right of inheritance,[5] he devoted himself to improving his estates and interest but does not appear to have tried to enter Parliament in 1780.

He stood for Forfarshire in 1782 at a by-election, and was returned against Sir David Carnegie (q.v.), who petitioned on the ground that Douglas as a claimant to the earldom of Angus should be disqualified. Elected on 11 Feb. Douglas did not take his seat for at least six weeks, possibly to avoid embarrassment while the Ayr Bank affairs were again before the House, but primarily to delay committing himself for or against the tottering North Administration. On the crucial division of 15 Mar. Robinson listed him among the 'persons who stayed away' although he was believed to be in London.[6] Douglas, however, was still in Edinburgh on 21 Mar.,[7] and may not have attended until shortly before the hearing of Carnegie's petition on 16 Apr. Closely connected with Lord Graham, he seems to have followed Henry Dundas in politics; voted 18 Feb. 1783 for the peace preliminaries, and in March was listed by Robinson under Shelburne. He did not vote in the division of 27 Nov. on Fox's East India bill; and on the change of Administration was counted pro-Pitt. Before the general election Robinson assumed that he would come in again for Forfarshire and 'be steadily *for*'; but Dundas thought he might probably bring in a friend there and himself stand for Roxburghshire against Sir Gilbert Elliot, the Opposition candidate.[8] In the event Douglas retained his Angus seat and assisted to secure the return of Sir George Douglas for Roxburgh. In the new Parliament he continued to support Pitt and remained faithful during the Regency crisis, 1788–9. No speech of his is recorded.

Created a British peer in 1790, he lived in great magnificence in London and in his Scottish castles. He died 26 Dec. 1827.

[1] For Archibald's early life and Steuart family corresp. see Sir W. Fraser, *Red Book of Grandtully*; Sir W. Fraser, *Douglas Book*, ii. 523–538. [2] A. Stuart to Duchess of Argyll, 26 June 1773, *Intimate Society Letters*, i. 146–7; Jas. Abercrombie to Loudoun, 21 May 1773, Loudoun mss; Laprade 6, 19. [3] *Private Pprs.*, xi. 147. [4] Graham to R. M. Keith, 28 Apr. 1778, Add. 35513, f. 274. [5] Douglas to his half-bro. Sir John Steuart, 30 Mar. 1779, *Red Book of Grandtully*, ii. 372. [6] Fortescue, v. 390. [7] Boswell, *Private Pprs.* xv. 71. [8] Laprade, 101, 104.

E.H.-G.

## DOUGLAS, Lord Charles (1726–56), of Kellwood, Dumfries.

DUMFRIESSHIRE 1747–18 Nov. 1755

*b.* 17 July 1726, 2nd s. of Charles, 3rd Duke of Queensberry [S] and 2nd of Dover [GB], by Lady Catherine Hyde, da. of Henry, 4th Earl of Clarendon. *educ.* Winchester 1734–41; Westminster 1742; Ch. Ch. Oxf. 1745. *unm.* *suc.* bro. Henry in the courtesy title of Earl of Drumlanrig 19 Oct. 1754.

From early in 1752 Lord Charles's health was precarious,[1] but he stood for re-election in 1754 and was returned unopposed, being listed by Dupplin as a Government supporter. On 19 Oct. 1754 he was travelling south from Scotland with his parents and Lord and Lady Drumlanrig, when his brother accidentally shot himself. Lord Charles thereby became the eldest son of a Scottish peer, but the question of his disqualification as a Scottish M.P. seems to have been held in abeyance until it was certain that no posthumous heir would be born to Drumlanrig's widow, and a new writ was not issued until 18 Nov. 1755.

He died 24 Oct. 1756.

[1] Duchess of Queensberry to Lady Bute, 7 June 1752, Bute mss.

E.H.-G.

## DOUGLAS, George (1754–1821), of Springwood Park, Roxburgh.

ROXBURGHSHIRE 1784–1806

*b.* 1 Mar. 1754, 1st s. of Sir James Douglas, 1st Bt. (q.v.). *m.* 16 Oct. 1786, Lady Elizabeth Boyle, da. of John, 3rd Earl of Glasgow [S], 1s. 2da. *suc.* fa. as 2nd Bt., 2 Nov. 1787.

Ensign 25 Ft. 1771, capt. lt. and capt. 1778; lt. and capt. 1 Ft. Gds. 1780; ret. 1788.

Douglas was returned in 1784 as an Administration supporter, on the interest of the Duke of Roxburgh. He consistently supported Pitt, except on parliamentary reform, but is not known to have spoken in the House before 1790.

He died 4 June 1821.

E.H.-G.

## DOUGLAS, James (1703–87), of Springwood Park, Roxburgh, and St. Olla, Orkney.

ORKNEY AND SHETLAND 1754–1768

*b.* 1703, s. of George Douglas of Friarshaw, Roxburgh by Elizabeth, da. of Sir Patrick Scott, 2nd Bt., of Ancrum. *m.* (1) 1753, Helen (*d.*1766), da. of Thomas Brisbane of Brisbane, Ayr, 4s. 3da.; (2) 25 Sept. 1768, Lady Helen Boyle, da. of John, 2nd Earl of Glasgow [S], *s.p.* Kntd. 16 Oct. 1759; *cr.* Bt. 27 June 1786.

Entered R.N. 1715; lt. 1732; capt. 1744; r.-adm. 1762; c.-in-c. West Indies 1763–5; v.-adm. 1770; c.-in-c. Portsmouth 1773–6; adm. 1782.

James Douglas sat on the Earl of Morton's interest for Orkney and Shetland, a constituency which supplied many recruits to the Royal Navy. Absent from Parliament for long periods on naval duty, he followed his patron's line and was counted by Dupplin in 1754 among the Scots Members attached to Newcastle rather than to Argyll.

In 1756 he was one of the three naval M.P.s appointed to the court martial on Admiral Byng, and like Morton had no qualms of conscience on the sentence. When on 2 Mar. 1757 the members of the court were examined at the bar of the House of Lords, he emphatically answered 'No' to the questions as to whether he knew of anything which would show the sentence to be unjust, and whether he wished the bill dispensing with the oath of secrecy to pass into law.[1] During the negotiations for a new ministry after Pitt's dismissal, Newcastle listed him among the Scots Members personally attached to himself.[2] He voted on 2 May with Newcastle's friends on the Minorca inquiry.[3]

Thereafter until nearly the end of the war he was almost continuously absent from Parliament on active service: in 1756 at Rochfort; 1759, at Quebec; 1761, in command of the squadron which captured Dominica; 1762, with Rodney at Martinique and with Pocock at Havana. He was absent at the general election of 1761 when the Morton interest in Orkney and Shetland had to face a contest.

He returned from the West Indies in time to attend the opening of the parliamentary session in November 1762.[4] Although his name does not appear in Fox's list of Members favourable to the peace preliminaries, he did not vote against them. In 1763 he was again posted to the West Indies. He had apparently returned by the summer of 1765, when Rockingham counted him among his supporters. After a division on 7 Feb. 1766 (on Grenville's motion to address the King to enforce all laws in America) James West reported to Newcastle:[5] 'I perceived no Scots with us but Sir Alexander Gilmour and Sir James Douglas.' Again in a division list of 18 Feb. (almost certainly about America) sent by Gilmour to Newcastle he is numbered among the Scots voting with the Administration.[6] But in the crucial division of 22 Feb. on the repeal of the Stamp Act he voted with the Opposition. During the Chatham Administration, although listed by Charles Townshend in January 1767 as a Government supporter, he voted against the Administration in the land tax division on 27 Feb.

In 1766 Morton sold Orkney and Shetland to Sir Lawrence Dundas, and at the 1768 election the seat passed into the control of the Dundas family. Douglas did not apparently attempt to re-enter Parliament, but devoted himself to his naval career. He died 2 Nov. 1787.

[1] Walpole, *Mems. Geo II*, ii. 364. [2] Add. 32995, f. 383. [3] Add. 33034, f. 232. [4] *CJ*, 26 Nov. 1762. [5] Add. 32973, f. 375. [6] Add. 32974, f. 24.

E.H.-G.

**DOUGLAS, John St. Leger** (c.1732–83), of Springfield Place, nr. Chelmsford, Essex.

HINDON 1768–1774
WEOBLEY 1774–23 May 1783

*b.* c.1732, 1st s. of John Douglas of St. Kitts, West Indies by Susanna, da. of Michael Lambert, lt-gov. of St. Kitts, wid. of Richard Holmes. *educ.* Westminster Jan. 1743, aged 10; Trinity, Camb. 22 Oct. 1748, aged 17. *m.* (1) (*d.*11 June 1764), 2s. 1da.; (2) 30 Dec. 1765, Caroline Otway, issue. *suc.* fa. 1747.

Douglas was returned for Hindon after a contest; he probably purchased the seat from the Calthorpe family. In Parliament he was a regular Government supporter. He was connected with Richard Rigby, a great friend of Lord Weymouth, on whose interest Douglas was returned in 1774 at Weobley. Only one speech by him is recorded: on 5 Dec. 1775 in support of the American prohibitory bill. Another West Indian, Nathaniel Bayly, having said that it would materially affect his property in the West Indies, Douglas replied that he too 'had a considerable estate in the West-Indies . . . nevertheless he thought the present bill a very wise and salutary measure . . . it was better to suffer temporary inconveniences than sacrifice the British Empire in America to the local interests of any of its constituent parts'.[1] And on 14 Dec. A. M. Storer, himself a West Indian, wrote to Lord Carlisle that even 'moderate West Indians' foresee total ruin for themselves—'every West Indian, except Jack Douglas, is in the utmost consternation'.[2]

Douglas died 23 May 1783.

[1] Almon, iii. 252. [2] *HMC Carlisle*, 311.

J.A.C.

**DOUGLAS, William** (c.1731–83), of Kelhead, Dumfries.

DUMFRIES BURGHS 1768–1780

*b.* c.1731, 1st s. of Sir John Douglas, 3rd Bt., M.P., by Christian, da. of Sir William Cunningham, 2nd Bt., of Caprington, Ayr. *educ.* Glasgow Univ. 1745–7. *m.* 11 Mar. 1772, Grace, da. and coh. of William Johnstone of Lockerbie, Dumfries, 5s. 4da. *suc.* uncle Charles Douglas in Breconwhat estate, Dumfries 13 Dec. 1770; and fa. 13 Nov. 1778.

Lt. Scots brigade in Holland 1747–?58; cornet 2 Drag. 1759–64.

Douglas's father was 'the chief director of his friend the Duke of Queensberry's country affairs and parliamentary interest in the county of Dumfries' but 'Sir John was no economist . . . he run aground and as he likewise had been nibbling to serve the Jacobite party . . . this added to the distraction and confusion of his affairs.'[1] In 1745, when no money was left for education, the family tutor, James Hogg, took his four pupils to Glasgow, supported them out of his own 'little patrimony', and sent the two eldest to the university. 'This he continued all the next year also when Sir John was sent to the Tower of London for rebellious practices.'[2] On Sir John's release in March 1748, the Duke of Queensberry 'got his estate put under trustees . . . himself lent money . . . and had his creditors thereby pacified'.[3] Meanwhile, in June 1747, William had obtained a commission in the regiment raised by Queensberry's son, Lord Drumlanrig, for the Dutch service and after the regiment's disbandment in 1752, continued to serve in the Scots Brigade; he returned home about 1758,[4] and shortly afterwards received a commission in the 2nd Dragoons. By 1762, when James Boswell met him, the family were again in financial trouble by Sir John's extravagant 'improvements' which had 'burthened his estate with about £30,000'.[5] At the end of the war William apparently retired from the army, and became a member of Queensberry's household.

In 1768 Queensberry brought him into Parliament where he supported Administration, but is not known to have spoken. His father, imprisoned for debt in January 1778, died in November, shortly after the death of his patron Queensberry, who had long treated William as his eventual heir to the marquessate of Queensberry, failing male issue by his immediate successor Lord March.[6] Sir William's uncle, Sir Alexander Dick, recorded in his 'Memoranda':

> The Duke shortly before his death, having a warm attachment to my nephew Sir William, whom he sincerely loved from his proper behaviour to him while in Parliament, and considering that he had [children] . . . to provide for, he left him £16,000 in money for their behalf . . . On the worthy Duke's death . . . this new unkindly and ungenerous Duke refused to pay the money . . . My nephew seeks my approbation for suing the Duke in the court of session.

And at the general election of 1780 the new Duke refused to return him to Parliament.

His action before the court of session for £20,000 (£16,000 plus interest) was successful; and on 30 Apr. 1783 Queensberry's appeal was dismissed by the Lords. Sir William was so overjoyed by the news that he had an apoplectic fit while playing with his children, and died 16 May 1783.[7]

[1] Memoranda by Sir Alex. Dick, W. Douglas's uncle, *Curiosities of a Scots Charta Chest*, ed. Forbes, 223. [2] Alex. Carlyle, *Autobiog.* 106. [3] Sir Alex. Dick's Memoranda. [4] *Scots Mag.* 1747, p. 351; *Scots Brigade in Holland* (Sc. Hist. Soc.), ii 390–1, 412, 414. [5] Boswell, *Private Pprs.* i. 87. [6] Jas. Chas. Sholto Douglas (William's bro.) to R. M. Keith, 7 Dec. 1775, Add. 35509, f. 274. [7] *Curiosities*, 270.

E.H.-G.

## DOWDESWELL, William (1721–75), of Pull Court, Worcs.

| | |
|---|---|
| TEWKESBURY | 1747–1754 |
| WORCESTERSHIRE | 1761–6 Feb. 1775 |

*b.* 12 Mar. 1721, 1st s. of William Dowdeswell of Pull Court by Amy, da. of Anthony Hammond of Somersham, Hunts.[1] *educ.* Westminster 1730; Ch. Ch. Oxf. 1737; Leyden (with John Wilkes and Hon. Charles Townshend qq.v.); Grand Tour (Italy and Greece). *m.* 6 Nov. 1747, Bridget, da. of Sir William Codrington, 1st Bt., sis. of Sir William Codrington, 2nd Bt. (q.v.), 6s. 9da. *suc.* fa. 1728.

P.C. 10 July 1765; chancellor of the Exchequer July 1765–July 1766.

The Dowdeswells were an old Worcestershire family with a strong electoral influence at Tewkesbury. William Dowdeswell was a country gentleman who made no mark in his first Parliament, and did not stand in 1754. In 1761 he was returned for Worcestershire as a Tory, and held his seat without a contest until his death. His first recorded vote in the Parliament of 1761 was against the peace preliminaries, December 1762. He became a frequent speaker in the House, and his political conduct can be traced in James Harris's reports of parliamentary debates.

Dowdeswell was a curious mixture of Whig and Tory. He supported the commemoration of Charles I's execution (which none but Tories did), yet heartily disliked the militia (a favourite Tory measure). The most constant theme of his speeches was the need to reduce Government expenditure and lower taxation. He wanted the army and navy reduced and the land tax lowered from its wartime figure of four shillings in the pound. He commended Grenville's scheme for lowering the rate of interest on Government loans, 13 Mar. 1765, but objected to his budget proposals, 27 Mar. 1765. Government expenditure was too high; 'as to our new taxes, [he] talked of the danger of provoking our colonies, and by duties on exports hinted the danger that foreigners may be induced to supply themselves elsewhere'. On Wilkes and general warrants he voted against the Grenville Administration, but did not identify himself with the Opposition: he did not belong to their club, and Newcastle on 10 May 1764 classed him as only a 'doubtful' friend. On 9 May 1765 he spoke for Administration on the Regency bill. It was as an opponent of the cider tax that he became really conspicuous. 'Dowdeswell . . . was the chief opponent', wrote Harris on 9 Mar. 1763, 'and had taken great pains'; and on 24 Jan. 1764 Dowdeswell moved for a committee to consider the tax, in a speech which Harris describes as 'decent, temperate, and reasonable'. On 31 Jan. he criticized the method of raising the tax by an excise on the maker—'he then entered into a detail of the grievances of the excise laws upon ignorant countrymen, the enormity of the penalties, the trials without juries, the partiality of what he called revenue injustices, the dreaded consequences that were these laws extended commissioners of excise might nominate Members for the cider counties'.

In July 1765 Dowdeswell was appointed chancellor of the Exchequer in the Rockingham Administration. The appointment was a surprising one and it is not certain who recommended it. But Charles Townshend, his close friend and successor, wrote to him on 28 Oct. 1766: 'I hope you will not be unmindful that I had more pleasure in contributing to your late situation than I had or have in my own succession.'[2] Horace Walpole described Dowdeswell as 'so suited to the drudgery of the office, as far as it depends on arithmetic, that he was fit for nothing else. Heavy, slow, methodical without clearness, a butt for ridicule, unversed in every graceful art, and a stranger to men and courts, he was only esteemed by the few to whom he was personally known.'[3] This unkind estimate is supported by an anecdote told by Mrs. Thrale:[4] 'When Warburton saw Lord Lyttelton going to dinner at Dowdeswell's—there, says he, goes a man who cannot tell that two times two is four going to dine with a man who knows nothing else.'

In fact, Dowdeswell was an honest country gentleman, passionately interested in finance, and neither a wit nor a great parliamentarian. He was not a regular member of the Cabinet but was consulted by Rockingham on American affairs.[5] In the debates on the repeal of the Stamp Act Dowdeswell took little part. Indeed, Harris noted, following his report of the great debate of 21–22 Feb.: 'Chancellor of the Exchequer said not a word. Some say he was in his private sentiments rather for a modification than a repeal.' When Chatham took office in July 1766 Dowdeswell was replaced at the Exchequer by Townshend, and declined an offer of the place of joint paymaster general or first lord of Trade. He wrote to his wife on 30 July, describing his last audience with the King:

> I begged his Majesty would give me leave to express my feelings as a man, and my hopes that in what his Majesty might intend for me he considered the high station to which he had already raised me and the manner in which I had discharged my office to his satisfaction, and I persuaded myself with no small degree of public approbation. I said that it might be the misfortune sometimes to have been raised too high. Men could not after being much exalted stoop to certain offices which they might have at first accepted.
> His Majesty approved very much what I said to him.

Dowdeswell now joined his political fortunes to those of Rockingham, and a close friendship developed between them: Dowdeswell became the leader of the Rockingham group in the Commons, and Rockingham's trusted adviser. He took part in the conference between the Bedfords and the Rockinghams on 20 July 1767 to draw up the outlines of a new Administration to be submitted to the King. On 21 July Bedford, to break the deadlock, proposed Dowdeswell for leader of the House of Commons instead of Conway; but Dowdeswell declined, 'for many reasons which he then gave, and for many more which he kept in his own breast'.[6] Conway now invited the Rockinghams to join Chatham's Administration; in a memorandum dated 23 and 24 July, Dowdeswell advised Rockingham to decline, unless 'the King should send for him to give him powers from his own mouth without any of his ministers'. He went on to outline the conditions on which Rockingham should form an Administration (conditions which Burke afterwards developed in his pamphlet *Thoughts on a late 'State of the Nation'*). Rockingham should endeavour to form as wide a coalition as possible—only a 'broad and comprehensive' Administration would be strong enough to stand up against 'the intrigues of the Closet'; but he 'must consider himself as the former of an Administration and answerable for its success, and would therefore preserve in all offices of business a manifest superiority for his own friends'. These principles were to guide Rockingham for the next fifteen years and foreshadow the coalition of 1783. What should be done, Dowdeswell finally asked, should such a coalition be found impracticable?

> Nothing but to finish with honour. We have hitherto acted with the strictest honour. If our friends will not join us it is impossible for us to join them . . .
> I confess that I see no fair prospect before us. Standing still is the only thing we can do. This may possibly weaken us as a party, it depends upon the virtue of our friends whether it will nor will not, but I am sure it will do us honour as individuals.

> In these unhappy times, when we find ourselves well in the opinion of mankind, the wisest thing we can do is to stand still and enjoy the reputation we have, not risk it for something new, the chances of which are so much against it.

Many a passage from Rockingham's letters during the American war reads like an echo of this.

On America Dowdeswell's views were conservative. In a long letter of 14 Aug. 1768 to Rockingham he discussed the American reaction to the Townshend duties.[7]

> A repeated opposition from that side of the water [he wrote] upon a principle directed against all duties for revenue must be met. It must either be admitted, which is timidity, weakness, irresolution, and inconsistency; or it must be resisted, and the arms of this country must be exerted against her colonies.

If the Americans petitioned against the Townshend duties, they would in effect be petitioning against all duties laid for revenue.

> If they succeed in such a petition they obtain a great charter, depriving this country in all future times and in all future circumstances of the power of raising any revenue there for the general support of its own authority, a power which the experience of these times will render this country extremely cautious of making use of, but which no human wisdom can foresee it may not, some time or other, and in some change of circumstances on both sides of the water, be equitable as well as necessary to exert.

Dowdeswell recognized that for Great Britain to abandon the right of taxation would be to abandon sovereignty over the colonies. Nor was there any reason to expect that the Americans would act in 'a temperate and wise manner'. If British authority were resisted, 'there are but two things left, either to fight to the last, in which case this country will be undone, or to treat with the contending party, depart from your own dignity, weaken your authority, and by giving up in time a part of your rights preserve the rest'. He concluded:

> This leads me to my decision for much moderation. I could find much to say against any dissent that any man could offer, but upon the whole moderate measures are less dangerous, and if we come off at last with a loss those must answer for it who have wantonly and unnecessarily revived the question, and I believe now profess that these duties were laid merely as a test to the Americans.

Henceforth until his death Dowdeswell directed the strategy of the Rockingham party, and his lead was unchallenged. 'I am sure', wrote Burke to Rockingham on 7 Jan. 1773, ' . . . we cannot find a leader whom a man of honour and judgment would so soon choose to follow.' One of the most frequent speakers in the Commons, his political life is the history of the Rockingham party. The defection of the Grenvilles in 1771 and the break with Chatham (whom Dowdeswell distrusted and found difficult to work with) made his task a dreary one. 'Impossibility of doing good in opposition', he wrote to Rockingham on 8 June 1774, 'and despair of being able to do it if we were again called into Administration, has long left me hopeless in politics.' In the summer of 1774 he fell ill, apparently with tuberculosis, and was ordered abroad. 'I am really not very sanguine in my expectations of his recovery', wrote Burke to Rockingham, 18 Sept. 1774; and Dowdeswell died at Nice, 6 Feb. 1775.

Burke, asked by Mrs. Dowdeswell to compose her husband's epitaph, wrote to her on 13 June 1775:

> I am indeed very incapable of doing justice to his memory. I have however some pretensions to it which I should not suffer many persons living to dispute with me. I think I knew him perfectly; and I am very sure that in proportion as I knew I loved and honoured him. You know that we lived for near nine years in the closest participation of councils, in affairs that were delicate, and in a time which was critical and difficult. In all that time, and in all those affairs, we have scarcely ever had a difference in opinion. From that, perhaps, my deference to his thoughts secured us— but this was not all; we never had a momentary coldness of affection; no disgust; no peevishness; no political or personal quarrels; no reconciliations. There never was a soul so remote as his from fraud, duplicity, or fear; so perfectly free from any of those little passions or from any of that capricious unevenness of temper which embitters friendships and perplexes business. Of all the men I ever knew he was the best to act with in public and to live with in private, from the manly decision and firmness of his judgment and the extreme mildness and pleasantness of his temper.

The epitaph which Burke composed was inscribed on Dowdeswell's monument in Bushley Church, Worcestershire.[8]

[1] C. W. Dowdeswell to Edmund Burke, 16 June 1775, Add. 16569, f. 76. [2] Dowdeswell mss, William L. Clements Lib. [3] *Mems. Geo. III*, ii. 139. [4] *Thraliana*, ed. Balderston, 2. [5] Add. 32973, ff. 3, 11–13. [6] Dowdeswell's account of the negotiations of July 1767 and his memorandum of 23 and 24 July, Rockingham mss. [7] Dowdeswell mss. [8] Nash, *Worcs.* i. 183.

J.B.

**DOWNE, Viscts.,** *see* **DAWNAY**

**DOWNING, Sir Jacob Garrard,** 4th Bt. (c. 1717–1764), of Putney, Surr. and Gamlingay Park, Cambs.

DUNWICH   1741–1747, 21 June 1749–1761, 29 Apr. 1763–6 Feb. 1764

*b.* c.1717, o.s. of Charles Downing of Bury St. Edmunds, Suff, comptroller of customs at Salem, Mass. (s. of Sir George Downing, 1st Bt.), by Sarah, da. and coh. of Jacob Garrard (1st s. of Sir Thomas Garrard, 2nd Bt., of Langford, Norf.). *educ.* Emmanuel, Camb. 1734. *m.* 17 May 1750, Margaret, da. of Rev. John Price of Barrington, Glos., *s.p. suc.* fa. ('vastly rich')[1] 16 Apr. 1740, and his cos. Sir George Downing in baronetcy and estates 10 June 1749.

Downing was returned for his cousin's pocket borough (which he inherited in 1749), and generally voted with the court.

He was closely connected with Lord Hardwicke.[2] 'As to my interest in this county', he wrote to Hardwicke from Gamlingay on 27 July 1753, 'it is undisputably at your disposal, and while I have the protection of your patronage I shall always think myself a man of consequence.' In 1754, at Newcastle's request, he returned for Dunwich Soame Jenyns, a friend of the Yorkes,[3] and Newcastle promised to try to obtain a peerage for Downing.[4] On 11 Nov. 1755 Downing wrote to him:[5]

> The current report of some gentlemen being very soon to be created peers, and having nothing from your Grace, has given me great uneasiness; as I can't tax myself with any one action in my whole life that has not been with the warmest and most sincere attachment to the present happy establishment and ministry, and will not suffer myself to think that I am to be laid aside, as I have had so many assurances of your Grace's intention to serve me.

Moreover, he had 'never asked any place, pension or employment', and so had 'been very little troublesome to any part of Administration'.[6]

Newcastle failed to obtain for him the peerage, and Downing (probably most unjustly) held him responsible. When the Newcastle-Pitt Administration was being formed, Downing wrote to Hardwicke, 16 June 1757, that while his feelings for Hardwicke remained unchanged, he could by no means think of acting with Newcastle, and did not desire to have 'the most distant appearance of the least connexion' with him; and on 18 June 1758, that he would not re-elect Soame Jenyns, but would return a Member 'that has as little reason as myself to be satisfied with the Duke of Newcastle'. On Jenyns vacating the seat in November 1758, Downing placed it at Fox's disposal. His friendship with Fox was now very close, and on 4 May 1759 he told him that the borough of Dunwich would 'during your life be absolutely under your directions and consequently the choice of the Members in your option.'[7]

In June 1762 Fox described Downing as 'very infirm';[8] yet when Fox was created a peer, Downing had himself returned again for Dunwich. But Fox, when asked by Sandwich, before the autumn session of 1763 to secure Downing's support, replied: 'Sir Jacob Downing I fear can't attend an hour.'[9]

He died 6 Feb. 1764.

[1] *Gent. Mag.* 1740, p. 204. [2] See corresp. between them in Add. 35679. [3] Add. 32995, ff. 63–67, 138–41. [4] Downing to Hardwicke, 25 June 1759. [5] Add. 32860, f. 450. [6] Downing to Hardwicke, 5 Apr. 1759. [7] Henry Fox mss. [8] Fox to Bute, 11 June 1762, Bute mss. [9] Sandwich to Holland, 26 Sept. 1763 (printed in Ilchester, *Letters to Hen. Fox*, 179–84, omitting in the postcript the list of 'Members to be applied to by Lord Holland'); Holland to Sandwich, 2 Oct., Sandwich mss.

L.B.N.

**D'OYLY, Christopher** (c.1717–95), of Walton-on-Thames, Surr.

WAREHAM       1774–1780
SEAFORD     4 Dec. 1780–1784

*b.* c.1717, 1st surv. s. of Christopher D'Oyly of Banbury, Oxon., an attorney in the court of common pleas, by Susanna. *educ.* I. Temple 1741, called 1744. *m.* 2 Dec. 1765,[1] Sarah, da. of George Stanley of Paultons, sis. and coh. of Hans Stanley (q.v.), *s.p. suc.* to an estate at Walton-on-Thames, Surr. under will of Adria, da. of William Drake of Amersham, wid. of Denton Boate 1754; his w. and Mrs. Welbore Ellis suc. to Paultons on d. of Hans Stanley 1780.

1st clerk, War Office, 1761–2; dep. sec. Jan. 1763–Jan. 1772; under-sec. in the colonial dept. May 1776–Feb. 1778; commissary gen. of musters May 1776–Sept. 1780.

Christopher D'Oyly is not a dim figure but is seen only in bits: like a landscape from an aeroplane through breaks in thick cloud. He retired from practice at the bar on inheriting the Walton-on-Thames estate in 1754. The reason for his entering the War Office is not known. He owed his promotion to Welbore Ellis, whose sister-in-law he married three years later; and his place was taken by his friend Philip Francis. When Charles Townshend died leaving his financial affairs in utter confusion, Lady Mary Coke, who was staying with his widow, noted in her diary on 17 Sept. 1767: 'Mr. D'Oyly came about 8 o'clock. I am glad she has so sensible and so worthy a man to assist her in her business.'[2]

On 21 Dec. 1771 D'Oyly wrote to Francis:[3] 'This morning, my dear Francis, I desired Lord Barrington's permission to retire from the War Office. My request was readily and, which is mortifying, without one civil speech, granted. I am persuaded whenever you please you may obtain the same permission on as easy terms.' Francis's resignation or dismissal followed—the reasons of neither are clear. And 'Veteran' (pseudonym of Francis-Junius) asserted in the *Public Advertiser*, 23 Mar. 1772, that Barrington had driven them both out of the War Office.

When Clive went to the continent early in 1774, he left his election affairs in the hands of John Walsh, George Clive, Henry Strachey (all three M.P.s), and of D'Oyly.[4] The origin of D'Oyly's connexion with Clive has not been ascertained, but he appears afterwards as close to Strachey. Similarly Francis, when he left for India in February 1774, made D'Oyly one of his trustees during his absence.[5] Moreover on 28 Feb., the eve of his departure, he wrote to the executors of John Calcraft (q.v.) who had desired Francis to be returned for his borough of Wareham:[6]

As my absence from England will prevent my immediately availing myself of the benefit and honour intended me by Mr. Calcraft, it is my earnest desire and request to you, that you will employ the interest vested in you by his will, to return my intimate friend Christopher D'Oyly . . . as Member for the borough of Wareham, at the next general election or at the first vacancy that may happen, instead of myself. He is a man whom Mr. Calcraft highly esteemed, and to whom there can be no objection on any account. My own particular reason for wishing that he may be elected in my room is, because I can depend upon his honour that if, on my return from India, I should require of him to vacate his seat, he will be ready to do so; and that in the meantime he will supply my place in Parliament with the greatest honour and ability.

Accordingly D'Oyly was returned in October 1774. In 1779 the *Public Ledger* wrote about him: 'A placeman of very good character. He is a private friend of Mr. Rigby, and has likewise a great regard for the two Howes.' It was as late deputy secretary at war 'and a particular friend of Howe' that D'Oyly, according to his then colleague William Knox, 'had the entire conduct of the military business', and together with Burgoyne settled the plan and instructions for Burgoyne's expedition.[7]

In January 1778 D'Oyly protested against Germain's treatment of the Howes: that his letters 'were so cold and dry in respect to Sir William Howe's successes in Pennsylvania, and left him in doubt as to his continuance in the command, which he thinks will have made him more fully bent upon quitting', and that 'it is necessary to consider how to persuade them to remain in the command, if it is intended that they should be continued in it'.[8] And on 19 Feb. 1778 D'Oyly wrote to Francis:[9]

I had last Friday asked and obtained leave to retire from my situation in Lord G. Germain's office, and at this moment various are the speculations upon it, as it is not in general known that leave is gone to Howe to give up his command. My reasons for giving up are many, but must not be trusted in a letter. The friends of Opposition increase, and we are now in the midst of an inquiry into the state of the nation; in short, we are in a damned bad way.

Still, he retained his post at the War Office, but even so his support of Government became less whole-hearted. He was used as an intermediary with Lord Howe.[10] But when after the division of 3 Mar. 1779 on Sandwich's naval administration, in which Government mustered only 204 votes against 170 of the Opposition (and from which D'Oyly and Strachey were absent), the list of the House of Commons was carefully scrutinized, the King hoped that the two had been 'strongly spoke to'.[11] After the further division of 8 Mar. on the state of the navy, Jenkinson wrote to the King: 'Admiral Keppel and Lord Howe . . . must be considered as enemies. Mr. D'Oyly and Mr. Strachey who are to be considered as Lord Howe's friends, were both present some part of the day, but neither voted.'[12] But in the divisions

February–April 1780 D'Oyly voted regularly with the Government.

None the less his position may possibly have been irksome to him. By the time Robinson drew up his survey in July 1780, D'Oyly's continuance in Parliament was doubtful; and in an additional note on 31 July Robinson stated that D'Oyly desired 'to quit Parliament on account of health'. On 4 Sept., three days after Parliament had been dissolved, North wrote to D'Oyly:[13]

> You are as you wished out of Parliament and I suppose that it continues to be your resolution never to come into Parliament again . . . While you are leaving the House of Commons Mr. Bowlby is resolved to undertake a parliamentary life . . . As you are changing your political situation, I do not see why you should not change places at the same time. The place he now fills [comptroller of army accounts] is not tenable with a seat in the House of Commons, your place ought always to be held by a Member of Parliament.

According to an endorsement by D'Oyly, North's letter did not reach him till 25 Sept.; but as Bowlby's election was fixed for 11 Sept., the exchange of places was gazetted on the 6th.[14] But D'Oyly declined the place assigned to him, and on 4 Dec. 1780 was returned for Seaford after a contest, on the Treasury interest. His reasons for re-entering the House are not known, nor the Government's in returning him. In February 1781 he was classed as no more than 'hopeful', and was absent from the critical divisions of 12 Dec. 1781 and of February–March 1782. On 18 Feb. 1783 D'Oyly voted against Shelburne's peace preliminaries, and was classed by Robinson as a friend of North. But he did not vote in the divisions on Fox's East India bill, nor in those of January–March 1784. He did not stand again in 1784. There is no record of his having spoken in the House.

He died 19 Jan. 1795.

[1] Par. reg. Rotherwick, Hants. [2] *Jnl.* iii. 128. [3] Parkes & Merivale *Mems. of Francis*, i. 274. [4] Minute of 'a Meeting of Lord Clive's Attorneys on Sunday, 24 Apr. 1774', Clive mss, Salop R.O. [5] Parkes & Merivale, i. 349. [6] Ibid. 344–5. [7] *HMC Var.* vi. 277. [8] North to the King, 10 Jan. 1778, Fortescue, iv. 9. [9] Parkes & Merivale, ii. 133. [10] Fortescue, iv. 293–4. [11] Ibid. 299. [12] Ibid. 469–70. Correct date, 9 Mar. 1779. [13] *Gent. Mag.* 1829, i. 506–7. [14] T52/69/64–65.

L.B.N.

**DRAKE, Sir Francis Henry,** 5th Bt. (1723–94), of Buckland and Nutwell Court, Devon.

BERE ALSTON     1747–6 Jan. 1771, 1774–1780

*b.* 29 Aug. 1723 1st s. of Sir Francis Henry Drake, 4th Bt., M.P., by Anne, da. of Samuel Heathcote of Clapton House, Hackney, Mdx., sis. of Sir William Heathcote of Hursley, 1st Bt., M.P. *educ.* Winchester 1734–9; Eton 1740; Corpus Christi, Camb. 1740–4; L. Inn 1740. *unm. suc.* fa. 26 Jan. 1740.

Ranger of Dartmoor forest 1752–*d*; clerk comptroller of the Board of Green Cloth 1753–1770; master of the Household 1771–*d*.

At the first general election after Drake had come of age, he was returned for the seat which by then had for a century been 'practically an appanage of the Drakes of Buckland'.[1] A good summary of his parliamentary career was given by the *Public Ledger* in 1779: 'He is a silent, eccentric man, votes always with the ministry . . .' There is no record of a speech by him during his 30 years in the House, and only of one vote against an Administration (although it is hard to believe that he did not vote against the cider bill if present). Drake's father and his uncle Samuel Heathcote, who held the family seat at Bere Alston during Drake's minority, had both been Walpolians; and Drake adhered to the Pelhams—there is a 'State of the borough of Exeter', dated 6 Sept. 1753, which Drake drew up at Pelham's request, and transmitted to him 'at the earnest request of the principal Whigs there'.[2] 'Busts of George II and Frederic, Prince of Wales, have long been amongst the adornments of the hall at Buckland Abbey', writes Lady Eliott-Drake;[3] and F. H. Drake seems soon to have fallen in with the new court: in July 1761 he was sent with Lord Harcourt to bring Princess Charlotte, the future Queen, over to England.[4] In Bute's parliamentary list, compiled in December 1761, he is marked 'Bute and Government', to which 'Talbot' (the new lord steward) is added. Even Newcastle, in his list of 13 Nov. 1762, concedes Drake as 'contra'; and Fox, early in December, places him among those favourable to the peace preliminaries. In the autumn of 1763 Jenkinson marked him as 'pro'; and when on 18 Feb. 1764, over general warrants, Drake gave his not unrecorded Opposition vote, he is listed by Jenkinson among 'persons who voted with the minority' but 'are friends or nearly so'.

When the Rockingham Government was being formed, Drake was at first listed among those to be replaced,[5] but by 9 July he was reprieved,[6] and in Rockingham's parliamentary list of July 1765 appeared as 'pro'—and he did not vote against the repeal of the Stamp Act. Under the Chatham Administration he was counted in all parliamentary surveys as a Government supporter, and, although a country gentleman, voted with them even for the higher land tax, 27 Feb. 1767. In the next Parliament his name appears in only one of the three division lists on Wilkes and the Middlesex election in which the names of the Government side are given; and when his appointment as master of the Household, 6 Jan. 1771, vacated his seat, he did not seek re-election but returned his brother Francis William (q.v.). In 1774 he re-entered Parliament, and his name appears in every division list which names those voting with the Government. Averse to standing again, Drake sold his share in the borough of Bere Alston to the Duke of Northumberland before the next general election.[7]

During the office reshuffles of June 1779 Drake's resigning his office seems to have been considered;[8] but he retained it even after having left the House. When in 1782 Grafton was in search of a place for a friend, Rockingham wrote to him about Drake and his office: '*He is no Member of Parliament*—and as I understand from his Majesty was active and useful in assisting the late Lord Talbot *in his reforms.*'[9] And George Selwyn writing to Lord Carlisle, 9 Dec. 1775, about an enclosure bill in which Carlisle was interested, referred to Drake as 'the most conscientious man in the House in questions of this nature'.[10] Obviously he was attentive to matters within the range of his real interests; but he was no politician.

Drake died 19 Feb. 1794.

[1] Lady Eliott-Drake, *Fam. & Heirs of Sir F. Drake*, ii. 315. [2] Newcastle (Clumber) mss. [3] Op.cit. ii. 301. [4] See ibid. 301–2; also John Secker to Sir John Cust, 9 July 1761, *Recs. Cust Fam.*, iii. 195. [5] See e.g. lists of 2 and 5 July 1765, Fortescue, i. 131, 137. [6] Ibid. 154. [7] Drake to Ld. Buckinghamshire, 3 June 1780, *HMC Lothian*, 366. [8] Fortescue, iv. 353. [9] 3 May 1782, Grafton mss. See also Shelburne to the King, 7 Oct. 1782, Fortescue, vi. 140. [10] *HMC Carlisle*, 310.

L.B.N.

## DRAKE, Francis William (1724–87), of Hillingdon, Mdx.

BERE ALSTON    29 Jan. 1771–1774

*bap.* 22 Aug. 1724, 2nd surv. s. of Sir Francis Henry Drake, 4th Bt., and bro. of Sir F. H. Drake, 5th Bt. (q.v.). *m.* 3 Nov. 1763, his cos. Elizabeth, da. of Sir William Heathcote, 1st Bt., M.P., 2da.

Entered R.N. bef. 1740, capt. 1748; gov. Newfoundland 1752–4; r.-adm. 1778; v.-adm. 1780.

Drake served under Knowles in the West Indies, 1748; under Rodney in Newfoundland 1751, succeeding him as governor; under Boscawen at Lagos, 1759. At various times his career seems to have been impeded by ill-health. N. Rowe, a close friend of the Drake family, wrote about him to Sir Francis Drake in March 1750:[1]

He's an honest young fellow, who, though he has seen the world abroad, wants to be better acquainted with that at home. A perfect harmony between you, which I greatly wish, may be a great means thereto; I need not mention to you the obligation. His health is better than I expected, and would be more so if he'd use the means.

He retired on half pay in 1763, but in 1766 was given command of a guardship at Plymouth.[2] His elder brother, who on being appointed master of the Household did not choose to seek re-election, returned Francis William to Parliament in his place, 29 Jan. 1771. He does not, however, appear in the

two division lists of February–March 1771, and on 8 Mar. 1772, is marked in Robinson's survey on the royal marriage bill as 'pro, sick, absent'. Over the petition of naval captains on half-pay he voted against the Government, but is marked as a 'friend'. Otherwise he voted with the Government. No speech of his is recorded; and after the dissolution of 1774 he did not again stand for Parliament.

In August 1780, while holding the command in the Downs, he was offered by Sandwich employment under Rodney, but had to decline it from the 'shattered condition of my constitution', and for fear that 'his Majesty's service there might suffer from my bodily inability'.[3] A short time later, crippled by gout, he quitted his station.[4] He died in December 1787.

[1] Lady Eliott-Drake, *Fam. and Heirs of Sir F. Drake*, ii. 258. [2] Ibid. ii. 306. [3] *Sandwich Pprs.* iii. (Navy Rec. Soc. lxxv), 227. [4] Charnock, *Biographia Navalis*, vi. 61.

L.B.N.

## DRAKE, William (1723–96), of Shardeloes, nr. Amersham, Bucks.

AMERSHAM    26 Feb. 1746–1796

*b.* 12 May 1723, 1st surv. s. of Montague Garrard Drake, M.P., of Shardeloes by Isabella, da. and h. of Thomas Marshall. *educ.* Westminster 1738; B.N.C. Oxf. 1739. *m.* 9 Feb. 1747, Elizabeth, da. of John Raworth of Basinghall St., London, 5s. 3da. *suc.* fa. 1728.

The Drakes of Shardeloes, a very old Buckinghamshire family, controlled both seats at Amersham. William Drake was classed as a Tory in Dupplin's list of 1754, and again in Bute's list of December 1761, with 'well inclined' added in Bute's own hand. He appears in Fox's list of Members favourable to the peace preliminaries. In the division of 18 Feb. 1764 on general warrants he voted against the Grenville Administration, but is not known to have done so in any other division. Rockingham in July 1765 classed him as 'contra', and he voted against the repeal of the Stamp Act, 22 Feb. 1766. He voted against Chatham's Administration on the land tax, 27 Feb. 1767.

On Wilkes and the Middlesex election he was uncertain: voted with the Opposition on Wilkes's petition, 27 Jan. 1769, with the ministry on the motion to expel Wilkes, 3 Feb. 1769, but against them on the petition against the seating of Luttrell, 8 May 1769. On Dowdeswell's motion about the Middlesex election, 25 Jan. 1770, and the Spanish convention, 13 Feb. 1771, he was again with Opposition; was classed by Robinson on the royal marriage bill, March 1772, as 'doubtful'; but supported the court on the renewal of the Middlesex question, 26 Apr. 1773, and although he voted for making Grenville's Election Act permanent, 25 Feb. 1774, was classed in the King's list as normally a friend to Government.

At first he supported North on the American war: his name occurs in none of the six minority division lists, 1775–8. He voted with Opposition on measures concerned with economy or the reduction of the influence of the Crown: the contractors bill, 12 Feb. 1779, the motion for an account of pensions, 21 Feb. 1780, for the abolition of the Board of Trade, 13 Mar. 1780, and Dunning's motion, 6 Apr. 1780; but with the court on the motion about prorogation, 24 Apr. 1780. In 1779 the *Public Ledger* wrote about him: 'A respectable independent gentleman, a Tory in principle, and a great admirer of Lord North, votes with the ministry in general, but sometimes in the minority.' And Robinson in his survey for the general election of 1780: 'Mr. Drake senior is oftener with Government than against: in ministerial questions he may be against, but in the great constitutional points he will always be with, if the questions are to affect the government or constitution.' His monumental inscription describes him as 'attached to no party, [but] supporting such measures as appeared to him constitutional and expedient'.[1]

Drake voted with the ministry on Lowther's motion to end the war, 12 Dec. 1781, but in the five divisions February–March 1782 with Opposition: he had at first doubted, but eventually Yorktown convinced him it was impossible to continue the war. He voted for Shelburne's peace preliminaries, 18 Feb. 1783, and against Fox's East India bill, 27 Nov. 1783; and was classed by Robinson in January 1784 as 'very hopeful'. He appears in no division list for the 1784 Parliament, but in the consolidated list on the Regency is listed as having voted with Pitt. There is no record of his having spoken in the House before 1790.

He died 8 Aug. 1796.

[1] Lipscomb, *Bucks.* iii. 170.

J.B.

**DRAKE, William** (?1747–95), of Shardeloes, nr. Amersham, Bucks.

AMERSHAM 1768–18 May 1795

*b.* ?1747, 1st s. of William Drake (q.v.). *educ.* Westminster 1759–64; B.N.C. Oxf. 20 June 1765, aged 17; Grand Tour. *m.* (1) 17 Feb. 1778, Mary (*d.*23 Oct. 1778), da. of William Hussey (q.v.), *s.p.*; (2) 20 Aug. 1781, Rachel Elizabeth, da. and h. of Jeremiah Ives of Norwich, 2da.

In the Parliament of 1768 Drake's voting pattern closely resembled his father's. He is known to have spoken three times, all in February 1774; 14 Feb., on Woodfall's case; 15 Feb., in favour of shorter Parliaments; and 25 Feb., for making Grenville's Election Act permanent.

In the Parliament of 1774 his attitude towards North's Administration hardened; and he voted against them in divisions on the civil list debts, 16 Apr. 1777, America, 2 Feb. 1778, the contractors bill, 12 Feb. 1779, and in four of the divisions February–April 1780. The *Public Ledger* wrote of him in 1779: 'A very independent, conscientious man, votes on each side, but most usually in the minority'; and Robinson in his survey for the general election of 1780 wrote that Drake was 'not of such sound principles as his father'. Drake did not vote in the division of 12 Dec. 1781 on Lowther's motion against the war, but voted against Administration in four out of the five divisions February–March 1782 (he was absent from the one of 15 Mar.). Like his father he voted for Shelburne's peace preliminaries, 18 Feb. 1783, and against Fox's East India bill, 27 Nov. 1783.

On 16 Jan. 1784 he spoke on Lord Charles Spencer's motion of censure against Pitt's ministry[1] (his first recorded speech since 1774—a curious silence for one who later spoke so often).

> He said he wished that there might always be an honourable Opposition; it was right to keep up in that House a proper jealousy of Administration to make them wary and prudent . . . He . . . mentioned the violence of the late East India bill, commended the moderation of the present, [and] advised the House by no means to agree to a motion calculated to disgrace an Administration just come into office.

He was a member of the St. Alban's Tavern group which tried to bring about a union between Fox and Pitt.

After this had failed he supported Pitt, whom he described as 'as good a minister as ever this country had'. But he voted against Pitt on Richmond's fortifications plan, 27 Feb. 1786, and on Bastard's motion to inquire into naval promotions, 18 Apr. 1788. He voted with Pitt on the Regency, although he disagreed with some of his proposals. In this well-reported Parliament he is recorded as having made over sixty speeches. His subjects varied a good deal, but taxation was his favourite topic ('in all matters of public expenditure his maxim was waste not, want not'). 'Mr. Drake possesses a most powerful voice', wrote Stockdale, 'and always speaks uncommonly loud.' He talked sense, and his speeches were ornate: he was fond of a Latin quotation, and liked to show his knowledge of French affairs (he once called Pitt 'the Necker of this country').[2]

Drake died *v.p.* 18 May 1795. 'He has left an immense property', wrote the *Gentleman's Magazine*

(1795, p. 445), 'partly acquired by marriage, and partly by some collateral branches. Had he lived to inherit that of his father, he would have been one of the richest men in the country.'

[1] Debrett xii. 587. [2] Stockdale, xii. 1-2; xv. 59-60; xvii. 412.

J.B.

### DRAX, Edward (c.1726–91), of Wareham, Dorset.

WAREHAM    24 Nov. 1755–1761

*b.* c.1726, 2nd s. of Henry Drax, and bro. of Thomas Erle Drax (qq.v.). *educ.* Eton 1742; Hertford, Oxf. 1743. *m.* 15 Apr. 1762, Mary, da. of Awnsham Churchill of Henbury, Dorset, 1da.

One of the terms of the compromise at Wareham in 1754 seems to have been a promise by Newcastle to find an office for Edward Drax. On 9 June 1756 his mother asked Newcastle to appoint Drax groom of the bedchamber in the household then being formed for the Prince of Wales.[1] Newcastle was willing to do so, but on 22 Oct. Drax wrote to him:[2] 'I take the liberty of returning your Grace thanks for the great honour intended me, but as it will be attended with a closer confinement than my private affairs will admit of, beg leave to be excused accepting it.'

He contested Shaftesbury in 1761, but was badly beaten.

He died in April 1791.

[1] Add. 32865, f. 241. [2] Add. 32868, f. 384.

A.N.N.

### DRAX, Henry (? 1693–1755), of Charborough, Dorset, and Ellerton Abbey, Yorks.

WAREHAM      28 Mar. 1718–1722
LYME REGIS      1727–1734
WAREHAM      1734–26 Jan. 1748, 25 Jan.
             1751–1754, 30 Dec. 1754–
             24 May 1755

*b.* ? 1693, 1st s. of Thomas Shatterden (afterwards Drax), of Pope's Common, Herts. and Barbados by Elizabeth, da. of Edward Ernle of Etchilhampton, Wilts. *educ.* Eton 1706–7; Magdalene, Camb. 1710. *m.* 1720, his 1st cos. Elizabeth, da. and h. of Sir Edward Ernle, 3rd Bt., M.P., and gd.-da. and h. of Thomas Erle, M.P., of Charborough, 3s. 5da.
    Sec. to Frederick, Prince of Wales 1744–51.

Henry Drax inherited electoral influence at Wareham through his wife's grandfather, Thomas Erle, of Charborough. In 1754 he and his son were opposed at Wareham by the Pitts of Encombe. A double return was made, but, on a compromise arranged by Newcastle, Henry Drax took his seat. He died 24 May 1755.

A.N.N.

### DRAX, Thomas Erle (? 1721–89), of Charborough, Dorset.

CORFE CASTLE   7 Dec. 1744–1747
WAREHAM              1747–26 Jan. 1748, 1761–
                    1768

*b.* ? 1721, 1st s. of Henry Drax, and bro. of Edward Drax (qq.v.). *educ.* Ch. Ch. Oxf. 1740. *m.* 16 Oct. 1754, Hon. Mary St. John, da. of John, 11th Baron St. John, *s.p. suc.* fa. 1755.

In 1754 Drax and his father stood at Wareham against the Pitts of Encombe; after a double return a compromise was arranged by which Thomas Erle Drax withdrew.

In 1761 he was returned without a contest, and received Newcastle's whip through Robert Nugent (q.v.), who had married his sister. In Bute's list of 1762 he is classed as 'Tory' and 'Bute', and he supported Bute's and Grenville's Administrations.

On 21 June 1764 Nugent wrote to Grenville:[1] 'As I see in the public papers that some Irish peers have been now created, I must beg leave to put you in mind of Mr. Drax's wishes upon this subject. He does not know that I ever mentioned them to you.' Grenville replied on 24 June:[2] 'I understood from you that Mr. Drax wished this, but was far from being very eager about it, which made me avoid entering upon the subject unless I had thought it very likely to succeed.'

When the Rockinghams took office Drax followed Nugent into Opposition, and voted against the repeal of the Stamp Act, 22 Feb. 1766. Nugent took office under Chatham, and Drax supported his Administration.

In 1766 or 1767 he sold his interest at Wareham to John Calcraft (q.v.), and in 1768 he did not stand.

He died December 1789.

[1] Grenville mss (JM). [2] Grenville letter bk.

A.N.N.

### DRAX, *see also* GROSVENOR, Richard (*d.*1819)

### DROGHEDA, Earl of, *see* MOORE, Charles

### DRUMLANRIG, Earl of, *see* DOUGLAS, Lord Charles

### DRUMMOND, Adam (1713–86), of Lennoch and Megginch, Perth.

LYMINGTON              1761–1768
ST. IVES              1768–11 Dec. 1778
ABERDEEN BURGHS   11 Jan. 1779–1784
SHAFTESBURY           1784–17 June 1786

*b.* 31 Jan. 1713, 1st s. of John Drummond, M.P., of Lennoch and Megginch by Bethia, da. of James

Murray of Deuchar, Selkirk. *educ.* Leyden 1733; adv. 1736. *m.* 4 Feb. 1755, Catherine, da. of Harry Powlett, 4th Duke of Bolton, wid. of William Ashe, M.P., *s.p. suc.* fa. 1752.

Entered army 1739; lt. 47 Ft. 1741, capt. 1745; half-pay 1753; ret. 1756.

Inspector gen. of the annexed estates 1780.

Drummond left the Scottish bar to join the army, served in the '45, was captured at Prestonpans, and was afterwards in America. Shortly after his marriage, he set up as a merchant. In 1761 he was returned for Lymington on the Bolton interest, but did not follow his brother-in-law into opposition, and was listed by Fox among those favourable to the peace preliminaries. When Grenville in 1763 gave Sir George Colebrooke and Arnold Nesbitt 'notice to quit',[1] Drummond and his partner Sir Samuel Fludyer applied for their contract for victualling the troops in North America. James Stuart Mackenzie wrote to Charles Jenkinson, 21 Dec. 1763:[2]

> I understand that nothing is yet settled about the contract in which Mr. Drummond and Sir Samuel Fludyer are concerned . . . my only concern in it is about Drummond, whom I wish Mr. Grenville would pay some attention to, as he is extremely well inclined to support Government, notwithstanding the powerful drawback he has to divert him from it in his brother-in-law the Duke of Bolton, and he (I will be answerable for it even to the King himself) will have no influence on Drummond if Mr. Grenville will take the least pains to prevent it, for I know him to be a most honest worthy man.

Drummond adhered to the Government, and in April 1764 he, Fludyer, and their American partner Moses Franks were awarded the contract.[3] In July 1764 Drummond, in partnership with Fludyer and Anthony Bacon secured a 30 years lease of 'all the coals on Cape Breton Island'[4] and in 1767 a large land grant for himself in St. John's Island.[5]

On the formation of the Rockingham Administration, George Colebrooke, asked by Newcastle 'if there was anything upon the change of ministry which occurred to him to have', wrote, 15 July 1765:[6]

> Now, my Lord, you will be pleased to observe that Mr. Drummond is brother-in-law to the Duke of Bolton, and though Sir Samuel Fludyer has no pretension to be well considered by the present Administration, yet Mr. Drummond I doubt not will have the protection of the noble Duke above mentioned, who will expect to see him continued in this thing, or that he should be considered in something else . . . If Mr. Drummond is to be provided for, or in other words, the Duke of Bolton will be satisfied with Mr. Drummond's removal to something else, I shall be very well pleased to return again to my place and stand contractor again with Mr. Franks.

Cancellation of Fludyer's and Drummond's contract did not take effect until July 1766, when, Colebrooke having withdrawn, the new victualling contract was awarded to Nesbitt, Drummond and Franks.[7]

Drummond, from his connexion with Bolton, was listed 'pro' by Rockingham, July 1765, and did not vote against the repeal of the Stamp Act. Next he adhered to the Chatham Administration; and received in November 1767 an additional contract for victualling the troops in Illinois.[8] Returned at the general election on Bolton's interest for both Lymington and St. Ives, he chose to sit for St. Ives. He supported the Grafton Administration on Wilkes and the Middlesex election.

On 20 Nov. 1770 the Treasury gave Nesbitt, Drummond and Franks 12 months' notice of the termination of their Illinois contract, although their terms were no higher than those of 'the merchants of the country'.[9] Drummond apparently turned to other American enterprises,[10] but continued to support North's Administration.

Although he had suffered reverses in business by the loss of his army contracts and, as a partner in the Bank of Ayr, in the crash of 1772, his financial standing was not seriously affected. In 1775 Thomas Coutts the banker, having dissolved his partnership with his brother James, took Drummond into the business. He wrote 24 Aug. 1775 to his friend Colonel J. W. Crawfurd of Crawfurdland:[11]

> I am so teased about taking a partner that I have concluded with Mr. Adam Drummond . . . He is to live in the house in the Strand. I could not have the benefit of my brother's advice . . . but I wished, if I could, to find a man who I thought might prove agreeable to him. Drummond is his old acquaintance and a good humoured man, and I hope will continue to live in friendship with him.

To Lord Stair, Coutts was more explicit:[12]

> I felt so fearful of the dissipated manners of the young people of the present age, that I believe I shall be thought to have gone to the other extreme in taking Mr. Adam Drummond the member for St. Ives, but I could only choose from among such as offered and the objections to him . . . were not so capital as to any of the others . . . His being in the Ayr Bank was an objective [sic], though in the way their affairs are settled, and Mr. Drummond having got from the Dukes of Buccleuch and Queensberry the most ample relief they could give for all consequences, I got over the difficulty. Besides on six months notice I may part with him if necessary.

In Parliament Drummond supported North's American policy and spoke on 22 Mar. 1775 against Burke's conciliation motion.[13] In 1776 he, Nesbitt and Franks were given a contract for victualling 12,000 troops in America.[14] Opposed to Bolton in politics, he vacated his St. Ives seat, 11 Dec. 1778, and was returned on 11 Jan. 1779 for Aberdeen Burghs with Government support.

In 1780 Thomas Coutts asked for Drummond's

resignation. He wrote to Col. Crawfurd, 24 June 1780:[15]

> I have thought it expedient on account of Mr. Drummond being a partner in the Ayr Bank that he should retire from my house and partnership, which he has accordingly done. It is not proper that any partner in a banker's shop should in any shape be liable to payments which he cannot answer on demand . . . We are perfectly in good friendship.

Drummond remained with North to the end, and voted with him against Shelburne's peace preliminaries, 18 Feb. 1783. He voted for Fox's East India bill but was among those early won over to the Pitt Administration.[16]

Robinson, in his electoral survey of 1784, wrote of Aberdeen Burghs:[17]

> If Mr. Adam Drummond should come in again he would be *pro* it is apprehended. His attachment to Lord North made him go for the East India bill though averse to it.

When it became obvious that Drummond would not prevail against the Opposition candidate, Sir David Carnegie, Robinson listed him among the Pittites who might 'probably choose to come in upon purchase',[18] and he was returned for Shaftesbury.

He died 17 June 1786.

[1] Namier, *Structure*, 51–53. [2] *Jenkinson Pprs.* 239–40. [3] T54/39, pp. 273–6. [4] *Bd. Trade Jnl. 1764–7*, p. 50; *APC Col. Unbound Pprs.* 10 July 1764; ibid. *1745–6*, p. 661. [5] *APC Col. 1766–83*, p. 63. [6] Add. 32967, ff. 434–6. [7] T29/38, p. 75. [8] T29/39, p. 28. [9] T29/40, pp. 414–15. [10] *Bd. Trade Jnl. 1768–75*, p. 288. [11] E. H. Coleridge, *Life of Thomas Coutts*, i. 75. [12] Ibid. 77. [13] Fortescue, iii. 188. [14] T29/45, pp. 30–32. [15] *Life of Coutts*, i. 131. [16] Laprade, 54. [17] Ibid. 98. [18] Ibid. 124, 127, 128.

E.H.-G.

**DRUMMOND, Hon. Henry** (1730–95), of Charing Cross, London, and The Grange, Hants.

WENDOVER 24 Dec. 1774–1780
MIDHURST 1780–1790

*b.* 1730, 4th surv. s. of William, 4th Visct. Strathallan [S], by Margaret, da. of William Murray, 2nd Lord Nairne [S]. *m.* 21 Mar. 1761, Elizabeth, da. of Hon. Charles Compton (q.v.), 1s. 1da.

In 1744 Lord Strathallan sent his younger sons Robert and Henry as apprentices to his brother Andrew Drummond the London banker.[1] In 1746 Strathallan was killed at Culloden on the rebel side, and was declared attainted. On suspicion of Jacobitism the Government temporarily closed the bank, but Andrew Drummond vindicated his loyalty. At the bank Henry handled a considerable amount of American business, acting in 1763 as financial agent for New Jersey.[2] In 1759 he became army agent for the 42nd and 46th Foot (commanded by his Murray relatives), and by 1761 for the 87th Regiment (Robert Murray Keith) and the 89th (Staats Long Morris). In 1765 he entered into partnership

with Richard Cox, and, the firm having acquired a number of Calcraft's agencies, by 1771 had 18 regiments on their books.

In 1770 he succeeded his cousin John Drummond (q.v.) as partner of Thomas Harley in the contract for army remittances to North America;[3] and in 1772, when John's health failed, Robert persuaded his brother Henry to give up his army agency business and return to the bank as third partner.[4] During the financial crisis of 1772–3, although the Drummonds had set on foot a subscription of £100,000 to support the credit of Sir George Colebrooke, they were not affected by his bankruptcy but, 'able to stand the call of half the world', emerged with enhanced prestige.[5]

Henry Drummond was a member of an intimate social group, known as 'The Gang', which included Anthony Chamier, Lord Frederick Campbell, Thomas Bradshaw, Rigby, Thomas Harley, Sir John Sebright, William Amherst, and R. M. Keith. Drummond, who looked after Keith's financial affairs, wrote to him, 18 Oct. 1774:[6]

> We had a busy time lately by the dissolving of Parliament . . . I . . . tried to keep up a family interest at Northampton where I offered to have paid Lord Northampton's debts amounting to about £3,000 and would have given the town as far as £1000 more towards paving their town and some public work, but would not give a guinea to individuals . . . I . . . told them I never should think a family interest worth preserving that was to be bought by money . . . found it would not do without money, therefore gave it up immediately . . . Things at present bear but a gloomy aspect with regard to North America . . . I daresay it will all come right but it is disagreeable in the operation.

In December 1774 Drummond purchased a seat at Wendover from Lord Verney. An intimate friend of Lord Suffolk, he consistently supported North's Administration, and on 3 Mar. 1775 wrote to Keith:[7] 'I think things look very favourable for our settling matters with America . . . Lord North and his coadjutors have infinite merit if they bring it about.' But by 1777 he had become disillusioned. His business relations with North were strained. In June 1777 the Treasury gave Drummond and Harley 12 months' notice of the termination of their contract.[8] Moreover Keith, during his visit home 1775–6, had lent to North, on Drummond's advice, a considerable part of his small fortune, repayment of which North repeatedly deferred. Drummond wrote to Keith, 20 Feb. 1778:[9]

> Yesterday I spoke to his Lordship, when he assured me he considered your business as an obligation that he was bound to pay . . . Although it is not the most agreeable thing to be constantly boring a great man . . . I shall continue to do it till I procure payment of the principal and interest . . . I have no heart to write

to you about politics, we are not only shamefully beat by the surrender of Burgoyne, but the panic has I think seized us here and we are now undoing . . . by giving up taxation, the very object of the war and . . . inviting a French war rather than avoiding it by the pusillanimity of our parliamentary conduct.

And again, 3 Apr. 1778:[10]

The despair of the country with *all ranks of men* has been such . . . that exceed all belief . . . Stocks have sunk to a price unknown in this country . . . want of confidence and opinion has produced the whole; . . . there is nothing so dangerous for a Government as to be wavering . . . How all this is to end God knows . . . some change of consequence must take place.

In June 1778 Harley and Drummond secured a renewal of their contract for North America, and in August an extension to the West Indies, if required.[11] To Keith, Drummond wrote, 2 Apr. 1779:[12]

I had a full and explicit conversation with the Great Man upon the old subject of the debt which he is indebted to *us*, for I will still keep him to that ground that it is an affair between *us* and *him*, and I must own, provoked and angry as I have been with him . . . he did show an honest and I think sincere feeling for the great loss you have sustained and once more assured me some steps would be *immediately taken* for the payment of the money.

Still, he did not trust even specific promises by North concerning repayment till assured by 'the confidential secretary' that he could depend on its being done.

At the general election of 1780 Drummond purchased a seat at Midhurst 'at Lord North's recommendation'.[13] To cover the expenses of that general election North, on 7 Dec. 1780, by the King's orders, borrowed from Drummonds' £30,000, at 5 per cent, and gave them a promissory note which the King had seen and approved.[14] But after the fall of the North Administration the King at first repudiated responsibility for all but £13,000 of this sum; in the end the King repaid the debt.[15]

Rigby wrote to Keith, 21 Jan. 1781:[16]

I live much and in great cordiality with the Drummonds who are the best people in the world. I tell Bob he is of the party I describe, an opposition to the Opposition, which is his case. Harry is a better courtier, for he has one of the best contracts that ever man had and I rejoice that it is so.

Profitable it may have been, but at times the two partners felt uneasy when they had to advance money to the Government; still, they retained the contract till the end of the war.

The Drummonds were also very big subscribers to Government loans, but how much they subscribed for themselves and how much for clients cannot be established. When on 26 Mar. 1781 Savile made a motion concerning the recent loan, its terms

and distribution, George Byng stated that while 'Mr. Drummond's house is put down for £84,000' (unexpectedly little seeing their credit character), subscriptions in the names of their clerks—the list was read out by him—'stood to the amount of £438,000'.[17]

Drummond supported North till his fall, voting in every division for which a list is extant; voted with North against Shelburne's peace preliminaries, 18 Feb. 1783; but was absent from the divisions on Fox's East India bill. Friendly with Henry Dundas,[18] (whose daughter Anne married his son in 1786), Drummond may well have followed his lead in politics, and by March 1784 was listed among Pitt's supporters. Re-elected for Midhurst, he henceforth followed Pitt. No speech by Drummond is recorded.

He died 24 June 1795.

[1] Strathallan to Robert, 12 Jan. 1745, Drummond's Bank mss. [2] *N.J. Archives 1757-67*, p. 445; *Jnl. N.J. Gov. and Council 1769-75*, p. 57. [3] T54/41/390-3. [4] Ex. inf. Drummond's Bank. [5] *Mems. and Corresp. R. M. Keith*, i. 364, 402; Add. 35505, f. 127. [6] Add. 35508, f. 69. [7] Add. 35509, f. 1. [8] T 29/46/193. [9] Add. 35513, f. 108. [10] Ibid. f. 225. [11] T 29/47/216, 296. [12] Add. 35516, f. 79. [13] Fortescue, v. 480. [14] Laprade, 55-56; Fortescue, v. 472, 481; vi. 6-7. [15] Fortescue, vi. 27; North to Robinson, 3 Sept. 1782, the King to Robinson, 19 Aug., 24 Oct. 1784, Abergavenny mss. [16] *Keith Mems.* 120-1. [17] Debrett, ii. 329. [18] Richard Atkinson to John Robinson, 14 Mar. 1783, 4 Sept. 1783, Abergavenny mss.

E.H.-G.

**DRUMMOND, John** (1723-74), of Stanmore, Mdx.

THETFORD 1768-25 July 1774

*b.* 27 April 1723, o.s. of Andrew Drummond, banker, of Charing Cross and Stanmore by Isabella, da. of Alexander Strachan, London-Scottish merchant; cos. of Henry Drummond (q.v.). *educ.* Westminster 1735. *m.* 22 Dec. 1744, Charlotte, da. of Lord William Beauclerk by Lady Diana de Vere, da. and h. of Aubrey, 20th and last Earl of Oxford, 2s. 2da. *suc.* fa. 2 Feb. 1769.

Director, Sun Fire Office 1763-*d.*

Drummond's marriage into the St. Albans family, of which his father was extremely proud, brought increased business to Drummonds' bank and important political connexions. 'A man of much parts and address', he made in 1764 a bid to enter Parliament for Hereford, counting upon the support of his wife's Beauclerk uncles, Lord Vere and Lord James, bishop of Hereford, and of the Earl of Oxford with whose brother Thomas Harley he was associated in business. Although Oxford had 'voluntarily assured . . . Mr. Drummond that he would assist him in everything in his power', he unexpectedly withdrew his support; on this the St. Albans family abandoned the contest and in January 1764 Lord Vere informed Grenville of 'Mr. Drummond's intention not to stand at Hereford'.[1]

In March 1767 he and Sir Samuel Fludyer (q.v.)

secured the contract for remitting money to the army in America.[2] On Fludyer's death in 1768, Thomas Harley became joint contractor with Drummond who shortly afterwards, on succeeding his father as head of the bank, resigned in favour of his cousin Henry (q.v.).[3]

Returned in 1768 for Grafton's borough of Thetford, he consistently supported the Grafton and North Administrations on Wilkes and the Middlesex election, was listed 'pro, present' on the royal marriage bill, March 1772, but did not vote on Grenville's Act 25 Feb. 1774. There is no record of his having spoken in the House. He died at Spa 25 July 1774.

[1] Grenville mss (JM). [2] T29/38/285; T54/40/204-6. [3] T54/41/390-2.

E.H.-G.

## DRUMMOND, John (1754–1835), of Lennoch and Megginch, Perth.

SHAFTESBURY 5 July 1786–1790

b. 1754, 1st s. of Colin Drummond by Katherine, da. of Robert Oliphant of Rossie, Perth. educ. Westminster 1765. m. 20 July 1788, Lady Susan Fane, da. of John, 9th Earl of Westmorland, 1s. 1da. suc. uncle Adam Drummond (q.v.) in the Lennoch and Megginch estates 17 June 1786.

As a youth John Drummond went to Canada where his father had settled in 1765, as distributor of stamps and Quebec agent for Fludyer, Adam Drummond and Franks, contractors for victualling the troops in North America.[1] In 1768 Colin Drummond was appointed a member of the Quebec council, and was commissary general and paymaster to the forces in Canada until his death in 1776. His son John succeeded him on the council and was appointed a deputy commissary and paymaster.[2]

In August 1779 Drummond obtained leave of absence, and in April 1781 resigned his office as deputy commissary, but seems to have remained deputy paymaster until June 1782.[3]

On the death of his uncle Adam Drummond, he succeeded him as Member for Shaftesbury, and voted with Administration to the end of the Parliament. He is not known to have spoken in the House. He stood for Perthshire in 1790 but was defeated.

Apparently in financial difficulties, he sold the Lennoch estate shortly after his succession, and in 1795 made over Megginch to his brother Robert, a captain in the East India Company marine service. He died 13 May 1835.

[1] John Watts Letter Bk. (N.Y. Hist. Soc. Coll.), 373, 376-7; Gage Corresp. ii. 266, 418. [2] Canadian Archives. Docs. relating to Constitutional Hist. 1759-91, i. 301, 395, 396, 401; ii. 595, 697; Bd. Trade Jnl. 1776-82, pp. 46-47. [3] T29/49/375; T29/57/275; T52/69/329; Laprade, 37.

E.H.-G.

## DUCKETT, Thomas (1713–1766), of Hartham, Wilts.

CALNE 1754—June 1757, 1761–Mar. 1766

b. 10 Feb. 1713, 2nd s. of George Duckett, M.P. for Calne, by Grace, da. and h. of Thomas Skinner of Dewlish, Dorset. m. 31 Mar. 1765, Miss Farrier of Haverfordwest, s.p.

The Duckett family owned the manor of Calne and Calstone, and eight of their name represented the borough between 1584 and 1766. Thomas Duckett was a merchant trading to Portugal, and appears in London commercial directories at various addresses, 1752–64. He was returned unopposed in 1754, and politically connected himself with Lord Sandwich who reported to Newcastle, 24 Dec. 1755, that he had learnt from Robert Jones (q.v.) that Duckett had 'attended and voted in every question this sessions in support of the measures of the Government'. Duckett 'was a great sufferer' in the Lisbon earthquake of that year,[1] which possibly caused him in June 1757 to vacate his seat in Parliament, then required by the Government, against a secret service pension of £500 p.a. 'till an office of that value can be found for him'.[2] Meantime the question of Duckett's selling Calne manor had arisen. 'Mr. Duckett', wrote John Bull, the local election manager,[3] to Lord Shelburne, 30 Oct. 1756, 'had an uncle prepossessed with a mistaken notion that his being elected Member for Calne was expensive to him, and therefore often desired he would sell his manor here in order to prevent his having any connection with his borough, and nothing that Mr. Duckett could say, could undeceive him.' The uncle died lately, 'and has given him his estate about £600 p.a. after his widow, upon condition he'll sell this manor, otherwise he has given it to his next brother'. The manor secured to its owners 'a natural interest in this borough . . . near half the burgesses being their tenants'. 'Whether Mr. Duckett is obliged to sell immediately, or stay till his aunt's death, I don't know . . . though if a good purchaser offered, I believe he would do it immediately.'[4] The matter was discussed, but nothing came of it; and in 1761 Duckett was determined to stand again for Parliament. Henry Fox wrote to Lord Fitzmaurice, 24 Jan. 1761:

Mr. Duckett has been with me. He has so often and so lately declared to the electors of Calne that he will stand, that he shall be looked upon as a very fickle and silly man if he should not. But if a year or two hence I make any proposal to him he shall be very glad to resign to any friend of yours and mine; or, if ever he thinks of it himself we shall have the refusal. This was all I could get out of him.

And Sandwich wrote to Newcastle, 29 Jan.: 'I have sounded Mr. D. as to his present political creed', and found him disposed 'to concur in everything that can support or strengthen your Administration'.[5] In Bute's list of 1761 Duckett is marked 'Government'; he is not in Fox's list of Members favourable to the peace preliminaries in December 1762; but does not appear in any minority list either; is marked by Jenkinson in the autumn of 1763 as 'pro', and by Rockingham in the summer of 1765 as 'contra'; but by that time he was hardly capable of attending Parliament. There is no record of his having spoken in the House.

In September 1762 the question of purchasing Duckett's estate reappears in Bull's letters to Shelburne; in February–March 1763 an agreement was concluded, the price being £28,637. On 5 Mar. 1764 Bull suggested to Shelburne to examine whether in view 'of the precariousness of Mr. Duckett's health', it might not be advisable for him to inform his friends at Calne that he had purchased Duckett's estate, and hoped they would give him 'leave to recommend a gentleman upon that interest'. But the purchase does not seem to have been as yet completed. On 31 Mar. 1765 Duckett married a girl of 20; the next day Bull paid them a visit; and found it difficult to form a judgment of Duckett's mental condition as he had 'so far lost his speech by the palsy in his tongue and mouth, that nobody but those about him know what he says'. If the marriage settlement affected Shelburne's purchase, and her concurrence is required, 'the completion of that affair must be postponed till she's of age'. And on 10 Feb. 1766, Bull wrote to Shelburne who wished to return John Calcraft (q.v.) in Duckett's place:

> In regard to Mr. Duckett his affairs are at present so circumstanced, that if he quits his seat in Parliament, he is sure to be in a gaol in a week afterwards, unless he had a few thousands to answer some of his voracious creditors, which is not in his power to advance till he receives his purchase money of your Lordship; therefore I can't think of proposing to him to vacate his seat in Parliament till the affair with your Lordship is completed, or a further sum *advanced* sufficient to make his creditors easy.

Duckett died in March 1766. His executors refused at first to complete the sale; 'so infirm that he could not express himself in correct words', he was understood to have denied having sold Calne or having got married;[6] but his brother William stepped in and the sale was soon afterwards concluded.

[1] See 'Mr. Bowman's Abstract and Observations' in Sir G. Duckett's *Duchetiana*, 66. [2] W. Pitt to Newcastle, 26 June 1757, Add. 32871, f. 406; for payments of that pension see Namier, *Structure*, and 'Thomas Duckett and Daniel Bull', *Wilts. Arch. Mag.* xliv. 2. [3] About him see Namier, *Structure*, 146. [4] Lansdowne mss. [5] Add. 32918, f. 110. [6] See memo. by Sir George (Jackson) Duckett (q.v.) in *Duchetiana*, 65–66.

L.B.N.

DUCKETT, *see also* JACKSON, George

DUFF, Hon. Arthur (1743–1805), of Orton, Elgin.

ELGINSHIRE   1774–Mar. 1779

> *b.* 1743, 5th surv. s. of William Duff, M.P., 1st Earl Fife [I], and bro. of James, 2nd Earl (q.v.). *educ.* St. Andrews Univ. 1757; Glasgow Univ. 1759; adv. 1764; Leyden 1769. *unm.*   *suc.* fa. in the Orton estate 1763.
> Comptroller of Excise in Scotland Apr. 1779–1804.

On his father's death, Duff's brother Lord Fife tried without success to obtain for him a place at court in the household of Prince William.[1] Thereafter Arthur seems to have made little effort to distinguish himself at the Scottish bar, but concerned himself mainly with farming and the legal and electoral affairs of the family.

When his cousin James Grant (q.v.) decided not to contest Elginshire at the general election of 1768, Lord Fife wrote to Grenville, 20 Oct. 1767:[2]

> Mr. Grant, the Member for Murray . . . without consulting me put up his uncle [Francis Grant] for the county, and in my absence secured several votes that have always gone with me; my brother upon that declared himself a candidate; upon my return to the country I found myself obliged to support my brother in opposition to the other; we have a good chance to carry the election . . . at any rate they have put an end to their interest afterwards, for I can certainly make the county, it could not have been in doubt at present had they not gained advantage by unhandsome surprise.

The brother was apparently George, but it seems that Arthur had been considered.[3] Fife reported to Grenville, 28 Apr. 1768:[4] 'My brother . . . is beat, owing to his being too late in starting and all the power of [the] present Administration exerted against him.'

After his return from Leyden in 1769, Duff as prospective candidate took a leading part in the campaign against the Grants in Elgin and in Banff and their allies the Gordons in Aberdeenshire. He was praeses of the 1772 Michaelmas head court of Elgin, whose legality was established when the House of Lords reversed the decision of the court of session favouring a rival meeting dominated by the Grants.[5] After the 1773 head court, Admiral Robert Duff congratulated Fife on having 'defeated the combination of Gordons, Grants and Gardens with all their following—truly a great victory'.[6] At the general election, after a 'very near run contest',[7] Duff was returned, and in Parliament for a time followed his brother's lead. He voted with the Opposition on Wilkes, 22 Feb. 1775, and looked forward to 'some fun from Wilkes . . . and the Liberty Boys in the streets'.[8]

Assiduous in attending the House, he reported to his mother by almost every post on personal and political affairs. Nevertheless Fife, censorious of the drinking habits which undermined his health, had little hesitation in proposing in 1776 to sacrifice Arthur's parliamentary career to his own political schemes for a compromise with the Gordons. As a result, both Arthur and his mother quarrelled with 'His Majesty of Fife', who on 7 Feb. 1777 wrote from London to his factor, W. Rose: 'I have been making a great many visits—first to the Duke and Duchess of Gordon . . . I did not see them. Mr. Arthur Duff did me the honour to pass me without taking notice, so I did put no stop in his way, and yet, though I shall never probably wish him in my company, I would do him good.'[9]

Having now nothing to lose, Duff, irrespective of his brother's views, continued to support North. On a rumour that a French war would result in a change of Administration he wrote to his mother, 19 Feb. 1778:[10]

I have so good an opinion of Lord North's integrity that I should most sincerely regret his loss. But I will not allow myself to believe it, although I confess my spirits are a few *pegs* down upon the occasion.

Lord Fife, after voting for the Opposition motion to tax all places above a certain value, wrote to Rose 10 Mar. 1778:[11] 'I was in a majority 100 to 85. Lord North and all the ministry in the minority . . . Arthur voted against, in order I suppose to do him honour.'

Although Fife's negotiations with the Gordons and Grants were now well advanced, Duff still refused to co-operate. On 10 Mar. Fife informed Rose that he had arranged a conference with the Duke of Gordon:

I fancy it will land in my taking peace and quiet in Banffshire and giving the interest of the other counties. Arthur to be provided in something not under £500 a year. *What a poor ungrateful fellow it is and a burden and drawback on me, doing nothing for himself.*

While his fate was being decided Duff continued to support Administration through many exhausting night sittings, but is not known to have spoken. In December 1778 he wrote to his mother:

The present minority would be in every sense contemptible but that their abandoned principles rouses other emotions; many of them do not scruple to avow that they wish to see the country a province to France to mark the imbecility of the present Administration and make the nation regret when too late that they had not been called into power. From such patriots— Good Lord deliver us.[12]

On 29 Mar. Fife wrote to Rose:

It is settled that my brother Arthur vacates his seat and he is to have the office of comptroller of the Excise. Lord William Gordon offers himself as candidate for Moray. I have agreed to give him my vote and interest.

The brothers were now apparently reconciled. Fife wrote to Rose, 1 Apr.:

Can you suppose that I felt a little in making the motion for a new writ for the county of Elgin in room of the Hon. Arthur Duff, steward of his Majesty's manor of East Hendred . . . Considering the trouble I had to bring him in, I felt a little at being the engine to turn him out. Arthur seems very sensible of the trouble I have taken for him, but so was he before.[13]

Duff never attempted to re-enter Parliament but spent the rest of his life in Scotland, living with his mother at Rothiemay until her death in 1788, and thereafter at Orton. The beloved bachelor uncle of numerous nephews and nieces, adviser and mediator in family crises and disputes, he died 2 June 1805, lamented by Lord Fife as his 'favourite brother'.

[1] G. Grenville to Fife, 24 Nov. 1764, Grenville letter bk. [2] Grenville mss (JM). [3] If a letter from Arthur to Fife of 27 Aug. refers to this year: A. & H. Tayler, *Book of the Duffs*, i. 159. [4] Grenville mss (JM). [5] *Morayshire M.P.s*, 27; Alex. Mackenzie to Sir Roderick Mackenzie, 24 Feb. 1773, Add. 39190, f. 193; *LJ*, i, 3, 11, 31 Mar., 27 May, 8 June 1773. [6] *Morayshire M.P.s*, 27. [7] Laprade, 6. 20. [8] *Book of the Duffs*, i. 160. [9] A. & H. Tayler, *Ld. Fife & his Factor*, 97, 99, 123. [10] *Book of the Duffs*, i. 161. [11] *Ld. Fife & his Factor*, 106. [12] *Book of the Duffs*, i. 162, 163. [13] *Ld. Fife & his Factor*, 113, 114.

E.H.-G.

**DUFF, Hon. James** (1729–1809), of Duff House, Banff. and Mar Lodge, Aberdeen.

BANFFSHIRE 1754–1784
ELGINSHIRE 1784–1790

*b.* 28 Sept. 1729, 1st surv. s. of William Duff, M.P., of Braco, 1st Baron Braco [I] and 1st Earl Fife [I], by his 2nd w. Jean, da. of Sir James Grant, 6th Bt., of Grant and sis. of Ludovick and Francis Grant (qq.v.). *educ.* St. Andrews Univ.; Grand Tour. *m.* 4 June 1759, Lady Dorothea Sinclair (sep. 1771), da. and h. of Alexander, 9th Earl of Caithness [S], *s.p.* Styled Visct. MacDuff 1759–63; *suc.* fa. as 2nd Earl Fife [I] 30 Sept. 1763; *cr.* Baron Duff of Fife [GB] 5 July 1790. Ld. lt. Banff 1795–*d.*

Duff's father, head of a family which by trade and money-lending had acquired great wealth and property in the shires of Banff, Elgin, and Aberdeen, was M.P. for Banffshire 1727–34 and was created by Walpole an Irish peer in 1735. James, having become his father's heir in March 1753, stood for Banffshire at the general election of 1754 when his uncle, Col. James Abercrombie, the sitting Member and Argyll's friend, was obliged to withdraw.

Listed by Dupplin among 'Whigs—doubtful', Duff soon declared himself. At the Elgin Burghs by-election in autumn 1754, he agreed to transfer the Duff interest from Abercrombie to Andrew Mitchell, Newcastle's protégé,[1] requesting in return the office of sheriff of Banff for David Ross.[2] 'It is the first favour I have asked since I came into Parliament, and I am in such a way in the world as to have little or no occasion to trouble your Grace with demands.'[3]

Newcastle had already promised it to Lord Findlater for George Cockburn, but anxious to gain Duff, 'a very considerable man and well worth obliging',[4] insisted that Findlater should withdraw his nomination. Findlater, bitterly offended,[5] protested to Hardwicke:[6]

> Braco and his son saying they will ask nothing more, nobody that knows them can believe . . . Although it is very right to be civil to new converts, I cannot think it for the public good to please them at the expense of old firm friends.

The 'new convert' did not long remain faithful. In May 1755 he set off on an extensive European tour[7] and shortly after his return joined Pitt and the Grenvilles in opposition. As a result Newcastle deprived Ross of the sheriffship and gave it to Cockburn in October 1756.[8] On the formation of the Devonshire-Pitt Administration in November, Duff jubilantly reported to his father that Pitt, unsolicited, had offered to recommend Braco for an Irish earldom.[9] He was disappointed both in this and in his hopes of securing Cockburn's dismissal. He voted 2 May 1757 against Newcastle over Minorca,[10] and remained personally attached to the Grenvilles, who under the united Administration importuned Newcastle in 1758 to obtain the Irish earldom. Bedford, the lord lieutenant, very reluctantly agreed to recommend it to the King, but the affair hung fire until March 1759, when Newcastle 'with great difficulty procured his Majesty's consent'.[11]

Shortly afterwards Duff, now Viscount MacDuff, married an heiress with £40,000, but whose claims to the estates and earldom of Caithness were finally rejected in 1767.

Over the Scottish militia question he avoided committing himself; did not reach London until early April 1760, and although he did not vote against the bill, was clearly anxious not to offend Newcastle, whose support he sought for the candidature of his brother-in-law Alexander Duff of Hatton in Aberdeenshire.[12] Shortly afterwards he applied to Newcastle, without success, for a place as lord of the bedchamber to the young Duke of York, with whom he was now on intimate terms.[13]

Returned unopposed in 1761, MacDuff attached himself to Grenville and henceforth remained his faithful supporter. On succeeding to the earldom, Fife increased his pretensions, lived magnificently, purchased a mansion in Whitehall, and from his overweening sense of his own importance was nicknamed by his brothers 'His Majesty of Fife'. In the summer of 1764 he violently protested to Grenville against the 'affront' his interest had suffered by James Stuart Mackenzie's appointment of a successor to Cockburn as sheriff of Banff, attributing it

to malice against Grenville's friends.[14] Furiously angry, Grenville, assuming that the affair was a continuation of the Fife-Findlater feud, strongly reprimanded Mackenzie for favouring Findlater and attacking Fife, a constant Government supporter, and his personal friend. Having promised Fife that he 'would do his utmost' to cancel the appointment, Grenville was disconcerted to find that there was no feud with Findlater and little evidence of Mackenzie's animosity. He was obliged to accept Mackenzie's explanation of his nomination of John Erskine, 'a neutral man', and acknowledged his mistake. 'But let me still wish that this unlucky appointment, which may very possibly throw an independent man into opposition, had never happened.' Fife had to accept the *fait accompli* but, bitterly resentful, wrote to Grenville, 4 Aug. 1764:

> Mr. Mackenzie may put it on any footing he please . . . Mr. Cockburn, the former sheriff, was put in here by the Duke of Newcastle at a time when my conduct in Parliament and my *friends*' was in opposition to his Grace. I did not *then* complain, it was rather doing me an honour for his Grace to mark me out in so public a manner. Mr. Erskine's appointment is just in the same style.

In September, when Erskine, pursued by Fife's hostility, applied for another place, Fife immediately nominated as sheriff his brother-in-law Keith Urquhart, to whose appointment Mackenzie, under extreme pressure from Grenville, was eventually induced to withdraw his objections.[15]

Confirmed in his attachment, Fife lost no opportunity of fanning Grenville's jealousy of Bute and Mackenzie.[16] In March he pressed Grenville to secure for his brother George the office of secretary to the Order of the Thistle; Grenville at once sought out Mackenzie who, after long argument, would promise only to submit Duff's name to the King with those of other competitors. When the King, disregarding Grenville's personal recommendation, appointed Bute's friend, Sir Harry Erskine, Grenville hotly argued Duff's claims in 'a very improper and passionate conversation' with the King, but failed to alter his decision.[17] Grenville's resentment eventually forced Mackenzie's dismissal in June, but before the political crisis Fife had gone abroad on a prolonged European tour. Grenville, disconcerted by his proposal to winter in Paris, wrote to him on 22 Nov. 1765:[18]

> I had depended upon . . . having your . . . assistance . . . in a crisis . . . from which I cannot think it right, for your own sake, that you should be absent . . . As you tell me . . . that if you foresaw anything likely to come before the public in which I am particularly interested, you would come to take part in it, I cannot conceal from you that . . . it is intended to attack . . . almost every public measure which I promoted during

the two former sessions and which I look upon myself as interested . . . to support to the utmost of my power.

Fife, however, remained abroad[19] and was absent from the Stamp Act debates. He voted against the Chatham Administration on the land tax, 27 Feb. 1767, and against printing the East India Company's papers.[20]

In the new Parliament Fife's attitude over Wilkes was at first uncertain; on 2 Feb. 1769 he voted with the Opposition, the following day with Administration,[21] but from March followed Grenville's lead, and voted with the Opposition. After Grenville's death in 1770, he remained uncommitted until 1771 when with other Grenvillites he adhered to North. In Spring 1772 he supported Government on the royal marriage bill; but was against them on the naval captains' petition, 9 Feb. 1773. Increasingly uneasy about the American situation and relations with France, he wrote to his factor, William Rose, 20 Apr. 1773: 'In the present times of low credit, avert war, say I. Stock jobbers, Jews, and contractors make by that, but you and I are out of pocket.' Always a strong supporter of Grenville's Election Act, he voted with the Opposition on 25 Feb. 1774 for its continuance, but at the end of the Parliament was counted by Robinson as a Government supporter.[22]

At the general election he secured his own return for Banffshire and that of his brother Arthur for Elginshire against strong opposition. He supported North in 'asserting the sovereignty of this country over America',[23] but on Wilkes again voted with the Opposition on 22 Feb. 1775. His application for the Order of the Thistle was firmly rejected by the King, 21 Apr. 1775, on the ground that as an Irish peer, 'his obtaining it would give the noblemen of Scotland real cause of displeasure'.[24] Although resenting North's attitude to the abortive Scottish militia bill in 1776,[25] he remained pro Administration but by 1778 had become highly critical of the conduct of the American war. On the appointment of the conciliation commission he wrote to Rose, 24 Feb. 1778:[26]

I pray God that punishment may fall on the heads of those who have made so bad a use of the great exerted force of this country and misspent so much blood and treasure . . . I fear we are even too late with this humiliating offer as I daresay France is beforehand with us.

In March 1778 he voted against the ministry in support of a tax on places, but on 19 Apr. 1779 against the Opposition motion to remove his friend Sandwich. But in the new session, he declined North's request to attend before Christmas, and next voted with the Opposition on pensions, econo-

nomical reform, and the abolition of the Board of Trade (21 Feb., 8 and 13 Mar. 1780). Absent from the division of 6 Apr. on Dunning's motion (probably out of respect for the King), he voted with Administration on the prorogation, 24 Apr.; but nevertheless at the end of the Parliament was counted 'contra' by Robinson.

In the new Parliament Fife was absent as usual from the autumn session; voted 20 Feb. 1782 with the Opposition on the censure of the Admiralty; with Administration, 22 Feb., on Conway's motion against the war; but again with Opposition in the division on 27 Feb.; attended (1 Mar.) the presentation of the Commons Address for peace, and remained hostile to North until his fall.

In May Fife, hearing that 'in these troublesome times . . . the Irish may dispute the rights of peers that do not take their seats', went to Dublin, was 'duly seated', left for Scotland in June, and never visited Ireland again.

He supported the Shelburne Administration, rejoiced at the prospects of peace, but was deeply concerned, particularly after the mutiny of the Atholl Highlanders, about the possible effects of unemployment following demobilization. Dreading disturbances in the Highland counties, he submitted proposals to Shelburne, Conway, and later to Dundas.[27]

After the division on the peace preliminaries, 18 Feb., he wrote to Rose:

I was in the minority with the ministers . . . I have no connexion with them, but I love peace; . . . abuse came but ill from a set of men who has brought the bad peace on us, for I think whatever is humiliating in it, is owing to the war-makers and not to the peace-makers.

Fife was an impatient observer of the negotiations for a new ministry. 'I wish to God party was at an end and that they would care for the country. I care not a twopence for either of them.' On the formation of the Coalition Administration, he wrote to Sir James Grant (q.v.): 'Thank God I am connected with no faction or party and I wish those now come in may do public service well. I have fear they won't long agree.' He voted (7 May) against Pitt's reform bill. 'I wish to God they would reform themselves and let the honest old constitution stand—the reformation within doors is more wanted. All is gambling and dissipation.'[28]

He returned with relief to Scotland, and was still at Duff House in December, when news reached him of the change of administration. Robinson wrote in December 1783:

Banffshire—Lord Fife will come in again; he is not a great attender but was formerly attached to Mr. Grenville; he varies and is uncertain without explanation and therefore he is classed doubtful, although he may be more steady. Mr. Dundas says *pro*.

In January 1784 Robinson listed him 'Hopeful. Quere if up. Absent'. When Fife remained weatherbound in Banff, organizing election campaigns, his son James, observing that he and James Wemyss were the only Scots M.P.s still absent, wrote to William Rose: 'I hope my Lord will leave you as soon as the snow will allow him. Hurry him. In these times every man ought to stand forth and take a part.' Fife did not attend until the end of February, remained until the dissolution, and then returned home. At the general election he gave up Banffshire to his son, and after a violent contest was returned for Elginshire. Back in London at the end of April he voted as a Westminster elector against Fox.[29]

Fife had no sympathy with the Opposition, admired Pitt, took pains to inform himself on his Irish propositions which he eventually supported, but voted against his reform bill, 18 Apr. 1785. Still essentially 'unconnected', he sponsored George Skene at the Aberdeenshire by-election against the Dundas-Gordon candidate, James Ferguson, and wrote to Pitt, 25 Dec. 1785:

I do not wish to put you to any trouble in supporting my friend, all I am to request is that it may be left to the free choice of the country gentlemen . . . I am sensible that the support I have given you as a minister has been of very little importance, yet it was perfectly independent.[30]

Absent from the division on Richmond's fortification plans, 27 Feb. 1786, Fife did not attend until March, when he made his only recorded speech, on settling the date of the hearing of Ferguson's petition against Skene.[31] Within a year, professing firm attachment to Pitt, he entered into negotiations with Dundas to secure peace among the rival proGovernment interests in Elgin, Banff, Aberdeenshire, and Elgin Burghs.[32]

During the debates on Hastings's impeachment, 1787 and 1788, Fife was convinced, on the evidence, of his guilt. 'I blessed God that I had not Asiatic wealth, for such a forfeit of conscience as these nabobs must feel.' But, as the trial progressed, he conceived great admiration for Hastings and 'abhorrence of the illiberal persecution which came from the managers' box'. On excellent terms with the King, he deplored the motion on the Prince of Wales's debts and wrote, 1 May 1787: 'I shall certainly support parental authority and feel a duty not to squander public money at the present time.'

'Racked by anxiety' about the King's madness, he hastened to London in December 1788 to attend the Regency debates, and support Pitt. 'God forbid that I should give a vote that did not mark my feelings for the King's right and to preserve it entire if it pleases God to recover him.' So strong was his loyalty that, when his own son took the opposite view, he insisted that he should vacate his seat, and thereafter cut off all communication with him for over four years.

On 10 Mar. 1789 Fife described his first interview with the King after his recovery:

I went to Kew yesterday . . . I saw him mount his horse . . . His eye catched me. He called out before all present, 'Lord Fife . . . I am glad to see you. Come to me.' I went forward . . . and returned my grateful thanks. He then called out, 'Lord Fife, you are no gambler, you are no rat.' I then forgot all distance betwixt King and subject, took him by the thigh, prayed the Almighty to bless him.

He retained to the end of his life the affectionate friendship of the King, who in 1790 conferred upon him a British peerage. A generous patron of the arts, Fife was essentially a countryman of spartan habits and remarkable hardihood, happiest when deer stalking in the Highlands, a considerate landlord, astute in business, but charitable to the poor. Ruthless in preserving his electoral interest, he sought neither ministerial office nor parliamentary fame.

My wishes are to support Government, and I never differ with them when I think in my mind I can support them—this is my old-fashioned way and I care not whether it meets with approbation—it gives selfsatisfaction which is one good thing.

Blind for the last nine years of his life, Fife died 24 Jan. 1809.[33]

[1] Mitchell to Newcastle, 5 Oct. 1754, Add. 32737, f. 43. [2] Duff to Newcastle, 8 Oct. 1754, ibid. f. 83. [3] Duff to Newcastle, 6 Nov. 1754, ibid. f. 292. [4] Newcastle to Argyll, 19 Oct. 1754, ibid. f. 162; and to Deskfoord, same date, f. 173. [5] Findlater to Mitchell, 29 Oct. 1754, ibid. f. 227. [6] Add. 35448, f. 224. [7] Duff to Newcastle, 10 May 1755, A. & H. Tayler, *Book of the Duffs*, 198. [8] Ld. Milton to Gilbert Elliot, 2 May ?1759, Minto mss; Duff to Grenville, 2 Aug. 1764, Grenville mss (JM). [9] *Book of the Duffs*, 170 (misdated Mar. 1759). [10] Add. 33034, f. 232. [11] *Bedford Corresp.* ii. 346, 353, 372; *Grenville Pprs.* i. 257. [12] MacDuff to H. V. Jones, 7 Apr. 1760, enclosing memorandum for Newcastle, Add. 32904, ff. 243, 245. [13] Add. 32905, f. 43. [14] The corresp. on the sheriff of Banff, 20 June–4 Aug. 1764, between Grenville, Fife, Charles Jenkinson, Stuart Mackenzie and others, is to be found in Grenville mss (JM); Grenville letter bk.; *Grenville Pprs.* ii. 382–4, 387, 388; *Jenkinson Pprs.* 309, 312; Stuart Mackenzie to Bute, 15 July 1764, Bute mss. [15] Fife to Grenville, 13 Sept., 6 Dec. 1764, Grenville mss (JM); *Jenkinson Pprs.* 334–5, 397; Grenville to Fife, 11 Oct., Grenville letter bk.; *Caldwell Pprs.* ii(1), p. 275. [16] *Grenville Pprs.* iii. 222. [17] Ibid. iii. 124–6; *Jenkinson Pprs.* 397. [18] Grenville letter bk. [19] *Walpole's Corresp. with Mme du Deffand* (Yale ed.) v. 270, 271, 286, 294; A. & H. Tayler, *Ld. Fife & his Factor*, 23–28. [20] Ibid. 40. [21] Fortescue, ii. 86. [22] *Ld. Fife & his Factor*, 70–71, 78, 81. [23] Fife to Rose, 21 and 25 Jan. 1775, ibid. 86–87. [24] Fortescue, iii. 207. [25] H. Dundas to Buccleuch, 16 Mar. 1776, Buccleuch mss. [26] *Ld. Fife & his Factor*, 105. [27] Ibid. 106, 115–16, 118, 139, 141–3, 148, 150, 158. [28] Ibid. 150, 152, 158; W. Fraser, *Chiefs of Grant*, ii. 480–1. [29] *Ld. Fife & his Factor*, 160, 161–2, 164; Laprade, 99. [30] *Ld. Fife & his Factor*, 166–7, 171, 176. [31] Debrett, xix. 411. [32] *Ld. Fife & his Factor*, 185–7; 'Fair Statement of Northern Politics' (1786), NLS, Melville mss; Dundas to T. Steele, 2 Sept. 1788, Chatham mss. [33] *Ld. Fife & his Factor*, 188, 189, 192, 196, 201, 258.

E.H.-G.

**DUFF, Sir James** (1753–1839), of Kinstair, Aberdeen.

BANFFSHIRE    1784–Dec. 1788

*b.* 1753, 1st illegit. s. of James, 2nd Earl Fife (q.v.), by Margaret Adam. *educ.* Keith acad.; Aberdeen Univ., M.A. 1771. *m.* 12 Aug. 1785, Basilia, da. of James Dawes of Rockspring, Jamaica, 1s. 3da. Kntd. 30 Apr. 1779.
Ensign 1 Ft. Gds. 1769, lt. and capt. 1775, capt. and lt.-col. 1780, col. 1790; maj.-gen. 1794; col. 50 Ft. 1798–*d.*; lt.-gen. 1801; gen. 1809.

Lord Fife was the father of three children by a Keith woman of humble origin from whom they were taken at an early age and placed under the direction of William Rose, Fife's factor. James was a handsome youth on whom his father lavished affection, making him his constant companion, purchasing his advancement in the army, and giving him a small estate in Aberdeenshire and voting qualifications in Elgin and Banff. In 1779, when Fife's friend James Harris, minister at St. Petersburg, was created K.B., Duff acted as his proxy at the installation, and for that purpose was himself knighted. His grandmother Lady Fife thereafter referred to him caustically as 'the nominal knight'.[1]

At the general election of 1784 Fife gave up his Banffshire seat to his son, and himself stood for Elginshire. From Fife's uncertain politics and Duff's connexion with the Duke of York,[2] neither Government nor Opposition was sure of their allegiance and classed both as 'doubtful'. By his marriage in the summer of 1785 to a West Indian heiress Duff acquired a sugar plantation in Jamaica, and became financially less dependent on his father.[3]

Nominated on 29 Mar. to the select committee on the Nairnshire election, he inadvertently caused a discussion on procedure by absenting himself through a misunderstanding. His apology to the House is his only recorded speech.[4] Fife, hitherto 'happy in a son who studied to exceed his wishes', differed profoundly from Duff on the Regency question. Although listed as voting with Administration in the division of 16 Dec. 1788, Duff wrote to Rose, 19 Dec.:[5]

I was never more distressed than I am at present respecting my conduct in Parliament. The Prince of Wales has sent to me, requesting I will give him my support in case of any attempt of restricting him of his natural rights. I have answered that I will not give my countenance to any measure where he is personally concerned. I am afraid Lord Fife will act contrary to this, but it is impossible for me to give offence to a young Prince coming to the throne, under whose protection as a military man I so immediately stand. I shall act in this . . . to the best of my judgment and abide by the consequences.

In a further letter Duff described the dispute with his father:[6]

On my informing him of my difference of sentiment on the present state of politics, my disapproving of Mr. Pitt's conduct, and resolution not to take any active part in opposition to the Prince of Wales, every art of persuasion and flattery of which he is master were put in practice to dissuade me from it, but, if I could not bring myself to vote for Mr. Pitt, imploring me, as the greatest service I could do him, to resign my seat. I took two days to consider on the subject of our conversation. I then wrote him that, anxiously wishing to do everything in my power I consistently could, I, in compliance with his request, was willing to vacate my seat.

Despite his father's 'numerous professions of friendship and affection', Duff was not surprised when the following day Fife deliberately avoided him in the street. All communication between them ceased; and Fife immediately nominated James Ferguson of Pitfour for Banffshire. Duff wrote to Rose: 'I could never have thought of holding a place of that nature when I was totally debarred from having an opinion of my own, not even where I think my interest is concerned.' After the King's recovery Duff, at Rose's suggestion, wrote to Lord Findlater justifying his parliamentary conduct,[7] but made no approach to his father. The breach between them remained complete until February 1793 when, on the eve of Duff's departure for active service in Holland, Fife sent him 'a kind note' wishing him a safe return. Much moved, Duff replied: 'My dear Lord, my heart is relieved by your kind letter. But much too agitated at present to say more than assure you of the eternal gratitude of your devoted James Duff.'[8]

Cordial relations being now restored, Fife proposed that Duff should succeed Sir James Grant in Banffshire. But as Dundas was unsympathetic,[9] and Sir James himself reluctant, Fife failed in his objective, and Duff did not re-enter Parliament.

He died 5 Dec. 1839.

[1] A. & H. Tayler, *Ld. Fife & his Factor*, 115–16, 163–4. [2] Adam, *Pol. State of Scotland*, 3. [3] A. & H. Tayler, *Book of the Duffs*, ii. 512. [4] Debrett, xx. 2. [5] *Ld. Fife & his Factor*, 195. [6] *Book of the Duffs*, ii. 511. [7] Ibid. 512. [8] *Ld. Fife & his Factor*, 241, 242. [9] Ibid. 247; H. Furber, *Hen. Dundas*, 240.

E.H.-G.

**DUKE** (formerly **HEATH**), **John** (?1717–75), of Otterton, Devon.

HONITON    1747–1754, 1761–1768

*b.* ?1717, s. of Staplehill Heath by Anne, da. of Thomas Duke of Otterton. *m.* 1745 (lic. 17 May), Susanna, da. and h. of William Gill of Honiton, *s.p. suc.* to estates of his uncle Richard Duke, and took name of Duke 1751.

Duke was defeated at Honiton in 1754, and returned in 1761 after a contest; in 1761 he also contested Ashburton. In Bute's list he was classed as a Tory, but was sent Newcastle's whip for the session of 1761. He appears in Fox's list of Members favourable to the peace preliminaries, and voted with the Grenville Administration on general warrants, 6 and 18 Feb. 1764.[1] Rockingham in July 1765 classed him as 'doubtful', in November 1766 as 'Swiss' (prepared to support every Administration), and Townshend in January 1767 as 'doubtful'. His only other known vote was against the Chatham Administration on the land tax, 27 Feb. 1767. There is no record of his having spoken in the House. He was defeated at Honiton in 1768.

He died 3 Nov. 1775, aged 58.[2]

[1] In the Grenville mss (JM) there is a paper by Duke, apparently intended as a letter to his constituents, justifying his vote in the division of 18 Feb. 1764. [2] *Devon & Cornw. N. & Q.* xiv. 293.

J.B.

## DUMMER, Thomas (c.1739–81), of Cranbury, Hants.

| | |
|---|---|
| NEWPORT I.o.W. | 26 Dec. 1765–1768 |
| YARMOUTH I.o.W. | 19 Jan. 1769–1774 |
| DOWNTON | 1774–14 Feb. 1775 |
| WENDOVER | 14 Mar. 1775–1780 |
| LYMINGTON | 1780–3 June 1781 |

*b.* c.1739, o.s. of Thomas Lee Dummer (q.v.). *educ.* Westminster 1749, still there 1754; L. Inn 1760. *m.* 5 June 1766, Harriet, da. of Sir Cecil Bisshopp, 6th Bt. (q.v.), *s.p. suc.* fa. 6 Oct. 1765.

On 18 Aug. 1765 Newcastle wrote to the Duke of Cumberland about electoral alignments in the Isle of Wight:[1]

Mr. Powell [q.v.] is now quite united with Mr. Holmes, Lord Holmes's heir and successor, Mr. Leigh (who has great weight in the Isle of Wight), Sir John Barrington [q.v.] and Mr. Dummer [Dummer's father, q.v.]; this united interest is sure of carrying five, if not the whole six Members in the Isle of Wight.

On 14 Oct. 1765 Hans Stanley (q.v.) wrote to George Grenville: 'On the death of Mr. Dummer . . . Mr. Holmes, who appears wholly devoted to the new Administration . . . promised his son the vacant seat at Newport',[2] for which he was duly returned. In November 1766 he was classed by Rockingham as a Whig which suggests that he voted with the Rockinghams when in office. But he did not vote on the land tax, 27 Feb. 1767, and on 2 Mar. appears in Newcastle's list among the 'doubtful or absent'. He voted, however, with Opposition on the nullum tempus bill, 17 Feb. 1768.

At the general election of 1768 Dummer stood again on the Holmes-Government interest for Yarmouth, and was seated on petition. But next over Wilkes and the Middlesex election he voted three times with Opposition, 27 Jan. and 2 Feb. 1769, and 25 Jan. 1770, and never with Government. He again voted with Opposition over the Spanish convention, 13 Feb. 1771, and over Grenville's Election Act, 25 Feb. 1774, and on that occasion is not marked by North, as are 84 other Members, as a friend voting against. In 1774 he was returned for Downton on the Duncombe interest but unseated on petition. In 1774 Lord Verney's private circumstances compelled him to have 'those stand for Wendover . . . who can bear the charge which that borough is to him',[3] but why and how Joseph Bullock vacated his seat there in March 1775 to let in Dummer is not clear. Possibly Bullock was still returned on easy terms—'Mr. Bullock is indeed accidentally of some use [to Verney]; we are of none at all', wrote Burke when explaining why Verney had to drop him [Burke]. And perhaps now Bullock vacated the seat to enable Verney to sell it to better profit; and it was sold to one who henceforth steadily voted with Government: there are none but minority lists for 1775–9, but Dummer never appears in them; and in the five divisions, February–April 1780 for which there are full division lists, he voted with Government. The *Public Ledger* wrote about him in 1779: 'gave £5,000 for his seat for this borough, and votes constantly with Government', and the *English Chronicle*, in 1780 or 1781, that Bullock was '*prevailed* upon to vacate his seat for the very purpose, as it was supposed, of introducing this opulent substitute'. Robinson, in his survey for the general election of 1780, counted Dummer as a friend to Government; wrote that Verney will not bring him in again; and put against Lymington, where two opponents were to be ousted, that 'two good friends of Government' would be brought in —Dummer was one of them. The *English Chronicle* starts its long, and not altogether accurate, note on Dummer by describing him as 'one of the richest, the obscurest, the most independent, and the most implicit Members in the House'; who for reasons incomprehensible to the writer, steadily voted with the Government—

He has fewer inducements than almost any man in the House, for his price (if he had one) could not consist in pecuniary temptations—he is too opulent for that; it could not arise from a wish for employment—he is too indolent for that; and besides if his intentions had had that tendency, they would doubtless have been indulged long ago; it could hardly proceed from ambition of titular consequence as he is too old . . . and has no relation sufficiently near . . . There is not, therefore, one motive to be assigned for this implicit conduct in Mr. Dummer; and as he cannot, of course, come under the predicament of a dependent, in the bad sense of the term, there is, perhaps but one way of getting rid of the difficulty, and that is, to call it a *paradox*, and wonder at it in ignorant taciturnity.

Although the point about the absence of titular ambitions is hardly convincing, and is probably adduced to round off the argument, it is a fact that no application has been found from Dummer for titles or honours; and he never held any office; and the idea that the American war brought over a Member to the Government side on perfectly honest and honourable grounds, seems to have been as incredible to contemporary as to latter-day 'Whigs'. But there undoubtedly was a paradox about a Member who in 1768–74 voted against the Government after having been returned on its interest, and in 1774–80 with it, while holding a seat purchased from Lord Verney. Also the concluding sentence of the note in the *English Chronicle* has retained its validity: the one peculiarity characterizing Dummer is 'of being at once one of the richest, and the most unknown individuals in the kingdom'. He died on 3 June 1781, and it is the disposal of his property in his will that brings him into contemporary correspondence. A. M. Storer wrote to Lord Carlisle, 18 June 1781:[4]

> Mr. Dummer . . . left nothing to either of the Pentons [qq.v.] who are his nearest relations, but has left all his [e]state to Ned Chamberlayne, who acted for him as his steward.

And Joseph Farington wrote that Dummer 'bequeathed his great property, an estate of £6 or £7,000 a year, besides an estate of about £100,000 in the hands of the accomptant-general, after the death of Mrs. Dummer' to Chamberlayne, his solicitor; and he adds the curious remark: 'the late Mr. Dummer was a very weak man, and did not appear to have partiality for Mr. Chamberlayne'.[5] Lastly, the Rev. M. Lort wrote to Bishop Percy, 24 June 1785: 'There is a very capital collection of Greek, Roman, and English coins coming to market, belonging to the late Mr. Dummer.'[6] Otherwise hardly anything is known about the man, whose estates are repeatedly referred to as 'immense', suggesting sums much higher than those named above.

[1] Add. 32969, f. 74. [2] The letter is printed in *Grenville Pprs*, iii. 98–99, but this passage is omitted, and is taken from the original in Sir John Murray's possession. [3] E. Burke to Rockingham, 16 Sept. 1774. [4] *HMC Carlisle*, 501. [5] *Farington Diary*, i. 56. [6] Nichols, *Lit. Illustrations*, vii. 470.

L.B.N.

**DUMMER, Thomas Lee** (?1712–65), of Cranbury, Hants.

SOUTHAMPTON    10 June 1737–1741
NEWPORT I.o.W.            1747–6 Oct. 1765

> b. ?1712, s. of Thomas Dummer, sometime dep. keeper of the great wardrobe, by Alathea Holland. *educ.* Westminster Feb. 1723, aged 10; B.N.C. Oxf. 1728.

> *m.* Elizabeth, da. of John Penton of Winchester, 1s. *suc.* fa. 24 Sept. 1749.
> Clerk of the great wardrobe c.1730–d.

A steady Government supporter, Dummer was returned by Thomas Holmes (q.v.) for Newport on the recommendation of the Pelhams, and adhered to Newcastle even after his resignation; voted against the peace preliminaries, December 1762; and with Opposition over Wilkes and general warrants in each of the five divisions 15 Nov. 1763–18 Feb. 1764 for which a list is extant. He was a member of Wildman's Club, and was classed as a 'sure friend' by Newcastle, 10 May 1764. On 2 Oct. 1764 Hans Stanley (q.v.) wrote from Paris to his nephew Hans Sloane (q.v.):[1] 'I hear from Spa, that the Duke of Devonshire is past recovery, and I conceive that Mr. Dummer's opposition most probably will expire with him.' And to George Grenville, 9 Dec. 1764:[2]

> I have it from one of his most intimate friends that his opposition came entirely from the Duke of Devonshire and this person thinks that any advances to him relative to the Isle of Wight would be kindly received. He has expressed himself very civilly as to yourself.

'It would be both easy and prudent', Stanley wrote again on 15 Dec., 'to inform him that it will still depend upon himself to be considered as a friend.' But Dummer was not gained over, and in the summer of 1765 Rockingham classed him as 'pro'. There is no record of his having spoken in Parliament.

Dummer died 6 Oct. 1765. He was reputed to have had an income of over £20,000 p.a.[3]

[1] Sloane-Stanley mss. [2] Grenville mss (JM). [3] Wilks, *Hist. Hantsi ii. 99.

L.B.N.

**DUNCANNON, Visct.,** *see* **PONSONBY, Frederick,** *and* **PONSONBY, William**

**DUNCOMBE, Henry** (1728–1818), of Copgrove, nr. Knaresborough, Yorks.

YORKSHIRE    1780–1796

> b. 1728, 3rd s. of Thomas Duncombe of Duncombe Park by Sarah, da. of Sir Thomas Slingsby, 4th Bt., of Scriven. *educ.* Westminster 1737–45; Lincoln, Oxf. 1745; M. Temple 1747. *unm.*

Henry Duncombe was one of the Yorkshire gentlemen who in September 1770 called a meeting to consider what further measures should be taken about petitioning the Crown on the Middlesex election. 'At our meeting I had the misfortune to differ from my associates', he wrote to Christopher Wyvill in December 1779, 'as things seemed then to me to carry too much the air of a party spirit which I totally disclaimed.'[1] In 1779 he made this his excuse for at first withholding his name from

Wyvill's campaign for economical reform, though he wrote to Wyvill:

> I wish with you that there may be spirit enough yet found in the county to express a proper resentment and sense of the insanity of Administration and to lead the first steps to the amendment of an almost ruined constitution.

In spite of his initial hesitation, he soon became a member of the Yorkshire committee of association, and on 28 Mar. 1780, at a county meeting seconded Wyvill's proposals for shorter Parliaments and an increase in the number of county Members.[2] Later that year Duncombe became a candidate for Yorkshire, standing jointly with Sir George Savile, with the support of both the association and Rockingham. Their opponent, Edwin Lascelles, withdrew before the poll and they were returned unopposed.

In the House Duncombe naturally voted with Opposition. His first reported speech, 15 Feb. 1781, was to second Burke's bill for regulating the civil list revenue. On 2 Apr. 1781 he presented the petition for economy from delegates of the associated counties, and on 19 May wrote to Wyvill: 'I am more than ever convinced that the only hopes of security to our liberties and of redress of our grievances, are to be derived from the integrity of Parliaments and a juster representation of the people.'[3] Duncombe voted for Shelburne's peace preliminaries, 18 Feb. 1783.

Presenting a petition from the Yorkshire association, 24 Feb. 1783, he delivered a panegyric on Pitt and censured North for opposing reform, declaring that he never would support any Administration in which North held office.[4] He spoke and voted in support of Pitt's parliamentary reform proposals of 7 May 1783. 'The true source whence our calamities are derived', he wrote to Wyvill, 20 Oct. 1783, 'is the very inadequate state of the representation of the people, by which the salutary restraints originally interposed against the errors, the weakness, and the wickedness of ministers have been baffled and defeated.'[5]

Duncombe voted against Fox's East India bill, 27 Nov. 1783, which, he declared, was 'accompanied with a wanton violation of charters . . . with what would have totally destroyed the liberties of this country, the patronage of 100 millions'.[6] In the debate of 1 Dec. 1783 he said of Fox that the 'confidence without which no minister in this country could ever be successful, was in respect to him no more. The people, whose rights he had so ably, so faithfully, and so effectually defended were sorry to be convinced of his desertion.'[7] Henceforth he was an ardent supporter of Pitt. At the general election of 1784, in company with William Wilberforce,

Duncombe stood as a Pittite candidate, and was returned unopposed, their opponents having withdrawn in face of a canvass showing an overwhelming majority for Duncombe and Wilberforce.

A letter of 14 Dec. 1784[8] from Wyvill suggests that Duncombe was now advocating a more cautious approach to reform, but in February 1785 he supported a further Yorkshire petition, and on 14 Apr. seconded Pitt's reform proposals. During the rest of the Parliament his speeches were infrequent and mainly on matters of local interest, but on 4 Mar. 1790 he complimented Henry Flood on his proposed bill for parliamentary reform, 'assuring him that at a more proper period he would vote in its favour'.[9]

Wyvill described Duncombe as 'in his temper mild and benevolent, in his principles firm and steady, in his political friendships warm and confidential'.[10]

He died 10 Apr. 1818.

[1] *Wyvill Pprs.* iii. 140. [2] Ibid. i. 155. [3] Ibid. 347-8. [4] *Debrett*, ix. 380, 381. [5] *Wyvill Pprs.* ii. 270-1. [6] Ibid. 336. [7] *Debrett*, xii. 267. [8] *Wyvill Pprs.* iv. 394-6. [9] *Debrett*, xvii. 59; xxvii. 219. [10] *Wyvill Pprs.* iv. 396-7 n.

I.R.C.

## DUNCOMBE, Thomas (?1724–79), of Duncombe Park, Yorks. and Barford Park, Wilts.

| | |
|---|---|
| DOWNTON | 22 Apr. 1751–1754 |
| MORPETH | 1754–1768 |
| DOWNTON | 1768–14 Feb. 1775, 8 Sept.–23 Nov. 1779 |

*b.* ?1724, 1st s. of Thomas Duncombe, M.P., of Duncombe Park, and bro. of Henry Duncombe (q.v.). *educ.* Westminster, Dec. 1732, aged 8; Ch. Ch. Oxf. 18 May 1742, aged 17. *m.* (1) 9 Feb. 1749, Lady Diana Howard (*d.*6 Mar. 1770), da. of Henry, 4th Earl of Carlisle, 2da.; (2) 24 Feb. 1772, Anne (*d.*24 July 1777), da. of Sir Philip Jennings Clerke, 1st Bt. (q.v.), 1da.; (3) 25 June 1778, Charlotte, da. of William Hale of King's Walden, Herts.; she m. (2) Thomas Onslow (q.v.). *suc.* fa. 1746; and kinsman Lord Feversham 1763.

Duncombe sat for Morpeth on the Howard interest; and in 1754 was classed by Dupplin as a Tory but in 1761 was sent Newcastle's parliamentary whip. He appears neither in Fox's list of Members favourable to the peace preliminaries nor in any list of the minority against them; voted against general warrants in one division, 15 Feb. 1764; and was classed by Rockingham in July 1765 as 'doubtful'. His parliamentary attendance was irregular, and nobody knew what to make of him: Rockingham in November 1766 classed him as 'Whig', Townshend in January 1767 as 'Government', and Newcastle in March as 'doubtful or absent'. He voted with Opposition on the nullum tempus bill, 17 Feb. 1768.

On the death of his cousin Lord Feversham in 1763 he inherited an interest at Downton, and in 1768 was returned unopposed. His first recorded vote in this Parliament, 6 Feb. 1772, was for the petition of the clergy against the 39 Articles. In Robinson's first survey on the royal marriage bill he is classed as 'doubtful, present'; in the second, as 'contra, present'; and he voted against the commitment of the bill on 11 Mar. 1772. His only other vote in this Parliament was for Grenville's Election Act, 25 Feb. 1774, when he was classed in the King's list as normally a friend of Government.

In 1774 his control of Downton was challenged by Lord Radnor, and Duncombe was unseated on petition. He was returned unopposed in 1779, but died a few weeks later, 23 Nov. 1779. There is no record of his having spoken in the House.

J.A.C.

## DUNDAS, Charles (1751–1832), of Barton Court, Berks.

| | |
|---|---|
| RICHMOND | 6 Jan. 1775–1780 |
| ORKNEY AND SHETLAND | 23 Feb. 1781–1784 |
| RICHMOND | 1784–Jan. 1786 |
| BERKSHIRE | 16 Sept. 1794–11 May 1832 |

*b.* 5 Aug. 1751, 2nd s. of Thomas Dundas of Fingask; bro. of Thomas Dundas, jun., and nephew of Lawrence Dundas (qq.v.). *educ.* Edinburgh h.s.; Edinburgh Univ. 1768; Trinity, Camb. 1769–73; M. Temple 1774, called 1777. *m.* (1) 16 Feb. 1782, Anne (*d.*29 Nov. 1812), da. and h. of Ralph Whitley of Aston Hall, Flints., 1 da.; (2) 25 Jan. 1822, his cos. Margaret, da. of Hon. Charles Barclay Maitland, wid. of (a) Charles Ogilvy of Inchmartin, (b) Archibald Erskine of Venlaw. *cr.* Baron Amesbury 11 May 1832.
Counsellor to Prince of Wales as great steward of Scotland 1785–1820.

Dundas was brought into Parliament by his uncle Sir Lawrence Dundas who, having returned his son Thomas for Richmond in 1774, made over the seat to Charles when Thomas opted to sit for Stirlingshire. Charles, almost wholly dependent upon his uncle, financially and otherwise, invariably voted at his direction; supported Administration until 1779, when at the opening of the new session Sir Lawrence informed him that though 'he hated Opposition' he could no longer support Government and would not attend;[1] nor did Charles, until in Spring 1780 he went over to the Opposition with his relations, voting against Administration on economical reform, 8 Mar. 1780, and in every subsequent recorded division to the end of the Parliament.

In consequence Lord Advocate Henry Dundas organized in 1780 strong opposition to Sir Lawrence's Scottish interest. To meet the challenge in

Orkney, Charles was transferred from Richmond to replace his brother Thomas (absent on active service). He was defeated but in February 1781 was seated on petition; and on 12 June 1781 spoke briefly in support of Fox's motion on the necessity for peace with America.[2]

After his uncle's death he remained closely attached to his cousin Sir Thomas and the Rockinghams; voted 12 Dec. 1781 for Lowther's motion against the war, but, from family friendship for Sandwich, voted with Government in the Admiralty debate of 7 Feb. 1782.[3]

On 16 Feb. 1782 Charles, hitherto an undistinguished barrister with little money of his own, obtained great estates by his marriage to the Whitley heiress. For at least a month thereafter Charles does not appear to have attended Parliament; did not vote on the censure motion against the Admiralty, 20 Feb., nor on Conway's motion of the 22nd; and was paired in the three recorded divisions of 27 Feb., 8 and 15 Mar. resulting in North's fall.

On Rockingham's death he again followed his cousin in attaching himself to Fox, and voted against Shelburne's peace preliminaries, 18 Feb. 1783. He voted, 7 May 1783, for parliamentary reform, and for Fox's East India bill, 27 Nov. 1783; and on the change of Administration opposed Pitt.

In 1784 he surrendered Orkney to his brother, and was returned for Richmond. In the new Parliament he again voted for parliamentary reform, 18 Apr. 1785, but otherwise remained opposed to Pitt's measures. A cipher in politics, he was persuaded by his cousin to vacate his seat in January 1786 in favour of a more effective Member, Sir Grey Cooper (q.v.).

Dundas resumed his legal practice, acted as business adviser to his brother, was consulted by Sir Thomas during the Regency crisis, and devoted himself to his Berkshire estates and to county affairs.[4] He died 30 June 1832.

[1] Robinson to Jenkinson, 20 Nov. 1779, Add. 38212, ff. 227–32.
[2] Debrett, iii. 545–6. [3] I. R. Christie, *End of North's Ministry*, 312.
[4] M. I. Dundas, *Dundas of Fingask*, 71–72, 93.

E.H.-G.

## DUNDAS, Henry (1742–1811), of Melville Castle, Edinburgh.

| | | |
|---|---|---|
| EDINBURGHSHIRE | | 1774–July 1782 |
| NEWTOWN I.o.W. | 16 Sept. | 1782–Dec. 1782 |
| EDINBURGHSHIRE | 2 Jan. | 1783–1790 |
| EDINBURGH | | 1790–24 Dec. 1802 |

*b.* 28 Apr. 1742, 2nd surv. s. of Robert Dundas M.P., of Arniston, Edinburgh, by his 2nd w. Anne, da. of Sir William Gordon, 1st Bt., of Invergordon; half-bro. of Robert Dundas (q.v.). *educ.* Dalkeith g.s.; Edinburgh h.s.; Edinburgh Univ.; adv. 1763. *m.* (1)

16 Aug. 1765, Elizabeth (div. 1778), da. of David Rennie of Melville, 1s. 3da.; (2) 2 Apr. 1793, Lady Jean Hope, da. of John, 2nd Earl of Hopetoun [S], *s.p.   cr.* Visct. Melville 24 Dec. 1802.

Solicitor-gen. [S] Apr. 1766–May 1775; ld. advocate May 1775–Aug. 1783; jt. keeper of the signet [S] Mar. 1777–June 1779, sole keeper June 1779–1800; P.C. 31 July 1782; treasurer of the navy Aug. 1782–Apr. 1783, Dec. 1783–June 1800; ld. of Trade Mar. 1784–Aug. 1786; commr. of Board of Control Sept. 1784–June 1793; Home sec. June 1791–July 1794; pres. of Board of Control June 1793–May 1801; sec. for war July 1794–Mar. 1801; privy seal [S] June 1800–*d.*; 1st ld. of Admiralty May 1804–Apr. 1805.

Henry Dundas came from a distinguished legal family, his father and half-brother having been president of the court of session. He began to practise law in 1763, and three years later was appointed solicitor-general for Scotland. 'Harry Dundas', wrote George Dempster to William Carlyle, 7 June 1766, 'is a great acquisition . . . he appears to me to have an exceeding good capacity and a very good heart.'[1] In 1770 Dundas warned Sir Alexander Gilmour, the sitting Member, that he intended to offer himself for Edinburghshire at the next general election,[2] and on 2 Nov. 1771 wrote to Lord North:[3]

> Before the expiry of the present Parliament I shall have been nine years in his Majesty's service, and shall be glad if, by being in Parliament, I can be more extensively useful in the service of my country. I flatter myself that none who are acquainted with the principles I hold with regard to government . . . will entertain any doubt what will be the line I shall pursue.

Supported by the Duke of Buccleuch, Dundas defeated Gilmour in 1774 without difficulty.

In the House of Commons, Dundas revealed himself at once as a most effective debater. His speech was broad Scots; his manner, like that of his friends Rigby and Thurlow, vigorous and forthright. Wraxall wrote of him:[4]

> His figure tall, manly, and advantageous, his countenance, open, cheerful, and pleasingly expressive, though tinged with convivial purple, prejudiced in his favour . . . His voice, strong, clear, and sonorous, enabled him to surmount the noise of a popular assembly, and almost to enforce attention at moments of the greatest clamour or impatience. Far from shunning the post of danger, he always seemed to court it; and was never deterred from stepping forward to the assistance of ministers by the violence of Opposition, by the unpopularity of the measure to be defended, or by the difficulty of the attempt. His speeches, able, animated, and argumentative, were delivered without hesitation and unembarrassed by any timidity.

In his first speech, delivered in the debate of 20 Feb. 1775 on North's conciliation proposals, he declared that 'he could never accede to any concessions whatever . . . until the Americans did, in direct terms, acknowledge the absolute supremacy of this coun-

try', and he maintained this uncompromising attitude until after Yorktown. On 27 Oct. 1775 he told the House:

> It would be ridiculous in Administration to recede, or to listen, at present, to conciliatory measures, whilst America was making so effectual a resistance; that all Europe would say we had felt our inability to enforce our rights . . . it was not uncommon for Great Britain to be unsuccessful in the beginning, and victorious in the progress and conclusion of her wars.[5]

His abilities were soon recognized and after less than a year in the House he was appointed lord advocate. Well aware of the value of his support, he pressed hard for reward. In March 1777 he was made joint keeper of the signet with Andrew Stuart, but held aloof from the ministry, spending much of his time on legal business in Scotland, and intervening only occasionally in debate. On 20 Feb. 1778 Dundas spoke against North's proposal to send commissioners to treat with the Americans: 'everything, he feared, was mismanaged, and the present measure would complete all'.[6] The King was full of indignation:[7]

> The more I think on the conduct of the advocate of Scotland the more I am incensed against him; more favours have been heaped on the shoulders of that man than ever was bestowed on any Scotch lawyer, and he seems studiously to embrace an opportunity to create difficulties; but men of talents when not accompanied with integrity are pests instead of blessings to society, and true wisdom ought to crush them rather than nourish them.

But Dundas was too useful to be crushed. The elevation of Thurlow to the Lords in the summer of 1778 removed one of North's legal watchdogs from the Commons, and the other, Wedderburn, was discontented and unreliable. On 21 Apr. 1779, the King wrote to North: 'Let the lord advocate be gained to attend the whole session', and in June Dundas was appointed sole keeper of the signet. 'The arrangement', wrote the King, 'arose that Lord North might be certain of an able debater at all times in the House of Commons.'[8] During the remainder of the Parliament Dundas spoke frequently, particularly in support of the American war: 'We ought to go on with spirit', he declared, 11 June 1779, 'and be reduced to the last resource, before we submit to acknowledge the independency of America.' On 8 Mar. 1780 he opposed economical reform: 'If the influence of the Crown was so excessive, why did the minister carry his questions by so small majorities?', and on 6 Apr. he condemned Dunning's motion as 'a mere naked, unconnected, abstract proposition'.[9] By the end of his first Parliament he had established himself in the front rank as a parliamentary speaker: 'My friend the advocate had made a very brilliant figure', wrote Sir William Gordon in June 1780;

'he is really a fine, manly fellow, and I like a decided character. He speaks out and is afraid of nobody.'[10]

The next step Dundas had set himself was to have the signet for life. North assured him that the King had a rule against making life appointments. Dundas was greatly irritated when he discovered that one of Loughborough's nephews had been given a life appointment, and complained of North's disingenuousness: 'It seems . . . that mine is the only Scotch office—or rather I am the only Scotch person —to which this rule is to be applied.' North had to coax him back to take his part in the House in February 1781. In April he was appointed chairman of the committee to investigate the war in the Carnatic, and began his long connexion with Indian affairs. But he was by no means satisfied, and chose the occasion of Yorktown to make another demonstration. He was now convinced, he told his brother, 29 Nov. 1781, that any further attempt to recover America was doomed:

> I for one should certainly oppose it [even] if the consequence should be a forfeiture of all the favour I have hitherto enjoyed, and of all the views of ambition I may have looked to in future. If I voted for such a proposition, I should not lay my head any night upon my pillow, without thinking that I had sent an army of my fellow subjects to be massacred . . . I spoke in a manner last night in the House of Commons which must soon compel Administration to take their ground one way or another. I believe they felt it as the severest bomb ever thrown among them. I was happy they did, as I meant they should.

This declaration, coming from one who had been such a strenuous supporter of the war, made a great impression on the House. Horace Walpole interpreted it as aimed against Lord George Germain, whom Dundas was urging North to remove as an obstacle to peace. When Germain was given a peerage in February 1782, North considered appointing Dundas his successor: 'Ability, spirit, eloquence he has in perfection', he wrote to the King, 21 Jan. 1782, 'but there are great difficulties in placing him in such a situation as to enable me to draw from him the support I want.' Dundas brought up his grievance about the signet, writing to his brother:

> The present bustle has enabled me to hold the language I do, which is, that if his Majesty does not choose I should have the signet for life, I take it for granted he considers my aid in public life to be of no material service to him, and that for the future I may confine myself to my professional line.

The King was willing to offer him the treasurership of the navy, but not the signet for life:

> I am clear that the trouble he has given this winter is not a reason for my rendering him independent, and great as his desires seem to be, the best English House of Commons office and one of two thousand per annum in Scotland during pleasure are no small recompenses.

Though Dundas refused the treasurership on these terms, he continued to speak in support of North until the end: after the debate of 8 Mar. 1782, when the ministry's majority dropped to nine, North, according to Dundas, 'was all gratitude, and even attributes to me the small majority he had'. When North resigned, he made one more attempt to induce the King to grant Dundas the signet for life. When the King refused, Dundas talked of resigning, but was dissuaded by Thurlow: 'I had nothing to do but coolly and temperately to lay by, and that within a month I would be courted by both parties.'[11]

When the Rockinghams took office, Dundas continued as advocate. Fox had already gone out of the way to flatter him, declaring in the House that 'he should think it strange indeed if anybody should think of forming a new Administration without taking the aid of the great talents he possesses', and Dundas's sister wrote: 'From what I hear he may be in when he pleases.' Most of the summer Dundas was occupied with Indian affairs, particularly with the charges against Sir Thomas Rumbold; and on 28 May he moved to recall Warren Hastings. On the formation of the Shelburne ministry, he was offered the treasurership and the signet for life, and accepted. To enable his re-election to go through as quickly as possible, he was brought in for Newtown, though he soon resumed his seat for Edinburghshire. At the beginning of 1783 he sought to bring about an understanding between North and Shelburne, but a meeting with North in the first week of February led to a quarrel. When the peace preliminaries came up for debate on 17 Feb. 1783, Dundas denounced the Coalition's opposition as factious:

> Let them remember that the noble lord in the blue ribband [North] had said, early in this session, that peace was much to be desired; let them remember that the honourable gentleman in his eye [Fox] had urged the necessity of peace still more strongly.

Though he anticipated defeat, he was not unduly alarmed about his own future. To his brother, he confided: 'with the signet and my profession I feel myself very much upon velvet'. When Shelburne resigned, Dundas tried hard to persuade Pitt to take power as first lord of the Treasury. When that failed, and the Coalition came in, Dundas resigned his treasurership, though he continued as lord advocate until August, when he was dismissed.[12]

Dundas was now a key figure in the Opposition. On 1 Dec. 1783 he spoke against Fox's India bill as creating 'a new, inordinate, and unexampled influence, which it placed in the hands of the minister of the present day, and his party, for five years together'. 'I am apt to believe that my speech against the India bill was the best I ever made in Parliament', he wrote later.[13] In December 1783 Pitt, Robinson and Richard Atkinson met at his house to concert plans for the overthrow of the Coalition, and when Pitt took office Dundas resumed his post as treasurer of the navy. During the spring of 1784 he shared with Pitt the brunt of the Opposition's attack in the House of Commons, maintaining that the King had an undoubted right to choose his ministers. When the general election came he was in charge of the Government's arrangements for Scotland.

Dundas's political eminence was now established. He was second man on the Government side in the House of Commons, on the closest terms, public and private, with Pitt, and could look forward with confidence to a seat in the Cabinet. In addition, he was virtually minister for Scotland, and soon took complete command of Indian affairs. His position was the result of his ability in the House. On 5 Feb. 1784, in answer to the accusation that he and Pitt were undermining the constitution by remaining in office, Dundas replied:[14]

> Those who know what I was, and what I am, will never think that I, of all men, could ever entertain a design to lessen the dignity of this House; for whatever little consequence and distinction I have, if I have any, I derive entirely from this House; and I know that if the House of Commons was to cease to be what it is now, a branch of the legislature, and a check and control upon the executive power, I must again return to the obscurity of a dull and laborious profession.

For the next twenty years Dundas held high office almost continuously, with particular responsibility for the conduct of the war against revolutionary France.

He died 2 May 1811.

[1] *Letters Geo. Dempster*, 221. [2] *Arniston Mems.* ed. Omond, 183. [3] H. Furber, *Hen. Dundas*, 190–1. [4] *Mems.* i. 425. [5] Almon. i. 207; iii. 54. [6] *Gazetteer and New Daily Advertiser*, 23 Feb. 1778. [7] Fortescue, iv. 41. [8] Ibid. 328. 384. [9] Almon, xii. 369; xvii. 268, 465. [10] C. Matheson, *Hen. Dundas*, 65. [11] Ibid. 66, 74, 77, 79, 80; Fortescue, v. 336. [12] Matheson, 78, 82, 90; Debrett, ix. 265. [13] Debrett, xii. 282; Matheson, 102. [14] Debrett, xiii. 79.

J.A.C.

**DUNDAS, James** (1721–80), of Dundas, Linlithgow.

LINLITHGOWSHIRE  27 Mar. 1770–1774

*b.* 18 June 1721, 1st surv. s. of George Dundas of Dundas, M.P., master of the King's works in Scotland, by Alison, da. of Brig.-Gen. James Bruce of Kennet. *educ.* prob. Dalmeny sch. *m.* 22 Apr. 1748, Jean Maria, da. of William, 14th Lord Forbes [S], 1s. 4da. *suc.* fa. May 1762.

Capt. Scots brigade in Holland, 1745; capt. 25 Ft. 1747–8; col. 94 Ft. 2 Mar. 1780–d. Burgess of Edinburgh 3 Oct. 1770.

As a young man James Dundas joined the Scots brigade in Holland, obtaining the captaincy of a new

company in Mackay's Regiment in 1745, but left the Dutch service in 1747 on accepting a captain's commission in the British army.[1] After his marriage and the reduction of his regiment at the end of the war he seems to have abandoned a military career.

When his father succeeded to the Dundas estates his title to the headship of the Dundas family was disputed by Thomas Dundas of Fingask (father of Thomas and Lawrence Dundas, qq.v.), whose claim was rejected by the court of session in 1758.[2] When James succeeded as 24th of his line in 1762 his right as 'the undoubted male representative of this most ancient family' was apparently not challenged.

In 1768 James contested Linlithgowshire, which his father had represented 1722–7 and 1741–3. Since 1743 the seat had been held by Charles Hope Weir (q.v., brother of John, 2nd Earl of Hopetoun), who in 1768 stood down in favour of his son John Hope (q.v.). Both sides created new votes which were the subject of litigation in court of session and House of Lords, but Hope was returned by a vote of 20–15. Dundas was seated on petition. He voted with Administration on Brass Crosby's case, 27 Mar. 1771, but, unlike the rest of the Dundas connexion, was classed as an opponent of Government on the royal marriage bill, March 1772, and voted against them on the Middlesex election, 26 Apr. 1773.

By 1774 Lord Hopetoun had regained control of Linlithgowshire, and Dundas stood no chance there. Supported by Sir Lawrence, he unsuccessfully contested Linlithgow Burghs in opposition to Sir James Cockburn (q.v.). He brought a petition which was subsequently dropped, and did not re-enter Parliament.

During the invasion alarm of 1779 he raised a regiment, the 94th or Dundas's Foot, and sailed with his troops when they were ordered to the West Indies in 1780. Arriving in St. Lucia in July in the sickly season, the transports were sent on to Jamaica with many casualties from fever aboard.[3] Dundas was among those who died on the voyage, on 20 July 1780.[4]

[1] *Scots Brigade in Holland* (Sc. Hist. Soc.), ii. 230. [2] M. I. Dundas, *Dundas of Fingask*, 43–49. [3] Fortescue, *Hist. British Army*, iii. 296, 347. [4] *Gent. Mag.* 1780, p. 494.

E.H.-G.

**DUNDAS, Sir Lawrence,** 1st Bt. (c.1710–81), of Kerse, Stirling and Aske, nr. Richmond, Yorks.

| | |
|---|---|
| LINLITHGOW BURGHS | 1747–16 Mar. 1748 |
| NEWCASTLE-UNDER-LYME | 27 Dec. 1762–1768 |
| EDINBURGH | 1768–1780 |
| RICHMOND | 1780–March 1781 |
| EDINBURGH | 23 Mar.–21 Sept.1781 |

*b.* ?1710, 2nd s. of Thomas Dundas of Fingask, Stirling and Edinburgh by Bethia, da. of John Baillie of

Castlecarry, Stirling, and bro. of Thomas Dundas (q.v.). *educ.* ?Edinburgh h.s. *m.* 1738, Margaret, da. of Brig.-gen. Alexander Bruce of Kennet, 1s. *cr.* Bt. 20 Oct. 1762.

Burgess of Edinburgh 1739; commissary for bread and forage in Scotland 1746-8, for stores and provisions in Flanders 1747-9, of stores in Scotland 1748-57; keeper of magazines of forage 1757-8; commissary of bread for foreign troops in Germany 1759; contractor for horses and wagons for the Hanoverians 1760-1; further contracts 1761-2.[1] Gov. R. Bank of Scotland 1764-77. P.C. 9 Oct. 1771.

The younger son of an impoverished branch of the Dundas family, Lawrence on leaving his father's drapery shop in the Luckenbooths set up in business as a merchant contractor.[2] During the '45, with the help of his friend James Masterton (q.v.), he obtained contracts for supplying the army of Cumberland, by whose favour he was appointed commissary in Scotland, and subsequently in Flanders.

In 1754 he again contested Linlithgow Burghs against the combined interests of Pelham, Argyll, and Hyndford, and early began 'his work of treating and bribing'.[3] Distrusted by almost everyone, including his kinsmen of Arniston and Dundas, he carried his feud with Argyll and the Campbells into Stirlingshire, where he gave his family interest, augmented by the purchase of the Kerse estate, to the Haldanes and 'prevailed upon the Duke of Montrose to act against Captain Campbell.'[4] The ministerial interest was solidly against him, and 'after violent scenes and vast expenditure',[5] 'the Forager', 'much hipped', lost Linlithgow Burghs to John Murray of Philiphaugh.

In the seven years' war Dundas recouped his losses by contracts and commissariat appointments for supplying the troops in Germany. Despite disputes with Thomas Orby Hunter (q.v.),[6] the commissaries of control,[7] and Prince Ferdinand (who, according to Walpole, 'had been on the point of hanging him' for not fulfilling a contract to time[8]) he acquired considerable reputation and a fortune estimated at £6–800,000.

Disappointed of a seat at the 1761 election, he approached Shelburne, whom he had known in Germany, through his Scots military friends, James Edgar[9] and James Masterton. Edgar wrote to Shelburne, 17 Oct. 1761:[10]

I have had a letter from Lawrie Dundas to say that he is very desirous of coming into Parliament under your Lordship's protection . . . he submits the terms to your Lordship, his object is to get in.

Dundas followed this up by a letter to Shelburne from Bremen, 28 Oct.:

Col. Masterton wrote me lately he had taken the liberty to inform your Lordship of the disappointment I had

met with about my seat in Parliament, and acquainted me how ready you was in offering your assistance with your friends to bring me in upon the first vacancy.

Expense being no object, Dundas preferred to be under obligation to Shelburne rather than 'to people he did not know', and on his return home in 1762, discussions took place during which Shelburne 'gave him the confidence' of his financial affairs and accepted a substantial loan.[11] On 19 Aug. 1762 Shelburne wrote to Henry Fox:[12] 'Dundas, the Nabob of the North, writes me to desire I'll get him made a baronet; this made me go to Lord Bute yesterday.' On 20 Oct. Dundas duly received his baronetcy, and having purchased the estates of Upleatham and Aske, made sure of a seat in future by acquiring the borough of Richmond. Shelburne consulted Bute, Fox, Calcraft, and the Bedfords on obtaining an immediate vacancy for the 'rich Scotch commissary'; suggested Hindon;[13] but eventually agreement was reached on Lord Gower's borough of Newcastle-under-Lyme. On 18 Dec. Dundas wrote to Shelburne:[14]

I have just now seen Mr. Calcraft who informed me what had been determined concerning my coming into Parliament, and that Lord Gower was to call upon me this forenoon and settle everything, I am afraid my Lord, that you have made a point of this in a stronger manner than I have any pretensions to or reason to expected [sic].

His 'German pillage', his extravagance and his gambling were the subject of much comment.[15] On 3 May 1763 Lord Hardwicke wrote to Lord Royston:[16] 'Sir Lory Dundas, who extends his conquests from North to South, has purchased Moor Park [from Lord Anson's heirs] for £25,000. He has contracted in his own great way; takes everything as it stands.' A few months later he bought Lord Granville's London house for about £15,000.[17]

About this time he sold out Government stock: of his subscription to the loan of 1760 he had retained £25,000, of 1761 nearly £50,000, and of October 1762, £50,000[18]—how much more he had obtained for 'stagging' is not known (on 15 Sept. 1762 Shelburne wrote to Bute: 'Dundas . . . will be obliged to you for a million of your subscription'). Further he pressed Shelburne in June 1763 for repayment of his loan,[19] and although he professed to be 'hurt in the extreme to think there could be a possibility of putting any other construction upon his letter', he was clearly unsettled by Bute's resignation. He wanted his son to replace James Campbell in Stirlingshire and appealed in July 1763 to Bute, to whom he professed great attachment both in and out of office, to persuade Campbell to quit Parliament or exchange Stirlingshire for Dundas's borough of Richmond.[20] This scheme having failed, he was further chagrined when the commissioners for German demands queried his accounts.[21]

Having loyally supported Grenville's Administration and come from a sickbed 'brought in on men's shoulders' to vote, 18 Feb. 1764, on general warrants, he was bitterly offended when on 12 Apr. the Treasury approved, despite his protest, the steps taken by the German commissioners to make 'a hypothetical charge' against him.[22] On 18 Apr. Sandwich warned Grenville:[23] 'I wish you may have an opportunity of saying something friendly to Sir Lawrence Dundas . . . as I think there is danger of losing him which a little well-timed civility will prevent.' Grenville replied the same day:[24] 'I saw Sir Lawrence Dundas yesterday and said to him all that I possibly could on this subject as friendlily as I was able and as I am really disposed to him.' By his son's marriage to Rockingham's niece, Dundas had a connexion with the Opposition, and while the Treasury continued to dispute his accounts, and refused an immediate settlement,[25] there was good reason to fear the commissary might change his allegiance. James Stuart Mackenzie sought to placate him by recommending against his better judgment his brother-in-law Bruce of Kennet for promotion to the Scottish bench.[26] Although forced to accept a reduction of £17,000 in his claims,[27] Dundas decided to remain faithful to Grenville, followed him into opposition, and voted against the repeal of the Stamp Act.

His interests were now concentrated, according to his critics, on achieving power in Scotland comparable to the former Argyll dictatorship. In July 1766 he purchased the Orkneys and Shetlands from the Earl of Morton for £63,000, thereby obtaining control of the county representation and a leading interest in Tain Burghs. He had long been nursing Stirlingshire for his son Thomas. Lavish expenditure would secure Stirling Burghs which he intended for his friend Robert Haldane. He still maintained an interest in Linlithgow Burghs and Linlithgowshire. In Fife he had considerable influence which he gave to James Wemyss of Wemyss. For himself he reserved the representation of the city of Edinburgh.

During the Chatham Administration he remained in opposition, closely associated with the Bedfords and Grenvilles. He voted with them on the land tax, 27 Feb. 1767, and on 8 Mar. spent the entire day negotiating with Rockingham, Rigby, and Grenville on the organization of a united opposition to the proposal to print the East India papers.[28] But when the alliance between the Bedfords and the Grenvilles was wearing thin, Alexander Wedderburn warned Whately in September 1767:[29] 'I wish Mr. Grenville would take some opportunity of writing to Sir

Lawrence Dundas; the Bedfords are extremely attentive to him, and he is apt to be taken with attentions.' All parties were interested in Dundas and the eight or nine Members he was expected to bring into the next Parliament, but Dundas did not commit himself; and neither he nor his son voted on the nullum tempus bill, 17 Feb. 1768. They were more immediately concerned with creating their Scottish 'empire', courting popularity, and promoting the Forth and Clyde canal.

Sir Lawrence was now about to reap his reward. At the general election, his brother Thomas was returned for Orkney, his son Thomas for Stirlingshire, his friend Masterton (in place of the deceased Robert Haldane) for Stirling Burghs. He himself having been returned for both Richmond and Edinburgh, vacated his English seat in favour of William Norton. The other Richmond Member was Alexander Wedderburn, brought in, it was said, as 'an able and well tongued friend' to act as spokesman for the Dundas group.[30]

By the autumn Dundas had still not decided whether to join Grenville in opposition, or Bedford and the court. Whately wrote to Grenville, 14 Oct. 1768:[31]

I have a letter from Wedderburn who asks whether you have written lately to Sir Lawrence Dundas. Though he is more satisfied than ever with his language yet he wishes a civility were now and then thrown in to prevent any impression by the great attention paid him from another quarter.

On 5 Nov. Rigby wrote to Bedford:[32]

It remains still doubtful whether I shall prevail with my friend Sir Lawrence to be steady with Government and to-night he will determine with Sir Fletcher Norton and Wedderburn whether to be friends or foes. I think them a material set of people at this juncture and have taken great pains to secure them. The Duke of Grafton will give no promise to Sir Lawrence's favourite point and without that, if Sir Lawrence determines to give his support to the Administration, he declares he does it for no other reason but the personal regard he bears to your Grace. Grenville and Lord George Sackville try heaven and earth to get him but I think I parted with him just now favourably disposed.

Dundas's 'favourite point' was a peerage. The King refused, but Dundas, despite his disappointment, from the beginning of 1769 consistently voted with Administration, parting company with Wedderburn on 8 May 1769 over Luttrell and the Middlesex election. Wedderburn vacated his seat, and the loss of 'the ablest man in Britain' was long remembered in Scotland as a blow to the parliamentary influence of Dundas with his 'eight or nine dead votes at his heels'.[33] Although Dundas never obtained office either for himself or his followers it was generally believed that 'without the name of minister' he had 'the disposal of almost everything in Scotland'.[34] While his critics claimed that his patronage only extended to 'ordinary' appointments in Scotland and the East India Company, and 'scraps' for 'his minions and dependants',[35] Garlies certainly resented his political interest: 'The Duke of Queensberry or Lord Marchmont . . . generally ask and get almost everything to be disposed of in Scotland, except what is given to Sir Lawrence Dundas.'[36] As governor of the Royal Bank, 1764–77, he exercised great influence in the financing of new projects, notably the Forth and Clyde canal, and steered the bank through the crisis arising from the collapse of the Bank of Ayr.[37] His wealth and financial acumen were useful to Administration at whose behest in 1769 he bought up holdings of East India stock to the value of over £100,000 for splitting to provide qualifications at the 1770 election of directors.[38]

On the formation of the North Government Dundas once more asked for his reward, presumably a peerage, which was again refused. 'I wish to know' wrote the King, 16 Feb. 1770, 'in what manner Sir Lawrence Dundas has received the answer I authorized you to give him in consequence of his very unreasonable and unseasonable application.'[39] North reassured the King, 17 Feb.: 'All Sir Lawrence's friends were at the House yesterday and would have voted with us if there had been any division.' During 1771 Sir Lawrence was in poor health and proposed to winter at Nice. Before going abroad he pressed North 'for the dignity of a Privy Councillor'; although North 'wished that the request had not been made', the King consented 'if Lord Gower had no objection', and the honour was accordingly granted.[40] Both he and his son were listed 'pro—absent' (presumably abroad) during the debates on the royal marriage bill, March 1772.

He was still neither liked nor trusted, the Scottish nobility in particular resenting the extension of the 'upstart's' influence. Argyll's interest in the west of Scotland was a principal object of attack by Dundas, who in 1774 opposed the Glasgow and Clyde navigation bill not on its merits but because it was supported by Argyll. John Craufurd (whom Dundas had offered to bring into Parliament if he failed in Renfrewshire) told William Mure[41] that it 'became a kind of trial of strength' between them, but the affair was so mishandled that in the end 'the shabby Sir Lawrence' divided against his friends.

In the constituencies Dundas had acquired new allies. Argyll wrote to Mure, 24 Feb. 1774:[42]

I hope that you . . . will not come under any engagement with Sir Lawrence Dundas as to the new Hamilton votes in Stirlingshire being neutral; Sir Lawrence Dundas has found means to have such influence with the Elphinstones, that if you do not keep him in order with these votes, he will have them [the Elphinstones] against Duke Hamilton and me both in Dunbartonshire and Clydesdale . . . I don't see that you have anything to fear in Linlithgow as Sir James Cockburn is ready to meet Sir Lawrence there with his own weapons without putting Duke Hamilton to any expense.

In Edinburgh Dundas's popularity had waned. He was criticized for neglecting the city's affairs,[43] and for his non-residence, which he rectified by building a mansion in St. Andrew's Square. None the less he was re-elected in 1774 against strong opposition. His posse was diminished by the loss of Stirling Burghs, and although his interest had secured Clackmannan, Ralph Abercromby declined his whip. The rest of the group followed their leader in supporting Administration.

Sir Lawrence now had to face the rivalry of his distant connexion Henry Dundas, with whose family he had long been on bad terms, and who in alliance with the Duke of Buccleuch openly challenged his interest. From 1776 violent struggles took place for control of the Edinburgh town council, scores of vituperative handbills appeared attacking 'the stout Earl of the German Plains', ridiculing his origins, his ostentation, his pretensions to a coronet. Although Sir Lawrence gained prestige in 1778 by presenting Edinburgh's loyal address and promoting the raising of the Edinburgh Regiment,[44] it became obvious that he could expect little from a ministry which permitted its lord advocate to oppose him.

By 1779 his loyalty began to be suspect. All his group were absent from the division on the contractors bill, 12 Feb. 1779, and their support was no longer taken for granted. Reporting to the King on the Keppel debates of 3 Mar., Sandwich particularly mentioned that Sir Lawrence 'with all his friends' had voted with Administration, and subsequently told Jenkinson 'that Sir Lawrence Dundas and his connexion would attend on every question in which he [Sandwich] was personally concerned'.[45] But on 20 Nov. 1779 Robinson wrote to Jenkinson[46] that Rigby 'had seen a letter from Sir Lawrence Dundas to his nephew in which he said that he hated opposition but that the conduct of Administration was so weak and bad that he could not support them and would not attend'. He seems to have kept his word. And his next recorded vote on 8 Mar., on economical reform, was against the Government. Thereafter he continued in opposition, making on 10 May 1780 his only recorded speech during nearly twenty years in Parliament: on the malt tax bill in support of Dempster's amendment complaining of an injustice to Scotland.[47]

Listed 'contra' in Robinson's survey of 1780, Sir Lawrence had to face contests in almost every part of his 'empire'. 'The court', wrote Rockingham, 'have been most alert and violent against him, not only in Edinburgh but wherever they could in boroughs and counties where he was concerned.'[48] Sir Lawrence showed considerable generalship against Henry Dundas's organized attack. He transferred his nephew Charles from Richmond to Orkney, to replace his absent brother Thomas and meet Baikie's opposition. To secure his son's return for Stirlingshire he made an agreement whereby in exchange for the Montrose interest he brought in the Marquess of Graham for Richmond. He bargained and intimidated, exchanged votes and interest, made new allies.[49] He had himself returned for Richmond as an insurance against defeat in Edinburgh where the Henry Dundas-Buccleuch party was as unscrupulous as himself in election tactics. Rockingham wrote to him during the campaign:[50]

I shall not condole with you that you are become an object of the malice and the intrigues of a time serving court party in Scotland ... I have heard that my friend Dempster and you have been deemed *traitors in Scotland* for having voted that the influence of the Crown was increased, was increasing and ought to be diminished.

Sir Lawrence was defeated in extraordinary circumstances, but promptly petitioned against William Miller's return.

During the contest James Boswell, formerly an opponent of Sir Lawrence, but now united with him in antagonism to Henry Dundas, met him for the first time.[51]

It was adding a new distinguished character to my collection. He appeared to me not a cunning shrewd man of the world as I had imagined, but a comely jovial Scotch gentleman of good address but not bright parts ... I liked him much. I even felt for him as a man ungratefully used in his old age.

In March 1781 Sir Lawrence won his petition but, crippled with gout, died 21 Sept. 1781, leaving an estate worth £16,000 p.a. and a fortune of £900,000 in personal and landed property.[52] Henry Dundas wrote to Robinson, 8 Oct. 1781:[53]

When Sir Lawrence Dundas laid out twenty thousand pounds to build a house in Edinburgh and submitted for these fifteen years to every species of disagreeable meanness to establish an interest in the town of Edinburgh, did he ever imagine that he would not only die without a coronet but that within a few months of his breath being out there should not remain in any of his family the vestige of that interest which cost him so much? And yet in truth that will be the case.

[1] T29/30/371; T52/45/7, 43; T29/32/136, 432; T54/36/377; T52/48/215; T29/33/40, 302; T29/34/181, 275; Add. 33038, f. 328; 32896, ff. 5-6; 32928, f. 280. [2] Edinburgh handbills, *Reply to 'a Citizen' by an Old Magistrate*, 28 Sept. 1776; *A Dramatic Interlude: The Humour of the Town*, 1 Oct. 1776. [3] Argyll to Pelham, 4 Sept. and 15 Oct. 1753, Newcastle (Clumber) mss. [4] Same to same, 6 Nov.

1753, ibid. [5] Letters from Andrew Pringle, *HMC Hamilton*, ii. 177-8. [6] Dundas to Newcastle, 20 Sept. 1759, Add. 32896, ff. 5-6. [7] Dundas to Col. Peirson, 10 Sept. 1761, Add. 32928, f. 280. [8] *Mems. Geo. III*, iii. 214. [9] See memorandum from Shelburne to Bute on Edgar's career, 20 Nov. 1761, Bute mss. [10] Lansdowne mss. [11] Gibbs Crawfurd to Shelburne, 11 June 1763. [12] Henry Fox mss. [13] Shelburne to Bute, 11 Dec. 1762, Bute mss. [14] Lansdowne mss. [15] Lady Barrymore to Bedford, 30 Jan. 1764, Bedford mss; James Harris's memoranda, 22 May and 24 July 1763, Malmesbury mss. [16] Add. 35352, f. 343b. [17] Alex. Forrester to Andrew Mitchell, 12 Sept. 1763, Add. 30999, ff. 16-17. [18] Bank of England recs. [19] Gibbs Crawfurd to Shelburne, 11 June 1763, Lansdowne mss. [20] Sir Harry Erskine to Bute, ?19 July 1763, Bute mss. [21] Dundas to Jenkinson, 18 Nov. 1763, Add. 38201, f. 248. [22] T29/35/361. [23] Grenville mss (JM). [24] Grenville letter bk. [25] T29/35/449; Grenville to Dundas, 14 July 1764, Grenville letter bk. [26] Mackenzie to Bute, 28 May and 3 June 1764, Bute mss. [27] T29/36/209, 304, 341; Jenkinson to Grenville, 21 Mar. 1765, Grenville mss (JM). [28] Rockingham to Newcastle, Newcastle to Rockingham, 8 Mar. 1767, Add. 32980, ff. 220-1, 226-7. [29] *Grenville Pprs*. iv. 160-2. [30] Edinburgh pamphlet, *A Rhapsody*, 9 Sept. 1777, p. 9. [31] Grenville mss (JM). [32] Bedford mss. 57, f. 220. [33] *A Rhapsody*. [34] Ramsay of Ochtertyre, i. 154. [35] *A Rhapsody*. [36] *Cal. Home Office Pprs. 1766-9*, pp. 506-7. [37] Neil Munro, *Hist. Royal Bank of Scotland*, ch. x. [38] Whately to Grenville, 2 and 15 June 1769, Grenville mss (JM); L. S. Sutherland, *E. I. Co. in 18th Cent. Politics*, 183; Lady Mary Coke, *Jnl.* iii. 134. [39] Fortescue, ii. 130. [40] North to Gower, 30 Sept. 1771, *HMC 5th Rep.* 208. [41] *Caldwell Pprs.* ii(2), pp. 231-2. [42] Ibid. 230. [43] *Letter of the Incorporated Trades to Thomas Dundas*, 9 Sept. 1771. [44] Fortescue, iv. 16-19. [45] Ibid. 298, 300. [46] Add. 38212, f. 227. [47] Almon, xvii. 693. [48] Rockingham to Frederick Montagu, 22 Oct. 1780, Rockingham mss. [49] See John, 9th Duke of Argyll, *Intimate Society Letters*, ii. 438, on the Dunbartonshire situation. [50] Rockingham mss. [51] Boswell, *Private Pprs.* xiv. 121-2, 123, 126. [52] *Gent. Mag.* 1781, p. 444. [53] H. Furber, *Hen. Dundas*, 197.

E.H.-G.

## DUNDAS, Robert (1713-87), of Arniston, Edinburghshire.

### EDINBURGHSHIRE 1754-May 1760

*b.* 18 July 1713, 1st surv. s. of Robert Dundas, M.P., of Arniston, ld. pres. of the court of session, by his 1st w. Elizabeth, da. of Robert Watson of Muirhouse, Edinburghshire; half-bro. of Henry Dundas (q.v.). *educ.* Edinburgh Univ.; Utrecht, Frankfurt, Paris 1733-7; adv. 1738. *m.* (1) 17 Oct. 1741, Henrietta Baillie (*d.*13 May 1755), da. and h. of Sir James Carmichael, 4th Bt., of Bonnington, Lanark, 1s. *d.v.p.* 4da.; (2) 7 Sept. 1756, Jean, da. of William Grant, Lord Prestongrange (q.v.), 4s. 2da. *suc.* fa. 26 Aug. 1753.

Solicitor-gen. [S] Aug. 1742-Jan. 1746; dean of faculty of advocates 1746-54; ld. adv. Aug. 1754-60; trustee for fisheries and manufactures 1755; ld. pres. of court of session June 1760-*d.*

Dundas, the fourth of a line of distinguished lawyers, was brought up as an anti-Walpole Whig, sharing his father's antipathy to Islay as manager for Scotland. A high-spirited, sociable young man, he returned home in November 1737 after four years' study abroad with little taste for literature or metaphysical subtleties, but a keen determination to gain fame and fortune at the Scottish bar. His marriage to an heiress worth £2,000 p.a. was a turning point in his career. 'In money it made me independent, set me out in a high sphere of life and laid the foundation of all my future success.'[1]

On Walpole's fall he obtained, through his father's connexion with Tweeddale, the office of solicitor-general under the Wilmington Administration, working in close harmony with his friend Andrew

Mitchell. After the outbreak of the '45 he was obliged to flee from Edinburgh to Berwick; he returned in November 1745 but, bitterly at odds with Lord Justice Clerk Milton and the Argyll party, resigned with Tweeddale in January 1746, much against his father's wishes.[2]

He resumed his lucrative bar practice and, disgusted with politics, refused to stand for Edinburghshire at the 1747 election. Connected through his wife with Hyndford and Findlater, hitherto inimical to his father, Dundas did not share his dislike of Newcastle and Pelham, but again in 1750 declined to contest Lanarkshire, though assured by Charles Hope Weir of Pelham's support.[3] After his father's death, however, Dundas accepted the offer of the sitting Member for Edinburghshire to stand down in his favour at the general election, and having secured the approval of Pelham and Hardwicke, also sought to placate Argyll, who wrote to Pelham, 15 Oct. 1753:[4]

> Mr. Dundas of Arniston and I are in all human appearance on a very good footing; he was so good as to say . . . that he would not stand unless I approved of it. He came to see me at Edinburgh and I then returned the compliment by begging him to stand . . . We have since corresponded . . . [on] the great utility it would be to the Government if we could make peace and prevent quarrels among the Whigs of distinction; he seems to be a sensible pretty kind of man; but some of his own friends say he is as hot as his father, though I think that cannot be true to such an extent.

After Dundas's unopposed return, his friend General Bland, commander-in-chief in Scotland, urged Hardwicke and Newcastle to promote William Grant to the bench and appoint Dundas his successor as lord advocate. 'The business of the Crown suffers by not having an able man . . . who is solely attached to the King and owes his preferment purely to the English ministers and not to any of the leading men here.' On receiving the office Dundas showed his anti-Jacobite zeal by a tour of investigation in the Highlands, and wrote to Hardwicke, 14 Sept.: 'I have the satisfaction of believing myself detached from every private party or faction.'[5] He remained in Scotland until his unopposed re-election in December, maintained a close correspondence with Hardwicke and Newcastle, and though outwardly in concert with Argyll was soon involved with Bland and Findlater's son Deskford in the 'English' ministry's intrigues to increase their influence in Scotland at the expense of the 'Viceroy.' When Dundas left for London after Christmas Bland sent to Newcastle a glowing tribute to his 'unusual spirit and success' in office:[6]

> Neither the favours nor frowns of the great men in this country can bias him from telling the truth . . . He is

free from the underhand low cunning peculiar to his countrymen, an enemy to the jobbing so much practised . . . to the destruction of justice and the ruin of this kingdom.

Newcastle and Hardwicke, equally impressed by Dundas's competence, concerted with him the Scottish legislation for the session. His chief task was to introduce and carry through the Government bill for continuing indefinitely the expiring Act of 1747, under which sheriffs depute were appointed during pleasure. Dundas himself had originally been opposed to the principle but for some two years past had been convinced of its necessity. But when he ably moved the bill on 20 Feb. 1755 the occasion was not a triumph for him but for Gilbert Elliot, whose brilliant opposition forced the ministry to a compromise. Alarmed by the support gained by 'the Scotch Cabal', the ministry dropped three other controversial bills which Dundas was to have introduced, but expressed 'entire satisfaction' with his conduct. Hardwicke wrote to Lord President Craigie, 1 Apr. 1755:

> His great knowledge, politeness and candour have amply recommended him to all friends of Government and gained him a thorough confidence; and in the House of Commons he has succeeded beyond expectation for so short a time.[7]

At the end of March Dundas was summoned home by the illness of his wife, whose death in May deprived him of control of the Baillie-Carmichael fortune. 'In an awkward and ticklish situation', with his paternal estate encumbered with debt, Dundas applied to the Government for provision for his stepmother and her family, as compensation for his father's losses in the '15.[8] Relying upon his English patrons, he made no compromise with his Scottish critics. Violently anti-Jacobite, narrowly Presbyterian, Dundas by his illiberal views made many enemies among the moderate church party and the *literati*.[9] Well aware that his secret reports on the jobbery not only of the ruling Argyll party, but of the Marchmonts, Dalrymples and other groups, would 'if discovered render him obnoxious',[10] Dundas urged Newcastle and Hardwicke to bolster his own prestige. He made almost a test case of his recommendation for the place of King's apothecary against Argyll's candidate, and wrote to Newcastle, 24 June 1755:[11]

> This being given to one known to be under my influence increases . . . your Grace's interest and weight . . . It is well known that I have declared my principles of promoting your Grace's interest and influence . . . and that I depend entirely on your countenance and support. Since my return to Scotland these declarations are not agreeable to many.

He was bitterly chagrined when Newcastle, alarmed

by the gathering opposition to the subsidy treaties, called off all attempts to undermine Argyll's authority, and instructed Dundas to wait upon the Duke and 'give him full assurance of acting in concert with him to strengthen Administration and cultivate harmony among all the King's servants in Scotland'.[12] He had, however, his reward. With the backing of Argyll, once more unchallenged 'viceroy' in the reconstructed Administration, he secured provision for his family out of Scottish revenues.[13]

In the new session Dundas spoke on 2 Dec. against the Opposition bill for speedily manning the navy, refuting charges made by Gilbert Elliot concerning the Scottish press gangs. A fluent and forceful speaker, he was listed by Walpole among the 30 outstanding orators in the House, but few speeches of his are recorded.[14]

He retained his office under the Devonshire-Pitt Administration, but remained faithful to Newcastle and voted in his defence in the debate of 2 May 1757 on the loss of Minorca. Under this Administration he concentrated on his official work in Scotland, and in Church affairs further incurred the enmity of the liberal minded by his condemnation of Rev. John Home as the author of 'Douglas', and of the clergymen who attended theatrical performances. Alexander Carlyle attributed his conduct to bigotry, 'want of taste, . . . a certain violence of temper which could endure no one that did not bend to him', and to his jealousy of Sir Gilbert Elliot and Milton, warm partisans of Home.[15]

Dundas was absent from Parliament for most, if not all, of the 1757–8 session;[16] obtained permission from Newcastle to remain in Scotland during the winter of 1758; but attended in February 1759, and on 14 May spoke well in support of the bill for the augmentation of judges' salaries.[17]

During the summer of 1759 Dundas, although not concerned in the Bute-Argyll quarrel, became alarmed by Charles Townshend's attempts to make capital out of the affair, and to gain through Milton an ascendancy in Scottish affairs, particularly when the Dundas interest in Midlothian was threatened by a proposal to set up John Dalrymple, Townshend's friend, as candidate at the next election.[18] Once more he appealed to Newcastle for support:[19] 'Without obtaining some . . . reward to those who serve me I shall soon be forsaken by others.'

Disapproving from its inception the agitation for a Scottish militia bill, which he believed would provide arms for the disaffected, he did not openly oppose it.[20] He did not attend the autumn session and was still absent in Scotland when the militia motion was moved on 4 Mar. 1760. When his own county freeholders demanded a meeting to concert

plans for carrying the bill, Lauderdale the high sheriff was obliged to agree, otherwise, Lauderdale wrote to Newcastle, 'they would have got the lord advocate for the sake of their votes to prevail on the sheriff substitutes to call a meeting without consulting me'.[21] It had long been known that Dundas, having declined an ordinary gown, aimed at the lord presidency of the court of session. When Lord President Craigie fell ill in February 1760 Dundas had at once written to Hardwicke putting in his claim to the succession,[22] and immediately Craigie died, posted to London. Arriving on 13 Mar., he conferred with Hardwicke and Newcastle who, with Argyll's conditional approval, were ready to press his promotion with the King.[23] By 15 Mar. he had obtained his objective[24] and at once threw himself into Newcastle's campaign to fling out the militia bill. In the debate of 15 Apr., in defiance of his own constituency's instructions, he spoke strongly against the bill, the only Scot to do so.[25] 'Universally applauded' by the Newcastle party for his 'great firmness and dignity', he was bitterly attacked and lampooned in Scotland where his speech was regarded as the price paid for the presidency.[26] Kinnoull wrote to Newcastle, 10 July 1760:[27]

> Our friend the advocate is a man of that spirit and resolution that he will always speak his opinion whatever the consequences . . . But as I love the man I cannot but think the conjunction was unfortunate, and I should be sorry if those who do not wish him well succeed in making people in general think that the part he acted proceeded more from motives of interest than conviction. Whatever unpopularity may arise from his opposition to the militia bill his . . . upright conduct in the seat of justice will in a short time acquire him the good opinion of his fellow subjects.

Dundas proved, indeed, the most able and energetic president of the century. He remained connected with Newcastle, who in 1765 offered him the management of Scotland 'in some shape or other' under the Rockingham Administration. This Dundas declined as 'improper for any judge'.[28] Yet he did not scruple to exert all the influence of his office in intervening in Scottish elections, extended his family's interest in numerous constituencies and laid the foundations of the 'empire' exercised by his half brother Henry Dundas.

He died 13 Dec. 1787.

[1] G. W. T. Omond, *Arniston Mems.* 168. [2] Ibid. 138–41. [3] Ibid. 146–9. [4] Newcastle (Clumber) mss. [5] Add. 35448, ff. 120, 156. [6] Add. 32737, f. 483. [7] Add. 35448, ff. 174, 245. [8] *Arniston Mems.* 167. [9] *Letters of D. Hume*, ed. Greig. i. 165–7, 210, 212. [10] Dundas to Hardwicke, 4 June 1755, Add. 35448, f. 259. [11] Add. 32856, f. 173. [12] Dupplin to Dundas, 30 July 1755, Add. 32857, f. 470. [13] Add. 33055, ff. 135, 137, 254, 255. [14] *Parlty. Hist.* xv. 561–5; Walpole, *Mems. Geo. II*, ii. 79–80, 144. [15] Carlyle, *Autobiog.* 334. [16] Add. 32876, f. 234; 35449, f. 86. [17] Add. 32891, f. 129. [18] John Campbell to Townshend, 25 Sept.; Dalrymple to Townshend, 5 Oct.; Sir Alex. Dick to Townshend, 4 Oct. 1759, Buccleuch mss. [19] Add. 32894, f. 183. [20] Elibank to Townshend, 21 Dec. 1759, 7 Jan. 1760,

Buccleuch mss. [21] Add. 32903, f. 106. [22] Add. 35449, f. 210. [23] Add. 32903, ff. 128, 272. [24] *Arniston Mems.* 162. [25] Add. 32904, f. 392. [26] Carlyle, *Autobiog.* 419-20. [27] Add. 32908, f. 165. [28] *Arniston Mems.* 177-9.

E.H.-G.

## DUNDAS, Thomas (c.1708-86), of Fingask and Carronhall, Stirling.

ORKNEY AND SHETLAND     1768-Dec. 1770

*b.* c.1708, 1st s. of Thomas Dundas of Fingask and bro. of Sir Lawrence Dundas (q.v.). *educ.* ?Edinburgh h.s. *m.* (1) 1737, Anne, da. of James Graham of Airth, judge of the Scottish court of Admiralty, *s.p.*; (2) 1744, Lady Janet Maitland, da. of Charles, 6th Earl of Lauderdale [S], 2s. 5da. *suc.* fa. 1762.
Burgess of Edinburgh 1734; dep. Lyon king of arms 1744-54; commr. of police Dec. 1770.

His father, merchant and bailie of Edinburgh, kept a woollen-draper's shop in the Luckenbooths, where Thomas and his brother Lawrence began their business careers selling cloth and stockings. Bailie Dundas was the representative of the family of Fingask, whose Perthshire lands had been alienated in the seventeenth century. He purchased estates in Stirlingshire, which in 1730 were by charter erected into a barony under the name of Fingask.[1] Thereafter the bailie's fortunes suffered a reverse but were restored in part through the successful financial career of Lawrence, on whose advice Thomas left the business to act as his brother's agent. Appointed deputy Lord Lyon in 1744, married to an earl's daughter, the proprietor of Carronhall estate (purchased in 1749), Thomas increased his pretensions. It was probably at his instigation that his father in 1757 instituted proceedings before the court of session challenging the title of George Dundas of Dundas to be served heir as chief of the 'name'. During the hearing it was stated that Thomas the younger of Fingask was 'well known to have made an idol of this headship of the family' and that while he was deputy Lyon king of arms he had fraudulently entered the arms of Dundas of Dundas in the Lyon books under his own family name.[2] The Fingask claim was dismissed in 1758 and Thomas later applied in 1769 to the Lyon office to have his arms differenced from those of Dundas of Dundas.

His career in business and politics was largely dependent on that of his brother Lawrence. He wrote to his son Thomas (q.v.), 27 Oct. 1777:[3]

I began life by marrying early. My parents could not spare me a separate subsistence for my family. I followed business and was happy and independent by your mother's frugal attention to our situation. Your uncle my brother's engagements with public business involved my time and engaged my attention too much for my own situation. From 1744 to 1761 I was his agent and correspondent. After he had acquired his large fortune I was made to believe my family would

benefit. I had at his desire given up my own business in town and retired to the country.

In 1768 Thomas was returned, apparently unopposed, on his brother's interest for Orkney and Shetland. He supported Administration until, on his appointment in December 1770 as a commissioner of police,[4] he vacated his seat in favour of his son.

Although the place had been obtained by Sir Lawrence's influence, Thomas did not think that he had been sufficiently rewarded for his services. 'My greatest error', he wrote in 1777, 'has been trusting so long to my brother's affection and promises. I am deceived and my credit has suffered by his conduct.'[5]

In financial difficulties in 1773, he sold one of his estates (Letham) to Lawrence, and from 1777 he repeatedly asked his son Thomas to leave the army and come home to supervise the family affairs, which were in disorder, the lands encumbered by debts, and the colliery on the estate mismanaged. Thomas assisted him to a considerable extent but declined to give up his military career, and his father's financial position continued to deteriorate. A sick and fretful old man when his son left for Nova Scotia in 1785, he died during his absence on 16 Apr. 1786. 'I fear' wrote his son, 'his life has been a very distressing scene since I left the country.'[6]

[1] Collins, *Peerage*, viii. 384; Anderson, *Scottish Nation*, ii. 95. [2] M. I. Dundas, *Dundas of Fingask*, 43-49, 236. [3] Ibid. 57. [4] *Cal. Home Office Pprs. 1770-2*, 179. [5] *Dundas of Fingask*, 58. [6] Ibid. 58, 62-63, 72.

E.H.-G.

## DUNDAS, Thomas (1741-1820), of Castlecary, Stirling and Aske, nr. Richmond, Yorks.

RICHMOND               16 Mar. 1763-1768
STIRLINGSHIRE          1768-13 Aug. 1794

*b.* 16 Feb. 1741, o.s. of Sir Lawrence Dundas (q.v.). *educ.* Eton 1753-6; St. Andrews 1756. *m.* 14 May 1764, Lady Charlotte Fitzwilliam, da. of William, 1st Earl Fitzwilliam, 6s. 5da. *suc.* fa. as 2nd Bt. 21 Sept. 1781; *cr.* Baron Dundas of Aske 13 Aug. 1794.
Lt.-col. Fauconberg's regt. 1779-83; councillor of state [S] to the Prince of Wales 1783-*d.*; ld. lt. and v.-adm. of Orkney and Shetland 1794-*d.*

Dundas was an amiable, unassuming young man, completely dominated by his ambitious father, who, having purchased control of Richmond, offered Lord Ancram £4,000 to vacate his seat in favour of Thomas.[1] Marriage in 1764 to Rockingham's niece had little effect on Thomas's politics; dutifully following his father, he was a silent supporter of the Grenville Administration; and voted against the repeal of the Stamp Act, 22 Feb. 1766. During the winter of 1766-7 he, like Sir Lawrence, was counted among the Bedfords, voted with Opposition on the land tax, 27 Feb. 1767, but was chiefly concerned in furthering his father's Scottish interests, notably in connexion with the Forth and Clyde canal. He supported the Grafton and North Administrations.

In 1766 Sir Lawrence, shortly after purchasing the controlling interest in Orkney, proposed his son as candidate at the next election;[2] at the same time he was creating a powerful interest in Stirlingshire, which secured Thomas's return in 1768, when Orkney was turned over to Sir Lawrence's brother Thomas.

In 1774 Thomas was returned for Richmond, but having secured re-election for Stirlingshire relinquished Richmond to his cousin Charles. Both he and Charles had been indirectly involved in a controversy in the burgh of Stirling resulting in the exposure of a system of corruption which occasioned the town's disfranchisement.[3] The case was still before the courts when Thomas was elected chairman of the parliamentary select committee on the notorious Hindon election, and made his first recorded speech on 27 Apr. 1775 for an inquiry into the corruption of witnesses.[4]

This probably marks the beginning of Dundas's interest in parliamentary and burgh reform, despite his father's notoriety in election affairs. In 1777 Sir Lawrence, violently attacked in Edinburgh by Henry Dundas and the Buccleuch interest, deputed Thomas to vindicate his conduct, and even the scurrilous pamphleteers found little to defame in 'Tommy's' personal conduct.[5]

In Parliament he supported Administration until 1779, when his father became disgusted with North's mismanagement of the war. During the summer Thomas helped to raise a regiment, with Lord Fauconberg as colonel and himself as lieutenant-colonel.[6] Absent from the division on pensions of 21 Feb. 1780, Thomas voted with his father against Administration over economical reform on 8 Mar. His family connexion with Rockingham now became a political alliance; he voted with Opposition in every recorded division to the end of the Parliament.

Re-elected unopposed for Stirlingshire, on a compromise with Lord Graham, Thomas assisted and advised his father in Edinburgh and the other contested elections in which the family interest was engaged. In the new Parliament Sir Lawrence, while remaining hostile to North and Henry Dundas, sought to maintain his personal connexion with Sandwich, to whom Thomas wrote on 22 Sept. 1781, immediately after his father's death:[7] 'May I flatter myself with the continuance of that friendship, the good effects of which I have so often experienced from the earliest part of my life.' Rumour suggested that 'Tommy Dundas' when at

Windsor had been 'so distinguished by the civility of both the King and Queen, that when Sir Lawrence died the Opposition had very little hopes of his continuing to vote against the Court'.[8] These suspicions proved unfounded: Sir Thomas took over his father's policies, and the direction of the family interest; voted with Opposition on 12 Dec. 1781 on Lowther's motion against the war, but from friendship to Sandwich voted with Administration on the censure of the Admiralty on 7 and 20 Feb. 1782. This incurred comment that 'the Dundasses' were 'veering about very fast',[9] but Thomas voted with Opposition on Conway's motion on 22 Feb. and in every further recorded division until North's fall.

After Rockingham's death Sir Thomas adhered to Fox, and voted against Shelburne's peace preliminaries, 18 Feb. 1783. He voted for Pitt's parliamentary reform bill on 7 May 1783, and thereafter directed his main efforts to the internal reform of Scottish burghs.

In August 1783 he obtained from Portland the office of lord advocate for his boyhood friend Henry Erskine,[10] with whom he maintained an intimate and semi-official correspondence on political and electoral affairs, and, as a fellow councillor of state to the Prince of Wales, transmitted to him the Prince's instructions on his Scottish establishment.[11] Strongly supporting Fox's East India bill, he was consulted by Portland and Fox on countering Pitt's attacks, and at their direction urged Erskine to 'send up' every Government supporter for the debate of 27 Nov. Enraged by the Lords' rejection of the bill and by Pitt's assuming office, Dundas, anticipating an immediate dissolution, concerted with Erskine plans for a general election, confident that 'the game was up with this still-born Administration'. When Pitt, nevertheless, maintained his minority Government in office, Dundas diligently prepared for his election campaign, and procured from Erskine and others detailed 'states' of the situation, sharing in effect the Scottish Opposition management with William Adam.[12]

At the general election he secured Stirlingshire for himself, Orkney for his cousin Thomas, and Tain Burghs for Charles Fox. Patrick Graeme, the sheriff of Orkney, wrote to a friend:[13]

> I know Sir Thomas from being at College with him. I regard and esteem him and both his cousins as among the most gentlemanly and good-tempered people I ever knew . . . he has it not in his nature a wish to oppress or injure any one.

Sir Thomas, in conformity with his liberal views, was 'very well inclined' to bring on to the electoral roll the hitherto unrepresented freeholders of Shetland, whatever their political attitude.[14] In the new

Parliament, distressed by reports of the famine in Scotland, which he himself had done his best to alleviate, he moved on 1 July 1784 for a committee of inquiry.[15]

He voted for Pitt's reform proposals, 18 Apr. 1785, but otherwise opposed his measures, voted against his Irish propositions, 13 May 1785, as detrimental to Scottish interests, and against Richmond's fortifications plan, 27 Feb. 1786. An active committee man, Dundas rarely spoke in the House, and then only on Scottish or Yorkshire concerns.[16] He strongly supported, on 17 June 1788, Sheridan's motion to bring in a bill to reform Scottish burghs.[17] During the Regency crisis Dundas, as a close friend of the Prince of Wales, was intimately concerned in consultations for a new Administration.[18]

'Beloved by men of all parties in Scotland' for his 'respectable and independent character',[19] Sir Thomas went over to Pitt with Portland in 1794 and was rewarded with a peerage. He died 14 June 1820.

[1] Newcastle to Devonshire, 23 Dec. 1762, Add. 32945, f. 345.
[2] P. N. Sutherland Graeme, *Parlty. Rep. Orkney and Shetland 1754–1900* (*Orkney Misc.* 1953), p. 66. [3] Stirling Guildry Bk. 115, 117, 137; *Scots Mag.* 1775, pp. 163, 731. [4] Almon, i. 443, 444. [5] Edinburgh Pamphlets 1776–7, e.g. *A letter . . . to Thomas Dundas of Castlecary*, 9 Sept. 1777. [6] Fortescue, iv. 407, 408, 551. [7] Sandwich mss. [8] James Hare to Ld. Carlisle, 5 Jan. 1782, *HMC Carlisle*, 564. [9] Same to same, 11 Feb 1782, ibid. 575. [10] Portland to Erskine, 15 Aug. 1783, Alex. Fergusson, *Hen. Erskine*, 239. [11] Dundas to Erskine, 1 Dec. 1783, ibid. 260. [12] Ibid. 248–9, 250–3, 254–7. [13] *Orkney Misc.* 1953, 70. [14] Ibid. 71. [15] Debrett, xv. 309. [16] Stockdale, xiii. 177, 183; xiv. 95. [17] Ibid. xv. 191–2. [18] M. I. Dundas, *Dundas of Fingask*, 92–93. [19] *Pol. State of Scotland*, 243, 322.

E.H.-G.

## DUNDAS, Thomas (1750–94), of Fingask and Carronhall, Stirling.

ORKNEY AND SHETLAND 31 Jan. 1771–1780, 1784–1790

*b.* 30 June 1750, 1st s. of Thomas Dundas of Fingask, bro. of Charles and nephew of Sir Lawrence Dundas (qq.v.). *educ.* Edinburgh h.s. *m.* 9 Jan. 1784, Lady Eleonora Elizabeth Home, da. of Alexander, 9th Earl of Home [S], 1s. 6da. *suc.* fa. 16 Apr. 1786.

Cornet 1 Drag. Gds. 1766; capt. 63 Ft. 1769, maj. 1776; lt.-col. 80 Ft. 1777; col. 1782; half pay 1783–93; commr. for loyalist claims 1783–90; dep. gov. Guernsey Jan. 1793, gov. May 1793; maj.-gen. 1793; col. 68 Ft. 1794; gov. Guadeloupe May 1794.

Thomas Dundas owed his first commission to his uncle Sir Lawrence. He was a captain in the 63rd Ft. stationed in Ireland when on 31 Jan. 1771, a few months before he was of age, he replaced his father as Member for Orkney and Shetland. In Parliament he joined his uncle's group in support of North's Administration. He is not known to have spoken in the House.

He obtained his lieutenant-colonelcy in a new regiment raised by the city of Edinburgh, and in April 1779 sailed with his regiment for South Carolina. His reputation as an officer stood high. The mother of one of his ensigns wrote to her son:

Always take Col. Dundas's advice. He has seen much of the world . . . everybody speaks well of him and whatever character he gives of the officers of his regiment will be believed before anybody.

He was present at the siege and capture of Charleston in 1780, served with Tarleton and Cornwallis in Virginia and the Carolinas, and in October 1781 was one of the commissioners appointed to arrange the surrender at Yorktown. As an absentee, who in any case had little contact with his constituency, he was replaced by his brother at the general election of 1780.

In June 1783, shortly after his return, he accepted from Lord John Cavendish a place on the board to examine the claims of the American loyalists. At the general election of 1784 he was again returned for his former constituency.

On 18 Apr. 1785 he voted with his brother and Sir Thomas in support of Pitt's motion for parliamentary reform, but all three voted against the Irish propositions in the following month. In September 1785 he sailed for Nova Scotia to examine the claims of loyalists settled there. He wrote from Halifax on 29 Nov. 1785 to his man of business, John Dundas, of his 'cruel situation . . . forced by conviction and a sense of duty to leave my father in the state he was, and my mother and wife who both required my assistance; but my coming here was unavoidable, my future prospects and character depended upon it.' Joined by his wife in 1786, he spent the next two years in Nova Scotia (on whose constitution he prepared elaborate notes), New Brunswick, and Canada.

His return to England in 1788 coincided with the political crisis over the King's insanity. Resuming his seat in Parliament, he voted on 16 Dec. 1788 and 16 Feb. 1789 with the Opposition on the Regency question. On 28 Jan. 1789 Sir Thomas Dundas wrote to Col. Dundas a secret and confidential letter, informing him that as soon as the Regency was settled the office of commander-in-chief would be given to the Duke of York, who planned to appoint 'a military man as confidential secretary' and would offer the post to Col. Dundas. But Dundas was unwilling to accept. Sir Thomas, exasperated at his cousin's 'diffidence', wrote to Charles, 3 Feb. 1789: 'It is but a bad compliment to the understanding of the Duke of Portland, Lord Fitzwilliam, William Adam and myself, that he puts his own opinion in competition with ours.'

Col. Dundas was essentially a soldier, not greatly interested in a parliamentary career. At the general election of 1790 he was defeated for Orkney and Shetland and did not seek to re-enter Parliament.

He died of yellow fever on the expedition to Guadeloupe, 3 June 1794.[1]

[1] M. I. Dundas, *Dundas of Fingask*, 61, 63, 64, 69–70, 93–94. For an account of Dundas's life and death in the West Indies, see *Gent. Mag.* 1843, ii. 155–160, 249–256.

E.H.-G.

## DUNGARVAN, Visct., *see* BOYLE, Hamilton

## DUNNING, John (1731–83), of Ashburton, Devon.

CALNE 1768–Mar. 1782

*b.* 18 Oct. 1731, o. surv. s. of John Dunning of Ashburton by Agnes, da. of Henry Judsham of Modbury, Devon. *educ.* Ashburton g.s.; M. Temple 1752, called 1756. *m.* 31 Mar. 1780, Elizabeth, da. of John Baring of Larkbear, Devon, sis. of John and Francis Baring (qq.v.), 2s. *suc.* fa. 1 Dec. 1780; *cr.* Baron Ashburton 8 Apr. 1782.

Recorder, Bristol 1766–*d.*; bencher, M. Temple 1768, reader 1776, treasurer 1779; solicitor-gen. Jan. 1768–Jan. 1770; P.C. 27 Mar. 1782; chancellor of the duchy of Lancaster Mar. 1782–*d.*

John Dunning began his legal career in the office of his father, a country attorney, and ended as the foremost advocate of his day. Shelburne, his political patron, wrote of him:[1]

He had the greatest power of reasoning which can be conceived, and such a habit of it that he could not slight a cause, no more than an able artist could suffer a piece of work to go imperfect from his hands. He could not pass a link in the chain, and had such a faculty of arrangement that he would take an absolute chaos of matter and return it to you in an instant so clear and distinct as of itself to present a proper judgment without need of discussion . . . His industry, his liberality, his acuteness added to his capacity, procured him the personal confidence, reverence, and attachment of almost all the great families, who always found him no less a gentleman than he was a lawyer. The only doubt was whether he excelled most at equity or common law. There was none as to anybody's coming up to him in either.

Chatham, who met him for the first time in December 1770, had an equally high opinion. 'Mr. Dunning . . . is another being from any I have known of the profession', he wrote to Shelburne on 3 Dec. 1770.[2] ' . . . Mr. Dunning is not a lawyer, at the same time that he is the law itself.'

Dunning became prominent in 1764 as a result of the law cases which followed Wilkes's arrest, and about this time he became friendly with Shelburne. On 9 Nov. 1765 he wrote to inform Shelburne that he had been offered through a friend (presumably authorized by the Rockingham Administration) a silk gown and a seat in Parliament—'your Lordship's wishes will determine mine either to do so [accept] or break off the treaty entirely', he wrote.[3] 'I would certainly lay hold of the opportunity', re-

plied Shelburne,[4] 'if either measures are fully explained as to leave no room for any future difference of opinion, or if you are left entirely at liberty without any engagement even implied.' But nothing came of this.

Dunning's appointment in January 1768 to be solicitor-general surprised contemporaries, for Shelburne's influence in the Administration was declining rapidly. It probably owed a good deal to Camden, who was Dunning's close friend. At the general election of 1768 Dunning was brought into Parliament by Shelburne, but did not resign with Shelburne and Barré in October. He hesitated a good deal, consulted Barré, talked about his wishing to resign, and finally allowed himself to be persuaded by Camden to stay.[5]

He remained for over a year in office under Grafton, an awkward and anomalous position, for Shelburne was in open Opposition. On 8 Nov. 1768 he made his first recorded speech in the House.

Both Grenville and Burke attacked the chancellor violently [Rigby reported to Bedford[6]] as having with Lord Chatham been the principal cause of the American disturbances. Dunning defended his friend, but not with such abilities as I think promise to make so great a figure in the House of Commons as he does at the bar.

Similarly, Walpole writes that his 'fame did not rise . . . in proportion to the celebrity he had attained at the bar';[7] and Wraxall:[8] his speeches 'resembled more the pleading of the bar than the oratory of the senate'. His appearance was unprepossessing and his voice husky, yet he was listened to with attention and respect.

When in December 1768 the affair of Wilkes's libel was about to come before the House, Dunning, writes Grafton,[9]

differed in opinion with most of the King's servants as to the mode of conducting the accusation. This offended Lord North much more than it need have done: he complained to me the next day most bitterly, and entreated me to desire Lord Camden to see Mr. Dunning upon it; which I did, though very reluctantly, seeing that Lord North was so much affected.

Camden took Dunning's part; but, continues Grafton:[10]

The prejudice of Lord North against Mr. Dunning was not removed by this explanation of ours, nor could he be brought to treat him with that confidence which the situation of the other had a right to expect from the minister of the House of Commons.

North had good reason to complain, for Dunning gave little assistance in the House of Commons; and when he did speak was trimming and inconclusive.[11] On the Middlesex election he neither spoke nor voted: like Camden, he disapproved of Government's proceedings, yet retained his office.

On 9 Jan. 1770, when the Middlesex question was renewed after the re-emergence of Chatham, Dunning voted with Opposition and shortly afterwards resigned. Henceforth he adhered strictly to Shelburne. During the greater part of North's Administration Dunning and Barré were Shelburne's only followers of consequence in the Commons. Dunning, though an inferior debater to Barré, was of great weight in the House, and seems to have reserved himself for the more important debates. Yet he never quite attained the front rank of parliamentary speakers.

After the defeat of Burke's economical reform bill in March 1780, Dunning took the lead in the Commons of the movement to reduce the influence of the Crown. On 6 Apr. he introduced two resolutions, designed to secure the widest measure of support: 'that the influence of the Crown has increased, is increasing, and ought to be diminished' (the famous 'Dunning's motion');[12] and 'that it is competent for this House to reform the civil list or any part of the public expenditure'. 'If the committee [of the whole House] should agree with me in the resolutions', he said,[13] 'I mean to follow them up with real, substantive, practicable measures.' The first was carried against Administration by 233 votes to 215, the second without a division; and on 10 Apr. Dunning carried two further resolutions for reform of the Household and the civil list. But his motion of 24 Apr., that Parliament should not be prorogued until measures had been taken to reduce the influence of the Crown, was lost by 254 to 203.

On 25 Mar. 1782 Dunning announced to the House the formation of the Rockingham Administration.[14] The same day he wrote to Shelburne:[15]

I have always given myself the credit enough with your Lordship to have it believed, and not imputed to a silly affectation, that instead of desiring I have a perfect dread of any office of any sort, proceeding from a perfect satisfaction with my present situation, an apprehension that I cannot change it with credit to myself or advantage to my friends, and that as far as such talents as mine can be of any use they may be better employed where I am.

But Shelburne's wishes prevailed. Dunning was made a peer and entered the Cabinet; and the duchy of Lancaster, with a pension of £4000 p.a., was conferred on him until the chief justiceship of the King's bench should become vacant. His acceptance of a pension was criticized in the House, and his profession of disinterestedness, made when he was in opposition,[16] brought up against him.

In the interregnum following Shelburne's defeat in Feb. 1783 Ashburton was frequently consulted by the King.[17] He withdrew from the Cabinet on the formation of the Fox-North Coalition; and died on 18 Aug. 1783.

[1] Fitzmaurice, *Shelburne*, ii. 318-19. [2] *Chatham Corresp.* iv. 41. [3] Lansdowne mss. [4] 10 Nov. 1765, ibid. [5] There are two letters, undated, from Barré to Shelburne in the Lansdowne mss, reporting conversations with Dunning about his expected resignation. One was written before 28 Oct. 1768, the other probably on 28 Oct. See also Camden to Grafton, 4 Nov. 1768, Grafton, *Autobiog.* 225. [6] 9 Nov. 1769, Bedford mss 57, f. 224. [7] *Mems. Geo III*, iii. 145. [8] *Mems.* ii. 39-40. [9] *Autobiog.* 227. [10] Ibid. 227-8. [11] See his speeches of 26 Jan. 1769, *Cavendish's Debates*, i. 203; 8 Feb. 1769, ibid. 218; and 24 Feb. 1769, ibid. 249-50 .[12] About this motion, see Fitzmaurice, ii. 318. [13] Almon, xvii. 447-54. [14] Debrett, vi. 510. [15] Fitzmaurice, ii. 90. [16] 21 Feb. 1780, Almon, xvii. 136. [17] See his memo., Fitzmaurice, ii. 253-61.

J.B.

**DUNTZE, John** (c.1735-95), of Rockbeare, nr. Exeter, Devon.

TIVERTON    22 Feb. 1768-5 Feb. 1795

*b.* c.1735, s. of John Duntze of Exeter, merchant, by Elizabeth, da. of James Hawker or Hawkes of Luppitt, Devon, wid. of Nicholas Munckley of Exeter. *m.* in or bef. 1765, Frances, da. of Samuel Lewis, 3s. 3da. *cr.* Bt. 8 Nov. 1774.

Duntze was an Exeter clothier and general merchant. Before 1776 his name does not appear in the London trade directories; in 1776 he founded a bank in London with John Halliday (q.v.) and William Mackworth Praed, which in 1781 became Halliday, Duntze, Saunders, and Hamilton, and seems to have been dissolved in 1782. He held no Bank of England stock, and did not invest in Government loans. In short, he was a provincial merchant, with few City connexions.

He first appeared at Tiverton in 1764 as an ally of the Barings, but quarrelled with them and began to build up his own interest. In 1765 he was elected to the corporation, and represented the borough in Parliament without a contest.

In the House he twice voted against the court over Wilkes in 1769, and on the Spanish convention, 13 Feb. 1771. He voted for Meredith's motion on the 39 Articles, 6 Feb. 1772. In John Robinson's surveys for the royal marriage bill he is noted as an opponent. His first speech seems to have been on 26 Jan. 1773, against Sawbridge's motion for annual Parliaments.

He got his baronetcy through Nathaniel Ryder, his colleague at Tiverton and a supporter of Administration, and presumably gave assurances about his conduct in Parliament. 'The vanity is all my own and not my wife's', he wrote to Ryder on 29 Nov. 1774.[1] On 5 Apr. 1775 he spoke for the bill to restrain the trade of the American colonies, using commonplace and familiar arguments:[2]

The Americans had by their open violence and repeated acts of disobedience forfeited the goodwill and protection of this country; and that it therefore became necessary for us to retaliate, in order to bring them back to a proper sense of their duty and dependence.

Bad health prevented his regular attendance: Philip Thicknesse, who treated him for gout, said that 'scarce any man has suffered more from the disorder';[3] and Robinson wrote in his survey for the general election of 1780: 'Sir John Duntze will come in again if his health will permit.' He was absent from the critical divisions of 1781–2 until 15 Mar., when he voted for the court in the last division of North's ministry.

He did not vote on Shelburne's peace preliminaries, 18 Feb. 1783, and was classed by Robinson as a follower of North. Nor did he vote on Fox's East India bill. Robinson before the general election, and William Adam after it, classed him as an opponent of Pitt, but his only known vote after 1784 was for Pitt on the Regency.

He died 5 Feb. 1795.

[1] 'Tiverton Letters and Papers', *N. & Q.* clxx. 204. [2] Almon, i. 421. [3] *Gent. Mag.* 1786, p. 108.

J.B.

**DUPPLIN, Visct.,** *see* **HAY, Thomas** (*d.* 1787)

**DURAND, John** (?1719–88), of Woodcote Lodge, Carshalton, Surr.[1]

| | |
|---|---|
| AYLESBURY | 1768–1774 |
| PLYMPTON ERLE | 7 Feb. 1775–1780 |
| SEAFORD | 1780–1784 |

Sheriff, Surr. 1767–8; commr. of Greenwich Hospital 1781–*d.*; e. bro. of Trinity House 1775–*d.*; director, French Hospital 1769–*d.*

Durand served as a captain in the East India Company's merchant service; returned to London with a 'handsome fortune' in or about 1762; and became a London merchant with premises at 51 Lime Street. He was also a partner in the firm of Durand and Nixon, Greenland Dock, Rotherhithe.

In 1767 he began to look round for a seat in Parliament. 'What think you of Mr. Durand?' wrote John Walsh (q.v.) to Lord Clive, 25 Nov. 'He has had folly and impertinence enough to talk loudly about Worcester: he is now set out for Totnes.'[2] He was not a serious candidate at either place, though he was said to have offered £4,000 for a borough seat before he went to Aylesbury. There he had 'established himself' strongly enough a few weeks before the election to discourage any opposition. On 23 Feb. 1768 Eyre Coote (q.v.), who had thought of standing, wrote to Sir William Lee that Durand was 'fully determined to get into the House at any rate, provided money can effect it'.[3] His first recorded votes were with Opposition over Wilkes on 27 Jan.

1769, and again on 2 Feb., but the next day he voted with Administration on the expulsion of Wilkes, and continued to support them for the rest of the Parliament.

In 1769 he applied for a contract for victualling troops in the ceded West Indian islands, and in 1770 took it over from Anthony Bacon, his colleague at Aylesbury. In 1771 he obtained a contract for supplying the navy with masts, and during the American war received half a dozen other contracts in America and the West Indies.[4]

In 1774 Durand again stood at Aylesbury, but was defeated, and seems to have attempted to intervene at Honiton. In 1775 he was returned as a Government candidate on Lord Edgcumbe's interest at Plympton. During this Parliament John Robinson in an undated letter to Sandwich complained that Durand was 'remarkably *slack*' and could not be depended on; but in 1780 he appears in the five extant division lists, each time voting with Administration.[5] No provision seems to have been made by the Treasury for bringing Durand in again at the general election, and he had to shift for himself. He planned to oppose the Fane candidates at Lyme, but was warned that North would take such an intervention 'extremely ill'.[6] He was eventually returned on the Treasury interest for Seaford, in circumstances which have not been explained.[7]

Durand continued to vote with North till his fall, though Sandwich, two days before the division on Conway's motion against the war, 27 Feb. 1782, told Robinson he would write to Durand—'all the rest of my friends are so orthodox that any application from me seems superfluous'.[8] He voted against Shelburne's peace preliminaries, 18 Feb. 1783, and was classed by Robinson, March 1783, as a follower of Sandwich. He did not vote on Fox's East India bill, 27 Nov. 1783, but was classed as 'contra' by Robinson in January 1784, and 'absent' by Stockdale. He did not stand again in 1784. There is no record of his having spoken during his fifteen years in Parliament. The *English Chronicle*, an Opposition newspaper, wrote of him in 1780: 'No man understands the *Multiplication Table* with more comprehensiveness and precision of intelligence; but in the laws of his country, or in the duties of a legislator, there is perhaps no individual more completely ignorant.'

He died 30 July 1788, aged 69.[9]

[1] He does not appear in the Durand pedigrees in the French Hospital coll., Univ. Coll., London. There is a note by Wagner that he was unable to trace Durand's background and parentage. [2] Clive mss. [3] Lee mss, Bucks. RO. [4] T29/40/72, 318; T29/41/55; T29/42/ 362, 442; T29/46/385; T29/48/399; T29/58/327; T29/61/369; T54/41/153, 480; T54/42/183–5, 475, 571; T54/43/435. [5] Geo. Jackson to Sandwich, n.d., Sandwich mss. [6] North to Robinson, 7 Sept. 1780, Abergavenny mss. [7] See SEAFORD constituency. [8] Abergavenny mss. [9] Manning & Bray, *Hist. Surr.* ii. 547.

M.M.D.

**DURANT, George** (1731–80), of Tong Castle, Salop.

EVESHAM 1768–1774

*bap.* 20 Nov. 1731,[1] 2nd s. of Rev. Josiah Durant, rector of Hagley, Worcs. by Anne, da. of George Hand of Lichfield.[2] *educ.* St. Edmund Hall, Oxf. 1750. *m.* July 1773, Maria, da. of Mark Beaufoy, a Quaker, and niece of Henry Beaufoy (q.v.), 1s. 1da.

Durant's grandfather, father, and brother were rectors of Hagley, but he fell foul of the Lyttelton family: about 1756 he had an affair with Elizabeth, wife of George Lyttelton (q.v.)—one cause of their separation.[3]

Durant was a clerk in the Pay Office, 1757–Feb. 1762, from 1762, first clerk; in a list sent on 1 Apr. 1761 to James West (q.v.) by George Munro, who was trying 'to get a footing' in the Office, the value of Durant's employment appears as £250 p.a.[4] In 1758 Durant acted as deputy-paymaster to the expedition against Guadeloupe. John Calcraft (q.v.) explained to Peter Taylor (q.v.) on 19 Oct.[5] that even had it been possible to send his son, R. Paris Taylor (q.v.), it would not have been thought advisable—'the money is to be issued in Spanish silver, and what is more, the climate to which they are destined not very healthy . . . so Durant of the Office goes.'

On 13 Jan. 1762, Henry Fox wrote to his friend J. L. Nicholl of the Pay Office: 'Mr. Durant has asked to go paymaster [to the expedition against Havana]; Mr. West . . . recommends Mr. Munro.'[6] And on 15 Feb. 1762 to Lord Albemarle:[7]

I wish Mr. Lechmere had taken his determination to decline the deputy paymastership a little sooner . . . The very short time he has left me has made it extremely difficult to find a proper person . . . I have appointed Mr. Durant, who is first clerk in my office, well acquainted with the business and was employed in the same capacity with the expedition to Guadeloupe; he behaved himself very well in that service . . . I have promised him he shall remain with the troops as long as they continue abroad; it would not have been worth his while to have undertaken this employment on any other conditions.

From that expedition Durant returned a rich man. In 1764 he purchased the Tong estate from the Duke of Kingston,[8] 'demolished all but the main block of Sir Harry Vernon's castle built in 1500, and encased the remaining portion of it in stone according to a fanciful design of his own, a mixture of Gothic and Moorish architecture',[9] spending large sums on thus 'embellishing' the Castle and improving the estate.[10] But how had he managed to amass that fortune? A search of the War Office records[11] has shown that over £300,000 of Government money passed through his hands. There was also the enormous prize money of that expedition: after deducting the share of the commander-in-chief and

his second-in-command, £221,000 was left for the army. Here was a chance of pickings: owing to heavy mortality and sickness, only a small proportion of the soldiers were alive or present to draw their share. Even so, the size of Durant's fortune, and the short time in which it was amassed, remain a puzzle.

At the Southwark by-election of 1765 Durant canvassed the borough against Henry Thrale (q.v.), although outsiders stood little chance in it. Between 23 Sept. and 5 Oct. Durant's advertisement appeared in the *Public Advertiser*, and he conducted a strenuous canvass in the borough, but gave it up on 15 Oct.

He next attempted Evesham. Mark Beaufoy, whose family was connected with the borough, wrote on 1 Sept. 1767 to Sir John Rushout—Sir John and his son were the sitting Members:[12]

Having been informed by letters from Evesham of thy resolution not to stand a contested election for that borough, I take the liberty, on behalf of Mr. Durant, to renew my proposal, made when I had the pleasure of waiting upon thee at Northwick, viz. That in consideration of thy interest, Mr. Durant will pay the expense of Mr. Rushout's return, provided Mr. Durant becomes one of the sitting Members.

Rushout's reply is not extant, but even if accepted, the offer could not have been openly avowed—James West (q.v.) reported to Newcastle about Evesham on 11 Oct.:[13]

There will probably be a very warm contest: Sir John Rushout has declined on account of age, and the town where are 900 voters were so angry at his bringing in two last time, that Mr. Rushout has been obliged to declare, he will not join any one and in that light only is his security. Mr. Durant without one gentleman in the country to support him, spends money, yet I think my son must succeed at last for in the turn things have taken there and the number and nature of the electors, nothing can be certain till the time of election.

In the end West's son did not stand but Sir John Rushout re-appeared as candidate—was it a feint to keep away others? On 24 Mar. 1768 West wrote to Newcastle:[14] 'I am sorry to tell your Grace Sir John Rushout on the morning of the election declined at Evesham and Mr. Durant and his son Rushout were chose.'

There is no record of Durant having spoken in the House. On 3 Feb. 1769 he is listed as voting for the expulsion of Wilkes, and on 8 May for seating Luttrell. But on 6 Dec. 1770 he is reported to have voted with Opposition for Glynn's motion for a committee on the administration of justice—he may, however, have been confused with Thomas Durrant, whose recorded votes were all with Opposition and who does not appear in that list. Over the royal marriage bill, March 1772, Durant was classed by

Robinson as 'pro, present'. No further votes of his are recorded; but again it is possible that some vote of his was assigned to John Durand, another Government supporter.

Durant stood again for Evesham in 1774 but was badly defeated. In July 1780 John Robinson noted in his survey against Evesham: 'Mr. Durant who represented it in the last Parliament it is said will stand again and with success, he was found a good friend to Government.' But he died on 4 Aug., two months before the general election; and is buried in St. Bartholomew's church at Tong, among the eight magnificent tombs of the Vernons whose castle he destroyed.

¹ Hagley par. reg. ² A. L. Reade, *Johnsonian Gleanings*, iv. 198. ³ M. Wyndham, *Chrons. of 18th Cent.* ii. 271–2, 280. See also T. Frost, *Life of Ld. Lyttelton*, 38–43. ⁴ Add. 34728, f. 74. ⁵ Add. 17494, ff. 36–37. ⁶ Hen. Fox mss. ⁷ Albemarle mss. ⁸ S. Bagshaw, *Hist. Salop*, 487. ⁹ Griffiths, *Guide to Tong Church*, 66. ¹⁰ H. F. J. Vaughan, 'Some Account of the Rickley Grange Estate, Salop', *Shropshire Arch. Soc. Trans.* 1878–9, pp. 213–72. ¹¹ T. H. McGuffie, 'A Deputy Paymaster's Fortune', *Jnl. Army Hist. Res.* 1954. ¹² G. Beaufoy, *Leaves from a Beech Tree*, 113. ¹³ Add. 32985, ff. 443–4. ¹⁴ Add. 32989, f. 252.

L.B.N.

**DURRANT, Thomas** (?1733–90), of Scottow, Norf.

ST. IVES 1768–1774

*b.* ?1733, 1st s. of Davy Durrant of I. Temple by Margaret, da. and h. of Thomas Durrant of Scottow. *educ.* Horstead; Caius, Camb. 17 Apr. 1752, aged 18. *m.* 1773, Susanna, da. of Hambleton Custance of Weston, Norf., 2s. 1da. *suc.* mother 1740; *cr.* Bt. 22 Jan. 1784.
Sheriff, Norf. 1784–5.

In 1768 Durrant successfully contested the expensive borough of St. Ives on the interest of his Norfolk neighbour Lord Buckinghamshire. In Parliament all his reported votes were with Opposition, though Robinson's second survey on the royal marriage bill, March 1772, lists him as 'pro, present'. There is no record of his having spoken in the House. He did not stand again in 1774.

Durrant died 6 Sept. 1790.

M.M.D.

**DUTTON, James** (1744–1820), of Sherborne, Glos.

GLOUCESTERSHIRE 24 Jan. 1781–1784

*b.* 22 Oct. 1744, 2nd s. of James Lenox Dutton of Sherborne by his 2nd w. Jane, da. of Christopher Bond of Newland, Glos. *educ.* Eton 1755–62; Ch. Ch. Oxf. 1763. *m.* 7 July 1774, Elizabeth, da. of Wenman Coke (q.v.) of Holkham, Norf., 1s. 3da. *suc.* half-bro. 29 Aug. 1771; *cr.* Baron Sherborne 20 May 1784.
Sheriff, Glos. 1779–80.

Dutton was returned for Gloucestershire as the candidate of the Beaufort interest. His first recorded vote was for Lowther's motion against the war,

12 Dec. 1781. He did not vote in the divisions of February 1782. On the censure motions of 8 and 15 Mar. he voted with Administration. In Robinson's list of March 1783, drawn up after the division on Shelburne's peace preliminaries, he is marked as 'abroad'. He voted for Fox's East India bill, 27 Nov. 1783, but subsequently supported Pitt. He did not stand in 1784, having received a promise of a peerage. There is no record of his having spoken in the House.

He died 22 May 1820.

I.R.C.

**DYSON, Jeremiah** (?1722–76), of Stoke, nr. Guildford, Surr.

YARMOUTH I.o.W. 28 Dec. 1762–1768
WEYMOUTH AND
  MELCOMBE REGIS 1768–1774
HORSHAM 1774–16 Sept. 1776

*b.* ?1722, 1st s. of Jeremiah Dyson of Bartholomew Close, London. *educ.* Edinburgh Univ.; Leyden 1742; L. Inn 1740, called 1746. *m.* June 1756, Dorothy, da. of his cos. Ely Dyson, 3s. 4da. *suc.* fa. 1730.
Clerk of the House of Commons 1748–62; sec. to Treasury May 1762–Apr. 1764; ld. of Trade Apr. 1764–Dec. 1768; ld. of Treasury Dec. 1768–Mar. 1774; P.C. 9 Mar. 1774; cofferer of the Household Mar. 1774–*d.*

According to Horace Walpole, Dyson was the son of a tailor.¹ But his father was a wealthy man, and Dyson inherited estates in Hertfordshire, Buckinghamshire, and Bedfordshire.² He was educated as a Dissenter.³

After having held a subordinate place in the clerical service of the House of Commons, in 1748 he bought the clerkship from Nicholas Hardinge (q.v.) for £6,000. 'His tenure of the clerkship . . . is mainly notable for his memorandum of 1751 which finally regulated the system by which fees on private bills were calculated, and for his contriving to obtain an official residence for the clerk of the House in the precincts of the palace of Westminster.' On his retirement in 1762 he refused to sell the office, as had hitherto been the custom, 'which example his successors felt bound to follow'.⁴ John Hatsell, Dyson's deputy and later clerk of the House, dedicated to him his *Precedents of Proceedings in the House of Commons* (1776), and wrote of his 'universal knowledge upon all subjects which relate to the history of Parliament'.⁵

In May 1762 Dyson became one of Bute's secretaries to the Treasury, and in December was brought into Parliament by Administration. 'His parts were excellent', wrote Walpole.⁶ 'He was quick, subtle, shrewd, clear both in conception and delivery, and was master of argumentative eloquence.' Grenville, in a conversation with James Harris on 1 Aug. 1763,[7]

> mentioned Secretary Dyson's being about to leave us on account of his health. That when he accepted the office from Lord Bute it was on condition that he might quit if he found the fatigue too great . . . Mr. Grenville spoke of him with great praise; and mentioned in particular how exactly our minute books had been kept, as well as every other sort of business transacted. He certainly deserves this character, for never was a man of more integrity and knowledge or freer from vanity and official insolence.

Dyson held office continuously during his membership of the House of Commons, and was the great authority on procedure. Harris described him as 'our great master of order',[8] and the King as 'so thorough a master of form';[9] while Charles Yorke wrote on 1 Jan. 1766 about a paper by Dowdeswell which required revision:[10] 'If Dyson is well disposed I would settle it with him in two or three hours, as conversant in the forms of Parliament and wording questions for the House.' A pedant dedicated to the worship of parliamentary procedure, rigid, dry, and unresponsive to ideas or events, he saw the House of Commons as a machine working with almost mechanical regularity—'There are persons in the world', said Burke referring to Dyson,[11] 'whose whole soul is a previous question and whose whole life is the question of the adjournment.' Proud of his knowledge and experience and contemptuous of sciolists,[12] he grew irritable if insufficiently courted.[13] Except during the Rockingham Administration, he rarely gave an opinion on procedure against the Government.[14]

On the formation of the Rockingham Administration, Thomas Whately (q.v.) wrote to Grenville:[15]

> Dyson's situation is said to be doubtful, but I understand that his sentiments are not so, and that whatever may be their determination he will not think himself much obliged to them: if he should stay, I shall be apt to attribute it to Lord Dartmouth's wish to keep him, which he could not at first succeed in.

Dyson voted against Administration on the Anstruther election petition,[16] and opposed the repeal of the Stamp Act. On 5 Feb. 1766 he made a motion against Government on the Stamp Act riots;[17] and on 6 Feb. spoke for Grenville's motion for an address to enforce it.[18] On 24 Feb. he moved resolutions against the American Congress and the nonimportation agreement—'Mr. Dyson acted with his usual parliamentary sagacity', wrote George Onslow to Pitt,[19] 'and endeavoured to embarrass us all he could.' This kind of sniping, and Dyson's attempts to trip up ministers on points of order, caused great annoyance; which was aggravated by his opposition, purely on grounds of procedure, to granting an

additional income to the King's brothers.[20] After Dyson had forced a division against the Government, 3 June 1766, Rockingham asked for an explanation of his conduct. Here is Dyson's account of his conversation with Rockingham on 5 June:[21]

> The conference lasted full two hours. It began with expressing great disappointment at the part I had acted, and proceeded to an enumeration in great detail of many of the causes of offence given through the whole session, descending even to such little circumstances of aggravation as had escaped my own observation. Before I entered upon any particulars I begged to know what was meant by the word *disappointment*. He readily acquitted me of any professions or other engagements than what must be understood to be implied by a man's continuance in office. This I admitted as amounting to an obligation not to go into Opposition without notice, but that whatever was expected beyond that must depend upon the measures and the degree in which they were communicated. I then went through the particulars one by one. The business of the last day[22] had been much misrepresented to him, and upon that article and that only I thought I made some little impression upon him, for . . . it was easy for me to show him how much more offensively it might have been handled. He then told me that at the Board too I had always set myself to throw difficulties in the way of Government. This I own was quite unexpected, and I could not answer it without some warmth . . . He left the subject of what was past, and said the situation of Government was become such that it was necessary for the King's servants to know what they might expect or depend upon for the future . . . I said that it was impossible for me to make any profession than that of acting up to my principles . . . But whether the continuance in office or the removal of a man acting upon those principles would be most for his Majesty's service belonged more properly to his Lordship's consideration than to mine.

Rockingham wrote to the King that evening:[23]

> The difference of opinion which Mr. Dyson professes even in regard to the great commercial regulations and improvements which have been so much the object of the business this session, and will naturally both during the summer and at the meeting of Parliament occupy the attention and consideration of his Majesty's servants, will certainly occasion great want of harmony; and, as Mr. Dyson's conduct during great part of the session and even to the last day has rendered the cordiality of his intentions towards those now in your Majesty's service very doubtful, Lord Rockingham can foresee nothing but disquiet and uneasiness in Mr. Dyson's remaining at this time in his Majesty's service.

The King consulted Northington, who advised him to dismiss Dyson only if he intended to continue the Administration;[24] and Dyson remained in office.

According to Dyson, Chatham, on taking office in July 1766, had intended to remove him, but was dissuaded from doing so by Hillsborough.[25] The new Administration, Dyson thought in August, did not promise much stability. At the meeting of 'the men of business' on 6 Dec. 1766[26] he joined with Charles

Townshend in opposing the East India inquiry. 'Mr. Dyson's behaviour cannot be acquiesced in', wrote Chatham;[27] and Dyson did not attempt to repeat under Chatham the conduct which had provoked Rockingham. As Conway and Townshend disapproved of the Government's East India policy, it was left to Dyson to introduce the dividend bill into the House of Commons on 8 May 1767 and pilot it through the House.[28]

Over the Wilkes case Grafton leaned heavily on Dyson. Shortly after Wilkes's return for Middlesex, Dyson prepared a paper, 'drawn up with great knowledge of the proceedings of the House of Commons', wrote the King,[29] 'and an uncommon precision in conveying the most efficacious as well as most proper mode of effecting the expulsion'. At the meeting of the men of business of the House of Commons on 25 April he 'stated the precedents of expulsion',[30] and after the discussion undertook 'to settle the mode' that would 'best take in all the different opinions'.[31] In the debate of 17 Feb. 1769 he foreshadowed the action which was ultimately taken:[32]

> I take the parliamentary law to be this: that no man who has been expelled shall sit again in that Parliament . . . It has been supposed that the county of Middlesex will continue to return Mr. Wilkes . . . If that county shall think proper to vote for Mr. Wilkes and another is returned by twenty freeholders only, the rest will have given their votes unnecessarily.

'I should have been justly blameable', wrote Grafton subsequently,[33] 'if I, who had been . . . the instigator of his labours for the public service on the nicest and most important points of business, had left the King's service without soliciting for him some reward.' Dyson and Bradshaw, secretary to the Treasury, were the two men for whom Grafton obtained pensions shortly before his resignation in January 1770—for Dyson one of £1,000 p.a. on the Irish establishment for his life and those of his three sons.[34] The Irish Parliament, citing a promise made by the King that he would grant no pensions for life on their establishment,[35] refused to provide for it; but a Treasury letter of 29 Dec. 1774 authorized payment and the pension was eventually agreed to by the Irish Parliament on 15 Nov. 1775.[36]

Dyson lost a good deal of consequence when North, a commoner, became head of the Treasury. In October 1771 he was reported 'extremely ill',[37] and after his recovery spoke much less frequently in the House of Commons. On 14 Oct. 1774 North wrote to the King:[38] 'Poor Mr. Dyson was this morning attacked by a stroke of the palsy, has lost the use of one side, and lies most dangerously ill at his house in Clifford Street.' He never fully recovered, and, though returned as a Government

candidate at the general election, seems henceforth to have taken no part in Parliament.

He died 16 Sept. 1776, aged 54.

[1] *Mems. Geo. III*, i. 316. [2] These, formerly the property of Sir W. Stanhope (q.v.), are mentioned in Dyson's will, PCC 385 Bellas. [3] See letter about Dyson from Geo. Hardinge (q.v.) to John Nichols, 19 June 1813, Nichols, *Literary Anecs.* viii. 522. [4] O. C. Williams, *Clerical Organization of House of Commons, 1661–1850*, pp. 64, 66. [5] Hatsell, *Precedents*, i. pp. viii–ix. [6] *Mems. Geo. III*, i. 317. [7] Harris's 'Memoranda', Malmesbury mss. [8] 'Debates', 16 Mar. 1764. [9] The King to North, 7 May 1771, Fortescue, ii. 248. [10] To Rockingham, Add. 35430, f. 25. [11] 25 Feb. 1774, Cavendish's 'Debates', Egerton 252, p. 212. [12] Dyson to Gilbert Elliot, 23 Aug. 1766, Minto mss. [13] Calcraft to Chatham, 26 Jan. 1770, Chatham mss; Egerton 3711, pp. 114–16. [14] Add. 32966, ff. 55–57. [15] Grenville *Pprs.* iii. 73–74. [16] Conway to the King, 1 Feb. 1766, Fortescue, i. 249. [17] Ryder's 'Debates', Harrowby mss. [18] Conway to the King, 7 Feb. 1766, Fortescue, i. 266–7. [19] *Chatham Corresp.* ii. 394–5. [20] For the grounds of his objection, see his letter to Gilbert Elliot of 23 Aug, 1766, Minto mss, and Conway to the King, 3 June 1766, Fortescue, i. 353. [21] Dyson to Elliot, 23 Aug. 1766, Minto mss. [22] The increased allowances to the King's brothers. [23] Fortescue, i. 354–5. [24] Northington to the King, 5 June 1766, ibid. 356. [25] Dyson to Elliot, 23 Aug. 1766, Minto mss. [26] For this meeting, see Brooke, *Chatham Administration*, 76. [27] Grafton, *Autobiog.* 110. [28] Walpole, *Mems. Geo. III*, iii. 36. [29] To Grafton, 16 Apr. 1768, Fortescue, ii. 19. [30] Bradshaw to Grafton [25 Apr. 1768], Grafton mss. [31] North to Grafton, 26 Apr. 1768 (misdated 28 Apr.), ibid. [32] *Cavendish's Debates*, ii. 234. [33] Grafton to Ld. Townshend, 7 Jan. 1772, Townshend mss in possession of W. S. Lewis. [34] *Cal. Home Office Pprs.* 1770–2, p. 175. [35] King to North, 24 Aug. 1774, Fortescue, iii. 124–5. [36] *Cal. Home Office Pprs.* 1773–5, p. 308. [37] John Ley to Hatsell, 7 Oct. 1771, Ley mss. [38] Fortescue, iii. 145.

J.B.

## EAMES, John (c.1716–95).

YARMOUTH I.o.W.     18 Jan. 1765–1768
NEWPORT I.o.W.      1768–May 1773

*b.* c.1716, s. of John Eames of Stoke, Northants. *educ.* Oriel, Oxf. 1733; I. Temple 1734, called 1739. *m.* (his o. da. and h. *m.* 25 Aug. 1782, Hon William Fitzwilliam, s. of Richard, 6th Visct. Fitzwilliam [I].)

Recorder, Newport 1741–*d.*; steward to dean and chapter of Winchester from 1761; master in Chancery 1764–*d.*; commr. for sale of prizes 1756–64; commr. of taxes 1773–*d.*

Harcourt Powell (q.v.) wrote to the Duke of Newcastle, 29 Jan. 1761, asking him to recommend Eames to the dean and chapter of Winchester: 'He is recorder and one of the corporation of Newport, and a most particular and serviceable friend . . . This letter from your Grace will secure the place about £150 p.a.; which though of little consideration by its connexions will be serviceable to Mr. Eames in his profession.'[1]

Lord Holmes (q.v.) died on 21 July 1764, and after a brief period of uncertainty, the Grenville Administration agreed to continue working with the Rev. Leonard Holmes, his nephew and heir.[2] A candidate had now to be picked for Holmes's seat, and on 14 Oct. Lord Northington wrote to Grenville:[3]

> Mr. Eames whom I made the last master in Chancery . . . informs me that Holmes and Lee [Leigh] have made up their Yarmouth dispute, and that they are for the future to take one and one. The present vacancy to be Mr. Holmes's and that Mr. Holmes intends to bring in Mr. Eames which latter hopes for your

approbation . . . You may be sure I have a good opinion of this gentleman's sense and principles, as I gave him unsolicited so considerable a mark, and as he now hath professed this attachment to the King's government, I should think no man more proper to succeed there.

Grenville, already informed by Powell of Holmes's recommendation, replied that he had always 'heard a very good character of Mr. Eames', and accepted the choice. Eames was returned unopposed. Although in Rockingham's list of July 1765 he was classed as 'pro', on 22 Feb. he voted against the repeal of the Stamp Act, and in Rockingham's list of November 1766, and in Townshend's and Newcastle's lists of 1767, is marked as a supporter of Administration, with whom he voted over the land tax, 27 Feb. 1767. In 1768 he had to fight an election against the Worsley-Oglander interest. In the new Parliament he was absent from the divisions 1768–1773, but in Robinson's surveys on the royal marriage bill appears as 'pro, present'. In November 1772 he was placed by the Government on its list of the secret committee to inquire into the affairs of the East India Company, and was returned in the ballot of 28 Nov. In May 1773 he was appointed commissioner of taxes. His only recorded speeches were delivered 21 and 29 Mar. and 24 Apr. 1765, when a bill concerning the masters in Chancery was before the House.

He died a rich man, 13 May 1795.

¹ Add. 32918, f. 118. ² Grenville mss (JM). ³ Grenville letter bk.

L.B.N.

**EARDLEY, Sir Sampson,** afterwards Baron Eardley, *see* **GIDEON**

**EARLE, William** (1728–74), of Malmesbury, Wilts.

CRICKLADE 8 Oct.–25 Nov. 1774

*bap.* 24 Apr. 1728, 3rd s. of Rev. Thomas Earle, vicar of Malmesbury, by his 2nd w. Grace. *m.* (1) c.1749, Katharine, *s.p.*; (2) 18 Dec. 1766, Anne, da. of Edmund Estcourt of Burton Hill, Malmesbury, *s.p.*

Inspector of baggage in port of London, 1752–*d.*; dep. commissary of musters in South Britain 1755–*d.*; steward of Chelsea Hospital Apr. 1761–*d.*; receiver of land tax for North Wilts. 1761–May 1765, Nov. 1765–*d.*

Earle and his father were among Henry Fox's chief supporters at Malmesbury, William acting as deputy steward of the borough under him, September 1750–September 1762; it was under Fox's wing that William Earle made his official career. When urging Newcastle to appoint Earle receiver of the land tax for North Wilts., Fox wrote, 14 May 1761: 'I would not thus importune your Grace if I were no more than ordinarily desirous to pre-

vail . . .'¹ Earle was dismissed from that post by George Grenville to make room for E. Wilkins, a Howard supporter at Malmesbury, but through Lord Holland's intervention was restored by Rockingham.²

In January 1765, on a false report of the death of Lord Tylney, Member for Malmesbury, Earle declared himself candidate;³ in 1768 the Suffolk party was in the ascendant, and in 1774 the one seat available to the Fox family was required for C. J. Fox. Earle stood for Cricklade, but as he was too ill to make an appearance, his wife canvassed for him. He was returned top of the poll, but died six weeks later without having taken his seat.

He is often confused with his distant cousin, William Rawlinson Earle (q.v.).⁴

¹ Add. 32929, f. 340. ² Rockingham to Cumberland, 20 Oct. 1765, Albemarle, *Rockingham Mems.*i . 240; *Glocester Jnl.* 18 Nov. 1765. ³ *Glocester Jnl.* 21 Jan. 1765. ⁴ *Wilts. Arch. Mag.* lviii. 29.

J.A.C.

**EARLE, William Rawlinson** (1702–74), of Eastcourt House, Crudwell, Wilts.

| | |
|---|---|
| MALMESBURY | 1727–1747 |
| CRICKLADE | 1747–1761 |
| NEWPORT I.o.W. | 7 Apr. 1762–1768 |

*b.* 7 Apr. 1702, 1st s. of Giles Earle, M.P., by Elizabeth da. of Sir William Rawlinson of Hendon House, Mdx., wid. of John Lowther of Lowther, Westmld. *m.* 4 Jan. 1731, Susanna, da. and h. of William White of Somerford, Wilts., 1s. 3da. *suc.* fa. 20 Aug. 1758.

Clerk of deliveries to the Ordnance 1732–40; clerk of the Ordnance 1740–72.

In 1727 William Rawlinson Earle joined at Malmesbury his father Giles Earle who had sat for it since 1722, and they held the borough until their defeat in 1747. William Rawlinson Earle then contested Cricklade, where he fought contests in 1747, 1754, and 1761.

Newcastle described his defeat in 1761 as 'very severe usage . . . after having expended near five thousand pounds'.¹ Earle had to be found a seat: Newcastle first thought of Fowey, then, on a vacancy at Newport, recommended him to Lord Holmes (q.v.) as 'a very deserving man and a very good friend'.² Holmes objected, 17 Mar. 1762:³

You assured me it should be some person in high station that would be agreeable to the electors . . . How a person with a little place in the Ordnance will go down, I don't know, but must beg the favour your Grace will excuse me from having anything to do with it.

Newcastle, surprised and concerned, replied, 20 Mar. 1762:⁴

The gentleman I recommend is of an unexceptionable character; has indeed the honour to serve the King in the Board of Ordnance in the very next office of rank to the Marquess of Granby.

Bute also supported Earle, and Holmes somewhat reluctantly acquiesced.

Earle appears in Henry Fox's list of Members favourable to the peace preliminaries (Walpole's statement[5] that he voted against the preliminaries and was then dismissed is incorrect), and voted with Grenville's Administration over general warrants, 6 Feb. 1764. Classed 'pro' by Rockingham in July 1765, he did not vote against the repeal of the Stamp Act. In November 1766 Rockingham classed him as 'Bute', and Newcastle in March 1767 as 'Administration': he voted with the Government over the land tax, 27 Feb. 1767 and nullum tempus, 17 Feb. 1768. He did not stand at the general election of 1768, and died 10 Aug. 1774.

[1] To Ld. Holmes, 20 Mar. 1762, Add. 32935, f. 497. [2] 15 Mar. 1762, ibid. f. 400. [3] Ibid. f. 435. [4] Ibid. ff. 497–8. [5] *Mems. Geo. III*, i. 185.

J.A.C.

**EDEN, Sir John,** 4th Bt. (1740–1812), of Windleston and West Auckland, co. Dur.

DURHAM CO.        1774–1790

*b.* 16 Sept. 1740, 1st s. of Sir Robert Eden, 3rd Bt., by Mary, da. of William Davison of Beamish, co. Dur., and bro. of William Eden (q.v.). *educ.* Eton 1755–8; Trinity, Camb. 1759. *m.* (1) 26 June 1764, Catherine (*d.*12 Mar. 1766), da. of John Thompson of Kirby Hall, Yorks., *s.p.*; (2) 9 Apr. 1767, Dorothea, da. and h. of Peter Johnson, recorder of York, 2s. 6da. *suc.* fa. 25 June 1755.

Eden was returned unopposed for co. Durham in 1774, and supported North's Administration. On 29 Aug. 1776 he wrote to his brother William (q.v.):[1]

I am confident our cause is good, and trust that by God's assistance we shall overcome all our enemies. I heartily wish we could begin by hanging a score or two of patriots as they are called . . . out of the Houses of Parliament and the city of London, for to them we are indebted for this horrid rebellion.

In division lists between 1779 and 1780 Eden appears regularly as a Government supporter, and was classed 'pro' by Robinson. He did not vote on Lowther's motion against the war, 12 Dec. 1781, and paired for the important divisions of February and March 1782. In 1780 or 1781 the *English Chronicle* commented: 'He holds the business of the House in great contempt, generally comes down after dinner, and is always the first to call for the question.' He voted against Shelburne's peace preliminaries, 18 Feb. 1783; did not vote on Fox's East India bill, 27 Nov. 1783, but in Stockdale's list of 19 Mar. 1784 appears among those who had voted against Pitt, and continued in opposition even after his brother had crossed over to Pitt's side. He seems to have found parliamentary attendance a tiresome interruption of his hunting, and on 4 Dec. 1788, at the time of the Regency crisis, wrote to his brother William: 'Came down yesterday to attend the call of the House this day . . . There were not I apprehend less than five hundred Members yesterday, many of whom like myself much displeased to be brought to town too soon.' He voted against Pitt's proposals in the first debate, and on 15 Dec. wrote to his brother: 'I have paired off for three weeks and go northward to-morrow morning. Before the expiration of that time the business will be somehow settled, but I much doubt whether it will be well settled.'[2] There is no record of his having spoken in the House.

In 1789 Eden became anxious about his seat and on 20 Apr. asked Lord Lisburne for his support against 'an *alien banker* [who], upon the idea of supporting Mr. Pitt has offered himself for the county'.[3] On 30 Dec. Dr. John Carr[4] wrote: 'Lord Auckland, I am told, is endeavouring to kick out his brother . . . Sir John's political sin, you know, was an adherence to Lord North.' Eden was defeated at Durham at the general election of 1790—it is not clear whether Auckland was responsible for his defeat.

He died 23 Aug. 1812.

[1] Add. 34413, f. 76. [2] Ibid. ff. 318, 349. [3] Egerton 2137, f. 37. [4] Nichols, *Lit. Anecs.* viii. 311.

L.B.N.

**EDEN, William** (1744–1814), of Beckenham, Kent.

NEW WOODSTOCK      1774–1784
HEYTESBURY          1784–22 May 1793

*b.* 3 Apr. 1744, 3rd s. of Sir Robert Eden, 3rd Bt., and bro. of Sir John Eden (q.v.). *educ.* Durham sch. 1755–8; Eton 1758–62; Ch. Ch. Oxf. 1762–5; M. Temple, called 1768. *m.* 26 Sept. 1776, Eleanor, da. of Sir Gilbert Elliot, 3rd Bt. (q.v.), 6s. 8da. *cr.* Baron Auckland [I] 18 Nov. 1789; Baron Auckland of West Auckland [GB] 22 May 1793.

   M.P. [I] 1780–3.

   Under-sec. of state 1772–8; ld. of Trade 1776–82; commr. for conciliation with America 1778–9; sec. to ld. lt. [I] 1780–2; P.C. [I] 23 Dec. 1780; P.C. 17 Apr. 1783; jt. vice-treasurer [I] Apr.–Dec. 1783; envoy to France on special commercial mission 1785–8; ambassador to Spain 1788–9, to the United Provinces 1789–93; jt. postmaster gen. 1798–1804; pres. Board of Trade 1806–7.

Eden first contemplated a career at the bar, began practice on the northern circuit, and in 1773 published a book on penal law; but he soon decided that politics offered more chance of advancement. Through Alexander Wedderburn he obtained the post of under-secretary to Lord Suffolk. About this time he told Wedderburn: 'I love politics better than law (and this not from caprice, for I feel it to be the natural bent of my inclination).' In fact he found the law hard going and uncongenial. 'I have a turn for business, none for oratory.'[1] His willingness and his 'most insinuating gentle manner'[2] soon made him a favourite with Suffolk, who did his best to advance him and praised him without stint in letters to the King.[3]

Seeking a seat in Parliament Eden showed extraordinary caution. He refused offers from Clive (not a good life) and also from Suffolk,[4] probably because he did not wish to have all his eggs in one basket. Instead he accepted Marlborough's offer of nomination for Woodstock, exploiting the intimate friendship with the Spencers which he had cultivated from his acquaintance with Lord Robert at Oxford. Soon afterwards the illness of John Robinson provided a new opportunity. Eden, while still holding his appointment under Suffolk, took over the conduct of much of the secret service business for North, who, like Suffolk, fell under the spell of his charm. After Robinson's recovery, Eden still kept this business in his hands, and was rewarded with his appointment to the Board of Trade.[5] After the outbreak of the American war, much of the intelligence received by the British government about American negotiations at Paris passed through his hands,[6] and his reports on it were prepared with skill. 'Mr. Eden', the King once commented, 'writes a short, clear and intelligent style, and has stated all that is necessary.'[7]

Eden fully supported the American war. He wrote, in December 1777:[8]

When I first came into Parliament . . . there was at that moment no alternative but 'war or separation'. All retrospect to the causes of such an alternative were idle; it was necessary to take a choice; and in doing so, I was not influenced either by the popular cry or by political connexions. As an individual of a family possessing considerable interests both in Great Britain and America I was naturally indisposed to a separation evidently mischievous to both countries, but still further as an English gentleman, inheriting my share of that English pride which I never wish to lose, I could not bear to see a dismemberment of the Empire without running every hazard to prevent it.

And in another letter:[9]

We have full conviction, indeed, that the Americans are no cowards, but that is no reason with us against fighting them, and all the world if necessary, in a just and honourable cause.

Though he took little part in debate, except to support in 1776 a criminal law amendment bill in which he was interested, he increasingly gained North's confidence. After Saratoga, he, with Wedderburn, was called into consultation about future tactics in Parliament.[10] He acted as a go-between in negotiations for a reconstruction of the ministry planned by Suffolk, Wedderburn, and himself, by which Chatham and his friends were to be brought in (and Wedderburn was to get personal

advancement).[11] In February 1778 North pressed him to accept a place on the America conciliation commission. Professing reluctance, Eden at heart was delighted. His spirits and ambition rose to the challenge: 'It is an enterprise of the great kind, we must hope it will end well.' 'My commission is the full appointment of ambassador in every respect.' So far as was possible the arrangements were planned to open the way to a great personal triumph. Carlisle, at the head of the commission, would be dependent on Eden's industry. Of the appointment of the third commissioner, Eden wrote:

The change made in the commission was my own private negotiation, and gives me much better hopes than I had before. Governor Johnstone is particularly favourable in his opinions towards me personally, is manly and right-headed on the points in question, is of much weight among the most violent Americans, and in his whole character active, decisive, and bold.[12]

Wedderburn 'was very desirous his friend should succeed in the negotiations, and the instructions were most liberally framed for that purpose, so diametrically against his former conduct'.[13] Always ready to press for present advantage, Eden also tried to get the commissioners made privy councillors.[14]

After going with such high hopes to America, Eden's indignation was beyond all bounds when he found, on arrival at Philadelphia, that the ministers had secretly sent instructions for its evacuation, as part of the new dispositions in consequence of the French entry into the war. On this sole point Eden afterwards blamed the failure of the commission, since he claimed that it made it impossible for the commissioners to negotiate from strength. His animus was kindled particularly against Germain and Sandwich. On his return home his anger increased, when he found no inclination on the ministers' part to defend the activities of the commission or to show approval by giving promotion to its members. In order to force the ministry to pay due attention to his pretensions he threatened to call in Parliament for papers relating to the withdrawal from Philadelphia, a move which, it was understood, would draw the support of Carlisle and Marlborough. He told Marlborough that Sandwich and Germain ought to be forced out of office. But he did not disclose to him the personal motives for his actions, which were apparent enough in the ultimatum he sent to North:

I certainly have not deserved the insinuation conveyed in your letter, that the proposed measure is adopted on a speculation that your Government is sinking—unless you admit at the same time that I have with the warmest and most honourable attachment to you suggested, urged, and attempted everything that might establish it on a firmer foundation . . . The long letter which I wrote on the subject near four weeks ago to the attorney-general . . . is a very sufficient proof that I arrived in England with a disposition to labour in your service to the last gasp of our political lives. The sentiments however which were then allowed to be so just and proper (and so pressing too in point of time) have not produced the slightest effect either public or personal; on the contrary our public embarrassment and every personal cause of complaint have been suffered to grow worse, and at this moment I am to choose among the three following lines of conduct.

1. I may continue in possession of a very inconsiderable office and greatly lowered from the situation which I held before I left England and answer through the session all such unpleasant questions as may be asked me; precluded from giving the only answers that may do credit to myself and justice to the public expectations. In short I may embrace various disadvantages and disgraces as the volunteer of a Government for which I have already sacrificed much and hazarded more, and for which I have met with nothing in return but disregard and neglect; and from a Government too, which, constituted as it now is, will I believe in my conscience tend very fast to its own dissolution after adding more calamities to those under which the King's fortunes at present labour.

2. If that Government were really . . . so circumstanced in the state of national parties, that it cannot be strengthened by the fairest attempts of your Lordship to strengthen it, I might not unnecessarily say, 'I will not on the one hand impair the very small chance that I see remaining in favour of the public, on the contrary I will concentrate to improve that chance by suggesting anything that may do good and by labouring to give energy and activity wherever I can.' But in return I expect (not as a matter of favour but of fair pretension) before I proceed one step in so hazardous a path to have my own situation made both creditable and secure and to see those with whom I am connected in this discussion previously satisfied.

3. I may take the manly part of bringing before the public a question which is the key to all my conduct in America, which leads to great consequences in every point of view, and upon which so far as it respects either measures or men, I should have the concurrence and countenance of the kingdom.

Three days later he told North that the price of his silence was an office or reversion worth £600 p.a., and satisfaction for Carlisle and Johnstone. His insistence that the Government ought to be re-shaped and strengthened hardly camouflaged his implication, that he was open to persuasion that this was impracticable, and would then give support—provided his demands were satisfied. To the King's disgust, he tried to secure a pension for life, in the name of his wife. This was refused, and he agreed to accept one at pleasure. At the end of February he made some show of finding a successor to Sandwich at the Admiralty—either Keppel or Howe—but soon found that this was impracticable. For the rest of 1779 his efforts were largely spent in trying to force North to provide immediate promotion for Wedderburn and to appoint a secretary of state in succession to Suffolk, more vigorous than Hills-

borough to whom North had promised the place. This campaign was abandoned in November, after promises of satisfaction had been made to Wedderburn. During 1779, in pamphlets published as 'Four Letters to the Earl of Carlisle', he defended the Government's policy.[15]

In January 1780, Lord Buckinghamshire, lord lieutenant of Ireland, asked that Eden be sent over as his secretary. Eden declined this opening, telling North, 'my situation here was not unpleasant, and my hopes of advancement not low, and that I could not therefore think it to my happiness or interest to engage in so very precarious and difficult a situation'.[16] During the spring he continued to intrigue on behalf of Wedderburn, and in the summer he was one of those who pressed strongly for an early general election.[17] In July, when Carlisle accepted the lord lieutenancy, Eden agreed to accompany him as secretary, but proceeded to set his price as high as possible.[18] North wanted him to go—he was ready to help him on, in reason, out of personal esteem, thought him 'clever' and a suitable person for Ireland, and probably also looked forward to being quit of him for a time at least.[19] From July to September Eden stood out for an appointment to the Treasury Board (if only for a few weeks) before he went to Ireland: 'I should then have gone to Ireland after having passed through the Boards, and if my zeal and discretion in Ireland should be such as to engage his Majesty's future favour, I might have entertained a reasonable expectation upon my return to England to be promoted to a Privy Council office.' He also tried unsuccessfully to secure immediate promotion to the Privy Council, and to get the promise of appointment to the first Privy Council office that should fall vacant after his return from Ireland, greatly irritating the King with his persistence.[20] The King standing firm, and Loughborough warning Eden that 'it was not our interest to hurt him [North] or to make an absolute quarrel', he at last accepted the secretaryship on the promise that he would, on returning, be considered as having passed the Treasury Board.[21]

From December 1780 till April 1782 Eden was in Ireland. He was brought into the Irish House of Commons for Dungannon, and set himself with immense zeal, and no little success, to the task of Irish parliamentary management. He worked loyally but took care to remind North of his merits and of the great expenses he felt bound to incur out of his own pocket. Despite his success with the Irish politicians, he ended his term in Ireland with the conviction that Irish constitutional demands would have to be conceded.[22]

On Rockingham's succeeding North, Eden at first

refused co-operation in Irish matters; but this was purely because of the new ministry's affront to Carlisle in dismissing him from his Yorkshire lord lieutenancy; and when Carlisle was found a court place, Eden ceased to be troublesome. He even voted for the contractors bill.[23] Deprived of most of his official salaries, owing to Carlisle's withdrawal from Ireland and the suppression of the Board of Trade, he trod warily, till he should see 'further light into the system' he should adopt.[24] After Rockingham's death his attitude to the Shelburne ministry was determined by his feeling that it could not endure. He agreed with Loughborough that a coalition between North and Fox offered the only prospect of a strong and lasting ministry, under which it would be profitable to enlist, but that the time was not yet ripe—an early move against Shelburne would be premature: 'The Portland set, as it is to be called, would not be quite what any reasonable man could bear, if they were now to come in as a triumphant party.' He gave non-commital replies to approaches from Shelburne, and considered 'the game would be completely in the hands of Lord North and his friends, if Lord North were formed to manage such a business'.[25] During the last months of 1782 he pressed his views on North and bolstered up his decision to remain aloof, ready to exploit the situation.[26] In the opening weeks of 1783 he and Loughborough exerted all their influence to bring about North's junction with Fox, and Eden made contact with Fox about the planning of their moves in the House of Commons.[27] 'It is', Robinson wrote, 'by . . . perpetual teasing and writing, that Eden gets his influence.'[28] In February Eden joined in the attack on Shelburne's peace preliminaries. Shortly after he explained his political position to his complaisant parliamentary patron, Marlborough.

> It happened to me originally to be engaged in Lord North's line of politics . . . [and] to receive several occasional favours through his friendship . . . believing him (as I do) to be both a good and a wise man, and knowing him always to mean well . . . I should reproach myself if I were capable of deserting him.

Whenever North should choose, or be obliged, to quit politics,

> there is no longer a claim on me from any party whatever, for I have not, nor do I mean to have a party connexion with the other branch of what is called the Coalition.

On the formation of the Coalition Eden obtained the coveted rank of Privy Councillor, but was disappointed to find himself fobbed off with a sinecure instead of 'an office of business'; nevertheless he made protestations to Fox of his loyalty.[29] He found consolation in being brought on to the ministry's

select committee on East India affairs.[30] He was also made chairman of a parliamentary committee to investigate smuggling.[31] Work on this body, which presented two important reports in March 1784, gave Eden a wide and valuable insight into the working of the revenue system, which he exploited to the full during the sessions of 1784 and 1785. In November 1783 he strongly approved of Fox's East India bill, on all counts, including the control of patronage it conferred. In a conversation with John Courtenay he 'expatiated with great zeal and party confidence on the infinite advantage of this politic expedient for infallibly securing the permanency of the . . . Administration for seven years at least, by their possessing such an unbounded and lucrative patronage'.[32]

When the Coalition was dismissed Eden promptly resigned his sinecure,[33] and joined in the attack on Pitt with the utmost energy. From December 1783 till July 1785 he was one of the most frequent and vigorous Opposition spokesmen; and on at least one occasion Fox was stung to a sharp rejoinder by Eden's complaint that he was not taking the game sufficiently seriously.[34] After the general election of 1784 he saw no hope except in 'the probability of the *imprudent use* which Pitt may make *of his great power and his obsequious Parliament*'.[35] Intent to exploit any ministerial errors, Eden made trade and finance his particular province: on these he 'ranked far above any individual composing the party of the Opposition'. On him, wrote Wraxall, 'principally devolved the task of dissecting, answering, and refuting, the arguments, calculations, or propositions brought forward by the Government', while North, Fox, and Sheridan were content to make Pitt the butt of their wit and eloquence. His style of speaking was described as 'neither glowing, nor elevated, nor impassioned, but . . . correct, with digression, always directed to the subject under discussion'.[36] But Eden was out of his element in Opposition. Even in the spring of 1784 he accepted Pitt's invitation to be re-elected to the select committee on East India affairs, now with Dundas as leading spirit.[37] As early as August 1784 Pitt seems to have hoped to win him over.[38] His close friend, Lord Sheffield, reporting in July 1785 a conversation in which his conduct in the Commons was highly praised, remarked unwittingly, 'I did not mention a word of your being so infernally civil that you do not appear to be in earnest, or that your only defect is not being as violent as myself.'[39] All through 1785 Eden was in contact with the ministers, and there were tentative efforts to detach him from Opposition, his Irish friend, John Beresford, acting at times as go-between. At an early stage he hinted at the Speakership of the Commons, a position which might not have meant a complete break with the Opposition; but perhaps for this reason, the suggestion was not acceptable to Pitt.[40] A new office with responsibility for reforming the revenue services was also considered between them but put aside as unsuitable. His acceptance in December 1785 of the post of special envoy to France to negotiate a commercial treaty was the climax of twelve months of negotiation. In his view politics had 'nothing to do with the foreign line', and he believed this offer would avoid any breach with his old friends: 'It is not fairly objectionable on any grounds of party.'[41] Indeed, while North and Fox resented his action, Fox and his friends attacking it in the Commons to deter waverers, others saw in it nothing disreputable and continued their private friendship with him.[42] His change of sides was regarded as important, both for itself and as an example. Robert Hobart wrote: 'He is a great acquisition and the fittest man in England for the appointment he has accepted; his example will, I make no doubt, be followed by as many of the Opposition as Mr. Pitt chooses to purchase.'[43]

Eden's appointment virtually ended his career in the Commons. Though he remained a Member for another eight years, he is not known to have spoken there again, and he was almost constantly out of the country on diplomatic duties. About September 1786, when the successful negotiations with France were approaching completion, he was offered the vice-treasurership of Ireland but declined it. In December Orde, the Irish secretary, wrote: 'I do not wonder that he should have refused . . . because he really seems to have lost all temper and decency in the wildness of self-complacency and pretensions'; and added his impression that Eden was being cossetted on the supposition that he might bring Carlisle, Loughborough, and Stormont over to the court.[44] Whether or not for these reasons Eden, though refused posts at home of the kind he wanted,[45] obtained other diplomatic appointments after 1787; but an inherent suspicion of him on Pitt's part is perhaps indicated by the fact that in 1793, by which time Pitt's political position was impregnable, he was given a peerage and dropped from the service.

He died 28 May 1814.

¹ Add. 34412, ff. 145, 202. ² HMC Var. vi. 265–6. ³ Fortescue, iii. 143; iv. 539. ⁴ L. Scott, 'Under-Secretaries of State, 1755–75' (Manchester Univ. M.A. thesis, 1950), pp. 72, 80. ⁵ HMC Var. vi. 265–6. ⁶ Add. 34413, 34414. ⁷ Fortescue, iii. 527. ⁸ Add. 46490–1, pkt. 2. ⁹ Countess of Minto, Mem. Hugh Elliot, 132. ¹⁰ Add. 34415, f. 422. ¹¹ Fortescue, iv. 59–60, 68, 115. ¹² Add. 34415, ff. 247, 325. ¹³ HMC Var. vi. 265–6. ¹⁴ Fortescue, iv. 44. ¹⁵ Add. 34416, ff. 241–2, 245, 248, 251, 264–6, 267–8, 269–70, 278; 38564, f. 1; 34416, ff. 285–288, 367, 372, 508, 391–2, 463; 38567, ff. 8–9; 38212, ff. 231–2; Fortescue, iv. 304, 327, 328, 330, 342, 343, 349. ¹⁶ Add. 38213, ff. 89–92; 34417, f. 98. ¹⁷ Fortescue, v. 45; Christie, End of North's Ministry, 1780–82, p. 31. ¹⁸ See corresp. in Add. 34417 and Fortescue, v. 115, 117, 124. ¹⁹ Abergavenny ms 266; Fortescue, v. 117. ²⁰ Add. 34417, ff. 135, 139–41; Add. 38567, f. 163; Fortescue v. 124. ²¹ Add. 29475, f. 17; 34417, ff. 208–9; Beresford Corresp. i. 144–5; Add. 34419, f. 144; Fortescue, v. 132. ²² HMC Lothian, 382, 390; HMC Charlemont, i. 147–8, 319, 390–1; Beresford Corresp. i. 188–9; Debrett, vii. 2–6. ²³ Add. 34418, ff. 407–8; Walpole, Last Jnls. ii. 442. ²⁴ Add. 34418, f. 460. ²⁵ Auckland Corresp. i. 5–14, 15–16; Mem. Hugh Elliot, 254–5. ²⁶ Auckland Corresp. i. 36; Add. 38567, ff. 107–112; Abergavenny ms 478. ²⁷ Add. 34419, ff. 105, 124; Auckland Corresp. i. 46–47; Last Jnls. ii. 478, 480. ²⁸ Add. 38567, ff. 123–4. ²⁹ Add. 34419, ff. 122, 147. ³⁰ Debrett, xv. 60. ³¹ J. E. D. Binney, British Public Finance & Admin. 1774–92, p. 69. ³² John Courtenay, Incidental Anecs. & Biog. Sketch (1809), pp. 135–8. ³³ Add. 34419, f. 315. ³⁴ Ibid. f. 357. ³⁵ HMC Dropmore, i. 230. ³⁶ Wraxall, iv. 227–9. ³⁷ Debrett, xv. 60. ³⁸ HMC 11th Rep. VII, 53. ³⁹ Auckland Corresp. i. 348. ⁴⁰ Eden to Pitt, 12, 21 Oct. 1785, Chatham mss; Auckland Corresp. i. 89. ⁴¹ Auckland Corresp. i. 70–71 and n.; Beresford Corresp. i. 295–6. ⁴² Auckland Corresp. i. 362. ⁴³ HMC Rutland, iii. 270–1. ⁴⁴ Ibid. 344, 348, 363. ⁴⁵ Eden to Pitt, 19 May 1787, Chatham mss.

I.R.C.

## EDGCUMBE, Hon. George (1720–95), of Mount Edgcumbe, nr. Plymouth.

FOWEY    30 July 1746–10 May 1761

b. 3 Mar. 1720, 2nd surv. s. of Richard, 1st Baron Edgcumbe, by Matilda, da. of Sir Henry Furnese, 1st Bt., M.P., of Waldershare, Kent, and bro. of Hon. Richard Edgcumbe (q.v.). educ. ?Eton 1732. m. 6 Aug. 1761, Emma, da. of Rt. Rev. John Gilbert, abp. of York 1757–61, 1s. suc. bro. as 3rd Baron Edgcumbe, 10 May 1761; cr. Visct. Mount Edgcumbe 5 Mar. 1781; Earl of Mount Edgcumbe 31 Aug. 1789.
  Lt. R.N. 1739; capt. 1744; r.-adm. 1762; c.-in-c. Plymouth 1765–71; v.-adm. 1770; adm. 1778; v.-adm. Cornw. 1782.
  Clerk of the duchy of Lancaster 1747–62; ld. lt. Cornw. 1761–d.; P.C. 26 July 1765; treasurer of the Household July 1765–Nov. 1766; jt. vice-treasurer [I] 1770–2 and 1784–93; capt. of gent. pens. 1772–82.

Edgcumbe was returned for Fowey on his family interest. Like the rest of his family he was an Administration supporter, but he seems rarely to have attended the House, being absent at sea for long periods; he served in the Mediterranean under Byng, with Boscawen at the capture of Louisburg in 1758, and with the Channel fleet under Hawke in 1759. There is no record of his having spoken in the House.

He died 4 Feb. 1795.

M.M.D.

## EDGCUMBE, Hon. Richard (1716–61).

PLYMPTON ERLE    4 Dec. 1742–1747
LOSTWITHIEL           1747–1754
PENRYN                     1754–22 Nov. 1758

b. 2 Aug. 1716, 1st surv. s. of Richard, 1st Baron Edgcumbe, and bro. of Hon. George Edgcumbe (q.v.). educ. Eton 1725–32. unm. suc. fa. 22 Nov. 1758.
  Mayor, Lostwithiel 1744, 1756, recorder 1759–d.; recorder, Plympton 1759–d.
  Ld. of Trade Apr. 1753–Dec. 1755; ld. of Admiralty Dec. 1755–Nov. 1756; P.C. 19 Nov. 1756; comptroller of the Household Dec. 1756–d.; ld. lt. Cornw. 1759–d.

Edgcumbe's family position compelled him to sit

in Parliament and engage in elections, but he took little interest in either. He was a wit, a patron of the arts, and most of all a gambler. 'Edgcumbe who thinks nothing important that is not to be decided by dice', Horace Walpole wrote to Richard Bentley, 13 Dec. 1754; and 16 Apr. 1761, to George Montagu: 'What parts, genius, and agreeableness, thrown away at a hazard table.' In politics he followed his father, and adhered to the Pelhams. But he did not make his mark, and there is no record of his having spoken in the House. In a letter to Enys c. 7 Oct. 1753,[1] having discussed election affairs, he added:

So lest you should fall into the same mistake that he [Lord Edgcumbe] has done, and think that because I enter a little into burgizing (as we call it here) I may come to take to it, I shall quit the subject, with declaring that my hatred of it increases with my experience. But as I have assured my father that, hateful as it is, he may ever command my assistance from my duty, so likewise may you.

On the death of Edgcumbe's father, Richard Rigby wrote to the Duke of Bedford, 5 Dec. 1758:[2]

Lord Edgcumbe writes word to Mr. Fox that his father has left him everything in his power, which everything will suffice to pay all his debts, and leave him a very handsome income. They say the estate is above £4,000 a year, and that the old man had twenty thousand ready.

He had also one of the greatest borough interests in Great Britain: eight seats under his control—two each at Lostwithiel and Grampound, and one at Penryn, Fowey, Bossiney, and Plympton; besides a part-interest at Mitchell. When on his death Grampound transferred their allegiance to Edward Eliot and William Trevanion, Edgcumbe wrote to Newcastle:[3]

These are two stirring young gentlemen and, may be, think to take advantage of me, as one of an opposite character. But the world shall see that if I have been idle, it was only because I had nothing to do.

But in reality he was half-hearted in 'burgizing': he hesitated whether to assert his claims at Bossiney (alias Tintagel) or renounce them. He wrote to Newcastle, 12 Oct. 1760: 'They quarrelled with my father, and at his death abjured me.' On 15 Dec.: he must fight it out at Tintagel, or else people might conclude that they had merely to attack for him to give up. Dec. 16: 'it was my father's advice in his last illness, that I should not put myself to any expense, nor to much trouble about it, any more than at Grampound'; but 'an exertion at Tintagel . . . will strengthen me in other places'. In the end no Edgcumbe candidate was returned at Tintagel in 1761.[4]

Edgcumbe died without legitimate issue 10 May 1761.

[1] Autograph Coll., R. Institution of Cornw. [2] Bedford mss 38, f. 168. [3] Add. 32886, f. 76; Namier *Structure*, 353. [4] Add. 32913, ff. 75–76; 32916, ff. 90, 123–4.

L.B.N.

## EDGCUMBE, Hon. Richard (1764–1839).

| FOWEY | 13 Feb. 1786–1790 |
| LOSTWITHIEL | 1790–Mar. 1791 |
| FOWEY | 7 Mar. 1791–4 Feb. 1795 |

*b.* 13 Sept. 1764, o.s. of George, 3rd Baron Edgcumbe (q.v.). *educ.* Harrow 1774–80; Ch. Ch. Oxf. 1781; Grand Tour (France, Germany, Italy) 1783–5.[1] *m.* 21 Feb. 1789, Lady Sophia Hobart, da. and coh. of John, 2nd Earl of Buckinghamshire, 3s. 2da. *styled* Visct. Valletort from 31 Aug. 1789; *suc.* fa. as 2nd Earl of Mount Edgcumbe 4 Feb. 1795.

Edgcumbe was returned for Fowey on the family interest as a Government supporter; voted, however, against Richmond's fortifications plan, 27 Feb. 1786; but with Pitt during the Regency crisis, 1788–9. According to Mrs. Boscawen, widow of the admiral, he attended the House 'most assiduously'.[2] At the opening of the session, 21 Jan. 1790, Valletort moved the Address, this being his only recorded speech in his first Parliament.

He died 26 Sept. 1839.

[1] See his *Musical Reminiscences* (1824). [2] To Mrs. Delany, ?July 1786, *Autobiog. & Corresp.* vi. 376.

L.B.N.

## EDMONSTONE, Archibald (1717–1807), of Duntreath, Stirling.

| DUNBARTONSHIRE | 10 Dec. 1761–1780 |
| AYR BURGHS | 1780–1790 |
| DUNBARTONSHIRE | 1790–1796 |

*b.* 10 Oct. 1717, 1st s. of Archibald Edmonstone, M.P. [I], of Duntreath, Stirling, and Red Hall, co. Antrim, by his 2nd w. Anne, da. of Hon. John Campbell of Mamore, sis. of John, 4th Duke of Argyll (q.v.). *educ.* Glasgow Univ. 1732; M. Temple 1737, called 1745. *m.* (1) 4 Oct. 1753, Susanna Mary (*d.*1776), da. of Roger Harenc, London merchant (*b.* Paris, naturalized 1725) of Foot's Cray Place, Kent, 5s. 3da.; (2) Apr. 1778, Hester, da. of Sir John Heathcote, 2nd Bt., of Normanton, Rutland, *s.p. suc.* fa. 1768; *cr.* Bt. 20 May 1774.

Gent. usher of the black rod [I] 1763–5.

Edmonstone came of an ancient and strongly Presbyterian family which, during the plantation of Ulster, purchased the estate of Broad Island, co. Antrim, and thereafter divided their interests between Ireland and Scotland.[1] His father acquired additional property in Dunbartonshire, but resided mostly in Ireland.

Lord Chesterfield wrote to Solomon Dayrolles, 21 Sept. 1753:

> Your friend Mademoiselle Harenc is to be married . . . to one Mr. Edmonstone, a Scotch gentleman, whose father has an estate in Scotland and Ireland of about £1500 a year. He is . . . under the protection of the Duke of Argyll, by whom he expects to be brought into Parliament. He is strong, well set, and promises to make a considerable husband. Harenc gives £10,000 down with his daughter.

Edmonstone's hopes of a seat at the 1754 election were disappointed. He seems to have entered business with his father-in-law,[2] and was not mentioned as a candidate in 1761 until, by the death of Argyll during the general election, Edmonstone's uncle succeeded as 4th Duke, and Dunbartonshire thereby became vacant. Bute hoped for 'time . . . to look about us',[3] but the Campbells' hands were forced by the appearance of Robert Haldane as a candidate. The new Duke wrote to Bute, 6 May 1761:[4]

> I am in hopes of hearing soon from you on the subject of the plan I proposed towards bringing my nephew Mr. Edmonstone into Parliament for the county of Dumbarton, meantime—as Mr. Haldane has been in the county with a view to offering his service I thought no time was to be lost by taking some measures to secure it for the interest of our families . . . I have accordingly recommended my nephew which I am hopeful will be agreeable to your Lordship. He is a man of considerable property both in Dumbarton and Stirlingshire and I have good reason to believe will follow my advice and consequently your Lordship's.

Haldane having withdrawn, Edmonstone was returned unopposed. Bute now took the Duntreath Edmonstones into favour and obtained for Archibald's brother Campbell the lieutenant-governorship of Dumbarton castle.

Edmonstone loyally supported the Bute and Grenville Administrations, and in the summer of 1763, having been appointed gentleman usher of the black rod, accompanied Northumberland, the new lord lieutenant, to Ireland. In anticipation of the Wilkes debates, Grenville asked Northumberland, 22 Sept. 1763,[5] to send Edmonstone, 'whom I have reason to believe as well inclined as possible', over to England. He returned and voted with Administration in the division of 15 Nov. Listed as 'doubtful' by Rockingham in the summer of 1765, he lost his place, and went into opposition. Albemarle wrote to Rockingham, 16 Feb. 1766:[6] 'Mr. Edmonstone will vote against you and go with the young Campbells, if the Duke of Argyll, who chooses him, does not lay his commands upon him.' Edmonstone voted with his cousins Lord Lorne and Lord Frederick Campbell against the repeal of the Stamp Act on 22 Feb.

He voted with the Chatham Administration on the land tax, 27 Feb. 1767, and on nullum tempus, 17 Feb. 1768.

Edmonstone was a conscientious Member, frequently appointed to committees, particularly on road bills; piloted the Glasgow roads bill through the House in 1766; and from 1762 was actively concerned in the transactions for paving Westminster streets.

In the new Parliament he continued to support Administration. He intervened in the debate of 15 Apr. 1769 on the Middlesex election;[7] and in March 1771 on the printers' case.[8] In September 1771 the Argyll interest obtained from North the place of receiver general of Scottish customs, worth £1500 p.a. A London newsletter records:[9] 'It is to be divided between Mr. Edmonstone of Duntreath and Colonel Campbell of Finab who is to go out of Parliament.' At the general election of 1774 he was returned after a contest with George Keith Elphinstone, who brought a petition, subsequently dropped, claiming that Edmonstone was ineligible 'because he enjoyed part of the profits of the office of receiver general of customs in Scotland held in the name of another person'.

At the 1780 election the Elphinstone opposition, backed by the Duke of Montrose's interest, constituted a dangerous threat. The Argyll family set up Lord Frederick Campbell as a stronger candidate for Dunbartonshire and moved Edmonstone to Ayr Burghs.

Edmonstone transferred his allegiance to successive Administrations. He voted, 18 Feb. 1783, for Shelburne's peace preliminaries, and, 27 Nov. 1783, for Fox's East India bill. Robinson, in his survey prepared shortly before Pitt took office, wrote of Ayr Burghs:[10]

> Sir Archibald Edmonstone will probably come in for these boroughs again unless there happens to be some agreement with the Bute family for the next turn. Sir Archibald very properly *votes now* with the present Government but would undoubtedly [do] so, as properly, with the next in a future Administration.

Counted 'hopeful' in early January 1784, Edmonstone was among the first to transfer his allegiance to Pitt. Returned apparently unopposed, he spoke against the coal tax (2 July) and the window tax (10 Aug.) as adversely affecting Scotland. Both speeches were uttered in so low a tone as to be inaudible.[11]

He had sold his Irish property by 1783 when he purchased for £41,000 the Kilsyth estates in Stirlingshire;[12] he also had interests in the East India Company,[13] in which his son Neil Benjamin subsequently had a distinguished career.

He died 20 July 1807.

[1] Sir Archibald Edmonstone, *Genealogical Account Fam. of Edmonstone of Duntreath*, 45–50; *The Montgomery Mss*, ed. Hill. [2] Edmonstone to Chas. Yorke, 17 May 1763, Add. 35636, f. 338. [3] Bute to W. Mure, 15 Apr. 1761, *Caldwell Pprs*. ii(1), p. 127. [4] Bute mss. [5] *Grenville Pprs*. ii. 128. [6] Rockingham mss. [7] Walpole, *Mems. Geo. III*, iii. 237. [8] Cavendish's 'Debates', Egerton 226, pp. 27, 369; Brickdale's 'Debates'. [9] Newsletter from Mrs. Anderson of the British Coffee House, 9 Oct. 1771, Loudoun mss. [10] Laprade, 102. [11] Stockdale, ii. 262; iii. 447. [12] Edmonstone, op. cit. 8, 68. [13] C. H. Phillips, *E.I. Co. 1784–1834*, p. 304.

E.H.-G.

### EDWARDES, William (c.1712–1801), of Johnston, Pemb.

HAVERFORDWEST    1747–1784, 6 Feb. 1786–13 Dec. 1801

*b.* c.1712, 3rd s. of Francis Edwardes of Johnston, M.P. for Haverfordwest, by Lady Elizabeth Rich, da. of Robert, 5th Earl of Warwick, 2nd Earl Holland and Baron Kensington, aunt and h. of Edward, 7th Earl of Warwick. *m.* (1) his cos. Rachel (*d.*14 Aug. 1760), da. of Owen Edwardes; (2) 10 June 1762, Elizabeth, da. and coh. of William Warren of Longridge, Pemb., 1s. *suc.* bro. Edward Henry in Warwick estates inc. considerable property in Kensington 18 Mar. 1738; *cr.* Baron Kensington [I] 28 July 1776.

Sheriff, Pemb. 1747–8.

Edwardes was returned to nine Parliaments without a poll; sat in the House 52 years and not a single speech by him is recorded; after 1760 he is not known ever to have voted against any Government; but, as he put it in a 'Memorial' to Lord Sandwich in October 1779, he 'never asked or received place, pension or any other emolument for himself'.[1]

In 1754 Edwardes had the best interest at Haverfordwest; the next best interest was in Sir John Philipps of Picton Castle. Before the general election there was a danger of a clash between them,[2] but the matter must have been accommodated, and subsequently while Edwardes supported the Philippses in the county, they supported him in the borough. When Richard Philipps was returned for Pembrokeshire on his father's death, 'I congratulate you', wrote George Grenville to Edwardes, 23 Feb. 1764, 'on an event which must be so agreeable to you.'[3]

Henry Fox leased from Edwardes Holland House 1745–68, when he bought it;[4] and when asking in June 1753 for some patronage on Edwardes's behalf, wrote that he, 'I make no doubt, may be brought to oppose Sir John Philipps' principles everywhere'.[5] Still, in 1754 he was classed as a Tory by Dupplin, and in February–March 1755 even by Fox himself;[6] and in 1760 was a member of the Society of Sea Serjeants, a club of Tory gentry in south-west Wales.[7] In 1761, however, Newcastle treated him as one of Fox's group; sent him the parliamentary whip in October 1761 through Fox; and wrote him off as 'contra' in November 1762. Edwardes's support was secured by Fox for the peace preliminaries, and next for the Grenville Administration.[8] Rockingham, both in 1765 and in 1766, and Townshend in January 1767, listed Edwardes as 'doubtful'; and Newcastle in March as 'Administration'. During the years 1765–79 his attendance in Parliament seems to have been rather poor: even though fewer division lists name those voting on the Government side than on the Opposition side, there are ten, of which only one names Edwardes. Besides, in Robinson's survey on the royal marriage bill, March 1772, he is listed as 'pro, present', and on the contractors bill, 12 Feb. 1779, as 'pro, out of town'. Still, when applying for a British peerage, Edwardes wrote to Sandwich, 12 Oct. 1779:[9]

I have worn out near five Parliaments in the service of Government under a laborious and expensive attendance, but particularly since the time of general warrants and through the whole of Lord North's Administration, I have attended his Lordship late and early in his minorities as well as in his majorities with warmth and zeal upon all occasions, and I believe I can say that during the whole time, till last winter, there was not a division happened in the house that concerned Administration, at which I was not present, and then I was prevented by Lady Kensington's health and my own, in return for which his Lordship, contrary to my repeated request to put me upon the list of English peers or to leave me remain in my then situation, his Lordship popped me off at the fag end of the Irish, I demurred . . . an indignity to the family set and a disadvantage to myself.

Unwearied attendance was with Edwardes much more of a forecast for the future: between 21 Feb. 1780 and 15 Mar. 1782 his name appears in 10 out of 11 division lists, always on the Government side; and there he remained however much Governments changed: he voted for Shelburne's peace preliminaries; for Fox's East India bill; and next he adhered to Pitt's Government.

In 1780 Robinson wrote about Haverfordwest: 'The same again. A contest started but compromised.' And in December 1783 about Edwardes: 'Against now, but may with civility perhaps be classed hopeful. He was entangled with some securities to the customs.'[10] But at the general election Edwardes stood down for Richard Philipps, now Lord Milford; and only resumed his seat when it was vacated by Milford in January 1786.

In 1794 and 1796 he again applied for a British peerage but died a commoner in England, 13 Dec. 1801.

[1] Sandwich mss. [2] H. Fox to Pelham, 12 June 1753, Newcastle (Clumber) mss. [3] Grenville letter bk. [4] Ilchester, *Hen. Fox*, i. 141; ii. 326. [5] Newcastle mss. [6] Add. 33002, f. 438. [7] R. Fenton, *Hist. Tour through Pemb.* 255. [8] Sandwich to Fox, 26 Sept. 1763, Hen. Fox mss; Fox to Sandwich, 2 Oct., Sandwich mss. [9] Sandwich mss. [10] Laprade, 97.

L.B.N.

**EDWARDS, Gerard Noel** (1759–1838), of Welham Grove, Leics. and Exton Park, Rutland.

MAIDSTONE    1784–June 1788
RUTLAND    15 July 1788–May 1808, 9 May 1814–
    25 Feb. 1838

*b.* 17 July 1759, o.s. of Gerard Anne Edwards of Welham Grove, by Lady Jane Noel, da. of Baptist, 4th Earl of Gainsborough. *educ.* Eton 1770–4; St. John's, Camb. 1776. *m.* (1) 21 Dec. 1780, Diana (*d.*12 Apr. 1823), da. and h. of Sir Charles Middleton (q.v.),12s. 6 da.; (2) 4 May 1823, Harriett (*d.* 11 Aug.) 1826), da. of Rev. Joseph Gill, vicar of Scraptoft, Leics., *s.p.*; (3) 11 Aug. 1831, Isabella, wid. of Raymond Evans, *s.p.*    *suc.* fa. 1773; and to estates of his uncle, Henry, 6th Earl of Gainsborough 1798, and took name of Noel in place of Edwards; *suc.* fa.-in-law under sp. rem. as 2nd Bt. 17 June 1813.

Edwards's only connexion with Maidstone seems to have been through his uncle, Sir Horace Mann (q.v.), whom in 1784 he succeeded as M.P. for the borough. He supported Pitt, voted for parliamentary reform, 18 Apr. 1785, and spoke occasionally in the House. On the death of his cousin, Thomas Noel (q.v.), he vacated his seat at Maidstone and was returned unopposed for Rutland, where the Gainsborough estates principally lay. He was a member of the group which in May 1788 tried to form a third party independent of both Pitt and Fox. On the Regency he spoke and voted against Pitt.

In an obituary notice he is described as 'in early life a partner in a banking house in Westminster',[1] which seems to have been Davison and Co. of Stratford Place, Oxford St.[2]

He died 25 Feb. 1838.

[1] *Gent. Mag.* 1838, i. 657. [2] F. G. Hilton Price, *Handbook of London Bankers*, 50–51.

    J.B.

**EDWARDS FREEMAN, Thomas** (?1726–1808), of Batsford, Glos.

STEYNING    1768–1780

*b.* ?1726, 1st s. of Walter Edwards of St. Dunstan's, London by Mary, da. of Richard Freeman of Batsford, Glos., ld. chancellor [I] 1707–10. *educ.* Queen's, Oxf. 3 Feb. 1744, aged 17. *m.* 23 July 1753, Elizabeth, da. of Henry Reveley of Newby Wisk, Yorks., 1s. *suc.* uncle Richard Freeman in Batsford estates March 1742 and assumed add. name of Freeman. Director, South Sea Co. 1769.

Freeman was returned for Steyning on the interest of Sir John Honywood, 3rd Bt., to whom he was distantly related. He seems to have been completely independent, to the point of self-contradiction in his votes and speeches: he voted with Administration on Wilkes and the Middlesex election, 3 Feb. and 15 Apr. 1769; but the following year, 27 Jan. 1770, voted for the pointed Opposition

motion that 'in matters of elections the House is bound to judge according to the law of the land'. Two years later on the motion for leave to bring in a bill to secure the rights of the electors of Great Britain, 25 Feb. 1772, he said he considered himself a member of 'a very respectable, and honourable body' which had been 'injured and traduced . . . I think we have the authority of Parliament for what we did, agreeable to the law of the land and customs of Parliament'; and opposing the same motion, 26 Apr. 1773, he argued that 'motions of this nature may tend to the renewal of unhappy divisions which distracted this whole country for a length of time'. In Robinson's first survey on the royal marriage bill, March 1772, Freeman is classed as 'doubtful, present', and in the second, 8 Mar., as 'pro, present'; but Cavendish reported, 16 Mar., that 'Mr. Freeman' thought the bill would not work, for it was 'not founded in the law of this country'. Freeman in a later debate on the bill, 24 Mar., declared that 'succession . . . may depend upon the arbitrary will of a single [man]', and concluded: 'I dissent to the third reading and passing.' He voted with the Opposition on Grenville's Election Act, 25 Feb. 1774, but appears in the King's list as a Government supporter. Robinson in his survey of 1774 classed him as 'pro'.[1]

Freeman does not appear in the five minority lists, February 1775–February 1778, spoke in support of the Address, 26 Oct. 1775, but voted with Opposition on the conciliatory mission, 4 Dec. 1778, and was listed as 'contra, present, friend' on the contractors bill, 12 Feb. 1779. He voted with Opposition in four of the five divisions, February–April 1780; but supported Administration on the motion against prorogation, 24 Apr. Robinson wrote in his survey of July 1780: 'Mr. Freeman is mostly with us', and classed him as 'pro'. Freeman did not stand again in 1780.

He died 15 Feb. 1808, aged 81.

[1] Cavendish's 'Debates', Egerton 234, p. 184; 237, p. 141; 239 pp. 139–40; 245, pp. 311–12.

    M.M.D.

**EDWARDS FREEMAN, Thomas** (1754–88).

STEYNING    9 Aug. 1785–23 Mar. 1788

*b.* 1754, o.s. of Thomas Edwards Freeman (q.v.). *educ.* Queen's, Oxf. 31 Dec. 1772, aged 18. *m.* Mary (*d.*1781), da. of John Curtis of Butcombe, Som., 1da.

Freeman was returned on the Honywood interest at Steyning. His only reported vote was with Opposition on Richmond's fortifications plan, 27 Feb. 1786. There is no record of his having spoken in the House. He died *v.p.* 23 Mar. 1788.

    M.M.D.

**EDWARDS FREEMAN,** *see also* **MITFORD, John**

**EDWIN, Charles** (c.1699–1756), of Llanmihangel Plas, Glam.

WESTMINSTER 31 Dec. 1741–1747
GLAMORGAN 1747–29 June 1756

*b.* c.1699, o.s. of Samuel Edwin of Llanmihangel Plas, M.P. (and gd.-s. of Sir Humphrey Edwin, ld. mayor of London 1698), by Lady Catherine Montagu, da. of Robert, 3rd Earl of Manchester. *m.* 1 May 1736, Lady Charlotte Hamilton, da. of James, 4th Duke of Hamilton [S], *s.p. suc.* fa. 1722; to estates of his uncle Thomas Edwin in Surr., Suss. and Northants. 1735.
Sheriff, Northants. 1739–40.

Returned unopposed for Glamorgan in 1754, Edwin was classed by Dupplin as Tory. He died 29 June 1756.

A.N.N.

**EDWIN** (formerly **WYNDHAM**), **Charles** (*d.* 1801), of Llanmihangel Plas and Dunraven Castle, Glam.

GLAMORGAN 1780–Aug. 1789

1st s. of Thomas Wyndham of Cromer, Norf. by his 2nd w. Anne, da. of Samuel Edwin, M.P., sis. and h. of Charles Edwin (q.v.). *m.* (1) 25 Jan. 1762, Eleanor, da. of James Rooke (q.v.), 1s.; (2) Charlotte, da. of Robert Jones of Fonmon Castle, Glam., wid. of Thomas Ashby of Isleworth, Mdx., and of Col. Charles Mawhood. *suc.* fa. 1752, and uncle on *d.* of Lady Charlotte Edwin 1776, and took name Edwin.

In 1780 Edwin was returned for Glamorgan without a contest, and shortly afterwards the *English Chronicle* wrote about him:

This gentleman possesses a large fortune in the county of Glamorgan, and it was probably due to the influence of that consideration alone that he owed the honour of his parliamentary delegation, as he is not distinguished for any other circumstances, than the omnipotent one of enjoying ten thousand pounds a year, and being the modern Nimrod of the neighbourhood where he resides. He is a new Member—is above corruption, and as far as a *silent* vote can go, will, in all probability, prove the sincere friend of the minister.

Possibly to begin with Edwin did vote with Administration, but in the first division after his election for which there is a list (12 Dec. 1781, on Lowther's motion against the American war) he voted with Opposition. On 16 Feb. 1782 Sandwich, in preparation for the motion of censure against the Admiralty, sent John Robinson a list of Members who might be persuaded to vote with Government or not to attend; Edwin's name is included, with the comment: 'Sir S. Gideon (q.v.) has promised to try him'. Yet Edwin again voted with Opposition in this division, 20 Feb., and also on 22 and 27 Feb.; but was absent from the divisions of 8 and 15 Mar.

He did not vote on Shelburne's peace preliminaries or on Fox's East India bill. Robinson, in preparation for the general election, wrote about Glamorgan: 'Same again; thought doubtful'; and Edwin was again returned without a contest. In both the list of 19 Mar. and William Adam's list of the new Parliament he is classed as a supporter of Pitt. The only votes he is known to have given in this Parliament were for the impeachment of Sir Elijah Impey, 9 May 1788, and for Pitt's Regency proposals. No speech by him is recorded. He vacated his seat in favour of his son, Thomas Wyndham.

He died 16 June 1801.

J.B.

**EGERTON, John William** (1753–1823), of Albemarle St., London.

MORPETH 20 Feb. 1777–1780
BRACKLEY 1780–8 Mar. 1803

*b.* 14 Apr. 1753, 2nd but 1st surv. s. of Rt. Rev. John Egerton, bp. of Durham, and gt.-gd.-s. of John, 3rd Earl of Bridgwater by Lady Anne Sophia Grey, da. and coh. of Henry, 1st Duke of Kent. *educ.* Eton 1764–8, Ch. Ch. Oxf. 1770. *m.* 14 Jan. 1783, Catherine Anne, da. and h. of Samuel Haynes (q.v.), *s.p. suc.* his 2nd cos. Francis, 3rd Duke of Bridgwater, as 7th Earl of Bridgwater, 8 Mar. 1803.
Cornet 7 Drag. 1771, capt. 1776; maj. 22 Lt. Drag. 1779; lt.-col. 7 Drag. 1790; col. in army 1793; maj.-gen. 1795; col. 14 Lt. Drag. 1797–*d.*; lt.-gen. 1802; gen 1812.

Egerton was returned unopposed for Morpeth on the interest of his distant relative, Lord Carlisle. In Parliament he, like Carlisle, regularly supported Administration until the fall of North.

At the general election of 1780 he was returned by the Duke of Bridgwater for his pocket borough of Brackley. He voted against Shelburne's peace preliminaries, 18 Feb. 1783; in Robinson's list of March 1783 he was counted as a follower of North. He did not vote on Fox's East India bill, 27 Nov. 1783; was classed as a supporter of Pitt in Robinson's list of January 1784, Stockdale's of 19 Mar., and by Adam in May, and though his first recorded vote was against Administration on Pitt's Irish proposals, 13 May 1785, his other recorded votes were in support of Administration.

Egerton is only twice reported to have spoken in the House: on 22 Feb. 1779[1] against Barne's motion for limiting the time of army service, and on 20 Nov. 1780, when he denied that the riots at Coventry had swayed the election results.[2]

He died 31 Mar. 1823.

[1] Fortescue, iv. 287. [2] Debrett, i. 119.

L.B.N.

**EGERTON, Samuel** (1711–80), of Tatton Park, nr. Knutsford, Cheshire.

CHESHIRE 1754–10 Feb. 1780

*b.* 28 Dec. 1711, 2nd s. of John Egerton of Tatton Park (gd.-s. of John, 2nd Earl of Bridgwater), by Elizabeth, da. of Samuel Barber. *m.* Beatrix, da. and coh. of Rev. John Copley of Batley, Yorks., 1 da. *suc.* bro. 1738.

Egerton was returned unopposed at all his elections. In 1754 he was classed by Dupplin as a 'Tory', but on 1 Oct. 1759 applied to Newcastle for ecclesiastical preferment for his brother, and though the Duke refused, wrote a polite letter of compliments and thanks.[1] In Bute's list he was classed as a 'Tory', but in September 1762 is in Newcastle's list of persons to be sent to; he declared his adherence to Newcastle;[2] voted against the peace preliminaries, and against the Grenville Administration, and was listed by Newcastle, 10 May 1764, as a 'sure friend'. Rockingham, July 1765, classed him as 'pro', and as 'Whig' in November 1766; he voted with the Opposition on the land tax, 27 Feb. 1767; yet Newcastle, 2 Mar. 1767, again classed him as 'Tory'. Egerton voted in opposition on the Middlesex election, 8 May 1769, and appears in both Robinson's surveys on the royal marriage bill, March 1772, as 'contra, present'. No other vote of his is recorded, though on the contractors bill, 12 Feb. 1779, Robinson listed him as 'pro, absent. Query, pro'. But these divisions may not have been typical of his normal voting. The *Public Ledger* wrote about him shortly before his death:

> A very wealthy country gentleman, and a Tory in principle. He votes constantly with Government when he attends Parliament, and professes a great veneration for Lord North.

Egerton's one reported speech was on the Chester navigation bill, 22 Apr. 1771.

He died 10 Feb. 1780.

[1] Add. 32986, ff. 188, 248, 356. [2] Add. 33000, ff. 278–9.

M.M.D.

**EGERTON, Sir Thomas,** 7th Bt. (1749–1814), of Heaton, nr. Lancaster.

LANCASHIRE 4 Feb. 1772–1784

*b.* 14 Feb. 1749, o.s. of Sir Thomas Grey Egerton, 6th Bt., of Heaton by Catherine, da. of Rev. John Copley of Batley, Yorks. *educ.* Westminster 1764. *m.* 12 Sept. 1769, Eleanor, da. and coh. of Sir Ralph Assheton, 3rd Bt., of Middleton, Lancs., 2s. *d.v.p.* 3 da. *suc.* fa. 7 Aug. 1766; *cr.* Lord Grey de Wilton, 15 May 1784; Earl of Wilton, 26 June 1801, with sp. rem. to 2nd and yr. sons of his da. Eleanor, m. 1794 to Robert Grosvenor, Visct. Belgrave (q.v.).

Egerton was returned unopposed in 1772, and at each subsequent election. At first he voted in

opposition: on the naval captains' petition, 9 Feb. 1773, Grenville's Act, 25 Feb. 1774, and Wilkes, 22 Feb. 1775; but on the American war he supported Government. In 1778 he raised a regiment of foot at Manchester for service in America,[1] and voted with North's Administration to the end.

Most of his speeches were on matters concerning Lancashire, and he was particularly sensitive about Lancashire's trade or industry. In 1778 he opposed North's proposals for opening Irish trade, and suggested a committee of inquiry.[2] But in 1780, when the situation in Ireland was critical, he said of North's further proposals:[3]

> It was no longer a question of commerce but a question of great national importance, for which reason the several places in the kingdom likely to be affected . . . thought it more decent and dutiful to remain silent and trust altogether to the wisdom and justice of Parliament.

On 26 Apr. 1781, fearing the effect of proposed bounties on linen goods, he asked for an adjournment to consult his constituents; and on 21 May proposed that cotton goods should receive the same bounty as linen.[4]

Egerton voted against Shelburne's peace preliminaries, 18 Feb. 1783; was classed by Robinson as 'North, doubtful', and on the formation of the Coalition was considered for some promotion, probably a peerage.[5] He did not vote on Fox's East India bill, but on 20 Jan. 1784 announced his support of Pitt,[6] and on 28 Jan. wrote to the King:[7] 'I . . . do assure your Majesty that I have had no view whatever in my political life, but to support and maintain the true principles of the Constitution.' He did not stand at the general election, and a month later was created a peer.

He died 23 Sept. 1814.

[1] Fortescue, iv. 392–3. [2] Stockdale, viii. 207. [3] Almon, xvii. 58. [4] Debrett, iii. 171, 371–2. [5] Fortescue, vi. 275; cf. list in J. C. Wedgwood, *Staffs. Parlty. Hist.* ii. 307. [6] Debrett, xii. 614. [7] Royal archives, Windsor.

J.B.

**EGERTON, William** (c.1730–83).

BRACKLEY 1768–1780

*b.* c.1730, 2nd s. of Hon. Henry Egerton, bp. of Hereford, by Lady Elizabeth Bentinck, da. of William, 1st Earl of Portland, and gd.-s. of John, 3rd Earl of Bridgwater. *educ.* Eton 1742–5. *m.* 15 Aug. 1751 Mary, da. of Robert Kirke, 2s. 3 da.

Sub-brigadier 2nd Troop Horse Gds. 1755, exempt and capt. 1764, cornet and major 1771, 2nd lt. and lt.-col. 1773; ret. 1779.

Gent. usher to Princess Dowager of Wales 1761–72; yeoman and clerk of jewel office 1761–*d.*; lt.-gov. Scilly Isles 1776–9.

Egerton sat for Brackley on the Bridgwater interest; voted with the court (his one known vote in opposition was on the naval captains' petition, 9 Feb. 1773); and is not known to have spoken in the House.

He died 26 May 1783.[1]

[1] Foster, *Lancs. Peds.*; *Gent. Mag.* 1783, p. 273, gives 16 Mar.; Collins *Peerage*, 26 Mar.

M.M.D.

**EGERTON** (formerly **TATTON**), **William** (1749–1806), of Tatton Park, Cheshire.

| | |
|---|---|
| HINDON | 1784–1790 |
| NEWCASTLE-UNDER-LYME | 15 Sept. 1792–1802 |
| CHESHIRE | 1802–21 Apr. 1806 |

*b.* 9 May 1749, o.s. of William Tatton of Wythenshawe, Cheshire by Hester, da. of John Egerton of Tatton Park, sis. and h. of Samuel Egerton (q.v.). *educ.* Manchester g.s. 1759; B.N.C. Oxf. 1767. *m.* (1) 27 Feb. 1773, Frances Maria (*d.*9 Jan. 1777), da. of Very Rev. John Fountayne, dean of York, 2s. 1da.; (2) 26 Oct. 1780, Mary (*d.*13 Nov. 1784), da. of Richard Wilbraham Bootle (q.v.), 3s. 1da.; (3) 1 June 1787, Anna Maria (*d.*4 Sept. 1799), da. of Sir George Armytage, 3rd Bt. (q.v.), 1s.; (4) 1 Nov. 1803, Charlotte Clara, da. of Thomas Watkinson Payler of Ileden, Kent, *s.p.* *suc.* mother in Egerton estates 1780, and took name of Egerton.
Sheriff, Cheshire 1778–9.

In 1784 Egerton successfully contested Hindon on the Calthorpe interest. In William Adam's list of May 1784 he was classed as 'Administration', and though his first recorded vote was against Pitt's Irish proposals, 13 May 1785, he supported Pitt over the Regency, 1788–9. Two speeches by Egerton are reported before 1790, both on Lancashire affairs.[1]

He died 21 Apr. 1806, said to be worth '£20,000 a year and upwards.'[2]

[1] Stockdale, v. 216, 229, reports these speeches as by 'Mr. Egerton', which is more likely to have been William than John William, who was an army officer, and seems to have had no connexion with Lancashire. [2] *Gent. Mag.* 1806, p. 391.

M.M.D.

**EGLETON**, *see* **KENT, Sir Charles**

**EGMONT, Earl of,** *see* **PERCEVAL, John**

**ELCOCK**, *see* **WEDDELL**

**ELIOT, Edward** (1727–1804), of Port Eliot, Cornw.

| | |
|---|---|
| ST. GERMANS | 12 Dec. 1748–1768 |
| LISKEARD | 1768–1774 |
| ST. GERMANS | 1774–Nov. 1775 |
| CORNWALL | 15 Nov. 1775–13 Jan. 1784 |

*b.* 8 July 1727, 1st s. of Richard Eliot, M.P., by Harriet, illegit. da. of James Craggs jun., M.P.; she m. (2) Nov. 1749, Capt. John Hamilton, R.N. (their s. was J. J. Hamilton, q.v.). *educ.* Liskeard sch.; St. Mary Hall, Oxf. 1742; Grand Tour (with Philip

Stanhope, q.v.) 1746–8. *m.* 25 Sept. 1756, Catherine, da. and h. of Edward Elliston of Gestingthorpe, Essex by Catherine, sis of Edward Gibbon sen. of Buriton, Hants, 4s. *suc.* fa. 19 Nov. 1748; *cr.* Baron Eliot 13 Jan. 1784.
Receiver gen. of duchy of Cornwall 13 May 1749–*d.*; ld. of Trade Dec. 1759–Mar. 1776.

Eliot succeeded his father in 1748 as M.P. for St. Germans and receiver general of the duchy of Cornwall. After the death of the Prince of Wales in 1751, Eliot joined the Pelhams, with Robert Nugent, his uncle by marriage, for political mentor. At the general election of 1754 Eliot chose his candidates in understanding with Administration[1] but from among his own friends: Edmund Nugent, Philip Stanhope, and Anthony Champion.

On 20 Oct. 1755 Newcastle asked Eliot, then in France, to attend the opening of the session if his health permitted, and anyhow to send across Champion. Eliot replied, 7 Nov., that, having received Newcastle's letter at Lyons, he set out for home, but this 'has brought back a return of my spitting of blood', and he therefore let Champion proceed to London alone.[2]

On 5 Oct. 1756 Eliot applied to Newcastle for a place at the Board of Trade,[3]

which is the lowest Board; where I hope to get such information as may enable some of us young people who act together to put in execution the resolution we have formed, of endeavouring to speak in the House of Commons upon points of business . . . I believe I can be of as much use towards carrying on his Majesty's business both as to interest and elections in the country, and as to the House of Commons in town, as any body whatsoever to whom your Grace can give the Board of Trade.

He pressed for an explicit answer, 'for it is high time that I should be in some certain track of life, my age will not admit of delays as to my outset'. Newcastle had only a slight acquaintance with Eliot, but knew that he did 'make as many Members of Parliament as any of them'. 'He is a pretty young man', he wrote to Hardwicke on 10 Oct., 'I saw him at Hanover. He looks high; but he seems a peremptory gentleman. Lord Chesterfield has a great opinion of him.'[4] To Eliot Newcastle replied with promises, often to be repeated.[5] In June 1757 Eliot reminded the Duke of his 'former kind intentions' and of the lost opportunities of obliging him. And on 15 May 1759:[6]

I desire *to stake my whole credit* (for the present and to come) with your Grace on this point, and I shall make it my final criterion whereby to judge your Grace's intentions towards me.

A week later, in a bitter, threatening letter:[7]

I am in a worse situation (with respect to office) a great deal now than I was ten years ago. I have lost some of the best years of my life—which is irrecoverable, and it does not appear unlikely but that I am condemned to lose more.

And on 28 Oct. 1759:[8]

Three or four years ago, indeed, my Lord Duke, you might have given me a seat at the Board of Trade with an extreme good grace, and I should have accepted it with joy. At present I have waited so long, and have seen so many people . . . preferred before me, that I should be insincere if I said that either my ambition or my vanity *could be flattered* with my being the last at the lowest Board.

Appointed in December 1759, he looked back at three wasted years, 'a loss, in point of business, which I shall never retrieve'.[9] He can hardly be said to have tried: his attendance at Board meetings from 1760–73 was poor, and *nil* 1773–6; and what was to have been his 'outset' was the only place of business he ever held.

Thus by 1760 relations between Eliot and New-castle were strained: Eliot resented any suggestion of being directed by him; and Newcastle wrote of the 'many instances' he had had 'of that gentleman's extraordinary way of thinking'.[10] Eliot would still approach Newcastle on matters arising in the Trea-sury,[11] and offer him his parliamentary interest in Sussex, but was turning to Bute, and tried 'to re-commend himself, his offices, and his Cornwall affairs' to Bute's protection.[12]

In 1761 Eliot had six seats to fill, Grampound having attached itself to him in 1758. There was, however, a difference in the way he filled up his boroughs. Counting the four seats at St. Germans and Liskeard, 1754–90, as 144 year-seat units, mem-bers of the Eliot family held 54, close friends another 54, and strangers only 36; i.e. on an average one seat only in four was filled by a stranger; while at Gram-pound Eliot invariably returned strangers.

Eliot's charge for a seat rose from the £2,000 he demanded from Fanshawe at Grampound in 1761[13] to the flat rate of £3,000 in 1780: which followed the general price level. But Gibbon in 1774 was returned on exceptionally easy terms, and so probably was Langlois. Looking back at nearly half a century of borough patronage, Eliot wrote to Pitt on 7 Oct. 1797:[14]

In election transactions I have never received what in the one town or the other I had not previously laid out. Such receipts were matters of necessity—I have never submitted to them without a feeling of reluct-ance. Often I have received nothing, and not in-frequently have thereby suffered very considerable personal inconvenience.

In 1761 the Members returned by Eliot for the family boroughs were he himself, Champion, and Stanhope, and Philip Stephens recommended to him on a vacancy in 1759 by Anson:[15] at Grampound he re-elected the two Administration candidates re-turned in 1754. When in October 1761 Newcastle sent out his parliamentary whip, the attendance of only Champion and Stanhope was to be secured by Eliot.[16]

In Bute's parliamentary list of December 1761 'Nugent and Government' is put against Eliot. Early in December 1762 Fox did not include him among the Members favourable to the peace pre-liminaries; and Eliot was absent from the two divi-sions of 9 and 10 Dec., while Champion voted against them. On 11 Dec. Fox, when sending Bute the lists of the minority, remarked:[17]

You'll observe Mr. Champion in both lists. Nugent says he is not the proper person to write to Eliot, who stays in the country, but he thinks without any ill will, notwithstanding this symptom of Champion's vote.

Although an office-holder, and generally well-inclined to the Grenville Government—he was marked 'pro' by Jenkinson in the autumn of 1763—Eliot was as irregular in his attendance in Parliament as he was independent in his voting when present. He was absent from the important division of 15 Nov. 1763; voted with the Government on general warrants, 6 Feb.; but against them over the Cider Act, 10 Feb.[18] and with the Opposition over general warrants, 15 and 18 Feb.

Nugent, who hung back for a fortnight after Grenville's dismissal, when informing him on 24 July 1765 of having resigned, added that he had engaged himself in honour to Eliot to do so; and on 8 Aug.: 'I explained to Lord Temple what I meant by my engagement to Eliot'[19]—puzzling statements, especially as Eliot himself did not resign. In a paper of June 1765 on a plan of the new Government, Rockingham wrote:[20]

Edward Eliot—should not be removed—brings in two or three Members—has been very well inclined—and has taken opportunities of showing it—and is a man of abilities and character.

In 1766 and 1767 both Rockingham and Newcastle placed him among the supporters of the Chatham Administration, and even over the land tax he voted with the Government.

The general election of 1768, though coming at the end of full seven years, found Eliot unprepared —it was his nature to hesitate and worry and tie himself into knots. For Grampound he again re-turned Government candidates: Grey Cooper, secretary to the Treasury, and C. W. Cornwall, a friend of Shelburne's. For both his family boroughs he returned himself and his friend Samuel Salt, obviously in order to gain a further eight months in which to decide on his choice of the other two Members. Benjamin Langlois, a close friend, was one applicant; and Rockingham, Portland, and some of their supporters, thought that Eliot's nomination might be obtained for Opposition candidates. On 30 July 1768 Portland wrote to Burke that, not knowing what Eliot's engagements were to Langlois, he had not written to Eliot yet, but was very willing to do so on behalf of Burke's brother Richard, and thus procure 'for the cause . . . an additional support in Parliament from your family'. And on 16 Aug. Rockingham wrote to Burke: 'I have not yet wrote again to Mr. Eliot which I must do. I don't expect success.' Eliot replied to Portland on 18 Nov., apologizing for the long delay:[21]

> I sincerely wish I could have thought myself at liberty to obey your Grace's and Lord Rockingham's commands. I was not in the least aware that either the one or the other would have imagined me to be wholly unengaged so late, or would have had a friend unprovided with a seat, whom you each have it so much at heart to bring into Parliament.
>
> Although I have been what is called successful, yet many circumstances have fallen out so unfortunately with regard to me at this general election, that I have felt much more uneasiness and concern from it than pleasure or satisfaction. The not being able to comply with your Grace's and Lord Rockingham's applications add much to that uneasiness and concern. At the same time that I can truly assure your Grace and his Lordship that I look upon myself as very much and very particularly honoured by having *had* those applications.

He went on to explain his reasons for returning Langlois, and said nothing about the other seat, for which he had returned George Jennings, a Government supporter.

Here is the net result of the 1768 election in Eliot's boroughs: of the Members for Grampound, after Chatham and Shelburne had resigned, C. W. Cornwall went into opposition—so that his vote and Cooper's cancelled out each other; of the Members for Eliot's family boroughs, Salt from the very outset regularly voted with the Opposition, obviously left free by Eliot to take his own line; Jennings, with similar regularity, voted on the Government side; Langlois did not return from Vienna till 1771, and then, in need of a place, voted with the Government; while Eliot himself is not known ever to have spoken or voted in that Parliament—he seems to have grown indifferent to politics, and to have spent most of his time in the country.

Gibbon, who even while enjoying Eliot's hospitality and friendship spoke of him in a carping manner, wrote to his step-mother from Port Eliot on 10 Sept. 1773:

> Our civil landlord possesses neither a pack of hounds, nor a stable of running horses, nor a large farm, nor a good library. The last only would interest me; but it is singular that a man of fortune, who chooses to pass nine months of the year in the country, should have none of them.

The library may not have satisfied Gibbon's requirements, but the impression this passage gives is hardly fair to Eliot, a member of the Literary Club and one of the 'most familiar and valued friends' of Sir Joshua Reynolds.[22] Elsewhere Gibbon speaks of Eliot's 'indolence'—he was hesitant and inclined to fret, and the result therefore often fell short of the effort. Yet he took a prominent part in county affairs; in June 1771 was one of the founders of the Cornish Bank; and in an age of extravagant expenditure looked carefully, or even anxiously, after his financial affairs.

On 9 Sept. 1774, before the dissolution of Parliament was announced, Eliot, who had in his will made Gibbon an executor and guardian to his children, offered him 'an *independent* seat' on very favourable terms, replacing Jennings. The other Members in Eliot's family boroughs remained the same, while at Grampound he again returned strangers designated by Government—'I set you down for Mr. Eliot's borough of Grampound', wrote North to Joseph Yorke, 16 Sept.[23]

At a by-election, on 15 Nov. 1775, Eliot was returned unopposed for Cornwall—a signal mark of popularity: as a rule counties were averse to placemen, and Cornwall to the big borough owners. 'I am amazed how he condescended to accept it', wrote Gibbon on 4 Dec. 'The Member of St. Germans might lurk in the country, but the knight of Cornwall must attend the House of Commons.' Henceforth Eliot's name re-appears in division lists. Opposed to the American war, he voted on 11 Mar. 1776 against a motion for army extraordinaries, 'and soon after resigned his employment'.[24] On 8 May 1780, Thomas Pitt wrote to William Lemon:[25]

> I must say that Mr. Eliot both by the independent line he has taken in Parliament, and by the zeal with which he has assisted every object of the county since he has been one of its representatives, has in my opinion entitled himself to our support and confidence at the next election.

For his own seat at St. Germans, Eliot returned in November 1775 John Pownall, secretary to the Board of Trade; and when in 1776 Pownall was appointed commissioner of the Excise, Eliot, though in opposition, returned another Government supporter, John Peachey: because Pownall, 'an intimate friend of mine for many years, had set his heart on being made commissioner', and could not be if this lost a vote to Government.[26] He similarly re-elected Langlois on his promotion, 3 June 1778, and Gibbon on his obtaining office, 12 July 1779.

Robinson in his electoral survey of July 1780 wrote against St. Germans:

> Mr. Eliot has been seen relative to this and his other boroughs, but he has not been explicit, saying he must

consult his friends in the county and at present it seems doubtful whether he will bring in the friends of Government. He is violent against Administration.

When Dr. Richard Williams offered, at a price, to act as intermediary, North wrote to Robinson, 13 Aug. 1780:[27]

As to seeing Mr. Eliot, I always told you that it did not appear to me likely to be of any service; if he would serve us at all he would in his conversation with you have given you reason to expect it . . . Dr. Williams . . . will not find us ungrateful for any successful negotiation he may have with Mr. Eliot . . . Employ him on that commission; he is much more likely to succeed than I should be.

Robinson thought Williams's terms unacceptable, and meant to seek some other approach to Eliot, though with 'little hopes' of success.[28] In the end North accepted Williams's conditions. 'I have yesterday sent a man down post to Cornwall to sound Eliot', Robinson wrote to Jenkinson on 21 Aug., 'a man Eliot has confidence in, and has trusted in his election jobs.' And the next day:[29] 'Langlois may do some good with Eliot, and as soon as I well dare venture I will talk to him, but Gibbon I understand is not so well with Eliot as he was.' After this nothing more appears about Government attempts to secure Eliot's electoral support. By that time he was fully committed to the Opposition leaders, and was not going to re-elect even Gibbon and Langlois. On 17 Aug. Rockingham asked Portland to inform Eliot that John Christian declined, but '*all the others* for whom I particularly spoke are decisively fixed to accept'; he himself would write to Eliot 'immediately after York races'.[30] On 20 Aug. Eliot wrote to Portland on the choice of candidates.

I have not the least objection to either of the three names you mention, unless the baronet is a North Briton . . .
Had I time, were I in the way, and could absolutely pick and choose . . . I should wish to have one candidate of talents, one that was likely to make a public speaker, and not very likely to get a seat elsewhere. Mr. Windham of Norfolk, and Mr. Jones (a candidate for Oxford) have both come into my head.

He had never seen either, but what he 'conceived of their principles and abilities', brought them to his mind.

On the sudden dissolution of the House on 1 Sept., Rockingham wrote to Portland:

I have furnished Mr. Eliot with four good candidates. First Mr. Lucas, president of Guys Hospital, by the recommendation of our friend Mr. Scudamore. My second is Sir John Ramsden (half brother to Lady Rockingham). My third Dudley Long Esq. My fourth *Charles Duncombe Esq. of Duncombe Park Yorkshire. This latter must be a secret. Indeed the whole transaction* in regard to all of them must be secret.

Portland replied on 3 Sept., greatly lamenting Rockingham's long silence,

not only from apprehensions of the effect it may have had upon Eliot's mind, but from the embarrassment which it has occasioned and may still create in his parliamentary arrangements, and the disappointment which may ensue to your fourth candidate, which . . . I greatly fear is now become unavoidable.

He added that Salt doubted 'his being any longer a part of Mr. Eliot's corps'. Rockingham's delays and Salt's 'refinements and irresolution' were undoubtedly embarrassing when only about ten days intervened between the dissolution and the elections in Eliot's boroughs. But there was something more to Eliot's choice for the fourth seat: he accepted for it Wilbraham Tollemache, a candidate recommended to him by Shelburne.[31] On 22 Sept. Rockingham wrote to Portland in high glee:[32]

The enemy have lost *five* Members and the friends of their country have got a reinforcement of five. A difference of ten gained at one haul is a comfortable event.

Eliot himself was re-elected for the county unopposed. Jeremy Bentham, who met Eliot at Bowood in August 1781,[33] describes him as

a modest, civil, good kind of man; sensible enough; but without those pretensions which one would expect to find in a man whose station in his country is so commanding, and political influence so great. He is modest enough in his conversation about politics, but desponding. He says he scarce ever looks into a paper, nor dares he, for fear of ill news.

—an attitude toward British disasters widely different from that of some of the other Opposition leaders.

In the new Parliament Eliot and his group of six Members regularly acted with the Opposition till the fall of North.

While the new Government was being formed, towards the end of March 1782, Shelburne wrote about Eliot in an undated memorandum for the King:[34]

He looks to peerage. He returns *seven* Members of Parliament, has a very great fortune, and uncommon personal weight in Cornwall, where the King wants an able person of influence; would humbly recommend him to your Majesty's remembrance when peers are made . . .

When in July 1782 the split occurred between Shelburne and Rockingham's political heirs, Eliot came out on Shelburne's side, and Edward James Eliot took office as a lord of the Treasury. But besides them, Lucas alone of Eliot's group voted on 18 Feb. 1783 for Shelburne's peace preliminaries; and all five, including Tollemache, adhered to the Coalition. They were dropped by Eliot at the general election of 1784, at which he returned his two sons and his half-brother J. J. Hamilton and three other steady followers of Pitt. He himself had on 13 Jan.

1784 been created a baron. He adhered to Pitt till the end of his life. He died 17 Feb. 1804.

[1] Eliot to H. Pelham, 12 Feb. 1754, Newcastle (Clumber) mss; Add. 32734, f. 275; 32735, f. 599. [2] Add. 32860, ff. 107, 408. [3] Add. 32868, ff. 96–97. [4] Ibid. f. 173. [5] Add. 32871, f. 356; 32872, f. 95. [6] Add. 32891, f. 142. [7] Ibid. ff. 237–8. [8] Add. 32895, ff. 446–7. [9] Add. 32900, f. 145. [10] Add. 32915, ff. 168–9. [11] Add. 32914, f. 217; 32919, f. 529. [12] Gilbert Elliot to Bute, 11 Mar. 1761, Bute mss. [13] Add. 32917, f. 359. [14] Chatham mss. [15] Anson to Eliot, 13 Nov. 1759, Eliot mss. [16] Add. 32929, ff. 303–11. [17] Bute mss. [18] Harris's 'Debates'. [19] Grenville mss (JM). [20] Rockingham mss. [21] Portland mss. [22] Leslie & Taylor, Life & Times of Reynolds, ii. 431. [23] Add. 35370, f. 275. [24] Walpole, Last Jnls. i. 533. [25] Lemon Pprs. Royal Institution of Cornwall. [26] Eliot to Gibbon, 24 Aug. 1780, Add. 34886, ff. 111–12. [27] Abergavenny mss. [28] To North, 14 Aug., ibid. [29] Add. 38567, ff. 59, 61. [30] Portland mss. [31] Eliot to Shelburne, 14, 16 Sept. 1780, Lansdowne mss. [32] Portland mss. [33] Works, ed. Bowring, x. 96. [34] Fortescue, v. 431.

L.B.N.

## ELIOT, Hon. Edward James (1758–97), of Port Eliot, Cornw.

ST. GERMANS 1780–1784
LISKEARD 1784–20 Sept. 1797

b. 24 Aug. 1758, 1st surv. s. of Edward Eliot, and bro. of Hon. John Eliot (qq.v.). educ. Pembroke, Camb. 1775. m. 24 Sept. 1785, Lady Harriet Pitt, da. of William, 1st Earl of Chatham, 1da.
   Ld. of Treasury July 1782–Apr. 1783, Dec. 1783–1793; commr. of Board of Control 1793–d.; King's remembrancer 1785–d.

Edward James, following his father's lead, voted with Opposition till the fall of North, and in July 1782 adhered to Shelburne. Gibbon, ill-disposed to the Eliot family, criticized his early promotion to a seat at the Treasury Board, describing him to Dorothea Gibbon, 10 Aug. 1782, as 'a very unmeaning youth'. Eliot acted as teller against Fox's East India bill, 27 Nov. 1783. In December, Pitt, a close friend of his, restored him to his Treasury post, and on the eve of his marriage with Pitt's sister Harriet, appointed him King's remembrancer. Thomas Orde wrote to the Duke of Rutland, 23 Sept. 1785: 'The office . . . is given to Lady Harriet Pitt as her portion upon her marriage to-morrow with Mr. Eliot. It is worth £1,500 p.a. net. Old Lord Eliot will, it is hoped, be softened by this accession of income.'[1] Similarly Mrs. Edward Boscawen, the admiral's widow, to Mrs. Chase Price, hinting at the father's supposed parsimony:[2] 'Lady Harriet Pitt if she goes on as she begins will be a fine fortune, and Lord Eliot who I hear has not taken out his purse upon this occasion will soon swear "there is no need".' But Edward James's 'first act on his appointment to that lucrative place was to restore to its regular course the succession to the places of the sworn-clerks, which, before, was open to be purchased by a fixed premium'.[3] In the House Eliot followed Pitt, and acted as teller for his proposals for parliamentary reform, 18 Apr. 1785. Only two unimportant interventions in debate by him are reported before 1790.[4]

He died v.p. 20 Sept. 1797.

[1] HMC Rutland, iii. 224. [2] Chase Price mss. [3] Gent. Mag., 1797, ii. 896. [4] 6 Mar. 1783 and 14 Feb. 1785.

L.B.N.

## ELIOT, Hon. John (1761–1823), of Port Eliot, Cornw.

LISKEARD 1784–17 Feb. 1804

b. 30 Sept. 1761, 2nd surv. s. of Edward Eliot, and bro. of Hon. Edward James Eliot (qq.v.). educ. Pembroke, Camb. 1780. m. (1) 9 Sept. 1790, Caroline (d.26 July 1818), da. of Charles Yorke (q.v.), s.p.; (2) 19 Aug. 1819, Harriet, da. of Reginald Pole Carew (q.v.), of Antony, Cornw., s.p. suc. fa. as 2nd Baron Eliot 17 Feb. 1804; cr. Earl of St. Germans 26 Nov. 1815.

John was Gibbon's favourite in the Eliot family. He wrote to Dorothea Gibbon, 15 May 1780: 'I see my young friend John . . . and was indeed astonished by the sense and propriety of his behaviour without embarrassment and without forwardness.' He played no prominent part in his first Parliament. A steady supporter of Pitt, he voted with him in all divisions 1784–90, including that on parliamentary reform, 18 Apr. 1785. During this period no speech of his is recorded, unless that of 14 Feb. 1785 was his.

He died 17 Nov. 1823.

L.B.N.

## ELLIOT, Gilbert (1722–77), of Minto, Roxburgh.[1]

SELKIRKSHIRE 13 Dec. 1753–May 1765
ROXBURGHSHIRE 20 June 1765–11 Jan. 1777

b. Sept. 1722, 1st s. of Sir Gilbert Elliot, 2nd Bt., M.P. of Minto, S.C.J. (Lord Minto), by Helen, da. of Sir Robert Steuart, 1st Bt., of Allanbank, Berwick, and bro. of John Elliot (q.v.). educ. Dalkeith 1732; Edinburgh Univ. 1735; adv. 1743; Leyden; tour in Holland and Germany 1744–5. m. 15 Dec. 1746, Agnes, da. and h. of Hugh Dalrymple Murray Kynynmound of Melgund, Forfar, and Lochgelly and Kynynmound, Fife, 4s. 2da. suc. fa. as 3rd Bt. 16 Apr. 1766.
   Sheriff-depute Roxburghshire Mar. 1748–Nov. 1753; ld. of Admiralty Nov. 1756–Apr. 1757, June 1757–61; ld. of Treasury Mar. 1761–May 1762; treasurer of the chamber May 1762–Mar. 1770; P.C. 14 July 1762; keeper of the signet [S] Dec. 1766–d.; treasurer of the navy Mar. 1770–d.

Elliot's father and grandfather, staunch 'Revolution Whigs', both owed their promotion to the bench to their close friendship with John, Duke of Argyll. Gilbert, after a frugally restricted European tour, returned to Edinburgh in June 1745, 'a fine gentleman and polite scholar' with a taste for poetry, history, and philosophy, but little zest for the

Scottish bar. 'Nature', he wrote, 'never meant me for a lawyer.' [2] Nevertheless he soon gained a great reputation, and attracted the notice of Archibald, Duke of Argyll.

When in London he attended Commons debates, conceived an admiration for Pitt, an ambition to join his friends William Mure, James St. Clair, George and Charles Townshend, in Parliament, and particularly to emulate James Oswald.[3] Possessed through his marriage of an independent income, he became a leader of Edinburgh literary society, and an intimate of David Hume.

Argyll encouraged his hopes of a parliamentary seat and on a vacancy in Selkirkshire gave him his interest and obliged John Murray to retire. Argyll wrote to Pelham, 4 Sept. 1753:[4]

> Mr. Elliot . . . is sure of his election. I believe this young gentleman will be above the common run; he has more of an English manner at the bar than any I see in Scotland.

Elliot made no attempt to speak in the House until the new Parliament, when he confidently intervened in November on the Stirlingshire election, in which Argyll's interest was concerned.[5] A protagonist of Scottish constitutional rights, he strongly opposed the Government bill to perpetuate the system of appointing sheriffs-depute during pleasure, and insisted that, under the terms of the Act of 1747, they should now be appointed for life. His brilliant speech on 20 Feb. 1755 created a parliamentary sensation.[6] He wrote to his wife, 22 Feb.:

> I impute the notice I have met with very much to its being a thing a little uncommon, from Scotland, for a young man, supported by none of the great, to take up a point of the constitution upon as high a key as any English Member of Parliament.

Backed by Pitt and the Townshends, Elliot eventually obliged Administration to concede appointment for life after an interval of 15 years. 'So' wrote Eliot on 4 Mar., 'we had the triumph of preventing their being declared for ever during pleasure, which is called saving the Revolution principle.'[7]

During the winter Elliot had formed an 'affectionate attachment' for Bute, who now sought his mediation in effecting an alliance with Pitt,[8] henceforward Elliot's chief political aim. Argyll, at odds with Newcastle who was scheming with Robert Dundas to undermine his 'viceroyalty', supported Elliot's nominee as sheriff of Selkirk against Dundas's uncle; but when a crisis arose over the subsidy treaties, Newcastle dropped his intrigues and informed Dundas: 'Mr. Elliot must be obliged.' Argyll wrote to Newcastle, 5 Oct. 1755: 'Mr. Elliot is a rising young man and I was very desirous of

fixing him under your Grace's protection.'[9] Nevertheless, while Argyll and Oswald adhered to the Newcastle-Fox Administration, Elliot joined Pitt and Bute's friends in opposition and in the new session 'shone' as a speaker against the treaties.[10]

On the formation of the Devonshire-Pitt Administration Elliot was offered a choice of appointments. While Argyll and Bute advised a seat on the Board of Trade, Pitt and Temple persuaded him to accept higher rank as a lord of the Admiralty. 'I mean to make a business of it more than I ever did of a profession', he wrote to his wife.[11] On the dismissal of Temple and Pitt he at once resigned; declined offers made to him by Fox;[12] and voted 2 May 1757, against the former Newcastle-Fox Administration over Minorca. Throughout the negotiations Elliot, while loyal to Pitt, acted as confidential adviser to Bute,[13] his influence strengthened by the appointment of his friends John Home as Bute's secretary and William Mure as the manager of his Scottish interests. Nevertheless, when in June 1757 Elliot was restored to his Admiralty place, Bute described him as 'entirely Pitt for parliamentary and public considerations'.[14]

Since autumn 1755 Elliot had been resentful of Oswald, against whose nomination to the Treasury Board in 1759 Bute unsuccessfully protested to Newcastle.[15] The Prince and Bute were at odds with the 'old court', and with Argyll in Scottish affairs. Charles Townshend, fishing in troubled waters, was aiming at the future management of Scotland and intriguing against Elliot.[16] But the three rivals sank their differences when in March 1760 Elliot moved for a Scottish militia bill, was seconded by Oswald, and 'thirded' by Townshend. Elliot wrote to his father, 15 Mar.:[17]

> I find several persons in power not satisfied with the part I have already taken in this affair . . . I do not trouble myself about consequences, and I must hope you will never disapprove of my holding the same conduct in Parliament upon which I set out and upon which I must either act or not act at all.

At the second reading on 15 Apr. Elliot's bill was overwhelmingly defeated, but his well-reasoned, impassioned speeches brought him immense prestige in Scotland.[18]

Elliot was deeply concerned over Pitt's bad relations with Bute, who in April 1760 unsuccessfully employed him to seek a reconciliation.[19] Although privy to Bute's attempts to 'raise the Prince's standard in Scotland', Elliot made no open appearance in the dispute with Argyll, on whom his own election largely depended, and left Bute's electoral affairs to Mure and Sir Harry Erskine.

On the accession of George III, Elliot on personal

and constitutional grounds regretted Bute's decision to 'remain behind the curtain',[20] and was delighted when in March 1761 he accepted office as secretary of state.[21] In February Bute reproached Newcastle for not promoting Elliot, and proposed that either Oswald or some other be displaced from the Treasury Board to make room for him. Newcastle, incensed, complained to Hardwicke: 'To impose upon me a creature of his own at my Board, that is not a pleasant circumstance.' In the event Elliot attained his goal, but did not succeed in ousting Oswald.[22]

On Argyll's death on 15 Apr. 1761, Newcastle and Hardwicke were convinced that 'Elliot would be the man' for the management of Scotland. Bute, however, aware that a writer's grandson would be unacceptable to the Scottish nobility,[23] dismissed the suggestion on the ground that, as a lord of the Treasury, Elliot would be fully occupied; but employed him in negotiations over the disposal of Argyll's offices[24] and, from May, as acting Scottish manager until the return of Stuart Mackenzie from Turin in August when, without apparent reluctance, Elliot surrendered his function.[25] He was probably by temperament unsuited for the distribution of patronage. In office he gradually developed a cool reserve towards place-hunters and strangers, which was interpreted as pride and selfishness in Scotland where 'the higher he rose the less was he liked by his countrymen'.[26]

Grieved by Pitt's resignation, Elliot wrote to Bute, 2 Oct. 1761:

> It is the last pang of a favourite system, the final separation of your Lordship and Mr. Pitt, whose union . . . while it seemed at all practicable, I ever most earnestly cherished as the surest ground of the tranquillity of his Majesty's Government.

To Pitt he wrote: 'It will be the greatest happiness of my life to recollect that I made a part . . . of your Administration'; but, after a moving farewell interview, gave his undivided devotion to Bute; he was rewarded with the reversion of Lord Milton's place as keeper of the signet. He spoke against Pitt on 9 and 11 Dec. on the German war and the Spanish papers, 'with great freedom . . . but decent and parliamentary'. In March 1762 he urged Bute to sponsor a Scottish militia bill: 'People must comply if you desire it'. Bute rebuked him for this 'very improper language': 'Whether I could force your bill down the throats of a powerful party is one consideration, whether it would be prudent . . . is another; of that I will be the judge.' In consequence the scheme came to nothing.[27]

When Bute took the Treasury Elliot, disappointed of Cabinet office, was given the lucrative treasurer-ship of the chamber which, he said, he preferred, as leaving him free for Commons business and 'attendance on the King'.[28] During the crisis over Grenville's attitude to the peace negotiations, Elliot was one of Bute's 'real council' with Halifax, Oswald, and Stuart Mackenzie;[29] reluctantly concurred in the alliance with Fox; but when the peace had been secured was one of his critics in March in the debate on public accounts.[30] Long aware of Bute's intention to resign, he was commissioned to communicate to Grenville Bute's 'final determination' to choose him for successor.[31] Elliot received no preferment for himself but the reversion of the office of lord justice clerk for his father.

Loyally supporting Grenville's Administration, he was shocked by Bute's negotiation with Pitt in August 1763. He wrote to his father, 30 Aug.:[32]

> I knew not the least syllable of this transaction till the Saturday when Mr. Pitt was with the King . . . When I heard what the propositions were . . . I immediately declared (though I had some reason to believe I was not comprehended in the general sweep) I should certainly resign my situation and retire from a government where I must contradict, if I stayed, all my professions for two years past, and besides be charged with privity to what I disclaimed.

Elliot and Jenkinson went to see Bute at Kew on Sunday, 28 Aug., when 'they terrified him so much upon the consequences of the step he had persuaded the King to take, that he determined to depart from it and to advise his Majesty to send for Mr. Grenville'.[33] Elliot wrote to his father:

> As I have acquitted myself in a public light . . . so I pay what duty I can to private friendship and am much with Lord Bute and shall be so till he leaves this place. My friendship with Mr. Grenville is confirmed and if Mr. Pitt has any candour he has no right to complain of me; but that is more than I expect or indeed desire as I find our ideas of the public so very opposite.

This transaction marks a stage in Elliot's disillusionment with politics and detachment from party connexion except as a 'King's friend'. Having escorted Bute to 'absolute retirement' in Bedfordshire, and temporarily disarmed Grenville's suspicions, Elliot was a prominent supporter of Administration over Wilkes and general warrants. In July 1764 he rebuked David Hume for his bitterness at English antagonism to the Scots:

> We are both Englishmen; that is true British subjects. Am I not a Member of Parliament with as much liberty to abuse ministers . . . as if I had been born in Wapping? . . . Had it not been for the clamour of 'a Scot', perhaps indeed I might have been in some more active but not more honourable or lucrative situation. This clamour . . . will in time give way to some other equally absurd.

Nevertheless Elliot and Bute's friends were

accused of 'caballing'—not always unjustly. When Grenville, having insisted upon Stuart Mackenzie's dismissal, resumed office, Elliot categorically refused his demand for firm guarantees of loyalty in any future crisis, asserting the 'right of the Crown to name its own officers' and his own duty to 'oppose improper measures in a parliamentary way'.[34]

In June Elliot transferred from Selkirk to Roxburghshire, where the principal Minto estates lay. On the formation of the Rockingham Administration in July, Elliot was retained in office, but gave no explicit assurances of support. He wrote to Jenkinson, 26 Aug. 1765:[35]

> I think I love the public and I am sure I love my friends . . . but as for that partial spirit which gave so much energy to business . . . it is by me totally irrecoverable. I will never be angry with ministers because they are incapable of a true confidential friendship.

The ministry were disturbed by Elliot's attitude: while affirming support in general, he reserved judgment over American affairs. Consulted by Conway on the Address, he insisted upon some reference to parliamentary authority over the colonies, but in the debate on 17 Dec. spoke against the violent terms of Grenville's amendment.[36] After his vote on 31 Jan. 1766 against Administration on the Anstruther election, Conway complained that it might have been attributed to local connexion but for 'a previous appearance of separation' from Government.[37] In the debates on the repeal of the Stamp Act Elliot was extremely critical of Pitt, favoured modification, and, when this was rejected, strongly opposed repeal.[38] He wrote to his father, 1 Mar. 1766:[39]

> I spoke and voted in the minority agreeably to the plan I have followed and the explanation I early made . . . In other matters I have supported Government, and in some instances with effect . . . I hear we'll also have the old questions on general warrants and the cider bill, in which case I shall also act consistently with my former opinions.

On Grafton's resignation, Rockingham and Newcastle tried to sound the King on what Elliot and Oswald would do, and to insist that unless 'those two' gave 'absolute and active support on all occasions' the ministry would resign.[40] The King wrote to Bute, 3 May 1766:[41]

> They mean to lay their not going on at your door and that of your friends; this day they named their surprise at those gentlemen not having spoke . . . I said I was not surprised for whilst they were barely tolerated it could not be expected they would with ardour step forward, unasked, to support the ministers.

When Chatham's Administration was formed Elliot was in Scotland on business consequent upon his father's death. He retained his place, but, 'cool and indifferent', remained at home[42] until the autumn session, when he challenged the legality of a recent corn embargo proclaimed without parliamentary sanction; but agreed to an indemnity bill,[43] and otherwise supported Administration; voted with them on the land tax, 27 Feb. 1767; and spoke 'admirably' in the East India debate, 9 Mar.[44] He voted with Administration on nullum tempus, 17 Feb. 1768.

Returned unopposed at the general election, he early took a strong line on Wilkes and the Middlesex election; on 12 May 1768 at a meeting of the Government men of business he 'insisted' that he would move for Wilkes's expulsion and reluctantly agreed to postponement. In the new session he repudiated on 23 Nov. Beckford's strictures on the previous Parliament's proceedings on Wilkes; advocated a union of parties against 'licentious men'; spoke, 3 Feb. 1769, for Wilkes's expulsion, and consistently voted with Administration; but according to Grenville 'was idle and not very strongly affected to them'. Critical of Grafton's 'weakness', and finding himself 'much neglected', he now seldom spoke except 'on occasions of emergency'.[45]

On Grafton's resignation Elliot, summoned to a meeting with North on 29 Jan. 1770, promised support to his Administration; spoke 31 Jan. in the debate on Wilkes and was offered the treasurership of the navy, which 'though hazardous' he accepted at the King's desire. During 1770–1 he was a leading Government speaker on the Falkland Islands question, on East India military forces, and the printers' case; and pressed North to take rigorous action against the city and Brass Crosby. Elliot's relations with North deteriorated; he began 'to act the part of discontent', but continued to vote with Administration. In February 1772 he was bitterly offended when the King concurred with North and Barrington in refusing his son Hugh a captain-lieutenancy in the Guards on the ground that the nominal commission obtained, illicitly, for him in 1762, when aged 10, gave no claim to rank. The presence of the first minister in the House of Commons made Elliot of less consequence in the House.[46]

In American affairs he remained a protagonist of the authority of Parliament and its right to impose colonial taxes; these principles being conceded, he favoured lenity. He spoke, 19 Apr. 1774, against the repeal of the tea duty, but on 22 Apr. in supporting the Massachusetts bill was no extremist.[47] In the new Parliament he continued to favour a firm American policy; but when, on 20 Feb. 1775, North's conciliatory proposals aroused violent controversy, Elliot, by his argument that the motion was complementary and not contradictory to the repressive terms of the Address, persuaded the ministerial dissidents to 'rally under their proper standards'.[48] Henceforward Elliot in his rare speeches upheld North's prestige; refuted on 27 Oct. 1775 William Adam's criticisms of his indolence,[49] although privately thinking him 'fat and lazy as ever' and Government mismanagement 'terrible';[50] and supported him in the army debate, 1 Nov. 1775, and on 20 Feb. 1776 over the demand for the inquiry into the ill-success of British arms.

Elliot's last major speeches were made in March 1776, in support of Mountstuart's Scottish militia bill, on which he argued with something of his old fire, but was again disappointed.

After assisting at his son's Morpeth election, Elliot fell ill, did not return for the autumn session, and died in France 11 Jan. 1777.

[1] This biography is based upon research by Rosemary Mitchison. [2] Ramsay of Ochtertyre, i. 364–5; Elliot to Mure, June 1745 (misdated 1742), *Caldwell Pprs.* ii(1), p. 29. [3] G. F. S. Elliot, *Border Elliots*, 331–2; *Mems. James Oswald*, 289. [4] Newcastle (Clumber) mss. [5] *Border Elliots*, 337. [6] Ibid. 337–8; Walpole, *Mems. Geo. II*, ii. 4–5. [7] Minto mss. [8] *Border Elliots*, 342. [9] Add. 32854, f. 93; 32857, f. 390; 32859, ff. 240, 396. [10] Walpole to G. Montagu, 20 Dec. 1755; *Caldwell Pprs.* ii(1), p. 110. [11] *Border Elliots*, 352, 353, 354. [12] Ibid. 357; Add. 32870, f. 377. [13] Elliot to Bute, June 1757, Bute mss. [14] Bute to Stuart Mackenzie, July 1757, Bute mss. [15] Dodington, *Diary*, 413–14. [16] John Dalrymple to Townshend, 5 Oct. 1759, Buccleuch mss. [17] *Border Elliots*, 360. [18] Hume to Minto, 1 May 1760, *Letters*, i. 525. [19] Namier, *England in Age of American Rev.* 104–9. [20] Dodington to Bute, 25 Dec. 1760, Bute mss. [21] Elliot to Bute, March 1761, ibid. [22] Add. 32918, ff. 465–6, 500–13; 32919, ff. 402–4. [23] Geo. Middleton to Bute, 24 Apr., ? July 1761, Bute mss. [24] Add. 32922, ff. 3–6, 15–24, 108–10, 131, 168–9. [25] Elliot to Bute, 30 Aug. 1761, Bute mss. [26] Ramsay, i. 368; T. Somerville, *Life & Times*, 121. [27] Minto mss; Patrick Craufurd to Mure, 17 Dec. 1761, *Caldwell Pprs.* ii(1), p. 152. [28] *Border Elliots*, 374; *Caldwell Pprs.* ii(1), p. 152. [29] Newcastle to Devonshire, 10 Oct. 1762, Add. 32943, f. 144. [30] The King to Bute, c. 5 Mar. 1763, Sedgwick, 197. [31] *Border Elliots*, 375. [32] Ibid. 378. [33] *Grenville Pprs.* ii. 197. [34] *Border Elliots*, 387, 394. [35] *Jenkinson Pprs.* 383. [36] Harris's 'Debates'. [37] Conway to the King, 1 Feb. 1766, Fortescue, i. 249. [38] *Caldwell Pprs.* ii(2), p. 72; Fortescue, i. 267–8. [39] Minto mss. [40] Egmont to the King, 4 May 1766, Fortescue, i. 303–6. [41] Sedgwick, 247. [42] Dyson to Elliot, 10 Oct. 1766, Minto mss. [43] *Border Elliots*, 401; *Grenville Pprs.* iii. 384; Fortescue, i. 422. [44] Hume, *Letters*, ii. 127. [45] Brooke, *Chatham Admin.* 359; Walpole, *Mems. Geo. III*, iii. 182–3, 198. [46] *Border Elliots*, 406–8; Fortescue, ii. 128, 316. [47] Walpole, *Last Jnls.* i. 436. [48] Almon, i. 207; Walpole, *Last Jnls.* i. 436. [49] Almon, iii. 68. [50] Elliot to his s. Hugh, 31 Aug. 1775, Lady Minto, *Mem. Hugh Elliot*, 78.

E.H.-G.

**ELLIOT, Gilbert** (1751–1814), of Minto, Roxburgh.

| | |
|---|---|
| MORPETH | 16 July 1776–Feb. 1777 |
| ROXBURGHSHIRE | 27 Feb. 1777–1784 |
| BERWICK-UPON-TWEED | 21 Sept. 1786–1790 |
| HELSTON | 23 Dec. 1790–June 1795 |

*b.* 23 Apr. 1751, 1st s. of Gilbert Elliot (q.v.). *educ.* La Pension Militaire, Fontainebleau 1764–6; Edinburgh Univ. 1766–8; Ch. Ch. Oxf. 1768; L. Inn 1769, called 1774. *m.* 3 Jan. 1777, Anna Maria, 1st da. of Sir George Amyand, 1st Bt. (q.v.), 4s. 3da. *suc.* fa. as 4th Bt. 11 Jan. 1777; mother in her Fife and Forfarshire estates 28 Dec. 1778, and assumed add. names of Murray Kynynmound; *cr.* Baron Minto 20 Oct. 1797; Earl of Minto 24 Feb. 1813.

Civil commr. to Toulon and P.C. 25 Sept. 1793; minister to the Italian States Mar.–May 1794; viceroy of Corsica 1794–6; envoy to Vienna 1799–1801; pres. of Board of Control Feb.–July 1806; gov. gen. India 1806–13.

Elliot inherited his father's temperament and ability, without his brilliance, and, always diffident of his own oratorical powers, aimed at a legal rather than a political career. Having gained considerable reputation, in July 1776 he was offered a seat at Morpeth by Lord Carlisle. Returned unopposed, Elliot never sat in Parliament with his father, on whose death he disconcerted Carlisle by transferring to Roxburghshire.[1] He made his maiden speech on 18 Nov. 1777 when, though 'vastly terrified', he ably seconded the Address.[2] But he did not follow up his initial success as a speaker. His mother wrote of him in January 1778:[3] 'Nothing can exceed the excellence of his heart and head; all he wants is a further stimulus to exertion . . . He is in a degree independent and I am sure very much unconnected except with the King and Lord Suffolk.'

He was a friend but no admirer of North, and was closely attached to his brother-in-law William Eden. By the spring of 1778 he had become convinced that 'the prospect of recovering America by war was certainly at an end', but that 'if new exertions have but a chance of recovering any part of our authority . . . and redeeming the honour of our country it is our duty to make them'.[4] On the outbreak of the French war he resisted his first impulse to join Buccleuch's regiment: 'It would at once knock up my law.'[5] He wrote on 5 Oct. 1778 to Eden, then in America as a member of the conciliation commission:

> I am glad I do not second the Address this year and perhaps you are not sorry you do not pen it; I think we want a dictator, a master mind, to rectify these disjointed times. The nation certainly does not want spirit and I hope has resource still. But it is natural to be wearied of seeing both these wasted.

Despising the Opposition for openly rejoicing at British defeats, he remained a silent supporter of Administration; occupied himself mainly with a bill for prison reform; and became increasingly detached from party.[6]

Carried away by Burke's eloquence he voted for an account of pensions, 21 Feb. 1780, but recanted and on 8 Mar. voted with Administration on economical reform, and on 13 Mar. against the abolition of the Board of Trade. He had decided that he could not in conscience join Opposition in forcing reforms, however admirable, upon a harassed Government, which still retained popular confidence, and whose efforts to restore British prestige he was resolved to support. Nevertheless he remained warmly attached to Burke, admired his liberal principles, and though the son of a 'King's friend', voted with Opposition on Dunning's motion, 6 Apr. 1780. He voted with Administration on the prorogation, 24 Apr., and at the end of the Parliament was counted 'pro' by Robinson.

In the new Parliament he remained a silent, unenthusiastic Government supporter; continued his interest in penal reform, and was appointed one of the three supervisors of the new penitentiaries.[7] Nominated, 14 Feb. 1781, to the select committee on the Bengal judiciary, Elliot was an active Member, assiduous in attendance. Over Indian affairs he was faced with conflicting loyalties: his brother Alexander (d.1778) had been the beloved private secretary of Hastings, whom both he and his father as East India proprietors had supported during the 1776 controversies,[8] and for whom he still expressed 'regard . . . founded not less on public than on private considerations'.[9] In consequence, while actively co-operating with Burke on the select committee, he took no part in the secret committee appointed to investigate the causes of the Carnatic war with which Alexander, as Hastings's negotiator, had been concerned in 1778.

From extensive travels abroad during the recess Elliot brought back an impression that 'all Europe favoured the independency of America and looked to the chance of some advantage from such a revolution'.[10] In the new session he voted, 12 Dec., with Government on Lowther's motion against the war; and also with them, 20 Feb. 1782, on the censure of the Admiralty. But he was now convinced that the American war was impracticable and, differing from almost all his family and friends, voted with Opposition on Conway's motion to end the war, 22 Feb.; and on 27 Feb. broke a long silence to support Conway's second motion:[11] 'He now plainly saw that the nation, the House of Commons, and the ministers had been for a long time in the wrong and he could no longer with justice to his constituents support their measures.' Loughborough wrote to Eden, 1 Mar.:[12]

> Sir Gilbert got up professing himself unsatisfied, though a hearty friend in general to Administration . . . The effect . . . was to fix all the wavering well-wishers in the same line with Sir Gilbert. I have no patience with him.

Now that 'the grand principle of . . . separation between parties' over America had been removed, he hoped for a coalition—'all the ability of the country united to direct all the resources of the country to one good end'; he could not bring himself to censure a ministry whose 'principles respecting America' had so long been 'agreeable to the people and those of the Opposition offensive to them'; and voted with Administration on Cavendish's censure motion of

8 Mar. When Elliot voted, 15 Mar., with the Opposition on Rous's motion of no confidence, Loughborough dismissed such fine distinctions as mere inconsistency.[13]

On the formation of the Rockingham Administration Elliot wrote to his brother Hugh, envoy at Berlin, 22 Apr. 1782:

> I shall support the present ministry with more cordiality and therefore I hope with more exertion than ever I could the last. The reforms with which their Government opens, you know I formerly approved . . . and I like them the better for the facility with which they may now be carried without those convulsions which could have alone produced them as the measures of Opposition, and which naturally, and I think deservedly, gave great scandal when they were attempted to be forced on Parliament by the means of popular distraction during a war which rendered all distractions fatal.

He neither expected nor received reward. When Fox recalled Hugh and did not fulfil his promises of alternative employment, Gilbert repudiated his brother's suspicions:

> I cannot bring myself to suspect Mr. Fox's sincerity . . . it would be contrary to his general character and . . . why should he use any art with me whom he certainly cannot fear? . . . To importunity I have myself an insurmountable aversion and if the business is to be decided on those principles I fear I shall be an unsuccessful agent.

Eden wrote to Hugh:

> [Gilbert's] politics are so pure that no individual interests can exist in their atmosphere . . . The world may misjudge him; but his conduct at the close of Lord North's Government was in its appearance most unsteady and in its effects most unkind to his natural and old friends and connexions. His subsequent conduct has been inefficient; for whether he had acted right or wrong he certainly was entitled to expect from the Rockingham ministry immediate, and solid protection both for you and for Mr. Elliot of New York.

Gilbert, however, 'was not disposed to think anything wrong that Charles Fox could do'; he knew little personally of Shelburne, but that little, 'added to the voice of the world', he disliked, and on the formation of the new ministry wrote to his wife, 8 July:

> I have declared myself to Charles Fox . . . I am thoroughly satisfied with my choice and am sure I have done right, not for myself and children, but for the sake of my precious soul and my poor country.[14]

He refused offers of preferment from Shelburne, who had suggested him for the Admiralty Board.[15] 'I told him frankly that I preferred his rivals.'[16] Nevertheless Shelburne gave the Copenhagen embassy to Hugh, who was amazed at his brother's continuing devotion to Fox, 'the demi-god of the blackguards'.[17]

Shortly afterwards Elliot fell gravely ill, left for France in October, and did not return until early August 1783. Reunited with his friends Eden and Loughborough in support of the Fox-North Coalition, he was consulted by Burke and Fox over the East India bill under which he was named one of the seven parliamentary commissioners. Astonished at the change of Administration in December and angered at the constitutional implications, Elliot despised Pitt's Government as 'a set of children playing at ministers', but nevertheless was too diffident to intervene in the debates. 'If', wrote Eden, 'his passions were equal to his abilities, he would play a leading part.'[18]

At the general election Elliot lost Roxburghshire and failed to secure another seat: he tried Leominster, Bridgwater, Berwickshire, and Forfarshire, and (at a by-election in August) Newtown. 'My philosophy or my indolence', he wrote, 'makes me well satisfied with the prospect of some leisure for self improvement.'[19]

By 1785 he was in acute financial difficulties by Treasury demands for immediate repayment of his father's balances, totalling some £10,000. He obtained a deferment with the assistance of Eden, who was now contemplating an accommodation with Pitt, in which Elliot could not concur. He wrote to Eden, 16 Oct. 1785:

> There are points so fundamental . . . that though hopeless they must be stuck to . . . Of this sort I consider the great constitutional questions in which Mr. Pitt is so implicated and where the mischief he has done is so deadly that the . . . talents . . . which may atone for common crimes . . . are inadmissible in his case . . . I do not know how many even of our friends may . . . carry it so far; but this is my own creed at present in which however I am not such a bigot as to want charity for other persuasions.[20]

In September 1786 Elliot, though still financially embarrassed, successfully contested Berwick to the delight of Burke, who urged him to undertake the management of a charge in the proceedings against Hastings. 'You *must* be less modest . . . You must be all you can be, and you can be everything.' Elliot declined the offer, but agreed to 'move and conduct the impeachment' of Sir Elijah Impey. On 12 Dec. 1787 he moved the impeachment in a speech which despite his acute nervousness was a brilliant success. During the next months he subordinated all his activities to attendance at Hastings's trial and the preparation of the case against Impey. At the hearing of the first charge on the trial and execution of Nuncomar, Elliot's opponents embarrassed him by producing documents, indicating that Impey's conduct had been approved by Alexander Elliot who, according to Sir Gilbert, had acted only as inter-

preter at the trial. In the debate of 28 Apr. 1788, Elliot in a 4½ hour speech defended his brother and justified his own changed opinion of Hastings; he resumed his attack on Impey on 7 and 9 May in equally long speeches, which exhausted the House and himself, but failed to carry the Nuncomar charge by 73 to 55. He wrote to his wife, 10 May: 'Our defeat is very like a victory . . . Pitt never exposed himself and his profligacy in so great a degree before.' He was chagrined when on 27 May the second charge against Impey was postponed.[21]

During the Regency crisis he was frequently consulted by Portland, at whose request he drafted the Duke's letter to the Prince, restoring good relations, strained during the dispute in 1787 over the Prince's debts. Although his legal knowledge and facility of expression were frequently employed by the Opposition leaders, Elliot did not speak in the Regency debates. On Cornwall's death he was nominated, 5 Jan. 1789, for the Chair, but was defeated 213-144. In the Opposition plan for a new ministry, Elliot was proposed as a possible chancellor of the Exchequer. During the attempts to effect a reconciliation between the Prince and the King, Elliot prepared the Prince's memorial justifying his conduct, but his draft of the accompanying letter, although approved by the Prince, was rejected on 25 June by the Whig leaders as likely to exacerbate the dispute.[22]

On 8 June 1789 he was again the Opposition candidate for the Chair but was again defeated. Meanwhile he had continued active in India affairs; spoke 4 May 1789 against the censure motion against Burke, and was so disgusted with the decision of the House that he resolved to 'drop Impey entirely'.[23]

During the recess Elliot, having already declined to seek re-election at Berwick,[24] decided for family and financial reasons to retire from active parliamentary life, but was persuaded by Portland to change his mind. His career as diplomat and administrator, on which his fame rests, was still before him.

He died 21 June 1814.

[1] *HMC Carlisle*, 319. [2] His sis. Isabella to Hugh Elliot, 28 Nov. 1777, Lady Minto, *Mem. Hugh Elliot*, 130. [3] Ibid. 137. [4] Elliot to Hugh, 10 Feb. 1778, ibid. 142. [5] Same to same, 31 Mar. 1778, ibid. 143. [6] Add. 34416, ff. 39, 301. [7] Add. 34417, f. 336. [8] L. S. Sutherland, *E.I. Co. in 18th Cent. Politics*, 306; S. Weitzmann, *Warren Hastings and Philip Francis*, 261, 265. [9] Elliot to Hastings, 31 May 1781, Add. 38871, f. 10. [10] Elliot to Jas. Harris, 5 Mar. 1782, Minto mss. [11] Debrett, vi. 329. [12] Add. 34418, f. 337. [13] Add. 34418, f. 361; *Mem. Hugh Elliot*, 233-8. [14] *Mem. Hugh Elliot*, 238-9, 242, 248-9, 254; *Life and Letters*, i. 81. [15] Fortescue, vi. 78. [16] Elliot to Hugh, 8 Aug. 1782, *Mem. Hugh Elliot*, 249. [17] Ibid. 250. [18] Ibid. 283, 284; *Life and Letters*, i. 89-91. [19] *Mem. Hugh Elliot*, 284. [20] Add. 34420, ff. 108, 129. [21] *Life and Letters*, i. 114, 175-84, 199-200, 201; Stockdale, xiii. 105-8, 151-2, 180, 209; xiv. 158-68; Wraxall, v. 49, 100. [22] *Life and Letters*, i. 162, 241-2, 260, 323, 332-4. [23] Stockdale, xvii. 144; *Life and Letters*, i. 306. [24] *Life and Letters*, 168, 355-6.

E.H.-G.

## ELLIOT, John (1732–1808).

COCKERMOUTH    9 Jan. 1767–1768

*b.* Apr. 1732, 4th s. of Sir Gilbert Elliot, 2nd Bt., M.P., and bro. of Sir Gilbert Elliot, 3rd Bt. (q.v.). *unm.* Entered R.N. 1745; lt. 1756; capt. 1757; r.-adm. 1787; v.-adm. 1790; adm. 1799.
Gov. Newfoundland 1786.

Elliot owed his promotion as lieutenant to the influence of his brother, who was now in Parliament, and through him was introduced to Sir James Lowther who brought him in for Cockermouth. In 1768 he contested Carlisle as one of Lowther's candidates, but was defeated, and does not seem to have stood again.

His only reported vote was with Administration on the land tax, 27 Feb. 1767. There is no record of his having spoken in the House.

He died 20 Sept. 1808.

J.B.

## ELLIS, John Thomas (1756–1836), of Wyddial Hall, Herts.

LOSTWITHIEL    1784–1790

*b.* 28 Sept. 1756, o.s. of Brabazon Ellis of Wyddial Hall. *educ.* L. Inn 1775. *m.* 15 Jan. 1786, Marianne, da. of John Heaton of Bedfords, Essex, 4s. 1da. *suc.* fa. 1780.
Sheriff, Herts. 1784–5.

In 1784 Ellis was returned unopposed for Lostwithiel, a borough placed at the disposal of Government by Lord Mount Edgcumbe. The seat cost £3,000, and in George Rose's secret service accounts[1] appears the entry: 'Mr. Ellis—Lostwithiel—above £1,500 paid to Lord Mount Edgcumbe—£500'—presumably Ellis himself had to pay only £1,000 from his own pocket. Naturally, he supported Pitt. On 18 Apr. 1785 he voted for parliamentary reform. His only recorded speech, 23 Jan. 1787, was in favour of a tax on hawkers and pedlars. He is not known to have stood in 1790.

Ellis died 6 Oct. 1836.

[1] Royal archives, Windsor.

M.M.D.

## ELLIS, Welbore (1713–1802), of Tylney Hall, Hants.

| | |
|---|---|
| CRICKLADE | 24 Dec. 1741–1747 |
| WEYMOUTH AND MELCOMBE REGIS | 1747–1761 |
| AYLESBURY | 1761–1768 |
| PETERSFIELD | 1768–1774 |
| WEYMOUTH AND MELCOMBE REGIS | 1774–1790 |
| PETERSFIELD | 29 Apr. 1791–13 Aug. 1794 |

*b.* 15 Dec. 1713, o. surv. s. of Rt. Rev. Welbore Ellis, bp. of Kildare and (1731) Meath, by Diana, da. of Sir John Briscoe of Boughton, Northants. and Amberley, Suss. *educ.* Westminster 1727–32; Ch. Ch. Oxf. 1732. *m.* (1) 18 Nov. 1747, Elizabeth (*d.* 1 Aug. 1761), da. and h. of Sir William Stanhope (q.v.), *s.p.*; (2) 20 July 1765, Anne, da. of George Stanley of Paultons, Hants, sis. and coh. of Hans Stanley (q.v.), *s.p. suc.* fa. 1 Jan. 1734; *cr.* Baron Mendip 13 Aug. 1794.

Ld. of Admiralty 1747–Dec. 1755; jt. vice-treasurer [I] Dec. 1755–Dec. 1762; P.C. 20 Mar. 1760; sec. at war Dec. 1762–July 1765; jt. vice-treasurer [I] Apr. 1770–June 1777; treasurer of the navy June 1777–Feb. 1782; sec. of state for America Feb.–Mar. 1782.

Welbore Ellis came of a Yorkshire family, but was born in Ireland (where his father was for more than thirty years a bishop) and acquired property in Dublin.[1] Without any parliamentary interest of his own he sat in the House of Commons for over fifty years, and held office for over thirty. Ambitious and industrious, his name became a byword for a placeman prepared to serve any Administration—which is hardly fair to him.

In 1754 he was the chief Admiralty spokesman in the House, and was provided with a seat by Administration at Weymouth and Melcombe Regis. He was a close friend of Henry Fox, who, on becoming secretary of state in September 1755, included Ellis among those for whom he demanded office. 'I have told Harry Fox that he may do as best suits his affairs with me', wrote Ellis to Devonshire on 20 Dec. 1755,[2] 'and that I will cheerfully acquiesce in what shall be settled.' Fox tried to have Ellis succeed him at the War Office, which proved impracticable;[3] and next he was considered for a seat at the Treasury Board. 'I endeavoured underhand as much as possible . . . to avoid it', wrote Ellis to Devonshire on 3 Feb. 1756,[4] and professed to like 'very well' the employment of joint vice-treasurer of Ireland which he eventually obtained. On the formation of the Pitt-Devonshire Administration he was again proposed for secretary at war (probably by Devonshire), but the King preferred Barrington.[5]

Ellis was Fox's chief manager during the Minorca inquiry, and on 2 May 1757 moved the amendment exonerating the Fox-Newcastle Administration.[6] He nearly lost his place when Pitt joined with Newcastle in June. Lady Kildare, Fox's sister-in-law, wrote on 17 June:[7]

> Poor Mr. Fox is vastly anxious for his friends; it is thought by some they will be all turned out . . . others say that it will be only Ellis, or some one very much marked person as his friend.

But Rigby to Bedford on 18 June:[8] 'Ellis, though he has been pushed at, is to remain where he is.' Through application to Newcastle, he got himself made a Privy Councillor in March 1760.[9] In November he again narrowly escaped being turned out to make room for Sir Thomas Robinson, and saved himself by timely application to Bute. Even Fox had no high opinion of him. 'Ellis', he wrote, 'had by my friendship and accident, got into a place much above his pretensions, and he was the only man in England who did not think so.'[10]

At the general election of 1761 Dodington, patron of Weymouth and Melcombe Regis, accepted Bute's nominees for the borough; and Ellis had to find a seat elsewhere. Fox advised him to try Aylesbury, an expensive and difficult constituency, where his father-in-law Sir William Stanhope had considerable interest;[11] and Newcastle promised Treasury support. Ellis was returned unopposed, but his election cost him £2,000.[12]

Ellis now directed his applications for advancement to Bute:[13] 8 Apr. 1761, to become one of the plenipotentiaries at the proposed peace conference; 19 Aug. 1762, to be chancellor of the Exchequer should Dashwood become a peer; 8 Apr. 1763, for 'the feather of being a Cabinet counsellor'. In June there was a rumour that he was to go as ambassador to The Hague,[14] in September to Vienna.[15] In December 1762 he succeeded Charles Townshend at the War Office, an onerous and difficult post: 'to have the principal hand in reducing a large army', wrote Rigby,[16] who had been considered for the office, ' . . . is a most irksome and unpleasant task'. Yet Ellis acquitted himself well. James Harris wrote of his speech of 4 Mar. 1763 on the army estimates:[17]

> Mr. Ellis . . . was more than an hour in opening this subject, but did it in so masterly a way, with such order, elegance, and perspicuity that he never lost the attention of the House, but was heard to the last with the greatest approbation. His detail of the proper position of troops in America . . . was a complete union of military and geographical knowledge. Some small sprinklings of philosophy, sparingly but judiciously applied, served, like salt, to give a seasoning to the whole.

In conversation with Harris on 26 June[18] Ellis gave his ideas on future military arrangements in America:

> [He] thinks the dominions of North America and the West Indies less liable to revolt by being placed under many governments, jealous of and hating each other, than if under one government. [He] thinks that America should pay its own troops . . . that the sum (perhaps £200,000) should be settled by Parliament here, and the quota for each island and province settled by the same authority, and that then the several governments there to adjust the method of raising their own taxation.

And about the agitation against the cider tax: 'He thinks . . . that 'tis best for Government (having the King, the Parliament, and an army) to stand it out and not comply; that compliance only begets an opinion of their superiority in the multitude . . . and thence more insolence, more proneness to oppose

and clamour'—an attitude he later held on the taxation of America.

Having been informed by Grenville of the abortive attempt to change the Administration in August 1763, Ellis replied, pledging himself 'fully and strongly' to Grenville and the King, and asking for the office of first lord of the Admiralty.[19] During the next two years he supported Administration loyally, but never identified himself with the ministers. 'I would serve your Majesty in the station of your footman to procure your ease of mind or to promote the good of your affairs', he told the King on 21 May 1765. And on 9 July, on being dismissed by the Rockingham Administration:

> I have neither intrigued nor caballed; I have in a great degree secluded myself from company to avoid all suspicion and misrepresentation, and have rested with a most resigned confidence in your Majesty's goodness to me; and having assured your Majesty that I was only your's, I have carefully avoided every other connexion and support.

The King assured Ellis that he would not be forgotten. Hearing a report that he was to be made joint paymaster-general, he protested that to accept this 'divided office' would be 'lowering me in the opinion of all mankind'.[20] 'Ellis is to have Rigby's place [of joint vice-treasurer of Ireland]', wrote Charles Fox to his father on 13 July;[21] and Lord George Sackville to Irwin on 14 Sept.:[22] 'They have not yet filled up the vice-treasurers' employments. Ellis pushes hard to be one.' On 7 Dec. he inquired of the King if this rumour were true,[23] but presumably received a discouraging reply.

On 22 Feb. 1766 Ellis spoke and voted against the repeal of the Stamp Act. In the proposed reconstruction of the ministry following Grafton's resignation, May 1766, the King pressed for his inclusion. 'Poor man', he told Rockingham,[24] 'he belongs to nobody, and therefore nobody [is] for him.' On 12 July the King named Ellis to Pitt (with Northumberland, Norton, and le Despenser) as 'men I wished brought again into office'.[25] Pitt replied that 'they were very fit persons . . . but as they brought no share of abilities with them, they must wait a little'.

On 9 Dec. 1766 Ellis spoke against Chatham's East India inquiry;[26] but voted with Administration on the land tax, 27 Feb. 1767, and the nullum tempus bill, 17 Feb. 1768. He supported Administration on the Middlesex election, and in April 1770 returned to office.

Wraxall wrote about Ellis:[27]

> In his figure, manner, and deportment the very essence of form, he regularly took his place on the Treasury bench dressed in all points as if he had been going to the drawing room at St. James's.

Walpole called him 'Don Welbore Ellis';[28] and Selwyn wrote of his appointment to the American department:[29] 'Ellis has added another footman to his chariot, and is a minister in form and fact and pomp and everything.' His precise and formal manner was the reflection of a rigid and authoritarian mind, unable to adapt itself to new ideas. He 'always had a dislike to doing anything which altered the constitution';[30] and his conception of the constitution was static and literal, taking no account of new trends. 'He did not think the House of Commons an assembly calculated for the discussion of state affairs', he said on 25 May 1778.[31] 'It was the business of Parliament to raise supplies, not to debate on the measures of Government.' He opposed the reporting of parliamentary debates;[32] took the lead in the proceedings against Oliver and Crosby for breach of privilege; opposed Grenville's bill for the trial of contested elections; and spoke against parliamentary reform.[33]

'All the confusion that has taken place [in America]', he said on 5 Mar. 1770,[34] 'is . . . totally owing to the repeal of the Stamp Act'; and he opposed all further concessions to the colonies, even when proposed by Government. He spoke against North's motion for the partial repeal of the Townshend duties, 5 Mar. 1770, and opposed his conciliatory resolutions of February 1775 'without an express and definitive acknowledgement from the Americans of our supremacy'.[35] ('Mr. Ellis, who differed from us upon a real conviction that our measure was wrong', wrote North to the King,[36] 'spoke against us in the most friendly terms, and behaved, as indeed he has always done, as a man of honour and a conscientious friend of Government.') On 16 Nov. 1775 he 'replied to Mr. Burke, and added that the greater disposition Great Britain showed towards conciliation the more obstinate, rebellious, and insolent America would become'. On 20 Feb. 1776, he said

> that gentle, moderate measures were unhappily pursued when the situation of America called for the most strong and decisive. Thank God this mistaken system is now at an end. A powerful fleet and a powerful army are now going out, and I have not the slightest doubt that they will be sufficient to crush the rebellious Americans.[37]

On Germain's resignation in February 1782 Ellis was offered the place of secretary of state for America. North wrote to the King on 5 Feb.:[38]

> Lord North has the honour of informing his Majesty that Mr. Ellis is ready to obey his Majesty's commands upon any occasion. That he does not desire to make any condition, but expressed the same wish that Lord Hillsborough gave me a hint of—that when he shall receive his Majesty's commands to retire he may be raised in dignity, and have his title granted in re-

mainder to his nephew. Mr. Ellis however repeated very strongly that this was only a wish of his, and that he was very far from presuming to make any condition.

'It becomes a man to lay aside all thoughts of self', wrote Ellis to Edmund Sexton Pery, Speaker of the Irish House of Commons, on 21 Feb.[39] ' . . . The object of all my wishes is that I may in any degree contribute to the salvation of my country.' But Wraxall wrote of his appointment:[40] 'It seemed difficult to have made a selection in consequence of which less strength would be acquired on the side of Administration.'

Ellis inherited a discredited policy, and joined a Cabinet tottering to its fall: no one could have saved North's Administration. On 22 Feb. he declared in the House of Commons that he had

> never entertained an idea . . . that America was to be reduced to obedience by force. His idea always was that in America we had many friends, and that by strongly supporting them we should be able to destroy that party or faction that wished for war.

'He was not now so sanguine in his hopes of success as he had been some time ago'; still the war must be continued because 'it was France, not the Congress, that was fighting in America'. In the debate of 15 Mar. he supported Dundas's idea for 'a coalition of parties'; and begged the House

> not to send his Majesty's ministers from their seats until this much desired coalition was formed, for by their going out before this was done they would leave the affairs of the public in confusion.

North's resignation a few days later ended Ellis's official career.[41]

During the remainder of 1782 and in 1783 Ellis spoke rarely in the House and avoided contentious political issues. He voted against Shelburne's peace preliminaries, 18 Feb. 1783, and was classed by Robinson as a follower of North. His ambition was a peerage, and his hopes were high when North returned to office with the Coalition. 'I have been in Parliament forty-two years', he wrote to the King about this time,[42] 'and in this long course of service I can say what few can, that I never was a part of any concerted system of Opposition.' On 11 July 1783 North wrote to Northington, lord lieutenant of Ireland, who had also been pressing Ellis's claims:

> The character and the merit, the long and faithful services of Mr. Ellis, would probably place him among the peers of Great Britain were the King disposed at this time to make any addition to the British peerage. But, although no such addition can be made in the present moment, his Majesty expressed himself repeatedly in the most gracious manner with respect to Mr. Ellis's personal worth and pretensions.

'Welbore Ellis's [peerage] is refused', wrote William Windham to Northington on 17 July, 'so you may imagine no one else has much chance.'[43]

Ellis voted for Fox's East India bill, and in a speech of 4 Mar. 1784 came out against Pitt.[44] In the Parliament of 1784-90 he voted regularly with Opposition, and was a frequent speaker (e.g., on the Westminster scrutiny, the French commercial treaty, and the Regency). 'He is a steady, honourable, old gentleman', wrote Sir Gilbert Elliot (q.v.) to his wife on 6 Mar. 1787,[45] 'but seems out of his place in a hopeless Opposition.'

Ellis broke with Fox over the French Revolution, and obtained his peerage in 1794 (at the age of 80) when the Portland Whigs went over to Pitt.

He died 2 Feb. 1802.

[1] Ellis to Edmund Sexton Pery, 31 Dec. 1784, *HMC 14th Rep. IX*, 184. [2] Devonshire mss. [3] Ilchester, *Hen. Fox*, i. 272. [4] Devonshire mss; Walpole, *Mems. Geo. II*, ii. 141. [5] Temple to Pitt, 9 Nov. 1756, *Chatham Corresp.* i. 188. [6] Walpole, *Mems. Geo. II*, iii. 7. [7] *Leinster Corresp.* i. 48. [8] *Bedford Corresp.* ii. 251. [9] Add. 32901, ff. 24-25. [10] Fox's memoir, *Life & Letters of Lady Sarah Lennox*, i. 15. [11] Fox to Ellis, 24 Nov. 1760, Hen. Fox mss. [12] W. Ellis to Holland, 20 Aug. 1765, Hen. Fox mss. [13] Bute mss. [14] Barrington to Newcastle, 13 June 1762, Add. 32939, f. 326. [15] Shelburne to Fox, 18 Sept. 1762, Ilchester, *Letters to Hen. Fox.* 161. [16] To Bedford, 16 Dec. 1762, Bedford mss 46, f. 148. [17] Harris's 'Debates'. See also James West's opinion, Add. 32947, ff. 265-6. [18] Harris's 'Memoranda'. [19] *Grenville Pprs.* ii. 112-14, 115, 16. [20] Fortescue, i. 109, 151. [21] *Letters to Hen. Fox*, 233. [22] *HMC Stopford-Sackville*, i. 102. [23] Fortescue, i. 196-9. [24] Add. 33001, f. 227. [25] Fortescue, i. 176. [26] Ibid. 425. [27] *Mems.* i. 425. [28] To Lady Upper Ossory, 3 Jan. 1780. [29] *HMC Carlisle*, 580. [30] Almon, i. 317. [31] Stockdale, viii. 300. [32] *Cavendish's Debates*, ii. 381-2. [33] Debrett, ix. 725. [34] *Cavendish's Debates*, ii. 497. [35] Almon, i. 206-7. [36] Fortescue, iii. 178. [37] Almon, iii. 186, 331-2. [38] Fortescue, v. 361. [39] *HMC 14th Rep. IX*, 163. [40] *Mems.* ii. 173. [41] Debrett, vi. 263-7, 474. [42] In an undated letter in the Royal archives, Windsor. [43] Add. 33100, ff. 195, 204. [44] Debrett, xiii. 254. [45] *Life & Letters of Sir G. Elliot*, i. 134.

J.B.

## ELPHINSTONE, Hon. George Keith (1746-1823).

DUNBARTONSHIRE    14 Feb. 1781-1790

STIRLINGSHIRE        1796-15 Dec. 1801

*b.* 7 Jan. 1746, 3rd surv. s. of Charles, 10th Lord Elphinstone [S] by Lady Clementina Fleming, da. and h. of John, 6th Earl of Wigtown [S] and niece of George Keith, 9th Earl Marischal [S]. *m.* (1) 10 Apr. 1787, Jane (*d.*13 Dec. 1789), da. and coh. of William Mercer (formerly Nairn) of Aldie, Kinross, 1da.; (2) 10 Jan. 1808, Hester Maria, da. and coh. of Henry Thrale (q.v.), 1da. K.B. 13 Apr. 1794; *cr.* Baron Keith of Stonehaven Marischal [I] 16 Mar. 1797 and [GB] 15 Dec. 1801; Baron Keith of Banheath (with sp. rem. to his elder da.) 17 Sept. 1803; Visct. Keith 1 June 1814.

Entered R.N. 1761; discharged 1766; acting lt. R.N. 1769; lt. 1770; cdr. 1772; capt. 1775; half-pay Jan. 1783-Jan. 1793; r.-adm. 1794; v.-adm. 1795; adm. 1801.

Sec., chamberlain and keeper of the signet of the principality of Scotland June 1783; treasurer and comptroller of household of Duke of Clarence 1789.

Elphinstone's parents, though owning great estates in Stirlingshire, Dunbartonshire and Lanarkshire, were harassed by debt and could make little provision for their numerous children. 'To acquire his education and business together and

without expense', Elphinstone entered the navy as an able seaman,[1] serving until December 1766 when, discharged at his own request, he shipped as third mate on the *Triton*, East Indiaman, commanded by his elder brother William. He returned home in 1768, after profitable trading ventures in India and China, and obtained a commission in the fleet commanded by Sir John Lindsay bound for the East Indies. Invalided home from India in 1771, he was subsequently posted to the Mediterranean, where in April 1774 he was deputed to negotiate with the Dey of Algiers.[2]

While on leave in October 1774 he unsuccessfully contested Dunbartonshire, with the support of Sir Lawrence Dundas, against Sir Archibald Edmonstone. Before his petition was heard he was sent to sea, and despite the efforts of his agent and friends the House, on a division, refused an extension of the time limit for receiving it. After serving on convoy duty and in American waters, he was sent by Howe in 1778 to defend East Florida, and distinguished himself in the operations leading to the capture of Charleston in May 1780, after which his ship was ordered home.

During his absence his brother William, Sir Lawrence Dundas, and the Marquess of Graham had concerted plans to support his candidature for Dunbartonshire against the Argyll interest.[3] A violent contest developed with Lord Frederick Campbell, and Elphinstone was returned on petition. He was then about to sail with a convoy for America, where at the end of 1781 Prince William Henry was placed in his care. In September 1782 Elphinstone fell ill and returned home.

Arriving in November 1782, he joined his brother-in-law William Adam in opposition to Shelburne and voted against the peace preliminaries, 18 Feb. 1783. He became a favourite of the Prince of Wales, who in June appointed him to succeed Sir John Gordon as his Scottish secretary. In December 1783 he followed his friends into opposition, but was a member of the St. Alban's Tavern group favouring a union of parties. Henry Dundas believed that at the general election in 1784 Elphinstone would 'certainly be turned out and a friend brought in',[4] but by agreement between his brother Lord Elphinstone, and Lord Graham, both Pittites, it was arranged that he should retain his seat for one Parliament only and thereafter withdraw in favour of a Graham candidate.

His only recorded speech in this Parliament was on 11 June 1788 when, during the trial of Warren Hastings, he protested against the closing of certain passages giving access to Westminster Hall.[5] His close connexion with the royal princes was confirmed in June 1789 when his former shipmate William, Duke of Clarence, appointed him comptroller of his household.

He died 10 Mar. 1823.

[1] Sir W. Fraser, *Elphinstone Fam. Bk.* i. 270. [2] For his naval career see *Keith Pprs.* (Navy Rec. Soc.) and Alex. Allardyce, *Mems. of Elphinstone.* [3] Duke of Argyll, *Intimate Society Letters* of *18th Cent.* ii. 438. [4] Laprade, 100. [5] Stockdale, xv. 169, 170.

E.H.-G.

## ELWES, John (1714–89), of Marcham, Berks. and Stoke, Suff.

### BERKSHIRE            30 Dec. 1772–1784

*b.* 7 Apr. 1714, o.s. of Robert Meggott, Southwark brewer, and gd.-s. of George Meggott, M.P. for Southwark 1722–3, by Amy, da. of Sir Gervase Elwes, 1st Bt., M.P. *educ.* Westminster 1722–9; Geneva. *unm.* *suc.* fa. c.1718; gd.-fa. 1723; took name of Elwes 1750; *suc.* to Stoke estates of his uncle, Sir Hervey Elwes, 2nd Bt., M.P., 1763.

'During the life time of Mr. Elwes', states Edward Topham, journalist and playwright, 'I said to him, more than once, "I would write his life." His answer was—"there is nothing in it, sir, worth mentioning."' But Topham persisted, and produced, in the words of Horace Walpole, 'one of the most amusing anecdotal books in the English language';[1] it went through 12 editions; and made 'Elwes the miser' into a stereotype and legend—he appears under this description in the *DNB*, and even in the British Museum catalogue of manuscripts. The biography is written with a professed moral purpose—to demonstrate 'the perfect vanity of unused wealth'; and having traced avarice as a family failing of the Elweses, deals with it in John Elwes with abundant repetition and elaboration. Here is a typical passage:

> In the penury of Mr. Elwes there was something that seemed like a judgment from heaven. All earthly comforts he voluntarily denied himself: he would walk home in the rain, in London, sooner than pay a shilling for a coach: he would sit in wet clothes sooner than have a fire to dry them: he would eat his provisions in the last stage of putrefaction sooner than have a fresh joint from the butcher's; and he wore a wig for above a fortnight, which I saw him pick up out of a rut in a lane where we were riding.

Yet he was generally credited with other qualities not usually associated with the character of a miser: he was a daring rider, keeping a remarkable stable of hunters; he was gentle and courteous, and would put himself to considerable inconvenience to help others; he would lend money but never on usurious terms; and at one time he 'played deep', but became disinclined to it 'from paying always, and not always being paid'. 'His avarice', says Topham, 'consisted not in hard-heartedness, but in self-denial.' There was austerity in his character, and a probity which commanded respect. The *Gentleman's Magazine*

wrote about him in its obituary notice: 'In such high estimation was he held for his love of justice, that numberless disputes amongst his constituents and others were left to his sole arbitrement.'[2] And similarly Topham states that his qualities as a magistrate earned him the offer of election to Parliament for the county.

When before the general election of 1754 a party at Abingdon opposed to John Morton asked Lord Fane to recommend to them a candidate, he thought in the first place of Elwes, and the Duke of Bedford directed Richard Neville Aldworth to find out whether Elwes would be prepared to stand.[3] Aldworth replied on 2 Apr. that Elwes, 'who is certainly a very proper person for the purpose in question, has already declared to me in confidence and in the most positive terms his resolution . . . not to stand at Abingdon, and though at the time he told me so he seemed sorry he had ever made that promise, yet he added he was determined to keep it'. Nothing more is known about Elwes standing for Parliament until 1772.

In 1772, writes Topham, there was 'the prospect of a contested election betwixt two most respectable families in Berkshire', when Lord Craven proposed Elwes as a third person unobjectionable to both sides; 'he was to be brought in by the freeholders for nothing.' And one of the few known letters from Elwes confirms Topham's account—he wrote to his London steward on 7 Jan. 1772:[4]

> I suppose you see that I am raised to great honour by my kind countrymen, by which an opposition in the county was prevented, which is so very much to the disadvantage of all ranks of people.

In 1772 Elwes's was something of a freak election; and in 1774 Robinson doubted whether it would be repeated.[5] But it was. 'A more respectable Member never sat in Parliament', wrote the *Gentleman's Magazine* in 1789. And the *Public Ledger* in 1779: 'A most worthy and respectable country gentleman, votes perfectly according to his conscience on each side, but generally with Opposition.' And Topham: 'In every part of his conduct, and in every vote he gave, he proved himself . . . an *independent* country gentleman . . . Wishing for no post, desirous of no rank, wanting no emolument, and being perfectly conscientious, he stood aloof from . . . temptations.'

At the outset Elwes sided with North, 'from no other motive . . . than a fair and honest belief' that his measures were right. The first division list in which his name appears, that of 25 Feb. 1774 on the Grenville Act, confirms this account: Elwes voted with the Opposition but is marked by North as one of those 'who generally vote with [the Government] and are friends'. He voted again with the Opposition over Wilkes's motion on the Middlesex election, 22 Feb. 1775. 'Both parties', writes Topham, 'were equally fond of having him as a nominee on their contested elections; frequently he was the chairman; and he was remarkable for the patience with which he always heard the counsel.' There is no record of his having spoken in the House, except when reporting as chairman of a committee. His name does not appear in the minority lists 1775–9. But Robinson's description of Elwes in his survey for the general election of 1780 marks the transition: 'Mr. Elwes though not against yet mostly is so' (a way of expressing in the language of the time that although not prejudiced against the Government, Elwes as a rule opposed it). He now came to vote regularly with the Opposition: in all the ten division lists available between March 1779 and the fall of the North Government. On 18 Feb. 1783 Elwes voted against Shelburne's peace preliminaries; but he was one of the four Members who, having seen that the Opposition 'was levelled not at the *measures* of Government, but at the *man*', next voted with the minister. On 7 May 1783 Elwes voted for Pitt's parliamentary reform.

Elwes adhered to the Coalition, and voted for Fox's East India bill; 'though I have talked with Mr. Elwes frequently upon the subject', writes Topham, 'I never could really learn why he supported it'. And John Sinclair wrote about him in a list which he drew up for Pitt about the end of December 1783:[6] 'I believe voted for the bill, being of Smith's select committee. He could not resist Mr. Pitt's personal solicitation.'

He died November 1789; his entailed estates valued at £7,000 a year descended to a great nephew; his personal estate, near £300,000, to his two illegitimate sons, John and George Elwes.

[1] *Life of the late John Elwes, Esq.* (1790). [2] 1789, p. 1149. [3] Bedford mss. 29, ff. 37–39. [4] Add. 38855, f. 201. [5] Laprade, 20. [6] Sinclair mss.

L.B.N.

**ELWILL, Sir John,** 4th Bt. (*d.*1778), of Englefield Green, Surr.

GUILDFORD  1747–1768

s. of Sir Edmund Elwill, 3rd Bt., of Exeter, comptroller of the Excise, by Anne, da. of William Speke of Beauchamp, Som. *educ.* Eton. *m.* 30 Nov. 1755, Selina, da. of Peter Bathurst (q.v.) of Clarendon Park, Wilts., wid. of Arthur Cole, 1st Baron Ranelagh [I], 1da. *suc.* fa. 2 Feb. 1740. His sis. Mary m. 1741 Richard, 3rd Baron Onslow.

Elwill sat for Guildford on the Onslow interest, and while Newcastle was in office supported the court. He appears in Henry Fox's list of Members favourable to the peace preliminaries, but over

Wilkes and general warrants voted with the Opposition. He was classed by Rockingham in July 1765 as 'doubtful', but did not vote against the repeal of the Stamp Act. Rockingham in November 1766, Townshend in January 1767, and Newcastle in March 1767 all class him 'doubtful'. He did not stand in 1768.

He died 1 Mar. 1778.

J.B.

**EMERSON,** *see* **AMCOTTS, Wharton**

**ERLE DRAX GROSVENOR,** *see* **GROSVENOR, Richard** (*d.*1819)

**ERSKINE, Sir Henry,** 5th Bt. (?1710–65), of Alva, Clackmannan.

AYR BURGHS                          29 Dec. 1749–1754
ANSTRUTHER EASTER BURGHS      1754–9 Aug. 1765

*b.* ?1710,[1] 2nd s. of Sir John Erskine, 3rd Bt., M.P., by Hon. Catherine St. Clair, da. of Henry, 10th Lord Sinclair [S]. *educ.* ?Eton 1725; L. Inn 1728. *m.* 16 May 1761, Janet, da. of Peter Wedderburn, Lord Chesterhall, S.C.J., and sis. of Alexander Wedderburn (q.v.), 2s. 1da. *suc.* bro. as 5th Bt. 2 July 1747.

Ensign 22 Ft. 1735, lt. 1736; capt. 1 Ft. 1743; dismissed Jan. 1756; reinstated as maj.-gen. with effect from June 1759; col. 67 Ft. 1760–1; col. 25 Ft. 1761–2; col. 1 Ft. 1762–*d.*; lt.-gen. 1765.

Surveyor of the King's private roads 1757–60; sec. of the order of the Thistle Apr. 1765–*d.*

Erskine was the son of a Jacobite leader in the '15, who dissipated his fortune and was compelled to sell his estate. Erskine joined the 22nd Foot commanded by his uncle James St. Clair (q.v.), on whose generosity he was largely dependent during his early career.

At the general election of 1754 he opposed Philip Anstruther, an old enemy, in Anstruther Easter Burghs. When Anstruther successfully appealed to Pelham for support, St. Clair wrote to James Oswald, 26 Jan. 1754:[2]

[Anstruther] has taken ample care to render both me and my nephew his implacable enemies . . . he sent his agents to insinuate that as we were descended from Jacobite families we must be looked on as disaffected to his Majesty and his Government. This malicious insinuation . . . I never will forgive . . . I never will desist. I will endeavour to place my nephew in that situation where he may be able to show his zeal for the present happy establishment and his attachment to the present administration. Mr. Pelham knows I undertook to answer for him, and since he is now certain of a seat in Parliament, Mr. Pelham will find he will adhere inviolably to the engagements I entered into for him.

In the constituency Sir Harry's lively personality and courtly manners won him great popularity,[3] and when Argyll declared in his favour his success was assured.

Listed by Dupplin among Government supporters attached to Argyll, Erskine's political attachments really lay elsewhere. While Argyll maintained good relations with Fox, Erskine fostered the alliance between Bute and Pitt, whom he greatly admired. He voted, 13 Nov. 1755, against the Address, and on 10 Dec. spoke in support of Potter's motion against the subsidy treaties. In January 1756 he was dismissed from the army by order of the King. On 29 Jan. 1756 Pitt raised the question of his dismissal in the House:[4] 'You have just broken a brave officer, distinguished with marks of two wounds, and by the applause of the Duke [of Cumberland]; and who was cashiered for nothing but his vote in Parliament.' After heated exchanges between Fox and Pitt, Erskine himself intervened: 'He did not complain of his dismission: a civil or a military life was indifferent to him, yet he could wish if there were any other cause than his vote, that Mr. Fox would declare it.' He spoke on 18 Feb. against the Swiss regiment bill, and again on 29 Mar.[5] against Lord George Sackville's motion for bringing over Hanoverian troops.

In face of the King's hostility the Devonshire-Pitt Administration could procure no favours for Erskine. George Dempster wrote on 26 Nov. 1756:[6] 'Sir Harry Erskine never will get into the army, but he is named for some civil employment.' He received nothing. On 2 May 1757 he voted against exonerating the Newcastle-Fox Administration for the loss of Minorca; took a considerable part, as Bute's representative, in the negotiations for a new Administration,[7] and was listed by Newcastle at the head of the six Scots attached to 'the last ministry or Mr. Pitt'. Shortly after the formation of the Coalition, Bute secured for him the office of surveyor of the King's private roads—this atonement for unjust and cruel treatment, wrote Bute to J. S. Mackenzie, he had demanded by express orders of the Princess of Wales who looked upon Erskine 'as a sacrifice for his attachment to the late Prince'.[8] Erskine was now established as one of Bute's principal confidants. He took a leading part in the Scottish militia bill, as one of the six Members nominated by the Edinburgh committee to consult on its introduction,[9] spoke strongly for it, 15 Apr. 1760, and was a teller in the division. 'All Scotland' he declared, 'would come and demand it at the bar of the House.'[10] Subsequently he received the thanks of the convention of royal burghs for his efforts.

On George III's accession Erskine was offered full restoration in the army, a regiment, a governorship, or, if he preferred it, civil employment—the King had promised 'to restore him to his rank when he should come to the Crown'.[11] Erskine chose the army, both for military honour and financial security. He wrote to Bute, 3 Nov. 1760:[12]

I have long looked forward to the late important event, as the only period that could restore me to it . . . Officers who were younger lt.-colonels than me have been fortunate enough to have the command of armies . . . and thence perhaps my Lord, my attachment to the military line of life has been increased. Nor has it been diminished by comparing that line with the line of civil employment . . . Multitudes of competitors; paucity of offices; immense jealousy of those who rise . . . the instability of human affairs, and my being born in North Britain, deter me from turning my eyes to that prospect . . . When I was dismissed from the service, Lord Barrington told me by way of comfort, that whenever anyone was restored . . . he was always restored to his former rank . . . The Duke of Argyll who is conversant in army matters saw no difficulty in my being re-established.

He hoped for the rank he might have expected had he remained in the army, but was unwilling to leave the decision to Ligonier, whom he considered prejudiced against him.

Imagination flattered me with a military life, whenever his present Majesty should succeed to the Crown; in the prospect of that event I addressed myself to a young lady, assuring her that I would aspire to her hand as soon as I should be in such circumstances as to be enabled to support the expenses of a married state.

Rather than give up Janet Wedderburn he was prepared to accept less than justice.

As 'favourite of the Favourite' Erskine now became, as he styled himself, *sous ministre* to Bute,[13] handling requests for favours and intervening in elections on behalf of Bute's friends. He consulted Lord George Sackville on securing the Dorset interest for William Mayne in Canterbury, and advised Bute against antagonizing the Kent Whigs by supporting Sir Roger Twisden in the county.[14] He supplied Bute with information about the Clive opposition in Penryn; recommended as election agent in Cornwall John Richmond Webb, who also consulted him on the choice of candidates for Exeter; and discussed with Pryse Campbell and his father electoral prospects in Inverness and Inverness Burghs.[15] His chief concern however was the settlement of the Argyll-Bute dispute over Ayr Burghs in September 1759. He had given early warning of Argyll's opposition to Bute's candidate, Patrick Craufurd,[16] and in the spring of 1761 was largely responsible for the compromise which led to the withdrawal of Sir Adam Fergusson in favour of Lord Frederick Campbell in the burghs, and the withdrawal of Loudoun's candidate, Mure Campbell, in Ayrshire.

While in Scotland for his own election, Erskine reported to Bute the defeat of the Argyll party at Edinburgh, and his own intervention in Stirling Burghs on behalf of his cousin, Robert Haldane.[17] When Haldane offered to transfer his interest to someone acceptable to Bute, Erskine nominated Wedderburn, but explained to Bute that he had not committed him to support Haldane in his petition against the Bridport return. Shortly after Argyll's death Bute informed Erskine of his intention to bring home Stuart Mackenzie from Turin. Erskine replied, 21 Apr. 1761:

> I was just going to sit down to entreat your Lordship to prevail on Mr. Mackenzie to return to Britain when I was honoured with your letter. Your Lordship knows too well the small extent of my abilities to be of use to you, but you know also the anxiety which I feel to do all in my poor power to endeavour to serve what it appears to me to be in your interest . . . Gratitude . . . and affection will ever prompt me not only to execute your orders but to prevent them by guessing at your inclinations.

When Haldane's Bridport petition was debated, 2 Mar. 1762, Bute's friends were committed to its support. Walpole writes:[18] 'Sir Henry Erskine, a creature of the Favourite, had the indecency and folly to call the English party in the House of Commons *a profligate* majority.' This so antagonized the House that Harris, Jenkinson and North, among others, abstained from voting.[19] He again roused national feeling on 26 Mar. 1762 when he moved for a Treasury grant for a bridge over the Tweed at Coldstream, 'from this amazing argument, the use it would be to draw cannon over'. Harris commented: 'It went. Lord Bute had issued his mandate and the Treasury obeyed. To carry a cannon into Scotland —why not to import thistles into England—a mere job.'

Still, Erskine retained Bute's full confidence. When on 14 June 1762 he reported that an 'association' had been formed against Bute consisting of Cumberland, Newcastle, Devonshire, Pitt, etc., Bute at once informed the King.[20] When he complained of a 'slight' to his brother-in-law, Major David Wedderburn, and attributed it to the machinations of Townshend or Shelburne, Bute and the King were duly incensed.[21] His interest was sought by naval and military acquaintances, by 'Ossian' Macpherson and the poet Gray, by his friend David Hume in his claim for half pay as judge advocate at L'Orient, etc.

After 1761 Erskine had little direct contact with electoral affairs, but was always ready to recruit new 'friends' for his patron. In November 1761 he urged George Dempster to attach himself to Bute; in August 1762 he recommended Locke, a neighbour's son, to Jenkinson as candidate for the Grimsby by-election; and in February 1763 passed on to Jenkinson a long letter from a correspondent on the management of the Isle of Wight boroughs.[22]

In November 1762 General St. Clair died, leaving his entailed estates to his heir, but 'his ready money to Sir Harry Erskine',[23] who in fulfilment of the King's long-standing promise succeeded his uncle as colonel of the Royals.

Violently partisan in support of Bute's Administration, he went so far as to oppose on 7 Mar. 1763 an address to the King on providing for half pay officers, on the ground that it implied 'a sort of reflection upon the King'. He was called to order and 'Mr. Pitt managed the point very properly and strongly against him'.[24] Shortly before Bute's resignation Erskine made a strong plea for the rehabilitation of his friend George Sackville.

Erskine supported the Grenville Administration throughout the debates on Wilkes and general warrants, but deplored the breach between Bute and Grenville. In ill-health during the summer of 1764 he wrote from Spa to Jenkinson, 23 Sept.:[25]

> I wished that your attempts for thorough conciliation had been attended with more success . . . 'Tis with regret I perceive we are to open the next campaign in the same situation in which we were the last. There has been so much time for conciliation 'tis pity it has elapsed in so fruitless a manner.

Before leaving England he had asked Grenville for any military governorship that should become vacant, and on 3 Jan. 1765 applied without success for the governorship of the ports of the north of Scotland.

Prevented by illness from regular attendance at the House, Erskine again wrote to Grenville, 25 Mar. 1765, asking for the vacant office of secretary of the Thistle: 'As it is a Scotch office . . . my obtaining it cannot produce the least murmur from anyone back in England.'[26] Grenville, who intended the office for Lord Fife's brother, had a long talk on the subject with Stuart Mackenzie, with whom he was already at odds over Scottish patronage. When Mackenzie refused to commit himself, and when the King 'spoke kindly of Sir Harry Erskine' and gave him the appointment over Grenville's protests, 'a very improper and passionate conversation' took place between Grenville and the King.[27] This incident, which still further embittered Grenville's relations with the King and Mackenzie, played a part in the Government crisis of April–May 1765.

Erskine died at York 9 Aug. 1765 when returning from Scotland after his re-election consequent upon his appointment. Remembered as a faithful friend, a wit and a minor poet,[28] 'he was', wrote Alexander

Carlyle, 'a truly honest man, but his views were not extensive nor his talents great'.

[1] His e. bro. Charles was *b.* 7 May 1709, *Sc. Hist. Soc. Misc.* ii. 400. [2] *Memorials of James Oswald,* 330. [3] *Letters of D. Hume,* i. 190. [4] Walpole, *Mems. Geo. II,* ii. 159-63. [5] Newdigate's 'Debates'. [6] James Fergusson, *Letters of G. Dempster to Sir Adam Fergusson,* 13-14. [7] Letters from Erskine in Add. 36796 and Bute mss. [8] Undated (1757), Bute mss. [9] Andrew Fletcher, Lord Milton to C. Townshend, 23 Feb. 1760, Buccleuch mss. [10] Walpole, *Mems. Geo. II,* iii. 280. [11] Dodington, *Diary,* 502. [12] Bute mss. [13] *HMC Var.* vi. 267. [14] *HMC Stopford-Sackville,* i. 45; Erskine to Bute, February 1761, Bute mss. [15] Namier, *Structure,* 311; letters from Campbell, Webb and Erskine, Bute mss. [16] *Caldwell Pprs.* ii(1), p. 120. [17] Erskine to Bute, 7, 13, 18 Apr. 1761, Bute mss. [18] *Mems. Geo. III,* i. 110. [19] Harris's 'Debates'. [20] Sedgwick, 160. [21] Erskine to Bute, 22 Aug. 1762, Bute mss; Sedgwick, 162-3. [22] Add. 38199, f. 187; *Jenkinson Pprs.* 126-9. [23] *Oswald Memorials,* 271. [24] Harris's 'Debates'. [25] *Jenkinson Pprs.* 153. [26] Grenville mss (JM). [27] *Jenkinson Pprs.* 398; *Grenville Pprs.* ii. 126. [28] Boswell, *Private Pprs.* xii. 27; xviii. 23.

E.H.-G.

## ERSKINE, Sir James, 6th Bt. (1762–1837), of Alva, Clackmannan.

CASTLE RISING    25 May 1782–1784
MORPETH              1784–1796
DYSART BURGHS     1796–2 Jan. 1805

*b.* 6 Feb. 1762, 1st s. of Sir Henry Erskine, 5th Bt. (q.v.). *educ.* Edinburgh h.s.; Eton 1772–7. *m.* 4 Nov. 1789, Henrietta Elizabeth (*d.*1810), 1st da. of Hon. Edward Bouverie (q.v.), 2 surv. s. 1da. *suc.* fa. 9 Aug. 1765; *suc. cos.* James Paterson St. Clair in the Rosslyn and Dysart estates, 14 May 1789, and assumed name of St. Clair before Erskine, 9 June 1789; *suc.* uncle Alexander Wedderburn (q.v.) as 2nd Earl of Rosslyn, 2 Jan. 1805.
    Lt. 21 Lt. Drag. 1778; capt. 19 Lt. Drag. 1780; capt. 14 Lt. Drag. 1781; maj. 8 Lt. Drag. 1783; lt.-col. 12 Lt. Drag. 1792; col. 1795; maj.-gen. 1798; col. 9 Drag. 1801–*d.*; lt.-gen. 1805; gen. 1814.

Erskine's early career was directed by his uncle Alexander Wedderburn who lost no opportunity of advancing the interests of his sister and her children. When in 1779 Wedderburn was raising demands against Government, he extracted from North a promise of a reversion for his nephew.[1] A few months later, Loughborough's friend Lord Carlisle, as lord lieutenant of Ireland, appointed Erskine one of his aides-de-camp extraordinary. Shortly after the fall of North, Erskine, although under age, was returned for Castle Rising, through Loughborough's interest with the Suffolk family. During the summer of 1782 he remained in Ireland attending to his military office as assistant adjutant-general and, according to William Eden, 'doing extremely well'.[2] On his return he joined the Opposition and voted against Shelburne's peace preliminaries, 18 Feb. 1783; supported the Coalition; and opposed Pitt. In 1784 Loughborough accepted Lord Carlisle's offer to return Erskine for Morpeth, on the understanding that he should be free to contest Fife at the first vacancy.[3]

In the new Parliament Erskine made his mark as a forceful Opposition speaker. He intervened in the Westminster election debate, 8 June 1784; spoke on the military and financial provisions of the East India bill; and warmly defended Fox against Pitt.[4] He strongly supported Sheridan's amendment to Pitt's Irish propositions commending Ireland's large contribution to defence.[5] A member of the group of young Whigs surrounding Burke, he took an effective part in the East India debates of March 1786, and was allotted a role by Burke in the proceedings against Warren Hastings.[6] On 15 Mar. 1787 Erskine opened the charge against Hastings relating to contracts.[7] Burke congratulated his pupil:[8] 'He had never heard a more business like speech nor a more masterly detail of facts: it was a wonderful display of ability from so young a man.' On 3 Apr. Erskine was among the seven managers appointed to prepare the articles of impeachment against Hastings. He was thus actively engaged when Fife fell vacant by the death of Robert Skene on 19 May, and although he seems to have made a last minute effort to oppose the Government candidate,[9] he shortly afterwards renounced his Scottish ambitions. Loughborough wrote to Lord Carlisle, 13 Oct. 1787:[10]

> Sir James Erskine is at present in Holland but I saw him at Newcastle, and I think nothing can have happened to alter the disposition he then had to disengage himself entirely from his contest in Scotland. It will always be my wish that he should think of Morpeth only, while you are so good as to think of him for that place . . . For supposing his success in Scotland could be ensured, I am satisfied it would be better for his fortune and his constitution and his political situation even to fight Morpeth under your auspices . . . than to take the charge and burthen of a large county with all its claims upon him. My former adoption of that project was entirely from complaisance to his cousin who wished to support a family interest without being at the trouble of it.

In the new session he was almost wholly engrossed in East India affairs, was a teller in the division, 11 Dec., on Fox's motion to add Francis to the managers of Hastings's impeachment, and was nominated a manager in the impeachment of Sir Elijah Impey. With an eye to his Fife interest he intervened occasionally on Scottish affairs; spoke on the distillery bill, 12 Feb. 1788, and opposed on 17 June Sheridan's motion for a bill to reform Scottish burghs, 'strongly protesting against the existence of the evils complained of'. During the Regency debates he spoke at least twice.[11]

He died 18 Jan. 1837.

[1] Fortescue, v. 9. [2] *Auckland Corresp.* i. 14. [3] *HMC Carlisle,* 651. [4] Debrett, xv. 80, 124, 315, 319, 400. [5] Stockdale, vi. 328–9. [6] Lady Minto, *Life & Letters of Sir G. Elliot,* i. 119; Debrett, xxi. 269–70. [7] Ibid. 430–8. [8] Stockdale, x. 478. [9] H. Furber, *Hen. Dundas,* 221. [10] *HMC Carlisle,* 652. [11] Stockdale, xiii. 181–2; xv. 193; xvi. 316, 415.

E.H.-G.

## ERSKINE, Hon. Thomas (1750–1823), of Hampstead, Mdx.

PORTSMOUTH 28 July 1783–1784

*b.* 10 Jan. 1750, 3rd s. of Henry David, 10th Earl of Buchan [S], by Agnes, da. of Sir James Steuart, 1st Bt. of Goodtrees. *educ.* St. Andrews g.s.; St. Andrews Univ. 1762–3; Trinity, Camb. 1776; L. Inn 1775, called 1778. *m.* (1) 29 Mar. 1770, Frances (*d.*26 Dec. 1805), da. of Daniel Moore (q.v.), 4s. 4da.; (2) 12 Oct. 1818, Sarah Buck (sep. 1821), 1s. *cr.* Baron Erskine, 10 Feb. 1806; K.T. 23 Feb. 1815.
R.N. 1764–8; ensign 1 Ft. 1768, lt. 1773, ret. 1775.
K.C. 1783; attorney-gen. to the Prince of Wales 1783–92; chancellor, duchy of Cornwall 1802–6; ld. chancellor Feb. 1806–Apr. 1807.

Erskine's parents, after providing for their elder sons, were too poor to afford either the university education Erskine desired, or the purchase price of an army commission.[1] He therefore reluctantly joined the navy but, disappointed of promotion, left it in 1768, and with the legacy bequeathed him by his father purchased a commission in the army. He further embarrassed his finances by a runaway match at the age of twenty. He served in Minorca from 1770 to 1772, when he obtained six months' leave, became a popular member of London literary circles, and published a pamphlet on 'abuses in the British army', protesting against low pay and promotion by purchase and influence.

In 1775, after consulting Mansfield, he decided to sell his commission and read for the bar. Three years of industrious penury were rewarded by spectacular success. As counsel in a series of celebrated cases involving attacks upon the ministry, he won the admiration of Sheridan, Fox and other Opposition leaders, through whom he became an intimate of the Prince of Wales.

In July 1783 the Coalition, by arrangement with Sir William Gordon (q.v.) and the Carter family,[2] brought him into Parliament for Portsmouth. A friend commented, 3 Nov. 1783:[3]

> Everybody says that Erskine will be solicitor-general . . . whether he is or not he will have had the most rapid rise that has been known at the bar . . . he has cleared £8,000 or £9,000 besides paying his debts—got a silk gown and business of at least £3,000 a year—a seat in Parliament—and over and above has made his brother lord advocate . . . I have great doubts whether his coming into Parliament was a wise thing. He sacrificed his House of Commons business . . . He has several of Burke's defects . . . and the expectation from him will be too great to be satisfied. We expect a match between him and Pitt.

Erskine's maiden speech on 20 Nov. on Fox's East India bill was a failure; and he was mortified by Pitt's contempt. He spoke with better effect on 27 Nov., pledging himself to stand or fall with Fox. Inveighing against 'secret influence' and the change

of administration, he moved the motion of 17 Dec. and the address to the King, 22 Dec., against a dissolution. After the recess he concentrated his satire on Pitt, sneered at Dundas's 'mysterious conversion', and repudiated allegations of bribery made against his brother, the ex-lord advocate. Attacking Pitt's East India measure on 23 Jan. as a 'mere piece of patchwork', he took a prominent part on 16 Feb. in defence of the Commons resolution limiting the payment of East India bills, and condemned the 'tricks' of the ministry in procuring popular addresses vilifying the Coalition.[4]

At the general election he unsuccessfully contested Truro on the interest of Sir Francis Basset. Resuming his parliamentary legal practice, he was Fox's counsel on the Westminster scrutiny, and was censured by the House for his insolent language. During the Regency crisis the Opposition intended him for the attorney-generalship in a new Administration. He differed from his friends over Hastings's impeachment, but remained a devoted adherent of Fox, to whom he owed his appointment as lord chancellor in 1806.

He died 17 Nov. 1823.

[1] Erskine to Lady Steuart of Goodtrees, 4 Nov. 1763, Campbell, *Lives of the Lord Chancellors*, vi. 372. [2] Laprade, 88. [3] Campbell, vi. 415. [4] Debrett, xii. 89, 189–94, 447–8, 463–70, 495–501, 536–9, 568, 627–31; xiii. 125–30; Wraxall, *Mems.* ii. 436.

E.H.-G.

## ESTCOURT, Thomas (1748–1818), of Estcourt House, nr. Tetbury, Glos.

CRICKLADE 20 Mar. 1790–1806

*bap.* 7 Oct. 1748, 1st surv. s. of Matthew Estcourt of Cam, Glos. by Lydia, da. of John Halling. *educ.* St. John's, Oxf. 1766. *m.* 6 Oct. 1774, Hon. Jane Grimston, da. of James, 2nd Visct. Grimston, 2s. 2da. *suc.* to estates of his kinsman Walter Estcourt 1750, and fa. bef. 1782.
Sheriff, Glos. 1774–5.

Estcourt was returned unopposed, pledged to a conduct 'founded on independence and guided by integrity'.[1]

He died 2 Dec. 1818.

[1] *Glocester Jnl.* 29 Mar. 1790.

J.A.C.

## ESTWICK, Samuel (?1736–95), of Berkeley St., London, and Barbados.

WESTBURY 20 Mar. 1779–19 Nov. 1795

*b.* ?1736, 3rd but o. surv. s. of Richard Estwick of Barbados by Elizabeth, da. of John Rous of Barbados. *educ.* poss. Eton; Queen's, Oxf. 10 Oct. 1753, aged 17; I. Temple 1752. *m.* (1) bef. 24 Mar. 1763, Elizabeth (*d.*1766), da. of Lt.-Col. John Frere, gov. of Barbados,

2da.; (2) 11 May 1769, Grace, da. and coh. of Jonas Longford of Antigua, 4s. 3da. *suc.* fa. 1753.

Assistant agent for Barbados 1763–78; agent 1778–1792; dep. paymaster-gen. Aug. 1782–Apr. 1783, 1784–*d.*; registrar of Chelsea Hospital, and searcher of the customs at Barbados, Mar.–?Apr. 1783, Jan. 1784–*d.*

Samuel Estwick first became known through his political pamphlets. These included: *A Vindication of the Ministry's Acceptance of the Administration* (1765), *Considerations on the Negro Cause* (1772), and *A Letter to the Rev. Josiah Tucker* (1776)—which last, in addition to the usual reasons against the American war, argued that 'Great Britain without America can neither support nor protect the West India islands.' 'Connected with no party of men of any description whatever', he wrote, 'I enjoy the solid comfort of independence.' Yet he clearly inclined towards Chatham, whom he described as 'this statesman *unique*'.

As a result of this pamphlet Estwick became acquainted with Lord Abingdon,[1] who held similar opinions and who brought him into Parliament for Westbury. His first speech, 23 Jan. 1781, was when presenting a petition from Barbados for relief for the sufferers in a hurricane. Two other speeches followed in this session, both on matters connected with Barbados. In 1780 or 1781 the *English Chronicle* wrote about him:

> He does not possess the gift of oratory, and never delivers his opinion in the House upon any but mercantile subjects, but constantly attends his duty, and votes upon all questions, with Opposition. He enjoys very large possessions in the West India islands, and is said to have been included as a very considerable sufferer in the dreadful calamity which has recently taken place in that quarter. He has not distinguished himself in the political world by any other circumstance, than by the zeal of his opposition to the measures of the present Administration.

It is also stated that he was a West India merchant, which is not substantiated by the trade directories— he seems to have been a planter only; nor has evidence been found for the further statement that he had rejected the offer of a share in a rum contract.

On the change of Administration in March 1782 Abingdon applied to Shelburne on Estwick's behalf: his hitherto 'sufficient and independent fortune' was now much reduced by the 'calamities of the times', and Abingdon asked for him to be appointed under-secretary of state.[2] Shelburne was already engaged but offered Estwick a place abroad, which he declined. However, when Barré became paymaster general in August 1782 he appointed Estwick his deputy. And on 18 Aug. Estwick wrote to Shelburne:[3]

Mr. Barré informed me of your Lordship's providing more permanently for me upon the expected vacancy at the customs. My noble friend the Earl of Abingdon gave me the same information and I had his Lordship's approbation for my acceptance of this provision, though my seat in Parliament was not tenable therewith; his Lordship seeing that whilst a numerous offspring would thereby be taken care of, I might more effectually serve your Lordship as well as the public in such a situation.

Shortly before Shelburne left office he secured further provision for Estwick, compatible with a seat in Parliament.

Estwick voted for Shelburne's peace preliminaries, 18 Feb. 1783, and against Fox's East India bill, 27 Nov. 1783; and supported Pitt. On 3 June 1783 he intervened in the debate on Burke's pay office bill, the last time he is known to have spoken in the House before 1790.

He died 19 Nov. 1795.

[1] Abingdon to Shelburne, 23 Mar. 1782, Lansdowne mss. [2] Ibid. [3] Ibid.

J.A.C.

## EUSTON, Earl of, *see* FITZROY, Augustus Henry, *and* FITZROY, George Henry

## EVELYN, John (1706–67), of Wotton, Surr.

*b.* 24 Aug. 1706, 1st s. of Sir John Evelyn, 1st Bt., M.P., by Anne, da. of Edward Boscawen, M.P., sis. of Hugh, 1st Visct. Falmouth, and gd.-da. of Sir Francis Godolphin. *educ.* Eton 1718; Queen's, Oxf. 1725. *m.* 17 Aug. 1732, his cos. Mary, da. of Hugh, 1st Visct. Falmouth, 2s. 3da. *suc.* fa. as 2nd Bt. 15 July 1763.

Groom of the bedchamber to Frederick, Prince of Wales 1733–51; clerk of the Green Cloth to George, Prince of Wales 1756–60, to George III 1760–*d.*

Evelyn sat for Helston on the Godolphin interest, and for Penryn on the Falmouth interest. In Bute's list he is classed as 'Newcastle and Government'. He does not appear in Henry Fox's list of Members favourable to the peace preliminaries nor in any list of those who voted against them. Jenkinson in the autumn of 1763 marked him as 'pro' and so did Rockingham, July 1765, but in November 1766 as 'Swiss' (prepared to follow any Administration). Townshend, January 1767, listed him as 'Government', and he voted with Administration on the land tax, 27 Feb. 1767. There is no record of his having spoken in the House. He died 11 June 1767.

J.B.

## EVELYN, William (*d.*1766), *see* GLANVILLE

**EVELYN, William** (1723–83), of Send, Surr.

HELSTON   1 July 1767–1774

> *b.* 10 Feb. 1723, 6th s. of Sir John Evelyn, 1st Bt., M.P., and bro. of Sir John Evelyn, 2nd Bt. (q.v.). *educ.* Westminster 1731–7. *unm.*
> Ensign 2 Ft. Gds. 1739, lt. 1744, capt. lt. 1754, capt. and lt.-col. 1754; col. 1762; col. 29 Ft. 1769–*d*; maj.-gen. 1770; lt.-gen. 1777.

Evelyn was returned unopposed for Helston on the Godolphin interest. He voted with Administration on Wilkes and the Middlesex election; does not appear in any of the minority lists between 1770 and 1772; was classed as 'pro, present' in both Robinson's surveys on the royal marriage bill, March 1772; and as a Government supporter who voted for Grenville's Act, 25 Feb. 1774. There is no record of his having spoken in the House.

Evelyn did not stand again in 1774. In 1780 he was elected for Helston on a double return, but in 1781 the House of Commons decided against him. He died 15 Aug. 1783.

J.B.

**EVELYN, William** (?1734–1813), of St. Clere, nr. Sevenoaks, Kent.

HYTHE   1768–1802

> *b.* ?1734, 1st s. of William Glanville (q.v.), formerly Evelyn, by his 2nd w. *educ.* Westminster 1744–51, aged 10. *m.* 2 Aug. 1760, Susanna, da. and coh. of Thomas Barrett of Shoreham, Kent, 2s. 3da. *suc.* fa. 19 Oct. 1766.

In 1766, when the newly appointed lord warden of the Cinque Ports, Lord Holdernesse, was searching for a suitable candidate to oppose the Sackville interest at Hythe at the general election, William Deedes, whose estate gave him some interest in the borough, suggested that William Evelyn should stand. Evelyn wrote to Deedes, 8 Dec. 1766:[1]

> I thought it would be but to little purpose to make any pretensions to succeed my father at Hythe . . . I certainly will make use of the hints you have given me . . . by seeing Lord Holdernesse and by offering to fight his battles for him, for believe me there is hardly anything I would not do to eradicate that haughty fellow [Lord George Sackville] though I can hardly believe he hath taken root here yet.

He was returned after a contest. In Parliament he supported Administration (but voted with the Opposition on Grenville's Election Act, 25 Feb. 1774). Four speeches of his are reported during this Parliament—none of much interest.

In 1774 Evelyn was again returned for Hythe after a contest. He continued to support Administration till the fall of North, and voted against Shelburne's peace preliminaries, 18 Feb. 1783. In 1784 he once more successfully contested Hythe, where

he had now established a personal interest. He opposed Pitt's Administration till the outbreak of the war with France. No speech by him is reported 1774–90.

He died 3 Nov. 1813, aged 79.

[1] Wilks, *Barons of the Cinque Ports*, 114.

M.M.D.

**EVELYN,** *see also* **SHUCKBURGH**

**EWER, Thomas** (*d.*1790), of Lincoln's Inn Fields.

DORCHESTER   4 July 1789–18 Jan. 1790

> 5th surv. s. of Henry Ewer, and bro. of William Ewer (q.v.).

Ewer was a London merchant in partnership with his brother William, at whose death he was returned for Dorchester on the Shaftesbury interest. Nothing is known of his conduct in the House: Parliament sat only five weeks while he was a Member. He died 18 Jan. 1790.

M.M.D.

**EWER, William** (c.1720–89), of Richmond, Surr.

DORCHESTER   23 Dec. 1765–23 June 1789

> *b.* c.1720, 4th surv. s. of Henry Ewer of The Lea, Herts., by his w. Hester Dunster. His aunt Jane Ewer *m.* Anthony, 3rd Earl of Shaftesbury. *unm. suc.* uncle Charles Ewer, M.P., grocer and alderman of London 1742; and bro. Anthony Ewer 1755.
> Director, Bank of England 1763–*d*, dep. gov. 1779–1782, gov. 1782–3; treasurer, Levant Co.

William Ewer and his brother Thomas (q.v.) inherited the grocery business of their uncle Charles Ewer, and continued trading at his premises. They also carried on business as Turkey merchants.

In 1765 William Ewer was returned unopposed for Dorchester on the interest of his cousin Lord Shaftesbury, governor of the Levant Company. In Rockingham's list, November 1766, Ewer is classed as 'doubtful', and in Townshend's, January 1767, as 'Government'. He voted with the Opposition on the land tax, 27 Feb. 1767.

In 1768 he successfully contested Dorchester on the Shaftesbury interest. During this Parliament he regularly voted with the court, except on Grenville's Election Act, 25 Feb. 1774, when he is described in the King's list as normally a friend.

After 1771 Ewer subscribed very large sums to Government loans, and before 1781 his one recorded speech was on 26 May 1774 to defend the method of alloting subscriptions to the current loan.

Returned after a contest in 1774 and unopposed in 1780, he voted with the court till the fall of North, except on the division for an account of pensions, 21 Feb. 1780, when he voted with Opposition.

In 1781 he advised the Government on the loan, and on 12 Mar. made a short speech explaining and defending its terms. He spoke on the renewal of the Bank's charter on 6 and 13 June 1781 when at some length he justified the bargain which as deputy governor he had helped to make. On 26 June 1782 he opposed the part of Burke's bill for regulating the pay office which affected the Bank. His only other recorded speech in this Parliament was on the receipts tax, 5 June 1783. Ewer voted for Shelburne's peace preliminaries, 18 Feb. 1783; and for Fox's East India bill, 27 Nov. 1783. In Robinson's list of January 1784 he was described as 'doubtful'. He was one of the St. Alban's Tavern group which tried to unite Pitt and Fox; after its failure he went over to Fox, and remained in opposition. He made two other speeches: on the establishment of the sinking fund, 6 Apr. 1786; and presenting a petition of London merchants claiming the benefits to the country of the slave trade, 28 May 1788.

He died 23 June 1789.

M.M.D.

## EYRE, Anthony (1727–88), of Rampton, nr. East Retford, Notts.

BOROUGHBRIDGE　1774–1784

*b.* 9 Jan. 1727, 1st surv. s. of Anthony Eyre by Margaret, da. of Charles Turner of Kirkleatham, Yorks. *educ.* Ch. Ch. Oxf. 1745. *m.* 1755, Judith Letitia, da. and h. of John Bury of Grange, nr. Grantham, and gt.-niece and h. of Sir Hardolf Wasteneys, 4th Bt., of Headen, Notts., 4s. 2da. *suc.* fa. 1748.

Eyre was returned for Boroughbridge on the interest of the Duke of Newcastle. 'A country gentleman of good fortune who submits to be a —— of the Duke of Newcastle', the *Public Ledger* wrote of him in 1779. On the contractors bill, 12 Feb. 1779, he was listed as 'con, present, friend', but his only three recorded votes during this Parliament were with the Administration—on Keppel, 3 Mar. 1779; economical reform, 8 Mar. 1780; and the motion against prorogation, 24 Apr. No vote by Eyre is recorded in the division lists of 1781 and 1782. He voted against Shelburne's peace preliminaries, 18 Feb. 1783, but separated from Newcastle by voting for Fox's East India bill, 27 Nov. 1783, and against Pitt's Administration. He wrote to Newcastle, 24 Mar. 1784:[1]

I am . . . extremely happy the differing in politics just now is not likely to injure me in your good opinion. It hurt me much the not being able to comply with your Grace's wishes. My conduct before I hope had been agreeable. In this last business I felt myself so much engaged by the part I took before Christmas (without knowing that I was acting contrary to your inclinations) that I could not with honour to myself alter my conduct.

I am extremely obliged to you for all your favours . . . I assure your Grace it was not my expectation to be again brought into Parliament by you.

It seems unlikely that he ever spoke in the House: ten speeches by 'Mr. Eyre', reported between 1781 and 1783, are almost certainly by Francis Eyre (q.v.).

Anthony Eyre died 14 Feb. 1788.

[1] Newcastle (Clumber) mss.

M.M.D.

## EYRE, Francis (1722–97), of Colesborne, Glos.

MORPETH　　　　　　　1774–27 Jan. 1775
GREAT GRIMSBY　　　1780–1784

*bap.* 28 June 1722, o. surv. s. of Francis Eyre, shoemaker of Truro, by his w. Elizabeth Pascoe. *m.* Sarah Prescott, 1da.

Articled in 1737 to a Truro attorney, Eyre qualified in 1744 and subsequently practised in London, specializing in cases concerned with trade and plantation affairs. During the seven years' war, as part owner of at least three ships engaged in privateering, he acquired a considerable fortune, and invested large sums in estates in Jamaica, Gloucestershire and Dorset.

In 1766, having 'for some time past entertained thoughts of coming into Parliament',[1] Eyre heard from a friend, John Spottiswoode, that members of the corporation of Morpeth were seeking a candidate to oppose the Carlisle interest, which was being maintained by restricting the creation of freemen in the borough. On 12 Aug. 1766 Spottiswoode wrote to Robert Trotter, one of the leaders of the opposition in the borough, about Eyre, who, he declared,

would on no consideration submit to represent a venal mercenary body whose only attachment is gold, and who are always at market to be bought and sold . . . Allow me, therefore, to recommend this gentleman as a person of strict honour and probity, a benevolent heart, and blest with a sufficient fortune, one who would cheerfully undertake all your battles against power and riches; and his knowledge in the law, which he has studied and practised for many years, joined with his natural spirit, activity and address, points him out to me as the person you wish for and ought to have.[2]

After some hesitation Eyre agreed to stand, and at his own expense instituted legal proceedings on behalf of the excluded freemen.

The expense and uncertainty [he wrote to Spottiswoode, 11 Nov. 1766] would be alarming and deter perhaps any man alive but the man who does it. He has spoke to several who are very anxious about a seat in Parliament, but they shudder at it . . . however, the greater the danger the greater the honour.[3]

Despite strong opposition from the Carlisle connexion, the rights of the excluded burgesses were established by the court of King's bench, and at a canvass taken late in 1767 Eyre and his colleague Richard Fuller received a 'fair majority'.[4] Eyre was then approached by the Carlisles but at first ignored what he described as their 'soothings, immense promises and threatenings'.[5] However when, shortly before the election, doubts were cast on the legality of votes by freemen chosen less than a year before the election, a compromise was reached, by which Fuller withdrew and Eyre was to be returned with Peter Beckford, the Carlisle candidate. This arrangement was upset by the last minute candidature of Sir Matthew White Ridley, who with Beckford was declared elected by the returning officer. After petitioning unsuccessfully, Eyre began to campaign for the next election. At the poll in 1774 the returning officer once more declared Carlisle's candidates elected, but finally, intimidated by the threats of Eyre's supporters, agreed to return Eyre in place of William Byron. On 8 Dec. 1774, shortly after taking his seat, and while a petition from Byron was pending, Eyre wrote to Trotter that he had spoken in the House,[6]

> very coolly relative to Mr. Grenville's bill, and the public say I got much honour by it as I succeeded. However, I rather lost my temper when I spoke upon my own affair, but it had its effect and got me many friends—Lord John Cavendish, Sir Edward Astley, Mr. Fuller, Mr. Mackworth etc. etc. who all spoke for me.

But on 27 Jan. 1775 he was unseated. In June 1776 Byron died and Eyre immediately prepared for another contest, but he received little encouragement from Trotter, and being already involved in financial difficulties and lawsuits in connexion with his West Indian estates, he withdrew from the contest, and made no further attempt at Morpeth.

Increasingly embarrassed financially, Eyre was forced to sell his Gloucestershire estates, and from 1777 was frequently a defendant in pleas of debts, while in 1777 and 1778 he was imprisoned in the Marshalsea. According to the *English Chronicle*, writing in 1780 or 1781, before the general election of 1780 Eyre, hearing that Charles Anderson Pelham, patron of Grimsby, 'was not decided as to his choice of any particular individual . . . rode post to Grimsby, and paid his compliments to his unknown patron', and having gained Pelham's support was returned unopposed.

In Parliament Eyre voted regularly with Administration till the fall of North; voted against Shelburne's peace preliminaries, 18 Feb. 1783, and for Fox's East India bill, 27 Nov. 1783. In Robinson's list of January 1784 he is classed as 'very hopeful', but in Stockdale's of 19 Mar. as a Foxite. Eyre spoke several times on a variety of subjects, but with parti-

cular reference to West Indian and American affairs.

Eyre did not stand again in 1784, nor apparently at any subsequent election. His fortunes continued to decline, and having disposed of all his estates, he died comparatively poor on 13 Mar. 1797.

[1] Spottiswoode to Trotter, 12 Aug. 1766, Woodman Coll., Blackgate Mus., Newcastle-upon-Tyne. [2] Ibid. [3] Ibid. [4] Fuller to Trotter, 24 Sept. 1767, ibid. [5] Eyre to Trotter, 22 June 1768, ibid. [6] Ibid.

J.M.F.

**EYRE, Samuel** (?1729–95), of New House, nr. Salisbury, Wilts.

SALISBURY    6 Feb. 1765–1768

*b.* ?1729, 1st s. of Kingsmill Eyre, treasurer of Chelsea Hospital, by Susanna Atkinson, wid. of Samuel Keilway. *m.* (1) bef. 1755, Stewart (*d.*2 Jan. 1769), da. of John Russell, consul-gen. at Lisbon, 2da.; (2) 25 June 1769, Margaret Brewster of Bath, *s.p. suc.* fa. 1743, cos. Robert Eyre 1762.

The Eyres were an old Wiltshire family, and had sat in Parliament since Henry VIII's reign for several Wiltshire constituencies. Samuel Eyre was returned for Salisbury in 1765 'after a severe and expensive contest, which occasioned the dismemberment of a considerable portion of family property'.[1] In his election address he promised to be 'steady, uniform, and independent, not biassed by interest, not attached to party'.[2] Rockingham, in his list of July 1765, first classed him as 'doubtful', but next added: 'Lord Folkestone says pro.'

In February 1766 Eyre was reported to be 'very bad with the gout in both his feet at the Bath', and in April 'not yet able to attend Parliament'.[3] His only recorded vote was with the Opposition on the land tax, 27 Feb. 1767. In August 1767 he informed the corporation of Salisbury that owing to ill-health he would not stand at the next general election.[4]

Eyre died 8 Apr. 1795, aged 65.

[1] Hoare, *Wilts* v(2), p. 60. [2] *London Chron.* 7–9 Feb. 1765. [3] Hen. Wyndham to H. P. Wyndham, 9 Feb. and 15 Apr. 1766, Wyndham mss. [4] *Salisbury Jnl.* 31 Aug. 1767.

J.A.C.

**FAIRFAX, Hon. Robert** (1707–93), of Leeds Castle, Kent.[1]

MAIDSTONE    15 Jan. 1740–1741, 1747–1754
KENT                              1754–1768

*b.* 1707, 3rd s. of Thomas, 5th Lord Fairfax [S], by Hon. Catherine Colepeper, da. and h. of Thomas, 2nd Lord Colepeper. *m.* (1) 25 Apr. 1741, Martha (*d.*Sept. 1743), da. and coh. of Anthony Collins of Baddow, Essex, 1s. *d.v.p.*; (2) 15 July 1749, Dorothy, da. of Maudistly Best of Chilham, Kent, sis. of Thomas Best (q.v.), *s.p. suc.* bro. as 7th Lord Fairfax 12 Mar. 1782.
    Cornet, R. Horse Gds. 1726; capt. 1 Life Gds. by July 1739; maj. 1 Life Gds. May 1742; res. Nov. 1745.

In 1754 Fairfax stood for Kent on a joint interest with Lewis Watson, Henry Pelham's son-in-law, against Sir Edward Dering, who had represented the county since 1734. Fairfax was generally regarded as the Duke of Dorset's candidate, and both Dorset and Newcastle had to assist him financially. Henry Pelham guaranteed a loan of £2,000 'on a bad security'[2] and during March 1754 Newcastle had to speak to the King about his affairs.

On 26 July 1759, after repeated appeals to Newcastle for assistance, Fairfax wrote:[3]

> I have been near eighteen years in Parliament, have stood two contested elections . . .which has run me into such difficulties and distress that I shall have an execution next week in my house at Leeds Castle, which will be my absolute ruin and destruction and oblige me to leave the country for ever . . . I therefore most humbly intreat your Grace if you think proper to recommend me to his Majesty's favour and protection for some assistance. I hope my conduct both in Parliament and private life will in some degree induce your Grace to think me worthy of being named to his Majesty, as I have never been troublesome or asked anything for myself but on this occasion.

Newcastle immediately obtained a gratuity of £500 for Fairfax, and a further £500 on 27 May 1760. On 9 Dec. 1760, when candidates for the next election were being considered, Sir George Oxenden wrote to Hardwicke: 'Everyone speaks of Mr. Fairfax as not being capable of being chose on account of the oath [that he possessed £300 p.a. in landed property] to be taken in the House.'[4] Oxenden himself was 'not in a humour to spend money for Mr. Fairax',[5] but liked the other potential candidates less, and it soon became clear that the only way to preserve the peace of the county was to nominate Fairfax again. 'One difficulty now is to qualify Fairfax',[6] wrote Lord George Sackville on 9 Feb.; but by 19 Feb. Fairfax had declared 'that he was qualified to stand for the county', and both the old Members were re-elected unopposed.[7]

Fairfax wrote to Newcastle on 8 Dec. 1761:

> Your Grace has long been acquainted with the unhappy situation of my affairs. Permit me therefore to tell you that they are now come to a crisis, and unless your Grace will please to give me your immediate assistance, I must sink under the weight of my misfortunes, I am neither able to stay here nor go home to my house in the country.[8]

On 10 Dec. Fairfax received £500, and another £500 on 25 May, the day Newcastle resigned.

Fairfax supported the Bute Administration, and in 1763 moved unsuccessfully for an address from Kent approving the treaty of Paris. 'Nobody can wonder at what he did', commented Hardwicke.[9]

Dorset's death in 1765 removed one of his patrons, and Fairfax did not stand in 1768. In the list of pensions drawn up in 1782 he appears as receiving £500 p.a., with a note in Shelburne's hand: 'Has applied for an addition.'

He died 15 Aug. 1793.

[1] Namier, *Structure*, 409–17. [2] Add. 32995, ff. 239–40. [3] Add. 32893, f. 293. [4] Add 35692, f. 434. [5] Add. 32917, f. 263. [6] To Sir H. Erskine, Bute mss. [7] Oxenden to Newcastle, 19 Feb. 1761, Add. 32919, f. 116. [8] Add. 32932, f. 56. [9] Ibid. f. 45.

A.N.N.

**FAIRFORD, Visct.,** *see* **HILL, Arthur**

**FALKLAND, Master of,** *see* **CARY, Lucius Ferdinand**

**FANE, Charles,** 2nd Visct. Fane [I] (after 1707[1]–1766), of Basildon, nr. Reading, Berks.

TAVISTOCK    1734–1747
READING      1754–1761

> *b.* after 1707, 1st s. of Charles, 1st Visct. Fane [I], by Mary, da. of Alexander Stanhope, sis. of James, 1st Earl Stanhope. *m.* 7 June 1749, Susanna, da. of John Marriott of Sturton Hall, Suff., wid. of Sir William Juxon, 2nd Bt., of Little Compton, Glos., *s.p. suc.* fa. 7 July 1744.
> Minister to Tuscany 1734–9.

Fane had for many years been connected with the Duke of Bedford, on whose interest he was returned for Tavistock, and whose political line he followed in the House. In 1754 Fane, whose estates were near Reading, contested the borough, and was returned by a majority of one vote over the Administration candidate John Dodd. When Dodd petitioned against Fane's return, Bedford immediately began organizing support, and on 19 Nov. 1754 wrote to Lord Upper Ossory:[2]

> The great personal friendship I have for Lord Fane, and the great opinion I have of his honesty and abilities, must always make me look upon those who engage at my request in this just defence of his cause, against the arbitrary power of a minister, as personal friends to myself.

Pitt told Fane that if his health permitted, 'there was no cause he would more willingly attend',[3] and on 1 Nov. 1754[4] wrote to Lord Temple:

> I had conversation this day at Reading, with Lord Fane . . . His Lordship I have known from boy's age, and his worth and honour inferior to none. His language is very manly: to your humble servant very obliging upon my public situation.

And on 26 Nov. 1754 John Calcraft wrote to Lord Digby (qq.v.):[5] 'At night was the first committee of elections. Mr. Pitt got up to move for a day for Reading, in order, as is guessed, to make a panegyric on Lord Fane, which he did very finely.'

In Dupplin's list of 1754 Fane is classed as an Opposition Whig. When, towards the end of 1755, Bedford made his peace with Administration Fane followed. Yet he voted with Opposition on the Minorca inquiry, 26 Apr. 1757.[6] There is no record of his having spoken in the House.

Fane did not contest Reading at the general election of 1761, having promised to withdraw if Dodd were chosen (presumably at a borough meeting). He does not seem to have attempted to re-enter Parliament elsewhere. In the remaining years before his death on 24 Jan. 1766 he appears to have been short of money. His nephew Charles de Salis wrote to his mother on 16 Apr. 1766: 'I am afraid . . . all the personal and real estates subject to the payment of Lord Fane's debts do not amount to much more than the lists of debts we have got in.'[7]

[1] His parents were married 12 Dec. 1707. [2] Bedford mss 30, f. 104. [3] Fane to Bedford, 3 Oct. 1754. [4] Grenville Pprs. i. 130. [5] HMC 8th Rep. pt. 1. 225b. [6] Add. 35877, f. 363. [7] Fane de Salis mss.

M.M.D.

**FANE, Francis** (c.1698–1757), of Brympton, nr. Yeovil, Som.

| TAUNTON | 1727–1741 |
| PETERSFIELD | 1741–1747 |
| ILCHESTER | 1747–1754 |
| LYME REGIS | 1754–27 May 1757 |

b. c.1698, 1st s. of Henry Fane of Bristol by Anne, da. of Thomas Scrope, a Bristol merchant, sis. and coh. of John Scrope, M.P., sec. to the Treasury; bro. of Henry and Thomas Fane (qq.v.). educ. King's, Camb. 1715; M. Temple 1714, called 1721. unm. suc. fa. 1726; to estates of his uncle John Scrope 1752.

K.C. 1727; bencher M. Temple 1727; counsel to Board of Trade 1725–46; solicitor-gen. to the Queen 1730–7; chairman of ways and means 1739–51; ld. of Trade 1746–56.

Fane inherited from his uncle a large fortune and the control of both seats at Lyme Regis. From 1757 till at least 1782 the family received £100 p.a. from secret service funds in support of their interest at Lyme Regis.

In 1754 Fane apparently planned to seek re-election at Ilchester, and on 8 Aug. 1753 wrote to Pelham[1] that he found Thomas Lockyer (q.v.), who had command of the borough, willing to stand jointly 'upon condition that I should bear the whole expense'. Fane was ready to pay his own share, 'be it ever so great', but hoped Pelham would not expect him 'to bear the whole expense of keeping this borough out of bad hands', since he feared that with the approaching election at Lyme his expenses would amount to at least £3,000—'a very great sum considering I have no further views and only wish to be in Parliament to give you my poor assistance to support you and your measures'. Fane now moved to Lyme, where he was returned unopposed; and in 1756 he was again employed by Newcastle to negotiate with Lockyer for the return of a Government

candidate at Ilchester. In 1756, when a place was required for Henry Fox's friend W. G. Hamilton, Fane vacated the Board of Trade, and was given a secret service pension of £200 a year for his brother Thomas.

He died 27 May 1757, aged 59.

[1] Newcastle (Clumber) mss.

M.M.D.

**FANE, Francis** (1752–1813), of Spettisbury, nr. Blandford, Dorset.

| LYME REGIS | 11 June 1777–1780 |
| DORCHESTER | 1790–1807 |

b. 5 Dec. 1752, 3rd s. of Henry Fane sen. (q.v.) by his 3rd w. Charlotte Luther. educ. Corpus Christi, Camb. 1768. m. Anne Cooke, s.p. suc. fa. in Somerset and Dorset estates 1777.

Fane was classed as 'pro, absent' on the contractors bill, 12 Feb. 1779, and voted with Administration over Keppel, 3 Mar. 1779. His only other recorded vote was with Opposition on the motion against prorogation, 24 Apr. 1780, but Robinson in his survey of July 1780 described him as 'pro'. He is not known to have spoken in the House during this period.

He died 10 Nov. 1813.

M.M.D.

**FANE, Henry** (1703–77), of Wormsley, nr. Watlington, Bucks.

| LYME REGIS | 13 June 1757–31 May 1777 |

bap. 16 Oct. 1703, 3rd s. of Henry Fane of Bristol, and bro. of Francis and Thomas Fane (qq.v.). m. (1) 17 July 1735, Charlotte (d.29 Sept. 1739), da. of Nicholas Rowe, poet laureate, 1da.; (2) 10 May 1742, Ann (d.1744), da. of Rt. Rev. John Wynn, bp. of Bath and Wells, 1da.; (3) Sept 1748, Charlotte, da. of Richard Luther of Ongar, Essex, sis. and coh. of John Luther (q.v.), 4s. 1da.

Chief clerk of the Treasury 1742–57; clerk to the Privy Council 1756–64.

Fane consistently supported successive Administrations throughout his parliamentary career. On 29 May 1762, three days after Newcastle's resignation, he wrote to the Duke thanking him for the payment for Lyme:[1] 'As he is not well versed in the political system of this country, he cannot tell what to say on the late changes he hears of amongst the great; but wishes his Lyme friends may meet with so good a paymaster as his Grace has been to them.' But he supported Bute's and Grenville's Administrations.

On 16 May 1764 he informed Bedford, president of the Council, that he wished to resign his place as clerk of the Council and to nominate his successor:[2]

As to the thing itself I cannot in honour keep it, as every one will look on me as a person of a mean spirit, to hold such an employment without any other emoluments, when every one of those who *have been* in it, have always enjoyed many other lucrative places; and if in 40 years service to the Crown, no better office has fallen to my lot, it will be imagined that I have behaved myself very ill, to be deserving of no greater favour.

I was bred in the Treasury under Sir Robert Walpole and Mr. Scrope, gentlemen of understanding, and the many years I served under them, made the business of that office very easy to me, and I can never forget it. But I was thrust out from thence, by having people put over my head, without knowledge, and without capacity for what they undertook.

Bedford replied that he regretted the decision, but disclaimed responsibility for 'any want of attention'. Fane wrote again 20 May 1764:[3]

My going out is quite voluntary, free from spleen and malice and purely for the sake of quiet. When I was in the Treasury my uncle set me a pattern of honour which I strictly followed, and could look every suitor in the face, as I was contented with my bare fees, nor was I ever concerned in Exchange Alley; but being contented with a little, and living within my income, with some advantages which accrued to me by marriages, and from my friends at their deaths, I have sufficient to live with independency.

He continued to vote with the court until his death on 31 May 1777.

[1] Add. 32939, f. 93.   [2] Bedford mss 49, f. 186.   [3] Ibid. f. 190.

M.M.D.

**FANE, Hon. Henry** (1739–1802), of Fulbeck, nr. Grantham, Lincs.

LYME REGIS   27 Jan. 1772–4 June 1802

*b.* 4 May 1739, 2nd s. of Thomas, 8th Earl of Westmorland, and bro. of John, Lord Burghersh (qq.v.). *m.* 12 Jan. 1778, Anne, da. and h. of Edward Buckley Batson, London banker, of Avon Tyrell, Hants, 9s. 5da. *suc.* to Fulbeck estate 1787.
    Clerk in the Treasury 1757–62; keeper of the King's private roads 1772.

In 1762 Fane's father unsuccessfully attempted to have him appointed to the commissionership of taxes vacated by his brother.

In Parliament he regularly supported Administration till the fall of North; voted against Shelburne's peace preliminaries, 18 Feb. 1783; was classed as a follower of North by Robinson, March 1783, and voted for Fox's East India bill, 27 Nov. 1783. Robinson in his electoral survey of December 1783 wrote that Lord Westmorland's family was 'in future likely to be more than hopeful with civility and management',[1] but in the Stockdale list of 19 Mar. and in Adam's list of May 1784 Fane appears as 'contra'. He voted against Administration on Richmond's fortifications plan, 27 Feb. 1786; but with them on the Regency, 1788–9. There is no

record of his having spoken in the House before 1790.

He died 4 June 1802.

[1] Laprade, 85.

M.M.D.

**FANE, John,** Lord Burghersh (1728–74), of Apethorpe, Northants.

LYME REGIS   1 Dec. 1762–12 Nov. 1771

*b.* 5 May 1728, 1st s. of Thomas Fane and bro. of Hon. Henry Fane (qq.v.). *educ.* Westminster 1739–45. *m.* (1) 26 Mar. 1758, Augusta (*d.*4 Feb. 1766), da. of Lord Montagu Bertie, gd.-da. of Robert, 1st Duke of Ancaster, 2s. 1da.; (2) 28 May 1767, Lady Susanna Gordon, da. of Cosmo George, 3rd Duke of Gordon [S], 1s. 3da. *suc.* fa. as 9th Earl of Westmorland 12 Nov. 1771.
    Commr. of taxes 1760–2.

Fane supported Administration throughout his parliamentary career. He is not known to have spoken in the House of Commons.

He died 26 Apr. 1774.

M.M.D.

**FANE, Thomas** (1700–71), of Bristol.

LYME REGIS   19 Jan. 1753–26 Aug. 1762

*bap.* 8 Mar. 1700, 2nd s. of Henry Fane of Bristol, and bro. of Francis and Henry Fane (qq.v.). *educ.* M. Temple 1729, called 1759. *m.* 8 Aug. 1727, Elizabeth, da. of William Swymmer, Bristol merchant, wid. of Samuel Kentish, clerk of the court of Chancery, 2s. 2da. *suc.* bro. in Somerset estates 1757; and distant cos. as 8th Earl of Westmorland 26 Aug. 1762.

Fane in his earlier years was an attorney, and clerk to the society of merchant venturers of Bristol.

He supported Administration in the House of Commons, and continued to do so after succeeding to the peerage in 1762. The pension of £200 p.a. given him in 1756[1] he waived after one payment probably in return for the £100 a year which was paid to Lyme. After his brother's death he took his place as Newcastle's intermediary at Ilchester.

He died 25 Nov. 1771.

[1] See FANE, Francis (*d.*1757).

M.M.D.

**FANE, Hon. Thomas** (1760–1807), of Brympton, Som.

LYME REGIS   1784–March 1806

*b.* 6 July 1760, 2nd s. of John Fane, Lord Burghersh (q.v.), by his 1st w. Lady Augusta Bertie. *educ.* Westminster 1772–4. *m.* 27 July 1789, Ann, da. of Richard Lowe of Locko House, Derbys., 2s.
    Ensign 61 Ft. 1775; lt. 1 Ft. 1778; capt. 2 Ft. 1779; maj. 2 Ft. 1783; capt. 2 Ft. Gds. and lt.-col. 1783; ret. 1793.
    Groom of the bedchamber 1793–*d.*

Fane was classed as 'Opposition' in William Adam's list of May 1784. He voted against Pitt on Richmond's fortifications plan, 27 Feb. 1786; but with him on the Regency, 1788–9. There is no record of his having spoken in the House before 1790.

He died 15 Apr. 1807.

M.M.D.

**FANSHAWE, Robert** (1740–1823), of Stone Hall, nr. Plymouth.

PLYMOUTH   1784–Jan. 1790

*b.* 4 Jan. 1740, 2nd s. of R.-Adm. Charles Fanshawe by Elizabeth, da. of Sir John Rogers, 2nd Bt., of Blackford, Devon. *m.* 5 Dec. 1769, Christiana, da. of John Gennys of Whitleigh Hall, Devon, 3s. 9da.
Lt. R.N. 1759; cdr. 1762; capt. 1768.
Commr. of Plymouth dockyard 1790–1815.

Fanshawe was returned for Plymouth on the Admiralty interest as a supporter of Pitt. His only known votes were with Pitt on the Regency; no speech by him is recorded. He vacated his seat on being appointed commissioner of Plymouth dockyard. James Gardner in his *Recollections* describes Fanshawe as 'one of the first seamen in the navy, and one of the bravest officers that ever did honour to the service, a rigid disciplinarian, and to sum up all, a tight hand of the watch, as the saying is'.[1]

Fanshawe died 4 Feb. 1823.

[1] *Navy Rec. Soc.* xxxi. 197–8.

J.B.

**FANSHAWE, Simon** (1716–77), of Fanshawe Gate, Derbys. and Dengie Hall, nr. Southminster, Essex.

OLD SARUM    22 Nov. 1751–1754
GRAMPOUND    1754–1768

*b.* 4 Mar. 1716, 1st s. of Thomas Edward Fanshawe of Great Singleton, Lancs. by Elizabeth, da. of William Snelling of Bromley St. Leonards, by Bow, Mdx. *m.* 10 Oct. 1753, his cos. Althea, da. of his mat. uncle William Snelling of Holborn 1s. 3da. *suc.* fa. 1726.
Comptroller of the household to the Prince of Wales 1756–60; comptroller of the Board of Green Cloth 1761–7.

Fanshawe, one of Lord Lincoln's friends, was returned by Government for Old Sarum. Promised an easy election in 1754, he was nominated by the Treasury for Grampound, paying £1,000 towards the cost of his election. Before the formation of the Prince of Wales's household Lord Waldegrave wrote about him to the Duke of Newcastle, 27 Feb. 1756:[1]

I shall certainly not think of recommending him as a groom of the bedchamber, and he exceeds the weight of an equerry by at least ten stone.
But he is a very proper person to keep his Royal

Highness's cooks under good discipline, to speak with authority to purveyors, wine merchants, cellar men etc., and consequently well qualified to be a clerk of the Green Cloth . . .
. . . I can recommend him as a gentleman who may be depended on, whose conduct in Parliament has ever been clear and uniform, of whom Mr. Pelham had a thorough good opinion, and who I know both in his private and political capacity, to be an honest man and a man of honour.

In 1761 Edward Eliot, now patron of Grampound, demanded £2,000 for returning Fanshawe, who wrote to Newcastle on 16 Jan. 1761: 'I did not believe you designed I should be at such an expense.'[2] But no money was available from the Treasury, and presumably Fanshawe had to pay the £2,000. He was appointed comptroller of the Board of Green Cloth in November.

In Bute's list of 1761 he was described as 'Government, Newcastle', and Newcastle wrote 27 Oct. 1762: 'I have all the reason in the world, from the strongest assurances which he has often given me, to depend upon my good friend Simon Fanshawe.'[3] Yet Newcastle was uneasy about him; in fact Fanshawe's name appears in Fox's list of Members secured for the peace preliminaries, and he remained a constant Government follower; Sandwich described him to Grenville, 12 Mar. 1764, as a 'good politician' with 'great merit'.[4] His only known Opposition vote was on the repeal of the Stamp Act, 22 Feb. 1766. There is no record of his having spoken in Parliament.

In December 1767 Fanshawe was removed from the Board of Green Cloth (Sir William Musgrave supposed, because he could not bring himself into Parliament) and George Selwyn wrote to Lord Carlisle: 'this greasy cook dismissed with a sop, but of what sort I know not'.[5] He received a secret service pension of £800.[6] When Fanshawe did not stand at the general election of 1768, George Selwyn commented: 'so there is so much money saved to him, and his pension consequently in greater security'.[7]

Fanshawe died 1 Jan. 1777.

[1] Add. 32863, ff. 85–86. [2] Add. 32917, f. 359. [3] Add. 32944, f. 106. [4] Grenville mss (JM). [5] HMC Carlisle, 223, 224. [6] Fortescue, v. 467. [7] HMC Carlisle, 227.

M.M.D.

**FARNABY** (afterwards **FARNABY RADCLIFFE**), **Sir Charles,** 3rd Bt. (?1740–98), of Kippington, nr. Sevenoaks, Kent.

EAST GRINSTEAD   30 Dec. 1765–1768
KENT             15 Feb. 1769–1774
HYTHE            1774–20 Oct. 1798

*b.* ?1740, 1st s. of Sir Thomas Farnaby, 2nd Bt., by Mary, da. of Rev. Montagu Lloyd. *educ.* prob. Eton

1747–54. *m.* 12 Aug. 1762, Penelope, da. of John Radcliffe of Hitchin Priory, Herts. sis. and coh. of John Radcliffe (q.v.), wid. of Richard Charlton, London merchant, *s.p. suc.* fa. 24 Mar. 1760. Assumed add. name of Radcliffe 1784.

Farnaby was returned for East Grinstead on the interest of Lord George Sackville, whose politics he followed during this Parliament, voting against the repeal of the Stamp Act, 22 Feb. 1766, and against the higher land tax, 27 Feb. 1767. Newcastle, 2 Mar. 1767, classed him as a friend.

In 1768 Sackville, who claimed a dominant interest at Hythe, and Farnaby jointly contested the borough, but were defeated. In 1769 Farnaby was returned unopposed for Kent in place of John Frederick Sackville, now Duke of Dorset. He no longer followed Lord George's political lead in Parliament; his only reported votes during this Parliament were with Administration—on Brass Crosby, 27 Mar. 1771, and Wilkes, 26 Apr. 1773, and he was listed as 'pro, present' in both Robinson's surveys on the royal marriage bill, March 1772. Farnaby was classed as 'pro' by Robinson in 1774. At the general election that year, and again in 1780 and 1784, he contested Hythe, with ministerial support, and each time topped the poll. Farnaby consistently voted with the Administration till the fall of North, and opposed Shelburne's peace preliminaries, 18 Feb. 1783. He did not vote on Fox's East India bill, 27 Nov. 1783. Robinson, in his survey of December 1783, wrote that Farnaby was 'very steady and always well inclined to support Government': and Farnaby supported Pitt's Administration. There is no record of his having spoken during his 25 years in the House before 1790.

He died 20 Oct. 1798.

M.M.D.

## FARNHAM, Baron, Visct., Earl, *see* MAXWELL

## FARRER, Thomas (1744–97), of Clapham, Yorks.

WAREHAM 1780–1790

*b.* 4 Feb. 1744, 3rd s. of James Farrer of Ingleton, Yorks. by Mary, da. and h. of Thomas Harrison of Ingleton. *unm.*

Farrer was trained as a solicitor in London, where he set up in practice. In 1774 he went to India as private secretary to Colonel Monson, one of the newly appointed members of the supreme council of Bengal. On arrival he started practice as a barrister in the new supreme court of Bengal, and in 1778 returned to England with a fortune said to be £60,000.[1]

II—O*

In 1780 Farrer, recommended by Administration, negotiated his return for Wareham on the Calcraft interest. In Parliament he voted with Opposition on Lowther's motion against the war, 12 Dec. 1781; the censure motion against the Admiralty, 20 Feb. 1782; and Conway's motion against the war, 22 Feb.; but with Administration on Cavendish's censure motion, 8 Mar. Yet on 15 Mar., on Rous's motion, he again voted with Opposition. He voted against Shelburne's peace preliminaries, 18 Feb. 1783; did not vote on Fox's East India bill, 27 Nov. 1783; was classed as 'doubtful, some hope' in Robinson's list of January 1784, and as a Pittite in Stockdale's of 19 Mar. and Adam's of May.

Farrer's only recorded vote in the new Parliament was with Pitt on the first division on the Regency, 16 Dec. 1788, but in the consolidated list drawn up in February 1789 he is counted as having voted with the Opposition. His only reported speeches were on 7 and 11 Feb. 1788, during the debates on the impeachment of Impey, when he told the House that 'he had it in his power to throw more light upon the business of the first charge than any other man could', and agreed to give evidence as an impartial witness but 'would on no account consent to be considered as witness either of the accusers or the accused'.[2]

Farrer died 12 Mar. 1797.

[1] T. Cecil, 2nd Baron Farrer, *Some Farrer Memorials*, 136 seq.
[2] Stockdale, xiii. 171.

I.R.C.

## FAZAKERLEY, Nicholas (?1685–1767), of Prescot, Lancs.

PRESTON 24 Jan. 1732–Feb. 1767

*b.* ?1685, 1st s. of Henry Fazakerley of Fazakerley, Lancs. *educ.* ?Eton 1698; B.N.C. Oxf. 12 Mar. 1702, aged 17; M. Temple 1700, called 1707. *m.* 10 Oct. 1732, Anne, da. of Sir Thomas Lutwyche, M.P., 1s. *d.v.p.* 1da.

Bencher L. Inn 1736, treasurer 1747; counsel to Cambridge Univ. 1738–57; recorder, Preston 1742–67.

In 1754 Fazakerley, an able and successful lawyer, was re-elected for Preston unopposed. Dupplin's list, drawn up shortly afterwards, classes him as 'Tory, against'. Horace Walpole reports that at a meeting of Tories held at the Horn Tavern on 4 Mar. 1755, Fazakerley

informed them that they were to take measures for acting in a body on the Mitchell election: he understood that it was not to be decided by the merits, but was a contest for power between Newcastle and Fox: whoever carried it would be minister: that he for every reason should be for the former.[1]

His only reported speech during this Parliament was on the prize bill, 4 May 1759, when he expressed doubts about some words in a clause, 'and therefore' wrote Hugh Valence Jones to Newcastle, '(after he was gone away) Mr. Attorney-General . . . did with a compliment to Mr. Fazakerley's age and understanding move for leaving out those words as not being necessary, and they were accordingly omitted'.[2]

In Bute's list of December 1761 he was classed as a Tory; he does not appear in Henry Fox's list of Members favourable to the peace preliminaries, but he did not vote against. Jenkinson in the autumn of 1763 classed him as 'doubtful', but on 29 Nov. 1763 Harris, after listing several prominent lawyers who had spoken against allowing privilege for criminal libel, reported that 'Fazakerley should have been added to this list' since he had told a common friend 'that nothing but a violent cold should have hindered him attending the House, and speaking on the subject' on the Administration side. During the debate of 17 Feb. 1764 on general warrants Fazakerley drew on his experience of the King's bench to defend general warrants.[3] In Rockingham's list of July 1765 he was classed as 'contra', and in that of November 1766 as 'Tory'. He died in February 1767.

[1] *Mems. Geo. II*, ii. 12. [2] Add. 32890, f. 488. [3] Harris's 'Debates'.

M.M.D.

## FEILDE, Paul (1711–83), of Stanstead Abbots, Herts.

HERTFORD     15 Jan. 1770–1780

*bap.* 6 Oct. 1711, 4th s. of Edmund Feilde of Stanstead Abbots by Martha, da. of James Paul of Braywick, Berks. *educ.* Westminster 1722; L. Inn 1724, called 1737. *m.* 12 Feb. 1763, Jane, da. of John Wowen, sugar refiner, of Hackney, Mdx., *s.p. suc.* bro. 1762.
Recorder, Hertford 1762–*d.*

Feilde's father was a cousin of Thomas Plumer Byde, M.P. for Hertfordshire 1761–8; and his great-grandfather had represented Hertford under Charles II. Feilde was a practising barrister, at least until he succeeded to the family estates, and a London magistrate. He was returned for Hertford in 1770 after a contest, presumably with the support of the corporation and probably also of the Dissenters.[1]

According to his monumental inscription in Stanstead church:[2]

He was an assiduous and able Member of Parliament, actuated by the purest patriotism, attached to no party, until a firm conviction engaged him in an early and strenuous opposition to the American war.

Isaac Barré, reporting to Chatham the debate of 7 Mar. 1771 on Dowdeswell's jury bill,[3] described Feilde as 'a friend of the Rockinghams'. But Feilde had not hitherto voted with the Opposition, was never claimed by Rockingham as a follower, and in this debate took a line opposite to that of the Rockinghams. Robinson, in his first survey on the royal marriage bill, classed him as 'doubtful, present', in the second as 'contra, present'. In the remaining divisions of this Parliament for which lists are available, Feilde voted with the Opposition; and in September 1774 was classed by Robinson as 'contra'. He was an advocate of the booksellers' right to perpetual copyright, and introduced the unsuccessful bill of March 1774.

Feilde was returned unopposed at the general election of 1774. 'He approved of the principles of the Declaratory Act', he said on 6 April 1778,[4] but condemned the subsequent conduct towards America; and on 14 April spoke for Savile's motion for the repeal of the Quebec Act. His last recorded speech in the House was on 15 April 1778, and his last recorded vote on 4 Dec. (on Coke's motion on the conciliation commission). Early in 1780 he was reported to be in bad health; did not stand at the general election; and died on 2 Feb. 1783.

[1] Feilde to Charles Yorke, 24 Sept. 1769, Add. 35639, f. 124. [2] Clutterbuck, *Herts.* iii. 249. [3] *Chatham Corresp.* iv. 110. [4] Stockdale, viii. 205.

J.B.

## FEILDING, William Robert, Visct. Feilding (1760–99).

BERE ALSTON     2 Dec. 1780–1790
NEWPORT                    1790–1796

*b.* 15 June 1760, 1st s. of Basil, 6th Earl of Denbigh, by Mary, da. and coh. of Sir John Cotton, 6th Bt. *m.* 26 Apr. 1791, Anne Catherine, da. of Thomas Jelf Powys of Berwick House, Salop., 3s. 3da.
Lt. 7 Ft. 1777; capt. 75 Ft. 1778; capt. 3 Drag. Gds. 1779; lt.-col. 22 Lt. Drag. 1782; raised 22 Regt. of Lt. Drag. 1794, of which he was col. –*d.*; maj.-gen. 1795.

At the by-election of December 1780 Feilding, while under age, was returned unopposed for Bere Alston on the Duke of Northumberland's interest. In Parliament he steadily supported North's Administration till its fall. On 8 May 1781, in his first reported speech, he condemned the Yorkshire reform petitions as 'a very dangerous spirit of innovation . . . He did not think the object of the reform, even if quietly effected, a subject so much to be desired; it must at least be done with great caution.' Nor did he believe that ministerial influence had increased, in fact 'a new third party' had

sprung up in that House, unknown to former periods. He meant the country gentlemen; the balance of power in that House was taken out of the hands of the minister, and placed in those of the country gentlemen . . . men neither to be frowned into servility nor hussaed into faction; by the support of these men, and not as had been asserted, by the low arts of corruption, did the present minister stand.[1]

According to Horace Walpole,[2] Feilding was to have moved the Address of thanks for the King's speech in November 1781, but when its optimistic tone was scarcely modified at the news of Cornwallis's defeat at Yorktown, he 'avoided being as ridiculous as the royal speech by excusing himself'. Feilding voted for Shelburne's peace preliminaries, 18 Feb. 1783, and did not vote on Fox's East India bill, 27 Nov. 1783. He was classed as an Administration supporter in Robinson's list of January 1784, in Stockdale's of 19 Mar., and Adam's in May. At the general election he was again returned for Bere Alston by Northumberland. On 27 Nov. 1787 Feilding praised Pitt's successful policy in Holland, declaring that he 'exulted in the respectable figure Great Britain had made in the eyes of Europe by her well-timed and successful exertions'.[3] But although Lord Lovaine, who in 1786 had inherited Bere Alston from his father, the 1st Duke of Northumberland, sided with Pitt, Feilding voted with the Opposition over the Regency, 1788-9, and on 22 Dec. 1788 suggested that 'an immediate declaration be made of the Prince of Wales, Regent'—

> A Prince born among us, whose filial tenderness and natural goodness of heart had already endeared him to all who knew him, and gave the best promise of being as anxious with the legislature in securing his father's rights as . . . Parliament could wish or expect.[4]

In 1790 he was returned for Newport, by Lovaine's brother, the 2nd Duke of Northumberland, who was in opposition to Pitt.

Feilding died *v.p.* 8 Aug. 1799.

[1] Debrett, iii. 222-5. [2] *Last Jnls.* ii. 378. [3] Stockdale, xiii. 8-10. [4] Stockdale, xvi. 151-2.

M.M.D.

### FELLOWES, Coulson (1696-1769), of Ramsey Abbey, Hunts.

HUNTINGDONSHIRE    1741-1761

> *b.* 12 Oct. 1696, 1st s. of William Fellowes of Eggesford, Devon by Mary, da. and h. of Joseph Martin of London. *educ.* Ch. Ch. Oxf. 1716; L. Inn 1714, called 1723; Grand Tour (France, Italy) c.1724. *m.* 20 Apr. 1725, Urania, da. of Francis Herbert, M.P., of Oakley Park, Salop, sis. of Henry Arthur Herbert, M.P., 1st Earl of Powis, 2s. 3da. *suc.* fa. 19 Jan. 1724.
> Sheriff, Devon 1727-8.

Fellowes's grandfather and great-grandfather were London merchants, and he himself a comparative newcomer in Huntingdonshire. In 1754 he was returned unopposed for the county, together with Sandwich's candidate, Lord Carysfort. In Dupplin's list Fellowes was classed as an Opposition Whig.

What line he followed after the Bedfords had rejoined the Government at the end of 1755, is uncertain: not one speech or vote of his is recorded in this Parliament.

In 1761 Lord Mandeville, son of the Duke of Manchester, having come of age, was a candidate; and on 12 July 1759 both Sandwich and Carysfort wrote to Bedford about the danger of a contest, and asked for his support.[1] Sandwich claimed that they both had told Fellowes 'that if he chose to stand [presumably against Mandeville] we were ready to support him to the utmost of our power; this proposal he absolutely declined, and as I understood told me he would not stand at all, but wait for a more favourable opportunity'. Now he seemed inclined to join Manchester—'I could get nothing more from him than that I had misunderstood him as to his intention of standing, and that he could not promise he would not join the other party.' Thus released of 'any tenderness for Mr. Fellowes', they both thought 'that a negotiation shall be tried to compromise things with the Duke of Manchester; for the trouble and expense of a contest is what we both dread.' Bedford, who had long been on good terms with Fellowes, would not decide against him without first hearing him, nor oppose the son of Manchester, with whose electoral interest he had to count in Bedfordshire; but always ready to support one candidate of Sandwich's for Huntingdonshire, Bedford wished for an agreement between him and Manchester. This was concluded, and Carysfort and Mandeville were returned unopposed; Fellowes did not stand either in 1761 or after, but the greatest care was taken by Sandwich to retain his support.[2]

A highly laudatory, yet not uncritical, character sketch of Coulson Fellowes, written toward the end of his life, was printed by John Nichols[3] from the mss of the Rev. John Jones (1700-70):[4]

> He is a gentleman of great worth in all respects . . . a man of extensive knowledge in almost all parts of learning . . . well acquainted with the real interests of these kingdoms, their connexions in trade, commerce, and interest with other nations . . .
> Mr. Fellowes is generally allowed to be one of the best politicians in this kingdom, and an excellent calculator in matters of loss and profit. His successful management in regard to the public funds, where his own interest is concerned, demonstrates this. He is said to be (and very probably is) immensely rich. The principal fault which is ascribed to him is too much parsimoniousness . . .
> He travelled, in his younger days, into foreign parts; and was at Rome at the same time with Dr. [Conyers] Middleton,[5] whom he often accompanied in viewing the curiosities of that city and the country surrounding it . . . He is both ingenious, lively, cheerful, and extremely well versed in history, ancient and modern . . . has also a considerable command of the classics.

He is uncommonly absteminous . . . drinks only water . . .

He died 23 Feb. 1769.

[1] Bedford mss 39, f. 252; 40, f. 8. [2] Sandwich to Wm. Fellowes, 7 Dec. 1765, Sandwich mss. [3] *Literary Anecs.* i. 589–90 [4] About him see *DNB.* [5] For his travels see Nichols, v. 410–11.

L.B.N.

## FELLOWES, William (?1726–1804), of Ramsey Abbey, Hunts.

LUDLOW 1768–1774
ANDOVER 11 Aug. 1784–1796

*b.* ?1726, 1st s. of Coulson Fellowes (q.v.). *educ.* Dalston; St. John's, Camb. 26 June 1744, aged 17. *m.* 17 May 1768, Lavinia, da. and coh. of James Smyth of St. Audries, Som., 3s. 2da. *suc.* fa. 23 Feb. 1769. His sis. m. 1763, John Wallop, 2nd Earl of Portsmouth.

Sheriff, Hunts. and Cambs. 1779–80.

Fellowes was returned unopposed at Ludlow on the interest of his uncle Lord Powis. On 2 Feb. 1769, over Wilkes's libel, he voted with the Opposition, but next day supported Administration over his expulsion, and henceforward consistently voted with them except on the petition of the naval captains, 9 Feb. 1773, when he appears in George III's list as a friend voting against. He did not stand in 1774, but in return for supporting Lord Hinchingbrooke in Huntingdonshire, received a promise from Lord Sandwich 'that if . . . upon any vacancy made by his means, Lord Hinchingbrooke should not be a candidate for the county, you will be entitled to his and my interest in his stead, and to every effectual support he or I can give you'.[1] No such vacancy occurred before 1792, and in 1784 Fellowes was returned unopposed for Andover on the interest of his brother-in-law Lord Portsmouth. His only reported vote in this Parliament was with Administration over the Regency, 16 Dec. 1788. There is no record of his having spoken in the House.

He died 4 Feb. 1804.

[1] Sandwich mss.

M.M.D.

## FENTON CAWTHORNE, John (1753–1831), of Wyreside, Lancs.

LINCOLN 27 Jan. 1783–2 May 1796
LANCASTER 1806–1807, 1812–1818, 1820–
1 Mar. 1831

*b.* 5 Jan. 1753, 1st s. of James Fenton, recorder of Lancaster 1758–91, by Elizabeth, sis. and coh. of John Cawthorne of Wyreside. *educ.* Queen's, Oxf. 1771; G. Inn 1792. *m.* 22 Aug. 1778, Frances, da. and coh. of J. H. Delaval (q.v.). *suc.* to Cawthorne estates 1781 and took add. name of Cawthorne; and fa. 1791.

Recorder, Lancaster 1791–6; col. Westminster militia 1791, cashiered for embezzlement 1796.

After unsuccessfully contesting Preston in 1780, Cawthorne was returned for Lincoln on the interest of his father-in-law, J. H. Delaval, whose political lead he followed. Cawthorne supported North; voted against Shelburne's peace preliminaries, 18 Feb. 1783, for Fox's India bill, and against Pitt's Government; and after the general election of 1784 was listed by William Adam with Opposition. But when in the new House Delaval declared his adherence to Pitt, Cawthorne again followed him; defended Delaval when attacked by Philip Francis (q.v.) for changing sides, 16 July 1784;[1] and on 21 Jan. 1790 in a few sentences seconded the Address.[2] Before 1790 only two other interventions of his in debate are noted, on technical points concerning election petitions.

Cawthorne died 1 Mar. 1831.

[1] Debrett, xvi. 72; Stockdale, iii. 95. [2] Stockdale, xix. 5.

L.B.N.

## FENWICK, Thomas (?1729–1794), of Kentmere, Westmld.

WESTMORLAND 1768–1774

*b.* ?1729, 2nd s. of Thomas Wilson, attorney, of Kendal by Dorothy, da. of John Fenwick of Nunriding, Northumb., sis. of Robert Fenwick M.P., of Burrow, Lancs. *educ.* Sedbergh; St. John's, Camb. 27 Feb. 1749, aged 19; L. Inn 1751, called 1756. *unm. suc.* 1757, on *d.* of his bro. to estates of his maternal uncle, and took name of Fenwick.

Fenwick was suggested by Lord Suffolk as a candidate for Westmorland as early as July 1767; opposition from leading families prevented his immediate nomination, but in March 1768 he was approached by a group of Carlisle gentlemen who were willing to subscribe 'a pretty considerable sum' towards his expenses if he would stand for Westmorland against Sir James Lowther's candidates. He also was promised the Duke of Portland's backing and financial support, and agreed to stand. He was returned by a majority of 81 votes over Lowther's second candidate. In spite of financial help Fenwick found his election expenses far greater than he had expected, and wrote to Portland, 11 Mar. 1769, that he was forced to apply 'for any sum which your Grace may think proper to give me a draught for'.[1]

All Fenwick's reported votes were with the Opposition. But he does not appear in the minority lists of 1770 and 1771; and in Robinson's first survey on the royal marriage bill, March 1772, is described as 'contra' with the note 'may attend, sick', in the second, 8 Mar., as 'contra, sick, present'. He voted with the Opposition on Grenville's Election Act, 25 Feb. 1774, and was classed by Robinson as 'contra', September 1774. He is not known to have spoken in the House.

In 1774 Fenwick again stood for Westmorland in opposition to Sir James Lowther, but he had damaged his never very strong position in the county by unjust claims to the property of his brother's widow, and this time did not receive support from the Carlisle gentlemen. He was defeated, and apparently never again stood for Parliament.

He died 3 Apr. 1794.

[1] Portland mss.

M.M.D.

## FERGUSON, James (1735–1820), of Pitfour, Aberdeen.

BANFFSHIRE            22 Jan. 1789–1790
ABERDEENSHIRE            1790–6 Sept. 1820

*b.* 25 May 1735, 1st s. of James Ferguson of Pitfour, S.C.J. (Lord Pitfour), by Hon. Anne Murray, da. of Alexander, 4th Lord Elibank [S]. *educ.* Edinburgh Univ.; adv. 1757; Grand Tour 1758. *unm. suc.* fa. 25 June 1777.

Ferguson's father, a distinguished lawyer, purchased in 1764 part of Earl Marischal's estates and thus acquired a major interest in Banffshire and Aberdeenshire. His son, a boon companion of Henry Dundas, was mentioned in Robinson's survey of 1780 as candidate for either Elginshire or Aberdeenshire, should Alexander Garden withdraw. On Garden's death in 1785 Ferguson unsuccessfully contested Aberdeenshire, with the support of Dundas and the Duke of Gordon, against Lord Fife's candidate, George Skene. Negotiations followed for an electoral compromise between Gordon and Fife, in consequence of which Ferguson was returned on Fife's interest at a by-election for Banffshire in January 1789.

William Adam in 1788 described Ferguson as an able man, 'of real good sense, but indolent', who wished for a judge's gown rather than a political career.[1]

Ferguson died 6 Sept. 1820.

[1] *Pol. State of Scotland*, 9, 54.

E.H.-G.

## FERGUSSON, Sir Adam, 3rd Bt. (1733–1813), of Kilkerran, Ayr.

AYRSHIRE            1774–1780, 2 Apr. 1781–1784
EDINBURGH            31 Aug. 1784–1790
AYRSHIRE            1790–1796

*b.* 7 May 1733, 1st surv. s. of Sir James Fergusson, 2nd Bt., M.P., of Kilkerran, S.C.J. (Lord Kilkerran), by Jean, da. of James, Visct. Maitland and gd.-da. of John, 5th Earl of Lauderdale [S]. *educ.* Maybole sch.; Edinburgh Univ.; adv. 1755; Brussels 1756–7; Grand Tour 1757–8. *unm. suc.* fa. 20 Jan. 1759.
    Ld. of Trade July 1781–May 1782.

Fergusson was an able, sober, scholarly young man of high moral character and attractive, if somewhat humourless, personality. On succeeding to his paternal estates he, like his close friend George Dempster, became ambitious of entering Parliament, and by the end of 1759 was the Argyll candidate for Ayr Burghs in opposition to Patrick Craufurd, supported by Bute. His success seemed assured until, in the new reign, Argyll and Bute composed their quarrel and agreed to sponsor a candidate acceptable to them both. Fergusson's refusal to withdraw embarrassed Argyll and enraged Eglintoun and other Bute supporters against 'that absurd boy',[1] who, despite strong pressure and the persuasions of his friend Lord Loudoun, did not give way until ten days before the election.[2] Mortified by this experience, Fergusson for some years abandoned political ambitions, devoted himself to his estates and to his bar practice in which he gained great reputation as counsel for the Hamiltons in the Douglas cause and for his ward, the young Countess of Sutherland, in her claim to the peerage. Although 'talked of' as a candidate for Ayrshire at the 1768 election,[3] Fergusson made no attempt to stand, but from 1770 launched a vigorous campaign in the county and 'began beating about for an independent party'.[4] Loudoun's alliance with Eglintoun and Cassillis offended many freeholders, and Fergusson now stood forth as 'a champion of the county against aristocratic influence'.[5] He was backed by Lord President Robert Dundas and his brother Henry Dundas who, to provide his friend with a seat in any event, negotiated an agreement between Buccleuch and the Hamilton interest to bring him in for Linlithgow Burghs if defeated in Ayrshire.[6] Fergusson also stood for Wick Burghs; but these precautions proved unnecessary. He was triumphantly returned for Ayrshire on the votes of his independent 'democratical coalition'.

In Parliament Fergusson, although in general a Government supporter, showed a certain independence. In his first recorded speech, 26 Oct. 1775, he advocated strong measures against America, urging that in defence of the authority of Parliament all party divisions should be laid aside; but on 24 Nov., as a strict constitutionalist, insisted that the Government must seek indemnity for sending Hanoverian troops to Gibraltar and Minorca without consent of Parliament.[7] Although an infrequent speaker, Fergusson acquired a reputation as an active and industrious committee man and, closely allied with Dundas, was mentioned in 1776 as a member of the group who 'were called or called themselves' the Scotch ministry.[8] A consistent advocate since 1759 of a Scottish militia, he with Dundas and William Pulteney revised the draft of Mountstuart's bill,[9] and in the debates of 5 and 12 Mar. 1776 vigorously opposed the suggestion that Scotland should pay for her own militia, urging the abolition of all national distinctions.[10]

Fergusson voted against Administration, 12 Feb. 1779, on the contractors bill, and also on 3 Mar. over Keppel. He spoke on 8 Mar. in support of the bill for the relief of Protestant Dissenters, contrasting the toleration allowed Episcopalians in Scotland with that of Presbyterians in England. Thereafter he intervened more frequently in debate; opposed, 26 Mar., Hartley's motion to refuse money for army extraordinaries, while advocating a committee to consider better methods of dealing with public accounts; supported the bill to prevent adultery, 4 May 1779; and caused the Government some embarrassment on 2 July 1779 by raising the constitutional issue of whether the Lords had any right to amend a militia bill which, he maintained, was essentially a money bill.[11]

In a rare intervention in a major American debate he opposed on 17 June 1779 Cavendish's motion for concentrating all available forces against France and thereafter does not appear to have wavered in his loyalty to Administration. He spoke on 22 Mar. 1780 in defence of William Fullarton after his duel with Shelburne, opposed Crewe's bill for disfranchising revenue officers, 13 Apr., and warmly justified concessions to Scotland on the malt tax.[12]

At the general election Fergusson's claim to independence was scorned by Sir Lawrence Dundas, who asserted he was 'as hackney a ministerial Member as ever went from Scotland'.[13] Although invited to stand for Glasgow Burghs,[14] Fergusson remained faithful to Ayrshire where the peers' coalition had set up Hugh Montgomerie against him. Despite the friendship of North and Dundas he was defeated, but returned on petition.

Having already shown concern about the government of India and submitted plans to North for its reform,[15] he was nominated a member of the secret committee appointed under the chairmanship of Dundas to inquire into the causes of the war in the Carnatic. When in July Dundas secured his appointment to the Board of Trade, Sir Adam was again faced with a contested election, which was only averted by the direct intervention of North, who wrote to Loudoun, 19 July:[16]

> I thought it my duty to the King to acquire for his service so able and respectable a man as Sir Adam Fergusson, and I think it my duty to Sir Adam to do everything in my power to prevent his being involved in difficulties . . . I should therefore feel it as the most sensible obligation if you and your noble friends will permit Sir Adam to be re-elected upon this occasion without opposition.

Similar letters to Eglintoun and Cassillis resulted in the reluctant withdrawal of Montgomerie, and on 16 Aug. Sir Adam was returned unopposed. His tenure of office was brief, but from 25 Jan. 1782 he was assiduous in attendance at the Board until its last meeting on 1 May.

A silent supporter of North until his fall, Fergusson under the Rockingham Administration confined his contributions in debate to such matters as the effect on Scotland of the turnpike tax bill, the prohibition of home grown tobacco, and the new soap duties. In Indian affairs he continued active on the secret committee, unsuccessfully opposed on 24 Apr., with his friends Dempster and Pulteney, the select committee's resolution to censure Laurence Sulivan; and was righteously indignant when the East India Company rejected the Commons resolution for the recall of Warren Hastings.[17]

Under the Shelburne Administration he took a line over the peace treaty independent of Dundas; pleaded the cause of the loyalists and supported the motion for copies of the instructions given to Richard Oswald concerning them. He did not vote in the division of 18 Feb. but on 21 Feb. declared his view that the King had gone further than he had any authority to do by ceding part of Quebec and Nova Scotia to the Americans.[18] In March Robinson listed him as attached to North, but 'doubtful'.

Under the Coalition he remained for a time apparently uncommitted; spoke frequently in the budget debates in support of Scottish interests, and while professing impartiality on the question of the tellership of the Exchequer granted to Dundas's friend Chancellor Thurlow, 'reasoned shrewdly' on 7 July 1783 that it was unjust to include his office in the projected Exchequer reforms. He supported Lord John Cavendish's motion for a new commission to inquire into loyalist claims, but feared lest if Parliament gave relief the Americans might evade their obligations under the peace treaty.[19]

His views were undoubtedly influenced by his friendship with Dundas, whom he eventually followed into opposition, voting against Fox's East India bill, 27 Nov. 1783. On the dismissal of the Coalition he supported Pitt; condemned on 27 Feb. the obstructive tactics of the Opposition, and on 5 Mar. attacked Fox for delaying the passage of the mutiny bill.[20]

At the general election Fergusson was again opposed by Montgomerie and, after negotiations between Dundas and the Ayrshire peers, decided to withdraw under an agreement that he should represent the county in the following Parliament and meanwhile be returned for a safe seat. Dundas duly arranged the retirement of James Hunter Blair from

Edinburgh City and secured the seat for Fergusson in August 1784.

While his connexion with Dundas gave him a certain importance, he received no office. He voted 18 Apr. 1785 for parliamentary reform, and for Pitt's Irish propositions; but his rare speeches were concerned mainly with questions of parliamentary procedure, election and Scottish affairs. His legal arguments in favour of hawkers and pedlars, of a reduction in the coal tax, of the Scottish malt distillery, were 'able and ingenious', but only on such questions did he venture to disagree with Administration.[21] From the formation of the British Fishery Society in 1786 he was active in furthering the establishment of settlements in the Hebrides and increased his reputation as an astute businessman and practical humanitarian.[22]

On the Regency question he voted, 16 Dec. 1788, with Administration, but in January 1789 on at least one occasion divided with Opposition. His bitter enemy, James Boswell, wrote, 23 Jan.:[23] 'Sir Adam Fergusson's having gone against Pitt is *capital* as the phrase is. He means to prevent the regency ministry from being against him in Ayrshire.' Fergusson however redeemed this aberration by his vote of 11 Feb., and remained a consistent Government supporter until the end of the Parliament.

He died 25 Sept. 1813.

[1] W. Mure to Bute, 1 Apr. 1761, Bute mss. [2] Sir Harry Erskine, Eglintoun, Mure, Loudoun, Argyll to Bute, February–April 1761, Bute mss; Loudoun's corresp. with Fergusson, Frederick Campbell, and others, Loudoun mss. [3] Loudoun to Bute, 28 Aug. 1766, Bute mss; Fergusson to Loudoun, 14 Nov. 1767, Loudoun mss. [4] Stair to Loudoun, 28 July 1771, ibid. [5] Boswell, *Johnson*, v. 354; James Fergusson, 'Making Interest in Scottish County Elections', *SHR* 1947, pp. 128–9. [6] Corresp. on Linlithgow Burghs 1774, Buccleuch mss. [7] Almon, iii. 10–14. [8] Boswell, *Private Pprs.* xi. 163. [9] Dempster to Carlyle, undated (early 1776), Carlyle mss, Edin. Univ. Lib. [10] Almon, iii. 397, 413. [11] Ibid. xii. 107–8, 256, 398; xiv. 539, 549. [12] Fortescue, iv. 360; Almon, xvii. 409, 507, 522, 642, 693. [13] Boswell, *Private Pprs.* xiv. 132–3. [14] Letters of G. Dempster, 110. [15] S. Weitzman, *Warren Hastings & Philip Francis*, 138. [16] Loudoun mss. [17] Debrett, vii. 75, 229, 244, 264, 279. [18] Ibid. ix. 210, 316. [19] Ibid. 124, 231, 267; x. 206, 308. [20] Ibid. xii. 222, 257. [21] Stockdale, viii. 360–70; ix. 137; xiii. 133, 180; xv. 52. [22] *Letters of G. Dempster*, 153, 163, 169–71, 176–8. [23] *Private Pprs.* xvii. 139.

E.H.-G.

## FETHERSTONHAUGH, Sir Henry, 2nd Bt. (1754–1846), of Uppark, Suss.

PORTSMOUTH 5 June 1782–1796

*b.* 22 Dec. 1754, o.s. of Sir Matthew Fetherstonhaugh, 1st Bt. (q.v.). *educ.* Eton 1766–71; Univ. Coll. Oxf. 1772; Grand Tour (Geneva, Italy, Paris) 1775–6. *m.* 12 Sept. 1825, when over 70, Mary Ann Bullock, his head dairy maid, aged 18, *s.p.* *suc.* fa. 18 Mar. 1774.

Edward Gibbon, a friend and neighbour of the family, wrote about Henry Fetherstonhaugh a month after his father's death: 'At present everything carries the appearance of sobriety and economy. The baronet, instead of flying to Paris and Rome, returns to his college at Oxford, and even the house at Whitehall is to be let.'[1] But on 31 Jan. 1775, after a visit to Uppark: 'Sir Henry is very civil and good-humoured. But from the unavoidable temper of youth I fear he will cost many a tear to Lady F. She consults everybody, but has neither authority nor plan.' Emma Hart—'Nelson's Emma' —was established near Uppark as his mistress in 1780, an early and rather short stage in her chequered career. In August 1784 Mrs. Elizabeth Montagu wrote to her sister Sarah Scott:[2]

The Prince of Wales has been at Sir Henry Fetherstone's. He stayed three days, during which they had races of all sorts, fine horses, ponies, cart-horses, women, and men in sacks, with various other divertimenti fit for children of six foot high. I hear he was much delighted, and said that Newmarket races were dull in comparison. They were within three or four miles of us, but no one except servants went from hence, nor do I find that any ladies of fashion in the town were at them. Poor Lady Fetherstone, Sir Harry's mother, fled from the riot to Mr. Iremonger's.

Fetherstonhaugh being a minor at his father's death, Joshua Iremonger, half-brother of his mother, contested Portsmouth; he had the support of the Dissenters and Radicals led by John Carter but was defeated by the Government candidate at the by-election of 29 Mar. 1774 and at the general election in October, as was Henry Fetherstonhaugh at the by-election of 26 Nov. 1777 and in 1780. The fall of the North Administration gave the whip hand to the opposition party at Portsmouth, and to Fetherstonhaugh his chance on a vacancy in May 1782. Keppel, first lord of the Admiralty, promised him Government support; and Rockingham wrote to him on 23 May: 'My opinion indeed was, even before your application, that from *many* circumstances which had passed, that *you* had a strong claim and was entitled to have preference at this time.'[3] Fetherstonhaugh was returned unopposed.

In July 1782 he adhered to Charles James Fox; voted against Shelburne's peace preliminaries; for Pitt's parliamentary reform, 7 May 1783; did not vote on Fox's East India bill; but remained one of his supporters. 'The electors', wrote Robinson in December 1783, 'will again, it is apprehended, choose Sir H. Fetherstone';[4] Administration therefore ran only one candidate; and the election was unopposed. Fetherstonhaugh, adhering to the Prince of Wales, remained in opposition to Pitt; voted against his Irish propositions, 13 May 1785; and when these came once more before the House, the Prince wrote to Fetherstonhaugh from Brighton, 20 July:[5]

If you have not already got a pair off in this business I would go to London as tonight and endeavour to get one tomorrow morning, which means you will be back again with us in the evening and ready for the terrible

terrible work with the high bred cattle [horse races] that is to ensue the next morning. Pray take [Thomas] Onslow with you upon the same errand.

Even during the Regency crisis Fetherstonhaugh seems to have found steady attendance excessively irksome. He paired on 16 Dec. 1788; and on Friday the 19th Portland, having heard that Fetherstonhaugh meant 'to go into the country and leave the business of the Regency', expostulated with him: 'many important questions must arise . . . and . . . the resistance which our friends will make to them will probably be successful if they but think it worth while to oppose them in full force of numbers'.[6]

There is no record of Fetherstonhaugh having spoken in the House.

He died 24 Oct. 1846.

[1] To his stepmother, 23 Apr. 1774. [2] R. Blunt, *Mrs. Montagu*, ii. 181. [3] Fetherstonhaugh mss at Uppark. [4] Laprade, 88. [5] Fetherstonhaugh mss. [6] Ibid.

L.B.N.

## FETHERSTONHAUGH, Sir Matthew, 1st Bt. (?1714–74), of Uppark, Suss.

| | |
|---|---|
| MORPETH | 29 Nov. 1755–1761 |
| PORTSMOUTH | 1761–18 Mar. 1774 |

*b.* ?1714, 1st s. of Matthew Fetherstonhaugh, merchant, hostman and twice mayor of Newcastle-upon-Tyne, by Sarah, da. and h. of Robert Browne. *m.* 24 Dec. 1746, Sarah, da. of Christopher Lethieullier, sis. of Benjamin Lethieullier (q.v.), half-sis. of Joshua Iremonger of Wherwell, Hants, 1s. *suc.* 1746 to the estates in Essex, Herts., Mdx. and the City of London, of Sir Henry Fetherston, 2nd and last Bt., said to be worth £400,000; purchased Uppark 1747 for £19,000. *suc.* fa. in estates in Northumb., Kent and Mdx. 1762; *cr.* Bt. 3 Jan. 1747.

Fetherstonhaugh and his wife spent 1749–52 travelling in France, Italy, and Austria. Horace Mann wrote to Thomas Pelham on 17 Oct. 1750, about an invitation he had to dine with them:[1]

Perhaps you do not know who the Fetherstones are. Sir Matthew is a very sick baronet . . . my lady is sister to Mr. Iremonger and Mr. Lethieullier who are here and occupying your house. They are all vastly rich.

From the journey Fetherstonhaugh brought back valuable collections of pictures, tapestries, china, etc. In 1754 he built for himself a house in Whitehall, now the Scottish Office, for nearly £6,000.

The same year he stood for Parliament at Andover where Iremonger had a considerable interest; Fetherstonhaugh was going 'to try what his friends can do for him', and had the fullest support from Newcastle. He failed, and wrote to Newcastle on the death of William Hay in June 1755, asking to succeed him at Seaford.[2] On being told that the seat was promised to James Peachey he seemed piqued at that preference and uncertain

whether he would wish to come in for another place;[3] and when on 1 Nov. Newcastle informed him through John Page of an expected vacancy at Tiverton where 'there can be no doubt of success with very little expense', Fetherstonhaugh did not relish the idea, nor, wrote Page, was likely to relish the suggestion of any other constituency: 'I think he is vexed with himself for having stooped to ask what he finds he has not weight enough to carry.' But when, on Robert Ord being appointed chief baron of the Exchequer in Scotland, Newcastle suggested that Fetherstonhaugh should succeed him at Morpeth (on Lord Carlisle's interest), Fetherstonhaugh replied, 17 Nov., that next to Seaford nothing could be 'more satisfactory than the serving for one in Northumberland'. Still, he would not spend more than £500 or £600, and wished to avoid a journey to Northumberland: or else the expense should be included in the sum named above. Newcastle replied on the 19th:

My Lord Carlisle has sent me word by Mr. Ord that the expense is £600 and no more. Mr. Ord says there must be a dinner, which can't exceed £20. Upon that we shall not differ . . . you need not give yourself the trouble of a journey.

Fetherstonhaugh was returned unopposed, 29 Nov. 1755.[4]

In April 1759, on a vacancy in the county representation of Essex, Fetherstonhaugh was offered the seat by a group of leading Essex Whigs, but declined standing, or undertaking to stand at the next general election.[5]

On 5 Oct. 1759 Robert Ord, who was one of Lord Carlisle's executors, wrote to Newcastle that at Morpeth some Yorkshire militia officers had offered 'money for the choosing of a Member the next election'; this forced him to put up immediately two candidates not disagreeable to the voters; at the same time Lady Carlisle's chief manager proposed to her Thomas Duncombe and Ord's son for candidates, and she agreed; the voters would not have accepted Fetherstonhaugh; and it was necessary to act immediately. Newcastle, much surprised, forwarded the letter to Fetherstonhaugh.

I shall certainly [he wrote, 13 Oct.] acquaint my Lord Chief Baron that I think myself very unkindly used by his Lordship. What effect that may have upon him who has such obligations to me, I know not.

But he assured Fetherstonhaugh of a seat in the next Parliament.[6]

Fetherstonhaugh replied that he had previous warning 'of the secret contrivances for this change'.[7] The Carlisle manager had told a friend of his that he could not be elected again—

that the freemen were offended, and resolved not to choose a person they had never seen; and that to preserve the interest of the Carlisle family he was obliged to humour the freemen, who had been tampered with by an attorney or two, and a great sum of money offered them.

Fetherstonhaugh did not doubt that the alleged discontent among the freemen had not arisen 'without instigation'.

Newcastle kept his promise, and on his recommendation to Anson, Fetherstonhaugh was returned with Admiralty support at Portsmouth.[8] On 1 Apr. Fetherstonhaugh wrote to Newcastle[9] thanking him for having

> recommended me to so worthy a set of gentlemen as this corporation seems to consist of; for everything was done with great order and decency; and after the election was over we finished the evening with great mirth and jollity.

He received his parliamentary whip direct from Newcastle both in October 1761 and 1762; was classed in Bute's parliamentary list of December 1761 as 'Newcastle'; does not appear in Fox's list of Members favourable to the peace preliminaries; but did not vote with the minority either.

In the autumn of 1763 Fetherstonhaugh was classed by Jenkinson as 'contra'; under the Grenville Administration voted steadily in opposition; and was counted by Newcastle among his 'sure friends . . . to be sent to upon any occasion'. In Rockingham's list of the summer of 1765 he was classed as a friend, and on 2 June 1766 was named by Newcastle among those 'proposed to be made peers'; he again appears as a friend in Rockingham's list in the winter of 1766–7 and in Newcastle's of 2 Mar. 1767; and in Townshend's of January 1767 as a 'Rockingham'. He voted with Opposition on the land tax, 27 Feb. 1767, over payment of the King's debts, 3 Mar. 1769, in the divisions over Wilkes and the Middlesex election, 8 May 1769 and 25 Jan. 1770, and the Spanish convention, 13 Feb. 1771.[10] In Robinson's two surveys on the royal marriage bill, March 1772, he is marked 'contra, sick, present'; but he did not vote on 11 Mar. The Duke of Richmond wrote to Edmund Burke, 2 Dec. 1772:[11]

> I . . . went to Up Park to my friend Sir Matthew Fetherstone . . . I found that all idea of getting him to London was vain. He has been in a very dangerous illness for several months. He is now better . . . but fears, and with great reasons, that if he was to venture out . . . it might cost him his life.

There is no record of Fetherstonhaugh having spoken in the House.

Fetherstonhaugh was among the biggest holders of East India and (at various times) of Bank of England stock, but never was a director of either. His holdings in East India stock averaged about £16,000, and when split represented considerable

voting strength: he supported Clive in 1763, 1764 and 1769;[12] in 1772 was inclined to temporize. He was also, together with John Sargent, Thomas Walpole (qq.v.), Samuel Wharton and Benjamin Franklin, one of the foremost promoters of the scheme for an interior colony, 'Vandalia', on the Ohio river, commemorated by a folly in the park, known as Vandalia Tower.

Fetherstonhaugh was a man of wide interests and reading, the owner of a fine library, and author of two manuscript volumes on 'natural philosophy' (with a chapter on electricity).

He died 18 Mar. 1774 aged 59. In the will which he made on his deathbed, he appointed his widow and Benjamin Lethieullier guardians to his only son Harry.

[1] Add. 33087, f. 54. [2] Add. 32995, ff. 199–200; 32735, f. 72; 32856, f. 313. [3] J. Page to Newcastle, 25 Oct. 1755, Add. 32860, ff. 161–3. [4] Ibid. ff. 289–90, 410–11; 32861, ff. 9, 25. [5] Jas. West to Newcastle, 7 Apr. 1759, Add. 32889, f. 394. [6] Add. 32896, f. 306; 32897, f. 59. [7] Add. 32897, ff. 156–7. [8] J. Clevland to Newcastle, 12 Mar. 1761, ibid. f. 135. [9] Add. 32921, f. 254. [10] Add. 32956, ff. 190–1; 33001, f. 264; Fortescue, ii. 86. [11] See also Gibbon to his step-mother, 7 Aug. 1772. [12] L. S. Sutherland, E. I. Co. in 18th Cent. Politics, 107, 121, 188, 240–1.

L.B.N.

## FIFE, Earl, *see* DUFF, Hon. James

## FILMER, Sir John, 4th Bt. (1716–97), of East Sutton, Kent.

### STEYNING    12 Feb. 1767–1774

*bap.* 30 Sept. 1716, 1st surv. s. of Sir Edward Filmer, 3rd Bt., by Anne, da. of John Wallis of Soundness, Oxon. *educ.* Univ. Coll. Oxf. 1734; G. Inn 1735; M. Temple 1738, called 1741. *m.* Apr. 1757, Dorothy, da. of Rev. Julius Deedes of Great Mongeham, Kent, prebendary of Canterbury, *s.p.*  *suc.* fa. 10 Feb. 1755. His sis. was 2nd w. of Sir John Honywood, 3rd Bt.

Filmer was returned for Steyning on the interest of his brother-in-law, Sir John Honywood. He was classed by Rockingham, November 1766, as 'Tory, Bute'; voted with Opposition on the land tax, 27 Feb. 1767; and was classed by Newcastle, 2 Mar. 1767, as 'Tory'. He voted with Administration on Wilkes, 3 Feb. and 15 Apr. 1769; was classed as 'doubtful, present' by Robinson in his first survey on the royal marriage bill, March 1772; as 'pro, present' in the second, 8 Mar. 1772; and he voted with Administration on the Middlesex election, 26 Apr. 1773. He voted with Opposition on Grenville's Election Act, 25 Feb. 1774, but appears in the King's list as normally a government supporter. Robinson, September 1774, classed him as 'doubtful'. There is no record of his having spoken in the House. Filmer did not stand again in 1774.

He died 22 Feb. 1797.

M.M.D.

## FINCH, Hon. Charles (1752–1819).

CASTLE RISING 2 Feb. 1775–May 1777
MAIDSTONE 16 May 1777–1780

*b.* 4 June 1752, 2nd s. of Heneage, 3rd Earl of Ayles-ford (q.v.), and bro. of Hon. Edward Finch and Heneage, Lord Guernsey (qq.v.). *educ.* Westminster; Ch. Ch. Oxf. 1769; L. Inn 1772. *m.* 28 Dec. 1778, Jane, da. and coh. of Watkin Wynne of Voelas, Denb., 1s.

Charles Finch sat for Castle Rising on the interest of his cousin, Lord Suffolk; and on his brother's succeeding to the peerage vacated his seat to contest Maidstone. He was a regular Government sup-porter, voting with them in every division for which a list is available. There is no record of his having spoken in the House. In 1780 he was defeated at Maidstone, and is not known to have stood again.

He died 17 Dec. 1819.

J.B.

## FINCH, (afterwards FINCH HATTON), Hon. Edward (?1697–1771), of Kirby Hall, nr. Rockingham, Northants.

CAMBRIDGE UNIVERSITY 1727–1768

*b.* ?1697, 5th surv. s. of Daniel, 2nd Earl of Notting-ham and 7th Earl of Winchilsea, by his 2nd w. Hon. Anne Hatton, da. and h. of Christopher, 1st Visct. Hatton; bro. of Hon. Henry and Hon. William Finch (qq.v.). *educ.* Trinity, Camb. 10 Oct. 1713, aged 16. *m.* 6 Sept. 1746, Elizabeth, da. and coh. of Sir Thomas Palmer, 4th Bt., of Wingham, Kent, 2s. 3da. *suc.* to estates of his gt.-aunt the Hon. Anne Hatton 1764 and took add. name of Hatton.

Minister to the Imperial Diet 1724–5; to Poland 1725–7; envoy to Sweden 1728–39; minister to Poland Apr.–May 1740; envoy to Russia 1740–42; groom of the bedchamber 1742–56; master of the robes 1757–1760; surveyor of the King's private roads 1760–d.

At the general election of 1754 Finch was re-elected unopposed for Cambridge University, while unsuccessfully contesting Rutland. In Dupplin's list he is classed as an Administration supporter, and on 12 Dec. 1755, in debate on the subsidy treaties he spoke on the Government side.[1] On the formation of the Devonshire-Pitt Administration he went out of office with Newcastle, but on his return to power the following year obtained another place. Finch was classed as an Administration supporter in Bute's list of December 1761 and by Jenkinson in the autumn of 1763. In the division on general warrants of 18 Feb. 1764 he was listed by Jenkinson as an 'absent friend'. Rockingham in his list of July 1765 classed him as 'pro', but in that of November 1766 as 'Swiss' (prepared to follow any Administration). In Townshend's list of January 1767 and in New-castle's of 2 Mar. 1767 he was counted as 'absent',

and on 22 Feb. he told Newcastle he wished to leave Parliament at the general election:[2]

> The state of my health (were I to settle again in London) would never allow me to attend the House of Commons on great business and consequently big days. My age, way of thinking, and a 25th of October [the date of George II's death] have therefore deter-mined my choice of retirement and quiet.

He died 16 May 1771.

[1] Add. 32861, f. 290. [2] Add. 32980, f. 155.

A.N.N.

## FINCH, Hon. Edward (1756–1843).

CAMBRIDGE 11 May 1789–Nov. 1819

*b.* 26 Apr. 1756, 5th s. of Heneage, 3rd Earl of Ayles-ford (q.v.), and bro. of Hon. Charles Finch and Heneage, Lord Guernsey (qq.v.). *educ.* Westminster 1766–73; Trinity, Camb. 1773. *unm.*

Cornet 20 Drag. 1778; lt. 87 Ft. 1779; lt. 2 Ft. Gds. and capt. 1783; capt. and lt.-col. 1792; col. 1796; maj.-gen. 1801; lt.-gen. 1808; col. 54 Ft. 1808–9; col. 22 Ft. 1809–d.; gen. 1819.

Edward Finch was a cousin of Charles, 4th Duke of Rutland, and sat for Cambridge on the Rutland interest.

He died 27 Oct. 1843.

E.A.S.

## FINCH, Heneage, Lord Guernsey (1715–77).

LEICESTERSHIRE 20 Dec. 1739–1741
MAIDSTONE 1741–1747, 1754–29 June 1757

*b.* 6 Nov. 1715, 1st s. of Heneage, 2nd Earl of Ayles-ford, by Mary, da. and h. of Sir Clement Fisher, 3rd Bt., of Packington, Warws. *educ.* Westminster 1728–1732; Univ. Coll. Oxf. 1732. *m.* 6 Oct. 1750, Lady Charlotte Seymour, da. of Charles, 6th Duke of Somerset, 8s. 4da. *suc.* fa. as 3rd Earl 29 June 1757.

Lord Guernsey was returned unopposed for Maidstone in 1754 and was classed by Dupplin as a Tory. He was connected with George Grenville, and on 13 Nov. 1755 voted against the subsidy treaties.

He died 9 May 1777.

A.N.N.

## FINCH, Heneage, Lord Guernsey (1751–1812).

CASTLE RISING 10 June 1772–1774
MAIDSTONE 1774–9 May 1777

*b.* 4 July 1751, 1st s. of Heneage, 3rd Earl of Aylesford (q.v.), and bro. of Hon. Charles Finch and Hon. Edward Finch (qq.v.). *educ.* Westminster; Ch. Ch. Oxf. 1767. *m.* 18 Nov. 1781, Hon. Louisa Thynne, da. of Thomas, 3rd Visct. Weymouth, 4s. 3da. *suc.* fa. as 4th Earl 9 May 1777.

Ld. of the bedchamber 1777–Dec. 1783; P.C. 31 Dec. 1783; capt. of the yeomen of the guard Dec. 1783–1804; ld. steward 1804–d.

Lord Guernsey was returned for Castle Rising on the interest of his cousin, Lord Suffolk. He was normally a Government supporter, but on 25 Feb. 1774 acted as teller against Administration on the motion to make Grenville's Election Act permanent. In 1774 he was returned for Maidstone after a contest. Only two speeches by him are recorded: on 13 Jan. 1774 he moved the Address, and on 29 Nov. 1774 proposed Sir Fletcher Norton for Speaker.

He died 21 Oct. 1812.

J.B.

**FINCH, Hon. Henry** (?1695–1761).

MALTON    27 Nov. 1724–26 Apr. 1761

*b.* ?1695, 4th surv. s. of Daniel, 2nd Earl of Nottingham and 7th Earl of Winchilsea, and bro. of Hon. William Finch and Hon. Edward Finch afterwards Hatton (qq.v.). *educ.* Eton 1707; Christ's, Camb. 19 Aug. 1712, aged 17, fellow 1713–49. *unm.*

Receiver gen. of the revenues of Minorca 1729–43; surveyor gen. of works 1743–60; groom of the bedchamber 1742–*d.*

Finch was returned for Malton on the interest of his nephew, Lord Rockingham. He is not known ever to have given a vote against Government, or to have spoken in the House. In December 1760 his place of surveyor general of works was required for Thomas Worsley, a friend of the King and Bute. And here is the summary of a letter from Count de Viry to Bute of 23 Dec. 1760:[1] 'Lord Rockingham will resign on his arrival if Mr. H. Finch is not employed. Recommends a hint to this effect being thrown out to Newcastle or Hardwicke.' Finch was given a secret service pension of £900 p.a.[2]

He died 26 Apr. 1761.

[1] 'Register of Corresp. of the Earl of Bute', Add. 36796, f. 62.
[2] Namier, *Structure*, 217.

J.B.

**FINCH, Savile** (c.1736–88), of Thrybergh, Yorks.

MAIDSTONE    6 Dec. 1757–1761
MALTON    11 Dec. 1761–Dec. 1780

*b.* c.1736, o. s. of Hon. John Finch, M.P. (2nd s. of Heneage, 1st Earl of Aylesford), by Elizabeth, da. and h. of John Savile, M.P., of Methley, Yorks. *m.* 12 Dec. 1764, Judith, da. of John Fullerton of Dorset, *s.p. suc.* fa. 1739.

Finch was a small man, a client of aristocratic patrons, who made no mark in Parliament. He sat at Maidstone on the interest of his cousin, Heneage, 3rd Earl of Aylesford, and at Malton on Lord Rockingham's interest. He is not known to have spoken in the House, and is hardly mentioned in contemporary correspondence. He did not vote on the peace preliminaries (December 1762), but henceforth voted regularly with the Rockinghams. His standing

can be seen from a letter he wrote to Rockingham on 3 Apr. 1769:[1]

I was very sorry I could not have the pleasure of seeing your Lordship before I left London. Hope my attendance in Parliament won't be absolutely necessary for the time I shall be absent, as this is the only time I can get to go to Bath and Mrs. Kendall has desired my wife and me to come immediately to her at Bath as she is going to her house in the country very soon. Your Lordship may be assured of my coming to town as soon as possible.

And here is the description of him in 1779 in the *Public Ledger*:

A quiet Member of Parliament, and one of the Rockingham party.

He retired from Parliament in 1780 when his seat was required for Edmund Burke.

He died 20 Sept. 1788.

[1] Rockingham mss.

J.B.

**FINCH, Hon. William** (1691–1766), of Charlewood, Herts.

COCKERMOUTH    31 Jan. 1727–1747, 11 Dec. 1747–1754
BEWDLEY    5 Feb. 1755–1761

*b.* 18 Jan. 1691, 2nd surv. s. of Daniel, 2nd Earl of Nottingham and 7th Earl of Winchilsea, and bro. of Hon. Henry Finch and Hon. Edward Finch (qq.v.). *educ.* Ch. Ch. Oxf. 4 Mar. 1707, aged 16. *m.* (1) 25 Jan. 1733, Lady Anne Douglas (*d.*26 Oct. 1741), da. of James, 2nd Duke of Queensberry [S], *s.p.*; (2) 9 Aug. 1746, Lady Charlotte Fermor, da. of Thomas, 1st Earl of Pomfret, 1s. 4da.

Envoy to Sweden 1720–4; envoy to Holland 1724–8 and minister 1733–4; P.C. 13 July 1742; vice-chamberlain 1742–65.

In 1754 Newcastle suggested that Finch should contest Taunton on the interest of Lord Egremont, nephew and co-heir of Algernon, 7th Duke of Somerset; but Finch, wrote Newcastle to Egremont, was 'afraid of the expense'.[1] He was eventually returned for Bewdley on the Lyttelton interest. In 1761 he did not stand.

In July 1765, now 'grown by age something between mad and foolish',[2] he was removed from his post and given a pension.[3]

He died 25 Dec. 1766.

[1] 18 July 1754, Add. 32736, ff. 49–50. [2] Mrs. Montagu to Mrs. Vesey, 19 Nov. 1765, Blunt, *Mrs. Montagu*, 132. [3] Walpole to Mann, 12 July 1765.

J.B.

**FINCH HATTON, George** (1747–1823), of Eastwell Park, nr. Ashford, Kent.

ROCHESTER    18 Sept. 1772–1784

*b.* 30 June 1747, 1st s. of Hon. Edward Finch (q.v.), afterwards Finch Hatton. *educ.* Westminster; Christ's,

Camb. 1765. *m.* 10 Dec. 1785, Hon. Elizabeth Mary Murray, da. of David, 7th Visct. Stormont [S], 2s. 3da. *suc.* fa. 16 May 1771.

Finch Hatton was returned after a contest in 1772. Lord North, on 24 Aug. 1772,[1] sent the King a warrant for £3,000 secret service money

which is much wanted at present, as Mr. Calcraft died yesterday, and Mr. Hatton set out at night to offer himself a candidate to succeed him at Rochester. He stands on the interest of Government, but, if he meets with opposition, will, I am afraid want pecuniary support.

The King replied the same day: 'The death of Calcraft will I trust bring the borough of Rochester into its ancient hands.'

Although on 26 Apr. 1773 Finch Hatton voted with the Opposition on the Middlesex motion, Robinson, in his survey of September 1774, classed him as 'pro', and he again had Government support in his election contest. On 31 Oct. 1776, the Address in reply to the King's Speech having been moved, 'Mr. Hatton seconded the motion'—which is all that appears about him in the parliamentary reports for nearly 12 years. Over the contractors bill, 12 Feb. 1779, he was listed by Robinson as 'pro, absent'. Only toward the end of this Parliament did his attendance improve: he voted with the Government in the four divisions of March–April 1780; and was again classed as 'pro' in Robinson's survey of July 1780. His re-election, however, seemed doubtful. Sandwich wrote to Robinson, 23 Apr. 1780, that he had heard 'Mr. Hatton was not liked';[2] and Commissioner Proby, of Chatham, to Sandwich, 31 July 1780, that Hatton would 'be excluded' for 'any gentleman who be declared a candidate'.[3] Returned again after a contest, he voted with the North Government in each of the six divisions 12 Dec. 1781–15 Mar. 1782; continued with North, voted against Shelburne's peace preliminaries, 18 Feb. 1783; for Fox's East India bill; and was classed with the Opposition in Stockdale's list of 19 Mar. 1784. He was defeated at the general election of 1784, and did not stand again. He died 17 Feb. 1823.

[1] Fortescue, ii. 382–3. [2] Abergavenny mss. [3] Sandwich mss.

L.B.N.

**FIREBRACE, Sir Cordell,** 3rd Bt. (1712–59), of Long Melford, Suff.

SUFFOLK    5 Mar. 1735–28 Mar. 1759

*b.* 20 Feb. 1712, o.s. of Sir Charles Firebrace, 2nd Bt., of Stoke Golding, Leics. by Margaret, da. of Sir John Cordell, M.P., 2nd Bt., of Long Melford, sis. and h. of Sir John Cordell, M.P., 3rd Bt. *educ.* St. John's, Oxf. 1729. *m.* 26 Oct. 1737, Bridget, da. of Philip Bacon of Ipswich, wid. of Edward Evers of Ipswich, *s.p. suc.* fa. 2 Aug. 1727.

Firebrace was returned unopposed in 1754, and was classed by Dupplin as a Tory. Although no speech by him is recorded after 1754—only an intention in May 1755 to move an address against the King's journey to Hanover, 'prevented by a sudden adjournment',[1] he is included in Newcastle's list of 'speakers and efficient men' (30 May 1757), and is placed in Pitt's group.[2] He died 28 Mar. 1759.

[1] H. Walpole to R. Bentley, 6 May 1755. [2] Add. 32997, ff. 203–4.

L.B.N.

**FISHER, Brice** (*d.*1767), of South Hill, Berks. and Follifoot, Yorks.

MALMESBURY       1754–1761
BOROUGHBRIDGE    1761–28 May 1767

Yst. s. of Walter Fisher, clothier, of Colham Mill, nr. Castle Combe, Wilts., by his w. Mary. *m.* June 1732 Anne de la Chambre, 1s.
    Director, South Sea Co. to 1754, Sun Fire Office 1734–*d.*

A glimpse of Fisher's background is obtained from the monument which, well pleased with himself, he put up in 1764 in Castle Combe church, to the memory of his 'valuable and respectable parents' who 'left behind them six sons and four daughters, all decently formed for the world by their industrious care and tenderness'. At his marriage he is described as 'Blackwell Hall factor', i.e. wholesale clothier; and he was in partnership first with one of his brothers, and afterwards with his nephew Nicholas Pearse, to whom he handed over the business in the early 60s. A friend of Lord Granby, Fox, and John Calcraft, he held army contracts for clothing; and was one of the packers in ordinary to H.M.'s great wardrobe. He also supplied cloth in a big way to the East India Company—but on 1 Nov. 1754 John Yorke wrote to his brother Lord Royston:

The ministers have had a meeting with the directors [of the East India Co.]; who, it seems, have lately discovered a very gross fraud in their trade, committed by the person who supplies the Company with English cloth, whose name is Brice Fisher, a Member of our honourable House, and a drinking companion of Lord Lincoln's. The fraud upon the Company is supposed to amount to a very large sum, and the injury to our trade in those parts . . . may be as fatal as anything we have to fear from French intrigues. Yet, it is said, that a party among the directors were against prosecuting this man; but *melior pars* was also *major* in this instance. The knavery is supposed to lie in . . . over-straining the cloth; which spoils the quality and substance of the manufacture, while it enables the person, who is guilty of it, to cheat in the quantity.[1]

The case opens in the East India court book[2] on 18 Sept. 1754 with a report by the inspector of cloth; Fisher was pressed to disclose the names of the makers, which he finally did; and when the matter came up for final decision, 28 Feb. 1755, the small clothiers were duly punished: no cloth made by them was to be offered in future for sale to the Company; but on the resolution declaring Fisher guilty 'of a great neglect' the votes were equal, and it was withdrawn. Still, henceforth Fisher disappears from the court books of the Company in which he previously figured as recipient of large sums in payment of cloth; his closest associates, Nicholas Linwood and Sir William Baker, drop out of the directorate; and he himself out of that of the South Sea Company. But Newcastle averred that 'there was not the least foundation in justice for any run upon Mr. Fisher',[3] and continued to favour him.

A share for him in the Minorca-Gibraltar contracts caused Newcastle unpleasantness with other merchant Members who thought they had a better right to them. Peter Burrell sen. (q.v.) died 16 Apr. 1756; 'at the earnest request of my Lord Lincoln' wrote Newcastle,[4] '(and it is not a great favour considering how he stands related to me) . . . Brice Fisher succeeds to Mr. Burrell'; but Peter Burrell jun. protested: 'What great merits this gentleman may have I cannot say, that so many emoluments should be heaped on him, for I am informed he has already the clothing of the army.'[5] Next, Minorca was lost, and four regiments were added to the garrison at Gibraltar. Newcastle now wanted Fisher and Bristow, the other Minorca contractor, to be given the victualling contracts for these regiments. But the Gibraltar contractors, the two Fonnereaus, Merrick Burrell, and Thomas Walpole, all of them M.P.s, protested. An accommodation was finally reached; Fisher and Bristow had, moreover, the remittance of money for the garrison.[6] But Fisher no longer held any of these contracts when the purge of Newcastle's friends occurred in 1762. Perhaps his last deal with Government was a share of £40,000 in the loan 'for the service of the year 1762'.[7]

Fisher's first constituency, Malmesbury, lay in the neighbourhood of his native Castle Combe; he owed his seat to Newcastle's recommendation to Henry Fox, who at that time ran the borough on the King's money, and to whom Fisher was no doubt an agreeable candidate. When differences arose between Newcastle and Fox, Fisher, a close friend of Newcastle's nephew and heir, Lord Lincoln, adhered to Newcastle. 'Fisher', wrote Calcraft on 7 Apr. 1757, ' . . . did not when tried stick to us . . . I am too much connected with politics not to feel angry when deserted.' By December 1760 Fox was running Malmesbury on his own account, and Fisher could not expect re-election. He now begins to appear in Newcastle's lists of unplaced candidates: is thought of for Fonnereau's borough of Aldeburgh or for Fane's Lyme Regis. Lastly, in an undated list of 'persons who have applied to be brought into Parliament' in Newcastle's own hand: 'Mr. Brice Fisher turned out of Parliament by Mr. Fox—recommended by Lord Lincoln—Aldborough or Boroughbridge [Newcastle's own pocket boroughs].' He was finally returned for Boroughbridge. 'Depend upon it, my dearest Lord', wrote Lincoln to Newcastle on 7 Apr. 1761, 'I feel as I *ought*, this *last obligation* I owe you in choosing Fisher.' Lincoln and Fisher became co-responsible with Newcastle for the £20,000 which he borrowed from Fisher's friend, Governor Watts, for the general election of 1761.[8]

Fisher was now in the fullest sense Newcastle's Member; voted against the peace preliminaries in December 1762; joined Wildman's Club; and was at Newcastle's beck and call: 'I am very much out of order', he wrote on 3 Feb. 1764, 'and by no means equal to the fatigue of the House, I will however at your Grace's desire go down there today, and see Sir William Baker.' He voted with Opposition over Wilkes and general warrants, 15 Nov. 1763, and 14 and 18 Feb. 1764; was listed by Newcastle among his 'sure friends . . . to be sent to upon any occasion'; and by Rockingham as 'pro' in July 1765. But he adhered to Lincoln when the break occurred between him and Newcastle; disappears from the lists of Newcastle's friends; and in March 1767 was classed by Newcastle as 'Government'. There is no record of his having spoken in the House.[9]

The connexion with Lincoln seems to have been the pivot of Fisher's social and political life. A drinking companion of his, and a 'racing associate' of Granby's,[10] with a fine sense for social strategy, Fisher bought in 1751 the estate of South Hill, near Ascot; and in the names of two of his racehorses he seems to have unconsciously epitomized his thoughts on his incursion into titled society—one was called ' Why Not', and the other 'Small Hopes'.[11] From 1758 till 1764 there was a break in his racing activities, and in 1758 he sold South Hill to Governor Watts for £7,730.[12] He moved to Follifoot in Yorkshire where he continued to entertain— 'my example *even* keeps *him* sober' wrote Lincoln to Newcastle from Follifoot, 15 June 1762. 'I like him as a companion', wrote Calcraft even after politics had come between them.[13] He was also a friend of Wilkes and of John Hall Stevenson, of 'Crazy Castle' fame.[14]

After Fisher's retirement from active business he still continued his interest in the Sun Fire Office, and moved to Craig's Court which was their headquarters; and together with Sir William Baker and

Nicholas Linwood held extensive property in South Carolina and in Georgia.[15]

Fisher died 28 May 1767. In his will he enjoined that he should be 'buried at night in the church of such parish where I shall happen to die in the most private and least expensive manner'.

[1] Add. 17493, ff. 27, 56, 144; 17494, f. 131; 35374, ff. 107–8. [2] India Office Lib. [3] Add. 32868, ff. 170–1. [4] Ibid. [5] Add. 32864, ff. 298–9. [6] See Namier, 'Brice Fisher, M.P.', *EHR*, Oct. 1927. [7] Add. 33040, ff. 290–1. [8] Add. 17493, f. 56; 32999, ff. 156, 202, 218; 33067, f. 282. [9] Add. 32957, f. 109; 32956, ff. 190–1. [10] W. E. Manners, *John Manners, Mq. of Granby*, 35. [11] See R. Heber's *Historical List of Horse Matches Run for 1753*; also for 1755, '58, '64, '66 and '67; also J. Pond's *Sporting Calendar* for 1753. [12] Private Act 14 Geo. III, c. 18. [13] Add. 32939, f. 362; 17493, f. 56. [14] Namier, 'Brice Fisher'. [15] H. A. M. Smith, 'The Baronies of S. Carolina', *S. Carolina Hist. and Gen. Mag.* 1913, p. 63; also Private Act, 8 Geo. III, c. 36, for their sale.

L.B.N.

**FITZHERBERT, Thomas** (?1746–1822), of Stubbington Lodge, Portsea, Hants, and later Pitt Place, Epsom, Surr.

ARUNDEL 1780–1790

*b.* ?1746. *m.* 26 Nov. 1789, Anna, da. of Rev. Robert Pye, and niece of Sir Thomas Alston, 5th Bt. (q.v.).

Fitzherbert's antecedents are unknown, but an account of his later career given by the *English Chronicle* in 1780 or 1781 states that twelve years before he was 'measuring coals to the labourers in the dock-yard at Portsmouth at thirteen pence a bushel', and adds that during the contest for Portsmouth at the general election of 1774 he took such an active part on behalf of the Admiralty candidates 'as . . . to attract the notice of the first lord of the Admiralty [Lord Sandwich], who from that time, honoured him with his patronage and gave him a promise of the first *good thing* that became vacant'. Between 1775 and 1782 he obtained contracts for supplying waggons for the Army in America, iron-work for gun-carriages, musket stocks, small-arms and gunpowder, and for the hire of horses employed on the fortifications at Portsmouth.[1]

Before the general election of 1780 Fitzherbert seems to have informed John Robinson, the secretary of the Treasury, that he was anxious for a seat and was willing to pay £3,000;[2] at Robinson's suggestion he stood for the expensive and corrupt borough of Arundel, where he was returned after a contest. In Parliament he supported North's Administration till the end. During the debate of 23 Jan. 1782 on Fox's motion for an inquiry into the conduct of Lord Sandwich, Fitzherbert declared that British weakness at sea did not arise 'from a neglect in the particular officers, but . . . was owing to the want of shipwrights'. He spoke from his experience at Portsmouth,

because he lived in its neighbourhood and had more frequent occasion to visit its dockyard than any other;

and although he was well aware of the evil tendency of raising the price of wages in this country, yet he could not but be of opinion that sufficient encouragement was not given to old and deserving shipwrights.[3]

Fitzherbert voted against Shelburne's peace preliminaries, 18 Feb. 1783. His contract for supplying horses having expired, it was not renewed by Shelburne's Administration, and when on 10 Mar. 1783 their estimates showed a considerably decreased payment to the new contractor, Fitzherbert, claiming this was not feasible,

gave a succinct and clear detail of the first contract . . . from the year 1757 to the expiration of that he held, and showed that it had been by no means so lucrative as the public had been given to imagine, but that, on the contrary, it had been attended with great inconvenience and great risk.[4]

Fitzherbert did not vote on Fox's East India bill, 27 Nov. 1783, and in both Robinson's list of January 1784, and Stockdale's of 19 Mar. he was described as absent.

At the general election of 1784 Fitzherbert was returned unopposed for Arundel. In May Adam counted him as an Administration supporter, but on 21 July 1784 he attacked the Government's fortifications bill, and on 21 Feb. 1785, during the debate on the Westminster scrutiny, he declared that an 'end should be put to so shameful, so aggressive and so arbitrary a measure . . . the minister talking of a reform in the representation whilst such a glaring absurdity as this was suffered to exist was idle in the extreme'.[5] Fitzherbert voted against Pitt's Irish proposals, 13 May 1785; against Richmond's fortifications plan, 27 Feb. 1786, and with the Opposition over the Regency, 1788–9. He did not stand again for Arundel in 1790.

Fitzherbert died 30 Jan. 1822, aged 75.

[1] WO 47/86/93, 251; Add. 33116, ff. 155–61. [2] Robinson to North, 14 Aug. 1780, Abergavenny mss. [3] Debrett, v. 254–5. [4] Ibid. ix. 467–469. [5] Ibid. xvii. 222.

M.M.D.

**FITZHERBERT, William** (1712–72), of Tissington Hall, nr. Ashbourne, Derbys.

BRAMBER 1761–Apr. 1762
DERBY 5 May 1762–2 Jan. 1772

*b.* 1712, 1st. s. of William Fitzherbert of Tissington Hall, recorder of Derby, by Rachel, da. and h. of Thomas Bagshaw of Bakewell, Derbys. and gd.-da. and h. of Thomas Alleyne of Barbados. *educ.* Derby; Emmanuel, Camb. 1732; I. Temple 1732, called 1739. *m.* 23 June 1744, Mary, da. of Littleton Poyntz Meynell of Bradley, Derbys. sis. of Hugo Meynell (q.v.), 5s. 2da. *suc.* fa. 1739.

Gent. usher of the privy chamber 1759–63; ld. of Trade July 1765–*d.*

The Fitzherberts and Bagshaws were important families in Derbyshire, and were closely associated with the Cavendishes. In January 1754 William Fitzherbert applied to Lord Hartington for the Cavendish interest at Derby; and, when that was given to G. V. Vernon, 'for any other vacancy in the same place, or in any other in the manner the friends of the Government and ministry are brought in'.[1] Nothing was done for him then, but in 1759 he was appointed by Devonshire to court office. On 29 Nov. 1760 Newcastle wrote to Devonshire about the forthcoming general election: 'I have been told that Mr. Fitzherbert comes in for Derby—is it so?'; to which Devonshire replied: 'There is no possibility of bringing in Mr. Fitzherbert for Derby, he relies upon your Grace's assistance.'[2] Newcastle arranged a seat for him at Bramber which he vacated a year later to stand for Derby, where he was returned unopposed.

Rather surprisingly he seems to have adhered to the court after Devonshire's dismissal. He is in Fox's list of Members favourable to the peace preliminaries, but also in one of the four lists in the Newcastle papers of those who voted against them (not, however, in the list in the *History of the Late Minority*, nor in that of Fox in the Bute mss). He turned against the court over Wilkes, voted in opposition on 15 Nov. 1763, and on 25 Nov. was mentioned by the King as one who had 'gone steadily against us' and should be dismissed.[3] This was done, and henceforth Fitzherbert voted against the Grenville Administration and was classed by Newcastle as a 'sure friend'. Though most zealous on Wilkes's behalf, he spoke rarely in the House. James Harris noted about the debate on Wilkes's expulsion, 19 Jan. 1764: 'Fitzherbert made a sort of dying speech for Wilkes . . . in which as in all other parts of the debate he was prompted by Lord Temple.' Fitzherbert collected and transmitted the subscriptions given by the Opposition leaders for Wilkes's support.

He was appointed by the Rockingham Administration to the Board of Trade, and took his duties very seriously: his average attendance works out at over 90 per cent, and in the years 1768–71 he attended all except 13 of the Board's 235 meetings. He described his West Indian interests as 'considerable' and upon which 'my family must depend in a great measure',[4] and in 1765 there was a rumour that he was to go as governor of Barbados.[5] In October 1766 Shelburne suggested him to Chatham for governor of Jamaica—'I know Mr. Fitzherbert . . . in general looks that way.'[6] 'Lord Chatham . . . is inclined to think that upon the whole the gentleman . . . may do extremely well', was Chatham's reply;[7] but it is not known whether Fitzherbert was ever offered the appointment.

He did his best both with Rockingham and Grafton to arrange for Wilkes's pardon and return to England. 'I have constantly endeavoured to bring your affair to a crisis', he wrote to Wilkes on 15 July 1766; and on 27 July: 'If you are served I care not by whom.'[8] When Wilkes did come back, without the promise of a pardon, it seems to have been against Fitzherbert's advice; and Fitzherbert took alarm when Wilkes began to stir up the London mob.[9] The strikes and riots in London in the summer of 1768 frightened him. 'No civil magistrate could execute his warrant without the assistance of the military', he told the House on 17 May; and on 23 Nov.: 'Mr. Fitzherbert, speaking of the civil power, said *that* part of our constitution is worn out, the military is the real support of this country.'[10]

He did not vote on the motion to expel Wilkes, 3 Feb. 1769; but on 17 Feb., when Wilkes was declared ineligible for re-election, repudiated him and censured his conduct. He said he had told Wilkes that 'quietness . . . was the only chance of his coming in again', and then went on:

> I would have gone upon my knees for his pardon. He would not come in upon his knees but upon the people's shoulders. I began to consider . . . whether my desire to serve him or Government was to prevail . . . I love him, but in the light he stands I will do as much as any man in England to oppose him.[11]

On 15 Apr. and 8 May Fitzherbert voted for the seating of Luttrell.

He seems to have felt the need to defend his conduct in accepting a place and abandoning Wilkes. 'I am a private gentleman in employment', he said in the House on 14 Dec. 1770, 'without connexion, without hopes, without fears. I am independent from temper . . . I shall never be ashamed to say what I think.' And on 12 Mar. 1771 he described himself as 'from disposition and temper as independent a man as any in the House'.[12]

There was no need for this self-justification: he was liked and respected in all circles, and by political opponents as well as friends. Lord Hyde wrote to Grenville, 14 Oct. 1764, when transmitting a request for patronage:[13]

> There are few men I would sooner oblige than Fitzherbert. His parts, his knowledge, his humanity, and utility make the foundation of my esteem. I might add his moderation notwithstanding his warmth for Wilkes which I believe was kindled by the coolness of others in seeing that unhappy man in jeopardy. I know few second-rate men that could be better employed by one in power.

Perhaps the best account of him was given by Johnson:[14]

> There was no sparkle, no brilliancy in Fitzherbert; but I never knew a man who was so generally acceptable.

He made everybody quite easy, overpowered nobody by the superiority of his talents, made no man think worse of himself by being his rival, seemed always to listen, did not oblige you to hear much from him, and did not oppose what you said. Everybody liked him; but he had no friend, as I understand the word, nobody with whom he exchanged intimate thoughts.

On 2 Jan. 1772 he committed suicide.[15]

He went to see the convicts executed that morning [wrote Walpole to Lady Upper Ossory, 5 Jan. 1772]; and from thence, in his boots, to his son, having sent his groom out of the way. At three, his son said, 'Sir, you are to dine at Mr. Buller's; it is time for you to go home and dress.' He went to his own stable and hanged himself with a bridle. They say his circumstances were in great disorder.

But according to Johnson[16] his suicide 'was owing to imaginary difficulties in his affairs, which, had he talked with any friend, would soon have vanished'.

[1] Fitzherbert to Vernon, 21 Jan. 1754, and to Hartington, 3 Mar. 1754, Devonshire mss. [2] Add. 32915, ff. 166, 272. [3] Grenville Pprs. ii. 166. [4] Fitzherbert to Ld. Hyde, 12 Oct. 1764, Grenville mss (JM). [5] David Garrick to Edmund Burke, 17 July 1765. [6] Chatham Corresp. iii. 92. [7] Chatham to Shelburne, 6 Oct. 1766, Lansdowne mss. [8] Add. 30869, ff. 55, 65. [9] Whateley to Grenville, 18 Apr. 1768, Grenville Pprs. iv. 271. [10] Cavendish's 'Debates', Egerton 215, ff. 73, 235. [11] Ibid., Egerton 217, ff. 347–9. [12] Ibid., Egerton 223, f. 270; 226, f. 36. [13] Grenville mss (JM). [14] Boswell, Johnson, iii. 148–9. [15] Three different dates are given for his death: 1 Jan. (Walpole to Lady Upper Ossory, 5 Jan. 1772); 2 Jan. (Gent Mag. 1772, p. 46); and 3 Jan. (Mrs. Thrale, in Thraliana, i. 63). [16] Boswell, ii. 228.

J.B.

**FITZMAURICE, Hon. Thomas** (1742–93), of Llewenny Hall, Denb.

CALNE                          29 Dec. 1762–1774
CHIPPING WYCOMBE                1774–1780

b. July 1742, 2nd s. of John Fitzmaurice (afterwards Petty), 1st Earl of Shelburne [I], and bro. of William, Visct. Fitzmaurice (qq.v.). educ. Eton 1755–8; Glasgow 1759; St. Mary Hall, Oxf. 1761; M. Temple 1762, called 1768. m. 21 Dec. 1777, Lady Mary O'Brien, da. of Murrough, 5th Earl of Inchiquin [I], by Mary, s.j. Countess of Orkney [S] (from whom she inh. the title in 1790), 1s.

Sheriff, Denb. 1781–2.

In August 1762, shortly after Fitzmaurice came of age, his brother, Lord Shelburne, arranged his return for Calne in place of Daniel Bull who was bought off with an office. In Parliament Fitzmaurice naturally followed Shelburne's lead; in February 1764 he was included by Harris among 'deserters this session': he voted against Grenville's Administration. He is only twice reported to have spoken during this Parliament: on 23 Jan. 1765 he defended the conduct of Shelburne 'who . . . did not retire to faction but adhered to his principles';[1] and, 29 Jan. 1765, on general warrants. About this William Baker jun. commented: 'Mr. Fitzmaurice . . . gave us a speech on I know not what which he had studied all the summer at his looking glass.'[2] He supported the Chatham Administration of which his brother was a leading member. In 1768 Fitzmaurice canvassed

Oxford University, but withdrew some time before the poll, and was again returned unopposed for Calne. During this Parliament he voted regularly with Opposition. In a series of speeches he opposed attempts to obtain relief from subscription to the 39 Articles, maintaining that 'established religion must be dependent in a very high degree upon it'. On 24 Mar. 1772 Fitzmaurice condemned the royal marriage bill as 'totally unnecessary'; nobody understood it, and he found it 'disgustful, unconstitutional, in all its parts repugnant to the spirit of our constitution'.[3]

In 1774 Fitzmaurice was returned unopposed on his brother's interest at Wycombe. His attendance at the House now became infrequent and by 1779 had ceased altogether. Instead, faced with unproductive Irish estates and financial difficulties, he set up as a linen merchant, and established a bleaching factory at Llewenny, the Welsh estate which he purchased in 1776. He wrote to Shelburne, 26 Nov. 1779, to explain that his prolonged absence from Wycombe, which had annoyed his constituents, was caused by 'the complicated distressed situation of Irish affairs . . . and my own very particular concerns in the linen trade'. In January 1780 Shelburne told Fitzmaurice that he could only continue at Wycombe if he could give the place more attention, but added: 'I wish it were in my power to bring you in where attention might not be requisite, which your distance and possible avocations render inconvenient to you.' But this could only be arranged at considerable expense. On 1 Feb. 1780 Fitzmaurice wrote that he was aware of 'the impropriety and unfairness of my continuing longer than for the present Parliament an indolent dog upon your parliamentary interest'. He regretted that it was necessary to give up his seat but 'anything like regular attendance' at the House would almost certainly be impossible for some time to come.

Upon these accounts, as well as upon a much more material one, namely my very great distress for money, I cannot help being of opinion that purchase of a seat for the ensuing Parliament would be except as to worldly appearance as useless as the advancement of a sum sufficient would . . . be embarrassing.[4]

He hoped that in a few years his circumstances would have improved enough to enable him to re-enter Parliament; but he does not seem ever to have stood again. On 20 July 1785 Richard Twining wrote to his brother about Fitzmaurice:[5]

He has plunged himself into a business which might make even a tradesman tremble. He is a bleacher of linen. The buildings which he has erected, and the machines and apparatus which he has placed in them are really astonishing. He has a shop at Chester at which he sells his linen when it is bleached.

In 1790 his wife succeeded to her mother's estate of Cliveden in Buckinghamshire, and Fitzmaurice seems to have made his home there. A picture of him in the last year of his life, broken in health and in reduced circumstances, is given by his nephew Lord Wycombe, who wrote to his father on 10 Apr. 1792:[6]

> I think him on the whole dejected and disgusted, not so much with the fatiguing business to which he is so unaccountably attached as with the world at large. His London and his foreign business he intends to sacrifice, but will not I believe be willingly prevailed on to give up the rest. In the meantime he says his plans are those of strict economy, and that he now designs to let his house at Cliveden; and to retrench to such a pitch as to pay off £5,000 a year. He told me that he rather wished for death, and that he thought his life was not to be of long duration. He also talked to me about a future state and of the education of his son; I was not fortunate to comprehend his reasoning on either of these subjects.

After his death on 28 Oct. 1793 the *Gentleman's Magazine* wrote (1793, p. 1053): 'He formerly lived on the most intimate terms with Johnson, Hawkesworth, and Garrick . . . He was the gentleman who from his extensive concerns in the linen manufactory, was called the Royal Merchant.'

[1] Harris's 'Debates'. [2] To a Mr. Talbot, 4 Feb. 1765, Baker mss. [3] Cavendish's 'Debates', Egerton 244, pp. 214–20; 239, pp. 151–4. [4] Lansdowne mss. [5] *Pprs. of Twining Fam.* ed. R. Twining, 115–16. [6] Lansdowne mss.

M.M.D.

## FITZMAURICE, *see also* PETTY

**FITZPATRICK, John,** 1st Earl of Upper Ossory [I] (?1719–58), of Ampthill, Beds.

BEDFORDSHIRE    5 Dec. 1753–23 Sept. 1758

*b.* ?1719, 1st s. of Richard, 1st Baron Gowran [I], by Anne, da. and coh. of Sir John Robinson, 2nd Bt., of Farmingwoods, Northants. *educ.* Queen's, Oxf. 6 June 1735, aged 15. *m.* 30 June 1744, Lady Evelyn Leveson Gower, da. of John, 1st Earl Gower, sis. of Gertrude, w. of John, 4th Duke of Bedford, 2s. 2da. *suc.* fa. as 2nd Lord Gowran [I], 9 June 1727; and mother in the estates of Farmingwoods and Ampthill 1744; *cr.* Earl of Upper Ossory [I] 5 Oct. 1751.

On 30 June 1753 Lord Hardwicke wrote from London to his son Philip about the by-election in Bedfordshire:[1] 'If the Duke of Bedford sets up any Whig it is my opinion that you should concur with him, and if it should be my Lord Upper Ossory, that will do best of all, for I don't find that his Lordship is a disagreeable man to our friends here.' Lady Hardwicke described Ossory as 'a very agreeable and a very moderate man'.[2] He was proposed by Yorke, and returned unopposed; and again unopposed in 1754.

He was regarded as a loyal follower of Bedford.

But once at least he tried to assert his independence. When before the session of 1754 Bedford was seeking support for his follower Lord Fane, against whose election for Reading a petition had been presented, Ossory's declaration that he would attend no election petitions angered Bedford who wrote to him on 19 Nov.:

> I find myself obliged . . . to state to you by letter the obligations I think you are under in a public light to your constituents, and in a private one to me, by whose means you have been introduced to those constituents . . . how will you answer to me your non-attendance in a point which so nearly interests me? . . . the great personal friendship I have for Lord Fane, and the great opinion I have of his honesty and abilities, must always make me look upon those who engage at my request in this just defence of his cause, against the arbitrary power of a minister, as personal friends to myself, as on the other hand I must undoubtedly think myself very ill used by those who have been under any obligations to me who shall refuse to give my Lord Fane any assistance that may be justly in their power to give.

Ossory replied 24 Nov.:

> Though I had determined . . . never to engage in committees of election yet as your Grace thinks yourself equally pushed at with him [Fane] and makes such a point of this affair, I will attend it in the manner your Grace desires; but am resolved for the future never to engage in a thing of this kind upon any account whatever.[3]

Ossory died 23 Sept. 1758.

[1] Add. 35351, ff. 228–9. [2] Chas. Yorke to Philip Yorke, 28 July 1753, Add. 35360, ff. 228–30. [3] Bedford mss 30, ff. 104, 108.

L.B.N.

**FITZPATRICK, John,** 2nd Earl of Upper Ossory [I] (1745–1818), of Ampthill, Beds.

BEDFORDSHIRE    7 Apr. 1767–9 Aug. 1794

*b.* 2 May 1745, 1st s. of John, 1st Earl of Upper Ossory [I], and bro. of Hon. Richard Fitzpatrick (qq.v.). *educ.* Westminster c.1754–60; Trinity, Camb. 1760. *m.* 26 Mar. 1769, Anne, da. of Henry Liddell, 1st Baron Ravensworth, div. w. of Augustus Henry, 3rd Duke of Grafton, 1da. *suc.* fa. 23 Sept. 1758; *cr.* Baron Upper Ossory [GB] 9 Aug. 1794.
Ld. lt. Beds. 1771–*d.*

A friend of Charles Fox and one of the fashionable set, Ossory, according to Horace Walpole, could 'live with macaronies and be in fashion without folly', and do 'everything right and proper so naturally, that both the sensible part of the world and the absurd part think he is just what he ought to be'.[1]

In 1767, on the death of his cousin Lord Tavistock, he was returned unopposed for Bedfordshire. In Parliament he, like his father, was influenced by his uncle John, 4th Duke of Bedford, and in the autumn of 1767 acted for him during the negotiations with the Grafton ministry.[2] But he seems to have been little interested in politics: he was, writes the 3rd Lord Holland, 'a man of sense, reflection, and prudence, and not much liable to be swayed by party feelings, or much disposed *bracchia tendere contra torrentem*. He had little ambition, though very desirous, from a dislike of the turmoil, and still more of the expense of elections, to obtain an English peerage.'[3] In January 1768, after the Bedfords had entered the Administration, it was rumoured that this ambition was to be realized,[4] but nothing more was heard of the matter, nor was he more successful when in August 1770 he applied for the embassy to Spain.

After Grafton's resignation Ossory continued to support Administration till the outbreak of the American war, though in 1773 he was associated with Rockingham and other leading members of the Opposition in protesting to North about the threatened Irish absentee land tax.[5] He continued to hope for a peerage, and on 9 Jan. 1774 asked his uncle Lord Gower to support his request, his 'only political ambition'.[6] At the general election of 1774, though his own seat was safe, Ossory spent large sums in securing the re-election of Robert Henley Ongley, a fellow supporter of Administration. But he had serious misgivings about the Administration's American measures, and told Gower it was only out of respect for him that he had withheld his criticism, but, he wrote on 5 Nov. 1775: 'After a great deal of reflection, being perfectly convinced of the fatal consequences of the war (from which I can see no prospect of advantage even if we are the conquerors) I have, I confess, contracted a most ardent wish for pacification, and a desire to concur in measures that might lead to it.'[7] And on 16 Nov. he supported Burke's conciliatory proposals, declaring 'he disapproved of the dangerous experiment of fomenting civil war and the obstinacy, if not worse, of prosecuting it at so great a risk and at such enormous expense'.[8] Thereafter he voted with the Opposition till the fall of North. On 20 Feb. 1776, seconding Fox's motion for a committee to inquire into the causes of defeat in America, he said 'he could not perceive how any Member in that House, who was unconnected with the ministry, and at the same time wished success to the American war, could be against it'.[9] Apart from this, only one intervention by Ossory was reported before 6 Dec. 1779, when he introduced a motion censuring the 'shameful inattention and criminal neglect of ministers, who might have in the early stages of the miseries of that kingdom, granted the Irish substantial relief'.[10] He voted with Opposition on the measures for economical reform, February–March 1780, but, writes Horace Walpole, when the petitioning counties were sending deputies to a convention in London, Ossory 'could not be prevailed to send any from Bedfordshire'.[11]

After the fall of North Ossory supported the Rockingham Administration, and once more applied for a British peerage, but seems to have had a non-committal reply from his brother-in-law, Lord Shelburne.[12] When, on the death of Rockingham in July 1782 Shelburne took office, he wrote to Ossory on the 4th: 'I am desirous of getting my own Board filled not merely with politicians, but friends, and I shall be happy if you will add to it in the character of a relation.' After declining, Ossory wrote: 'I assure you it is not from any political motives, not having had any concert with anybody, or taken any engagement since this event.'[13] He seems to have been unwilling to commit himself openly to supporting Shelburne's Administration. On 15 Sept. he wrote to his sister:[14] 'I wish his Administration exceedingly well but at the same time am free to own that I shall be exceedingly . . . disappointed if I don't find his inclinations the same still [as] they were upon the first change . . . You know I am no boaster, but I really think my being pleased or out of humour is of some consequence to Lord Shelburne as a minister.' In reply Lady Shelburne pressed him to declare his support openly: 'It will be impossible for him [Shelburne] to urge what you so much wish without the most distinct and avowed previous support—otherwise we shall feel in a very awkward situation.'[15] But Ossory's attitude remained ambiguous. His brother Richard wrote to him after the division on the peace preliminaries, 18 Feb. 1783:[16]

> I am not very sorry your indolence prevailed upon you to stay in the country, as I should have feared your *pacific* disposition and that general partiality to peace might have inclined you to follow the example of some of your brother country gentlemen . . . and to have voted in favour of a ministry you wished to destroy.

On the formation of the Coalition Ossory applied to Fox about his peerage, but was informed that the King had refused to create any. In November he was persuaded by Fox to move the Address, but this was his last reported speech in the House. He voted for Fox's East India bill, 27 Nov. 1783. Ossory was classed as a Foxite in Robinson's list of January 1784, in Stockdale's of 19 Mar., and by Adam in May.

At the general election of 1784, though safe himself, Ossory organized the Bedford interest, and after the contest claimed at least £7,000 for expenses from Bedford's agent.[17] He voted with the Administration over Pitt's Irish proposals, 13 May 1785,[18] but with Fox over the Regency, 1788-9.

Ossory died 1 Feb. 1818.

[1] To Lady Ossory, 7 Oct. 1773. [2] Grafton, *Autobiog.* 172–3. [3] *Corresp. C. J. Fox,* i. 464. [4] Ibid. [5] Walpole, *Last Jnls.* i. 254 [6] Granville mss, PRO. [7] Ibid. [8] Almon, iii. 187. [9] Ibid. 330. [10] Ibid. xvi. 99–101. [11] *Last Jnls.* ii. 292. [12] Fortescue, v. 431. [13] *Fox Corresp.* i. 462–3. [14] Lansdowne mss. [15] 18 Sept., Ossory mss, Nat. Lib. Ireland. [16] *Fox Corresp.* ii. 16. [17] Robt. Palmer to Ossory, 8 July 1784, 5 Feb. 1785, to Bedford, 18 July 1784, 16 Jan. 1785, Palmer's letter bk. Bedford Estates Office. [18] *HMC Rutland,* iii. 205.

M.M.D.

## FITZPATRICK, Hon. Richard (1748–1813).

| | |
|---|---|
| OKEHAMPTON | 20 Oct. 1770–1774 |
| TAVISTOCK | 1774–1807 |
| BEDFORDSHIRE | 1807–1812 |
| TAVISTOCK | 1812–25 Apr. 1813 |

*b.* 24 Jan. 1748, 2nd s. of John, 1st Earl of Upper Ossory [I], and bro. of John, 2nd Earl (qq.v.). *educ.* Westminster c.1764; Caen military acad. 1767. *unm.*

Ensign 1 Ft. Gds. 1765, lt. and capt. 1772, served in America 1777–8, capt. and lt.-col. 1778; col. 1782; maj.-gen. 1793; lt.-gen. 1798; gen. 1803; col. 11 Ft. 1806–7, 47 Ft. 1807–*d.*

Sec. to ld. lt. [I] Mar.–July 1782; M.P. [I] 1782–3; P.C. 14 Apr. 1783; sec. at war Apr.–Dec. 1783, Feb. 1806–Mar. 1807; lt.-gen. of the Ordnance Feb. 1806–Mar. 1807.

Celebrated for his wit and charm, Fitzpatrick was an intimate friend of Fox and a notable figure in the fashionable world. He was, writes Wraxall, 'tall, manly, and distinguished . . . No man's society was more eagerly courted among the highest orders by persons of both sexes. He possessed no mean poetic talents, peculiarly for compositions of wit, fancy, and satire.'[1]

In 1770 he was returned for Okehampton on the interest of his uncle, the 4th Duke of Bedford, and subsequently represented the Bedford borough of Tavistock. Like the rest of the Bedford group he voted with Administration for the remainder of the 1768 Parliament. But gambling rather than politics was his main preoccupation. Horace Walpole, who found Fitzpatrick 'an agreeable young man of parts', noted that in November 1772 he was already 'overwhelmed with gaming debts' and reports that in moving the Address (26 Nov.), his criticism of the East India Company was 'not well taken from a young man of so light a character'.[2] In March 1775, on the Duchess of Bedford's applying for a place at court for Fitzpatrick, the King replied: 'I do not choose to fill my family with professed gamesters.'[3]

Though a boon companion of Fox, Fitzpatrick did not follow him into opposition till after the outbreak of the American war. During the debate of 16 Nov. 1775 on Burke's conciliatory proposals, having 'declared his good opinion of the gentlemen in Administration with whom he had acted till that day', he said 'that he now must differ from them, because he was convinced their measures were

ruinous and the object impracticable'. And on 20 Feb. 1776, supporting Fox's motion for an inquiry into British defeats in America, he

> insisted that the whole of the American business from the very beginning had been planned in absurdity, accompanied by negligence, and executed in a manner which evinced the very excess of ignorance, incapacity, and misconduct.[4]

Fitzpatrick does not seem to have spoken again during this Parliament, nor is any vote by him recorded.

During the winter of 1776–7 on a visit to Paris with Fox, his gambling activities were severely censured by Madame du Deffand, who nevertheless commented to Walpole, 19 Jan. 1777: 'Le Fitzpatrick est silencieux, mais je crois qu'il a plus de bon sens que le Fox, et que sans ce dernier il serait raisonable.'

Shortly after this Fitzpatrick, who, according to Selwyn, had by then accumulated debts amounting to £40,000,[5] was ordered to America with his regiment. He was absent from March 1777 till June 1778. During that time Fitzpatrick, according to Walpole, 'distinguished himself by his gallant behaviour' and was 'mentioned with praise by General Howe to the King'. But his experience reinforced his opposition to the war, and Walpole reports that he had written to his brother 'saying he was far more rooted in his principles from admiration of the noble behaviour of the Americans, and their love of freedom; and was disgusted with the army, who were grown to abhor the name of *Whigs* and had lost all attachment to liberty'.[6] Fitzpatrick seems to have written in a similar vein to Fox, who replied on 3 Feb. 1778:[7] 'What a scene of folly it has been. But it has not yet had all the effect here that you at a distance imagine it would have. I think you are too violent in some of your ideas.' Fox was nevertheless eagerly awaiting Fitzpatrick's return: 'I really want you at present to a great degree . . . it would be a great satisfaction to have you here, who I know would be of my opinion.' Fitzpatrick returned to England on 1 June, and attended the House on the 2nd when, writes Walpole, he

> rose and gave a strong account of the extreme dissatisfaction the conciliatory plan had occasioned in the royal army, and contempt in the Americans. He complained that the army had been promised 20,000 recruits and had been deceived, commended General Howe, and complained bitterly how ill that General, Burgoyne and Carleton had been treated by the Administration.[8]

During the summer of 1779, when an attempt was made to bring Fox into the Administration, Fitzpatrick was considered by North for a place, possibly at the Board of Green Cloth.[9] Fitzpatrick now seems to have attended the House more frequently, and was one of the leading figures in the Westminster Committee of Association. Though he still rarely spoke in the House, he supported an Opposition amendment to the Address, 6 Nov. 1780, and 'after a good deal of strong irony' about the Administration's methods of obtaining a majority in the new Parliament, 'represented the impolicy of the present war in America and recommended the withdrawing our troops from thence and concentrating our force . . . against the House of Bourbon'. On 5 Mar. 1781 he seconded Sheridan's motion for an inquiry into the use of the military during the Gordon riots, and referring to his own distasteful experience of this as a soldier, hoped that 'some mode would be established to put the police of this great city on so respectable a footing as to render the intervention of the military in the cases of riot, unnecessary'.[10] 'As a Member of the House of Commons', writes Wraxall,[11] 'he obtained no distinction for eloquence, though he never betrayed any want of ideas, language or ability.'

Early in 1781, hoping to repair their disordered finances, Fitzpatrick and Fox set up a faro bank at Brooks's. 'The play . . . is exorbitant as I hear', wrote Selwyn to Carlisle on 24 Mar. 'Richard is high in cash.' And on 21 May he reported that on visiting Brooks's he had 'found Richard in his faro pulpit where he had been alternately with Charles since the evening before . . . The bank ceased a few minutes after I was in the room; it was a little after 12 at noon, and it had won 3,400 or 3,500g . . . But . . . Richard's horses were taken the other day with his coach.' The bank was still going in December, and on Christmas day Selwyn wrote to Carlisle:

> Charles, or Richard if he is there, never fail; and at their own bank they will lose a thousand in one deal, and win them back in the other; but Richard, as I was told, lost *tout de bon* 7,000 the other night to this bank. The whole manœuvre, added to their patriotism, their politics etc. etc. are incredible.

On 29 Dec. James Hare (q.v.), who also owned a share in the bank, wrote to Carlisle: 'You will be surprised when I tell you that Richard is our most valuable punter, and has lost this year full as much as his share of the winnings . . . Last night he lost £13,000.' During the weeks before the fall of North Fitzpatrick's open jubilation was a sore trial to Selwyn who, foreseeing the loss of his place, wrote angrily to Carlisle, 27 Mar.: 'Richard has provoked me beyond measure by his insolence and unfeelingness about everybody and everything.'[12]

On 9 Apr. 1782 Fitzpatrick, then on the point of leaving for Ireland to take up his duties as secretary to the Duke of Portland, the lord lieutenant, told the House that

he had been prevailed upon to accept of that office in the firm persuasion and confidence that his Majesty's present ministers were sincere in their professions, and that they were earnestly disposed to make such concessions to Ireland as should quiet their jealousies and give satisfaction to their minds. If he had not had this opinion of the King's ministers, no circumstances upon earth should have induced him to take a situation, which at any time he would not have coveted, and which only such opinion and confidence would have made him endure.[13]

But while his experiences in Ireland confirmed his belief in the necessity for concessions, Fitzpatrick's relations with his brother-in-law and political superior, Lord Shelburne, became increasingly strained: Fitzpatrick found Shelburne's attitude to Ireland ambiguous, while Shelburne believed that Fitzpatrick was far too willing to give way to Irish demands. Still, on 22 June 1782, having talked to Fitzpatrick who had just come over 'to answer questions or give any information which may be required', Shelburne informed the King that Fitzpatrick had talked 'so sensibly and with so much good humour upon both men and things in Ireland that it's impossible to remember that he has been a principal actor in all the absurdities which have been passing there'. To which the King replied: 'The account Lord Shelburne gives of Lt. Col. Fitzpatrick's language on Ireland shows what indeed but too often appears in life—that men may be able to discuss points with apparent judiciousness, and when called into action, be totally void of good conduct.'[14] And on 1 July, considering the changes on the death of Rockingham, the King wrote to Shelburne: 'From the language of Mr. Fitzpatrick it would seem that Lord Shelburne has no chance of being able to coalesce with Fox.'[15] Fitzpatrick was an active opponent of Shelburne's Administration and according to the subsequent account of Lord John Townshend (q.v.), during the negotiations for the Coalition, 'Fitzpatrick's aid was invaluable, his excellent judgment mainly contributing to the success of the measure and removing unexpected difficulties that occasionally arose. No one's opinions . . . *had half so much weight* with Mr. Fox.'[16] Of Fitzpatrick's appointment as secretary at war, Wraxall writes:[17]

> Though his talents always appeared to me to be of a description more elegant than solid, more adapted to entertain and delight than fitted for the desk or cabinet, yet I have been assured that he gave great as well as general satisfaction while he held that employment.

After the dismissal of the Coalition Fitzpatrick was active in his opposition to Pitt; he was one of the principal authors of the *Rolliad*; spoke against the Westminster scrutiny, 18 and 21 Feb. 1785; criticized Pitt's Irish commercial propositions, 23 May

1785; and in several speeches on military affairs condemned Administration policy.

After Fitzpatrick's death on 25 Apr. 1813, the *Gentleman's Magazine* wrote of him (1813, i. 672):

> Instructed by observation that the proper world of a rational being is his own circle, Fitzpatrick had formed perhaps the truest estimation of popular acclaim; and to the 'crowd below' his philosophy made him almost indifferent . . . With a temper divested of everything abrupt and inflammable, his quiescent nature peculiarly qualified General Fitzpatrick to survey with clearness and judge without passion . . . His liberal knowledge extended to everything but he pretended to nothing. There was not an atom of foppery in his whole character. Natural, easy, unaffected, supremely well-bred, Fitzpatrick . . . neither sought nor shunned any particular subject . . . He laboured at nothing except where labour was wholly invisible—his poetry.

[1] *Mems.* iii. 57. [2] *Last Jnls.* i. 160. [3] Fortescue, iii. 190. [4] Almon, iii. 187, 331. [5] Selwyn to Carlisle [Feb. 1777], *HMC Carlisle*, 320. [6] *Last Jnls.* ii. 148. [7] *Corresp. C. J. Fox*, i. 167. [8] *Last Jnls.* ii. 185. [9] Fortescue, iv. 352. [10] Debrett, i. 29–31; ii. 106. [11] *Mems.* iii. 57. [12] *HMC Carlisle*, 475, 484, 552, 554, 608. [13] Debrett, vii. 27. [14] Fortescue, vi. 63, 64. [15] Fitzmaurice, *Life of Shelburne*, ii. 149. [16] *Corresp.* i. 448. [17] *Mems.* iii. 57.

M.M.D.

## FITZROY, Augustus Henry, Earl of Euston (1735–1811), of Euston, Suff.

| | |
|---|---|
| BOROUGHBRIDGE | 10 Dec.–21 Dec. 1756 |
| BURY ST. EDMUNDS | 21 Dec. 1756–6 May 1757 |

*b.* 28 Sept. 1735, 1st surv. s. of Lord Augustus Fitzroy (3rd s. of Charles, 2nd Duke of Grafton) by Elizabeth, da. of Col. William Cosby, gov. of New York. *educ.* Hackney; Peterhouse, Camb. 1751; Grand Tour (France, Switzerland and Italy). *m.* (1) 29 Jan. 1756, Hon. Anne Liddell (div. 23 Mar. 1769), da. and h. of Henry, 1st Lord Ravensworth, 3s. 1da.; (2) 24 June 1769, Elizabeth, da. of Rev. Sir Richard Wrottesley, 7th Bt., 5s. 8da. *suc.* gd.-fa. as 3rd Duke of Grafton 6 May 1757; K.G. 20 Sept. 1769. Ld. of the bedchamber to the Prince of Wales 1756–7; ld. lt. Suff. 1757–63, 1769–90; P.C. 10 July 1765; sec. of state, northern dept. July 1765–Apr. 1766; 1st ld. of Treasury July 1766–Jan. 1770; chancellor of Cambridge Univ. 1768; ld. privy seal June 1771–Oct. 1775, Mar. 1782–Feb. 1783.

Lord Euston was returned almost at the same time for Boroughbridge and Bury St. Edmunds, and chose to sit for the family borough. His career in the Commons was too short for him to make any mark. His only known vote was with Pitt on the Minorca inquiry.[1]

The most important years of his political career were from 1765 to 1770, when he was secretary of state under Rockingham and first lord of the Treasury in the Chatham Administration. Immature, sensitive, and uncertain, he feared responsibility and lacked authority; as first minister after Chatham's resignation he held a post for which he was totally unsuited, and his Administration was a disgrace to himself and a disaster for the nation.

In his old age he composed an autobiography, parts of which, based on contemporary correspondence and memoranda, are of great value.

Grafton died 14 Mar. 1811.

[1] *Autobiog.* 8.

J.B.

## FITZROY, Hon. Charles (1737–97), of Highgate, Mdx.

| | |
|---|---|
| ORFORD | 20 Dec. 1759–1761 |
| BURY ST. EDMUNDS | 1761–1774 |
| THETFORD | 1774–1780 |

*b.* 25 June 1737, 2nd surv. s. of Lord Augustus Fitzroy, and bro. of Augustus Henry, Earl of Euston (q.v.). *m.* 27 July 1758, Anne, da. and coh. of Adm. Sir Peter Warren, M.P., of Warrenstown, co. Meath, 9s. 7da. *cr.* Baron Southampton 17 Oct. 1780.

Ensign 1 Ft. Gds. 1752, lt. and capt. 1756, capt. and lt.-col. 1758; served in Germany as aide-de-camp to Prince Ferdinand of Brunswick 1759–62; col. 119 Ft. 1762–3; 14 Drag. 1765–72; 3 Drag. 1772–*d.*; maj.-gen. 1772; lt.-gen. 1777; gen. 1793.

Groom of the bedchamber 1760–2; vice-chamberlain to the Queen 1768–82; groom of the stole to the Prince of Wales 1780–*d.*

Fitzroy was returned for Orford on the Government interest, but played no part in politics until 1762 when, on his return from Germany, he resigned his place at court and joined his brother in opposition. During the negotiations between Cumberland and Pitt in May 1765 he was Grafton's intermediary with Pitt; and he was appointed to a regiment by the Rockingham Administration.

Naturally he supported the Chatham-Grafton Administration, and became vice-chamberlain to the Queen in 1768, but in 1770 refused the office of vice-chamberlain to the King.[1] Hitherto he had always followed Grafton, but now began to go his own way; and after 1775, when Grafton resigned and reverted to Opposition, Fitzroy continued to support North and in 1780 was rewarded with a peerage.

He died 21 Mar. 1797.

[1] Fortescue, ii. 128–9.

J.B.

## FITZROY, Lord Charles (1764–1829), of Wicken, Northants.

| | |
|---|---|
| BURY ST. EDMUNDS | 5 Feb. 1787–1796, 1802–1818 |

*b.* 14 July 1764, 2nd surv. s. of Augustus Henry, 3rd Duke of Grafton (q.v.) by his 1st w., and bro. of George Henry, Earl of Euston (q.v.). *educ.* Harrow 1774–6; Hackney; Trinity, Camb. 1781. *m.* (1) 20 June 1795, Frances (*d.*9 Aug. 1797), da. of Edward Miller Mundy (q.v.), 1s.; (2) 10 Mar. 1799, Lady Frances Stewart, da. of Robert, 1st Mq. of Londonderry [I], 2s. 3da.

Ensign 3 Ft. Gds. 1782; capt. 43 Ft. 1787; equerry to Duke of York 1788; capt. and lt.-col. 3 Ft. 1789; col. 129 Ft. 1795-9; half pay [I] 1795; maj.-gen. 1798; col. commandant 20 Ft. 1799–1805; col. 48 Ft. 1805–*d.*; lt.-gen. 1805; gen. 1814.

Lord Charles Fitzroy, like his father and brother, voted with Pitt on the Regency. There is no record before 1790 of his having spoken in the House. He died 20 Dec. 1829.

J.B.

## FITZROY, Hon. George Ferdinand (1761–1810), of Highgate, Mdx.

BURY ST. EDMUNDS    1784–Jan. 1787

*b.* 7 Aug. 1761, 1st s. of Hon. Charles Fitzroy (q.v.). *educ.* Eton 1775–6. *m.* (1) 2 July 1784 (after a previous surreptitious marriage in Scotland), Laura (*d.*10 June 1798), da. of Hon. Frederick Keppel, bp. of Exeter 1762–78, 2da.; (2) 2 Dec. 1802, Frances Isabella, da. of Lord Robert Seymour Conway (q.v.), 1s. 2da. *suc.* fa. as 2nd Baron Southampton 21 Mar. 1797.
    Lt. 3 Drag. 1778; capt. 14 Ft. 1780; capt. 41 Ft. 1787; maj. 51 Ft. 1792; lt.-col. 2 Ft. Gds. 1793; col. 1796; col. 34 Ft. 1797–*d.*; maj.-gen. 1801; lt.-gen. 1808.
    Groom of the bedchamber to the Prince of Wales 1783–97.

Fitzroy was returned for Bury St. Edmunds after Henry Seymour Conway, Grafton's first choice, had been rejected by the borough. There is no record before 1790 of his having spoken in the House, and his name appears in no division list. He vacated his seat for Grafton's second son, Lord Charles Fitzroy. He died 24 June 1810.

J.B.

## FITZROY, George Henry, Earl of Euston (1760–1844).

THETFORD              6 Apr. 1782–1784
CAMBRIDGE UNIVERSITY         1784–14 Mar. 1811

*b.* 14 Jan. 1760, 1st s. of Augustus Henry, 3rd Duke of Grafton (q.v.) by his 1st w., and bro. of Lord Charles Fitzroy (q.v.). *educ.* Harrow c.1770–6; Trinity, Camb. 1776. *m.* 16 Nov. 1784, Lady Charlotte Waldegrave, da. and coh. of James, 2nd Earl Waldegrave, 6s. 4da. *suc.* fa. as 4th Duke 14 Mar. 1811; K.G. 20 Dec. 1834.
    Ld. lt. Suff. 1790–*d.*; ranger of Hyde Park and St. James's Park 1794–1807.

Lord Euston was a Cambridge contemporary, close friend, and political adherent of William Pitt. In 1780 he was a candidate for Cambridge University, but withdrew because he would not have been of age at the general election; in 1784 he owed his success largely to Pitt's support. In November 1784 he declined Pitt's offer of the place of vice-chamber-

lain.[1] His only recorded speech was on 5 Jan. 1789, when he proposed W. W. Grenville for Speaker. He died 28 Sept. 1844.

[1] Pitt to the King, 8 Nov. 1784, Royal archives, Windsor.

J.B.

## FITZROY SCUDAMORE, Charles (?1713–82), of Holme Lacy, Herefs.

| | |
|---|---|
| THETFORD | 1 Feb. 1733–1754 |
| HEREFORD | 1754–1768 |
| HEYTESBURY | 1768–1774 |
| THETFORD | 1774–Mar. 1782 |

*b.* ?1713, illegit. s. of Charles Fitzroy, 2nd Duke of Grafton. *educ.* Westminster, Nov. 1721, aged 8, left 1730. *m.* 1749, Frances, da. and h. of James, 3rd and last Visct. Scudamore, div. w. of Henry Somerset, 3rd Duke of Beaufort, 1da. Assumed add. name of Scudamore 22 Mar. 1749.
    Capt. 5 Ft. 1735; capt. and lt.-col. 1 Ft. Gds. 1740; second maj. 1747; ret. 1748.
    Master of the King's tennis courts 1733–62; groom porter 1743–62; deputy cofferer of the Household 1765–70.

Charles Fitzroy, through his marriage in 1749 to the heiress of the old and wealthy Scudamore family of Holme Lacy, acquired large estates near Hereford and an interest in the borough. In 1754 he transferred to Hereford from Thetford, where he had sat on his father's interest, and topped the poll after a contest. He continued to support Administration throughout this Parliament. In 1761 he again topped the poll at Hereford. His nephew, the 3rd Duke of Grafton, now began to take an active interest in politics, and Scudamore henceforward appears to have followed the Duke's line very closely. He voted with Opposition on the peace preliminaries, 1 Dec. 1762; was dismissed from office, and voted regularly against the Bute and Grenville Administrations. In 1765, when Grafton was approached by Cumberland about joining a new Administration, he asked to have Scudamore, as a sufferer on his account, 'replaced'.[1] In Newcastle's plan of the new Administration, 15 May 1765, Scudamore was to be restored to his previous office; next he was considered for a clerkship of the Green Cloth, but finally was appointed deputy cofferer,[2] in which office he was continued under Chatham and Grafton. When in 1768 a strong opposition seemed likely at Hereford, Grafton found a seat for him at Heytesbury where he was returned unopposed. After 1770, like Grafton, Scudamore supported North's Administration till the outbreak of the American war, when he followed the Duke into opposition. In 1779 the *Public Ledger* wrote of him that 'though very weak and infirm, he attends constantly to vote with his Grace and his friends in opposition'. But from the important divisions of March and April 1780 he was absent because of ill-health, and though again returned for Thetford at the general election of 1780, does not seem to have attended Parliament, apparently acting merely as stop-gap till the coming of age of Grafton's son, Lord Euston, for whom he vacated his seat in March 1782. Scudamore died 22 Aug. the same year.

[1] Grafton, *Autobiog.* 43. [2] Fortescue, i. 93, 127, 131, 138.

M.M.D.

## FITZWILLIAM, Hon. George (1757-86).

RICHMOND 9 Apr. 1781-1784

*b.* 28 Feb. 1757, 2nd and posth. s. of William, 1st Earl Fitzwilliam [GB], by Lady Anne Watson Wentworth, da. of Thomas, 1st Mq. of Rockingham, sis. and coh. of Charles, 2nd Mq. *educ.* Eton 1766-9; Trinity Hall, Camb. 1771. *unm.* His sis. Charlotte m. 1764, Thomas Dundas (*d.*1820, q.v.).

Sub-lt. 1 Troop Horse Grenadier Gds. 1776; sold out 1782.

In August 1780 Fitzwilliam's brother, Earl Fitzwilliam, was approached by Charles Anderson Pelham about the choice of a candidate at Grimsby. Fitzwilliam immediately wrote to his uncle, Lord Rockingham, suggesting that they should propose George Fitzwilliam and defray the expenses of his election between them. Rockingham refused, thinking it too costly and risky a venture, and no other seat was found for Fitzwilliam at the general election.[1] In 1781 Fitzwilliam was returned for Richmond on the interest of his sister's father-in-law, Sir Lawrence Dundas, whose choosing to represent Edinburgh had caused a vacancy at Richmond. In Parliament Fitzwilliam voted consistently with Opposition till the fall of North; against Shelburne's peace preliminaries, 18 Feb. 1783; against parliamentary reform, 7 May 1783; and for Fox's East India bill, 27 Nov. 1783. There is no record of his having spoken in the House.

In November 1783 Lord Fitzwilliam planned to nominate his brother at the York by-election, but was informed that a considerable part of the Rockingham Club were 'violent associators' for parliamentary reform, and had it 'fresh in their minds that Mr. Fitzwilliam voted against the reform bill'.[2] On 10 Nov., Peregrine Wentworth, one of Fitzwilliam's Yorkshire friends, wrote: 'If Mr. Fitzwilliam put up it would divide your Lordship's interest in such a manner that it would not be itself again.' After this Fitzwilliam did not nominate his brother. In 1784 Lord Fitzwilliam again suggested his brother as

a candidate at York, but was dissuaded on the same grounds.

George Fitzwilliam died 6 May 1786.[3]

[1] I. R. Christie, *End of North's Ministry*, 116. [2] Peregrine Wentworth to Fitzwilliam, York, Monday 12 o'clock, Fitzwilliam mss. [3] Collins, *Peerage*, iv. 399; Burke gives 8 May.

M.M.D.

## FITZWILLIAM, Hon. John (1714-89), of Merrion, co. Dublin, and Richmond, Surr.

NEW WINDSOR 1754-1768

*bap.* 28 Mar. 1714, 3rd s. of Richard, 5th Visct. Fitzwilliam [I], by Frances, da. of Sir John Shelley, 3rd Bt. *educ.* Westminster 1724. *m.* 17 Oct. 1751, Barbara, da. of Dr. Edward Chandler, bp. of Durham, wid. of Lord William Cavendish.

Ensign R. Horse Gds. 1732, lt. 1739, capt. 1745, col. 1755; col. 2 Ft. 1755-60; col. 2 Horse 1760-*d.*; maj.-gen. 1759; lt.-gen. 1761; gen. 1778.

Groom of bedchamber to Duke of Cumberland 1746, on his staff in Flanders 1747.

Returned on Cumberland's interest at Windsor in 1754, Fitzwilliam invariably followed his lead in politics. On 28 Feb. 1757 he questioned Admiral Keppel about Admiral Byng's court martial—the only time he is known to have spoken in the House.[1] His only recorded votes were with Opposition over the peace preliminaries, 9 Dec. 1762, when the message from the Duke ordering him not to vote did not reach him in time;[2] over Wilkes on 15 Nov. 1763, and over general warrants, 18 Feb. 1764. In July 1765 Rockingham classed him as 'pro', but in November 1766, after Cumberland's death, as 'Swiss' (ready to support any Administration), while in March 1767 Newcastle described him as 'doubtful or absent'.

He did not stand at the general election of 1768. He died 31 July 1789.

[1] Walpole, *Mems. Geo. II*, ii. 347. [2] Harris's 'Debates'.

M.M.D.

## FLEMING, John (1743-1802), of Stoneham, Hants.

SOUTHAMPTON 1774-1780, 1784-1790

*b.* 1743, 2nd s. of Thomas Willis by his 2nd w. Frances Robinson of Cranesley, Northants, and gd.-s. of Browne Willis, the antiquary. *educ.* Eton 1758-64. *m.* 1774, Elizabeth, da. of Valentine Knightley (q.v.) of Fawsley, Northants. *s.p. suc.* half-bro. Thomas in the Fleming estate of Stoneham 1767, and assumed name of Fleming.

In 1774, Fleming, 'a neighbouring gentleman of considerable fortune and independent principles, raised so formidable an opposition' at Southampton[1] that Hans Stanley, who for the last 20 years had represented the borough with Government support, agreed to their standing jointly, both being treated as 'friends of Government'; and the opposition which Lord Charles Montagu was offering to Fleming, was discountenanced by Lord North. In the division over Wilkes's motion of 22 Feb. 1775, Fleming voted, however, with Opposition, as did a number of independent country gentlemen. Still, his name does not appear in the next four extant minority lists, and in Robinson's division list on the contractors bill, 12 Feb. 1779, he was classed as an absent friend. He was again absent from the two divisions on Admiral Keppel, 3 and 8 Mar. 1779, voted with Opposition over the list of pensions, 21 Feb. 1780; was absent on 8 and 13 Mar. (abolishing the third secretary and the Board of Trade); and voted with Opposition on Dunning's motion, 6 Apr., and on the motion concerning prorogation, 24 Apr. 1780. In 1779 the *Public Ledger* described him as 'a country gentleman of Tory principles' who 'never votes against the minister'. But Robinson in his electoral survey compiled in July 1780 classed him as 'contra', and clearly wished to see him ousted—which he was at the general election.

In 1784 he stood with the support of the Pitt Administration; was classed in William Adam's list as 'doubtful'; was absent from the division on Richmond's fortifications plan, 27 Feb. 1786; and voted with Pitt over the Regency bill, 1788–9. He did not stand again in 1790. There is no record of his having spoken in the House.

He died 28 Feb. 1802.

¹ *English Chron.* in its note on Hans Sloane.

L.B.N.

**FLEMING, Sir Michael le,** 4th Bt. (1748–1806), of Rydal, Westmld.

WESTMORLAND 1774–19 May 1806

*b.* 10 Dec. 1748, o.s. of Sir William Fleming, 3rd Bt. (q.v.). *educ.* Eton 1760–5. *m.* 23 Nov. 1782, Lady Diana Howard, da. of Thomas, 14th Earl of Suffolk and 7th Earl of Berkshire, 1da. *suc.* fa. 31 Mar. 1757.

Fleming (the 'le' was added at his baptism) was a ward of Sir James Lowther, and in 1774 contested Westmorland jointly with him. On 17 Dec. 1774 Fleming wrote to a friend:¹ 'What is to be done to our *good* subjects on the other side of the Atlantic I cannot say, but I think it should not be made a party matter of, as the crisis is at hand which must determine whether we are to have colonies or not.' Like Sir James, he voted regularly with Opposition till the fall of North; supported Shelburne's peace preliminaries, 18 Feb. 1783, and voted against Fox's East India bill, 27 Nov. 1783. Fleming voted for both Pitt's parliamentary reform

bills, 7 May 1783 and 18 Apr. 1785, and at first supported his Administration, but like the other Lowther Members, voted with Opposition on the Regency, 1788–9.

Only one speech by Fleming is reported before 1790—against a proposal to suppress hawkers and pedlars, 9 June 1785.²

Fleming was described by his friend James Boswell as 'a very fashionable baronet in the brilliant world', who had a great love of literature.³ He died 19 May 1806.

¹ *HMC Le Fleming,* 359. ² For evidence of a second speech see *Scots Mag.* xliii. 188. ³ *Johnson,* i. 461.

M.M.D.

**FLEMING, Sir William,** 3rd Bt. (*d.*1757), of Rydal, Westmld.

CUMBERLAND 19 May 1756–31 Mar. 1757

o.s. of Michael Fleming, M.P., by Dorothy Benson. *m.* 1745, Elizabeth, da. of Christopher Petyt of Skipton-in-Craven, Yorks, 1s. 5da. *suc.* uncle as 3rd Bt. 2 July 1747.
Ensign in Howard's Regt. of Ft.
Sheriff, Cumb. 1754–5.

On the death of Sir William Lowther, Fleming was persuaded to offer himself for the vacant seat and hold it in trust for Sir James Lowther till he should come of age. He was recommended by Lowther in a circular letter as 'a person most heartily attached to his Majesty', and was returned unopposed. Even so the election cost Lowther over £550, £200 being paid to the needy Sir George Dalston (q.v.) for organizing it.

Fleming died 31 Mar. 1757.

¹ B. Bonsall, *Sir James Lowther,* 36–37.

L.B.N.

**FLETCHER, Andrew** (1722–79), of Saltoun, Haddington.

HADDINGTON BURGHS 1747–1761
HADDINGTONSHIRE 1761–1768

*b.* 1722, 1st s. of Andrew Fletcher of Saltoun, S.C.J. (Lord Milton), by Elizabeth, da. of Sir Francis Kinloch, 2nd Bt., of Gilmerton. *educ.* Glasgow Univ. 1735; Ch. Ch. Oxf. 1739. *m.* 1764, Jeanie, da. of Sir Robert Myreton, 2nd Bt., of Gogar, Edinburgh., *s.p. suc.* fa. 1766.
Clerk of the pipe in the Scottish Exchequer 1746–1751; sec. to Duke of Argyll as keeper of the great seal, 1748–61; auditor gen. of the Scottish Exchequer 1751–*d.*

From his youth, Fletcher was trained in political discretion by his father, Lord Milton, 'confidential friend and deputy' to Archibald, Duke of Argyll in the management of Scotland.¹ Fletcher became Argyll's secretary and constant companion, living with him in London, and attending him on his annual visits to Edinburgh and Inveraray. 'Though not a man who produced himself in public life', wrote Alexander Carlyle,[2] he was 'sufficiently knowing and accomplished to be a very amiable member of society'. In politics a loyal and self-effacing subordinate, he relied on his father and Argyll to fight his battles. Thus when Milton in 1754 demanded that Sir Hew Dalrymple should resign Haddingtonshire in Fletcher's favour, and 'take his turn' of representing the Burghs, Fletcher himself declined to press the matter; and when in 1760 the quarrel over representation came to a head, it was Argyll and Milton who were the principals in the complicated negotiations with Dalrymple, resulting in Fletcher's transfer to the county in the Parliament of 1761.

Over the Scottish militia bill of 1760, on which Argyll's attitude was equivocal, Fletcher, under his father's direction, took an active part, being one of the inner group nominated by the Edinburgh committee (under Milton's presidency), to concert how the bill should be brought into Parliament.[3]

Owing to Argyll's dislike of letter-writing Fletcher was entrusted with much confidential business. In 1760 he was employed by Argyll in an attempt to patch up his quarrel with Bute. Newcastle wrote to Hardwicke, 6 Sept. 1760:[4]

[Argyll] told me . . . that he had sent Fletcher to my Lord Bute, his Lordship having objected extremely to Mr. [Samuel] Martin. That Fletcher had not succeeded better, that he complained to him of sending Mr. Martin and letting *the English* into their dispute.

After Argyll's death, although Bute proffered friendship,[5] Milton's control of Scottish affairs rapidly declined, and his withdrawal from public life, followed by his physical and mental breakdown, left his son without a political mentor.

Fletcher supported the Bute Administration on the peace, and the Grenville Administration on general warrants, but after 1765 practically ceased to attend Parliament. He was absent in Scotland from the divisions on the repeal of the Stamp Act in February 1766, and does not appear in any subsequent division list. In January 1767 Townshend classed him as absent. He maintained a connexion with Grenville, to whom he explained on 9 Mar. 1768[6] that 'a sad variety of distress' had greatly impaired his health, rendering him 'unable to attend to his own affairs, much less the House'. His father's mental collapse and his death in December 1766 were the primary causes of this distress, which was aggravated by the opposition raised in his constituency by Sir Hew Dalrymple and Sir George Suttie. When Grenville, at Dalrymple's instigation,

urged him on 16 Feb. 1768[7] to agree to a junction of the Fletcher and Dalrymple interests to defeat Suttie, Fletcher replied[8] that owing to ill-health 'he thought it honest to decline coming into Parliament', but could not forgive Dalrymple for his unfriendly conduct in 1766, 'at the time of his greatest distress'. Despite pressure from Grenville, and probably also from Bute and Loudoun, Fletcher decided neither to stand nor to 'meddle'.

Fletcher retired to his Saltoun estate, devoting himself to agricultural improvement and the cultivation of his nurseries of exotic trees and shrubs, which had long been famous. He died 24 May 1779.

[1] About Milton, see Ramsay of Ochtertyre, i. 86–90. [2] *Autobiog.* 261. [3] Milton to C. Townshend, 23 Feb. 1760, Buccleuch mss. [4] Add. 32911, f. 101. [5] Carlyle, 414; Milton to Loudoun, 22 Apr. 1761, Loudoun mss. [6] Grenville mss (JM). [7] Grenville letter bk. [8] Mar. 1768, Grenville mss (JM).

E.H.-G.

**FLETCHER, Henry** (c.1727–1807), of Clea Hall, Cumb.

CUMBERLAND    16 Dec. 1768–1806

*b.* c.1727, 7th s. of John Fletcher of Clea Hall by his 2nd w. Isabella, da. and coh. of John Senhouse of Netherhall, Cumb. *m.* 20 Oct. 1768, Catherine, da. and h. of John Lintot of Southwater, Suss., 1s. 1da. *suc.* bro. 1759; *cr.* Bt. 20 May 1782.
Director, E.I. Co. 1769, 1771–5, 1777–80; dep. chairman Apr.–July 1782; chairman July 1782–Nov. 1783.

Fletcher was an officer in the naval service of the East India Company, from which he retired in 1766. In 1768 he stood for Cumberland on the antiLowther interest, backed by the Duke of Portland; and though he obtained a majority on the poll the sheriff rejected sufficient of his votes to enable Lowther to be returned. Fletcher was seated on petition. In Parliament he voted consistently with the Rockingham party, and seems to have been regular in his attendance. Before 1782 he is known to have made only one speech: 5 June 1780, on the Cumberland petition; and at the county meeting of 1780 his opponents charged him with being 'by no means equal to the important trust of a Member of the House of Commons' because 'he never spoke upon any question whatsoever'.[1]

As chairman of the East India Company in 1782–3, Fletcher had much to do with Shelburne's peace negotiations. In spite of his close connexion with Portland and Fox he defended the East India articles of Shelburne's peace preliminaries, said they were acceptable to the directors, and in the division of 18 Feb. 1783 abstained from voting. Between February and November 1783 he made 15 speeches in the Commons, all on East Indian affairs.

Francis Baring (q.v.), who probably knew as much

about the East India Company as anyone, wrote to Shelburne on 20 Nov. 1783:[2]

> In the state which Mr. Fox gave of the Company's affairs he made several capital mistakes, but which I do not wonder at, as he received his information from Fletcher, who is neither capable of forming accounts himself nor of digesting those which are formed by others: the blunders which Sir Henry has made in some commercial arrangements during the present Administration are far more injurious although not obvious to the public eye, but under his management will the great commercial concerns of the Company fall.

In Fox's East India bill Fletcher was nominated one of the seven commissioners for Indian affairs. On 24 Nov., as chairman of the Company, he presented a petition against the bill; then resigned, as he told the Commons on 27 Nov., 'that his mind might be free and open to judge of a question of such great importance'.[3] His judgment was that the bill was a good one, and he both spoke and voted for it.

Fletcher after his resignation lapsed into insignificance. Although he remained connected with Portland and Fox and voted with them in opposition to Pitt, he took no part in the impeachment of Warren Hastings—which is surprising in view of his long East Indian experience. Between 1784 and 1790 only one speech by him is recorded, 12 July 1784, on a matter concerning Cumberland.

He died 29 Mar. 1807, aged about 80.

[1] T. Benson to the Duke of Portland, 11 Sept. 1780, Portland mss. [2] Lansdowne mss. [3] Debrett, xii. 199–202.

J.B.

**FLETCHER, Sir Robert** (c.1738–76), of Ballinasloe, co. Roscommon and Lindertis, Angus.

CRICKLADE     1768–1774

*b.* c.1738,[1] 1st s. of Robert Fletcher of Ballinasloe by Elizabeth, da. of William Lyon of Carse, Angus. *m.* 17 Dec. 1774, Anne, da. of John Pybus, banker, of Cheam, Surr., *s.p.* Kntd. 29 Dec. 1763. Ensign Bengal army 1757, capt. 1760, maj. 1764, lt.-col. 1765, col. 1769, brig.-gen. 1774.

Fletcher's father served in the '45 as a major in Lord Ogilvy's regiment, and was reported to have escaped after Culloden to Bergen.[2] He returned to Scotland soon after 1754.

Fletcher's career was brief but stormy. Appointed a writer at Madras in May 1757, he transferred to the army four months later. He was dismissed the service when a lieutenant for insolence, but Eyre Coote secured his reinstatement. He then rose rapidly in his profession, and on his return to England in 1763 was knighted for gallantry in action. Sent out to India once more in command of a brigade, he was involved in the 'batta' mutiny against Clive in 1766, court-martialled, and again

cashiered. He then sailed to England to get the sentence quashed.

At the general election he was first reported to be canvassing Bridport,[3] but moved on to stand at Malmesbury, where he and Sir William Mayne were defeated by the Howard candidates. He then presented himself at the neighbouring borough of Cricklade, and though 'an entire stranger', took over an interest abandoned by Clive's brother-in-law, and secured his return.[4] It was said to have cost him £4,000.[5]

In the House he voted at first with Opposition, to which most of his friends belonged. But his main interest was to secure restoration to the Company's service. His first attempt was frustrated by Clive's friends; John Walsh described the Company's general court in a letter to Clive, 8 Apr. 1768:

> The court was over at four by the previous question being put on the motion for thanking and reinstating Fletcher. The thanking part he before had modestly moved to be withdrawn. We carried it by about thirty majority, though Sir Robert had been very industrious in mustering friends.

Fletcher then persuaded George Grenville to ask Clive not to maintain his opposition, and Clive agreed.[6] On 15 Dec. 1769 Fletcher was appointed to Madras as colonel, though he did not sail until the summer of 1771. In the meantime he had moved over to Administration, voting with the majority over Brass Crosby on 27 Mar. 1771, and attacking Barré.

Within a few months of his return to India he was again embroiled, this time with the governor, Josias Dupré. By January 1773 they were 'at daggers drawn',[7] and Dupré dismissed him from the council and ordered him to Trichinopoly, where he could do no mischief. In this situation Sir Robert recollected that he had duties to his constituents at home, and sailed for England in March 1773.[8] He arrived in time to take an active part in the House in the spring of 1774. On 25 Feb. he spoke and voted against the motion to perpetuate the Grenville Act, and three days later gave notice that he would move for an inquiry into the affairs of the Company.

In April 1774 the Company re-appointed him to Madras with the rank of brigadier-general. He remained in England until after the general election, when he canvassed Cricklade, but was forced to decline the day before the poll.[9]

He arrived once more in India in June 1775 to take up his old command, and was soon involved in conspiracy. This time he kidnapped the new governor, Lord Pigot (q.v.), and confined him to prison. His own explanation was:[10]

> Opposition in our council ran to such violence between the majority, of which I was a member, and the minority, led by Lord Pigot, that matters came at

length to mutual suspension, or rather expulsion, of each side. Lord Pigot expelled first the majority, and took possession of the Fort. We, to prevent bloodshed, were obliged to arrest his person.

Fletcher was now increasingly ill with tuberculosis, and left in October 1776 in the *Greenwich* on a voyage to restore his health. He died at Mauritius on 24 Dec. 1776. The King, not knowing of Fletcher's death, wrote in April 1777 of his part in the *coup*: 'Sir Robert Fletcher appears with his usual inclination to disputes.'[11]

The large fortune which he left was the subject of litigation, and in 1778 his friend George Dempster wrote:[12]

Few fortunes acquired in the East will bear a very minute investigation . . . Will it become his executors to tell the chancellor in open court that the nabob had promised the commander-in-chief of the Company's forces ten thousand pound about the time that the Company's governor, and that governor Lord Pigot, was by the intrigues of that very nabob deprived of his government, of his liberty, and in consequence of his life? . . . would one wish to see Colonel Capper giving his public testimony of the means by which Sir Robert obtained a parcel of the most valuable pearls of India from the same nabob? . . . To keep the whole of this matter as quiet as possible is a duty we all owe to Sir Robert.

[1] His parents were m. in 1736. [2] *Sc. Hist. Soc.* viii. 210-11. [3] Jesse, *Selwyn*, ii. 275. [4] Letter of T. Carter, 14 Apr. 1771, Powis mss. [5] J. Walsh to Clive, 8 Apr. 1768, ibid. [6] Grenville to Clive, 28 Mar. 1769, ibid. [7] A. Owen to Orme, 31 Jan. 1773, Orme mss. [8] *HMC Palk*, 216. [9] *Bath Chron.* 13 Oct. 1774. [10] *HMC Stopford-Sackville*, i. 356. [11] Fortescue, iii. 440. [12] *Letters of G. Dempser*, ed. Fergusson, 102.

J.A.C.

**FLOOD, Henry** (1732–91), of Farmley, co. Kilkenny.

WINCHESTER    17 Oct. 1783–1784
SEAFORD          26 Apr. 1786–1790

*b.* 1732, illegit. s. of Warden Flood, chief justice of Ireland 1760–4, by Miss Whiteside[1] whom he subsequently married. *educ.* Trin. Dublin 1747; Ch. Ch. Oxf. 1750; I. Temple 1750. *m.* 16 Apr. 1762, Lady Frances Beresford, da. of Marcus, 1st Earl of Tyrone [I], *s.p. suc.* fa. 1764.
    M.P. [I] 1759–76, 1777–83.
    Jt. vice-treasurer [I] 1775–81; P.C. [GB and I] 1776, struck off both 1781.

As early as 1768 Flood seems to have been trying to enter the British Parliament.[2] And on 7 Oct. 1776, shortly after Flood had gone over to Administration, John Robinson wrote to the King:[3]

Mr. Flood's views are now strongly bent to get into the British Parliament. He has expressed his wishes for this to Lord North, and repeated them frequently . . . His Lordship has given him no hopes of his assistance, but leaves it to his Majesty's consideration.

Nothing further is known of Flood's Westminster ambitions till 1783, when he was returned for Winchester on the Duke of Chandos's interest. On 8 Dec. 1783 he attended the House for the first time, when Fox's East India bill was debated, and began with an apology for venturing to speak 'totally unacquainted as he was with the subject of Indian concerns, not having read the reports on the table, and knowing no more of their contents than he had heard at a distance . . . He thought it however, an indisputable act of parliamentary duty to say something upon the occasion.'[4] He went on to attack the bill, and the unprecedented powers which Fox was attempting to acquire. John Burgoyne reported to Lord Northington, lord lieutenant of Ireland, 9 Dec.:[5]

At four in the morning when the House had been long in clamour for the question [Flood] rose to speak . . . He began unluckily professing himself unattached to any party, and equally unconnected with ministry and Opposition; this created a diversion in the House, and whether that circumstance diverted him, or the fatigue of his journey, or the heat of the House had exhausted him, it is certain from the avowal of all parties that his speech was not only below mediocrity, but upon a class with the very lowest form in parliamentary speaking . . . In short Flood has made a *début* . . . of the most discouraging kind.

His only other long speech in this Parliament was against the sending of troops to Ireland, 10 Dec. 1783. He was classed by Robinson in January 1784 as a supporter of Pitt, and again in Stockdale's list of 19 Mar.

During his first months in Parliament Flood continued on very friendly terms with the Duke of Chandos who wrote to him at length, professing great admiration for what he was doing in Ireland, and concern for his well-being. At Christmas, when a dissolution seemed imminent, it was agreed that he should again come in for Winchester. But at the dissolution in March, while Flood was in Ireland, Chandos returned his brother-in-law Richard Gamon. In the dispute that followed Chandos maintained that Flood had undertaken to retire whenever his seat was wanted for Gamon, while Flood asserted that 'not a hint ever fell that his Grace had any intention to have Mr. Gamon returned for Winchester'.[6] He now claimed that Chandos was obliged to find him a seat elsewhere which Chandos denied; Flood, infuriated, sent him a challenge which he ignored, merely reiterating his readiness 'to give Mr. Flood every assistance in his power to procure him a seat'.

Flood next stood for Seaford in March 1785. The previous election there had been declared void, and Flood was introduced by T. H. B. Oldfield with a view to overthrowing the Treasury interest. Though Flood topped the poll, the returning officer brought in the Treasury candidates. Again the election was declared void. Flood once more topped the poll, and again two Treasury candidates were returned; but on 26 Apr. 1786 Flood was seated on petition.

The same day Daniel Pulteney (q.v.) wrote to the Duke of Rutland: 'This man will attempt some mischief, I suppose, as soon as he can'; but on 18 Jan. 1787: 'I think Mr. Flood is so low that I might safely enough abuse him, if ever he introduces Irish subjects in an English House of Commons.' When on 15 Feb. 1787 Flood discoursed against the commercial treaty with France, inquiring why such concessions should be granted to France and denied to Ireland, his language, wrote Pulteney, was 'so barbarous to an English ear, his manner of arguing so abstracted and void of illustration, and his *tout ensemble* somehow or other so disgusting, that he fell infinitely below my expectations, and will never make the slightest impression on our side', nor even 'gain much confidence with the Opposition.'[7] His one recorded vote was with Pitt over the Regency, 1789.

On 4 Mar. 1790 in a speech on parliamentary reform Flood proposed that one hundred new Members be added, elected by a 'numerous and new body of responsible electors; namely the resident householders in every county'. This would add 'a body of responsible constituents of such number that the majority of the people may have the exercise of the franchise', without interfering with existing borough ownership.[8] His scheme received no support from Pitt, and was negatived by a motion to adjourn the House. Flood did not stand in 1790.

He died 1 Dec. 1791.

[1] Warden Flood, *Mems. of Hen. Flood*, 4. [2] Copeland, *Burke Corresp.* i. 338; *Letters to Hen. Flood*, 48. [3] Add. 37833, f. 67. [4] Debrett, xii. 398. [5] Add. 33800, f. 448. [6] Flood to Chandos, 10 Apr. 1784, Chandos Pprs., Huntington Lib. [7] *HMC Rutland*, iii. 213, 292 366. [8] Wyvill, *Pol. Pprs.* ii. 537–63.

M.M.D.

**FLUDYER, George** (1761–1837), of Ayston Hall, Rutland.

CHIPPENHAM 28 Feb. 1783–1802
APPLEBY 23 June 1818–Apr. 1819

*b.* Sept. 1761, 2nd s. of Samuel Fludyer, and bro. of Sir Samuel Brudenell Fludyer (qq.v.). *educ.* Westminster 1771; Grand Tour with his bro. Samuel. *m.* 16 June 1792, Lady Mary Fane, da. of John, 9th Earl of Westmorland, 3s. 4da.

Fludyer entered Parliament on the family interest at Chippenham; was classed by Robinson in March 1783 as 'country gentleman; doubtful'; voted for Fox's East India bill; but next went over to Pitt and was classed as 'pro' by Robinson in January 1784, and as 'Administration' by Stockdale, 19 Mar. He

voted with Pitt during the Regency crisis. No speech by him is recorded before 1790.

He died 15 Apr. 1837.

J.A.C.

**FLUDYER, Sir Samuel Brudenell,** 2nd Bt. (1759–1833), of Lee, Kent.

ALDBOROUGH 8 June 1781–1784

*b.* 8 Oct. 1759, 1st s. of Samuel Fludyer (q.v.). *educ.* Westminster 1771; Grand Tour. *m.* 5 Oct. 1786, his cos. Maria, da. of Robert Weston, gd.-da. of James Brudenell, 1s. 2da. *suc.* fa. 18 Jan. 1768.

There is no evidence to show whether either Fludyer or his younger brother George was ever an active partner in their late father's firm, though both presumably kept an interest in it.

Fludyer was connected through his mother with a family prominent at court and with which Lord North had an indirect family connexion. He was brought in for Aldborough by the 2nd Duke of Newcastle as a Government supporter; voted with them on 12 Dec. 1781 and 22 Feb. 1782, and possibly also on 20 Feb; but was absent from the divisions of 27 Feb. and 8 Mar., and on the 'no confidence' motion, 15 Mar., voted with Opposition. Robinson classed him that day among 'Persons who were hopeful, who now came and voted against'; and wrote about him in August 1782: 'was much the friend of Mr. Fox and acted with him'. He did not, however, vote on Shelburne's peace preliminaries; was again classed by Robinson in March 1783 as a supporter of Fox; but in the published lists appears as absent from the divisions on Fox's East India bill. In the second week of December Robinson wrote: 'Sir S. Fludyer is always against [i.e. with Fox]; . . . Sir Samuel will scarce be brought in again.' But John Sinclair wrote in a paper drawn up sometime between 18 Dec. 1783 and 10 Jan. 1784: 'Sir Samuel, Member for Chippenham, and his brother both voted for the bill, but Mr. Brudenell might still have an influence over them to alter their opinion.' This probably happened, as Fludyer was classed as 'pro' in Robinson's list of January 1784, and as 'Administration' in Stockdale's list of 19 Mar. He did not stand again in 1784. There is no record of his having spoken in the House.

He died 17 Feb. 1833.

[1] Sandwich mss; Abergavenny mss; Fortescue, v. 390; Laprade, 40, 43, 86; Sinclair mss.

I.R.C.

**FLUDYER, Samuel** (?1704–68), of Lee, Kent.

CHIPPENHAM 1754–18 Jan. 1768

*b.* ?1704, 1st s. of Samuel Fludyer, London clothier (originally of Frome, Som.), by Elizabeth, da. of

Francis de Monsallier, a Huguenot. *educ.* Westminster. *m.* (1) Jane Clerke (*d.* 15 Mar. 1757), of Westminster, 1da.[1]; (2) 2 Sept. 1758, Caroline, da. of Hon. James Brudenell, M.P., sis. of George Bridges Brudenell (q.v.), and niece of George, 3rd Earl of Cardigan,[2] 2s. Kntd. 19 Sept. 1755; *cr.* Bt. 14 Nov. 1759.

Common councillor, London 1734–51, alderman 1751, sheriff 1754–5, ld. mayor 1761–2.

Director, Bank of England 1753–5, 1756–8, 1759–1762, 1763–6; dep. gov. 1766–*d.*

Fludyer was born a Dissenter, but, according to Ezra Stiles, president of Yale, his second marriage and his baronetcy led him away from his Church.[3] He joined his father's business which he greatly developed; became one of the foremost cloth merchants; and from 1738 till his death appears in the London directories in partnership with his brother Thomas as warehouseman, of Basinghall Street. In a list of merchant M.P.s compiled about 1754, in the Lowther mss, he is described as a 'great dealer in North and West country cloths'. This helped him to establish a parliamentary interest at Chippenham where in 1754, at a cost of £1,500,[4] he was returned unopposed. In Newcastle's lists of 1754 he is classed as Government supporter; though over the Mitchell election petition, which was not strictly a party matter, he voted on the Fox-Sandwich side.[5] In the first part of his career he was, however, neither a Government contractor nor a large subscriber to Government loans.

At the general election of 1761 Fludyer stood for the City of London as one of the four who had a majority on a show of hands at the meeting of the livery at Guildhall on 4 Mar.; and he signed a joint address with Thomas Harley, William Beckford, and Richard Glyn;[6] but was defeated on the poll, 26 Mar.–2 Apr. He complained to Lord Kinnoull on 30 Mar. that there were letters from the Ordnance and the Board of Works in Beckford's favour only, who 'will certainly carry it if he gets this interest'. And Kinnoull, forwarding the letter, wrote to Newcastle:

> The Whigs seem to be cutting one another's throats. The Dissenters divided. Dr. Chandler [a leading nonconformist minister] polled against Fludyer as he tells me . . . The Ordnance and the Board of Works *single Beckford*. That is surprising. It is not unreasonable to ask that they should be for Fludyer *not exclusive of Beckford*; surely that cannot give offence anywhere [i.e. to Pitt].[7]

And here is the account of the election sent to Newcastle by one of his City agents, Joseph Watkins:[8]

> If I am rightly informed Sir Samuel was greatly to blame for, by acting secretly against Mr. Harley, he flung the whole weight of the merchant interest on a person whom they were determined to fling out, and whose corporation interest was nothing without the

merchants' support, a mortifying circumstance to him but he acknowledged the fact.

Fludyer was re-elected at Chippenham; in Bute's parliamentary list of December 1761 was marked as a supporter of Newcastle, who still classed him as such in his list of 13 Nov. 1762. But the bidding had already started—Lord Harcourt wrote to Charles Jenkinson on 5 Nov.:[9]

> We find that great pains have been taken to bring Sir Samuel to a right way of thinking, every kind of civility and complaisance has been exerted by a great man whose Lady is related to Lady Fludyer [Henry Fox]. I fancy it will have its effect. Notwithstanding which I hope your Lord [Bute] will have an opportunity of explaining matters to him which will set everything right.

Fludyer appears in Fox's list of Members favourable to the peace preliminaries with a query against his name. But presumably he voted with the majority, for in a paper drawn up after 10 Dec. Fox writes: 'Sir Samuel Fludyer has my promise . . . of some share in contracts and remittances that remain in peace.'[10]

Fluyder appears as subscriber of £19,000 to Bute's loan of £1,100,000 in 1762;[11] and again as subscriber to the 3½ million loan of March 1763, on which a profit of about 10 per cent was netted; but he was not among the biggest subscribers enumerated in the *North Briton*, No. 42, and to Fox's appeal for an increased allocation for Fludyer, Bute replied, 2 Mar.:[12]

> Sir Samuel Fludyer stood with me on the same footing that every other person does, whose subscription I promised to receive; the few excepted, who were immediately to take upon themselves the chance of carrying my plan into execution, and of them none have half what they desired . . . I have no private list (as they call it); every man is welcome to see it, and to see that justice, not favour, has made the arrangement.

Also under the Grenville Administration Fludyer was one of the leading Government financiers.[13] But his subscriptions were for a quick turn-over only: £10,000 in annuities, held from April 1766 till his death, is the most substantial holding of Fludyer's in the Bank of England records.

For victualling contracts he had to wait till the existing ones expired. He and Adam Drummond signed one for the troops in West Florida, but gave it up in order to replace George Colebrooke and Arnold Nesbitt, merchant Members who adhered to Newcastle, in much bigger contracts for America and Quebec. These were not signed till April 1764.[14] Fludyer also obtained in February 1764 a contract for remittances to several West Indian islands;[15] and together with Anthony Bacon, the Fludyer-Drummond partnership applied in 1764 'for the lease of all coals on the island of Cape Breton'—Bacon, a big and experienced coal operator being obviously the future manager, while Fludyer was cashing in on his political influence and connexions.[16]

In the autumn of 1763 Fludyer was classed by Jenkinson as a Government supporter, but in the crucial division on general warrants, 18 Feb. 1764, appears in the list of 'absent friends'. In Newcastle's lists preparatory to the formation of the Rockingham Government, Fludyer is among the contractors to be removed; but in Rockingham's parliamentary lists of July he is once classed as 'pro' and another time as 'query'; he did not vote against the repeal of the Stamp Act. Nevertheless notice to terminate his American contracts was given to him on 11 July 1766 by a moribund Treasury.[17] Next Fludyer adhered to the Chatham Administration; was classed as such by Rockingham, Newcastle and Townshend; voted with Government on the land tax, 27 Feb. 1767, the last division in his lifetime for which lists are extant; and received a new victualling contract in March.[18] No speech by Fludyer is recorded during his 14 years in the House.

The following account appears in a biographical sketch of Fludyer published in 1800.[19] 'An unfortunate moment of avarice . . . clouded his reputation, and is supposed to have shortened his life.' He was assignee of a bankrupt, and when the business was heard before Lord Camden, the discovery was made of a contraband trade which Fludyer 'had carried on in scarlet cloth, to the detriment of the East India Company. The lord chancellor reprehended his conduct in the most severe terms, and decreed against him. Sir Samuel, who was present in court, sunk as it were beneath the chastisement, and did not long survive it.'

Fludyer died 18 Jan. 1768, 'reputed worth £900,000'.[20]

[1] Add. 32921, ff. 184, 190. [2] *Leinster Corresp.* i. 413. [3] Stiles to Dr. Alison, 5 Sept. 1766, Stiles mss at Yale. [4] Namier, *Structure,* 200 n. 3; Add. 32995, f. 114. [5] E. Boscawen to Newcastle, 12 Mar. 1755, Add. 32853, f. 260. [6] *British Chron.* 2–4 Mar. 1761; *Gent. Mag.* 1761, p. 137; Beaven, *Aldermen of London,* i. 280. [7] Add. 32921, ff. 190, 184. [8] Add. 32922, f. 187. [9] Jucker, *Jenkinson Pprs.* 81. [10] Add. 40758, f. 279. [11] Bute mss. [12] Ilcaester, *Letters to Hen. Fox,* 172. [13] Jucker, 351–2. [14] T54/39/273–6; Namier, *Structure,* 51; Jucker, 239–40. [15] T29/35/301. [16] Add. 38337, f. 284; 38338, ff. 24–27. [17] Fortescue. i. 128; T29/38/75. [18] T54/40/304–6. [19] *City Biog.* 23. [20] *Gent. Mag.* 1768, p. 47.

L.B.N.

**FLUDYER, Sir Thomas** (1711–69), of Lee, Kent.

GREAT BEDWYN    2 Dec. 1767–Jan. 1768
CHIPPENHAM      29 Jan. 1768–19 Mar. 1769

*b.* 1711, 2nd s. of Samuel Fludyer, and bro. of Samuel Fludyer (q.v.). *m.* 27 Mar. 1742, Mary, da. of Sir George Champion, M.P., London alderman, 1da. Kntd. 9 Nov. 1761.

Fludyer goes through life as junior partner to his

brother, in business and in politics. In Kent's *London Directory* for 1736 a Thomas Fludyer 'druggist', Leadenhall Street, is mentioned, but his identity is uncertain; from 1738 till 1768, Samuel and Thomas Fludyer appear together as 'warehousemen, Basinghall Street'. The first time Thomas appears in Newcastle's lists of parliamentary candidates it is as 'Fludyer's brother',[1] and on the monument in the graveyard of St. Margaret's church at Lee, he is still 'Brother to Sir Samuel Fludyer Bart.' Under his brother's wing he stood for Devizes: canvassed the borough in 1761; was defeated at the by-election in January 1765; and canvassed the borough once more before another by-election in May. Later in the year he thought of standing for New Shoreham—George Grenville wrote to John Sargent on 20 Oct. 1765: 'With regard to Sir Thomas Fludyer's application to you for your recommendation at Shoreham you know that I gave him all the assistance in my power when he was candidate last spring for Devizes and therefore can have no objection to him now supposing that Sir Samuel and he are still in the same sentiments towards me which they were then in.' But on 28 Oct. Grenville wrote to another possible candidate, Topham Beauclerk, that Thomas Fludyer was 'unwilling to appear at all without the certainty of success'.[2] In December 1767 he was brought in for Great Bedwyn by Lord Bruce, whose cousin Samuel Fludyer had married; but six weeks later, on his brother's death, Thomas vacated the seat in order to preserve the family interest at Chippenham. No vote or speech of his in Parliament has been recorded.

He was presumably with his brother a big subscriber to Government loans; and at his death held nearly £30,000 of Government stock.

He died 19 Mar. 1769.

[1] Add. 32916, f. 66. [2] Grenville letter bk.

L.B.N.

**FOLEY, Andrew** (?1748–1818), of Newport, Herefs.

DROITWICH    7 Apr. 1774–28 July 1818

*b.* ?1748, 3rd s. of Thomas Foley (*d.*1777), and bro. of Edward and Thomas (qq.v.). *educ.* B.N.C. Oxf. 11 June 1768, aged 19. *m.* 7 May 1773, Elizabeth, da. and h. of Boulter Tomlinson, 1s. 4da.

Andrew Foley, like his brothers, was connected politically with Charles James Fox: he opposed North, supported the Coalition, and opposed Pitt. There is no record of his having spoken in the House before 1790.

He did not share his brothers' passion for gaming

and was not involved in their debts. Mrs. Delany wrote about his marriage:[1]

> The young people have liked one another some time. Mr. Foley settles on them in present his house and estate at Newport, which is now above £1000 a year, and Miss Tomlinson's fortune, exclusive of what she will have after her mother's death, is £7000 and £400 a year. It is a great match for him according to his present income; but Mr. Foley intends *doing more* if they behave well ... He says his son Andrew has always shown him a *proper regard*, is very well-disposed, and has withstood all the snares that have been laid for him.

Lord Foley showed his confidence in his youngest son by making him a trustee of his will.

Andrew Foley died 28 July 1818.

[1] *Autobiog. and Corresp.* (ser. 2), i. 492–3.

J.B.

**FOLEY, Edward** (1747–1803), of Stoke Edith, Herefs.

DROITWICH 1768–May 1774
WORCESTERSHIRE 30 May 1774–22 June 1803

*b.* 16 Mar. 1747, 2nd s. of Thomas Foley (*d.*1777), and bro. of Andrew and Thomas (qq.v.). *educ.* Westminster 1764; B.N.C. Oxf. 1764; L. Inn. 1768. *m.* (1) 24 Oct. 1778, Lady Anne Margaret Coventry (div. 21 May 1787), da. of George William, 6th Earl of Coventry, 1s. *d.v.p.*; (2) 21 Mar. 1790, Elizabeth Maria, da. and h. of Thomas Hodgetts of Prestwood, Staffs., 3s. 2da.

Foley sat on the family interest at Droitwich; and at the by-election of 1774 was returned unopposed for Worcestershire, as he was again at the general elections of 1774, 1780, and 1784. In Parliament he conformed to the family pattern of voting: opposed North, supported the Coalition, and opposed Pitt. There is no record of his having spoken in the House before 1790.

Like his brother Thomas he became overwhelmed by gambling debts, and participated with his brother in the attempt to upset their father's will.

Foley died 22 June 1803.

J.B.

**FOLEY, Thomas** (1716–77), of Stoke Edith, Herefs. and Witley, Worcs.

DROITWICH 1741–1747, 9–16 Dec. 1747, 1754–1768
HEREFORDSHIRE 1768–20 May 1776

*b.* 8 Aug. 1716, o.s. of Thomas Foley, M.P., by his 1st w. Hester, da. and h. of Thomas Andrews of London. *educ.* Westminster 1724–32; Trinity, Camb. 1732. *m.* 29 Mar. 1740, Hon. Grace Granville, da. and coh. of George, 1st Baron Lansdowne, 3s. 4da. *suc.* fa. 1749; to estates of his cos. Thomas, 2nd Baron Foley, 1766, when the title became extinct; *cr.* Baron Foley 20 May 1776.

The Foleys had large estates in Herefordshire and Worcestershire, and exerted considerable political influence in both counties. Throughout this period they controlled one seat at Droitwich, and for the most part two. In 1754 Thomas Foley was classed by Dupplin as a Tory. In George III's reign he generally voted with the Whig Opposition.

He is not in Fox's list of Members favourable to the peace preliminaries, nor did he vote against them. In the autumn of 1763 Jenkinson marked him as 'pro', but he voted against the Grenville Administration on Wilkes and general warrants (15 Nov. 1763, and 15 and 18 Feb. 1764)—on the last occasion included by Jenkinson in his list of those who were normally friends; and he was classed by Newcastle as a 'doubtful friend'. He opposed Administration on the cider duty (as did most West country Members), acted once as a teller against them, 10 Feb. 1764, and twice spoke for its repeal, 13 Mar. 1763 and 7 Mar. 1764—his only recorded speeches.[1]

In July 1765 Rockingham classed Foley as 'pro', but he voted against the repeal of the Stamp Act. This did not prevent Rockingham proposing him for a peerage—he wrote to the King, 5 June 1766:[2]

> Mr. Foley's hopes are grounded on some expectation that the late Lord Foley had of being created a peer with a higher title than baron and with limitation to the present Mr. Foley.
> The present Mr. Foley in point of family estate, and weight is certainly very proper for the honour of peerage.

George III replied that he adhered to his previous 'intention of not at least for the present increasing the peerage'.

Foley voted against Chatham's Administration on the land tax, 27 Feb. 1767. In 1768 he was returned unopposed for Herefordshire. He voted against Administration over the Middlesex election, 15 Apr. and 8 May 1769, and in 1769 tried to promote a petition in Herefordshire against the seating of Luttrell—he was very friendly with Dowdeswell, the leader of the Rockingham group in the Commons. Foley voted against the Spanish convention, 27 Mar. 1771, and his next recorded vote (on Grenville's Election Act, 25 Feb. 1774) was also against Administration. Yet Robinson in September 1774 classed him as 'hopeful'.

In the contested election for Herefordshire in 1774 Foley came out head of the poll. His only other recorded vote was for Wilkes's motion on the Middlesex election, 22 Feb. 1775. His peerage was included in the batch of ten created in 1776—although during the 28 years he had spent in the

Commons he appears in no division list as having voted with the court.

He died 18 Nov. 1777.

[1] Harris's 'Debates'. [2] Fortescue, i. 354–5; Albemarle, *Rockingham Mems.* i. 347.

J.B.

## FOLEY, Thomas (1742–93).

HEREFORDSHIRE 18 May 1767–1774
DROITWICH 1774–18 Nov. 1777

*b.* 24 June 1742, 1st s. of Thomas Foley (*d.*1777), and bro. of Andrew and Edward (qq.v.). *educ.* Westminster 1753; Magdalen, Oxf. 1759. *m.* 20 Mar. 1776, Lady Harriet Stanhope, da. of William, 2nd Earl of Harrington (q.v.); 2s. 2da. *suc.* fa. as 2nd Baron Foley 18 Nov. 1777.
Jt. postmaster gen. Apr.–Dec. 1783.

Foley was returned unopposed for Herefordshire in 1767, and again at the general election of 1768. From 1768 to 1772 he voted with Opposition, appearing in eight out of eleven division lists for that period. In the three divisions for which lists are extant, 1772–4, he did not vote; and Robinson in 1774 classed him as 'hopeful'.

He did not stand for Herefordshire in 1774 but was returned for the family borough of Droitwich. On 22 Feb. 1775, on Wilkes's renewal of the Middlesex question, and on 26 Oct. 1775, on the Address, he voted against the court. According to Walpole[1] he wished to stand for Herefordshire at the by-election following his father's elevation to the peerage, but North refused him the Chiltern Hundreds. This seems probable, since the King hoped that Thomas Harley would succeed to the vacant seat;[2] but the rest of Walpole's story—that Foley in order to vacate his seat asked Lord Harrington to appoint him his regimental agent, and that North threatened if this were done to dismiss Harrington from his regiment—lacks confirmation.

Foley was a close friend of Charles James Fox, a gambler, and a racing man. Mrs. Delany wrote in 1773:[3] 'Mr. T. Foley has *lost* at Newmarket etc. fifty thousand pounds. He has now entered into an agreement with his father, that if he will pay his debts he *will* entirely leave off gambling.' But in Nov. 1775 George Selwyn wrote to Lord Carlisle:[4] 'Old Foley pays another £70,000 of debt, and settles, I hear today, £4,000 in present upon his son, and £6,000 a year more at his death.' And according to Walpole (to Mann, 11 Aug. 1776), Foley and his brother Edward were faced with the payment of £18,000 per annum interest on their debts.

Lord Foley in his will authorized his trustees to pay a sum not exceeding £6000 per annum for the maintenance of his two eldest sons. The remainder of the income from the family estates was to be used for the payment of their debts. When these had been settled, the Witley estate (worth £11,500 a year) was to go to Thomas, and Stoke Edith (worth £3500 a year) to Edward. Thomas and Edward promoted a private bill to enable the estates to be sold for the payment of their debts. The judges who were ordered to report on the bill estimated that these amounted to £220,000, and under the terms of the will would be repaid in 27 years. In spite of intense lobbying by the two elder Foleys, the Lords rejected the bill.[5]

Thomas Foley died 2 July 1793.

[1] *Last Jnls.* i. 508–9. [2] Fortescue, iii. 360. [3] *Autobiog. and Corresp.* (ser. 2), i. 492–3. [4] *HMC* Carlisle, 304. [5] Walpole, *Last Jnls.* ii. 133–135; *LJ*, xxxv. 341–4, 466–9.

J.B.

## FOLJAMBE, Francis Ferrand (1750–1814), of Aldwark, nr. Rotherham, Yorks.

YORKSHIRE 1 Jan.–25 Mar. 1784
HIGHAM FERRERS 13 Nov. 1801–1807

*b.* 17 Jan. 1750, o.s. of John Moore of Hull by Anne, da. of Francis Foljambe of Aldwark. *educ.* St. John's, Camb. 1768. *m.* (1) 30 June 1774, Mary Arabella (*d.*28 Dec. 1790), da. of John Hewett (q.v.), by Arabella, sis. and coh. of Sir George Savile, 8th Bt. (q.v.), 5s. 2da.; (2) 12 June 1792, Lady Mary Arabella Lumley, da. of Richard, 4th Earl of Scarbrough, by Barbara, also sis. and coh. of Sir George Savile, *s.p. suc.* uncle Thomas Foljambe 1758, and took name of Foljambe; and fa. 1768.
Sheriff, Yorks. 1787–8.

Foljambe was a member of the Yorkshire Association of 1780 and took a prominent part in its activities. When his wife's uncle, Sir George Savile, retired from the representation of the county in November 1783, Foljambe, though comparatively young and untried, was chosen to succeed him. He received the support of the Association and of Lord Fitzwilliam, both of whom were trying to make capital out of Savile's popularity.

Foljambe's first vote, 16 Jan. 1784, was for Lord Charles Spencer's motion for the dismissal of Pitt. Mason and Wyvill, the leaders of the Association, who had come out strongly in favour of Pitt, now regretted having supported Foljambe for the county. Mason wrote about him to Wyvill, 22 Jan.:[1]

I have known him from his infancy; I may justly say that I have been a father to him; yet on many trying occasions I have seen him close and reserved where he ought to have been open and explicit, rash and determined where he should have been deliberate or dubious, and always too soon cooled in his pursuits if the expected success did not immediately attend him . . . We must now hope no more from him than a mere support of parliamentary reform, if ever that question should chance to be agitated. This will not satisfy me, nor do I think it will you.

After the county meeting of 25 Mar., when Wyvill succeeded in obtaining an address in support of Pitt, Foljambe resigned from the Association; and at the general election stood with William Weddell as Fitzwilliam's candidate. Their canvass was unfavourable, and the evening before the poll they withdrew.

Foljambe remained loyal to Fitzwilliam, but refused Fitzwilliam's request to stand again in 1788. He died 13 Nov. 1814.

¹ Wyvill, *Political Pprs.* iv. 353-4.

E.A.S.

## FOLKESTONE, Visct., *see* PLEYDELL BOUVERIE

## FONNEREAU, Martyn (1741–1817), of Leadenhall St., London.

ALDEBURGH    30 Mar. 1779–1784

*b.* 19 Mar. 1741, 2nd s. of Zachary Philip Fonnereau, and bro. of Philip Fonnereau (qq.v.). *unm.*
Director, Bank of England 1771–83.

He succeeded his uncle Thomas at Aldeburgh; adhered to the North Government, voting with them in every division for which a list is extant; voted against Shelburne's peace preliminaries; for Fox's East India bill; and against Pitt. There is no record of his having spoken in the House. He did not stand again in 1784.

He died 18 May 1817.

L.B.N.

## FONNEREAU, Philip (1739–97).

ALDEBURGH    1761–1768

*b.* 17 June 1739, 1st s. of Zachary Philip Fonnereau, and bro. of Martyn Fonnereau (qq.v.). *educ.* ? Trinity Hall, Camb. 1755; L. Inn 1753, called 1765. *m.* 15 Dec. 1763, Mary, da. of Armstead Parker (q.v.) of Peterborough, 1s. 3da. *suc.* fa. 1778.

Returned for Aldeburgh together with his father, he is likewise marked in Bute's list: 'Newcastle, contra'. He voted together with his uncle and his father against the Government on 1 Dec. 1762, and also with his uncle on 9 Dec. After that he again followed them in adhering in turn to each successive Administration. He did not stand in 1768 nor at any subsequent election. There is no record of his having spoken in the House.

He died 17 Feb. 1797.

L.B.N.

II—P*

## FONNEREAU, Thomas (1699–1779), of Ipswich, Suff.

SUDBURY    1741–1768
ALDEBURGH    13 May 1773–20 Mar. 1779

*b.* 27 Oct. 1699, 1st s. of Claude Fonnereau, Hamburg merchant, by his 1st w. Elizabeth, da. of Philip Bureau of La Rochelle, and bro. of Zachary Philip Fonnereau (q.v.). *unm.* *suc.* fa. 5 Apr. 1740.

Fonnereau's father, a Huguenot naturalized in 1693, was a Hamburg merchant, and is stated to have made his fortune in the linen trade. He left large landed estates to Thomas, and considerable money legacies to him and the other children.¹

Thomas, in 1754 a regular Government supporter, had an interest at Sudbury and Aldeburgh. With his brother Zachary Philip he had a share in the contract for victualling the Gibraltar garrison. The Fonnereaus were also big subscribers to Government loans: in 1757 Thomas applied for £30,000; in 1759 he underwrote £250,000, and in 1762 £350,000. These large subscriptions covered many customers, while Fonnereau's permanent holdings in Government stock, as entered in the Bank of England records, were not considerable.²

Before 1761 only two interventions of Thomas Fonnereau in debate are recorded, on the budget, 28 Apr. 1758, and over the bill for restraining privateers, 4 May 1759, when he was 'upon his feet but did not say much'.³

From 1760 onwards Fonnereau was engaged at Sudbury in a bitter struggle with Thomas Fenn, receiver general of the land tax in that part of Suffolk, who was originally appointed at Fonnereau's recommendation, but afterwards turned against him; favoured, however, by powerful protectors, foremost the Duke of Grafton, he retained his office, undermining Fonnereau's influence in the borough.

In Bute's list of December 1761 Fonnereau was marked 'Newcastle, contra'; in Newcastle's list of 13 Nov. he and his brother still appear as friends; and they voted with the Opposition for postponing consideration of the peace preliminaries, 1 Dec. Thomas also voted against the preliminaries on Thursday, 9 Dec., but did not vote the next day. How the Fonnereaus were got over to the Government side appears from an account by Newcastle of his talk with Zachary Philip on 16 Dec. As it was Zachary Philip who had talked both to Bute and Newcastle the story is told in his biography although Newcastle believed that it was 'Tom Fonnereau who has done this with his brother'. Henceforth they steadily adhered to Government, and were among its leading financiers.⁴ But after the Grenville Administration had been dismissed, Temple wrote to Grenville, 8 Aug. 1765: 'All the little Fonnereaus . . .

have been performing the eastern adoration of that rising sun, Lord Rockingham, at his levee.'[5] Rockingham in his list of July classed them as 'pro', and in November 1766 as 'Swiss' (prepared to support every Administration), and both Townshend in January and Newcastle on 2 Mar. again as Government followers. Thomas voted with the Government on the land tax, 27 Feb. 1767.

The approaching general election of 1768 soured relations between Fonnereau and Government: at Sudbury an opposition was raised to him by men friendly to the Government and by Fenn, whom he could not get dismissed, and similarly at Aldeburgh the opposition to the Fonnereaus boasted of Government support. When on 17 Feb. 1768 Beckford's bill against bribery in elections was discussed in committee,

> Fonnereau, [writes Horace Walpole] a peevish man, who had all his life been a court tool, complained that Chauncy Townsend, a brother dependant, but more favoured, had so much interest with the ministers, that one Bennet, parson of Aldeburgh, and attached to Townsend, had vaunted that he could obtain the dismission of any officer of the revenue who should vote for Fonnereau.[6]

To this Harris adds that Fonnereau complained of Townsend's agent offering £200 a man to the Aldeburgh voters.[7] Bradshaw, Grafton's secretary to the Treasury, 'having been concerned in the business' at Aldeburgh, writes Walpole, 'the Opposition hoped to reach the Duke himself, and ordered the parson to their bar'. Dunning, the new solicitor-general but not yet in Parliament, appeared for Bennet.

> Fonnereau, to save £40, for he was a very miser, had refused counsel, and behaved so obstinately and absurdly that though Grenville, Wedderburn, and Dowdeswell supported, and gave him hints, with all their parliamentary craft, he counteracted his own witnesses; and it came out that he had not only been more criminal himself than the clergyman, but for a series of years had established and profited of ministerial influence in the borough in question.[8]

He turned the House against himself, and the parson was acquitted by 155 to 39.

At the general election Thomas Fonnereau stood for Sudbury and was defeated both on the poll and on his petition. At Aldeburgh, he put up his brother Zachary Philip and his friend Nicholas Linwood, who was rich and in favour with Grafton; and they were returned unopposed. Thomas Fonnereau himself was now out of Parliament till returned for Aldeburgh on Linwood's death. In 1774 he stood both for Sudbury and Aldeburgh, and was returned for both; but having been unseated on petition at Sudbury, he sat for Aldeburgh.

On 25 Feb. 1774, on Grenville's Election Act, he voted with Opposition. His name does not appear in the Opposition list over Wilkes, 22 Feb. 1775, nor on Lord John Cavendish's amendment to the Address, 26 Oct. 1775; but he voted with them over payment of the King's debts, 16 Apr. 1777, and in two divisions on America, 2 Feb. 1778 and 3 Mar. 1779.

He died 20 Mar. 1779.

[1] Agnew, *Protestant Exiles from France*, ii. 399, 400, 485; *Gent. Mag.* 1740, p. 203. [2] Add. 32866, ff. 393–4; 32868, ff. 170–1; 32901, f. 238; 33040, ff. 290–1; Devonshire mss. [3] Add. 32879, f. 331; H. V. Jones to Newcastle, Add. 32890, f. 488. [4] *Jenkinson Pprs.* 353. [5] Grenville mss (JM). [6] *Mems. Geo. III*, iii. 112–13; Add 32988, f. 361. [7] Add. 32988, f. 355. [8] *Mems. Geo. III*, iii. 114, corrected from original.

L.B.N.

**FONNEREAU, Zachary Philip** (1706–78), of Sise Lane, Bucklersbury, London.

ALDEBURGH 1747–1774

*b.* 31 Jan. 1706, 4th *s.* of Claude Fonnereau, and bro. of Thomas (q.v.). *m.* 13 Apr. 1738, Margaret, da. and coh. of George Martyn of Odington, Glos., 10s. 3da. Director, E. I. Co. 1753, 1754.

Fonnereau supported Administration, and together with his brother Thomas was a Government contractor. In January 1754 the candidature of the two sitting Members for Aldeburgh, Windham and Fonnereau, was approved by Pelham, and was subsequently taken over by Newcastle. When the case against Brice Fisher (q.v.) was brought before the directors of the East India Company, Fonnereau, together with Nicholas Linwood (q.v.) and Chauncey, took his side; after this the three dropped out from the directorate, though Fonnereau seems to have retained a certain standing in East India House.[1]

In Bute's list of December 1761 he is marked 'Newcastle, contra'. Together with Thomas he voted with Opposition on 1 Dec., but not on the 9th—it was he who was negotiating with Bute. On 17 Dec. Newcastle wrote to Thomas Walpole, Fonnereau's partner in the Gibraltar contract:[2]

> Yesterday morning I had a long conversation with Mr. Zachary Fonnereau, by which it appears, and by his own confession, that he is entirely gone over to my Lord Bute. The fact, as he states it, is this, that he acquainted Mr. [Samuel] Martin, that if my Lord Bute desired it, he was ready to be concerned in the loan for raising the money, *this year*, as he had been formerly; that voluntary offer on his part produced (as he certainly intended it should) some farther discourse with Mr. Martin; and ended in my good *friend's* having some conference with my Lord Bute himself; in which Mr. Fonnereau gave his Lordship such assurances that Fonnereau himself apprehended that his voting with us, as he did one night, might be (as to be sure it was) inconsistent with the assurances which

he had before given to my Lord Bute; and Mr. Fonnereau thought himself obliged to come to explain himself to my Lord Bute; and that, as I find, ended by Mr. Fonnereau's engaging himself, his brother, and his son absolutely to my Lord Bute.

I talked very civilly but very strongly to him, of his behaviour to me, after the assurances he had given me. He owned very plainly that it was interest; that he had a family; his brother and he had spent thirty thousand pounds in elections; that he had got but little from my brother and me, and that he must look out to his interest. I suppose his price is some valuable remittances to Minorca etc.; when a man knows himself that he is bought, one has nothing to say to him.

I then supposed that if I should be personally attacked, I might there depend upon his assistance. He eventually said, yes, but with some sort of hesitation; which makes me believe they have endeavoured to secure him in that also. This is the man that was represented to me as a friend and as honest a man, as any in the city . . .

I wish you would go as a friend and talk this matter over with Mr. Fonnereau, show him the figure he will make; and that possibly this may not finally turn out for his interest . . . I believe it is Tom Fonnereau, who has done this with his brother.

Zachary Fonnereau's politics continued to coincide with those of his brother: he supported Administration whoever it was that held office. So also in the Parliament of 1768–74, from which Thomas was absent, Zachary's name appears in the extant division lists steadily on the Government side. He did not stand again in 1774. There is no record of his having ever spoken in the House during the 27 years he sat in it.

He died 15 Aug. 1778.

[1] Add. 32995, ff. 63–67; 32866, ff. 393–4; *Jenkinson Pprs.* 272.
[2] Add. 32945, ff. 301–2.

L.B.N.

## FORD, Richard (1758–1806), of the Inner Temple.

EAST GRINSTEAD    27 Feb. 1789–1790
APPLEBY    1790–May 1791

*b.* 1758, 4th s. of Dr. James Ford, physician to Queen Charlotte, of Albemarle Street, London by his w. Anne Hole. *educ.* ?Westminster 1765–74; L. Inn 1777, called 1782. *m.* 7 Apr. 1794, Marianne, da. and coh. of Benjamin Booth, director, E.I. Co., of the Adelphi, London, 2s. 1da. Kntd. 16 Dec. 1801.
Chief magistrate at Bow Street 1800.

In 1789 Ford was returned for East Grinstead by the Duke of Dorset, presumably as a supporter of Pitt. No vote by him appears in this Parliament, but three speeches of his are reported. He commented on the legal aspects of Warren Hastings's petition, 1 May 1789; on the bill to prevent vexatious removals of the poor, 15 May, opposed a clause which 'took away the possibility of a settlement'—'was pleasant on his own profession . . . he did not know but he might fall into the situation of a person to become

chargeable';[1] his third speech was in the debate on army estimates, 5 Feb. 1790.

He died 3 May 1806, aged 47.

[1] Stockdale, xvii. 235.

M.M.D.

## FORDWICH, Visct., *see* COWPER, George Nassau Clavering

## FORESTER, Brooke (1717–71), of Dothill Park and Willey Park, Salop.

WENLOCK    14 Feb. 1739–1768

*b.* 7 Feb. 1717, 1st s. of William Forester, and bro. of Cecil Forester (qq.v.). *m.* (1) 4 May 1734, Elizabeth (*d.*Mar. 1753), da. and h. of George Weld of Willey Park, Wenlock, 4s.; (2) 1760, Elizabeth, da. of Robert Barnstone of Chester, 1da. *suc.* fa. 12 Nov. 1758. Resided at Willey Park 1734–59, at Dothill 1759–*d.*

Brooke Forester supported the Walpole Administration, and became one of the old corps of Whigs. Like his father, he followed Lord Powis, and was counted by Newcastle among his surest supporters. When asking the Duke, 15 Mar. 1759, that his brother Cecil be made aide-de-camp to the King, he could write: 'the long steady attachment my family has always showed, and the few favours we have solicited . . .' And in Bute's list of the House, December 1761, the remark is placed against his name: 'By Whiggism attached to Lord Powis as head of that party in Shropshire, but soliciting very few favours of Government.' Forester adhered to Newcastle even after Powis's defection, and on 9 Dec. voted against the peace preliminaries; he did not vote on the 10th. He voted steadily with the Opposition over Wilkes and general warrants, but did not join Wildman's Club. On 10 May 1764 he was listed as a 'sure friend' by Newcastle, who on 21 Mar. 1765 wrote from Bath to George Onslow, Member for Surrey:[1]

I have . . . had a great deal of discourse with the two Foresters: the Stag [Brooke Forester[2]] and his brother the Colonel. I believe neither of them will come up. The Stag is very zealous, as he always was, and ever will be; I think he has still some correspondence with his old friend, my Lord Powis; though he resents extremely the part he takes; and has a good deal of partiality for my Lord Granby. But, when he came to the point, he said (what all the world say, except a very, very narrow clique) 'that we have no *Head*; nobody to lead them, etc.' . . . In short I see we shall have no assistance from the very best set of men I ever knew in Parliament, what we used to call *the Shropshire Gang.*

A rather different light is thrown on Forester's doubts and complaints by two letters.[3] On 29 Jan. 1765 Powis 'with great pleasure' informed George Grenville that Forester and his brother would stay away that day from the House (where general warrants were discussed once more); and on 27 Feb. Forester wrote to Lord Gower:

> When your Lordship honoured me with a letter the beginning of last sessions, wherein you mentioned your desire of my supporting the present Administration, I at that time thought myself under the strictest obligations to the Duke of Devonshire, who I had always been connected with for upwards of five and twenty years. But since his death, I think myself now as free from all political connexions both private and public, as if I came but yesterday into Parliament, exclusive of the principles I ever have, and ever will support, as a Whig. Now, my Lord, as I have a favour to ask of the Government and there is no person I would so soon choose to be obliged to as your Lordship, hope you'll excuse the liberty I take in begging your assistance in behalf of my youngest son.

His son was a major on half-pay, and Forester asked to have him put again on full pay. This was done, but by then the Grenvilles were out of office—before Forester had time to attach himself to them; and in Rockingham's list of July 1765 he is listed 'pro'; in November 1766 as 'Whig'; by Townshend in January 1767 as 'doubtful'; and by Newcastle, on 2 Mar., as a 'friend'. No vote of his is recorded during those years; and no speech during nearly 30 years in the House. He retired at the general election of 1768, and died 8 July 1771.

¹ Add. 32889, f. 86; 38333, f. 93; 32966, ff. 79-80. ² On Brooke Forester's nickname, see Namier, *Structure*, 297 n. 1. ³ Grenville mss (JM).

L.B.N.

## FORESTER, Cecil (?1721-74), of Rossall, nr. Shrewsbury, Salop.

WENLOCK 1761-1768

*b.* ?1721, 2nd s. of William Forester, and bro. of Brooke Forester (qq.v.). *educ.* Westminster Apr. 1733 (aged 12)-1737. *m.* Anne, da. and coh. of Robert Townshend of Christleton, Cheshire, 5s. 2da.
Cornet 4 Drag. 1739; maj. 46 Ft. 1748, lt.-col. 1752; lt.-col. 11 Ft. 1755; sold out 1760.

Forester's elder brother, Brooke, when asking the Duke of Newcastle, 15 Mar. 1759, that Cecil be made aide-de-camp to the King, added: 'As my brother has been ill used, if he is not preferred he is determined to give up immediately.' The secretary at war, Lord Barrington, noted in his 'Military Paper' of 28 Mar. that Forester was 'high on the list of lieutenant-colonels'; and from now onwards he continued to appear in the Duke's memoranda, and in his correspondence with Lord Powis; to whom Newcastle wrote in despair on 12 Aug. 1759:

> Your Lordship knows my zealous wishes for Colonel Forester's service; the King knows them; my Lord Ligonier knows them. It is not in my power to make

any absolute promise of any military preferment; and therefore I should be extremely to blame to promise what it may not be in my power to perform.

Yet nothing happened, and Forester left the army.[1]

In the House he presumably followed his brother. On 9 Dec. 1762 he appears as voting against the peace preliminaries in the list published in the *History of the Late Minority*, but not in that sent by Fox to Bute. Otherwise not a single vote, and not a single speech, by him is recorded during his seven years in Parliament; in the division lists on general warrants, 6 and 18 Feb. 1764, he is marked as 'absent'; and together with his brother, at Lord Powis's instance, stayed away from the House on 29 Jan. 1765. He did not stand again for Parliament, and died on 22 Aug. 1774, aged 53.

¹ Add 32889, ff. 86, 283-4; 32894, f. 103.

L.B.N.

## FORESTER, George (1735-1811), of Willey Park, Salop.

WENLOCK 8 Dec. 1758-1761, 1768-1780, 9 Dec. 1780-1784, 9 Aug. 1785-1790

*b.* 21 Dec. 1735, 1st s. of Brooke Forester (q.v.). *educ.* Peterhouse, Camb 1753.[1] *unm. suc.* mother Mar. 1753; fa. 8 July 1771.

George Forester succeeded to his grandfather's parliamentary seat in 1758, and replaced his father in 1768. In the three earliest division lists extant for the new Parliament, 27 Jan. and 2 and 3 Feb. 1769, all three on Wilkes, he appears on the Opposition side; and on 13 June, the common and burgess hall of Wenlock, having thanked their Members for their past conduct in the House, voted instructions to them[2] which probably expressed the Members' views at least as much as those of their constituents. They were asked to

> promote and concur in all such measures as tend
>
> 1st. To preserve the electors of this realm the sole choice of their representatives in Parliament . . .
> 2nd. To protect all the subjects of this realm from arbitrary and illegal seizure of their papers and imprisonment of their persons . . .
> 3rd. To promote to the utmost frugality of the public treasure . . .
> 4th. To restore the tranquility and promote the commerce of our American colonies by redressing their grievances in such a manner as to preserve in its full force the unquestionable control of the British Legislature over there.
> 5th. To preserve and extend the manufactures and commerce of this kingdom by reducing the present high price of provisions and taking off the additional duty on beer so severely felt by the industrious poor of this populous and extensive franchise.

Forester seems to have voted with Opposition whenever present, but appears only in two out of the ten division lists, March 1769–May 1774: on the Spanish convention, 13 Feb. 1771, and the royal marriage bill, 11 Mar. 1772. He also seems to have intervened in two debates during those early years: on 22 Jan. 1770, he expressed regret that Thomas Townshend jun. should have refused the Chair—'an union of sentiments upon the present occasion might have been the occasion of an union that might have healed the present breaches and divisions'; and on 16 Feb. 1770, spoke in the debate of censure on the Speaker.[3] No other speech by him is recorded during his 23 years in the House.

In the Parliament of 1774–80 Forester appears in none of the five division lists 1775–8, and over the contractors bill, 12 Feb. 1779, is listed by Robinson as 'contra, absent'; of the remaining six division lists, four name him. He did not stand at the general election of 1780. Six division lists are extant for the period between Forester's re-entry in December 1780 and the fall of North: Forester voted in one division, possibly in a second,[4] and was paired in three. Siding with Fox, he voted against Shelburne's peace preliminaries, 18 Feb. 1783, and for Fox's East India bill, 27 Nov. 1783; but supported Pitt over parliamentary reform, a non-party measure, 7 May 1783. He did not stand in 1784 when two Bridgemans, like him Foxites, were returned for Wenlock unopposed; so was he himself at the by-election of August 1785, at a total cost of £364, almost all on entertaining his constituents.[5] He voted with Fox in the Regency crisis of 1788–9. In 1790 he retired in favour of his cousin and heir, Cecil Forester, son of Cecil Forester (q.v.).

The *English Chronicle* wrote about George Forester in 1781 that he owed his repeated elections

> to the general good opinion that is entertained of him by the electors, of his feelings and liberalities as a man, and his attention and ability as a magistrate. He is eminently distinguished for the two prescriptive characteristics of an English gentleman, an attachment to the chase, and a generous hospitality at the conclusion of it. . . . These are qualities of no great importance as a senator; but in a period when it is fashionable to despise the old and respectable criteria of our national character, it is peculiarly pleasing to see an individual of consequence bold enough to deviate into *ill-bred* familiarity and antiquated hospitality.

He is credited with 'a strong attachment to the fair sex', of which there is 'a variety of *living* witnesses' in the country. Affluent and independent, he neither fears nor courts any minister.

> He is a Whig in his principles, and so perfectly sincere in the vindication of his favourite tenets, . . . that he would relinquish his dogs for freedom, and sacrifice even his strong beer (for which, by the by, he is famed beyond any modern competitor) to the rigid preservation of our most excellent constitution.

George Forester died 13 July 1811.

[1] T. A. Walker, *Adm. to Peterhouse*, 306. [2] Copy of Much Wenlock Borough Minutes (made in or after 1816) in Forester mss at Willey Park. [3] Cavendish's 'Debates', Egerton 3711, pp. 79–80; 220, pp. 143, 146. [4] I. R. Christie, *End of North's Ministry*, 379. [5] Forester mss.

L.B.N.

**FORESTER, William** (1690–1758), of Dothill Park, Salop.

WENLOCK   1715–1722, 1734–1741, 1754–12 Nov. 1758

*b.* 1690, 1st s. of Sir William Forester, K.B., M.P., of Dothill by Lady Margaret Cecil, da. of James, 3rd Earl of Salisbury. *m.* 1714, Catherine, da. and h. of William Brooke of Clerkenwell, 3s. 3da. *suc.* fa. Feb. 1718.

Thirteen Foresters[1] sat for Wenlock between 1529 and 1885 (not counting relatives returned by them), and no Forester in the 18th century sat for any other constituency. Wenlock, without being a pocket borough, was identified with the Forester family, as they were with it; and they have continued to this day to supply mayors to the borough.

William Forester's parliamentary career lies for the most part outside our period. He was a strong Whig: one of those 'I have under my care', wrote Lord Powis to the Duke of Newcastle in October 1754.[2] No vote or speech of Forester's is recorded in the Parliament of 1754. He died 12 Nov. 1758.

[1] G. T. O. Bridgeman, 'Some Account of the Family of Forester', *Trans. Shropshire Arch. Soc.* (ser. 2), iii. 172; Namier, *Structure*, 235–298. [2] Add. 32737, ff. 33–34.

L.B.N.

**FORRESTER, Alexander** (?1711–87), of Lincoln's Inn.

| | |
|---|---|
| DUNWICH | 2 Dec. 1758–1761 |
| OKEHAMPTON | 1761–1768 |
| NEWCASTLE-UNDER-LYME | 1768–1774 |

*b.* ?1711, s. of Alexander Forrester (s. of Andrew Forrester and Jean Cunningham). *educ.* I. Temple 1727, called 1731. *unm.*

Forrester came of a Scots Jacobite family who had followed James II into exile. His uncle, John Forrester,[1] was a trusted agent who went to Scotland in the '15, escaped capture, and returned to France to serve in the Duke of Berwick's regiment. Of Forrester's father nothing certain is known. His mother was probably a Frenchwoman, and Forrester was almost certainly born in France. The family had connexions in Angus with the Maules of Panmure, who were also 'out' in the '15.

Forrester became a successful counsel, and in 1741 published *Cases in Equity during the time of Lord Talbot*. From 1741 he frequently appeared before the Board of Trade, and occasionally before the Privy Council, in colonial cases; but after about 1758 he seems to have specialized in cases before the House of Lords (among them Scottish election appeals). Alexander Wedderburn repeatedly appeared as his junior, and he associated in his cases with men like Charles Yorke, Lord Frederick Campbell, Fletcher Norton, and Pratt.

On a vacancy at the Duke of Bedford's borough of Tavistock, William Beckford appealed to the Duke, 4 June 1754, 'as the head of an opposition, founded on true patriot principles', to return 'Counsellor Forrester, whose steadiness, honour, and elocution, are not exceeded by many in these kingdoms'.[2] This seems to have been the first introduction of Forrester to his future patron; that time the Duke had another candidate in view. But when in May 1758 Lord George Bentinck, M.P. for Malmesbury, was supposed to be dying, Bedford 'mentioned that succession' to Forrester:[3] the nomination to the borough was then in Henry Fox. Bentinck did not die till March 1759, and on 2 Dec. 1758 Forrester was returned for Dunwich by Sir Jacob Downing, a friend of Fox.

About the same time Forrester was recommended by Baron Maule (brother of Lord Panmure) to the Duke of Argyll as candidate for the city of Edinburgh; and although Forrester was unpopular as an Anglicised Scot resident in England—'too much an Englishman'—such was Argyll's majority on the town council that his election was generally expected. But Charles Townshend, who was trying to prepare the ground for his own return at Edinburgh, helped to drive him 'off the field': in a speech at a city dinner, on 18 July 1759, he lessened him 'so much in their eyes by his fine vein of ridicule that the dislike of the town council was increased to aversion'. In the end even Argyll's party did not dare to nominate him. He was returned by Bedford for Okehampton.[4]

On 12 Oct. 1761 Forrester applied to Bedford to recommend him to the ministers for the vacant Chair of the House of Commons.[5] 'I am, indeed, astonished at my own presumption' (as he well might be); but he hoped possibly to attain the Chair 'in the light of your Grace's most devoted friend and servant (the most glorious and desirable to myself)'. He admitted the objections he was liable to: 'the short time of my sitting in Parliament, and my ignorance of the forms'. But he drew an ingenious analogy with the case of every new chancellor in the Lords. He referred to his 30 years at the bar, and his position there, which nevertheless left him outdistanced by juniors: 'by a peculiar fatality [I] have constantly had wind and tide against me, nor ever in my life met with any the most

distant offer of advancement, until your Grace was . . . pleased to take me by the hand'. Bedford refused; he had already recommended Rigby; and beside the short time Forrester had been in the House, those unfriendly would urge against him his being a Scotsman, and his former connexions with the Tories.[6]

When in December 1761 a vacancy was impending in the post of solicitor-general, Forrester again applied to Bedford, who recommended him to Bute and Newcastle. Bute replied that the King's choice was already 'in a manner fixed'; and Newcastle that he was committed to Fletcher Norton.[7] 'The peculiar fatality', which pursued the Anglicised Scot, persisted, and advancement was to elude him even during the years when the Bedfords were in office.

Forrester's speech in the debate on the Address, 13 Nov. 1761, in which he followed Eliab Harvey, was that of a 'still shrewder lawyer': he slurred over the issues of the German and Spanish wars and the militia, and hoped that 'the night's mail would not carry to the continent news of disunion in the new Parliament'.[8] Harris, reporting several of his subsequent interventions in debate on minor points, remarks that he 'spoke well'.[9] In a way most remarkable is that on 23 Nov. 1763, when objections were raised to proceeding with the question of Wilkes's parliamentary privilege in his enforced absence. Harris thus summarizes Forrester's speech: '*audi alteram partem*—contra.' Grenville reported to the King that the authority of Wilbraham 'weighed so much with several gentlemen of the law', Forrester among them, that they supported putting off the question. And Walpole: 'Forrester . . . reckoned no squeamish lawyer, spoke for procrastination, and voted against the court.' If so, this was the only recorded occasion of Forrester dissociating himself from the Bedford group. Later on, he spoke frequently on Wilkes and general warrants and always on orthodox lines. Most of his interventions were on legal questions; and like so many Scotsmen, and especially Scots lawyers, he usually took an authoritarian view. Thus on 4 Mar. 1765, about the power of the attorney-general to grant informations *ex officio* in the King's bench: 'every power is liable to abuse but there must be powers . . . The Crown has no more power than it wants for the support of its authority.' And according to Harris: 'in these days of licence, not ashamed to be called a prerogative lawyer'.[10]

In July 1765 Forrester followed Bedford into opposition. Sandwich wrote to Grenville, 14 Aug. 1765: 'I dined on Sunday last at Sir John Cotton's . . . I met Forrester there who is eager beyond imagination.' Several speeches of his are recorded during the debates on America and the Stamp Act: on 17 Dec. 1765 he supported Grenville's amendment to the Address declaring the colonies in rebellion; on 5 Feb. 1766 he spoke for Nugent's amendment requiring the colonial assemblies to recompense sufferers in the Stamp Act riots; on 7 Feb. he supported Grenville's motion for enforcing laws in America; and he naturally voted against the repeal. Over the land tax, 27 Feb. 1767, he seems to have voted against the Chatham Administration —his name appears in two out of three extant division lists.[11]

On 28 Feb. 1768 the Duke of Bedford informed Thomas Brand that he had reserved for him a seat at Okehampton 'in the place of Mr. Forrester, who Lord Gower, at my request, chooses at Newcastle-under-Lyme'. On 6 Dec. 1770 Forrester said when opposing Glynn's motion for an inquiry into the administration of justice:

> What I see . . . has not given me so high an idea of the liberty of the press, as it did in my youth. I am not so concerned for the fate of the booksellers. There is too much learning already. We should be better men, if we had less books . . . My independence is known. I have no obligation to any one set of men or another, nor ever will.

This was his last major speech in the House. Also his attendance at divisions became poor: his name appears in only three out of seven division lists, 1768–74, which give the names of the Government side. Perhaps he felt his years—on 1 May 1769, pleading for an earlier meeting of the House, he said: 'At my time of life, I am not over fond of the hours of the present age, either for business or amusement'; possibly also he was disappointed at the lack of preferment. He did not stand again in 1774, though there seems then to have been no estrangement between him and Lord Gower, to whom Forrester in his will dated 20 Feb. 1778 left the wines in his cellar 'in remembrance of our former many convivial meetings' (but revoked the bequest in a codicil, dated 9 July 1783). He died 2 July 1787, aged 76, naming Lord Frederick Campbell as his residuary legatee. He directed all his papers to be destroyed.[12]

¹ Ruvigny, *Jacobite Peerage*, 52, 191. ² *Bedford Corresp*. ii. 150. ³ Rigby to Bedford, 1 June 1758, ibid. 243 (misdated). ⁴ Carlyle, *Autobiog*. 289, 387; Walpole, *Mems. Geo. III*, i. 47. ⁵ Bedford mss 44, f. 200. ⁶ *Bedford Corresp*. iii. 54–55. ⁷ Bedford mss 44, ff. 284, 288. ⁸ Walpole, *Mems. Geo. III*, i. 73. ⁹ 25 Feb., 8 Apr. 1762. ¹⁰ Fortescue, i. 61; *Mems. Geo. III*, i. 258; Newdigate mss. ¹¹ Grenville mss (JM); Fortescue, i. 202, 267; Newdigate mss. ¹² Bedford mss 57, f. 16; Cavendish's 'Debates', Egerton 223, ff. 82–84; Cavendish, *Debates*, i. 405; Esdaile, *Temple Church Monuments*, 90.

L.B.N.

### FORTROSE, Lord, *see* MACKENZIE, Kenneth
(*d*.1761)

### FORTROSE, Visct., *see* MACKENZIE, Kenneth
(*d*.1781)

### FORTESCUE, Hon. Hugh (1753–1841).
BEAUMARIS 1784–10 July 1785

*b*. 12 Mar. 1753, 1st s. of Matthew, 2nd Baron Fortescue, by Anne, da. of John Campbell (q.v.) of Calder, Nairn, and of Stackpole Court, Pemb. *educ*. Eton 1764–9; Univ. Coll. Oxf. 1770. *m*. 10 May 1782, Hester (*d*.26 May 1812), da. of George Grenville (q.v.), 2s. *suc*. fa. as 3rd Baron 10 July 1785; *cr*. Earl Fortescue 1 Sept. 1789.

Returned for Beaumaris by Lord Bulkeley (q.v.), a great friend of the young Grenvilles, Fortescue adhered to Pitt. There is no record of his having spoken or voted in the House of Commons during the year he sat in it.

He died 16 June 1841.

L.B.N.

### FOSTER, Thomas (1720–65), of Egham, Surr.
BOSSINEY      12 May–11 Dec. 1741, 18 Mar. 1742–1747
DORCHESTER    1761–20 Oct. 1765

*b*. 1720, 1st s. of Col. John Foster of Elim, Jamaica by his w. Elizabeth Smith of Barbados. *m*. 2 June 1741, Mary, da. and h. of John Helden of St. Kitts and Egham House, Surr., *s.p.*[1] His sis. m. W. M. Burt (q.v.). *suc*. fa. 1731.

Foster had considerable estates in Jamaica, but seems to have lived permanently in England.

In Shelburne's list of constituencies for the general election of 1761[2] there is a note under Dorchester: 'Mr. Foster, West Indian, opposes present Member'. He was returned without a poll. He appears in Henry Fox's list of Members favourable to the peace preliminaries, December 1762, but little seems to have been known about him, and in all the lists for this period he is classed as 'doubtful'. His only reported votes were with Opposition over general warrants, February 1764. There is no record of his having spoken in the House. He died 20 Oct. 1765.

¹ *Gent. Mag.* 1741, p. 331; *Caribbeana*, iii. 375. ² Lansdowne mss.

M.M.D.

### FOWLE, *see* MIDDLETON, William

### FOWNES LUTTRELL, Francis (1756–1823).
MINEHEAD 1780–Mar. 1783

*b*. 9 Feb. 1756, 5th s. of Henry Fownes Luttrell, and bro. of John Fownes Luttrell (qq.v.). *educ*. Eton 1770–2; Queen's, Oxf. 1773; M. Temple 1770, called 1782. *m*. 21 Apr. 1788, Charlotte, da. of Francis Drewe, sis. of w. of his bro. John, 5s. 7da.

Commr. of taxes 1784–93, of customs 1793–1819; chairman, Bd. of Customs 1813–19.

Returned for Minehead with his elder brother, he voted with Government on Lowther's motion, 12 Dec. 1781, but for peace with America, 27 Feb. 1782; and again with Government on the vote of no confidence, 15 Mar. On 18 Feb. 1783, he voted, together with his brother, for Shelburne's peace preliminaries. In March he resigned his seat to Henry Beaufoy for £3,000.[1]

He died 24 Apr. 1823.

[1] *Eng. Hist. Docs.* xi. 243.

L.B.N.

## FOWNES LUTTRELL, Henry (?1722–80), of Dunster Castle, Som.

MINEHEAD 1768–Dec. 1774

*b.* ?1722, 1st s. of John Fownes of Nethway, Devon by his 2nd w. Anne, da. of Samuel Maddock of Tamerton Foliott. *educ.* Queen's, Oxf. 21 Apr. 1741, aged 17. *m.* (1) 16 Feb. 1747 his 2nd cos. Margaret (*d.*13 Aug. 1766), da. and h. of Alexander Luttrell, M.P., by Margaret, da. of Sir John Trevelyan, 2nd Bt., M.P., of Nettlecombe, Devon, 6s. 4da.; (2) 1771, Frances, da. of Samuel Bradley of Dunster. Assumed add. name of Luttrell 1747.

The Luttrells of Dunster had represented Minehead in almost every generation since the borough first sent Members to Parliament in the sixteenth century. In 1753 Henry Fownes Luttrell was trying to sell the manor of Minehead but finding no purchaser at his own price of £30,000, finished by supporting a stranger, Henry Shiffner, stipulating, however, that he should stand on 'the country interest', and should not join either of the two other candidates without Luttrell's consent. Shiffner was defeated by a narrow margin; but in 1757 Luttrell, who was now carefully nursing his interest in the borough, came to an agreement with Lord Egremont at the next general election to divide its representation between them. Still not anxious to enter Parliament, Luttrell returned Shiffner in 1761. But after the death of his wife he wrote about November 1766 to Leonard Herring, vicar of Minehead:[1]

> The late severe loss I have sustained has made home become very dull and insipid to me, and therefore I have some thoughts of changing the scene and going into Parliament. If I persevere in my present intentions, I shall of course offer myself for Minehead at the ensuing election . . . I purpose to communicate this intended scheme of mine soon to Mr. Shiffner, that he may look out for some other borough in case I should carry it into execution.

He had already declared that he neither intended 'to ask for more than one vote, or even countenance another candidate', unless agreeable to the Minehead electors.[2] He countered attempts of a group of

Minehead electors to raise Government-sponsored opposition to him, by going to London and obtaining from the Government 'the immediate patronage of all offices at Minehead';[3] possibly on a promise of his giving them general support. Returned to Parliament he certainly never appears voting with the Opposition; but in the five divisions for which lists of the Government majority are available, his name is not among them either; nor is there any record of his having spoken in the House.

By 1774 Luttrell was able to fill both seats at Minehead, and chose to return himself and his eldest son John Fownes Luttrell. There seems to have arisen a misunderstanding with regard to that election: Lord North was under the impression that Luttrell was willing to accept his recommendation for one seat in the borough, and in writing to Robinson, 6 Oct. 1774, named Thomas Pownall for Minehead.[4] Luttrell seems to have taken umbrage at their treating Minehead as if it were a Government borough, and Robinson being too ill to answer his letter, North did so himself on 22 Oct.[5] 'From the time that you explained to me that the borough was entirely in your hands', he wrote, 'I have always disposed of the offices there at your recommendation.' Charles Whitworth (q.v.) was warned not to interfere at Minehead. 'It was from your own suggestion that I first thought of recommending a candidate at Minehead . . . This, I solemnly declare, is all I have done with respect to Minehead, and I cannot conceive how you can form, from any part of this conduct, an idea that I look upon it as a Government borough. If you have changed your opinion, and, instead of bringing in a gentleman at my recommendation, as you seemed inclined to do when I last heard from you, are now determined to represent Minehead yourself, I do not complain of it.'

Luttrell, once he was satisfied that there had been no undue Government interference at Minehead, was ready to vacate his seat, and did so, apparently on favourable terms, in December 1774. But in 1780 Robinson classed both future Members for Minehead as 'doubtful'—the Government had no hold either on Luttrell or his borough.

Luttrell died 30 Oct. 1780.

[1] H. C. Maxwell Lyte, *Hist. Dunster*, i. 245. [2] Draft of an address 'to the Minehead gentlemen', Dec. 1766, Luttrell mss at Dunster Castle. [3] Maxwell Lyte, 249. [4] Laprade, 24. [5] Luttrell mss.

L.B.N.

## FOWNES LUTTRELL, John (1752–1816).

MINEHEAD 1774–1806, 14 Jan. 1807–Feb. 1816

*bap.* 24 June 1752, 1st s. of Henry Fownes Luttrell, and bro. of Francis Fownes Luttrell (qq.v.). *educ.* Eton

1765; Queen's, Oxf. 1770. *m.* 2 Aug. 1782, Mary, da. of Francis Drewe of Grange, Devon, 5s. 4da.

The *Public Ledger* wrote about Luttrell in 1779: 'Appears to be an independent country gentleman, and votes sometimes one way, and sometimes another.' By 1780 he voted as a rule with Opposition: on Dunning's motion alone, 6 Apr. 1780, he voted with Government. He was absent from all the crucial divisions preceding the fall of the North Government, and Robinson in his survey of 8 Mar. 1782 noted about him 'will not attend'. On 18 Feb. 1783 he voted in favour of Shelburne's peace preliminaries, but was absent from the divisions on Fox's East India bill. In the new Parliament he was classed by Adam as a follower of Pitt, but his name does not appear in any of the division lists—he was absent even from those on the Regency bill.

He died in February 1816.

[1] Abergavenny mss.

L.B.N.

## FOX, Hon. Charles James (1749–1806), of Wimbledon, Surr.

| | |
|---|---|
| MIDHURST | 1768–1774 |
| MALMESBURY | 1774–1780 |
| WESTMINSTER | 1780–1784 |
| TAIN BURGHS | 1784–4 Mar. 1785 |
| WESTMINSTER | 4 Mar. 1785–13 Sept. 1806 |

*b.* 24 Jan. 1749, 2nd s. of Henry Fox, 1st Baron Holland, and bro. of Hon. Stephen Fox (qq.v.). *educ.* Wandsworth sch.; Eton 1757–64; Hertford, Oxf. 1764; L. Inn 1764; Grand Tour (France, Italy, Switzerland). *m.* 28 Sept. 1795, Elizabeth Bridget Armistead, *s.p.*

Ld. of Admiralty Feb. 1770–Feb. 1772, of Treasury Jan. 1773–Feb. 1774; P.C. 30 Mar. 1782, struck off 9 May 1798, restored 5 Feb. 1806; sec. of state for foreign affairs Mar.–July 1782, Apr.–Dec. 1783, Feb. 1806–*d.*

The parliamentary careers of Henry and Charles James Fox span more than seventy years: before the fall of Walpole, Henry Fox was a man of standing in the House of Commons, and his son lived to see Napoleon Emperor of the French. At first glance it seems hardly possible to imagine two careers more dissimilar. Henry Fox spent twenty-five years in the service of the Crown and never once went into declared opposition; Charles James was a junior minister for a little over three years, had three spells as foreign secretary (each of only a few months), and spent nearly thirty years in opposition. Henry conceived politics primarily in terms of jobs and honours, Charles James of party and principle. The one exalted the power of the Crown, the other did all he could to diminish it.

Charles James Fox was his father's favourite

child; caressed, adored, and spoilt; and treated as a man when he was little more than a boy. When only nineteen he was brought into Parliament for Midhurst by an arrangement between Lord Holland and Lord Montagu, patron of the borough. Following the line marked out for him by his father, he voted steadily with Government, and as a speaker became noted for his self-assurance and aggressiveness. In February 1770, a month after his twenty-first birthday, he was given a place at the Admiralty Board, an extraordinary appointment for one so young, particularly as he had not served an apprenticeship at the Board of Trade, the lowest rung of the Government ladder. Already he was becoming notorious for the reckless gambling which was to cause his parents so much unhappiness. But in his political conduct he was a model son, pursuing his father's vendettas and taking up the causes for which Holland had fought in vain. 'I am ill-natured enough to be very sorry whenever I hear there is any chance of the Bedfords being pleased', he wrote to George Macartney on 6 Aug. 1767, echoing his father's dislike of the Bedford party, who had used him ill. And in January 1772 he gave notice that he would move the repeal of Hardwicke's Marriage Act, against which his father had fought a long and bitter campaign. But probably Holland's greatest resentment at this time was against the King, who had refused him the earldom he so dearly coveted and showed an unfeeling ingratitude for Holland's services. In a letter to his son of 24 July 1767, Holland quoted the couplet:

Of all court service know the common lot,
Today 'tis done, tomorrow 'tis forgot.

'Don't ever, Charles', he continued, 'make any exception or trust as I did.' And throughout his life Charles Fox showed an inveterate hostility towards George III, which was fully reciprocated by the King.[1]

On 20 Feb. 1772 Fox resigned his place at the Admiralty. 'He had not any one particular reason for this step', wrote John Craufurd to Lord Ossory, 'but upon the whole he thought Lord North did not treat him with the confidence and attention he used to do.' But Fox himself gave a deeper reason: 'I should not have resigned at this moment merely on account of my complaints against Lord North, if I had not determined to vote against this *Royal Family Bill* . . . I think myself very safe from going into Opposition.'[2] The royal marriage bill was introduced at George III's express command, and Fox was one of its bitterest opponents. Yet in December 1772 there was 'a new disposition of places', according to Walpole[3] 'arranged solely to make room for Charles Fox at the Treasury'.

Fox's attendance at the Admiralty Board had been very poor, and it was not much better at the Treasury. There was some justification for George III's comment in 1783 that he 'wanted application and . . . the fundamental knowledge necessary for business'.[4] The excitement of politics or gambling enthralled him but not the routine work of administration, and his upbringing had not conditioned him to self-discipline. At this stage in his life he found it difficult to adapt himself to team work. He took a leading part against Clive in the East India inquiry of 1773, and was exasperated by North's refusal to commit Administration. On 25 May he wrote to the Duke of Buccleuch:[5]

You will have heard before this of the disgraceful end of all India inquiries in the House of Commons. I really did not [think] it possible for me to be so much out of humour about any political event as I am about this. But the strange irresolution shown in this affair .. . leaves one no hopes of any plan being ever carried on with spirit and perseverance. Lord Clive is not only unpunished and uncensured, but a vote passed in his praise.

Strongly self-centred, Fox needed to feel superior to those about him and was irritated by having to accept a subordinate role. Increasingly dissatisfied with North's dilatoriness and placidity, he ceased to attend the Treasury board; defied North's authority in the House of Commons; and in February 1774 was dismissed. 'That young man', the King wrote on 16 Feb.,[6] 'has so thoroughly cast off every principle of common honour and honesty that he must become as contemptible as he is odious.'

George III's dislike of Fox began before the American war, and did not originate in political differences. To some extent it was a continuation of the King's dislike of Lord Holland, and was certainly accentuated by Fox's manner of life. In November 1773 Holland agreed to pay his son's debts, 'not exceeding the sum of one hundred thousand pounds',[7] yet there is no evidence that Fox was in any way repentant or concerned for his father's feelings. Holland's death in July 1774 was followed six months later by that of his eldest son, when Fox inherited the sinecure of clerk of the pells in Ireland which he exchanged for a pension of £1700 per annum for thirty-one years.[8] 'I was told today', wrote James Harris on 28 Nov. 1775,[9] 'that Charles Fox was not worth a farthing, and [had] nothing to live upon'; and in November 1776: 'I heard it said that Charles Fox had spent £175,000.' But his aunt Lady Sarah Bunbury told her sister the Duchess of Leinster on 23 Oct. 1776 that Fox's finances were 'somewhat better than ever'.[10] 'He won enormously last year, and as fast as ever he got the money he paid and paid away till he reduced his debt to about £1000 or £1200. He does not game now but in horse racing, which is such a passion of his . . . that I doubt he will never give it up.' Nor did he altogether give up cards: in 1781, when leader of the Opposition in the Commons, he was running a faro bank at Brooks's and the bailiffs were in his house. There is a ludicrous description of him at Brooks's in March 1782, when North's Administration was on its last legs and Fox was already being solicited by Members of Parliament:[11]

I own [wrote George Selwyn (q.v.)] that to see Charles closeted every instant at Brooks's by one or the other, that he can neither punt nor deal for a quarter of an hour but he is obliged to give an audience, while Hare [q.v.] is whispering and standing behind him, like Jack Robinson [q.v.], with a pencil and paper for memorandums, is to me a scene la plus parfaitement comique que l'on puisse imaginer.

It took Fox a long time to live down the reputation he had made for himself, and he possibly never realized the harm it did to his party.

Selwyn, who knew Fox well, wrote about his 'determination never to put himself under the disagreeable restraint of one minute', and describes him as 'intoxicated with the all sufficiency, as he imagines, of his parts'.[12] As a young man he was the idol of the jeunesse dorée. Horace Walpole wrote in 1771:[13]

The faculties of his mind were genuine, strong, and mature. He conceived, digested, and replied at once. His reasoning and elocution were equally impetuous . . . Such an amazing burst of parts, that wanted no ripening and anticipated instruction, produced as rapid effects; in others admiration and envy, in himself excess of vanity and presumption, beyond what even flattery and intoxication could warrant. Bold, spirited, and confident, he behaved as if already in possession of all the triumphs he aspired to, and familiarized himself with pre-eminence before he was known enough to have published even his pretensions. Thus at twenty-two he acted and was hated as a leader of a party; his arrogance, loquacity, and intemperance raising him the enemies of a minister before he had acquired the power of one.

And Selwyn in 1774:

Two or three inconsiderate people of Almack's . . . have imbibed such a belief of the necessity of Charles's being the first man of this country, and the necessity also to the well-being of this country that it should be so, that they cannot conceive there should be the least impediment to it, arising either from his own conduct or that of others.

His 'infinite contempt' for what Selwyn calls the 'qu'en dira-t-on, upon every point which governs the rest of mankind' is seen in the matter of his personal appearance. Henry Beaufoy [q.v.] describes a visit he paid to Fox about 1779 in company with Dr. Kippis, the dissenting minister:[14]

There we accordingly knocked, and were told by the servant that his master was not up but that he would take our names to him, and in the meantime we were conducted to a handsome room in which was a portrait of an opera girl, a small table with an ordinary breakfast service for one person, a dirty sofa, and three or four chairs. After we had waited a few minutes Mr. Fox came in. His complexion was of the dirtiest colour and tinged with a yellowish hue; his hair was exceedingly black, uncombed, and clotted with the pomatures and small remnants of powder of the day before; his beard was unshaved, and together with his bushy eyebrows increased the natural darkness of his skin; his nightgown was old and dirty; the collar of his shirt was open and discovered a broad chest covered with hair; the knees of his breeches were unbuttoned; his stockings were ungartered and hung low upon his legs; his slippers were down at the heels; his hands were dirty; his voice was hoarse like that of a hackney coachman who is much exposed to the night air. Yet under all these various disadvantages his countenance was mild and pleasing.

In 1781 Selwyn told Fox that a writer in the *Public Advertiser* had described his figure as 'squalid and disagreeable'. Fox replied that 'he never cared what was said of his person. If he was represented ugly and was not so, those who knew him would do him justice, and he did not care for what he passed in that respect with those who did not.'[15]

The lack of feeling Fox showed towards his father was reproduced in other relationships; and Selwyn, Philip Francis, and his cousin Lady Susan O'Brien all complained of his failure to help them at their moment of need. Selwyn wrote in 1782:[16]

Charles, I am persuaded, would have no consideration on earth but for what was useful to his own ends. You have heard me say that I thought he had no malice or rancour; I think so still and am sure of it. But I think he has no feeling, neither, for anyone but himself.

'The essential defect in his character', wrote Francis after his death,[17] 'and the cause of all his failures, strange as it may seem, was that he had no heart.' Together with poverty in human relationships (except where his own supremacy was uncontested) went a lack of judgment which was fatal to his success as a politician. A man so self-centred could not adapt himself to changes of mood; and at moments of crisis he was apt to be hesitant and perplexed. Gilbert Elliot wrote at the time of the Regency crisis in 1789 that Fox had 'great difficulty or backwardness in *resolving*, as if he had no interest or no judgment in the affairs that are depending, and at last he lets anybody else decide for him, so measures are often the production of chance instead of wisdom'.[18] Moreover, Fox was unable to sense mass opinion with which he himself was not in sympathy.

But no analysis of Fox's character can reveal the qualities which so attracted his contemporaries. The charm of his conversation could not survive, and the brilliance of his speeches is but faintly visible in the imperfect parliamentary reports. 'Charles Fox . . . is one of the pleasantest men in the world', wrote Burke in 1777,[19] 'as well as the greatest genius that perhaps this country has ever produced . . . the British dominions cannot furnish anything beyond him.' And Wilberforce, a political opponent, wrote during one of Fox's absences from the House:[20] 'You cannot imagine how insipid and vapid our debates are without Fox.' Without possessing Burke's intellectual distinction, he was a much greater parliamentarian: vigorous, persevering, and with a clear and lucid mind, which could simplify and resolve complex problems; excelling alike in set speeches or in debate; and able to win both personal affection and political loyalty.

A month after Fox's dismissal in February 1774, North introduced his punitive measures against the American colonies. Fox supported the Boston port bill as essential if law and order were to be maintained in America, but he warned the House that no plan for America would do any good unless it included the repeal of the tea duty. 'A tax laid merely to maintain a right is very improper', he said.[21] ' . . . To combat with the prejudices of a whole people for trifles is very impolitic. As far as this measure goes I think it will do good, but I hope it's not all that is meant.' On 19 Apr. he supported Rose Fuller's motion for the repeal of the tea duty:

Experience is better than all reasoning, and from experience one may conclude that by leaving America untaxed she would be useful and obedient and by taxing her that she would be contrary . . . I think we should be content to tax them virtually by regulating their trade. If soldiers are to collect the taxes in America, I doubt this country will be little benefited by what may be raised there.

His attitude towards the American problem remained the same throughout the conflict. 'Countries should always be governed by the will of the governed', he said in the debate of 19 Apr. 1774; and when America declared her independence, Fox was one of the first to urge that Britain should accept the inevitable. The right of peoples to choose for themselves their form of government became part of his political creed.

In September 1774 Fox was counted by Administration as in declared opposition; by the end of the next session of Parliament he was on the way to becoming the acknowledged leader of the Opposition in the House of Commons. His friendship with Burke brought him into touch with the Rockinghams; he was close to Grafton and Camden; with Chatham and Shelburne, alone of the Opposition leaders, he seems to have had little contact. In addition he built up a following among the independent Members, drawn by his character and parliamentary talents. Chatham died in 1778 and Rockingham became more and more a titular leader of Opposition, with Fox as the real driving force in the House of Commons. Moreover Fox was able to make an appeal to the nation at large and to capture their imagination as no other politician could. He identified himself with the programme of the association movement; became chairman of the Westminster Association; and in 1780 was triumphantly elected, free of expense, M.P. for Westminster.

On the fall of North, Fox took office in a Cabinet of which Rockingham was the nominal leader but Shelburne the man whom the King trusted. Fox became minister in the House of Commons and the first holder of the office of secretary of state for foreign affairs. As such he had charge of peace negotiations with France, Spain, and Holland, while the negotiations with America were the responsibility of Shelburne, secretary for home and colonial affairs. The struggle for power between Fox and Shelburne began the moment they took office; and Rockingham reigned impotent over a divided Cabinet. To sharpen Fox's resentment was the recollection of Shelburne's quarrel with Lord Holland in 1763. Fox had taken over another of his father's old feuds.

Fox and Shelburne first clashed over patronage, and then over their respective shares in the peace negotiations. Each secretary had his envoy in Paris, and the envoys took up and accentuated the quarrels of their masters. The struggle for power came to a head over the recognition of American independence. Fox, following the line he had taken since 1776, demanded the immediate recognition of the independence of the United States (which would have placed the whole of the peace negotiations in his department); Shelburne, equally faithful to a policy he and Chatham had consistently advocated, wished to grant independence only as a condition of peace. On 28 June Fox complained to Grafton 'of the decided opinions against everything proposed by him, and added that it would be impossible to go on in such a way'.[22] The issue was fought out at a Cabinet meeting on 30 June, and Fox was defeated. He declared his determination to resign, but postponed his resignation because of Rockingham's illness. Rockingham died the next day.

The King had decided before Rockingham's death that Shelburne should succeed to the Treasury. 'Charles . . . will move heaven and earth to resist the appointment', wrote Richard Fitzpatrick to his brother, Lord Ossory, on 3 July.[23] Fox claimed that the new head of the Treasury should be chosen by the Cabinet, and should possess the confidence of the Rockingham party. But the Rockinghams were not a majority in the Cabinet, and when Fox resigned Lord John Cavendish was the only Cabinet minister to accompany him. In the House of Commons on 9 July Fox justified his resignation by his distrust of Shelburne.[24] He spoke of his differences with Shelburne over America; accused him of treating 'with the utmost contempt' the policy of reducing the influence of the Crown; and of being inclined 'to screen from justice and punishment those delinquents who had destroyed our possessions in the East'. With Shelburne as minister, Fox declared, the principles of the Rockingham Administration would be thrown over, and the King would have a minister pledged to maintain the influence of the Crown—a minister worse even than North.

Fox could not conceal behind a declaration of political principles, sincere though they were, his hatred of Shelburne and the King. To George Selwyn in March 1782 he 'talked of the King under the description of Satan', a comparison, added Selwyn, 'which he seems fond of and has used to others'.[25] Such had been his sentiments for some time. 'It is intolerable', he wrote to Fitzpatrick on 9 Sept. 1781, referring to the King, 'that it should be in the power of one blockhead to do so much mischief.'[26] And Lord Carmarthen reports Fox having said on the day he received the seals as secretary of state: 'Certainly things look well, but he (meaning the King) will die soon, and that will be best of all.'[27] Behind Fox's politics were deep obsessional hatreds, which distorted his judgment and perverted his sense of reality.

Shelburne, with the support of the Crown, had won the first round; it was now Fox's business to make himself master of the House of Commons and drive out Shelburne. An alliance between Fox and North would bring obvious advantages to both parties, and soon after Parliament met in December 1782 negotiations began. By the time Shelburne's peace preliminaries came before the House the alliance was complete, and in the debate of 17–18 Feb. 1783 Fox virtually avowed it:[28]

> It is neither wise nor noble to keep up animosities for ever. It is not just nor candid to keep up animosity when the cause of it is no more. It is not my nature to bear malice, nor to live in ill will. My friendships are perpetual, my enmities not so . . . When a man ceases to be what he was, when the opinions which made him obnoxious are changed, he then is no more my enemy but my friend.

But had North ceased to be what he was, or had he changed his opinions? Certainly it was understood by both parties that there was to be no more economical reform, and no attempt to reform Parliament. In 1779 Fox seems to have been in favour of impeaching North, or at least, in Burke's words, of 'a criminal process of some kind or other, of more or less rigour, against some of those who had been the principal managers of our affairs'.[29] And on 5 Mar. 1782 Fox had denounced North's Administration in the bitterest terms:[30]

> From the moment when he should make any terms with one of them he would rest satisfied to be called the most infamous of mankind. He could not for an instant think of a coalition with men who in every public and private transaction as ministers had shown themselves void of every principle of honour and honesty. In the hands of such men he would not trust his honour even for a minute.

Fox has been more criticized for making the coalition with North than for any other action of his life. Yet there is much to be said in his defence. Shelburne's Administration was weak, and a coalition of some kind was almost inevitable in 1783. Moreover, the coalition satisfied a deep psychological need in Fox's party: it brought to a triumphant conclusion the feud which they had waged since 1766 against Shelburne and Chatham; and to force an Administration on the King was the logical culmination of the policy of reducing the influence of the Crown.

At this crisis in his career Fox failed to sense the reaction of public opinion. Independent Members, highly respected in the Commons and not unfavourably disposed to Fox, such as Sir George Savile and Thomas Powys, were shocked that he could so lightly pass over his declarations against North. The association movement, still powerful in the north of England, could not forgive him for what they regarded as his betrayal of parliamentary reform. To independent men it seemed that Fox had thrown over his principles for the sake of office.

Shelburne was defeated on the peace preliminaries and at once resigned. For nearly seven weeks George III twisted and turned, and tried every expedient rather than accept the Coalition. But no man would take upon himself the responsibility for conducting Administration against Fox in the House of Commons; and the King had eventually to capitulate. The ill-grace with which he accepted the Coalition should have been a warning to Fox that their tenure of office was on a very insecure footing. But Fox made no attempt to salve the King's wounded feelings; George III was compelled to accept a Cabinet not one member of which he could call his own. Fox reigned supreme: North feared responsibility and was not likely to challenge his authority, and the Duke of Portland, the nominal head of Administration, was a mere convenience.

Undoubtedly the Coalition commanded the confidence of the House of Commons. There was a general desire for stability in Administration, and the Coalition was far more broadly based than the ministries of Rockingham or Shelburne. Had Fox been able to win the confidence of the King as he had done that of the Commons, he would have consolidated his power. Soon after taking office he wrote to George III:[31]

> Mr. Fox . . . begs leave most humbly to implore your Majesty to believe that both the Duke of Portland and he have nothing so much at heart as to conduct your Majesty's affairs, both with respect to measures and to persons, in the manner that may give your Majesty the most satisfaction, and that, whenever your Majesty will be graciously pleased to condescend even to hint your inclinations upon any subject, that it will be the study of your Majesty's ministers to show how truly sensible they are of your Majesty's goodness.

But how much feeling was there behind these words? Instead of attempting a reconciliation, Fox seemed to do everything possible to antagonize the King. His friendship with the Prince of Wales evoked memories of past divisions in the royal family, and gave the Coalition the appearance of the 'Prince's ministry'; which was strengthened by Fox's injudicious attempt to increase the Prince's establishment. Emotionally he sympathized with the son against the father, with the subject against the sovereign, with the rebel against authority. With his politics based on such a foundation, he could not hope to win the King's favour; he counted instead on the support of public opinion, and he blundered into losing that.

Peace having been concluded and parliamentary reform shelved, India was the most urgent problem facing the Coalition. Fox and Burke held similar ideas about the settlement of India, and it matters little what were their respective shares in the drafting of Fox's East India bill. The bill was based on three premises: that the East India Company could no longer govern India with efficiency and justice; that some sort of public control over the government of India was essential; and that it would be dangerous to vest this control in the Crown. The Company was to be relieved of its territorial responsibilities, which were to be entrusted to a body of seven commissioners, named in the bill, to hold office for four years. The Crown was to fill up vacancies and to nominate future commissioners. The head of the commission was to be Lord Fitzwilliam, Rockingham's nephew and heir; and all seven commissioners were close political friends of either Fox or North. For at least the next four years Fox would govern India and control the patronage of the Company. The India bill was the last measure in the movement to limit the influence of the Crown, and it came when a reaction in favour of the Crown was just beginning.

Fox had a strong hand in the autumn of 1783; it is astounding how badly he played it. With a majority in the Commons such as no minister had possessed since North at the height of his power, he lost the game through his lack of judgment, his failure to sense public reaction to his policy. He introduced the India bill in November, a time of year when the House was always thin and controversial measures never brought forward—thus giving substance to the charge that he was trying to rush the bill through the Commons. Lord Fitzwilliam, to be entrusted with the leading share in the government of India, had no experience of its affairs and had never held public office before: men knew him only as Rockingham's nephew and a devoted follower of Fox. The presence of even one commissioner, independent of the Coalition, would have helped to rebut the charge that Fox was trying to monopolize the patronage of the Company. Such was the view even of men who admired Fox greatly and wished to act with him in politics. Lord Camden wrote to his son-in-law, 19 Dec. 1783:[32]

> Mr. Fox . . . formed a plan . . . to get possession of the East India patronage by vesting it in seven of his own friends, by which means the parliamentary influence of a private man would have been almost equal to the great power of the prerogative . . . This possession would have made him too powerful to have been turned out, and consequently the private being united to the ministerial influence would have made him perpetual dictator.

The King determined to profit by Fox's mistakes, and, with a complete lack of scruple, which indicates the depth of his hatred of Fox, plotted the Coalition's downfall. He could not prevent the India bill from passing the Commons, but he let it be known that all who voted for it in the Lords would be regarded as his enemies. This had its effect. On 16 Dec. Administration were beaten on a motion to adjourn, and again the next day on the motion to commit the bill. On 18 Dec. Fox and North were dismissed.

'We are beat', wrote Fox, ' . . . by such treachery on the part of the King, and such meanness on the part of his friends in the House of Lords, as one could not expect either from him or them . . . However, we are so strong that nobody can undertake without madness, and if they do I think we shall destroy them almost as soon as they are formed.'[33] It was a grave over-estimate of his own strength, and entirely neglected the force of public opinion. As Pitt held on to office, the House of Commons slowly turned in his favour: on 12 Jan. 1784 Fox had a majority of 39; by 8 Mar. it was reduced to a bare one. Richard Fitzpatrick, probably Fox's closest

friend, had compared George III's conduct on the India bill to that of Charles I in 1641;[34] and a similar parallel seems to have run through Fox's mind. Just as Pym in 1641 could not entrust Charles I with the command of an army to put down the Irish rebellion, so Fox could not entrust George III with the patronage of the East India Company. But there was no parallel between Charles I's attempt to arrest the five Members and George III's intervention against the India bill. Fox's tactics pre-supposed the existence of a revolutionary situation in England; in fact, public opinion was behind the King, and it was Fox, not George III, who was accused of having attempted to overturn the constitution.

'Is George III or Charles Fox to reign?', asked Lord Fauconberg at the meeting of Yorkshire freeholders on 25 Mar. 1784. At the general election Fitzwilliam sponsored two Foxite candidates for Yorkshire against two followers of Pitt. Here are some of the reports of his agents as they canvassed the county: 'The cry against Mr. Fox is most astonishing' (Stephen Croft, 6 Mar.); 'The people have no idea but that Mr. Fox wants to get the better of the King and be the lord protector' (John Carr, 8 Mar.); 'They [the merchants of Wakefield] are so hot at present and angry with Charles Fox upon his India bill that many of them are not to be talked to' (Peregrine Wentworth, 11 Feb.); 'The received notion amongst the inferiors in many parts is that Mr. Fox was attempting to dethrone the King and make himself an Oliver Cromwell' (R. Parker, 26 Apr.); etc. In the open constituencies, where the force of public opinion could be felt, Fox's friends fared badly; and Fox himself had a hard fight at Westminster, where Pitt's Administration strained every nerve against him. Fox was elected after a prolonged scrutiny, and in the meantime he sat for Tain Burghs on the interest of his friend, Sir Thomas Dundas.

And so Fox began another long period of opposition, longer even than that of the American war. Sir Andrew Hamond, an ambitious naval officer, wrote to William Eden on 10 Dec. 1785:[35]

> As to Charles Fox, though I admire his abilities as much as anybody can, yet I am perfectly convinced that nothing but the death of the King can bring him forward, and therefore I consider him destined to pass the greatest part of his life in opposition. I have heard the King speak of him with that indignation that I really believe he would sacrifice everything than allow him to come forward.

Fox, the man of the people, had made opposition to the influence of the Crown the nucleus of his political programme; and it was a supreme stroke of irony that only through the favour of the Crown did he appear likely to achieve office again. When

George III became insane in 1788 and Fox's friend the Prince of Wales seemed about to become Regent, Fox was driven to defend the rights of the Crown against Pitt's attempt to limit the powers of the Regency. 'Surely Mr. Fox will not call his doctrine a Whig one?' wrote Richard Hopkins to the Duke of Grafton on 11 Dec. 1788, after Fox had declared in the Commons that the Prince of Wales had a clear and express right 'to assume the reins of government and exercise the powers of sovereignty' during the King's incapacity.[36]

After 1784 Fox matured a great deal. Under the impact of the French Revolution his politics lost their emotional colouring, and he became the advocate of a political ideal, far different from that of his friend Burke. More than any other man, he may be deemed the founder of the Whig party of the early nineteenth century.

Fox died 13 Sept. 1806.

[1] *Corresp. C. J. Fox*, i. 36, 41. [2] Ibid. 72-73. [3] *Last Jnls.* i. 164. [4] Buckingham, *Courts & Cabinets Geo. III*, i. 213. [5] Buccleuch mss. [6] Fortescue, iii. 69. [7] Add. 35068, f. 12. [8] T14/15/342-5. [9] Memorandum, Malmesbury mss. [10] *Leinster Corresp* i. 204. [11] *HMC Carlisle*, 586. [12] Ibid. 264, 277. [13] Unprinted passage of *Mems. Geo. III.* [14] Beaufoy's memoir, Hants RO. [15] *HMC Carlisle*, 506. [16] Ibid. 591. [17] Parkes & Merivale, *Mems. Francis*, ii. 459. [18] *Life and Letters of Sir G. Elliot*, i. 257. [19] Burke to Garret Nagle, 26 Oct. 1777. [20] *HMC Kenyon*, 527. [21] Brickdale's 'Debates'. [22] Grafton, *Autobiog.* 322. [23] *Corresp. C. J. Fox*, i. 459. [24] Debrett, vii. 292-7, 300-6, 308-311. [25] *HMC Carlisle*, 599. [26] *Corresp. C. J. Fox*, i. 267. [27] *Pol. Memoranda Duke of Leeds*, ed. Browning, 66. [28] Debrett, ix. 283. [29] Burke to Rockingham, 17 Oct. 1779. [30] Debrett, vi. 367. [31] Fortescue, vi. 357. [32] Camden mss. [33] *Corresp. C. J. Fox*, ii. 221. [34] Ibid. 220. [35] *Eden Corresp.* i. 362. [36] Stockdale, xvi. 12-13.

J.B.

**FOX, Henry** (1705–74), of Holland House, Kensington.

| | |
|---|---|
| HINDON | 28 Feb. 1735–1741 |
| NEW WINDSOR | 1741–1761 |
| DUNWICH | 1761–17 Apr. 1763 |

*b.* 28 Sept. 1705, 2nd surv. s. of Sir Stephen Fox of Farley, Wilts. by his 2nd w. Christian, da. and coh. of Rev. Francis Copes, rector of Haceby and Aswarby, Lincs. *educ.* Eton 1713; Ch. Ch. Oxf. 1720. *m.*[1] 2 May 1744, Lady Georgiana Caroline Lennox (*cr.* Baroness Holland of Holland 3 May 1762), da. of Charles, 2nd Duke of Richmond, 4s. (1 *d.* in infancy). *cr.* Baron Holland of Foxley 17 Apr. 1763.

Surveyor gen. of works 1737–43; ld. of Treasury 1743–6; P.C. 23 July 1746; sec. at war 1746–Oct. 1755; Cabinet councillor Dec. 1754; sec. of state, southern dept. Oct. 1755–Oct. 1756; granted Apr. 1757 reversion to sinecure post of clerk of the pells [I] for his life and those of his two elder sons (suc. to it July 1762); paymaster gen. June 1757–May 1765; 'Cabinet councillor and H.M.'s minister in the House of Commons', Oct. 1762–Apr. 1763.

Henry Fox sat 28 years in the House of Commons; seemed as parliamentary manager in direct line of succession to Walpole and to Henry Pelham; was several times within reach of the premiership, actual or virtual, but then had not the spirit to undertake it. First given office in 1737, never (barring October 1756–June 1757) was he without it; and never in declared opposition to any Government; but in all these years he held front-rank office during 18 months only: as secretary of state, 1755–6, and as leader of the House of Commons, October 1762–April 1763—a meagre record for a man of Fox's political eminence and connexions. And never was he his own master: in middle age he acted under the Duke of Cumberland; and he finished as parliamentary manager for Bute. 'Mr. Fox', writes Shelburne, 'was not formed to be a man *sui juris*, else he would have been so.'[2]

Yet he was neither pliable nor submissive but independent and with a 'warmth and impetuosity of temper' which sometimes led him into capital mistakes.[3] He was an organizer and manager and not a leader; not an orator but a debater. 'A great hesitation in his elocution, and a barrenness of expression' he conquered by 'a vehemence of reasoning and closeness of argument that beat all the orators of the time'; he 'always spoke to the question . . . to carry the question'.[4] 'Quick and concise replication' was 'his peculiar excellence'.[5] He had 'an extraordinary degree of shrewdness and sagacity'; 'a great spirit of order, arrangement, and economy in regulating everything that came before him'; was 'infinitely able in business, clear, penetrating, confident and decisive in all his dealings with mankind, and of most extraordinary activity'.[6]

He was benevolently cynical: 'every set of men are honest', he argued; 'it's only necessary to define their sense of it to know where to look for it.' And on 29 Dec. 1761 he wrote to Shelburne:[7]

A man who follows his own interest, if he makes no undue sacrifices either private or public to the worship of it, is not dishonest or even dirty. . . . Whoever goes on with what I have left off (ambition) must wish for such supporters, and it would be an additional curse on that cursed trade, to have a constant bad opinion of one's most useful friends and most assiduous attendants.

Probably more than any other statesman even of his period, Fox thought of power and employment primarily in terms of patronage and profits; when assuming or leaving office he would produce lists of preferments for friends, attaching cardinal importance to trivial matters. Shelburne calls his ambition narrow, interested, and mean; 'never daring to look high', he was 'timid, with a certain dread of the public'. His attention was to individuals; he was 'extremely honest in all his dealings' with them; tried to 'secure them each by particular services of consequence'; and was 'apprehensive of such . . . as were unsecured by bribes and promises, which being far the greatest part, his very conduct made him afraid of the public, if he was not naturally so, which . . . there is the greatest reason to believe'. Horace Walpole describes Fox as 'dark and troubled—yet . . . an agreeable man';[8] and in Hogarth's expressive portrait, in spite of a certain massive grandeur, he appears anxious, almost hagridden.

Waldegrave wrote about him c.1757:[9]

> Few men have been more unpopular; yet when I asked his bitterest enemies what crimes they could allege against him, they always confined themselves to general accusation; that he was avaricious, encouraged jobs, had profligate friends and dangerous connexions; but never could produce a particular fact of any weight or consequence.

Among the great, Fox had many friends, including men of the highest character: the Duke of Devonshire, writing to him on 14 Oct. 1762,[10] speaks of 'the long friendship I have had for you, as well as the strongest love and regard'. But Fox picked Rigby, a political buccaneer, and Welbore Ellis, a professional placeman, for his closest associates, and for dependants men like John Calcraft, Peter Taylor, or Samuel Touchet (qq.v.), with whom politics, administration, and finance merged into shameless money making. Lady Caroline, with a sense of human values, was not partial to these friends—

> They don't improve upon acquaintance [she wrote to Lady Kildare[11]] . . . I don't like any of them in private life . . . Mr. Fox with all his good sense does not know people's characters at all, and . . . admires people too much for being good company and clever.

Still, there was another side to Fox's dealings with individuals: he was humane and helpful to those in need of him, to the obvious under-dog. He was capable of friendship and attachment, and sought friendship (and perhaps protection). But frustration would bring out a bitter vindictive strain in his character; and frustration is writ large over Fox's career after 1754, years during which his power drive soon turned into despondency and self-effacement, and his ambition became fixed on the level of jobs and honours, for himself, his family and friends. The determining factor in this political fade-out was Pitt, a man of unbounded courage and in most things the opposite of Fox who feared and hated him, talked of him as a madman, but in reality was 'conscious of his own inferiority'.[12]

Pitt, solitary and aloof, had more of a real following in the House than Fox who assiduously tried to gain supporters but never could raise a standard to which men would rally. A very rough survey of Members whom Fox was supposed to influence can be obtained from Dupplin's parliamentary lists compiled after the general election of 1754, from Newcastle's lists of October 1761 specifying through whom to send circular letters inviting attendance at the opening of the session, and from Bute's parliamentary list of December 1761.[13]

While the Duke of Cumberland was captain-general, i.e. before October 1757, nine or ten army Members, closely connected with him, were directed by Fox, to whom the distribution of military preferment gave also a wider, numerically indefinable, influence in a House including another forty-odd army officers. But the prejudice caused by these 'dangerous connexions' perhaps outweighed the benefit Fox derived from them: he was described as 'a proper minister to overturn the constitution, and introduce a military government';[14] and even Mansfield, though friendly to him, warned George II in June 1757 of a general apprehension that the intended Administration under Fox 'was founded in violence and would be supported by *violence*'.[15]

Barring this professional group the Members assigned to Fox were in each list a variegated collection. He had no fixed borough interest of his own, only the temporary management of two boroughs (Malmesbury and Stockbridge); occasionally the nomination to seats controlled by friends (e.g. Dunwich); and he helped to manage some elections in which he was not personally concerned—Members thus in various degrees beholden to him for their seats appear in these lists. Besides, there are personal friends such as Horace Walpole, George Selwyn, Welbore Ellis, Sir John Wynn, etc.; Fox's nephew Lord Digby, and Tudway, Digby's colleague at Wells; Fox's brothers-in-law, Thomas Conolly and Charles Bunbury; Members returned by Selwyn for Ludgershall and by the Duke of Marlborough for Woodstock; William Edwardes, Fox's landlord at Holland House; etc. But no political principle or cohesion can be discerned in any of these different groupings: each is tentative, a jumble. There was no such thing as Fox's own party; and his following, built up on personal friendship or personal advantage or a combination of the two, was potential more than actual: with the extensive connexions he had among the leading peers, and his known skill as political manager, it could have been quickly and powerfully enlarged had he obtained control of court and Treasury patronage.

When Pelham died on 6 Mar. 1754, among commoners Fox seemed his most likely successor; and, with more eagerness than subtlety, within a few hours was calling on possible rivals and supporters, and sending 'very humiliating and apologizing messages' to Lord Hardwicke, whom he had recently offended.[16] But instead of the Treasury he was offered a secretaryship of state, though he had never taken interest in foreign affairs. 'Now what do you think of this new secretary of state?' wrote Fox to Lord Digby[17] on 12 Mar. 'Why that he is got into the place in England that he is most unfit for. So he thinks I can assure you.' He accepted on the assumption that placed 'at the head of the House of Commons' he would have its management (and that of the imminent general election). When he found that Newcastle meant to retain all effective power, he begged to be continued at the War Office; and (except at Malmesbury, under a previous arrangement) had no share in managing the Government interest at the general election. He himself was returned unopposed for Windsor, where he had Cumberland's support.

Fox, keeping at this juncture in close touch with Pitt (similarly excluded from power), hovered on the brink of opposition, yet was averse to plunging into it; and acting under Cumberland, attended to the business of his office, without giving general support to the Government in a House which had no real leader. After some perfunctory *pourparlers* in the summer of 1754, negotiations with him were resumed towards the end of the year—he was desired to act with Government on all occasions, and not relative to the army only. What he himself apparently wished for was to have his post at the War Office turned into a third secretaryship of state (an unprecedented arrangement) which would have left him the military patronage, and, without burdening him with the conduct of foreign affairs, made him leader of the House. But finally all he asked was to be enabled 'to speak like one well informed and honoured with your Majesty's favour', i.e. to be admitted to the Effective Cabinet; which was conceded with the limitation that it should not 'derogate from the priority' of the secretary of state in the Commons: a half-hearted compromise productive of further intrigues and negotiations.[18] All connexion between Pitt and Fox was now broken off: Pitt, adhering to Leicester House, passed into sharp opposition, while at the end of September Fox was appointed secretary of state in charge of the House of Commons; and Newcastle was relieved when Fox stipulated for preferment for five Members only (William Sloper, Sir John Wynn, George Selwyn, W. G. Hamilton, and Welbore Ellis).

As soon as Fox was in the saddle, he gained the adherence of the Bedfords to Government; and during the first session things went surprisingly well. But in 1756 foreign affairs and 'difficulties at home occasioned by the war' gained paramount importance. 'As to the first', wrote Newcastle on 30 May, 'he [Fox] is totally ignorant, and Pitt must

be his master.'[19] And Fox to Devonshire, 31 July, after the loss of Minorca:

> The rage of people and of considerable people . . . increases hourly . . . when the Parliament meets the scene of action will be the House of Commons and I being the only figure of a minister there, shall of course draw all the odium on me.

By 4 Aug. he was willing to give way to Pitt 'and yet join with him'—'I think my situation like that of the public, bad but incapable of being mended.' And on 12 Aug.:

> I do not . . . think my offer with regard to Pitt in the least generous. For this Administration has, I think, lost the good will and good opinion of their country . . . and without them who can wish to be in Administration?

Two months later, when Digby was omitted from the Prince of Wales's 'family', and eight Members were placed in it without Fox's previous knowledge, he resigned, complaining of having 'his full share of odium of every measure or misfortune', 'more trouble in Parliament than any other man', and no share 'in the distribution of favours there'. But he was ready to serve 'in any other employment, not of the Cabinet or Court'. In a 'plan of ministry' he sent to Devonshire on 1 Nov., he named Pitt for secretary of state, and himself for paymaster general—'I would do anything to join Pitt', he wrote, 28 Oct.; but on the 30th: 'Pitt . . . refuses to act with me a minister.'[20] The King had wanted Fox to form a Government: which Fox did not dare to attempt. And when omitted from the Pitt-Devonshire Government he pressed Devonshire for a peerage for Lady Caroline.[21] Pay office and peerage now became the two objects of his ambition.

The King had reluctantly accepted Pitt and Temple for ministers; and soon, to get rid of them, was ready to 'throw all in' to Fox.[22] But in Fox's schemes of Government it was again the pay office which he by preference claimed for himself, regarding the Treasury as 'a most disagreeable and perhaps untenable post'. Nor did he want any other office in which he would be 'supposed, as formerly, to have a share in measures and power'.[23] When Temple and Pitt were dismissed (5 and 6 Apr.), Fox received the King's promise of the pay office, and conducted several tangled negotiations for a new Government. But Pitt would not have him for colleague, nor Newcastle undertake office without Pitt. Early in June a scheme of Government was discussed with Waldegrave for figurehead, and Fox for minister. But after a meeting at Devonshire House on 12 June, attended by Granville, Gower, Bedford, Winchilsea, Waldegrave, Fox, and Devonshire, Bedford whispered to Waldegrave, 'that it would be to no purpose to give ourselves further trouble: for we could not possibly go on without a principal actor in the House of Commons, and that Fox had not spirit to undertake it'.[24] In the Newcastle-Pitt Government Fox, through the King's intervention, obtained the pay office, 'the situation of all others I like best'.[25] He was to hold it for the next eight years, but even after that was able, for technical reasons, to retain in his hands vast sums of public money (about £500,000 between 1768 and 1774) which he employed to his own advantage; and while the official income of the paymaster was about £3,000 p.a., Fox's unofficial profits during the seventeen years 1757–74, as calculated from his ledgers, amounted to about £400,000, half of which he laid out in landed property.[26]

Between June 1757 and the end of the Parliament Fox seldom attended the House, and no speeches by him are recorded; and he himself in his 'Memoir'[27] speaks in 1762 of his 'five years silence in Parliament'. In the new reign Lady Caroline wrote to Lady Kildare, 30 Oct. 1760, that to remain in the pay office 'is all his ambition as well as mine'.[28] But he still craved for the peerage for her, 'an honour I had long and indeed beyond measure been ambitious to obtain for my family'.[29] He tried through Cumberland; and next placed himself through Lord Fitzmaurice at the service of the new court, especially in regard to the general election. And when Lady Caroline was omitted from the new creations, 'I am ashamed', wrote Fox to Fitzmaurice on 20 Feb. 1761, 'of . . . the little resolution with which I bear this disappointment'.[30] His exasperation rose still more when on Pitt's resignation Lady Hester was created Baroness Chatham (and George Grenville made leader of the House of Commons—'put over my head, *sans dire gare*'); but he was pacified by assurances 'of obtaining the favour before the end of the next session', and agreed to support Grenville, to forward Bute's wishes, and 'enter no sort of engagement with any one else'.[31] He was once more politically active though even now he rarely spoke in the House; and

> I tell you once for all [wrote Lady Caroline to Lady Kildare, 27 Jan. 1762] . . . Mr. Fox is to have no employment but paymaster. Mr. Fox wants nothing but the peerage. Mr. Fox will not be desired to be minister or have any responsible place, and Mr. Fox would not be it if he was desired.[32]

On 6 May Lady Caroline was created Lady Holland.

Even after Newcastle had been removed from office in May 1762, active employment was not offered to Fox; but when in September Bute ran into difficulties with Grenville over the peace terms and the management of the Commons, Fox was called out from his country retreat, and on 7 Oct.

was pressed by the King to accept Grenville's place as secretary of state and leader of the House—'He believed I was . . . the only proper person to take upon me his support in the House of Commons.'[33] Fox replied that his declining health would not admit of 'taking the seals and acting a busy part in the House of Commons'; and that his being minister would 'greatly add to the unpopularity of which Lord Bute had full enough already', and might put off 'many, particularly of the Tories', otherwise willing to support Bute. But the King persisted, though indulging Fox in his objection to the seals. 'Short of being secretary of state I am, for the necessary time, at his Majesty's service', wrote Fox to Shelburne,[34] and in a tentative and round-about way suggested himself for the Treasury—an idea which Bute did not relish.[35] On 13 Oct. Fox was appointed 'Cabinet councillor and his Majesty's minister in the House of Commons'.[36]

Why did he accept? Asked by his brother whom this would benefit, he replied, 9 Oct.:[37] 'To the King and the public it would be useful and should be meritorious. To my nearest friends (I want nothing for myself) it would certainly be useful too.' The personal disclaimer is hardly convincing—he did expect reward for 'meritorious' service but named no precise terms. Moreover, after six years of effacement here was revenge on its authors: he would be instrumental in excluding Pitt from power and Newcastle from patronage, and at last have the management of the House with the resources of the Crown at his disposal. He now addressed himself to individual Members and omitted no chance of gaining a supporter or eliminating a possible opponent. Of his most extraordinary activity there is plentiful evidence in his extant correspondence, especially with Bute and Shelburne. But being 'apprehensive of such as were unsecured by bribes and promises', Fox went further than was required. Hardwicke, in a letter to Newcastle, 27 Nov., having referred to 'the *motives*, which prevail in general',[38] added:

> Yet we ought not to deceive ourselves. We ought not to ascribe the whole to such causes; for I am persuaded . . . that the burden and tedium of the war and the desire of peace, are so strong in the generality of the Parliament, and of the nation (abstracted from the interested or wild part of the City of London), that the very name of peace is agreeable to them, and they would have been content with terms rather lower than all we have yet been told of these preliminaries.

Lord Strange, one of the most upright and independent Members, wrote to Fox on 1 Nov. that a good peace was the most desirable thing for the nation, and it should not be too good, for 'none that is not reasonable can be durable'; and the list drawn up by Fox c. 3 Dec. of Members favourable to the peace preliminaries, though incomplete, contains the names of a great many independent and utterly incorruptible Members.[39] Yet Fox's reputation and his feverish exertions produced an impression fixed in Walpole's oft-quoted (and misquoted) account of how 'in a single fortnight a vast majority was purchased to approve the peace'.[40]

On 27 Nov. Fox wrote to a friend:[41]

My success has fully answered my activity. And the Duke of Newcastle will appear, as I ever thought he would, nothing without a court; provided my advice is taken, to pursue the victory, without delay; and without . . . lenity.

And to Bute, 30 Nov.:

Upon my word, my Lord, I have been asked by several today whether the Duke of Newcastle has any chance of coming to court again. Strip him of his three lieutenancies immediately, I'll answer for the good effect of it, and then go on to the general rout. But let this beginning be made immediately.

And after the signal victories of 9 and 10 Dec.:[42] none of the numerous dependants of their conquered enemies should be left in lower employments; if no leniency is shown they will for safety flock to Bute in their thousands; which is the only way to make the rest of the King's reign easy. 'I . . . am willing to take upon myself all the odium of the advice . . . And I don't care how much I am hated' for doing 'such honest and essential service to the King'. But the King himself warned Bute[43] of 'the many harsh things' Fox will try to drive him into— 'no man should be dismissed' on Fox's evidence alone.

Victory earned Fox no friends and brought him no joy: it left him bitter and irritable. 'He has been . . . nervous lately and slept . . . ill', wrote Lady Holland to Lady Kildare on 5 Jan.[44] In the House he experienced humiliations. He received scant support from his own side when on 11 Feb. 1763 Sir John Philipps moved for a commission of accounts, of which Fox 'was most unaccountably afraid . . . insomuch that he could not conceal it from anybody';[45] and a further debate on 4 Mar. made him remark in a rage to George Onslow, 'though an enemy, "Did you ever see a man so treated in my situation?"'[46] Similarly on 23 Mar., over a petition from Newfoundland presented by him, which was a copy and was described as a forgery, he was treated with such disrespect that he withdrew the petition and left the House, although the cider bill, 'so much a measure of Government', was next debated.[47]

Bute, about to retire, early in March recommended Fox for his successor at the Treasury. The King objected: Fox was 'a man void of principles' —'it is not prejudice but aversion to his whole mode of government'. As a half-measure he was consulted about the new Government without being asked to form it. His paper of 11 Mar.[48] seems to suggest that he was once more playing with the idea of the Treasury for himself. When pressed by Bute, the King agreed to appointing Fox if no other solution was possible,[49]

but I own from the moment he comes in I shall not feel myself interested in the public affairs and shall feel rejoiced whenever I can see a glimmering of hope of getting quit of him.

The offer was made to him on 14 or 15 Mar.: the supreme prize of political life was within his easy reach. 'Mr. Fox', wrote Calcraft, 'is plainly . . . much inclined to the Treasury, but Lady Holland . . . much against it.'[50] He refused—was it not because she voiced his own deepest fears and feelings?

On 17 Mar. he sent Bute a second plan of Government, naming George Grenville, no friend of his own, for the Treasury.[51] But this raised new fears in his mind: that he might have to settle his pay office accounts with a perhaps unfriendly Treasury; which made Nicholl, a pay office official, suggest, and Fox consider, his taking the Treasury after all.[52] And now his closest friends, Calcraft, Rigby, and Shelburne insisted that on becoming a peer he was expected to relinquish the pay office. The conflict over it finished by producing a complete breach between them and Fox,[53] and some friction even between Fox and Bute. In the end Fox retained the pay office, and on 17 Apr. was created Baron Holland—but he had expected a viscountcy and had hoped for an earldom. His going into the House of Lords, wrote Lady Holland on 12 Apr.,[54] was against her opinion. 'I can't help feeling mortified at his ceasing to be of consequence, though I would neither have him in power nor in opposition. . . . However, if he is happy I shall soon get over that.'

But happy he was not. 'I have lost too many friendships, which I had spent my life in deserving', he wrote to Selwyn, 2 Dec. 1766.[55] And the earldom, already the hallmark of leading ministers in retirement, eluded him and became well-nigh an obsession. He courted anyone who he thought could help; continued to cultivate Bute; through his old friend Sandwich kept in with the Grenville Administration (by whom, however, he was deprived of the pay office in May 1765 on suspicion of having been concerned in the recent attempt to displace them); in October 1765 tried an approach to the Duke of Cumberland and Rockingham;[56] and next turned to Grafton. But to no avail. 'I am humbled, and shall endeavour to conform to my fate', he wrote to

Selwyn on 23 Dec. 1767; and on 27 Jan. 1768, referring to various new creations and his own 'absolute insignificance': 'I cannot help sometimes asking myself . . . why I am in such disgrace with the King? Have I deserved it?'[57]

His last years were embittered by the extravagance and callousness of his two elder sons. He died 1 July 1774.

[1] For the story of his reputed first marriage see Ilchester, *Hen. Fox*, i. 35–37. [2] Fitzmaurice, *Shelburne*, i. 135; Dodington, *Diary*, 374–5. [3] Waldegrave, *Mems*. 24. [4] Walpole, *Mems. Geo. II*, i. 94; ii. 148–9. [5] Waldegrave, 25. [6] Fitzmaurice, i. 130–2. [7] Ibid. 101. [8] *Mems. Geo. II*, 148. [9] *Mems*. 24. [10] Ilchester, *Letters to Hen. Fox*, 162. [11] 15 June 1759; *Leinster Corresp*. i. 227–8. [12] Fitzmaurice, i. 133; Lady Ilchester and Lord Stavordale, *Life & Letters of Lady Sarah Lennox*, 57–59. [13] Add. 33034, ff. 173–4; 32995, f. 170; 32929, ff. 303–11; 38333, ff. 74–106. [14] Waldegrave, 22. [15] Add. 32871, ff. 298–9. [16] Yorke, *Hardwicke*, ii. 205–8. [17] *HMC 8th Rep.* pt. 1, p. 220. [18] Ilchester, *Hen. Fox*, i. 212–31, 234, 236–7, 364–5. [19] Add. 32865, f. 205. [20] Devonshire mss; Ilchester, *Hen Fox*, ii. 3, 5. [21] 11 Nov., Devonshire mss; Ilchester, ii. 15. [22] Hardwicke to Newcastle, 7 Jan. 1757, Add. 32870, f. 58. [23] Ilchester, *Hen. Fox*. ii. 38, 45. [24] Waldegrave, 128; Walpole, *Mems. Geo. II*, iii. 29; *Leinster Corresp.* i. 47. [25] Ilchester, *Hen. Fox*, ii. 61–62. [26] L. S. Sutherland and J. Binney, 'Henry Fox as Paymaster General of the Forces', *EHR*, 1955. [27] *Lady Sarah Lennox*, 71. [28] Ilchester, *Hen. Fox*, i. 300. [29] *Lady Sarah Lennox*, i. 24. [30] Fitzmaurice, i. 86. [31] Fitzmaurice, i. 89–96; Ilchester, *Hen. Fox*, i. 147–52; Add. 32929, ff. 255, 258. [32] *Leinster Corresp.* i. 310, 315. [33] Ilchester, *Hen. Fox*, ii. 190. [34] Hen. Fox mss; Fitzmaurice, i. 120–1. [35] Namier, *England in Age of American Rev.* 352–3. [36] Fox to Bedford, 13 Oct., *Bedford Corresp.* iii. 134. [37] Ilchester, *Hen. Fox*, ii. 193. [38] Add. 32945, f. 166. [39] *Hen. Fox mss*. [40] *Mems. Geo. III*, i. 157; Namier, *Structure*, 181–4. [41] J. L. Nicholl, *Henry Fox mss.* [42] To Bute, 11 Dec., Bute mss. [43] Sedgwick, 187. [44] *Leinster Corresp.* i. 357. [45] Fitzmaurice, i. 140. [46] Walpole, *Mems. Geo. III*, i. 196. [47] Harris, 'Debates'. [48] Fitzmaurice, i. 142–5; Ilchester, *Hen. Fox*, ii. 225–9. [49] Sedgwick, 200. [50] Fitzmaurice, i. 146–7. [51] Fitzmaurice, i. 148–9; Ilchester, *Hen. Fox*, ii. 231–2. [52] Ilchester, *Hen. Fox*, ii. 234, 237; Fitzmaurice, i. 159. [53] See CALCRAFT, John and RIGBY, Richard. [54] *Leinster Corresp.* i. 365. [55] Jesse, *Selwyn*, ii. 371, misdated 1769. [56] Albemarle, *Rockingham Mems.* i .238–44. [57] Jesse, ii. 209, 247.

L.B.N.

## FOX, Hon. Stephen (1745–74), of Winterslow, nr. Salisbury, Wilts.

SALISBURY      10 Nov. 1768–1 July 1774

*b.* 20 Feb. 1745, 1st s. of Henry Fox, 1st Baron Holland, and bro. of Hon. Charles James Fox (qq.v.). *educ.* Eton 1756–9; Grand Tour 1760–5. *m.* 20 Apr. 1766, Lady Mary Fitzpatrick, da. of John, 1st Earl of Upper Ossory [I] (q.v.), 1s. 3da. *suc.* fa. as 2nd Baron 1 July 1774.
   Clerk of the pells [I] 1 July 1774–d.

Stephen Fox was the favourite child of his mother, as Charles James was of his father; he had most of his brother's faults but little of his ability. 'I fear, let his future fortune be ever so great,' wrote his tutor George Macartney to Holland on 16 Dec. 1762,[1] 'he will always be distressed in his circumstances.' On his marriage Holland wrote, in a document drawn up for the Duke of Bedford, Lady Mary Fitzpatrick's guardian:[2]

> Lord Holland proposes to give his son immediately all his landed estate, except that in Somersetshire and in Kent, which are intended for Charles.
> The landed estate which he proposes to give his son immediately is almost all in Wiltshire . . . It is very considerable, and will not produce less than three thousand five hundred pounds a year immediately,

and soon a thousaud pound a year more. His house in town, the income of a large sum of money, and place of clerk of the pells in Ireland, will come to him on Lord Holland's death.

By 1769 Fox owed over £20,000; by 1773, over £100,000. Holland paid his debts, as well as Charles's. 'You have already among you had almost our all,' wrote Lady Holland to Fox in November 1773. And in an undated letter, about the same time:[3]

> Lord Holland is much the same; better, I fear, I must never expect to see him. Oh! Ste., this last attack, whatever it was, I'm confident has been owing to the disagreeable business he has of late been engaged in on your account. Lord Holland's ill state of health, I'm persuaded, is solely owing to the vexations of his mind, which have been too powerful for a benevolent, friendly-feeling heart like his. Rigby, Calcraft, etc., began; the Duke of Leinster, Lord Hillsborough, Sarah greatly contributed; and Charles and you have put the finishing stroke. How painful this idea must be to you I know. Charles does not yet feel it, but he will severely one day; so he ought. And indeed, Ste., fondly as I once loved you both, I do not scruple distressing you by telling you how much you are in the wrong; indeed, indeed, you ought to feel it, and let it be deeply imprinted on your mind.

Fox was returned for Salisbury after a contest. In politics he followed the same line as his brother. He supported Administration 1768–72; opposed the royal marriage bill; voted for the naval captains' petition, 9 Feb. 1773, but was classed in the King's list as a friend; and voted with Administration on Grenville's Act, 25 Feb. 1774. At first he supported North's punitive measures against America. He told the House, during the debate on the bill to regulate the government of Massachusetts Bay, 28 Mar. 1774, that he 'approved vigorous measures, but said the disorders had arisen neither from the Stamp Act nor its repeal, but that all colonies as they acquire strength look with a jealous eye on the mother country'.[4] Still on 6 May 1774 he voted against the bill to regulate the administration of justice in Massachusetts Bay. Over 30 speeches by him are recorded.

He died 26 Nov. 1774.

[1] Ilchester, *Hen. Fox*, ii. 263. [2] Bedford mss 53, f. 96. [3] Ilchester ii. 353, 355. [4] Walpole, *Last Jnls*. i. 323.

J.B.

## FOX LANE, George (?1696–1773), of Bramham Park, Yorks.

HINDON                        1734–1741
YORK            21 July 1742–1761

*b.* ?1696, 1st surv. s. of Henry Fox, by his 2nd w. Frances, da. of George Lane, 1st Visct. Lanesborough [I]. *m.* 12 July 1731, Harriet, da. and h. of Robert Benson, 1st Baron Bingley, 1s. *d.v.p.* 1da. *suc.* fa.

1719; to estates of his uncle James, 2nd Visct. Lanesborough and took add. name of Lane 1751; cr. Baron Bingley 13 May 1762.

In 1754 Lane was returned unopposed for York on the corporation interest. He was always counted as a Tory. In 1758 he attempted to extend the interest which he had cultivated at York by having his son returned for the second seat, but this was unpopular even with his staunch corporation supporters and Robert Lane was defeated. In 1761 George Lane stood down in favour of Robert, and in 1762 was made a peer, largely through the efforts of his son's father-in-law, Lord Henley.[1]

He died 22 Feb. 1773, aged 76.

[1] Henley to Bute, 23 Apr. 1762, Bute mss.

J.B.

## FOX LANE, see also LANE

## FOX STRANGWAYS, Henry Thomas, Lord Stavordale (1747–1802).

MIDHURST 1768–1774

b. 10 Aug. 1747, 1st s. of Stephen Fox Strangways, 1st Earl of Ilchester, by Elizabeth, da. and h. of Thomas Strangways Horner of Mells Park, Som. educ. Eton 1760–4; Ch. Ch. Oxf. 1765. m. (1) 26 Aug. 1772, Mary Theresa (d.14 June 1790), da. and h. of Standish O'Grady of Cappercullin, co. Limerick, 2s. 6da.; (2) 28 Aug. 1794, Mary, da. of Very Rev. William Digby, dean of Durham, 3s. suc. fa. as 2nd Earl 26 Sept. 1776.
Cornet 1 Horse 1770; capt. 24 Ft. 1771; sold out 1775.

Lord Stavordale seems to have been hardly less afflicted with the passion for gambling than his cousins, Charles James and Stephen Fox. Horace Walpole wrote to Mann about him on 2 Feb. 1770:

Lord Stavordale, not one and twenty, lost eleven thousand . . . last Tuesday, but recovered it by one great hand at hazard: he swore a great oath—'Now if I had been playing deep I might have won millions.'

And George Selwyn to Lord Carlisle, November 1775:[1] 'Stavordale . . . told me himself the other night that this last trip to town had cost him £4,000 . . . He is the most framed to be a victim of any young man I ever saw.'

Stavordale was returned unopposed for Midhurst, which in 1768 was placed by its patron, Viscount Montagu, at Lord Holland's disposal. In the House of Commons he was of little consequence. His first recorded vote was with Administration on Brass Crosby's case, 27 Mar. 1771. On the royal marriage bill he voted with his cousins in opposition; and his only other recorded vote was with Administration on the revival of the Middlesex question, 26 Apr. 1773. In 1774 Holland had lost control of Midhurst,

and Stavordale is not known to have stood anywhere else.

He seems also to have taken his military career very lightly; and when in 1775 his regiment was ordered to America, he resigned his commission.[2]

He died 5 Sept. 1802.

[1] HMC Carlisle, 304. [2] Selwyn to Carlisle, 12 Dec. 1775, ibid. 310.

J.B.

## FRANCIS, Philip (1740–1818), of East Sheen, Surr.

| YARMOUTH I.o.W. | 1784–1790 |
| BLETCHINGLEY | 1790–1796 |
| APPLEBY | 1802–1807 |

b. 22 Oct. 1740, o.s. of Rev. Philip Francis by his w. Elizabeth Rowe. educ. St. Paul's Sch. m. (1) 12 Feb. 1762, Elizabeth (d. 5 Apr. 1806), da. of Alexander Mackrabie, 1s. 5da.; (2) Dec. 1814, Emma, da. of Rev. Henry Watkins, s.p. suc. fa. 5 Mar. 1773. cr. K.B. 29 Oct. 1806.

Philip Francis, senior, a clergyman of the Church of Ireland and translator of Horace, came to London about 1747, and from 1756 'almost lived at Holland House',[1] being chaplain to Lady Caroline Fox and employed by Henry Fox in pamphleteering and other confidential duties. In 1756 Philip Francis, junior, was given employment by Fox in the secretary of state's office; in 1758, through the friendship of John Calcraft and Robert Wood, he was made secretary to General Bligh on the Cherbourg expedition; and in 1760 to Lord Kinnoull on a special embassy to Portugal. On his return he acted temporarily as amanuensis to William Pitt, and in 1762 became first clerk at the War Office, where he became a close friend of the deputy clerk, Christopher D'Oyly. When D'Oyly resigned this position in December 1771, Francis, three months later, followed his example in circumstances which remain exceedingly obscure, as does his whole conduct at this period. A case of some strength has been made out for his being the author of the anonymous letters of Junius published between 1769 and 1772; he was in close contact with John Calcraft, who was working for the return of Chatham to power during the Falkland Islands dispute 1770–1 (in 1771 Calcraft promised to return him for Wareham in the next Parliament) and he lost £500 in speculation on the outbreak of war over this incident.

His resignation and the death of Calcraft nine months later left him in serious straits, though Calcraft had left him £1,000 in a codicil to his will and instructed his executors to implement his intention of returning Francis for Wareham. In June 1773, however, he was offered a place on the council to the governor general of Bengal which was to be set up under North's Regulating Act, a place which he owed chiefly to the failure to attract other candidates and the support of his former chief, Lord Barrington.

He left for India on 1 Apr. 1774, having persuaded Calcraft's executors to let Christopher D'Oyly hold the seat at Wareham in his absence. He did not return until 19 Oct. 1781. During his service in India he became well-known for the leading part he took in the contest between the governor general, Warren Hastings, and the majority of his council, and for his virulent opposition to Hastings after the death of his two colleagues.[2]

On his return, with a fortune of over £3,000 p.a.,[3] he devoted all his energies to the attempt to obtain the recall and disgrace of Hastings, at first hoping to achieve this through the North Administration, but soon throwing in his lot with those of the Rockingham Administration who were members of the select committee set up in 1781 to investigate Bengal affairs. Chief among them was Edmund Burke, with whom he was already acquainted, and over whom he acquired a great influence. Though shortly after his arrival he tried to enter the House,[4] he did not obtain a seat until the general election of 1784, when he was returned for Yarmouth on the Holmes interest.

By this time a strong supporter of the Foxite Opposition, he at first confined his activities to East India affairs, making his speeches an opportunity to justify his own actions in India and to condemn those of Hastings. He first spoke on East India affairs on 16 June 1784, on the finances of the Company, made a long speech in the debate of 2 July, and was active in the debates on Pitt's East India bill in the same month. He was prominent in the events leading to the impeachment of Warren Hastings and in the drawing up of the articles, but he was embittered by the refusal of the House on 5 Dec. 1787 to include him among the managers of the impeachment. From 1787 he took a considerable part in debates on a variety of non-Indian measures, supporting the Foxite Opposition in all major issues.

An ambitious, arrogant and vindictive man, his public life was undoubtedly, as he himself admitted, a failure, for which faults of character and lack of practical political acumen were responsible.

He died 23 Dec. 1818.

[1] Francis's autiobiog., printed in Parkes & Merivale, *Mems. of Francis*, i. 360. [2] Ibid. 263, 343, 363, 366–7. [3] Ibid. ii. 211. [4] Francis to E. Wheler, 25 Dec. 1781, Francis mss, India Office Lib.

L.S.S.

**FRANKLAND, Thomas** (1718–84), of Kirby Hall, Berks. and Thirkleby, nr. Thirsk, Yorks.

THIRSK    12 May 1747–1780, **3** Apr.–21 Nov. 1784

*b.* 26 June 1718, 2nd s. of Henry Frankland, gov. of Fort William, Bengal by Mary, da. of Alexander Cross, merchant, and bro. of William Frankland (q.v.). *m.* 27 May 1743, Sarah, da. of Judge Rhett, c.j. and gov. of South Carolina, 5s. 8da. *suc.* bro. as 5th Bt. 11 Jan. 1768, and his uncle's wid. in possession of Thirkleby estates 1783.

Entered R.N. 1731; capt. 1740; r.-adm. 1755; v.-adm. 1759; adm. 1770.

In 1754 Frankland was brought in for the family borough of Thirsk, and was classed by Dupplin as a Government supporter. As agent for the sale of captured ships in the West Indies he had dealt in very large sums of money, and in 1760 he became involved in a bitter dispute with the Treasury. He was threatened with prosecution if he did not pay £40,000, the balance remaining in his hands from the sale of prizes. On his refusal, the Treasury brought an action against him which lasted till 1766, when a compromise was reached: Frankland agreed to pay £30,000, and the case was dropped.[1]

In Bute's list of December 1761 Frankland is marked 'doubtful', but is included in Henry Fox's list of Members favourable to the peace preliminaries, December 1762. He did not vote against the Grenville Administration over general warrants, 18 Feb. 1764, nor is he known to have been absent. Classed 'pro' in July 1765 by Rockingham, he did not vote against the repeal of the Stamp Act; classed 'Government' by Charles Townshend in January 1767, he voted with the court on the land tax, 27 Feb. 1767, but against on the nullum tempus bill. In 1769 over Wilkes and the Middlesex election he went with the Opposition; became connected with Rockingham (in January 1770 he was one of those who presented the Yorkshire petition to the King); and remained in opposition throughout the Parliament.

He decided not to stand again in 1780, and on 28 July Rockingham wrote to the Duke of Portland:[2]

I have heard for some time that Sir Thomas Frankland had been offering to barter his boroughs for [the governorship of] Greenwich Hospital. I don't doubt but that if he sells the seats he will get the best price he can, and that the difference between *pounds* and *guineas* will weigh more than the difference between Whig and Court Tory. I wish nevertheless that we could get at the knowledge of the price he would ask for *one* of the *two* seats . . . It might be suggested that perhaps *some creditable Yorkshire gentleman* might be found, and a little hint that £3,000 was a good fair price.

'Being disappointed of Greenwich Hospital', Frankland returned Thomas Gascoigne and Beilby Thompson, both wealthy Yorkshiremen and followers of Rockingham.

In 1784 Frankland was again returned for Thirsk, and traded his other seat to Pitt. There is no record of his having voted in this Parliament, but he made two speeches in which he 'complained loudly that all subordination and discipline were lost in the navy', and condemned the appointment of very young men as ships' commanders.[3] He died 21 Nov. 1784.

[1] T29/30/333; T29/34/101–2; T29/37/299, 417, 445. [2] Portland mss. [3] Stockdale, ii. 114–16.

M.M.D.

## FRANKLAND, Thomas (1750–1831), of Thirkleby, nr. Thirsk, Yorks.

THIRSK 1774–1780, 1796–Oct. 1801

*b.* 18 Sept. 1750, 1st surv. s. of Sir Thomas Frankland, 5th Bt. (q.v.). *educ.* Eton 1761–7; Merton, Oxf. 1768; L. Inn 1772. *m.* 7 Mar. 1775, his cos. Dorothy, da. of William Smelt of Bedale, Yorks., 2s. 3da. *suc.* fa. as 6th Bt. 21 Nov. 1784.

Frankland consistently voted in opposition till he left Parliament in 1780. There is no record of his having spoken during his first period in the House. The family historian records that he was 'distinguished as author, artist, scientist, mechanician, and classical scholar. A learned botanist and florist, an excellent naturalist and well known authority on British sports.'[1]

He died 4 Jan. 1831.

[1] Sir R. F. Payne-Gallwey, *Ped. Frankland of Thirkleby.*

M.M.D.

## FRANKLAND, William (1720–1805), of Muntham Court, Suss.

THIRSK 1768–1774

*b.* 1720, 3rd s. of Henry Frankland, and bro. of Sir Thomas Frankland, 5th Bt. (q.v.).

Frankland spent twenty years in Bengal in the service of the East India Company. He travelled extensively in the East, journeying through Persia alone and in disguise.[1] He followed his brother in politics, and voted consistently in opposition throughout his parliamentary career. He spoke on East India affairs, 18 and 21 May 1773, but there is no record of any other speech. According to his obituary notice in the *Gentleman's Magazine* (1805, p. 1242): 'In his latter years his habits were recluse and studious, and his attention principally directed to improvements in science, and the application of mechanics to manufacturing processes.'

He died 28 Dec. 1805.

[1] Sir R. F. Payne-Gallwey, *Ped. Frankland of Thirkleby.*

M.M.D.

## FRASER, Archibald Campbell (1736–1815), of Lovat, Inverness.

INVERNESS-SHIRE 28 Mar. 1782–1784

*b.* 16 Aug. 1736, 3rd s. of Simon, 11th Lord Lovat [S], by his 2nd w. Primrose, da. of Hon. John Campbell, M.P., of Mamore, and sis. of John Campbell (q.v.), 4th Duke of Argyll; half-bro. of Simon Fraser (q.v.). *educ.* under the parish minister of Petty, Inverness 1745–6; Glasgow Univ. 1750–2; acad. in London 1753. *m.* 1763, Jane, da. of William Fraser of Leadclune, Inverness, 5s. (all *d.v.p*). *suc.* half-bro. Simon 8 Feb. 1782.

Consul at Tripoli 1764–6, Algiers 1767–76.

Fraser, after his father's execution in 1747, was educated by his mother, who sent him to Glasgow, 'a place of known loyalty'.[1] He was granted an award of some £55 p.a. from the forfeited Lovat estates for his maintenance. Subsequently he became a merchant.

On his half-brother's death in 1782 he succeeded to the restored Lovat estates, which had been vested in trustees until all debts should be paid off. Fraser resented this 'injustice', which reduced his electoral interest and gave the trustees 'more to say with their name than the present lord'.[2] However, he was returned unopposed for Inverness-shire.

During his two years in the House some ten speeches by Fraser are reported, mainly on economic and Scottish affairs. In his maiden speech, on 17 June 1782, he seconded Lord Graham's motion to repeal the Act prohibiting Highland dress, as a 'kindness' likely to discourage emigration.[3] 'Every effort is laudable', he wrote on 1 July, 'whose motives have a tendency to divert transatlantic notions.'[4] He voted against Shelburne's peace preliminaries, 18 Feb. 1783, and spoke and voted for Fox's East India bill, 27 Nov. 1783.

Robinson in December 1783 classed Fraser as an opponent of Pitt's Administration, but in January 1784 as a supporter. Fraser belonged to the St. Alban's Tavern group which tried to unite Pitt and Fox, and in the House on 12 Jan. declared that 'he was not pledged to vote on either side' but 'would defend the constitution and the present royal family of Hanover with his life'.[5] In Stockdale's list of 19 Mar. he was noted as absent.

He did not stand in 1784 but gave his interest to Lord William Gordon.

He died 8 Dec. 1815.

[1] *Forfeited Estates Pprs.* (Sc. Hist. Soc.), 32–34, 46. [2] C. Fraser Mackintosh, *Antiquarian Notes* (ser. 2) 8; Adam, *Pol. State of Scotland 1788*, p. 173. [3] Debrett, vii. 235–7. [4] C. F. Mackintosh, *Letters of Two Centuries*, 344. [5] Debrett, xii. 522.

E.H.-G.

## FRASER, James (*b.*?1740), of Golden Sq., London.

GATTON 26 Feb. 1787–1790

Poss. s. of James Fraser, merchant and apothecary of 'Mariebone St.', nr. Golden Sq.'[1] and a kinsman of Simon Fraser, London merchant and E.I. Co. director.

Fraser 'received a regular education as a merchant'[2] and by 1767 was established in business in Bengal where he became a close friend of George Graham (q.v.). From his headquarters at Patna he conducted 'extensive dealings', and in 1772, 'having for some time made the navigation of the Ganges his study', applied to Warren Hastings for a three years' contract for supplying boats for the transport of troops and military stores.[3] In 1773-4 he was associated with Col. Gabriel Harper and Col. Alexander Hannay (brother of Sir Samuel, q.v.) in a contract for supplying elephants to the Nabob of Oude, the accounts for which were still unsettled at Hannay's death in 1782. In 1783, Fraser, having amassed a considerable fortune, prepared to return home, called in his debts, and thereby became involved in a bitter dispute with Hannay's brothers and executors, Ramsay and Johnstone, over a note of hand for 10,000 rupees and the elephant contract accounts. Accused by them of fraud, Fraser admitted he had 'by mistake' charged the cancelled note against the estate. The 'elephant' dispute was referred to arbitrators one of whom, Capt. Robert Stewart, became Fraser's bitter enemy, and on their return to England publicly denounced him in 1785 as unfit for membership of the Bengal Club. Six arbitrators appointed to investigate the charges signed an 'award' acquitting Fraser of intent to defraud, but 'his inaccuracies in his accounts were sufficient to have misled Capt. Stewart'. Stewart thereafter went abroad, but on his return in 1786 threatened to publish a 'Narrative' of Fraser's misdeeds. Fraser, who had embarked upon his canvass for election to the East India directorate, suspecting that Stewart 'had come over from India on purpose to be an evidence against Mr. Hastings', had allegedly threatened Stewart's life, and had had Stewart watched by a spy, who, when arrested in June 1786, revealed the full plot.

While Stewart was in Scotland, Fraser was brought in for Gatton on the interest of his friends the Graham family and their uncle William Mayne, Lord Newhaven, presumably intending to support Hastings. Fraser had secured nomination on the East India Company house list of directors, but a few days before the election Stewart published his *Narrative*. Fraser records:

> On the close of a laborious canvass for the India direction when by the most flattering exertions of private friendship and the public recommendation of the court of directors . . . nothing seemed wanting to my success but the mere form of election . . . I found myself on a sudden publicly accused of a gross and intentional fraud . . .

Fraser failed of election by 5 votes.[4] He then published his *Answer* to the charges, together with testi-

monials to his good character from old Indian friends and supporters in the general court including George Vansittart, Dalhousie Watherston, and George Graham (qq.v.). Stewart thereupon printed his *Reply* with further damaging evidence.

Thus discredited, Fraser made little mark in Parliament. He is not known to have spoken but voted with Administration on Impey's impeachment, 9 May 1788, and in the Regency debates.

The date of his death has not been ascertained.

[1] Add. 28234, ff. 277, 395; 28235, f. 404. [2] The information contained here has been compiled from two pamphlets published in 1787, *The Answer of James Fraser M.P. to the charges made against him by Robert Stewart Esq.*, and *A Reply to the Answer of James Fraser Esq. by Robert Stewart Esq.* [3] Add. 29133, f. 180. [4] *Gent. Mag.* 1787, p. 361.

E.H.-G.

## FRASER, Simon (1726-82), of Lovat, Inverness.

INVERNESS-SHIRE      1761-8 Feb. 1782

*b.* 19 Oct. 1726, 1st s. of Simon, 11th Lord Lovat [S], by his 1st w. Margaret, da. of Ludovick Grant of Grant, M.P. [S]. *educ.* St. Andrew's Univ. 1743-5; Glasgow Univ. 1748; adv. July 1752; M. Temple 1752, called 1756. *m.* in Portugal, ?1765, Catherine, da of John Bristow (q.v.), *s.p.*

Lt.-col. commandant 78 Ft. (Fraser's Highlanders) Jan. 1757; col. 1762; brig.-gen. (local rank in Portugal) 1762; maj.-gen. Portuguese forces and gov. of a province 1763; maj.-gen. British army 1772; col. 71 Regt. (which he raised) 1775-*d.*; lt.-gen. 1777.

Deputed by Lord Lovat in 1745 to raise the clan in rebellion, Fraser, on discovering that he was a pawn in his father's intrigues, decided to leave Scotland for Leyden, but, browbeaten into tearful submission, eventually accepted his role of scapegoat and joined the Highland army.[1] A fugitive after Culloden, and attainted by Act of Parliament, Fraser surrendered in August 1746, and was imprisoned in Edinburgh castle. After his father's execution Newcastle issued a warrant for his release on condition that he lived in Glasgow.[2] Having rejected the Pretender's offer of a regiment in the French service,[3] Fraser began to study law at Glasgow University and in 1750 was granted a full pardon and an allowance of £300 p.a.[4] He qualified as an advocate, and formed a lasting friendship with Alexander Wedderburn, who followed him to the English bar.

In September 1753 the ministry was dismayed to find that Fraser was standing for Inverness-shire. Norman Macleod wrote to Newcastle, 6 Oct.:[5]

> Mr. Fraser has been some little time here and had a very kind reception from all of us . . . I am most willing to yield in his favour, and really he has got it so much in his head that it will be a mean to make his fortune, that I shall be sorry if he's baulked.

This 'revival of Jacobite clanship' was strongly

opposed by Hardwicke, Pelham, Newcastle, and Argyll, who wrote to Pelham, 15 Oct.:[6]

> I have lost no time in letting everybody know how much I abhor the measure, both for the sake of the young man and of the public; if he really intends to stand I think his head must be turned.

Argyll summoned Fraser to Inveraray and reported to Pelham, 28 Oct.:[7]

> I instantly . . . attacked him about his standing, he protests to me that . . . he always declared it was subject to the opinion and direction of those to whom he owed the favours he has received; he then went on with the history of himself in such a manner as that I must have been void of common humanity not to be affected by it. I said what I could to comfort him but persisted in a positive negative to his standing, so that I take it for granted that affair is over.

After being called to the English bar in 1756 Fraser was 'in very good business for his standing',[8] when by Argyll's interest with Pitt[9] he was offered the command of one of the two new battalions to be raised in the Highlands. Recruiting in record time, Fraser sailed with his regiment for America in April 1757, served with distinction at Louisbourg, under Wolfe and Murray in Canada where he was twice wounded, and returned home in the spring of 1761.

His friends meanwhile had been canvassing his candidature for Inverness-shire, which Argyll and the ministry again vetoed. After Argyll's death the electors defied the ministry and unanimously chose Fraser on 2 May, the day after he arrived in London from America. On receiving the news, Fraser at once wrote to Bute, 12 May:[10]

> I do upon my honour assure your Lordship I was totally ignorant when I arrived in London twelve days ago of everything here [his friends] had done . . . I am persuaded their motives for choosing me were founded on no other attachment but personal friendship and the honour I have of commanding a regiment of the King's troops raised in that county . . . I have always avoided the least appearance of encouraging that attachment of clanship and for seven years avoided going to that part of the country till I had the sanction of Government for making use of that attachment to raise a thousand men for the King's service . . . You, my Lord, have too much humanity not to be sensible how distressing the being at this time objected to must [be] and will pardon my anxiety. If the affair should reach the King's ear, you are too just to decline representing in the most favourable light the part I have acted and my dutiful readiness to obey his Majesty's commands.

Bute, wrote Newcastle to Hardwicke on 14 May, 'seems much offended'.[11]

> He says the principal electors have wrote to him (Lord Bute) . . . they say they are independent gentlemen, have no places, no employments and that nothing but Col. Fraser's own request, which they had not had, could have prevented their choosing him. Nothing I

think could be more insolent to the King or more renouncing his Majesty's influence than this letter to his minister. His Lordship told me Mr. Pitt took part with Col. Fraser and wondered how the Duke of Newcastle could object to him who had acted meritoriously in North America . . . Lord Bute said he should have no objection to Col. Fraser's being in Parliament but not for the shire of Inverness.

Under this cloud of suspicion Fraser went to court. Many years later he wrote to Barrington:[12]

> I can never forget that the first time I appeared at St. James's after my return from America in 1761, your Lordship was pleased, in a circle of the great officers of state . . . to say you thought it incumbent upon you to thank me in this public manner for the services I had done with my regiment to my King and country . . . As I desired to leave Canada only because the war was at an end there, my only request when I returned was to be again employed wherever there was actual service, of which his Majesty was pleased to express his approbation in the most gracious terms and to name me to go to Portugal as brigadier.

After serving with the British forces in Portugal until the peace, Fraser, rather than retire on half-pay, transferred to the Portuguese army on the understanding that 'it would be considered as British service', and eventually attaining the chief command, spent most of the next ten years abroad.

He was almost continuously absent from Parliament from early in 1762 to February 1766. Though listed by Sir Alexander Gilmour 'absent in Portugal' in the division of 17 Feb.,[13] he voted against the repeal of the Stamp Act on 22 Feb. Closely associated with Wedderburn, he became an intimate friend of Grenville, to whom he wrote, 10 June 1766,[14] asking for an assurance that Lord Temple was not responsible for *The History of the Late Minority* which had 'nettled' Bute and his friends and might militate against a Grenville-Bute alliance. Uneasy about his re-election, which was 'more likely to be disputed on account of the change of ministry', Fraser in July 1766 consulted Grenville and Whately on purchasing for £2,000 an English borough seat.[15] From Scotland, when 'hardly sober' after his welcome home by the clan, he pursued the question, but in October, having secured Inverness-shire by an agreement with the Gordon interest, returned to London, thanked Grenville 'for the kindness intended him',[16] and by November was again attempting to negotiate an alliance between Bute, Grenville and Temple.[17] At the end of the year he went back to Portugal.

Fraser returned home in 1771, when war seemed imminent; voted with Administration on Brass Crosby, 27 Mar.; but presumably returned to Portugal before the royal marriage bill of March 1772 when he was listed 'pro, absent'. Back in

England about the end of 1772 he decided to resign his Portuguese command, applied without success for a vacant colonelcy in February 1773, and was considered for a command in India, but in June, 'very handsomely and without the least hesitation relinquished his pretensions' when North informed him of the difficulties which had arisen with other generals.[18] Having taken a house in Downing Street, he became an intimate friend of North, who supported his memorial of 1773[19] for the recovery of the forfeited Lovat estates and obtained the King's recommendation for his successful petition to Parliament in 1774.[20] Nevertheless, his re-election was uncertain, in view of his 1766 agreement to stand down in favour of the Gordon family,[21] who in 1772 had already announced the candidature of Lord George Gordon. But, by agreement with North, Fraser purchased a seat at Ludgershall for Lord George,[22] and was returned apparently unopposed.

Through North's favour Fraser, in 1775, secured approval of his proposal to raise a new Highland regiment of two battalions,[23] and made his first recorded speech in the House on 22 Nov. 1775 in explanation of his choice of officers.[24] He himself remained in London where he was deeply involved in the intrigues of Philip Francis against Warren Hastings. The appointment by Francis in 1775 of Fraser's brother-in-law, John Bristow, as resident at Oude, in preference to Frederick Stuart, Bute's son, aroused considerable controversy.[25] Fraser, having presented Bristow's case to North and Suffolk, disarmed the Bute family's opposition by nominating Charles Stuart as major in his new regiment. Corresponding with Francis on Bengal affairs, Fraser worked behind the scenes to further his and Bristow's interests with the ministry, and in 1779 evolved a 'delicate and dangerous' plan to replace Hastings by Francis as governor general.[26] In these affairs he frequently consulted his friend Wedderburn, for whom he acted in May–June 1778 as agent in his negotiations with North and the King for high office and a peerage.[27]

Fraser is not known to have spoken on Indian affairs, but confined himself to America and the army. On 24 Feb. 1778, 'in a long and animated speech' on the conciliation bills,[28] he 'reviewed the whole subject of the American dispute', maintained that, as the repeal of the Stamp Act was a 'virtual renunciation of the exercise of the right of taxation . . . it should not have been again taken up', and, 'lamenting the despondency of the ministry', urged that, if the concessions were rejected, the rebellion must be rigorously subdued. Although he continued to support North, according to a notice of him in

the *English Chronicle* in 1781 he voted for Fox at the Westminster election of 1780.

He died 8 Feb. 1782.

[1] Alex. Mackenzie, *Hist. Frasers of Lovat*, 377–490; *Trial of Lord Lovat*, ed. D. N. Mackay; *Chiefs of Grant*, ii; *More Culloden Pprs.* iv, v. [2] Argyll to Pelham, 11 Aug. 1747, Newcastle (Clumber) mss; *Chiefs of Grant*, ii. 269. [3] Fraser's memorial of 1773, *Forfeited Estates Pprs.* 104. [4] T52/45/278. [5] Add. 32733, f. 28. [6] Newcastle (Clumber) mss. [7] Ibid. [8] *Forfeited Estates Pprs.* 104. [9] J. Calcraft to Alex. Mackay, 31 Dec. 1756, Add. 17493, f. 24b. [10] Bute mss. [11] Add. 32923, f. 70. [12] 15 Feb. 1773, Fortescue, ii. 454. [13] Add. 32974, f. 24. [14] *Grenville Pprs.* iii. 244. [15] Whately to Grenville, 30 July, Grenville mss (JM). [16] Same to same, 16 Sept., 13 Oct. 1766, ibid. [17] *Grenville Pprs.* iii. 280. [18] Fortescue, ii. 454–5, 496–7. [19] *Forfeited Estates Pprs.* 103–5. [20] Fortescue, iii. 77–78. [21] Laprade, 5. [22] A. & H. Tayler, *Ld Fife & his Factor*, 108. [23] Fortescue, iii. 249, 268, 287; *HMC Laing*, ii. 480, 482–4; *HMC Royal Institution*, i. 24, 66. [24] Almon, iii. 206–7. [25] Parkes & Merivale, *Mems. of Francis*, ii. 21. [26] Ibid. 166–7, 179; S. Weitzman, *Warren Hastings & Philip Francis*, 285–6, 309. [27] Fortescue, iv. 163. [28] Almon, vii. 399.

E.H.-G.

## FREDERICK, Charles (1709–85), of Hammersmith, Mdx.

| | |
|---|---|
| NEW SHOREHAM | 1741–1754 |
| QUEENBOROUGH | 1754–1784 |

*b.* 21 Dec. 1709, 3rd *s.* of Sir Thomas Frederick, gov. of Fort St. David and director of the South Sea Co., by Mary, *da.* and *h.* of William Moncrieff; *bro.* of John Frederick (q.v.). *educ.* Westminster 1719–20; New Coll. Oxf. 1725; M. Temple 1728; Grand Tour with his bro. John 1737–9 (Italy, Constantinople, Nr. East, France[1]). *m.* 18 Aug. 1746, Hon. Lucy Boscawen, *da.* of Hugh, 1st Visct. Falmouth, 4s. 2da. *cr.* K.B. 23 Mar. 1761.

Clerk of deliveries of the Ordnance 1746–50; surveyor gen. of the Ordnance 1750–82.

Charles Frederick was an eminent antiquary, a scholar, artist, and civil servant, rather than a politician. He collected early French coins which he engraved 'in 36 quarto plates';[2] and made drawings of churches, monuments, views, etc. for Smart Lethieuller's folio volumes, 'the work of many years' tours about England, on which Sir Charles Frederick spent near £500'.[3]

In 1754 he was put up for Queenborough 'where the fleet and the Ordnance have great influence . . . and therefore their dependants want to nominate [the Members]'.[4] Still, there were difficulties because of 'the strange fellow at the head of the corporation', and apparently New Shoreham was kept open for Frederick if he failed at Queenborough.[5] In 1761 he was returned unopposed; and again in 1768. He was marked in Bute's list of December 1761 'Falmouth. Bute. Government. Pro'; was included in Fox's list of Members favourable to the peace preliminaries; and was counted by Newcastle, 13 Nov. 1762, as 'contra'.

In the reshuffle of offices, December 1762–January 1763, Shelburne, who wanted the surveyorship of the Ordnance for Barré, suggested that Frederick should be made receiver general of the customs.[6] Fox saw Frederick about it. 'He seemed to like the offer', Fox wrote to Bute on 13 Jan., 'and if what he said of the profits of his present place and of his own circumstances is strictly true, he will undoubtedly be thankful for the exchange.'[7] And Bute to Fox, 14 Jan.: 'Sir Charles Frederick was with me, but did not seem so fond of the idea as I could have wished. He has taken till Monday to give his answer. However I believe I have a lure to tempt him if necessary.'[8] But nothing more is heard of it—possibly he was too much attached to the office in which he had already served sixteen years, and remained there another twenty.

He retained the character of a civil servant, even in the House—his very few recorded interventions in debate were all on technical matters concerning his department. Two letters from Frederick to Lord Townshend,[9] since October 1772 master general of the Ordnance, deal with his constituency. On 15 Sept. 1774 he writes about a late clerk of the Ordnance who threatened to destroy Frederick's interest at Queenborough:

He talks ignorantly though he is a voter; for he must know I can have no interest there, but from the support of the master general.

This time the borough was contested, Piercy Brett, the Admiralty Member in the previous Parliament, having been dropped, and now standing against the official candidates. A month after the election, 8 Nov., Frederick wrote to Townshend:

All under your Lordship (except two or three) behaved with uncommon firmness and disinterestedness ... The dissolution of the Parliament was so very secret and sudden, and my election being four days after the dissolution, I had not time to apply to you for your commands. Sir Walter Rawlinson who was chose with me, was the person sent by Lord North and Lord Sandwich, and who I never saw till an hour before we got into a post chaise for Queenborough; it is to the master general's interest I owe my seat, and therefore return your Lordship my sincere thanks for permitting me to be chose there.

In 1779 the *Public Ledger* wrote about Frederick: 'A superannuated placeman. He just continues to crawl to the House, to keep a debate out, and give his vote.' This he did with great regularity. But he was too ill to attend the crucial divisions of February 1782; his physician told Sandwich that going out would kill him—'you will however see', wrote Sandwich to Robinson, 16 Feb. 1782, 'that he is very hearty in our cause, and that therefore we must not give him up'; he voted with the Government on 8 Mar. and wrote to Sandwich on the 13th: 'You may be assured, notwithstanding the weak state of my health, I will attend on Friday next, and shall at all times when in my power be happy to obey your commands.'[10]

On the fall of North he was removed from office. Pleading 'extreme poverty' he applied to the new Administration for a pension,[11] but begged to be allowed to retain his seat in Parliament: 'he was so poor he was afraid of the Fleet or King's bench prison'. On 18 Feb. 1783 he voted against Shelburne's peace preliminaries, his first recorded vote against any Administration. He adhered to the Coalition; was granted by them a pension of £500 p.a.; and opposed Pitt. He did not stand in 1784. He is commemorated in *Fox's Martyrs*:

If he had persisted in the constant line of worship which he had so long shown to the minister of the day ... he would not (to invert the scripture penalty) have been cast *out* of the furnace of the Woolwich foundery, nor possibly would he have been rejected by the electors of Queenborough.

He died 18 Dec. 1785.

[1] E. H. Fellowes, *Family of Frederick*, 43–44. [2] J. Nichols, *Literary Anecs.* vi. 383. [3] Gough's account quoted in Yale ed. of H. Walpole's *Corresp.* ii. 238. [4] H. Pelham to Newcastle, 24 July 1753, Add. 32732, f. 348. [5] Same to same, Add. 32733, f. 138. [6] Fox to Shelburne, 25 Dec., Lansdowne mss; and Shelburne to Bute, n.d., Bute mss. [7] Bute mss. [8] Ilchester, *Letters to Hen. Fox*, 171. [9] WO46/9/47–9. [10] Abergavenny mss. [11] About this, see Stockdale, viii. 91–94.

L.B.N.

**FREDERICK, John** (1708–83), of Burwood Park, Walton-on-Thames, Surr.

NEW SHOREHAM   24 Nov. 1740–1741
WEST LOOE      10 Dec. 1743–1761

*b.* 28 Nov. 1708, at Fort St. George in India, 2nd s. of Sir Thomas Frederick, and bro. of Charles Frederick (q.v.). *educ.* Westminster 1719–20; New Coll. Oxf. 1725; M. Temple 1729; Grand Tour with his bro. Charles 1737–9 (Italy, Constantinople, Nr. East, France). *m.* 22 Oct. 1741, Susanna, da. of Sir Roger Hudson of Sunbury, Mdx., and sis. and h. of Vansittart Hudson, 2s. 3da. *suc.* bro. Thomas at Burwood 24 July 1740; his cos. as 4th Bt. 16 Dec. 1770.

Commr. of Customs Mar. 1761–Mar. 1782.

John Frederick sat at West Looe as a Government candidate. During the years 1755–60 he repeatedly applied to Newcastle for office: a clerkship of the Green Cloth (25 Feb. 1755, and 1 May 1759), a place at the Board of Trade (20 May 1756, and 7 May 1759), the keepership of the records at the Tower (24 June 1755), etc.;[1] and he pleaded years of 'implicit obedience to his Majesty's service attended with great expenses', 'without emolument or favour', and his steady attachment to Newcastle and his family 'in every instance'. On 27 May 1757:[2]

I am credibly informed the Administration is to be formed tomorrow, which must occasion many vacancies. I can no longer forbear to put your Grace in mind that I expect at this time performance of the repeated promises you have given me and which you must be conscious of. I have been your faithful friend, and I cannot now be amused by specious words. To be neglected I neither deserve, or can I submit to it. Your Grace's answer will determine me.

And on 1 May 1759:[3] 'no one has shown more zeal and attachment . . ., and hitherto I have spent many and many years in cruel disappointment and vexation'.

Meantime he was trying to establish an interest of his own at West Looe against the Bullers, the Government managers who came more and more to control the borough. He was worsted,[4] and during the months preceding the general election of 1761 his name appears in Newcastle's lists of candidates in need of seats; in one undated list[5] with the remark: 'Turned out of Parliament by Mr. Buller. Has had long expectations and constant disappointments.' Finally his name is crossed out, the word 'Customs' having been put against it: he obtained his consolation prize in a commissionership worth £1,000 a year, which he retained till the winding up of the North Administration when the place was required for Sir Stanier Porten. In exchange Frederick received a pension of £1,000 p.a. during pleasure.[6]

He died 9 Apr. 1783.

[1] Add. 32852, f. 621; 32856, f. 179; 32864, f. 118; 32891, f. 23; 32900, f. 266. [2] Add. 32871, f. 149. [3] Add. 32890, f. 436. [4] Namier, *Structure*, 326–8. [5] Add. 32999, f. 222. [6] T52/70/458.

L.B.N.

**FREDERICK, John** (1750–1825), of Burwood Park, Surr.

NEWPORT            30 Dec. 1774–1780
CHRISTCHURCH       29 Jan. 1781–1790
SURREY             7 Nov. 1794–1807

*b.* 18 Mar. 1750, o. surv. s. of John Frederick (q.v.). *educ.* Westminster 1760–5; Trinity, Oxf. 1767; Grand Tour 1769–72. *m.* 15 Oct. 1778, Mary, da. and coh. of Richard Garth of Morden, Surr., 6s. 5da. *suc.* fa. as 5th Bt. 9 Apr. 1783.

Frederick was returned for Newport by Humphry Morice as a follower of Administration. Morice having sold his boroughs, no other seat was found for Frederick at the general election of 1780. In 1781 he was returned at Christchurch by Edward Hooper: 'From the interest on which he procured his seat', wrote the *English Chronicle*, 'we may venture to predict he will be the close friend of the minister.' And Frederick consistently voted with the North Administration till its fall. He voted against Shelburne's peace preliminaries, 18 Feb. 1783; for Fox's East India bill, 27 Nov. 1783; and he opposed Pitt till he went out of Parliament in 1790.

The *Public Ledger* wrote about Frederick in 1779: 'This gentleman is no speaker'; and there is no record of his having spoken in the House before 1790.

He died 16 Jan. 1825.

M.M.D.

**FREEMAN, Sambrooke** (c.1721–82), of Fawley Court, Henley-on-Thames, Berks.

PONTEFRACT    1754–1761
BRIDPORT      1768–1774

*b.* c.1721, 2nd s. of John Cooke (who assumed name of Freeman on succeeding to estates of his uncle, William Freeman of St. Kitts and Fawley) by Susanna, da. of Sir Jeremy Sambrooke. *educ.* Univ. Coll. Oxf. 1739. *m.* Dec. 1757, Sarah Winsford of Glasshampton, Worcs.

Freeman was returned unopposed at Pontefract on the interest of his friend George Morton Pitt, M.P., and was classed by Dupplin as a country gentleman, supporting Administration. He did not stand in 1761, but in 1768 was returned unopposed for Bridport, possibly introduced there through his West Indian connexion. He voted with Administration on the Middlesex election, 8 May 1769, but does not appear in any other list until March 1772, when, in Robinson's first survey on the royal marriage bill he was described as 'doubtful, present', and in the second as 'pro, present'. He voted for Administration on the Middlesex election, 26 Apr. 1773, but on the bill for perpetuating Grenville's Election Act, 25 Feb. 1774, appears in George III's list as a friend voting for the bill and twice spoke against the Government, 'though sorry to differ in opinion from the noble lord [North] for whose opinion [he had] the greatest regard'. His only other recorded speech was on the Reading canal bill, 21 Feb. 1771, when he explained he was 'so unused to speak in this House if I should not acquit myself so cleverly'.[1]

Freeman stood again at Bridport in 1774 but was defeated.

He died 21 Sept. 1782.

[1] Cavendish's 'Debates', Egerton 252, p. 185; 225, p. 150.

M.M.D.

**FREEMAN,** *see also* **EDWARDS FREEMAN** *and* **MITFORD, John**

**FRENCH, Jeffrey** (*d.*1754), of Argyle Buildings, London.

MILBORNE PORT        1741–1747
TAVISTOCK            24 Apr.–14 May 1754

6th s. of Arthur French of Cloonyquin, co. Roscommon, by his 2nd w. Sarah, da. and h. of Ulick Burke of Clare, co. Galway, wid. of Iriel Farrell of Cloonyquin. *educ.* M. Temple 1719, called 1724. *m.*

Catherine, da. of Richard Lloyd of Croghan, co. Roscommon, speaker of the upper house of assembly and c.j. Jamaica; issue.

French was a practising barrister, and owned a plantation in Jamaica. In 1754 he and Richard Rigby unsuccessfully contested Newport (Cornwall) on the Duke of Bedford's interest; and were returned by Bedford for Tavistock. French was too ill to attend at Newport until the day before the poll, and died on 14 May before Parliament met. He left his Jamaica plantation or 'about £900 per annum in the county of Roscommon' to James Plunkett, son of his sister Mary.[1] According to Horace Walpole,[2] French had paid Bedford £1,500 for his seat at Tavistock, and Plunkett sued the Duke for the return of the money, 'who paid it, rather than let the cause be heard'. A slightly different story is told by Charles Townshend:[3] Plunkett applied to Bedford for the vacant seat, and on being refused 'brought a bill in equity for the recovery of the purchase money', to which Bedford replied that 'the contract was merely personal and strictly performed on his part'.

[1] Jesse Foote, *Life of Arthur Murphy*, 12. [2] *Mems. Geo. II*, ii. 124–125. [3] Draft of a pamphlet written in 1763 or 1764, Buccleuch mss.

L.B.N.

## FULLARTON, William (1754–1808), of Fullarton, Ayr.

| | |
|---|---|
| PLYMPTON ERLE | 8 Apr. 1779–1780 |
| HADDINGTON BURGHS | 22 June 1787–1790 |
| HORSHAM | 24 Oct. 1793–1796 |
| AYRSHIRE | 30 Nov. 1796–Mar. 1803 |

*b.* 12 Jan. 1754, o.s. of William Fullarton of Fullarton, by Barbara, da. of William (Scot) Blair of Blair, Ayr. *educ.* Edinburgh Univ. 1768; Grand Tour 1769–71; L. Inn 1774. *m.* 18 June 1792, Hon. Marianne Mackay, 2nd da. of George, 5th Lord Reay [S], 1da. *suc.* fa. 7 Sept. 1758.
Sec. at British embassy in Paris 1775–8.
Lt.-col. commandant (temp. rank) 98 Ft. May 1780–85; col. (local rank, East Indies) June 1782; raised 23 Drag. (Fullarton's Light Horse) 1794, and 101 Ft. 1800. First commr. for govt. of Trinidad 1802–3.

As a child Fullarton succeeded to great estates and the headship of a family with extensive East Indian connexions. He was brought up in Edinburgh with William Adam, and after the Grand Tour he began to read for the bar. But at the age of 21 he was appointed principal secretary to Lord Stormont, then ambassador in Paris, by whose interest with North he was brought in for Plympton. Described by the *Public Ledger* in 1779 as 'a hungry Scotchman . . . willing to do anything he is —[paid] to do', Fullarton consistently supported

Administration. When William Adam fought his duel with Fox in November 1779 he borrowed Fullarton's pistols,[1] and chose for his second Major Thomas Mackenzie Humberston, elder brother of Francis Humberston Mackenzie (q.v.). Humberston and Fullarton had already launched a plan, backed by friends, to fit out four privateers manned by troops raised by themselves to cruise in the Pacific and attack the coast of Mexico. 'Willing to hazard under Government direction £70,000–£80,000', they asked ministerial support and a ship of 64 guns. On 20 Jan. 1780 Fullarton submitted the scheme for Cabinet approval through Lord George Germain, who warmly recommended it and suggested a complementary expedition to the Spanish Main.[2] When both men obtained lieutenant-colonels' commissions to raise regiments for the expedition, Shelburne and Richmond violently attacked Fullarton's appointment, ridiculing this 'embassy clerk, this *commis*' with no military experience, now 'by ministerial caprice' raised to a command in a buccaneering expedition.[3] Fullarton, having pressed Jenkinson to afford him an opportunity to reply,[4] on 20 Mar. in an angry speech defended himself and his corps, abused Shelburne by name for his 'aristocratic insolence', and was called to order for breach of parliamentary usage.[5] When Fullarton published further provocative comments, a duel resulted on 22 Mar. in which Shelburne was wounded.[6] Sir James Lowther immediately pressed for an inquiry; Adam and Sir Adam Fergusson stoutly defended their friend, and, after a heated debate on the possible effect of this and the Adam-Fox duel on the freedom of debate, the question was deferred until Fullarton should be present.[7] The affair aroused considerable anti-Scottish feeling;[8] and when the new regiments were discussed in the army estimates debate of 5 Apr. the full force of the objections of the Opposition and the regular army officers was concentrated upon Fullarton, whose disinterested zeal was warmly praised by Jenkinson and Lord George Germain. On a division the separate estimate for Fullarton's corps was passed in committee by 102 to 66, but the attack was renewed on 11 Apr., particularly on the question of Fullarton's rank.

Fullarton did not seek re-election in 1780. The Cabinet having finally approved the South Sea expedition in August, Fullarton and Humberston were authorized to double the size of their regiments; but on the outbreak of the Dutch war the force was diverted, first to the Cape of Good Hope and eventually to India.[9] Here Fullarton confounded his critics by brilliant military leadership which earned for him in May 1783 the command of the army south of the Coleroon. After further successful campaigns (during which he advanced considerable sums from his own funds to native princes) Fullarton left India in December 1784 and on his return home published in 1787 an account of his campaigns and a pamphlet, *A View of the English Interests in India.*[10]

Having maintained his attachment to North, Stormont, Adam, and other Opposition leaders, Fullarton became connected with the Prince of Wales; and when in 1787 his friend Francis Charteris was obliged to vacate Haddington Burghs, Fullarton succeeded him as an Opposition candidate.

An able debater, he spoke with authority on Indian affairs, and opposed the declaratory bill on 5 Mar. 1788 as unfair to East India Company officers. On 9 May he 'inveighed against Impey as a criminal of the most atrocious description whose ermine was steeped in human blood'. He was an equally effective Opposition speaker in the Regency debate of 16 Jan. 1789. An uncompromising critic of Hastings, in the debate of 15 Mar. 1790 on the execution of Mustapha Khan he maintained that no British officer was obliged to obey a cruel, illegal order.[11]

He lost his seat in 1790. He died 13 Feb. 1808.

[1] Walpole to Mann, 8 Apr. 1780. [2] *HMC Stopford-Sackville*, ii. 282; James Paterson, *Hist. Ayr*, ii. 19–20. [3] Stockdale, xiv. 198–207. [4] Add. 38213, ff. 206, 218. [5] Almon, xvii. 372–4. [6] Walpole, *Last Jnls.* ii. 288–92; Walpole to Mason, 22 Mar. 1780. [7] Almon, xvii. 407–14. [8] E. H. Coleridge, *Life of T. Coutts*, i. 127–8. [9] Fortescue, v. 106–8; H. D. Love, *Vestiges of Old Madras*, iii. 259–60. [10] Stockdale, xix. 176; Fortescue, *Hist. British Army*, iii. 484, 493; Add. 38410, f. 93. [11] Stockdale, xii. 289–94; xiv. 342–69; xvi. 253–60; xix. 187–91.

E.H.-G.

## FULLER, John (1706–55), of Brightling, Suss.

BOROUGHBRIDGE    20 Dec. 1754–1 Feb. 1755

*bap.* 8 Feb. 1706, 1st s. of John Fuller, M.P., of Brightling by Elizabeth, da. of Fulke Rose of Jamaica; bro. of Rose Fuller (q.v.). *educ.* Trinity, Camb. 1723; M. Temple 1724. *m.* Miss Darell, *s.p.*

At the general election of 1754 Fuller had meant to stand for Sussex, and was said to have the support of Lord Middlesex.[1] But on 14 Mar., 'with the greatest regard to the peace and quiet of the county', he acquainted the Duke of Newcastle that he would not stand.[2] And this is how Fuller described the sequel in a letter to a friend:[3] The Duke called in Lord Ashburnham, and said: 'My Lord, one civility deserves another, I will never be outdone'; and made Ashburnham witness to his voluntary offer that Fuller 'shall be in the next Parliament chosen by me without expense, and without any constraint upon his actions. He shall come into the House as free and independent as any

Member there.' On a vacancy occurring in Newcastle's pocket borough of Boroughbridge, Fuller was returned, 20 Dec. 1754, *in absentia*, his 'infirm state of health' not permitting attendance.[4] He died 1 Feb. 1755.

[1] Halifax to Newcastle, 12 Mar. 1754, Add. 32734, f. 227. [2] Newcastle to Ld. Northampton, 15 Mar., ibid. f. 255. [3] Fuller to H. Dodson, 19 Mar. 1754, ibid. f. 289. [4] Newcastle to the burgesses of Boroughbridge, 6 Dec. 1754, Sir T. Lawson-Tancred, *Recs. of a Yorkshire Manor*, 293–4.

L.B.N.

## FULLER, John (1732–1804), of Lewes, Suss.

TREGONY    1754–1761

John Fuller was a Sussex man, but unconnected with the Fullers of Rose Hill. The following identification is probable.[1]

*bap.* 2 Sept. 1732, 2nd s. of Joseph Fuller of East Hoathly, nr. Lewes, by Mary Attwood. *m.* Ann (surname not known), *s.p.*

John Fuller was a small man, who made himself a nuisance to Newcastle at Lewes. To keep him quiet, Newcastle in 1754 arranged for him to be brought into Parliament for Tregony, and £1455 for his expenses was paid out of secret service funds.[2] In Dupplin's list he is naturally classed as a supporter of Administration. No vote or speech by him is recorded.

By 1760 he was again on bad terms with Newcastle. To a list of 'persons to be brought into Parliament the next election', dated 8 May 1760, Newcastle added: 'To be left out absolutely—Mr. John Fuller of Lewes.'[3] Still, Fuller does not seem to have interfered in Lewes at the general election of 1761. A report, however, in the Stowe papers[4] (unsigned and undated but placed by internal evidence in the second half of 1762) examining how Newcastle's influence could be destroyed in Sussex and its boroughs, points to Fuller as an 'unexceptionable candidate' for Lewes.

He would warmly enter into any opposition both from a spirit of revenge (arising from some slights), and the hopes of success. He lives in the town and has the interest of all the malcontents there.

And at the by-election of Feb. 1763 Henry Fox was prepared to back him had there been any chance of success.[5] But nothing was done, and at the next by-election, in December 1766, Fuller, though described by Newcastle as his 'great antagonist', informed the Duke that he would not interfere, and apparently never did so again.[6]

He died 26 Jan. 1804.

[1] *Misc. Gen. & Her.* (ser. 4), iii. 168; *Gent. Mag.* 1804, p. 184. [2] Namier, *Structure*, 200. [3] Add. 32999, f. 4. [4] Huntington Lib. [5] Fox to J. L. Nicholl [Feb. 1763], Henry Fox mss. [6] Add. 32978, ff 321, 358.

J.B.

## FULLER, John (c.1756–1834), of Rose Hill, Suss.

| | |
|---|---|
| SOUTHAMPTON | 29 Jan. 1780–1784 |
| SUSSEX | 16 July 1801–1812 |

*b.* c.1756, o.s. of Rev. Henry Fuller by a da. of Thomas Fuller of Catsfield. *educ.* Eton 1767–74. *unm. suc.* his uncle Rose Fuller (q.v.) at Rose Hill and in Jamaica plantations 1777.

Fanny Burney wrote in 1779 about Fuller and his interest in the militia:

> Captain Fuller . . . has an estate of £4000 or £5000 a year, is but just of age, has figure, understanding, education, vivacity, and independence, and yet voluntarily devotes almost all his time, and almost all his attention to a company of light infantry.

Mrs. Thrale described him in *Thraliana* (29 Jan. 1781) as 'wild, gay, rich, loud'; and wrote in a letter to Fanny Burney, 7 Feb. 1781: 'Captain Fuller flashes away among us. How that boy loves rough merriment! the people all seem to keep out of his way for fear.'[1]

On the death of Hans Stanley, his cousin and heir Hans Sloane, who was married to Fuller's sister, returned him on the Stanley interest at Southampton; and at the general election the same year the two were returned on a joint interest with Government support. In the House Fuller voted regularly with the North Administration to the very end. He voted for Shelburne's peace preliminaries, 18 Feb. 1783, and was listed by Robinson in March 1783 among the country gentlemen of 'doubtful allegiance.' Absent from the first division on Fox's East India bill, he voted against it in the second division; and appears as a friend of Pitt in the list of 19 Mar. 1784. Yet he was opposed by the Government at Southampton at the general election, and withdrew without a contest. Only two interventions of his in debate are recorded, both in his first session (9 Feb. and 5 June 1780) and both on minor personal points.

He died 11 Apr. 1834.

[1] *Diary and Letters,* i. 223, 461.

L.B.N.

## FULLER, Richard (c.1713–82), of Dorking, Surr.

| | |
|---|---|
| STEYNING | 9 Feb. 1764–1768 |
| STOCKBRIDGE | 1768–1774 |

*b.* c.1713, 3rd s. of Rev. Joseph Fuller of Harwell, Berks., Baptist minister, by his w. Martha. *m.* Susanna Barnard, 5s. 3da.

Fuller was a banker originally in partnership with Frazer Honywood (q.v.) and subsequently head of the banking firm of Fuller, Baker, and Halford, in Cornhill. At one time he held over £20,000 in Bank of England stock, and was a considerable speculator in Government stock.

In 1764 Frazer Honywood died, and his heir, Sir John Honywood, agreed to recommend Fuller at Steyning. James West commented to Newcastle:[1] 'As the correspondence of the shop is very great . . . the very postage of their letters would amount to near £800 p.a., and it is otherwise thought to be of great service to the house to have one of the partners in Parliament.' Newcastle had suggested another candidate, but now declared he would 'readily concur' in the recommendation of 'Mr. Fuller, who is a very honest man, and a very good friend of mine'.[2] Fuller was returned unopposed, 9 Feb. 1764; voted in opposition on general warrants, 18 Feb.; was listed as a 'sure friend' by Newcastle, 10 May 1764, and 'pro' by Rockingham in July 1765. His next recorded vote was with Administration on the land tax, 27 Feb. 1767, but he voted against them on the nullum tempus bill, 17 Feb. 1768.

In 1768 Fuller was introduced at Morpeth by Francis Eyre (q.v.), and stood on a joint interest with him. On 15 Jan. 1768, he wrote to Robert Trotter, a Presbyterian clergyman, and one of the leaders of the opposition to the Carlisle interest:

> As I am enlisted under the banner of liberty, the cause in which I have had the happiness to be educated, let me say that no consideration upon earth shall tempt me to deviate from it, and if my poor endeavours should be conducive to establish the freedom and independency of your borough I shall esteem it the happiest event of my life.

But on 12 Mar., from London:

> The general opinion which has prevailed in this part of the world is that Mr. Eyre and myself stood no chance of being the sitting Members for Morpeth, though we had no doubt of a fair majority from the great encouragement we met with on the canvass. Therefore in order to secure the freedom of the town and Mr. Eyre's election I have been induced by a compromise to give up any pretensions of my own as I never presumed an equal merit with Mr. Eyre.[3]

He was returned unopposed at Stockbridge. He continued in opposition until he left Parliament. His only recorded speeches were on the corn bill, 3 Feb. 1772, and on the East India Company loan bill, 15 June 1773.[4]

He died 2 Jan. 1782.

[1] Add. 32955, f. 320. [2] Add. 34728, ff. 89–90. [3] Woodman mss 1, ff. 443–4, 458, Soc. of Antiquaries, Newcastle-upon-Tyne. [4] Cavendish's 'Debates', Egerton 232, pp. 88–89; 250, p. 325.

M.M.D.

## FULLER, Rose (?1708–77), of Rose Hill, Suss.

| | |
|---|---|
| NEW ROMNEY | 8 Dec. 1756–1761 |
| MAIDSTONE | 1761–1768 |
| RYE | 1768–7 May 1777 |

*b.* ?1708, 2nd s. of John Fuller, M.P., of Brightling, Suss., and bro. of John Fuller (q.v.). *educ.* Leyden

26 Apr. 1729, aged 20; graduated M.D. Camb. 1732. *m.* Apr. 1737, Ithamar (*d.*22 Apr. 1738), da. of Richard Mill, receiver gen. and c.j. Jamaica, *s.p.* *suc.* to Rose property in Jamaica 1746, and bro. 1755.

Rose Fuller studied medicine at Leyden University, but there is no evidence that he ever practised. His father made over to him the family estates in Jamaica, and before 1735 Fuller settled there. In 1735 he was elected to the assembly, in 1737 was called to the council, and about the same time made judge of the supreme court. Disputes with Governor William Trelawny led in 1740 to his removal from the council and in 1746 from the bench, and in 1749 he was back in England.[1] He returned to Jamaica c.1752 when Charles Knowles succeeded Trelawny, and was appointed chief justice. His brother John wrote to Newcastle, 15 July 1753,[2] that Knowles wished Rose Fuller to have 'a dormant commission for lieutenant-governor of the Island in case of . . . the governor's death or absence'; and Halifax, president of the Board of Trade, said

> that he had a most extraordinary character of my brother, not only from Mr. Knowles, but from several other people of that island, and that his being made chief justice was with the absolute approbation of the whole island.

But on 14 Jan. 1754 Knowles wrote to the Board of Trade 'complaining of the tyrannical proceedings of Dr. Fuller in his capacity of judge', and on 15 Feb. about Fuller's 'indecent behaviour' in leading the opposition to the plan to move the seat of government from St. Iago to Kingston.[3] Fuller resigned his post of chief justice, and complained of Knowles's conduct to the Board of Trade. In 1755, on the death of his elder brother, he returned to England.

He was now a wealthy man—landowner and ironmaster in Sussex and one of the biggest planters in Jamaica—and determined to enter Parliament. In August 1756 he stood for New Romney. William Sotheby, who had married Fuller's niece, wrote to Hardwicke, 18 Sept. 1756:[4]

> Mr. Fuller is a real friend to our constitution and wishes very well to the present Administration, and if in Parliament will always vote with them in any measures that ought to be supported, but is of too much property to desire to be brought in by any interest that should entirely restrain the freedom of his vote.

A contest seemed probable; Fuller spent heavily on treats and presents, and in the end was returned without a poll.

In Parliament Fuller was one of the principal spokesmen for Jamaica. On 8 Feb. 1757 his dispute with Governor Knowles was settled when the Board of Trade disallowed the act transferring the seat of government (the part he played in the Commons

inquiry into Knowles's conduct is uncertain). Fuller was occasionally consulted by the Board of Trade on Jamaica, and in 1764 his brother Stephen, a London merchant, became agent for the colony; he himself, while retaining his interests in Jamaica, seems never to have revisited it.

He attached himself politically to Newcastle, and spoke frequently in the House on various subjects. He took great pains to make his interest at New Romney more secure, but he had no property there and could not prevent Sir Edward Dering acquiring control of the borough. In the autumn of 1760 Fuller told Newcastle he stood no chance of being returned for New Romney at the general election, and Newcastle promised to find him another constituency. Then Fuller accepted an offer of a seat at Midhurst from Sir William Peere Williams; when a contest threatened and it seemed doubtful whether Williams would prevail, Fuller wrote to Newcastle, 6 Jan. 1761:[5] 'if I should not be the sitting Member for that borough, which I am engaged and resolved to try my utmost to be, I have no other resource for a seat in Parliament but your Grace's promise.'

On 1 Mar. 1761 Newcastle, in a list of 'persons to be brought into Parliament', put down Fuller for Plympton. The same day Fuller wrote to him on election affairs in Sussex—'you have my influence, advice, and purse to support your interest everywhere'; then continued:

> I go tomorrow at six of the clock to Maidstone where I have had an interview, countenanced by your nephew Sondes and [Robert] Fairfax. I did not give you previous notice of it for certain reasons you can guess.[6]

The 'certain reasons' were no doubt that Newcastle had promised to support the Tory candidates, Gabriel Hanger and William Northey.[7]

> I am sorry I cannot approve of your going to Maidstone [Newcastle wrote to Fuller on 3 Mar.[8]] because the little interest I have there . . . must be against you. I love and esteem you most sincerely, but if I do not keep my promise and my word I am sure you would not esteem me . . . I see the reason you did not mention your intention to me, but if you had I think I should have persuaded you not to attempt it.

Fuller replied, 12 Mar. 1761:[9]

> I was . . . invited to offer myself at that town by the Whig interest, which before I was twenty years of age I was convinced was the only one by which the religion, power and internal peace of this nation could be preserved . . . Upon these principles I set out and have continued to act upon and shall persevere in to the end of my life. I attached myself to your Grace because I knew these principles were rivetted in your soul, and not upon account of your birth, riches or power.

Despite the Treasury interest being against him he was returned head of the poll.

On 14 Aug. 1761 Lord Boston wrote to Bute about an application for Church patronage from Fuller's brother, Henry:[10] 'The favour asked seems to me to be an affair of no great difficulty, and if you should think it proper to interfere in it your Lordship will lay the family of the Fullers under an obligation to you.' In Bute's list of December 1761 Fuller is marked: 'Newcastle. But not certain. Supposed Government.' He appears in Newcastle's list, 27 Sept. 1762, of 'persons to be sent to' for the opening of Parliament; about which Newcastle wrote to Thomas Pelham on 23 Oct.: 'I wish you would convey my desire also to Rose Fuller; but say nothing about the meeting at the Cockpit to him. It is reported that Rose Fuller talks oddly; I think I may depend upon him after all he has said to me.'[11] But Fuller is included in Henry Fox's list of Members favourable to the peace preliminaries; voted with Administration on the motion to postpone their consideration, 1 Dec.; and does not appear in any list of those who voted against them, 9 and 10 Dec.

Yet he voted consistently against the Grenville Administration; spoke against them in the debate on general warrants of 17–18 Feb. 1764; belonged to Wildman's Club; and was classed by Newcastle, 10 May 1764, as one of his 'sure friends'. When Grenville announced his intention to lay a stamp tax on America, 9 Mar. 1764, Fuller 'got up to express his satisfaction in the plan';[12] but in the debate on the Stamp Act resolution of 6 Feb. 1765 spoke and voted against it, and on 15 Feb. presented a petition against it from merchants trading to Jamaica. On 1 Apr. he spoke against a bill to allow troops in America to be quartered upon private houses. He was also active in the debates on the Regency bill, proposed that the Queen should be appointed, 9 May 1765, and spoke 'though in very moderate terms' against the amendment to include the Princess Dowager among those capable of becoming Regent, 10 May.[13]

On the formation of the Rockingham ministry Newcastle wrote to Rockingham, 12 July 1765:[14] 'I would most earnestly recommend for the public service Mr. Rose Fuller'; and suggested he might go to the Board of Trade. No offer seems to have been made, but Fuller did good service as chairman of the committee of the whole House which considered American affairs. He was also a prominent member of the committee of West India merchants and planters, and helped to reach agreement between them and the North American committee about the proposed free port in Dominica. 'I send you the agreement of the West India committee,' wrote James West to Newcastle on 8 May 1766,[15]

'which Rose and Stephen Fuller have had infinite merit in procuring.'

In March 1766, two years before the general election was expected, Fuller asked Newcastle for his support at Rye—a borough normally under Treasury control but which had remained faithful to Newcastle and which he regarded as his own. Newcastle readily agreed, but took offence when Fuller asked that the matter be put in writing and the local manager and the Treasury be informed—he feared, with reason, that Fuller was hoping to establish his own interest at Rye. Fuller supported the Chatham Administration even after Newcastle had gone into opposition, which increased Newcastle's dissatisfaction with him; still he remained his candidate at Rye, and in 1768 was returned unopposed. He built up an interest in the borough, in 1774 was again returned unopposed, and at his death was succeeded by his niece's husband, William Dickinson.

On 2 Feb. 1769 he spoke and voted against the court over Wilkes's libel, but voted with them in three other divisions this year over Wilkes and Middlesex. Generally he supported Administration, but took a different line on America—'the most important business that can come before the House'. On 8 Feb. 1769 he warned the Commons that coercion in America would achieve nothing: 'Where do gentlemen wish to end? Do they expect that before it is ended the Americans should in their assemblies declare the power of taxing them to be in this country?'[16] And on 5 Mar. 1770 he spoke for the repeal of the tea duty.

In Robinson's first survey on the royal marriage bill Fuller was classed as 'doubtful'; in the second, 8 Mar. 1772, as 'contra'. On 23 Mar. he moved to confine the bill to the duration of the King's life: 'He had talked, he said, with men of all sides, and all thought that the Act ought to be but temporary.'[17] He voted with the court on the naval captains' petition, 9 Feb. 1773, and the Middlesex motion, 26 Apr. 1773, but against them on Grenville's Election Act, 25 Feb. 1774.

In the spring of 1774 he opposed the measures taken against America. On 21 Mar. 1774 he said on the second reading of the Boston port bill:

> I am from the bottom of my heart convinced that if this bill passes as it now is it will ruin this country. I would alter the mode of the bill for it destroys all trade. I would lay a large fine . . . I am sure it would be complied with. If they did not pay it by such a day I would have this bill take place.

And on the third reading, 25 Mar.: 'Had I in the course of this debate learnt that the tea duty would have been repealed, I would have voted for it. But as I have rather had the contrary intimated I must vote against it, for I think a rebellion will be raised.' He said of the tea duty, 28 Mar.: 'I know it is the genuine foundation of our evils'; and on 19 Apr. moved its repeal (when Burke made his celebrated speech on American taxation):

> I mean it as an olive branch to show that the House means to act just and reasonably towards the Americans. The Boston Port Act we passed the other day will be looked on by the Americans as a very cruel one . . . The bill we have now before us for regulating the colony will not be less relished; they may and I think will resist the execution of them by violence or by confederacy . . . and America as they are now united will be difficult to overcome.[18]

On 6 May he was one of the 24 who voted against the third reading of the Massachusetts Bay bill. Yet Robinson, in his electoral survey, September 1774, classed him as a Government supporter.

On 19 Dec. 1774 he made his last recorded speech in the House:[19]

> Mr. Rose Fuller said that we were too precipitate in our last measures; and that was the chief reason why they miscarried; that he foresaw at the time they would answer no end but to inflame; nor ever would while they were continued to be directed to the same end; on which account he would be much better pleased that the affairs of America . . . were taken up on mature deliberation, and discussed with coolness, in order, in the end, to come to a wise, deliberate, and rational decision.

But on 12 Jan. 1775 Burke wrote to Rockingham about a petition on America:

> Mr. [John] Ellis [agent for Dominica] has done a great deal towards bringing the West India merchants and planters to a right sense of their situation. He would have succeeded better, if your Lordship's old withered Rose, who in his best was no better than a dog rose, had not, within these few weeks, totally altered his hue. He has seen his brother, and he has seen Lord North. He had drawn a set of resolutions as the basis of a petition, in which no shadow of censure was thrown upon any of the Acts; nor did he admit the most remote allusion to the advantages derived from your Lordship's repeal . . . But I showed Ellis the Journals yesterday morning, where Rose Fuller was in the chair of the committee for repealing that Act, one of the tellers on the division, and a principal actor and zealous manager in the whole. It seems our Rosicrucian philosopher had lost all memory of this transaction. Ellis instantly called on him, revived his recollection, and for the mere sake of consistency he consented to admit a hint concerning the repeal.

He seems to have reverted to Administration; and his name does not appear in any of the four minority division lists between 22 Feb. 1775 and his death on 7 May 1777.

[1] Add. 19038, ff. 44–45. [2] Add. 32732, ff. 270–1. [3] *Bd. Trade Jnl.* 1754–8, pp. 39, 58. [4] Add. 35692, f. 374. [5] Add. 32917, f. 155. [6] Add. 32919, ff. 344, 348. [7] Namier, *Structure*, 113–18. [8] Add. 32919, ff. 410–11. [9] Add. 32920, ff. 121–2. [10] Bute mss. [11] Add. 33000,
ff. 129–35; 32943, ff. 402–3. [12] Harris's 'Debates'. [13] Grenville to the King, 11 May 1765, Fortescue, i. 87. [14] Add. 32967, f. 349. [15] Add. 32975, f. 114. [16] Cavendish's 'Debates', Egerton 217, ff. 248–9. [17] Walpole, *Last Jnls.* i. 65. [18] Brickdale's 'Debates'. [19] Almon, i. 26.

J.B.

## FURNESE, Henry (d.1756), of Gunnersbury, Mdx.

| DOVER | 20 Dec. 1720–1734 |
| MORPETH | 18 May 1738–1741 |
| NEW ROMNEY | 1741–30 Aug. 1756 |

o.s. of George Furnese, an East India factor. *unm.*
Sec. to Treasury July–Dec. 1742; ld. of Treasury Dec. 1755–d.

Apprenticed as a young man to a London merchant, Furnese, though of a Kentish family, seems to have owned no significant estate in the county, but was originally returned for Dover on the interest of his cousin, Sir Robert Furnese, M.P. On the death of Sir Robert's son Henry in 1735, Furnese acted as a trustee of his estates, which commanded a considerable interest at New Romney.

In 1754 he was closely connected with George Bubb Dodington, and was classed by Dupplin as 'doubtful'. As part of the bargain concluded between Dodington and Newcastle in October 1755 Furnese was appointed to a seat at the Treasury Board, with full liberty to oppose the subsidy treaties, and on 13 Nov. 1755 he voted with Dodington against them.[1] He died 30 Aug. 1756.[2]

[1] Dodington's *Diary*, 499. [2] *Gent. Mag.* 451; *London Mag.* 452 gives 28 Aug.

M.M.D.

## GAGE, William Hall (1718–91), of Firle, Suss. and High Meadow, Glos.

| SEAFORD | 9 May 1744–1747, 1754–1780 |

b. 1 Jan. 1718, 1st s. of Thomas, 1st Visct. Gage [I], by his 1st w. Benedicta Maria Theresa, da. and h. of Benedict Hall of High Meadow, Glos. *educ.* Westminster 1728–35. *m.* 3 Feb. 1757, Elizabeth, da. of Sampson Gideon, and sis. and coh. of Sir Sampson Gideon, 1st Bt. (q.v.), *s.p. suc.* fa. as 2nd Visct. 21 Dec. 1754; *cr.* Baron Gage of Firle [GB] 17 Oct. 1780; Baron Gage of High Meadow [GB], with sp. rem. to his nephew, 1 Nov. 1790.
Equerry to Prince of Wales 1742–51; paymaster of pensions 1755–63, July 1765–Mar. 1782.

William Gage came of an old Sussex family, whose estate at Firle gave them a natural interest at Seaford. A former follower of the Prince of Wales, Gage joined the Pelhams after the Prince's death; and in 1754 with Newcastle's support was returned unopposed for Seaford. In 1755 he was appointed paymaster of pensions, and on 2 Nov. 1756, shortly before Newcastle resigned, wrote to him:[1] 'I am ready to follow your Grace and your fortune and shall have more satisfaction in laying down my employment to serve you than I felt pleasure, when his Majesty honoured me with it.' Newcastle did not wish him to resign, and the new Administration had no intention of dismissing him. When in 1762 Newcastle went into opposition, Gage proved faithful; voted against the peace preliminaries, 9 and 10 Dec. 1762; and was dismissed. In the four divisions over Wilkes and general warrants, 1763-4, for which lists are extant, Gage voted with the Opposition, and Newcastle wrote to him on 18 Sept. 1764: 'I have had so many and such constant proofs of your tender affection for me, scarce to have been paralleled by anybody.'[2] On the formation of the Rockingham Administration in July 1765 Gage was reinstated in his old office.

Henceforth his politics were directed by two aims: to retain office and to obtain a British peerage. In June 1766 Rockingham supported his claim to a peerage, and the King promised to consider Gage when new peers were made.[3] In November Rockingham classed him as 'Swiss' (prepared to support every Administration), and Townshend, in January 1767, as 'Government'; but Newcastle for some time continued to believe that Gage would be directed by him. Thus he asked Gage to vote against Administration on the land tax, which Gage refused to do. 'I have had such an answer from my Lord Gage that I shall write to him no more upon these subjects', wrote Newcastle to Thomas Pelham on 22 Feb. 1767.[4] Gage in fact voted with the court in this division. 'I look upon him as entirely *gone to the court* in political sentiments', wrote Rockingham to Newcastle, 4 Feb. 1768.[5]

Early in 1768 Gage expected to receive his British peerage at the dissolution of Parliament, and began discussing with Newcastle his successor at Seaford. But when he did not obtain his peerage he stood again at Seaford, and was returned unopposed. At a by-election in November Gage was invited by the Duke of Richmond and Lord Pelham to stand for the county, and at first accepted. But a week before the county meeting he informed Richmond that he must decline: 'he says', wrote Richmond to Pelham, 22 Nov. 1768, 'he is sure that no man will refuse to let him off his engagement to the meeting when he tells him his story. That every man he has spoke to says he is perfectly in the right.'[6] His reasons for declining are nowhere explained—possibly he feared it would affect his interest at Seaford.

Henceforth Gage voted consistently with Administration and eventually received his British peerage. Only two speeches by him are recorded during nearly 30 years in the House of Commons: for a motion on Hanoverian troops, 29 Mar. 1756,[7] and against having his brother's letter about quartering troops in America laid before the House, 2 Apr. 1765.[8]

He died 11 Oct. 1791.

[1] Add. 32868, f. 544. [2] Add. 32962, f. 131. [3] Fortescue, i. 355 [4] Add. 32980, f. 230. [5] Add. 32988, f. 165. [6] Add. 33088 f. 319 [7] Newdigate mss. [8] Harris's 'Debates'.

M.M.D.

## GALE, Wilson, *see* BRADDYLL

## GALLY KNIGHT, John (?1741-1804), of Langold Park, Yorks.

ALDBOROUGH  20 Jan. 1784-1796

*b.* ?1741, 1st s. of Rev. Henry Gally (of Huguenot descent), rector of St. Giles-in-the-Fields, London by Elizabeth, da. of Isaac Knight of Langold Park, sis. and h. of Ralph Knight (*d.*1768). *educ.* Eton 1753-7; Trinity Hall, Camb. 1756, called 1765. *unm. suc.* fa. 1769. Took add. name of Knight on succeeding to the Langold estate.

Fellow of Trinity Hall, 1764; bencher, L. Inn 1795.

Henry Gally and Ralph Knight were connected with the 1st Duke of Newcastle in Nottinghamshire affairs, and John Gally Knight seems to have had a similar connexion with the 2nd Duke, who brought him into Parliament for Aldborough. Knight supported Pitt's Administration. There is no record before 1790 of his having spoken in the House.

He died 20 Oct. 1804, aged 63.

M.M.D.

## GALWAY, Visct., *see* MONCKTON, William, *and* MONCKTON ARUNDELL

## GAMON, Richard Grace (1748-1818), of Minchenden House, Mdx.

WINCHESTER  1784-1812

*b.* 14 Aug. 1748, o.s. of Richard Gamon of Datchworthbury, Herts. by Elizabeth, da. of John Grace of The Grange, Queen's Co. *educ.* Winchester. *m.* (1) Grace (*d.*10 Aug. 1794), da. of James Jeffreys by Elizabeth, da. of William Cosby, wid. of Lord Augustus Fitzroy and mother of Augustus Henry, 3rd Duke of Grafton, *s.p.*; (2) 2 July 1796, Amelia, da. of John Murray, 3rd Duke of Atholl[S], wid. of Thomas Ivie Cooke, 1da. *cr.* Bt. 17 May 1795, with sp. rem. to his cos. Richard Grace of Queen's Co.

Cornet 1 Horse Gds. 1769, lt. 1771; disappears from army list 1774.

Collector of Basse Terre, St. Kitts; sec. to Board of Excise 1777-84; commr. of salt duties Jan.-Apr. 1784.

On 25 July 1782 Gamon's brother-in-law, the Duke of Chandos, unsuccessfully recommended him to Shelburne for a 'permanent situation of £1,000', explaining that he lost 'a clear annual income' of £1,200 when St. Kitts was taken by the French and was unable to continue at the Excise Board because of his health.[1] In September 1783

Chandos meant to bring him in at Winchester, but ultimately returned Henry Flood. Gamon was appointed commissioner of the salt duties in January 1784, but resigned in March to stand for Winchester.

In Parliament Gamon followed Chandos's lead and supported Pitt. He spoke several times; on 4 July 1788 he opposed Dolben's bill to regulate the shipment of slaves to the West Indies, where he owned estates; and on 6 Feb. 1789 he defended Chandos against an attack by Burke.[2]

He died 8 Apr. 1818.[3]

[1] Lansdowne mss. [2] Stockdale, xv. 222, 224; xvi. 378. [3] *GEC Baronetage. Gent. Mag.* 1818, i. 570 gives 9 Apr.

M.M.D.

## GARDEN, Alexander (1714–85), of Troup, Banff.

ABERDEENSHIRE 1768–21 Dec. 1785

*b.* 1714, 1st s. of Alexander Garden of Troup, adv., by Jean, da. of Sir Francis Grant, S.C.J., 1st Bt., of Cullen, Banff. *educ.* Edinburgh; King's Coll. Aberdeen. *unm. suc.* fa. 22 July 1740.

Garden inherited an ample fortune and great estates in Banff and Aberdeen. A staunch Hanoverian in the '45, he acted as liaison between the King's ships in the Moray Firth and Cumberland's army on its march to Culloden, and thereafter was elected convener of the county of Banff.[1] An astute business man, Garden bought up forfeited estates in Kincardine and Aberdeenshire, increased his fortune to £3,000–£4,000 p.a., but continued to live, without ostentation, at Troup, 'a most amiable and respected country gentleman',[2] and a considerate landlord, sharing the interest of his brother Lord Gardenstone, S.C.J., in agricultural and social improvement. In 1768 the Aberdeenshire freeholders, many of whom were his kinsmen or intimate friends, returned him apparently unopposed, and continued, despite the rivalry of the Fife and Gordon interests, to support him to the end of his life.

An independent in politics, who is not known to have spoken in the House, he supported Administration on Wilkes and the Middlesex election in 1769, on Brass Crosby, 27 March 1771, and the royal marriage bill, March 1772, but voted against them on the naval captains' petition, 9 Feb. 1773, on the Middlesex election, 26 Apr. 1773, and on Grenville's Act, 25 Feb. 1774. Robinson nevertheless counted him 'pro' at the end of the Parliament and expected his re-election. Garden's personal popularity overcame any opposition contemplated by Lord Fife or the Duke of Gordon. Lord Adam Gordon wrote to a Ross-shire friend, 20 July 1774:[3] 'Troup stands for this county and I think will have no opposer. He is a worthy respectable man and means well.'

In the Parliament of 1774–80 no vote by Garden is recorded. The *English Chronicle* wrote about him in 1781:

> He possesses a very large fortune, and many of the very first connexions in the shire; but it was not to the influence of either of these that he has owed the successive compliment of these repeated representations. The freeholders have long been unanimous in this determination, to prefer honesty to talents, and an old acquaintance, though distinguished for no splendid endowments, to any stranger, however ingenious or popular . . . He is very moderate in his political conduct—is, in general subjects, a friend to Government, but has uniformly opposed them in the particular and important question of the American war. He is very old and infirm, but nevertheless always makes it a point to execute the efficient duty of a Member of Parliament by staying to give his vote, unless the division takes place after eight o'clock, at which hour he generally leaves the House . . . Amongst all his good qualities he is distinguished for nothing so much as this, *that he is the only Scotch Member who never asked a favour.*

Garden was listed 'pro' in Robinson's survey of 1780, but as it was doubtful whether he would seek re-election, his friend Henry Dundas suggested either James Ferguson or Lord William Gordon as his successor. Garden, however, despite his infirmities, agreed to continue. He did not vote on Lowther's motion against the war on 12 Dec. 1781, voted with Administration on 20 Feb. 1782 on the censure of the Admiralty, but against them two days later on Conway's motion against the war. On 27 Feb., possibly at North's request, he abstained,[4] but in the final division on 15 Mar. voted for Rous's no confidence motion.

He voted for Shelburne's peace preliminaries, 18 Feb. 1783, and in March was listed by Robinson as connected with Shelburne and Dundas. He did not vote on Fox's East India bill, 27 Nov. 1783, and in mid-December was counted as a follower of Pitt by Robinson, who wrote:[5]

> If Mr. Garden wishes to come in again it is apprehended he may, but at his age it is a question; attached to Mr. Dundas who can best tell what would happen if Mr. Garden should decline.

Lord Fife's supporters forecast a 'hard-run battle', but Garden again agreed to stand and was returned. He voted, 18 Apr. 1785, for Pitt's parliamentary reform bill; but was absent from the budget debate. Lord Fife wrote to his factor, 10 May: 'Troup was away yesterday, so you see how Aberdeen is represented and yet there is no complaints.'[6]

Before the end of the session he went home to Troup House where he died 21 Dec. 1785. Lord Gardenstone wrote of him in 1790:[7]

> My eldest brother . . . was always esteemed a truly independent country gentleman, and he was for . . . pure motives of integrity and public duty, a firm

friend to Mr. Pitt's Administration, indeed his friends and family have ground to believe that Mr. Pitt has still a generous remembrance of his sincere attachment and honourable services.

[1] *House of Forbes*, ed. A. & H. Tayler, 351, 399; *Recs. County of Banff.* 417. [2] Ramsay of Ochtertyre, *Scotland & Scotsmen*, i. 376. [3] Add. 39190, f. 202. [4] I. R. Christie, *End of North's Ministry*, 332 and n.5. [5] Laprade, 98. [6] *Ld. Fife & his Factor*, 161, 174. [7] Chatham mss.

E.H.-G.

## GARDINER, see WHALLEY GARDINER

## GARDNER, Alan (1742–1809).

PLYMOUTH        1 Feb. 1790–1796
WESTMINSTER                1796–1806

*b.* 12 Apr. 1742, 3rd s. of Lt. Col. William Gardner by Elizabeth, da. of Valentine Farington of Preston, Lancs. *m.* 20 May 1769, Susanna Hyde, da. and h. of Francis Gale of Jamaica, wid. of Samuel or Sabine Turner, 9s. 1da. *cr.* Bt. 9 Sept. 1794; Baron Gardner of Uttoxeter [I] 23 Dec. 1800; Baron Gardner [GB] 27 Nov. 1806.
    Entered R.N. 1755; lt. 1760; cdr. 1762; capt. 1766; r.-adm. 1793; v.-adm. 1794; adm. 1799; ld. of Admiralty Jan. 1790–5.

Gardner was returned for Plymouth on the Admiralty interest shortly after being appointed to the Board of Admiralty. There is no record of his having spoken before the dissolution in June 1790. He died 1 Jan. 1809.

M.H.P.

## GARFORTH, see BAYNES GARFORTH

## GARLIES, Visct., see STEWART, John (d. 1806)

## GARRARD, Benet (?1704–1767), of Lamer, Herts.

AMERSHAM    1761–1 July 1767

*b.* ?1704, 3rd s. of Sir Samuel Garrard, 4th Bt., M.P., by his 2nd w. Jane, da. of Thomas Benet of Salthrop, Wilts. *unm. suc.* bro. as 6th Bt. 1 Dec. 1761.

The Garrard family were of City origin, and had been settled at Lamer since the 17th century. Sir Benet Garrard's father was lord mayor of London 1709–10, and M.P. for Amersham 1701–10. They were related to its patrons, the Drakes of Shardeloes; and Sir Benet left his estates to Charles Drake, 2nd s. of William Drake, sen. (q.v.).

In Bute's list Garrard was classed as 'Tory', to which was added (in Bute's hand): 'well inclined'. He appears in Fox's list of Members favourable to the peace preliminaries, and seems also to have supported Grenville's Administration: his name appears in none of the minority division lists 1763–5, and he voted with Administration, 10 Feb. 1764, on the repeal of the cider duty.[1] In July 1765 Rockingham classed him as 'contra'; yet he did not vote against the repeal of the Stamp Act. Nothing further is known of his political conduct, and there is no record of his having spoken in the House. He died 1 July 1767, aged 63.

[1] Harris's 'Debates'.

J.B.

## GARTH, Charles (c.1734–84), of Brownston House, Devizes, Wilts.[1]

DEVIZES    15 Jan. 1765–21 Nov. 1780

*b.* c.1734, 1st s. of John Garth (q.v.). *educ.* Merton, Oxf. 1750; I. Temple 1752, called 1758. *m.* 29 Nov. 1764, Fanny, da. of John Cooper of Camberwell, 3s. 4da. *suc.* fa. 1764.
    Recorder, Devizes 1765–*d.*; Crown agent for Georgia Nov. 1763–Jan. 1765; provincial agent for South Carolina 1762–75; agent for Maryland assembly 1766–75; commr. of Excise Nov. 1780–*d.*

Garth was intended for the bar, and he presumably practised, for in May 1765 his name was included in a list of possible readers sent by the Inner Temple to Clement's Inn. But before he could 'shift for himself' his father asked Newcastle to provide for him in some employment.[2] Newcastle was willing to help but awaited suggestions from Garth, who found that vacancies were mostly filled up before he came to know of them. His requests were therefore usually in general terms, while his specific applications ranged from the postmaster at Devizes or keeper of the records at Westminster Abbey to clerk to the Privy Council or commissioner of the victualling office.[3] When Newcastle left the Treasury, 26 May 1762, Charles Garth was still unplaced; but in July 1763 his father obtained for him from Grenville the Crown agency for Georgia,[4] a sinecure 'principally confined to receiving and issuing the money granted by Parliament to defray the expenses of the government'.[5]

Far more vital for Garth's career was his appointment in June 1762 to the colonial agency of South Carolina, to which he had been recommended by his cousin and its governor, Thomas Boone, as yet on cordial terms with the assembly. He took up his duties with real zeal not free of fussiness which, in the early stages, produced letters of prodigious length. He thoroughly identified himself with the interests of South Carolina; 'I . . . as minister of the province' was the view he took of his position. 'I believe few agents have taken more pains or been more indefatigable' (30 July 1763). His salary was £200 p.a., plus expenses and additional payment for more considerable transactions which 'generally account one year with another to about £160 more'.[6]

At first his work was mainly of a commercial and financial character; he usually concerted his measures with merchants trading to America, and had the support of his cousins, Charles Boone and J. E. Colleton who, friendly with Grenville, had promised him 'all the assistance in his power in parliamentary business', and of Sir William Meredith, Member for Liverpool. Garth's position became more difficult when he had to represent the assembly in its conflict with Governor Boone; but they trusted his 'alertness and diligence as agent', while he was scrupulously careful in the discharge of his duties—'in the situation I stand, I had rather be thought to err in doing too much than too little' (20 July 1764).

In March 1764 Charles Garth, not yet a Member, followed from the gallery the debates on the budget resolutions of which the fifteenth foreshadowed the Stamp Act; but by the time it came up as a bill, in 1765, he had, on his father's death, been returned for Devizes, after a bitter contest against Thomas Fludyer, who had the support of Government. Writing to South Carolina, 5 Apr. 1765, he could therefore claim to hold an 'independent seat', especially as he had resigned the Crown agency, incompatible with membership of the House. On 6 Feb. 1765 he was one of the 49 who voted against the Stamp Act, and on 15 Feb. he presented a petition against it. Over the mutiny bill in March–April 1765: 'I have taken every opportunity of giving it all the opposition in my power'; and on 4 Apr. he presented a petition against it from Montagu, agent for Virginia.[7] On 15 May 1767 he moved that the resolutions passed on the 13th relative to New York for having disobeyed the Mutiny Act be recommitted.[8] Further, in March 1769, he moved an amendment to the mutiny bill, approved by Trecothick and Barré, and in May 1770 one to the paper currency bill.[9] But most of his activities were of an extra-parliamentary character.

His membership of the House enabled him to watch developments, and make early reports on them to South Carolina. He was very active over the repeal of the Stamp Act, but even then acknowledged the difficulties which arose for him as both M.P. and agent 'from the diversity of opinions' on the two sides—the colonial doctrine concerning taxation 'has not been pleasing to country gentlemen in the House', while palliatives 'will be as little acceptable in America'. But he obviously sympathized with the argument put to him by Conway that 'the great object of solicitude being the repeal', and many country gentlemen 'wavering in opinions and others easily inflamed', the Government's difficulties should not be aggravated by too much stressing the point of right. Altogether Garth's reports were objective and moderate, and aimed at

healing the breach. He wrote, 6 June 1766, after sittings which 'turned night into day': 'I have given my best attention, time, and endeavours . . . I have nothing more at heart than to promote . . . the united interest and happiness of the Mother Country and her colonies'—somewhat flat, as he usually was, but sincere.

Again over the Townshend duties, Hillsborough told the agents in December 1768 that a request for repeal would be well received if placed on grounds of inexpediency only, but must be rejected if an exclusive right of taxation was claimed for the colonies. This proposition, wrote Garth to South Carolina, must await their decision, as agents must not waive a point which 'their constituents appear to adhere to'; still, 'if a repeal of this law can be obtained on any ground, it would be a right measure for both countries and tend to heal the unhappy breach . . . after a repeal of a second Revenue Act, future legislatures would be tender of the like attempt'. In March 1769 the agents in fact asked Franklin to prepare the draft of a petition 'to be as near as might be agreeable to the sentiments of America, and yet not exceptionable at home'; Garth favoured it, but finally 'it seemed prudent to wait for the sense of our constituents'. He sent them the draft, and received a severe rebuke: they were 'almost to a man . . . extremely concerned to find' that he should have thought himself warranted to give his assent to such a petition. After that Garth seems to have performed his day-to-day duties in an un-political manner.

A thorough change was also coming over his position in the House. At no time does he seem to have enjoyed the esteem of the Opposition: although he voted with the Rockinghams over American problems 1765–6, and over the land tax, 27 Feb. 1767, he was listed as 'Swiss' (prepared to vote with any Administration) by Rockingham in November 1766, and as 'Administration' by Newcastle in March 1767. He voted again with the Opposition on the nullum tempus bill, 17 Feb. 1768, and on the Middlesex election, 8 May 1769 and 25 Jan. 1770; but was absent from the divisions on the naval captains' petition, 9 Feb. 1773, and on the Grenville Act, 25 Feb. 1774, in which even many regular followers of Administration voted with Opposition. On the eve of the general election of 1774 John Robinson listed him as 'pro' Administration. When Burke refused to wait on Lord Dartmouth with the petition from the American congress, which he and other agents were asked to present, William Baker, trying to secure a sufficient representation, wrote on 22 Aug. 1775: 'Consider further, that Mr. Garth (a dependant of the ministry) will hardly attend';[10]

which, in fact, he did not. Garth's name does not appear in any of the minority lists 1774–80; but he is known to have voted five times with Government 1778–80; and over the contractors bill, 12 Feb. 1779, is listed by Robinson as 'pro, absent', with the mark of 'placeman' against his name: he held a secret service pension of £500 p.a. which ceased 'on his quitting Parliament and being provided for in the Excise' (the date of its commencement is unknown).[11] Robinson wrote in his electoral survey of July 1780: 'Mr. Garth will not come in again as he expects to take office.' But apparently to make sure of getting it he stood again, and was returned. On 21 Nov. 1780 North sent the King the warrant appointing Garth commissioner of the Excise, and the King, having signed, instantly returned it 'as it may be useful to have his seat vacated this day'.[12] About the middle of December 1783 Robinson noted against Devizes: 'Mr. Garth must be seen and talked to about this at the proper moment'[13]—by now he obviously could be expected to serve any Administration.

He died 9 Mar. 1784.

[1] This biography is largely based on Namier 'Charles Garth and His Connexions', *EHR*, July and Oct. 1939; on transcripts of Garth's letter-books in the possession of Mr. A. Godsal at Haines Hill, Berks.; and on corresp. between Garth and the assembly of S. Carolina published by J. W. Barnwell and T. D. Jervey in *S. Carolina Hist. & Gen. Mag.* xxvi, xxviii–xxxi, xxxiii. [2] 15 May 1755, Add. 32854, f. 530. [3] See among others, Add. 32864, ff. 60 and 263; 32870, f. 95; 32916, f. 214; 32926, f. 59; and 32934, ff. 229, 365. [4] Add. 34713, f. 120. [5] Garth to committee of corresp. of S. Carolina, 7 Jan. 1764. [6] Garth to Maryland, 14 Feb. 1767. [7] Harris's 'Debates'. [8] W. S. Johnson to Gov. W. Pitkin, 16 May 1767, *Trumbull Pprs.* (Mass. Hist. Soc. Colls. ser. 5, ix), 232–3. [9] Garth to S. Carolina, 17 Mar. 1769 and 14 May 1770. [10] Burke, *Corresp.* (1844), ii. 46. [11] Laprade, 50. [12] Fortescue, v. 154. [13] Laprade, 112.

L.B.N.

## GARTH, John (1701–64), of Garth House, Devizes, Wilts.

DEVIZES    26 Feb. 1740–24 Dec. 1764

*b.* 1701, 2nd s. of Thomas Garth of Harrold, Beds. (yr. bro. of Sir Samuel Garth, physician to George I and author of *The Dispensary*) by Elizabeth, da. of Thomas Colleton of Barbados. *educ.* Clare, Camb. 1719; L. Inn 1718; I. Temple 1727, called 1728. *m.* 1730, Rebecca, da. and coh. of John Brompton of Whitton, Mdx., 3s. 3da. *suc.* fa. 1731.

Recorder, Devizes 1732–*d.*

John Garth sat for Devizes on his own interest, and adhered in the House to the 'old corps' of Whigs. In 1756 he could speak of 'fifteen years' of 'constant attendance and steady concurrence in support of the measures of Government in Parliament without any assistance or return'.[1] Even that year, he bought for his second son George an army commission, which he might perhaps have obtained without payment had he applied to Henry Fox. But in a letter of 15 May 1755 he asked of Newcastle

some employment for his son Charles 'not incompatible with his profession, that may take him off my hands till he can shift for himself'. He received only promises.

In 1759 John Garth 'had a stroke of palsy' and was 'not expected to recover'. He survived, but his illness produced prospective candidates for his seat in Parliament, foremost Thomas Fludyer, brother of Sir Samuel Fludyer, Bt., M.P. for Chippenham. Garth wrote to Newcastle, 30 June 1760:

> The general election is approaching, and . . . myself advancing to a time of life when a retreat from the hurry of business may neither be unpleasant, nor, considering the number of children I have to provide for, improper . . . Many years are now past since I first presented a petition in behalf of my son, as many since I had the honour of all the assurances from your Grace on that score I could flatter myself with, as yet nothing is done for him. The expense of attendance in Parliament and supporting my seat therein against the intrigues of a faction has been very heavy to one circumstance as I am.

Charles Garth wrote to Newcastle in December 1760: 'notwithstanding Sir Samuel Fludyer's opposition and interest with the clothiers, I canvassed for my father a majority of 26 voices to 8'; and in February 1762, that supporting their parliamentary interest at Devizes 'has already been attended with no inconsiderable expense, at least £5,000 as my father has often assured me'.

It is not certain whether John Garth ever attended the Parliament of 1761: to Newcastle's circular letter he replied on 20 Oct. that he was too ill to travel, and in Newcastle's lists of December 1763 and February 1764 he is classed as 'absent'; in those used by Bute and Grenville in December 1761 and November 1763 he is left unclassified; and his name appears in none of the division lists. But in July 1763 he applied to George Grenville to make his son Charles Crown agent for Georgia, and in the Administration list of the division on general warrants, 18 Feb. 1764, his name appears among 'friends, absent'. He died 24 Dec. 1764.

[1] For authorities, see Namier, 'Charles Garth and his Connexions', *EHR*, July and Oct. 1939.

L.B.N.

## GARTH TURNOUR, Edward Turnour, 1st Baron Winterton [I] (1734–88), of Shillinglee Park, Suss.

BRAMBER    4 Dec. 1761–14 Feb. 1769

*b.* 1734, o.s. of Joseph Garth by Sarah, da. and h. of Francis Gee of Shillinglee Park, and gd.-da. of Sir Edward Turnour, lord chief baron of the Exchequer 1661–75. *educ.* Trinity, Oxf. 28 Oct. 1752, aged 18. *m.* (1) 13 Mar. 1756, Anne (*d.*20 June 1775), da. of Thomas, 1st Lord Archer, 6s. 8da.; (2) 18 Feb. 1778, Elizabeth, da. of John Armstrong of Godalming,

Surr., 2s. 2da. *suc.* mother to Turnour property in Suss. and took add. name of Turnour 1744; *cr.* Baron Winterton [I] 10 Apr. 1761; Earl Winterton [I] 12 Feb. 1766.

In 1756 Turnour unsuccessfully applied to Newcastle for an Irish peerage; to obtain it was henceforth his dominant aim. In 1760 his father-in-law, Lord Archer, named him as candidate at Bramber, but next asked Newcastle to make him an Irish viscount, 'upon which he should not stand at Bramber', and offered the nomination in return for the peerage.[1] Newcastle agreed to these terms, and by 15 Mar., ten days before the election, had obtained a peerage for Turnour, who did not stand. But when his brother-in-law, Andrew Archer, who had been returned for Bramber and Coventry, elected to sit for Coventry, Turnour, now Lord Winterton, was returned for Bramber.

In Parliament Winterton was a faithful follower of Newcastle, and voted consistently against Bute and Grenville. On the formation of the Rockingham Administration, Newcastle, apparently in recognition of Winterton's fidelity, obtained for him an Irish earldom. He voted against the higher land tax, 27 Feb. 1767; was classed by Newcastle as a friend, 2 Mar. 1767; and voted with Opposition on nullum tempus, 17 Feb. 1768. There is no record of his having spoken in the House.

In 1768 Winterton, in conjunction with Charles Lowndes, stood again at Bramber in opposition to two candidates nominated by Lord Granby, who since 1761 had acquired an interest in the borough. Winterton and Lowndes were returned but unseated by a party vote in the House of Commons. Winterton apparently did not stand again for Parliament.

He died 10 Aug. 1788, aged 54.

[1] Add. 32919, f. 17.

M.M.D.

## GASCOIGNE, Sir Thomas, 8th Bt. (1745–1810), of Parlington, Yorks.

| THIRSK  | 1780–1784       |
| MALTON  | Apr.–Aug. 1784  |
| ARUNDEL | 11 Feb. 1795–1796 |

*b.* at Cambrai, 7 Mar. 1745, 3rd s. of Sir Edward Gascoigne, 6th Bt., by Mary, h. of Sir Francis Hungate, 4th Bt., of Hudleston.[1] *educ.* Grand Tour with George Damer 1765.[2] *m.* (1) 1772, Miss Montgomery, *s.p.*; (2) 4 Nov. 1784, Mary, da. of James Shuttleworth of Gawthorp (q.v.), wid. of Sir Charles Turner, 1st Bt., of Kirkleatham (q.v.), 1s. *d.v.p. suc.* bro. as 8th Bt. 10 Jan. 1762.

Bred a Catholic, Gascoigne became an Anglican in the summer of 1780. At the general election he

was returned for Thirsk by Sir Thomas Frankland, probably by arrangement with Rockingham.[3] He voted regularly against North's Government until its fall; was regarded as a probable opponent by Shelburne, but did not vote on the peace preliminaries, 18 Feb. 1783. He voted for Pitt's proposals for parliamentary reform, 7 May 1783, and for Fox's East India bill, 27 Nov. 1783. After the dismissal of the Coalition in December 1783, he went into opposition. In 1784 Frankland returned an Administration supporter, and Gascoigne was returned for Lord Fitzwilliam's borough of Malton, but vacated his seat to make way for another old Rockinghamite, William Weddell. Gascoigne's only reported speech was on a motion for licensing horse dealers, 20 July 1784.[4] He remained one of the leading supporters of Fitzwilliam and the Opposition in Yorkshire, and in 1788 became chairman of a committee to organize this interest for the next general election.

Gascoigne died 11 Feb. 1810.

[1] *Genealogist*, n. s. xxv. 188. [2] See DAMER, Hon. George. [3] *Annual Reg.* 1780, p. 215; Rockingham to Portland, 28 July 1780, Portland mss. [4] Debrett, xvi. 139.

I.R.C.

## GASCOYNE, Bamber (1725–91), of Bifrons, Barking, Essex.

| MALDON   | 1761–20 Apr. 1763 |
| MIDHURST | 16 Jan. 1765–1768 |
| WEOBLEY  | 28 Dec. 1770–1774 |
| TRURO    | 1774–1784         |
| BOSSINEY | 1784–Apr. 1786    |

*bap.* 22 Feb. 1725, 1st s. of Sir Crisp Gascoyne, brewer, ld. mayor of London 1752–3, by Margaret, da. and coh. of John Bamber, M.D., of Bifrons, Barking. *educ.* Felsted; Queen's, Oxf. 1743; L. Inn 1745, called 1750. *m.* 24 Jan. 1757, Mary, da. and coh. of Isaac Green of Childwall Abbey and Hale Hall, Lancs., 4s. 1da. *suc.* maternal gd.-fa. 8 Nov. 1753; fa. 28 Dec. 1761.

Ld. of Trade Apr. 1763–Aug. 1765, Feb. 1772–July 1779; ld. of Admiralty July 1779–Mar. 1782; receiver gen. of customs Apr. 1786–d.

Gascoyne, intent on being a country gentleman, in a letter to his friend John Strutt (q.v.), 13 Apr. 1759, discussed the impending Essex county by-election with a show of Toryism, talking of Whigs, 'Quakers, Presbyters, the Devils, etc.'[1] In 1761, with Strutt's support, he contested Maldon against Newcastle's candidates, and topped the poll—which 'was occasioned', he wrote in 1773, 'by two incidents: Colebrooke and Bullock could not raise cash and I was young and industrious'. Industrious he remained throughout life, 'an active, bustling man' with a well-nigh obsessionist persistence and perseverance.

In Bute's parliamentary list of mid-December 1761, Gascoyne was classed as 'Tory' and 'Pitt'; and on 30 Dec. 1762 Henry Fox still referred to him as 'Tory, which he is'.[2] When on 11 Dec. 1761 George Cooke, seconded by Beckford, moved for Spanish papers (to document Pitt's demand for war against Spain), Gascoyne supported the motion; allowed 'royal prerogative to negotiate, but insisted on that of the House to inquire': if necessary, through a secret committee. There was, he said, 'faction in the ministry'; Whig and Tory had been destroyed, but *personal* parties substituted in their stead'.[3] 'He himself had never been in a minister's house, nor ever intended it.'[4] Again, on 29 Jan. 1762, he supported Beckford over the Spanish papers 'with many words, and a voice rather audible, than melodious'. He often intervened in debates: over the Liverpool bill, 23 Mar.; the game bill 23 and 29 Mar.; 'did well' over the Durham election petition, 11 May; and altogether kept in the foreground.[5] In August 1762, Fox, when advising Bute to make sure of Members before the House met, wrote: 'I would try at Bamber Gascoyne; though I fear it is too late, and therefore with caution.'[6]

It was left to Fox to make the attempt. Temple wrote to Lady Chatham in November 1762: 'Gascoyne has been here: much dealing with Fox; but I think he is firm.'[7] Then on Tuesday, 30 Nov., in a talk with Fox, Gascoyne agreed to take office; but next day wrote to him: 'I find it incompatible with my happiness in life to part with the freedom I enjoy, I am therefore determined to remain independent.' Fox replied: 'I cannot tell whether my surprise or concern is greatest.' On 2 Dec. Gascoyne wrote to Strutt enclosing copies of his correspondence with Fox:

This will somewhat surprise you . . . On Tuesday I partly accepted, but I never had a moment's easiness in my mind till I had quitted it again, my heart was uneasy, I never slept. The words of persons accosting me in the street hurt me, I therefore wrote a letter to Mr. Fox the next morning, I have herewith sent his answer. Mr. W. [unidentified] . . . will . . . to-morrow . . . assure him that against the Duke of Newcastle I will act with him. That as to the Crown I will support it against every faction and that he may command me when he pleases to open any measures . . . and that time may come when the civility offered may be accepted with less difficulty—thus I left it. Indeed I am a coward and my conscience never was at rest.

On 9 Dec. Gascoyne spoke and voted against the peace preliminaries, but was absent on the 10th.[8] On 21 Dec. Fox wrote to Bute:[9]

Mr. Gascoyne is your declared friend, and will come to your Lordship to-morrow with a letter from me, desiring for him the disposition of King's waiter at Maldon. Luckily his inclination squares with our convenience, and he likes the promise of the Board of Trade in the course of the sessions better than the possession now.

And Gascoyne to Bute, the same day: 'At the request of Mr. Fox and with my own inclination I am to wait on your Lordship'; but he protested: 'I am no attendant on levees.'[10] On the 22nd, presumably after the visit to Bute, he wrote to Pitt:[11]

The offer of coming into the Board of Trade is now made me without conditions, and in a more eligible manner than before offered . . . I have attached myself to you upon principle, gratitude, and respect; and could I flatter myself that my going into office was likely to impede any operation of yours, I should never forgive myself.

He asked for Pitt's opinion or wish in this matter; and received the reply which he probably expected:

I cannot offer you any advice. Your own sense of things must alone guide you . . . I never in my life expressed my wish to any friend, either for their accepting or declining office.

Gascoyne's appointment to the Board of Trade in the Grenville Administration was declared on 20 Apr. 1763—Fox thought him 'a proper person in the House to treat any opponent roughly and coarsely who should deserve it';[12] and he promised Gascoyne that Administration would 'bring him into Parliament if he failed in his election at Maldon'.[13] But strenuous efforts were made in good time to secure it;[14] and on 23 Apr. Gascoyne told Strutt: 'I verily believe I should show you a better appearance than the last election, the Treasury hath fully exerted itself.' Three days later, Huske, a tough adventurer of American origin, defeated him by 438 to 254 votes (in 1761 Gascoyne had received 400). Gascoyne was crestfallen. He wrote to Strutt, 9 May: 'I have often sat down to write to you, and as often declined it by not knowing where to begin . . . I have been in a perturbed state ever since I left you and yet I still think mine enemies will not triumph over me.' He felt deceived and sold; was ruminating on instances of 'hypocrisy and ingratitude'; on how 'to recover the lost game'; also on the bills which his 'good friends' had run up against him—he had to borrow money from Strutt which it took him years to repay. Vindictive and aggressive, he conceived a relentless hatred of Huske; and by a long-drawn series of lawsuits he managed to destroy the corporation which had contrived his defeat, and made the borough forfeit its charter—no mean achievement.

While waiting to re-enter Parliament, Gascoyne assiduously attended to his official duties—in 1764 he was present at 103 out of 131 meetings of the Board.[15] On a vacancy in the representation of Essex, he wrote to Strutt, 12 June 1763, that even if assured of being well supported he was 'determined never to stand another contested election'; and yet in the same letter speculated on his chance of 'jumping in' without publicly offering himself. But even his friends were agreed that his 'little popularity' would render the attempt 'arduous' and 'improper' —'Gascoyne *can never do*'.[16] He was not to hold an Essex seat again: self-righteous and constantly engaged in litigation ('sometime,' he wrote to Strutt, 12 Nov. 1770, 'I am determined to have revenge by law which I never find strong enough for my resentment'), he was not liked in the county.

Fox (now Lord Holland) wrote to Sandwich from France, 23 Sept. 1763: 'If you can get Bamber Gascoyne brought into Parliament Mr. Grenville knows I think he will be a very useful man.'[17] But when a vacancy was impending at Midhurst where Holland had the nomination, he pleaded a previous engagement; Gascoyne appealed to Grenville 'with a concern equal to that I suffer from my present situation';[18] and Grenville reminded Holland of the promise which Gascoyne was urging 'in the strongest terms'.[19] After somewhat acrimonious correspondence Gascoyne was returned for Midhurst, 16 Jan. 1765.

On 29 Jan. he voted with the Government on the renewed motion on general warrants, but did not speak: 'There were speakers enough and I did not seek applause nor desire to be more unpopular than I am.' He criticized the Opposition's mismanagement of their motion on *ex officio* informations by the attorney-general: 'My fetters galled me much . . . had I been free . . . I had shook the House or carried the question' (16 Mar.). Further limitations were imposed on him by his official duties: 'I never can attend till 2 o'clock and have scarce ever time to be prepared.'

Gascoyne left London for Childwall early in July 1765, and was absent when the Grenville Administration was replaced by Rockingham's. In Newcastle's preparatory lists Gascoyne invariably appears among those to be removed: and that he would be, he was told by Grenville on 27 July.[20] But he himself thought the new ministry in tribulation over it: 'too prudent to write to me . . . they have some doubts and fears as to displacing me and yet they think it imprudent to keep me in without knowing my mind'—'poor as I am, I will not act with them or under them'.[21] And on 11 Aug.: 'these wretched and feeble statesmen'; 'nothing shall ever tempt me . . . to spend my days with Whigs, Presbyters, and Pelhamites'. When told by a friend that the Bedford connexion were being dismissed (the Duke having 'personally affronted the King'), but that there was no intention of discharging him unless

he meant to act against the new Government, he claims to have replied that nothing should divert him 'from openly and boldly vindicating the late Administration and opposing the present'. But when invited by Lord Gower to Trentham to meet the Dukes of Marlborough and Bridgwater, and other friends of Bedford,

> I thought it was as well to avoid appearance of attaching myself so much to this connection and therefore under pretence of being obliged to watch Liverpool for political purposes I put off this visit; since this I have received a letter from Lord Hillsborough congratulating me on my discharge.

He turned squire; cared not 'when Parliament meets' (15 Oct.); 'amusements of the field in the morning', and cards at night; and 'much uneasiness' at the impending return to the political stage. He did not attend the December session, though urged by Grenville.[22] But on 14 Jan. 1766 he was the first Opposition speaker[23]—'I stepped forth not to oppose the Address but to speak of the state of the nation and abuse our new masters, declaring my hearty approbation of my dismission as I never yet acted with them nor ever would.'[24] When on 7 Feb. Grenville's motion for enforcing laws in America was defeated by 274 votes to 134, Gascoyne wrote to Strutt:

> It appeared very strange even to me who have seen the vicissitudes in political matters that there should be such an alteration in men's minds. At the breaking up of the last session when the minority was 35, and the person whom the then majority supported has not had the direction of any one act since by which he could by any means forfeit the opinion of those who had voted with him in that very measure, now condemned and in every other measure.
>
> I now fear the Stamp Act will be repealed in the Commons . . . Faction not principle has divided us and the enemies to our established constitution in church and state wish to increase the flame.

He spoke again on the third reading of the repeal, 4 Mar.[25]

But even more of Gascoyne's time and energy during the session was devoted to local problems; foremost, that of the Chelmer navigation which cut across political divisions in the county. The enthusiasm for the venture 'all came from those living in the neighbourhood of Chelmsford, whose trade had everything to gain from the navigation, while the reluctance was all on the side of Maldon which had everything to lose in the way of wharf, warehouse and harbour dues'.[26] Strutt was prominent in the Maldon interest, and Gascoyne its chief spokesman and manager in the House. His many and very long reports to Strutt supply an almost unique picture of the way in which such business of considerable local interest was transacted in the House, and of how much time and energy was devoted to it—it looms large in the journals of the House, sometimes in local newspapers, but neither in the metropolitan press nor in reports of parliamentary debates. Similarly Gascoyne took a very active part in debates on the corn trade—in the spring of 1765, in February 1766, November 1767, and again in 1771; and he complained of the ineffectiveness of the country gentlemen over a question of so much importance to the landed interest. During the debates on the indemnity bill for the embargo placed on the export of corn, December 1766, he took 'a spirituous part in opposition'—[27]

> and had my intentions been lucrative the alarm I have sounded is not in vain, but I still remain fixed as when I saw you last and have returned for answer that I am rivetted to Mr. Grenville, not for favours received or hopes but for measures.

By whom the offer was made, and with how much authority does not appear—Gascoyne was apt to over-rate the awe and consideration in which he was held.

As the Parliament of 1761 was approaching its term, the problem of a seat arose for him once more —Midhurst was at the disposal of the Government. What Gascoyne craved for he admitted when disappointed of it (15 Mar. 1768): 'To have represented the county would have been the highest honour and I should have made it the greatest task of my life.' But late in 1767 he protested to Muilman, a merchant of Dutch extraction settled in Essex:

> I have no intention of seeking another seat in Parliament as I own I am much dispirited when I think how few advocates the landed interest will have and how many it will want; I have done my duty and I have been much abused for so doing and ungratefully treated.

And to Strutt, 26 Dec.: 'Muilman . . . rebukes me for deserting Parliament, assures me Essex is open'; 10 Feb. 1768: everything is shaping well but 'of candidates I know not'. And Bramston (q.v.) wrote to Strutt on the 12th: Gascoyne had been plaguing him 'all this week', discoursing on the support their side could secure, and the poor state of their opponents—

> All this and a vast deal more I heard, it ended with— we have only to find a candidate and the thing is done . . . Gascoyne plainly called upon me as far as he could without speaking quite out, to ask him to stand. I do think he would be a useful man but I have private objections I cannot get over and besides I verily believe he would not go down; but who will tell him so.

Finally Gascoyne declared his candidature; and when Eliab Harvey, who in February 1767 had voted for the higher land tax, was preferred to him,

Gascoyne wrote to Strutt on 12 Mar. in an outburst of passion:

> There was but one thing agreed on by the company . . . that I was the only objectionable man in the room. The basis of our opposition was public principle which we have now deserted; my ears were tickled with the general approbation of my conduct in every act in Parliament, and he whose conduct was reproachable was preferred unanimously before me because it was thought this conduct had rendered me in some places with some persons unpopular. Constructive errors in private life were used to damn my public conduct; nay I was sold before I offered and for this I was called out of Lancashire, for this my labours were incited and multiplied, my private business neglected and my abilities magnified and my services magnified that I might assist a proud and malevolent enemy to stride over me.

But having calmed down, he honestly worked for the candidates; and on 13 Apr., after their defeat, wrote to Strutt:

> I feel a vast comfort when I reflect that neither the cause or the candidates can lay any misconduct at my door . . . I now take my leave of all elections and party meetings . . . I am determined to oppose no more but make the yoke easy by rending myself agreeable to them in private, for I think it more eligible to live with Whigs than act with Tories diametrically opposite to principle and reason. So adieu to the old interest.

Gascoyne meant to work his way back into Parliament and office. He made up his differences with the Whig lord lieutenant of Essex—'you are not acquainted with the friendship Lord Rochford bears me', he wrote to Strutt, 2 Jan. 1769, 'I am taught to believe I am high in his esteem'. He was one of the promoters of the loyal address passed at the Chelmsford assizes and presented to the King on 6 Mar.[28] On the 13th he wrote to Strutt: 'The King hath spoke very graciously and very frequently of my services and he hath thought of reinstating me but how far his minister will permit that I cannot say.' Hillsborough, back at the Board of Trade, favoured the reinstatement of Gascoyne who next waited on Grafton;[29] he told the Duke: 'my ambition in office was no higher than where I stood before; I wished to be in Parliament', and 'thought myself entitled to ease in that respect as I had wasted too much of my private fortune in attempts of that kind already'. Grafton promised to serve Gascoyne when opportunity offered; but was under some previous engagements with regard to the Board of Trade.

It reached Gascoyne that Hillsborough had told Grafton 'he had nobody to do business for him or with him and that since I had been turned out he had lost his right hand'. 'This man is . . . wonderfully good to me . . . he works night and day to get me in.' Toward the end of May, at his suggestion,

Gascoyne tried to obtain from Thomas Bradshaw, secretary to the Treasury, 'some certain advice' as to his situation, and again received assurances for the future. 'I correspond with Bradshaw at his desire', Gascoyne wrote to Strutt at the end of October; but he still knew nothing for certain about his 'political state'. When early in December there seemed a possibility of Camden's obtaining a repeal of 'the revenue laws in America', and of Hillsborough resigning, Gascoyne wrote to Strutt: 'until I see what measures are resolved on, I will not embark'. When he again took up the matter, 'I have no doubt of the wishes and intentions of your friends', replied Bradshaw, 20 Dec., 'but at present there is no opportunity for carrying them into execution.' 'If nothing happens soon', Gascoyne remarked to Strutt, 'I will take my leave of London and these cursed courtiers. As to public business I will withdraw myself from it as fast as I can, for it is not in my power to do any good, I only draw vexation on myself and hatred from others.'

On 6 Feb. 1770: 'the resignation of the Duke of Grafton made no room for me . . . Lord Hillsborough continues his perseverance and friendship in my interest but I think there are many young men in Parliament that will be attended to in preference.' 6 Mar.: 'All things remain as to my situation just as they did. No news, nor no appointments.' After long searching for a constituency Gascoyne was returned on 28 Dec. by Lord Weymouth for Weobley, as part of an arrangement connected with Weymouth's resignation.[30] 'I knew not that I was chosen till this moment', Gascoyne wrote from Hillsborough's London house, 2 Jan. 1771. There was also a vacancy at the Board of Trade—but 'a treaty is on foot for advantage of Government to which I shall most willingly accede . . . in or out that is my plan'. And in his New Year resolutions on re-entering Parliament (to Strutt, 10 Jan.):

I have well considered my situation, I know it to be nice and dangerous, therefore it will much behove me to be sparing in my speech, cautious in my words, and cool in my temper; not only the humour of the times requires this, but my own time is changed much since I first went into Parliament. Ten years is an age that works alterations . . . There is great difference betwixt speaking as a young man, or a new Member and an old one . . . now I am fixed and espoused by one side and *hated* by the other. Therefore I must confine myself to measures and not engage with men. Few things shall tempt me even to speak to measures unless on such subjects as my education and practice have made me master of.
I know the factious phalanx are alarmed at my return and the whole host will be ready to rise at the first opportunity . . . For these reasons I am not very pressing to accept the Board of Trade . . . There is a treaty on foot with a small party who are called

Grenville's friends; to one of which [Thomas Whately], if this treaty takes place, the place at the Board of Trade would be acceptable. I have therefore declared I am in no haste to accept nor shall in any ways be disgusted if any disposition of that is made to the strengthening his Majesty's Government. This is taken kindly . . . I think being the first sessions in Parliament without being in place will render me more respectable and consequently more serviceable than if in place and to speak plain, if Lord Hillsborough was not concerned I should not be satisfied with the Board.

When toward the end of May, North offered Gascoyne the office of keeper of the King's roads and he refused it as a mere sinecure, an exchange was settled with Whately; but as Weymouth wished his borough 'not to be vacant six months', it was arranged for Whately to draw the keeper's salary, and Gascoyne Whately's, even before the appointments were declared: 'The pay runs on as if I had kissed hands.'[31] He also started to function unofficially at the Board—he wrote, 11 Sept. 1771: 'Some disturbances among our pious brethren at Boston called me to office three times last week and this day, as there was no real lord in town and Lord Hillsborough desired me to assist.' The official appointment followed on 10 Feb. 1772.

After his return to the House Gascoyne was a fairly frequent speaker: during the remaining $3\frac{1}{2}$ years of that Parliament, interventions by him in 38 debates are recorded. They covered a wide diversity of subjects, yet mostly within the range of his real interests and knowledge: trade, especially the corn bills, provisions, etc.; the Africa Company and East Indian affairs; legal matters: salaries of Welsh judges, the Gray's Inn petition, etc.; the poor bill (' I mean to give my opinion as a practising justice only'). He grew passionate over the motion for the attendance of the lord mayor on the committment of a messenger of the House sent to arrest a printer (18 Mar. 1771): the question 'must be determined, or you destroy the very existence of Parliament'; 'the charters of the City of London we know nothing of. I know the privileges of this House'; 'if you yield . . . you are the most nugatory body of people on earth'.[32] On 23 Mar. 1774 he spoke in support of the Boston port bill;[33] and in June supported the Quebec bill. At the Board of Trade (where his attendance at meetings was 80–90 per cent) he exerted considerable influence on American affairs. John Pownall, under-secretary to Lord Dartmouth who in August 1772 succeeded Hillsborough as secretary of state for the colonies and at the Board of Trade, wrote to William Knox, the other under-secretary, 23 July 1773:[34]

Our business has hitherto been as light as you could wish, and I think it is likely to continue so, for what can Lord Dartmouth have to do whilst Bamber Gascoyne is minister for America at the Board of Trade and Lord Suffolk at the Council Office, where they will not let us have anything to say, all Councils for American business being in Lord Gower's absence held by Lord Suffolk.

In the House Gascoyne regularly supported the Government; but, as an old Grenvillian, voted with the Opposition for making permanent Grenville's Election Act, 25 Feb. 1774.

As the Parliament of 1768 was drawing to an end, the question of a seat for Gascoyne arose once more: the arrangement at Weobley was for the one Parliament only. Gascoyne wrote to Strutt in November 1773: 'I never sat so pleasant in Parliament as when I knew I sat by suffrages and not by power'; but he had to sit 'by power', i.e. on the Government interest; and this too meant expense. On 6 Sept. 1774: 'My own seat is uncertain without some cash and I will not give any. I shall not dislike to quit London and public business . . . what little attachment I may have to measures and men, it will soon be eradicated by ill usage.' On 30 Sept., the day Parliament was dissolved: 'They are still squeezing me . . . I am not hurt at departing from public business. You will soon see my [London] house advertised.' And on 4 Oct.:

> Before we meet my resolution and orbit will be fixed and at this time of life, now in the 49th year of my age, I look upon my situation more critical than at any other period . . . The conditions offered to me, will not go down, for however repudiated I may be for being a placeman yet God be thanked I have been a freeman—however this I will own—had I not been a placeman I had been a better man.

And North wrote to Robinson, 6 Oct.: 'I think Gascoyne should have the refusal of Tregony if he will pay £1,000, but I do not see why we should bring him in cheaper than any other servant of the Crown'; and further on: 'Tell Gascoyne that if we can bring in Jenkinson for less than £1,000 we will not require so much of him. He had better venture, as we are much disposed to serve him.'[35]

On 13 Oct. Gascoyne was returned at Truro for a seat placed by Lord Falmouth at the disposal of the Government. In the new Parliament a dozen speeches by him are reported, none of much interest. In the reshuffle in offices, June–July 1779, he was promoted to a seat at the Admiralty Board, and henceforth dealt in the House mostly with its departmental business, again regularly voting with the Government. Unfortunately after 1775 his letters to Strutt, now himself in Parliament, are few; there may also have been a cooling off in their relations (after calling him for tens of years 'Dear Jack', Gascoyne towards the end addressed him 'Dear Strutt').

Gascoyne left office with North; spoke repeatedly on the Opposition side (against the Crewe bill disfranchising revenue officers, 23 Apr.; against Barré's pension, 9 July 1782; etc.); and voted against Shelburne's peace preliminaries, 18 Feb. 1783. In March 1783 he was classed by Robinson as 'North, doubtful'; he held no office under the Coalition; and voted against Fox's East India bill, which he described as 'imprudent, impudent, damnably wicked'. 'The seals are this day sent for by the King from Lord North and Fox. God send that they may never see them again.'[36] As for himself: 'I had retired with a full determination not to attend but on great events.' He stood again in 1784: about 25 Mar. Robinson included him among 'friends . . . who may choose to come in upon purchase', and in April among 'old Members who will probably pay if they do not get in again for their present seats'.[37] Gascoyne had written to Strutt, 19 Dec.: 'As to Truro I will not visit it'; and he was returned at Bossiney for a seat placed by Lord Mount Edgcumbe at the disposal of Government, which covered half of the £3,000 it cost from secret service funds.[38] In the new Parliament Gascoyne spoke several times (on 30 Mar. 1786 against an extension of the Crewe Act); and voted with the Government even on Richmond's fortifications plan, 27 Feb. 1786. In April 1786 he was appointed receiver general of customs, which vacated his seat.

Gascoyne died 27 Oct. 1791, never having attained a position commensurate to his abilities and effort. An effective speaker, a relentless worker, rough and not easily intimidated, though often almost morbidly depressed, he was defeated by his own temper and capacity to make enemies: he was disliked, and was fully conscious of it.

According to the *Gentleman's Magazine* (1791, p. 1066), he left his eldest son entailed estates in Essex and Lancashire worth near £4,000 p.a.

[1] Strutt mss at Terling. [2] Bute mss. [3] Add. 33035, ff. 32–38. [4] Walpole, *Mems. Geo. III*, i. 91. [5] Harris's 'Debates'. [6] Fox to Shelburne, 16 Aug., Shelburne to Bute, 19 Aug., Lansdowne mss. [7] *Chatham Corresp.* ii. 193. [8] Add. 33000, ff. 223–4; Fox's list of these two divisions, Bute mss. [9] Bute mss. [10] Add. 5726 D. f. 25. [11] *Chatham Corresp.* ii. 204–6. [12] Harris's memorandum, 14 Apr. 1763. [13] Grenville to Holland, 3 Apr. 1764, Grenville letter bk. [14] Rochford to Bute, 22 Feb., Bute mss. [15] A. H. Bayse, *Board of Trade 1748–82*, p. 225. [16] Bramston to Strutt, 12 June 1763; Keeling to Strutt, 13 June 1763. [17] Sandwich mss. [18] 3 Mar. 1764, Grenville mss (JM). [19] 3 Apr. letter bk. [20] Ibid. [21] To Strutt, c.18 July. [22] Grenville letter bk., 9 Nov. 1765. [23] Fortescue, i. 224. [24] To Strutt, 16 Jan. [25] Walpole, *Mems. Geo. III*, ii. 216. [26] Chas. Strutt, *Strutt Fam. of Terling, 1650–1873*, p. 21. [27] To Strutt, 5 Dec. 1766. [28] *Gent. Mag.*, 1769, p. 163. [29] Letter to Strutt, undated. [30] Gascoyne to Strutt, 7 Dec. 1769, 14 Oct. and 2 Nov. 1770; Fortescue, ii. 183. [31] To Strutt, n.d. (but about the end of May), and 11 and 15 June 1771. [32] Cavendish's 'Debates', Egerton 226, pp. 176–81. [33] Brickdale's 'Debates'. [34] *HMC Var.* vi. 110. [35] Laprade, 24, 25. [36] To Strutt, 19 Dec. 1783. [37] Laprade, 124, 128. [38] Royal archives, Windsor, no. 5715, election disbursements.

L.B.N.

## GASCOYNE, Bamber (?1758–1824), of Childwall Hall, Liverpool.

LIVERPOOL    1780–1796

*b.* ?1758, 1st s. of Bamber Gascoyne (q.v.). *educ.* Magdalen, Oxf. 1 July 1775, aged 17; Grand Tour (Netherlands) 1778–9. *m.* 24 July 1794, Sarah, da. and h. of Chase Price (q.v.), 1da. *suc.* fa. 27 Oct. 1791.

The Childwall Hall estates of Gascoyne's mother gave him a considerable interest at Liverpool, and in 1780 he was returned after a contest. In the House he followed his father's line. He consistently supported Administration till the fall of North; voted against Shelburne's peace preliminaries, 18 Feb. 1783, but also against Fox's East India bill, 27 Nov. 1783; and next adhered to Pitt.

Gascoyne spoke frequently in the House, especially on matters affecting Liverpool. In May 1788, in a debate on the slave trade, Gascoyne and his fellow Member, Lord Penrhyn, were the only two Members who attempted to justify the African trade. Abolition Gascoyne thought 'unnecessary, visionary and impracticable', though he admitted that 'some regulations might be beneficially adopted'.[1] But on 26 May, after consulting his constituents, he declared that the regulating bill 'was not likely to be productive of any good consequences whatever', and on 4 July said that if the bill 'would not quite ruin the trade, it would so cramp and fetter it, that it would in all probability throw it into the hands of our natural rivals'.[2] Henceforth he spoke frequently in defence of the trade; denied that any abuses existed, and on 12 May 1789 said that he was persuaded that the slave trade 'might be made a much greater source of revenue and riches to this country, than as it stood at present'.[3]

He died 17 Jan. 1824.

[1] Stockdale, xiv. 284–5; Wraxall, v. 120. [2] Stockdale, xv. 224–5. [3] Ibid. xvii. 216–17.

M.M.D.

## GASHRY, Francis (1702–62), of Hollybush House, Parson's Green, London.[1]

ALDEBURGH    30 Mar.–27 Apr. 1741
EAST LOOE     1741–19 May 1762

*b.* 14 Nov. 1702, s. of Francis Gascherie, perfumer, of Lamb's St., Stepney by his w. Susanna, both natives of La Rochelle.[2] *m.* bef. 1747, Martha, sis. of Burrington Goldsworthy (consul at Leghorn, and subsequently at Cadiz), aunt of Philip Goldsworthy (q.v.), wid. of Charles Bolton (nephew of Adm. Charles Wager, M.P.),[3] *s.p. suc.* through his w. to manor of Rotherhithe, and to Kilmenath, nr. Looe, on *d.* of Wager's wid. 1748.

Inspector of the captains' journals, sec. to Sir Charles Wager (first ld. of Admiralty 1732–42), and commr. for sick and hurt seamen 1737; asst. sec. to the Admiralty 1738; commr. of the navy 1741–7; comptroller of victualling accounts 1744–7; director, South Sea Co. 1749–*d.*; treasurer and paymaster of Ordnance 1751–*d.*

Gashry's father was naturalized in 1709 as 'Gascherye';[4] in the books of the Sun Fire Office in 1710 the name is anglicized into 'Gashery'. Francis Gashry started his official and parliamentary career under the auspices of Sir Charles Wager; and became the intermediary between Administration and the Trelawny family at East Looe[5] and also agent for Edward Trelawny, governor of Jamaica. Newcastle wrote about the Looes on 15 Mar. 1754: 'Mr. Roberts is ordered to talk with Mr. Gashry concerning the state of these boroughs.'[6] Gashry informed Newcastle of Pelham's engagements to the Trelawnys, and obtained office for John Buller, heir to Governor Trelawny's electoral interest.

In October 1761 Newcastle left it to Gashry to secure the attendance of the Members for the two Looes at the opening of the session. In the House Gashry can be presumed to have voted with the Administration; there is no record of his having spoken.

As director of the South Sea Company and treasurer of the Ordnance, Gashry was consulted by Newcastle on financial matters, and he was a subscriber to Government loans.[7] After having 'long been in a declining state'[8] Gashry died 19 May 1762. Executor under his will was the Rev. William Buller, brother of James, John and Francis Buller (qq.v.). Gashry left a mourning ring to Richard Rigby (q.v.).

[1] *Ex inf.* F. E. Hansford, chairman, executive committee, Fulham Hist. Soc. [2] *Reg. of the Church of La Patente, Spitalfields, 1689–1785* (Huguenot Soc. xi), 35. [3] *VCH Surr.* iv. 88–89. [4] *Denizations and Naturalizations of Aliens in England & Ireland, 1701–1800* (Huguenot Soc. xxvii), 84. [5] Namier, *Structure*, 205, 443. [6] Add. 19038, ff. 44–45, 48–51; 32995, ff. 63–67. [7] Add. 32893, f. 481; 33039, f. 258; 33040, ff. 290–1; Devonshire mss 512, f. 10; Bank of England recs. [8] H. B. Legge to Newcastle, 20 Feb. 1762, Add. 32934, f. 490.

L.B.N.

## GERMAIN, *see* SACKVILLE, Lord George

## GIBBON, Edward (1737–94), of Bentinck St., London; Buriton, Hants; and Lenborough, Bucks.

LISKEARD        1774–1780
LYMINGTON    25 June 1781–1784

*b.* 27 Apr. 1737, o. surv. s. of Edward Gibbon, M.P., by his 1st w. Judith, da. of James Porten, merchant, of Putney, Surr. *educ.* Kingston g.s. 1746; Westminster 1748–50; Magdalen, Oxf. 1752; in Lausanne 1753–8; Grand Tour (France, Switzerland and Italy) 1763–5. *unm. suc.* fa. 1770.

Ld. of Trade June 1779–May 1782.

In 1719 Gibbon's grandfather, army contractor and director of the South Sea Company, bought

Buriton, the manor of Petersfield, and an interest in the burgages; Gibbon's father represented the borough 1734-41, but in 1739 sold his interest to John Jolliffe. When Gibbon returned from Lausanne in 1758 his father gave him hopes of a seat in Parliament, and 'fifteen hundred pounds were mentioned as the price of the purchase'. Shortly before the general election of 1761 Gibbon asked his father to reconsider the matter.[1]

This design [he wrote] flattered my vanity, as it might enable me to shine in so august an assembly. It flattered a nobler passion; I promised myself that by the means of this seat I might be one day the instrument of some good to my country. But I soon perceived how little a mere virtuous inclination, unassisted by talents, could contribute towards that great end; and a very short examination discovered to me, that those talents were not fallen to my lot . . . I never possessed that gift of speech, the first requisite of an orator, which use and labour may improve, but which nature can alone bestow. That my temper, quiet, retired, somewhat reserved, could neither acquire popularity, bear up against opposition, nor mix with ease in the crowds of public life. That even my genius . . . is better qualified for the deliberate compositions of the closet than for the extemporary discourses of the Parliament. An unexpected objection would disconcert me; and as I am incapable of explaining to others what I do not thoroughly understand myself, I should be meditating while I ought to be answering. I even want necessary prejudices of party and of nation.

He did not yet realize that the 'gift of speech' or 'prejudices of party' were needed only by those who aimed at the front bench, and life in Parliament was not necessarily uncongenial to a reserved and scholarly nature. But Gibbon had set his heart on going to Italy, 'a country which every scholar must long to see', and resented the diversion of energy or money to any other purpose.

Yet his father set him up as candidate at the general election. On 20 Mar. 1761, the day Parliament was dissolved, Gibbon, at Dover with the militia, was summoned to Buriton. Next day, with a letter from Sir Thomas Worsley of Appuldercombe, Isle of Wight, he waited on Lord Fitzmaurice, a friend of Bute and Henry Fox. Here is the entry in Gibbon's journal for 22 Mar.:[2]

Some freeholders of Petersfield had persuaded my father to stand against Jolliffe's interest upon the supposition he could not transfer any of his votes, having settled them upon his wife. My father declined in my favour. I had never any opinion of the affair, and was only comforted by the reflexion that it cost hardly anything. One Barnard of Alresford made me lose the election or rather gave me an opportunity of giving it up with honour.

And on 1 Apr.:[3] 'The election came on. I in a set speech thanked my friends, abused Barnard, and declined a poll.'

On 8 July Shelburne (as Fitzmaurice had now become) sent Bute a copy of Gibbon's first book, the *Essai sur l'Etude de la Littérature*, published the previous day. Shelburne wrote in a covering letter:[4]

He has . . . been an enthusiast in the militia, and my acquaintance with him was on account of his election at Petersfield, where he failed, which prevented my mentioning him to you. He since comes to me to give me this book written in French, and to desire me to present another copy to your Lordship, which he is very anxious should be understood by you as a mark of respect for your public character, and not an interested one—having nothing to ask.

In January 1763 Gibbon set out again for the continent, intending to spend a year at Lausanne before making the tour of Italy. He was apprehensive lest financial difficulties might curtail or prevent the tour, and received with 'much uneasiness' his father's suggestion to mortgage Buriton.

The advantages for me would be [he wrote to his father from Lausanne on 10 Sept. 1763] your being able to bring me into Parliament, increasing my annuity, and enabling me to continue my travels. Give me leave to say, dear sir, that the first has very little weight with me. I find my ambition diminish every day, and my preference of a quiet studious life to hurry and business grow upon me. Besides . . . if I was in, what could I do? Whether I consulted principle or prudence, everything seems so unsettled that I might find myself very soon at the tail of an opposition; (and as a total change seems to be the modern maxim of every new ministry) in case I had got anything I should be reduced to my former situation, with the added mortification of having just tasted a little more power and plenty.

Italy, not Parliament, was his 'great object'. 'When I am just in view of Italy', he wrote, 'to be obliged to give up a scheme which has been always a favourite, would afflict me to the greatest degree.'

1763 to 1765 were formative years in Gibbon's life: at Lausanne in August 1763 he met John Baker Holroyd (q.v.) and began a friendship that lasted till death; and at Rome on 15 Oct. 1764 he 'conceived the first thought' of the *Decline and Fall*. His enjoyment of his Italian tour however was marred by the need to practise parsimony and he had to abandon his plan of a tour through southern France. He spent the next five years between Buriton and London, but after his father's death in 1770 made London his home. Here he found 'that unity of study and society' which best suited his temperament; began the *Decline and Fall*; and turned his thoughts towards entering Parliament. His friends and neighbours were in the House of Commons; his letters touched more and more on political affairs; and he began to sense and relish the atmosphere of the House. He felt towards it as he had towards the Italian tour ten years earlier.

He had no electoral interest or political connexion, and could not afford to buy a seat. But Edward Eliot, husband of his cousin Catherine, had six seats at his disposal. It seems that it was Eliot who suggested sending Gibbon to Lausanne in 1753; his sons were Gibbon's nearest male relatives; yet Gibbon had no strong liking for him. In the spring of 1773 Gibbon meditated a visit to Port Eliot with his stepmother. He wrote to her on 25 Mar.:

> With regard to the Cornish journey . . . as we are often tempted to sacrifice propriety to inclination, I am afraid that I should have deferred it another summer in favour of Derbyshire. Your company has fixed me . . . I fancy my stay at Port Eliot will hardly be so long as yours.

On 5 May he wrote: 'I have seen the Eliots several times, and think he and I take to each other very well this year.' And again on 31 July: 'The Eliots testify a strong inclination to see us in Cornwall, a passionate one indeed. I hope we shall like one another.'

The visit was deferred until the autumn, and on 10 Sept. Gibbon wrote to Holroyd from Port Eliot: 'In general our time rolls away in an equal kind of insipidity'; Eliot possessed neither hounds, horses, nor a good library.

> One possession he has indeed most truly desirable [Gibbon continued] but I much fear that the Danae of St. Germans has no particular inclination for me, and that the interested strumpet will yield only to a golden shower.

During the next twelve months Gibbon hardly refers to Eliot in his correspondence, but in August 1774 Eliot asked Gibbon to become executor to his will and guardian to his children and then—

> Yesterday morning, about half an hour after seven [Gibbon wrote to Holroyd on 10 Sept.] as I was destroying an army of barbarians, I heard a double rap at the door, and my Cornish friend was soon introduced. After some idle conversation he told me, that if I was desirous of being in Parliament, he had an *independent* seat very much at my service. You may suppose my answer, but my satisfaction was a little damped when he added that the expense of the election would amount to about £2,400, and that he thought it reasonable that we should share it between us. I paused, and recovering myself, hinted something of parental extravagance, and filial narrowness of circumstances and want of ready money, and that I must beg a short delay to consider whether I could with prudence accept of his intended favour, on which I set the highest value. His answer was obliging, that he should be very much mortified if a few hundred pounds should prevent it, and that he had been afraid to offend me by offering it on less equal terms. His behaviour gave me courage to propose an expedient, which was instantly accepted with cordiality and eagerness, that when his second son John (who is now thirteen) came of age I would restore to him my proportion of the money.

'This is a fine prospect opening upon me' he concluded, 'and if next spring I should take my seat and publish my book, it will be a very memorable era in my life.' He recognized that Eliot had acted 'in the most liberal manner': indeed Gibbon was fortunate to secure a safe and independent seat for only £1,200 and that on deferred payment.

Gibbon attended the eve of the session meeting as a Government supporter; on 5 Dec. he voted for the first time—with Government on the amendment to the Address, but 'resisted the premature temptation to speak'. He took pains to become acquainted with American affairs. On 31 Jan. 1775 he wrote to Holroyd:

> I think I have sucked Mauduit [agent for Massachusetts Bay] and Hutchinson [late governor] very dry; and if my confidence was equal to my eloquence, and my eloquence to my knowledge, perhaps I might make no very intolerable speaker. At all events, I fancy I shall try to expose myself . . . I am more and more convinced that we have both the right and the power on our side, and that, though the effort may be accompanied with some melancholy circumstances, we are now arrived at the decisive moment of persevering or of losing forever both our trade and Empire.

And on 8 Feb.: 'I am more and more convinced that with firmness all may go well; yet I sometimes doubt Lord North.' Though he supported Government on America, he voted against them on 22 Feb. 1775 when Wilkes moved to rescind the decision on the Middlesex election. Walpole described him in 1776 as 'whimsical . . . because he votes variously as his opinion leads him'.[5] And here is his character as given in the *Public Ledger* in 1779:

> A most ingenious and learned gentleman. He follows the dictates of his own opinion, voting sometimes with Government, and sometimes against, and lives in good friendship with all parties.

But in the House he remained 'a mute'. 'It is more tremendous than I imagined', he wrote to Holroyd on 15 Feb. 1775, 'the great speakers fill me with despair, the bad ones with terror.' He felt he had come into Parliament too late in life to exert 'the talents of an orator'. Still the House of Commons, he wrote to his step-mother on 30 Mar. 1775,

> is, upon the whole, an agreeable improvement in my life, and forms just the mixture of business, of study, and of society, which I always imagined I should, and now I find I do, like.

It was 'a very agreeable coffee house'.

He had no doubt of the justice of the British case, yet did not imagine the war would be quickly or easily won, and was frequently critical of its conduct. On 16 Dec. 1777, on the news of Burgoyne's surrender at Saratoga, he wrote:

> What will be the resolutions of our governors I know not, but I shall scarcely give my consent to exhaust

still further the finest country in the world in the prosecution of a war from whence no reasonable man entertains any hopes of success. It is better to be humbled than ruined.

On 27 Jan. and 2 Feb. 1778 he voted with Opposition on motions directed against the conduct of the war, and on 28 Feb. wrote to Holroyd about North's conciliatory proposals:

> You are mistaken in supposing that the bills are opposed . . . in the *only* division I voted with Government. Yet I still repeat that in my opinion, Lord North does not deserve pardon for the past, applause for the present, or confidence for the future.

The entry of France into the war and the failure of the conciliatory mission convinced Gibbon that the only course was to support Government. He had no confidence in the Opposition; he silenced his doubts about the vigour and ability of ministers; and henceforth voted regularly with the court.

About this time his financial affairs were causing him considerable uneasiness. Negotiations for the sale of Lenborough, in progress for some years, broke down; he was forced to sell his shares in the New River Company; Buriton was causing him expense; moreover he had to provide for his stepmother.

> My desires have always been moderate [he wrote to her on 7 Jan. 1779] and my domestic economy has been conducted with tolerable prudence. Yet my income has never been quite adequate to my expenses, and those expenses, unless I retired from Parliament, from London, and from England, it would be impossible for me to retrench. When I look back I cannot find much to censure or regret in my own conduct, but when I look forwards I am sometimes alarmed and perplexed.

But he had a good friend and patron in Alexander Wedderburn, attorney-general, and by his interest hoped soon to achieve 'an honourable and advantageous post either at home or abroad'. This, he wrote on 21 Mar., 'would remove every difficulty and supply every want'. On 20 June the King consented to the appointment of 'the attorney-general's friend' to the Board of Trade, although, he wrote to North, it 'will I fear, and not without reason, greatly offend the clergy'.[6]

Next he had to sound Eliot, now in opposition, about his re-election.

> My answer [to Wedderburn's offer] was sincere and explicit [he wrote on 20 June 1779]. I told him that I was far from approving all the past measures of Administration, even some of those in which I myself had silently concurred; that I saw with the rest of the world many essential defects in the character of ministers, and was sorry that in so alarming a crisis the country had not the assistance of several able and honest men who are now in opposition. But . . . that I did not discover among them such a superiority either of measures or abilities as could make it a duty

for me to attach myself to their cause; and that . . . opposition could not tend to any good purpose and might be productive of much serious mischief. That in this view of public affairs I saw no reason which ought to prevent me from accepting office . . . But that he must be sensible that it was impossible for me to give a decisive answer till I had consulted the person to whose generous friendship I was indebted for my seat in Parliament . . . That from my knowledge of your dislike to the present system it was not in my power to determine whether you might not feel some reluctance to replace me in a situation, in which I could never oppose and must *generally* support the measures of Government. But the experience of your friendship inspired me however with a lively hope that you would not refuse on this interesting occasion to renew and confirm the obligation you had already conferred upon me.

He concluded:

> Your answer will decide whether I may continue to live in England or whether I must speedily withdraw myself into a kind of philosophical exile in Switzerland . . . The addition of the salary which is now offered will make my situation perfectly easy; but I hope you will do me the justice to believe that my mind would not be so, unless I were sincerely persuaded that I could accept the offer with honour and integrity.

Eliot agreed to re-elect Gibbon, although it was 'highly unpleasant to him'.

Gibbon was conscientious in his attendance at the Board; his duties did not unduly interfere with his work on the *Decline and Fall*, although the post was no sinecure; and it gave him an insight into the workings of the Government machine. In July 1779, at the request of Weymouth and Thurlow, he wrote the *Mémoire Justificatif* against the conduct of France and Spain. 'Though I will never make myself the champion of a party', he told his step-mother on 10 Dec. 1779, 'I thought there was no disgrace in becoming the advocate of my country against a foreign enemy.'

He was now at work on the second and third volumes of the *Decline and Fall*, and frankly admitted that if it were not for his place he would retire 'without regret' from Parliament—'that scene of noise, heat and contention'. But what would happen at the dissolution, now expected?

> I am totally ignorant of the designs of the electors of Liskeard [he wrote on 15 May 1780]. My great constituent grows warmer in patriotism, but he still expresses the same regard for me, and though I have no motives for confidence, I have not any reasons for fear. He is perfectly silent on the subject, and I am prepared for the worst.

He had taken few pains to cultivate Eliot: in spite of invitations to visit Cornwall he had not done so since 1773. On 11 Aug. 1780 he wrote to Eliot about the approaching election:

> Unless I obtain a seat in the next Parliament, I cannot flatter myself with a hope of remaining at the Board

of Trade; such is the unpleasant state of my private affairs, that I must resign with my office all prospect of living in England, and the discontinuance of your favours will therefore be a sentence of banishment from my native country.

He concluded:

Various circumstances of public and private distress have hitherto prevented me from disposing of my Buckinghamshire estate, from whence I may expect to derive a considerable supply, and I shall find myself under the necessity of soliciting your indulgence till I can discharge what I shall always esteem a very small part of my obligations.

What he did not tell Eliot was that on 1 June, less than six weeks earlier, he had sold the copyright of the second and third volumes of the *Decline and Fall* for £4,000.[7]

Neither was Eliot frank with Gibbon: he did not disclose that he had placed the available seats in his boroughs at the disposal of Opposition. His reply, dated 24 Aug. 1780,[8] was long, rambling, and shuffling: he was plainly concerned and embarrassed. More than half the letter sought to demonstrate that Administration would find Gibbon a seat in Parliament anyway. And here is the reason he gave for not returning Gibbon:

The most zealous friends I have in Liskeard declare decidedly against choosing you again, so that if I were ever so desirous of prevailing on them it is out of my power.

'Mr. Eliot', wrote Gibbon in retrospect in his *Autobiography*, 'was now deeply engaged in the measures of Opposition, and the electors of Liskeard are commonly of the same opinion as Mr. Eliot.' And in his reply of 8 Sept. 1780, a masterpiece of irrefutable argument delicately phrased, he wrote that he would not 'presume to arraign the consistency of the electors of Liskeard, whom you so gravely introduce'.

He offered a dignified defence of his parliamentary conduct:

I may fairly rest my apology on the truth of one single assertion, that I have never renounced any principle, deserted any connexion, or violated any promise. I have uniformly asserted . . . the justice of the American war. I have constantly supported in Parliament the general measures of Government, except at one particular crisis while it was doubtful . . . whether they would offer terms to the rebels. I agreed with you in a speculative opinion, almost equally rejected by both parties, that after the substance of power was lost, the name of independence might be granted to the Americans. I have often and severely censured the faults of Administration, but I have always condemned the *system* of opposition: and your judgment will allow that in public life every man is reduced to the necessity of choosing the side which upon the whole appears to him the least reprehensible.

He concluded, as Eliot had done, with an avowal that political differences should not mar private friendships.

Eliot's 'civil ambiguous silence' had prevented him from applying to Administration for a seat; now he hastened to do so. Loughborough (as Wedderburn had now become) wrote to him on 4 Sept.: 'It would be bad policy in Administration to suffer . . . you . . . to wait long for a seat because it behoves a Government to show that no protection was so powerful as theirs.' Eden too encouraged him to apply to 'the powers above'. Gibbon told North that he could bear but a small part of the expense, and asked for 'an almost gratuitous seat'. He was returned on the Burrard interest at Lymington on 25 June 1781. His seat cost the Government £3,000, towards which Gibbon made an immediate contribution of £800—presumably the rest was paid later.[9]

The second and third volumes of the *Decline and Fall* had been published in March 1781, and Gibbon now decided to continue his work to the fall of the Eastern Empire. He had lost his taste for Parliament and was concerned only for the safety of his place. He supported North's Administration to the end, and in May 1782 was dismissed from the Board of Trade. 'I am heartily tired of the scene', he wrote on 4 May.

He could expect nothing from Rockingham or his successor.

If Lord Shelburne should be the man [he wrote on 3 July 1782] as I think he will, the friends of his predecessor will quarrel with him before Christmas. At all events, I foresee much tumult and strong opposition, from which I should be very glad to extricate myself, by quitting the House of Commons with honour and without loss.

He watched with detachment and almost indifference the game that followed: yet 'from honour, gratitude, and principle' attached himself to North, and on 18 Feb. 1783 voted against Shelburne's peace preliminaries.

North's return to office with the Coalition seemed to be favourable to his prospects.

Notwithstanding their apparent neglect [he wrote on 5 May 1783], I have reason to think them well inclined to me, and have even received some assurances, but as everything that depends on ministers is precarious and uncertain, I would not raise too much either your hopes or my own.

He had resumed work on the *Decline and Fall* and now wished to retire to Lausanne to complete it. On 20 May he informed his friend Deyverdun of his plan. But Lord Sheffield (as John Baker Holroyd had become) and his English friends urged him to try to obtain a place, and he agreed to make the effort. He told Deyverdun that success was uncertain, and he did not know if he wanted it.

In truth, his heart was set on Lausanne and completing his history, and on 10 July he wrote to Sheffield:

> The source of pensions is absolutely stopped, and a double list of candidates is impatient and clamorous for half the number of desirable places. A seat at the board of customs or excise was certainly the most practicable attempt, but how far are we advanced in the pursuit? . . . Have we received any promise of the *first* vacancy? How often is the execution of such a promise delayed to a second or third opportunity? When will those vacancies happen? Incumbents are sometimes very tough . . .
>
> But I will take a more favourable supposition, and conceive myself, in six months, firmly seated at the board of customs; before the end of the next six months, I should infallibly hang myself. Instead of regretting my disappointment, I rejoice in my escape; as I am satisfied that no salary could pay me for the irksomeness of attendance, and the drudgery of business so repugnant to my taste, (and I will dare to say) so unworthy of my character.

It was his 'IRREVOCABLE resolution' to be in Lausanne by the beginning of October. Sheffield and Loughborough, while regretting his departure, agreed he could do no other.

On 27 Aug., almost on the eve of Gibbon's departure, George Maddison, secretary of the embassy at Paris, died. John Craufurd (q.v.), intimate with Fox, solicited the post on Gibbon's behalf, but Gibbon probably neither expected nor desired success. There is in his papers a list written in double columns, of reasons 'for and against accepting'.[10] The first three reasons 'for' were: 'The credit of being distinguished and stopped by Government, when I was leaving England'; 'The salary of £1,200 a year'; 'The society of Paris'. Against these he put the disappointment of Deyverdun who was expecting him, his inexperience in diplomacy, the lack of permanency, and (number four) 'Giving up the leisure and liberty for prosecuting my history'. On 4 Sept. Portland sent to the Duke of Manchester, ambassador at Paris, a list of candidates,[11] and invited his comments. Fox was no friend to Gibbon, and could not have been displeased to learn that Gibbon was *persona non grata* with the French court.

> One person only (Mr. Gibbon) [wrote Manchester to Fox on 11 Sept. 1783[12]] has, I am told, rendered himself obnoxious here by an expression in his book, in which he talks of the French sceptre slumbering in the hands of Arcadius or Honorius.[13] The King formally took notice of the expression.

Gibbon left England on 17 Sept., before Storer's appointment was decided.

He entrusted Sheffield with the disposal of his seat in Parliament and the sale of Lenborough.

Negotiations were opened in respect of his seat, which Gibbon hoped would bring him a thousand guineas. But Sir Harry Burrard proved difficult, and when the Coalition was dismissed Gibbon, not expecting Parliament to be dissolved or Pitt's Administration to last, yet anxious to be rid of his seat, lowered his price by half. On 2 Feb. he gave Sheffield *carte blanche* to obtain the best price he could. He had now come round to a different view of Pitt's prospects.

> Fox drives most furiously [he wrote] yet I should not be surprised if Pitt's moderation and character should insensibly win the nation, and even the House, to espouse his cause.

By the end of April he had little hope of getting anything for the seat. 'Can nothing, nothing be done', he wrote, 'in any way by direct or indirect, by humble or strenuous measures?' He did not know that Parliament had been dissolved on 25 Mar.

'The eight sessions that I sat in Parliament', wrote Gibbon in his *Autobiography*, 'were a school of civil prudence, the first and most essential duty of a historian.' War, the intrigues of parties, and the government of nations are the staple themes around which Gibbon wove the rich fabric of the *Decline and Fall*; and he had been militia officer, Member of Parliament, and lord of Trade. 'The deliberate compositions of the closet' were enriched by experience of 'the extemporary discourses of the Parliament'.

Gibbon died 16 Jan. 1794. He left the bulk of his fortune (over £20,000) to cousins on his mother's side, Charlotte and Stanier Porten. Lady Eliot, he wrote, 'is my nearest relation on the father's side: but her mother was so favourably treated by our common grandfather, and her three sons are in such prosperous circumstances, that I may well be excused for withholding from them a small addition, which they cannot desire and have never solicited.'

¹ All quotations, unless otherwise stated, are from *Letters of Edward Gibbon*, ed. J. E. Norton. ² *Gibbon's Jnl.* ed. D. M. Low, 23. ³ Ibid. 24. ⁴ Bute mss. ⁵ Walpole to Mason, 18 Feb. 1776. ⁶ Fortescue, iv. 364. ⁷ J. E. Norton, *Bibliog. Gibbon*, 45. ⁸ Add. 34886, ff. 111–12. ⁹ I. R. Christie, *End of North's Ministry*, 100. ¹⁰ Add. 34882, f. 256. ¹¹ *HMC 8th Rep.* pt. 2, p. 131. ¹² *Corresp. C. J. Fox*, ii. 157–8. ¹³ In 'General Observations on the fall of the Roman Empire in the west', following ch. 38 of the *Decline and Fall*.

J.B.

## GIBBONS, John (c.1717–76), of Stanwell Place, Mdx.

STOCKBRIDGE 1754–1761
WALLINGFORD 1761–1768

*b.* c.1717, 1st s. of Sir William Gibbons, 1st Bt., of Barbados, speaker of the house of assembly, master gen. of the Ordnance and lt. gen. of the island, by Frances, da. of Robert Hall of Barbados. *m.* Martha, da. of Rev. Scawen Kenrick, vicar of St. Martin-in-the-Fields, 5s. 1da. *suc.* fa. as 2nd Bt. 11 Apr. 1760; *cr.* K.B. 23 Mar. 1761.

From 1745 till at least 1768 Gibbons was a member of the Barbados assembly; and apparently retained an active interest in island affairs when settled in England.[1] In 1754 he was returned unopposed at Stockbridge. He was described in Dupplin's list as 'doubtful'. On 13 Dec. 1760 George Cooke wrote to Newcastle that Gibbons, who owned 'an immense fortune in land and money', wished for a knighthood,[2] and on 23 Mar. 1761 he was created K.B. According to a suppressed passage in Walpole's *Mems. Geo. III* he confessed having 'purchased a red ribbon' through Miss Vansittart, maid of honour to the Princess Dowager, whom Walpole describes as 'her agent for the sale of honours'.

In 1761 Gibbons was returned unopposed at Wallingford. He was included in Henry Fox's list of Members favourable to the peace preliminaries but voted in opposition in the divisions of 1, 9 and 10 Dec. Gibbons was classed in Bute's list as his follower and on 22 Apr. 1763 asked Bute to recommend him for an Irish peerage, declaring himself 'already much obliged'.[3] In the autumn of 1763 Jenkinson classed Gibbons as 'doubtful'. James Harris notes that in the debate on Wilkes and the *North Briton*, 15 Nov. 1763, Gibbons 'vociferated', and that 'Wilkes said, when he first heard him, that he was a greater West India monster than Beckford himself'. He is not in the minority list of this debate, but voted in opposition on general warrants, 6, 15 and 18 Feb. 1764; and on 10 May 1764 was counted by Newcastle as a 'sure friend'. On 6 Feb. 1765 he spoke against Grenville's proposals for taxing America; is classed by Rockingham in July 1765 as 'pro', in November 1766 as 'doubtful'. On 27 Feb. 1767 he voted with the court on the land tax; and was listed by Newcastle as 'Administration', 2 Mar. 1767.

In 1768 Gibbons was defeated at Wallingford. He did not stand again, and died 9 July 1776.

[1] Gibbons to Jenkinson, 2 Apr. 1763, Bute mss. [2] Add. 32916, f. 41. [3] Bute mss.

M.M.D.

## GIDEON (afterwards **EARDLEY**), Sir Sampson, 1st Bt. (1745–1824), of Spalding, Lincs.

| | |
|---|---|
| CAMBRIDGESHIRE | 22 Nov. 1770–1780 |
| MIDHURST | 29 Nov. 1780–1784 |
| COVENTRY | 1784–1796 |
| WALLINGFORD | 1796–1802 |

*b.* 10 Oct. 1745, o.s. of Sampson Gideon, the Jewish financier, of Stepney by Jane, da. of Charles Ermell, an English Protestant. *educ.* Tonbridge 1752–60; Eton 1761–3; Ch. Ch. Oxf. 1763; L. Inn 1762. *m.* 6 Dec. 1766, Maria, da. of Sir John Eardley Wilmot, c.j. of the common pleas, 2s. *d.v.p.* 3da. *cr.* Bt. 21

May 1759; *suc.* fa. 17 Oct. 1762; took name of Eardley instead of Gideon 17 July 1789; *cr.* Baron Eardley [I] 24 Sept. 1789.

Gideon's father was one of the chief financial advisers of the Pelhams, very active in connexion with Government loans to which he heavily subscribed.[1] Because of his religion his application for a baronetcy in 1757 was refused by George II— 'therefore', wrote Charles Frederick to Lord George Sackville, 'his son is to be one, who eats pork and is a Protestant.'[2] Sampson Gideon junior, who thus became a baronet at the age of thirteen, inherited his father's fortune, estimated at about half a million pounds, while still under age. He does not appear to have entered business himself though he was a heavy subscriber to Government loans, and by 1789 held £200,000 of stock.[3] He early embarked on a political career. On 7 Jan. 1768 Lord Bessborough wrote to the Duke of Bedford: 'He wants a seat, he has a great deal of money';[4] and suggested that Gideon might be a suitable purchaser of the Duke's Hampshire estates. In February 1768 Gideon's brother-in-law, Lord Gage, recommended him to Newcastle for a seat at Seaford, but the Duke refused to accept him because he 'was disposed to be with Administration'.[5] In the end he did not stand in 1768.

In 1770 a vacancy occurred in the county representation of Cambridgeshire where Gideon's father, shortly before his death, had purchased Lord Lincoln's estates. When neither the Yorkes nor the Manners produced a candidate, Gideon offered himself, and was nominated with Lord Hardwicke's support in opposition to Thomas Brand. After an expensive canvass Brand agreed to withdraw, receiving £1,000 compensation from Gideon, whose expenses were said to have been 'not less than £5,000'.[6] In Parliament Gideon faithfully supported Administration till the fall of North. His only reported speech during this Parliament was in support of the motion that the printer be ordered to attend in the Horne libel case, 11 Feb. 1774. At the general election of 1774 Gideon was re-elected without a contest.

Early in 1780 a county meeting was called to consider a petition to the House for economical and parliamentary reform. Gideon and his fellow Member, Sir John Hynde Cotton, attended, but, since neither was enthusiastic, the meeting voted that Crisp Molineux, M.P. for King's Lynn, should present the county petition to Parliament.[7] Gideon, in his one reported speech during this Parliament,[8] told the House, 6 Apr. 1780, that

he had attended the meeting with an intention of supporting the petition to the House, recommending a faithful and economical expenditure of public money; but that he was much surprised and disappointed to find so necessary and salutary measure was accompanied with other matters, which he could by no means assent to . . . when associations and committees purposely established to control and direct the proceedings and judgment of that House, formed a part of it, he thought it his duty to express dissent.

In 1780 Gideon again stood for Cambridgeshire, but at this election the Duke of Rutland's brother and Lord Hardwicke's nephew, both recently come of age, were candidates. Gideon's property in the county was not equal to theirs, nor had he made a particularly favourable impression in the county while its representative. Some years later Hardwicke referred to Gideon's 'indolence and showing no capacity for common business' as a warning to his nephew Philip Yorke. Yorke himself wrote on 30 Apr. 1780:

It is rather remarkable to see how violently the common freeholders are prejudiced against Sir Sampson Gideon. I went to pay my compliments to a room full of them . . . and they all declared they would choose their countrymen for their Members, and not a Jew. Besides, said one, he is so great a fool, so weak a man, he is always asleep and never did any business in his life.

And on 5 May:

I wish Sir Sampson would give up, it would save an enormous deal of money, and his will be thrown away, as he stands no chance whatever of succeeding, and will in all probability meet with an unpleasant reception at the nomination meeting.

But Gideon persisted and, according to Yorke (writing to Hardwicke, 6 May), angered by rumours of a junction between his opponents,

made rather an imprudent declaration . . . to the printer of the Cambridge paper, that he had an hundred thousand pounds ready to spend upon this election. That was very imprudent and will do him infinitely more harm than good.[9]

Gideon's former colleague, Sir John Hynde Cotton, also believed that opinion was against him: 'Indeed I much wish he would give up, for these enormous sums of money spending in every town and almost village through the county have and will have a most shocking effect among us.'[10] It was even rumoured that Gideon left 'commissions with tailors . . . to make suits of clothes for freeholders, and that he lends money to indigent farmers upon their own notes of hand at two per cent'.[11] Gideon's extravagant canvass continued till polling started, and he only withdrew when at the end of the first day's poll he was far behind the other two candidates.

In November 1780 Gideon was returned unopposed for Midhurst as an Administration candidate. After the fall of North he continued to adhere to Administration; voted for Shelburne's peace preliminaries, 18 Feb. 1783, and for Fox's East India bill, 27 Nov. 1783. In January 1784 he was classed by Robinson as 'very hopeful'. At the general election he stood for Coventry on the corporation interest and was returned after an expensive contest. His only reported speech during this Parliament was in support of the Address, 24 May 1784; and he faithfully adhered to Pitt. When in July 1786 Pitt suggested to the Irish Administration that 'two or three' Englishmen should be included in the next creation of Irish peers, Gideon's name was mentioned. Thomas Orde commented to the Duke of Rutland that it was objectionable, 'but being asserted to be as good and generous a Christian as any, the best friend of his Government, Mr. Pitt is extremely anxious to gratify him'. When Pitt was informed of Rutland's 'objections and apprehensions about Sir Sampson', he expressed concern, but he had 'absolutely promised' to recommend him. 'I am afraid that Judaism will not be admitted as an obstacle to his success', wrote Orde, 12 Aug. 1786,

for Mr. Pitt observed that *he* had never been a Jew, and that he *had been* a Member for a county, and of course a good candidate for the peerage. Sir Sampson has taken a ridiculous step to remove some part of the prejudice against him. He has applied for leave to change his name to Eardley, but has made it but a *half* measure, for the cloven foot is sadly exposed by the preservation of *Sampson*.[12]

In fact Gideon did not change his name for another three years, and had to wait the same length of time for his peerage. Wraxall writes of him:[13]

Sir Sampson . . . if he was one of the richest, was likewise one of the most benevolent men who has appeared in our time. His hand was never shut to distress or closed against human suffering.

He died 25 Dec. 1824.

[1] L. S. Sutherland, 'Sampson Gideon and the Reduction of Interest, 1749-50', *Econ. Hist. Rev.*, 1946. [2] *HMC Stopford-Sackville*, i. 55. [3] Bank of England recs. [4] Bedford mss 57, f. 4. [5] Add. 32988, ff. 154-6. [6] Add. 35680, f. 286. [7] Add. 35626, f. 130. [8] Almon, xvii. 445. [9] Add. 35381, f. 202; 35379, ff. 70, 87, 91. [10] Add. 35681, f. 269. [11] P. Yorke to Hardwicke, 9 June 1780, Add. 35379, f. 120. [12] *HMC Rutland*, iii. 323, 333. [13] *Mems.* v. 121.

M.M.D.

**GILBERT, Thomas** (?1719-98), of Cotton, Staffs.

NEWCASTLE-UNDER-LYME 22 Nov. 1763–1768
LICHFIELD 1768–Dec. 1794

*b.* ?1719, 1st s. of Thomas Gilbert of Cotton. *educ.* I. Temple 1740, called 1744. *m.* (1) 24 Dec. 1761 or 27 Jan. 1762,[1] Miss Philips (*d.*22 Apr. 1770), 2s.; (2) Mary, da. of Lt.-Col. George Crauford.

Paymaster of the charity for the relief of widows of naval officers 1753–*d.*; comptroller of the great wardrobe 1763-82; chairman of ways and means 1784-94.

Bencher, I. Temple 1782, reader 1787, treasurer 1789.

'Mr. Gilbert', wrote the *Gentleman's Magazine*, (1798, p. 1146), 'to improve a small estate by the profession of the law . . . was called to the bar, but with no great success.' He held a commission in the regiment raised by Lord Gower during the '45; became Gower's land agent; and through his influence was appointed to a semi-sinecure office. Granville, 2nd Earl Gower, brought Gilbert into Parliament for Newcastle-under-Lyme, and subsequently for Lichfield; and procured for him a place at the great wardrobe.

Through his connexion with Gower he belonged to the Bedford party. His first recorded speech on a political issue was against the repeal of the Stamp Act, 21 Feb. 1766. He voted against Chatham's Administration on the land tax, 27 Feb. 1767. Neither in December 1766 nor December 1767 did Bedford ask for an office for Gilbert, nor, after the Bedfords joined Administration, is there any record of his applying for office.

Gilbert early began the work which was to become the main interest of his career. His first poor law bill, which grouped parishes into unions, passed the Commons in April 1765 but was rejected by the Lords. Further attempts to improve the poor law followed, and in 1776 he was responsible for an Act requiring overseers to make returns of sums raised by the poor rates. Canals and roads also occupied his attention; and his Act of 1773, consolidating the law relating to turnpikes, is regarded as a landmark in the history of English highway administration.

After the Bedfords took office in December 1767 Gilbert regularly voted with Administration. Until 1778 he rarely spoke on political questions, and the speech he made on 2 Mar. 1778 took the House by surprise. Concerned at 'the expenditure of public money, particularly the exorbitant contracts and abuses of office . . . he declared his resolution . . . to propose a tax of one fourth upon the incomes of all placemen'.[2] 'Lord Gower and the Duke of Bridgwater', wrote Horace Walpole,[3] 'had taken great pains to dissuade him, but he said he could not be easy in mind without proposing it.' He declared he did so 'the better to enable his Majesty to vindicate the honour and dignity of his Crown and the dominions thereunto belonging'.[4] The motion was successful in the committee of supply, but was rejected on report.

James Harris, in a letter to his son of 10 Mar. 1778,[5] calls Gilbert 'a kind of demi-courtier, demi-patriot'. On the contractors bill, 12 Feb. 1779, he was classed by Robinson as 'pro, out of town'; and he voted with Administration on the censure motion over Keppel, 3 Mar. 1779. But when Burke introduced his economical reform bill, 15 Dec. 1779,

Gilbert 'expressed the warmest approbation of Mr. Burke's propositions, and said that if he had not got the start of him he proposed to do something of the same kind himself'. In the divisions on economical reform of February and March 1780 he voted with Opposition; but on Dunning's motion, 6 Apr., and the motion against proroguing Parliament, 24 Apr., with the court. On 28 Apr. he opposed as 'indelicate' Burke's attempt to reform the civil list by Act of Parliament, 'rather wishing his Majesty would be pleased to make the necessary reformations . . . by his own authority'.[6] Of his own place in the Household he said: 'That with the assistance of the master of the wardrobe he had reformed such abuses in the office as fell under his inspection as comptroller, and had saved his Majesty £900 p.a.' When asked by Sir Philip Jennings Clerke on 26 Apr. 1781 if he intended to re-introduce his motion for a tax on places, he replied 'that he had not the most distant intention of reviving the bill'.[7]

Gilbert voted against Lowther's motion to end the war, 12 Dec. 1781. But by February 1782 his attitude towards North's Administration had changed. On 16 Feb. Sandwich, trying to win support in view of the forthcoming motion of censure against the Admiralty, wrote to Robinson:[8] 'The Duke of Bridgwater . . . has spoke to Gilbert, and has told him that he is sure those who bring him into Parliament do not approve of his absenting himself.' Gilbert voted with Administration in this division, 20 Feb.; but in those of 22 and 27 Feb., both on motions by Conway against the war, with Opposition. In the debate on Rous's motion of no confidence in North's Administration, 15 Mar., he said:[9]

> He was quite undetermined how he should vote; he did not believe all his Majesty's ministers were bad, but some of them undoubtedly were; he thought if there was a coalition of parties a good Administration might be formed that would be a means of saving this country if it was not too far gone.

He voted with Administration.

On 22 May 1781 Gilbert had proposed another bill 'for the better relief and employment of the poor', the well known 'Gilbert Act' of 1782. This gave parishes increased power to combine to build workhouses for the support of children and those unable to work; and sanctioned the practise of giving outdoor relief to the able-bodied. It was, wrote Sidney and Beatrice Webb,[10] 'the most carefully devised, the most elaborate and perhaps the most influential, for both good and evil, of . . . poor law statutes between 1601 and 1834'. Sir Gregory Page Turner said in the Commons, 9 May 1787, that Gilbert 'ought to have his name written in letters of gold, for the uncommon pains he had taken to assist the poor'.[11]

In August 1782 Gilbert was asked by Shelburne to conduct an inquiry into the value of places and pensions, for which he was paid £700:[12] 'in consequence of his report . . .', he afterwards said,[13] 'a great number of salaries had been diminished, and many sinecure places entirely abolished'. He voted for Shelburne's peace preliminaries, 18 Feb. 1783, and against Fox's East India bill, 27 Nov. 1783; was a member of the St. Alban's Tavern group which tried to bring about a union between Pitt and Fox; and supported Pitt. Much of his time in the Parliament of 1784 was taken up by his work as chairman of the committee of ways and means; but he continued his endeavours to reform the poor law both in Parliament and by pamphlets.

Gilbert died 18 Dec. 1798, 'in his 79th year'.

[1] *Gent. Mag.* 1761, p. 603; 1762, p. 45. [2] Almon, viii. 421. [3] *Last Jnls.* ii. 129–30. [4] Stockdale, viii. 95. [5] *Letters of 1st Earl of Malmesbury*, i. 380. [6] Almon, xvi. 198; xvii. 590. [7] Debrett, iii. 164. [8] Abergavenny mss. [9] Debrett, v. 465. [10] *Hist. Eng. Poor Law* i. 171. [11] Stockdale, iii. 35. [12] T29/54/114. [13] Stockdale, ii. 134.

J.B.

## GILMOUR, Sir Alexander, 3rd Bt. (c.1737–92), of Craigmillar, Edinburgh.

EDINBURGHSHIRE    12 Jan. 1761–1774

*b.* c.1737, o.s. of Sir Charles Gilmour, 2nd Bt., M.P. for Edinburghshire 1737–50, by Jean, da. of Sir Robert Sinclair, 3rd Bt., M.P. [S], of Longformacus, Berwickshire. *educ.* St. John's Camb. 1753. *m.*, *s.p.*[1] *suc.* fa. 9 Aug. 1750.
Ensign 1 Ft. Gds. 1756, lt. and capt. 1760; res. 1765.
Clerk comptroller, Board of Green Cloth 1765–75; clerk 1775–9.

Gilmour served in 1758 in the expedition against Cherbourg and St. Malo, and was captured at St. Cas, 11 Sept.;[2] on 11 Oct. he and Lord Frederick Cavendish 'arrived at court on their paroles of honour to settle the exchange of prisoners'.[3] On 21 Oct. 1759 he wrote to Newcastle asking for promotion—'I need not . . . mention . . . that staying in the army to rise in a man's own turn would be loss of time to any one who can live without it.'[4]

Informed in advance of the vacancy in Edinburghshire caused by the appointment of Lord Advocate Robert Dundas to the presidency of the court of session, he wrote, 25 May 1760, to Andrew Mitchell, his former guardian: 'I am a candidate with the entire approval of Mr. Dundas to whose protection I have been recommended by the Duke of Newcastle . . . Mr. Dalrymple, Sir William's son . . . has already declined it, so that I may very probably meet with no opposition.'[5] His unopposed return both at the by-election and the general

election was regarded as proof that the Arniston interest had been little affected by the 'clamour about militia',[6] and Gilmour took no part in the renewed militia agitation of 1762.

His application for military promotion having been rejected by the King in February 1762 as presumptuous,[7] he was subsequently recommended by Sir Henry Erskine, who proposed that he be appointed deputy adjutant in Ireland with the rank of lieutenant-colonel.[8] The negotiation apparently hung fire; and in October Gilmour, having decided to join his friends Grafton, Cornwallis and George Onslow in Opposition, applied through Grafton for the post of deputy quartermaster general in Germany. On 17 Oct. 1762 Grafton wrote to Newcastle,[9] asking for his support with Granby, the secretary at war having

promised to facilitate matters on his side as soon as he hears it would not be disagreeable to Lord Granby . . . Sir Alexander has too much honour, and too right a way of thinking to apply for assistance (though in the most material and critical point in his life) to any but those to whom he would be happy to profess his obligation.

Newcastle at once wrote to Granby, enclosing Gilmour's own application:

I have now a very great favour to ask . . . It is in favour of a most worthy young man, a very particular friend of mine, Sir Alexander Gilmour . . . You will see by the enclosed letter from the Duke of Grafton how much it would oblige him . . . My nephew and friend Charles Townshend has promised to do it if you will send him your consent.

Granby agreed; but Bute, acting on Erskine's proposal, early in November had recommended to the King Gilmour's appointment as deputy adjutant in Ireland; when, however, Gilmour voted against the peace preliminaries, the King wrote to Bute, 10 Dec. 1762:

Sir Alexander Gilmour has no right now to what he wished in Ireland, for he had no occasion to attend Parliament this day he being on guard, consequently was forced to ask my leave to attend the House this day, which was never before asked when intending to oppose Government.[10]

The only Scots M.P. whom Newcastle, in April 1763, counted among his 'sure friends', Gilmour became uneasy about the effect in Scotland of his parliamentary conduct. After the session he and Cornwallis arranged to travel north together, with letters from Newcastle to Kinnoull, Hopetoun and Dundas. Newcastle wrote to Hardwicke, 2 June 1763:

My friend, Sir Alexander Gilmour, who is as worthy a man as ever was born and is zealously and constantly with us in everything, was here with me the other day . . . My Lord Bute is so enraged with him that he has declared he shall never more come in for the county of Edinburgh where our friend the president of the session has the chief interest. Sir Alexander Gilmour owned to me that he was afraid that the reports spread in Scotland of our being enemies to Scotland and having put our opposition upon that, had made *some impression* upon our two good friends my Lord Hopetoun and the president of the session. But, however, they were so thoroughly attached to the Duke of Newcastle and my Lord Hardwicke, that letters from us by him would set all right.[11]

In July Gilmour and Cornwallis reported to Newcastle on their mission. Hopetoun and Dundas would continue their electoral support of Gilmour, but while remaining attached to Newcastle declined open opposition; no arguments could persuade Kinnoull to emerge from his retirement.[12]

After the Wilkes debate of 15 Nov. 1763, James Stuart Mackenzie wrote to William Mure:[13] 'On the second division, the most important one, Sir Alexander Gilmour voted with us . . . Gilmour only arrived after the first division was over.' But on general warrants, 6, 15 and 18 Feb. 1764, Gilmour voted with the Opposition; was a member of Wildman's Club; and was again listed among Newcastle's 'sure friends' (10 May). On 19 Mar. 1764 he seconded Lord Strange's motion for regulating Scottish banks,[14] and seems to have replaced Kinnoull as Newcastle's principal Scottish adviser. In August 1764 he was once more entrusted with the interpretation of Newcastle's views to his Scottish friends.[15]

John Dalrymple, who proposed, as soon as Gilmour left for London, to launch a campaign against him, wrote to Mackenzie, 24 Nov. 1764:[16]

Men's minds being irritated against Sir Alexander Gilmour at present, on account of his parliamentary conduct, *now is the time* to make advantage of it; a delay . . . may lose the opportunity of securing this . . . first county of Scotland to the interests of his Majesty and your family.

But Mackenzie, while anxious to turn out Gilmour, was reluctant to sponsor a candidate so indiscreet as Dalrymple.

In Parliament Gilmour made his position clear. He spoke, 29 Jan. 1765,[17] in support of Meredith's motion to declare general warrants illegal but added: 'if not a Scot [he] should say more against Wilkes'. During the negotiations of June and July 1765 Gilmour was one of Newcastle's confidants, but in the lists for places in the Rockingham Administration his name was either omitted or crossed out, and after a visit from Gilmour Newcastle wrote to Rockingham, 14 July, complaining that his recommendations were disregarded: 'Sir Alexander Gilmour is very importunate, as so are many other deserving friends.' Impatiently awaiting the outcome of Newcastle's interview with Rockingham, Gilmour wrote, 14 July:

Your Grace cannot I am sure be surprised at my being so anxious on a subject which so nearly concerns me, especially as I must again repeat that its not being done at present, will in the eyes of all men in my own country and indeed of those of many in this part of the island, imply either my having a very small share of the esteem and protection of those whose principles and conduct I not only have approved but pursued, or their having as little sense of gratitude as a just attention to those who are their real friends at all times in contradistinction to such as are only friends to themselves. If I am again to be told that what is not done to-day may be done another day, I shall only return the same answer as I did before, that I will accept of nothing from those I have reason to complain of; ill usage from those I dislike I despise; when it comes from those whose friendship I think myself entitled to, I own it hurts me, but at the same time forces me to change my opinion of those I always wished to conceive the highest opinion of and to stand as high in my idea of private integrity as public.

In the event Gilmour received the lucrative Green Cloth appointment, and throughout the Rockingham Administration continued to act as Newcastle's Scottish adviser. On Sir Henry Erskine's death he recommended Sir John Anstruther as candidate for Anstruther Burghs, and with Thomas Walpole was mainly responsible for negotiating the withdrawal of the petition against Anstruther's return.[18]

He spoke in favour of repealing the Stamp Act, and on 18 Feb. sent Newcastle a list indicating how Scottish Members had voted on the repeal.[19] Newcastle wrote to Hopetoun, 27 Feb.: 'Our good friend Sir Alexander Gilmour is always steady in the good cause and of great use to it.'[20]

His influence apparently waned on the resignation of Grafton, whose admiration for Pitt he now shared,[21] and whom he followed into the Chatham Administration. At the opening of Parliament, 11 Nov., he seconded the Address. Attentive to Scottish interests, he was particularly thanked by the committee of the Royal Burghs for his support of the Forth and Clyde canal project and for 'introducing and conducting the flax bill through the House of Commons and recommending it to the Duke of Grafton'.[22]

Re-elected in 1768, with Dundas support, Gilmour uniformly supported the Grafton Administration on Wilkes and the Middlesex election; spoke several times, and seconded Onslow's motion, 15 Apr. 1769, that Luttrell should have been returned. 'I have never shown myself but as a sincere friend of liberty and an avowed contemner of seditious and licentious men.'[23]

On Grafton's resignation he supported North but by the autumn of 1770 was heavily in debt and, aware of Henry Dundas's designs on the county, uncertain of re-election. On 26 Sept. 1770 Dundas told Gilmour that he intended to stand for Edinburghshire at the next general election.[24] Gilmour denied any desire to set up a separate interest, but hoped Dundas would not insist on contesting Edinburghshire 'if the consequence thereof should be a total exclusion of him from Parliament'. To this Dundas would agree only if an alternative constituency could not be found.

> In that case my desire not to divide the county . . . and my regard for him . . . would incline me to leave the representation of the county with him, rather than that he should be put in a situation (I mean out of Parliament) which I knew as his affairs were circumstanced would be highly inconvenient for him.

But the proposed agreement broke down, and in 1774 Gilmour engaged in a contest with Henry Dundas, who obtained North's support. Unable to find a safe alternative seat, in 1773 he applied without success for the governorship of Jamaica.[25]

In 1774, defeated in Edinburghshire, he desperately sought another seat; replaced his friend Patrick Warrender as candidate for Haddington Burghs, and at the last moment replaced James Masterton, Sir Lawrence Dundas's candidate, at Stirling Burghs. His petitions were supported by the Bute family, with whom he had been on intimate terms for some years.[26] Gilmour lost his Haddington petition on 8 May 1775 and withdrew his Stirling petition on 5 Feb. 1776. In September 1776 North failed to persuade Lord Irwin to bring him in for Horsham.[27] Deprived of parliamentary immunity, Gilmour went abroad to escape his creditors, and in 1779 lost his place at the Board of Green Cloth. In 1780 and 1781 he received occasional doles from secret service funds, amounting in all to £500.[28]

On 29 July 1782 he wrote to Shelburne asking to be recommended to the King for relief from his 'dreadful situation', the details of which Henry Dundas, who delivered the letter, was authorized to explain.[29] And on 30 Aug. he wrote to the King:[30]

> Your Majesty's known humanity and benevolence will . . . plead my excuse for presuming humbly to make known to your Majesty the very distressed situation in which I at present feel myself, owing most assuredly, in the first instance to my own folly and imprudence, of which . . . I have sufficiently repented and for which I hope your Majesty will think I have been sufficiently punished, by having been four years banished in solitude from the society of the world. And before returning to it, I made every compensation to my creditors which the settlement of my estate would permit of . . . I hope after having had the honour of serving your Majesty nine years in the Guards and fourteen at the Green Cloth . . . Your Majesty will be graciously pleased to take my melancholy situation into your consideration . . .

His plea seems to have been in vain; he was obliged to live abroad, mainly at Boulogne, for the rest of his life. George Dempster wrote to Sir Adam Fergusson, 28 June 1784:[31]

> I thank you for enabling me to satisfy poor Sir Alexander Gilmour's curiosity [probably on Edinburgh election affairs], the only one of his wants that I fear we shall ever be able to satisfy. I am sorry to say the very generous exertion of his friends to extricate him from difficulties in this island have only served to involve him in new ones on the Continent. He furnishes a strong confirmation of the truth of the maxim that all the noble virtues are often useless unless accompanied by that dirty one, economy.

He died at Boulogne, 27 Dec. 1792.

[1] For evidence as to his marriage, see *Gent. Mag.* 1780, p. 102. [2] Fortescue, *Hist. Army*, ii. 349. [3] *Gent. Mag.* 1758, p. 501. [4] Add. 32897, f. 275. [5] Add. 6860, f. 286. [6] Hardwicke to Dundas, 31 Aug. 1760, G. W. T. Omond, *Arniston Mems.* 165. [7] Sedgwick, 84. [8] Add. 38339, f. 190. [9] Add. 32943, f. 272. [10] Ibid. ff. 301, 355-6; 32945, f. 13; Sedgwick, 154, 173. [11] Add. 32948, f. 140; 32949, ff. 1, 9-10. [12] Add. 32949, ff. 412, 436, 447. [13] *Caldwell Pprs.* ii (1), p. 199. [14] Harris's 'Debates'. [15] Add. 32961, f. 298. [16] *Caldwell Pprs.* ii (1), pp. 281, 283. [17] Harris's 'Debates'; Newdigate's 'Debates'. [18] Add. 32967, ff. 75, 390, 417; 32969, f. 209; 32974, f. 187. [19] Add. 32973, f. 321; Add. 32974, f. 24; Walpole, *Mems. Geo. III*, ii. 204. [20] Add. 32974, f. 101. [21] Add. 6860, ff. 288, 290, 207. [22] *Recs. Convention Royal Burghs* 1759-79, pp. 243, 269, 272. [23] Cavendish's 'Debates', Egerton 219, p. 224. [24] *Arniston Mems.* 183. [25] *Corresp. Sir R. M. Keith*, i. 371. [26] *Caldwell Pprs.* ii (2), p. 195; Boswell, *Private Pprs.* x. 202, 207. [27] Walpole, *Last Jnls.* i. 572. [28] Royal archives, Windsor. [29] Lansdowne mss. [30] Fortescue, *Corresp. Geo. III*, vi. 118-19. [31] Jas. Fergusson, *Letters of Geo. Dempster to Sir Adam Fergusson*, 133.

E.H.-G.

**GIPPS, George** (c.1728–1800), of Harbledown, nr. Canterbury.

CANTERBURY 1780–1796, 12 May 1797–13 Feb. 1800

*b.* c.1728, 3rd s. of John Gipps, staymaker, of Ashford, Kent by his w. Sarah née Flint. *m.* (1) 2 Aug. 1755, Elizabeth Johanna (*d.*1775), da. of John Roberts of Harbledown, *s.p.*; (2) 27 Nov. 1780, Sarah (*d.*2 June 1789), da. of William Stanton, Spanish merchant, 1s.; (3) 18 Jan. 1792, Elizabeth, da. of Thomas Lawrence, M.D., 1s.

Gipps, according to the *English Chronicle* in 1780, was originally 'an apothecary in the city of Canterbury, and not at all distinguished either for the extent of his practice, or the affluence of his fortune'. Later 'he relinquished pharmacy and became a very extensive and fortunate speculator in the hop trade';[1] in 1784 he appears in Bailey's *British Directory* as a hop merchant; but by 1790 had given up the trade and entered banking as partner in the firm of Gipps, Simmons, and Gipps of Canterbury.

In 1780 he stood for Canterbury on an independent interest in opposition to Lord Newhaven, and was head of the poll. He voted against North's Administration; supported Shelburne's peace preliminaries, 18 Feb. 1783; voted for parliamentary reform, 7 May 1783; and against Fox's East India bill, 27 Nov. 1783. Returned in 1784 after a contest, he supported Pitt; but in 1788 signed the third party manifesto. There is no record of his having spoken before 1790.

He died 13 Feb. 1800.

¹ *Gent. Mag.* 1800, p. 190.

J.B.

**GISBORNE, John** (?1717–79), of Derby, and Yoxall, Staffs.

DERBY    30 Jan. 1775–8 Feb. 1776

*b.* ?1717, o.s. of Thomas Gisborne of Derby by Temperance, da. of Robert Packer, M.P., of Shillingford, Berks. *m.* Anne, da. of William Bateman of Derby, 2s. 2da. *suc.* fa. 9 Dec. 1760.

Gisborne came of an old-established Derby family and possessed an influence in the town which he seems for years to have exerted on behalf of the Cavendishes. In 1775 he stood for the town, probably with Cavendish support, in opposition to D. P. Coke; was returned, but unseated as a result of petitions complaining of his 'undue influence' over the mayor. No vote or speech by him is reported.

He died 13 Feb. 1779, aged 62.

M.M.D.

**GLANVILLE, William** (c.1686–1766), of St. Clere, nr. Sevenoaks, Kent.

HYTHE    22 Feb. 1728–19 Oct. 1766

*b.* c.1686, 5th s. of George Evelyn, M.P., by his 3rd w. Frances, da. of Andrew Bromehall. *m.* (1) c.1718, Frances (*d.*1719), da. and h. of William Glanville, M.P.,¹ 1da., who m. 1742 Hon. Edward Boscawen (q.v.); (2) bef. 1733, Bridget, da. and h. of Hugh Raymond of Langley, Kent, 2s. 3da. c.1718 took the name of Glanville. His da. Sarah m. Chase Price (q.v.). Commr. of revenue in Ireland, c.1735–47.

Returned for Hythe by the Duke of Dorset, Glanville voted regularly with Administration. Little is known of him after 1754, and he appears in no division list after 1761. In 1761 he was included by Newcastle among those to whom the whip was to be sent, but without indicating through whom it was to go; does not appear in Fox's list of Members favourable to the peace preliminaries; and was classed 'doubtful' by Rockingham in July 1765. He died 19 Oct. 1766.

¹ H. Evelyn, *Hist. Evelyn Fam.* 220.

A.N.N.

**GLANVILLE**, *see also* **EVELYN, William** (*d.*1813)

**GLOVER, Richard** (?1712–85), of Exchange Alley, London.

WEYMOUTH AND MELCOMBE REGIS    1761–1768

*b.* ?1712, s. of Richard Glover, a Hamburg merchant of London, by Mary, da. of Richard West, London

merchant, sis. of Richard West, M.P., lawyer and playwright. *educ.* Cheam, Surr. *m.* (1) 21 May 1737, Hannah Nunn (div. Feb. 1756), 2s.; (2) unascertained.

As a young man Glover became an active member of his father's firm in the City; but at the same time pursued his own literary interests, wrote poetry, and dabbled in politics. He early became connected with Cobham and his 'cubs'—Lyttelton, the Grenvilles, and Pitt; and when in 1737 he published an epic poem *Leonidas* (dedicated to Lord Cobham) it was enthusiastically received by the Opposition, who praised Glover for his 'patriot' sentiments. Glover was active in stirring up City opinion against Walpole; in 1740 opposed his candidate for lord mayor, and in 1742 drew up the merchants' complaints against the Administration's inadequate protection of trade. These, according to the 1st Earl of Egmont, he 'summed up [at the bar of the House] in a remarkable good speech of two hours long'.¹ Glover's activities between 1742 and 1757 are related in his *Memoirs* which, though often inaccurate on political events and full of vastly inflated self-importance, at least give an indication of his activities and opinions during these years. He appears to have continued with his Opposition friends after Walpole's fall, but writes that by 1744 he had realized that Pitt, Lyttelton, and others were 'a party founded on the base desire of pecuniary emoluments, partly on the more extensive views of procuring the whole ministerial power to themselves'. And after they joined with Henry Pelham: 'I had intimacies to a degree of friendship with most of them; but as these intimacies were contracted on the public account, when that cause was deserted by them, their society was abandoned by me.' He was by this time in financial difficulties.

> Forsaken by fortune [he writes] yet in the day of distress, I returned not to those powerful friends who were really willing and able to assist me: but I opened a new scene, repaired my losses, and maintained my independence.²

It is uncertain when Glover re-entered politics. He states that in 1754 he co-operated with Charles Townshend on 'a plan of operation in North America', which was put before Newcastle;³ and in October 1755 it was reported that he was being used by Leicester House to 'stir up a clamour in the City' against the Hanoverian subsidies.⁴ John Yorke, writing to his brother Lord Royston on 1 Nov. 1755, called Glover 'Dodington's trumpeter'.⁵ Glover himself writes that he knew that Dodington was 'trimming between Pitt and Fox, though assuring me that he would unite with no cabal but stand on his own bottom, and publicly declare his sentiments unbiassed. This I encouraged, wishing sincerely well to a man whose company gave me pleasure.' He records that his reconciliation with his former friends, the Grenvilles and Pitt, took place during the ministerial crisis of 1756: 'It was now twelve years at least', he writes, 'since my own reserved behaviour and unpliant principles had kept me remote from this my once intimate and most favoured society. They received me with embraces.'[6] As a result he drew up a memorandum for Pitt about conditions of accepting office, particularly the establishment of a strong militia. Glover was strongly opposed to the country becoming involved in a German war, and appears to have believed that Pitt felt the same.

After the accession of George III Dodington noted in his diary that though Glover 'was full of admiration of Lord Bute', and 'applauded his conduct and the King's', he was 'not determined about political connexions', but 'I believe he will come to us'.[7] At the general election Glover was returned for Weymouth and Melcombe Regis on Dodington's interest. Disapproval of the German war was the theme of one of his first speeches, 10 Dec. 1761, described by Horace Walpole as 'most heroic fustian but not without good argument';[8] by Newcastle as 'long and dull';[9] and as 'elaborate and to the purpose' by Harris who adds: 'being delivered too slowly, and filled with a multiplicity of dates, numbers of ships, of men etc. it was not heard as it deserved, and would have made a better pamphlet than it did a speech'. Glover seems to have been known for his long speeches. James West wrote to Newcastle on 10 Dec. 1761: 'Mr. Glover is now up and may speak an hour.'[10]

Glover subscribed £20,000 to the loan of 12 millions for the year 1762, in which Henry Fox and his friends did so well. Newcastle, on 20 June 1762, included Glover with Salvador and 'Mr. Fox's particular friends' as 'the only persons they [the Administration] have in the City'. Glover supported the peace preliminaries, and on 10 Dec. 1762, made 'an elaborate speech . . . proving by many facts that our trade had suffered by war'. Harris comments: 'it was a well drawn performance, and full of more matter than could well be comprehended in one hearing'. Glover was admitted to a large share of the subscription to the Government loan of 1763. According to Sir Francis Dashwood he had £60,000 and had 'got a great deal by it'.[11] But in March 1763 Glover joined in the Opposition clamour against the cider tax. Charles Jenkinson reported to Bute on 11 Mar.:[12]

Glover got up meaning to be against the tax, and made the strangest enthusiastic speech against excises in general I ever heard . . . the House was in a laugh;

he was the only person serious in it. Not a word however of what he said had any relation to cider.

He appears to have drafted the City of London's petition against the tax; and on 24 Mar. the King wrote to Bute:[13]

Mr. Glover's conduct now exceeds the bounds that his opinion of my dear friend ought to keep him; and his having wrote so inflammatory a petition as the minutes of yesterday's debate represents gives me much reason to believe that the desire of popularity will make him a tool of Opposition.

In fact, Glover seems to have followed an independent line. He was classed by Jenkinson in the autumn of 1763 as 'pro', but appeared as voting with Opposition in all the extant division lists on general warrants, February 1764. He wrote to Grenville, 16 Feb. 1764:[14]

Give me leave to say with some confidence that Sir William Meredith's motion will pass, unless you snatch that occasion out of the hands of Opposition by an amendment, and secure to yourself all the credit which else will remain with them.

And he concluded by suggesting an amendment to the effect that general warrants were illegal. He again voted with Opposition on the following day, but was counted by Jenkinson as a friend. No other votes by him are reported. Newcastle (10 May 1764), and Rockingham (July 1765 and November 1766) both class him as 'doubtful'. He remained on friendly terms with Grenville after the latter left office, and was classed 'Bedford and Grenville' by Townshend in January 1767.

Glover did not stand again in 1768, and seems henceforth to have played no part in City or national politics, but rather to have concentrated on his own commercial interests. On the failure of the Ayr bank in June 1772 he took a prominent part in settling its affairs. In March and April 1774 he appeared before the House of Commons as an agent for the English linen merchants, and in 1775 supported a petition from West Indian merchants.

Glover died 25 Nov. 1785.

[1] *HMC Egmont Diary*, iii. 258. [2] *Mems. of a Celebrated Lit. and Pol. Figure.* [3] Ibid. For the plan see Add. 32736, ff. 510–13. [4] Add. 35374, ff. 126–7. [5] Ibid. f. 131. [6] *Mems.* [7] *Diary*, 20 Dec. 1761. [8] *Mems. Geo. III*, i. 89. [9] Add. 32932, ff. 107–8. [10] Ibid. ff. 109–10. [11] Harris's memoranda, 23 Mar., 22 May 1763. [12] Bodl. North mss. [13] Sedgwick, 204. [14] *Grenville Pprs.* ii. 265.

M.M.D.

**GLYN, Sir Richard** (1711–73), of Gaunts, nr. Wimborne, Dorset.[1]

LONDON        30 Nov. 1758–1768
COVENTRY      1 Dec. 1768–1 Jan. 1773

*bap.* 13 June 1711, 2nd s. of Robert Glyn, drysalter, by Ann Maynard, niece of Sir William Lewen, ld. mayor of London 1717–18. *educ.* poss. Westminster. *m.* (1) 8 June 1736, Susanna (*d.* 5 Feb. 1751), da. and

h. of George Lewen of Ewell, Surr., 3s.; (2) 23 Mar. 1754, Elizabeth, da. of Sir Robert Carr, silk mercer, of Ludgate Hill, 3s. *suc.* fa. 1746; kntd. 22 Nov. 1752; *cr.* Bt. 29 Sept. 1759.

Alderman of London 1750-*d.*, sheriff 1752-3, ld. mayor 1758-9; original director, Equitable Life Ass. Soc. 1762, vice pres. 1762-4, pres. 1764; director, Million Bank 1764.

Glyn at first followed his father's profession as a drysalter or oilman, and carried on a successful business in Hatton Garden. At the end of 1753 he entered into partnership with Joseph Vere, banker, and with Thomas Hallifax (q.v.), chief clerk at Martin's bank, and founded the banking firm of Vere, Glyn, and Hallifax in Lombard Street.[2]

Glyn unsuccessfully contested London at the general election of 1754. In 1758-9, as lord mayor, he led the City in support of the Administration, and the same year was returned unopposed for London at a by-election. In 1761 he came out fourth on the poll. Lady Grey wrote to Lord Royston after the election: 'I have heard it supposed that when Beckford was secure himself, he made common cause with, and assisted Sir Richard.' In Bute's list he is marked as 'Tory' with a query, and as 'Pitt'. He was among the aldermen who in October 1761 supported a proposal in common council that Pitt should be thanked for his 'eminent and great services'.[3] But early in December 1762 he appears in Fox's list of Members favourable to the peace preliminaries; and he did not vote with the minority on 9 and 10 Dec. Jenkinson in the autumn of 1763 classed him as 'pro'; he was absent from the division of 6 Feb. 1764 on general warrants, but voted with Opposition in the divisions of 15 and 18 Feb. The political leaders did not know what to make of him: he was classed as 'doubtful' by Newcastle on 10 May 1764, by Rockingham in July 1765, and by Townshend in January 1767; but as 'Tory' by Rockingham in November 1766, and by Newcastle, on 2 Mar. 1767. He voted with Opposition on the land tax, 27 Feb. 1767.

When at the general election of 1768 Glyn again stood for the City in opposition to Wilkes and Barlow Trecothick, his former colleagues, Beckford, Harley, and Ladbroke, canvassing jointly, seem to have formally dissociated themselves from him. In a fierce election campaign he was attacked as a follower of Bute, and ridiculed as 'a man of heavy temper, rotundity of form, and vacuity of look, and therefore not a proper person to represent the City of London in Parliament'; while his speech before the livery was condescendingly reported: 'There was not much in what he said, but upon the whole it was very well, and exactly what might be expected from such a good-natured little man.'[4] Glyn was defeated by a narrow margin. In December 1768 he

contested the expensive borough of Coventry with the support of the Treasury in opposition to the corporation interest, and was returned by a large majority. In Parliament he voted with Administration over the expulsion of Wilkes, 3 Feb. 1769, and the Middlesex election, 15 Apr. and 8 May 1769; he does not appear in any of the minority lists 1769-1772 and was listed by Robinson as 'pro, present' in both his surveys on the royal marriage bill in March 1772. Glyn's only reported speech was on 27 Feb. 1771 when a stranger found voting in a division claimed to know him; he replied 'I knew him at the general election . . . originally a merchant of Bermuda.'[5]

In 1772 Glyn's bank was seriously affected by the Ayr bank failure and stopped payment on 22 June. He and his partners were able to restore their credit, and re-opened on 6 Aug. But when Glyn died on 1 Jan. 1773, his death, so soon after the failure of 1772, gave rise to rumours of suicide, which were denied in the press by his physician.

[1] We are indebted to Mr. S. W. Shelton, archivist of Glyn Mills & Co., for biographical information about this Member. [2] R. Fulford, *Glyn's, 1753-1953*. [3] Add. 35376, f. 47; 32929, f. 442. [4] *Gazetteer*, 16, 19 Mar. 1768. [5] Cavendish's 'Debates', Egerton 225, f. 137.

M.M.D.

## GLYNN, John (1722-79), of Cardinham, Cornw.

MIDDLESEX 14 Dec. 1768-16 Sept. 1779

*bap.* 3 Aug. 1722, 2nd surv. s. of William Glynn of Cardinham by Rose, da. of John Prideaux of Padstow, Cornw. *educ.* Exeter, Oxf. 1738; poss. Leyden 1746; M. Temple 1741, called 1748. *m.* 21 July 1763, Susanna Margaret, da. of Sir John Oglander, 4th Bt., of Nunwell, I.o.W., 3s. 1da. *suc.* nephew at Cardinham 1762.

Sergeant-at-law 1763; recorder of London 1772-*d.*

Glynn was a radical both in politics and religion, a member of the Essex St. group of Unitarians and of the Bill of Rights Society. He was counsel for the printers of the *North Briton* in 1764, for Wilkes in 1768, and for James Townsend in 1772. 'A most ingenious, solid, pleasing man', wrote Chatham on their first meeting in 1770,[1] 'and the very spirit of the constitution itself'; and Horace Walpole described him as 'a man of unexceptionable character'.[2]

In 1768 he stood for Newtown, I.o.W., on the Worsley–Oglander interest, but was defeated. Encouraged by Dunning and Shelburne, with whom he had been connected since the early 60s, he decided to petition.[3] But before the case could be considered a vacancy occurred in Middlesex; and Glynn, sponsored by Wilkes, was elected after a riotous and expensive contest.

He made his first speech in the House, on Wilkes's petition, 23 Jan. 1769. Six other speeches are reported for that session, all connected with Wilkes's case; and in the conduct of this difficult and intricate business he acquitted himself well. Walpole wrote of the debate of 27 Jan. that he 'spoke with a clearness, argument, decency, and propriety that was applauded by both sides'; and of his speech on Wilkes's expulsion, 3 Feb.: 'Serjeant Glynn gained great fame by the candour of his conduct on the whole proceeding'.[4] He was sincere, earnest, and disinterested; and though so closely connected with Wilkes, they had little in common and never became friends.

On 6 Dec. 1770 Glynn introduced a motion to inquire into the administration of justice, and he was a member of the committee which drew up the bill of 1772 reducing the number of capital offences. Nearly all his interventions in debate were on constitutional questions or radical motions: and only twice (28 Apr. 1774 and 25 Apr. 1776) is he recorded as having spoken on America. After 1774 his health deteriorated, and his speeches were less frequent. In the debate on Wilkes's motion concerning the Middlesex election, 22 Feb. 1775, 'he spoke in great pain, being at that time afflicted with a severe fit of the gout';[5] and the *Public Ledger* wrote of him in 1779: 'His ill health prevents him from seconding his colleague.' He died 16 Sept. 1779.

[1] *Chatham Corresp.* iii. 483. [2] *Mems. Geo. III*, iii. 190. [3] Gibbon to his stepmother, 18 Apr. 1768. [4] *Mems. Geo. III*, iii. 211, 219. [5] Almon, iii. 494.

J.B.

**GLYNNE, Sir John,** 6th Bt. (1712–77), of Hawarden Castle, Flints.

FLINTSHIRE                    1741–1747
FLINT BOROUGHS   28 Nov. 1753–1 June 1777

*b.* 3 Jan. 1712, 4th s. of Sir Stephen Glynne, 3rd Bt., by Sophia, da. and coh. of Sir Edward Evelyn, 1st Bt., of Long Ditton. *educ.* Queen's, Oxf. 1730. *m.* (1) 23 Jan. 1732,[1] Honoria (*d.*10 Feb. 1769), da. and h. of Henry Conway of Bodrhyddan, Flints., 6s. 8da.; (2) 27 Mar. 1772, Augusta Beaumont, governess to his children, *s.p. suc.* bro. as 6th Bt. Aug. 1730; built Hawarden Castle 1752.
Sheriff, Flints. 1751–2.

After Glynne re-entered Parliament in 1753 Mrs. E. Conway wrote to George Grenville, 4 Jan. 1754:[2]

I don't believe Sir John had any thoughts of standing before Mr. Williams' death gave him so fair an opportunity, for he has always declared he would have nothing to do in a contested election . . . I have a great esteem for Sir John, both as a relation and a deserving man, and one that I think won't inflame but endeavour to keep all parties in peace.

An agreement between Sir Thomas Mostyn and Glynne secured for them uncontested elections in county and boroughs. In Newcastle's list of candidates in March–April 1754 Glynne is marked 'Tory, moderate'; and in the lists drawn up after the general election he is included among 'Tories, against'. He was a frequent speaker in the House, and even for the very poorly reported Parliament of 1754–61 there are a few traces of his intervention, then as later on the orthodox Tory lines. Thus Roger Kenyon reported on 25 Feb. 1758 to Lloyd Kenyon: 'John Glynne has speeched it away last week in support of the triennial bill, and they say pretty sensibly, but the motion was rejected again by a great majority.' And again, on 25 June 1759: 'The behaviour of Sir J. Glynne raised my indignation not a little . . . He is, I find, a great condemner of Mr. Pitt, and little better than a chattering caff [sic].'[3]

He continued in the new reign the pursuit of lost causes of the Tory type, with a peculiar anti-Pitt twist of his own. On 1 Dec. 1761 he

moved for a book to register alphabetically the qualifications; insinuated they might be withdrawn; hinted the difficulty of inspecting them as they stood.[4]

When on 11 Dec. Pitt's friends moved for the Spanish papers, Glynne spoke against it:

That that time twenty years had been famous for calling for papers; with intention then to condemn a minister; now it was with a view to applauding one. A paper had been produced at that time which the King of Prussia never forgave. Himself had never seen any benefits arise from motions of that sort.[5]

Glynne is included in Fox's list of Members favourable to the peace preliminaries, December 1762; was counted by Jenkinson as an Administration supporter in the autumn of 1763; and was pro-Administration in his speeches. He is reported by Jenkinson to have spoken in favour of North's resolution against privilege for seditious libel, 24 Nov. 1763,[6] though Harris describes his intervention as a 'little burlesque' with no bearing on the debate. And reporting the debate of 6 Feb. 1764 on Wilkes's complaint of breach of privilege, Harris notes merely that Glynne 'gets up and jokes', though Walpole included him with Members who 'debated the question for the court'. Glynne was anxious for the Commons to reconsider the marriage bill, which he considered 'had separated man and wife, and instead of preventing clandestine marriages, had increased them';[7] and when on 9 Feb. 1764 he re-introduced the matter, Harris reports, apparently with surprise, that Glynne was 'not amiss nor ludicrous', and on 6 Mar. made 'a set speech part of it very well, where he addressed first the young men and then the old ones, showing how far each of them were interested against the bill'. During the debate of 11 May 1765 on the Regency Glynne spoke on the side of Administration. In Rockingham's list of July 1765 he was classed as an opponent; and he spoke and voted against the repeal of the Stamp Act, 21–22 Feb. 1766. He voted against Administration on the land tax, 27 Feb. 1767; spoke and voted with Administration on the expulsion of Wilkes, 3 Feb. 1769, and again voted with Administration on the Middlesex election, 15 Apr. 1769. In Robinson's first survey drawn up for the royal marriage bill, March 1772, Glynne is marked 'pro, sent to'; in the second, of 9 Mar., as 'pro, present'; and on 11 Mar. he spoke in support of the bill.[8] After that no other vote or speech by him is reported. He died 1 June 1777.

[1] *Genealogists' Mag.* vii. 69; *Gent Mag.* gives 17 Aug. 1731. [2] Grenville mss (JM). [3] *HMC Kenyon*, 495–6. [4] Harris's 'Debates'. [5] Walpole, *Mems. Geo. III*, i. 91. [6] Namier, *Add. & Corr. to Fortescue*, 85. [7] Harris's 'Debates', 27 Jan. 1764. [8] Cavendish's 'Debates', Egerton 236, p. 177.

P.D.G.T.

## GODDARD, Ambrose (?1727–1815), of Swindon, Wilts.

WILTSHIRE 21 Aug. 1772–1806

*b.* ?1727, 3rd s. of Ambrose Goddard by Elizabeth, da. of Ambrose Awdry of Seend, Wilts., and bro. of Thomas Goddard (q.v.). *educ.* Winchester 1743–5. *m.* 16 Aug. 1776, Sarah, da. and h. of Rev. Thomas Williams of Pilrowth, Carm., 3s. 7da. *suc.* bro. 1770.

The earlier part of Goddard's life was, according to the *Gentleman's Magazine* (1815, ii. 275), 'passed in mercantile engagements in Lisbon, till, by the death of his elder brother, he succeeded to the paternal inheritance in Wiltshire'. Until 1772 he was agent at Lisbon for the Post Office.

In 1772 he was nominated by the Wiltshire gentry 'not for the affluence of fortune, or pre-eminence of talents, but . . . the probity of his principles and character',[1] and was returned by a large majority after a fierce contest against Henry Herbert. The election was said to have cost £20,000;[2] a subscription opened for Goddard brought in £8,250, of which he donated £1,000.[3] In Parliament he consistently opposed North's Administration; voted for Shelburne's peace preliminaries, 18 Feb. 1783, and for Fox's East India bill, 27 Nov. 1783. In January 1784 he was classed by Robinson as 'very hopeful'. He was a member of the St. Alban's Tavern group which attempted to bring about a union between Pitt and Fox; after this failed he 'generally though not invariably'[4] supported Pitt, his only recorded votes being with Opposition on Richmond's fortifications plan, 27 Feb. 1786, and with Administra-

tion over the Regency. The *Gentleman's Magazine* states that Goddard's 'diffident habits and the state of his nerves precluded him from public speaking', and no speech by him is reported before 1790.

He died 19 June 1815, aged 88.

[1] *Gent. Mag.* [2] *Wilts. Mag.* xxi. 328. [3] Awdry mss, Wilts. RO. [4] *Gent. Mag.*

M.M.D.

## GODDARD, Thomas (1722–70), of Swindon, Wilts.

WILTSHIRE 24 Mar. 1767–12 Aug. 1770

*bap.* 6 Mar. 1722, 1st s. of Ambrose Goddard of Swindon, and bro. of Ambrose Goddard (q.v.). *educ.* M. Temple 1742. *unm.* *suc.* fa. 1755.

Goddard belonged to an old Wiltshire gentry family, and a kinsman of his had represented the county in the Parliament of 1722. He himself was returned unopposed for Wiltshire in 1767 and 1768. All his reported votes were with Opposition. There is no record of his having spoken in the House. He died 12 Aug. 1770.

M.M.D.

## GODOLPHIN, Francis (1706–85), of Baylis, Bucks.

HELSTON 1741–17 Jan. 1766

*bap.* 2 Nov. 1706, o.s. of Rev. Henry Godolphin, dean of St. Paul's 1707–26 and a yr. bro. of Sidney, 1st Earl of Godolphin, by Mary, da. and h. of Sidney Godolphin, gov. of Scilly Isles. *educ.* Eton 1718–21; Queen's, Oxf. 1723. *m.* (1) 18 Feb. 1734, Lady Barbara Bentinck (*d.* 13 Apr. 1736), da. of William, 1st Earl of Portland, *s.p.*; (2) 28 May 1747, Lady Anne Fitzwilliam, da. of John, 2nd Earl Fitzwilliam [I], *s.p. suc.* fa. 1733; and cos. as 2nd Baron Godolphin 17 Jan. 1766.
    Recorder, Helston 1766–*d.*; lt. gov. Scilly Isles 1739–66, gov. 1766–*d.*

Godolphin sat on the family interest at Helston. Under George II he counted as a Whig, and Dupplin in 1754 classed him as a country gentleman supporting Administration. In Bute's list of the Parliament of 1761 he is marked 'Newcastle' and then 'convert'—presumably he went over to Bute. But he appears neither in Fox's list of Members favourable to the peace preliminaries nor in any list of those voting against them. In the autumn of 1763 Jenkinson classed him as 'doubtful'; he voted against general warrants, 15 and 18 Feb. 1764; was classed by Newcastle as a 'sure friend', 10 May 1764; and by Rockingham as 'pro', July 1765. There is no record of his having spoken in the Commons, nor was he prominent in the Lords.

He died 25 May 1785.

J.B.

## GOLDSWORTHY, Philip (c.1737–1801).

WILTON    2 Feb. 1785–Jan. 1788, 15 Feb. 1794–
4 Jan. 1801

*b.* c.1737, s. of Burrington Goldsworthy, consul at
Leghorn and subsequently Cadiz, by Philippia, da.
of Capt. Philip Vanbrugh, R.N., yst. bro. of Sir John
Vanbrugh the architect. *educ.* Westminster 1749–
c.1754; Trinity, Camb. 1755; L. Inn. 1755. *unm.*
*suc.* to estates of his aunt Martha, wid. of Francis
Gashry (q.v.), 1777.

Cornet, 1 Drag. 1756, lt. 1760, capt. 1768, maj.
1776, lt.-col. 1779; col. 1784; maj.-gen. 1793; col.
1 Drag. 1794–*d*; lt.-gen. 1799.
Equerry 1779 and clerk marshal 1788 to the King.

Goldsworthy served with Lord Herbert in the
regiment commanded by Lord Pembroke, and was
returned for Wilton when Herbert was appointed
vice-chamberlain. 'Though Goldsworthy was very
proper for the time', wrote Pembroke to Herbert on
21 Sept. 1787,[1] 'I do not of course mean him to be
the fixed Member here.' Herbert now wished to
return to Parliament, and Goldsworthy, though
anxious to remain in the House, was prepared to
vacate his seat. Herbert approached Pitt, who
appeared willing to bring in Goldsworthy when a
vacancy occurred, and was himself ready to wait till
that took place. But no other constituency was found
and in January 1788 Goldsworthy vacated his seat.
He was returned again in 1794 when Herbert succeeded to the peerage. There is no record of his
speaking in the House, and his only known vote
during his first term in Parliament was for Administration on the Duke of Richmond's fortifications
plan, 27 Feb. 1786.

Goldsworthy was for many years an equerry in
the royal household, 'warmly and faithfully attached
to the King and all the royal family'.[2] Fanny Burney
described him as 'a man of little cultivation or literature, but delighting in a species of dry humour'
which greatly entertained the King; he was 'the wag
professed among the equerries', and privileged to
say what he pleased. When 'perfectly at his ease,
pleased with every individual in his company, and
completely in good humour' he would joke about
court life:

> After all one's labours, riding, and walking, and stand-
> ing, and bowing—what a life it is! Well! it's honour!
> that's one comfort; it's all honour! royal honour!—
> one has the honour to stand till one has not a foot left;
> and to ride till one's stiff, and to walk till one's ready
> to drop,—and then one makes one's lowest bow, d'ye
> see, and blesses one's self with joy for the honour.

But she also describes him as a man of moods whose
'sport and humour . . . ceases wholly if the smallest
thing happens to disconcert him'. A brother officer,
Major J. Floyd, called him 'a very good fellow' and
'a most excellent officer'.[3]

He died 4 Jan. 1801.

[1] *Pembroke Pprs.* ii. 360. [2] *Diary and Letters of Mme D'Arblay*, ed.
Dobson, iii. 64–65, 258. [3] *Pembroke Pprs.* i. 348; ii. 66.

M.M.D.

## GOODRICKE, Henry (1741–84), of York.

LYMINGTON    4 Dec. 1778–1780

*b.* at Boulogne, 6 Apr. 1741, o.s. of Sir John Goodricke, 5th Bt.(q.v.). *m.* 31 Jan. 1761, Levina Benjamina,
da. of Peter Sessler of Namur (and continued for some
years to live at Groningen in Holland), 3s. 4da.

Goodricke was returned unopposed on the Burrard interest at Lymington. He was listed as 'pro,
present' on the contractors bill, 12 Feb. 1779; on
22 Feb. spoke for Barré's motion for limiting the
time of service of the soldier, but again voted with
Administration on Keppel, 3 Mar. 1779. On 28 Apr.
1779 he supported the bill for granting relief to
Dissenters, and spoke of 'the necessity and sound
policy of freedom in religion; there ought to be no
tie on men's professions of faith'. He voted with
Opposition for an account of pensions, 21 Feb. 1780,
supporting the motion 'with some very judicious and
pertinent observations', and henceforth continued
in opposition till he left Parliament.[1]

He died *v.p.* 9 July 1784.

[1] Almon, xii. 353; xvii. 138.

M.M.D.

## GOODRICKE, Sir John, 5th Bt. (1708–89), of
Ribston, nr. Knaresborough, and Bramham Park,
Yorks.

PONTEFRACT              1774–1780
RIPON              21 Dec. 1787–3 Aug. 1789

*b.* 20 May 1708, 1st s. of Sir Henry Goodricke, 4th
Bt., by Mary, da. of Tobias Jenkyns of Grimston,
Yorks., and gd.-da. of Charles, 1st Duke of Bolton.
*educ.* Trinity, Camb. 1725. *m* 28 Sept. 1731, Mary
Benson (formerly Johnson), illegit. da. of Robert
Benson, 1st and last Baron of Bingley (of the 1st
creation), 1s. 2da. *suc.* fa. 21 July 1738; and in 1773
to Bramham Park estate of George Fox Lane (q.v.),
1st Baron Bingley (of the 2nd creation), who had m.
a legit. da. of Robert, Lord Bingley.

Resident at the court of Brussels 1750, but did not
go there. Appointed minister to Sweden 1758, he
remained at Copenhagen till admitted to Sweden in
Apr. 1764, and was there as envoy 1764–73.

Goodricke relinquished his Stockholm appointment on succeeding to the Bramham Park estate, and
in 1774 successfully contested Pontefract on the
joint Walsh and Galway interests. He supported
Administration on the American war. Writing on
16 July 1775 to Lord Hardwicke on the flourishing
state of the north country, he described himself as
'one of those singular persons who think we can do

much better without the Americans than they can without us, and if artificial riots are not stirred up among the people, they will not suffer for want of work merely on account of the continental colonies not taking our goods'; and he concluded that 'English ministers never gave themselves much trouble to justify the national conduct against mis-representation, so that the world is always pre-judiced against us: it is so in this dispute'. On 14 Sept. 1777 he wrote that he could not

as Mr. Burke and his sheriffs do, feel exactly the same whether the Americans get a victory or the English troops, or whether they ruin us or we them by cap-tures; with Mr. Burke's leave I suppose I ought to feel in a different manner for the fortune of my son than I should for the misfortunes of one of the descendants of my family whose ancestors sprung from it in Queen Elizabeth's time.[1]

Goodricke was listed as 'pro, present' on the con-tractors bill, 12 Feb. 1779, which to him was 'an innovation in the constitution and narrowed the elective powers of the people': no arguments had been produced for excluding contractors from the House of Commons any more than others in lucra-tive employments, including officers in the army and navy.[2] He voted with Administration on Keppel, 3 Mar. 1779. On 10 Mar. 1779 he supported Hogh-ton's motion for granting further relief to Protestant Dissenters, because 'union was much wanted throughout the kingdom, and this would promote it'.[3] Goodricke does not appear in any of the other division lists for the remainder of the Parliament, but was among the Yorkshire gentlemen who met at Lord North's house, 24 Dec. 1779, to express dis-approval of the York meeting calling for economical reform.[4] He did not stand again at the general election, but in 1787 was returned for Ripon on the Lawrence interest. He did not vote on the Regency, 1788–9, and died 3 Aug. 1789.

[1] Add. 35425, ff. 264, 281. [2] Almon, xii. 128. [3] Ibid. 108. [4] Pol. Memoranda of the Duke of Leeds, 19.

M.M.D.

**GORDON, Lord Adam** (?1726–1801), of Cuttie-shillock, Aberdeen, and The Burn, Kincardine.

ABERDEENSHIRE 1754–1768
KINCARDINESHIRE 1774–Apr. 1788

b. ?1726, 4th surv. s. of Alexander, 2nd Duke of Gordon [S], by Lady Henrietta Mordaunt, da. of Charles, 3rd Earl of Peterborough. educ. Eton 1742–3. m. 2 Sept. 1767, Jane, da. of John Drummond, M.P., of Megginch, wid. of James, 2nd Duke of Atholl, sis. of Adam Drummond (q.v.), s.p. suc. mother to Preston Hall estate, Edinburgh, 11 Oct. 1760.
Ensign, 2 Drag. 1741, lt. 1743; capt. 18 Ft. 1746; capt. 3 Ft. Gds. and lt.-col. 1756; col. 1762; col. 66 Ft. 1763–75; maj.-gen. 1772; col. 26 Ft. 1775–82;

lt.-gen. 1777; gov. Tynemouth castle 1778–96; col. 1 Ft. 1782–d.; c.-in-c. Scotland 1789–98; gen. 1793; gov. Edinburgh castle 1796–d.

In 1754 Lord Adam Gordon stood for Aberdeen-shire against the sitting Member Andrew Mitchell. After Pelham's death Lord Cathcart wrote to Loudoun, 26 Mar. 1754:[1]

The Duke of Argyll . . . told me . . . that everything was to go on as concerted in Mr. Pelham's time, in so much that the Duke of Newcastle, who protected Mr. Mitchell's interest against Lord Adam Gordon, who was supported by the Duke of Argyll and Mr. Pelham, has sent him word that he must not stand for Aberdeenshire as he is resolved to carry everything out on his brother's plan.

Nevertheless Mitchell joined forces with the third candidate Sir Archibald Grant, and both resigned in favour of Col. Robert Dalrymple Horn, who, how-ever, withdrew when the accession of the Duffs of Braco made Lord Adam's victory certain.[2]

Gordon was listed by Dupplin in 1754 among those personally connected with Argyll, but during the negotiations of March 1757 on Argyll's position in a new Government, Newcastle, hopeful of attach-ing Gordon to himself, counted him among those 'not to be relied on at present—to be treated with'. Lord Adam voted on 2 May 1757 with Newcastle's supporters on the Minorca inquiry.[3] In 1758 he served in the expedition to the French coast, and distinguished himself in the rearguard action at St. Cas on 10 Sept.[4]

In 1761 Gordon was faced with an opposition in Aberdeen from the Duffs of Braco, but was returned 'by a very creditable majority'.[5] He attached himself to Bute with whom in 1762 he sought to intervene on behalf of his friend Lord George Sackville.[6] He was not listed by Fox among those favourable to the peace preliminaries, but did not vote against them. He supported the Grenville Administration, and in April 1764 he sailed with his regiment for Jamaica. In his 'Journal of an Officer's travels in America and the West Indies, 1764–5'[7] he recorded his impres-sions of an extensive tour, the purpose of which is not stated. He was attracted by the prospect of becoming a great landowner in America and possibly obtaining a colonial governorship, particularly as his parliamentary future was uncertain. His absence abroad indeed seemed to confirm rumours that he had given up the county of Aberdeen.[8]

After visiting Antigua and St. Kitts, and inspect-ing his corps in Jamaica, he sailed for West Florida, which did not impress him. For East Florida, how-ever, he shared the enthusiasm of Governor James Grant. 'Was I ever to apply for any land in America, it should be in this province.' Of Virginia he wrote: 'Was it the case to live in America this province in

point of company and climate would be my choice.'
His observations in Maryland and Pennsylvania
confirmed his objections to proprietary governments.

> I cannot help wishing that . . . every . . . proprietary
> government in America was re-annexed to the Crown
> and governed by royal governors whose salaries ought
> to be permanent and independent of the fickle will and
> fancy of those they are sent to superintend; till this . . .
> take place Americans will never cordially unite or be
> induced to act warmly and effectively either towards
> their own defence or to such other purposes as may
> equally tend to their own and to the honour and
> advantage of Great Britain.

By the time he reached New York in May 1765
his views on American hostility to the recently
passed Stamp Act had crystallized. 'He seems to be
as sanguine about laying it thick upon the Colonies
as they are to throw off everything', wrote his friend
John Watts on 1 June 1765.[9] Gordon sailed up the
Hudson to Albany and thence to the Mohawk
Valley to visit Sir William Johnson, superintendent
of Indian affairs. Continuing his tour to Fort
Niagara and the Great Lakes, Gordon deplored the
general neglect of the back country communications
and defences. 'It would be for the good of the public
to give the charge and government of what I may
now be allowed to call back America, to some man
of sense and service who should reside in it and be
empowered to act as circumstances should require.'
After visiting Montreal and Quebec he recorded
'some thoughts relative to Canada'.

> I would by Act of Parliament vest all the religious
> property of Canada inalienably in the King . . . I
> would throw into this fund all other King's revenues,
> whether customs, stamps etc. . . . I would have a
> brigade of militia . . . [which] would be a useful
> nursery in a future war either against Spain or any
> of our own provinces that might wish to shake off their
> dependence on Britain . . . I would have an open and
> free toleration of all Christian religions throughout
> Canada and the two Floridas and all the back country.

He returned to Johnson Hall, negotiated with Sir
William Johnson about a land grant, and thereafter
travelled through New England to Boston where a
delegation waited upon him with an address:[10]

> Humbly to request your kind representations and
> influence in favour of this town and province as your
> Lordship's wisdom and justice shall direct; parti-
> cularly with regard to the new parliamentary regu-
> lations . . . which have created universal uneasiness
> among his Majesty's most loyal subjects on this
> continent.

Gordon gave a non-committal reply:

> What little influence I . . . have shall ever be cheer-
> fully employed where the interests of Great Britain
> and America are concerned, which to me seem in-
> separable: having ever been of opinion that any man
> who could wish to see a distinction or endeavour to

create a difference between them must be an enemy of
both.
Unsympathetic to Boston's 'ancient rugged spirit of
levelling', he recommended in his journal 'a thorough
alteration in their charter . . . putting it . . . on the
footing of a royal government'. After visiting Rhode
Island he returned to New York, sailed for home on
14 Oct. 1765,[11] and on 20 Nov. 'had a conference
with his Majesty's secretaries of state' on the American situation.[12] Sir William Johnson, reporting
Gordon's letter of 14 Dec., wrote to Cadwallader
Colden:[13]

> Lord Adam says nothing to me of his being appointed
> to any American government . . . nothing could then
> be determined upon and the ministry were not
> expected to hold their places.

In the debates of January–February 1766 Gordon
made use of his American experience; spoke on
17 Jan. in support of Dowdeswell's motion to
rescind the order for printing the American papers
lest it expose to danger those who had supplied
information;[14] but he was among those 'particularly
remarked' by Conway as voting against Administration on the Anstruther Burghs election petition on
31 Jan.[15] He spoke in the American debate on 5 Feb.
'to justify the Quakers';[16] on 17 Feb. on West
Indian trade;[17] and on 22 Feb. voted against the
repeal of the Stamp Act.

In association with Charles Townshend he applied
for a land grant in East Florida,[18] and became chairman and spokesman of a group of prospective
Florida proprietors.[19] He also acquired, through Sir
William Johnson, 10,000 acres in the New York
back country and in 1767 sent out two Lincolnshire
farmers to report on the land, with the intention, in
collaboration with certain 'noble associates', of settling 300 families there as his tenants.[20] He had therefore personal as well as military reasons for opposing
Grenville's motion of 18 Feb. 1767 to withdraw
troops from American frontier posts on the ground
of expense.[21] During the winter of 1766–7 he was
listed by Rockingham as connected with Bute, by
Newcastle as pro Administration, but by his associate Townshend as 'doubtful'. He did not vote on the
land tax, 27 Feb. 1767, but voted with Administration on nullum tempus, 17 Feb. 1768.

Gordon failed to obtain a seat in 1768. Out of
Parliament he maintained his interest in America
and the West Indies. His New York associate John
Watts wrote to Sir William Johnson, 16 Jan. 1769:[22]
'Lord Adam . . . says his friends upbraid him with
his friendship for America'; and Gordon wrote to
Johnson, 21 July 1771:[23]

> I see Governor Grant has arrived from East Florida
> . . . My property there lies just as it did when I got it.
> Marriage put a great stop to my American plans of

improvement and quickened those at home . . . Two or three seasons more will complete the plan of everything I possess in Britain. It consists of about 750 acres and I am hopeful to bring it to a neat £1,000 per annum, after which I shall be more free and more able to do something in America.

Although he took out his patent and paid his quit-rent on his New York lands, his hopes of revisiting America were disappointed.

In 1772–3 Lord Adam was invited by a majority of the freeholders to stand for Kincardineshire, where 'he had no fortune', and was returned unopposed in 1774.[24] In Parliament he consistently supported Administration, but failed to obtain an active military command either in America or India.[25] On 7 Apr. 1778 North wrote to the King enclosing Lord Adam's application for the governorship of Tynemouth castle:[26]

Lord North . . . begs leave to repeat, what he has often taken the liberty of mentioning to his Majesty before, that no Member of the House of Commons has been more uniform and zealous in support of Government than Lord Adam.

The King replied:

There is a very improper warmth in Lord Adam Gordon's letter that undoubtedly would be a good reason never to promote him, but I am above remembering improprieties when men have good qualities.

In this Parliament only two speeches of Gordon's are recorded: one in support of Administration in the American debate of 23 Jan. 1775, the other on 14 Dec. 1778 in favour of the augmentation of the army.[27]

In the Parliament of 1780 he continued to support North. He was absent from the division of 22 Feb. 1782 on Conway's motion against the war, but at Sandwich's request was sent for by Amherst and voted in the division of 27 Feb.[28] He was also absent from the division of 8 Mar. on Cavendish's censure motion, but was again summoned, and voted on 15 Mar. against Rous's motion of no confidence.

Deeply concerned by reports of loyalists' hardships, Gordon voted against Shelburne's peace preliminaries on 18 Feb. 1783. He spoke during the loyalist debate of 24 June and again on 27 June in support of North's motion for half pay for officers of American provincial corps, mentioning particularly the vast losses suffered by Sir William Johnson's son, Sir John:[29]

It was one among the ill effects of the late peace . . . that it left us no other power to reward the provincial officers but half pay . . . by giving the Americans so much of the continent we had effectually deprived ourselves of rewarding the brave officers by grants of land.

He did not vote on Fox's East India bill on 27 Nov. 1783 and shortly afterwards Robinson and Dundas were 'hopeful' that he would support a Pitt Administration.[30] By January 1784 he was counted 'pro', and at the general election was returned as a Government supporter. On 4 Aug. 1784, on instructions from his constituents, he opposed the partial abolition of franking; on 15 Feb. 1785 spoke in support of retaining on the establishment four regiments including his old corps, the 66th,[31] but thereafter his parliamentary career is obscure. He did not vote on the Duke of Richmond's fortifications plan on 27 Feb. 1786, and in April 1788 vacated his seat. Appointed c.-in-c. Scotland the following year, he became closely connected with Henry Dundas and the Duke of Gordon in Scottish politics.[32]

He died 13 Aug. 1801.

[1] Loudoun mss. [2] Add. 32735, ff. 3, 36, 74; Aeneas Mackintosh to Loudoun, 10 May 1754, Loudoun mss. [3] Add. 33034, f. 232. [4] Anderson, *Scottish Nation*, ii. 319. [5] G. Middleton to Bute, 24 Apr. 1761, Bute mss. [6] Same to same, Aug. 1762, Bute mss. [7] Copy in the King's mss (B.M.), including comments added after the imposition of the Townshend duties. [8] A. & H. Tayler, *Ld. Fife & his Factor*, 21. [9] *Letter Bk. of John Watts* (N.Y. Hist. Soc. Colls.), 355–6. [10] *Mass. Gaz.* 19 Sept. 1765. [11] *N.Y. Col. Docs.* vii. 765–6. [12] *Pennsylvania Gaz.*, 13 Feb. 1766. [13] *Colden Pprs.* 103. [14] Harris's 'Debates'. [15] Fortescue, i. 250. [16] Ryder's 'Debates', Harrowby mss. [17] Harris's 'Debates'. [18] *APC Col.* 1745–66, p. 815; *Unbound Pprs*, no. 688. [19] *Bd. of Trade Jnl.* 1764–7, p. 383. [20] *Johnson Pprs.* v. 391, 767–9, 587–8, 799. [21] Fortescue, i. 453 (misdated). [22] *Johnson Pprs*, vi. 587. [23] Ibid. viii. 196. [24] Laprade, 6, 19; Add. 39190, ff. 197, 199. [25] Fortescue, iii. 162, 439. [26] Fortescue, iv. 99–100. [27] Fortescue, iii. 169; Almon, xi. 155. [28] Sandwich to Robinson, 25 Feb. 1782, Abergavenny mss. [29] Debrett, x. 211–12, 245. [30] Laprade, 102. [31] Debrett, xvi. 344; xvii. 175, 178. [32] H. Furber, *Hen. Dundas*, 81 168–70, 268, 271–2.

E.H.-G.

**GORDON, Cosmo** (c.1736–1800), of Cluny, Aberdeen, and Kinsteary, Nairn.

NAIRNSHIRE        1774–Mar. 1777

*b.* c.1736, 1st s. of John Gordon of Cluny, Aberdeen. *educ.* Marischal Coll. Aberdeen 1749–53; adv. 1758. *m.* 30 June 1786, Mary, da. of Henry Baillie of Carnbroe, Lanark, *s.p.* *suc.* fa. 14 Sept. 1769.

Baron of the Scottish court of Exchequer 1777–*d.*; trustee for fisheries and manufactures in Scotland 1778; rector Marischal Coll. 1782–3, 1786–7.

Gordon's father was factor to Cosmo George, 3rd Duke of Gordon, and, as tacksman (or lessee) of the Spey salmon fishings, amassed a fortune with which he purchased the estate and castle of Cluny. In 1763 the Kinsteary estate was sold to Cosmo Gordon for £4,200 by its bankrupt owners whose electoral interest in Nairnshire was finally extinguished in 1772.[1] In 1774 Gordon stood for the county with the support of old John Campbell of Calder, to whom the principal interest belonged. Opposed by William (Johnstone) Pulteney, sitting Member for Cromarty (which alternated with Nairn in representation), Gordon was returned by 11 votes to 2, and Pulteney's petition was subsequently dropped.

In Parliament he supported North's American policy, and in the debate of 2 Feb. 1775 spoke strongly 'against any compromise or lenient measures with America till she entirely submitted'.[2] In the debate, 3 Nov. 1775, on the ministry's action during the recess in sending Hanoverian troops to garrison Gibraltar and Minorca, he asserted that the measure was certainly illegal, but condemned Sir James Lowther's motion as an 'abstract proposition' which might 'carry too severe a censure upon an act which he was convinced was well meant and very expedient'. He suggested that the question of illegality might be emphasized by altering the terms of the preamble to the indemnity bill introduced by North, and accordingly moved the previous question. Burke ridiculed his argument: 'The Hon. Member knew the measure was illegal yet he would vote in favour of it . . . it is an argument of the majority'. But, when the Commons majority allowed no alteration in the preamble, and when the Lords entirely rejected the bill, Gordon 'condemned the conduct of the minister, respecting the indemnity bill and disapproved of introducing foreigners into the dominions . . . without the consent of Parliament'.[3] Retaining, however, his faith in North's respect for the constitution, he refuted Thomas Townshend's charge that the ministry had intended to vote funds for the payment of foreign troops in Ireland. Had he believed it, 'no man would be more ready to join in a vote of disapprobation and censure'.

When on 25 Apr. 1776 Lowther again raised the question of the employment of foreign troops in America and elsewhere, Gordon maintained that while he did not entirely approve the measure, 'it was an improper time to take any step which might have the appearance of censuring H.M. ministers', since he believed that they 'always acted according to the King's inclinations'.[4]

In March 1777 Gordon received from North the appointment of baron of the Scottish Exchequer which vacated his seat.

A man of 'character and ability'[5], Baron Gordon was a leading member of Edinburgh's legal, literary, and philosophical circles—a close friend of Lord Monboddo and of James Boswell. Possessed of great wealth, he was an enthusiastic agricultural improver, and in politics maintained to the end his connexion with the Campbells of Calder, the Duke of Gordon, and Henry Dundas. He died 19 Nov. 1800.

[1] G. Bain, *Hist. Nairnshire*, 336. [2] Almon, i. 141. [3] Ibid. iii. 319. [4] Ibid. iii. 493. [5] Adam, *Pol. State Scotland 1788*, p. 238.

E.H.-G.

## GORDON, Lord George (1751-93).

LUDGERSHALL 1774-1780

*b.* 26 Dec. 1751, 3rd s. of Cosmo, 3rd Duke of Gordon [S], by Lady Catherine Gordon, da. of William, 2nd Earl of Aberdeen [S], and bro. of Lord William Gordon (q.v.). *educ.* Eton 1758-65. *unm.*
Entered R.N. 1766; lt. 1772; ret. 1777.

Lord George Gordon was given the rank of ensign in his stepfather's regiment, the 89 Foot, in 1759, but on leaving Eton joined the navy. From 1766 to 1769 he was in the American colonies. For some years before the general election of 1774 he cultivated an interest in Inverness-shire. The sitting Member, General Fraser, bought him off with a seat at Ludgershall, George Selwyn's pocket borough.[1]

From the first Gordon attended regularly and voted with Opposition. He did not speak, however, until after he had resigned his commission, which he did in 1777. Sir James Douglas, writing to Sandwich, 5 Feb. 1777, offered the following explanation:[2]

Mr. Stephens informed me that Lord George Gordon had desired to quit the service, which perhaps may be owing to what passed one evening in my house, where there was a gentleman from Maryland, who had last year been drove from his house in a barbarous manner by the rebels, for which he did not spare to give them the epithets they deserved. Lord George said so much in their defence that the gentleman said he was a good deal surprised at hearing a King's officer, who wore his uniform, say anything in their favour, and that he ought to take it off first.

He neither spoke nor voted against Sir George Savile's bill, 14 May 1778, to release Roman Catholics from certain penalties, though this was the immediate cause of the anti-Catholic agitation which followed. His first reported intervention in debate was on 13 Apr. 1778, and was a characteristic mixture of violence and piety: he appealed to North to 'call off his butchers and ravagers from the colonies —to turn from his wickedness and live; it was not yet too late to repent'. He made several more speeches in 1778, all of them extravagant, incoherent, and irrelevant, but shot through with flashes of genuine debating skill. He was still capable of some effort to control himself: on 26 Nov. 1778, warning the House of the danger of a revolt at home, he continued: 'I am afraid, Sir, I speak too loud, as that may give an appearance of passion to what I assure the House are my most deliberate sentiments.'[3]

In the course of 1779 he went to Scotland, where he was hailed with enthusiasm by the various Protestant Associations that had sprung up to oppose Savile's bill. From this time onwards, alarming tendencies began to reveal themselves in his parliamentary utterances. In May 1779 he told the House that the Scots were ripe for rebellion: 'they would prefer death to slavery, and perish with arms in their hands, or prevail in the contest'. In the debate on the King's speech, 25 Nov. 1779, he boasted that he had 'one hundred and twenty thousand men at his back': the Scots, he declared, 'are convinced in their own minds that the King is a papist'.[4]

His interruptions in debate were now tediously frequent. On 24 Jan. 1780 he insisted on reading the whole of a long pamphlet, 'much to the dislike of the House, which, from near 200 Members, soon thinned to less than fifty'. The following day he attempted to read the pamphlet again, explaining that it was 'really so excellent that it ought to be read every day in the week': frustrated in this design, he contented himself with quoting copiously from newspapers, and was engaged in reading, for the second time, the Declaratory Act of 1718, when the Members all left the chamber. On 15 Feb. he was dissuaded from another harangue by his friends, who told him that the Speaker was too ill to bear it. By this time, his remarks were blood-curdling: on 8 Mar. 1780 'he told the House he had 160,000 men in Scotland at his command, and that if the King did not keep his coronation oath, they would do more than take away his civil list revenue, they were determined to cut off his head'.[5] It was clear to most people that his mind was deranged, but the House, out of consideration for his rank and concern for the freedom of debate, was reluctant to restrain him. The King, too, was remarkably indulgent. In January 1780, Gordon had insisted on an audience, and began reading a pamphlet: according to Horace Walpole,

The King had the patience to hear him do so for above an hour, till it was so dark that the lecturer could not see. His Majesty then desired to be excused, and said he would finish the piece himself. 'Well', said the lunatic apostle, 'but you must give me your honour that you will read it out.' The King promised, but was forced to pledge his honour. It is to be hoped this man is so mad that it will soon come to perfection.[6]

In the debate of 11 Apr. 1780 he was in the middle of a description of popery in Ireland in 1626 when Charles Turner interrupted him:

He could not sit still and hear the noble lord run on at that rate. The noble lord was perpetually interrupting business and introducing matters directly personal. The noble lord had got a twist in his head, a certain whirligig which ran away with him if anything relative to religion was mentioned, and made him expose himself perpetually . . . He could not bear to see the noble lord render himself a laughing stock, and become the make game of the whole House. He respected the noble lord, and the House ought to respect him on account of his noble family.

Gordon then continued by reading yet another newspaper, and assured the House that his supporters 'had not yet determined to murder the King and put him to death: they only considered they were absolved from their allegiance'.[7]

In November 1779 the committee of the Protestant Association in London had invited Gordon to become its president, and on 26 May 1780 he gave notice that he would present their petition to Parliament. On 2 June a crowd of 60,000 gathered to accompany him to Westminister: many of them broke into the lobby of the House of Commons, and defied all attempts to get them to leave. Gordon kept up a running commentary for their benefit, telling them who was speaking in the debate, and whether in support of the petition. One witness described Gordon's behaviour when le Fleming begged him to leave the lobby:[8]

As soon as Lord George Gordon turned round and saw who it was, he called out to the people, 'This is Sir Michael le Fleming, he has just been speaking for you.' His Lordship seemed to me remarkably pleased with Sir Michael, he patted or stroked his shoulder, and expressed a kind of joy in his countenance which I hardly know how to describe: it seemed to me extravagant, and, if I may use the expression, childish.

Events were now beyond Gordon's control. That evening rioting and looting broke out, and for six days London was in the hands of the mob. The Protestant Association hastily issued an appeal to its supporters to 'refrain from unconstitutional proceedings', and Gordon himself offered North his services in restoring law and order. More than 450 persons were killed or injured. On Friday, 9 June, Lord George was arrested and sent to the Tower, charged with high treason.[9]

The trial came on in February 1781. Gordon was fortunate in having the services of two excellent lawyers, Lloyd Kenyon and Thomas Erskine. His defence was that he had made every effort to ensure that the meeting would be properly conducted, but that criminal elements, in no way connected with the Protestant Association, had seized their chance to begin plundering. Sir Philip Jennings Clerke testified that the original petitioners had been 'the better sort of tradesmen: they were all well dressed, decent sort of people', and Sir James Lowther told the court that he had heard Gordon shout to the mob outside: 'go home, be quiet, make no riot nor noise'. Kenyon, in a masterly cross-examination, exposed the prosecution's first witness as a rascal, while Erskine's closing speech was acclaimed on all sides as brilliant. In reply to the argument that Gordon should have realized that the crowd would get out of hand, he explained:

Gentlemen, we are not trying whether he might or ought to have foreseen mischief, but whether he wickedly and traitorously preconcerted and designed it.

After a retirement of half an hour, the jury found Gordon not guilty.[10]

Though out of Parliament, he continued to hover on the sidelines of political life. In the autumn of 1781 he announced his intention of standing for the City of London, but soon withdrew. He pestered the King, North, Shelburne, and Pitt with letters and requests for interviews. The megalomaniac strain in his character was more apparent than ever. In August 1783 he published a grandiose letter to the Jews of Portugal and Germany beginning:[11]

> The eyes of all Israel are upon you. America is in confusion. No wise man wonders at it. There is no prospect of a peace. The peace was ratified. The definitive treaty was ratified. The preliminary articles were ratified. The whole negotiation was ratified. The negotiators themselves are ratified. Shemah Israel! All Europe is in confusion . . .

In May 1785, convinced that the Pope had sent two Jesuits to poison him, he wrote to Lord Carmarthen, the foreign secretary, to demand protection.[12] Three months later he wrote to Joseph II of Austria to point out that 'if you had paid due attention to the remarks I made on your ordinance against the Jews on the 14th of March 1782 . . . you and your subjects would not have been in such a state of distraction and plague as at this hour'.[13]

Early in 1788 he was sentenced to five years imprisonment for a libellous pamphlet entitled 'A petition to Lord George Gordon from the prisoners at Newgate' and two paragraphs which he had had inserted in the *Public Advertiser* attacking the Queen of France and the French ambassador. The rest of his life was spent in Newgate, where he observed the Jewish faith. He was allowed visitors, entertained well, and was regarded as the most distinguished inmate. This was perhaps the happiest period of his life. Although his sentence expired in January 1793, he was unable to secure guarantors, and died in prison, 1 Nov. 1793.

[1] *Morning Post*, 18 July 1780. [2] Sandwich mss. [3] Stockdale, viii. 247; xi. 14. [4] Ibid. xii. 400; xvi. 17. [5] Ibid. xvii. 62, 66, 128, 236. [6] Walpole to Lady Upper Ossory, 29 Jan. 1780. [7] Almon, xvii. 490, 527; *Morning Post*, 15 Apr. 1780. [8] *State Trials*, xxi. 525. [9] Add. 42129, Ld. Geo. Gordon's Narrative. [10] *State Trials*, xxi. 485–652. [11] P. Colson, *Hist. Ld. Geo. Gordon*, 157. [12] Add. 27915, f. 9. [13] Colson, 142.

J.A.C.

**GORDON, James** (?1758–1822), of Moor Place, Herts., and Knockespock, Aberdeen.

STOCKBRIDGE    31 Jan. 1785–1790
TRURO             1790–1796
CLITHEROE    27 Jan. 1808–1812

*b.* ?1758, o.s. of James Brebner (who took name of Gordon 1768), chief justice of the Ceded Islands

(1767), by Anne, da. of Judge Lavington of Antigua. *educ.* Winchester; St. John's, Camb. 13 Oct. 1775, aged 17; L. Inn 1775, called 1780. *m.* 10 July 1789, Harriet, da. of Samuel Whitbread (q.v.). *suc.* fa. 1807.

Gordon came of a Scottish family with extensive connexions in the West Indies. His father for many years practised as a barrister in Antigua, but in 1768, on succeeding to his uncle James Gordon's estates in Hertfordshire, Aberdeenshire, and the West Indies, came to England and settled in Hertfordshire.

In 1785 Gordon stood as a Government candidate for the venal and expensive borough of Stockbridge and was returned unopposed. He voted for parliamentary reform, 18 Apr. 1785, and supported Pitt's Administration. There is no record of his having spoken during this Parliament.

He died 18 Feb. 1822.

L.B.N.

**GORDON, Sir John,** 2nd Bt. (?1707–83), of Invergordon, Cromarty.

CROMARTYSHIRE    30 Dec. 1742–1747, 1754–1761

*b.* ?1707, 1st s. of Sir William Gordon, M.P., 1st Bt., of Invergordon by Isobel, da. of Sir John Hamilton, S.C.J., of Hallcraig, Lanark. *m.* (1) Miss Raines (*d.* 20 Aug. 1729), gd.-da. of Sir Richard Raines, *s.p.*; (2) 18 Feb. 1739, Mary Weir, ? his cos., wid. of Hon. George Ogilvie, *s.p.* *suc.* fa. 9 June 1742.
     Sec. for Scottish affairs to the Prince of Wales 1745–51; sec. and chamberlain to the principality of Scotland 1753–*d.*

Gordon's father was a London–Scottish merchant and banker, owning considerable property in Sutherland, Ross and Cromarty, but who afterwards fell into financial difficulties. John Gordon, on his father's death, succeeded to his seat and his close connexion with the Prince of Wales. On the Prince's death he attached himself to the Pelhams, who obtained for him a place.

In 1754 he was returned for Cromarty, apparently unopposed, and also took an active and aggressive part in the Ross-shire election, in support of James Stuart Mackenzie. Listed 'pro' by Dupplin, he sought further favours.[1] Although, during the negotiations of 1757, Gordon was listed by Newcastle among his Scots supporters, he voted 2 May 1757 against Newcastle on the Minorca inquiry; and as his finances improved, showed his true colours. In October 1757 he recorded in his diary:

> Thank God I still have between £800 and £900 per annum, subject to a debt only of about £7000, besides the salary of my office . . . I [am] now able to stand against ministerial close fistedness for [I am] not obliged to be equal dependent as formerly when my situation subjected [me] to slights at their hands . . . Disgustful to be always soliciting . . . The cloud of private anxieties is now wearing off. I could stir in

business if encouraged . . . I [am] said to be losing ground; not to be well in the closet . . . My sole connexion and attachment are to the Prince's family. I owe them much, though I have also suffered much by 'em.

Gordon maintained friendly relations with the Hardwicke family. In April 1758, during the debates on the habeas corpus bill, he wrote to Philip Yorke proposing a review of Scots law affecting the liberty of the subject. Hardwicke consulted Lord Advocate Robert Dundas, who replied, 16 Nov. 1758, listing his objections:

> But as I am well informed that Sir John said in a pretty remarkable place that he etc. etc. were resolved to push it this session of Parliament, my intention is to prepare to defend against attack, particularly in concert with our president and some other of the judges.

In June 1760 Gordon again showed his active interest in law when he submitted papers to Hardwicke on the rights of vassals of the principality of Scotland.[2]

In preparation for the general election Gordon began his campaign for Tain Burghs against Sir Harry Munro in 1757. The real contest, however, lay between Colonel John Scott and Gordon, who after violent controversy was defeated but continued the battle in the courts. His election lawsuits were still before the House of Lords in 1766,[3] by which time Gordon was engaged in an equally bitter and unsuccessful campaign to carry Cromarty in 1768 against William (Johnstone) Pulteney. An opponent wrote on 10 June 1768: 'Sir John . . . has almost ruined himself by the immense expense he has run into, litigating every point with Mr. Pulteney.'[4]

Embittered and cantankerous, pursuing his personal and political opponents with violent abuse and frequent lawsuits, Gordon never succeeded in re-entering Parliament, but remained extremely active in the affairs of Ross and Cromarty, and in 1780 had the satisfaction of assisting Henry Dundas to secure the return for Ross-shire of his nephew John Mackenzie, Lord Macleod, whom he had made his heir.

He died 25 May 1783.

[1] Gordon's diary, J. M. Bulloch, *Gordons of Invergordon*, 87. [2] Add. 35353, f. 246; 35449, ff. 133, 236. [3] Gordon's letters to his solicitor David Ross, SRO. [4] George Gun Munro to James West, West mss.

E.H.-G.

**GORDON, John** (1750–1840), of Kenmure, Kirkcudbright Stewartry.

KIRKCUDBRIGHT

STEWARTRY    6 Apr. 1781–6 Feb. 1782

*b.* 1750, 2nd s. of John Gordon of Kenmure (s. of William, 6th Visct. Kenmure [S], attainted 1716), by

Lady Frances Mackenzie, da. of William, 5th Earl of Seaforth [S] (attainted 1716), and sis. of Kenneth Mackenzie (q.v.). *m.* 1791, Sarah Ann Morgan, *s.p. suc.* bro. 1772; 17 June 1824, on reversal of attainder, resumed title as 7th Visct. Kenmure.

Ensign 17 Ft. 1770, lt. 1772; capt. lt. 54 Ft. 1775; capt. 14 Lt. Drag. 1775; ret. 1779.

Gordon's family connexions and estates gave him considerable interest in Kirkcudbright Stewartry, where he stood in 1780 as a Government candidate backed by the Duke of Queensberry. The Catholic relief bill of 1778 was a vital issue at the election (Gordon's mother was a Catholic); and Gordon was defeated. The election, however, was declared void, and at the new election Gordon was successful against Peter Johnston. But Johnston brought a petition, claiming that Gordon had concluded a corrupt bargain with Alexander Stewart, and on 6 Feb. 1782 Gordon was unseated. His only recorded vote in Parliament was with Administration on 12 Dec. 1781 on Lowther's motion against the American war.

His determined efforts to enter the House may have been inspired in part by a desire to acquire parliamentary immunity from his creditors, for his financial position was desperate. In May 1781 he executed a trust deed empowering the trustees to sell part or all of his lands to meet his debts. A considerable part of his other properties was, however, saved, including Kenmure castle.

He died 21 Sept. 1840.

E.H.-G.

**GORDON, Sir William** (1726–98), of Garendon Park, Leics.[1]

PORTSMOUTH    26 Nov. 1777–July 1783

*b.* 1726, 1st s. of William Gordon, merchant and planter of St. Mary's, Kingston, Jamaica, by Susanna Gordon. *educ.* Glasgow Univ. 1739–45; Leyden 1745–6; Grand Tour 1746–?7. *m.* 2 July 1776, Mary, da. of Thomas Allsopp of Ashbourne, Derbys., wid. of Samuel Phillipps of Garendon. K.B. 3 Feb. 1775.

Minister to the Diet at Ratisbon Apr. 1764–5; envoy to Denmark 28 June 1765; minister at Brussels Nov. 1765–77; clerk comptroller, Board of Green Cloth, Sept. 1780–Mar. 1782.

Gordon was born in Jamaica of Aberdeenshire parents, cousins of the Gordons of Hallhead. At Leyden he was a fellow student of Charles Townshend, John Wilkes, James Johnstone, William Dowdeswell and Alexander Carlyle, but was 'too young and too dissipated' to attend their serious discussions.[2] With Dowdeswell he made the tour of Italy, Sicily and Greece; after further travels in France and Germany he probably went home to Jamaica, but after his father's death disposed of his interest in the family plantations and mercantile concerns to his two brothers, and settled in London. He may have been the William Gordon of Marlborough Street who unsuccessfully contested Sudbury in 1761 and, claiming friendship with 'Sir Harry Erskine, Mure and Campbell', applied to Bute for support in his petition.[3]

*Bon viveur*, rake, and humorist, he was an intimate friend of Lord Sandwich who in 1764 appointed him envoy to Ratisbon. Despite his ribald comments on his own mythical qualifications, Gordon 'really liked the trade he had taken by the hand', and was anxious to earn the approval of his patron, who early in January 1765 offered to obtain his transfer from Ratisbon to Copenhagen.[4] Gordon wrote to Under-Secretary Richard Phelps, 14 Jan. 1765:[5] 'Copenhagen is damned expensive and I am damned poor . . . but as that place may lead to preferment I am ready to go there or anywhere else.' Shortly before Sandwich's dismissal, Gordon was appointed assistant to the Copenhagen minister,[6] but did not take up duty, and in November received from the Rockingham Administration a better post in Brussels.

In England in 1776 he married a wealthy widow whose first husband had left her £7,000 a year and all his estates for life. He wrote to Sandwich, 13 July 1776:[7] 'May Heaven long preserve Lady Gordon say I . . . I have been pretty active all my life . . . but the getting to Garendon Park is the best thing I have yet done.' Unwilling to return to Brussels, he pressed North for preferment, and sought to enter Parliament.

Will Suffolk, will North, force me to quit this charming abode? . . . Before I left town I swore to them both I would not after 14 years banishment be thrown aside like an old slipper; *reste à voir* what they will do for me.[8]

Hearing that Peter Taylor was dying, he urged Sandwich in July to carry out his friendly intentions and ask North for the Government interest at Portsmouth. But Taylor did not die; and Gordon wrote to Sandwich, 26 Sept. 1776:

I have adhered to the advice that both you and Weymouth gave me, which was not to give up my post, but always to say I was ready to go abroad, for if I once gave it up without getting something I should be *sur le pavé* . . . But one thing is very clear to me that my Principal will either make me resign or go abroad very soon unless my friends interfere and save me.

A few days later he was officially informed that he was destined for Sweden; but managed to avoid the Swedish appointment; seems to have returned for a time to Brussels; resigned in 1777; and on Taylor's death entered Parliament.

Long hostile to 'those canting hypocritical rebellious scoundrels of Bostonians',[9] Gordon in his maiden speech on 5 Dec. 1777 advocated coercive measures until 'America had laid aside her claim to independence'.[10] Horace Walpole records that in the debate on North's conciliatory proposals, 17 Feb. 1778:[11]

Governor Johnstone . . . called on Sir William Gordon . . . who had been in America, to testify that the Americans had not formerly thought of making themselves independent. Sir William, a man of very blundering head, thus unexpectedly called on, had one of those momentary inspirations which sometimes light on idiots . . . and ridiculed him with much humour, wondering that the Governor who so boldly attacked the highest personages, should descend to him.

Gordon remained closely attached to Sandwich, reporting to him parliamentary gossip and trends of opinion, but by the end of 1779 had lost faith in North, who had disregarded his claims for preferment. He wrote to Sandwich, 18 Jan. 1780:

I am no stranger to the views of the Opposition . . . They are dangerous to particulars, they are dangerous to the Constitution . . . It is now therefore become the duty of every man in the community to stand forth and counteract their schemes. But, my dear Lord, can a few Members in the House of Commons do this without a leader that is active, resolute, and decisive? Has Lord North a friend in office (one or two excepted) that is not lukewarm in his cause? Will his *Majority of Mutes* save him . . . He must alter his conduct or he must sink himself and those that are joined with him. I will say nothing with regard to his behaviour to me; you have called upon me and I will most certainly be in town at the meeting of Parliament, and when there will give him all the active assistance I can, for I cannot act a lukewarm part. But I will be candid and honest to declare that the first Member of the House of Commons that kisses hands I shall ask for the Chiltern Hundreds.

Sandwich sent this letter to Robinson, who replied 22 Jan. 1780:[12]

Sir William Gordon is impatient, indeed too much so, for impatience might defeat the best intentions which are held for him. I return you his letter because I think it would injure him to show it to our friend.

Gordon continued to support Administration, and in 1780 was returned again on the Government interest for Portsmouth. On 5 Sept., a few days before the election, he received the lucrative place of clerk comptroller of the Green Cloth, and his loyalty to North was assured. He spoke, 20 Nov. 1780, against the vote of thanks to the former Speaker, Sir Fletcher Norton,[13] and consistently voted with Administration to the end except on the censure motions of 8 and 15 Mar. 1782 when he was absent through illness.

Under the new Administration Gordon's place was abolished. In August 1782 he had several conferences at Buxton with Loughborough, whose scheme for a Fox-North Coalition he approved, but thought impracticable. Loughborough reported to William Eden that Gordon held Shelburne 'in great contempt' and believed that 'the country gentlemen . . . bitterly repented their folly and would rally under Lord North's standard if he would set it up'.[14]

Gordon voted against Shelburne's peace preliminaries, 18 Feb. 1783, and supported the Coalition. In July he vacated his seat so that the Coalition might bring in Thomas Erskine. His price was a pension 'on the foreign ministers' list' of £1000 p.a., and although the King was believed to be unwilling to grant it, the warrant was passed 17 Oct. 1783.[15]

Gordon retired to Garendon where he and his wife were active enclosers and, taking full profit from their liferent possession, cut down trees to the value of £9,500, which they invested for their own benefit.[16] When his wife died in 1796 he lost control of the estate.

Gordon died 26 Jan. 1798.

[1] *Scottish N. & Q.* (ser. 3) ix. 170, 188. [2] Carlyle, *Autobiog.* 168, 176. [3] 1 Apr. 1761, Bute mss. [4] Gordon to Sandwich, 6, 23 July 1764, Sandwich mss; Stowe mss 258, ff. 188, 213; 259, f. 54; J. M. Bulloch, *Gay Gordons*, 207–19. [5] Stowe mss 260, f. 120. [6] Sandwich to Walter Titley, 28 June 1765, Stowe mss 261, f. 80. [7] Sandwich mss. [8] Ibid. 13 July 1776. [9] Gordon to Sandwich, 25 Aug. 1775. [10] Debrett, viii. 130. [11] *Last Jnls.* ii. 117. [12] Sandwich mss. [13] Debrett, i. 107. [14] *Auckland Corresp.* i. 18, 19. [15] T. Orde to Shelburne, 17 July 1783, Lansdowne mss; T52/72/502. [16] Nichols, *Leics.* iii. 802, 844, 855, 906, 919, 1017, 1022.

E.H.-G.

**GORDON, William** (?1735–76), of Bully Hill, Rochester, Kent.

ROCHESTER    1768–Feb. 1771

*b.* ?1735, s. of George Gordon, wine merchant, mayor of Rochester 1755 and 1759. *m.* 11 June 1761, his cos. Elizabeth, da. and h. of Thomas Gordon of Bully Hill, 1da.[1] *suc.* fa. 28 Dec. 1759.[2]
Sheriff, Kent 1763–4; commr. of the victualling office 1772–d.

When Calcraft stood for Rochester in 1765, Rockingham wrote to Newcastle, 26 Nov.: 'I understand that Gordon, a wine merchant at Rochester, is the occasion.'[3] He was apparently at the head of the independent interest. When in 1768 Calcraft had Government support, and Fordyce the banker could not be persuaded to stand, Gordon did so himself, and carried his election through his influence with the local artisans and shopkeepers. In Parliament he voted with the Opposition in each of the six divisions on Wilkes and Middlesex, 27 Jan. 1769–25 Jan. 1770. There is no record of his having spoken in the House. Together with Calcraft and Sawbridge he was instrumental in carrying the Kent petition to the King for a dissolution of Parliament, 27 Nov. 1769.[4] But on 25 Feb. 1771 Sandwich wrote to John Robinson about Rochester: 'I think you may on very reasonable terms get a bad man out and a

good man in his room into Parliament'; and next, Gordon accepted the Chiltern Hundreds; for what immediate consideration is unascertained. He now served the Government, and wrote to Sandwich, 16 Oct. 1771:

> As I find with certainty that the lord mayor of London [Brass Crosby] with the sheriffs [Frederick Bull and Richard Oliver] are to be here on Friday or Saturday next in order to take up their freedoms, it seems the opinion of our friends that it will be better for me at that time not to be absent. With this view I will presume to take the liberty of attending your Lordship in the following rather than the present week.
> It is not impossible but these same people may attempt more honorary freedoms, but I think, this attempt will be effectually over-ruled.

And Sandwich to Robinson, 20 Oct.:

> I judge from the enclosed that what you and I have lately written has had the proper effect; I should think it would not be amiss (if you had prepared your book and are otherwise ready) that we should have an interview with Mr. Gordon.[5]

Gordon was appointed to the victualling office, 28 Oct. 1772. He died 29 Mar. 1776, aged 40.[6]

[1] Hasted, *Kent*, iii. 447; iv. 162. [2] Father's M.I., St. Nicholas, Rochester. [3] Add, 32972, ff. 62–63. [4] Calcraft to Chatham, 27 Nov. 1769, Chatham mss; *St. James's Chron.* 30 Nov. Abergavenny mss. [6] M.I., St. Nicholas, Rochester.

L.B.N.

**GORDON, Hon. William** (1736–1816), of Fyvie, Aberdeen.

NEW WOODSTOCK    8 June 1767–1774
HEYTESBURY                         1774–1780

*b.* 1736, 2nd surv. s. of William, 2nd Earl of Aberdeen [S], by his 3rd w. Lady Anne Gordon, da. of Alexander, 2nd Duke of Gordon [S]. *educ.* Glasgow Univ. 1748. *m.* his housekeeper Isobel Black, by whom he had previously had a son.
Cornet 11 Drag. 1756; capt. 16 Drag. 1759; lt.-col. 105 Ft. 1762; half-pay 1763; col. 1777; col. 81 Ft. 1777–83; maj.-gen. 1781; col. 71 Ft. 1789–1803; lt.-gen. 1793; gen. 1798; col. 21 Ft. 1803–d.
Groom of the bedchamber 1775–1812.

In 1767 Gordon was returned for Woodstock by his friend the Duke of Marlborough. He did not vote on the nullum tempus bill, 17 Feb. 1768. In the new Parliament his attendance also seems to have been poor: he voted with Administration but appears in only three out of seven division lists giving the names of their side; all three being on Wilkes and the Middlesex election (3 Feb. and 15 Apr. 1769, and 26 Apr. 1773). Over the royal marriage bill, March 1772, Robinson listed him 'pro—sent to'; and at the end of the Parliament classed him no higher than 'hopeful'.

In 1774 Gordon was brought in for Heytesbury by Marlborough, who in April 1775 obtained for him the place of groom of the bedchamber with permission to retain his half-pay in addition to his salary.[1] A bitter enemy later wrote:[2] 'Never was a more perfect prototype of Polonius than our groom of the bedchamber, and though the King sometimes hit him rather hard, yet he was a great favourite.' In 1777 Gordon took advantage of his position to steal a march on his nephew the Duke of Gordon, whose offer to raise a regiment hung fire because of the King's objections to the Duke's discredited brother Lord William as its commander. The Duke wrote to his agent, 1 Jan. 1778:[3]

> The King, having absolutely refused to give Lord William Gordon the rank, Fyvie was appointed, after having assured Lord George Germain that he was to have my interest and support—and indeed he was sure of it had he behaved properly—but he had named most of his officers and before he was sure whether he or Lord William was to command the battalion . . . and you will see that he had an eye to Aberdeenshire in the list he has named . . . When Sandy Gordon [later Lord Rockville] delivered me Fyvie's letter at Edinburgh with the list . . . I was very angry and said I was surprised at his brother's conduct in having got a regiment through my interest and not giving me the nomination of one officer. He answered in a huff: 'Well, by God, we can raise it without you!'

The Duke complained to Germain and to North, who wrote 30 Dec. 1777 to the King:[4]

> Colonel Gordon, by taking this method has made it HIS regiment and not the *Duke's*, and has obliged many of the Duke's friends in order as he [the Duke] supposes, to gain their interest at a future political contest if [he] should again oppose, as he has already done once, the Duke's candidate for the county of Aberdeen.

After an interview with the Duke, the King instructed Germain to reprimand Gordon, whose reply seemed to Germain 'so proper that the Duke of Gordon ought to be satisfied' and Gordon commended for his attention to the King's wishes.[5] But the Duke was not satisfied and the King reluctantly gave him permission to raise a regiment of his own, 'The Northern Fencibles'. Competition in recruiting resulted in violent disputes in Aberdeenshire and a lasting breach between the two branches of the Gordon family.[6]

In Ireland with his 'Aberdeenshire Highlanders' from June 1778, Gordon was listed 'pro, abroad' on the contractors bill, 12 Feb. 1779, but returned shortly afterwards and voted with Administration on Keppel, 3 Mar. He returned to Ireland during the summer but was back in London by January 1780 seeking military promotion,[7] and voted with Administration in every recorded division to the end of the Parliament. On 2 June 1780, when his nephew Lord George Gordon presented the petition of the Protestant Association and harangued the mob besieging the House, Gordon wrote the *Annual Register*

(p. 258), went up to him and accosted him in the following manner: 'My Lord George, do you intend to bring your rascally adherents into the House of Commons? If you do—the first man of them that enters I will plunge my sword not into his but into your body.'[8]

Gordon was not returned for Heytesbury at the general election of 1780, and, despite the Duke of Gordon's suspicion of his intentions, apparently did not contest Aberdeenshire.

He died 25 May 1816.

[1] Fortescue, iii. 189–90; *Cal. Home Office Pprs. 1773–5*, p. 563. [2] J. M. Bulloch, *Territorial Soldiering in the North East*, 37, quoting Pryse Lockhart Gordon, *Personal Mems.* [3] Ibid. 39. [4] Fortescue, iii. 531. [5] *Territorial Soldiering*, 40–41; Fortescue, iv. 16. [6] *Territorial Soldiering*, 37–57. [7] HMC *Lothian*, 362. [8] See also MURRAY, James (1734–94).

E.H.-G.

## GORDON, Lord William (1744–1823), of Mamore, Inverness.

| | |
|---|---|
| ELGINSHIRE | 29 Apr. 1779–1784 |
| INVERNESS-SHIRE | 1784–1790 |
| HORSHAM | 10 Mar. 1792–1796 |

*b.* 15 Aug. 1744, 2nd s. of Cosmo George, 3rd Duke of Gordon [S], and bro. of Lord George Gordon (q.v.). *educ.* Harrow 1757; Eton 1758–60; Grand Tour 1762–3. *m.* 1 Mar. 1781, Hon. Frances Ingram Shepherd, da. and coh. of Charles, 9th Visct. Irwin [S] (q.v.), 1da.

Lt. 89 Ft. 1759; capt. 37 Ft. 1764; res. 1769.

Dep. ranger St. James's and Green Parks 1778–*d.*; v.-adm. Scotland 1782–95; receiver gen. duchy of Cornwall 1817–*d.*

While still a schoolboy Lord William was given a commission in the regiment of his step-father, Staats Long Morris, but preferred fashionable London life to military duty. Handsome, popular, and 'esteemed by the British court, one of the most accomplished young noblemen of the age',[1] he resigned from the army in January 1769 when he eloped to Scotland with Lady Sarah Bunbury, wife of Sir Charles Bunbury (q.v.) and sister of the Duke of Richmond.[2] After a few months Lady Sarah returned in disgrace to her brother's house, and Lord William, lampooned in the scurrilous press and ostracized by society, left England in August 1770 vowing never to return. With 'his hair cut close, a knapsack on his back, and no other companion than a very big dog', he intended walking to Rome, and his movements for the next three years are uncertain.[3] By 1774 he had returned to London and resumed his life as a man of fashion with Lord March and his friends.[4] He had little money and was largely dependent on his brother the Duke of Gordon, who was anxious to rehabilitate him and bring him into Parliament. But when the Duke, in 1777, offered to raise a regiment under the command of Lord William, the

King contemptuously vetoed the appointment:[5] 'I can never think of giving Lord William Gordon the rank of lieutenant colonel . . . he has not the smallest claim to military rank.'

When William Gordon of Fyvie (q.v.) 'stole a march' on his kinsmen, and secured the regiment for himself, the Duke, highly incensed, protested to North and the King, and offered to raise another corps. To placate him North, in February 1778, secured the King's approval of a scheme to purchase for Lord William the place of deputy ranger of St. James's and Green Parks from the incumbent, Captain Shirley, 'a bargain', wrote Horace Walpole, 'so very advantageous to the latter, that it was supposed the Government really paid the charge to soothe Lord William and the Duke, his brother, for the refusal of their new regiment to the other'.[6] Eventually, in April 1778, North prevailed upon the King to approve the raising of a Fencible corps with the Duke as colonel and his brother second in command.

In April 1779 Gordon at last obtained a seat, when after long negotiation between the Duke and Lord Fife he succeeded Arthur Duff in Elginshire. His only recorded speech was made on 23 June 1779 when he spoke 'against parts of the bill for augmenting the militia, although approving the principle'.[7] A consistent supporter of Administration, he was acutely distressed by the conduct of Lord George; visited him in the Tower after the riots and during his trial in 1781, and seemed by his harassed and dishevelled appearance more of a gallowsbird than his brother.[8]

His own position was not affected, and he was returned unopposed for Elgin in 1780. The *English Chronicle* wrote of him in 1781:

> He possesses that kind of ability with which nature has benevolently supplied the more impotent order of her beings . . . a quick perception in all the modes of applicable adulation, and an intuitive sagacity in discerning the most direct and effectual roads to preferment . . . He is a constant attender at St. James's on every vacancy, and is polite enough to be on all occasions the *most obedient humble servant to command* to the premier and all his colleagues in Administration.

A heavy gambler, deep in debt, he achieved financial stability in 1781 by his marriage to an heiress, a ward in Chancery, despite the opposition of Lord Chancellor Thurlow.[9] In 1782 his fortunes were further improved. On the death of Simon Fraser, North, fearing that the Duke of Gordon would try to bring in Lord George for Inverness-shire, suggested to the King that Lord William might be transferred there from Elgin:[10]

> If his Majesty would permit Lord William to hold the office of vice-admiral of Scotland, his seat would

be vacated and the family could not in that case refuse an arrangement to exclude Lord George.

Lord William's mother-in-law, Lady Irwin, urged that the office be held by him personally and not in the name of the Duke, but the King objected: 'The appointment . . . will give well grounded disgust to the peerage of Scotland, he not being one of them and certainly his private character not being much in his favour.' Nevertheless, in view of North's anxiety to ensure the support of Henry Dundas and his Gordon connexions, the King was prevailed upon to agree and Lord William kissed hands on 1 Mar. On North's fall he did not transfer to Inverness-shire but was re-elected for Elgin, 25 Apr. 1782.

Gordon did not vote on Shelburne's peace preliminaries, 18 Feb. 1783, nor on Fox's East India bill, 27 Nov. Robinson, in his survey prepared in December shortly before the change of Administration, wrote under Elgin:[11]

> Lord William Gordon will certainly come in again. He acts at present and with propriety with the present Administration . . . But . . . there are hopes that in a future Parliament, holding the offices he does, he would be *pro*, and it may reasonably be expected that he would give his assistance, with attention, to get the seats at Horsham.

Shortly after Pitt took office Lord William went over to Administration; at the general election he did not contest Elginshire, but by a compromise with the Fraser interest was returned for Inverness-shire. He voted with Pitt on the Regency.

He died 1 May 1823.

[1] *Scots Mag.* 1770, p. 515. [2] *Life & Letters of Lady Sarah Lennox,* i. 223. [3] *Scots Mag.* 1770, p. 515; *Gent. Mag.* 1770, p. 390; J. M. Bulloch, *Gay Gordons,* 103–23. [4] A. & H. Tayler, *Ld. Fife & his Factor,* 82–83; Boswell, *Private Pprs.* x. 147. [5] Fortescue, iii. 529. [6] Walpole, *Last Jnls.* ii. 105, 113. [7] Fortescue, iv. 372. [8] Walpole, *Last Jnls.* ii. 312; *HMC Carlisle,* 453. [9] Walpole to Lady Upper Ossory, 16 Aug. 1780; *HMC Carlisle,* 458; *Scots Mag.* 1781, p. 110. [10] Fortescue, v. 362–3. [11] Laprade, 101.

E.H.-G.

**GORE, Charles** (?1711–68), of Tring, Herts.

| | |
|---|---|
| CRICKLADE | 21 Nov. 1739–1741 |
| HERTFORDSHIRE | 1741–1761 |
| TIVERTON | 14 May 1762–15 Feb. 1768 |

*b.* ?1711, 1st s. of William Gore, M.P., by Lady Mary Compton, da. of George, 4th Earl of Northampton; nephew of John and Thomas Gore (qq.v.). *educ.* Ch. Ch. Oxf. 12 July 1729, aged 18. *m.* 3 Dec. 1741, Ellen, da. of Sir William Humphreys, 1st Bt., M.P., sis. and coh. of Sir Orlando Humphreys, 2nd Bt., 3s. 5da. *suc.* fa. 1739.

In 1754 Gore stood for Hertfordshire on a joint interest with Paggen Hale, and was returned after a contest. There was another contest in 1761, when Gore stood jointly with Jacob Houblon, but having lost the support of the Dissenters, he was beaten. In May 1762 Newcastle, then in his last days at the Treasury, recommended Gore, apparently against the King's inclination, to Nathaniel Ryder for a seat at Tiverton. 'His Majesty talked very oddly about the borough of Tiverton', wrote Newcastle to Hardwicke on 10 May,[1] 'that it was a court borough. But thank God, that is over, and I hope Mr. Gore chose.' Yet if Newcastle expected Gore to follow him into Opposition he was disappointed: in December 1762 Gore's name is in Fox's list of Members in favour of the peace preliminaries, and it appears in none of the minority division lists of 1763 or 1764. On 17 Dec. 1763 Newcastle wrote to Ryder:[2] 'I have an account from good hands that Mr. Charles Gore . . . is in a very bad state of health and not likely to hold out long'; and went on to recommend his successor. Gore spent the winter of 1764-5 in France, returned to England in May,[3] and in Rockingham's list of July 1765 was classed 'pro'. He does not appear in the division lists 1765-8 and his political conduct at this period is not clear: Rockingham in November 1766 classed him 'doubtful', Townshend in January 1767 'Bedford' (there is no evidence that he was ever claimed by the Bedfords as one of their group), and Newcastle in March 1767 'Administration'. He is not known to have spoken in the House. He died 15 Feb. 1768.

[1] Add. 35421, ff. 259-60. [2] 'Tiverton Letters and Papers, 1724-1843', N. & Q. clxx. 171. [3] Ibid. 189.

J.B.

**GORE, John** (c.1689-1763), of Bush Hill, Mdx.

GREAT GRIMSBY 1747-1761

b. c.1689, 2nd s. of Sir William Gore, merchant and director of the Bank of England, by Elizabeth, da. of Walter Hampton, London merchant. m. Hannah, da. of Sir Jeremy Sambrooke, 4th Bt., M.P., of North Mimms, Herts., 1s. d.v.p. 3da.: Catherine m. Joseph Mellish (q.v.) and Anne m. his bro. William Mellish, M.P.

John Gore carried on business in Bishopsgate Street in partnership with Joseph Mellish, later his son-in-law, with whose support he was returned for Grimsby. He began as a Hamburg merchant, but his concerns grew more widespread: he was one of the original directors of the South Sea Company; held extensive Government contracts for remittances and victualling troops;[1] was a large subscriber to Government loans; and one of the City men consulted by Newcastle on Treasury affairs. Gore and Mellish suffered considerably in the Lisbon earthquake of 1755, Gore's loss being estimated at £30,000.[2]

He died 3 Aug. 1763.

[1] Namier, Structure, 47, n. 1. [2] Mrs. Delany's Autobiog. iii. 379-80.

J.B.

**GORE, Thomas** (?1694-1777), of Dunstan Park, nr. Newbury, Berks.

| CRICKLADE | 1722-1727 |
| AMERSHAM | 17 Feb. 1735-Feb. 1746 |
| PORTSMOUTH | 3 Mar. 1746-1747 |
| BEDFORD | 1747-1754 |
| CRICKLADE | 1754-1768 |

b. ?1694, 3rd. s. of Sir William Gore, and bro. of John Gore (q.v.) educ. I. Temple 1711; Ch. Ch. Oxf. 4 June 1714, aged 19. m. 15 Sept. 1748, Mary, da. of Sir William Humphreys, 1st Bt., M.P., sis. and coh. of Sir Orlando Humphreys, 2nd Bt., wid. of (1) William Ball Waring, (2) John Honywood; s.p. Commissary-gen. of musters, 1746-d.

After taking office, Gore supported every Administration in turn. There is no record of his having spoken in the House during this period. In 1761 he was mentioned as a candidate for Speaker, but Newcastle considered him to be 'too old and infirm'.[1] He survived a three-cornered contest at Cricklade in 1761, but was forced to decline at the general election of 1768.

Gore died 17 Mar. 1777.

[1] Newcastle to Bedford, 10 Oct. 1761, Bedford mss.

J.A.C.

**GORGES, Richard** (c.1730-80), of Eye, nr. Leominster, Herefs.

LEOMINSTER 1754-1761

b. c.1730,[1] 1st s. of Richard Gorges of Eye by Elizabeth, da. of John Rodd of Hereford. m. Frances, da. of Thomas Fettiplace of Sevenbrook, Oxon., 2s. 5da. Sheriff, Herefs. 1768-9.

Richard Gorges came of a Herefordshire gentry family. His father had contested Leominster in 1747; he himself was returned without a poll in 1754, after a threatened opposition was withdrawn. In Dupplin's list he was classed as a Tory. No vote or speech by him is recorded. He did not stand in 1761.

He died in 1780.

[1] R. Gorges, Story of a Fam. 205-6.

J.B.

**GORING, Charles** (1743-1829), of Wiston, nr. Shoreham, Suss.

NEW SHOREHAM 1774-1780

b. 1743, 2nd s. of Sir Charles Matthew Goring, 5th Bt., by his 2nd w. Elizabeth, da. of Sir Robert Fagge, 3rd Bt., of Wiston, and sis. and coh. of Sir Robert Fagge, 4th Bt., M.P. educ. Magdalen, Oxf. 27 Mar. 1762, aged 18. m. (1) 20 Apr. 1779, Sarah (d.6 Dec. 1797), da. of Ralph Beard of Hurstpierpoint, Suss., s.p.; (2) 7 June 1798, Elizabeth (d.8 Aug. 1811), da. of Edward Luxford, 3da.; (3) 7 May 1812, Mary, da. of Rev. John Ballard, rector of Great Longford, Wilts., 2s. 1da.

Members of the Goring family sat for various Sussex constituencies since the sixteenth century. Charles Goring inherited property near Shoreham through his mother, and his political influence was 'always very great in the Western part of Sussex'.[1] In 1774 he stood for Shoreham which in 1771 had been enlarged by an Act throwing it into the rape of Bramber and enfranchising about 1200 freeholders. He topped the poll. In Parliament he voted consistently with Opposition. Only one speech by him is reported—on the bill for disfranchising Hindon voters, 29 Mar. 1775, when he sided with Opposition. Goring declined to stand again in 1780.

He died 3 Dec. 1829 aged 86. The *Gentleman's Magazine* wrote in his obituary notice: 'He was a singular specimen of an old English gentleman . . . of a hearty vigorous constitution and great hospitality. His fortune amounted to £12,000 a year.'

[1] *Gent. Mag.* 1830, i. 87.

M.M.D.

**GOUGH** (afterwards **GOUGH CALTHORPE**), **Sir Henry,** 2nd Bt. (1749–98), of Edgbaston, Warws.

BRAMBER 1774–1796

*b.* 1 Jan. 1749, 1st s. of Sir Henry Gough, 1st Bt., M.P., by his 2nd w. Barbara, da. of Reynolds Calthorpe, M.P., of Elvetham, Hants. *educ.* Eton 1762–7; Oriel, Oxf. 1767. *m.* 1 May 1783, Frances, da. and coh. of Gen. Benjamin Carpenter, 6s. 2da. *suc.* fa. 8 June 1774; and to estates of his uncle Sir Henry Calthorpe, and took add. name of Calthorpe 1788; *cr.* Baron Calthorpe 16 June 1796.

Gough inherited control of one seat at Bramber in 1774, and was returned unopposed at the general election.

His parliamentary attendance seems to have been irregular, and his voting independent. He voted with Opposition on Wilkes, 22 Feb. 1775; was marked as 'contra, present, friend' by Robinson on the contractors bill, 12 Feb. 1779; voted with Opposition on the abolition of the Board of Trade, 13 Mar. 1780, and on Dunning's motion, 6 Apr. 1780, but with Administration on the motion against prorogation, 24 Apr. 1780. Robinson in his 1780 survey classed him as 'pro'. During the last critical months of North's Administration only one vote by Gough is recorded: with Opposition on Conway's motion against the war, 22 Feb. 1782. He voted against Shelburne's peace preliminaries, 18 Feb. 1783, and for Fox's East India bill, 27 Nov. 1783, but Robinson, in his survey of December 1783, wrote: 'Sir Henry Gough is in inclination generally with Government', and George III wrote to Pitt, 1 Jan. 1784: 'I have good hopes of Sir Henry Gough.'[1]

Gough was a member of the St. Alban's Tavern group which met in January 1784 to try and bring about a union of parties. Stockdale, 19 Mar. 1784, and Adam, May 1784, classed him as 'Administration'. His only recorded votes in this Parliament were with Pitt over the Regency, 1788–9; and on 25 Mar. 1789 he wrote to Pitt soliciting a peerage.

Gough's one recorded speech before 1790, was against a bill for licensing a theatre at Birmingham, 29 Apr. 1777: he thought 'there was no necessity Birmingham should have any theatre at all; a strolling company might now and then come here, but the magistrate would judge if it was proper for them to perform or not'.[2]

He died 16 Mar. 1798.

[1] Chatham mss. [2] Almon, vii. 139.

M.M.D.

**GOULD,** (afterwards **MORGAN**), **Charles** (1726–1806), of Ealing, Mdx.

BRECON 23 Apr. 1778–June 1787
BRECONSHIRE 20 June 1787–1806

*b.* 25 Apr. 1726, 1st s. of King Gould, dep. judge-advocate gen., by Elizabeth, da. of Charles Shaw of Besthorpe, Norf. *educ.* Westminster 1735; Ch. Ch. Oxf. 1743; L. Inn 1743, called 1750, K.C. 1754. *m.* Feb. 1758, Jane, da. of Thomas Morgan (q.v.) of Tredegar, Mon., sis. and ult. h. of Thomas, Charles, and John Morgan (qq.v.), 3s. 2da. Kntd. 5 May 1779; *suc.* bro.-in-law John Morgan 28 June 1792, and took name of Morgan 16 Nov. 1792; *cr.* Bt. 15 Nov. 1792.

Dep. judge-advocate gen. c.1753–69; judge-advocate gen. 1769–*d.*; P.C. 2 Sept. 1802.

Soon after Charles Gould began to practise at the bar he succeeded his father as deputy judge-advocate general. In 1756 Thomas Morgan, judge-advocate general, applied to Newcastle on Gould's behalf for a seat at Dover:[1]

I should not be so pressing but that I have the pleasure of knowing Mr. Gould many years, and can assure your Grace that he is sincerely attached to the present royal family and likewise the present Administration . . . I must beg leave to acquaint your Grace that Mr. Gould's father has a very great interest at Dover and has upon all occasions exerted it in your Grace's interest, and I am very certain that Mr. Gould will be very acceptable to that port as a candidate . . . I do assure your Grace he is a young gentleman of great merit, and likewise will shine whenever he has the honour to be in the House.

The application was unsuccessful, as was also a second one in 1759.[2]

Meanwhile Gould had married Morgan's daughter, but he had to wait twenty years before he found a seat in Parliament. In 1778 he was returned on the Morgan interest at Brecon. In Parliament he consistently supported North's Administration, and voted for Shelburne's peace preliminaries, 18 Feb.

1783, and Fox's East India bill, 27 Nov. 1783. His few speeches in the House all dealt with the business of his office. Unlike his brothers-in-law he supported Pitt. On the Regency he seems to have hedged: in the division of 16 Dec. 1788 he voted with Opposition, in that of 11 Feb. 1789 with Pitt, and in the consolidated list appears with Opposition.

He died 6 Dec. 1806.

¹ Add. 32864, f. 372. ² Add. 32891, ff. 453, 457–8.

P.D.G.T.

## GOULD (afterwards MORGAN), Charles (1760–1846), of Ealing, Mdx.

| BRECON | 6 Dec. 1787–1796 |
| MONMOUTHSHIRE | 1796–1831 |

*b.* 4 Feb. 1760, 1st s. of Charles Gould (q.v.). *educ.* Westminster 1771. *m.* 6 Apr. 1791, Mary Magdalen, da. and h. of Capt. George Stoney, R.N., 4s. 4da. Took name of Morgan 16 Nov. 1792. *suc.* fa. as 2nd Bt. 6 Dec. 1806.

Ensign 2 Ft. Gds. 1777, lt. and capt. 1781, capt. and lt.-col. 1790; ret. 1792.

Gould was on active service during the war of American independence, and in 1781 was taken prisoner at Yorktown. He entered Parliament for the Morgan pocket borough of Brecon, vacated by his father on moving to the county. In all three lists on the Regency he appears as voting with Opposition—the only evidence of his political line during his first Parliament.

He died 5 Dec. 1846.

P.D.G.T.

## GOWER, *see* LEVESON GOWER

## GOWLAND, Ralph (c.1722–c.1782), of Durham City and Laleham, Mdx.

| DURHAM | 12 Dec. 1761–11 May 1762 |
| COCKERMOUTH | 30 Jan. 1775–1780 |

*b.* c.1722, s. of Samuel Gowland, attorney, of Cook's Court, Lincoln's Inn, by his w. Averil Skinner,¹ and gd.-s. of Ralph Gowland, Durham attorney and antiquary. *m.* 25 July 1749, Ann, da. of John Darby of Foots Cray, Kent, 1s.

During the seven years' war Gowland served with Lord Darlington in the militia, and at the general election of 1761 unsuccessfully contested Durham City as Darlington's candidate. He stood again at the by-election of December 1761 and was returned, but unseated on petition. Neither in wealth nor in popularity could he rival the Lambtons and Tempests, and he had difficulty in meeting the expense of the elections and the petition. According to R. S. Ferguson, *Cumberland and Westmorland M.P.s,* he 'became insolvent in 1775'.

Before the Cockermouth by-election of January 1775 Gowland was recommended by George Johnstone to Sir James Lowther in the most extravagant terms:²

If you have not communicated your intentions to Major Gowland I shall presume to bring an image to your mind that has disturbed me all night. Genius, generosity, fortitude, and affability are painted on his mien, loving and beloved by all men of worth and real virtue. Known and esteemed by the first characters for the extent of his knowledge, with an elocution capable of enforcing his opinions. Talbot raised Thompson, Hertford, David Hume, Rockingham, Burke. But you have a prize in your power superior to all three and your glory and advantage would be in proportion.

Gowland's career in the House scarcely accords with this encomium: he appears on the Opposition side in the division lists available for February 1775–February 1779, after which he is marked on the extant division lists as absent, too ill to attend; and there is no record of his having spoken in the House. The *Public Ledger* in 1779, though partial to those voting with Opposition, has nothing to say about him except that 'he pins his political faith' on Sir James, and votes with him. Gowland did not stand again in 1780, and died soon after.³

¹ Sharp, *Knights & Burgesses of Durham,* 43. ² 20 Jan., *HMC Lonsdale,* 134–5. ³ Ferguson, 365.

L.B.N.

## GRAEME, David (1716–97), of Braco and Gorthy, Perth.

| PERTHSHIRE | 23 Mar. 1764–May 1773 |

*b.* 2 Feb. 1716, 1st s. of James Graeme of Braco by Catherine, da. of Sir William Stirling, 2nd Bt., of Ardoch. *m.* ?1747, Catherine, 1st da. of James Hepburn of Keith, Haddington, sis. of Robert Rickart Hepburn (q.v.), 1da. (who m. 13 June 1768 Thomas Hampden, q.v.). *suc.* fa. 1736, and his cos. Mungo Graeme, M.P., in Gorthy estate 1754.

Served in the Scots brigade in Holland; capt. 1745; lt.-col. 1752; col. British army 1761; col. 105 Ft. 1761–3; maj.-gen. 1762; col. 49 Ft. 1764–8, 19 Ft. 1768–*d;* lt.-gen. 1772; gen. 1783.

Sec. to the Queen Aug. 1761–Jan. 1774; comptroller of the Queen's Household Oct. 1765–Jan. 1774.

Burgess of Edinburgh 1762.

Graeme's father was 'out' in the '15, escaped abroad, and lived for some years in Flanders;¹ and Graeme as a young man joined the Scots brigade in Holland. Sent in February 1745 with a recruiting party to Scotland, he became involved in Jacobite intrigues with John Murray of Broughton;² but returned to Holland in June, thus narrowly missing involvement in the rebellion, of which his mother was an ardent supporter.

In London in 1758 Graeme managed to ingratiate himself with Bute, with whose support he applied, jointly with Richard Oswald, for a contract for supplying the British and Hessian troops in Germany. But Commissary Boyd reported to Samuel Martin: 'When I mentioned to the Prince [Ferdinand] Mr. Oswald's proposal of sending a lieutenant-colonel in the character of a contractor, he immediately objected that we could not treat this gentleman as we might a common undertaker in case the contract was not complied with.' Martin wrote to Bute, 24 Aug. 1758:[3]

> I . . . acquaint your Lordship on the first opportunity with Prince Ferdinand's sentiments upon the employment of that gentleman who appears to me as he does to you a very unexceptionable man in his character.

Nevertheless Graeme secured army contracts; but in 1760 Oswald and Graeme were disgraced and their contracts cancelled.[4] Lord North told James Harris in 1764[5] that 'Graeme . . . was a man of low and contemptible character, during the late war being concerning [sic] as an undertaker but dismissed.'

This view was not shared by Bute and George III, who in June 1761 sent Graeme on a secret mission to Germany to ask for the hand of Princess Charlotte of Mecklenburg-Strelitz; and on acceptance, to make arrangements for Harcourt's official embassy and the journey of the Princess to England.[6] His tactful handling of the situation delighted the King, who wrote to Bute:[7] 'The more I see of this affair the more I feel my obligations to my dearest friend in having pointed out Graeme to me.' On his return with the Queen, Graeme was appointed her secretary, and colonel of the Queen's Own Royal Regiment of Highlanders; and as her supposed confidant, he freely used her name in private to obtain political influence and further his friends' interests.

In March 1764, when John Murray succeeded as Duke of Atholl, Graeme stood for Perthshire, with 'the entire approbation of his Majesty's servants', and the support of Bute, Charles Townshend, and Breadalbane.[8] He was unexpectedly opposed by George Drummond, the Atholl candidate. James Stuart Mackenzie wrote to William Mure, 11 Feb. 1764:[9]

> To raise a flame in the country . . . is in my mind as absurd a project as ever I heard of . . . Let me add too . . . that all this bustle and opposition is to be made to the first person belonging to —[the Queen] who has yet appeared among us as a candidate, and that person more peculiarly circumstanced than any other servant can be.

North deplored Graeme's advancement, particularly 'his turning out the Duke of Atholl's friend'.[10]

During the crises of 1765–6 Graeme played his own hand—it is unlikely that the Queen had any knowledge of his intrigues. When Grenville resumed office on 23 May 1765, having forced the King to disclaim Bute and dismiss Stuart Mackenzie, 'General Graeme came to Mr. Grenville's levee (28 May 1765) and made profession of wishing him well and desired to speak with him the first day that was convenient'; but a few days later cancelled the appointment. While listed 'pro' by Rockingham in July 1765, Graeme remained in touch with Temple through his Perthshire friend Robert Mackintosh, a dubious figure, and acting, it was presumed, on behalf of the Queen, embarked upon a secret negotiation. Humphrey Cotes reported to Temple, 13 Oct.:

> Our friend Mackintosh . . . told me of the conversation had with General Graeme, secretary to her Majesty, and showed me the notes he had taken to preserve precision. I in turn acquainted him with the particulars which your Lordship gave me in charge.[11]

At Graeme's request Cotes and Mackintosh prepared a paper, expressing Temple's sentiments: praising 'the Queen's amiable qualities and prudent conduct', he declared his willingness 'to undertake public service' if assured of the King's full 'cordiality and confidence'. Cotes continued: 'Mr. Graeme had not an opportunity of conveying the written paper to the Queen till last Tuesday night when he gave it into her own hand, together with a letter he wrote himself upon the subject.' But nothing more appears about it. Next, under date of 9 Feb. 1766,[12] Bedford wrote in 'Minutes' for the Duke of York:

> Sir Lawrence Dundas desired to speak to me apart to inform me that a friend of his whom he did not name, but I suppose to be Col. Graeme, had told him that morning, viz. that he usually went to the King after the debates in each House to report them and the numbers on the divisions. He told them the King was greatly affected at the result of the last great majority in the House of Commons and that he wished to change his Administration. This Sir Lawrence desired Mr. Grenville and I should be informed of.

Walpole believed that Graeme instigated the meeting on 12 Feb. 1766 between Bute, Bedford and Grenville, arranged by Eglintoun in an attempt to form a united Opposition. 'Certain it is that Colonel Graeme, the Queen's secretary, and much a confidant, had indirectly and by an oblique channel opened a kind of negotiation.'[13] That Graeme wished to have these things believed is more than probable; but what foundation of truth there is to them is very uncertain: there is not a shred of evidence to confirm these stories.

Graeme voted against the repeal of the Stamp Act; and supported the Chatham Administration. His prestige in Scotland stood high. He was active in support of the linen industry and the Forth and Clyde canal; Patrick Craufurd's son James was 'made equerry to the Queen entirely by General Graeme's interest';[14] Lord George Sackville sought his support for General Irwin in Kinross;[15] his interest with Findlater and the Bute connexion secured Kincardineshire for his brother-in-law Robert Rickart Hepburn.[16]

During the negotiations of July 1767, Graeme was privately in touch with Grenville; and next came up against Grafton.[17] On 24 Aug. 1767 Whately wrote to Grenville that Grafton 'has contrived lately to offend the Queen . . . for that, on the vacancy of the place of vice-admiral of Scotland, she expressed her wish that the King might on that occasion bestow a mark of his favour on General Graeme'; but 'Grafton carried the point for Lord March'.

Henceforth Graeme was openly connected with Temple and Grenville; joined with them in supporting Robert Mackintosh, Clive's candidate for Perth Burghs against George Dempster, canvassed for him in Scotland in October 1767, and on his return acted as Mackintosh's confidant and adviser in the complicated legal and parliamentary proceedings arising from Dempster's arrest for alleged bribery.[18] Graeme conferred with the Grenvilles and Clive's agent, John Walsh, who gladly handed over to him Mackintosh's 'vast packets' on election matters and 'desired him to take the general management of the affair'.[19]

In November 1767 General Irwin told Grenville a 'surprising anecdote':[20]

That General Graeme told him that he, General Graeme, had leave from the Queen to go into open Opposition to the present Administration if he chose it; that he had talked much to him of the King's . . . feeling the weakness and insufficiency of the present ministry but not knowing well how to get rid of them . . . that everybody saw and knew that it must end in the King's sending for Mr. Grenville; to which General Irwin said he thought his Majesty was angry and displeased at Mr. Grenville. The General answered him, that had been so but all was forgot and that matters would go very easy with regard to Mr. Grenville and more so with Lord Temple.

Grenville commented: 'Words like these are . . . frequently circulated possibly with no other meaning than to keep up a degree of good humour'; but when after his conversation with Bedford on 4 Dec. Grenville realized that Bedford intended joining Administration, first Temple, and next Whately immediately discussed the situation with Graeme. Whately reported to Grenville, 4 Dec. 1767:[21]

He thinks you were never in so respectable a situation as now, that you preserve all your importance without the support of party, and he feels the liberty you enjoy upon being freed from such party connexions.

Graeme voted with Government on Wilkes and the Middlesex election. But Alexander Carlyle records that in the spring of 1769[22] he found

Graeme talking strongly against Administration for not advising the King to yield to the popular cry . . . I drew an inference, which proved true, that he had been tampering with her Majesty, and using political freedoms, which were not long afterwards the cause of his disgrace. Graeme was a shrewd and sensible man, but the Queen's favour and his prosperity had made him arrogant and presumptuous and he blew himself up.

In May 1773 he decided to resign his seat in favour of his kinsman Thomas Graham of Balgowan. But North, who had always disliked him, seized the opportunity by 'an uncommon exertion of ministerial influence',[23] to restore the Atholl interest. There is no record of Graeme having spoken in the House.

When next on a vacancy the office of Queen's treasurer was in January 1774 secured by North for Lord Guilford, Graeme 'declined to continue in the inferior office'.[24] He 'retired into obscurity in Scotland for the rest of his days', living on estates encumbered with debts he had incurred by his 'large hearted' spending and extravagant life at court.[25] His attempts in 1775 and 1779 to return to favour and 'manifest his zeal for his Majesty's service' met with no success;[26] and he did not try to re-enter Parliament, but at every election exerted his interest against the Atholl family's control of Perthshire.

He died 19 Jan. 1797, mainly remembered as the man 'who brought over the Queen from Germany'.

[1] *HMC Stuart*, i. 495-9; ii. 202, 234, 268. [2] *Scots Brigade in Holland*, ii. 230, 261-2, 282, 294; *Murray of Broughton's Memorials*, 133, 139. [3] *Bute mss*. [4] Add. 17495, f. 150b. [5] Harris's memorandum, 22 Sept. 1764. [6] Sedgwick, 55-62; Graeme's letters in Add. 36796. [7] Sedgwick, 58. [8] *HMC Laing*, ii. 442. [9] *Caldwell Pprs*. ii (2), p. 235. [10] Harris's memorandum, 22 Sept. 1764. [11] *Grenville Pprs*. iii. 92-93, 96-97, 190, 192. [12] *Bedford Corresp*. iii. 327. [13] *Mems. Geo. III*, ii. 208. [14] P. Craufurd to W. Mure, 11 Dec. 1766, *Caldwell Pprs*. ii(2), p. 96. [15] Sackville to Irwin, 27 Mar., 27 June, 27 July 1766, Germain mss, Clements Lib., Ann Arbor. [16] Add. 38205, ff. 138, 139, 142. [17] *Grenville Pprs*. iv. 123, 157. [18] G. Clive to Ld. Clive, 8 Oct. 1767; Mackintosh to Graeme, 16 Nov., Clive mss. [19] Walsh to Clive, 22 Dec. 1767, ibid. [20] *Grenville Pprs*. iv. 233-4. [21] Grenville mss (JM). [22] *Autobiog*. 515. [23] Strathmore to Portland, 20 July 1773, Portland mss. [24] Harris's memoranda, 12 Jan. 1774, 16 May 1778. [25] Carlyle, *Autobiog*. 515; L. G. Graeme, *Or and Sable*, 478-81. [26] Add. 38306, ff. 107, 109.

E.H.-G.

## GRAFTON, Duke of, *see* FITZROY, Augustus Henry

## GRAHAM, George (1730-1801), of Kinross, Kinross-shire.

KINROSS-SHIRE 1780-1784, 1790-1796

*b.* 17 May 1730, 2nd s. of John Graham, Edinburgh merchant, by his 1st w. Agnes, da. of Rev. Robert MacFarlane, minister of Buchanan. *unm.*

Burgess of Edinburgh 1777; ld. lt. Kinross 1794–*d.*

Graham's father's second wife was Helen, sister of Robert and Sir William Mayne (qq.v.), who obtained appointments in the East India Company's service for Graham's half-brothers, John and Thomas. In 1765 George Graham was settled as a planter in Jamaica, but, failing to prosper, decided in 1770, on the advice of Sir William Mayne, to seek his fortune in India. There, having secured a contract for supplying the troops in Bengal, and engaging in private trade (in association with the House of Mayne in Lisbon), within four years he acquired 'a competency to enjoy the rest of his days'.[1]

He owed his position mainly to his brother John, a member of the Bengal council, and a close associate of Warren Hastings. When, after the arrival of the new councillors under North's Regulating Act, John Graham resigned, George accompanied him to England. Settling in London as a merchant in association with Robert Mayne, he engaged in an extensive trade in wine and East India goods between Lisbon, China and India.

In 1777 he purchased the estate of Kinross, which gave him the controlling interest in a county in which his only considerable rival was John Adam of Blair Adam, whose son William then represented Gatton on Sir William Mayne's interest. Returned unopposed at the general election of 1780, Graham was thus described in the *English Chronicle* in 1781:

> He is a man of moderate principles but not without discernment, and has more sober sense than many men who make a greater bustle in the world. He is likely to be ministerial as most of his connexions incline that way; although if Opposition could once get hold of him it would be a difficult matter to alter his opinion, of which he is tenacious perhaps to obstinacy.

He supported the North Administration to the end, but thereafter his political affiliations were uncertain. He did not vote on Shelburne's peace preliminaries, 18 Feb. 1783; and voted for Fox's East India bill, 27 Nov. 1783. On the formation of the Pitt Administration Robinson and Dundas were 'hopeful' of his support, and although Robinson shortly afterwards counted him among the converts,[2] in Stockdale's list of 19 Mar. 1784 he was listed among Pitt's opponents. In 1784 Graham was mentioned as a candidate for Clackmannan, which alternated with Kinross in representation, but was not returned.

He died in London 18 Dec. 1801, leaving his estates to his illegitimate son James, on condition that he married his cousin Anna Maria, daughter of Thomas Graham, M.P., who, failing this marriage, succeeded to Kinross.[3]

[1] J. Graham sen. to G. Graham, 1 Feb. 1765, Sir W. Mayne to G. Graham, 10 Aug. 1771, Kinross House mss, SRO. [2] Laprade, 54. [3] L. G. Graeme, *Or and Sable*, 597–8.

E.H.-G.

## GRAHAM, James, Mq. of Graham (1755–1836).

RICHMOND 1780–1784
GREAT BEDWYN 1784–23 Sept. 1790

*b.* 8 Sept. 1755, o.s. of William, 2nd Duke of Montrose [S] and Earl Graham [GB], by Lady Lucy Manners, da. of John, 2nd Duke of Rutland. *educ.* Eton 1765–72; Trinity, Camb. 1773; Grand Tour. *m.* (1) 3 Mar. 1785, Lady Jemima Elizabeth Ashburnham (*d.*17 Sept. 1786), 1st da. of John, 2nd Earl of Ashburnham, 1s. *d.v.p.*; (2) 24 July 1790, Lady Caroline Maria Montagu, 1st da. of George, 4th Duke of Manchester, 2s. 5da. *suc.* fa. as 3rd Duke of Montrose 23 Sept. 1790. K.T. 14 June 1793; resigned when appointed K.G. 31 Mar. 1812.

Ld. of Treasury Dec. 1783–9; vice-pres. Board of Trade July 1789–90; jt. paymaster gen. July 1789–91; P.C. 1 Aug. 1789; master of the horse 1790–5; commr. for Indian affairs 1791–1803; ld. justice gen. of Scotland 1795–*d.*; pres. Board of Trade and jt. postmaster gen. 1804–6; master of the horse 1807–21; ld. chamberlain 1821–7, 1828–30.

Ld. lt. Hunts. 1790–3, Stirling 1794–*d.*, Dunbarton 1813–*d.*

On his return from the grand tour in February 1778, Graham reported to Robert Murray Keith in Vienna his concern at the 'lethargic torpor' at home in face of the disasters in America, and, fascinated by Fox's eloquence, contrasted his energetic leadership with ministerial irresolution. The threat of French invasion having prevented his return to Vienna, he wrote to Keith, 28 Apr. 1778:

> Scotland has at least the merit of indefatigable efforts —about 12,000 volunteers have not sufficed to blunt the edge of martial prowess, or the refusal of a militia some time ago . . . to prevent the rising of the inhabitants for . . . internal defence. My humble opinion was that this was the moment to press Administration for a national and legal body of troops . . . subject to English militia laws.

He offered to raise a regiment of light dragoons, but his offer was refused. Professing no party connexions, he sent Keith his 'unbiassed judgment' on 14 Dec. 1778:

> Internal confusion and disunion of our leading men, the effect of want of success, and a determined Opposition openly declaring its intention to clog the wheels of Government in weakening our own efforts, chiefly constitute the strength of France.

Without a seat in the Commons, 'though eagerly wishing it', Graham joined a social set which included members of the Opposition. He wrote to Keith, 8 Apr. 1779:

> Pleasure is my resource, 'tis to that I am carried by taste and driven to by necessity . . . As soon as I have an opportunity, believe me, you shall hear of me, how I cannot tell but to do good or some harm I am determined.

When in 1779 his father gave him control of his Scottish estates, Graham proceeded to restore the family electoral interest. In Dunbartonshire he attacked the Argyll interest and at the general election secured the return (on petition) of his friend George Keith Elphinstone against Lord Frederick Campbell. In Stirlingshire he so successfully challenged the interest of Sir Lawrence Dundas that Dundas, to avoid the defeat of his son Thomas, was forced to agree to bring in Graham for Richmond, with no obligation to join the Dundases in Opposition.[1]

Listed 'doubtful' by Robinson in 1780, Graham for a time was more prominent in society than in politics. The *English Chronicle* commented in 1781: 'He is a young nobleman of very promising abilities and admirable address . . . he will undoubtedly prove a most important acquisition whichever party he espouses.' By the winter of 1781 he had allied himself with Henry Dundas; voted with Government, 12 Dec., on Lowther's motion against the war; but a few days later was concerned in Dundas's schemes to oust Sandwich. When Dundas, having secured the removal of Germain, agreed to support Government on the censure of the Admiralty on 20 Feb. 1782, Graham followed suit; but on 22 and 27 Feb. voted with Opposition on Conway's motions against the war. He voted with North on the censure motions of 8 and 15 March. Under the Rockingham Administration Graham seized the opportunity provided by Shelburne's circular letter on arming the people to move on 15 May 1782 for a Scottish militia, as 'a shield to the constitution against the turbulent grasp of democracy and the encroachments of the Crown'. The bill reached its third reading on 10 June, when the secretary at war, supported by the commander-in-chief, moved for a clause permitting the regular army to recruit from the Scottish militia. Graham indignantly rejected any such discrimination between England and Scotland, and when the motion was carried against him withdrew the bill. On 17 June he successfully initiated legislation to repeal the Act prohibiting the wearing of Highland dress, and during the recess was publicly thanked for his efforts by a meeting in Edinburgh. He took the lead in raising a corps of Edinburgh volunteers, 'on Lord Shelburne's plan', to be 'clothed in Highland dress and called the Caledonian Band' with himself as colonel.[2]

Graham voted for Shelburne's peace preliminaries on 18 Feb. 1783, and in March was listed as attached to him and Lord Advocate Dundas, whose lead he followed under the Coalition. On 19 May he joined Pitt and Dundas in opposing the proposal to discharge the motion for papers on the case of Powell and Bembridge; and on 2 June supported Dundas's motion that the proceedings against Sir Thomas Rumbold be not discontinued by any prorogation of Parliament. On 5 June he seconded Dempster's proposals for relief for the famine-stricken districts of Scotland, and on the 24th 'spoke long and ably' in favour of assistance for the cotton and linen manufactures. On 27 Nov. 1783 he attacked Fox's East India bill 'in terms of the greatest acrimony', and on the dismissal of the Coalition was appointed a lord of the Treasury in Pitt's Administration.[3]

At the general election of 1784 Graham, through his connexion with Dundas and Archibald Douglas, was brought in for Great Bedwyn by Lord Ailesbury, uncle of the Duke of Buccleuch. In the new Parliament he increased his reputation as a fluent and forceful speaker on Scottish questions. In August 1784 he strongly supported the bill for the restoration of the forfeited estates, and backed Dempster's motion for improving the lot of Scottish fishermen; took a prominent part in 1785 in obtaining redress of Scottish grievances on distilling; but in 1788 supported Pitt's view that the Act of 1786 should be amended as giving the Scots an unfair advantage over English distillers. On 9 May 1788 he voted with Administration on Impey's impeachment and challenged the managers of Hastings's impeachment to explain their objections to an examination of their accounts. He was an effective Government speaker during the Regency debates.[4]

In May 1789 when Warren Hastings protested to the Commons against Burke's reference to him at his trial as the instigator of the 'murder' of Nunducomar, Graham insisted that, irrespective of precedent, the shorthand writer be examined about the speech. On 4 May, declaring that Hastings was entitled to the protection of the House against unsubstantiated allegations, he moved that no directions had been given to the managers 'respecting the condemnation or execution of Nunducomar'. Fox at first acquiesced, but when he insisted that no censure of Burke be implied, Graham amended his motion to the effect that Burke should not have spoken the words complained of. Fox violently attacked Graham; angry scenes followed; and on a division Graham's amended motion was carried. On 1 June 1789 he again crossed swords with Fox when he proposed Henry Addington as Speaker.[5]

His services were rewarded by the appointments of vice-president of the Board of Trade and joint paymaster. When the Marquess of Buckingham resigned the lord lieutenancy of Ireland he recommended Graham to succeed him as 'decidedly the fittest of all' and 'more eligible' than Westmorland, who was, however, eventually appointed.[6]

He died 30 Dec. 1836.

[1] Add. 35513, ff. 77, 274; 35515, f. 131; 35517, f. 90; Robinson's survey of 1780. [2] Boswell, *Private Pprs.* xiv. 209, 211, 212, 231–2; Walpole, *Last Jnls.* ii. 371, 392; I. R. Christie, *End of North's*

*Ministry*, 331; Debrett, vii. 152, 162–3, 221–2, 235; *Scots Mag.* 1782, pp. 275, 322–3, 387–8, 444, 501, 666; Kay, *Edinburgh Portraits*, 284–289. [3] Debrett, x. 36, 109, 119, 120, 217; xii. 183–4. [4] Stockdale, iii. 355, 393; v. 279–80; xii. 132–3, 180–1; xiv. 273; xv. 48; Debrett, xvi. 327. [5] Stockdale, xvii. 121, 133, 148–58, 286–7. [6] HMC Fortescue, i. 525.

E.H.-G.

**GRANBY, Mq., of,** *see* **MANNERS, Charles,** *and* **MANNERS, John** (*d.*1770)

**GRANT, Sir Alexander,** 5th Bt. (*d.*1772), of Dalvey, Elgin.

INVERNESS BURGHS    1761–1768

1st s. of Sir Patrick Grant, 4th Bt., by Lydia, da. of William Mackintosh of Borlum. *m.* (1) Elizabeth, da. of Robert Coote of Jamaica, *s.p.*; (2) 1764, Margaret, da. of Alexander Grant of Auchterblair, *s.p.* *suc.* fa. 10 Apr. 1755.

Like others of his family group, impoverished in the Jacobite cause, Grant sought his fortune abroad and as a young man seems to have settled in Jamaica. By the early 1740s he was a leading West India merchant in Billiter Lane, and proceeded to restore his family influence in Scotland, purchasing extensive estates in the shires of Elgin and Nairn, as well as property in the Inverness district of burghs,[1] which he unsuccessfully contested in 1754.

On friendly terms with Lord Loudoun, Lord Home, and their regimental agent John Calcraft, Grant, during the war, held army contracts, his business interests extending from the Mediterranean to the West Indies, America, Africa, and India. As an authority on colonial commerce, he attended the Board of Trade on 29 Feb. 1760 to give his views on Jamaica currency,[2] and acted as agent for his friends in America in their dealings with the Board.

In politics he attached himself to Bute and with a view to the next election strengthened his interest in Inverness Burghs and the neighbouring counties. On the accession of George III he wrote to Bute, 4 Nov. 1760:[3]

> I have firmly secured my election into next Parliament for the boroughs of Inverness, Fortrose, etc. etc. As a Member of Parliament and a merchant of eminence and credit in London I most humbly offer myself to his Majesty's service and to your Lordship's direction. I hope I know the sphere I move in, out of which I aspire not to be elevated. In it I am a useful subject, as I annually pay many thousand pounds to his Majesty's revenue and have for some years been (not an insignificant) supporter of and contributor to the public credit. I am to come up soon at the head of many hundreds of merchants of great opulency and zealous as myself to present our Address of duty and cordial obedience to our revered young King, whom your Lordship was pleased to honour me with an introduction to, some years ago, which has ever since procured me his gracious notice whenever I appear before him . . . My rank and situation in life gives me

all the honour and felicity I wish to have, except my Sovereign's countenance.

Grant's opponent was Captain D. Brodie, who applied for support to Newcastle, who referred him to Bute.[4] After Bute also had refused to interfere, Brodie appealed again to Newcastle for his interest against Grant, a 'purse-proud citizen too vain to be ever warmly attached to his Grace'. 'I wish', wrote Brodie, 'there may not be too many of his stamp endeavouring to get into Parliament.'[5]

Receiving no encouragement, Brodie withdrew and Grant was unanimously elected. In Parliament he remained faithful to Bute and was among those classed by Fox as favourable to the peace. His claim in October 1763 that the Grenville Administration had no more 'zealous supporter' than himself,[6] was justified by his division record. For his vote of 15 Nov. 1763 condemning the 'North Briton' he was attacked by the Wilkes mob assembled at the Royal Exchange who, recognizing him as a City merchant, shouted '*He* voted for it. Pelt him', and, as Sir Alexander reported to the House, 'he was pelted accordingly'.[7]

He supported the ministry throughout the Wilkes debates and the agitation for the repeal of the cider tax, and spoke strongly in favour of the 'self denying ordinance' introduced 8 Mar. 1764 to curtail the parliamentary privilege of merchant M.P.s by making them liable to bankruptcy proceedings.[8]

After Grenville's fall Grant's political affiliations were uncertain. Though classed by Rockingham in July 1765 as friendly to the new Administration, he voted against the repeal of the Stamp Act. During the Chatham Administration he continued his association with Bute, but in Townshend's parliamentary list of January 1767 was counted as a 'doubtful' Government supporter. To his friend James Grant of Grant he sent on 3 Mar. 1767 an account of the Government's defeat on the land tax.[9] Although himself voting with Administration, he wrote approvingly of the 'eloquence and spirit' of George Grenville and Dowdeswell, and unsympathetically of Townshend and 'the Dictator' Chatham.

In his constituency Grant was faced with serious opposition. Provost of Fortrose from 1762–5, he lost control of the burgh in 1766 to the Munros; and in Nairn he was involved in a lawsuit with the magistracy over estate and burgh boundaries. At the general election of 1768 he was defeated.

He died 1 Aug. 1772.

[1] G. Bain, *Hist. Nairnshire*, 301–3. [2] *Bd. Trade Jnl.* 1759–63, p. 91. [3] Bute mss. [4] Add. 32920, f. 218. [5] Add. 32921, f. 86. [6] Add. 38201, f. 168. [7] Harris's 'Debates', 8 Dec. 1763. [8] Ibid. 10 Feb., 8 Mar.1764. [9] Sir W. Fraser, *Chiefs of Grant*, ii. 447.

E.H.-G.

## GRANT, Francis (1717–81), of Dunphail, Elgin.

ELGINSHIRE    1768–1774

*b.* 10 Aug. 1717, 3rd surv. s. of Sir James Grant, 6th Bt., M.P., by Anna, da. and h. of Sir Humphrey Colquhoun, 5th Bt., of Luss, Dunbarton; bro. of Sir Ludovick Grant (q.v.). *m.* 17 Mar. 1763, Catherine Sophia, da. of Joseph Cox of Stanford Vale, Berks. 3s. 3da.

Entered army 1739; lt.-col. 42 Ft. 1755; lt.-col. commandant 90 Ft. 1761; col. 1762; col. 63 Ft. 1768–*d.*; maj.-gen. 1770; lt.-gen. 1777.

Grant was a favourite nephew of Simon, Lord Lovat, on whose advice he joined the 42nd Ft. (the Black Watch).[1] He served with them in Flanders and in Scotland during the '45; commanded his regiment in America from 1756, fought at Ticonderoga 1758, and served under Amherst in the campaigns of 1759–60, returning home in 1760.[2] He, or his brother Charles, was mentioned as a possible candidate for Inverness-shire at the general election;[3] but in 1761 Grant went to the West Indies, and was present at the taking of Havana in 1762.[4] After James Grant (q.v.) became lieutenant-colonel of the 40th Foot in July 1760, the career of Francis is frequently confused with his kinsman's. In November 1762 a friend, reporting news from Havana, wrote:[5] 'The two Colonel Grants . . . will share high in prize money. Francis will have upwards of £25,000.'

Nevertheless Francis was in serious financial difficulties by 1767 when his nephew James Grant, yr. of Grant (q.v.), proposed to stand down in his favour as candidate for Elginshire at the 1768 general election. Lord Fife, another nephew, indignant at not having been consulted, set up his brother against him, and when Grant won with ministerial support, wrote about him to Grenville:[6]

The Member returned has not a foot of property in this island, or any part of his Majesty's dominions, and the half of the votes that returned him are in the same state with himself.

James Grant, now governor of East Florida, irritated by the behaviour of his nephew Major W. Grant of Ballindalloch (also a nephew of Francis Grant) wrote from St. Augustine to a friend in Scotland, 14 Sept. 1769:[7]

I don't interfere in Major Grant's affairs . . . but I was rather surprised to hear that he had joined the Duffs at last election in opposition to his uncle Colonel Grant, who at that time was rather in a situation which claimed and entitled him to help and assistance from his friends and relations; the poor Colonel at first starting had rather been lucky in the service, but by an imprudent step of quitting an old regiment, at the end of the war, when he was beginning to get on in life and drawing towards fifty, he found himself with additional charge of a wife and children, reduced to live upon such a trifle as could barely furnish him and

them with the necessaries of life—in those circumstances he was attacked in his election by his nephews the Duffs, and Major Grant joined them, not only to keep his uncle out of Parliament but to take the shire of Moray [Elgin] out of the hands of the Grant family. God knows they never were and never will be able to do me any service, in fact I want none from them, but I wrote to Mr. Grant of Grant that if they were pressed . . . I would buy fifty or a hundred pounds a year in the shire of Moray to entitle me to a vote.

In November 1768 the King fulfilled his promise to give Grant the first vacant regiment on the Irish establishment, and appointed him colonel of the 63rd Ft.[8]

Grant voted consistently with Administration, except on the naval captains' petition, 9 Feb. 1773. He is not known to have spoken in the House. In 1774 the Duffs, having gained control of Elginshire, ousted Grant, who after that did not apparently seek to re-enter Parliament.

He died 30 Dec. 1781.

[1] *Chiefs of Grant*, ii. 377, 379–80. [2] *Corresp. of W. Pitt with Colonial Govs.* (ed. Kimball), ii. 128, 129; Add. 25412, f. 83. [3] Sir Harry Erskine to Bute, 21 Apr. 1761, Bute mss. [4] A. M. Delavoye, *Recs. 90th Regt.* p. iii. [5] R. Grant, London merchant, to R. Grant of Tammore, 4 Nov. 1762, Add. 25412, f. 164. [6] 28 Apr. 1768, Grenville mss (JM). [7] Add. 25412, f. 301. [8] *Cal. Home Office Pprs. 1766–9,* p. 1047.

E.H.-G.

## GRANT, James (1720–1806), of Ballindalloch, Banff.

TAIN BURGHS             26 Apr. 1773–1780
SUTHERLANDSHIRE    1 Aug. 1787–1802

*b.* 1720, 2nd s. of Lt.-Col. William Grant of Ballindalloch by Anne, 2nd da. of Ludovick Grant of Grant, M.P. [S]; cos. of Sir Ludovick and Francis Grant (qq.v.). *educ.* Edinburgh Univ. 1736–40. *unm. suc.* nephew as laird of Ballindalloch 12 July 1770.

Ensign 1st Royal Regt. 1741, capt. 1744; maj. 77 Ft. 1757; lt.-col. 40 Ft. 1760; col. 1772; col. 55 Ft. 1775–91; maj.-gen. (in America) 1776; maj.-gen. 1777; lt.-gen. 1782; col. 11 Ft. 1791–*d.*; gen. 1796. Gov. East Florida 1763–73; gov. Stirling castle 1789–*d.*

Grant was educated in the care of Patrick Grant, Lord Elchies, S.C.J., on whose advice he studied law, but, preferring a military career, obtained a commission in his brother's regiment, commanded by James St. Clair (q.v.).[1] He served in Flanders from 1743, fought at Fontenoy, and returned to England in autumn 1745 with St. Clair, who appointed him and Sir Harry Erskine (q.v.) his aides-de-camp for the expedition intended against Canada. Expecting to leave he unsuccessfully appealed to his brother, the laird of Ballindalloch, to 'make him of more consequence in the country' by giving him electoral qualifications in Elginshire and Banffshire.[2] When the American venture was cancelled, Grant, with Erskine and David Hume, served in the L'Orient expedition under St. Clair, who also appointed them his aides-de-camp during his diplomatic mission to Vienna and Turin in 1748.[3] After the peace Grant continued to act as aide-de-camp to St. Clair, who in April 1752 sent him abroad as travelling tutor to his grand-nephew William, 17th Earl of Sutherland. In the spring of 1755 St. Clair ordered him to rejoin his regiment, in expectation of active service.[4]

Through St. Clair and Argyll Grant obtained a major's commission in the new Highland regiment, commanded by Archibald Montgomerie (q.v.); recruited two companies of Grants; and sailed for Charleston, South Carolina, in 1757.[5] In June 1758 the regiment took part in the campaign against Fort Duquesne, during which Grant 'sacrificed with good grace his repugnance for serving under colonial officers for the good of the service'.[6] Taken prisoner in September 1758, he was sent to Montreal and released in November 1759:[7]

In 1760 he served against the Cherokees in South Carolina. Contemptuous of South Carolina's war effort, he had a violent quarrel with Col. Middleton, the provincial commander, over the merits of their respective troops.[8] In 1762 he served in the expeditions against Martinique and Havana. He returned to London in February 1763, renewed his friendship with Sir Harry Erskine, Bute's favourite, and shortly afterwards was appointed governor of East Florida.

An able, if autocratic, administrator, he vigorously promoted the development of communications, agriculture and settlement; took a firm line on 'land grabbing'; and maintained good relations with the Indians, claiming that American backwoodsmen were often the aggressors. On one occasion, in fulfilment of his pledge that 'red and white rogues' be equally punished, he ordered the execution of a white man convicted of having murdered an Indian. Proud of his colony, he wrote to Robert Grant of Tammore, 8 Jan. 1768:[9]

This province, which was a desert when I came to it, though inhabited by Spaniards at least 200 years, will soon be a fruitful and plentiful country, it fills faster with inhabitants than I could well have expected.

In 1770, by the death of his nephew, Grant became laird of Ballindalloch. Hillsborough at once offered him 15 months leave, which Grant however postponed accepting:[10]

People are accustomed to me and will go on as they have begun while I remain with them, but I am afraid of trusting them to themselves. Dissension might creep in if there was a change of measures to mine, and East Florida, which I have taken so much pain about for seven years, would dwindle to nothing.

He wrote to Brigadier Haldimand in West Florida, 20 Oct. 1770:[11] 'I think I shall hardly leave the province for two years, though my friends at home will think me mad, more so when I return from Europe to Florida, which I shall certainly do for a year or two.'

Ill health, however, induced Grant to go home in the early summer of 1771.[12] He now had to face considerable criticism. An opponent wrote: 'Governor Grant may be an excellent officer but he is a most tyrannical governor.' Another complained of his injustice in granting land and 'his persecution shown to those who refuse to submit to his . . . caprices'.[13] Shortly after Dartmouth had succeeded Hillsborough Grant was displaced, and he never again went back to Florida.

In April 1773 he was returned unopposed for Tain Burghs on the Sutherland interest. He voted with Administration, and at the general election of 1774 was re-elected after a contest. While a petition was pending against him, Grant made a violent speech on 2 Feb. 1775, ridiculing what he considered American religious cant, the poor quality of colonial troops, and boasting that with 5,000 regulars he could march from one end of America to the other.[14] Americans present at the debate were incensed.[15] Ralph Izard of South Carolina wrote to George Dempster: 'Lord Sandwich and Colonel Grant have persuaded all ranks of people that Americans are base abject cowards.'[16]

Grant was not interested in a parliamentary career. He wanted another governorship or a high military command; and in the spring of 1775 was sent to America with the rank of brigadier. He served at Boston until the evacuation, and distinguished himself at the capture of New York. After his successful operations on Long Island he wrote to Richard Rigby, 2 Sept. 1776:[17]

You will be glad and Lord North not displeased that we have had the field day I talked of . . . and if a good bleeding can bring those bible-faced Yankees to their senses, the fever of independence should soon abate . . . These cursed saints put me in the newspapers as being killed and rejoiced exceedingly at getting rid of a man who had abused them in Parliament . . . They may from compulsion become dutiful subjects for a time, but they will never be cordial and affectionate . . . In the course of the winter the commissioners will probably be able to bring things to an accommodation, for I don't look for another campaign.

He was wrong. He spent the next two years on active service in New Jersey, fought at Brandywine, took part in the capture of and withdrawal from Philadelphia, and was highly commended by Howe and Clinton, who in 1778 appointed him to command the land forces in the expedition to St. Lucia.

After the capture of the island Grant, crippled by gout and fever, sailed for England, and on his arrival was attacked in the Lords by Shelburne on 25 Nov.

1779,[18] and in the Commons by Sir Charles Bunbury and others on 8 Dec. He defended himself in 'a faithful narrative of his conduct and motives';[19] and when Temple Luttrell taunted him with 'his former gasconades' on American cowardice, claimed that he had referred only to untried, ill disciplined men, and that now, after battle experience, 'he never saw better troops than some of the rebel regiments were'.

At the general election of 1780 Grant lost Tain Burghs and unsuccessfully contested Elgin Burghs. North in 1782 mentioned him to the King as a possible candidate for Inverness-shire or Elginshire.[20] He was an intimate friend of Henry Dundas, whose politics he followed, but who failed to secure his return in 1784 for Elgin Burghs.[21] In 1787 he re-entered Parliament for Sutherland. He voted with Pitt on the Regency, and in 1789 obtained through Dundas the governorship of Stirling castle.[22]

He continued in Parliament until the age of 82, a corpulent, amiable, eccentric old gentleman, well known in London society as a *bon viveur* and *gourmet*. Every summer he travelled north, with his retinue of attendants and his black cook, in his state coach, to his Ballindalloch estates. Here he spent immense sums on improving agriculture, building roads and bridges, dispensing vast hospitality, and ruled his tenants with the same firm but benevolent paternalism which had characterized his government of Florida.

He died 13 Apr. 1806.

[1] Macpherson Grant, *Gen. James Grant of Ballindalloch*, 24–31. [2] Add. 25408, f. 174. [3] Ibid. f. 323; J. Kay, *Edinburgh Portraits*, ii. 22. [4] Add. 25411, f. 98. [5] Add. 17493, f. 28; 25411, ff. 231–6, 253. [6] H. Bouquet to Gen. Forbes, 20 Aug. 1758, Macpherson Grant, 53. [7] *Pprs. of Henry Bouquet*, ii. 499–504, 517–21, 537; *Corresp. of W. Pitt with Colonial Govs.* (ed. Kimball), i. 370–1; *N.Y. Col. Docs.* x. 902–3; *Gent. Mag.* 1759, pp. 173, 223. [8] E. McCrady, *S.C. under Royal Govt.* 350–2; D. D. Wallace, *Life of H. Laurens*, 51. [9] Add. 25412, f. 301. [10] Macpherson Grant, 79. [11] Add. 21729, f. 169. [12] Add. 25412, f. 345. [13] *HMC Dartmouth*, ii. 83, 185. [14] Almon, i. 135. [15] W. A. Duer, *Life of Ld. Stirling* (N.J. Hist. Soc.), 162–4. [16] *Corresp. of Ralph Izard*, ed. A. Deas, 79. [17] Macpherson Grant, 85. [18] Almon, xv. 45–46. [19] Ibid. xvi. 155–6, 162. [20] Fortescue, v. 362. [21] Laprade, 102. [22] Macpherson Grant, 106.

E.H.-G.

## GRANT, James (1738–1811), of Castle Grant, Elgin.

ELGINSHIRE    1761–1768

BANFFSHIRE    1790–June 1795

*b.* 19 May 1738, o.s. of Sir Ludovick Grant (q.v.), 7th Bt., by his 2nd w. Lady Margaret Ogilvie. *educ.* Westminster 1747–55; Christ's, Camb. 1756–8; Grand Tour 1758–60. *m.* 4 Jan. 1763, his 2nd cos. Jean, da. and h. of Alexander Duff of Hatton, 7s. 7da. *suc.* fa. as 8th Bt. 18 Mar. 1773.

Gen. cashier of Excise in Scotland 1795–d.; ld. lt. Inverness 1794–1809.

At school and at Cambridge, Grant's closest friend was Thomas Robinson (q.v.), his companion for part of his European tour. After studying at Geneva, Grant travelled extensively in Italy, whence, in the summer of 1760, he was summoned home by his father to contest Elginshire. On his return journey he sent Robinson his reflections upon 'the character most consistent with the man of honour as representative of his country in the House of Commons':

> He should have studied . . . every form of government . . . he should be master of the law of nations in general, as well as of . . . particular treaties. He should be capable of distinguishing when . . . to incline the balance towards the executive part of the government and when to the people . . . He should consider any bill that is offered in Parliament in the most extensive light . . . He should be a father to his family and tenants . . . he should be as cool and unprejudiced in his determinations, as expeditious and resolute in executing them: to sum up . . . he should be slave to his *country*, subject to his *King*, and friend to all mankind . . . There are many who have these principles really at heart but few act up to them. We have a notion that one must attach themselves to one party, and vote always for them, which is the same thing as to say he must not make use of the liberty given him by the constitution.[1]

Grant entered public life under the wing of his mother's cousins Lord Kinnoull and the archbishop of York,[2] friends of Newcastle. On 1 Nov. 1762 Lord Findlater, in great concern over political divisions, wrote to Hardwicke recommending his grandson, Grant, to his protection:

> He appears to me a young man of good principles and dispositions, zealous for our royal family and the constitution, and vastly desirous to promote industry and right sentiments in his father's large Highland estate. Although he has been universally well beloved by all his contemporaries at Westminster, Cambridge, Geneva etc. yet he is not forward and needs to be encouraged . . . I flatter myself his capacity and good sense may some time or other make him useful to this country and particularly to that part of it to which he belongs.

Newcastle, in view of Findlater's attitude, could not count upon Grant's following him into opposition, and on 13 Nov. 1762 listed him as 'doubtful'; early in December Fox counted him among those favourable to the peace.[3]

Grant supported Bute on the cider tax,[4] and was not mentioned by Stuart Mackenzie among the Scots 'scabby sheep' voting against Administration on Wilkes in November 1763; but in the divisions of 15 and 18 Feb. 1764, on general warrants, he voted with Opposition although normally counted a Government supporter. In May 1764 Newcastle again listed him as 'doubtful'. A diligent but inconspicuous Member, he conscientiously carried out the instructions sent to him by his constituency on Scottish and local affairs.[5]

After his father had made over to him the family estates in 1763 his main interest lay in agricultural and social improvement, in settlement schemes for disbanded soldiers, and from 1765 in founding his new town of Granton.[6] As a result he was absent from Parliament for most of the 1765 session.[7] Listed 'pro' by Rockingham in the summer of 1765, he voted with Administration on the repeal of the Stamp Act.[8] In April 1766 he sought, through Newcastle, a place for his father, as a friend of Administration.[9] During the winter of 1766-7 he was listed by Rockingham 'doubtful', by Townshend 'Government', and by Newcastle 'friend'. In fact he was absent in Scotland, and when in February 1767 a call of the House was ordered, asked his kinsman Sir Alexander Grant to make his excuses. Sir Alexander replied, 3 Mar. 1767:[10]

> Attendance is now more strictly insisted than you or I have heretofore known it to be—party and Opposition running very high indeed. [The Speaker] allowed the reasons for your absence to be cogent, but . . . advised me to move for leave of the House, which I did for a month, and it is granted, so that your non-attendance [sic] is legally dispensed with.

It is doubtful whether he put in many more attendances in Parliament; he decided during the summer of 1767 to give up his seat at the next election to his uncle Francis Grant.

His costly projects of 'peopling and planting' had greatly increased the family debts, which after his father's death in 1773 were estimated at £130,000. To extricate himself 'from a most perilous situation', Sir James was obliged to retrench and sell large parts of his estates. In 1781, with the assistance of his brother-in-law Henry Mackenzie ('the Man of Feeling') and Thomas Robinson (now Lord Grantham), he petitioned the Treasury for repayment of debts incurred by his predecessors in Government service during the Revolution, the '15 and the '45, but got little encouragement. Warned by Grantham that 'without parliamentary interest applications were not much attended to', Sir James tried to obtain a seat after the death of Simon Fraser in February 1782, but was disappointed. In 1784 he stood for Inverness-shire, but, refusing to make use of fictitious votes as 'illegal and no less ruinous to the title-deeds of families than hurtful to the Constitution', was defeated by Lord William Gordon.[11]

He died 18 Feb. 1811.

[1] *Chiefs of Grant*, ii. 432. [2] Add. 32911, f. 117. [3] Add. 35449, ff. 345, 346. [4] *Chiefs of Grant*, ii. 434-5. [5] *HMC Laing*, ii. 443. [6] *Scots Mag.* 1763, p. 346; *Chiefs of Grant*, ii. 447. [7] Ibid. ii. 446. [8] Sir Alex. Gilmour to Newcastle, 18 Feb. 1766, Add. 32974 f. 24. [9] Add. 32974, f. 286. [10] *Chiefs of Grant*, ii. 447. [11] Ibid. i. 450-2; ii. 474-7, 481-2.

E.H.-G.

**GRANT, John** (c.1720-1804), of Waltham Place, Berks.

FOWEY 1784-Feb. 1786

*b.* c.1720, 3rd s. of Rev. John Grant, rector of Nolton, Pemb. *m.* (1) 1767, Alicia (*d.*16 Nov. 1785), da. of Dr. Robert Gilbert, canon of Salisbury, 1s.; (2) 30 June 1788, Hon. Charlotte Bouverie, da. of Jacob, 1st Visct. Folkestone, sis. of William and Edward Bouverie (qq.v.), *s.p.*

According to an obituary note in the *Gentleman's Magazine* (1804, p. 91) Grant was 'a native of Scotland'; went out as a regimental surgeon in the service of the East India Company; rose to the rank of major; and made a fortune in India. A correspondent, 'M.S.', claiming to correct the note (ibid. p. 104), states his parentage as given above; and says that Grant 'accompanied Sir Eyre Coote, in 1739 [should be 1759], in the 84th regiment to India; and in 1762, under Major Adams, was greatly instrumental to the re-establishment of Jaffier Ali Cawn . . . in Bengal'. But his name does not appear in the army list among the officers of the 84th regiment nor in Hodson's *Officers of the Bengal Army, 1758-1834*. Still, in Parliament he was usually referred to as Major Grant. Speaking in the House, 4 Aug. 1784, he claimed to have been 'almost the only officer who served the Company, and gained nothing by it'.[1] He became a partner in Pybus & Co., bankers, of Old Bond Street, London; and in 1776 purchased Waltham Place, in Berks.[2]

In 1780 Grant nibbled at Cricklade, for which Robert Fletcher, another East India officer (married to Ann Pybus), had sat 1768-74. In 1784 he was returned to Parliament as Government candidate on the Edgcumbe interest at Fowey, his seat being listed by Robinson in December 1783 among the six to be obtained from Lord Edgcumbe at £3,000 each.[3] He voted for Pitt's parliamentary reform proposals, 18 Apr. 1785; and intervened in four debates: in three on Pitt's East India bill (19 July, and 2 and 4 Aug. 1784), and in one on the budget, 9 May 1785.[4] Whether his vacating his seat when Lord Edgcumbe's eldest son came of age was prearranged is unascertained, and so are its financial terms.

He died 8 Jan. 1804.

[1] Debrett, xvi. 341. [2] *VCH Berks*. iii. 174. [3] Laprade, 108. [4] Debrett, xvi. 132, 133, 136, 319, 341; xviii. 230.

L.B.N.

**GRANT, Sir Ludovick**, 7th Bt. (1707-73), of Castle Grant, Elgin.

ELGINSHIRE 1741-1761

*b.* 13 Jan. 1707, 1st surv. s. of Sir James Grant, M.P., 6th Bt., and bro. of Francis Grant (q.v.). *educ.* St. Andrews and Edinburgh Univs.; *adv.* 1728. *m.* (1)

6 July 1727, Marion (*d.*Jan. 1735), da. of Sir Hew Dalrymple, 1st Bt., of North Berwick, ld. pres. of the court of session, 1da.; (2) 31 Oct. 1735, Lady Margaret Ogilvie, da. of James, 5th Earl of Findlater [S], 1s. 7da. *suc.* fa. 16 Jan. 1747.

*Commr. of police Dec. 1737–Apr. 1741.*

In 1754 Sir Ludovick Grant was returned unopposed for Elginshire with the support of Administration. The place of commissioner of police he had surrendered in 1741 to be held in trust for him by a kinsman, and he was anxious to obtain further preferment. At odds with Argyll, he tried to ingratiate himself with Newcastle. But despite his subservience he received few favours. He had little influence in Parliament, where he is not known to have spoken, and was distrusted by many of his fellow Scots. His obsession with money and property involved him in frequent lawsuits and in intrigues even against relations and old friends.[1]

During the change of Administration Grant seems to have sat on the fence. In 1757, while counted by Newcastle among the Scots attached to himself, he was absent from the division of 2 May on the loss of Minorca. Although not prominent in the Scottish militia agitation, he was appointed to the parliamentary committee for preparing the bill, and presumably voted for it since he was not listed by Newcastle among those who might be persuaded to abstain.

As the general election approached, Grant plunged into intrigues. Lord Deskfoord warned Newcastle, 6 Mar. 1760:[2]

> Sir Ludovick Grant is set out for London where he will have some favours to ask and I think your Grace should previously to your granting them, stipulate with him that he should give his interest in Elgin [Burghs] at next election to Mr. [Andrew] Mitchell. If this point is not fixed he may possibly give your Grace's friends some trouble.

By this time his avarice and self-seeking had brought him into disrepute even with many of his clan, who welcomed the proposal that he should withdraw from Elginshire in favour of his son. A kinsman wrote, 24 Aug. 1760:[3]

> Mr. Grant of Grant . . . is much more esteemed in England than his father and by what I hear would have more interest were he to try . . . I think the name is but in little favour at court at this time. Sir Ludovick ought either to make himself more or less respected, I am in great hopes his son will. It's only at such times as this that he has it most in his power, but for the sake of a dirty pension he can sacrifice his interest and have no more regard paid to him than to his servant.

Sir Ludovick, having agreed to support Mitchell in Elgin Burghs, informed Newcastle of his intention to bring in his son for Elginshire. He himself proposed standing for Inverness Burghs, which Sir

Alexander Grant (q.v.) had been nursing for years.[4] Sir Alexander, however, refused to withdraw in favour of his chief, and 'Sir Lud. with ane apology for past conduct' eventually gave him his support.[5] Sir Ludovick had earlier intended to set up his brother Francis Grant (q.v.) for Inverness-shire, while another brother contested Dunbartonshire. Sir Harry Erskine commented to Bute, 21 Apr. 1761:[6] 'Too great a number of one family, and especially of Grants, is what I presume your Lordship would not be solicitous to have in Parliament.'

In poor health and permanently lame from a riding accident, Sir Ludovick retired from Parliament to his estates which, with all their accumulated debts, he made over to his son in 1763. Having lost his 'dirty pension' by the removal of his kinsman from the Board of Police in October 1761, he sought to obtain from the Rockingham Administration the lucrative place of receiver-general of the land tax in Scotland. James Grant wrote to Newcastle, 1 Apr. 1766:[7]

> Your Grace, knowing my father's services to Government, his extensive interest . . . in the country and his constant attachment to the principles of the present Administration, will think it proper that he should now receive some mark of his Majesty's favour. And you will think it more proper as he has of late years, without, I am sure, deserving it, been discountenanced, which to an old and faithful subject can never be agreeable.

Sir Ludovick was again disappointed. He died 18 Mar. 1773.

[1] *Chiefs of Grant*, ii. [2] Add. 32903, f. 110. [3] Add. 25412, f. 83 [4] Add. 32911, f. 117. [5] Sir A. Grant to Sir Rob. Gordon of Gordonstoun, 29 Dec. 1760 (misdated), *HMC Laing*, ii. 458. [6] Bute mss. [7] Add. 32974, f. 286.

E.H.-G.

**GRANT, William** (1701–64), of Prestongrange, Haddington.

ELGIN BURGHS  18 Feb. 1747–Nov. 1754

*bap.* 4 May 1701, 2nd s. of Sir Francis Grant (Lord Cullen S.C.J.), 1st Bt., of Cullen of Buchan, Banff, by Jean, da. of Rev. William Meldrum, Tolbooth Kirk, Edinburgh. *educ.* Edinburgh Univ.; M. Temple 1721; adv. 1722. *m.* c.1729, Grizel, da. and h. of Rev. John Miller of Neilston, Renfrew, 4da.

*Procurator for Church of Scotland and principal clerk of assembly 1731–46; solicitor-gen. for Scotland 1737–42; commr. for fisheries and manufactures 1738; lord adv. Feb. 1746–Aug. 1754; raised to Scottish bench as Lord Prestongrange 14 Nov. 1754; commr. for annexed estates 1754.*

Grant was a hard working lawyer, of 'virtuous integrity',[1] owing his political advancement to Archibald, Duke of Argyll, whose personal affection he retained despite his attachment to the interests of his clan and kinsmen, whom Argyll disliked.

In July 1754 Newcastle, anxious to see Robert

Dundas as lord advocate, secured for Grant promotion to the Scottish bench, and on the appointment being formally gazetted in November, Grant vacated his seat in the House.[2] In 1760 he unsuccessfully pressed his claims to the presidency of the court of session in opposition to Dundas, by then his son-in-law.[3]

He died 23 May 1764.

[1] Brunton & Haig, *Senators of College of Justice*, 519–20; Ramsay of Ochtertyre, *Scotland & Scotsmen*, i. 121–7. [2] Add. 32736, ff. 225, 276. [3] Add. 32903, f. 77.

E.H.-G.

### GRAVES, Thomas (1725–1802), of Thanckes, Cornw.

EAST LOOE    2 Jan.–May 1775

*b.* 23 Oct. 1725, 2nd s. of R.-Adm. Thomas Graves by Elizabeth, da. of Rev. Gilbert Budgell; bro. of William Graves (q.v.). *m.* 22 June 1771, Elizabeth, da. and coh. of William Peere Williams of Cadhay, Devon, 2s. 3da. *cr.* Baron Graves [I], with a pension of £1,000 p.a. 24 Oct. 1794.
Lt. R.N. 1743; cdr. 1754; capt. 1755; r.-adm. 1779; v.-adm. 1787; adm. 1794.
Gov. Newfoundland 1761–3.

On 5 Oct. 1774, ten days before the general election, North wrote to Robinson: 'I have promised Mr. Graves that he shall come in for East Looe, as soon as we can place Sir Charles Whitworth in any other seat'; and the next day: 'I promised Mr. Buller that if we could find a seat for Sir Charles Whitworth even before the election, Mr. Graves should come in for East Looe.'[1] No Christian name was given in either letter, and neither of the brothers was returned at the general election; but Thomas Graves in January replaced Whitworth at East Looe, and Buller's long connexion with the Admiralty seems to suggest that his candidate was the naval officer. Yet Thomas Graves held the seat for four months only, possibly as a stop-gap for William.

There is no record of Thomas Graves having voted or spoken in the House, nor does he appear to have stood for Parliament at any other time.

He died 9 Feb. 1802.

[1] Laprade, 24.

M.M.D.

### GRAVES, William (?1724–1801), of Thanckes, Cornw.

WEST LOOE           1768–1774
EAST LOOE    5 June 1775–Nov. 1783, 1784–May
                         1786, 1796–Apr. 1798

*b.* ?1724, 1st s. of R.-Adm. Thomas Graves, and bro. of Thomas Graves (q.v.). *educ.* Balliol, Oxf. 20 Nov. 1741, aged 17; M. Temple 1739, called 1747.
Master in Chancery 1761; bencher M. Temple 1782, reader 1790, treasurer 1794.

In 1768 Graves was returned on the Buller interest at West Looe. His first recorded vote was with Administration on the Middlesex election, 8 May 1769, but in the division of 25 Jan. 1770 he voted against them; remained in opposition till the end of the Parliament, and in 1774 was classed by Robinson as 'contra'. Before the general election Robinson noted that Graves's seat at West Looe, now managed by John Buller jun., would be available for an Administration candidate, and showed no intention of transferring him to East Looe or finding him another seat. In June 1775, when his brother Thomas vacated his seat at East Looe, William Graves was returned on the interest of John Buller sen., and henceforth consistently voted with North's Administration till its fall.

During his first Parliament Graves spoke frequently on a variety of subjects, but after 1775 made fewer speeches and their substance is generally not reported; his only known departure from a mild pro-ministerial line was over the bill for new modelling the supreme court of judicature of Bengal, 19 June 1781, when he declared 'he felt the greatest indignation at seeing such a bill patronized or defended by any one; it militated against every principle of justice and equity . . . was of so unjust a nature, he should hold himself unworthy of the name of a legislator if he should give his consent to any part of it'.[1] It was his last recorded speech before 1790.

In 1784 Graves was again returned for East Looe. In William Adam's list of May 1784 he was classed as 'Administration', but no vote by him is recorded before he vacated his seat in May 1786.

He died 30 Apr. 1801, aged 77.

[1] Debrett, iii. 639.

M.M.D.

### GRAY, Charles (1696–1782), of Holly Trees, Colchester, Essex.

COLCHESTER    26 Feb. 1742–13 Mar. 1755, 1761–
                              1780

*bap.* 20 Sept. 1696, s. of George Gray, glazier and alderman of Colchester, by his w. Elizabeth. *educ.* Colchester g.s.; G. Inn 1724, called 1729. *m.* (1) 1726 Sarah (*d.*June 1751), da. of John Webster, wid. of Ralph Creffield, 2da. *d.v.p.*;[1] (2) 1755 Mary, da. of Randle Wilbraham (q.v.), *s.p.*
Alderman, Colchester 1734; bencher G. Inn 1737, treasurer 1755; recorder, Ipswich 1761–76; trustee of the British Museum.

Gray was disinherited by his father, and it was from the family of his first wife that he derived a great part of his substance. As a barrister he had a large practice, and he was moreover 'steward of many local manors, very lucrative appointments'.[2]

In Newcastle's 'State of Elections', March 1754, the note is placed against Gray: 'A Tory, who will probably succeed, though strongly contested.' He was returned on scrutiny and unseated on petition. In 1761 he was returned unopposed on a compromise with I. M. Rebow. He did not receive Newcastle's summons at the beginning of the autumn session. But on 1 Nov., Lord Barrington, asked by Newcastle to consider who in the Commons 'would make proper commissioners of accounts', named Gray among the unexceptionable men who 'will do you no harm'.[3] Fox listed him in December 1762 among those favourable to the peace preliminaries. As a Tory and completely independent, he was marked by Jenkinson in the autumn of 1763 as 'doubtful'; but no vote of his against the Grenville Government is recorded. In July 1765 Rockingham classed him as 'contra'; and he voted against the repeal of the Stamp Act, 22 Feb. 1766. In November 1766 Rockingham listed him as 'Tory, perhaps not ministerial', which was accurate: Gray voted against the Government on the land tax, 27 Feb. 1767. 'No partisan of either side can be a judge of the state of the nation', wrote to him his friend and relative, T. Falconer, 20 Jan. 1770. 'Your cool judgment will determine rationally.' And on 4 Apr.: 'As you regard all parties with an equal eye . . .'[4]

In 1768 Gray and Rebow were re-elected after an expensive contest against the Scottish banker Alexander Fordyce. On 4 Apr. 1770 Falconer was grieved to hear that Gray's health suffered from the strain of the session, which suggests both that he attended Parliament and that he no longer felt equal to it. In 1774 he seems to have considered retiring—Falconer wrote to him, 6 May 1775:[5]

> The town of Colchester had the best reasons to persist in its former choice, and your declining the first offer was a happy circumstance to make their selection of you more honourable than any preceding one.

At the end of the Parliaments of 1768-74 and 1774-1780, Gray was classed by Robinson as 'pro'; over the royal marriage bill, March 1772, as 'pro, present', and over the contractors bill, 12 Feb. 1779, as 'pro, out of town'. Yet during the 12 years 1768-80 he does not appear in a single division list, though 14 name those voting on the Government side. The *Public Ledger* wrote about him in 1779: 'A very old man, who has not attended these two years.' And Robinson in his electoral survey of July 1780: 'It is apprehended Mr. Gray is too infirm and too old to stand again.' He now retired, having already in 1776 resigned the recordership of Ipswich 'on account of his age and infirmities'.[6]

Only four speeches definitely known to be his are recorded 1761-80: 29 Mar. 1762, on the game bill

(see extracts from his parliamentary notebook, *HMC 14th Rep. IX, Round*); 7 Feb. 1764, when Gray proposed, 'reduced into a question', a scheme put forward by his father-in-law, Randle Wilbraham for amending the Cider Act;[7] 6 Apr. 1770, to move to bring in a bill to empower the Speaker to order writs during a vacation;[8] and 16 May 1774, for a duty on hawkers.[9] The original notebook, which has not been traced, might disclose more about his parliamentary activities; the printed extracts show a preponderant interest in legal questions and election petitions.

Falconer's letters indirectly point to interests which they had in common: they were Hebrew and classical scholars, antiquaries and numismatists; humanitarians with a real feeling for the poor, for their condition and education, and for the suffering of negro slaves and the condition of indentured labour; interested in the propagation of Christianity, and painfully aware of the barrier which the ill-treatment of natives by white settlers raised against it. Altogether Gray was a cautious, conservative reformer; as is also shown by the pamphlet he published in 1751, *Considerations on Several Proposals lately made for the Better Maintenance of the Poor*. He even favoured a modest measure of electoral reform.

Gray died 12 Dec. 1782.

[1] *Baptisms in Dutch Church at Colchester* (Huguenot Soc. xii), 76. [2] *Essex Review*, lvii. 184; lxi. 92-6. [3] Add. 32930, f. 257. [4] *HMC 14th Rep. IX, Round*, 303, 304. [5] Ibid. 306. [6] Add. 25335, f. 65. [7] Harris's 'Debates'. [8] Harris to Hardwicke, 6 Apr. 1770, Add. 35609, f. 173. [9] Cavendish's 'Debates', Egerton 259, f. 58.

L.B.N.

## GRAY, George (c.1710-73).

WINCHELSEA    26 Jan. 1759-Mar. 1760

> b. c.1710, 2nd s. of Sir James Gray, 1st Bt., by Hester Dodd, and bro. of Sir James Gray, 2nd Bt., the diplomat. m. Charlotte, da. of Maj.-Gen. Robert Hunter, sis. of Thomas Orby Hunter (q.v.), s.p. suc. bro. as 3rd Bt. 9 Jan. 1773.
> Ensign 2 Ft. 1730; ensign 1 Ft. Gds. 1734; capt. 47 Ft. 1741; capt. 18 Ft. 1743, maj. 1745; lt.-col. 1st Troop Horse Gds. 1749; col. 1759; col. 61 Ft. 1759-1768; col. 37 Ft. 1768-d.; lt.-gen. 1770.

Gray held the seat at Winchelsea while his brother-in-law Thomas Orby Hunter was in Germany as commissary of supplies to the army with Prince Ferdinand. He wrote to Newcastle, 29 June 1759:[1]

> You was pleased . . . to think me worthy of sitting in the House of Commons, in place of Mr. Hunter . . . I have that obligation to your Grace, and as I am sincerely attached to your person and Administration, could wish I might lie under an obligation to no one but yourself. My situation at present is very particular and critical. The eldest lieutenant-colonel in the army,

in the list given in by Lord Ligonier to his Majesty, thirty years an officer, ten years in the post of lieutenant-colonel, paid £1,000 for my commissions, served in Minorca, in Flanders last year, and in Scotland during the rebellion: I hope such pretensions with the assistance of your Grace may procure me the rank of colonel . . . Upon these considerations, and my connexions with my brother Mr. Hunter, in whose place I now stand, and whom I know has your Grace's esteem, I hope for your protection.

His promotion followed on 19 July 1759, and he vacated his seat on Hunter's return in 1760.

He died 14 Feb. 1773.

[1] Add. 32892, f. 322.

M.M.D.

**GRAY,** see also **GREY**

**GREATHEED, Samuel** (c.1710–65), of Guy's Cliffe, nr. Warwick.

COVENTRY 28 Dec. 1747–1761

*b.* c.1710, 1st surv. s. of John and Frances Greatheed of St. Mary Cayon, St. Kitts. *educ.* Bradford; Trinity, Camb. 1730; L. Inn 1730. *m.* (1)[1]; (2) 21 Feb. 1748, Lady Mary Bertie, da. of Peregrine, 2nd Duke of Ancaster, 2s.

Greatheed, after rejoining his family in St. Kitts for a few years,[2] settled in England; in 1743 rented Guy's Cliffe, a mile from Warwick, and bought it in 1750. In 1754 he contested Coventry on Lord Archer's interest and was returned head of the poll. In Dupplin's list he was classed as a supporter of Administration. He did not stand again in 1761. Henry Fox, writing to Egremont, 20 Feb. 1763, refers to Greatheed as 'a great friend' of his.[3] In January 1764 Greatheed applied to Grenville to be made commissioner for the sale of lands in the conquered islands, but the post had already been filled.[4]

He died 2 Aug. 1765.

[1] *Caribbeana*, ed. V. L. Oliver, v. 50. [2] *An Englishman in Paris: 1803. The Journal of Bertie Greatheed*, ed. J. P. T. Bury and J. C. Barry, p. x. [3] Wyndham mss. [4] Grenville letter bk.

L.B.N.

**GREGG, Francis** (1734–95), of Mitcham, Surr.

MORPETH 14 Sept. 1789–Dec. 1794

*b.* 1 Sept. 1734.[1] *m.* 26 Oct. 1758, Elizabeth Wellford, 3s. 3da.
Clerk to the Skinners' Co. 1759–*d.*

When in 1773 Lord Carlisle's extravagance, together with his rashness in having stood surety for Stephen and Charles Fox, had brought him to the brink of ruin, he turned to Francis Gregg for advice.[2] Gregg, an attorney by profession, took charge of Carlisle's affairs, restored them to some order, and even recovered from Charles Fox a large proportion of his debt. Gregg also became a close

friend of Carlisle and his political associates, who frequented his house at Mitcham.[3] In 1789 he was returned on Carlisle's interest at Morpeth to hold the seat till Carlisle's heir came of age. There is no record of his having spoken in the House.

Gregg died 29 Mar. 1795.

[1] Ms pedigree, Soc. of Genealogists. [2] *HMC Carlisle*, 252, 254–6. [3] Ibid. 448, 455, 467, 513, 535.

E.A.S.

**GREGORY, Mark** (*d.*1793), of King's Arms Yard, Coleman St., London.

NEWTOWN I.o.W. 30 Aug. 1784–1790

Gregory was a London corn and flour merchant with correspondents at Leith, Liverpool, and Lynn. He also traded with Spain and Turkey, and was partner in a commercial house at Barcelona.

Gregory did not stand at the general election of 1784, nor does he appear in Robinson's lists of those for whom seats were to be found,[1] but in August 1784 was returned for Newtown I.o.W., which Robinson before the election had listed as 'available for money',[2] and for which James Worsley had been returned apparently as a stop-gap till a suitable candidate could be found.

No vote by Gregory is reported before 1788 when he voted with Pitt over the Regency. There is no record of his having spoken in the House. He seems to have been on friendly terms with Charles Jenkinson, and was on several occasions consulted by him about the Spanish and Turkey trades. Gregory was anxious to destroy the monopoly of the Turkey Company, and campaigned for its abolition.[3]

He did not stand again in 1790; seems to have gone to the Continent some time in 1791 or 1792; spent a considerable time touring French industrial towns; and died in Paris 1 May 1793.

[1] Laprade, 126–9. [2] Ibid. 108. [3] Add. 38228 f. 1; 38391, f. 170.

M.M.D.

**GREGORY, Robert** (?1729–1810), of Valence, Kent; Rolls Park, Essex; and Coole Park, co. Galway.

MAIDSTONE 1768–1774
ROCHESTER 1774–1784

*b.* ?1729, s. of Henry Gregory of Galway by Mary, da. of Robert Shaw of Newford, co. Galway. *m.* Maria Nimmo, da. of an East India merchant, 3s. 1da.
Director, E. I. Co. 1769–73, 1775–9, 1780–2, chairman Apr.–July 1782.

Gregory went out to Bengal about 1747 as a free merchant, and, having made his fortune, returned to England in 1766 and settled in Kent. In 1767 he gave evidence before the House in committee on

East India affairs. On 4 Mar. 1768 Rockingham wrote to Newcastle:[1]

> Lord Aylesford through Lord Winchelsea conveyed to me a day or two ago that he wanted much a candidate to set up at Maidstone and yesterday he came to me about it . . .
> Mr. Gregory, a gentleman of good fortune, acquired really in a very honourable manner in the East Indies, and whose character and abilities I think well of, had some time ago conveyed to me his wishes of coming into Parliament. He particularly desired that where he stood it might be with the countenance of the neighbouring gentlemen and some old and known interest, as thinking that ground was better and freer from the accusation of coming as an adventurer. Mr. Gregory met Lord Aylesford . . . and in short likes the appearance so much that he embarks . . . Gregory's political inclinations are certainly with us. Lord Aylesford takes it so . . .
> I shall try to do all the service I can for Mr. Gregory as I really like him from the conversations I have had with him on India matters, and have found him very intelligent and able on that matter.

Gregory had started late and there were already two candidates, but he came second on the poll with a comfortable majority.

In Parliament he voted consistently with the Opposition, and was consulted by Rockingham on East India affairs. He is recorded as having made over 30 speeches, almost all in debates covering the East India Co. He was a member of the secret committee of 1772 and of Burgoyne's select committee, and was genuinely concerned for the welfare of India as well as of the Company. He said in the House on 5 Apr. 1773:[2]

> Most of the gentlemen now in India are my particular friends, but I am willing to do all I can for the ease of the inhabitants of India. A place without law can never be happy. I shall prefer the happiness of seventeen millions of souls to the emoluments of my friends, and shall be glad to give all the information I can from my long residence in India.

In 1774 he was defeated at Maidstone, and elected after a contest at Rochester. He opposed the American war, and in every recorded division 1780–2 voted against North's Administration. 'Though strongly attached to Fox and to the party acting with him', writes Wraxall,[3] 'Gregory disdained to be considered a devoted partisan.' On 9 Apr. 1781, during a debate on East India affairs, Gregory 'expressed a willingness' to support North 'in whatever measure should appear to him to have for its object the mutual interests of the public and the Company.'[4] Burke, who followed him, pledged himself, Gregory, and 'those in Opposition with whom he had conversed on the subject' to support North 'in everything that should appear to them conducive to the joint interest of the Company and the kingdom'.

Mr. Gregory got up again; and with warmth observed that as no man was more ready to support the noble Lord in everything reasonable than he was, yet he requested the honourable Member would only pledge himself, and nobody else, for the support of the measures that might be proposed; he said he stood connected with no party, nor with the honourable Member who had spoken last; he would give his opinion freely, and his support where he thought it due; but still regardless of the promises of others, he being as independent in his principles and his seat as any man in the House.

'Mr. Burke was hurt . . . and observed that as the honourable gentleman thought proper to renounce any connection with him, he was very welcome to do it.'

On 30 Apr. 1781, when North moved for a committee of secrecy on the war in the Carnatic, Gregory 'trusted that it would not be a mockery of justice, nor mixed with party interests and party friendships'.[5] The committee was chosen by ballot, and Gregory 'was placed out of all competition at the head of the committee, he uniting the suffrages of the ministerial as well as of the Opposition sides of the House'.[6] He obtained 249 votes, 88 more than the second Member chosen.

In 1782 he had a serious illness: in July he resigned his post as chairman of the East India Co.; and in Robinson's list of March 1783, drawn up after the division on Shelburne's peace preliminaries, he is included amongst those who were 'ill or cannot attend'. Yet he was named one of the commissioners for Indian affairs in Fox's East India bill, and his last speech in the House, 1 Dec. 1783, was in defence of that measure:[7]

> Mr. Gregory declared that though the bill then under consideration appeared to him to be by far the best system that he had yet seen or heard of, yet he hoped there would ever continue a respectable Opposition in that House who would narrowly watch the commissioners' conduct and exercise a rigorous control over their proceedings.

In Robinson's list of January 1784 and Stockdale's of March he is classed as an opponent of Pitt. He did not stand at the general election.

He died 1 Sept. 1810, aged 81.

[1] Add. 32989, ff. 29–30. [2] Brickdale's 'Debates'. [3] *Mems.* ii. 108. [4] Debrett, iii. 155–56. [5] Ibid. 184. [6] Wraxall, ii. 107. [7] Debrett, xii. 275–6.

J.B.

## GRENVILLE, George (1712–70), of Wotton, Bucks.

BUCKINGHAM 1741–13 Nov. 1770

*b.* 14 Oct. 1712, 2nd s. of Richard Grenville, M.P., by Hester, da. of Sir Richard Temple, 3rd Bt., M.P., and sis. and h. of Richard, 1st Visct. Cobham (she suc. by sp. rem. to his viscountcy in Sept. 1749 and was cr. Countess Temple in October). *educ.* Eton 1725–8; Ch. Ch. Oxf. 1730; I. Temple 1729, called 1735, bencher

1763, *m.* May 1749, Elizabeth, 2nd da. of Sir William Wyndham, 3rd Bt., M.P., 4s. 5da.

Ld. of Admiralty 1744-7; of Treasury 1747-54; P.C. 21 June 1754; treasurer of navy, Mar. 1754–Nov. 1755, Nov. 1756–Apr. 1757, June 1757–May 1762; sec. of state May–Oct. 1762; first ld. of Admiralty Oct. 1762–Apr. 1763; first ld. of Treasury Apr. 1763–July 1765.

George Grenville, during his first 20 years in politics, was overshadowed by his rich and domineering brother, Lord Temple, on whose interest he sat at Buckingham (and who could have cut him out of the entail), and by William Pitt, since 1754 his brother-in-law, to whom he played second fiddle in the Commons. They treated him with patronising benevolence, but neither greatly exerted himself on his behalf.

In the reshuffle on Pelham's death in March 1754, Pitt thought that Grenville should have the Exchequer or the War Office; when he was made treasurer of the navy, hoped this would lead on to the Exchequer; and wrote to Temple on 8 Apr.:[1] 'George Grenville's turn must come for greater things; there I lay the stress.' And to Hardwicke on 4 Apr.:[2] 'Mr. Grenville is universally able in the whole business of the House and, after Mr. Murray and Mr. Fox, is among the very first, if not the best Parliament-man in the House.' Yet he was suffered by Pitt and Temple, when they were in office during the next seven years, to remain treasurer of the navy.

In October 1756, when Pitt was negotiating with Hardwicke for a re-entry of their group into the Government, 'he informed us', writes Grenville, 'that he had stated me for the office of paymaster . . . and that it was consented to without any difficulty'. But a few weeks later Pitt let the pay office be divided between Potter and Dupplin.[3] In May 1757 he proposed Grenville for chancellor of the Exchequer, but in the end agreed to his being merely restored to his previous place. Meanwhile Grenville was doing Pitt's chores in the House, accounted an excellent man of business but hardly a statesman. By 1760 he wished to withdraw from active politics to the Speaker's Chair, for which he was eminently qualified. But before the election came on in November 1761, a change occurred not wholly unforeseen.

Grenville was a favourite with the new court, addressed by Bute as 'Dear George'. 'The King commended George Grenville extremely', wrote Newcastle to Hardwicke, 9 Jan. 1761; 'approved him very much [for Speaker], if he liked it; but would himself have rather kept him for some employment of greater consequence.'[4] This made Newcastle fear a further attempt to foist Grenville

on him as chancellor of the Exchequer. On 11 Feb. Bute informed Grenville that he would be of the [Nominal] Cabinet—'Let me congratulate you, my worthy friend, on this additional honour; may I see many added to it.'[5] But this did not give Grenville the circulation of Cabinet papers; and Bute (told by Gilbert Elliot on 26 Feb. that he had found Grenville uninformed by 'any of his own family' of what was transacting[6]), when appointed secretary of state, immediately ordered his private secretary, Charles Jenkinson, confidentially to communicate to Grenville 'all things of importance'[7].

On Pitt's resignation, 2 Oct., Bute offered his place to Grenville who declined it; even so the King pressed him to assume the leadership of the House. But Grenville, frightened of Pitt and distrustful of Newcastle and Fox, begged the King to let him 'go into the Chair, which situation was on many accounts far the most eligible to him'; and stated his own want of support and the danger of being finally abandoned 'in the midst of his enemies'.[8] To reassure him Bute, on 13 Oct. sent Elliot with a letter which he was to show to Grenville but return to Bute because of its disparaging remarks about Newcastle. After Elliot had left, Grenville dictated to his wife a summary of some 600 words;[9] the original is among the Bute mss.

> You desired me at parting [wrote Bute in the opening paragraph] to think on the painful discourse that we had had together, painful to me indeed beyond description wherein I saw manifestly all the symptoms of a mind extremely agitated turning every incident in the blackest light and viewing with an eye of despondency every part of your intended situation.

Yet even then Grenville was already subconsciously cutting out Bute as a superior intervening between himself and the King—this is shown by two omissions in his summary, significant because unintentional. Bute wrote:

> Your eyes will see and from you I shall hear the transactions of each day. Part of your duty will be to report to the King the conduct of these gentlemen. The King will be informed. That is sufficient. For when you know him better you will find a firmness extremely calculated to support his own authority delegated by him to others.

But this is how Grenville remembered it—'myself' being Grenville:

> Information from myself of what passed: daily representation by myself in the Closet of the conduct and proofs which I should daily receive from experience of the King's resolution.

Daily reporting by him to the King but none to Bute. Again in Bute's letter:

> . . . from the minute you are there, your honour my honour, your disgrace, my disgrace is his, to all intents and purposes . . .

But in Grenville's summary:

> ... that the King ... would support me to the utmost, my honour his honour, my disgrace his disgrace ...

Once more Bute is eliminated, and Grenville remains alone with the King: long shadows of a future as yet unperceived.

Grenville was nearly 50, and had never stood alone. Now Temple forbade him the house, and Pitt treated him with cold contempt: he felt unnerved. Could he assume the leadership of the House without parliamentary backing of his own? When Bute secured for him Fox's support,

> What a figure shall I make? [Grenville said to Newcastle] Mr. Fox has superior parliamentary talent to me; Mr. Fox has a great number of friends in the House of Commons, attached strongly to him; Mr. Fox has *great connections*, I have none; I have no friends; I am now unhappily separated from my own family.[10]

So Bute, 'teased out of his life', had now to save Grenville from being eclipsed by Fox's support. 'Mr. Fox will attend every day', wrote Shelburne to Bute,[11] 'and will either by silence or by speaking as he finds it prudent ... do his best to forward what your Lordship wishes.' Grenville's brother-in-law, Lord Egremont, succeeded Pitt as secretary of state, and he himself, while remaining treasurer of the navy, became minister for the House of Commons with a seat in the Effective Cabinet, the only Commoner in it. An unrelenting worker, in action he gradually recovered from the anxieties and self-doubt which, acute at this turn in his career, he had avowed, but which, cautious and formal in his approach, he was usually able to repress, or at least to disguise.

An illuminating sketch of Grenville is given by his cousin and devoted but not uncritical follower, Thomas Pitt jun.[12]

> Mr. Grenville ... was of all the heads of party the worst patron ... he weighed every favour in the nicest scale; but I knew my honour would be always safe with him ... He had nothing seducing in his manners. His countenance had rather the expression of peevishness and austerity ... He was to a proverb tedious ... he was diffuse and argumentative, and never had done with a subject after he had convinced your judgment till he wearied your attention—the foreign ministers complained of his prolixity which they called amongst each other, the being *Grenvilisé*. The same prolixity rendered him an unpleasant speaker in the House of Commons ... Yet though his eloquence charmed nobody, his argument converted ... The abundance of his matter, his experience of the forms and practice of the House ... his accurate knowledge of the laws and history of his own country ... his wariness never to suffer himself to be drawn out beyond the line he had prescribed to himself ... his skill upon all matters of finance, of commerce, of foreign treaties, and above all the purity of his character ... gave him ... weight ... He never took notes; he never quitted his seat for refreshment in the longest debates, and generally spoke the last, when his strength and his memory served him to recollect every argument that had been used, and to suffer scarce a word of any consequence to escape his notice ... He was a man born to public business, which was his luxury and amusement. An Act of Parliament was in itself entertaining to him, as was proved when he stole a turnpike bill out of somebody's pocket at a concert and read it in a corner in despite of all the efforts of the finest singers to attract his attention. Order and economy were so natural to him that he told me from the first office he ever held till he became minister he had made it an invariable rule to add the year's salary to his capital contenting himself with carrying the interest the succeeding year into his expenses. His prudence rather bordered upon parsimony.

During the session Nov. 1761–May 1762, as leader of the House Grenville had to face Pitt in debates on foreign affairs. Bute's congratulations on 10 Dec. were warm but condescending: 'this will do, my dear friend, and shows you to the world in the light I want.'[13] By intervening in Treasury business, which his position as leader of the House enabled him to do, Grenville was instrumental in forcing Newcastle from office. But when Bute, though ignorant of finance, was about to assume the Treasury, Grenville would not serve as his chancellor of the Exchequer—his 'mind revolting against what [Bute] had ever looked upon as fixed'.[14] 'I am inclined to think ...', the King had written to Bute on 6 May, 'that Grenville is weak enough to think he may succeed the Duke of Newcastle.' He looked to a post 'where he could ... figure more than as an assistant in a Board'.[15] After having thrust Grenville into the front rank, the King and Bute were taken aback at his enhanced self-esteem.

Grenville succeeded Bute as secretary of state, for which post he was ill-qualified. In the summer further differences arose between them: Grenville insisted on peace terms higher than Bute 'could be brought to consent to'; and as manager of the House desired authority to talk to the Members 'upon their several claims and pretensions', which Bute would not concede. Consequently a Government reshuffle was undertaken, but Grenville was informed only after things had been fixed:[16] Fox replaced him as leader of the House, and Halifax as secretary of state. Grenville, relegated to the Admiralty, tamely submitted, and on 14 Oct. 'with good humour delivered up the seals'.[17]

'Grenville has thrown away the game he had two years ago', wrote the King to Bute, 14 Mar. 1763, when discussing who should succeed him at the Treasury.[18] But Fox, having declined it, on 17 Mar. 'very reluctantly' recommended Grenville; Shelburne, however, was to replace Egremont as secretary of state.[19] Although the King himself was averse to Shelburne, his appointment was pressed on Grenville when on 24 Mar. Bute offered him the Treasury—'if Lord Egremont's quitting the seals, or Shelburne having them' are insurmountable obstacles to him, wrote Bute to Grenville the next day, 'I must in a few hours put other things in agitation'. Grenville replied in a very long and submissive letter: he did not 'presume to suggest who is the most proper for that high office', but thought it his duty before he 'entered upon such a situation' to state his opinion 'upon those parts of the system which have been opened' to him. And further: 'If your Lordship had allowed me to consult with some of those who must bear the greatest share in it . . .'—a unique performance in Government making.[20] Even Grenville's own Board was being fixed for him by Bute; and the King told him 'that I received him in the Treasury as recommended by my dear friend [Bute] and as such should support him'.[21]

One reason for Bute's wishing to remove Egremont had been that, in order to preserve the King's independence, men 'too much allied' should not hold 'the active posts of Government'. The King agreed, but hoped that 'Grenville's coming into the Treasury will so hurt Halifax that it will dissolve his union' with the two brothers-in-law.[22] When Halifax and Egremont were re-appointed secretaries of state, they and Grenville were enjoined by Bute and the King to preserve 'a strict union' not only among themselves but with all defenders of Government, 'as the only means of supporting the King's independency'. The emphasis was really on union with those others, Shelburne being specifically mentioned;[23] but 'a strict union' among themselves to the exclusion of the other ministers, became the practice of the Triumvirate,[24] a most anomalous formation: which can be viewed as the premiership in commission or as the narrowest Effective Cabinet on record. Hardwicke noted as early as 8 Apr. that the two secretaries 'talked in the style of *the ministers*';[25] and one of them told a foreign minister 'in form' that the three were the ministry, and 'that everything *important* was to be determined by their *unanimous* opinion'.[26] Grenville admitted them even to an equal share in patronage: an unprecedented procedure which shows how weak he felt as head of the Government. Perhaps that uncertainty made him, when taking the Treasury, stipulate for the reversion of a teller's place for his son and £3,000 p.a. for himself when out of office—'a shameful thing, never heard of before', wrote Newcastle on 3 June;[27] and the King to Bute, 27 Apr.: 'I told him . . . for his own sake he had better not have

wished it now, but his avarice overcame his prudence.'[28]

Bute haunted the new Administration: had he never again interfered in government, the part of 'minister behind the curtain' would still have been ascribed to him; and within a month the ministers were saying that they would quit if they found him acting it.[29] Their minds became 'cankered with the most violent jealousies against him', wrote the King,[30] who, to break up the Triumvirate, offered the vacant presidency of the Council to Hardwicke. On his refusing, the King embarked, early in August, on wider schemes of Government reconstruction, next rendered inevitable by Egremont's sudden death on the 21st. In these negotiations Bute was a prime mover; why they failed is not altogether clear even now. But their failure, and the accession of the Bedfords, strengthened Grenville's position; and Bute himself wrote to the King that he desired to retire absolutely from all business and even absent himself from the King till the Administration was firmly established. Of this the King informed Grenville when asked by him on 28 Aug. to let in future 'no secret influence whatever' prevail against the advice of his ministers; and the next day read out to him part of Bute's letter:[31] whereupon Grenville, without first asking the King's leave, repeated in an account of the crisis circulated to his friends, that Bute would retire even 'from the presence and place of residence' of the King.[32] Public use of what Bute 'intended should have remained a secret', was greatly resented by him,[33] and no doubt also by the King, despite consent obtained from him *post factum*. Tactless and insensitive, Grenville little realised, and still less foresaw, the impression or impact of his actions on others.

To follow up the history of Grenville's Administration would by far transcend the scope and limits of this biography: only certain aspects characteristic of him and of his position especially with regard to the King, colleagues, and the House of Commons, can be touched upon. In the new Government Bedford was president of the Council, and Sandwich and Halifax secretaries of state, and the three formed with Grenville an Inner Cabinet or *junta* within the Effective Cabinet: when in January 1764 they decided to dine together once a week, the King's suggestion (he wanted an observer at these meetings) that the chancellor should be included, was ignored.[34] Yet a common front with the three against Bute did not stop Grenville from appealing to the King for support against them.

The conversation with the King as related in the Grenville diary on 8 Sept. 1763, the day before the new ministers kissed hands, gives the *leitmotif* of many a later entry. Grenville started by trying to rechew the story of the late crisis.

> The King said . . . let us not look back, let us only look forward; nothing of that sort shall ever happen again. Mr. Grenville said he hoped not; that he put himself entirely upon his Majesty's protection.

He had advised the King to call to his Government Bedford and Sandwich in order to strengthen it—

> these might prove too strong for him, his only reliance was upon his Majesty's truth and honour, and on that he trusted he might depend. The King assured him he might; that he would never fail him, nor forget his services. His Majesty again dropped something of Lord Bute's retreat not being necessary, or at least might be shortened.
> Mr. Grenville dissented, and spoke again of the great uneasiness and ferment there was against him.

Within a week of joining the Government Bedford raised the question of 'the disposal of offices'; a month later, Halifax and Sandwich suggested that Grenville should continue with them the Triumvirate's partnership in patronage. But Grenville's invariable reply was that while he was understood to manage the King's business in the House of Commons, he would never consent that any offices tenable by Members 'should go through any channel but his own';[35] and he told Halifax on 13 Oct. that while Bedford, Holland, and Sandwich 'had been forming a party for themselves for these twenty years', he had none, and therefore had to 'reap what aid he could from patronage'. This, in fact, he extended through Treasury control far beyond the House of Commons. The King, to separate Grenville from his colleagues, encouraged his claim to exclusive patronage; expressed disapproval 'of the factions of great lords who are making parties for themselves'; and declared that 'it was necessary to lodge the power of Government in one man alone . . . Mr. Grenville', through whom 'all recomendations and appointments should come'.[36] The King talked 'a good deal of Lord Sandwich, with whom he always seems displeased'; and complained also of Halifax and Bedford.[37] He went even further: told Grenville 'that the rest of the ministers acted against him'; and that Sandwich and Halifax 'do not act fairly' by Grenville.[38] And on 26 Feb. 1764, 'I know the difference between you and the rest of my servants; they have many purposes to serve, you have none but my service, and that of the public.' Grenville readily lapped up such remarks; and on 13 Aug. 1764, finding the King graciously disposed towards him, asked for the grant of a lighthouse (to become available in four years), a sinecure worth about £2500 p.a., 'as a provision for his younger children, who, from various circumstances relating to the unhappy state of his family, might be left in

difficulties'.[39] Even by the standards of the time Grenville's behaviour, as avowed in his diary, failed to uphold the dignity of his office.

Nor did he realize how much his manner and discourses irritated George III, and with obtuse pertinacity he tried to force his way into the King's private life and favour. In September 1763 he pressed the King to let him succeed Bute as keeper of the privy purse, which the King refused: Bute had held it not as first lord of the Treasury but as 'his immediate friend', and the King 'claimed the right of disposing of an office so immediately about his person'.[40] Again, in April 1764 Grenville asked the King to let him inhabit the New Lodge in Richmond Park (obviously to be near the King even there); and when the King (not to be *Grenvilisé* in his leisure hours) refused, Grenville invoked the intercession of Bute who, to the dissatisfaction of ministers, had come up to London.[41] But by mid-1764 Grenville was becoming aware of failure as would-be favourite—he said to James Harris on 11 June[42] that

> his years compared to the King (52 to 26) did not promise any great degree of intimacy as a favourite, that if it were feasible to become so, he had not time for that character, and to do the public business—that he was perfectly well with Lord Bute.

By the end of the year there were expostulations and 'pretty strong' remonstrances on Grenville's part, while the King was cold, distant, and embarrassed.[43] Grenville complained of inferior persons about the King who indisposed him 'to his principal servants'; of 'lukewarm friends to Government' who, while professing attachment to the King, 'thought themselves at liberty to oppose his measures and ministers'; and of 'want of a thorough support and countenance from the King to his principal servants'.[44] What brought about the change is uncertain: most probably questions of patronage and a renascent suspicion that Bute was interfering. There were frequent disputes between Grenville and Bute's brother, James Stuart Mackenzie, about Scottish appointments. Early in 1765 Grenville warned Charles Townshend that 'if he wished to attain any situation in the King's service through any channel but Mr. Grenville's . . . Mr. Grenville would quit that moment'; and Townshend assured Grenville that 'he was in no communication with Lord Bute'.[45] Lastly there is the incident with Thomas Worsley, an intimate friend of Bute's. George III wrote in a memorandum in the autumn of 1765:[46]

> No office fell vacant in any department that Mr. Grenville did not declare he could not serve if the man he recommended did not succeed. A very strong instance of this insolence appeared in his sending for Mr. Worsley, the surveyor of the works, and abusing

him for my having curtailed the painter's office, and he used this very remarkable expression, that if men presumed to speak to me on business without his leave that he would not serve an hour; had I followed my own inclinations I certainly should have dismissed him the moment I heard this.

It was typical of Grenville that he raged over the curtailing of a painter's office, but did not object in the least when about an important talk which Sandwich had with the Austrian ambassador he spoke to the King before acquainting Grenville with it.[47] In fact, foreign affairs engaged his attention mainly when they bore on finance—witness his differences with Bedford, Halifax, and Sandwich in 1764 over the outstanding accounts with the French. Bute had described him to Charles Yorke in April 1763 as 'a very worthy and able man . . . whose turn lay towards the revenue, and to that public economy, which was so much wanted'.[48] He reduced the unfunded debt; tried to reform the revenue; insisted on its officials, many of whom had considered their salaries as sinecures, attending to their duties; boasted of having 'saved great sums' in contracts he had made; and of having 'never quartered a person on a place . . . nor . . . suffered a place to be sold'.[49] And in one of his expostulatory discourses to the King: 'that he had neither pressed him for grants, honours, nor pensions, that the secret service money was by a great deal less than under any other minister'[50] (the grants and pensions he had obtained for himself and his family he conveniently forgot). The orderly routine of Grenville's administration was appreciated by officials—thus Sir James Porter, minister to Brussels, wrote to Sir George Amyand on 11 Sept. 1764: 'Mr. Grenville will deserve a statue from all the King's servants, especially those abroad. I see we shall now be paid regularly.'[51]

Opponents as well as friends paid tribute to Grenville's budget of March 1764: Horace Walpole wrote that Grenville opened it fully, 'for brevity was not his failing; but he did it with art and ability';[52] and Harris that the speech of $2\frac{3}{4}$ hours 'was perfectly well heard the whole time, and gained the applause of the *whole* House'. Country gentlemen, many of whom had voted against the Government over general warrants, and who had never attended ministerial levees, met at his 'by agreement'[53] because they appreciated his care of the tax-payer's money, an attitude not encountered for years past. Even the great blunder of that budget, the scheme for taxing America, was meant to relieve the unfair burden of the British tax-payer, and did not spring from a desire to assert Britain's supremacy over the Colonies. But Grenville, being of a legalistic turn of mind—himself bred to the law—failed to see why this country should not avail itself of a power of

which he thought it duly possessed. Similarly over Wilkes and general warrants he merely followed the opinion of the law officers, without entertaining any of the arbitrary notions ascribed to him. He thought in terms of administration and law rather than of policy. Yet by the end of 1764 his Government seemed firmly established in office, in line of succession to Walpole's and Pelham's.

Relations between the King and his ministers were, however, already moving toward a crisis when his illness in Feb.–Mar. 1765 caused him, on recovering, to propose a Regency bill in which he reserved to himself the power to appoint the Regent without naming the person in the Act. This revived anti-Bute suspicions, and the attempt of the ministers to exclude the Princess Dowager from the Regency (in which Halifax and Sandwich involved the King) hardened his determination to change the Government. During these tense weeks Grenville, feeling the ground slip from under his feet, plied the King with exhortations and reproaches: 'with a firm and steady countenance' he complained of being shown little 'confidence and communication' upon the subject of the bill; of the King having visibly withdrawn 'even his approbation from him'; and he engaged in long self-laudatory discourses.[54] When the King, having failed to form a new Government, on 21 May asked him to continue in office and 'pressed for a categorical answer', Grenville expatiated on the sacrifices he had made for the King's service, on the promises he had received, etc. The terms which the ministers, obsessed by the idea that Bute had been the prime mover in the crisis, imposed on the King as conditions of their resuming office included the dismissal of J. S. Mackenzie from the Scottish privy seal which the King had promised him for life; and they insisted on it although according to Grenville's own account the King told him 'he should disgrace himself if he did'.[55] And here is George III's account to Egmont:[56]

That he told him [Grenville] he saw evidently that they were not satisfied with his parting with his power, but that nothing would content him, but his parting with his honour too—bid him take notice what he told him—and earnestly and in great anger bid him take notice of this—more than once—that he had forced him to part with his honour—that as a King for the safety of his people he must submit.

Thereupon Grenville, according to his diary, begged the King rather to dismiss him 'than to put him under the cruel dilemma of thinking that he was forcing his inclination'.

Dismissed he was seven weeks later without a chance of return. When on 10 July he surrendered the seal of his office, he went once more over the story of his official career (the summary of his discourse in the diary exceeds 1700 words). The King 'was civil, imputing no blame, but giving no word of approbation throughout the whole conversation'. George III recalled Pitt and Newcastle after having vowed never to employ them again; but not Grenville. Lord Holland wrote to George Selwyn, 27 Aug. 1765:[57]

> I am persuaded, Selwyn, that the King, who we can see can swallow anything almost, could not, however, bear his conversation. A dose, so large and so nauseous, often repeated, was too much for any body's stomach.

In October 1761, and even in April 1763, Grenville was without a following of his own; in July 1765 quite a respectable array of Members went with him into opposition. Most of these could, however, hardly be classed as followers: there were the Bedfords who under the Rockingham Administration invariably went with Grenville, but began to waver under Chatham; similarly, unconnected office-holders, displaced by the Rockinghams and gradually reinstated 1766–8. Grenville's personal followers (to whom Grenville's reconciliation with Temple in May 1765 added none in the Commons) were a small and heterogeneous group, dwindling and neglected by him once it became clear that he would not return to office.[58] But perhaps most significant is the position which Grenville had established for himself among the so-called Tory country gentlemen. Harris wrote in a memorandum on the crisis of May–July 1765, under date of 23 May:[59]

> Great encomiums of Mr. Grenville by all persons. The persons of the first rank and credit at the Cocoa Tree declared for him. On Tuesday last [21 May] he had a very full levée, when were Sir James Dashwood, Sir Charles Tynte, Sir Robert Burdett, Sir Walter Bagot, and many others.

And as their support was disinterested, it was more enduring—in January 1767 Charles Townshend, in an incomplete list places against 14 of them 'Grenville', to whom several others could certainly be added. They respected Grenville's character, approved of his economy, and also of his American measures.

Grenville in his last talk with the King, on 10 July, besought him[60]

> not to suffer any one to advise him to separate . . . his British and American dominions; that his Colonies was the richest jewel of his Crown; that for his own part he must uniformly maintain his former opinions both in Parliament and out of it; . . . that if any man ventured to defeat the regulations laid down for the Colonies, by a slackness in the execution, he should look upon him as a criminal and the betrayer of his country.

The defence of his American policy, especially of the Stamp Act, stood now in the centre of Grenville's

parliamentary activities: an amendment to the Address declaring America in rebellion, 17 Dec.; a motion for American papers, 19 Dec.; a speech on 14 Jan. 1766 insisting, as usual, on the 'strict dependence' of America; on 17 Jan. against rescinding the order to print the American papers ('very angry', Conway put against his name in a list of speakers sent to the King):[61] erudite speeches transfused with passion. Thus on 7 Feb., when moving for an address to the King for enforcing all laws in America:[62]

> America would not have been in this condition if they had believed that we would enforce the law . . . Whoever advises the King to give up his sovereignty over America is the greatest enemy to this country and will be accused by all posterity.
> Says he finds the Americans disputing the authority of this country and was willing to try how far their disobedience could reach . . .
> Let those who encourage America and have raised and increased this condition by such encouragement extricate us out of it, and God grant that they may meet with success.

He was ready to join anyone, even Bute, in an attempt to defeat the repeal of the Stamp Act; and avidly listened to any gossip alleging that this was also the wish of the King—who might have favoured enforcing the Act had it not been Grenville's (see the King's ironic remarks to Grafton, 17 Dec. 1765,[63] on Grenville's 'great care' and 'wise regulations' in that matter).

Under the Chatham Administration Grenville from the outset favoured sharp Opposition, while his allies, the Bedfords, oscillated between Opposition and negotiations for a re-entry into Government. With Pitt removed to the House of Lords, Grenville grew in stature—he was, wrote Walpole, 'confessedly the ablest man of business in the House of Commons, and, though not popular, of great authority there from his spirit, knowledge, and gravity of character'.[64] He took a leading part in the campaigns over the corn embargo, East India affairs, for the reduction of the land tax, etc. But again American affairs were his foremost concern; and he 'never forgot the Stamp Act, never forgave those who repealed it, and never ceased to urge the policy he had initiated'.[65] It was his motion on 26 Jan. 1767 which brought Townshend's schemes for Colonial taxation into the open. But even Townshend's speech of 13 May and the repressive measures proposed, did not satisfy Grenville—'no moderation was to be suffered, when the authority of Parliament was resisted'.[66]

Two things became obvious in the negotiations for a Government reconstruction in July 1767: that the King gave 'an implied exclusion' to Grenville; and that, because of Stamp Act memories, Grenville could never join in office with the Rockinghams. With the accession of the Bedfords to the Chatham Administration in December 1767, the last, illusory, hopes of his return to office vanished, and with them his interest in parliamentary manoeuvres: henceforth it was his man of business, Thomas Whately (q.v.), rather than Grenville, who looked after what remained of their group in the House.

Detachment from struggles for office added dignity to Grenville's position as foremost senior statesman among commoners. In February 1768 all debate on the principle of a bill was deferred to the third reading on account of Grenville's absence, 'who sent word that he had some objections to the preamble'.[67] Urged to stand for Buckinghamshire in 1768, he replied that 'after having had the honour to serve the King and the kingdom in the highest public situation it would not become me at my time of day to be running about and canvassing for a county election'.[68] In September 1769 Whately explained to Burke Grenville's keeping aloof from the petitioning movement by the peculiarity of his situation, 'being the only commoner in opposition who had been at the head of his Majesty's affairs'; and Burke admitted that this 'must restrain him upon many occasions'.[69] In the House, however, during the years 1766-9, Grenville was one of the most frequent speakers.

On 5 Dec. 1769 he suffered a grievous loss through his wife's death. 'I know you wish to avoid every attendance [in the House] which the occasion does not call for,' wrote Whately to him, 12 Jan. 1770.[70] His last important measure was a bill in March–April 1770 to reform the trial of election petitions in the House. These were being decided by favour or party, the House substituting its vote for that of the electors no less than in the case of Wilkes. By transferring the examination of election petitions to committees chosen by lot, Grenville secured for them a fairer judicature: an effective reply to the grievances arising from the Middlesex election. The bill 'was generally liked', and a Government motion to put it off for two months, was defeated by 185 to 133.[71]

Seriously ill in the summer, in October Grenville was brought to London 'in a state of languor and debility'; and died on 13 Nov. 1770. A *post mortem* disclosed an advanced condition of decay of several ribs and the skull.[72]

In Grenville's will estates are mentioned which he had purchased in Eastern Florida; and in 1770 he secured through Thomas Pitt and Samuel Wharton a share in the Vandalia scheme on the Ohio River.[73]

---

[1] *Grenville Pprs.* i. 107, 111, 119, 120. [2] Yorke, *Hardwicke*, ii. 215. [3] Narrative, dated 12 Apr. 1762, *Grenv. Pprs.* i. 422-39. [4] Add. 32917, ff. 203-4. [5] *Grenv. Pprs.* i. 359. [6] Bute mss. [7] *Grenv. Pprs.* i. 361. [8] Grenville's narrative, ibid, 409-15. [9] Ibid. 395-7. [10] Newcastle to Devonshire, 31 Oct., Add. 32930, ff. 225-6. [11] Fitzmaurice, *Shelburne*, i. 95-96. [12] 'Family Characters and Anecdotes' by Lord Camelford, Fortescue mss at Boconnoc. [13] *Grenv. Pprs.* i. 418. [14] Bute to Grenville, 22 May, ibid 446. [15] Sedgwick, 100, 104-5. [16] *Grenv. Pprs.* i. 449-53, 482-5. [17] The King to Bute, 14 Oct., Sedgwick, 147. [18] Ibid. 200-1. [19] Fitzmaurice, *Shelburne*, i. 147-9. [20] *Grenv. Pprs.* ii. 32-40. [21] Sedgwick, 209-10. [22] Ibid. 203-4. [23] Bute to Grenville, *Grenv. Pprs.* ii. 40-41; Grenville to Bute, Bute mss, both 1 Apr.; the King to Bute, 4 Apr., Sedgwick, 209-10. [24] Sedgwick, 228. [25] Add. 32948, ff. 54-57. [26] Newcastle to Jos. Yorke, 13 Apr., ibid. ff. 120-2. [27] Add. 32949, f. 15. [28] Sedgwick, 230-1. [29] Hardwicke to Newcastle, 13 May, Add. 32948, f. 275. [30] Fortescue, i. 163. [31] *Grenv. Pprs.* ii. 200-1. [32] Ibid. ii. 104-7, 117, 203; *Jenkinson Pprs.* 394. [33] *Jenkinson Pprs.* 394-5. [34] *Grenv. Pprs.* ii. 256, 489, 498, 503, 506, 515. [35] Grenville diary (printed in *Grenv. Pprs.*) 15, 28 Sept., 11 Oct., 12 Nov. [36] Ibid. 15, 28 Sept., 5 Dec. 1763, 23 Mar. 1764. [37] Ibid. 6, 14 Mar., 3, 22, 26 Sept. [38] Ibid. 8 June, 5 Dec. 1764. [39] Ibid. 13 Aug. 1764. [40] Ibid. 26 Sept.-1 Oct. 1763. [41] Sedgwick, 237; *Jenkinson Pprs.* 396. [42] Malmesbury mss. [43] *Grenv. Pprs.* ii. 523-4; iii. 112-16. [44] Diary, 19 Dec. 1764; 25, 27 Jan. 1765. [45] Diary, 23 Feb., 3 Mar. 1765. [46] Fortescue, i. 164. [47] Diary, 24, 25 Dec. 1763. [48] Add. 32948, ff. 92-98. [49] Memo. of conversations by Jas. Harris, 16 Nov., 20 Dec. 1763, Malmesbury mss. [50] Diary, 1 May 1765. [51] *HMC 12th Rep. IX.*, 342. [52] *Mems. Geo. III*, i. 309. [53] Newdigate diary, 21 Feb. 1764, Newdigate mss, Warws RO. [54] Diary, 28 Apr., 1 May. [55] Ibid. 22 May. [56] Fortescue, i. 115. [57] Jesse, *Selwyn*, i. 405-6; Walpole, *Mems. Geo. III*, ii. 115. [58] Brooke, *Chatham Admin.* 262-75. [59] Malmesbury mss. [60] Diary, *Grenv. Pprs.* iii. 215-16. [61] Fortescue, i. 236. [62] Ryder's 'Debates', Harrowby mss. [63] Grafton mss. [64] Walpole, *Mems. Geo. III*, iv. 125. [65] Brooke, *Chatham Admin.* 26. [66] *Mems. Geo. III*, iii. 26. [67] Burke to Chas. O'Hara, 20 Feb. 1768. [68] To J. Morton, 15 Oct. 1767, Grenville letter bk. [69] *Grenv. Pprs.* iv. 446-7. [70] Ibid. 505. [71] Walpole, *Mems. Geo. III*, iv. 74. [72] Camelford, 'Family Characters'; Walpole, *Mems. Geo. III*, iv. 125. [73] Grenville to T. Pitt, 9 and 29 July 1770, Grenville mss (JM).

L.B.N.

## GRENVILLE, George (1753-1813).

BUCKINGHAMSHIRE 1774-11 Sept. 1779

*b.* 17 June 1753, 1st s. of George Grenville (q.v.), and bro. of Thomas and W. W. Grenville (qq.v.). *educ.* Eton 1764-70; Ch. Ch. Oxf. 1770; Grand Tour (Italy and Austria) 1774. *m.* 16 Apr. 1775, Lady Mary Elizabeth Nugent, da. and coh. of Robert, 1st Earl Nugent [I] (q.v.), 2s. 2da. *suc.* fa. 13 Nov. 1770; and his uncle as 3rd Earl Temple 11 Sept. 1779 and took names of Nugent-Temple before that of Grenville; *cr.* Mq. of Buckingham 4 Dec. 1784; K.G. 2 June 1786.

Teller of the Exchequer Mar. 1764-*d.*; ld. lt. Bucks. 1782-*d.*; P.C. 31 July 1782; ld. lt. Ireland July 1782–June 1783, Nov. 1787–Oct. 1789; sec. of state for foreign affairs 19-22 Dec. 1783.

In 1774 Grenville was returned unopposed for Buckinghamshire. His first recorded vote in the House was with Opposition on the Address, 5 Dec. 1774, which supported Administration's coercive measures in America—'in effect', wrote Horace Walpole, 'against his own father's famous Stamp Act'. In fact Grenville was thoroughly independent, but during the next few years was involved in a struggle to reconcile his father's views on American taxation with the subsequent course of events. On 2 Feb. 1775, when Fox 'threw some reflections' on Grenville's father as author of the Stamp Act, Grenville, according to Walpole,

defended his father both with spirit and decency, and gained great favour with the House by his pleasing manner. Yet he would not, he said, blame those who had repealed the Stamp Act, and owned the charter bill had united all America against us.[1]

And though he 'spoke very well in support of the legislative power and controlling power of Parliament', he 'entirely disapproved of the present measures, as every way improper, intemperate and impolitic', and abstained from voting.[2] On 29 Feb. 1776 he observed that 'he had scarcely been long enough in public life to fix before now his sentiments relating to America. That he had no doubt of the right of Parliament to tax America, and consequently must concur in the coercive measures. He was far from approving all the steps the ministry had taken', but he believed the most important step now was to recover British sovereignty over America.[3] The news of Saratoga, which reached England in December 1777, increased Grenville's dilemma: at the beginning of February 1778 he told Rockingham that 'though he could never depart from the principle of England's right of taxation, yet he totally disagreed with ministers on every other part of the war'.[4] In the House on 11 Feb. 1778 he declared that

he should ever continue to think, be the outcome of the present contest what it may, that Parliament had a right to have a control over America, to levy taxes, to regulate its trade, and secure the monopoly of its commerce . . . it was upon these principles that he had supported the war . . . These principles were now merely matter of speculation, such as they were, however, he should ever retain them: he therefore did not mean by his vote of that day to abandon them, but meant to consider the question of expediency which must decide upon the war.

Though he deplored the circumstances 'he must yield, but . . . hoped the day of retribution would come, when ministers might be called to severe account for the infamy which they have brought upon this country'. And he suggested that Chatham should be recalled.[5]

On 27 Nov., while still 'of the opinion that America might be regained', he urged the removal of the ministry as 'an indispensable preliminary to any overtures for a reconciliation'.[6] At length, on 8 Mar. 1779, he declared:[7]

he was now convinced that the measures respecting America were wrong at the outset; that they were worse conducted, that instead of resting the claims of this country over her colonies on grounds truly constitutional, we had set up demands, which if attended with success, must have terminated in tyranny and oppression. That instead of putting an end to the first complaints, by adopting measures of persuasion and of a lenient nature, we increased the public discontents, and irritated and inflamed; that when things arose afterwards to the alarming height they did, we fed the disease by weak and irresolute measures, instead of acting with vigour; and that finally, when we resolved to adopt a conduct, which if proper or necessary at all, should have taken place much earlier, we found ourselves totally inadequate to the task.

As a peer he adhered to Shelburne and next to Pitt. In November 1783 he carried the notorious message of George III to the Lords declaring against Fox's East India bill.

He died 11 Feb. 1813.

[1] Last Jnls. i. 413, 428. [2] Almon, i. 135; Last Jnls. i. 428–9. [3] Almon, iii. 353–4. [4] Last Jnls. ii. 99. [5] Almon, viii. 364–6. [6] Parl. Hist. xix. 1369. [7] Almon, xii. 91–93.

M.M.D.

GRENVILLE, Henry (1717–84), of Shrub Hill, Dorking, Surr.

BISHOP'S CASTLE 15 Feb. 1759–1761
THIRSK 1761–June 1765
BUCKINGHAM 1768–1774

b. 15 Sept. 1717, 4th s. of Richard Grenville, M.P., and bro. of Richard, 2nd Earl Temple, and of George and James Grenville (qq.v.). educ. Eton 1728–32. m. 11 Oct. 1757, Margaret Eleanor, da. of Joseph Banks of Revesby Abbey, Lincs., 1da.

Gov. Barbados 1746–56; ambassador to Constantinople 1761–5; commr. of customs 1765–6.

In 1746 Grenville obtained the governorship of Barbados through the influence of his brother George. He returned to England in 1755 and resigned the following year. On 18 Nov. 1756 Dodington noted in his diary (p. 391):

Mr. Tucker [M.P. for Weymouth and Melcombe Regis] had agreed with Mr. George Grenville to be paymaster of the marines and for Governor Grenville to be chosen in his place. The King sent to Fox to know if he could prevent it, and if he thought I would interpose. Mr. Fox said he supposed, if his Majesty commanded me, I would. The King ordered Fox to speak to me—he did, and I stopped it. This is the first step towards turning out Lord Temple.

In February 1759 George Grenville arranged that Walter Waring, M.P. for Bishop's Castle and patron of the borough, should resign in Henry's favour: 'Mr. Waring's interest and Mr. Pitt's popularity united seemed to me invincible there',[1] Henry wrote on 22 Feb. after an uncontested return. In 1761 he was returned on the Frankland interest at Thirsk, but almost immediately was appointed ambassador to Constantinople and does not appear to have taken his seat in Parliament before leaving for Turkey where he remained for more than three years; and thus was not involved in the family quarrel. When on 3 Jan. 1765 he wrote to George Grenville of the 'uneasiness of his situation . . . [in Constantinople] and his earnest wish to be recalled',[2] his brother immediately offered him a commissionership of customs; 'which as it would oblige him to vacate his seat in Parliament would exempt him from involving himself in the unhappy differences in his own family'.[3] In fact these were resolved before his appointment was confirmed in June, and Henry did not return to England till the autumn. On 7 Aug. 1766 Lord Townshend wrote to Bute: 'H.

Grenville has resigned the customs; Lord Temple has given him a house and land.'[4]

In 1768 Grenville was returned unopposed at Buckingham on Temple's interest. In Parliament he now voted consistently with Opposition. There is no record of his having spoken in the House. In April 1774 Temple requested Grenville to resign his seat and proposed to return their nephew George Grenville jnr. in his place as soon as he came of age in June. But on young George's protesting that he did not wish to supplant his uncle before the general election and that 'it was never understood that he held it in trust for me',[5] Temple relented, and Henry retained his seat till the end of the Parliament, but did not stand again.

He died 22 Apr. 1784.

[1] *An 18th Cent. Corresp.* ed. Dickens & Stanton. [2] *Grenville Pprs.* iii. 117. [3] Grenville's diary, 12 Feb. 1765, ibid. [4] Bute mss. [5] *Grenville Pprs.* iv. 559.

M.M.D.

**GRENVILLE, James** (1715–83), of Butleigh Court, Som.

| | |
|---|---|
| OLD SARUM | 5 Jan. 1742–May 1747 |
| BRIDPORT | 25 May 1747–1754 |
| BUCKINGHAM | 1754–1768 |
| HORSHAM | 1768–Mar. 1770 |

*b.* 12 Feb. 1715, 3rd s. of Richard Grenville, M.P., and bro. of Richard, 2nd Earl Temple, and of George and Henry Grenville (qq.v.). *educ.* Eton 1728–32; I. Temple 1734, called 1738. *m.* 1740, Mary, da. and h. of James Smyth of South Elkington, Lincs., 2s.

Dep. paymaster of forces May 1745–1755; ld. of Trade 1746–Dec. 1755; ld. of Treasury Nov. 1756–Apr. 1757, July 1757–Mar. 1761; cofferer of the Household Mar.–Oct. 1761; P.C. 3 Apr. 1761; jt. vice-treasurer [I] Aug. 1766–Jan. 1770.

In 1754 Grenville was returned unopposed on Lord Temple's interest. Throughout his parliamentary career he was a faithful supporter of William Pitt; resigned with him in October 1761, and vigorously opposed Bute's Administration and that of his own brother George Grenville. Though he spoke fairly often in the House, his speeches, which seem to have been tedious, were usually but briefly mentioned. Still, when on 24 Nov. 1763 Richard Rigby condemned Lord Temple as the instigator of Wilkes and the mob, James Grenville, according to Horace Walpole,[1]

> rose, in amazing heat, to defend his brother and vomited out a torrent of invectives on Rigby ... the bitterest terms flowing spontaneously from him who had ever been the most obscure and unready speaker; and what added to the outrage of the diction was, that sitting on the bench immediately above Rigby, and dashing about his arm in the air, he seemed to aim blows at the latter, who was forced to crouch lest he should receive them.

In 1765, during negotiations for a new Administration, James Grenville was mentioned on 15 May as treasurer of the navy or secretary at war, and on 30 June and 5 July as joint vice-treasurer of Ireland.[2] According to Horace Walpole, Grenville genuinely regretted the necessity to refuse the Rockinghams' offer of this post;[3] and even in November Newcastle had hopes that he would accept.[4] In July 1766 Chatham offered Grenville the joint vice-treasurership of Ireland, and subsequently the presidency of the Board of Trade or the pay office; and at his own request he was appointed joint vice-treasurer.[5]

James Grenville's adherence to Pitt after the latter's estrangement from Temple prevented him from standing again at Buckingham in 1768, and Grafton arranged for his return at Horsham on the Irwin interest. His political enthusiasm seems by this time to have waned: no votes or speeches by him are reported during this Parliament, and when early in January 1770 he resigned office it was, according to Walpole, 'unwillingly, to gratify the violence of his brothers'.[6] Next he decided to leave Parliament, and on 16 Jan. Grafton wrote to Lord Irwin: 'Mr. James Grenville was with me to-day wishing to accept of some office in order to clear himself from the political difficulties in which he found himself entangled'; on 20 Jan. Irwin was informed by his agent that Grenville had declared that 'family connexions etc. had made it unavoidable'.[7] On 19 Feb. 1779 Grenville wrote to Lady Chatham:[8]

> I have long pursued the path of private life, and have adhered to that plan. I chose it under circumstances many years past, from knowing myself of too little capacity or consequence to do good, and from having an invincible dislike to doing harm.

He died 14 Sept. 1783.

[1] *Mems. Geo. III*, i. 260. [2] Fortescue, i. 93, 126, 137. [3] *Mems. Geo. III*, ii. 140. [4] Add. 32971, f. 289. [5] *Chatham Corresp.* ii. 466. [6] *Mems. Geo. III*, iv. 37. [7] *HMC Var.* viii. 184, 185. [8] *Chatham Corresp.* iv. 423.

M.M.D.

**GRENVILLE, James** (1742–1825), of Butleigh Court, Som.

| | |
|---|---|
| THIRSK | 26 Dec. 1765–1768 |
| BUCKINGHAM | 26 Nov. 1770–Dec. 1790 |
| BUCKINGHAMSHIRE | 27 Dec. 1790–June 1797 |

*b.* 6 July 1742, 1st s. of James Grenville (q.v.). *educ.* Eton 1754–8; Ch. Ch. Oxf. 1759; L. Inn 1760. *unm. suc.* fa. 14 Sept. 1783; *cr.* Baron Glastonbury 20 Oct. 1797.

Ld. of Treasury Mar. 1782–Mar. 1783; P.C. 26 Dec. 1783; member of Board of Trade 1784–*d.*

When in 1765 a seat at Thirsk was vacated by Henry Grenville, James was returned in his place 'in consequence of a former agreement made with

Mr. Frederick Frankland'.[1] Like his father he supported the Chatham Administration and voted with them on the land tax, but against them on nullum tempus, 17 Feb. 1768. He did not stand at the general election of 1768, but in 1770, on the death of George Grenville, was returned for Buckingham on Lord Temple's interest. During this Parliament he followed an independent line: voted with Opposition on the Spanish convention, 13 Feb. 1771; was classed by Robinson as 'contra, present' in his first survey on the royal marriage bill, March 1772; voted with Opposition on the naval captains' petition, 9 Feb. 1773, when he was marked in the King's list as a friend; voted with Opposition on the Middlesex election, 26 Apr. 1773, and on George Grenville's Act, 25 Feb. 1774, when he again appears in the King's list as a friend; but in Robinson's list of September 1774 he is classed as 'contra'. Grenville spoke several times during this Parliament, apparently always on matters about which he felt strongly. After Grenville's first speech on 7 Mar. 1771 Barré reported to Chatham:[2] 'His manner had all the modesty of his character; his language had not the smallest appearance of being studied; it was spirited and nervous. He was universally applauded.' Grenville supported Sir William Meredith's motion concerning subscription to the 39 Articles at the universities, declaring on 23 Feb. 1773 that 'no subscription to these Articles should be exacted from any layman whatever'.[3] On 21 May 1773 he supported Clive, not only because of his 'eminent services to the whole nation' but because 'we are now proceeding by an *ex post facto* resolution to punish an action which we have constituted a crime, but it was not such when it was committed . . . This . . . is contrary to every rule of justice, contrary to every rule of policy.'[4] He strongly supported the motion to perpetuate George Grenville's Election Act, 25 Feb. 1774. He disapproved of the American war. The *Parliamentary Register*[5] reports that on 27 Oct. 1775, 'with that modesty, ability and candour for which he is remarkable', he

> gave his reasons for not going on against America, because the Americans did not mean to render themselves independent of this country, and because he judged it impracticable to reduce them by force. He concluded by showing with much feeling propriety, that he did not mean to throw any reflection upon the conduct of his late relation Mr. George Grenville.

Grenville now voted consistently with Opposition, and criticized the Administration with increasing vehemence. On 12 Dec. 1781 he supported Lowther's motion to end the war, and quoted Chatham when after Saratoga he called upon Parliament to 'relinquish this mad war'.[6]

Grenville, who was appointed a lord of the Treasury by Rockingham, retained the post under Shelburne, having 'declined in the most positive manner' to become either chancellor of the Exchequer or secretary at war in the new Administration. Shelburne wrote to the King on 9 July that he was 'obliged . . . in a very particular manner to the assistance of Mr. James Grenville' who had persuaded his cousin Lord Temple to go to Ireland instead of having the secretaryship for home affairs which he had hoped for. The King replied the same day: 'I am glad Mr. James Grenville has been of use; I hope he will be cultivated. He is certainly a worthy man.'[7] Grenville voted against Fox's East India bill, 27 Nov. 1783. Only one vote by him is reported during the Parliament of 1784, with the Administration on Richmond's fortifications plan, 27 Feb. 1786, and there is no record of his having spoken.

Horace Walpole described Grenville as 'an amiable and ingenious man, who had improved parts, and a most pleasing manner'.[8] He died 26 Apr. 1825.

[1] *Grenville Pprs.* iii. 192. [2] *Chatham Corresp.* iv. 109. [3] Egerton 244, pp. 196-9. [4] Egerton 248, pp. 206-14. [5] Almon, iii. 58. [6] Debrett, v. 133. [7] Fortescue, v. 77, 79. [8] *Last Jnls.* i. 301.

M.M.D.

## GRENVILLE, Richard (1742–1823).

### BUCKINGHAM 1774–1780

> *b.* 6 July 1742, 2nd s.[1] of James Grenville (q.v.) *educ.* Eton 1754–8. *unm.*
> Ensign 1 Ft. Gds. 1759; capt. 24 Ft. 1761; capt. and lt-col. 2 Ft. Gds. 1772; col. 1779; maj.-gen. 1782; col. 23 Ft. 1786–*d.*; lt.-gen. 1796; gen. 1801.
> In charge of Prince Frederick Augustus's establishment in Hanover, c.1781–7,[2] and comptroller and master of the Household to him as Duke of York 1788–*d.*

Grenville was returned for Buckingham on the family interest. During 1775 he joined his brother and cousin in supporting a motion for expunging from the journals the proceedings against Wilkes, and a bill for disfranchising electors of Hindon on grounds of corruption.[3] These are the only occasions on which he is known to have spoken or voted. Robinson wrote of him in July 1780:

> It is said to be doubtful whether Lord Temple will bring Mr. Richard Grenville in again, and thought that he may bring in his younger brother . . . but if Mr. Richard Grenville comes in, he may be reckoned hopeful, because he never votes against Government.

It seems probable that at the general election Grenville withdrew voluntarily in favour of Temple's brother-in-law, Richard Aldworth Neville.

Grenville died 22 Apr. 1823.

[1] If the date of birth given in *Eton Coll. Reg.* is correct, Richard and his bro. James were twins. [2] Grenville's corresp. with Sir R. M. Keith, 1783–7, Add. 35528–35537. [3] Almon, i. 230, 395.

M.M.D.

## GRENVILLE, Thomas (1755–1846).

BUCKINGHAMSHIRE  25 Oct. 1779–1784
ALDEBURGH   1790–1796
BUCKINGHAM   1796–Dec. 1809
BUCKINGHAMSHIRE  6 Mar. 1813–1818

*b.* 31 Dec. 1755, 2nd s. of George Grenville (q.v.), and bro. of George and William Wyndham Grenville (qq.v.). *educ.* Eton 1764–71; Ch. Ch. Oxf. 1771; L. Inn 1774. *unm.*

Ensign 2 Ft. Gds. 1778, lt. 1779, ret. 1780.

Envoy to Paris May–July 1782; minister extraordinary (with Lord Spencer) to Vienna 1793; chief justice in eyre South of Trent 1800; pres. Board of Control July–Oct. 1806; first ld. of Admiralty 1806–7.

Grenville succeeded his brother George as Member for Buckinghamshire. Until North's fall he voted steadily with the rest of his family in opposition. In April 1780, resenting refusals to promote him, he attacked the ministry for discriminating against him in military promotions; and on this ground left the army.[1] In November 1780, probably owing to the close friendship he had formed with Fox, he was chosen to move the amendment to the Address:[2] his only reported speech during this Parliament. Initially a member of the Westminster Committee of Association, he took no part in its proceedings once its objects were switched to parliamentary reform.

On the formation of Rockingham's ministry, Fox chose Grenville as envoy to conduct peace negotiations at Paris. During this mission Grenville shared Fox's resentment at the way in which Shelburne asserted control over negotiations with the Americans, and this seems to have been the main reason for his refusal, after Rockingham's death, to serve under Shelburne despite Temple's urgent appeal.[3] In 1783 he did not criticize the peace preliminaries in debate—'Tom, to my infinite joy, did not speak', W. W. Grenville informed Temple[4]—but he voted against them, and thereafter gave full support to the Coalition. According to one account Fox thought of him for governor general of India.[5] At the end of 1783 Grenville voted for the motion implying censure upon the sending of messages from the King to the peers about the East India bill. This led to a complete breach with Temple, and reconciliation was delayed till 1785.[6] Deprived in 1784 of the support of the family interest, Grenville did not stand at the general election and was out of the next Parliament.

Grenville died 17 Dec. 1846. A bibliophile, and a trustee of the British Museum, he bequeathed to it his library of over 20,000 volumes, valued at the time at more than £50,000.

[1] Almon, xvii. 497–8. [2] Debrett, i. 28–29. [3] Buckingham, *Courts & Cabinets Geo. III*, i. 50–53, 57–58; Fortescue, vi. 81–82. [4] Buckingham, i. 155. [5] *Gent. Mag.* 1847, i. 197. [6] Buckingham, i. 308–10.

I.R.C.

## GRENVILLE, William Wyndham (1759–1834).

BUCKINGHAM   19 Feb. 1782–1784
BUCKINGHAMSHIRE   1784–25 Nov. 1790

*b.* 25 Oct. 1759, 3rd s. of George Grenville (q.v.), and bro. of George and Thomas Grenville (qq.v.). *educ.* Eton 1770–6; Ch. Ch. Oxf. 1776–80; L. Inn. 1780. *m.* 18 July 1792, Anne, da. of Thomas Pitt, 1st Baron Camelford (q.v.), *s.p. cr.* Baron Grenville 25 Nov. 1790.

P.C. [I] 15 Sept. 1782; chief sec. to ld. lt. [I] Sept. 1782–June 1783; P.C. 31 Dec. 1783; paymaster gen. Jan.–Mar. 1784, jt. paymaster gen. Mar. 1784–Sept. 1789; member of Board of Trade Mar. 1784–Aug. 1789, vice-pres. 1786–9; member of Board of Control Sept. 1784–Mar. 1790, pres. Mar. 1790–June 1793; Speaker of the House of Commons Jan.–June 1789; Home sec. June 1789–June 1791, foreign sec. June 1791–Feb. 1801; auditor of the Exchequer 1794–*d.*; first ld. of Treasury Feb. 1806–Mar. 1807.

Returned for Buckingham on his brother's interest, Grenville voted with the Opposition in the crucial divisions before the fall of North. Like his brother George, 3rd Earl Temple, he supported Rockingham's Administration, and on the formation of Shelburne's in July 1782 became chief secretary to Temple as lord lieutenant of Ireland. Edward Cooke, private secretary to Grenville's predecessor, commenting unfavourably on the appointment of so young and inexperienced a man to lead the Irish House of Commons, nevertheless conceded that he seemed 'sensible and perfectly well-disposed, and ... laborious'.[1] In November 1782 he was sent to London to discuss Irish policy with the ministers, and during the next few months laboured to obtain a renunciating bill to allay Irish fears of English interference in their judicature. Cabinet divisions and procrastinations exasperated him: on 20 Dec. he wrote to Temple asking permission to remain in London till the bill was presented

to prevent their being frightened ... into any weakening of the preamble, and to goad them on to do something. For you see ... the objection was not so much to the taking any particular step, as to doing anything at all.[2]

And on the 24th about Shelburne: 'Is it not inconceivable that a man will hazard so much ... without its being possible for one to discover any one object under heaven which he is to gain by the delay?' During this period his only two reported speeches in the House were on Irish affairs. On 21 Jan. 1783 he at length felt able to report to Temple that 'considering all the circumstances ... the whole has not gone off ill'.

After the publication of the peace preliminaries Grenville wrote to Temple on 6 Feb.:

I own I cannot think it so bad, all things considered ... and I see no reason for being at all confident that another campaign would have put us in a better situation to negotiate. In this line, I had intended to have stated my ideas on the day of debate in the House of Commons; but I am deterred by reading your opinions, and by a fear . . . that you will take an active part the other way . . . If it had not been for this, I think it would have had a handsome appearance in the hour of their distress.

Instead, in reply to a request from Pitt to move an address of approbation, he hedged: while he preferred 'such a peace to such a war' and felt 'obliged to that Government, who have, at any rate, put a stop to the progression of evil', it was 'still too humiliating to Great Britain to admit of very sanguine expressions of exultation', and he was very hesitant about moving such an address.[3] In the end he avoided doing so, though he voted with Administration on the preliminaries, 18 Feb.

At the beginning of March, when Temple announced his intention to resign, Grenville followed, but with characteristic prudence restrained his brother from leaving the country 'with an appearance of fretfulness and intemperance' before the appointment of his successor. During the next few weeks, acting on Temple's behalf, he saw the King several times and acted as a restraining influence on his brother's impetuosity. On the 28th he reported that the King having referred to the possibility of Temple's forming an Administration, he had pointed out the difficulty of finding a manager for the House of Commons. Various names were discussed but rejected, and, he wrote, as far as he himself was concerned,

> even if equal in other respects, which I very unaffectedly know I am not, still I am much too young, and too little versed in the navigation of that tempestuous sea to venture out in such a hurricane as this.

On 1 Apr., informing Temple of the King's acceptance of the Coalition, he obviously considered it a very temporary measure: the King, he wrote, was anxious

> that those who act with us should hold themselves apart from such government, in order that he may have something else to look to whenever circumstances allow of it . . . our ground I think clear—honourable to ourselves, consistent with our principles and professions, and holding out to us the fairest prospects of honest ambition.

On 20 Nov. 1783 Grenville attacked Fox's East India bill. 'In a speech of great length and greater ability', wrote Wraxall,[4] he 'gave promise of those vigorous powers of mind which he has since unfolded.'

But though Grenville obtained office on the formation of Pitt's Administration, he does not at first seem to have been active in the House: his only reported speech during the following critical months was on 22 Dec. 1783 to announce and defend his brother's resignation. On 16 June 1784 he attacked

the principle of parliamentary reform, though paying tribute to Pitt who, he declared, did not expect 'a servile compliance with his particular sentiments on every great and important question'.[5] He now spoke more frequently in the House; on 5 Apr. 1785 he moved for leave to bring in a bill to amend his father's act for trying controverted elections; and more than once defended Pitt's Irish propositions. Wraxall, writing of 1785, declared that Grenville had

> the second place in Pitt's favour and friendship at this period of his political career. The ties of consanguinity cemented every other motive derived from mental endowments. Nature had bestowed on him no exterior advantages. His person was heavy, and devoid of elegance or grace, his manners destitute of suavity. Even his eloquence partook of these defects. In debate he wanted Pitt's copious pomp of words, his facility and majesty of expression.[6]

Grenville now seems to have thought of applying for a peerage, but hesitated about leaving the Commons:

> I am so much pleased with my present situation [he wrote to his brother, 12 Dec. 1786] that I am unwilling to quit it so soon . . . I shall, I am confident in the next session, by the help of my present situation, be able to put myself much more forward in the House than I have hitherto done, which appears to me a great object to attain previous to accepting of what, after all, I fear, will wear the appearance of putting myself *hors de combat*. I am not in the same mind about it for any ten minutes together.

When in July 1787 war with Holland appeared imminent, Grenville was sent to the Hague to investigate, and shortly after his return in September, to Paris, to advise William Eden about the dispute. On 23 Sept. 1787 Pitt wrote to him: 'Let me know what you think of all this. Even in these two days I felt no small difference in not being able to have your opinion on things as they arise.'[7] On 1 Apr. the following year, on Lord Howe's resigning the Admiralty, Grenville told his brother that Pitt had appeared much disposed to give him the office—

> but I must confess my mind has never gone to it at all. The situation would unquestionably have been highly flattering to me at my time of life . . . But . . . I think it is not prudent for a person who has already been put forward beyond what many people think his pretensions entitle him to and who has still much way to make for himself, to incur the risk of shocking and revolting the feelings of almost everyone . . . Besides I am unwilling—after having been endeavouring for four or five years to qualify myself, in some degree for almost any other line of public service—that my first ostensible debut should be in one where I should have the first ABC to learn.

He hoped eventually to obtain the Home Office, and had mentioned it to Pitt, who had replied he was unwilling to move Lord Sydney abruptly without being able to compensate him, 'but that, whenever any such opportunity offered, he should willingly and eagerly embrace it ... I am by no means desirous that the interval should be so much shortened as to make the appointment immediate. I am in the train of making myself fitter for it.' In the meanwhile Grenville hoped to obtain a reasonable sinecure post, and finding difficulties in securing a life grant of the master of the rolls in Ireland, finally settled for the reversion of the office of chief remembrancer. On 23 June 1788, reporting changes in Administration to his brother, he wrote: 'For my own part ... the circumstances of my present situation in almost every point of view, particularly the confidence with which I am treated, leave me very little to look to, or to hope for, from any change that can arise.' But in January 1789, on the death of the Speaker at the height of the Regency crisis, Grenville agreed to take his place.

> Upon the whole, I think the decision I have made is clearly right [he wrote to Buckingham, 2 Jan.]. If the King recovers before Parliament is dissolved, it is clearly understood that my acceptance of this situation is not to prejudice my other views ... If the Regent goes on without dissolving, I am then in a situation which, though perhaps not perfectly pleasant, is nevertheless respectable, and will give me occupation.
> If they dissolve and carry the Chair against me in the new Parliament I do not see how I stand worse, in any respect, for having held this office.

He was elected on 5 Jan. on a party vote. On the 16th he made a long speech in committee supporting Pitt's Regency proposals. Less than six months later he resigned from the Speakership, having at last obtained the office of Home secretary; the following year he went to the Lords, and as Lord Grenville achieved the highest office.

'He loved business as his father did', wrote the *Gentleman's Magazine* (1834, i. 237) after his death on 12 Jan. 1834,

> it was not merely the result of his ambition, but his amusement; the flowers of imagination, or the gaieties of society never seduced him astray. There was nothing to dissipate his ideas, and he brought his mind to bear on the subjects before him with its full force.

¹ *Auckland Corresp.* i. 336. ² Letters from Grenville to Temple quoted in this biography, unless otherwise stated, are in Buckingham, *Courts & Cabinets of Geo. III.* ³ *HMC Fortescue*, i. 193–4. ⁴ *Mems.* iii. 161. ⁵ *Debrett*, xv. 213. ⁶ *Mems.* iv. 101. ⁷ *HMC Fortescue*, iii. 429.

M.M.D.

## GREVILLE, Hon. Charles Francis (1749–1809).

### WARWICK   21 Jan. 1774–1790

*b.* 12 May 1749, 2nd s. of Francis, 1st Earl of Warwick, by Elizabeth, da. of Lord Archibald Hamilton; bro. of George, Lord Greville and Robert Fulke Greville (qq.v.). *educ.* Edinburgh 1764–7;¹ Grand Tour. *unm.* Ld. of Trade Jan. 1774–Sept. 1780; ld. of the Admiralty Sept. 1780–Mar. 1782; treasurer of the Household Apr.–Dec. 1783; vice-chamberlain 1794–*d.*

In January 1774 Greville was returned for the seat at Warwick vacated by his brother's succeeding to the earldom; and at the same time took over his place at the Board of Trade. 'A violent and tedious fever' for several months prevented him from taking his seat either at the Board or in the Commons,² but when in June he eventually did so, his attendance, at the Board at least, seems to have been fairly regular. He voted consistently with North's Administration. His only reported speech during his first Parliament was on the Address, 26 Nov. 1778. In 1779 Greville was considered as a possible treasurer of the Household,³ and was offered the first vacant seat at the Admiralty Board, which 'from the increase in income ... was considered as superior to the Board of Trade'.⁴ He was still hoping for promotion the following year, but was anxious that it should come at the time of the dissolution, 'to save me the revival of a contest which I am anxious to avoid'. He was unwilling to press North about it, and told Lord Sandwich: 'Although I have a desire to get forward, I confess I cannot seek promotion or favour for myself by dint of importunity.'⁵ He was appointed to the Admiralty Board, 6 Sept., and returned at Warwick after a contest a few days later. Greville voted against Shelburne's peace preliminaries, 18 Feb. 1783, and in April 1783, on the formation of the Coalition, accepted office as treasurer of the Household. In December 1783, on the dismissal of the Coalition, Greville immediately resigned. His opposition to Pitt brought him into conflict with his brother Lord Warwick, and at the general election of 1784 he stood at Warwick in opposition to his brother's candidate. He wrote to his younger brother, Robert Fulke Greville:⁶

> Fortunately for me I have had no politics since I have canvassed, for the politicians were my late friends, and those I have now to support me have not yet the refinement of trusting their politics to a man they do not esteem in preference to a man they profess to esteem, because he has varied in one point which they take up on the present occasion. I never had a more agreeable canvass ... and never thought that I was so well in the opinion of the low orders ... none of my gentle friends have polled for me.

He was returned again, and continued in opposition till he left Parliament. Only one speech by him is recorded during this Parliament—on the hawkers and pedlars bill, 1 July 1785.

Wraxall wrote of him:⁷

> Possessing like his uncle, Sir William Hamilton, an elegant mind and a taste for many branches of the fine arts, which pursuit carried him into expenses beyond the bounds of severe prudence, his resignation ... could not ... be to him in any sense a matter of indifference ... He retired during several years from court and from public life into comparative obscurity.

In fact Greville, who had a very small income, seems by 1784 to have been seriously embarrassed financially, and in December approached the Duke of Rutland about selling him the collection of pictures and sculpture 'which has taken me twelve years to make, and during which I have had the pickings of several collections which were sold in Italy, through the assistance of Mr. Hamilton at Rome, and Sir William Hamilton at Naples'.[8] Greville's economies included giving up his liaison with Emma Hart—he sent her out to Naples where his uncle Sir William Hamilton (whom she subsequently married) was minister.

Greville seems to have canvassed Warwick at the general election of 1790, but retired before the poll. He died 23 May 1809.

[1] Mrs. Delany, *Autobiog. & Corresp.* (ser. 2), i. 110. [2] Add. 35507, f. 58. [3] Fortescue, iv. 353. [4] Greville to Sandwich, 9 Aug. 1780, Sandwich mss. [5] Ibid., undated (Apr. 1784). [6] Add. 40714, ff. 204–206. [7] *Mems.* iii. 206–7. [8] *HMC Rutland*, iii. 269.

M.M.D.

## GREVILLE, George, Lord Greville (1746–1816).

WARWICK 1768–6 July 1773

*b.* 16 Sept. 1746, 1st s. of Francis, 1st Earl of Warwick, and bro. of Hon. Charles Francis and Robert Fulke Greville (qq.v.). *educ.* Eton 1753–4; Ch. Ch. Oxf. 1764; Edinburgh Univ.; Grand Tour. *m.* (1) 1 Apr. 1771, Georgiana (*d.*1 Apr. 1772), da. of Sir James Peachey, 4th Bt. (q.v.), 1s.; (2) 14 July 1776, Henrietta, da. of Richard Vernon (q.v.) of Hilton, Staffs., 2s. 6da. *suc.* fa. 6 July 1773.

Ld. of Trade April 1770–Jan. 1774; ld. lt. Warws. 1795–*d.*

Greville was returned unopposed for Warwick on his family interest. His first recorded vote was with Opposition over Wilkes's petition, 27 Jan. 1769, but during the rest of his time in the Commons he voted with Administration. Only one speech by him is reported—moving the Address at the beginning of the session, 13 Nov. 1770.

The *Royal Register* described him in 1780 as 'a quiet inoffensive character, little known but by persons of taste and *virtu*'.[1]

He died 2 May 1816.

[1] Quoted *CP.*

M.M.D.

## GREVILLE, Hon. Robert Fulke (1751–1824).

WARWICK 1774–1780
NEW WINDSOR 1796–1806

*b.* 3 Feb. 1751, 3rd s. of Francis, 1st Earl of Warwick, and bro. of George, Lord Greville and Charles Francis Greville (qq.v.).[1] *educ.* Edinburgh Univ. 1764–7.[1] *m.* 19 Oct. 1797, Louisa, *s.j.* Countess of Mansfield, da. of Charles, 9th Lord Cathcart [S], wid. of David, 7th Visct. Stormont and 2nd Earl of Mansfield, 1s. 2da.

Cornet 10 Drag. 1768, lt. 1772; lt. and capt. 1 Ft. Gds. 1775; capt. and lt.-col. 1 Ft. Gds. 1777.

Equerry to the King June 1781–97; groom of the bedchamber 1800–18.

Greville was returned for Warwick on his brother Lord Warwick's interest. 'Lord Warwick is a steady supporter', George III wrote to Lord Barrington, 18 Mar. 1774, 'his brother a very pretty young man and a Member of Parliament, and the oldest ensign [sic] only of 1769', and should therefore be considered for promotion.[2] Greville consistently supported North's Administration. There is no record of his having spoken in the House. In 1780 he stood again at Warwick, but was defeated. His brother Charles wrote to R. M. Keith, 15 Sept. 1780:[3] 'A banker's purse has obtained a seat which my brother ought to have had and which it is but small consolation to see must be his again.' In fact, Greville seems to have had no ambition for a political career, and was content with the court place which he obtained the year after his defeat. His diaries detail with obvious satisfaction his daily routine at court, and he describes his first attendance as an equerry as 'the happiest month of my life'.[4] When in 1784 his two elder brothers quarrelled about politics and opposed each other at Warwick, he himself kept out of the contest. Fanny Burney, who always refers to him as 'Colonel Wellbred', and thought him 'so elegant' and 'so pleasing' that it was impossible not to 'see him with approbation, and speak of him with praise', wrote of his situation in the family:[5]

He loves them both, and with both keeps well; but while he has a place that devotes a fourth of the year to the King, his residence for the rest of it is with the brother who is in opposition to the Government. Not small must be the difficulties of such circumstances and his preferment is probably checked by this determined fraternal amity, though his moderation and uprightness secure him the esteem and force the good word of both parties, as well as both brothers.

Greville died 27 Apr. 1824.

[1] Mrs. Delany, *Autobiog. & Corresp.* (ser. 2), i. 110. [2] Barrington mss. [3] Add. 35519, f. 236. [4] *Diary of R. F. Greville,* ed. Bladon, 67. [5] *Diary & Letters of Mme D'Arblay,* ed. Dobson, iii. 385; iv. 357.

M.M.D.

## GREY, Hon. Booth (1740–1802), of Budworth Magna, Cheshire.

LEICESTER 1768–1784

*b.* 15 Aug. 1740, 2nd s. of Harry 4th Earl of Stamford, by Lady Mary Booth, da. and h. of George, 2nd Earl of Warrington; bro. of George Harry, Lord Grey (q.v.). *educ.* Queens', Camb. 1758. *m.* 10 May 1782, Elizabeth, da. of Charles Manwaring of Brombrough, Cheshire, 1s. 1da.

Grey stood for Leicester in 1768 on a joint interest with his friend Eyre Coote, supported by the Rutland interest but against the corporation; they were successful, but the contest was protracted and expensive. In 1774 and 1780 he was returned without a contest. He voted with the Rockinghams but had no influence in the party. He was absent from the division on Shelburne's peace preliminaries, 18 Feb. 1783; was classed by Robinson as 'Fox' and voted for Fox's East India bill, 27 Nov. 1783. In December 1783 Robinson noted about Leicester: 'Probably the same Members'; Grey canvassed the borough, but faced with the prospect of an expensive contest and with the loss of the Rutland interest, withdrew. He never stood for Parliament again.

He died 4 Mar. 1802.

J.B.

## GREY, Charles (1764–1845), of Howick, Northumb.

| NORTHUMBERLAND | 6 July 1786–1807 |
| APPLEBY | 25 May 1807–July 1807 |
| TAVISTOCK | 20 July 1807–14 Nov. 1807 |

*b.* 13 Mar. 1764, 1st surv. s. of Charles Grey of Howick (*cr.* Earl Grey 1806) by Elizabeth, da. of George Grey of Southwick, co. Dur.; nephew of Sir Henry Grey, 2nd Bt. (q.v.). *educ.* St. Marylebone; Eton 1773–81; Trinity, Camb. 1781; M. Temple 1783; Grand Tour. *m.* 18 Nov. 1794, Mary Elizabeth, da. of Henry Brabazon Ponsonby (*cr.* Baron Ponsonby of Imokilly 1806), 6s. 10da. *suc.* fa. as 2nd Earl Grey 14 Nov. 1807; K.G. 27 May 1831.

P.C. 5 Feb. 1806; first ld. of Admiralty Feb.–Sept. 1806; sec. of state for foreign affairs Sept. 1806–Mar. 1807; first ld. of Treasury 1830–4.

Sir Edward Blackett wrote to his son, William, 12 June 1786:[1]

The Duke of Northumberland is dead, so Lord Algernon goes into the House of Lords. Sir Henry Grey is now making interest for his nephew, and writing circular letters; and young Grey is sent for in a great hurry from Italy.

Charles Grey was elected without opposition and *in absentia*. About his first speech Sir Gilbert Elliot wrote to his wife, 22 Feb. 1787:[2]

I heard yesterday the first speech of a young Member Mr. Grey, for Northumberland, excessively good indeed, and such as has given everybody the highest opinion both of his abilities and his character. He was brought in for that county by the Northumberland interest as ministerial, which is the side of all his friends and family, but he has taken the other line himself, at least in the only business of this session [the French commercial treaty] . . . He professes not to be of a party, but I think he has a warm leaning to us in general.

By his speech of 30 Apr. 1787 on the Prince of Wales's debts he aligned himself with Fox, and set the course of his career.

Grey died 17 July 1845.

[1] Blackett mss at Matfen. [2] *Life & Letters of Sir G. Elliot*, i. 130.

J.B.

## GREY, George Harry, Lord Grey (1737–1819).

STAFFORDSHIRE 1761–30 May 1768

*b.* 1 Oct. 1737, 1st s. of Harry, 4th Earl of Stamford, and bro. of Hon. Booth Grey (q.v.). *educ.* Leicester; Queens', Camb. 1755. *m.* 28 May 1763, Lady Henrietta Bentinck, da. of William, 2nd Duke of Portland, 4s. 5da. *suc.* fa. as 5th Earl of Stamford 30 May 1768; *cr.* Earl of Warrington 22 April 1796. Ld. lt. Cheshire 1783–*d.*

Lord Grey's father was a close friend of Lord Gower, whom he made a trustee of his will. Grey was returned unopposed for Staffordshire in 1761 as Gower's candidate, and through him was sent Newcastle's parliamentary whip. Yet in December 1762 he voted against the peace preliminaries. His marriage brought him close to the leaders of the Opposition. He wrote to his brother-in-law Portland, 9 Nov. 1763:[1]

Prayers and entreaties innumerable have been thundered into my ears to prevent me going up to the meeting of the Parliament. My disobedience I am certain would be the means of an open breach with all my family; I have therefore determined to lay aside all thoughts of it. The arguments you made use of to prevail upon me carried with them great weight, but when my dear friend considers that the peace of a family is at stake he will, I hope, think that I have acted the most prudent part. My sentiments I can with great truth assure him are not in the least altered, nor shall I on any account desert the good cause I have espoused.

Thus he does not appear in the list of the minority of 15 Nov. 1763. But in the three divisions over general warrants, 6, 15 and 18 Feb. 1764, he voted with the Opposition; was classed by Newcastle, 10 May 1764, as a 'sure friend'; and belonged to Wildman's Club. He supported the Rockingham Administration; and voted against the Chatham Administration on the land tax, 27 Feb. 1767, and the nullum tempus bill, 17 Feb. 1768.

He was again the Gower candidate for Staffordshire at the general election of 1768, in spite of their divergence in politics; and was returned unopposed. There is no record of his having spoken in the House of Commons.

In the Lords Stamford voted with the Rockinghams; and after Rockingham's death with the Portland Whigs. He died 23 May 1819.

[1] Portland mss.

J.B.

## GREY, Sir Henry, 2nd Bt. (1722–1808), of Howick, Northumb.

NORTHUMBERLAND 1754–1768

*bap.* 15 Nov. 1722, 1st s. of Sir Henry Grey, 1st Bt., M.P., of Howick by Hannah, da. of Thomas Wood of Falloden. *unm.* *suc.* fa. May 1749.

Grey, 'a young man of great family and fortune',[1] was returned unopposed in 1754 with the support of Lord Northumberland and the Pelhams; and again in 1761. In Dupplin's list of 1754 he was classed as a Government Whig. Under George III he adhered to Bute,[2] and presumably to Grenville; while Rockingham in July 1765 classed him as 'pro'. But no vote by him is recorded during this period. Edward Blackett wrote to Captain Henry Tulip, 27 Mar. 1767:[3]

> I was told that the doorkeeper of the House of Commons refused Sir H. Grey admittance t'other day, taking him for a stranger; and that some Members of his acquaintance were forced to be called out of the House to vouch for him that he was a Member. A long absence had made him be forgot, even by the doorkeeper.

In Townshend's list of January 1767 and Newcastle's of March he is classed as absent. He did not stand in 1768.

Grey died 3 Apr. 1808.

[1] Northumberland to Newcastle, 30 June 1753, Add. 32732, ff. 129-30. [2] John Craufurd to C. Jenkinson, 3 Apr. 1763, Bute mss. [3] Blackett mss at Matfen.

J.B.

**GREY, Hon. John** (c.1724-77), of Enville Hall, nr. Stourbridge, Staffs.

BRIDGNORTH 1754-1768
TREGONY 1768-1774

*b.* c.1724, 2nd s. of Harry, 3rd Earl of Stamford, by Dorothy, da. of Sir Nathan Wright of Caldecote Hall, Warws., lord keeper 1700-5. *educ.* Westminster Apr. 1733 (aged 8) -1740; Emmanuel, Camb. 16 June 1740, aged 17. *m.* 24 May 1748, Lucy, da. of Sir Joseph Danvers, 1st Bt., of Swithland, Leics., *s.p.*

Clerk of the Board of Green Cloth 1754-*d.*

Grey, wrote Lord Gower to Newcastle, 17 June 1752, was 'at his first appearance in the world introduced into bad company by his cousin Lord Ward [John Ward, M.P., a prominent Jacobite] and some females of his family', but he had now been presented at court 'by which step he has highly incensed all his old friends against him, and is I believe fully determined for the future to adhere to the family upon the throne'.[1]

In 1754 and 1761 Grey was elected unopposed on the Whitmore interest at Bridgnorth, where he himself was no stranger: Enville Hall is 8 miles from the borough, and Grey's sister was married to Richard Acton of Aldenham, 3 miles from it. In Bute's list Grey was classed as 'Government', but does not appear in Henry Fox's list of Members favourable to the peace preliminaries, December 1762, and after the divisions of 9 and 10 Dec. Fox wrote to Bute: 'Mr. Grey of the Green Cloth went away and did not

vote with us in either division.'[2] But henceforth he voted with every Administration; was returned as a Government candidate in 1768; and retained his office after leaving Parliament. There is no record of his having spoken in the House.

Grey died 25 Feb. 1777.

[1] Add. 32728, f. 7. [2] Bute mss.

M.M.D.

**GREY,** *see also* **DE GREY** *and* **GRAY**

**GRIFFIN, Sir John Griffin** (1719-97), of Audley End, Essex.

ANDOVER 28 Nov. 1749-3 Aug. 1784

*b.* 13 Mar. 1719, 1st s. of William Whitwell of Oundle, Northants, by Hon. Anne Griffin, da. and h. of James, 2nd Baron Griffin (by Lady Essex Howard, da. and h. of James, 3rd Earl of Suffolk and Lord Howard de Walden). *educ.* Winchester 1734-6. *m.* (1) 9 Mar. 1749, Anna Maria (*d.* 18 Aug. 1764), da. of John, Baron Schutz, *s.p.*; (2) 11 June 1765, Catherine, da. of William Clayton (q.v.) of Harleyford, Bucks., *s.p.* *suc.* fa. 1755, and on *d.* of his uncle Edward, 3rd Baron Griffin, to Audley End 1742, and took name of Griffin 1749; K.B. 3 May 1761; the abeyance of the barony of Howard de Walden terminated in his favour 3 Aug. 1784; *cr.* Baron Braybrooke 5 Sept. 1788, with sp. rem. to his second cos. once removed, Richard Aldworth Neville (q.v.).

Ensign 3 Ft. Gds. 1739, capt. 1743, capt. and lt.-col. 1747; col. 1756; maj.-gen. 1756; col. 33 Ft. 1760-6; lt.-gen. 1761; col. 1 Troop Horse Grenadier Gds. 1766-88; gen. 1778; col. 4 Drag. 1788-*d.*; f.m. 1796.

Griffin served under the Duke of Cumberland in Flanders, 1747-8. Returned for Andover on the interest of his uncle, John Wallop, 1st Earl of Portsmouth, his first political connexion was with Henry Fox, secretary at war and Cumberland's right-hand man. In Dupplin's list of the Parliament of 1754 Griffin is included in Fox's group; and when in 1755 Fox wished to secure Portsmouth's support for Sir Edward Winnington at Bewdley, he approached him through Griffin. 'You, my Lord', wrote Griffin to Portsmouth on 19 Sept. 1755,[1] 'are not unacquainted with the civilities I have received from Mr. Fox and the farther obligations I am likely to owe him and I am persuaded will, if you can on this occasion, give me a fresh proof of your friendship.'

He served on the expeditions to St. Malo and St. Cas in 1758, and on his return claimed to have met with 'a reception from the King and court . . . far I own beyond anything that my own merit could entitle me to'.[2] He applied to Newcastle for the Order of the Bath, 26 Nov. 1758; a second application was made on 17 June 1759 and one to Pitt on 28 Aug. 1759.[3] He served in Germany 1759-60, where he was 'in three different affairs (and wounded in the last two of them)'.[4] On the accession of George III he renewed his application for the Bath, this time to Bute and with success.[5]

He received Newcastle's whip in 1761 through Lord Barrington, secretary at war, and in Bute's list was classed 'Government'. He supported Bute and applied to him for favours (unsuccessfully) through Jenkinson—a military governorship, 18 July 1762, the lieutenant governorship of the Isle of Wight, 19 Aug., an office about the Queen, 7 Nov.; and obtained from Sandwich promotion in the navy for his brother.[6]

A letter to Pitt of 27 Oct. 1763 is the first suggestion of his leaving Government: he requested 'the honour of a few minutes conversation' before the meeting of Parliament, which Pitt, professing himself 'extremely flattered', granted.[7] On 23 Nov., on a point of procedure, he voted against Government over Wilkes; and on 19 Jan. 1764 said in the House that 'he should vote his own way and according to evidence, though not only one general and one colonel, but a dozen had been broke'.[8] Yet he voted against the Opposition motion to postpone considering Wilkes's case—'he was', wrote James Grenville to Lady Chatham, 'much more an intimidating, than an intimidated voice, but the effect was not the less important against us'.[9] In the division of 18 Feb. he voted against Government.

Rockingham in July 1765 classed Griffin 'pro', and courted him 'in an obliging, *unsolicited* and friendly manner'.[10] Griffin applied for a vacant regiment which had been already promised elsewhere, and Conway, most anxious to propitiate him, wrote on 7 Sept.:

I own among others I should be particularly happy that you showed us so much friendship as not to let the world say you were among the refuters and for our sakes among the dissatisfied, which I feel would with justice hurt us, and I should almost flatter myself you would even at the expense of a slight disadvantage wish to serve us were it the case.

And Rockingham the same day: 'I trouble you with a letter lest you should feel any uneasiness, which I am sure would not only be very disagreeable to me but critical I may say to all of us.'[11] On 13 Sept. a grant of the revenues of five lighthouses on the coasts of Norfolk and Suffolk, which he held for 36 years, was further extended; and in March 1766 he was appointed to the command of a troop of Horse Grenadier Guards.

Griffin, though sensible of his obligations to Rockingham, welcomed Chatham's return to office, and on 15 Aug. 1766, barely a fortnight later, applied to him for a peerage. Chatham, anxious to 'proceed with the sincerity of a real friend', felt obliged to

inform Griffin that 'his Majesty will probably not be easily moved to create many'.[12] Griffin repeated his application on 31 Aug.:

May I not be allowed to say that those whose expectations have been raised only by applications to former ministries cannot have quite so much reason to hope for the accomplishment of them under your Lordship's Administration as I had flattered myself I had had for mine?

On 26 Oct. he inquired if Chatham desired the 'close attendance of your particular friends' at the meeting of Parliament.[13] On 28 Nov., after the Rockinghams had broken with Chatham over Lord Edgcumbe's dismissal, he expressed to Chatham his 'concern at the present situation of affairs' and asked 'the honour of a very few minutes conversation'.[14] Obviously, he was uneasy about Chatham's treatment of the Rockinghams. He voted with Government over the land tax, 27 Feb. 1767, yet kept on friendly terms with Rockingham, who, though careful to stand well with him, treated him as a follower of Chatham.

Griffin voted with Opposition over Wilkes on 2 and 3 Feb. 1769; pressed by Rockingham to attend the division of 8 May, which confirmed Luttrell in his seat for Middlesex, he declared himself 'no friend to the resolution of the House of Commons which gave Colonel Luttrell his seat there', but 'particular business' prevented his attendance.[15] On 15 July 1769 he congratulated Chatham on the recovery of his health,[16] and on 9 and 25 Jan. 1770 voted with Opposition over the Middlesex election. He voted against the Spanish convention, 13 Feb. 1771.

No correspondence between Griffin and Chatham after 1769 survives, and they seem to have lost touch with each other. When Chatham and Rockingham quarrelled in March 1771 Rockingham tried to make sure that Griffin would be on his side, yet Griffin maintained his independence. Rockingham wrote on 23 Feb. 1771[17] for Griffin's support on Dowdeswell's jury bill (the occasion of the quarrel)—'the *best* mode, and I believe I may also say the *only* mode' of resolving 'the doubts and controversies which have arisen on the power of juries', in spite of the 'difference of opinion in some considerable persons'. His next request for Griffin's attendance was on the royal marriage bill, 7 Mar. 1772. Griffin, though he disliked the bill, thought it 'indelicate' to oppose what was 'a personal point to his Majesty';[18] and did not vote against the bill on 11 Mar. On 25 Feb. 1774 he voted for Grenville's Election Act.

Early in 1774 Lord Richard Cavendish wrote to Rockingham:[19]

I take the liberty of giving you this trouble at the request of Dr. [Richard] Watson to inform you that in a conversation he had the other day with Sir John Griffin, he seemed disposed to come over to the opinions of Opposition about America and expressed a great desire, of communicating his sentiments to you, and of knowing yours in the present turn of affairs. Dr. Watson thinks that an application of any sort from you would be agreeable to him, and could not fail to have a good effect on his conduct.

On 24 Feb. 1775, in the debate on the bill to prohibit the colonists from fishing off Newfoundland, Griffin expressed 'his sincere wishes to see a happy conclusion put to the American disputes without bloodshed': the operation of the bill should be delayed 'to such a period as ought to give those so inclined time to return to their duty', so that 'none but the unrelenting and untractable could feel its influence'.[20]

Confronted with the choice between abandonment of British sovereignty or war, Griffin hesitated and was unwilling to decide. On 22 Oct. 1775 Rockingham urgently requested his attendance at the opening of Parliament;[21] he did not vote for the Opposition amendment against the Address on 26 Oct., but on 1 Nov. spoke in debate on the naval estimates.[22]

He declared that he had hitherto supported Government on principles, without regard to men; thinking it his duty as an honest man so to do, as long as the true interest of the country appeared to be consulted, and the public affairs conducted to the credit or honour of the nation; denied that to be the case at present . . . adding, he should ill deserve to sit there any longer, if he continued to afford his support to men, the effects of whose mistaken and pernicious measures had reduced us to so shameful and dishonourable a situation. Professed himself an advocate for the supreme legislative authority of this country over its colonies; disclaimed however on the one hand vindicating the rash and indiscreet measure of having taxed the Americans, as he did on the other, their mode of resistance.

He opposed 'coercion and conquest', the use of foreign troops, the increase of the army, and the calling out of the militia,

instead of which, he added, tender of conciliation on terms suited to the true spirit of the British constitution ought to be preferred and held out to the Americans, which, if found not to prevail, to relinquish all connections with them; or otherwise, if practicable, to harass them with your fleets, by interrupting their trade, till at length they might perhaps be brought to sue for protection.

He remained independent, friendly with Rockingham but not of his party, more courted than courting. When, on 9 May 1777, Sir James Lowther moved for an address to the King to increase his brothers' incomes, Griffin, 'objecting to the propriety of the motion, and urging the difficulty of

discussing a subject of so delicate a complexion', moved the previous question.[23] And he wrote to Rockingham on 11 Apr. 1778[24] about a motion by Thomas Powys which would have authorized the conciliation commissioners to grant American independence:

If those gentlemen, my Lord, who are of opinion that the Americans will not treat but on the footing of independence should prove to be right, I must confess, all circumstances considered, it nevertheless does not appear to me necessary nor in sound policy prudent in this first instance to begin by acknowledging their independence.

He was more concerned for the welfare of the Empire than to see Administration defeated, and closer in spirit to Chatham than to Rockingham—predestined to follow the younger Pitt.

From 1780 till the fall of North's Administration he voted in every recorded division with the Opposition. He voted for Shelburne's peace preliminaries, 18 Feb. 1783, and against Fox's East India bill, 27 Nov. 1783, and received his peerage from the younger Pitt.

He died 25 May 1797.

[1] Essex RO, Braybrooke mss. [2] Griffin to Newcastle, 5 Feb. 1760, Add. 32902, f. 74. [3] Add. 32886, f. 25; 32892, f. 129; Chatham mss. [4] Add. 32902, f. 74. [5] Bute to Griffin, 8 Jan. 1761 (misdated 1760), Braybrooke mss. [6] Add. 38199, ff. 38, 156; 38200, f. 97; Sandwich to Griffin, 6 Sept. 1763, Braybrooke mss. [7] Braybrooke mss. [8] Harris's 'Debates'. [9] Chatham Corresp. ii. 274–5. [10] Griffin to Pitt, 14 Sept. 1765, Chatham mss. [11] Braybrooke mss. [12] Ibid. [13] Chatham mss. [14] Braybrooke mss. [15] Rockingham mss. [16] Chatham mss. [17] Braybrooke mss. [18] Griffin to Rockingham, 8 Mar. 1772, ibid. [19] Rockingham mss. [20] Almon, i. 233. [21] Braybrooke mss. [22] Almon, iii. 87–88. [23] Ibid. vii. 165. [24] Rockingham mss.

J.B.

**GRIFFIN, Thomas** (c.1700–71), of Dixton Hadnock, nr. Monmouth.

ARUNDEL    1754–1761

*b.* c.1700.
    Entered R.N. c.1711; lt. 1718; capt. 1731; r.-adm. 1747; v.-adm. 1748; adm. 1757.

In 1750 Griffin was tried by court martial for failing to engage the enemy while commander-in-chief in the East Indies 1746–8; was found guilty, and suspended from his rank and employment. In 1752 he was reinstated, but saw no further service.

At Arundel in 1754 he seems to have stood jointly with Sir George Colebrooke, who had an interest in the borough, and with the support of the Treasury. He was returned after a contest, and classed by Dupplin as a supporter of Administration. No vote or speech by him is known. He did not stand in 1761.

Griffin died 23 Dec. 1771.

J.B.

**GRIFFITH, Christopher** (?1721–76), of Padworth, Berks.

BERKSHIRE 1774–12 Jan. 1776

*b.* ?1721, s. of Christopher Griffith of Winterbourne, Glos. by Mary, da. of Loftus Brightwell of Padworth. *educ.* Queen's, Oxf. 31 May 1738, aged 17; L. Inn 1737, called 1744. *m.* (1) 1 Mar. 1756, Anne, da. of Richard Chicheley, *s.p.*; (2) 26 Nov. 1759, Catherine, da. and coh. of Sir William St. Quintin, 4th Bt., M.P., of Harpham, Yorks., *s.p. suc.* gd.-fa. in Padworth estate 1738.

Griffith was returned unopposed. His only reported vote was with Opposition on Wilkes, 22 Feb. 1775. He is not known to have spoken in the House. He died 12 Jan. 1776.

M.M.D.

**GRIGBY, Joshua** (?1731–98), of Drinkstone, Suff.

SUFFOLK 1784–1790

*b.* ?1731, o.s. of Joshua Grigby, 'eminent solicitor', and town clerk of Bury St. Edmunds, of Gonvile, Wyndham, Norf. by Mary, da. of Richard Tubby of Brockdish, Norf. *educ.* Bury g.s. 1739; Clare, Camb. 1748; G. Inn 1749, called 1756. *m.* bef. 1759, Jane Bird of Coventry, 3s. 5da.

Bencher, G. Inn 1770, treasurer 1778.

In 1780 Grigby contested Ipswich, but was heavily defeated, and 'disclaimed all future attempts to represent the borough'.[1] In 1784 he stood for the county as an opponent of the Coalition and an advocate of parliamentary reform, and defeated Fox's friend, T. C. Bunbury. He voted for parliamentary reform, 13 May 1785; against Richmond's fortifications plan, 27 Feb. 1786; but with Pitt over the Regency, 1788–9.

Three speeches by Grigby are reported.[2] On a motion to repeal the shop tax, 2 Mar. 1786, he declared 'that, old fashioned as the custom appeared, he was determined to obey the instructions of his constituents . . . he had consulted them, and . . . they were generally satisfied with the tax'. On 30 Mar. 1786 he spoke on a motion to disfranchise voters employed by the Navy and Ordnance Boards, and on 9 May 1788 in favour of the abolition of the slave trade.

Grigby did not stand in 1790. He died 26 Dec. 1798, aged 67. The *Gentleman's Magazine* (1829, p. 374) described him as 'a zealous advocate for civil and religious liberty'.

[1] Add. 25336, f. 1. [2] Debrett, xix. 285.

M.M.D.

**GRIMSTON, Hon. James** (1711–73), of Gorhambury, Herts.

ST. ALBANS 1754–1761

*b.* 9 Oct. 1711, 1st surv. s. of William Grimston, M.P., 1st Visct. Grimston [I], by Jean, da. of James Cooke of London. *m.* 19 June 1746, Mary, da. of William Bucknall of Oxhey Place, Watford, Herts., 3s. 5da. *suc.* fa. as 2nd Visct. 15 Oct. 1756.

James Grimston, whose father had represented St. Albans in four Parliaments 1710–22 and 1727–1734, was a candidate at the by-election of 1743, but refused to offer any bribes and was defeated by a narrow margin. He hesitated at first whether to stand at the general election of 1754—his father apparently was against it[1]—but finally declared himself a candidate on 29 Dec. 1753, and was returned unopposed on an agreement with the Duke of Marlborough, acting for his nephew John Spencer: Grimston promised to support Spencer or his nominee at the next general election. No vote or speech by him in the House is recorded. He did not stand again for Parliament, and died 15 Dec. 1773.

[1] Add. 34734, f. 64.

L.B.N.

**GRIMSTON, James Bucknall**, 3rd Visct. Grimston [I] (1747–1808), of Gorhambury, Herts.

ST. ALBANS 29 Dec. 1783–1784
HERTFORDSHIRE 1784–1790

*b.* 9 May 1747, 1st s. of Hon. James Grimston, and bro. of Hon. William Grimston (qq.v.). *educ.* Eton 1761–6; Trinity, Camb. 1766–9. *m.* 28 July 1774, Henrietta, da. of Edward Walter (q.v.) of Stalbridge, Dorset, 1s. 2da. *suc.* fa. as 3rd Visct. [I] 15 Dec. 1773; *cr.* Baron Verulam [GB] 6 July 1790.

Grimston inherited a strong interest in Hertfordshire and at St. Albans. In 1774 he stood unsuccessfully for Hertfordshire, but failed to secure the indispensable support of Lord Salisbury.[1] Later this aid was promised, and Grimston's cousin, Lady Forrester, urged him to try again at the next vacancy—'Unite with Lord Salisbury and nothing can shake your interest'[2]—but Grimston did not stand in 1780, probably because Lord Salisbury was then on his deathbed. In December 1783 he came in for St. Albans on the death of his family's nominee, John Radcliffe. In the next weeks he voted with Pitt, and presented the address from St. Albans thanking the King for having dismissed the Coalition.[3]

At the general election of 1784 Grimston canvassed St. Albans, but having already decided to stand for Hertfordshire withdrew at the last moment in favour of his brother, William.[4] With Lord Salisbury's support Grimston stood for Hertfordshire as an opponent of the Coalition and for 'the rights of the King and the People', and was returned after a contest. In Parliament he was an independent supporter of Pitt's Government. In 1785 he was informed about Irish discontent at Pitt's commercial propositions,[5] but did not vote against them. In 1786 he was absent from the division on Richmond's fortifications plan. He supported Pitt during the Regency crisis, explaining to one of his constituents:[6]

> You are not unacquainted that I am a wellwisher of Mr. Pitt and his Administration, and I hope you are equally convinced that I would not upon any terms give any support to a grand constitutional question which I thought subversive of our common rights in compliance to any party whatever.

And he made sure that his brother also voted.

Grimston did not stand in 1790. His alliance with Lord Salisbury bore further fruit in the British peerage of Verulam; and in return he brought in Lord Salisbury's friend, John Calvert, for St. Albans in place of his brother.

In 1796 Grimston inherited from his maternal uncle, John Askell Bucknall, a fortune said to be over £150,000.[7]

He died 30 Dec. 1808.

[1] HMC Verulam, 124. [2] Ibid. 126. [3] Ld. Spencer to his mother, 19 Feb. 1784, Spencer mss. [4] Lady Spencer to Ld. Spencer, 2 Apr. 1784, ibid. [5] HMC Verulam, 132. [6] Ibid. 135. [7] Gent. Mag. 1796, pp. 792-3.

L.B.N.

## GRIMSTON, Hon. William (1750–1814).

ST. ALBANS      1784–1790
APPLEBY     21 Jan. 1791–1796

b. 23 June 1750, 2nd s. of Hon. James Grimston, and bro. of James, 3rd Visct. Grimston (qq.v.). educ. Eton 1763–8; Christ's, Camb. 1768–70; L. Inn 1767. m. 7 Feb. 1783, Sophia, da. and coh. of Richard Hoare of Boreham, Essex, 1da.

Grimston was brought in on the family interest at St. Albans, his brother, Lord Grimston, withdrawing in his favour on the morning of the election. In 1786 he voted against Richmond's fortifications plan, but he usually followed his brother's political line, acting as an independent supporter of Government, and he voted with Pitt on the Regency crisis. He did not stand in 1790, his brother requiring the seat for Lord Salisbury's friend, John Calvert.[1]

He died 25 Apr. 1814.

[1] Ld. Spencer to his mother, 11 June 1790, Spencer mss.

L.B.N.

## GROSVENOR, Richard (1731–1802), of Eaton Hall, nr. Chester.

CHESTER    1754–1761

b. 18 June 1731, 1st s. of Sir Robert Grosvenor, 6th Bt., and bro. of Thomas Grosvenor (qq.v.). educ. Oriel, Oxf. 1748. m. 19 July 1764, Henrietta, da. of Henry Vernon (q.v.) of Hilton Park, Staffs., 4s. suc.

fa. as 7th Bt. 1 Aug. 1755; cr. Baron Grosvenor 8 Apr. 1761; Earl Grosvenor 5 July 1784.

Richard Grosvenor, like his father, was a Tory. But when Pitt took office Grosvenor became one of his strongest supporters; and on 23 Nov. 1758, when seconding the Address, described the Newcastle-Pitt Administration as 'the glory of this country', and 'ended with particular compliments to Mr. Pitt, who was the shining light or rather the blazing star of this country'.[1] Pitt flattered him, and Grosvenor responded. 'If you think it necessary for me to be at the meeting of the Parliament', he wrote to Pitt on 31 Oct. 1759,[2] 'a summons from you shall be immediately obeyed by your most sincere friend and servant.' To which Pitt replied:[3] 'As you are manifesting your zeal for his Majesty and for your country in so essential a manner where you are [with the militia], it would be unpardonable selfishness in me to express the regret which losing the pleasure of seeing [you] must always occasion.' Grosvenor obtained his peerage on Pitt's recommendation.

In the Lords he did not follow Pitt. He seconded the Address of thanks for the peace preliminaries, 9 Dec. 1762, protested against the repeal of the Stamp Act, and supported the American war. His great object was to become lord lieutenant of Cheshire—'this is a thing I am very earnest about', he told Bute in 1761;[4] and when again refused the office in 1780, felt slighted and hung back from supporting North. But William Knox assured North there was no fear of Grosvenor's going into opposition, 'for the family principles are too strongly monarchical to allow of a combination with republicans; and, besides, his Lordship does not forget, as some others have done, that he owes his peerage to the grace of his present Majesty'.[5] He voted against Fox's East India bill, and received his earldom at the recommendation of the younger Pitt.

He died 5 Aug. 1802.

[1] James West to Newcastle, 23 Nov. 1758, Add. 32885, f. 524. [2] Chatham mss. [3] Duke of Westminster's mss. [4] Bute mss. [5] HMC Var. vi. 165.

J.B.

## GROSVENOR, Richard (1762–1819), of Swell Court, Som.

EAST LOOE     4 Sept. 1786–Apr. 1788
CLITHEROE    15 Sept. 1794–1796
CHESTER      15 Dec. 1802–1807
NEW ROMNEY   18 June 1818–8 Feb. 1819

b. 5 Oct. 1762, 1st s. of Thomas Grosvenor (q.v.). educ. Westminster 1773; Ch. Ch. Oxf. 1779. m. 11 Mar. 1788, Sarah Frances, da. and h. of Edward Drax (q.v.) of Charborough, Dorset, and took names of Erle Drax before Grosvenor, 1s. 1da. suc. fa. 1795.

Grosvenor was returned for a Government seat, which he vacated when his cousin Lord Belgrave came of age. No vote or speech by him is recorded during his first term in Parliament.

He died 8 Feb. 1819.

J.B.

**GROSVENOR, Sir Robert,** 6th Bt. (1695–1755), of Eaton Hall, nr. Chester.

CHESTER    24 Jan. 1733–1 Aug. 1755

*b.* 7 May 1695, 4th s. of Sir Thomas Grosvenor, 3rd Bt., M.P. for Chester, of Eaton Hall by Mary, da. and h. of Alexander Davies of Ebury, Mdx. *educ.* Eton; B.N.C. Oxf. 1712; I. Temple 1716. *m.* 21 May 1730, Jane, da. and h. of Thomas Warre of Swell Court and Shepton Beauchamp, Som., 2s. 4da. *suc.* bro. 31 Jan. 1733.

Grosvenor, one of the most prominent of the Tory country gentlemen, was in Parliament for 20 years before our period. He is not known ever to have given a vote for any Administration. He died 1 Aug. 1755.

J.B.

**GROSVENOR, Robert,** Visct. Belgrave (1767–1845), of Eaton Hall, nr. Chester.

EAST LOOE    22 Apr. 1788–1790
CHESTER                 1790–5 Aug. 1802

*b.* 22 Mar. 1767, o. surv. s. of Richard Grosvenor (q.v.). *educ.* Westminster 1777; Harrow 1780; Trinity, Camb. 1783; Grand Tour 1786–8. *m.* 28 Apr. 1794, Hon. Eleanor Egerton, da. and h. of Thomas, 1st Lord Grey de Wilton, 3s. 1da. *suc.* fa. as 2nd Earl Grosvenor 5 Aug. 1802; *cr.* Mq. of Westminster 13 Sept. 1831; K.G. 11 Mar. 1841.
Ld. of Admiralty 1789–91; P.C. 21 June 1793; member, Bd. of Control 1793–1801; ld-lt. Flints. 1798–*d.*

Lord Belgrave was returned for a Government seat at East Looe almost immediately he had come of age, and a few months later was given office. He remained throughout with Pitt.

He died 17 Feb. 1845.

J.B.

**GROSVENOR, Thomas** (1734–95), of Swell Court and Shepton Beauchamp, Som.

CHESTER    10 Dec. 1755–12 Feb. 1795

*b.* Mar. 1734, 2nd s. of Sir Robert Grosvenor, 6th Bt., and bro. of Richard Grosvenor (qq.v.). *educ.* Westminster 1749–51; Oriel, Oxf. 1751; I. Temple 1750. *m.* 21 Sept. 1758, Deborah, da. and coh. of Stephen Skynner of Walthamstow, Essex, 4s. 2da.

Thomas Grosvenor was proposed for Chester almost immediately after his father's death. At first there was some opposition because of his youth and because the other seat was held by his brother, but it came to nothing and Grosvenor was returned with-

out a poll. Like his father and brother he was always classed as a Tory. On 1 Dec. 1762 he voted to postpone taking into consideration the peace preliminaries. This seems to have been of no political significance, for he appears in Fox's list of Members favourable to the peace and on 3 Dec. Shelburne assured Bute that Grosvenor 'speaks very decidedly for you'.[1]

On 15 Nov. 1763 he voted against Administration over Wilkes, and on 10 Feb. 1764 spoke for the repeal of the cider duty. On 15 Feb. over general warrants, he again voted against Administration. Great efforts were made by the court to win him for the debate of 17 Feb. On 16 Feb. Lord Grosvenor wrote to Grenville:[2]

Lord Grosvenor . . . knows his brother's intention is to attend the House to-morrow, and as it is his inclination to support Administration whenever he can do it with propriety, hopes he will find sufficient reason in the course of the debate to justify his doing it to-morrow.

Grosvenor again voted with Opposition, but was listed by Jenkinson as a friend who normally supported.

In July 1765 Rockingham classed Grosvenor as 'doubtful', and he voted against the repeal of the Stamp Act. In the divisions on the land tax, 27 Feb. 1767, and the nullum tempus bill, 17 Feb. 1768, he voted against the court, as did so many other country gentlemen. In five divisions between 1769 to 1771 (four on the Middlesex election and one on the Spanish convention) he voted with Opposition; on the royal marriage bill he was classed by Robinson as 'doubtful'; by the King on the naval captains' petition, 9 Feb. 1773, as 'friend', and again by Robinson on the eve of the general election of 1774 as 'doubtful'. In short, he was thoroughly independent.

From the beginning of the American troubles he consistently supported North's policy. He said during the debate on the Boston port bill, 14 Mar. 1774:[3] 'I am of opinion all this trouble proceeds from the repeal of the Stamp Act. We shall I hope be of one mind to agree with this bill.' From 1775 to 1778, when only minority lists are available, he does not appear in them, and presumably voted with the court; on the contractors bill, 12 Feb. 1779, he is marked as 'pro, absent'; and in the five divisions February to April 1780 the only votes he gave were for the abolition of the Board of Trade, 13 Mar., and with the court on the motion against prorogation, 24 Apr. Towards economical reform he took an attitude different from the politicians' or the country gentlemen's, and while concerned for economy was not prepared to reduce the dignity and influence of the

Crown. On 13 Mar. 1780 (in the only speech he is known to have made during the American war) he welcomed 'the abolition of useless places' but protested against 'the appropriation of the savings to public uses'.[4]

> He did not see any reason why Parliament should proceed without any proof of previous abuse to deprive the Crown of those grants which had been made in lieu of revenues, which the King formerly enjoyed, and which were taken up in consideration of the present civil list establishment.

Even those who opposed his politics respected him. The *English Chronicle*, a newspaper friendly to the Opposition, having described him in 1781 as 'a most confirmed and uniform friend to the measures of the present Administration', continued:

> The constancy of his attachment does him honour, whatever judgment may be entertained of the object of it. In the catalogue of his virtues, a warm gratitude towards his constituents, and a sincere interest in their general and individual concerns, may be fairly and truly enumerated.

'In these times Grosvenor is a man to whom attention should be paid', wrote Charles Jenkinson in December 1781.[5] On 20 Feb. 1782 Grosvenor voted for the censure motion against the Admiralty; but on the three motions against continuing the war (22 Feb., 27 Feb., and 8 Mar.) voted with Administration. On Rous's no confidence motion of 15 Nov. he paired on the Administration side. Then, on 18 Mar., North wrote to the King:

> Mr. Grosvenor to-day in the House of Commons desired me to appoint him an hour to-morrow morning, as he had a matter of importance to communicate to me, and I have since learned from good authority, that it is his intention to represent to me, in his own name, and in those of some other country gentlemen *'that, being now convinced that the present Administration cannot continue any longer, they are of opinion that vain and ineffectual struggles tend only to public mischief and confusion, and that they shall think it their duty henceforward to desist from opposing what appears to be clearly the sense of the House of Commons'.*

Next day Grosvenor saw North and agreed to vote with the court on 20 Mar., but said, North wrote to the King, 'he would be against us to-morrow if he conceived that we were determined to persevere in the struggle'.[6] The defection of Grosvenor and the group he represented finally convinced North that he could no longer retain office.

Grosvenor voted for Shelburne's peace preliminaries, 18 Feb. 1783, and against Fox's East India bill, 27 Nov. 1783; and in Robinson's list of January 1784 was classed as a follower of Pitt. On 26 Jan. he took the chair at a meeting at the St. Alban's Tavern, 'of such Members of the House of Commons as wish to promote a union of parties'. Well-meaning and naïve, he seemed to imagine that if only Pitt and

Fox could have a full and frank conversation there was no difficulty which given goodwill on both sides could not be overcome. Both Pitt and Fox professed to welcome the idea, but Fox demanded that Pitt should first resign, which Pitt refused to do, and nothing resulted except pious resolutions. On 2 Feb. Grosvenor moved in the House 'that the present arduous and critical situation of public affairs requires the exertion of a firm, efficient, extended, united Administration', which passed unanimously. It was followed by another resolution, moved by Thomas Coke, 'that the continuance of the present ministers in power . . . is an obstacle to a firm, efficient, extended and united Administration', which was carried against Pitt. It is not known how Grosvenor voted on Coke's resolution, but in Stockdale's list of the House of Commons, 19 Mar. 1784, he is classed as a supporter of Pitt.

In 1784 Grosvenor was returned head of the poll at Chester. During the next four years four speeches by him are recorded, none of any significance, and no votes. In 1786 he accepted a seat for his son in a Government borough, and in 1788 applied for a peerage. He voted with Pitt over the Regency, and described Pitt's plan as 'wise, distinct, discreet, prudent, and loyal'.[7]

Grosvenor died 12 Feb. 1795.

[1] Bute mss. [2] Grenville mss (JM). [3] Brickdale's 'Debates'. [4] Almon, xvii. 294. [5] Add. 38217, f. 204. [6] Fortescue, vi. 394, 397. [7] Stockdale, xvi. 420-1.

J.B.

## GROVE, William (1702–67), of Coventry and Honiley, nr. Warwick.

COVENTRY 1741–1761

*b.* 14 Dec. 1702, 1st s. of William Grove of Coventry, attorney, by Hannah, da. of Nathaniel Harryman, alderman of Coventry. *educ.* M. Temple 1713. *m.* 2 Oct. 1739, Mary, da. of Thomas Bayley of Madeley, Staffs., wid. of John Saunders of Honiley; 1s. 3da. *suc.* fa. 1734.

Grove was a Tory, and had to stand a contest in all his three elections, 1741, 1747, and in 1754, when he received the support of a discontented section of the corporation.[1]

In 1761 Grove, who wished to retire because of his age, was with reluctance persuaded to stand against the corporation candidate, but the opposition 'got together a great part of Mr. Grove's friends before the poll began and kept them drunk till it was over',[2] and Grove withdrew on the last day of the poll.

He died 1 May 1767.

[1] For accounts of the 1754 and 1761 elections see Sir Roger Newdigate's diaries, Warws. RO. [2] T. W. Whitley, *Parlty. Rep. Coventry*, 162.

M.M.D.

## GROVE, William Chafin (c.1731–93), of Zeals, Wilts.

SHAFTESBURY                     1768–1774
WEYMOUTH AND MELCOMBE REGIS    1774–Apr. 1781

*b.* c.1731, 1st s. of Chafin Grove of Zeals by his w. Ann Amor. *educ.* Sutton; St. John's, Camb. 30 Apr. 1750, aged 18; M. Temple 1750, called 1756. *m.* 7 Oct. 1776, his distant cos. Elizabeth, da. of John Grove of Ferne House, nr. Shaftesbury, 1s. *suc.* fa. 31 Jan. 1761.

Recorder, Weymouth 1774–86; sheriff, Wilts. 1784–5.

In 1768 Grove was returned for Shaftesbury after a contest. In Parliament he voted consistently with Opposition. In 1774 he declined to contest Shaftesbury because of the expense; and was returned unopposed for Weymouth and Melcombe Regis, where he had some property. On the outbreak of the American war he went over to Government. The *English Chronicle* in 1780 wrote of him:

An invariable and inveterate advocate for Administration, but not distinguished in any particular degree for any other quality either good or bad.

But on the contractors bill, 12 Feb. 1779, he was classed by Robinson as 'contra, absent, query doubtful', and he voted against Dunning's motion, 6 Apr. 1780. Robinson in his survey for the general election of 1780 classed him as 'hopeful'.

He vacated his seat in April 1781; and died 27 Jan. 1793, aged 62.

J.B.

## GUERNSEY, Lord, *see* FINCH, Heneage (*d.*1777), *and* FINCH, Heneage (*d.*1812)

## GUISE, Sir William, 5th Bt. (1737–83), of Elmore and Rendcombe, Glos.

GLOUCESTERSHIRE   6 Aug. 1770–6 Apr. 1783

*bap.* 26 July[1] or 19 Aug.[2] 1737, o. surv. s. of Sir John Guise, 4th Bt., by Jane, da. of John Saunders of Mongewell, Oxon. *educ.* Queen's Oxf. 1754; L. Inn 1754; Grand Tour (Italy) 1763–5. *unm.* *suc.* fa. 1769.

Gibbon met Guise at Lausanne in 1763, and found him 'a very sensible well-bred man'.[3] 'He . . . has seen a good deal of the world', he wrote, 'and without being a profound scholar is far from wanting either parts or knowledge.'[4] Together they made the Grand Tour of Italy 'in great harmony and good humour',[5] and their friendship continued after their return to England.

Guise, with the support of the Berkeley interest, represented Gloucestershire without a contest. In Parliament he voted against North's Administration; the *Public Ledger* in 1779 describes him as 'a very independent man'. He voted for Shelburne's

peace preliminaries, 18 Feb. 1783. Guise is only twice reported to have spoken in the House: on militia affairs, 25 Apr. 1780, and in favour of sending a relief fund to Barbados, 24 Jan. 1781.

He died 6 Apr. 1783.

[1] GEC, *Baronetage.* [2] Pedigree of Guise in *Trans. Bristol & Glos. Arch. Soc.* iii. 72. [3] Gibbon to his stepmother, 18 June 1763. [4] Same to same, 7 Dec. 1763. [5] Gibbon to his fa., 4 June 1764.

J.B.

## GULSTON, Joseph (c.1694–1766), of Ealing Grove, Mdx.

TREGONY   2 Mar. 1737–1741
POOLE              1741–May 1765

*b.* c.1694 at Lisbon, 1st s. of Joseph Gulston, merchant. *m.* c.1733, Maricas Sylva, da. of a Portuguese merchant, 2s. 2da.

Director, South Sea Co. 1742–60.

Gulston's father 'never was in England'; he himself was head of a mercantile house at Lisbon, presumably inherited from his father.[1] The family moved to England some time before 1730, and Joseph Gulston carried on business as a City merchant.

With Poole, where Gulston established an enduring parliamentary interest, he was probably connected through his extensive trade with both North and South America. In Parliament he regularly adhered to the Government, from whom he held contracts during the war of the Austrian succession, and when war re-started in 1755 Gulston felt indignant at not being immediately re-employed as a money remitter. He wrote to James West, 6 Nov. 1755, that some time ago he had spoken about it to the Duke of Newcastle, who seemed surprised at his early application; but next Gulston 'found others employed therein'; 'I am turned out of my post (if I may so call it) without having done anything to deserve it . . . I have a sort of right to be employed again and indeed upon an equal footing with any body else the most favoured, which I expect, perhaps more out of a point of honour than profit.' The Duke had directed him to West, and he now asked for 'an explicit answer from the Duke, for if it be in the negative, I shall not trouble his Grace any more, which next to granting my request is the greatest favour he can do me'.[2]

In his elections at Poole, a difficult constituency, he had Government support, which was important both because of a group of placemen who could turn the balance between competing candidates, and also because of the favours which a mercantile community with extensive trading interests had to solicit from the Government. There are hints in letters from Sir Peter Thompson, a leading Poole merchant, to James West[3] that Gulston was thought to have been remiss in watching over the borough's interests in Parliament, and that he gradually lost popularity. And although he would sometimes excuse his absence from the borough by the need of attending Parliament, that attendance too seems to have fallen off towards the end. Newcastle, in his list of 13 Nov. 1762, classed Gulston as 'pro'; but early in December Fox included him in that of Members in favour of the peace preliminaries; and only in Newcastle's division lists for 9 and 10 Dec. does he appear as voting with the minority, but in none of the others. In the autumn of 1763 Jenkinson listed Gulston as a Government supporter; he was absent from the division of 6 Feb. 1764 on general warrants; 'Mr. Gulston is infirm, but perhaps may come down, and take somebody off', wrote Edward Kynaston to Jenkinson, 16 Feb. 1764;[4] but he was again absent on 17–18 Feb.; and 10 May was classed by Newcastle as 'doubtful'. There is no record of his having spoken in the House. On 4 May Thompson reported to West a letter from Gulston to the Poole corporation 'that through frequent fits of the gout he was unable to attend his duty in Parliament, therefore he hoped his friends would give him leave to resign in favour of his son'. A severely contested election ensued during which Gulston greatly exerted himself on behalf of his son—Thompson wrote to West on 25 May: 'Mr. Gulston has returned from London, he was gone from hence but 56 hours, very extraordinary for one of 75.' The election was won by the narrowest margin.

Gulston was indeed a sick man, and died on 16 Aug. 1766. According to his daughter, 'he left in the funds £250,000 . . . ; an estate in Hertfordshire of £1500 a year; Ealing-grove, and the house in Soho-square'.

[1] The story of the family is told by Gulston's da. Elizabeth, Nichols, *Literary Illustrations*, v. 1–59. [2] Add. 32860, f. 393. [3] West mss. [4] *Jenkinson Pprs.* 266 (misdated).

L.B.N.

## GULSTON, Joseph (?1744–86), of Ealing Grove, Mdx.

POOLE 30 May 1765–1768, 1780–1784

b. ?1744, 1st s. of Joseph Gulston (q.v.). *educ.* Worcester 1750–6; Eton 1756–9; Ch. Ch. Oxf. Feb. 1763, aged 18. *m.* 24 June 1767, Bridgetta, da. of Sir Thomas Stepney, 6th Bt., sis of Sir John Stepney, 7th Bt. (q.v.), 1s. 1da. *suc.* fa. 16 Aug. 1766.

Gulston, a sickly child, was 'spoiled intolerably' by his Portuguese mother; when he was six, his father 'very wisely' sent him to school at Worcester; and next to Eton.[1] There he 'was indolent in the extreme', and showed no application, while his younger brother John 'found it no *trouble* to learn.'

Their father meant to make John his heir, and 'sent his eldest son to Hamburg to learn business; but . . . business was the only thing he did not learn'. He took to music and gave concerts to the town. The statement that on John's dying at Eton their father recalled Joseph from Hamburg and sent him to Oxford is hardly correct: John died in 1764, and Joseph matriculated at Oxford in February 1763.

In May 1765 old Gulston vacated his seat at Poole in his son's favour, and by a considerable effort carried his election. When in July 1765 Rockingham compiled his parliamentary list, Gulston had not yet taken his seat but had already applied for a tidesman's place at Poole: evidence that he was a well-wisher to Government; which he remained also under their successors: at the end of 1766 Rockingham classed him, with a query, as 'Swiss' (prepared to support every Administration), Townshend in January 1767 as 'Government', but Newcastle, 2 Mar. 1767, as 'friend'. There is no vote or speech of his on record during those years. In 1768 he stood for Poole on a joint interest with Thomas Calcraft but was defeated; petitioned against Joshua Mauger's return, which was declared void, 10 Feb. 1769; but the petition itself did not ask for Gulston to be seated in his place. Both stood at the ensuing by-election, but Gulston withdrew the night before the poll. Calcraft's friends who had supported him called his behaviour shameful, base, and dastardly:[2] they feared the consequences in case the counter-petition against Thomas Calcraft's return succeeded, especially as many voters who had expected money from Gulston were disappointed. Was there some underhand agreement between Gulston and Mauger? 'I have been misinformed if he did not see Mauger before he declined the poll', wrote Mrs. Pike. And Thomas Hyde: 'Mauger's party . . . at times . . . talk of bringing down Gulston [as candidate if Calcraft was unseated], but I can't think that any persuasion would tempt him to that.' The most probable explanation is that he despaired of success and cut his losses—even those who condemned his action credited him with only 43 votes against 44 for Mauger.

Gulston now settled at Ealing Grove; converted it into an Italian villa at a cost of £30,000 ('more taste could not be displayed than he exhibited on the lovely spot'); and his wife being equally artistic and extravagant in her tastes, the study of the day of the giddy pair 'seemed to be who should spend the money the fastest'. 'He began in 1768 the magnificent collection of books and prints which he lived to complete unrivalled, and also just lived long enough to see them dispersed . . . Mr. Granger was always at Ealing, there compiled his work.' William

Cole, in a letter to Horace Walpole, 20 Nov. 1772, describes a visit from Gulston, whom he had only just met:

> On a very slight offer of accommodating him with such prints or heads as he had not, he absolutely has taken 187 of my favourite and most valuable heads, such as he had not, and most of which he had never seen, and all this with as much ease and familiarity as if we had been old acquaintance. I must do him the justice to say that I really did offer him . . . to take such as he had not, but this I thought would not have exceeded a dozen or thereabouts. He has absolutely gutted and garbled my collection.

Walpole replied, 15 Dec., lamenting the plunder 'by that Algerine hog':

> The beast has no sort of taste neither—and in a twelvemonth will sell them again . . . This Muley Moloch used to buy books, and now sells them. He has hurt his fortune, and ruined himself to have a collection, without any choice of what it should be composed.

And on 11 Apr. 1775: Gulston has sold Ealing Grove to the Duke of Marlborough (for £12,000). 'I suppose he will not keep his prints long.' He moved to Smedmore, near Wareham, and next to a cottage at Corfe Mullen, six miles from Poole.

When in 1780 he stood once more for Poole, on a joint interest with W. M. Pitt, Robinson, who expected his return, described him as 'a warm friend'. Gulston wrote to his mother, 7 Sept.: 'My election, which will be next Saturday, is perfectly safe; but we have a petition against us, which will be very expensive, so the whole will cost near £700; but it is all for the good of my son, so must do the best I can.' Gulston was returned, and the petition was rejected. During the critical months before the fall of North, Gulston seems to have attended the House regularly; never spoke; but appears in each of the six division lists, December 1781–March 1782, always with the Government. The very night North resigned, 'he sent Mr. Gulston the place of collector of the customs in Newfoundland for Mr. Bouth, an American loyalist, who had lost £4,000 a year in America, and was at that time clerk to a merchant at Poole, at £50 a year'. From the divisions in 1783 and early in 1784, Gulston was absent, apparently owing to ill-health, but was reckoned a follower of the Fox-North Coalition, and as such stood in 1784, when he was defeated. This the biographical sketch ascribes foremost to 'his ill-judged generosity' in having helped in 1780 Pitt, an opponent of his in local affairs.

> Notwithstanding his near residence to the town, which exposed his irregularities too much to the view of the burgesses, and this imprudent measure of bringing in adverse interest, so much was he really loved, that he lost his election by only five votes, and they were a Quaker family; and . . . he lost these because he

would not get out of his bed till after the good people had dined, and take the trouble of asking for their votes; the name of this family was White.

Gulston was ruined financially; in June 1784 sold his books; and his prints and portraits in 38 nights, 16 Jan.–13 Mar. 1786, besides more than 20 volumes of works of great masters, 18,000 foreign and 23,500 English portraits, 11,000 English caricatures and political prints, and 14,500 topographical prints. But all the sale produced was £7,000.

> Many years of Mr. Gulston's life were spent in the compilation of a Biographical Dictionary of all the foreigners who had ever been in England, forming a Supplement to Granger. At his death the voluminous manuscript was sold for little.

Gulston died 4 July 1786, aged 41.

[1] Quotations and statements, unless otherwise stated, are taken from the biographical sketch of Joseph Gulston jun. in Nichols, *Lit. Illustrations*, v. 1–60. [2] Letters to John Calcraft from Mrs. O. Pike, 20, 23, and 27 Feb., from John Oliver 20 Feb., and from Thomas Hyde 25 Feb. 1769, Calcraft mss at Rempstone.

L.B.N.

## GWILLYM, Robert Vernon Atherton (?1741–83), of Atherton Hall, nr. Manchester

NEWTON 1774–1780

> b. ?1741, 2nd s. of Robert Gwillym of Langstone, Herefs. by Elizabeth, da. and h. of Richard Atherton of Atherton Hall. m. Jan. 1763, Henrietta Maria, da. and coh. of Peter Legh (q.v.) of Lyme Hall, 2s. 4da. suc. bro. 1771; took name of Atherton 1779.[1]

Gwillym was returned for Newton on his father-in-law's interest. He suffered from bad health and seldom attended the House: his one recorded vote, 22 Feb. 1775, was for Wilkes's Middlesex resolution, and he is not known ever to have spoken. In 1780 Robinson classed him as 'contra'. He did not stand at the general election.

He died in France 9 July 1783.

[1] Ormerod, *Cheshire*, iii(2), 678.

J.B.

## GWYNNE, Howell (1718–80), of Garth in Llanleonfel, Brec.

RADNORSHIRE 11 Mar. 1755–1761
OLD SARUM 1761–1768

> b. 16 Apr. 1718, 1st s. of Marmaduke Gwynne[1] by Sarah, da. of Daniel Evans of Peterwell. educ. Ch. Ch. Oxf. 1736. m. 1751, Mary, da. and coh. of Sir Thomas Powell, 1st Bt., wid. of Sir John Rudd, 4th and last Bt., 1s. His sis. Sarah m. in 1749 Charles Wesley. suc. fa. 13 Apr. 1769.
> Ld. lt. Rad. Dec. 1755–66.

At the general election of 1754 Gwynne unsuccessfully contested Breconshire. But the previous year, when a vacancy was expected in Radnorshire, Henry Pelham had consulted Lord Powis, and Gwynne 'was fixed upon as a proper candidate';[2]

and when it occurred in February 1755, he was recommended to Newcastle by Powis and his friends as 'a gentleman of known zeal for his Majesty and his royal family, and of very considerable property in the county'.[3] An opposition was threatened by Sir Richard Chase, supported by Lords Oxford and Carnarvon and the Tories, but on his declining, Gwynne was returned unopposed; the very moderate expense of £173 was paid out of secret service money.[4]

On 15 Dec. 1755 Powis wrote to Newcastle:[5]

Your Grace was pleased to tell me that I must take care of Mr. Howell Gwynne ... And I have the pleasure to assure your Grace that his conduct in Parliament has hitherto been agreeable to your wishes. I am under a necessity now of putting him into your Grace's hands, recommending to your Grace in my turn, *that you will take care of him.*

Gwynne wished his brother to be made customer of the port of Milford—'on easier terms, your Grace could scarce desire it, and it will oblige him'.

At the end of the month Gwynne was appointed lord lieutenant of Radnorshire, to the indignation of Carnarvon who on the accession of George III set out to supplant Gwynne both in his parliamentary seat and in the lord lieutenancy. Gwynne seems to have been anxious not to offend the new court, and in the ensuing transactions appears much more as a pawn in the hands of his friends than as a principal. Early in March 1761 an agreement was reached whereby Gwynne was to relinquish Radnorshire to Carnarvon for this Parliament, be returned elsewhere free of expense, and retain the lord lieutenancy for the next five years.[6] He was placed by Newcastle at Old Sarum.

In October 1761 Gwynne still received Newcastle's parliamentary whip through Powis, and in Bute's list of December 1761 was first marked 'Newcastle'; but next 'Fox': he is included in Fox's list of Members in favour of the peace preliminaries. In the autumn of 1763 Jenkinson classed him as 'pro', and his name does not appear in any of the minority lists under the Grenville Administration. Marked as 'contra' by Rockingham in July 1765, he voted against the repeal of the Stamp Act. There is no record of his having spoken in the House. Dim and independent, he was listed by Rockingham in November 1766 as a Grenvillite, by Charles Townshend in January 1767 as a Rockingham, and by Newcastle in March 1767 as a follower of Administration. He did not vote either on the land tax, 27 Feb. 1767, or on nullum tempus, 17 Feb. 1768.

Chase Price wrote (to the Duke of Portland) in September 1765 about Gwynne 'canvassing hourly' in Radnorshire; and Price's brother Richard reported to him on 13 Oct. that Carnarvon had informed Gwynne he would not stand again in 1768.[7] But next Chase Price declared his candidature, and although Gwynne was supported by Lords Powis, Oxford and Bateman, Price established such superiority on the canvass that Gwynne declined the poll. He did not stand again, and died in 1780.

[1] G. J. Stevenson, *Memorials Wesley Fam.* 427–30; Add. 39746 f. 290. [2] Geo. Rice to Newcastle, 7 Feb. 1755, Add. 32852, f. 388. [3] Newcastle to Ld. Carnarvon, 8 Feb. 1755, ibid. f. 404. [4] Namier, *Structure*, 255, 436. [5] Add. 32861, ff. 316–17. [6] Namier, 168–79. [7] Portland mss.

L.B.N.

**GYBBON, Phillips** (1678–1762), of Hole Park, Rolvenden, Kent.

RYE 2 Dec. 1707–12 Mar. 1762

*b.* 11 Oct. 1678, 1st surv. s. of Robert Gybbon of Hole Park by Elizabeth, da. of John Phillips. *m.* Catherine, da. of Honor Bier, 1da. *suc.* fa. 1719.

Surveyor gen. of the land revenues 1726–30; ld. of Treasury 1742–4.

Gybbon had considerable estates on the Kent-Sussex border which gave him an interest at Rye. Originally one of Pulteney's lieutenants in opposition to Walpole, he became reconciled to the Pelhams, and in 1754 and 1761 was returned unopposed with Newcastle's support. No vote or speech by him is reported between 1754 and 1762. On 9 Dec. 1760 Sir George Oxenden suggested to Lord Hardwicke that Gybbon should stand for Kent at the general election:[1] 'I dare say it would go down very well, and he might sit at home, at his age, and be chosen in his great chair.' In July 1761 Gybbon was reported to be 'very infirm',[2] and he died on 12 Mar. 1762.

When shortly before his death Gybbon learnt that John Norris had 'made application to supply the vacancy at Rye', he begged Newcastle and Hardwicke to secure the succession to his son-in-law Philip Jodrell. Hardwicke, forwarding Gybbon's letters to Newcastle (and unsuccessfully pleading his cause) described him as 'an old humble servant of your Grace, and an old friend of mine';[3] and after Gybbon's death, as 'so old and faithful a servant of the public'.[4]

[1] Add. 35692, ff. 434–5. [2] Add. 32925, ff. 247–8. [3] Add. 32934, ff. 293, 295–6, 314. [4] Add. 32935, ff. 340, 364, 366–7.

M.M.D.

**HADDOCK, Nicholas** (1723–81), of Wrotham, Kent.

ROCHESTER 26 Jan. 1754–1761

*b.* 1723, 1st surv. s. of Adm. Nicholas Haddock, M.P., by his w. Frances. *unm. suc.* fa. 1746.

Haddock, whose father had sat for Rochester

1734–46, was returned on the Admiralty interest. No vote or speech by him is recorded.

He died 19 July 1781.

A.N.N.

**HALDANE, George** (1722–59), of Bearcrofts, Stirling and Gleneagles, Perth.

STIRLING BURGHS   1747–Jan. 1758

*bap.* 10 July 1722, o.s. of Patrick Haldane, M.P., of Bearcrofts and Gleneagles, jt. solicitor-gen. [S] 1746–55, by Margaret, da. of William, 4th Lord Forrester of Corstorphine; nephew of Robert Haldane (q.v.). *unm.*
    Ensign 3 Ft. Gds. 1740, capt. and lt.-col. 1749; col. 1758.
    Gov. Jamaica Jan. 1758–*d.*

At the 1754 general election the Haldanes, with lavish expenditure, prepared to oppose ministerial candidates in three constituencies: in Stirlingshire Robert attacked Argyll's protégé Sir James Campbell; in Stirling Burghs George sought to outbid Robert Cuninghame; and also contested Perth Burghs against Thomas Leslie, Pelham's pensioner, 'for no other reason than to distress Administration', wrote the Duke of Argyll.[1]

After Pelham's death, George was prepared to come to terms with Administration. Thomas Leslie wrote to Newcastle, 24 Mar. 1754:[2]

> Colonel Haldane desired me . . . to mention to you that he and his friends had no inclination to oppose the measures of his Majesty or his ministers; that if your Grace would see him, he would endeavour to satisfy you; at the same time, in consequence of that, proposed to give me no further trouble.

After negotiations, Haldane withdrew his opposition to Leslie in Perth Burghs, and was himself returned for Stirling Burghs. But Robert Haldane did not desist in Stirlingshire, and Argyll remained implacably hostile to the family.

Haldane was classed by Dupplin as a supporter of Administration, and was not slow to solicit rewards for his allegiance. Even before his election he unsuccessfully applied for the place of baron of the Exchequer for his father, and on his retirement as solicitor-general in April 1755 secured for him a pension of £400 per annum. On Mungo Haldane's death in June 1755, when his father succeeded to Gleneagles, George promptly applied for his uncle's salary as commissioner of police; and when refused, suggested as a mark of favour army promotion, a place in the Prince of Wales's household, or any office worth £400 p.a. Newcastle was friendly, but not wishing to offend Argyll put Haldane off.[3]

Committed to support the Newcastle-Fox Administration, Haldane spoke in the debates on the bill for the encouragement of seamen, and defended the Russian and Hessian treaties, testifying to his experience of Hessian troops in action.[4] Despite Newcastle's promises of favour, he failed to secure preferment either as commissary to the Russian troops, or as a member of the Board of Ordnance. Nevertheless he remained faithful. He wrote to Newcastle, 2 Apr. 1757:[5] 'I beg leave . . . to assure your Grace that changes in Administration make no alteration in my way of thinking, and that you may command my single vote.' But he was absent through illness from the division of 2 May 1757 on the loss of Minorca.

Under the Pitt-Devonshire Administration Haldane desperately continued his search for preferment; when refused the governorship of New York he offered to serve in the Rochfort expedition 'as adjutant or quartermaster general even without rank', and resented Wolfe's promotion. 'I have been longer an officer than he . . . and seen as much service as Mr. Wolfe or any other officer of my age in the army.'[6] His importunities were at last rewarded by his appointment on 27 Jan. 1758 as governor of Jamaica, at a salary of £2,500 p.a., with additional emoluments to be voted by the colonial assembly.

He vacated his seat in favour of his uncle Robert Haldane, and in anticipation of future profits recklessly contracted further debts, to meet which his father pledged his family estates. Having taken the oath as governor and been promoted colonel, he was appointed brigadier-general in October to serve in the expedition against Martinique, with instructions to proceed afterwards to Jamaica. His extravagant pretensions had long made him ridiculous. Allan Whitefoord wrote to Loudoun, October 1758:[7]

> The new expedition and general staff are all extraordinary and . . . Lt.-Col. Haldane (now Brig.-Gen.) not the least. I do not despair if I live a few years to see an excellent new farce acted on the stage by that name.

After serving at Martinique and at Guadaloupe, Haldane arrived in Jamaica in April 1759 but died at Spanish Town, 26 July. He left a vast accumulation of debts which brought his father to financial disaster and forced the sale of Gleneagles in 1760 to Robert Haldane.[8]

[1] Add. 32737, f. 340. [2] Add. 32734, f. 334. [3] Add. 35448, f. 88; 32854, f. 202; 32855, f. 475; 32858, f. 83. [4] *Parl. Hist.* xv. 544–8, 611–16; Walpole, *Mems. Geo. II*, ii. 128. [5] J. A. L. Haldane, *Haldanes of Gleneagles*, 167. [6] Ibid. 167–8. [7] Loudoun mss. [8] Breadalbane to Hardwicke, 17 Nov. 1759, Add. 35450, f. 289.

E.H.-G.

**HALDANE, Robert** (1705–67), of Plean and Airthrey, Stirling.

STIRLING BURGHS   3 Mar. 1758–1761

*b.* 16 Mar. 1705, 10th s. of John Haldane of Gleneagles, M.P., by his 2nd w. Helen, da. of Sir Charles

Erskine, 1st Bt., of Alva; uncle of George Haldane (q.v.). *m.* 29 Sept. 1742, Elizabeth, da. of Sir William Oglander, 3rd Bt., of Nunwell, I.o.W., wid. of Capt. Robert Holmes, R.N., *s.p.*

Haldane entered the sea service of the East India Company.[1] He returned home with a great fortune and, an arrogant, ambitious, purse-proud man, at the general election of 1754 stood for Stirlingshire against the Argyll candidate, was defeated, and petitioned. Argyll, who hated the Haldane family, wrote to Newcastle, 10 Nov. 1754:[2] 'I know none of this country who call themselves Whigs, so obnoxious to Mr. Pelham as this India captain was.' In 1755 his nephew George introduced him to Newcastle, then intriguing against Argyll, to discuss withdrawing the petition if Robert could be brought in elsewhere. When nothing was done Haldane threatened to revive his petition, which Newcastle, having been reconciled to Argyll, declined to support. Eventually Haldane was induced to abandon his claims, and did not obtain a seat until he succeeded his nephew in Stirling Burghs in March 1758.[3]

His parliamentary career is obscure; no speech of his is recorded. His main concern was to secure re-election in 1761 through his great wealth and the interest of his cousin Sir Henry Erskine with Bute. By the purchase of Airthrey, Gleneagles, and property in Dunbartonshire, he increased his interest in three counties; practised extensive bribery in Stirling Burghs; and also cultivated Perth Burghs.

At the general election he stood for Bridport, was defeated, and appealed through Lord Fitzmaurice to Bute, to whom he offered to give up all his Scottish pretensions in return for support in his petition.[4] He then went to Scotland; withdrew from Perth Burghs; relinquished his claims in Stirling Burghs to Alexander Wedderburn;[5] contested Perthshire but withdrew the day before the election. On the news that, by the succession of John Campbell of Mamore as Duke of Argyll, Dunbartonshire was vacant, Haldane at once offered himself as candidate[6] but soon gave up the contest, and concentrated on his Bridport petition. Despite the efforts of Erskine and the Bute connexion, 'the Scots were beaten by three to one'[7] on 2 Mar. 1762, and Haldane having 'gone all round the compass'[8] was left without a seat.

He intended to stand again for Bridport at the general election of 1768, and also for Stirling Burghs with the support of his friend Sir Lawrence Dundas,[9] but died 31 Dec. 1767.

[1] J. A. L. Haldane, *Haldanes of Gleneagles*, 293-4. [2] Add. 32737, f. 340. [3] Add. 32860, ff. 78, 262, 486. [4] Fitzmaurice to Bute, Apr. 1761, Bute mss; Bute to Fitzmaurice, Apr. 1761, Lansdowne mss; Haldane to Bute, 6 Apr., Bute mss. [5] Sir Hen. Erskine to Bute, 13 Apr. 1761, Bute mss. [6] Haldane to Bute, 23 Apr. 1761, Argyll to Bute, 6 May 1761, Bute mss. [7] Walpole, *Mems. Geo. III*, i. 110.

[8] Bute to Fitzmaurice, Apr. 1761, Lansdowne mss. [9] Jenkinson to Grenville, Feb. 1765, G. Chalmers to Grenville, 5 Jan, 1768, Grenville mss (JM).

E.H.-G.

**HALE, Francis** (c.1758-1827).

MITCHELL 22 Sept. 1779-1784

*b.* c.1758, s. of Gen. Bernard Hale by Martha, da. of Richard Rigby, sen. of Mistley, Essex. *educ.* prob. Eton 1768-73; Lausanne 1773-9.[1] *m.* 3 Mar. 1785, Frances, da. of Sir Thomas Rumbold 1st Bt. (q.v.), 1da. *suc.* uncle Richard Rigby (q.v.) to the Mistley estate, and took name of Rigby 8 Apr. 1788.

Hale was brought in for Mitchell in 1779 probably by arrangement between his uncle Richard Rigby, the Treasury, and Lord Falmouth. He followed Rigby's line in politics, supporting North's ministry till March 1782, and voting on 18 Feb. 1783 for Shelburne's peace preliminaries, but after April 1783 supporting the Coalition. He accordingly lost his seat in 1784. No speech by him is reported.

He died 17 Aug. 1827.

[1] Rigby to Newcastle, 1, 20 Aug. 1776, Newcastle (Clumber) mss.; *Pembroke Pprs.* i. 181.

I.R.C.

**HALE, Paggen** (c.1715-55), of King's Walden, Herts.

HERTFORDSHIRE 1747-3 Apr. 1755

*b.* c.1715, 2nd s. of William Hale of King's Walden, M.P., by Catherine, da. of Peter Paggen of Wandsworth, Surr. *educ.* G. Inn 1732, called 1739. *m.* 20 Nov. 1742, Elizabeth, da. of Humphry Morice, M.P., dep. gov. of Bank of England, and sis. of Humphry Morice jun. (q.v.), *s.p. suc.* bro. William 1742.

In 1754 in a contested election Hale stood on a joint interest with Charles Gore and came out head of the poll. Dupplin classed him among the 'country gentlemen' supporting the Government. He died 3 Apr. 1755.

L.B.N.

**HALES, Sir Philip,** 5th Bt. (c.1735-1824), of Bekesbourne, Kent.

DOWNTON 14 Feb. 1775-1780
MARLBOROUGH 1784-1790

*b.* c.1735, 6th s. of Sir Thomas Hales, 3rd Bt., and bro. of Sir Thomas Pym Hales, 4th Bt. (qq.v.). *m.* 27 Jan. 1775, Elizabeth, da. and h. of Thomas Smith of Keyworth, Notts., 1da. *suc.* bro. as 5th Bt. 18 Mar. 1773.

Groom of the bedchamber 1771-1812.

Hales contested Canterbury in 1774 but was badly defeated, receiving only 177 votes out of a poll of over 1000. He was defeated also at Downton, where he stood on the Radnor interest, but seated on petition. He consistently supported Administration.

By 1780 the Radnor family had lost control of Downton, and Robinson considered that Hales would make a 'good candidate' at Dover. But he did not stand, and was out of Parliament until 1784 when he was returned for Marlborough on the Bruce interest. His only known vote after 1784 was with Pitt on the Regency. He is not known to have spoken in the House.

He died 12 Apr. 1824.

J.A.C.

**HALES, Sir Thomas,** 3rd Bt. (?1694–1762), of Bekesbourne, Kent.

| | |
|---|---|
| MINEHEAD | 1722–1727 |
| CAMELFORD | 1727–1734 |
| GRAMPOUND | 1734–1741 |
| HYTHE | 3 Dec. 1744–1761 |
| EAST GRINSTEAD | 8 Dec. 1761–6 Oct. 1762 |

*b.* ?1694, 1st s. of Sir Thomas Hales, 2nd Bt., M.P., by Mary, da. of Sir Charles Pym, 1st Bt., M.P. *educ.* Oriel, Oxf. 1711; I. Temple. *m.* 22 June 1723, Mary, da. of Sir Robert Marsham, 4th Bt., M.P., 6s. 7da. *suc.* fa. 7 Jan. 1748.
Clerk of the Board of Green Cloth to the Prince of Wales c.1719–27, to the King 1727–60; lt. Dover castle 1728–50; vice-warden of the Cinque Ports 1750–*d.*

Hales was a follower of the Duke of Dorset, and a supporter of Walpole and the Pelhams. He sat on Dorset's interest at Hythe and East Grinstead.

On the accession of George III he lost his place in the Household, and applied to Newcastle for a pension. On 11 Mar. 1761 Newcastle noted about Hales: 'Two sons and four daughters. Hopes to have £800 per annum amongst them till something may fall to provide for some of them.' And on 19 Mar.: 'Pension for Sir Thomas Hales's children. £600 for his son.' He was given a pension of £600, and applied for the first half-yearly instalment on 25 Nov. 1761: 'There is now', he wrote to Newcastle, 'half a year due of the small sum your Grace promised me in lieu of so large a one which I was so hardly deprived of.' He received two payments of £300 from Newcastle, on 17 Feb. and 27 Apr. 1762.[1] He died 6 Oct. 1762.

[1] Namier, *Structure*, 221, 478, 479; Add. 32930, f. 30.

L.B.N.

**HALES, Thomas Pym** (c.1726–73), of Bekesbourne, Kent.

| | |
|---|---|
| DOWNTON | 1 Feb. 1762–1768 |
| DOVER | 20 Jan. 1770–18 Mar. 1773 |

*b.* c.1726, 1st s. of Sir Thomas Hales, 3rd Bt., and bro. of Sir Philip Hales, 5th Bt. (qq.v.). *educ.* Wadham,

Oxf. 1743. *suc.* fa. as 4th Bt. 6 Oct. 1762. *m.* 11 Oct. 1764, Mary, da. of Gervase Heyward of Sandwich, wid. of George Coussmaker of Staple, Kent, 5da.

Returned at Downton on the interest of his brother-in-law Lord Feversham, Hales supported Administration until February 1764 when he was 'carried into the minority'[1] by Lord George Sackville, and voted with Opposition over general warrants, 6 and 18 Feb. Described as 'doubtful' in Rockingham's list of July 1765, he did not vote against the repeal of the Stamp Act; but in Rockingham's list of November 1766 and Townshend's of January 1767 was classed 'Grenville', presumably because of Sackville. He voted with Opposition on the land tax, 27 Feb. 1767. There is no record of his having spoken in the House.

Hales did not stand at the general election of 1768, and re-entered Parliament in 1770 as a follower of Administration. At Dover in 1770 he was judged 'the most acceptable person the court could recommend':[2] he had financial support from the Government and was backed by the Yorke interest. The contest was 'violent' and his victory 'was entirely owing to the votes of the out dwellers, many of whom were brought from a distance at a very heavy expense'.[3]

He does not appear in any divisions in this Parliament but in Robinson's first survey on the royal marriage bill he is marked 'pro, absent, sick'. He died 18 Mar. 1773.

[1] Walpole to Lord Hertford, 6 Feb. 1764. [2] North to Hardwicke, Add. 35424, ff. 19–20. [3] Hales to C. Yorke, 2 Jan. 1770, and North to Hardwicke, Add. 35639, f. 163.

J.A.C.

**HALLIDAY, John** (?1709–54), of Yard House, nr. Taunton, Som.

| | |
|---|---|
| TAUNTON | 15 Apr.–8 June 1754 |

*b.* ?1709, 1st s. of John Halliday of Yard House by Mary, da. of Edmund Trowbridge of Lipyeate, Som. *m.* 1737, Mary, da. of Isaac Welman of Poundisford Park, Som., 3s. 4da. *suc.* fa. 1737.
Sheriff, Som. 1746–7.

Halliday came of a gentry family with estates in Somerset and Wiltshire. He was returned unopposed for Taunton at the general election of 1754. He died on 8 June 1754, a week after the new Parliament had assembled, aged 44.

M.M.D.

**HALLIDAY, John** (?1737–1805), of Yard House, nr. Taunton, Som.

| | |
|---|---|
| TAUNTON | 16 Mar. 1775–1784 |

*b.* ?1737, 1st s. of John Halliday (q.v.). *educ.* I. Temple 1756. *unm. suc.* fa. 1754.

About 1770 Halliday founded the banking firm of Halliday and Co. in Lombard Street, and in 1776 went into partnership with Sir John Duntze (q.v.).

In 1774 he contested Taunton; was defeated, but returned on petition. He at first voted with Opposition, but over the contractors bill, 12 Feb. 1779, was listed as 'pro, absent. Query hopeful', and henceforth supported Administration till the fall of North. He voted against Shelburne's peace preliminaries, 18 Feb. 1783, for parliamentary reform, 7 May 1783, and for Fox's East India bill, 27 Nov. 1783, but was classed as 'pro' by Robinson, January 1784, and in Stockdale's list of 19 Mar. There is no record of his having spoken in the House.

Halliday did not stand at the general election of 1784, hoping instead to obtain a vacant commissionership of taxes. To this end he exerted himself to get an Administration supporter returned at Taunton ('by which [zeal] I greatly endangered my life at a time when I had been confined to my bed by the gout', he later wrote to Pitt),[1] and at the same time 'relinquished a partnership in the banking house of Sir John Duntze and Co. which would . . . since have been very profitable to me on purpose to remove any objection to the appointment then promised me'. But he did not get it. In 1790 he again stood at Taunton but was defeated.

He died 21 Apr. 1805, aged 68.

[1] 20 July 1792, Chatham mss.

M.M.D.

## HALLIFAX, Sir Thomas (d.1789), of Gordon House, Enfield, Mdx.[1]

| | |
|---|---|
| COVENTRY | 29 Dec. 1780–27 Feb. 1781 |
| AYLESBURY | 1784– 7 Feb. 1789 |

3rd s. of John Hallifax, clockmaker of Barnsley, by Anne, da. of George Archdale of Pilley, nr. Barnsley. m. (1) 27 Apr. 1762, Penelope (d.6 Dec. 1762), da. of Richard Thomson of Ewell, Surr., s.p.; (2) 1 Nov. 1772, Margaret, da. and coh. of John Saville, linen draper, of Clay Hill, Enfield, Mdx., 2s.; her sis. m. Christopher Atkinson (q.v.). Kntd. 5 Feb. 1773.

Alderman of London 1766–d., sheriff 1768–9, ld. mayor 1776–7.

Hallifax, who was indentured to a Barnsley grocer while still very young, left before his apprenticeship was completed, and went to London where he became a clerk in the banking house of John Martin and Co. He quickly rose to be chief clerk, and at the end of 1753 left Martin's to found a banking house in partnership with Joseph Vere, a banker, and Richard Glyn, a city merchant.

Alderman since 1766, and in 1768 one of the sheriffs, he acted as returning officer for the last three of the four Wilkes Middlesex elections, upholding the rights of free election; and in his cap-

acity as sheriff, in company with the mayor and other members of the corporation, presented a petition to the King against the seating of Luttrell. But when on 6 Mar. 1770 a second petition was presented by some of the aldermen, led by William Beckford, Hallifax, no longer in office, publicly dissociated himself from it. The Ayr bank disaster of 1772 seriously affected Glyn and Hallifax, and in June they suspended payment, but were able to re-open in August. In October 1772 Hallifax stood as court candidate for lord mayor in opposition to Wilkes. He was defeated, and though encouraged by the King and North to demand a scrutiny, seems quickly to have abandoned the idea.[2] When in 1776 he at last became lord mayor he 'invited the ministers to his feast to which they had not been asked for seven years'.[3] But though Hallifax supported the Administration in opposing Wilkes, he seems to have become increasingly inclined towards the Opposition. During his term of office he gained considerable popularity by taking a vigorous stand against press gangs in the City.

Hallifax was now anxious to find a seat in Parliament, and according to Henry Beaufoy's account[4] of his own attempts to enter the House, 'though in general a most cautious man . . . was defrauded of £1,000 by an attorney whose services I had declined, and who seems to have owed his better success with Mr. Hallifax to the alderman's penurious solicitude to obtain a seat in Parliament for much less than the customary price'. In October 1779, in conjunction with Lord Mahon, a regular Opposition supporter, he was mentioned at a freeholders' meeting as a possible candidate for Middlesex.[5] The suggestion received no support, but in 1780 Hallifax and a fellow banker, Thomas Rogers, stood for Coventry on the corporation interest against the Administration supporters Edward Roe Yeo and Lord Sheffield. A violent contest ended in the closure of the poll by the sheriffs without a return. After a debate in the House of Commons in which Charles James Fox supported Hallifax and Rogers, a new writ was ordered. Hallifax and Rogers were returned but unseated on petition.

In 1784 Hallifax was returned unopposed at Aylesbury. He was classed as an Administration supporter by Adam in May 1784, and his one recorded vote on the Regency, 16 Dec. 1788, was in support of Pitt. There is no record of his having spoken in the House, and during his Coventry election campaign he was labelled 'the Dumb Knight'.[6] He died 7 Feb. 1789. His fortune was estimated at £100,000.

[1] This biography is based on an essay by Mr. S. W. Shelton, archivist of Glyn Mills & Co. [2] Fortescue, ii. 397, 401. [3] Walpole,

*Last Jnls.* i. 588. *English Hist. Docs.* xi (ed. Aspinall & Smith), 242. *Fortescue,* iv. 451. *Whitley, Parlty. Rep. Coventry,* 183.

M.M.D.

## HALSEY, Thomas (?1731–88), of Great Gaddesden, Herts.

HERTFORDSHIRE 1768–1784

*b.* ?1731, 2nd s. of Charles Halsey of Great Gaddesden by Agatha, da. of Frederick Dorrien of London. *m.* 18 Mar. 1784, Sarah, da. of John Crawley of Stockwood, Beds., 1da. *suc.* bro. 1762.

Halsey came of an old Hertfordshire family: his grandfather represented the county 1708–15; his father, a younger son, was a London merchant in the Hamburg trade, but in 1739 inherited the family estates on the death of his elder brother. Halsey himself followed his father into the Hamburg trade. In 1759 or before, as a member of the firm of Hanbury and Halsey, he went out to Hamburg, and in 1760 while still out there, was appointed a commissary of control to the army under Prince Ferdinand. His job was mainly to examine the execution of contracts, at a stipend of £3 a day. In 1762 he succeeded to the family estates on the death of his brother, and in February 1763 returned to England where he seems to have settled down as a country gentleman.[1]

In 1768 he was returned unopposed for Hertfordshire. Before the election Sir John Sebright wrote to Lord Spencer, 15 Feb.:[2] 'Mr. Halsey has seen the Duke of Grafton; and . . . enjoys his Grace's good wishes . . . as far as I can form an opinion the present Administration . . . will not hereafter find cause to repent of any support he may derive from them.' But all Halsey's reported votes were with Opposition; he was present at the Opposition dinner of 9 May 1769, and in September 1774 was classed by Robinson as 'contra'. In 1780 he was returned again after a contest and continued to vote with Opposition. *The English Chronicle* wrote of him:

His infirm state of health prevents him from all attention to his parliamentary duty, sometimes for a whole sessions together. This amiable character, however, in private life, has so endeared him to his constituents, that notwithstanding several gentlemen of the first opulence in the country have attempted to supplant him, and have promised a stricter attention to the duties of so important a trust; their efforts have, hitherto, proved totally nugatory . . . Mr. Halsey resides mostly in the country, where his humanity and generosity, and a friendly familiar intercourse with his neighbours, have gained him the most universal esteem.

Halsey's name appears in all the crucial divisions reported 1781–2, each time with Opposition. He voted for Shelburne's peace preliminaries, 18 Feb. 1783, and for parliamentary reform, 7 May 1783, but was absent from the division on Fox's East India

bill, 27 Nov. 1783. Robinson in January 1784 classed him as 'doubtful, desperate', and Stockdale's list as 'Opposition'. He stood for Hertfordshire again in 1784, but was defeated.

He died 9 Oct. 1788, aged 57.

[1] T52/50. [2] Spencer mss at Althorp.

M.M.D.

## HAMILTON, Lord Archibald (1740–1819), of Ashton Hall, Lancs.

LANCASHIRE 1768–Jan. 1772

*b.* 15 July 1740, 2nd s. of James, 5th Duke of Hamilton [S], by his 3rd w. Anne, da. and coh. of Edward Spencer of Rendlesham, Suff.; she m. (2) 1751, Richard Savage Nassau (q.v.). *educ.* Eton 1753; Grand Tour.[1] *m.* 25 May 1765, Lady Harriet Stewart, da. of Alexander, 6th Earl of Galloway [S], 2s. 3da. *suc.* to estates of Charles Gerard, 2nd Earl of Macclesfield, and Digby Gerard, 5th Baron Gerard, on *d.* of paternal gd.-m. 1744; to estates of his gd.-fa. Edward Spencer 1771; and his nephew as 9th Duke of Hamilton and 6th Duke of Brandon 2 Aug. 1799.

Hamilton was elected for Lancashire without a contest. He voted for Wilkes's expulsion, 3 Feb. 1769, but against the seating of Luttrell, 15 Apr. 1769, against Government on the Middlesex election, on 9 Jan. 1770, and against the Spanish convention, 13 Feb. 1771. He does not appear to have spoken in the House, and the circumstances of his leaving Parliament are not known.

He died 16 Feb. 1819.

[1] Mann to Walpole, 22 Nov. 1760.

J.B.

## HAMILTON, Sir Charles, 2nd Bt. (1767–1849), of Iping, nr. Midhurst, Suss.

ST. GERMANS 1 Feb.–11 June 1790
DUNGANNON 21 Nov. 1801–1802, 9 June 1803–1806
HONITON 1807–1812

*b.* 25 May 1767, 1st s. of Sir John Hamilton, 1st Bt., by Cassandra Agnes, da. of Edmund Chamberlayne of Maugersbury, Glos.; he was descended in the junior line from James, 1st Earl of Abercorn. *educ.* R. N. Acad. Portsmouth 1777. *m.* 19 Apr. 1803, Henrietta Martha, da. of George Drummond, banker, of Stanmore, Mdx., 1s. *suc.* fa. 24 Jan. 1784; K.C.B. 29 Jan. 1833.

Entered R.N. 1776; lt. 1781; capt. 1790; r.-adm. 1810; v.-adm. 1814; gov. Newfoundland 1818–24; adm. 1830.

When his cousin J. J. Hamilton succeeded to the earldom of Abercorn, Charles Hamilton replaced him at St. Germans, a stop-gap until the impending dissolution of Parliament. He did not sit again during our period.

He died 14 Sept. 1849.

M.M.D.

## HAMILTON, James, 2nd Earl of Clanbrassill [I] (1730–98), of Dundalk, co. Louth.

HELSTON 1768–1774

*b.* 23 Aug. 1730, o. surv. s. of James, 1st Earl of Clanbrassill, M.P., by Lady Henrietta Bentinck, da. of William, 1st Earl of Portland. *m.* 21 May 1774, Grace, da. of Thomas Foley (q.v.), *s.p. suc.* fa. 17 Mar. 1758. K.P. 5 Feb. 1783.

Chief remembrancer of the court of Exchequer [I] 1757–*d.*; P.C. [I] 4 July 1766.

Clanbrassill's mother wrote to her brother, Count William Bentinck,[1] 27 May 1760, that her son, having inherited his estate with a large debt on it, has not, these last two years, 'acted with economy'. Now he has determined 'to stint himself to a certain sum, to part with his horses, to stop all works here, and to go over to England'. She did not feel sure that he would carry through his resolve. 'He is careless and thoughtless, but he is good natured and generous', and honest; though 'pinched in his affairs' has never yet thought of marrying for money nor of 'selling places in his office by which last means he might certainly get pretty considerably'. And he is not a gambler.

In 1768 he was returned for Helston, unopposed, on the interest of Francis, 2nd Baron Godolphin, whose first wife was a sister of Clanbrassill's mother. In the House, Clanbrassill voted with the Administration. North wrote of him to Harcourt, lord lieutenant of Ireland, 23 June 1774:[2]

I had always the greatest reason to be thankful to him for his conduct in Parliament. He brought himself into the House of Commons without the assistance of Administration; has never asked a single favour; but has been constant in his attendance and uniform in his support in Parliament.

He is not known to have spoken in the House.

Mrs. Delany, a cousin of Clanbrassill's wife, met him at the time of his wedding, and formed a very favourable opinion of him; and she was assured by a friend who knew him well that 'he was free from *every vice in the world*'. He 'looks old of his age (having lost all his fore teeth), but he is tall, genteel, and *very well bred*'; 'nothing can have been more generous and polite than Lord Clanbrassill's behaviour, and he is of an age as well as his lady to know their minds'. And a year later: 'I like him mightily; he is good humoured, easy, well-bred, and *deep* in search of *botany* . . . he takes notice of everything.'[3]

On 18 Nov. 1774 she wrote to Mrs. Port:[4]

Lord Clanbrassill not in Parliament; depending on *Lord Godolphin's* interest made no other, and *he* was under obligation to give his to Lord Carmarthen. It seems strange that his father, Mr. Foley, did not bring him in; but there is no accounting for narrow minds.

And on 14 Jan. 1775, to her brother Bernard Granville:[4] she had a letter from Lady Clanbrassill from Dundalk—'she seems happy, but hankering after her English friends, and much chagrined at her lord's not being brought into the English Parliament'. He never re-entered it. He died 6 Feb. 1798.

[1] Egerton 1722, ff. 69–71. [2] *Harcourt Pprs.* ix. 209. [3] Mrs. Delany, *Autobiog. & Corresp.* (ser. 2), i. 580, 591; ii. 134–5. [4] Ibid. 67, 93.

L.B.N.

## HAMILTON (formerly DALRYMPLE), John (1715–96), of Bargany, Ayr.

WIGTOWN BURGHS 1754–1761
WIGTOWNSHIRE 1761–Feb. 1762
WIGTOWN BURGHS 15 Apr. 1762–1768

*b.* 4 Feb. 1715, 2nd s. of Sir Robert Dalrymple, adv., of Castleton, Haddington by his 1st w. Johanna, da. and h. of Hon. John Hamilton, 1st s. of John, Lord Bargany [S]; bro. of Sir Hew Dalrymple, 2nd Bt., (q.v.). *educ.* North Berwick; adv. 1735; M. Temple 1735; Leyden 1738. *m.* (1) contract 25 Apr. 1746, Lady Anne Wemyss (*d.c.*1760), da. of James, 4th Earl of Wemyss [S], *s.p.*; (2) contr. 4 July 1769, Margaret, da. of Alexander Montgomerie of Coilsfield, Ayr, and sis. of Hugh Montgomerie (q.v.). *suc.* to Bargany estates and changed his name to Hamilton on *d.* of James, 4th Lord Bargany 1736.

Hamilton was a younger son of the Dalrymple clan of jurists, soldiers and politicians, headed by John, 2nd Earl of Stair. A man of vigorous personality and pawky humour, he attached himself to Frederick, Prince of Wales, became an intimate friend of the Grenvilles,[1] and interfered with zest in the political intrigues of any constituency where he or his numerous connexions had an interest. In Ayrshire in 1754, pre-engaged to his friend Patrick Craufurd, he opposed his relation James Mure Campbell and the Loudoun-Argyll interest. Electioneering in Wigtown Burghs in the interest of his kinsman Captain John Dalrymple of Stair, he took advantage of the confused situation to play his own hand; and by a compromise with Lord Galloway secured his own return, against the Argyll candidate. Hamilton's 'impetuosity' was deplored by his relations.[2] His brother-in-law, W. Duff, wrote to Loudoun, 22 Apr. 1754:[3] 'I cannot say that Bargany's being Member will give me the least joy, as I do not see that it will be for his advantage to be in Parliament.'

Dupplin, in his parliamentary lists of 1754, counted Hamilton among ministerial supporters connected with Argyll, but in 1755 he followed Pitt into opposition, and supported his Administration 1756–7, when Scottish placehunters sought to make use of his 'particular friendship and intimacy' with the Grenvilles.[4] On Pitt's fall Newcastle, when negotiating for a new Administration, listed Hamilton among the Scots 'not to be relied on at present —to be treated with'.[5] But on 2 May 1757 Hamilton 'unexpectedly' voted against Newcastle and Fox in the debate on the loss of Minorca.[6]

In the Scottish militia agitation Hamilton took an active but not a leading part; attended the meeting at Ayr on 12 Oct. 1759 to address the King, and was a member of the Commons committee to prepare the bill.

In Ayrshire Hamilton by about 1758 had joined his relations in supporting the Argyll-Loudoun candidate against Archibald Montgomerie, brother of the Earl of Eglintoun, who in retaliation allied himself with Galloway, secured his brother's return for Wigtown Burghs, and opposed Hamilton's candidature in Wigtownshire. Hamilton was returned with the backing of Bute, but was obliged to accept a compromise with the Galloway interest, vacated the county seat, and in April was returned for the Burghs.

He supported Bute, and was equally constant to Grenville, who repudiated Garlies's demand that Hamilton should be excluded from any share in Wigtown Burghs patronage.[7] Soon afterwards an opportunity to reward Hamilton occurred when the office of master of works fell vacant in February 1764. The place was not officially filled until 4 July 1765, shortly before Grenville's fall, when it was given to Hamilton in the name of James Duff of the Middle Temple.[8]

Listed 'doubtful' by Rockingham in July 1765, Hamilton followed Grenville into opposition and voted against the repeal of the Stamp Act, 22 Feb. 1766. After the formation of the Chatham Administration Grenville believed that Hamilton was still 'inclined' to follow him;[9] but in the winter of 1766-7 Rockingham listed him under 'Bute', and Townshend in January 1767 counted him 'doubtful'. Although he voted with Grenville on the land tax, 27 Feb. 1767, Newcastle, in March, counted him an Administration supporter. Nevertheless in March 1768 Hamilton lost his place to James Pringle.[10] He is not known to have spoken in the House.

From 1766 Hamilton had been seeking another seat. He proposed standing for Ayrshire but was dissuaded by Loudoun.[11] On 26 Oct. 1766 Loudoun warned Bute of a rumour that Hamilton was canvassing in one of the Ayr Burghs: 'He would be a formidable enemy if supported elsewhere.'[12] Timorous of contesting Wigtownshire, he eventually negotiated an agreement with William McDowall, offered him the Stair interest, and stood down.[13] By his second marriage in 1769 he became connected with his old enemies, the Eglintoun family,

but in 1772 wrote to Loudoun roundly denying a rumour that he was 'an apostate' to his interest or intended standing for Ayrshire as the Eglintoun candidate: 'I have no views for myself and am thankful my ambition that way is satisfied.'[14]

He died 12 Feb. 1796.

[1] Hamilton to Bute, 30 Nov. 1761, Bute mss. [2] Dalrymple of Stair to Loudoun, 21 and 28 Apr. 1754, Lord Dumfries to Loudoun, 15 Jan. 1760, Loudoun mss. [3] Ibid. [4] Archibald Cunningham to Mure Campbell, 13 Dec. 1756, Patrick Boyle to Mure Campbell, 29 Nov. 1756, 12 Jan. 1757, ibid. [5] Add. 32995, f. 383. [6] Fox to Devonshire, 3 May 1757, Devonshire mss; Add. 33034, f. 232. [7] Grenville to Bedford, 27 Dec. 1763, Bedford mss 48, f. 226. [8] Cal. Home Office Pprs. 1760-5, p. 689. [9] Grenville to Temple, 24 Oct. 1766, Grenville mss (JM). [10] T17/20/35. [11] Loudoun to Bute, 28 Aug. 1766, Bute mss. [12] Loudoun mss. [13] John Dalrymple to Loudoun, 18 Nov. 1767, Chas. Dalrymple of Orangefield to Loudoun, 31 Dec. 1767, 9 Jan., 26 Feb. 1768, ibid. [14] Sir John Dalrymple to Loudoun, 8 Jan. 1772, Ld. Dumfries to Loudoun, 15 Sept. 1772, Hamilton to Loudun, 10 May 1772, ibid. See also DALRYMPLE, Hew.

E.H.-G.

## HAMILTON (formerly NISBET), John (1751-1804), of Pencaitland and Saltcoats, Haddington.

HADDINGTONSHIRE    24 July 1786–Nov. 1795

b. 22 Dec. 1751, 2nd s. of William Nisbet of Dirleton by Mary, da. and h. of Alexander Hamilton of Pencaitland and Saltcoats (d.1758); bro. of William Hamilton Nisbet (q.v.). m. 1782, Janet, da. of Robert Dundas (q.v.), ld. pres. of court of session, s.p. As heir (by entail, 1747) to Pencaitland assumed name of Hamilton.

Receiver of land tax in Scotland 1795.

Hamilton owed his seat in Parliament mainly to Henry Dundas, his wife's uncle, who gave him private and prior notice of the vacancy. William Nisbet wrote to Dundas, 11 May 1786:[1] 'I mentioned to you at Wimbledon that I was ready to produce the cash to bring my brother in Parliament (as this seemed what you wished for him) whenever you pointed out a place.' Although Dundas withheld open support until he had sounded local opinion Hamilton was elected unopposed.

In Parliament he supported Administration on the Regency, 1788-9.

He died 25 Dec. 1804.

[1] H. Furber, Hen. Dundas, 219-20.

E.H.-G.

## HAMILTON, John James (1756-1818).

EAST LOOE      1 Dec. 1783-1784
ST. GERMANS    1784-9 Oct. 1789

b. July 1756, posth. s. of Capt. Hon. John Hamilton, R.N., by Harriet, illegit. da. of Rt. Hon. James Craggs, wid. of Richard Eliot, M.P., of Port Eliot, Cornw.; half-bro. of Edward Eliot (q.v.), and gd.-s. of James, 7th Earl of Abercorn [S]. educ. Harrow 1770-1; Pembroke, Camb. 1773; I. Temple 1773. m. (1) 20 June 1779, Catherine (d. 13 Sept. 1791), da. of Sir Joseph Copley, 1st Bt., of Sprotbrough, Yorks., 2s. 4da.; (2) 4 Mar. 1792, his 1st cos. Lady Cecil Hamilton (div. Apr. 1799), da. and coh. of Hon. and Rev. George Hamilton, dean of Windsor, 1da.; (3) 3 Apr. 1800, Anne Jane, da. of Arthur Saunders Gore, 2nd Earl of Arran [I], wid. of Henry Hatton of Great Clonard, co. Wexford, *s.p.* *suc.* uncle as 9th Earl of Abercorn [S] 9 Oct. 1789; *cr.* Mq. of Abercorn [GB] 15 Oct. 1790; K. G. 17 Jan. 1805.

P.C. [I] 1794.

In the late summer of 1783 Hamilton returned to England after two years' absence abroad; and on 1 Dec. was elected unopposed at East Looe on the interest of John Buller sen., an uncle of his wife. On 5 Dec. he voted against Fox's East India bill, and on the 8th, in his maiden speech,[1] rejoiced that even at this last stage he had an opportunity of expressing his abhorrence of a measure 'which he verily believed would completely overturn the constitution'. He still hoped the Commons would reject the bill, but if not 'trusted that the other House would interpose, and by rejecting the bill, preserve the country from the fetters that were forging for it'. Horace Walpole commented to Lord Strafford, 11 Dec. 1783: 'Though his first essay, it was not at all dashed by bashfulness and though he might have blushed for discovering so much personal rancour to Mr. Fox, he rather seemed impatient to discharge it.' Hamilton from the first attached himself to Pitt, with whom he had been at Pembroke, Cambridge; in Robinson's survey of mid-December 1783 is marked as 'strongly for', and on 1 Mar. 1784, in reply to Fox's motion for Pitt's removal, 'praised the constancy of the ministers, and urged them to persevere'.[2]

At the general election of 1784 Hamilton was returned for St. Germans by his half-brother, Edward Eliot. On 24 May he moved the Address. Daniel Pulteney reported to the Duke of Rutland on 27 May that he 'spoke long and very well, though rather too pompous for the House of Commons'.[3] After drawing a highly laudatory picture of Pitt, with whom 'the fondest hopes of the people were reposed',[4] Hamilton, according to Wraxall,[5] showed 'his aversion to the Opposition leader . . . in a manner scarcely compatible either with the rules of debate or with the forms of decorum'. Without actually naming Fox he castigated those 'who having dissipated their fortune, ruined their constitution, and prostituted their powers, had entered those walls for the purpose of political traffic, for the purpose of repairing their finances, or from motives of ambition and aggrandisement'.[6] Hamilton voted for Pitt's proposals for parliamentary reform, 18 Apr. 1785. He was a vigorous champion of Warren Hastings. Wraxall writes[7] that

ardently attached as he was to the chancellor of the Exchequer, yet possessed great independence of mind

joined with a haughty inflexibility of character. Deeply impressed with a sense of Hastings's services to the state, he disdained to follow the crowd of ministerial dependants who alternately acquitted or condemned him as their leader dictated.

When on 21 June 1786 the House was about to rise for the summer recess, with charges against Hastings unresolved, Hamilton moved for a call of the House 'with a view to go on with the charges against Mr. Hastings, so as to completely finish them in the course of the present session'; individual inconvenience was an insignificant object when 'opposed to what was due to the feelings of a persecuted and accused man . . . if Mr. Hastings were ultimately to be deemed criminal, let him be proved such and then be punished, but let condemnation precede punishment, and his punishment not be suspense'.[8] But when on 27 Mar. 1787 Hastings's impeachment was to be moved in the House, Hamilton endeavoured to gain more time, and, according to Wraxall[9]

equally regardless of the effect which his speech might produce on Pitt or Burke, though connected by the closest ties of friendship with the former, in the imperious and dictatorial tone natural to him, he expressed his astonishment at the indecent precipitation which characterized their deliberations.

Reminded by Dundas that he had the previous year pressed the House to continue sitting the whole summer in order to do Hastings justice as speedily as possible, he 'desired the House to recollect the difference between using dispatch in deciding upon preliminary charges and precipitately coming to a determination on the great question of impeachment'.[10] Hamilton was a keen supporter of the abolition of the slave trade, and on 21 May 1788 opposed Sir William Dolben's proposals for the regulation of the shipping of slaves because 'by such a bill that House would, for the first time, sanction that most abominable traffic, unauthorized by divine law, and so repugnant to human feeling'.[11]

Wraxall gives the following picture of Hamilton:[12]

Of a dark complexion, with very intelligent and regular features, he resembled more a Spaniard than a native of Britain; and his arrogant solemnity of manner augmented by the peculiarities of his demeanour, obtained for him from Sheridan the name of 'Don Whiskerandos', the lover of Tilburina in his own 'Critic'. Mr. Hamilton's abilities, though not of the first order, might have qualified him for public employment . . . if he had emulated to obtain office; but pleasure rather than business, enjoyment and not application or renunciations, seemed principally to occupy his mind.

He died 27 Jan. 1818.

[1] Debrett, xii. 354. [2] Laprade, 83; Debrett, xiii. 243. [3] *HMC Rutland*, iii. 97. [4] Debrett, xv. 26. [5] *Mems.* iii. 387. [6] Debrett, xv. 26. [7] *Mems.* iv. 346. [8] Debrett, xx. 396. [9] *Mems.* iv. 432. [10] Debrett, xxi. 511–13, 520–1. [11] Stockdale, xv. 72. [12] *Mems.* iii. 387.

M.M.D.

## HAMILTON, William (1730–1803).

*b.* 13 Dec. 1730, 4th s. of Lord Archibald Hamilton, bro. of James, 4th Duke of Hamilton [S], by his 3rd w. Lady Jane Hamilton, da. of James, 6th Earl of Abercorn [S]. *educ.* Westminster 1740. *m.* (1) 25 Jan. 1758, Catherine (*d.*25 Aug. 1782), da. of Hugh Barlow (q.v.) of Lawrenny Hall, Pemb., 1da.; (2) 6 Sept. 1791, Emma, da. of Henry Lyon of Nesse, Great Neston, Cheshire (Nelson's Lady Hamilton). K.B. 15 Jan. 1772.

Ensign 3 Ft. Gds. 1747, lt. 1753, ret. 1758.
Envoy to Naples 1764–1800.

In 1761 Hamilton was nominated with Edward Harvey on the Browne interest at Midhurst which had been offered to the court. Two candidates were also put forward on the interest of Sir William Peere Williams, but a compromise was arranged: each side was to nominate one candidate and provide £1,000 to help to bring in the others elsewhere. It was suggested that Hamilton should go to Leominster but he refused to leave Midhurst, and Lord Waldegrave wrote to Newcastle, 22 May 1761: 'Mr. Harvey gave way to Mr. Hamilton, not because Hamilton had better pretensions, but because Harvey had greater regard to the convenience of his friends.'[1] Apparently Hamilton did not pay his share of the money either, for on 20 Mar. Fox wrote to Fitzmaurice that according to Browne, Hamilton would refuse to pay, in which case he and Waldegrave would pay it for him.[2]

There is no record of his having spoken in the House. He was described in Bute's list of December 1761 as 'pro', and appears in Henry Fox's list of Members favourable to the peace preliminaries.

In April 1763 Hamilton wrote to Charles Jenkinson asking for the embassy at Naples, in case of a vacancy, 'on account of Mrs. Hamilton's ill-health and my own situation'.[3] Hamilton was appointed in August 1764, over a year after the vacancy occurred. It was understood that he would vacate his seat in Parliament. He remained in Naples until 1800, making a large collection of antiquities which was eventually acquired by the British Museum.

He died 6 Apr. 1803.

[1] Add. 32923, f. 220. [2] Bute mss. [3] *Jenkinson Pprs.* 139.

M.M.D.

## HAMILTON, William Gerard (1729–96), of Hampton Court, Mdx.

*b.* 28 Jan. 1729, 1st surv. s. of William Hamilton, barrister, of Lincoln's Inn, by his 1st w. Helen, da. of David Hay of Woodcockdale, West Lothian. *educ.* Harrow 1742–5; Oriel, Oxf. 1745; L. Inn. *suc.* fa. 1754. *unm.*

M.P. [I] 1761–8.

Ld. of Trade 1756–61; chief sec. to ld. lt. [I] 1761–1764; chancellor of the Exchequer [I] 1763–84 when he exchanged the office for pension of £2,000 p.a.

Hamilton sat at Petersfield on the Jolliffe interest, and was counted by Dupplin in April 1754 as a supporter of Administration. In the spring of 1755, 'with a frank abruptness', he 'offered his service to Mr. Fox, telling him that he foresaw he must one day be very considerable; that his own fortune was easy and not pressing; he did not disclaim ambition, but was willing to wait'.[1] When Fox joined Newcastle, he included Hamilton among those for whom he wanted places. In the debate on the Address, 13 Nov. 1755, Hamilton made his maiden speech and 'succeeded admirably': 'his voice, manner, and language were most advantageous; his arguments sound though pointed; and his command of himself easy and undaunted.'[2] 'His figure is advantageous', wrote Walpole,[3] 'his voice strong and clear, his manner spirited, and the whole with the ease of an established speaker.' And on 4 Mar. 1756: 'The young Hamilton has spoken and shone again.' In December 1755, disappointed of preferment, he had threatened to leave Fox and join Pitt;[4] and in April 1756 he was made a lord of Trade.

On 11 Jan. 1761 Lord Fitzmaurice wrote to Bute:[5]

As to the affair of Hamilton 'twas thus. Mr. Fox I believe made him lord of Trade—Hamilton finding himself much pushed about getting into Parliament consulted him, whether it would be right to apply to your Lordship . . . He [Fox] told him his sentiments of your Lordship, and further advised him to it as the most advantageous way certainly he could compass it, as it would be at the same time probably securing your protection in his place.

Possibly Bute recommended him to Lord Galway, patron of Pontefract. In March 1761 Lord Halifax, Hamilton's chief at the Board of Trade, was appointed lord lieutenant of Ireland and took him as his secretary.

As in the English Parliament, so in the Irish, he soon made a reputation as a speaker. George Montagu, Halifax's cousin, wrote to Walpole on 6 Feb. 1762: 'Hamilton's speech for an augmentation of forces was the best he ever made'; and Walpole himself adds that the motion was carried 'by the sole power of his eloquence'.[6] When Halifax was appointed first lord of the Admiralty, Hamilton wrote to his friend, John Hely Hutchinson, prime serjeant in Ireland, 2 Aug. 1762: 'Nothing I think is more probable than that my being secretary will be imposed as a condition upon any one who applies for the lord lieutenancy, and in that nomination it is also likely that I should be consulted.' And on 9 Aug. 1762: 'Nothing is more evident to me than that my continuance in Ireland, instead of retarding, will very essentially promote my progress in England; and that these two situations will assist each other, and will enable me to assist my friends.' With Hutchinson's help, he had visions of great influence in Ireland:

Nothing is more evident to me [he wrote to Hutchinson on 10 Nov. 1762] than, that if I was to return to you again as secretary, I might continue in possession of that employment so long as we pleased; and I am clear that advantages more extensive and on a much wider plan might be obtained in Ireland, than has hitherto been projected by anyone in your situation or mine. It has often struck me that such a body of friends might be made in Parliament, and attached particularly to ourselves . . . as would form, with the power inseparable from Government, a body which under our conduct would be very respectable . . . Let me know your opinion as soon as you have formed it. I can only say I am willing to risk anything, and to embark in anything.

His immediate aim was much less grandiose: to secure for himself the rich sinecure of chancellor of the Exchequer of Ireland. But as time passed, and no lord lieutenant was appointed, he no longer felt so certain of remaining chief secretary. Then on 30 July 1763, after Lord Northumberland had been named, and he had at last obtained the Exchequer, he wrote to Hutchinson: 'There may be an appearance of vanity in the declaration, but it is literally fact that by my own personal friends I obtained the government both for Lord Halifax and Lord Northumberland, as much as ever I procured . . . the chancellorship of the Exchequer for myself.' Yet he begged Hutchinson

to convey to each of the [lord] justices separately an idea how great an obligation I shall consider it, if upon their first interview with my lord lieutenant . . . they would express strongly their approbation of my returning in my present situation, and their opinion of the utility which would arise from it to his Excellency's Administration . . . Would Malone, the attorney, the solicitor, and Patterson, as servants of the Crown (and with whom perhaps by that time I may be friends) declare their particular satisfaction at being able to act in conjunction with me . . . I will tell you the use I propose to make of this, and the benefit which I think must arise from it. Lord Northumberland will write a letter to the secretary of state to be laid before the King, stating the prodigious satisfaction which everybody expresses (and which nobody but you and one more will feel) upon my returning in the office I now hold. When this is once done, it will be impossible to ascribe any part of the miscarriages of Government to a person whom they just before approved of.[7]

He was too clever by half. 'Mr. Hamilton', wrote Montagu to Walpole on 15 Nov. 1763, 'always

treated the great people of Ireland with contempt . . . and the primate could never endure him.' On 15 Mar. 1764 Northumberland complained to Bedford 'of the uneasiness that Mr. Hamilton's conduct brought upon me, on the first opening of the session here, and of my entire disappointment in the hopes I had conceived from his assistance to me'.[8] Halifax, now secretary of state, did not protect Hamilton, and in May he was dismissed.

His dismissal hurt; he felt isolated and ill at ease in the English Parliament; and professed contempt for English politicians. On 7 Mar. 1765 he wrote to Edmund Pery, later Speaker of the Irish House of Commons:

You judge perfectly right in thinking that it requires but little fortitude to deliver any opinion in the English House of Commons. There are a few, and but a very few, men of extraordinary talents. The herd are wretched beyond conception, and parliamentary abilities were upon the whole, I believe, never at a lower ebb. And I sometimes wish you would take a view of our Parliament, you would return so very highly satisfied with your own.

However little fortitude it may have required, Hamilton never again spoke in the House of Commons, though he sat there for another thirty years.

He claimed to have received 'proposals from the Administration, and professions, the only thing they had to offer, from the Opposition'. He had confidence in neither, and believed that Bute was still the power behind the throne.

I am neither for accepting an employment under every Administration [he wrote[9]] or for refusing one under all. Till I can unite the influence, the rank, and the emolument of office with public character and public good opinion, I will take no situation—and when I can do that, it will be indifferent to me what situation I take.

He attached himself politically to Lord Temple, and on 22 Feb. 1766 voted against the repeal of the Stamp Act. In 1766 and 1767 he sent Temple frequent and detailed reports of political events— 'Your Lordship may rely upon it', he wrote on 22 July 1767, 'that in these active and interesting times the *Bee* will be even more industrious than usual.' Intelligent and searching analysis is mingled with gullibility and gush: in July 1767 he realized that the King had no wish to change his Administration and that Rockingham 'was applied to, not to be the successor, but the auxiliary of the Duke of Grafton', yet professed to believe that Bute still had power and would eventually recommend Temple to the King.[10]

At the same time he was sending John Calcraft similar accounts and reports of debates in Parliament. To Calcraft he slighted George Grenville, professed not to desire office, and took a line on

America the direct opposite to Temple's (and to his own vote on the repeal of the Stamp Act).

> For my own part [he wrote about the Americans[11]] I think you have no right to tax them, and that every measure built upon this supposed right stands upon a rotten foundation, and must consequently tumble down, perhaps, upon the heads of the workmen.

He voted against Chatham's Administration on the land tax, 27 Feb. 1767, and the nullum tempus bill, 17 Feb. 1768; and in 1768 was returned for Old Sarum by Thomas Pitt, a close friend of Grenville.

In 1769 and 1770 Hamilton voted against Administration in every known division, and attended the Opposition dinners at the Thatched House Tavern in May 1769 and January 1770. He voted with Opposition on the Spanish convention, 13 Feb. 1771, and Grenville's Election Act, 25 Feb. 1774. In 1774 he was returned for Wareham on the Calcraft interest, and until 1779 voted regularly with Opposition.

In 1780 he was returned for Wilton by Lord Pembroke. His name does not appear in any division list between 1779 and 1781; he voted with Opposition on 20 Feb. 1782; and paired with a Government supporter on 27 Feb. and 15 Mar.

In July 1782 he refused Shelburne's offer of the secretaryship at war. 'Mr. Hamilton's view goes to no active employment whatever', wrote Shelburne to the King on 9 July,[12] 'but looks to some sinecure situation.' And William Eden wrote to Loughborough about Hamilton on 8 Aug.:[13] 'I do not believe . . . that he would refuse the vice-treasurership of Ireland, if it were offered to him; but he is as decided as we can be, in his opinion that the present frame of Government will not do.' He did not vote in the division on Shelburne's peace preliminaries, and in Robinson's list of March 1783 is classed among 'Mr. Fox's connexions'. He did not vote on Fox's East India bill but in Stockdale's list of 19 Mar. 1784 is classed as a supporter of Pitt, and William Adam after the general election of 1784 counted him with Government. His name appears in no division list between 1784 and the Regency question.

In December 1788 he voted against Pitt on the Regency, and shortly after approached Lord Herbert about his seat at Wilton in case of a dissolution. Pembroke, who was in Venice and behindhand with English news, informed Hamilton he would be returned again, but Herbert protested:

> I am very sorry you have written to Hamilton, and I still trust that you cannot intend to bring him in, if his intention is to support Opposition against the present Government, nor can I conceive that he expects you to bring him in in that case.

'I had not . . . the least idea', replied Pembroke on 6 Apr. 1789, 'of his being in Opposition, as whatever he has ever dropped to me confirmed me in the idea that he was not only a political, but a personal friend of Mr. Pitt's . . . and I am much vexed at it; for I have wrote him yes.'

Here is the account Herbert sent to his father on 3 May of a conversation with Hamilton:

> He allowed that at the time the agreement was made between you, he was both a political and personal friend of Pitt's, but that he never bound himself to vote this way or that way, that he is not bound now to vote with any party, but probably shall with the present Opposition, of which he has indeed given pretty good proof. He was very sore and rounded with me respecting my motives for urging you not to bring him into Parliament which I told him I should continue to do with all my might and power, in answer to which he said he should write to counteract as much as possible what I wrote . . . I cannot fully give credit to what Hamilton seemed to insinuate, that there was no period fixed for the termination of the agreement, for if so, it can be broke but by the death of one or the other.

Hamilton persuaded the Prince of Wales to write to Pembroke on his behalf, but Pembroke refused to return him again.[14]

'My attachment to nobody', Hamilton wrote to Eden on 17 Nov. 1781, 'lays open to me the society of everybody.'[15] Few men had such a wide social and political acquaintance and made so little of it. He was Burke's first patron and Johnson's lifelong friend; he began in politics as a protégé of Henry Fox, was connected with both Grenville and Chatham when they were at odds with each other, had links with both Opposition and Government during the American war, was offered office by Shelburne in 1782, was a friend of Pitt in 1788, and in 1789 of the Prince of Wales. He sat for six constituencies, each under a different patron. This wide circle of friends indicates social charm and political ambitions, but also inability to take a straight political line. He had too many powerful friends, and could not become too closely attuned to one for fear of offending the others. The political ambitions of the 60's had by 1782 turned into a wish for sinecure office only, and the nickname 'Single Speech' Hamilton reflects talents, ambition, and ultimate failure.

He died 16 July 1796.

[1] Walpole, *Mems. Geo. II*, ii. 44. [2] Ibid. 51. [3] To Conway, 15 Nov. 1755. [4] Add. 32861, ff. 334, 336. [5] Bute mss. [6] *Mems. Geo. III*, i. 111–112. [7] *HMC Donoughmore*, 233–52. [8] Bedford mss 49, f. 78. [9] *HMC 8th Rep*. pt. 1, 191. [10] *Grenville Pprs*. iv. 37, 92. [11] *Chatham Corresp*. iii. 203. [12] Fortescue, vi. 77. [13] *Jnls. & Corresp*. i. 22. [14] *Pembroke Pprs*. ed. Herbert, ii. 405, 408, 421–2. [15] Add. 34418, f. 174.

J.B.

**HAMILTON DALRYMPLE,** see **DALRYMPLE, Hew**

## HAMILTON NISBET, see NISBET, William

## HAMMET, Benjamin (?1736–1800), of Taunton, Som.

TAUNTON    20 Mar. 1782–22 July 1800

*m.* Louisa, da. of Sir James Esdaile, London banker, 3s. 5da. Kntd. 11 Aug. 1786.
Alderman of London 1785, sheriff 1788–9.

Hammet, a self-made man, variously reported to have been the son of a Taunton serge manufacturer[1] and of a Taunton barber,[2] is said to have started his London career as a porter in a bookshop on Fish-street Hill.[3] By 1763 he was established as a merchant on the corner of Change Alley. He himself told the House of Commons on 16 Apr. 1783 that he had been in America and was 'formerly concerned with their affairs',[4] but gives no indication of his business there or of the date of his visit. In 1781 he became a partner in the London bank of his father-in-law, Sir James Esdaile, he having previously established a banking house at Taunton, where he had also acquired considerable property. He took a leading part in attempts to improve the borough, and in 1769 became a trustee of the progressive Market House Society, an association of local tradesmen who were mainly Dissenters. Largely through his efforts the centre of Taunton was cleared of ruinous and disreputable property and a fine new street bearing his name built instead. In 1782 Hammet successfully contested Taunton with the support of the Market House Society and of Government.

He was a frequent speaker in the House. In his first reported speech on 6 Dec. 1782 he stated that he had no connexion with any ministers.[5]

> [He] rose with great warmth, to reprobate the language of gloom and despondency which he had heard held the preceding day in the House . . . We had beat the French in the West Indies, baffled them in the East, disgraced them in Europe . . . As to the funds and resources of this country he was convinced that rather than submit to the cession of Gibraltar, and to other ignominious terms, the people of this country would carry on the war for ten years and spend two hundred millions more . . . His professional habits and knowledge of the resources of the country gave him, he observed, a right to say what he had done.

Hammet voted for Shelburne's peace preliminaries, 18 Feb. 1783; for Pitt's parliamentary reform proposals, 7 May 1783; and against Fox's East India bill, 1 Dec. 1783. On 19 Dec. 1783 he told the House that he 'liked those ministers who were gone out, and those who were coming in; he was really sorry that such divisions prevailed in the House', and he wished that 'a coalition, taking in the abilities of all parts of the House might take place'. He was a

member of the St. Alban's Tavern group which in January 1784 attempted to bring about a union of parties, but on 2 Feb. 1784 he declared that Pitt 'possessed . . . the confidence and affection of the people at large in as eminent a degree as any minister had ever done'. Hammet was classed in Stockdale's list of 19 Mar. and by William Adam in May 1784 as an Administration supporter. But he himself told the House on 28 July 1784 that he was 'totally unconnected with any party; he never had received or solicited the smallest favour from any ministers whatever'.[6] He strongly criticized measures of which he did not approve, particularly the shop tax which he continuously attacked till its repeal, but on major issues regularly supported Pitt's Administration.

Hammet died 22 July 1800, aged 64.

[1] Burke, *L. G.* 1749, suppt. 15. [2] *City Biog.* 136. [3] *Gent. Mag.* 1800, p. 798. [4] Debrett, ix. 445–6. [5] Ibid. ix. 53. [6] Ibid. xii. 458; xiii. 47–48; xvi. 275.

M.M.D.

## HAMMOND, William (d.1763), of Goat Yard, St. Margaret's Hill, Southwark.

SOUTHWARK    1754–1761

Hammond was a Southwark brewer, and in his will[1] mentions his brewery in Goat Yard; in a list in the Lowther mss drawn up between April 1754 and March 1755 he is described as a surgeon and justice of the peace in Southwark. He was classed in Dupplin's list of 1754 as 'pro'. He seems to have been on friendly terms with Joseph Mawbey and Henry Thrale (qq.v.), to whom he left rings in his will. In 1761 he again contested Southwark, but was defeated.

He died 22 May 1763, leaving a widow and one son.

[1] PCC 285 Caesar.

M.M.D.

## HAMPDEN, Hon. Thomas (1746–1824), of Glynde, nr. Lewes, Suss.; and Hampden House, nr. Wendover, Bucks.

LEWES    1768–1774

*b.* 11 Sept. 1746, 1st s. of Robert Trevor (who in 1754 took the name of Hampden), subsequently 4th Baron Trevor and 1st Visct. Hampden, by Constantia, da. of Peter Anthony de Huybert, Lord van Kruyningen, of The Hague. *educ.* Ch. Ch. Oxf. 1763. *m.* (1) 13 June 1768, Catherine (*d.*24 May 1804), da. of David Graeme (q.v.), of Braco, Perth., *s.p.*; (2) 11 June 1805, Jane Maria, da. of George Brown, said to be of Ellistoun, Scotland, *s.p.* *suc.* fa. as 2nd Visct. 22 Aug. 1783.

The Trevors were an old Sussex family and represented several Sussex constituencies in the 17th and early 18th centuries. Robert Trevor Hampden, 4th Baron Trevor, was descended from the famous John Hampden, and inherited the family estates in Buckinghamshire and Bedfordshire. He was joint postmaster general in Grenville's Administration and after 1765 remained politically connected with Grenville. His brother Richard, bishop of Durham 1752–71, was a close friend of Newcastle; and it was as a compliment to the bishop that Newcastle in 1768 selected his nephew, Thomas Hampden, to stand on the Pelham interest at Lewes, where he was returned head of the poll.

Hampden voted with Opposition in the divisions of 1769 on Wilkes and the Middlesex election, but did not attend the Opposition dinners of May 1769 and January 1770. His name is rarely mentioned in the correspondence of Opposition leaders, yet he seems to have achieved a certain prominence—possibly through his father's close connexion with Grenville. On 25 and 31 Jan. 1770 he seconded the Opposition motions in the committee on the state of the nation, but his speeches are not reported in Cavendish's very full notes of these debates.

In 1770 Hampden apparently went abroad and did not return until 1772, during which time Grenville died and most of his followers went over to the court. In Robinson's survey on the royal marriage bill, March 1772, Hampden is listed as 'doubtful, present'. And here is Lady Temple's report of his speech of 11 Mar. on the bill:[1]

> Mr. Hampden spoke against the whole of the bill, said he was an independent man, had seen very few people since his return, that he found some of his friends in a very different situation from that he left them in, he did not know how it came about. That he found himself so happy in a marriage of choice that he could not but think it the greatest hardship to debar a person from making their own felicity, that he could not understand the King ever had a right to break or hinder marriages, that his consent might be asked in form just as his Dutch relations sent to him for his consent whenever they married . . . That he was very much hurt to vote contrary to his father, but his conscience would not let him do otherwise. Then run into vast encomiums of his father's ability and services to the state, and seemed to think that he had not been paid for them. In short, he talked a great deal too much of his father and himself, but they gave him a good hearing, and thought it upon the whole a spirited speech.

In the divisions of 26 Apr. 1773 (Wilkes) and 25 Feb. 1774 (Grenville's Act) he voted against the court; and in Robinson's list of September 1774 was classed as 'contra'.

In 1774 he unsuccessfully contested Bedfordshire while his brother contested Lewes; and in 1779 stood for Buckinghamshire but withdrew before the poll. As a peer he voted for Fox's East India bill, and opposed Pitt until the French Revolution.

He died 20 Aug. 1824.

[1] To Ld. Temple, 12 Mar. 1772, Grenville mss (JM).

J.B.

## HANBURY, Capel (1707–65), of Pontypool, Mon.

LEOMINSTER 1741–1747
MONMOUTHSHIRE 1747–7 Dec. 1765

*b.* 2 Dec. 1707, 2nd surv. s. of John Hanbury, M.P., by Bridget, da. and coh. of Sir Edward Ayscough of South Kelsey, Lincs.; bro. of Charles Hanbury Williams (q.v.). *educ.* Ch. Ch. Oxf. 1723. *m.* 7 Oct. 1743, Hon. Jane Tracy, da. of Thomas Charles, 5th Visct. Tracy, 1s. 2da. *suc.* bro. 1 Oct. 1739.

Hanbury inherited from his brother large estates in Monmouthshire, to which he added considerably, and forges, furnaces, and iron works at Pontypool,[1] started by his family in the 16th century. In Parliament, Hanbury was an 'Old Whig' voting steadily with the Government. In 1761 he received Newcastle's parliamentary whip through Andrew Stone; in September 1762 he is again marked as 'to be sent for' by 'Duke of Newcastle, Mr. Stone'; and in the list of 13 Nov. is counted by Newcastle as on his side. He was absent from the divisions on the peace preliminaries—he wrote to James West from Pontypool, 23 Jan. 1763: 'I have now been nine weeks in my bed, and am but just . . . recovered so much as to sit up.'[2] Both in this letter and another of 1 Feb. he mentions having had letters from Henry Fox (a friend of his brother Charles Hanbury Williams), who was obviously trying to gain him over to the Government side. On 17 Mar. 1763, Fox, when recommending Hanbury's nominee for surveyor of the port of Chepstow, wrote to Bute: 'Mr. Hanbury has great right to ask favour of this kind having come to town in a very bad state of health on purpose to attend.'[3] Soon after that a difference must have arisen between them: Fox left for abroad on 11 May, and in the parliamentary list drawn up for Bute in December 1761 but used by Jenkinson till November 1763, the remark appears against Hanbury: 'Fox has quarrelled with him'; and a 'doubtful' is added in Jenkinson's hand. In fact, he joined the Opposition over Wilkes and general warrants; appears as voting with them in all four extant division lists (15 Nov. 1763 and 6, 15, and 18 Feb. 1764); and on 10 May is included by Newcastle among his 'sure friends'. Rockingham classed him in July 1765 as 'pro'.

Although not a Dissenter, he sympathized with them and, during Newcastle's tenure of the Treasury, drew from secret service money £100 a year 'for the Dissenting ministers in Monmouthshire'.[4]

The bounty was not applied for under the Bute and Grenville Administrations.[5] On 12 Oct. 1765 Newcastle included it among payments 'particularly recommended' to Rockingham, marking that none had been received since he left the Treasury,[6] but no such payment appears in Rockingham's secret service accounts—possibly because Hanbury's death intervened. He died 7 Dec. 1765.

[1] A. A. Locke, *Hanbury Fam.* i. 165–7. [2] West mss at Alscott. [3] Bute mss. [4] Namier, *Structure*; Add. 32906, f. 88. [5] List at Windsor in C. Jenkinson's handwriting of persons who have not applied for 'private salaries'. [6] Add. 32970, f. 296.

L.B.N.

## HANBURY, John (1744–84), of Pontypool, Mon.

MONMOUTHSHIRE   9 Jan. 1766–6 Apr. 1784

*b.* 6 Aug. 1744, o.s. of Capel Hanbury (q.v.). *educ.* Eton 1753. *m.* 12 Feb. 1774, Jane, da. of Morgan Lewis of St. Pierre, Mon., 3s. *suc.* fa. 7 Dec. 1765.

The Hanburys had large estates in Monmouthshire and were proprietors of extensive ironworks at Pontypool. The family had held a county seat since 1720, and John Hanbury's election on his father's death was popular and unanimous.[1] In Parliament Hanbury, like his father, was one of the independent Members attached to the Rockingham group, and he voted steadily with Opposition from 1766 until the fall of the North ministry in 1782. Surviving division lists indicate that he attended regularly at times of crisis: he was in the minority in all five divisions on Wilkes in 1769, and was present at the Opposition dinner at the end of the session; he was present at four of the five important divisions in 1780, and at all five in 1782. That Hanbury had inherited also his father's sympathy with nonconformists is suggested by his vote of 1772 in the minority over the 39 Articles.

Hanbury doubtless supported the Rockingham ministry of 1782, but his independence was shown when Fox led the former Rockinghams into opposition to the Shelburne Administration. Hanbury voted for that ministry over the peace on 18 Feb. 1783, although John Robinson in the next month reckoned him a follower of Fox. Hanbury, too, was one of the Coalition supporters who voted on 7 May for Pitt's proposals on parliamentary reform. He was absent during the important session of 1783–4, Robinson carefully noting the reason:[2] 'Mr. Hanbury is in a very ill state of health, and for that and other causes he is gone abroad. His life has been thought precarious for some time.'

He died at Rouen on 6 Apr. 1784, two days before his fifth unopposed return for Monmouthshire.

[1] NLW, Tredegar mss 66/6. [2] Laprade, 68.

P.D.G.T.

## HANBURY WILLIAMS, Sir Charles (1708–59), of Coldbrook, Mon.

MONMOUTHSHIRE   6 Mar. 1735–1747
LEOMINSTER                1754–2 Nov. 1759

*b.* 8 Dec. 1708, 3rd surv. s. of John Hanbury of Pontypool, Mon. and bro. of Capel Hanbury (q.v.). *educ.* Eton 1720; Grand Tour (Belgium, Switzerland, Italy) 1724–1726. Assumed add. name of Williams in 1729 in accordance with will of his godfa. Charles Williams, whose property he inherited. *m.* 1 July 1732, Lady Frances Coningsby, da. and h. of Thomas, 1st Earl of Coningsby, 2da. K.B. 20 Oct. 1744.

Paymaster of marines Nov. 1739–47; ld. lt. Herefs. July 1742–7; envoy at Dresden 1747–9, 1751–5; envoy at Berlin 1750–1; ambassador at St. Petersburg 1755–7.

Hanbury Williams was well-known as a diplomatist and man of letters. He was returned for Leominster, where he was high steward, on the interest of his wife's estate of Hampton Court, Herefordshire. He left England in August 1754, before the new Parliament assembled, and when he returned in February 1758 was insane and unable to take any part in public life. After a partial recovery in the summer of 1758, he became ill again in the December, and died by his own hand on 2 Nov. 1759.

J.A.C.

## HANGER, Gabriel (1697–1773), of Cannon Place, Bray, Berks. and Kempsford Hall, Glos.

MAIDSTONE     25 Apr. 1753–1761
BRIDGWATER   21 Nov. 1763–1768

*b.* 9 Jan. 1697, 1st surv. s. of Sir George Hanger of Driffield Hall, Glos., Turkey merchant, by Anne, da. and coh. of Sir John Beale, 1st Bt., of Farningham, Kent. *m.* 18 Jan. 1736, Elizabeth, da. and h. of Richard Bond of Cobrey Court, Herefs., 3s. 1da. *suc.* fa. 1731, and to Coleraine estates on *d.* of his cos. Anne, wid. of Henry Hare, 3rd Baron Coleraine [I] 1754; *cr.* Baron Coleraine [I] 26 Feb. 1762.

Entered Bengal establishment of E.I. Co. 1714, factor 1718, junior merchant 1722, senior merchant 1724.

Hanger resigned from the East India Company on the death of his elder brother in 1725 and returned to England. He first stood for Parliament in 1753 at Maidstone, where he had some local connexions, but he seems to have owed his election to Lord Romney. At the general election Hanger stood jointly with Lord Guernsey, defeating Abraham Hume, who was supported by Newcastle. He was classed by Dupplin as a Tory, and was one of the Tories who voted with Newcastle's friends, 12 Mar. 1755, on the Mitchell election petition.

On 12 Dec. 1760 Hanger applied to Newcastle for the peerage of Coleraine to be re-created in his favour:[1]

No one can be more zealously attached to his Majesty and his most illustrious family than I am, and

I have a fortune equal to that or almost any title of nobility whatever. I have been in Parliament near ten years, and propose being in it again and never did ask your Grace or anybody for anything yet.

He stood again at Maidstone in 1761 on Lord Romney's interest, but was defeated. On 14 Apr. 1761 he renewed his claim for a peerage, this time to Bute:[2] 'I have been in two Parliaments, and never once to the best of my knowledge all the time, ever gave a vote that I thought was contrary to the true interest of my country.' Before the end of the year he was promised the title of Coleraine.

He commenced an election petition for Maidstone, but dropped it; and on 18 Dec. 1761 sounded Bute on the chances of Government support at Bath.[3] In April 1763 he began a canvass of Gloucestershire, but withdrew when he found how little support he would receive. He wrote to Bute on 6 May, just after his resignation:[4]

I shall detain your Lordship only to ask the favour of you to mention me to the gentlemen in Administration as very desirous of coming into Parliament, cost what it will, on purpose to show my duty to his Majesty and my attachment to his measures, in opposition to that wicked cabal and seditious train of libels that are every day publishing to destroy the quiet of the best Prince and the rights and privileges of the happiest people under heaven.

He was recommended to Lord Egmont by Grenville for the seat at Bridgwater.[5]

Coleraine voted for the repeal of the cider tax on 10 Feb. 1764, but with Administration over general warrants on 18 Feb., and in July 1765 was classed by Rockingham as 'contra'. He does not appear in the printed list of those who voted against the repeal of the Stamp Act on 22 Feb. 1766, but is included in the second of Sir William Meredith's lists of the minority. On 28 Apr. and 12 May 1766 he voted against the window tax, and on 9 Dec. 1766 spoke against Chatham's East India proposals. He voted against the land tax, 27 Feb. 1767.

He did not stand at the general election of 1768, and died 24 Jan. 1773.

[1] Add. 32916, f. 15. [2] Bute mss. [3] Egremont to Bute, 25 Apr. 1761, ibid. [4] Ibid. [5] Grenville to Egmont, 1 Nov. 1763, Grenville letter bk.

A.N.N.

## HANGER, Hon. William (1744–1814).

| EAST RETFORD | 2 Feb. 1775–Feb. 1778 |
| ALDBOROUGH | 6 Mar. 1778–1780 |
| MITCHELL | 1780–1784 |

*b.* 6 Aug. 1744, 2nd surv. s. of Gabriel, 1st Baron Coleraine [I] (q.v.). *educ.* Reading sch.; Queen's, Oxf. 1761. *unm. suc.* bro. 4 Dec. 1794.

Cornet R. Horse Gds. 1763, lt. 1765, capt. 1772; ret. July 1776.

Hanger, a rake and gambler, owed his seat in

Parliament to his friendship with Henry Pelham Clinton, Duke of Newcastle, and may have obtained it to avoid his creditors. In August 1774 George Selwyn wrote to Lord Carlisle:[1] 'The Duke of Newcastle is to bring Will Hanger into Parliament, but what is to pay for his chair to go down to the House the Lord knows; they tell me that there is absolutely not a shilling left.' He was not elected until February 1775, apparently on the understanding that he would vacate the seat whenever Newcastle wished.[2] In 1778 he resigned in favour of Lord John Pelham Clinton, probably an arrangement to reinforce the Newcastle interest at East Retford before the general election, and was brought in immediately for Newcastle's pocket borough of Aldborough. During this Parliament Hanger attended regularly and consistently supported Administration, but is not known to have spoken.

In 1780 Hanger was returned by Lord Falmouth at Mitchell as a Government candidate. He supported North's Administration until the end, voted against Shelburne's peace preliminaries, and in Robinson's list of March 1783 was described as of Lord North's connexion. He voted with Pitt on parliamentary reform, 7 May 1783, and for Fox's East India bill, 27 Nov. 1783. Late in 1783 Robinson wrote in his survey that Lord Falmouth might 'probably be prevailed on to bring in a friend vice Hanger', and Hanger, who was classed as a Foxite by Robinson in January 1784 and in Stockdale's list of 19 Mar., did not stand at the general election of 1784.

He died 11 Dec. 1814.

[1] *HMC Carlisle*, 279. [2] Wm. Mellish to Newcastle, 8 Dec. 1776, Newcastle (Clumber) mss.

M.M.D.

## HANMER, Walden (1717–83), of Simpson, Bucks.

SUDBURY    1768–1774, 22 Mar. 1775–1780

*bap.* 19 Mar. 1717, o.s. of Job Hanmer, bencher of L. Inn, by Susanna, da. and h. of Thomas Walden of Simpson, Bucks. *educ.* Balliol, Oxf. 1736; L. Inn 1732, called 1741, bencher 1758. *m.* bef. 1747, Anne, da. and coh. of Henry Vere Graham of Holbrook, Suff., 5s. 1da. *suc.* fa. 1739, and to Hanmer estates in Flints. on *d.* of his cos. Humphrey Hanmer 1773. *cr.* Bt. 21 May 1774.

In 1761 Hanmer, with the support of part of the corporation, stood at Bedford in opposition to Francis Herne, but declined after the first day's poll. In 1766 he unsuccessfully applied to George Grenville for a Welsh judgeship.[1] He considered standing for Bedford again in 1768, and seems to have been well received by the Duke of Bedford,[2] but eventually stood for Sudbury and was returned after a contest. In Parliament he regularly voted with the Administration. In 1774 he again contested Sudbury, and, defeated at the poll, was seated on petition. He again supported Administration, but towards the end of the Parliament seems to have attended infrequently. There is no record of his having spoken in the House. He did not stand again in 1780, and died 20 Oct. 1783.

¹ Grenville to Hanmer, 19 Jan. 1766, Grenville letter bk. ² Same to same, 27 Sept. 1767, ibid.

M.M.D.

**HANNAY, Sir Samuel,** 3rd Bt. (c.1742–90), of Kirkdale, Kirkcudbright, and Philpot Lane, Fenchurch St., London.

CAMELFORD 5 July 1784–11 Dec. 1790

*b.* c.1742, 2nd s. of W. Hannay of Kirkdale by Margaret, da. of Rev. Patrick Johnston of Girthon, Kirkcudbright. *m.* 1768, Mary, da. of Dr. Robert Meade, 1s. 2da. 26 Sept. 1783 served heir to Sir Robert Hannay, 1st Bt., who *d.* 1658, the baronetcy having been dormant since 1689.

The *Gentleman's Magazine* (1790, p. 1151), in Hannay's obituary note, describes him as 'formerly an eminent chemist'; in the London directories, from 1765 onwards, he appears merely as a merchant; but in 1790 in partnership with William Duncan as a drug merchant. His brother Alexander was a lieutenant-colonel in the Indian army; another brother, Ramsay, was in trade from India to China. Samuel Hannay himself had important Indian (City and shipping) interests; he was one of the creditors of the Nawab of Arcot.¹

In 1784 Hannay was on the list of Government candidates recommended by Richard Atkinson, and was one of those willing to pay £2,000 or £2,500 or perhaps £3,000.² He stood at Ilchester but was defeated; next, Jonathan Phillips vacated for him the seat at Camelford. He voted with Pitt over Richmond's fortifications plan, 27 Feb. 1786, and the impeachment of Impey, 9 May 1788, but left him during the Regency crisis together with his colleague at Camelford, James Macpherson, 'both of whom were annoyed because Pitt had refused to allow Sir John Macpherson to return to India'.³ 'Sir John Macpherson', wrote James Grant to Lord Cornwallis, 18 Mar. 1789, ' . . . took the opportunity of going over to the Rising Sun in the first boat . . . he carried off his namesake and Sir Samuel Hannay.'⁴

Hannay died 11 Dec. 1790.

¹ C. H. Philips, *E.I. Co. 1784–1834*, p. 30. ² Laprade, 126–9. ³ Philips, 64. ⁴ *Cornwallis Corresp.* i. 448.

L.B.N.

**HARBORD, Harbord** (1734–1810), of Gunton Hall and Suffield, Norf.

NORWICH 8 Dec. 1756–21 Aug. 1786

*b.* 15 Jan. 1734, 1st s. of William Morden of Gunton (later Sir William Harbord, 1st Bt., M.P.) by Elizabeth, da. of Robert Britiffe of Baconsthorpe, Norf. Took name of Harbord 1742 under will of his gt.-uncle Harbord Harbord, M.P. *educ.* Christ's, Camb. 1752. *m.* 7 Oct. 1760, Mary, da. and coh. of Sir Ralph Assheton, 3rd Bt., of Middleton, Lancs., 3s. 3da. *suc.* fa. as 2nd Bt. 17 Feb. 1770; *cr.* Baron Suffield 21 Aug. 1786.

Harbord came of a rich and influential Norfolk family, and in 1756 was returned unopposed for Norwich with the support of his cousin the second Lord Buckinghamshire. 'It is true indeed my son is very young', wrote Sir William Harbord to Newcastle, 30 Sept. 1756,¹

but bred in the same principles with his father who for many years together in Parliament invariably supported the measures of the then Administration, may he have an opportunity of performing the same with regard to the present.

In fact throughout his parliamentary career Harbord followed his own thoroughly independent line. In 1761 Newcastle after some hesitation marked him as doubtful.² He does not appear in Fox's list of Members favourable to the peace preliminaries, December 1762, nor did he vote against them. Bute, believing that he would follow Buckinghamshire in supporting Administration, in December 1762 offered to make him a groom of the bedchamber, but Harbord declined on the grounds that his accepting might 'foment divisions' amongst his constituents.³ In the autumn of 1763 he was classed by Jenkinson as an Administration supporter, and he does not appear in the minority list on Wilkes, 15 Nov. 1763; but he voted with the Opposition over general warrants, 6, 15 and 18 Feb. 1764; was included in Newcastle's list of 'sure' friends, 10 May 1764, and in Rockingham's lists of July 1765 and November 1766 as a supporter. He voted against the Administration on the land tax, 27 Feb. 1767. Before the general election of 1768 Buckinghamshire suggested that Harbord should decline, but apparently did not press the point, and he topped the poll with a large majority. Henceforth he voted regularly with the Opposition.

Harbord was returned unopposed in 1774. In 1780, though deserted by some of his original supporters, his personal influence was sufficient to return him at the top of the poll with a large majority. *The English Chronicle* wrote of him shortly afterwards:

In private life he is a kind of rustic *despot*—rigid to his tenants, tyrannic and lofty to his immediate adherents, and exact to a degree of puerility, in all the *game laws*; but as a compensation for these defects he is in his public conduct the friend to *freedom*, and votes invariably on the side of liberty and patriotism.

Harbord voted for Shelburne's peace preliminaries, 18 Feb. 1783; and for Pitt's proposals for parliamentary reform, 7 May 1783. He did not vote on Fox's East India bill, 27 Nov. 1783, but in Robinson's list of January 1784 was classed as 'pro', and henceforth supported Pitt's Administration.

Less than half a dozen speeches by Harbord, on minor matters, are reported during his thirty years in the House.

He died 4 Feb. 1810.

¹ Add. 32867, ff. 482–3. ² Add. 33000, ff. 153–61. ³ Harbord to Bute, 6 Jan. 1763, Bute mss.

B.H.

## HARCOURT, George Simon, Visct. Nuneham (1736–1809).

ST. ALBANS 1761–1768

*b.* 1 Aug. 1736, 1st s. of Simon, 1st Earl Harcourt, by Rebecca, da. and h. of Charles Samborne le Bas, of Pipewell Abbey, Northants. *educ.* Westminster 1746–1748; Grand Tour (Germany and Italy) 1754–6. *m.* 26 Sept. 1765, his 1st cos. Hon. Elizabeth Venables Vernon, da. of George, 1st Lord Vernon (q.v.), *s.p. suc.* fa. as 2nd Earl 16 Sept. 1777.

Master of the horse to the Queen 1790–d.

Lord Nuneham was returned after a contest on the Spencer interest at St. Albans. His father was a courtier: had been governor to George III when Prince of Wales, was sent to Mecklenburg in 1761 to escort the future Queen to England, and was appointed her master of the horse. Naturally Nuneham was expected to adhere to the court. In Bute's list of 1761 he is marked 'Bute', and he appears in Fox's list of Members favourable to the peace preliminaries. On 7 Nov. 1762 Harcourt wrote to Charles Jenkinson:

I have wrote to Lord Bute about Lord Nuneham, but my letter to his Lordship is far from being pressing. I have expressed my desire to see Lord Nuneham in his Majesty's service but I have left it entirely at large, to take place now, or hereafter, whichever may be most convenient to his Majesty or his Administration.

Nuneham received no appointment, and probably did not desire one. He was of little political consequence. Harcourt said in December 1762 'that Lord Nuneham did not open his mouth in the House', and there is no record of his speaking afterwards.¹

He supported the Grenville Administration, but in the division of 18 Feb. 1764 on general warrants voted against them. The same day Harcourt wrote to the King:²

I am under such perturbation of mind, and so completely unhappy on account of Lord Nuneham who

(I find) has taken a part in the last question so contrary to your Majesty's interest, so contrary to the wellbeing of this country, and so diametrically to my own principles, that I think myself called upon in duty and honour to declare my disapprobation of it.

Lord Nuneham has hitherto attended so little to affairs of Government that I fear he has allowed himself to be imposed upon by those who have but too well succeeded in making him and other unwary people the dupes of faction and the tools of ambition.

The King assured Harcourt that no blame should be laid to his account, and the incident passed over without doing father or son any harm. It does not appear that Nuneham ever repented his vote, but he took care not to offend again. After his marriage in September 1765 he went abroad, and did not return to England until the end of 1766. His only other recorded vote in the Commons was with Administration on the land tax, 27 Feb. 1767.

Horace Walpole wrote³ about Nuneham after he had become a peer:

The new Earl was a most honest man, and, being by principle averse to the measures of the court, had quitted the House of Commons because he would not support the measures and would not differ with his father.

'I have neither spirits nor constitution', wrote Nuneham to Harcourt, 10 June 1772,⁴ 'to engage in the hurry and bustle, nor to support the constraint of a public scene.' But he had political opinions: he was a friend of Mrs. Catherine Macaulay, the Radical, and an admirer and correspondent of Rousseau. His first vote in the House of Lords was against the court on the Address, 20 Nov. 1777, and he consistently opposed the American war. Neither he nor his wife went to court until December 1783, when Harcourt refused the offer of the embassy to Spain but accepted for his wife a place in the Queen's bedchamber. Then, writes Walpole (but this was after he had quarrelled with Harcourt),⁵ 'she and her Lord became a proverb even to courtiers, of the most servile attachment to their Majesties'. The attachment, at least, is proved by the number of letters addressed to them by members of the royal family.⁶

Harcourt died 20 Apr. 1809.

¹ *Jenkinson Pprs.* 82, 101. ² Ibid. 267. ³ *Last Jnls.* ii. 75. ⁴ *Harcourt Pprs.* iii. 113. ⁵ Note by Walpole on his letter to Mason of 2 Feb. 1784, Yale ed. xxix. 332. ⁶ *Harcourt Pprs.* vi.

J.B.

## HARCOURT, John (*d.*?1826), of Wall Hall, Kent.

ILCHESTER 8 Feb. 1785–22 Feb. 1786, 1790–1796
LEOMINSTER 1812–1818, 15 Feb. 1819–1820

*m.* c.1790, Mary ?Ainslie,¹ 2s.

Harcourt was described as a banker, and 'related to the noble family of the same name'² (a Harcourt was a partner in the banking house of Sansom and

Co. of Lombard Street from 1791 to 1801). In 1784 Harcourt unsuccessfully contested Ilchester, where he had 'purchased nominally' a 'considerable property in land', in opposition to the Lockyer interest. He tried again on a vacancy in February 1785, and 'having the returning officer he prevailed by a gross and illegal procedure'.[3] A petition was lodged against his return; and he protested in the House on 28 Feb. 1785 that the day chosen for the hearing was inconvenient. Fox supported his case; and that order was discharged on the motion of William Eden by 130 votes to 97. He was nevertheless finally unseated.

It was alleged that the real owner of the Ilchester properties was a London attorney, Richard Troward; and from 1785 he and Harcourt were engaged in highly dubious transactions for their sale to Samuel Smith (q.v.), who had succeeded to the Lockyer interest. Nevertheless in the general election of 1790, Harcourt again secured his return for the borough.

He died at St. Omer, France, in December 1825 or January 1826.[4]

[1] The two sons, John Johnson and George Simon, used the surname Ainslie until 1816 and 1825 respectively: see *East India Register* and *Army Lists*. They and their mother are mentioned in Harcourt's will. [2] J. Wilson, *Biog. Index of House of Commons* (1808), pp. 87, 298. [3] Chatham Pprs. Memorandum by Samuel Smith. [4] PCC 157 Sawbey.

M.H.P.

## HARCOURT, Richard (?1714–77), of Wigsell, Suss.

SUSSEX 9 Dec. 1768–1774

*b.* ?1714, o.s. of Richard Harcourt, barrister, of Pendley, Herts. by his cos. Elizabeth, da. of Sir Philip Harcourt, sis. of Simon, 1st Visct. Harcourt. *educ.* Westminster 1721, aged 7; B.N.C. Oxf. 6 June 1729, aged 15; I. Temple 1729, called 1737. *m.* Phoebe, da. of Charles Palmer, sis. of Sir Charles Palmer, 5th Bt., 2da. *suc.* fa. 1728.

Harcourt, returned unopposed for Sussex at a by-election, was a comparative newcomer in the county. From 1768 to 1772 no vote by him is recorded, but he voted with the court on the naval captains' petition, 9 Feb. 1773, and on Grenville's Act, 25 Feb. 1774, and on the eve of the general election was classed by Robinson as 'pro'. There is no record of his having spoken in the House.

By 1774 he seems to have become very unpopular in Sussex. At a county meeting on 27 Sept. a motion to thank him for his 'upright conduct in Parliament' and inviting him to stand again was rejected; and the *Sussex Weekly Advertiser* of 3 Oct. announced his withdrawal.

He died 2 May 1777.

J.B.

## HARCOURT, Hon. William (1743–1830).

OXFORD 1768–1774

*b.* 20 Mar. 1743, 2nd s. of Simon, 1st Earl Harcourt, and bro. of George Simon, Visct. Nuneham (q.v.). *m.* 3 Sept. 1778, Mary, da. of Rev. William Danby of Swinton, Yorks., wid. of Thomas Lockhart of Craig House, nr. Edinburgh, *s.p. suc.* bro. as 3rd Earl 20 Apr. 1809.

Ensign 1 Ft. Gds. 1759; capt. 16 Lt. Drag. 1759, 3 Drag. 1760; lt.-col. 31 Ft. 1764, 4 Lt. Drag. 1765, 16 Lt. Drag. 1768; col. 1777; col. 16 Lt. Drag. 1779–*d.*; maj.-gen. 1782; lt.-gen. 1793; gov. Fort William 1794–5, Hull 1795–1801; gen. 1798; gov. R. Military Coll. 1801–11, Portsmouth 1811–26; f.m. 1821; gov. Plymouth 1826–*d.*

Groom of the bedchamber 1766–1808; master of the robes 1808–9; master of the horse to the Queen 1809–18.

William Harcourt was returned for Oxford after a contest in 1768. In 1769 he voted with Administration over Wilkes and the Middlesex election; was classed by Robinson as 'pro, present' on the royal marriage bill; and his only other recorded vote was for the naval captains' petition (he was classed, however, as a friend to Government). There is no record of his having spoken in the House, and he seems to have shown little interest in politics. His father wrote about him from Paris to Charles Jenkinson, 24 Jan. 1770:

If the colonel was not a lazy fellow he would send me some accounts of what is passing. But so great is his aversion to writing that without an absolute necessity he never sets pen to paper.

He did not stand in 1774. Lord Harcourt wrote to Jenkinson, 10 Jan. 1775:

I am much obliged to you for apprizing me of Mr. Harcourt Powell's intention to offer his seat in Parliament to the colonel, who is less anxious about it than I am. Till I know what consideration he may expect for what he offers to give up, it is no easy matter to foresee the turn that this affair may take.

Possibly Powell asked too much; at any rate nothing came of this plan.[1] William Harcourt served in America 1776–7, and won great *éclat* by capturing the American general Charles Lee. In later years he lived near Windsor, and in 1787 Pitt suggested him to the King as a possible candidate for New Windsor.[2] But a dispute Harcourt had had with the corporation made him unsuitable, and the idea was dropped.

Harcourt died 17 June 1830.

[1] Add. 38206, f. 204; 38208, f. 123. [2] Pitt to the King, 24 June 1787, Royal archives, Windsor.

J.B.

## HARDINGE, George (1743–1816), of Pyrton, Wilts.

OLD SARUM 11 Mar. 1784–1802

*b.* 22 June 1743, 1st surv. s. of Nicholas Hardinge (q.v.). *educ.* Eton 1753–60; Trinity, Camb. 1761; M. Temple 1764, called 1769. *m.* 20 Oct. 1777, Lucy, da. and h. of Richard Long of Hinxton, Cambs., *s.p.*

K.C. 1782; bencher, M. Temple 1782, reader 1789, treasurer 1791.

Sec. of commissions to Lord Chancellor Camden 1766–70; commr. of bankruptcy 1771–82; solicitor-gen. to the Queen Apr. 1782–94, attorney-gen. 1794–1816; c.j. Brec. 1787–*d.*

Lord Camden, having on 16 Dec. 1783 heard Hardinge speak at the bar of the House of Lords as counsel for the directors of the East India Company, wrote to his daughter, Fanny Stewart:[1]

> I . . . am able to pronounce upon my judgement that in language wit and voice he has no superior at the bar . . . His fortune is made, let him take care he does not spoil it by levity and indiscretion.

And on 19 Mar. 1784, to her husband:

> That young man is mounting rapidly—he is brought into Parliament by Lord Camelford, and if he can learn a little discretion cannot fail of making a considerable figure.

To others Hardinge, over forty, was no longer a 'young man'; and his 'levity' in the end prevented him from reaching the front rank of politics or of the law, or, for that matter, even in literature.

In the House he was a frequent speaker, of uneven quality. Daniel Pulteney, a good parliamentary observer, wrote on 1 June 1786 that Hardinge spoke 'very ably . . . better indeed than I could have ever imagined, as I have heard him very indifferent two or three times before'.[2] In politics he followed Camden and Pitt, but preserved a measure of independence towards them, and still more so toward his borough patron, Camelford. Having on 16 June 1784 voted for Sawbridge's motion in favour of parliamentary reform, the Member for Old Sarum offered his one and only 'constituent' to resign his seat.[3] When on 25 Jan. 1785 Pitt adumbrated his reform proposals, Hardinge again declared to Camelford his own 'democratical principles'.

> If, from your general wish to support that minister [replied Camelford] or from your attachment to Lord Camden, or from a conscientious opinion upon the subject, you cannot think as I do, at least absent yourself upon this occasion, and do not distress me so far as to make me appear to hold two languages, at the same time that you oppose one of the most decided political tenets I can ever form, and oppose it with the weapon I have put into your hands.

In the end Camelford left him free to act upon his own feeling, and in the crucial division of 18 Apr. 1785 Hardinge voted for reform.

When Mansfield's impending resignation opened a prospect of legal promotions, Camden wrote, on 1 June 1786, to Robert Stewart:[4]

> If poor George should get a Welsh judgeship in the scramble, he has not the spirit to push at any thing greater. Is it not strange he has fine parts and is the best speaker at the bar, yet will always be kept down below his merit, because he does not know how to feel his own importance or to improve his capacity by discretion. I am sorry for it—he has a great many good qualities and the best disposition in the world.

There was even more to him as shown by the letter he wrote to Sir Lloyd Kenyon on 29 June 1787:[5]

> I have a serious disagreement with my dear Lord Camden, whom I love and revere with more than filial affection . . . in offending him I have made a painful sacrifice to public honour . . . He has pressed me to supersede an able and useful officer . . . for the sake of a new appointment in favour of a person recommended by him. Usage in modern times . . . is uniform against any such removals . . . To say the truth, if usage could justify it upon my circuit, I would not act upon it, but would endeavour to begin a usage the other way.

When in 1789 the lord chancellorship of Ireland was about to fall vacant, Camden pressed Hardinge's candidature for it. But Buckingham, the lord lieutenant, refused to have him—'this arrangement is openly talked of here and with the contempt it merits.'[6]

In December 1788 Hardinge strongly supported Pitt over the Regency bill. None the less Camelford wrote to him that should Pitt be dismissed and a dissolution follow, and Pitt then call on him to return for Old Sarum 'two *public men*, who are necessary to him in Parliament, and for whom he can find room nowhere else', he would have to drop Hardinge who could give but one answer, and in fact had to be persuaded to continue at Old Sarum at the next general election.

He died 26 Apr. 1816.[7] Perhaps the best appraisal of the man is that of the *Annual Biography and Obituary* (1817, i. 299):

> So various were his powers that he was a judge, a Member of Parliament, a poet, a prose writer, and a writer of sermons. He occasionally exhibited great eloquence; no one had a finer choice of words and few a more graceful delivery. His voice was also sonorous, his imagery rich and classical, his narrative clear and perspicuous. He was possessed of abilities of the highest order, and great expectations were formed as to his career in the legal profession, but his natural indolence, blended with his intense regard for poetry, doomed these to failure.

[1] 25 Jan. 1784, Camden mss at Bayham Abbey. [2] *HMC Rutland*, iii. 306. [3] 58 letters from Camelford to Hardinge are printed in Nichols, *Lit. Illustrations*, vi. [4] Camden mss. [5] *HMC Kenyon*, 523–4. [6] *HMC Fortescue*, i. 465. [7] A great many letters from Hardinge on literary and biographical subjects are printed by Nichols in his *Lit. Anecs.* and *Lit. Illustrations*. A collection of his *Miscellaneous Works* in 3 vols. was printed in 1818 with intro. by John Nichols. The ms of Hardinge's unfinished biography of Lord Camden is among the Bayham Abbey mss.

L.B.N.

## HARDINGE, Nicholas (1699–1758), of Kingston-upon-Thames, Surr.

EYE 15 Feb. 1748–9 Apr. 1758

*b.* 7 Feb. 1699, 1st s. of Rev. Gideon Hardinge, vicar of Kingston-upon-Thames, by his w. Mary Westbrooke. *educ.* Eton c.1711–18; King's, Camb. 1718, fellow 1722; M. Temple 1721, called 1725. *m.* 19 Dec. 1738, Jane, da. of Sir John Pratt, l.c.j. of the King's bench 1718–25, sis. of Charles, 1st Earl Camden (q.v.), 9s. 3da.

Clerk of House of Commons 1731–48; law reader to the Duke of Cumberland 1732; attorney-gen. to the Duke 1733; jt. sec. to Treasury 1752–*d.*

Hardinge, a scholar and an antiquary, sat at Eye on the interest of Lord Cornwallis. According to John Nichols, he had 'no talents or courage for eloquence', but as secretary to the Treasury was 'laborious, able, zealous and so honest that he had many enemies'.[1] He died 9 Apr. 1758.

[1] *Lit. Anecs.* v. 339–40.

L.B.N.

## HARDMAN, John (c.1694–1755), of Allerton Hall, nr. Liverpool.

LIVERPOOL 1754–6 Dec. 1755

*b.* c.1694, 2nd s. of Richard Hardman of Liverpool merchant, by Elizabeth, da. of James Fernyside. *m.* a lady named Kockshead, *s.p.*

Hardman was a Liverpool merchant, and during the decade preceding his entry into Parliament he repeatedly attended or addressed the Board of Trade on behalf of the corporation of Liverpool or of Liverpool merchants. A ship-owner, he was engaged in the triangular trade between England, West Africa, and the West Indies,[1] and had considerable knowledge of African and American trade, though, as he stated when giving evidence before the House of Commons, 7 Mar. 1750, he had 'never been abroad'.

In 1754 he was returned head of the poll, and was classed by Dupplin as a Government supporter. But he was a sick man—'I was very poorly at London,' he wrote to Robert Nugent, 15 Apr. 1755, 'and my health deprived me of all spirits.'[2] He died 6 Dec. 1755.

[1] *CJ,* xxii. 567. [2] C. Nugent, *Mem. Earl Nugent,* 263.

L.B.N.

## HARDY, Sir Charles (c.1714–80).

ROCHESTER 23 Mar. 1764–1768
PLYMOUTH 10 Aug. 1771–19 May 1780

*b.* c.1714, 2nd s. of V.-Adm. Charles Hardy by Elizabeth, da. of Josiah Burchett, M.P., sec. of the Admiralty. *m.* (1) July 1749, Mary, da. of Bartholomew Tate of Delapré, Northants., *s.p.*; (2) 4 Jan. 1759, Catherine, da. of Temple Stanyan, 3s. 2da. Kntd. 20 Apr. 1755.

Capt. R. N. 1741; r.-adm. 1756; v.-adm. 1759; adm. 1770.

Gov. New York 1755–7; gov. Greenwich Hosp. 1771–*d.*; c.-in-c. Channel fleet 1779–80.

After an unsuccessful expedition to Louisbourg in 1757, Hardy took part in its capture by Boscawen in 1758. In 1759 he was appointed second to Hawke in command of the Channel fleet; served at the battle of Quiberon Bay, and continued under Hawke till the end of the war.

In 1764 Hardy was returned unopposed for Rochester on the recommendation of Lord Halifax.[1] He was classed by Rockingham in July 1765 as 'contra'; voted for the Opposition motion for American papers, 18 Dec. 1765; and in the debate of 18 Feb. 1766 on the repeal of the Stamp Act, gave an account of the illicit trade of America 'which the merchants and ministry by no means approved';[2] but he does not appear in the lists of those voting against the repeal, 22 Feb. 1766. Hardy voted with Opposition on the land tax, 27 Feb. 1767, and nullum tempus, 17 Feb. 1768. He does not seem to have tried to re-enter Parliament at the general election, but in 1771 was returned unopposed at Plymouth, and henceforth consistently supported North's Administration.

On 9 Mar. 1779, towards the end of Keppel's court martial, the King wrote to North that Hardy had 'been with Lord Sandwich to offer in the most ardent manner his services' and 'rather than not serve would resign the government of Greenwich Hospital';[3] and on Keppel's resignation he took over command of the Channel fleet. He was also offered a seat at the Admiralty Board, but, wrote North to Sandwich, 9 Apr. 1779,[4]

declines . . . unless he can at the same time enjoy the commission of lieutenant-general of marines, as Sir Hugh Palliser did. He said that upon the return of peace he with his large family would feel very sensibly the diminution he would suffer by having exchanged the government of Greenwich Hospital for a seat at the Board of Admiralty. He added that he should be very happy to have both the offices . . . I did not offer him the marines, so cannot say whether he would not accept of that employment, but the Admiralty he declined.

Hardy's appointment as commander-in-chief was used by the Opposition as further ammunition against Sandwich and the Administration, and on 30 Mar. 1779 the Duke of Richmond declared in the House of Lords:[5]

The nation has lost Lord Howe and Admiral Keppel, the nation in their stead has got Sir Charles Hardy, the governor of Greenwich Hospital, whom they have dragged from his final retreat to the public service. What was the consequence? The whole body of officers was disgusted at so extraordinary arrangement of command.

Sir Charles Hardy had not been at sea for almost twenty years. He was arrived at a period of life little calculated for active service.

Hardy's own senior captain, Richard Kempenfelt, wrote to his friend Charles Middleton on 6 Aug.:[6]

We are every day from morning to night plagued with minutiae, whilst the essentials are totally neglected. An odd obstinacy and way of negating everything proposed makes all advice useless. There is a fund of good nature in the man, but not one grain of the commander-in-chief . . . My God, what have your great people done by such an appointment?

On the appearance of the combined Spanish and French fleets, superior in numbers to the British, Hardy, according to Charnock,[7]

prudently resolved to act merely on the defensive instead of risking an encounter, which, if unsuccessful, would have been productive at least of the greatest national alarm, if not actual misfortune. The event, if not glorious, was not unfortunate.

But Hardy was severely criticized, and in the House on 1 Dec. 1779 James Luttrell demanded an inquiry. Hardy, in his only reported speech during this Parliament, replied with a long account of the affair:[8]

On the whole he could affirm that although he did not force them to action, battle was offered to them, and if they declined it, it might with equal truth be said that the combined fleet fled from the British as the British from the combined fleet.

Hardy struck his flag at the close of the season but was about to resume command when he died on 19 May 1780.

[1] Add. 32972, f. 61. [2] Harris's 'Debates'. [3] Fortescue, iv. 49, misdated 1778; *Sandwich Pprs.* (Navy Rec. Soc. lxxi), ii. 235. [4] *Sandwich Pprs.*, ii. 248. [5] Almon, xiv. 205. [6] *Barham Letters* (Navy Rec. Soc. xxxii), 293. [7] *Biog. Navalis*, v. 103. [8] Almon, xvi. 72.

M.M.D.

## HARE, James (1747–1804).

| STOCKBRIDGE | 5 May 1772–1774 |
| KNARESBOROUGH | 3 July 1781–17 Mar. 1804 |

*bap.* 9 Apr. 1747 at Somerton, Som., 2nd s. of Joseph and Frances Hare. *educ.* T. Hodgkinson's sch. at Exeter; Eton 1760–5; King's, Camb. 1765, fellow 1768–74; L. Inn. 1768. *m.* 21 Jan. 1774, Hannah, da. of Sir Abraham Hume, 1st Bt., sis. of Sir Abraham Hume, 2nd Bt. (qq.v.), 1 da. Hare and his wife soon separated; he had several children by subsequent liaisons.

A widely accepted identification of Hare, started by the obituary in the *Gentleman's Magazine* which placed him at Oxford, and elaborated by Foster who made him matriculate at Oxford six years after entering Parliament, is disproved by Austen-Leigh, Venn, and the Lincoln's Inn *Register*. However, the statement that his father was an apothecary was current among contemporaries. Martin Whish, who was with him at Eton, is quoted as saying that Hare was 'son to an apothecary at Wells in Somersetshire,

and had not a shilling of fortune'.[1] Mrs. Thrale, in *Thraliana*, 7 Mar. 1778:

The famous Mr. Hare is the son of an apothecary; remarkably lean, and has an odd way of dancing country dances, popping up, and popping down; this fellow, says George Selwyn, puts one for ever in mind of his father's pestle and mortar.

And Wraxall writes:[2] 'Hare was, I believe, like myself, a native of Bristol, and as I have been assured, of obscure origin.'

Unfavoured in his beginnings, Hare, a brilliant scholar, formed his connexions at Eton and Cambridge: and there emerged 'the Hare and many friends' (a saying of the Duchess of Gordon, repeated in almost every note on Hare). 'The child of whim'[3] and no toady, always looked after by friends —Charles Fox, Lord Carlisle, the Duke of Devonshire, etc.—he lived in the most fashionable set, doing no work and empty of achievement. It is impossible to recapture social charm or the flavour of warmed-up witticisms; but Wilberforce spoke of his 'captivating manner and charm'; Sir Thomas Lawrence described him as 'excelling all others in conversation'; and Horace Walpole, when a joke of Hare's was ascribed to him, protested: 'He has a great deal too much wit for me to presume to deck myself in his plumes, I who am a jackdaw to him.'[4] His company was in demand, and he was courted. Carlisle, in July 1772, felt hurt when Hare failed to visit Castle Howard—'one whom I have always looked upon and always treated as the warmest friend';[5] and a favourable opinion from him was valued by Georgiana Devonshire 'because . . . he has got good sense and good taste, but a difficulty in liking, that doubles the price of a praise'.[6]

Charles Fox, when warmly congratulated on his maiden speech, is said to have replied: 'Wait till you hear Hare';[7] but when returned for Stockbridge (probably on a remnant of the Fox interest in the borough) Hare 'wondered how any man could open his mouth in that place or keep it shut out of it'.[8] In the very full parliamentary reports for 1772–4 there is no trace of his having even attempted to speak; and his only recorded vote was given with the Government minority against perpetuating Grenville's Act—but this was the last time that Fox still voted with North. In 1774 Hare, jointly with Fox, stood on a hopeless interest at Pontefract; and Hare had no safe constituency for a hedge.

How Hare supported the expense of elections or of life in London is a mystery. On 18 Jan. 1774, three days before his marriage to the sister of Sir Abraham Hume, Selwyn wrote to Carlisle:[9]

If I was to credit his own insinuations, Hare is upon the point of bringing his affair to a conclusion . . . He drives about in an old chariot . . . with a servant of his own in livery; and this occasions so much speculation, that his great secret *diu celari non potest*. I would advise him to conclude as soon as he can this business; *sans cela la machine sera derangée.*

Wraxall's statement that the marriage 'brought him a very considerable fortune' is probably a guess; anyhow, it was not equal to the occasion. Selwyn wrote to Carlisle, 30 July 1774:

> There is reason . . . to fear for Hare. Boothby assures me that as yet no prejudice has been done to his fortune. I have my doubts of that, but am clear that he runs constant risk of being very uneasy. But there is no talking to him; he has imbibed so much of Charles's *ton* of *qu'importe, que cela peut mener a l'hôpital.*

And on 5 Dec. 1775 Carlisle inquired of Selwyn:

> What is Hare about? Lose much I hear he cannot; therefore, if he is not winning your money, I hope he is successful.

Selwyn replied on 9 Dec.:

> You ask what is Hare about? He is about town; he plays at night, but not very extravagantly; *il joue pourtant*, and what will be the end of him God knows . . . We should have been all better pleased, *s'il n'avoit jamais sorti de son état* . . . that he has been deluded, that he has been precipitated into what both his head and heart condemn, is what I am very sorry for . . . And yet . . . there is one spot which will be totally indelible . . . I . . . mean . . . in regard to his wife, for that is the heaviest charge against him.[10]

The next chapter in Hare's career was an attempt to obtain a diplomatic appointment.

> I have lost a great deal this winter [he wrote to Selwyn on 18 May 1779[11]] and, in considering my resources, very naturally looked to Carlisle . . . We could think of no better scheme than his asking Lord North to appoint me to fill one of the vacancies, either to Warsaw or Munich. He applied to Lord North; the chancellor seconded his application; and Eden, who sees Lord North frequently and familiarly, promised to give the thing as favourable a turn as he could. As yet we can get no answer, and I have found out that the old Fish [John Craufurd jun.] is trying to get the same appointment for the Colonel [James Craufurd].
> If I could get this appointment, it would be a comfortable provision till some of my friends are able to serve me at home . . . Carlisle . . . has acted with a degree of zeal and kindness that I never shall forget.

After long delays Hare obtained the appointment, but when he was to have kissed hands for it, was not in town.[12] Next, Hare obtained permission for personal reasons to defer his departure for Warsaw, and, on 26 Apr. 1780, he wrote again to Lord Stormont, secretary of state for the northern department:[13]

> I had flattered myself that I should have been by this time ready to . . . set out for Warsaw; but the extreme confusion of my affairs obliges me . . . to desire your Lordship's . . . indulgence, as it is quite impossible for me at present either to leave the country honourably, or to support myself suitable to my future abroad.

He was allowed a 'further lease' of two months, but when it expired, and he still found himself 'surrounded by the same embarrassments', his resignation was accepted, an event foreseen by his friends.[14]

In February 1781 Carlisle, now lord lieutenant of Ireland, offered Hare the Black Rod, in case of its becoming vacant; but Hare declined—the Duke of Devonshire, on hearing of Boyle Walsingham's death, offered to return Hare for Knaresborough, preferring him to 'many other competitors'.

> To any one in my circumstances [wrote Hare to Carlisle, 13 Feb.[15]] personal security is a great object, and grows every day more necessary; I did not therefore hesitate to accept this offer, which, though it by no means bids fair to enable me to live comfortably, will at least keep me out of jail. The Duke of Devonshire is so little subject to caprice, that I need not fear his leaving me out in the next Parliament; but, without being very sanguine, I may reckon on a seat for Knaresborough as a seat for life.
> I had much rather, on many accounts, remain out of Parliament, and the privilege of freedom from arrests is the only one I care a farthing for. There is no chance of my taking any pains to make myself master of the business that comes before the House, and in my opinion nothing can be more irksome than the attendance there to a person who takes no active part.

In London Hare shared with Fox a house in St. James's Street; and at Brooks's helped him and Fitzpatrick to hold a faro bank. 'Hare is . . . indefatigable', wrote Selwyn on 31 May 1781. 15 June: the bank won £2,300; Hare's share was one-twelfth, besides six guineas an hour for dealing. 18 June: 'the bank turns out to Hare better than an embassy to Warsaw'.[16] On 3 July, a week before the House was adjourned, Hare was returned for Knaresborough; left London in 'opulent circumstances'; stayed at Foxley; but having returned to London in October, 'lost near £4,000 in three nights to a set of fellows' whom he had never seen before.[17]

In the House he voted with the Opposition in the divisions which brought down the North Government; but his most sustained effort was at Brooks's, 'in his semi-circular niche at the faro table, improving his fortune every deal'. He wrote from Foxley, 5 Jan. 1782: 'It is very pleasant to have such a retreat from the fatigue of dealing at faro, and the late hours that it occasions.' When the House re-assembled, and the political crisis thickened, even more of the 'drudgery of dealing' fell on Hare. On 1 Mar. Selwyn wrote to Carlisle:

> I own that to see Charles closeted every instant at Brooks's by one or the other, that he can neither punt nor deal for a quarter of an hour but he is obliged to give an audience, while Hare is whispering and standing behind him, like Jack Robinson, with a pencil and paper for mems., is to me a scene *la plus parfaitement comique que l'on puisse imaginer.*

Selwyn never liked Hare; but to hear Hare talk of 'executions' among placemen made him for once burst out about Hare to Carlisle.

> When people of low birth [he wrote on 30 Mar.] have by great good luck and a fortunate concurrence of events been able to obtain, from lively parts only, without any acquisitions which can be useful to the public, such situations as are due only to persons of rank, weight, and character, it is surely an easy task *not to be* insolent. It is all I require of them.[18]

Hare came out of the change of Administration empty-handed; and at the end of July he congratulated Fox 'on coming from the service of the King of England, once more to attend the King of Egypt'.[19] Nor did Hare obtain office under the Coalition; but he steadily voted with Fox both before and after: over Shelburne's peace preliminaries, the East India bill, and even in favour of Pitt's proposals of parliamentary reform, both 7 May 1783 and 18 Apr. 1785. He did not vote in the divisions on the Regency, 1788–9.

Hare died 17 Mar. 1804.

[1] *Farington Diary*, vii. 216. [2] *Mems.* iii. 384. [3] Duchess of Devonshire to her mother, Lady Spencer, 17 Oct. 1786, *Georgiana*, ed. Ld. Bessborough, 111. [4] *Farington Diary*, vi. 122, vii. 8; Walpole to Lady Ossory, 9 Sept. 1783. [5] Jesse, *Selwyn*, iii. 30. [6] *Georgiana*, 166. [7] *Gent. Mag.* 1804, p. 287. [8] *Farington Diary*, ii. 122. [9] *HMC Carlisle*, 263. [10] Ibid. 273, 308; Jesse, iii. 124. [11] Jesse, iv. 141–2. [12] Ibid. 223, 292. [13] SP 88/114. [14] *HMC Carlisle*, 436. [15] Ibid. 457. [16] Ibid. 488, 499, 501. [17] Hare to Carlisle, 29 Dec. 1781, ibid. 554. [18] Ibid. 564, 580, 586, 613. [19] *Auckland Corresp.* i. 15.

L.B.N.

## HARLEY, Edward, Lord Harley (1726–90).

HEREFORDSHIRE    1747–11 Apr. 1755

*b.* 2 Sept. 1726, 1st s. of Edward, 3rd Earl of Oxford, by Martha, da of John Morgan, M.P., of Tredegar, Mon.; bro. of Hon. Thomas Harley (q.v.). *educ.* Westminster 1735–44; Ch. Ch. Oxf. 1744. *m.* 11 July 1751, Susanna, da. of William Archer, M.P., of Welford, Berks., *s.p. suc.* fa. as 4th Earl 11 Apr. 1755.

High steward, Hereford 1755–*d.*; ld. of the bedchamber 1760–*d.*; ld. lt. Rad. 1766–*d.*

Harley was the only courtesy lord among the Tories returned in 1754. He had spoken repeatedly in his first Parliament, but no speech or vote of his is recorded during the year 1754–5.

He died 8 Oct. 1790.

J.B.

## HARLEY, Robert (?1706–74), of Eywood, Herefs.

LEOMINSTER    1734–1741, 29 Mar. 1742–1747
DROITWICH    1754–15 Mar. 1774

*b.* ?1706, 2nd s. of Edward Harley, M.P., of Eywood by Sarah, da. of Thomas Foley, M.P., of Witley, Worcs.; nephew of Robert, 1st Earl of Oxford and bro. of Edward, 3rd Earl. *educ.* Westminster c.1715–19; Ch. Ch. Oxf. 5 Mar. 1723, aged 16; L. Inn 1724, called 1730. *unm.*

Recorder, Leominster 1732–*d.*; bencher L. Inn 1751; recorder, Tewkesbury 1756–60 and 1764–*d.*

Harley was returned for Droitwich in 1754 on the Foley interest, and was classed by Dupplin as a Tory. He was not sent Newcastle's whip in 1761, but on 1 Nov. was recommended to Newcastle by Barrington for the commission of accounts as an 'unexceptionable man' who would do Newcastle 'no harm'.[1] In Bute's list he was also classed 'Tory', and in November 1762 was suggested by Bute to Fox as suitable to second the address of thanks for the peace preliminaries. Fox replied on 23 Nov.:[2]

> Mr. Harley has been here; I never saw a more sensible behaviour or a more obliging one. He thinks he can be of more use where he lives and that he has been of use by declaring himself unengaged. The seconding this motion he thought an honour, it was unexceptionable, that he wished to do all the service he could, and really did not think this the likeliest way to do it, and that was his only objection.

On 15 Feb. 1764 he voted against Grenville's Administration—his only known vote in the divisions over Wilkes and general warrants. Rockingham in July 1765 classed him as 'doubtful', and he voted against the repeal of the Stamp Act. In November 1766 Rockingham classed him 'Tory—Bute', and Newcastle in March 1767 'Tory'; yet he voted against Administration on the land tax, 27 Feb. 1767, and the nullum tempus bill, 17 Feb. 1768—measures on which the general opinion of the country gentlemen was against Administration. After 1768 he voted regularly with Administration. He is not known to have spoken in the House. He died 15 Mar. 1774.

[1] Add. 32930, f. 257. [2] Bute mss.

J.B.

## HARLEY, Hon. Thomas (1730–1804), of Berrington, Herefs.

LONDON    1761–1774
HEREFORDSHIRE    22 May 1776–1802

*b.* 24 Aug. 1730, 4th s. of Edward, 3rd Earl of Oxford, and bro. of Edward, Lord Harley (q.v.). *educ.* Westminster 1738–48. *m.* 15 Mar. 1752, Anne, da. of Edward Bangham, M.P., 2s. 5da.

Alderman, London 1761–*d.*, sheriff, 1763–4, ld. mayor 1767–8; P.C. 27 May 1768.

Harley set up as a wine merchant in Aldersgate St. c.1752. In the trade directories of 1763 he is still described as a wine merchant, but by then he had also entered other fields. Lord Oxford wrote to Sir John Cust, 31 Dec. 1760:[1] 'My brother, Mr. Thomas Harley, who is ... to be concerned in clothing some of the militia regiments, has desired me to mention his name to you, if you ... should think proper to employ him.'

In 1761 Harley was proposed as candidate for London by a committee of merchants under the chairmanship of Richard Glover, and was returned after a contest. He made his first speech on 11 Mar. 1762. He appears in Fox's list of Members favourable to the peace preliminaries, but like most West country Members he opposed the cider tax, March 1763. Over general warrants he at first supported Grenville's Administration, and in the debate of 14 Feb. 1764 spoke for them; but in the decisive division of 18 Feb. voted with Opposition—doubtless a concession to popular sentiment in the City of London. He voted against the repeal of the Stamp Act, 22 Feb. 1766. He supported Chatham's Administration, but voted against them on the land tax, 27 Feb. 1767.

In 1768 he was returned for London head of the poll. As lord mayor during the riots of May 1768 he exerted himself to restore law and order; his conduct won general praise, and an address was voted by both Houses asking the King to confer 'some mark of distinction' upon him. He was made a Privy Councillor but refused a pension, asking instead for 'something in the way of his profession'.[2] In November 1768 he was given a share in the contract to remit money to the troops in North America.

In the division on Wilkes's expulsion, 3 Feb. 1769, Harley voted with the court, but on the seating of Luttrell, 15 Apr. 1769, with the Opposition—which was explained by Opposition newspapers, probably correctly, as a sop to popular feeling in the City. Harley consistently supported North's Administration, and became the leader of the court party in the City. In 1772 he was chairman of the secret committee on East India affairs, and as such introduced the bill to restrain the Company from sending out supervisors to India. He made several speeches on East India affairs, but always in his capacity as chairman of the committee; and seems to have had no personal interest in the Company.

In 1774 he refused to contest London; though had he stood, wrote Walpole,[3] 'Wilkes himself owned that . . . he . . . would have been the first on the poll'. Wishing to maintain his family's interest in Herefordshire he contested the county, but was defeated; he was returned after another contest at a by-election in 1776.

During the American war Harley's contract became extremely profitable, and he added others for remitting money to the West Indies and for supplying clothing and blankets to the troops in America. In 1778 he became a partner in the bank of Raymond, Harley, Webber, and Co., and principal subscriber to Government loans. He bought an estate in Herefordshire and built himself a mansion. He was sensitive about the correctness of his financial dealings with Government; and of the nine speeches he made between 1774 and 1782, eight are in defence of his own honesty and political probity (though neither was ever publicly attacked)—the ninth was on a turnpike bill.

> He wished that the contracts were strictly inquired into, [he said in the House, 13 Apr. 1778[4]] as he was conscious that . . . *his* would bear the test . . . he had always supported Government upon principle, and had even risked his person and life in support of Government . . . he could solemnly affirm his vote in Parliament was never influenced by any other consideration but the mere merit of the several questions as they arose.

Harley did not vote on Shelburne's peace preliminaries, and was classed by Robinson, March 1783 as a doubtful follower of North. But he voted against Fox's East India bill, 27 Nov. 1783, belonged to the St. Alban's Tavern group which tried to bring about a union between Pitt and Fox, and afterwards supported Pitt. However, he voted against Pitt's Irish commercial propositions, 13 May 1785, but supported him on the Regency.

Harley died 1 Dec. 1804.

[1] *Recs. Cust Fam.* ed. Cust, iii. 308. [2] Harley's speech of 12 Apr. 1782, Debrett, vii. 42. [3] *Last Jnls.* i. 404. [4] Stockdale, viii. 244.

J.B.

## HARPUR, Sir Henry, 6th Bt. (?1739–89) of Calke Abbey, Derbys.

### DERBYSHIRE 1761–1768

*b.* ?1739, 1st s. of Sir Henry Harpur, M.P., 5th Bt., by Lady Caroline Manners, da. of John, 2nd Duke of Rutland. *educ.* Westminster July 1749, aged 10. *m.* 17 July 1762, Lady Frances Greville, da. of Francis, 1st Earl of Warwick, 1s. *suc.* fa. 7 June 1748.

Harpur came of an old and influential Derbyshire family with estates said to be worth £10,000 a year.[1] In 1761 he was returned unopposed for the county and, in spite of his connexion with the Rutland family, as representative of the independent country gentlemen he was often counted as a Tory. He does not appear in Henry Fox's list of Members favourable to the peace preliminaries, December 1762, but was classed as 'pro' by Jenkinson in the autumn of 1763, and is not included in any of the minority lists during the Bute and Grenville Administrations. Rockingham, July 1765, classed him as 'contra'; he voted against the repeal of the Stamp Act, 22 Feb. 1766, and was listed as 'Tory, Bute' by Rockingham in November 1766, and as 'Tory' by Newcastle on 2 Mar. 1767. No other vote by him is known, and there is no record of his having spoken in the House.

In 1768 he again stood for Derbyshire, in opposition to Godfrey Bagnal Clarke, and was defeated after an expensive contest. In 1774 Georgiana, Duchess of Devonshire, reported to her mother that if Wenman Coke were returned for both Derby and Norfolk, Harpur would hold the seat at Derby till Thomas Coke was of age; but Coke was defeated, and Harpur did not stand again for Parliament.[2]

He died 10 Feb. 1789.

[1] Add. 6839, f. 273. [2] Spencer mss.

M.M.D.

## HARRIS, James (1709–80), of Salisbury, Wilts.

CHRISTCHURCH 1761–22 Dec. 1780

*b.* 20 July 1709, 1st s. of James Harris of the Close, Salisbury, by his 2nd w. Elizabeth, da. of Anthony, 2nd Earl of Shaftesbury. *educ.* Salisbury Cathedral sch.; Wadham, Oxf. 1726; L. Inn 1724. *m.* 8 July 1745, Elizabeth, da. and h. of John Clarke of Sandford, Som., 2s. 3da. *suc.* fa. 1731.

Ld. of Admiralty Dec. 1762–Apr. 1763, of Treasury Apr. 1763–July 1765; sec. and comptroller to the Queen 1774–*d.*

The Harris family had been settled in Wiltshire since the sixteenth century, and had lived in the Close, Salisbury, since 1660. James Harris was the first of the family to enter Parliament. His cousin Edward Hooper of Heron Court, near Christchurch, M.P. for Christchurch 1735–48 and a commissioner of customs 1748–93, had the chief influence in the borough, and it was on his interest that Harris was returned. Harris was also connected with the Yorkes: his father's first wife and the wife of Philip, 1st Earl of Hardwicke, were sisters.

Harris was a classical scholar of note, a lover of music and art, and a writer on philology and philosophy. His principal work *Hermes, or A Philosophical Inquiry concerning Universal Grammar*, was published in 1751 and dedicated to Lord Hardwicke. It had a great vogue at the time, but today appears dull, formal, and pedantic. Dr. Johnson described Harris as 'a sound, sullen scholar'; 'I looked into his book', he said, 'and thought he did not understand his own system.'[1] But others, who had perhaps studied Harris more carefully, had a higher opinion of his worth. Gibbon describes him as 'the learned and amiable Mr. Harris', who 'laboured to revive the studies of Grecian literature and philosophy'.[2] Harris was a born writer, never happy without a pen in his hand. From the day of his entering Parliament he began to keep a journal of the debates there, and apparently continued doing so until the end. Unfortunately, only the part from 1760–1766 appears to have survived (apart from fragments for 1779 and 1780). Still, this is the most important source yet discovered for debates in the Parliament of 1761. Harris was intelligent and accurate; he tried to summarize the arguments of the speakers fairly, and often succeeds in capturing typical phrases and turns of speech. In addition, he made careful memoranda of conversations and discussions during the time he was in Parliament, and these form a valuable supplementary source of information to the correspondence of that period.[3] A pleasing picture of Harris emerges from the reading of his papers: he had a lively mind, graced both with wit and humour, and his learning never obtrudes; firm in his political views and loyal in his allegiances, he also tried to be fair to the other side. He knew no secrets and makes no great revelations, but among the minor chroniclers of his age he deserves a high place.

Harris entered the House without any strong political views, except a general wish to support Administration; and at first looked towards Hardwicke as his political mentor. His only interventions in debate during his first session were on the Lichfield election petition—'I spoke, and was heard attentively', he wrote on 1 Feb. 1762. On 26 Nov. he was offered through Lord Shelburne a seat at the Board of Admiralty. Shelburne was a Wiltshire neighbour and old acquaintance, and presumably knew that Harris was well disposed towards the Bute Administration. Harris asked for time to consult his friends: his brother Thomas was doubtful, but Edward Hooper pressed him to accept. On 28 Nov. he informed Hardwicke of the offer, who advised him to decline; Legge gave the same advice; and on 2 Dec. Harris told Shelburne that he would not accept the place. Then, Harris's account continues:

> Things were in this situation, and I myself full of thought the remainder of the day and all the night following. When I got up the next morning [3 Dec.], and without saying a syllable to anyone what I proposed and where I was going, I went to Lord Shelburne's. My Lord was then going to Wycombe, his coach at the door, and [had] I come a quarter of an hour later I should have missed him. As soon as I saw him I asked whether I might have liberty to change my mind. He said I might. I then at once told him I was ready to accept the honour his Majesty had offered me of a place in the Admiralty, and to move the Address upon the Preliminaries. I gave my Lord the same reasons for doing this which had influenced myself: the contrariety of opinion among my friends and my own diffidence had at first made me decline, but that when I reflected how great an honour had been made me and in how generous a manner, unsought, unsolicited; when I reflected too that even though I refused a place, I so far approved the present measures of Government that I should certainly vote for them, I had come to a resolution contrary to my former and hoped my Lord would forgive me for being thus changeable, which I would not be any more he might be assured.

On 9 Dec. 1762 Harris moved the Address in favour of the peace preliminaries: the text of his speech is among his papers, and it contains little except what might have been said by anyone on such an occasion. (Horace Walpole, a political opponent, writing of this debate, calls Harris a 'wretched orator'.[4]) On 16 Dec. Harris talked with George Grenville, first lord of the Admiralty. 'Mr. Grenville', he wrote, ' . . . expressed his good opinion of me, and of his early desire . . . that I should be taken into employment; that Lord Bute approved it, knowing me by character though not personally.' In April 1763, when Grenville moved to the Treasury, he took Harris with him, and a warm friendship developed between the two men. Harris came to respect Grenville as he did no other politician, and in his pages a picture of the statesman emerges such as is not found elsewhere: an efficient and tireless man of business, concerned only for the public welfare, and a loyal and disinterested friend, able to evoke real warmth of feeling. Harris shared Grenville's political fortunes; was dismissed with him in July 1765; followed him into opposition to the Rockingham Administration; and remained attached to Grenville to the end. He had no liking for Wilkes and in 1769 could not bring himself to vote with Grenville on the Wilkes case; he voted for the expulsion of Wilkes, 3 Feb. 1769, and in the divisions on the Middlesex election abstained. Similarly in January 1770, pressed by Grenville to attend the committee on the state of the nation when the Middlesex election was to be again debated, Harris did not arrive in London until the division had been taken.[5]

The death of Grenville in November 1770 released Harris from his nominal allegiance to the Opposition, and henceforth he steadily supported North. His speeches in the House were infrequent, and mostly on uncontentious topics. One cause he did have much at heart—the relief of Protestant Dissenters, and in February 1772 and March 1773 he spoke in their favour.[6] He supported North's American policy without any reservations. By August 1772 he was soliciting office from North, and in January 1774 was offered the post of comptroller and secretary to the Queen. ''Tis a place more of honour than of profit', wrote Mrs. Harris to her son, 'but it suits him in all respects more than a place of business.'[7] And Harris himself wrote about his place: 'They were two offices, required no duty, were worth together £500 a year (£25 deducted), were regularly paid, and the duty done by deputy . . . all I had to do was to sign receipts.'

In other respects also this office was ideal for Harris. He had a profound reverence for the royal family, amounting almost to worship, and to be about the court and to take part in royal ceremonies,

gave him intense pleasure. He carefully described his first audience with the Queen when she presented him with the seals of office—'an easy and familiar conversation, which lasted at least twenty minutes'. They began by talking about music. 'I told her Majesty', writes Harris, 'that for the honour of Germany it had the best scholars, the best soldiers, the best musicians, and the best painters now in Europe.' Then the conversation passed to artists and to writers. 'She honoured me with mention of my works. I lamented that the subjects being philosophical were some of them difficult. She politely said there were parts intelligible.' The Queen 'fell into an encomium upon the King's worth and goodness', in which Harris joined, and added his own praise of the Queen. 'Thus ended this extraordinary conference, in which I had the strongest proofs of the Queen's excellent understanding and goodness of heart.' The first royal ceremony which Harris attended was the christening of the King's sixth son, Prince Frederick Adolphus, on 24 Mar. 1774. The ceremony took place in the Queen's bedchamber in the presence of the King, the ladies of the bedchamber, maids of honour, officials of the Queen's court, foreign ministers, peers and peeresses, etc.

> The Queen was in her state bed, her head decorated with jewels, and her hair without powder . . . At the bottom of the bed was a table with four gold candlesticks and a gold ewer with water. There was a desk and cushion for the Archbishop just by it, who soon began reading the office. The King stood by the Archbishop. The child was delivered by Lady Charlotte Finch to Lady Effingham, who with Lords Hertford and Jersey were the sponsors. The name was Frederick Adolphus. The child cried aloud great part of the time.

After the ceremony Harris was the last to leave the room. 'The Queen did me the honour to speak to me', he writes, 'asked when I expected my son home from Berlin, and how my gout did. I replied, such a sight was enough to cure any complaint.'

Harris died 22 Dec. 1780.

[1] Boswell, *Johnson*, iii. 345. [2] Notes 58 and 69 to ch. lii. of *Decline & Fall*. [3] All these mss are now in the possession of the Earl of Malmesbury. [4] *Mems. Geo. III*, i. 178. [5] Add. 35608, f. 334; *Letters of 1st Earl of Malmesbury*. ed. Malmesbury, i. 186–7, 189. [6] Cavendish's 'Debates', Egerton 233, pp. 267–8; 243, pp. 261–3, 349–51. [7] *Malmesbury Letters*, i. 279.

J.B.

**HARRIS, James** (1746–1820), of Salisbury, Wilts.

CHRISTCHURCH    20 Nov. 1770–1774, 1780–19 Sept. 1788

*b.* 21 Apr. 1746, o. surv. s. of James Harris (q.v.). *educ.* Salisbury Cathedral sch.; Winchester 1757–62; Merton, Oxf. 1763; Leyden; Grand Tour (France, Holland, Prussia, Poland) 1766–8. *m.* 28 July 1777

Harriet Maria, da. of Sir George Amyand, 1st Bt. (q.v.), 3s. 2da. K.B. 24 Feb. 1779; *suc.* fa. 22 Dec. 1780; *cr.* Baron Malmesbury 19 Sept. 1788; Earl of Malmesbury 29 Dec. 1800.

Sec. of embassy in Spain 1768–71, chargé d'affaires 1769–71, minister 1771–2; envoy to Prussia 1772–6; ambassador to Russia 1776–83; P.C. 3 Sept. 1784; envoy to Holland 1784–8, ambassador 1788–9; on special mission to Prussia and Holland 1793–4; on mission to Brunswick to negotiate the marriage of the Prince of Wales 1794–5; ambassador to France to negotiate peace 1796–7.

James Harris was the foremost diplomat of his age, and his membership of the House of Commons during most of this period was purely nominal. He was appointed to his first diplomatic post by Lord Shelburne in 1768, at the request of his father, who, though in opposition, was on friendly terms with Shelburne.[1] As chargé d'affaires at Madrid he won a great reputation by his handling of the Falkland Islands crisis. In 1770 he had been returned at Christchurch on the interest of his father's cousin, Edward Hooper, but it is doubtful whether he ever took his seat in his first Parliament.

He was not a candidate in 1774, but in 1780 was returned again while absent in St. Petersburg. He came home in September 1783, and the next few months seem to have been the only time when he attended the House of Commons. He was a follower of Fox; but such was his standing as a diplomat that he was appointed by Pitt to the critical post at The Hague. On being raised to the rank of ambassador in 1788 he was created a peer.

He died 21 Nov. 1820.

[1] Jas. Harris sen. to Shelburne, 9 June 1768, and Ld. Hyde to Shelburne, 7 Sept. 1768, Lansdowne mss.

J.B.

**HARRIS, John** (?1690–1767), of Hayne, Devon.

HELSTON          1727–1741
ASHBURTON    1741–5 Oct. 1767

*b.* ?1690, 2nd but 1st surv. s. of Christopher Harris by his w. Jane. *educ.* L. Inn 1706, called 1713. *m.* (1) Margaret (*d.* 13 Mar. 1754), da. of Roger Tuckfield of Raddon, Devon, wid. of Samuel Rolle of Heanton Satchville, Devon, *s.p.*; (2) 10 Mar. 1755, Anne, da. of Francis Seymour Conway, 1st Baron Conway, and sis. of Henry Seymour Conway (q.v.), *s.p.*

Paymaster of the Board of Works by June 1738–Sept. 1740; master of the Household 1741–*d.*

Harris, through his first marriage, obtained control of Ashburton, where he was returned unopposed in 1754; and after his wife's death shared the borough interest with his step-daughter Lady Orford. When before the general election of 1761 an opposition was threatened by Nathaniel Newnham, Harris wrote to Newcastle asking him to prevent Newnham from standing:[1]

'Twould be very hard upon me, an old servant of the Crown, to be opposed in a place where I have for three Parliaments brought in myself and my friend without a shilling expense to the Government, and a trifle to those I recommended. I must beg your Grace to rank me among the number of your best friends.

Newnham withdrew, but Laurence Sulivan forced a contest in which Harris was returned second at the poll. Newcastle wrote to Charles Yorke on 14 Feb. 1762 that Sulivan had petitioned, whereupon 'the Duke of Devonshire's whole family, and all the old friends of Sir Robert Walpole . . . pressed me so strongly in favour of Mr. Harris that it has been absolutely impossible for me to avoid declaring for him'.[2] In Parliament Harris steadily supported each successive Administration till his death on 5 Oct. 1767, aged 77. No speech of his is recorded 1754–67.

[1] Add. 32908, f. 359.  [2] Add. 32934, f. 337.

M.M.D.

**HARRIS, John** (1703–68), of Pickwell Manor, Devon, and Wrotham, Kent.

BARNSTAPLE    1741–1747, 1754–1761

*bap.* 6 Sept. 1703, s. of William Harris of Pickwell Manor by Honor, da. of R. Scott Bickford of Dunsland. *educ.* I. Temple 1724. *m.* 1731, Dorothy, da. of Francis Herbert of Oakley Park, Mont., sis. of Henry Arthur, 1st Earl of Powis, 2s. 2da. *suc.* fa. bef. 1724.

At the general election of 1754 Harris stood for Barnstaple, where the Government candidate was George Amyand, and the manager, John Clevland, himself possessed influence in the borough. Lord Powis sounded Harris about his attitude towards Administration, and wrote to Pelham, 30 May 1753:[1]

An answer I have had, which is very satisfactory in relation to his future conduct in Parliament. He has put himself into my hands, and since he has done so, I wish now, with all my heart, that Mr. Clevland's friend and Mr. Harris could be brought to join their forces in support of each other . . . Mr. Harris has certainly the best interest in that borough of any of the candidates; and by what I can learn, the best single interest that any man has. This is the circumstance you said would be required by you . . . I have added another . . . (viz) that I will be answerable for his public conduct. Under this assurance, I shall be glad to settle this affair to your's and Mr. Clevland's satisfaction, on the part of Mr. Harris . . . The other candidates will probably give up the point.

John Fortescue did not; but Harris and Amyand were returned after a contest. Harris's feelings toward Clevland appear, however, from his letter to James Buller, 13 Oct. 1753:[2]

I hear Clevland is opposed at Saltash, I hope you will strenuously join in that opposition. It is very surprizing that in so opulent a country as Cornwall, that persons unknown to them, nay the very scrubs of the earth, should carry off their boroughs triumphantly.

In Dupplin's list of 1754 Harris was classed as a 'country gentleman, for'. But when Edward Boscawen, a very independent Whig, to Newcastle's great embarrassment came forward as candidate for Cornwall, Harris wrote to James Buller, in a style indistinguishable from that of a Tory country gentleman in sharpest opposition to Government:[3]

> Permit me, Sir, in the first place, to express my surprise that ministerial influence should now take such bold strides in your county, as not only to carry all your boroughs but to attempt even the county itself; I always thought that the first was owing to the want of true spirit in gentlemen of fortune in your county that have it in their power to enforce there a natural and true interest. I am glad however to find that you are determined to oppose such proceedings, as to the latter; and be assured that you command absolutely the little interest I can make in your country.

He did not stand again in 1761 and died in February 1768.

[1] Newcastle (Clumber) mss. [2] Buller mss at Antony, Cornw. [3] Ibid.

L.B.N.

## HARRISON, George (1680–1759), of Balls Park, Herts.

HERTFORD    23 Jan. 1727–1734, 1741–2 Dec. 1759

*b.* 10 Feb. 1680, 2nd surv. s. of Richard Harrison, M.P., by Audrey, da. of George Villiers, 4th Visct. Grandison [I]. *educ.* Charterhouse 1695–7; Wadham, Oxf. 1697. *m.* 12 June 1737, Mary, da. of Edward Feilde of Stanstead Abbots, Herts., *s.p. suc.* bro., Edward Harrison, M.P., 1732.

In 1754 Harrison was returned unopposed for Hertford, where his family had considerable influence. When Newcastle took over the Treasury Harrison was already in receipt of a secret service pension of £500 p.a.[1] of which the origin is unascertained. Harrison drew the yearly instalments in 1754 and 1755,[2] but although further payments were intended they were apparently never claimed or made.[3] There were no compelling reasons for him to draw them. He was well-to-do; in 1753 he invested £4,500 in Bank of England stock; at the time he made his will, December 1755, he had £5,000 owing to him from an estate in which he had a life interest; and he left a further £3,000 in legacies. His principal estate went to Lady Townshend, wife of the 3rd Viscount and mother of George and Charles Townshend, with the proviso that it was to be free from any 'intermeddling' from her husband. He died 2 Dec. 1759.

[1] Add. 33038, f. 415. [2] Namier, *Structure*, 432, 438. [3] Add. 32997, ff. 64, 237, 330.

L.B.N.

## HARRISON, John (1738–1811), of Norton Place, Lincs.

GREAT GRIMSBY    1780–1796
THETFORD          1796–1806

*b.* 1738, o. surv. s. of John Harrison of Norton Place by Elizabeth, da. of William Dealtry of Gainsborough, wid. of Philip Jenkinson of Lincoln. *educ.* Eton 1753–6; Trinity, Camb. 9 June 1756, aged 18; M. Temple 1760, called 1766. *m.* 7 Nov. 1766, Catherine, da. of Rev. Robert Pinder of Owston Hall, Lincs., 3da. *suc.* fa. 1768.

Harrison was returned unopposed for Grimsby in 1780 on the interest of Charles Anderson Pelham. 'A young man of genteel though not ample fortune', wrote the *English Chronicle* in 1781, '[he] . . . is the first of his family who ever aspired to the high honour of a British legislator.' Until the fall of North he voted consistently with Opposition. Four speeches are recorded 1780–2, all on America.

After July 1782 he supported Fox, and voted against Shelburne's peace preliminaries, 18 Feb. 1783. He voted for parliamentary reform, 7 May 1783; and is described in his obituary (*Gent. Mag.* 1811, i. 196) as 'invariably the friend of popular rights and . . . celebrated for his inflexible opposition to the Administration of his day'. He was a noted agriculturist and supporter of enclosures.

He died 7 Feb. 1811, aged 78.

I.R.C.

## HART, William Neville (1741–1804), of Westminster.

STAFFORD    12 Apr. 1770–1774

*b.* 27 Dec. 1741, 1st s. of Lewis Augustus Blondeau, gentleman usher to King George II, by Denise Gougeon (who m. (2) Sir William Hart, banker). *m.* (1) 7 Jan. 1765, Elizabeth (*d.*30 Oct. 1766), da. of Caesar Hawkins, serjeant-surgeon to the King, *s.p.*; (2) 6 Oct. 1767, Elizabeth, da. of Stanhope Aspinwall, 2s. 4da. *suc.* step-fa. 1765, and took name of Hart.

Hart seems early to have entered the banking firm of Backwell, Hart, Darell, and Croft, of Pall Mall; and in 1765, on the death of his step-father, became a partner. He retired in 1772 or 1773.

He was returned at Stafford in 1770 without opposition, on what interest is not known. His first recorded vote, 6 Dec. 1770, was for Glynn's motion for an inquiry into the administration of justice. His first recorded speech was against the commitment of Oliver over the printers' case, 27 Mar. 1771: 'As a citizen of London and a Member of Parliament I think what has been done to Oliver has been wrong. I should have done as he has.'[1] On 6 Feb. 1772 he voted for the petition of the clergy against the 39 Articles. But on the royal marriage bill he spoke for the court; and he voted with them over the

Middlesex question, 26 Apr. 1773, and Grenville's Act, 25 Feb. 1774. In all, seven speeches by him are recorded. He did not stand in 1774.

In later life Hart is said to have been chamberlain to Stanislaus Augustus, King of Poland, and to have received the Polish Order of St. Stanislaus. He died 23 Oct. 1804.

[1] Brickdale's 'Debates'.

J.B.

**HARTLEY, David** (c. 1730–1813), of Putney, Surr.[1]

KINGSTON-UPON-HULL 1774–1780, 6 June 1782– 1784

*b.* c. 1730, 1st s. of David Hartley, physician and philosopher, of Bath by his 1st w. *educ.* Sherborne; C.C.C. Oxf. 6 Apr. 1747, aged 17; Leyden, 26 July 1757, aged 26; L. Inn 1759. *unm. suc.* fa. 1758.

The portrait of David Hartley painted by Romney in 1783[2] shows him in simple, unadorned dress, sitting by a table on which rests a copy of the peace treaty with America. His eyes loom large behind his spectacles; earnestness, honesty, and naïvety are written in his features; it is the face of a man wrapped up in his ideas and caring little for those of others. 'Though destitute of any personal recommendations of manner', wrote Wraxall,[3] '[he] possessed some talent, with unsullied probity, added to indefatigable perseverance and labour.' In the House of Commons 'the intolerable length, when increased by the dullness of his speeches, rendered him an absolute nuisance even to his own friends'. And Anthony Storer wrote, after listening to one of Hartley's speeches:[4] 'No one can have a complete idea of a bore who has not been in Parliament.' John Adams wrote of his 'consummate vanity'.[5] Yet his benevolence was unquestioned, and many of his ideas were far beyond his time.

Hartley had studied medicine at Leyden; was an expert on public finance; and a scientist of note. He was the intimate friend of Sir George Savile, and well known to Rockingham and Portland. In 1764 he published a pamphlet criticizing Grenville's finance, and in July 1765 was offered the post of secretary to the Treasury in the Rockingham Administration. 'I know that I have [neither] talents nor inclination for the common train and routine of office business', wrote Hartley to Rockingham;[6] in addition:

The treatment which so many persons have so lately received as to their reputation as well as their fortunes has, I confess, in my mind destroyed all confidence in the service of Government. Every man's fortune and good name . . . is to depend upon the caprice and villainy of parties.

This did not prevent him from laying down a plan of finance for Rockingham's guidance, including the injunction that the land tax must be reduced. 'The stubborn, uncompromising spirit of Mr. Hartley's political sentiments', wrote his friend, Richard Warner,[7] 'had not escaped his Lordship's notice, and he was perfectly aware could not harmonize with his own views.'

In 1768 Hartley stood with John Bentinck, and backed by the Duke of Portland, for Callington, against candidates supported by Lady Orford, patron of the borough.[8]

For my own part [he wrote to Portland on 14 Mar. 1768] I am entirely . . . indifferent about Parliament. If I may have the happiness to be connected with you and to contribute our joint labours to the public stock, I don't care whether I am in the House or out . . . I shall have but one object in view, to consent to nothing that is unbecoming or wrong, that might make either my friends or myself have any proceedings to be ashamed of.

He went down to Callington, only to find that the borough could not be carried without bribery; and abandoned the enterprise when it became clear that he and Bentinck would be overborne by the faggot votes.

In 1774 he stood at Hull with Savile's recommendation, and was returned after a contest. Nearly a hundred parliamentary speeches by him are reported, all on finance or the American war; and between 1775 and 1779 he made eight motions for conciliation with the colonies. His proposals varied according to circumstances, but his assumptions were always the same: the British Government was bent on tyrannizing the colonists, and whatever the Americans did was justifiable. In his pamphlet, *Letters on the American War*, published in 1778, he wrote about the British Government:

The motives which I impute to them . . . are a design to establish an influential dominion to be exercised at the pleasure of the Crown, and to acquire from America an independent revenue at the disposition of the Crown, uncontrolled, and not accountable for to Parliament.

Sense and nonsense were mixed together in his American proposals: always lacking was an understanding of what was possible both in Britain and America. On 7 Dec. 1775 he said:[9]

Even if you could make out your right to tax America, yet justice . . . requires that you should abandon that supposed right . . . If we boast that taxation by representation is the prerogative blessing of our own constitution, reason and justice demand that we should have given the same to every part of the empire.

He proposed that 'the Americans contribute to the general defence of the empire by way of requisitions'; if so, 'there can be no doubt but that this country will think them entitled to relaxations in trade in proportion as they contribute'. In short, he was proposing an entirely new system of imperial affairs. 'I have long seen', he wrote to Franklin on 22 July 1775,[10] 'the terms of parent state over children as very misleading in themselves; if we must have allegorical terms let us change them for brethren and friends.' Few in the House of Commons had such insight.

His proposals of December 1775 were a tribute both to his benevolence and naïvety:

Let the Americans be replaced where they were in 1763 if they will admit and register in their assemblies such an Act of Parliament as they themselves shall confess that they would have admitted in 1763 . . . the Act to be proposed to America as an auspicious beginning to lay the first stone of universal liberty should be what no American should hesitate an instant to comply with, that every slave in North America should be entitled to his trial by jury in all criminal cases. America cannot refuse to accept and enrol such an Act as this, and thereby to re-establish peace and harmony with the parent state. Let us all be re-united in this as a foundation to extirpate slavery from the face of the earth.

It never occurred to Hartley that even if the British Parliament could be induced to pass such an Act, it would merely be regarded in America as one more example of British tyranny.

After 1776 Hartley favoured the recognition of American independence, but with a 'mutual naturalization' between the two countries.[11] The American alliance with France, he wrote in 1778, was a 'reluctant act of self-defence'; and would be abandoned if the British Government would drop its aggressive policy. Franklin, with whom Hartley corresponded throughout the war, tried in vain to disabuse him. In April 1778 Hartley, with North's privity but with no authority from the British Government, saw Franklin and Vergennes, the French foreign minister, in Paris. 'He seemed to consider our treaty with France as a nullity', wrote John Adams, 'that we might disregard at our pleasure, and treat with England separately or come again under her government.'[12] It was once more explained to him that America would stand by her treaty with France; and the cession of Canada and Nova Scotia was also demanded. Yet Hartley, on his return home, professed to have found a basis for negotiation. He said in the House on 22 June 1779:[13]

America will doubtless perform all her contracted engagements; but whenever the British ministry can be prevailed upon . . . to abate their hostilities towards America, the common interests . . . and all the ancient ties of friendship and consanguinity between us will again emerge into operation, and lead the two countries to peace and reunion with each other.

It was unwise of North to have sanctioned Hartley's visit, which did no good.

At the general election of 1780 Hartley was defeated at Hull, which he attributed to his opposition to the American war (but Wilberforce, elected in his place, also opposed the American war). Anticipating his defeat, he had hinted that Portland might like to provide him with a seat in the House; and his request was supported by Savile after the general election.[14] But Rockingham wrote to Portland on 22 Sept.:

Sir George Savile . . . came here on Wednesday night . . . He was in good spirits and good humour, except when anything brought up any thought about the *loss* he *sustained* by Hartley's not being in Parliament . . . I did not attempt to contend, but I neither would nor could afford any encouragement to raise any expectation that it could be accommodated.

Hartley was out of Parliament until returned again for Hull in June 1782.

When Rockingham took office in 1782, Savile applied to him on Hartley's behalf. Hartley wished to be employed in the peace negotiations, and the office Rockingham suggested for him (which has not been ascertained) was not acceptable. In a reproachful letter to Rockingham of 28 Mar.,[15] Savile wrote: 'I cannot wonder at the decision he is come to. The business of the office in question would have been ill suited to his particular talents, to the course of his studies, or indeed to the whole plan and object of his life.' But Rockingham was not disposed to give him a second choice.

Hartley voted against Shelburne's peace preliminaries, giving as his reason that Shelburne had yielded too much to the Bourbon powers.[16] He had an old friendship with North and disliked Shelburne; and, against Savile's advice, adhered to the Coalition.[17] In April 1783 he went to Paris to negotiate the definitive treaty with the United States and to try to reach a trade agreement; but, after four months' negotiations, no agreement on trade was reached and the preliminary treaty was accepted as final.[18]

In 1784 Hartley stood again at Hull, and was defeated. It was his last attempt to enter Parliament. The remainder of his life he passed in retirement at Bath, mostly engaged on scientific experiments. He died 19 Dec. 1813.

[1] See G. H. Guttridge, *David Hartley*. [2] Reproduced in Guttridge, 320. [3] *Mems.* iii. 124. [4] *HMC Carlisle*, 315. [5] Guttridge, 283. [6] Undated, Rockingham mss. [7] *Lit. Recollections*. ii. 223. [8] About this election, see corresp. of Hartley, John Peters, and David Maitland, Portland mss. [9] Almon, iii. 256–68. [10] Guttridge, 247. [11] Stockdale, viii. 212–22. [12] Guttridge, 262–4, 284. [13] Almon, xiii. 553–64. [14] 7 Aug., 16 Sept. 1780, Portland mss. [15] Rockingham mss. [16] Almon, ix. 294. [17] See under SAVILE, Sir George. [18] Guttridge, ch. iv.

J.B.

**HARTLEY, Winchcombe Henry** (?1740–94), of Bucklebury, Berks. and Little Sodbury, Glos.

BERKSHIRE    21 Feb. 1776–1784, 1790–12 Aug. 1794

*b.* ?1740, 2nd s. of David Hartley, physician, of Bath by his 2nd w. Elizabeth, da. of Robert Packer, M.P., of Bucklebury; half-bro. of David Hartley (q.v.). *educ.* C.C.C. Oxf. 11 Nov. 1757; L. Inn 1756. *m.* (1) Mary, *d.s.p.* 15 Apr. 1786;[1] (2) 24 Aug. 1787, Anne, da. of Samuel Blackwell (q.v.) of Williamstrip Park, Glos., 1s. *suc.* to estates of uncle Henry Packer of Bucklebury 1746.

Hartley owned large estates in Berkshire and Gloucestershire, and was returned for Berkshire in 1776 and 1780 without a contest. In politics he followed his brother and consistently opposed North's Administration. He 'sometimes speaks', wrote the *Public Ledger* in 1779, 'which he had better let alone'; his speeches, though not as long as those of his half-brother, are flat and empty.

Hartley voted against Shelburne's peace preliminaries, 18 Feb. 1783, and for Fox's East India bill, 27 Nov. 1783. He voted for Pitt's scheme of parliamentary reform, 7 May 1783. In 1784 he was defeated in Berkshire; he also stood for Gloucestershire, but retired after the first day's poll.

He died 12 Aug. 1794, aged 54.

[1] Her M.I. in Bucklebury church is in A. L. Humphreys, *Bucklebury*, 176.

J.B.

**HARVEY, Edward** (1718–78), of Cleveland Court, Westminster.

GATTON     5 Dec. 1761–1768
HARWICH        1768–27 Mar. 1778

*b.* 1 Aug. 1718, 3rd s. of William Harvey, M.P., of Chigwell by Mary, da. and h. (coh.?) of Ralph Williamson of Berwick, Northumb; bro. of Eliab and William Harvey (qq.v.). *educ.* Westminster 1727–35; L. Inn 1736. *m.*, 1s.
Cornet 10 Drag. 1741, lt. 1744; capt. 7 Drag. 1747, maj. 1751; lt.-col. 6 Drag. 1754; col. 1760; maj.-gen. 1762; col. 12 Drag. 1763–4; col. 3 Horse 1764–75; adjutant-gen. of the forces 1765–d.; lt.-gen. 1772; gov. of Portsmouth 1773–d.; col. 6 Drag. 1775–d.

Harvey's advancement after the accession of George III seems to have been furthered largely by the efforts of his brother William, a friend of Fitzmaurice and Bute. In December 1760, when Harvey was appointed aide-de-camp to the King, John Calcraft wrote to him: 'Let me tell you to whom alone you are obliged for this: Lord Bute, Lord Fitzmaurice, and your brother Will. Lord Bute got you rank at the instance of the two latter.' At the same time William was negotiating a seat for his brother, and declared to Calcraft that he himself 'would be security for the £2,000 it must cost if the opportunity could be found'. On 9 Dec. Calcraft informed

Edward Harvey that Fox would return him at Dunwich 'upon such terms as you or any independent man may accept it'. In fact Fox subsequently decided to nominate Harvey and William Hamilton for Midhurst, the Browne interest there having been offered to the court. This arrangement broke down: Harvey withdrew and Hamilton was returned, as Lord Waldegrave commented to Newcastle, 'not because Hamilton had better pretensions, but because Harvey had greater regard to the convenience of his friends'. No seat was found for him at the general election, but on 22 May 1761 Waldegrave wrote to Newcastle: 'Mr. [William] Harvey by his connexion with the Colebrooke family has hopes of bringing in the Colonel for Gatton, and is ready to give a good price. Sir G. Colebrooke has told Mr. Harvey that he should be guided by your Grace . . . [Harvey] is esteemed a good man, as well as a good officer.' He was returned at the by-election in December.[1]

In Bute's list of December 1761 Harvey was classed 'Fox, pro', but absence in Germany prevented his voting on the peace preliminaries.[2] He did not vote with the minority on Wilkes, 15 Nov. 1763, but James Harris records that on the 23rd, after a speech by Grenville, 'Beckford, Cooke, and Edward Harvey followed, all of the other side'.[3] He did not vote in opposition in any of the divisions of 1764, nor does his name appear in lists of absentees. He was classed 'pro' in Rockingham's list of July 1765, but voted against the repeal of the Stamp Act, 22 Feb. 1766, and in November 1766 was classed 'Bute' by Rockingham. Described as 'Government' in Townshend's list of January 1767, he voted with Administration over the land tax.

In 1768 he was returned by Government at Harwich, and from this time regularly voted with the court—with one known exception: the division on the sending of troops to St. Vincent, 15 Feb. 1773. According to Horace Walpole, ' General Harvey . . . had threatened to condemn in Parliament the embarkation of troops at so improper a moment', and the King had ordered him to be moderate, but Harvey voted in opposition.[4]

Harvey spoke rarely in the House, and generally on military matters. He told the House that he considered that 'an adjutant-general who would not give every military assistance possible [on] every military question that may be asked, from a fifer to the highest in commission, is unworthy his office'.[5] As adjutant-general he had considerable influence over military appointments. Lord George Sackville wrote to General Irwin, 24 Oct. 1767: 'General Harvey . . . knows more of the real intentions of his Majesty as to military affairs than any one man about court;

and the only right things which are recommended by Lord Granby are the effects of General Harvey's influence over him.'[6] But according to Thomas Whately, Harvey himself declared:[7]

> If it were not for the reviews the army would go to ruin, for want of a proper authority, which the King would not, Lord Granby would not, and he in his subordinate situation could not exercise; that he had represented to the King, that if his Majesty received equally well the deserving and undeserving officers, it would be impossible to preserve a distinction between them; but that his representations had not all the effect he could wish; and the emulation of reviews alone now kept up attention to discipline.

Walpole described Harvey as 'a personal military favourite of the King',[8] and that he thought highly of Harvey is shown in a letter to Lord Barrington, 15 July 1773, in which the King ordered the governorship of Portsmouth to be given to Harvey 'whose ability and integrity make me happy of this occasion of rewarding him'.[9]

No speeches of Harvey's are recorded after 1773, and though his name appears in existing majority lists, his preoccupation was with army affairs. He died 27 Mar. 1778.

[1] Add. 17495, ff. 179, 181; 32923, f. 220. [2] *HMC Rutland*, ii. 279. [3] Harris's 'Debates'. [4] *Last Jnls.* i. 172. [5] Cavendish's 'Debates', Egerton 244, pp. 99–101. [6] *HMC Stopford-Sackville*, i. 124. [7] *Grenville Pprs.* iv. 305. [8] *Last Jnls.* i. 172. [9] Barrington mss.

M.M.D.

## HARVEY, Eliab (1716–69), of Claybury Hall, Barking, Essex.

DUNWICH    1761–1768

*b.* 23 May 1716, 2nd s. of William Harvey, M.P., and bro. of Edward and William Harvey (qq.v.). *educ.* Westminster 1724; Trinity, Camb. 1734; I. Temple 1733, called 1741. *m.* 20 Nov. 1756, Mary, da. of Richard Benyon of Gidea Hall, Essex, sis. of Richard Benyon (q.v.).

K.C. 1758; reader, I. Temple 1766, treasurer 1767.

Harvey was nominated by Henry Fox at Dunwich, for which place his brother Edward had been originally selected. On 17 Feb. 1761 Fox wrote to Fitzmaurice:[1] 'Mr. Eliab Harvey will be chose at Dunwich and keep his seat there, if the Colonel [Edward Harvey] keeps his at Midhurst. If not the Counsellor will give way to the Colonel.' Consequently when a compromise at Midhurst left Edward Harvey without a seat, Eliab was offered the chief justiceship of Ireland in lieu of Dunwich. 'Surely he should accept what will secure him a fortune', wrote Fox to a friend,[2] 'and if he lives ten years, a peerage and head of the law in Ireland.' But Harvey refused. 'He says his fortune is easy', wrote Richard Rigby to Newcastle, 10 Mar. 'and his practice in his profession increasing, and therefore he does not choose leaving his own country.'[3] He

was returned unopposed at Dunwich, and Edward was left without a seat.

Harvey was a frequent speaker on a diversity of subjects. Horace Walpole thought that his speech against the war in Germany, 13 Nov. 1761, was 'very sensible';[4] and Lord George Sackville reported that he spoke 'ably and like a gentleman and was attended to accordingly'.[5] James Harris noted that as a speaker he had 'force and precision'.[6]

Classed in Bute's list of December 1761 as a follower of Fox, he appears in Fox's list of Members favourable to the peace preliminaries, December 1762. He was present at the meeting at Sir Francis Dashwood's, 25 Feb. 1763, of '60 or 70 persons, Tories and others', met to give the King their opinion about troops in Ireland, and declared 'that an augmentation in Ireland could not be made without an Act of Parliament'.[7] Harvey is not known to have voted in opposition till 1766, when he opposed the repeal of the Stamp Act, 22 Feb. He voted with Chatham's Administration on the land tax, 27 Feb. 1767.

Harvey did not stand again for Dunwich in 1768, the interest there no longer being at the disposal of Government. He was nominated for Essex at a meeting of country gentlemen discontented with the sitting Members, but came bottom of the poll, with 1792 votes against 2035 for Jacob Houblon, the other unsuccessful candidate. He died 23 Oct. 1769.

[1] Lansdowne mss. [2] Hen. Fox mss. [3] Add. 32920, f. 74. [4] *Mems. Geo. III*, i. 73. [5] *HMC Stopford-Sackville*, i. 86. [6] Harris's 'Debates'. [7] Add. 32947, ff. 92–93.

M.M.D.

## HARVEY, Eliab (1758–1830), of Chigwell, Essex.

MALDON    27 May 1780–1784
ESSEX        1802–1812, 1820–20 Feb. 1830

*b.* 5 Dec. 1758, 4th s. of William Harvey (q.v.) and bro. of William Harvey, jun. (q.v.). *educ.* Westminster 1768; Harrow 1770–5. *m.* 15 May 1784, Lady Louisa Nugent, da. and coh. of Robert, 1st Earl Nugent (q.v.), 2s. 6da. *suc.* bro. 1779; G.C.B. 17 Jan. 1825.

Lt. R.N. 1779; cdr. 1782; capt. 1783; r.-adm. 1805; v.-adm. 1810.

Returned unopposed for Maldon at the by-election of 1780 and again at the general election, Harvey was probably brought in on the interest of his fellow Member John Strutt, in return for paying two-thirds of the election expenses.[1] Harvey supported Lord North's Administration to the end, voted for Shelburne's peace preliminaries, 18 Feb. 1783, but does not appear in the division on Fox's East India bill. In Stockdale's list of 19 Mar. 1784 he is counted as a supporter of Pitt.

The *English Chronicle* wrote of him in 1781: 'We never heard of Mr. Harvey's abilities in the House

as a speaker, he being content to give a silent vote
. . . Though little heard of in his legislative capacity,
he has made some noise in the gay world, having, it
is said, not long ago actually lost all his fortune to
Captain O'Bourne at cards who suffered him to
regain the whole again, excepting only the trifling
sum of *ten thousand pounds*.'[2]

Harvey did not stand in 1784. He died 20 Feb.
1830.

[1] C. R. Strutt, *Strutt Fam. of Terling*, 19. [2] See also Walpole to
Mann, 6 Feb. 1780.

M.M.D.

## HARVEY, William (1714–63), of Chigwell, Essex.

ESSEX 1747–11 June 1763

*b.* 9 June 1714, 1st s. of William Harvey, M.P., and
bro. of Edward and Eliab Harvey (qq.v.). *m.* 13 Aug.
1750, Emma, da. and coh. of Stephen Skynner of
Walthamstow, Essex, 5s. 4da. *suc.* fa. 1731.

All Harvey's returns for Essex were unopposed.
He was invariably classed as a Tory. While himself
an independent country gentleman, Harvey was
seeking promotion for his brothers: he tried to have
Eliab made a K.C., and was offended when a junior
barrister was preferred. Informing Newcastle of it,
Lord Talbot wrote on 23 Jan. 1758 that he 'wished
that during the time whilst the constellation is in the
ascendant, under the influence of which the Members of Tory counties may dare to receive marks of
ministerial regard, that Mr. William Harvey might
receive a favour and the Duke of Newcastle bestow
it'; and when on 22 Apr. 1758 Newcastle reported
the King's approval of Eliab Harvey's receiving silk,
Talbot wrote the same day: 'you have greatly
obliged a very valuable family'.[1]

Harvey was closely connected with Fitzmarice and
Bute, through whom he secured promotion for his
brother Edward; and he appears in Henry Fox's list
of Members favourable to the peace preliminaries,
December 1762. There is no record of his having
spoken in the House.

He died 11 June 1763. Gilly Williams wrote to
George Selwyn: 'Will Harvey died of an apoplexy
at Wanstead. He had hunted in the morning, and
was in a boat on the water, talking to Mr. G. Grenville, when he was taken speechless, and expired
presently.'[2]

[1] Add. 32817, ff. 216–17, 269. [2] Jesse, *Selwyn*, i. 226.

M.M.D.

## HARVEY, William (1754–79), of Chigwell, Essex.

ESSEX 28 Nov. 1775–24 Apr. 1779

*b.* 10 Sept. 1754, 1st s. of William Harvey (q.v.), and
bro. of Eliab Harvey jun. (q.v.). *educ.* Trinity, Camb.
1771. *unm.*

'Unanimously approved' at a meeting of the
county held while he was abroad,[1] Harvey was
returned unopposed. His one recorded vote was
with Administration on the motion on sending
Keppel to sea, 3 Mar. 1779. There is no record of his
having spoken in the House. He died 24 Apr. 1779.

[1] J. Eyre to R. Newdigate, 13 Oct. 1775, Newdigate mss.

M.M.D.

## HARVEY THURSBY, John (?1711–64), of Abing-
ton, Northants.

WOOTTON BASSETT 1741–1747
STAMFORD 1754–1761

*b.* ?1711, 1st surv. s. of Robert Harvey, barrister, of
Stockton, Warws. by Mary, da. and h. of Thomas
Thursby, London merchant. *educ.* Charterhouse;
Pembroke, Camb. 9 Nov. 1727, aged 16. *m.* (settle-
ment dated 12 June 1731) Honor, da. of Robert
Pigott, M.P., of Chetwynd, Salop, 6s. 5da. *suc.*
fa. 1726; on inheriting estates of Richard Thursby,
1736, took add. name of Thursby.

In 'Minutes of Conversations' 16–19 Mar. 1754,
dated Newcastle House, 19 Mar., the note against
Stamford reads: 'Mr. Barber [q.v.] or Mr. Thoresby
chosen by Lord Exeter. Mr. Barber thinks Mr.
Thoresby a Tory might be got over.'[1] But in
Dupplin's lists drawn up after the general election,
Thursby was placed among the Tory opponents.
He is not known to have spoken in the Parliament of
1754–61.

He died 1 June 1764, aged 54.

[1] Add. 32995, f. 102.

L.B.N.

## HARWOOD, *see* HILL, Noel, *and* HILL (formerly HARWOOD), Thomas

## HATTON, *see* FINCH, Hon. Edward (d.1771), *and* FINCH HATTON

## HAWKE, Sir Edward (1710–81), of Scarthingwell Hall, Yorks.

PORTSMOUTH 28 Dec. 1747–20 May 1776

*b.* 21 Feb. 1710, o.s. of Edward Hawke, barrister, of
L. Inn by Elizabeth, da. of Nathaniel Bladen of Hems-
worth, Yorks., wid. of Col. Ruthven. *m.* 1737,
Catherine, da. and h. of Walter Brooke of Burton Hall,
nr. Hull, gd.-da. and coh. of William Hammond of
Scarthingwell Hall, 3s. 1da. *suc.* fa. 1718; K.B.
14 Nov. 1747; *cr.* Baron Hawke 20 May 1776.

Entered navy 1720; lt. 1729; cdr. 1733; capt. 1734;
r.-adm. 1747; v.-adm. 1748; adm. 1757; adm. of the
fleet 1768.

P.C. 10 Dec. 1766; first ld. of Admiralty Dec. 1766–
1771.

Hawke's first great naval success was in October
1747, when he attacked a French convoy off Belle

Isle and captured seven out of nine ships. For this he was created K.B. Shortly afterwards he was returned to Parliament on the Admiralty interest at Portsmouth. In 1754 he was returned again without a contest. But on 11 Apr. 1755 Vice-Admiral Edward Boscawen wrote to his wife from Portsmouth:[1] 'Vice-Admiral Sir Edward Hawke is become very unpopular here and, though Member for and alderman of the town, yet is despised.'

In 1755 Hawke commanded a squadron in the Mediterranean, and in 1756 was sent to relieve Byng off Minorca. In August 1757 Lord Anson, first lord of the Admiralty, wished to appoint Hawke to a seat at the Board; Pitt was in favour, but Newcastle claimed that he had promised it to Hans Stanley, and told Anson 'that he would go into the Closet and settle it for Mr. Stanley, or he would never go to the Treasury again'.[2] Newcastle promised Hawke his support for the next vacancy, to which Hawke replied on 27 Aug.:[3] 'I am greatly concerned that I should be the means of giving your Grace so much trouble . . . and I beg your Grace will pardon my freedom in telling you that I think it too late for me to come to that Board at all.'

He was now appointed naval commander of the expedition preparing against Rochfort. On 25 Sept. in a council of war held off Rochfort, Hawke gave his opinion that the landing could be effected but refused 'to be a judge of land operations';[4] however, the attack was abandoned, and Hawke returned with the fleet to England. Sir John Mordaunt, who commanded the land forces, was court martialled for his part in this fiasco, but Hawke escaped censure: Anson was satisfied with his behaviour, and the King gave him 'a good reception'.[5]

At the end of 1757 he was appointed to command a squadron in the Channel, but in May 1758 struck his flag when ordered to detach ships to another squadron. In May 1759 he was entrusted with the task of preventing the invasion which France was known to be preparing. For six months he blockaded Brest, but in November 1759 bad weather forced him to return to England and the Brest fleet escaped. Hawke put to sea again, overtook the French fleet, and in Quiberon Bay almost annihilated it. Newcastle described this victory as 'the most glorious event that has happened, at least this century, for this country at sea';[6] and Sir John Knox Laughton as 'the greatest victory at sea since the defeat of the Spanish Armada'.[7] Hawke received the thanks of the House of Commons, and was given a pension of £2,000 p.a. on Ireland.

Hawke remained at sea till September 1762, when he struck his flag for the last time. He does not appear in Henry Fox's list of Members favourable to the peace preliminaries, December 1762, but did not vote against them, 9 and 10 Dec. He seems to have been counted as a Government supporter by Grenville, and voted with Administration on general warrants, 6 Feb. 1764, though Augustus Hervey wrote to Grenville, 15 Feb. 1764: 'Sir Edward Hawke—divided against us [on] divisions to adjourn and supposed not to enter into the consequence'.[8] Rockingham in July 1765 classed him as 'pro'. In December 1766 he was appointed first lord of the Admiralty by Chatham who was determined the office should no longer be a mere political prize. The appointment gave Hawke Cabinet rank, but he carried no weight except in business of his own department; and during a Commons debate on East India affairs, 6 Mar. 1767, he embarrassed his Cabinet colleagues by blurting out that they were seriously divided on the subject.[9] Horace Walpole wrote that Hawke 'though so brave and fortunate a commander, had never been a man of abilities', and by 1770 was 'worn out, grown indolent, and . . . almost superannuated, paying so little attention to the fleet, that the ships were rotted in harbour'.[10] There was a good deal of criticism of the state of the navy during the Falkland Islands crisis, and on 12 Dec. 1770 it was suggested that there should be an inquiry before more money was voted. Hawke replied:[11]

> Everything is in more forwardness than I ever knew in any war . . . Ships are now getting ready to be manned if wanting—people are apt to misrepresent things . . . The ships are better now than in 1765. I never knew such ships . . . This is the true state of things. I have drudged in this service not to fill my pockets.

On 5 Jan. 1771 Thomas Bradshaw wrote to the Duke of Grafton:[12]

> I *know* he [Hawke] is very ill, and that Lord North has now a letter from him to Lord Rochford, in his possession, in which the poor old man tells him that he finds himself unable to attend Cabinets, or St. James's; and that, if he does not very soon find an alteration in his health for the better, he shall endeavour to creep once more to St. James's; and there thanking the King for all his kindnesses to him, lay his office at his feet.

No vote by Hawke is reported after his resignation in January 1771. Robinson's survey on the royal marriage bill, March 1772, lists him as 'pro, sick, present', but before the general election in 1774 he was classed 'doubtful'. Nevertheless he was continued on the Admiralty interest at Portsmouth until created a peer.

He died 17 Oct. 1781.

[1] *Naval Misc. iv.* (Navy Recs. Soc.), 171. [2] Anson to Hardwicke, 10 Aug. 1757, Add. 35359, ff. 399–400. [3] Add. 32873, f. 309. [4] Minutes of the council of war, Chatham mss. [5] Add. 35359, f. 401; *Grenville Pprs.* i. 213–14. [6] Add. 32899, f. 196. [7] *DNB.* [8] Grenville

mss (JM). [9] Brooke, *Chatham Admin.* 113. [10] *Mems. Geo. III*, iv. 137. [11] Brickdale's 'Debates'. [12] Grafton, *Autobiog.* 260.

J.B.

## HAWKE, Martin Bladen (1744–1805), of Scarthingwell Hall, Yorks.

SALTASH  1768–1774

*b.* 20 Apr. 1744, 1st s. of Sir Edward Hawke (q.v.). *educ.* Eton 1754–6; Queen's Oxf. 1764; L. Inn 1766. *m.* 6 Feb. 1771, Cassandra, da. of Sir Edward Turner, 2nd Bt. (q.v.), 2s. 4da. *suc.* fa. as 2nd Baron Hawke 17 Oct. 1781.

In 1768 Hawke was returned on the Admiralty interest for Saltash, and generally voted with Administration. He spoke several times in the House, and on a motion to inquire into the state of the nation, 9 Jan. 1770, 'gave the characters of the Opposition, describing them to be factious and ambitious'.[1] In a long speech on the motion about half-pay naval captains, 9 Feb. 1773, he dwelt on the difficulties and dangers of life at sea and voted against Administration, appearing in the King's list of the division as a friend for once voting in opposition. During the examination of papers and witnesses on the St. Vincent expedition, 12 Feb. 1773, Hawke queried the advisability of campaigning at that time of year, and asked about the number of deaths resulting from the expedition. He voted against Administration on Grenville's Act, 25 Feb. 1774, and was classed by Robinson in September 1774 as 'doubtful'. He contested York at the next general election, but was defeated.

He died 27 Mar. 1805.

[1] Cavendish's 'Debates', Egerton 3711, p. 12.

M.M.D.

## HAWKINS, Christopher (1758–1829), of Trewithen, Cornw.

| | |
|---|---|
| MITCHELL | 21 June 1784–Apr. 1799 |
| GRAMPOUND | 28 July 1800–1807 |
| PENRYN | 1818–1820 |
| ST. IVES | 26 May 1821–Feb. 1828 |

*b.* May 1758, 1st surv. s. of Thomas Hawkins, M.P., by Anne, da. of James Heywood of Austin Friars, London. *educ.* ?Eton 1769–73.[1] *unm.* *suc.* fa. 1 Dec. 1770; *cr.* Bt. 28 July 1791.

Sheriff, Cornw. 1783–4.

Hawkins stood for Mitchell in 1784 on Lord Falmouth's interest against that of Sir Francis Basset; a double return was made, Hawkins tying for second place with Basset's candidate Roger Wilbraham. The issue was ultimately decided in favour of Hawkins, 21 June 1784.

Hawkins does not appear to have spoken in the House before 1790. He voted for parliamentary reform, 18 Apr. 1785; signed the third party circular,

1 May 1788; and on the Regency question, 1788–9, supported Pitt.

He died 6 Apr. 1829.

[1] *Etoniana*, xciv. 696.

M.H.P.

## HAY, Adam (*d.*1775), of Soonhope, Peebles.

PEEBLESSHIRE  31 Dec. 1767–1768, 17 June–15 Nov. 1775

2nd surv. s. of John Hay of Haystoun, sheriff-depute of Peebles, by Grizel, da. of Rev. James Thomson, minister of Peebles.[1] *m.* (1) Miss Britland of Nottingham; (2) Caroline, da. of Sir Henry Harpur, M.P., 5th Bt., sis. of Sir Henry Harpur, 6th Bt. (q.v.), *s.p.*

Ensign 25 Ft. 1747, lt. 1755; capt. 104 Ft. 1760; half pay 1763; capt. 6 Ft. 1766; ret. 1768.

Apprenticed in 1742 to Archibald Wallace and James Stewart, a firm of Edinburgh merchants,[2] after a few years Hay abandoned a commercial career and obtained a commission in the army. He was returned to Parliament in 1767 on Lord March's interest as a stop-gap for James Montgomery, who took his place at the general election of 1768.

After his brief parliamentary experience Hay apparently became ambitious of establishing himself as a landed proprietor. His brother, Dr. James Hay, had succeeded in 1762 to the estate of Haystoun. Adam now proceeded to acquire the nearby lands of Soonhope, formerly the property of his family, and built a mansion near Peebles called Hay's Lodge.[3] These transactions strained his resources, and it seems probable that he was also involved in the financial disasters of 1772. By 1775 he was in serious difficulties.

In May 1775 James Montgomery vacated his seat, and on 17 June Hay was unanimously elected in his place. He may have hoped, as an M.P., to escape his creditors until the end of the Parliament.

It is not known whether he took his seat in the new session beginning 26 Oct. On 15 Nov. 1775 he died in London. George Selwyn wrote to Lord Carlisle, 16 Nov. 1775:[4]

Adam Hay, Lord March's Member for Peebles, died yesterday, I am afraid to say suddenly because it is a suspicious word, and will be more so in his case, as I believe fortune has not been favourable to him. But I do not believe anything of that sort; his general state of health has been bad for some time and I was told that his last and fatal attack was in his bowels.

Hay's affairs were in such confusion that his property had to be sold to pay his debts, and his estate of Soonhope was bought by his brother, Dr. James Hay of Haystoun, in 1778.

[1] J. W. Buchan & H. Paton, *Hist. Peeblesshire*, ii. 357. [2] *Reg. Edinburgh Apprentices, 1701–55* (Sc. Rec. Soc.), 41. [3] Buchan & Paton, ii. 349–350. [4] *HMC Carlisle*, 302.

E.H.-G.

## HAY, George (1715–78).

| | |
|---|---|
| STOCKBRIDGE | 1754–Nov. 1756 |
| CALNE | 12 July 1757–1761 |
| SANDWICH | 1761–1768 |
| NEWCASTLE-UNDER-LYME | 28 Nov. 1768–6 Oct. 1778 |

*b.* 25 Jan. 1715, s. of Rev. John Hay, rector of St. Stephen's, Coleman St., London. *educ.* Merchant Taylors' 1724; St. John's, Oxf. 1731; Doctors' Commons 1742. *unm.* Kntd. 11 Nov. 1773.

Chancellor of the diocese of Worcester 1751–64; King's advocate gen. Mar. 1755–May 1756, Nov. 1756–July 1764; vicar gen. to abp. of Canterbury 1755–64; ld. of Admiralty Nov. 1756–Apr. 1757, July 1757–July 1765; chancellor of the diocese of London 1764–78; judge of the prerogative ct. of Canterbury and dean of the arches 1764–78; judge of the high ct. of Admiralty 1773–8.

Hay was returned for Stockbridge on the interest of Sir Robert Henley as a Government supporter; and when appointed advocate general solicited and received through Newcastle from the archbishop of Canterbury the office of vicar general—which was 'a necessary support to a station attended with small emolument though of such high rank at the Bar'.[1] But half a year later he joined Pitt and Legge in opposing the subsidy treaties to Hesse and Russia. 'I have . . . sought out Dr. Hay and secured him in the strongest manner', wrote his friend Thomas Potter to George Grenville in September 1755.[2] And Lord Dupplin expressed to Newcastle his surprise at Hay's conduct, and concern 'because he has great abilities'.[3] (Horace Walpole counted Hay among the 28 foremost speakers in the House.[4]) When the House met, 13 Nov., Hay spoke and voted against the Address approving the treaties;[5] and on 10 Dec. against the Russian treaty.[6] He was dismissed from his office of King's advocate in May 1756, but reinstated by the Devonshire-Pitt Administration: 'It was insisted upon in a manner not to be withstood', wrote Holdernesse to Newcastle, 15 Nov. 1756,[7] 'and though it appeared unreasonable in the closet, was yielded to but with reluctance.' Moreover he was appointed a lord of the Admiralty. A difficulty arose over his re-election: he was told by Henley that what interest he had had at Stockbridge was now 'not at his but at Mr. Fox's disposal'.[8]

When Dr. Hay knew this [wrote Fox to Devonshire on 26 Nov.[9]] . . . I might have been applied to for my interest; but I have never yet been applied to from Dr. Hay's quarter; nor from your Grace, till since Mr. Pitt and George Grenville made it a matter of public complaint. Now, my Lord, if it had been asked of me as a favour, refusing to choose Hay might show ill humour; but, on the other side to have chose him unasked, would have been meanness.

And when Bedford wrote on 22 Nov. to Fox

deprecating his action as liable 'to exasperate men's minds', and make him appear against the King's measures and ministers, Fox added to his complaint about the ministers that 'the King . . . is mightily pleased that I oppose Dr. Hay'.[10]

When next the Government wished to return Hay in Admiral Byng's place at Rochester, the King insisted on choosing Admiral Smith, who however declined. 'But his Majesty is sturdy', wrote Rigby to Bedford, 21 Mar. 1757, 'and rightly says it shall nevertheless not be Dr. Hay.'[11] A fortnight later Hay was dismissed from the Admiralty together with Temple, but was reinstated by the Newcastle-Pitt Administration. 'I wish', wrote Newcastle to Pitt, 24 June, 'you would consider with Dr. Hay of a person and place to be vacated for his election.' Pitt replied: 'We have found a person to vacate, who is Mr. Duckett, and ready to accept a pension of £500 p.a. till an office of that value can be found for him.'[12] Hay was now a prominent speaker on the Government side, especially on legal and naval matters (habeas corpus bill, March 1758; judges salaries, June; privateer bill, April–May 1759; etc.).

In 1761 he was returned by Newcastle for Sandwich on the Admiralty interest. When before the opening of Parliament the choice had to be made of a new Speaker, Hardwicke wrote to Newcastle, 9 Oct. 1761:

I have thought again of Dr. Hay. He has certainly more talents for it than any other person that has been named. The chief objections are that he is too low, and a Scotchman; and . . . I doubt whether he would quit his profession for it.[13]

In the new House Hay adhered to the Government as such, and early in December 1762 both Newcastle and Fox listed him as gained for the peace preliminaries. But during the Bute period Hay's interventions in debate were merely on legal or naval questions.

In the next session, on 2 Dec. 1763, Hay moved the Admiralty estimates; on 9 Feb. supported his friend Charles Yorke over the Marriage Act—a tender point with the Yorkes; and spoke repeatedly in the debates on general warrants and Wilkes with whom he admitted, on 17 Feb., to have 'lived in friendship . . . till his violent and profligate behaviour made him quit him'.[14] On this, the decisive day in the Opposition campaign, Hay took a prominent part on the Government side, moving an amendment to the Opposition motion. Nevertheless, when the office of dean of the arches fell vacant in May, Yorke urged the archbishop to appoint him and pressed Newcastle for support: he himself had 'always lived in friendship' with Hay, 'especially since his reconciliation with your Grace, my father and Lord Anson'; and Hay was the first in his profession. Newcastle admitted so much—'But I know also that, after I had *singly* made him vicar general . . . he left me' for Pitt and Legge, and them for Bute. Finally Newcastle gave in, though conscious that this would not 'be approved by any one friend of mine *but yourself*'. 'Standing as we all must do on public ground', Thomas Walpole wrote to Newcastle on 15 June, 'it is more necessary you consult the humour of the public than that of any private man whatever.'[15] But when the archbishop told Hay that he owed his appointment to Newcastle, Hay replied that being in the King's service he could not ask or accept a favour through Newcastle but 'should always acknowledge Mr. Yorke's friendship', to which alone he thought himself indebted for it. In turn Hay negotiated for Yorke his patent of precedency with the Government in November 1764.[16]

When on 29 Jan. 1765 general warrants were once more discussed in the House, Hay spoke 'with much and able subtlety',[17] but asserted that 'there is a law superior even to the law of the land, the law of government by public safety'[18] and was blamed for introducing concepts of Roman law alien to common law. (Thus again by Pitt, on 4 Mar. 1766, for adopting 'arbitrary notions from the civil law',[19] and by Serjeant Adair over the prohibitory Act bearing 'a much nearer affinity to the civil law than the common law of England'.[20]

Hay went into opposition with the Grenvilles; spoke repeatedly on the anti-American side,[21] and voted against the repeal of the Stamp Act; and spoke and voted against the Government over the land tax, 27 Feb. 1767. Nevertheless, Camden was prepared to help him at the general election. Hay wrote to Samuel Martin, 16 Dec. 1767: 'A seat in the next Parliament must certainly be very acceptable to me. But I would much rather submit to the mortification of being excluded than lose your good opinion by forgetting my obligations to Mr. Yorke with which both you and my lord chancellor are well acquainted.' And on 21 Dec. 1767 he told Martin 'that he could not accept of lord chancellor's help to a seat in the next Parliament; he said he could not tell whether he should sit there or not, and must take his chance'.[22]

Hay had kept up his connexion with Oxford University. Influential at St. John's, he had been talking of standing for the University since 1759; and encouraged by Thomas Frey, president of St. John's, an eccentric supporter of Wilkes and liberty, did so in 1768; but he found himself at the bottom of the poll, with less than one-third of the votes of Charles Jenkinson, the other defeated candidate. He was returned unopposed in November 1768 on Lord

Gower's interest at Newcastle-under-Lyme, and re-elected in 1774. He was now with the Government whenever his vote is recorded; but he was not a frequent speaker: only nine interventions of his in debate are noted 1768–74, none of much importance; and only four in the next Parliament, the last in December 1775. On 5 Dec. he spoke in favour of the prohibitory bill: 'No man in his senses could doubt that America was in rebellion', and rebels should be treated with severity. And again, on 8 Dec. he called the Admiralty courts in America 'the wisest and most salutary measure . . . for compelling the rebellious Americans to return to their duty'.[23] However, if Horace Walpole's statement is correct, he was asked in March 1778 to serve on the conciliation mission to America, but 'positively refused'.[24]

In May he fell ill, and on the 11th Horace Walpole prematurely registered his death.[25] By August he was known to be 'lunatic';[26] and the terms were settled for his quitting his offices.[27] In a postscript to a letter of 28 Sept.–5 Oct., James Hare wrote to Lord Carlisle, then with the conciliation mission in America: 'Sir George Hay, who has been confined for madness some time, yesterday escaped from his keepers and drowned himself.'[28]

Bishop Butler, a close friend of Legge's, wrote to Lord Onslow about Hay on 17 May 1778:[29]

> He had a better temper, a better understanding and a better character, than he was willing the world should see. It required much knowledge of him to perceive this . . . His conduct in politics was much blamed. The true account of it was that he had no opinion of any cause, but considered them all as the pretences under which men carry on their selfish schemes; yet he was a friend to liberty, and did not think it in danger in any hands. When he joined Lord Bute's party, for which I among others censured him, his apology was that Mr. Legge was declining in health, and that he liked neither Mr. Pitt nor any of the set, and thought the public full as safe in the feeble hands of Lord Bute as in theirs.

[1] Hay to Newcastle, 1 Mar. 1755, Add. 32853, f. 19. [2] *Grenville Pprs.* i. 138–9. [3] Add. 32860, f. 116. [4] *Mems. Geo. II*, ii. 144. [5] Add. 32860, f. 476; 33034, f. 208. [6] Add. 32861, f. 271; Newdigate's 'Debates'. [7] Add. 32869, f. 49. [8] Fox to Bedford, 23 Nov. 1756, Bedford mss 32, f. 107; Fox to Devonshire, 24 Nov., Devonshire mss. [9] Devonshire mss. [10] *Bedford Corresp.* ii. 220, 222. [11] Ibid. 241. [12] Add. 32871, ff. 383, 406. [13] Add. 32918, ff. 293, 338; 32929, ff. 143–5. [14] Harris's 'Debates'; Walpole, *Mems. Geo. III*, i. 296. [15] Add. 32959, ff. 3, 28, 98, 401. [16] *Grenville Pprs.* ii. 531. [17] *Mems. Geo. III*, ii. 38. [18] Ryder's 'Debates'. [19] Walpole, *Mems. Geo. III*, ii. 215. [20] Almon, iii. 273. [21] Fortescue, i. 236, 246, 267; Add. 32965, f. 311. [22] Add. 41354, f. 119. [23] Almon, iii. 250, 273. [24] *Last Jnls.* ii. 129. [25] Ibid. 174. [26] John Baker, *Diary*, ed. Yorke, 464. [27] Add. 41335, f. 229. [28] *HMC Carlisle*, 372. [29] Onslow mss at Clandon.

L.B.N.

**HAY, Thomas,** Visct. Dupplin (1710–87).

SCARBOROUGH 26 Jan.–21 Apr. 1736
CAMBRIDGE 1741–29 July 1758

*b.* 4 June 1710, 1st s. of George, 8th Earl of Kinnoull [S], by Abigail, da. of Robert Harley, 1st Earl of Oxford. *educ.* Westminster 1718; Ch. Ch. Oxf. 1726. *m.* 12 June 1741, Constantia, da. and h. of John Kyrle Ernle of Whetham, Wilts., 1s. *d.v.p. suc.* fa. as 9th Earl of Kinnoull 29 July 1758.

Commr. of revenue [I] 1741–6; ld. of Trade 1746–1754; chairman of committee of elections and privileges 1747–58; ld. of Treasury 1754–5; jt. paymaster gen. 1755–7; P.C. 27 Jan. 1758; chancellor of the duchy of Lancaster 1758–62; recorder of Cambridge 1758–*d.*; ambassador to Portugal 1759–62; chancellor of St. Andrews Univ. 1765–*d.*

Lord Dupplin was successively the faithful servant of Sir Robert Walpole, Henry Pelham, and the Duke of Newcastle. In 1754 he was returned unopposed for Cambridge, a borough managed for Government by Dupplin and Lord Montfort. He had been employed by Pelham on election business and in 1754 had to explain to Newcastle all Pelham's plans for the forthcoming general election. After the election he drew up for Newcastle a list of the House of Commons arranged according to political allegiances. He was also an expert on finance, and in this also he was Newcastle's mentor at the Treasury. 'Lord Dupplin aimed at nothing but understanding business and explaining it', wrote Horace Walpole, reviewing in 1755 the leading speakers in the House of Commons.[1]

But Kinnoull (as Dupplin became in 1758) was not made for Opposition and knew it. On Newcastle's resignation he told George III he would support whatever minister the King should name. When the Duke of Devonshire was dismissed, Kinnoull resigned his office from his 'inviolable friendship' to Devonshire, but refused to go into opposition.[2] He retired to Scotland and ceased to concern himself with politics; in July 1765, much to Newcastle's chagrin, he refused to become Government manager for Scotland under the Rockingham Administration.

He died 27 Dec. 1787.

[1] *Mems. Geo. II*, ii. 144, 146. [2] Sedgwick, 106, 162.

J.B.

## HAY, Thomas (1733–86), of Glyndebourne, Suss.

LEWES 1768–1780

*b.* 3 July 1733, 1st s. of William Hay (q.v.). *educ.* Westminster 1747; Göttingen Univ. *unm.*

Cornet 9 Drag. 1751; lt. 7 Drag. 1755, capt. 1757, maj. 1761; served on the expedition to Cherbourg 1758; in Germany 1759–63, as aide-de-camp to Granby; lt.-col. 1765; unattached list 1771.

In 1768 Hay was selected by Newcastle as candidate for Lewes, after having given an assurance that he would follow Newcastle in Parliament. A fortnight later Newcastle changed his mind; his re-

lations in Sussex were uneasy at the choice of Hay; it would be 'a perpetual exclusion of all of the name of Pelham for the future';[1] and he recommended instead Thomas Miller. But it was too late: Hay had already canvassed the town and had obtained promises from many of Newcastle's tenants, and was elected. In 1774 he stood on his own interest; in 1780 he stood again but was defeated; he did not stand in 1784.

Hay voted with the Opposition in Parliament, but there is no record that he ever spoke in the House. He was described by George Hardinge as 'a modest, virtuous, respectable, and sensible man; with no brilliancy of talent, but with a high sense of honour'.[2]

He died 9 Feb. 1786.

[1] Newcastle to Hay, 1 Mar. 1768, Add. 32989, f. 1. [2] Nichols, *Lit. Anecs.* viii. 520.

J.B.

## HAY, William (1695–1755), of Glyndebourne, Suss.

SEAFORD 25 Jan. 1734–19 June 1755

*b.* 21 Aug. 1695, o. surv. s. of William Hay, M.P., of Glyndebourne, by Barbara, da. of Sir John Stapley, 1st Bt., of Patcham, Suss. *educ.* Lewes g.s. 1710–12; Ch. Ch. Oxf. 1712; L. Inn; M. Temple; Grand Tour; called M. Temple 1723. *m.* 1731, Elizabeth, da. of Thomas Pelham, M.P., of Catsfield Place, Suss., 3s. 2da. *suc.* fa. 1695.

Commr. for victualling the navy 1738–47; keeper of the records in the Tower of London 1754–*d.*

William Hay married a cousin of Newcastle, electioneered on behalf of Newcastle's candidates, and was returned to Parliament by Newcastle. 'An acute and very intelligent speaker', wrote George Hardinge;[1] he voted consistently with Administration; and was particularly interested in poor law reform, on which he wrote copiously and introduced two bills into Parliament.

'His temper was not austere;' wrote Nichols, 'he willingly mixed in company and conversation, and sometimes made himself agreeable to his young friends by little pieces of poetry.' Deformed and scarcely five feet high, he wrote an *Essay on Deformity*—'a masterpiece of humour, wit, ingenuity, elegant style, fancy, and good sense . . . the portrait of a most amiable mind'.[2]

He died 19 June 1755, and on 29 June Newcastle wrote to Holdernesse:[3]

His Majesty has lost a very faithful and useful servant in the House of Commons, who in twenty-two years attendance there was scarce ever absent at one question and never gave a wrong vote, to the best of my remembrance.

[1] Nichols, *Lit. Anecs.* viii. 520. [2] Ibid. vi. 349; viii. 520. [3] Add. 32865, ff. 167–8.

J.B.

**HAYES, James** (1715–1800), of Hollyport, Berks.

DOWNTON    12 May 1753–June 1757, 1761–1768,
11 Feb. 1771–1774

*bap.* 27 Oct. 1715, 1st s. of James Hayes of Hollyport,
receiver of the land tax for Berks. 1744–50, by Mary,
da. of Richard Aldworth of Stanlake, Berks. *educ.*
Eton 1725–34; King's, Camb. 1734, fellow 1737–50;
M. Temple 1732, called 1740, bencher 1768, reader
1777, treasurer 1781. *m.* 20 Mar. 1750, Jane, da. of
James Croxton of Cheshire, 3s. 2da. *suc.* fa. 1750.
2nd. justice of Anglesey 1761–78, c.j. 1778–1793.

Hayes was a close personal friend of Lord Feversham, patron of Downton; and after his death an
executor of his will and trustee for his children. Like
his father and grandfather he was a practising
barrister, but not apparently of any great distinction.
When in 1756 Feversham solicited to have Hayes
made second justice of Chester, Hardwicke commented:[1] 'He urges his great merit, of which I can
say nothing because it has not come much in my
way.' Nor was he prominent in the House, and only
one speech by him is recorded (on the Minorca
inquiry, 26 Apr. 1757).

On the formation of the Devonshire-Pitt Administration, Hayes offered his seat to Pitt (who could
not expect to be re-elected at Aldborough); 'I am
sensible of how much more consequence it is to the
public that you should be in Parliament than myself
. . . and I entirely depend on your honour to consider what return you will think proper to make
me.'[2] Pitt found a seat elsewhere; but the next year
Hayes repeated his offer in favour of Charles Pratt,
his contemporary at Eton, appointed attorney-
general in the Newcastle-Pitt Administration. Pratt
accepted, and wrote to Pitt, 30 June 1757:[3] 'This
generous behaviour . . . deserves a suitable return,
and you will concur with me in thinking such a man
should not be deceived or disappointed.' In March
1761 he was appointed a Welsh judge, and at the
general election was returned again for Downton.

Fox wrote about him to Fitzmaurice, 15 Mar.
1761:[4] 'I hear he is a very gentlemanlike worthy
man, bred to the law, and a man of fortune. He
is through the attorney-general much attached I
believe to Mr. Pitt, but I don't know it'; and
Barrington to Newcastle, 1 Nov. 1761:[5] 'Hayes, who
though made a Welsh judge by Pitt, is your friend.'
Hayes does not appear in Fox's list of Members
favourable to the peace preliminaries. Pitt 'is always
great', he wrote of the debate of 9 Dec., 'and in some
parts of his speech on this occasion as great as ever
he was in his life'; but Hayes voted for the preliminaries.[6]

He is not in the list of those who voted against the
Grenville Administration over Wilkes, 15 Nov.

1763; but Harris includes him among those who 'left
the minority' on the division of 19 Jan. 1764—
which suggests he had previously voted with
Opposition, as he did again on 15 Feb. He was
absent from the division of 18 Feb., and was classed
by Newcastle, 10 May 1764, as a 'doubtful friend'.
In July 1765 Rockingham classed him as 'contra',
but he did not vote against the repeal of the Stamp
Act. He supported the Chatham Administration,
and voted with them on the land tax, 27 Feb. 1767.

As a trustee of Feversham's Wiltshire estate,
Hayes was involved in the struggle between Thomas
Duncombe and Lord Radnor for control of Downton; and seems to have supported Radnor. At the
general election of 1768, when Duncombe controlled
the borough, he was dropped; and it is not clear why
he was returned in 1771. In his last spell in Parliament he supported Government. He did not stand
in 1774, when Radnor first challenged Duncombe's
hold on the borough.

Hayes died 9 Sept. 1800.

[1] Add. 32868, f. 122. [2] Hayes to Pitt, 26 Nov. 1756, Chatham mss.
[3] Ibid. [4] Lansdowne mss. [5] Add. 32930, f. 257. [6] *Bedford Corresp.* iii.
168.

J.A.C.

**HAYLEY, George** (*d.*1781), of London.

LONDON    1774–30 Aug. 1781

1st s. of George Hayley (whose fam. came from Shropshire) by Hannah Hopkins (of a Herefordshire fam.).
*m.* Mary, da. of Israel Wilkes, malt distiller of Clerkenwell, wid. of Alexander Stock, merchant of London,
sis. of John Wilkes (q.v.), 2s. 2da.
Alderman of London 1774, sheriff 1775–6.

In 1781 the *English Chronicle* wrote about Hayley:

He was originally a clerk to the house in which he is
now the principal, and by a fortunate marriage with
his present amiable consort, with whom he received
a dower of £15,000, and by the exertions of honest
industry has so increased his fortune as to be deemed,
at this time, one of the wealthiest merchants in the
city. He is not very well calculated by endowments,
nor inclined by disposition, to take an active share in
the political bustle of the times, but is singularly exact
in his payments, upright in his general transactions,
and independent in his parliamentary conduct, which
has always entirely coincided with that of his patriotic
cynosure, the present chamberlain [John Wilkes].

In January 1775 Hayley took a leading part in the
organization of a petition to Parliament from the
merchants trading with America against the Government's American measures.[1] During this year he
spoke occasionally on questions concerning the
colonies, but he was not a good speaker. Frederick
Bull, commenting to Wilkes on a newspaper report
of a debate, remarked: 'Brother Hayley's speech was
short. I hope he did not stop in the middle. I think
he told the House that if it had not been for his

instructions he would not have troubled himself about the Americans.'[2]

In 1778 Hayley was one of the committee appointed by the common council to petition the King to make peace with America,[3] and the same year, as representative of his ward, signed an association 'for lawfully labouring to secure a more equal parliamentary representation'.[4] He was returned again in 1780, standing jointly with Bull, John Sawbridge and John Kirkman as a declared opponent of the Government.

He died 30 Aug. 1781.

[1] Walpole, *Last Jnls.* i. 417. [2] Add. 30871, f. 228. [3] *Last Jnls.* ii. 124. [4] *General Evening Post,* 9-12 Sept. 1780.

I.R.C.

## HAYNES, Samuel (1735-1811), of Sunning Hill, Berks.

BRACKLEY    6 July 1789-Dec. 1802

*bap.* 20 Mar. 1735, 1st surv. s. of Rev. Hopton Haynes by his w. Margaret.[1] *m.* Elizabeth, 1 da. (Charlotte Anne, m. 1783 J. W. Egerton, q.v.).

Haynes was returned for Brackley on the interest of the Duke of Bridgwater, whom his son-in-law J. W. Egerton succeeded in 1803 as 7th Earl of Bridgwater. Being of that connexion Haynes adhered to Pitt.

He died 18 June 1811.

[1] *Genealogist,* n.s. xx. 280-1.

L.B.N.

## HAYWARD, Thomas (1706-81), of Quedgeley, Glos.

LUDGERSHALL    1741-1747, 1754-1761

*bap.* 2 Aug. 1706,[1] 1st s. of William Hayward of Quedgeley by Margaret, da. of William Selwyn of Matson, Glos. *educ.* L. Inn 1723, called 1729. *m.* bef. 1733, Mercy, da. of Charles Parsons of Bredon, Worcs., 3s. 1da. *suc.* fa. 1709.

In 1754 Hayward was returned on the interest of his cousin George Augustus Selwyn. In Dupplin's list of 1754 he was classed as 'pro' among the group of Henry Fox's friends. On 16 Feb. 1758 he unsuccessfully applied to Newcastle to make his brother dean of Gloucester: 'I have attended the service of my country with great assiduity for one whole Parliament and half another, which may be presumed to have some merit, nor have I troubled your Grace before.'[2] Hayward did not stand again in 1761.

He died 14 Mar. 1781.

[1] Parish recs. printed *Glos. N. & Q.* iii. [2] Add. 32877, f. 472.

J.A.C.

## HEADLEY, Lord, see ALLANSON WINN

## HEATH, see DUKE

## HEATHCOTE, Sir Gilbert, 3rd Bt. (c.1723-85), of Normanton, Rutland.

SHAFTESBURY    1761-1768

*b.* c.1723, 1st s. of Sir John Heathcote, 2nd Bt., by Bridget, da. of Thomas White, M.P., of Wallingwells, Notts., sis. of John White (q.v.). *educ.* Queens', Camb. 1741. *m.* (1) 1 June 1749, Margaret (*d.* 10 Aug. 1769), da. of Philip Yorke, 1st Earl of Hardwicke, *s.p.*; (2) 26 Dec. 1770, Elizabeth, da. of Robert Hudson of Teddington, Mdx., 3s. 1da. *suc.* fa. 5 Sept. 1759.

In November 1756 Heathcote was offered by Newcastle a seat at Aldborough, without trouble or expense, but declined because of 'very particular objections' to being in the House: 'the attendance . . . would be very disagreeable to me', he wrote to Hardwicke, 22 Nov., 'and what I don't think I should ever perform as I ought to do'.[1]

In June 1760 Lord Exeter wrote to solicit Heathcote's support in Rutland for T. C. Cecil and Thomas Noel—Lord Winchilsea was running a candidate against them. Heathcote consulted Hardwicke, and Hardwicke Newcastle: he would not have Heathcote 'take such a part now, as, by an absolute submission, may exclude him for ever from taking advantage of the great property which he has in the county'. Newcastle offered to find a borough for Heathcote who should now, against a future election, try to form a connexion with one 'of the noble families in the county which his father had neglected'.[2] Meantime Heathcote returned to Exeter a reply drafted for him by Hardwicke:[3] having but lately come into a considerable property in the county, he must have a reasonable attention to any interest that may properly fall to his own share; and therefore 'be excused from taking any engagement on this occasion'. Two months later he still adhered to his neutrality 'as none of the parties have hinted anything relating to him'.[4] Negotiations between Exeter and Hardwicke followed in December.[5] Exeter dangled before him the chance that Cecil would withdraw soon; but Hardwicke did not relish the prospect of a by-election after a borough seat had been secured. Heathcote agreed: he would stand now if Cecil withdrew; otherwise he would give them his interest on a promise of support at a future election.

On 3 Feb. 1761 Newcastle wrote to Hardwicke offering Heathcote a seat at Shaftesbury on Lord Shaftesbury's interest. 'But the expense will be very great . . . viz. £2,000.'[6] Hardwicke and Heathcote thought 'the sum exorbitant'; yet 'he is ready to give it, provided he may be excused from going down to Shaftesbury and any personal attendance. He lays more weight upon the trouble and disagreeableness than upon the money.'[7] Although there was a contest, Heathcote's presence was dispensed with, and he was returned on 27 Mar.

And then on 4 Apr. Lady Grey wrote to her husband, Lord Royston:[8]

> The strangest event that has happened since you left us, is the desperate resolution Sir Gilbert has taken to go down and vote in Rutlandshire, for which he sets out with an aching heart, sleepless nights, and trembling nerves (God willing) tomorrow morning, and leaves *my lady* and *the steeds* to the protection of the fates for four or five whole days. It would tempt one to do something very riotous, carry off the former and turn the *latter* out to grass, if a cold on her part and a great deal of sobriety on ours, did not secure him.

In Parliament Heathcote voted against the peace preliminaries, 9 and 10 Dec. 1762; opposed Grenville's Administration; and supported Rockingham. He did not vote on the land tax, 27 Feb. 1767, but was classed by Newcastle as a friend, 2 Mar. 1767, and voted with Opposition on the nullum tempus bill, 17 Feb. 1768. There is no record of his having spoken in the House. He did not stand again, either for a borough or for Rutland.

He died 2 Nov. 1785.[9]

[1] Add. 35594, ff. 344, 347. [2] Add. 32907, ff. 157, 159, 235, 253–4. [3] Ancaster mss, Lincs. RO. [4] Hardwicke to Newcastle, 3 Aug., Add. 32909, ff. 239–40. [5] Hardwicke to Heathcote, 4 Dec. 1760, Ancaster mss; Add. 35596, ff. 197–201. [6] Add. 35420, f. 177. [7] Add. 32918, f. 228. [8] Add. 35376, f. 47. [9] *GEC Baronetage;* but *Gent. Mag.* gives 2 Dec.

L.B.N.

**HENDERSON, John** (1752–1817), of Fordell, Fife.

| | |
|---|---|
| FIFE | 7 Feb.–1 Sept. 1780 |
| DYSART BURGHS | 1780–1784 |
| SEAFORD | 29 Mar. 1785–13 Mar. 1786, 21 Mar.–26 Apr. 1786 |
| STIRLING BURGHS | 1806–1807 |

*b.* 8 Jan. 1752, 1st s. of Sir Robert Henderson, 4th Bt., by Isabella, da. of Archibald Stuart of Torrance, Lanark, wid. of George Mackenzie of Fairnie. *educ.* St. Andrew's Univ. 1764; Ch. Ch. Oxf. 1771; adv. 1774. *m.* May 1781, Anne Loudoun, da. of General James Robertson of Newbigging, Fife, 1da. *suc.* fa. as 5th Bt. 19 Oct. 1781.

Provost of Inverkeithing 1791–1807.

A non-practising lawyer, of an ancient Fife family, Henderson began his chequered political career in 1776, under the auspices of his uncle Andrew Stuart and Henry Dundas, when he unsuccessfully contested Fife. In 1779 Henderson stood again, was defeated, but seated on petition. He voted with Administration, and was counted 'pro' in Robinson's survey of 1780.

At the general election he was returned for Dysart Burghs, supported North until his fall, and followed

him into opposition, voting against Shelburne's peace preliminaries on 18 Feb. 1783. Divided in his loyalties between Dundas and Andrew Stuart, he was listed by Robinson in March 1783 among 'Lord North's connexions—doubtful', voted with Dundas in May 1783 for Pitt's reform motion, but remained absent in Scotland during the debates on Fox's East India bill.

On the formation of the Pitt Administration Robinson and Dundas were first 'hopeful', then 'very hopeful', of winning him over, mainly through the influence of his father-in-law, General Robertson, who 'on a hint' from Dundas 'advised him, at the period of the India bill, to leave his affairs in Scotland and come to London'. 'On his arrival, when the voice even of a single Member was of consequence', Robertson's counsels prevailed,[1] and by March 1784 he was listed as a Pitt supporter. Robinson expected him to 'come in again and be pro',[2] but he lost Dysart Burghs and was also defeated in Fife.

In 1785 Henderson secured, presumably through Dundas, the Treasury nomination for Seaford, and with Sir Peter Parker was returned 29 Mar. 1785. He voted for parliamentary reform, 18 Apr. 1785. Unseated on 13 Mar. 1786, he and Parker were re-elected 21 Mar., but again unseated on 26 Apr.

On the death of Robert Skene in May 1787 Henderson was a candidate against William Wemyss who proposed vacating his Sutherland seat to represent his native Fife. Both applied for support to Dundas who, reversing the policy of a decade, gave his interest to the Wemyss family, his former antagonists.[3] General Robertson protested to Dundas, 29 May 1787:[4]

> [Sir John] was much mortified at seeing Mr. Wemyss desire to change his seat with your approbation, to the destruction of his (Sir John's) favourite wish to support Administration in the county where he was born, which he had represented in Parliament and where his friends were numerous. He is now disposed to obey their call to support his own and their consequence by standing for the election.

While bound to 'aid a son-in-law and a friend', Robertson undertook 'to remind him of his interest and duty' to support Administration whatever the election result, and not to break with Dundas, but, embittered by defeat, Henderson rejected his advice. 'This', wrote Dundas in 1802, 'has procured me the inveterate opposition of Sir John ever since.'[5]

For a time Henderson thought of abandoning parliamentary ambitions, and in 1788 'wanted to go abroad as a foreign envoy'.[6] He was not then listed among active Opposition supporters, but hatred of Dundas soon led him to align himself with Henry Erskine in national as well as local politics.

He died 12 Dec. 1817.

[1] Robertson to Dundas, 29 May 1787, Melville mss, NLS. [2] Laprade, 102. [3] H. Furber, *Hen. Dundas*, 276. [4] Melville mss. [5] Furber, 276. [6] Adam, *Pol. State of Scotland 1788*, p. 123.

E.H.-G.

## HENEAGE, *see* WALKER HENEAGE

## HENLEY, Robert (c.1708–72), of The Grange, Alresford, Hants.

BATH 1747–30 June 1757

*b.* c.1708, 2nd s. of Anthony Henley, M.P., by Mary, da. and coh. of Hon. Peregrine Bertie, 2nd s. of Montagu, 2nd Earl of Lindsey. *educ.* Westminster 1720; St. John's, Oxf. 1724; fellow of All Souls 1727; I. Temple 1729, called 1732. *m.* 19 Nov. 1743, Jane, da. of Sir John Huband, 2nd Bt., of Ipsley, Warws., sis. and coh. of Sir John Huband, 3rd Bt., 3s. 5da. *suc.* bro. 1746; kntd. 29 Oct. 1756; *cr.* Baron Henley 27 Mar. 1760; Earl of Northington 19 May 1764.

K.C. 1751; bencher, I. Temple 1751; recorder of Bath 1751; solicitor-gen. to Prince of Wales 1751–4, attorney-gen. to him 1754–6; attorney-gen. Nov. 1756–June 1757; P.C. 30 June 1757; ld. keeper June 1757–Jan. 1761; ld. chancellor Jan. 1761–July 1766; ld. lt. Hants 1764–71; ld. pres. of the Council July 1766–Dec. 1767.

Henley, an ambitious lawyer, was a former Leicester House man who went over to the Pelhams after the Prince of Wales's death in 1751. When Sir Richard Lloyd was made solicitor-general in 1754, Hardwicke instructed Charles Yorke to write to Henley explaining the reason for this appointment, and adding:

> With respect to yourself, you were not forgotten, and I have lord chancellor's direction to tell you that he was not wanting to do you justice to the King and that he persuades himself he has possessed his Majesty with an opinion of you which will make him open to future applications in your favour.

The letter went on to assure Henley of Hardwicke's support for his claim to succeed to the vacant post of attorney-general to the Prince of Wales, to which he was duly appointed, being succeeded as the Prince's solicitor-general by Charles Yorke.[1]

On the death of Lord Chief Justice Ryder in 1756 Henley wrote to Hardwicke:[2]

> The great kindness I received from your Lordship (when on a late occasion you were pleased to mention your favourable intention towards me) induceth me on this great event in the profession . . . to throw myself on your Lordship's protection. I can, my Lord, say nothing for myself, but that my principles with regard to his Majesty and the public are such as your Lordship would approve, and that my morals will ever retain a most unalterable sense of gratitude for your Lordship's protection at this critical juncture.

On Hardwicke's recommendation Henley was made attorney-general in succession to William Murray and over the head of Sir Richard Lloyd.

Henley retained his post till the formation of the Pitt-Newcastle Coalition, when Pitt insisted that Charles Pratt should be attorney-general. Meanwhile the Great Seal, in commission since Hardwicke's resignation, had been refused by Mansfield and the master of the rolls, Sir Thomas Clarke, while Lord Chief Justice Willes was unwilling to take it without a peerage. In these circumstances, on Hardwicke's advice, it was conferred upon Henley, with the style of lord keeper, together with the reversion of a tellership of the Exchequer for his son and a pension of £1,500 p.a. till the tellership fell in. In accordance with precedent, Henley also became Speaker of the House of Lords, without the right to speak or vote there. Hardwicke regarded the appointment[3]

> as the best disposition [of the Great Seal] that could be made at present and much better approved at Westminster Hall than a commission, which is always disliked and should never be continued long. Sir Robert Henley has abilities and law and I hope will do very well, if his health permits of it.

Owing to George II's aversion to granting peerages, Henley remained for nearly three years, as he put it to Newcastle, in a 'very disagreeable situation . . . with respect to that rank in which (by his Majesty's grace only) I am placed in the House of Lords',[4] where his decisions in Chancery were liable to be reversed before his face without his being empowered to defend them. At last in 1760 he received a peerage to enable him to officiate as lord high steward at the trial of Lord Ferrers. He was not a regular member of the Effective Cabinet, attended by Hardwicke and Mansfield, till made lord chancellor, 16 Jan. 1761.

He died 14 Jan. 1772.

[1] Add. 35633, f. 352. [2] Add. 35594, f. 59. [3] Phillimore, *Lyttelton*, 593–4. [4] Walpole, *Mems. Geo. II*, iii. 274.

L.B.N.

## HENLEY, Robert, Lord Henley (1747–86).

HAMPSHIRE 1768–14 Jan. 1772

*b.* 3 Jan. 1747, o. surv. s. of Robert Henley (q.v.). *educ.* Westminster; Ch. Ch. Oxf. 1763. *unm.* *suc.* fa. as 2nd Earl of Northington 14 Jan. 1772; K.T. 18 Aug. 1773.

Teller of the Exchequer 1763–*d.*; clerk of the hanaper 1771–*d.*; P.C. 30 Apr. 1783; ld. lt. [I] June 1783–Feb. 1784.

Henley was returned for Hampshire without a contest, Richard Mill standing down for him. He supported the court, and his only recorded speech was on 8 Nov. 1768 when he moved the Address.

He died 5 July 1786.

M.M.D.

**HENLEY ONGLEY, Robert** (c.1721–85), of Old Warden, Beds.

BEDFORD       1754–1761

BEDFORDSHIRE   1761–1780, 1 July 1784–19 May 1785

*b.* c.1721, 3rd s. of Robert Henley of St. Clement Danes, London by Anne, da. of [?Thomas] Merryam, niece of Sir Samuel Ongley, M.P. *educ.* Ch. Ch. Oxf. 1741; M. Temple 1737, called 1744. *m.* 4 May 1763, Frances, da. and coh. of Richard Gosfright of Langton Hall, Essex, 2s. 4da. *suc.* to Old Warden estate of cos. Samuel Ongley and assumed add. name of Ongley 1747; *cr.* Baron Ongley [I] 30 July 1776.

Sir Samuel Ongley was a linen draper in Cornhill, a director of the East India Company and of the South Sea Company, 'very rich, said £10,000 per annum, 5 to be sure'.[1] His heir, Samuel Ongley, was M.P. for Bedford from 1734 till his death on 15 June 1747—Old Warden is about six miles from Bedford. Besides landed estates Robert Henley Ongley inherited an interest in East Indian affairs and City connexions; he frequently dabbled in Government stock, as subscriber or purchaser, usually in partnership with City men.

When the Duke of Bedford agreed to bring in Ongley for Bedford, Lord Hardwicke wrote from London to his son Philip, 22 Aug. 1753: 'It is strongly affirmed here that your neighbour Mr. Ongley is a determined Tory, but I thought you had told me otherwise.'[2] In the House he acted with the Bedford group, but guarding a measure of independence. His one reported speech in his first Parliament, 8 May 1760, was 'against the militia in general'.[3] Returned in 1761 for Bedfordshire with the Duke's support, he spoke on 9 Dec. 1761 against the German war: he had heard 'a great many words . . . but no one real argument' in its support—'I never approved of that measure from the first beginning.'[4] Harris notes: ' 'twas late and he was ill heard'. He took up subjects of interest to country gentlemen: spoke on the game bill, and was co-author of a bill concerning the powers of justices which none of the lawyers to whom Harris showed it approved of.[5] In December 1762 Fox listed him as favourable to the peace, and in the autumn of 1763 Jenkinson marked him as a Government supporter. On 15 Feb. 1764 Ongley wrote to Bedford:[6]

> As it has ever been my desire to see the administration of affairs in the hands of those who have the greatest stake in the country, so I shall always be extremely happy never to differ in opinion from your Grace, and will do everything in my power to assist Government when in such hands; always endeavouring to act in matters of great consequence according to the best of my judgment. I have not divided in any question with the minority, but I must own that I am far from

being clear, at present, that a secretary of state has, or ought to have, the power to seize persons and papers, in matters relative only to misdemeanours . . . I will, my Lord, attend the House on Friday, and . . . do everything which I can answer to my own judgment.

That Friday, 17 Feb., he spoke and voted with the Opposition, and was listed by Jenkinson among the straying 'friends'; while Newcastle marked him for the future merely as 'doubtful' (10 May).

In July 1765 Ongley followed Bedford into opposition. He repeatedly spoke against the repeal of the Stamp Act,[7] and voted accordingly. When Sir George Osborn, on 30 July 1766, asked Bedford for his support in the county at the next general election, the Duke replied that Ongley's parliamentary conduct had been so agreeable to him that he would be very sorry if the county was not willing to re-elect him.[8] On 27 Feb. 1767 Ongley spoke and voted against the Government on the land tax. He was returned unopposed in 1768.

In the Parliament of 1768–74 Ongley very frequently intervened in debate but his speeches were seldom on major political topics and none was of much weight. The description given of him in the *Public Ledger* in 1779 is about correct: 'He is a very narrow-minded, selfish man, and a tedious, bad speaker.' On 29 Nov. 1768 his speech on Wilkes's petition as reported by Cavendish is unclear, and so is the pattern of his subsequent voting: he was not with the Opposition on 27 Jan. 1769; voted with them on Wilkes's libel and expulsion (2 and 3 Feb.); and then, on 8 May, surprisingly, voted for declaring Luttrell duly elected. On 12 Dec. 1770 he spoke for postponing consideration of the land tax till after the Christmas recess: wherein he acted with the 'Bedford squadron', temporarily discontented with Lord North.[9] Over the printers' case and the commitment of the lord mayor to the Tower, he spoke and voted with the Government. He deprecated unauthorized publication of debates as leading to misrepresentation, 12 Mar. 1771; or admitting anyone into the gallery, 14 May 1777— 'he knew no business strangers had there'.[10] He supported the royal marriage bill.

In December 1770 he acted as nominee for Sir Thomas Rumbold over the New Shoreham by-election; and he frequently spoke on East India affairs. On 6 Dec. 1768 he opposed a petition for opening the East India trade: the national credit would be affected, and monopoly may be beneficial to trade. In May 1773 he supported Burgoyne's resolutions against Clive, and, disclaiming all animosity against him, remarked: 'I have riches enough and I envy not those of Lord Clive.' His attitude to those who had none, appears over the bill to prevent the vexatious removal of the poor, 2 Mar. 1774:

> This bill would be the most pernicious . . . Justices should have a discretionary power . . . Men should be confined to districts where they would be known . . . Working men will extort wages from their employers.[11]

And on the Act respecting imprisonment of debtors, 24 Feb. 1780: 'he verily believed 19 out of 20 debtors now in jail were fraudulent debtors.'[12]

In 1774 Ongley stood as a Government supporter, strongly backed by the Woburn interest, and was returned after a hot contest. Walpole, writing to Lady Ossory, 14 Nov. 1774, remarks on her husband's 'flinging away so much money on an election, and not for himself, who was sure of his own seat': besides being purse-proud, Ongley seems to have been parsimonious. He was one of the 18 Irish peers created in July-August 1776. He was a determined advocate of coercion toward America. Thus on 9 May 1777: 'He was satisfied the nation . . . was a match for all her foreign and domestic enemies, whether in America or Europe'; and her situation forbade her to make any concessions 'unbecoming her dignity, or short of her constitutional supreme rights over all the dominions of the British Crown'. On 28 Nov.: 'it is but reasonable that when we shall compel the colonies to their duty', they should be made to contribute to the support of the Government. When North moved his conciliatory proposals, 11 Feb. 1778, Ongley opposed 'any measure of accommodation, short of compelling America . . . to acknowledge the supreme right of Parliament'. But he supported the bill to exclude Government contractors from the House, 12 Feb. 1779. Over Keppel he still voted with the Government, 3 Mar. 1779; and on 11 Feb. 1780 objected to the Bedfordshire petition for economical reform. But an extraordinary change occurred on the 21st: Ongley voted with the Opposition on a motion calling for an account of pensions. Similarly on 8 Mar., over Burke's motion for economical reform. Almon's reporter states, however, that 'Lord Ongley spoke in very strong terms against the motion', which was probably a guess from past experience: judging by the brevity with which his speeches were reported, he was hardly listened to. Thus on Dunning's motion on the influence of the Crown, 6 Apr. 1780: 'Lord Ongley spoke in support of the original motion.' On Crewe's bill for disfranchising revenue officers, 13 Apr.: 'Lord Ongley spoke in favour of the bill.' On both occasions he again voted with the Opposition. Was it from conviction or with a view to securing in the county the continued support of the Woburn interest, directed

by Ossory and the Duchess, now both siding with the Opposition? Only in the last division of 24 Apr., against prorogation, Ongley again voted with the Government; and Robinson, in his survey of July 1780, put him down as 'pro',

> because he generally is so except in some of the questions of economy and reformation and I think he may be mostly depended upon, if attended to and humoured a little, for I have generally on trial found him practicable.[13]

At the general election of September 1780 the Woburn interest backed St. Andrew St. John against Ongley, who declined after canvass; on 16 Sept. the Rev. Hadley Cox, archdeacon of Bedford, had written to Hardwicke, who supported Ongley, that 'he will never carry the day . . . except he will untie the *hard knot* of his purse strings'.[14] But next, 'not being fond of an idle life', he appealed to Sandwich to remember him 'if any reasonable opportunity should offer of coming into Parliament'.[15] In 1784 Ongley stood for Bedfordshire as an adherent of Pitt; was defeated by one vote; was seated on petition, 1 July 1784; and unseated on a counterpetition, 19 May 1785. He died 23 Oct. 1785.

[1] Le Neve, *Knights* (Harl. Soc. viii), 508. [2] Add. 35351, ff. 265-6. [3] Jas. West to Newcastle, 8 May 1760, Add. 32905, f. 339. [4] Add. 38334, ff. 25-26. [5] Harris's 'Debates', 27 Apr. 1762. [6] Bedford mss 49, f. 46. [7] Fortescue, i. 205, 247; Harris's 'Debates', 24 Feb. 1766. [8] Bedford mss 53, f. 208. [9] Walpole, *Mems. Geo. III*, iv. 151. [10] Almon, vii. 194. [11] Brickdale's 'Debates'. [12] Almon, xvii. 179. [13] Ibid. vii. 173; viii. 367; xvii. 92, 278, 522. [14] Add. 35693, f. 367. [15] 31 Oct. 1780, Sandwich mss.

L.B.N.

**HENNIKER, John** (1724–1803), of Stratford House, West Ham, and Newton Hall, Dunmow, Essex.

SUDBURY      1761–1768
DOVER        1774–1784

> *b.* 15 June 1724, 1st s. of John Henniker of London, freeman of Rochester and Russia merchant, by Hannah, da. of John Swanson, London merchant. *m.* 24 Feb. 1747, Anne, da. and coh. of John Major (q.v.), 3s. 1da. *suc.* fa. 1749; and fa.-in-law by sp. rem. as 2nd Bt. 16 Feb. 1781; *cr.* Baron Henniker [I] 31 July 1800.
>
> Sheriff, Essex 1757-8; director, London Assurance Co. 1758.

Until about 1770 Henniker's City address is given as Janeway's coffee house; after that, Bank coffee house, Bank Street; and next Threadneedle Street. He continued the business of his father, who had been 'the greatest importer . . . of masts from Norway, Riga and Petersburg for his Majesty's navy';[1] was a big shipbuilder on the Medway;[2] had considerable shipping interests; and engaged in the Greenland white fishery.

In February 1754 Henniker was invited to stand

at Rochester,[3] but declined. On 6 Dec. 1760 he wrote to Newcastle:[4]

> Encouraged by your Grace's obliging promise of assistance in the next Parliament (after I had quitted Rochester at the desire of Mr. Pelham) I beg leave to offer my best services wherever your Grace may be pleased to direct—with probability of success. In Rochester I have a native interest and have been desired by some to offer myself a candidate. I will decline that without your Grace's full leave and permission.

Should Newcastle be already engaged everywhere, Henniker asked to be allowed to seek a seat in the best manner he could. This he did at Sudbury; and the following note appears against his name in Bute's parliamentary list of December 1761:

> Has a natural interest in the town of Rochester and very often has been indulged with building a man of war there. Supported in his election by a very considerable sum of money and the Duke of Newcastle, £5,500.

Fox, trying to secure a majority for the peace preliminaries, wrote to Sandwich on 12 Nov.: 'Pray, my Lord, send Mr. Major, Mr. Henniker, Mr. Stephenson, and, if you can, Lord Clive, to me next Tuesday' (16 Nov.).[5] The grouping suggests an East India House background to Sandwich's connexion with Major and Henniker. Newcastle, in his list of 13 Nov., still classed the two as his friends; but soon became aware of what was brewing—in his 'Memorandums' of 23 Nov. he linked their names with Sandwich's. However, on 1 Dec. they voted with the Opposition for postponing consideration of the preliminaries, and were not in Fox's list of Members secured in their favour. In the end both voted for them.[6] By 17 Dec. Newcastle had written off both.[7]

They now claimed their reward. On 7 Jan. 1763 Henniker wrote to Jenkinson asking for allotments in the loan for 1763: £50,000 for himself, and £30,000 for Major; and on 8 Jan. to Bute: he heard 'that Mr. Walpole was to quit the share of the contract he has with Mr. Fonnereau' (at Gibraltar), and asked to succeed him.[8] Although unsuccessful in this particular application, they obtained a contract for the victualling of troops in West Florida, and another for remitting money thither;[9] and grants of land in Nova Scotia, 20,000 acres each; last but not least, a baronetcy for Major with special remainder to Henniker—the warrant for it was signed on 5 July 1765,[10] five days before the Grenville Administration, to which the two had adhered, was dismissed from office. In July 1765 Rockingham classed Henniker 'contra'; but he did not vote against the repeal of the Stamp Act; and in November 1766 was listed by Rockingham as 'Swiss' (prepared to

support every Administration); by Townshend in January 1767 and by Newcastle on 2 Mar. as 'doubtful'. How he voted over the land tax, 27 Feb. 1767, is uncertain—one list places him on the Government side, another with the Opposition. After July 1765 the line taken by him no longer coincides with that of Major as much as it did before, but on one occasion they both voted with the Opposition: 9 Mar. 1767, over the printing of the papers of the East India Company.[11]

In 1768 Henniker did not stand again for Sudbury, but about a fortnight before the election declared his candidature for Maldon, a difficult and expensive borough. A stranger to it, he was guided by Bamber Gascoyne and John Strutt, who were inveterate opponents of John Huske. When defeated Henniker was unwilling to petition—'He is a poor creature', wrote Gascoyne to Strutt, 'and fit for nothing but the use we have made of him, and I wish we may hold him for another time.'[12] But Henniker was through with Maldon: the London voters alone cost him £800, 'and there are not fifty in number'.[13]

In 1774 he was returned as Government candidate for Dover, yet another difficult and expensive borough. During the war, 1776–82, he held considerable victualling contracts for troops in America.[14] Robinson wrote in his electoral survey of July 1780: 'Mr. Henniker would stand again and can well afford his share of an hearty contest, both from his fortune and the honey he eats from Government without much labour.' The return was unopposed; and Henniker's name again appears regularly in the lists on the Government side to the very end of the North Administration. But while his attendance was steady, only two speeches of his are recorded during his 17 years in the House, and both were on naval matters.[15] Henniker stuck to North even after his fall: voted against Shelburne's peace preliminaries; adhered to the Coalition; voted for Fox's East India bill; and against Pitt. He did not stand again in 1784. When his son entered the House in 1785 it was as a supporter of Pitt; and Henniker was one of the 16 Irish peers created on 31 July 1800.

Henniker had inherited a substantial fortune from his father, which he increased himself. When asking George Grenville for the baronetcy for his father-in-law with remainder to himself, he claimed to hold unencumbered landed estates worth near £3,000 p.a.; and those of John Major, to which his wife was co-heir and which were ultimately entailed on his son, he put at about £5,000 p.a.[16]

He died 18 Apr. 1803.

[1] John, 2nd Baron Henniker, *Some Account Fams. of Major & Henniker*, 3. [2] Add. 38340, f. 94. [3] *London Evening Post*, 9-12, 12-15 Feb. [4] Add. 32915, f. 330. [5] Sandwich mss. [6] Jas. Marriott to Bute

5 Feb. 1763, Bute mss; Newcastle's 'Mems' of 11 Dec., Add. 33000, f. 278. [7] Add. 32945, ff. 301–2. [8] Add. 5726 D. ff. 118–19. [9] T29/35/394; T54/39/300–6. [10] *Cal. Home Office Pprs. 1760–5*, p. 656. [11] Add. 32980, f. 248. [12] Strutt mss. [13] Gascoyne to Strutt, 21 Dec. 1773, ibid. [14] T54/42/176–8, 470–5; T54/43/134, 306, 435. [15] 21 Apr. 1766, Newdigate's 'Debates'; 30 Apr. 1776, Almon, iii. 501. [16] Henniker to Grenville, 2 May, 2 July 1765, Grenville mss (JM).

L.B.N.

## HENNIKER, John (1752–1821), of Worlingworth Hall, Suff.

| | |
|---|---|
| NEW ROMNEY | 7 June 1785–1790 |
| STEYNING | 3 Feb. 1794–1802 |
| RUTLAND | 31 Jan. 1805–1812 |
| STAMFORD | 1812–1818 |

*b.* 19 Apr. 1752, 1st s. of John Henniker and gd.-s. of John Major (qq.v.). *educ.* Eton 1764–8; St. John's, Camb. 1769; L. Inn 1768, called 1777. *m.* 21 Apr. 1791, Emily, da. of Robert Jones of Duffryn, Glam., *s.p. suc.* on *d.* of his mother 1792, to estates of his maternal gd.-fa., and took name of Major after that of Henniker. *suc.* fa. as 2nd Baron Henniker [I], 18 Apr. 1803.

In 1780 Henniker unsuccessfully contested his father's first constituency of Sudbury, but is not known to have stood anywhere in 1784. In 1785 he was returned at New Romney on the interest of Sir Edward Dering (q.v.), and in the House he was an independent supporter of Pitt. In one of the divisions on Richmond's fortifications plan he voted against Government: his name does not appear on either side in the only extant list, that of 27 Feb. 1786, but speaking on the army estimates, 10 Dec. 1787, he 'boasted to have been one of those who gave a vote against the system of fortifications, which had been proposed . . .' In doing so he claimed to have done 'essential service' to Pitt, 'and stood forward, with many other of his friends, to shield him from the consequence of a measure, that . . . must have brought mischief on himself and the country'. He now supported the Government proposals, and spoke of Pitt as a minister who 'had brought the country to an elevation of glory from a depressure of despondency'.[1] In the Regency crisis of 1788–1789 Henniker went with Pitt. His contributions to debates were sometimes exotic: thus, on Wilberforce's motion regarding the slave trade, 21 May 1789, Henniker, having declared that 'proper regulations might answer every necessary end of humanity, and that the trade might still be maintained', to illustrate the cruelties of native rulers he read out a letter of about 3,500 words written in 1726 by an African King to George I—'if we did not take the slaves off their hands, the miserable wretches would suffer still more severely'.[2] He concluded with a quotation from Cicero.

He left a few antiquarian studies, among them an 'Account of the Families of Henniker and Major'. He died 4 Dec. 1821.

[1] Stockdale, xiii. 65–66. [2] Ibid. xvii. 251–2.

L.B.N.

## HEPBURN, Robert Rickart (1720–1804), of Rickarton, Kincardine and Keith, Haddington.

| | |
|---|---|
| KINCARDINESHIRE | 1768–1774 |

*b.* 1720, 1st s. of James Hepburn (or Hepburn Rickart) of Keith, by Katharine, da. and h. of David Rickart of Rickarton. *educ.* Edinburgh h.s.; Edinburgh Univ. 1735. *m.* Magdalen, da. of Col. William Murray, 2s. 3da. *suc.* fa. in Keith estate, and mother in Rickarton. Cornet 6 Drag. 1743, capt. 1745, maj. 1755, lt.-col. 1763; sold out 1768. Burgess, Edinburgh 1762.

His grandfather, originally Congalton of that ilk, on succeeding to the Keith estate changed his name to Hepburn and relinquished to his next brother the Congalton estate, which subsequently passed out of the family. His father was 'out' in the '15, fled abroad, but eventually returned to Scotland where he lived in close friendship with Robert Keith (later ambassador) and his family.

At Edinburgh University Robert Rickart Hepburn was a contemporary of John Home and Alexander Carlyle. He was serving with the Inniskillings in Flanders when, on the outbreak of the '45, his father again joined the rebels.[1] Hepburn's military career was not materially affected by his father's Jacobitism. He commanded the Inniskillings at Minden and, with Robert Murray Keith, was called as a witness for the defence by Lord George Sackville at his court-martial.

Soon after Hepburn's brother-in-law David Graeme entered Parliament, he took steps with the support of Lord Findlater and the Bute connexion to secure Hepburn's return for Kincardineshire.[2] In Parliament Hepburn was a constant, though silent, Government supporter; his only recorded Opposition vote was on Grenville's Act, 25 Feb. 1774. Although there is no evidence that Hepburn was involved in Graeme's political intrigues, North's hostility to Graeme barred Hepburn's re-election in 1774, when the Kincardineshire gentlemen 'offered the county' to Lord Adam Gordon.

Having bought back the ancestral seat of Congalton, Hepburn retired there, unable to afford the London life he preferred. He wrote, 29 Mar. 1783, to Robert Murray Keith:[3]

It is natural for people who can afford it to get near the seat of Government; in England . . . you feel you are in a better country . . . amongst a richer and happier people . . . All this strikes one with a damp whenever you cross the Tweed, and everything relating to the Government here seems things . . . that we have little concern in. The only objects of the common people is to be free of patronage . . . and of the gentlemen a good or bad crop . . . We are only fit to supply England with inhabitants and very few of those that can help it will ever return except for a visit.

He sought Keith's interest in obtaining preferment for his son, and a place for himself as commissioner of Excise,[4] and, a disillusioned observer, sent him critical comments on political events.

He seems to have made no attempt to re-enter Parliament and died 24 May 1804.

[1] Carlyle, *Autobiog.* 31, 54, 232–3, 265. [2] Add. 38205, ff. 138, 142. [3] Add. 35528, f. 141. [4] Add. 35527, f. 110; 35529, f. 141; 35539, f. 173; 35541, f. 170.

E.H.-G.

**HEPBURNE SCOTT**, *see* **SCOTT, Hugh**

**HERBERT, Charles** (1743–1816), of Heath, nr. Wakefield, Yorks.

WILTON    20 Feb. 1775–1780
1806–5 Sept 1816

*bap.* 28 May 1743, 2nd s. of Hon. William Herbert, and bro. of Henry Herbert (qq.v.). *educ.* ?Eton 1753–4. *m.* 13 July 1775, Lady Caroline Montagu, da. of Robert, 3rd Duke of Manchester.
     Lt. R.N. 1761; cdr. 1765; capt. 1768.
     Groom of the bedchamber 1777–*d.*

Herbert regularly voted for North's Administration. He spoke in the House on 25 Feb. 1777, and may be the 'Mr. Herbert' who spoke on 10 Dec. 1778.[1] In 1780 Robinson did not expect Lord Pembroke, now in opposition, to return Herbert again.

He died 5 Sept. 1816.

[1] Almon, vi. 302; ix. 131.

J.B.

**HERBERT, Edward** (?1700–70), of Muckross, co. Kerry.

LUDLOW    10 Dec. 1754–26 Sept. 1770

*b.* ?1700, 1st s. of Edward Herbert of Muckross by Agnes, da. of Patrick Crosbie of Tubrid, co. Kilkenny. *educ.* Pembroke, Oxf. 1 Mar. 1722, aged 21; M. Temple 1722, called 1734. *m.* 1723, Hon. Frances Browne, da. of Nicholas, 2nd Visct. Kenmare [I], 3s. 6da.
     M.P. [I] 1749–60.

The Herberts of Muckross, who had settled in Ireland in the seventeenth century, were descended from the Herberts of Powis. They do not seem to have been of high standing in Ireland, and the marriage with Edward Herbert was vigorously opposed, on social as well as religious grounds, by Frances Browne's Catholic family, who considered the Herberts 'a poor sort of people'.[1] Also by the English Herberts, with whom Edward Herbert kept

up a connexion, he seems to have been regarded as a poor relation. In 1736 he was appointed agent to the Kenmare estate by Henry Arthur Herbert (created Earl of Powis 1748), then guardian of the 4th Viscount Kenmare, but in 1747, when Kenmare came of age, was dismissed with 'a present of £4000, balance of money due from him to me as my agent'. Kenmare later wrote of the Herberts: '[I] recommend it to such as succeed me upon no account to . . . have any dependence on the honesty or professions of their family.' He subsequently seems to have modified his opinion about the Herbert family, adding in October 1767: 'I have since that time been under some obligations to the old gentleman and his son Tom for services rendered me in providing for a youth in the East Indies' and for 'their zeal in an appeal' he had in court.[2]

In 1754 Herbert settled in England as agent to Lord Powis, and in September, after the death of Powis's brother, Richard Herbert, was returned in his place for Ludlow. In Parliament Herbert supported Administration, and in July 1761 was unsuccessfully recommended by Powis to Newcastle for the post of auditor general to the Queen. Like Powis, he supported Bute and Grenville, and opposed Rockingham, voting against the repeal of the Stamp Act, 22 Feb. 1766. He voted against the higher land tax, 27 Feb. 1767, but supported Administration on nullum tempus, 17 Feb. 1768. In the new Parliament he voted with Opposition in three divisions on Wilkes and the Middlesex election, 27 Jan., 2 and 3 Feb. 1769. There is no record of his having spoken in the House. He died 26 Sept. 1770.

[1] *Irish HMC Kenmare*, 124. [2] Notebook of Thos. 4th Visct. Kenmare, ibid. 189–90.

M.M.D.

**HERBERT, George Augustus,** Lord Herbert (1759–1827).

WILTON    1780–17 Nov. 1784, 9 Feb. 1788–26 Jan.
1794

*b.* 10 Sept. 1759, o.s. of Henry, 10th Earl of Pembroke, by Lady Elizabeth Spencer, da. of Charles, 3rd Duke of Marlborough. *educ.* Harrow 1770–5; Grand Tour 1775–80. *m.* (1) 8 Apr. 1787, his 1st cos. Elizabeth (*d.*1793), da. of Topham Beauclerk by Lady Diana Spencer, da. of Charles, 3rd Duke of Marlborough, 3s. 1da.; (2) 25 Jan. 1808, Catherine, da. of Count Vorontsov of Russia, 1s. 5da. *suc.* fa. as 11th Earl 26 Jan. 1794. K.G. 17 Jan. 1805.
     Ensign 12 Ft. 1775;[1] capt. 75 Ft. 1778; capt. 1 Drag. 1778; maj. 22 Drag. 1781; lt.-col. 2 Drag. Gds. 1782; col. 1793; maj.-gen. 1795; col. 6 Drag. 1797–*d.*; lt.-gen. 1802.
     P.C. 17 Nov. 1784; vice-chamberlain of the Household 1784–94; ld. lt. Wilts. 1794–*d.*

Herbert started on his Grand Tour in November

1775 with the Rev. William Coxe (later Archdeacon Coxe, the historian) for tutor, and Major Floyd for travelling companion. They stayed at Strasbourg till April 1777, except for the summer of 1776, spent in Switzerland. 'I think history the most essential of all studies for his Lordship', wrote Coxe to Lady Pembroke, 15 Feb. 1776, 'for which reason I shall make that my principal aim.' And on 7 Mar.: 'He has got the better of his indolence, which I once began to despair of.' 30 June: 'He has received a bad education . . . is not in the least fond of poetry, nor has he any inclination for polite literature. He has no great ambition to make a figure . . . He has uncommon good principles, and is possessed of very amiable qualities.' During the next three years Lord Pembroke, while preaching economy, made them traverse Europe in various directions. Belgium and Holland, May–July 1777; Potsdam, Berlin, Breslau, Prague, Dresden, back to Berlin, Leipzig, Prague, Vienna, Aug.–Oct. 1777; the winter in Vienna; and then, on 7 Apr. 1778: 'I hope you will see Pressburg, and part of Hungary, . . . Warsaw, Stockholm, . . . and Copenhagen, in your way to Petersburg . . . I much wish you would reach Venice before the winter . . . I seriously desire you will follow the cheapest way of travelling . . . for you cannot conceive how much I am really distressed.' 27 July, Moscow is added to the itinerary, 'with as little expense as possible, for I am poor beyond description'. Having gone by Moscow, they returned from Petersburg by Finland, Sweden, and Copenhagen, Lübeck, Hamburg, and Munich, reaching Vienna once more in June 1779; to Venice and Milan, where Coxe left them; Naples, August 1779. 'You will be a Parliament man by the time you return,' wrote Pembroke to him, 30 Sept. And Lady Pembroke, 20 Oct.: 'Lord Pembroke is distressed for money . . . it is your constant moving that made the expense . . . he orders you to travel . . . eternally . . . and is all the time preaching to you to spare money.' With the country at war, Herbert wanted to join his regiment; 'your madness to return', Pembroke called it, 23 Nov. 1779. Finally he agreed: but Herbert was to return by way of Spain and Portugal. On 1 Jan. 1780: 'I . . . consent to your return home without visiting those two countries, provided that you will promise me to do it the first opportunity.' After a few months in Turin, and a tour of France, he reached England in June 1780.

At the general election of 1780, a day after having come of age, Herbert was returned, in his own words 'to represent our worthy constituents of our worthy corporation of Wilton borough'. 'I wish you would muster up your oratorical powers', wrote Pembroke on 14 Oct., ' . . . and give that *canaille une bonne*

*salade* in St. Stephen's Chapel.' But Herbert was trying for an appointment in the household of the Prince of Wales, and the King and Queen were friendly—'you should not this time vote against the Address', wrote Lady Pembroke on 24 Oct., 'so immediately after asking a favour, whether granted or not, as they have been as civil as they can about it.' And Floyd, on the 30th, the day before Parliament met: 'I guess . . . some of your reasons for not being very anxious about continuing in Parliament, or attending it assiduously . . . your opinion on political topics may not always coincide [with his father's], and that will be awkward enough.' And after his first three weeks in Parliament, Herbert wrote to Sir Robert Murray Keith, then minister to Vienna:

> I have lately discovered what has long been known, that in this blessed country nobody sits on principle, being all biassed by connexions, either friendly or family interest etc. For my part I have been on three divisions in the House and out of those three times have only voted once according to my opinions, and did that *en cachet* for fear my *family connexions* should get hold of it. And after all this the world are pleased to call me a free Englishman and a member of a free Parliament.

As a rule, therefore, he can be assumed to have adhered to 'family connexions' and voted against the Government: on his being refused a company of the Guards, 'favours in any profession', wrote Lady Pembroke on 10 Oct. 1781, 'are not to be expected when in red hot opposition to Government'; and in the division lists of December 1781–March 1782, he is seen voting regularly with the Opposition. He voted for Shelburne's peace preliminaries, 18 Feb. 1783; and for parliamentary reform 7 May. When in the summer his parents went abroad, Pembroke insisted that either he himself or Herbert must stay at home—because of possible difficulties at Wilton in case of a dissolution. But Herbert left for France in October 1783; was away during the critical months November 1783–March 1784; and was returned for Wilton in his absence. He landed at Dover on 17 Aug., three days before Parliament was adjourned; and when appointed vice-chamberlain to the King, 17 Nov. 1784, did not seek re-election, but returned his friend Goldsworthy for his seat. 'By this time', wrote Pembroke from Rome on 16 Feb. 1785, 'ye have probably settled your parliamentary business; if to your own mind, it is certainly so to mine.'

Herbert may have left the House for reasons of health: 'I am glad ye are not sitting in the bad House of Commons air', wrote his father, 11 Jan. 1786, 'but sorry to hear *any* physician thinks it necessary to advise you against it.'

On 21 Sept. 1787, Pembroke wrote to Herbert from Wilton House:

> Do you mean to be a Parliament man again? I am inclined to believe not. At any rate I wish ye would be rechosen again, or that we should take some other step; for, though Goldsworthy was very proper for the time, I do not, of course, mean him to be the fixed Member here.

Herbert replied that Goldsworthy 'certainly did not consider himself as the settled representative of Wilton'; but as Pitt was willing to bring him in on a vacancy, Herbert preferred 'remaining out till that took place'.

The subject of Parliament came up once more in January 1788. Pembroke, writing from France, suggested that Herbert might secure Pitt's agreement to being called up to the House of Lords; 13 Feb.: 'the House of Commons . . . is particularly unwholesome for you, stink, heat and late hours, etc.' Herbert replied, 3 Mar.: 'The House of Commons is certainly neither an agreeable or wholesome place for me, but I am so much better in health now than I have been for three or four years, that a common decent attendance there cannot, I think, do me harm.' During the Regency crisis he voted with Pitt, whom he followed and greatly admired. He was not, however, a strong party man and did not relish the violent animosities which developed during those years. Nor is he known to have spoken in the House.

He died 26 Oct. 1827.

[1] Lord Herbert, *Pembroke Pprs.* i. 49, from which all quotations are taken.

L.B.N.

**HERBERT, Henry** (1741–1811), of Christian Malford, Wilts. and Highclere, Hants.

WILTON 1768–July 1772, 7 Dec. 1772–1780

*b.* 20 Aug. 1741, 1st s. of William Herbert, and bro. of Charles Herbert (qq.v.). *educ.* Eton 1753–9; Ch.Ch. Oxf. 1760; Glasgow Univ. 1762. *m.* 15 July 1771, Lady Elizabeth Wyndham, da. of Charles, 2nd Earl of Egremont, 7s. 1da. *suc.* fa. 1757; *cr.* Baron Porchester 17 Oct. 1780; Earl of Carnarvon 3 July 1793. P.C. 12 Feb. 1806; master of the horse 1806–7.

Herbert sat for Wilton on the interest of his cousin, Lord Pembroke. He voted with Opposition over Wilkes and the Middlesex election, and in 1770 introduced a bill to allow a Member expelled from the House to take his seat if re-elected. He is described by Horace Walpole as 'a young man of great fortune and good principles', and 'a very conscientious young man'.[1] He was a frequent speaker in the House; never attached himself to any party; and judged issues on their merits.

On 6 Dec. 1770 he opposed a motion by John Glynn, Wilkes's friend, to inquire into the administration of justice—an Opposition measure founded on no real grievance; but on 7 Feb. 1771 he spoke for Sir George Savile's bill to secure the rights of electors—which had some popular feeling behind it. He did not vote with the Opposition over the Spanish convention, 13 Feb. 1771. On 18 Mar. 1771, during a debate on the printers' case, he warned the House against engaging 'in another contest with the people, more difficult and more dangerous' than the Middlesex election—'It will be no disgrace to give up a little dignity absurdly engaged'.[2] He voted for the petition of the clergy against subscription to the 39 Articles, 6 Feb. 1772, and against the royal marriage bill, which he said 'ought to be entitled an act to encourage adultery and fornication'.[3]

In July 1772 Herbert vacated his seat at Wilton and contested Wiltshire at a by-election. On 25 July he wrote to Shelburne asking for his interest in the county. Shelburne replied:[4]

> I should be very glad to obey your commands as well on account of the good disposition which I am informed you have shown in Parliament as of some persons you stand connected with for whom I have a great regard. But it's impossible for me on this occasion to separate myself from those who . . . made strenuous though hitherto ineffectual efforts for the redress of grievances, to which I must think a temporary opposition insufficient.

The election was hard fought, and Herbert was defeated. In December he was re-elected for Wilton where the vacancy had not been filled. About 1774 he began to build up an interest at Cricklade; and between 1779 and 1782, when the borough was reformed, controlled one seat.

He voted for Grenville's Election Act, 25 Feb. 1774, and for Wilkes's motion on the Middlesex election, 22 Feb. 1775, but supported the court over the American war. He seems at this time to have been losing interest in Parliament: between 1768 and 1774 eighty speeches by him are reported by Cavendish, but for 1774–80 Almon's *Parliamentary Register* prints only two. When defeats came he blamed the conduct of the war: on 3 Mar. 1779 he voted with Opposition on the motion of censure against the Admiralty, and on 26 Nov. 1779 criticized the state of the defence at Plymouth. He did not vote in the divisions of February–April 1780 for which lists are available—again an indication that his interest in Parliament had waned.

On 21 Aug. 1780 John Robinson wrote to Charles Jenkinson: 'Unless Henry Herbert will stand for Hampshire, I fear no candidate tolerably on our side will step forward. Herbert will with encouragement.'[5] Shortly afterwards Herbert learnt that Lord

Pembroke, now in opposition, would not return him again for Wilton; but still he did not contest Hampshire. Perhaps he already had a promise of a peerage. He died 3 June 1811.

[1] *Mems. Geo. III*, iv. 73; *Last Jnls.* i. 62. [2] *Brickdale's' Debates'.* [3] *Last Jnls.* i. 44. [4] *Lansdowne mss.* [5] *Add. 38567, f. 59.*

J.B.

**HERBERT, Henry Arthur** (1756–1821), of Muckross, co. Kerry.

EAST GRINSTEAD    19 Feb. 1782–Feb. 1786
KERRY                          1806–1812
TRALEE                        1812–June 1813

*b.* 1756, 1st s. of Thomas Herbert (q.v.). *educ.* ?Harrow 1774–6; St. John's, Camb. 1774; M. Temple 1776. *m.* 28 Oct. 1781, Elizabeth, da. of Lord George Germain (q.v.), 2s. 1da.

Herbert was returned for East Grinstead in place of his father-in-law, created Viscount Sackville; followed his lead in politics, voted with North in the five crucial divisions, 20 Feb.–15 Mar. 1782, and spoke against Conway's motion to end the war, 27 Feb. 1782. On 8 Apr. 1782 he opposed a motion for Irish legislative independence.[1] He voted against Shelburne's peace preliminaries, 18 Feb. 1783, and spoke and voted against Fox's East India bill, 27 Nov. 1783. In December 1783 Herbert was offered an appointment at the Admiralty Board by Pitt who hoped that Sackville, by allowing Herbert to accept, would show his 'disposition in favour of the present Government'.[2] Sackville explained that Lord Carmarthen's appointment as secretary of state made him refuse, otherwise he would have been 'happy in seeing Mr. Herbert at the Board of Admiralty as a mark of favour to him and attention to me'.[3] Nevertheless Herbert and Sackville supported Pitt's Administration, and in 1785 Herbert, through the Duke of Dorset, approached Pitt about an Irish peerage, and apparently received a favourable reply.[4] Herbert resigned his seat in 1786; his reasons for doing so have not been ascertained. In 1789 he applied to Pitt directly about the peerage which he claimed had been promised him, but was unsuccessful.

He died 21 June 1821, aged 65.

[1] Debrett, vii. 17. [2] Pitt to Sackville, 29 Dec. 1783, *HMC Stopford-Sackville*, i. 81. [3] Sackville to Ld. Sydney, 30 Dec. 1783, ibid. 82. [4] H. A. Herbert to Pitt, 6 Sept. 1789, Chatham mss.

M.M.D.

**HERBERT, Hon. Nicholas** (c.1706–75), of Great Glemham, Suff.

NEWPORT    22 Jan. 1740–1754
WILTON        17 Apr. 1757–1 Feb. 1775

*b.* c.1706, 7th s. of Thomas, 8th Earl of Pembroke, by

his 1st w. Margaret, da. and h. of Robert Sawyer of Highclere, Hants; bro. of Robert Sawyer and William Herbert (qq.v.). *educ.* ?Eton 1725; Ch. Ch. Oxf. 1726. *m.* 19 July 1737, Anne, da. of Dudley North, M.P., of Great Glemham, Suff., 2da.

Cashier and accountant to the treasurer of the navy 1742–5; treasurer to Princess Amelia 1757–60; sec. of Jamaica 1765–*d.*

Herbert sat at Wilton on the interest of his nephew Henry, 10th Earl of Pembroke. On the accession of George III he lost his place as treasurer of the Household to Princess Amelia, and on 20 July 1761 wrote to Newcastle:[1]

> I flattered myself from your Grace's answer to her Royal Highness's strong recommendation of me, that some proper employment would have been given me before the breaking up of the last Parliament and was not a little mortified at finding no sort of notice taken of me, not even with a promise upon a first vacancy, while several were preferred to the Board of Trade and even much higher offices, who I have pride enough to think, considering my family and connexions, have less pretensions than myself, even though I had not been recommended to your Grace by her Royal Highness, and I think my pretensions still greater as I am almost the only person in Parliament who has lost a place in consequence of his late Majesty's death, who has not had an equivalent by some other employment.

An opportunity is afforded by 'the list now making out of servants for the Queen that is to be'; if Newcastle would not endeavour to help, he should say so frankly. Newcastle replied that he was 'greatly concerned and indeed a little surprised' at Herbert's letter. 'My situation at present at court is such as gives me very few opportunities of being useful to men to whom I wish very well. My promise to you could only extend to my power . . . I heartily wish you would apply to others, who may be more able to serve you.'[2]

Herbert again wrote to Newcastle on 1 Nov. 1761, asking for Andrew Stone's place at the Board of Trade, and added:[3]

> I do not withdraw myself from your Grace's levee out of any disrespect to your Grace's person, but out of regard to my own . . . I have too much spirit to attend there as an unsuccessful beggar, to be sneered at as many others have been upon like occasions, by the company present for my folly and credulity.

Herbert does not appear in Henry Fox's list of Members favourable to the peace preliminaries, yet he did not vote against them. He is not known to have voted against any Administration nor ever to have spoken in the House. He died 1 Feb. 1775.

[1] Add. 32925, f. 207. [2] Ibid. f. 209. [3] Add. 32914, f. 15.

L.B.N.

**HERBERT, Richard** (*d.*1754).

LUDLOW    11 Feb. 1727–1741, 30 Dec. 1743–17 May 1754

s. of Francis Herbert of Oakley Park, Salop, by Dorothy, da. of John Oldbury, London merchant; bro. of Henry Arthur Herbert, 1st Earl of Powis. *unm.*

Richard Herbert sat at Ludlow on the interest of his brother, Lord Powis. For some time before 1754 Powis had been trying to secure some provision for him. But it was only after Henry Pelham's death that Newcastle was able to satisfy Herbert with the offer of the wardenship of the mint. But as a second vacancy on the Board of Green Cloth had been simultaneously set aside for John Grey, who was not even in Parliament at that time, Herbert considered it beneath his dignity to accept the wardenship unless the salary was made equal to Grey's.[1]

Eventually, on 2 Apr., this was agreed upon and a private addition of £400 p.a. arranged. But the long sought for preferment was not long enjoyed, for, one month after the general election, Herbert died, 17 May 1754.[2]

[1] Add. 32995, ff. 110, 126, 130, 180. [2] *Mont. Colls.* viii. 6.

L.B.N.

## HERBERT, Hon. Robert Sawyer (1693–1769), of Highclere, Hants.

WILTON 1722–1768

*b.* 28 Jan. 1693, 2nd s. of Thomas, 8th Earl of Pembroke, and bro. of Hon. Nicholas and Hon. William Herbert (qq.v.). *educ.* Ch. Ch. Oxf. 1709. *m.* Mary, da. of John Smith, Speaker of the House of Commons, *s.p. suc.* to mother's estates 1706.

Groom of the bedchamber 1723–7; commr. of revenue [I] 1727–37; ld. of Trade 1737–51; ld. lt. Wilts. 1750–2; surveyor of Crown lands 1751–*d.*

Herbert is not known ever to have given a vote against Administration or to have made a speech in the House; and was correctly classified by Rockingham in November 1766 as 'Swiss' (prepared to serve any Administration).

He died 25 Apr. 1769.

J.B.

## HERBERT, Thomas (?1727–79), of Muckross, co. Kerry.

LUDLOW 3 Nov. 1770–1774

*b.* ?1727, 1st s. of Edward Herbert (q.v.). *educ.* Hackney; St. John's, Camb. 12 July 1744, aged 17; M. Temple 1743, called 1750. *m.* (1) 7 May 1755, Anne, da. of John Martin (q.v.), 2s. 5da.; (2) Agnes, da. of Rev. Francis Bland of Killarney, 2s. 2da.

Herbert was returned in place of his father on the Powis interest at Ludlow. Robinson in his first survey on the royal marriage bill, March 1772, listed him as 'pro, present', and as 'pro' before the general election of 1774, but there is no record of any vote

or speech by him. Herbert did not stand again in 1774.

He died May 1779.

M.M.D.

## HERBERT, Hon. William (c.1696–1757).

WILTON 1734–31 Mar. 1757

*b.* c. 1696, 5th s. of Thomas, 8th Earl of Pembroke, and bro. of Hon. Nicholas and Hon. Robert Sawyer Herbert (qq.v.). *m.* bef. 1741, Catherine Elizabeth Tewes of Aix-la-Chapelle, 3s. 2da.

Lt. 1 Life Gds. 1722; capt. and lt.-col. 1 Ft. Gds. 1738; col. 1745; a.d.c. to Geo. II; col. 14 Ft. 1747–53; col. 6 Marines Feb.–Dec. 1747; col. 2 Drag. Gds. 1753–*d.*; maj.-gen. 1755.

Groom of the bedchamber 1740–*d.*; paymaster to the garrison at Gibraltar 1740–*d.*

In all available division lists Herbert is found voting with Administration, and was classed as 'for' in Dupplin's list of 1754. He died 31 Mar. 1757.

L.B.N.

## HERNE, Francis (c.1702–76), of Luton Hoo, Beds. and Harrow-on-the-Hill, Mdx.

BEDFORD 1754–1768
CAMELFORD 1774–26 Sept. 1776

*b.* c.1702, s. of Francis Herne, Spanish merchant, by his w. a Miss or Mrs. Flatman. *educ.* Harrow 1714–20; Caius, Camb. 1720. *suc.* to Luton Hoo estates of his kinswoman Miss Frances Napier 1751.

Sheriff, Beds. 1753–4.

Herne was returned in 1754 on a compromise with the Duke of Bedford and with the support of the corporation at a cost of 'about £460'.[1] Dupplin in 1754 classed him as Tory; Bute in December 1761 as 'Bedford, Tory'; Rockingham in November 1766 and Townshend in January 1767 as 'Bedford'. He does not, however, appear to have acted in Parliament with the Bedfords, nor was he ever claimed by them as one of their party. His name is not included in Henry Fox's list of Members in favour of the peace preliminaries. In the autumn of 1763 Jenkinson marked him as 'doubtful'; he is not in any minority list on Wilkes; and on 16 Feb. 1764, during the debates on general warrants, Edward Kynaston, writing to Jenkinson, included Herne among 'such gentlemen, that perhaps a line from you or Mr. Grenville may engage their attendance tomorrow', though he was one of those who 'very seldom stay out a long day'.[2] His one recorded vote was with Opposition on the land tax, 27 Feb. 1767.

In 1763 Herne sold Luton Hoo to Lord Bute, and in 1768 did not stand for Bedford. The circumstances of his election for Camelford in 1774 have not been ascertained. He was presumably nominated by Administration, though it is not clear why they should have chosen one apparently independent of them. There is no record of his having spoken in the House. He died 26 Sept. 1776.

[1] T. Woodward to R. Butcher, 25 Apr. 1754, Bedford mss (unbound). [2] Add. 38202, f. 91.

M.M.D.

**HERRIES, Sir Robert** (1730–1815), of Richmond, Surr.

DUMFRIES BURGHS 1780–1784

*b.* 1730, 1st s. of William Herries of Halldykes, Dumfries, by his 1st w. Katherine, da. of John Henderson of Broadholme, Dumfries. *m.* (1) his cos. Grace (*d.* 1773), da. of John Henderson of Broadholme, *s.p.*; (2) 12 Aug. 1777, Catherine, da. of Rev. Francis Hender Foote of Charlton Place, Kent, wid. of John Ross, *s.p. suc.* fa. 1777; kntd. 25 Feb. 1774.

Herries[1] was the son of a prodigal father, whose brother Robert, a Rotterdam merchant, rescued the family from ruin, took young Robert into his business in 1747, and purchased the Halldykes estate in 1751.[2] When his uncle retired to Scotland, Herries remained in Holland in partnership with another uncle until c.1753, when with the assistance of Hope and Company of Amsterdam he established himself as a wine merchant in Barcelona. Subsequently he extended his interests to Valencia and Montpelier, and developed trade connexions in America, France, and the Mediterranean. In 1762 he accepted the invitation of Thomas and James Coutts to become principal partner in their father's banking and commercial firm, John Coutts and Company of Edinburgh and London, withdrew from all his enterprises except that at Barcelona, and established his headquarters in London. In 1771 the Coutts brothers severed all connexion with the firm, leaving Herries and his partners Sir William Forbes and James Hunter Blair in control, who then, in association with Herries's relations and Sir William Pulteney, founded the London Exchange Banking Company for handling the 'circular exchange notes' (prototype of travellers' cheques) which Herries had invented. Through the Hopes, the Company established a network of exchange facilities extending from Lisbon to Moscow.

Herries successfully intrigued against Thomas Walpole and the Edinburgh firm of William Alexander and Sons to obtain the lucrative tobacco-purchasing contract of the French farmers general, secured the Scottish contract in 1771, the London contract in 1774, and also control of the outport funds. His commercial speculations with the vast French balances so disturbed his Edinburgh associates, Forbes and Hunter Blair, that in 1775 they withdrew from the partnership; his private tobacco

deals also offended the farmers general and almost lost him his contract which nevertheless he retained until the war with France.[3]

Herries's wide knowledge of the City, of European, West Indian, and American affairs made him useful to the North Administration who in 1774 obtained for him a knighthood. He was consulted by North on the prospects of opposing Frederick Bull at the London by-election 1773;[4] in June 1776 he sent to Germain a letter from a Philadelphia correspondent, probably Robert Morris, on the American situation, warning him confidentially that unless Herries could devise means of shipping American tobacco to France, he would be obliged to yield to the planters' demands and himself contract for it with the farmers general.[5] Thereafter Herries exerted himself to save his contract and block the American tobacco negotiations in Paris, harassing the Government for permission to trade with America despite the blockade laws. On 2 Mar. 1777 Robinson wrote to Dartmouth condemning Herries's 'extraordinary' propositions, but on 3 Mar. was chagrined to find that despite North's disapproval Germain had given letters of protection to Herries's agent to go to British occupied areas in America in an attempt to purchase tobacco.[6] In 1778 his memorial on his French tobacco interest was recommended by Germain to the British conciliation commissioners with instructions to further his affairs.[7]

For some time Herries had recognized that a parliamentary seat would be a useful asset. Through his numerous relations and his friendship with Pulteney, he had considerable influence in Dumfriesshire, and when in 1780 Queensberry withdrew his interest from Sir William Douglas, Herries received the nomination and was returned unopposed. In Parliament he consistently voted with North to the end of his Administration. Although not known to have been concerned in the East India Company, he submitted to Jenkinson on 2 May 1781[8] 'Propositions for the renewing the charter of the East India Company', which included the establishment of branches at Bristol, Liverpool, Edinburgh, and Hull, the appointment of a committee of war and finance including eight M.P.s, and direct trade between India and the American colonies.

He voted against Shelburne's peace preliminaries, 18 Feb. 1783; and on 11 Mar., in his first reported speech, opposed the bill for renewing trade with America, although its over-generous terms would be to his own advantage:

He had a house at Barcelona for thirty years and another at Ostend and by these might make an immense fortune. But as a Member of Parliament and a good citizen he must condemn the bill.

But he was also critical of Fox's bill abolishing the regulations requiring American ships to produce bonds and other documents, protesting that certificates of lading and of health were essential, and that America should conform to the same rules as other nations. In general, however, he was a silent supporter of the Coalition. His only other reported speech was made on 4 Dec. 1783 when he opposed the expulsion of Christopher Atkinson, proclaimed his belief in his innocence, and offered to stand bail for his appearance.[9]

He voted for Fox's East India bill on 27 Nov. 1783, but in December, shortly before Pitt took office, Robinson listed him 'doubtful' and believed he would eventually swing over to Pitt.[10] Herries, however, remained faithful to the Coalition to the end of the Parliament and lost his seat at the general election.

He did not apparently seek to re-enter Parliament but concentrated on his commercial interests, travelled widely, kept closely in touch with foreign affairs, and lived for considerable periods in Paris.[11] In 1798 he retired from business to Cheltenham, where he died 25 Feb. 1815.

[1] For the information concerning Herries's business career we are indebted to Dr. J. M. Price. [2] *Misc. Gen. et Her.* (ser. 4), iv. 301–5, 378–82. [3] Sir W. Forbes, *Mems. of a Banking House*, 9, 17–36, 45–53. [4] Fortescue, iii. 20. [5] *HMC Stopford-Sackville*, ii. 21–23. [6] *HMC Dartmouth*, ii. 434. [7] *HMC Carlisle*, 398. [8] Add. 38405, f. 120. [9] Debrett, ix. 482, 642; xii. 329, 330. [10] Laprade, 100. [11] Add. 36495, f. 386.

E.H.-G.

## HERVEY, Hon. Augustus John (1724–79).

BURY ST. EDMUNDS    26 May 1757–Feb. 1763
SALTASH             1 Dec. 1763–1768
BURY ST. EDMUNDS    1768–18 Mar. 1775

*b.* 19 May 1724, 2nd s. of John, Lord Hervey (and gd.-s. of John, 1st Earl of Bristol), by Mary, da. of Brig.-Gen. Nicholas Lepell; bro. of Hon. William Hervey (q.v.). *educ.* Westminster 1733. *m.* 4 Aug. 1744, Elizabeth, da. of Col. Thomas Chudleigh (she m. bigamously, 8 Mar. 1769, Evelyn, 2nd Duke of Kingston), 1s. *d.v.p. suc.* bro. as 3rd Earl of Bristol 18 Mar. 1775.
    Entered R.N. 1735; lt. 1740; cdr. 1746; capt. 1747; r.-adm. 1775; v.-adm. 1775.
    Groom of the bedchamber 1763–75; chief sec. to ld. lt. [I] 1766–7; ld. of Admiralty 1771–5.

Well born, with powerful connexions, but a younger son with small expectations, Hervey was sent to sea at the age of eleven. For nearly twenty years he served continuously, engrossed by his career afloat and his amatory exploits ashore—'I cared very little about anything but my pleasures in these days till I got to sea, and then my profession

was all my pleasure.'[1] His abilities and flamboyant courage brought him some renown, yet he never reached the front rank he sought.

In 1754, while serving in the Mediterranean, Hervey was nominated for Bury St. Edmunds by his brother, Lord Bristol, and was elected on a double return, but in December 1754 his opponent was seated by the House.

Touchy and critical of his superiors, Hervey bitterly disliked Lord Anson, and after the outbreak of war with France, became increasingly indignant about his handling of the fleet. In May 1756, after the battle of Mahon, he wrote to Henry Fox blaming the Administration for its lack of support. When in 1757 he was recalled to give evidence at the court martial of his friend Byng, he was zealous in his defence, and after the sentence approached everyone he could 'to show a face against such an infamous violation of justice'. He commented bitterly that

it was easily perceived there was a sullen determination in the King, the Duke of Cumberland, Lord Anson, and the Duke of Newcastle (which was artfully conducted by *that determined* implacable villain, Mr. Fox) to sacrifice Admiral Byng in order to screen themselves from the just resentment of the people for the loss of Minorca and other infamous conducts.[2]

During his campaign for Byng he felt the disadvantage of not being in the Commons, but when the seat at Bury became vacant, merely noted in his journal: 'I did not stir in it as my brother was abroad';[3] and soon afterwards went to sea, only learning from an English newspaper on 30 June that he had been returned for Bury in May. That he would support Administration was taken for granted by Bristol, who informed Newcastle that he had reminded his brother 'of the many professions he has made of adhering steadily to me and my friends, of which list I have placed your Grace at the head; I hope I may congratulate you upon having an additional friend in the House of Commons'. On 19 Oct. Bristol wrote again: 'My brother Augustus has not long since confirmed to me his former assurances of having no other connexion than mine, and has particularly mentioned his resolution to serve your Grace.'[4]

In January 1759 Hervey at last took his seat, and though he writes that he was 'too much dissipated to mind much of what was going on in public business', he attended the debates on the supply, and when on 2 Feb. Alexander Hume introduced a bill against pressing, he 'took a very warm part against the whole'. After attending one of Newcastle's levees he noted in his journal that the Duke repeated former promises (presumably about promotion) 'with the same false grinning countenance', and, he wrote to Bristol, 'how little I relied on anything his Grace said'.[5] But on 27 Mar. he wrote:[6]

I have little to hope for obtaining anything but from your Grace's goodness towards me, nor shall I seek it through any other channel, as that is the most acceptable to my brother Bristol and will always be preferable to myself.

Soon afterwards he returned to sea, and for the next few months kept watch on the French fleet at Brest, without returning to harbour. When finally fatigue forced Hervey to return to England, Hawke wrote: 'He has given such proofs of diligence, activity, intrepidity, and judgement that it would be doing injustice to his merit as an officer not to acknowledge that I part with him with the greatest regret.'[7]

Between 1761 and 1762 Hervey served in the West Indies, and in 1762 distinguished himself at the taking of Havana, returning to England with the news in October 1762. He now retired from active service at sea, though remaining in the navy and retaining a keen interest in its affairs. In Parliament, to which he had again been returned during his absence in 1761, he supported Bute's Administration, while his brother adhered to Pitt. Relations between the brothers, always delicate, now reached a crisis. On 30 Nov. 1762 Fox mentioned to Bute that Bristol had written Hervey 'two cruel letters indeed', and on 20 Jan. Augustus himself wrote to Bute that his position was so awkward that he would be grateful for

any little stewardship that will vacate my present seat in Parliament, that according to my first and determined resolution I may make use of it, unless my Lord Bristol on my acquainting him again therewith, and finding it in my power, should then leave me at liberty to take that part which he before prevented me, and which from every principle and motive I am inclined to.[8]

Hervey resigned his seat in February, and, a vacancy having occurred at Saltash during the summer prorogation, was returned there by Administration. In the meantime he had at the Government's request abandoned a voyage to the Mediterranean with the Duke of York. 'A person of your parts and activity is not to be spared in these critical times',[9] Lord Sandwich wrote to him on 7 Sept. Hervey himself wrote to Grenville on 16 Sept.[10]: 'I . . . hope this additional proof I have given of my zeal for the support of his Majesty's Administration will give me some merit; believe me, Sir, I have in many senses been a great loser in this last affair.' He was rewarded with a post in the bedchamber.

During the debates of February 1764 on general warrants Hervey exerted himself in support of Administration, and sent Grenville information about the attitude of various Members;[11] but few

speeches by him are reported, and those almost invariably on points of order. Throughout his life he was a frequent contributor of political articles to the newspapers under assumed names. His personal relations with Grenville were close, and in May 1765 he succeeded in effecting a reconciliation between Grenville and Temple. On the formation of the Rockingham Administration, Hervey wrote to Grenville of his 'unalterable' attachment—'I am neither ungrateful nor a weathercock.'[12] Yet he did not feel it necessary to resign his post at court, and while he criticized Administration and constantly avowed his connexion with Grenville, he avoided plunging deep into opposition. James Harris reports[13] that in September 1765 Hervey had told him he thought

very meanly of the present Administration—said that all business stood still, and that they did nothing—wondered what Pitt meant by standing off, that he ought to come in—that Mr. Grenville and his friends would support his measures—if not, then let Lord Temple try—each at the head of the Treasury. If not that, then let them support Mr. Grenville there.

At the beginning of 1766, when the repeal of the Stamp Act was mooted, Hervey, declaring that he intended to vote against it, requested the King's permission to resign,[14] but with the King's blessing remained in office, while warning the House of the 'consequences that would ensue from that puerile, pitiful, and baneful measure'.[15]

By July 1766 good relations were restored with Bristol. 'I have the pleasure to tell you my brother has requested of me *to be for Bury* next Parliament', Hervey wrote to Grenville, 10 July 1766, 'and with the assurance that I am *ever* to be at *my own liberty as to what measures I shall pursue*; you will easily imagine how glad I was to prove my desire of giving him the preference to any other place I could be brought in for.'[16] When almost immediately after this Pitt came into power, Hervey, assuming that Lord Temple would 'have the settling all with Mr. P.' wrote 'to lightly throw my wish of the Admiralty before him'.[17] Temple's withdrawal dashed his hopes, but another chance seemed imminent when Pitt wrote to Bristol 'inviting him *in* and to everything he can wish and desire'. Whereupon, Hervey wrote to Grenville, Bristol had said to him:[18]

If I accept I hope you'll take a seat at the Admiralty as I know you wish it. I beg to be excused. I said, brother, I wished it had my friends come in with yours. But all I desire is that I may not be offered it, because I'll refuse. If this is asked you or if you intended to make this your terms too, assure yourself you'll only hurt me. I am determined to take nothing whatever. But if you go in, I'll not oppose, and by that means show that 'tis for you alone.

—and considerably more in the same vein. In fact no such offer was made, but finally Bristol was appointed lord lieutenant of Ireland and asked his brother to go with him as his secretary. Hervey, protesting loudly, accepted, writing to Grenville on 30 Aug.:[19]

> Ill health, inabilities, *and other things* had made me determine not to go, and to remain quiet as I was. I told him this and declined it, but had you seen the effect of it and how impossible it was for me to persist after what he said, you would both applaud and pity the determination. So there I am embarked in what I know nothing of, nor like.

Yet in October Hervey suggested that Sandwich, one of Grenville's allies in the Bedford group, should be offered the embassy at Madrid ,'as a friend to Administration, he thought it might accelerate further arrangements'.[20]

In November 1766 Hervey was asked to second the Address, and according to Grenville, 'induced by Lord Bristol's earnest and peremptory solicitation (though very much against his will)'[21] agreed to do so. Finally, on 11 Nov., the principal Administration speaker having defaulted, Hervey moved the Address, in what Grenville described as 'a direct Opposition speech'. Hervey did not vote on the land tax, 27 Feb. 1767. Relations with Bristol were again precarious, and, at the beginning of April, Hervey, then at Bath for his gout, was summoned back to London. Informing Grenville of this on 4 Apr., he wrote that he had been warned by Bristol

> that the closet canvassed over rigidly every absentee, and that it became me to act with more circumspection and more vigour than the rest, lest I should be suspected to be waiting the cast of the die, when it was so well known I was so strongly and avowedly attached to those two brothers who were the declared antagonists of that one which he was determined to support.

To this Hervey had replied:

> that even my friend Mr. Grenville knows and approves my determination to support my brother in preference to himself, and he, (my brother) knows it is to support Mr. Grenville in preference to every one else but my brother.

On 1 July, referring to the 'very great alteration' in Bristol's conduct, he at last offered his resignation. He would, he wrote to his brother, continue to support Administration—'I think myself wounded by your suffering it to be insinuated that your conduct to me proceeds from my not supporting the King's Administration, which is false in whoever dare to tell you the untruth or propagate it.'[22]

During the negotiations of July 1767, Hervey professed to believe that Grenville and Temple would be approached, and wrote to Grenville on the 21st that Grafton had declared he 'knew no man so fit to be at the head of our House' as Grenville. To which Hervey had replied that he knew nothing of Grenville's intentions 'but that I knew you had several friends who, like myself, were determined only to act as we saw you should approve; that I for one made no secret of declaring that I wanted nothing but the Admiralty, which I thought I had a right to after those I had seen there, but that I never desired it till you came in, or supported the Administration'.[23] By September 1767, when the general election was in sight, Hervey became reconciled with his brother once more, and an agreement was reached which left him 'totally at liberty' in Parliament. Which, wrote Grenville to Hervey,[24] is 'the best proof Lord Bristol can give that he has no essential blame to impute on you, and the most honourable justification of your own conduct towards him'. Hervey voted with the Opposition on nullum tempus, 17 Feb. 1768, and in a letter of 21 Oct. wrote despairingly of the 'melancholy scene' presented by Administration—'How can a Grafton supply the seat of a Walpole or a Grenville'.[25] But contrary to Grenville's opinion he spoke several times in support of Administration over Wilkes, and voted with Administration on the Middlesex election, 8 May 1769. No votes or speeches by him are reported during the following year.

In 1771, after Grenville's death, Hervey with other Grenvillites was taken into Administration, at last obtaining a place at the Admiralty Board. His infrequent speeches were henceforth mainly on naval matters, but on 6 Feb. 1775 he spoke at considerable length on the American crisis:[26]

> That America . . . ought to be subordinate to the authority of Great Britain is beyond a doubt . . . From the moment I had a seat in this House, I thought it my duty to study the conduct and opinions of those whose abilities and attachment to their country justly entitled them to a preference, and very early attached myself to that good, wise, and able minister, Mr. Grenville . . . I will not prove myself undeserving the friendship and confidence that minister honoured me with, by deviating this day by one single iota from what I am confident would have been his conduct . . . and therefore, as far as my voice goes, I will never consent to the rescinding, the discharging, or the repealing of any one resolution, order, or act, that either the last or any former Parliament has passed for the declaring, maintaining, enforcing the legislative authority of Great Britain over all its colonies.

On succeeding to the peerage in 1775 Hervey resigned his offices. He seems to have been ambitious for the post of first lord of the Admiralty; during the last years of his life, joining the Opposition in its criticism of naval matters, he became a vigorous champion of Keppel and a violent critic of the first lord, his former friend Lord Sandwich. He died 22 Dec. 1779.

[1] *Augustus Hervey's Jnl.* ed. D. Erskine, 294. [2] Ibid. 235, 236, 320. [3] Ibid. 232. [4] Add. 32871, f. 464; 32875, f. 190. [5] *Jnl.* 297, 298.

[6] Add. 32889, f. 270. [7] Quoted *Jnl.* 304. [8] Bute mss. [9] Sandwich mss. [10] Grenville mss (JM). [11] Hervey to Grenville, 15 Feb. 1764, ibid. [12] 26 June 1765, ibid. [13] Malmesbury mss. [14] Walpole, *Mems. Geo. III*, ii. 183. [15] See his speech of 6 Feb. 1775, Almon i. 146–50. [16] Grenville mss (JM). [17] Hervey to Grenville, 19 July 1766, ibid. [18] To Grenville, 21 July, ibid. [19] Ibid. [20] Shelburne to Chatham, 28 Oct., *Chatham Corresp.* iii. 122. [21] *Grenville Pprs.* iii. 382. [22] Grenville mss (JM). [23] *Grenville Pprs.* iv. 69. [24] 27 Sept., Grenville mss (JM). [25] *Grenville Pprs.* iv. 385. [26] Almon, i. 146–50.

M.M.D.

## HERVEY, Hon. Felton (1712–73), of Bury St. Edmunds, Suff.

BURY ST. EDMUNDS    1747–1754, 9 Dec. 1754–1761

*b.* 12 Feb. 1712, 10th s. of John, 1st Earl of Bristol, by his 2nd w. Elizabeth, da. and h. of Sir Thomas Felton, 4th Bt., of Playford, Suff. *educ.* Bury St. Edmunds g.s.; Eton 1727–30. *m.* 25 Dec. 1740, Dorothy, da. of Solomon Ashley, M.P., wid. of Charles Pitfield of Brixton, 1s. 3da.

Equerry to the Queen 1736–7; groom of the bed-chamber to the Duke of Cumberland 1737–56.

At the general election of 1754 Hervey, having quarrelled with his nephew, Lord Bristol, contested Bury St. Edmunds in opposition to Bristol's brother Augustus. After a double return Felton was seated by the House on 9 Dec., and Augustus's election was declared void.

In 1756 Felton Hervey resigned his place with the Duke of Cumberland.

> Besides that my health would not permit me to give the same attendance I had done for seventeen years together [he wrote to Newcastle on 3 Oct. 1756] it was very inconvenient for me to be going backward and forwards, three or four times in a summer, and some-times to be in waiting a year together.[1]

He claimed that Henry Pelham had often thanked him for his 'constant attendance', and had promised 'to do something' for him 'very soon'; he now applied (unsuccessfully) for a seat at the Board of Trade. In 1760, through the good offices of Lady Yarmouth, he obtained the reversion of the place of remembrancer of the Exchequer for himself and his son.[2]

He died 16 Aug. 1773.

[1] Add. 32868, f. 58. [2] Add. 32887, f. 258.

J.B.

## HERVEY, John (1696–1764), of East Betchworth, nr. Reigate, Surr.

REIGATE           16 Feb. 1739–1741
WALLINGFORD      1754–30 July 1764

*bap.* 25 June 1696, 1st s. of Stephen Hervey, M.P., justice of Anglesey, by his cos. Anne, da. of John Hervey of St. Mary-at-Hill, London, Turkey mer-chant and treasurer of the Levant Co.[1] *educ.* M. Temple 1709, called 1723, bencher 1745, treasurer 1753. *m.* c.1731, Anne, da. of Sir Christopher Des Bouverie, 2s. *suc.* fa. 1707.

Justice of Brecon 1745–d.

At the general election of 1754 Hervey stood at Wallingford against the Government candidates, Thomas Sewell and Lord Castlecomer, the other Opposition candidate being Richard Neville Ald-worth, a Bedford Whig. 'The affair of Mr. Hervey at Wallingford has given me a great deal of concern', wrote Hardwicke, a close friend, to Newcastle on 4 Oct. 1753.[2] He first heard of it from Henry Pelham and then talked

> in the strongest style possible to the gentleman con-cerned. No person dependent upon, or connected with, the Administration had any hand in it; and Mr. Hervey, though a Welsh judge, with an estate of near three thousand pounds a year, might see himself in a different situation from what he was before, though he made a very weak and wrongheaded inference from it.

And here is the account which Hervey gave to Hard-wicke of 'the Wallingford affair' in a letter of 10 Jan. 1753.[3] He knew but one man in the corporation, 'a person of unquestionable attachment to the Govern-ment', who suggested that Hervey should stand for Wallingford and shortly before Christmas brought a paper 'signed by 24 of the chamber' that they would support him and Aldworth as candidates at the next election.

> I asked my friend the political principles of these gentlemen . . . he told [me] that about half was for, and half against, the Administration, that they never in any instance had been unanimous before, and added that the motive of this resolution was to recover the credit of the borough, and to get it out of the hands of the lower people.

Finding on inquiry that the signatories were 'men of the best credit and substance at Wallingford' he accepted their invitation and went down with Aldworth, 'a stranger to me', to solicit votes.

> I declared to Mr. Aldworth that in case I was returned for Wallingford I should vote in Parliament on the side of the Administration . . . Indeed, my Lord, it would have prejudiced my interest, if I had publicly declared my attachment to the Ministry, but it was so under-stood, which made some not so zealous in my interest as otherwise they would have been.

And on 20 Jan.:[4]

> This morning I saw Mr. Pelham. We talked over the affair of Wallingford and I made him all the assurances I could, and sincerely, of my steady attachment to the Administration. He said he was persuaded it was so, but that I was so unhappily linked he must oppose me. At parting he called to me in this manner—Hearken, Hervey, we'll fight it out in the country, and be good friends in town.

Hervey and Aldworth won the election, although Sewell was heavily financed by Administration, and according to Aldworth there was heavy bribery.[5] Consequently Wallingford was entered in New-castle's election accounts as a loss, and Hervey as 'doubtful'. But by 1761 he was accepted by

Newcastle, and in October 1761 was sent the parliamentary whip through Hardwicke. In Bute's list of December 1761 he was first entered as 'Newcastle'; but this was crossed out by Bute who marked him as 'independent'. On 9 Dec. 1762 Hervey voted against the peace preliminaries (which none of the Yorkes did), and he also voted against the Grenville Administration on Wilkes and general warrants. He died 30 July 1764.

[1] *N. & Q.* (ser. 9), iv. 51. [2] Add. 32733, f. 16. [3] Add. 35592, ff. 6–7. [4] Ibid. f. 23. [5] Bedford mss 30, f. 26.

L.B.N.

## HERVEY, Hon. William (1732–1815).

BURY ST. EDMUNDS    24 Feb. 1763–1768

*b.* 13 May 1732, 4th s. of John, Lord Hervey, and bro. of Hon. Augustus John Hervey (q.v.). *educ.* Westminster 1745–7; Corpus Christi Camb. 1751. *unm.*

Lt. 44 Ft. 1755, capt. 1756; capt. and lt.-col. 1 Ft. Gds. 1766; col. 1777; maj.-gen. 1782; lt.-gen. 1793; gen. 1798.

William Hervey served in North America 1755–1763, and was returned to Parliament *in absentia*. At first he followed his brother, Lord Bristol, a friend of Pitt, and in the divisions over Wilkes of 15 Nov. 1763 and 6 and 15 Feb. 1764 voted with Opposition. But on 17 Feb., the day of the critical debate on general warrants, Lord Sandwich wrote about Hervey to Grenville: 'He has absolutely quarrelled with Lord Bristol; his brother Augustus thinks if you would speak a civil word or two to him if you see him in the House he will certainly vote with you today.'[1] However, he voted again with Opposition.

Brother Augustus reconciled him to Administration, but he was indifferent about Parliament and not sorry to find a way of getting out. On 18 Dec. 1764 Augustus wrote to Grenville:[2]

I cannot resist acquainting you that my brother William . . . still persists in his determination to acquaint the House of his having given up his qualification, and . . . tells me *if he finds himself obliged to go abroad he will then acquaint the Speaker by letter and desire the sense of the House*; but I hope when I see him to make him forgo this silly and very wrong idea. I have just wrote the strongest letter to him on that head, for his brother exacts nothing of him, only desires he will keep his seat, and act as he pleases . . . I have represented it in the worst of lights to him, and told him he would certainly be questioned for taking his oath and subscribing to it of his being qualified, and then giving that up undesired, unobliged, and only to vacate his seat. I have painted to him the appearance it must have to every one, his doing it at a time that he was soliciting preferment, in such a manner as gave room to suspect he was not acting a very open and right part by those who were so kind in their attentions to his requests.

He remained, and seems to have attended regularly, but there is no record that he ever spoke. From 1765

to 1768 his politics closely followed Bristol's: he did not vote against the repeal of the Stamp Act, 22 Feb. 1766, and voted with Chatham's Administration on the land tax, 27 Feb. 1767, but against them on the nullum tempus bill, 17 Feb. 1768. He did not stand in 1768.

After he left Parliament he spent much time travelling about England, and recorded his experiences in his journal. He does not mention his unsuccessful contest at Bury St. Edmunds in 1775, and his entry for the contest of 1780 reads simply:[3] 'Election at Bury—22–18–13'.

His mother's account of him, written in 1766, seems to be near the truth:[4]

He is now captain in the first regiment of guards, with the rank of lieutenant-colonel, and a promise of the first company that falls . . . though I know not a man in the world more indifferent about money than himself; when he has it he makes use of it; when he has it not he suits his mind to his situation; walks home at night in the rain with as much content and cheerfulness as if he was carried in his coach; eats his mutton cutlet and drinks his glass of water with the same good humour and content as he could feast on turkey or drink Burgundy. He has one of the happiest contented tempers I know; and, added to that, loves reading and improvements of all kinds; is a curious observer and an accurate relater. He is beloved by all the company he keeps.

He died 15 Jan. 1815.

[1] Grenville mss (JM). [2] Ibid. [3] *Jnls. Hon. Wm. Hervey*, 299. [4] Ibid. p. xxvi.

J.B.

## HEWETT, *see* THORNHAGH

## HEWITT, James (1712–89), of Alveston, Warws.

COVENTRY    1761–Nov. 1766

*b.* 28 Apr. 1712, 1st s. of William Hewitt, mercer and draper of Coventry, by his w. Hannah Lewis. *educ.* M. Temple 1737, called 1742. *m.* (1) 18 May 1749, Mary (*d.* 1765), da. and coh. of Rev. Rice Williams of Stapleford Abbots, Essex, 4s.; (2) 15 Dec. 1766, Ambrosia, da. of Rev. Charles Bayley of Navestock, Essex, 1s. 2da. *suc.* fa. 22 Nov. 1747; *cr.* Baron Lifford [I] 9 Jan. 1768; Visct. Lifford [I] 8 Jan. 1781.

Serjeant-at-law 1755; King's serjeant 1759; justice of the King's bench Nov. 1766–Jan. 1768; ld. chancellor [I] Jan. 1768–*d.*

Hewitt's father was a member of the Coventry corporation, and in 1744 mayor. Hewitt was articled to an attorney before being called to the bar. He contested Coventry in 1754; and in 1761, as corporation candidate and with the support of the Archer interest, came out head of the poll.

He appears in Fox's list of Members favourable to the peace preliminaries, December 1762, and in autumn 1763 was classed by Jenkinson as 'pro'. But over Wilkes and general warrants he turned against the Government; and became one of the most frequent Opposition speakers on a pre-eminently legal subject. According to Walpole,[1] he was 'much despised for his deficiency of parliamentary talents'. James Harris wrote that in the debate of 6 Feb. 1764 Hewitt was 'heard with difficulty and by the friendly interposition of those he opposed'; and of a speech he made on 7 Mar. 1764: 'Serjeant Hewitt followed—hoarse murmurs filled the House—he was *seen*, not *heard* to speak—the words jury and liberty were sometimes audible.'

When the Rockingham Administration was being formed, Hewitt wrote to Newcastle:[2]

> Serjeant Hewitt, who has nothing to ask of Government for himself and who had never received any beneficial mark of public favour, begs leave to recommend his brother, Mr. William Hewitt, for something at home or abroad which may carry some public mark of respect to the Serjeant and therein do him credit.

William Hewitt was appointed a commissioner for the sale of ceded lands in the West Indies.

In February 1765 Hewitt had been one of the few who had spoken against the introduction of the Stamp Act; a year later he also opposed the Declaratory Act. Contemporaries said that it was his support of Chatham's American policy which induced Camden, then lord chancellor, to appoint him a judge. On 20 Oct. 1767 Camden, when asked to advise on candidates for the post of lord chancellor of Ireland, wrote to Grafton about Hewitt:[3] 'Though a good lawyer and an honest man, [he] will probably be thought not of sufficient eminence to be recommended at this time.' The Cabinet wanted an English lawyer; no chief justice could be induced to take the post; and Hewitt was chosen. Lord Mansfield, according to Grenville,[4] 'spoke with great derision of the appointment'.

Yet it proved to be no bad one. John Hely Hutchinson, an ambitious Irish lawyer and politician who rarely spoke well of anyone, wrote to W. G. Hamilton, in 1773:[5]

> In answer to your question about the chancellor . . . he does his business very ably and expeditiously and to the general satisfaction of suitors and practisers in this country where he is much respected and a very popular character, and is in his private and public deportment a most worthy, honest and amiable man.

He died 28 Apr. 1789.

[1] *Mems. Geo. III*, iii. 79. [2] Add. 32972, f. 300. [3] Grafton, *Autobiog.* 165. [4] *Grenville Pprs.* iii. 232. [5] *HMC 12th Rep. IX*, 276.

J.B.

**HEY, William** (c.1733–97), of Coxheath, Kent.

SANDWICH 1774–31 Oct. 1776

*b.* c.1733, s. of Thomas Hey, formerly a merchant in Venice, by Elizabeth, wid. of (1)—Markham, (2) Sir

Thomas Palmer of Wingham, 4th Bt., M.P. *educ.* Eton 1748; Corpus Christi, Camb. 1750; M. Temple 1750, called 1756. *m.* (2)[1] 5 Apr. 1783, Miss Paplay of Jamaica,[2] *s.p.*

Recorder, Sandwich 1763–6; dep. recorder, Dover 1763–6; c.j. Quebec 1766–76; commr. of customs 1776–*d.*

In July 1763 Sir Wyndham Knatchbull recommended Hey to Lord Hardwicke, nominally steward (i.e. recorder) of Dover for his deputy: he 'attends always on this circuit', and is reputed to have 'very good abilities'.[3] Hardwicke's friends at Dover agreed in thinking Hey 'the properest person'—'a gentleman . . . with extreme good natural parts, very ready and capable of business, but has not applied to it so much as his friends could have wished'—which he now proposed to do, settling at Canterbury.[4] When Hardwicke died in 1764, Hey showed 'genteel behaviour' in desiring Charles Yorke to succeed, while he himself might 'be appointed deputy as before'.[5]

Early in 1766 Charles Yorke, then attorney-general, recommended Hey for chief justice of Quebec;[6] Hey sailed from Plymouth on 23 June and arrived at Quebec on 8 Sept.[7] In the absence of a legislative assembly and as first member of the governor's council, he played a considerable part in organizing the administration and framing the laws of the province, and earned the reputation of an upright and able judge.[8] On 10 Apr. 1773 he received permission to return home on leave on account of ill-health.[9] In London he assisted Alexander Wedderburn, attorney-general, in framing certain parts of the Quebec Act,[10] and on 25 Jan. 1774 submitted 'A Plan for the Administration of the Laws in the Province of Canada'.[11] On 2 June he was examined in the House of Commons on certain aspects of the Quebec bill, especially the system of laws to be established and the question of introducing juries and a legislative council; but professed to have only a superficial acquaintance with the bill as a whole, to be 'perfectly indifferent to it' and 'very unable to form an opinion'.[12]

At the general election of October 1774 he was returned unopposed for Sandwich on the government interest. On 27 Sept. he had sent in his resignation as chief justice,[13] obviously refused by Dartmouth, colonial secretary, who on 10 Dec. had 'the satisfaction' to inform the governor of Canada that Hey was

> resolved to return to Quebec in the character of chief justice although he should be under the necessity of relinquishing his seat in Parliament, which, however, we hope and think may be avoided.[14]

In fact, he did not mean to return for long, and his stay was cut down still further: on 28 Aug. he wrote to Lord Chancellor Bathurst on the prospects in Quebec 'as gloomy . . . in point of security and in the ill humours and evil dispositions of its inhabitants . . . as can be imagined'; he hoped that

> ten years honest, however imperfect, endeavours to serve the Crown in an unpleasant and something critical situation deserve to be compensated with moderate and reasonable means of retirement.

In postscripts of Sept. 11 and 17 he described the province as about to fall into rebel hands: 'I hold myself in readiness to embark for England where I possibly may be of some use . . . I can be of none here.'[15] Back in England he resigned his office. On 20 Feb. 1776 he made his only recorded speech in the Commons, in defence of the Quebec Act.

On 3 Oct. 1776 John Robinson wrote to the King referring to a commissionership of customs about to fall vacant, that when Hey 'came in for Sandwich it was understood that he was soon after to quit Quebec and have office . . . he has strenuously pressed for one of the commissionerships of excise or customs especially since he has been superseded in his office of chief justice of Quebec.'[16] On 31 Oct. 1776 Hey was appointed commissioner of customs, which vacated his seat.

He died 3 Mar. 1797.

[1] For evidence as to the first marriage, see W. S. Wallace, *Maseres Letters, 1766–8.* [2] *Caribbeana*, v. 40, 41. [3] Add. 35692, ff. 483, 487. [4] Michael Russell to Hardwicke, 15 Aug. 1763, ibid. f. 489. [5] Mayor of Dover to H. V. Jones, 27 Mar. 1764, Add. 35636, f. 443; Hey to Chas. Yorke, 10 Sept. 1764, Add. 35637, f. 29. [6] Add. 35915, f. 334. [7] Wallace, 41. [8] F-J. Audet, *Les Juges en Chef de la Province de Quebec 1764–1924*; W. S. Wallace, *Dict. Canadian Biog.*; Le Jeune, *Dict. Gén. du Canada.* [9] A. Shortt & A. G. Doughty, *Docs. relating to the Const. Hist. of Canada, 1759–91*, pt. i, 256, 272, 273. [10] Ibid. 536. [11] *HMC Dartmouth*, i. 347. [12] Cavendish, *Debates on Government of Quebec Bill*, 153. [13] *HMC Dartmouth*, i. 363. [14] Shortt & Doughty, ii. 285–6. [15] Ibid. 668–72. [16] Add. 37833, ff. 67–68.

L.B.N.

**HEYWOOD, James Modyford** (?1729–98), of Marystow, nr. Tavistock, Devon.

FOWEY 1768–1774

> *b.* ?1729, o.s. of James Heywood of Marystow and Jamaica by Mary, da. of Sir Abraham Elton, 2nd Bt., M.P. *educ.* Eton 1742–7; Trinity, Camb. 8 June 1747, aged 17. *m.* Catherine, da. and coh. of Gen. Chiverton Hartopp of Welby, Leics., 1s. 5da. Her sis. Mary m. 1758 Richard, 4th Visct. Howe (q.v.). *suc.* fa. 1738. Ld. of Admiralty Dec. 1783–Mar. 1784.

Heywood was returned on the Edgcumbe interest after a contest. No vote by him is recorded before February 1774, but Thomas Davenport wrote to the Duke of Portland, 10 Feb. 1770, that Heywood would have Administration support at the next election.[1] John Robinson's first survey on the royal marriage bill listed him as 'doubtful, present', but even when voting with Opposition on Grenville's Election Act, 25 Feb. 1774, he is marked in the King's list as a friend, and before the general elec-

tion was classed by Robinson as 'pro'. There is no record of his having spoken in the House. He did not stand again for Parliament.

On 30 Dec. 1783 Pitt wrote to the King:[2]

> Mr. Pitt flatters himself that the Admiralty commission is expedited, the name of Mr. Heywood, a relation of Lord Howe, out of Parliament, had been added to fill the vacancy for the present.

Heywood died 22 Apr. 1798.

[1] Portland mss. [2] Royal archives, Windsor.

M.M.D.

**HILDYARD, Sir Robert,** 3rd Bt. (1716–81), of Winstead, Yorks.

GREAT BEDWYN 1754–1761

> *bap.* 15 July 1716, posth. s. of Rev. William Hildyard, rector of Rowley St. Peter, Yorks., by Nancy, da. of Thomas Croft of Stillington, Yorks. *educ.* Peterhouse, Camb. 1731. *m.* May 1738, Maria Catherine, da. and h. of Henry Darcy of Sedbury, Yorks., 2s. 1da. *suc.* uncle as 3rd Bt. 30 Nov. 1729.

Hildyard was mentioned in November 1753 as a possible candidate for York at the forthcoming general election,[1] but nothing came of it. He was returned for Great Bedwyn as the joint candidate of Lords Bruce and Verney, and paid £2,000 for his seat. He was classed in Dupplin's list as Whig country gentleman. His only recorded vote was against Newcastle and Fox on the Minorca inquiry, 3 May 1757.[2]

He is not known to have stood again for Parliament. He firmly opposed the American war, and was one of the original members of the committee of the Yorkshire Association. He died 1 Feb. 1781.

[1] W. Murray to Rockingham, 27 Nov. 1753, Rockingham mss. [2] West to Newcastle, 3 May 1757, Add. 32871, f. 13.

J.B.

**HILL, Arthur,** Visct. Fairford (1753–1801).

LOSTWITHIEL 1774–1780
MALMESBURY 1780–1784

> *b.* 23 Feb. 1753, o. surv. s. of Wills Hill, 1st Earl of Hillsborough and 1st Mq. of Downshire [I] (q.v.). *educ.* Magdalen, Oxf. 1771. *m.* 29 June 1786, Mary, da. and h. of Col. Martin Sandys, and h. of her uncle Edwin, 2nd Baron Sandys (q.v.), 5s. 2da. *suc.* fa. as 2nd Mq. of Downshire 7 Oct. 1793.
> M.P. [I] 1776–93; P.C. [I] 7 Nov. 1793–18 Feb. 1800.

Lord Fairford was brought into Parliament by Administration in 1774 and 1780. The *English Chronicle* wrote about him in 1781:

> Son to the Earl of Hillsborough, a great railer against the Opposition. He adores his father's *great political character*, and next to him thinks Bamber Gascoyne [q.v.] the wisest, the best, and the honestest man alive.

Two speeches by Fairford are recorded: 14 Feb. 1780, in defence of a speech by his father in the Lords; and 26 Apr. 1781, in the committee on the linen manufacture.

He did not vote on Shelburne's peace preliminaries or Fox's East India bill. He was classed by Robinson in January 1784 and by Stockdale in March as a supporter of Pitt. In 1784 he unsuccessfully contested St. Albans on the interest of his brother-in-law, Lord Salisbury.

He died 7 Sept. 1801.

J.B.

## HILL, John (1740–1824).

SHREWSBURY 29 Oct. 1784–1796, 10 June 1805–1806

*b.* 21 July 1740, 2nd s. of Sir Rowland Hill, 1st Bt., and bro. of Richard Hill (q.v.). *educ.* Shrewsbury sch. *m.* 27 Sept. 1768, Mary, da. and coh. of John Chambré of Petton, Salop, 8s. 5da. *suc.* bro. as 3rd Bt. 28 Nov. 1808.

In October 1784 Hill was returned for Shrewsbury unopposed, as a follower of Pitt with whom he voted over parliamentary reform, 18 Apr. 1785, and during the Regency crisis. There is no record of his having spoken in the House before the dissolution in 1790. He died 21 May 1824.

L.B.N.

## HILL, Noel (1745–89), of Tern, Salop.

SHREWSBURY 1768–1774
SHROPSHIRE 1774–1784

*b.* Apr. 1745, o. surv. s. of Thomas Hill (formerly Harwood) of Tern (q.v.). *educ.* St. John's, Camb. 1759; I. Temple 1763. *m.* 18 Nov. 1768, Anna, da. of Henry Vernon (q.v.), 3s. 3da. *suc.* fa. 11 June 1782; *cr.* Baron Berwick 19 May 1784.
Mayor of Shrewsbury 1778–9.

Lord Powis wrote to the Duke of Newcastle, 18 July 1761, that Thomas Hill was extremely solicitous for his son to be made a gentleman-usher and secretary to the Queen—'he is a good scholar and master of languages'. Newcastle included him in his recommendations but apparently without success.[1]

Thomas Hill, in his letter to the Shrewsbury corporation, 15 Jan. 1768, declining for reasons of health to seek re-election, recommended to them his son Noel. Noel Hill and Lord Clive stood on a joint interest, and when William Pulteney declared his candidature, it was against Clive only. Hill was returned top of the poll. He was thoroughly independent, and voted with Opposition over Wilkes's petition, 27 Jan. 1769, and the civil list debt, 2 Mar. 1769;[2] but with Administration on the Middlesex election, 15 Apr. and 8 May 1769, and 26 Apr. 1773.

Over the royal marriage bill, March 1772, Robinson listed him as 'doubtful, present'; he voted with Opposition over the naval captains' petition, 9 Feb. 1773 and Grenville's Act, 25 Feb. 1774, but was each time marked in the King's list as a friend, and at the end of the Parliament was classed by Robinson as 'pro': which suggests unreported votes on the Government side.

In 1774 and 1780 he was returned unopposed for the county. During the years 1775–8, for which only five Opposition lists are extant, he appears voting with them once only: again on the civil list debts, 16 Apr. 1777; and over the contractors bill, 12 Feb. 1779, is marked by Robinson 'contra, present, friend', which once more suggests his having voted as a rule on the Government side. The *Public Ledger*, not always a reliable source, wrote about him in 1779: 'A Tory in principle, who professes himself an independent man, and terms an implicit obedience to every inconsistent, contradictory measure of ministers, *steadiness*.' But no vote by him is recorded on the Government side in the six lists, March 1779–April 1780, which give the names on both sides, and in the four last divisions, from 8 Mar. 1780 onwards, he voted steadily with Opposition. But even as late as 6 Apr., over Dunning's motion, he is included by North in a list of 'Persons generally with who went against';[3] and at the end of the Parliament Robinson classed him merely as 'doubtful'. In the first four division lists of the new Parliament Hill again voted with Opposition, 12 Dec. 1781–27 Feb. 1782; but was absent on 8 Mar., and again on the 15th when in Robinson's list the remark 'stayed away at request' appears against his name;[4] he was back on 20 Mar. to support the Opposition motion for the removal of the ministers[5] (forestalled by North's resignation). Hill voted for Shelburne's peace preliminaries, against Fox's East India bill, and adhered to Pitt, to whom he wrote on 15 Feb. 1784:[6]

I am yet so ill, that I am forbid stirring out, but a Mr. Cotes, a warm friend of the other side, has paired off with me for this day or I should otherwise have run all risks to have attended the House.

He did not stand again at the general election of 1784, having obviously been promised a peerage.[7] Not one speech of his is recorded during his 16 years in the House. He died 16 Jan. 1789.

[1] Add. 32925, ff. 167, 211. [2] Fortescue, ii. 86. [3] Ibid. iii. 419 (misplaced). [4] Ibid. v. 390. [5] I. R. Christie, *End of North's Ministry*, 376. [6] Chatham mss. [7] Geo. III to Pitt, 28 Mar. 1784, ibid.

L.B.N.

## HILL, Richard (1733–1808), of Hawkestone, Salop.

SHROPSHIRE 1780–1806

*b.* 6 June 1733,[1] 1st s. of Sir Rowland Hill, 1st Bt., of Hawkestone by his 1st w. Jane, da. of Sir Brian Broughton, 3rd Bt. *educ.* Shrewsbury; Westminster 1744–8; Magdalen, Oxf. 8 Dec. 1750, aged 17; Grand Tour 1755–7.[2] *unm. suc.* fa. as 2nd Bt. 7 Aug. 1783.

Hill's father, a strong Tory, was a nephew of Sir Richard Hill, Kt., diplomatist and statesman, from whom he inherited Hawkestone, and thus a first cousin of Thomas Hill of Tern (q.v.) who, failing male issue, was named in the remainder to Sir Rowland's baronetcy.

Richard Hill, prominent among the religious revivalists of his time, was a man of deep piety, whose writings and meditations show sincerity and zeal, though not much originality of thought. He engaged in theological controversy; wrote in 1768 a pamphlet, *Pietas Oxoniensis,* in defence of six students expelled from St. Edmund Hall, Oxford, as Calvinist Methodists; and championed Whitfield against Wesley. There is nothing to suggest an interest in politics before he entered the House, though relevant references may have been omitted by his biographer, a mid-19th century Evangelical, as 'neither interesting nor beneficial to the general reader'. Hill's election, to which 'there was not even the least shadow of an opposition',[3] was the more remarkable as the other seat was already held by Noel Hill, and choosing two members of the same family for a county was unusual. His subsequent elections were similarly unopposed: he was highly respected, a country gentleman of Tory antecedents, and at the same time a patron of Methodists and tolerant of Dissenters. Wraxall writes:[4]

> . . . Sir Richard Hill was one of the most upright, disinterested, and honest men who ever sat in Parliament . . . but his religious cast of character laid him open to . . . ridicule. His manners were quaint and puritanical, his address shy and embarrassed. He possessed, however, a most benevolent disposition, together with a great estate, which enabled him to gratify his generous and philanthropic feelings.

A Member, unnamed, quoted by Sidney (p. 303), says that he could find nothing to disapprove in Hill's conduct, except 'his introducing religion, or quoting Scripture in some of his speeches'.

> In every other respect, I think Mr. Hill's conduct is, and has been, that of an upright, conscientious Member of Parliament, who is biased by no party, and who wishes always to act as he judges right. Nor do I know any one Member of the House who thinks otherwise of him.

Yet, 'his enthusiastic turn in matters of religion' was hardly the main reason for the ridicule he often incurred. Even his admiring biographer admits that Hill 'at times unnecessarily exposed himself to it' when, to prove that religion does not generate 'moroseness and gloom', he gave 'vent to a flow of natural humour, which it would often have been more prudent to have restrained, especially at those times when he allowed it to mingle with discussions of the most serious importance'. Besides, his speeches were long, laboured and whimsical, adorned with similes and parables, mixing classical and literary quotations with biblical precepts and exhortations. In the debate of 15 Mar. 1782, which overthrew North, Hill quoted Gibbon on the withdrawal of the Roman troops from Britain, drew an analogy with the present situation, and recommended to the nation, 'if it wished to be saved, to turn to Jehovah, and appease his wrath'. The motion condemning the recall of Rodney (30 May) he opposed 'in a vein of pleasantry'. As last speaker in the debate on Shelburne's peace preliminaries, 21 Feb. 1783, he 'kept the House in a continual roar of laughter'; compared the union of Fox and North to a mixture of an acid and an alkali, of Herod and Pontius Pilate. His speech on Fox's East India bill was a typical performance; possibly there was in it a streak of self-irony, more probably a great fund of self-deception: 'He was never long-winded, as the House knew. *Multum in parvo* was a maxim he wished to follow; and if unhappily he failed in that, he would be careful to avoid a *nihil in multo.*' The bill was a stab to the English constitution; 'he was ready to cry out, *Et tu Brute!* or, to change classical for scriptural ground, he could not help calling to mind the conduct of Joab to Amasa.' On 8 Mar., when Fox moved a representation to the King on the constitutional position, 'Sir Richard Hill made a humorous speech, and read some verses that he had made, being the answer from the King that he supposed Mr. Fox would have dictated'.[5] This according to Sidney, who reproduces the doggerel (pp. 342–3), caused 'extreme amusement'. Yet comic turns ill accorded with moral exhortations and the regard which his character and actions amply deserved.

While personally respectful to North, Hill considered that peace with America was the predominant concern, and that 'the safety of the state required new men'. He consequently voted against the Government in the six divisions, 12 Dec. 1781–15 Mar. 1782, for which lists are extant. On 18 Feb. 1783 he voted for Shelburne's peace preliminaries; on 7 May with Pitt for parliamentary reform; but on the 16th against Sawbridge's motion for shorter Parliaments.[6] He spoke and voted against Fox's East India bill, was a steady supporter of Pitt, and was re-elected as such at the general election. On 26 Oct. 1784, a few months after his cousin Noel Hill had been made a peer, Richard Hill wrote to Sir Lloyd Kenyon[7] that the elevation of one 'who could not have had the smallest pretensions to such an honour but what were derived from that family whose name his father had taken, and whose arms he bore, whilst the elder branch and only male lineal heir seemed to be passed over and forgotten', was causing astonishment and dissatisfaction. He (Richard Hill), 'so far from being envious', rejoiced in the advancement of an upright man who will support the dignity with credit; nor had he himself ever asked for a peerage though he does not undervalue such distinctions; but 'as I am *now* circumstanced really do not wish it'; yet sometime he might; and so on, in a rigmarole of about 2,500 words—*parvum in multo*. There is, however, one clear statement, borne out by Richard Hill's further conduct: that this would in no way be affected by such matters. He continued to support Pitt; and again voted for parliamentary reform, 18 Apr. 1785. Humane and austere, an enemy of corruption and luxury, he repeatedly pleaded for taxing the amusements of the rich and especially 'places of public diversions', and for freeing from taxation the necessaries of the poor and the business of the industrious.[8] On 15 May 1789 he spoke in favour of the new bill to prevent vexatious removals of the poor,[9] and generally supported measures calculated to improve their lot.

He died 28 Nov. 1808.

[1] *Gent. Mag.* 1733, p. 325. [2] E. Sidney, *Life of Sir Richard Hill*, 18. [3] Jonathan Scott to Richard Hill, 7 Oct. 1780, Sidney, 278. [4] *Mems.* iii. 268. [5] Debrett, vi. 462; vii. 204; ix. 368; x. 382–6; xiii. 277. [6] Ibid. vii. 182. [7] Chatham mss. [8] Sidney, 299, 353–63, 493–5. [9] Stockdale, xvii. 234.

L.B.N.

**HILL, Thomas** (1721–76) of Court of Hill, nr. Ludlow, Salop.

LEOMINSTER   1774–23 Aug. 1776

*bap.* 28 Sept. 1721, o. s. of Thomas Hill by Martha, da. of Edward Hammond. *educ.* M. Temple 1755. *m.* 29 Dec. 1757, Lucy, da. of Francis Roche of Whitton, 2da. *suc.* fa. 14 Oct. 1724.

The Hills of Court of Hill had a common ancestor with the Hills of Hawkestone *temp.* Henry VI, and were settled at Court of Hill since the 16th century.[1] Mrs. Philip Lybbe Powys wrote in 1771, after a visit to Court of Hill:[2]

Their manner of living . . . is always in the superb style of ancient hospitality, only their winters are spent in London. You see generosity blended with every elegance of fashionable taste; but they have a vast fortune and only two children, both girls . . .

The circumstances of Hill's election for Leominster are unascertained. There is no record of any vote or speech of his in the House. He died 23 Aug. 1776.

[1] Burke, *Landed Gentry*, 5th ed. (1871). [2] *Passages from the Diary of Mrs. P. L. Powys*, ed. Climenson, 128.

L.B.N.

**HILL** (formerly **HARWOOD**), **Thomas** (1693–1782), of Tern, Salop.

SHREWSBURY   9 Mar. 1749–1768

*b.* 1693, 1st s. of Thomas Harwood, Shrewsbury draper, by Margaret, da. of Rowland Hill of Hawkstone, sis. of Rt. Hon. Richard Hill, diplomatist and financier. *m.* (1) 14 Feb. 1723, Anne (*d.*21 Dec. 1739), da. of Richard Powys of Hintlesham, Suff., 1s. *d.v.p.*, 2da.; (2) 3 May 1740, Susan Maria, da. and coh. of William Noel (q.v.), 2s. 2da. Assumed name of Hill 1712. *suc.* to a substantial part of Richard Hill's estates 1727; to Attingham on *d.* of his mother 1734; fa. 1739; to Shenstone Park on the *d.* of his cos. Samuel Hill 1758.

Hill received a mercantile education on the continent directed by his uncle, Richard Hill; his letter books, 1740–59,[1] show him engaged in extensive financial transactions on his own account, and possibly for others. He is seen lending nearly £8,000 to George Crowle, and considerable sums to Lord Lincoln, Velters Cornewall and others. On 1 Dec. 1753 he sent a message to Sir Edward Leighton: 'I have not such a sum as £9,000 but if he pleases I will do my endeavours to procure it for him'; and on 17 Aug. 1754 wrote to his cousin Samuel Hill (another of Richard's heirs) advising him to lend £20,000 to 'a very honest gentleman', Sir Thomas Mostyn. In October 1753, having consulted Bartholomew Burton, Hill invested £14,000 in Bank of England stock;[2] and there is further correspondence with Burton and with Child and Backwell about other English stocks and even French 'actions'—finance in great style carried on from Shrewsbury.

There is in the summer and autumn of 1753 a lengthy correspondence between Lord Powis and Hill about election prospects at Shrewsbury, where Hill had been returned unopposed in 1749. An opposition was apprehended from a 'few capital merchants of commanding interest' supported by country gentlemen under the leadership of the Windsor family. 'I understand', wrote Powis on 15 July, 'that Windsor is now going to put his favourite scheme to a trial, (viz.) the getting a number of low people assessed, to suit his purposes. This must be prevented.' Hill tried to influence the Tories through his nephew, Edward Kynaston; and wrote to him, 30 Aug.: 'My Lord [Powis] cannot be persuaded but the leading gentlemen of the party' might stop the opposition to his friends 'if they were in earnest'; unless they do, he will immediately retaliate in the county. On 1 Sept. Powis announced his intention to 'take such measures, as shall be most proper for the support of the Whig interest, and for their service in particular'—he obviously treated Hill as a 'Whig'. On 5 Sept. Hill reported to Powis that a delegation from 'a large body of burgesses' had offered him 'their votes and interest' if he joined another candidate in opposition to the corporation, which he refused to do.

After Sir Richard Corbett had declined to stand again, Thomas Hill and Robert More were on 27 Oct. 1753 unanimously adopted candidates. Hill now looked after the Tories, and More, an arch-Whig by family tradition, after the Dissenters. Thus on 3 Dec. Hill told Richard Lyster that had his and Sir John Astley's 'intimate friends . . . promised Mr. More and me their votes upon condition that the county Members . . . were not to be disturbed it would have set a good example'—with which Lyster agreed; and on 19 Jan. Lyster thought he could 'answer for all the gentlemen his friends that they will strictly adhere to the compromise'.[3] In turn, when in February 1754 Benjamin Bathurst, hitherto Member for Gloucester, was in search of another seat, two friends of his, one a Dissenting minister, came to Shrewsbury and proposed to the Dissenters that if they voted for Bathurst, the Tories 'would give an equal number of their votes to Mr. More'. But while they found support with the Windsor group, the Dissenters told them, wrote Edward Elisha to Hill on 23 Feb., that 'they came here on a wrong errand for that they all had promised to vote for you and Mr. More and would keep their words'.[4] On 16 Apr. Hill and More were returned unopposed, with Lyster and Astley attending in support.

In the House Hill was a regular follower of Powis, receiving through him Newcastle's parliamentary whip. Thus on 10 May 1754, when only formal business was expected, Powis wrote: 'It is therefore at your option whether you will be at the trouble of a journey to London on this occasion, or not.' But on 16 Oct. 1755: 'Give me leave to say, that though I doubt not of your present intention of attending the meeting of the Parliament on the first day, I shall be extremely glad to see you there accordingly, and shall take it as a favour if you will be so good as to let me know I shall certainly have that pleasure.'

When in 1759 More decided not to stand at the next general election, and a struggle ensued between Robert Clive, backed by Powis, and Lord Pulteney, son of Lord Bath, Hill again followed Powis. 'I am informed Lord Pulteney is come to Pateshall', wrote Powis to him, 1 Aug. 1759. 'I long to hear what part the Tory party take on the present occasion.' And when on 4 Aug. 1760 Clive gave a dinner to the Shrewsbury burgesses, Hill, together with other members of the Powis group, was asked to attend. Receiving scant support from any quarter, Bath gave up, and Hill and Clive were returned unopposed.

And here is a summons of 13 Jan. 1761 to support Powis when attacked by Bath:

Lord Powis sends his compliments to Mr. Hill and acquaints him that the Shropshire gentlemen will meet tomorrow morning at the Bedford Coffee House in Covent Garden at nine o'clock (and Mr. More will be there) in order to proceed to the Duke of Newcastle's from thence.

In Bute's parliamentary list of December 1761 Hill is marked: 'Tory, hitherto connected with Lord Powis'; and next, 'Bute'—he probably went over to the court together with Powis in November 1762. In the autumn of 1763 Jenkinson classed him as 'pro'.

When during the struggle over general warrants Edward Kynaston was whipping up Members on the Government side, he wrote of Hill that he very seldom stayed out a long day;[5] and he was absent from the division of 18 Feb. 1764. Again, during the crisis over the repeal of the Stamp Act, Powis wrote to George Grenville, 16 Feb. 1766:[6] 'I will certainly use my best endeavours to obey your commands tomorrow in regard to Mr. Hill. I can generally engage his attendance on business, but I am not so fortunate at all times in regard to his staying it out and taking a part in the division.' His name does not appear on 22 Feb. among those voting against the repeal; nor again in the division on the land tax, 27 Feb. 1767. Rockingham in his list of July 1765 classed Hill as 'doubtful', in that of November 1766 as 'Tory, perhaps not ministerial'; and Newcastle in March 1767 as 'Tory'. There is no record of Hill's having spoken in the House.

On 15 Jan. 1768 Hill addressed a letter to the mayor, aldermen, and burgesses of Shrewsbury: 'from my infirm state of health I find myself obliged to decline offering myself again, not being able to attend my duty there as I ought to do'; he recommended his son Noel for his successor. It was on Noel's behalf that Hill fought the bitterly contested election of 1768 at Shrewsbury. He died 11 June 1782.

[1] Attingham mss, Salop RO, from which all quotations, unless otherwise stated, are taken. [2] Bank of England recs. [3] Hill to Powis, 4 Dec. 1753, 19 Jan. 1754. [4] More to Hill, 23 Feb.; Elisha to Hill, 11 Mar. [5] *Jenkinson Pprs.* 265-6. [6] Grenville mss (JM).

L.B.N.

**HILL, Wills,** 1st Earl of Hillsborough [I] (1718–93), of North Aston, Oxon.

WARWICK 1741–17 Nov. 1756

*b.* 30 May 1718, o. surv. s. of Trevor, 1st Visct. Hillsborough [I], by Mary, da. and h. of Anthony Rowe of North Aston, Oxon., wid. of Sir Edmund Denton, 1st Bt., of Hillesden, Bucks. *m.* (1) 1 Mar. 1748, Lady Margaret FitzGerald (*d.*25 Jan. 1766), da. of Robert, 19th Earl of Kildare [I], sis. of James, 1st Duke of

Leinster [I], 2s. 3da.; (2) 11 Oct. 1768, Mary, *suo jure* Baroness Stawell, da. of Edward, 4th Baron Stawell, wid. of H. B. Legge (q.v.), *s.p.* *suc.* fa. as 2nd Visct. Hillsborough [I] 5 May 1742; *cr.* Earl of Hillsborough [I] 3 Oct. 1751; Baron Harwich [GB] 17 Nov. 1756; Earl of Hillsborough [GB] 28 Aug. 1772; Mq. of Downshire [I] 20 Aug. 1789.

P.C. [I] 27 Aug. 1746; comptroller of the Household May 1754–Dec. 1755; P.C. [GB] 21 June 1754; treasurer of the chamber Dec. 1755–Nov. 1756; first ld. of Trade Sept. 1763–July 1765 and Aug.–Dec. 1766; jt. postmaster-gen. Dec. 1766–Jan. 1768; sec. of state for the American dept. Jan. 1768–Aug. 1772, for the southern dept. Nov. 1779–Mar. 1782.

Hillsborough sat at Warwick on the interest of Lord Warwick. He had very little property in England, but was one of the largest Irish landowners and controlled nine seats in the Irish Parliament. His political career was passed almost entirely in England, and his wish to become lord lieutenant of Ireland was never fulfilled.

He entered Parliament as an Opposition Whig, and went over to the Pelhams about 1750. He was first given office in the Newcastle Administration in May 1754. He was then politically connected with Henry Fox, but also on friendly terms with Pitt.[1] On 13 Nov. 1755 he moved the Address on the subsidy treaties. Horace Walpole thus reports his speech:

> The question was opened disadvantageously for the court by the imprudence of Lord Hillsborough, who arrived so late that the Speech was read before he came: instead of veiling, he pointed out the tendency of the treaties as a Hanoverian measure; and seemed to describe, while he meant to defend, the weakness of the Government.

Yet Walpole considered him at this time to be one of the foremost speakers in the House.[2] When the treaties were considered on 10 Dec. Hillsborough spoke again—'very well', reported Andrew Stone to Newcastle.[3] On Newcastle's resignation in November 1756, he was created through the influence of Fox with Devonshire a British peer.

The most important part of his career was spent under George III. During this period he was a leading political figure, and twice held office as secretary of state. Yet the King had a low opinion of his abilities. 'I do not know a man of less judgment than Lord Hillsborough', he wrote to Robinson on 15 Oct. 1776;[4] and to North on 27 Mar. 1782:[5] 'Lord Hillsborough always put things off to the last minute, and though an amiable man [is] the least man of business I ever knew.' He died on 7 Oct. 1793.

[1] Dodington's *Diary*, 320. [2] *Mems. Geo. II*, ii. 49–50, 144. [3] Add. 32861, f. 275. [4] Abergavenny mss. [5] Fortescue, v. 418.

J.B.

**HILLSBOROUGH, Earl of,** *see* **HILL, Wills**

**HINCHINGBROOKE, Visct.,** *see* **MONTAGU, John** (*d.* 1814)

**HOBART, Hon. George** (1731–1804), of Nocton and Blyborough, Lincs.

| St. Ives | 1754–1761 |
| Bere Alston | 1761–1780 |

*b.* 8 Sept. 1731, 4th s. of John, 1st Earl of Buckinghamshire, by his 2nd w. Elizabeth, da. of Robert Bristow, M.P., of Micheldever, Hants; bro. of Hon. Henry Hobart, and half-bro. of John, Lord Hobart (qq.v.). *educ.* Westminster 1739. *m.* 16 May 1757, Albinia, da. and coh. of Lord Vere Bertie (s. of Robert, 1st Duke of Ancaster), 4s. 4da. *suc.* half-bro. as 3rd Earl of Buckinghamshire 3 Sept. 1793.

Hobart sat for St. Ives and Bere Alston on the interest of Lord Buckinghamshire. He early wished to be employed abroad, and in 1756 applied to Newcastle for the post of resident at Hamburg.[1] In August 1762 he went with Lord Buckinghamshire to St. Petersburg as secretary of embassy. But he did not like it there. 'My brother is a good deal out of spirits', wrote Buckinghamshire on 21 Oct. 1762.[2] And on 27 Dec.: 'Poor George . . . is convinced that this climate will not agree with him and is therefore determined to ask leave to return to England.'[3] He arrived in July 1763.

In Parliament Hobart followed Grenville, and went over to the court after his death. But he seems to have taken little interest in politics, and there is no record of his having spoken in the House. He did not stand in 1780. He was better known in social life as the promoter of the opera in the Haymarket.[4]

He died 14 Nov. 1804.

[1] Add. 32866, f. 355. [2] *Despatches & Corresp. of Ld. Buckinghamshire*, ed. d'Arcy Collyer, i. 76. [3] *HMC Lothian*, 171. [4] Walpole to Mann, 22 Feb. 1771; *Malmesbury Letters*, i. 216.

J.B.

**HOBART, Hon. Henry** (1738–99), of Intwood, Norf.

| Norwich | 16 Sept. 1786–9 Mar. 1787 |
| | 28 Mar. 1787–10 May 1799 |

*b.* 1738, 5th s. of John, 1st Earl of Buckinghamshire; bro. of Hon. George Hobart and half-bro. of John, Lord Hobart (qq.v.). *educ.* Ch. Ch. Oxf. 1756; L. Inn 1757; Geneva 1757–9. *m.* 22 July 1761, Anne Margaret, da. of John Bristow (q.v.), 1s. 3da.

At the general election of 1768 Hobart considered standing for Exeter, where his brother had some interest, and for Norfolk, but soon withdrew. He does not appear to have made any other attempt until 1784, when he unsuccessfully contested Norwich. In 1786 he was returned for Norwich as an Administration supporter, was unseated on petition the following year, and returned once more at the ensuing by-election. In Parliament he supported Pitt. His only reported speech during this Parliament was on the wool bill, 1 May 1788, upholding the position of the Norwich manufacturers.

He died 10 May 1799.

B.H.

## HOBART, John, Lord Hobart (1723–93), of Blickling, Norf.

### NORWICH    1747–22 Sept. 1756

*b.* 17 Aug. 1723, 1st surv. s. of John, 1st Earl of Buckinghamshire, by his 1st w. Judith, da. of Robert Britiffe of Baconsthorpe, Norwich; half-bro. of Hon. George and Hon. Henry Hobart (qq.v.). *educ.* Westminster 1732–9; Christ's, Camb. 1739. *m.* (1) 14 July 1761, Martha (*d.* 30 Dec. 1769), da. and coh. of Sir Thomas Drury, 1st Bt., M.P., 4 da.; (2) 24 Sept. 1770, Caroline, da. of William Conolly, M.P., sis. of Thomas Conolly (q.v.), 3s. *d.v.p.* 1 da. *suc.* fa. as 2nd Earl 22 Sept. 1756.

Comptroller of the Household Dec. 1755–6; P.C. 27 Jan. 1756; ld. of the bedchamber Nov. 1757–Nov. 1767; envoy to Russia 1762–5; ld. lt. [I] 1777–80.

Hobart sat for Norwich on his family interest. He was a Government supporter, and one speech of his is recorded during the two years he sat in the Parliament of 1754: in support of the motion for Hanoverian troops, 29 Mar. 1756.[1]

A picture of his personality, not altogether favourable, emerges from his letters to his brother-in-law, Charles Hotham, in the Hotham papers. He died 3 Sept. 1793.

[1] Newdigate's 'Debates'.

L.B.N.

## HOBART, Hon. Robert (1760–1816).

### BRAMBER    15 Dec. 1788–1790
### LINCOLN           1790–1796

*b.* 6 May 1760, 1st surv. s. of Hon. George Hobart (q.v.). *educ.* Westminster 1770; Strasbourg military acad. 1776–7.[1] *m.* (1) 4 Jan. 1792, Margaretta (*d.*7 Aug. 1796), da. and coh. of Edmund Bourke of Urrey, wid. of Thomas Adderley of Innishannon, co. Cork, 1s. (*d.* inf.), 1 da.; (2) 1 June 1799, Eleanor Agnes, da. of William Eden, 1st Baron Auckland (q.v.), *s.p. cr.* Lord Hobart of Blickling 30 Nov. 1798; *suc.* fa. as 4th Earl of Buckinghamshire 14 Nov. 1804.

M.P. [I] 1784–97.

Ensign 59 Ft. 1776; went out to America Aug. 1777; capt. 30 Ft. 1778; maj. 18 Lt. Drag. 1783; ret. 1784. P.C. [I] 21 Apr. 1789; chief sec. to ld. lt. [I] 1789–1793; P.C. [GB] 1 May 1793; gov. Madras 1793–8; sec. of state for war and colonies, Mar. 1801–4; chancellor of duchy of Lancaster Jan.–July 1805, May–June 1812; jt. postmaster gen. 1806–7; pres. Board of Control 1812–*d.*

Hobart, like some other members of his family, cultivated 'pretty ladies', an affected style, and went in for theatricals. In April 1786, when a vacancy was

expected at Lincoln, the Duke of Rutland recommended him to Pitt;[2] and on 8 June Rutland wrote to Thomas Orde[3] that when Pitt was approached, he pleaded a prior engagement:

> But if . . . on a vacancy he should find himself disengaged, let him know that Major Hobart will have my utmost support, and that I am certain I shall have his. I hope Mr. Pitt, on all my election views, will not contend to prevent my ability of serving him.

On 15 Dec. 1788 Hobart was returned for Bramber on the Rutland interest, and on 16 Dec., in the division on the Regency bill, voted with Government.

He died 4 Feb. 1816.

[1] Hobart to Sir Chas. Hotham, 29 July, 9 Oct. 1776, 13 Apr. 1777, Hotham mss, East Riding RO. [2] *Corresp. bet. W. Pitt and Charles Duke of Rutland*, ed. John, Duke of Rutland, 3 (misdated). [3] *HMC Rutland*, iii. 306–8.

L.B.N.

## HOGHTON, Sir Henry, 6th Bt. (1728–95), of Hoghton Tower, nr. Blackburn, Lancs.

### PRESTON    29 Nov. 1768–9 Mar. 1795

*b.* 22 Oct. 1728, 1st s. of Philip Hoghton by his 1st w. Elizabeth, da. of Thomas Slater of Denham, Lancs; gd.-s. of Sir Charles Hoghton, 4th Bt. *educ.* Northampton acad.[1] *m.* (1) 23 June 1760, Elizabeth (*d.* 19 May 1761), da. and h. of William Ashurst of Hedingham Castle, Essex, 1 da.; (2) 8 July 1766, Fanny, da. and coh. of Daniel Booth, director of the Bank of England, of Hutton Hall, Essex, 2s. *suc.* uncle as 6th Bt. 23 Feb. 1768.

Hoghton 'was educated a Dissenter . . . and continued invariably in communion with that body'.[2] His family, one of the oldest in Lancashire, first represented the county in 1322; and for 53 years between 1710 and 1802 held one seat at Preston. In 1768 Hoghton stood on a joint interest with Lord Derby's candidate, John Burgoyne; and after one of the most violent contests of the century, was seated on petition.

Wraxall described him as 'a rigid Presbyterian, of ample fortune, adorned with the mildest manners', and 'without stain of any kind'.[3] An independent inclined to support Administration, he nevertheless between 1768 and 1774 voted four times against them: on the Middlesex election, 15 Apr. 1769; the royal marriage bill, 11 Mar. 1772; the naval captains' petition, 9 Feb. 1773; and Grenville's Election Act, 25 Feb. 1774. He always appears in their lists as a friend. He was a frequent speaker especially on matters concerning Lancashire, and tried several times (1772, 1779, 1787, 1789, 1790) to obtain relief for Protestant Dissenters.

He supported the American war; acted as a teller for the court on the contractors bill, 12 Feb. 1779 —which was unusual in an independent Member—

and voted with North to the end. Even in May 1781 'he was persuaded . . . that a majority of the inhabitants of North America were willing . . . to return to obedience to the British Government'.[4] He is known to have given only one vote against North —on the motion for an account of pensions, 21 Feb. 1780.

Hoghton voted for Shelburne's peace preliminaries, 18 Feb. 1783, and for Fox's East India bill, 27 Nov. 1783; and in January 1784 was classed by Robinson as 'very hopeful'. He was a member of the St. Alban's Tavern group which tried to unite Pitt and Fox, and when this broke down, supported Pitt. Although he sat for the constituency with the widest franchise in Great Britain, he did not vote for parliamentary reform in either 1783 or 1785. He died 9 Mar. 1795.

[1] H. McLachlan, *Warrington Acad.* (Chetham Soc. n.s. cvii), 112. [2] *Gent. Mag.* 1795, pp. 260–1. [3] *Mems.* iv. 437. [4] Debrett, iii. 444.

J.B.

## HOLBURNE, Francis (1704–71).

STIRLING BURGHS 1761–1768
PLYMOUTH 1768–15 July 1771

*b.* 1704, 3rd s. of Sir James Holburne, 1st Bt., of Menstrie, Clackmannan by Jean, da. of Alexander Spittal of Leuchat. *educ.* Inverkeithing. *m.* c. 1750, Frances, da. of Guy Ball, member of Barbados council, wid. of Edward Lascelles, collector of customs, Barbados, 1s. 2da.; stepfa. of Edward Lascelles (q.v.).
Entered R.N. 1720; lt. 1727; capt. 1740; r.-adm. 1755; v.-adm. 1757; c.-in-c. Portsmouth Dec. 1755–1767; adm. Jan. 1768; r.-adm. of Great Britain 1770; ld. of Admiralty Feb. 1770–Jan. 1771; gov. Greenwich Hospital Jan. 1771-*d.*
Burgess of Edinburgh 1740.

Holburne owed his advancement in the navy to Lord Morton, an intimate family friend, and to Archibald, Duke of Argyll, who 'took him by the hand in his younger days and made him a captain'.[1] He made his name in 1742 by the capture of a Spanish ship; held a number of commands, serving in the West Indies, the Channel and the Bay of Biscay, until the peace of 1748; and in 1749 was sent to Barbados to help secure the execution of the treaty terms. There he married a rich widow, and returned home in 1752.

In 1755 Holburne, considered by Newcastle 'a very good man',[2] was sent to reinforce Boscawen's fleet off Louisburg. Boscawen wrote to his wife, 26 June:[3]

I believe you never heard of this Admiral Holburne before . . . He is a Scot, you know I don't think well of that nation for upper leather, nor was he ever thought much of in our service; he is rich and has contrived to insinuate himself into the good graces of Lord Anson, made an admiral and sent here to my

assistance. You see by this I don't like him, nor ever did, having known him from my first entering into the service . . . As soon as he joined me, [he] was laying schemes for making a job immediately. I cut him short and told him I sent him to Halifax to fill his water, and join me here as soon as possible. I don't expect to see him again very soon, but I shall soon be after him.

For most of 1756 Holburne served with his squadron off Brest, and in December was appointed a member of the court martial which tried Byng; strongly attached through Morton to Newcastle and Hardwicke, he took no part in the moves to mitigate the sentence, though he signed the court's original recommendation to mercy. When, on 2 Mar. 1757, the members of the tribunal were examined before the House of Lords, 'all the court martial seemed terrified . . . except old Admiral Holburne, who cursed and swore at the bar of that House, because Byng was not shot out of the way, without giving him the trouble of coming from Portsmouth'.[4] In February 1757 he was appointed to command the fleet sent to support Loudoun in his attack on Louisburg. When Loudoun, in consequence of a report on the strength of the French forces, decided to abandon the attempt, Holburne concurred in his view.[5] Walpole commented: 'Admiral Holburne, one of the sternest condemners of Byng, wrote . . . that he having but seventeen ships and the French nineteen, he dared not attack them'; and Hardwicke to Newcastle, 5 Sept. 1757: 'They all proceed upon the Byng principle'.[6]

Shortly after Holburne's return in December he was appointed port admiral at Portsmouth, and never held a sea command again. While he apparently lost favour with Anson, who considered him a mischief maker,[7] he remained closely attached to Loudoun and his patron Argyll, who suggested in 1758 that he should contest Stirling Burghs at the general election.[8]

Holburne immediately began his campaign in the burghs against Robert Haldane but, hampered by his duties at Portsmouth, besought Loudoun to make interest for him with Lord Cathcart.[9] Cathcart wrote to Loudoun, 14 Sept. 1760:[10] 'The Admiral . . . is a very worthy and serviceable man, and his station in the navy together with his good disposition ought to make him an agreeable representative and a useful one to those burghs, who are so much connected with seafaring people.' At the crucial burgh council elections of Michaelmas 1760, Holburne made unscrupulous use of his position, especially at Inverkeithing, which 'he looked upon as his *natale solium*' and where he stood for provost. He brought in armed press gangs, entered a trades meeting with drawn sword, and by intimidation and bribery secured the return of his party. When

Haldane successfully brought an action before the court of session for reduction of the Inverkeithing election, Holburne appealed to the House of Lords.[11] He urged Loudoun to attend the hearing and 'to let the Duke of Argyll know his situation'. 'It is a cursed thing to be brought to this and such an expense, and your Lordship knows well that had it not been for the encouragement I met with from the Duke I had never undertaken this.'[12]

Although his appeal was rejected, 11 Feb. 1761, Holburne was returned in April against Alexander Wedderburn, who had replaced Haldane as candidate. Deprived by Argyll's death of a powerful friend, he now sought the patronage of Bute[13] who, although committed to support Wedderburn, was prepared to compromise. Newcastle wrote to Rockingham, 24 Nov. 1761:[14]

Lord Bute was in very good humour . . . He complained but very modestly that the Duke of Devonshire and I were against him in the only two elections where he concerned himself . . . that it would have a very unpleasant appearance if we two and he should differ; and for that reason he had made up the first, Admiral Holburne's, and that Holburne was to continue this Parliament.

As a result Wedderburn's petition was withdrawn. Although Newcastle and his friends 'rejoiced that Holburne sits this Parliament',[15] the Admiral, having won Bute's favour and retained his post at Portsmouth, showed no inclination to join them in opposition and was listed by Fox among those favourable to the peace preliminaries. On the formation of the Grenville Administration, Holburne wrote to Sandwich, first lord of the Admiralty, 28 Apr. 1763:[16]

Permit me to mention my desire of continuing in this command, it having been intended so, as I have been confined here most of the war very contrary to my inclinations, having frequently requested to serve at sea, but here have I been confined, fitting most of the navy for younger officers to go and command them and make fortunes in. I hope your Lordship will think of continuing me.

His request was granted, and he remained a supporter of the Grenville Administration.

Listed 'pro' by Rockingham in July 1765, he retained his Portsmouth appointment, but voted against the repeal of the Stamp Act, 22 Feb. During the Chatham Administration he was listed by Rockingham as attached to Bute, and by Townshend and Newcastle as pro Administration; he voted with Government on the land tax, 27 Feb. 1767. Having lost or relinquished his Portsmouth post, he unsuccessfully tried, through Sandwich, to obtain an appointment at Trinity House in July 1767.[17]

In 1768 he stood for Plymouth on the Admiralty interest. A friend wrote to Lord Barrington, 16 Jan. 1768:[18]

We were almost unanimous for your Lordship and Admiral Holburne . . . My friend, the Admiral, would at least have had some witticisms on him if he had not been named with your Lordship, such is the advantage of good company.

In the new Parliament he supported Grafton on Wilkes and the Middlesex election. He was made a lord of the Admiralty in the North Administration, holding office until appointed governor of Greenwich Hospital in January 1771. Ten years a Member, he is not known to have spoken in the House.

He died 15 July 1771, remembered for protecting his seamen from brutality, but otherwise having a reputation 'variously represented by his friends and enemies'.[19]

[1] Holburne to Bute, Apr. 1761, Bute mss. [2] Newcastle to Hartington, 17 May 1755, Devonshire mss. [3] Naval Misc. iv. (Navy Recs. Soc.), 194. [4] Edw. Owen to Edw. Weston, 5 Mar. 1757, HMC 8th Rep. pt. 1 (1881), 313. [5] Add. 29589B, ff. 19, 20, 22; Charnock, Biographia Navalis, v. 37-39. [6] Mems. Geo. II, iii. 40; P. C. Yorke, Hardwicke, iii. 171. [7] Ibid. 215. [8] Holburne to Loudoun, 10 May 1759, Loudoun mss. [9] Holburne to Loudoun, 18 Jan., 10 May 1759, ibid. [10] Ibid. [11] Add. 36166, f. 308; W. Stephens, Hist. Inverkeithing, 224. [12] Holburne to Loudoun, 5 Feb. 1761, Loudoun mss. [13] Holburne to Bute, Apr. 1761, Bute mss. [14] Add. 32932. ff. 258-9. [15] Add. 32931, ff. 317-20; Rockingham to Devonshire, 28 Nov. 1761, Devonshire mss. [16] Sandwich mss. [17] Bedford to Sandwich, 31 July 1767, Bedford mss. [18] Barrington mss. [19] Charnock, v. 41-42.

E.H.-G.

## HOLDSWORTH, Arthur (c.1757-87), of Widdicombe, Devon.

DARTMOUTH    1780-21 Aug. 1787

b. c.1757, o.s. of Arthur Holdsworth, gov. of Dartmouth castle, by Rebecca, da. of Joseph Taylor of Ogwell, Devon. educ. Eton 1766-74; Trinity, Camb. 1775. m. Elizabeth, da. of Robert Holdsworth, a Dartmouth merchant, 3s. and other issue. suc. fa. 1777.

Gov. Dartmouth castle 1777-d.

The Holdsworths were an old Dartmouth merchant family. The interest which Holdsworth's father had established in the borough as governor of the castle and parliamentary manager for the Government passed on his death, together with his functions, to his son, who was hardly of age. As Robinson admitted both in 1780 and in 1784, the choice of Members rested with Holdsworth rather than with the Treasury. In the House Holdsworth attached himself to the Opposition; voted with them in the five divisions in February–March 1782 for which lists are available; voted for Shelburne's peace preliminaries, 18 Feb. 1783, and with Pitt for parliamentary reform, 7 May 1783; opposed the Coalition, and voted against Fox's East India bill; supported Pitt's Government from the very outset; paired in favour of his parliamentary reform proposals, 18 Apr. 1785; but, thoroughly independent as he was, he voted against Richmond's fortifications plan, 27 Feb. 1786. A fairly frequent speaker, he almost invariably dealt with subjects of which he had real knowledge. Five interventions of his in debate recorded before the fall of North's Administration are all concerned with abuses in the dockyards, malpractices in the sale of ships and naval stores, with 'the shameful prodigality of the public money'. In 1785 he took a prominent part in favour of a bill concerning Newfoundland's trade with the United States, which he described, 14 Feb., as a compromise between the views of all the parties interested in it: the merchants of London, of Poole and Dartmouth, and of Canada.[1] He 'defended his constituents, acknowledging that it was to the Newfoundland trade carried on from Dartmouth, that he stood indebted for his seat in that assembly'. In the same session he was very critical of the Government scheme of fortifications; described the Ordnance as 'the source of more profusion than any other department'; asked for an inquiry into their expenses; and called attention to cases where owners had been obliged to give up lands to the Ordnance, 'after expending considerable sums on them', only to have them returned after purchasing others.[2] His last reported speech was in support of a bill 'to prevent frivolous and vexatious suits in ecclesiastical courts' —'this arbitrary, this infernal court' (23 Feb. 1787).[3]

He died 21 Aug. 1787. There was a suggestion of a pension to Mrs. Holdsworth, 'on account of her husband's services and her distress'.[4]

[1] Stockdale, iv. 86, 170, 199. [2] Ibid. 317, 338–40. [3] Ibid. x. 342. [4] Geo. Rose to W. Pitt, 26 Aug. 1787, Chatham mss.

L.B.N.

**HOLLIS,** *see* **BRAND HOLLIS**

**HOLME SUMNER,** *see* **SUMNER**

**HOLMES, Charles** (1711–61).

NEWPORT I.o.W.   1 June 1758–21 Nov. 1761

*bap.* 19 Sept. 1711, 5th s. of Henry Holmes, and bro. of Thomas Holmes (q.v.). *unm.*

Lt. R.N. 1734; capt. 1748; in the West Indies 1741–1748; in N. America 1756–8; commanded a squadron on the rivers Weser, Elbe, and Ems, and took town of Emden 1758; r.-adm. 1758; in expedition to Quebec 1759; c.-in-c. in Jamaica 1760–*d.*

On the death of Ralph Jenison, Newcastle wrote to Thomas Holmes, 16 May 1758, that he meant to recommend to Holmes 'a very honest gentleman' but must speak to the King before naming him. This letter crossed one from Holmes written from Newport the same day: 'my brother, Capt. Charles Holmes, by the united desire and approbation of the

corporation and myself, intends offering himself as candidate in the room of Mr. Jenison'. Newcastle replied that nobody could be more agreeable to him than Charles Holmes—'a proof to you how much I desire and depend upon your friendship and of both your brothers. It will be necessary for me to mention this affair to the King, before I can in form give you an answer.' The King approved, and Newcastle wrote on 20 May to Lord Portsmouth, governor of the Isle of Wight:

> I know the Commodore extremely well, and have a very good opinion of him, and he has given all the assurances I can desire of attachment to the King and his service. I acquainted his Majesty yesterday with this affair, and the King agrees with me that it will be for his services that Commodore Holmes should come in at Newport.

On 2 June Holmes reported that his brother had been elected unanimously.[1]

On 16 Dec. 1758, Holmes, ordered to join Saunders and the Western Squadron, wrote to Newcastle to remind him of a promise of the Jamaica Command, in which he feared he might be supplanted in his absence—'no person is better acquainted with the station of Jamaica than I am; or will, I believe, be more agreeable to the gentlemen of the island'.[2]

He died in Jamaica, 21 Nov. 1761.

[1] Add. 32880, ff. 106, 109–10, 126, 160, 162, 307. [2] Add. 32886, ff. 344–5.

L.B.N.

**HOLMES, Henry** (1703–62).

NEWTOWN I.o.W.   1741–1747
YARMOUTH I.o.W.   1747–11 Aug. 1762

*bap.* 28 Feb. 1703, 2nd s. of Henry Holmes, and bro. of Thomas Holmes (q.v.). *m.* his cos. Anne, da. of Nicholas Lysaght of Mountnorth, co. Cork, by Grace, yst. da. of Col. Thomas Holmes, *s.p.*

Ensign 28 Ft. 1721, lt. 1723, capt. 1727, maj. 1740, lt.-col. 1743; col. 1746; col. 31 Ft. 1749–*d.*; maj.-gen. 1756; lt.-gen. 1759; lt.-gov. I.o.W. 1754–*d.*

Henry Holmes was the nominee of his brother Thomas, the government manager of the Isle of Wight boroughs, and regularly followed his line in politics. He died 11 Aug. 1762.

L.B.N.

**HOLMES, Thomas** (1699–1764), of Yarmouth I.o.W.

NEWTOWN I.o.W.   1727–25 Apr. 1729, 1734–1741
YARMOUTH I.o.W.   1747–21 July 1764

*bap.* 2 Nov. 1699, 1st s. of Henry Holmes, M.P. for Yarmouth 1695–1717 and lt.-gov. of I.o.W., by Mary, illegit. da. of Sir Robert Holmes, uncle of Henry Holmes, M.P. for Newport 1678–90 and gov. of I.o.W. 1667–90. *m.* (1) Anne (*d.* 1743), da. of Henry Pleyer

of Alverstoke, Hants, wid. of Colby Apsley, 1s. *d.v.p.*;
(2) Catherine, da. of John Leigh of Shorwell, I.o.W.,
*s.p.* *suc.* fa. 1738; *cr.* Baron Holmes [I] 11 Sept. 1760.
Gov. I.o.W. Apr. 1763–*d.*

Against Thomas Holmes's name in Bute's list of
December 1761 appears the note:

Opponent to Sir Robert Walpole, afterwards attached
to him on condition that he should have the Government interest to make the boroughs of the Isle of
Wight. On the same condition swore fealty to Pelham,
at his death on the same condition to Newcastle.

And this is how he was 'making' two of the
boroughs:[1]

Lord Holmes ever since he had the management of
affairs in that corner of the kingdom has followed the
same sure policy at Newport which secured him Yarmouth. Upon every vacancy of a burgess he filled his
place with a relation of his own; at this time his relations make a very considerable body in the corporation,
and if he continues this practice two or three years
longer (as there are several very old burgesses) he will
have such a determined majority in his own family,
that he may return such Members as are agreeable to
himself only.

Hans Stanley, who succeeded Holmes as governor of
the island, in a letter of 24 Aug. 1764,[2] incidentally
remarks that Holmes 'was secured by very lucrative
contracts in the brewing business at the docks'.

On 14 Mar. 1754 Ralph Jenison, who served as
intermediary between Holmes and the Government
whenever Holmes was out of London, gave Newcastle a list of candidates for the Isle of Wight
boroughs 'settled by Mr. Pelham'.[3] And on 23 May
1756 Holmes wrote to Newcastle:[4]

As the care and expense of the three boroughs in the
Isle of Wight rests entirely on me, the governor never
expending one shilling or ever going there, and no
place in the Ordnance or castles giving any aid as
usual, I flatter myself your Grace will not think it
unreasonable to allow me £200 yearly for each borough
amounting in the whole to £600, and as I have been
for some years at a great expense, hope at least one
year's income may be paid directly.

His request was granted without any of the usual
delays, and on 21 July 1756 the first payment of
£600 was made to Jenison for Holmes from secret
service funds. When Jenison died, 15 May 1758,
Holmes asked the Duke to have some one pay the
money into his account at Hoare's bank, 'and send
me their receipt as he used to do . . . I don't choose
my brothers [both M.P.s] or any other person should
be acquainted with the affair'.[5] In the same letter:
'I can assure your Grace that I can choose here
[Newport] any two persons I please and shall take
care they shall always be in your interest.'

Holmes's next application, 9 May 1760, was for
an Irish peerage—not 'from any desire of self
emolument, of grandeur', but to 'enable me . . . to
secure an interest in the country so much entrusted

to my management alone'.[6] And in a further letter to
Newcastle on 23 May 1760:[7]

Were I to communicate to your Grace the estates I
have in England, Ireland, and Wales, besides money
in the stocks and other securities, you would see my
fortune is equal to those honours; the annual thing I
asked as I have no employment was only to repay me
the money I am out of pocket in the several services we
support. I never meant it should tie me down from
receiving some honourable mark of distinction for
having brought a factious part of the country over to
his Majesty's interest. Every one knows I have a greater
weight in the Island of Wight than any governor or
any other person ever had; my gratitude for the favours
my brothers have received from you and your family
will oblige me to secure the boroughs for your interest,
but shall not choose to concern myself in any other
affairs unless what I have requested is granted, for I
think the person that is first in interest and fortune
ought not to be the lowest in rank and quality.

On 19 July 1760 Newcastle was able to inform
Holmes that his request had been granted.

'Being confined most part of the winter by illness
and having frequent returns', Holmes had written to
Newcastle, 5 June 1759, 'made me afraid of crossing
the water to attend Parliament'; should his illness
continue, he was prepared to give up his seat to a
friend of the Duke.[8] On 22 Mar. 1762:[9] 'I am . . .
very ill . . . I sincerely wish my friends would consent for me to vacate my seat, for I know I shall
never be able to attend any more.'

The question of Holmes's allegiance was brought
up soon after Newcastle's resignation by the death
on 11 Aug. 1762 of his brother Henry, lieutenant-
governor of the Isle of Wight and M.P. for Yarmouth. Shelburne wrote to Bute in an undated
letter, docketed 'August 1762':[10]

Lord Holmes . . . is but a poor creature—but his
boroughs and his being direct, where he professes
himself attached, makes him considerable . . . Government and he . . . joining bring in every Member but
one in the Isle of Wight. I have taken the properest
method with regard to him, only your Lordship will
take care, the government [lieutenant-governorship] is
not given to his nephew [Lt.-Col. Troughear] till you
hear further of it.

On 15 Sept. Shelburne reminded Bute of Holmes—
''tis well if a thing is resolved on, to do it soon, which
. . . doubles the obligation'. On 17 Oct. Newcastle
asked Harcourt Powell if he had heard what Holmes
intended at Yarmouth; he himself in his present
situation did not think it proper to apply to Holmes
—'it would certainly have no effect'. But possibly
Holmes 'may bring in a good man himself; and that
would be the best of all'.[11]

Lord Portsmouth, governor of the Isle of Wight,
died 22 Nov. 1762, and on the 24th Fox wrote to
Bute to 'advise strongly' against the office being
given to the Duke of Bolton:[12]

His uncle destroyed the interest of the Crown in that county; he would do the same. I have likewise advice to give, which if approved would tend to present and future security, and very extensively. Three boroughs depend chiefly on Lord Holmes, he will not keep it long, he is so infirm, he will bring in Mr. Dyson instantly [for Yarmouth] and I have several other things to say in his behalf.

On 30 Nov.: 'I could not succeed with Lord Holmes without saying more than I was authorized to say. But there cannot fail of an opportunity for Mr. Dyson very soon.' On 18 Dec.: 'Lord Holmes will choose Mr. Dyson.' Early in December Fox had included Holmes in the list of Members favourable to the peace preliminaries.

On 6 Apr. 1763 Holmes kissed hands as governor of the Isle of Wight. 'I will answer for him', Fox had written to Bute on 27 Mar.[13] He continued Government manager for the Isle under Grenville; but there is no record of his having received any payments from secret service funds toward the management after Newcastle had left the Treasury.

Holmes was absent from the divisions on general warrants in February 1764 owing to ill-health. But Grenville wrote to him on 12 Apr.:[14]

No one is more sensible than myself of your steady zeal for the public service and of your particular attention to me in the very obliging offer which your Lordship makes of supplying your seat in Parliament. This proposition will I flatter myself be rendered wholly unnecessary by the recovery of your health.

He died on 21 July 1764, and was succeeded in his estates and his parliamentary interest by his nephew, the Rev. Leonard Troughear, who assumed the name of Holmes.

[1] John White to Sir Harry Erskine, 1 Feb. 1763, *Jenkinson Pprs.* 128. [2] Sloane-Stanley mss. [3] Add. 32995, f. 94. [4] Add. 32865, f. 100. [5] Add. 32880, f. 307. [6] Add. 32905, ff. 377-8. [7] Add. 32906, f. 188. [8] Add. 32891, f. 437. [9] Add. 32936, ff. 50-51. [10] Bute mss. [11] Add. 32943, f. 240. [12] Bute mss. [13] Hen. Fox mss. [14] Grenville letter bk.

L.B.N.

## HOLROYD, see BAKER HOLROYD

## HOLT, Rowland (?1723–86), of Redgrave Hall, Suff.

SUFFOLK   20 Apr. 1759–1768, 18 Dec. 1771–1780

*b.* ?1723, 1st s. of Rowland Holt by his w. Elizabeth Washington.[1] *educ.* Magdalen, Oxf. 23 Dec. 1740, aged 17; Grand Tour (Italy) c.1746. *unm. suc.* fa. 25 July 1739.

Holt's great-uncle, Sir John Holt, L.C.J., purchased Redgrave Hall; the Holts were merchants and lawyers. Rowland Holt, when in Rome in 1746, is reported to have paid court publicly to the Pretender, and to have dined with him.[2] In the House he ranked as a Tory. When Sir John Rous thought of standing for Suffolk at the general election of 1761,

Holt complained to his colleague, John Affleck, that he feared T. C. Bunbury and Rous 'would both greatly out-number him, and that he should be laid aside after being made use of by the county for two years only', as a stop-gap on the death of Cordell Firebrace. A compromise was then arranged, whereby Rous stood down on the understanding that room should be made for him at the latest in 1768, and the election was uncontested.

In October 1761 Newcastle did not send Holt his parliamentary whip, and on 13 Nov. 1762 marked him as 'contra'; but on 9 Dec. Holt voted against the peace preliminaries. In the autumn of 1763 Jenkinson classed him as 'pro'; but in the three divisions on general warrants, 6, 15, and 18 Feb., Holt voted with Opposition, and on 10 May was listed by Newcastle as a 'sure friend'. Rockingham, however, in July 1765 put him down as 'contra' and he voted against the repeal of the Stamp Act. In January 1767 Charles Townshend classed him as 'Administration', but on 27 Feb. 1767, over the land tax, he voted against the Government. In short, he was an independent Tory country gentleman, voting in accordance with his convictions: 'he accepted of no place, or applied for any'.[3]

As the general election of 1768 drew near neither of the sitting Members was prepared to abide by the agreement of 1761, and as Rous was determined to stand, all three were nominated at the county meeting on 6 Nov. 1767. But three days later Holt, reflecting on having at the meeting been forsaken by gentlemen on whose support he had counted, in a letter to the electors took his 'final leave' of them, adding:

Gentlemen, be assured you will never receive any further application from me, as a private station of life will become everyday more eligible to a person at my time of life, and of my disposition.

And a further long letter, dated 15 Nov., in which he argued his case and defended his action, he concluded by asking leave for the future to build his enjoyments 'with more durable materials than the popular breath of such folks as constitute a majority at most public meetings'.[4]

Nevertheless on the death of Sir John Rous, 31 Oct. 1771, he stood, apparently with support from Grafton and the Administration, against Rous's son, who, at the county meeting at Stowmarket, 13 Nov., withdrew from the contest. Holt was returned unopposed. Over the royal marriage bill Robinson classed him in March 1772 as 'pro, present'; and a vote on the Opposition side on making the Grenville Election Act permanent, 25 Feb. 1774, is the only one by him recorded in this Parliament. But at its close he was classed by Robinson as 'pro'. In 1774 he was again returned unopposed, and in the new Parliament Holt seems as a rule to have sided with Government, although in the division list of 22 Feb. 1775, on the Middlesex election, consistently with his previous attitude, he voted with Opposition; similarly on 21 Feb. 1780, on Fox's motion for an account of pensions. Over the contractors bill, 12 Feb. 1779, he was listed by Robinson as 'pro, present', and in the lists of the four divisions, March–April 1780, he appears as voting with Government. But a list among George III's papers at Windsor, marked 'persons generally with who went against', and clearly relating to Dunning's motion on the influence of the Crown, 6 Apr. 1780,[5] includes his name though with a query against it. Robinson, in his survey of 1780, classed Holt as 'pro', and forecast that Rous would stand against him; but in a postscript of 31 July noted that Holt stood higher in the county than Bunbury, and therefore expected him to succeed. But Holt, who at all times seemed unwilling to engage in contested elections, withdrew, and never stood for Parliament again. There is no record of his having spoken in the House during the 18 years he was a Member.

Very little is known about his personal life: he is hardly ever mentioned in contemporary correspondence; the pamphlet on the four Suffolk elections, which on the whole seems biassed against him, suggests that he was parsimonious; and he is said to have been nicknamed 'Tyrant of Manors' for too strictly enforcing his manorial rights.[6] He died 12 July 1786.

[1] HMC Portland, vi. 151. [2] Mann to Walpole, 4, 18 Jan. 1746. [3] Hist. Last Four Elections for Suff. (1772), p. 18. [4] Ipswich Jnl. 14, 28 Nov. 1767. [5] Fortescue, iii. 419. [6] K. F. Doughty, Betts of Wortham, 213n.

L.B.N.

## HOLTE, Sir Charles, 6th Bt. (?1721–82), of Aston Hall, nr. Birmingham.

WARWICKSHIRE    1774–1780

b. ?1721, 2nd s. of Sir Clobery Holte, 4th Bt., of Aston Hall by Barbara, da. and h. of Thomas Lister of Whitfield, Northants. educ. Magdalen, Oxf. 13 Feb. 1739, aged 17. m.1754, Anne, da. of Pudsey Jesson of Langley, Warws., 1da. suc. bro. as 6th Bt. 21 Apr. 1770.

Sir Charles Holte came from an old Warwickshire family who first represented the county in 1661. He was returned in 1774 after a contest, and voted with Opposition. His attendance was not very good, and he appears in only five out of the 14 division lists for this Parliament. The English Chronicle wrote about him in 1780:

The bad state of health under which Sir Charles had long laboured, incapacitating him for the arduous duty

of inspecting, with necessary vigilance and attention, the various interests of an opulent, respectable, and commercial county, he intimated, towards the conclusion of the last Parliament a positive determination to resign.

There is no record of his having spoken in the House.

He died 13 Mar. 1782.

J.B.

## HOME, Patrick (1728–1808), of Billie and Wedderburn, Berwick.

BERWICKSHIRE    1784–1796

b. 22 May 1728, 2nd s. of Rev. Ninian Home of Billie by his 2nd w. Margaret, da. of George Home of Wedderburn. Adv. 1755. m. May 1771, Jane, da. of John Graham, adv., of Dougalston, s.p. suc. to Billie bef. 1754; to Wedderburn 1766.

His father Ninian Home, parish minister of Sprouston, Roxburghshire, deposed 1718 for drunkenness and Jacobitism,[1] became the proprietor of Billie and Wedderburn by buying up the debts of their impoverished owners. Denounced by his detractors as 'Old Ringan Griphard', he rightly regarded himself as the preserver of the Wedderburn fortunes and in due course returned their lands, under certain financial obligations, to the dispossessed family. Ambitious of allying his own comparatively humble line with theirs, he married Margaret, daughter of George Home, and by her had a large family. In 1733 he drew up an elaborate entail, settling the Wedderburn estate on George Home's sons. Only after the heirs of all these had failed were the estates to descend to his own family by Margaret Home.[2]

Patrick Home inherited £1,000 on his father's death in 1744. In 1766 he succeeded to Wedderburn on the death of the last of the Wedderburn line designated by Ninian Home in his entail. He had for many years spent much time at Wedderburn Castle and had acquired a reputation for whimsical humour or even eccentricity.[3] Although he had a strong electoral interest in Berwickshire, for many years he pretended an indifference to politics; but in 1784, at the age of 56, he was returned unopposed for Berwickshire with the support of Henry Dundas.

In Parliament Patrick Home followed Pitt, and on 18 Apr. 1785 voted for his parliamentary reform proposals. He is not known to have spoken in the House before 1790.

He died 19 Dec. 1808.

[1] Hervey Scott, Fasti, ii. 5, 89–90. [2] E. E. Hume, 'A Colonial Scottish Jacobite Family', Virginia Mag. of Hist. and Biog. (1930). [3] HMC Home; SRO, Dunglass mss.

E.H.-G.

**HOME**, see also **HUME**

**HONYWOOD, Filmer** (c.1745–1809), of Hull Place, Kent and Marks Hall, Essex.

STEYNING    1774–1780
KENT        1780–1796, 1802–1806

*b.* c.1745, 3rd s. of Sir John Honywood, 3rd Bt., by his 2nd w. Dorothy, da. of Sir Edward Filmer, 3rd Bt., of East Sutton, Kent. *educ.* B.N.C. Oxf. 1762. *suc.* to estates of his distant cos. Philip Honywood (q.v.) 1785.

Honywood was returned unopposed on the family interest in 1774. All his recorded votes in this Parliament were with Opposition. He spoke twice, on each occasion as seconder to a motion proposed by Charles Marsham.

In 1780 in conjunction with Marsham he was 'nominated at a patriotic meeting' for the county of Kent, and returned unopposed. He again voted regularly in opposition; on 8 May 1781 spoke in favour of a petition for the reduction of the power of the Crown; and on 15 Mar. 1782 in support of Sir John Rous's motion of no confidence. He voted for Shelburne's peace preliminaries, 18 Feb. 1783, for Pitt's parliamentary reform proposals, 7 May 1783, and against Fox's East India bill, 27 Nov. 1783; but in Stockdale's list of 19 Mar. 1784 he appears as an opponent of Pitt, and he voted against Pitt 1784–1790, though he again supported Pitt on parliamentary reform, 18 Apr. 1785. He spoke several times in favour of disfranchising employees of the navy and the Ordnance Board, and on 12 Mar. 1789 supported a resolution to repeal the County Elections Act.

He died 2 June 1809.

M.M.D.

**HONYWOOD, Frazer** (*d.*1764), of Malling, Kent.

STEYNING    10 Feb. 1759–27 Jan. 1764

*o.s.* of Isaac Honywood of Hampstead by his w. Mary Frazer.[1] *m.* 5 May 1736, Jane, da. of Abram Atkyns of Clapham, London merchant, 1s. *d.v.p.* *suc.* fa. 1740.

Honywood was a wealthy banker, in partnership with Richard Fuller (q.v.). He dabbled extensively in Government loans, subscribing to them and selling shortly after.

He was unsuccessful candidate at the Shaftesbury by-election of 1747. In 1750 Sir Hugh Smithson, M.P. for Middlesex, who had just succeeded as Earl of Northumberland, recommended him 'as a proper person to stand for the county . . . he has a very good estate, and is a very active zealous Whig'.[2] He was defeated, and does not appear to have stood again until 1759 when he was returned unopposed at Steyning. In 1761 he was returned again after a contest in which he headed the poll. Bute's list of 1762 classes him 'contra' with the additional comment: 'once Newcastle, now discontented with his

Grace'; nevertheless he continued in opposition until his death.

There is no record of his having spoken in the House. He died 27 Jan. 1764.

[1] P. C. Yorke, *Diary of John Baker*, 260. [2] Bedford mss.

M.M.D.

**HONYWOOD, Sir John**, 4th Bt. (c.1757–1806), of Evington, Kent.

STEYNING     1784–July 1785, 17 Apr. 1788–1790
CANTERBURY   1790–1796, 10 Mar. 1797–1802
HONITON      1802–29 Mar. 1806

*b.* c. 1757, 1st s. of William Honywood by Elizabeth, da. of Thomas Clack of Wallingford, Berks., and gd.-s. of Sir John Honywood 3rd Bt. *educ.* C.C.C. Oxf. 1775. *m.* 13 Dec. 1779, Frances, da. of William, 2nd Visct. Courtenay, 1s. 6da. *suc.* gd.-fa. as 4th Bt. 26 June 1781.

Honywood was returned unopposed for Steyning, his family borough, in 1784, but in 1785, for reasons unascertained, took the Chiltern Hundreds. In April 1788, after the death of his successor at Steyning, Thomas Edwards Freeman, he was again returned.

He voted with Pitt on parliamentary reform, 18 Apr. 1785, and on the Regency, 1788–9. And in a letter to Pitt, 4 Oct. 1791, asking for the place of receiver of the land tax for Kent, he declared 'when my parliamentary support was necessary to you, I never even debated on the propriety of the measure'.[1]

There is no record of his having spoken in the House before 1790.

He died 29 Mar. 1806.

[1] Chatham mss.

M.M.D.

**HONYWOOD, Philip** (c.1710–85), of Marks Hall, Essex and Howgill Castle, Westmld.

APPLEBY    1754–10 Feb. 1756, 4 Mar. 1756–1784

*b.* c.1710, 5th s. of Sir Robert Honywood of Marks Hall by Mary, da. of Sir Richard Sandford, 2nd Bt., sis. and h. of Sir Richard Sandford, 3rd Bt., of Howgill Castle. *m.* 22 Apr. 1751, Elizabeth, da. of John Wastell of Tower Hill, 1s. *d.v.p..* *suc.* bro. 1755.
Cornet 11 Drag. 1735; capt.-lt. 3 Drag. 1739, capt. 1741, maj. 1741, lt.-col. 1743; severely wounded at Dettingen; col. 1752; col. 20 Ft. 1755–6; col. 9 Drag. 1756–9; maj.-gen. 1758; col. 4 Horse 1759–82; lt.-gen. 1760; gov. Hull 1766–85; gen. 1777; col. 3 Drag. Gds. 1782–*d.*

In 1754 Honywood was returned for Appleby on Lord Thanet's interest after a fierce contest with Sir James Lowther's candidates. In February 1756 the election was declared void by the House, but on 4 Mar., Thanet and Lowther having compromised, he was again returned.

In Dupplin's list of 1754 he was classed 'for', in

Bute's of 1761 'Thanet and Government', and he appears in Fox's list of Members favourable to the peace preliminaries. On 18 Feb. 1764 he voted against general warrants, on 10 May was classed as a 'sure friend' by Newcastle, and 'pro' by Rockingham in July 1765. He did not vote against the repeal of the Stamp Act, and in Rockingham's list of November 1766 was classed as 'Whig'. He voted in opposition on nullum tempus, 17 Feb. 1768, and over the Middlesex election, January 1770. No other vote by him is recorded until the division on Grenville's Election Act, 25 Feb. 1774, when he appears in George III's list as a friend voting for once with opposition. He voted for Fox's motion to send no more regular troops out of the kingdom, 2 Feb. 1778, and continued in opposition until the fall of North. He did not vote on Shelburne's peace preliminaries, 18 Feb. 1783; was classed as a follower of Fox in Robinson's list of March 1783, but did not vote on Fox's East India bill, 27 Nov. 1783. He is not known to have spoken in the House. He died 21 Feb. 1785.

M.M.D.

## HOOD, Alexander (1726–1814), of Crickett St. Thomas, Som.

BRIDGWATER        1784–1790
BUCKINGHAM        1790–1796

*b.* 2 Dec. 1726, 2nd s. of Rev. Samuel Hood, vicar of Butleigh, Som. by Mary, da. of Richard Hoskins of Beaminster, Dorset; bro. of Samuel, 1st Baron Hood (q.v.). *m.* (1) 1761, Mary (*d.* 12 Sept. 1786), da. of Rev. Richard West, prebendary of Winchester, *s.p.*; (2) 26 June 1788, Mary Sophia, da. and h. of Thomas Bray of Edmonton, *s.p.* *cr.* K.B. 7 May 1788; Baron Bridport [I] 14 Nov. 1794; Baron Bridport [GB] 13 June 1796; Visct. Bridport [GB] 16 June 1800.
Entered R.N. 1741; lt. 1746; cdr. 1756; capt. 1756; r.-adm. 1780; v.-adm. 1787; adm. 1794.

Both in the navy and in Parliament Hood was overshadowed by his brother. He was elected for Bridgwater after a contest, and like his brother was a supporter of Pitt. His first recorded speech was on 23 June 1784; and three or four others followed during his first Parliament (the exact number cannot be given because of confusion with his brother in the printed *Debates*), all on matters of naval interest and none of much consequence.
He died 3 May 1814.

J.B.

## HOOD, Samuel, 1st Baron Hood [I] (1724–1816), of Catherington, Hants.

WESTMINSTER      4 Mar. 1785–July 1788
REIGATE          18 Aug. 1789–1790
WESTMINSTER                 1790–1796

*b.* 12 Dec. 1724, 1st s. of Rev. Samuel Hood, and bro. of Alexander Hood (q.v.). *m.* 25 Aug. 1749, Susanna, da. of Edward Linzee of Portsmouth, 3s. *cr.* Bt. 20 May 1778; Baron Hood [I] 12 Sept. 1782; Visct. Hood [GB] 1 June 1796.
Entered R.N. 1741; lt. 1746; cdr. 1754; capt. 1756; r.-adm. 1780; v.-adm. 1787; adm. 1794.
Ld. of Admiralty 1788–95.

Hood was created an Irish peer for his services as second-in-command to Rodney in the West Indies. In June 1782, while still at sea, he was nominated without his consent candidate for Westminster, at the by-election following Rodney's elevation to the peerage; but his son withdrew his name. Letters written by Hood after hearing this illustrate his attitude at this time towards Parliament and the service.[1]

What a lucky escape have I had in the affair of Westminster! [he wrote to Sir Charles Middleton, 1 Feb. 1783] . . . poor as I undoubtedly am, I would sooner have given £500 than have stood a contest . . . A seat in the House of Commons, I have no ambition after, and will never offer myself for it anywhere. If . . . any corporation in England . . . make choice of me as its representative, from perfect free will of the electors, well! If not, I shall be full as well satisfied. I shall ever most carefully and studiously stand clear . . . of all suspicion of being a party man; for if once I show myself of that frame of mind . . . I must . . . expect to lose every degree of consideration in the line of my profession . . . the first and greatest object of my wishes . . . I . . . acknowledge myself totally unfit to fight the battles of a minister in a House of Parliament; and . . . I think it an employment derogatory to the true character of a sea officer.

Hood was connected with Pitt through the marriage of his brother to Pitt's aunt; and in 1784 stood at Westminster as ministerial candidate with Sir Cecil Wray in opposition to Fox. The election was prolonged ('the most arduous and unpleasant business I ever took in hand', wrote Hood to the Duke of Rutland, 24 Aug. 1784[2]), and though Hood came out top of the poll the return was delayed for almost a year.

Hood's first recorded vote, 18 Apr. 1785, was for Pitt's parliamentary reform proposals. His first speech, 23 May 1785, was against the proposed shop tax—much disliked by his constituents, many of them small shopkeepers. He became Pitt's spokesman in the Commons for naval affairs, and as such spoke in the debate of 27 Feb. 1786 on Richmond's fortifications plan.

On 12 Jan. 1786 he wrote to Pitt, applying for the appointment of major-general of marines:[3]

The situation of my finances (which the King is fully apprized of) stands in great need of assistance, as the being so much in town the last two years and the consequences of my election for Westminster have embarrassed me much, and unless Government does something for me I shall be obliged from dire necessity to retire and take a final leave of London at the close of the next sessions of Parliament.

He did not get the appointment for which he asked, but was given the command at Portsmouth.

His most notable speech was on 2 Mar. 1787, against the impeachment of Warren Hastings.[4]

Lord Hood called the serious attention of the House to the consequences of proceeding with too scrupulous a nicety to canvass the conduct of those who had filled stations abroad of high difficulty and important trust . . . Should the fear of an impeachment by Parliament be hung out to every commander in whose hands was placed the defence of our national possessions, it must necessarily operate as a dangerous restraint to their exertions.

'Every word that he uttered', wrote Wraxall,[5] 'was devoured by the audience'; and Sir Gilbert Elliot, one of Hastings's opponents, described Hood's speech as 'very well delivered'.[6]

When Hood stood for re-election at Westminster in 1788 after being appointed a lord of the Admiralty he was unexpectedly defeated; and was out of Parliament until a seat was found for him on the Cocks interest at Reigate.

Hood died 27 Jan. 1816.

[1] To Maj.-Gen. de Bude (wrongly attributed to Sir W. Fawcett), 16 Jan. 1783, Fortescue, vi. 208–12; to Sir Chas. Middleton, 1 Feb. 1783, *Barham Pprs*, i. 246–51; to Geo. Jackson, 29 Jan. 1783, *Letters by Sir Sam. Hood*, 155–61. [2] *HMC Rutland*, iii. 134. [3] Chatham mss. [4] Stockdale, x. 394–5. [5] *Mems*. iv. 416. [6] *Life & Letters*, i. 133.

J.B.

## HOPE, John (1739–85), of Craigiehall, Linlithgow.

LINLITHGOWSHIRE   1768–27 Mar. 1770

*b*. 7 Apr. 1739, 2nd surv. s. of Hon. Charles Hope Weir (q.v.) by his 1st w. Catherine Weir. *educ*. Enfield sch. c.1749–52. *m*. 2 June 1762, Mary, da. of Eliab Breton of Enfield, Mdx., 3s.
Chamberlain of Ettrick forest 1761–8.

In 1752 Hope was sent to Holland to be initiated into business in the great house of the Hopes of Amsterdam, his distant kinsmen. His seven years' residence abroad were, he believed, the formative part of his life, setting him apart from the majority of Scottish politicians. He wrote in 1780:[1]

I was early used to the customs of a republic . . . They on the contrary have chiefly studied the imperial law and have been educated in a country where it is regarded as a kind of treason to speak of the measures of Government with the smallest contempt.

Returning home in 1759, a younger son with little capital, he set up in business in the City; and through his father's influence obtained a place in Scotland. But in 1767 a tragedy occurred from which Hope never fully recovered: his wife, whom he had married without her parents' consent, committed suicide; and in deep 'dejection of spirits', Hope went

home to Scotland.[2] At the general election of 1768 his father stood down in his favour as candidate for Linlithgowshire. After a bitter contest, during which his cousin Lord Hope acted as his election manager, Hope was returned against James Dundas of Dundas, who petitioned. Having surrendered his place to his father, Hope was compensated by an allowance from his uncle Hopetoun of £400 p.a. for parliamentary expenses.

Hope entered Parliament with a considerable knowledge of public affairs, finance, and trade, but an inconvenient political conscience. The Hopetoun family's immediate concern was Dundas's petition, against which they sought the assistance of all parties. Every week Hope sent to Hopetoun House reports of the proceedings in Parliament, which he afterwards published in justification of his conduct.[3] He attended the Wilkes debate of 23 Jan. 1769 but during the debate on America on the 26th was taken ill and went home. Although he confessed 'I never could get over the tremor which affects me on making any public oration',[4] from his sickbed he entertained his cousin with the pro-American speech he might have made. He was absent through illness from the Wilkes debates of 27 Jan. and 2 and 3 Feb., but his comments on Administration were by no means favourable. His account of the debate of 17 Feb. on the Middlesex petition showed sympathy with the Opposition case, but did not state how he had voted. In the debate on the civil list on 28 Feb. he found the Opposition arguments 'so plain and convincing' that he did not stay for the division.

How far [the Government] arguments will justify us to the people for voting away their money to the King without knowing how it is employed, a little time will show . . . an additional weight will be given to the instructions coming from all parts of the country to examine into the number of pensioners and to petition for a shorter duration of Parliament.

His only consolation was that Dundas's petition had been postponed until next session, and that he could in conscience vote with Administration against Burke's motion of 8 Mar. for an inquiry into the St. George's Fields riots. He could not concur in the resolution of 15 Apr. that Luttrell should have been returned for Middlesex. He wrote to Hopetoun, 18 Apr.:

Having debated the point within myself, I resolved not to give my vote to such a resolution, and therefore did not attend the House. Had I attended I must have spoken to explain myself, as being attached to no party, and this I was uncertain if I should have the courage to do . . . It is such an infringement on the liberties of every freeholder in Great Britain, that I am very much mistaken if the people above have not, by this measure, placed a match to that combustible matter which has this twelvemonth past been accumulating in every part of the country.

In the division of 8 May on the Middlesex petition against Luttrell's return, he had the courage of his convictions; and wrote to Hopetoun, 13 May:

> Your Lordship will by this time have supposed on which side I voted . . . So much was said by the ablest speakers on the nature of the question being entirely separate from the cause of Mr. Wilkes, that, without making any apology for differing with my friends on this occasion, I sided with the minority of 152 to 221. I am very sorry when I cannot with the conviction of my own mind conform to the opinions of my friends and I shall be particularly concerned if by my vote . . . I have forfeited their esteem. I wish the county had been called to give me instructions . . . for I have ever been of opinion that every representative in Parliament is *in conscience* bound to follow the instructions given him by his constituents.

Hope seems temporarily to have pacified Hopetoun, in the belief that a change of government was probable; but when Grafton threatened to withdraw support on the Linlithgowshire petition, Hopetoun fell into line and expected Hope to conform.

When Parliament reassembled Hope voted, 9 Jan. 1770, with Administration on the Address; but in the debate of 25 Jan. on the Middlesex election with the Opposition. The Hopetoun family, in dismay, arranged with a certain lord (unidentified) to reason with him. Hope wrote to his cousin Lord Hope, 10 Feb.:

> Lord . . . expostulated with me that the question now was not whether this or that ministry should be in, but . . . whether this constitution should be continued or a republic founded on its ruins . . . He was sure . . . I was acting contrary to Lord Hopetoun's principles and what the Duke of Grafton was given to expect; that I was losing the support of Government and was doing myself little good with the other people unless I meant to side with them at once.

Hope argued that the constitution was less endangered by the mob than by a servile Parliament and an arbitrary government, and declared his faith in the 'independent power in the counties of Britain' and the 'virtue and strength of the middling classes'.

> As to my acting against the inclinations of Lord Hopetoun . . . I was sensible that in Parliament I was but a creature of his making, but still I considered myself as a free agent and one of the representatives of the Commons and not of the peers of Great Britain.

He dismissed Hopetoun's adherence to the Government as mere time-serving:

> His Lordship was for supporting the ministers for the time being; now the divisions in the House of Commons running so near as forty, and the late Duke of Cumberland's friends with whom I thought his Lordship mostly connected, being the people that might be among the ministers next, I was rather inclined to side with them.

Charles Hope Weir now arrived from Scotland to advise his son. 'My father told me', wrote Hope, 'Lord Hopetoun was so provoked with my conduct that he declared he would have nothing to do with the petition against me', now due to be heard in March. Hope now realized that as an independent he had little chance of success. He wrote to Lord Hope, 28 Feb.:

> I had been offered support by the heads of the Opposition without solicitation or condition; if I must go through thick and thin with either party for a month, I thought it most honourable with them, because I approve of their present patriotical notions and was left at liberty to act hereafter as I pleased . . . The ministry . . . had already withdrawn from me their support, and to procure it again I must solicit, must vote against my conscience on their side, and must promise to be for ever in future a ministerial man.

Recommended by Sir George Colebrooke to Rockingham,[5] Hope was none the less dissuaded from accepting Opposition support by his father's arguments. He wrote to Lord Hope:

> He was of opinion I was acting wrong; because the ministry . . . could give me the greatest support; that they had not yet retracted their promise of it; and that my friends would rather have me lose my seat than be under obligation for it to the other people . . . that I was not the principal concerned . . . for the honour of the family interest in the county was the chief purpose of giving me the seat in Parliament . . . I ought therefore to have done nothing without their advice and approbation . . . This reasoning . . . altered my proceeding . . . I now think it incumbent on me to be passive; at least till the petition is over; and then, if my Lord your father should find that . . . I am going contrary to his political principles, it certainly will be just that I should resign to somebody who in conscience can vote entirely with them. Your Lordship knows . . . that I think myself responsible for my public conduct to the whole people of Great Britain and that is what all the representatives of the Commons *ought to be*; but in effect they are not so . . . and it is but equitable that your father should have his additional share in the legislature as well as other peers.

In this mood Hope remained 'passive'; but on 27 Mar. 1770 Dundas won his petition and Hope was unseated. Hopetoun did not forgive the blow to his family interest and completely disowned his nephew, who in 1772 published the correspondence in explanation of the breach.

> To have great relations and to be forsaken by them, is more disadvantageous to a man's fortune than to have no relations alive in the whole world; it carries . . . a presumption . . . that he has been guilty of some very criminal or dishonourable action.

Thrown upon his own resources in a not very prosperous business, Hope openly declared his Opposition principles and in 1772 suggested to Wilkes that he should move a vote of thanks to him in the Society of the Bill of Rights for his disinterested conduct in Parliament, which had cost him his seat and Hopetoun's annuity of £400 p.a.

'I don't mean by it to rival you in your patriotic fame, but to make my relations ashamed of their behaviour.'[6] He turned to journalism and under the pseudonyms of 'the Leveller' and 'the Advocate of the People' contributed to the newspapers essays on a wide variety of topics, ranging from politics and finance to horsemanship, architecture, seabathing, and children's health. These 'Thoughts in Prose and Verse' he collected and published in 1780. In his preface he wrote:

I did not determine to put my name to this book until I read in the parliamentary debates that of the 33 Scotch Members who were present . . . when Mr. Dunning's motion was put to the vote . . . 28 of them voted against it. As one who once had the honour of sitting in that House, I now willingly risk the acquiring the name of a bad author, that I may increase the small number of constitutional Scotsmen . . . This is no time when any friend of freedom should be hid.

Strongly opposed to North and the American war, he became almost republican in his political thinking, and although he remained on good terms with his father, had little affection for Scotland or Scotsmen, preferring to be considered a 'citizen of the world'. He died 21 May 1785.

[1] Preface to his *Thoughts in Prose and Verse*. [2] Ibid. 268–70. [3] *Letters on Certain Proceedings in Parliament during . . . 1769 and 1770* (1772). [4] *Thoughts in Prose and Verse*, 8. [5] Colebrooke to Rockingham, Feb. 1770, Rockingham mss. [6] Add. 30871, ff. 132–3.

E.H.-G.

**HOPE WEIR, Hon. Charles** (1710–91), of Craigiehall, Linlithgow and Blackwood, Lanark.

LINLITHGOWSHIRE 13 May 1743–1768

*b.* 8 May 1710, 2nd surv. s. of Charles Hope, 1st Earl of Hopetoun [S], by Henrietta Johnstone, da. of William, 1st Mq. of Annandale [S]. *educ.* Glasgow Univ. 1724; Leyden 1728; Grand Tour. *m.* (1) 26 July 1733, Catherine (*d.* 5 Dec. 1743), da. and h. of Sir William Weir or Vere, 2nd Bt., of Blackwood, Lanark, 6s. 2da.; (2) 20 Mar. 1746, Anne Vane (div. May 1757), da. of Henry, 1st Earl of Darlington, 2s.; (3) 2 Apr. 1766, Helen, da. of George Dunbar of Leuchold, Linlithgow, 1s. 3da. *suc.* uncle 2nd Mq. of Annandale in the Craigiehall estate 1730; on m. acquired Blackwood estate and assumed add. name of Weir.

Gov. Blackness castle 1744–*d.*; commissary gen. for musters [S] 1744–59; trustee for fisheries and manufactures 1755–84; commr. for the forfeited estates 1755; chamberlain of Ettrick forest 1768–*d.*

From his youth, Hope Weir travelled extensively in Europe, and became known as a connoisseur of the arts.[1] Re-elected unopposed in 1754, he was absent abroad from September 1754 to May 1756. On his return, faithful to Newcastle, he voted on his side in the division of 2 May 1757 on the loss of Minorca,[2] and was counted among his personal supporters during the negotiations for a new Administration. In 1760 Hope Weir took the unpopular course of siding with the ministry against

his fellow Scots over the Scottish militia bill. Newcastle commented in his 'Memorandum for the King', 15 Apr.:[3] 'Mr. Hope—If he is the single man, he will oppose it. He knows it is not the sense of Scotland.' In the decisive division, the same day, Hope Weir and Lord Advocate Robert Dundas were the only Scots to vote against the bill. As a result Hope Weir was immediately faced with a violent opposition in Linlithgowshire. He appealed to Newcastle for help and, although opposed by family tradition to Argyll's vice-royalty, also approached Argyll;[4] Robert Dundas at the same time sought Hardwicke's intervention on his ally's behalf.[5] At the general election of 1761, after an intensive campaign, he was re-elected by a majority of one vote.

The Hopetoun family, badly shaken, were thereafter unwilling to take political risks. Hope Weir did not follow Newcastle into opposition, but supported Bute, and in December 1762 was listed by Fox among those favourable to the peace. After Bute's resignation the Hopetoun family apparently kept a foot in either camp. Cornwallis, reporting on 'the Whig cause' in Scotland, wrote to Newcastle, 29 July 1763,[6] that although 'Charles Hope abandoned his friends so shamefully last winter in Parliament', his brother Hopetoun was considered 'pretty right'.

Under the Grenville Administration Hope Weir's name does not appear in any of the Opposition lists on Wilkes and general warrants. Counted 'pro' by Rockingham in July 1765, Hope Weir voted with the Government in the division of 17 Feb. 1766,[7] and almost certainly on the repeal of the Stamp Act. On the formation of the Chatham Administration he again swung over to 'the ministers for the time being'. Although absent from the land tax division, 27 Feb. 1767, he voted with Government on nullum tempus, 17 Feb. 1768. Shortly afterwards, on 10 Mar., he succeeded his son John as chamberlain of Ettrick forest and stood down in his favour at the general election.

Hope Weir is not known to have spoken in the House. He disliked London[8] and regarded parliamentary attendance as a tedious duty necessary for the honour and interest of his family.

He died 30 Dec. 1791.

[1] J. P. Wood, *Cramond*, 67–68; *Letters of Hume* (ed. Greig), i. 239. [2] Add. 33034, f. 232. [3] Add. 32904, f. 388. [4] Add. 32906, f. 283. [5] Add. 35449, f. 234. [6] Add. 32949, f. 437. [7] Add. 32974, f. 24. [8] Add. 6861, f. 314.

E.H.-G.

**HOPKINS, Benjamin** (c.1734–79), of Lydd, Kent.

GREAT BEDWYN 29 Jan. 1771–1774

*b.* c.1734, 2nd surv. s. of Edward Hopkins, M.P., of

Coventry by Anne Maria, da. of Hugh Chamberlain of Alderton Hall, Suff.; bro. of Richard Hopkins (q.v.). *m.* 20 Sept. 1761, Mary, da. of Mark Skinner, of Lydd, *s.p.*

Director, Bank of England 1765-7, 1768-71, 1772-1775, 1776-*d*; alderman of London 1773-6; chamberlain 1776-*d*.

Hopkins is described in trade directories as 'Bank director and merchant', of 58 Old Broad St. In 1765 he held £3,000 of Bank stock and, at the time of his death, £12,000. His main interest was insurance; he told the Commons on 11 Mar. 1773:[1] 'I have for many years followed the business of an underwriter'.

Lord Bruce returned Hopkins for Great Bedwyn on the death of his brother-in-law, William Northey, a neighbour of Bruce's and connected with him in politics. His maiden speech on 29 Apr. 1771 was in support of a bill to restrain stock jobbing. 'I never sell stock,' he said,[2] 'and I am not possessed of, nor do I buy, what I can't pay for.' He concluded: 'Before I sit down I will return my sincere thanks to the House for their kind indulgence. I do assure them I will not often trouble the House or expose myself.' Eight of his speeches are reported in Cavendish's Debates, all on commercial subjects and all sensible. He voted with Government over Brass Crosby's case, 27 Mar. 1771, and over Wilkes, 26 Apr. 1773, and against them on the naval captains' petition, 9 Feb. 1773, and on Grenville's Election Act, 25 Feb. 1774: but in both these lists he is marked as normally a Government supporter. He was one of Government's foremost supporters in the City, and thrice defeated Wilkes in the election for chamberlain.

He did not stand at the general election of 1774, and died 9 Nov. 1779.

[1] Cavendish's 'Debates', Egerton 245, f. 7. [2] Ibid. Egerton 231, ff. 97-101.

J.B.

## HOPKINS, Richard (c.1728-99), of Oving, Bucks.

| DARTMOUTH | 7 Feb. 1766-1780 |
| THETFORD | 1780-1784 |
| DARTMOUTH | 1784-1790 |
| QUEENBOROUGH | 1790-1796 |
| HARWICH | 1796-19 Mar. 1799 |

*b.* c.1728, 1st s. of Edward Hopkins, M.P., of Coventry, and bro. of Benjamin Hopkins (q.v.). *educ.* Queens', Camb. 1746. *unm. suc.* fa. 1735.

Clerk of Board of Green Cloth 1767-77; ld. of Admiralty, Mar. 1782-Apr. 1783, Apr. 1784-91; ld. of Treasury 1791-7.

Hopkins was connected with the Fitzroy family and a personal friend of the 3rd Duke of Grafton. On 27 June 1755, when the 2nd Duke was alive, Hopkins wrote to Newcastle about a vacancy at Seaford:[1] 'I should not presume to put your Grace

in mind of me upon the vacancy . . . but that I have the Duke of Grafton's orders to do so.' But he had to wait eleven years before entering Parliament: when the 3rd Duke was secretary of state Hopkins was returned on the Government interest for Dartmouth. In 1767 Grafton appointed him a clerk of the Green Cloth, and he remained a supporter of Administration until October 1775 when Grafton resigned over American policy.

On 26 Oct. 1775 Hopkins voted against the Address, yet retained his place until 1777. On 9 Dec. the King wrote to North:[2] 'I don't think Mr. Hopkins of consequence enough to have notified to him his dismissal.' It is surprising that he should have held office so long after he had gone into opposition. Henceforth he voted regularly against 'the absurd, detestable, and damnable' American war, as he described it in the Commons on 9 Dec. 1779.[3] At the general election of 1780 he was returned by Grafton for Thetford.

In 1782-3 his conduct closely followed Grafton's: he held office under Rockingham and Shelburne, but refused to join the Coalition in spite of his liking for Fox. He voted against the East India bill on 27 Nov. 1783, yet wrote to Grafton on 16 Dec.:[4] 'Though I rejoice that the bill is thrown out, I am not yet ready to say that the overthrow of the ministry at this moment is a desirable event'; and on 1 Mar. 1784 spoke in the Commons for agreement between Fox and Pitt. Only after the attempt to reconcile Pitt and Fox had failed did he take office; and at the general election of 1784 he was again returned as a Government candidate.

He died 19 Mar. 1799.

[1] Add. 32856, f. 315. [2] Fortescue, iii. 505. [3] Almon, xvii. 165. [4] Grafton, *Autobiog.* 384-5.

J.B.

HOPKINS, *see also* BOND HOPKINS *and* PROBYN

## HOTHAM, Beaumont (1737-1814).

WIGAN 1768- May 1775

*b.* 5 Aug. 1737, 4th s. of Sir Beaumont Hotham, 7th Bt., by Frances, da. and coh. of Rev. Stephen Thompson of Welton, Yorks.; bro. of Charles Hotham (q.v.). *educ.* Westminster 1745; Trinity Hall, Camb. 1753; M. Temple 1753, called 1758. *m.* 6 June 1767, Susanna, da. of Sir Thomas Hankey, alderman of London, gd.-da. of Sir John Barnard (q.v.), wid. of James Norman of East Molesey, Surr., 3s. 3da. Kntd. 17 May 1775. *suc.* bro. William as 2nd Baron Hotham [I] and 12th Bt. 1 or 2 May 1813.

Baron of the Exchequer 1775-1805; commr. of the great seal Apr.-Dec. 1783.

Hotham, a school fellow and close friend of William Henry, 3rd Duke of Portland, was legal adviser and auditor of the Duke's estates (also, after 1775, of those of the Duke of Devonshire). He was returned on Portland's interest for Wigan, where he had also old family connexions. Before the general election of 1774 he offered to stand down in favour of Lord Edward Bentinck; and when Portland refused, wrote on 24 Oct.:[1]

> I beg to repeat, that nothwithstanding what you have said, I shall consider myself as holding it in trust for Lord Edward (if he comes in nowhere else) to be resigned to him, whenever you or he shall entertain the most distant wish that it should be so . . . I owe you this, and a great deal more, more than I shall ever be able I am sure to repay you or your family.

In the debates 1768–75, 24 speeches or interventions of his are recorded (in March 1772 he spoke five times against the royal marriage bill, a subject about which the court was very touchy). His name appears in ten division lists, and every time on the Opposition side. Yet when in May 1775 the place of baron of the Exchequer was about to fall vacant, Hotham was given the appointment as part of a deal between Portland and the Administration, and in return the seat vacated by Hotham at Wigan was given to John Morton, an Administration supporter. Hotham was appointed on the 10th, and on the 15th the King wrote to North: 'I thoroughly approve of the arrangement in consequence of the declining state of Baron Perrott; Mr. Hotham's character qualifies for this promotion; and Mr. Morton will prove a more agreeable attender in his room.'[2]

In April 1777, when Portland's financial difficulties were acute, Hotham wrote to him waiving further payments for his services

> for I am sure that every little must now be material to you, and I owe so much to your unexampled friendship and generosity towards me that I cannot feel happy without doing everything in my power to relieve your distress.[3]

He continued to act for the Duke without pay. Hotham died 4 Mar. 1814.

[1] Portland mss. [2] Fortescue, iii. 209. [3] A. S. Turberville, *Hist. Welbeck Abbey*, ii. 155.

L.B.N.

**HOTHAM, Charles** (1729–94), of Dalton Hall, Yorks.

ST. IVES 1761–1768

*b.* 18 June 1729, 1st s. of Sir Beaumont Hotham 7th Bt., and bro. of Beaumont Hotham (q.v.). *educ* Westminster 1741–5; M. Temple 1742. *m.* 21 Oct. 1752, Lady Dorothy Hobart, da. of John, 1st Earl of Buckinghamshire, 1da. *suc.* fa. Sept. 1771, and to Thompson estates in Yorks. 1772 and took name of Thompson; resumed name of Hotham 1787. K.B. 15 Jan. 1772.

Ensign 1 Ft. Gds. 1746, lt. 1750, capt. and lt.-col.

1758; col. army 1762; col. 63 Ft. 1765–8, 15 Ft. 1768–1775; maj.-gen. 1772; ret. 1775.

Groom of the bedchamber 1763–94.

At the general election of 1761, Hotham was in his absence returned for St. Ives on the interest of his brother-in-law, Lord Buckinghamshire, and at his expense. Hotham's father, writing to him 7 Apr. 1761,[1] thought this a right, promising measure, 'productive of more advantages than . . . franking letters.'

> Though for the first session or two at least there seems little prospect, luckily for this country, of much altercation or debate, yet there are days of common business which an observing and sensible man may gather good information and materials from.

Hotham himself wrote, 26 Aug. 1782, in his autobiographical notes:

> When I first knew the House of Commons, it was a noble school for young men. I wish it were so still, and that it may become so again.

But in fact, the army and the court, and not Parliament and politics, were at the centre of Hotham's interests. He was therefore greatly disappointed when in 1763, on a change in the office of adjutant-general, he was passed over in favour of Isaac Barré. 'Lord Bute . . . had it conveyed to me that it was not his doing, that he had resisted it to the utmost of his power.' He offered Hotham the secretaryship to Buckinghamshire's embassy to Russia, which he refused.

> I had been but a few days at Bath, when I received an official notification that the King had appointed me one of the grooms of his bedchamber, and that being the office of all others, I was always the most desirous of, though I never applied for it, I thought it full amends for the mortification I had sustained . . . The only unpleasant circumstance was the necessity of my re-election, which cost me above £1200.

A favourite of the King and sincerely devoted to him, Hotham voted as a rule with the court; and on 7 May 1765 spoke for committing the Regency bill. When on the Anstruther election petition, 31 Jan. 1766, he voted against the Rockinghams (who, unjustly, suspected George III of being behind that move), Conway next day mentioned Hotham in his pointed list of 'those who were particularly remarked on this occasion'.[2] He did not vote against the repeal of the Stamp Act.

On 30 Aug. 1765 Hotham had written to Lord Barrington complaining of several officers junior to him having been made colonels while he had only a company in the Guards:

> A few days afterwards the King sent for me into the closet and said 'I have only sent for you, Colonel Hotham, that I might have the pleasure of wishing you joy of being colonel of the 63rd Regiment. I have long wished for an opportunity of showing my regard for you, and I do assure you I never did anything that gave me more pleasure.'

Hotham adds that Rockingham and Grafton 'fairly owned' to him that 'they had exerted all their strength in favour of Lord Cornwallis'.

On 25 June 1766 Buckinghamshire wrote to Hotham that he had asked his agent to send Hotham 'the state of affairs at St. Ives'.

> The expense of my parliamentary interest has been so great as to make it necessary for me to determine for the future never in any shape whatsoever to engage myself upon any other occasion. Before however I offer the seat at St. Ives to any other person upon the terms of their furnishing the money, I cannot omit giving you the refusal of it.

Hotham replied that not having been able 'to answer the common expenses of an election without a contest, so much less certainly am I able to think of it with the prospect of an opposition'. He was therefore not going to stand for St. Ives again.

> I gave the King my reasons for it, which he entered so much into, and so entirely approved of, that my mind was quite at ease on that subject.

When Hotham's father succeeded as 7th Baronet, October 1767, and Hotham settled at Dalton Hall, about 4 miles from Beverley, he was invited to stand there at the forthcoming general election.

> The same motive produced the same resolution, being besides by no means in love with the House of Commons, though perhaps my father might, and I believe would have assisted me for that particular borough our family had so often represented, had I been eager about it. But I did not think it fair to wish him to be at such an expense, before he was well in possession of his estate. I rather bent my thought to improving it, and rescuing the place from ruin.

Before Hotham left the House two more votes of his are recorded: with the Government on the land tax, 27 Feb. 1767; but against them on Savile's nullum tempus bill, 17 Feb. 1768—a signal act of independence on the part of one so close to the King.

Out of Parliament, he busied himself with the house at Dalton which he built and furnished at a cost of £30,000; with enclosures on his estates, and other improvements.

> In addition to all this I found myself under the disagreeable necessity of engaging in an election at Beverley. My friends, and the world were incessantly sounding in my ears that it depended upon me to re-establish the family interest there . . . The whole of the gentlemen of the county, and all the principal inhabitants of the town, with few exceptions, urged me to stand in the gap between them and strangers. So that I saw I must either devote myself to the trial, or lie under the imputation of want of spirit in having deprived the family as it would have been said (indeed was said) of that borough. And as an accidental piece of business the corporation engaged me in, brought it forward, almost whether I would or not.

The business here referred to concerned proposed quays on the River Hull which the burgesses and corporation feared might expose their lands to flooding. They asked Hotham to intervene on their behalf, and he went to see Lord North and Grey Cooper, but in a letter of 3 Mar. 1774 remarked that such intervention had best come from their Members—and he expressed regret that he could not speak as such. The corporation having replied how sensible they would be of the credit and honour of being represented by him, he addressed them in form on the subject, 14 Mar. On 25 Mar. three leading burgesses, but not the mayor, wrote to him:

> We, as individuals . . . beg leave to assure you of our fidelity and attachment to your interest, but at the same time, it is highly necessary to inform you, as our borough corporate consists of 26 members, a great majority of whom are dependent upon trade and business, it will not be in our power to prevail on them to enter into any engagement of this kind so long beforehand, as they know not at present, how their connexions and interests may then be affected.

And here is the story of the election as told by Hotham in his autobiographical memoranda:

> The Parliament being dissolved that year, the election went on. Sir James Pennyman, Mr. Tuffnell . . . and I were the candidates. The Bar Interest, as it is called, secured Sir James, so that the struggle was between Mr. T. and me. He had all the rabble. I, as I said before, the whole of the respectable people, almost to a man. His friends, I must do them the justice to say, behaved always to me with the greatest respect, and fairly told me, their opposition was not owing to any disregard to me personally, much otherwise. But that unless they united against me, that is, said they, against the gentlemen, they never should have any chance for a third man. Their numbers, as I always foresaw, prevailed. And to my infinite satisfaction gave me a fair excuse to free myself of all trouble on that score for the rest of my life. It cost me near £1000. But I thought it therefore money well bestowed.
>
> And here, I cannot help offering it as my most serious and earnest advice to those who shall succeed me, to suffer no consideration to induce them to be drawn in to become representatives of Beverley or Scarborough. They are both too near their places of residence, and will entail upon them a slavery and expense that will know no end. If they will be in Parliament, which perhaps it may be wiser never to think of, it should be much farther from home.

In 1775 Hotham retired from the army. He saw no chance of being employed in America—'three younger general officers than me, Howe, Clinton, and Burgoyne being appointed on that staff'. He did not expect war in Europe, and did not want to draw emoluments and stand in the way of other officers' promotion while himself unemployed. Lastly, 'the first great requisite of a soldier is health'—'with a broken constitution, and a delicate mind' he obtained the King's permission to resign his regiment. Much pressed by the King in 1776 to become sub-governor to the Prince of Wales, he declined the post (which he secured however for his younger brother George).

On 22 Aug. 1780, Lord North wrote to Hotham:

> When I sent to you, I had received intelligence from Beverley that the electors there were not well pleased with their present Members, and as I have no great reason to be more pleased with them than the electors, I wished to know whether it would be agreeable to you to declare yourself a candidate upon that opening, as I suppose that no man in Great Britain is so likely to succeed there as you are.

Hotham replied, 27 Aug.:

> After what passed at the last election I could not stoop to solicit the favours of a set of people who might have recollected with some degree of gratitude the very long connection . . . between them and my predecessors.

He similarly refused to stand when invited by a number of Beverley burgesses.

He died 25 Jan. 1794.

¹ All quotations, unless otherwise stated, are from the Hotham mss, E. Riding RO. ² Fortescue, i. 59, 249.

L.B.N.

## HOTHAM, Sir Richard (?1722–99), of Merton Place, Surr.

SOUTHWARK    1780–1784

*m.* (w. *d.* 4 Feb. 1777), *s.p.* Kntd. 12 Apr. 1769.
Sheriff, Surr. 1770–1.

Hotham is variously reported to have begun life as a hatter at Southwark and as a hosier.¹ He subsequently 'ventured into the commercial world, and particularly in the property of shipping for the East India Company. Being a man of strong judgment, with a mind invariably directed towards business, he in time acquired very large property.'² In 1774 he published *A Candid State of Affairs Relative to East India Shipping*, in which he suggested ways of preventing abuses.

Hotham had by this time acquired an estate in Surrey and, in association with other business men, became active in county politics. At the general election of 1780 he took a leading part in organizing the campaign to secure Admiral Keppel's election, while he himself contested Southwark in opposition to Henry Thrale, and was returned at the head of the poll. In Parliament he voted consistently with the Opposition till the fall of North, and against Shelburne's peace preliminaries, 18 Feb. 1783. He voted for parliamentary reform, 7 May 1783, and for Fox's East India bill, 27 Nov. 1783, and was classed by Robinson in January 1784 as 'contra'. Sir John Sinclair in his list drawn up in January, noted against Hotham: 'Could speak to him if necessary. He might be converted.'³ Hotham was a member of the St. Alban's Tavern group which attempted to bring about a union of parties, and after its failure was

classed in Stockdale's list of 19 Mar. 1784 as 'Opposition'. Only two speeches by him are reported (5 and 11 June 1783), both on the receipts tax which he opposed on instructions from his constituents; the second very short, since 'the House had heard so much about it from his worthy colleague'.⁴ Hotham did not stand at the general election of 1784, but again contested Southwark at the by-election of June 1784 when he was defeated by a very narrow margin.

Hotham's great interest during the latter part of his life was in the development of Bognor as a seaside resort. He was reported to have spent £160,000 on this scheme, having 'in the course of a few years . . . made large purchases of land, and erected spacious houses', but when, after his death on 14 Mar. 1799 (aged 76), the property was sold by his heir, it apparently realized only £64,000.⁵

¹ *Gent. Mag.* 1799, p. 345; *Candid State of Affairs.* ² *Gent. Mag.* ³ Sinclair mss, Thurso East Mains. ⁴ Debrett, x. 151. ⁵ Dalloway, *West. Div. Suss.* i(2), p. 46; *Gent. Mag.*

M.M.D.

## HOUBLON, Jacob (1710–70), of Hallingbury, Essex.

| | |
|---|---|
| COLCHESTER | 20 Mar. 1735–1741 |
| HERTFORDSHIRE | 1741–1747, 1761–1768 |

*b.* 31 July 1710, o. surv. s. of Charles Houblon, Portugal merchant, by Mary, da. and h. of Daniel Bate, London merchant and vintner. *educ.* Corpus Christi, Camb. 1725; Emmanuel 1730. *m.* 31 July 1735, Mary, da. of Sir John Hynde Cotton, 3rd Bt., sis. of Sir J. H. Cotton, 4th Bt. (q.v.), 2s. 1da. *suc.* fa. 20 Mar. 1711, and his fa.'s cos. Sir Richard Houblon 13 Oct. 1724.
Sheriff, Herts. 1757–8.

The Houblons came over from Flanders as Protestant refugees in the time of Elizabeth I, and became very considerable London merchants.¹ But Jacob Houblon was a country gentleman and never went into business. The old Houblons had been Whigs; Jacob Houblon was returned for Colchester as a Tory; was a member of the Cocoa Tree Club; and by his marriage with John Hynde Cotton's daughter became connected with the more extreme Tories. In 1761 he stood on a joint interest with Charles Gore, a Pelhamite: Houblon was returned but not Gore. Houblon is not in Fox's list of December 1762 of Members favourable to the peace preliminaries, but did not vote against them. He remained an independent. In the autumn of 1763 he was classed by Jenkinson as 'pro', but in at least one division on general warrants, 15 Feb. 1764, voted with Opposition. Rockingham, in the summer of 1765, correctly classed him as 'contra': he voted against the repeal of the Stamp Act, 22 Feb. 1766.

As a Tory country gentleman he voted against the Chatham Government over the land tax, 27 Feb. 1767. He did not stand again in 1768—his son was to be a candidate in his place,[2] but finally stood for Essex and was defeated. There is no record of Houblon having spoken in the House.

He died 15 Feb. 1770.

[1] Lady A. Archer-Houblon, *Houblon Fam.* [2] Bamber Gascoyne to John Strutt, 9 Feb. 1768, Strutt mss.

L.B.N.

## HOWARD, Hon. Sir Charles (d.1765).

CARLISLE 1727–1761

2nd s. of Charles, 3rd Earl of Carlisle, by Lady Anne Capel, da. of Arthur, 1st Earl of Essex. *unm.* K.B. 2 May 1749.

Ensign 2 Ft. Gds. 1715, capt. 1717, capt. and lt.-col. 1719; col. 1734; col. 19 Ft. 1738–48; maj.-gen. 1743; lt.-gen. 1747; col. 3 Drag. Gds. 1748–*d.*; gen. 1765; lt. gov. Carlisle 1724–49, gov. 1749–52; gov. Inverness 1752–*d.*

Howard, a regular Government supporter, sat on the family interest at Carlisle. He did not see active service during the seven years' war, but in 1760 he presided over the court martial of Lord George Sackville. He stood for Carlisle again in 1761, but withdrew when a contest threatened.

He died 26 Aug. 1765.

A.N.N.

## HOWARD, Charles, Earl of Surrey (1746–1815).

CARLISLE 1780–31 Aug. 1786

*b.* 15 Mar. 1746, o.s. of Charles, 10th Duke of Norfolk, by Catherine, da. and coh. of John Brockholes of Claughton, Lancs., and gd.-s. of Charles Howard of Greystoke, Cumb. *educ.* in France. *m.* (1) 1 Aug. 1767, Marian (*d.*28 May 1768), da. and h. of John Coppinger of Ballyvolane, co. Cork, *s.p.*; (2) 2 Apr. 1771, Frances, da. and h. of Charles Fitzroy Scudamore (q.v.), *s.p. suc.* fa. as 11th Duke 31 Aug. 1786.

Ld.-lt. Yorks (W.R.) 1782–98; ld. of Treasury Apr.–Dec. 1783.

Surrey, born and bred a Roman Catholic, conformed to the Church of England in 1780. He stood for Carlisle at the general election on his own interest but with the support of the Duke of Portland. He wrote to Portland on 16 July:[1]

Your Grace's kind intimation to me about a public declaration of my religious opinions, I take as one more to the many instances of friendship already received. I am very decided and have been for some time . . . I am ready to declare my religious conformity on all proper occasions, but would wish to avoid an *ostentatious* declaration, that I might give as little mortification as possible, to a set of men who are labouring under persecution and have lately been cruelly marked as the objects of odium and outrage.

On election day he 'addressed the freemen in a very

gentleman-like manner',[2] and was returned unopposed. 'I perceived a heartfelt satisfaction in Lord Surrey's countenance', wrote George Mounsey, Portland's agent, 'which even his powers of eloquence (which were great on the occasion) could not express.'

In Parliament he spoke frequently and voted regularly with the Opposition. On 20 Mar. 1782 he was to have moved a motion of no confidence in North's ministry, which North prevented by announcing his resignation. Surrey, however, threatened

in case any deception should be practised . . . and any part of the present Administration remain, he would, on Monday, come forward with a motion, not the same as that he had intended to have moved . . . but a very, very different motion indeed.

On 7 May he spoke in favour of parliamentary reform and on 16 May supported Sawbridge's motion for shorter Parliaments.[3]

On 31 July Surrey wrote to Shelburne (now head of Administration):[4]

Having had no intimation of the secret causes that produced the late changes . . . I have not presumed to form an opinion of them. I do not mention this with a desire of knowing them, it being my present resolution to keep unconnected till the meeting of Parliament, presuming Government to be right until I think I see error . . . The parliamentary reform in the boroughs is the object in which I am most sanguine. In regard of your Lordship's Administration, I beg leave to repeat when I come to town I mean to be *thoroughly explicit* in what and how far I mean to support it.

On 9 Sept. Shelburne offered Surrey the lord-lieutenancy of the West Riding of Yorkshire (which Fitzwilliam had declined). Surrey accepted on 17 Sept., and concluded his letter to Shelburne:

Since I saw your Lordship [I] have met with some friends of Mr. Fox and the late Lord Rockingham who much regretted Lord Fitzwilliam's refusal, which confirms one in the propriety of it's having been offered to him as a measure which would tend to conciliate, which your Lordship may depend it will be my endeavour to promote.

'I . . . am glad he seems now heartily in the cause', commented the King.[5] In Shelburne's list, drawn up in October 1782, he was classed as 'pro'.

In December 1782 Shelburne offered him the post of ambassador to the United States. Surrey replied on 16 Dec.:[6]

Should the provisional treaty now pending come to a happy issue the appointment of ambassador to ratify it and adjust the terms of a federal commercial union that might in consequence take place, would be very flattering to my ambition, and . . . I have no doubt from the candour I have experienced from your Lordship and the similarity of our ideas on the subject, that the lesser arrangements would with great ease be settled to our mutual satisfaction, but as I cannot bring my mind to the resolution of leaving England for a longer time than may be necessary for settling the greater objects of the two agreements, which I do not suppose will extend to the limits of one year, I must leave it entirely to your Lordship to determine whether it is worth while to consider me farther in this matter.

He did not speak in the debate on Shelburne's peace preliminaries, 17–18 Feb. 1783, but voted with Government, and was naturally classed by Robinson in his list of March 1783 as 'Shelburne'. But on 22 Mar. Robinson described him as 'now violent Fox',[7] and on 24 Mar. he seconded Coke's motion for a new Administration. On 27 Mar. he told the House:

> In case . . . no arrangement of Administration . . . should soon be made, he desired to be understood as giving notice, that he would on Monday next move for an inquiry into the causes that had so long prevented an arrangement's taking place.

He moved this motion on 31 Mar., and, when taunted about the coalition with North, whom a year ago he had threatened to impeach, replied:

> He had exerted his endeavours to turn the noble Lord out of office last year, because he then thought his measures tended to the ruin of the country; he was now anxious for an Administration, without any consideration who was to form it, because he was convinced the country would be ruined unless some one was soon appointed.

He held office as lord of the Treasury under the Coalition. On 7 May 1783 he voted for Pitt's motion on parliamentary reform. 'He had hoped', he said, 'the burgage tenures would have been abolished, and the rotten boroughs disfranchised.'[8] He voted for Fox's East India bill, 27 Nov. 1783, and was dismissed with the Coalition, December 1783.

Surrey now became a great borough monger. In 1784 he was elected for Carlisle, Arundel, and Hereford; and secured the return of a candidate on his interest at Gloucester. From 1786 he began buying burgages at Horsham. In the Parliament of 1784 he was one of Fox's staunchest supporters and a constant advocate for parliamentary reform. 'He never shrunk from any exertion', wrote Wraxall, 'however rough or personal.'[9] 'A lively, affable, talking man', wrote Boswell, 'with very good sense and competent knowledge.'[10]

He died 16 Dec. 1815.

[1] Portland mss. [2] Geo. Mounsey to Portland, 19 Sept. 1780. [3] Debrett, vi. 509; vii. 134, 182. [4] Lansdowne mss. [5] Fortescue, vi. 137. [6] Lansdowne mss. [7] Add. 38567, ff. 137–40. [8] Debrett, ix. 540, 583, 732. [9] Mems. iii. 56. [10] Private Pprs. xiii. 137.

J.B.

**HOWARD, George** (1718–96), of Stoke, Bucks. and Great Bookham, Surr.

LOSTWITHIEL 1761–March 1766
STAMFORD 1768–16 July 1796

bap. 20 June 1718, 1st s. of Lt.-Gen. Thomas Howard (nephew of Francis, 5th Baron Effingham) of Great Bookham by Mary, da. of Rt. Rev. William Moreton, bp. of Meath 1705–16, sis. of Sir William Moreton (q.v.). educ. Westminster 1729; Ch. Ch. Oxf. 1735. m. (1) 16 Feb. 1747, Lady Lucy Wentworth (d.27 Apr. 1771), da. of Thomas, 1st Earl of Strafford, sis. and coh. of William, 2nd Earl, 1s. 2da.; (2) 21 May 1776, Elizabeth, da. of Peter Beckford of Jamaica, sis. of Julines, Richard and William Beckford (qq.v.), wid. of Thomas, 2nd Earl of Effingham, s.p. suc. fa. 1753. K.B. 3 Aug. 1774.

Ensign 24 Ft. 1725, lt. 1736, capt.-lt. 1736, capt. 1737; capt. 3 Ft. 1739, lt.-col. 1744; col. 1749; maj.-gen. 1750; lt.-gen. 1760; col. 7 Drag. 1763–79; gen. 1777; col. 1 Drag. Gds. 1779–d.; f.m. 1793.

Gov. Minorca 1766–8, Chelsea hospital 1768–95, Jersey 1795–d; P.C. 29 July 1795.

Howard fought at Fontenoy, Falkirk, and Culloden; served on the expedition to Rochfort in 1757; and commanded a brigade in Germany, 1760–2. He was returned for Lostwithiel on Lord Edgcumbe's interest, and received Newcastle's whip in 1761 through the Duke of Devonshire. In Bute's list he is marked as a Government supporter. He was not included in Fox's list of Members favourable to the peace preliminaries, nor did he vote against them; he was probably still absent in Germany. He was classed by Jenkinson in the autumn of 1763 as pro-Administration, but voted against general warrants, 18 Feb. 1764. On 29 Jan. 1765 he reaffirmed his opposition to them; and in Rockingham's list of July 1765 was classed 'pro'.

On 7 Feb. 1766 during the debate on Grenville's motion for an address to enforce the laws in America, he said 'he hoped in God it would not suceed, for in all likelihood he might be ordered to execute it, and before he would imbrue his hands in the blood of his countrymen who were contending for *English* liberty, he would if ordered draw his sword, but would soon after sheathe it in his own body'.[1]

Soon afterwards his appointment as governor of Minorca vacated his seat. On 7 Feb. 1768 George Selwyn wrote to Lord Carlisle:[2]

> G. Howard has Chelsea in the room of Sir R. Rich. Lord Exeter brings him into Parliament; he exchanged it with Mostyn [John Mostyn, q.v.], who has Minorca, which . . . is 500 more, but Mr. Howard chose to be in Parliament.

He voted for Wilkes's expulsion, 3 Feb. 1769, but did not vote on the motion to seat Luttrell, 15 Apr., and in the division list of 8 May, on the motion to consider the Middlesex petition against Luttrell's election, is placed among the 'absent friends'. He voted against Administration in the division on the Middlesex election of 25 Jan. 1770, but henceforward supported Administration till the fall of North, though he paired in opposition for the motion to make Grenville's Election Act permanent, 25 Feb. 1774.

William Baker, a follower of Rockingham's, wrote to his mother-in-law, Lady Juliana Penn, on 30 June 1775:[3]

> Gen. Howard has many good qualities but he and I do not think quite alike respecting America. I can however make many allowances for his thinking as he does. The blood of Howard is of so deep a dye, that it looks almost like the crimson of royalty. It is no wonder then that it should boil at the idea of resistance in republicans . . . The prejudice too of education and the regard he bears to the honour of the profession to which he has been bred may weigh something.

He spoke sensibly in Parliament, mostly on matters of military administration, but rarely on policy or the conduct of the war.

Howard voted against Shelburne's peace preliminaries, 18 Feb. 1783, and against Fox's East India bill, 27 Nov. 1783. During the debate on the third reading of the bill, 8 Dec., he told the House 'he should vote against the bill; but declared, as he was a man of honour, from no other motive than from not being able to reconcile himself to the principle of the bill'.[4] He supported Pitt's Administration.

Horace Walpole described him as 'one of those sort of characters who are only to be distinguished by having no peculiarity of character.'[5] 'Sir George is pompous', wrote Fanny Burney in 1786, 'yet . . . good-humoured in his manners.'[6]

He died 16 July 1796.

[1] Conway to the King, 7 Feb. 1766, Fortescue, i. 267; *Massachusetts Hist. Soc. Colls.* (ser. 7), ix. 139-43. [2] *HMC Carlisle*, 238. [3] Baker mss formerly at Bayfordbury. [4] Debrett, xii. 394. [5] *Mems. Geo. II*, iii. 50. [6] *Diary & Letters of Mme d'Arblay*, ii. 407.

J.B.

## HOWARD, Hon. Richard (1748–1816).

STEYNING 1784–1790

*b.* 21 Feb. 1748, 2nd s. of Thomas, 2nd Earl of Effingham, by Elizabeth, da. of Peter Beckford of Jamaica, sis. of Julines, Richard, and William Beckford (q.v.); stepson of Sir George Howard (q.v.). *educ.* Eton 1755–62. *m.* 14 June 1785, Harriet Elizabeth, da. and coh. of John Marsh, of Waresley Park, Hunts., *s.p. suc.* bro. as 4th Earl 19 Nov. 1791.

Lt. 1 Horse Gds. 1768; ret. 1771; sec. and comptroller to the Queen 1784–1814; treasurer to the Queen 1814–*d.*

Howard sat for Steyning on the interest of Sir John Honywood, who was connected politically with Lord Effingham. He voted for Sir Elijah Impey's impeachment, 9 May 1788, and with Pitt on the Regency, and is not known to have spoken in the House.

He died 10 Dec. 1816.

L.B.N.

## HOWARD, Hon. Thomas (1721–83), of Ashtead Park, Surr.

CASTLE RISING 1747–1768
MALMESBURY 1768–1774
MITCHELL 29 Dec. 1774–10 Aug. 1779

*b.* 11 Jan. 1721, 5th s. of Henry Bowes, 11th Earl of Suffolk and 4th Earl of Berkshire, by Catherine, da. of Col. James Graham of Levens, Westmld. *educ.* Eton 1732; St. John's, Oxf. 1738; I. Temple 1742, called 1744, bencher 1779. *m.* 13 Aug. 1747, Elizabeth, da. of William Kingscote of Kingscote, Glos., 1da. *suc.* gt.-nephew as 14th Earl of Suffolk and 7th Earl of Berkshire 10 Aug. 1779.

In 1754 Howard appears in Dupplin's list as a practising lawyer, but he left the bar before 1769.[1] He sat for Castle Rising on the interest of his nephew Henry, 12th Earl of Suffolk; was counted as a Tory; and appears in Henry Fox's list of Members favourable to the peace preliminaries, December 1762. From 1763 to 1771 he followed Suffolk (who was closely allied with Grenville), and voted against the repeal of the Stamp Act. Charles Townshend in January 1767 marked him as 'Grenville', but Rockingham in November 1766 and Newcastle in March 1767 still listed him as Tory.

He was returned on Suffolk's interest for Malmesbury in 1768. In a speech of 31 Jan. 1769[2] he said he had 'never troubled the House but three times' in over twenty-one years; but between 1768 and 1779 he was a more frequent speaker. In 1769–70 he voted four times against the Government on the Middlesex election, and claimed to have been the first man to sign the Surrey petition against Luttrell's return.[3] When Suffolk and most of the Grenvilles went over to the court in February 1771, Howard remained in opposition. On 25 Feb. 1774 he voted to make Grenville's Election Act permanent, and in June spoke twice against the Quebec bill—'this most tyrannous proposition . . . to introduce slavery and oppression into the colonies'.[4]

Howard was left out by Suffolk in 1774. He was thought of as candidate for Surrey,[5] but stood down in favour of James Scawen, another Opposition Member, on whose interest he was returned at Mitchell after Scawen had been elected for Surrey. Howard remained in opposition until he succeeded to the peerage. His opposition seems to have had a personal edge against the King; on Suffolk's death he 'declined' to deliver in person the ensigns of the Garter.[6] But as a peer he took little part in politics.

He died 3 Feb. 1783.

[1] Cavendish's 'Debates', Egerton 216, f. 237. [2] Ibid. [3] Ibid., Egerton 3711, f. 30. [4] Ibid., Egerton 262, f. 4. [5] Howard to the Duke of Newcastle, 10 Oct. 1774, Newcastle (Clumber) mss. [6] The King to North, 22 Mar. 1779, Fortescue, iv. 307.

J.B.

**HOWE, George Augustus,** 3rd Visct. Howe [I] (?1724–58), of Langar, nr. Nottingham.

NOTTINGHAM    1747–6 July 1758

*b.* ?1724, 1st surv. s. of Emanuel Scrope, 2nd Visct. Howe [I], M.P., by Mary Sophia Charlotte, da. of John Adolph, Baron von Kielmansegge (by Charlotte Sophia, *suo jure* Countess of Darlington, mistress of George I); bro. of Richard, 4th Visct., Hon. Thomas, and Hon. William Howe (qq.v.). *educ.* Westminster Nov. 1732, aged 8; Eton c. 1734. *unm. suc.* fa. 29 Mar. 1735.
     Ensign 1 Ft. Gds. 1745, lt. and capt. 1746, capt. and lt.-col. 1749; col. 1757; col. commandant 3 Btn. 60 Ft. Feb.–Sept. 1757; col. 55 Ft. Sept. 1757–*d.*; brig.-gen. in America 1757.

Howe was returned after a contest for Nottingham in 1754. On 13 Nov. 1755 he voted against the Address. He was killed in action near Fort Ticonderoga, 6 July 1758.

                                                        J.B.


**HOWE, Richard,** 4th Visct. Howe [I] (1726–99), of Langar, nr. Nottingham.

DARTMOUTH    23 May 1757–20 Apr. 1782

*b.* 19 Mar. 1726, 2nd surv. s. of Emanuel Scrope, 2nd Visct. Howe [I] M.P., bro. of George Augustus, 3rd Visct., Hon. William, and Hon. Thomas (qq.v.). *educ.* Westminster 1732–3; Eton 1735–40. *m.* 10 Mar. 1758, Mary, da. and coh. of Chiverton Hartopp of Welby, Leics., 3da. *suc.* bro. as 4th Visct. 6 July 1758; *cr.* Visct. Howe [GB] 20 Apr. 1782; Earl Howe [GB] 19 Aug. 1788; K.G. 2 June 1797.
     Entered R.N. 1739; lt. 1745; capt. 1746; r.-adm. 1770; v.-adm. 1776; adm. 1782; adm. of the fleet 1796. Ld. of Admiralty Apr. 1763–July 1765; P.C. 26 July 1765; treasurer of the navy July 1765–Apr. 1766, July 1766–Jan. 1770; naval c.-in-c. America Feb. 1776–July 1778; first ld. of Admiralty Jan.–Apr. 1783, Dec. 1783–July 1788.

During the seven years' war Howe served on the expeditions to Rochfort, St. Malo, and Cherbourg; and fought with distinction at Quiberon Bay. His courage and powers of leadership won him high reputation in the navy. In 1757 he was returned to Parliament on the Admiralty interest at Dartmouth, and counted as a regular Government supporter. He was at sea when the peace preliminaries were debated, and his attitude to Bute's Administration is not known. Under the Grenville Administration he took office as a lord of the Admiralty.

There was a strong vein of independence in Howe's character; taciturn and reserved, he had no close political connexions. The politician he most admired was Pitt, the great war leader. He spoke frequently in the House, and was heard with respect. He supported the Opposition in the debate on general warrants of 17–18 Feb. 1764—'Lord Howe's speaking as well as leaving us had a bad effect',

wrote James Harris; but this was an isolated vote— he attended the meeting at Grenville's house on 8 Jan. 1765 as one of the Government men of business. He was promoted by the Rockingham Administration treasurer of the navy; which he resigned at the end of April 1766, 'declaring he could not co-operate unless Mr. Pitt was minister'.[1]

He was restored by Pitt in July 1766, and voted regularly with the Chatham and Grafton Administrations: on the land tax, 27 Feb. 1767, the nullum tempus bill, 17 Feb. 1768, and the Middlesex election. When Chatham returned to Opposition in January 1770, Howe resigned; but never recanted his vote on the Middlesex election, as did some followers of Chatham. On the royal marriage bill, March 1772, he was classed by Robinson as 'doubtful'. On 9 Feb. 1773 he presented the petition of the naval captains on half-pay, but was classed in the King's list of the division as a friend to Government; and similarly on 25 Feb. 1774, when he voted for making Grenville's Election Act permanent.

Howe supported the Government's punitive measures against the colonies; and described the bill to restrain the trade of New England 'as the only moderate means of bringing the disobedient provinces to a sense of their duty without involving the Empire in all the horrors of a civil war' (6 Mar. 1775). On 20 Nov. 1775 he declared in the House that 'if it was left to his choice he certainly should decline to serve' in the war; 'but if he was commanded, it was his duty to obey and he could not refuse to serve'.[2] In fact Government had already approached him about taking a command in America.

Two difficulties stood in the way of his accepting. He objected to Shuldham's appointment to a separate command in the St. Lawrence.

> Lord Howe looks upon this measure [North wrote to the King on 2 Feb. 1776[3]] as materially disgraceful to him, and is very jealous of Lord Sandwich, thinking that he does not wish him well, and doubtful that he would not give him a proper support if he took the command of the fleet. The appointment of Lord Howe, which begun to get wind, had a very good effect in the public, but, if it is now laid aside, the consequences will be much worse than if it had never been in agitation.

The King persuaded Sandwich to agree to Howe's wishes: his promotion was ante-dated, and he was appointed sole naval commander-in-chief in North American waters.

The second difficulty arose from the Government's wish to send a commission to negotiate with the Americans. Howe insisted that he and his brother William (who was to command the army in America), should be appointed sole commissioners, and disagreed with Germain about their instructions. He wrote to Germain on 26 Mar. 1776:[4]

Lord Howe always flattered himself the intentions of Government were that he should be authorized upon his arrival to hold forth to the Americans, in the mildest though firmest manner, the most favourable terms that Government mean to grant, in order to induce them to lay down their arms and return to their duty.

But observing that a method directly the reverse is now ordered to be pursued, it is with infinite concern he finds himself obliged to confess that he is disqualified from engaging as a commissioner in the execution of instructions framed on that plan.

'If Lord Howe would give up being a commissioner', the King wrote to North on 13 Apr.,[5] 'I should think it better for himself as well as the service.' But Howe was insistent, and Wedderburn intervened with Germain in his favour, 24 Apr. 1776:[6]

I am persuaded Lord Howe will have the commission for this reason if there were no other, because at this moment . . . no other person has been thought of. I believe, too, that he wishes to have it . . . Except the point of being sole commissioner, in which he has prevailed, every other point that he has contended for affords some reasons for relying on his honour in the discharge of it, for he would not be very anxious about the terms of his instructions if he did not mean to be guided by them . . . If Lord Howe means to execute as far as he can the intentions of Government, it is the best measure to place confidence in him.

Howe arrived in America after the Declaration of Independence had been signed, which vitiated all prospect of his success as commissioner. There was some criticism of his inactivity as naval commander, but success at sea would not have ended the American war. He gained no *éclat* from his command, and it was no surprise that he asked to be recalled with his brother.

Howe returned to England in October 1778, and joined with his brother in a demand for an inquiry into their conduct in America. In December 1778, when it was proposed to appoint Sandwich secretary of state, Howe was suggested for first lord of the Admiralty. It 'seems much for the advantage of my service', the King wrote to North on 12 Dec.; and on 28 Dec., with reference to the inquiry: 'It would remove all that altercation which, if he is not during the recess satisfied, will take up the time of Parliament from business more useful.' On 19 Jan. 1779 North wrote to the King:

Lord Clarendon told Lord North yesterday at court that Lord Howe's most earnest wish was to see some military preferment or distinction conferred upon his brother, which might mark that his Majesty did not disapprove of his services. He added that such a promotion would he believes put all ideas of inquiry out of his head as well as his brother's.[7]

On 4 Feb. North was authorized to offer Howe the Admiralty. 'I must expect', wrote the King, 'an explicit declaration that he will zealously concur in prosecuting the war in all the quarters of the globe.' North had a conversation of two and a half hours with Howe that evening, but the result was unsatisfactory. 'I think I clearly see he means to decline', wrote the King to Weymouth on 6 Feb. Howe named 'four circumstances which he thought necessary to enable him to be of use to his Majesty's service'.[8] What these were is not stated but it is probable that they included the dismissal of Germain and the abandonment of offensive warfare in America. After a further long conversation with North on 8 Feb., Howe definitely declined.

Howe had not hitherto intervened in the dispute between Keppel and Palliser, although on 16 Dec. 1778 he had given some indication of his opinion when he seconded the bill to allow Keppel's court martial to be held on shore. On 19 Feb. 1779 he came out into the open, and seconded Admiral Pigot's motion for an address to the King to dismiss Palliser. Yet at the end of February the Admiralty was again offered to him, and again rejected.[9] On 3 Mar. he spoke for Fox's motion on Keppel, and on 8 Mar. made an important contribution to the debate on Fox's motion of censure against the Admiralty. The Admiralty's measures, he said, were 'weak, incapable, and if longer permitted or pursued must terminate in the destruction of the naval power of this country'. He protested that 'he was deceived into his command, that he was deceived while he retained it, that, tired and disgusted, he desired permission to resign'; and declared he would not serve again while the present ministers were in office.[10] 'Lord Howe may now be ranked in Opposition', wrote the King to North on 9 Mar.[11]

Howe voted regularly with Opposition until the fall of North. He aided his brother in the conduct of the inquiry into their command in America, and his speeches in the House were nearly all on naval questions. At the general election of 1780 Arthur Holdsworth, hitherto Government manager at Dartmouth but now in control on his own account, returned Howe against the wish of Government. The tone of Howe's speeches against the Admiralty became increasingly bitter, but he continued to remain aloof from both Opposition parties. On 6 Feb. 1782 he

urged that the navy could not have been worse managed than it had been under the present commission; but still, if the first commissioner should be replaced in consequence of a vote of censure passed by the House, he did not see by whom he should be replaced.

He ended his speech by stressing 'the necessity of union'.[12]

When the Rockingham Administration was formed in March 1782 Howe was created a British peer and appointed commander-in-chief of the Channel fleet. His greatest naval triumphs were yet to come—his relief of Gibraltar in 1783, and his victory on 'the glorious first of June' in 1794. Though generally reckoned unsuccessful as an administrator, he ranks with Anson, Hawke, and Rodney as one of the greatest seamen of the century.

Howe died 5 Aug. 1799.

[1] Walpole, *Mems. Geo. III*, ii. 231. [2] Almon, i. 291; iii. 200. [3] Fortescue, iii. 335-6. [4] *HMC Stopford-Sackville*, ii. 26. [5] Fortescue, iii. 351. [6] *HMC Stopford-Sackville*, ii. 29. [7] Fortescue, iv. 231, 239, 261. [8] Ibid. 267-8. [9] Ibid. 293. [10] Almon, xii. 76-78. [11] Fortescue, iv. 302. [12] Debrett, v. 427.

J.B.

## HOWE, Hon. Thomas (c.1728-71).

NORTHAMPTON    14 Feb. 1769-14 Nov. 1771

*b.* c.1728, 3rd surv. s. of Emanuel Scrope, 2nd Visct. Howe [I], M.P., and bro. of George Augustus, 3rd Visct., Richard, 4th Visct., and Hon. William (qq.v.). *unm.*

Howe contested Northampton on the Spencer interest, and was returned on petition. His only known vote was with Administration on the Middlesex election, 8 May 1769. There is no record of his having spoken in the House. He died 14 Nov. 1771.

J.B.

## HOWE, Hon. William (1729-1814).

NOTTINGHAM    1 Dec. 1758-1780

*b.* 10 Aug. 1729, 4th surv. s. of Emanuel Scrope, 2nd Visct. Howe [I], and bro. of George Augustus, 3rd Visct., Richard, 4th Visct., and Hon. Thomas (qq.v.). *educ.* Eton 1742. *m.* 2 June 1765, Frances, da. of Thomas Conolly of Castletown, co. Kildare, sis. of Thomas Conolly (q.v.), *s.p. suc.* bro. as 5th Visct. 5 Aug. 1799; K.B. 13 Oct. 1776.

Cornet 15 Drag. 1746, lt. 1747; capt.-lt. 20 Ft. 1750, capt. 1750; maj. 60 Ft. 1756; lt.-col. 58 Ft. 1757; col. 1762; col. 46 Ft. 1764-75; maj.-gen. 1772; c.-in-c. in America 1775-8; col. 23 Ft. 1775-86; lt.-gen. 1777; col. 19 Lt. Drag. 1786-*d*.; gen. 1793; gov. Berwick 1795-1808, Plymouth 1808-*d*.

P.C. 21 June 1782; lt.-gen. of the Ordnance 1782-1804.

William Howe was returned unopposed for Nottingham in 1758 on the death of his brother George Augustus, 3rd Viscount. During the seven years' war he served in Canada, and with the expeditions to Belle Isle and Havana. In politics he followed his brother, and generally supported Government; but, like Lord Howe, voted against the Grenville Administration on general warrants, 18 Feb. 1764. Before 1778 there is no record of his having spoken in the House.

In 1775 he was one of the three major-generals sent to America when war seemed imminent, and on the recall of Gage was appointed commander-in-chief. For the next three years he held the crucial post in the conduct of the American war.

On 25 Sept. 1775 Lord Howe (who had not yet assumed his appointment as naval commander-in-chief) informed Germain that his brother considered that an army 30,000 strong would be required to restore peace in America—'If Government is unable to furnish the force he suggests . . . he then thinks it better policy to withdraw the troops entirely from the delinquent provinces, and leave the colonists to war with each other for sovereignty.'[1] Every effort should also be made to conciliate the revolted provinces and attract the support of the loyalists. The British Government did all they could to comply with Howe's wishes; Lord Howe was given power to act as a conciliator, and the troops his brother demanded were sent. Howe wrote to Germain on 8 June 1776:[2]

> I cannot take my leave from your Lordship without expressing my utter amazement at the decisive and masterly strokes for carrying such extensive plans into immediate execution as have been effected since your Lordship has assumed the conducting of this war, which is already most happily experienced by those who have the honour of serving here under your guidance.

Howe 'showed throughout his command a growing pessimism, a feeling that military achievement, no matter how brilliant, would bring by itself no decisive results in the struggle'.[3] His hopes of conciliating the colonists were ended by the Declaration of Independence, and he relied too much on loyalist support. He failed to bring Washington to decisive battle, and would not risk his army in the attempt. His mood varied between pessimism and optimism equally ill-founded; and he pressed constantly for more troops, which the Government found great difficulty in raising. On 26 Apr. 1776, after the evacuation of Boston, he wrote to Germain:

> The scene here at present wears a lowering aspect, there not being the least prospect of conciliating this continent until its armies shall have been roughly dealt with; and I confess my apprehensions that such an event will not be readily brought about.

But on 31 Dec. he informed Germain that if France could be prevented from interfering and sufficient reinforcements sent, 'it would in my opinion put a stop to the rebellion'. On 2 Apr. 1777: 'My hopes of terminating the war this year are vanished'. 7 July: 'A corps of Russians of ten thousand effective fighting men I think would ensure the success of the war to Great Britain in another campaign'.[4]

When after two years of war, and in spite of the capture of New York and Philadelphia, the end was still not in sight, relations between Howe and Germain began to deteriorate. Each blamed the other for lack of success: Howe complained that he had not been sufficiently reinforced, Germain that Howe failed to inform him of his plans. On receiving the news of Burgoyne's surrender at Saratoga, Howe wrote to Germain, 22 Oct. 1777:[5]

> From the very little attention, my Lord, given to my recommendations since the commencement of my command, I am led to hope I may be relieved from this very painful service, wherein I have not the good fortune to enjoy the necessary confidence and support of my superiors . . . By the return of the packet I humbly request I may receive his Majesty's permission to resign the command.

'Sir William Howe's complaint of want of support is very unjust', wrote Germain to the King on 1 Dec.,[6] 'but his desire of being recalled does not come unexpected.' On 25 May 1778 Howe handed over his command to Clinton, and sailed for England.

On 3 July Howe had 'a very long conversation' with the King, 'the substance of which was his very strongly declaring that nothing shall make either his brother or him join Opposition, but that Lord G. Germain and his secretaries . . . have everywhere loaded him with obloquy, that he must therefore be allowed some means of justifying himself'.[7] In the House of Commons on 4 Dec. he spoke about his resignation:[8]

> He declared that it had been in consequence of a total disregard to his opinions, and to his recommendations of meritorious officers. The war had not been left to his management; and yet when he applied for instructions he frequently could not get them. The noble lord at the head of the Treasury had indeed supported; but the noble secretary for the American department had not used him well . . . He concluded with saying that whatever orders are sent to America for the conduct of the war he was sure they never could be executed to the satisfaction and advantage of this country while they go through the hands of the noble lord who holds the American department.

He demanded a parliamentary inquiry into his conduct in America, which North, against Germain's advice, granted. It was opened on 29 Apr. 1779 with a long speech by Howe;[9] occupied a good deal of time that session of Parliament; and ended inconclusively. An inquiry on the scale Howe demanded was impossible, nor was the House of Commons a fit tribunal to judge of the conduct of military operations.

On the contractors bill, 12 Feb. 1779, Howe was classed by Robinson as 'pro, present'. But all his subsequent recorded votes were with Opposition. Like Burgoyne in similar circumstances he repeatedly told the House of Commons the tale of his campaigns; but his criticism of Government was confined to alleged misconduct of the war.

He stood again for Nottingham at the general election of 1780. But he and his brother had aroused strong opposition in the town. Frederick Montagu wrote to Portland on 22 Aug.:[10] 'Half the town abhor them for going to America, and the other half detest them for doing so little there.' The *Political Magazine* wrote about this election:[11]

> The most respectable people in the town waited on the brothers, and acquainted them that the electors of Nottingham had formerly . . . revered the name and family of Howe; but that reverence had lately been obliterated by other sentiments: they saw the present distresses of their country: they imputed them to the conduct of the General and noble Lord when in America: therefore the General could have no hopes of carrying his election.

Upon this Howe withdrew.

In March 1782, he was appointed lieutenant-general of the Ordnance through his brother's influence, but saw no further service. He died 12 July 1814.

[1] *HMC Stopford-Sackville*, i. 9. [2] Quoted T. S. Anderson, *Command of Howe Bros. during American Rev.* 123. [3] Ibid. 107. [4] *HMC Stopford-Sackville*, ii. 30, 54, 63, 71. [5] Ibid. 80. [6] Fortescue, iii. 501. [7] The King to North, 3 July 1778, ibid. iv. 176. [8] Almon, xi. 111. [9] Ibid. xii. 319–50. [10] Portland mss. [11] Quoted I. R. Christie, *End of North's Ministry 1780–2*, p. 146.

J.B.

**HOWELL, David** (?1751–1804), of Lanbaren, Cornw.

MITCHELL 1784–1796

*b.* ?1751, 2nd s. of Rev. Joshua Howell, rector of Lanreath, Cornw., by Dunetta, da. and h. of David Haweis of Treworgey, Cornw. *m.* Eliza Parsons, 1s. 1da.

Cornet 16 Lt. Drag. 1774, lt. 1777, capt. 1781–9; capt. 36 Ft. 1790; capt. 10 Ft. 1791; disappears from army list 1792.

In 1784 Howell successfully contested Mitchell on the interest of Sir Francis Basset. In Parliament he regularly voted against Pitt's Administration. There is no record of his having spoken before 1790. He died in 1804.

M.M.D.

**HOWORTH, Henry** (c.1746–83), of the Inner Temple.

ABINGDON 21 Dec. 1782–11 May 1783

*b.* c.1746, s. of Rev. Henry Robert Howorth of Maesllwch, and gt.-nephew of Sir Humphrey Howorth (q.v.). *educ.* Westminster 1764; L. Inn 1764, called 1769. *unm.*

K.C. 1780; recorder Abingdon 1780.

Howorth voted for Shelburne's peace preliminaries, 18 Feb. 1783, and was classed a few weeks later as a follower of his; possibly Howorth's return for Abingdon, in place of John Mayor, was arranged by Administration. Only one speech by him is reported, in a debate on the vagrancy laws. An enthusiastic amateur yachtsman, he was drowned in a sailing accident, 11 May 1783. The *Gentleman's Magazine* (1783, i. 453) described him as 'one of the first Crown lawyers in practice', and as having made 7,600 guineas during the previous year.

I.R.C.

**HOWORTH, Sir Humphrey** (c.1684–1755), of Maesllwch, Rad.

RADNORSHIRE 1722–4 Feb. 1755

*b.* c.1684, s. of Humphrey Howorth of Maesllwch. *m.* (1) Sibel (*d.*4 Mar. 1742), da. of Roger Mainwaring, 1s. 1da.; (2) Mary, da. of John Walbeoffe of Llanhamlach, Brec., wid. of Henry Williams of Gwernyfed, Brec. Kntd. 21 Aug. 1715.

Receiver of Crown rents in Cheshire 1714–30.

Howorth's estate of Maesllwch gave him considerable electoral influence in Radnorshire, but this required constant vigilance and great expense. He was returned unopposed in 1754, but the expense of earlier contests (in 1722, 1734, and 1741) had made inroads into his capital; and the situation was not improved when he was ordered to pay into the Treasury £3,000 arrears from the Crown rents he had collected in Cheshire between 1714 and 1730.[1] He was compelled to sell much of his estate to his tenants; and he left Maesllwch encumbered by a mortgage of £26,000, and by the claim from the Treasury which, with interest, must have amounted to over £5,000. He died 4 Feb. 1755.

[1] Chase Price to Duke of Portland, 12 Sept. 1765, Portland mss.

L.B.N.

**HUDSON, Giles** (*d.*1783), of Putney, Surr.

CHIPPENHAM 1780–19 Feb. 1783

*m.* (1) 2 Jan. 1772, Miss Deschamps of Bucklersbury,[1] several s. and poss. 1 da.;[2] (2) Catherine.

Hudson appears in the London directories 1769–1782 as a partner in Fludyer, Marsh and Hudson, warehousemen, 79 Basinghall Street. He dealt at times in Government stock, but never held much for any length of time and does not appear among the subscribers to the two loans of 1780–1.

He was returned for Chippenham on the Fludyer interest and in succession to his partner Samuel Marsh, the young Fludyers being still under age. He voted with Administration on Lowther's motion against the war, 12 Dec. 1781; it is uncertain whether he voted on the censure motion against the Admiralty, 20 Feb. 1782; and he was absent from the divisions of 22 and 27 Feb. and 8 Mar.; but voted with Administration on the 'no confidence' motion of 15 Mar., when Robinson placed him

among the 'new persons who did not vote before'. In a list sent to Sandwich on 15 Mar. Robinson added after Hudson's name: 'ill, query whether able to stay it out'.[3] In his will made in November 1782,[4] Hudson speaks of himself as 'of indifferent health of body'; he was absent from the division on Shelburne's peace preliminaries, and died the next day, 19 Feb. 1783.

[1] *Gent. Mag.* 1772, p. 46. [2] See Foster, *Al. Ox.* and *Register L. Inn* under Henry Hudson. [3] Sandwich mss. [4] PCC 130 Cornwallis.

J.A.C.

**HUMBERSTON, Thomas** (c.1730–55), of Humberston, Lincs.

BRACKLEY 1754–22 July 1755

*b.* c. 1730, 1st surv. s. of Matthew Humberston by his w. Rebecca who m. (2) Benjamin Pryse. *suc.* fa. 1736.

Humberston was returned after a contest in which he defeated Henry Vernon, one of the Duke of Bridgwater's candidates. The Duke, patron of Brackley, was a minor and on his Grand Tour, and an opposition appears to have been assiduously organized during his absence. The Duke of Bedford, Bridgwater's guardian, believed that the plot had been 'a good while in agitation' and discontent had been 'raised by individuals in the borough in order to stir up for their own advantage an opposition';[1] and on 13 Apr. 1754 Vernon told Bedford that he thought the scheme had been 'laid and encouraged by persons that do not at present appear in it'. Of Humberston himself Bedford wrote to Bridgwater: 'I could not find for a long time any one that knew such a person, and it was the opinion of many I spoke with that this was only a phantom conjured up, to create an expense'; but Robert Wood, Bridgwater's tutor, replied from Lyons, 18 May:

> [Humberston] must I think be an old acquaintance of mine who his Grace and I met last summer in our tour through Savoy;[2] if so his fortune is by no means equal to such a scheme and should he attempt to establish an interest at Brackley, it must be as injurious in the end to himself as it is now disagreeable to the Duke.

According to Vernon, Humberston was a member of the Society of Dilettanti.

Bedford, seeing 'no possibility of carrying two Members for Brackley, but by outbidding them', and thinking 'the Duke of Bridgwater's future interest in that borough may run great risk of being totally lost', authorized Bridgwater's agent to 'go as far as two thousand pounds . . . towards the obtaining the secure election of the two candidates in his Grace's interest'. If this was unsuccessful he advised a compromise with Humberston. But Vernon did not think there was any possibility of succeeding: 'Our opponents are kept constantly in a body at breakfast, dinner and supper, and their wives have been bribed so high that they will neither let us see them, or hearken to any proposals.' Bedford himself then went to Brackley but found Humberston had been so alert, that his election could not be prevented. Marshe Dickinson received 33 votes, Humberston 18, and Vernon 15.

Humberston was intent on establishing a lasting interest at Brackley. Bedford wrote to Bridgwater on 29 Apr. 1754:

> Mr. Humberston . . . intends to try at law with your Grace the right of nomination in the steward of your court and the mayor, of two persons to be elected into the body upon vacancies occasioned by the death of any of the 33 members of the corporation, and that he has likewise established a weekly club of your opposers to which he allows a guinea a week.

Humberston was also a candidate at Grimsby in 1754 but there is no record of a poll, and he probably withdrew before the election.

In Dupplin's list of the Parliament of 1754 he was classed as 'For, of various connexions', but nothing is known of the part he took in the House.

He was concerned with improving his estates and in his will he enjoined his heirs to continue the work which he had 'already begun and made great progress in'. He died 22 July 1755.

[1] 29 Apr. 1754. This and following quotations are from Bedford mss. [2] See also Gibbon to his father, 30 July 1753.

M.M.D.

## HUME, Abraham (1703–72), of Wormleybury, Herts.

STEYNING     1747–1754
TREGONY     1761–1768

b. 1703, 4th s. of Robert Home (subsequently Hume) of Ayton, Berwick, by Hannah Curtis of Mile End, Mdx.; bro. of Alexander Hume (q.v.). m. 2 Oct. 1746, Hannah, da. of Sir Thomas Frederick, gov. of Fort St. David, sis. of Sir John Frederick, 4th Bt. and of Sir Charles Frederick (qq.v.), 2s. 1da. His w.'s sis. Mary m. Alexander Hume. suc. bro. 15 Sept. 1765; cr. Bt. 4 Apr. 1769.
  Director, South Sea Co. and Exchange Assurance Co.; commissary to the forces abroad Dec. 1742; commissary gen. of stores at home and abroad Dec. 1746–7, 1756.[1]

Hume was a merchant holding some Government contracts. In 1754 he resigned his seat at Steyning to his brother Alexander, and unsuccessfully contested Maidstone, at a cost of at least £1,600.[2]

His brother-in-law, Sir Charles Frederick, was married to a daughter of Hugh, 1st Viscount Falmouth, and Hume was returned for Tregony on the Falmouth interest in 1761. He is marked as an Administration supporter in Bute's list, and by Jenkinson in the autumn of 1763. Like his brother, he did not vote in the division on general warrants,

18 Feb. 1764, and was included by Jenkinson in his 'List of Friends Absent'; but so he was also by Newcastle. No vote by Hume in any division in this Parliament is recorded, nor any speech; but Newcastle listed him in March 1767 as 'Administration'. He did not stand again in 1768.

He died 10 Oct. 1772.

[1] Cal. Treasury Pprs. 1742–5, p. 421; T29/30/449; T29/33/40; Add. 33039, f. 149. [2] Add. 33055, ff. 265–7; 32995, f. 173.

L.B.N.

## HUME, Sir Abraham, 2nd Bt. (1749–1838), of Wormleybury, Herts.

PETERSFIELD     1774–1780
HASTINGS     1807–1818

b. 20 Feb. 1749, 1st s. of Sir Abraham Hume, 1st Bt. (q.v.). educ. Eton 1758–65; Trinity, Camb. 1766. m. 25 Apr. 1771, Amelia, da. of Rt. Rev. John Egerton, bp. of Durham, 2da. suc. fa. 10 Oct. 1772.

Hume stood for Southwark at the general election of 1774. In order to make sure of a seat in the House, he arranged through Lord North to be returned at Petersfield for a seat which William Jolliffe had placed at the disposal of Administration. In Southwark he was badly beaten. North wrote to the King on 11 Oct.: 'Sir Abraham Hume's poll has been much prejudiced by its being known that he has secured to himself a seat at Petersfield.'[1]

The Public Ledger described him in 1779 as 'a very honest, conscientious man, and votes as he thinks right'. He seems at first to have supported Administration and to have turned against them after Saratoga. 'I am no friend in general to the connexions of the present Administration', he wrote to Lord Macartney on 3 Nov. 1780.[2] In 1780 he stood no chance of being returned again at Petersfield, and tried to obtain a seat through the Opposition. Portland recommended him to Rockingham for one of Edward Eliot's boroughs, but Rockingham 'appeared not to relish the idea of his coming in, upon a doubt of his patriotic principles'.[3]

He is known as a great collector of paintings and of precious stones; also of minerals—he was one of the founders of the Geological Society, and a director of the British Institution. He died 24 Mar. 1838.

[1] Fortescue, iii. 144. [2] Macartney mss. [3] Portland to Rockingham, 14 Aug. 1780, Rockingham mss.

L.B.N.

## HUME, Alexander (c.1693–1765), of Wormleybury, Herts.

SOUTHWARK     30 June 1743–1754
STEYNING     1754–1761
SOUTHWARK     1761–15 Sept. 1765

b. c.1693, 1st s. of Robert Home (subsequently Hume)

of Ayton, Berwick, and bro. of Abraham Hume (q.v.). *m.* 5 Apr. 1733, Mary, da. of Sir Thomas Frederick, gov. of Fort St. David, sis. of Sir John Frederick, 4th Bt. and of Sir Charles Frederick (qq.v.), 1da. *d.v.p.* His w.'s sis. Hannah m. Abraham Hume. *suc.* fa. 1732. Bought Wormleybury 1739.

Director, E.I. Co. 1737-40, 1742-5, 1747-8.

In 1754, because of ill-health, Hume did not contest Southwark, but claimed subsequently[1] that 'by his influence' William Hammond was returned there 'to the satisfaction of the Duke of Newcastle'. On his giving up Southwark Newcastle recommended him for Steyning 'in the room of his brother who willingly resigned to make room for him', and he was returned there unopposed at a cost of £1,400.[2] During this Parliament he spoke against the prize bill 'as it was drawn',[3] 4 May 1759, and against the distillers bill, 25 Mar. 1760.[4]

On 10 Mar. 1760, having discovered that Newcastle intended to nominate another candidate at Steyning, Hume submitted a long memorandum to the Duke summarizing his parliamentary career, and concluding:

> Mr. Hume is ignorant of what may have offended the Duke of Newcastle; he very seldom differed from him in Parliament; he carried all his elections at his own expense; with the very few exceptions enumerated, his conduct in Parliament always conformed with the wishes of the Government.

On 24 Dec. 1760 he wrote to Newcastle that his friends had invited him to stand for Southwark; he did not propose to join either of the other candidates 'unless directed to do so by a majority of the electors who declared themselves my friends in so distinguished a manner'. He asked for the Duke's assistance with the officers of the Customs and Excise; presumably he received a favourable reply; but on 24 Feb. 1761 complained that 'not a single person belonging to the Customs hath hitherto been applied to'; again on 27 Mar.: 'not one of them . . . had the least hint given them as yet to be in my interest'; he must therefore struggle on unaided after having counted on such help. He was returned second on the poll.[5]

In Bute's list of 1761 Hume is counted as an Administration supporter, and appears in Fox's list drawn up early in December of Members favourable to the peace preliminaries. In the autumn of 1763 Jenkinson classed him as 'doubtful'; he voted with Opposition over general warrants, 6 Feb. 1764; and when absent from the division on 18 Feb. 1764 was listed as an 'absent friend' by Newcastle who, however, on 10 May 1764 counted him as 'doubtful'. Rockingham marked him as 'pro' in July 1765.

Hume was wealthy and independent; he held no Government contracts himself, though he sometimes acted in them for others,[6] and occasionally subscribed to Government loans, e.g. £20,000 in 1762; and while he was generally well disposed to Government, after 1761 neither side seems to have been certain of him. At India House he was a friend of Clive's, and there are a good many letters from him among the Clive papers.

He died 15 Sept. 1765, leaving his estate to his brother Abraham, besides more than £25,000 in Government stock.

[1] Memorandum to Newcastle, 10 Dec. 1760, Add. 33055, ff. 265-7. [2] Add. 32995, f. 172. [3] H. V. Jones to Newcastle, Add. 32890, f. 488. [4] James West to Newcastle, 24 and 25 Mar. 1760, Add. 32903, f. 497 and 32904, f. 26. [5] Add. 33055, ff. 265-7; 32916, f. 304; 32919, f. 265; 32921, f. 119. [6] Cal. Treasury Pprs. 1742-5.

L.B.N.

**HUME CAMPBELL, Hon. Alexander** (1708-60), of Birghamsheil, Berwick.

BERWICKSHIRE    1734-19 July 1760

*b.* 15 Feb. 1708, 2nd surv. s. of Alexander, 2nd Earl of Marchmont [S], lord clerk register, by Margaret, da. and h. of Sir George Campbell of Cessnock, lord justice clerk; twin bro. of Hugh, 3rd Earl. *educ.* private sch. London 1716-?21; Holland (Utrecht and Francker) 1721-?5; Edinburgh Univ.; adv. 1729; I. Temple, called 1731. *m.* 16 July 1737, Elizabeth Pettis of Savile Row, London, *s.p.*

Solicitor-gen. to Prince of Wales Dec. 1741-Jan. 1746; lord clerk register Jan. 1756-*d.*

Hume Campbell's politics were influenced by three considerations: jealousy of Argyll (Islay) as 'viceroy' of Scotland, family pride, and devotion to his brother. For most of the period 1734-1754 he was in opposition, during which time he also built up a considerable practice at the English bar.

In the 1754 Parliament Hume Campbell almost at once 'took a very active part . . . in support of the King's measures',[1] and was prepared to connect himself with Newcastle. In return for assistance against Pitt over the subsidy treaties, the brothers demanded full support for their Berwickshire interest at the expense of Lord Home, Argyll's protégé.[2] Employed by Newcastle in the autumn of 1755 to win over Gilbert Elliot and Sir George Lee,[3] Hume Campbell formulated proposals for his own advancement. Newcastle wrote to Hardwicke, 18 Oct. 1755:[4]

> Hume Campbell . . . made me an absolute offer of himself, to quit his profession entirely . . . to apply himself singly to the House of Commons, to take an active part in everything and to have difficulties in nothing. His condition was to be made chancellor of the duchy of Lancaster with the salary . . . made up to £2000 a year . . . It is certain he will be of vast use in the House of Commons. His manner of talking is what we want at present.

With the King, however, 'Hume Campbell would not go down at all'.[5] While alternative offices were under consideration Campbell supported the

Address on 13 Nov., but almost spoilt his chances by offending Hardwicke, who wrote to Newcastle, 5 Dec.:[6]

> Unless Mr. Hume Campbell shall come to me and ask my pardon . . . I shall think myself obliged to oppose this promotion to the utmost of my power, for though I can connive at many things I cannot submit to be insulted.

Hardwicke having been placated, Hume Campbell on 9 Dec. was offered the place of lord clerk register with a salary made up to £2,000 p.a.;[7] the following day he led for the Government in defence of the Russian and Hessian treaties. Walpole records:[8]

> The Duke of Newcastle . . . had selected another champion who was equal to any philippic and whom he would for that purpose have made paymaster if Fox had not withstood it. This was Hume Campbell, who for some time had deserted Opposition and almost Parliament and applied himself entirely to his profession of the law, which he was at once formed to adorn and suit, for he was eloquent, acute, abusive, corrupt, and insatiable.

Hume Campbell's 'masterly speech' provoked Pitt to a savage personal attack upon the 'servile lawyer', once his intimate friend.[9] 'Hume Campbell was annihilated,' wrote Walpole,[10] and made no reply. His 'want of manhood'[11] was not redeemed by his belated explanation on 12 Dec. of his personal and political conduct.[12] The ministry did not consider their champion 'annihilated', and proceeded to implement their promises. 'Notwithstanding any objections his Majesty may have', wrote Newcastle to Fox on 12 Dec., 'his abilities make him a useful and necessary man in these circumstances'.[13]

According to Walpole,[14] Campbell, after his preferment 'never provoked Pitt's wrath, and repaid this munificence with one only scrap of an ignorant speech on the plate tax' on 3 Mar. 1756.

On Fox's resignation the brothers were 'disconcerted with the change of ministry'[15] which brought in Pitt, and were 'deadly angry'[16] when in April 1757 Argyll obtained through Devonshire the lord lieutenancy of Berwickshire for Lord Home. Hume Campbell sought to act as peacemaker between Fox and Newcastle,[17] and took a leading part in the Minorca inquiry in defence of his friends.[18] During the negotiations for a new Administration, 'Hume Campbell modestly asked the treasurership of the navy . . . in addition to his office of lord register', and when it was denied, the duchy of Lancaster for life.[19] Hardwicke wrote to Newcastle, 1 June 1757:[20]

> The difficulty still rests . . . in finding proper persons to carry on . . . the business of the House of Commons . . . I thought Sir George Lee and Mr. Hume Campbell had been more sanguine upon that essential point . . . though . . . I doubted their forces for it . . . I perceive now that both these gentlemen draw back as to undertaking [it] independently of Mr. Fox.

In the final settlement of the Pitt-Newcastle coalition Hume Campbell received no office; deeply chagrined, the brothers returned to Scotland and began 'an extraordinary correspondence' with Newcastle, 'full of professions outwardly, but really most severe reproaches, not unmixed with threats',[21] demanding as the 'touchstone' of his friendship the removal of Home as lord lieutenant. Dupplin, after consulting John White (q.v.) suggested an explanation:[22]

> Mr. White fears . . . that Lord Halifax will be set at the head of a connection of weight and ability in which . . . Lord Marchmont will join as well as his brother, upon the plan of opposing Pitt as distinguished from your Grace.

When the ministry reached a settlement with Halifax, Dupplin thought the brothers would now 'change their language':[23]

> Their chief apprehension is of a defeat (and what they will think a disgrace) in the county election . . . Mr. White says that Lord Register will never forgive Pitt's personal abuse and all that can be expected is to keep them quiet, which they may possibly be when they see no standard set up to which they can resort.

Hume Campbell, perforce, renewed his attachment to Newcastle,[24] supporting him in any controversy with Pitt or Argyll, subject always to the overriding claims of his family and Scottish interests.[25] On the Scottish militia question the brothers' attitude was equivocal; they were ready to sponsor a county defence force but not one commanded by Home and his deputy lieutenants. When requested by Lord Milton, chairman of the Edinburgh committee, to co-operate in furthering a bill similar to the English Militia Act, Hume Campbell privately suggested to Newcastle that regiments of light horse and foot 'would do better than any militia whatever'.[26] In the debate of 4 Mar. 1760 he hedged,[27] but was appointed to the committee to prepare the bill. Afraid of offending either the King or Scottish opinion,[28] in the final vote on 15 Apr. 1760 'Lord Register was not in the House'.[29]

He died 19 July 1760. Hardwicke commented to Newcastle, 22 July:[30]

> I rejoice in no man's death but I hope your Grace has not suffered great loss in Mr. Hume Campbell. He certainly had abilities of a certain sort, but I fear he had no principles or courage. You have tried him in this united Administration and had tried him before . . . Have you found any real use for him in either?

[1] Newcastle to Holdernesse, 27 June 1755, Add. 32856, f. 302. [2] Add. 32855, f. 526; 32448, f. 269; 32856, ff. 223, 484; 35448, f. 277; 32860, f. 56. [3] Add. 32858, f. 299; 32859, ff. 237, 242; 32860, ff. 86–88. [4] Add. 32860, ff. 88–89. [5] Newcastle to Hardwicke, 7 Nov. 1755, Add. 32860, f. 269. [6] Add. 32861, f. 200. [7] See the Minute approved by Campbell, Add. 35448, f. 317. [8] *Mems. Geo. II*, ii. 107. [9] Ibid. 114. [10] Walpole to R. Bentley, 17 Dec. 1755. [11] Alex. Carlyle, *Autobiog.* 276. [12] *Mems. Geo. II*, ii. 141. [13] Add. 32861, f. 284; see also Fox to Newcastle [16 Dec.], ibid. 339. [14] *Mems. Geo. II*, ii. 143, 179. [15] *Ridpath's Diary* (Sc. Hist. Soc.), 103. [16] John Calcraft to Loudoun,

9 Apr. 1757, Add. 17493, f. 58. [17] Yorke, *Hardwicke*, ii. 380, 382; *Mems. Geo. II*, ii. 377; iii. 6. [18] *Mems. Geo. II*, iii. 7, 9, 23; Add. 35877, f. 359. [19] *Mems. Geo. II*, iii. 23. [20] *Hardwicke*, ii. 397. [21] Marchmont to Newcastle, 20 Sept. 1757; Newcastle to Dupplin, 28 Sept., Add 32874, ff. 183, 253. [22] Dupplin to Newcastle, 24 Sept. 1757, ibid. f. 264. [23] 8 Oct. 1757, ibid. 479. [24] Marchmont to Newcastle, 27 June 1758, Add. 32881, f. 88. [25] Add. 32879, f. 276; John Dalrymple to Chas. Townshend, 20 Jan. 1760, Buccleuch mss; Add. 32903, f. 497. [26] Memo. to the King, 27 Feb. 1760, Add. 32902, f. 431. [27] John Yorke to Hardwicke, 4 Mar. 1760, Add. 32903, f. 75. [28] Marchmont to Hardwicke, 1 Apr. 1760, Add. 35449, f. 220. [29] Add. 32904, f. 392. [30] Add. 32908, f. 439; for another assessment of him see Carlyle, *Autobiog.* 275-7.

E.H.G.

## HUNGERFORD, *see* PEACH HUNGERFORD

## HUNT, George (?1720–98), of Lanhydrock, nr. Bodmin, Cornw.

BODMIN 19 Jan. 1753–1784

*b.* ?1720, 2nd s. of Thomas Hunt of Mollington, Cheshire by Mary Vere, da. of Russell Robartes, M.P., sis. and h. of Henry, 3rd Earl of Radnor; bro. of Thomas Hunt (q.v.). *educ.* Queen's, Oxf. 10 Mar. 1738, aged 17. *unm.* *suc.* uncle at Lanhydrock 1741.

Having secured control of Bodmin corporation,[1] Hunt was returned at a by-election in 1753. He even thought of putting up his brother Thomas for the other seat at the next general election, but gave up the attempt which would have been very unpopular with the borough and with neighbouring country gentlemen. Elected in 1754 without a contest he is classed in Dupplin's lists as a Government supporter.

In June 1760 Thomas Jones, Edgcumbe's Cornish election agent, wrote about Bodmin: 'Mr. Hunt hath met with great difficulties of late and 'tis still a question whether his interest is well established.'[2] He was again returned unopposed; in October 1761 received his parliamentary whip direct from the Duke of Newcastle; and in Bute's list of December 1761 is marked 'Without connexion of Government otherwise than inclination.' His name appears in Fox's list of Members in favour of the peace preliminaries; and on 26 Dec. 1762 Hunt wrote to Bute when recommending his brother for some employment: 'I take this opportunity of making the strongest professions to your Lordship of my attachment to his Majesty's person and Government; as also of my hearty concurrence in support of the present system.'[3] It can therefore be taken as certain that he had voted for the peace preliminaries on 9 and 10 Dec. He went, however, into opposition over Wilkes and general warrants, and voted with the minority on 15 Nov. 1763, and 6, 15, and 18 Feb. 1764. Newcastle therefore counted him among his 'sure friends' (10 May 1764); and, on 12 July 1765, wrote to Rockingham, when his Administration was being formed, suggesting office for Hunt because of his 'steadiness, and invariable attachment to our friends

and the Whig cause'.[4] But there is no evidence that Hunt desired office, and he never held any. In Rockingham's list, November 1766, he is classed as 'Whig'; in Charles Townshend's of January 1767 as 'Administration'; and in Newcastle's, March 1767, as 'doubtful or absent'. His name does not appear either in the division lists on the land tax, 27 Feb. 1767, or on the nullum tempus bill, 17 Feb. 1768.

In 1768 Hunt topped the poll, and in the ensuing Parliament, over Wilkes and the Middlesex election voted consistently with Opposition, present in almost every division for which a list is extant; similarly on Grenville's Election Act, 25 Feb. 1774. In the next Parliament he again voted steadily with Opposition, and was mostly present at important divisions. The *Public Ledger* wrote of Hunt in 1779: 'A very upright Member of Parliament, of Whig principles, and generally votes in the minority.'

John Robinson naturally classed him as an opponent, and in his survey of July 1780 wrote about Bodmin: 'It is said that Mr. Hunt will be thrown out', but added he feared that 'Sir James Laroche may fall'—which did happen. The *English Chronicle* wrote in 1780:

> *George Hunt, Esq.* is a gentleman of independent fortune, and resides in the neighbourhood of this borough, in which he possesses sufficient influence to command an exclusive nomination for at least one Member. He has had the honour of representing it above thirty years, during which period he has never condescended to accept any favour, nor to become the creature of any Administration. He is attached to no set of political tenets in particular, but following the dictates of an independent and upright mind, has uniformly voted for or against such a system as he thought any way advantageous or inimical to the real interests of his country. Since the commencement of the American war, he has been a steady opponent to all the measures of ministry, and has taken a very active part both in town and country in resisting the effect of measures, in his estimation, so eminently injurious to the State. He can neither be said to possess the shining qualities necessary for constituting a public orator, nor the systematic solidity requisite in a great statesman, but is nevertheless eminently qualified for the important trust he holds, viz. the honest representative of a free people.

He voted with the Opposition in the decisive divisions 1781–March 1782; for Shelburne's peace preliminaries, 18 Feb. 1783; but also for Fox's East India bill, 27 Nov. 1783; and against Pitt in the divisions preceding the dissolution of 1784. He did not stand again at the general election but ceded his seat to his brother Thomas. No speech of his is recorded during his 31 years in the House.

He died 8 Nov. 1798.

[1] Hunt to Edw. Eliot, 2 May 1752, Eliot mss at Port Eliot. [2] Add. 32907, ff. 461–2; Namier, *Structure*, 302. [3] Add. 5726D, f. 158. [4] Add. 32967, f. 349.

L.B.N.

## HUNT, Thomas (c.1723–89), of Mollington, Cheshire.

BODMIN 1784–11 Oct. 1789

*b.* c.1723, 3rd s. of Thomas Hunt, and bro. of George Hunt (q.v.). *educ.* Queen's Oxf. 1739; M. Temple 1737; I. Temple 1746, called 1747. *m.* 11 Dec. 1765, Mary, da. of Peter Bold (q.v.) of Bold Hall, Lancs., 2da.

Returned for Bodmin in a contested election, Hunt was classed as a follower of the Portland-Fox Opposition both in William Adam's list of 1784 and in North's list of 1788. He voted steadily against Pitt. On 2 Dec. 1788, R. Burton wrote to Lord Sandwich[1] that his 'Western friend'[2] had said the following words which he allowed Burton to write down and send to Sandwich:

> that he should be for the sole Regency of the Prince of Wales and that he hoped in any Administration under that Regency, he should always vote in support of their measures.

He further authorized Sandwich 'to acquaint the Prince of Wales with this determination'.

There is no record of his having spoken in the House. He died 11 Oct. 1789.

[1] Royal archives, Windsor. [2] Identified in Sandwich's covering letter of same date, ibid.

L.B.N.

## HUNTER, John (?1724–1802), of Gubbins, nr. Potter's Bar, Herts.

LEOMINSTER 1784–June 1797

*m.* a wid., Anne (*d.*1780).[1]
Director, E.I. Co. 1781–4, 1786–9, 1791–4, 1796–9, 1801–2; dep. chairman 1794–5.
Sheriff, Herts. 1780–1.

Hunter, 'by long success in trade as a free merchant in the East Indies . . . raised a very ample fortune, upwards of £100,000, and arrived to a seat in the East India direction'.[2] In July 1777 he bought the estate of Gobions or Gubbins in Hertfordshire, and in 1780 unsuccessfully contested Milborne Port in opposition to the Medlicott interest. Before the general election of 1784 Hunter appears as a candidate of George Rose's in Robinson's lists of those for whom seats were to be found, and willing to pay £2,000, or £2,500, or perhaps £3,000.[3] He was returned for Leominster after a contest. He supported Pitt's Administration and voted for parliamentary reform, 18 Apr. 1785. There is no record of his having spoken in the House before 1790.

He died 16 Dec. 1802, aged 78.

[1] Cussans, *Herts.* 13–14, 297; *Gent. Mag.* 1803, p. 88; Hunter's will, PCC 39 Marriott. [2] *Gent. Mag.* loc. cit. [3] Laprade, 128–29.

M.M.D.

## HUNTER, Thomas Orby (c.1716–69), of Crowland, Lincs. and Waverley Abbey, Surr.

WINCHELSEA 1741–Jan. 1759, 5 Apr. 1760–20 Oct. 1769

*b.* c.1716, o.s. of Maj.-Gen. Robert Hunter, gov. of New York 1710–19 and of Jamaica 1729–34, by Elizabeth, da. and h. of Sir Thomas Orby, 1st Bt., of Crowland, wid. of Lord John Hay. *m.* 4 Apr. 1749, Jacomina Caroline, gd.-da. of Hon. William Bellenden, gd.-da. of John, 2nd Lord Bellenden [S], 4s. 3da. *suc.* to Crowland Abbey and other estates of his uncle Sir Charles Orby, 3rd Bt., Feb. 1724; and fa. 31 Mar. 1734.

Dep.-paymaster of the forces in Flanders 1742–8; commissary to treat with France 1748; ld. of Admiralty Nov. 1756–Apr. 1757, July 1757–Apr. 1763; superintendent of supplies to the allied armies in Germany Dec. 1758–Apr. 1760; ld. of Treasury Apr. 1763–July 1765.

Hunter was connected politically with Pitt, who in 1746 became his chief at the pay office. On 13 Nov. 1755 he followed Pitt in voting against the Address. When the Pitt-Devonshire Administration was being formed in October 1756, H. B. Legge told Sir Robert Wilmot 'that something must be done for two or three of his friends', and mentioned Hunter and Samuel Martin.[1] Hunter was appointed a lord of the Admiralty, which office he retained under the Pitt-Newcastle Administration.

He was really a man of business, and not an effective parliamentarian (he rarely spoke in the House). In December 1758 he undertook the exacting and important post of superintendent of supplies to the armies in Germany, which vacated his seat in Parliament (it was held for him by his brother-in-law, George Gray). Pressed by Newcastle to keep down expenses and by Pitt to ensure that the army never went short, he seems to have done a difficult job admirably—an honest man amongst the shady crew of commissaries. He wrote to Newcastle on 31 Jan. 1759:[2]

> I do with great truth assure your Grace that though I rise every morning at six o'clock and give a constant and close attention to my business till midnight, I find the time too short to despatch what is already under my care.

'He is a very sensible, able man, and does his duty very well', wrote Newcastle to Granby on 14 Aug. 1759;[3] and Peter Taylor told James Harris in 1763 'that Mr. Hunter had acted honourably and kept down the expenses'.[4]

When on 21 Mar. 1759 Hunter applied to Newcastle for a pension for his mother-in-law (recently left a widow), he pleaded 'the distress I was obliged to leave my family in to obey your Grace's commands'.[5] Towards the end of the year his health deteriorated, and he asked leave to come home at the close of the campaign. But to Harris in May 1763 he gave a different reason for relinquishing his employment:[6]

> Mr. Hunter in talking over the German war said as usual that Pitt opened the flood-gates of expense, [and] gave Prince Ferdinand powers to call for what men and money he pleased; that Pitt . . . did this to make his court to the old King, contrary to the sentiments and endeavours of the Duke of Newcastle . . .; that he (Hunter), who was sent over to regulate expenses and who did it at first with some success, finding all his endeavours after the battle of Minden vain, determined from that time to resign.

In Bute's list of December 1761 Hunter was classed as his follower. In December 1762 Henry Fox offered him the place of receiver-general of the customs, said to be worth £2,500 per annum, but incompatible with a seat in Parliament. To Bute, Fox wrote on 18 Dec.:[7]

> Mr. Hunter has just left me. He has no thought of quitting Parliament, and you can not have a worthier friend than he is in it. He is much obliged by the offer though he declines it. He wishes to be surveyor of the woods, and I wish you could contrive it for him.

This proved impracticable, but when the Grenville Administration was formed Hunter was promoted to the Treasury Board.

In July 1765 he followed Grenville into opposition; voted against the repeal of the Stamp Act, 22 Feb. 1766; and against the Chatham Administration on the land tax, 27 Feb. 1767 and the nullum tempus bill, 17 Feb. 1768. At the general election of 1768 he stood at Winchelsea with Lord Thomond on the Egremont interest, and was returned after a contest. He remained a follower of Grenville to the end, but there is no record of his having voted in the Parliament of 1768. He died 20 Oct. 1769.

[1] Wilmot to Devonshire, 22 Oct. 1756, Devonshire mss. [2] Add. 32887, f. 414. [3] Add. 32894, f. 157. [4] Harris's memorandum, 24 July 1763, Malmesbury mss. [5] Add. 32889, f. 179. [6] Harris's memorandum, 20 May 1763, Malmesbury mss. [7] Bute mss.

J.B.

## HUNTER BLAIR, James (1741–87), of Dunskey, Wigtown.

EDINBURGH    29 Oct. 1781–Aug. 1784

*b.* 21 Feb. 1741, 2nd s. of John Hunter of Milnholm and Brownhill, merchant, by Anne, da. and coh. of William Cunninghame of Brownhill, Ayr. *educ.* Ayr sch.; Edin. Univ. *m.* 12 Dec. 1770, Jane, da. of John Blair of Dunskey, niece of David Kennedy (q.v.), 10th Earl of Cassillis [S], 10s. 4da. After 1777, when his w. suc. her bro. to Dunskey estates, assumed add. name of Blair. *cr.* Bt. 27 June 1786.

Ld. provost Edinburgh 1784–6.
Jt. King's printer and stationer 1785.[1]

Hunter began his business career at the age of 15, as an apprentice in the Coutts bank in Edinburgh. In 1762 he became a partner when the firm was reorganized under Robert Herries as senior partner.[2]

In 1763 Hunter was brought on to the Edinburgh town council by Lord Milton to support the interest of James Coutts, who wrote to William Mure, 9 Sept. 1763:[3] 'Hunter . . . is, I think, one of the most promising young men I ever knew; it would be a pity politics should do him any hurt.' Hunter lost his seat on the council in 1768 and thereafter was immersed in business. The firm's activities included the formation of the London Exchange Banking Company in 1771 for the issue of travellers cheques, an undertaking which led to a breach with the Couttses. 'Cheerful and fond of society, . . . ever ready to promote the interest' of his friends, and 'capable of the most unwearied application', Hunter had a high reputation. But his partner Sir William Forbes records:

> In his temper there was a degree of warmth . . . which . . . in the heat of an argument occasionally bordered on vehemence and impetuosity . . . In his notions of right and wrong he was rigid and even stern, and he had no allowance to make [for] . . . any departure from the standard he had formed of propriety of conduct.

After Herries obtained the tobacco contract from the French farmers general in 1771 Hunter, 'who managed the department of the tobacco purchases, did not always take the best method of smoothing matters' with the Glasgow merchants. When the firm almost lost the contract in 1774 Hunter and Forbes, disliking Herries's speculative business methods, dissolved the partnership, relinquished their share in the London Exchange Bank, and thereafter confined their activities to the Edinburgh banking business.[4]

Re-elected to the Edinburgh town council in 1777, Hunter supported the party of Sir Lawrence Dundas, and at the 1780 general election strongly opposed the return of William Miller, the Government candidate. When Sir Lawrence, after winning his petition in March 1781, died in the following September, Henry Dundas wrote to John Robinson, 8 Oct. 1781:[5]

> I was much relieved by receiving a message . . . that Mr. Hunter Blair would be unanimously chosen if my friends would concur with him, and that he was to come in under the previous declaration of acting cordially with Government . . . I believe him perfectly sincere in all this; at the same time, the party by which he is chosen and which in truth is the party left by Sir Lawrence Dundas must be broke and the town of Edinburgh brought under some respectable patronage on which Government can rely . . . I have . . . told [Mr. Hunter Blair] plainly that he must lay his account that the interest of the Duke of Buccleuch in Edinburgh is what Government will continue to support . . . This being steadily adhered to, you may be

perfectly assured that before twelve months is over Mr. Hunter Blair himself and the whole council of Edinburgh will be completely and permanently placed, as they used to be, in the hands of Government.

Hunter Blair accepted the situation with some reservations. Opposed to the continuance of the American war, in his speech at his election dinner on 29 Oct. he said:[6]

> I am determined in the present embarrassing conjuncture to support very earnestly every measure of Administration which my judgment shall approve. At the same time I give you the fullest assurance that the prosperity of the British Empire, of this great city, and of you my constituents, shall be the constant object of my attention.

His first recorded vote, 20 Feb. 1782, was with Administration on the censure of the Admiralty, but he voted with the Opposition on 22 and 27 Feb. on Conway's motion against the war. He again divided with the Government on 8 and 15 Mar. on Cavendish's censure motion and Rous's motion of no confidence. He voted for Shelburne's peace preliminaries, 18 Feb. 1783; did not vote on Fox's East India bill; and in December 1783 was listed 'doubtful' by Robinson. By January Hunter Blair was listed as a supporter of Pitt and was returned at the general election as an Administration candidate. A few months later he vacated his seat to make way for Dundas's friend, Sir Adam Fergusson. Only one speech of his is recorded—on 4 Aug. 1784 when he opposed the new duties on linen and cotton and 'proved his extensive knowledge of the trade and manufactures of Scotland. His arguments were pointed and conclusive.'[7]

At Michaelmas he was elected lord provost of Edinburgh and during his two year term of office actively promoted the rebuilding of the University and the construction of the South Bridge over the Cowgate. He died 1 July 1787. Sir William Forbes wrote of him:

> As a magistrate he was active and zealous . . . as a senator he was honestly independent . . . Too early and too deeply immersed in business, he . . . was therefore but little acquainted with books or literature; but he possessed . . . great knowledge of the world and an almost intuitive discernment of the characters of men.[8]

[1] *Scots Mag.* 1785, p. 624. [2] Sir W. Forbes, *Mems. of a Banking House*, 15–19. [3] *Caldwell Pprs.* ii (1), p. 192. [4] Forbes, 29–36, 45, 66. [5] H. Furber, *Hen. Dundas*, 195–7. [6] *Scots Mag.* 1781, p. 55. [7] Stockdale, iii. 391. [8] Forbes, 65–66.

E.H.-G.

## HUSKE, John (1724–73).[1]

MALDON        26 Apr. 1763–Oct. 1773

*b.* 3 July 1724, at Portsmouth, New Hampshire, s. of Ellis Huske by Mary, da. of Ichabod Plaisted, judge of probate, N.H. *educ.* at Boston. *unm.*

Chief clerk and deputy to the treasurer of the chamber Dec. 1756–Mar. 1761.

Huske's father, a brother of Lt.-Gen. John Huske, settled at Portsmouth, N.H., and through his brother-in-law Samuel Plaisted, who was married to a daughter of Benning Wentworth, governor of New Hampshire 1741–67, became connected with the 'Wentworth political dynasty'. A member of the New Hampshire provincial council 1733–55, justice of the superior court 1739–49, and chief justice 1749–54, he was also postmaster of Boston 1734–54, and deputy postmaster general for the colonies, in which office he preceded Benjamin Franklin. He died at Boston 24 Apr. 1755, bankrupt.

John Huske started as a merchant in Boston,[2] and came over to England in 1748. At the general election of 1754 he appears at Great Bedwyn as agent for Roger Townshend (younger brother of George and Charles Townshend) against the candidates of the patrons of the borough Lord Bruce and Lord Verney—'they join in interest', read Newcastle's election notes, 'and all the neighbouring gentlemen concur, and yet an opposition is apprehended'. 20 Mar.: 'Mr. Huske, General Huske's relation, makes great opposition.' 'General Huske to be spoken to by Lord Cardigan.' 21 Mar.: 'Mr. Huske is gone down making great expense.' On 25 Mar., three candidates were named, Robert Brudenell, Roger Townshend, and William Sloper: 'It is supposed, the two last are supported by an unknown hand.'[3] Finally the original candidates, Brudenell and Metcalfe, quitted, but so did Roger Townshend; and nothing more appears about this first electoral adventure of Huske's.

When Charles Townshend was appointed treasurer of the chamber in December 1756, he made Huske his deputy: theirs became a standing connexion.

Huske's next recorded exploit was in a by-election at Hull, of which the most coherent account appears in a letter of 4 July 1757 from Lord Downe to the Duke of Devonshire:[4]

> I came last night from Hull, where I was detained longer than I expected by an alarm that Sir George Metham received by one Huske coming down as agent to Roger Townshend with a letter of recommendation from Charles Townshend of him to the mayor, which letter met with nothing but the contempt it deserved and thus Mr. Huske finding that he could make no impression even upon the mob which I had secured, and which he expected great matters from, thought it yesterday most prudent to retire which saved us the trouble of throwing him into the Humber which would most undoubtedly have been his fate had he attempted anything. The election was to have been this morning.

In the 'Schedule of papers sent from Downing Street to Sudbrook'[5] after Charles Townshend's death, a now missing bundle is mentioned of 'Letters from Lady Townshend to Mr. Huske, written in the summer 1757'; and a few references to the Hull adventure occur in Charles Townshend's letters to his mother.[6] On 13 July he sent Lady Townshend 'a letter to the mayor of Hull, and also letters upon the same subject to Lord Downe, Lord Carlisle, and such persons of the county as I have any pretence to write to'; for her to post if she approved of them—obviously some kind of *post mortem* on the affair. On 2 Aug.:

Your Ladyship has probably heard from Mr. Huske an exact account of his wild project at Hull, to which I was no party, and from which I ordered him to desist as soon as I knew he was engaged in it . . . I am distressed . . . that every step I shall take to punish the author will oblige me to expose, if not ruin, Mr. Huske, whose behaviour to me would indeed well justify what my temper is nevertheless unwilling to bring upon him.

And on 6 Sept.:

I hope you will keep Lord Downe's letter and apply it as your Ladyship pleases, for I am sure it is your goodness to me makes you desire to have it. The mayor of Hull had not as yet sent me a copy of Mr. Huske's letter to him, but enclosed you receive Lord Carlisle's answer.

The matter long continued to rankle—'after the vexatious affair of Hull', wrote Lady Townshend to Charles in June 1760, 'I am always *apprehensive* of Mr. *Hurst's* [Huske's] *mistakes*'.[7]

General Huske died 3 Jan. 1761, leaving nearly £42,000 to friends, servants, and relatives, but nothing to his nephew.[8] There were constant ups and downs in the financial position of Huske, a tough, unscrupulous adventurer.

Charles Townshend wrote to Chase Price (q.v.), another plunger, on 4 Oct. 1765:[9]

I should hope you have heard Huske's loss exaggerated, at least I am told he has not yet suffered much. He is incurable; he was easy; he has been in infinite distress, and yet neither the knowledge of misery or the enjoyment of affluence have had the power to prevent him returning to play for the whole of his fortune. At least I am told this is true.

Nothing is known of Huske's having stood at the general election of 1761, which can be accounted for by financial distress only; and in April 1763 Bamber Gascoyne refers to Townshend having relieved Huske 'from his distresses when deservedly disinherited by his father' (in fact Huske's father did not disinherit him[10]). When, however, in December 1762 Welbore Ellis, Townshend's successor at the War Office, had to seek re-election, 'Mr. Huske', wrote Fox to Bute on the 21st, 'is gone to Aylesbury to oppose Ellis, with a great sum of money'.[11] But apparently Huske did not stand the poll.

When c.17 Apr. 1763 Gascoyne was appointed to office, at the ensuing Maldon by-election Huske intervened with a mixture of mob-raising ability and ruthlessness. Gascoyne immediately turned to George Grenville who replied by assuring him of Government support.[12] Next he wrote to Charles Jenkinson, secretary to the Treasury, 21 Apr.:[13]

I have herewith sent you a list of the freemen of Maldon who are in office under the Government, to desire an immediate conveyance to them that they are to assist me; for I am sorry to tell you, that they are to a man almost against me. The opposition to me is carried on with a great violence and open bribery. Ribbons with 'Liberty, property and *no excise*' are the ornament of my opponents' booths and carriages, and some other devices of this sort which I do not choose to mention. Guineas and scraps of *North Britons* are scattered all over the town and I can assure you that the opposition is founded by that ingenious gentleman Mr. Wilkes and his crew and is more immediately at Government than me.

Besides, Gascoyne appealed to Townshend who was amazed at Huske's rashness and 'ignorant of his intentions'; and gave Gascoyne a letter to send to Huske—'you will see how strongly it is worded', wrote Gascoyne to John Strutt; also one to John Bullock. 'If these do not do I know not what will.'

Meantime John Bindley (q.v.), commissioner of the Excise, explained to Jenkinson how the canvassing of the excisemen, an affair 'of the most delicate nature', had to be done, and William Hunter of the custom house, on 26 Apr., how his own had been 'strictly upright and consistent with the freedom of elections'.[14] For Huske had taken action. He wrote to Grenville complaining of Gascoyne having declared to the officers of the revenue who were freemen at Maldon that Grenville had written him a letter which 'commands them to vote for him upon a penalty of losing their places immediately'. Grenville denied having authorized Gascoyne to make such a declaration, and, while enclosing Huske's letter, remarked to Gascoyne that he looked upon these 'extraordinary and unjustifiable assertions' as 'mere election artifice'.[15] Gascoyne, in reply, assured Grenville of the 'falsity' of the charge:[16]

I was yesterday to my great surprise sent for by Huske to the custom house of this place and when I came there among a multitude of people I was charged by Mr. Huske with having used the unwarrantable means alluded in his. I immediately denied the assertion and called on him to produce his authority which he refused. Lord Tylney, Sir Robert Long and Mr. Houblon were present. The wrath of this gentleman and his friends was very great when they thought they should lose the Government interest, and therefore wrote that letter by way of getting that kind of answer which might induce the placemen to vote for them, which would much injure my election.

Anyhow, Huske's 'election craft' did the trick. Gascoyne, who in 1761, without Government support, had topped the poll with 400 votes, now obtained only 254 against Huske's 438. Still by June 1763, Edward Richardson,[17] a City agent of Jenkinson's, named Huske as one of his 'new acquisitions' to Government, his mind having been freed from wrong 'surmises'—'all Gasconade'. And in none of the divisions over Wilkes and general warrants is Huske found voting against the Government, not even on 18 Feb. 1764, though Charles Townshend did so.

In the House Huske was during his first session a fairly frequent speaker, almost exclusively on American revenue and trade—'a wild, absurd man, very conversant with America', Walpole called him.[18] On the Address, 16 Nov. 1763, notes Harris, Huske 'was short, but spoke well upon American revenue'; 31 Jan. 1764, 'proposed an entire new bill of his own—a capitation tax, I think—to be extended through Scotland, Ireland and America'; on 9 Mar., 'gave us ample detail of America, and of our funds there, that were to raise £500,000' (and 'fell on the West Indians', which made Beckford fall on Huske 'as a North American'); on the 22nd spoke for reducing the 3d. tax on molasses imported to America; on the 23rd spoke about the King's quit rents in America, and 'opposed and prated' over the drawback on linens and calicoes exported to America; on the 26th, still on the American bill, 'was *seen*, not *heard*, to talk for near an hour'. Thus much from James Harris's parliamentary reports; to which an important addition is made by Charles Garth, not yet a Member but who as agent for South Carolina carefully followed debates on American affairs. On 17 Apr. 1764 he wrote to the committee of the Commons House of South Carolina about the 15th resolution of the American bill for levying stamp duties, an 'alarming proposition to all concerned in or for the plantations':

> The chancellor of the Exchequer at first proposed it as a measure to take place this sessions, but Mr. Alderman Beckford and Mr. Huske signifying their wish to have the colonies apprized of the intention of Parliament, Mr. Grenville readily acquiesced, declaring it was far from his inclination to press any measure upon any part of the dominions without giving them time to be heard, should they have objections thereto.[19]

This certainly runs counter to assertions widely believed that Huske was a supporter, or even originator, of the Stamp Act. As such he was burnt in effigy at Boston, and reviled in a poem, *Oppression*, printed in London, and twice reprinted in 1765 at Boston and New York.[20]

There is no record of Huske having spoken in the House during January–March 1765; not even when the Stamp Act was before the House in February—he may have been abroad: 'I congratulate you upon the arrival of Mr. Huske into this kingdom who made his appearance at the House on Monday last [25 Feb.]', wrote Gascoyne to Strutt on the 28th.[21] Was he pre-occupied with a shady law-case in which he was then involved? In Michaelmas term 1764 an information against him was moved for having been concerned with others in a fraud in October 1762: he was indicted in 1765, and tried on 12 June before Lord Mansfield. It is difficult to obtain a clear picture of the case from the materials in the Public Record Office,[22] while Gascoyne's running commentary on it in letters to Strutt is too virulently hostile to be of full value. According to him Huske tried to circumvent the prosecution, and even to avail himself of parliamentary privilege, but gave in, 'Mr. Sandys and Lord Warkworth having spoke to him that they should move the House to enforce him, and the Speaker also assured him that he had no privilege in such a case.'[23] In the end the accused were acquitted, the plaintiff's behaviour having also been shady.

In April 1765 Huske was again prominent in debates on America: 'flamed' against an American mutiny bill; called for extracts from Gage's letter about quartering soldiers; and 'battled clause by clause' against the bill, 'though totally disarmed of its offensive clause, the quartering soldiers'.[24] Although Huske was on friendly terms with the Grenville Administration, and at times seems to have aspired to employment,[25] he switched over quickly to the Rockinghams—Charles Lloyd, Grenville's secretary, wrote to Jenkinson on 24 Aug. 1765: 'Huske is talked of to succeed Mellish as secretary to the Treasury.'[26] And when on the reassembly of Parliament, Grenville, on 17 Dec. 1765, moved an amendment to the Address declaring the American provinces in rebellion, Huske spoke against it.[27] He spoke again on 14 Jan. 1766 'on the impracticability of the Stamp Act'; 17 Jan., for rescinding the order to print the American papers; on 28 Jan., for receiving the petition from the Stamp Act Congress (Pitt and his followers spoke for it but the Rockinghams mainly against it); on 3 Feb.—against Grenville.[28] On 7 Feb. once more against Grenville on his motion for 'enforcing' laws in America.[29] Lastly, on 24 Feb., he spoke for the repeal of the Stamp Act.[30] In short, his record during these months was irreproachable from the American point of view, and it seems certain that there was no tergiversation on his part with regard to the Stamp Act: had there been any, Harris, a thoroughgoing Grenvillian, would not have failed to point it out in his notes. In the budget debate on 18 Apr. 1766 Huske spoke again on the Government side: 'wild and saucy', writes Harris.

On the advent of the Chatham Administration with Townshend at the Exchequer Huske received no office—the relations between the two seem to have been less close than before: in November 1766 Rockingham listed Huske as 'doubtful', and not as a sure follower of Administration, as which he was, however, listed by Townshend in January and by Newcastle in March 1767. Among the Townshend papers at Dalkeith House there is only one important letter from Huske, dated 9 Apr. 1767, which shows that he was consulted about the American duties, as he had been by the Rockinghams, but that some essential information concerning Townshend's intentions he had only at second-hand. He starts by stating what duties he had proposed to lay on wine, oil, and fruit imported into America.

These duties were judged too high by Lord Rockingham; and that Administration had agreed to admit those articles into America direct from the place of their growth, at a much inferior duty, but I cannot recollect what rates they fixed. You may have them from Mr. Dowdeswell, or from Mr. Rose Fuller who took a copy of them at a meeting I was on at the occasion at Mr. Dowdeswell's. Mr. Cooper can give them to you. They are necessary for you to see as they were communicated to the American agents and by them sent to America, or at least by some of them; but they were never proposed in the committee of supply, though Mr. Dowdeswell carried them to the House for that purpose, which was owing to the difficulties which arose about the free-ports.

Permit me to remark to you, that it is certain that by a regulation of the trade of America for the reciprocal interest of both mother and children, you may have a sufficient revenue to pay all Great Britain's expense for her colonies and in a manner perfectly agreeable to both under your conduct; but be assured no regulation or measure that is to raise money can be agreeable or practicable in the continent colonies till you give them a currency. Till then you are demanding brick without straw. A bill for this purpose was drawn up by Mr. Franklin and myself last year; and I moved to bring it in with the *seeming* approbation of the ministers; but Mr. Dyson and Lord Clare opposing it, though they knew not one tittle of the plan, or of the nature of a good or bad paper currency, nor never will know any more of it than I do of the Mogul's cabinet, it was carried to postpone it to this session when to this moment nothing is brought into the House about it.

I have been told to-day by a gentleman, who said he had it from you, that you intended to impose a duty upon *salt* imported into America! . . . permit me, Sir, to assure you that a more fatal imposition to both Great Britain and her colonies could not be devised . . . I shall conclude with saying your account will be finished as soon as I can stand and move without assistance.

It is not clear what account he refers to, but the most likely would be of the treasurer of the chamber, the only office dealing with finance in which he was engaged with Townshend.

No detailed reports having been found for the last two years of the 1761–8 Parliament, it is not possible to follow Huske's part in debates during the Chatham Administration. He was absent through illness from the division on the land tax, 27 Feb. 1767, but voted with the Government on the nullum tempus bill, 17 Feb. 1768.

In 1768 Gascoyne and his friend John Strutt did their best to raise an opposition at Maldon against Huske who stood on a joint interest with John Bullock; and naturally a good many voters were 'desirous for an opposition . . . chiefly for what they can get'. But Huske secured re-election. In the new House he is not known to have spoken or voted on Wilkes and the Middlesex election. His most important interventions were again on American questions. When in September 1768 the Pennsylvania assembly sent through its agents, Benjamin Franklin and Richard Jackson, petitions to the Crown, Lords, and Commons against being taxed by the British Parliament, Jackson thought that 'what he had to say in support of it, would have more weight if it were *offered* by another';[31] which was done, on 7 Dec., by Huske. When the petition met with considerable opposition, Huske remarked: 'The agent who gave me the petition has received positive orders to present it to this House . . . what will be the consequence of giving no relief to any petition from America? The inhabitants of Pennsylvania would not come into the desire of New York of stopping the use of manufactures, they did this a second time.'[32] Finally he withdrew the petition saying that if it was rejected 'it would probably be the last ever offered them from any colony on any occasion'. He continued co-operating with the colonial agents—thus on 21 Jan. 1769, W. S. Johnson, agent for Connecticut, mentions having met him together with Jackson and Barlow Trecothick and several agents 'on American affairs'.[33]

Huske's last recorded speech in the Commons was on 8 Mar. 1769 when he divided the House over Burke's motion on the St. George's Fields riots. England was getting too hot for him: on 11 Dec. 1768 Gascoyne wrote to Strutt[34] about an 'intended benevolence to Mr. Huske'—'a place in America'; and when this fell through, Huske decamped to Paris. John White, Strutt's election agent at Maldon, wrote to him on 1 June 1770 that early in the year Townshend's widow tried to have Huske arrested 'if found in England'.

You must know, Sir, the Government has demanded of that lady between 30 and 40 thousand pounds due from Mr. Townshend at the time when Huske was secretary to him. It appears by the books that Huske defrauded Mr. Townshend of chief parts of the money. The lady was determined to bring him to justice if he could be found. She offered Brownton a thousand pounds if he could procure him. He did come to England about the time but made a very short stay. He returned in a day or two after they began to seek him . . . He is a complete villain . . . Mr. Clark tells me he heard in London last week there was an extent out against him and, farther, that he and two more such had actually opened a banker's shop in Paris. Upon the whole I do imagine he will never appear in the House of Commons again . . . I have lately stuck up at the town hall his last dying speech.

White's allegation of Huske's default is borne out by an entry in the accounts of the treasurer of the chamber, which refers to vouchers and books 'in the possession of Mr. Huske . . . who absconded with them and resided abroad and died there'.

O'Gorman, recommended by Huske to Franklin, wrote to Franklin from Paris, 4 Jan. 1773, that Huske expected soon to return to London.[35] But apparently he did not, and died in Paris in October 1773.[36]

On 22 Dec. 1777, W. Hayes, who had once been *valet de chambre* to Huske, wrote to Franklin on behalf of Huske's 'orphan son' apprenticed to Hooper of Wilmington, North Carolina, asking him 'to recommend the young man to some of his friends in that part of the world'.[37]

[1] Our thanks are due to Whitfield J. Bell jun., associate editor of the Benjamin Franklin Papers, for help in our researches into Huske's American antecedents. [2] F. S. Drake, *Dict. Am. Biog.* 469. [3] Add. 32995, ff. 81, 105, 111, 127. [4] Devonshire mss. [5] Townshend mss in the possession of the Duke of Buccleuch. [6] Townshend mss at Raynham. [7] Buccleuch mss. [8] *Gent. Mag.* 1761, p. 22. [9] Hatfield mss. [10] Gascoyne to Strutt, Strutt mss at Terling Place, Essex. For Ellis Huske's will see *Probate Recs. of N.H.* (State Ppr. ser. xxxiv), iv. 184-5. [11] Bute mss. [12] Grenville letter bk. [13] Add. 38200, f. 312. [14] *Jenkinson Pprs.* 148-50. [15] Grenville to Huske, Grenville letter bk. [16] Grenville mss (JM). [17] *Jenkinson Pprs.* 69. [18] *Mems. Geo. III*, ii. 213. [19] In transcripts of Chas. Garth's letter books, in the possession of Capt. W. Godsal, at Haines Hill, Berks. [20] *N. & Q.* (ser. 12), viii. 217, 335. [21] Strutt mss. [22] A. Pickersgill, 'Parlty. Elections in Essex 1759-74' (Manchester Univ. M.A. thesis). [23] Gascoyne to Strutt, 26 Apr. 1765, Strutt mss. [24] Harris's 'Debates', 1, 2, 30 Apr. 1765. [25] Gascoyne to Strutt, 26 Apr. 1765. [26] *Jenkinson Pprs.*, 380-1. [27] Harris's 'Debates'. [28] Fortescue, i. 226, 236, 247; Newdigate's 'Debates'. [29] Fortescue, i. 267. [30] Harris's 'Debates'; Newdigate's 'Debates'; Add. 32974, f. 79. [31] Franklin to Joseph Galloway, 9 Jan. 1769; C. van Doren, *Franklin's Autobiographical Writings*, 183-9 and *Franklin-Jackson Corresp.* 22. [32] Cavendish's 'Debates', Egerton 215, f. 283. [33] Diary of W. S. Johnson, Bancroft Transcripts, N.Y. Pub. Lib. [34] Strutt mss. [35] I. M. Hays, *Cal. Pprs. Benjamin Franklin*, i. 131; iii. 143. [36] Pickersgill, 65. [37] Hays, iii. 323.

L.B.N.

**HUSSEY, Richard** (?1715-70), of Truro, Cornw.

MITCHELL 24 Mar. 1755-1761
ST. MAWES 1761-1768
EAST LOOE 1768-11 Sept. 1770

*b.* ?1715, s. and h. of John Hussey, town clerk of Truro 1722-7. His mother was a Gregor, prob. of fam. of Trewarthenick, nr. Tregony. *educ.* Balliol, Oxf. 30 Oct. 1730, aged 15; M. Temple 1731, called 1742. *unm.*

Counsel to duchy of Cornw. 1752, to Admiralty 1757; K.C. 1760; bencher M. Temple 1760; attorney-gen. to the Queen 1761-Jan. 1770; auditor to duchy of Cornw. 1768.

On 12 Sept. 1753 Henry Pelham wrote about Mitchell to Lord Hardwicke:[1]

Mr. Hussey is a young lawyer greatly attached to the Boscawen family, and one who has a good personal interest in many parts of Cornwall. Lord Falmouth and the Admiral [Edward Boscawen] desired in the beginning of last winter that they might choose this gentleman in one of their boroughs. I told them in the room of one of themselves with all my heart, but I could not think of removing any of those recommended by the King to introduce a stranger, though never so worthy a man. With this they seemed contented, but I heard afterwards that Mr. Hussey had one or two places in view, in one he was to oppose Lord Edgcumbe's interest [Grampound], and in the other my own. This your Lordship may imagine I greatly objected to, and the Admiral promised to use his interest with Mr. Hussey to give it over, which he did at that time, but being I think Parliament mad he then sends me word that he was invited and could certainly carry it for Mitchell.

In a paper of 22 Mar. 1754, docketted 'Lord Falmouth's state of the borough of Mitchell',[2] Hussey is described as having 'the undoubted interest and majority at Mitchell'. He stood on a joint interest with Simon Luttrell, backed by Edgcumbe and Falmouth, and supported by Newcastle; and after a long and bitter struggle in the House was seated on petition.

In 1761 he was returned on the Falmouth interest for St. Mawes, and was classed in Bute's list as 'Admiralty and Government'. His stature as a lawyer was such that in December 1761 he was considered for the post of solicitor-general. Newcastle opposed his appointment, though he admitted Hussey was 'a very good and a very amiable man'; while Bute considered he 'had lately had great things done' for him.[3] Hussey appears in Fox's list of Members favourable to the peace preliminaries, and in the autumn of 1763 was classed by Jenkinson as 'pro'.

He turned against Grenville's Administration over Wilkes. He did not vote with the Opposition in the division of 15 Nov. 1763, but his speech in the debate on Wilkes's privilege, 24 Nov., was described by George Onslow as 'the finest . . . that ever was made for us'.[4] 'He was copious and learned, and reasoned well', wrote James Harris. 'No one on his side the question made so able a figure.' Like most West country Members he supported the attempt to repeal the cider duty. He voted against Administration over general warrants, 15 and 18 Feb. 1764, but with them on Nicolson Calvert's motion on *ex officio* informations, 4 Mar. 1765;[5] and was classed by Newcastle as a 'doubtful friend'.

Rockingham in July 1765 classed Hussey as 'doubtful', but in one of Newcastle's lists he is put down for the office of attorney-general.[6] On American policy he took a point of view nearer to that of the Rockingham Administration than of his friends Camden and Pitt. 'If the Stamp Act is illegal that of Navigation is illegal', he said on 3 Feb. 1766.[7] 'The obligation to obey must be entire or it cannot exist at all.' On 24 Feb. he spoke 'very finely indeed' both for repealing the Stamp Act and maintaining the right of taxation.[8]

When the Chatham Administration was formed it was generally expected that Hussey would be given a more responsible office. 'I am anxious to know Mr. Hussey's sentiments on the present system', wrote Grafton to Chatham, 17 Oct. 1766; to which Chatham replied: 'That gentleman's ability and weight are great indeed, and my esteem and honour for his character the highest imaginable', and referred Grafton to Camden.[9] According to Walpole,[10] Hussey refused 'any preferment', but he supported Chatham's Administration; and in 1768 was given a Government seat at East Looe.

On 25 Apr. 1768 Hussey attended a meeting of men of business to discuss the expulsion of Wilkes. 'Mr. Hussey was strongly against a second expulsion for the same offence, *in being the author of a political libel*', wrote Bradshaw to Grafton; and North: 'Mr. Hussey will certainly be against expelling Wilkes, though he declared he had not formed his opinion entirely.'[11] Yet Hussey voted for both the expulsion of Wilkes, 3 Feb. 1769, and the seating of Luttrell, 8 May 1769. On America he maintained his opinions: the Townshend duties, 'however inexpedient and impolitic', were neither an innovation nor unjust. 'When the Americans see you are resolute and determined', he said on 26 Jan. 1769,[12] 'they will . . . acknowledge their error, and own the supreme power of the mother country.'

When Camden was dismissed in January 1770 Hussey resigned his office of attorney-general to the Queen. Whether he followed Camden into opposition is not clear, for no further speeches by him are recorded; and he died 11 Sept. 1770.

Hussey was an able lawyer, but not a great parliamentary figure. He was universally respected. Walpole describes him as 'a very honest man'.[13] Lord John Cavendish wrote:[14] 'Of all the lawyers in the House of Commons he seems to me the ablest and the honestest'; and North:[15] 'He is a most amiable estimable man, and gives a credit to every question he supports.'

[1] Add. 35423, f. 162. [2] Add. 35592, ff. 290–1. [3] Add. 32932, ff. 238–239, 278. [4] Add. 32953, f. 37. [5] Harris's 'Debates'. [6] Fortescue, i. 128. [7] Newdigate's 'Debates'. [8] Add. 32974, f. 79. [9] *Chatham Corresp.* iii. 111; Grafton, *Autobiog.* 108. [10] *Mems. Geo. III*, ii. 269. [11] Grafton mss. [12] *Cavendish's Debates*, i. 197–8. [13] *Mems. Geo. III*, ii. 269. [14] To Portland, 1 Jan. 1768, Portland mss. [15] To Grafton, 26 Apr. 1768, Grafton mss.

J.B.

**HUSSEY, William** (1725–1813), of Upper Eldon, Hants, and Salisbury, Wilts.

| | |
|---|---|
| St. Germans | 11 June 1765–1768 |
| Hindon | 1768–1774 |
| Salisbury | 1774–26 Jan. 1813 |

*bap.* 1 Jan. 1725, s. of John Hussey, mayor of Salisbury in 1737, by his 2nd w. Margery, wid. of Richard Rumsey of Salisbury. *m.* (1) 9 Oct. 1752, Mary (*d.*21 May 1754), da. of John Eyre of Landford Lodge, Wilts., 1da.; (2) 5 Apr. 1758, Jane, da. of Robert Marsh, London merchant and gov. of Bank of England, 1s. 1da. (who m. 1778 William Drake jun., q.v.). *suc.* fa. 1739.

Hussey, who as a boy inherited considerable property in Wiltshire and Dorset from his father, became a clothier at Salisbury and made a fortune to which he added by his two marriages. In 1755 he became a common councillor at Salisbury, in 1756 an alderman, and in 1759 mayor. At the general election of 1761 he contested Hereford, but was overwhelmingly defeated. He declared himself a candidate at the Salisbury by-election of January 1765, but withdrew before the poll. Later the same year Hussey was recommended by Grenville to Edward Eliot for St. Germans, Lord Sandwich having persuaded Philip Stanhope to resign in favour of 'a very good friend to Government' who would pay him £500 compensation, and also 'the usual consideration' of £1,000 to the borough.[1] In Parliament Hussey seems at first to have followed Grenville; appears in Sir William Meredith's two lists of Members voting against the repeal of the Stamp Act, 22 Feb. 1766, though not in the printed list; was classed by Rockingham in November 1766 as 'Grenville', and as 'doubtful' by Townshend in January, and by Newcastle in March 1767.

At the general election of 1768 Hussey seems to have been invited to contest Hindon by an independent group in the borough, and was returned after a contest. In 1774 he achieved his ambition and was returned for his native borough of Salisbury which he continued to represent till his death.

Hussey now followed an independent line; he opposed North's Administration from the beginning, and strongly disapproved of the American war. 'In his political principles he is by no means violent' wrote the *English Chronicle* in 1781, 'but no man is more active against the measures of Administration, whom he opposes with vigour, but without rudeness or enthusiasm.' He supported Rockingham's Administration, declaring on 29 Apr. 1782 that 'he had the fullest reliance on the integrity of the present ministry; and as they came into place on a thorough conviction of being averse to the destructive measures which had for many years been pursued, those abuses, he trusted, would soon be abolished'. He voted for Shelburne's peace preliminaries, 18 Feb. 1783. After the formation of the Coalition he continued to criticize North, but voted for Fox's East India bill, 27 Nov. 1783, stating, however, that he did so merely because 'he thought some bill immediately necessary'. In Robinson's electoral survey drawn up in December 1783 he was classed as 'doubtful', and in the list of January 1784 as 'contra'. He was a member of the St. Alban's Tavern group which attempted to bring about a union between Pitt and Fox, and on 11 Feb. 1784 urged 'gentlemen on both sides . . . by such concessions as they could make, cordially and manfully [to] give way not to each other only, but to the calls and exigencies of their country'. And on 27 Feb. as 'one of those independent country gentlemen, who had never attached themselves to any party', again called for union.[2] After the failure of these attempts Hussey regularly voted with Opposition, though he seems always to have been considered completely independent.

During his first years in the House Hussey spoke on several occasions, and towards the end of North's Administration became one of the most frequent back-bench speakers, concentrating mainly on financial matters. Wraxall, who found him 'a dull debater, destitute of all the graces of elocution, tedious, and labouring under impediments of enunciation', conceded that he 'thoroughly understood all financial questions'; and was 'of recognized integrity', and 'exceedingly tenacious of the national purse'.[3] The *English Chronicle* also commended his abilities as financier, adding:

> The minister [North] always gives the strongest testimony on the communication of his taxes, by addressing himself to Mr. Hussey with pointed attention, watching his approbation, and replying by anticipation to such objections as this Member by the taciturn indications of his countenance seems to convey.

And on 31 Jan. 1781 North, replying in the House to Hussey's financial criticisms, 'acknowledged that he had frequently received great assistance and information from his abilities'. But though Hussey constantly advocated strict economy and supervision of all Government expenditure, he pressed for generous treatment of the navy which should be increased and strengthened, not 'by driblets', but by as many as 20,000 men. He thought that the House should 'know something of its management and its state'; and he himself had 'made it his business to go into the opportunities, and the efforts of the naval department'. He vigorously attacked the principle of fortifications; and pressed for the encouragement of the fishing industry—'an excellent nursery for the navy'.[4]

Hussey, who was a shareholder in the East India Company, frequently intervened in debates on its affairs; constantly criticized their management; opposed high dividends; and on 28 May 1782 'wished the whole of the direction and management of the East India Company was fixed in the hands of the ministers, that responsibility and influence might go together': 'it would be better for this country, if they had no possessions in the East Indies, than that they should remain governed as they were'. On 21 June 1786, he advocated throwing open the whole of the East India Company's trade.[5]

Hussey, who in 1780 was a member of the Wiltshire Committee of Association, declared on 3 June 1784 that he was 'a sincere well-wisher to such a reform as would give the people a more complete representation within these walls'.[6] Yet he did not vote for either of Pitt's reform proposals, 7 May 1783 and 18 Apr. 1785.

Hussey's 'spirit, consummate probity, and . . . independence'[7] seem to have gained him general respect, and he was described by Burke in 1790 as 'one of the most upright, able, and industrious members of the House'.[8] He died 26 Jan. 1813.

[1] See STANHOPE, Philip. [2] Debrett, vii. 74; ix. 634; xii. 189; xiii. 93, 223. [3] *Mems.* ii. 91; v. 123. [4] Debrett, i. 376, 183–5; v. 97; xx. 252. [5] Ibid. vii. 198; xx. 396. [6] Ibid. xv. 68. [7] *English Chron.* 1781. [8] Stockdale, xv. 157.

M.M.D.

## HUSSEY DELAVAL, *see* DELAVAL, John

## HUSSEY MONTAGU, Sir Edward (1721–1802),
of Ditton Park, Bucks. and Westown, co. Dublin.

TIVERTON 29 June 1758–11 May 1762

*b.* 1721, 1st s. of James Hussey of Westown by Catherine, da. of Richard Parsons, 1st Visct. Rosse [I]. *m.* secretly c.1743, Isabella, da. and coh. of John, 2nd Duke of Montagu, wid. of William, 2nd Duke of Manchester, 1s. 1da. (both *d.v.p.*). On *d.* of his fa.-in-law 1749, took add. name of Montagu. *suc.* fa. 1759. K.B. 27 Aug. 1753; *cr.* Baron Beaulieu 11 May 1762, Earl of Beaulieu 8 July 1784.

Edward Montagu lived in the shadow of his proud and wealthy wife: she, daughter and widow of dukes, was determined that her husband's rank should correspond to her fortune. Montagu was returned for Tiverton at Newcastle's recommendation, and himself seems never to have applied for a peerage. That was left to his wife, but her success in 1762 was short of what she had hoped: three days before her husband was created a peer, the family title of Montagu was given to the son of her younger sister, Lady Cardigan; and in 1766 the dukedom of Montagu was revived for Lord Cardigan. On this Lord Beaulieu went into opposition and his wife ceased to attend at court.

When in 1776 the Duke of Montagu was to be created Earl of Montagu with remainder to his daughter, Lady Beaulieu protested that she had been promised this title for her husband. But, the King wrote to North on 30 May 1776,

> she never had any promise from me, and no other proof can be necessary than her manifest appearances of neglect in never coming to court since the Duke of Montagu was advanced, which conduct has uniformly been followed by her son, and the political part Lord Beaulieu has taken if the others are not proofs sufficient show none of the family placed any hopes on me.

North recollected that he had given such a promise in 1772, but the King would not go back on his word to the Duke of Montagu. The affair blew over when Montagu waived his claim to the earldom.[1] Beaulieu was created an earl in 1784 by Pitt; even so, the title of Montagu was withheld from him.

He died 25 Nov. 1802.

[1] Fortescue, iii. 365-7.

J.B.

## HUSSEY MONTAGU, Hon. John (1747-87).

NEW WINDSOR    9 Nov. 1772-25 June 1787

*b.* 18 Jan. 1747, o.s. of Sir Edward Hussey Montagu (q.v.). *educ.* Eton 1762-5. *unm.* Styled Lord Montagu 1784-7.

Montagu was returned unopposed for Windsor in 1772 with the support of Administration.[1] In 1779 the *Public Ledger* wrote that he 'seldom attends the House, but when he does he votes with Opposition. He is no speaker.' This, though otherwise correct, seems hardly fair to Montagu in the matter of his attendance: between 1774 and 1782 he voted in 11 out of the 17 divisions for which lists are available. He voted for Shelburne's peace preliminaries, 18 Feb. 1783; did not vote on Fox's East India bill, 27 Nov. 1783; and supported Pitt.

He died 25 June 1787.

[1] North to Guilford [June 1776], Bodl. North mss.

J.B.

## HUTCHINGS (afterwards HUTCHINGS MEDLYCOTT), Thomas (c.1728-95), of Ven House, Milborne Port, Som.

MILBORNE PORT    22 Nov. 1763-May 1770
                 1780-Nov. 1781

*b.* c.1728, o.s. of John Hutchings of Lovestreet, Dorset by Elizabeth, da. of James Medlycott, M.P., sis. of Thomas Medlycott (q.v.). *m.* 21 Sept. 1766, Jane, da. of William Coles of Salisbury, 2s. 1da. *suc.* fa. 1737; uncle 21 July 1763, and took add. name of Medlycott.

Medlycott inherited his uncle's interest at Milborne Port, and succeeded him in the representation of the borough. His political conduct during his first spell in Parliament was variable and unpredictable. He voted with Opposition on general warrants, 18 Feb. 1764, was classed by Jenkinson as normally friendly to Government, but by Newcastle, 10 May 1764, as a 'sure friend' to Opposition. In July 1765 Rockingham classed him as 'doubtful'; and in November 1766 as 'Whig', but with a query; and he voted with the Chatham Administration on the land tax, 27 Feb. 1767, and the nullum tempus bill, 17 Feb. 1768. In the next Parliament his only known vote was with Opposition on the expulsion of Wilkes, 3 Feb. 1769.

In May 1770 Medlycott retired from Parliament, probably by arrangement with Administration, in favour of Lord Catherlough, who is said to have paid £3,000 for the seat. In 1772 the compromise with Edward Walter (q.v.), by which each recommended to one seat at Milborne Port, broke down; and at the by-election of that year Medlycott's candidate was defeated at the poll but returned on petition. In 1774 Medlycott and Walter each named two candidates and after a hard contest Medlycott again won on petition. But he had been put to considerable expense; and in 1779 accepted an offer from North to advance the money to buy out Walter, in return for one seat at Milborne Port being placed at the disposal of Government.[1]

At the general election of 1780 Medlycott returned himself and a Government candidate. On 8 Mar. 1781 he made his only reported speech:[2] a defence of Lord North's loan, which reads as if he himself had been consulted about it. In this speech he revealed that four years before he had subscribed to a loan—the only evidence of his engaging in such transactions. In November 1781 he vacated his seat in favour of another Government supporter. At the general election of 1784 Robinson classed Milborne Port among the 'open boroughs where seats may probably be obtained with expense';[3] in fact the sitting Members, both of whom supported Pitt, retained their seats.

Medlycott died 15 May 1795.

[1] See LUTTRELL, Hon. Temple Simon. [2] Debrett, ii. 216. [3] Laprade, 109.

J.B.

## HYDE, Lord, *see* VILLIERS, Hon. Thomas (*d.*1824)

## INCHIQUIN, Earl of, *see* O'BRIEN

## INGRAM, Charles (1727-78), of Templenewsam, Yorks.

HORSHAM    1747-14 Apr. 1763

*b.* 19 Mar. 1727, 1st s. of Col. the Hon. Charles

Ingram (s. of Arthur, 3rd Visct. Irwin [S]), by Elizabeth, da. and coh. of Charles Scarborough of Windsor, wid. of Francis Brace. *educ.* Westminster 1737–43. *m.* 28 June 1758, Frances Gibson, illegit. da. of Samuel Shepherd, M.P., London merchant, of Exning, Suff., 5da. *suc.* uncle as 9th Visct. Irwin [S] 14 Apr. 1763.

Groom of the bedchamber to the Prince of Wales 1756–60, to the King 1760–3.

Scottish representative peer 1768–*d.*

Ingram was returned for Horsham by his uncle, Viscount Irwin, who controlled both seats. Like him Ingram supported Administration, and was appointed groom of the bedchamber through Newcastle's influence. He is not included in Henry Fox's list of Members favourable to the peace preliminaries, December 1762, but a connexion of his, Thomas Ramsden, informed Jenkinson, 20 Nov. 1762, that Ingram was well inclined to support the Administration, and suggested that he should be summoned to the eve of session meeting of Parliament.[1]

On 5 Nov. 1763, Irwin, as he had now become, wrote to Pitt:[2] 'My inheriting a peerage has made a vacancy in Parliament for the borough of Horsham; and it is my great ambition, that you will do me the honour to name some friend of yours to supply my place.' Pitt nominated Robert Pratt, whom Irwin accepted, and had re-elected in 1768. But in 1774 Irwin returned two Administration candidates. He died 19 June 1778.

[1] *Jenkinson Pprs.* 90. [2] *Chatham Corresp.* ii. 266.

M.M.D.

## INNES, William (1719–95), of Lime Street Sq., London, and Blackheath, Kent.

ILCHESTER 1774–4 Dec. 1775

*b.* 29 July 1719, s. of Alexander Innes of Cathlaw, West Lothian, banker and merchant of Edinburgh, by Johanna, da. of Alexander Ainslie, Edinburgh merchant. *m.* 19 May 1753, Ann Wintle, *s.p.*

In 1749 Innes was established as a London merchant, trading with the West Indies where he had extensive family connexions.

In 1774 he was returned at Ilchester on the interest of Thomas Lockyer. There is no record of his having voted in the House, but on 8 Nov. 1775 he spoke at length in a debate on the army estimates.[1] He advocated a strong army to deal with America: 'You laid on the Stamp Act without power to enforce it: you were so weak to repeal it, without giving time to try what effect it might have in the ordinary course of things, owing to your own unsteady and factious pursuits at home.' Vigorous measures should be taken against the colonists: 'If our forefathers have been so negligent as not to give stability to the authority of this country over her

colonies, it is high time we should do it'; though peace

was recommended by some right honourable gentlemen who tell you the Declaratory Act (an Act passed while they themselves were in office) means nothing. That Act certainly meant something at the time it was made; the intention of it must at least have been a deception on this country to palliate the disgrace of repealing the Stamp Act.

Those advocates for a paltry and inglorious peace seem to depend too much on their rhetorical abilities; they wantonly sport with the constitution of this great nation, merely with a view to overturn the present ministry, under the pretence of rescuing their country from imminent danger . . . Let the Americans trust them, if they will; but . . . it would be the height of folly in this country to put confidence in such men a second time.

Innes is reported to have made one other speech, 13 Nov. 1775,[2] when he supported an increase in the land tax 'as it did not affect him'—to which Joseph Mawbey replied that he would be glad to know what was Innes's qualification for a seat.

The defeated candidates at Ilchester petitioned against Innes and his fellow Member Peregrine Cust, and on 4 Dec. the election was declared void. Innes did not stand again for Parliament.

He died 14 Jan. 1795.

[1] Almon, iii. 136–47. [2] Ibid. 162.

M.M.D.

## INSKIP, *see* LADE

## IRBY, Sir William, 2nd Bt. (1707–75), of Whaplode, Lincs.

| | |
|---|---|
| LAUNCESTON | 24 Mar. 1735–1747 |
| BODMIN | 1747–1761 |

*b.* 8 Mar. 1707, o.s. of Sir Edward Irby, 1st Bt., of Whaplode, Lincs. by Dorothy, da. of Hon. Henry Paget of Dublin, yr. s. of William, 7th Lord Paget. *educ.* Westminster 1719–22. *m.* 26 Aug. 1746, Albinia, da. of Henry Selwyn of Matson, Glos., 2s. 1da. *suc.* fa. 11 Nov. 1718; and to unsettled estates of his cos. Henry Paget, 1st Earl of Uxbridge, 1743; *cr.* Baron Boston 10 Apr. 1761.

Page of honour to the King 1724–8; equerry to the Prince of Wales 1728–36; vice-chamberlain to the Princess of Wales 1736–51, chamberlain 1751–72; chairman of committees in the House of Lords 1770–*d.*

In 1747 Irby, returned by Thomas Pitt for both Old Sarum and Bodmin, chose to sit for Bodmin. In 1752 he advanced £1,000 to Pitt against a promise to return him for Old Sarum at the general election, or else to have the money repaid 'by the person who came in'.[1] But by the spring of 1753 Irby's thoughts were again turning toward Bodmin where his colleague George Hunt, possessed of a 'natural' interest in the borough, was planning to run his brother Thomas for Irby's seat at the general election, alleging that Irby was obnoxious to Henry Pelham. Irby therefore, in a letter of 3 May 1753,[2] appealed to Pelham for his recommendation —'you may depend firmly on my attachment to your interest in all respects'. He had received letters (two of which he enclosed)

> from that borough and the neighbouring gentlemen to it, that the offer of my future services would be agreeable to a majority in the corporation, and that numbers of the electors were determined not to choose both the Hunts . . . [They] I find are inclined to choose me again, nothing can prevent it in all probability but your disapprobation of my standing for it, on which account I would not positively declare myself a candidate, before I had consulted you, and knew your mind.

Nor did he think that Hunt would then persist 'in his chimerical notions . . . in particular when he perceives the corporation won't choose him, and his brother together'. Irby, having apparently received Pelham's approval (which left both seats at Old Sarum at Pelham's disposal), was returned unopposed. The election 'cost me the same money I had laid down for Old Sarum', he wrote on 19 Mar. 1755 when claiming refund of his £1,000: which was made from secret service money on 8 May.[3] Irby did not stand again in 1761; gave his interest at Bodmin to Bute's candidate, John Parker; and having been created a peer, wrote on 19 May 1761:[4]

> I have laboured long, I have served five apprenticeships in the vineyard of a court, it was time for me to taste some of the good wine it produced, and I might with reason hope I should receive some reward besides the penny a day bestowed on the other labourers in it . . . I have not been forgot, and I am very content, though I have not yet reaped in a lucrative manner a share in the loaves and fishes distributed amongst the multitude of the hungry in such profuse proportions.

He died 30 Mar. 1775.

[1] Add. 32853, ff. 378-9. [2] Newcastle (Clumber) mss. [3] Namier, *Structure*, 437. [4] Add. 5718, f. 86.

L.B.N.

## IRNHAM, Baron, *see* LUTTRELL, Simon

## IRVINE, Alexander (c.1754–89), of Berners St., Marylebone, London.

EAST LOOE   24 May 1786–24 Dec. 1789

*b.* c.1754, 1st s. of George Irvine of Artamford, New Deer, Aberdeen. *educ.* ?Eton 1763. *m.* 30 Nov. 1782, a da. of George Peters, London banker and a director of the Russia Company, 1s.
  Ensign 1 Ft. 1770, lt. 1774, capt. 1778; lt. and capt. 1 Ft. Gds. 1782.

Irvine's family was closely related to the Irvines of Drum. A number of his Irvine relations were prominent London and Aberdeen merchants trading to France and Sweden. After serving in America, Irvine sold his Artamford estate, made a wealthy

marriage, and settled in London. In May 1786 he was brought into Parliament for East Looe, as a Government supporter. He voted with Administration on the Regency question, but is not known to have spoken in the House. He died 24 Dec. 1789.[1]

[1] J. F. Irvine, *Irvines of Drum and Collateral Branches*, 168.

E.H.-G.

## IRVINE, *see also* IRWIN *and* RAMSAY IRVINE

## IRWIN (IRWINE, IRVINE), John (c.1728–88).

EAST GRINSTEAD   30 Nov. 1762–Apr. 1783

*b.* c.1728, o.s. of Lt.-Gen. Alexander Irwin by his w. Catherine (possibly of fam. of Irvine of Drum). *educ.* Ireland; Grand Tour (Holland and France). *m.* (1) 16 Dec. 1749, Elizabeth (*d.*Apr. 1750), da. of Hugh Henry of Dublin, *s.p.*; (2) Apr. 1753, Anne (*d.*1767), da. of Sir Edward Barry of Dublin, *s.p.*; (3) Caroline, 2 ch. *suc.* fa. 1752; K.B. 15 Dec. 1775.
  Ensign 5 Ft. 1736, lt. 1738, capt. 1745, maj. 1751, lt.-col. 1752; col. 1761; col. 74 Ft. 1761–2; maj.-gen. 1762; gov. Gibraltar 1765–7; col. 57 Ft. 1767–80; lt.-gen. 1772; c.-in.-c. [I] 1775–82; col. 3 Horse 1780–*d.*; gen. 1783.

John Irwin was page of honour to Lionel, 1st Duke of Dorset, lord lieutenant of Ireland 1730–7; and thus began a connexion with the Sackville family which lasted throughout his life. He was returned to Parliament on the Sackville interest at East Grinstead; and became the closest friend of Lord George Sackville, whose political line he followed implicitly, voting with Opposition till 1774 and afterwards with Government. Only one speech by him (on a trivial matter) is recorded.[1]

Burke called him 'a good humoured, well behaving man';[2] Charles James Fox thought him a fop, 'but good-humoured'.[3] Wraxall wrote of him:[4] 'His person, manners, and conversation were all made for the drawing-room, where he seemed to be in his native element . . . It was impossible to possess finer manners, without any affectation, or more perfect good breeding.' He is said to have been a favourite with George III, and he was also well known in French society.

He saw service on the coast of France in 1758, and later with Prince Ferdinand in Germany. His regiment was disbanded in 1762, and for three years he was without military employment. On 19 June 1765 Thomas Whately wrote to Grenville:[5]

> General Irwin has been offered to go to Gibraltar: he is much mortified at this turn . . . as it is a situation very different from that he hoped for, and he fears may be given him instead of a regiment. It has, however, been put to him in such a way that he finds he must accept it.

He was promoted to a regiment on his return in November 1767, and at the general election of 1768 unsuccessfully contested Kinross. In 1775, probably through the influence of Lord George Germain (as Sackville had become), he was given the command in Ireland. When affairs became difficult in that country, North wrote to the King, 27 June 1779:

> Lord North thinks himself obliged to repeat to his Majesty that he finds in every quarter that Sir John Irwin, though well esteemed as a gentleman, is in no great estimation as a general, and the world is very uneasy about his having the command in Ireland in such a perilous moment as the present.

To remove him, thought the King, 'would be disgracing an amiable man'; but 'if the advice had been to send a good general below him to his assistance that might have deserved attention. Irwin is practicable and would hear advice.'[6] No change was, however, made; and Irwin handled a dangerous situation better than might have been expected.

'No income, however large', wrote Wraxall,[7] 'could survive for his expenses, which, being never restrained within any reasonable limits, finally involved him in irretrievable difficulties.' And Lord Carlisle, lord lieutenant of Ireland, to Gower, 30 June 1781:[8] 'You have sent our commander-in-chief over . . . in a great scrape as to money matters, for the other day some official letters were laid before me addressed to Sir J. Irvine to repay a large sum owing to Government, which I fear he is by no means prepared for.' The loss of his appointment in March 1782 ruined him financially, and he was obliged to go and live in France. In April 1783, with no hopes of being able to return to England, he retired from Parliament. From a letter of 4 July 1784 to his old friend Sir Charles Hotham, he appears to have been in great poverty;[9] the King is said to have sent him £1,000;[10] but he was obliged to remove to Parma, where he died in May 1788. George III sent his widow £500 to enable her and her children to return home.[11]

[1] Walpole, *Last Jnls.* i. 25. [2] Burke to Chas. O'Hara, 20 Apr. 1775. [3] Fox to Geo. Selwyn, 19 Nov. 1770, Jesse, *Geo. Selwyn*, ii. 402. [4] *Mems.* iii. 91–93. [5] *Grenville Pprs.* iii. 52. [6] Fortescue, iv. 379, 380. [7] *Mems.* iii. 91. [8] *HMC Carlisle*, 510. [9] Hotham mss, Northallerton RO. [10] Wraxall, *Mems.* iii. 94. [11] Caroline Irwin to Hotham, 23 Aug. 1788, Hotham mss.

J.B.

## ISHAM, Sir Edmund, 6th Bt. (1690–1772), of Lamport, Northants.

NORTHAMPTONSHIRE    31 Mar. 1737–15 Dec. 1772

*b.* 18 Dec. 1690, 4th s. of Sir Justinian Isham, M.P., 4th Bt., by Elizabeth, da. of Sir Edmund Turner of Stoke Rochford, Lincs. *educ.* Rugby 1699–1707; Wadham, Oxf. 1707. *m.* (1) 17 Feb. 1735, Elizabeth (*d.*19 July 1748), da. of Edward Wood of Littleton, Mdx., *s.p.*; (2) 4 May 1751, Philippa, da. of Richard Gee of Orpington, Kent, *s.p. suc.* bro. as 6th Bt. 5 Mar. 1737.

Fellow of Magdalen, Oxf. 1720–35; adv. Doctors' Commons 1724; judge adv. for ct. of Admiralty 1731–41.

Sir Justinian Isham and two of his sons, Justinian and Edmund, represented Northamptonshire continuously from 1698 to 1772. During the 35 years Sir Edmund sat for the county he never had a contest nor was his hold on the seat seriously threatened.

The family were Tories, and Sir Edmund was always classed as such. He does not appear in Fox's list of Members in favour of the peace preliminaries; nor did he vote against them. In the autumn of 1763 he was classed by Jenkinson as 'pro'; he did not vote against Grenville's Administration over general warrants, and opposed the repeal of the cider tax, 10 Feb. 1764.[1] Rockingham in July 1765 classed him as 'contra', and he voted against the repeal of the Stamp Act, 22 Feb. 1766. On 27 Feb. 1767 he seconded Dowdeswell's motion for the reduction of the land tax. Only two other speeches by him are recorded: 3 Mar. 1756, on the plate tax;[2] and 1 Mar. 1762, on the militia.[3]

In the Parliament of 1768 no vote by Isham is recorded, but he was listed as 'contra, present' in Robinson's first survey on the royal marriage bill. He died 15 Dec. 1772.

[1] Harris's 'Debates'. [2] Newdigate's 'Debates'. [3] Harris's 'Debates'.

J.B.

## JACKSON, George (1725–1822), of Hartham House, Corsham, Wilts.

WEYMOUTH AND
MELCOMBE REGIS    27 Mar. 1786–Dec. 1788
COLCHESTER    15 Dec. 1788–6 Apr. 1789
    1790–1796

*b.* 24 Oct. 1725, 1st surv. s. of George Jackson of Richmond, Yorks. by Hannah, da. of William Ward of Guisborough, Yorks. *m.* (1) 24 Sept. 1745, his cos. Mary (*d.*1754), da. of William Ward of Guisborough, 3s. 3da.; (2) 9 Sept. 1775, Grace, da. and h. of Gwyn Goldstone, merchant, of Goldstone, Salop by Grace, da. of George Duckett of Hartham House, Wilts., wid. of Robert Neale of Shaw House, Melksham, Wilts., 1s. *suc.* fa. 1758; *cr.* Bt. 28 July 1791; assumed name of Duckett 3 Feb. 1797, in accordance with the will of his w.'s uncle Thomas Duckett.

Second sec. to Admiralty Nov. 1766–June 1782; judge adv. to the fleet 1769–*d.*

Jackson entered the navy office as a clerk about 1743. In 1766 on Chatham's recommendation he was transferred to the Admiralty by Sir Charles Saunders, and in 1769 became judge advocate and second secretary to the Board. After the fall of North's Administration he retained his post as judge advocate, but was dismissed from his secretaryship with a pension of £400 a year. 'The strange conduct of the Admiralty' in dismissing 'probably the most useful man at the Board' was raised in the House of Commons, 12 May 1783, by John Buller senior, who declared that 'a more able and honest man never served the public'.[1]

Before the general election of 1784 Jackson appears in Robinson's lists of those to be brought in, and willing to pay '£1,500, or perhaps somewhat more'.[2] He was tentatively put down for Rochester, but eventually stood as the Government candidate at Penryn, where he was defeated. In 1786 he was returned for Weymouth and Melcombe Regis in place of its patron, Gabriel Steward, who took the Chiltern Hundreds. No vote or speech by Jackson is reported during this Parliament. Towards the end of 1788 he vacated his seat and with Government support contested the expensive borough of Colchester.[3] He was returned, but the following year was unseated on petition.

Jackson was keenly interested in improving inland waterways, and according to the *Gentleman's Magazine* (1822, ii. 644) 'employed his leisure hours in making the river Stort navigable'. He died 15 Dec. 1822.

[1] Debrett, x. 4. [2] Laprade, 126-9. [3] Add. 35641, f. 192.

M.M.D.

## JACKSON, Richard (?1721-87), of Weasenham, Norf.

| WEYMOUTH AND | |
|---|---|
| MELCOMBE REGIS | 1 Dec. 1762-1768 |
| NEW ROMNEY | 1768-1784 |

*b.* ?1721, o.s. of Richard Jackson of Weasenham, Norf., London merchant, director South Sea Co. and dep.-gov. 1764-8, by Elizabeth, da. of Edmund Clarke. *educ.* Queens', Camb. 1739; L. Inn 1739, called 1744. *unm. suc.* fa. 11 Jan. 1768.

Agent for Connecticut May 1760-70, for Pennsylvania Apr. 1763-1770; sec. to chancellor of Exchequer 1763-July 1765; counsel to South Sea Co. 1764-7; agent for Massachusetts Apr. 1765-70; counsel to Board of Trade Apr. 1770-1782; bencher I. Temple 1770; counsel to Camb. Univ. 1771-*d.*; ld. of Treasury July 1782-Apr. 1783.

Jackson, 'from his extraordinary stores of knowledge . . . styled *omniscient*',[1] was a scholar rather than a politician, and though esteemed by leading statesmen, very rarely appears in their correspondence. His failure to cut a figure in public life was largely due to 'his lack of personal ambition, his solitary habits, his nervous, if not neurotic, modesty, and the diffusion of his interests over an enormous range of knowledge'.[2] Eminent in his own profession, he was also versed in economics and finance, in science and agriculture, had travelled intelligently in Europe, and was deemed an expert on colonial

problems. His attitude toward America was basically that of a Dissenter (which he was by birth),[3] thinking in non-hierarchical terms; and his aim was to preserve the union of the two branches of the English nation. With this in view, and not for personal gain, he tried for a time to keep a foot in either camp, but was never accused of double-dealing by anyone who knew him.

He became connected with Benjamin Franklin through Peter Collinson, the naturalist, whose letter of 26 Sept. 1751 gives an early glimpse of him:[4]

I have prevailed on our worthy, learned, and ingenious friend Mr. Jackson to give some dissertations on the husbandry of Norfolk, believing it may be very serviceable to the Colonies. He has great opportunities of doing this, being a gentleman of leisure and fortune, being the only son, whose father has great riches and possessions, and resides every year, all the long vacation, at his father's seat in Norfolk.

During Franklin's stay in England, 1757-62, they were much together, and Franklin furnished Jackson with materials for his *Historical Review of the Constitution and Government of Pennsylvania*, published anonymously in June 1759; and Jackson assisted Franklin over his pamphlet on *The Interest of Great Britain* with regard to Canada and Guadeloupe, published in 1760.

In 1759-60 Jackson bought a farm of 700 acres in Connecticut; and next, together with Franklin, engaged in schemes for new western colonies, including the Vandalia project. In 1764 he obtained a grant of 20,000 acres in Nova Scotia.[5]

On the vacancy caused at Weymouth by the death of John Olmius, 1st Baron Waltham, Fox wrote to Bute, 17 Nov. 1762: 'Lady Waltham does not intend her son, but one Mr. Jackson.'[6] Though not a Government candidate, a fortnight later he was included by Fox in the list of Members favourable to the peace preliminaries. 'A seat in Parliament', wrote Jackson to Franklin, 4 Apr. 1763, 'in this kingdom is (you know) usually built on negotiations, and those negotiations (in the course of which I met with some trouble) took up most of my last summer.' And Franklin's satisfaction at Jackson having 'at length got into Parliament', points to an old ambition.[7]

On 24 Mar. 1760 Jackson was chosen by the Connecticut assembly agent in Great Britain, to act jointly with Jared Ingersoll during his stay in London;[8] and in April 1763 Franklin, returning home, caused him to be appointed agent for Pennsylvania. In Massachusetts he was in April 1762 Governor Francis Bernard's candidate but his being already agent for Connecticut, with whom Massachusetts had disputes, was considered an 'insuperable obstacle'; the governor was none too popular with the assembly; and Jackson's belonging to the

Church of England counted against him.[9] Even when elected, on 24 Jan. 1765, it was merely by a majority vote; and on 5 Nov. the house of representatives appointed Dennys De Berdt, a Dissenter, their special agent in England, while Jackson remained agent for the province. 'Mr. Jackson', wrote De Berdt to the Speaker of the assembly on 27 Dec. 1765, 'assures me of all the assistance in his power both in and out of the House [of Commons].' And on 1 Mar. 1768: 'we have always maintained a friendly correspondence'.[10]

Before accepting the Massachusetts agency Jackson, by then secretary to the chancellor of the Exchequer, asked for Grenville's views—'his own inclination', wrote Jenkinson to Grenville, 11 Apr. 1765, 'rather led him to decline it and yet if his acceptance of it would be of service to Government he was ready to take it'. The date of Jackson's appointment to the Exchequer is uncertain, though most probably it was soon after Grenville himself had taken office: Jackson's letter to Jenkinson of 18 Sept. 1763 suggests an official connexion between them; so does the remark to Franklin, 27 Dec. 1763, that he has 'a good deal of access' to Grenville, and has 'received a very considerable mark of his good will and esteem, and what is generally too deemed a mark of his confidence'. The description often given of him as 'private secretary' to Grenville is misleading (it was Charles Lloyd), and the relation between them was never close; in the mass of Grenville correspondence there is not one letter from or to Jackson; and on 21 Apr. 1768 Grenville wrote to Lord Halifax that he scarce ever exchanged a word with Jackson since leaving the Exchequer, 'and he has I think in every vote acted differently from me'.[11]

Jackson had hoped while 'in favour with Administration' to do effective service to the Colonies and the mother country—'I consider their interests as inseparable'.[12] He was disappointed. On 26 Jan. 1764, having told Franklin that numerous American questions were to come before Parliament, he wrote:[13]

> I am ... employed not only in attending the House, but in combating what I deem the most dangerous errors in American politics in 100 places ... I have access to almost every place any friends of the colonies would wish to have access to, but I am not sensible of my making any impression proportioned to my endeavours.

And when Franklin, on 25 June 1764, referred to 'letters from people at home to their American friends ... mentioning in the strongest terms your zeal for the welfare of the Colonies, and the success attending it', Jackson replied that in fact he had 'very little weight or influence'. This is not the style

of a self-seeking or self-important person; nor did he value the agencies for their emoluments. He left it to the Connecticut assembly whether any salary should be paid to him for the four years while Ingersoll was still in England, and it was the assembly, 'fully sensible of the great pains taken and good services rendered' by him and 'in full confidence of his future friendship', who desired him to charge it from 30 May 1760.[14] With regard to the Massachusetts agency, De Berdt wrote on 1 Mar. 1768 that he was glad Jackson 'has at last been rewarded'.[15]

Jackson's first reported speech in the House was on the American bill, 22 Mar. 1764, pleading for a lower duty on molasses. Over Wilkes and general warrants he supported the Government: on 28 Jan. 1765, the night before the subject came up once more in the House, he was at the meeting of 'men of business' at Grenville's house. On 2 Feb., together with other colonial agents, he waited on Grenville, to remonstrate against the impending stamp bill, and 'told him plainly' what consequences he foresaw from 'the measure now pursuing'.[16] On 6 Feb. he spoke and voted against the stamp bill: he argued that though the British Parliament had an undeniable right to tax America, it would be wrong to impose internal taxes while she was unrepresented. The short reports of his speech by Harris and Ryder perhaps unduly stress the opening admission; his own reports[17] give both parts of the argument. On 15 Feb. Jackson and other Members connected with the Colonies presented petitions against the stamp bill, which the House refused to receive. On the 27th, on the third reading, according to Harris, he spoke 'though against the bill yet for Admiralty courts'. Also in his correspondence with his American constituents, Jackson invariably pleaded for moderation.[18]

In the summer of 1765 Jackson, who left the Exchequer with Grenville, was wrongly classed by Rockingham as 'contra'. He supported the repeal of the Stamp Act; and on 27 Feb., writing to Connecticut about the forecasts by opponents that it would produce further disorders in America, warned them that 'the credit of the best friends America ever had is pledged that this will not be the case'. On 18 Apr. 1766, in a debate on the budget, he spoke on the Government side against Grenville.

Next, Jackson adhered to the Chatham Administration; it included Shelburne who, when at the Board of Trade, had wanted him for its counsel,[19] and in November 1767 named Amherst, Franklin, and Jackson as 'the best authorities for anything that related to America'.[20] On 26 Jan. 1767 Jackson spoke against Grenville's motion that troops in America should be paid for by the Colonies;[21] and on 7 Dec. 1767, in support of the petition from Pennsylvania complaining of taxation without representation.

In 1768, Lord Waltham being of age, Jackson had to give up the seat at Weymouth, and was returned for New Romney, a borough at the disposal of the Treasury. On 19 Apr. 1769 Jackson made his last recorded speech on America, in support of Pownall's motion for a repeal of the Townshend duties: 'I consider the preservation of America to depend upon the repeal of this act. Laws cannot be carried into execution, countries cannot be well governed, when there is universal discontent among the people.'[22] In April 1770 Jackson was appointed counsel to the Board of Trade, and consequently resigned his colonial agencies. In October 1771 the Connecticut assembly resolved to thank him 'for his services and for the great care and faithfulness and steady attention he has ever paid to the true interest of the Colony', and to present him with an inscribed piece of plate.[23]

Jackson, agreeing with the principle of parliamentary sovereignty over the Colonies, must have found his position as colonial agent increasingly awkward. Still, it is difficult to explain how he henceforth reconciled himself to supporting the Government, whose American policy he condemned but on whose interest he was re-elected in 1774 and 1780. He did not speak again on America except in June 1774 on some technical aspects of the Quebec bill,[24] with which he had to deal as counsel to the Board of Trade: 'I have always observed', wrote Burke to James Delancey, 2 Aug. 1773, 'that his report has, as it ought to have, great weight with the Board; and indeed in most cases is decisive.' Chosen on 28 Nov. 1772 member of the secret committee on East India affairs, both in 1773 and in 1783 he took part in debates on them. Half a dozen other speeches by him are reported; but his only known reference to America concerns his own votes—a puzzling subject. On 13 June 1781, Charles James Fox having incidentally remarked he wished Jackson 'had voted oftener, as he had told the House he thought that the last system of government was pernicious', Jackson

> declared he had uniformly voted for the repeal of the Stamp Act, against the Boston port bill, and the other bills, which he had declared both in public and private, to be the cause of our misfortunes. But he had voted for a supply, because as the country was in a state of war, he did not wish to leave it without fleets and armies.[25]

In a letter of 30 Nov. 1784 to a Connecticut friend, W. S. Johnson, he even claimed to have voted against all legislation concerning America,[26] which is not borne out by the voting records for 1774–82:

Jackson's name does not appear in the list of Members voting against the Massachusetts Judicature bill, 6 May 1774, or for the amendment to the Address on America, 20 Oct. 1775, or for Fox's motion against sending the 'old corps' of the army to America, 2 Feb. 1778. In fact, during those years not a single vote of his against the Government is recorded; and he still voted with them on the two censure motions of 20 Feb. and 8 Mar. 1782; but he was absent from the divisions on the American war, 12 Dec. 1781, 22 and 27 Feb. 1782, and 'stayed away' when on 15 Mar. Rous moved the vote of no-confidence which overthrew the North Administration.[27]

In February–April 1778 there was an opening for Jackson to take an active part in American affairs: he was invited by the Government to join Lord Carlisle and William Eden in the conciliatory mission. Carlisle wrote about him to a friend:[28]

> I bent to the persuasion that his accurate knowledge of the country to which we were to repair, and his long and familiar acquaintance with her interests, would outbalance the insignificancy of his situation and the obscurity of his name.

And Jackson wrote to Eden on 28 Feb.:[29]

> I assure you with great truth, nothing could have contributed more to my acceptance of the honour intended me, than your making one of the commission; that will at least make the passage agreeable. No objection that I have to the bill (though I have at least one that weighs much with me), no inconvenience that can happen to my affairs in England, shall prevent me from going, if named: but you must be sensible that the instructions make a material part of the plan; you will recollect that I expressed a wish the other day that they might be full and precise. I am not afraid of being too much straitened, in point of discretion: though it is true on the other hand that I can conceive them drawn so as to exclude all hope of good effect, which last, I do not believe will be the case; believing however, as I do, that the ends of the plan will be otherwise frustrated.

He went on with reservations and apprehensions, and concluded:

> The commencement of the American war always appeared to me an impolitic measure, the continuance of it cannot be less than ruin to this empire, and will be an object that I cannot be near without an anxiety that will be too much for me to bear.

Equally expressive of his unfitness for the task was a further short letter to Eden on 1 Mar.:[30]

> I could almost wish you did not consider me as having accepted . . . difficulties insurmountable may arise from the instructions, I wish to be entrusted with no discretion unless it be accurately limited and defined at both ends. I certainly have not accepted, but upon the supposition that I find myself sufficiently instructed, and that too in a manner not likely to defeat the end.

During March Jackson grew increasingly averse

to going; raised objections which, when surmounted he 'repeated with a fresh addition of difficulties';[31] and, as Eden wrote on 30 Mar.,[32]

> said . . . that we should proceed immediately to give independence to the Colonies—that he had made a great subscription to the loan which was still unsettled—that he should wish soon to come back—that he could not go this month and even then should leave all his affairs at sixes and sevens—that it did not signify when they arrived—and was of no consequence except to satisfy the people of this country—that his seat in Parliament might be vacated—'and such a deal of skimble-skamble stuff etc.'
>
> Upon the whole he has convinced me that he does not mean to go—and also that he ought not to go.

When North reported the matter to the King, George III replied on 1 Apr.: 'I am very clear he ought not to be allowed to go.'[33] Carlisle and Eden felt relieved to be rid of 'a person who, with the best intention in the world, would have driven us mad with doubts and digressions before we had got to Portsmouth'. And Archbishop Markham wrote to Eden, 11 Apr.:[34] 'Jackson may be a good index, but I am much mistaken if you would have found him an efficient man.' Jackson himself, recounting the story of those years, told W. S. Johnson in a letter of 30 Nov. 1784 that even after the outbreak of hostilities he kept up intercourse with American friends, hoping to contribute to stopping the calamity.

> That intercourse continually lessened until upon my declining to go out a commissioner to America with emoluments to the amount of £6 or £7,000 sterling, the little intercourse that remained ceased, and first I began to remit in my attendance on Parliament and afterwards to give way to a resolution to have little to do with public affairs.

But he would refuse taking part in them only when convinced that he could be of no use.

> This conviction I was under in 1778, and I got the better of the *most earnest* solicitation—but I was convinced . . . that the commission could only operate by reconciling the people of this country to a continuance of the war. The event proved my judgment to be true.

When Shelburne included Jackson in his Treasury list on 9 July 1782,[35] 'not decided' was put against him—signifying doubts on one side or perhaps on both. There is no evidence of Jackson's having played any part in the peace negotiations with America, and, although a member of the Government, he did not speak in defence of the preliminary treaty. Even after 1783 he envisaged the English nation as one, 'whether resident in Europe or America . . . *a common origin, manners and language* make a *nation*, though different parts of it may be governed by distinct and independent sovereignties'.[36]

He did not seek re-election in 1784, and died 6 May 1787, aged 65.

[1] Boswell, *Johnson*, iii. 19. [2] C. Van Doren, *Letters & Pprs. Ben. Franklin and Jackson 1753–85*, intro. [3] Note by Ezra Stiles, later president of Yale, dated 26 Dec. 1765, on a letter from Dr. J. Eliot of 21 Aug. 1761, Stiles mss. Yale Univ. [4] Van Doren, 3. [5] *APC Col.* 1745–66, p. 816. [6] Bute mss. [7] Van Doren, 94, 97–98. [8] *Fitch Pprs.* ii. (Conn. Hist. Soc. Coll. xviii), 55–56. [9] *Jasper Mauduit* (Mass. Hist. Soc. Coll, lxxiv), 31, 36, 78, 124, 128, 179n. [10] *Mass. Col. Soc. Trans.* 1910–11, pp. 309, 331. [11] *Jenkinson Pprs.* 191–2, 359; Van Doren, 122; Grenville letter bk. [12] To Franklin, 27 Dec. 1763, Van Doren, 122. [13] Ibid. 138. [14] *Public Recs. Conn.* xii. 256. [15] *Mass. Col. Soc. Trans.* 1910–11, pp. 328, 331. [16] Ingersoll to T. Fitch, gov. Conn. 11 Feb. 1765, *Fitch Pprs.* ii. 324. [17] Ibid. ii. 316–17; Van Doren, 194–6; *Connecticut Gaz.* 9 Aug., quoted Bancroft, v. 238. [18] See e.g. his letters to Fitch, 5 June, 9 Nov. 1765, 11 Jan., 27 Feb. 1766. [19] Harris's Memorandum , 9 May 1763, Malmesbury mss. [20] Smyth, *Corresp. Franklin*, v. 67. [21] Fortescue, i. 451 (misdated). [22] *Cavendish's 'Debates'*, i. 400. [23] *Public Recs. Conn.* xiii. 518. [24] Cavendish's 'Debates', Egerton 259, pp. 196–8, 205; 262, p. 133. [25] Debrett, iii. 600. [26] Bancroft transcripts, N.Y. Pub. Lib. [27] Fortescue, v. 390; Robinson to Sandwich [16 Mar. 1782], Sandwich mss. [28] *HMC Carlisle*, 377. [29] Add. 34415, f. 151. [30] Ibid. f. 231. [31] *HMC Carlisle*, 378. [32] Quoted Van Doren, 28–29. [33] Fortescue, iv. 91, 93. [34] Add. 34415, f. 337. [35] Fortescue, vi. 78. [36] Jackson to W. S. Johnson, 30 Nov. 1784, Bancroft transcripts; Van Doren, 200–2.

L.B.N.

## JAMES, William (?1721–83), of Park Farm Place, Eltham, Kent.

### WEST LOOE 1774–16 Dec. 1783

*b.* ?1721, poss. s. of a miller at Bolton Hill, nr. Haverfordwest.[1] *m.* by 1765, Anne, da. and coh. of Edmond Goddard of Hartham, Wilts., 1s. 1da.[2] *cr.* Bt. 25 July 1778.

Director, E.I. Co. 1768–72, 1773–7 (dep. chairman 1776–7), 1778–83 (dep. chairman 1778–9, chairman 1779–80, dep. chairman 1781–2).

Wraxall, who 'knew Sir William James with great intimacy', writes:[3]

> His origin was so obscure as almost to baffle inquiry, and he had derived no advantage from education, but he possessed strong natural abilities, aided by a knowledge of mankind.

James entered the East India Company's navy in about 1747; by 1751 he was commodore, and in 1755 and 1756 commanded expeditions which destroyed the immensely rich pirate strongholds, Severndroog and Gheriah. In 1759 he returned to England with a fortune; became closely associated with Lord Sandwich, and from 1769 was one of his leading supporters in the East India Company directorate.

In 1770 James was a candidate at the notorious New Shoreham by-election, but was defeated by an overwhelming majority. He was returned in 1774 at West Looe on the Buller interest, and as a follower of Sandwich he naturally supported North's Administration till its fall. In 1780 James was again returned at West Looe by John Buller junior who, hoping to gain control at Saltash, nominated there James and himself in opposition to the Administration candidates; they were defeated, and their petition was dismissed. James opposed Shelburne's Administration and voted against the peace preliminaries, 18 Feb. 1783. On 1 Apr. 1783 a report from the select committee on Bengal affairs was put before the House alleging that James had been associated with Laurence Sulivan in altering the East India Company's records and attempting to deceive the committee about communications to India. James opposed a motion to print the report, which 'unaccompanied by a defence' would create a bias against Sulivan and himself, and begged that Members would

> not condemn them unheard; for the other gentleman and he would be able to bring the most satisfactory evidence to prove that if there had been made an alteration or an erasure in the records of the company, it was wholly without his knowledge or that of Mr. Sulivan.

On 19 May he again maintained that the charge was 'absolutely false and groundless', and on 28 May, in his last reported speech, told the House that 'he was that moment prepared to meet any charge that could be brought against him'.[4] James was absent from the division of 27 Nov. 1783 on Fox's East India bill. On 30 Nov. Fox commented to Sandwich, with whom James remained on very close terms: 'It is as much as could be expected from him, all circumstances considered.'[5] James died on 16 Dec. 1783, aged 62, of a stroke which was generally believed (erroneously, according to Wraxall) to have been brought on by indignation at the bill.[6]

[1] N. & Q. (ser 2), xii. 244–5. [2] For the story of a previous marriage see Naval Chron. xiii. 89. [3] Mems. iii. 168. [4] Debrett, ix. 583, 590; x. 12, 13, 97. [5] Sandwich mss. [6] Mems. iii. 168.

M.M.D.

## JEFFREYS, John (1706–66), of The Priory, Brecon, and Sheen, Surr.

BRECONSHIRE 1734–1747
DARTMOUTH 1747–Jan. 1766

b. 1706, 1st surv. s. of John Jeffreys, M.P., by Elizabeth, da. of Anthony Sturt of London. unm. suc. fa. 20 Oct. 1715.
Jt. sec. of the Treasury Nov. 1742–May 1746; sec. to chancellor of the Exchequer May 1752–Apr. 1754; warden of the mint July 1754–d.; dep. ranger of St. James's and Hyde Parks Dec. 1757–d.

'Little Jeffreys', as he was known, was a gamester, a member of White's, and of the set of Lord Lincoln, Newcastle's nephew and heir and Henry Pelham's son-in-law. He soon ran through his private fortune; and his political career is the record of his struggle to keep his head above water at the public expense.

Henry Pelham had provided for Jeffreys by appointing him to the sinecure of secretary to the chancellor of the Exchequer, and billeting him for £800 p.a. on Nicholas Hardinge, junior secretary to the Treasury. On Pelham's death in 1754 the new chancellor of the Exchequer, Legge, refused to retain Jeffreys as his secretary but Newcastle was almost at once able to make good the loss by appointing him warden of the mint. Two years later Newcastle and West went out of office for a short time, during which Hardinge replaced West as senior secretary and Jeffreys was transferred to the new junior secretary, Samuel Martin. When in July 1757 West returned to the Treasury, replacing Martin, Hardinge refused to resume paying Jeffreys, who appealed to Newcastle:

> Your Grace well knows I have been oft obliged to plague and trouble your Grace about Mr. Hardinge's payment from the Treasury, and had I not been necessitated to take it I would not have received it from him because he has used me so ill. I therefore must entreat your Grace that if you please to appoint him my paymaster he may be told to pay Mr. West for me.[1]

Under pressure from Lord Lincoln and Lord Ashburnham Newcastle did his best to persuade one or other of the secretaries to accept liability for Jeffreys, and eventually fell back on a payment of £500 from the secret service funds.[2] Lord Ashburnham, as ranger of St. James's and Hyde Parks, also helped by appointing Jeffreys his deputy; and in 1761 he was given a regular secret service pension of £500 p.a.

As soon as Newcastle was forced out of office in 1762 Jeffreys got the Duke of Bedford to represent his 'situation in a kind and compassionate manner' to Bute. When Newcastle went into open opposition George III heard that 'little Jeffreys . . . was to be ordered by the D. of N. to retire, he must then starve, being these many years a bankrupt'.[3] He did not retire but continued to support and be supported by successive Governments till the formation of the Rockingham Administration, when he wrote to Newcastle from Bath, where he was recuperating from a severe illness, 'to congratulate your Grace and the public on this most agreeable and happy change in the Administration' and 'to beg the favour of your Grace to recommend me to Lord Rockingham's protection. I now receive £1,100 per annum, in your Grace's Administration it was £200 more.'[4]

He had no occasion to congratulate yet another minister, for he died in January 1766.

[1] Add. 32875, f. 275. [2] Namier, Structure, 403–4. [3] Sedgwick, 163–164. [4] Add. 32907, f. 385.

L.B.N.

## JEKYLL, Joseph (1754–1837).

CALNE 20 Aug. 1787–Feb. 1816

b. 1 Jan. 1754, 1st s. of Capt. Edward Jekyll, R.N., of Haverfordwest by Elizabeth, da. of Thomas Walker of Killiver, Carm. educ. Westminster 1766–70; Ch. Ch.

Oxf. 1771; L. Inn 1769, called 1778. *m.* 20 Aug. 1801, Maria, da. of Hans Sloane (q.v.), 2s.

Bencher, I. Temple 1805; solicitor-gen. to Prince of Wales and K.C. 1805; reader, I. Temple 1814, treasurer 1816; commr. of lunacy and master in Chancery 1816.

Jekyll was returned for Calne on Lord Lansdowne's interest; voted with the Administration on Impey's impeachment and during the Regency crisis; and spoke a few times in the House, 1789–1790, mainly on legal matters. In the *Dictionary of National Biography* W. P. Courtney classes him as a 'wit'. But Lady Susan O'Brien, having dined in his company during the Dorchester assizes, wrote in her 'Journal' on 25 July 1806: 'quite disagreeable, such endless attempts at wit and spinning every idea *threadbare* as to be quite wearisome to the hearers'.[1] Some of his *jeux d'esprit* have been reproduced, but it requires an effort to read them.[2]

Jekyll died 8 Mar. 1837.

[1] Lord Ilchester's mss. [2] *N. & Q.* (ser. 1), x. 172; Fitzmaurice, *Shelburne,* ii. 416–18.

L.B.N.

**JENISON, Ralph** (1696–1758), of Walworth Castle, co. Dur.

NORTHUMBERLAND    16 Apr. 1724–1741
NEWPORT I.o.W.    20 June 1749–15 May 1758

*bap.* 23 Dec. 1696, 1st surv. s. of Ralph Jenison of Elswick and Walworth by Elizabeth, da. and h. of Cuthbert Heron of Chipchase, Northumb. *educ.* Christ's, Camb. 1719–20. *m.* 10 Dec. 1751, Susan, da. of Thomas Allan of the Flatts, co. Dur., 1s. *d.v.p.* *suc.* gd.-fa. Robert Jenison 1714.

Sheriff, Northumb. 1717–18; freeman of Newcastle-upon-Tyne 1718.

Master of the buckhounds 1737–44, 1746–57.

Jenison was of an old family of Newcastle merchants, and was politically connected with Charles, 2nd Earl of Tankerville. Possibly he owed his introduction to the Isle of Wight to Tankerville, whose brother-in-law and friend, Lord Portsmouth, was its governor in 1749. There he became the intermediary between the Pelhams and Thomas Holmes, their manager for the Isle of Wight boroughs; was in his confidence and usually collected for him the secret service subsidy he had for those boroughs, and which Holmes kept a secret from his brothers, their Members. About his own seat at Newport, Jenison wrote to Pelham on 18 Feb. 1754:[1] 'The people of that place have taken the opportunity of paving their town against a general election and Mr. Holmes says the candidates are to pay for it, that and the expense at the day of election and some gratuities to particular people, will amount to six hundred pounds for each candidate, which Mr. Holmes desires may be paid into his hands before he

leaves London.' On 14 May £700 of secret service money was paid to Jenison, presumably for election expenses. On the re-arrangement of offices in July 1757 Jenison had to give up the buckhounds, and was offered as compensation a secret service pension of £1,500 p.a.[2] Because of the uncertainty of such a pension he asked that £1000 be placed on the Irish establishment. 'The Duke of Newcastle has been a father to me', he wrote to Lord Lincoln on 3 July 1757,[3] '... All my wishes can be for nothing further than a security after his Majesty's decease.' Finally the secret service pension was fixed at £1,800 but Jenison drew only £1,350 of it, as he died on 15 May 1758.

[1] Add. 32734, ff. 148–9. [2] Namier, *Structure,* 202, 218–19. [3] Newcastle (Clumber) mss.

L.B.N.

**JENKINSON, Charles** (1729–1808), of Addiscombe, Surr.

| COCKERMOUTH | | 1761–Dec. 1766 |
|---|---|---|
| APPLEBY | 20 Jan. | 1767–July 1772 |
| HARWICH | 7 Aug. | 1772–1774 |
| HASTINGS | | 1774–1780 |
| SALTASH | | 1780–21 Aug. 1786 |

*b.* 26 Apr. 1729, 1st s. of Col. Charles Jenkinson (3rd s. of Sir Robert Jenkinson, 2nd Bt., M.P.) by Amarantha, da. of Capt. Wolfran Cornwall, R.N.; bro. of John Jenkinson and cos. of Charles Wolfran Cornwall (qq.v.). *educ.* Charterhouse 1740; Univ. Coll. Oxf. 1746; L. Inn 1747. *m.* (1) 9 Feb. 1769, Amelia (*d.*7 July 1770), da. of William Watts of Southall, Berks., gov. of Fort William, Bengal, 1s. (Robert Banks Jenkinson, 2nd Earl of Liverpool, prime minister 1812–27); (2) 22 June 1782, Catherine, da. of Sir Cecil Bisshopp, 6th Bt. (q.v.), wid. of Jenkinson's cos. Sir Charles Cope, 2nd Bt., 1s. 1da. *suc.* fa. June 1750; *cr.* Baron Hawkesbury 21 Aug. 1786; *suc.* cos. in the baronetcy and family estates 22 July 1790; *cr.* Earl of Liverpool 1 June 1796.

Private sec. to Lord Holdernesse 1758–61; under-sec. of state Mar. 1761–May 1762; private sec. to Bute as first ld. of Treasury, and treasurer of the Ordnance May 1762–Apr. 1763; jt. sec. to Treasury Apr. 1763–July 1765; auditor to the Princess Dowager July 1765–1772; ld. of Admiralty Dec. 1766–Dec. 1767, of Treasury Dec. 1767–Jan. 1773; jt. vice-treasurer [I] Jan. 1773–Oct. 1775; P.C. 5 Feb. 1773; clerk of the pells [I] 1775–*d.*; sec. at war 1778–Mar. 1782; member of the Board of Trade 1784, pres. 1786–1804; chancellor of duchy of Lancaster 1786–1803.

Charles Jenkinson belonged to a younger branch of an old Oxfordshire family.[1] Two of his uncles, his grandfather, and great-grandfather had represented the county as Tories. He was intended for the Church, but, after taking part on the Whig side in the Oxfordshire election of 1754, he turned his mind towards politics. His first patron was Lord Harcourt, who introduced him to Lord Holdernesse, secretary of state. Holdernesse, wrote Jenkinson to George Grenville on 15 Nov. 1756,[2]

> was so good as to employ me both at his own house and in the secretary's office, without any profit or emolument to myself, but with the design alone of instructing me in foreign affairs and the business of that office, and qualifying me for anything of which my friends might hereafter think me worthy.

To Grenville, a man of similar mind and outlook, Jenkinson looked for advancement; but Grenville was unable to obtain for him an official situation, and it was not until 1760 that his services were recognized by the award of a pension of £250 per annum.[3]

In March 1761 Bute, newly appointed secretary of state, took Jenkinson at Grenville's recommendation as his under-secretary. 'I am absolutely in love with Lord Bute', Jenkinson wrote to Grenville on 24 Mar., 'his goodness shows itself to me more and more every day.' And on 26 Mar.:[4] 'His Lordship . . . has been so good as to assign me a particular apartment [in his house] where I shall live and be always at hand.' At the general election of 1761 Jenkinson was returned for Cockermouth on the interest of Sir James Lowther, Bute's prospective son-in-law. He conceived a regard and esteem for Bute such as he afterwards felt for no other minister; though cold and cautious by nature, he could show deep loyalty once his friendship had been won. When Bute took the Treasury Jenkinson became his private secretary (the place at the Ordnance was given to provide him with a salary). At the centre of power and secure in the confidence of his chief, he had every prospect of further advancement.

On Bute's resignation, Jenkinson became one of Grenville's secretaries to the Treasury, concerned both with parliamentary and financial business. In the autumn of 1763, using Bute's list of 1761, he classified the Members of the House of Commons according to their presumed political allegiance. He conducted the correspondence with Griffith Davies, the Treasury manager at Harwich, and had charge of the Government interest in the Cinque Ports. Routine patronage and financial business also occupied his attention, and he was concerned with the plan for a stamp tax in the colonies. As early as September 1763 he was taking advice about the drafting of the bill, and on 2 July 1764 wrote to Grenville:[5]

> In the last session of Parliament you assigned as a reason for not going on with the Stamp Act that you waited only for further information on that subject. This having been said, should not Government appear to take some step for that purpose? I mentioned this to you soon after the Parliament was up. I remember your objections to it; but I think the information may

be procured in a manner to obviate those objections, and without it we may perhaps be accused of neglect.[2]

Jenkinson wished to remain on friendly terms with Bute, and to smooth away any friction that might occur between Bute and Grenville. In August 1763, after Bute had opened negotiations with Pitt for a new Administration, Jenkinson and Gilbert Elliot persuaded him to advise the King to recall Grenville; and in December Jenkinson conveyed a friendly message from Bute to Grenville. Jenkinson remained loyal to Grenville but their relationship lost something of its friendly character: Jenkinson felt that Grenville's suspicion of Bute's influence was excessive, and Grenville mistrusted Jenkinson's friendship with Bute. Jenkinson never quite threw off the odium of being Bute's agent in Administration, and in 1766 his acceptance of office under Chatham was regarded by the Opposition as a sign of Bute's continued influence at court. In fact Bute played little part in politics after July 1766, and Jenkinson had to steer his course alone.[6]

Jenkinson lost office with Grenville in July 1765, but a few days later was appointed to a place in the household of the Princess Dowager—by whose recommendation is not easy to say. Replying to Grenville's letter of congratulation, he wrote:[7]

> The office conferred on me is very agreeable to me, as I owe it to no minister whatsoever and it leaves me unconnected and free to act that part which my honour and conscience dictates. I think it a happiness to have no concern in the politics of the present hour.

Politically timid, Jenkinson attached himself to the Crown as the one stable element in the political scene; a born bureaucrat, of restricted sympathies, his passion was for the detail of office. He never felt the excitement of the parliamentary game, and feared responsibility for policy. He held the typical eighteenth-century view that government was mainly a matter of precedent and law. With such ideas, he naturally followed Grenville in opposing the repeal of the Stamp Act. 'The present time', he said in the debate of 21–22 Feb. 1766,[8] '[was] the properest to tax the colonies, when they were grown able to bear it and not yet strong enough to resist it.' Rigid in his ideas and authoritarian in his outlook, he lacked the breadth of vision to understand American aspirations.

When Chatham took office in July 1766 many who had been in opposition to the Rockingham Administration reverted to the court. In November Jenkinson told Grenville that he could not separate himself from his patron, Sir James Lowther, 'being brought into Parliament by him, and knowing no other person who would give him a seat there'—a clear hint of what was to follow. On 3 Dec. Jenkinson informed Grenville that he had been appointed to the Admiralty Board, 'to which Mr. Grenville returned no answer, and forbid his porter ever to let him into his house again'.[9] Henceforth Jenkinson adhered to each successive Administration until the fall of North, but took care not to attach himself too closely to any political leader. At the general election of 1768 he was returned for Lowther's borough of Appleby, but, like all Lowther's clients, found it impossible to maintain a dignified and tolerable relationship with his over-bearing patron. On 8 Aug. 1772 Jenkinson wrote to Gilbert Elliot:[10]

> You will be surprised to hear that I have vacated my seat at Appleby and been chosen for Harwich. I have for some time had a squabble with Sir James . . . I have endeavoured to make him reasonable but in vain, and, finding I could not, I determined to change my seat, as I have done. I believe you will think me neither unwise nor unfortunate on this occasion.

At Harwich, and later at Hastings and Saltash, Jenkinson sat on the Government interest. He progressed steadily up the ministerial ladder, without achieving any post of real consequence. In the House he was a frequent speaker but not a good debater: his style was precise, formal, and pedantic, and he relied on the strength of his reasoning to convince. James Harris wrote about his speech on the repeal of the Stamp Act, 21 Feb. 1766: 'No speech was more fraught with matter nor more accurately put together, but from defect of voice was ill-heard, though perhaps the best worth hearing of any speech for argument and information.'

Throughout the American war Jenkinson was generally credited with an influence at court and in Administration beyond that to which he was entitled by his office. Horace Walpole believed him to be the 'sole confidant' of the King and 'the director or agent of all his Majesty's secret counsels';[11] and Burke wrote to Rockingham on 5 Jan. 1775:

> I have great reason to suspect that Jenkinson governs everything. But it would be right to know this a little more clearly. A trusty person set at his door to follow him in his motions would give great lights. Surely it is so far from mean or trifling that nothing is more worthy of a general than to get good intelligence of the enemy's motions.

But Jenkinson himself wrote to Lord Harcourt on 29 Dec. 1777:[12]

> The world are so obliging as to give me the credit of much more influence than I really have, and when I deny it I have seldom the good fortune to be believed. In the management of public affairs it is true that I sometimes have a share, I am always ready to give any assistance I am able, but I never intrude it, and to say the truth it is never called for but in emergencies when they cannot do without me.

The springs of policy during the North Administration are exceedingly difficult to trace, but it is clear that by 1778 Jenkinson, together with John Robinson, Charles Wolfran Cornwall, and Grey Cooper, belonged to the inner circle of North's confidential advisers. In this there was nothing extraordinary: all were servants of the Treasury, or, in Jenkinson's case, had long experience of Treasury matters. In December 1778 Jenkinson became secretary at war, an office which gave him direct access to the King, and henceforth his influence was out of all proportion to his departmental standing. The King recognized that in Jenkinson he had an able and loyal servant, and began to rely upon him for information about the state of his Administration which could not be obtained from ministers in the closet. 'I think it right that your Majesty should in the present moment be informed of everything that passes', wrote Jenkinson on 20 Nov. 1779; and on 16 Mar. 1782: 'I shall continue in town that I may have an opportunity of observing all that passes, and be able to render every service in my power.' He sent information about Lord Gower's attitude towards Administration, North's doubts and indecisions, the conduct of ministers in the House of Commons, rumours of divisions among Opposition leaders, the intrigues of Wedderburn and Eden, etc. From supplying information it was but one step to giving advice: on how to treat Keppel, how to handle Wedderburn, how North should conduct the military inquiry in the House of Commons, etc. In 1779 Jenkinson was consulted by the King on the appointment of a secretary of state and on the terms to be offered for the support of Opposition.[13] With John Robinson, North's confidential secretary to the Treasury, he had an old friendship, and the two worked closely together. Jenkinson had no qualms about the policy to be pursued towards America, and supported the King's attempt to buttress his weak Administration. He wrote to the King, 7 Nov. 1779, about admitting the Opposition to office provided they would support the American war:[14]

> I highly approve of your Majesty's conduct in everything you have said and done, of your resolution to resist the evil [the break-up of North's Administration] as long as you possibly can, and of your determination to convince the world that whatever may happen is not owing to want of fortitude in your Majesty or of attachment to those principles which you approve. I always think that when a man pursues this line of conduct Providence will support him and lead him out of the difficulties in which he is involved.

Jenkinson was aware of the delicacy of his position and took care to prevent his communications to the King from being known. On 4 Nov. 1779 he ended a letter: 'I thought it better to write all this to your Majesty than to come to court and have an audience, which might create suspicion.' And on

30 Nov.: 'I received your Majesty's note just as I was going to the House of Commons, where I had a motion to make that would not admit of delay; I thought it best therefore to go, that I might not occasion suspicion.'[15] In August 1779 he agreed 'to prepare something for the consideration of Parliament on Irish affairs'—'not that I would have ever given an opinion on what ought to be done for the relief of that kingdom', he added in a letter to Robinson, 'which is a task for which I confess I am wholly unequal'.[16] But the matter leaked out and Jenkinson refused to undertake it—'as the condition I made of not being known to have any concern in this business is thus already broken', he wrote, 'I must beg Lord North's permission to decline having any further share in it'. Still, Jenkinson did take up the business again. 'Lord North . . . is glad that you approve of his amendments to the Irish addresses', wrote Robinson on 23 Oct.; and on 29 Oct.: 'I really wish to get you the Irish papers . . . as you will want them for your judgment on what is done.' When in October 1779 Robinson asked Jenkinson to look over the Government's proposals to the East India Company, he added: 'You may be assured that I will not let slip from me the least thing tending to show that you have been so good as to take up the business.'[17] In short, Jenkinson occupied an important place at the centre of government, was consulted on important Government business, and did not wish his activities to be known. Yet there is little evidence that he initiated or directed policy, and it is very doubtful whether he could have led North or the King in a direction they did not wish to go.

Perhaps North was the person from whom Jenkinson desired most to conceal his activities. Their relations, though apparently friendly, were equivocal. Jenkinson looked with contempt on North's hesitations and vacillations, and did not believe that he was sincere in wishing to give up his office.[18] North, however, tried to bring Jenkinson into a more important situation. In October 1778 and in February 1779 he proposed to resign the Exchequer to Jenkinson—'by much the fittest person in England to have the direction of the finances', but nothing came of the proposal. Similarly a suggestion in October 1779 that Jenkinson should be admitted to the Cabinet, though backed by North, Sandwich and Robinson, came to nought. It is difficult to say why: the King confided so much in Jenkinson that he would hardly have objected to his being in the Cabinet. Perhaps the objection came from Jenkinson himself. In January 1782 he refused a categorical offer from North of the secretaryship of state for the American department. Cautious, timid, and re-

served, he preferred to work behind the scenes, and it is no wonder that the Opposition ascribed to him an unconstitutional influence at court. Still, in spite of these offers Jenkinson professed to believe that North was jealous of him. In July 1781 he had a quarrel with North about a trifling affair of patronage. 'I will not ask in order to be refused and slighted', he wrote to Robinson. 'There is not one man in his Government of any consideration that he treats in the same manner . . . The plan is to make as much use of me as possible, but to keep me as low as he is able both in rank and consideration.'[19] And to the King, 22 Jan. 1782, after having refused the American department: 'I entertain great doubts whether his intentions were ever very favourable to me, notwithstanding what he says.'[20]

On North's resignation in March 1782, Jenkinson was at hand to strengthen the King's resolve not to capitulate to the Opposition. They seem to have discussed a plan for an all-party Administration, and Jenkinson talked to Gower and Thurlow about it.[21] But North declared that no such Administration could command the confidence of the Commons; the King had to yield to Rockingham; and Jenkinson lost his office. He wrote to Robinson on 13 June:[22] 'I have thought it most advisable to absent myself wholly from the House of Commons, unless my friends should desire my attendance'; and during the period of the Rockingham Administration he was not in touch with the King. But Shelburne, even before Rockingham's death, informed the King that he wished to see Jenkinson in office; and soon after taking the Treasury, opened communications with him. 'Lord Shelburne certainly must and shall have my fullest support,' wrote the King to Jenkinson on 13 July. 'I therefore desire Mr. Jenkinson will give him every degree of assistance.' To which Jenkinson replied: 'I will accordingly give every support and assistance in my power to Lord Shelburne . . . My attachment has ever been to your Majesty and ever will be; and for this reason I did not think it right to enter into any new engagement till I had received your Majesty's commands on this subject.'[23] But it is not clear what assistance Jenkinson gave to Shelburne. He received no office; and spoke only twice in the House during the period of Shelburne's Administration (he voted for the peace preliminaries but did not speak in the debate). Nor was Shelburne the man to allow Jenkinson a share of the royal confidence.

On Shelburne's fall, Jenkinson was again prepared to advise the King. 'Mr. Jenkinson has thought much of the subject of possible arrangements', wrote Thurlow to the King, 1 Mar. 1783.[24] ' . . . I submit it to your Majesty that it would be useful to hear from himself his ideas.' But nothing Jenkinson could suggest could get round the fact that Fox was master of the House of Commons, and the Coalition was another period of eclipse for Jenkinson. He spoke and voted against Fox's East India bill, and seems at this time to have been again in contact with the King. 'You may be assured', he wrote to Robinson on 5 Dec., 'that the King sees the bill in all the horrors that you and I do.' And on 14 Feb. 1784, after Pitt had taken office: 'You may be assured that a certain person is firm, so that nothing will shake his resolution.'[25]

In December 1783 Pitt was in no position to reject offers of support, from whatever quarter they came. But he was very shy about taking Jenkinson into his Administration, and preferred to win him by fair words and promises. 'Mr. Pitt intends to write to you a very strong letter', wrote Robinson to Jenkinson on 25 Dec. 1783, 'expressing his opinion of you, his wish to show you every attention, and giving you assurances of his regard.' And later the same day: 'Fears and doubts, makes difficulties to your having office at the moment.'[26] By the end of 1784 Pitt was firmly established in power and nothing had yet been done for Jenkinson. 'I am no ways solicitous about myself', he wrote to Robinson on 7 Dec. ' . . . I do not choose to give up the game as yet entirely, but I pursue it with great coolness and without anxiety for the event.'[27] In March 1784 he had been appointed a member of the newly-constituted Board of Trade, an honorary appointment but one where he did useful work; and some of Pitt's supporters were apprehensive that this was the prelude to further advancement. Grafton wrote to Camden on 31 Dec. 1785:[28]

> We have here a report to which I can give no credit, although it is confidently asserted, concerning Mr. Jenkinson's advancement to our House and to the Cabinet. Your Lordship would, I am confident, if no other friend interposed to keep the minister from a step which would ruin his credit with the nation and make him soon feel that he was playing only a second part to *others*. Surely it can never be.

Pitt probably appreciated Jenkinson's expert knowledge of commercial and financial problems. In August 1786, when the Board of Trade was again reconstituted, Jenkinson became president and was created a peer. In 1791 he entered the Cabinet and in 1796 obtained an earldom. He left the Cabinet in 1804 and died 17 Dec. 1808. By temperament more suited to be a permanent official than a politician, it was his lot to live in an age when the civil service had not yet separated itself from Parliament. Hence much of the confusion of his career.

[1] *Jenkinson Pprs. 1760–6.* [2] *Grenville Pprs.* i. 180. [3] Namier, *England in Age of American Rev.* 75; T52/50/413. [4] *Grenville Pprs.* i.

359, 361. [5] Add. 35911, ff. 17–18; *Grenville Pprs.* ii. 373. [6] *Grenville Pprs.* ii. 197, 231; iii. 220; *Jenkinson Pprs.* 393–400. [7] 22 July 1765, Grenville (JM) mss. [8] Ryder's 'Debates'. [9] Grenville diary, *Grenville Pprs.* iii. 381, 393. [10] Minto mss. [11] *Mems. Geo. III*, iv. 89–90. [12] *Jenkinson Pprs.* pp. xxiv–xxv. [13] Jenkinson's corresp. with Geo. III, Fortescue, iv, v. [14] Fortescue, iv. 476. [15] Ibid. 472, 503. [16] Add. 38307, f. 19. [17] Add. 38212, ff. 137–8, 191, 201–2. [18] Fortescue, iv. 500, v. 338. [19] 29 July 1781, Abergavenny mss. [20] Fortescue, v. 338. [21] Ibid. 391, 393–4, 401–2. [22] Add. 38309, f. 63. [23] Fortescue, vi. 69, 74, 84, 85, 88. [24] Ibid. 253. [25] Abergavenny mss. [26] Add. 38567, ff. 175, 177–8. [27] Abergavenny mss. [28] Camden mss.

J.B.

## JENKINSON, John (?1734–1805).

### CORFE CASTLE 1768–1780

*b.* ?1734, 3rd s. of Col. Charles Jenkinson, and bro. of Charles Jenkinson (q.v.). *educ.* Charterhouse. *m.* 1778, Fanny, da. of Adm. John Barker, 4s. 1da.

Page to the King Apr. 1748–52; gentleman usher to the Queen 1761–*d.*; second (or Ulster) sec. to the ld. lt. [I] 1773–5, and jt. sec. to the ld. lt. in England 1775.

Cornet 2 Horse 1752, capt. 1762; capt. 12 Drag. 1765; ret. 1773.

Jenkinson's great-grandmother was a Bankes, relations between the two families were close, and in March 1764 John and Henry Bankes considered the possibility of returning Jenkinson for Corfe Castle, which they did in 1768 and 1774 without contest.

Jenkinson owed his original appointment at court probably to Lord Harcourt, a friend of his family; his career in the army, Parliament, and in office mainly to his brother Charles. It was to him that he was indebted for his promotion in 1762,[1] and again 1765.[2] In 1768 Charles applied for him to Lord Townshend;[3] and on 14 Oct. 1769 wrote to Lord Granby:[4] 'I have frequently before now mentioned my brother to you; though he was page to the late King, and has served in the army, at least 18 years, he has not yet attained any higher rank than that of captain.'

John Jenkinson was offered the Irish post by Harcourt within a month of Harcourt's being offered the lord lieutenancy.[5] Godfrey Lill, Irish solicitor-general, wrote to George Macartney, 21 Aug. 1773:[6] 'Mr. Jenkinson is come here . . . he is reserved but seems to have got some good lessons under his brother and I think will through him make his way here.' But on 5 Nov.: Jenkinson seems hurt at his situation, being 'a British Member but an under-secretary here'; and is 'going in a few days to England without any intention to return till next sessions'. Harcourt, writing to the secretary of state Lord Rochford, on 27 Nov. described Jenkinson as 'a most prudent and sensible man' who 'has attended the business of the session most assiduously, and from an accurate, good understanding will be able to give your Lordship the clearest insight into our affairs'.[7] Still, Jenkinson seems never to have settled down in Ireland; did not enter the Irish Parliament; and on 20 June 1774 wrote to his brother hoping

Charles would obtain for him 'a seat at a Board on this side of the water and particularly at the lower ones', or at least 'a small Irish pension'—'I have surely claim enough on Lord North to expect his consent, and there seems ground . . . to think that Lord Harcourt would do such a favour for me.'[8] In 1775 he was appointed joint secretary to the lord lieutenant in England, with a salary of £400 per annum, and a prospect of its rising shortly to £600; and a 'very easy' attendance on the business of the office which, moreover, did not vacate his seat.[9]

In Parliament Jenkinson always voted with the Government. During his twelve years in the House only two speeches are reported: 31 Jan. 1772, on a motion of Thomas Townshend jun. about the export of horses; and an intervention in the debate of 6 Feb. 1772 on the 39 Articles.[10] By September 1780 Henry Bankes jun. had come of age, and the seat at Corfe Castle was required for him. Jenkinson did not stand again. He died 1 May 1805, aged 70.

[1] Calcraft to Shelburne, 30 Oct. 1762, Lansdowne mss. [2] *Jenkinson Pprs.* 350–1. [3] Add. 38206, f. 36. [4] Rutland mss. [5] Add. 32807, f. 139. [6] Macartney mss, PRO Northern Ireland. [7] *Cal. Home Office Pprs. 1773–5*, pp. 107–8. [8] Add. 38208, f. 80. [9] Harcourt to Chas. Jenkinson, 22 May 1775, ibid. f. 148. [10] Cavendish's 'Debates', Egerton 232, pp. 102, 116.

L.B.N.

## JENNINGS, George (?1721–90), of Newsells, Herts.

WHITCHURCH     8 Mar. 1757–1768
ST. GERMANS     14 Dec. 1768–1774
THETFORD        1784–9 June 1790

*b.* ?1721, o.s. of Adm. Sir John Jennings, M.P., by Alice, da. of Francis Breton of Wellington, Herefs. and 1st cos. of Phillip Jennings, fa. of Philip Jennings (q.v.). *educ.* Westminster July 1730, aged 9; Corpus, Camb. 1737. *m.* 30 Apr. 1741, Lady Mary Burke, da. of Michael, 10th Earl of Clanricarde [I], 1s. *d.v.p.* 1da. (who m. 1784 John Peachey q.v.). *suc.* fa. 1743.

Before the general election of 1754 Jennings applied to the Pelhams to bring him into Parliament; they tried to place him but failed.[1] In 1757 he was returned for Whitchurch on the interest of Lord Portsmouth. Newcastle in 1758 described him as 'a gentleman of great consideration in Hertfordshire and a very zealous friend'.[2]

He appears in Fox's list of Members favourable to the peace preliminaries, early December 1762, but according to Newcastle's list voted against them. He voted against the Grenville Administration on Wilkes and general warrants; belonged to Wildman's Club; and was classed by Newcastle, 10 May 1764 as a 'sure friend'. When the Rockingham Administration was being formed Jennings wrote to Newcastle, 13 July 1765:

The many assurances I have had of your Grace's good-will towards me encourages me to beg the favour of your recommendation to Lord Rockingham for some employment . . . I waited on his Lordship this morning and mentioned my wishes to be at the Board of Trade . . . My wish for being at one of the Boards proceeds from my liking business.

Newcastle included Jennings in a list, 15 July 1765, of persons to be given office, and applied to Rockingham on his behalf. On 22 Aug., when most of the vacant places had been filled, Jennings wrote again to Newcastle: 'I by no means waive my claim, and hope that in case of a vacancy at the Board of Green Cloth or elsewhere I shall still be honoured with your Grace's protection.' Rockingham, in his list of July 1765 classed Jennings as 'pro', but seems to have made no effort to provide for him. 'I . . . am truly concerned', wrote Newcastle to Jennings, 17 June 1766, 'that I have hitherto been able to be of such little service to you.' Without doubt he was sincere.[3]

After Chatham had taken office Newcastle wrote from Claremont to Rockingham, 31 Aug. 1766:[4] 'Offley and George Jennings are now here. The first, I think, is equally forgot by everybody. My friend George Jennings is wiser. My Lord Chatham has secured for him his son to be groom of the bed-chamber to Prince Henry, whose family is to be established in November next.' Rockingham in November classed Jennings as 'Whig' (i.e. as Rockingham Whig), but Townshend in January 1767 as 'Administration'; and Jennings voted with Administration on the land tax, 27 Feb. 1767, and nullum tempus, 17 Feb. 1768. At the general election of 1768 his seat at Whitchurch was required for a brother of Lord Portsmouth, and he is not known to have stood elsewhere. In December he was returned at St. Germans by Edward Eliot, presumably at the request of Administration. On the evidence of division lists 1768–74 he was a regular Government supporter, but Robinson in his electoral survey of September 1774 classed him as 'doubtful'. At the general election he was dropped by Eliot. In 1776 he thought of standing for Cambridge, but withdrew and canvassed for Thomas Plumer Byde; and nothing is known of any further attempt by him to enter Parliament until 1784, when he was returned for Thetford on the Duke of Grafton's interest. He voted against Pitt on Richmond's fortifications plan, 27 Feb. 1786, but with him on the Regency. There is no record of Jennings having spoken in the House. He died 9 June 1790.

[1] Add. 32995, ff. 63–67, 90, 138–41, 122. [2] Add. 32879, f. 337. [3] Add. 32967, ff. 381, 423; 32969, f. 155; 32975, f. 424. [4] Add. 32976, ff. 511–14.

J.B.

**JENNINGS, Philip** (1722–88), of Duddleston Hall, Salop, and Lyndhurst, Hants.

TOTNES   1768–14 Jan. 1788

*b.* 1722, 1st s. of Philip Jennings of Duddleston Hall by his 2nd w. Dorothy, da. of George Clerke. *educ.* Westminster, Jan. 1733, aged 10; Oriel, Oxf. 7 Nov. 1739, aged 17. *m.* bef. 1756, Anne, da. of Col. Richard Thompson of Jamaica and Coley Park, Reading, 2s. 1da.   *suc.* to estates of his uncle Sir Talbot Clerke, 6th Bt., 1774, and took add. name of Clerke; *cr.* Bt. 26 Oct. 1774.

Lt. 36 Ft. 1741; capt. 8 Ft. 1744; maj. 1 Troop Horse Gds. 1746, lt.-col. 1761; ret. 1770.

Jennings was connected in politics with Harry Powlett, 6th Duke of Bolton, and sat on his interest at Totnes. Bolton professed himself a follower of Chatham, and from 1768 to 1774 Jennings was in opposition. He was a frequent speaker, and attended the Opposition dinner at the Thatched House Tavern, 9 May 1769.

In March 1774 he spoke strongly against the Government's punitive legislation against Massachusetts Bay: the Boston port bill would 'punish the innocent';[1] the annulment of the charter was 'tyranny and oppression';[2] the bill to regulate the administration of justice was 'unnecessary, unlawful, unjust'.[3] But on 7 June Lord Sandwich wrote to his son Lord Hinchingbrooke:[4]

> I saw Colonel Jennings the day I left London and I must do him the justice to say that no man could talk more sensibly or more explicitly than he did upon political matters . . . I have no doubt of his sincerity, because I see that he with great propriety perceives that the nicest measure he can pursue is to engage the Duke of Bolton in a close connection with you and me. I would therefore advise you to cultivate the Colonel as much as you can . . . and you will do well to tell him that I am much pleased with his sensible language and behaviour in our late interviews, and that I am determined to lose no opportunity of improving our acquaintance.

And in a postscript: 'If you see Lord North it would not be amiss if you was to tell him how well Colonel Jennings behaves.'

On 29 Sept. North wrote to the King:[5]

> The Duke of Bolton having declared himself a friend to Government, and being about to bring in three persons who will be favourable to us, asks it as a favour that Colonel Jennings may be made a baronet. The Colonel himself who will be one of the Duke's Members wishes for it. Lord North humbly recommends to his Majesty that it will be of service at this time to grant that favour.

In the debate on the Address of 18 Nov. 1777, Jennings Clerke (as he now was) said:[6]

> Having constantly opposed the American war from the commencement of it as thinking it might and ought to have been avoided, and for other reasons which I have frequently offered in this House . . . it will not be wondered at that I should now refuse to give my assent

to those parts of the Address which are to convey assurances to the Throne of our intentions to furnish means of prolonging and continuing the war.

The first part of this sweeping statement is not borne out by the extant records of debates and divisions 1774–7. The one speech on America which he is known to have made, 27 Feb. 1775, during this period was critical of the Government but not hostile;[7] and he did not vote against them in the division of 26 Oct. 1775 on American policy. But from November 1777 he voted consistently against the war.

On 13 Apr. 1778 he introduced a bill to exclude from the House Government contractors, except those who held their contracts as the result of public auction. In his speech he said:[8]

> Members of Parliament would not be contractors, if extraordinary and improper advantages were not given them . . . giving these contracts to Members was an arrant job, and did create a dangerous influence in that House, which must operate much to the injury of the nation.

The bill was defeated on 4 May by 113 to 109, but became a favourite Opposition point, and was introduced each year. In 1779 it was again defeated; in 1780 it passed the Commons but was rejected by the Lords; and in 1781 was defeated in the Commons. Towards the end of the American war Jennings Clerke became the spokesman of those who complained of excessive Government expenditure: on 21 Mar. 1781 his main argument for the contractors bill was that Government contractors gained excessive profits; on 21 May he proposed a tax on placemen in the Commons; and on 28 May moved for an account of the money spent on the American loyalists.

He introduced his contractors bill for the fifth time on 1 Mar. 1782. Three weeks later North's resignation and Rockingham's accession to power ensured that the bill would become law. It received the royal assent on 19 June, after a conference between Lords and Commons at which the Lords withdrew their amendments. Its effect on the composition of the House was much less than its sponsor had professed to believe.

Jennings Clerke voted for Shelburne's peace preliminaries, 18 Feb. 1783; opposed Pitt's proposals for parliamentary reform, 7 May 1783, but supported Sawbridge's motion for shortening the duration of Parliaments, 15 May 1783;[9] and voted for Fox's East India bill, 27 Nov. 1783. After 1783 only two speeches by him are recorded, and his only known vote was for parliamentary reform, 18 Apr. 1783—why he changed his opinion is not known. He died 14 Jan. 1788.

[1] Cavendish's 'Debates', Egerton 254, f. 190. [2] Brickdale's 'De-

bates'. [3] Cavendish's 'Debates', Egerton 256, ff. 95-96. [4] Sandwich mss. [5] Fortescue, iii. 135. [6] Almon. viii. 15-16. [7] Ibid. i. 247. [8] Stockdale, viii. 243. [9] Debrett, x. 26.

J.B.

**JENYNS, Soame** (1704–87), of Bottisham, Cambs.

| | |
|---|---|
| CAMBRIDGESHIRE | 1741–1754 |
| DUNWICH | 1754–Nov. 1758 |
| CAMBRIDGE | 29 Nov. 1758–1780 |

*b.* 1 Jan. 1704, o.s. of Sir Roger Jenyns of Bottisham by Elizabeth, da. of Sir Peter Soame, 2nd Bt., of Hayden, Essex. *educ.* St. John's, Camb. 1722. *m.* (1) his cos. Mary (*d.*30 July 1753), da. of Col. Soame of Dereham Grange, Norf., *s.p.*; (2) 26 Feb. 1754, his cos. Elizabeth, da. of Henry Grey of Hackney, *s.p. suc.* fa. 22 Sept. 1740.
Ld. of Trade 1755–80.

Soame Jenyns led a sheltered orderly existence. His patrons, Lord Montfort and Lord Hardwicke, arranged his elections for him, and the post at the Board of Trade, which he held for 25 years, brought him £1,000 p.a. He supported every Administration in turn, busied himself about Cambridge affairs, and maintained a prolific output of light verse and writings on political, economic and religious subjects. He was bland and amusing, 'with the most even temper and undisturbed hilarity of all the good companions whom I ever knew', wrote Richard Cumberland.[1] William Cole the antiquary, a close friend, described him as 'rather of a finical and beauish turn, and not at all made for canvassing and caballing at elections':

> If a person who did not know him was to be asked on seeing him dressed what was his profession, I think it is ten to one but that he would say he was a dancing master. He has the misfortune to be extremely short sighted, a circumstance not unusual with eyes formed as his are, which are very projecting, and though he has a large wen in his neck, which a grave and even no very large wig would cover and hide, yet the predominancy for dress is such that a small little bag or pig-tail wig is preferred, by which means the aforesaid blemish is visible to everyone. Mr. Jenyns is a man of a lively fancy and pleasant turn of wit; very sparkling in conversation, and full of merry conceits and agreeable drollery, which is heightened by his particular inarticulate manner of speaking through his broken teeth, and all this is mixed with the utmost good nature and humanity, having hardly ever heard him severe upon any one.[2]

In 1747 he had been returned for Cambridgeshire with Philip Yorke, Lord Hardwicke paying half his expenses. There was some discontent in the county at both the representatives being members of the Yorke group, and in 1753 Lord Granby declared himself a candidate. Lord Hardwicke was unwilling to face the 'monstrous expense' of a contest on Jenyns's behalf: 'he cannot argue or suppose that it is reasonable that things should go on upon the

unequal foot they were upon'. Jenyns had to be 'laid aside', though assured that he would certainly be taken care of'. When the general election came, Montfort arranged with Newcastle for him to be returned for Sir Jacob Downing's borough of Dunwich: Jenyns paid £500, and the Treasury found the other £500. He was also given a secret service pension of £600 p.a., presumably until a place could be found for him, and in December 1755 was appointed a lord of Trade. But by 1758 Downing had quarrelled with Newcastle, and wrote to Hardwicke that he was not prepared to re-elect Jenyns. In vain Hardwicke protested to Downing, 22 June 1758:

> I took a real pride in thinking that you had brought him in at Dunwich in a great measure as a friend of mine and not of anybody else's. He had no attachment to the Duke of Newcastle. His dependence is upon me, and to me he owed his place.

Having eased Jenyns out of the county seat, Hardwicke felt it his duty to find him a haven. The opportunity came a month later, when Lord Dupplin, the Member for Cambridge, succeeded his father as Earl of Kinnoull. To Philip Yorke Jenyns wrote, 21 Sept. 1758:

> Lord Kinnoull said it was the Duke of Newcastle's opinion as well as his own that nothing would so firmly establish the interest at Cambridge as my being his successor, and Lord Hardwicke thought that it would be the surest method for me to get an established seat in Parliament and in the end the least expensive.

He accordingly vacated his seat at Dunwich, and was returned unopposed for Cambridge.[3]

Jenyns made no figure in the House of Commons. His interventions in debate were brief and infrequent, though he was useful to Administration as a pamphleteer. In *The Objections to Taxation of our American Colonies considered* (1765), he argued neatly against the Chathamite view that Parliament had no right to tax the Americans because they were unrepresented. Jenyns pointed out that the vast majority of Britons were also unrepresented, yet no one suggested they could not be taxed: if the argument of 'indirect representation' were brought forward, it applied equally to Britons and Americans. When the Rockinghams came in, he was marked down to be removed from his office, but his friendship with the Yorkes must have saved him. In 1768 he was returned for Cambridge unopposed, but in 1774 there was a strong contest. Canvassing the borough he spent 'the most disagreeable and fatiguing week I ever passed', and polling day was worse, with wild rioting. He retired at the general election of 1780, having nearly shared the fate of Cinna the poet; William Cole told Richard Gough, 24 May 1780:

Mr. Soame Jenyns told me that he did not mean to offer his services for the town any more . . . all the time I was with him seemed much frightened, as he had escaped being trampled to death by the mob in the Castle-yard . . . I observed one side of his face was much bruised by his fall. He is not fit to go among a mob; his age, slight make, and short-sightedness should have warned him against it.[4]

In the most celebrated of his writings, *View of the Internal Evidence of the Christian Religion* (1776), Jenyns maintained that the ethics of the New Testament were more pure than any previously enunciated. His mild tone was in keeping with the spirit of the period, and the work went through several editions. His political views were unadventurous. He rejected any suggestion of a reform of Parliament: a House of Commons where there was no 'attractive influence' would be quite unmanageable.[5] 'The chief business of a government', he insisted, 'is to hinder those who are under its care from doing mischief to themselves.'[6] Opposition he regarded as faction—'a most unpromising school'—and he took care to avoid it.

Jenyns died 18 Dec. 1787.

[1] *Mems.* 247. [2] Add. 5873, f. 51. [3] Add. 35351, ff 228, 245; 35679, ff. 267, 268; 35631, f. 24; Namier, *Structure*, 429, 437. [4] Fortescue, i. 93, 130; Add. 35351, f. 138; Nichols, *Lit. Anecs.* i. 685–6. [5] *Thoughts on a Parliamentary Reform.* [6] *Reflections on Several Subjects.*

J.A.C.

**JERVIS, Sir John** (1735–1823).

| | |
|---|---|
| LAUNCESTON | 31 Jan. 1783–1784 |
| GREAT YARMOUTH | 1784–1790 |
| CHIPPING WYCOMBE | 1790–Jan. 1794 |

*b.* 9 Jan. 1735, 2nd s. of Swynfed Jervis of Meaford in Stone, Staffs., solicitor to the Admiralty and treasurer of Greenwich Hosp., by Elizabeth, da. of George Parker of Park Hall, Staffs. *educ.* Burton-on-Trent g.s. *m.* 5 June 1783, his cos. Martha, da. of Sir Thomas Parker, chief baron of the Exchequer 1742–72, *s.p.* K.B. 28 May 1782; *cr.* Earl of St. Vincent 23 June 1797.

Entered R.N. 1749; midshipman 1752; lt. 1755; capt. 1760; r.-adm. 1787; v.-adm. 1793; adm. 1795; adm. of the fleet 1821.

P.C. 20 Feb. 1801; first ld. of Admiralty 1801–4.

Jervis saw considerable action with the fleet off North America during the seven years' war. He served under Sir Charles Saunders on the expedition against Quebec; was on friendly terms with Wolfe, and with Col. Barré with whom he was later connected politically. After intermittent service between the wars, Jervis became captain of the *Foudroyant* in 1775, but remained inactive till 1778 when he joined Keppel's fleet, and took part in the action off Ushant. Sandwich in his list of 'Officers of Admiral Keppel's fleet' drawn up in November 1778 wrote of him: 'a good officer, but turbulent and

busy, and violent as a politician attached to Mr. Keppel'.[1] Jervis's capture in April 1782 of the powerful French ship *Pégasse* brought him renown and a knighthood. Charnock (v. 409) states that in January 1783 he was 'appointed commodore of a small squadron . . . intended for a secret expedition' but the project was abandoned on the conclusion of the peace.

In January 1783 he was returned for Launceston on the Duke of Northumberland's interest at the request of Shelburne, a friend and correspondent of Jervis. Jervis voted for Pitt's parliamentary reform proposals, 7 May 1783, and against Fox's East India bill, 27 Nov. 1783. In Robinson's list of January 1784 and in Stockdale's list of 19 Mar. he was classed as 'pro'. At the general election Jervis was returned for Great Yarmouth as an Administration candidate. He again voted for parliamentary reform, 18 Apr. 1785. He voted against Richmond's fortifications plans, 27 Feb. 1786, which he had already opposed as a member of a commission of inquiry; but with Pitt over the Regency, 1788–9. Jervis's infrequent speeches in the House were invariably connected with naval matters: that of 2 Mar. 1786, in which he exposed the inefficiency of naval maintenance and told the House of his 'disposition . . . to root up and totally prevent the growth of evils so enormous and alarming',[2] foreshadowed his great work of naval reform, which with his improvements in naval discipline and his victory at St. Vincent were to establish him as one of the great naval figures of his time.

After his death on 13 Mar. 1823, the *Gentleman's Magazine* (1823, p. 371) wrote of him:

He was a man of strong and acute mind, resolute in what he undertook and unbending in his ideas of discipline and subordination. The British navy has been incessantly improving by those rules which he had prescribed for its management.

[1] Fortescue, iv. 226. [2] Debrett, xix. 255.

M.M.D.

**JERVOISE,** *see* **CLARKE** (afterwards **CLARKE JERVOISE**) *and* **CLARKE JERVOISE**

**JOHNES, Thomas** (c.1721–80), of Croft Castle, Herefs.

RADNORSHIRE 29 July 1777–May 1780

*b.* c.1721, 1st. s. of Thomas Johnes of Llanfair, Card. by Mary Anne, da. and h. of Jeremiah Powell of Cumelan. *educ.* I. Temple 1738. *m.* c.1746, Elizabeth, da. and h. of Richard Knight of Croft Castle, Herefs., 2s. 2da.

Custos rot. Card. 1741–*d.*; ld. lt. Carm. 1779–*d.*

In his youth Thomas Johnes cut a figure in

London society, and among his guests at Llanfair were Sir Charles Hanbury Williams, Henry Fox, and Richard Rigby. Although he lived in Herefordshire after his marriage, Johnes was active in Cardiganshire politics for many years. He was a candidate for the county in 1741 and 1747, but withdrew on both occasions. Later he acted as election manager for the Lloyds of Peterwell, negotiating the election of John for the county in 1754 and of Herbert for the boroughs in 1761.[1] His family was Whig by tradition, and he boasted to Newcastle early in 1760 that he had always shown attachment to Government.[2] During this period, too, Johnes had been connected with Lord Powis, who in 1765 backed a patronage request of his to Grenville with the assertion, 'If I can depend upon anyone I am persuaded I can depend upon Mr. Johnes.'[3]

In the 1774 election, when his son Thomas contested Cardigan Boroughs, Johnes was defeated for Radnorshire, but he was returned unopposed at the by-election of 1777. During his three years in Parliament Johnes supported the North ministry. He died May 1780.

[1] Add. 32856, f. 612; 32893, f. 300. [2] Add. 32901, f. 359. [3] Powis to Grenville, 14 Feb. 1765, Grenville mss (JM).

P.D.G.T.


## JOHNES, Thomas (1748–1816), of Hafod, Card.

| | |
|---|---|
| CARDIGAN BOROUGHS | 7 Dec. 1775–May 1780 |
| RADNORSHIRE | 26 June 1780–1796 |
| CARDIGANSHIRE | 1796–23 Apr. 1816 |

*b.* 20 Aug. 1748, 1st s. of Thomas Johnes (q.v.). *educ.* Shrewsbury; Eton 1760; Edin. Univ.; Grand Tour 1768–9. *m.* (1) 26 Aug. 1779, Maria (*d.*1 Apr. 1782), da. and h. of Rev. Henry Burgh of Monmouth, *s.p.*; (2) 1783, his cos. Jane, da. of John Johnes of Dolaucothi, Carm., 1s. 1da. (both *d.v.p.*). *suc.* fa. May 1780.
Auditor of the King's land revenue in Wales, May 1781–*d*; ld. lt. Card. July 1800–*d*.

Thomas Johnes contested Cardigan Boroughs on the Peterwell interest of John Adams and was seated on petition. On his father's death in May 1780 he vacated his seat to stand for Radnorshire.

In Parliament he supported North's Administration, and in 1780 was given a secret service pension of £500. In May 1781, at North's recommendation, he was appointed auditor of the land revenue in Wales, and his pension then ceased.[1] Thereafter he supported each successive Administration. There is no record of his having spoken in the House in our period.

Johnes died 23 Apr. 1816.

[1] Secret service accounts, Royal archives, Windsor.

P.D.G.T.


## JOHNSTON, Peter (1749–1837), of Carnsalloch, Dumfries.

| | |
|---|---|
| KIRKCUDBRIGHT STEWARTRY | 1780–5 Mar. 1781, 6 Feb. 1782–July 1786 |

*b.* 5 Aug. 1749, 1st s. of Alexander Johnston of Carnsalloch, by Janet, da. of James Gordon of Campbelton, Kirkcudbright. *educ.* Eton 1762–6; Trinity Hall, Camb. 1766–9; L. Inn 1769, called 1775. *unm. suc.* fa. 15 Nov. 1775.
Bankruptcy commr. 1784–1831.

Johnston was a family friend and protégé of James Murray of Broughton, on whose recommendation he was returned in 1780 for Kirkcudbright on the joint Murray-Galloway interest.[1] The following March the House declared the election void. At the by-election Johnston was defeated but seated on petition.

Directed in politics by Keith Stewart and Henry Dundas, he supported North's Administration to the end; voted for Shelburne's peace preliminaries, 18 Feb. 1783, and against Fox's East India bill, 5 Dec. In January 1784 he was counted by Robinson as a supporter of Pitt.

At the general election Murray, having decided to stand himself for Kirkcudbright, accused Johnston of base ingratitude for not withdrawing in his favour, and resentfully acquiesced in an agreement to share the Parliament with Johnston and Alexander Stewart. Johnston was therefore returned on the understanding that at the end of two sessions he would vacate in Murray's favour. By May 1785 Murray was pressing Johnston to fulfil the agreement before the end of the current session and declined to concede further time for Galloway and Keith Stewart to solicit an employment for him. In July, however, Murray eloped abroad with Johnston's sister, and resigned his pretensions to Alexander Stewart. Johnston, having failed to obtain an office in India, denied any obligation to vacate his seat for Alexander Stewart; but when confronted with a copy of the agreement signed by Keith Stewart (which he had not previously seen) was prepared to negotiate. Eventually he agreed to retire at the end of the 1786 session.[2] He died 3 Oct. 1837.

[1] Murray to Keith Stewart, 28 Jan. 1784, 12 June 1784, Seaforth mss, SRO. [2] Letters from Murray and Johnston to Keith and Alexander Stewart, May 1785–Jan. 1786, ibid.

E.H.-G.


## JOHNSTONE, George (1730–87).

| | |
|---|---|
| COCKERMOUTH | 24 May 1768–1774 |
| APPLEBY | 1774–1780 |
| LOSTWITHIEL | 1 Dec. 1780–1784 |
| ILCHESTER | 22 Feb. 1786–Feb. 1787 |

*b.* 1730, 4th s. of Sir James Johnstone, 3rd Bt., M.P.,

of Westerhall, Dumfries, by Barbara, da. of Alexander Murray, 4th Lord Elibank [S]; bro. of Sir James and John Johnstone and William (Johnstone) Pulteney (qq.v.). *m.* at Lisbon 31 Jan. 1782, Charlotte Dee, 1s.
  Lt. R.N. 1755; capt. 1762.
  Gov. West Florida 1763–7; director, E.I. Co. 1784–1786.

Johnstone went to sea as a boy, in the merchant service, and subsequently entered the Royal Navy. He served with distinction during the war of the Austrian succession and the seven years' war, and in 1763 was placed on half pay. In November, at Bute's recommendation, he was appointed governor of West Florida.[1] There he displayed energy and enterprise, established civil government, encouraged immigration, and fostered trade. But his pride and lack of tact brought him into conflict with the military authorities, whose prior responsibilities to the commander-in-chief in America he refused to recognize. In January 1767, after he had begun to make plans for a punitive war against the Creek Indians, which ran counter to government policy, he was recalled.[2]

Johnstone now became connected with Sir James Lowther (q.v.), Bute's son-in-law. At the general election of 1768 he stood as Lowther's candidate at Carlisle and was defeated, but shortly afterwards was returned for Lowther's pocket borough, Cockermouth. In the House he quickly displayed his energy and ability, and became a frequent and effective speaker. At first he seems to have been with Administration: he is listed as having voted with them on the expulsion of Wilkes, 3 Feb. 1769; but he voted with the Opposition on the Middlesex election in both 1769 and 1770. It is extraordinary that Lowther, who at this time was a Government supporter, should have allowed Johnstone to take an independent line in Parliament, a privilege he never accorded to any other of his Members. But Johnstone did not vote with the Opposition on the Spanish convention, 13 Feb. 1771; on the royal marriage bill, March 1772, was classed by Robinson as merely 'doubtful'; and when he voted for making the Grenville Act permanent, 25 Feb. 1774, was listed as one who normally supported Government. He took an active part in the politics of East India House, where he opposed any suggestion of Government interference in the affairs of the Company,[3] and was thus drawn into co-operation with the Rockingham party.

North's American policy drove Johnstone back into opposition, and he was one of the few who spoke against the Boston port bill.[4] He carried on his opposition to the measures directed at Massachusetts Bay, and condemned the Quebec bill as an attempt to destroy the constitution.[5] At the general election of 1774 Lowther returned Johnstone for two constituencies: Appleby and Cockermouth; and Johnstone chose to represent Appleby. Johnstone, through his friendship with Burke, now tried to bring Lowther, who was veering away from Government, into contact with the Rockingham group.[6] In Parliament he urged that conflicting rights should not be pushed to the point of civil war—'the whole art of government consists in preserving to each one his established rights'; and after war had broken out, warned the Government of the dangers of Bourbon intervention.[7]

The decision of the Rockinghams to support the recognition of American independence, and the approach of war with France, brought about a radical change in Johnstone's political position. In February 1778 he approached the Government, through Wedderburn, about a command at sea.[8] The following month he declared in the House of Commons that 'he always had been and still was against the independence of America'.[9]

> He was extremely sorry to see the idea adopted by gentlemen with whom he had acted; that if he found he had been acting with gentlemen who were ready to give up the supremacy of this country over America . . . he would sooner cross the floor and join those whose measures he had always disapproved.

He now accepted a place on the Carlisle peace commission to America, a step which aroused much ridicule after Johnstone's earlier criticism of Carlisle's appointment.[10]

Before leaving, Johnstone re-affirmed his opposition to independence: he thought the repeal of the Quebec Act and the Declaratory Act would be sufficient to reconcile America.[11]

> Whatever the people in power may wish and aim at, the great body of the people do not wish to change the government of Britain for that of Congress. The people of old settled interest and property do not wish for independency, they rather dread it.

He hoped to negotiate a settlement which would preserve some form of Anglo-American union. In America Johnstone tried to supplement the formal negotiations between the commission and Congress by private ones with individual American leaders, and on their failure returned home in advance of the other commissioners.[12] His view of the situation after the commission's failure appears in a letter he wrote to his friend Lord Granby, 5 Nov. 1778:[13]

> Lord Chatham's death I consider as the greatest evil that has yet befallen us. My ideas are the same as he held: do ample justice to all your fellow citizens but maintain your own indisputable rights . . . The ill success of Howe and Keppel (who were my darlings as superior sea officers) against an equal if not inferior force confounds all my sense and sickens my very soul. Something must be done. We cannot submit that

France shall dictate the terms on which this nation shall hold her dominions. It is a vain thought to imagine that granting the unjust claim of independence to the united colonies of America, that this will dissolve the power of our enemies or separate France and America. We shall lose a great deal and gain nothing but contempt by such a proceeding. Whereas by perseverance, if there was any head to direct or to execute the most obvious operations, our success seems certain.

Johnstone now opened negotiations with Government. He was very bitter against Lord Howe, whom he blamed for the failure of naval operations in America; 'thought Lord George Germain and Lord Sandwich must go out'; and offered a tempting prospect of substantial gains from the Opposition.[14]

> He did nothing without the consent of Sir James Lowther, who would also in that case accept some small trifling office to mark his connexion; that he thought he could bring Charles Fox in, and that the Duke of Grafton and all his friends would come in with Lord Camden and the Grenvilles; and he rather thought also the Shelburnes might.

North may well have been sceptical of Johnstone's ability to bring over to Government all these members of the Opposition; in the event none of them came. Johnstone received no political office, but was appointed to the command of a ship with a promise of a bigger command later.[15]

At the general election of 1780 Lowther left out Johnstone in the first arrangement of his boroughs, and Lord Loughborough urged John Robinson to provide him with a Government seat.[16]

> It would be idle to enlarge upon the advantage of bringing in so powerful and active a friend, who you know does nothing feebly and would be most warmly attached to Lord North if he felt an obligation to him. I have reason to think that Sir James still intends to offer him a seat upon the second cast of his Members, which in his present disposition Johnstone will refuse, but I hope and trust that I am not too late in suggesting to you to anticipate the reconciliation which would probably take place between them.

The advice was acted upon, and Johnstone was found a seat at Lostwithiel. During the next eighteen months he was mostly absent at sea. Early in 1781 he was given command of an expedition to the Cape of Good Hope, but failed to reach the Cape before the arrival of French reinforcements had made his undertaking impracticable. He returned to England in time to vote with North's Administration in the last two divisions before its fall.

In May 1782 Johnstone criticized the Rockingham Administration for their recall of Rodney, and praised Rodney's unorthodox tactics in breaking the line at the battle of the Saints.[17] About this time he was drawn once more into East India affairs in association with Laurence Sulivan, John MacPherson, Richard Atkinson (qq.v.), and the so-called 'Old Interest' at India House.[18] He wished to leave the patronage of the Company in its own hands, and to restrict Government control to the minimum; he was strongly opposed to Burke and Dundas, who in their separate ways wished to impose public control over the Company. On America, Johnstone remained fixed against granting independence and he voted against Shelburne's peace preliminaries, 18 Feb. 1783. But Indian affairs brought him into opposition to the Coalition. He became chairman of a committee of proprietors entrusted with the defence of the Company's interests, and in January 1784 was elected a director. He supported Pitt's Administration, having previously voted for his parliamentary reform proposals. He contested Ilchester in 1785, was defeated, but returned on petition in 1786. By then he was in poor health,[19] and in February 1787 he took the Chiltern Hundreds. He died 24 May 1787.

Wraxall wrote about Johnstone:[20]

> Nature had cast his person in a coarse but vigorous mould . . . irascible, intemperate, violent, he was a warm and zealous friend but an implacable enemy. He possessed a species of ardent, impetuous, half-savage eloquence, restrained by no delicacy of language, yet capable of powerfully affecting his hearers by the display of information, by his energetic appeal to their passions, and even by his gesticulations.

His generosity and lack of rancour is indicated by the fact that, though a Scot, he lent money to Wilkes —and was apparently never repaid.[21] George Dempster (q.v.), an old friend and a sensible man, thought him of 'strict integrity, real worth, and unsullied honour'.[22]

[1] *Jenkinson Pprs.* 157–9. [2] C. Johnson, *British West Florida, 1763–1783*, pp. 24–60. [3] Sutherland, *E.I. Co. in 18th Cent. Politics*, 196, 217–18, 231, 246–7. [4] Brickdale's 'Debates', 25 Mar. 1774. [5] Walpole, *Last Jnls.* i. 335. [6] Johnstone to Burke, 25 May 1775, 4 June 1775; *HMC Lonsdale*, 135. [7] Almon, i. 111–15, 174–5; iii. 14–30, 105–16. [8] Wedderburn to North, 19 Feb. 1778, Abergavenny mss. [9] *Parlty. Hist.* xix. 915. [10] Wedderburn to Eden, 21 Mar. 1778, Abergavenny mss; Walpole, *Last Jnls.* ii. 157; Fortescue, iv. 91; *HMC 8th Rep.* pt. 1, 196. [11] Stockdale, viii. 240–1. [12] *Annual Reg.* 1779, pp. 19–21. [13] Rutland mss. [14] Robinson to North, 31 Jan. 1779, Abergavenny mss. [15] Thurlow to Sandwich, March 1779, Sandwich mss; Fortescue, iv. 302, 320–1, 323; *Sandwich Pprs.* ii. 245–6. [16] Loughborough to Robinson, 8 Sept. 1780, Abergavenny mss. [17] Debrett, vii. 207–9. [18] Sutherland, 380. [19] Add. 29169, f. 56. [20] *Mems.* ii. 68. [21] Add. 30873, f. 4. [22] Debrett, iii. 653.

I.R.C.

## JOHNSTONE, Sir James, 4th Bt. (1726–94), of Westerhall, Dumfries.

| | |
|---|---|
| DUMFRIES BURGHS | 1784–1790 |
| WEYMOUTH AND MELCOMBE REGIS | 17 June 1791–3 Sept. 1794 |

*b.* 23 Jan. 1726, 1st s. of Sir James Johnstone, 3rd Bt., M.P., and bro. of George and John Johnstone and William (Johnstone) Pulteney (qq.v.). *educ.* Leyden 1745–6. *m.* bef. 3 July 1759, Louisa Maria Elizabeth Colclough wid. of Rev. John Meyrick, vicar of Edwinstowe, East Retford *s.p. suc.* fa. 13 Dec. 1772.

2nd lt. Marines 1748; capt. Scots Brigade in Holland

1747–56; capt. 19 Ft. 1756; capt. 66 Ft. 1758; maj. 1761; maj. commandant 101 Ft. Nov. 1762; half pay 1763; lt.-col. 1772.

Johnstone was the head of a Whig family, closely related to the Marquis of Annandale. He may have been the 'Major James Johnstone' who unsuccessfully contested St. Ives in 1768. At the general election of 1774 he attempted to challenge the very strong Queensberry interest in Dumfriesshire, but eventually withdrew in favour of Alexander Fergusson of Craigdarroch, who was unsuccessful. But Johnstone increased his interest in the county at the expense of the unpopular 4th Duke, and at the general election of 1784 successfully contested Dumfries Burghs.

Johnstone was expected by William Adam to support Administration; in fact, he was a highly independent Member, unconventional as a speaker in both manner and matter. Wraxall writes:[1]

> Sir James . . . realized our ideas of these hardy Scots, the companions . . . of Robert the Bruce, cast as he was in a Herculean mould, of an uncouth aspect, rude address and almost gigantic proportions . . . [but] who concealed under . . . unpolished manners great integrity directed by common sense.

His sonorous voice, which compelled attention, was first heard on 28 May 1784 when, 'as an old man but a young Member', he unsuccessfully urged the House to disregard fatigue and continue its sitting on the Westminster election. On 7 June he was the centre of an acrimonious scene when he charged Fox's counsel, Thomas Erskine, with vilifying the House. His frequent interventions that session ranged over the Ordnance estimates, finance, West Indian trade, East India affairs, the militia, game licences, and the plight of Scottish fishermen. In the East India debate of 21 July he insisted that if returning Company servants were required to declare their fortunes, naval and military officers should in fairness do the same. With difficulty he found a seconder for his motion which, after acrimonious exchanges, was lost.[2]

On all questions Johnstone followed his own judgment, resenting pressure from any quarter, and his vote was unpredictable. He supported Pitt on the Westminster scrutiny, voted for his parliamentary reform proposals of 18 Apr. 1785, and commended the commercial treaty with France. He later declared that he had voted against Richmond's fortifications plan, but his name does not appear in the division list of 27 Feb. 1786. He was no respecter of persons: in a debate on naval promotions he called Howe, first lord of the Admiralty, 'a mere driveller'; and on 15 May 1787 objected to any limitation of the Post Office inquiry, merely because the postmaster-general was involved. 'He would suspect whom he

pleased. He would suspect the Speaker, the bishops, every man in the House. He was sent there to suspect them and he dared to do his duty.' On East India affairs he tended to go with the Opposition. On 2 Mar. 1787 he declared 'upon his conscience and upon his stumps, which were almost gone', that he was convinced of Warren Hastings's guilt and would vote for his impeachment. Thereafter he never wavered in his determination to bring Hastings to a fair trial, 'for the honour of the nation', regardless of expense. Similarly, on 9 May 1788 he supported the impeachment of Impey. 'We have beheaded a King, we have hanged a peer, we have shot an admiral, we are now trying a governor-general, and I can see no reason why we should not put on his trial a judge and a chief justice.'[3]

Johnstone had real sympathy for the burdens of the poor and repeatedly pleaded their cause: on the candle tax, the duties on hawkers and pedlars, and the improvement of seamen's conditions. He objected to the extension of the penal laws, advocated universal toleration (though himself favouring Presbyterianism as 'the least expensive road to Heaven'), and supported the abolition of the slave trade. In Scottish affairs he was an individualist, advocating complete uniformity between England and Scotland in law and taxes, and frequently alleging the gross partiality of Scottish juries, sheriffs and even judges. On 17 Apr. 1787 he moved for a bill limiting Scottish sheriffs' discretionary powers at elections in conformity with English practice. His zeal did not, however, extend to the reform of Scottish burghs: he vehemently opposed Sheridan's bill in 1788 and again in 1789, despite petitions from his own constituency and Sheridan's appeal to his love of civil liberty. He supported Pitt on the Regency. 'He had never been at St. James's since 1761 nor at Carlton House in his life. A man might be a good Member of Parliament . . . without cringing at court or sacrificing to the rising sun.' At the general election of 1790 he was defeated for Dumfries Burghs.[4]

Johnstone died 3 Sept. 1794.

[1] *Mems.* iii. 404; v. 111. [2] Ibid. iii. 404; Stockdale, i. 103–4, 308; iii. 323; Debrett, xv. 246, 266, 291–2; xvi. 143, 147, 150–1, 368; xvii. 286. [3] Debrett, xxi. 358, 361, 470, 503; xxii. 42, 81, 365; Stockdale, xiii. 201–2; xiv. 138, 253–4, 309; xviii. 76; Wraxall, *Mems.* v. 111. [4] Stockdale, ii. 385–6; vi. 440, 520; xiv. 56; xv. 189; xvi. 179; xvii. 64, 190, 242, 275, 346–7, 428–9; xviii. 85; xix. 254; Debrett, xxi. 470; xxii. 489.

E.H.-G.

**JOHNSTONE, John** (1734–95), of Denovan and Alva, Stirling.

DYSART BURGHS 1774–1780

*b.* 28 Apr. 1734, 5th s. of Sir James Johnstone, 3rd Bt., M.P., and bro. of George and Sir James Johnstone and

William (Johnstone) Pulteney (qq.v.). *m.* 1 Sept. 1765, in Calcutta, Elizabeth Caroline, da. of Col. Keene, and niece of Sir Benjamin Keene, minister at Madrid, 1s. 1da.

Johnstone went to Bengal c.1750 and by 1756, when the East India Company settlements were overrun, was a writer in Dacca, where he was captured but released and took shelter in the French factory. He returned with Clive to Calcutta, served in the artillery at Plassey, and subsequently accompanied Eyre Coote on his expedition up the Ganges. In October 1757 he was recalled to the civil branch of the Company's service.[1]

While at Dacca he had been befriended by a fellow prisoner, Mrs. Warwick, who, on the presumed death of the family heir, bequeathed to Johnstone her fortune of £100,000. Johnstone, intending to go home, instructed his relations to negotiate for an estate in Scotland, but on the appearance of the missing Warwick heir surrendered his fortune and remained in the East India Company service. In 1761 he was appointed chief in Burdwan and a member of the Bengal council. A shrewd and unscrupulous business man, profitably engaged in private commerce, he resented the loss of privilege incurred by the Company's proposals to regulate the inland trade, and was a leader in 1763 of the rebels in the Bengal council who, by rejecting the agreement made by Henry Vansittart with the nabob Mir Kassim, helped to create a situation leading to the outbreak of hostilities.[2]

When the news reached London the Company dismissed Johnstone from their service, despite the efforts of his brothers and George Dempster (q.v.). The Johnstone group, having supported Clive at India House against Laurence Sulivan in the contest for control of the direction, were deeply chagrined when Clive did not stipulate for John's reinstatement as a condition of accepting the command in India, but none the less secured their objective in May 1764.[3] Before Clive arrived in India, Johnstone, newly reinstated on the council, had taken the lead in negotiating terms with the new nabob and, ignoring the Company's regulations, had secured for himself presents amounting to some £50,000. Clive, on reaching Calcutta in May 1765, indignantly rebuked the council for their 'shameless' proceedings; and Johnstone, charged with disobedience to the Company's orders, resigned the service.[4]

He sailed for home in October 1765 with a fortune estimated at £300,000, and on his arrival aimed at acquiring Scottish estates and parliamentary interest. He negotiated with John Murray for some of his Selkirkshire property; with Lord Morton for the Orkneys; and eventually made his first purchases in Stirlingshire.[5]

Faced with a prosecution by the East India Company over his ill-gotten gains, Johnstone published his *Letter to the Proprietors* justifying all his actions. At India House his friends, led by Dempster and supported by the Sulivan party, campaigned on his behalf, and at the general court in May 1767, despite opposition both from the direction and the ministry, secured the withdrawal of the prosecution.[6]

At the general election of 1768 Johnstone unsuccessfully contested Haslemere; and in 1774 stood for Dysart Burghs and by his immense wealth succeeded in ousting James Townsend Oswald. In Parliament he voted with the Opposition; spoke 'very severely' on 17 Feb. 1775 against the bill debarring New Englanders from the Newfoundland fishing; voted 22 Feb. against Administration on Wilkes; and on 30 Oct. opposed North's bill for assembling the militia. Consistently pro-American, he supported, 7 Nov., Luttrell's plea for conciliation; and on 11 Dec. seconded George Johnstone's motion against including Georgia in the general prohibition of trade. On 25 Feb. 1777 he seconded George Johnstone's demand for firm action against Spanish attacks on British ships in the Bay of Honduras, deplored Britain's humiliating situation, and urged an inquiry 'to rouse us . . . from romantic dreams of American conquest and legislative supremacy'. He voted consistently with Opposition to the end of the Parliament.[7]

At the general election of 1780 he lost his seat to John Henderson, a Government supporter. Out of Parliament he continued to extend and improve his estates, acquired most of the Philiphaugh lands in Selkirkshire, but though 'immensely rich' was unpopular and had little personal following either there or in Stirlingshire.[8] Having purchased an estate in his native Dumfriesshire, he made an unsuccessful attempt in 1790 to stand for the county.[9] He died 10 Dec. 1795.

[1] John Johnstone, *Letter to the Proprietors of E.I. Stock* (1766); C. L. Johnstone, *Hist. Johnstones*, 178; S. C. Hill, *Recs. Bengal*, i. 70, 173; iii. 75; *Fort William-India House Corresp. 1757-9*, pp. 88, 284, 312. [2] Forrest, *Life of Clive*, ii. 225-44. [3] L. S. Sutherland, *E.I.Co. in 18th Cent. Politics*, 131. [4] *Bengal Past & Present*, iii. 390-3; Forrest, ii. 261-7. [5] John Pringle to Gilbert Elliot, 17 May 1766, Minto mss. [6] Sutherland, 144-6, 171. [7] Almon, i. 193; iii. 77, 129, 279; vi. 291. [8] Adam, *Pol. State Scotland 1788*, pp. 315, 317, 333. [9] Sir W. Maxwell to Buccleuch, 27 Apr. 1790, Buccleuch mss.

E.H.-G.

**JOHNSTONE,** *see also* **PULTENEY, William** (*d.*1805)

**JOLLIFFE, John** (c.1697–1771), of Petersfield, Hants.

PETERSFIELD 1741–1754, 1761–1768

*b.* c.1697, 3rd s. of Benjamin Jolliffe of Cofton Hall, Worcs. by Mary, da. of John Jolliffe, London merchant, sis. of Sir William Jolliffe, M.P., Turkey merchant. *educ.* Westminster; Univ. Coll. Oxf. 1712; M. Temple 1714; I. Temple 1720. *m.* (1) 30 Mar. 1731, Catherine (*d.*24 June 1731), da. and h. of Robert Michell of Petersfield, *s.p.*; (2) June 1744, Mary, da. and coh. of Samuel Holden, M.P., a leading Dissenter, gov. of the Bank of England and of the Russia Co., 3s. 1da.

Commr. for wine licences Dec. 1720–June 1741; receiver-gen. of the duchy of Lancaster Aug. 1738 for life, but resigned 1751.[1]

Jolliffe controlled both seats at Petersfield. The reasons for his not standing in 1754 and for returning William Beckford (and when Beckford made his election for the City of London, John Philipps) are not known—they could hardly have been financial: besides the fortune inherited from his first wife, he had received a share in Samuel Holden's considerable estate, and also in that of his uncle Sir William Jolliffe. He was cut out of the will of his elder brother, Thomas, who died in 1757: this 'alienation of Cofton and all the old family property' was a disappointment to him but 'chiefly of a sentimental character, for . . . John was himself a wealthy man'.[2]

At the general election of 1761 Jolliffe intended to return himself and Beckford. On 31 Mar. Beckford wrote to him: 'I must desire you will nominate me for a candidate for I am far from being secure for London. If the poll turns out very favourable this day, Mr. Pennant will be with you on the morrow by eight of the clock, and you will then be pleased to nominate him in my place'[3]—which was done on 1 Apr. Edward Gibbon, who had been persuaded to stand for Petersfield, withdrew before the poll.

Jolliffe did not receive Newcastle's parliamentary whip in October 1761, and in Bute's list of December is marked 'Tory, Pitt'—presumably because of his connexion with Beckford and Philipps, and because nothing more was known about him. Although he does not appear in Fox's list of Members favourable to the peace preliminaries, in Newcastle's list of 13 Nov. he is classed as a Government supporter. He was absent from the division on general warrants, 18 Feb. 1764, but was classed by Jenkinson as a friend; appears in the printed list of the minority voting against the repeal of the Stamp Act, 22 Feb. 1766, but not in Newcastle's lists; is classed by Rockingham in November 1766 as 'Swiss' (prepared to vote with every Administration); by Charles Townshend in January 1767 as 'Grenville'; and by Newcastle in March 1767 as 'Administration, doubtful'. He probably voted with the court over the land tax, 27 Feb. 1767, and he was absent from the division on the nullum tempus bill, 17 Feb. 1768. There is no record of his having spoken in the House.

In the few surviving papers of John Jolliffe[4] is a letter from Lord Holland, 4 July 1767, trying to arrange a meeting between him and Welbore Ellis (whom Jolliffe returned for Petersfield in 1768); and when on the death of Sir Ellis Cunliffe, 16 Oct. 1767, Pennant vacated his seat to stand for Liverpool, Holland wrote, 4 Nov., recommending George Macartney to Jolliffe: 'Be so kind as to draw on Mr. Powell [Holland's man at the pay office] for what you choose should be the expense of it.' And Macartney, enclosing this letter on 11 Nov.: 'Mr. Pennant . . . wishes me extremely well . . . And the Duke of Grafton has assured me that he interests himself much in my success.' But having kissed hands as ambassador to Russia, 20 Nov., Macartney wrote to Jolliffe countermanding his candidature: 'I have wrote to Mr. Pennant by the Duke of Grafton's desire to inform him of this change in my situation and to tell him that his Grace would take it as a favour if he would be so good as to recommend Mr. Croftes to you for the seat at Petersfield'; and he added that Holland will be 'infinitely indebted' for it. The origin of Jolliffe's connexion with Holland is again unknown.

Jolliffe did not stand in 1768, but returned his son William and Welbore Ellis. When William married, 28 Aug. 1769, his father made over to him the Petersfield estate reserving to himself the nomination of one Member for his life.[5]

John Jolliffe died 31 Jan. 1771.

[1] H. G. H. Jolliffe, *Jolliffes of Staffs.* 45. [2] Ibid. 47. [3] Jolliffe mss, in the possession of Lord Hylton. [4] Ibid. [5] Jolliffe, 45–46.

L.B.N.

## JOLLIFFE, Thomas Samuel (1746–1824), of Trotton Place, Suss.

PETERSFIELD 1780–Feb. 1787

*b.* 22 June 1746, 2nd s. of John Jolliffe, and bro. of William Jolliffe (qq.v.). *educ.* Winchester; Grand Tour. *m.* 23 June 1778, Ann, da. and h. of Rev. Robert Twyford of Kilmersdon, Som., 3s. 1da.

Sheriff, Som. 1792–3.

Returned by his brother, Jolliffe faithfully followed him in the House; voted with North till his fall in March 1782; against Shelburne's peace preliminaries; for Fox's East India bill; against Pitt both before and after the general election of 1784. There is no record of his having spoken. The reasons for his vacating his seat in 1787 are uncertain. The *Gentleman's Magazine* (1824, ii. 91) wrote in Jolliffe's obituary: 'Of the disinterested and upright principle which universally governed his conduct, he early in life gave an evident proof, by resisting a very flattering overture, which embraced high hereditary rank as well as pecuniary emolument, rather than desert those connexions whose political views he had conscientiously adopted.' Nothing about such an offer is known from any other source; possibly there is confusion between him and William Jolliffe.

After the death of his mother-in-law in 1788, Jolliffe settled in Somerset, and in the following year started building Ammerdown House. He died 6 June 1824.

L.B.N.

## JOLLIFFE, William (1745–1802), of Petersfield, Hants.

PETERSFIELD 1768–20 Feb. 1802

*b.* 16 Apr. 1745, 1st s. of John Jolliffe, and bro. of Thomas Samuel Jolliffe (qq.v.). *educ.* Winchester; B.N.C. Oxf. 1764. *m.* 28 Aug. 1769, Eleanor, da. and h. of Sir Richard Hylton, 5th Bt., of Hayton Castle, Cumb., 5s. 6da.

Ld. of Trade Feb. 1772–June 1779; ld. of the Admiralty Apr.–Dec. 1783.

Jolliffe writes in an autobiographical memorandum: 'On my first coming into Parliament, by the advice of my father I supported the then Administration of the Duke of Grafton, and on his soon quitting the office of first minister I continued my support of Lord North.'[1] No speech or vote by him on Wilkes and the Middlesex election is recorded, but on 12 Dec. 1770, in a debate on the land tax, he declared that, though 'very independent' and under no obligation to Government, he generally voted with them.[2] On 27 Mar. he spoke and voted for committing the lord mayor to the Tower; and in February 1772 was appointed to the Board of Trade. On the death of Sir Matthew Fetherstonhaugh (18 Mar. 1774), he thought of standing for Portsmouth with 'no other view but ambition to represent the borough',[3] but he failed to secure the support of the corporation. In 1774, at Lord North's recommendation, he nominated for his colleague Sir Abraham Hume, and they were returned on a poll, the only one at Petersfield 1754–90.

Speaking on 6 Feb. 1775 on Lord North's motion for enforcing obedience in the Colonies, Jolliffe strongly pleaded for conciliation;[4] argued that if successful Britain's gain would merely be 'an abject submission of the Colonies through fear' which 'must end in rebellion'; and that America must soon rise above any apprehensions of Britain's power; but he did not even feel confident of short-term success. Later on he supported the Government over America, speaking on their side on 26 Oct. 1775 and 29 Feb. 1776.[5] 'I have been thought inconsistent,' he said on 23 Feb. 1778, 'in giving my support to the continuance of what I had disapproved in the commencement.' But though in favour of concilia-

tion before hostilities were commenced, once independence was declared, he rallied to the Government which could not have 'pursued any other line but that of vigorous hostility'.

> In questions of small importance, if every man was to follow his own caprice, no government could last a day, the business of this empire would be anarchy and confusion; but when the fate of thousands is at stake, when millions may be wasted, and an empire lost, he ill deserves to sit here, who can from any motive sacrifice his opinion. It is not in the power of the Crown to bribe a man of property on such occasions.

Vigour having failed, 'peace on almost any terms must now be obtained'; and whatever concessions are to be made, should be made immediately. 'Instead of suspending the obnoxious Acts . . . repeal them . . . We are not in a condition to haggle: we have lost an empire; it is an humiliating consideration; but we are in the state of suppliants . . . I trust we are not an undone people; but our greatness is vanity; that vanity has been our ruin.' Mere suspension 'wears the face of insidiousness'. He called on Parliament 'to be open and liberal' and to remember 'that the fate of the empire depends on this Act'.

This, and his speech of 19 Mar. on Burgoyne's expedition and surrender, hardly seem to justify the description given in a character sketch of him in the *English Chronicle* of 9 Apr. 1781: 'He sometimes speaks in the House, but there is a disgusting stiffness in his orations, as well as in every other part of his character, that deprives them of the small merit they might inherently possess, and him of all attention from the House.' Yet there was unconscious self-criticism in his own remarks on a man who follows 'his own caprice'. And here is another self-revealing passage from that speech:

> Sir, I am sorry on this, as on other occasions, to observe, the noble Lord [North] so blends every proposition with much that I like, and something that I dislike, that although he gains my assent, I am unable to give him my hearty support. As at the commencement of the war, the address was such a mixture that it deprived me of giving my vote; so at this period, though I approve what is intended to be done, I disapprove the mode of doing it.

Whimsical and cantankerous, he quarrelled with his relatives; with his superiors in the militia— Gibbon writes about 'his extravagant behaviour, which was much worse than anything you saw in the papers';[6] with his neighbours at Petersfield. 'They asked more than I could grant; alleging that my house was undertaxed, I made bread at home, bought groceries in London, in short, was not so devoted as they expected . . . Every trifling object of mine was opposed, I was not suffered to plant some trees in the churchyard, and I was opposed in building a wall near my own garden.'[7] He finished by buying the Merstham estate near Gatton, and pulling down 'his father's fine house at Petersfield' (but none the less retained his electoral hold on the borough).

In June 1779 he resigned his place at the Board of Trade. Answering some obscure innuendoes in the *English Chronicle* he wrote: 'I have ever considered an employment in the service of my country, as honourable, and not disgraceful. I therefore accepted a seat at the Board of Trade in the early part of my life, and I quitted it, as you truly state, because I did not care a farthing for it, in competition with my parliamentary independence.' But the concrete meaning of this phrase is not clear. In his autobiographical fragment he says that Wedderburn was pressing North to give an appointment to Gibbon, and 'to accomplish that arrangement I resigned but acted as before in support of Government'. In divisions on pensions and economical reform (21 Feb. and 8 and 13 Mar. 1780) he voted with the Government; and speaking on the bill for regulating the King's civil list revenue, 26 Feb., he is stated to have said 'that his constituents, he believed, were unanimously against the bill, and for that reason he should vote against it' (a flight of imagination on his part or on that of the reporter?). On the re-arrangement of offices before the general election of 1780 he was considered for a place at the Board of Admiralty.[8]

Robinson, having marked in his survey in July 1780 that Jolliffe and his brother would be returned for Petersfield, wrote: 'Mr. Jolliffe has very handsomely supported since his being out of the Board of Trade, it is hoped that he will continue to do the like and that his brother will be a friend'; to which he added later on: 'as he has an object and to him a great one, to attain'. To have the abeyance of the barony of Hylton determined in favour of his wife now became his ambition. He hoped to achieve it through Lord North, whom he supported in the crucial divisions of 1781—March 1782. But after North's fall Jolliffe continued to support him; voted against Shelburne's peace preliminaries, 18 Feb. 1783; and adhered to the Coalition; was placed by them at the Admiralty Board; voted for Fox's East India bill; and continued his support of them after their dismissal in spite of offers from Pitt.[9] 'Much will depend upon the appearance of the House on the 12th of this month', wrote North to Jolliffe on 2 Jan. 1784. ' . . . We are sending all over the kingdom to ask our friends to give us their attendance.'[10] And in his memorandum Jolliffe writes: 'On my arrival in London Mr. Robinson earnestly requested me to avoid going to the House, and I have no

doubt was authorized to give me full assurances of the attainment of my wishes . . . I went immediately and gave my vote . . . with the Opposition.' He returned himself and his brother for Petersfield in 1784, and besides joined Lord Verney in a hopeless attempt at Wendover.

In the new Parliament he continued to support the Opposition, speaking frequently on their side; and when by 1788 North's following was reduced to a mere 17 Members, Jolliffe was one of them.

He died 20 Feb. 1802.

[1] H. G. H. Jolliffe, *Jolliffes of Staffs.* 55. [2] Brickdale's 'Debates'. [3] To John Carter, 24 Mar. 1774, Jolliffe mss. [4] There is only a very short summary of it in Almon's report on that debate (i. 153) but Jolliffe himself sums it up in his speech of 23 Feb. 1778 (Almon, viii. 394–5) from where the above is taken. [5] Almon, iii. 44, 353. [6] To his stepmother, 29 Sept. 1778. [7] Jolliffe, 59–60. [8] Fortescue, v. 114–15. [9] Jolliffe, 56. [10] Jolliffe mss.

L.B.N.

## JONES, Henry (*d.*1792).

DEVIZES 28 Nov. 1780–1784

s. of William Jones of Argyll St., London. *m.* 13 Jan. 1777, Harriet, da. of Alderman Nathaniel Thomas of Ratton Lodge, Suss.

Described as 'a merchant and cloth buyer at London',[1] Jones was returned unopposed at Devizes. He supported North's Administration to the end, did not vote on Shelburne's peace preliminaries, 18 Feb. 1783, and appears in Robinson's list of the 'ill or cannot attend' in March 1783. He did not vote on Fox's East India bill, but in Stockdale's list of 19 Mar. 1784 was classed as a supporter of Pitt. There is no record of his having spoken in the House. He did not stand at the general election of 1784.

He died 1 Oct. 1792.

[1] B. H. Cunnington, *Annals of Devizes* ii. 260.

L.B.N.

## JONES, Hugh Valence (1722–1800), of Dover, Kent.

DOVER 6 May 1756–June 1759

*b.* 9 Dec. 1722, 1st s. of Charles Valence Jones of Penrose, Cornw., by Mary, da. of Philip Yorke of Dover, sis. of Philip, 1st Earl of Hardwicke. *unm.*

Clerk in sec. of state's office 1740; under-sec. of state 1750–4; solicitor to the Treasury 1754–90; commr. of revenue [I] 1759–71; comptroller of customs 1780–*d.*

Jones's father, a barrister, 'who doth not practice, nor hath he exerted himself',[1] died practically bankrupt in 1737, leaving his wife and family dependent on Hardwicke who recommended Hugh Valence Jones to Newcastle. In 1747 he became Newcastle's confidential amanuensis, and retained the post till the Duke's resignation in 1762. Nothing but a subordinate clerk (although he kept the secret service accounts 1757–62), Jones never played any part in the management of patronage or elections (as did for instance Roberts under Pelham and Jenkinson under Bute); and the idea of returning him to Parliament did not originate with Newcastle but with Jones's fellow townsmen at Dover, who disliked having all the time strangers 'named, sent down and recommended' to them by the ministry.[2] Newcastle, although he had another candidate in view, acceded to the request, and Jones was returned unopposed.

When Newcastle left the Treasury in November 1756, Jones was given the reversion to the comptrollership of the customs, to which in 1759 Newcastle wanted to add a pension on the Irish establishment. But as Hardwicke objected, lest people should say that it was held by Jones in trust for him,[3] Jones was appointed commissioner of the revenue in Ireland which vacated his seat in Parliament.

With places worth over £1,600 a year and a reversion of £1,200, Jones still pressed Newcastle for an additional appointment in the customs 'reputed £2,000 per annum'. Newcastle wrote to Hardwicke on 13 Sept. 1760:

> I perceived for these two last days an alteration in him; and as I always do with my friends I spoke to him and I found him harping or still muttering about the holding both places . . . I have experience enough in these matters to know that a man that talks so *is not pleased*, and what is my situation if Mr. Jones is not *now* pleased with me?

Hardwicke replied the next day:

> Your Grace does him the honour and justice to say you know his good heart and so do I. He is very honest and nobody can possible have more duty and gratitude to your Grace or be more sensible of his infinite obligations to you.[4]

His advice was 'not to take the least future notice of it'.

Jones remained solicitor to the Treasury after Newcastle's resignation in 1762, and, in 1771, exchanged his commissionership of the revenue in Ireland for a pension of £725 on the Irish establishment; when in 1780 his reversion of the comptrollership of the customs fell in, this gave him an additional £1,085 per annum. He died 9 Jan. 1800.

[1] Isaac Minet, Apr. 1737, W. Minet, *Huguenot Fam. of Minet*, 66. [2] Add. 35692, f. 360. [3] Rigby to Bedford, 29 May 1759, Bedford mss 39, f. 180. [4] Add. 32911, ff. 272, 301.

A.N.N.

**JONES, Robert** (*d.*1774), of Clement's Lane, Lombard St., London, and Babraham, Cambs.

HUNTINGDON      1754–17 Feb. 1774

*m.*, 1da.
Director, E.I. Co. 1754–8, 1765–9.

G.F. Grand, apprenticed c.1765 to Jones, states that he started as 'captain of a Lisbon trader'.[1] In August 1743 Jones entered into partnership at Gibraltar with Thomas Tierney, father of George Tierney (q.v.).[2] In a list of Members 1754–5[3] he is described as 'wine merchant intimate with Captain Montagu': who may be Lord Sandwich's brother William, M.P. for Huntingdonshire 1745–7, or possibly John Montagu, of the Manchester branch, M.P. for Huntingdon 1748–54; both were naval captains. The origin of the connexion with Sandwich, the decisive factor in Jones's public career, is unascertained. He sat in Parliament on Sandwich's interest, and acted as his man of business both in national politics and in East India House.

Sandwich, having taken office, reported to Newcastle, 24 Dec. 1755, that Jones had 'attended and voted in every question this sessions in support of the measures of the Government'; and on 23 June 1758, when forwarding Jones's application to be employed in remittances to America:

> If he had the honour of being more known to your Grace, you would find him a very honest, intelligent, and useful friend, in which light his own inclination, and my advice makes him wish to be considered.

It was probably as a favour to Jones that in February 1759 his brother John was appointed receiver of the land tax for Berkshire.[4]

When in April 1761 Sandwich tried to detach Clive from Pitt,[5] he used Jones as intermediary—'I can entirely depend on Jones's discretion and address', he wrote to Newcastle, 24 Apr. 1761.[6] In July 1762 Jones appears as employed in remittances to Portugal.[7] When in 1763 merchant Members faithful to Newcastle were being deprived of their contracts, Jones, in partnership with Peregrine Cust, obtained a share in remittances to Gibraltar; also to Goree.[8] After the return of the Bedfords to office, he held a victualling contract for troops in Nova Scotia, 1770 till his death.[9] At times he dealt heavily in Government loans—over £100,000 was entered in his jobbing account at the Bank, 1760–3.[10] He was one of the financiers consulted when Grenville was at the Treasury.[11]

Jones went into opposition with Sandwich; voted against the repeal of the Stamp Act, 22 Feb. 1766; and against the Chatham Administration over the land tax, 27 Feb. 1767. On 9 Mar. 1767, during the debates on the affairs of the East India Company, he 'presented a petition to the House from the court of directors praying that the papers called for by the House might not be printed':[12] his only recorded intervention in debate during 20 years in the House. His attendance in divisions was fairly regular.

When in September 1768 Sandwich showed

dissatisfaction at his 'subordinate situation' as postmaster general, Jones discussed the matter with Grafton's secretary to the Treasury, Thomas Bradshaw: a remarkable example of top negotiations through political henchmen. On 12 Sept. Jones reported to Sandwich that Bradshaw had called on him, thanked him for his assistance over East India affairs,

and asked if I could point anything that his Grace could oblige me in. This gave me an opportunity to exercise the authority your Lordship gave me at Epsom. I told him I had but one wish, and that was to see my best friend happy, pointing at your Lordship's picture. He desired me in confidence to explain. I told him I could not presume to say much on so delicate a subject, but my opinion was your Lordship would be happy to be in a more active situation to assist his Grace in administration. He desired my private thoughts on what would be most agreeable to your Lordship, which led me to the Admiralty. We had a long conversation, in which Lord Hinchingbrooke was not forgot. He appeared to be much in earnest, and assured me that he could communicate the whole to the Duke, with his best wishes. He told me in confidence that Lord Shelburne would soon be out of office.[13]

On the 14th Sandwich wrote to Rigby, who showed the letter to Jones when on the 23rd they dined with the notorious Powell of the pay office.[14] 'The subject alarms him', wrote Jones to Sandwich on the 26th, 'and believe carries him and Lord Weymouth to Euston.' Meantime Jones told Bradshaw's brother-in-law, Anthony Chamier, who desired employment in the office of the secretary of state, 'how favourably your Lordship speaks of him and that he is the first person to be provided for when your Lordship has it in your power'. Two days later Bradshaw assured Jones of Grafton's 'good disposition' towards Sandwich, but 'the office of secretary of state was out of the question', and it was difficult to remove Hawke from the Admiralty. And here the matter rested for some time.

The most important sphere of Jones's activities was India House. Sandwich seems first to have concerned himself seriously in East India affairs when the Administration of which he was a member supported Clive against Sulivan in the election of directors of 1764. Jones, who had earlier been a director, but lost his seat when Sulivan rose to power, now re-entered East India politics as Sandwich's agent.[15] In 1765 he was again elected a director and was noted as one 'who would certainly follow Lord Sandwich on all occasions',[16] and until 1768 was the most prominent of the three directors owing him allegiance (the others being John Stephenson and George Wombwell). In 1769, though he was not eligible for election since he had

served four consecutive years, he organized the campaign for the election of directors for his patron. His role had won him some unpopularity in the Company, but it is not clear why he withdrew from its affairs at this time. In 1773 the ministry tried to press him on the Company[17] but without success, and his death prevented any further efforts.

In July 1770 Jones bought Babraham for £27,500,[18] and 'pulled down the old house which was built in the Italian style by Sir Horatio Pallavicini [Palavicino]'.[19] At his death, 17 Feb. 1774, the estate, with his improvements, was valued at £37,000, and the total of his properties and holdings in the funds at £88,000.[20] As his daughter had 'disobliged him in marrying' J. W. Adeane (q.v.), he made his grandson Robert Jones Adeane his chief heir.

[1] *Narr. Life Gent. long resident in India* (1910), p. 2. On this point Grand's evidence can probably be accepted; but the story of the 'bargain' between Jones and Sandwich, p. 11, is sheer nonsense. [2] Adeane Pprs. at Babraham. [3] Lowther mss. [4] Add. 32861, f. 427; 32881, ff. 25, 27; 38334, f. 206. [5] Namier, *Structure*, 286. [6] Add. 32922, ff. 181–2. [7] T29/34/336. [8] Add. 38338, ff. 109–11; T29/35/175; T29/36/212. [9] T54/41/89–93. [10] Bank of England recs. [11] *Jenkinson Pprs.* 352. [12] James West to Newcastle, 9 Mar., Add. 32980, f. 248. [13] Sandwich mss. [14] Rigby to Sandwich, 24 Sept. 1768, ibid. [15] L. S. Sutherland, *E.I. Co. in 18th Cent. Politics*, 120–5. [16] J. Walsh to Clive, 5 Apr. 1765, Clive mss. [17] L. Sulivan to W. Hastings, 28 Apr. 1775, Add. 29133, ff. 533–6. [18] Memorandum c.1774 in the Adeane Pprs. [19] J. Nichols, *Anecs. of Wm. Bowyer*, 95–96 n. [20] Memorandum cited above.

L.B.N.

## JONES SKELTON, Arnoldus (c.1750–93), of Branthwaite, Cumb.

EYE 1780–Mar. 1782

*b.* c.1750, s. of James Jones, capt. 3 Ft. Gds., by Jemima, da. of Col. Tullekens. His sis. Jemima m. 1768 Charles, 2nd Earl Cornwallis (q.v.). Took add. name of Skelton 1772 in accordance with will of his fa's benefactor Lt.-Gen. Skelton. *m.* Oct. 1775, Elizabeth, da. of William Hicks of Whitehaven and Papcastle, Cumb., 4s. 5da.
Ensign 3 Ft. Gds. 1772, lt. and capt. 1776; ret. 1779.

Returned by his brother-in-law, Lord Cornwallis, Skelton supported Administration in all five divisions of February–March 1782, but is not known to have spoken in the House. At the end of March he vacated his seat; and on 1 Apr. Lord Cornwallis's brother, the bishop of Lichfield and Coventry, wrote to William Cornwallis:[1] 'Skelton is to have or rather has a pension on the list, for it was done by Lord North . . . It was absolutely necessary for [Lord Cornwallis] to get rid of Skelton as he had entangled himself with him [presumably Lord North]'. But Skelton's pension has not been traced.

He died 23 Mar. 1793.

[1] *HMC Var.* vi. 329.

M.M.D.